HANDBOOK OF RESEARCH ON TEACHING

Third Edition

HANDBOOK OF RESEARCH ON TEACHING
Third Edition

A PROJECT OF THE AMERICAN EDUCATIONAL RESEARCH ASSOCIATION

Edited by

Merlin C. Wittrock

MACMILLAN PUBLISHING COMPANY
A Division of Macmillan, Inc.
NEW YORK

Collier Macmillan Publishers
LONDON

Macmillan Publishing Company
A Division of Macmillan, Inc.
866 Third Avenue, New York, N. Y. 10022

Collier Macmillan Canada, Inc.

Library of Congress Catalog Card Number: 85-4866

Printed in the United States of America

printing number
10

Library of Congress Cataloging in Publication Data
Main entry under title:

Handbook of research on teaching.

 "A project of the American Educational Research Association."
 Includes bibliographies and index.
 1. Education—Research—United States. I. Wittrock,
M. C. (Merlin C.), 1931–   . II. American
Educational Research Association.   III. Second handbook
of research on teaching.
LB1028.H315 1985   371.1′07′072   85-4866
ISBN 0-02-900310-5

Contents

Preface

Research on teaching has flourished since the publication of the *Second Handbook of Research on Teaching*. Since then, traditional lines of inquiry matured and emerging areas of research evolved. These old and new areas of research led to chapters in the third edition that have no counterparts in the two earlier editions of the *Handbook*. In addition, methods for studying, observing, and analyzing teaching and thought processes of learners grew and developed. From these areas of study and methods of research came data that added to our knowledge about teaching and to our interpretations of familiar concepts. In addition to these empirical advances, important conceptual approaches opened lines of inquiry that led to an understanding of the cognitive processes of teachers and learners that mediate the effects of teaching upon student achievement. These recent advances in empirical research, combined with improved conceptualizations, advanced our understanding of teaching and our ability to explain and to demonstrate how teaching can be improved.

Historical Notes

These strong statements about data, methods, and conceptualizations of research, especially about the significance of research on teaching, indicate progress made since the publication of the last edition of the *Handbook*. In the preface to the *Second Handbook of Research on Teaching*, Robert Travers discussed his disappointment in the lack of advance in substantive knowledge about teaching. He described the difficulty chapter authors had in finding significant research to report in the *Handbook*, a difficulty even greater than that encountered by the chapter authors of the first edition of the *Handbook of Research on Teaching*. He also mentioned that the research on teaching was often not cumulative across areas of study or even within an area, lacking the coherence of integrative theories and models of teaching.

On a more positive note, Travers discussed the then new areas of research on teaching that offered promise. He mentioned the technology of classroom management. He wrote also of the influence of educational sociology, and of the contributions of the following areas of study. Behavior modification was beginning to affect teaching. Piagetian concepts about learning were also beginning to make their way into research on teaching. The study of preschool educational programs offered significant findings and promise, as did the research on computer assisted instruction.

At the time he wrote, the young field of research on teaching was growing rapidly. Theories of teaching were attempting to catch up with it, organize it, and develop conceptualizations and models of it. Dunkin and Biddle's influential book, *A Study of Teaching*, was soon to be published. Process-product research on teaching was the dominant research program. Programmed instruction was a popular instructional technique, and behavioristic models of learning were the most common conceptualizations of how teaching influenced achievement. The study of cognition had not yet made much impact on research on teaching.

Recent Advances in Research

In the *Handbook of Research on Teaching, Third Edition*, none of the chapter authors had difficulty in finding significant work to report either in substantive areas or in the methodologies of research. Some of the significant research they report occurs in areas that have no analogues in chapters of the earlier editions of the *Handbook*. The chapter "Teachers' Thought Processes," for example, reports data and a conceptualization of teaching that emphasize how teachers' thoughts mediate between classrooom processes and student behaviors. Most of the work in this area began in 1973.

Another chapter, "Students' Thought Processes," also has no parallel in the earlier editions of the *Handbook*. In this chapter, research on student cognitive and affective processes, such as attention, motivation, and comprehension, offers new interpretations of teaching processes, such as practice, time-on-task, teacher praise, reinforcement, and the active role of learners in constructing meaning from classroom teaching. For example, teacher praise seems to influence the attention of many students in the classroom. By observing one child being rewarded, many students learn the teachers' objectives and intentions. From the study of student attributional processes, reinforcement seems to function, not automatically, but primarily when learners attribute it to their own activity. Research on learning from text and on reading and writing indicates that comprehension involves students actively building relations between knowledge or experience and the text.

Other chapters report related data and models. The chapter "The Teaching of Learning Strategies" discusses the mental processes learners use to remember and to understand information and subjects taught in school. The chapter on teaching in the armed forces introduces research on intelligent computer-assisted instruction, including beginning attempts to model or simulate learning using the computer to represent our knowledge about a learner's responses to teaching. In the chapter on mathematics learning, which is, of course, not a new chapter topic, research on learner's strategies of adding and subtracting is described and used to imply how teaching might be improved using this knowledge. The chapter on written composition studies related processes and their implications for the teaching of writing.

In the section on theory and methods of research on teaching, methodological advances are presented. In the chapter "Measurement of Teaching," for example, the authors present methods for measuring students' and teachers' thought processes. In the chapter on quantitative methods, sophisticated techniques of multivariate analyses of teaching are summarized. In the chapter "Qualitative Methods in Research on Teaching," we read about the influence of anthropology upon the methods of research on teaching. Last of all, the newly emerging programs and paradigms of research on teaching are discussed in the first chapter of the *Handbook*. This chapter on research programs provides an excellent introduction into the concepts and models that underlie the recent and encouraging progress in the research on teaching reported throughout the *Handbook*.

The Development of the Handbook

Frank Farley, President of AERA, asked me to edit the *Handbook of Research on Teaching, Third Edition*. With his advice, and after talking with numerous people in AERA, especially in the field of research on teaching, I nominated and President Farley appointed the *Handbook* Editorial Board: Marianne Amarel, Beverly Armento, David Berliner, Geraldine Clifford, Walter Doyle, Frank Farley, Gary Fenstermacher, Thomas Good, Reginald Jones, Richard Shavelson, and Lee Shulman. After several months of preliminary work, in August of 1981 this Editorial Board met for three days to design the *Handbook*, to set policies for its preparation, to suggest chapter authors, and to make recommendations about the obligations of the *Handbook* publisher.

Among the more important recommendations and policies of the Editorial Board were the following. First, the board suggested structuring the *Handbook* to best represent the advancing state of knowledge about teaching, including the incorporation of new chapters needed to reflect recent and important lines of inquiry. Second, the board asked me to appoint at least one, usually two, reviewers for each chapter. These reviewers, as do their counterparts in other AERA publications, would provide comments and feedback to the chapter authors from colleagues specializing in their same fields of research.

After the meeting of the Editorial Board, the authors of the *Handbook* chapters were promptly invited, as were the reviewers for each chapter. Each chapter author and each chapter reviewer was told that we had four objectives or intentions for each chapter. First, we wanted the chapter to include, but also to go beyond, the important function of summarizing or reviewing research, theories, and methods of research on teaching. We wanted chapter authors to emphasize a conceptual understanding of the research on teaching that will show the readers how the studies, theories, and findings relate to one another. We wanted to provide an integrated discussion of research.

Second, we wanted to convey what is known about research on teaching, and, where appropriate, what is known about teaching. Third, we wanted to provide useful theoretical explanations of the research findings. Fourth, we wanted to provide an organized coverage of the appropriate subject matter. All chapters were developed according to these criteria.

ACKNOWLEDGMENTS

The preparation of this *Handbook* involved excellent work by many people. I am greatly indebted to them for all of their contributions to the *Handbook*. I thank Frank Farley for his guidance in the planning of the *Handbook*. The members of the Editorial Board deserve full credit and special recognition for all of their contributions to the focus and structure of the *Handbook*, for their suggestions about the chapter authors and reviewers, and for the development of the policies that guided the preparation of this volume.

The chapter authors and the chapter reviewers, of course, deserve thanks for preparing the manuscripts that comprise the *Handbook*.

Anita King, Amy Shaunessey, and William Russell, of AERA, contributed to the preparation of the *Handbook* from its conception to its completion. Elyse Dubin and Charles Smith, of Macmillan Publishing Company, supervised the publication of the book. Elyse Dubin and her staff worked carefully, transforming the edited manuscripts into the finished volume.

I also want to thank people at UCLA, including Deans John Goodlad and C. Wayne Gordon for their support. Special thanks go to Christine Carrillo, Barbara Trelease, and Joyce Amslow for their help over several years with all the correspondence regarding the preparation of the *Handbook*, and to Nancy Wittrock for the many hours she donated to the editing of the *Handbook*.

Merlin C. Wittrock
Los Angeles, California

HANDBOOK OF RESEARCH ON TEACHING
Third Edition

Part 1
Theory and Method of Research on Teaching

I.
Paradigms and Research Programs in the Study of Teaching: A Contemporary Perspective

Lee S. Shulman
Stanford University

Introduction and Overview

This is a chapter about alternatives. It deals with the alternative ways in which the women and men who study teaching go about their tasks. We conduct research in a field to make sense of it, to get smarter about it, perhaps to learn how to perform more adeptly within it. Those who investigate teaching are involved in concerted attempts to understand the phenomena of teaching, to learn how to improve its performance, to discover better ways of preparing individuals who wish to teach. This handbook presents the approaches and results of research on teaching, both to inform readers regarding the current state of theoretical knowledge and practical understanding in the field and to guide future efforts by scholars to add to that fund of understanding.

The purpose of this chapter is to serve as a reader's guide to the field of research on teaching, especially to the research programs that direct, model, or point the ways for research on teaching. The premise behind this chapter is that the field of research on teaching has produced, and will continue to yield, growing bodies of knowledge. But knowledge does not grow naturally or inexorably. It is produced through the inquiries of scholars — empiricists, theorists, practitioners — and is therefore a function of the kinds of questions asked, problems posed, and issues framed by those who do research. To understand the findings and methods of research on teaching, therefore, requires that the reader appreciate the varieties of ways in which such questions are formulated. The framing of a research question, like that of an attorney in a court of law, limits the range of permissible responses and prefigures the character of possible outcomes. Simply put, to interpret the findings of the many studies summarized in this volume, it is essential that the reader understand the questions that have been asked and the manner in which those questions have been framed, both conceptually and methodologically. Research on teaching, like most other fields of study, is not the work of individual scholars working alone and idiosyncratically. Indeed, most research is conducted in the context of scientific communities, "invisible colleges" of scholars who share similar conceptions of proper questions, methods, techniques, and forms of explanation. To understand why research is formulated in a particular fashion, one needs to locate the investigation among the alternative approaches to inquiry that characterize a field. A goal of this chapter will be to describe the diverse communities of scholars, practitioners, and policymakers that comprise, or in whose interests are defined, the activities and universe of research on teaching.

The term most frequently employed to describe such research communities, and the conceptions of problem and method they share, is *paradigm*. The term has been used in several ways. In his chapter "Paradigms for Research on Teaching" prepared for the first *Handbook of Research on Teaching* under his editorship, Gage referred to paradigms as "models, patterns, or schemata. Paradigms are not theories; they are rather ways of thinking or patterns for research that, when carried out, can lead to the development of theory" (Gage, 1963, p. 95). Writing during the infancy of this field of research, Gage drew most of his models from psychology or other behavioral sciences, rather than from the study of teaching itself. He was describing how models might be used in the study of teaching, not how they had already been employed. An important sign of the vigor of the field Gage was then fathering is the multiplicity of models from the study of teaching itself that we can now describe some

The author thanks reviewers Richard Shavelson (U.C.L.A.) and N. L. Gage (Stanford University) and editorial consultants Walter Doyle and Marianne Amarel for their helpful suggestions.

twenty years later. More recently, Doyle (1978; 1983) has written lucidly on the paradigms for research on teaching.

The most famous use of "paradigm" is that of Thomas Kuhn, whose *Structure of Scientific Revolutions* (1970) is a classic of contemporary history of science that has become part of the common parlance and prevailing views of nearly all members of the social and natural science communities. Since one of his friendliest critics (Masterman, 1970) identified some twenty-two different uses of "paradigm" in Kuhn's book, I will refrain from attempting a succinct definition at this point. I prefer to employ the concept of a research program (Lakatos, 1970) to describe the genres of inquiry found in the study of teaching, rather than the Kuhnian conception of a paradigm. Nevertheless, the two terms are used interchangeably in most of the chapter.

The argument of this chapter is that each of the extant research programs grows out of a particular perspective, a bias of either convention or discipline, necessarily illuminating some part of the field of teaching while ignoring the rest. The danger for any field of social science or educational research lies in its potential corruption (or worse, trivialization) by a single paradigmatic view. In this manner, the social sciences and education can be seen as quite different from Kuhn's conception of a mature paradigmatic discipline in the natural sciences, which is ostensibly characterized by a single dominant paradigm whose principles define "normal science" for that field of study.

I will therefore argue that a healthy current trend is the emergence of more complex research designs and research programs that include concern for a wide range of determinants influencing teaching practice and its consequences. These "hybrid" designs, which mix experiment with ethnography, multiple regressions with multiple case studies, process-product designs with analyses of student mediation, surveys with personal diaries, are exciting new developments in the study of teaching. But they present serious dangers as well. They can become utter chaos if not informed by an understanding of the types of knowledge produced by these different approaches. However, the alternative strategy that reduces the richness of teaching to nothing more than the atomism of a multiple variable design may be even worse. This chapter will thus discuss several alternative ways of thinking about "grand strategies" for research on teaching, for programs of research properly construed rather than individual, one-shot investigations.

The chapter will begin with a discussion of the general character of research programs or paradigms, those conceptions of problem and procedure that members of a research community share and in terms of which they pursue their inquiries and exercise their gatekeeping.

After examining the general conception of research programs, a synoptic map of research on the teaching field will be presented. In terms of that map, the various research programs that constitute the field will be described and discussed. This general model will be followed by detailed discussions of the dominant competing (and complementary) research programs currently pursued in the study of teaching.

The next section will discuss the prospects for this field of study, in light of its current progress and present dangers, and in the spirit of contemporary critiques of social science method and theory as exemplified in the work of Cronbach (1975;

1982). Finally, a set of recommendations and anticipations regarding future research programs will be presented. We begin with the matter of research programs or paradigms.

Paradigms and Research Programs

How should teaching be studied? Where does one begin? In what terms can questions be put? Although logically the range and diversity of answers to these questions is vast, in practice, any given scholar appears to operate within a fairly limited repertoire of alternatives. Thus, some researchers always begin with the assumption that their task is to relate, whether experimentally or descriptively, variations in the measured achievement or attitudes of pupils to variations in the observed behavior of teachers. Additional wrinkles may be added to the design — use of individual pupil data as against classroom mean scores, use of pupil- or teacher-characteristic data as mediating variables — but the fundamental character of the questions remains unchanged. Other scholars are equally focused on still other formulations, whether involving classroom discourse, teacher cognitions, the sense pupils make of instruction, or the social organization of classrooms via task or activity structures. Once committed to a particular line of research, the individual scholar seems rarely to stray from it. A research program has been adopted.

Within the terms of such a research program, we can expect that certain kinds of research will be deemed relevant, will be carefully followed and cited by the investigator. A community of like-minded scholars will likely develop, exchanging papers, citing one another's work, using similar language and sharing both assumptions and styles of inquiry. They will agree on the starting points for inquiry. What is problematic? What are sources of wonder or dismay? What are the key topics, the strategic sites, for research? What are the implicit definitions of schooling, of teaching, of learning? What are the units of analysis? What methods of observation and analysis are legitimate? As the answers to such questions evolve, usually without much explicit debate, a kind of paradigm may be inferred to have developed.

A word on paradigms is in order. The concept of a paradigm became part of the working vocabulary of social scientists under the influence of Thomas Kuhn (1970). In Kuhn's sense of the term, a paradigm is an implicit, unvoiced, and pervasive commitment by a community of scholars to a conceptual framework. In a mature science, only one paradigm can be dominant at a time. It is shared by that community, and serves to define proper ways of asking questions, those common "puzzles" that are defined as the tasks for research in normal science. Members of the community acknowledge and incorporate the work of perceived peers in their endeavors. Kuhn would expect members of such a group to be relatively incapable of communicating meaningfully with members of other communities. (Quite literally, the ability to *communi*cate is a central definer of *communi*ty membership.) Moreover, they would have difficulty comprehending why members of another paradigmatic community would find the particular puzzles they pursue of either importance or value.

A research program not only defines what can be legitimately studied by its advocates, it also specifies what is necessarily excluded from the list of permissible topics. For example, in their landmark *The Study of Teaching*, Dunkin and Biddle (1974) explicitly exclude certain kinds of research from their review. In doing so, they leave out all studies that do not employ quantifiable measures of process or product. Ironically, the work of Jackson (1968) in *Life in Classrooms* is explicitly left out of consideration, even though it is among the most frequently cited references in their conceptual analysis of teaching.

In examining the effects of paradigms on the activities of researchers, we should distinguish between two general ways in which the term can be employed. The first sense, that which Kuhn intended in his characterization of the history of physics and other natural sciences, limits a discipline to but a single dominant paradigm during any particular epoch. He reports (Kuhn, 1970, pp. vii–viii) that he was drawn to that view during a year spent at the Center for Advanced Study in the Behavioral Sciences when, for the first time, he found himself in extended colleagueship with a community of social scientists. He observed that they seemed to argue, even when from the same discipline, about basic matters of theory and method that physical scientists tended to take for granted. It was then he realized that they failed to share a common conception of their fields so characteristic of the more "mature" disciplines. He called that network of shared assumptions and conceptions a paradigm, and concluded that the social sciences were, therefore, "preparadigmatic" in their development.

There is a second, weaker sense of paradigm I prefer to use in this chapter. Social scientists pursue their research activities within the framework of a school of thought that defines proper goals, starting points, methods, and interpretive conceptions for investigations (see Schwab, 1960/1978). These schools of thought operate much like Kuhnian paradigms or Lakatosian research programs insofar as they are relatively insular and predictably uniform. However, in no sense are social science fields necessarily dominated by a single school of thought. Indeed, as Kuhn observed, what distinguishes the social from the natural sciences is this very absence of a single dominant paradigm.

Where Kuhn erred, I believe, is in diagnosing this characteristic of the social sciences as a developmental disability, a state of preparadigmatic retardation. Indeed, it is far more likely that for the social sciences and education, the coexistence of competing schools of thought is a natural and quite mature state. In this matter, I agree fully with Merton's observations about sociology:

> The chronic crisis of sociology, with its diversity, competition and clash of doctrine, seems preferable to the ... prescription of a single theoretical perspective that promises to provide full and exclusive access to the sociological truth. ... No one paradigm has even begun to demonstrate its unique cogency for investigating the entire range of sociologically interesting questions. And given the variety of these questions, the past prefigures the future. (Merton, 1975, p. 28)

Merton argues for the superiority of a set of competing paradigms over the hegemony of a single school of thought. He asserts that theoretical pluralism encourages development of a variety of research strategies, rather than premature closure of investigation consistent with the problematics of a single paradigm. Different paradigms alert research workers to differ-

ent phenomena of interest, different conceptions of problem, and different aspects of events likely to be ignored within a single perspective. He advocates the virtues of "a plurality of theoretical orientations ... in the form of a 'disciplined eclecticism'" (ibid., p. 51).

> The cognitive problems of coexisting paradigms call for discovering the capabilities and limitations of each. This involves identifying the kinds and range of problems each is good for (and noting those for which it is incompetent or irrelevant), thus providing for potential awareness of the respects in which they are complementary or contradictory. ... Many ideas in structural analysis and symbolic interactionism, for example, are opposed to one another in about the same sense as ham is opposed to eggs: they are perceptibly different but mutually enriching. (Merton, 1975, pp. 50, 31)

The philosopher of science Feyerabend (1974) puts the matter even more directly in his essay "How to Be a Good Empiricist: A Plea for Tolerance in Matters Epistemological":

> You can be a good empiricist only if you are prepared to work with many alternative theories rather than with a single point of view and "experience." This plurality of theories must not be regarded as a preliminary stage of knowledge which will at some time in the future be replaced by the One True Theory. (p. 14)

This is also the view of the present chapter regarding the proper treatment of the alternative research programs to be discussed presently.

Gage (1963) presented a comprehensive review of paradigms for research on teaching in the first *Handbook of Research on Teaching*, compiled under his editorship. He reviewed a host of exemplars of paradigms from other social sciences that might prove valuable for studies of teaching, then proceeded to explore those that had been used for research on classroom teaching itself. By far the most influential source of paradigms for the study of teaching came from psychology, especially the behavioristic, experimental, functional perspective within that discipline. He defined "criterion-of-effectiveness" paradigms that specified criteria for judging the success with which a teacher had performed his or her tasks and related that criterion to a variety of potential correlates to discern those that were most consistently and powerfully associated with achievement of the criterion.

Potential Correlates → Criterion of Effectiveness

Gage distinguished among several types of effectiveness criteria (and microcriteria, specific outcome variables rather than general ones) as well as types of design. He then discussed "teaching process" paradigms, where the emphasis of the research was on characterizing the observable teacher and student behaviors in the classroom as they related to measures of pupil growth. Summarizing across the several models of teaching process research, he found four common elements. These were (a) the perceptual and cognitive processes of the teacher, which eventuate in (b) action elements on the teacher's part. The teacher's actions are followed by (c) perceptual and cognitive processes on the pupil's part, which in turn lead to (d) actions on the part of pupils (Gage, 1963, p. 127).

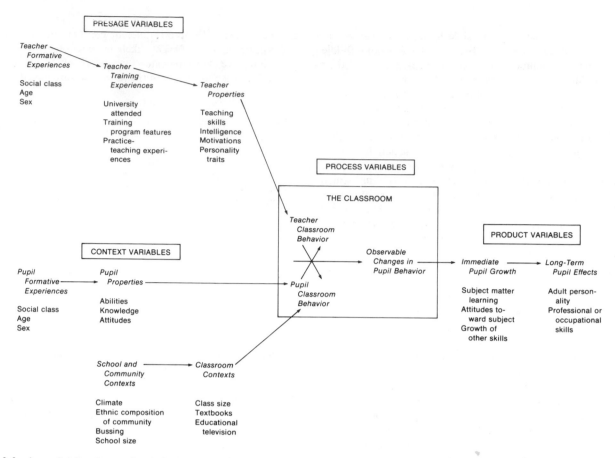

Fig. I.I. A model for the study of classroom teaching. From *The study of teaching* (New York: Holt, Rinehart, and Winston) by M. J. Dunkin and B. J. Biddle, 1974. Reprinted by permission.

It is somewhat ironic that in this important and early characterization of research paradigms, the cognitive and affective internal states of both learners and teachers are given equal weight with the observable actions of each. As the field continued to develop, the interest in those perceptual and cognitive states that are hypothesized to produce and mediate observable behavior waned. The dominant research program for the study of teaching combined a microcriterion of effectiveness (tested academic achievement) and teaching process correlates.

Gage recognized the limitations of these paradigms. He commented on the importance of classrooms as places where teachers must deal with more than one pupil at a time, a fact often ignored by then-extant models. He also observed that the unit of interaction connoted by those paradigms was typically the "single interact," ignoring the larger and more complex exchanges that constituted the important features of classroom process. On the other hand, it was important to begin the enormously difficult job of studying classroom behavior, and a number of simplifications were necessary. Those simplifications were provided by the early models and made possible the important first steps in the development of the field.

Some 10 years later, in *The Study of Teaching*, Dunkin and Biddle (1974) constructed a model for research on teaching based on an earlier formulation by Mitzel (1960). They posited four classes of variables: presage variables (teacher characteris-

tics, experiences, training, and other properties that influence teaching behavior), context variables (properties of pupils, of the school and community, and of the classroom), process variables (observable actions of teachers and students in the classroom), and product variables (immediate and long-term effects of teaching on pupil growth intellectually, socially, emotionally, and the like). While it is unfair to characterize such a sophisticated and prescient work too simply, their formulation had an enormous impact on the field. The emphasis on studies relating processes to products did not begin with their reviews. But their book gave strong impetus to the process-product work and helped embed it in a more comprehensive theoretical matrix. Moreover, they provided the working vocabulary for those who followed to describe what they were studying and how they were going about it.

The next section shall present a more general model for research on teaching, reflecting changes in the field, both observed and needed, during the last decade.

A Synoptic Map of Research on Teaching

In asserting that no single research program can capture the full set of educational events, I imply that the insufficiencies of particular programs can be overcome through proper blending with the insufficiencies of other programs. This image of a yoking of inadequacies to produce a hybrid more vigorous than either of its parents is certainly not alien to the practice of agriculture, but it has not been widely touted in the social sciences.

Two matters can be mentioned at this juncture. First, while most disciplines or fields of study become identified with narrowly defined methods, others have developed traditions of eclecticism, a penchant for employing a variety of methods for both acquiring information and subjecting it to analysis and interpretation. Among the traditional disciplines, most prominent is history, whose activities are so diversely puzzling to many outsiders that there is often debate over whether history is more properly classified among the social sciences or the humanities. Yet it is, I shall argue, precisely because history so readily defies categorization (or so comfortably accepts multiple affiliation) that it may serve as a useful analogy for the kind of multiple paradigmatic inquiry I shall advocate in this chapter. Moreover, it manages its several faces while surviving as both a form of fundamental investigation and as a significant source of guidance for both policy and practice — at least for those who do not choose to ignore it.

I begin with the assumption that there is no "real world" of the classroom, of learning and of teaching. There are many such worlds, perhaps nested within one another, perhaps occupying parallel universes which frequently, albeit unpredictably, intrude on one another. Each of these worlds is occupied by the same people, but in different roles and striving for different purposes simultaneously. Each of these contexts is studied by social scientists and educators, becoming the subject of theoretical models and treatises. Each has its own set of concepts and principles and, quite inevitably, its own set of facts, for facts are merely those particular phenomena to which our questions and principles direct our attention.

We become involved in these different worlds as elements of our puzzle because we most often must make a particular level or strand the subject of empirical study, but then we attempt to infer properties of other strands from the one we have investigated. Thus, for example, we conduct studies of how individual students learn to perform certain complex school tasks, and then infer principles for the learning of similar tasks by groups of students. Similarly, we may study classrooms of youngsters and then use the data to recommend policy for a school or school district. The essence of the puzzle lies in recognizing that no benevolent deity has ordained that these parallel lives be consistent with one another, nor that the principles found to work at one level must operate similarly at others.

Indeed, I would contend that our most reasonable hypothesis is that each of these lives must be studied in its own terms. We must attempt to capture the essential features of each strand in one or more middle-range theories (Merton, 1967) which render accounts of the teaching-learning episodes that characterize that level. These episodes provide the dramatic material for lives in that context, and define the strategic research sites (Merton, 1959) within which we make theoretical sense of what occurs there. Since those strategic research sites are different in each strand, so must be the strategic investigations, hence the facts, principles, and theories that emerge from those investigations. It is unlikely that any single theoretical frame can encompass the diversity of sites, events, facts, and principles that cross all those levels.

Any claim that the worlds of teaching, of schools and classrooms, of pedagogues and pupils, are so complex that no single perspective can capture them should be treated with skepticism. Like our suspicions of the mythical sociologist who asserts that all generalizations are false, we must ask how the claim can be made. It is fashionable to recall the ancient image of the blind men who provide alternative portrayals of an elephant whose unseen bulk is not perceptible to any one of them. Yet that tale presupposes the talents of a sighted observer who possesses knowledge of the total pachyderm and can thus grasp the futility of each assessment from the blind inquirers. Likewise in a field of scholarship, the observer who claims to possess precisely the kind of knowledge that he asserts is, in principle, unavailable to his fellows makes a claim we must find suspect. For those who conduct research on teaching are not blind, and relative to my fellow scholars I can claim no special gift of insight.

Given that my rationality is as limited as anyone else's, I have attempted to piece together a more comprehensive portrayal of the field through incorporating reports arriving from many vantage points (or touching points, in the case of our metaphor). By combining these separate accounts of teaching from different families of researchers, accounts much like the tales of early mariners regarding the geographic wonders they encountered on their journeys, we can begin to fashion a broader picture of our phenomena.

This map, however, cannot be a comprehensive *theory* of teaching. It is a representation of the variety of topics, programs, and findings of the field of research on teaching, related to one another as usefully as possible. For it to be useful, we must attempt to construct a map of the full domain of research on teaching (or several alternative maps, each highlighting different features, analogous to political subdivisions, the physical features and elevations, climatic conditions, and the like), a map sufficiently broad and encompassing that we can locate upon it not only the particular sections of terrain well captured by particular programs but also those left out. Moreover, we must seek to construct maps that themselves have some coherence or order, so our analyses can go beyond a mere shopping list of topics *qua* ingredients, some of which just happen to be omitted from any one particular treatment.

The fundamental terms in my analysis are the primary participants — teacher(s) and student(s) — who may be studied as individuals or as members of a larger group, class, or school. Teaching is seen as an activity involving teachers and students working jointly. The work involves the exercise of both thinking and acting on the parts of all participants. Moreover, teachers learn and learners teach. Both those functions of each actor can be considered an essential part of the inquiry.

The potential determinants of teaching and learning in the classroom are the three significant attributes of the actors — capacities, actions, and thoughts. *Capacities* are the relatively stable and enduring characteristics of ability, propensity, knowledge, or character inhering in the actors, yet capable of change through either learning or development. *Actions* comprise the activities, performances, or behavior of actors, the observable physical or speech acts of teachers and students. *Thoughts* are the cognitions, metacognitions, emotions, purposes — the tacit mental and emotional states that precede, accompany, and follow the observable actions, frequently foreshadowing (or reflecting) changes in the more enduring capacities. Both thoughts and behavior can become capacities (in the form, for example, of knowledge and habits or skills).

The activities of teaching can take place in a number of contexts, "surrounds" which define, in part, the milieu in which teaching occurs — individual, group, class, school, community. Within each of these nested levels (See Barr & Dreeben, 1983a; 1983b), the two sorts of transactions that comprise classroom life are occurring. Two sorts of agendas are being followed, two sorts of curriculum are being negotiated. One agenda is the organizational, interactional, social, and management aspect of classroom life, sometimes dubbed the hidden curriculum, though its visibility has improved dramatically as it has been studied. The second band of transmission is the academic task, school assignment, classroom content, and manifest curriculum. The contents of these two agendas, these forms of pedagogical transmission, are at the very heart of the educational enterprise, because they define what schools are for, what purposes they are designed to accomplish. The dual general purposes of transmitting mastery of the contents of a curriculum, comprising many subjects, skills, and attitudes, and of socializing a generation of young people through the workings of the classroom community define the core of classroom life.

Since the events we are coming to understand occur in classrooms and schools, they invariably occur in the service of teaching *something*. That something is usually capable of characterization as the content of a subject (e.g., Shakespeare's *Hamlet*, quadratic equations, diagraming sentences, word-attack skills, Boyle's Law), a particular set of skills, strategies, processes or understandings relative to the subject matter, or a set of socialization outcomes. The content ought not be viewed as only a "context variable" (Dunkin & Biddle, 1974), comparable to class size or classroom climate. The content and the purposes for which it is taught are the very heart of the teaching-learning processes. Smith (1983) put it clearly when he asserted that the "teacher interacts with the student in and through the content, and the student interacts with the teacher in the same way" (p. 491). Although the content transmitted for particular purposes has rarely been a central part of studies of teaching, it certainly deserves a place in our comprehensive map, if only to remind us of its neglect.

Central to any discussion of content is the unit of instructional activity that serves as the starting point for analyses of teaching. Is it the individual interchange between student(s) and teacher, the episode (e.g., quelling a particular behavioral disturbance, or explaining a new concept), the lesson (say, a 20-minute reading group session), the unit (e.g., a six-day sequence on the Age of Jackson in a U.S. history course), the semester course, or the year of work? If it is a longer analytic unit, is it assumed to be decomposable into an aggregation of discrete interchanges or episodes, or is it dealt with as a totality in itself? These are certainly critical choices for the researcher. In addition, conceptions of content itself are important. These include those deriving from philosophers of education (e.g., the distinction between substantive and syntactic structures [Schwab, 1962/1978]), from instructional psychologists (e.g., facts, con-

cepts, principles, cognitive strategies), or from cognitive psychologists (schemata, scripts, metacognitions, etc.).

Finally, the perspective taken by the research can be that of an outside observer attempting to discover the lawful relationships among the observable features, or the emphasis can be on discovering the meanings constructed by the participants as they attempt to make sense of the circumstances they both encounter and create. These two aspects are sometimes called the positivistic and the interpretive, or the *etic* and the *emic* (following the tradition in linguistics of distinguishing between phon*etic* and phon*emic* analyses).

The drawing of Figure 1.2 attempts to portray the relationships among these units of inquiry. Almost all research on teaching examines the relationships among features, be they capacities, actions, or thoughts as evidenced by the participants conceptualized in some fashion. Research programs differ in the particular features chosen for analysis, the direction of causality implied by the discussion (e.g., teacher → student; students → teacher; students ↔ teacher, reflexively or interactively caused joint behavior of students and teacher), the agendas to which they attend, the level of aggregation or context at which relationships are sought, and the perspective taken with respect to the activities or experiences of the participants.

Thus, for example, research in the tradition of teacher characteristics typically examined the relationships between indicators of teacher capacities (e.g., teacher test scores, years of experience, personality measures) and of student capacities (e.g., achievement test scores, attitudes toward self or school). At other times, teacher capacities were related to student actions (e.g., student ratings of course satisfaction).

The process–product tradition studies the relationships of teaching performance and subsequent student capacities. The Academic Learning Time program relates teaching performance to student actions, as inferred from the time allocations made by students. The student mediation program focuses on student thoughts and feelings, usually in relation to teacher actions and subsequent student actions or capacities. The teacher cognition program examines the relationships of teacher thought to teacher action (e.g., studies of judgment policies and teachers' assignments of pupils to reading groups). The classroom ecology program examines the reflexive influences of teacher and student actions, frequently illuminated by aspects of thought. Different patterns of interaction may subsequently be related to changes in students' capacities.

The study of teaching usually involves coming to understand the relationships, in the forms of causes or reasons, among these different aspects of teaching and learning. But such a model alone does not portray those research efforts. Different research programs for the study of teaching select different parts of the map to define the phenomena for their inquiries. There are also other sorts of choices that determine the manner in which research on teaching is conducted. These include predilections for qualitative as against quantitative research methods, disciplinary or interdisciplinary orientation, preference for the characterization of behavior as against the representation of thought — behaviorism versus mentalism, to use somewhat older terms — and, most broadly, the conception of one's craft as a science in search of laws or as an exercise of interpretation in search or meanings.

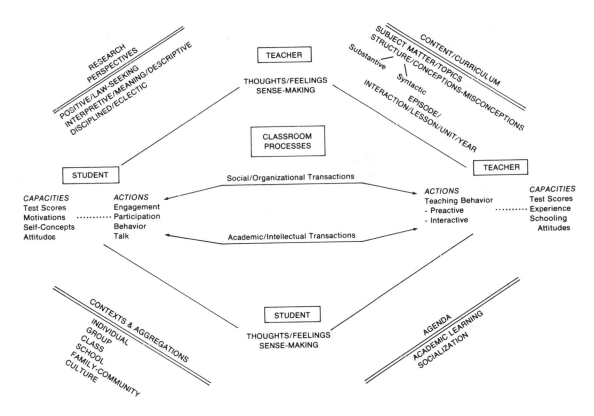

Fig. 1.2. Synoptic map of research on teaching.

The Major Research Programs

In the sections that follow, the major research programs that organize the bulk of research on teaching will be presented, described, analyzed, contrasted, and criticized. It will not be the purpose of this chapter to review the literature of each program, or even to summarize its central findings fully. Indeed, the many chapters which follow in this handbook are devoted to this demanding task. As each program is presented, I shall attempt to outline its central organizing questions, the topics and paths in the synoptic model it occupies, the prototypical designs and methods it employs, and the types of findings it generates.

I shall emphasize in particular the manner in which research programs have developed in response and reaction to other programs. Quite typically, new research programs did not develop as alternative ways to accomplish the research objectives of existing programs. Instead, investigators reacted against particular aspects of an existing program — the report of findings that were not believable, the extrapolation to policies that were ideologically or politically unacceptable, the use of methods that were considered questionable. This conception of the research-on-teaching field as a Great Conversation, an ongoing dialogue among investigators committed to understanding and improving teaching, is central to the discussion that follows.

We will begin with the central and most active program in research on teaching, process–product research, followed by its close cousin, albeit occasional critic, the program of research on academic learning time. We will see how the student mediation program occupies a position midway between the perspectives of process–product research and studies of classroom processes as ecological systems or as language communities. The study of teacher cognition will be examined in parallel to examinations of pupil cognition in several programs. We turn first to process–product research.

Process–Product Research

Easily the most vigorous and productive of the programs of research on teaching during the past decade has been the teaching effectiveness approach, also known as the process–product program in the terminology of Mitzel (1960) and of Dunkin and Biddle (1974). Its key contributors have been Gage (1978), Soar (e.g., Soar & Soar, 1979), Brophy (e.g., 1983), Evertson, Emmer (e.g., Evertson, Emmer, Sanford, & Clements, 1983), Bennett (e.g., Bennett, Jordan, Long, & Wade, 1976), Good (e.g., 1979), Stallings (e.g., Stallings & Kaskowitz, 1974), Kounin (e.g., 1970), and others, with periodic review papers by Rosenshine (e.g., 1983) serving to consolidate the body of work into conceptions of direct instruction or, more recently, active teaching (Good, Grouws, & Ebmeier, 1983). Work in this program is reviewed by Brophy and Good, Good and Brophy, and by Rosenshine and Stevens, all in this volume. Those studies dealing predominantly with classroom management are discussed by Doyle, also in this volume. The basic tenets of process–product research were described by Anderson, Evertson, and Brophy (1979)

...to define relationships between what teachers do in the classroom (the processes of teaching) and what happens to their students (the products of learning). One product that has received much attention is achievement in the basic skills. ... Research in this tradition assumes that greater knowledge of such relationships will lead to improved instruction: once effective instruction is described, then supposedly programs can be designed to promote those effective practices. (p. 193)

In a similar fashion, McDonald and Elias (1976) observed:

A major goal was to estimate the effects of teachers' actions or teaching performances on pupil learning. The assumption was made that differences among teachers in how they organize instruction, in the methods and materials they use, and in how they interact with pupils would have different effects on how much children learned. ... The major analyses of this study were of the relations of the scores representing differences in teaching performances to differences in pupil learning. (p. 6)

The teaching effectiveness studies are typically conducted in existing classrooms that function normally during the periods of observation (the term "naturalistic" is used, though "natural" is a more accurate description.) Observers ordinarily use categorical observation scales, typically of the "low inference" variety (tallying the occurrence of observable events rather than judging or evaluating the quality of observed activities, which would be deemed "high inference") and most often spread a set of observation occasions (as few as four to as many as twenty) across most of the school year.

The units of analysis are generally the school day (or whatever portion of the day constituted the observation period) and the actions of the teacher and students. These actions can be treated alone (frequency of teacher asking higher-order questions; incidence of calling on pupils in a predetermined order) or as chains or sequences of teacher action → pupil response → teacher reaction (e.g., higher-order question → correct pupil response of particular sort → teacher praise). The subsequent analyses nearly always disaggregate the observed classroom processes into the categories employed in the observation instrument (or composites constructed subsequently) and then combine those observations across observational days and across all teachers observed. Thus, incidents of teacher questioning or praise in Classroom A will be aggregated across all *n* days of observation in that classroom to investigate the effectiveness of such questioning, as well as combine with the results for such questioning observed in all other teachers.

In contrast to some other research programs, the effectiveness of teaching is seen as attributable to combinations of discrete and observable teaching performances per se, operating relatively independent of time and place. Scholars in this tradition regularly speak of controlling for "context variables." These are usually fairly static categories like subject matter, age and sex of students, ability levels of students, type of school, and so forth. Data from early in an observational hour are combined with data from late on the same occasion. Data from fall may be combined with data from spring. Data from a unit on natural selection combines with data from a unit on the circulation of the blood. All these are seen as instances of teaching, an activity that transcends both individual teachers and specific situations.

It is not surprising that one of the leading figures in this tradition, N. L. Gage (1978), advocates the "meta-analysis" of research findings from process–product studies to discover more stable relationships between teaching behavior and pupil performance. In quest for a mode of analysis that would provide better-grounded inferences regarding the relationships of teaching and achievement than can be gleaned from single studies examined individually, he urges

...converting the exact probability value of the result of any single study into a value of the statistic called chi square. Then the values of chi square are summed over studies, and the significance, or probability, of the sum is determined. In essence, the technique provides an estimate of the statistical significance, or "non-chanceness," of the whole cluster of independent findings that are considered by the research reviewer to deal with a specified process variable, or aspect of teacher behavior or teaching method. (Gage, 1978, p. 29)

Meta-analysis thus serves as the cross-investigation equivalent of the logic of process–product research itself. We are urged to sum statistics across studies, just as we have summed the values of individual teachers' behavior across both situations and the observed behavior of other teachers. There is assumed to be an underlying "true score" for the relationship between a given teacher behavior and a pupil outcome measure. There is a parameter or law which can be estimated. The problem is to get beyond the limitations of particular teachers, particular classrooms, particular studies to a more stable generalization.

What accounts for the vigor of the process-product research program? Why have its central constructs — teacher effectiveness, direct instruction, active teaching, time-on-task — been so readily accepted and applied by practitioners and policy makers? After many decades during which the study of teaching and learning *in vivo* (rather than in the laboratory) was either pursued only by evaluators (e.g., the classroom observations of the Eight-Year Study) or essentially ignored, why did it rise phoenix-like from the ashes of educational research? But why, especially, has this particular school of thought gained such dominance in the field?

The process-product research program has had many virtues. First, the approach was responsive to the important topics being discussed in the Great Conversation. Within educational policy circles, the Coleman Report (Coleman, et al., 1966) had created a sensation, especially with its apparent claim that teachers, or more accurately variations among teachers, do not make a difference in school achievement. But Coleman's findings were based on a classic input-output production function analysis of schools and included no data on the actual teaching events of classroom life. A number of classroom researchers (whose work was summarized by Good, Biddle, & Brophy, 1975) were motivated to study teacher effectiveness to provide a more stringent test of Coleman's assertion. One of the most significant sets of findings from process-product research on teaching entailed the demonstration that teachers *did* make a difference. Variations in teacher behavior were found to be systematically related to variations in student achievement, a finding that was only possible from a research design relating teaching *processes* to student *products*.

Another central topic in the late 60s was teacher expectations, an interest that resulted from the publication of the provocative and controversial study *Pygmalion in the Classroom*

(Rosenthal & Jacobson 1968). Without directly documenting teacher behavior, the authors claimed that teachers were subtly communicating their expectations to pupils through patterns of praise, questioning, tones of voice, and opportunities to learn. Was there really an expectation effect? Did teachers act differently toward students for whom they held different expectations? Toward children of different gender or race? Were such differences, if detected, related systematically to variations in student performance? These types of research questions demanded meticulous descriptions of teacher behavior in relation to individual students. In turn, those descriptions could be related to student characteristics and to eventual student achievement as well. They were a significant impetus for the development of process–product research (Brophy & Good, 1974). Thus, this form of research first gained credence because of its value in dealing with major questions addressed by educators in relation to the effectiveness of teachers and the power of their expectations.

Second, process–product research was consistent with a strong existing research tradition—applied behavioristic psychology and its task-analytic, training tradition wherein the decomposition of complex tasks into their components followed by the assessment and retraining of individuals on the components themselves had a demonstrably successful track record (e.g., Glaser, 1962; Gagné, 1970). If the decomposition of a complex skill worked for radar technicians, aircraft mechanics, second-language learners, and other skilled performers, why not for teachers? The metaphor of teaching as skill, or bundle of skills, deployed across variations in setting, was both compelling and well understood within the educational research and practice communities.

Third, unlike the laboratory tradition for the study of learning, this program of research was carried out in naturally occurring classrooms. The teachers who were observed were performing normally, carrying out their duties in the natural context of instruction. Therefore, the generalizations about teaching effectiveness were not based on a "test-tube" classroom, but on the real thing. It would be impossible to claim that the findings could not be applied because such behavior was impractical. Indeed, the behavior has already been observed in typical classrooms with enough frequency to have been identified as effective or ineffective.

Fourth, the implications of the research program for practice and policy were frequently seen as straightforward. Those who read the research often saw it as having clear implications for practice and policy. The research frequently identifies large numbers of teacher behaviors, discrete variables that were correlated with student outcomes and that defined the key elements of teaching effectiveness. These, in turn, lent themselves to lists of "teachers should" statements that were handy to those who wished to prescribe or mandate specific teaching policies for the improvement of schools. Moreover, the work was tied to an indicator that both policy makers and laypersons took most seriously as a sign of how schoolchildren were doing: standardized achievement tests.

The sign rapidly evolved into the signified, the indicator into the end in itself. The raising of test scores became a goal of instruction. Teaching performances that were observable could both be evaluated and serve as the basis for training and staff development. The competency-based teacher education movement flourished energetically for several years, and though on the wane in schools of education is reemerging at the state level in programs for beginning teachers and/or for evaluating teachers for certification, tenure, or merit increases. This dual advantage of ready association with observable results for pupils and the appearance of clear implications for evaluation, training, and policy, made the process–product approach attractive indeed. Although a number of process–product researchers actively opposed the oversimplification of their findings, warning against the premature application of results, others seemed to encourage the development of teacher education or evaluation systems that employed the findings of their studies as a framework for assessing teacher quality. Process-product researchers were surely not alone in seeing their work so used. The work on Academic Learning Time lent itself even more readily to naive misuse by policy makers, whose prescriptions of "more time-on-task," longer school days, and extended school years would typically cite research as the basis for their recommendations.

Finally, the approach worked. The studies conducted under its programmatic direction accomplished the sorts of important aims outlined for them. Teachers who consistently were associated with higher achievement gains tended to behave differently from those who were not. The data accumulated across correlational studies and survived experimental field tests. Teachers seemed capable of learning to perform in the manners suggested by the research program and the performances tended to produce higher achievement among their pupils. Within the limits of whatever activities standardized achievement tests were measuring, the program was palpably successful. Not only were the proposed interventions effective, they were typically acceptable and credible to experienced teachers. The dictates of direct instruction or the principles of active teaching made sense to most teachers, at least to those not ideologically wedded to images of open classrooms and progressive education. Along with conceptions of "time-on-task" and the heavy emphasis on strong teacher control and management, the program produced scientific support for approaches to instruction with which the majority of teachers, administrators, and parents felt intuitively and professionally comfortable.

The timing of the research program was also fortunate, coming as it did during the national reaction against the laissez-faire character of the youth culture during the late 1960s and early 1970s. The concern over test-score declines, adolescent misbehavior, and poor school discipline produced an emphasis on a return to the basics, both in behavior and in curriculum. The educational climate was ripe for a return to traditional values —back to basics, to discipline, to phonetics, to computation, to penmanship, to homework, to teachers in charge of kids, and principals in charge of their schools, to less down-time and more time-on-task—in short, back to an image of schooling in which there was less question about who was in charge and what was to be learned.

The contrast to the late 1950s is fascinating, for although the threat of Russian science was a significant goad to national educational and curriculum reform, the emphasis on beefing up the subject matter was matched with strong concern for inquiry, discovery, and problem solving, for student-initiated activities and divergent thinking, for ascending the heights of Bloom's taxonomy. The opinion leaders were less concerned with the basics than with those more elevated understandings that are needed to be scientifically literate and competitive. The process–product work conducted at the time, Flanders's (1970) pioneering efforts studying classroom interaction with categorical observation instruments, did not lead to the conclusion that direct instruction was best. In fact, Flanders had concluded that "indirect teaching" was the most effective approach to classroom instruction.

(An interesting footnote may be added here. Barr and Dreeben (1978) reanalyzed Flanders's tables because of the apparent contradiction between his earlier findings and those of the process–product researchers of the 1970s. While this discrepancy could certainly have been another example of Cronbach's (1975) "decade-by-treatment interactions," a simpler explanation was offered. Flanders defined his "indirect teaching" score as a ratio between indirect and direct teaching. Barr and Dreeben found that those teachers who had the highest ratio also displayed the largest *amount* of teaching overall. They not only did more indirect teaching. They simply did more teaching. Therefore, the apparent contradiction melted away.)

The major findings from the teaching effectiveness literature produced in the process–product program are summarized by Brophy and Good (this volume). The program of research contains many variants. Most of the research is descriptive and correlational, with several field experiments in recent years. In some cases, teachers are preselected as unusually effective based on analysis of their class achievements during the previous one to three years. In other cases, effectiveness is measured only after the fact by the performance of students at the end of the year, and then retrospectively correlated with each of the observational categories. In some cases, the frequency of types of teacher behavior is tallied without regard to the particular pupils who were targets for the behavior. In other studies, differences in the behavior of the same teacher vis-à-vis individual pupils are examined.

Overall, the findings take the form of propositions describing those forms of teacher behavior that are associated with gains in student performance, often conditioned on grade level and subject matter. That aspect of teacher behavior usually described is either classroom management behavior (responses to misbehavior, allocating of turns, establishment of rules) or generic instructional behavior (use of lower- or higher-order questions, frequency of praise or criticism [treated as feedback], wait-time), rather than behavior describing the *substantive* subject-specific content of instruction (e.g., choice of examples, sources of metaphors, type of subtraction algorithm employed, reading comprehension strategy demonstrated and explained, and the like).

As time passes, the process–product program seems surprisingly to be losing intellectual vigor within the research community. Though at the levels of practice and policy it remains the most widely used and cited body of work (exemplified especially by the impressive studies of direct instruction or active classroom teaching, e.g., Good, Grouws, & Ebmeier, 1983, and those of classroom management, e.g., Emmer, Evertson, & Anderson, 1980), the other research programs to be described in this chapter have gained the interest and investment of the newer generation of scholars on teaching. Why has this been the case?

There are several reasons to consider. First, the program has succeeded relative to its own goals. So often when a program succeeds, that very success leads critics to consider goals beyond those envisaged by the program and to criticize the program for failing to accomplish them. The program's leaders understandably respond with great frustration, since their success in accomplishing their proposed goals is inadequately acknowledged when the criticisms grow most strident. Moreover, the funds needed to conduct large-scale process–product research have diminished considerably.

Second, while the claim could be made that the program studied naturally occurring behavior and therefore met the ultimate reality tests, in principle, the manner in which individual behavioral elements were aggregated into patterns or styles of teaching performance did not necessarily meet this criterion. Gage (1978), explains the distinction between styles as naturally occurring patterns and styles as composites in the following passage:

> Before we proceed, we should note the difference between two methods of research. The first compares intact patterns of teaching, such as direct and open styles. This method studies the relationship between these patterns of teaching and what pupils learn. The second method deals with many specific dimensions, or variables, of teaching styles or methods. Here the investigators study the relationships between each of hundreds of variables within various teaching styles and what pupils learn. *From the hundreds of correlations, especially the significant ones, the investigators and reviewers then synthesize the style or pattern of teaching that seems to be associated with desirable kinds of pupil achievement and attitude.* (p. 31; italics added).

Thus the bulk of process–product research, while based on naturally occurring correlations, defined effective teaching through an act of synthesis by the investigator or reviewer, in which the individual behaviors associated with desirable pupil performance were aggregated into a new composite. There was little evidence that any observed teacher had ever performed in the classroom congruent with the collective pattern of the composite.

A most important development in this program was the series of field experiments in which the composites were translated into experimental teacher training treatments. Studies such as Anderson, Evertson and Brophy (1979), or Good, Grouws, and Ebmeier (1983), as summarized and interpreted by Gage and Giaconia (1981), and Gage (in press) reported on naturalistic field experiments in which teachers who had been trained using the composites typically produced higher achievement gains among their students than did their control counterparts. Even in these cases, however, it was typically found that the teachers in the experimental treatments did not always engage in the "desired" behaviors more frequently than did their control counterparts. Moreover, not all the trained behaviors continued to correlate with the student achievement criteria in the field experiments. This further suggests that all the elements in the composite were not needed for effective performance. Although Gage and Giaconia (1981) demonstrated a relationship between degree of implementation and degree of association with performance, what tended to remain unexplained was *why* particular combinations of teacher behavior led to gain and others did not, a question of theory. And this question leads to the most serious problems of process-product research.

A third, and most important reason for the erosion of the process-product program was its unabashedly empirical and nontheoretical tenor. Even as it moved to experimental treatments, the emphasis was pragmatically on what worked, rather than on why it worked. Causes were sought in behaviors, not in theoretically meaningful mechanisms or explanations. The perspective was that of engineering rather than that of science, or even of history. But, paraphrasing Aristotle, man (at least the non-Skinnerian among the scholarly species) is a theoretical animal. Humans seek to identify mechanisms or processes that will *explain why* stimuli elicit responses, why behaviors are associated with performances, and most compellingly, why some do under some circumstances and not under others. Even experiments that may help somewhat in distinguishing causes from co-occurrences do not necessarily explain. And the best scientific theory is not necessarily the one that predicts or controls best, but indeed that which renders the most comprehensive and compelling account consistent with the available evidence (Toulmin, 1961).

It is thus no surprise that the critics who found the process-product program wanting did so on theoretical grounds, not because it failed to yield significant correlations or *F* ratios. The problems associated with an absence of explanatory theory had been anticipated by Dunkin and Biddle (1974, e.g., pp. 428-430). Nearly a decade later, they were acknowledged by leaders in the process-product tradition, such as Good et al. (1983). Within the broad purview of process-product psychologists, critics typically sought to develop programs in which explanatory mediating variables were posited to intervene between teacher behavior and pupil performance, in the form of process → mediator → product. These mediators took several forms, which will be discussed thoroughly in the sections to follow.

The earliest was the Beginning Teacher Evaluation Study (BTES) search for the mechanism that would explain why direct instruction worked (Fisher et al., 1978). Their solution, guided by John Carroll's (1963) model of school learning, was *allocated time* and *task engagement*. They shifted the emphasis from the activities of teachers as causes to the activities of pupils as explanations, interpreting the latter as the intervening events that accounted for what direct instruction could accomplish that other forms of teaching (or nonteaching) did not. This research program will be discussed in the section that follows.

The student mediation program also sought for a mechanism of explanation, and its proponents were not satisfied with time as a mediator. What were pupils doing with that time? How were they engaged? Engaged in what? These scholars drew from several neighboring fields to guide their work. Some took the information-processing perspectives of cognitive science and examined the ways in which pupils used time to reduce the complexity and make sense of the curriculum content presented. The active model of the learner as assimilator, as transformer, as apprehender of knowledge-as-presented (echoing Herbart's conception of the apperceptive mass) was applied to the classroom and the image began to develop of an active

learner interacting with active teaching. What sense do pupils make of different forms of instruction? Rowe's (1974) work on wait-time took on renewed significance as the complex forms of information processing necessary for students to transform instruction were studied.

Other student mediation scholars sought their explanations not from cognitive psychology, but from social psychology and sociology, from the traditions of W. I. Thomas's "definition of the situation" as cloaked either in self-concept theory or, more recently, in Becker, Geer and Hughes's (1968) metaphor of the "performance-grade exchange." They directed the attention of the research community away from a focus on the classroom as a site for cognitive teaching and learning, as well as from traditional notions of pedagogy. Instead they looked at the classroom as a stage on which roles were played and the pupil's goals were to perform in ways that attracted good grades, high status, and minimum hassle. These perspectives from sociology served to connect the work on student mediation to research in the sociolinguistic and ethnographic traditions as well.

In their still-formidable work entitled *The Study of Teaching*, Dunkin and Biddle (1974) observed that while the process-product research had already been the most fruitful of the approaches reviewed (and this before the program's effort had really peaked), two aspects of that work were already perceptibly problematic. These were the continuing reliance on standardized achievement tests as the ultimate criterion of effectiveness and the overly molecular units of classroom analysis.

With respect to the measurement of achievement, they commented:

> This is not only an insensitive variable, but it may be offmark for our purposes. Consider the finding that teacher use of higher cognitive demand leads to lower pupil achievement. It seems possible to us that lower cognitive demand is more efficient for putting across facts, while higher cognitive demand encourages independence of thought. The latter, of course, is not measured by standardized achievement tests. Hypotheses of this sort cannot be tested until more sensitive product criteria are developed and used in research on teaching. (p. 409)

Their views of the units of analysis were also critical:

> It appears to us that any meaningful analysis of teaching must involve sequential elements. Indeed, perhaps *the greatest single flaw* [italics added] in much of the research we have reviewed is the persistent assumption that appears to underlie much of it — that teaching can somehow be reduced to a scalar value that can be indicated by a frequency of occurrence for some teaching behavior. We suspect, with Taba, that this simply is not true. Rather, effective teaching must consist of sequences of presentations that are planned carefully and conducted sensitively. Moreover, we find the sequential concepts we have reviewed to be insightful, exciting, suggestive. ... [But] even the clearest discussions of sequence are couched in murky, intuitive, analogistic phrases suggesting that investigators are still groping toward solutions to these complex problems. Thus, we can find relatively little evidence to back up our belief that the real breakthroughs in research on teaching should involve sequence. (ibid., p. 353)

Thus the volume that has served as the most powerful framer of the questions for the process-product research program via its comprehensive presage-context-process-product model found serious problems in the manner in which both processes and products are characterized. It may be recalled that Gage recognized similar limitations 10 years earlier. In spite of these misgivings, the process-product program has been conducted apace during the intervening years. Nevertheless, the possibility that the truncated, molecular conceptions of process fit uniquely well with the limited measures of product — thus inventing a classroom reality that "works" only within the confines of this research program — is an issue worth pondering.

As we shall see, many of the research programs that follow were stimulated by the desire to repair some flaw in the process-product paradigm, or to attend to phenomena ignored or invisible to its scholars. However, in contrast to the conception of paradigm shifts and scientific revolutions found in Kuhn, these more recent approaches rarely attend to everything treated in the process-product work *or* the missing aspect of teaching they have identified. Some of the newer approaches represent supplementary programs that examine particular aspects of teaching or learning in great detail while often themselves ignoring features of teaching highlighted in process-product work. Others, such as the classroom ethnographers, take a totally different perspective on teaching, but in so doing also lose sight of many aspects of the phenomenon of teaching highlighted in the older paradigm, As Merton (1975) led us to anticipate, the alternative research programs do not supplant one another so much as provide opportunities to examine particular aspects of teaching more closely. Each paradigm highlights a particular neighborhood on the synoptic map, leaving other territories dark and unexplored. No one has all the lines in the Great Conversation.

Time and Learning

Even as the process-product program was picking up speed in the early 1970s, a most significant variation on that program, dedicated to identifying the key mediators of teacher behavior in the activities of pupils, was initiated. The research staff of the Far West Regional Educational Laboratory was conducting the third phase of the Beginning Teacher Evaluation Study (BTES). Under the leadership of David Berliner, Charles Fisher, Leonard Cahen, and their colleagues, they were seeking an indicator of teacher effectiveness they could locate in the observable performance of pupils without waiting for end-of-year achievement tests. They were motivated to find such an indicator for two reasons. They wished to transfer the attention of the research-on-teaching community from concern for teacher behavior alone to more balanced consideration of the coordinate and immediate pupil responses to teaching. In addition, they felt that variations in some pupil indicator would provide a more sensitive estimate of the effects of teaching than the more distal product of achievement-test performance.

Consistent with our view that the field of research on teaching should be viewed as an ongoing dialogue or conversation among scholars, the starting point for their analysis was a critique of the adequacy of the logic of the process-product program. Note that their critique did not rest on a failure of the program's empirical findings nor on an empirical anomaly. In Berliner's (1979) words:

The investigators [in BTES] became increasingly dissatisfied with the process-product approach since it appeared that certain illogical elements were inherent in the design of a process-product study of classroom teaching. For example, how could the number or percentage of teacher verbal communications coded as praise statements in November influence results on achievement test items given in May? ... How could anyone expect to discover a relationship between a variable such as time spent lecturing on ecology and achievement test items that measure dictionary usage? The latter occurs when investigators use instruments that code teacher behavior of various sorts and correlate that behavior with broad-spectrum tests of reading achievement.

At first it appeared that correlational approaches using the process-product research paradigm were inherently deficient. Some of our colleagues argued that only by recourse to true experiments could the situation be remedied. But true experimental designs used in the investigation of teaching and learning in classrooms also have certain flaws. The most serious of these are that such designs do not reflect the complexities of the classroom, with its myriad interactions; they do not reflect the dynamic quality of the classroom, with its ever-changing events; nor can they, typically, develop an appropriate time perspective since the acquisition of knowledge in the classroom is best conceived of as a multiyear process. Thus, experimental designs that reflect the process-product framework often suffer from problems of ecological validity.

If correlational studies were to be conducted in natural classroom environments, which would appear to give them more potential external validity, then the logical and hypothetical causal flow of events in the process-product model needed to be modified. Researchers on the Beginning Teacher Evaluation Study proposed a simple modification to the process-product approach to the study of classroom learning. The modification is based on the belief that what a teacher does at any one moment while working in a circumscribed content area affects a student primarily at only that particular moment and in that particular content area. The link between teacher behavior and student achievement is, therefore, the ongoing student behavior in the classroom learning situation. The logic continues in this way. What a teacher does to foster learning in a particular content area becomes important only if a student is engaged with *appropriate* curriculum content. Appropriate curriculum content is defined as content that is logically related to the criterion and is at an easy level of difficulty for a particular student. ... The variable used in BTES research is the accrued engaged time in a particular content area using materials that are not difficult for the student. This complex variable is called Academic Learning Time (ALT). ...

In this conception of research on teaching, the content area the student is working on must be specified precisely, the task engagement of the student must be judged, the level of the difficulty of the task must be rated, and time must be measured. The constructed variable of ALT, then, stands between measures of teaching and measures of student achievement. (pp. 122–125)

Berliner locates the BTES research on Academic Learning Time at the intersection of three research programs: the process-product tradition of research on teaching; the work of Carroll (1963), of Bloom (1968; 1976), and of Harnischfeger and Wiley (1976), all deriving from Carroll's model of school learning; and the literature of instructional design, especially programed instruction, with its concern for the control of error rates.

The decision to take the conception of error control from the field of instructional design led to the most significant weakness in the program. It is certainly true that error control is important in skill acquisition. Low error rates are particularly important because of the nature of standardized achievement tests as criteria. The observation that high error rates are associated with poor performance can be nearly tautological. The tasks of classroom life are themselves a sample of the same universe of questions from which are drawn the items of the standardized tests. In that sense, classroom discourse is a series of achievement tests in dialogue or in seatwork. (In fact, numerous studies have demonstrated that most teaching involves very little explicit instruction by the teacher. Instead, assignments are distributed and subsequent student work is monitored.) The youngster with high error rates is not simply learning less because of his errors. His errors are a signal that he is learning less. Moreover, the estimation of task difficulty has become one of the most troublesome in the ALT research program, and has generally been given far less attention in both the research and policy literatures than has the conception of academically engaged time.

In this work as well, the extent to which the significance of relationships is ultimately tethered to performance on standardized achievement tests remains troubling. At least two recent studies, by Armbruster, Stevens, and Rosenshine (1977) at the Center for the Study of Reading, and by Freeman et al. (1983) at the Institute for Research on Teaching, have demonstrated the extent of the mismatch between what is taught in schools and what is measured on standardized tests. Doyle (1983) summarized the results of the study by Armbruster et al. thus:

> They found that the overlap between the texts and the standardized tests was low. The reading curricula tended to emphasize "comprehension skills that appear to require inference, interpretation, identification of relationships, and synthesis." ... The tests, on the other hand, tended to focus on "factual items entailing locating information in the presented text." (p. 181)

Given the demonstrated mismatch between the texts of instruction and the tests of achievement, will curricular relevance within the ALT program be defined by correspondence with instructional goals and materials, or by correlation with test-measured long-term outcomes? The answer is significant, not only for the ALT program, but for all other programs that employ outcome measures in their work.

Most important in the theoretical aspect of this work is the influence of Carroll's model of school learning and its choice of *time* as the central construct for the teaching–learning transaction. Carroll's model posits five variables which, in their direct effects and interactions, account for the amount learned on particular school tasks. Three of these constructs describe attributes of the learner—ability, aptitude, and perseverance. Two constructs describe attributes of the instruction—opportunity to learn and quality of instruction. Most important, the values of three of the variables can be expressed as units of time. Thus, *aptitude* is defined as the amount of time needed by a learner to achieve mastery of a particular school task. *Opportunity* to learn is defined as the amount of time provided by the teacher for the learning of a particular task by a particular student. *Perseverance*, the student analogue of opportunity, is the amount of time a learner devotes to the job of mastering the task in question.

The other two constructs, ability and quality of instruction, are defined in more qualitative terms. *Ability* describes the individual's mode or style of learning relative to the task at hand. *Quality of instruction*, so central to any research on teaching, remains frustratingly elusive. It represents the extent to which the instruction provided adequately matches the character of the student's ability. Berliner's treatment of task difficulty appears to be an indirect way of representing this important concept of instructional quality. Certainly the discussion of curriculum-appropriate tasks is also relevant to this notion. But the continuing difficulty among both process–product investigators and the ALT proponents in dealing adequately with the issues of substantive instructional quality remains a nagging weakness in these research programs. In fact, as we shall see in the course of this chapter, it is the common flaw in all the extant programs of research on teaching.

Though it was initiated by a critique of the process–product program, we can see that the ALT program itself continues to employ many of its predecessor's characteristic tactics and distinctions. It is concerned with the relationships among *variables*, it focuses on individual students (rather than the collectivity of the classroom) as units of analysis, its conception of student learning remains a rather passive one (compared to the active processing view of contemporary cognitive psychology or the ethnography of communication), and it continues the disaggregation of the events of classroom life. That is, despite Berliner's eloquent attack on the process–product paradigm's inability to capture the "complexities of the classroom, with its myriad interactions" and "the dynamic quality of the classroom, with its ever-changing events," the ALT program as well falls short of that richness. ALT remains a more explanation-oriented, mediational variant of process–product research. It certainly has forsaken its parent's home in some significant ways, but it remains an unmistakable member of the extended family. Gage (1978) had criticized the ALT emphasis on engaged time with the observation that time is an empty vessel. Unless a better account could be rendered of how that time was being used by students, the addition of another layer of variables could hardly make the claim of theoretical progress. But the BTES's identification of the need to fill the gap between teaching and academic achievement with a representation of how and what students were processing served to formulate the next critical task for the field of research on teaching—a task most directly addressed by those who labor in the research program we call the student mediation of instruction, to which we now turn.

Pupil Cognition and the Mediation of Teaching

The Academic Learning Time research program shifted the emphasis of researchers away from the study of relationships between the actions of the teacher and the distant outcomes of pupil achievement. Its scholars brought attention to the inferred thought processes of the pupils themselves. Yet, consistent with the traditions of psychological behaviorism, the ALT program relied wholly on observed teacher and student behavior, and on the characteristics of task performance, as the bases for these inferences.

In the student mediation programs, reviewed by Wittrock in this volume, we encounter for the first time the influence of several new perspectives on the study of teaching. From within psychology, the effect of the cognitive revolution can be observed, in particular studies of social cognition. We also can detect influences from the psychology of personality and the study of self-concept. From other disciplines, we observe the influence of sociology, both in theoretical formulation and in choice of methods. We shall see that this research program comprises the potential bridge between the traditional quantitative psychological perspectives of the process–product and ALT approaches and the predominantly qualitative strategies of classroom ecology research, with its strong links to sociolinguistics and ethnography.

The overriding questions for those who pursue the student mediation program are "How do students make sense of the instruction they encounter in the classroom? What are the immediate and intermediate-term processes engendered in students by teaching?" It should be recalled that the concept of mediation arose out of the stimulus–response (S–R) paradigm in psychology as learning theorists like Tolman and Osgood attempted to understand what processes mediated between the S and the R. Similarly, the fundamental process of teaching is assumed in process–product research to be a link between teacher behavior and eventual student performance. When you attend to the possibility that the action is not direct, that it is not im-mediate, not unmediated, you then posit an intervening process through which the initial cause is transformed into its eventually observed effect. For the time-on-task researcher, Academic Learning Time serves as the proxy for such an intervening process. For those who seek to fill the "empty vessel" of time with more descriptive accounts of what is happening in the minds of learners between the input of instruction and the output of achievement (hence, the *mediating* processes that occupy that middle ground), a fuller account is needed. A proxy will not do. A direct account of the mediating mechanisms is the goal of research.

In the pupil mediation literature, two sources for these accounts can be identified. Mehan (1979) has observed that the complexity of classroom life for students is twofold. "Participation in classroom lessons involves the integration of academic knowledge and social or interactional knowledge" (p. 34). These two kinds of accomplishment are the topics of research on the social mediation and the intellectual mediation of classroom life, respectively. The first, and thus far the more popular, emerges from the sociological traditions in which classroom work is seen as an exchange of performance for grades (Becker et al., 1968) or some equivalent underlying process not immediately obvious to the observer who views classroom settings as occasions for teaching and learning. This approach to analysis emerges, at least in part, from the distinction between manifest and latent functions, or between anticipated and unanticipated consequences, both distinctions presented by Merton to explain some of the complexities of social processes. In these analyses, the sociologist is asked to peer beneath the apparent surface meanings and purposes of participants in a social setting to discern the underlying processes, goals, and perspectives. This tradition has been the source for the important efforts regarding the "hidden curriculum" of the school and classroom, wherein what is hidden are precisely those latent features not explicitly treated in the apparent curriculum.

One example of such work is a study by L. Anderson (1984). She examines the ways in which primary-grade children cope with seatwork, that ubiquitous element in the life of schoolchildren. Whereas the process–product researcher would have correlated frequency of seatwork (or proportion of classroom time spent in seatwork) with student achievement, and the Academic Learning Time scholar would have observed the proportion of seatwork time during which the student was apparently engaged along with the degree of difficulty of the tasks with which the student was working, Anderson proceeds to record student comments to themselves and to classmates during assignments and to interview the students about their assignments after observing them at work. Her focus is on what the students are thinking and feeling as they work on their tasks, on what these phenomena reveal about the mediation of instruction by the students.

"There! I didn't understand that, but I got it done," offers one 6-year-old. "I'm almost done—just two more," or "How far are you?" are typical of the most frequently overheard student exchanges, rather than "What answer did you get?" In general, Anderson remarks on the frequency with which the essential goal of the students is to complete an assignment rather than to comprehend a task. They are exchanging performance for evaluation and approval.

She also detects differences between low and high achievers in the strategies employed to complete the work. Low-achieving students are observed to employ any strategy available to complete an assignment whether or not the completed page makes sense. They do not appear to have developed the metacognitive strategies needed to identify whether their work is correct. Confusion is such a constant companion during seatwork that they appear to assume that confusion is supposed to accompany all academic work. They rarely seek help to allay the difficulty. In contrast, when high-achieving students get confused, they treat that state as problematic and seek help immediately.

Anderson's study exemplifies both the strengths and weaknesses of work on student mediation. Characterization of student thought processes and motivations surrounding school tasks is accomplished with a sensitivity unavailable in other research programs. But trade-offs are necessary. The tasks themselves are not carefully described. We get too little sense of how variations among tasks, or among forms of teaching, relate to differences in how students mediate those instructional presentations. As with the paradigms discussed earlier, far too little attention is devoted to differences in the content of subject matter being taught. In focusing down on the description of how students respond to teaching, the scholar in this approach provides quite incomplete portrayals of other aspects of the teaching situation. We thus learn important new things about teaching from this research, but also forgo parts of the portrayal available from the work in other research programs.

The second stream of work on the pupil mediation of instruction has developed from the current applications of cognitive psychology to the learning of school subjects. This work has been grounded in the recognition that in even the most simple of cognitive tasks, learning is not a passive process in which the learner incorporates veridical representations of what has been taught. Indeed, the essence of any act of learning or problem solving is the active role played by the learner in transforming the ostensible message (the nominal stimulus in the language of S–R psychology) of instruction into the learner's own cognitive structures. Whether discussed in the language of nominal and functional stimuli, or of the Piagetian's balance between assimilation and accommodation, or of Ausubel's advance organizers and subsumptions, or the information-processing psychologist's task environment and its transformation into a problem space, or of Herbart's appreciative mass, the central message is always the same. The learner does not respond to the instruction per se. The learner responds to the instruction as transformed, as actively apprehended. Thus, to understand why learners respond (or fail to respond) as they do, ask not what they were taught, but what sense they rendered of what they were taught. The consequences of teaching can only be understood as a function of what that teaching stimulates the learner to do with material.

We can thus envision two parallel streams of action traversing between teacher and learner. Teaching is mediated by the sense the learner makes of the social context of the classroom situation — the way turns are distributed, the character of praise and blame, the implicit standards of performance, the cues employed to signal opportunities to participate, or changes of task and the like. Parallel to the learner's active interpretation of the social reality of the classroom, there exists a mental representation and construction of the cognitive content of what is being taught. New concepts are constantly compared to and assimilated within older ones; metacognitive strategies are deployed, accurately or not, to direct and monitor intellectual skills and specific pieces of knowledge needed for understanding a new principle or perspective. The schematic figure below, abstracted from the larger synoptic model presented earlier, represents the simultaneity of the two processes in the learner. Unquestionably, both processes are occurring concurrently in the minds of students. Ironically, the research community has seemed capable of thinking about only one of these at a time. With the signal exception of the empirical and theoretical work of Walter Doyle (1983), the two streams of mediational processes — social and intellectual — have been pursued by quite separate communities of investigators.

TEACHING→SOCIAL MEDIATION→COGNITIVE MEDIATION→ LEARNING

To understand the parallel between the social mediation and the cognitive information-processing perspectives, it is useful to compare key statements of theoretical propositions from central figures in each domain: Clifford Geertz (1973), the social anthropologist, and Herbert Simon (1957), the information-processing psychologist. Geertz (1973) asserts:

> The concept of culture I espouse ... is essentially a semiotic one. Believing with Max Weber that man is an animal suspended in webs of significance he himself has spun, I take culture to be those webs, and the analysis of it to be therefore not an experimental science in search of law but an interpretive one in search of meaning. It is explication I am after, construing social expressions on their surface enigmatical. (p. 5)

In a similar vein, Simon (1957) defines the concept of bounded rationality:

> The capacity of the human mind for formulating and solving complex problems is very small compared with the size of the problem whose solution is required for objectively rational behavior in the real world — or even a reasonable approximation to such objective reality. ... the first consequence of the principle of bounded rationality is that the intended rationality of an actor requires him to construct a simplified model of the real situation in order to deal with it. He behaves rationally with respect to this model, and such behavior is not even approximately optimal with respect to the real world. To predict his behavior, we must understand the way in which this simplified model is constructed, and its construction will certainly be related to his psychological properties as a perceiving, thinking, and learning animal. (pp. 198–199)

The two conceptions are remarkably parallel, each arguing that the construction of reality, whether sociocultural reality in the form of webs of significance or cognitive reality in the form of problem spaces, is the central process explaining human behavior and choice. To understand why individuals behave as they do, one must understand both the grounds on which they render their simplifications or constructions, and the particular constructions they create. The difference between the psychologist's account and the sociologist's is the grounds. For the psychologist they have to do with the species-general cognitive limitations and predispositions of the individual information processor, as well as with the intellectual history of that individual that shows up as schemata, scripts, preconceptions, prototypes, metacognitive strategies, expectations, attributions, subjective probabilities, and the like. For the sociologist, they are properties associated with the groups of which the individual is a member — SES, ethnicity, occupation, religion, and the like. They may also be called expectations, attributions, or roles (concepts which, like the cognitive psychologist's scripts, are simply parallel metaphors from the theater), but the theoretical explanation for their sources is different. In that sense, the sociologist and the anthropologist will often look alike, although the latter will work harder to see the world from the perspective of the phenomenological categories that function to parse the world of the subjects themselves.

For the microethnographer, or constitutive ethnographer, whose work will be discussed in the next section of the chapter, the most important reality may be that of the group or setting within which the individual and his colleagues function. They will have established rules by which the group members interact, rules that define the legitimate and illegitimate, allowable and forbidden activities of group members. These certainly function within limits set by the larger cultural and social groups of which members are a part, but the smaller school or classroom groups define further rules of the game.

For both the cognitive psychologist and the social anthropologist, therefore, the task of explaining the life of classrooms, the fate of instructional activities, and the social interactions that accompany them, is a matter of discovering the simplification and reconstruction of reality employed by the participants to transform the world as presented into a world with which they can work. The question is not what teaching is most effective, but what meaning is given to the teaching (or is given by teacher and students to the events of classroom life) and what are the grounds for those constructions.

Most of the social psychological work on student mediation of instruction has not followed the format of the Anderson research cited earlier. Instead, investigators (e.g., Weinstein, 1983) have attempted to understand the more stable ways in which students regularly interpret teacher comments and actions. Those student mediations are treated almost like enduring states, like traits, perceptions, attributions, or evaluations employed to make sense of one's own behavior as well as that of others. The studies rarely trace such mediations through to the outcomes of particular instructional episodes. Instead, the ostensible mediators are treated as ends in themselves.

In contrast, those engaged in the study of cognitive mediators of instruction (e.g., Peterson & Swing, 1982; Winne & Marx, 1982) generally use interviews or stimulated recall to collect reports of student thought processes during and immediately after instruction. They may also conduct experiments in which students are taught to use the hypothesized mediators and the effects of such use on achievement are monitored. In most such cases, the mediators studied are generic, at the level of strategies, attentional focus, broad schemata, and the like. They rarely get to the subject-specific level of student thought processes studied by cognitive psychologists of learning. Important findings from all this work indicate the unreliability of judgments regarding student attention made by outside observers. Students who look as if they are attending may not be mediating the instruction productively.

As indicated earlier, the work of Doyle stands out as an exception to the observation that cognitive and social mediation are never studied together. In his essay on academic work (Doyle, 1983), he presents an analysis of the relationships between the cognitive difficulties presented by a task and the challenges of accomplishing such tasks in the social and evaluative environment of classrooms. His work serves not only as a conceptual bridge between these two islands in the student mediation research program, but as a provocative link to the research on classroom ecology, a research program deriving mainly from disciplines outside of psychology, to be discussed in the next section.

Classroom Ecology

The approaches to the study of classroom teaching we have reviewed thus far share a fundamental family membership in the process–product tradition. All except the social perception stream of the mediational program derive from psychology. But as we enter the world of research on classroom ecology, we encounter an utterly different set of intellectual traditions. Not only are these more often qualitative than quantitative methodologically, but their parent disciplines are more frequently anthropology, sociology, and linguistics. The emphasis of process–product research on the essential role of achievement outcomes, on the relative decontextualization of analyses, on the objectification of data in the search for positive laws, is typically missing in this family of research. Missing also, however, are the propositions that can be readily translated into principles for policy or maxims for practice. For those concerned with the value of research for guiding practice through the aggregation and accumulation of usable knowledge, the yield of research in this program is questionable. For those committed to a view of social science as a source of criticism and new questions rather than practical answers, the yield is considerable.

This is an extended family of inquiries, not a simple, tightly knit one. The family includes ethnographers like Erickson (1973), Heath (1983), Wolcott (1973) or Phillips (1983); sociologists like Delamont (e.g., Delamont & Atkinson, 1980), or Lightfoot (1983); psychologists like Jackson (1968) or Smith (Smith & Geoffrey, 1968); sociolinguists like Cadzen (this volume), Mehan (1979), or Green (1983); curriculum and teaching specialists like Doyle (1977). Even these classifications are difficult to make because the work so readily crosses disciplinary boundaries in the social sciences and even the humanities.

Studies within this research program range from the microanalysis of interactions, both verbal and nonverbal, within a single reading group lesson (McDermott, 1976) or over several sessions of a morning "show and tell" in a kindergarten/first grade, using videotape to preserve the smallest units of interactional detail (Florio, 1978), to the macroanalysis of an entire high school with data gathered over a two-week period (Lightfoot, 1983) or of a full community in relation to its high school, with data gathered over an entire year (Peshkin, 1978).

It is important to appreciate the differences between the kinds of questions posed and propositions offered by scholars in this general tradition and those whose work we have considered thus far. The most articulate spokesperson for this research program is the distinguished anthropologist Clifford Geertz, whose work I have briefly cited earlier. I shall quote from two of his writings: "Thick Description" (Geertz, 1973) and "Blurred Genres" (1983), in which he strives to contrast these two traditions of investigation, the positive and the interpretive, as well as to explain to those of us who have been raised in the positivist milieu what constitutes the interpretive research program. In a statement quoted earlier in the chapter, Geertz (1973) observes:

> The concept of culture I espouse ... is essentially a semiotic one. Believing with Max Weber that man is an animal suspended in webs of significance he himself has spun, I take culture to be those webs, and the analysis of it to be therefore not an experimental science in search of law but an interpretive one in search of meaning. It is explication I am after, construing social expressions on their surface enigmatical. (p. 5)

Geertz thus sees the purpose of his investigations to be "an interpretive one in search of meaning" rather than "an experimental science in search of law." A number of years later, he wrote an essay in which he observed that the boundaries between traditional scholarly genres had become blurred, and not only within the anthropological field. Geertz (1983) asserts that "many social scientists have turned away from a laws and instances ideal of explanation toward a cases and interpretations one.... Analogies drawn from the humanities are coming to play the kind of role in sociological understanding that analogies drawn from the crafts and technology have long played in physical understanding" (p. 19). Geertz (1983) characterizes the vocation of social scientists as "trying to discover order in collective life":

> Interpretive explanation ... trains its attention on what institutions, actions, images, utterances, events, customs, all the usual objects of social scientific interest, mean to those whose institutions, actions, customs, and so on they are. As a result, it issues not in laws like Boyle's, or forces like Volta's, or mechanisms like Darwin's, but in constructions like Burckhardt's, Weber's or Freud's: systematic unpackings of the conceptual world. . . .
>
> The manner of these constructions itself varies: Burckhardt portrays, Weber models, Freud diagnoses. But they all represent attempts to formulate how this people or that ... makes sense to itself and, understanding that, what we understand about social order, historical change, or psychic functioning in general. Inquiry is directed at cases or sets of cases, and toward the particular features that mark them off; but its aims are as far-reaching as those of mechanics or physiology: to distinguish the materials of human experience.
>
> ... In the social sciences, or at least in those that have abandoned a reductionist conception of what they are about, the analogies are coming more and more from the contrivances of cultural performance than from those of physical manipulation—from theater, painting, grammar, literature, law, play. What the lever did for physics, the chess move promises to do for sociology. (p. 21)

In the research programs we have been discussing thus far, certain shared assumptions have been apparent in spite of the contrasts drawn among them. The teacher has been very much the center of classroom life, the source or starting point for teaching. Whether the teacher's verbal or physical behavior has been seen as the immediate cause of learning, as in the process-product tradition, or as the agent whose messages are mediated, as in the ALT or student mediation programs, that it is the starting point for analysis has not been a matter for controversy. In the research programs that collectively define the study of classroom ecology, however, this matter of causal direction is itself problematic.

Green's (1983) review of the linguistic perspective in research on teaching captures some of the central assumptions of this program:

> Central to this conceptualization is the view of classrooms as communicative environments in which the events that make up everyday life are constructed as part of the interactions between teachers and students. . . . From this perspective, events evolve during interactions as teachers and students work together to meet instructional goals. Therefore, classroom events ... are dynamic activities constructed by teachers and students as they process, build on, and work with both their own and others' messages and behaviors. . . .
>
> The goal of this work is to understand the nature of teaching-learning processes from the perspective of the participants and to identify those factors that support learning and communicative performance that may lead to evaluation of student ability. (pp. 355, 357)

In an article in the same volume, Hamilton (1983) argues that there are four criteria for ecological research, criteria that bear strong similarity to those enunciated by Green. These characteristics are (a) attention to the interaction between persons and their environments, especially in reciprocal terms rather than in terms of simple directional causality from teachers to students; (b) treating teaching and learning as continuously interactive processes rather than isolating a few factors in the system and labeling them as "cause" and "effect"; (c) seeing the classroom context as nested within other contexts—the school, the community, the family, the culture—all of which influence what can be observed in the classroom itself; and (d) treating unobservable processes, such as thoughts, attitudes, feelings, or perceptions of the participants, as important sources of data.

A number of chapters in this volume treat the growing body of work that participates in this research program. These include the chapters by Erickson, Cazden, and Evertson and Green. I run the risk of lumping together what many participating investigators view as distinct research enterprises. Surely the disciplinary traditions from which participants derive are diverse. They range from anthropology and sociolinguistics to sociology and ecological psychology. They include in their number both ethnomethodologists and symbolic interactionists. Yet, when contrasted with the psychologists, whether behaviorist or mentalist, whose work has dominated the programs reviewed earlier (and the study of teacher cognition to be discussed in the next section), they constitute a distinctive family of inquiry.

Most of these research programs derive from disciplinary roots much older, and certainly independent of, the mainstream research-on-teaching traditions represented by process-product programs. Nevertheless, within the recent history of research on teaching, they have jointly played a critical role in the great conversation, a role in which they raise questions about the findings and assumptions of the dominant tradition. They are especially interested in circumstances wherein the generalizations of process-product studies may fail to hold for social or cultural minorities, or under particular circumstances, both concerns deriving from the strong anthropological and sociological perspectives of these researchers. When process-product researchers summarize the results of their studies in general prescriptive terms such as "increase engaged time" or "increase wait-times" or "begin the school year with clearly formulated rules," the classroom ecology researchers ask how teachers might concretely and locally accomplish such ends. Here again, they are also wont to ask under what cultural conditions these general prescriptions will be found incomplete or even dead wrong.

Researchers in this program have somewhat different perspectives on the concept of "effectiveness" as well. Process-product researchers focus predominantly on criteria of effectiveness lying outside the immediate classroom setting being observed, that is, achievement measured by end-of-year standardized achievement tests or end-of-unit norm-referenced performance tests. Classroom ecology researchers tend to look for criteria of effectiveness within the situation. These include equality of opportunities to participate (rather than participation frequencies as a function of social class, ethnicity, or prior academic standing); indicators of clear communications of meaning between teacher and students (especially focal in multiethnic classrooms where teacher and students may be from different cultural backgrounds); or smoothness of interchanges, transitions, or other commonplace classroom events.

In addition, they are particularly sensitive to what students do in order to convey the *appearance* of understanding or correct performance. They are concerned about poor students being so judged because they have not learned to "look smart" or "talk smart." The complex interplay between the hidden and manifest curriculum is apparent in these analyses of how learning the presentation of self as a good student relates to being treated as one. That treatment, in turn, can lead to subsequent opportunities to learn (e.g., placement in a higher reading group, more frequent opportunities to respond) that ultimately produce higher achievement and more positive self-esteem.

The most frequent misunderstanding of this research program occurs when it is characterized as "qualitative" and the other programs are deemed "quantitative." This view assumes that the different research programs are essentially looking at the same phenomena for similar purposes, but that process-product or positivistic scholars use larger samples and carefully prepared observation schedules subsequently to be analyzed quantitatively. Interpretive or sociolinguistic or ethnographic researchers employ lined yellow pads, write down everything they see for extended durations of time in very few (frequently only one) classrooms with the intention of summarizing their findings in narrative form. The contrast is erroneously drawn between quantitative science and qualitative story-telling.

As can be learned in the several chapters on this topic found in the present volume (Erickson; Cazden; Evertson & Green) the most important differences between the research programs are substantive rather than methodological. While it may well be true that interpretive classroom process researchers are likely to eschew observation scales for open-ended observations, the important differences lie in the conceptions of learning, classrooms, and teaching held by the investigators, as well as the implicit perspectives on the goals of educational research and the interests served by such activity.

While process-product researchers view classrooms as reducible to discrete events and behaviors which can be noted, counted, and aggregated for purposes of generalization across settings and individuals, interpretive scholars view classrooms as socially and culturally organized environments. Individual participants in those environments contribute to the organization and to the definition of meanings. They are actively engaged in "making sense" in the setting, taking both senses of that phrase. They both discern the meanings intended by other actors and they engage in the continuing invention and reformulation of new meanings.

Those personal meanings become the focal point for inquiry, in contrast to the behaviors that focus the effort of the process-product scholars. Here we see the work of the student mediation program intersecting with that of the classroom process, interpretive, sociolinguistic scholars. This program is concerned with the significance of events to the actors themselves, both those shared by all participants in a context and those that are interpreted differently by individuals in the setting who come from very different social, linguistic, and/or cultural backgrounds.

This program is thus comparative in at least two ways. Every context is seen as embedded or nested within other contexts. Life in classrooms is understood as a function, not only of the jointly produced local meanings of the particular classroom group, but also as influenced by the larger contexts in which the class is embedded — the school, the community, the society, the culture. Moreover, since children of different backgrounds move in and out of the classroom from contrasting social and language communities, they will be making sense of classroom life employing different frames of reference.

Reflecting the influence of anthropology and linguistics, this program is also comparative in a second sense. Studies are often conducted in settings that are culturally different from the typical American school, and contrasts are drawn with schools and classrooms in other cultures. This frequently reflects not only the value of contextual contrasts in clarifying the interpretation of a phenomenon under study, but the tendency of scholars in this program to be particularly concerned with the special problems encountered in the educational systems by pupils (and even teachers) who are relatively powerless.

Research is thus often conducted for the purpose of showing how "the system" fails to serve the children of the poor, the linguistically or culturally different, ethnic minorities, and other disadvantaged populations. Through meticulous examination of the most commonplace events of classroom life — turn allocations, modes of explanation, nonverbal messages of praise and blame, and the like — classroom ecology researchers show how a hidden curriculum to which the less advantaged are not privy can control access to success with the manifest curriculum. In this way, much research in this tradition takes on a more radical or critical political tone relative to the process-product approaches.

The study of particular instances of classroom failure — the Anglo teacher who misunderstands and is misunderstood by Hispanic youngsters; the native Hawaiian reading group that fails because the participation structure violates principles of discourse learned in the home; the native American reservation classrooms in which achievement does not rise until native American teachers are brought in to teach; the South Boston kindergarten/first grade where the Italian-American child cannot figure out how to get a turn — often are the focal points of the cases carefully described by classroom process researchers. The implicit logic of the inquiries is that analysis of occasions where the typical flow of instruction breaks down or falters presents a strategic site for research. Much like the approach of neuroanatomists, who study the effects of brain lesions in order better to understand the normal workings of the brain, or of personality psychologists who investigate deviant behavior as a way of discovering general principles, the classroom ethnographer studies concrete, particular cases where what is typical or expected is likely to be violated. But he has interest not only in characterizing that particular setting, but in discovering universals as well.

In this regard, the classroom ethnographer frequently has his or her own perspective on teacher effectiveness, and will even accede to using the standardized test score as criterion. Instead of locating effectiveness in the specific behaviors of the teacher, the classroom process researcher looks for the "independent variable" in the reflexive participation structures produced jointly by the teacher and students. Although the effectiveness criterion is the same one employed by the process-product researchers, the essential conception of process is different.

Erickson (this volume) makes a strong argument that the

logic of inquiry for the interpretive researcher is from the concrete particular to the universal. Where this differs from the inductive positivist is that the interpretive researcher does not sample instances or elements across a wide range of concrete particulars as the basis for inferring universals. Instead, he studies a concrete particular case in detail, aiming to develop as full a model as possible of the situation and the contexts in which it is nested. From analysis of concrete cases and examination of commonalities across detailed particularizations of them, generalizations are sought and tested. This approach contrasts with the characterization of positivist researchers who employ partial specifications of a setting that are sampled far more widely across instances of the same sort of setting.

It is thus the ecosystem of learner, classroom, teacher, school, and community that serves as the theoretical ideal unit of inquiry for the interpretive researcher. It is not the behavior or thought of the individual teacher or student. The participants are seen as jointly constructing the meanings in those situations, and those meanings are subject to continuous renegotiation and revision. Individual behavior, interpretations, meanings, or motives can be understood only in the context of the more general system of organized relations.

How well do interpretive researchers achieve the ideal they seek? What problems do they encounter as they attempt to understand the complexities of classroom life? Although our discussion of research in the classroom ecology program is not yet complete, it is perhaps judicious to examine it critically at this point. The ambition of the classroom ecology program has not always been matched by its accomplishments. It is, unfortunately, far easier to speak of the importance of capturing reflexively constructed social realities, or of documenting the consequences of nested contexts, than it is to conduct the research. The challenges of producing a fully specified model of a classroom situation, of eschewing generalization for particularization, or of portraying the world from the perspectives of the participants rather than that of researchers, are formidable. It is especially difficult to pursue interpretive studies with appropriate levels of reliability and precision. Those who pursue research in the classroom ecology program are prone to no fewer problems of both substance and method than are their colleagues who conduct research in the other paradigms we have reviewed.

A major problem is the tendency toward ambivalence with respect to generalization from case to case and from a particular case to the world at large. Although Geertz speaks wisely of generalizing within rather than across cases in ethnographies, too frequently we find educational researchers making sweeping general statements based on woefully limited data. Inferences that demand careful cross-site analyses, for example, are based on examination of a single case, or on several cases whose variations do not reflect principles of theoretical sampling.

Despite the criticisms that process-product researchers are guilty of looking at the complexities of classroom life only superficially, a few variables at a time, many classroom ethnographers limit themselves to examining particular features of classrooms in meticulous detail (e.g., participation patterns, uses of language), while themselves ignoring other central aspects of teaching, subject matter, or instructional tasks entirely. Contexts outside the classroom are too often described in the most general terms, subsequently to be ignored, or given short shrift, in the explanations of classroom interaction that follow. This occurs in spite of rhetoric regarding the importance of understanding the multiplicity of layered environments within which individuals and groups function. Research methods are often documented poorly or incompletely, leaving the reader to guess how certain data were collected or how frequently particular observations or interviews were conducted. The logic of inferences from data to conclusions is not always specified, thus leaving the reader either to trust in the integrity and wisdom of the researcher or to reject the claims entirely. These are a few of the problems that can beset research in the classroom ecology program.

Since this perspective is somewhat alien to the majority of researchers on teaching who have, like the author, been raised as psychologists (or at least with the unquestioned assumptions of positivist and reductionist social science), it may be helpful to think of an analogy from biology. It is certainly possible to argue that the natural starting point for biological inquiry and discourse is the individual cell, for it is the building block of all other forms of life or biological structures. Biology is therefore the study of cells, their characteristics and functions, and the ways cells aggregate to form organs, organ systems, and organisms.

Alternatively, it can be asserted that the organism, that entity capable of independent existence and functioning, is the appropriate unit of analysis. Starting from the organism, one would then ask how individual organs function to enable the organism's activities and how equilibrium among the various components of the organism's total structure is maintained. One would thus ask how the parts of the organism are organized into the functioning whole which is the organism itself.

Finally (though by no means exhaustively), one could posit that neither cells nor organisms are adequate as units of inquiry, for each is no more than a part of the natural whole, which is the community or ecosystem. It is as impossible to understand the workings of any individual organism independent of its ecosystem as it is impossible to define the functions of a cell independent of the organized system of organs and organ systems to which it contributes.

This example is presented simply to illustrate a biological analogue to the units-of-inquiry problem encountered in the study of teaching and learning in classrooms. Whether the individual teaching behavior, the coordinated activity of a teacher (or a learner) over an extended period of time, or the ecosystem of a total classroom — teacher and pupils viewed as reflexively causing one another's behavior — is the proper starting point for inquiry is, in principle, not answerable. Each starting point is a legitimate consequence of contrasting disciplinary and methodological assumptions. Each carries consequences for the questions that can be asked and the issues that can be entertained. For the present discussion, this starting point has been selected quite differently in the process-product and the interpretive/ethnographic research programs.

We can therefore see how the various characteristics of the interpretive/qualitative/ethnographic/sociolinguistic research program of the classroom ecology genre are linked together. Definition of the unit of inquiry, emphasis on the personal perspectives of the participants, focus on concrete and particular, identification with the powerless, a particular view of verification and generalization, and a comparative orientation are all features of these approaches. Surely there are sharp battles among members of this broad research program, who often see the differences separating them as serious and profound. But compared to the assumptions and methods shared by most of the research programs discussed earlier, the differences are relatively small.

CLASSROOM PROCESS AND COGNITIVE SCIENCE RESEARCH

There is a striking similarity between some aspects of research in the traditions of school ethnography and of cognitive science. Both approaches ascribe substantial cognitive and/or social organization to the participants in their studies, and assume that prior knowledge, experience, or attitude frames the new encounters and their interpretation. Moreover, both approaches assume that the performances being viewed are rule governed. One of the central goals of research in both traditions is to analyze the observed behavior in meticulous detail in order to infer an underlying set of rules which would explain the observed variations. The system of rules for the cognitive scientist is often expressed in the form of a computer simulation program, or if memory organization and processes are in focus, as a semantic network or flow diagram. The system of rules for the ethnographer is typically presented in narrative form, or as a set of propositions.

It is likely that the similarity is due to a common source for research in both traditions. Both cognitive science and sociolinguists (which underlies much of what we currently call classroom microethnography) were born in the middle 1960s under the influence of Chomsky's (1957) transformational grammar. Miller, Galanter, and Pribram's (1960) *Plans and the Structure of Behavior* provides a clear report of the influence on the emerging field of cognitive psychology. Chomsky posited the distinction between performance and competence, offering the notion that variations in observed performance must be understood as generated by an underlying set of rules—grammatical competence—adequate to produce those variations. The logic of research involved detailed documentation of observable variation in language use, equally meticulous examination of language experience, and the *positioning* of a set of rules adequate to account for the differences between language that had been experienced and language that could be generated. The emphasis of contemporary sociolinguistics on a similar research paradigm is no coincidence.

As indicated earlier, these research programs are certainly not free of faults. Among the most serious has been the tendency to ignore the *substance* of classroom life, the specific curriculum content and subject matter being studied. One can read the meticulous detail of many classroom ethnographies and never discover the simple facts, concepts or principles, skills or understandings, being taught. One is overwhelmed with details of conversational alterations, body tonus modifications, distributions of speaking turns, patterns of individual and overlapping speech and chartings of pupil and teacher movements through the classroom. Even one of the leaders of the classroom ethnography field felt obliged to ask somewhat plaintively

where were the stories of learning and teaching in ethnographic accounts of classrooms in a paper titled "Taught Cognitive Learning in Its Immediate Environment: A Neglected Topic in the Anthropology of Education" (Erickson, 1982b). Thus, for all of its emphasis on the particularities of context as the hallmark of research in the interpretive program, that context was defined by the research agenda of general sociolinguistics and microethnography which did not treat curriculum or instructional content as a core feature of context, as a feature worthy of characterization in detail. If process–product scholars were guilty of generalizing without due restraint across decontextualized molecular features of teaching processes, interpretive researchers were equally guilty of treating talk as talk, turns as turns, task as task, regardless of the subject matter under study by the participants.

Another problem of interpretive research lay in its commitment to the powerless, its strong tendency to locate its portrayal of personal meanings in the pupils in the classroom, especially those from ethnic or linguistic minorities, while often ignoring the perspective of teachers. While acknowledging that teachers, too, are often powerless in the school organization when compared to administrators or board members, in the ethnography of individual classrooms they become the oppressors or the tools of oppression, and the minority youngsters are the helpless victims. Too many of these portrayals thus present teachers as insensitive, uncaring, without skills or adequate understanding of the subtleties of cultural differences. The cognitive and emotional strain of teaching, the limits of teachers' capacities to respond to increasing complexity or diversity, the reasons why their behavior makes sense to them, all are likely to be ignored. The accounts are emic with respect to the pupils, but etic and even hostile in relation to the teacher. Here again, what is often a virtue of the interpretive program, an orientation toward seeing the world from the perspectives of those least likely to be understood in traditional research endeavors, becomes a liability with reference to the study of teaching.

There are at least two provisos to be offered in relation to this last criticism. First, a program should perhaps not be criticized for taking the interests of pupils as primary and those of teachers as secondary. Contemporary forms of a social history have injected a breath of fresh air into the study of history by supplementing with the heroic tales of white male politicians, business tycoons, and generals making power, money, and war with the history of women, minorities, and the poor. Similarly, a history of research on teaching that has portrayed classroom life only as seen by teachers might well be fruitfully enriched by new accounts providing the hitherto untold story of teaching from the perspective of the disadvantaged learner.

A second proviso emerges from the comment by Cadzen toward the end of her chapter in this volume. She speculates that the most useful kind of feedback to give teachers who have participated in research on discourse in their classrooms may well be accounts of what their pupils were doing, saying, thinking, and feeling, rather than detailed analyses of their own behavior. The portrayal of pupil responses to teaching may be more productive of positive changes in the teachers, and less likely to breed defensiveness and denial, than would descriptions of the teachers themselves. It is a researchable point and one worth taking seriously.

Finally, although the logic of inference and generalizability has attracted the attention of leaders in the interpretive program (e.g., Erickson, Heath) and although the tactics and strategies of data analysis, data reduction, and data use for inferences have now been examined in careful detail (Miles & Huberman, 1984), exemplars of this research program are far too often characterized by sloppy procedures, inadequate precision and control, and glib generalizations, from poorly and incompletely specified classroom particulars to assertions about the world of schools writ large. Geertz (1973) has observed:

> I have never been impressed by the argument that, as complete objectivity is impossible in these matters (as, of course, it is), one might as well let one's sentiments run loose. As Robert Solow has remarked, that is like saying that as a perfectly aseptic environment is impossible, one might as well conduct surgery in a sewer. (p. 30)

Research in the interpretive programs has injected a healthy note of criticism into the process–product-dominated conversations about teaching effectiveness. Now they must become concerned about the discipline of their own methods.

Teacher Cognition and Decision Making

The phrase "teacher behavior" rolls trippingly off the tongue. Those two words, *teacher* and *behavior*, have been paired almost automatically for many years in academic discussions of research on teaching, and even in more applied deliberations on teaching policy. When Gage defined research on teaching in the first *Handbook of Research on Teaching* as "research in which at least one variable consists of a behavior or characteristic of teachers" (Gage, 1963, p. 97), certainly no feelings of shock were elicited. Research was surely a process that involved the measurement and manipulation of *variables*, and an emphasis on behavior had been the cornerstone of American psychology since Watson. Since the studies of teacher characteristics, while certainly popular for many years, continued to produce few replicable findings, the emphasis fell increasingly on the description of what teachers did in the classroom, how their behavior related to student behavior, and how that behavior could best be shaped by training.

In Dunkin and Biddle (1974), teacher process variables were at the very heart of the teaching model, and those process variables were composed of observable teacher behavior. What preceded and accompanied behavior were presage variables — for example, teacher characteristics — and context variables — for example, the subject matter, grade, or class size. Yet even as the research on teacher processes flourished, some scholars urged that other aspects of teaching, less immediately observable, more clearly associated with notions of thought, judgment, or decision making, be investigated. These researchers, such as Shavelson (1973) and Shulman and Elstein (1975), argued that the field of research on teaching was still embedded in a style of psychological language and theory that was already losing its hegemony in the behavioral sciences. Those disciplines were rapidly becoming "cognitive" in response to repeated demonstrations of the insufficiencies of behaviorist explanations. Yet research on teaching was being pursued as if teaching and thought were mutually incompatible. The only reference to

teachers' thinking among all the studies cited in Dunkin and Biddle was an oblique one in their summary of Dahloff's (1971) and Lundgren's (1972) work on "steering groups."

The new emphasis on teacher cognition developed from several sources. First, beginning in the mid-1950s, the cognitive critique of behaviorism took hold in psychology, through the efforts of information-processing psychologists and psycholinguists. *Plans and the Structure of Behavior* (Miller et al., 1960) synthesized research and theory from the still-new fields of information-processing psychology (e.g., Newell & Simon, 1956) and transformational grammar (Chomsky, 1957) in a devastating critique of the adequacy of behaviorist explanations for complex human cognitive and skilled performance. During the same period, the work of Piaget, though dating back to the 1920s, first began to catch hold among American psychologists and educators. Translation of several of Piaget's later books, such as *The Origin of Intelligence in Children* (Piaget, 1952), brought the Swiss psychologist's work on cognitive development to the attention of an American audience now somewhat more sympathetic to his conceptions (if not yet to his methods). When Bruner, Goodnow, and Austin (1956) introduced notions of concept-attainment strategies and cognitive strain in their *Study of Thinking*, yet another legitimating study was added to the critique of behaviorism and the emergence of a new cognitive psychology. The trend was so powerful that, by the 1970s, one of the long-term leaders of behavioristic learning theory, Gregory Kimble (1975), observed:

> How far we have come in the past ten years; that the white rat and the pigeon no longer provide the majority of our data, that complex mazes are rarely used these days, that S–R has been deposed as king of the theoretical hill, that "mind" is no longer a dirty four-letter word. (p. 613)

It was no surprise then to find a generation of psychologists raised on the new information-processing and cognitive psychology beginning to train those lenses on the field of research on teaching. That field of research had certainly remained immune to the cognitive revolution Kimble found sweeping through psychology. The mental life of the teacher had not become a central topic of teaching research.

Shavelson (1983) has defined the purposes and rationale for this research program in the following manner:

> First, teachers are rational professionals who, like other professionals such as physicians, make judgments and carry out decisions in an uncertain, complex environment. ... teachers behave rationally with respect to the simplified models of reality they construct. ... teachers' behavior is guided by their thoughts, judgments and decisions. (pp. 392–393).

Therefore, to understand adequately the choices teachers make in classrooms, the grounds for their decisions and judgments about pupils, and the cognitive processes through which they select and sequence the actions they have learned to take while teaching, we must study their thought processes before, during, and after teaching.

Following Shulman and Elstein (1975), reviewers have tended to distinguish among three fundamental types of cognitive process research on teaching — studies of judgment and policy, of problem-solving, and of decision making. Each of the three genres of research presupposes a different form of task for teachers and a different type of research method for investigators. If anything, the influence of the psychological research models has been too strong, for they may have driven this program of research into a dead end.

Several strategic research sites have emerged in this program. Consistent with Jackson's (1968) distinction between preactive and interactive phases of teaching (roughly synonymous with planning and actively instructing, respectively) substantial research has focused on the cognitive processes observed in the course of teacher planning. Given the speed of normal classroom events, this strategy of studying the rare reflective moments during the life of a teacher was attractive. Thinking-aloud techniques were normally employed, with the teacher using his or her actual materials and/or planbook, or simulated materials prepared by the investigators. Protocols of the thinking aloud would be collected, perhaps followed by classroom observations and debriefing, perhaps not. The major research questions focused on descriptions of what teachers thought about as they planned for instruction, and the major finding identified most teachers as concentrating on content and activities in their planning, rather than formal objectives and individual characteristics of students. These findings regarding the contrast between current practices and the normative principles of planning typically espoused by instructional specialists constituted a serious indictment of conventional wisdom in teacher education. That is, if it is so clearly desirable to plan on the basis of considering the objectives of instruction and the characteristics of learners, why did no one practice that way?

A second major genre of research was the study of interactive thought, which had to employ methods of stimulated recall because thinking aloud is not possible in the conventional classroom while instruction is underway. Using video- or audiotapes of the classroom session recently completed, the participant is asked why he or she engaged in the observed behavior. Studies of interactive thought were far more difficult to conduct than were those of preactive teaching. The methods of stimulated recall had originally been developed by Bloom (1953) for study of student thought processes during college classes. They had been elaborated by Kagan, Krathwohl, and Miller (1963) for work with psychological counselors and subsequently, by Kagan, for work with other members of helping professions. Elstein and Shulman (with Kagan's collaboration) had applied the methods to the study of physician thought (e.g., Elstein, Shulman, & Sprafka, 1978; Shulman & Elstein, 1975). Chapters in this volume by Shavelson, Webb, and Burstein, as well as Clark and Peterson, discuss the methodological challenges of such techniques as thinking aloud and stimulated recall.

The forms taken in these studies varied enormously. In some studies (e.g., Peterson & Clark, 1978), preactive and interactive thinking was monitored for individual lessons during simulated microteaching sessions. The Alberta studies (e.g., MacKay & Marland, 1978) generally followed teachers in their actual classrooms for several days. Shroyer (1981) likewise studied interactive thought in teachers' natural classrooms for the duration of an entire unit of elementary mathematics. In his study of teacher planning, Yinger (1977) worked with the same teacher for nearly a year, again monitoring her actual second-grade classroom.

A third major genre of research used the methods of judgment and decision-making research to render mathematical models of teachers' cognitions about students. Shavelson and his students (Cadwell, Borko, Russo, Stern) applied the methods of "policy capturing" to model teacher judgments about pupils, using regression equations to represent the weights teachers implicitly gave to alternative sources of information in making decisions about pupil placements, evaluations, groupings, and the like.

Two serious problems beset the research program for the study of teacher cognitions. The first is the limited range of teaching activities about which teacher thoughts have been investigated. Other than the findings regarding teacher planning (findings that contrast observed planning emphases with those normative positions on teacher planning advocated by proponents of behavioral objectives and rational teaching models patterned after instructional design), little that is remarkable has emerged from the research studies. Moreover, most of the controversies among teacher cognition researchers themselves, such as the discussions over how many "real" decisions teachers make in a typical instructional hour, are of little practical or theoretical interest (unless one is only prepared to take teachers seriously as thinkers and professionals if it can be demonstrated that they make many decisions hourly rather than few). Most of the teaching activities have been tied closely to the process–product program, asking how teachers think about those behavioral performances identified as critical for effectiveness. These include assignments of pupils to groups, giving praise or criticism, setting and modifying pacing, allocating turns, and the like. These are important, and their importance will be discussed presently, but they represent a severely attenuated menu of teacher cognitions, a limited perspective on what it might be important for teachers to think about.

The second problem is the growing distance between the study of teacher cognition and those increasingly vigorous investigations of cognitive processes in pupils. The initial stimulus for research on cognition came from psychological approaches to the study of judgment, problem solving, and decision making. Models of research, ways of formulating questions, and general research paradigms were borrowed from previous psychological work in those areas. Thus studies of judgment policies in college admissions committees (Dawes, 1971) or of clinical problem solving in physicians (Elstein et al., 1978) established the templates for studies of cognition in teachers. But the central cognitive psychological work of the early 1970s was not the most important source of applications to the cognitive psychology of education in the late 1970s and the 1980s. Work in the psychology of instruction had moved toward the study of learning and problem solving in specific subject areas. Resnick (1981) summarizes the situation well in her chapter for the *Annual Review of Psychology*:

> First, there is a shift toward studying more and more complex forms of cognitive behavior. This means that many of the tasks and processes of interest to cognitive psychologists are ones that can form part of a school's curriculum. Psychological work on such tasks is naturally relevant to instruction. Second . . . is a growing interest in

the role of *knowledge* in human behavior. Much effort is now directed at finding ways to represent the structure of knowledge and at discovering the ways in which knowledge is used in various kinds of learning.... Finally, today's assumptions about the nature of learning and thinking are interactionist. We assume that learning occurs as a result of mental constructions of the learner. These constructions respond to information and stimuli in the environment, but they do not copy or mirror them. This means that instruction must be designed not to put knowledge into learners' heads but to put learners in positions that allow them to construct well-structured knowledge. (p. 660)

Studies of the cognitive psychology of instruction concentrate on how students use their knowledge and conceptions to apprehend what they are taught. In the spirit of Herbart's (1895) conception of the appreciative mass, cognitive psychologists assume that all learners approach instruction actively. They already possess extensive bodies of knowledge, organized in particular ways. When presented with new knowledge by texts or by teachers, they actively process the information in that instruction through the filters or lenses of their prior understanding.

The essential task for the teacher, therefore, is to appraise, infer, or anticipate these prior cognitive structures that students bring to the learning situation. Teachers must organize the content of their instruction in terms of those preconceptions, actively working to reveal and transform them when they would interfere with adequate comprehension of the new material to be taught. The language of this research program includes such key terms as *schema, script, frame, metacognitive strategy,* and other words to describe those mental tools or structures employed by learners to make sense of what they are being taught.

Quite centrally, the thrust of the cognitive research program in learning is subject matter specific rather than generic. That is, the schemata used to make sense of instruction on photosynthesis in a biology class are completely different from those used to understand the concept of inertia in physics.

With the exception of research programs of Leinhardt (e.g., 1983) and of Anderson and Smith (1984), most of the cognitive research on teaching has ignored the teacher's cognitive processes in this sense. There have been no studies of teachers' knowledge, of the schemata or frames they employ to apprehend student understandings or misconceptions.

Leinhardt's most recent work (e.g., Leinhardt & Smith, 1984) is exceptional in her application of the methods of cognitive science, not only to the representation of understanding in the minds of students, but also to the representation of and instruction in the same topics by the teachers. Classrooms are described in some detail and the cognitive understandings manifested by the participants, both teacher and students, are carefully mapped and analyzed.

Another interesting group of studies, deriving from roots in curriculum research and teacher education rather than cognitive psychology, has examined teachers' practical knowledge (e.g., Elbaz, 1981). In these studies, teachers are interviewed at length about their activities and choices, as well as the grounds for those choices. The researchers then develop a theory for practical pedagogical knowledge from the interview data and coordinated observations. This work is summarized by Feiman-Nemser and Floden (this volume).

As intimated earlier, most others who study teacher thought have implicitly accepted the process–product model of teaching, as exemplified in the Dunkin–Biddle model, and have treated teachers' thoughts as processes that precede teacher behavior. Since the behavior in question is the same behavior deemed important in the process–product program, then the kinds of thoughts that are understood become those germane to the predominantly classroom-management behavior of teachers studied by that program.

Indeed, even the style of analysis resembles that of process–product research. Teachers are asked to think aloud while planning or to describe their thoughts and feelings during stimulated recall of interactive teaching. The resulting self-report protocols are then analyzed by counting the frequency of verbalizations under particular categories. Do teachers use objectives in planning? Count the relative frequency of references to objectives, activities, pupil characteristics, or specific content in the protocols and you have your answer: Teachers make very few references to objectives. How frequently do teachers make "in-flight" decisions during interactive instruction? Count the number of explicit decisions teachers recall making and you have your answer. The complexity and subtlety of cognitive science studies of learners is absent in such work, as are the theoretical constructs that make the cognitive psychology of instruction the most exciting single research program in educational psychology today.

There are, therefore, several kinds of cognitive studies of teachers being pursued. First, there are the studies of teachers' preactive and interactive thoughts in relation to the generic processes of teaching investigated by the process–product researchers. These are summarized and discussed by Clark and Peterson (this volume). Second, there are the studies of teachers' practical knowledge reviewed in this volume in the chapter by Feiman-Nemser and Floden. Research on subject matter understanding and representation by teachers as they instruct particular topics in specific subject matters is in its infancy. This work is closest in its orientation to the cognitive psychology of learning and will be discussed in greater detail presently. Additional studies of cognition in classrooms can be found in the work of the classroom process researchers employing sociolinguistic methods. Though they do not claim to be studying teacher cognition, much of their work throws significant light on how teachers and students jointly produce the rules of classroom life, and how teachers' understandings or misconstrual of the meanings communicated by children of different backgrounds can influence the choices teachers make and the interpretations and decisions they render.

A Missing Program. Where the teacher cognition program has clearly fallen short is in the elucidation of teachers' cognitive understanding of subject matter content and the relationships between such understanding and the instruction teachers provide for students (Shulman, 1984a). The general public and those who set educational policy are in general agreement that teachers' competence in the subjects they teach is a central criterion of teacher quality. They remain remarkably vague, however, in defining what sort of subject-matter knowledge they have in mind—basic skills, broad factual knowledge, scholarly depth—and the research-on-teaching community has been of little help with this matter.

In this discussion, I shall distinguish among three kinds of content knowledge: subject matter knowledge, pedagogical knowledge, and curricular knowledge. *Subject matter knowledge* is that comprehension of the subject appropriate to a content specialist in the domain. Thus it is the knowledge of physics expected of a successful university physics major, or the knowledge of Shakespeare's plays appropriate for a college English literature major. *Pedagogical knowledge* refers to the understanding of how particular topics, principles, strategies, and the like in specific subject areas are comprehended or typically misconstrued, are learned and likely to be forgotten. Such knowledge includes the categories within which similar problem types or conceptions can be classified (what are the ten most frequently encountered types of algebra word problems? least-well-grasped grammatical constructions?), and the psychology of learning them. *Curricular knowledge* is familiarity with the ways in which knowledge is organized and packaged for instruction, in texts, programs, media, workbooks, other forms of practice, and the like. It is the pedagogical equivalent of the physician's knowledge of *materia medica*, of the diversity of treatment alternatives.

How do we establish the state of these different forms of teaching knowledge? How much should teachers know, and about what? What are the consequences for teaching of different levels of these kinds of teaching knowledge? How are such forms of knowledge acquired from subject-matter courses in high school and in the subject-matter departments of the university? In professional education courses? From both supervised and unguided practical teaching experiences?

In a program of research only recently begun, my colleagues and I (Shulman, Sykes, & Phillips, 1983) are pursuing such questions. What are the sources of teacher explanations in particular instructional situations? When students have difficulty understanding a short story by Faulkner, or the principles of photosynthesis, where do teachers turn for their explanations, their examples, the analogies, metaphors, or similes employed to clarify the obscurity? Under what circumstances is depth of subject matter knowledge an apparent disadvantage to the teacher, and what strategies can remedy the problem? How does the character of the subject-matter knowledge possessed by teachers affect the cognitive quality of their teaching? How do different types of undergraduate subject-matter learning experiences in college result in different organizations of understanding for subsequent teaching? How do teachers approach the teaching of material they have never themselves learned before and how does this differ from their teaching of highly familiar material? How do teachers' general epistemic beliefs, their generic conceptions of knowledge, and their understanding of knowledge in their own discipline relate to the manner in which the subject is taught? In general, we are interested in examining in detail what most laypersons assume is the central question of teacher education. How much and what should teachers know of what they teach? Where is such knowledge acquired and how can it be improved or changed?

This research is pursued through a combination of oral intellectual histories, repeated interviews over a 1- to 2-year period of teacher education and beginning teaching, systematic observations of teacher planning, teaching, and retrospective assessment, analyses of simulated tasks involving the selection and critique of new teaching materials, and both observation and interviews in a variety of other settings.

One of the contentions of those who pursue research on teacher cognition has been that proper examination and reform of teacher education will be contingent upon progress in understanding teacher thought. This has certainly been the view of Fenstermacher (1978) and others who have analyzed how research results can be used by teachers. Ironically, little is known about such matters empirically because these questions have fallen between the cracks in the research-on-teaching field. Nevertheless, new and emerging research programs, in which studies of teacher knowledge development are closely articulated with investigations of teacher education, promise to remedy those deficiencies in the coming years.

Although research on teacher cognition may have yielded less than was anticipated in its first decade, it remains an area of immense promise. Changes in both teaching and teacher education will become operational through the minds and motives of teachers. Understanding how and why teachers plan for instruction, the explicit and implicit theories they bring to bear in their work, and the conceptions of subject matter that influence their explanations, directions, feedback and correctives, will continue as a central feature of research on teaching. A comprehensive understanding of teaching will include explanations of both thought and action in teachers as well as students.

Summary and Prognosis

We come to the end of our discussion of the research programs in the study of teaching. The chapter began with a discussion of the concept of a research program and a clarification of how our treatment of this topic differed from the Kuhnian notion of a paradigm. The intrinsic incompleteness of social science research programs was discussed as well as some ways in which those insufficiencies might complement one another. That topic will be developed further in this section.

A synoptic map of the research-on-teaching field was then presented. It was schematic, necessarily leaving out important research initiatives. Programs were seen as making choices among a host of alternative units of inquiry for studying teaching. These units included *participants* (teacher, students, group-as-unit), *attributes* of those participants (capacities, thoughts, actions), *context* or levels of contextual aggregation (individual, group, class, school), *content* (topics, type of structure, duration of instructional unit), *agenda* (academic tasks, social organization) and foci within that agenda (subject matter content, participant structures), and *research perspective* (positivist/law-seeking or interpretive/personal meaning oriented). These choices resulted in strikingly different research programs, and hence strikingly different narratives about teaching, its antecedents and consequences.

Choices among research programs were not made so rationally, however. Investigations did not ponder the trade-offs among approaches and deliberately select that particular style of investigation that suited them optimally. Instead, they were driven by their individual disciplinary roots (and propensities within the discipline, as reflected in the differences between behaviorists and mentalists in psychology), their educational or political ideologies, their respective commitments to technical improvement or "scientific" explanation, and most of all, to the stage in which they became part of the Great Conversation. More than anything else, research programs were influenced by the dialogues and debates among scholars. Whether these occurred in print, in large national or regional meetings, or in the face-to-face sessions of invisible colleges, researchers reacted to each other's work. And since, in the modern era (since 1965), the process–product program represented the mainstream of research on teaching, it also served as the focal point for most of this conversation. Whether to elaborate and refine that model through specifying the influences mediating between process and product, or to demonstrate the putative insufficiency of the formulation, the other participants in the dialogue focused their attention on the mainstream approach. It became the most frequent source for guiding policymakers and teacher educators, and also the favorite target of critics from other perspectives in the field. It doubtless receives more than its fair share of criticism in this chapter as well.

The chapter continued with extensive discussions of the major research programs themselves, beginning with the process–product approach and continuing with a number of others. In portraying as members of a single program investigations that were distinguishable in significant ways, it did disservice to many studies and their authors. This is always the danger when the goal is broad classification and characterization. Moreover, there are doubtlessly significant portions of the research-on-teaching field that have been substantially ignored in this review, owing to lack of adequate understanding on my part.

In this final section of the chapter, I shall discuss a number of issues that cut across many of the programs discussed earlier. These will include the types of knowledge produced in research on teaching, the conceptions of effectiveness implicit in different approaches, the role of ideology in the personal predilections of investigators for particular research programs, the contrasting implications for both educational policy writ large and teacher education in particular that flow from these research programs, and the conceptions of social science research and scientific progress that characterize the different programs.

I shall conclude the section with a discussion of the prognosis for the near future, with special reference to the search for "grand strategies" (Schwab, 1960/1978, pp. 220–225) that might overcome the limitations of the individual research programs we have reviewed.

Types of Knowledge

Different programs of research are likely to produce different types of knowledge about teaching, knowledge of interest to theoreticians, policymakers, and practitioners. There is no simple one-to-one correspondence between a particular research program and the knowledge produced within it. Moreover, in some research programs the knowledge is produced before any empirical work is conducted, and the empirical activities serve to test, refine, confirm, or elaborate the earlier conceptual work.

The following scheme is far from exhaustive, but is presented to suggest the range of types of knowledge to consider as we review the programs of research on teaching.

- *Empirical propositions.* These are generalizations that derive directly from empirical findings. They are most frequently found in discussions of process–product research, but can as easily be generated from research in any of the other programs. Examples include the most frequent statements of association in process–product work, for example, higher academic performance is associated with the use of ordered turns in first-grade reading groups.
- *Moral propositions.* These are normative generalizations that derive from value positions, ethical analyses, or ideological commitments. They frequently underlie other, ostensibly empirical analyses. For example, all the studies of teachers' expectation effects, whether conducted in the process–product tradition or in the classroom ecology approach, rest on moral propositions regarding equity and equality of opportunity.
- *Conceptual inventions, clarifications, and critiques.* These are conceptual developments that may derive from empirical work, but involve a far longer leap from the data, or the inventive combining of empirical generalizations from diverse sources. Examples include Carroll's model of school learning, the concepts of direct instruction or active teaching, and Academic Learning Time. As Rosenshine has pointed out regarding the instructional technologies or protocols (to be discussed presently), these conceptual inventions do not derive directly from findings in any simple way. They are acts of scholarly imagination in which theoretical understanding, practical wisdom, and empirical generalizations are likely to combine into a more general formulation. The most important findings of Jackson's *Life in Classrooms* were a set of conceptual inventions (eg., preactive and interactive teaching) that were to enlighten much of research on teaching for the next decade.
- *Exemplars of practice or malpractice.* These are normally case descriptions of teachers, classrooms, or schools. They do not necessarily claim empirical generalizability. They are presented as instances or exemplars, documenting how education was accomplished (or stymied) by a particular group of teachers and students in a particular place. Florio's (1979) account of the teacher who taught writing through the creation of a simulated town, Erickson and Mohatt's (1982) descriptions of teaching in a North American Indian reservation school, or Smith and Geoffrey's (1968) analysis of teaching in a particular classroom are instances of this type.
- *Technologies or procedural protocols.* These are systematic approaches to instruction in which the sequence of desirable instructional events is specified. These include mastery learning, active mathematics teaching, and other procedural protocols described by Rosenshine and Stevens (this volume). Like conceptual inventions, they represent combinations of empirical generalization, practical experience, useful cases as exemplars, and the intuitions of a designer.

As indicated earlier, the types of knowledge do not map in a simple way onto the research programs. Both ethnographers and process–product researchers may offer empirical generalizations or conceptual inventions. Process–product researchers may even present case descriptions to exemplify aspects of their findings, though they are unlikely to present the personal inter-pretations of participants. Moral propositions are likely to lie undetected beneath most forms of research program.

Conceptions of Effectiveness

Contrasting conceptions of effectiveness accompany the differ-ent programs discussed in this chapter. All programs in which effectiveness was assessed as a function of empirically dem-onstrable relationships with academic achievement measures (or attitude scales, interest inventories, and the like) can be considered to employ *pragmatic* or *correlative* conceptions of effectiveness. Those practices or performances are effective that correlate with an outcome deemed desirable. This criterion of effectiveness is characteristic of both the teaching effectiveness and effective-schools approaches (Brophy & Good; Good & Brophy; Rosenshine & Stevens, all in this volume) to the study of teaching, as well as some more ethnographic studies of class-room process (e.g., Shulman, 1980).

A distinctive alternative is the *normative* conception of effec-tiveness, in which a given exemplar of instruction is compared to a model or conception of good teaching derived from a theory or ideology. This criterion of effectiveness uses *cor-respondence* rather than *correlation* as its test.

For example, Dewey argued that a central purpose of schools is to prepare citizens to function effectively in a democratic society. Therefore, classrooms and schools ought to be settings that, on inspection, provide opportunities for students to learn, the skills of democratic citizenship. One need not develop a test of democratic-skill outcomes to ascertain whether the oppor-tunities for participation, shared decision making, group delib-eration, and the like are presented. Flanders' (1970) research was initiated precisely for that reason, to study the extent to which the features of democratic societies were present in the typical classroom.

Effectiveness by correspondence can be found in many con-temporary studies of teaching as well. When Durkin (1981) studied the teaching of reading comprehension in elementary schools, she did not measure the effectiveness of observed in-struction against tests of reading comprehension. Instead, she began with an a priori normative model of reading comprehen-sion instruction and used that as a template against which to measure the adequacy of the teaching and learning she ob-served. Similarly, when Erickson views the interactions between teacher and students, he uses a conception of effective teaching as accomplishing a match between the linguistic and cultural forms employed by the students and those encouraged, re-warded, and used by the teacher. His match/mismatch ex-amination of classroom life uses an implicit normative criterion of effectiveness. These are both instances of effectiveness as-sessed by correspondence to a normative model rather than correlation with an empirical outcome.

It should be clear that no use of correlative criteria can be free of normative choices. Indeed, the selection of a particular em-pirical criterion instead of all other possibilities, the choice of a particular length of time or extensiveness of teaching episode as the unit of inquiry, all imply normative or value choices. Those who employ correlative criteria, such as standardized achieve-ment tests, frequently avoid explicit consideration of the values or norms underlying their commitments. They must examine the outcome measures employed as indicators of product and determine whether *what* is measured adequately corresponds to the normative definitions of educational outcome to which they subscribe.

Similarly, those who would employ correspondence criteria must be prepared to demonstrate that the appearance of ap-propriate classroom organization, teacher explanations or in-structional practices has been adequately documented. They may ultimately have to link their judgments of correspondence to claimed consequences of educational worth, whether in the form of measured student performance or predictions about the future character of a particular classroom or school. Thus, al-though pragmatic and normative criteria represent different ap-proaches to judging the value of educational activities in the short run, a fully adequate program of research on teaching may well require the use of both kinds of assessment.

Unlike Dunkin and Biddle (1974), I do not encourage scholars to forego their normative commitments as they study teaching. Indeed, I find that the popularity of pragmatic or cor-relative criteria has too often led to mindless studies of teaching effectiveness. Especially when research begins once again (as it must) to study teaching in particular subject areas, conceptions of how knowledge ought to be represented in those areas will become central to judgments of effectiveness. Experts in those areas should not defer to existing standardized achievement tests as the appropriate criteria for measuring the adequacy of teaching. The tests should be adapted and modified until their measurements correspond to the judgment of experts in both the subject field and the cognitive psychology of learning.

Having devoted substantial attention to normative questions in the discussion of knowledge types and conceptions of effectiveness, we shall now turn to the role of ideology gener-ally, as exemplified in the alternative ways scholars choose to study teaching.

Ideology

A number of the controversies reviewed earlier have rested on underlying differences of ideology. Some of these ideological differences are rooted in contrasting conceptions of education in general and teaching in particular; others around political commitments; yet others in relation to perspectives on proper forms of inquiry, whether dubbed scientific or not. Research programs are often adopted because of their consistency with favored ideological stances. Even more typically, programs are actively criticized or resisted because critics detect within them ideological implications the critics find offensive.

Dunkin and Biddle (1974) were critical of the tendency for researchers to employ their studies of teaching processes in the service of an ideological "commitment." They were particularly critical of the pioneering work of Flanders (e.g., 1970), whose commitment to the value of democratic classroom processes (in the spirit of Lewin, Lippitt, & White, 1939) lent a taint of advo-cacy to his research.

More recently, the ideological debates have swirled around the generic conflict between, broadly (and inaccurately) speak-ing, behaviorists and humanists. The humanists claim that process–product research and its Academic Learning Time offshoot derive from a "technological orientation" (e.g., Zumwalt, 1982) to both education and teaching. This orientation is said to focus on particular techniques or behaviors that can be practiced by teachers, leading to prescriptive standards of practice. Such standards "de-skill" the teaching profession, place undue emphasis on achievement gains as measured by standardized tests, and thereby render teaching merely technical rather than "deliberative" and require continuing decision making and artfulness by teachers.

Asserting that sin, like beauty, is often in the eye of the beholder, Gage (in press) argues that the search for lawful relationships between teaching and learning does not necessarily reflect a technological orientation, and surely does not inexorably lead to the teacher as robot. Indeed, reminding readers of his choice of title, "The Scientific Basis of the Art of Teaching" (Gage, 1978), he maintains that his perspective simply calls for the artful practice of teaching to be grounded in scientific propositions as much as possible, and surely not in technical maxims that have been substituted for pedagogical judgment.

Nevertheless, policies and programs for teacher selection and certification at the local and state levels have often taken the results of process–product research and translated them into rather inflexible evaluative standards (Shulman, 1983). Commissions have taken research on engaged time and prescribed longer school days or school years as a solution to low academic achievement. Contrary to the intentions of most leaders in the process–product program, the conception of teaching as a precisely prescribable set of behaviors for increasing pupil gain scores has flourished among designers of some teacher evaluation and staff development programs.

In teacher education, there has been a similar ideological conflict. Those who have pursued the program of teacher cognition and decision making have a strong commitment to a view of teaching as a profession populated by autonomous and learned professionals, much like medicine or law. Those whose studies have focused on the teaching career have generally shared that commitment to a body of research that will enhance teacher autonomy rather than restrict it. Hence, we can appreciate Zumwalt's (1982) unease with those process–product studies that incorporate "shoulds" for teachers into their experimental treatments or their statements of findings. The fact that such maxims are often commonplace in fields of medicine and law without doing great damage to their professionalism is rarely discussed. Ironically, however, it has been precisely the research programs that have been replete with such "shoulds" that have typically been found most valuable by those developing programs of professional development for experienced teachers, even from the vantage point of the teachers' unions (e.g., AFT, 1983).

I have not discussed research on teacher education or the teaching career thus far because it falls outside the bounds of the synoptic model presented earlier. I shall comment on the topic quite briefly at this point. *Teaching* is a beautifully ambiguous term. It describes a process engaged in by individuals in classrooms. That is the sense in which we have been using the term thus far in the chapter. But teaching is also the name for an occupation, a role that occupies the energies and commitments of many people over the course of their adult lives. Teaching is a set of understandings and skills, an occupation, a profession, a career. Teacher education is the process of being prepared to engage in the activities of that career.

We find in the study of teacher education and teaching a set of research programs roughly parallel to those already found in the study of classroom teaching. There are those who view teacher education from a process–product perspective and define research in teacher education as studies in which experimental treatments are manipulated with changes in teaching behavior seen as the outcomes. Others view teaching in the interpretive tradition and describe the experiences of being socialized into the teaching field from the perspectives of the initiates. Such is the work of Lacey (1977) in England, Zeichner (1983) and his colleagues in the United States, and many others whose work is presented by Lanier and Little (this volume).

Among those who study the occupation of teaching and the cultures that characterize it (Feiman-Nemser and Floden, this volume), there are those who treat the career as an unfolding, developmental pattern intrinsic to an occupation, following the traditions of professional socialization in medicine pioneered by Becker et al. (1961) and by Merton, Reader, and Kendall (1957). Others are much more attuned to the interaction between teachers and the particular organizational settings in which they work, concerned less with the universals of professional socialization than with the particulars of work in a context. Much of the work on the teaching profession falls into the interpretive/descriptive mode.

Conceptions of Social Science

At the heart of much of the debate over research programs have been differences in the fundamental conception of social science. This is not unique to the study of teaching. The world of social science and educational research has been rife with debates about the proper conceptions of inquiry in those fields. While the natural science models have dominated the first century of contemporary social science, severe doubts are now being expressed about the appropriateness of those models. Lee Cronbach (1975; 1982) has been among the most powerful of the critical voices. He has seriously questioned the separation of the social sciences from one another as well as from the humanities. He has called for a reduction in concern over methodological orthodoxies and urged that the most important criterion for good social research be the clarity with which it illuminates specific problems in particular contexts of both place and time. He raises serious doubts that inquiries disciplined by the experimental and quantitative procedures of the social sciences can lay claim to achieving significant levels of generalizability:

> All social scientists are engaged in case studies. The 1980 census is no less a case study than is Erikson's *Young Man Luther*. The observations take meaning from their time and place, and from the conceptions held by those who pose the questions and decide how to tabulate. (Cronbach, 1982, p.75)

In his characterization of social science research, Cronbach asserts that "social inquiry reports on events in one or more sites during one slice of time. It can be viewed as quantitatively assisted history" (Cronbach, 1982, p.74). This comparison between social science and educational research, on the one hand,

and history on the other, is provocative. I have earlier remarked that I found the methodological catholicism of history, the manner in which a whole host of both disciplinary perspectives and methodological predilections can coexist in that one field of study, an important model for the study of teaching. In that spirit, I would like to consider some perspectives on the doing of history and consider their implications for our own work.

We have observed that a key feature distinguishing programs of research is their relative emphases on behavior or thought, on the observable and/or directly measurable actions and capacities of individuals or on the stated or inferred intentions, reasons, strategies, attitudes, feelings, expectations, goals or other cognitive states. The two emphases clearly connect to distinctive scholarly traditions.

One way to think about these two alternative perspectives, sometimes called the *etic* and the *emic* in the anthropology and the linguistic literatures, is through a discussion on the doing of history by one of our most eminent philosophers of history, R. G. Collingwood.

Collingwood (1946) contrasts the doing of history with the doing of natural science in a manner that highlights differences among researchers on teaching with regard to their perspectives on what kind of scholarship they pursue:

The historian, investigating any event in the past, makes a distinction between what may be called the outside and the inside of an event. By the outside of the event I mean everything belonging to it which can be described in terms of bodies and their movements: the passage of Caesar, accompanied by certain men, across a river called the Rubicon at one date, or the spilling of his blood on the floor of the senate-house at another. By the inside of the event I mean that in it which can only be described in terms of thought: Caesar's defiance of Republican law, or the clash of constitutional policy between himself and his assassins, The historian is never concerned with either of these to the exclusion of the other. He is investigating not mere events (where by a *mere* event I mean one that has only an outside and no inside) but *actions*, and an action is the unity of the outside and inside of an event....

In the case of nature, this distinction between the outside and the inside of an event does not arise. The events of nature are mere events, not the acts of agents whose thought the scientist endeavors to trace. It is true that the scientist, like the historian, has to go beyond the mere discovery of events; but the direction in which he moves is very different. Instead of conceiving the event as an action and attempting to rediscover the thought of its agent, penetrating from the outside of the event to its inside, the scientist goes beyond the event, observes its relation to others, and thus brings it under a general formula or law of nature. (pp. 213–214)

Collingwood's observations about the doing of history are instructive in two ways. They help us see more clearly the difference between the two research perspectives we have earlier distinguished, the positivist, law seeking, and the interpretive, meaning oriented. Additionally, Collingwood argues that, while distinctly different, the two approaches are not, in principle, incompatible. In fact, the proper work of the historian requires the commingling of the two orientations. This need to describe both events and their correlations as well as actions and their meanings is what makes history the fascinating methodological hybrid of the social sciences. (Or is it the humanities?)

Another question worth pursuing is whether the natural science perspective alone allows scholars to talk about "causes," while the interpretive researcher must be content to render explanatory accounts, that is, to tell compelling stories. Here again, Collingwood offers an insightful argument on the role of causal explanation in history:

This does not mean that words like "cause" are necessarily out of place in reference to history; it only means that they are used there in a special sense. When a scientist asks "Why did that piece of litmus paper turn pink?" he means "On what kinds of occasions do pieces of litmus paper turn pink?" When an historian asks "Why did Brutus stab Caesar?" he means "What did Brutus think, which made him decide to stab Caesar?" The cause of the event, for him, means the thought in the mind of the person by whose agency the event came about: and this is not something other than the event, it is the inside of the event itself. (pp. 214–215)

Collingwood would thus argue that it is not only legitimate to combine the positivist and interpretive perspectives in the same field of study, it is an essential marriage in any truly comprehensive piece of historical (and, perhaps, educational) inquiry. We will examine some conceptions for combining such different approaches to research in the final section of this chapter.

Conceptions of Scientific Progress. Among many researchers, there is a view of scientific progress that we may call Newtonian, based on the observation often attributed to that great mathematician that if we can see far it is because we are as dwarfs standing on the shoulders of giants. (For an extraordinary discussion of the sources for that aphorism, see Merton, 1965.) In this view, science progresses additively, the work of more recent scholars aggregating with that of their predecessors to produce progress in scientific knowledge from generation to generation. The perspective is well expressed in a statement by Clark Hull (1943) describing the conditions for progress in learning theory:

Progress ... will consist in the laborious writing, one by one, of hundreds of equations; in the experimental determination, one by one, of hundreds of empirical constants contained in the equations; in the devising of practically usable units in which to measure the quantities expressed in the equations ... in the rigorous deduction, one by one, of thousands of theorems and corollaries from the primary definitions and equations; in the meticulous performance of thousands of critical quantitative experiments. (pp. 400–401)

This is a perspective on the cumulative character of scientific knowledge that fits well with the process–product program and its derivatives. Certainly the emphasis upon the meta-analysis of findings from disparate studies to establish empirical relationships more firmly is consistent with this view of cumulative progress. From this vantage point, it is difficult to understand how much of the research in the classroom ecology or teacher cognition programs can be construed as progressing, much less scientifically enlightening.

Kuhn's (1970) view of progress is quite different. Progress occurs as old paradigms are found wanting and new ones are invented to replace them. Often there are not adequate empirical grounds for choosing between competing paradigms. When a new paradigm emerges it often leaves behind, unanswered, many of the research questions that were at the heart of earlier paradigms. They are no longer critical puzzles. As Dewey (1898) observed in another context, speaking of the way in which Darwinist conceptions replaced the Aristotelian problem formulations that had preceded them, "we do not solve them; we get over them."

The sense of progress found in the work of interpretive researchers contrasts dramatically. Clifford Geertz (1973) expresses the view eloquently:

> Cultural analysis is intrinsically incomplete. And, worse than that, the more deeply it goes the less complete it is. It is a strange science whose most telling assertions are its most tremulously based...
>
> The fact is that to commit oneself to ... an interpretive approach to the study of [culture] is to commit oneself to a view of ethnographic assertion as, to borrow W.B. Gallie's by now famous phrase, "essentially contestable." Anthropology, or at least interpretive anthropology, is a science whose progress is marked less by perfection of consensus than by a refinement of debate. What gets better is the precision with which we vex each other. (p. 29)

To the extent that this sense of progress indeed characterizes the work of those who conduct interpretive research on teaching, the ideological conflict regarding the goals and functions of science becomes clear. It is also apparent why the results of positivist research are more typically employed to guide policy while those of interpretive researchers most frequently are employed to criticize and question, to vex with precision.

This becomes a source of great frustration for policymakers who want research to point the way to correct practices and procedures. Kenneth Prewitt (quoted in Cronbach, 1982) attempted to alleviate those frustrations (though not entirely to relieve them) in his testimony before the House Subcommittee on Science, Research, and Technology:

> The complexities of the problems for which the social and behavioral sciences might be helpful are always going to be one step ahead of the problem-solving abilities of those sciences. ... They are sciences whose progress is marked, and whose usefulness is measured, less by the achievement of consensus or the solving of problems than by a refinement of debate and a sharpening of the intelligence upon which collective management of human affairs depend. (p.75)

Views of Teaching and Teacher Education

How can these alternative perspectives on the study of teaching be resolved? How can we be guided with respect to what constitutes the knowledge base of teaching and how it grows? What does a teacher need to know and to do in order to function well? And how does that knowledge relate to the results of research on teaching? Agreeing with Gage (1978) and others, Schwab (1983) defines teaching as an art. He proceeds to discuss the characteristics of an art:

> Every art, whether it be teaching, stone carving or judicial control of a court of law ... has rules, but knowledge of the rules does not make one an artist. Art arises as the knower of the rules learns to apply them appropriately to the particular case. Application, in turn, requires acute awareness of the particularities of that case and ways in which the rule can be modified to fit the case without complete abrogation of the rule. In art, the form must be adapted to the

matter. Hence the form must be communicated in ways which illuminate its possibilities for modification. (p. 265)

If teaching is an art, its practice requires at least three different forms of knowledge: These are knowledge of rules of principles, knowledge of particular cases, and knowledge of ways to apply appropriate rules to properly discerned cases. Most successful process-product research produces propositional rules. Such general rules include propositions about assigning praise or blame, allocating turns, sequencing instruction, checking for understanding, and the like (see Rosenshine & Stevens, this volume). There are also general maxims that do not necessarily derive from research on teaching, but are part of the traditional wisdom of the practitioner.

In this regard, medicine is often proposed as a proper model for education. The results of basic and clinical medical research provide general principles that guide clinical choices in particular circumstances (or at least indicate that the practice should be consistent with those principles). Medical students learn that portion of the knowledge base during their premedical and preclinical education. They then proceed to clinical clerkships and graduate residency education to acquire knowledge of cases and opportunities for supervised practice in applying rules to such cases.

The ambiguity of the term "case" can be problematic. In teaching, the term not only represents types of individual children (the typical referent for a "case" study), but also types of classrooms or schools, and types of subject-matter content to be taught. These elements would produce many conjunctions of child, class, and subject. I use "types" purposely since I do not view cases as unique events, but as instances of a broader class. To call something a case is to make the claim that it is a "case of something." Even in an idiographic enterprise, cases must have some generalizability or their potential value in the knowledge base is severely limited.

An alternative to the medicine-like view of the knowledge base of teaching may be the analogy of law and legal practice. In medicine, the claim is that the general propositions derive from scientific processes of observation, experimentation, interpetation, and generalization—the use of empirical methods of inductive inquiry. The general rules then act in the manner of major premises from which clinical practices are deduced, as mediated by observations of particular circumstances that serve as minor premises. In law, however, there is no body of empirically demonstrated generalizations forming the knowledge base of the field. Instead, there are general normative principles dealing with such generic concepts as justice, property, individual rights, and social obligations, These typically take the form of laws, regulations, or statutes. Legal education is a process of learning to find one's way through the thicket of documented cases to find proper precedents for the current problem. Instead of reasoning deductively from general principles to particular cases, the attorney or judge typically reasons analogically from other cases qua precedents to the particularities of the case at hand. Alternative candidates for the status of precedent are weighed in light of the features of the present case and in regard to the normative principles germane to the case until a justifiable judgment or decision can be rendered. That judgment is then entered into the cumulative record that aggregates into the body of case law. Learning the knowledge base of law requires repeated opportunities to practice the classification and retrieval of cases and the analogical combining of rules and cases.

An image of the teaching art such as this one is provocatively parallel to that of Fenstermacher (1978). Following Green (1971), Fenstermacher argues that educating a teacher is not a matter of inculcating a knowledge base in the form of a specific set of teaching skills and competencies. Rather, to educate a teacher is to influence the premises on which a teacher bases practical reasoning about teaching in specific situations. In Green's terms, these are the premises of the practical argument in the mind of the teacher. These premises are derived, in part, from the generalizations of empirical research on teaching. The premises serve to ground the decisions, not determine them.

Yet another analogy can be drawn to architecture, where the practitioner simultaneously derives guidance from two bodies of knowledge, the physics, mathematics, and chemistry of engineering and materials science and the accumulated wealth of cases from the Acropolis to the Transamerica Building, from a Navajo Indian village to Levittown. The scientific principles of construction, heating, lighting, and the like will progress in a Newtonian or Kuhnian manner. In that sense, Frank Lloyd Wright had a larger-principled knowledge base than Sir Christopher Wren, as did Mies van der Rohe relative to Bramante. But the accumulated exemplars of architectural design form the case literature for practitioners. (See Soltis, 1975, for a similar analysis.)

In all these senses, we can view the study of teaching progressing. Both our scientific knowledge of rules and principles (properly construed as grounds, not prescriptions) and our knowledge of richly described and critically analyzed cases combine to define the knowledge base of teaching. The guided and supervised practice needed to learn how to apply, adapt, and, when necessary, invent rules for particular cases understood as instances of classes of events, that practice constitutes another component of the knowledge base. And this base must incorporate rules and cases for subject matter content and its pedagogy as well as for the organization and management of instruction.

While it has been inspiring to state the case for learning from cases, the fact is that we have little idea of how such a process works. How do practitioners learn vicariously from the documented experiences of others? We know from the literature on human judgment and decision making (e.g., Tversky & Kahneman, 1974; Nisbett & Ross, 1980) that most individuals find specific cases more powerful influences on their decisions than impersonally presented empirical findings, even though the latter constitute "better" evidence. Although principles are powerful, cases are memorable, and lodge in memory as the basis for later judgments. But why this is the case, and how to make this kind of process work to the advantage of reflection and intelligent practical reasoning, rather than as one of the "idols of the mind" (Bacon, 1620), is a serious problem for those who study the education of teachers.

Search for a Grand Strategy

If any one program of research is in principle insufficient, is there no alternative to conducting research that is limited in its perspectives or applications? Schwab (1960, 1978) has discussed this as the question or a "grand strategy" (1978, pp. 220-221). Having dismissed the possibility of any one strategy being best, Schwab (1978) asserts that a circumstance much like we confront in research on teaching may well be a blessing rather than a sign of weakness:

> We need not, therefore, *make* a virtue of the necessity of pursuing enquiry through men who are moved by numerous preferences to work in different ways toward differing specifications of their common goal. It *is* a virtue.
>
> Yet, as long as resources for research are limited, there is an itch to believe that one of the several strategies available to science is the best one.... I have tried to show that this hope must betray us. Consensus on a single pattern of choices will merely enable us to overlook what we have not done in our enquiry.... This leaves the possibility that some particular *order* of different strategies, constituting a grand strategy, may be better than all other orders. (p.221)

Several researchers on teaching have advocated versions of a grand strategy. The most popular of these is the "descriptive-correlational-experimental loop." Gage (1978) among others has advocated an order of studies in which general qualitative description of a small number of cases is the first stage of research. After important variables and constructs have been identified using those descriptive studies (exemplars leading to conceptual inventions), large-scale process–product correlational studies are conducted to identify discrete relationships between individual teacher behaviors and student outcomes at a level of specificity and precision unavailable through qualitative work (leading to empirical generalizations). Scholars then organize the array of empirical generalizations into composites (more conceptual invention) for purposes of field testing. The last stage of research is controlled experimentation to establish causal links between those composite models of teaching (now in the form of instructional technologies or teaching protocols) and student learning outcomes. Gage (in press) maintains that this has been the pattern followed in the successful process–product program. Moreover, he urges that the descriptive-correlational-experimental loop become the basis for a new era of collaboration between those involved in process–product work and those in the ethnographic/sociolinguistic program.

Another view of grand strategy moves in exactly the opposite direction from the descriptive-correlational-experimental loop. Ethnographers such as Erickson (this volume) have argued that the empirical propositions emanating from process–product work are too general to provide adequately concrete guidance to teachers unless they are followed by much more thickly described interpretive work. Thus Erickson claims that any stage of generalization, whether produced through correlational studies or experiments, must be followed by the particularization of concrete detail characteristic of classroom ethnographies. Both arguments appear sound. Two alternative grand strategies have been proposed, and each will be germane under the correct circumstances. How might we think about such circumstances?

Evertson and Green (this volume) advocate thinking about observational research on teaching in terms of programs of research that blend approaches traditionally labeled quantitative or qualitative as appropriate for the particular phenomena under investigation. They provide extremely useful heuristics for determining how to combine methods of observation in a sequence of studies forming a program of research.

Cronbach (1982) also argues for an eclectic strategy:

What research styles and objectives follow from the intent to advance understanding? A mixed strategy is called for: censuses and laboratory experiments, managerial monitoring and anthropological *Einfühlung*, mathematical modeling and unstructured observation. A few maxims can be offered even for eclectic social science. (p. 73)

Although Cronbach's call for eclecticism is one with which I can surely resonate in principle, the practice of such combined strategies is complex indeed. One of the strategies more frequently encountered these days could best be called the "goulash" or "garbage can" approach. It is a form of eclecticism run wild, with little or no discipline to regulate the decisions. In these studies, many forms of research are incorporated and thrown together with little thought for the differences in their purposes, assumptions, or perspectives. Systematic observations are conducted randomly throughout the year for thirty minutes each as is typical for the process–product study. Case studies of particular classes are thrown in for purposes of "thick description," but nothing about the resulting descriptions is either thick or interpretively descriptive. They are simply impressionistic descriptions written in the etic style of process–product research, but without its characteristic precision. Undisciplined eclecticism is no virtue when compared to carefully conducted research within a particular research program's tradition. Indeed, it is probably worse.

Nevertheless, we need not give up on the notion of research programs conducted in the spirit of disciplined eclecticism. A new generation of educational scholars is being prepared who are truly research methodologists, that is, capable of employing alternative approaches to problems as they are formulated, rather than the orthodox research methodists of an earlier generation (Shulman, 1984b). Moreover, the development of research centers and institutes in which representatives of distinctly different research programs and traditions can work collaboratively shows promise for the development of healthy new hybrid programs. It may be that in many cases individual studies cannot be pursued jointly, the canons of each research program must be allowed to function, thus to discipline the inquiry as it is pursued. But when investigators have learned to speak each other's languages, to comprehend the terms in which other programs' research questions are couched, then processes of deliberation over findings can yield the hybrid understandings not possible when members of individual research programs dwell in intellectual ghettos of their own construction.

With respect to the concept of a grand strategy, my own view is that, while the concept is heuristically useful, there exists no particular sequence or order of approaches that is generally optimal. The order selected will reflect the particular propensities or styles of the investigators, the ways in which the research problem is cast as influenced by prior research or by policy issues. Most important, the order will be determined by the dialogue in the Great Conversation, with the excitement engendered or horror elicited by recently conducted pieces of

research. The responses they elicit from among other members of the research community will determine which studies are appropriate to pursue next.

Zumwalt (1982, pp. 232–233) reported that after the excitement associated with publication of the first *Handbook of Research on Teaching*, authors for the *Second Handbook* found little to crow about. Travers, editor of the 1973 volume, observed that "those who participated in the first *Handbook* would never have guessed that, a decade later, authors of the *Second Handbook* would be having even greater difficulty in finding significant research to report than did their predecessors" (Travers, 1973, pp. vii–viii).

This is certainly not the case some 12 years later as we examine the present third edition. Findings have proliferated. Many have been replicated and extended. Policymakers and practitioners alike take the research seriously and apply its results to their activities. No contemporary field of applied social science research has attracted the range and diversity of disciplinary efforts in the pursuit of its questions as has research on teaching. The absence of a single research paradigm is not a sign of pathology in the field. The presence of active, occasionally even acrimonious, debate among investigators does not signal danger for the field of study. The publication of this edition finds research on teaching in a state of admirable vigor and promising progress. It is not Newtonian progress, to be sure, but it is precisely the kind of development appropiate to educational inquiry. Its benefits are manifold for they promise to lead to a deeper theoretical understanding of teaching, a continuing documentation of its many forms and functions, and the likelihood of more enlightened future approaches to the entire teaching enterprise.

REFERENCES

American Federation of Teachers. (1983). Final Report, Research Dissemination Project. Washington, DC: National Institute of Education.

Anderson, C., & Smith, E. (1984). Children's preconceptions and content-area textbooks. In G. Duffy, L. Roehler, & J. Mason (Eds.), *Comprehension instruction: Perspectives and suggestions*. New York: Longman.

Anderson, L. (1984). The environment of instruction: The function of seatwork in a commercially developed curriculum. In G. Duffy, L. Rochler, & J. Mason (Eds.), *Comprehension instruction: Perspectives and suggestions*. New York: Longman.

Anderson, L., Evertson, C., & Brophy, J. (1979). An experimental study of effective teaching in first-grade reading groups. *Elementary School Journal, 79*(4), 193–223.

Anderson, L., Evertson, C., & Emmer, E. (1980). Dimensions of classroom management derived from recent research. *Journal of Curriculum Studies, 12*, 343–356.

Armbruster, B. B., Stevens, R. J., & Rosenshine, B. (1977). *Analyzing content coverage and emphasis: A study of three curricula and two tests* (Tech. Rep. No. 26). Urbana–Champaign: University of Illinois, Center for the Study of Reading.

Au, K. (1980). Participation structures in a reading lesson with Hawaiian children. *Anthropology and Education Quarterly, 11*(2), 91–115.

Bacon, F. (1902). *Novum organum.* (J. Dewey, Ed.). New York: P. F. Collier. (Original work published 1620).

Barr, R., & Dreeben, R. (1978). Instruction in classrooms. In L. S. Shulman (Ed.), *Review of research in education* (Vol. 5). Itasca, IL: F. E. Peacock.

Barr, R., & Dreeben, R. (1983a). *How schools work.* Chicago: University of Chicago Press.

Barr, R., & Dreeben, R. (1983b). School policy, production, and productivity. In L. S. Shulman & G. Sykes (Eds.), *Handbook of teaching and policy*. New York: Longman.

Becker, H. S., Geer, B., & Hughes, E, (1968). *Making the grade: The academic side of college life*. New York: John Wiley.

Becker, H. S., Geer, B., Hughes, E., & Strauss, A. (1961). *Boys in white: Student culture in medical school*. Chicago: University of Chicago Press.

Bennett, N., Jordan, J., Long, G., & Wade, B. (1976). *Teaching styles and pupil progress*. Cambridge MA: Harvard University Press.

Berliner, D. C. (1979). Tempus educare. In P. L. Peterson and H. J. Walberg (Eds.), *Research on teaching*. Berkeley, CA: McCutchan.

Bloom, B. S. (1953). Thought-processes in lectures and discussions. *Journal of General Education, 7*(3), 160–169.

Bloom, B. S. (1968). Learning for mastery. *Evaluation comment*. UCLA—CSEIP, 1, n.p.

Bloom, B. S. (1976). *Human characteristics and school learning*. New York: McGraw-Hill.

Brophy, J. E. (1983). Classroom organization and managment. *Elementary School Journal, 83*(4), 265–286.

Brophy, J. E., & Good, T. L. (1974). *Teacher-student relationships: Causes and consequences*. New York: Holt, Rinehart and Winston.

Bruner, J. S., Goodnow, J. J., & Austin, G. A. (1956). *A study of thinking*. New York: John Wiley.

Carroll, J .B. (1963). A model for school learning. *Teachers College Record, 64*(8), 723–733.

Chomsky, N. (1957). *Syntactic structures*. Hawthorne, NY: Mouton.

Clark, C. M., & Yinger, R. J. (1979). Teacher thinking. In P. L. Peterson & H. J. Walberg (Eds.), *Research on teaching*. Berkeley, CA: McCutchan.

Coleman, J. S., Campbell, E. Q. Hobson, C. J.. McPartland, J. Mood, A. M., Weinfeld, F. D., & York, R. L. (1966). *Equality of educational opportunity*. Washington, D.C.: U.S. Government Printing Office.

Collingwood, R. G. (1946). *The idea of history*. New York: Oxford University Press.

Cronbach, L. J. (1975). Beyond the two disciplines of scientific psychology. *American Psychologist, 30*(2), 116–127.

Cronbach, L. J. (1982). Prudent aspirations for social inquiry. In L. Kruskal (Ed.), *The future of the social sciences*. Chicago: University of Chicago Press.

Dahloff, U. (1971). *Ability grouping, content validity, and curriculum process analysis*. New York: Teachers College Press, Columbia University.

Dawes, R. M. (1971). A case study of graduate admissions: Application of three principles of human decision making. *American Psychologist, 26*(2), 180–188.

Delamont, S., & Atkinson, P. (1980). The two traditions in educational ethnography: Sociology and anthropology compared. *British Journal of Sociology of Education, 1*, 139–152.

Dewey, J. (1910). The influence of Darwinism on philosophy. In J. Dewey, *The influence of Darwinism on philosophy, and other essays*. New York: H. Holt & Co. (Original work published 1898).

Doyle, W. (1977). Learning the classroom environment: An ecological analysis. *Journal of Teacher Education, 28*, 51–55.

Doyle, W. (1978). Paradigms for research on teacher effectiveness. In L. S. Shulman (Ed.), *Review of research in education* (Vol 5). Itasca, IL: F. E. Peacock.

Doyle, W. (1983). Academic work. *Review of Educational Research, 53*(2), 159–199.

Doyle, W. (in press). Paradigms for research on teaching. In T. Husen and T. N. Postlethwaite (Eds.), *International encyclopedia of education: Research and studies*. Oxford: U.K.: Pergamon.

Dunkin, M. J., & Biddle, B. J. (1974). *The study of teaching*. New York: Holt, Rinehart and Winston.

Durkin, D. (1981). Reading comprehension instruction in five basal reading series. *Reading Research Quarterly, 16*(4), 515–544.

Elbaz, F. (1981). The teacher's "practical knowledge": Report of a case study. *Curriculum Inquiry, 7*(1), 43–71.

Elstein, A. S., Shulman, L. S., & Sprafka, S. A. (1978). *Medical problem solving: An analysis of clinical reasoning*. Cambridge, MA: Harvard University Press.

Emmer, E., Evertson, C., & Anderson, L. (1980). Effective classroom management at the beginning of the school year. *Elementary School Journal, 80*, 219–231.

Erickson, F. (1973). What makes school ethnography ethnographic? *Council of Anthropology and Education Newsletter, 2*, 10–19.

Erickson, F. (1982a). Classroom discourse as improvisation: Relationships between academic task structure and social participation structures in lessons. In L. C. Wilkinson (Ed.), *Communicating in the classroom*. New York: Academic Press.

Erickson, F. (1982b). Taught cognitive learning in its immediate environment: A neglected topic in the anthropology of education. *Anthropology and Education Quarterly, 13*, 149–180.

Erickson, F., & Mohatt , G. (1982). Cultural organization of participant structures in two classrooms of Indian students. In G. D. Spindler (Ed.), *Doing the ethnography of schooling: Educational anthropology in action*. New York: Holt, Rinehart and Winston.

Evertson, C., Emmer, E., Sanford, J., & Clements, B. (1983). Improving class management: An experiment in an elementary classroom. *Elementary School Journal, 84*(2), 173–188.

Fenstermacher, G. D. (1978). A philosophical consideration of recent research on teacher effectiveness. In L. S. Shulman (Ed.), *Review of research in education, Vol. 6* (pp. 157–185). Itasca, IL: F. E. Peacock.

Feyerabend, P. (1974). How to be a good empiricist — A plea for tolerance in matters epistemological. In P. H. Nidditch (Ed.), *The philosophy of science* (pp. 12–39). Oxford: Oxford University Press.

Fisher, C., Filby, N., Marliave, R., Cahen, L., Dishaw, M., Moore, J., & Berliner, D. (1978, June). *Teaching behaviors, academic learning time, and student achievement. Beginning teacher evaluation study* (Phase III-B, final report). San Francisco: Far West Labotatory.

Flanders, N. A. (1970). *Analyzing teacher behavior*. Reading, MA: Addison-Wesley.

Florio, S. (1978). *Learning how to go to school*. Unpublished doctoral dissertation, Harvard University.

Florio, S. (1979). The problem of dead letters: Social perspectives on the teaching of writing. *Elementary School Journal, 80*(1), 1–7.

Freeman, D. J., Kuhs, T. M., Knappen, L. B., Floden, R. E., Schmidt, W. H., & Schwille, J. R. (1983). Do textbooks and tests define a natural curriculum in elementary school mathematics? *Elementary School Journal, 83*(5), 501–514.

Gage, N. L. (Ed.), (1963). *Handbook of research on teaching*. Chicago: Rand McNally.

Gage, N. L. (1978). *The scientific basis of the art of teaching*. New York: Teachers College Press, Columbia University.

Gage, N. L. (in press). Hard gains in the soft sciences: The case of pedagogy. *Phi Delta Kappa Monographs*.

Gage, N. L. & Giaconia, R. (1981). Teaching practices and student achievement: Causal connections. *New York University Education Quarterly, 12*(3), 2–9.

Gagné, R. M. (1970). *The conditions of learning* (2nd ed.). New York: Holt, Rinehart, and Winston.

Geertz, C, (1973). Thick description: Toward an interpretive theory of culture. In C. Geertz, *The interpretation of cultures* (pp. 3–30). New York: Basic Books.

Geertz, C. (1983). Blurred genres: The refiguration of social thought. In C. Geertz, *Local knowledge*. New York: Basic Books.

Glaser, R. (Ed.), (1962). *Training research and education*. Pittsburgh: University of Pittsburgh Press.

Good, T. L. (1979). Teacher effectiveness in the elementary school: What we know about it now. *Journal of Teacher Education, 30*, 52–64.

Good, T. L. (1983). Classroom research: A decade of progress. *Educational Psychologist, 18*(3), 127–144.

Good, T. L., Biddle, B. J. & Brophy, J. E. (1975). *Teachers make a difference*. New York: Holt, Rinehart and Winston.

Good, T. L., Grouws, D. A., & Beckerman, T. (1978). Curriculum pacing: Some empirical data in mathematics. *Journal of Curriculum Studies, 10*(1), 75–82.

Good, T. L., Grouws, D. A., & Ebmeier, H. (1983). *Active mathematics teaching*. (Research on Teaching Monograph Series). New York: Longman.

Green, J. L. (1983). Teaching and learning: A linguistic perspective. *Elementary School Journal, 83*(4), 353–391.

Green, T. F. (1971) *The activities of teaching*. New York: McGraw-Hill.

Hamilton, S. F., (1983). The social side of schooling: Ecological studies of classrooms and schools. *Elementary School Journal, 83*(4), 313–334.

Harnischfeger, A., & Wiley, D. E. (1976). The teaching–learning process in elementary schools: A synoptic view. *Curriculum Inquiry, 6*(1), 5–43.

Heath, S. B. (1983). *Ways with words*. Cambridge: Cambridge University Press.

Herbart, J. F. (1895). *The science of education, its general principles deduced from its aim and the aesthetic revelation of the world* (Trans. from German by Herluf & Emme Felkin). Boston: D. C. Heath.

Hull, C. L. (1943). *Principles of behavior*. New York: Appleton.

Jackson, P. W. (1968). *Life in classrooms*. New York: Holt, Rinehart & Winston.

Kagan, N., Krathwohl, D. R., & Miller, R. (1963). Stimulated recall in therapy using video tape—a case study. *Journal of Counseling Psychology, 10*(3), 237–243.

Kimble, G. A. (1975). Required reading for the profession [Review of E. Hilgard & G. Bower, *Theories of learning* (4th ed.)]. *Contemporary Psychology, 20*(8), 613–614.

Kounin, J. (1970). *Discipline and group management in classrooms*. New York: Holt, Rinehart & Winston.

Kuhn, T. S. (1970). *The structure of scientific revolutions* (2nd ed. enlarged). Chicago: University of Chicago Press. (Original work published 1964).

Lacey, C. (1977) *The socialization of teachers*. London: Methuen.

Lakatos, I. (1970). Falsification and the methodology of scientific research programmes. In I. Lakatos & A. Musgrave (Eds.) *Criticism and the growth of knowledge*. Cambridge: Cambridge University Press.

Leinhardt, G. (1983). Novice and expert knowledge of individual students' achievement. *Educational Psychologist, 18*(3), 165–179.

Leinhardt, G., & Smith, D. (1984, April). Expertise in mathematics instruction: Subject-matter knowledge. Paper presented at the annual meeting of the American Educational Research Association, New Orleans.

Lewin, K., Lippitt, R., & White, R. (1939). Patterns of aggressive behavior in experimentally created "social climates." *Journal of Social Psychology, 10*, 271–299.

Lightfoot, S. L. (1983). *The good high school*. New York: Basic Books.

Lundgren, U. P. (1972). *Frame factors and the teaching process: A contribution to curriculum theory and theory on teaching*. Stockholm: Almgrist and Wiksell.

MacKay, A., & Marland, P. (1978). Thought processes of teachers. Presented at the meeting of the American Educational Research Association, Toronto.

Masterman, M, (1970). The nature of a paradigm. In I. Lakatos & A. Musgrave (Eds.), *Criticism and the growth of knowledge*. Cambridge: Cambridge University Press.

McDermott, R. P. (1976). *Kids make sense: An ethnographic account of the interactional management of success and failure in one first-grade classroom*. Unpublished doctoral dissertation, Stanford University, Stanford, CA.

McDonald, F., & Elias, P. (1976). *The effects of teacher performance on pupil learning. Beginning teacher evaluation study* (Phase II, final report, Vol. I). Princeton, NJ: Educational Testing Service.

Mehan, H. (1979). *Learning lessons: Social organization in the classroom*. Cambridge, MA: Harvard University Press.

Merton, R. K. (1959). Notes on problem finding in sociology. In R. K. Merton, L. Broom, & L. S. Cottrell, Jr. (Eds.), *Sociology today* pp. ix–xxxiv. New York: Basic Books.

Merton R. K. (1965). *On the shoulders of giants: A Shandean postscript*. New York: The Free Press.

Merton, R. K. (1967). On sociological theories of the middle range. In R. K. Merton, *On theroretical sociology* pp. 39–72. New York: The Free Press.

Merton, R. K. (1975). Structural analysis in sociology. In P. Blau (Ed.), *Approaches to the study of social structure*. New York: The Free Press.

Merton, R. K., Reader G. G., & Kendall, P. (Eds.). (1957). *The student physician: Introductory studies in the sociology of medical education*. Cambridge, MA: Harvard University Press.

Miles, M. B., & Huberman, A. M. (1984). *Qualitative data analysis: A sourcebook of new methods*. Beverly Hills: Sage Publications.

Miller, G. A., Galanter, E., & Pribram, K. H. (1960). *Plans and the structure of behavior*. New York: Holt, Reinhart & Winston.

Mitzel, H. E. (1960). Teacher effectiveness. In C. W. Harris (Ed.), *Encyclopedia of educational research* (3rd ed., pp. 1481–1486). New York: Macmillan.

Newell, A., & Simon, H. A. (1956). The logic theory machine: A complex information processing system. *I.R.E. Transactions on information theory, 2*, 61–79.

Nisbett, R. E., & Ross, L. (1980). *Human inference: Strategies and shortcomings of social judgement*. Englewood Cliffs, NJ: Prentice-Hall.

Peshkin, A. (1978). *Growing up American: Schooling and the survival of community*. Chicago: University of Chicago Press.

Peterson, P. L., & Clark, C. M. (1978). Teachers' reports of their cognitive processes during teaching. *American Educational Research Journal, 15*(4), 555–565.

Peterson, P. L., & Swing, S. R. (1982). Beyond time on task: Students' reports of their thought processes during classroom instruction. *Elementary School Journal, 82*(5), 481–491.

Phillips, S. U. (1983). *The invisible culture: Communication in classroom and community on the Warm Spring Indian Reservation*. New York & London: Longman.

Piaget, J. (1952). *The origin of intelligence in childen*. New York: International Universities Press.

Resnick, L. B. (1981). Instructional psychology. *Annual Review of Psychology, 32*, 659–704.

Rosenshine, B. (1983). Teaching functions in instructional programs. *Elementary School Journal, 83*(4), 335–351.

Rosenthal, R., & Jacobson, L. (1968) *Pygmalion in the classroom*. New York: Holt, Rinehart and Winston.

Rowe, M. B. (1974). Relation of wait-time and rewards to the development of language, logic, and fate control: Part II – Rewards. *Journal of Research in Science Teaching, 11*(4), 291–308.

Schwab, J. J. (1960). What do scientists do? *Behavioral Science, 5*(1), 1–27. (Reprinted in Schwab, 1978).

Schwab, J. J. (1962). The concept of the structure of a discipline. *Educational Record, 43*, 197–205. (Reprinted in Schwab, 1978).

Schwab, J. J. (1978). *Science, curriculum, and liberal education* (selected essays). Chicago: University of Chicago Press.

Schwab, J. J. (1983). The practical 4: Something for curriculum professors to do. *Curriculum Inquiry, 13*(3), 239–265.

Shavelson, R. J. (1973). What is *the* basic teaching skill? *Journal of Teacher Education, 24*(2), 144–151.

Shavelson, R. J. (1983). Review of research on teachers' pedagogical judgements, plans and decisions. *Elementary School Journal, 83*(4), 392–413.

Shroyer, J. C. (1981). *Critical moments in the teaching of mathematics: What makes teaching difficult?* Unpublished doctoral dissertation, Michigan State University, East Lansing.

Shulman, L. S. (1983). Autonomy and obligation: The remote control of teaching. In L. S. Shulman & G. Sykes (Eds.), *Handbook of teaching and policy* (pp. 484–504). New York: Longman.

Shulman, L. S. (1984a). The missing paradigm in research on teaching. Lecture presented at the Research and Development Center for Teacher Education, Austin, TX.

Shulman, L. S. (1984b). The practical and the eclectic: A deliberation on teaching and educational research. *Curriculum Inquiry, 14*(2), 183–200.

Shulman, L. S., & Elstein, A. S. (1975). Studies of problem solving, judgement, and decision making: Implications for educational research. In F. N. Kerlinger (Ed.), *Review of research in education* (Vol 3). Itasca, IL: F. E. Peacock.

Shulman, L. S., Sykes, G., & Phillips, D. (1983, November). *Knowledge growth in a profession: The development of knowledge in teaching*. Proposal submitted to the Spencer Foundation, Stanford University School of Education, Stanford, CA.

Simon, H. A. (1957). *Models of man: Social and rational: Mathematical essays.* New York: John Wiley.

Smith, B. O. (1983). Some comments on educational research in the twentieth century. *Elementary School Journal, 83*(4), 488–492.

Smith, L. H., & Geoffrey, W. (1968). *The complexities of an urban classroom: An analysis toward a general theory of teaching.* New York: Holt, Reinhart and Winston.

Soar, R. S., & Soar, R. M. (1979). Emotional climate and management. In P. L. Peterson & H. J. Walberg (Eds.), *Research on teaching.* Berkeley CA: McCutchan.

Soltis, J. (1975). Philosophy of education: Retrospect and prospect. *Education Theory, 25*(3), 211–222.

Stallings, J. A., & Kaskowitz, D. (1974). Follow through classroom observation evaluation. 1972–73. Menlo Park, CA: Stanford Research Institute.

Toulmin, S. E., (1961). *Foresight and understanding: An enquiry into the aims of science.* Bloomington, IN: Indiana University press.

Travers, R. M. W. (Ed.). (1973). *Second handbook of research on teaching,* Chicago: Rand McNally.

Tversky, A., & Kahneman, D. (1974). Judgement under uncertainty: Heuristics and biases. *Science, 185,* 1124–1131.

Weinstein, R. S. (1983). Student preceptions of schooling. *Elementary School Journal, 83*(4). 287–312.

Winne, P. H., & Marx, R. W. (1982). Students' and teachers' views of thinking processes for classroom learning. *Elementary School Journal, 82*(5), 493–518.

Wolcott, H. F. (1973). *The man in the principal's office.* New York: Holt, Rinehart and Winston.

Yinger, R. (1977). *A study of teacher planning: Description and theory development using ethnographic and informal processing methods.* Unpublished doctoral dissertation, Michigan State University, East Lansing.

Zeichner, K. M. (1983). Alternative paradigms of teacher education. *Journal of Teacher Education, 34*(3), 3–9.

Zumwalt, K. K. (1982). Research on teaching: Implications for teacher education. In A. Lieberman and M. W. McLaughlin (Eds.), *Policy making in education. Eight-first yearbook of the National Society for the Study of Education.* Chicago: University of Chicago Press.

2.
Philosophy of Research on Teaching: Three Aspects

Gary D Fenstermacher
University of Arizona

This chapter makes use of three different enterprises within philosophy: concept analysis, philosophy of social science, and moral theory. These three aspects of philosophical enquiry are employed, not so much to show how philosophy works, but to argue for a particular kind of connection between research on teaching and the profoundly moral task of educating fellow human beings. This connection will be apparent as the three sections of the chapter unfold.

The first section sets forth an analysis of the concept of teaching. The point of this analysis is to distinguish the root or generic meaning of 'teaching' from the elaborated meanings that often appear in empirical studies of teaching. The second section uses some recent work in philosophy of science to differentiate knowledge production from knowledge use, and to establish the value of different research methods for the study of teaching. The third section shows how research on teaching can be brought to bear on the moral and rational foundations of teaching, thereby enhancing the teacher's capacity to educate.

I believe that research on teaching has contributed to the improvement of teaching and learning, and may continue to do so. Good research on teaching not only advances our understanding of the phenomena of teaching, it adds to our ability to teach in morally defensible and rationally grounded ways. Future contributions will be enhanced if researchers undertake their work with informed regard for the philosophical aspects of the concepts and methods they use, as well as for the moral properties inherent in the activity of education. The purpose of this chapter is to assist the researcher with work that is productive of the nobler ends of education.

A Concept of Teaching

Anyone engaged in the study of teaching undertakes that study with some concept of what he or she is studying. The concept may be implicit, as when a certain notion of teaching is presupposed or unconsciously assumed, or it may be explicit, as when a specific definition or set of criteria is set forth by the researcher. In the case of standard, quantitative methods of research, any attempts to be explicit about definitions are usually controlled by the demands of operationalization. That is, the researcher is required to specify the concept in ways that make it measurable, and as a continuous variable when and where possible. Hence many researchers are not familiar with other ways of getting at the meaning of 'teaching', particularly ways that render the concept as faithfully as possible in the language of everyday discourse.

A linguistic analysis of the concept of teaching should reveal its central features, and those features that are "attached" to the concept as a result of the way the term is used in specific contexts. In this section, I try to tease out the basic meaning of the concept and then show how researchers elaborate on this basic meaning as they study the activities of teaching. The analysis that follows shows how easily we can confuse the basic or generic meaning with its elaborated forms, such as good teaching and successful teaching. The analysis also reveals the naiveté that often characterizes the connections we make between teaching and learning.

Consider yourself an observer of some activity. What must there be about this activity for you to call it teaching? This

The author thanks reviewers David Berliner (University of Arizona), Thomas Green (Syracuse University), Virginia Koehlar (University of Maryland), Richard Shavelson (U.C.L.A.), and Lee Shulman (Stanford University). The author acknowledges their patient counsel and helpful insight.

question initiates what Soltis (1978) calls a "generic-type analysis," wherein the task is to tease out the root meaning of the term 'teaching'. For example, think of a parent teaching a child to set the dinner table, a youngster teaching a friend to shoot baskets, or a spouse teaching her mate to play bridge. There are features of each of these activities that, if carefully examined, would provide purchase on the concept of teaching.

One obvious feature is that, in each case, two persons are involved in the activity. Another feature is that the two persons are engaged in a particular way. On looking at the nature of this engagement, one notes that one person knows, understands, or is able to do something that he is trying to share with the other person. That is, the person in possession of the knowledge or skill *intends* to convey it to the other person. It is not clear from these brief examples whether the other person wants to or is trying to acquire the knowledge or skill, so let us leave this matter unresolved for the moment. So that the two persons may easily be distinguished, the first one will be P, the *possessor* or *provider* of the knowledge or skill. The second person will be known as R, the *receiver* or *recipient* of the knowledge or skill.

The conveying of something from P to R is clearly the occasion for their engagement. As anything from knowledge, understanding, and skills to beliefs, emotions, and traits of character can be conveyed from P to R, we can — crudely but usefully — lump these together under the general heading C, for *content*. Let us now say that P wants R to acquire C, and that P and R establish a relationship to effect this acquisition. Expressing the point in this way indicates another feature of the relationship: there is an imbalance between P and R concerning C. The relationship begins with R lacking C and presumably ends with R in possession of C. Looking back at the example of a child learning to set the table, we see that the child begins ignorant of C. The parent already knows how to set the table, and conveys this knowledge to the child, such that there is no longer an imbalance between P and R with regard to C.

Thus far, the following features of the activity called "teaching" have been isolated:

1. There is a person, P, who possesses some
2. content, C, and who
3. intends to convey or impart C to
4. a person, R, who initially lacks C, such that
5. P and R engage in a relationship for the purpose of R's acquiring C.

Returning to the question that initiated this inquiry (what must there be about an activity to call it 'teaching'?), one answer is that there must be at least two persons, one of whom possesses some knowledge, skill, or other form of content and the other does not, and the possessor intends to convey the content to the one who lacks it, leading to the formation of a relationship between them for this purpose.

Even with this very simple analysis there are problems of considerable difficulty. Almost nothing has been said about R's state of mind. Must he want (intend) to acquire C before P can be said to be teaching? In other words, must R act with the intention to learn before P is teaching? Another difficulty is with self-teaching. Must two persons always be involved before an activity can properly be called 'teaching', or is the case of learning by oneself a proper instance of teaching? A third prob-

lem involves the distinction between telling and teaching (Scheffler, 1960). How is it possible to distinguish the telling or reporting of, say, a television newscaster from the teaching of a television tutor such as Alistair Cooke or Carl Sagan? Finally, must P actually be in possession of C (in the sence of having it in one's head, or is it sufficient that P simply have informed access to C? The short analysis of teaching offered above is simply too weak to help with these questions.

These difficulties will have to be resolved eventually, but doing so now will introduce confounding detours. I shall let them be for the moment, with the promise of returning soon enough. At this juncture it is important to be clear about what makes up the root or generic meaning of the term 'teaching'. Despite the difficulties just mentioned, I want to argue that the five characteristics listed above constitute a generic concept of teaching. Any additions to these five characteristics are simply extensions or elaborations on this generic concept. There are many ways to elaborate on the generic notion. One might do so organizationally, examining the concept within the context of schooling. The concept might be elaborated behaviorally, which is what educational psychologists often do when they study the concept. Or it could be elaborated morally, as educational philosophers are wont to do (and as I will do later). Anthropologists make cultural elaborations, sociologists make structural and functional elaborations, and so it goes for the many different approaches to the study of teaching. Before becoming enmeshed in any of these disciplinary elaborations, we ought to understand more about the root or generic concept.

No features of the generic meaning of 'teaching' touch upon whether the performance is a good one, or whether it is successful. This is as it should be, for it is important not to confound the root meaning of the term with elaborations regarding the success or goodness of the activity. The question, What is teaching? is different from the questions, Is this good teaching? and, Is this teaching successful? We can ask of some activity, "Is that teaching?" (in contrast to, say, entertaining or reporting), without asking whether that activity is good teaching or successful teaching. The generic conditions provide the basis for answering whether or not some activity is teaching (as opposed to something else), but not whether it is good or successful teaching.

This last point bears a bit more exploration. Some may argue that, in order for P to be teaching at all, R must acquire what P is teaching. That is, there can be no teaching without learning. As will be shown in a moment, there is a very tight connection between teaching and learning. but it is not the kind of connection that supports the claim that there can be no teaching without learning. To argue that there is no teaching without learning confuses the generic conditions with what might be called the appraisal conditions for teaching. That P is successful or unsuccessful at the task of teaching is determined by elaborations on the generic conditions, not the generic conditions themselves. It makes no more sense to require learning in order to be teaching than it does to require winning in order to be racing, or finding in order to be looking.

But suppose R never learns C as a result of his association with P. Can it still be maintained that P is teaching R? Yes. Take an analogous set of concepts, racing and winning. I can race until the end of time, never win, and yet still be racing. And though I need never win in order to race, the concept of racing would be meaningless in the absence of any concept of winning. That is, if *no one ever* won, then whatever it is that people do on a track, it would not be called racing. There is a special semantic relationship between the terms 'racing' and 'winning', such that the meaning of the former is, in many ways, dependent on the existence of the latter concept. I call this relationship ontological dependence.

The notion of ontological dependence helps to explain why most of us perceive such a tight connection between teaching and learning. If no one ever learned, it is hard to imagine that we would possess the concept of teaching. For, if learning simply never occurred, what point would there be in teaching? The connection between the two concepts is tightly woven into the fabric of our language. So tightly, in fact, that it is easy to mistake ontologically dependent relationships for causal relationships. Because the concept of teaching is dependent on a concept of learning, and because learning so often occurs after teaching, we may easily be lulled into thinking that one causes the other.

The temptation to infer a causal relation is further strengthened when we note that variations in teaching often yield variations in learning. Thus we detect not just the conceptual relationship that the meaning of teaching is dependent on the occurrence of learning, but also the empirical relationship that variations in the activity of teaching are often followed by variations in what the learner acquires. From these connections it seems even more defensible to conclude that teaching causes learning. If we do draw this conclusion, it could be because we are being fooled by a complex semantic relationship that also happens to exhibit some very deceptive empirical properties. On the other hand, the causal nexus could be the most useful and revealing one for further inquiry. Digging a little deeper into the analysis may settle the issue.

Think for a moment of the ways teaching and learning differ. Learning can be done by oneself; it occurs within one's head. Teaching, on the other hand, is most often done with at least one other person present; it is not something that occurs within the head of a single individual. Another difference is that though one may learn about morality, one does not learn morally or immorally. Yet teaching can be done morally or immorally. Learning involves acquiring something; teaching involves giving something. Wherever one looks, there is almost no parallel structure between the concepts of teaching and learning. They are two radically different kinds of phenomena. Are they really ontologically dependent, much less causally related?

There seems little doubt about the ontological dependence of teaching on learning. Without the concept of learning, there would be no concept of teaching (though, as suggested above, the dependence does not work in reverse). Those who argue for a causal relation between teaching and learning are, I believe, misled by the ontologically dependent relationship between the two. The ontological dependence leads the researcher to infer causality from observed correlations, when indeed it is possible to explain these correlations in other ways. The empirical correlations can, in fact, be accounted for in ways other than positing them as precursors for tight, direct causal connections. These correlations can be explained as outcomes of the teacher's improving the student's abilities and capacities to be a student.

The concept of studenting or pupiling is far and away the more parallel concept to that of teaching. Without students, we would not have the concept of teacher; without teachers, we would not have the concept of student. Here is a balanced ontologically dependent pair, coherently parallel to looking and finding, racing and winning. There are a range of activities connected with studenting that complement the activities of teaching. For example, teachers explain, describe, define, refer, correct, and encourage. Students recite, practice, seek assistance, review, check, locate sources, and access material. The teacher's task is to support R's desire to student and improve his capacity to do so. Whether and how much R learns from being a student is largely a function of how he students.

It certainly seems odd to use the word 'student' as an intransitive verb. The strangeness is probably due to the fact that we make the term 'learning' do double duty, sometimes using it to refer to what the student actually acquires from instruction (achievement), and other times using it to refer to the processes the student uses to acquire content (task). Because the term 'learning' functions in both a task and achievement sense, it is easy to mix the two and thus contend that the task of teaching is to produce the achievement of learning, when it in fact makes more sense to contend that *a central task of teaching is to enable the student to perform the tasks of learning.*

This discussion of ontological dependence is intended as groundwork for the view that learning is an upshot of studenting, not an effect that follows from teaching as a cause. The task of teaching is to enable studenting; to teach the student how to learn. The old cliché that the teacher's task is to teach the learner how to learn is close to the mark. Were we dealing exclusively with tutorial relationships, it might be entirely on the mark. In the context of modern schooling, however, there is much more to studenting than learning how to learn. In the school setting, studenting includes getting along with one's teachers, coping with one's peers, dealing with one's parents about being a student, and handling the nonacademic aspects of school life. Though one of the more immediate tasks of the teacher is to enable the student's learning of academic content, the secondary tasks just mentioned are nearly as critical; they often determine whether the immediate and longer-range tasks will be fulfilled.

Having replaced the bringing about of learning with the improvement of studenting as one of the central tasks of teaching, let us return to the generic and appraisal conditions of teaching to assess how well they apply to this new task. Recall that teaching was generically defined as two or more people, one of whom knows or is able to do more than the other, engaged in a relationship for the purpose of conveying knowledge or skill from one to the other. As a result of the ontologically dependent pair analysis, the generic view requires some modification, for it, too, was framed on the presupposition that learning is the achievement of teaching. On the revised view, the teacher does not convey or impart the content to the student. Rather the teacher instructs the student on how to acquire the content from the teacher, text, or other source. As the student becomes skilled at acquiring content, he or she learns.

The teacher's tasks include instructing the learner on the procedures and demands of the studenting role, selecting the material to be learned, adapting that material so that it is appropriate to the level of the learner, constructing the most appropriate set of opportunities for the learner to gain access to the content (it is within this task that I would include motivation), monitoring and appraising the student's progress, and serving the learner as one of the primary sources of knowledge and skill. These tasks sound much like those already advanced in the literature as the proper tasks of teaching. There is, however, an important difference. On this new scheme, the teacher is held accountable for the activities proper to being a student (the task sense of 'learning'), not the demonstrated acquisition of content by the learner (the achievement sense of 'learning'). Thus a learner who fails a reasonably valid and reliable test of content covered in instruction must accept a major share of the responsibility for this failure. To the extent the student lacks the skills of studenting needed to perform well on this test, is given no opportunity to exercise these skills, or is in no helpful way encouraged to engage the material to be learned, the teacher must accept a major share of responsibility for the student's failure.

With the view that one of the major achievements of teaching is the attainment on the part of the student of those rules, procedures, and skills of studenting that properly fall within the purview of the teacher (not all aspects of studenting are within the teacher's range of concern), some of the puzzles left unresolved at the beginning of the analysis can now be examined. What of the learner's state of mind? Must he want to acquire the skills and insights of studenting in order for teaching to be occurring? I think not. It seems unlikely that students will acquire the characteristics of learners unless they want to, and thus an extraordinary demand is placed upon teaching if the students' intention to learn must be formed before it can be said that teaching is occurring. The most we may be able to do here is to determine that the teacher is indeed executing the tasks of teaching mentioned in the previous paragraph, and is doing nothing to discourage or inhibit learners from acquiring the pertinent skills, procedures, and rules of studenting.

(Some readers of a draft of this chapter found the paragraph above very disturbing. They chastised me for relieving the teacher of all responsibility for motivation and in turn requiring that the student come to class with a mind prepared for instruction. I am not quite so heartless. Recall that it is the generic notion of teaching that is under scrutiny here. I am arguing that learners need not want or desire to student before teachers may be said to be teaching, *in the generic sense of the term*. On the other hand, if the appraisal conditions are introduced as elaborations on the generic concept, then it would be the case that good teaching requires the teacher to accommodate the readiness of learners to learn, and to encourage their interest in the material.)

What about self-teaching? It seems to me that the generic meaning of teaching will always require two or more persons, as the notion of teaching oneself would not make any sense were we not first familiar with one person teaching another. In other words, the idea of self-teaching is understandable only as an analogue of one person teaching another. Furthermore, much of the time the expression is used, we mean by it that we *learned* the content without the assistance of a physically present teacher. The notion of self-teaching is most applicable when it refers to the actions of persons preparing to learn something on their own. They go out looking for the right texts, find assistance at the appropriate level of difficulty, and guide themselves through trial-and-error stages of development. Because these are the things a teacher frequently does for a learner, we are at ease speaking of teaching oneself.

Must teachers have the content in their heads before they can be said to be teaching? The question itself is misconceived, as it is founded on a conception of teaching that has learning as its achievement. Teachers may have what is to be learned in their heads, or it might be in a book, on a film or computer program, in the head of a guest lecturer, or even already in the head of the person being taught. The task of teachers is not necessarily to possess the content and convey it to the student, but is rather to enable the student to take possession of the content wherever it is found. For reasons that will be clear in the third section of this chapter, teachers are far more likely to succeed at this task if they have previously taken possession of the content themselves.

With many of the details now in place, it may be useful to point out that many of the implications of this analysis are not radically different from what is already implied in extant research on teaching. For example, the work of Amarel (1982, 1983), Carew and Lightfoot (1979), Cusick (1983), Doyle (1979a, 1979b, 1983), Green (1983), and Weinstein (1983) is already highly focused on the activities of students in classrooms. This work is teaching us a great deal about what students do in classrooms and how they undertake, succeed, and fail at the activities of learning. Even the process–product research, as closely tied to the behaviorist program as it is, contains the seeds for studying the effects of teachers on students rather than on learning. Notions of academic learning time, engaged time, and time-on-task all pertain to activities of studenting. It is, of course, believed (many researchers would say it is empirically established) that the concepts of on-task and off-task time are intervening variables between teaching behaviors and student learning. Yet only a slight shift in perspective is needed to fix the notion that learning follows directly from studenting, not teaching.

This analysis has concentrated on the generic conditions of teaching, and the elaborations we employ to determine what counts as successful teaching. There are many other elaborations. One that is special to the philosopher of education concerns the question of what counts as good teaching. The use of 'good' here is not simply a synonym for success, such that successful teaching is good teaching, and vice versa. On the contrary, 'good' has both moral and epistemological force in this context. To ask what is good teaching in the moral sense is to ask what teaching actions are justified on moral principles, and evocative of principled action on the part of students. To ask what is good teaching in the epistemological sense is to ask whether what is taught is rationally defensible, and ultimately worthwhile for the student to know, believe, or understand.

No research on teaching with which I am familiar takes account of issues dealing with good teaching. That is, research on teaching has not, to my knowledge, specifically addressed aspects of moral worth reflected in the teacher's actions, or considerations of epistemic worth in the selection and reconstruction of content. In a way, this absence of moral consideration is not surprising, given the passion of many scientists to undertake inquiry untainted by moral or axiological commitment. However, with our increasing understanding that science is replete with ideology and commitment, there is less concern about the possibility of moral and axiological bias in the scientific community. Hopefully newer conceptions of philosophy of science will encourage more educational researchers to investigate activities of teaching that are solidly based on the various theories, such as those described by Maxine Greene (this volume).

In this first section I have tried to distinguish a generic notion of teaching from the many possible elaborations on that notion. As the analysis developed, it became apparent that the concept of teaching implicit in much of the research literature is rooted in the generic notion *combined with* the appraisal conditions for successful teaching. The particular notion of success evident in much of the literature is founded on the view that there is some sort of causal connection between teaching and learning. This presumption of causality is probably best explained by the ontological dependence of teaching on learning, though as the argument shows, ontological dependence does not justify causal inference. Conceptually, the notion of studenting or pupiling appears a far more coherent relative of teaching than does the notion of learning. Thus it was argued that research on teaching would reflect more conceptual integrity were it not tied to a concept of teaching rooted in the standard appraisal conditions of success. Instead, the research should be based on a notion of teaching that has as its point the performance of certain kinds of tasks and activities by students.

The analysis presented in this section makes only passing mention of good teaching, in contrast to successful teaching. One of the thorny issues that researchers face is the degree of their obligation to work with theoretically sophisticated, *prescriptive* concepts of teaching, set within a morally explicit context. That is, must research on teaching account for what is believed to be good teaching? Would research on teaching be better research if it dealt only in morally and epistemically sound conceptions of teaching? To answer these questions, I turn to a consideration of the methods of research on teaching. In this second section, it is argued that research has a contribution to make to good teaching, though not always in the way educational philosophers have argued in the past.

Methods for Research on Teaching

The purpose of this section is to argue for a particular connection between the ways teaching is studied and how teaching can be done better. I do this by showing how different ways of studying teaching can contribute to the ways teachers think about what they do. The argument begins quite far from the conclusion, however. It starts with the issue of the merit and compatibility of different research methods, especially those methods typically grouped under the headings of quantitative and qualitative. From there the argument proceeds to examine how these different methods bear on the distinction between producing knowledge and using knowledge. It is contended that research is the act of producing knowledge, while teaching is an act of using knowledge. The researcher helps the teacher by producing knowledge that the teacher can use, though the

researcher is not under any blanket obligation to produce useful knowledge. Indeed, there is a sense in which all reliable knowledge is useful; it is more a matter of finding the occasion for use. But I am getting ahead of the argument. The first task is to examine some central ideas about research methods.

It will be helpful to begin with the notion of a research tradition. This notion was developed by Laudan, following the work of Lakatos (1970). Laudan (1977) adopts the following as a working definition: "*A research tradition is a set of general assumption about the entities and processes in a domain of study, and about the appropriate methods to be used for investigating the problems and constructing the theories in that domain*" (emphasis in original, p. 81). Behaviorism is clearly a research tradition in psychology. Other contenders are cognitive psychology and humanistic psychology, although the latter is less developed as a research tradition.

Note that as part of the definition, Laudan refers to "the appropriate methods to be used for investigating the problems and constructing the theories in that domain." Educational research currently makes use of a number of different methods, many of them classifiable as either quantitative or qualitative. Depending on how they are applied in specific contexts, quantitative methods are also known as confirmatory, hypothesis testing, or predictive methods. Qualitative methods are also often known as exploratory, hypothesis generating, descriptive, or interpretive methods. Among the techniques of quantitative methods are the experiment, quasi-experiment, correlational study, and survey research. These methods typically employ both logical design and statistical techniques as controls for the collection, analysis, and interpretation of data. Among qualitative methods are the techniques used in ethnography, ethnomethodology, and what Doyle (1979a) and, on different grounds, Bronfenbrenner (1979) call ecological research.

Quantitative methods have reigned supreme in educational psychology for most of this century. These methods are highly congruent with notions of scientific psychology, especially the behaviorist tradition, which — until recently — has been the dominant research tradition in educational psychology. Over the last two decades, however, the pristine splendor of the experiment has accumulated more tarnish than patina. There are a number of reasons for the markedly diminished use of quantitative methods, not all of them worthy.

Perhaps the most damaging attack on quantitative methods came from the critics of behaviorism, who saw the experiment, the covering law (hypothetico-deductive) model of explanation, the generalizibility criterion, and many of the other trappings of predictive inquiry as part and parcel of the research tradition of behaviorism. There is indeed a tight link between the theories propounded by behaviorists and the methods they employ to study psychological phenomena; that link is the result of social scientists taking seriously the methodological demands of the physical sciences. As behaviorists sought to make their inquiries "truly scientific," they adopted the procedures and controls that brought them as close as possible to methodological isomorphism with the natural sciences.

The problems with this approach are now rather well known among social scientists. The methods of the physical sciences are grounded in presuppositions and assumptions that pertain to events, activities, and phenomena generally without will and purpose; things like atoms, molecules, ball bearings, and planets. As psychologists adopted these physical science methods, they also imported the presuppositions and assumptions undergirding them (e.g., causal regularities, law-like generalizations, predictability, and near-perfect confirmation). To make these methods work, behaviorists either had to ignore the telic properties of human behavior, or deny that human beings had the capacity to act with purpose (including the capacity to act stupidly or inconsistently).

Few psychologists denied these human capacities, though many chose to ignore them for purposes of research and theory construction. So long as this research and theory remained within the confines of the science itself, there were few consequences for the everyday lives of outsiders. But the research and the theory did not remain within research laboratories or arcane journals. They spilled over, in great waves, into the workaday lives of educators because so many of them were completing courses in educational psychology or being held accountable (albeit in very loose ways) for the knowledge produced by psychology. Thus, for many educators, behaviorism and psychology became synonyms, and the quantitative methods of research became behaviorist methods of research.

The reaction to behaviorism, at least in its more stringent forms, was so vituperative that the baby of quantitative methods may have been tossed out with the bathwater of behaviorism. In an extended critique of social science methods, Louch 1966) wrote that "triviality, redundancy, and tautology are the epithets which I think can be properly applied to the behavioural scientist" (p. 9). the British philosopher, John Wilson, became so exasperated with the behaviorist program and the seeming willingness of educators to give it credence that he wrote: "*Most people (even researchers) will do anything rather than think*, and this is particularly obvious in educational research" (1972, p. 129). The philosopher of education, James McClellan, impugned not only the program, but the behaviorist as well (McClellan, 1976). Condemning what he calls pedagogical behaviorism, "the doctrine that teaching can be defined and described in terms which are purely behavioral in reference" (p. 8), McClellan wrote:

the closer one gets to the source of pedagogical behaviorism, the more one is inclined to believe that it is mostly a reflection of the nihilistic, skeptical, cynical system of power in our society. One is also inclined to regard persons who advocate pedagogical behaviorism as either knaves or fools, either persons who are grasping for power or willing helpers of others who are. These inclinations must be understood and then transcended, for behaviorists, even pedagogical behaviorists, are human beings whose only crime is holding a set of false and confused beliefs. (p. 8)

Going to bed with behaviorism was not the only stigma for quantitative methods. The attacks on logical positivism taking place in philosophy seriously weakened methodological assumptions and presuppositions about verifiability and explanatory power (see Phillips, 1981). Finally, psychologists themselves became disillusioned with what they had long assumed to be the promise of quantitative methods (uniform regularities, predictability, control, etc.). In his now-classic paper, Cronbach (1975) concluded:

The goal of our work ... is not to amass generalizations, atop which a theoretical tower can someday be erected. ... the special task of the social scientist in each generation is to pin down the contemporary facts. Beyond that he shares with the humanistic scholar and the artist in the effort to gain insight into contemporary relationships, and to realign the culture's view of man with present realities. To know man as he is is no mean aspiration. p. 126)

As the researcher's belief in conventional quantitative methods shifted from doctrinaire commitment to restrained confidence, the way was cleared for the introduction of qualitative methods. The entry was not an easy one, for there were those researchers who pooh-poohed qualitative methods, contending that they were fine for persons who did not know what the problems were. (Supposedly qualitative methods were problem *finding*, while quantitative methods were problem *solving*. Were this actually the case, qualitative methods would have risen to quick domination, for perhaps the most difficult step in research is locating a worthwhile problem.) Other researchers resisted using qualitative methods on the grounds that they would not yield lawful generalizations. This objection softened when it was understood that not even quantitative methods yield the valid and reliable social science generalizations it was once supposed they might. Concern also diminished as those employing qualitative methods turned out research that the users of quantitative methods found provocative and illuminating (such as the work of Cusick, 1983; Doyle 1979a, 1979b, 1983; Erickson, 1982; Erickson & Mohatt, 1982; Lightfoot, 1983; Ogbu, 1978; Willis, 1977; and Wolcott, 1977, 1982). Qualitative methods made further inroads with the evident willingness of many qualitative researchers to address the problems of validity and generalizability (Kidder, 1981; Le Compte & Goetz, 1982; Miles & Huberman 1984; Spradley, 1979, 1980).

Now that qualitative research has established itself as a worthy means for undertaking scholarly inquiry in education, the question of its relation to quantitative method arises. Under the general heading of naturalistic inquiry, Guba (1978) was among the first educational theorists to examine the differences between the two major forms of inquiry. Smith (1983) analyzed the differences recently, concluding that the two positions are not compatible. He goes on to say that the absence of compatibility does not mean that "the two approaches can never be reconciled, only that at the present time the actual divisions are more notable than the possibilities for unification" (p. 12). Shulman (1981) acknowledges the apparent incompatibility of various research methods, but points to the potential rather than the problems that differences present. After noting the variety of methods comprising educational research, Shulman contends that "each is demanding and rigorous and follows disciplined rules or procedures. Taken together these approaches build a methodological mosaic that is the most exciting current field of applied social research — the study of education" (p. 12).

I believe Shulman's support of methodological pluralism in educational research is correct, though there are some difficult problems with this position (which are further explored in his chapter, this volume). Strict empirical methods, such as those usually associated with behaviorism, deny or dismiss (depending on whose view of behaviorism is at issue) the intentional, purposive nature of human behavior. This dismissal is a serious problem, for it gives rise to research in education that does violence to morally grounded conceptions of education (see Greene, this volume; Fenstermacher, 1979). On the other hand, quantitative methods, considered apart from the behaviorist program, are replete with mechanisms for intersubjective appraisals of validity and generalizability—making them extremely valuable tools for disciplined inquiry. In contrast, qualitative methods are not burdened with a history of attempts to achieve isomorphic dependence on the physical sciences. These methods can accommodate the telic properties of persons in ways that do not do violence to morally grounded theories of education. Yet qualitative methods do lack established mechanisms for intersubjective appraisals of validity and generalizability. How should this apparent dilemma be resolved? Is it really possible to contain the best of both worlds?

I believe that it is, but not in the ways typically propounded. Not by merger, reduction, or synthesis of quantitative and qualitative methods. Nor by custodial forays into each of the methodological camps to clean up errors and sins. Rather, methodological pluralism in educational research becomes a feasible and justified position when a clear distinction is made between the production or generation of knowledge, and the use or application of knowledge. This distinction is derived from Aristotle's differentiation between theoretical wisdom and practical wisdom, and might be expressed as the logic of knowledge production and the logic of knowledge application. The logic of knowledge production consists of statements or propositions about the world. This logic terminates in assertions, in claims about events, states, or phenomena. These assertions are testable using such disciplined methods as are available to the researcher. The logic of knowledge use also consists of statements, but arguments in this logic terminate in actions rather than propositions. Compare, for example, these two arguments:

Knowledge Production Argument Type

> Learning is more likely to occur in well-managed classrooms.
>
> There is evidence that direct instruction is an effective form of classroom management.
>
> Therefore, learning is more likely to occur in classrooms that incorporate direct instruction.

Knowledge Use Argument Type

> As a teacher, I want to teach in ways that yield as much student learning as possible.
>
> Well-managed classrooms yield gains in learning.
>
> Direct instruction is a proven way to manage classrooms.
>
> My students and I are together in this classroom.
>
> ACTION: (I am organizing my class according to the principles of direct instruction.)

The truth of the premises in these arguments is of no interest at this time. For the moment, note only the form of the arguments. The knowledge production argument consists entirely of assertions, and terminates in a statement that is tightly connected to the preceding premises. The conclusion can be more precisely phrased and its terms operationalized, then tested with standard methods. The knowledge use argument also con-

tains assertions, some of them empirically testable; this argument, however, ends in an action—in a description of an agent doing something consistent with the premises that precede the action description. This form of argument first appears in the work of Aristotle (*Metaphysics*, Book 7: *De Motu Animalium*; *Nicomachean Ethics*, Book 7). It is later discussed by Kant (*Metaphysics of Morals* and *Critique of Practical Reason*), and Hume (*A Treatise on Human Nature*). It is fundamental to the philosophy of pragmatism, and to current Continental philosophy in the areas of critical theory and hermaneutics. Practical reasoning has also been extensively explored by the ordinary language philosophers, particularly around the 1960s (Anscombe, 1963; Hare, 1971; Kenny, 1966; Jarvis, 1962; von Wright, 1963). Writing at the time when there was a rich debate on the topic, Rescher (1973) describes the supporting rationale for practical reasoning:

> Our knowledge answers to two categories of purpose, the theoretical and the practical. The theoretical sector of purpose is *pure* and the practical is *applied* in orientation. The theoretical relates to the strictly intellectual interests of man, the acquisition of descriptive information and explanatory understanding (to *what* and *why*); the practical relates to the material interests of man that underlie the guidance of human action.... The functional role of our knowledge encompasses both the intellectual/theoretical aspect of the purists' knowledge for knowledge's sake and the activist/practical aspect of knowledge as a guide to life. (pp. 3–4)

The position I want to advance here is that this distinction between the logic of knowledge production and the logic of knowledge use permits the educational researcher to employ any method of inquiry that meets criteria of adequacy imposed by the disciplines or methodological analysis, without concern for the practical, pedagogical effects of the inquiry. The basis for this methodological freedom is that *the benefit of educational research to educational practice is realized in the improvement of practical arguments, not in programs of performance deduced from the findings of research.* An explicit educational formulation of this essentially Aristotelian idea has been developed by Green (1976). He takes up the notion of practical reasoning in an effort to determine the competencies required for successful instruction. In his view, the competencies needed by a successful teacher can be determined "by identifying what is required to change the truth value of the premises of the practical argument in the mind of the child, or to complete or modify those premises or to introduce an altogether new premise into the practical argument in the mind of the child" (p. 252).

Adapting Green ever so slightly, I am arguing that the value of educational research for educational practice is the help it provides in "identifying what is required to change the truth value of the premises of the practical argument in the mind of the [teacher], or to complete or modify those premises or to introduce an altogether new premise into the practical argument in the mind of the [teacher]." Research bears on practice as it alters the truth or falsity of beliefs that teachers have, as it changes the nature of these beliefs, and as it adds new beliefs. Consider this practical argument in the mind of the teacher:

1. It is better for children to be treated as unique individuals than as members of a group.

2. Allowing children to pace their own learning is a good way to honor their individuality.

3. If I present new material to the whole class, drill them as a group, then assign the same seatwork to all of them at the same time, I prevent them from proceeding at their own pace, and thus deny their individuality.

4. If I do these things with smaller groups of children, I come closer to honoring their individuality.

5. If I create independent work stations, with varied tasks and differing amounts of time for completion, and allow children to schedule their activities at these stations, I come as close to honoring their individuality as I possibly can.

6. There will soon be children in my class awaiting the assignment of tasks I design for them.

ACTION: (I am preparing independent learning centers, with a full range of materials at each center).

This practical argument is a slight paraphrase of one actually offered by a classroom teacher who was asked why she made such extensive use of work stations and learning centers. The teacher based her action on moral convictions about the proper treatment of children. She clearly believes in choice and individualization, and tried to design her classroom to reflect these commitments. As it turns out, her students were not scoring well on end-of-year standardized examinations. The teacher was concerned about the scores, yet also strongly committed to individualization practices. She would not change her practices if the new practices meant a complete overthrow of her beliefs about the nature of teaching. On further inquiry, she stated that, though she had reservations about standardized examinations, her students ought to do better than they did — and she wished they would.

On further discussion, it became apparent to the teacher that she had at least two major objectives: honoring the unique aspects of each learner, and each learner's acquiring the material presented. She assumed that classroom procedures for individualization would gain both these ends. The data she had on hand (standardized test scores) did not support this assumption, though she was reluctant to reconsider the premises in her practical argument for individualization. With reservation, she began to read the process–product literature on teaching effectiveness (see Brophy & Good, this volume). The evidence derived from this line of research shows with a fair degree of clarity that the practices this teacher used to effect individualization are not practices typically correlated with uniform gains in acquisition of content assigned.

The effect of this evidence from teacher effectiveness research was to initiate the process of modifying the premises of the practical argument in the mind of the teacher. The exact outcome in this case is irrelevant, for my point in offering it is only to illustrate a process, not to offer empirical justification for this view. However, empirical studies of the practical arguments in the minds of teachers, and how and why changes take place in these arguments would be extremely valuable. The teacher decision-making research done by Shavelson and his students (Borko, Cone, Russo, & Shavelson, 1979; Shavelson, 1983; Shavelson & Stern, 1981) provides an excellent springboard for inquiry into the practical arguments of teachers, as does the

conceptual–analytic work in teacher education done by Buchmann (1984), Nemser (1983), and their colleagues at the Institute for Research on Teaching. Teachers themselves determine whatever new practices follow from modifications they make to their practical arguments. New practices are not determined by deducing strict rules of action from research findings. William James (1899) remains the authority on this matter: "You make a great, a very great mistake, if you think that psychology, being the science of the mind's laws, is something from which you can deduce definite programmes and schemes and methods of instruction for immediate classroom use" (p. 23).

It is on this view of the nature and use of practical arguments that I argue for methodological pluralism in educational research. For the purpose of advancing our knowledge of the phenomena that scientists study, or solving puzzling empirical or theoretical problems, any research method that meets criteria of adequacy developed within the discipline where that method is housed is an acceptable method for the study of education. Whether that method is a good method, in the sense of being valuable or worthwhile, is determined by still another set of criteria. These latter criteria are shaped by scholars in the several disciplines and by theorists concerned with the philosophy of social science. Methods that conform to such criteria are the critical components of knowledge production. However, they are not methods appropriate for knowledge use or application (though they may be used to study knowledge use). Practical arguments, or some similar way of acknowledging purposive, passionate, intuitive, and moral properties of human action, are the methods for transforming what is empirically known and understood into practice.

Educational research may stand on its intrinsic merits — such as these may be — without necessity for proving its worth on the basis of improving educational practice. However, *when it is argued that research has benefit for practice, the criterion of benefit should be the improvement of practical arguments in the minds of teachers and other practitioners.* As researchers cast about for interesting problems, they may seek problems that bear on the practical arguments in the minds of teachers, or they may ignore these arguments. The relevance of research for teaching practice can be understood as a matter of how directly the research relates to the practical arguments in the minds of teachers.

To return to the matter of quantitative and qualitative methods of research with which this section began, it will now be clear, I hope, that the divisive issue is not whether one or the other produces more valid and reliable implications for pedagogical practices. As Shulman argues, both orientations to the study of teaching are valuable for the different understandings they provide. Their adequacy as methods for knowledge production is determined within the disciplines that house them and allied disciplines (such as philosophy). They are not adequate methods for the logic of knowledge use, as they are not designed for this purpose. Their value for knowledge use or application is in the quality of knowledge and understanding they generate for consideration by the practitioner.

There are a number of aspects of this argument that need further exploration. To make it a bit more enjoyable, this exploration will be carried out by looking at the work of others in relation to the argument advanced here. Before commenting on others, however, some self-criticism is in order. Five years ago I (Fenstermacher, 1979) claimed that researchers ought to seek research methods that conform to the telic properties of human behavior. I specifically called for research programs that were formulated out of normative (prescriptive) theories of education. I now believe that call to be wrongheaded. Given the interaction between research methods and practical arguments described in this chapter, the formulation of normatively grounded research methods is not a moral prerequisite for doing research on teaching. Rather, the normative considerations are accounted for in the practical argument, not in the research, obviating the need for research methods to reflect morally grounded theories of education. I agree with Ericson and Ellett (1982):

> Try as it may, empiricist educational research cannot break out of the web of interpretation. Insofar as it rests on the teleological language—purposive language—of intention, belief, emotion, and so forth, rather than the mechanistic language of genes and phenotypes, it will doubly fail: first, to discover any laws of human behavior; and, second, to elucidate plausible (though not lawlike) readings of the meanings that human beings attach to their lives and to their social institutions—all that is of *human* importance. (p. 508)

To call on empirical research (behaviorism or any other form of empirical research) to found its methods on normative theories of education is, as Ericson and Ellet show, a double curse. It neither improves the methods nor succeeds in capturing the essence of being human. I do not wish to argue that it is conceptually impossible to devise an empirical research program that is grounded in a morally sophisticated conception of education. Indeed, the recent work by Novak and Gowin (1984) may be of just this type. Yet until such conceptions have been fully explored, I believe we are best served by holding research methods accountable to internal criteria of adequacy and worth, and reserving consideration of the normative aspects of education for the practical arguments in the minds of teachers.

In another variation on the theme of links between researchers and practitioners, Tuthill and Ashton (1983) argue that science will not progress in education unless scientists and practitioners work together within the same universe of discourse. Basing their notions on Kuhn's concept of paradigms, they espouse the hope that "as members of the same paradigmatic communities, educational scientists and practitioners would share common values, assumptions, goals, norms, language, beliefs, and ways of perceiving and understanding the educational process" (p. 9). This call for collaboration is based, in my view, on a profound misconception of the tasks and aims of science on the one hand and professional practice on the other. As I have tried to show, the work of science is not necessarily improved when it is structured by the phenomenologies of practitioners, nor are practitioners advantaged by conceiving of their tasks and purposes in the language of science. Enormous advances in philosophy of social science and disciplinary methods of inquiry would have to occur before calls for collaboration of the kind Tuthill and Ashton make can be justified as both good science and good practice.

Eisner (1984) comes close to making the same kind of call when he contends:

> If educational research is to inform educational practice, researchers will have to go back to the schools for a fresh look at what is going on there. We will have to develop a language that is relevant to educational practice, one that does justice to teaching and learning in educational settings, and we will need to develop methods of inquiry that do not squeeze the educational life out of what we study in such settings. (p. 451)

Eisner's dissatisfaction with strictly controlled forms of empirical inquiry leads him to call for "the construction of our own unique conceptual apparatus and research methods" (p. 451). As in the case of Tuthill and Ashton, this call does not account for the critical differences between the logic of knowledge production and the logic of knowledge use. To use well the knowledge that any controlled form of research provides, that knowledge must be placed into the specific context of teachers' actions, taking its place alongside what scientific inquiry cannot provide—passion, intuitive insight, purpose, and morality. I believe Eisner can gain far more of what he seeks by sorting carefully between knowledge production and knowledge use, keeping the two separate and holding each accountable only for what it is possible and appropriate for each to do. The yield of the logic of knowledge production is neither designed nor intended for straight-line application to practice. Given his good work in the development of naturalistic inquiry, it is curious that Eisner would criticize empirical research for not succeeding at what it cannot and should not do.

Finally there is the recent work of Buchmann (1984), who contends that practical arguments have a force of their own, independent of research findings that may bear upon these arguments. Her argument, grounded in Schwab's (1978) studies of the practical, offers a number of reasons why research findings might properly be set aside as teachers determine what actions best accord with the educative interests of their students. In words that capture well the distinction between the inquiries of researchers and the practices of teachers, Buchmann says that "research knowledge is only a fragment of human awareness—precious, no doubt, but not created for the purposes of action nor sufficient to determine them" (p. 422). Her argument clearly shows that research findings have no compelling priority over other well-justified considerations; research does not automatically outrank experience, faith, and ethics. One of the key reasons I argue for a clear distinction between research and practical reasoning is as a means of preserving the value and force of experience, ethics, passion, and so forth in the work of teachers. The findings of research are one among a number of bases for appraising and changing the practical arguments in the minds of teachers. As Feyerabend (1981) says, "*Science is just one of the many ideologies that propel society and it should be treated as such*" (emphasis in original, p. 162).

Education and the Manner of the Teacher

The previous section offered a view of research methodology that was argued primarily on epistemological grounds. I held that many different research methods are appropriate for the investigation of educational phenomena. This claim was based on the view that any appropriate and minimally adequate method has the potential to generate knowledge or understanding, which in turn might be valuable for changing the truth value of premises in a practical argument, or for modifying, adding, or deleting premises in a practical argument. In this third and final section, a moral argument is added to the epistemological argument for methodological pluralism and practical arguments. This argument is grounded in a particular view of education, one that incorporates the concept of teaching advanced in the first section of the chapter. The argument is initiated with this question: What does it mean to participate instrumentally in the education of another human being?

There are several ways to answer this question, some of them primarily empirical, others primarily normative. Empirical answers are framed from actually *looking at* education taking place. Whatever the investigator says about education as a result of this inquiry is descriptive. That is, he is saying something about what is going on in the world; he is describing what is happening when persons are gathered for what is obviously an educative reason. Normative answers are framed from thinking about what *ought to be going on* when persons are engaged with one another for educative reasons. Normative answers are prescriptive. They point us in directions that are good places to be headed, they help determine if we have lost sight of the point of our labors; they give that larger, human meaning to the workaday tasks of teaching and learning.

Normative answers are usually formulated from specific theories of teaching, such as those examined by Greene (this volume). These normative theories employ philosophical inquiry and wisdom to stipulate what is in the educative interest of the learner and how, in general, teachers might act to insure the learner's education. The desire of most philosophers of education is to have one or perhaps a few of the more carefully articulated theories of teaching provide the foundational premises for most or all of the practical arguments in the minds of teachers. When this occurs, we speak of the teacher's actions as justified on normative grounds.

All normative theories of teaching that have passed the philosopher's review place a premium on rational processes, moral deliberation, and virtuous action (this claim must be set in the context of developed Western nations, though its range of application may extend much farther). No theory known to me permits indoctrination, mere recitation and rote, conditioning (at least not without informed consent), drill and practice without reflection and analysis, or conformity to rules without deliberation on the rightness of these rules. When all is said and done, most normative theories of teaching make extraordinarily sophisticated demands on teachers. The following working definition is one among several possible ways of summing up these demands: Education is the provision of means to fellow human beings enabling them to structure their experience in ways that continually enlarge knowledge, reasonable belief, understanding, autonomy, authenticity, and sense of place in the past, present, and future of the human race.

To educate a fellow human being is to provide that person with the *means* to structure his or her own experiences in ways that keep on expanding what the person knows, has reason to doubt or believe, and understands, as well as the person's capacity for autonomous and authentic action, and the person's sense of place in history. It is not supplying the knowledge, the

reasonable beliefs, and so on, but rather supplying the means to gain access to and continue the enlargement of knowledge, understanding, and so forth. To initiate this process it is usually necessary to "prime the pump," to begin by supplying the content that the learner is to acquire. As the learner comes to understand what is happening (which the teacher must help the learner to see), *the learner becomes a student*, capable of gaining independent access to content. The teacher's responsibility quickly shifts from serving as supplier of "raw" content to supplier of the means to structure experience (both everyday experience and the experience of advanced inquiry in any number of fields).

How is this conception of education applicable to teachers as learners? The same end is sought: to supply teachers with the means to structure their experiences in ways that continually enlarge their knowledge, reasoned belief, understanding, autonomy, authenticity, and sense of place. In the case of pedagogical competence, one of the first tasks is to assist teachers in framing the practical arguments undergirding their actions, for many of these are not likely to be consciously known by the teacher. The next step is to assist in the teacher's appraisal of the premises in the practical argument. A critical part of this appraisal is determining the bearing of empirical evidence on premises that make assertions about the world. Consider this practical argument:

1. It is extemely important for children to know how to read.

2. Children who do not know how to read are best begun with primers.

3. All nonreaders will proceed through the primers at the same rate (the importance of learning to read justifies this standardization).

4. The skills of reading are most likely to be mastered by choral reading of the primers, combined with random calling on individual students.

5. This is a group of nonreaders for whom I am the designated teacher.

   ACTION: (I am distributing primers and preparing the class to respond in unison to me).

There are a number of premises in this argument that make assertions about empirical phenomena, particularly Numbers 2 and 4. The growing base of research in reading instruction should lead this teacher to doubt these premises. However, my point is not to explore the facts. The point is to illustrate an argument supporting pedagogical behavior that is inconsistent with the evidence presently available. By assisting the teacher to formulate the practical argument supporting these instructional practices, and presenting the evidence that bears on the relevant premises, the teacher's teacher enables the teacher to see what could not be seen before. This process of teaching, repeated again and again, makes the teacher a student of his or her own practices. Muir (1980) is an excellent autobiographical account of a teacher engaged reflexively in just this process. Muir is a teacher who changed the organization and management of her classroom after becoming acquainted with the Beginning Teacher Evaluation Study (Berliner, 1979). While she does not describe her changes as alterations in the premises of practical arguments, the essay is written so that these changes are easily detected.

To teach teachers in this way is to exhibit a *manner* of a certain kind. This manner is as much a part of the content to be conveyed to the student as the facts, theories, arguments, and insights of the subject being taught. The well-known British philosopher of education, R. S. Peters, has dealt extensively with this aspect of education. He argues as follows (Peters, 1973):

> The discipline imposed by the teacher, the equality of consideration with which he treat individuals, the respect and degree of liberty which he accords to them, are, on the one hand, rules which are necessary for the distribution and organization of education. But, on the other hand, an essential part of the moral education of children is that they should make these principles, which form the framework of their explorations, their own. They will develop as moral beings if they treat the principles immanent in such procedures as content which is subtly imparted to them. (p. 25)

After making this point about how the manner of the teacher contributes or detracts from the moral development of the student, Peters continues with an analysis of how the teacher's manner also imparts to the student the nature of the discipline under study:

> There are those principles of procedure which are presuppositions of worth-while activities such as science or history. There must be respect for evidence and a ban on 'cooking' or distorting it; there must be a willingness to admit that one is mistaken; there must be non-interference with people who wish to put forward objections; there must be a respect for people as a source of argument and an absence of personal invective and contempt for what they say because of who they are. To learn science is not just to learn facts and to understand theories; it is also to learn to participate in a public form of life governed by such principles of procedure. (p. 25)

To be engaged in education as a normative enterprise one must have and exhibit the manner appropriate to this activity. One must not only possess and exhibit the manner of an educator, writ large, but also the manner that best accords with the specific content areas one is opening up to students. This manner consists primarily of moral and intellectual virtues pertinent to education. Of the moral virtues pertinent to education, one thinks immediately of fairness, respect, openness, and honesty—to name just a few. Of the intellectual virtues, humility, creativity, reflectivity, dispassionateness (at the proper place and time), and honesty come quickly to mind. The manner of one who possesses these traits of character is learned by modeling, by being around persons who are like this, and by being encouraged to imitate these persons and adapt your actions to the demands of these traits. As Ryle (1975) says,

> What will help to make us self-controlled, fair-minded or hardworking are good examples set by others, and then ourselves practising and failing, and practising again, and failing again, but not quite so soon and so on. In matters of morals, as in the skills and arts, we learn first by being shown by others, then by being trained by others, naturally with some worded homily, praise, and rebuke, and lastly by being trained by ourselves. (pp. 46–47)

The teacher learns the manner of an educator from being taught by a person who possesses the manner of an educator. An educator in possession of manner that is founded on a rationally grounded and morally defensible theory of education will not simply toss research findings at teachers with the expectation that these findings will, come what may, show up in practice. Rather the educator will assist teachers to identify and clarify their practical arguments, then to assess the bearing of research evidence on the premises in these arguments. Teachers who teach in this way are themselves students of teaching.

A critic may counter here with the claim that all the teacher need be is a student of some subject in order to teach another that subject. The critic's view is that there is no need for a teacher to be both a student of teaching and a student of some subject to be a teacher of that subject. This counterargument is an old one; it raises all sorts of ghosts and goblins: whether teaching is a profession, whether there need be teaching methods courses, whether teachers should be required to take more work in their academic areas, and so forth. There are two ways of responding to this criticism. The first is to acknowledge it as a sane and sensible position, save that the complexity of modern schooling requires special training for those who teach there. This first response in effect supports the critic, saying that were it not for the complex institutionalization of education in our society (in the form of schools, classrooms, textbooks, grades, marks, SATs, etc.), all that would be necessary to teach is mastery of the subject taught.

A different response is that the purpose of teaching a student some subject is not simply to make him an expert or specialist in that subject. The purpose is to make available the knowledge and understanding of that subject so that the student can use it to free himself further from the constraining forces of dogma, stereotype, and convention. The subject is not taught to prepare the student to be a specialist in it, but to increase the student's capacity to understand and gain influence over his world. This is the notion of liberal education, of education undertaken to liberate or free the mind. It is education that requires more than subject matter mastery; it requires the manner of a liberated person. To liberate the mind of another, the teacher must know how to teach in a manner that liberates as well as know the subject matter to be taught.

Education is liberation in the profoundest sense of the term. To educate another one must be liberated, and carry the manner of liberation to the learner. It is the teacher who must possess the manner of a liberated scholar, this manner to serve as model for learners on their way to becoming students. The notion of practical argument and its relation to research is a good scheme for treating teachers in the manner we hope teachers will treat their students.

The argument of this chapter, in a nutshell, is that we simplify matters too much if we argue simply that the value of educational research is the improvement of educational practice. That is a misleading construction. The value of educational research, when it is done well, is to help us know and understand a certain limited range of educational phenomena. This knowledge and understanding gained from the research *may* improve educational practice, if it bears fruitfully on the premises of practical arguments in the minds of teachers. If researchers intentionally decide or just happen to pick out research problems whose investigation bears fruitfully on practical arguments, then the educational researcher is making an important contribution to the education of the teacher. But the simple production of knowledge about teaching does not in itself constitute the education of the teacher. Rather this knowledge must be picked up by a student of teaching, who uses it in the manner of an educator — and, in so doing, imparts to the teacher the manner of an educator. The student of teaching who teaches teachers may be the researcher whose work is under consideration, a person designated as an educator of teachers, or some other who is "to the manner made." The goal of anyone who sets out to teach teachers is to enable these teachers to become students of their teaching. Having become students of their work, they may then, by their manner, enable those in their custody to become students themselves.

Because, in education, we deal with persons, with entities that possess purpose and passion, we cannot have a science that treats us as if we were atoms, molecules, ball bearings, or planets. Yet this difference does not entail that we cannot have a science at all. We can and we must. However, it is important that we understand how science works when it deals with telic beings who are constituted in part by their emotions and feelings. I have tried, in this chapter, to show how science can work in education, in ways that educate. I approach science in this way because I believe that science should be understood as a contributor to what Nozick (1981) envisions as

a humanistic philosophy, a self-consciously artistic one, sculpting ideas, value, and meaning into new constellations, reverberative with mythic power, lifting and ennobling us by its content and by its creation, leading us to understand and to respond to value and meaning — to experience them and attain them anew. (p. 647)

REFERENCES

Amarel, M. (1982). The reader and the text — three perspectives. In W. Otto & S. White (Eds.), *Reading expository material* (pp. 243–257). New York: Academic Press.

Amarel, M. (1983). An education for commercial artists. *Daedalus, 112*(3), 29–58.

Anscombe, G. E. M. (1963). *Intention* (2nd ed.). Ithaca, NY: Cornell University Press.

Berliner, D. C. (1979). *Tempus educare.* In P. L. Peterson & H. J. Walberg (Eds.). *Research on teaching: Concepts, findings, and implications* (pp. 120–135). Berkeley, CA: McCutchan.

Borko, H., Cone, R., Russo, N. A., & Shavelson, R. J. (1979). Teachers' decision making. In P. L. Peterson & H. J. Walberg (Eds.). *Research on teaching: Concepts, findings, and implications* (pp. 136–160). Berkeley, CA: McCutchan.

Bronfenbrenner, U. (1979). *The ecology of human development.* Cambridge, MA: Harvard University Press.

Buchmann, M. (1984). The use of research knowledge in teacher education and teaching. *American Journal of Education, 92,* 421–439.

Carew, J. V., & Lightfoot, S. L. (1979). *Beyond bias: Perspective on classrooms.* Cambridge, MA: Harvard University Press.

Cronbach, L. J. (1975). Beyond the two disciplines of scientific psychology. *American Psychologist, 30*(2), 116–127.

Cusick, P. A. (1983). *The egalitarian ideal and the American high school.* New York: Longman.

Doyle, W. (1979a). Classroom tasks and students' abilities. In P. L. Peterson & H. J. Walberg (Eds.), *Research on teaching: Concepts, findings, and implications* (pp. 183–209). Berkeley, CA: McCutchan.

Doyle, W. (1979b). Making managerial decisions in classrooms. In D. L. Duke (Ed.), *Classroom management. Seventy-eighth yearbook of the National Society for the Study of Education* (pp. 42–74). Chicago: University of Chicago Press.

Doyle, W. (1983). Academic work. *Review of Educational Research, 53,* 159–199.

Eisner, E. W. (1984, March). Can educational research inform educational practice? *Phi Delta Kappan,* pp. 447–452.

Erickson, F. (1982). Classroom discourse and improvisation: Relationships between academic task structure and social participation structures in lessons. In L. C. Wilkinson (Ed.), *Communicating in the classroom* (pp. 153–182). New York: Academic Press.

Erickson, F., & Mohatt, G. (1982). Cultural organization of participation structures in two classrooms of Indian students. In G. Spindler (Ed.), *Doing the ethnography of schooling* (pp. 132–174). New York: Holt, Rinehart & Winston.

Ericson, D. P., & Ellett, F. S., Jr. (1982). Interpretation, understanding, and educational research. *Teachers College Record, 83,* 497–513.

Fenstermacher, G. D. (1979). A philosophical consideration of recent research on teacher effectiveness. *Review of Research in Education, 6,* 157–185.

Green, T. F. (1976). Teacher competence as practical rationality. *Educational Theory, 26,* 249–258.

Green, J. L. (1983). Research on teaching as a linguistic process: A state of the art. *Review of Research in Education, 10,* 151–252. Washington, DC: American Educational Research Association.

Guba, E. G. (1978). *Toward a methodology of naturalistic inquiry in educational evaluation.* Los Angeles: Center for the Study of Evaluation.

Hare, R. M. (1971). *Practical inferences.* London: Macmillan.

James, W. (1899). *Talks to teachers on psychology: And to students on some of life's ideals.* New York: W. W. Norton, 1958.

Jarvis, J. (1962). Practical reasoning. *Philosophical Quarterly, 12,* 316–328.

Kenny, A. J. (1966). Practical inference. *Analysis, 26,* 65–75.

Kidder, L. H. (1981). Qualitative research and quasi-experimental frameworks. In M. B. Brewer & B. E. Collins (Eds.), *Scientific inquiry and the social sciences* (pp. 226–256). San Francisco: Jossey-Bass.

Lakatos, I. (1970). Falsification and the methodology of scientific research programmes. In I. Lakatos & A. Musgrave (Eds.), *Criticism and the growth of knowledge* (pp. 91–195). Cambridge: Cambridge University Press.

Laudan, L. (1977). *Progress and its problems: Towards a theory of scientific growth.* Berkeley: University of California Press.

LeCompte, M. D., & Goetz, J. P. (1982). Problems of reliability and validity in ethnographic research. *Review of Educational Research, 52,* 31–60.

Lightfoot, S. L. (1983). *The good high school: Portraits of character and culture.* New York: Basic Books.

Louch, A. R. (1969). *Explanation and human action.* Berkeley: University of California Press.

McClellan, J. E. (1976). *Philosophy of education.* Englewood Cliffs, NJ: Prentice-Hall.

Miles, M. B., & Huberman, A. M. (1984). Drawing valid meaning from qualitative data: Toward a shared craft. *Educational Researcher, 13*(5), 20–30.

Muir, R. (1980). A teacher implements instructional changes using the BTES framework. In C. Denham & A. Lieberman (Eds.), *Time to learn* (pp. 197–212). Washington, DC: National Institute of Education.

Nemser, S. F. (1983). Learning to teach. In L. S. Shulman & G. Sykes (Eds.), *Handbook of teaching and policy* (pp. 150–170). New York: Longman.

Novak, J. D., & Gowin, D. B. (1984). *Learning how to learn.* Cambridge: Cambridge University Press.

Nozick, R. (1981). *Philosophical explanations.* Cambridge, MA: Harvard University Press.

Ogbu, J. (1978). *Minority education and caste: The American system in cross-cultural perspective.* New York: Academic Press.

Peters, R. S. (1973). Aims of education — a conceptual inquiry. In R. S. Peters (Ed.), *The philosophy of education* (pp. 11–29). London: Oxford University Press.

Phillips, D. C. (1981). Post-Kuhnian reflections on educational research. In J. F. Soltis (Ed.), *Philosophy and education. Eightieth yearbook of the National Society for the Study of Education* (pp. 237–261). Chicago: University of Chicago Press.

Rescher, N. (1973). *The primacy of practice.* Oxford: Basil Blackwell.

Ryle, G. (1949). *The concept of mind.* New York: Barnes & Noble.

Ryle, G. (1975). Can virtue be taught? In R. F. Dearden, P. H. Hirst, & R. S. Peters (Eds.). *Education and reason, Part 3* (pp. 44–57) London: Routledge & Kegan Paul.

Schwab, J. J. (1978). The practical: A language for curriculum. In I. Westbury & N. J. Wilkof (Eds.), *Science, curriculum, and liberal education.* Chicago: University of Chicago Press.

Shavelson, R. J. (1983). Review of research on teachers' pedagogical judgments, plans, and decisions. *Elementary School Journal, 83,* 392–413.

Shavelson, R. J., & Stern, P. (1981). Research on teachers' pedagogical thoughts, judgments, decisions, and behavior. *Review of Educational Research, 51,* 455–498.

Shulman, L. S. (1981). Disciplines of inquiry in education: An overview. *Educational Researcher, 10*(6), 5–12.

Smith, J. K. (1983). Quantitative versus qualitative research: An attempt to clarify the issue. *Educational Researcher, 12*(3), 6–13.

Soltis, J. F. (1978). *An introduction to the analysis of educational concepts* (2nd ed.). Reading, MA: Addison–Wesley.

Spradley, J. P. (1979). *The ethnographic interview.* New York: Holt, Rinehart & Winston.

Spradley, J. P. (1980). *Participant observation.* New York: Holt, Rinehart & Winston.

Tuthill, D., & Ashton, P. (1983). Improving educational research through the development of educational paradigms. *Educational Researcher, 12*(10), 6–14.

von Wright, G. H. (1963). Practical inference. *The Philosophical Review, 72*(2), 159–179.

Weinstein, R. S. (1983). Student perceptions of schooling. *Elementary School Journal, 83,* 287–312.

Willis, P. (1977). *Learning to labor.* New York: Columbia University Press.

Wilson, J. (1972). *Philosophy and educational research.* Slough, Berkshire, England: National Foundation for Education and Research in England and Wales.

Wolcott, H. F. (1977). *Teachers versus technocrats: An educational innovation in anthropological perspective.* Eugene: University of Oregon, Center for Educational Policy and Management.

Wolcott, H. F. (1982). Mirrors, models, and monitors. Educator adaptations of the ethnographic innovation. In G. Spindler (Ed.), *Doing the ethnography of schooling: Educational anthropology in action* (pp. 70–95). New York: Holt, Rinehart & Winston.

3

Measurement of Teaching

Richard J. Shavelson, Noreen M. Webb, and Leigh Burstein
University of California, Los Angeles

Introduction

This is the first time in the *Handbook*'s distinguished history that a separate chapter has been devoted to the broad topic measurement of teaching. To be sure, previous volumes have not ignored measurement. Medley and Mitzel's classic chapter (1963), for example, not only provided methods for systematically observing and measuring attributes of teacher behavior, but it also presented elements of a measurement theory to go along with these methods. (Indeed, our chapter picks up the threads of that measurement theory in the form of generalizability theory.) Moreover, measurement concerns could be found sprinkled throughout the more substantive chapters. Just what, then, is the domain of measurement of teaching?

Domain of Measurement of Teaching

Charting the measurement-of-teaching domain depends importantly on how the field of research on teaching is conceived (see Shulman's chapter in this volume). As a heuristic for mapping the domain, one possible view of the field is sketched briefly.

THE FIELD OF RESEARCH ON TEACHING

We conceive the field as encompassing studies of teacher planning, classroom processes, teaching outcomes, and the multilevel contexts that form the environment for teaching (e.g., classrooms, schools). Studies of *planning* are carried out in the "empty classroom" and focus on teachers' thoughts, judgments, and decisions in selecting curricular materials, grouping students, or developing lessons (see Clark & Peterson's chapter in this volume). Studies of classroom *process* bring a wide variety of methods to bear on teacher–student and student–student interactions in the classroom (see Evertson & Green's chapter in this volume), and on teachers' decisions during interactive teaching (see Clark & Peterson's chapter). Studies of teaching *outcomes* typically examine relations between measures of teacher behavior and student achievement. More recently, they have included randomized experiments that examine the effect of systematic variations in teaching behavior on student achievement (see Brophy & Good's chapter in this volume). And studies of teaching *context* examine the effects of classroom and school characteristics on classroom processes and teaching outcomes (see Feiman-Nemser & Floden, Lanier & Little, and Good & Brophy, all in this volume.)

Research on teaching typically focuses on the human teacher. The field, however, is not restricted to human teachers; it also includes, for example, studies of textbooks and computers as teachers. Further, teachers are not necessarily the sole focus of this research. Students' (and others') perceptions of teaching, of the teacher, and of the behavior of their teachers and classmates clearly fall within the domain (see Shulman's chapter in this volume).

MEASUREMENT-OF-TEACHING DOMAIN

Traditionally, the field of educational and psychological measurement covers instrument construction, scaling and metrics, reliability, and validity. We define the *measurement-of-teaching domain* by linking each of these topics with each area of research on teaching. For example, by linking the area of teacher planning with validity, the domain includes questions such as whether teachers' verbal reports of their cognitive processes reveal anything about those processes. By linking the area of reliability with classroom process measurements, we raise questions about, for example, the dependability of measures of teacher behavior over observers, time, and subject matters. When we combine the area of scaling and metrics with the measurement of student outcomes, questions arise about how best to create students' scores from their responses to achievement test items or from their responses on self-concept questionnaires.

The authors thank reviewers Donald M. Medley (University of Florida), William H. Schmidt (Michigan State University), and Philip H. Winne (Simon Fraser University).

These few examples illustrate the enormity of the measurement-of-teaching domain. Only a small portion can be treated adequately in a single chapter. We delimit the domain by selecting three areas of research that have, in our opinion, substantially shaped the field of research on teaching, measurement, or both, over the past decade. One area—research on teacher effectiveness—contributed importantly to the policy debate on educational excellence and to practical matters of teacher selection, training, and evaluation. The second area, generalizability theory (Cronbach, Gleser, Nanda, & Rajaratnam, 1972), is one of the most important advances in measurement theory during the 1970s. By applying this theory to measures of classroom process, we come full circle to one of this chapter's predecessors (Medley & Mitzel, 1963). The third area—research on teachers' thoughts, judgments, and decisions—significantly reconceptualized the field. It introduced an entirely new set of research methods and, not surprisingly, measurement issues.

There are glaring omissions in this chapter. One is the Beginning Teacher Evaluation Study's measurement of *time-on-task*. Although the BTES will not receive the attention due its importance, some aspects of the study will nevertheless be touched upon. The tack of ignoring instrumentation seemed reasonable; this topic is treated in other *Handbook* chapters. Less defensible is the decision to ignore scaling, in particular, the important contributions of item-response theory (Lord, 1980). Item response theory is simply too new (in its fullest version) to have made a significant impact on teaching research. Perhaps the *Handbook*'s next volume will feature IRT as this chapter has done with generalizability theory.

Overview of the Chapter

The remainder of this chapter takes up three topics: measurement of teacher effectiveness, classroom processes, and teachers' cognitive processes. The section on the measurement of teacher effectiveness critically examines current practice and proposes more sensitive and sensible measurement methods. In particular, we argue that the measurement of effectiveness must be linked closely to the content of instruction and to the multilevel nature of the classroom. The following section presents the rudiments of generalizability (G) theory and shows how the theory can be used to determine the dependability of classroom process measurements. It matches prototypical designs for collecting process data with the appropriate analysis using G theory. The last section examines the reliability and validity of measures of teachers' judgments, decisions, and thought processes. It addresses questions such as: Under what conditions can dependable measures of covert mental processes be obtained? What pitfalls, such as unwarranted interpretations of measurements, await the uninitiated researcher?

This ordering of topics was chosen to reflect the range of research on teaching, from the macro policy-relevant studies of

teacher effectiveness and studies of classroom processes as explanations for effective teaching to the micro studies of the "mental life" of teachers (and students) as explanations for observed classroom processes and teaching outcomes. A more pragmatic reason for this sequence is to move the reader gently from the familiar process-product (effectiveness) research to the unfamiliar cognitive-process research.

The Measurement of Teacher Effectiveness

Certainly the years 1972 through 1978 can be viewed as the heyday of process-product research on teaching. Although a substantial number of studies relating teacher behavior to student achievement had been conducted in earlier years (see reviews by Dunkin & Biddle, 1974; Medley, 1977; Rosenshine & Furst, 1973), this research paradigm did not generate consistent evidence until this period. Or possibly research on teaching simply took on new meaning and emphasis as classroom researchers scrambled to refute overinterpretations and overreactions to the negative findings from the school effects research exemplified by the Coleman Report (Coleman, Campbell, Hobson, McPartland, Mood, Weinfeld, & York, 1966).

Process-product research tended to follow a common general paradigm. In each study, measures of teacher behavior ("process") and teacher effectiveness ("product," later called "outcome") were gathered from a large sample of classrooms (typically more than 20 but fewer than 100) at one or more grade levels (typically lower primary). In virtually all the studies, the measures of teacher behavior were derived from systematic observation of classroom interactions of teachers and students on multiple occasions throughout the school year.[1] Measures of teacher effectiveness were based on gains in student achievement. Earlier studies were correlational. Later on, findings from correlational research were used to develop instructional packages, and experimental field studies were conducted using essentially the same data collection procedures.

We will not review the results from the main body of research on teacher effectiveness. Extensive thoughtful and thorough reviews already abound (e.g., Brophy, 1979; Good, 1979, n.d; Medley, 1977; Rosenshine, 1979, 1983; Rosenshine & Berliner, 1978). Moreover, this task falls within the purview of several chapters in this volume.

This section focuses on the measurement of teacher effectiveness by achievement tests and what this choice indicates about the dominant conception of teaching that guided the work. We will also consider whether the measurement choice introduced its own set of problems; in particular, whether it potentially masked the effects of certain teaching activities and almost preordained that others would demonstrate consistent impact.

We will contend that the ways in which scores from standardized achievement tests were typically used as outcomes in teacher effectiveness studies reflected a flawed conception of

---

[1] Researchers use different criteria to identify process-product or teacher effectiveness studies. The correlational studies cited most often in the major reviews are Brophy & Evertson (1974), Evertson, Anderson, & Brophy (1978a, 1978b), Fisher, Filby, Marliave, Cahen, Dishaw, Moore, & Berliner (1978), Good & Grouws (1975), McDonald & Elias (1976), Soar & Soar (1972), Stallings & Kaskowitz (1974), and Tikunoff, Berliner, & Rist (1975). The most frequently cited experimental field studies are Anderson, Evertson, & Brophy (1978), Good & Grouws (1979), and Program on Teaching Effectiveness (1976).

how teaching can influence student learning. The concern here goes beyond the obvious narrowing of the goals, functions, and purposes of education, and the explicit preoccupation with achievement in basic skills in reading, mathematics, and the language arts in elementary schools. The flaws stem from a limited view of the role of the teacher and of teaching in the instruction–learning process.

Toward the end of the 1970s, process–product studies widened in scope. The concept of time as a resource was reintroduced. Also, curriculum, subject matter, and learning strategies were included as both the substance of instruction and the direct antecedents of learning from instruction. By the time these changes occurred, research on teaching had expanded its methods to include small-scale naturalistic intensive examinations of the teaching process (e.g., see Green & Smith, 1983 as well as chapters by Erickson and by Evertson & Green, in this volume) and its focus to include teacher and student thoughts, judgments, and decisions (see Clark & Peterson, this volume; Marx, 1983; Shavelson, 1983) and the social ecology of the classroom (see Hamilton, 1983).

In contrast to the evolution cited above, recent advances in the handling of classroom achievement data have not been evident in new research on teaching. Although most teacher effectiveness research roughly paralleled developments in achievement testing, especially criterion-referenced measurement with its focus on representing the content and objectives of instruction, and the developments in cognitive psychology with its information-processing models of learning (e.g., Anderson, Spiro, & Montague, 1977; Snow, Federico, & Montague, 1980), analyses of the total scores on norm-referenced achievement tests dominated this literature. Perhaps the ideas presented in this chapter anticipate the applications of better models of the instruction–learning process in research on teaching and better measurement of learner knowledge and skills.

Operationalizing Teacher Effectiveness

In our review we will concentrate on the common, though often implicit, definition of teacher effectiveness in process–product research. According to Good, "Teacher effectiveness refers to the ability of a classroom teacher to produce higher-than-predicted gains on standardized achievement tests" (1979, p. 53). Operationally, effective teaching was equated with (measured by) large mean residual gains for a teacher's class. Such gains were computed from standardized achievement test scores as either posttest minus pretest mean, or observed posttest mean minus the posttest mean predicted from pretest. Some investigators established more stringent criteria by equating effectiveness to gains in both reading and mathematics, or to

stable gains across multiple classes or multiple years (Brophy, 1973; Emmer, Evertson & Brophy, 1979; Veldman and Brophy, 1974). Once evidence of differential effectiveness had been ascertained, an attempt was then made to find its correlates among the set of teaching behaviors measured by classroom observation instruments.

To begin to understand the problems of outcome measurement in process–product research, it is necessary to examine more closely what the numbers from the typical measure of teacher effectiveness actually mean. According to the paradigm, a teacher is *effective* if, within the time period studied, students, *averaged* over the *whole class*, answered *more* questions *correctly* on *multiple-choice standardized achievement* tests than expected, based on the pretest performance. Under these conditions, the students in the effective teacher's class are said to have *learned more* than expected.

When stated in the above fashion, it is clear that the standard operationalization of effectiveness in process–product research has the following properties.:

1. Effectiveness assumes commonality of curriculum goals, objectives, and content coverage across classrooms because one standardized achievement test is used to judge the effectiveness in all classrooms.
2. Effectiveness is strictly summative in its measurement of subject matter knowledge. It is not what students know or don't know that matters, but the accumulated quantity of their knowledge in comparison with students in other classrooms.
3. Performance on the effectiveness measure is equated with knowledge or skill in subject matter. There is no notion of "less than best effort," guessing, partial knowledge, or test-taking skill.
4. Effectiveness is strictly aggregative across students within a classroom. Operationally, regardless of how student performance is distributed within the classroom, the class average is chosen to represent class performance.

Although there are other features of the operationalization that might warrant our attention,[2] the above-mentioned properties—match of curriculum, instruction, and test; mode of representation of test performance; extraneous testing conditions; and the representativeness of measures of group-level performance—are most likely to influence what will or will not appear to be the instructional determinants of effectiveness. In the sections that follow, we consider the nature of current practice with respect to each property, its limitations, and possible alternative practices that may warrant further investigation and application in teacher effectiveness research.

---

[2] Examples of such topics are methodological problems in the use of gain or residual gain scores and in the applications of variance partitioning procedures in research on teaching. Chapter 4 of this handbook covers these topics to some degree. Recent work (e.g., Rogosa, Brandt, & Zimkowski, 1982) has caused some revision of negative views about gain scores, but conclusions from that work do not resolve the issue addressed here.

Discussions of "variance accounted for" in teacher effectiveness research are misguided almost from the start. The confusion is especially troubling because, even ignoring measurement errors, four sources of total variation in scores have been used as outcomes in the literature. These four sources are *between-student* variation in *posttest* scores, *between-student* variation in *gain* scores, *between-classroom* variation in *average posttest* scores, and finally, *between-classroom* variation in *average gain* scores. An investigator can cause the percentage of variance accounted for by a given teacher variable to be larger or smaller depending on the choice among these four measures.

The Assumption of a Common Curriculum

There are historical precedents to support the choice of standardized achievement tests as outcomes in process-product research. Such tests have been widely used for purposes of local monitoring in school districts for decades. They also routinely serve as indicators for informing state and national education policy. At the national and state level, standardized achievement tests were used as outcomes in virtually all of the major large-scale evaluations of educational programs (e.g., Projects Head Start and Follow Through, the ESEA evaluations, the Sustaining Effects Study), and in studies of school effects and educational productivity such as Coleman et al. (1966).

Standardized tests are designed to reflect curriculum over a broad array of schools and districts using different textbooks, syllabi, and instructional methods. Their content and the scores they typically generate cover lightly a variety of objectives within a content area. As such these tests represent a common standard by which to measure progress during a year of instruction.

LIMITATIONS OF CURRENT PRACTICE

But strengths for some purposes represent weaknesses for others. The intent of these tests to cover the broad spectrum of local orientations invariably means that the content of the tests imperfectly aligns with the curricular goals of any local district, and yet more imperfectly with the specific instructional goals and content in a particular classroom.

The potential consequences of the mismatch between content of a standardized test and what is taught in a teacher's classroom are well known. First, a number of studies (e.g., Floden, Freeman, Porter, & Schmidt, 1980; Hoepfner, 1978; Jenkins & Pany, 1976; Schmidt, 1983) indicate that standardized achievement tests and textbooks exhibit substantial variation in content coverage. Thus when the teachers within a study use different textbooks, the correspondence of their instruction with test content is bound to vary within the study beyond whatever mismatches characterize the district's curriculum and the test's content.

Second, the amount of overlap between what is taught and what is tested is strongly related to how well students perform on tests (Barr and Dreeben, 1983; Cooley & Leinhardt, 1980; Husen, 1967; Leinhardt, 1983; Leinhardt & Seewald, 1981); programs emphasizing a particular set of curriculum objectives do better on tests designed to measure those objectives than programs with different emphases (e.g., Walker & Schaffarzik, 1974). This generalization is robust. It fits across a wide variety of grade levels and subject matters. It also holds for different ways of measuring overlap although the relationship appears to be stronger when the overlap measure more nearly approximates the actual instructional experience of the student (Leinhardt, 1983; Leinhardt & Seawald, 1981; Schmidt, 1983).

Given the evidence that content coverage matters in performance on standardized achievement tests, it is somewhat surprising that so few of the major studies actually controlled for curriculum variations. With notable exception, the large-scale correlational studies rarely observed classrooms covering the same content, measured content coverage explicitly, or otherwise ensured that their outcome measures were aligned with the curriculum delivered in the classrooms being observed. Even in the experimental studies in which teachers were trained to employ specific behaviors or strategies, curricular homogeneity was neither explicitly planned nor generally examined (Anderson, Evertson & Brophy, 1979; Emmer, Evertson, Sanford, & Clements, 1982; Evertson, Emmer, Sanford, & Clements, 1982; Good & Grouws, 1979). As Good (n.d.) concludes, "broader issues of *what is taught* and *how appropriately* have been largely ignored" (p. 31).

Only in those studies that connect research on teaching with the work on models of school learning (Bloom, 1976; Carroll, 1963; Harnischfeger & Wiley, 1976) does the notion of differential opportunity to learn enter into consideration. For example, Cooley and Leinhardt (1980; Leinhardt & Seewald, 1981) directly measured what they called "curriculum overlap" in several ways along with observations of other "opportunity-to-learn" aspects of the instructional environment, the environmental motivators that encourage student learning, the structure of instructional material, and the quality of instructional activities. Opportunity-to-learn effects were clearly the major determinants of performance on the standardized achievement tests they used (Cooley, 1981).

The Beginning Teacher Evaluation Study (BTES) conducted by researchers at the Far West Laboratory (e.g., Fisher et al., 1978) was responsive to the curriculum-test overlap issue in several ways. These researchers developed their own test battery based on items (partly taken from existing standardized tests) that were shown to be sensitive to instruction during the pilot phase of the study (Filby & Dishaw, 1976). Moreover, the investigation focused directly on the time individual students spent in instruction within specific reading and mathematics content areas. Curriculum-test overlap per se was not examined nor were teachers' instructional choices constrained. As a result, the BTES researchers found that both within and between classrooms, students varied as to the amount of time they spent in a given content area, and these time differences were associated with differential performance gains.

INCORPORATING CURRICULUM

This new emphasis on time-on-task definitely reflects a greater awareness of the role of curriculum content and coverage. But one would hope that at some point the content of instruction itself would be a central element in research on teaching. Even in its most refined form, the academic learning time (ALT) measure from the BTES study—the amount of time students are judged to be engaged in learning content at a level of difficulty appropriate for them—is operationalized in terms of the student's level of functioning rather than in terms of the inherent characteristics of content per se.

Bringing curriculum into the study of teaching will not be a straightforward task. The measurement of content will necessarily need to function at two levels. First, a direct accounting is needed of the *specific topics actually taught*, perhaps along the lines of the work at the Institute for Research on Teaching (IRT) on content coverage (e.g., Floden, et al., 1980; Schmidt, 1983) or Leinhardt's measurement of overlap. Such accountings can be made more or less precise depending on specificity of the content domain of a given topic (e.g., whether addition and sub-traction of fractions are treated separately or are both classified within the domain of fractions). Regardless of specificity, trans-lating topic coverage into measures suitable for relating to gen-eral performance measures will involve complicated choices (e.g., Schmidt, 1983).

On the second level, researchers will need to identify the *curriculum processes* emphasized by teachers. The term curriculum processes is used here to encompass a number of approaches to classifying the content of instruction into generic forms of knowledge (e.g., concepts, principles, procedures) that cut across topics. The processes dimension of Bloom's taxonomy of educational objectives is a classic attempt to capture this di-mension though it is unlikely to serve the purposes required in teaching research (e.g., see Kropp, Stoker, & Bashaw, 1966).

Modern work combining cognitive psychology with notions of curriculum structures to yield a cognitive structure of know-ledge (Anderson, 1977; Baker & Herman, 1983; Calfee, 1981; Curtis & Glaser, 1983; Davis & McKnight, 1976, 1979; Doyle, 1983; Glaser, 1978; Haertel & Calfee, 1983; Resnick & Ford, 1981; Romberg, 1983) is promising. Its emphasis on higher-level cognitive processes, meaning, and knowledge structures and its distinction of various stages or levels in learning (e.g., expert vs. novice) provide both the impetus and the focus for examining teaching strategies that can enhance the develop-ment of fundamental and hopefully enduring skills. Such efforts can potentially move classroom research toward understanding what teachers do that encourages "learning how to learn." Un-fortunately, much of this modern work still remains beyond the scope of practical research on naturally occurring instruction.

Returning to the major theme of this section, recent work on the relationship of content coverage and time-on-task to test performance clearly indicates that standardized achievement tests fail as common measures of teacher effectiveness. Berliner (1980) argued convincingly that these tests cannot be "fair" measures of effectiveness "as long as teachers have the freedom to choose what areas to emphasize and what materials they will use" (p. 193).

We generally agree with Berliner's assessment of the inade-quacy of standardized achievement tests for measuring the con-sequences of teaching. Certainly questions regarding their specific content and format are central to dissatisfaction with their past use in teacher effectiveness research. Yet the major limitation of using standardized achievement tests is that the virtual absence of information about curriculum content and processes from process–product research provides an inade-quate basis for judgments about the plausible sources of per-formance gain that may be associated with teaching practices. Are the quantity of topics covered and the quality of curriculum strategies employed the primary determinants of learning or do general classroom organization principles and practices and task structuring also play a key role? These questions simply cannot be answered without explicit attention to curriculum issues in research on teaching. As Smith points out:

> The performance of the teacher is shaped by many variables ... among these is the content of instruction. ... The teacher interacts with the student in and through the content, and the student inter-acts with the teacher in the same way. (1983, p. 491)

There seems to be no sound basis for ignoring subject matter and its "interactions" with the processes and outcomes of in-struction.

The Adequacy of Summative Evidence About Students' Knowledge and Skills

Assume for the moment that all teachers covered the same ma-terial and some standardized test measured that material. Also assume that students' responses to test questions at both the pretest and the posttest represent what they believe to be the correct answers. That is, students tried to answer each question correctly and did not guess randomly at the answer. Under these conditions what can be wrong with simply calculating a summary score (either of correct responses or the increase in the number correct) and letting that value represent how much students learned, and consequently, their teacher's effective-ness? The problems with such scores as measures of knowledge and skills and an alternative means of treating the test data are discussed below.

MEASURING THE COGNITIVE CONTENT AND COGNITIVE STRUCTURE OF KNOWLEDGE

In our view an important aspect of students' learning is missed when only summary scores are considered. Instruction affects both the cognitive content and cognitive structure of student knowledge. Student responses to test items should reflect their knowledge and thus should be responsive to instruction (a prin-ciple that the evidence cited in the previous section certainly supports). Measures of teaching outcomes, then, should tell us something about the kinds of questions students can answer and the kinds of mistakes they made on the questions missed. Such information is necessary to identify effective and ineffec-tive aspects and components of instructional events. Yet sum-mary scores provide no direct information for this purpose.

The possible impact of instruction on the cognitive structure that students have for approaching test tasks (e.g., Kropp et al., 1966; Shavelson, 1972) points to another problem with sum-mary scores as measures of teacher effectiveness. Even when pretests and posttests contain the same questions, some test items retain their meaning over both occasions while others change in terms of the content of students' cognitive structure or the cognitive strategies students employ to accomplish the task. As an example, a paraphrase-type question from a reading comprehension test might be answered correctly at the pretest by those students familiar with the topic of the passage. After instruction that enhances comprehension processing (Rumel-hart & Ortony, 1977), those students who successfully mastered the instruction would now answer correctly regardless of prior exposure to passage content, and even those students familiar with the passage content could tap new skills to generate their responses.

Summary scores cannot reflect these changes in students' cognition associated with instruction. Instead, tests need to be designed and analyzed in a manner that directly attends to this purpose (e.g., Baker & Herman, 1983; Curtis & Glaser, 1983; Tatsuoka, 1983). Even the best of currently available tests fall short by this criterion.

STUDENTS' RESPONSE PATTERNS: AN
ALTERNATIVE TO SUMMARY SCORES

Even when multiple-choice achievement tests have not been especially designed to tap either curriculum content, the tasks students are asked to perform on the curriculum, or the students' understanding of the task, there still remains a means of gathering useful information about certain consequences of instruction. This information is obtained by examining the patterns of students' responses to test items across occasions and across classes. In a classroom where most students cover the same topics (although pacing and depth might vary), the typical change in the pattern of responses from incorrect to correct answers and the types of wrong answers that persist from pretest to posttest can reflect the consequences of teaching. In these response patterns, differences between classrooms can be particularly informative.

A reanalysis of selected test item data from the BTES study suggests how response patterns might provide information about teaching differences. Miller (1981, 1984) examined the answers chosen by 123 students from 21 fifth-grade classrooms to the 15 items from the fractions subtest on two occasions (prior to [Occasion B] and following [Occasion C] most instruction in this subject area). He classified the test items into four subtopics: adding of fractions, subtracting of fractions, equating fractions, and solving fractions with algebraic unknowns (e.g., $x/3 = 6/9$. What is x?).

Several distinctive class-level patterns emerged. Students in most classes did best on the addition and subtraction items and poorest on algebraic unknowns. There were, however, several classes with high performance on the last topic. The students in one class actually mastered only this topic. In another class, the students did well with algebraic unknowns but missed virtually all of the addition items. Even if these students had scored only at the mean in the addition area, the class average total score at Occasion C would have moved from tenth place to sixth among the 21 classrooms because of their relative performance in algebraic unknowns.

When Miller studied the response choices on the two occasions, other instruction-related patterns emerged. In most classrooms that did well on addition and subtraction but poorly on the remaining topics, student responses on the latter topics had approximately the same scatter across alternatives within classes at both occasions. This suggests that the teachers in these classrooms simply did not teach these topics during the period of instruction between test occasions.

Changes in the patterns of incorrect responses to addition items were also informative. At Occasion B a substantial number of students, distributed across all classrooms, chose alternatives that involved summing both numerators and denominators (e.g., $1/2 + 1/3 = 2/5$). While the proportion of incorrect responses to addition items at Occasion C was significantly smaller (53% incorrect at Occasion C versus 75% at Occasion B), the students in a few classes were still making the same fundamental mistake. These teachers either did not teach fractions at all, followed an atypical pattern of topic coverage, or simply failed to notice that students did not understand the concept.

The possible implications of response patterns for teacher ef-

fectiveness research depend to some degree on how well the curricular issues discussed earlier are addressed in a particular investigation. If study classrooms are supposed to be teaching the same material and the chosen tests adequately represent the intended curriculum, then atypical class-level response patterns presumably reflect teacher deviations from prescribed goals or ineffective instruction. The collection of additional information about actual instructional coverage — through teacher, observer, and student reports of topic coverage, strategy, ordering, and emphasis keyed to test content — can further pinpoint the basis for performance patterns. Then, depending on the operable components of "effective teaching" in a given study, these data (performance patterns plus curriculum coverage) represent either direct evidence of effectiveness (e.g., the ability to cover the intended curriculum in an instructionally appropriate manner) or a means of controlling for a major confounding or nuisance variable in examining other aspects of teaching. In the absence of a common intended curriculum and direct measurement of actual instructional coverage, conditioning interpretations on an examination of performance patterns may be the only means to introduce controls for factors viewed to be irrelevant (or relevant) to identifying generic or specific teaching processes associated with effectiveness.

The above examples barely scratch the surface of possibilities since the BTES study did not provide content coverage data for specific subtopics in fractions or any other topic, for that matter. Currently, cognitive psychologists and psychometricians have begun to construct tests and develop analytical methods that use response patterns to identify procedures students use in responding to test items. One value of these methods is that they can help diagnose procedural bugs (Baker & Herman, 1983; Birenbaum & Tatsuoka, 1980; Brown & Burton, 1978; Curtis & Glaser, 1983; Davis, 1979; Harnisch, 1983; Harnisch & Linn, 1982; Tatsuoka, 1983; Tatsuoka & Linn, 1982; Tatsuoka & Tatsuoka, 1982, 1983) that result from lack of instruction or poor instruction. At some point the developments from this work will be organized in a form that classroom researchers can use to help identify what has been taught, how it has been taught, and perhaps even how well it has been taught.

*The Distinction Among Knowledge,
Effort, and Test-Wiseness*

There are good reasons for not accepting standardized test scores of students as necessarily indicative of their knowledge. Students may answer certain questions correctly for which they lack the necessary knowledge and yet miss others which they "know."

Both cognitive and affective explanations are possible for the lack of isomorphism between knowledge and test performance. Student affect toward the test task can contribute to performance. Most standardized testing has no direct bearing on students' normal functioning within the classroom because these tests are infrequently given and thus are not part of the normal routine. Furthermore, these tests rarely have a direct bearing on student grades (e.g., see Dorr-Bremme, 1982). In fact, while curriculum-embedded and teacher-made tests of various types are routine classroom events, the formal standardized testing with its large number of multiple-choice items typically disrupts normal classroom practices.

Under the conditions described above, it is quite plausible that some students will not be motivated sufficiently to perform well on the standardized tests used as outcomes in teacher effectiveness research. Some students may not perceive the test as a task requiring their best effort. Others may perceive it as strictly an aversive condition which lacks the feedback mechanisms and consequences necessary for either intrinsic or extrinsic motivation.

From another perspective, taking a standardized test is a cognitive task that has different meanings for different students. Some view it as an application of their problem-solving skills, attempting to figure out what the test tasks require and apply their reasoning skills as well as knowledge to arrive at the best (or most likely) answer to individual items. Others simply cycle through test questions applying their full but perhaps partial knowledge to each. There are yet others for whom standardized tests are a bewildering maze. They may have sufficient knowledge to provide correct answers or make intelligent guesses but become confused by the extraneous information provided by the alternatives (distractors) or by the format and layout of the test. Finally, students differ in their propensity to guess; that is, students vary with respect to the amount of partial knowledge (the number of alternatives that need to be eliminated) they require before choosing an answer.

These "extra-knowledge" influences on test performance are important in teacher effectiveness research for at least two reasons. First, like content coverage and instructional strategy, the motivation to do well on standardized tests and the attainment of test-taking skills necessary to make best use of one's knowledge can be affected by instruction. Teachers faced with classes that are similar in ability composition and prior test-taking experiences and skills nonetheless differ in their success at providing an atmosphere and the prior task preparation conducive to maximum student performance. Thus skill at establishing conditions for maximum test performance is potentially a legitimate and separable component of effective teaching, one that possibly should be considered in teacher effectiveness research.

Second, regardless of one's interest in test motivation and preparation as teaching skills, it is still useful to separate this influence on scores from the knowledge and skill acquisition component of performance. Otherwise, gain scores will confound the direct impact of teaching on student knowledge with the effects of student effort and test-taking skills and thereby hinder the identification of instructional practices related to the former.

There is not much that one can recommend researchers do psychometrically with their achievement tests that would make them impervious to the "extra-knowledge" influences of motivation and prior preparation. Adequate standardization and control of administration conditions are essential, but efforts to apply formulas to adjust for guessing and psychometric techniques that measure, and perhaps credit, partial knowledge barely scratch the surface of the problem. Even worse, these efforts devote research resources to the wrong aspects of the issues.

What may be more useful is to enhance or expand the classroom process and context information collected in ways that might capture the prevalence and salience of effort and test-wiseness conditions existing in a given study. Augmentations might include attitudinal information from teachers and students about their testing-related perceptions (e.g., their valuing of standardized tests, preparations to take them, and anxieties about the experience), observations of test administration and test-taking, and probes of teachers' and students' thoughts, judgements and decisions relevant to testing. Thus investigators interested in improving effectiveness research with respect to this property might consider the literature on recent developments in methods for measuring classroom conditions and processes (e.g., Clark & Peterson, this volume; Green & Smith, 1983; Hamilton, 1983; Shavelson, 1983; Weinstein, 1983). So far, however, this new classroom research relevant to test conditions other than content has been limited to portions of the work on student perceptions conducted by Weinstein (1983) and IRT's policy capturing research on teachers' testing policies and practices (e.g., Floden, Porter, Schmidt, Freeman, & Schwille, 1981, Schwille, Porter, Belli, Floden, Freeman, Knapper, Kuhs, & Schmidt, 1983).

Aggregation of Scores Across Students

The tendency in teacher effectiveness research has been to focus analyses on the correlates of the *average* gain across students in the classroom, regardless of the distribution of performance within classrooms at either the pretest or the posttest. The primary statistical analyses in virtually all the major studies were conducted at the classroom level. This choice was typically a consequence of the research focus on the teacher. But this choice also certainly reflected prevailing statistical wisdom as well (e.g., Glass & Stanley, 1970); observations in the statistical analysis needed to be independent, and observations on students within classrooms typically are statistically dependent.

This is not the place to reopen the debate about choosing the appropriate unit of analysis (e.g., see Burstein, 1980; Hopkins, 1982; Slavin, 1983) nor is this even the right question. Rather, what is important is whether the substantive intent of teacher-effectiveness research is well served by concentrating on mean gains. In our judgment the aggregation of the experiences and performances across pupils within a classroom may mask the effects of the quality of teaching in much the same way as others (e.g., Good, 1979; Veldman & Brophy, 1974) have argued about the consequences of aggregating across teachers in school effects research.

LIMITATIONS OF CLASS MEANS

Stated in its simplest form, class mean gains hide important information about the within-class variability in student performance and experiences. Concentrating on class means thus misses evidence of a teacher's differential effectiveness. Mean gain scores cannot indicate who learned what or how much within the class; moreover, they are insensitive to the organization and setting of instruction. Distributions of student attributes, opportunities, experiences, and performance within the classroom and the teacher's impact on these distributions matter and should not be overlooked.

The limitations of mean gains become clearer when we concentrate directly on instruction in elementary school classrooms. Under every configuration for organizing academic instruction, the target group—the group of students that determines the choice of topics, the time devoted to them, the level and pace at which material is covered—is seldom, if ever, the whole class. This is true regardless of the overall distribution of instructional time among whole-class, large-group, small-group, and seatwork and tutorial settings. Even whole class instruction is directed toward a "steering group" within the classroom (Dahllof, 1971; Lundgren, 1972).

When instruction is viewed from the student perspective, instead, there are yet other drawbacks of mean gains. Even if it were possible for the teacher to "target" the whole class, or more likely, be oblivious to the consequences of ignoring student differences in presenting a lesson, students would nevertheless vary in their responses. That is, student attributes such as ability, personality, and motivation interact with instruction to yield differential gains. Some students work best under highly structured conditions while others benefit more from less structure (e.g., Peterson, 1977). This evidence of a teacher's differential effectiveness is missed by concentrating on class means.

Work on student mediation of instruction (e.g., Doyle, 1977, 1983) and student perceptions of schooling (Weinstein, 1983) also suggests sources of differential responsiveness to teaching. (See Wittrock's chapter in this volume.) Obviously a conception of the teaching–learning process that incorporates such intervening student-level mechanisms cannot be properly depicted nor investigated using class mean gains.

ANALYTICAL ALTERNATIVES

Barr and Dreeben (1977) contend that "school events should be observed where they occur: school, track, classroom, or whichever ... a full range of organizational levels and their interconnections" (pp. 101–102). In making a case for a multi-level perspective in investigating educational effects, Burstein (1985) states:

> What is needed is an appropriate model of the educational phenomena of interest and analytical strategies that disentangle effects from a variety of sources so that the interface of individuals and the "groups" to which they belong and the implications of this interface for educational effects can be examined. (p. 14; see also Burstein, 1980)

In the context of teacher effectiveness research, both of these recommendations translate into analyses that attend to the organization of instruction in classrooms and differences in students' reactions to it.

In the remainder of this section, we briefly describe examples of approaches to enhancing the analytical sensitivity of effectiveness research to the phenomena identified by Barr and Dreeben and by Burstein. Attempts to improve the sensitivity of effectiveness analyses to instructional organization and student differences have followed two general approaches. Some investigators adopt an outcomes-based approach to examine the possibility of teachers' differential effectiveness. A broader, potentially more sensitive array of statistical indices is considered to enhance the chances of identifying various aspects and antecedents of effectiveness. The approach taken by other researchers is to start with a model of classroom organization and instructional activities and let the analytical procedures mirror

this model. While the actual statistical techniques might be the same, the impetus of the analytical efforts is clearly instructional organization and processes rather than outcomes.

In moving away from class means as the sole indicator of teacher effectiveness, a variety of choices emerge. The simplest strategy has been to consider measures of the distribution (e.g., variance, proportion of students above or below a certain standard) of class performance (e.g., Block & Burns, 1976; Burstein & Linn, 1981; Cooley & Lohnes, 1976; Linn & Burstein, 1977; Lohnes, 1972). Analysis of additional statistical descriptors expands the possibility for detecting additional class-level variation in performance and its correlates. But these alternative indicators of class outcomes are no better attuned to a model of the educational phenomena in the classroom than are means. The effects they detect may still arise from either the initial composition of abilities in the classroom, the differential impact of a teacher's general instructional methods on individual students, or the consequences of a teacher's efforts to adapt instruction to the differential needs of students. Thus the payoff of this form of analytical enhancement depends heavily on the nature and quality of information about classroom conditions, student composition, and the organization and emphasis of instructional activities.

Studies in which the experiences and outcomes of subgroups of students are investigated (e.g., Wiley, 1970) employ another outcome-based alternative. Virtually any attribute of students can be used to define contrasting groups, but ability and personality characteristics are the most likely candidates. The analytical focus would then be on subgroup contrasts (e.g., mean differences) in student experiences and outcomes and the variance of outcome contrasts as a function of instruction. The main complication would be how to select consistent, defensible rules for forming subgroups. Yet the potential payoff from such an approach is clearly suggested by Webb's (1980, 1982) studies of variation in participation and learning in small groups as a function of student ability and group composition.

The analysis of subgroup differences as described in the previous paragraph reflects one attempt to capture directly the consequences of within-class processes for different types of students (e.g., Burstein, 1980; Burstein, Miller, & Linn, 1981; Wiley, 1970). Still another approach to studying within-class variation while focusing on instructional effects is to study between-class variation in the relationships of student attributes to student outcomes (Burstein, Linn, & Capell, 1978; Burstein, Miller, & Linn, 1981; Corno, 1979; Greene, 1980; McDonald & Elias, 1976; Schneider & Treiber, 1984.) Analytically, this approach treats the slopes from the regression of student outcomes on their entering characteristics for each class as statistical measures that may vary as a function of between-class differences in teaching methods. Conceptually, this strategy follows naturally from attempts to investigate aptitude treatment interactions in classroom research (Cronbach, 1976; Cronbach & Snow, 1977; Cronbach & Webb, 1975). Either differential student responsiveness to common instructional strategies or instruction specifically adopted to individual differences yields slope heterogeneity, and thus focusing on classroom antecedents of this heterogeneity makes theoretical sense. Unfortunately, very little evidence about the measurement and analytical viability of this approach exists.

The "slopes-as-outcomes" strategy described above is an attempt to move from an outcomes-based method of examining teacher effectiveness to one more in accord with naturally occurring instruction and its consequences. In what follows we describe various attempts to link analytical methods more directly to a model of classroom instruction.

A primary example of analyses driven by a model of instruction is provided in the classroom research by the economists Brown and Saks (1980, 1981, 1983). They started with a theoretical formulation wherein (a) teaching affects student learning; (b) teachers vary in their preferences for different student outcomes and thus distribute instructional resources among class members accordingly, and as a consequence, (c) the relationship between student attributes and student outcomes will vary according to teacher preferences. In their reanalyses of the BTES data, Brown and Saks (1983) found that teachers varied in their use of time as a resource and that the relationship of ability to performance varied systematically with time across classrooms. Their analytical machinery was sophisticated by the normal standards of teacher effectiveness research. Nonetheless, their findings clearly suggest the benefits of matching methodology to theoretical formulation and moving away from mean performance measures.

In certain respects, Brown and Saks's formulation and analyses represents the application of procedures from a purportedly mature branch of social and economic sciences to a field where both theory, and the measurement and analytical machinery to investigate it, are less well developed. At the developmental stages of a formulation, less-advanced measurement and analytical alternatives might be warranted. In teacher effectiveness research, analyses that directly decompose variation in student experiences and outcomes according to the organization of instruction can be particularly valuable.

By fortuitous coincidence, two recent classroom studies of beginning reading (Barr & Dreeben, 1983; Martin, Veldman, & Anderson, 1980) decomposed instruction and performance measures into variation among classrooms, among reading groups within classrooms, and among students within reading groups. Barr and Dreeben (1983) focused on content coverage as an instructional variable and found that its variation was mainly between reading groups and not between teachers. Not surprisingly, student performance on both content-referenced learning measures and standardized achievement tests also varied primarily between reading groups.

In the Texas First Grade Reading Group Study, the focus was on teaching behavior variables including teachers' selection of students to read measures (e.g., nonvolunteer selection, callouts), types of student responses to teacher questions (correct, incorrect, no response) and teacher feedback (praise, criticism, asking a new question). In their analyses, Martin et al. (1980) decomposed achievement variation into effects of teacher behaviors at three levels: students within reading groups, reading groups within classes, and classes. Very few behaviors were found to have significant relationships only at the class level; rather, most of the significant relationships were for students within reading groups, especially among the student response variables. There was also some indication of teachers changing their selection strategies across the reading groups within their class. Here again, conducting a multilevel analysis combined with theory-guided interpretations helped to clarify what appeared to be inconsistencies. An analysis of class means only (a "class-level" analysis) would have missed the effects of teachers' differential activities across reading groups and the differential impact of teacher behaviors on the members of specific reading groups.

The alternatives to concentrating on class mean gains certainly can complicate matters. The choice of appropriate indicators of performance and procedures for detecting variation in performance will require more thought about instruction and more sophistication in detecting its consequences. Moreover, the interpretations warranted by the results of more thorough, possibly multilevel analyses may appear to be less clear cut as the trade-offs of higher gains to some students for lower gains to others are likely to be more evident. Yet, once again, these conditional conclusions about the efficacy of specific teaching practices perhaps better reflect the reality of classroom choices and consequences. Such messages should not be ignored.

Distal Versus Proximal Measurement: A Conceptual Problem

It should be clear by this point that the major flaws with the standardized test scores used as measures of teacher effectiveness have little to do with the inherent psychometric properties of the test instruments. What the tests are expected to measure and how test data are used to reflect the consequences of teaching activities are more central issues in improving measurement in teacher effectiveness research. The fundamental problem with the typical way of measuring teacher effectiveness and its antecedents is that it is devoid of a clear conception of how teaching can directly influence test scores. Improvements in the conceptual foundation for teacher effectiveness research are possible through greater attention to what Doyle (1983) characterizes as "academic work and how that work is experienced by students in classrooms" (p. 159). According to Doyle, the core of the curriculum is a collection of *academic tasks* which "are defined by the answers students are required to produce and the routes that can be used to obtain these answers" (1983, p. 161). Actions by teachers that affect the accomplishment of academic work would seem to be the primary basis for judging effectiveness.

The tests used as outcomes in teacher effectiveness research should measure the quality of academic work in classrooms. If this is the case, then teachers can directly affect test performance through the following activities:

1. Selection and coverage of content;
2. Presentation of topics in a manner that enables students to understand academic tasks and that helps students develop cognitive structures for responding to related and future tasks;
3. Provision of a cognitive framework through which students can respond to tasks presented in specific formats and testing situations;
4. Establishment of a classroom atmosphere that motivates students to perform their best and promotes the necessary self-esteem in students to accomplish test tasks within the range of their cognitive knowledge and skills;

5. Adoption of sufficient variation in topic coverage and strategy to accommodate differences in styles and abilities regarding student learning.

These are the aspects of the teaching process that are proximal to student performance. Traditionally, the focus of teacher effectiveness research has been on general teaching behaviors, such as the frequency and types of questions and the amount of praise, that may be only distally connected with the core of academic work. As classroom research moves toward more proximal measurement of the aspects of the teaching process that can influence academic work, perhaps more defensible notions for the measurement of teacher effectiveness will follow.

Measurement of Classroom Processes

In the *First and Second Handbook of Research on Teaching*, Medley and Mitzel (1963), in "Measuring Classroom Behavior by Systematic Observation," and Rosenshine and Furst (1973), in "The Use of Direct Observation to Study Teaching," questioned the ways in which the reliability of classroom process measures, most notably teaching behavior, was estimated and interpreted. Medley and Mitzel pointed out that observer agreement is only one aspect of reliability, and that variations in behavior across situations and occasions may be far greater than disagreements among observers. Rosenshine and Furst (1973, p. 169) voiced concern about reliability cast as "representativeness": "whether a sample of observed classroom transactions is a trustworthy representative sample of total behavior. Decisions to make two, four, or more observations on each teacher in a study have little empirical basis."

These concerns point out the need to assess multiple sources of variation in measurements of classroom processes — observers, occasions, settings — to obtain generalizable samples of behavior. Generalizability theory (Cronbach, Gleser, Nanda, & Rajaratnam, 1972; Cronbach, Rajaratnam, & Gleser, 1963; see also Brennan, 1983; Shavelson & Webb, 1981) is a measurement theory designed to address these issues. Generalizability theory uses analysis of variance to partition sources of variation in behavioral measurements. The results of a generalizability study show the relative influence of (say) observers, occasions, and settings on a measure of teacher behavior, and can be used to determine the number of observations needed to attain maximum generalizability in prespecified varieties of teaching situations.

This section introduces generalizability theory by describing a study with multiple sources of variation in observations of teaching behavior. Following a sketch of generalizability theory, we present illustrative generalizability studies. Finally, some unresolved issues in the measurement of classroom processes are discussed. It should be noted that although the literature on classroom processes typically focuses on teacher behavior, this section also considers the behavior of students.

*Setting the Stage: A Study of Teacher
Behavior over Observers and Occasions
of Observation*

To show the advantage of generalizability (G) theory over most conventional approaches for determining reliability, this section describes a typical study of teacher behavior. Within the context of this study, conventional approaches for estimating reliability are described, followed by a discussion of how G theory might be applied. Finally, this section describes the issues that cannot be addressed by conventional approaches but can easily be addressed with generalizability theory.

Peterson, Marx, and Clark (1978) investigated the relationship of teacher planning to teacher behavior and student achievement. A major question in their study was whether teachers' behavior in the classroom corresponded to their planning decisions. To answer this question, Peterson et al. calculated correlations between teachers' scores on planning categories (e.g., the "cognitive" level at which teachers planned to deal with the subject matter) and their behavior in class (e.g., the actual "cognitive" level of the classroom discussions).

Prior to performing the analyses linking teacher planning and teacher behavior, it was necessary to ensure that ratings of teacher planning and behavior used in the analyses were reliable. To examine the reliability of the ratings, Peterson et al. (1978) collected information on teacher behavior on multiple occasions using multiple observers. Nine observers coded the videotapes of two teachers who were each taped on two days. In analysis-of-variance terminology, the design underlying these observations was "fully crossed": Both teachers were observed by all nine observers on both occasions. One of the teacher behavior variables examined by Peterson et al. was the frequency of lower-order discussion of subject matter. A hypothetical data matrix for this variable appears in Table 3.1. This hypothetical data matrix presents the frequency counts of three teachers by two observers on two occasions. For simplicity of exposition, two rather than nine observers are used. Furthermore, because observation studies typically focus on more than two teachers, three teachers are used in this hypothetical example. Each frequency is the number of lower-order interchanges between teacher and students during a 45-minute class period.

Conventional approaches for determining reliability would examine stability over time and consistency over observers separately. The most common method for determining the stability of teacher behavior over time is to observe teachers' behavior on two occasions and correlate the scores. For the hypothetical data in Table 3.1, the conventional approach would calculate correlations between the frequency counts at Occasion 1 and Occasion 2. Because there are two observers in

Table 3.1. Hypothetical Data on Three Teachers for Two Observers and Two Occasions[a]

	Occasion 1	Occasion 2
Teacher 1		
Observer 1	13	9
Observer 2	17	12
Teacher 2		
Observer 1	10	11
Observer 2	12	14
Teacher 3		
Observer 1	6	10
Observer 2	9	12

[a] Number of lower-order interchanges between teacher and students during a 45-minute class period.

Table 3.1, the correlations between occasions could be calculated for each observer separately or for the average of the two observers' frequency counts. For Observer 1, the stability coefficient across the two occasions is $-.43$. For Observer 2, the correlation is $-.14$. For the average of the two observers' frequency counts, the correlation between Occasions 1 and 2 is $-.20$.

A problem with many studies of the stability of teacher behavior over time is that, unlike the Peterson et al. (1978) study, the occasion of observation often cannot be separated from (is confounded with) other sources of variation, such as the characteristics of the students and subject matter taught. Shavelson and Dempsey-Atwood (1976), in their review of 11 studies that produced over 250 stability coefficients for 12 categories of teacher behavior, stressed that the confounding of occasion of observation with other sources of variation made the results of any one study equivocal. The students taught on different occasions were not always the same nor were they always drawn from the same population. Furthermore, the lessons taught on different occasions sometimes focused on the same general content area (although typically on different topics), but at other times differed in content area (e.g., mathematics on one occasion and social studies on another). When stability coefficients are low, it is impossible to determine without further study whether the instability is in teacher behavior per se, or due in part to differences in student populations, content over time, or both. Among the solutions to this problem are holding constant student population and content over occasions of observation, as Peterson et al. did, or systematically varying them, for example, by observing multiple content areas for each teacher on several occasions.

The most common method used to assess consistency over observers, often called interrater agreement or consistency, is percent agreement. Percent agreement indices include simple percent agreement, Scott's coefficient, Flanders' or Garrett's modifications of Scott's coefficient, and Cohen's kappa (see Frick & Semmel, 1978). These indices have been used to evaluate the interrater consistency of many teacher and student behavior variables at many grade levels (Anderson et al., 1979; Evertson et al., 1978a; Good, Cooper, & Blakey, 1980; Good & Grouws, 1977; Karweit & Slavin, 1981).

Observer reliability can be estimated by correlating scores across observers. In the hypothetical data set in Table 3.1, the correlations between observers' frequency counts could be calculated for each occasion separately or for the average of each observer's frequency counts over occasions. The correlations between observers' frequency counts on each occasion are .97 and .87; the correlation between observers' average counts over both occasions is .98.

While observer agreement contributes to reliability of observational measures, observer agreement coefficients are *not* reliability coefficients. Agreement coefficients focus on consistency of *observers'* behavior, rather than on the consistency of *teachers'* behavior. Yet, many studies have mistakenly referred to observer agreement as reliability. Reliability concerns the accuracy of measurement (Cronbach et al., 1972) and the extent to which differences between the objects of the measurement can be dependably discriminated by the observational measure (Frick & Semmel, 1978). While high reliability necessitates high

observed agreement, high observer agreement is not sufficient for high reliability. Medley and Mitzel (1963; see also McGaw, Wardrop, & Bunda, 1972) pointed out several situations in which observer agreement is high but reliability may be low. First, if individual differences in behavior of teachers or students are small, estimates of reliability will be low regardless of the degree of interrater agreement. Second, estimates of reliability will be low when behavior is unstable from one occasion to another, even if observers agree highly on each occasion (as in the data in Table 3.1).

Another method often used to assess the stability of teacher behavior over time and the consistency over observers is the intraclass correlation, which can be applied when there are more than two observers or more than two occasions (for formulas, see Allen & Yen, 1979; Guildford & Fruchter, 1978; Lord, 1980). Under some conditions (when the variances of scores of teachers are the same for each occasion), the intraclass correlation is equivalent to the average of the correlations between pairs of observers. To calculate the estimated reliability for observers in the Peterson et al. (1978) study using this approach, one would perform a two-way analysis of variance (ANOVA) with teachers crossed with observers. The two-way ANOVA could be performed separately for each occasion or for the average over occasions. The intraclass correlation calculated from the two-way ANOVA of teachers crossed with observers would indicate the average correlation among the observers' frequency counts.

In the hypothetical data set in Table 3.1, the intraclass correlation for observers is .96 using the data for Occasion 1, is .86 using the data for Occasion 2, and is .95 for the average over the two occasions. Similarly, the intraclass correlation for occasions is $-.22$ for Observer 1, is $-.08$ for Observer 2, and is $-.14$ for the average over the two observers. The intraclass correlation coefficient has been used in many studies, for example, to assess the reliability of measures of student engaged time, variation in teachers' task assignments, grouping arrangements, group activities, interactions between adults and children, and the physical environment of the classroom (Evertson, Emmer, & Clements, 1980; Evertson & Hickman, 1981; Marliave, Fisher, & Dishaw, 1978; Stallings, 1976; Stallings & Kaskowitz, 1974).

Generalizability theory enables the researcher to estimate influences of multiple sources of variation in observations simultaneously, rather than consecutively, as is necessary with conventional approaches. The basis of a generalizability (G) study is an analysis of variance incorporating as "factors" the multiple sources of variation in scores. In the Peterson et al. (1978) study, the ANOVA would have three factors; teachers, observers, and occasions. In their fully crossed design, there are seven sources of variation: (a) teachers, (b) observers, (c) occasions, (d) the interaction between teachers and observers, (e) the interaction between teachers and occasions, (f) the interaction between observers and occasions, and (g) a residual source of variation which includes the three-way interaction among teachers, observers, and occasions, and unsystematic error. It is useful to describe these seven sources of variation as three main effects and four interaction effects.

The three main effects concern variation across teachers, variation across observers, and variation across occasions. The variation for teachers shows individual differences among teachers in their behavior. In the hypothetical data set in Table 3.1, the teacher effect refers to the differences among Teachers 1, 2, and 3 in their use of lower-order discussion. When one averages over observations and occasions, Teacher 1 uses the most lower-order discussion (mean = 12.75), Teacher 2 exhibits an intermediate level (mean = 11.75), and Teacher 3 uses the least (mean = 9.25). The variation across observers shows whether observers are using the same criterion when counting teacher behavior (i.e., whether some observers "see" more behavior than others). When the scores in Table 3.1 are averaged over teachers and occasions, the mean for Observer 1 is 9.83 and the mean for Observer 2 is 12.67. These means indicate that Observer 2 tends to see more lower-order discussion than Observer 1, even though both observed the same teachers at the same time.

The third main effect, variation over occasions, shows whether teacher behavior, averaged over teachers and observers, changes from one occasion to the next. The means for Occasion 1 and 2 are 11.17 and 11.33, respectively, showing that, on the average, the frequency of lower-order discussion is similar at Occasions 1 and 2.

The interaction effects can also be interpreted using the hypothetical data in Table 3.1. The interaction between teachers and occasions shows whether teachers are rank-ordered differently across occasions in their use of lower-order discussion.[3] Averaging over observers, teachers are rank-ordered differently from one occasion to the next. On Occasion 1, Teacher 1 shows the most lower-order discussion, whereas on Occasion 2, Teacher 2 shows the most lower-order discussion.

The interaction between teachers and observers indicates whether observers rank-order teachers differently in their use of lower-order discussion. Averaging over occasions, in Table 3.1, both observers rank-order Teacher 1 the highest and Teacher 3 the lowest in lower-order discussion.

The interaction between observers and occasions shows whether observers are consistent across occasions. Averaging over teachers in Table 3.1, each observer shows nearly identical counts on Occasions 1 and 2, indicating that observers are very consistent across occasions.

Finally, the residual source of variation reflects both the three-way interaction and other sources of variation in teacher behavior counts (for example, grouping arrangement and subject matter), that were not in the design. Unfortunately, the three-way interaction is confounded with these other sources of variation and cannot be interpreted separately.

The magnitudes of the sources of variation can also be used to determine the number of occasions and observers that are needed to obtain reliable measures of teacher behavior, and to help guide decisions about how data on teacher behavior should be collected. The effects involving observers can be used to determine whether several observers are needed and whether different observers can be used to rate different teachers or whether the same observers must rate all teachers. For the data

in Table 3.1, since both observers rank-ordered teachers in the same way (a small interaction between teachers and observers), it would not be necessary to have more than one observer rate each teacher. But, since some observers produced higher scores than others for the same teachers, it would be important that all teachers be observed by the same observer.

Similarly, the effects involving occasions would indicate whether teachers need to be observed on multiple occasions and whether the occasions should be the same for all teachers. In Table 3.1, the fact that teachers were rank-ordered differently across occasions (a large interaction between teachers and occasions) indicates that a teacher's average rating across several occasions will be more reliable than the rating on one occasion. The similar mean level of lower-order discussion on Occasions 1 and 2 (a small main effect for occasions) suggests that, although teachers must each be observed on several occasions, they need not be observed on the same occasions.

As will be discussed in the next section, the magnitudes of these sources of variation can be used to estimate the exact number of observers and occasions needed for reliable measurement of teacher behavior. In their generalizability study of the frequency of lower-order discussion, Peterson et al. (1978) found that two occasions and nine observers yielded an estimated generalizability coefficient of .86. In their analyses linking teacher planning and teacher behavior, then, each teacher's score was the average rating over two occasions and nine observers.

Sketch of Generalizability Theory

Generalizability (G) theory (Cronbach, Gleser, Nanda, & Rajaratnam, 1972) evolved out of the recognition that the concept of undifferentiated error in classical test theory provided too gross a characterization of the multiple sources of variation in a measurement. The multidimensional nature of measurement error can be seen in how a measurement of teacher behavior is obtained. For example, a teacher might be observed by one of many observers, on one of many possible occasions, and in one of several subject matters. Each of these choices — observer, occasion, and subject matter — is a potential source of error in the ratings of teacher behavior. G theory assesses each source error in order to characterize the measurement and improve its design.

A particular behavioral measurement is a sample from a universe of admissible observations. This universe is characterized by one or more sources of error variation or *facets* (e.g., observers, occasions, subject matters). This universe is typically defined as all combinations of the levels (called *conditions* in G theory) of the facets. In the Peterson et al. (1978) generalizability study described in the previous section, the universe was characterized by two facets, namely, observers and occasions. The admissible universe of observations consisted of ratings of teachers by all combinations of observers and occasions. The ratings by the nine observers on two occasions in the G study

---

[3] Technically, an interaction could also occur when teachers have identical rank orders across occasions *and* the distances between teachers' scores are different on each occasion (an ordinal interaction). An interaction with reversals in rank order (a disordinal interaction) is more common and, for simplicity, will be used to describe interactions throughout this section.

Table 3.2. Equations for Scores and Coefficients in Generalizability Theory

Equation

1   Decomposition of Observed Score

$$X_{tro} = \mu \text{ (grand mean)}$$
$$+ \; \mu_t - \mu \text{ (teacher effect)}$$
$$+ \; \mu_r - \mu \text{ (rater effect)}$$
$$+ \; \mu_o - \mu \text{ (occasion effect)}$$
$$+ \; \mu_{tr} - \mu_t - \mu_r + \mu \text{ (teacher} \times \text{rater effect)}$$
$$+ \; \mu_{to} - \mu_t - \mu_o + \mu \text{ (teacher} \times \text{occasion effect)}$$
$$+ \; \mu_{ro} - \mu_r - \mu_o + \mu \text{ (rater} \times \text{occasion effect)}$$
$$+ \; X_{tro} + \mu_t + \mu_r + \mu_o - \mu_{tr} - \mu_{to} - \mu_{ro} - \mu \text{ (residual)}$$

2   Variance of Observed Score

$$\sigma^2_{X_{tro}} = \sigma^2_t + \sigma^2_r + \sigma^2_o + \sigma^2_{tr} + \sigma^2_{to} + \sigma^2_{ro} + \sigma^2_{tro,e}$$

3   Error Variance for Relative Decisions

$$\sigma^2_{\text{Rel}} = \frac{\sigma^2_{tr}}{n'_r} + \frac{\sigma^2_{to}}{n'_o} + \frac{\sigma^2_{tro,e}}{n'_r n'_o}$$

4   Error Variance for Absolute Decisions

$$\sigma^2_{\text{Abs}} = \frac{\sigma^2_r}{n'_r} + \frac{\sigma^2_o}{n'_o} + \frac{\sigma^2_{tr}}{n'_r} + \frac{\sigma^2_{to}}{n'_o} + \frac{\sigma^2_{ro}}{n'_r n'_o} + \frac{\sigma^2_{tro}}{n'_r n'_o}$$

5   Generalizability Coefficient for Relative Decisions

$$E\rho^2_{\text{Rel}} = \frac{\sigma^2_t}{\sigma^2_t + \sigma^2_{\text{Rel}}}$$

6   Generalizability Coefficient for Absolute Decisions

$$E\rho^2_{\text{Abs}} = \frac{\sigma^2_t}{\sigma^2_t + \sigma^2_{\text{Abs}}}$$

---

represented a sample from the universe of admissible observations. The results of this study were intended to generalize to the entire universe of admissible observations. Since different measurements may represent different universes, G theory speaks of universe scores rather than true scores, acknowledging that there are different universes to which decision makers may generalize. Likewise, the theory speaks of generalizability coefficients rather than of the reliability coefficient, realizing that the computed value of the coefficient may change as the definition of the universe changes.

In G theory, a measurement is decomposed into a component for the universe score (corresponding to the true score in classical test theory) and one or more error components. To illustrate this decomposition, we consider a two-facet, $t \times r \times o$ (teacher by rater by occasion) crossed design such as the Peterson et al. (1978) study described earlier. (Throughout this section we are using the terms observers, raters, and coders interchangeably.) The object of measurement, here teachers, is not a source of error and, therefore, is not a facet. The rating of, say, the teacher's use of lower-order discussion (X_{tro}) for a particular teacher (t) for a particular rater (r) on a particular occasion (o) can be decomposed into eight components as shown in Equation 1 in Table 3.2.

The single observed rating X_{tro} and each component other than μ in Equation 1 has a distribution. For all teachers in the universe of raters and occasions defined by the investigator, the distribution of $\mu_t - \mu$ has a mean of zero and a variance denoted by σ^2_t. This variance is called the universe score variance. Similarly, there are variances associated with each of the other

components; they are called variance components. For example, the variance of $\mu_r - \mu$ is denoted by σ^2_r. The variance of the collection of X_{tro} for all teachers, raters, and occasions included in the universe, then, is the sum of all of the variance components in Equation 2 (see Table 3.2). In other words, the variance of the ratings can be partitioned into independent sources of variation due to differences between teachers, raters, occasions, and their interactions.

Numerical estimates of the variance components can be obtained from the analysis of variance by setting the expected mean squares for each component equal to the observed mean squares and solving the set of simultaneous equations as shown in Table 3.3. In this example, the variance component for teachers (σ^2_t) represents universe score variance and the remaining components represent error variance. Generalizability theory focuses on the variance components. The relative magnitudes of the components provide information about particular sources of error in scores assigned to a teacher's behavior.

Generalizability theory recognizes that certain studies (generalizability studies) are associated with the development of a measurement procedure, for example, to determine how many observers and occasions are needed to obtain reliable ratings of teacher behavior, while others—decision (D) studies—then apply the procedure, for example, to investigate the link between teacher behavior and student achievement. The universe of observations in the G study is defined as broadly as possible within practical and theoretical constraints. In most cases, Cronbach et al. (1972) recommended using a crossed G study design so that all of the variance components can be estimated.

Table 3.3. Estimates of Variance Components for a Two-Facet, Crossed Design

Source of Variation	Mean Square	Expected Mean Square	Estimated Variance Component
Teacher (t)	MS_t	$\sigma_{tro,e}^2 + n_r\sigma_{to}^2 + n_o\sigma_{tr}^2 + n_r n_o\sigma_t^2$	$\hat{\sigma}_t^2 = (MS_t - MS_{to} - MS_{tr} + MS_{res})/n_r n_o$
Rater (r)	MS_r	$\sigma_{tro,e}^2 + n_t\sigma_{ro}^2 + n_o\sigma_{tr}^2 + n_t n_o\sigma_r^2$	$\hat{\sigma}_r^2 = (MS_r - MS_{ro} - MS_{tr} + MS_{res})/n_t n_o$
Occasion (o)	MS_o	$\sigma_{tro,e}^2 + n_t\sigma_{ro}^2 + n_r\sigma_{to}^2 + n_t n_r\sigma_o^2$	$\hat{\sigma}_o^2 = (MS_o - MS_{ro} - MS_{to} + MS_{res})/n_t n_r$
tr	MS_{tr}	$\sigma_{tro,e}^2 + n_o\sigma_{tr}^2$	$\hat{\sigma}_{tr}^2 = (MS_{tr} - MS_{res})/n_o$
to	MS_{to}	$\sigma_{tro,e}^2 + n_r\sigma_{to}^2$	$\hat{\sigma}_{to}^2 = (MS_{to} - MS_{res})/n_r$
ro	MS_{ro}	$\sigma_{tro,e}^2 + n_t\sigma_{ro}^2$	$\hat{\sigma}_{ro}^2 = (MS_{ro} - MS_{res})/n_t$
tro, e	MS_{res}	$\sigma_{tro,e}^2$	$\hat{\sigma}_{tro,e}^2 = MS_{res}$

Note: n_t = number of teachers; n_r = number of raters; n_o = number of occasions.

The results of the generalizability study provide information for optimizing the design of the decision study. If the results of the G study show that some sources of variation are very small, then the decision maker may reduce the number of levels of a facet, may select and thereby control one level of a facet, or may ignore a facet. For example, if a G study with teachers, raters, and occasions showed that raters were consistent in their ratings of teacher behavior, the decision maker might use only one rater in the D study. This permits a smaller—and presumably less costly—design for the decision study than that used in the G study. If, however, raters disagreed in their rankings of teachers (an outcome signified by a relatively large variance component for the interaction between teachers and raters, σ_{tr}^2) the decision maker could choose to have several raters observe each teacher and use the average of their ratings in further analyses (for example, in process-product studies).

The variance associated with the *average* of the raters' scores is the variance associated with the raters divided by the number of raters. Hence, the variance component for the interaction of teachers and raters, averaging over raters, is denoted as σ_{tr}^2/n_r', where n_r' is the number of raters to be sampled in the D study. Similarly, multiple occasions could be sampled and the ratings averaged over occasions. The variances of the components concerning occasions would correspondingly be divided by n_o', the number of occasions to be sampled in the D study.

G theory recognizes that decision makers may use the same rating in different ways. Some interpretations may focus on individual differences between teachers (relative decisions). For example, the decision maker may be concerned mainly with the generalizability of the rank ordering of teachers over raters and occasions (as would be the case in process-product correlational studies). Other interpretations may focus on the level of a teacher's behavior itself, without references to other teachers' performances (absolute decisions). The written examination for a driver's license is an analogy: Your score is interpreted by its level, not by how you do relative to others taking the exam. A decision maker, then, may be concerned with the absolute level of a teacher's score on some behavior over raters and occasions, perhaps by itself or in addition to the generalizability of individual differences between teachers.

Measurement error is defined differently for each of these proposed interpretations. For *relative decisions*, the error variance consists of all variance components representing interactions with the object of measurement, here teachers. The error variance for relative decisions is shown in Equation 3 (Table 3.2).

The error variance for relative decisions reflects disagreements among raters and occasions about the ordering of teachers on some behavior variable such as "use of feedback with elaboration." These disagreements are error in this case because they do not reflect true differences in teacher behavior, but reflect differences in raters' perceptions of the same behavior.

For *absolute decisions*, the error variance consists of all variance components except that for universe scores (see Equation 4, Table 3.2). The error variance for absolute decisions reflects differences in mean ratings of teachers across raters and occasions as well as disagreements about the ranking of teachers on their use of feedback with elaboration. When the decision maker is concerned with the absolute level of teaching behavior, the variance components associated with effects of raters and occasions (σ_r^2, σ_o^2, and σ_{ro}^2) are included in error variance. The lenience of one rater as compared with another will influence a person's score, as might the date on any particular occasion (e.g., near a holiday). That is, perceptions of the particular raters that observe a teacher and the events occurring during the particular occasions will influence the observed score and, hence, the decision maker's estimate of the teacher's universe score. Thus, it is important to obtain ratings of teacher behavior on several occasions and to use several observers so that these influences will average out. For relative decisions in a crossed design, however, the effect of rater and occasion are constant for all teachers and so do not influence the rank-ordering of them. Consequently, the three components associated with only rater and occasion are not included in error variance for relative decisions. Since the decision maker determines the types of decision to be made in any specific application, he or she defines which sources of variation constitute error variation and which do not.

While stressing the importance of variance components and error variances, G theory also provides a coefficient analogous to the reliability coefficient in classical theory. The generalizability coefficient for relative decisions is given in Equation 5 (Table 3.2). In Equation 5, the symbol for the generalizability coefficient, $E\rho^2$, indicates the expected value of the squared correlation between observed scores and universe scores. An analogous coefficient can be defined for absolute decisions as in Equation 6 (Table 3.2).

The generalizability coefficient, $E\rho^2$, indicates the proportion of observed score variance ($\sigma_t^2 + \sigma_{Rel}^2$) or ($\sigma_t^2 + \sigma_{Abs}^2$) that is due to universe score variance (σ_t^2). It ranges from 0 to 1.00 and, like the reliability coefficient in classical test theory, its magnitude is

Table 3.4. Facets Investigated in Observational Studies of Classroom Processes

Study	Classroom (CL) or Teacher (TE)	Student (ST)	School (SC)	Observer (OB)	Occasion (OC)	Time (TI)	Section or Class (CL)	Grouping or Context (CO)	Subject Matter (SM)	Population Characteristic	Approximate Design[a]
Anderson (1981)		✓			✓					Sex Achievement level (ACH)	$OC(ST(Sex \times ACH))$
Anderson, Evertson, & Brophy (1979)	✓			✓	✓					Experimental vs. Control (Group)	$OC(OB(TE(Group)))$
Anderson, Morgan, Evertson, & Brophy (1978)	✓							✓		Experimental vs. Control (Group)	$TE(Group(CO))$
Brophy & Evertson (1977)	✓		✓		✓	Year				SES	$OC(TE(School(SES \times Year))$
Colbert (1979)	✓					Day of week		✓	✓		$Day \times TE \times SM \times CO$
Cooley & Leinhardt (1980)	✓								✓	Grade level	$CL(Grade) \times SM$
Cornbleth & Korth (1979)		✓			✓	Day of week			✓		$OC(ST(CL \times SM \times Day))$
Crawford, Brophy, Evertson, & Coulter (1977)	✓			✓	✓			✓			$TE \times CO \times OC(OB)$
Crawford & Stallings (1978)	✓				✓						$OC(TE)$
Eggert (1978)	✓				✓				✓	Grade level	$OC(CL(Grade) \times SM)$
Evertson, Anderson, Anderson & Brophy (1980)	✓			✓	✓		✓		✓		$OC(OB(CL(TE(SM))))$
Fiedler (1975)	✓				✓						$OC(TE)$
Fitzgerald, Wright, Eason, & Shapson (1978)	✓				✓	Time of day Month of year			✓		$OC(TE \times Time) \times SM$
Good & Beckerman (1978)		✓	✓				✓	✓	✓	Achievement level (ACH) Sex	$ST(ACH \times Sex \times CL(SC)) \times CO \times SM$

Study					Month / Semester		Facet	Design
Good, Cooper & Blake (1980)	✓		✓			✓		$CL \times OC(Time) \times CO$
Good & Grouws (1977)	✓		✓			✓	Effectiveness (EFF)	$OC(TE(EFF))$
Good & Grouws (1979)	✓		✓			✓	Experimental vs. Control (Group)	$OC(TE(Group))$
Karweit & Slevin (1981)		✓	✓		✓	✓		$(ST \times OC) : CL$
Leinhardt (1978)	✓	✓	✓			✓		$SC(TE) \times OB$
Luce & Hoge (1978)	✓		✓		✓	✓		$OC(CL \times SM \times CO)$
Marliave, Fisher & Dishaw (1978)	✓	✓	✓		✓	✓	Grade level	$(ST(CL \times OB) : Grade \times SM$
McConnell & Bowers (1979)	✓					✓	Semester	$OC(TE \times Semester)$
Stallings (1976)	✓					✓	Grade level / City	$OC(TE(Grade \times City))$
Wright & Nuttall (1970)	✓					✓		$OC(TE)$
Generalizability Studies								
Borich, Malitz & Kugle (1978)	✓		✓			✓		$OC(TE) \times OB$
Calkins, Borich, Pascone & Kugle (1977)	✓		✓			✓		$OC(TE) \times OB$
Erlich & Borich (1979)	✓					✓		$OC(TE)$
Erlich & Shavelson (1978)	✓		✓			✓		$OC(TE) \times OB$
Peterson, Marx and Clark (1978)	✓		✓			✓		$TE \times OB \times OC$
Peterson & Janicki (1979)		✓	✓			✓		$ST \times OB \times OC$
Webb (1982)		✓	✓			✓		$ST \times OB \times OC$

[a] Approximate design based on description of data collection in method section.

influenced by variation among teachers' scores and the number of observations made. The number of observations is taken into account in much the same way as in the Spearman-Brown prophecy formula in classical theory. Using the Spearman-Brown formula, one can estimate the reliability of a test of any length from the reliability of the original test. In Equations 3 and 4, the denominator indicates the number of observations (number of raters and the number of occasions). As the number of observations increases, the error variance (σ^2_{Rel} or σ^2_{Abs}) decreases and the generalizability coefficient (Ep^2) increases.

A major contribution of generalizability theory is that it allows the researcher to pinpoint the sources of measurement error (e.g., rater, occasion, or both) and increase the appropriate number of observations accordingly so that error "averages out." The researcher can estimate how many conditions of each facet are needed to obtain a certain level of generalizability. If, for example, variation due to occasions is large relative to variation due to teachers, and variation due to raters is small, then increasing the number of occasions would produce a lower estimate of error variation and consequently a higher generalizability coefficient (see Equation 4), whereas increasing the number of raters would have little effect on the estimates of error variation and generalizability.

Illustrative Generalizability Studies

The results of a generalizability study enable the researcher to answer the following kinds of questions. First, which facets and how many levels of each need to be sampled to obtain reliable estimates of teacher behavior? Second, can different raters be used to observe different teachers or must the same raters observe all teachers? This question concerns the use of a nested versus a crossed design. Third, can the decision maker generalize over all possible subject matters or must generalization be restricted to teacher behavior in mathematics? This question concerns whether facets should be treated as random or fixed. Finally, is it reasonable to generalize over different subgroups in the population (e.g., experienced vs. inexperienced teachers) or must conclusions be drawn separately for each subgroup? This question concerns the study of multifaceted populations.

This section presents generalizability studies to illustrate each of these issues. Designs with one facet are described first, followed by designs with two facets. For both one-facet and two-facet designs, nested and crossed designs are considered.

Designs with a fixed facet are discussed next. Finally, the issue of multifaceted populations is addressed. Although the designs described in this section are fairly simple, the discussion readily extends to more complicated designs.

To further illustrate generalizability theory, we also describe designs that have been used in observational studies of teaching but did not examine their measurements with G theory. This enables us to show the variety of facets that might be investigated. The studies listed in Table 3.4, then, were selected to represent a variety of designs. A checkmark appears where multiple conditions of a facet (for example, occasions) have been sampled.

TEACHERS OBSERVED BY MULTIPLE
OBSERVERS OR OBSERVED ON MULTIPLE
OCCASIONS: ONE-FACET DESIGNS

A one-facet design includes teachers and one source of error variation—e.g., observers or occasions. It may be crossed, as when each teacher is observed under every condition of the facet (e.g., occasions or observers). In a nested design, the teachers are not observed on the same occasions; e.g., some were observed during third period on Tuesday and some were observed during first period on Friday. Nor are they observed by the same observers; for example, Mr. Jones was observed by Tom and Sally, while Ms. Smith was observed by Mary and Dave.

Teachers Observed on Different Occasions or by Different Sets of Observers: Nested Designs. The one-facet nested study is presented first to describe the procedures for analyzing a simple design, and to show the equivalence of this design to the ANOVA approach to reliability in classical test theory. The Erlich and Borich (1979) study of classroom interaction provides a concrete illustration of this design. They observed 17 second- and third-grade classrooms each on five occasions. Because "teachers were observed at different times of day, on different days and teaching what may be considered different lessons," Erlich and Borich (1979, p. 12) treated Occasions as Nested Within Teachers (we write $O:T$).

The results of the generalizability analysis for the behavior "teacher asks a new question following a correct response to the teacher's previous question," appear in Table 3.5, including the estimated variance components and generalizability coefficients for decision studies with different numbers of occasions.

Table 3.5. Results of One-Facet Nested Generalizability Study for Different Numbers of Occasions (n_o) ($O:T$ Design)

Source of Variation	$\hat{\sigma}^2$	n'_o					
		1	2	3	4	5	6
Teachers (t)	$\hat{\sigma}^2_t$	11.70	11.70	11.70	11.70	11.70	11.70
Occasions: Teachers ($o:t$)	$\hat{\sigma}^2_{o,to,e}$	22.73	11.36	7.58	5.68	4.55	3.79
$\hat{\sigma}^2_{Rel}$		22.73	11.36	7.58	5.68	4.55	3.79
$\hat{\sigma}^2_{Abs}$		22.73	11.36	7.58	5.68	4.55	3.79
$\hat{\rho}^2_{Rel}$ [a]		.34	.49	.61	.67	.72	.76

Note: The data are from Erlich & Borich (1979).
[a] In this design, $\hat{\rho}^2_{Rel} = \hat{\rho}^2_{Abs}$.

Because occasions are nested within teachers, the analysis can isolate only two sources of variation. One is teachers. The other source of variation, occasions, is confounded with the interaction between teachers and occasions and unsystematic variation. Since the teacher is the object of measurement in this study, the variance component for teachers represents universe score variation ($\hat{\sigma}_t^2$). The remaining component is error variation ($\hat{\sigma}_{o,to,e}^2$). In this design there is only one error term. Because ($\hat{\sigma}_o^2$) is confounded with ($\hat{\sigma}_{to,e}^2$), the error variance for relative decisions ($\hat{\sigma}_{\text{Rel}}^2$) is the same as the error variance for absolute decisions ($\hat{\sigma}_{\text{Abs}}^2$).

As can be seen in Table 3.5, error variance decreases as the number of occasions increases (see Equations 3 and 4 in Table 3.2). The decrease in error variance is great from one to two occasions (a reduction of 50%) but starts to level off with a large number of occasions (increasing the number of occasions from five to six results in only a 17% reduction in error variance). Similarly, the increase in estimated generalizability (see Equations 5 and 6) is greatest from one to two occasions. Table 3.5 can be used to identify the number of occasions needed for a desired level of generalizability. Teachers need to be observed on five occasions to produce a level of generalizability that exceeds .70.

As a consequence of the confounding of the variation for occasions with the interaction between teachers and occasions, the one-facet nested generalizability study is equivalent to the analysis-of-variance approach to reliability in classical test theory. The classical approach considers only between-teacher and within-teacher variation. Between-teacher variation is considered true score variation and within-teacher variation is considered error variation. In a one-facet *crossed* design (teachers × occasions, say), the within-person component is the interaction between teachers and occasions. Classical theory ignores the main effect of occasions because the assumption of parallel measures implies that the means of measures on different occasions are equal and so the variance component will be zero. Only in a one-facet *nested* design is the main effect for occasions included as within-person variation. As a consequence of the equivalence of generalizability theory and classical test theory for a one-facet nested design, the estimated generalizability coefficients presented in Table 3.5 are identical to intraclass correlation coefficients in classical theory (see Allen & Yen, 1979; Guildford & Fruchter, 1978; Magnusson, 1966.)

Teachers Observed on the Same Occasions or by the Same Observers: Crossed Designs. If, in the Erlich and Borich (1979) study, teachers were observed by the same set of observers, the design would have teachers crossed with observers. Similarly, if teachers were observed on the same days teaching the same (or similar) lessons, one could argue that teachers were crossed with occasions.

The decision about whether to treat occasions as crossed with teachers or nested within teachers is not always straightforward. In many situations, it is impossible to observe teachers on exactly the same occasions. For example, when one observer is performing all of the observations, it is physically impossible for the observer to be in multiple classrooms at the same time. Even if the observer were to switch classrooms every 5 minutes, teachers would not be observed at the same time.

Some investigators have treated occasions as crossed with teachers when the time interval between observations of teachers on one occasion is much smaller than the time interval between occasions. For example, if all teachers are observed on the morning of October 1 and then are observed again on the morning of December 1, it may be reasonable to consider teachers as having been observed on the same occasions. In general, it is reasonable to treat occasions as crossed with teachers when features of the occasion are similar for all teachers (for example, when it is assumed that teacher behavior at 9:00 on Monday is the same as that at 11:00 on Monday). However, even this decision may depend on the behavior variables being examined. For example, if teachers teach reading at 9:00 and social studies at 11:00, then for the behavior variable "use of small groups," it would be unreasonable to assume that 9:00 for one teacher and 11:00 for another teacher are the same occasion. For the behavior variable, responding to incorrect answers with an elaborated response, on the other hand, it may be more reasonable to treat 9:00 and 11:00 on the same day as the "same" occasion.

The choice of a nested versus a crossed design has implications for the estimation of measurement error and reliability. The crossed design has three separate sources of variation: teachers, occasions, and the interaction between teachers and occasions. The nested design, as seen above, has only two sources of variation: teachers and occasions confounded with the interaction between teachers and occasions. Because the usual notion of reliability concerns the stability of the ordering of teachers' scores over occasions, measurement error would consist of the interaction between teachers and occasions. Because the nested design confounds occasion variation with the interaction between teachers and occasions, error variation in a nested design will be larger than that in a crossed design whenever occasion variation is nonzero. As a result, a lower estimated generalizability coefficient is obtained from a nested design than from an equivalent crossed design.

TEACHERS OBSERVED BY MULTIPLE OBSERVERS ON MULTIPLE OCCASIONS: TWO-FACET DESIGNS

Teachers Evaluated by the Same Raters on the Same Occasions. Crossed Designs. The generalizability study by Marzano (1973; described by Shavelson and Dempsey-Atwood, 1976) illustrates a two-facet crossed design. As described by Shavelson and Dempsey-Atwood (1976):

Each teacher was audiotaped while teaching one lesson during each of five 1-week segments. The five taping segments were equally spaced throughout a 6-month period (October to March) so that lessons taught from Books A, B, and C of the *Distar Language 1* program were observed. The dependent variable was the degree to which the teacher followed the Distar format in group activities and individual activities. (p. 556)

The design of Marzano's study, then, was fully crossed: Teachers were crossed with occasions and books. Because the time interval between audiotaping of teachers on any one occasion was much smaller than the time interval between

Table 3.6. Results of Two-Facet Crossed Generalizability Study for Different Numbers of Occasions and Books ($T \times O \times B$ Design)

Source of Variation	$\hat{\sigma}^2$	$n'_o =$ 1 $n'_b =$ 1	2 1	5 1	2 2
Teachers (t)	$\hat{\sigma}^2_t$	.450	.450	.450	.450
Occasions (o)	$\hat{\sigma}^2_o$	—[a]	—	—	—
Books (b)	$\hat{\sigma}^2_b$	—[a]	—	—	—
to	$\hat{\sigma}^2_{to}$	.030	.015	.006	.015
tb	$\hat{\sigma}^2_{tb}$	.030	.030	.030	.015
ob	$\hat{\sigma}^2_{ob}$	—[a]	—	—	—
tbo, e	$\hat{\sigma}^2_{tbo,e}$	.350	.175	.070	.088
	$\hat{\sigma}^2_{Rel}$	.410	.220	.106	.118
	$\hat{\rho}^2_{Rel}$	.52	.67	.81	.79

Note: The data are from Marzano (1973; see Shavelson & Dempsey-Atwood, 1976). n'_o = number of occasions. n'_b = number of books.
[a] Data not available.

occasions, and topics were the same over teachers at any occasion, it is reasonable to analyze the data as though teachers were each taped on the same occasion. That is, it is reasonable to treat occasions as crossed with teachers.

The results of the two-facet crossed design for individual activities are presented in Table 3.6, including estimated variance components, estimates of error variance, and generalizability coefficients for decision studies with different numbers of occasions and books. In this study, teachers are the object of measurement and $\hat{\sigma}^2_t$ represents universe score variation. The other variance components in Table 3.6 represent error variation. In Table 3.6, the relatively small variance components for the interaction between teachers and occasions ($\hat{\sigma}^2_{to} = .03$) and the interaction between teachers and books ($\hat{\sigma}^2_{to} = .03$) indicate that the rank orders of teachers in their tendency to follow the Distar format in individual activities were very similar across occasions and across books. The relatively large residual variance component ($\hat{\sigma}^2_{tro,e} = .35$ vs. $\hat{\sigma}^2_t$, $\hat{\sigma}^2_{to}$, and $\hat{\sigma}^2_{tb}$) indicates either a large three-way interaction among teachers, occasions, and books or a large variation due to sources of variation that are unidentified in the design, or both.

The results presented in Table 3.6 show that the optimal design for a D study has equal numbers of occasions and books, in terms of total number of observations per teacher, other factors—such as cost—being equal. A level of generalizability of .79 can be obtained with two occasions and two books necessitating a total of four observations per teacher. If only one book were to be used, it would take five observation occasions for each teacher to reach a similar level of generalizability.

Very few observational studies have used a fully crossed design. The only fully crossed design in Table 3.4 is Colbert's study of instructional organizational patterns. Colbert observed the behavior of four elementary school teachers in five subject matters (reading, language, mathematics, science, and social studies) on 2 days of the week (Monday, Friday) for four sizes of instructional group (whole-class, central group, small group, individual). In Colbert's design, then, teachers were crossed with subject matter, days of the week, and size of the instructional group.

Teachers Evaluated on Different Occasions by the Same Raters: Nested Designs. Erlich and Shavelson (1976) used a two-facet partially nested design to examine the generalizability of measures of teacher behavior in the Beginning Teacher Evaluation Study (BTES). Five fifth-grade teachers had been videotaped on three occasions; the occasions were different for each teacher. Three trained raters coded each of the 15 videotapes. The design, therefore, had occasions nested within teachers, and raters crossed with occasions and teachers. Erlich and Shavelson conducted generalizability analyses for 76 teacher behavior variables; the results for the teacher variable, "direction to try again," are presented in Table 3.7.

There are only five variance components in this nested design, in contrast to the seven components in Marzano's (1973) fully crossed two-facet design. This occurs because the nested design confounds the variation attributed to occasions with the interaction between teachers and occasions, and the rater–occasion interaction with the three-way interaction among raters, occasions, and teachers. As can be seen in Table 3.7, the effect of raters ($\hat{\sigma}^2_r$, $\hat{\sigma}^2_{tr}$) is less than that of occasions ($\hat{\sigma}^2_{o,to}$). The optimal decision study, therefore, will have fewer raters and more occasions. A level of generalizability of at least .70 can be obtained with one rater and seven occasions (a total of 7 observations per teacher), two raters and four occasions (8 observations), or three raters and three occasions (9 observations). To obtain a

Table 3.7. Results of Two-Facet, Partially Nested Generalizability Study for Different Numbers of Occasions and Raters ($R \times (O : T)$ Design)

Source of Variation	$\hat{\sigma}^2$	$n'_o =$ 1 $n'_r =$ 1	5 1	7 1	8 1	4 2	3 3	2 5
Teachers (t)	$\hat{\sigma}^2_t$	8.29	8.29	8.29	8.29	8.29	8.29	8.29
Raters (r)	$\hat{\sigma}^2_r$	1.06[a]	1.06	1.06	1.06	.53	.35	.21
Occasions : Teachers ($o : t$)	$\hat{\sigma}^2_{o,to}$	4.62	.92	.66	.58	1.16	1.54	2.31
tr	$\hat{\sigma}^2_{tr}$	1.54	1.54	1.54	1.54	.77	.51	.31
ro, tro, e	$\hat{\sigma}^2_{ro,tro,e}$	9.07	1.81	1.30	1.13	1.13	1.01	.91
	$\hat{\sigma}^2_{Rel.}$	15.23	4.27	3.50	3.25	3.06	3.06	3.53
	$\hat{\rho}^2_{Rel.}$	.35	.66	.70	.72	.73	.73	.70

Note: The data are from Erlich & Shavelson (1976).
[a] Hypothetical data generated for this table. Original data not available.

similar level of generalizability observing teachers on only two occasions, it would be necessary to use five raters (10 observations).

Not only does the information in Table 3.7 help the decision maker determine how many raters and occasions are needed for dependable measurement of teaching behavior, but it also can be used to assess the consequences of using different raters for different teachers (raters nested within teachers or teachers nested within raters). In this study, because raters tended to use similar standards of observation (indicated by a small $\hat{\sigma}_r^2$) and tended to rank-order teachers similarly (indicated by a small $\hat{\sigma}_{tr}^2$), it would be reasonable to use different raters for different teachers. If, however, raters had used different standards, that is, if some raters had "seen" more behavior than other raters for the same teacher on the same occasion (a large $\hat{\sigma}_r^2$), or if raters had rank-ordered teachers differently (a large $\hat{\sigma}_{tr}^2$), then using different raters for different teachers would not be sensible. In the latter case, the ratings of some teachers would not be comparable to the ratings of other teachers.

Nearly all of the observational studies in Table 3.4 involved nesting. Most designs were partially nested, that is, they had crossed and nested facets. For example, Good, Cooper, and Blakey (1980) observed each classroom approximately 16 times during each of 3 time blocks during the year (October/November, January/February, and April/May) in each of two contexts (seatwork, whole-class instruction). Their design, then, was partially nested with occasion of observation nested within time block while the rest of the design crossed teachers with time blocks and contexts.

A few designs in Table 3.4 were fully nested. Evertson et al. (1980), for example, observed two classes for each teacher. Each class was observed 20 times during the year. Since observers alternated visits to each class, the occasions were different for each observer. Furthermore, some teachers taught English while others taught mathematics. In this design, then, occasions were nested within observers, observers were nested within classes, classes were nested within teachers, and teachers were nested within subject matter.

The choice of a nested versus a crossed design depends on whether the focus is on assessing sources of measurement error (G study) or on making decisions (D study). To maximize information about separate sources of error in the measurement (the G study), a crossed design is preferable to a nested design. In the fully nested design of Evertson et al. (1980), it would be impossible to separate variation of teacher behavior over occasions from variation over observers and classes. If occasions and observers were important sources of variation in the observations of teacher behavior, the confounding created the potential for larger error variances and, consequently, lower generalizability coefficients. If the measures of teacher behavior were not generalizable, then the correlations between teacher behavior and student achievement (process–product correlations) would be attenuated. Furthermore, a higher level of generalizability for some teacher behavior variables than for others could lead to higher process–product correlations for some teacher behavior variables than for others, even if the true relationships are similar.

To determine the degree to which confounding of sources of variation in the design may lower the generalizability of the ratings of teacher behavior, it would be advantageous to introduce crossing into the design. Although some sources of variation were necessarily nested by definition in the Evertson et al. (1980) study—for example, classes nested within teachers—normally it would be possible to introduce some crossing into the design. For example, it would be possible to cross observers with occasions, classes, and teachers. That is, the same observers could be present on each occasion for each class of each teacher. The investment of resources to accomplish this need not be large. In a small pilot study, two observers could visit three teachers' classes twice. This design would provide unambiguous information about the sources of measurement error due to observers, and the interactions between observers and occasions, classes, and teachers.

If observers were found to be a negligible source of error variation, then it would be reasonable in the larger decision study to nest observers within occasions, classes, and teachers without sacrificing much information about sources of variation in observations. This nested design, with different observers on each occasion, for each class, and for each teacher, would be more efficient and possibly more cost-effective than a crossed design and so would be a preferable design for the decision maker.

TEACHERS OBSERVED IN MULTIPLE SUBJECT MATTERS AND TEACHING CONTEXTS: DESIGNS WITH A FIXED FACET

All of the designs discussed so far in this section assume that the facets were random. That is, the conditions used in the G study (e.g., the particular occasions of observation) were assumed to be a randomly selected subset of all occasions in the universe and the results were assumed to be generalizable over all occasions, not just those used in the G study. If occasions turned out to be a major source of variation in teacher behavior, the recommendation from a G study would be to observe teachers on several occasions and use the average over occasions in substantive analyses.

In many studies of teacher behavior, however, sources of variation are selected systematically and may not be reasonably considered random. Two common examples are subject matter and teaching context. It is not reasonable to assume that mathematics and reading are random selections from all subject matters, nor is it reasonable to assume that all the teacher behavior observed in mathematics and reading generalize to social studies, spelling, and science. Furthermore, observations of teacher behavior in seatwork and small groups probably do not generalize to teacher behavior in other teaching contexts, such as whole group lecture and large group discussion. Both of these facets, subject matter and teaching context, then, should be considered fixed.

Generalizability theory treats fixed facets differently from random facets. Rather than asking how many subject matters are needed for reliable measurement (as in the case of occasions above), G theory examines whether it is reasonable to average over subject matters or whether generalizability should be examined separately for each subject matter.

G theory treats a fixed facet most frequently by averaging scores over the conditions of the fixed facet and examining the generalizability of this average over the random facets. For example, in Erlich and Shavelson's (1978) generalizability study of teaching behavior, teachers were observed while teaching reading and mathematics. Subject matter was treated as fixed, and teachers' scores were averaged over reading and mathematics lessons. This information might be useful to elementary school principals who are interested in a teacher's behavior in general and would be willing to use an average over reading, mathematics, and other subject matters. Averaging over those two subject matters, however, may distort the phenomena being observed because teaching behavior can be quite different during reading and mathematics. A preferable strategy, in this study, might have been to examine the generalizability of the reading and mathematics data separately. Or, to provide the most comprehensive information, it may be reasonable to present the results for each condition of a fixed facet separately *and* in combination (averaged over the conditions).

The analysis of a design with a fixed facet might proceed in two stages (see Shavelson & Webb, 1981). The first stage would be a generalizability study with all facets, including subject matter, treated as random to assess the variability of teacher behavior across subject matter. (Since G theory averages scores over the conditions of a fixed facet—here, subject matter—it would not be possible to obtain an estimate of the variability in teaching behavior across subject matters if subject matter were treated as a fixed facet. The only way to ascertain the variability of teacher behavior across subject matters is to treat the facet as random. By definition, variance components apply only to random facets.) In an analysis with all facets random, large components of variance associated with subject matter would suggest that teaching behavior differs across subject matters. A large variance component for the interaction between teachers and subject matters would indicate that teachers behave (are rank-ordered) differently in teaching different subject matters. If we suspect that teacher behavior differs across subject matters, it makes sense to analyze the data separately for each subject matter. The second stage, then, would be separate generalizability analyses for each subject matter. If teacher behavior does not differ across subject matters, indicated by small variance components associated with subject matter, then the average score over subject matter (e.g., reading and mathematics) would accurately represent teacher behavior. The second stage in this case would be a generalizability analysis averaging over subject matters.

As can be seen in Table 3.4, many studies have observed teachers in multiple subject matters. Most of them reported only mean levels of teacher or student behavior for each subject matter or for all subject matters combined. Few of them examined the interactions between subject matter and other facets in the design.

One could argue that several other facets in Table 3.4, such as teaching context and time, should be treated as fixed in most studies. Some studies were concerned with the type of lesson—slow-paced questioning and answering without individual materials provided to students, workbook or worksheet activities, and reading new material from basal textbooks (Anderson, Morgan, Evertson, & Brophy, 1978)—while others were concerned with group size—whole-class and small-group instruction (Brophy, Evertson, Crawford, King, & Senior, 1975;

see also Crawford, Brophy, Evertson, & Coulter, 1977). It would be difficult to argue a priori that these teaching contexts were selected randomly and so teaching context should probably be treated as fixed in a generalizability study. The resulting variance components for teaching context would show whether it is reasonable to average teacher behavior over the teaching contexts used in the study or whether to examine the generalizability of teacher behavior for each teaching context separately.

A few studies have recognized that the month of the year, the day of the week, and the time of day might exert important influences on behavior. For example, Good et al. (1980) sampled three 2-month intervals and Evertson and Veldman (1981) observed students and teachers every month from November to April. Since it is probably unreasonable to substitute observations in the fall for those obtained in the winter, the month of observations should probably be treated as a fixed facet.

Four studies explicitly varied the day of the week (Mondays and Fridays, Colbert, 1979; Tuesdays, Wednesdays, and Thursdays, Wright & Nuthall, 1970; Monday through Friday, Cornbleth & Korth, 1980) or the time of day (mornings and afternoon, Fitzgerald, Wright, Eason, & Shapson, 1978) in their observations. The selection of days of the week in the first two studies was not random. In the last two studies, the entire universe of school days or times of day was observed. The conventional solution when the entire universe is sampled in the G study is to consider the facet as fixed because the decision maker is generalizing only to the conditions included in the G study. However, if the decision maker wants to generalize beyond the specific days sampled in the G or D study and believes that they are exchangeable for any other Monday, Tuesday, Wednesday, Thursday, or Friday, then days of the week might be considered random (see de Finetti, 1964; Shavelson & Webb, 1981, pp. 142–143).

Although the studies investigating time of observation (month, day, time of day) as a facet had ideal designs to determine the stability of behavior over time, none of them took full advantage of this potential. Rather, they were concerned mainly with occasion variation, that is, trends in teachers' mean behavior over time. What their results do not tell us, and what generalizability studies could easily provide, is information about the rank-ordering of teachers over time (the interaction of teachers and time). For example, even though teachers in the Colbert study facilitated learning more on Mondays than on Fridays, on the average, the teachers who were the most facilitative on Monday may not have been the most facilitative on Friday. The former finding would not contribute to measurement error or reliability when consistency of rank-ordering of teachers is at issue. The latter finding would.

THE STUDY OF MULTIFACETED POPULATIONS

The purpose of psychological measurement has typically been to differentiate individuals. The work of Cardinet, Tourneur, and Allal (1976a, 1976b, 1981), Cardinet & Tourneur (1974, 1977), Tourneur (1978), and Tourneur & Cardinet (1979) recognizes, however, that the focus of measurement may change depending on a particular decision maker's purpose. In the study of teaching behavior, an important focus may be population subgroups. In particular, the decision maker can systematically investigate whether there are differences in the behavior of different subgroups in a population or whether the population can be considered homogeneous.

For example, if a population consists of subjects nested within sex and socioeconomic status (SES), it is important to know whether the behavior of females and males differs and whether the behavior of high-SES persons differs from that of low-SES persons. In a G study, variance components can be estimated for the fixed facets sex and SES by treating them initially as random. If the variance components for sex and SES are negligible, the decision maker can assume a homogeneous population and ignore these attributes in the design of the D study. If the components are sizeable, the decision maker should maintain distinctions between the subgroups in the population. One feature distinguishing studies of multifaceted populations from others, then, is the focus on subgroups rather than on individuals. When the investigator's interest concerns differences between the subject populations, individual differences between *persons* within each subject population would be considered error variation.

This approach should be applied to studies of teacher or student behavior whenever the investigator wants to compare the behavior of subgroups of teachers or students or wants to draw conclusions generalizing over subgroups. Some of the population characteristics investigated by studies listed in Table 3.4 include teaching effectiveness (Good & Grouws, 1977), student achievement level (Anderson, 1981; Good & Beckerman, 1978), and grade level (Cooley & Leinhardt, 1980; Eggert, 1978; Marliave et al., 1978; Stallings, 1976).

A generalizability study of multifaceted populations would show whether they can be treated as a single homogeneous population, or should be treated as separate populations. In Anderson's (1981) study of high-achieving and low-achieving students, for example, a generalizability study could be conducted with students nested within achievement level (high, low) and other facets of measurement (e.g., raters, occasions). Large variance components associated with achievement level (and the interaction between achievement level and other facets in the design) would indicate that high-achieving and low-achieving students do not constitute a single homogeneous population. In this case, the decision maker cannot make the same interpretation about behavior of high-achieving students as about behavior of low-achieving students. Therefore, the next step in a measurement study would be to investigate reliability of behavior separately for high-achieving and low-achieving students.

Generalizability (or other reliability) studies that do not take into account population characteristics may yield erroneous interpretations about the dependability of measurements. When there are sizeable effects due to population characteristics (e.g., achievement level), the estimates of universe score variance and error variance in Equations (5) and (6) may be falsely inflated. Differences between population subgroups would be incorrectly attributed to differences between individuals. Similarly, interactions between population characteristics and facets of error would be incorrectly attributed to interactions between individuals and facets. For example, a large variance component for the interaction between students and raters might result (in whole or in part) from the interaction of student achievement level and raters (when raters disagree in their ordering of the behavior of high-achieving and low-achieving students: some raters rate high-achieving students higher than low-achieving students while others rate low-achieving students higher than high-achieving students). Without including the population characteristic in the study, it is impossible to determine which effects are inflated, and by how much. Consequently, the estimated dependability of the measurement is affected in unknown ways: it could be overestimated or underestimated.

Loose Strings

Although generalizability theory is a powerful tool for assessing multiple sources of variation in the measurement of teaching behavior, a number of measurement issues outside of G theory have not been resolved. These include consistency of composites of teacher behavior, length of periods for observing teaching behavior versus number of observation periods, the bidirectionality of teacher–student interaction and influence, the assumption of steady-state versus changing behavior over time (linear, nonlinear, unsystematic), and dichotomous observation data.

INTERNAL CONSISTENCY OF COMPOSITES

Often a category of behavior can be broken down into component behaviors. For example, "shows affection for a pupil" may be subdivided into more specific behaviors such as "smiles at pupil" and "puts arm around pupil." Since the component behaviors can probably be coded more objectively than the single global category, the accuracy of the composite may be higher than that of the single category. It is possible to treat the component behaviors as levels of a facet in a generalizability study. The results would show whether teachers' frequency of behavior is consistent across the component behaviors and would help guide decisions about the number of component behaviors that need to be observed. Large variation in teachers' ratings across component behaviors would indicate low consistency of teacher behavior and would suggest that many component behaviors should enter the composite.

What a generalizability study would not provide is information about *which* component behaviors should enter the composite. Multivariate generalizability theory (see Shavelson & Webb, 1981; Webb & Shavelson, 1981; Webb, Shavelson, & Maddahian, 1983) can be used to obtain weighted combinations of the component behaviors with maximum generalizability. Using this approach, however, the *data*, rather than the investigators, define the composites with maximum generalizability, and the resulting composites may not be interpretable. A preferable approach to determining composites of behavior that conform to psychological theory or practice may be confirmatory maximum-likelihood factor analysis (Joreskog, 1969). The decision maker can form composites on the basis of the theory and can test their fit to the data.

LENGTH VERSUS NUMBER OF OBSERVATIONS

Many observational studies described in this chapter investigate the variability of teacher and student behavior over observation occasions. In order to obtain reliable measurements, attention focuses, in part, on the *number* of occasions needed for dependable measurement, and, in part, on the *length* of the observation periods. The only attempt thus far to estimate the effect on reliability of varying the length *and* number of observation periods is the work of Rowley (1976, 1978). He described the effects of varying number and length of observations separately and simultaneously. Since observations obtained on one occasion may be correlated (called linked by Cronbach et al., 1972; Cronbach & Furby, 1970), Rowley pointed out that increasing the number of independent samples of behavior would likely produce a more representative set of observations than would increasing the length of fewer observation periods. He proposed a formula to estimate the effects on reliability of increasing length and number of observation periods simultaneously. His formula takes into account the higher correlation between observations obtained on the same occasion than that between observations obtained on different occasions. Rowley (1978) compared the estimates of reliability produced by his formula to actual reliability coefficients calculated from observation periods of varying length and number and obtained a fairly good match.

Although Rowley's approach provides a way of considering length and number of observation periods simultaneously, there are more general issues that need to be addressed. First, Rowley's approach assumes that all observations obtained during the same occasion are correlated to the same degree. Webb (1980; see Shavelson & Webb, 1981, p. 153) has shown different degrees of correlation between student behavior within a time period as short as five minutes. The issue here is how to take into account the differing correlations between observation periods occurring closer or further in time. Second, procedures have not yet been developed for estimating error variance and reliability in a study investigating other facets of error variation (for example, rater, teaching context) in addition to length and number of observation periods.

BIDIRECTIONALITY OF TEACHER–STUDENT INTERACTION AND INFLUENCE[4]

Most of the research on teacher behavior has tended to focus on the teacher's influence on the student. When observational studies do examine student behavior, they tend to focus on the student's response to a teacher's behavior (for example, the student's response to a teacher's question). Rarely have observational studies measured the influence of students on teachers. Rarer still are studies of the bidirectionality of teacher–student interaction or influence.

The few studies to investigate the influence of student behavior on teacher behavior have found evidence that such influence does occur. Sherman and Cormier (1974), for example, systematically altered the behavior of disruptive students. The improved behavior of the target students produced changes in the teachers' responses to them. Klein (1971) manipulated the behavior of students by instructing them how to respond to invited lecturers. Among the results that Klein observed was the tendency of teacher behavior to be more positive when student behavior was positive or neutral than when students behaved negatively. (Other examples are provided by Noble and Nolan, 1976; Haller, 1975; and Copeland, 1979).

In one of the only studies to examine the bidirectionality of teacher-student influence, Fiedler (1975) compared the effectiveness of attempts by both teachers and students to influence classroom procedures and activities. Fiedler looked at four categories of influence by teachers and students: attempts to influence another person, compliant responses to another person's request or suggestion, refusals to modify one's behavior in response to a request or suggestion, and responses that were not clear or not performed. She reported that both students and teachers made regular efforts to influence one another, and that both teachers and students tended to comply with attempts at influence.

The studies described above suggest that a unidirectional model of influence from teachers to students or from students to teachers is an inadequate characterization of classroom interaction (see Shulman's chapter in this volume). But the measurement issues involved in assessing reciprocal interaction—especially the nonindependence of sequences of behavior—have not been addressed.

STEADY STATE VERSUS CHANGING BEHAVIOR

Nearly all of the approaches to studying the stability of teacher and student behavior assume that the phenomenon being studied remains constant over observations, that is, is in a steady state. Both classical reliability theory and generalizability theory make this assumption. Assessment of stability or reliability is much more complex when the behavior changes over time. Among those investigating time-dependent phenomena are Bock (1976), Bryk and colleagues (Bryk, Strenio, & Weisberg, 1980; Bryk & Weisberg, 1977), Rogosa and colleagues (Rogosa, 1980; Rogosa, Brandt, & Zimkowski, 1982; Rogosa, Floden, & Willett, in press), and Plewis (1981).

Rogosa et al. (in press) consider generalizability theory as one method for assessing the stability of teacher behavior over time. Their approach is to formulate two basic questions about stability of behavior:

(a) Is the behavior of an individual teacher consistent over time? And
(b) are individual differences among teachers consistent over time?

For an individual teacher, consistent behavior is defined as absolutely invariant over time (true behavior is constant over time; see also Wohlwill, 1973, Figure 12-2). They characterized inconsistency in the behavior of an individual teacher in several ways; unsystematic scatter around a flat line, a linear trend (with or without unsystematic scatter), and a nonlinear trend

---

[4] We would like to thank Richard Cohen for his major contribution to this section.

(with or without scatter). Changing teacher behavior over time has important implications in generalizability theory for the estimation of a teacher's universe score. When behavior changes systematically over time, the estimate of a teacher's universe score will be time dependent.

The second, and more common, question about stability of teacher behavior is the consistency of individual differences among teachers. Perfect consistency of individual differences occurs whenever the trends for different teachers are parallel, whether the teachers' individual data are flat, linear, or nonlinear.

A generalizability analysis with occasions as a facet is described by Rogosa et al. (in press) as one method for assessing the consistency of individual differences over time. The variance component that reflects the stability of individual differences over time is the interaction between teachers and occasions. A small component for the interaction (compared to the variance component for teachers) suggests that teachers are rank-ordered similarly across occasions; that is, their trends are parallel. It says nothing about whether individual teacher behavior is changing over time: As described above, the behavior of *all* teachers could be changing over time in the same way (a nonzero main effect for occasion). A relatively large value of the component for the teacher × occasion interaction (compared to the component for teachers) shows that teachers are ranked differently across occasions. This could be the result of unsystematic fluctuations in individual teachers' behavior over time, the usual interpretation made in G theory under the steady state assumption. But it could also reflect differences in systematic trends over time for different teachers: The behavior of some teachers (e.g., the number of reprimands) may systematically increase over time, while that of other teachers systematically decreases or remains flat over time. Furthermore, the systematic changes could be linear or nonlinear.

Clearly, we must be able to specify the process by which teacher behavior changes in order to model it. Rogosa et al. (in press) provide excellent steps in that direction by describing analytic methods for assessing the consistency of behavior of individual teachers and the consistency of individual differences among teachers. At the least, their exposition is valuable for clarifying the limited ability of generalizability theory to distinguish between real changes in teacher behavior over time and random fluctuations over time that should be considered error.

Although the analytic models for investigating time-dependent changes in behavior are important, they do not alleviate the investigator's responsibility to define the appropriate time interval for observation using relevant theory. In studying the dependability of the measurement, it is necessary to restrict the time interval so that the observations of, say, teacher behavior can be reasonably expected to represent the same phenomenon. Just as no one would interpret the change in student achievement scores from the fall testing to the spring testing as representing random fluctuations rather than systematic changes, one would not expect teacher behavior to remain constant over a long period of time.

There are other developments in the field that examine the changing behavior of teachers or students over time, such as models of change based on Markov processes (e.g., Plewis,

1981). However, since these developments do not follow our philosophy of isolating multiple sources of measurement error, and do not provide much information about how measurement error might be characterized or estimated, they are not discussed here.

DICHOTOMOUS OBSERVATION DATA

Analysis of variance approaches to reliability, including generalizability theory, assume that the scores being analyzed represent continuous random variables with normal distributions. When the scores are dichotomous (for example, a teacher uses or does not use small groups for a particular lesson), analysis of variance methods produce inaccurate estimates of variance components and reliability (Cronbach et al., 1972; Bock & Lieberman, 1970; Brennan, 1980). In analyses of achievement test data with dichotomously scored items, L. Muthen (1983) found that the ANOVA approach for estimating variance components tended to overestimate error components and underestimate reliability. She found that a covariance structure analysis model, a combination of factor analysis and analysis of variance (see Bock, 1960; Bock & Bargmann, 1966; Joreskog, 1974; B. Muthen, 1978, 1983; B. Muthen & Christoffersson, 1981; Schmidt, 1969; Wiley, Schmidt, & Bramble, 1973), produced estimates of variance components and generalizability coefficients that were closer to the true values than those from the analysis of variance.

Although this approach has not been applied to the study of teacher behavior, several applications are possible. For example, in a design with multiple observers coding teachers' use of small groups on different occasions, it would be worthwhile to investigate whether covariance structure analysis would produce more accurate estimates of variance components and, hence, generalizability coefficients than the traditional ANOVA method described throughout this section.

Response to Critics

The use of generalizability theory in classroom research has its critics. Most criticisms of G theory concern practical limitations. One concern is that studies of teacher and student behavior usually examine many different behavior variables, and it is possible that generalizability analyses of the variables would lead to different recommended designs, in terms of numbers of observations of each teacher, kind of observation design, or both. Another concern is that generalizability studies may be expensive and leave few resources for the substantive studies.

Although both of the above concerns are valid, they are not insurmountable. First, if different generalizability analyses suggest different optimal decision studies, the investigator can choose between a common design for all observation variables or use different designs for different variables (for example, observing some variables on a subset of occasions). Second, the expenditure of resources on a G study need not be great. A comprehensive study can be conducted with a small sample of teachers or students. Moreover, a generalizability study can help the investigator to optimize the use of resources in the decision study and minimize waste. For example, without a G study, an investigator may have several observers rate all the teachers, whereas the results of a G study may show that only one observer is needed for any teacher and that teachers can be rated by different observers. The latter design could result in substantial savings.

Brophy (1979) has stated that "it appears that investigators' degrees of success in making sure that they collect enough data *per classroom* to allow meaningful study of a given process variable will continue to depend on their familiarity with the classrooms of interest, the process variable itself, and the context factors that affect it" (p. 740). Generalizability theory provides an excellent way of increasing investigators' knowledge about the context factors that influence behavior. With a generalizability study, the investigator can objectively assess the influence of the occasion of observation (whether hour, day, month, or year), the observer, the subject matter, the teaching context, the school, the student population, the teacher population, and a variety of other factors, on the behavior of teachers and students. With this information, the investigator can then collect dependable data on teacher and student behavior.

Measurement of Teachers' Cognitive Processes

Just as Gage's "paradigms" chapter in the first *Handbook* ushered in an era of research on teacher behavior, publication of Shulman's "Teaching as Clinical Information Processing" (National Institute of Education, 1975; see also Shulman & Elstein, 1975) and Shavelson's "What Is *the* Basic Teaching Skill?" (1973; see also Shavelson, 1976) signaled an era of research on teachers' cognitive processes—their pedagogical thoughts, judgments, and decisions. (For reviews, see Clark & Peterson, this volume; Shavelson, 1983; Shavelson & Stern, 1981).

One version of the cognitive approach assumes that teaching is a process by which teachers make reasonable descisions with the intent of helping students reach worthwhile educational outcomes, and learn from the consequences of these decisions in order to improve their teaching. Although teachers' thoughts, judgments, and decisions do not always match this description, it seems to apply to many goal-oriented teaching situations, especially during instructional planning. Teachers, then, are seen as active professionals who, for example, select textbooks, assign students to groups, plan instructional sequences, and choose among many teaching skills and techniques at their disposal to help students reach some goal (e.g., Shavelson & Stern, 1981). Based on classroom experience, they adjust their judgment and decision policies.

This *cognitive* research on teaching has characteristic methods that differ markedly from those in the correlational and experimental studies of previous process–product research. These methods purportedly produce data on mental processes and so use more or less direct probes of teachers' thoughts, judgments, and decisions. The names of some of these methods are, admittedly, novel to most researchers on teaching: "policy capturing," "lens modeling," "process tracing," "stimulated recall," and a potpourri of case study and ethnographic methods (Shulman & Elstein, 1975). We treat measurement issues surrounding the four methods just named in three subsections—regression modeling, process tracing, and their comparison—and leave the case study and enthnographic

methods to Evertson and Green, and to Erickson (both in this volume).

Regression Modeling

Teachers repeatedly make the same or similar kinds of decisions about teaching. Choosing textbooks and adjunct instructional materials, grouping students for instruction, deciding whether to challenge a student during classroom discourse, and grading students are but a few of such important judgments and decisions. When professionals make judgments time and again, we expect to find some underlying "rules of thumb" that guide them. That is, we expect teachers to have *policies* for arriving at decisions that are based on their training, past experience, and values.

One research tool used to measure these policies is called *regression modeling*. Regression modeling attempts to identify the kinds of information teachers use and the ways in which they combine or integrate this information to reach pedagogical judgments and decisions.

One version of this technique is called *policy capturing*. With this procedure, different pieces of information available to teachers are treated as predictors of their judgments or decisions. The resulting linear prediction model is often interpreted as the teacher's decision policy. A second version of regression modeling compares a teacher's judgments with judgments made by experts in a curricular area or preferences of students in the teacher's class. This technique is called *lens modeling*, for reasons explained below.

POLICY CAPTURING

Policy capturing studies are typically performed using simulated cases or vignettes (e.g., Borko & Cadwell, 1982; Floden et al., 1981; Shavelson, Cadwell, & Izu, 1977), although they need not be (Pullis & Cadwell, 1982). For example, Borko and Cadwell (1982) presented descriptions of 32 hypothetical students to 46 elementary teachers. These hypothetical students differed in sex, general achievement, rule-following behavior, ability to work independently, social competence, and self-confidence. (The 2^6 design produced 64 vignettes; each teacher received a balanced half.) For example,

> Joyce often has difficulty making friends with other students. She seems unsure of herself in most situations. Joyce recently took a standardized achievement test and received a score about one year above grade level. She generally behaves appropriately in the classroom. She usually works without the teacher's supervision when given individual assignments. (p. 600)

The teachers were asked to judge the likelihood that each student would master the skills and concepts typically included in a fifth-grade curriculum.

The teachers' judgments were then regressed on the students' characteristics and the resulting multiple-regression equation was interpreted as a model of the teachers' procedures or "policy" for judging students' mastery. Typically each teacher makes a set of judgments based on the information provided. Then the data for each teacher are pooled in a regression analysis and something like an average (mean) policy is obtained.

When Borko and Cadwell did this, they interpreted the results of their linear model to mean that "teachers utilized at least five of the six student variables in making each of the judgments" (p. 602). However, when the regression models for individual teachers were compared with one another, they found that "teachers either utilized different information or, if they used the same information, tended to use it in different ways" (p. 604). Thus the average equation was misleading.

Floden et al. (1982) provided another good example of policy capturing. They attempted to determine the relative impact of external pressures that might influence teachers' decisions about the content to be covered in fourth-grade mathematics. Sixty-four vignettes systematically manipulated the presence or absence of six sources of pressure: district tests, mandated textbooks, district instructional objectives, other teachers' opinions, the principal's opinion, and parents' opinions. For each vignette, teachers indicated on a seven-point, Likert-type scale their willingness to add or delete topics from their mathematics curriculum when "pressured" to do so. Each teacher's judgments were regressed on the six sources of pressure in order to capture that teacher's policy. Then the policies of individual teachers were aggregated by counting the number of teachers that were influenced by each piece of information (i.e., by counting the teachers with a statistically significant regression coefficient for a particular piece of information).

How were policy capturing results interpreted? Floden et al. (1982) found that each pressure significantly affected teachers' decisions about content to be covered: "Perhaps the most striking result ... is the degree to which teachers see themselves going along with whatever pressures are administered. Even with only a single pressure present, teachers on the average project that they would be fairly certain to teach requested topics" (p. 139). The authors correctly warned the reader that either the results can be taken as a first approximation of the effects of external pressures on teachers' content decisions, or these verbal reports might not mirror teachers' actual behavior at all. In the end, they concluded that "one should not be so naive as to think that a projected response perfectly mirrors actual behavior. But neither should one be so cynical as to consider expressed prediction as unrelated to future actions" (p. 139).

LENS MODELING

Lens modeling is a technique that grew out of Egon Brunswik's research on human perception. Just as a lens focuses light from or reflected by an object, Brunswik was interested in (a) the way the decision maker or judge brings into focus only certain pieces of the vast information available, and (b) the accuracy of this judgmental process.

Perhaps the easiest way to introduce the technique is with a concrete example. Byers and Evans (1980) used lens modeling to capture a teacher's policies for selecting books for her students' leisure reading and to compare those policies with her students' policies for making the same selections. Elementary school teachers were presented with a set of brief descriptions of books for leisure reading and asked to select those each student might like. Their students were also asked to select the books they would like to read. As might be expected, the accuracy of teachers' predictions of their students' choices varied widely

from one teacher to another. "The discovery of large variations in accuracy of judgments," Byers and Evans pointed out, "provides researchers with conditions for learning about how teachers use the information available to them to make judgements and decisions" (p. 3).

This lens modeling study has three major components: the student's choices of books (the criterion state), the teacher's judgments about which books each student might like, and the set of attributes (called *cues* in lens modeling) on which the books varied. Byers and Evans characterized the attributes of leisure-reading books along five dimensions: type (e.g., poetry, biography), theme (e.g., fantasy, heroism), main character (e.g., animal, parent, child), reading level, and physical characteristics (e.g., size, type font). The attributes, if not already measured on a scale (e.g., reading level, book size), were quantified as to their presence or absence.

The components of the lens model are shown in Figure 3.1. In this figure, the lens is in the middle. Just as a lens focuses light emanating from or reflected by an object, Brunswik's lens model focuses information about the environment on a student's choices and on the teacher's judgments.

The correlation between a student's book selections (yes = 1, no = 0) and his teacher's selections $(1, 0) - r_{YJ}$ — is called *response validity*. It represents the accuracy of the teacher's judgments. By regressing the student's book selections (using logistic regression with the dichotomos variable Y in Fig. 3.1) on each of the attributes (e.g., cues score 0, 1 of the books, X, in

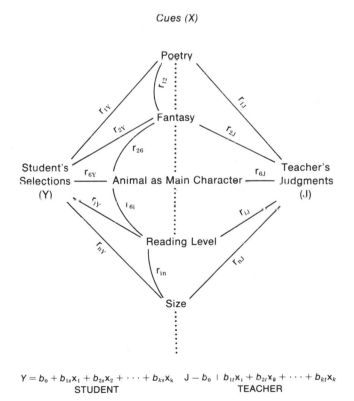

Cues (X)

$$Y = b_0 + b_{1s}x_1 + b_{2s}x_2 + \cdots + b_{ks}x_k \qquad J = b_0 + b_{1t}x_1 + b_{2t}x_2 + \cdots + b_{kt}x_k$$
STUDENT   TEACHER

Fig. 3.1. Lens model characterizing the book selection task. (To improve clarity, not all correlations among cues are shown.)

Figure 3.1), weights are obtained in the form of regression coefficients. They provide a measure of the extent to which "the cue values . . . are used to predict the child's selection [sic] in much the same manner as high school rank, G.P.A., and SAT scores are used to predict high school seniors' college performance" (Byers & Evans, 1980, p. 5). The multiple correlation between the cues and the student's choices is termed *cue* or *ecological validity* of the judgment task. If the cue validity is low, the accuracy of the teacher's judgments must also be low, assuming that the cues adequately reflect the important attributes of the books.

By regressing the teacher's judgments (J) on the presence or absence of the cues (Xs), an attempt is made to capture that teacher's policy for selecting books for a particular student. The regression weights are interpreted as the *cue utilization* in the judgment task. (This is analogous to cue validity, but from the teacher side of the model, not the criterion—i.e., student—side.) The extent to which the teacher uses the same cues with the same weights attached to them as the student does determines the maximum value of the teacher's predictive accuracy.

Cue validity and cue utilization, then, provide indicators of the "goodness of fit" of the model. If the predicted value for each book based on the linear model characterizing the student's responses is correlated with the teacher's predicted values, this correlation provides a measure of "the teacher's *knowledge* of the student's interest" (Byers & Evans, 1980, p. 7).

The lens model captures both the teacher's policy for judging reading material for a student and the student's policy for selecting books. The model of the student is taken to be the criterion against which the teacher's judgments are compared. In laboratory settings, both the student and the teacher would be "fully informed as to what the attributes (cues) were, [and] the maximum value of accuracy would be strictly determined by the product of *cue validity, cue utilization, and knowledge*" (Byers & Evans, 1980, p. 7). However, in realistic tasks such as those naturally occurring in classrooms, the cues are not specifically given. In this case, both student and teacher may use cues other than those selected by the researcher (Figure 3.1). Then judgmental accuracy might be higher than the product of validity, utilization, and knowledge. Byers and Evans, following Einhorn, dubbed the correlation between the residuals from the child's and teacher's selections the missing cue weighting. "If this correlation . . . is neither zero nor close enough to zero that the discrepancy can be attributed to chance, it suggests that attributes are being used which are not included in the model" of cues selected by the researcher (1980, p. 8).

The results of part of the Byers and Evans study are presented in Table 3.8. The multiple correlation between students'

selections and the cues (cue validity) considered with the teachers' judgments and the cues (cue utilization) were reasonably high (.67 and .68, respectively). However, students tended to select different books for themselves than did their teachers (r = .23 and .31, or the average correlation between students' and teachers' observed choices, and the average correlation between their predicted choices, respectively). Finally, a very small proportion of the variation shared between students' and teachers' selections was due to unmeasured cues (r = .16).

RELIABILITY OF MEASUREMENTS

With regression modeling, a teacher makes repeated judgments or decisions based on information. Often this information is presented in the form of vignettes, that systematically vary one or more independent variables. Suppose, within the task, several vignettes that repeat exactly the same information are randomly interspersed among the others. To what degree would a teacher's judgments be consistent on identical or "equivalent" vignettes? To what degree would a teacher's judgments on the same vignettes vary from day to day or week to week? To what degree would a teacher's judgments vary over both occasions and equivalent versions of the same vignette? All of these questions refer to the dependability of the judgments, i.e., the generalizability from a particular observed score (e.g., rating judgment) to a universe of scores that would constitute equally admissible observations to a researcher (cf. Cronbach et al., 1972). In classical theory terms (e.g., Lord & Novick, 1968), how reliable are measures of teachers' judgments and decisions?

Perhaps surprisingly, systematic studies of the reliability of teachers' judgments and decisions in regression modeling tasks have not been carried out. Moreover, only a handful of studies —mostly dissertations—have reported reliability information. They do so, typically, by randomly inserting five to ten of the same or equivalent vignettes into the task. Judgmental ratings on replicate or equivalent vignettes are then correlated to arrive at a reliability coefficient. Borko (1978), for example, repeated identical and randomly parallel vignettes in a policy capturing task in which each teacher judged hypothetical students' *aptitudes* (academic competence, motivation, and classroom behavior) and then made seven *preinstructional decisions* (about instructional plans, tutoring, testing, and long-term objectives).

The reliability of the teachers' judgments of students' aptitudes was determined from the correlations between either a pair of exact replicate vignettes (only the student's name was changed), or a pair of randomly parallel replicative vignettes. (The student's name, the sentences representing each cue, and the order of cues were randomly determined.) The reliabilities of exact replicates, averaged over teachers, were .51, .54, and .47 for judgments of competence, motivation, and behavior problems. For the randomly parallel replicates, the corresponding reliabilities were .44, .28, and .63.

The reliabilities for the preinstructional decisions were, on average, considerably higher than the aptitude judgments, with little difference between exact replicates and randomly parallel replicates. For example, the reliabilities for exact replicates ranged from .53 to .82 with a median of .69 for the seven decisions, while the average reliability of the randomly parallel

Table 3.8. Estimates of Lens Model Parameters
(Averages over Teachers)

Parameter	Sample Value	Standard Deviation	Standard Error
Judgmental Accuracy	.23	.19	.01
Cue Validity	.67	.09	.01
Cue Utilization	.68	.09	.01
Knowledge	.31	.24	.02
Missing Cues	.16	.23	.02

replicates ranged from .28 to .81 with a median of .74. These findings are consistent with reliabilities reported by Russo (1978) for teachers' judgments of students' reading and mathematics abilities, and by Cone (1978) for decisions regarding how to deal with classroom behavior problems.

The importance of examining the reliability of teachers' judgments is further highlighted by a series of studies of teachers' diagnoses of reading problems conducted by Vinsonhaler (1979, 1983) and his colleagues (Gil, 1980; VanRoekel & Patriarca, 1979; Weinshank, 1980). Although not properly considered regression modeling, these studies are nevertheless germane to a discussion of the reliability of teachers' judgments.

Vinsonhaler (1979, 1983) created four simulated cases (and four replicates) representing hypothetical students' reading problems of sight-word deficiencies, inadequate structural and phonetic analysis skills, inadequate fluency of oral reading, and poor comprehension. For each simulated case, a file of material based on an actual case was created. The file contained background information, test data including both standardized test scores and a variety of special diagnostic test scores, report cards, interview data from teachers and parents, and other information commonly found in a student's diagnostic file. Eight diagnosticians were asked to diagnose three cases each, that is, two original cases and a replicate of one of the two. They could select as much of this information as they wanted and in any order. The mean within-diagnostician consistency coefficient between replicates was .13 with a range of .04 to .27 over the four cases and their replicates. Vinsonhaler's method for measuring diagnoses, however, is much more complicated than the ratings commonly used in regression modeling tasks. Several steps are needed to translate diagnosticians' diagnostic write-ups into scores; errors may arise at each step of the way.

These findings lead us to stress that studies of clinical information processing—including regression modeling studies—should be more concerned with reliability. Indeed, inconsistencies within clinicians across equivalent cases, and the sensitivity of judgments and decisions to minor changes in the task (e.g., Payne, 1982) suggest that measurements of teachers' judgments may fall prey to multiple sources of error. Some of the more important error sources are: *occasions* —teachers' judgments vary from one presentation of a vignette to its next presentation; *equivalence*—simple changes in the wording of information in parallel vignettes, no matter how carefully done, seem to give rise to inconsistencies in judgments; and *sequence* of vignettes—teachers' judgments may vary unsystematically due to (say) off-task thoughts stimulated by a chance pairing of two vignettes or systematically due to boredom, fatigue, or change in judgmental strategy. Generalizability theory is particularly well suited to examining the influence of most of these sources of measurement error.

VALIDITY OF COGNITIVE INTERPRETATIONS OF REGRESSION MODELS

The regression equation relating a teacher's judgments or decisions to a set of independent variables—whether based on the policy-capturing or lens-modeling approach—is usually interpreted as reflecting the extent to which each type of information (independent variables) influences that teacher's judgments.

More specifically, the regression coefficients are typically interpreted as indicating: (a) which types of information influence teachers' judgments (i.e., statistically significant coefficients) and which do not, (b) the direction of the relationship, and (c) the relative magnitude of the influence.

This interpretation of regression equations as reflecting teachers' decision policies is evident in the studies reviewed earlier. For example, Floden et al. (1981, p. 139) found that "*low* [regression] *coefficients* [italics added] for pressure from textbook was [sic] particularly notable" because teachers are well known to "base their instruction firmly on the text they use." Similar interpretations can be found throughout the literature on teachers' decision policies. Studying the influence of children's temperament characteristics on teachers' instructional decision making, Pullis and Cadwell (1982) concluded that "temperament consistently entered the regression equation even when controlling for ratings of [student's] ability, motivation, and social interaction" (p. 178). Indeed, information about temperament was used to make management decisions "more than any other type of information. This was the case both in terms of the number of teachers that used the temperament information, as well as the magnitude of the regression weights" (p. 178).

Just exactly what is the inference being made about teachers' cognitive processes from the policy capturing data? Is the claim that teachers, with or without awareness, mentally calculate the sum of a weighted set of information and then judge or make decisions depending on the magnitude of this sum? Or is the claim that the regression equation merely provides a method for *predicting* teachers' judgments and decisions without telling anything about their cognitive processes?

Hoffman (1960) argued that the regression equation was *not* isomorphic with the decision maker's cognitive processes. It was, instead, a *paramorphic* model; a model that *simulated* the decision maker by performing like one. However, Hoffman (Hoffman, Slovic, & Rorer, 1968) and researchers studying teaching (e.g., Borko & Cadwell, 1982; Byers & Evans, 1980; Floden et al., 1981; Shavelson et al., 1977; Yinger, Clark, & Mondol, 1981) slip into talking as if the regression model at least indicates which variables the decision maker is using, the direction of the relation, and the relative weighting (cf. Shulman & Elstein, 1975). To what extent are these claims valid?

CONCEPTUAL BASIS FOR CAPTURING POLICIES WITH REGRESSION MODELING

We begin by examining the use of a linear model to capture a teacher's policy. This practice, to the uninitiated, may appear curious. In the absence of some conceptual underpinnings that justify the use of linear models, it should be. Teachers (and other decision makers) often report using complex and nonlinear strategies. There is, however, a theoretical basis for using linear models. It explains, in large part, why linear models fit policy capturing and lens modeling data so well.

The theory is Brunswik's (1943). It attempts to explain human adaptation and adjustment to a probabilistic environment. Adjustment is achieved primarily through what Postman and Tolman (1959) called vicarious functioning: "Cues can be used interchangeably so that different patterns of cues can lead to equivalent results. Similarly, different motor responses can result in equivalent behavioral achievements. This is the principle of vicarious functioning which is the essential underpinning of adjustment to an environment which remains partly erratic" (p. 553).

The person's ability to substitute and make trade-offs among cues is essential in adjusting to the environment. This adjustment is aided by the fact that environmental cues are correlated with one another. As a consequence, decision makers in a cue-redundant environment can (a) extract considerable information about their environment without extensive search because the few observed cues correlate with the unobserved ones, (b) attend to information selectively with only minor loss of generality for the same reason, (c) avoid information overload because correlated cues reduce the dimensionality of the complex environment, (d) substitute cues for one another because of their correlation, and (e) minimize cue unreliability because the few observed cues are correlated and provide multiple measures of the same cue variable (Einhorn, Kleinmuntz, & Kleinmuntz, 1979).

The consequences of Brunswikian theory for the application of linear models to capture judgment and decision processes are the following, as enumerated by Einhorn et al. (1979).

(1) The additive combination function of linear models implies a fully compensatory system as envisioned by Brunswik.
(2) "The *B* weights are determined by considering all of the cues and their particular levels in the situation."
(3) "Cue redundancy is incorporated in the model since the *B* weights are determined by the correlational structure of cues (and the correlation of cues with the judgment)."
(4) The inconsistency and random error in judgment, resulting from the lack of cognitive control in executing one's strategy ... is explicitly defined and measured within regression procedures." (pp. 467–468)

Statistical Caveats when Capturing Policies with Regression Models. Even though the linear model can be linked with an underlying conception of human behavior, a number of caveats are in order. The first pertains to common practice in capturing a teacher's policy—using standard regression analysis packages with ordinary least squares (OLS) to estimate teachers' policies and then aggregating policies (i.e., regression coefficients) over teachers. Cadwell (1979; Borko & Cadwell, 1982) has pointed out that this seemingly reasonable approach may rest on a number of possibly untenable assumptions regarding teachers' decision strategies. One assumption is that the teacher applies a consistent strategy for making decisions over a sequence of vignettes—i.e., the regression coefficients remain constant *within* a teacher. This implies that the teacher does not have a decision strategy that changes over time, that the teacher does not change strategies due to boredom or fatigue, and that the teacher does not change strategies as a consequence of learning. "Even random fluctuations in the coefficients, resulting from subjects' inability to maintain a consistent weighting of the information, are not allowed" (Cadwell, 1979, p. 11). This is tough medicine to swallow since many policy capturing tasks are time consuming and inherently repetitive in order to maintain control over the independent variables.

Table 3.9. Alternative Estimation Procedures When Regression Coefficients Are Not Fixed

Type of Variation	Source of Variation	
	Within-Teacher	Between-Teacher
Systematic	Introduce explanatory variables for variation in parameter (e.g., time)	Find homogeneous groups of teachers Introduce moderator variables
Random	Use a random coefficient model (e.g., Hildreth & Houck, 1968)	Use a random coefficient model (e.g., Swamy, 1970)

Note. Adapted from Cadwell (1975, p. 15).

A second assumption about between-teacher homogeneity is made when data are pooled over more than one teacher to obtain estimates of the "average" judgment/decision policy. That is, all teachers are assumed to apply the same policy. Borko and Cadwell (1982), for example, have shown that this is not the case. Indeed, they found that even subgroups of teachers sharing the same policy were hard to find.

If regression coefficients are not fixed, either due to within-teacher variability or between-teacher variability, OLS may produce biased estimates of the regression coefficients, depending especially on whether the variation is systematic or random. Table 3.9 summarizes this discussion and presents some options recommended by Cadwell (1979).

A second caveat concerns the seemingly good fit of linear models to the policy capturing data. Linear models can account for a substantial portion of the variability in teachers' judgments and decisions, perhaps so much so that the results might be overinterpreted. "One reason ... that linear models perform so well is that they have been investigated in contexts in which the true relationships, whatever they are, tend to be conditionally monotone" (Dawes & Corrigan, 1974, p. 98). That is, no matter how they score on other variables, students who score high on published achievement tests are more likely to do better in classroom achievement situations. Teachers' judgments and decisions reflect this relation. Furthermore, say Dawes and Corrigan,

variables that do not have a conditionally monotone relationship to the criterion variable tend to have a single peak relationship that is easily converted to a monotone relationship by changing from raw units to units of worth or predictability. ... An intelligence test may then be rescored in terms of the absolute distance from 100—that is, rescaled to measure "intellectual mediocrity." (1974, p. 99)

A second reason why linear models fit so well is that regression weights are not affected by error in the criterion variable. Errors of measurement in the independent variables can increase the magnitude of some regression coefficients while decreasing the magnitude of the others as a complex function of the reliabilities of each of the variables and their interrelations. Measurement error also "tends to make optimal functions more linear — that is, curves separating values on the dependent variable tend to become flatter" (Dawes & Corrigan, 1974, p. 99).

Parenthetically, we should point out that, historically, regression models were developed not to represent cognitive processes but to *predict* judgments of a skilled clinician. This use of linear models was called "bootstrapping." The intent was to develop a simple actuarial model that rendered judgments as well as or better than the clinician. And indeed the linear model did, and a lively controversy has ensued ever since (see Goldberg, 1976; Gough, 1962).

ECOLOGICAL VALIDITY OF REGRESSION MODELS

Linear models aside, there are several other threats to the validity of interpretations of regression models as providing a "simulation" of (teachers') "real-world" judgments and decisions (see Einhorn & Hogarth, 1981; Ebbesen & Konecni, 1980). Perhaps the most problematic threat is that most studies are artificial; they do not examine judgments and decisions *in vivo*. They often employ factorial designs such that the cues (independent variables) in the vignettes are uncorrelated. In actual classroom settings, however, most cues are correlated. The teacher does not have to live with judgments and decisions made in a laboratory task; the decisions themselves are abstractions of actual decisions teachers might make. Furthermore, teachers' classroom decisions usually are not "once and for all." Rather, they are made incrementally and adjusted on the basis of subsequent information (feedback).

Regression modeling studies, then, do not provide a "high fidelity" simulation of actual teaching decisions. This is not to say that researchers have been remiss in selecting variables, constructing stimulus materials, and so on; the internal validity of most of these studies is impeccable. Rather, it means that generalizing from the results of regression modeling studies to teaching practice or recommendations for teacher education may be hazardous. (But see Shavelson, 1976 and Borko & Shavelson, 1983 for potential applications of policy capturing simulations to teacher training; see Hammond & Adelman, 1976, for an application resolving a conflict over local government policy.)

A second, related problem has to do with the fact that much of the hard part of decision making has been accomplished by the time the teacher arrives at the laboratory. Researchers select variables that teachers, prior research, and theory say should be important in the judgmental or decision process. In order to make tasks manageable, they have pared the number of variables. However, in making classroom decisions, teachers have to seek information themselves, avoiding pitfalls of irrelevant or misleading information. Furthermore, many regression modeling studies present what originally might be quantitative information in the form of qualitative or ordered information. For example, a student might be described as a year below grade level rather than by a raw score or a grade equivalent score. Much of the information processing is done before the teacher begins the laboratory task. Some regression modeling studies, then, may tell us more about *the demands of the experimental task* than about what information teachers use to arrive at pedagogical judgments and decisions.

Regression modeling is a delicate instrument for capturing teachers' policies. Its statistical and design foibles are severe enough to make skeptical even its strongest proponents. Nevertheless, used wisely, regression modeling has demonstrated its utility in identifying key variables and the direction of their relation with judgments and decisions. When designed well and interpreted in light of its remaining methodological uncertainties, the regression modeling technique can provide important information on teachers' judgments and decisions.

Process Tracing

Process tracing refers to verbal report methods that attempt to obtain data on the "intellectual processes used by subjects as they render judgments and make decisions or solve problems" (Shulman & Elstein, 1975, p. 4; see also Slovic, Fischhoff, & Lichtenstein, 1977). Although process tracing has been used to refer to a variety of methods (Shulman & Elstein, 1975), it most commonly describes research in which a subject is asked to (a) "think aloud" or "talk aloud" while performing a task, (b) recall thoughts after having completed a task, or (c) think aloud while viewing a videotape of himself performing a task. The first method is usually called a "think aloud" method; the second is often called a retrospective interview; and the third is called stimulated recall.

Each method produces a verbal protocol (and sometimes accompanying written material). The protocol is interpreted as a series of mental operations that the researcher infers that the subject used to reach a judgment, decision, or problem solution. It may serve as the basis of a verbal characterization of a subject's thought processes, as data for a content analysis, or as data for the development of a computer program that attempts to simulate the subject's decision making or problem solving.

In a study of instructional planning, for example, Peterson et al. (1978) asked each of 12 experienced teachers to "think aloud" as they planned their social studies lessons for three different classes of eight randomly assigned junior high students. "The teachers first listened to a model 'think aloud' tape as an introduction to the procedure. Then they were asked to talk into the tape recorder while planning their lessons" (p. 421).

The audiotapes were replayed and coded using the "Teacher Planning Coding System" (Peterson et al., 1978, p. 421). The coding system contained five substantive dimensions — objectives, subject matter, instructional process, materials, learner — and a "miscellaneous" category "for utterances that did not fit one of the five substantive categories" (p. 421). Peterson et al. interpreted the planning statements in the "think aloud" protocols as indicative of "one aspect of the *mental life* [italics added] of the teacher" (p. 431).

Teachers cannot "think aloud" while conducting a class discussion, presenting a lecture, or helping an individual student. To study teachers' thoughts, judgments, and decisions during interactive teaching, then, classroom interactions must be captured and stored until the students have left and the teacher can think aloud while reviewing the events recorded earlier. The method for doing this is *stimulated recall* (Bloom, 1953; for a technical exposition of the method applied to research on teaching, see Tuckwell, n.d.-a, n.d.-b). According to Bloom (1953):

> The basic idea underlying the method of stimulated recall is that a subject may be enabled to relive an original situation with vividness and accuracy if he is presented with a large number of cues or stimuli which occurred during the original situation. ... With cues such as these to furnish the framework, a great many associations will return—many with great vividness. Since the individual is a participant in an event ... this type of investigation can be carried on in such a way as to have only minimal effect on the nature of the original situation. (p. 161)

Today stimulated recall typically involves video- or audio-taping a lesson. This tape, replayed as soon as possible after the lesson, then serves as a stimulus to elicit the teacher's thought processes. The technique assumes that teachers can and will recall and articulate their thought processes, and do so completely and accurately.

Peterson and Clark (1978; see also McNair, 1978–79), for example, videotaped four brief (2–3 minute) segments of a social studies lesson. The first and fourth segments included the initial and last 2–3 minutes of the lessons, respectively; the other two segments covered randomly determined points in between. After viewing each segment, each teacher's answers to the following questions were tape-recorded: (a) What were you doing and why? (b) What were you noticing about the students? How were the students responding? (c) Were you thinking of any alternative actions or strategies at that time? And (d) did any students' reactions cause you to act differently than you had planned? A group of coders categorized the teachers' audio-taped responses as reflecting one of four alternative sequences of decisions about whether or not to change their behavior.

RELIABILITY OF PROCESS-TRACING DATA

Questions can be raised about the reliability of the verbal report data themselves, the reliability of the researcher's coding of the data, or both. In fact, reliability is seldom mentioned, let alone estimated in process-tracing studies.

In the case of the verbal report data, the absence of reliability studies is understandable. What would constitute evidence of reliability? Certainly two verbal protocols based on a subject's performance on two strictly equivalent tasks will not be identical. Words, sentences, and "paragraphs" will differ because thought processes may be expressed in different ways, and the sequence of these thought processes may not be exactly the same. If verbal protocols based on equivalent vignettes can be expected to vary, then perhaps the same decision or problem-solving processes should be evident in the protocols. But at this point, reliability estimates would refer to the consistency with which a particular coding scheme can be applied—one that records, say, the kinds and numbers of statements about processes. Questions about the reliability of the verbal report data themselves, then, must be resolved by determining their validity in, for example, predicting behavior on similar tasks using (say) a computer simulation. We are willing to infer minimally adequate reliability if validity can be demonstrated.

Reliability of coders' counts or ratings from protocols can readily be estimated; generalizability theory is particularly well

Table 3.10. Generalizability of Coders' Counts of Teachers' "Think Aloud" Statements
[Teachers (Random) × Coders (Random) × Days (Fixed)]

Category	Statements About	G Coefficient
Objectives	Student outcomes of instruction	.79
Subject Matter	Material contained in text, or concepts, principles (etc.) derived from text material	.99
Questions		
Lower-Order	Material stated verbatim from text	.92
Higher-Order	Material interpreted from text	.76
Instructional Process	Activity or tactic teacher intends to take during instruction	.99
Materials	Instructional and noninstructional materials and other aspects of the physical environment	.85
Learner	Attributes of student cognitive development, ability, affect	.75
Miscellaneous	Other statements	.48
Productivity	Total number of statements	.99

Note: Adapted from Peterson et al. (1978, p. 422).

suited for the task. Peterson et al., for example, examined the generalizability of coders' counts of teachers' statements falling into one of the five substantive categories, a miscellaneous category, and a "productivity" category. The generalizability coefficients in Table 3.10 are estimated from a mixed model design that crossed coders, assumed to be a random facet, and days (the three lessons each teacher taught), assumed to be a fixed facet. In general, the data indicated adequate levels of reliability for most uses of process-tracing data.

In their stimulated recall study, Peterson and Clark (1978) had coders tally, for each teacher, the occurrence of each of four decision sequences over three 50-minute lessons (days). For their two-facet mixed design—coders (random) by days (fixed)—the generalizability (reliability) coefficients ranged from .57 to .92.

VALIDITY OF COGNITIVE INTERPRETATIONS OF PROCESS-TRACING DATA

Process tracing produces verbal report data that are still branded as a suspect source of evidence because they are *introspective*. "As Lashley (1923) said in a vigorous and widely cited attack on the method, 'introspection may make the preliminary survey, but it must be followed by the chain and transit of objective measurement'" (Ericsson & Simon, 1980, p. 216).

One reason the debate over introspection has ebbed and waned for more than 50 years is because, lacking guidelines distinguishing legitimate verbal report data from suspicious introspections, proponents and opponents of verbal reports could talk past one another. On what grounds, for example, would behaviorists accept as valid a subject's "yes" or "no" to a stimulus, but reject other forms of verbalization as illegitimate? A second reason the debate thrived is that the validity of the data produced by different methods for eliciting verbal reports—for example think aloud, retrospective interview, stimulated recall—has not been evaluated. The absence of guidelines on methods encouraged some to reject verbal report data whole-sale.

Characterization of Process-Tracing Measurements. A first step in examining the validity of process-tracing measurements is to characterize differences among them. An analysis of these methods following on Ericsson's and Simon's (1980) seminal work shows that process-tracing protocols vary along at least four dimensions. The first dimension is *time* — verbal reports are given concurrently with task performance in the think aloud method but retrospectively in a retrospective interview or stimulated recall. The second dimension is the *form* of the information being processed in the task — verbal or nonverbal (e.g., pictures, imagery). The third is the *demands* placed on the respondent by the researcher's probes. The think-aloud-and-tell-all method asks for information normally available. However, it is also possible to request information not normally available, as when the subject is asked to edit information in a particular way. And the fourth dimension is the *breadth* of the event reported. The verbalization in think aloud and stimulated recall methods might report on cognitive processes during a specific and well-circumscribed event while performing a task. Or a retrospective interview might be general and broad, asking for reports on cognitive processes after a lengthy task has just been performed. Sometimes subjects are even asked to report on the cognitive processes they would use while performing a *similar* task, or on their cognitive strategy in carrying out the task. Variations among process-tracing methods along these four dimensions are summarized in the first column of Table 3.11.

Having distinguished among verbal report methods, our next step is to draw out the consequences of their similarities and differences for the validity of process-tracing data. Specifically, we seek to distinguish these methods as to their effect on the completeness of the data, on the time needed to perform the task itself, and on the structure and course of the cognitive processes revealed (see Table 3.11). In short, we seek a theory that explains the data obtained by each of these methods, a theory of the measuring instrument. Ericsson and Simon (1980) define the problem thus:

> The expansion of theories to include a theory of the measuring instruments is commonplace in physics. ... experiments that record verbal responses of any kind need at least a rudimentary theory of how subjects produce such responses — in what memories the response information has been stored, what demands the response makes on short-term memory, whether responses can go on in parallel with other behaviors, and so on. (p. 216)

ERICSSON AND SIMON'S THEORY

Ericsson and Simon provided just such a theory. We will briefly outline it here in order to provide grounds for evaluating the validity of process-tracing protocols. The theory has as its central component a psychological model of how humans process information. It assumes that human cognition can be represented as "a sequence of internal states [that are] successively

Table 3.11. Validity of Verbal Protocols as a Function of Reporting Technique

Techniques for Eliciting Verbal Protocols	Name	Effect on Verbal Protocol		
		Completeness	Time to Process	Structure and Course of Cognitive Process
I. *Concurrent*[a] report of *verbal* information:				
(1) *Normally* available (nondirective probe)	Think (talk) aloud	As complete as possible	Negligible	No distortion
(2) *Not normally* available (directive probe)	Think (talk) aloud with probe constraint	Slight decrement	Increase	Possible change, distortion
II. *Concurrent* report of *nonverbal* information:				
(1) *Normally* available (nondirective probe)	Think (talk) aloud	Slight decrement	Slight increase	No distortion
(2) *Not normally* available (directive probe)	Think (talk) aloud with probe constraint	Decrement	Increase	Possible change, distortion
III. Retrospective report using:				
(1) Clear, specific (short-term) probes immediately afterwards	Retrospective/ specific	Slight decrement	None[b]	Possible distortion
(2) Unclear probes of task in general	Retrospective/ general	Inaccurate	None[b]	Distortion
(3) Probes unrelated to the task	Retrospective/ unrelated	Inaccurate	None[b]	Distortion
IV. Retrospective report based on extensive retrieval cues eliciting:				
(1) Information normally available	Stimulated recall[a]	Some decrement	None[b]	Some distortion
(2) Information not normally available (specific probes)	Stimulated recall	Decrement	None[b]	Distortion

[a] Concurrent reports and reports based on stimulated recall are, by definition reports of specific events as they occur.
[b] Retrospective reports of cognitive processes do not, of course, affect processing time when it originally occurred.

transformed by a series of information processes" (p. 223). Information is retained ("stored") in several, not necessarily separate, memories, each having different capacities and methods for assessing characteristics of the information. For our purposes, the two most important memories are short-term memory (STM) and long-term memory (LTM). STM is a limited-capacity memory of relatively short duration (if its contents are not rehearsed) containing information most recently attended to (i.e., "heeded"). LTM is a large-capacity memory with relatively permanent storage. Considerably more time is required to store information in it than in STM.

The model assumes that information recently acquired is stored in STM and is directly available for further processing, such as for solving a problem or *producing verbal reports*. The attractiveness of the "think aloud" method is that the protocols are obtained, more or less directly, from STM and are believed to be closely linked to ongoing cognitive processes. More specifically, if the task involves manipulation of verbal stimuli (e.g., assigning students to reading groups on the basis of classroom behavior, reading ability, and so on), verbal reports may be more or less direct. If the task involves nonverbal stimuli (e.g., pictures, images), these nonverbal stimuli need to be translated into verbal form. This translation process makes modest demands on STM's processing capacity, perhaps slowing up cognitive processes but probably not distorting them (Ericsson & Simon, 1980). If the person has overlearned the task (e.g., multiplying two single-digit numbers), cognitive processes become highly automated and the verbal protocol may be sketchy. Nevertheless cognitive processing will probably not be slowed or distorted.

The model hypothesizes that before some of the contents of STM are lost, they are transferred to LTM. Information in LTM sometimes can be retrieved at a later point in time, but data retrieved retrospectively from LTM is considerably more limited because (a) when stored, the contents of LTM reflect only a portion of the contents of STM; (b) the data retrieved from LTM depend on the adequacy of search of LTM; and (c) the person may reconstruct, or even invent this information, in part, by replacing gaps inferentially. Hence, the model may distinguish think aloud data retrieved from STM from retrospective or stimulated recall data retrieved after a search of LTM.

Some process-tracing techniques have people report only some portion of their thinking, usually that part related to the researcher's hypotheses. The greater the constraints placed on the person by these probes, the greater their potential for interrupting ongoing cognitive processes, altering their sequences, increasing processing time, and producing incomplete information.

How accurate is this theory of verbal report data? To answer this question, Ericsson and Simon (1980) reviewed a large number of studies employing a wide variety of techniques for eliciting verbal reports. Their theory was used to predict characteristics of verbal report data when different methods are employed. The characteristics predicted are; *completeness*, the *structure* and *course* of cognitive processes revealed, and their impact on the *time* needed to complete the task. The methods might vary as to whether (a) concurrent and retrospective verbalizations were used — that is, think aloud versus retrospective methods, (b) probes were used, (c) data sought by the researcher would not be heeded in the normal course of processing, and (d) the task involved visual rather than verbal processing. Based on Ericsson and Simon's theory and review, we drew implications about the validity of process-tracing data commonly collected in research on teaching. These implications are summarized in the body of Table 3.11.

Predictions Based on the Theory. The think aloud method is characterized by reporting Techniques 1 and 2 in Table 3.11. Technique 1, the think aloud method applied to verbal tasks, theoretically provides the most valid data on cognitive processes. According to theory, it produces verbal protocols as complete as possible, has a negligible effect on processing time, and does not distort the structure and course of cognitive processes. Note that we do not claim that verbal report data reflect actual (neural) cognitive processes. Rather, we claim that they should provide the best data for constructing as-if models or simulations of these processes. Such models are expected to predict actual behavior better than models based on less trustworthy verbal report data.

Technique 2 provides concurrent reports of processes involving nonverbal information. It appears to increase processing time but not otherwise to distort the data. However, incorporating probes into the think aloud method runs the risk of lengthening processing time and distorting the structure and course of cognitive processes.

Retrospective methods — especially retrospective interviews — fare considerably less well. What evidence is there to support a cognitive-process interpretation of retrospective interviews? Although clear, specific probes immediately after a short-term event may provide data having only minor distortion and a slight decrement in completeness, unclear probes or probes unrelated to the task (e.g., "Would you use the same thinking processes in a similar task?") are likely to produce inaccurate data. In particular, the respondent is likely to fill gaps of missing information by inference, thereby reporting a version of cognitive activity that is not necessarily accurate in reflecting the structure and course of cognitive processes.

Stimulated recall presents an important alternative to retrospective interviews and a necessary alternative to think aloud methods in studying interactive teaching. With its rich source of stimuli — namely, replay of the teaching event — certainly the cues are available with which to improve the search of long-term memory and retrieval of the particulars of the past event. What evidence is there, then, to support the validity of a cognitive-process interpretation of stimulated recall data?

Bloom and his students (e.g., Gaier, 1954) assumed that a subject's ability to recall cognitive processes using stimulated recall could be indexed by his ability to recall overt behavior. Bloom (1953) reported that subjects were sometimes able to recall overt behavior such as classroom activities, specific talk, or particular gestures with as high as 95% accuracy up to 2 days afterwards: "The inference that the recall of one's own private, conscious thoughts approximates the recall of the overt, observable events has led to the anticipation that the accuracy of the recall of conscious thought is high enough for most studies ... if the interviews are made within a short time after the event" (p. 162; cf Gaier, 1954). To link recall of cognitive processes with recall of overt behavior required a heroic leap of faith since no adequate bridge between the two had been built.

To begin to bring evidence to bear on the validity of cognitive-process interpretations of stimulated recall data, we apply Ericsson and Simon's (1980) theory of the measuring instrument. Stimulated recall is retrospective; teachers are asked to reveal what they were thinking after completing a lesson. The fact that the videotape is potentially rich in detail permitting the teacher to "relive" the teaching event does not make the recall "concurrent"; thought processes one or more hours old are recalled from long-term memory. In Ericsson and Simon's terms, some part of the information regarding the teacher's thought processes must be stored in LTM and subsequently must be retrieved and placed into STM for the teacher to report this information. The videotape, by providing a recreation of the teaching event, provides a rich set of cues for retrieving cognitive-process information for a precisely delimited event. This means that the information retrieved will be at least somewhat incomplete and so invite the teacher to "fill in" the gaps (see Table 3.11).

The probes used to elicit information from the teacher in stimulated recall may vary greatly. McNair (1978–1979), for example, first asked teachers, "What were you thinking at that point?" Peterson and Clark (1978), in contrast, asked teachers about what they were doing, what they were perceiving (etc.), and then they probed very specifically about thinking—"Were you thinking of any alternative actions or strategies at that time?"—a probe directly related to hypotheses guiding their study. To the extent that the probes are specific and unrelated to ongoing cognitive processes, the structure and course of events may be distorted, and processing time will be increased (see Table 3.11).

In sum, stimulated recall is a technique for gathering retrospective reports of verbal and nonverbal thought processes under conditions of explicit and informationally rich recall cues regarding a well-circumscribed event. The technique, therefore, is limited to that information about cognitive processes that has been stored in LTM. This information is likely to be incomplete. As such, it invites the teacher to reconstruct and fill in memory gaps. (Tuckwell, n.d.-a went to some length in distinguishing data on teachers' thoughts from their editorializing or theorizing, but he did so on intuitive and empirical grounds. He observed that content analyses of protocols from stimulated recall sessions always contain both types of information.) The extent to which the limited amount of information on thought processes is retrieved undistorted depends on the nature of the probes used by the researcher. Probes such as McNair's "tell me what you're thinking" ask the teacher to report information normally available. Probes such as Peterson and Clark's "were you thinking of any alternative actions" require the teacher to search for specific information that might not normally be heeded and so may distort the thought processes reported.

Technique 4 in Table 3.11 evaluates the impact of retrospective reports of cognitive processes from well-circumscribed events. Classification (1) seems to come closest to stimulated recall in which the teacher is asked to report his thoughts. In this case, a slight decrement in the completeness of

the report should be expected because not all information in STM is transferred to LTM for later recall. This technique may distort data on the structure and course of cognitive processes due to the teacher's filling in of the informational gaps. However, this distortion can be reduced by carefully analyzing the teacher's recall data to distinguish information about cognitive processes from the teacher's attempts to fill gaps in the information. Stimulated recall with probes is expected to decrease the completeness of the data and distort them.

The descriptions presented in Table 3.11, however, do not bear on the relation between reports of cognitive processes and overt behavior. Yet this is the crux of the controversy involving verbal reports as legitimate data on cognitive processes (Nisbett & Wilson, 1977). What does the information-processing model predict and what has been found on this score?

RELATIONSHIP BETWEEN PROCESS-TRACING DATA AND OVERT BEHAVIOR

The model predicts with substantial accuracy (Ericsson & Simon, 1980) that two processes can produce verbal reports inconsistent with behavior. "First, cues used to access LTM, if too general, could retrieve information related to, but not identical with, the information that was actually sought" (Ericsson & Simon, 1980, p. 243). The second source of inconsistency arises when respondents attempt to fill in informational gaps by inferring missing information. Ericsson and Simon concluded that "in most of the cases in which inconsistency has been observed or claimed, the verbal reports were retrospective" (p. 243).

Perhaps the most impressive demonstration of the link between data on cognitive processes and behavior comes from artificial intelligence research (e.g., Newell & Simon, 1972). Think aloud data—those data predicted by Ericsson and Simon's theory of the measuring instrument to be most valid for representing cognitive processes (see Table 3.11)—have been used to construct a computer simulation of how a person solves, for example, cryptoarithmetic problems (Newell & Simon, 1972), how a physician diagnoses a patient's illness (e.g., Duda & Shortliffe, 1983), or how a reading teacher diagnoses a student's reading problems (Vinsonhaler, 1983). The goal is to create a computer program that behaves like the person in the problem-solving situation, that is, able to solve some problems, not others, make the same types of errors, and so on. For well-circumscribed tasks such as cryptoarithmetic and solving the Tower of Hanoi problem, computer simulations of actual performance have been remarkably accurate. Simulations of more complex tasks such as medical diagnosis (Duda & Shortliffe, 1983), geometry problem solving (Greeno, 1976), and diagnosis of reading problems (Vinsonhaler, 1979, 1983) have also provided reasonably accurate, if incomplete, analogs to actual behavior.

Comparison of Regression Modeling and Process-Tracing Methods

Intuition suggests that regression modeling and process-tracing methods are quite different. Although both methods purport to measure some aspects of cognitive processing, the former takes a "black box" approach to inferring these processes while the latter attempts to describe them as directly as possible (Shulman & Elstein, 1975). However, such a cursory comparison begs an underlying conception of the judgment or decision process and so is superficial. Here we briefly present one possible conceptualization of this process, compare the two methods with respect to that conceptualization, and briefly review two studies that have empirically compared the methods.

One possible conception of the judgment/decision process (cf. Cadwell, 1979; Einhorn et al., 1979) assumes that there is information relevant to the decision and independent of the decision maker. The decision maker seeks, selects, and internally represents this information. In order to make a judgment or reach a decision, the decision maker combines or integrates the diverse information through a sequence of information-processing transformations. An early view of such a process was put forth by Ben Franklin, who recommended adding up the positive and negative pieces of information for each alternative. The result of this integrative process is then transformed into overt behavior judgment, or a decision. Franklin recommended choosing the alternative where the pluses most outweighed the minuses. Feedback, based on the outcome of a judgment or decision, serves to modify the preceding processing components. While this description is linear, the decision-making sequence may not be; later steps in the process can influence earlier ones as the decision maker cycles back and forth. The components of the judgment/decision-making conceptualization are enumerated in Table 3.12.

Most research on judgment and decision making focuses on the information integration process. This is true of both regression modeling and process tracing. In this research, information search, selection, and representation are often skipped by assuming a one-to-one correspondence between the objective information presented and that acquired by the decision maker. Such an assumption is more characteristic of regression modeling approaches than of process tracing since the researcher exerts greater control over both the stimuli and the responses with the former than with the latter. For this reason, process tracing is clearly richer in detail. According to Einhorn et al. (1979), this sense of richness is further "strengthened by the fact that the process-tracing model has been developed inductively, whereas the regression model has been derived deductively" from Brunswik's theory of judgment (p. 470).

Response processes are often skipped by assuming that the judgment or decision reached covertly is identical to the observed response. This again is more characteristic of regression modeling than of process tracing (Table 3.12). The feedback/ learning component of decision making is inherent in both methods but often is considered a nuisance—in regard to its instability in the application of a decision policy—more than an object of study (however, see Einhorn & Hogarth, 1978).

Based on this conception of judgment and decision making, there are a number of factors on which the methods differ. First, process tracing, unlike regression modeling, preserves some of the details of the decision maker's search for information. This information search can be carried out in, for example, the teacher's natural environment, not necessarily in a laboratory. Furthermore, process tracing sheds some light on how decision

Table 3.12. Comparison of Regression and Process-Tracing Methods on Their Ability to Access Components of a Model of Decision Making

Components of Judgment/Decision Processes	Process Tracing	Regression Modeling
Information search	Yes	No
Information selection	Yes	Limited
Information representation	Yes	No
Information combination	Yes	Yes
Response processes	Yes	No
Feedback/learning	Yes	Yes

makers internally represent this information. (But see the discussion of verbal reports of nonverbal information above.) Second, process tracing provides richer detail on the process of reaching a judgment or decision. It attempts to find general rules based on a verbal protocol taken from specific tasks whereas regression modeling captures a general strategy embellished in a theory of judgment. Third, regression modeling "smooths over" fluctuations that arise when individuals apply different strategies to information that has (roughly) the same relation with the outcome. This statistical modeling, then, is less likely than process tracing to identify these different strategies. Fourth, regression modeling has the tendency to identify either more variables underlying a decision than are actually used (Ebbesen & Konecni, 1982) or to identify variables that are not actually present in subjects' verbal protocols (Cadwell & Leary, 1982). Fifth, regression modeling provides a stochastic model of judgment and decision making—a characteristic component of decision makers' behavior—while the process tracing approach usually yields a deterministic model.

Process tracing and regression modeling, then, are clearly different approaches to studying cognitive processes of decision makers. However, are they different in kind or just in level of abstraction? Should they be considered alternative methods for measuring the same construct or measures of different constructs?

Einhorn et al. (1979) argue pursuasively that "although the models that result from each seem quite different, the difference is not with respect to the *underlying process* [italics added] uncovered but rather with each model's different emphasis and descriptive level of detail" (p. 465). In measurement terms, these alternative methods measure the same construct albeit at different levels of abstraction.

Data reported by Einhorn et al. (1979) and Cadwell and Leary (1982) generally support the interpretation that both methods measure some important aspects of cognitive processes. Cadwell and Leary, for example, presented three teacher consultants (experts in learning disabilities) information about the intelligence, reading, and mathematics achievement, classroom behavior, sex and socioeconomic status of 50 hypothetical students and asked them to place each student into one of three classrooms—a regular classroom, a classroom for educationally disabled students, or a classroom for learning-disabled students. These teacher–consultants were asked to think aloud as they placed the first (randomly ordered) 25 students; the last 25 served cross-validation purposes.

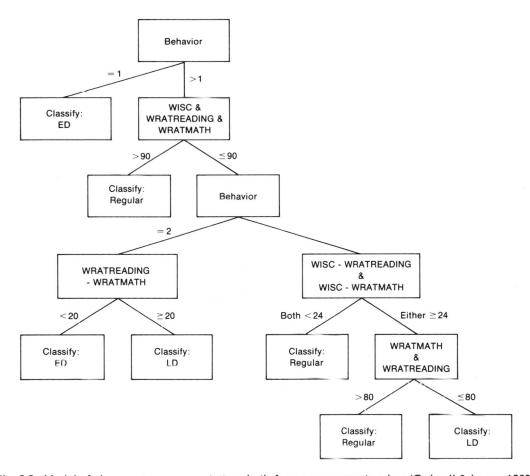

Fig. 3.2. Model of placement recommendations built from process tracing data (Cadwell & Leary, 1982).

From the verbal protocols, an analysis was made of each teacher–consultant's decision process and charted. Figure 3.2 shows a flow chart for one teacher–consultant's placement decisions. The flow chart indicates the order in which the teacher requested information: behavior rating, IQ, achievement, sex, and SES. The behavior variable predominated, entering the decision process in two ways: (a) first as an overall screen—if behavior is potentially dangerous to the student or other students (= 1) then classify him or her as educationally disabled; and (b) as an indicator, along with low reading and mathematics achievement, for classifying the student for special education.

From this flow chart, a computer program was written to simulate each consultant's decision processes. The decisions based on the computer program for each of the 50 students were compared with the teacher's placement decisions. For the 25 students for whom verbal report data were collected and upon whom the simulation was based, the model and the teacher–consultant agreed on 88% of the placement decisions. For the remaining 25, 85% agreement was obtained. According to Cadwell and Leary:

An examination of those profiles over which there was disagreement indicated that the disagreement resulted more from the subject's [teacher–consultant's] inconsistent use of a strategy than an inade-

quacy in the process model. ... However, since process-tracing models do not contain an error component, there was no means for incorporating the subject's inconsistencies when applying the placement policy." (1982, p. 10)

(Here we disagree. The computer program could have incorporated a stochastic process reflecting these inconsistencies. The problem is to ascertain the magnitude and function of this process.)

The teacher–consultant's placement decisions also were discriminated on the information about student intelligence, achievement, sex, and SES using discriminant analysis. The most important variable in discriminating among the teacher–consultant's placements, far and away, was evidence of problematic behavior. In addition, reading, mathematics achievement, and sex also reliably discriminated among placements. The statistical model placed 82% of the hypothetical students into the same classrooms as did the teacher–consultant.

Both methods, then, were similar in identifying what information was needed to simulate the teacher–consultant's judgment. Both replicated the teacher–consultant's placement decisions with about the same accuracy, above 80%.

The models, however, disagreed about some variables used to make the placement decisions and the way in which information was combined to reach those decisions. First, the statistical model included the variable, sex, while the process-tracing data gave no indication that the teacher–consultant considered this information. And the statistical model ignored data on intelligence while the process-tracing model included it. Second, the statistical model applied the same strategy to all data while the process-tracing model used different placement strategies for different levels of problematic behavior. And third, the computer model did not contain an error component reflecting variation in the consistency with which the teacher–consultant applied strategy, while the statistical model did.

The two methods, then, are similar in that they show a reasonable amount of consistency in the variables identified for decision making, the relative importance of these variables, and, with notable exceptions, how those variables were combined (Table 3.12).

In the abstract, the two methods appear to measure the same construct. Nevertheless, one caveat is in order. The similarity between the two methods might be as much as function of the requirements of simple computer programs such as those used by Cadwell and Leary (1982) and Einhorn et al. (1979) as they are of the abstract similarity of data obtained with the methods. This is because such programs require data to be segmented into components and integrated back into a sequential, stepwise process. As Cadwell and Leary (1982) pointed out, their program did not capture the categorization processes that their teacher–consultants might reasonably be expected to use, both because of the requirement to report their thoughts verbally (words and linear sequences of words) and the need to translate the protocols into a simple sequential rather than a more complicated categorization program for the computer.

Concluding Remarks

Normally a chapter on measurement would contain relatively pure psychometrics, presenting the latest developments in metrics and scaling (e.g., item response theory), reliability (e.g., generalizability theory or item response theory), and validity (e.g., construct validation theory). However, in originally conceiving the chapter in this manner, we discovered inadequacies. In the end, we realized that any discussion of psychometrics cannot, and should not, be divorced from the phenomena they are used to model. As we hope we have made quite clear, substantive knowledge is a precursor to measuring the attributes of teaching. If not, psychometrically sophisticated analyses are likely to miss their target.

This chapter treats just the tip of the measurement iceberg for a number of reasons. First, the domain of measurement in research on teaching is enormous; far too broad for us to treat in any depth. Hence, our decision to deal with just three areas — measurement of teacher effectiveness, classroom process, and teacher cognition.

Second, each topic within the domain is terribly complex. This chapter raises as many questions about the measurement of effectiveness, process, and cognition as it answers.

Third, attempting to review the literature on the measurement of teaching is like trying to hit a moving target. Research is already underway using measurement techniques we have presented here and exploiting many of the measurement issues we raised (e.g., the various lines of instructional content

research, the research of Rogosa et al. (in press) on teacher behavior, and Cadwell's work on teacher ratings).

Finally, research on teaching is a psychometrician's nirvana and nemesis at the same time. As the research progresses into new areas at an explosive rate, measurement issues abound. There is practically no limit to the measurement problems in need of solution. But the problems are not easily dealt with by straightforward psychometric techniques based on simplified assumptions. Rather, these techniques must be built on a bedrock of substantive knowledge and the complexities that such knowledge reveals.

REFERENCES

Allen, M. J., & Yen, W. M. (1979). *Introduction to measurement theory.* Monterey, CA: Brooks/Cole Publishing Company.

Anderson, L. M. (1981). Short-term student responses to classroom instruction. *The Elementary School Journal, 82,* 97–108.

Anderson, L. M., Evertson, C. M., & Brophy, J. E. (1978). The First-Grade Reading Group Study: Technical report of experimental and process–outcome relationships (Report No. 4070). Austin TX: University of Texas, R & D Center for Teacher Education.

Anderson, L. M., Evertson, C. M., & Brophy, J. E. (1979). An experimental study of effective teaching in first-grade reading groups. *Elementary School Journal, 79,* 193–223.

Anderson, L. M., Morgan, R. O., Evertson, C. M., & Brophy, J. E. (1978). *Context effects and stability of teacher behaviors in an experimental study of first grade reading group instruction.* Paper presented at the Annual Meeting of the American Educational Research Association, Toronto.

Anderson, R. C. (1977). The notion of schemata and the educational enterprise: General discussion of the conference. In R. C. Anderson, R. S. Spiro, & W. E. Montague (Eds.), *Schooling and the acquisition of knowledge.* Hillsdale, NJ: Lawrence Erlbaum.

Anderson, R. C., Spiro, R. S., & Montague, W. E. (1977). *Schooling and the acquisition of knowledge.* Hillsdale, NJ: Lawrence Erlbaum.

Baker, E. L., & Herman, J. L. (1983). Task structure design: Beyond linkage. *Journal of Educational Measurement, 20,* 149–164.

Barr, R., & Dreeben, R. (1977). Instruction in classrooms. In L. S. Shulman (Ed.), *Review of Research in Education* (Vol. 5). Itasca, IL: F. E. Peacock.

Barr, R., & Dreeben, R. (1983). *How schools work.* Chicago: University of Chicago Press.

Berliner, D. C. (1980). Studying instruction in the elementary classroom. In R. Dreeben and J. A. Thomas (Eds.), *The analysis of educational productivity: Vol. 1. Issues in microanalysis.* Cambridge, MA: Ballinger.

Birenbaum, M., & Tatsuoka, K. K. (1980). *The use of information from wrong responses in measuring students' achievement* (Research Report 80-1 ONR). Urbana: University of Illinois Computer-Based Education Research Laboratory.

Block, J. H., & Burns, R. B. (1976). Mastery learning. In L. S. Shulman (Ed.), *Review of research in education* (Vol. 4). Itasca, IL: F. E. Peacock.

Bloom, B. S. (1953). Thought processes in lectures and discussions. *Journal of General Education, 7,* 160–170.

Bloom, B. S. (1976). *Human characteristics and school learning.* New York: McGraw-Hill.

Bock, R. D. (1960). Components of variance analysis as a structural and a discriminal analysis for psychological tests. *British Journal of Statistical Psychology, 13,* 151–163.

Bock, R. D. (1976). Basic issues in the measurement of change. In D. N. M. de Gruijter & L. J. T. van der Kamp (Eds.), *Advances in psychological and educational measurement.* New York: Wiley.

Bock, R. D., & Bargmann, R. E. (1966). Analysis of covariance structures. *Psychometrika, 31,* 507–533.

Bock, R. D., & Lieberman, M. (1970). Fitting a response model for N dichotomously scored items. *Psychometrika, 40,* 5–32.

Borich, G. D., Malitz, D., & Kugle, C. L. (1978). Convergent and discriminant validity of five classroom observation systems: Testing a model. *Journal of Educational Psychology, 70,* 119–128

Borko, H. (1978). *Factors contributing to teachers' preinstructional decisions about classroom management and long-term objectives.* Unpublished doctoral dissertation, University of California, Los Angeles.

Borko, H., & Cadwell, J. (1982). Individual differences in teachers' decision strategies: An investigation of classroom organization and management decisions. *Journal of Educational Psychology, 74,* 598–610.

Borko, H., & Shavelson, R. J. (1983). Speculations on teacher education: Implications of research on teachers' cognitions. *Journal of Education for Teaching, 9,* 210–224.

Brennan, R. L. (1980). Applications of generalizability theory. In R. A. Berk (ed.), *Criterion-referenced measurement: State of the art.* Baltimore: Johns Hopkins Press.

Brennan, R. L. (1983) *Elements of Generalizability Theory.* Iowa City, IA: The American College Testing Program.

Brophy, J. E. (1973). Stability in teacher effectiveness. *American Educational Research Journal, 10,* 245–252.

Brophy, J. E. (1975). *The student as the unit of analysis* (Report No. 75-12). Austin: University of Texas, Research and Development Center for Teacher Education.

Brophy, J. E. (1979). Teacher behavior and its effects. *Journal of Educational Psychology, 71*(6), 733–750.

Brophy, J. E., Coulter, C. L., Crawford, W. J., Evertson, C. M., & King, C. E. (1975). Classroom observation scales: Stability across time and context and relationships with student learning gains. *Journal of Educational Psychology, 67*(6), 873–881.

Brophy, J. E., & Evertson, C. M. (1974). *Process–product correlations in the Texas Teacher Effectiveness Study: Final report* (Report No. 74-4). Austin: University of Texas, R & D Center for Teacher Education.

Brophy, J. E., & Evertson, C. M. (1977). Teacher behavior and student learning in second and third grades. In G. D. Borich & K. S. Fenton (Eds.), *The appraisal of teaching: Concepts and process.* Reading, MA: Addison-Wesley.

Brophy, J. E., Evertson, C. M., Crawford, J, King, C., & Senior, K. (1975). Stability of measures of classroom process behaviors across three different contexts in second and third grade classrooms. *Catalog of Selected Documents in Psychology, 5,* 338.

Brown, B. W., & Saks, D. H. (1980). Production technologies and resource allocations within classrooms and schools: Theory and measurement. In R. Dreeben & J. A. Thomas (Eds.), *The analysis of educational productivity: Vol. I. Issues in microanalysis.* Cambridge, MA: Ballinger.

Brown, B. W., & Saks, D. H. (1981). Microeconomics of schooling. In D. C. Berliner (Ed.), *Review of research in education* (Vol. 9). Washington, DC: American Educational Research Association.

Brown, D. W., & Saks, D. H. (1983). *An economic approach to measuring the effects of instructional time on student learning.* Paper presented at the annual meeting of the American Educational Research Association, Montreal.

Brown, J. S., & Burton, R. R. (1978). Diagnostic model for procedural bugs in basic mathematical skills. *Cognitive Science, 2,* 155–192.

Brunswik, E. (1943). Organismic achievement and environmental probability. *Psychological Review, 50,* 255–272.

Bryk, A. S., Strenio, J. F., & Weisberg, H. I. (1980). A method for estimating treatment effects when individuals are growing. *Journal of Educational Statistics, 5,* 5–34.

Bryk, A. S., & Weisberg, H. I. (1977). Use of the nonequivalent control group design when subjects are growing. *Psychological Bulletin, 84,* 950–962.

Burstein, L. (1980a). The role of levels of analysis in the specification of educational effects. In R. Dreeben and J. A. Thomas (Eds.), *Analysis of educational productivity: Vol. I. Issues in microanalysis* (pp. 119–94). Cambridge, MA: Ballinger.

Burstein, L. (1980b). Analyzing multilevel educational data: The choice of an analytical model rather than a unit of analysis. In E. Baker and E. Quellmalz (Eds.), *Design, analysis, and policy in testing and evaluation* (pp. 81–94). Beverly Hill: Sage Publications.

Burstein, L. (in press). Units of analysis. In *International Encyclopaedia of Education: Research and Studies,* Oxford, U.K.: Pergamon.

Burstein, L., & Linn, R. L. (1981). *Analysis of educational effects from a multilevel perspective: Disentangling between- and within-class relationships on mathematics performance* (CSE Report Series 172). Los Angeles: University of California, Center for the Study of Evaluation.

Burstein, L., Linn, R. L., & Capell, F. S. (1978). Analyzing multilevel data in the presence of heterogeneous within-class regressions. *Journal of Educational Statistics, 3*(4), 347–383.

Burstein, L., Miller, M. D., & Linn, R. L. (1981). *The use of within-group slopes as indices of group outcomes* (CSE Report Series 171). Los Angeles: University of California, Center for the Study of Evaluation.

Byers, J. L., & Evans, T. E. (1980). *Using a lens-model analysis to identify factors in teaching judgement.* Research Series No. 73. East Lansing: Michigan State University, Institute for Research on Teaching.

Cadwell, J. (1979). *Regression models of teacher judgment and decision-making.* Unpublished doctoral dissertation, University of California, Los Angeles.

Cadwell, J., & Leary, L. F. (1982, March). The cognitive processes underlying the identification of children with learning and behavior problems. Paper presented at the annual meeting of the American Educational Research Association, New York.

Calfee, R. C. (1981). Cognitive psychology and educational practice. In D. C. Berliner (Ed.), *Review of research in education* (Vol. 9). Washington, DC: American Educational Research Association.

Calkins, D., Borich, G. D., Pascone, M., & Kugle, C. L. (1977). *Generalizability of teacher behaviors across classroom observation systems.* Paper presented at the annual meeting of the American Educational research Association, New York.

Cardinet, J., & Tourneur, Y. (1974, July–August). The facets of differenciation [*sic*] and generalization in test theory [shortened English version of the original test: Une theorie des tests pedagogiques]. Paper presented at the 18th Congress of the International Association of Applied Psychology, Montreal.

Cardinet, J., & Tourneur, Y. (1977). How to structure and measure educational objectives in periodic surveys. In R. Summer (Ed.), *Monitoring national standards of attainment in schools.* Slough, UK: National Foundation for Educational Research in England and Wales.

Cardinet, J., Tourneur, Y., & Allal, L. (1976a). The generalizability of surveys of educational outcomes. In D. N. M. De Gruijter & L. J. T. van der Damp (Eds.), *Advances in Psychological and Educational Measurement* (pp. 185–198). New York: Wiley.

Cardinet, J., Tourneur, Y., & Allal, L. (1976b). The symmetry of generalizability theory: Applications to educational measurement. *Journal of Educational Measurement, 13,* 119–135.

Cardinet, J., Tourneur, Y., & Allal, L. (1981). Extension of generalizability theory and its applications in educational measurement. *Journal of Educational Measurement, 18,* 183–204.

Carroll, J. B. (1963). A model for school learning. *Teachers College Record, 64,* 723–733.

Colbert, C. D., (1979). *Classroom teacher behavior and instructional organizational patterns.* Paper presented at the annual meeting of the American Educational Research Association, San Francisco.

Coleman, J. S., Campbell, E. G., Hobson, C. J., McPartland, J., Mood, A. M., Weinfeld, F. D., & York, R. L. (1966). *Equality of Educational Opportunity.* Washington, DC: U.S. Department of Health, Education, and Welfare, Office of Education.

Cone, R. (1978). *Teachers' classroom management decisions: A study of interactive decision-making.* Unpublished doctoral dissertation, University of California, Los Angeles.

Cooley, W. W. (1981). Understanding achievement test variables. In N. Sovik, H. M. Eikel & A. Lysne (Eds.), *On individualized instruction: Theories and research* (pp. 27–38). Oslo: Universitetsforlaget.

Cooley, W. W., & Leinhardt, G. (1980). The instructional dimensions study. *Educational Evaluation and Policy Analysis, 2,* 7–25.

Cooley, W. W., & Lohnes, P. R. (1976). *Evaluation research in education: Theory, principles, and practices.* New York: Irvington.

Copeland, W. D. (1979, March). *Teaching/learning behaviors and the demands of the classroom environment: An observational study.* Paper presented at the annual meeting of the American Educational Research Association, San Francisco.

Cornbleth, C., & Korth, W. (1979, April). *Instructional context and individual differences in pupil involvement in learning activity.* Paper presented at the annual meeting of the American Educational Research Association, San Francisco.

Cornbleth, C., & Korth, W. (1980). Context factors and individual differences in pupil involvement in learning activity. *Journal of Educational Research, 73,* 318-323.

Corno, L. (1979). A hierarchical analysis of selected naturally occurring aptitude-treatment interactions in the third grade. *American Educational Research Journal, 16*(4), 391-409.

Crawford, J., Brophy, J. E., Evertson, C. M., & Coulter, C. L. (1977). Classroom dyadic interaction: Factor structure of process variables and achievement correlates. *Journal of Educational Psychology, 69,* 761-772.

Crawford, W. J., & Stallings, J. (1978). *Experimental effects of in-service teacher training derived from process-product correlations in the primary grades.* Paper presented at the annual meeting of the American Educational Research Association, Toronto.

Cronbach, L. J. (with assistance of Deken, J. E. and Webb, N.) (1976). *Research on classrooms and schools: Formulation of questions, designs and analysis* (Occasional paper). Stanford, CA: Stanford Evaluation Consortium.

Cronbach, L. J., & Furby, L. (1970). How should we measure "change"—or should we? *Psychological Bulletin, 74,* 68-80.

Cronbach, L. J., Gleser, G. C., Nanda, H., & Rajaratnam, N. (1972). *The dependability of behavioral measurements: The theory of generalizability for scores and profiles.* New York: John Wiley.

Cronbach, L. J., Rajaratnam, N., & Gleser, G. C. (1963). Theory of generalizability: A liberalization of reliability theory. *British Journal of Statistical Psychology, 16,* 137-163.

Cronbach, L. J., & Snow, R. W. (1977). *Aptitudes and instructional methods.* New York: Irvington.

Cronbach, L. J., & Webb, N. (1975). Between-class and within-class effects in a reported aptitude × treatment interactions: Reanalysis of a study by G. L. Anderson. *Journal of Educational Psychology, 67,* 717-724.

Curtis, M. E., & Glaser, R. (1983). Reading theory and the assessment of reading achievement. *Journal of Educational Measurement, 20*(2), 133-147.

Dahllof, U. S. (1971). *Ability grouping, content validity, and curriculum process analysis.* New York: Teachers College Press, Columbia University.

Davis, R. B. (1979). *Error analysis in high school mathematics, conceived as information processing pathology.* Paper presented at the annual meeting of the American Educational Research Association, San Francisco.

Davis, R. B., & McKnight, C. (1976). Conceptual, heuristic, and algorithmic approaches in mathematics teaching. *Journal of Children's Mathematical Behavior, 1* (Supplement), 271-286.

Davis, R. B., & McKnight, C. (1979). Modeling the processes of mathematical thinking. *Journal of Children's Mathematical Behavior, 2,* 91-113.

Dawes, R. M., & Corrigan, B. (1974). Linear models in decision making. *Psychological Bulletin, 18,* 95-106.

de Finetti, B. (1964). Foresight: Its logical laws, its subjective sources. In H. E. Kyburg & G. E. Smokler (Eds.), *Studies in Subjective Probability.* New York: John Wiley.

Dorr-Bremme, D. (1982). Assessing students: Teachers' routine practices and reasoning. In J. Burry, J. Catterall, B. Choppin, & D. Dorr-Bremme (Eds.), *Testing in the nation's schools and districts: How much? What kinds? To what ends? At what costs?* (Report No. 194, pp. 18-51). Los Angeles: University of California, Center for the Study of Evaluation.

Doyle, W. (1977). Paradigms for research on teacher effectiveness. In L. Shulman (Ed.), *Review of research in education* (Vol. 5). Itasca, IL: F. E. Peacock.

Doyle, W. (1983). Academic work. *Review of Educational Research, 53*(2) 159-199.

Duda, R. O., & Shartliffe, E. H. (1983). Expert systems research. *Science, 220,* 261-268.

Dunkin, M., & Biddle, B. (1974). *The study of teaching.* New York: Holt, Rinehart & Winston.

Ebbesen, E. B., & Konecni, V. J. (1980). On the external validity of decision-making research: What do we know about decisions in the real world? In T. S. Wallsten (Ed.), *Cognitive processes in choice and decision behavior.* Hillside, NJ: Lawrence Erlbaum.

Eggert, W. (1978, March). *Teacher process variables and pupil products.* Paper presented at the annual meeting of the American Educational Research Association.

Einhorn, H. J., & Hogarth, R. M. (1978). Confidence in judgment: Persistence of the illusion of validity. *Psychological Review, 85,* 395-416.

Einhorn, H. J., & Hogarth, R. M. (1981). Behavioral desision theory: Process of judgement and choice. *Annual Review of Psychology, 32,* 53-58.

Einhorn, H. J., Kleinmuntz, D. N., & Kleinmuntz, B. (1979). Linear regression and process-tracing models of judgment. *Psychological Review, 86,* 465-485.

Emmer, E. T., Evertson, C. M., & Brophy, J. E. (1979). Stability of teacher effects in junior high classrooms. *American Educational Research Journal, 16*(1), 71-75.

Emmer, E. T., Evertson, C. M., Sanford, J., & Clements, B. S. (1982). *Improving classroom management: An experimental study in junior high classrooms.* Austin: University of Texas, R & D Center for Teacher Education.

Ericsson, K. A., & Simon, H. A. (1980). Verbal reports as data. *Psychological Review, 87,* 215-251.

Erlich, O., & Shavelson, R. J. (1976, September). *The application of generalizability theory to the study of teaching. Beginning teacher evaluation study* (Tech. Report No. 76-9-1). San Francisco: Far West Laboratory.

Erlich, O., & Shavelson, R. J. (1978). The search for correlations between measures of teacher behavior and student achievement: Measurement problem, conceptualization problem, or both? *Journal of Educational Measurement, 15,* 77-89.

Erlich, O., & Borich, G. (1979). Measuring classroom interactions: How many occasions are required to measure them reliably? *Journal of Educational Measurement, 16,* 11-18.

Evertson, C. M., Anderson, C. W., Anderson, L. M., & Brophy, J. E. (1980). Relationships between classroom behaviors and student outcomes in junior high mathematics and English classes. *American Educational Research Journal, 17,* 43-60.

Evertson, C. M., Anderson, L. M., & Brophy, J. E. (1978a). *Process-outcome relationships in the Texas junior high school study: Overview of methodology and rationale.* Paper presented at the annual meeting of the American Educational Research Association, Toronto.

Evertson, C. M., Anderson, L. M., & Brophy, J. E. (1978b). *Texas Junior High Study: Final report of process-outcome relationships* (Report No. 4061). Austin: University of Texas, R & D Center for Teacher Education.

Evertson, C. M., Emmer, E. T., & Brophy, J. E. (1980). Predictors of effective teaching in junior high mathematics classrooms. *Journal for Research in Mathematics Education, 11,* 167-178.

Evertson, C. M., Emmer, E. T., & Clements, B. S. (1980). *Junior high classroom organization study: Summary of training procedures and methodology* (Research and Development Report No. 6101). Austin: University of Texas, R & D Center for Teacher Education.

Evertson, C. M., Emmer, E. T., Sanford, J., & Clements, B. S. (1982). *Improving classroom management: An experimental study in elementary classrooms.* Austin: University of Texas, R & D Center for Teacher Education.

Evertson, C. M., & Hickman, R. C. (1981, March). *The tasks of teaching classes of varied group composition.* Austin: University of Texas, R & D Center for Teacher Education.

Evertson, C. M., & Veldman, D. J. (1981). Changes over time in process measures of classroom behavior. *Journal of Educational Psychology, 73,* 156-163.

Fiedler, M. L. (1975). Bidirectionality of influence in classroom interaction. *Journal of Educational Psychology, 67,* 735-744.

Filby, N. N., & Dishaw, M. M. (1976). Refinement of reading and mathematics tests through an analysis of reactivity. *Beginning teacher evaluation study* (Tech. Rep. No. III-b). San Francisco: Far West Laboratory.

Fisher, C., Filby, N., Marliave, R., Cahen, L. Dishaw, M., Moore, J., & Berliner, D. (1978). *Teaching behaviors, academic learning time, and student achievement. (Phase III-b, final report) Beginning teacher evaluation study.* San Francisco: Far West Laboratory.

Fitzgerald, J., Wright, E. N., Eason, G., & Shapson, S. (1978). *The effects of subject of instruction on the behavior of teachers and pupils.* Paper prepared for the annual meeting of the American Educational Research Association, Toronto.

Floden, R. E., Freeman, D. J., Porter, A. C., & Schmidt, W. H. (1980). Don't they all measure the same thing? Consequences of selecting standardized tests. In E. L. Baker & E. Quellmalz (Eds.). *Design, analysis and policy in testing and evaluation.* Beverly Hills: Sage Publications, 109–120.

Floden, R. E., Porter, A. C., Schmidt, W. H., Freeman, D. J., & Schwille, J. R. (1981). Responses to curriculum pressures: A policy-capturing study of teacher decisions about context. *Journal of Educational Psychology,* 73, 129–141.

Frick, T., & Semmel, M. I. (1978). Observer agreement and reliabilities of classroom observational measures. *Review of Educational Research,* 48, 157–184.

Gaier, E. L. (1954). A study of memory under conditions of stimulated recall. *Journal of General Psychology,* 50, 147–153.

Gil, D. (March 1980). *The decision-making and diagnostic processes of classroom teachers* (Research Series No. 71). East Lansing: Michigan State University, Institute for Research on Teaching.

Glaser, R. (Ed.). (1978). *Advances in instructional psychology* (Vol. 1). Hillsdale, NJ: Lawrence Erlbaum.

Glass, G. V., & Stanley, J. C. (1970). *Statistical methods in education and psychology.* Englewood Cliffs, NJ: Prentice-Hall.

Goldberg, L. R. (1976). Man versus model of man: Just how conflicting is that evidence? *Organizational Behavior and Human Performance,* 16, 13–22.

Good, T. L. (1979). Teacher effectiveness in the elementary school: What we know about it now. *Journal of Teacher Education,* 30(2), 52–64.

Good, T. L. (n.d.). Research on teaching, unpublished manuscript.

Good, T. L., & Beckerman, T. M. (1978). Time-on-task: A naturalistic study in sixth-grade classrooms. *Elementary School Journal,* 78, 193–201.

Good, T. L., Cooper, H. M., & Blakey, S. L. (1980). Classroom interaction as a function of teacher expectations, student sex, and time of year. *Journal of Educational Psychology,* 72, 378–387.

Good, T. L., & Grouws, D. A. (1975). *Process-product relationships in fourth-grade mathematics classrooms* (Final report, National Institute of Education Grant NEG-OO-3-0123). Columbia: University of Missouri, College of Education.

Good, T. L., & Grouws, D. A. (1977). Teaching effects: A process-product study in fourth-grade mathematics classrooms. *Journal of Teacher Education,* 28, 49–53.

Good, T. L., & Grouws, D. A. (1979). The Missouri Mathematics Effectiveness Project: An experimental study in fourth-grade classrooms. *Journal of Educational Psychology,* 71, 355–362.

Good, T. L., & Grouws, D. A. (1981, May). *Experimental research in secondary mathematics classrooms: Working with Teachers* (Final report of National Institute of Education Grant NIE-G-79-0103).

Green, J. L., & Smith, D. C. (1983). Teaching and learning: A linguistic perspective. *Elementary School Journal,* 83(4).

Greene, J. C. (1980). Individual teacher/class effects in aptitude treatment interactions. *American Educational Research Journal,* 17, 291–302.

Greeno, J. G. (1976). Indefinite goals in well-structured problems. *Psychological Review,* 83, 473–491.

Guilford, J. P., & Frutcher, B. (1978). *Fundamental statistics in psychology and education* (6th ed.). New York: McGraw-Hill.

Haertel, E., & Calfee, R. (1983). School achievement: Thinking about what to test. *Journal of Educational Measurement,* 20(2), 119–132.

Haller, E. (1975). Pupil influence on teacher socialization: A sociolinguistic study. *Journal of Educational Psychology,* 67, 735–744.

Hamilton, S. F. (1983). The social side of schooling: Ecological studies of classrooms and schools. *Elementary School Journal,* 83(4), 313–334.

Hammond, K. R., & Adleman, L. (1976). Science, values and human judgement. *Science,* 194, 389–396.

Harnisch, D. L. (1983). Item response patterns: Applications for educational practice. *Journal of Educational Measurement,* 20(2), 191–206.

Harnisch, D. L., & Linn, R. L. (1982). *Identifications of aberrant response patterns in a test of mathematics.* Paper presented at the annual meeting of the American Educational Research Association, Los Angeles.

Harnischfeger, A., & Wiley, D. E. (1976). The teaching-learning process in elementary schools: A synoptic view. *Curriculum Inquiry,* 6, 6–43.

Hildreth, C., & Houck, J. P. (1968). Some estimators for a linear model with random coefficients. *Journal of the American Statistical Association,* 63, 584–595.

Hoepfner, R. (1978). Achievement test selection for program evaluation. In M. J. Wargo & D. R. Green (Eds.), *Achievement testing of disadvantaged and minority students for educational program evaluation.* Monterey, CA: CTB/McGraw-Hill.

Hoffman, P. J. (1960). The paramorphic representation of clinical judgment. *Psychological Bulletin,* 57, 116–131.

Hoffman, P. J., Slovic, P., & Rorer, L. G. (1968). An analysis-of-variance model for the assessment of configural cue utilization in clinical judgment. *Psychological Bulletin,* 69, 338–349.

Hopkins, K. D. (1982). The unit of analysis: Group mean vs. individual observation. *American Educational Research Journal,* 19(1), 5–18.

Husen, T. (Ed.). (1967). *International study of achievement in mathematics: Comparison of twelve countries* (Vols. 1 & 2). New York: John Wiley.

Jenkins, J. R., & Pany, D. (1976). *Curriculum biases in reading achievement tests* (Tech. Rep. No. 16). Urbana-Champaign: University of Illinois, Center for the Study of Reading.

Jöreskog, K. G. (1969). A general approach to confirmatory maximum likelihood factor analysis. *Psychometrika,* 32, 443–482.

Jöreskog, K. G. (1974). Analyzing psychological data by structural analysis of covariance matrices. In D. H. Krantz, R. C. Atkinson, R. D. Luce, & P. Suppes (Eds.), *Contemporary developments in mathematical psychology* (Vol. 2). New York: W. H. Freeman & Company.

Karweit, N., & Slavin, R. E. (1981). Measurement and modeling choices in studies of time and learning. *American Educational Research Journal,* 18, 157–172.

Klein, S. S. (1971). Student influence on teacher behavior. *American Educational Research Journal,* 8, 403–421.

Kropp, F. F., Stoker, H. W., & Bashaw, W. L. (1966, February). *The construction and validation of tests of the cognitive processes as described in the Taxonomy of Education Objectives.* (U.S. Office of Education Contract OE-4-10-019). Tallahassee; Florida State University.

Lashley, K. S. (1923). The behavioristic interpretation of consciousness (Part 2). *Psychological Review,* 30, 329–353.

Leinhardt, G. (1978). Applying a classroom process model to instructional evaluation. *Curriculum Inquiry,* 8, 155–186.

Leinhardt, G. (1983). Overlap. Testing whether it's taught. In G. F. Madaus (Ed.), *The courts, validity, and minimum competancy testing.* Hingham, MA: Kluwer-Nijhoff Publishing.

Leinhardt, G., & Seewald, A. M. (1981). Overlap: What's tested, what's taught? *Journal of Educational Measurement,* 18, 85–96.

Linn, R. L., & Burstein, L. (1977). *Descriptors of aggregates* (CSE Report Series). Los Angeles: University of California, Center for the Study of Evaluation.

Lohnes, P. (1972). Statistical descriptors of school classes. *American Educational Research Journal,* 9, 547–556.

Lord, F. M. (1980). *Applications of item response theory to practical testing problems.* Hillsdale, NJ: Lawrence Erlbaum.

Lord, F. M., & Novick, M. R. (1968). *Statistical theories of mental test scores.* Reading, MA: Addison-Wesley.

Luce, S. R., & Hoge, R. D. (1978). Relations among teacher rankings, pupil-teacher interactions, and academic achievement: A test of the teacher expectancy hypothesis. *American Educational Research Journal,* 15, 489–500.

Lundgren, V. P. (1972). *Frame factors and the teaching process.* Stockholm: Almquist & Wiksell.

Magnusson, D. (1966). *Test theory.* Reading, MA: Addison-Wesley.

Marliave, R., Fisher, C. W., & Dishaw, M. M. (1978, February). *Academic learning time and student achievement in the B-C period. Beginning teacher evaluation study* (Technical Note Series, Technical Note V-2a, February).

Martin, J., Veldman, D. J., & Anderson, L. M. (1980). Within-class relationships between student achievement and teacher behaviors. *American Educational Research Journal*, 17(4), 479-490.

Marx, R. W. (1983). Student perception in classrooms. *Educational Psychologist*, 18(3), 145-165.

Marzano, W. A. (1973). *Determining the reliability of the Distar instructional system observation instrument.* Unpublished thesis, University of Illinois, Urbana-Champaign.

McConnell, J. W., & Bowers, N. D. (1979). *A comparison of high-inference and low-inference measures of teacher behaviors as predictors of pupil attitudes and achievements.* Paper presented at the annual meeting of the American Educational Research Association, San Francisco.

McDonald, F., & Elias, P. (1976). *The effects of teacher performance on pupil learning. Beginning Teacher Evaluation Study* (Phase II, final report, Vol. I). Princeton, NJ: Educational Testing Service.

McGaw, B., Wardrop, J. L., & Bunda, M. A. (1972). Classroom observation schemes: Where are the errors? *American Educational Research Journal*, 9, 13-27.

McNair, K. (1978-1979). Capturing inflight decisions: Thoughts while teaching. *Educational Research Quarterly*, 3, 26-42.

Medley, D. M. (1977). *Teacher competence and teacher effectiveness: A review of process-product research.* Washington, DC: American Association of Colleges for Teacher Education.

Medley, D. M., & Mitzel, H. E. (1963). Measuring classroom behavior by systematic observation. In Gage, N. L. (Ed.), *Handbook of Research on Teaching.* Chicago, IL: Rand McNally.

Miller, M. D. (1981). *Measuring between-group differences in instruction.* Unpublished doctoral dissertation, University of California, Los Angeles.

Miller, M. D. (in press). Item response and instructional coverage. *Journal of Education Measurement.*

Muthen, B. (1978). Contributions to factor analysis of dichotomous variables. *Psychometrika*, 43, 551-560.

Muthen, B. (1983). Latent variable structural equation modeling with categorical data. *Journal of Econometrics*, 22, 43-65.

Muthen, B., & Christoffersson, A. (1981). Simultaneous factor analysis of dichotomous variables in several groups. *Psychometrika*, 46, 407-419.

Muthen, L. (1983). *The estimation of variance components for dichotomous dependent variables: Applications to test theory.* Unpublished doctoral dissertation, University of California, Los Angeles.

Newell, A., & Simon, H. A. (1972). *Human problem solving.* Englewood Cliffs, NJ: Prentice-Hall.

Nisbett, R. E., & Wilson, T. D. (1977). Telling more than we can know: Verbal reports on mental processes. *Psychological Review*, 84, 231-259.

Noble, C. G., & Nolan, J. P. (1976). Effect of student verbal behavior on classroom teacher behavior. *Journal of Educational Psychology*, 68, 342-346.

Payne, J. W. (1982). Contingent decision behavior. *Psychological Bulletin*, 92, 382-402.

Peterson, P. L. (1977). Interactive effects of student anxiety, achievement orientation and teacher behavior on student achievement and attitude. *Journal of Educational Psychology*, 69, 779-792.

Peterson, P. L., & Clark, C. M. (1978). Teachers' reports of their cognitive processes during teaching. *American Educational Research Journal*, 15, 555-565.

Peterson, P. L., & Janicki, T. (1979). Individual characteristics and children's learning in large-group and small-group approaches. *Journal of Educational Psychology*, 71, 677-687.

Peterson, P. L., Marx, R. W., & Clark, C. M. (1978). Teacher planning, teacher behavior and student achievement. *American Educational Research Journal*, 15, 417-432.

Plewis, I. (1981). Using longitudinal data to model teachers' ratings of classroom behavior as a dynamic process. *Journal of Educational Statistics*, 6, 237-255.

Postman, L., & Tolman, E. C. (1959). Brunswik's probabilistic functionalism. In S. Kock (Ed.), *Psychology: A study of a science* (Vol. 1). New York: McGraw-Hill.

Program on Teaching Effectiveness (November 1976). *A factorially designed experiment on teacher structuring, soliciting, and reacting* (Research and Development Memo #47). Stanford Center for Research and Development in Teaching.

Pullis, M., & Cadwell, J. (1982). The influence of children's temperament characteristics on teachers' decision strategies. *American Educational Research Journal*, 19, 165-181.

Resnick, L., & Ford, W. (1981). *The psychology of mathematics for instruction.* Hillsdale, NJ: Lawrence Erlbaum.

Rogosa, D. E. (1980). Comparisons of some procedures for analyzing longitudinal panel data. *Journal of Economics and Business*, 32, 136-151.

Rogosa, D. E., Brandt, D., & Zimkowski, M. (1982). A growth curve approach to the measurement of change. *Psychological Bulletin*, 90, 726-748.

Rogosa, D. E., Floden, R., & Willett, J. B. (in press). Assessing the stability of teacher behavior. *Journal of Educational Psychology.*

Romberg, T. A. (1983). A common curriculum for mathematics, In G. D. Fenstermacher & J. I. Goodlad (Eds.). *Individual differences and the common curriculum: Eighty-second yearbook of the National Society for the Study of Education* (pp. 121-159). Chicago: University of Chicago Press.

Rosenshine, B. (1979). Content, time, and direct instruction. In P. Peterson and H. Walberg (Eds.), *Research on teaching: Concepts, findings, and implications.* Berkeley, CA: McCutchan.

Rosenshine, B. (1983). Teaching functions in instructional programs. *Elementary School Journal*, 83(4), 335-352.

Rosenshine, B., & Berliner, D. C. (1978). Academic engaged time. *British Journal of Teacher Education*, 4, 3-16.

Rosenshine, B., & Furst, N. (1973). The use of direct observation to study teaching. In R. M. W. Travers (Ed.), *Second Handbook of Research on Teaching.* Chicago: Rand McNally.

Rowley, G. L. (1976). The reliability of observational measures. *American Educational Research Journal*, 13, 51-59.

Rowley, G. L. (1978). The relationship of reliability in classroom research to the amount of observation: An extension of the Spearman-Brown formula. *Journal of Educational Measurement*, 15, 165-180.

Rumelhart, D. E., & Ortony, A. (1977). The representation of knowledge in memory. In R. C. Anderson, R. J. Spiro, & W. E. Montague (Eds.), *Schooling and the acquisition of knowledge.* Hillsdale, NJ: Lawrence Erlbaum.

Russo, N. A. (1978). *The effects of student characteristics, educational beliefs and instructional task on teachers' preinstructional decisions in reading and math.* Unpublished doctoral dissertation, University of California, Los Angeles.

Schmidt, W. H. (1969). *Covariance structure analysis of the multivariate random effects model.* Dissertation, University of Chicago.

Schmidt, W. H. (1983). Content biases in achievement tests. *Journal of Educational Measurement*, 20(2), 165-178.

Schneider, W., & Treiber, B. (1984). Classroom differences in the determination of achievement changes. *American Educational Research Journal*, 21(1), 195-211.

Schwille, J., Porter, A., Belli, G., Floden, R., Freeman, D., Knappen, L., Kuhs, T., & Schmidt, W. (1983). Teachers as policy brokers in the content of elementary school mathematics. In L. S. Shulman & G. Sykes (Eds.), *Handbook of teaching policy.* New York: Longman.

Shavelson, R. J. (1973). What is 'the' basic teaching skill? *Journal of Teacher Education*, 14, 144-151.

Shavelson, R. J. (1972). Some aspects of the correspondence between content structure and cognitive structure in physics instruction. *Journal of Educational Psychology*, 63, 225-234.

Shavelson, R. J. (1976). Teachers' decision making. In N. L. Gage (Ed.), *The psychology of teaching methods*, Seventy-fifth Yearbook of the National Society for the Study of Education (Part I). Chicago: University of Chicago Press.

Shavelson, R. J. (1983). Review of research on teachers' pedagogical judgments, plans, and decisions. *Elementary School Journal*, 83(4).

Shavelson, R. J., Caldwell, J., & Izu, T. (1977). Teachers' sensitivity to the reliability of information in making pedagogical decisions. *American Educational Research Journal*, 14, 83–97.

Shavelson, R. J., & Dempsey-Atwood, N. (1976). Generalizability of measures of teaching behavior. *Review of Educational Research*, 46, 553–611.

Shavelson, R. J., & Stern, P. (1981). Research on teachers' pedagogical thoughts, judgments, decisions, and behavior. *Review of Educational Research*, 51, 455–498.

Shavelson, R. J., & Webb, N. M. (1981). Generalizability theory: 1973–1980. *British Journal of Mathematical and Statistical Psychology*, 34, 133–166.

Sherman, T. N., & Cornier, W. H. (1974). An investigation of the influence of student behavior on teacher behavior. *Journal of Applied Behavior Analysis*, 7, 11–21.

Shulman, L. S., & Elstein, A. S. (1975). Studies of problem solving, judgment, and decision making: Implications for educational research. In F. N. Kerlinger (Ed.), *Review of Research in Education* (Vol. 3). Itasca, IL: Peacock.

Slavin, R. E. (1983). *Student level analysis in classroom experiments: An extension of the Cornfield-Tukey bridge*. Paper presented at the annual meeting of the American Educational Research Association, Montreal.

Slovic, P., Fischhoff, B., & Lichtenstein, S. (1977). Behavioral decision theory. *Annual Review of Psychology*, 28, 1–39.

Smith, B. O. (1983). Some comments on educational research in the twentieth century. *Elementary School Journal*, 83(4), 488–492.

Snow, R. J., Federico, P. A., & Montague, W. E. (Eds.), (1980). *Aptitude, learning and instruction* (Vols. 1 & 2). Hillsdale, NJ: Lawrence Erlbaum.

Soar, R. S., & Soar, R. M., (1972). An empirical analysis of selected follow through programs: An example of a process approach to evaluation. In I. Gordon (Ed.), *Early Childhood Education*. Chicago: National Society for the Study of Education.

Stallings, J. A. (1976). How instructional processes relate to child outcomes in a national study of follow through. *Journal of Teacher Education*, 27, 43–47.

Stallings, J. A., & Kaskowitz, D. (1974). *Follow through classroom observation evaluation 1972–1973*. (SRI Project URU-7370). Menlo Park, CA: SRI International.

Swamy, P. A. V. B. (1970). Efficient inference in a random coefficient regression model. *Econometrics*, 38, 311–328.

Tatsuoka, K. K. (1983). Rule space: An approach for dealing with misconceptions based on item response theory. *Journal of Educational Measurement*, 20(4), 345–354.

Tatsuoka, K. K., & Linn, R. L. (in press). Indices for detecting unusual patterns: Links between two general approaches and potential applications. *Applied Psychological Measurement*, 7(1), 81–96.

Tatsuoka, K. K., & Tatsuoka, M. M. (1982). Detection of aberrant response patterns and their effect on dimensionality. *Journal of Educational Statistics*, 7, 215–231.

Tatsuoka, K. K., & Tatsuoka, M. M. (1983). Spotting erroneous rules of operation by the individual consistency index. *Journal of Educational Measurement*, 20(3), 221–230.

Tikunoff, W., Berliner, D. C., & Rist, R. (1975). *An ethnographic study of the forty classrooms of the Beginning Teacher Evaluation Study known sample* (Tech. Rep. 75-10-5). San Francisco: Far West Laboratory.

Tourneur, Y. (1978). *Les Objectifs du domaine cognitif, 2me partie theorie des tests*. Ministere de l'Education Nationale et de la Culture Francaise, Universite de l'Etat a Mons, Faculte des Sciences Psycho-Pedagogiques.

Tourneur, Y., & Cardinet, J. (1979). *Analyse de variance et theorie de la generalizabilite: Guide pour la realisation des calceuls* [Doc 790. 803/ (CT/9)]. Universite de l'Etat a Mons.

Tuckwell, N. B. (n.d.-a). *Content analysis of stimulated recall protocols* (Occasional Paper Series Tech. Rep. #80-2-2, [a]). Edmonton, Canada: University of Alberta, Center for Research in Teaching, Faculty of Education.

Tuckwell, N. B. (n.d.-b). *Stimulated recall: Theoretical perspectives and practical and technical considerations* (Occasional Paper Series Technical Report 8-2-3, [b]). Edmonton, Canada: University of Alberta.

Van Roekel, J. L., & Patriarca, L. (April 1979). Do reading and learning disability clinicians differ in their diagnosis and remediation? Paper presented at the Annual Conference of the International Reading Association, Atlanta.

Veldman, D. J., & Brophy, J. E. (1974). Measuring teacher effects on pupil achievement. *Journal of Educational Psychology*, 66(3), 319–324.

Vinsonhaler, J. F. (1979). *The consistency of reading diagnosis*. Research Series No. 28. East Lansing: Institute for Research on Teaching, Michigan State University.

Walker, D. F., & Schaffarzik, J. (1974). Comparing curricula. *Review of Educational Research*, 44(1), 83–111.

Webb, N. M. (1980). Group process: The key to learning in groups. In K. H. Roberts and L. Burstein (Eds.), *Issues in aggregation, New directions for methodology of social and behavioral science* (Vol. 6), 77–87.

Webb, N. M. (1982). Group composition, group interaction and achievement in cooperative small groups. *Journal of Educational Psychology*, 74, 475–484.

Webb, N. M. (1980). *Implementation of BTES interaction activities in junior high school mathematics* (Final report submitted to the California Commission for Teacher Preparation and Licensing).

Webb, N. M., & Shavelson, R. J. (1981). Multivariate generalizability of general educational development ratings. *Journal of Educational Measurement*, 18, 13–22.

Webb, N. M., Shavelson, R. J., & Maddahian, E. (1983, June). Multivariate generalizability theory. In L. J. Fyans, Jr. (Ed.), *Generalizability theory: Inferences and practical applications* (New Directions for Testing and Measurement, No. 18). San Francisco: Jossey-Bass.

Weinshank, A. (June 1979). *An observational study of the relationship between diagnosis and remediation in reading*. Research Series No. 72. East Lansing: Institute for Research on Teaching, Michigan State University.

Weinstein, R. (1983). Perceptions of schooling. *Elementary School Journal*, 83(4), 287–312.

Wiley, D. E. (1970). Design and analysis of evaluation studies. In M. C. Wittrock & D. E. Wiley (Eds.), *The evaluation of instruction*. New York: Holt, Rinehart & Winston.

Wiley, D. E., Schmidt, W. H., & Bramble, W. J. (1973). Studies of a class of covariance structure models. *Journal of the American Statistical Association*, 1973, 68, 317–323.

Wohlwill, J. S. (1973). *The study of behavior development*. New York: Academic Press.

Wright, C. J., & Nuthall, G. (1970). Relationships between teacher behaviors and pupil achievement in three experimental elementary science lessons. *American Educational Research Journal*, 7, 477–492.

Yinger, R. J., Clark, C. M., & Mondol, M. M. (1979). *Selecting instructional activities: A policy-capturing analysis*. Research Series No. 103. East Lansing: Michigan State University, Institute for Research on Teaching.

4.

Quantitative Methods in Research on Teaching

Robert L. Linn
University of Illinois at Urbana–Champaign

The division of methods into the categories considered in this chapter and the following chapter on qualitative methods is convenient. Quantitative methods are generally associated with systematic measurement, experimental and quasi-experimental methods, statistical analysis, and mathematical models. Qualitative methods, on the other hand, are associated with naturalistic observation, case studies, ethnography, and narrative reports. It should be recognized, however, that the boundaries between the methods sometimes get blurred.

The person using quantitative methods must make many qualitative decisions regarding the questions to pose, the design to implement, the measures to use, the analytical procedures to employ, and the interpretations to stress. The person who relies on qualitative methods often finds certain quantitative summaries, classifications, and analyses a useful part of the research (cf. Light, 1973). Methods in both categories can contribute to what Cronbach and Suppes (1969) have described as "disciplined inquiry." Nonetheless the emphases, traditions, and ideals are different. The "two cultures" (Stenhouse, 1978) more often appear to be conflicting than complementary. Yet, results relying on both categories of methods contribute to the understanding of teaching and therefore have complementary value even if there is no deliberate effort of the type recommended by Saxe and Fine (1979) to make them complementary.

Although the title of this chapter provides a convenient distinction, it may suggest a more ambitious effort than was intended or undertaken. The scope is certainly much more limited than the gamut of available quantitative methods, the consideration of which would require a grandiose project indeed. Measurement is a crucial element in the use of quantitative methods. Fortunately, other chapters deal with measurement and while some measurement issues are also addressed here, the coverage is limited to issues as they relate to the analysis and interpretation of results. Properties of certain commonly used metrics for reporting achievement test data, for example, often affect interpretations and are reviewed for this reason. Similarly, measurement error plays an important role in explanatory models and attempts to adjust for preexisting differences between groups, and is discussed in those contexts. But no attempt is made to provide a comprehensive treatment of measurement theory or techniques.

Questions of design are central components of the topics covered in this chapter. But it is *not* a chapter on design, in the tradition of either Fisher (1925) or Campbell and Stanley (1963), though concepts from those traditions are heavily relied upon. The power of randomization is recognized, but greater attention is given to quasi-experimental designs that have more frequent applicability in research on teaching. The discussion owes much to the conceptualization provided by Campbell and Stanley (1963) and updates and extensions of that work (e.g., Cook & Campbell, 1976, 1979). Their types of validity and identification of threats to validity provide important logical underpinnings for the quantitative methods that are discussed. Here the emphasis is more on the quantification and analytical methods associated with the designs, however.

Statistical analysis is also a vital part of the discussion, but the chapter is not a survey of statistical techniques and developments, per se. Rather, the emphasis is on the logic of certain techniques and their utility for the analysis of data obtained in commonly used paradigms for the study of teaching and its effects.

The chapter starts with a section on considerations in the choice of a design, in which the emphasis is on trade-offs and the implications for analysis and interpretability. This is followed by the major section of the chapter, in which analyses of data from randomized experiments, various nonequivalent control group designs, single-group designs, and designs involving aggregate data are considered. The final section of this chapter is devoted to the quantitative analysis of summary results from previous research.

The author thanks reviewers Richard M. Jaeger (University of North Caroline—Greensboro) and David Rogosa (Stanford University).

Some Basic Considerations in Design, Interpretation, and Analysis: An Overview

Although description is sometimes the end goal, and always an important part of quantitative methods, causal inferences are of primary concern in this chapter. Some would question both the feasibility and the desirability of making causal inferences. Indeed, the editor of the *Second Handbook of Research on Teaching*, Robert M. W. Travers, has recently recommended (Travers, 1981) that we "drop that word *cause* and bring educational research out of the middle ages" (p. 32). Travers' recommendation was based upon his conclusion that "discussions of causal relationships in research are pre-Newtonian" (p. 32), i.e., based on "Aristotle's concept of *push from behind*" (.p. 32). He further argued that "modern scientists do not use the concept of cause, except during chatty moments" (p. 32). The idea of functional relationships was offered as one of the available substitutes that is better than the concept of cause.

Causation is a controversial topic. Philosophical debates about causation are plentiful. Cook and Campbell (1979, pp. 9–36) have discussed the relationship of their work to some of the philosophical traditions. That discussion will not be repeated here, nor will an analysis of the theoretical arguments be attempted. Such an analysis is left to others who are better equipped to undertake the task (cf. Ennis, 1973). Before proceeding to a discussion of methods, however, it is desirable to consider briefly the three major points made by Ennis (1982) in a rejoinder to Travers' recommendation that we abandon the concept of causality.

Ennis acknowledged that the analysis of the concept of cause remains quite controversial, but argued that the concept as ordinarily used is not limited to the mechanistic notion of a "push from behind." As Ennis argued, "it is legitimate and essential for educational researchers to have causal concerns" and to pursue "questions about what brings about, and what has brought about matters of educational significance" (Ennis, 1982, p. 27). Such investigations are concerned with general and specific causal statements, respectively, and need not involve the mechanistic notion of a physical push.

Ennis persuasively argued that we cannot eliminate the concept of cause merely by doing away with the word "cause." Investigations of whether reduced class size leads to improved student achievement, of whether peer tutoring helps either the tutor or the person being tutored, of who benefits from round-robin reading groups, or of teacher behaviors that increase time-on-task are all concerned with cause, whether or not the word is used. Of course, being concerned about cause is no guarantee of success, or that the causal statements are valid. Empirical assumptions are always required: Even the most tightly controlled experimental design cannnot eliminate all alternative explanations (Ennis, 1973, p. 9). Recognition of the fallibility of causal statements produced from the results of any design leads to an emphasis on the search for "plausible rival hypotheses" (cf. Cook and Campbell, 1979, pp. 20–25) and an emphasis on falsification (Popper, 1959). It is also important to distinguish between proximate and fundamental causes and to recognize that general causal statements need to be qualified by an indication of frequency by "specifying a condition that either sometimes is, often is, usually is, always is, etc., a sufficient condition for the bringing about of a specified sort of effect" (Ennis, 1973, p. 10).

A Comparison of Two Treatments

Whether judged by means of a randomized experiment, a quasi-experiment, or merely a "thought experiment" (Cronbach, 1982, p. 120), comparison of alternative conditions is fundamental to causal inferences. Rubin (1974) has provided a formulation for the comparison of treatments that defines a specific causal effect in a manner consistent with the ordinary meaning of the concept. His formulation is useful in analyzing the assumptions required in making causal inferences from comparative studies and in comparing alternative designs and analyses. Using E and C to denote the treatments to be compared, Rubin (1974) defined "the causal effect of the E versus C treatment on Y for a particular trial (i.e., a particular unit and associated times t_1, t_2) as follows:"

Let $y(E)$ be the value of Y measured at t_2 on the unit, given that the unit received the experimental Treatment E initiated at t_1; Let $y(C)$ be the value of Y measured at t_2 on the unit given that the unit received the control Treatment C initiated at t_1; Then $y(E) - y(C)$ is the causal effect of E versus C treatment on Y for that trial, that is, for that particular unit and the times t_1, t_2. (p. 689)

Rubin's definition provides a useful standard for evaluating designs for the comparison of two treatments. It is obvious, however, that it is impossible to measure directly the specific effect for any unit because only one of the two treatments can be introduced at t_1. If $y(E)$ is obtained for a particular unit (e.g., individual classroom, school) then $y(C)$ cannot be obtained for that unit, and vice versa. Two time intervals t_1 to t_2 and t_3 to t_4 might be used with, say, C introduced at t_1 and E at t_3 while $y(C)$ and $y(E)$ are obtained at times t_2 and t_4, respectively. But there are many plausible rival hypotheses (e.g., maturation, carryover effects) that must be eliminated in order for such a design to be a reasonable approximation to Rubin's conceptual definition.

The more common operational approximation to the definition is to assign E to one unit and C to another. But, of course, $y_1(E)$ may not equal $y_2(E)$ and $y_1(C)$ may not equal $y_2(C)$, where the subscripts identify the units. The outcome of the experiment is either $y_1(E) - y_2(C)$, or $y_2(E) - y_1(C)$. Neither quantity is necessarily equal to the specific causal effect for either unit, $y_i(E) - y_i(C)$; $i = 1$ or 2.

The dilemma of not being able to obtain $y(E)$ and $y(C)$ on the same unit led Rubin (1974) to define the "'typical' causal effect of the E versus C treatment for M trials ... [as] the average (mean) causal effect for the M trials" (p. 690). This average still cannot be directly assessed because some units receive E while others receive C, and no unit can receive both for a given t_1, t_2. If N units receive E and another N units receive C, $M = 2N$, then the "typical causal effect" is

$$\Delta = \frac{1}{2N} \sum_{i=1}^{2N} y_i(E) - \frac{1}{2N} \sum_{i=1}^{2N} y_i(C),$$

but the available data only allows for the calculation of

$$d = \frac{1}{N} \sum_{i=1}^{N} y_i(E) - \frac{1}{N} \sum_{i=N+1}^{2N} y_i(C),$$

where it is assumed that the units are ordered such that the first N receive E and the second N receive C.

RANDOMIZATION

Random assignment cannot guarantee that d will equal Δ. Only one of the $(2N)!$ possible allocations of the "randomization set" is observed, and none of the possible ds resulting from a particular allocation is necessarily equal to Δ. But there are, as Rubin has shown, two important benefits of randomization. First, d is an unbiased estimator of Δ, and, second, "precise probabilistic statements can be made indicating how unusual the observed" (Rubin, 1974, p. 693) d is under any hypothesized Δ. Without randomization, the possibility of bias due to prior differences on an uncontrolled "third variable" can seldom, if ever, be ruled out as an alternative explanation of the results. These important advantages of randomization identified by Rubin apply not only to the completely randomized experiment, but to randomized block designs in which $2N$ matched pairs are created and one member of each pair is randomly selected to receive E and the other to receive C. The latter design may also have an advantage of greater precision.

IMPROVING ESTIMATES

Blocking is one example of an approach to improving the estimate of Δ. To the extent that the variable(s) used to form matched pairs may increase the within-block homogeneity on Y, the precision of the estimates will be improved (cf. Feldt, 1958). For example, in a study where the dependent variable is student achievement, students with equal scores on a previously administered ability test would generally be expected to have more similar achievement than students with different ability test scores. By forming matched pairs on the ability test scores and randomly assigning one member of each pair to the E and C conditions, the effect can be estimated with greater precision. Often other adjustment procedures, e.g., use of gain scores or covariate adjustments, have great advantage, whether the adjustment variables causally affect Y or are only correlated with Y. The choice of variables (e.g., prior achievement, age, height) on which to make an adjustment, and the way in which those adjustments are to be made often involves trade-offs between desirable properties of unbiasedness and the magnitude of the error variance. Rubin (1974) shows that subtracting any prior score x_i from $y_i(E)$ or $y_i(C)$, depending on which treatment the unit receives, preserves the property of unbiasedness, but not all prior variables make sense. If y is a measure of achievement, then $x =$ prior achievement makes sense; running speed, pulse rate, and height do not.

"Clearly, in order to make an intelligent adjustment for extra information, we cannot be guided solely by the concept of unbiasedness over the randomization set. We need some model for the effects of prior variables in order to use their values in an intelligent way" (Rubin, 1974, p. 696). This conclusion of Rubin's may be illustrated by a simple example in which the values of $y_i(E)$ and $y_i(C)$ are assumed to be known, but different

Table 4.1. Hypothetical Values on a Prior Measure, X, and Outcomes Under Two Treatment Conditions for Four Experimental Units

Unit	x_i	$y_i(E)$[a]	$y_i(C)$[b]	$y_i(E) - y_i(C)$[c]
1	10	8	2	6
2	20	14	10	4
3	30	20	18	2
4	40	26	26	0

[a] $y_i(E) = .6x_i + 2$.
[b] $y_i(C) = .8x_i - 6$.
[c] The typical causal effect, Δ, equals $\frac{1}{4}(6 + 4 + 2 + 0) = 3$.

functions of a prior variable, x, are used. Values of x_i, $y_i(E)$, and $y_i(C)$ are listed in Table 4.1 for four hypothetical units. The functional relationships for the two treatments are $y_i(E) = .6x_i + 2$ and $y_i(C) = .8x_i - 6$, respectively. As can be seen in Table 4.1, the specific causal effects, assuming both $y_i(E)$ and $y_i(C)$, could be obtained for each unit range from 0 to 6, with the typical causal effect, Δ, equal to 3.

There are six possible allocations of units to treatments in the randomization set. Numerous estimates of the typical causal effect are possible for any given allocation, and the results for any estimation procedure will vary from one allocation to another over the randomized set. The results for three possible estimation procedures are summarized in Table 4.2 for each of the six possible allocations of units to treatments.

Estimate 1, denoted d_1, is the simplest and most obvious estimate; that is, the difference between the mean y for the two units in E and that for the two units in C, ignoring the available information on the prior measure. The estimates d_1 are unbiased, that is, the average value of d_1 over the six allocations in

Table 4.2. Outcomes of the Six Possible Randomized Experiments Based on the Hypothetical Values in Table 4.1.

Randomized Allocation	Units in E	Units in C	Estimates of Typical Causal Effect[a]		
			d_1	d_2	d_3
1	1, 2	3, 4	−11	9	5
2	1, 3	2, 4	−4	6	4
3	1, 4	2, 3	3	3	3
4	2, 3	1, 4	3	3	3
5	2, 4	1, 3	10	0	2
6	3, 4	1, 2	17	−3	1
Average Across Randomization Set			3	3	3
Maximum Estimate			17	9	5
Minimum Estimate			−11	−3	1

[a] The three estimates of the $E - C$ typical causal effect are:

$$d_1 = \frac{1}{2}\sum_{i\epsilon E} y_i(E) - \frac{1}{2}\sum_{i\epsilon C} y_i(C),$$

$$d_2 = \frac{1}{2}\sum_{i\epsilon E} (y_i(E) - x_i) - \frac{1}{2}\sum_{i\epsilon C} (y_i(C) - x_i),$$

$$d_3 = \frac{1}{2}\sum_{i\epsilon E} (y_i(E) - .8x_i + 6) - \frac{1}{2}\sum_{i\epsilon C} (y_i(C) - .8x_i + 6),$$

where E and C refer to the set of units in the E and C conditions, respectively.

the randomization set is 3, equal to Δ. But the range of possible estimates is quite large, from -11 to $+17$. That is, the results of any particular randomized allocation could be off by as much as 14 points.

In this hypothetical example, it is important to take the prior measure, x, into account. An obvious way of doing this is to subtract the value of x_i from $y_i(E)$ or $y_i(C)$ and compute the difference of the resulting $y - x$ averages for the two conditions. Such a procedure results in the estimates denoted d_2 in Table 4.2. As can be seen, d_2, like d_1, is an unbiased estimator (i.e., the mean over the six allocations of d_2 is 3). The range of d_2 (-3 to $+9$) is smaller than that of d_1. Hence, d_2 is clearly the better of the two estimators for these data.

Knowledge of the functional relationship between y and x in the C condition can be used to obtain still better estimates. The estimates denoted d_3 in Table 4.2 illustrate this fact. Rather than subtracting x_i from each observed y as was done for d_2, the value of y expected under the C condition based on the functional relationship, $y_i(C) = .8x_i - 6$, is subtracted from the ys observed under each condition. The resulting estimates, d_3, are again unbiased, but have a much smaller range ($+1$ to $+5$) than either of the previous estimates in Table 4.2. The use of the functional relationships for the C condition is predicted on the assumption that, in the absence of a treatment effect, the same relationship would hold for the E condition.

Though obviously contrived, this simple hypothetical example illustrates the potential advantages of taking prior information into account and using knowledge of functional relationships even in randomized experiments. These advantages may be even more pronounced in the nonrandomized designs that are the primary focus of this chapter.

Estimating Adjustment Parameters

Of course, it is easy to specify the adjustment parameter (slope equal .8 and intercept equal -6) in contrived situations such as the above. But strong models with widely accepted functional relationships are not available in educational research. Even if a researcher is willing to assume a linear model, the parameters will be unknown. Hence use of adjustment models requires estimation of the unknown parameters. When estimates of the parameters are obtained from the available data, "in general the average $E - C$ difference in adjusted scores is no longer unbiased over the randomization set" (Rubin, 1974, p. 696). Adjustment procedures may still be of considerable value, even when they yield biased estimates.

For the above hypothetical situation represented in Table 4.1, for example, a standard analysis of covariance yields estimates of the causal effect that are precisely equal to the typical causal effect Δ, despite the fact that the assumption of homogeneity of within-group slopes is violated. The slopes, adjusted means, and differences in adjusted means, d_4, are reported in Table 4.3 for each of the six possible allocations of units to treatments. As can be seen, $d_4 = \Lambda = 3$ for all six allocations. This pleasant albeit unrealistic outcome is a consequence of the linear functional relationships between x and y in the two treatments and the evenly spaced values of x.

If the last row of Table 4.1 were changed such that $X_4 = 50$, $y_4(E) = .6x_4 + 2 = 32$, and $y_4(C) = .8x_4 - 6 = 34$, while the first three rows were left unchanged, Δ would equal 2.5. The

Table 4.3. Analysis of Covariance Estimate of Pooled Within-Group Slopes, Adjusted Means, and Differences in Adjusted Means, for the Hypothetical Values in Table 4.1 ($\Delta = 3$)

Allocation	Units in E	Units in C	Slope	Adjusted Means[a] E	Adjusted Means[a] C	Difference[b] d_4
1	1, 2	3, 4	.7	18.	15.	3
2	1, 3	2, 4	.7	17.5	14.5	3
3	1, 4	2, 3	.62	17.	14.	3
4	2, 3	1, 4	.78	17.	14.	3
5	2, 4	1, 3	.7	16.5	13.5	3
6	3, 4	1, 2	.7	16.	13.	3

[a] The adjusted means are obtained in the usual manner, i.e., the observed group mean on Y minus the pooled within-group slope times the difference between the group mean and the overall mean on X.
[b] d_4 equals the adjusted Y mean for E minus the adjusted Y mean for C.

analysis of covariance results would yield biased estimates over the 6 samples in the randomization set. But, as can be seen in Table 4.4, the mean-square error (i.e., the average squared deviation of the estimates from Δ) for d_4 would be considerably smaller than the mean-square error for d_1 or d_2. The advantage of unbiasedness that d_1 and d_2 have over d_4 is clearly outweighed by the small variance of the latter, compared to those of d_1 and d_2 across samples in the randomization set.

Generalization

Inferences only to the set of units receiving either Treatment E or C are seldom the primary interest. The more typical goal is to generalize to a population of units from the sample included in the study. With random sampling of the $2N$ study units from a larger population of units (Rubin, 1974), noted:

the ability to generalize results to other trials seems relatively straightforward probabilistically. However, most experiments are designed to be generalized to *future* trials; we never have a random sample of trials from the future but at best a random sample from

Table 4.4. Estimates for the Six Allocations in the Randomization Set for the Hypothetical Results in Table 4.1 with Case 4 Altered to $x_4 = 50$, $y_4(E) = 32$ and $x_4(C) = 34$ ($\Delta = 2.5$)

Allocation	Units in E	Units in C	Estimates of Effect[a] d_1	d_2	d_3	d_4
1	1, 2	3, 4	-15	10	5	4.00
2	1, 3	2, 4	-8	7	4	3.08
3	1, 4	2, 3	6	1	2	2.94
4	2, 3	1, 4	-1	4	3	2.93
5	2, 4	1, 3	13	-2	1	3.08
6	3, 4	1, 2	20	-5	0	4.00
Average Across Randomization Set			2.5	2.5	2.5	3.34
Mean Square Error			142.92	39.38	2.92	.93

[a] d_1, d_2, and d_3 defined as in Table 4.2 and d_4 as in Table 4.3.

the present; in fact experiments are usually conducted in constrained atypical environments and within a restricted period of time. (p. 698)

Thus, the step from the results of any study, whether a true randomized experiment or a nonrandomized study, to conclusions of interest about general causal effects always depends on more than strict probabilistic reasoning.

Cronbach (1982) speaks of generalizations not only to a wider population, *U*, of units, but to domains, *T*, of treatments, and of "admissible procedures and conditions, *O*, for obtaining data on a certain variable" (p. 79). These domains or populations along with the setting *S*, that is, "the times and cultural conditions in which the study is made" (Cronbach, 1982, p. 78), define the domain *UTOS* for which generalizations are desired. The actual study is conducted on only a sample, whether random or not, of units and particular instances of the treatments and data-gathering procedure in the specified setting, denoted *utoS*.

Generalizations from *utoS* to *UTOS* may depend partially on strict probabilistic reasoning, for example, *u* is a random sample from *U*, as well as on subjective judgment, for example, the conclusion is not limited to the particular procedures *o* used to obtain the data. Generalizations to other settings, *S**, for example, the future or another culture, necessarily require more than probability theory. So too, do inferences based on study results about what will happen when the treatment is applied to a specific unit, for example, a particular school, teacher, or student.

In research on teaching, as well as in most educational or social science research, the choice of a design should include consideration of the various types of generalization desired and the threats to validity of each. A tightly controlled randomized experiment may provide the best basis for generalizing from *u* to *U* in Cronbach's scheme, but a very poor basis for equally, if not more important, generalizations from *o* to *O*, *t* to *T*, and *S* to *S**. In the terminology of Campbell and Stanley (1963), the greater internal validity of a randomized experiment often comes at the cost of lower external validity. Nonrandomized studies often have better representation of *UTOS* than randomized studies, but lack control for preexisting differences. Adjusting for the effects of uncontrolled variables is a major concern in the nonrandomized studies discussed below. Foolproof methods that necessarily provide the "right" adjustment cannot be expected. By emphasizing falsification and the search for and testing of plausible rival hypotheses, however, much can be learned from nonrandomized studies.

As shown above, variables other than the treatment that affect *Y* are important to consider in either a randomized or nonrandomized study. In either case, "the investigator should think hard about variables besides the treatment that causally affect *Y* and plan in advance how to control the important ones — either by matching or adjustment or both" (Rubin, 1974, p. 700).

Design and Analysis

Three general categories of designs are considered in this section: randomized experiments, nonrandomized control group studies, and single-group studies. Discussion of these three types of designs and associated analytical procedures is followed by a consideration of two special topics: aggregation and meta-analysis.

Randomized Experiments

For three reasons, the discussion of randomized experiments will be very brief. First, the logic and many of the benefits of a randomized experiment have already been discussed in the context of defining a causal effect in the two-group experiment involving experimental (*E*) and control (*C*) treatments. Second, there are many excellent sources that are familiar to researchers and students of statistics on the design and analysis of randomized experiments (e.g., Cochran & Cox, 1957; Kempthorne, 1952; Kirk, 1982; Scheffé, 1959; Winer, 1971). Third, randomized experiments are the exception rather than the rule in research on teaching. The limited attention is *not* intended to suggest that randomized experiments lack value for research on teaching. To the contrary, where feasible, a randomized experiment is the preferred design. But even the most elegant design and analysis are of little value unless relevant to the questions of interest.

SAMPLE SELECTION AND ASSIGNMENT

Random selection and assignment of units for a randomized experiment are conceptually straightforward but often complicated in practice. Requirements for informed consent not only reduce the population of all units of interest to a population of volunteers but may have differential effects by treatment condition. When refusals to participate are related to the treatment conditions, the logical advantages of random assignment are jeopardized

Reicken et al. (1974) have described three stages in an experimental design at which random assignment to treatments may occur (also see Cook & Campbell, 1979, pp. 356–359). First, random assignment may be made on the basis of an initial list of eligible participants. This is a common approach but has a danger that refusal rates will differ as a function of treatment when informed consent is sought. Without prior information on refusals it may be impossible either to evaluate fully the possible effects of differential refusals or make reasonable adjustments for their effects.

Reicken et al. (1974) place the second stage for random assignment after initial measurement of potential participants. Potential participants must first agree to the collection of the initial measures which are to be used as a baseline for all experimental groups. Random assignment to treatments is made after the initial measures have been obtained. Assignment at this second stage does not preclude the possibility that refusals to participate will be related to the treatment conditions, and thereby limit the external validity of the results. However, the measures obtained prior to assignment provide a basis for evaluating the possibility and making adjustments for differential refusal.

A possible third stage for assignment comes after initial measures are obtained and the experiment has been described. Consent to participate in any of the treatment conditions is sought and random assignment is made from among those who are willing to accept any of the treatment conditions. Assignment at this third stage avoids the possibility of differential refusals provided participants do not change their minds once they are assigned to a particular treatment condition. Assignment at stage three is generally preferable where feasible. It is apt to work best where treatments do not differ greatly in their perceived advantages or disadvantages for participants. There will often be a trade-off between providing sufficient information about the treatments to obtain informed consent to participate in any of them and providing so much information that the treatments may be partially contaminated. Knowledge of other treatment characteristics could lead participants to seek out information from another condition and thereby to a diffusion of effects. This danger is apt to be greatest where participants in different treatments have the opportunity to interact during the course of the experiment.

IMPLEMENTATION

Treatments designed to alter teacher behavior may consist of a variety of training materials and workshops. The major dependent variables of interest may be student performance. In such a situation, a simple comparison of the performance of students in classes whose teacher had one type of training with those in classes with teachers who had another is obviously relevant to the question of the differential effects on student performance. Such a "black-box" approach leaves unanswered questions of how or why differences or the lack of differences come about. Measures of implementation of the treatments are vital to addressing the latter questions. Also needed is a sound theory that incorporates a causal chain from intervention with teachers to changes in student behavior.

Logs, questionnaires, interviews. and observations may all serve useful purposes in measuring the implementation of treatments. It is obviously important that such measures be obtained for all treatments, controls as well as experimentals. Observation of one condition but not another would itself constitute a treatment difference and generate the possibility that any observed differences were the result of a "Hawthorne effect," that is, that the special attention given by means of observations and other activities, rather than the planned treatment, produced the observed effect. Of course if there is an interest in isolating the effect of the observation, then two control conditions, one with and one without observation, are needed. Ordinarily, however, the treatment effects will be more convincing when possible Hawthorne effects are as strong in the control as in the experimental condition.

An experimental study reported by Good and Grouws (1979) provides a good illustration of measuring implementation and the creation of what they call a "Hawthorne control condition" (p. 357). Teachers who were randomly assigned to the treatment condition were given training and a manual with detailed instructions for implementation in the fall of 1977.

Control teachers were told that they would not get details of the instructional program until February 1978. Furthermore, they were told that it was hoped that this information might be especially useful to them then because at that time they would receive individual information about their *own* classroom behavior and refined information about the program itself. Finally control teachers were told that their immediate role in the project was to continue to instruct in their own style.

Given that control teachers knew that the research was designed to improve student achievement, that the school district was interested in the research, and that they were being observed, we feel reasonably confident that a strong Hawthorne control was created. (pp. 356–357)

The results of the Good and Grouws study included clear evidence of differences between treatment and control group teachers on key implementation variables as well as in gains in student achievement. For example, the mean percentage of occurrence of "Did teacher conduct reviews?" was 91% for treatment teachers and 62% for control. Comparable figures for "Did teacher check homework?" were 79% and 20%, respectively (p. 358). The creation of a Hawthorne control helped justify the Good and Grouws conclusion that "the large magnitude of the treatment effect is important and offers convincing proof that it is possible to intervene successfully in school programs" (p. 362). The availability of the implementation measures and their relationship to student gains in achievement not only aided in the interpretation of the results, but the basis for hypotheses regarding the importance of particular variables "can only be evaluated in subsequent studies that delete certain aspects of the instructional program" (p. 362).

VARIATION IN IMPLEMENTATION

Although between-treatment comparisons of implementation variables and of dependent variables provide the strongest bases for inferences regarding effects, within-treatment variations in implementation variables and the relationship of these variables to dependent variables are also valuable sources of information. The large difference between groups in the checking of homework by teachers, cited above from the Good and Grouws study, is important in and of itself. But the differences in these variable gains additional importance when coupled with the finding that checking homework correlated .54 with residualized gain scores on the SRA Mathematics Test. As would be true of a straight correlational study, the latter result does not alone provide a good basis for causal inference. The correlation could be spurious. Nonetheless, such a result enriches the study findings and provides a plausible hypothesis for further study.

ATTRITION

A common, albeit too frequently ignored, threat to experimental studies is attrition. Attrition is apt to be an especially serious problem in studies that involve long periods of time and/or involve treatment conditions that differ in attractiveness to participants. Accounting for attrition and differences in attrition rates by treatment condition is a minimal requirement for any experimental study. Where partial information is available on units prior to attrition, analyses of these data by treatment condition, and the lost versus retained participants, is called for. Jurs and Glass (1971) provide a good example of such an analysis. A 2×2 analysis (treatment condition by attrition–nonattrition) illustrates the desired analyses of the pretest or other measures available prior to attrition. As summarized by Cook and Campbell (1979, p. 361), "a main effect of those who drop out versus those who remain can indicate a threat to external validity." That is, the target population, having once been redefined by the requirement of informed consent, is again systematically altered as the result of attrition. "A statistical interaction of the mortality and treatment factors suggests...a threat to internal validity, for the kind of unit dropping out of the experimental group is different from the kind of unit dropping out of the controls" (Cook & Campbell, 1979, p. 361).

Attrition can, and often does, convert a randomized experiment into a comparison of noncomparable groups. Where attrition may be unavoidable it is therefore important to prepare for the eventuality. Plans for alternate analyses of the types considered below in the section on nonequivalent control group designs are advisable. Where feasible, it is also desirable to plan for at least partial follow-up measurement of participants who drop out of the study. Teachers who decide they do not want to continue in an experiment may still be willing to allow researchers to analyze student achievement test data that is routinely collected by the school and that may serve as one of the study's dependent variables. While the inclusion of achievement results for teachers who do not complete the study with those of the groups to which they were initially assigned may dilute the magnitude of the treatment effect, it retains the probabilistic advantages of randomization. A more extended discussion of ways of dealing with the problems of attrition in randomized experiments is provided by Cook and Campbell (1979).

ENHANCING POWER

Studies of teaching must often be conducted with relatively small numbers of teachers. The number of students may be relatively large, but when the unit of interest and the unit of assignment are teachers, then the relevant sample size is the number of teachers. With small samples and an interest in small or modest-sized effects, statistical power can be a major concern. Under such conditions, the importance of obtaining premeasures that are expected to be highly related to the posttreatment measures of primary interest is especially great.

Blocking and the analysis of covariance (ANCOVA) can substantially enhance power where the blocking variable of covariate is highly related to the dependent variable. Feldt (1958) has shown that blocking is generally preferable to ANCOVA for pretest–posttest correlations of .4 or less, whereas ANCOVA is more powerful for correlations of about .6 or higher. Blocking can be more demanding in the sense that premeasures must be obtained and analyzed prior to assignment while assignment in ANCOVA is made without knowledge of pretest results. As noted above, however, assignment following the analysis of premeasures has the potential advantage of reducing problems caused by treatment differences in refusal. Blocking also depends on weaker assumptions than those required by ANCOVA.

A secondary advantage of blocking or ANCOVA over a posttest-only design is the ability to identify interactions between levels of the premeasure and the treatment condition. For more detailed discussion of blocking and/or ANCOVA see Cox (1957), Feldt (1958), and Kirk (1982).

Nonequivalent Control Group Designs

Comparison is fundamental not only to experimental studies but to all of the quasi-experimental and nonexperimental designs discussed below. The fundamental comparison between the observed outcome, $y(E)$, for units receiving an experimental treatment, to $y(C)$ for units receiving a control treatment, as described by Rubin (1974), is the logical goal even though the basis for estimating the later value may be quite tenuous. The designs considered below differ in the way in which comparison values of $y(C)$ are obtained and in the trustworthiness of those estimates.

NORMATIVE EXPECTATION

Informal comparisons to normative data have long been used in the interpretation of achievement test results and changes in achievement. Often the comparisons rest upon implicit, albeit not necessarily valid, assumptions regarding the meaning of the scale of measurement. For example, the ubiquitous grade equivalent (GE) scale has too frequently formed the basis for judging improvement. The common expectation of a year's increase in GE units in a year's time provided an informal basis of comparison in the early days of the evaluation of Title I of the Elementary and Secondary Education Act of 1965. For most students, however, such a comparison is clearly unreasonable. For students whose pretest scores are below grade level, the expectation of a year's gain in a year's time in the absence of a treatment effect is generally too high, whereas for students with pretest scores above grade level it is generally too low (cf. Linn & Slinde, 1977). As stated by Rosenshine and McGaw (1972), "a year's progress in a year's time means different things to a teacher whose class begins the year near or above grade level and a teacher whose class begins the year two or three years below grade level" (p. 640).

Linn and Slinde (1977) plotted the deviations from the nominal grade level of GE scores for students with precentile ranks of 20 and 80 at grades two through six for three commonly used reading and arithmetic tests. The size of the deviation varied noticeably from one test to another, but they all showed the same general trends. At the sixth grade, the student at the 80th percentile for his or her grade was roughly twice as many GEs above grade level as a second grade student with the same percentile rank. Similarly, students at the 20th percentile were farther behind grade level in grade six than at grade two by a factor of roughly two to one. Others have reported similar results. For example, Prescott (1973) found that a gain of .67 GEs per year would result in a constant percentile rank of 24 while David and Pelavin (1977) found that the empirical average growth rate for students eligible for certain compensatory education programs was .7 GEs per year as opposed to the naive expectation of 1.0. Clearly, the 1.0 GE unit gain per year provides an inappropriate basis of comparisons for most students or for groups of students whose starting position differs from the 50th percentile.

The lack of suitability of GE scores for purposes of providing a reasonable no-treatment expectation of gains against which to compare observed gains for students receiving a special program has led to a search for alternatives. Percentile ranks in norm groups relevant to the time of measurement is one possibility. However, as Linn reports (1979):

even if the assumption that normal growth is defined as maintaining a constant percentile rank is accepted, there are good reasons to prefer other metrics for analysis. By definition a distribution of percentile ranks is rectangular in the group for which they are derived. In order to achieve this distribution, raw scores in the middle of the distribution must be spread out while those at the extremes are squeezed together. For example, in one widely used test of math concepts, a single additional correct answer would result in an increase from the 50th to the 56th percentile rank. On the other hand, the same increase in percentile rank would require three additional right answers at the high and low ends of the distribution. The metric limitations of the percentile rank scale led Coleman and Karweit (1970) to the conclusion that the potential utility of this type of score is limited to indicating the direction of change compared to the norm. It is not considered appropriate for measuring the amount of change. (p. 93)

The perceived need to use normative data as the basis of comparison of program results for which reasonable control groups cannot be obtained, coupled with the limitations of GE scores and percentile ranks, led to the creation of the Normal Curve Equivalent (NCE) scores which have received widespread use in the context of Title I evaluations. NCEs became the required metric in the Title I Evaluation and Reporting System. These scores are simply normalized standard scores with a mean of 50 and a standard deviation of 21.06, ranging from a minimum of 1 to a maximum of 99. NCEs are commonly assumed to retain the major advantages of percentile ranks and have, in addition, the advantage of an equal interval scale (e.g. Tallmadge & Wood, 1976). The equal interval assumption is questionable, however.

Model A of the Title I Evaluation and Reporting System provides a simple means of estimating $y(C)$ in the absence of a control group. The "no-treatment expectation" for the average posttest NCE score is simply the average pretest NCE for the experimental group. Pretest and posttest NCEs must be obtained by comparison to norms based on test administration dates that are near those used for the experimental group. In other words, it is assumed that in the absence of the experimental treatment, or in the case of the Title I, the implementation of the Title I program, students would maintain a constant percentile rank, and therefore a constant NCE.

The idea of a constant percentile rank as a no-treatment expectation, coupled with the claimed properties of normalized standard scores, has considerable intuitive appeal and may be better than other available alternatives in many practical situations. However, "the model rests on strong assumptions for which there is no adequate basis" (Linn, 1981, p. 94). Its applicability is limited to standardized tests with empirical norms at the times desired for measuring the experimental group participants. The results can be expected to vary from one test to another (Jaeger, 1979); the quality of norms and comparability of, say, fall and spring norming groups is questionable (Baglin, 1981; Linn, Dunbar, Harnisch, and Hastings, 1982), and there is no guarantee that the norms are an appropriate comparison for students in the study. Norms defined in different ways, for example, local, state, or national; low income or general popu-

lation; urban or rural, can produce different "no-treatment expectations." Finally, the correspondence of the selected test to the instruction in the experimental treatment may differ from that provided to typical members of the norm group. (See Linn et al., 1982 for a discussion of these and other threats to the validity of the norm-group comparison model for deriving no-treatment expectations.) In general, normative comparisons provide a weak basis for conclusions regarding treatment effects.

Where random assignment is not feasible but different groups receive different treatments, there is always a question of comparability. Preexisting differences between groups on measured and unmeasured characteristics pose serious threats to the validity of comparisons. A variety of techniques such as matching, the use of gain scores, and the analysis of covariance are available. Each technique provides an adjustment for preexisting differences. These techniques, and approaches that rely on systematic assignment, for example, the regression discontinuity design, are reviewed below. It should be recognized at the outset, however, that "there simply is no logical or statistical procedure that can be counted on to make proper allowances for uncontrolled preexisting differences between groups" (Lord, 1967, P. 305).

DIFFERENCE SCORES

An intuitively reasonable approach to the problem of preexisting differences between groups is to focus on change rather than final status. In its simplest form, pretest scores are simply subtracted from posttest scores and the resulting difference scores are used in the analysis (e.g., an analysis of variance). Variations on this approach include residual gain scores (i.e., posttest minus the value of posttest predicted from a regression of the posttest on the pretest), estimated "true" change scores, and standarized change scores.

Much has been written about difference scores, which are variously called change scores and gain scores. The two most frequent criticisms of difference scores are (a) that they tend to be unreliable, and (b) that they tend to be correlated with initial status. Unreliability is of concern when difference scores are used to make decisions about individuals, but is *not* a major concern in the present context. Between-group differences in average change may be detected with considerable power despite the very low reliability of within-group change scores. Indeed the very property that tends to produce low reliability, that is, a high pretest–posttest correlation, is the same property that often enhances the power of a repeated measures analysis of variance. More precisely, power of repeated measures analysis of variance is high when individual differences in change are small within a treatment group, which is a result often, though not necessarily, associated with a high pretest–posttest correlation.

The second characteristic of change scores, that is, the correlation with initial status, is of more serious concern in the comparison of preformed groups. The correlation between change, $D = Y - X$, and initial status, X, is given by

$$\rho_{xd} = \frac{\rho_{xy}\sigma_y - \sigma_x}{(\sigma_x^2 + \sigma_y^2 - 2\rho_{xy}\sigma_x\sigma_y)^{1/2}},$$

where Y is the postmeasure, σ_x and σ_y are the standard deviations of X and Y, respectively, and ρ_{xy} is the correlation between X and Y. As can be seen from the above equation, ρ_{xd} will equal zero only if $\rho_{xy}\sigma_y = \sigma_x$. If the standard deviations of the pre- and postmeasures are equal, then the change scores will be negatively correlated with the premeasure. It is possible for the correlation to be positive, but only when the postmeasure standard deviation is larger than that of the premeasure. Scales such as grade equivalent scores which show an increasing standard deviation with grade level, for example, may result in a positive correlation between change and pretest.

A nonzero correlation between change and initial status in comparisons of preformed groups is a potential problem because individuals who start at different levels will have different expected amounts of change in the absence of a treatment effect. As noted by Rogosa, Brandt, and Zimowski (1982), a correlation of change with initial status is not a problem in itself since the observed change is an unbiased estimate of an individual's true change. If the groups are not equivalent initially, however, these differences in expected amounts of change will bias the estimates of the effects of the treatment on change. This pseudo effect may be illustrated by a simple example. Suppose that there is no treatment effect but that the treatment group has a mean pretest score that is half a standard deviation below the total-group mean, whereas the control group pretest mean is half a standard deviation above the total group mean. Further, suppose that the pretest and posttest have equal standard deviations and a correlation of .8. From the above equation, the correlation between change and the pretest for the total group is found to be $-.32$. From this correlation the expected mean change for the treatment group may be shown to be $+.16$ times the standard deviation of the change scores, whereas the corresponding value for the control group is $-.16$ times that standard deviation. The result is a biased estimate of the effect of the treatment that is equal to almost a third of a standard deviation.

The above example is admittedly rather extreme, but illustrates the problem. It is clear that simple difference scores cannot be counted on to make proper allowance for differences in the initial status of preformed groups.

STANDARDIZED GAIN SCORES

Kenny (1975) has proposed the use of standardized gain scores in place of raw gains for analysis. This approach is motivated by Campbell's (1967) fan-spread notion and is similar to the use of the normal curve equivalent scale, in that the latter has a constant mean and standard deviation for the norm group at each date of testing. The fan-spread hypothesis postulates that, in the absence of the experimental treatment effect, the rate of growth is greater for initially high-scoring than for initially low-scoring groups. By standardizing pretest and posttest scores the presumed natural tendency for scores to spread out with time is removed and treatment effects are judged in terms of changes in relative differences between groups.

The pooled within-group standard deviation is used to standardize scores obtained at each measurement point. This is equivalent to assuming that without an experimental treatment effect, the initial gap between groups would increase "in direct proportion to the pooled within-group standard deviation of the scores" (Cook & Campbell, 1979, p. 185). A positive experimental treatment effect is implied according to this model if

$$\frac{\bar{Y}_E - \bar{Y}_c}{S_y} > \frac{\bar{X}_E - \bar{X}_c}{S_x},$$

where the Ys and Xs refer to the posttest and pretest scores, respectively, Es and Cs to experimental and control groups, respectively, and the Ss denote pooled within-group standard deviations. Alternatively, a positive experimental treatment effect implies that

$$\rho_{yt} > \rho_{xt},$$

where t is a dichotomous variable coded 1 for members of the experimental group and 0 for members of the control group, and the correlations are estimated for the combined groups.

The validity of the standardized change score analysis obviously is dependent on the validity of the fan-spread hypothesis. As noted by Cook and Campbell (1979), "the fan-spread pattern is an explicit model of one very specific pattern of change which the data may or may not approximate. Obviously, when the data do not conform to this pattern, the standardized gain score analysis will be biased" (p.185). Linn and Werts (1977) have presented a model that illustrates bias resulting from analyzing standardized gain scores when the fan-spread pattern is inappropriate. A variation of the standardized gain score analysis in which scores are standardized using estimated true-score standard deviations rather than observed score standard deviations is also discussed by Kenny (1975).

RESIDUAL SCORES

The disadvantage of change scores discussed above led to use of residual scores, which by definition are uncorrelated with initial status (DuBois, 1957; Manning & DuBois, 1962). A residual score is obtained by first regressing the posttest on the pretest. The regression is used to compute predicted posttest scores. Residual scores are simply the differences between the observed posttest scores and their predicted values. Residual scores are often referred to as residual gains, but "one cannot argue that the residualized score is a 'corrected' measure of gain" (Cronbach & Furby, 1970, p.74; see also Rogosa et al., 1982, pp. 738–741). It merely provides an index of the degree to which an individual's posttest score is higher or lower than expected.

Residualized scores avoid the bias in estimates of treatment effects for nonequivalent groups that is inherent in simple difference scores due to the nonzero correlation of the latter scores with pretest scores. Residual scores do not guarantee that the proper or complete adjustment has been made for all preexisting differences between groups, however. Initial diffferences on other variables, whether measured or unmeasured, may affect posttest performance and, hence, the residual scores may still be biased in favor of one group over another in the absence of a treatment effect.

Use of the total-group regression to obtain residual scores ignores the possibility that the pretest–posttest relationship may be affected by treatment differences. Mean differences as a result of treatment effects are also confounded with the total-group regression. For these reasons, within-treatment regressions and residual scores need to be used for purposes of making comparisons among treatment conditions. Within-group regressions are, of course, the ones that are used in the analysis of covariance.

ANALYSIS OF COVARIANCE (ANCOVA)

In randomized experiments ANCOVA is a potentially useful means of increasing the power of the analysis. The gain in power is achieved as the result of reducing the error variance by accounting for that part of the error variance of an analysis of variance that is predictable from the within-group relationship of the covariate and the posttest. The covariate may be a pretest or some other measure, and multiple covariates may be used. Increased precision depends on the strength of the relationship between the covariate(s) and the posttest, and comes at the cost of a more elaborate model with additional assumptions. The additional assumptions made ANCOVA a more "delicate instrument" (Elashoff, 1969) than the analysis of variance. The reservations of Elashoff and others (e.g., Campbell & Erlebacher, 1970) are more serious in the use of ANCOVA in nonrandomized studies than in randomized experiments.

In nonrandomized studies, ANCOVA retains its potential utility as a means of increasing precision. But the primary motivation for using ANCOVA is to adjust for preexisting differences between groups. The latter purpose is only of secondary interest in randomized studies where the expected value on the covariate is the same for all treatment groups. The estimated adjusted mean for treatment group j in a simple one-way design with a single covariate is given by

$$adj\bar{Y}_j = \bar{Y} - \hat{\beta}(\bar{X}_j - \bar{X}.),$$

where $\bar{Y}_j$ is the mean for treatment group j on the posttest, $\bar{X}_j$ and $\bar{X}.$ are the treatment-group and total-group covariate means, respectively, and $\hat{\beta}$ is the pooled within-group slope of the regression of the posttest on the covariate, which is assumed to be homogeneous across all treatment conditions. The magnitude of the adjustment obviously depends on the estimated slope and the deviation of the treatment-group mean on the covariate from the total-group mean.

With random assignment, the expected value of $\bar{X}_j$ is equal to the expected value of $\bar{X}.$ for all j, and with reasonably large sample sizes the adjustment will generally be small and of little consequence. In nonrandomized studies, however, the expected value of the group means on the covariate are generally not the same, and consequently the adjustments may be sizeable. But there is no guarantee that the adjustments are appropriate. Campbell and Erlebacher (1970) have argued that measurement error and "uniqueness" in the covariate produce a bias in the direction of underestimating the absolute value of the slope and therefore result in an underadjustment for preexisting differences. Such an underadjustment would tend to favor the initially higher scoring group (i.e., the group with the higher mean on the covariate) assuming a positive slope. Cronbach, Rogosa, Floden, and Price (1977) have shown, however, that the adjustment is not necessarily too small. Both under- and overadjust-

ments are possible, depending on the relationship of the observed covariate with the "complete discriminant" and the ideal predictor. The latter concepts are elaborated below following a brief review of the assumptions of ANCOVA.

Elashoff (1969) lists seven assumptions of ANCOVA. The first of these is an assumption that units are randomly assigned to treatments. This assumption is obviously violated in the application of primary concern here. Without this assumption, however, one can never entirely rule out the possibility that there are variables other than the covariate(s) on which there are preexisting differences between groups and which may influence the results on the dependent variable. Ironically, violations of some of the other assumptions reviewed by Elashoff are also most serious when there is nonrandom assignment.

The second assumption is that the covariate is independent of the treatment. This assumption is best satisfied by using as covariates only variables that are measured prior to the start of the treatments. See Smith (1957) for a detailed discussion of interpretations of ANCOVA results in situations where the covariate is subject to treatments effects.

A third assumption, which is bound to be violated in research on teaching, is that the covariate is measured without error. Cochran (1968) provides a valuable review of the effects of measurement error in statistics, including ANCOVA. Under the usual assumptions of classical test theory, the slope of the regression of Y on a fallible covariate can be shown to be attenuated by a factor equal to the reliability of the covariate. More specifically, the slope for the fallible covariate is

$$\beta_{yx} = \beta_{yt}\rho_{xx'},$$

where t is the true score part of X and $\rho_{xx'}$ is the reliability of X.

With random assignment, the expected value of the difference between two adjusted treatment means is not biased as the result of measurement error in the covariate. With nonrandom assignment, however, the expected value of the difference in adjusted means for Treatments 1 and 2 is biased by a factor equal to

$$\beta_{yt}(1 - \rho_{xx'})(\mu_{x1} - \mu_{x2}),$$

where μ_{x1} and μ_{x2} are the population means on the covariate for treatment Conditions 1 and 2, respectively. Figure 4.1 illustrates the bias for a condition where there is no treatment effect and the true scores (solid line) on the covariate account for all the preexisting differences between the treatment groups that are relevant to the dependent variable. As can be seen, the measurement error in the covariate (dashed lines) results in a bias in favor of the treatment group with the higher scores on the covariate, a condition consistent with the conclusion of Campbell and Erlebacher (1970) cited above. The fact that the conclusion does not always hold is due to the possibility that T is not the only relevant variable on which the groups may differ.

Lord (1960) has developed a large-sample covariance analysis procedure for a fallible covariate, and Porter (1967; see also Porter & Chibucos, 1974) has provided an approximation procedure using an estimate of the reliability of the covariate, which worked well with simulated data. Porter's estimated true score analysis of covariance is an improvement over the usual

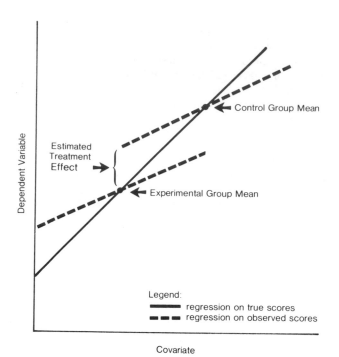

Fig. 4.1 Illustration of bias in estimated treatment effects due to errors of measurement in the covariate in the analysis of covariance.

ANCOVA for the analysis of results of nonrandomized studies, but requires parallel-form reliability estimates for the covariate and does not solve the logical problem of missing variables on which there are preexisting group differences or difficulties caused by other assumptions considered by Elashoff (1969).

The remaining four assumptions analyzed by Elashoff are linearity, homogeneity of the within-group regressions, normally distributed errors, and homogeneity of error variances. Nonlinearity reduces the effectiveness of the adjustment in randomized studies, but may, in addition, bias the estimates of treatment effects in nonrandomized studies. Differences in within-group regressions are testable, but the power of the test is limited for modest-sized studies. When found, differences in within-group regressions may be of substantive importance and are sometimes the major focus of research (e.g., aptitude-treatment interaction studies, Cronbach & Snow, 1976). ANCOVA is less robust than the analysis of variance with respect to violations of normality, especially when the distribution of the covariate is itself markedly nonnormal. Compared to the other limitations of ANCOVA for the analysis of data from preformed groups, however, violations of normality and of homogeneity of error variance are of relatively minor concern.

STRUCTURAL EQUATION MODELS

Recognition that errors of measurement in covariates can bias the estimates of treatment effects leads to an interest in models involving unmeasured latent variables. A distinction is made between a measurement model, in which observed variables are treated as fallible indicators of latent variables, and a structural model, in which the hypothesized causal relations among latent variables are specified. Although a more general model has

been proposed (Bentler, 1976), perhaps the best-known and most widely used analytical procedure for simultaneously incorporating measurement and structural models is Jöreskog's (1973) linear structural relations (LISREL) model. The most recent computer program for this general model is LISREL V (Jöreskog & Sörbom, 1981).

The application of LISREL to the analysis of data from a nonequivalent group design may be illustrated by Sörbom's (1981) reanalysis of the data taken from Barnow's (1973) analysis of the effects of a Head Start Summer Program (see also Bentler & Woodward, 1980; Magidson, 1977; and Jöreskog & Sörbom, 1981, for uses of LISREL with these data). Sörbom used results for a sample of 148 children who participated in Head Start summer programs and a sample of 155 comparison-group children who were matched to the Head Start group on sex and kindergarten attendance.

The study included two potential dependent variables (scores on the Metropolitan Readiness Test and scores on the Illinios Test of Psycholinguistic Abilities, which are denoted Y_1 and Y_2, respectively). Four potential covariates were available (mother's education, father's education, father's occupation, and family income, which are denoted X_1 thru X_4). The four "X" variables are assumed to be fallible indicators of a single construct, ξ, which is labeled socioeconomic status. Similarly, the two tests are assumed to be fallible indicators of a single cognitive ability construct, η. The structural model specifies cognitive ability in group j in terms of socioeconomic status in a manner analogous to ANCOVA. That is,

$$\eta_j = \alpha_j + \beta_j \xi_j + \zeta_j,$$

where β_j is the within-group slope, α_j is the intercept for group j, and ζ_j is the disturbance term, If η and ξ were directly measured, a standard ANCOVA could be used to test the equality of slopes:

$$\beta_1 = \beta_2,$$

and, given equal slopes, the treatment effect by testing the equality of the intercepts,

$$\alpha_1 = \alpha_2.$$

Since only fallible measures of ξ and η are available, the measurement models are used to specify these constructs. The ith X variable and the ith Y variable in group j are specified as follows:

$$X_{ij} = \gamma_i + \lambda_i \xi_j + \delta_{ij},$$
$$Y_{ij} = \gamma_i + \lambda_i \eta_j + \varepsilon_{ij},$$

where δs and εs are errors of measurement, the λs are slope parameters relating X to ξ or Y to η, and the γs and λs are not dependent on the group, whereas the other terms are. Because the scaling of η and ξ is arbitrary, one λ in the X set and one in the Y set are arbitrarily set equal to 1.0. In a similar fashion, the intercept in the structural model for one of the groups is set to zero, say $\alpha_1 = 0$. The estimate for the other group, α_2, then provides an indication of the differential treatment effect.

The actual specification for LISREL involves the use of dummy variables. The full model for the analysis is given in terms of matrix equations below:

(1) Measurement model for X in group j:

$$\begin{bmatrix} X_{1j} \\ X_{2j} \\ X_{3j} \\ X_{4j} \end{bmatrix} = \begin{bmatrix} 1 & \gamma_1 \\ \lambda_2 & \gamma_2 \\ \lambda_3 & \gamma_3 \\ \lambda_4 & \gamma_4 \end{bmatrix} \begin{bmatrix} \xi_j \\ l \end{bmatrix} + \begin{bmatrix} \delta_{1j} \\ \delta_{2j} \\ \xi_{2j} \\ \delta_{4j} \end{bmatrix},$$

(2) Measurement model for Y in group j

$$\begin{bmatrix} Y_{ij} \\ Y_{2j} \end{bmatrix} = \begin{bmatrix} 1 & \gamma_5 \\ \lambda_6 & \gamma_6 \end{bmatrix} \begin{bmatrix} \eta_j \\ 1 \end{bmatrix} + \begin{bmatrix} \varepsilon_{ij} \\ \varepsilon_{2j} \end{bmatrix}$$

(3) Structural model in group j.

$$\begin{bmatrix} \eta_j \\ \xi_j \\ l \end{bmatrix} = \begin{bmatrix} O & \beta_j & O \\ O & O & O \\ O & O & O \end{bmatrix} \begin{bmatrix} \eta_j \\ \xi_j \\ l \end{bmatrix} + \begin{bmatrix} \alpha_j \\ K_j \\ l \end{bmatrix} (1) + \begin{bmatrix} \zeta_j \\ \xi_j - K_j \\ O \end{bmatrix},$$

Where K_j is the expected value of ξ_j. As was true of α_1, K_1 is set equal to zero and K_2 then provides the mean between group difference in socioeconomic status.

The primary hypotheses of interest are: (a) Do the groups differ in mean socioeconomic status, that is, does $K_2 = O$? (b) Are the group slopes in the structural equation equal, that is, does $\beta_1 = \beta_2$? and (c) Given that $\beta_1 = \beta_2$, are the intercepts of the structural equation equal, that is, does $\alpha_2 = O$?

Using a slightly more complicated version of the above model, which allowed for a nonzero correlation between δ_{1j} and δ_j, Sörbom (1981) obtained the following estimates:

$\hat{K}_2 = -.382$ with standard error $= .103$,

$\hat{\beta}_1 = 2.295$ and $\hat{\beta}_2 = 2.026$, which were not significantly different, and with β_1 constrained to equal β_2 (estimated value = 2.135),

$\hat{\alpha}_2 = .182$ with standard error $= .376$.

From the above results it was concluded that the groups differed in socioeconomic status ($\hat{K}_2$ was more that twice its standard error with K_1 set to zero), the Head Start program did not alter the slope of the regression of cognitive ability on socioeconomic status ($\beta_1 = \beta_2$), and there is no evidence of a significant positive effect of Head Start on cognitive ability (α_2 was less than twice its standard error with $\hat{\alpha}_1$ set to zero).

While obviously more complex and less familiar, the Sörbom (1981) analysis has several advantages over a standard ANCOVA. It provides a single test of the effects using all the variables, as opposed to a separate ANCOVA for each dependent variable. More importantly, it allows for errors of measurement and thereby removes the bias in estimated treatment effects. It might be noted in this regard, that, although the estimated effect, $\hat{\alpha}_2 = .182$, is not significant, it is positive, whereas the original ANCOVA analysis with fallible covariates produced significantly negative estimates of the effect of Head Start, which were presumably an artifact of measurement error in the covariates. Other advantages of the LISREL approach include the tests of the measurement models and the flexibility of allowing for correlated errors of measurement as was done by Sörbom.

Although the above advantages of LISREL are notable, it is not a panacea. The model involves strong assumptions. Multiple measures of constructs are needed to gain the advantages of the model, and such multiple measurement is the exception rather than the rule. Implementation of the model is complex and at times controversial, as is illustrated by Bentler and Woodward's (1980) critique and reanalysis of results reported by Magidson (1977). Finally, and most importantly, there is no guarantee that the ξ constructs will capture all of the relevant preexisting group differences. This last caveat will be considered in the next two sections, albeit with different formulations.

SELECTION MODELS

A fundamental problem in the use of nonrandom samples is that the precise basis of selection is usually unknown and the selection effects can bias the estimates of population parameters of interest. The advantage of regression discontinuity designs, discussed below, derives from the fact that the basis of selection is known. With knowledge of the basis of selection, its effects can be taken into account in the analysis. As demonstrated by Goldberger (1972a) and Rubin (1977), explicit selection on the basis of a pretest (covariate) can be accounted for in the analysis and unbiased estimates of treatments effects can be obtained. Frequently, however, the basis for selection into a particular treatment condition is unknown. In such situations it is important to be able to model the selection process.

The problems caused by selectivity can most readily be seen by first considering a single group, the comparison group, and then turning to a consideration of the problems with multiple groups. Numerous discussions of selection effects and models for removing selectivity bias have appeared in recent years, particularly in the econometric literature (cf. Barnow, Cain, & Goldberger, 1980; Berk, Ray, & Cooley, 1982; Goldberger, 1981; Heckman, 1976, 1979, 1980; Muthén & Jöreskog, 1983; Olsen, 1980). Models of the selection process are the key to these approaches to the selectivity problem. Muthén & Jöreskog have provided a clear presentation of the basic problems caused by selectivity and a model for taking selectivity into account. Much of the discussion of the problem here follows their lead, except for changes in notation.

Suppose there is a systematic but unknown basis for selection into a comparison group, whether it is the result of self-selection, administrative selection, or, as is most common, some combination of the two. Whatever the basis of selection, it is assumed that it is systematically determined on the basis of an unmeasured variable, U. Units are included in the comparison group if U is greater than some critical value, which, since the scaling of the unmeasured variable is arbitrary, will be assumed to equal 0.

Now consider the regression of Y, the dependent variable of interest, on X, a covariate. The regression of interest is the one in the unselected population, that is,

$$y = \beta_o + \beta_1 X + e.$$

Assuming the regression in the unselected population is linear, the expected value of y given x is $\beta_o + \beta_1 X$. However, data can only be obtained from a sample from the selectable population, that is, units with $U > 0$. As shown by Muthén and Jöreskog (in press), the expected value of y given x for the selectable population is

$$E(y|x, U > 0) = \beta_o + \beta_1 X + E(e|U > 0),$$

where $E(e|U > 0)$ is the expected value of the error term for persons in the selectable population. The above conditional expectation of y is equal to the desired regression function in the unselected population only if $E(e|U > 0) = 0$. In general, however, $E(e|U > 0) \neq 0$. Consequently, the conditional expectation of Y in the selectable population is not the desired regression function in the unselected population.

In order to determine the conditions under which $E(e|U > 0)$ is equal to zero, it is useful to consider the regression of the unknown selection variable, U, on x,

$$U = \alpha_o + \alpha_1 x + g.$$

No causal interpretation is intended for this regression, only a descriptive relationship. Since the scaling of U is arbitrary, it may be assumed without loss of generality that the variance of the disturbance term, g, is equal to 1.0. It follows that the regression of e on g has a slope, ω, equal to the covariance between g and e. This regression is denoted

$$e = \omega g + h,$$

where h is the disturbance term.

With this notation, the expected value of e for the selectable population can be shown to be

$$E(e|U > 0) = \omega E(g > -\alpha_o - \alpha_1 x),$$

which will equal zero only when $\omega = 0$, that is, g is uncorrelated with e.

Under the special condition that g has a standard normal distribution, then the expected value of y given x in the selectable population may be expressed as follows:

$$E(y|\chi, U > 0) = \beta_o + \beta_1 X + \omega f(\lambda),$$

where $f(\lambda)$ is the ratio of the standard normal density function to that of the corresponding cumulative distribution function evaluated at $\lambda = \alpha_o + \alpha_1 x$. The true regression given by the above expectation is nonlinear. As shown by Muthén and Jöreskog (in press), the true regression function in the selectable population is also heteroscedastic, with conditional variance given by

$$\sigma^2(y|X, U > 0) = \sigma_e^2 - \omega^2 f(\lambda)[\lambda + f(\lambda)].$$

An illustrative example of the effects of selection on regression when the covariance between g and e is nonzero is shown in Figure 4.2. The solid straight line is the regression in the unselected population. The curved solid line is the resulting nonlinear regression in the selectable population and the dashed straight line is linear approximation to the regression in the

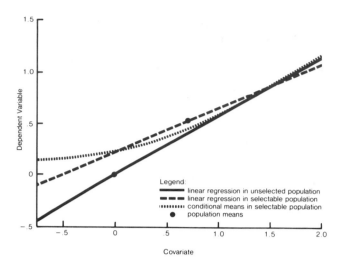

Fig. 4.2. Linear regressions in unselected and selectable populations and conditional means in selectable population.

selectable population. As can be seen, neither the nonlinear regression, nor its linear approximation in the selectable population corresponds to the desired regression function in the unselected population.

The linear regression for a sample from the selectable population would commonly be used as the basis for adjusting for group differences on x. That regression provides an estimate of the linear approximation to the regression function in the selectable group, which may be denoted

$$L(y|x, U > 0) = \beta_o^* + \beta_1^* x.$$

But the estimates are biased for the unselected population since in general

$$\beta_1^* \neq \beta_1,$$
$$\beta_0^* \neq \beta_0.$$

Thus, ordinary least squares regression of y on x does not provide the desired adjustment except under two special conditions. These are either (a) that g and e are uncorrelated, or (b) that g is equal to zero, which implies that U is a linear function of x. In either of these special cases, whatever relationship there is between the unmeasured selection variable, U, and the dependent variable, y, that relationship may be fully explained by x.

Several procedures have been proposed for estimating the regression parameters in the unselected population. Heckman's (1979) two-stage procedure uses a probit analysis in the first stage to estimate α_o and α_1, from which an estimate of $f(\lambda)$ may be computed. The latter estimate is used as an additional predictor in the second stage, in which the ordinary least squares regression of y on X and the estimated $f(\lambda)$ is obtained. Applications of this general approach to the two-group comparative study are described by Barnow et al. (1980) and by Goldberger (1979).

The two-stage probit analysis approach requires that χ scores are available for unselected as well as selectable units, while y scores are available only for selectable units. Situations where x

scores are available for $U \leq 0$ as well as $U > 0$ are referred to as *censored* selection. In some situations, however, neither x nor y are available for units with $U \leq 0$. The latter situation is referred to as *truncated* selection, and obviously poses more difficult estimation problems.

A more general model for J groups and a maximum likelihood estimation technique was developed by Muthén and Jöreskog (in press). Estimation techniques for both the censored and the truncated selection cases are provided. The basic features of the latter model are briefly described below for the simple case of a single dependent variable and a single covariate assuming a single selection relationship. As noted by Muthén and Jöreskog, generalizations to a multivariate system and multivariate selection relations are possible.

The causal model for the dependent variable in group j, $j = 1$, $2, \ldots J$, is:

$$y^j = \beta_o^j + \beta_1^j x + e^j.$$

Selection into group j occurs if an unmeasured selection variable, U^j, is greater than O, and the selection variable is related to the observed covariate by

$$U^j = \alpha_o^j + \alpha_1^j x + g^j,$$

for the jth group. As the result of the selection process, the covariance between g and e in any group may be nonzero, that is,

$$\sigma_{ge}^j \neq 0.$$

Muthén and Jöreskog (in press) used simulated data for two groups to evaluate their estimation procedure and compare it to an ordinary ANCOVA. Members of Group 1, the control group, were assumed to be randomly sampled from an unselected population in which the following causal model related y to x,

$$y = -.4 + .8x + e,$$

where the mean and variance of x were 0 and 1 respectively, and the variance of e was .9. The causal model for the experimental condition, group 2, was assumed to be

$$y = 0 + 1.0x + e,$$

and selection into the experimental group is based upon $U > 0$, where

$$U = 0 - 1.0x + g.$$

Variances of e and g are assumed to equal 1.0, the covariance between g and e to equal $-.5$ and x to be normally distributed. In other words, the simulated experimental treatment had an effect on y, changing both the slope and intercept of the regression, but the units selected for the treatment generally had lower values of x, since $g - x$ had to be greater than zero for a unit to be selected into the experimental group.

A standard analysis of covariance with 4000 simulated control units and 2037 experimental units showed no significant difference between treatments, with a pooled within-group slope of .81 and intercepts of .42 and $-.43$ for the control and experimental groups, respectively. In contrast, the Muthén and Jöreskog estimation correctly indicated a significant positive effect of the experimental treatment for both the censored and truncated selection situations. For the censored case, the estimates of the within-group slopes and intercepts were quite close to the original values of the simulation. Estimates assuming a truncated selection case were not as good, but were still considerably better than those from a standard ANCOVA.

Figure 4.3 shows the differences between the true simulation model regressions and the estimates obtained from three analyses for each treatment group. Panel A of Figure 4.3 shows differences for a standard ANCOVA while Panels B and C show the Muthén and Jöreskog differences for the censored and truncated selection situations, respectively. A perfect outcome would yield horizontal lines with a difference of zero for both treatment groups. As can be seen, the results for the censored case are quite satisfactory. Those for the ANCOVA are not.

COMPLETE DISCRIMINANT AND IDEAL COVARIATE

Cronbach et al. (1977) have presented a conceptual formulation that provides a basis for analyzing the potential sources of bias of various adjustments for preexisting differences between nonrandomly formed groups. They consider two hypothetical variables: the complete discriminant and the ideal covariate. The

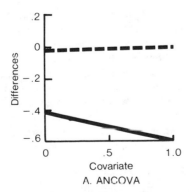

A. ANCOVA

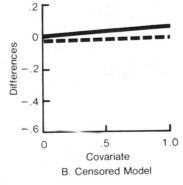

B. Censored Model

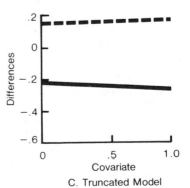

C. Truncated Model

Fig. 4.3. Difference between the true simulation model regressions and estimates obtained from three analyses (based on Muthén and Jöreskog, 1983). (Legend: ——— = experimental group; — — — = control group.)

complete discriminant, D, serves a role similar to U in the above formulation. It is the variable that contains the best possible information regarding selection differences between groups. In other words, no other variable would add to the ability to predict group membership beyond that possible from knowledge of D.

The ideal covariate, C, is the best possible predictor of the dependent variable without knowledge of treatment conditions. Within a treatment condition, prediction of the dependent variable could not be improved by the addition of any prior information to that contained in C. It is possible that C would differ from one treatment group to another, but this possibility will be ignored here.

If either D or C were known, it could be used as the covariate in ANCOVA to produce unbiased estimates of the treatment effect. In practice, of course, neither D nor C is known. Instead, some measures of variable, X, or set of variables, is available for use as the covariate. Substituting X for D or C generally leads to biased estimates of the treatment effects. The magnitude of the bias depends on the relationships of X to the unknown variables D and C.

The Cronbach et al. (1977) analysis shows that the bias in the estimates due to using X as a covariate may be in either direction rather than just in favor of the group with higher scores on X, as is often presumed. Their analysis also shows the limits on the amount of bias as a function of the relationship of X to the hypothetical variables D and C. As noted by Cook and Campbell (1979), "the implication is that knowledge about the relationship of an arbitrary covariate to both these constructs can be used to fix limits on the size of the bias" (p. 194).

In practice, the relationship of X with D and with C is uncertain. However, reasonable ranges of correlations of X with D and X with C may be hypothesized. The range of hypothesized correlations may, in turn, be used to set limits on the amount of bias in the treatment effect estimates. Thus, a range of estimates of the size of the treatment effect, rather than a point estimate, would be produced. This approach is illustrated by Reichardt (1979).

REGRESSION-DISCONTINUITY DESIGN

As is illustrated by the Cronbach et al. (1977) analysis, knowledge of the basis of assignment to treatment groups is the key to obtaining unbiased estimates of treatment effects. The surest way to gain such knowledge is to control the process of assignment. The regression–discontinuity design derives its strength from the fact that the basis of assignment is known. Units are assigned to treatments solely on the basis of a pretest or other measure obtained prior to treatment. Units below a cutting score on the premeasure are assigned to one treatment condition and those above are assigned to a second treatment condition. Commonly, the group with scores below the cutting score receives the experimental treatment and the higher-scoring group serves as the comparison, but logic applies as well to the opposite assignment or to any two treatments.

With assignment determined solely on the basis of the premeasure, that measure is necessarily the complete covariate in the terminology of Cronbach et al. (1977). If the assumptions of ANCOVA are satisfied, then using as the covariate the premea-

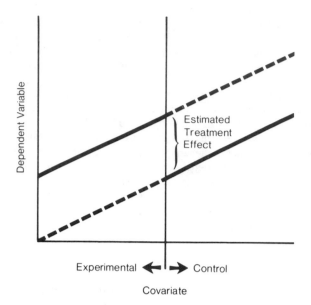

Fig. 4.4. Illustration of regression on discontinuity analysis. (Solid lines are the estimated within-group regressions for the observed range of scores in each group; dashed lines are extrapolations into the range of scores of the other group.)

sure on which assignment was based will yield unbiased estimates of the treatment effect (Goldberger, 1972a; Rubin, 1977). Measurement error in the covariate does not bias the ANCOVA estimates in a regression–discontinuity design. As stated by Cook and Campbell (1979) "it is knowledge of the selection process that makes the regression–discontinuity design so potentially amenable to causal interpretation" (p.138).

The logic of the regression–discontinuity design is illustrated in Figure 4.4. Units with pretest scores below the cutting score receive the experimental treatment and those above receive the comparison treatment. The solid lines represent the within-group regressions over the range of observed pretest scores within each group. The dashed lines show the extrapolations of those within-group regressions into the range of pretest scores of units receiving the other treatment. The estimated differential effect of the treatment is the difference in the predicted scores on the dependent variable evaluated at the cutting score of the pretest.

The example in Figure 4.4 is straightforward, but may be overly simplistic. There is, of course, no guarantee that the within-group regressions are parallel. Unequal slopes are not necessarily a problem; indeed, they may be of considerable substantive interest. However, they may also be the result of a potentially more difficult problem, that of nonlinearity. Floor and ceiling effects on the dependent variable can result in nonlinearity and can seriously distort the estimates based on a linear model. The potential for distortion is illustrated in Figure 4.5. The dashed line shows the true nonlinear regression assuming no treatment effect. The solid lines represent the fitted linear regression effect which erroneously suggests a positive effect of the treatment for the group with higher pretest scores.

Problems such as those illustrated in Figure 4.5 have been encountered in applications of the regression–discontinuity

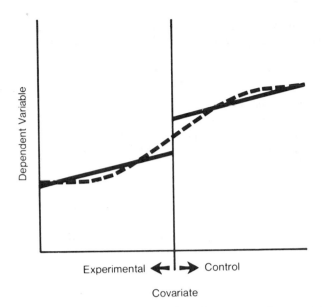

Fig. 4.5. Illustration of effects of nonlinearity in the regression–discontinuity design. (Solid lines are estimated linear regressions within groups; dashed line is the true nonlinear regression.)

design within the context of the Title I Evaluation and Reporting System (TIERS). Model C of Tiers is the regression–continuity design and was originally preferred to the more frequently used norm-referenced evaluation model, Model A (Tallmadge & Wood, 1976). Subsequent investigations of Model C, however, found that Model C often yields biased and erratic results (Stewart, 1980; Tallmadge & Wood, 1981). Nonlinearity resulting from floor effects for low-scoring Title I students and ceiling effects for high-scoring non-Title I students is a major factor in the unsatisfactory results of Model C.

In his analysis of designs where assignment to treatment conditions is based solely on a covariate, Rubin (1977) concluded that "if the conditional expectations are parallel and linear, the proper regression adjustment is the simple covariance adjustment. However, since the quality of the resulting estimates may be sensitive to the adequacy of the underlying model, it is wise to search for non-parallelism and nonlinearity in these conditional expectations" (p. 1). Checks for nonlinearity are greatly facilitated by having distributions of scores on the covariate overlap for the two groups, which is contrary to the usual regression discontinuity design. As stated by Rubin, "the most defensible analysis of the data requires the distribution of the covariate to overlap in the two groups; without overlap, the analysis relies on assumptions that cannot be checked using the data at hand" (1977, p. 22). This caution suggests a variation in the regression–discontinuity design in which scores on the covariate are used to define three regions: Units in the first region are assigned to the experimental treatment, units in the third to the control, and units in the middle region are randomly assigned to treatments. The existence of data for both treatments in the middle score range on the covariate provides a direct estimate of the conditional expectations without the need for extrapolation.

Single Group Designs

The absence of a comparison group severely limits the ability of the investigator to make causal inferences. On the other hand, premature experimentation can be costly and have little chance of payoff. Brophy (1979) put it stronger, in suggesting that premature experimentation can be "counterproductive." He went on to suggest that "before rushing to make a classroom process variable the independent variable to be manipulated in an experiment, it is worth exploring the correlational relation itself at greater length in order to develop 'grounded theory'... to guide experimentation" (Brophy, 1979, p. 740). This advice is similar to that given earlier by Rosenshine and Furst (1973), who argued for programmatic research starting with observation followed by correlational studies and experimental studies.

The potential range of variables is great. Correlational studies can often serve to narrow the range by identifying likely candidates for experimental manipulation. Dunkin and Biddle (1974) proposed a model with four categories of variables that need to be considered in studies of teaching. Their model provides a useful framework for organizing variables and guiding correlational studies. They distinguish between presage, context, process, and product variables. Included among presage variables are indicators of teacher formative experiences (e.g., SES, sex, and age), teacher training experiences (e.g., university, practice teaching, special training), and teacher properties (e.g., teaching skills, and ability and personality measures). Context variables include measures of student formative experiences, student properties (e.g., pretest scores), school and community contexts (e.g., school size, ethnic composition), and classroom contexts (e.g., size, facilities, materials). Process variables are measures of teacher and student classroom behaviors. Finally, product variables are short- and long-term measures of student knowledge, skills, and attitude (Dunkin & Biddle, 1974, pp. 36–48).

ZERO-ORDER CORRELATION COEFFICIENTS

Almost 30 years ago Herbert Simon (1954) aptly observed:

> Even in the first course in statistics, the slogan "Correlation is no proof of causation!" is imprinted firmly in the mind of the aspiring statistician or social scientist. It is possible that he leaves the course (and many subsequent courses) with no very clear ideas as to what *is* proved by correlation, but he never ceases to be on guard against "spurious" correlation, that master of imposture who is always representing himself as "true" correlation. (p. 467)

Simon goes on to discuss the usual alternative explanations of an observed correlation between X and Y: that X causes Y; that Y causes X; that X and Y are both caused by a third variable, Z; or that the "causal effect of X on Y (or vice versa) operates through Z" (Simon, 1954, p. 468). He then proceeds to present a detailed analysis of the standard approach to testing for spuriousness, by controlling for Z through partial correlations or other related approaches. Simon's analysis leads to the clear conclusion that whether one is dealing with zero-order correlations or partial correlations, causal interpretations necessarily rest on the acceptance of certain a priori assumptions. He concludes that "*correlation is proof of causation in the two-variable case if we are willing to make the assumptions of time precedence and non-correlation of error terms"* (Simon, 1954, pp. 472–473).

Of course, the catch is that these strong assumptions are seldom considered tenable. It is important to bear in mind, however, that strong assumptions are just as necessary in making causal interpretations from more complicated analysis, whether in the form of partial correlations, regression analyses, or structural equation models. Duncan (1975), who is well known for his contributions to causal modeling (cf. Duncan, 1966; Goldberger & Duncan, 1973), has cautioned that "one can *never* infer the causal ordering of two or more variables knowing only the values of the correlations (or even the partial correlations!)" (p. 20).

Causal reasoning must be in the other direction, from a model to implications for correlations which have causal interpretations only within the context of the model and its assumptions, as Duncan (1975) observed:

Knowing the causal ordering, or, more precisely, the causal model linking the variables, we can sometimes infer something about correlations. Or, assuming a model for the sake of argument we can express its properties in terms of correlations and (sometimes) find one or more conditions that must hold if the model is true but are potentially subject to refutation by empirical evidence.... Failure to reject a model, however, does not require one to accept it, for the reason ... that some other model(s) will always be consistent with the same set of data. (p. 20)

Given the limitations of causal modeling with correlational data, it is hardly surprising that some of the leaders in research on teaching eschew "simplistic models that 'explain' variance in student learning by entering predictor variables into multiple regression or path analysis" (Brophy, 1979, p. 741). Preference is given to using correlational analysis in simple form for the generation of hypotheses for experimental study. Simple correlations of individual process variables with student outcome (e.g., achievement) or change variables, or two-variable regressions with student pretest scores as the second predictor along with each process variable, are considered more useful for hypothesis generation in Brophy's judgment than more complex models. This approach is illustrated by Evertson, Anderson, Anderson, & Brophy's (1979, 1980) analysis of several hundred individual observation variables.

Subsequent experimental research by Emmer, Evertson, Sanford, & Clements (1982) illustrates the potential benefits of using the results of exploratory correlational analyses to provide hypotheses and focus for experimental studies. It is not obvious, however, that the search of hundreds of zero-order correlation coefficients or beta weights in two-predictor regressions had advantages over other correlational analysis strategies using more complex regression analyses and causal modeling. The inclusion of student pretest scores as a predictor, along with each individual process variable, in the search for relationships with student posttest scores reflects an implicit concern that the simple correlation between process and posttest may be spurious. But there are other potential variables in the presage and context categories described by Dunkin and Biddle (1974) that, if taken into account, might also lead to the conclusion that the relationship of a particular process variable

to student performance is spurious. The analytical procedures described below are intended to explore such possibilities.

MULTIPLE REGRESSION: PARTITIONING VARIANCE

Multiple regression and correlational (MRC) analysis is hardly new, but as Cohen (1982) recently observed, the view of MRC "has changed radically during the past decade when articles (e.g., Cohen, 1968; Darlington, 1968; Overall & Speigel, 1969) and later textbooks (e.g., Cohen & Cohen, 1975; Kerlinger & Pedhazur, 1973; McNeil, Kelly & McNeil, 1975; Namboodiri, Carter & Blalock, 1975; Ward & Jennings, 1973) appeared in which MRC ... was presented as a very powerful and flexible *general* data-analytic method" (p. 41). This "new look," as Cohen (1982) calls it, includes a number of features relatively unfamiliar a decade ago, such as uses of coded variables (e.g., dummy variables, effect codes), polynomial and product terms (cf. Glass, 1968; Cohen, 1978; Sockloff, 1976), hierarchical regression, and the partitioning of variance (cf. Mood, 1971; Wisler, 1969). Here the focus is on the latter of these: hierarchical regression and partitioning variance.

The Dunkin and Biddle (1974) categorization of variables is used to illustrate the partitioning of variance for hierarchical blocks of variables. Table 4.5 lists as "major blocks" of variables, Dunkin and Biddle's four major categories. Minor blocks are groups of variables within each major block and, finally, examples of individual variables within each block are listed. For simplicity, it is assumed that only one product variable, student achievement on a posttest, is of interest.

In order to partition the variance into portions unique to each block, joint for blocks of variables (also called common terms), and that portion due to error (or unexplained), a variety of multiple correlations are computed. Differences between squared multiple correlations are then used to partition the

Table 4.5. Blocks of Variables in Dunkin and Biddle's (1974) Model for the Study of Teaching

Major Blocks	Minor Blocks	Example of Individual Variables
A. Presage	a. Teacher Formative Experiences	a1. Social Class
		a2. Age
	b. Teacher Training Experiences	b1. University
		b2. Training Program
	c. Teacher Properties	c1. Teacher Skills
		c2. Teacher Ability
B. Context	d. Student Formative Experiences	d1. Social Class
		d2. Sex
	e. Pupil Properties	e1. Pretest
		e2. Student Attitude
	f. School & Community Contexts	f1. School Size
		f2. Ethnic Composition
	g. Classroom Contexts	g1. Class Size
		g2. Materials
C. Process	h. Teacher Classroom Behaviors	h1. Teacher Enthusiasm
		h2. Corrects Homework
	i. Student Classroom Behaviors	i1. Engaged Time
		i2. Student Questions
D. Product	j. Student Performance	j1. Posttest

Note. Adapted from Figure 3.1 of Dunkin & Biddle (1974).

Table 4.6. Illustration of the Partitioning of Variance for the Dunkin and Biddle (1974) Model

Component	Estimate	Results for Example[a]
Unique		
Block A: $U(A)$	$SMC(A, B, C) - SMC(B, C)$	.02
Block B: $U(B)$	$SMC(A, B, C) - SMC(A, C)$	.32
Block C: $U(C)$	$SMC(A, B, C) - SMC(A, B)$	.05
Joint		
Blocks A & B: $J(A, B)$	$SMC(A, B, C) - SMC(C) - U(A) - U(B)$	.06
Blocks A & C: $J(A, C)$	$SMC(A, B, C) - SMC(B) - U(A) - U(C)$	.03
Blocks B & C: $J(B, C)$	$SMC(A, B, C) - SMC(A) - U(B) - U(C)$	.13
Blocks A, B & C: $J(A, B, C)$	$SMC(A, B, C) - U(A) - U(B) - U(C)$ $- J(A, B) - J(A, C) - J(B, C)$	.19
Error or Unexplained	$1.0 - SMC(A, B, C)$	.20

[a] Results are computed assuming the following values of the relevant squared multiple correlations: $SMC(A) = .3$; $SMC(B) = .7$; $SMC(C) = .4$; $SMC(A, B) = .75$; $SMC(A, C) = .48$; $SMC(B, C) = .78$; $SMC(A, B, C) = .8$.

variance. Detailed rules for partitioning the variance are provided by Kerlinger and Pedhazur (1973, pp. 297–305) and by Pedhazur (1982, pp. 194–208), but here the procedure will be illustrated only by example. The technique is often referred to as commonality analysis. A major application of this technique is described in Mayeske et al. (1972).

The unique variance attributed to each of the three major blocks of predictors (pressage, context, and process) is the difference between the squared multiple correlation with all predictors included in the regression, $SMC(A,B,C)$ and the squared multiple correlation with all variables *except* those in the block of interest included. For example, the unique variance for the process block, $U(C)$, is

$$U(C) = SMC(A,B,C) - SMC(A,B).$$

Joint terms, or variance common to two blocks and not unique to either, and the error or unexplained variance are obtained from other combinations of squared multiple correlations, as shown in Table 4.6.

The last column of Table 4.6 shows results for a hypothetical example using the squared multiple correlations listed at the bottom of the table. From those numbers it would be concluded that, while 40% of the variance in posttest scores is predictable from process variables ($SMC(C) = .4$), only 5% of the variance is uniquely associated with that block of variables ($U(C) = .05$). The remaining 35% is common with A (3%), with B (13%), or with A and B (19%). Similar analyses could be conducted at the level of minor blocks of variables or individual variables. However, the number and interpretation of common terms would be quite unwieldy. Hence, the attention to minor blocks and/or individual variables is apt to be limited to the estimated uniquenesses.

A potential problem, not apparent in the hypothetical results in Table 4.6, is that negative estimates of common or joint terms can and often do occur. For example, if $SMC(A)$ were .5 instead of .3 but all other squared multiple correlations on Table 4.6 remained unchanged, the joint term for Blocks B and C, $J(B,C)$ would equal $-.07$. Such negative estimates of "variance accounted for" are uninterpretable.

PATH ANALYSIS/STRUCTURAL EQUATION MODELS

In the past ten or fifteen years the use of linear causal models, called path analysis or structural equation models, for analyzing correlational data has grown substantially. Duncan (1966) introduced the basic ideas of path analysis to many social scientists, and since that time causal modeling has been widely discussed and applied to a wide range of social science and educational problems (cf. Anderson, 1978; Anderson & Evans, 1974; Duncan, 1975; Goldberger, 1972b; Goldberger & Duncan, 1973; James, Mulaik, & Brett, 1982; Jencks et al., 1972; Kenny, 1979; Land, 1969; Wolfe, 1977). Although the estimation procedures that are now available (e.g., Jöreskog and Sörbom's LISREL V, 1981) are considerably more powerful and sophisticated than those available to early workers, the fundamental ideas of path analysis were rather fully developed in the 1920s by Sewall Wright (1921).

Path diagrams are useful representations of presumed models, which show, with arrows, the hypothesized causal connections between variables and underlying assumptions regarding disturbance terms. A simple, four-variable path diagram is illustrated in Figure 4.6. A single variable from each of Dunkin and Biddle's (1974) categories is posited for simplicity. The curved, double-headed arrow between the pressage and context variables represents a simple, unanalyzed correlation. That is, no casual direction is presumed and no attempt is made to explain this correlation as spurious. The straight single-headed arrows, on the other hand, depict presumed causal relations. Thus, process is seen to be presumed to be affected by both pressage and context, and product is affected by all three of the other variables. The fact that process is not completely determined by pressage and context is depicted by the unobserved variable U_1, which is known as a disturbance term. The disturbance term for product is U_2.

The fact that there is no direct connection between pressage or context and the disturbance terms or between the two disturbance terms corresponds to critical assumptions of this model, namely that U_1 and U_2 are uncorrelated with each other and with pressage and context. Using X_1, X_2, and X_3 for pressage, content and process, respectively, and Y for product, the path diagram in Figure 4.6 corresponds to the following two equations:

$$X_3 = p_1 X_1 + P_2 X_2 + q_1 U_1,$$

$$Y = p_3 X_1 + p_4 X_2 + p_5 X_3 + q_2 U_2,$$

where the ps and qs are path coefficients.

With a simple model such as in Figure 4.6, in which the Xs and Y are all observed variables, the path coefficients are simply equal to standardized partial regression coefficients. That is, p_1 and p_2 are the "beta" weights in the regression of X_3 on X_1 and X_2, and p_3, p_4, and p_5 are the beta weights in the regression of Y on X_1, X_2, and X_3. The qs are equal to the square roots of one minus the corresponding squared multiple correlations. There are often advantages, however, to using the corresponding unstandardized weights which, unlike the standardized weights, do not depend on sample variability (cf. Blalock, 1967; Boudon, 1968).

In more complicated models, where some of the variables are unobserved but data are available for fallible indicators, and/or there is reciprocal causation hypothesized in the model (e.g., achievement affects self-concept and self-concept affects achievement), estimation procedures other than ordinary least square regression are needed. For example, two-stage least squares (e.g., James & Singh, 1978) or the least squares or maximum likelihood analysis of covariance structures (e.g., Jöreskog and Sörbom, 1981) may be used in such situations. Before considering these complications, however, the basic procedure is illustrated by a numerical example for the simple model in Figure 4.6.

Intercorrelations among the four variables in the model in Figure 4.6 are listed in the top of Table 4.7 for a hypothetical example. Those correlations yield the multiple correlations and standardized partial regression coefficients (i.e., path coefficients) shown in the bottom half of Table 4.7. From those results, ignoring sampling error, it would be concluded that X_1 and X_2 each have a small positive effect on X_3, but that X_3 is largely determined by other factors, $q_2 = .966$. Both X_2 and X_3 are seen to have small positive effects on $Y(P_4 = P_5 = .1)$, while X_1 has a considerably larger effect ($P_3 = .5$). Again, however, other factors, not included in the model but depicted by the disturbance term, have still larger effects on $Y(q_2 = .817)$.

Correlations between observed variables are decomposed into a sum of products of path coefficients and unexplained cor-

Table 4.7. Intercorrelations, Standardized Partial Regression Coefficients, and Multiple Correlations for Hypothetical Example Corresponding to Figure 4.6.

Variables	Intercorrelations			
	X_1	X_2	X_3	Y
X_1	1.000	.400	.180	.558
X_2	.400	1.000	.240	.324
X_3	.180	.240	1.000	.214
Y	.558	.324	.214	1.000

Dependent Variable	Partial Regression Coefficients					Multiple Correlation
	X_1	X_2	X_3	U_1	U_2	
X_3	.1	.2	—	.966	—	.257
Y	.5	.1	.1	—	.817	.577

relations. The fundamental equation for recursive models (i.e., models in which the causal linkages run in only one direction) is

$$\rho_{yz} = \sum_i P y x_i \rho x_i z,$$

where the Ps are all the direct path coefficients to variable Y and the ρs are correlations. For example, the correlation between Y and X_1 is

$$\rho_{y1} = P_{y1} + P_{y2}\rho_{12} + P_{y3}\rho_{13}$$
$$= .5 + (.1)(.4) + (.1)(.18)$$
$$= .558$$

The correlation between X_1 and X_3 could also be decomposed into

$$\rho_{13} = p_{31} + p_{32}\rho_{12}$$
$$= .1 + (.2)(.4) = .18$$

but the correlation ρ_{12} is left unexplained. Thus, a complete decomposition of ρ_{y1} is

$$\rho_{y1} = P_{y1} + P_{y2}\rho_{12} + P_{y3}(p_{31} + p_{32}\rho_{12}).$$

All the arrows, except the curved arrow representing the unexplained correlation between X_1 and X_2, flow in one direction. That is, for example, there is no arrow pointing back from Y to one of the explanatory variables, X_1, X_2 or X_3. Such a model is called recursive. Nonrecursive models, which allow for reciprocal causation, are also possible, but as noted above, require more complex estimation procedures plus more complex decomposition. Nonrecursive models will not be considered here, but discussions and examples may be found in Anderson (1978), Duncan (1975), Jöreskog and Sörbom (1981), and Kenny (1979).

A model such as the one in Figure 4.6 suffers from a number of limitations. The path coefficients are consistent with, indeed they reproduce perfectly, the observed correlations among the variables. However, many other models would also fit the data. As was noted above, "one can *never* infer the causal ordering of

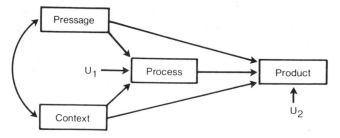

Fig. 4.6. Diagram based on Dunkin and Biddle's (1974) variable classification scheme.

two or more variables knowing only the values of the correlations" (Duncan, 1966, p. 20). Sometimes a model may be rejected, however, because it implies restraints on correlations which, if not satisfied, make that model untenable. For example, if it were assumed that there was no direct path from context to process in the model in Figure 4.6 (i.e., that $p_{32} = 0$, and the arrow from context to process was deleted), the correlation between process and context, ρ_{23}, would be implied to equal the product of two other correlations. Specifically,

$$\rho_{23} = \rho_{12}\rho_{13},$$

which is equivalent to saying that the partial regression weight of X_2 in the regression of X_3 on X_1 and X_2 is zero. If that partial regression weight were significantly different from zero, the modified model could be rejected. There is no way, however, to reject the original model on the basis of correlational data, because any set of correlations among four variables could be reproduced by the model. This is so because the model in Figure 4.6 is *just identified*; that is, there are no constraints of the values of any of the correlations imposed by the model. Hence, the model could not be rejected on the basis of correlational data.

The modified model with $p_{32} = 0$, on the other hand, is said to be *overidentified*. The implied constraint in the correlations stated above provides the potential means of rejecting the model. Overidentified models obviously provide greater potential for learning from the data than just-identified or *underidentified models* (i.e., models where there is not a unique solution for the model coefficients).

The model depicted in Figure 4.6 is also limited by the failure to take into account measurement error. Errors of measurement in the regressors lead to biased regression coefficients (Cochran, 1968). For example, if β_{yt} is the standardized regression weight for the regression of Y on an error-free measure, T, then the corresponding coefficient for the regression of Y on X, a fallible indicator of T, is

$$\beta_{yx} = \beta_{yt}\rho_{xx'},$$

where $\rho_{xx'}$, is the reliability of X. The above expression is based on the assumptions of classical test theory, that is,

$$X = T + E,$$

where E is the error of measurement and is assumed to be uncorrelated with both T and Y. Since the reliability of X is less than one, the regression coefficient for X is obviously less than the corresponding value for T. Thus, if the interest is in the effect of the construct T on Y, then that effect will be underestimated by β_{yx}.

With more than one regressor in the equation, errors of measurement will again result in biased coefficients, but the direction of the bias is not necessarily in the direction of underestimation. Some coefficients may be biased toward overstating the magnitude of an effect, while others tend to understate an effect. A measurement model must be added to the structural model to remove the biases due to errors of measurement.

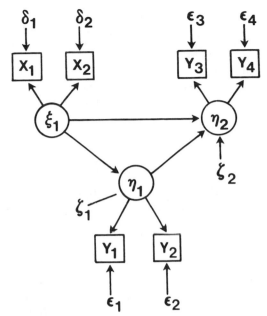

Fig. 4.7. Path diagram with latent variables, each measured by two fallible indicators.

MEASUREMENT MODELS WITH MULTIPLE INDICATORS

The LISREL model (Jöreskog and Sörbom, 1981) may be used to illustrate the use of measurement models in combination with a structural model involving unmeasured constructs. A simple model involving three unobserved constructs, each with two fallible indicators, is shown in Figure 4.7. Circled Greek letters represent the unobserved constructs, and the arrows connecting the circles show the presumed structural model. The observed fallible indicator variables are indicated by the letters in the squares. Uncircled δs and εs denote errors of measurement, which are assumed to be mutually uncorrelated and uncorrelated with all the unobserved constructs. Uncircled ζs are disturbance terms in the structural model.

To make the model in Figure 4.7 more concrete, X_1 and X_2 may be considered classroom means on two tests administered at the beginning of the year and are seen as indicators of average ability, ζ, Y_1 and Y_2 are two measures of teacher implementation of an instructional program, say, from teacher logs and classroom observations; and η_1 is the underlying implementation construct. Finally, Y_3 and Y_4 are classroom means on two posttests and η_2 is average achievement. The path of primary interest is between implementation, η_1, and achievement, η_2.

The measurement model in Figure 4.7 can be represented by the following six equations:

$$X_1 = \lambda_1\xi + \delta_1,$$
$$X_2 = \lambda_2\xi + \delta_2,$$
$$Y_1 = \lambda_3\eta_1 + \varepsilon_1,$$
$$Y_2 = \lambda_4\eta_1 + \varepsilon_2,$$
$$Y_3 = \lambda_5\eta_2 + \varepsilon_3,$$
$$Y_4 = \lambda_6\eta_2 + \varepsilon_4,$$

where the δs and εs are assumed to be mutually uncorrelated and uncorrelated with ξ and the ηs. Since the scale of ξ and the ηs is arbitrary, λ_1, λ_3, and λ_5 are set equal to 1.0 in order to identify the model. The remaining λs and variances of the δs and εs can then be estimated from the variances and covariances of the observed variables, the Xs and Ys.

The structural model is defined by the following two equations:

$$\eta_1 = \gamma_1 \xi + \zeta_1,$$

$$\eta_2 = \gamma_2 \xi + \beta \eta_1 + \zeta_2,$$

where the disturbance terms ζ_1 and ζ_2 are assumed to be uncorrelated with each other and with all other latent variables in the model. The estimate of β provides the desired estimate of the direct effect of program implementation on achievement. Parameter estimates for the above model could be obtained using LISREL V from the six-by-six variance-covariance matrix for the observed variables.

The use of multiple measures, as illustrated by the above model, has substantial theoretical advantages because it provides a means of avoiding distortions in the parameter estimates due to errors of measurement. From a practical point of view, however, it is the exception rather than the rule that multiple measures of each construct are feasible to obtain.

Aggregation and the Unit of Analysis

In studies of teaching, measures are typically obtained at two or more levels. There are at least measures of individual students within a classroom and of teachers and/or classroom-level variables. There may also be measures at other levels of aggregation, for example, school or school district characterizations, and community characteristics. The data are inherently multilevel. Too frequently, however, the hierarchical nature of the data is ignored in analysis.

Cronbach (1976) has forcefully argued that analyses of educational data often look at the wrong question and produce unjustified conclusions due to the failure to attend to questions of the unit of analysis and the hierarchical organization of the data. According to Cronbach (1976):

> The majority of studies of educational effects—whether classroom experiments, or evaluations of programs, or surveys—have collected and analyzed data in ways that conceal more than they reveal. The established methods have generated false conclusions in many studies. (p. 1)

The fact that correlation and regression analyses may yield quite different results when data are aggregated at different levels is hardly a new discovery. Warnings by Thorndike (1939) and Robinson (1950) that correlations between group means should not be interpreted as relationships at the level of individuals are well known. But there is less understanding of how to match the level of analysis to the question or how best to conduct multilevel analyses.

Brophy (1979) has proposed that studies of teacher behavior and its effects should "use the teacher as the unit of analysis (not the school or school district)" (p. 739). This is sensible ad-

vice; and better than the alternative, sometimes used, of attributing teacher and classroom characteristics to each student in a classroom and using the individual student as the unit of analysis. But, as was earlier recognized by Brophy (1975), some questions concern relationships within classrooms. The effects of variation of teacher–student interactions within a classroom are concealed by between-classroom analyses of means. As stated by Burstein (1980), "lumping together (through aggregation to the class level) data from different teacher–student interactions may mask the varying quality of the interactions in the same way that Veldman and Brophy (1974) argued that school-level analyses do for teacher differences" (p. 188).

Recognition that both between- and within-group analyses may be needed to address the questions of concern in a study of teaching has led several authors (e.g., Burstein, 1980; Cooley, Bond, & Mao, 1981; Cronbach, 1976; Cronbach & Webb, 1975) to recommend routine use of both types of analysis or a multilevel analysis that includes both between- and within-group effects. Cronbach (1976), for example, suggests that statistical analyses that pool individuals without regard to grouping are apt to be misleading. He goes on to suggest that "the more reasonable analysis is to relate variables *within* groups,... and then analyze group level variables across groups" (p. 1.3).

Burstein (1980) has summarized results of an application of Cronbach's analysis strategy that was conducted by Martin (1978). Martin reanalyzed data from Anderson, Everston, and Brophy's (1978) study of first-grade reading groups. Three levels: classrooms, reading groups within classrooms, and students within reading groups were used in Martin's reanalysis. Summary results from Martin's dissertation that were reported by Burstein (1980) show a significant effect for "new-question feedback" at the between-class level but not at the other two levels. "Nonvolunteer selection" into reading groups, on the other hand, had a sizeable significant effect at the level of reading groups within classes but no effect at the between-class or student-within-reading-group levels. Results such as these led Burstein (1980) to conclude that "one need not choose a 'correct' unit of analysis in teacher effectiveness research. On the contrary, analyses at multiple levels combined with theory-guided interpretations have much to offer the substantive researcher" (p. 191).

Cronbach (1976, pp. 3.1–3.11) proposed a decomposition of an individual's score on a dependent variable of interest into the following components:

1. the between-group predicted
2. the between-group residual
3. the common within-group predicted
4. the specific within-group predicted
5. the individual student residual

For example, if Y_{ij} is the score on a posttest for student i in group j, X_{ij}, the corresponding pretest score, and T_j a measure of the teacher in classroom j, then the five above components may be identified as follows:

1. $\bar{Y}.. + b_{BX}(\bar{X}._j - \bar{X}..) + b_{BT}(T_j - \bar{T}.)$,
2. $(\bar{Y}_j - \bar{Y}..) - b_{BX}(\bar{X}._j - \bar{X}..) - b_{BT}(T_j - \bar{T}.)$,
3. $b_w(X_{ij} - \bar{X}._j)$,

4. $(b_j - b_w)(X_{ij} - \bar{X}_{.j})$, and

5. e_{ij},

where means are denoted by bars and dots for the subscripts over which averages are taken, b_{BX} and b_{BT} are between-class regression coefficients, b_w is the pooled within-class regression coefficient, b_j is the regression coefficient within class j, and e_{ij} is the individual residual. If the teacher variables were measured specifically to each student, then terms involving T, parallel to those involving X, could be added to Components 3 and 4.

A between-class analysis would focus only on the first two components. For many studies this may be the most appropriate focus. Certainly, teacher effects as indicated by b_{BT} are of major interest in any study of teaching, as is the amount of residual variation between classes, indicated by the second component. The search for additional process variables at the classroom level that reduce the second component is an obvious part of research on teaching.

The third and fourth components are also of potential substantive interest, however, particularly if they include process variables that are linked to individual students. The pooled "within-group slope reflects the tendency, across all groups, of students above the group average to do better or worse on the outcome measure than the rest of the group" (Burstein, 1980, p. 217). The specific within-group slopes have the potential of reflecting differences in process between groups, that tend to increase or decrease the dependency of student outcomes on ini-

tial status. Hence, variation between classes in the specific within-group slopes is itself worthy of study and, if possible, explanation in terms of teacher behaviors (Burstein, 1980; Burstein, Linn, & Capell, 1978).

McDonald and Elias' (1976) beginning teacher effectiveness study included analyses of specific within-class slopes from regressions of posttest on pretest scores. They concluded that "there is substantial variability among classes with regard both to slopes and intercepts of the regression lines" (p. 615). An inspection of the within-class regressions shows a substantial range indeed. For 33 classes with reading data, the slopes ranged from a low of .60 to a high of 1.21. The corresponding figures for the 37 classes with mathematics test data are .06 and 1.44.

Ninety-percent confidence intervals for the within-class regressions for the 37 classes with mathematics test results are shown in Figure 4.8. The solid vertical line in the figure corresponds to the value of the pooled within-class slope. It is apparent from an inspection of Figure 4.8 that there is considerable instability in the specific within-group slopes due to the small number of students within a class. Consequently the confidence intervals for many classes are quite wide. Nonetheless, a few of the confidence intervals do not overlap and the pooled within-class slope is not included in the 90% confidence intervals for 5 of the classes. The important unanswered question is whether differences in within-class slopes may reflect differences in classroom process.

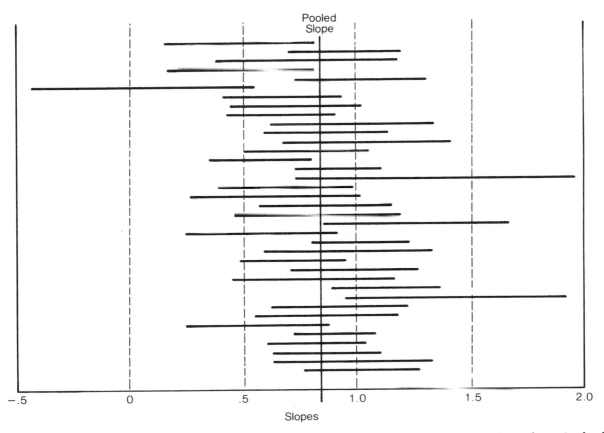

Fig. 4.8. Ninety-percent confidence intervals for regressions of posttest in mathematics on pretest in mathematics for 37 second-grade classrooms (data from McDonald and Elias, 1976).

Meta-Analysis

The quantitative methods discussed above are applicable to individual studies. The usefulness of quantitative analysis of data collected in a research study has long been recognized. Glass (1976) and others (e.g., Hunter, Schmidt, & Jackson, 1982; Jackson, 1980; Rosenthal, 1978) have persuasively argued that quantitative methods are just as important to the review and analysis of results across studies. According to Glass:

> most of us were trained to analyze complex relationships among variables in the primary analysis of research data. But at the higher level, where variance, non-uniformity and uncertainty are no less evident, we too often substitute literary exposition for quantitative rigor. The proper integration of research requires the same statistical methods that are applied in primary data analysis. (p. 6)

It is not easy to look at the results of 100 independent studies with varying and often apparently conflicting results and reach sound conclusions regarding effects and true variation in effects without the help of quantitative analysis. The problem is akin to trying to summarize the test results for 100 individuals in varying experimental conditions without the use of summary statistics. Yet, when Jackson (1980) randomly sampled 36 reviews in leading educational, psychological, and sociological journals, he found that only 3 of them cited summary statistics for the studies reviewed. In the last few years, however, Glass's notions of meta-analysis have gained much favor. The power of the approach and of related approaches developed independently by Schmidt and Hunter (1977) can be seen in the strength of the support provided for conclusions in a number of areas where previous reviews had yielded little (cf. Glass & Smith, 1979; Hartley, 1977; Hunter, 1980; Hunter, Schmidt, & Hunter, 1979; Kulik, Kulik, & Cohen, 1979; Pearlman, 1982; Smith & Glass, 1977). Two books (Glass, McGaw, & Smith, 1981; Hunter, Schmidt, & Jackson, 1982) on meta-analysis have recently been published. The reader interested in greater detail is referred to those two books and to McGaw (in press). See also Walberg's chapter in this volume for further discussion of meta-analysis.

Vote Counting

An early approach to quantification in reviews has come to be known as "vote counting." As described by Light and Smith (1971), studies are categorized as showing a significantly positive effect, a significantly negative effect, or no significant effect. "The number of studies falling into each of these three categories is then simply tallied" (Light & Smith, 1971, p. 433).

Vote counting is a step in the right direction and has been widely used, but it has limitations. As noted by Hunter, Schmidt, and Jackson (1982) it "is biased in favor of large sample studies which may show only small effect sizes" (p. 22). More importantly, Hedges and Olkin (1980) have shown that vote counting methods have very poor power that actually decreases as the number of studies increases.

p-Values

An alternative to vote-counting that was suggested by Rosenthal (1978) is to combine the probabilities (p-values) from inde-

pendent studies. This approach has an advantage over simple vote counting, in that it uses information available in p-values within either the range of "significant" or "nonsignificant" results. As noted by Rosenthal and Rubin (1979), "a p of .05 tells about the same story as a p of .06 if both results are in the same direction and the studies are of similar size (p.1165). In vote counting, however, the two studies would be tallied in different categories.

An obvious limitation of cumulation p-values is that they depend not only on effect sizes but on sample sizes. It is important to know not only the existence of an effect, but its size. Thus, it is desirable to go beyond probabilities, to estimates of the size and variability of effects across studies.

Another concern that applies not only to vote-counting and p-value methods but to the methods considered below, is the possibility that significant results are more apt to get published, and hence be available for review, than nonsignificant results. The "lost studies" might alter the probability and the estimate of the average effect size if they were available. Rosenthal (1979) has proposed an ingenious method for dealing with the question of studies that may have been conducted but never reported because the results were nonsignificant. He suggested that reviewers calculate the number of "new, filed or unretrieved" (p. 640) studies, which on average showed null results, and which would be required to bring the estimated overall probability of an effect down to a barely significant level. If the number of such studies is larger than could plausibly be expected to have been conducted, the conclusion based on the probability estimate from available studies is strengthened. Rosenthal and Rubin's (1978) estimate that about 65,000 lost studies would be required to lower the p-value to the barely significant level in their review of interpersonal expectancy effects, for example, makes the lost-study explanation of the findings entirely implausible.

Effect Sizes

Glass (1976, 1977, 1980) has emphasized the importance of estimating the effect size of each study and quantitatively analyzing the effect sizes across studies. The mean, variance, and relationship of effect sizes to coded study chracteristics provide the primary basis for synthesizing research findings and drawing conclusions. For studies comparing experimental and control groups, the effect size for study i, ES_i, is defined by

$$ES_i = \frac{\bar{Y}_E - \bar{Y}_c}{S},$$

where $\bar{Y}_E$ and $\bar{Y}_C$ are the sample means for the experimental and control groups, respectively, and S is the standard deviation in the control group or the pooled within-group standard deviation. Alternatively, correlations are used as estimates of effect sizes. Glass (1977) reports a variety of formulas that may be used to convert various statistics that may be available in the reports of individual studies into estimates of effect sizes.

Glass's meta-analysis approach has been applied to several areas of research relevant to teaching. Redfield and Rousseau (1981) found that, contrary to the mixed and inconclusive interpretations of a previous narrative review, the meta-analysis of

20 studies of teachers' use of higher cognitive questions had positive effects on student achievement. Hartley (1977) used the approach to synthesize the findings of studies of individually paced instruction and Kulik, Kulik, and Cohen (1979) have used it to analyze results of 75 studies of Keller's (1968) personalized system of instruction. Possibly the most elaborate application of the general approach is Glass and Smith's (1979) analysis of the effects of class size on student achievement. Despite a long history of inconclusive and conflicting reviews, the power of the quantitative analyses used by Glass and Smith enabled them to conclude that "a clear and strong relationship between class size and achievement has emerged" (1979, p. 15).

Recent statistical work related to the use of effect size estimates (e.g., Hedges, 1981, 1982; Rosenthal and Rubin, 1982) has moved beyond simple descriptive statistics based upon estimated effect sizes to provide statistical theory for the analysis. Distinguishing between population and sample estimates of effect sizes enabled Hedges (1981) to obtain a distribution of effect sizes, which he used to show that Glass's estimate has a small-sample bias. He also derived an unbiased estimator, which he showed has a smaller variance. More recently, Hedges (1982) presented a large-sample test for the homogeneity of effect sizes across studies. Rosenthal and Rubin (1982) have also provided an approximate significance test "of the heterogeneity of effect sizes for two or more independent studies for any type of effect size assuming estimates of its variance are available" (p. 503)

Explaining the Variance of Effect Sizes

Schmidt and Hunter (1977) independently developed methods of meta-analysis within the context of validity-generalization that share many of the features of Glass's approach (see, for example, Hunter, Schmidt, & Jackson, 1981; Linn & Dunbar, in press; Pearlman, 1982, for reviews of methodological developments and applications stemming from the Schmidt and Hunter approach to meta-analysis). The principal difference between the Schmidt-Hunter and Glass approaches is that the variance of the estimated effect sizes is typically unanalyzed in the Glass approach, whereas Schmidt and Hunter place considerable emphasis on explaining that variance in terms of various statistical artifacts. "These artifacts include: (1) sampling error, (2) study differences in reliability of independent and dependent measures, (3) study differences in range restriction, (4) study differences in instrument validity, and (5) computational, typographical and transcription errors" (Hunter, Schmidt, & Jackson, 1982, p. 28). A variety of methods have been developed for estimating the amount of variance in effect size estimates that is attributable to the first three of these artifacts (cf. Hunter, Schmidt, & Jackson, 1981; Linn & Dunbar, in press).

The meta-analysis techniques advocated by Schmidt and Hunter have had a profound effect on the interpretation of validity study results in personnel psychology. The approach has applicability in many other areas of research, including research on teaching. Applications of the Glass and Schmidt-Hunter meta-analytic techniques hold the promise of learning much more from previous research than has heretofore been feasible.

Conclusion

Quantitative analysis of primary research data and of results of previous research is a vital part of research on teaching. But quantitative methods cannot stand alone. Statistical adjustments are a poor substitute for adequate research design. The choice of what is worth studying and the appropriate reach of generalizations that almost always take us beyond the "limited reach of internal validity" (Cronbach, 1982, p. 112 ff.) necessarily involve qualitative judgments. The utility of highly quantitative causal modeling requires string theory that is often lacking. On the other hand, theories need the power of quantitative analysis in order to be refined. As Cooley et. al. (1981) noted:

This is a kind of chicken and egg situation. The more we understand phenomena, the better the models will be; the better the models, the better will be our understanding. The way to improve both is to use models in our educational research. Make them explicit. Get them out in the open so that they can be critically examined and improved as better thinking and better data are brought to bear on them. Through such an iterative process, we will finally begin to achieve the kinds of convincing models that are so desperately needed if we are to improve quantitative approaches to the study of educational phenomena. (p. 80)

REFERENCES

Anderson, J. G. (1978). Causal models in educational research: Nonrecursive models. *American Educational Research Journal, 15,* 81–97.

Anderson, J. G., & Evans, F. B. (1974). Causal models in educational research: Recursive models. *American Educational Research Journal, 11,* 29–39.

Anderson, L., Evertson, C., & Brophy, J. (1978). *The first grade reading group study: Technical report of experimental and process–outcome relationships.* Austin: University of Texas, R & D Center for Teacher Education.

Baglin, R. F. (1981). Does "nationally" normed really mean nationally? *Journal of Educational Measurement, 18,* 97–108.

Barnow, B. S. (1973). *The effects of Head Start and socioeconomic status on cognitive development of disadvantaged children.* Unpublished doctoral dissertation, University of Wisconsin, Madison.

Barnow, B. S., Cain, G. G., & Goldberger, A. S. (1980). Issues in the analysis of selectivity bias. In E. Stromsdorfer & G. Farkus (Eds.), *Evaluation Studies Review Annual* (Vol. 5). Beverly Hills: Sage Publications.

Bentler, P. M. (1976). Multistructure statistical model applied to factor analysis. *Multivariate Behavioral Research, 11,* 3–25.

Bentler, P. M. (1980). Multivariate analysis with latent variables; Causal models. *Annual Review of Psychology, 31,* 419–456.

Bentler, P. M., & Woodward, J. A. (1980). A Head Start reevaluation: Positive effects are not yet determined. In E. L. Baker & E. S. Quellmalz (Eds.), *Educational testing and evaluation: Design, analysis and policy.* Beverly Hills: Sage Publications.

Berk, R. A., Ray, S. C., & Cooley, T. F. (1982). *Selection biases in sociological data* (Project Report, National Institute of Justice Grant No 80-IJ-CX-0037). Santa Barbara: University of California.

Blalock, H. M., Jr. (1967). Causal inferences, closed populations, and measures of association. *American Political Science Review, 61,* 130–136.

Boudon, R. (1968). A new look at correlation analysis. In H. M. Blalock, Jr., & A. B. Blalock (Eds.), *Methodology in social research.* New York: McGraw-Hill.

Brophy, J. E. (1975). *The student as the unit of analysis* (Research Rep. No. 75-12). Austin: University of Texas.

Brophy, J. E. (1979). Teacher behavior and its effects. *Journal of Educational Psychology, 71,* 733–750.

Burstein, L. (1980). The analysis of multilevel data in educational research and evaluation. In D. C. Berliner (Ed.), *Review of Research in Education, 8,* 158–233.

Burstein, L., Linn, R. L., & Capell, F. J. (1978). Analyzing multilevel data in the presence of heterogeneous within-class regressions. *Journal of Educational Statistics, 3,* 347–383.

Campbell, D. T. (1967). *The effects of college on students: Proposing a quasi-experimental approach* (Research Report). Evanston, IL: Northwestern University.

Campbell, D. T., & Erlebacher, A. E. (1970). How regression artifacts in quasi-experimental evaluations can mistakenly make compensatory education look harmful. In J. Hellmuth (Ed.), *Compensatory education: A national debate: Vol. 3. Disadvantaged child.* New York: Brunner/Mazel.

Campbell, D. T., & Stanley, J. C. (1963). Experimental and quasi-experimental designs for research on teaching. In N. L. Gage (Ed.), *Handbook of research on teaching.* Chicago: Rand McNally.

Cochran, W. G. (1968). Errors of measurement in statistics. *Technometrics, 10,* 637–666.

Cochran, W. G., & Cox, G. M. (1957). *Experimental designs* (2nd ed.). New York: John Wiley.

Cohen, J. (1968). Multiple regression as a general data analytic system. *Psychological Bulletin, 70,* 426–443.

Cohen, J. (1978). Partialed products *are* interactions; partialed powers *are* curve components. *Psychological Bulletin, 85,* 858–866.

Cohen, J. (1982). "New-look" multiple regression/correlational analysis and the analysis of variance/covariance. In G. Keren (Ed.), *Statistical and methodological issues in psychology and social sciences research.* Hillsdale, NJ: Lawrence Erlbaum Associates.

Cohen, J., & Cohen, P. (1975). *Applied multiple regression/correlation analysis for the behavioral sciences.* Hillsdale, NJ: Lawrence Erlbaum Associates.

Coleman, J. S., & Karweit, N. (1970). *Measures of school performance.* Santa Monica, CA: Rand Corporation.

Cook, T. D., & Campbell, D. T. (1976). The design and conduct of quasi-experiments and true experiments in field settings. In M. Dunnette (Ed.), *Handbook of industrial and organizational psychology.* Chicago: Rand McNally.

Cook, T. D., & Campbell, D. T. (1979). *Quasi-experimentation: Design and analysis issues for field settings.* Chicago: Rand McNally.

Cooley, W. W., Bond, L., & Mao, B. (1981). Analyzing multilevel data. In R. A. Berk (Ed.), *Educational evaluation methodology: The state of the art.* Baltimore: Johns Hopkins University Press.

Cox, D. R. (1957). The use of a concomitant variable in selecting an experimental design. *Biometrika, 44,* 150–158.

Cronbach, L. J. (1976, July) *Research on classrooms and schools: Formulation of questions, design, and analysis* (Occasional paper). Stanford, CA: Stanford University, Stanford Evaluation Consortium.

Cronbach, L. J. (1982). *Designing evaluations of educational and social programs.* San Francisco: Jossey-Bass.

Cronbach, L. J., & Furby, L. (1970). How we should measure "change" — or should we? *Psychological Bulletin, 74,* 68–80.

Cronbach, L. J., Rogosa, D. R., Floden, R. E., & Price, G. G. (1977). *Analysis of covariance in nonrandomized experiments; Parameters affecting bias* (Occasional paper). Stanford, CA: Stanford University, Stanford Evaluation Consortium.

Cronbach, L. J., & Snow, R. E. (1976). *Aptitudes and instructional methods.* New York: Irvington.

Cronbach, L. J., & Suppes, P. (Eds.). (1969). *Research for tomorrow's schools: Disciplined inquiry for education.* New York: Macmillan.

Cronbach, L. J., & Webb, N. (1975). Between-class and within-class effects in a reported aptitude × treatment interaction: Reanalysis of a study by G. L. Anderson. *Journal of Educational Psychology, 67,* 717–727.

Darlington, R. B. (1968). Multiple regression in psychological research. *Psychological Bulletin, 69,* 161–182.

David, J. L., & Pelavin, S. H. (1977). *Research on the effectiveness of compensatory education programs: A reanalysis of data* (SRI Project Report URU-4425). Menlo Park, CA: SRI International.

DuBois, P. H. (1957). *Multivariate correlational analysis.* New York: Harper.

Duncan, O. D. (1966). Path analysis: Sociological examples. *American Journal of Sociology, 72,* 1–16.

Duncan, O. D. (1975). *Introduction to structural equation models.* New York: Academic Press.

Dunkin, M., & Biddle, B. (1974). *The study of teaching.* New York: Holt, Rinehart & Winston.

Elashoff, J. D. (1969). Analysis of covariance: A delicate instrument. *American Educational Research Journal, 6,* 383–401.

Emmer, E. T., Evertson, C., Sanford, J., & Clements, B. S. (1982). *Improving classroom management: An experimental study in junior high classrooms* (R & D Rep.) Austin: University of Texas, R & D Center for Teacher Education.

Ennis, R. H. (1973). On causality. *Educational Researcher, 2,* 4–11.

Ennis, R. H. (1982). Abandon causality? *Educational Researcher, 11,* 25–27.

Evertson, C. M., Anderson, C. W., Anderson, L. M., & Brophy, J. E. (1979). *Predictors of student outcomes in junior high mathematics and English classes* (Rep. No. 4066). Austin: University of Texas, R & D Center for Teacher Education.

Evertson, C. M., Anderson, C. W., Anderson, L. M., & Brophy, J. E. (1980). Relationships between classroom behaviors and student outcomes in junior high mathematics and English classes. *American Educational Research Journal, 17,* 43–60.

Feldt, L. S. (1958). A comparison of the precision of three experimental designs employing a concomitant variable. *Psychometrika, 23,* 335–353.

Fisher, R. A. (1925). *Statistical methods for research workers.* London: Oliver and Boyd.

Glass, G. V. (1968). Correlations with products of variables: Statistical formulation and implications for methodology. *American Educational Research Journal, 5,* 721–728.

Glass, G. V. (1976). Primary, secondary and meta analysis of research. *Educational Researcher, 5*(11), 3–8.

Glass, G. V. (1977). Integrating findings: The meta-analysis of research. *Review of Research in Education, 5,* 351–379.

Glass, G. V. (1980). Summarizing effect sizes. In R. Rosenthal (Ed.), *New directions for methodology of social and behavioral science: Quantitative assessment of research domains.* San Francisco: Jossey-Bass.

Glass, G. V., McGaw, B., & Smith, M. L. (1981). *Meta-analysis in social research.* Beverly Hills: Sage Publications.

Glass, G. V., & Smith, M. L. (1979). Meta-analysis of research on the relationship of class-size and achievement. *Educational Evaluation and Policy Analysis, 1,* 2–16.

Goldberger, A. S. (1972a). *Selection bias in evaluating treatment effects: Some formal illustrations* (Discussion paper). Madison: University of Wisconsin, Institute for Research on Poverty.

Goldberger, A. S. (1972b). Structural equation methods in the social sciences. *Econometrika, 40,* 979–1001.

Goldberger, A. S. (1979). *Methods for eliminating selection bias.* Madison: University of Wisconsin, Department of Economics.

Goldberger, A. S. (1981). Linear regression after selection. *Journal of Econometrics, 15,* 357–366.

Goldberger, A. S., & Duncan, O. D. (1973). *Structural equation models in the social sciences: Specification, estimation, and testing.* New York: Seminar Press.

Good, T. L., & Grouws, D. A. (1979). The Missouri Mathematics Effectiveness Project: An experimental study in fourth-grade classrooms. *Journal of Educational Psychology, 71,* 355–362.

Hartley, S. S. (1977). *Meta-analysis of the effects of individually paced instruction in mathematics.* Unpublished doctoral dissertation, University of Colorado, Boulder.

Heckman, J. J. (1976). The common structure of statistical models of truncation, sample selection and limited dependent variables and a simple estimator for such models. *Annuals of Economic and Social Measurement, 5,* 475–492.

Heckman, J. J. (1979). Sample selection bias as specification error. *Econometrika, 47,* 153–161.

Heckman, J. J. (1980). Sample selection bias as a specification error. In J. P. Smith (Ed.), *Female labor supply: Theory and estimation.* Princeton, NJ: Princeton University Press.

Hedges, L. V. (1981). Distribution theory for Glass's estimator of effect size and related estimators. *Journal of Educational Statistics, 6,* 107–128.

Hedges, L. V. (1982). Estimation of effect size from a series of independent experiments. *Psychological Bulletin, 92,* 490–499.

Hedges, L. V., & Olkin, I. (1980). Vote-counting methods in research synthesis. *Psychological Bulletin, 88,* 359–369.

Hunter, J. E. (1980). *Validity generalization for 12,000 jobs: An application of synthetic validity and validity generalization to the General Aptitude Test Battery (GATB).* Washington, D.C.: U.S. Department of Labor, U.S. Employment Service.

Hunter, J. E., Schmidt, F. L., & Hunter, R. (1979). Differential validity of employment tests by race: A comprehensive review and analysis. *Psychological Bulletin, 86,* 721–735.

Hunter, J. E., Schmidt, F. L., & Jackson, G. B. (1982). *Meta analysis: Cumulating research findings across studies.* Beverly Hills: Sage Publications.

Jackson, G. B. (1980). Methods for integrative reviews. *Review of Educational Research, 50,* 438–459.

Jaeger, R. M. (1979). The effect of test selection on Title I project impact. *Educational Evaluation and Policy Analysis, 1,* 33–40.

James, L. R., Mulaik, S. A., & Brett, J. M. (1982). *Causal analysis: Assumptions, models, and data.* Beverly Hills: Sage Publications.

James, L. R., & Singh, B. K. (1978). An introduction to the logic, assumptions and basic analytic procedures of two stage least squares. *Psychological Bulletin, 85,* 1104–1122.

Jencks, C., Smith, M., Acland, H., Bane, M. J., Cohen, D., Gintis, H., Hayns, B., & Michelsohn, S. (1972). *Inequality: A Reassessment of the Effect of Family and Schooling in America.* New York: Basic Books.

Jöreskog, K. G. (1973). A general model for estimating a linear structural equation system. In A. S. Goldberger & O. D. Duncan (Eds.), *Structural equation models in the social sciences: Specification, estimation and testing.* New York: Seminar Press.

Jöreskog, K. G., & Sörbom, D. (1981). *LISREL V: Analysis of linear structural relationships by maximum likelihood and least squares* (Research Rep. 81-8). Uppsala, Sweden: University of Uppsala, Department of Statistics.

Jurs, S. G., & Glass, G. V. (1971). The effect of experimental mortality on the internal and external validity of the randomized comparative experiment. *Journal of Experimental Education, 40,* 62–66.

Keller, F. S. (1968). Good-bye teacher. *Journal of Applied Behavior Analysis, 1,* 79–89.

Kempthorne, O. (1952). *The design and analysis of experiments.* New York: John Wiley.

Kenny, D. A. (1975). A quasi-experimental approach to assessing treatment effects in the nonequivalent control group design. *Psychological Bulletin, 82,* 345–362.

Kenny, D. A. (1979). *Correlation and causality.* New York: John Wiley.

Kerlinger, F. N., & Pedhazur, E. J. (1973). *Multiple regression in behavioral research.* New York: Holt, Rinehart & Winston.

Kirk, R. E. (1982). *Experimental design: Procedures for the behavioral sciences* (2nd ed.). Monterey, CA: Brooks/Cole.

Kulik, J. A., Kulik, C. C., & Cohen, P. A. (1979). A meta-analysis of outcome studies of Keller's personalized system of instruction. *American Psychologist, 34,* 307–318.

Land, K. C. (1969). Principles of path analysis. In E. F. Borgotta & G. W. Bohnstedt (Eds.), *Sociological Methodology 1969.* San Francisco: Jossey-Bass.

Light, R. J. (1973). Issues in the analysis of qualitative data. In R. M. W. Travers (Ed.), *Second handbook of research on teaching.* Chicago: Rand McNally.

Light, R. J., & Smith, P. V. (1971). Accumulating evidence: Procedures for resolving contradictions among different research studies. *Harvard Educational Review, 41,* 429–471.

Linn, R. L. (1981). Measuring pretest–posttest changes. In R. A. Berk (Ed.), *Educational evaluation methodology: The state of the art.* Baltimore, MD: Johns Hopkins University Press.

Linn, R. L., & Dunbar, S. B. (in press). Validity generalization and predictive bias. In R. A. Berk (Ed.), *Performance assessment: The state of the art.* Baltimore: Johns Hopkins University Press.

Linn, R. L., Dunbar, S. B., Harnisch, D. L., & Hastings, C. N. (1982). The validity of the Title I Evaluation and Reporting System. *Evaluation Studies Review Annual, 7,* 427–442.

Linn, R. L., & Slinde, J. A. (1977). The determination of the significance of change between pre- and posttesting periods. *Review of Educational Research, 47,* 121–150.

Linn, R. L., & Werts, C. E. (1977). Analysis implications of the choice of a structural model in the nonequivalent control group design. *Psychological Bulletin, 84,* 299–324.

Lord, F. M. (1960). Large-sample covariance analysis when the control variable is fallible. *Journal of the American Statistical Association, 55,* 307–321.

Lord, F. M. (1967). A paradox in the interpretation of group comparisons. *Psychological Bulletin, 68,* 304–305.

Magidson, J. (1977). Toward a causal model approach for adjusting for preexisting differences in the nonequivalent control group situation: A general alternative to ANCOVA. *Evaluation Quarterly, 1,* 399–420.

Manning, W. H., & DuBois, E. H. (1962). Correlational methods in research on human subjects. *Perceptual Motor Skills, 15,* 287–321.

Martin, D. (1978). *The unit of analysis problem in teacher effectiveness research.* Unpublished doctoral dissertation, University of Texas at Austin.

Mayeske, G. W., Wisler, C. E., Beaton, A. E., Jr., Weinfeld, E. D., Cohen, W. M., Okada, T., Proschek, J. M., & Tabler, K. A. (1972). *A study of our nation's schools.* Washington, DC: U.S. Government Printing Office.

McDonald, F. J., & Elias, P. J. (1976). *Beginning Teacher Evaluation Study: Vol. I. The effects of teaching performance on pupil learning* (Phase II, final report). Princeton, NJ: Educational Testing Service.

McGaw, B. (in press). Meta-analysis. In T. Husén & T. N. Postlethwaite (Eds.), *International encyclopedia of education: Research and studies.* Oxford: Pergamon.

McNeil, K. A., Kelly, F. J., & McNeil, J. T. (1975). *Testing research hypotheses using multiple linear regression.* Carbondale: Southern Illinois University Press.

Mood, A. M. (1971). Partitioning variance in multiple regression analyses as a tool for developing learning models. *American Educational Research Journal, 8,* 191–202.

Muthén, B., & Jöreskog, K. G. (1983). Selectivity problems in quasi-experimental studies. *Evaluation Review, 7,* 139–174.

Namboodiri, N. K., Carter, L. F., & Blalock, H. M., Jr. (1975). *Applied multivariate analysis and experimental designs.* New York: McGraw-Hill.

Olsen, R. (1980). Approximating a truncated normal regression with the method of moments. *Econometrika, 48,* 1099–1105.

Overall, J. E., & Spiegel, D. K. (1969). Concerning least squares analysis of experimental data. *Psychological Bulletin, 72,* 311–322.

Pearlman, K. (1982). *The Bayesian approach to validity generalization: A systematic examination of the robustness of procedures and conclusions.* Unpublished doctoral dissertation, Catholic University of America, Washington, DC.

Pedhazur, E. J. (1982). *Multiple regression in behavioral research: Explanation and prediction* (2nd ed.). New York: Holt, Rinehart & Winston.

Popper, K. R. (1959). *The logic of scientific discovery.* New York: Basic Books.

Porter, A. C. (1967). *The effects of using fallible variables in the analysis of covariance.* Unpublished doctoral dissertation, University of Wisconsin, Madison.

Porter, A. C., & Chibucos, T. R. (1974). Selecting analysis strategies. In G. D. Boruch (Ed.), *Evaluating educational programs and products.* Englewood Cliffs, NJ: Educational Technology Publications.

Prescott, G. A. (1973). *Manual for interpreting: Metropolitan Achievement Test.* New York: Harcourt Brace Jovanovich.

Redfield, D. L., & Rousseau, E. W. (1981). A meta-analysis of experimental research on teacher questioning behavior. *Review of Educational Research, 51,* 237–245.

Reichardt, C. S. (1979). *The design and analysis of the nonequivalent group quasi-experiment.* Unpublished doctoral dissertation, Northwestern University, Evanston, IL.

Reicken, H. W., Boruch, R. F., Campbell, D. T., Coplan, W., Glennan, T. K., Pratt, J., Rees, A., & Williams, W. (1974). Social experimentation: *A method for planning and evaluating social innovations.* New York: Academic Press.

Robinson, W. S. (1950). Ecological correlations and the behavior of individuals. *American Sociological Review, 15,* 351–357.

Rogosa, D., Brandt, D., & Zimowski, M. (1982). A growth curve approach to the measurement of change. *Psychological Bulletin, 92,* 726–748.

Rosenshine, B., & Furst, N. (1973). The use of direct observation to study teaching. In R. M. W. Travers (Ed.), *Second handbook of research on teaching.* Chicago: Rand McNally.

Rosenshine, B., & McGraw, B. (1972). Issues in assessing teacher accountability in public education. *Phi Delta Kappan, 53,* 640–643.

Rosenthal, R. (1978). Combining results of independent studies. *Psychological Bulletin, 85,* 185–193.

Rosenthal, R. (1979). The "file-drawer problem" and tolerance for null results. *Psychological Bulletin, 86,* 638–641.

Rosenthal, R., & Rubin, D. B. (1978). Interpersonal expectancy effects: The first 345 studies. *Behavioral and Brain Sciences, 3,* 377–415.

Rosenthal, R., & Rubin, D. B. (1979). Comparing significance levels of independent studies. *Psychological Bulletin, 86,* 1165–1168.

Rosenthal, R., & Rubin, D. B. (1982). Comparison effect sizes of independent studies. *Psychological Bulletin, 92,* 500–504.

Rubin, D. B. (1974). Estimating causal effects of treatments in randomized and nonrandomized studies. *Journal of Educational Psychology, 66,* 688–701.

Rubin, D. B. (1977). Assignment to treatment group on the basis of a covariate. *Journal of Educational Statistics, 2,* 1–26.

Saxe, L., & Fine, M. (1979). Expanding our view of control groups in evaluations. In L. Datta & R. Perloff (Eds.), *Improving evaluations.* Beverly Hills: Sage Publications.

Scheffé, H. (1959). *The analysis of variance.* New York: John Wiley.

Schmidt, F. L., & Hunter, J. E. (1977). Development of a general solution to the problem of validity generalization. *Journal of Applied Psychology, 62,* 529–540.

Schmidt, F. L., Hunter, J. E., & Pearlman, K. (1981). Task differences as moderators of aptitude test validity in selection: A red herring. *Journal of Applied Psychology, 66,* 166–185.

Simon, H. A. (1954). Spurious correlation: A causal interpretation. *Journal of the American Statistical Association, 49,* 467–479.

Smith, H. J. (1957). Interpretation of adjusted treatment means and regression in analysis of covariance. *Biometrics, 13,* 282–308.

Smith, M. L., & Glass, G. V. (1977). Meta-analysis of psychotherapy outcome studies. *American Psychologist, 32,* 752–760.

Sockloff, A. L. (1976). The analysis of nonlinearity via linear regression with polynomial and product terms. *Review of Educational Research, 46,* 267–291.

Sörbom, D. (1981). Structural equation models with structured means. In K. G. Jöreskog & H. Wold (Eds.), *Systems under indirect observation: Causality, structure and prediction.* Amsterdam: North Holland Publishing.

Stenhouse, L. (1978). Some limitations of the use of objectives. In D. Hamilton et al. (Eds.), *Beyond the numbers game.* Berkeley, CA: McCutchan.

Stewart, B. L. (1980). *The regression model in Title I evaluation.* Mountain View, CA: RMC Research.

Tallmadge, G. K., & Wood, C. T. (1976). *User's Guide: ESEA Title I evaluation and reporting system.* Mountain View, CA: RMC Research.

Tallmadge, G. K., & Wood, C. T. (1981). *User's Guide: ESEA Title I evaluation and reporting system.* Mountain View, CA: R.M.C. Research.

Thorndike, E. L. (1939). On the fallacy of imputing the correlations found for groups to the individuals or smaller groups composing them. *American Journal of Psychology, 52,* 122–124.

Travers, R. M. W. (1981). Letter to the editor. *Educational Researcher, 10,* 32.

Veldman, D. J., & Brophy, J. E. (1974). Measuring teacher effects on student achievement. *Journal of Educational Psychology, 66,* 319–324.

Ward, J. H., Jr., & Jennings, E. (1973). *Introduction to linear models.* Englewood Cliffs, NJ: Prentice-Hall.

Winer, B. J. (1971). *Statistical principles in experimental design* (2nd ed.). New York: McGraw-Hill.

Wisler, C. E. (1969). Partitioning the explained variation in a regression analysis. In G. W. Mayeske et al., *A study of our nation's schools.* Washington, DC: U.S. Department of Health, Education, & Welfare, Office of Education.

Wolfe, L. M. (1977). An introduction to path analysis. *Multiple Linear Regression Viewpoints, 8,* 36–61.

Wright, S. (1921). Correlation and causation. *Journal of Agricultural Research, 20,* 557–585.

5.
Qualitative Methods in Research on Teaching

Frederick Erickson
Michigan State University

> *General and abstract ideas are the source of the greatest errors of mankind.*
> *J. J. Rousseau*

> *What is General Nature? is there such a Thing?/What is General Knowledge?*
> *is there such a Thing?/Strictly Speaking All Knowledge is Particular.*
> *W. Blake*

Introduction and Overview

This chapter reviews basic issues of theory and method in approaches to research on teaching that are alternatively called ethnographic, qualitative, participant observational, case study, symbolic interactionist, phenomenological, constructivist, or interpretive. These approaches are all slightly different, but each bears strong family resemblance to the others.

The set of related approaches is relatively new in the field of research on teaching. The approaches have emerged as significant in the decade of the 1960s in England and in the 1970s in the United States, Australia, New Zealand, and Germany. Because interest in these approaches is so recent, the previous editions of the *Handbook of Research on Teaching* do not contain a chapter devoted to participant observational research. Accordingly, this chapter attempts to describe research methods and their theoretical presuppositions in considerable detail and does not attempt an exhaustive review of the rapidly growing literature in the field. Such a review will be appropriate for the next edition of this handbook.

From this point on I will use the term *interpretive* to refer to the whole family of approaches to participant observational research. I adopt this term for three reasons: (a) It is more inclusive than many of the others (e.g., ethnography, case study); (b)

it avoids the connotation of defining these approaches as essentially nonquantitative (a connotation that is carried by the term *qualitative*), since quantification of particular sorts can often be employed in the work; and (c) it points to the key feature of family resemblance among the various approaches — central research interest in human meaning in social life and in its elucidation and exposition by the researcher.

The issue of using as a basic validity criterion the *immediate and local meanings of actions*, as defined from the actors' point of view, is crucial in distinguishing interpretive participant observational research from another observational technique with which interpretive research approaches are often confused, so-called *rich description*. Since the last decades of the 19th century, the data collection technique of continuous narrative description — a play-by-play account of what an observer sees observed persons doing — has been used in social and behavioral research. The technique was first used by psychologists in child study and then by anthropologists and sociologists doing community studies.

It is important to emphasize at the outset that the use of continuous narrative description as a technique — what can less formally be called "writing like crazy" — does not necessarily mean that the research being conducted is interpretive or qualitative, in a fundamental sense. What makes such work

The author thanks reviewers Hugh Mehan (University of California at San Diego) and Raymond P. McDermott (Teachers College, Columbia University). Preparation of this chapter was supported in part through the Institute for Research on Teaching, College of Education, Michigan State University. The Institute for Research on Teaching is funded primarily by the Program for Teaching and Instruction of the National Institute of Education, United States Department of Education. The opinions expressed in this publication do not necessarily reflect the position, policy, or endorsement of the National Institute of Education. (Contract No. 400-81-0014).

interpretive or qualitative is a matter of substantive focus and intent, rather than of procedure in data collection, that is, a research *technique* does not constitute a research *method*. The technique of continuous narrative description can be used by researchers with a positivist and behaviorist orientation that deliberately excludes from research interest the immediate meanings of actions from the actors' point of view. Continuous narrative description can also be used by researchers with a nonpositivist, interpretive orientation, in which the immediate (often intuitive) meanings of actions to the actors involved are of central interest. The presuppositions and conclusions of these two types of research are very different, and the content of the narrative description that is written differs as well. If two observers with these differing orientations were placed in the same spot to observe what was ostensibly the "same" behavior performed by the "same" individuals, the observers would write substantively differing accounts of what had happened, choosing differing kinds of verbs, nouns, adverbs, and adjectives to characterize the actions that were described.

The reader should note that in making these assertions I am taking a different position from Green and Evertson (this volume), who emphasize certain commonalities across various approaches to direct observation. Their comprehensive review of a wide range of methods of classroom observation (including some of the methods discussed here) does not emphasize the discontinuities in theoretical presupposition that obtain across the two major types of approaches to classroom research, positivist/behaviorist and interpretive. This chapter emphasizes those discontinuities. Green and Evertson are relatively optimistic about the possibility of combining disparate methods and orientations in classroom observation. I am more pessimistic about that possibility, and have become increasingly so in the last few years. Reasonable people can disagree on such matters. The reader should compare the two chapters, keeping in mind the differences in perspective that characterize our two discussions, which run along lines that are somewhat similar but are nonetheless distinct.

From my point of view, the primary significance of interpretive approaches to research on teaching concerns issues of content rather than issues of procedure. Interests in interpretive content lead the researcher to search for methods that will be appropriate for study of that content. If interpretive research on classroom teaching is to play a significant role in educational research, it will be because of what interpretive research has to say about its central substantive concerns: (a) the nature of classrooms as socially and culturally organized environments for learning, (b) the nature of teaching as one, *but only one,* aspect of the reflexive learning environment, and (c) the nature (and content) of the meaning-perspectives of teacher and learner as intrinsic to the educational process. The theoretical conceptions that define the primary phenomena of interest in the interpretive study of teaching are very different from those that underlie the earlier, mainstream approaches to the study of teaching. These distinctive features of the interpretive perspective will be considered throughout this essay.

This is not quite to say that this is a situation of competing paradigms in research on teaching, if paradigms are thought of in the sense used by Kuhn (1962) to refer to an integrated set of theoretical presuppositions that lead the researcher to see the world of one's research interest in a particular way. A paradigm is metaphysical. A scientific theoretical view, according to Kuhn, becomes in practical usage an ontology. The current conflict in research on teaching is not one of competing paradigms, I would argue, not because the competing views do not differ ontologically, but simply because as Lakatos (1978) and others have argued for the natural sciences—and especially for the social sciences—paradigms do not actually compete in scientific discourse. Old paradigms are rarely replaced by falsification. Rather the older and the newer paradigms tend to coexist, as in the survival of Newtonian physics, which can be used for some purposes, despite the competition of the Einsteinian physics, which for other purposes has superseded it. Especially in the social sciences, paradigms don't die; they develop varicose veins and get fitted with cardiac pacemakers. The perspective of standard research on teaching and the interpretive perspective are indeed rival theories—rival research programs—even if it is unlikely that the latter will totally supersede the former.

I have not attempted a comprehensive review of the field, nor have I attempted to present a modal perspective on interpretive research. There is much disagreement among interpretive researchers about the proper conduct of their work and its theoretical foundations. Given this lack of consensus, which is greater than that in the more standard approaches to research on teaching, it would be inappropriate for me to attempt to speak on behalf of all interpretive researchers. Accordingly, this chapter emphasizes those aspects of theory and method that are most salient in my own work. In substance, my work is an attempt to combine close analysis of fine details of behavior and meaning in everyday social interaction with analysis of the wider societal context—the field of broader social influences —within which the face-to-face interaction takes place. In method, my work is an attempt to be empirical without being positivist; to be rigorous and systematic in investigating the slippery phenomena of everyday interaction and its connections, through the medium of subjective meaning, with the wider social world.

The chapter begins with an overview of interpretive approaches and the kinds of research questions that are of central interest in such work. The next section reviews the intellectual roots of interpretive research, the development of firsthand participant observation as a research method, and the underpinnings of that development in particular kinds of social theory and practical concern. The third section traces the implications of this general theoretical orientation for the study of classroom teaching. Then the discussion turns to consider issues of method. There is a section on data collection and analysis, and a section on data analysis and the preparation of written reports. These sections will address the reasons that data analysis inheres in the data collection phase of research as well as in the reporting phase. The chapter concludes with a discussion of implications of interpretive approaches for future research on teaching.

Overview

Interpretive, participant observational fieldwork has been used in the social sciences as a research method for about seventy years. Fieldwork research involves (a) intensive, long-term participation in a field setting; (b) careful recording of what happens in the setting by writing field notes and collecting other kinds of documentary evidence (e.g., memos, records, examples of student work, audiotapes, videotapes); and (c) subsequent analytic reflection on the documentary record obtained in the field, and reporting by means of detailed description, using narrative vignettes and direct quotes from interviews, as well as by more general description in the form of analytic charts, summary tables, and descriptive statistics. Interpretive fieldwork research involves being unusually thorough and reflective in noticing and describing everyday events in the field setting, and in attempting to identify the significance of actions in the events from the various points of view of the actors themselves.

Fieldwork methods are sometimes thought to be radically inductive, but that is a misleading characterization. It is true that specific categories for observation are not determined in advance of entering the field setting as a participant observer. It is also true that the researcher always identifies conceptual issues of research interest before entering the field setting. In fieldwork, induction and deduction are in constant dialogue. As a result, the researcher pursues deliberate lines of inquiry while in the field, even though the specific terms of inquiry may change in response to the distinctive character of events in the field setting. The specific terms of inquiry may also be reconstrued in response to changes in the fieldworker's perceptions and understandings of events and their organization during the time spent in the field.

Interpretive methods using participant observational fieldwork are most appropriate when one needs to known more about:

1. The specific structure of occurrences rather than their general character and overall distribution. (What does the decision to leave teaching as a profession look like for particular teachers involved?) What is happening in a particular place rather than across a number of places? (If survey data indicate that the rate of leaving teaching was lowest in a particular American city, we might first want to know what was going on there before looking at other cities with average teacher leaving rates.)
2. The meaning-perspectives of the particular actors in the particular events. (What, specifically, were the points of view of particular teachers as they made their decisions to leave teaching?)
3. The location of naturally occurring points of contrast that can be observed as natural experiments when we are unable logistically or ethically to meet experimental conditions of consistency of intervention and of control over other influences on the setting. (We can't hold constant the conditions that might influence teachers to want to leave teaching, and we can't try to cause them to want to leave.)
4. The identification of specific causal linkages that were not identified by experimental methods, and the development of new theories about causes and other influences on the patterns that are identified in survey data or experiments.

Fieldwork is best at answering the following questions (on these questions, and the ensuing discussion, see Erickson,

Florio, & Buschman, 1980, of which these remarks are a paraphrase):

1. What is happening, specifically, in social action that takes place in this particular setting?
2. What do these actions mean to the actors involved in them, at the moment the actions took place?
3. How are the happenings organized in patterns of social organization and learned cultural principles for the conduct of everyday life—how, in other words, are people in the immediate setting consistently present to each other as environments for one another's meaningful actions?
4. How is what is happening in this setting as a whole (i.e., the classroom) related to happenings at other system levels outside and inside the setting (e.g., the school building, a child's family, the school system, federal government mandates regarding mainstreaming)?
5. How do the ways everyday life in this setting is organized compare with other ways of organizing social life in a wide range of settings in other places and at other times?

Answers to such questions are often needed in educational research. They are needed for five reasons. The first reason concerns the *invisibility of everyday life*. "What is happening here?" may seem a trivial question at first glance. It is not trivial since everyday life is largely invisible to us (because of its familiarity and because of its contradictions, which people may not want to face). We do not realize the patterns in our actions as we perform them. The anthropologist Clyde Kluckhohn illustrated this point with an aphorism: "The fish would be the last creature to discover water." Fieldwork research on teaching, through its inherent reflectiveness, helps researchers and teachers to *make the familiar strange* and interesting again (see Erickson, 1984). The commonplace becomes problematic. What is happening can become visible, and it can be documented systematically.

A second reason these questions are not trivial is the *need for specific understanding through documentation of concrete details of practice*. Answering the question, "What is happening?" with a general answer often is not very useful. "The teacher (or students) in this classroom is (are) on-task" often doesn't tell us the specific details that are needed in order to understand what is being done, especially if one is attempting to understand the points of view of the actors involved. Nor is an answer like the following sufficient, usually: "The teacher is using behavior modification techniques effectively." This does not tell how, specifically, the teacher used which techniques with which children, nor what the researcher's criterion of effectiveness was. Similarly, the statement "The school district implemented a program to increase student time-on-task" does not tell enough about the extent and kind of implementation so that if test scores or other outcome measures did or did not show change, that putative "outcome" could reasonably be attributed to the putative "treatment." "What *was* the treatment?" is often a useful question in research on teaching. Interpretive fieldwork research can answer such a question in an adequately specific way.

A third reason these questions are not trivial concerns the need to consider the *local meanings* that happenings have for the people involved in them. Surface similarities in behavior are sometimes misleading in educational research. In different classrooms, schools, and communities, events that seem ostensibly the same may have distinctly differing local meanings. Direct questioning of students by a teacher, for example, may be seen as rude and punitive in one setting, yet perfectly appropriate in another. Within a given setting, a certain behavior like direct questioning may be appropriate for some children at one moment, and inappropriate at the next, from a given teacher's point of view at that time in the event being observed. When a research issue involves considering the distinctive local meanings that actors have for actors in the scene at the moment, fieldwork is an appropriate method.

A fourth reason these main research questions of fieldwork are not trivial concerns the *need for comparative understanding of different social settings.* Considering the relations between a setting and its wider social environments helps to clarify what is happening in the local setting itself. The observation "Teachers don't ask for extra materials; they just keep using the same old texts and workbooks for each subject" may be factually accurate, but this could be interpreted quite differently depending on contextual circumstances. If school system-wide regulations made ordering supplementary materials very difficult in a particular school district, then the teachers' actions could not simply be attributed to the spontaneous generation of local meanings by participants in the local scene — the "teacher culture" at that particular school. What the teachers do at the classroom and building level is influenced by what happens in wider spheres of social organization and cultural patterning. These wider spheres of influence must also be taken into account when investigating the narrower circumstances of the local scene. The same applies to relationships of influence across settings at the same system level, such as the classroom and the home. Behavior that may be considered inappropriate in school may be seen as quite appropriate and reasonable in community and family life. For example, children may be encouraged in the family to be generous in helping one another; in the classroom this may be seen by the teacher as attempts at cheating.

A fifth reason for the importance of this set of questions concerns the *need for comparative understanding beyond the immediate circumstances of the local setting.* There is a temptation on the part of researchers and school practitioners alike to think of what is happening in the standard operating procedures of everyday life as the way things must and ought to be, always and everywhere. Contrasting life in United States classrooms to school life in other societies, and to life in other institutional contexts such as hospitals and factories, broadens one's sense of the range of possibilities for organizing teaching and learning effectively in human groups. Knowing about other ways of organizing formal and nonformal education by looking back into human history, and by looking across to other contemporary societies around the world, can shed new light on the local happenings in a particular school.

The fieldworker asks continually while in the field setting, "How does what is happening here compare with what happens in other places?" Awareness of this does not necessarily lead to immediate practical solutions in planning change. The comparative perspective does inform attempts at planning change, however. By taking a comparative perspective people can distinguish the spuriously distinctive and the genuinely distinctive features of their own circumstances. That can lead them to be at once more realistic and more imaginative than they would otherwise have been in thinking about change.

To conclude, the central questions of interpretive research concern issues that are neither obvious nor trivial. They concern issues of human choice and meaning, and in that sense they concern issues of improvement in educational practice. Even though the stance of the fieldworker is not manifestly evaluative, and even though the research questions do not take the form "Which teaching practices are most effective?" issues of effectiveness are crucial in interpretive research. The definitions of effectiveness that derive from the theoretical stance and empirical findings of interpretive research differ from those found in the more usual approaches to educational research and development. The program of interpretive research is to subject to critical scrutiny every assumption about meaning in any setting, including assumptions about desirable aims and definitions of effectiveness in teaching. This critical stance toward human meaning derives from theoretical presuppositions that will be reviewed in considerable detail in the next section of this chapter.

Intellectual Roots and Assumptions of Interpretive Research on Teaching

Roots in Western European Intellectual History

Interpretive research and its guiding theory developed out of interest in the lives and perspectives of people in society who had little or no voice. The late 18th century saw the emergence of this concern. Medieval social theorists had stressed the dignity of manual labor, but with the collapse of the medieval world view in the 16th and 17th centuries the lower classes had come to be portrayed in terms that were at best paternalistic.

One sees this paternalism in baroque theater and opera. Peasants and house servants were depicted in a one-dimensional way as uncouth and brutish. They were not reflective, although they may have been capable of a kind of venal cleverness in manipulating their overseers, masters, and mistresses. Examples of this are found in the servant characters of Molière and in the farm characters of J. S. Bach's *Peasant Cantata,* written in 1742. Beaumarchais' *The Barber of Seville,* written in 1781, is distinctive precisely because it presented one of the first sympathetic characterizations of a servant figure. The dangerous implications of such a portrayal were immediately recognized by the French censors, who prevented its performance for three years after it had been written. The perspective represented by *The Barber of Seville* had been preceded in France by the writings of Rousseau. In England, this new perspective had been prefigured by the mid-18th-century English novelists.

Interest by intellectuals in the life-world (Lebenswelt) of the poor — especially the rural poor — continued to grow in the early 19th century as exemplified by the brothers Grimm, who elicited folklore from German peasants. Their work emerged simultaneously with the development of the early romantic movement in literature, in which commoners were positively portrayed. Folklore research presupposed that the illiterate country people who were being interviewed possessed a genuine aesthetic sense and a true folk wisdom, in spite of the peasants' lack of formal education and lack of "cultivated" appreciation of the polite art forms that were practiced among the upper classes. Concerns for social reform often accompanied this interest in the intelligence and talent of the untutored rural poor. Innovations in pedagogy were also related to this shift in the view of the poor, for example, the schools established in Switzerland by Pestalozzi to teach children who had hitherto been considered unteachable.

Later in the 19th century, attention of reformers shifted from the rural poor to the working-class populations of the growing industrial towns (for a parallel discussion of this development, see Bogdan and Biklen, 1982, pp. 4–11). In England, Charles Booth documented the everyday lives of children and adults at work in factories and at home in slum neighborhoods (see Webb, 1926). Similar attention was paid to the urban poor in the United States by the "muckraking" journalists Jacob Riis (*How the Other Half Lives*, 1890) and Lincoln Steffins (1904), and in the novels of Upton Sinclair, for example, *The Jungle* (1906).

Another line of interest developed in the late 19th century in kinds of unlettered people who lacked power and about whom little was known. These were the nonliterate peoples of the European-controlled colonial territories of Africa and Asia, which were burgeoning by the end of the 19th century. Travelers' accounts of such people had been written since the beginnings of European exploration in the 16th century. By the late 19th century such accounts were becoming more detailed and complete. They were receiving scientific attention from the emerging field of anthropology. Anthropologists termed these accounts *ethnography*, a monograph-length description of the lifeways of people who were *ethnoi*, the ancient Greek term for "others" — barbarians who were not Greek. Anthropologists had begun to send out their students to collect ethnographic information themselves, rather than relying for the information on the books written by colonial administrators, soldiers, and other travelers.

In 1914, one of these students, Bronislaw Malinowski, was interned in the Trobriand Archipelago by the British government while he was on an ethnographic expedition. Malinowski was a student at Oxford University and had been sent to the Britsh colonies by his teachers. He was also Polish; a subject of the Austro-Hungarian Empire. On that ground he was suspect as a spy by some officials of the British colonial administration. Forced to stay in the Trobriands more than twice as long as he had intended, during his detention Malinowski developed a closer, more intimate view of the everyday lifeways and meaning-perspectives of a primitive society than had any previous ethnographer, whether traveler or social scientist. Malinowski's account, when published in 1922, revolutionized the field of social anthropology by the specificity of its descriptive reporting and by the sensitivity of the insights presented about the beliefs and perspectives of the Trobrianders. Malinowski (1935, 1922/1966) reported insights not only about *explicit* cultural knowledge. Information on explicit culture had been elicited from informants by earlier researchers who used interviewing strategies derived from the work of the early folklorists. In addition

Malinowski reported his inferences about the Trobriander's *implicit* cultural knowledge — beliefs and perspectives that were so customary for the Trobrianders that they were held outside conscious awareness and thus could not be readily articulated by informants. By combining long-term participant observation with sensitive interviewing, Malinowski claimed, he was able to identify aspects of the Trobrianders' world view that they themselves were unable to articulate.

Many anthropologists attacked the claims of Malinowskian ethnography as too subjective and unscientific. Others were very taken by it. It squared with the insights of Freudian psychology that people knew much more than they were able to say. Freud's perspective, in turn, was consonant with the much broader intellectual and artistic movement of expressionism, which emphasized the enigmatic and inarticulate dark side of human experience, harking back to a similar emphasis among the early Romantics. Malinowski was a product of this late-19th-century intellectual milieu, and the postwar disillusionment with the values of rational liberal thinking made the 1920s an especially apt time for the reception of Malinowski's position.

Malinowski's intellectual milieu in his formative years was not only that of the late 19th century in general, but that of German intellectual perspectives in particular. These bear mention here, for they involve presuppositions about the nature of human society and consequently about the nature of the social sciences. German social theory, as taught in universities of the time, made a sharp distinction between natural science, *Naturwissenschaft*, and what can be translated "human science," or "moral science," *Geisteswissenschaft*. The latter term, which literally means, "science of spirit," was distinguished from natural science on the grounds that humans differ from other animals and from inanimate entities in their capacity to make and share meaning. Sense-making and meaning were the spiritual or moral aspect of human existence that differed from the material existence of the rest of the natural order. Because of this added dimension, it was argued, humans living together must be studied in terms of the sense they make of one another in their social arrangements.

The etymological metaphor of spirit as an entity that underlies this sharp distinction between the natural and the human sciences recalls an analogous metaphor in the term *psychology*, which in the Greek literally means "systematic knowledge about the soul." The terms *Geisteswissenschaft* and *psychology* remind us that in the mid-19th century, as social and behavioral sciences began to be defined as distinctive fields, there was as yet no commitment to define them as positive sciences modeled after the physical sciences. That came later.

The chief proponent of the distinction between the natural and the human sciences was the German historian and social philosopher Wilhelm Dilthey (1883/1976c, 1914/1976a). He argued (1914/1976b) that the methods of the human sciences should be *hermeneutical*, or interpretive (from the Greek term for "interpreter"), with the aim of discovering and communicating the meaning-perspectives of the people studied, as an interpreter does when translating the discourse of a speaker or writer. Dilthey's position was adopted by many later German social scientists and philosophers, notably Weber (1922/1978) and Husserl (1936/1970). A somewhat similar position was taken by Dilthey's contemporary, Marx, especially in his early writings, for example, the *Theses on Feuerbach* (1959 ed.). Despite Marx's emphasis on material conditions as determining norms, beliefs, and values, he was centrally concerned with the content of the meaning-perspectives so determined. Indeed, a fundamental point of Marx's is the historical embeddedness of consciousness—the assumption that one's view of self and of the world is profoundly shaped in and through the concrete circumstances of daily living in one's specific situation of life. Subsequent Marxist social theorists have presumed that profound differences in meaning-perspective will vary with social class position, and that presumption extends to any other special life situation, for example, that due to one's gender status, race, and the like.

We can assume that Malinowski was influenced by basic assumptions in German social theory of his day. Those assumptions were contrary to those of French thinkers about society, notably Comte and Durkheim. Comte, in the mid-19th century, proposed a positivist science of society, modeled after the physical sciences, in which causal relations were assumed to be analogous to those of mechanics in Newtonian physics (Comte, 1875/1968). Durkheim, Comte's pupil, may or may not have adopted the metaphor of society as a machine, but in attempting to contradict the notion that the individual is the fundamental unit of society, he argued that society must be treated as an entity in itself—a reality *sui generis*. Such a position can easily be interpreted as a view of society as an organism or machine. At any rate, what was central for Durkheim was not the meaning-perspectives of actors in society, but the "social facts" of their behaviors (Durkheim 1895/1958). This stands in sharp contrast to the German intellectual tradition of social theory. (On the relations of presuppositions in social theory to methodology in the social sciences, see the book-length comparative review of functionalist, interpretive, Marxist, and existentialist positions in Burrell & Morgan, 1979; and see also Winch, 1958, and Giddens, 1982.)

A final influence on American participant observational research was the development of American descriptive linguistics during the 1920s. In studying native American languages linguists were discovering aspects of language structure—sound patterns and grammar—that had never been considered in traditional grammar and philology based on Indo-European languages. These new aspects of language structure were regular and predictable in speech, but the speakers themselves were unaware of the structures they had learned to produce so regularly. Here was another domain in which was evident the existence of implicit principles of order that influenced human behavior outside the consciousness of those influenced.

This intellectual environment was the context for the training of Margaret Mead at Columbia University, with which she was associated for the rest of her career. Her study *Coming of Age In Samoa* (1928), again controversial as of this writing, can be considered the first monograph-length educational ethnography. It is significant that it dealt with teaching and learning outside schools.

By the mid-1920s, with the urban sociology of Robert Park at the University of Chicago, ethnography came home. Students of Park and Burgess (e.g., Wirth, 1928; Zorbaugh, 1929) used sustained participant observation and informal interviewing as a means of studying the everyday lives and values of *natural groups* of urban residents (mostly working class migrants from Europe), who in Chicago and other major American cities were distributed in residential territories defined by an intersection of geography, ethnicity, and social class. In the 1930s a whole American community, Newburyport, Massachusetts ("Yankee City"), was studied by Malinowskian fieldwork methods, under the direction of the anthropologist W. Lloyd Warner at Harvard (Warner & Lunt, 1941). In a study that was greatly influenced by Warner, Whyte (1955) identified another kind of natural group as a unit of analysis, a group of late adolescent males in an urban working-class Italian neighborhood. Here the community was studied out from the gang of young men, rather than the usual anthropologist's way of trying to study the *community as a whole*, which Whyte found to be theoretically and logistically impossible in an urban setting.

After World War II, ethnographers began to turn directly to issues of education, under the leadership of Spindler (1955) at Stanford and Kimball (1974) at Teachers College, Columbia. Both were influenced considerably by the work of Margaret Mead, and Kimball had been a student of Warner's. Chicago school sociology also made a significant contribution to ethnographic work in a study of a cohort of medical students under the direction of Everett Hughes (cf. Becker, Geer, Hughes, & Strauss, 1961). An institutionalized network for researchers with these interests was initiated in 1968, with the formation of the Council on Anthropology and Education as a member organization of the American Anthropological Association. Also during the 1960s much qualitative work on teaching was done in England, under the leadership of Stenhouse and his associates (Stenhouse, 1978; MacDonald & Walker, 1974; Walker & Adelman, 1975; Elliott & Adelman, 1976). The next major impetus for ethnographic study of education, and the last to be noted in this discussion, came in the early 1970s with the creation of the National Institute of Education. Key staff there established policies that not only allowed funding for ethnographic study, but which in some instances encouraged work to be done in schools along those lines. Often in that work the unit of analysis was the school community, with classroom teaching receiving peripheral attention. At the same time, however, studies were begun in which teaching in school classrooms was the central phenomenon of research interest. (For additional discussion of the role of NIE, see Cadzen, this volume).

To conclude where we began, it is important to remember that qualitative research that centers its attention on classroom teaching is a very recent phenomenon in educational research. The key questions in such research are: "What is happening here, specifically? What do these happenings mean to the people engaged in them?"

The specifics of action and of meaning-perspectives of actors in interpretive research are often those that are overlooked in other approaches to research. There are three major reasons for this. One is that the people who hold and share the meaning-perspectives that are of interest are those who are themselves overlooked, as relatively powerless members of society. This is the case for teachers and students in American public schools, as it was for the working class in postmedieval Europe. (See the discussion on the powerlessness of teachers in Lanier & Little, this volume). A second reason that these meaning-perspectives are not represented is that they are often held outside conscious awareness by those who hold them, and thus are not explicitly articulated. A third reason is that it is precisely the meaning-perspectives of actors in social life that are viewed theoretically in more usual approaches to educational research as either peripheral to the center of research interest, or as essentially irrelevant — part of the "subjectivity" that must be eliminated if systematic, "objective" inquiry is to be done.

In the section that follows we will explore further the significance to research on teaching of the meaning-perspectives of teachers and students, and we will consider reasons why standard educational research does not, for the most part, take account of these phenomena in the design and conduct of studies of teaching and learning in classrooms.

Theoretical Assumptions of Interpretive Research on Teaching

Let us begin by considering some well-documented findings from survey research — test data on school achievement and measured intelligence. These are perplexing findings. They can be interpreted differently depending upon one's theoretical orientation.

1. In the United States there are large differences across individuals in school achievement and measured intelligence, according to the class, race, gender, and language background of the individuals. Moreover, these differences persist across generations.
2. Test score data accumulated in the recent process–product research on teaching show differences across different classrooms in the achievement of elementary pupils who are similarly at risk for school failure because of their class, race, gender, or language background.
3. The same test data also show differences in achievement and measured intelligence among individual children in each classroom.

These findings from survey data suggest that while the likelihood of low school achievement by low-socioeconomic-status children and others at risk may be powerfully influenced by large-scale social processes (i.e., handicaps due to one's position in society) and individual differences (i.e., measured intelligence), the school achievement of such children is amenable to considerable influence by individual teachers at the classroom level. Teachers, then, can and do make a difference for educational equity. Finding Number 2 seems to argue against the contention of critics on the radical left that social revolution is a necessary precondition for improvement of school performance by the children of the poor in America. Finding Number 2 also contradicts the contention of liberals that environmental deprivation, especially the home child-rearing environment, accounts for the low school achievement of such pupils, since outside-school conditions presumably did not change for those students at risk who nonetheless did better academically with some teachers than with others. Findings Number 1 and 3 contradict the contention of moderate and radical conservatives that current school practices involve social sorting that is fair (i.e., assigning pupils to different curricular tracks on the basis

of measured achievement) and that the route to educational improvement lies in simply applying current sorting practices more rigidly.

The radical left, of course, can dismiss finding Number 2 on the grounds that the differences in measured achievement of pupils that can be attributed to teacher influence are only slight, and are thus trivial. The radical right can dismiss findings Number 1 and 3 on the grounds that children of low socioeconomic status (SES), or racial/linguistic/cultural minority background, or females are genetically inferior to white upper-class males, which accounts for their low achievement and measured intelligence. Both of these counterarguments, from the left and from the right, have been used to dismiss the significance of these three findings. If one does not dismiss the findings on those grounds, however, the three findings taken together are paradoxical. It would seem that children's achievement can vary from year to year and from teacher to teacher with no other things changing in those children's lives. Yet children at risk, overall, perform significantly less well in American schools than do children not at risk. Positive teacher influence on the achievement of children at risk seems to be the exception rather than the rule, and *risk* here refers to the children's social background, not to the individual child's intrinsic ability. (Indeed, from an interpretive perspective it is meaningless to speak of a child's intrinsic ability, since the child is always found in a social environment, and since the child's performance and adults' assessments of the child's performance both influence one another continually. Rather we can say that a child's assessed ability is socially constructed. It is a product of the child's social situation — the social system — rather than an attribute of that person.)

The findings from the United States are more paradoxical in the light of international school science achievement data (see Comber & Keeves, 1973, pp. 251, 259) which show that in some developed countries, such as Flemish-speaking Belgium, Italy, Sweden, and Finland, the correlation between social class background and school achievement is much lower than it is in the United States or Great Britain, and that the correlation is lower in Japan than in the United States or Britain although not so low in Japan as in the countries listed first in this sentence. How are we to understand why these survey data show the patterns that they do? Is the social construction of student performance and assessed ability different in Italy from that of the United States? What might we do to foster higher achievement by low-achieving groups of pupils in the United States? How are we to understand the nature of teaching in the light of these findings? The survey data themselves do not tell us. They must be interpreted in the context of theoretical presuppositions about the nature of schools, teaching, children, and classroom life, and about the nature of cause in human social life in general. These assumptions, we have already noted, differ fundamentally between the standard approaches to research on teaching and the interpretive approaches that are the topic of this chapter.

Perhaps the most basic difference between the interpretive and the standard approaches to research on teaching lies in their assumptions about the nature of cause in human social relations. This recalls the distinction made earlier between the natural sciences and the human sciences (*Naturwissenschaft* and *Geisteswissenschaft*).

In the natural sciences causation can be thought of in mechanical, or chemical, or biological terms. Mechanical cause, as in Newtonian physics, involves relationships between force and matter, and physical linkages through which force is exerted — one billiard ball striking another, or the piston in a combustion engine linked by cams to the drive shaft. Chemical cause involves energy transfer in combination between atoms of different elements. Biological cause is both mechanical and chemical. Relations among organisms are also ecological, that is, causal relations are not linear in one direction, but because of the complexity of interaction among organisms within and across species, cause is multidirectional. Thus the notion of cause and effect in biology is much more complex than that of physics or chemistry. But the differences in conceptions of cause in the natural sciences are essentially those of degree rather than of kind. Even in biology there is an underlying assumption of uniformity in nature. Given conditions *x*, a bacterium or a chicken is likely to behave in much the same way on two different occasions. The same is true in physics or chemistry, more or less, despite post-Einsteinian thinking. Under conditions *x*, one calorie of heat can be considered the same entity on the surface of the sun and on the surface of the earth, and under conditions *x*, one atom of oxygen and two of hydrogen will combine in the same way today as they do the next day.

The assumption of uniformity of nature, and of mechanical, chemical, and biological metaphors for causal relations among individual entities is taken over from the natural sciences in positivist social and behavioral sciences. Animals and atoms can be said to *behave*, and do so fairly consistently in similar circumstances. Humans can be said to behave as well, and can be observed to be doing so quite consistently under similar circumstances. Moreover, one person's behavior toward another can be said to cause change in the state of another person. Mechanical, chemical, and ecological metaphors can be used to understand these causal relations, thinking of humans in society as a machine, or as an organism, or as an ecosystem of inanimate and animate entities.

Classrooms and teaching have been studied from this perspective, especially by educational psychologists, and also by some positivist sociologists. Linear causal models are often employed, behavior is observed, and causal relations among various behavioral variables are inferred; for example, certain patterns of questioning or of motivational statements by the teacher are studied to see if they cause certain changes in test-taking behavior by children.

In educational psychology this perspective derives from a kind of hybrid behaviorism, in the sense that what counts is the researcher's judgment of what an observable behavior means, rather than the actors' definitions of meaning. Such behaviorist or "behavioralist" presuppositions about the fixed and obvious meanings of certain types of actions by teachers underlie the so-called *process–product* approach to research on teacher effectiveness (cf. Dunkin & Biddle, 1974), which was at first correlational and later became experimental.

In educational sociology an analogous perspective derived from the shift toward positivism that occurred in American sociology after World War II. Social facts were seen as causing other social facts, by relations akin to that of mechanical linkage. These linkages were monitored by large-scale correlational survey research (e.g., Coleman et al., 1966) and subsequent reanalyses of that data set (Mosteller & Moynihan, 1972, and Jencks et al., 1979).

The main guiding metaphors for most educational research on teacher and school effectiveness from the 1950s through the 1970s became the metaphor of the classroom as something like a Skinner box and the metaphor of school systems and the wider society as something like linked parts of a large, internally differentiated machine. In neither metaphor is the notion of mind necessary. The phenomenological perspective of the persons behaving is not a feature of the theoretical models the metaphors represent.

Interpretive researchers take a very different view of the nature of uniformity and of cause in social life. The behavioral uniformity from day to day that can be observed for an individual, and among individuals in groups, is seen not as evidence of underlying, essential uniformity among entities, but as an illusion — a social construction akin to the illusion of assessed ability as an attribute of the person assessed. Humans, the interpretive perspective asserts, create meaningful interpretations of the physical and behavioral objects that surround them in the environment. We take action toward the objects that surround us in the light of our interpretations of meaningfulness. Those interpretations, once made, we take as real — actual qualities of the objects we perceive. Thus, once a child is assessed as having low ability, we assume not only that the entity *low ability* actually exists, but that it is actually an attribute of that child. We do not question such assumptions, once made. We cannot do so, or as actors in the world we would always be inundated by masses of uninterpretable detail and would be continually tantalized by the need to hold all inference and background assumption in abeyance. We handle the problem of having to be, for practical purposes, *naive realists* — believers in the taken-for-granted reality we perceive at first glance — by continually taking the leap of faith that is necessary. We see the ordinary world as if it were real, according to the meanings we impute to it.

The previous discussion elaborates on the point made in the previous section on the emergence of a distinction between the natural sciences, *Naturwissenschaften*, and the human sciences, *Geisteswissenschaften*. This line of thinking, explicated by Dilthey, and continued with Weber (1922/1978) and Schutz (1971), is exemplified in current writing in the philosophy of social science by Berger and Luckmann (1967), Winch (1958), and Giddens (1976), among many others.

To be sure, there is much more apparent uniformity in human social life. Through *culture* humans share learned systems for defining meaning, and in given situations of practical action humans often seem to have created similar meaning interpretations. But these surface similarities mask an underlying diversity; in a given situation of action one cannot assume that the behaviors of two individuals, physical acts with similar form, have the same meaning to the two individuals. The possibility is always present that different individuals may have differing interpretations of the meaning of what, in physical form, appear to be the same or similar objects or behaviors. Thus a crucial analytic distinction in interpretive research is that between *behavior*, the physical act, and *action*, which is the physical behavior plus the meaning interpretations held by the actor and those with whom the actor is engaged in interaction.

The object of interpretive social research is action, not behavior. This is because of the assumption made about the nature of cause in social life. If people take action on the grounds of their interpretations of the actions of others, then meaning-interpretations themselves are causal for humans. This is not true in nature, and so in natural science meaning from the point of view of the actor is not something the scientist must discover. The billiard ball does not make sense of its environment. But the human actor in society does, and different humans make sense differently. They impute symbolic meaning to others' actions and take their own actions in accord with the meaning interpretations they have made. Thus the nature of *cause* in human society becomes very different from the nature of cause in the physical and biological world, and so does the nature of uniformity in repeated social actions. Because such actions are grounded in choices of meaning interpretation, they are always open to the possibility of reinterpretation and change.

This can be seen in examples of symbolic action such as public executions. Such an event is conducted with the aim not only to punish a particular offender but to coerce a confession of guilt or remorse in order to deter others from committing similar offences. The intentions are both physical and social: to kill the offender and to do so in such a way as to influence public opinion. The physical death that occurs can be seen to result from a physical cause that disrupts the biochemical organization of the body as a living system. The reactions of the offender and audience, however, are not "caused" by the physical intervention itself, but are matters of meaning interpretation, emanating from the various points of view of differing actors in the event.

Consider the case of Joan of Arc. Some soldier's hand thrust a lighted torch into the pile of wood whose subsequent combustion killed Joan, who was tied to a stake. Looking at the crude physical and behavioral "facts" in this sequence of events, one can say that the result of what the soldier did was a matter of physics, chemistry, and biology. But the soldier's behavior did not cause Joan to cry out, denying the charge of witchcraft, insisting that the voices she had heard were those of angels rather than demons. She persisted in justifying her military resistance to the English as a response to the will of God. Such persistence was social action, entailing a choice of meaning interpretation. Some of the witnesses at the scene accepted Joan's interpretation rather than that of her English judges. As the story of her death spread, French nobles and commoners united in intensified resistance to the English. French morale was increased rather than decreased, which frustrated the intent of the execution on grounds of witchcraft.

Meaning interpretations — rather than physical or chemical processes — were what were causal in this sequence of social actions and reactions. These interpretations were the result of human choices, made at successive links in the chain of social interaction. Had the soldier refused to light the fire because he was persuaded of Joan's innocence, the judges might have chosen to relent or to have executed the soldier as well. Had Joan admitted guilt to the charge of witchcraft, the reaction of the French armies might have been different. But even if she had confessed publicly, the witnesses and subsequent audience might have discounted her admission as the result of coercion. Thus the French might still have continued to resist the English, enraged by what they had come to see as a symbol of abhorrent injustice.

We can see how it makes sense to claim that prediction and control, in the tradition of natural science, is not possible in systems of relations where cause is mediated by systems of symbols. The martyr breaches the symbolic order of a degradation ceremony, turning the tables upon those whose intention is to degrade. Martyrs are exceptional but they are not unique. That martyrdom occurs at all points to the intrinsic fragility of the usual regularities of social life, grounded as they are in choices of meaning in the interpretation of symbols.

The case of the execution of Joan of Arc shows how interpretive sense-making can be seen as fundamentally constitutive in human social life. Because of that assumption, interpretive research maintains that causal explanation in the domain of human social life cannot rest simply upon observed similarities between prior and subsequent behaviors, even if the correlations among those behaviors appear to be very strong, and experimental conditions obtain. Rather, an explanation of cause in human action must include identification of the meaning-interpretation of the actor. "Objective" analysis (i.e., systematic analysis) of "subjective" meaning is thus of the essence in social research, including research on teaching, in the view of interpretive researchers.

The interpretive point of view leads to research questions of a fundamentally different sort from those posed by standard research on teaching. Rather than ask which behaviors by teachers are positively correlated with student gains on tests of achievement, the interpretive researcher asks "What are the conditions of meaning that students and teachers create together, as some students appear to learn and others don't? Are there differences in the meaning-perspectives of teachers and students in classrooms characterized by higher achievement and more positive morale? How is it that it can make sense to students to learn in one situation and not in another? How are these meaning systems created and sustained in daily interaction?"

These are questions of basic significance in the study of pedagogy. They put *mind* back in the picture, in the central place it now occupies in cognitive psychology. The mental life of teachers and learners has again become crucially significant for the study of teaching (Shulman, 1981, and Shulman, this volume), and from an interpretive point of view mind is present not merely as a set of "mediating variables" between the major independent and dependent variables of teaching — the inputs and outputs. Sense-making is the heart of the matter, the medium of teaching and learning that is also the message.

Interpretive, participant observational fieldwork research, in addition to a central concern with mind and with subjective meaning, is concerned with the relation between meaning-perspectives of actors and the ecological circumstances of action in which they find themselves. This is to say that the notion of the *social* is central in fieldwork research. In a classic statement Weber (1922/1978) defined social action: "A social relationship may be said to exist when several people reciprocally adjust their behavior to each other with respect to the meaning which they give to it, and when this reciprocal adjustment determines the form which it takes" (p. 30). Standing somewhere, for example, is a behavior. Standing in line, however, is social action, according to Weber's definition, because it is meaningfully oriented to the actions of others in the scene — others standing in the line, and in the case of a typical school classroom, the teacher in charge, who has told the children to stand in line. All these others in the scene are part of ego's social ecology. Patterns in that ecology are defined by implicit and explicit cultural understandings about relationships of proper rights and obligations, as well as by conflicts of interests across individuals and groups in access to certain rights. Thus, for example, in the standing-in-line scene, the official rights of the person occupying the status of teacher differ from the rights of those persons occupying the status of student. Moreover, there is an additional dimension of difference in rights and obligations, that between the official (formal) set of rights and obligations and the unofficial one. Officially, all children in the line have the obligation to obey the teacher's command to stand in line. Unofficially, however, some children may have rights to obey more casually than others. These differences among the children can be thought of as an unofficial, informal social system within which status (one's social position in relation to others) and role (the set of rights and obligations that accrues to a particular status) are defined differently from the ways they are defined in the official, formal system.

A basic assumption in interpretive theory of social organization is that the formal and informal social systems operate simultaneously, that is, persons in everyday life take action together in terms of both official and unofficial definitions of status and role. A basic criticism of standard research on teaching that follows from this theoretical assumption is that, to the extent that teacher and student roles are accounted for in the predetermined coding categories by which classroom observation is done, the category systems take no account of the unofficial, informal dimensions of role and status in the classroom. This is not only to miss the irony and humor of the paradoxical mixing of the two dimensions of classroom life, but to miss the essence of the social and cognitive organization of a classroom as a learning environment. Classrooms, like all settings in formal organizations, are places in which the formal and informal systems continually intertwine. Teaching, as instructional leadership, consists in managing the warp and woof of both dimensions in dealing with children and their engagement with subject matter. To attempt to analyze classroom interaction by observing only the warp threads and ignoring the woof threads is to misrepresent fundamentally the process of pedagogy.

The focus on social ecology — its process and structure — is intrinsic in interpretive social research on teaching. The researcher seeks to understand the ways in which teachers and students, in their actions together, constitute environments for one another. The fieldwork researcher pays close attention to this when observing in a classroom, and his or her fieldnotes are filled with observations that document the social and cultural organization of the events that are observed, on the assumption that the organization of *meaning-in-action* is at once the learning environment and the content to be learned.

All human groups have some form of social organization. While it is universal that regularly interacting sets of individuals possess the capacity to construct cultural norms by which their social ecology is organized — face to face, and in wider spheres up and out to the level of the society as a whole — the particular forms that this social organization takes are specific to the set of individuals involved. Thus we can say that social organization has both a local and a nonlocal character. Let us consider the local nature of social organization first, and then the nonlocal nature of it.

Interpretive social research presumes that the meanings-in-action that are shared by members of a set of individuals who interact recurrently through time are *local* in at least two senses. First, they are local in that they are distinctive to that particular set of individuals, who as they interact across time come to share certain specific local understandings and traditions — a distinctive microculture. Such microcultures are characteristic of all human groups whose members recurrently associate. These are so-called *natural groups*, which are the typical unit of analysis studied by fieldwork researchers. The ubiquity of these natural group-specific microcultures can be illustrated by the following example. Compare and contrast the daily routines of two upper-middle-class white American families, one of which is characterized by serious emotional pathology, and the other of which is not. As the family systems are viewed from the outside, on the surface, patterns in the conduct of everyday life may seem very similar. Both families live in the same suburb, next door to one another. Both houses have dining rooms. Both families use paper towels in the kitchen and buy Izod sports shirts for their children. Yet in one family there is deep trouble, and in the other there is not.

The microculture of one nuclear family regarding child-rearing and other aspects of family life differs in at least some respects from that of a family living next door that is identical to the first in ethnicity, class position, age of parents and children, and other general demographic features. These differences, although small, are not at all trivial. They can have profound significance for the successful conduct of daily life. This is attested to by the personal experience of marriage, in which ego learns that ego's in-laws and spouse hold somewhat different assumptions from those held by ego about the normal conduct of daily life, and that these others may be just as deeply convinced as is ego of the inherent rightness of their own customary ways of doing things.

The same is true for school classrooms. Interpretive researchers presume that microcultures will differ from one classroom to the next, no matter what degree of similarity in general demographic features obtains between the two rooms, which may be located literally next door or across the hall from one another. Just as the adjacent suburban families differed, so two classrooms can differ in the meaning-perspectives held by the teacher and students, despite the surface similarities between the two rooms. Almost every American elementary school classroom today has fluorescent lights. Regulations governing the amount of floor space that must be provided for a given number of children mandate that American classrooms will be roughly the same size. Regulations mandate a roughly similar ratio of adults to students. Entering virtually any elementary school classroom one will see arithmetic workbooks, a published basal reading series, a chalkboard, dittoed work sheets, some books to read, crayons for coloring, paste, and scissors. Roughly the same level of skills is taught at the various grade levels throughout the country. How then to account for the substantial differences in patterns of student achievement across different classrooms? It may be that the differences in organization that we need to be interested in are quite small indeed, and radically local — little differences in everyday classroom life that make a big difference for student learning, subtly different meaning-perspectives in which it makes sense to students to learn in one classroom and does not make sense to learn in another classroom, from a student's point of view.

Meanings-in-action are assumed by some interpretive researchers to be local in a second and more radical sense, that of the locality of moment-to-moment enactment of social action in real time. Today's enactment of breakfast in a family differs from yesterday's, and in conversation during today's breakfast, the content and process of one person's turn at speaking and the reaction of the audience to what is said will differ from that of the next turn at speaking, and audience reaction. Life is continually being lived anew, even in the most recurrent of customary events. This is assumed to be true of school classrooms as well.

Positivist research on teaching presumes that history repeats itself; that what can be learned from past events can generalize to future events — in the same setting and in different settings. Interpretive researchers are more cautious in their assumptions. They see, as do experienced teachers, that yesterday's reading group was not quite the same as today's, and that this moment in the reading group is not the same as the next moment. What constitutes appropriate and intelligible social action in classrooms and all other natural human groups is the capacity for a set of individuals to live together successfully in the midst of the current moment, reacting to the moment just past and expecting the next moment to come. This is the world of lived experience, the life-world (Lebenswelt). The life-world of teacher and students in a classroom is that of the present moment. They traverse the present moment together across time as surfboarders who ride the crest of a wave together with linked arms. It is a delicate interactional balancing act. If any one in the set wavers or stumbles, all in the set are affected.

Each individual in the set has a particular point of view from within the action as the action changes from moment to moment. During the course of the enactment of recurrent types of events (e.g., breakfast, math lessons) some of these individual perspectives come to be intersubjectively shared among the members of the interacting set. Members come to approximate one another's perspectives, in at least a rough correspondence among the individually differing points of view even though these are not identical. Since each individual in the set is unique, however, the specific content of shared understandings at any given moment and across moments and days is unique to that particular set of individuals. Thus within a given moment in the enactment of an event and during the overall course of shared life together, particular sets of individuals come to hold distinctive local meanings-in-action.

These meanings are also nonlocal in origin. Face-to-face social relations do indeed have a life of their own, but the materials for the construction of that life are not all created at the moment, within the scene. One nonlocal influence on local action is culture, which can be defined in cognitive terms as learned and shared standards for perceiving, believing, acting, and evaluating the actions of others (see the discussion in Goodenough, 1981, pp. 62ff.). Cultural learning profoundly shapes what we notice as well as what we believe, at levels outside conscious awareness as well as within awareness. Students in an ordinary American classroom speak English, a culturally learned language system that connects the students with the lives of others across space and time, back before the Norman Conquest. Much of what they know of the language is outside conscious awareness — that is, children come to school knowing how to use grammatical constructions of which they develop a reflective awareness only after some years of schooling. Students in American classrooms learn a particular cultural tradition of mathematical reasoning, and an arithmetic symbol system derived from Arabia. These cultural traditions are nonlocal in provenience.

Another source of nonlocal influence is the perception that local members have of interests or constraints in the world beyond the horizon of their face-to-face relations. In a school classroom these influences may come from the teacher next door, from parents, from the principal, from institutionalized procedures in the federal government regarding the allocation of special resources to the classroom. There is indeed a social structure within which classroom life is embedded. In that sense Durkheim was right — society is a reality in itself, and there are social facts of which local actors take account.

Here, however, the interpretive researcher parts company with Durkheim, for the issue is how to take account of the reality of nonlocal culture and society without assuming mechanistic causal linkages between these outside realities and the realities of social relations face to face. Interpretive research takes a somewhat nominalist position on this issue of ontology: Society and culture do exist, but not in a reified state. Social class position, for example, does not "cause" school achievement — people influence that, in specific interactional occasions. The structure of the English language system does not "cause" the way specific people speak — the speaker makes use of the system in individually distinctive ways. The principal's memo that an achievement test is to be given Friday morning does not "cause" the teacher's hand motions as he or she passes out the test booklets — that behavior is the result of meaning-interpretations and choices, deliberate and nondeliberate, that the teacher has made, including the choice not to ignore the memo's injunction.

The task of interpretive research, then, is to discover the specific ways in which local and nonlocal forms of social organization and culture relate to the activities of specific persons in making choices and conducting social action together. For classroom research this means discovering how the choices and actions of all the members constitute an enacted curriculum — a learning environment. Teachers and students in their interaction together are able to (a) make use of learned meaning acquired and shared through acculturation (not only language system and mathematical system, but other systems such as political ideology, ethnic and class subcultures, assumptions about gender roles, definitions of proper role relationships between adults and children, and the like); (b) take account of the actions of others outside the immediate scene, making sense of them as structure points (or better, as production resources) around which they can construct local action; (c) learn new culturally shared meanings through face-to-face interaction; and (d) *create meanings*, given the unique exigencies of practical action in the moment.

Some of these emergent solutions become institutionalized as distinct local traditions. Others of these created meanings are improvised in uniquely concerted ways, given the unique perspectives of *just that local set* of interacting individuals. Indeed, even what can be called "following rules" can be seen as involving more than passive compliance to external constraints. Individuals are not identically socialized automatons performing according to learned algorithmic routines for behavior (such blind rule followers are described by Garfinkel, 1967, as "judgmental dopes" and "cultural dopes," pp. 67–68). Rather, they are persons who act together and make sense, according to the cultural "rules" which as they enact, they vivify in situationally specific ways. Thus the local microcultures are not static. The microculture can be drawn upon by the members of the local group as they assign meanings to their daily action, but because of the constant, intense dialogue between the interpretive perspective provided by the microculture, the exigencies of practical action in the unique historical circumstances of the present moment, and the differences in perspective among members of the interacting group, the ways in which the evolving microculture can influence the actions of group members is a dynamic process in which change is constant.

From this perspective, in research on teaching it is the surface similarities across classrooms or across reading groups that seem trivial and illusory, rather than as in the standard perspective, in which the local differences we have been describing are seen as trivial — as uninterestingly "molecular" variation that can be ignored in the analysis of general characteristics of effective teaching. Mainstream positivist research on teaching searches for general characteristics of the analytically generalized effective teacher. From an interpretive point of view, however, effective teaching is seen not as a set of generalized attributes of a teacher or of students. Rather, effective teaching is seen as occurring in the particular and concrete circumstances of the practice of a specific teacher with a specific set of students "this year," "this day," and "this moment" (just after a fire drill).

This is not to say that interpretive research is not interested in the discovery of universals, but that it takes a different route to their discovery, given the assumptions about the state of nature in social life that interpretive researchers make. The search is not for *abstract universals* arrived at by statistical generalization from a sample to a population, but for *concrete universals*, arrived at by studying a specific case in great detail and then comparing it with other cases studied in equally great detail. The assumption is that when we see a particular instance of a teacher teaching, some aspects of what occurs are absolutely generic, that is, they apply cross-culturally and across human history to all teaching situations. This would be true despite tremendous variation in those situations — teaching that occurs outside school, teaching in other societies, teaching in which the teacher is much younger than the learners, teaching in Urdu, in Finnish, or in a mathematical language, teaching narrowly construed cognitive skills, or broadly construed social attitudes and beliefs. Despite this variation some aspects of what occurs in any human teaching situation will generalize to all other situations of teaching. Other aspects of what occurs in a given

instance of teaching are specific to the historical and cultural circumstances of that type of situation. Still other aspects of what occurs are unique to that particular event, and to the particular individuals engaged in it.

The task of the analyst is to uncover the different layers of universality and particularity that are confronted in the specific case at hand — what is broadly universal, what generalizes to other similar situations, what is unique to the given instance. This can only be done, interpretive researchers maintain, by attending to the details of the concrete case at hand. Thus the primary concern of interpretive research is particularizability, rather than generalizability. One discovers universals as manifested concretely and specifically, not in abstraction and generality (see the discussion in Hamilton, 1980). Among anthropologists this point is made in the distinction between *ethnography*, the detailed study of a particular society or social unit, and *ethnology*, the comparative study of differing societies, or social units. The basis for valid ethnological comparison, however, is the evidence found in detailed ethnographic case studies, not in data derived from surveys. (See the discussion in Hymes, 1982, who asserts that educational ethnology rather than ethnography is the most fundamental task for interpretive fieldwork research in education.)

In linguistics, from which the term *concrete universal* comes, the point is made in distinguishing between universal and specific structural features of human languages. One cannot study the topic of human language in general. One finds in nature only specific human languages. Only by detailed understanding of the workings of a specific language, followed by comparative analysis of each language considered as a system in its own right, can one distinguish what is universal from what is specific to a given language. One can begin to distinguish the universal from the specific by comparing languages with differing structural properties, for example, Navaho, Ojibwa, Urdu, Chinese, Yoruba, Finnish, Greek, English, but only if one understands very thoroughly the organization of each language as a distinct system, through developing a fully specified model of each system. Partial models of each system, and a sampling procedure that randomly selected a few sentences from each of the languages would not be an adequate empirical base for studying human language as a general category.

Interpretive social research on teaching presumes that the same obtains for teachers and classrooms. Each instance of a classroom is seen as its own unique system, which nonetheless displays universal properties of teaching. These properties are manifested in the concrete, however, not in the abstract. Such concrete universals must be studied each in its own right. This does not necessarily mean studying classrooms one by one. But it does presume that the discovery of fully specified models of the organization of teaching and learning in a given classroom must precede the testing of generalization of those models to other classrooms. The paradox is that to achieve valid discovery of universals one must stay very close to concrete cases.

For interpretive researchers, then, the central focus of process–product research on teaching on the production of generalizable knowledge seems inappropriate. The following quotation from Brophy (1979) illustrates the way in which the concern for generalization drives the enterprise to process–product research: "A study involving 20 classrooms studied for 20 hours each is almost certainly going to be more valuable than a study of a single classroom for 400 hours or a study of 400 classrooms for one hour each, other things being equal (i.e., sophistication of research design)" (p. 743). That could only be true if fully specified models had been developed, and if classrooms were generically similar enough that subtle variations across them were trivial in what for lack of better terms we can call the social and cognitive organization of teaching and learning.

The Mainstream Perspective in Research on Teaching

The history of mainstream positivist research on teaching for the past 20 years is one of analytical bootstrapping with very partial theoretical models of the teaching process, on the assumptions that what was generic across classrooms would emerge across studies, and that the subtle variations across classrooms were trivial and could be washed out of the analysis as *error variance*.

This approach to studying teacher effectiveness can be seen as a borrowing by American educational researchers of an applied natural science model for research and development exemplified by agricultural experimentation.

Research and development using a positivist natural science approach is possible in agriculture because of the uniformity of the phenomena that are considered. While the chemical composition of the soil may vary from one field to the next, and weather conditions may vary from year to year, the fundamental variables that are considered — chemicals, genetic structures of plants, the biochemistry of plant metabolism and growth — are constant enough in form and bounded enough in scope that it is possible to conduct research and development by the operations of repeated measurement, prediction, and controlled experimental intervention. This is research by means of the design and testing of "treatments" whose effects can be monitored and whose working can be explained by references to a theoretical apparatus of covering laws. In the first *Handbook of Research on Teaching* it was just such theory and research design that was called for in the introductory chapter by Gage (1963) — the positivist model of science borrowed from the natural sciences of psychology, with Hempel providing the fundamental rationale in philosophy of science (see the discussion in Smith, 1979). The first *Handbook* contained what since became the classic article on experimental design (Campbell & Stanley, 1966), according to which an agricultural kind of research and development could be conducted. Campbell extended these recommendations in later proposals for large-scale program development. These were interventions that could be studied as quasi-experiments (Cook & Campbell, 1979).

Twenty years later it seems that there is so much variation across classrooms, and so much variation in the implementation of "treatments" themselves that large-scale program evaluation by quasi-experimental methods is very problematic. As that became apparent in study after study Campbell himself (1978) and Cronbach (1975) called for the use of more naturalistic observational methods — case studies done by participant observers, or "documentation" studies, which would give a detailed view of the actual structure and process of program implementation. At the same time, Bronfenbrenner (1977) was calling for an "ecological" approach to the study of child development, considering the child in the context of family and community life. These approaches, while advocating the use of methods other than those of the experiment or the social survey (testing and measurement in education are considered here as one form of survey research), still did not consider going beyond the bounds of the fundamental natural science paradigm for educational research, with its underlying assumption of the uniformity of nature in social life.

A story similar to that for attempts at large-scale program evaluation can be seen in recent research on teacher effectiveness, in which the classroom was the unit of analysis, rather than the program. This so-called "process–product" research (the term is that of Dunkin & Biddle, 1974) developed during the late 1960s and early 1970s (see the review of major studies in Brophy & Good, this volume).

The last fifteen years of this work can be seen as a search for an increasingly specific look at causal linkages between teacher effectiveness, as measured by end-of-the-year student gain scores on standardized achievement tests, and particular teaching practices.

The teaching practices were monitored firsthand by observers who noted the occurrence of various types of predetermined teacher behaviors and student behaviors (e.g., teacher questions, teacher praise, teacher reprimand, student "on-task" behavior, student "off-task" behavior). In this approach, called *systematic classroom observation*, the types of behavior of interest for observation were chosen according to their theoretical significance. What was "systematic" was the use of predetermined categories themselves. This was to assure uniformity of observation (reliability) across times of observation in the same classroom and across different classrooms. The concern for reliability of measurement reflected the positivist assumptions behind the research.

As the work has progressed, coding categories for a while became more specific and differentiated. Then as certain variables (such as student on-task behavior) seemed to correlate highly with gains in student test scores across multiple studies, the observational systems focused more and more on theoretically salient types of student and teacher behavior, which were generalized functions.

Subsequent experimental "treatment" studies indicated that when teachers increased certain behaviors that were found in the correlational studies to be associated with increased student achievement gains, those gains occurred in the experimental classrooms. (See the review in Brophy & Good, this volume. Students in the classrooms receiving the experimental treatments in some cases achieved higher scores on standardized tests than did children in control group classrooms in which the frequency of the recommended teacher behaviors was much less.

This is hopeful news for educators. It suggests that an agricultural model for inquiry into educational productivity is an appropriate one. In the model the teacher, as Mother Nature, provides the fertilizer, light, and water that enable the students, as plants, to grow tall and strong.

All this seems quite straightforward. Why then might any other form of research on teaching be necessary? Interpretive participant observational research is very labor intensive, while observation by use of predetermined coding categories is much

less so. It would seem that there is no need for interpretive research, or any other. The findings on teacher effectiveness seem
to be all in.

That would be a premature conclusion, however. The case
for interpretive research is pointed to by some interesting
anomalies in the process–product work.

One such anomaly lies in the corpus of process–product data
itself. Apparently, in correlational studies of the same teacher
across school years, the stability of teacher effects on student
achievement is not high (see the discussion in Brophy and
Good, this volume. This could be due to a number of influences,
for which there is no evidence in the correlational data sets, for
example, teachers teaching somewhat differently with each new
set of students, stress in the teacher's life outside school (birth of
child, death in family, divorce, remarriage), stress or change in
the school itself (introduction of new reading series, change of
principal). The process–product data do not indicate why
teacher influence seems to vary from year to year. Another
anomaly is that in spite of evidence that indicates that certain
teacher behaviors can influence students to learn more, and in
spite of experience that shows that teachers can be trained to
use those behaviors more frequently, teachers do not always
persist in using the recommended behaviors. Sometimes they
do, but sometimes they do not. An example of this is Rowe's
finding (1974) that waiting longer for student answers produces
more reflective answers by students. Teachers can be told this,
and trained to pause for a longer "wait-time," yet after a few
months they go back to using shorter wait-time in lesson dialogue with students. One wonders if wait-time might not have
negative meaning to teachers in the concrete circumstances of
conducting classroom discussion. Such a concrete, enacted
meaning might override whatever more abstract and decontextualized meaning that wait-time behavior might have as generally correlated positively with student learning. How do
teachers make sense such that a behavior like wait-time seems
sociolinguistically inappropriate? What are the intuitions
about interaction against which doing wait-time behavior runs
counter? How might these intuitions be changed — or is there
another behavioral means that might provide a less counterintuitive route to the same ends? Those are questions about the
specifics of practice that derive from the perspectives of interpretive research.

These kinds of anomalies suggest that while the standard
work has produced some insights about general characteristics
of effective training, we may have learned about all that is possible by proceeding with that theoretical frame of reference, and
the methods that derive from it.

An Interpretive Perspective on Teacher Effectiveness

The use of predetermined coding categories by process–product
researchers presupposes uniformity of relationships between
the form of a behavior and its meaning, such that the observer
can recognize the meaning of a behavior time after time.
Imagine a student sitting at a desk, looking out the window.
What does this mean? Is the student on-task or off-task? We
must infer meaning from the observed behavior. What are the

grounds for such inferences? When they must be made in split-
second judgments by coders, what evidence do we have that
such inferences about meaning are valid? The fundamental
problem with the standard approach to observational research
on teacher effectiveness, from an interpretive perspective, is that
its evidence base is invalid. Surface appearances are taken as
valid indicators of intended meaning. In consequence, what are
claimed to be low-inference observational judgments are in fact
highly inferential. Once the data are coded there is no way to
retrieve the original behavioral evidence to test the validity of
the inferences made about the behavior's meaning (see the discussion on this point by Mehan, 1979). No matter how strong
the correlations appear to be in such data sets, a good possibilty
always exists that such correlations are spurious, if relationships between behavioral form and social meaning are as variable as interpretive researchers claim them to be. Moreover, if
such variability is inherent in social life and thus omnipresent in
classrooms, experiments that purport to manipulate teacher
and student behaviors, so globally defined, are likely to be shot
through with confounding relationships between putative
"treatment" conditions, "control" conditions, and "outcomes"
that invalidate the causal inferences that are made.

The standard research on teacher effectiveness could only
proceed as it has done on the presupposition of uniformity of
nature in social life that follows from adopting natural science
models for social scientific inquiry. Interpretive research makes
very different assumptions. It looks for variability in relationships between behavioral form and intended meaning in classroom interaction. Moreover, interpretive research on teaching
repeatedly discovers locally distinctive patterns of *performed
social identity*—of enacted statuses and their attendant role relationships, such that a phenomenon like time-on-task is locally
meaningful in terms of the particular performed social identities
of the actual students spending time on the academic tasks assigned to them. If Mary, a high achiever, is observed by the
teacher to be off-task at a given moment, this may mean something quite different from Sam, a problem student, being observed as off-task in the same moment. One of Sam's
obligations as a problem student (who is perceived as often being off-task) may be to be constantly on-task (since this will be
"good for him"). Mary, on the other hand, who as a high
achiever is perceived as (by definition) being on-task most of
the time, does not have Sam's obligation to be constantly on-
task. Indeed Mary has earned the right to take occasional
"breaks"—time off-task. One is reminded of the differences in
work rights and obligations between hourly wage employees,
who punch a time clock, and salaried workers, who do not. Yet
even the role distinction between Sam and Mary is not entirely
absolute. Some mornings, if Sam is having an unusually good
day (i.e., if he appears to be working diligently and constantly)
he may have earned, for that morning, the right to take a break,
like Mary, the salaried worker.

The contrast between the interpretive and the standard perspectives can be further illustrated by considering classroom
social organization in terms of the metaphor of a chess game.
Standard research on teacher effectiveness presupposes a standard board (curriculum and aims), a standard set of chess
pieces (statuses of teacher and student), and a standard set of
rules of procedure that govern the relations among the pieces

(roles of teacher and student) that are appropriate, that is, possible within the game. Interpretive researchers presume that the board itself, the number and shapes of its "squares" — places to be in the curriculum — will vary from one classroom to the next, although on the one hand, with the publication of textbooks for reading and arithmetic with teacher's manuals and accompanying worksheets for students, and on the other hand, with accountability systems for management by objectives and continual achievement testing, there seems to be more pressure for uniformity of curriculum and aims than there was a generation ago. Even if one grants a superficial uniformity of the board itself, when one comes to the direct observation of actual playings of the game — observation that is unmediated by predetermined coding categories — one finds that the types of pieces vary from game to game. In one game there are many pawns, few knights, and no bishops. In another game there are no pawns, many knights, and many bishops. Since each type of piece is allowed to move differently on the board, the system of possible movements — the system of social relations — changes from game to game. Moreover, some interpretive researchers would argue that the differences among games, as they are actually played, are even more profound than the differences that would obtain if it were only a matter of having a different board or different pieces from one game to the next. If within a given game, neither the board nor the pieces are themselves entirely fixed — if the definitions of aims, curriculum, and the social identities and roles of teachers and students are constantly emergent in negotiation within the action of teaching and learning itself — then the school classroom is indeed a fundamentally different kind of social universe than the stable, fixed, and unidimensional one presupposed by positivist research on teaching. It is as if in the chess game, the white bishop has a mistress, the red king knows this but the white king doesn't, and the red king chooses at some times to take advantage of his knowledge to pressure the white bishop through blackmail, while at other times the red king chooses to ignore the white bishop's secret. To see the school classroom as a chess game that is multidimensional, filled with paradox and contradiction from moment to moment and from day to day, is to see the school classroom, and teaching, as a game of real life. The study of classrooms, interpretive researchers would argue, is a matter of social topology rather than social geometry.

A central task for interpretive, participant-observational research on teaching is to enable researchers and practitioners to become much more specific in their understanding of the inherent variation from classroom to classroom. This means building better theory about the social and cognitive organization of particular forms of classroom life as immediate environments for student learning.

Conclusions drawn from process–product research can suggest in general terms what to do to improve student achievement, but these general recommendations give neither the researcher nor the practitioner any information about how, specifically, to do what is called for. Some examples of recommended teaching behaviors are found in a recent review article by Rosenshine (1983, p. 338):

- Proceed in small steps (if necessary) but at a rapid pace.
- Use high frequency of questions and overt student practice.

- Give feedback to students, particularly when they are correct but hesitant.
- Make corrections by simplifying questions, giving clues, explaining or reviewing steps, or reteaching lost steps.
- Ensure student engagement during seatwork (i.e. teacher or aide monitoring).

The teaching functions called for by Rosenshine are global; for example, give feedback, simplify questions to correct, insure student engagement during seatwork (i.e., insure time-on-task). The functions could be performed in a myriad of different ways, appropriately and inappropriately, on differing occasions. How to understand what might be appropriate and what not, in specific cases, goes beyond the bounds of standard research on teacher effectiveness.

In considering issues of teacher effectiveness interpretive researchers might ask, "How is time-on-task manifested in different classrooms and at different times by different students within a given room? What is clear feedback, from differing student points of view and teacher points of view? Does any one of the possible ways of giving clear feedback actually take place in the concrete circumstances of face-to-face communication or in writing between teacher and student? For that matter, if relationships between teacher and student are fully interactional (i.e., reciprocal), how do students give teachers clear feedback? How do student actions influence teacher productivity — the teacher's time-on-task?"

To conclude, there are three very serious problems with standard process-product research on relationships between classroom interaction and student achievement. The first problem is that the work proceeds from an inadequate notion of interaction — one-way causal influence as a behavioral phenomenon — rather than reciprocal exchange of phenomenologically meaningful action. The second problem is that the standard work gives an extremely reduced view of classroom process. Its use of predetermined coding categories as a means of primary data collection gives no clear detailed evidence about the specific classroom processes that are claimed to lead to desired outcomes. The third problem is that the product studied is too narrowly defined — usually as end-of-the-year achievement test scores. With the standard approach to the study of teacher effectiveness having provided so reduced and one-dimensional a view of classroom processes, classroom products, and classroom interaction itself, it is not unreasonable to claim that the final word has not been spoken on this issue in research on teaching.

From an interpretive point of view, teacher effectiveness is a matter of the nature of the social organization of classroom life — what we have called the enacted curriculum — whose construction is largely, but not exclusively, the responsibility of the teacher as instructional leader. This is a matter of local meaning and local politics, of teaching as rhetoric (persuasion), and of student assent as the grounds of legitimacy for such persuasion and leadership by a teacher. As Doyle (1979) puts it in a felicitous phrase, students in classrooms are not the "passive recipients of instructional treatments" (p. 203).

In sum, issues of local politics at the classroom level seem to be at the heart of educational decision making by teachers and by students. Moreover, one can use the notions of politics and persuasion to consider an essential activity of schools as institutions, that of social sorting.

Power, Politics, and the Sorting Functions of Teaching

The sorting activities of schools occupy central interest in interpretive research on teaching. In developed countries the availability of universal public schooling is a means justifying the allocation of individuals across generations across the range of occupational slots available in the society. Conservative sociologists, such as Parsons (1959), liberals such as Clignet and Foster (1966), and radical sociologists such as Willis (1977) and Bourdieu and Passeron (1977) agree on the importance of this sorting function. Opinion differs over whether or not a particular society's school sorting procedures are justifiable or not, on grounds of fairness to individuals and groups. According to liberal social theory, school sorting procedures would be fair if they were universalistic, that is, if sorting criteria applied to individuals as individuals, along dimensions of comparison that apply universally to all persons regardless of such attributes of status as gender, race, social class, or religious preference.

From the early work (e.g., Henry, 1963) through the recent work of Willis (1977), much fieldwork research in education has been concerned with identifying the particularistic bias inherent in the putatively universalistic standard operating procedures of schools. At the classroom level, fieldwork has investigated the particularistic bias that is implicit in the kinds of environments that are established by teachers. The presumption is that the low school achievement of social and cultural minority students is better explained by considering the character of the classroom learning environment than by attributing the typical pattern of school failure of those children to deficiencies in individual intelligence and motivation.

For anthropologists especially it has seemed odd that in developed societies the school failure rate is so high among the majority of the population, who are of working-class or underclass status. This pattern stands in sharp contrast to that found in various nonliterate societies, in which almost everyone in the society acquires the knowledge and skills necessary for survival according to the pattern of adaptation developed in the particular society. That may have been true in nonliterate societies for the five million years of human evolution. Wolcott (1982) quotes Gearing in a question to modern societies: "It's something of a wonder that anyone ever learns anything. But given that they do, then we can also ask why everybody doesn't learn everything?" (See also Gearing & Sangree, 1979, p. 1.) Is this because socialization of the young is done more effectively in nonliterate societies? Is the apparent difference in the success of teaching and learning somehow due to the difference in scale between large developed societies and small nonliterate ones? Or might this difference also have to do with something about the institutionalization of teaching and learning in the school as a formal organization? Or, because the school failure rate is highest among the lower classes, is there something wrong with them?

One possibility is that lower class and minority populations are genetically inferior; that across generations gene pools have developed in these populations that produce, on the average, an overrepresentation of individuals of lower intelligence than those found in populations of white, upper-middle-class Americans. This *genetic deficit theory* was proposed in the late 1960s by Jensen (1969).

Another possible explanation lies in a family *socialization deficit hypothesis.* If the life circumstances of the poor are difficult and if their vision of life possibilities is limited, families of the poor may not provide children with the amounts of intellectual stimulation and motivation for achievement that middle-class families provide. Socialization deficit hypotheses were proposed during the 1960s under the labels of "cultural deprivation," "linguistic deprivation," and "family disorganization" (e.g. Riessman, 1962). It was argued that school subjects and intelligence tests required abstract thought and that lower-class families developed only concrete reasoning skills in their children. Numerous studies were conducted by child development researchers in which invidious comparisons were made between the child-rearing patterns of lower class and middle-class families (e.g., Hess & Shipman, 1965).

In the United States and Great Britain a large body of literature developed that criticized the genetic and socialization deficit hypotheses, characterizing them as "blaming the victim" (see Keddie, 1973). The argument over socialization deficit hypotheses tended to be conducted across disciplinary lines. Much of the deficit-oriented research and the prescriptions for teaching practice that followed from it were done by psychologists in the fields of education and child development. Much of the critique of the deficit hypotheses came from anthropologists, sociologists, and linguists. Cole, a notable exception, was a cognitive psychologist who conducted cross-cultural research that showed that nonschooled people often simply did not know the point of school-like tasks used in intelligence tests, by which they could be assessed as mentally deficient when in fact they were just using a different way of making sense (Cole & Scribner, 1974; Scribner & Cole, 1981).

Anthropologists and sociologists with linguistic training found the school failure rate among low-SES and minority populations in developed societies especially odd, in light of what was coming to be known about the cognitive demands of first-language acquisition by children. It was apparent that virtually every child who is not severely impaired physically or neurologically comes to school at age 5 having mastered the basic structure of the language spoken at home, its grammar and sound system. Linguists had contended that less prestigious regional, social class, and racial dialects were no less cognitively complex than the standard language spoken in school (cf. Labov, 1972, and Erickson, 1984).

Modern language-acquisition theory viewed mastering the grammar and sound system of a language as necessarily requiring complex, abstract, cognitive abilities, even though the thinking that took place was outside conscious awareness. Given that mastery of the speaking knowledge of a language was far more cognitively complex than beginning to learn to read the written form of that language, how was it that many children appeared to have great difficulty with simple, beginning reading? Children of low SES and of ethnic, racial, and cultural minority background could be seen, in school and outside it in the home and local community, to be able to speak much better than they could read. What might account for this?

One line of explanation, proposed by anthropologists, linguists, and by some sociologists, was that subtle subcultural differences between the community and the school led to interactional difficulties, misunderstanding, and negative attributions between teachers and students in the classroom. The preponderance of this work identified specific cultural differences between teachers of majority group background and low-SES, minority group children. The cultural differences consisted principally in implicit assumptions, learned outside conscious awareness in everyday life in the home and in the community, about the appropriate conduct of face-to-face interaction. Some of the basic properties in the organization of interaction that were investigated (often through comparative studies of children's lives at home and at school) were *phonological and grammatical dialect features in children's speech* that teachers had difficulty understanding (Piestrup, 1973), children's means of showing attention and understanding through nonverbal behavior such as gaze and nodding (Erickson, 1979), and differences in the organization of turn-taking in conversation that lead to overlapping of speakers or to long pauses between turns (Watson-Gegeo & Boggs, 1977; Shultz, Florio, & Erickson, 1982).

Mehan (1979) published a study of question–answer sequences in school lessons that revealed the tremendous complexity involved in managing such conversation. His analysis suggested the possibility of miscommunication due to different cultural expectations for the fine tuning of classroom discourse. More global aspects of interaction patterns that differed between home and school were also identified. These had to do with the cultural organization of social relationships in communication, that is, with foundational definitions of appropriateness in leadership and followership, in adult roles and in child roles. Among the topics investigated were differing cultural assumptions about the appropriateness of indirectness and directness (a) in the exercise of social control and in the use of a "spotlight" of public attention by asking content questions of named individuals (Philips, 1982; Erickson & Mohatt, 1982; (b) in the very situation of an adult asking "teacher-like" questions of a child—questions the child can presume the adult already knows the answer to (Heath, 1982); (c) in the differences in assumptions about the appropriateness of competitiveness and in cultural definitions of students offering and receiving help from one another as *showing laudable concern for others*, or as *cheating*; and (d) in cultural notions of appropriateness of humor and mock aggression in discourse (Lein, 1975).

Taken together, cultural differences between home and school that have been identified at the level of basic structural properties in the organization of interaction, and at the level of global differences in assumptions about appropriate role relationships between adults and children, involve fundamental building blocks, as it were, of the conduct of classroom interaction as a medium for subject matter instruction and for the inculcation of culturally specific values—definitions of honesty, seriousness of purpose, respect, initiative, achievement, kindliness, reasonableness. When students act in ways that do not match the classroom teacher's cultural expectations, the children's behavior can be perceived by teachers as frustrating, confusing, and sometimes frightening. Given the teachers' and the students' recurring difficulties in interacting together from day to day, an adversarial relationship is likely to be set up between the teacher and the student. This would inhibit the teacher's ability to learn from the students—to assess accurately what the students know, what they want educationally, and what they intend interpersonally in social relations with the teacher.

Recent work in Alaska and Hawaii appears to support the cultural difference hypothesis. In both cases, as teachers have interacted with students in the classroom in ways that resemble those that are culturally appropriate in the home and community, student achievement on standardized tests increases dramatically. The Alaskan study (Barnhardt, 1982) reports the situation in a small village school in the Alaskan interior. Achievement by Athabaskan Alaskan native children of the village was low until Alaskan native teachers began to teach in the three classrooms of the school: Grades 1–2, 3–4, and 5–6. After the native teachers arrived student achievement rose dramatically in all three classrooms. Subsequent participant observation and videotape analysis revealed that the teachers organized instruction and interacted with students in ways that were culturally appropriate. Exercise of social control was for the most part very indirect, and the teachers usually avoided public reinforcement—not only avoiding negative reinforcement of children's actions, but avoiding overt positive reinforcement as well. These patterns are typical of child-rearing in the community, and resemble those reported in Oregon and Northern Ontario by Philips (1982) and by Erickson and Mohatt (1982). The patterns found in the Athabaskan classrooms resemble patterns documented in Alaskan Eskimo classrooms by Collier (1973).

From this study it is not absolutely clear that the cultural patterns of instruction were the main influence on increased student achievement, since the native teachers at the school were also lifelong residents of the village, and their presence in the role of teacher may have increased rapport with parents and changed the climate of family and community expectations for children's school achievement. Still the evidence is highly suggestive that not only were the new teachers local natives, but they also taught children in forms of interaction that resembled those that were appropriate in family and community life outside the school.

In the Hawaiian case, evidence supporting the cultural difference hypothesis is even more clear than in the Alaskan case. In an innovative school program developed for native Hawaiian children researchers discovered that when the children were allowed to use overlapping speech while discussing reading stories in reading groups, their reading achievement rose. Previous ethnographic research had established that overlapping speaking turns was characteristic of certain kinds of conversations in the community (Au & Jordan, 1980). In subsequent experimental research (Au & Mason, 1981), material of equivalent difficulty was taught under two different conditions of social organization of discourse. In one condition the teacher allowed the students to overlap one another's speaking turns while discussing the reading story. In the other condition the teacher did not allow overlapping speech during the discussion of the story. The children's achievement was clearly higher under the first condition, in terms of proximal indices of achievement, such as error rates during the lesson, and in scores on tests administered directly after the lesson. In subsequent development work this alternative procedure for teaching reading, which incorporates culturally congruent discourse patterns into the overall design for reading pedagogy, is now being implemented in public school classrooms with native Hawaiian children. Similar positive results in student achievement have occurred, as indicated both by proximal indices of achievement and in end-of-the-year scores on standardized tests.

What might account for these results, theoretically? One line of explanation concerns the nature of face-to-face interaction as a learning task environment. In interaction in school lessons a dimension of culturally patterned social organization (patterns for turn-taking, listening behavior, and the like) always coexists with the dimension of the logical organization of the information content of the subject matter. The two dimensions — social organization and subject matter organization — are always reflexively intertwined in the enactment of a lesson. (For full discussion, see Erickson, 1982b, 1982c.) One reason that cultural congruence in the social organization of interaction in lessons seems to lead to higher student achievement may be that when the social organization of lesson interaction happens in ways that are culturally customary — already mastered through overlearning in daily life outside school — this simplifies the task environment of the lesson, allowing children to concentrate more fully on the subject matter content. In other words, lessons may be easier for children when their social organization dimension is clear and familiar.

This theory of lesson interaction as a social and cognitive task environment may provide an alternative explanation to the finding that highly ritualized lesson interaction formats appear to lead to higher achievement by cultural minority children even if the lesson formats are not congruent with cultural patterns for the social organization of interaction that are found in the student's home and community. Stallings and Kaskowitz (1974) report this finding in the evaluation of alternative models for Follow Through. The DISTAR instruction format, highly ritualized and not culture-specific, seems to result in higher student achievement, even for cultural minority populations for which the lesson format is quite culturally alien, as in the case of native Americans. The DISTAR format may have this result, not because it happens to fit a direct instruction model, but because the format by its very ritualization is so clear and easy to learn that it is soon mastered by children. Once learned, the ritual format would simplify the lesson as a task environment.

Indeed, the communication of a teacher's expectations for the conduct of interaction in ways that are clear and predictable, and the establishment of implicit or explicit consensus between the teacher and students that these ways of interacting are just, may be the fundamental feature that characterizes both the culturally incongruent teaching strategies, such as DISTAR, and the culturally congruent ones, such as the Kamehameha reading program in Hawaii. If clarity is of the essence, and if clarity can be achieved by instructional means that are culture-specific and culturally congruent, as well as by means that are culturally incongruent, then a wider range of policy options becomes available for improving the academic performance of cultural minority students.

The cultural difference hypothesis assumes that differences in expectation for the conduct of interaction are a systematic source of breakdowns in interaction that is analogous to the notion of *linguistic interference* in second-language acquisition. When features of the grammar and sound system of two languages differ, one can predict the likely recurrence of certain types of structural errors. For example, if in some language other than English the /th/ sound does not occur, but the /d/ sound does occur, one can predict that a speaker will consistently say "dis" for "this" when speaking English. Or if in some language other than English gender reference is signaled by some means other than alternative pronouns, one can predict that the speaker will substitute "he" for "she"and vice versa when speaking English. Analogously, one can predict that a teacher who is not used to overlapping speech in conversation (such as that found among working-class native Hawaiians and Italian-Americans) will interpret the overlapping talk as interruption, even though the children do not interpret the behavior of overlapping talk as an interruption. It follows, then, that culturally congruent social organization of instruction can reduce the situations of interactional interference that occur in the classroom, and that the reduction of these interactional difficulties increases student opportunity to learn and decreases misunderstanding between teacher and student.

But if interactional interference, by itself, is the chief factor that inhibits student learning, how can one explain the results of the Follow Through Evaluation? How does one explain reports of other instances of culturally incongruent instruction that appear to raise student achievement? One such instance is reported in a case study of a residential school for Alaskan natives in which instruction was conducted in culturally incongruent ways and yet in which student motivation and achievement were high (cf. Kleinfeld, 1979). It would seem that interactional difficulty and miscommunication are not simply a matter of structural interference between cultural patterns of the community and of the school.

A possible explanation lies in considering as a political phenomenon the local microculture and social organization of classroom life and its relation to student learning. If we think of classroom teaching and learning as a matter of local politics, some relationships between cultural difference or similarity, social relationships among teachers and students, and student learning begin to appear. These relationships are much less clear when we think of teaching and learning as a matter of individual psychology (whether behaviorist, cognitive, or social), or even in terms of the sociology and anthropology of the classroom as an ecosystem. When we consider individual functioning in the context of a sociocultural ecosystem, we have a framework for an anatomy of classroom teaching and learning. When we consider the dynamic operation of the ecosystem as a political process we have a physiology of teaching and learning. Central to such a framework are the concepts of power, authority, influence, competing interest, legitimacy, assent, and dissent.

Power, as the ability to coerce the actions of others, is potentially possessed both by teachers and by students in the classroom. Authority, the legitimate exercise of power and focus of socially sanctioned knowledge and judgment, resides officially with the teacher. Influence, the unsanctioned capacity to exercise power, resides with students. Every person who has attempted to teach faces the reality of student influence in relation to teacher authority. Even in institutional arrangments of schooling that vest the teacher with virtually unchecked authority (traditional religious instruction being a vivid case in point), the exercise of that authority in the absence of student assent can at best lead to outward conformity to the teacher's will, that is, in a teaching situation the student always possesses the ability to resist by refusing to learn what the teacher intends should be learned. The teaching–learning transaction, then, can be seen as an inherently political and rhetorical situation, in which at least the implicit consent of the governed must be gained by the governor through persuasion. The teacher must somehow persuade the followers that his or her guidance is legitimate and in the student's own interest. If the student perceives his or her interest to be fundamentally in conflict with that of the teacher, and if the student resists the teacher by withholding learning, the teacher is unable to teach. Thus in the classroom social system as a political economy, the power to withhold the currency that is essential to the system — student learning — ultimately resides with the student. This is true even if student resistance is covert and the student does not engage in more overt forms of protest. The interactional sabotage we call "discipline problems" can be seen as a form of interactional judo — control of the ostensibly stronger party by the ostensibly weaker one.

A crucial question for educational research then becomes: What are the conditions of micropolitics in the social organization of classroom life that set off a contest of wills between teacher and students in which the students refuse to learn what the teacher intends to teach? Some student failure may indeed be due to lack of student ability or motivation that lies outside the teacher's ability to change it as the conventional wisdom of educators and educational psychologists suggests. But some student failure may be more accurately seen as a matter of micropolitical resistance. The overrepresentation of student failure to learn simple knowledge and skill among low-SES and cultural minority populations of students is suggestive in this regard.

The interpretation of school failure as evidence of self-defeating resistance rather than as evidence of inadequacy on the part of students has been most consistently maintained by British sociologists of education, who see the production of student failure in schools as necessary for the maintenance of the existing class structure in society. In a recent review (1983) Giroux surveys this work. He makes the critical point that it is important to restrict the notion of resistance and not use the term loosely to refer to any sort of inappropriate or self-defeating action by a student or by a teacher.

In the United States this position has been asserted in a series of papers by McDermott (1974, 1977) and McDermott and Gospodinoff (1981) that criticize both the family socialization deficit hypothesis and the cultural difference hypothesis as explanations for school failure. His argument derives in part from psychiatrists' theories accounting for the generation of psychopathology in family relationships. One of McDermott's principal sources was Scheflen's adaptation (1960) of Bateson, Jackson, Haley, and Weakland's (1956/1972) theory of the interactional "double bind" as the cause of schizophrenia in children. An analogue to Scheflen's position is found in the work of Laing (1970). In the pathological family certain family members

become locked in patterns of regressive relations with other family members. The situation is not caused by the action of any single individual. The entire family system — its locally negotiated and maintained system of statuses and roles — supports and maintains the adversarial relationship between the parties who are manifestly at odds. To return to the chess metaphor for the social organization of face-to-face relations, pawns, knights, and kings by their patterned actions enable each other to act in concert. We see similar situations in which individuals become locked into relationships that are mutually punitive or are mutually destructive in other ways: in bad marriages, in alcoholic or abusive families, in recurrent difficulties in relations between a supervisor and a subordinate in a work group. Over time, interpersonal conflict develops a history. It ramifies throughout the whole social unit of interacting individuals. McDermott contends that this is what happens in school classrooms, among teachers and students who, for the most part unwittingly, are mutually failing one another. The student can be seen as playing an active role in this as student and teacher collaborate in producing a situation in which the student achieves school failure (McDermott, 1974). Another source of McDermott's position comes from recent work on interethnic relations in two-person interview situations (Erickson, 1975, Erickson & Shultz, 1982). Shultz and I found that in interethnic and interracial interviews between junior college counselors and students, certain kinds of cultural differences in communication behavior (e.g., differences in signaling attention and understanding through nonverbal listening behavior) were associated with other kinds of interactional trouble and negative interpersonal attribution in some interviews, conducted by a given counselor, yet in other interviews conducted by that counselor with students whose ethnic or racial background and cultural communication style matched that of the students with whom the counselor had had trouble, the same features of culturally differing communication behavior that had led to trouble with one student did not lead to serious, ramifying interactional difficulty with another student. Even though momentary difficulty due to culturally differing behavior styles could be observed, the trouble that occurred was soon recovered from. It did not escalate the way it did in other interethnic or interracial interviews conducted by the same counselor. This suggested a micropolitics of cultural difference in interaction. (For a discsussion of the role of culture difference in the larger scale politics of interethnic relations see Barth, 1969.) Under some circumstances, cultural differences in communication patterns became a resource for interpersonal conflict, while in other circumstances the same kinds of behaviors were not reacted to and made use of as a resource for conflict. A simple interference explanation for the negative effects of cultural difference on the conduct of interaction was inadequate to explain our data.

The significance of cultural difference as an inhibiting factor in classroom teaching and learning may be that cultural difference can function as a risk factor. As a source of relatively small interactional difficulties, cultural differences can become resources for the construction of much more large-scale and widespread conflict between teachers and students. It is in this sense that cultural differences along the lines of social class, ethnicity, race, gender, and handicapping conditions can play a role in the creation of classroom situations in which some students withhold learning as a form of resistance to teachers.

To summarize, a wide range of explanations exist for the high rates of school failure in developed societies. At one extreme are explanations that presume a radical individual determinism. These explanations identify some deficit in the individual learner, whether due to genetic inheritance or to environmental socialization, as the primary cause of school failure by students. A related set of explanations identifies similar deficits in the individual teacher, identifying the teacher as primarily responsible for student failure. This is the implication of the process–product research on teaching which suggests as a policy conclusion that individual teachers who are instructionally ineffective need either to be retrained or to be removed from the classroom.

At another extreme are explanations that presume a radical contextual or societal determinism as the source of school failure. These explanations identify the inequitable distribution of power and privilege in society as the root cause of school failure of low-SES and cultural minority children. Schools function, these theorists argue, as passive sorting mechanisms that reproduce the social class position of individuals from one generation to the next. (See, e.g., Bowles & Gintis, 1976.) In the absence of widespread change in power relations along the lines of social class, race, and gender, school achievement patterns will not change and any minor changes in achievement at the classroom level that might result fron remedial work with teachers and students are at best trivial and at worst pernicious, since they would mask the need for fundamental social change. Currently the aim of boring drill and denial of opportunities for independent reasoning in classrooms is to produce a docile work force from the compliant students, and to justify the existence of a permanently unemployed underclass made up of noncompliant students, who resisted by refusing to learn.

A middle position is taken on this issue by many interpretive researchers. Such a position attempts to acknowledge the reality of individual differences in aptitude and motivation for learning, the reality of cultural differences and their micropolitical significance, as it varies from classroom to classroom, the reality of the sorting functions of schools, as well as the reality of the functions of schools to stimulate learning and broaden opportunity among students whose life circumstances are limited, and who are thus at risk for school failure. Many interpretive researchers acknowledge that the tension for the classroom teacher between the responsibility to be the student's impartial judge and the responsibility to be the student's advocate is an inherent source of tension in the role of the teacher as it is institutionally defined in the United States. This contradiction in the teacher role, identified more than a generation ago by Waller (1932), can be seen as genuinely inherent as a paradox that is not reducible. In Japan and in other educational systems in which examinations are centralized and are administered by an agency external to the classroom, the teacher's role is not so contradictory as it is in the United States. In Japan the teacher prepares the student for the examinations, functioning as the student's advocate throughout the process of elementary and secondary schooling (Vogel, 1965).

No univocal social theory, whether conservative, liberal, or radical, provides by itself an adequate explanation for phenomena of school achievement in the United States. According to conservative social theory the essential inferiority of the lower classes as less intelligent and hard working than the higher classes is evidenced by the manifest class differences in school achievement. According to liberal social theory, inequities currently exist in school sorting practices, but if sorting were done more objectively according to universalistic judgment criteria the schools could provide equality, or equity, of opportunity. According to radical social theory, changes in school sorting practices can only result after fundamental social change since the current sorting practices serve to legitimate current class division and are thus maintained at the school system and classroom level by pressures from the wider society.

Interpretive research accommodates the reality of the local organization of teaching and learning at the classroom level, together with the reality of external pressures on the organization of the classroom. Both levels of organization must be encompassed, theoretically and empirically, in an account of the micropolitics of classroom organization, within which low-SES minority children fare more or less well from one classroom to the next.

This suggests a set of issues and questions for future interpretive research on teaching. We must ask what are the specific features of social organization and meaning that arise on a given classroom ecosystem; the enacted hidden curriculum of social organization and the enacted manifest curriculum of subject matter organization, which must be considered together. We can ask about the relation of this enacted curriculum to the range of kinds and amounts of student learning that take place. *Learning* here can include cognitive learning of subject matter, but the notion of learning would not be limited to this single aspect. In order to study these issues it is necessary to ask what the specific conditions are by which teachers and students construct local social organization in ways that increase or decrease differing specific kinds and amounts of student resistance to learning the manifest curriculum. We can consider how this situationally embedded, locally produced resistance to learning (and other kinds of difficulty in learning) varies by class, race, ethnicity, and gender. We can consider the ways in which the situationally embedded informal classroom social system—the statuses and roles available to students in it, the locally produced resistance to learning and other sources of learning difficulty—is organized in relation to statuses external to the classroom, such as class, race, ethnic, and gender identity. We can consider how all the local social organization relates to nonlocal, external sources of influence and how the settings exterior to the classroom are influenced by what happens inside the room. We can ask how all this relates to student learning and to teacher morale.

Such study can begin with the assumption that learning and teaching are intrinsic to the biological and social foundations of human adaptation, within the life cycle and across generations. Learning, it can be assumed, is not optional for humans, and we would not expect it to be so for students in classrooms. The basic issue is not that some students learn and others do not. We can assume that all students are learning something. The basic issue is that many students, for a variety of different reasons, do not appear to be learning what the teacher and the school claim to be teaching. Both the claims regarding what is being taught and the claims regarding what is being learned need to be scrutinized, in the context of the wider societal influences and the local meaning systems that are created as teachers and students influence one another in the teaching and learning environment of enacted curriculum, the specifics of which must be identified because they vary from classroom to classroom as does student achievement. The core issues in teacher and student effectiveness concern meaningfulness—the grounds for legitimacy and mutual assent—rather than causation in a mechanical sense. The inquiry involves a search for interpretive understanding of the ways in which particular individuals engage in constructing patterns of action and meaning by which they enable one another to accomplish desired (or undesired) ends. The particular means they construct for collaboratively accomplishing those ends are expected to vary across each specific classroom, and within classrooms from year to year. There may be universal principles of organization by which people collectively foster or inhibit the accomplishment of their stated goals. These, it is assumed, can only be discovered by studying particular instances in close detail, since the universal principles are realized in ways that are locally unique.

Finally, such study must also link the immediacy of the local lives of students and teachers, inside and outside the classroom, to nonlocal and general aspects of social structure and culture. For the interpretive participant observational researcher, this must be done by looking out from the classroom to the wider world, as well as looking in to the classroom from the wider world, as functionalists and radical critics both tend to do.

One of the most immediate places to look outside the classroom is the student's own family and local community. Many claims are made about the influence of the home and community on the child's learning in the classroom. It may be that the main reason for differences in student achievement according to class and parents' educational background is that parents who are higher in SES and in education know how to coach their children in school subjects, while parents who are lower in SES and in experience with educational success themselves do not know how to do this coaching. It may be that parents who are higher in SES and in educational attainment model the meaningfulness and usefulness of knowledge and skill that are acquired in school, while parents of lower SES and educational attainment do not model this. It may be that, as Ogbu asserts (1978), parents and other members of a caste-like minority group with a pariah status in the society, such as American blacks, communicate a sense of hopelessness to their school-age children, while parents and other members of a non-caste-like minority group (such as the American Chinese) communicate the more hopeful belief that school success is the route to adult success. The caste-like minority student, according to Ogbu, by failing to strive, plays an active role in achieving school failure. (There is something that strikes one intuitively as realistic in this hypothesis, in its portrayal of the low-achieving student as an active agent in the construction of his or her own victim status. In that sense Ogbu's hypothesis is reminiscent of that of McDermott.)

Currently, however, there is no substantial body of empirical evidence against which to judge these claims. To test any of these assertions we would need specific knowledge of the life experiences of students who vary in educational achievement within the same classroom, and within class, racial, ethnic, and gender categories. There are a few studies that have begun to investigate students' lives outside school in relation to their lives inside school, notably Heath (1983), as well as studies mentioned earlier in this discussion. These studies have not focused specifically on variation in classroom achievement *within as well as between* demographic background factors such as class, race, ethnicity, and gender, among students from the same classroom. To test Ogbu's hypothesis, for example, we would need to follow high-achieving and low-achieving American black students from the same classroom, as well as high-achieving Chinese-American students from the same classroom, to see if the high-achieving black and Chinese-American students were receiving a qualitatively different set of implicit and explicit messages about achievement attribution than were the low-achieving black American students. It hardly seems possible that the low achievement pattern among low-SES black students is explained by so simple a matter as the presence of significant others who say to the student, implicitly or explicitly, "You can't make it no matter what you do." How consistent are such messages? How do they relate to the message in the meaning system of the classroom? How does Ogbu's hypothesis account for the fact that in some classrooms low-SES black students do better than they do in other classrooms? The relationships between what happens in students' lives outside and inside the classroom, and the relations between that and school achievement are not at all clear.

The same is true for teachers. In recent work, Cusick (1980) asserts that teachers in two public high schools he studied voted on curriculum issues differently depending on the ways in which a particular curriculum decision might affect a second job they held or a strong avocational interest they had. We do not know the ways in which teachers who are parents of children may be influenced in their teaching by the demands (and rewards) of family life, nor how this might vary with the age of the teacher's children, nor how the situation of teachers who are parents might contrast with that of teachers who are not parents. A host of new questions can be raised concerning the ways in which different kinds of teachers and students make sense of the differences between the concrete circumstances of their lives outside and inside school.

Data Collection

Of all the aspects of fieldwork research, data collection has been the most discussed in the literature on methods. In the interest of economy of exposition, this discussion of issues in data collection is kept to a minimum. I will review major themes and issues in data collection and will refer the reader to main sources in the literature for discussion at greater length.

One approach to data collection in the field is to make it as intuitive—or as radically inductive—as possible. The conviction is that with long-term, intensive participant observation in a field setting, begun with no prior conceptual expectations that might limit the fieldworker's openness to the uniqueness of experience in the setting, an intuitive sense of relevant research questions and of conclusions regarding pattern will emerge by induction. From this point of view, fieldwork is seen as an almost mystical process, essentially unteachable. The best preparation is solid grounding in substantive courses in anthropology and/or sociology. After learning relevant substantive theory and after reviewing empirical results of fieldwork research the novice researcher proceeds to the field and does fieldwork.

Anthropologists, especially, have set forth this mystical conception of fieldwork as unteachable. It is said of Alfred Kroeber that when a doctoral student came for advise on fieldwork research methods before embarking on a study of a native American society somewhere in California, Kroeber made the following comments:

1. First, find your Indians (i.e., don't study the wrong group by mistake).
2. Pads of paper and pencils are very useful.
3. Be sure to take a frying pan, but don't loan it to anyone; you may not get it back.

This is an extremely romantic notion of fieldwork. One enters the field with no preconceptions, and learns the methods by doing them (as one can learn to swim by being thrown in the pool). After tremendous emotional stress one finally induces grounded analytic categories. The likelihood of stress is increased if one experiences not only emotional trauma while in the field, but contracts an exotic, debilitating disease such as malaria. Only after returning home does one crack the code of local lifeways and solve the interactive analytic puzzle.

Another approach to data collection is to make the process as deliberative as possible. That is what is argued for here. There is no warrant, in contemporary philosophy of science and cognitive psychology, for the romantic conception of fieldwork, in which the fieldworker arrives in the setting with a *tabula rasa* mind, carrying only a toothbrush and hunting knife. One can argue that there are no pure inductions. We always bring to experience frames of interpretation, or schemata. From this point of view the task of fieldwork is to become more and more reflectively aware of the frames of interpretation of those we observe, and of our own culturally learned frames of interpretation we brought with us to the setting. This is to develop a distinctive view of both sides of the fence, what Bohannon (1963, pp. 7–8) has characterized as the *stereoscopic social vision* of the ethnographer.

When we consider fieldwork as a process of deliberate inquiry in a setting (cf. Pelto & Pelto, 1977; Levine, Gallimore, Weisner, & Turner 1980) we can see the participant observer's conduct of data collection as progressive problem solving, in which issues of sampling, hypothesis generation, and hypothesis testing go hand in hand. Fieldworkers' daily presence in the setting is guided by deliberate decisions about sampling and by intuitive reactions as well. When and where these observers go, whom they talk to and watch, with whom they participate in daily activities more actively and with whom they participate with a more distanced observational stance—all these involve strategic decisions about the nature of the key research questions and working hypotheses of the study.

All research decisions are not deliberate, however. Because of this the toothbrush and hunting-knife school has a valid point in reminding us of the importance of induction, intuition, and intensive firsthand presence in the setting. From the point of view of a more deliberative conception of fieldwork, however, the central issue of method is to bring research questions and data collection into a consistent relationship, albeit an evolving one. This is possible, we argue here, without placing shackles on intuition and serendipity. Framing research questions explicitly and seeking relevant data deliberately enable and empower intuition, rather than stifle it.

In the absence of a deliberative approach to fieldwork some typical problems of inadequate evidence emerge at the stage of data analysis after leaving the field. These are problems that might have been avoided had different strategic decisions been made at the stage of data collection, when midcourse correction was still possible. There are five major types of evidentiary inadequacy.

1. *Inadequate amounts of evidence.* The researcher has too little evidence to warrant certain key assertions. The fieldworker's daily round did not include the scenes in which evidence could have been collected that would have confirmed the assertion.
2. *Inadequate variety in kinds of evidence.* The researcher fails to have evidence across a range of different kinds of sources (e.g., direct observation, interviewing, site documents) to warrant key assertions through *triangulation*. The researcher did not seek triangulating data while in the field.
3. *Faulty interpretive status of evidence.* The researcher fails to have understood the key aspects of the complexity of action or of meaning perspectives held by actors in the setting. (Participation was not long enough or intensive enough in key recurrent scenes, and/or interviewing and direct observation did not complement one another, and/or the researcher was deceived by informants who lied and faked because they did not trust the researcher or did not agree with the researcher's aims.)
4. *Inadequate disconfirming evidence.* The researcher lacks data that might disconfirm a key assertion. Moreover, the researcher lacks evidence that a deliberate search was made for potentially disconfirming data while in the field setting. This weakens the plausibility of the absence of disconfirming evidence and leaves the researcher liable to charges of seeking only evidence that would support favorite interpretations. (The researcher, not having realized while in the field the relations between research questions and data collection, failed to identify a key assertion during fieldwork, and consequently failed to search for evidence that might disconfirm the assertion or that might stand as discrepant cases, whose analysis while in the field might shed new light on the assertion and its theoretical presuppositions.)
5. *Inadequate discrepant case analysis.* The researcher did not scrutinize the set of disconfirming instances, examining each instance (i.e., discrepant case) and comparing it with the confirming instances to determine which features of the disconfirming case were the same or different from the analogous features of the confirming cases. Such comparative feature analysis often reveals flaws in the original assertion, which if rewritten can account for the discrepant cases as well as accounting for those initially thought to have been confirming instances. The remaining members of the set of

disconfirming instances are genuinely discrepant cases that are not accounted for by the assertion. (Discrepant case analysis will be illustrated by classroom examples in the next major section of the chapter on data analysis and report writing. The point to be noted here is that discrepant case analysis enables the researcher to refine and adjust major assertions and their theoretical presuppositions. If such analysis is not done two types of errors can result: (a) the researcher rejects an assertion prematurely, by counting as similar all instances that seem, upon first analysis, to be disconfirming ones, and/or (b) the researcher fails to refine and adjust the assertions that appeared at the first analysis to be confirmed by the data.)

Issues of Site Entry and of Research Ethics

Potentially good fieldwork research can be compromised from the outset by inadequate negotiation of entry in the field setting. This leads to problems of data quality and of research ethics. The researcher's interest is in the broadest possible kinds and amounts of access. Given the potential problems of evidentiary adequacy noted above, the fieldworker wants ideally to be able to observe anywhere in the setting at any time, and to be able to interview any member of the setting on any topic. This may or may not be in the best interests of those in the setting. Issues of special interest and special risk arise, not only between members of the setting and its outside constituencies (school district staff and its local community, the state education department, federal education agencies); these issues of special interest and risk also arise within and across system levels in the organization (the interests of teachers in relation to a principal, the interests of students in relation to teachers).

Two basic ethical principles apply. Those studied, especially those studied as focal research subjects, need to be (a) as informed as possible of the purposes and activities of research that will occur, and of any burdens (additional work load) or risks that may be entailed for them by being studied. Focal research subjects also need to be (b) protected as much as possible from risks. The risks involved can be minimal. Their nature is not that of physical risk, as in some medical experiments. Psychological and social risks (embarrassment and/or liability to administrative sanction) are usually the kind entailed in fieldwork research. Still, the risks of psychological and social harm can be substantial when fieldwork is done by an institutionally naive researcher who has not adequately anticipated the range of different kinds of harm to which persons of varying social position in the setting are potentially liable.

Liability to risk is often greatest between members of differing interest groups in the local setting. Reporting to a general scientific audience usually does not expose local people to risk. Rather, it is reporting in the local setting that needs to be considered in the negotiation of access to information about individuals in the setting.

The researcher is in a perplexing situation. He or she needs to have done an ethnography of the setting in order to anticipate the range of risks and other burdens that will be involved for those studied. While it is not possible, at the outset, to antic-ipate all the ethical issues that will emerge, it is possible to anticipate many of them and to negotiate about them with those interest groups in the setting whose existence and whose circumstances are apparent at the outset. In school settings, these general classes of group interest are students, teachers, parents, principals, central administrators. Some of the differing interests of these differing classes can be identified in advance. It is usually wise, for example, to guarantee to teachers that certain kinds of information about their teaching will not be available to their immediate supervisors, and that information about a student's home life will not be available to teachers. Such information about teachers and about homes, however, might not expose individuals to risk if reported in the aggregate—all or many teachers, all or many homes.

In special local circumstances the usual risks attendant to a given institutional position may not exist. For example, the information that a teacher does not use the basal reader as directed by the system-wide mandates for the reading program might count against the teacher in one principal's eyes, while for another principal with another point of view that same information would count in the teacher's favor.

The researcher is wise to negotiate strict protection of information at the outset of a study. When special circumstances warrant, these agreements can be changed to be more flexible later in the research process. Usually, however, it is more difficult to restrict access of higher-ups in the system to certain kinds of information later in the research process.

The basic ethical principle is to protect the particular interests of especially vulnerable participants in the setting. Focal subjects are especially vulnerable, as are those who are single occupants of an institutional status (e.g., there is only one principal and many teachers, but only one kindergarten teacher). People who are not focal in a study may be less at risk. (For example, if one is studying low-achieving students who are girls, high-achieving boys in the room are less likely to be at risk. They would appear in descriptive reports as part of the background, not in the foreground of the report.) In a study I directed in a large urban school system, for example (Cazden, Carrasco, Maldonado-Guzman, & Erickson, 1980), we were conducting a full year's participant observation and videotaping with Hispanic bilingual teachers who were not fully certified. The teachers did not have tenure and were on annually renewable contracts. In that instance we negotiated an agreement with the building principal, the district superintendent, and an associate superintendent in the central office that not only would the researchers never be asked to show their field notes to an administrator, but that no administrator would ask the researchers for oral characterizations of the teachers being studied or for access to the videotapes for any purposes of evaluation. The researchers anticipated showing some videotape footage to the principal and the faculty in staff meetings, but planned to do this in a second year, after data had been collected, and after the teachers had reviewed the videotape footage to be shown and had given consent that others see the footage. In any event, no footage would ever be shown anyone but the research staff without the teachers' consent. In addition, however, we had negotiated written agreement with administrators that they would not even ask to see teacher-cleared footage until after the next annual contract had been signed by the teachers. This did not totally eliminate risk to the teachers, but it minimized the risk of informal coercion while the teachers were being studied. As it happened, no requests for information or tape viewing were made by administrators during the year, but it was prudent to have anticipated this in negotiating entry.

The researcher is wise to take great care in being explicit about uses of information and access to it, because it is in the researcher's interest to have as much access in the setting as is possible under conditions of high trust and rapport. Access in itself is of no use to the researcher without the opportunity to develop trust and rapport. The very process of explicit entry negotiation with all categories of persons likely to be affected by the research can create the conditions of trust that are necessary. In consequence, we can see that ethical responsibility and scientific adequacy must go hand in hand in fieldwork research. If research subjects consent freely to be studied and if they do so having been informed of the purposes of research and the possible risks to them, as well as the possible benefits, then deception and faking are minimized, as is passive resistance to the researcher's presence.

In sum, negotiation of entry is a complex process. It begins with the first letter or telephone call to the site. It continues throughout the course of research, and continues after the researcher has left the site, during later data analysis and reporting. Careful negotiation of entry that enables research access under conditions that are fair both to the research subjects and to the researcher establishes the grounds for building rapport and trust. Without such grounds mutual trust becomes problematic and this compromises the researcher's capacity to identify and analyze the meaning-perspectives of those in the setting. There is considerable discussion of entry negotiation in the literature of fieldwork research methods. See especially Agar (1980, pp. 42–62), Bogdan and Biklen (1982, pp. 120–125), Schatzman and Strauss (1974, pp. 18–33), and Wax (1971, pp. 15–20, 84–93, 143–174).

Developing a Collaborative Relationship with Focal Informants

Trust and rapport in fieldwork are not simply a matter of niceness; a noncoercive, mutually rewarding relationship with key informants is essential if the researcher is to gain valid insights into the informant's point of view. Since gaining a sense of the perspective of the informant is crucial to the success of the research enterprise, it is necessary to establish trust and to maintain it throughout the course of the study.

One source of difficulty with trust is the tendency for informants to assume, whatever the researcher's presentation of the purposes of research was during the initial stages of negotiation of entry, that the researcher's purposes are in some way evaluative. It is often necessary to reinterpret the purposes of research a number of times to the same informant. In addition, it is necessary to explain the purposes of the study to each new informant one meets. If the new informant is not a potential key informant, a brief recounting of the study's purposes may suffice, but it is often wise to give each new informant one meets a full explanation of the study's purposes because one cannot anticipate fully at the outset which informants will become key

later in the study. It is useful for the researcher to have virtually memorized a brief statement of the study's purposes, the procedures that will take place, and the steps taken to maximize confidentiality and minimize risk. If material cannot be kept confidential the informant(s) need to know that. If the researcher will be present in a given scene in the role of participant observer, the informants need to know that in that scene their actions and comments are "on the record," even if the researcher is not writing notes or making a recording. If informants wish actions to remain off the record they need to understand clearly that it is up to them to request that of the participant observer.

Informant concerns about the observer's evaluative perspective make great sense, given the ubiquity of observation for evaluative purposes in schools. In an ultimate sense, the researcher's purposes are indeed evaluative, for to portray people's actions in narrative reports is to theorize about the organization of those actions, and evaluation is inherent in any theory. We will return to this point in the next section of the chapter.

The researcher can expect that informants will test the assurances of confidentiality, nonjudgmental perspective, and other ethical considerations that were negotiated by the researcher. This testing usually happens early in the relationship with a new informant. The informant may ask for an evaluative comment, or may reveal some harmless piece of information to the researcher and then check the organization's rumor network to see if the researcher revealed the item of information to anyone else in the setting.

When doing team research it is very important for all members of the research team to adhere strictly to a basic ground rule: Never make comments to other team members about anything observed in the site, while you are at the site. Side conversations between research team members on site can be overheard by participants in the site, sometimes with disastrous consequences for the credibility of the research team.

An excellent way to establish and maintain trust in a setting is to involve the informants directly in the research, as collaborators with the researcher(s). Some issues of trust come up at the outset of attempts by the researchers to develop a partnership in research with key informants. The informants may perceive such attempts by researchers as manipulative, since the self-perception of classroom teachers, especially, is that they are not experts; if anyone is the expert in a partnership between researchers and classroom teachers, the teachers may assume that it is the researchers who are the experts. This perception on the part of the teachers may persist despite disclaimers by the researchers. In time, however, a genuine partnership can develop, in which the teacher and the researcher begin to frame research questions jointly and to collect data jointly. (On the process of collaborative fieldwork research on teaching, see Florio & Walsh, 1980.)

In developing initial rapport, as well as in establishing a collaborative relationship with key informants, it is necessary that the researcher have a clear idea of the major research questions guiding the inquiry, and the likely data collection procedures that will be used to pursue the lines of inquiry suggested by the study's guiding questions. This presupposes the deliberative conception of the fieldwork research process that was alluded to earlier in this discussion.

Data Collection as an Inquiry Process

Inquiry begins in the field with the research questions that guide the study. Three issues are crucial at the outset: (a) identifying the full range of variation in modes of formal and informal social organization (role relationships) and meaning-perspectives; (b) collecting recurrent instances of events across a wide range of events in the setting, so that the typicality or atypicality of certain event types with their attendant characteristic social organization can later be established; and (c) looking at events occurring at any system level (e.g., the classroom, the school, the reading group) in the context of events occurring at the next higher and next lower system levels. This means that if one were observing reading groups because a guiding research question led one to focus on issues in the teaching of reading, one would look at least at constituent events within the reading group event (sets of topically connected turns at speaking, teacher moves, student moves) and at events at the classroom level —for example, formal and informal status hierarchies of students in the classroom as a whole, characteristic ways the teacher has of organizing interaction with students in events other than reading. Ideally, one would wish to look at an even wider range of system levels for possible connections of influence—for example, building-level influences, exerted by other teachers and by the principal, that might affect the teacher's teaching, and influences from children's lives outside school in their homes and in other community settings that might influence their actions in the reading group. In fieldwork one never considers a single system level in isolation from other levels; that is a basic feature of the sociocultural theory from which participant observational methods derive.

In order to determine the full range of variation in social organizational arrangements, meaning-perspectives, and connections of influence within and across system levels in the setting and its surrounding environments, it is necessary to begin observation and interviewing in the most comprehensive fashion possible. Later in the research process one moves in successive stages to more restricted observational focus.

The progressive problem solving of fieldwork entails a process of sequential sampling. Because of the wide-angle view taken at the outset, it can be seen as "observing without any preconceptions," but that is a misleading characterization. Preconceptions and guiding questions are present from the outset, but the researcher does not presume at the outset to know where, specifically, the initial questions might lead next. In consequence the researcher begins with the most comprehensive possible survey of the setting and its surrounding environments. Concretely, that means that the researcher plans deliberately to spend time in particular places, at particular times. For example, in studying a classroom, one would first begin by seeking an overall sense of the neighborhood school community by collecting written information on the school community (e.g., census data), walking and driving around the community, and stopping in local shops. One would then enter the classroom, observing for complete days, from before the students arrive until they leave at the end of the day. Having identified the full range of events that occurred in the day, and having, through repeated observation, begun to establish the relative frequency of occurrence of the various event types, the researcher can be-

gin to focus on those events that are of central interest in the study. The researcher would begin to restrict the range of times and places at which observation occurred. Periodically, however, the researcher would want to return to more comprehensive sampling, in order to restore breadth of perspective, and in order to collect more instances of events across the full range of events that occurred in the setting. This provides additional warrant for claims the researcher might later want to make regarding the typicality and atypicality (high and low frequency) of certain event types, or of certain role relationships within an event or range of events.

As the researcher focuses on a more restrictive range of events within the setting, the researcher also begins to look for possible connections of influence between the setting and its surrounding environments. Unlike standard community ethnography, in which one begins with the whole community as the unit of analysis and moves progressively to investigate subunits within the community, in educational fieldwork one usually moves relatively quickly, after a brief general survey of the community, to continuous, focused study of a given educational setting (e.g., the classroom, the math lesson). After considerable study of the focal setting the researcher moves out again to investigate its surrounding environments. The analytic task is to follow lines of influence out the classroom door into the surrounding environments. Cues to these lines of influence are found in site documents (e.g., memos enjoining certain actions within the classroom) and in comments of members in the setting (teachers, students) about those aspects of their lives outside the immediate setting that influence what takes place there. Informants are usually not fully aware consciously of the full range and depth of these influences, which include culturally learned and taken-for-granted assumptions about proper conduct of social relations, content of subject matter, human nature, and attitudes that shape one's definitions of what *work*, *play*, *trustworthiness*, *academic ability*, and the like might look like when encountered in everyday life in the classroom.

With time, the fieldworker's notions of the phenomena that are most relevant to the study become clearer and clearer. In the final stages of fieldwork research, the focus may be very restricted indeed, as research questions and working hypotheses become more and more specific. The process of fieldwork research as deliberate inquiry has been described by some anthropologists (e.g., Agar, 1980; Dobbert, 1982; Dorr-Bremme, 1984; Goetz, & LeCompte, 1984; Levine et al., 1980; Pelto & Pelto, 1977), and by numerous sociologists (e.g., Glaser & Strauss, 1979; Lofland, 1976; Schatzman & Strauss, 1974). This process has been described for studies of teaching by Erickson (1973, 1977), and by Mehan (1979), among others. Limits of space preclude full discussion here. Some elaboration on the nature of the inquiry process itself, however, is appropriate.

The Boundedly Rational Process of Problem Solving in Fieldwork

In fieldwork the researcher is attempting to come to understand events whose structure is too complex to be apprehended all at once, given the limits on human information-processing capacity. These limits—what Simon (1957) calls *bounded rationality*—are compensated for in participant observation by spending time in the field setting.

The participant observer, present in particular spaces and times in the field setting, waits for particular types of recurrent events to keep happening (e.g., disputes over land tenure, deaths, births, preparing the main meal of the day, seeing the next client at the unemployment office, having a reading lesson, exchanging turns at reading aloud, handing in a written exercise). The researcher may seek out particular sites within a field setting where a particular type of event is most likely to happen. This gives the participant observer a situation analogous to that of the subject in a learning experiment—the opportunity to have multiple trials at mastering a recurringly presented task. In this case the task is that of learning how to observe analytically a particular type of event, and how to make records (field notes, audio and video recordings) of the actions that occur in the events, for purposes of more careful study later.

Across each trial at observing a recurrent event the participant observer can alter slightly the focus of analytic attention. each time attending to some features of what is occurring and not attending to others. The observer can also vary the focus of attention in rereading field notes taken during the event, and in writing these up in expanded form after the day's observation has been completed. A fundamental principle is that this subsequent reflection and write-up, which usually takes at least as long as the time spent initially in observation, needs to be completed before returning to the field setting to do further observation. This means that the researcher needs to anticipate spending time writing up notes—a full day's observation in a classroom would need to be followed by a full day's (or night's) period of write-up. Write-up stimulates recall and enables the researcher to add information to that contained in the unelaborated, raw notes. Write-up also stimulates analytic induction and reflection on relevant theory and bodies of research literature. There is no substitute for the reflection during fieldwork that comes from time spent with the original field notes, writing them up in a more complete form, with analytic insights recorded in them.

In spite of the limits on information-processing capacity, time over time observation and reflection enable the observer to develop an interpretive model of the organization of the events observed. These models are progressively constructed across a series of partial observations in a process that is analogous to a learning experiment in which the learner is presented a series of trials.

Two sets of procedural decisions by the fieldworker have special importance for correcting what is traditionally thought of as *bias* in sampling and observation—(a) the decisions the observer makes about where to be in space and in time in the field setting, and (b) the decisions the observer makes about the foci of attention in any one occasion of observation. The former decisions affect the overall sampling of events that the participant observer makes. The latter decisions affect the completeness and analytic adequacy of observations made cumulatively across a set of trials.

A major strength of participant observation is the opportunity to learn through active participation—one can test one's theory of the organization of an event by trying out various kinds of participation in it. A major limitation in fieldwork is the partialness of the view of any single event. There is, in consequence, a tendency toward bias in sampling that favors the frequently occurring event types since those are the ones one comes to understand most fully across time.

We will discuss the consequences of the bias in the next section of the paper. There is also another sense in which a bias toward the typical is present in fieldwork research. Given the limits on what can be attended to during any one observational trial, the observer may come to be dominated early on by a focus on an emerging theory of organization that is being induced. As that happens the fieldworker may attend, while observing, mainly to those aspects of action that *confirm* the induced theory, overlooking other aspects of action that might be noted as data according to which the emergent theory might be *disconfirmed*. Thus potentially disconfirming evidence is less likely to be recorded in the fieldnotes than is the potentially confirming evidence.

The researcher's tendency to leap to conclusions inductively early in the research process can be called the *problem of premature typification*. This problem makes it necessary to conduct (while in the field, and in subsequent reflection after leaving the field) deliberate searches for disconfirming evidence in the form of discrepant cases—instances of the phenomena of interest whose organization does not fit the terms of one's emerging theory. (On the importance of discrepant case analysis, see Mehan, 1979, and the classic statement of Lindesmith, 1974.)

Another way to reduce the bias of premature typification and the bias toward emphasis on analysis of recurrent events at the expense of analysis of rare events is to include machine recording in the research process. Audio or audiovisual records of frequent and rare events in the setting and in its surrounding environments provide the researcher with the opportunity to revisit events vicariously through playback at later times. Recording of naturally occurring interaction in events does not substitute for firsthand participant observation and recording by means of fieldnotes. Still, such recordings, subjected to systematic analysis, can provide a valuable additional data source in fieldwork research. It is appropriate to discuss briefly the special nature of machine recording and analysis in the process of fieldwork research. The discussion will anticipate slightly that to be covered in the next section on data analysis, but it is appropriate here to highlight contrasts with the kinds of progressive problem solving that are possible during firsthand participant observation in the field setting. The use of machine recording as a primary data resource in fieldwork research has been called "microethnography" by Erickson (1975, 1976, 1982a), "constitutive ethnography" by Mehan (1979), and "sociolinguistic microanalysis" by Gumperz (1982). The microethnographic research process has been described in detail by Erickson and Shultz (1977/81), by Erickson and Wilson (1982), and by Erickson (1982a).

Machine recording and analysis differ from participant observation in one crucial respect. Unlike the participant observer the analyst of audiovisual or audio documentary records does not wait in the setting for instances of a particular event type to occur. In reviewing the machine-recorded documentary evidence, the analyst is freed from the limits of the participant observer's embedding in the sequential occurrence of events in real time and space. The researcher indexes the whole recorded corpus, identifying all the major named events recorded (e.g., lessons, meetings, recess periods, parent-teacher conferences) and identifying as well the presence in certain events of key informants. Then the researcher searches back and forth through the entire recorded corpus for instances of frequent and rare events, moving as it were back and forth through time and space to identify analogous instances. This is analogous to the initial survey of the setting and its surrounding environments that the participant observer does by making choices of where to be in time and space in the setting. Then the researcher identifies a particular set of instances from the recorded corpus that are of special interest. The researcher at this point is able to revisit this set of instances vicariously by replaying them. The capacity to revisit the same event vicariously for repeated observations is the chief innovation made possible by the use of machine recordings in fieldwork research. The innovation has distinctive strengths and limitations.

The first strength is the *capacity for completeness of analysis*. Because of the (theoretically) unlimited opportunity for revisiting the recorded instance by replaying it, the instance can be observed from a variety of attentional foci and analytic perspectives. This enables a much more thorough description than those that can be prepared by a participant observer from field notes.

A second strength is the *potential to reduce the dependence of the observer on primitive analytic typification*. Because the instance can be replayed, the observer has opportunity for deliberation. She can hold in abeyance interpretive judgements of the functions (meanings) of the actions observed. Often in participant observation these interpretive inferences can be faulty, especially at the early stages of fieldwork.

In microethnographic analysis of a film or videotape the opportunity to look and listen more than once relieves the observer's tendency to leap too soon to analytic induction. This independence from the limits of real time in observation produces a profound qualitative difference in the conduct of inquiry. That difference is analogous to the contrast between spoken and written discourse, the latter being amenable to revision and to much more detailed preplanning than the former (on this contrast, see Goody, 1977; Ong, 1977).

A third strength, in the analysis of machine recordings, is that it *reduces the dependence of the observer on frequently occurring events as the best sources of data*. For the analyst of a machine recording, especially an audiovisual one, the rare event can be studied quite thoroughly through repeated reviewing. That opportunity is not available to the participant observer in dealing with rare events.

There are two main limitations in the use of machine records as a primary data source. The most fundamental limitation is that in replaying a tape the analyst can only interact with it vicariously. Thus the vicarious experience of an event which is microethnography's greatest strength is also its greatest weakness. The researcher has no opportunity to test emerging theories by trying them out as an active participant in the scenes being observed. That opportunity is one of the hallmarks of participant observation.

Another limitation in using machine recordings as a primary data source is that in order to make sense of the recorded material the analyst usually needs to have access to contextual information that is not available on the recording itself. The recorded event is embedded in a variety of contexts—in the life histories and social networks of the participants in the events, and in the broader societal circumstances of the events, including the relevance of ethnic, social class, and cultural group membership of the participants for the ways in which they organize their conduct together in the recorded event. Knowing the ways in which the event that occurs face to face fits into the web of influences within the setting and between the setting and its wider environments (including the total society in which the setting resides) can be crucially important in helping the researcher to come to an interpretive understanding of the immediately local organization of interaction within the event, or to an interpretive understanding of the significance of the event's having happened in a particular way rather than some other possible way. Sometimes the broader contexts around an event may not have much influence on the conduct of social relations face to face within the event. In such cases, an analysis is not invalidated by the absence of broader ethnographic framing. But when the influence of the wider world is strong on the immediate scenes of face-to-face interaction in the classroom, and when those influences place systematic constraint on the conduct of relations in the classroom, then the absence of broader contextual framing from general ethnographic fieldwork can invalidate the analysis.

Both limitations of microethnography—the absence of participation as a means of learning, and the absence of contextual information beyond the frame of the recording—can be overcome by combining regular ethnography with microethnography.

Data Analysis and Reporting

Writing the Report

There are nine main elements of a report of fieldwork research:

1. Empirical assertions
2. Analytic narrative vignettes
3. Quotes from fieldnotes
4. Quotes from interviews
5. Synoptic data reports (maps, frequency tables, figures)
6. Interpretive commentary framing particular description
7. Interpretive commentary framing general description
8. Theoretical discussion
9. Report of the natural history of inquiry in the study

Each of these elements will be discussed in turn. Separately and together they allow a reader to do three things. First, they allow the reader to experience vicariously the setting that is described, and to confront instances of key assertions and analytic constructs. Second, these elements allow the reader to survey the full range of evidence on which the author's interpretive analysis is based. Third, they allow the reader to consider the theoretical and personal grounds of the author's perspective as it changed during the course of the study. Access to all these elements allows the reader to function as a coanalyst of the case reported. The absence of any one of the elements, or inadequacy in any of them, limits the reader's ability to understand the case and to judge the validity of the author's interpretive analysis.

GENERATING AND TESTING ASSERTIONS

A report of fieldwork research contains empirical assertions that vary in scope and in level of inference. One basic task of data analysis is to generate these assertions, largely through induction. This is done by searching the data corpus — reviewing the full set of field notes, interview notes or audiotapes, site documents, and audiovisual recordings. Another basic task is to establish an evidentiary warrant for the assertions one wishes to make. This is done by reviewing the data corpus repeatedly to test the validity of the assertions that were generated, seeking disconfirming evidence as well as confirming evidence.

Here are some examples of the kinds of assertions that a fieldwork research report might include:

1. There are two major groups of children in the classroom, from the teacher's and the students' points of view: good readers and bad readers.
2. Usually, good readers receive higher-order skills emphasis in reading instruction (i.e., emphasis on comprehension) while bad readers receive lower-order skills emphasis in reading instruction (emphasis on decoding).
3. There are two main subgroups of bad readers; those who try, and those who don't try.
4. Not trying, from this particular teacher's point of view, consists in lack of persistence in small group reading lessons, and in lack of accuracy in doing reading seatwork. Not trying does not consist in not completing seatwork, nor in talking with other students during periods of seatwork. Such behavior is not conceived of by the teacher as not trying. Nor does making an occasional error in seatwork count as not trying. What counts as not trying in seatwork behavior is frequent small errors — frequent in each day's work, and from day to day.
5. The two subgroups of bad readers receive the same kind of reading instruction, but those who try get some of the same privileges that good readers get (e.g., a wider choice of books to read, taking a message to the office, an interesting assignment).
6. Bad readers who don't try are usually treated differently by classmates from bad readers who do try. Bad readers who don't try are often not chosen by classmates to play a game, or to trade food with at lunch time, while bad readers who do try are chosen for these relationships by their good reading classmates as often as the good readers choose fellow good readers.
7. Two exceptions to the pattern described in Assertion 6 are two boys who are physically adept and skilled in sports. These boys, both bad readers who do not try, are chosen often by other boys for sports teams on the playground.
8. With the bad readers who don't try the teacher has a regressive social relationship, that is, in almost every face-to-face encounter with the teacher, regardless of the subject matter, and in nonacademic activities as well, the teacher reacts to these children negatively in some way, and the children act inappropriately in some way. There is one ex-

ception to this. That child is a girl who comes from what the teacher considers to be a very disorganized family. The teacher suspects child abuse in this family but has not yet reported this to the principal.

These assertions about major lines of division in the class in *social identity* (status) and *role* (rights and obligations in relation to others) vary in scope and in level of inference. The assertion (1) that two major categories of students exist, good readers and bad readers, is broad in scope, but relatively low in level of inference. The assertion (4) about what, from this teacher's point of view, counts as not trying is relatively narrow in scope and low in inferential level. The assertion (8) that the teacher's relationship with the bad readers who don't try is regressive is both broad in scope and high in inferential level, since the assertion covers all sorts of encounters with the teacher that occur across the school day, and involves the inference that both parties are contributing to the trouble they are in.

Assertions such as these are generated during the course of fieldwork as noted in the previous section of this chapter. After the researcher has left the field site, such assertions are tested and retested against the data base: the corpus of fieldnotes, interview protocols, site documents (in this case including samples of students' written work), and perhaps audiotapes or videotapes of naturally occurring classroom events.

To test the evidentiary warrant for an assertion the researcher conducts a systematic search of the entire data corpus, looking for disconfirming and confirming evidence, keeping in mind the need to reframe the assertions as the analysis proceeds. For example, in testing Assertion 2 above, concerning the different kinds of reading instruction given to those students the teacher considers to be good readers and bad readers, the researcher would first search the data corpus for all instances of formal reading instruction. If the students were divided into different groups by skill level, all instances of formal reading instruction in those groups would be examined to see whether the teacher's emphasis was on higher-order or lower-order skills. Any discrepant cases, that is, higher-order skills instruction given to a low-performance reading group, or lower-order instruction given to a high-performance group, would be identified. If the discrepant cases outnumbered those that fitted the assertion, the assertion would not be warranted by the data. Even if most of the cases fitted the assertion, the discrepant instances would be noted for subsequent analysis. After reviewing the behavioral evidence, the researcher might also review other kinds of evidence. If the teacher had commented on formal reading instruction in interviews, the interview transcripts or audiotapes would be reviewed to see what they might reveal about the teacher's beliefs about the kinds of reading instruction that were appropriate for children at different skill levels.

In Assertion 3 the teacher distinguishes between two types of bad readers, those who try and those who don't try. To test this assertion and to discover the attributes that distinguish individuals in the two categories, interview data would be reviewed first. Did the teacher mention this distinction, in so many words, in formal interviews? What about in informal comments made to the researcher during transitions between classroom activities? Review of the fieldnotes would reveal this.

The fieldnotes might also show if the teacher invoked the distinction in addressing students in the classroom (e.g., "John, you're just not trying") or in writing a comment on a student's paper. The researcher would search the fieldnotes, videotapes, and samples of student written work for any instance of such action by the teacher. In addition the researcher would look for more subtle indicators of the teacher's perspective on *trying* and on *who trys*: tone of voice and facial expression in addressing those who don't try, amounts of time given to complete the work or to comply with a directive to close the book and line up for recess. Did the teacher, finally, not hold a *not-trying* student accountable for completing a task, or for not only finishing it, but doing it well?

Traces of evidence for these issues and questions would appear in the field notes. It should be emphasized that these are indeed traces—fragments that must be pieced together into mosaic representations that are inherently incomplete. Conclusive proof is often not possible, especially from data derived from fieldnotes. Yet some lines of interpretation can be shown to be more robust than others. On that admittedly shaky ground must rest the possibility of intellectual integrity and credibility in interpretive research.

Assertion 5 claims that all bad readers receive the same kind of formal reading instruction, but that those who try receive a different kind of informal reading instruction (a wider choice of books to read during free time, an interesting writing assignment). Assertion 5 also claims that bad readers who try also receive other privileges, such as taking a note to the office, leading a song, collecting student papers, while bad readers who do not try do not receive these privileges. To test the warrant for these claims, the researcher would look in the data corpus beyond the instances of formal reading instruction. Here the unit of analysis might be mention of individuals in the fieldnotes. The researcher might identify the full set of individuals who are bad readers who don't try, and the full set of those who do try, and search the fieldnotes for instances of description of what those children were doing. Then the researcher would compare what the notes reported for the two sets of bad readers—what were their differences in privileges, in access to activities that were positively valued by children in the room. Notice that the general concept of *privileges* would have to be specified in terms of local meanings that were distinctive to that classroom. There would need to be descriptive evidence in the fieldnotes, or in interviews with children, that such activities as taking a note to the office or collecting student papers were indeed valued positively. Descriptive evidence for this might consist of a number of instances reported in the fieldnotes in which many students volunteered for such activities, or expressed disappointment that they were not chosen. The researcher continues to assume that local meanings and values are not self-evident in the data, nor can they be assumed to generalize from one room to the next. It may be true that most grade-school-age children in America like to collect papers. That might not be true in this particular classroom, however, for some locally distinctive reasons.

As the data corpus is searched the researcher continually looks for disconfirming evidence. Are there any instances in which a bad reader who doesn't try receives privileges that are similar to those received by bad readers who do try? These discrepant cases are noted. After the general search is completed the researcher returns to the discrepant cases for closer investigation. The results of such an investigation are reported in Assertions 6 and 7, concerning the ways that students treat the bad readers who don't try. The general pattern was reported in Assertion 6; bad readers who don't try are usually treated negatively by their peers. Two students are treated positively, however, in special circumstances. These are athletically adept boys, who are chosen for team sports in the playground. Evidence for this assertion would come from the discrepant case analysis. There might have been many instances of these two boys being chosen. The circumstances would be limited to team sports in the playground, however, and the positive reaction of peers is easily explained in terms of the interests of building a winning team.

Another example of a finding from discrepant case analysis is seen in Assertion 8, concerning the one bad reader who doesn't try, with whom the teacher does not have a regressive relationship. The explanation for this case involves higher levels of inference than does the explanation for the athletically adept boys being chosen by their peers. Why would this girl be treated differently from the other bad readers who don't try? The answer lies not in a causal analysis—in a mechanical sense of causation—but in an exploration of the teacher's perspective. What does this child mean to the teacher? How does that differ from what other bad readers who don't try mean to the teacher? Various comparison cases can be identified. The researcher might consider all the other girls in the set *bad readers who don't try* to see what the child's gender status might mean to the teacher. The researcher might consider all the other children, boys and girls, for whom child abuse is suspected. If there were another bad reader who doesn't try who may be abused at home, that would be an appropriate comparison case. If that child were also a girl, and did not receive special privileges, that would form the ideal contrast set. In that case the researcher might ask, "What else might explain this?" Further investigation of the fieldnotes, teacher interviews, and videotapes might reveal that there are differences in general classroom demeanor between the two children—the one who does not receive special privileges is less polite than the other, or less funny, or less sad looking. The preceding discussion illustrates the kind of analytic detective work by which the researcher discovers the subtle shadings of distinctions in social organization and meaning—perspective according to which classroom life is organized as a learning environment for the children and for the teacher. Discrepant cases are especially useful in illuminating these locally distinctive subtleties. A deliberate search for disconfirming evidence is essential to the process of inquiry, as is the deliberate framing of assertions to be tested against the data corpus. This is classic analysis, termed analytic induction in the literature on fieldwork methods. Much of this induction takes place during fieldwork, but much of it remains to be discovered after leaving the field. A good rule of thumb is to plan to spend at least as much time in analysis and write-up after fieldwork as one spent in collecting evidence during fieldwork.

In reviewing the fieldnotes and other data sources to generate and test assertions the researcher is looking for *key linkages* among various items of data. A key linkage is key in that it is of central significance for the major assertions the researcher wants to make. The key linkage is linking in that it connects up many items of data as analogous instances of the same phenomenon. To have said, for example, that the teacher distinguishes between good readers and bad readers is to link all occurrences in the total data set in which the teacher treated bad readers differently from good readers, in reading instruction and in any other classroom activities. The distinction between bad and good readers is key because many instances of one kind of treatment by the teacher toward the bad readers and another kind of treatment toward the good readers can be linked together in the review of the fieldnotes. Instances from interviews can also be linked, in relation to this distinction, together with instances of teacher–student interaction from the fieldnotes.

In searching for key linkages the researcher is looking for patterns of generalization within the case at hand, rather than for generalization from one case or setting to another. Generalization within the case occurs at different levels, which differ in the scope of applicability of the generalization. In our example we saw that the distinction between good and bad readers generalized most broadly for formal reading instruction. This means that upon review of the data corpus it was apparent that there were no instances of higher-order formal instruction given to bad readers and no instances of lower-order formal instruction given to good readers. For informal instruction, however, the broadest generalization does not hold. A subsidiary distinction must be made to account for the patterns in the data; the distinction between bad readers who try and those who don't try. We found upon review of all instances of informal reading instruction (this set included certain kinds of writing assignments and privileges for choosing books for free reading) that the bad readers who tried were treated the same as good readers, while the bad readers who didn't try were treated differently from both the good readers and the bad readers who tried. Moreover that pattern of differential treatment generalized beyond informal reading instruction to many other instances of interaction between the teacher and the bad readers who didn't try, with some notable exceptions. But the exceptions were a

minority of instances, and they applied to a limited subset of the bad readers who didn't try.

An appropriate metaphor for this kind of pattern discovery and testing is to think of the entire data set (fieldnotes, interviews, site documents, videotapes) as a large cardboard box, filled with pieces of paper on which appear items of data. The key linkage is an analytic construct that ties strings to these various items of data. Up and down a hierarchy of general and subsidiary linkages, some of the strings attach to other strings. The task of pattern analysis is to discover and test those linkages that make the largest possible number of connections to items of data in the corpus. When one pulls on the top string, one wants as many subsidiary strings as possible to be attached to data. The strongest assertions are those that have the most strings attached to them, across the widest possible range of sources and kinds of data. If an assertion is warranted not only by many instances of items of data from the fieldnotes, but by items from interviews and from site documents, one can be more confident of that assertion than one would be of an assertion that was warranted by only one data source or kind, regardless of how many instances of that kind of data one could link together analytically. The notion of key linkage is illustrated in Figure 5.1.

It should be noted that this kind of analysis requires a substantial number of analogous instances for comparison. Rare events are not handled well by the method of analytic induction. In consequence, there is a bias toward the typical in fieldwork research at the stage of data analysis after one has left the field setting—a bias that is analogous to that discussed in the previous section, at the stage of progressive problem solving during data collection. It is important to remember that in this approach to research, frequently occurring events can come to be understood better than can rare events. Audiovisual recording of rare events can reduce this problem somewhat, since the recording permits vicarious "revisiting," but even this does not entirely eliminate the problem. In judging the validity of a researcher's analysis, then, it is important to keep in mind how

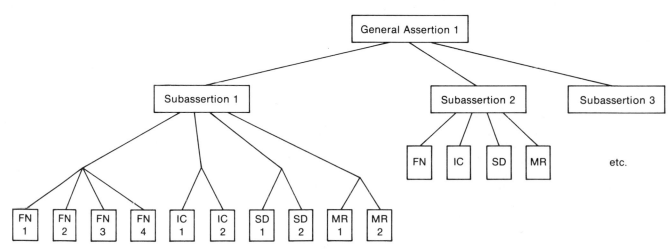

FN = Field Note Excerpt; IC = Interview Comment; SD = Site Document (memo, poster);
MR = Machine Recording (audiotape, videotape)

Fig. 5.1. Key linkages between data and assertions.

much of the author's argument hangs upon the interpretive analysis of rare events. The best case for validity, it would seem, rests with assertions that account for patterns found across both frequent and rare events.

In conducting such analysis and reporting it, the researcher's aim is not proof, in a causal sense, but the demonstration of plausibility, which as Campbell argues (1978) is the appropriate aim for most social research. The aim is to persuade the audience that an adequate evidentiary warrant exists for the assertions made, that patterns of generalization within the data set are indeed as the researcher claims they are.

Much fieldwork research can be faulted on this point. The analysis may be correct. It may even be believable on intuitive grounds, in the sense that we say "This rings true" after reading the report. If systematic evidence to warrant the assertions is not presented, however, the researcher is justly open to criticism of the analysis as merely anecdotal. Such criticism can be refuted by conducting the kind of systematic data analysis described here, and by reporting the evidence for the assertions in the ways that will be discussed in the sections to come.

It should be clear from this discussion that the corpus of materials collected in the field are not data themselves, but resources for data. Fieldnotes, videotapes, and site documents are not data. Even interview transcripts are not data. All these are documentary materials from which data must be constructed through some formal means of analysis. We will conclude the discussion of data analysis by describing the means by which the data resources are converted into items of data.

The process of converting documentary resources into data begins with multiple readings of the entire set of fieldnotes. Then the researcher may find it useful to make one or two photocopied sets of the whole corpus of fieldnotes. These copies can be used in the kinds of data searches described above. Analogous instances of phenomena of interest can be circled in colored ink. These may be instances of a whole event (e.g., a reading lesson), or of a constituent episode or phase within an event (e.g., the start-up phase of the reading lesson), or of a transaction between focal individuals (e.g., reprimand by the teacher to a bad reader who doesn't try). A number of searches through the notes can be made in this fashion, to identify evidence for or against the major assertions the researcher wishes to make, circling instances in different colors of ink, depending on the assertion the instance relates to. At this point some researchers cut up a second copy of the fieldnotes and tape the various instances to large file cards, which then can be sorted further as the analysis proceeds. One can easily envision the use of microcomputers at this stage, or at earlier stages in the review of fieldnotes. As of this writing the use of microcomputers in this kind of data analysis is just beginning and there seem to be no major discussions of this in the literature. It would seem wise, however, to use the computer for retrieval tasks later in the search process rather than at the outset. Reading through the actual notes page by page provides the researcher with a more holistic conception of the content of the fieldnotes than that which would be possible with the more partial view provided by computerized data retrieval. Reading the notes "by hand" provides more opportunity to encounter unexpected disconfirming evidence and to discover unanticipated side issues that can be pursued in subsequent readings.

To conclude, the basic units of analysis in the process of analytic induction are instances of action in events that take place between persons with particular statuses in the scene, and instances of comments on the significance of these commonplace actions, and on broader aspects of meaning and belief, from the perspectives of the various actors involved in the events. The instances of actions are derived from review of the fieldnotes and from review of machine recordings. The instances of comments are derived from analysis of formal and informal interviews with informants.

The basic units in the process of data analysis are also the basic elements of the written report of the study. Instances of social action are reported as narrative vignettes or as direct quotes from the fieldnotes. Instances of interview comments are quoted in interpretive commentary that accompanies the portions of analytic narrative that are presented. Reporting these details can be called *particular description*. This is the essential core of a report of fieldwork research. Without particular description to instance and warrant one's key assertions, the reader must take the author's assertions on faith. Particular description is supported by more synoptic surveys of patterns in the basic units of analysis. This can be termed *general description*. A third major type of content in a report of fieldwork research is *interpretive commentary*. Such commentary is interpolated between particular and general description to help the reader make connections between the details that are being reported and the more abstract argument being made in the set of key assertions that are reported.

The researcher has two main aims in writing the report: to make clear to the reader what is meant by the various assertions, and to display the evidentiary warrant for the assertions. The aim of clarification is achieved by instantiation in particular description. Analytic narrative vignettes and direct quotes from interviews make clear the particulars of the patterns of social organization and meaning-perspective that are contained in the assertions. The aim of providing evidentiary warrant for the assertions is achieved by reporting both particular description and general description. A single narrative vignette or a quote from an interview provides documentary evidence that what the assertion claimed to have happened did occur at least once. General description accompanying the more particular description provides evidence for the relative frequency of occurrence of a given phenomenon. General description is also used to display the breadth of evidence that warrants an assertion—the range of different kinds of evidence that speak to that assertion.

In the next sections we turn to consider the major types of content in a report on fieldwork research. Particular description is discussed first, then general description, and then the interpretive commentary that accompanies the presentation of descriptive evidence.

PARTICULAR DESCRIPTION: ANALYTIC NARRATIVE AND QUOTES

Analytic narrative is the foundation of an effective report of fieldwork research. The narrative vignette is a vivid portrayal of the conduct of an event of everyday life, in which the sights and sounds of what was being said and done are described in the natural sequence of their occurrence in real time. The moment-to-moment style of description in a narrative vignette gives the reader a sense of *being there* in the scene. As a literary form the vignette is very old; it was termed *prosographia* by Greek rhetoricians, who recommended that orators include richly descriptive vignettes in their speeches to persuade the audience that the orator's general assertions were true in particular cases.

In the fieldwork research report the narrative vignette has functions that are rhetorical, analytic, and evidentiary. The vignette persuades the reader that things were in the setting as the author claims they were, because the sense of immediate presence captures the reader's attention, and because the concrete particulars of the events reported in the vignette instantiate the general analytic concepts (patterns of culture and social organization) the author is using to organize the research report. Such narrative is analytic—certain features of social action and meaning are highlighted, others are presented less prominently or not mentioned at all.

This is an extremely important point; the vignette has rhetorical functions in the report. The task of the narrator is twofold. The first task is didactic. The meaning of everyday life is contained in its particulars and to convey this to a reader the narrator must ground the more abstract analytic concepts of the study in concrete particulars—specific actions taken by specific people together. A richly descriptive narrative vignette, properly constructed, does this. The second task of the narrator is rhetorical, by providing adequate evidence that the author has made a valid analysis of what the happenings meant from the point of view of the actors in the event. The particular description contained in the analytic narrative vignette both explains to the reader the author's analytic constructs by instantiation and convinces the reader that such an event could and did happen that way. It is the task of more general, synoptic description (charts, tables of frequency of occurrence) to persuade the reader that the event described was *typical*, that is, that one can generalize from this instance to other analogous instances in the author's data corpus. We will consider synoptic description more fully later in this discussion.

It follows that both the author and the critical reader should pay close attention to the details of the narrative and to features of its construction. The narrative vignette is based on fieldnotes taken as the events happened and then written up shortly thereafter. The vignette is a more elaborated, literarily polished version of the account found in the fieldnotes. By the time the vignette is written up the author has developed an interpretive perspective, implicitly or explicitly. The way the vignette is written up should match the author's interpretive purposes and should communicate that perspective clearly to the reader. The vignette fulfills its purpose in the report to the extent that its construction as a narrative presents to the reader a clear picture of the interpretive point the author intends by telling the vignette. Even the most richly detailed vignette is a reduced account, clearer than life. Some features are selected in from the tremendous complexity of the original event (which as we have already seen contains more information bits than any observer could attend to and note down in the first place, let alone report later) and other features are selected out of the narrative report. Thus the vignette does not represent the original *event itself*, for this is impossible. The vignette is an abstraction; an analytic caricature (of a friendly sort) in which some details are sketched in and others are left out; some features are sharpened and heightened in their portrayal (as in cartoonists' emphasis on Richard Nixon's nose and 5 o'clock shadow) and other features are softened, or left to merge with the background.

Two potential aspects of contrast in the narrative convey the empathetic caricature that highlights the author's interpretive perspective: (a) variation in the density of the texture of description (across a sequence of events in time, some of which are described in great detail and some of which are glossed over in summary detail), and (b) variation in the alternatively possible terms used for describing the action itself (selecting some particular nouns, verbs, adverbs, and adjectives rather than others, and by this selection pointing to the locally meaningful roles, statuses, and intentions of the actors in the event).

A story can be an accurate report of a series of events, yet not portray the meaning of the actions from the perspectives taken by the actors in the event. Here is a version of a familiar story in which the basic terms of a summary narrative do not convey meaningfulness, from the point of view of the characters in the story.

> A young man walked along a country road and met an older man. They quarreled and the young man killed the other. The young man went on to a city, where he met an older woman and married her. Then the young man put his eyes out and left the city.

This version does not tell us about roles, statuses, and the appropriateness of actions, given those roles and statuses. The older man was not just any older man, but was Oedipus' father and king of the city. The woman was queen of the city and Oedipus' mother. Thus, actions that generally could be described as killing and marrying entailed parricide and incest, at more specific levels of meaning.

In sum, richness of detail in and of itself does not make a vignette ethnographically valid. Rather, it is the combination of richness and interpretive perspective that makes the account valid. Such a valid account is not simply a description; it is an analysis. Within the details of the story, selected carefully, is contained a statement of a theory of organization and meaning of the events described.

We can see that the analytic narrative vignette, like any other conceptually powerful and rhetorically effective instrument, is a potentially dangerous tool that can be used to mislead as well as to inform. The interpretive validity of the form a narrative vignette takes cannot be demonstrated within the vignette itself. Such demonstration is the work of accompanying interpretive commentary, and of reporting other instances of analogous events. In an effective report of fieldwork, key assertions are not left undocumented by vignettes, and single vignettes are not left to stand by themselves as evidence. Rather, interpretive connections are made across vignettes, and between the vignettes and other more summary forms of description, such as frequency tables.

Direct quotes from those observed are another means of conveying to the reader the point of view of those who were studied. These quotes may come from formal interviews, from more informal talks with the fieldworker on the run (as when during the transition between one classroom event and the next the teacher might say, "Did you see what Sam just did?"), or in a chat at lunch. Quotes may also come from fieldnotes, from what was recorded about the speech of teacher or students, from audiotapes or videotapes made in fieldnotes, or from transcriptions of audiotapes or videotapes made in the classrooms.

Another form for reporting narrative vignettes is the written-up fieldnotes themselves. These can be quoted directly in the report, with the date they were originally taken included. Often a series of excerpts from the notes, written on different days, can warrant the claim that a particular way an event happened was typical—that the pattern shown in the first excerpt from the notes (or shown in a fully finished vignette) did in fact happen often in the setting. This demonstrates *generalizability within the corpus*, substantiating such statements as "Usually when Sam and Mary didn't finish their seatwork the teacher overlooked it, but when Ralph didn't finish he was almost always called to account."

Direct quotes from fieldnotes can also be used to show changes in the fieldworker's perspective across time. This use will be disscussed as we consider below the report of the evolution of inquiry in the study.

I have discussed the reporting functions of vignettes, quotes from fieldnotes, and quotes from the speech of participants studied. I have said that to tell a story in a certain way is to present a theory of the organization of the events described, and to portray the significance of the events to those involved in them. There is another purpose in choosing and writing up descriptive narratives and quotes. This is to stimulate analysis early on in the organization of data on the way to writing the report. Much has been written about the process of rereading fieldnotes and reviewing audiovisual records to generate analytic categories and to discover assertions and key linkages between one set of events observed and others observed (see Agar, 1980, pp. 137–173; Becker, 1958; Bogdan & Biklen, 1982, pp. 155–162; Dorr-Bremme, 1984, pp. 151–166; Goetz & LeCompte, 1984, pp. 164–207; Levine et al., 1980; McCall & Simmons, 1969; Schatzman & Strauss, 1974, pp. 108–127; see especially Miles & Huberman, 1984, pp. 79–283.)

The Leap to Narration. A way to stimulate the analysis is to force oneself, after an initial reading through of the whole corpus of fieldnotes and other data sources, to make an assertion, choose an excerpt from the fieldnotes that instantiates the assertion, and write up a narrative vignette reporting the key event chosen. In the very process of making the choices (first, of which event to report, second, of the alternative regarding descriptive density and the use of alternative descriptive terms) the author becomes more explicit in understanding the theoretical "loading" of the key event that was chosen. Later in the analysis the author may conclude that this was not the best instance of the assertion, or that the assertion itself was flawed in some way. Forcing oneself at the outset to make the choices entailed in jumping into storytelling can be a way of bringing to explicit awareness the analytic distinctions and perspectives that were emerging for the author during the course of the time spent in the field. This awareness can be pushed still further by rewriting the vignette in such a way that it makes an interpretive point that is substantially different from the point of the first version, while recounting the same events reported in the first vignette. Choosing a key event early in the analysis after

leaving the field, and then writing it up as two different vignettes that make two differing interpretive points, is a standard assignment when I teach data analysis and write-up. It teaches the skills of using alternative density of descriptive detail and deliberate choice of descriptive terms to highlight the interpretive point being made. It also forces the analyst to begin to make deliberate analytic decisions. By forcing the analyst to choose a key event, it brings to awareness latent, intuitive judgments the analyst has already made about salient patterns in the data. Once brought to awareness these judgments can be reflected upon critically.

GENERAL DESCRIPTION

The main function of reporting general descriptive data is to establish the generalizability of patterns that were illustrated in particular description through analytic narrative vignettes and direct quotes. Having presented a particular instance it is necessary to show the reader the typicality or atypicality of that instance—where it fits into the overall distribution of occurrences within the data corpus. Failing to demonstrate these patterns of distribution—to show generalization *within the corpus*—is perhaps the most serious flaw in much reporting of fieldwork research. The vignette shows that a certain pattern of social relationships can happen in the setting, but simply to report a richly descriptive, vivid vignette, or to assert in interpretive commentary that accompanies the vignette that this instance was typical or was significant for some other reason (e.g., it was an interesting discrepant case) does not demonstrate to the reader the validity of such assertions about the significance of the instance. This can only be done by citing analogous instances—linking the key event to others like it or different from it—and (a) by reporting those linked instances in the form of vignettes and (b) by showing in summary fashion the overall distribution of instances in the data corpus.

General descriptive data are reported synoptically; that is, they are presented so that they can be seen together at one time. One kind of synoptic reporting medium is the simple frequency table showing raw frequencies, whose patterns of distribution are apparent by inspection. Because the frequency data that are tabulated are often nominal rather than ordinal, two- and three-way contingency tables are often an appropriate way to show patterns to the reader. Fienberg (1977) recommends three-way contingency tables as an especially appropriate way to display these patterns.

Occasionally one may wish to apply inferential statistical tests of significance to the data. Usually, given the conditions of data collection, nonparametric tests, such as chi-square and the Mann-Whitney two-tailed test of rank-order correlation are more appropriate than are parametric statistics. The parametric approaches are usually inappropriate for an additional reason. In standard inferential statistics we assume as analysts that we do not know the pattern of distribution within a sample. One of the tasks of statistical manipulation is to discover what the patterns of distribution are. In the analysis of fieldwork data, pattern discovery is done qualitatively. The frequency tables presented to the reader are usually a tabulation of qualitative judgments using nominal scales (or of judgments on ordinal scales involving very low levels of inference in assigning rank or series position to a given instance). In preparing the table as a reporting medium the analyst already knows the pattern of frequency distribution. The analysis is already done; the table merely reports the results of analysis in a synoptic form. In consequence, manipulation of the data by elaborate inferential statistical methods such as multivariate analysis, multidimensional scaling, or other forms of factor analysis is usually not necessary or appropriate. One example of an appropriate use of multidimensional scaling is in a study whose multiple methods of data collection included a questionnaire survey of teenagers, some of whom had dropped out of schools, others of whom had not (see Jacob & Sanday, 1976.)

INTERPRETIVE COMMENTARY

Accompanying commentary frames the reporting of particular and general description. This commentary appears as three types: interpretation that precedes and follows an instance of particular description in the text, theoretical discussion that points to the more general significance of the patterns identified in the events that were reported, and an account of the changes that occurred in the author's point of view during the course of the inquiry.

The interpretive commentary that precedes and follows an instance of particular description is necessary to guide the reader to see the analytic type of which the instance is a concrete token. An instance of an analytic narrative vignette or an instance of an extended direct quote contains rich descriptive detail that is multivocal in meaning. Especially in the vignette, but also in quotes from interviews, there is much more semantic content in the text than can be seen at first reading by the audience. Interpretive commentary thus points the reader to those details that are salient for the author, and to the meaning-interpretations of the author. Interpretive commentary also fills in the information beyond the story itself that is necessary for the reader to interpret the story in a way similar to that of the author. Foreshadowing commentary, like a set of road signs encountered while driving, enables the reader to anticipate the general patterns that are to be encountered in the particulars of the narrative to come. Commentary that follows the particular vignette or quote stimulates the retrospective interpretation of the reader. Both the anticipatory and the subsequent commentary are necessary if the reader is not to be lost in a thicket of uninterpretable detail. Writing this commentary is necessary for the author as well, since it is precisely the reflective awareness that enables one to write such commentary that enables the writer to be an analyst as well as reporter. A key vignette is relatively easy to select and to write up. What is much more difficult is to probe analytically the significance of the concrete details reported, and the various layers of meaning contained in the narrative. Beginning fieldwork researchers find that the most difficult task in reporting is to learn to comment on the details of the narratives that are presented, using elaborated expository prose to frame the narrative contents of the report.

In fact, alternation between the extreme particularity of detail found in the vignette (or in an exact citation from fieldnotes, or in a direct quote from an interview) and the more general voice of the accompanying interpretive commentary is a difficult shift to become accustomed to as a reporter of fieldwork

data. It is often necessary in the space of a few adjoining paragraphs (or even sentences) to be very specific descriptively and quite general interpretively. Some beginning fieldworkers resolve this tension by presenting particular description only, with a minimum of interpretation, thus giving any reader but the author a case of semantic and conceptual indigestion — too much richness. Other students attempt to resolve the tension by adopting a voice of medium-general description — neither concrete enough nor abstract enough. This resembles somewhat the "scientific" discourse style of journals in which positivist research is reported. In this voice the author fails to ground the generalizations in particulars and fails as well to take the generalizations far enough theoretically.

NATURAL HISTORY OF INQUIRY

Very often, in article-length reports of fieldwork research, and even in monograph-length reports, the author does not include a discussion of the ways in which the key concepts in the analysis evolved or unexpected patterns were encountered during the time spent in the field setting and in subsequent reflection. This is an unfortunate omission from a report of fieldwork research, since the plausibility of the author's final interpretation is greatly enhanced by showing the reader that the author's thinking did indeed change during the course of study.

Fieldwork research presumes that distinctive local meanings will be present in the field setting. These are meanings that could not be fully anticipated by armchair theorizing ("operationalization of indicators of variables") before entering the setting. Because these unknown local meanings and unrecognized dimensions of the research problem cannot be known at the outset, fieldwork is necessary. But as we pointed out in the previous section, the fieldwork researcher is always guided by a general set of research interests, and often by a set of quite specific research questions. Given the complexity of the phenomena to be observed in the setting there is ample opportunity to be selective in collecting evidence — finding only those data that confirm the author's initial hunches and ideological commitments.

We have discussed the research process as the search for falsification. It is the author's responsibility to document this process for the reader, to show in considerable detail (a) that the author was open to perceiving, recording, and reflecting on evidence that would disconfirm the author's preconceived notions and commitments (as evidenced by the fact that the author's thinking and data collection did change during the course of the study); and (b) specific ways in which the changes in interpretive perspective took place. A good way to show this is by writing a first-person account of the evolution of inquiry before, during, and after fieldwork.

Primary evidence for this change in perspective comes from the corpus of fieldnotes and the original research proposed. If the notes contained formal statements of the research questions, dated quotes from the notes can reveal changes in the questions across time. The final set of research questions and issues can be contrasted with those found in the initial proposal. Dated analytic memos written "to the file" during the course of the research can be an additional source of evidence for changes in the researcher's interpretive perspective. A synoptic chart can be an effective way to display these changes in thinking. Another way in which the fieldnotes can be used to illustrate shifts in interpretive perspective is by analyzing the texture of description found in the notes before and after major intellectual turning points in the inquiry.

AUDIENCES AND THEIR DIVERSE INTERESTS

We have discussed generic issues of audience interest in the previous sections on data collection, analysis, and reporting. For any reader, the report must (a) be intelligible in the relations drawn between concrete detail and the more abstract level of assertions and arguments made by linked assertions; (b) display the range of evidence that warrants the assertions the author makes; and (c) make explicit the author's own interpretive stance and the grounds of that stance in substantive theory and in personal commitments. Presenting all this enables the reader to act as a coanalyst with the author.

In addition to these general concerns of a universal reader, there are more particular concerns of specific audiences that should be kept in mind by the researcher in preparing a report. There are at least four major types of audiences, each with a distinctive set of salient interests: (a) the general scientific community (fellow researchers), (b) policymakers (central administrators in the school district, state and federal officials), (c) the general community of practitioners (teachers, principals, and teacher educators), and (d) members of the local community that were studied (teachers, students, building principal, parents). It is often advisable to prepare different research reports to address the specific concerns of the different audiences. Let us review these differing kinds of concerns.

The most salient concerns of the general scientific community involve the scientific interest and adequacy of the study. If the problem addressed in the study is seen as intellectually significant and if the assertions and interpretations that were made seem warranted by the evidence presented, the interests of the scientific community are met. These interests are essentially technical.

The most salient concerns of policymakers have to do with generating policy options and making choices among them. Here the central interest is not in the technical adequacy or intrinsic scientific merit of the study, but in how the study can inform the current decision situation of the policymaker. Given the labor-intensive, long-term nature of fieldwork research, it might appear that this approach is usually of little use to policymakers in current decision making, since by the time the fieldwork study was completed, the decision situation would have changed considerably (cf. Mulhauser, 1975).

A more appropriate role for fieldwork research in relation to policy audiences is to inform the generation of options by pointing to aspects of the practical work situation that may have been overlooked by policymakers. A fieldwork research report can help the policymaker see what a specific aspect of the work of teaching looks like up close; what the practical constraints and opportunities for action are in the everyday world of life in a specific classroom, in a specific school building, in a specific community. This is why fieldwork studies of implementation have been useful; they identify unintended consequences of implementation, unanticipated barriers to it, unrecognized reasons why it was successful in a particular setting. Such reporting can help policymakers develop new conceptions of policy and generate a wider range of options than they had previously conceived of. To say to a policymaker caught in trying to decide between option x and option y that options a and b are also available can be of considerable benefit.

Lest the picture be painted too rosily, however, it should be noted that fieldwork research, by uncovering practical details of everyday work life that may be inhibiting or fostering the implementation of generally defined policies, can present information to policymakers that they find frustrating. Indeed, the core perspective of fieldwork research can be seen as fundamentally at odds with the core perspective of policymakers. The core perspective of fieldwork research is that fine shadings of local meaning and social organization are of primary importance in understanding teaching. The core perspective of general policymakers is that these fine shadings of local detail are less important than the general similarities across settings; at best this is insignificant random error, at worst it is troublesome noise in the system that needs to be eliminated if the system is to operate more effectively.

The conclusions of fieldwork research usually point to the rationality of what is often considered organizationally irrational behavior by administrators and policymakers. The main message of a fieldwork research report to a policy audience, then, is likely to be one of cognitive dissonance. It is important that the researcher realize this in designing a report for a policy audience.

The most salient concerns of a general audience of practitioners have to do with deciding whether or not the situation described in the report has any bearing on the situation of their own practice. The interests of practitioners can be pejoratively characterized as a desire for tips and cookbook recipes — prescriptions about "what works." This notion of what practitioners want is too simplistic. Practitioners may say they want tips, but experienced practitioners understand that the usefulness and appropriateness of any prescriptions for practice must be judged in relation to the specific circumstances of practice in their own setting. Thus the interest in learning by positive and negative example from a case study presupposes that the case is in some ways comparable to one's own situation.

Another way to state this is to say that a central concern for practitioners is the generalizability of the findings of the study. This is not a matter of statistical generalization so much as it is a matter of logical generalization (the distinction is that of Hamilton, 1980). The responsibility for judgment about logical generalization resides with the reader rather than with the researcher. The reader must examine the circumstances of the case to determine the ways in which the case fits the circumstances of the reader's own situation.

Practitioners can learn from a case study even if the circumstances of the case do not match those of their own situation. This is possible for the practitioner only if the circumstances of the case were described clearly and specifically by the researcher. Thus the problem of inadequate specificity mentioned in the previous section is a technical issue in data collection and reporting that affects the usefulness of the case study to audiences of practitioners.

For the last type of audience to be considered here, members of the local community that was studied, issues of central concern are of a different order from those of the previous types of audiences that have been considered. We use the term *community* loosely here to refer to the network of persons who interact directly, or no more than one or two steps removed from direct interaction, in the delivery of instruction to children. That set of persons includes the teachers and students themselves, the building principal and any other building-level staff, staff who visit the school to deliver instruction or to supervise teachers, and the parents of the children. In a small school district this set might also include the central office administrators, school board members, and leaders of key interest groups of citizens in the school district.

For these members of the local school community there are a variety of personal concerns with the information the fieldwork research report contains. They are not only concerned with the scientific interest and adequacy of the study. The issue of generalization to their own situation does not apply to them, since this is their case. What does apply, powerfully, is that individually and in various collectivities, their personal and institutional reputations are at stake in their portrayal by the researcher in the report. It is extremely important that the researcher keep this in mind in preparing a report, or a set of reports, to individuals and groups within the local community that was studied. If the information presented in the report is to be of use to them—if they are to be able to learn by taking a slightly more distanced view of their own practice—the reports must be sensitive to the variety of personal and institutional interests that are at stake in the kinds of information that are presented about people's actions and thoughts, and in the ways these thoughts and actions are characterized in the reports.

We can distinguish four major types of information that have different kinds of sensitivity in reports to audiences of members of the local community. These four types, or domains, of information lie along two major lines of contrast: (a) that between information that is news, or not news, and (b) that which if known would be positively or neutrally regarded, or negatively regarded.

The distinction between news and that which is not news involves conscious awareness by the audience of the information contained in the report. Much of what is contained in a report of fieldwork research that is written to a general, nonlocal audience is information that local members already know. Because of the transparency of everyday life to those involved in it, however, a good deal of the contents of the fieldwork report may be perceived as news by members of local audiences. What is news to one local member may not be news to another; for example, what the teacher knows as a commonplace reality of everyday work in the classroom may not be known at all (or may be understood in a different way) by the principal or by parents.

The distinction between information that might be negatively regarded and that which might be positively or neutrally regarded points to the differential sensitivity of different information to different actors in the local setting. One way to view social organization is in terms of patterns of access to or exclusion from certain kinds of information. In organization theory since Weber we have seen that lines of power and influence are

Fig. 5.2. Types of information in reports to local audiences.

drawn along lines of differential access to information. Thus basic political interests are at stake in the revelation or concealment of certain items of information among local audiences. The researcher needs to keep these interests in mind in preparing reports for local audiences.

Figure 5.2 can be a useful heuristic in making strategic decisions about what to include in a report to a local audience, and how to characterize what is presented in the report. The contingency table displays four major types of information across the two dimensions of contrast just discussed: Type 1 information is that which is already known to some or all of the members of the local setting, and which is either positively regarded, or is neutrally regarded, that is, not negatively regarded. This type of information is sensitive not because it might jeopardize the reputation of any individual or group in the setting; rather, Type 1 information puts the reputation of the researcher at risk, since it can be dismissed as trivial by local members, for whom this information is not news. They may see such information as unimportant, unless it is carefully framed in the report. An example of such information is the assertion that there are approximately 27 children to every adult in early grades classrooms in which the teacher does not have a full-time aide. On the face of it, this seems an obvious bit of information that is also trivial. One can imagine a local audience reading this in a report and thinking, "This researcher spent 6 months in our building, and that's all she has to say about what early grades classrooms are like? Of course, children vastly outnumber adults in classrooms; everyone knows that."

The fact that an early grade classroom is a crowded social space in which children vastly outnumber adults is not at all trivial. It is one of the most important social facts about classrooms, considered as an institutionalized set of relations among persons. In no other setting in daily life does one encounter such an adult–child ratio, sustained each day for approximately 5 hours. In addition, authority is radically asymmetric in these crowded conditions, as illustrated by an observation of Sommer (1969, p. 99) who notes that despite the crowding teachers have 50 times more free space than do students, and teachers also have more freedom to move about in their classroom territory. Profound realities about the daily work of teaching—realities involving information overload and what might be called person overload—are entailed in this statement about the adult–child ratio in the early grades classroom. To report such an item of information to a local audience without considerable interpretive framing to highlight the significance of the social fact, however, is to risk having the credibility of the researcher's work dismissed by the local audience. The researcher needs to attend to this when presenting Type 1 information in a report to the local audiences, and also when writing to general audiences of practitioners and policymakers.

Type 2 information is that which is already known to all or to some local members, and which is negatively regarded. This is perhaps the most sensitive type of information to present in a report to a local audience. Often members of the local community have developed informal or formal social organizations around such information—ways of avoiding dealing with it, ways of concealing it. This type of information is the proverbial skeleton in the closet that everyone knows is there. An example is an item of information regarding one reason teachers' work takes the form it does in a particular building is because the principal is an alcoholic. Everyone in the building knows this, and most of the staff are involved in covering for this principal. Considerable effort goes into this social organizational work, effort which could be made use of in more educationally productive ways.

For a general audience of practitioners or policymakers, information about the principal's addiction problem might be a social fact that is crucial to interpretation of social organization in the setting. Moreover, since alcoholism among school staff is not an isolated phenomenon, general audiences may find the opportunity to reflect on this issue in this case study very useful as a stimulus to taking a slightly more distanced view of the phenomenon of addiction and its influence on social organization in their own setting. If strict confidentiality can be maintained, the Type 2 information would not be at all inappropriate for reporting to a general audience. To a local audience—at least to some individuals and groups in the local setting—such information could be very provocative. Usually it seems wise to censor entirely such information in reports to local audiences, unless the information is essential to a key assertion or interpretation in the study. In that case, the information might be reported to some actors in the setting and not to others. It is impossible to stress too strongly the need for care in presenting Type 2 information in reports in the local setting.

Type 3 information is that which is not known by members of the local community and which, if known, would be positively regarded. This type of information presents the least problems in reporting of all the four types discussed here. Still, some strategic considerations apply in presenting Type 3 information. Members of the local community are pleased by this information; they discover things that work in their setting that they were not aware of, or they discover new aspects of what works, and this helps them think about the organization of other activities that don't work the way they want them to. Thus, the presentation of Type 3 information has important teaching functions in the report to a local audience.

One teaching function is that Type 3 material can be used as positive reinforcement in the report. Type 3 material is a reward to the reader who is a member of the local community—it can influence the reader to continue reading the report. Moreover, Type 3 information is justly rewarding. The researcher is not simply flattering those studied; they have a right to know this type of information about themselves. Because of the function of Type 3 material as positive reinforcement, and because it does not jeopardize the individual and collective self-esteem of members of the local community, Type 3 information can be alternated in the report with Type 4 information, which is negatively regarded, once known. Type 3 information can prepare the way for members of the setting to begin thinking about more unpleasant information, or to think about Type 1 information, which if properly framed can stimulate new insights into the taken-for-granted, but which, since it is not news, does not stimulate the pleasurable reaction that follows from learning Type 3 information. Since Type 3 material is genuinely good news it is an important pedagogical resource for the researcher in preparing a report for an audience of those who were studied.

Another more substantive function of presenting Type 3 material is that it can stimulate deeper reflection into everyday practice in the setting—new aspects of the organization of social relations and meaning-perspectives of participants that reduce student resistance to learning, or that make for greater clarity and comprehensiveness in the presentation of subject matter, or that foster greater justice in the relations between teacher and student, and among students, or that channel intrinsic interest and motivation on the part of students and teachers. These are basic issues in the organization of instruction in classrooms and in a school building as a whole that warrant reflection by participants in that setting. To stimulate this reflection Type 3 information should be highlighted in the report, possibly by reporting some of it first, possibly also by reporting Type 3 information on a topic that the researcher has discovered is of current interest in the setting. In the report the underlying organizational issues should be stressed, for example, the local definitions of justice in social relations, the local definitions of intrinsic interest, the features of presentation of subject matter that are locally regarded as clear and understandable. Having raised such issues by reporting items of Type 3 material, the researcher can then use those topics in the report as a bridge for the presentation of Type 4 material. Because of the connection between Type 3 and Type 4 material within a common topic, the sensitivity of Type 4 material can be reduced, by placing it in the context of information that is positively regarded.

Type 4 material is that which is not currently known in the setting, and which if known would be negatively regarded. This kind of information needs to be handled with care in the report, but it is by no means impossible to present to local audiences. It is not so potentially explosive as Type 2 material, since participants in the setting, being unaware of it, have not organized ways to keep it away from the light of scrutiny. Still, Type 4 information can at the least threaten the self-esteem of individuals and of networks of individuals in the setting. In some cases this information can be extremely sensitive. It may be wise to exclude some of this information from reports to some of the audiences in the setting. What one might say in a confidential report to the teacher that was studied, for example, one might want to leave out of the report that was to be read by the principal, or by parents. To make these kinds of strategic decisions the researcher needs to apply the same standards for assessing risk to those studied that were discussed in the previous section under the topic of negotiating entry. Those with the least power in a setting are usually those least at risk for embarrassment or administrative sanction by the revelation of Type 4 information—but not always. The researcher's basic ethnographic analysis of the setting can shed light on these strategic issues in reporting.

The researcher's role in the setting is also an important consideration in dealing with Type 4 information. If the researcher were doing advocacy research on behalf of a particular interest group in the setting (e.g., teachers, parents) one might present more Type 4 information, or one might handle it less tenderly than if one had negotiated access to the setting by agreeing to address the interests of a broader array of interest groups.

Even if Type 4 information is not especially sensitive for key individuals in the setting it still should be handled judiciously in a report to a local audience. The reasons for this are pedagogical as well as ethical. Some of these reasons were introduced in the discussion of Type 3 material. Generic issues that can be illustrated by negative example with Type 4 material can be presented first as positive examples by reporting Type 3 material. This makes the relatively bitter pill of Type 4 information easier to swallow, and can reduce the defensiveness of members of the local community to the more unpleasant aspects of the report. It would be pedagogically ineffective to introduce an important topic in the report by presenting a whole series of instances of Type 4 information, in vivid narrative vignettes and striking quotes from interviews. This would be hard for people to take, and when without dissimulation a researcher can present bad news in the context of good news, this seems the much wiser course.

To conclude, reporting to local audiences can be thought of as a process of *teaching the findings*. In doing so, the researcher takes an active stance toward the audience, considering the audience as client. As in any teaching, it is crucial to assess the current state of the learner's knowledge and to assess the sensitivity of the learning task—its potential for embarrassment or difficulty. All learning involves risk, and in designing instruction any teacher needs to consider the risks from the student's point of view. In this sense, teaching requires an ethnographic perspective toward the learners and toward the learning environment. Because of this the fieldwork researcher is in an unusually good position to be a teacher of the findings of the study, if he or she chooses to take on that role with audiences of those who were studied. The very process of data collection and analysis that makes it possible to report valid information at the end of a fieldwork study provides the data relevant to decisions about how to teach the findings.

In applied research, and especially in reporting to local audiences of those studied, the single report in the form of a monograph-length ethnography is probably obsolete. Multiple reports of varying length, each designed to address the specific interests of a specific audience, are usually more appropriate. Nor is writing the only medium of reporting. In the local setting oral reports at meetings, and mixing oral and written reporting in workshops, can be effective ways to teach the findings. For an individual teacher that was studied, reviewing a set of field notes or a videotape with the researcher can be a valuable experience in continuing education.

Whether the report to a local audience takes oral or written form the researcher should invite critical reactions from the audience. Dialogue between the researcher and those studied provides the researcher with an opportunity to learn as well as providing those studied an opportunity to learn. The validity check that comes from this dialogue can be of great value to the researcher. It can inform revisions in reports. It can stimulate the researcher to rethink the basic analysis itself. One of the problems in reporting to general audiences is that the writer does not usually get this kind of feedback. In teaching the findings to local audiences, such dialogue is intrinsic to the reporting process.

Conclusion: Toward Teachers as Researchers

Interpretive research is concerned with the specifics of meaning and action in social life that takes place in concrete scenes of face-to-face interaction, and that takes place in the wider society surrounding the scene of action. The conduct of interpretive research on teaching involves intense and ideally long-term participant observation in an educational setting, followed by deliberate and long-term reflection on what was seen there. That reflection entails the observer's deliberate scrutiny of his or her own interpretive point of view, and of its sources in formal theory, culturally learned ways of seeing, and personal value commitments. As the participant observer learns more about the world *out there* he or she learns more about himself or herself.

The results of interpretive research are of special interest to teachers, who share similar concerns with the interpretive researcher. Teachers too are concerned with specifics of local meaning and local action; that is the stuff of life in daily classroom practice. In a recent review article titled "Toward a More Effective Model of Research on Teaching," Bolster (1983) argues on the same grounds presented in this chapter. He uses the terms *sociolinguistic* and *symbolic interactionist* as labels for interpretive approaches to research on teaching, and argues that these approaches have special relevance for classroom teachers.

Bolster's argument is especially telling because of his situation as an experienced public school teacher who for 20 years was also simultaneously a university-based teacher educator. Bolster's career as a teacher has been a prototype for new roles for experienced teachers; he has shown one way of being a master teacher. He spent mornings as a junior high school social studies teacher in Newton, Massachusetts, and spent afternoons as a professor of education at Harvard University. For him the radically *local* character of classroom teaching was a compelling reality. He found that interpretive research took account of that dimension of teaching practice (Bolster, 1983):

> The more I became aware of and experienced with this methodology, the more I became convinced that of all the models of research I knew, this model has the greatest potential for generating knowledge that is both useful and interesting to teachers . . . this approach focuses on situated meanings which incorporate the various reactions and perspectives of students. In common with the teachers' perspective, it assumes the multiple causation of events: the class-

room is viewed as a complex social system in which both direct and indirect influences operate. Unanticipated contingencies potentially illuminate rather than confound understanding since reaction to the unexpected often highlights the salient meanings assigned to what is normal.

Most important of all, symbolic interactionist research in classrooms necessarily relies heavily on the teacher's interpretation of events. The relationship between teacher and researcher as colleagues, therefore, is more perceptive than political, and each has individual and professional reasons for nourishing and extending it. (pp. 305–306)

The inherent logic of the interpretive perspective in research on teaching leads to collaboration between the teacher and the researcher. The research subject joins in the enterprise of study, potentially as a full partner. In some of the most recent work (e.g. Florio & Walsh, 1980) the classroom teacher's own research questions — about particular children, about the organization of particular activities — become the focus of the study.

It is but a few steps beyond this for the classroom teacher to become the researcher in his or her own right. As Hymes notes (1982), interpretive research methods are intrinsically democratic; one does not need special training to be able to understand the results of such research, nor does one need arcane skills in order to conduct it. Fieldwork research requires skills of observation, comparison, contrast, and reflection that all humans possess. In order to get through life we must all do interpretive fieldwork. What professional interpretive researchers do is to make use of the ordinary skills of observation and reflection in especially systematic and deliberate ways. Classroom teachers can do this as well, by reflecting on their own practice. Their role is not that of the participant observer who comes from the outside world to visit, but that of an unusually observant participant who deliberates inside the scene of action.

A future for interpretive research on teaching could be that the university-based researcher gradually works him or herself out of a job. That is a slight rhetorical exaggeration; there is still a need for outsiders' views of classrooms and of teaching practice. In some ways the teacher's very closeness to practice, and the complexity of the classroom as a stimulus-rich environment, are liabilities for reflection. Kluckhohn's aphorism, mentioned at the outset of this chapter, can be recalled here at its close: The fish might indeed be the last creature to discover water.

The university-based researcher can provide valuable distance — assistance to the classroom teacher in making the familiar strange, and interesting. This can be done by the university-based researcher as a consultant, as a continuing educator of experienced teachers. The teacher, as classroom-based researcher, can learn to ask his or her own questions, to look at everyday experience as data in answering those questions, to seek disconfirming evidence, to consider discrepant cases, to entertain alternative interpretations. That, one could argue, is what the truly effective teacher might do anyway. The capacity to reflect critically on one's own practice, and to articulate that reflection to oneself and to others, can be thought of as an essential mastery that should be possessed by a master teacher.

Teachers in public schools have not been asked, as part of their job description, to reflect on their own practice, to deepen their conceptions of it, and to communicate their insights to others. As the teaching role is currently defined in schools there are external limits on the capacity of a teacher to reflect critically on his or her own practice. There is neither time available, nor an institutionalized audience for such reflection. The lack of these opportunities is indicative of the relative powerlessness of the profession outside the walls of the classroom.

This is not the case, to the same degree, in other professions. For physicians and lawyers, and even for some nonelite professions more similar to teaching such as social work, it is routine for practitioners to characterize their own practice, both for purposes of basic clinical research and for the evaluation of their services. For example, surgeons often dictate a narrative description of the procedures used during an operation. After this narrative is transcribed and filed it can be reviewed by colleagues for purposes of evaluation, and it is available as documentation in the event of a malpractice suit. The social worker writes process notes on interviews with clients; these notes are then available for evaluation and consultation by supervisors. By contrast, the teacher's own account of his or her practice has no official place in the discourse of schooling, particularly in teacher evaluation, staff development, and/or debates about the master teacher role and merit pay that have been stimulated by recent reports and proposals for educational reform (e.g., National Commission on Excellence in Education, 1983; Goodlad, 1984).

If classroom teaching in elementary and secondary schools is to come of age as a profession — if the role of teacher is not to continue to be institutionally infantilized — then teachers need to take the adult responsibility of investigating their own practice systematically and critically, by methods that are appropriate to their practice. Teachers currently are being held increasingly accountable by others for their actions in the classroom. They need as well to hold themselves accountable for what they do, and to hold themselves accountable for the depth of their insight into their actions as teachers. Time needs to be made available in the school day for teachers to do this. Anything less than that basic kind of institutional change is to perpetuate the passivity that has characterized the teaching profession in its relations with administrative supervisors and the public at large. Interpretive research on teaching, conducted by teachers with outside-classroom colleagues to provide both support and challenge, could contribute in no small way to the American schoolteacher's transition to adulthood as a professional.

It is appropriate to conclude with a narrative vignette and some interpretive commentary on it. During 1981 and 1982 a set of jokes became popular in the United States concerning activities that "Real Men" did or did not engage in, because the activities were considered effete and unmasculine. The first of the jokes to have currency was "Real Men don't eat quiche."

In the winter of 1982 a well-known practitioner of process-product research on teaching sent brief notes to colleagues around the country containing the following one-liner, which the researcher claimed to have found very amusing: "Real Men don't do ethnography."

On a winter morning as I arrived at the mailboxes of the staff of the Institute for Research on Teaching where I work, two of my IRT colleagues gleefully showed me the note, which had just arrived in the mail. I too found the joke amusing, but not for the same reasons as those that may have been held by the author of the note.

One reason the joke seemed funny to me was because of its apparent presuppositions about power in social research — presuppositions of which the author of the note seems to have been unaware. One presupposition is that of prediction and control as the aim of nomothetic science. Another presupposition involves the power relations that are presumed to obtain between the social scientist, as the producer of assertions whose authoritativeness rests on their predictive power, and the various audiences to which those assertions are addressed. In the case of research on teaching, these audiences include government officials, curriculum developers, school administrators, teachers, parents, and the general citizenry.

The primary role of researchers on teaching who are Real Men, as defined by the standard approach to educational research and dissemination, seems to be to make statements about the general effectiveness of various teaching practices. The primary audience for these statements is those placed in relatively high positions in the hierarchy of educational policy formation and implementation: federal and state officials, curriculum developers and publishers, local school administrators (especially central office staff who relate directly to the school board), and teacher educators. It is the role of these audiences to communicate the prescriptions of research on teaching regarding effective practice to the primary service deliverers in the school system — teachers and building principals. These service deliverers, in turn, are to communicate the prescriptions to individual parents as justifications for the classroom practices of the teacher who teaches their child.

Perhaps Real Men don't do interpretive research on teaching because they are unwittingly, or wittingly, committed to existing power relations between technical experts and managers, and the front-line service providers and receivers of services in the institution of American schooling. In those existing arrangements, statements about "what works" in general, derived from positivist research conducted across many classrooms, can carry considerable weight with audiences of higher-level decision makers. Even if such statements turn out in the long run to have been wrong, in the short run they serve to support belief in the fundamental uniformity of practice in teaching. Such belief is functional for decision makers, since it justifies uniform treatment by general policy mandates that are created by centralized decision making and implemented in "top-down" fashion within the existing social order. More decentralized, "bottom-up" decision making that granted more autonomy to front-line service providers in the system would change the current distribution of power in educational institutions. The appropriateness of such "bottom-up" change strategies is suggested in the theoretical orientations and in the growing body of empirical findings of interpretive research on teaching. Such research, while it does not claim to speak in a voice of univocal, positive truth, can make useful suggestions about the practice of teaching, since although no interpretive assertions can be conclusively proven, some lines of interpretation can be shown systematically to be false. Paradoxically, the chief usefulness of interpretive research for the improvement of teaching practice may be its challenge to the notion that certain truths can be found, and in its call to reconstrue fundamentally our notions of the nature of the practical in teaching.

Interpretive research on teaching, then, is not only an alternative method, but an alternative view of how society works, and of how schools, classrooms, teachers, and students work in society. Real Men may be justified in not wanting to do ethnography, for in the absence of general belief in social science as a means of determining positive truth it is difficult for the social scientist to operate in society as a mandarin, or philosopher-king. The key issue for that kind of Real Man in educational research may not be teacher effectiveness, but researcher effectiveness, narrowly construed.

Another view of the future is that it could be a place in which interpretive work is a creatively subversive activity in the field of education. Real Women and Men who were schoolteachers, principals, parents, and students, as well as those who were university-based scholars, might find themselves doing ethnography, or whatever one might want to call it, as a form of continuing education and institutional transformation in research on teaching.

REFERENCES

Agar, M. (1980). *The professional stranger: An informal introduction to ethnography*. New York: Academic Press.

Au, K. H., & Jordan, C. (1980). Teaching reading to Hawaiian children: Finding a culturally appropriate solution. In H. Trueba, G. P. Guthrie, & D. H. Au (Eds.), *Culture in the bilingual classroom*. Rowley, MA: Newbury House.

Au, K. H., & Mason, J. (1981). Social organizational factors in learning to read: The balance of rights hypothesis. *Reading Research Quarterly, 17*(1), 115-152.

Barnhardt, C. (1982). "Tuning-in": Athabaskan teachers and Athabaskan students. In R. Barnhardt (Ed.), *Cross-cultural issues in Alaskan education* (Vol. 2). Fairbanks: University of Alaska, Center for Cross-Cultural Studies.

Barth, F. (1969). *Ethnic groups and boundaries: The social organization of culture difference*. Boston: Little, Brown.

Bateson, G., Jackson, D., Haley, J., & Weakland, J. (1956). Toward a theory of schizophrenia. *Behavioral Science, 1*. (Reprinted in G. Bateson, Ed., *Steps toward an ecology of mind*. New York: Ballantine Books, 1972).

Becker, H. S. (1958). Problems of inference and proof in participant observation. *American Sociological Review, 23*, 652-660. (Reprinted in G. J. McCall & J. L. Simmons, Eds., *Issues in participant observation: A text and reader*, pp. 245-254. Reading, MA: Addison-Wesley, 1969).

Becker, H. S., Geer, B., Hughes, E. C., & Strauss, A. (1961). *The boys in white: Student culture in medical school*. Chicago: University of Chicago Press.

Berger, P., & Luckmann, P. (1967). *The social construction of reality*. New York: Anchor Books.

Bogdan, R. D., & Biklen, S. K. (1982). *Qualitative research for education: An introduction to theory and methods*. Boston: Allyn & Bacon.

Bohannon, P. (1963). *Social anthropology*. New York: Holt, Rinehart & Winston.

Bolster, A. S. (1983). Toward a more effective model of research on teaching. *Harvard Educational Review, 53*(3), 294-308.

Bourdieu, P., & Passerson, J. C. (1977). *Reproduction: In education, society and culture*. Beverly Hills: Sage Publications.

Bowles, S., & Gintis, H. (1976). *Schooling in capitalist America: Educational reform and the contradictions of economic life*. New York: Basic Books.

Bronfenbrenner, U. (1977). Reality and research in ecology of human development. *Proceedings of the American Philosophical Society, 119*(6), 439-469.

Brophy, J. E. (1979). Teacher behavior and its effects. *Journal of Educational Psychology, 7*(6), 733–750.

Burrell, G., & Morgan, G. (1979). *Sociological paradigms and organizational analysis.* London: Heinemann.

Campbell, D. T. (1978). Qualitative knowing in action research. In M. Brenner, P. Marsh, & M. Brenner (Eds.), *The social context of method.* New York: St. Martin's.

Campbell, D. T., & Stanley, J. C. (1966). *Experimental and quasi-experimental designs for research.* Chicago: Rand McNally.

Cazden, C., Carrasco, R., Maldonado-Guzman, A., & Erickson, F. (1980). The contribution of ethnographic research to bicultural bilingual education. In J. Alatis (Ed.). *Current issues in bilingual education.* Washington, DC: Georgetown University Press.

Clignet, R., & Foster, P. (1966). *The fortunate few: A study of secondary schools and students in the Ivory Coast.* Evanston, IL: Northwestern University Press.

Cole, M., & Scribner, S. (1974). *Culture and thought: A psychological introduction.* New York: John Wiley.

Coleman, J. S., Campbell, E. Q., Hobson, C. J., McPartland, J., Mood, A. M., Weinfeld, F. D., & York, R. L. (1966). *Equality of education opportunity.* Washington, DC: U.S. Government Printing Office.

Collier, J. (1973). *Alaskan Eskimo education.* New York: Holt, Rinehart & Winston.

Comber, L. C., & Keeves, J. P. (1973). *Science education in nineteen countries.* New York: John Wiley.

Comte, A. (1968). *System of positive polity.* New York: B. Franklin. (Original work published 1875)

Cook, T. D. & Campbell, D. T. (1979). *Quasi-experimentation: Design and analysis issues for field settings.* Chicago: Rand McNally.

Cronbach, L. J. (1975). Beyond the two disciplines of scientific psychology. *American Psychologist, 30*(2), 116–127.

Cusich, P. A. (1980). *A study of networks among the professional staffs of two secondary schools* (Final Tech. Rep. No. 400–79–0004). Washington, DC: National Institute of Education.

Dilthey, W. (1976a). The construction of the historical world in the human studies. In. H. P. Richman (Ed.), *W. Dilthey: Selected writings* (pp. 170–206). Cambridge: Cambridge University Press. (Originally published in W. Dilthey, *Gesammelte Schriften*, Vol. 7, pp. 79–88, 130–166. Leipzig, 1914).

Dilthey, W. (1976b). The development of hermeneutics. In H. P. Richman (Ed.), *W. Dilthey: Selected Writings* (pp. 247–260). Cambridge: Cambridge University Press. (Originally published in W. Dilthey, *Gesammelte Schriften*, Vol. 5, pp. 317–337. Leipzig, 1914).

Dilthey, W. (1976c). Introduction to the human studies: The relationship of the human studies to the sciences. In H. P. Richman (Ed.), *W. Dilthey: Selected writings* (pp. 163–167). Cambridge: Cambridge University Press. (Originally published in W. Dilthey, *Gesammelte Schriften*, Vol. 1, pp. 14–21. Leipzig, 1883).

Dobbert, M. L. (1982). *Ethnographic research: Theory and application for modern schools and societies.* New York: Praeger.

Dorr-Bremme, D. (1984) *An introduction to practical fieldwork from an ethnographic perspective* (Grant No. NIE-G-83-0001). Los Angeles: University of California, Center for the Study of Evaluation.

Doyle, W. (1979). Classroom tasks and student abilities. In P. L. Peterson & H. J. Walberg (Eds.), *Research on teaching: Concepts, findings, and implications.* Berkeley, CA: McCutchan.

Dunkin, M. J., & Biddle, B. (1974). *The study of teaching.* New York: Holt, Rinehart & Winston.

Durkheim, E. (1958). *The rules of sociological method.* Glencoe, IL: Free Press. (Original work published 1895).

Elliott, J., & Adelman, C. (1976). *Classroom action research* (Ford Teaching Project, Unit 2 Research Methods). Norwich, England: University of East Anglia, Centre for Applied Research in Education.

Erickson, F. (1973). What makes school ethnography 'ethnographic'? *Council of Anthropology and Education Quarterly, 4*(2), 10–19.

Erickson, F. (1975). Gatekeeping and the melting pot: Interaction in counseling encounters. *Harvard Educational Review, 45*(1), 44–70.

Erickson, F. (1976). Gatekeeping encounters: A social selection process. In P. R. Sanday (Ed.), *Anthropology and the public interest.* New York: Academic Press.

Erickson, F. (1977). Some approaches to inquiry in school/community ethnography. *Anthropology and Education Quarterly, 8*(3), 58–69.

Erickson, F. (1979). Talking down: Some cultural sources of miscommunication in inter-racial interviews. In A. Wolfgang (Ed.), *Research in nonverbal communication.* New York: Academic Press.

Erickson, F. (1982a). The analysis of audiovisual records as a primary data source. In A. Grimshaw (Ed.), *Sound-image records in social interaction research.* Special issue of the *Journal of Sociological Methods and Research, 11*(2), 213–232.

Erickson, F. (1982b). Classroom discourse as improvisation: Relationships between academic task structure and social participation structure in lessons. In L. C. Wilkinson (Ed.), *Communicating in the classroom.* New York: Academic Press.

Erickson, F. (1982c). Taught cognitive learning in its immediate environments: A neglected topic in the anthropology of education. *Anthropology and Education Quarterly, 13*(2), 149–180.

Erickson, F. (1984). Rhetoric, anecdote, and rhapsody: Coherence strategies in a conversation among Black American adolescents. In D. Tannen (Ed.), *Coherence in spoken and written discourse* (pp. 81–154). Norwood, NJ: Ablex.

Erickson, F., Florio, S., & Buschman, J. (1980). *Fieldwork in educational research* (Occasional Paper No. 36). East Lansing: Michigan State University, Institute for Research on Teaching.

Erickson, F., & Mohatt, G. (1982). The cultural organization of participation structures in two classrooms of Indian students. In G. Spindler (Ed.), *Doing the ethnography of schooling.* New York: Holt, Rinehart & Winston.

Erickson, F., & Schultz, J. (1981). When is a context? Some issues and methods in the analysis of social competence. In J. Green & C. Wallat (Eds.), *Ethnography and language in educational settings.* Norwood, NJ: Ablex. (Originally published in *The Quarterly Newsletter of the Institute for Comparative Human Development,* 1977, *1*(2), 5–10.)

Erickson, F., & Schultz, J. (1982). *The counselor as gatekeeper: Social interaction in interviews.* New York: Academic Press.

Erickson, F., & Wilson, J. (1982). *Sights and sounds of life in schools: A resource guide to film and videotape for research and education.* (Research Series No. 125). East Lansing: Michigan State University, Institute for Research on Teaching.

Flenberg, S. E. (1977). The collection and analysis of ethnographic data in educational research. *Anthropology and Education Quarterly, 8*(2), 50–57.

Florio, S., & Walsh, M. (1980). The teacher as colleague in classroom research. In H. Trueba, G. Guthrie, & K. Au (Eds.), *Culture in the bilingual classroom: Studies in classroom ethnography.* Rowley, MA: Newbury House.

Gage, N. L. (Ed.). (1963). *Handbook of research on teaching.* Chicago: Rand McNally.

Garfinkel, H. (1967). Studies of the routine grounds of everyday activities. *Studies in ethnomethodology.* Englewood Cliffs, NJ: Prentice-Hall.

Gearing, F., & Sangree, L. (1979) *Toward a cultural theory of education and schooling.* The Hague: Moulton.

Giddens, A. (1976). *New rules of sociological method: A positive critique of interpretive sociologies.* London: Hutchinson.

Giddens, A. (1982). *Profiles and critiques in social theory.* Berkeley: University of California Press.

Giroux, H. (1983). Theories of reproduction and resistance in the new sociology of education: A critical analysis. *Harvard Educational Review, 53*(3), 257–293.

Glaser, B., & Strauss, A. (1979). *The discovery of grounded theory: Strategies for qualitative research.* Hawthorne, NY: Aldine.

Goetz, J. P., & LeCompte, M. D. (1984). *Ethnography and qualitative design in educational research.* New York: Academic Press.

Goodenough, W. (1981). *Culture, language, and society.* Menlo Park, CA: Benjamin-Cummings.

Goodlad, J. I. (1984). *A place called school: Prospects for the future.* New York: McGraw-Hill.

Goody, J. (1977). *The domestication of the savage mind.* Cambridge, England: Cambridge University Press.

Gumperz, J. J. (1982). *Discourse strategies.* Cambridge, England: Cambridge University Press.

Hamilton, D. (1980). Generalization in the education sciences: Problems and purposes. In T. Popkewitz & R. Tabachnick (Eds.), *The study of schooling: Field-based methodologies in education research.* New York: Praeger.

Heath, S. B. (1982). Questioning at home and at school: A comparative study. In G. Spindler (Ed.), *Doing the ethnography of schooling.* New York: Holt, Rinehart & Winston.

Heath, S. B. (1983). *Ways with words: Language, life, and work in communities and classrooms.* Cambridge: Cambridge University Press.

Henry, J. (1963). *Culture against man.* New York: Random House.

Hess, R., & Shipman, V. (1965). Early experience and the socialization of cognitive modes in children. *Child Development, 34,* 869–886.

Husserl, E. (1970). *The crisis of European sciences and transcendental phenomenology* (D. Carr, Trans.). Evanston, IL: Northwestern University Press. (Original published 1936).

Hymes, D. (1982). Ethnographic monitoring. In H. T. Treuba, G. P. Guthrie, & K. H. Au (Eds.), *Culture in the bilingual classroom.* Rowley, MA: Newbury House.

Jacob, E., & Sanday, P. R. (1976). Dropping out: A strategy for coping with cultural pluralism. In P. R. Sanday (Ed.), *Anthropology and the public interest: Fieldwork and the theory.* New York: Academic Press.

Jencks, C., Bartlett, S., Corcoran, M., Crouse, J., Eaglesfield, D., Jackson, G., MClelland, K., Mueser, P., Olneck, M., Schwartz, J., Ward, S., & Williams, J. (1979). *Who gets ahead? The determinants of economic success in America.* New York: Basic Books.

Jensen, A. R. (1969). How much can we boost IQ and scholastic achievement? *Harvard Educational Review, 39*(1), 1–123.

Keddie, N. (1973). *The myth of cultural deprivation.* Harmondsworth, Middlesex: Penguin.

Kimball, S. T. (1974). *Culture and the educative process.* New York: Columbia University, Teachers College Press.

Kleinfeld, J. S. (1979). *Eskimo school on the Andreafsky.* New York: Praeger.

Kuhn, T. (1962). *The structure of scientific revolutions.* Princeton, NJ: Princeton University Press.

Labov, W. (1972). *Language in the inner city.* Philadelphia: University of Pennsylvania Press.

Laing, R. D. (1970). *Knots.* New York: Pantheon.

Lakatos, I. (1978). *The methodology of scientific research programmes.* Cambridge, England: Cambridge University Press.

Lein, L. (1975). You were talkin' though, oh yes, you was: Black migrant children: Their speech at home and school. *Anthropology and Education Quarterly, 6*(4), 1–11.

Levine, H. G., Gallimore, R., Weisner, T., & Turner, J. L. (1980). Teaching participant-observational methods: A skills-building approach. *Anthropology and Education Quarterly, 11,* 38–54.

Lindesmith, A. R. (1947). *Addiction and opiates.* Chicago: Aldine.

Lofland, J. (1976). *Doing social life: The qualitative study of human interaction in natural settings.* New York: John Wiley.

MacDonald, B., & Walker, R. (Eds.). (1974). *SAFARI: Innovation, evaluation, research, and the problem of control.* Norwich, England: University of East Anglia, Centre for Applied Research in Education.

Malinowski, B. (1935). *Coral gardens and their magic.* London: Allen & Unwin.

Malinowski, B. (1961). *Argonauts of the western Pacific.* New York: Dutton. (Original work published 1922).

Marx, K. (1959). Theses on Feuerbach. In S. Feuer (Ed.), *Marx and Engels: Basic writings on politics and philosophy.* Garden City, NY: Doubleday Anchor.

McCall, G. L., & Simmons, J. L. (1969). *Issues in participant observation: A text and reader.* Reading, MA: Addison–Wesley.

McDermott, R. P. (1974). Achieving school failure: An anthropological approach to illiteracy and social stratification. In G. D. Spindler (Ed.), *Education and culture process.* New York: Holt, Rinehart & Winston.

McDermott, R. P. (1977). School relations as contexts for learning in school. *Harvard Educational Review, 47,* 298–313.

McDermott, R. P., & Gospodinoff, K. (1981). Social contexts for ethnic borders and school failure. In H. T. Trueba, G. P. Guthrie, & K. H. Au (Eds.), *Culture and the bilingual classroom.* Rowley, MA: Newbury House.

Mead, M. (1928). *Coming of age in Samoa.* New York: Morrow.

Mehan, H. (1979). *Learning lessons: Social organization in the classroom.* Cambridge, MA: Harvard University Press.

Miles, M. B., & Huberman, A. B. (1984). *Qualitative data analysis.* Beverly Hills: Sage Publications.

Mosteller, F., & Moynihan, D. P. (Eds.). (1972). *On equality of educational opportunity.* New York: Random House.

Mulhauser, F. (1975). Ethnography and policy making: The case of education. *Human Organization, 34*(3), 311–315.

National Commission on Excellence in Education. (1983). *A nation at risk: The imperative for educational reform.* Washington, DC: U.S. Department of Education.

Ogbu, J. (1978). *Minority education and caste: The American system in cross-cultural perspective.* New York: Academic Press.

Ong, W. (1977). *Interfaces of the word.* Ithaca, NY: Cornell University Press.

Parsons, T. (1959). The school class as a social system. *Harvard Educational Review, 29*(4), 297–318.

Pelto, P., & Pelto, G. (1977). *Anthropological research: The structure of inquiry.* New York: Harcourt Brace.

Philips, S. U. (1982). *The invisible culture: Communication in classroom and community on the Warm Springs Indian Reservation.* New York: Longman.

Piestrup, A. (1973). *Black dialect interference and accommodation of reading instruction in first grade* (Monograph No. 4). Berkeley, CA: Language Behavior Research Laboratory.

Riessman, F. (1962). *The culturally deprived child.* New York: Harper & Row.

Riis, J. (1890). *How the other half lives.* New York: Scribner's.

Rosenshine, B. (1983). Teaching functions in instructional programs. *Elementary School Journal, 83*(4), 335–351.

Rowe, M. B. (1974). Wait-time and rewards as instructional variables. *Journal of Research in Science Teaching, 11,* 81–94.

Schatzman, L., & Strauss, A. (1974). *Field research: Strategies for a natural sociology.* Englewood Cliffs, NJ: Prentice–Hall.

Scheflen, A. E. (1960). Regressive one-to-one relationships. *Psychiatric Quarterly, 23,* 692–709.

Schutz, A. (1971). *Collected papers I: The problem of social reality.* The Hague: Martinus Nijhoff.

Scribner, S., & Cole, M. (1981). *The psychology of literacy.* Cambridge, MA: Harvard University Press.

Shulman, L. S. (1981). Recent developments in the study of teaching. In B. Tabachnik, T. S. Popkewitz, & P. B. Szekely (Eds.), *Studying teaching and learning.* New York: Praeger.

Shultz, J. J., Florio, S., & Erickson, F. (1982). Where's the floor? Aspects of the cultural organization of social relationships in communication at home and at school. In P. Gilmore & A. A. Glatthorn (Eds.), *Children in and out of school: Ethnography and education.* Washington, DC: Center for Applied Linguistics.

Simon, H. A. (1957). *Models of man.* New York: John Wiley.

Sinclair, U. (1906). *The jungle.* New York: Doubleday, Page.

Smith, L. M. (1979). An evolving logic of participant observation, educational ethnography, and other case studies. In L. Shulman (Ed.), *Review of research in education.* Itasca, IL: F. E. Peacock.

Sommer, R. (1969). *Personal space.* Englewood Cliffs, NJ: Prentice–Hall.

Spindler, G. D. (Ed.). (1955). *Education and anthropology.* Stanford, CA: Stanford University Press.

Stallings, J. A., & Kaskowitz, D. (1974). *Follow-through classroom observation evaluation 1972–1973.* Menlo Park, CA: Stanford Research Institute.

Steffens, L. (1904). *The shame of the cities.* New York: McClure, Phillips.

Stenhouse, L. (1978). Case study and case records: Towards a contemporary history of education. *British Educational Research Journal, 4*(2), 21–39.

Vogel, E. (1965). *Japan's new middle class.* Berkeley: University of California Press.

Walker, R., & Adelman, C. (1975). *A guide to classroom observation.* London: Methuen.

Waller, W. (1932). *The sociology of teaching*. New York: John Wiley.

Warner, W. L., & Lunt, P. S. (1941). *The social life of a modern community*. New Haven, CT: Yale University Press.

Watson-Gegeo, K. A., & Boggs, S. T. (1977). From verbal play to talk story: The role of routine in speech events among Hawaiian children. In S. Ervin-Tripp & C. Mitchell-Kernan (Eds.), *Child discourse*. New York: Academic Press.

Wax, R. H. (1971). *Doing fieldwork: Warnings and advice*. Chicago: University of Chicago Press.

Webb, B., (1926). *My apprenticeship*. New York: Longmans, Green.

Weber, M. (1978). The nature of social activity. In W. C. Runciman (Ed.). *Weber: Selection in translation* (pp. 7–32). Cambridge: Cambridge University Press. (Originally published in *Wirtschaft und gesellschaft*, Vol. 1, pp. 1–14. Tübingen, 1922).

Whyte, W. F. (1955). *Street corner society* (2nd ed.). Chicago: University of Chicago Press.

Willis, P. E. (1977). *Learning to labour: How working class kids get working class jobs*. Aldershot, Hampshire: Saxon House.

Winch, P. (1958). *The idea of a social science and its relation to philosophy*. London: Routledge and Kegan Paul.

Wirth, L. (1928). *The ghetto*. Chicago: University of Chicago Press.

Wolcott, H. (1982). The anthropology of learning. *Anthropology and Education Quarterly, 13*(2), 83–108.

Zorbaugh, H. (1929). *The gold coast and the slum*. Chicago: University of Chicago Press.

6.

Observation as Inquiry and Method

Carolyn M. Evertson
Peabody College, Vanderbilt University

Judith L. Green
The Ohio State University

Introduction

Observation, as an approach to study educational processes and issues, has a rich and varied history. One way to view this history is to consider the directions taken in past research. Using this approach, four overlapping phases can be identified. Phase One can be viewed as an exploratory phase in which the question of interest was whether teacher–student interactions and other related classroom and instructional behaviors could be reliably and validly identified (ca. 1939–1963). This phase begins with some of the earliest systematic studies of instructional processes (see Amidon & Hough, 1967) and ends with the publication of the chapter by Medley & Mitzel in the first *Handbook of Research on Teaching* (Gage, 1963a).

Phase Two can be characterized as a period of instrument development, and of descriptive, experimental, and training studies (ca. 1958–1973). This phase begins with the emergence of studies using category systems (Amidon & Hough, 1967; Simon & Boyer, 1970a; 1970b) and of issues about paradigms for the study of teaching (Gage, 1963b). It ends with publication of chapters by Rosenshine and Furst and by Gordon and Jester in the *Second Handbook of Research on Teaching* (Travers, 1973).

Phase Three is described as a period in which studies of teacher effects explored teacher behaviors that relate to student outcome performance generally on standardized tests (ca. 1973 to present). This phase was influenced by several events. The beginning of this phase is chronicled by Rosenshine and Furst in the *Second Handbook of Research on Teaching* (Travers, 1973), in which they called for systematic exploration of teacher behaviors related to student outcomes using a series of related descriptive, correlational, and experimental studies. This approach is often referred to as a process–product approach (Doyle, 1977; Dunkin & Biddle, 1974; Koehler, 1978). Another source of influence in this phase was the availability of funds for evaluation studies of Follow-Through projects from the U.S. Office of Education and for large- and small-scale studies of teaching from the newly formed National Institute of Education.

Phase Four parallels Phase Three in terms of time and can be defined as a period of expansion, alternative approaches, theoretical and methodological advances, and convergence across research directions in the use of observational techniques to study teaching (ca. 1972 to present). This phase has two beginning points: The publication of *Functions of Language in the Classroom* (Cazden, John, & Hymes, 1972) and the USOE/NIE panels on the study of teaching. The former resulted from a series of interdisciplinary conferences sponsored by the U.S. Office of Education (1965 & 1966) held for the purpose of suggesting priorities for research on children's language and its relationship to school success (Cazden, this volume; Cazden, John, & Hymes, 1972). Therefore, the publication of *Functions of Language in the Classroom* marks the beginnings of the linguistic approach to the study of teaching–learning processes. This approach was solidified in the panel reports with the publication of Report 5, *Teaching as a Linguistic Process in a Cultural Setting* (National Institute of Education, 1974b). The USOE/NIE panels on the study of teaching were convened to help the National Institute of Education set a research agenda for the

The authors thank reviewers Hermine H. Marshall (University of California — Berkeley) and Celia Genishi (The University of Texas — Austin).
Preparation of this chapter was supported in part by Peabody College, Vanderbilt, The Ohio State University, and the University of Delaware. The authors also wish to thank Rita Fillos, James Hiebert, Gladys Knott, Virginia Koehler, Daniel Neale, Don Sanders, and Cynthia Wallat for their comments on earlier drafts; however, the opinions expressed and any responsibility for errors or omissions belong solely to the authors.

next decade. These reports laid the groundwork for other perspectives on the study of teaching (e.g., human interaction, clinical information processing, theory development; see Berliner & Koehler, 1983). While Phase Four is continuing, its history has been chronicled recently in special issues of the *Elementary School Journal* and the *Educational Psychologist* ("Research on Teaching," 1983a, 1983b), and in chapters throughout this volume.

Across all four phases numerous methods have been described for use in observing teaching–learning processes in educational settings (e.g. Amidon & Hough, 1967; Barnes, Britton, & Rosen, 1971; Dunkin & Biddle, 1974; Erickson & Wilson, 1982; Evertson & Holley, 1981; Flanders, 1970; Genishi, 1983a; Gilmore & Glatthorn, 1982; Good, 1983; Gordon & Jester, 1973; Green, 1983b; Green & Wallat, 1981a; Hamilton, 1983; Heap, 1980b; 1983; Lundgren, 1977; Medley & Mitzel 1963; Mehan, 1979a; Rosenshine & Furst, 1973; Shavelson, 1983; Simon & Boyer, 1970a, 1970b; Sinclair & Coulthard, 1975; Spindler, 1982; Stallings, 1977; Stubbs & Delamont, 1976; Trueba, Guthrie, & Au, 1981; Weinstein, 1983; Wilkinson, 1982; Woods and Hammersley, 1977). However, little systematic discussion exists on the nature of observation both as method and as an inquiry process (Fassnacht, 1982). Given the varied nature of observational research and the expansion of methodological directions identified in Phase Four (1972–present), such a discussion is needed in order to guide the decision making of those interested in systematic observation in educational settings.

The purpose of this chapter is to explore the nature of observation as a research approach and to provide a framework for making informed decisions about design and implementation of observational research. That is, the intent of this chapter is to explore the nature of observational inquiry and methods related to this inquiry process. The framework was derived from a review of work on the nature of observation; consideration of observational tools used in past research; discussion of approaches to observation that have emerged in the last decade for use in the study of teaching–learning processes; and discussions between the authors of this chapter and groups of junior researchers — doctoral students at the University of Delaware and at The Ohio State University — interested in designing and implementing systematic observational research projects. This chapter is complemented by discussions of research methods and design processes presented in other chapters in this volume.

The information in the chapter is presented in two parts. Part One focuses on a discussion of generic and specific issues related to the nature of observation and observational tools. Part Two discusses observation as an inquiry process and describes the framework for selecting, designing, and implementing observation of educational practices and issues.

The Nature of Observation and Observational Tools

The answer to the question "What is observation?" depends on the purpose for which the person is asking the question. Is the person a classroom teacher interested in observing student performance during ongoing lessons? Is the person a teacher or counselor interested in observing student behavior in order to

supplement test information so that a comprehensive profile of ability and performance can be developed before placing a student in a special program? Is the person a researcher interested in using observation to study intellectual development, effective instruction, classroom climate, and so forth? Is the person a developmental psychologist interested in observing student ability to conserve?

Each of these people will engage in some form of systematic, deliberate observation; however, the specific observational process will vary. Different foci will be selected; observations will be conducted in different environments; different events will be sampled; the duration of the observation will vary; different means of recording data will be used; different rules for evidence will exist. In other words, the *program of research* (a series of conceptually and theoretically linked studies) will differ (see Shulman, this volume, for a discussion of "program of research").

The differing purposes lead to differences in strategies for observation, levels of systematization, and levels of formality. These factors lead to differences in design and implementation. In other words, the purpose of the observation influences what is observed, how it is observed, who gets observed, when observation takes place, where it takes place, how observations are recorded, what observations are recorded, how data are analyzed, and how data are used. In addition, the purpose of an observation is related to the theory, beliefs, assumptions, and/or past experiences of the person who is doing the observation. These factors form the *frame of reference* of the observer and influence the decision-making as well as the observational process (e.g. Dunkin & Biddle, 1974; Fassnacht, 1982; Power, 1977; Shulman, 1981).

While differences exist, generic issues and principles can be identified when the question of what is meant by observation and observational methods is explored on a general level. In the remainder of this section, the generic issues involved in doing observation in educational settings will be discussed. The issues involved in such observation will be considered separately from the theoretical or conceptual frame guiding specific studies or approaches. In the section on observation as inquiry, the relationship of the theoretical or conceptual frame and related methods will be considered. The separation of the discussion of method from theory guiding individual studies (a) permits the development of concepts about the nature of observation as a strategy for representing aspects of reality and (b) avoids issues related to the use of observation as a method of research in a given discipline or field of study. This approach was selected for heuristic purposes to avoid contrasts of a limited set of approaches (e.g. qualitative vs. quantitative; experimental vs. descriptive; normative vs. interpretive). The purpose of this approach is to highlight issues involved in doing adequate observation, to describe the complexity of those issues, to consider tools available, and to provide guidelines for what must be considered regardless of frame of reference.

Observation: A Multifaceted Phenomenon

Observation is an everyday event. It is part of the psychology of perception, and as such, it is a tacit part of the everyday functioning of individuals as they negotiate the events of daily life.

Not all observation that occurs in daily life is tacit. Observation also occurs more deliberately and systematically when the situation demands such behavior. For example, more deliberate and systematic observations are required of children playing baseball and other games. The player must observe the patterns of play, the direction of the ball, the actions of others, and the objects in the path of play in order to participate appropriately or navigate the field of play. These observations, while more systematic than ordinary observations in everyday life, are frequently tacit. This type of more systematic observation is also required in more formal situations such as classrooms. Students must observe the social and academic expectations of who can talk—when, where, how, and for what purpose—in order to participate appropriately in learning activities. Teachers must observe more systematically to maintain the flow of a lesson, the management of instruction, and the involvement of students, as well as to obtain informal and formative assessment of student performance, lesson development, and program direction.

In daily life, systematic observations are undertaken, not to answer specific questions, but to establish, maintain, check, suspend, and participate in everyday events (Blumer, 1969). Such observations are related to the demands of the situation. However, when observation is used to answer a stated question, it must be deliberate and systematic. In addition, it must be a conscious process that can be explicated so that others may assess its adequacy and understand the process. Observations used for research and overt decision-making processes in educational settings are more formal and externalized than observation in daily life. One way to think of these different aspects of observation is as a continuum in which everyday, tacit observations are the least formal; systematic situation-specific, everyday tacit observations are more formal, but are still not under overt, conscious control; and deliberate and systematic question-specific observations are the most formal of the three and under the most direct control.

This way of conceptualizing observation, illustrated in Figure 6.1, suggests that observation for research and decision making in educational settings (deliberate, systematic, question-specific observation) is both similar to everyday observational processes and different from such processes. One major difference is the reason for observing. Other differences will become evident in the sections that follow.

Observation as a Research and Decision-Making Process

As suggested previously, observation for research and decision-making purposes is closely tied to the question of why one observes. Observations for observation's sake (i.e., random observations) cannot be added together in the way children put beads on a string. Such observations are not cumulative and do not constitute evidence. The question would have to be raised: Why was the observation done? What purpose does it serve? Since observations are phenomena that occur in a specific context or setting, there would be no systematic means of aggregating information from such observations. The purpose of the observation guides what will be done, how it will be used, and what can be obtained. Karl Popper (1963), as cited in Stubbs, Robinson, and Twite (1979), makes the point:

> Twenty-five years ago I tried to bring home the same point to a group of physics students in Vienna by beginning a lecture with the following instructions: "Take pencil and paper; carefully observe, and write down what you have observed!" They asked, of course, what I wanted them to observe. Clearly the instruction "Observe!" is absurd. (It is not even idiomatic, unless the object of the transitive verb can be taken as understood.) Observation is always selective. It needs a chosen object, a definite task, an interest, a point of view, a problem. And its description presupposes a descriptive language, with property words; it presupposes similarity and classification, which in its turn presupposes interest, points of view, and problems. (p. 21)

Implicit in Popper's definition is the assumption that the observer is the first instrument of observation. In other words, the task or object selected, the observer's frame of reference, and the purpose of the observation, among other factors, will influence what will be perceived, recorded, analyzed, and ultimately described by the observer. While this is true, in observational research in the behavioral and social sciences, the observer often augments the observation process by using a tool or instrument to focus or guide observation (e.g., a sign system, a specimen record, category system, field notes). Another way to think about this is that the perceptual system of the observer is the first tool used by the observer and that this tool is influenced by the observer's own goals, biases, frame of reference, and abilities. An observation tool or lens (e.g., an observation instrument or system) further influences and constrains what will be observed, recorded, analyzed, and described. Therefore, observation is a mediated process on several levels—the level of the observer as a person with biases, beliefs, training, and ability, and the level of the instrument or tool used to make and record an observation. This tool also has a point of view, bias, structure, and so forth.

The issues related to the mediation and representation processes must be considered since as Fassnacht (1982) suggests:

> A statement about real events is always a statement mediated by a particular representational mechanism in a particular context. A representation can have many different qualities, depending on the mechanism or the organism involved in the representational process. (p. 7)

He goes on to conclude that because of these issues "absolute independence of a mechanism is a contradiction in terms." The

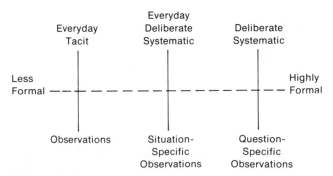

Fig. 6.1 Continuum of observation types.

issues raised above deserve further exploration since one purpose of observation in educational settings is to obtain a description or representation of events, processes, and phenomena as well as factors that influence these phenomena. Such information is necessary for understanding and improving schooling, instruction, and learning. The issues raised above require consideration of (a) observation as a means of representing reality in educational settings; (b) observation as a contextualized process; (c) mechanisms or tools for recording and storing observations; and (d) factors involved in observation: units of observation/aggregation of data; sampling; and sources of error.

Observation as a Means of Representing Reality

The remainder of this chapter will focus on observations that are systematic, deliberate, and question-specific. Such observations are formal in structure and situation-specific. As will be shown, such observations are undertaken in a variety of ways using a variety of representational systems. While others have viewed this diversity as chaos (Rosenshine & Furst, 1973), we argue that the variety of options is a potential strength for researchers interested in the study of teaching. Weinstein (1983) points to the value of such diversity:

It is difficult to maintain that one view of classroom events is more accurate than another. Rather, we must learn from each perspective, identify matches and mismatches among perspectives, and examine relationships between perceptions and behavior.... By investigating several perspectives in each study, we will improve our understanding of the social reality of classrooms. (p. 306)

Mead (1975) made a similar point when she suggested that one reason an anthropologist enters the field is to obtain "a" grammar, not "the" grammar of a people or an event. Fassnacht (1982) also made a similar point. He suggests:

Even the representational mechanism with the finest analysis now known does not guarantee that with a different mechanism a finer analysis of reality would not be possible. (p. 5)

What these scholars are suggesting is that any tool (mechanism) used or approach to observation of an event (process, set of behaviors, group context) provides only one representation or view of the phenomena under study. Weinstein (1983) suggests that this characteristic of observations and approaches be used as a strength and be incorporated into studies. Recently, this approach to integrating multiple perspective analysis in a single project has been undertaken by researchers from a wide variety of disciplinary groundings and perspectives interested in the study of teaching–learning processes (e.g. Bloome, 1983; Cole, Griffin, & Newman, 1979; Cook-Gumperz, in press; Evertson, Anderson, & Clements, 1980; Frederiksen, 1981; Green & Harker, 1982; Green, Harker, & Wallat, in press; Marston & Zimmerer, 1979; Morine-Dershimer & Tenenberg, 1981; Weinstien, 1983; among others). These studies demonstrate the richness of information and the complementarity of views that can be obtained by systematically building on differ-

ent approaches. They suggest that the selectivity issue need not be a detriment; they demonstrate what can be learned by acknowledging this issue and developing a program of observational research that incorporates a variety of perspectives.

The selectivity issue operates beyond the level of perspective or approach. Selectivity is an inevitable characteristic of any tool, representational system, or program of research. It is not possible to record all aspects of reality with any given system or tool or in any single research project. Selectivity is also reflected in the decisions a researcher or decision maker must make. For example, researchers and decision makers must select (a) *the question for study*; (b) *a setting in which to observe* (e.g. playground, classroom); (c) *a slice of reality to observe within the setting* (e.g. games played by boys vs. girls; reading groups; group discussions; question asking by teachers during language arts lessons; the first hour of school; the beginning of a lesson); (d) *a tool or combination of tools to record and store the segment of reality for study* (e.g., category system and narrative record; rating scale, category system, and checklist; field notes and videotape record; audiotape record, still camera pictures, and field notes); (e) *procedures for observing* (e.g., where to stand, when to observe, how many observers to use, in what order to use specified tools); (f) *the subjects to be observed or the locus of observation* (e.g., individual, group, event, behavior type, strategy); (g) *the analysis procedures appropriate for the question and the record obtained*; and (h) *the method of reporting the data and information extracted from the observation record* (e.g., written report, graphic representation, protocol tape). In other words, selectivity is a part of the entire decision-making, design, and implementation process involved in observational research.

Rather than control for selectivity that appears to be impossible, one strategy could be to report in more detail than exists presently in most studies the parameters of the study and the nature of the decisions made. Another way to think about these issues is to consider the reporting of decisions that contribute to selectivity as demographic information. This would provide a clearer picture of what was observed, how, where, when, and for what purposes (Herbert & Attridge, 1975; Shaver, 1983; see also Corsaro, 1985, for an illustrative example). This strategy may avoid some of the pitfalls that led to the lack of replication in studies of teaching reported in Dunkin & Biddle (1974). The information would provide the basis for determining whether two observational studies were indeed equivalent, and whether the variation observed across studies was a result of the procedures used in the study or the portion of reality selected.

Closely related to the selectivity issue is the fact that reality cannot be directly apprehended (Fassnacht, 1982). Since observations require a representational mechanism and the mechanism contains selective elements, the representation is mediated by the tool used as well as by the representational process. That is, the representation or description obtained is dependent on the instrument used to record the observation and the way in which the data were collected (e.g., length of observation; events sampled). In addition, the process surrounding the observation also provides a degree of mediation of reality (Stubbs et al., 1979). In other words, "Truth" can never be known. What the researcher and decision maker attempt to do is to collect sufficient and appropriate evidence to ensure that the description is as accurate as possible given the representational process used. (Additional information related to these issues will be considered in the section on sources of error.)

In this section, several factors that influence the nature of the description or representation of reality were discussed briefly. On a general level, description was shown to be related to both the system for recording the observations and the process of observational research itself. In the discussion below, a closer look at various aspects of the observational process will be considered. The purpose of this discussion is to describe options available and to clarify issues that influence the nature and quality of observational research.

Observation as a Contextualized Process

One factor that influences what is observed is the way in which a "context" is defined. A review of research on teaching suggests that a variety of definitions of context exist. That is, the issue of context has been discussed from a variety of perspectives (e.g., Barr & Dreeban, 1983; Bloome & Green, 1982; Brophy & Evertson, 1978; Cazden, 1983; Cook-Gumperz & Gumperz, 1976; Erickson & Shultz, 1981; Evertson & Veldman, 1981; Fishman, 1972; Good, Cooper, & Blakey, 1980; Green, 1983b; Hamilton, 1983; McDermott, 1976; Ogbu, 1981; Philips, 1972, 1982; Popkewitz, Tabachick, & Zeichner, 1979; Scribner & Cole, 1981; Taylor, 1983). From this work a series of issues related to ways of considering context can be extracted: local context as embedded in larger levels of context; historical context of the setting; historical context of the specific event under study; and context of the research approach.

Consideration of these issues related to context can (a) help researchers understand how individuals and groups acquire knowledge from everyday activities and events in both formal and informal educational settings, (b) help researchers determine factors constraining and supporting performance in a given context, and (c) lead to understandings of what makes two contexts functionally equivalent (Erickson & Shultz, 1981; Florio & Shultz, 1979). As will be shown below, the task is to match the question with the context and the instrument with the phenomenon, context, and question.

Local Context as Embedded in Broader Levels of Context. The discussion to this point has considered only the immediate event in the immediate setting. However, the context in the immediate or local setting (Erickson, 1979) is only one context that surrounds the observed event. If a systems approach is taken, the local context can be seen as embedded in and influenced by larger contexts (Barr & Dreeban, 1983; Bloome & Green, 1982; Carey, Harste, & Smith, 1981; Erickson & Shultz, 1981). The reading group is embedded in the classroom; the classroom is embedded in the school; the school in the district; the district in the community; and so forth. These other contexts occur simultaneously and impact on the immediate context. For example, they frame how people will participate (e.g., Au, 1980; Fishman, 1976; Michaels, 1981; Scollon & Scollon, 1984; Tannen, 1979), what resources people use and what resources are available (Barr & Dreeban, 1983; Heap, 1980b), and often how people will use or perceive what occurs (Anderson, 1981; Morine-Dershimer & Tenenberg, 1981; Morine-Dershimer, 1982;). In other words, links exist between micro and

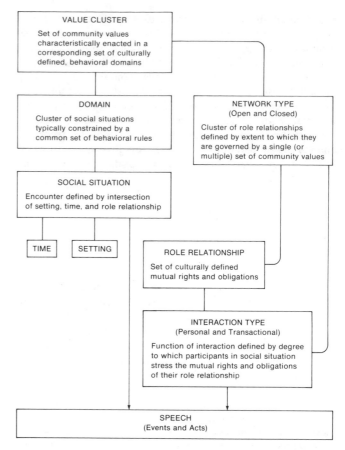

Fig. 6.2. Relationship among some constructs employed in sociolinguistic analysis. From "How Can We Measure the Roles Which a Bilingual's Languages Play in His Everyday Behavior?" by R. Cooper. Copyright 1976 by *La Linguistique*, P.U.F. Paris. Reprinted by permission.

macro levels of context and are signaled through performance, materials available, practices, and so forth. In Figure 6.2, Cooper (1968 [as cited by Fishman, 1976]) demonstrates the links between micro- and macro-constructs for a sociolinguistic analysis.

Cooper's example also relates to a previous point. Weinstein (1983) suggested the need to consider multiple perspectives to provide alternative descriptions or representations so that the matches and mismatches in perspective could be explored and more holistic representations of events obtained. Cooper suggests that the micro and macro factors and the links between these factors should be considered and that such considerations may require a full range of methods and analytic procedures. (For other discussions of micro–macro issues in education see Bloome & Green, 1982; Hamilton, 1983; Ogbu, 1981.)

This brief discussion highlights the need to consider multiple levels of context as well as the level of context used in a specific observational study. In addition, it suggests the need to account for relevant aspects of other contexts that impact on the specific context under study. The consideration of context issues is an important part of making inferences about processes and how those generalize.

Historical Context of the Setting. Another type of context that frames local ones is the historical context of the setting. For example, schools have histories and one way to view this history is as a set of expectations, traditions, networks, and lines of communication (Hymes, 1981; Little, 1981, 1982). The historical context of the setting is not directly observable. However, to answer the question of why an event or structure occurred where it did or when it did, the researcher may have to explore the historical context. For example, past practice or policy may determine why reading rather than mathematics instruction occurs from 9:00 to 10:00 in every classroom in a school. The decision may be based on past practice, because it has always been that way. In order to generalize about the time segmentation of the day in a particular school or about the meaning of an event, the history behind the observed phenomenon needs to be considered.

The Historical Context of the Event. Recent work on classroom processes has shown that events in classrooms have histories (e.g., Cazden, 1976; Cochran-Smith, 1984; Emmer, Evertson, & Anderson, 1980; Erickson & Shultz, 1981; Evertson & Emmer, 1982; Mehan, 1979a; Smith & Geoffrey, 1968; Wallat & Green, 1979, 1982). This work focuses on how processes (e.g., social norms, management of activities) unfold over time. It shows that the first few weeks of school are critical periods in the establishment of routines, expectations, classroom structures, and so forth. If the question is, What is reading? How does mathematics occur? What are the group practices? What is the nature of curriculum delivery, organization, and development? or similar questions about teaching-learning processes and relationships, then the development of these processes over time must be considered and the beginnings of the processes (events) must be captured.

The historical context of local events is important to consider given the findings that some processes (events, practices) remain stable over time while others vary (Eder, 1982; Evertson & Veldman, 1981; Good et al., 1980; Wallat & Green, 1982). That is, the students may be adhering to a set of rules, expectations, or procedures established prior to the day of observation. Some of these may be stable over time and, therefore, the observer recording these behaviors would get a representative set of behaviors. Some of the behaviors might be situation specific, content specific, or time specific. Without knowing which behaviors were stable and representative of the event under study, and which were idiosyncratic to the specific day and time, the researcher will be constrained in what can be generalized about this teacher, pupil, or class.

This work suggests that a match between sampling and the question must be carefully considered and that the behavior in any one context or event within a context may be related to prior experiences with similar events. The questions that need to be considered include, What are the ties between contexts? What behaviors are stable over time and therefore representative of the expectations (procedures, practices), and which vary? When should sampling be done and at what points, in order to know that observations are representative? In other words, the issue of context is related to the issue of sampling and the representativeness of the data and findings.

Exclusive Approaches ——————————— Inclusive Approaches

Fig. 6.3. Inclusive and exclusive approaches to context.

Context as Determined by the Research Approach. One last aspect of context will be reviewed. This aspect is related to the research approach, that is, different approaches may sample different amounts and levels of context, and the decisions about context sampling may be related to the theory used, the beliefs of the researcher, and the tools used, as well as the questions asked. One way to view this issue is as a continuum. On one end of the continuum, context factors are controlled or minimized. At the other end of the continuum, contexts are not controlled and as many aspects of the context as can be obtained are included in the data collection. Figure 6.3 provides a graphic representation of this continuum. Approaches toward the exclusive end seek to simplify what is collected, to reduce the "noise" in the system so that specific types of phenomena or behaviors are considered (e.g., question asking; teacher-student interactions). Researchers using approaches at this end of the continuum (e.g. category systems, checklists, rating scales) tend to be concerned with discerning behavioral laws or normative information. They seek to study a large number of classrooms with an efficient, reliable approach. Generally, what is observed is predetermined; rules for observation are routinized to permit interobserver agreement. At this end of the continuum, many of the cues that offer redundancy to interpretations (Snow, 1974) are reduced or eliminated in the measuring instrument. Selectivity at this end of the continuum is deliberate. That is, the researcher has made deliberate decisions about the unit used in the observation system (e.g., checklists or category systems have a limited number of items to observe and record). Only the items on the instrument are observed and recorded. Although instruments may be modified later as a result of what the investigator learns about the setting, no new units are added during the period of observation.

As the researcher moves toward the other end of the continuum, larger and larger segments of context and greater numbers of context variables are considered. At the farthest end, the inclusive end, no attempt is made to exclude any aspect of context on a deliberate basis. Rather, researchers attempt to sample a wide slice of everyday life or reality. They often attempt to sample multiple levels of context. Decisions about what to observe and record, when examining less than the total setting (e.g. group, culture, event over the year, etc.), are principled decisions (Heath, 1982). The decisions frame not only what slice of context will be sampled, but also what will be sampled within the context (e.g., Erickson & Wilson, 1982; Green, 1983b; Heath, 1982).

Recording at the inclusive end of the continuum is usually made by one or more tools including audiotapes, videotapes, movie cameras, still cameras, narrative records (Erickson & Wilson, 1982). Records at the inclusive end are more dependent upon technological advances to record and freeze segments of life and everyday events. In contrast, records at the exclusive end tend to reduce descriptions to categories of behavior recorded during the observation period (on-line recording). Selectivity at the inclusive end of the continuum, therefore, is less constrained. Coding or representation at this end is done retrospectively; the degree of distance from the "live" data is less at the inclusive end. Finally, rules for data collection are adaptive (Corsaro, 1985; Erickson, 1977; Heath, 1982; Spindler, 1982; Spradley, 1980). Principled decisions are made within the observational period and during the project, based on need identified during the project. A general set of guidelines exist governing observation. New techniques or combinations of techniques are selected and used to answer questions. While systematic, the observation process at this end is broader and more flexible than at the exclusive end of the continuum.

While the two ends of the continuum have tended to be mutually exclusive in the past, there is no theoretical reason that the two ends cannot work together. For example, from research at the inclusive end of the continuum, naturally occurring variables, patterns of behavior, and events can be identified. The investigator would then be able to construct a category system or checklist to focus observation on specific aspects within the context. The information obtained with the focused tool could then be examined at the more inclusive end. This procedure can allow the investigator to change lenses and to move back and forth across and within levels of context.

To pursue the lens notion, an analogy for the context issues above is a microscope (Green, 1983b). At the highest power, the microscope lens focuses on the details on the slide and the general field is obscured. As the power becomes weaker, more and more of the field or general context is included. At the lowest power, the details are obscured and the field becomes the focus. The different powers allow the investigator to explain different aspects of the phenomenon and move back and forth across powers. This procedure permits exploration of the observed phenomenon under different levels of focus. On the continuum, then, the exclusive end is often considered the higher power. It decontextualizes behaviors and focuses on the occurrence of specific behaviors. The field surrounding these behaviors is generally ignored except for general demographic information. As the researcher moves toward the inclusive end, more and more of the field or context is considered. The studies selected for indepth discussion in the section of this chapter dealing with observation as inquiry illustrate various aspects of the continuum and the way that researchers may move across the ends of this continuum.

The discussion of context above is meant to be illustrative rather than all-inclusive. The topic requires greater treatment, not only of context and selectivity issues, but of the levels of context and their relationship to analysis procedures and statistical treatment (e.g., Burstein, 1980; Martin, Veldman, & Anderson, 1980; Snow, 1974; and chapters in this volume). Other context issues that have been considered in recent research include intrapersonal versus interpersonal contexts (e.g., Bloome & Green, 1984; Cazden, 1983; Heap, 1980b), the interrelatedness of levels of context of schooling (Barr, in press; Barr & Dreeban, 1983), and functions of language used as context for instruction (e.g., Collins, 1983, in press; Marshall & Green, 1978; Mehan, 1979a; Pinnell, 1977).

By considering the different types and levels of context, future research can address more systematically questions of match and mismatch of performance in different contexts, of factors influencing performance in a given setting, and of differing perspectives and levels of description of a phenomenon.

Snow (1974), building on the work of Brunswik (1956), articulates the issues involved:

> Brunswik seems to have felt that intelligent human beings were active, flexible, adaptive processors of information available in a probabilistic, partially redundant environment. Above all, then, the experimenter must adapt his research methodology to fit this form of phenomenon, rather than trying to force the phenomenon to adapt to the experimenter. (p. 266)

Snow further states:

> Brunswik would say that we should continue to use systematic design for what it is good for. But he would note that we have so far failed to adjust that methodology to fit the adaptive, probabilistic functioning of human behavior or to derive molar descriptions of that behavior in multidimensional natural situations. (p. 269)

To paraphrase this point for observational research, the researcher's goal is to freeze everyday activities as well as experimental activities so that they can be examined systematically. To do this, the researcher selects a tool to obtain a representation of reality. The crucial point is to select a tool that fits the phenomenon under study and the level of context that is appropriate. In other words, a researcher must choose, construct, or adapt an observational tool, method, process, and program appropriate to the question asked, the context surrounding the phenomenon, and the nature of the phenomenon. In this case, the task is to use a tool that will permit the researcher to record and store the active, flexible, adaptive processes that occur in teaching–learning situations and to consider the contextualization cues (Cook-Gumperz & Gumperz, 1976; Corsaro, 1985) that form the basis of inference by both the participants in the situation and the researcher (e.g., verbal, nonverbal, and paralinguistic features of language). This information then becomes the basis for the construction of data, for the reconstruction of the event, and for the analysis of data.

Systems for Recording and Storing Observational Data

The systems used to record, store, and represent observations in this section are described in general terms. The intent of this section is not to review the literally hundreds of instruments/systems available or to prescribe which systems are best. That task has been addressed elsewhere (e.g. Dunkin & Biddle, 1974; Rosenshine & Furst, 1973; Simon & Boyer, 1970a, 1970b). Rather the purpose of the discussion that follows is to provide a way of classifying the major types of systems used, to describe their general characteristics, and to explore how data are collected.

However, before presenting the classification framework, the premises on which the classification is based will be discussed. Four premises underlie the classification of tools/instruments. First, the plethora of instruments can be sorted into a finite set of classes. For the purpose of this discussion, four classes of collection procedures have been identified: categorical systems, descriptive systems, narrative systems, and technological records. Second, each classification of systems/records can be identified by a unique set of characteristics which can then be used to discriminate among the different instruments (see Table 6.1). Third, all of the instruments are selective and all are used to freeze behavior, events, and processes for later analysis.

The key is not which is best but which is most suited for the question under study and which will adequately represent the segment of reality being observed. Fourth, the characteristics of the systems can be considered separately from the perspective or theoretical orientation that frames the particular study. In other words, the characteristics can be determined generically. This last premise means that the nature of the system is distinguished from the items in the system (e.g. verbal praise, teacher warmth, higher-order questions), since the items or units of observation are related to the perspective of the researcher. (For other classification systems for observational methods see Genishi, 1983a; Gordon & Jester, 1973; Rosenshine & Furst, 1973; Simon & Boyer, 1970a 1970b; Wright, 1960.)

The classification framework in Table 6.1 presents four types of information about each system: (a) general classification of the nature of the system; (b) types of systems; (c) methods of recording data found within each type of system, and (d) general goals of the users. Each of these will be considered in turn as they appear in Table 6.1. The order of presentation is related to the context continuum presented previously (see Figure 6.3). The systems listed at the far left of Table 6.1 would be placed at the far left or exclusive end of the context continuum. Systems to the right of categorical systems include larger and larger segments of context and, therefore, will be found at the more inclusive end of the continuum. Just as it is possible to move across or to consider different levels of context, it is possible to combine more than one system within the same study. (See the section on observation as inquiry for an illustration of this point.) The key is to match the type of system selected with the question and phenomena under study at the particular point in the study.

Nature of the System. The question of whether a system was a closed one or an open one was considered. Closed systems are those that contain a finite number of preset categories or units of observation (e.g. teacher criticism, student response to convergent questions). The categories for a closed system are mutually exclusive and defined in advance to reflect philosophical, theoretical, empirically derived, or experience-based beliefs about the nature of the process, event, or group under study (cf. Dunkin & Biddle, 1974). Observations are confined to identifying and recording behaviors contained within the system itself. The observation system is self-contained (i.e., no new categories may be added to the system during observation periods even though revisions of the system may be done later). Categorical systems are considered complete or closed systems.

Table 6-1. Ways of Recording and Storing Observations: Broad Classifications

	Category Systems	Descriptive Systems	Narrative Systems	Technological Records
Nature of Systems	Closed system Always has preset categories. Samples of behaviors, events, processes that occur within a given time period. Boundaries of events are often ignored. Focus on behavior in general.	Open system May have preset categories. Meaning is viewed as context specific. Boundaries of events are considered during as well as prior to observations. Samples behaviors, events, processes that occur with naturally occurring boundaries.	Open system No preset categories. Meaning is viewed as context specific. Boundaries of events are considered during as well as prior to observation for live recording. Samples behaviors that occur within naturally occurring boundaries.	Open system No preset categories. Meaning is viewed as context specific. Samples behaviors, events, processes that occur within a given time period or a given event. No attempt to filter or mediate what is observed.
Types of Systems	Category, sign, checklist, rating scales	Structured descriptive analysis systems	Specimen record, diaries, anecdotal records	Still pictures, videotape, audiotape
Methods of Recording	Selected behaviors coded on form using tallies, numeric representations, ratings. Records one behavior at a time. Used live and on line. Behaviors coded on special form.	Selected behaviors recorded using verbal symbols and/or transcription. Records multiple aspects of behaviors. Also considers broad segment of event. Generally used with permanent record (e.g., audiotape, videotape).	Broad segments of events recorded orally or in written form. Observation recorded in everyday syntax.	Potentially the widest "lens." An unfiltered record of all behaviors and events that occur in front of the camera or within pickup of microphone. Depending on the focus of the researcher the lens can be wide or narrow.
Goals of Users	Study a wide range of classrooms to obtain normative data, identify laws of teaching, generalized across cases. Less interest in individual variation within cases.	Obtain detailed descriptions of observed phenomena, explain unfolding processes, identify generic principles from explorations of specific situations, and generalize within cases as well as compare findings across cases.	Obtain detailed descriptions of observed phenomena, explain unfolding processes, identify generic principles and patterns of behavior in specific situations. Goal is to understand specific case and to compare findings across cases.	Obtain a permanent record of event to be recorded. Decisions on what to record are related to goals of researcher and questions under consideration. The purpose is to freeze the event in time for analysis at a later point in time.

An open system uses a wider lens. These systems may have a range of preset categories used to describe behaviors (or other types of phenomena), or may contain categories generated from observed patterns. The categories within an open system differ from those within the more closed systems. Individual behaviors/phenomena in an open system are often recorded using more than one category. For example, behaviors may have more than one function; therefore, the categories may be combined to reflect a variety of co-occurring functions (e.g. a teacher's message can focus students and simultaneously signal control; the delivery provides the multiple cues). Variables reflecting patterns of behavior are obtained (e.g. initiation-response–evaluation; cf. Mehan, 1979a). The patterns can be described in terms of both functions and effects.

Within the types of open systems, differences occur. Descriptive systems are more constrained than either narrative systems or technological records. Descriptive systems may have preset categories as described above and also categories generated by the data. The narrative systems and the technological records have no predetermined categories. The categories for these systems/records are derived from analysis of the data after observations, not during collection. Since permanent records are used (e.g. written, audio, or video), identification of categories of behavior, patterns of behavior, and construction of variables is possible retrospectively. Such variables can be reliably and validly identified (Erickson, 1979). Another way to view open systems is that they can be generative; that is, new variables can be identified throughout the analysis process. The number and type of variables are grounded in (suggested by) observed patterns in the data as well as the theoretical framework guiding analysis.

One difference, then, between closed and open systems can be seen in the point of identification of categories. First, in closed systems, categories are selected a priori. In the more open systems, categories are generally drawn from the raw data. In both systems, theoretical, philosophical, or experience-based decisions are used to construct the categories. A second difference is found in the role of the observer. The observer using a closed system is limited to recording only those items listed. With open systems, the observer captures a wider slice of context. The observer's perceptions, training, and framework determine what will be recorded. The notable exception to this is the technological records. Technological records augment the observation process by providing a permanent record of the events. At the point of analysis, the observer as the instrument of observation becomes a key factor. Whether one chooses an open or a closed system may depend upon the question, the philosophy, the theory, and/or the point of observation within the study. Each type of system/record serves different purposes and produces different descriptions.

Methods of Recording Data. The second factor that was considered in distinguishing between and in classifying the systems was the means of recording data. Data from categorical systems are recorded live and on line in general. That is, observed behaviors are recorded on the coding forms as they occur, either as ratings at the end of a set period of time, as numeric symbols for the behavior observed (e.g., 4 represents 'direct questions'; cf. Flanders, 1970), or as a tally on a checklist. Each behavior is generally recorded in only one category. As indicated in Table 6.1, behaviors, events, and processes are sampled during a given time period. Two types of boundaries for the *period of observation* have been used; time and event. When *time* is the sampling unit the boundaries of specific events are ignored. For example, the first hour of school might be recorded beginning at 9:00 and continuing until 10:00. When *event* is the sampling unit, the observation begins with the onset of the event and ends with its closure. That is, in the real time of the classroom, the observer uses the cues given by participants that the event has begun and ended. For example, recording begins when the teacher calls the Bluebirds to the reading group and ends when the teacher dismisses them.

Within the period of observation two other types of recording procedures are used. First, tallies are made of each occurrence of a specific behavior, event, or process. Only those behaviors designated within the category system or checklist are recorded. Second, the behaviors on the system are recorded at preset *time intervals* (e.g. Flanders, 1970 — every 3 seconds; Stallings, 1983 — alternating 5-minute segments during interactions). Table 6.2 summarizes the differences among instruments in this classification. Each type of recording procedure produces different types of raw data and leads to different descriptions. (See the section on units of observation for additional discussion of categorical systems.)

The *descriptive systems* are generally used in combination with technological records (e.g., audiotapes, videotapes). Descriptive systems are applied to such records in one of two ways. First, descriptive systems that have been formalized and have predetermined categories to guide description are applied to either the video record or to a combination of video record and transcript (e.g., Adelman, 1981; Bellack, Hyman, Smith, & Kliebard, 1966; Elliott, 1976; Frederiksen, 1981; Green & Wallat, 1979, 1981b; Mehan, 1979a; Sinclair & Coulthard, 1975; Stubbs, 1983). The behaviors are then recorded in a way that reflects the communicative or pedagogical structure of the unfolding event. Generally, this requires patterns of behavior to be identified and represented systematically. Second, transcriptions are made and usually linguistic symbols are used to identify stress patterns, turns, tied sequences, and so forth (e.g. Cochran-Smith, 1984; Collins, 1983; Erickson, 1982; Heap, 1983; Mishler, 1984; Ochs, 1979; Stubbs et al., 1979; Tannen, 1979). Both of these descriptive approaches use a retrospective analysis of specific aspects of the total recording. These systems, however, continually refer to the broader record of the event recorded by technological records. The period of observation may vary in length; however, data are recorded within naturally occurring boundaries of events or contexts. Meaning in these systems is considered to be situation specific. (See section on units of observation for additional discussion of descriptive systems.)

With *narrative systems* descriptions are recorded using spoken or written language. An observer either writes a narrative description of the unfolding event or orally records a verbal description on a tape recorder. The recordings can be made live, as in the case of critical incident records and specimen records, or can be reflective, as in the case of diaries or journal records. Table 6.3 describes the differences among the systems. The period of observation may vary depending upon the purposes of

Table 6.2. Categorical Approaches: Types of Recording Systems and General Characteristics

Category Systems	Checklist Sign Systems	Rating Scales
1. Contain preset categories in which all occurring behavior must be recorded in one of the categories.	1. Contain preset categories in which only the specified behaviors are recorded, not all occurring behavior.	1. Contain preset categories for which weighted judgements are required (e.g., 1 = low, 3 = moderate, 5 = high).
2. Essentially a classification system; nominal scale.	2. Essentially a classification system; nominal scale.	2. Essentially a system using interval scales (e.g., ordinal: determination of greater or lesser; interval: determination of equality of differences between points).
3. Generally used in settings as events unfold. Can be used with video or audio records.	3. Generally used in settings as events unfold. Can be used with video or audio records.	3. Generally used at the end of an observation period to summarize cumulative direct observations. Observer need not be in the setting when using.
4. Amenable to recording smaller units of behavior which require low inference.	4. Amenable to recording smaller units of behavior which require low inference.	4. Amenable to assessing high-inference or global constructs (e.g., teacher warmth; emotional intensity).
5. Time based in that behaviors are recorded at designated intervals. The period of time for recording multiplied by the number of tallies equals the approximate length of observation. (e.g. a 5-minute observation in which codes are assigned every 5 seconds yields 12 per minute and 60 per 5-minute observation). Events may be the locus of observation, but time sampling is the dominant procedure.	5. Can be time based or event based. That is, a general time period (period of observation) is set or an event in which observation will be undertaken is specified. Total number of tallies is not necessarily related to the length of the observation period.	5. Time for recording is not relevant except that too long an interval between observation and assessment can yield loss of information. (For an in-depth coverage of rating scales see Remmers, 1963; see Fassnacht, 1982 on dimensional scales.)

Table 6.3. Types of Narrative Systems

Diary/Journal Records	Critical Incident	Specimen Description	Field Notes/Descriptive Notes
1. Retrospective written records of either ones's own behavior/experience or that of others.	1. On-line or retrospective record used to record relevant behavior or incidents that address an area or topic of interest.	1. On-line, more systematic and intensive recording of events. Aim is to record all behavior during a designated time period in an uninterrupted stream and in detail.	1. Written account of what the investigator sees, hears, experiences, and thinks in the course of collecting and reflecting. Refers to all data collected in the field in the course of the study.
2. Useful for chronicling longitudinal information about individuals, groups, activities, and so forth.	2. Used to gain specific information in descriptive form that bears on a question or questions of interest (e.g., to monitor implementation of school-wide rules).	2. Useful for recording "everything" in sequence and unselectively about what subjects do, say, and what the situation is. May be less useful for recording longitudnal information unless many records are collected over time.	2. Used to record information obtained during participant observation.
3. No particular systematic training needed. Presumption of reasonable use of written language. Diarykeeper must understand the question of interest and the theoretical framework to record appropriate information.	3. Recorder is usually a person in the setting in a position to observe directly. Requires (a) definition of field of observation, person, place, situation, behavior to be set up in advance; (b) definition of behavioral criteria to determine which incidents are critical.	3. Requires an observer trained in the conceptual framework or tradition guiding the observations.	3. Requires an observer trained in field work techniques and in the conceptual framework or tradition guiding the observation. Training insures consistency of recording of observations.

the study. The duration of the observation can be a single event, a critical incident, or a longer period (e.g., the first day of school, the first hour of school, the first 2 weeks of school for the first hour). As in the case of descriptive systems, researchers using narrative systems consider meaning to be situation specific. The data recorded are constrained by the observer's perceptual framework, acuity, training, and written or oral fluency. (See the discussion on narrative systems in the section on units of observation for additional information.)

Technological records are live recordings of events, processes, and groups. Records are obtained by using electronic devices that make permanent records (e.g. videotapes, audiotapes, videodiscs). This record is raw data and must be acted upon systematically in order to construct data or representations of events. Technological records can be used in combination with any of the other systems depending upon the researcher's goals and questions. The decisions involved in placement of the camera, in gaining access, in selecting the locus of observation are some of the factors that influence the types of information that can be obtained from these records. (See Erickson & Wilson, 1982 for a comprehensive discussion.) Periods of recording will vary depending upon the question under study. (See the section on units of observation for additional information about technological records.)

General Goals of the User. The final class of distinctions that will be considered involve the goals of the investigator. Users of *categorical systems* are generally concerned with studying a wide range of classrooms in order to obtain normative data and to identify general laws of teaching. Little focus is given to individual cases, except to identify contrastive groups (e.g. more- and less-effective classroom managers). Within-case variations are less often considered.

Users of *descriptive systems* are generally concerned with obtaining a detailed description of observed phenomena in order to explain developing processes, and to identify generic principles by exploring specific processes. The purpose of this work is to explore both within and across occurrences (cases) of specific phenomena (type case analyses) and to contrast findings in one setting with those in other settings (Erickson & Shultz, 1981; Florio & Shultz, 1979; Green & Harker, 1982). Of concern are questions such as how two contexts are functionally equivalent; what behaviors are stable across situations; and which are situation specific. In other words, issues of functioning within a case and across cases from a comparative perspective are considered.

Narrative System users are also concerned with obtaining detailed descriptions of observed phenomena in order to explain unfolding processes and to identify generic principles and patterns of behavior within specific events. The goal is to understand not only what is occurring but to identify factors that influence the occurrence of this behaviors. Like descriptive systems, the key is to assemble a broad picture of the phenomena under consideration. Differences in intent influence what will be done and how it will be done (see Table 6.3). For example, a school psychologist using a specimen record or a critical incident technique will record behaviors to obtain data about a specific student who needs an intervention program or about an ongoing problem. In contrast, an ethnographer using a specimen record will record (e.g. descriptive field notes) different information, information about the nature of the classroom or phenomena as a social process or social system.

Finally, the goal of the user of the *technological record* is to obtain a permanent recording of an event or phenomenon so that it can be studied in greater depth at a later time. The goal and theoretical framework of the researcher as well as the question under study will influence what is recorded.

The observation systems described above are tools that can be used to study a wide variety of educational phenomena. Each system, however, will record a different segment of reality; each obtains a different level and type of description of the observed phenomena; each stores information in different forms; and each permits retrieval of different types of information. In other words, the structures of the different instruments constrain and influence the nature of the information that can be obtained about the observed phenomena. The range of different types of instruments described above means that the researcher has a variety of options. The task is to select from this range of methods or tools the one or ones best suited to both the question and the phenomena under study.

The Systems, Units of Observation, and Aggregation of Data

The discussion above described the general structure of observation instruments. In this section, the nature of these systems will be elaborated further and the nature of units of observation found within observational systems will be considered. The issue of what units of observation are is complex. Units of observation must be considered in a variety of ways. First, a diversity of units exists. For example, Fassnacht (1982), in an extensive treatise on observation theory and practice, identified nineteen different units. Table 6.4 provides a brief description of these.

The description of units in Table 6.4, while useful in demonstrating the diversity of units of observation, is not meant to be a definitive statement of units or a set of definitions for the discussion that follows. This discussion is meant to serve primarily as a point of departure for the discussion of units and their relationship to systems of observation.

Second, each unit of observation represents an independent variable in that it is not manipulated overtly. However, during data analysis any given unit can function as a dependent variable for analysis purposes. For example, in a correlational study, measures (units of observation) of student engagement and success in class activities could be correlated with certain teacher behaviors (Fisher et al., 1980). In a descriptive study the researcher could explore shifts in behaviors (e.g., ways of bidding for a turn at talk) within and across lessons to determine whether students had acquired a particular social rule or norm of behavior (Hammersley, 1974; Stoffan-Roth, 1981). Third, units of observation can be aggregated during the data analysis phase of the study to form larger classes of units. For example, praise (Brophy, 1979) and attention (May, 1981) have been found to be multifaceted phenomena. Fourth, by identifying patterns across units of observation, new descriptive units can

Table 6.4. Terms for Behavioral Units

Type of Unit	General Definition
1. Natural units	Detected through the perceptual system and reflected in natural language (Barker & Wright, 1955). Perceived as breaks in streams of behavior.
2. Units of behavior	Can be described as a natural unit also. Laws of perceiving forms are also valid for behavioral forms. Just as there are forms in the world of objects, there are dynamic and temporal configurations (e.g., direction or speed of movement, position of the body).
3. Inductive vs. deductive	Refers to the process by which units are constructed. For inductive units, one starts with the behavior and attempts to classify (e.g., ethology). For deductive units, units are derived from theory, hypotheses, or logical propositions.
4. Directly observable vs. inferred	Two types are distinguished: those that are on principle invisible (e.g. a person's intentions, emotions, thoughts), and those that are invisible due to circumstances (e.g., instances when the observer cannot see the behavior because of an obstacle). Both instances require inference. The issues involved here are not so much whether inference should be used but at what stage in the data collection.
5. Descriptive vs. evaluative	The former notes concrete behaviors and suspends judgments. The latter summarizes and assesses a series of behaviors (e.g., one can observe a child for 30 minutes and conclude he is angry, or one can record the concrete behaviors which could lead to that judgment.)
6. Phenomenological	Behaviors that have the same form (Brannigan & Humphries, 1972).
7. Morphological	Similar to a phenomenological unit with emphasis on the formal or structural aspects of the behavior as criteria for constructing.
8. Units based on factor analysis	Units are based on dimensions emerging from the statistical analysis (see Emmer & Peck, 1973).
9. Discrete vs. continuous	This refers to the extent to which it is possible to count or measure behaviors. The issue of discreteness vs. continuousness arises with the use of rating scales.
10. Simple vs. complex	Two views exist of these types of units. The first views the uniqueness of the human cortex to analyze complex events and relies on ratings of complex concepts (Langer, Schulz, & Thun, 1974). The second is the construction of complex units out of already observed simple ones (Richards & Bernal, 1972).
11. Indices as units	Composed of various indicators drawn together. Mentioned more frequently in the sociological literature than in the psychological literature.
12. Reductionist	These are the result of finding the smallest unit of meaning, not necessarily the smallest observable unit. To be meaningful, it must have a particular meaning for the observer of the behavior or evoke a particular response in a partner.
13. Causal	Behaviors with a common cause are regarded as identical.
14. Functional	A unit defined with respect to its effect or context. The emphasis is on the importance of the context.
15. Situations as units	If one is concerned with behavior which is to some extent rule bound and has recurrent elements, then situations can be viewed as units. More precisely such a unit should be comprised of both situation and behavior. Barker and Wright (1955) regard their "behavior setting" as such a unit.
16. Molecular	
17. Molar	Both terms are taken from Barker and Wright (1955). Molecular units are known as actones and molar units are actions (e.g., molecular: perspiration; molar: hurrying to school).
18. Time units	These refer to time intervals of time-sampling methods and to any time-derived measures used for behavior observation.
19. Action units or events	Conceptually similar to behavior unit and natural units, but is distinguished by its form and content.

Note. Adapted from *Theory and Practice of Observing Behaviour* (pp.76–81) by G. Fassnacht, 1982, London: Academic Press. Copyright 1982 by Academic Press. Reprinted by permission.

be constructed. For example, Mehan (1979a) identified a pattern of initiation–response–evaluation. This unit is composed of a series of smaller units, adjacency pairs (e.g., initiation–response; response–evaluation).

The issue of units of observation, therefore, is related to both data collection and data analysis. The units selected constrain what can be reported. They are lexical items (words/morphemes) in a system of language (Fassnacht, 1982.) The relationships between and among units, as specified by the framework guiding the systems, make up the grammar of the system. An observational system, therefore, is a language system. That is, it determines what can be described and which aspects of the phenomena are described. Fassnacht (1982) captures the issues succinctly:

> Decisions about units are of great importance insofar as they establish principles with regard to the statements that can be made about a topic before anything has been discovered about it. By deciding on certain units, the nature of the relationships that can subsequently be discovered is defined. One can neither discover nor construct anything beyond the limits imposed by these units. The unit defines, so to speak, the intellectual limits of possible statements and only allows relationships within the context. (p.57)

This statement highlights how the selection of units is a central issue in observational research. It also emphasizes the relationship between the choice of unit and the framework guiding the study as well as the relationship between the choice of unit and the nature of the description obtained. The choice of units depends on the theoretical, philosophical, experience, or commitment basis of the framework that guides the observational study (Dunkin & Biddle, 1974). Different frameworks require and lead to different units. These frameworks reflect different foci. Another way to think about this issue is that "different units emerge depending on whether one bases them on their structural or functional aspects, their content or the way they are collected, their purpose or their relationship with other units" (Fassnacht, 1982, p. 76). Before proceeding to the discussion of the relationship between different types of systems and units of observation, two additional facts about units uncovered during the exploration of this topic will be presented. These facts and the discussion above form a general frame for the considerations of units and systems that follow. First, no simple dichotomy or continuum can be used to classify or explore the different units. Units tend to overlap; they may represent different levels of context; different levels may exist within a general category (e.g. within natural units, behavioral units, deductive units); units may take a variety of forms and may include a range of different types of content. Second, some units are used to record information and are determined on an a priori basis. Other units are constructed from smaller recorded units to permit analysis of data. Still others are constructed during analysis and are products of the analysis.

To illustrate some of the points, one type of unit, natural units, will be explored without reference to specific instruments. The remainder of the units will not be considered individually, but will be considered by system type: categorical systems, descriptive systems, narrative systems, and technological records. No attempt will be made to cover each unit identified by Fass-

nacht (1982) presented in Table 6.4 or to adhere to those definitions. Rather they serve as a point of departure.

Natural units are defined by Fassnacht (1982) as breaks in streams of behavior (cf. Barker, 1963, 1968; Barker & Wright, 1955). Where the stream of behavior being observed is segmented depends on the theoretical orientation or the conceptualization of the process that frames the recording, analysis, and/or construction of the units of observation. Fassnacht (1982) argues that what makes a natural unit natural is not that it is reality itself, but that reality has determined the unit. Another way to view this type of unit is that it was not constructed by the observer first, but rather the observer described a naturally occurring event. A natural unit, therefore, is a phenomenon that is perceived by members of a particular social group or culture as real. For example, in many classrooms, reading groups are natural units. They are organized by teachers in the environment and are understood to be segments in the school day by all members of the classroom, school, and community. They exist in a particular time slot in the school day; they have specific rights and obligations for participation associated with them; they have specific content associated with them; they have particular configurations of participants from the total classroom group; and they have been created to meet specific goals. These units are defined by the reality of classroom life.

Such units can exist on both a micro/molecular level and a macro/molar level. The community, the school, the classroom, and even the reading group are molar units or micro units relative to each other and other segments of reality. In classrooms, reading groups may be seen as micro or macro. They are less than the total composite of a classroom, therefore, they do not reflect all of classroom life. The reading group defined this way is a micro unit. However, in contrast to a peer tutorial situation or an individual student working alone, reading groups would be molar units. In comparison to the community or the school, classrooms are micro units. The size of the unit varies with the focus selected. The same unit can be both micro or macro depending on the framework used and the way the unit is conceptualized. All of these units are natural units.

Natural units can also exist beyond the setting or episode level. A natural unit for a sociolinguist interested in studying classroom communication and classroom life might be narrative forms of discourse (e.g., Cazden this volume; Cochran-Smith, 1984; Cook-Gumperz, in press; Michaels, 1981; Scollon & Scollon, 1984), instances of requests (Wilkinson & Calculator, 1982), or ways students get help from teachers (Cooper, Ayres-Lopez, & Marquis, 1981; Merritt, 1982). They can also be sequences of talk, questioning patterns, norms for participation, the nature of peer interaction, and nonverbal behavior. (For examples, see edited volumes by Borman, 1982; Cazden et al., 1972; Cook-Gumperz, in press; Garnica & King, 1979; Gilmore & Glatthorn, 1982; Green, Harker, & Wallat, in press; Green & Wallat, 1981a; Hymes, 1981; Trueba et al., 1981; Wilkinson, 1982). Natural units can vary depending on the theoretical frame used. Natural units for the ecological psychologist (e.g., Barker, 1963, 1968; Barker & Wright, 1955; Gump, 1969; Moos, 1976) will differ from those used by the ethologist (e.g. Blurton-Jones, 1972; Lorenz, 1981). The units identified by researchers from these disciplines will differ from those units used by educational psychologists, linguists, social psychologists, clinical psychologists, sociologists, behaviorists, phenomenologists, and so forth.

The brief discussion above suggests that units can overlap and can co-occur. They are determined within the specific framework guiding the study or observation. They will differ in size, scope, content, level, function, and structure. In preparing for observation, careful consideration must be given to which units are used and to how they are to be determined and constructed. In the remainder of this section, different types of units associated with each of the different classifications of observation systems will be highlighted: categorical systems, descriptive systems, narrative systems, and technological records. This discussion is not intended to be all-inclusive; rather, illustrative examples of units from each of these systems will be provided. Also included will be a discussion of some of the issues related to units from the various systems. Before turning to the discussion of the units within each classification, one additional point should be made. The classification of systems presented in this chapter was constructed to provide a framework for distinguishing among the ways of recording observations that have been used in research on teaching. The first class of systems is usually referred to in the literature as "category systems" (categorical systems in the classification in this chapter) and the nature and structure of these has been well documented elsewhere (e.g., Dunkin & Biddle, 1974; Gordon & Jester, 1973; Rosenshine & Furst, 1973; Simon & Boyer, 1970). The other classes of systems were formulated to reflect the nature and structure of those systems. In addition, narrative and descriptive systems and technological records tend to be relatively recent developments in educational research and have not as yet received extensive treatment. For this reason the discussion of these systems is more elaborated than that for categorical systems.

UNITS AND CATEGORICAL SYSTEMS

As suggested in Tables 6.1 and 6.2, categorical systems are closed systems with units of observation specified on an a priori basis. A limited set of units is used with any particular instrument and units are tallied in some manner.

The units within a checklist, category system, or rating scale can be viewed in a variety of ways. First, the units are generally derived deductively. Researchers have used a variety of perspectives to select and/or construct the units for the system. While in the past units have generally been deductively derived, there is no theoretical or conceptual reason that units for a category system, checklist, or ration scale could not be determined inductively. That is, the items for these categorical systems could be derived from data from an earlier study or from a current study. If a technological record was used (e.g., videotape or audiotape) then a category system or checklist could be developed from inductively derived units. This inductively derived system could then be applied to the technological record. In this way the findings of one or more studies that identified a series of patterns could be used to design a category system, checklist, or rating scale.

Second, units in category systems and checklists generally reflect a behavioral stance (e.g., Berliner, 1978; Brophy & Good, 1970b). That is, dynamic, temporal configurations are perceived as behavior units (Fassnacht, 1982). Each behavioral unit tends to represent a wide variety of forms. For example, the verbal dimensions of teaching are reflected in a group of ten categories in the Flanders Interaction Analysis System (Flanders, 1970). Each category is a behavioral unit and represents a different, discrete type of behavior. For example, all student talk was placed in either a category labeled "Student initiation" or in one labeled "student talk." Other researchers have differentiated these categories to a greater degree (e.g., Ober, Bentley, & Miller, 1971). Teacher talk in Flanders' system was represented by seven categories. Four categories were assumed to represent teachers' indirect influence (e.g., accepts feelings, praises or encourages, accepts or uses ideas of students, and asks questions). Three categories were assumed to reflect teachers' direct influence (e.g., lectures, gives directions, and criticizes or justifies authority). The final category represented silence or confusion. This system was designed to be used on line (live). Regardless of content, all teacher and student behaviors were coded in one of the ten categories. While greater numbers of behaviors or units were used in other category systems, the format of these systems and the assumptions underlying many of them are similar to the Flanders' System (See Simon & Boyer, 1970a, 1970b for a general review of category systems; see Medley, Soar, & Coker, 1984; Hough, 1980a, 1980b, 1980c and Stallings, 1983 for examples of more recent systems.)

Third, units within category systems and checklists are also discrete units and simple units. Each behavior observed is coded in only one category. One exception, however, is with sign systems where the observer indicates all behaviors that apply. In addition, the units within these systems reflect only directly observed behaviors.

Finally, in contrast to category systems and checklists, rating systems include continuous rather than discrete units. For example, one type of rating scale uses a semantic differential format (Osgood, Suci, & Tannenbaum, 1957). This approach creates a continuous unit (e.g., individual attention by teacher to group instruction by teacher). The observer places a mark on a point between the two units to reflect which variable occurred most frequently or the intensity of the occurrence of the variable. (For examples of this approach see Marshall, Hartsough, Green, & Lawrence, 1977; Marshall & Weinstein, 1982; and Remmers, 1963 for a detailed discussion). Other types of rating scales require the observer to record a single rating (e.g., percentage of occurrence of a behavior; degree or intensity of occurrence—high, medium or low). Rating scales may also include units based on factor analysis (Emmer & Peck, 1973) and units that require some degree of observer inference.

To summarize, a variety of units of observation have been used for category systems in general: deductive units, behavioral units, and discrete units. Category systems and checklists have also included simple units, molecular units, and directly observable units. Rating systems add continuous units, units based on factor analysis, and inferred units. Additionally, they can include micro or molar units. As the foregoing discussion demonstrates, no single unit is related to all systems classified as categorical systems; rather, different units are found in various systems. While units vary by system, some aspects of categorical systems are the same. In categorical systems units are determined and the relationship between units is specified prior to data collection and analysis. Therefore, the construction of new units is not done during collection and rarely done during analysis.

As noted in Table 6.1, descriptive systems are open systems. While these may have preset categories, the categories can be combined in a variety of ways in order to construct systematic descriptions of evolving lessons and to segment streams of behavior. Streams of behavior (both verbal and nonverbal) are recorded using symbols of everyday language. In some instances, the verbal symbols are then translated into other types of symbols (e.g., dance notation, graphic forms) that reflect the actions, forms, or functions of the observed behaviors. Central to the descriptive system is the use of transcriptions of the flow of talk in the lesson or observed context.

The need to have transcriptions of talk and/or actions means that descriptive systems are not used for on-line recordings. Regardless of the ways data are coded or recorded in written form, all descriptive systems depend upon permanent records of observed events. That is, descriptive systems are used in conjunction with technological records. In most instances, the person who will be analyzing and coding data was also involved in making the technological record. The technological record provides the basis for (a) in-depth analyses of evolving streams of behavior, (b) identification of patterns of behavior within the ongoing sequences, (c) identification and construction of new units of observation, (d) testing of identified patterns across time and situations, and (e) analyses of data from a variety of complementary perspectives. In addition, the existence of a permanent record allows the researcher to use the record with participants in a stimulated recall format to obtain the participants' perspectives on what was occurring and to validate the observed patterns in a form of triangulation (e.g., Elliott, 1976; Morine-Dershimer, 1981, in press-a, in press-b).

Units of observation related to descriptive systems are both deductive and inductive. Such units can be selected on an a priori basis or derived from the analysis procedures. The a priori units are both natural and micro units. They are based on a conceptualization of what teachers do; that is, on what types of pedagogical moves they make (e.g., Bellack et al., 1966; Namuddu, 1982); on a theoretical perspective about the nature of communication (e.g., research on conversational analysis, ethnography of communication, ethnomethodology, sociolinguistics, and sociology of language); or on nonverbal actions (e.g., Birdwhistell, 1970; Duncan & Fiske, 1977; Duncan & Niederehe, 1974; Galloway, 1971, 1984; Hall, 1966; Harper, Wiens, & Matarazzo, 1978; Knapp, 1978; Scheflen, 1972; Woolfolk & Brooks, 1983). The units used to guide descriptions are drawn from theoretical research in different disciplines. In addition, the relationships between units are also specified on a conceptual or theoretical base. For example, from conversational analysis, discourse analysis, ethnography of communication, and sociolinguistics come the descriptors of linguistic elements of conversation. These elements become units of analysis on a micro level. Units include, but are not limited to, chunks of discourse (e.g., conversations or episodes, utterances/sentences, phrases, words, phonemes, speech events, speech

acts, etc.). Rules of discourse and syntax help specify the relationships between elements.

The type of unit and the relationship that exists between units are related to the question under study as well as the theoretical framework in which the analysis is grounded (e.g., conversational analysis, sociolinguistics, psycholinguistics). For example, using the construct of adjacency pairs in conversation, Mehan (1979a) found that many teacher–student interaction sequences had a structure that he labeled the I–R–E (initiation–response–evaluation) sequence. This unit may be a simple question, followed by a response which is then followed by an evaluative statement about the response or which can be a series of exchanges tied to each other through adjacency pairs (Sacks, Schegloff, & Jefferson, 1974). This sequence begins with an initiation and proceeds through a series of turns until the initiator receives the expected response as indicated by the nature of the evaluation (Mehan, 1979a, 1979b). The micro units are tied together in ways specified by communication or conversational theory (e.g., through cohesion ties, adjacency pairs, etc). In linguistically based descriptive approaches, then, the micro units are units constructed to allow researchers to talk about elements of conversation, and the relationships between the units are specified by the theoretical frame guiding the study. For a related discussion of linguistic units see the discussion of criteria for adequate observation at the end of the first section of this chapter.

Within descriptive systems, micro units are used to construct more molar units. (For examples of systematic work using this framework see Adelman, 1981; Au, 1980; Barnes & Todd, 1977; Barr, in press; Barr & Dreeban, 1983; Bellack et al., 1966; Bloome, 1981, in press; Cochran-Smith, 1984; Collins, 1983, in press; Edwards & Furlong, 1978; Frederiksen, 1981; Gilmore, in press; Green et al., in press; Green & Wallat, 1981b; Lundgren, 1977; Mehan, 1979a; Sinclair & Coulthard, 1975; Stubbs, 1983; Wilkinson, 1982.) In other words, the micro units are discrete units that can be combined to form more molar units that are inductively determined. The level of analysis depends on the theoretical framework guiding the individual study. However, as suggested above, all of the descriptive systems depend on permanent records and some form of transcriptions of these records.

Transcriptions of audio and videotape records contain both micro units and natural units. How the transcription is made depends on the theoretical requirements of the researcher. Transcription is a principled process (Cochran-Smith, 1984; Heap, 1980a; Mishler, 1984; Ochs, 1979; Stubbs et al., 1979). For example, some researchers require transcripts with detailed information about pauses, intonation patterns, stress patterns, false starts, hesitations, and other such paralinguistic and contextualization cues (e.g., Collins, 1983, in press; Cook-Gumperz & Gumperz, 1976; Corsaro, 1985). Others can use transcripts with less detail. For some researchers transcriptions can be made on a turn-by-turn-at-speaking basis. That is, notations are made on the transcript each time a new speaker begins to talk. For some researchers transcriptions must be made on less than a turn-by-turn level. That is, the transcriptions must reflect the propositional structure of talk (e.g., Frederiksen, 1975, 1981; Green & Harker, 1982; Harker, in press) or the individual social message units (e.g., Bloome, 1981; Green & Wallat, 1979,

1981b). The way in which the units in a transcript will be formalized will depend on the theoretical and conceptual needs of the researcher as well as the nature of the process and the level of the process under study. In addition, some transcription processes require the addition of nonverbal information. Aspects of the form as well as the content of the transcription are units of observation. Transcriptions are natural units and are also the basis for, or rather the data for, the construction of other types of units. In the process of transcription the way talk is displayed is a theoretical statement about what units are important and about the relationship of units.

A number of other units of observation are related to descriptive systems: functional units, situations as units, inferred units. First, functional units will be considered. One way to think about functional units is to consider the purpose the observed behavior serves. For example, not all talk presented in question form is a request for information or is meant to elicit information. Some questions actually serve an imperative function or are forms of indirect requests (Ramirez, in press; Sinclair & Coulthard, 1975; Wilkinson & Calculator, 1982). Consideration of how the talk unit is functioning permits construction of categories that become functional units. This view of functional units is constructed by exploring the goals of patterns of actions. When the goals of larger patterns of action are considered, situations as units can be identified (e.g, letter writing is occurring, students are playing a game). From this perspective, situations can be considered as constructed by what people are doing, how they are doing it, and what definitions they have of these actions. The structural and functional aspects of these units can be inferred by considering how participants hold each other accountable for the actions and meanings that occur (cf. Barker, 1963, 1968; Erickson & Shultz, 1981; McDermott, 1976; Philips, 1972, 1982). By considering the rights and obligations for participation and the structural aspects of situations, researchers are able to construct and explore situations as units of observation (e.g., Barker & Wright, 1955; Bossert, 1979; Erickson & Shultz, 1981; Florio & Shultz, 1979; Green & Harker, 1982; Philips, 1972, 1982; Wallat & Green, 1982).

The last units to be explored are inferred units. These units are a central part of the inquiry process used in conjunction with most descriptive systems. In most studies in which descriptive systems are used, higher level or molar units are constructed from groupings of micro/molecular units. The basis for such groupings may be theoretical or conceptual frameworks that specify the relationship between units, or they can be inferred from patterns of observed actions or behaviors. The process of making inferences is principled and the basis of such inferences is a part of the inquiry process related to the construction of grounded theory (cf. Glaser & Strauss, 1967). As suggested above, by observing ways people engage in everyday events, how tasks are structured, how people hold each other accountable, and what definitions they hold for tasks, researchers can extract natural units and develop descriptions of ongoing events. Inferred units, therefore, are a central part of descriptive systems. The differences in units are often due to the differences in the frameworks guiding the inferencing process (e.g., anthropology, cognitive science, linguistics, developmental psychology, ecological psychology, educational psychology,

social psychology, sociology, and phenomenology, among others.

To summarize, a variety of units of observation have been used with descriptive systems: inductive units, deductive units, natural units, discrete units, inferred units, units of behavior, molecular units, molar units, functional units, and situations as units. While not all-inclusive, this list is representative of the different units generally found in these relatively new types of observation and analysis systems. They are products of the current phase of observational studies, Phase Four: the expansion and consolidation phase referred to at the beginning of this chapter. Descriptive systems tend to be approaches in which units are both specified on an a priori basis and are constructed during the inquiry/observational process or analysis process. In other words, descriptive systems tend to be based on a retrospective analysis of recorded events. This approach to observation permits in-depth, detailed description and analysis of evolving events and conversations within events and exploration of the comparability of events, observations, and so forth. It also permits construction of variables and units of observation that can be used within the corpus of recorded events to explore the nature of observed phenomena and patterns within the data. Descriptive systems, therefore, are integrally tied to technological records.

NARRATIVE SYSTEMS

As noted in Tables 6.1 and 6.2, narrative systems are open systems, have no predetermined categories, and record broad segments of events or behaviors in oral or written form. While each of the types of narrative systems — diaries/journals, critical incident records, specimen records, and field notes — require oral and /or written records, the ways they are recorded or collected make the form, content, and scope of these systems different from both categorical systems and descriptive systems. Differences are related, in part, to the fact that the observer is the primary instrument of observation. That is, what is recorded is not necessarily specified on an a priori basis; rather what is recorded depends largely on the observer's perceptual system and ability to capture in everyday language what is observed. In other words, researchers' perceptions and training, as well as their oral and written language abilities, influence what will be recorded and how it will be recorded. The narrative approach, therefore, is dependent on the individual doing the observing.

Units of observation related to narrative systems are both similar to and different from those for categorical systems and descriptive systems. As in the case of categorical and descriptive systems, the locus of observation is predetermined. The observer decides who will be observed, what will be observed, and where and when observations will occur. The observer records information in everyday language. A narrative record, then, is a form of natural unit or rather a record of naturally occurring actions, events, behaviors, and so forth. In this way, a narrative record is more like a technological record than either a categorical system or a descriptive system. The observer in making a narrative record records a wide slice of life. No attempt is made to filter what occurred in any systematic way although a specific lens can be used (eg., management of events, sequences of teacher–student interaction). A narrative record, therefore, becomes a permanent record of what was observed (e.g., Becker, 1970; Corsaro, 1985; Denham & Lieberman, 1980; Evertson, Anderson, & Clements, 1980; Evertson, Emmer, & Clements, 1980; Marshall & Weinstein, 1982; McCall & Simmons, 1969; Pelto & Pelto, 1977; Sevigny, 1981; Spradley, 1980).

The locus of observation is a deductively derived unit. That is, the nature of the question, past research, and past units can be used to select macro level/molar units such as situations as units, actions as units, units of behavior, phenomenological units, and functional units. These units can serve as loci of observation within a given setting. They can also be derived inductively from the narrative records. The type of unit selected and the information recorded depend on the conceptual or theoretical framework guiding the observation.

Narrative records are constructed in two ways: during observation and after observation. Three of the four types of narrative systems described in Tables 6.1 and 6.2 use narrative records made during the period of observation: critical incident records, specimen records, and field notes. Diary or journal records and some forms of field notes are made after the event. Each of these will be considered in turn. Since there is a relationship between the way a record is made of the observation and the units that can be derived from the record, the discussion will explore issues in recording related to each system.

Critical incident records are made either on line or in a retrospective manner. The observer records information in narrative form about the implementation of a particular practice (e.g., a school-wide set of rules) or a particular type of behavior (e.g., disruptive behavior). The recorder uses a specific frame to guide what is recorded (e.g., the definition of behaviors to be observed). Discrete units such as place, person, situation, and type of behavior to be observed are set in advance. Patterns of behavior are recorded in everyday language. These patterns are extracted from the text to create observation units. Observation units are inferred from the behaviors recorded on the narrative record. These patterns become descriptors of the incident observed. The narrative record is a context for interpreting and inferring these units; the records are not data in and of themselves. Additionally, the patterns identified can be classified to construct more molar level units. Units, therefore, are both deductively and inductively derived. They can include behaviors, situations, actions, conversations, structure of phenomena, and so forth. The observer is the critical element, since the observer is the instrument of observation and recording. The structure of the record stems from the observer's training, theoretical perspective, and the type of information required in the study. The critical incident record, therefore, can be viewed as a constrained system that records a specific slice of reality, one defined in advance and guided by a specific framework or theory.

Specimen descriptions are more detailed than critical incident records. The aim of this type of recording is to obtain descriptions of events that are systematic and intensive on-line records. The observer records the behavior that occurs during a designated time period. The goal is to obtain an uninterrupted stream of behavior with as much detail as possible. Recording is not intentionally selective. The observer records what a selected subject does and says, as well as the information about the setting. Other individuals are recorded only in relationship to the person selected for observation. The recorder attempts to make a chronological record of all of the main steps in any action (e.g., goes to the blackboard; writes an answer to the problem correctly; returns to seat). Interpretation is avoided. Information is recorded from a participant perspective (cf. Barker & Wright, 1955).

Once the specimen record has been made, the observer segments the streams of behavior into episodes that reflect the action or situation. Episodes are constructed by viewing behaviors in an episode as having a consistent direction, as being goal directed (cf. Barker & Wright, 1955). Behaviors, therefore, are viewed as leading the "subject towards a particular behavioral goal" (Fassnacht, 1982, p. 175). Episodes are natural units. They can also be considered, or can contain, behavior units, action units, and/or situation units. As with categorical and descriptive systems, specimen records permit the identification and construction of a variety of types of units. Each contributes different information about the observed phenomena and each provides a different type and level of description.

Field notes, like specimen records and critical incident reports, depend on the observer as the instrument of observation to obtain narrative records. Field notes are generally associated with participant observation in anthropology (e.g, Pelto & Pelto, 1977; Sanday, 1976; Spradley, 1980) and in sociology (Becker, 1970; McCall & Simmons, 1969). Participant observation has been used in ethnographic studies of educational processes and settings.

To understand the types of units that can be identified or constructed from narrative records made during participant observation, a brief discussion of the nature of this method needs to be considered. Participant observation is used to study the ways of living of a culture or social group. Participant observation ranges from active to passive participation (Spradley, 1980). Active participation means that the observer becomes involved in events and records events after the fact. This type of participant observation allows the observer to capture the *insider's perspective*, to record the events as they were perceived by a participant in the event. Passive participant observation means that the observer does not participate in the events but remains an *outsider* to the event or the setting. In both instances, the observer records the ways of living of the social group under study.

What gets observed and recorded depends on both the framework guiding the participant observation and the type of ethnography used — e.g., comprehensive, topic centered, and hypothesis testing (Hymes, 1981). Comprehensive ethnography explores an entire society or social group and its relationship to the larger society (e.g., Ogbu, 1981). A topic-centered ethnographic approach focuses on an aspect of a social group or society — e.g., literacy (Collins, in press; Gilmore, in press; Heath, 1982, 1983; Szwed, 1977; Taylor, 1983) or schooling (Hymes, 1981; Noblit, 1982; Smith & Geoffrey, 1968; Spindler, 1982). Hypothesis-testing ethnography is an ethnographic study framed by a specific theory. For example, the Whitings (Whiting, 1963) used socialization theory to frame a study of socialization practices in six cultures. Cook-Gumperz, Gumperz, and Simons (1981) used discourse theory, reading theory, conversational analysis theory, and other related work to frame a study of communication in classrooms and the ways in which communication leads to evaluation of performance. (For additional information see the discussion on observation as inquiry later in this chapter.) While these types of ethnography may appear discrete, in reality they represent different points on a continuum. Additionally, they may co-occur. For example, a single study may have different levels of context sampled, use past theory to frame aspects of the study (e.g., communication between participants; reading processes), and select specific phenomena to explore in more depth (e.g., narrative performance, reading groups, playgrounds).

Each of these approaches uses narrative records to freeze the events being observed. However, given the difference in purpose, the type of information will vary to some degree. For example, those working with teacher–student communication will require more information about the type of talk that occurred. The observer focusing on teacher–student talk will want to supplement the narrative record of the event with a technological record. Participant observation, then, like the other narrative approaches and categorical and descriptive systems, is influenced by the questions being asked and the framework guiding the study.

Like specimen records, once the narrative records are made, the streams of behavior are indexed (e.g., Erickson, Cazden, Carrasco, & Guzman, 1978–1981; Griffin, as cited in Merritt & Humphrey, 1981). That is, events and episodes are identified. Information about who is participating, what contexts were created by participants, the nature of the events, and so forth are transcribed for each record. The indexing permits identification of potentially functionally equivalent events and processes (Erickson & Shultz, 1981; Florio & Shultz, 1979) across days and observations within the corpus. The indexed information may contain information on a variety of types of units: phenomenological units, situations as units, behaviors as units, action units. The specific types of units indexed will depend on the goals of the researcher. While indexing has been considered theoretically for field notes and technological records (audio- and videotapes), this procedure is an important step in all observational studies.

The units within narrative systems are dependent on the descriptions recorded. While general information recorded on field notes is information about the unfolding events, observers often record other information about the nature of the process (e.g., Corsaro, 1981; Scvigny, 1981). Corsaro (1981) reports taking four types of field notes: personal notes, methodological notes, theoretical notes, and descriptive notes. The latter type of notes, descriptive notes, are those reported above. *Methodological notes* refer to issues related to placement of equipment, positioning of the observer, gaining access to the setting, and recording information. The observer records all decisions made during the inquiry cycle. *Personal notes* refer to personal observations or reactions and to things to remember or consider. *Theoretical notes* refer to ties to theory and to observed patterns. The observer records hypotheses generated within the situation and makes notes on patterns observed in one event so that they can be explored in other situations. The four sets of notes help to provide systematic information about the inquiry process and help frame the analyses of the data.

Field notes, therefore, are records in everyday language of observed phenomena, methodological decisions, theoretical ob-

servations, and other relevant information. In anthropology and sociology, field notes also refer to historical records, and other information obtained in the field (e.g., Pelto & Pelto, 1977).

Units of observation are constructed from information recorded on the field notes. Units of observation, therefore, are generally derived inductively. A wide variety of units can be derived by extracting patterns of behavior or segments of goal-directed behavior. These patterns can be sequences of behavior, situations, actions, or structures. In addition, the units observed in one observation or setting can be used to guide decisions about what to observe in subsequent sessions.

While field notes are generally used within an anthropological or sociological perspective, recent work on the study of teaching has also begun to use this form of narrative record (e.g., Evertson, Anderson, & Clements, 1980; Evertson, Emmer, & Clements, 1980; Fisher et al., 1978; Marshall & Weinstein, 1982). More information will be presented about these approaches in the section on observation as inquiry.

The final records and their related units are *journals* and *diaries*. These records are made retrospectively. They are not recorded live but rather capture the person's recalled knowledge of the event recorded (Florio & Clark, 1982; Yinger & Clark, 1981). These records permit longitudinal studies of events and people. As suggested in Table 6.3, records tend to be written, but no theoretical or conceptual reason exists that they could not be oral records (audiotape records). As with the other types of narrative records, the frame guiding the journal or diary writer influences what will be recorded and the observations depend on the perceptions and the recall of the writer/observer.

Patterns of behavior or situations are extracted from the text, thus creating units inferred from the narrative records. Units that guide collections (e.g., who, what, when) are derived deductively from past work and from the framework guiding the recording of information. As it is in the case of other narratives, units can also be derived inductively. Which units can be identified depends on the frame of the person writing the journal and the purpose for keeping it.

In summary, narrative records record unfolding events in varying degrees of detail. They can be written on-line or live *in situ* or can be written after the event. The information is taken down in everyday language in a chronological manner. Variety of types of units can be derived from the data. They can be derived both inductively and deductively. Units include: natural units, deductive units, inductive units, behavior units, situations as units, phenomenological units, action units, directly observable units, and inferred units.

TECHNOLOGICAL RECORDS

As indicated in Table 6.1, technological records include audiotape, videotape or videodisc records, and camera records. These instruments are open systems and tend to capture the widest segment of reality with little intervention of the observer. Once the observer sets the system in motion (e.g., audiotape or videotape), the events that occur in front of the camera lens or around the pick-up of the microphone are collected unselectively. Records may be made of specific events or behaviors. Therefore, they would involve deductive units, behavior units, and situational units that are set on an a priori basis. They are also *potential* sources of other types of units. Which units will be derived depends on the nature of the analysis used and the framework guiding the study.

Technological records may be used in conjunction with all of the other systems presented previously. The technological record may be used *in situ* with the other systems or may be a record to which the other systems are applied. In general then, units described for the previous systems can be derived from technological records. The permanence of the record makes multiple analyses, approaches, and the identification of a wide variety of complementary units or variables possible (e.g., Morine-Dershimer, in press-a, in press-b; Ramirez, in press; Shuy, in press; Tenenberg, in press).

SUMMARY

In the sections above the range or options available for describing phenomena were presented briefly. Each provides a different interpretation and representation of reality, since reality can "only be apprehended indirectly via signs and mechanisms of representation" (Fassnacht, 1982, p. 64). As noted above, interpretations and representations are the products of the conceptual framework guiding the study (Brophy, 1983; Delamont & Hamilton, 1976; Doyle, 1977; Sanders, 1981; Shulman, 1981). As Hamilton (n.d.) points out, "different frames of reference create different patterns of explanation" (p. 8). Units from this perspective "are inventions, not discoveries; interpretations, not descriptions" (Hamilton, n.d., p. 5). Units can also be thought of as samples of different aspects of reality as well as different levels of reality. Units, therefore, are variables constructed to help the observer reflect on various aspects of observed phenomena.

Issues in Sampling

The discussion of units of observation is also related to a discussion of sampling issues because each unit represents a selected aspect of reality, not the whole of reality. In this section three additional ways of viewing sampling will be presented: (a) issues of what is sampled, when and where; (b) issues of when sampling decisions are made; and (c) time issues in sampling.

When and Where. Berliner (1976) notes that "part of the answer is knowing *when* and *where* to observe" (p. 8). The requirement is to select an appropriate time and place to observe within the curriculum or stream of behavior. Selection of the wrong time and place wastes time and can invalidate findings. The problem is to select the time, place, and locus of observation that match the question under study. Herbert & Attridge (1975) identify five areas of decision making and sampling: (a) number of subjects; (b) total length of time of observation; (c) distribution of observation time; (d) likelihood of observations being representative of the phenomena under study; and (e) alternatives/options. Each of these decisions needs to be informed by the theoretical framework, past research, and/or a pilot or "orientation to the setting" phase. As discussed in the following section, without the latter, the researcher cannot insure the representativeness of the sample. The issue of what is sampled and where is a part of the broader issues of validity.

The issues above are also related to variability and stability of the behavior or phenomena under study, the environment in which the observation takes place, the characteristics of the subjects, and the nature of the inquiry cycle adopted. Problems may arise at *all* stages of an investigation and each decision may alter the validity of information obtained at other points in a study (Herbert & Attridge, 1975). A study conceived of this way is not based on a static, rigid approach, but rather on a dynamic one with a series of decision points, each of which is related to and influences what is collected and how it is collected. This view of sampling decisions leads to the second issue to be considered: when sampling decisions are made. (Additional factors related to sampling issues are presented by Linn, this volume and by Erickson, this volume.)

When Sampling Decisions Are Made. The two factors presented below were extracted from the review of the different observational systems discussed previously. From this review two general inquiry approaches with different sampling procedures were identified. These approaches can be thought of as differences in the inquiry cycle used by investigators. The first approach involves decisions made on an a priori basis. The second involves decisions made throughout the inquiry process. These approaches do not form a dichotomy; rather they can be considered as different ends of a continuum, illustrated in Figure 6.4, similar to the exclusive and inclusive context continuum presented earlier in this chapter.

Investigators that make all decisions on an a priori basis select the units of observation, the locus of observation, and determine the length of time and place of observation in advance. Issues of timing of observations and selection of events occur prior to beginning the study. Researchers who use this approach must be familiar with the setting to insure that what will be observed is representative of the phenomena to be studied. In addition, the researcher must ascertain whether or not the phenomena will occur in the context selected for study, and if it does occur, whether or not it occurs with sufficient frequency to be reliably identified (Shavelson & Dempsey-Atwood, 1976). Without considering the setting and the frequency of occurrence of the events selected for observation, the researcher may encounter problems with the validity and stability of the findings. For example, Wallat, Green, Conlin, & Haramis (1981) report the case of a teacher who was asked to record for 20 minutes a day the time spent in whole-group instruction. The teacher complied and recorded the time spent with children evaluating progress in the learning centers and directing children to center work. This was the only period in which the teacher met with the total group. The researcher, who had never visited the class, concluded that the teacher was the most dogmatic and authoritarian teacher in the study. Had he visited the classroom, he would have seen the teacher operate skillfully in

All decisions are made on an a priori basis. ———————— Decisions are made throughout the study.

Fig. 6.4. Sampling continuum.

an open structure setting. While this incident is an exception, it serves to highlight the need to be familiar with the setting and to represent accurately the nature of the phenomena to be studied.

The inquiry cycle for those studies at the far left end of the continuum is one in which the locus of observation and the timing of the observations are set in advance. After these are set, the researcher then gains access to the site(s) needed to carry out the study in a reliable, valid way. This approach, like all observational studies, requires that the observer gain access to the site and develop a level of trust and rapport with the participants. The observer needs to negotiate a contract with safeguards for the participants, thereby coming to an agreement with the participants that includes general human subjects protection and specifies how the information will be used as well as who will have access to the data and the results (e.g., Erickson & Wilson, 1982; Kimmel, 1981). This procedure helps to avoid situations such as those reported by Wallat et al. (1981), cited above. The research process or cycle at the far left is a multistep process in which the steps are taken to insure the validity of the decisions and choices in sampling.

At the far right of the continuum, sampling issues are encountered at various points within the inquiry cycle. The researcher begins with a general question and selects the setting(s) for study. The researcher then seeks to gain access to the setting, to develop trust and rapport with the participants, and to negotiate a contract to insure confidentiality and validity. In this type of inquiry cycle, general questions are asked, instruments are selected, collection procedures designed, data collected, and analyses begun. This process is then used to refine questions, select or add new collection procedures and loci of observation, and guide continued analyses. The cycle is reflexive; that is, it is not linear. Rather these stages tend to co-occur and are used to inform each other (e.g., Spradley, 1980).

While there are many similarities between these two approaches, one of the major differences is the size of the general sample. The studies at the left end of the continuum tend to employ a larger number of cases than those at the far right. Investigators who engage in research at the far left are generally interested in testing hypotheses and in the identification of general laws of behavior or norms of performance. Therefore, they must sample a large enough number of cases in order to generalize to other populations and settings. In contrast, those at the far right are generally interested in in-depth studies of a small number of cases. The purpose of these studies is to explore selected processes or settings in as much detail as possible, to generate hypotheses about the nature of these processes/settings, and then to test what is occurring both within and across cases.

Studies have recently been undertaken that also combine these approaches. These studies tend to be longitudinal or programmatic in nature. In such studies substudies are added, various aspects explored, and questions generated and refined. Sampling decisions within such work vary with the component under exploration (e.g., Cole, Griffin, & Newman, 1979; see also various studies by Cook-Gumperz, Gumperz, & Simons, and Evertson et al. in the section of this chapter dealing with observation as inquiry). Another body of work that fits between two general approaches is work in which multiple studies are done on the same body of data. This work is a form of secondary analysis in which the first study can be approached from either end of the continuum. The later studies are grounded in the earlier study, but may explore additional aspects of the phenomenon. For example, Merritt (1982; Merritt & Humphrey, 1981) elected to explore how students obtained help from teachers and how teachers gave help in a variety of contexts. Merritt reanalyzed data collected under a broader ethnographic study (Shuy & Griffin, 1981).

Time Sampling. Whether the researcher uses a normative approach, an in-depth approach, or a combination with a recursive inquiry cycle, time sampling and event sampling are the two most frequently used ways of selectively recording information. Time is used in at least three ways. First, time is used to specify the general boundaries of the observation period (e.g., the whole day, 1 hour, or 30 minutes). Second, time is used to designate the specified interval of recording of certain behaviors with an on-line category system (e.g., every 5 minutes; cf. Stallings, 1983). Third, small segments of time can be designated within a general period of observation. All occurrences of observed behaviors or events are then recorded using a checklist or rating scale. In addition, rating scales can also register the intensity of a particular event as well as the frequency of occurrence.

The first time-sampling method, the *period of observation*, involves a series of decisions. The investigator must determine the length of a specific day's observations, the sequencing of observations, and the distribution of observations over time. This first time-sampling method, therefore, allows one to collect information over time and over many occasions. The periods of observation are kept stable. If the period of time is the same, depending upon the observational system, one can explore what kinds of events, behaviors, actions, demands, constraints, and processes occur in this time period. The nature of the period of observation will be determined by the question under study. For example, if the research question focuses on how school gets started, then the investigator must sample the beginning of the day of the first days of school. If the question concerns effective reading instruction, then the researcher would sample both formal and informal reading events in classrooms in which instruction occurred (e.g., Griffin, 1977). If the question has to do with the quality of teacher–pupil academic contacts, the period of observation must encompass a representative sample of academic activities both over the day and over the week. Finally, if the goal is to make a statement about the nature of the process on a general level, then the investigator would have to sample events over time (e.g., throughout the year). Longitudinal samples are needed to answer the question of variability and stability of behaviors.

The researcher must determine whether to sample a given period of time and ignore the boundaries of events or to sample within an event. The decision about this sampling issue will influence the type of system selected and the type of questions that can be explored. For example, some systems such as narrative and descriptive systems and technological records will permit ease of exploration of longitudinal questions. The category system or sign system, unless special adjustments and designations is made to note boundaries of events, are not as sensitive to these issues. In addition, coding strategies (e.g., reducing actions or behaviors to a symbol) do not readily permit exploration of detailed processes over time.

The second time-sampling method, *short-interval sampling*, permits exploration of the duration of time a specific behavior occurred (e.g., 70% of all talk was teacher talk; 20% higher-order questions were asked). It does not permit retrieval of the actual number of instances of a specific behavior. Therefore, we cannot tell whether a frequency code is a single instance of a behavior for 15 seconds or five instances each lasting 3 seconds. The distribution of specific behaviors and the shifts in distribution and influence are not retrievable (e.g., Bales & Strodtbeck, 1967). The second time-sampling method is related to the first approach in that the observer needs a length of time to record (e.g., 30 minutes), a specific point to begin (e.g., the beginning of school at 8:30), and an interval in which to record the frequency of behaviors (e.g., every 3 or 5 seconds). The problem for the researcher is to determine how many intervals must be sampled to be representative and how long the observation period should be.

Small segments of time sampled within the general period of observation through the use of checklists and rating scales permit exploration of the actual occurrence of a specific behavior or event (e.g., 45% or all behaviors observed were teacher-initiated questions; praise did or did not occur during the 10 minutes of observation of oral reading). This approach does not permit exploration of (a) the duration of a given behavior unless specifically indicated as an item (e.g, indicate how long attention to task lasted—2 minutes, 3 minutes, 4 minutes, 5 minutes, or more), or (b) what preceded or followed a given behavior or event. In other words, a given behavior is decontextualized from the stream of behavior. The problem for the investigator is to determine the number of sampling sessions within the overall period of observation, the length of these sessions, and which instruments to use.

Event Sampling. The final issue of sampling to be discussed is event sampling. In contrast to time sampling, event sampling specifies a locus of observation (e.g., reading groups, whole class activities) but does not specify the length of observation. The length of the observation period is determined by the naturally occurring boundaries related to the event in the ongoing situation of the classroom. Event sampling is a topic-centered approach. For example, if one is interested in the nature of children's oral reading in middle grades, it is not necessary to record the beginning of school. However, it will be necessary to sample all events in which oral reading occurs (e.g., reading groups, social studies lessons, story reading, music, science lessons, menu reading, etc.). The researcher must select a locus of observation and then determine all possible situations in which the phenomenon occurs. Once this has been determined, events can be sampled in a representative manner.

This discussion of sampling briefly illustrates the nature of the decisions that must be considered and the interrelatedness of many of these decisions. Sampling issues are related to issues of stability and validity. The way one samples within a given observation study is related to the questions asked and the framework guiding the observations. Finally, sampling is related to the degree of confidence that a reader can have in the interpretations and findings of the study. The question is, does the sample provide a high degree of confidence that reality has been represented validly?

Representative Sources of Error: Limits on Certainty in Observation

In previous sections, the general purpose of observation and generic factors involved in designing and implementing systematic observation were discussed. The goal of observational research was defined as the representation of specific segments of reality. The representational process was shown to be mediated by the mechanism or system selected as the means of representing reality. In this section, one last set of factors will be considered. These factors focus on the identification of sources of error and ways of reducing such errors.

The notion of sources of error was selected for consideration since it underlies issues of reliability, validity, and rigor in observation and places limits on certainty as to what can be obtained. Space does not permit in-depth discussion of each of these issues; therefore, a more general focus on the issue of sources of error was selected since reliability and validity have been addressed elsewhere in this volume. (See also Bracht & Glass, 1968; Cohen, 1960; Erickson, 1979; Flanders, 1967; Frick & Semmel, 1978; Genishi, 1983a; Heap, 1980a; Herbert & Attridge, 1975; Kugle, 1978; Light, 1971; McCutcheon, 1981; McDermott & Hood, 1982; Shavelson & Dempsey-Atwood, 1976; Snow, 1974, among others.) Reliability and validity will be considered within the general issue of sources of error.

SOURCES OF ERROR: AN OVERVIEW

The perspective on observational research as a means of representing and exploring reality adopted in this chapter means that the cause of error can never be found in the segment of reality. Sources of error are found in the representational system or process (cf. Fassnacht, 1982). Table 6.5 presents a synthesis of representative sources of error drawn from several sources (e.g. Erickson, 1979; Fassnacht, 1982; Frick & Semmel, 1978; Herbert & Attridge, 1975; McGaw, Wardrop, & Bunda, 1972; Miller, 1974).

This list, while not all-inclusive, represents the range of types of errors that can lead to false representations of reality and invalid descriptions. Analysis of this list suggests two things. First, the different systems described previously are subject to different types of errors. For example, issues of central tendency and leniency are applicable to categorical systems that base descriptions on on-line ratings or codings. On the other hand, logical errors and errors in sampling are applicable to all systems. Second, the list of errors can be categorized. Errors are related to (a) observers, (b) the system for obtaining the representation, (c) the framework or assumptions about the phenomena under study, and (d) the procedures used to collect data.

Fassnacht (1982) argues that errors are an inherent part of the perceptual process. This fact has led investigators to adopt a variety of measures in an effort to reduce the possibility of error, to insure rigor in observation, and to obtain an adequate representation of reality. Two such measures will be considered

Table 6.5 Sources of Error in Observational Research

Type of Error	Definition
1. Central tendency	When using rating scales, the observer tends toward the subjective midpoint when judging a series of stimuli.
2. Leniency or generosity	When using rating scales for which a "yes," "sometimes," "rarely," or "no" is required, the observer tends to be lenient or generous.
3. Primacy or recency effects	Observer's initial impressions have a distorting effect on later judgments.
4. Logical errors	Observer makes judgment errors based on theoretical, experiential, or commitment-based assumptions (e.g., the assumption that because a teacher shows warmth to a class, she/he is also instructionally effective).
5. Failure to acknowledge self	The influence of the observer on the setting is overlooked. The investigator's role may lead to the establishment of particular expectations. Judgments can be made in accordance with these expectations.
6. Classification of observations	Construction of macro categories loses fine distinctions. Such categories permit quantification, but lose information about the process and fine-grained differences.
7. Generalization of unique behavior	Judgments may be based on evidence from an unrepresentative sample. Can lead to false conclusions or incorrect classifications of people or events.
8. Nested interests and values of observer	Findings become value-laden or otherwise distorted because of unchecked personal bias.
9. Failure to consider perspective of the observed	For investigators interested in a clear picture of everyday life, failure to obtain participants' perspectives may leak to identification of unvalidated factors, processes, or variables (Erickson & Wilson, 1982).
10. Unrepresentative sampling	Errors may occur based on samples which do not represent the general group of behaviors, that do not occur frequently enough to be observed reliably, or are inconsistent with the theory guiding the observations.
11. Reactions of the observed	Reactions of participants being observed can distort the process or phenomena being observed (e.g., teachers who are anxious about being observed may behave differently than they would at a calmer time).
12. Failure to account for situation or context	Leads to incorrect conclusions from assumptions of functional equivalents (e.g., reading time 1 = reading time 2). Can lead to overlooking what is being taught, changes in activities, variations in rights and obligations for participation, hence can distort conclusions.
13. Poorly designed observation systems	Leads to problems with reliability and validity.
14. Lack of consideration for the speed of relevant action	Errors may occur based on the omission of crucial features because of the rapidity of actions in the classroom.
15. Lack of consideration for the simultaneity of relevant action	Errors may occur based on failure to account for more than one activity occurring at a time; more than one message being sent at a time (e.g., use of different channels—verbal and nonverbal); and more than one function of a message at a time.
16. Lack of consideration of goal-directed or purposive nature of human activity.	False conclusion that a behavior lacks stability because of failure to consider the purposes of human behavior.
17. Failure to insure against observer drift	Errors caused by changes in the way the observer uses a system as time goes on. Can lead to obtaining descriptions that do not match the original categories or that vary from each other (Kugle, 1978).

below: (a) measures of reliability and (b) proposed sets of criteria for various aspects of the observational process.

RELIABILITY: A SOURCE OF
POTENTIAL ERROR

Issues of reliability are complex and are tied to issues of validity (see Erickson's chapter, this volume for a discussion of validity). Herbert & Attridge (1975) define the relationship as follows:

> Generically validity refers to the degree to which the measures obtained by an instrument actually describe what they purport to describe; reliability refers to the accuracy and consistency with which they do so. (p. 6)

On a general level, reliability is involved with the reduction of possible sources of error, as will be shown in this section.

Given the diversity of systems, no single approach to reliability assessment is adequate. Rather a variety of issues must be considered. In Table 6.6, a set of questions extracted from the work of Frick & Semmel (1978) and others is presented to help clarify the issues in reliability.

As indicated in Table 6.6, different systems require different approaches to reliability. The two most general approaches were defined by Frick and Semmel (1978). They suggest that when considering reliability in observational research, it is important to make conceptual distinctions between two indices of reliability: reliability coefficients (score reliability) and observer agreement coefficients (percentage of agreement). Both of these indices are related to a quantitative approach to reliability and require the quantification of data before they can be determined. A discussion of the statistical treatment of each of these measures is beyond the scope of this discussion (see, for

Table 6.6. Questions and Issues in Reliability

Questions	Related Issues
When should observer agreement be measured?	1. Prior to data collection (Frick & Semmel, 1978).
	2. Training does not guarantee against observer skill deterioration as data collection proceeds (Frick & Semmel, 1978; Kugle, 1978).
	3. Calculations of degree to which observer disagreement limits reliability should be done after the study.
On what kinds of data should observer agreement be calculated?	1. Agreement should be computed on the same unit(s) of behavior that will be used in the data analysis.
	2. Agreement should be computed on subcategories of behavior as well as the larger, subsuming categories.
With whom should agreement be obtained?	1. High interobserver agreement may not mean agreement with the original categories, because systematic misinterpretation can exist even with high agreement.
	2. Observers' scores should also be compared with a criterion. This is known as criterion-related agreement.
Under what conditions should agreement be calculated?	1. Coding in the setting may differ from coding of unambiguous samples in a laboratory or training session (also see Johnson & Bolstad, 1973).
	2. Ways to heighten observer vigilance and maintain accountability should be considered.
How can agreement be measured?	1. *Intraclass correlation coefficients* Useful after a study is completed, but impractical during or before. Highly affected by the variance between subjects.
	2. *Simple percentage agreement.* Drawbacks are that low frequencies in some categories and high frequencies in others may make interpretations ambiguous. Does not account for false inflation due to chance agreement. (See Cohen, 1960; Flanders, 1967; Light, 1971; Scott, 1955 for examples of ways to compute agreement coefficients.)
Which agreement coefficient is appropriate?	1. Dependent upon the type of observation system, number of categories, type of data, unit(s) of analysis, and purpose.
	2. If nominal comparisons cannot be obtained, then marginal agreement methods should be used.
	3. If there are only a few categories and/or frequency distributions are unequal, then correction for chance agreement should be made.
	4. The definition of "items" changes with systems. The probability of occurrence of the items must be considered.

example, Cohen, 1960; Flanders, 1967; Light, 1971; McGaw et al., 1972); however, issues that affect the determination of this type of reliability are presented instead (e.g., observer drift, training, units used for reliability, frequency of occurrence of units). Consideration of the points raised in Table 6.6 can help eliminate or avoid errors in determination of both reliability coefficients and observer agreement coefficients.

Erickson (1979) proposes another type of reliability, reliability for descriptive studies. The first issue relates to the value of description for classroom research. He argues that the value of description

does not lie essentially in its "richness," nor in its capacity to evoke in us a vivid sense of "being there." Nor does the "discovery of new independent and dependent variables" in itself get us anywhere, necessarily. Before classroom research can proceed further, researchers need languages of description at the level of primary data collection which make contact with the theories of action that are being used in moment-to-moment decision making by participants in the events they observe and describe. (p. 4)

Erickson's first concern, therefore, relates to the interrelationship of description, theory, and language. This concern echoes a similar concern voiced by Popper (1963, as cited in Stubbs, Robinson & Twite, 1979; see p. 164 of this chapter). Popper suggests that all observation "and its description presupposes a descriptive language with property words; it presupposes similarity and classification which in its turn presupposes interest, points of view, and problems" (p. 21). For Erickson and Popper, therefore, issues of reliability are related to obtaining adequate description as well as validity.

Erickson elaborates the issues of reliability. He suggests that "descriptive *reliability* is indeed desirable in the interest of showing plausibility in judgment, even though ... descriptive *validity* is the logically antecedent problem in the construction of an adequate descriptive language" (p. 19). He notes two ways that reliability can be obtained for descriptive data. Since this area has received little or no treatment in the research field in general, this issue will be treated in greater detail than the other types of reliability discussed above.

First, when audiovisual records are made, the researcher can use an "instant replay" to demonstrate reliability in description. This approach, according to Erickson (1979), is analogous to the instant replay by a sports announcer on television.

The instant replay can be thought of as a "folk" means of demonstrating validity and reliability in description. In classroom research, the external memory of an audiovisual record, together with the running notes obtained as a participant observer, provide the researcher with the same evidentiary resource the television football announcer has in the instant replay. The audiovisual record and replay capability provide the qualitative researcher an opportunity to make the data base public. (p. 19)

This evidence, he suggests, can be shared with teachers and other participants working in partnership with the researcher. This approach is a form of triangulation of data or perspectives (also see Adelman & Walker, 1975 and Elliott, 1976).

Second, primary evidence can be shared with other researchers or with other members of the community (see Bloome, 1981 for an example of the use of a community advisory board to insure reliability and validity of data and inferences about data). With regard to this approach, Erickson (1979) states:

In the process of this sharing, descriptive research becomes no longer a matter of strictly private judgment and opinion. The epithets "mere journalism" or "fiction" may still be flung, but they can no longer stick, for the grounds of evidence can be made clear in the arena of public knowledge. The claims made in descriptive statements can be *disconfirmed*, at least at the level of inference involved in the language of primary data collection. The propositions involved in descriptive accounts are no longer incorrigible ones (and the incorrigibility of narrative description as reported in field studies has been a serious problem up to now, especially for educational researchers trained in a tradition of positivism in scientific research). The capacity for instant replay opens up the possibility of interactional research which is not positivistic, yet is still rigorously empirical. (pp. 19–20)

This discussion highlights a wide range of issues that must be considered when determining the reliability of a study. In addition, reliability was shown to be a possible source of error. That is, because a reliability coefficient is presented does not mean that the information is valid, that the coefficient was determined in an appropriate manner, or that the representation of reality is accurate. The consumer of observational research must go beyond the score and ask how reliability was determined and explore the relationship between reliability and validity, since it is possible to measure behaviors reliably that have low validity with regard to the question under study or the segment of reality observed. For example, one could conceivably construct an instrument to measure intelligence by having children throw stones as far as they could. It would be possible to obtain a high correlation between how far stones were thrown on one occasion and how far they were thrown on a second occasion, but this would hardly constitute a valid measure of intelligence.

The foregoing discussion of reliability can be thought of as a framework or set of guidelines for finding appropriate ways to determine reliability. That is, the questions and the related issues that were raised can guide the researcher in designing, selecting, and applying appropriate measures of reliability. For additional discussion of these and other issues (e.g., internal and external validity), see Le Compte and Goetz (1982); Hansen (1979); and Pelto and Pelto (1977), among others.

TOWARD CRITERIA FOR ADEQUATE OBSERVATION

As in the case of reliability, no single set of criteria exist to date to guide observation in general. Rather specific criteria have been proposed for different types of systems. The purpose of such criteria is to insure the rigor associated with a particular approach and to provide a framework for informed decision making for design and implementation of an observational study.

Regardless of the approach, the investigator must answer a general set of questions. The questions include: who, what, when, where, and how to observe as well as why to observe. While these questions appear obvious, what is not so obvious is how they are interrelated and how they are influenced by the

186 CAROLYN M. EVERTSON AND JUDITH L. GREEN

questions under study. Additionally, what is not evident in looking at these questions alone are the ways in which the theoretical (philosophical, experience-based, or commitment-based) perspective influences the questions asked, the data collected, the level(s) of analysis, and the descriptions obtained. To illustrate this relationship, the work of two researchers who have explored this issue will be considered (Genishi, 1983b; Hymes, 1977).

A graphic outline of these issues is provided by Genishi derived from her work in exploring verbal interactions in the classroom (Genishi & Di Paolo, 1982). Figure 6.5 shows the relationship among various aspects of the research process as conceptualized by Genishi (1983b).

As indicated in Figure 6.5, the questions asked affect the methods of data collection, the units of analysis, and the types of coding systems used as well as the level of transcription. This conceptualization provides a framework for making decisions about what to do and how to do it. While designed for analysis of verbal interaction in classrooms from a sociolinguistic, psycholinguistic, or child language framework, the relationships among parts and the decisions to be made are the same as for other disciplines. This framework, therefore, is a general one to guide decision making in observational studies.

Hymes (1977) demonstrates how the area of concern influences what questions will be asked and, therefore, what data will be collected and how those data will be analyzed. Writing for the research approach known as linguistic ethnography, he states that: If one begins with social life, then the *linguistic aspects of ethnography* require one to ask:

What are the communicative means, verbal and other, by which this bit of social life is conducted and interpreted?
What is their mode of organization from the standpoint of verbal repertoires or codes?
Can one speak of appropriate and inappropriate, better or worse, uses of these means?
How are the skills entailed by the means acquired, and to whom are they accessible? (p. 93)

In contrast, if one starts from *language* in one's study, the *ethnography of linguistic work* requires one to ask another set of questions:

Who employs these verbal means, to what ends, when, where, and how?
What organization do they have from the standpoint of patterns of social life? (p. 93)

While stated for linguistic approaches, the Hymes (1977) example suggests that a change in lenses leads to a shift in the focus of the questions or to another set of questions. The key is to match the questions and the behaviors observed. This is true whether the approach is behavioral, phenomenological, or ecological, and so forth.

The Genishi (1983b) and Hymes (1977) examples point out that one type of criteria that must be considered is the match between the focus, the research questions, the data collection, the manner of displaying data, and the analysis. In other words, they demonstrate the need to consider the internal as well as the external validity of the study. Another factor they point to is the

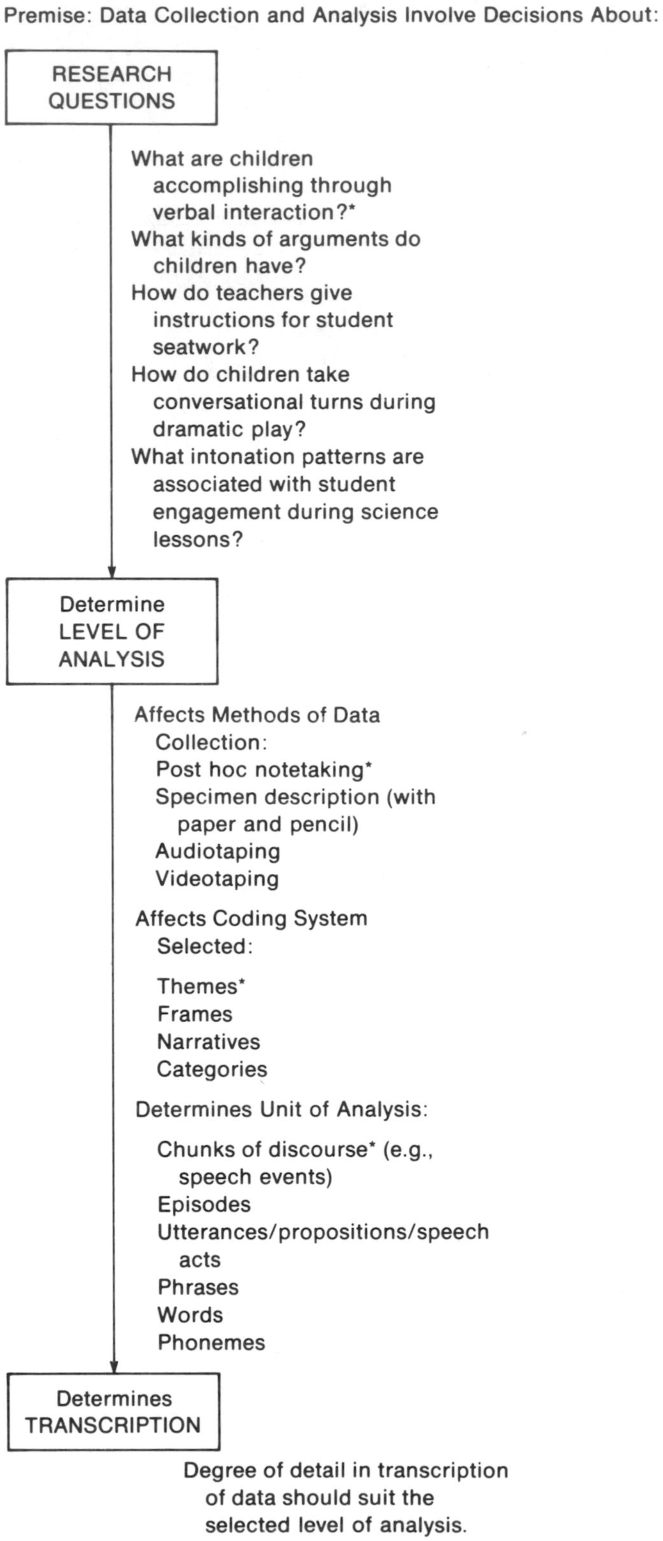

Premise: Data Collection and Analysis Involve Decisions About:

Fig. 6.5. Studying classroom verbal interaction. Adapted from Genishi (1983b).

*Examples are arranged from most global to most highly focused.

need to consider the level of analysis that is appropriate for the question under study. For example, if a researcher is concerned with identifying the relationship between classroom management procedures and student achievement (cf. Evertson and her colleagues), then detailed analyses of teacher–student talk may not be an appropriate beginning point. This level may be appropriate at a later point (e.g., Evertson, 1984; Green & Weade, 1984) when a contrast between effective and less effective classroom managers is desired in order to explore differences in models of management and management of lesson content. (For other examples see Barr & Dreeban, 1983; Burstein, 1980; Green et al., in press; Morine-Dershimer, in press-a, in press-b.) The issue of level of analysis has implications for factors such as sampling, units of observation, and the nature of the systems selected. These issues are also related to factors involved in secondary analyses (e.g., Koehler, in press; Rentel, in press).

The discussion to this point has dealt with general issues. In the remainder of this section, two specific sets of criteria will be presented. The first set by Herbert and Attridge (1975) are aimed at researchers whose approaches require the use of categorical systems, systems to the far left of the context continuum proposed in Figure 6.3. The second set by Spindler (1982) is aimed at investigators whose approaches require an ethnographic or more descriptive approach, systems that fall to the right of the context continuum. While contrasting on one level, these two sets of criteria can serve as a point of departure for researchers regardless of orientation. Each set of criteria is designed to insure that the observation will be systematic, that information will be obtained in a reliable and valid manner, that information will be easily transmitted to others, and that others can reconstruct the research process.

Herbert and Attridge (1975) have identified a series of criteria for use in designing and implementing categorical systems. In addition to the design issues, Herbert and Attridge address the process of training and coding manual development. Table 6.7 presents a summary of the criteria by area.

While this set of criteria was designed for use with categorical systems, many of the items are applicable to all types of observational studies. That is, many of the items in the validity section apply across approaches. For example, in all studies, terms should be clearly defined, the basis for the terms (theory or other bases) should be specified and used consistently, items should represent dimensions being studied, and ground rules for implementation and categorization for all units should be specified. All of the items in the section on inference can be applied to other systems. In contrast, the two items in the context section will be specific to approaches at the context-exclusive end of the continuum in Figure 6.3. These criteria can be viewed as points of departure rather than as a set of rules that are set in stone. Their goal is to assure rigor and internal and external validity of studies in addition to replicability.

The criteria or characteristics proposed by Spinder (1982) apply to studies at the context-inclusive end of the continuum. These criteria help to define anthroethnography (ethnography based on anthropological perspectives applied to the study of education). Spindler's criteria, therefore, serve both to define this approach and to clarify the relationship between perspective and data collection. Table 6.8 provides a summary of these characteristics/criteria.

The criteria above will guide data collection and help to specify the perspective guiding the approach. They also indicate the nature of the inquiry cycle. That is, they suggest that the observation has a specific *theoretical perspective* (transcultural sociocultural participant oriented); it is *goal driven* (to make explicit what is implicit in sociocultural knowledge generated in the setting); *questions and hypotheses are generated within the observation/ethnographic cycle—inquiry is dynamic* (instruments, codes, observation schedules, etc., are selected as needed within the study for the specific questions raised during the study), and *technical devices are used* in addition to other instruments, codes, and so forth.

The discussion above is illustrative rather than definitive. Different approaches will require different types of criteria. The fact that the majority of criteria presented in this section focus on linguistic or ethnographic approaches stems from the fact that these approaches are relatively recent to the study of the classroom and educational processes. Researchers who have used or developed these approaches, as with any new direction, have had to specify criteria for other investigators not grounded in the approaches. These criteria, however, raise a basic issue: What are the criteria for each approach? In order to examine observational research approaches, to develop a theory or theories of observation for research purposes, and to insure systematic observation, researchers need to address the issue of what makes observation systematic both within a specific approach, study, or program of research as well as across approaches. In this way, the consumer will be able to understand the segment of reality each addresses best. Additionally, such criteria will help researchers show how a particular method or instrument was used and adapted.

In the sections above, the argument was made that a method or tool could be described independently from the framework of its selection and the units of observation. The criteria presented confirm this but also suggest that within a specific approach a given tool (e.g. narrative, interview, technological record) will be used in specific ways; it will be adapted to the needs of the study. For example, stimulated recall was used to explore teachers' perceptions in one study by Morine and Vallance (1975) and adapted to collect both teacher and student perspectives in a later study by Morine-Dershimer and Tenenberg, (1981). Stimulated recall is a tool; the framework guiding it determines how it will be used and what information it will be used to collect.

Summary

The discussions above were designed to raise generic questions about the nature of observation and observational processes. The discussion began with the consideration of the nature of observation as an everyday process as well as a research- or question-directed process. Factors involved in using observation as a research approach were discussed: context of observation, systems for recording and storing observations, units of observation, sampling, and sources of error. Observation was shown to be a process mediated by a variety of factors. Observational research was shown to be a multifaceted process, a process in which different goals require different ways of recording and storing data. Finally, observation as a research

    CAROLYN M. EVERTSON AND JUDITH L. GREEN

Table 6.7. Criteria for Observation Systems and Manuals

Area	Subcategory	Criteria
1. IDENTIFYING: Enabling selection of appropriate instrument		1.1 Name of instrument should identify focus and purpose. 1.2 Instrument should be accompanied by a statement of purpose. 1.3 Behaviors, subjects, and content should be specified. 1.4 Intended applications should be stated. 1.5 Situations in which the instrument should not be used should be specified.
2. VALIDITY: Specifying the provisions of evidence that allow both developer and user to decide if the instrument represents the events it claims to	ITEM CHARACTERISTICS	2.1 All terms should be clearly defined. 2.2 If derived from theory, terms should be defined consistently with their use in the theory. 2.3 Items should be exhaustive of the dimension(s) of behavior under study. 2.4 Items should be representative of the dimensions of behavior under study. 2.5 Items should be mutually exclusive. 2.6 Ground rules for implementation and for categorization of borderline/unusual behaviors should be specified.
	INFERENCE	2.7 Items should be as low in degree of observer inference as the complexity of the behavior(s) will permit. 2.8 The degree to which observer inference is present and controlled should be explicated. 2.9 Guidelines as to the kinds of inferences that can and should be made should accompany the system to reduce unwarranted assumptions/applications of the findings. 2.10 Statistical and other methods of inferential treatment which are recommended for use should be specified.
	CONTEXT	2.11 The problems of context must be recognized and the degree and kind of context brought to bear in the instrument must be explicated. 2.12 Methods of reducing/controlling use of context by observers must be explicated.
	OBSERVER EFFECT	2.13 The effect of observers, equipment, and procedures on the observational setting should be explicated.
	RELIABILITY	2.14 The types of reliability assessed, meaning, and conditions under which they were determined should be recorded.
	VALIDITY	2.15 Instruments should be accompanied by methods used to test their validity, results obtained, and purpose for which they apply.
3. PRACTICALITY: Concerning the ease of implementation, its acceptability to those under study, complexity of data gathering mechanisms, training procedures, etc.	INSTRUMENT ITEMS	3.1 Items comprising the instrument should be relevant to its purposes. 3.2 Codes should be simple and easy to make. 3.3 Categories and codes should be easily learned.
	OBSERVERS	3.4 Special qualifications of observers should be noted. 3.5 Training procedures, steps, durations, and results should accompany instruments. Manuals, tapes, and training devices should be available.
	COLLECTION AND RECORDING OF DATA	3.6 Manuals should recommend number, location, and functions of observers, coders, technicians, and staff needed. 3.7 Data collection and recording procedures must accompany the instrument. 3.8 Observation unit recommended should be specified (e.g., length of time). 3.9 Coding unit recommended should be specified. 3.10 Procedures for analyzing data should be described. 3.11 Recommendations for data transmission and display techniques for the instruments should be described. 3.12 Costs likely to be incurred in use of instrument should be noted.

Note. From "A Guide for Developers and Users of Observation Systems and Manuals" by J. Herbert and C. Attridge, 1975, *American Education Research Journal*, 12(1), pp.1–20. Copyright by American Educational Research Association. Reprinted by permission.

Table 6.8. Criteria for Adequate Ethnography

Guidelines

1. Observations are contextualized.
2. Hypotheses and questions emerge as the study proceeeds in the setting selected for observation.
3. Observation takes place over a long period and is repetitive (1 year appears to be minimum).
4. The native view of reality is brought out by inferences from observation and by various forms of ethnographic inquiry.
5. A major part of the ethnographic task is to understand what sociocultural knowledge participants bring to and generate in the social setting being studied.
6. Instruments, codes, schedules, questionnaires, agenda for interviews, and so forth are generated in the field as a result of observations and ethnographic inquiry.
7. A transcultural perspective is present, though frequently as an unstated assumption.
8. The task is to make explicit what is implicit and tacit to informants and participants in the social setting being studied.
9. Inquiry and observation must disturb as little as possible.
10. The conversational management of the interview or eliciting interaction must be carried out so as to promote the unfolding of emic[1] cultural information in its most heuristic, natural form.
11. Any form of technical device that will enable the ethnographer to collect more live data—immediate, natural, detailed behavior—will be used, such as camera, audiotapes, and videotapes.

Note. Adapted from *Doing the Ethnography of Schooling* by G. Spindler. Copyright © 1982 by CBS College Publishing. Reprinted by permission.

[1] By "emic" is meant the view from within the culture, the folk view, in terms of native categories.

approach was shown to be a systematic process guided by the frame of reference of the researcher.

In the last section of this chapter, the question of observation as an inquiry process will be considered. Since the ways in which an observational study will be designed and implemented depend on the questions under consideration and the frame of reference guiding the study, no prescription for approaches is possible. Therefore, in the following section three different research approaches will be highlighted to demonstrate how frame of reference combines with methods/tools to create unique observational studies. Finally, in this section, a set of steps constructed by a group of young researchers attempting to design and implement their first observational studies will be described. This section, while it closes the chapter, will actually constitute a beginning. Therefore, in the section that follows, work will be presented that represents both advanced programs of research and beginning points for new researchers.

Observation as Inquiry

In the previous sections, the discussion of observation focused on methods and factors involved in the design and implementation of observational research. The discussion was generic in nature; that is, no consideration was given to observation used in specific studies or to the design and implementation of such studies. In this section, observation as a process of inquiry will be explored and examples of ways this process can be realized will be presented. The purpose of this section is to help the reader begin to make plans for conducting observational stud-

ies. To facilitate this process a series of concrete examples are presented.

The conceptualization of observation as an inquiry process, that is, as a systematic and appropriate approach to research on educational processes, events, and issues in educational settings, involves more than simply using a particular system. The design and implementation of an observational study requires the researcher to make a series of systematic decisions about who, what, when, and where to observe, in addition to answering the question of how. In addition, the researcher selecting observation as the principal way of collecting information about processes, events, and issues must be concerned about sampling, representativeness, and systematicity. These issues must be considered in all types of studies that use observation. In other words, whether one uses observation as a way of capturing and representing reality in, say, a statistical, hypothesis-testing study, a descriptive study, a correlational study, or an ethnographic study, the decisions will be similar. What will differ are the ways in which the studies will be designed, the theoretical grounding, the instruments used to sample and represent reality, the units of observation, the locus of observation, the sample size, the orchestration of collection procedures, and the sampling procedures.

The following discussion by Corsaro (1985) provides a concrete illustration of some of the major aspects of the decision-making process. The issues raised in this example will be applied to the representative examples of observational research presented in the remainder of this chapter. Therefore, this example serves as a general introduction to this inquiry section. In this example, factors discussed in the first section are highlighted.

Earlier I defined *interactive episode* as the collection or sampling unit. Actual sampling procedures involved decisions regarding which units (interactive episodes) to sample from the continuous flow of interaction in the nursery school. The interactive episodes recorded in field notes and on videotape were representative of typical activities in the setting and had potential for the development of theoretical propositions. In short, sampling decisions *were both representative and theoretical.*

When a sample is representative it captures the overall texture of the setting under study. Since it is impossible to record all interaction in a given setting, field researchers often attempt to insure representativeness by collecting data across several dimensions including people, places, time and activities (cf., Denzin, 1977; Mehan, 1979a; Reiss, 1971; and Schatzman & Strauss, 1973). A typical strategy is to draw up an inventory of the range and number of elements in each of the dimensions in early phases of field entry and then modify the inventory as needed at various points in data collection. When using more than one data collection technique (e.g., observational field notes, interviewing, audiovisual recording, etc.) data obtained at one point in time with one technique can serve as a basis for identifying dimensions in the setting which are then sampled using another technique later in the collection process.

I used data collected during the period of concealed observation to develop an inventory of the participants, activities, social-ecological areas and schedule of the nursery school. The inventory then guided the sampling of interactive episodes in participant observation during the next three months. At the end of this period, I reviewed the field notes, and added and deleted items to and from the inventory. The revised inventory was then used to guide sampling decisions in later participant observation and for the audiovisual recording of interactive episodes.

Once the videotaping phase of the research began, I checked the representativeness of the sample of audiovisual data in two ways. First, after each taping session, I reviewed and summarized the data. In the summaries, I specified the number of episodes, where and when they occurred, their duration, the participants, and the nature of the activity. At the end of each week, I compared the summaries with the sampling inventory and checked off items (features of behavior recorded in the episodes) as they were collected. Secondly, on several occasions, I asked the teachers to look over the summaries and to respond to their representativeness of typical activities in the school. The teachers' responses, as well as my comparison of the audiovisual data with field notes, resulted in the collection of additional videotaped episodes which improved the overall representativeness of the recordings.

… As I have pointed out, sampling procedures in field research should be both reliable and representative. But the nature of ethnographic research demands that sampling procedures also be reactive to developments in the course of research. As Hymes notes, "for many ethnographers, it is of the essence of the method that it is a dialectical, or feed-back (interactive–reactive) method. It is of the essence of the method that initial questions may change during the course of inquiry" (Hymes, 1978: 8). Thus, sampling procedures must, in part, reflect the dialectical nature of ethnographic research.

It is precisely along these lines that ethnographic research differs from hypothesis-testing approaches. It is not that field research is more theoretically oriented than hypothesis-testing approaches (i.e., surveys, experiments, etc.), but rather field research differs in that theoretical concerns guide sampling decisions both *initially and throughout the study*. The ethnographer must be sensitive to theoretical leads as they emerge, and pursue them through theoretically directed sampling procedures. (in press, pp. 32–34)

Corsaro has identified several issues that can be used to understand inquiry. First, decision points for sampling, instrumentation, and question generation and refinement may occur at different points. In ethnographic studies, these decisions occur prior to and throughout the study. In individual studies from other approaches (e.g., descriptive, sociolinguistic, narrative) this pattern of decision making can also be identified. This pattern can also be seen when programs of research are considered. That is, findings and procedures in one study may be used to inform those in another or as the basis for modification in later studies that are linked together to explore a question or set of equations systematically. The second issue raised by Corsaro is the question of the history of a study. In the ethnographic study, decisions had both *local histories*, histories within the study, and *distant histories*, histories of research approaches, questions, and findings from past work. The history of a single study must also be considered. In programmatic research, the history of a given study is the sum of preceding work as well as the theoretical grounding. For example, to understand why a particular instrument or data collection procedure was used may require knowledge of earlier work within the program.

The distinctions made by Corsaro about the differences in decision points for sampling and design in different types of studies suggests the need to extend the earlier discussions on this and related issues (see Figures 6.2 and 6.4). The issue is not simply when decisions are made within a single study but when and how decisions are made both within and across studies. When decision making is viewed from this broader perspective,

the varied approaches appear more similar than different. The key is to make decisions in systematic and principled ways, and to modify procedures based on questions, local context, and knowledge gained from past work (work either at an earlier point in the study or in an earlier study).

In considering the types of studies to include as examples of the inquiry process these distinctions were considered. The studies that were selected as illustrative examples had to meet several criteria. First, they had to represent different observational approaches to the study of teaching–learning processes in educational settings. Second, they had to represent programmatic research. Third, they had to represent different theoretical orientations. Fourth, they had to represent different research (e.g., experimental, descriptive, enthnographic, etc.). Fifth, they had to use multiple perspectives and multiple approaches to represent reality within a study; and sixth, they had to represent different types of decision making (e.g., initial cycles of decision making across studies, cycles of decision making within studies, and combinations of these approaches).

Four sets of studies were identified and serve as illustrations: work on classroom management and organization by Evertson (Peabody College, Vanderbilt University) and her colleagues, Jere Brophy and Linda Anderson (Michigan State University); Edmund Emmer et al. (Research and Development Center for Teacher Education, The University of Texas—Austin); work by Marshall and Weinstein on classroom processes and student perceptions (University of California—Berkeley); work on participant perspectives of classroom discourse by Morine-Dershimer (Syracuse University) and Tenenberg (California State University—Hayward) and their colleagues in a number of different institutions (e.g., Shuy, Georgetown; Ramirez, State University of New York); and work by Cook-Gumperz, Gumperz, and Simons and their colleagues (Michaels, Harvard; Collins, Temple; Murphy, University of California—Berkeley) on discourse processes within and across educational settings in the School/Home Ethnography Project at the University of California, Berkeley.

Each of these bodies of work will be explored; each serves to illustrate a variety of different aspects of the decision making and inquiry process involved in using observation as the primary means of representing reality. As a whole, the four sets of studies represent a range of ways of orchestrating a limited set of tools and procedures to match the question under study and to obtain representations of specific aspects of the reality of life in classrooms and other educational settings.

These studies highlight the design and implementation process and help to specify some of the aspects of the research process related to observation as inquiry. In addition, these studies represent extensively funded projects (all were funded by federal agencies USOE, NIE, & NIMH). They do not address the question of how to begin or what an *individual* researcher might do. Therefore, the final set of questions to be addressed in this section will be those relating to a general framework for conducting observational research. This framework was derived from consideration of the issues raised in this chapter and from work by a group of novice researchers at the University of Delaware and Ohio State University. These junior researchers explored both the steps involved in doing observational research and the ways to conceptualize these processes graphically.

*Example 1: The Descriptive-
Correlational-Experimental Cycle*

One way to view the work of Evertson and her colleagues across the various studies is to consider this set of studies as representing the descriptive-correlational-experimental cycle suggested by Rosenshine and Furst (1973). Figure 6.6 provides a brief graphic representation of this 15-year program. (For more detailed information about each study, the reader is referred to the citations provided.) While the cycles are presented linearly, each cycle itself is actually composed of two descriptive-correlational-experimental loops and a series of interactive-reactive decisions across studies (cf. Corsaro, 1985). These loops overlap; that is, they share studies in common and the decisions within Loop 1 influenced decisions in Loop 2. In addition, the questions raised in one study are explored in subsequent studies; methods used in a study are often modified and extended in studies that follow; and findings in one study are tested and/or explored in later studies at different grade levels. Therefore, as the researchers moved from one study to the next, they interacted with data, procedures, and questions, and reacted to the problems, issues and findings. This interactive-reactive process led to modifications in subsequent studies (e.g., instruments were modified, collection procedures added, and hypotheses generated and tested).

Background of the Studies. The cycle began as a response to several factors. First, the Coleman Report (Coleman et al., 1966) and later reanalyses of these data by Jencks et al. (1972) minimized the contributions of teachers to student academic achievement. Aside from statistical and methodological flaws which masked rather than revealed teacher effects, the studies contributed to the general attitudes that teacher effects on their students were less important than other factors such as socioeconomic status. The Coleman study did not include systematic observation of teacher behaviors, and findings were based on school measures, data available from school records, and averages across classrooms. In other words, individual teachers' contributions to student achievement were not considered. Second, relationships between teachers' classroom behaviors and student achievement had not been carefully explored. What appeared to be needed were systematic studies of teachers teaching in natural settings. Third, simultaneous with these research issues was the trend toward developing curricula that were "teacher-proof," that is, designed to convey the content regardless of the skill of the teacher. Fourth, earlier studies of teachers' classroom behavior showed a lack of stability from one year to the next (Rosenshine, 1970). This lack of stability appeared to be a major obstacle in developing a sound data base that related teacher behavior to student outcomes.

The response to the issues discussed above was the design and development of the Texas Teacher Effectiveness Project (TTEP) starting in 1970 (Brophy, 1973; Good, Biddle, & Brophy, 1975; Veldman & Brophy, 1974). The intent of the series of studies described in Loop 1 was to build a data base by conducting large-scale field studies of teachers' classroom behavior and relating these characteristics and processes to measures of student learning gain. In addition some of the methodological problems were addressed by developing new methods of observation and by identifying a stable group of teachers who had consistent effects on their students' achievement across years.

This brief discussion of the background of this cycle of studies demonstrates the need to consider the historical context in which the studies were developed. In order to understand a given study, it may be necessary to explore what was occurring historically in education and the broader society that influenced the development of a study. This information also serves as the framework for a given study or set of studies.

The historical perspective will also become clear as the different studies in the cycle are considered. This program can be divided into a series of loops, or related studies. Therefore, to understand what was done and why, it is important to trace the links between and across studies. Another way to think about an individual study is to consider it within a particular research loop that is grounded in a program of research. From this perspective, each study has a history and a place in history. To understand the findings and observational approaches in one study and to utilize these findings or approaches, it may be necessary to consider the study in its historical perspective (research history) as well as in the historical perspective of the times.

LOOP 1: RESEARCH ISSUES AND DESIGN
OF LATER INQUIRY

Space does not permit adequate discussion of each study; therefore the focus of the discussion of this set of studies and the remainder of the studies in this and subsequent sections will focus on the links between studies and factors contributing to decision making within a program of research. Loop 1 consists of the Texas Teacher Effectiveness Study (TTEP) and the First Grade Reading Group Study (FGRGS). The TTEP was the first descriptive-correlational study; the teachers observed were those identified as consistent in their effects on student achievement over a 3-4-year period. As indicated in both Figure 6.6 and Table 6.9, this study used a variety of data collection methods to obtain a representation of classroom behavior (Brophy & Evertson, 1974; 1976).

From the TTEP and research literature on teaching in preschool (Blank, 1973) as well as Jere Brophy's program development work at Southwest Educational Development Laboratory, a manual was developed delineating 22 principles for small-group management and instruction. These principles formed the basis for the treatment condition in the FGRGS. The FGRGS was the first experimental study in this program of research (Anderson, Evertson, & Brophy, 1979). The TTEP and FGRGS form the descriptive-correlational-experimental loop.

This loop ends with the FGRGS; however, the information obtained in this set of studies informs work in Loop 2. Three factors led to the cessation of Loop 1 and to modifications of work in Loop 2. First, one of the consistent findings across the TTEP and FGRGS was that management and organization factors were related to student achievement. Second, the use of category systems did not permit in-depth exploration of the managerial and organizational process. The behaviors and variables obtained from the category systems were decontextualized to a degree and contextual information could not be retrieved to help explain how the process itself was constructed. Third, the studies were undertaken beginning in October of the

Fig. 6.6. Descriptive-correlational-experimental inquiry cycle.

192

school year. This sampling procedure did not enable the researchers to explore *how* teachers established and maintained effective management and organization patterns and structures. In addition, with the exception of Smith and Geoffrey (1968) and Tikunoff, Ward, and Dasho (1978), little information existed on how teachers began school. These factors led to a modification of data collection procedures and to a change in observation systems. These changes are discussed again in Loop 2.

LOOP 2: DECISION MAKING AND SHIFTING LENSES IN AN INQUIRY CYCLE

Loop 2 also begins with the Texas Teacher Effectiveness Study (TTEP). In this way Loop 1 and Loop 2 overlap. Loop 2 consists of two patterns: (a) a set of linked descriptive-correlational studies that explored effectiveness in general terms at two different levels of schooling (elementary and secondary), and (b) a descriptive-correlational-experimental set that explored a more focused question, a question identified in Pattern 1 and in Loop 1.

Pattern 1, the descriptive-correlational studies that made up the Texas Teacher Effectiveness studies, showed the interactive-reactive nature of the studies in this program of research. The Texas Junior High School Study (TJHSS) (Evertson, Anderson, Anderson, & Brophy, 1980; Evertson, Anderson, & Brophy, 1978) was informed by the elementary TTEP. First, the observational systems were modified to fit the setting and to eliminate the problems identified in the elementary study. For example, within the first week, additional data collection was needed. Some observers were turning in coded sheets with few or no recordings in the teacher-student public interaction sections of the system. One of the major reasons for the lack of codes in these sections was that much of the coding system provided for recording only public or private verbal interaction between teachers and students. The classes in which some of the observers were recording information were ones in which there was limited verbal interaction and larger amounts of silent or seatwork. Therefore, in order to ascertain what was occurring when the teacher and students were not interacting verbally, all observers were asked to record brief narrative descriptions. This qualitative information was used to index what was occurring in classrooms where verbal interaction was limited. Also the descriptions provided a context, some academic content information, and some idea of the flow of events.

Second, two classes were observed for each teacher to explore the issue of teacher stability of effective practices. Third, student outcome measures were expanded. Two types were collected: student achievement measures (pre and post) and student ratings of their teachers. Student achievement was measured with a content-referenced test designed to align with the curriculum in the district. Student scores on the California Achievement Test were used as pretest measures. Estimates of student learning gain were then related to classroom process measures and teachers' classroom behaviors.

Once again, management and organization factors correlated with student achievement. As in the case of the studies in Loop 1, the category system did not permit exploration of the process of management and organization nor did the sampling procedures permit observation of the onset of these processes. These

limitations led to a further modification of instrumentation and collection procedures in Pattern 2, the set of descriptive-correlational-experimental studies.

Pattern 2, the Classroom Organization Study (COS), the first in the descriptive-correlational-experimental loop, was a more focused, in-depth look at management and organization procedures. This study was designed to capture events starting on the first day of school, therefore maximizing the opportunity to detect and explore the procedures teachers used to establish and maintain the organization and management of classrooms. A shift also occurred in the ways in which data were collected. Instead of designing a category system that counted behaviors, a series of procedures were adopted: (a) narrative records were made; (b) observer ratings focusing on lesson management, student behavior, class climate, and so forth, were obtained; and (c) time spent in various class activities was recorded. From this study, a series of principles for effective management and organization of classrooms was obtained (Emmer, Evertson, & Anderson, 1980; Evertson, Anderson, & Clements, 1980). These principles formed the basis for the pilot experimental field study and, ultimately, the Classroom Management Improvement Study (CMIS, 1980–1981; see Evertson, Emmer, Sanford, & Clements, 1983).

The Classroom Organization Study also led to a second descriptive-correlational study at the junior high school level. This study, like the Texas Junior High School Study (TJHSS), was designed to provide information about how effective processes were realized in a setting with older students. The junior high COS (JHCOS), therefore, was an extension of the COS and the TJHSS. The findings from this study, along with findings from the pilot experimental field study, formed the basis for the Classroom Management Improvement Study (CMIS).

The interrelatedness of the studies shows how the type of focusing cycle suggested in the Corsaro (1985) description of a research strategy can be realized over a series of studies. Rather than occurring within a single study as in the case of an ethnographic study, the decisions and modifications occurred across studies. Each new study builds on the ones before and informs the ones that follow. In this way this cycle is interactive and reactive in nature.

The descriptive-correlational-experimental loop does not end with the Classroom Management Improvement Study, however. In 1982–1983, Evertson, in cooperation with the Arkansas State Department of Education, conducted an action research study and tested the Texas training model in Arkansas. This study explored the question of exportation of a model developed in one region to another region. It used a modified version of the training model. The fact that the state and local districts provided the resources, rather than a funding agency, influenced both how the study was undertaken and the nature of the data collected. Training of observers was limited; observers used rating forms similar to those in the COS and CMIS and counts of student engagement. Observers took notes but did not use detailed narratives. Live audiotapes replaced narrative records.

This study involved a cooperative effort between state and local educators and Evertson, the consultant who trained observers and workshop leaders. This study, therefore, is a collaborative effort between researcher and school districts; it is an action research study, a study undertaken *in situ* and adapted to the needs and conditions of the local groups requesting the training.

LOOP 3: A QUALITATIVE–QUANTITATIVE MERGER

The Arkansas Classroom Management Training Study (ACMTS) is both the end of a cycle and the beginning of a new loop. This third loop is just underway with the study entitled Exploring Models of Management (1983–1984). This study, funded by NIE, is a collaborative effort between the Arkansas State Department of Education and a team of researchers (Evertson and Green). In this study, the focus on management models narrows even further. The lens shifts from a training model derived from a descriptive–correlational–experimental loop to an exploration of the nature of the models of management and organization of environment and content. To explore the models used by effective and less effective managers identified in the training study, an in-depth secondary analysis using a sociolinguistic ethnographic perspective (Green & Bloome, 1983) and a descriptive analysis system adapted from the work of Green (Green & Harker, 1982; Green & Wallat, 1981b) is being used. This study involves a secondary analysis of data and a shift in analytic approach. It merges qualitative and quantitative analyses. It also merges qualitative and quantitative with micro- and macro-levels of analysis.

Summary of the Decision-Making Process in a Descriptive–Correlational–Experimental Loop. As discussed above, in a systematic program of research over an extended period of time, decisions made in one study can be used to modify and inform later studies; that is, they can be used to determine a new focus, what is to be collected, and how it is to be collected, as well as when data are to be collected. In other words, decisions and the resulting research cycle become interactive–reactive (cf. Hymes, 1978). In this way decisions become principled and theoretically driven. The use of such decision-making strategies can lead to changes in ways of observing the segment of reality under study.

Table 6.9 shows the shift in instrumentation used in the Evertson et al. program of research. As in the case of the Corsaro approach, multiple collection procedures were used within and across studies; data collection procedures provided convergent information within and across studies; and data collection procedures were modified, added, and deleted when the question and situation required. Finally, issues of entry and intent influenced the types of information collected and available for analysis.

The inquiry cycle described above, therefore, is both linear and generative; that is, it contains both preset, a priori aspects of design and interactive reactive types of decision points. As the program of research developed, the approach used moved from the decontextualized (exclusive) end of the continuum presented in Figure 6.3 to the more context inclusive end of the continuum; it also moved from a preset format in decision making to one in which questions are generated throughout the study as described in Figure 6.4.

Example 2: Merging Perspectives in Collaborative Research

The second example illustrates how differing research programs and questions can be merged to form a unique and continuing program of research. Figure 6.7 graphically presents this program. As indicated in Figure 6.7, prior to 1979, Weinstein and Marshall each had their own programs of research. Weinstein was concerned with investigating the effect of teacher expectations and began studying teachers' differential treatment of students and students' perceptions of such treatment. This early work led to the development of a student mediation model of the processes by which patterns of teacher differential treatment result in differences in student achievement. This model suggests that students perceive, interpret, and act on information contained in teacher cues about expected achievement (Weinstein, in press). As a part of this research, Weinstein developed a student questionnaire to explore student perceptions of teacher treatment, the Teacher Treatment Inventory (Weinstein & Middlestadt, 1979). This work provided the background for the NIE study of Student Perceptions of Differential Teacher Treatment in 1979.

In the precollaborative stage, Marshall was involved in developing ways of exploring the nature of classroom structure and functioning across open and traditional classrooms and in identifying the characteristics of open classrooms (1972–1978). During this phase, Marshall developed the Dimensional Occurrence Scale (DOS), a low-inference, broad-range instrument, designed to capture a wide range of classroom structures and ways of functioning (e.g., grouping practices, time spent on various activities, types of materials available and in use, the types of strategies teachers used, etc.). This instrument included ratings and a sign system as the primary ways of capturing the similarities and differences in structuring and functioning (Marshall, 1976a; Marshall et al., 1977). Along with the DOS, Marshall used a categorical system, a revision of the Reciprocal Category System (Ober et al., 1971), modified to capture different contexts or types of language use (Marshall & Green, 1978). Marshall also used other coding systems designed to explore student engagement and teacher movement paths (Marshall, 1976b). In other words, Marshall was involved in studying open and traditional classrooms using multiple perspectives.

In 1979, Marshall joined Weinstein for the data collection and analysis stage of the NIE study of Student Perceptions of Differential Teacher Treatment. One contribution to this project was Marshall's knowledge of classroom structure and the literature on open–traditional education. A major hypothesis for this study was that students would perceive less differential teacher treatment in open than in traditional classrooms. This hypothesis was not supported, although the study did show large classroom differences in the amount of differential treatment perceived by students (Weinstein et al., 1982). Moreover teacher expectations were found to contribute more to the prediction of achievement in classrooms in which students perceived high degrees of differential teacher treatment as opposed to classrooms where students perceived low amounts of differential teacher treatment (Brattesani, Weinstein, & Marshall, 1984).

Table 6.9. Nature of Data Collected Throughout Inquiry Cycle

	Category System	Ratings	Checklist/Sign System	Narrative	Interviews	Technological	Outcome Measures
Texas Teacher Effectiveness Study (TTEP) 1970–1973	Expanded version of Brophy–Good Dyadic Interaction System	Observer ratings of teacher behaviors/ characteristics/ class climate, clarity, enthusiasm, etc.	Observer checklists of teacher methods, materials, time use, lesson presentation, feedback, etc.		Teacher interviews about methods, materials, use of rewards, beliefs, etc.		
Texas Junior High School Study (TJHSS) 1974–1975)	Expanded version of TTEP observation system with added categories for student questions/ comments	(See above)	Observer records of classroom time spent in various formats	Brief observer descriptions of class activities, format, content being presented	(See above)		Student achievement on California Achievement Tests used as a covariate with specially designed end-of-year test Student attitude measure
First-Grade Reading Group Study (FGRGS) 1974–1975	A specially developed category system capturing methods and materials, along with teacher student interaction and treatment implementation				Teacher interviews about reading methods and use of 22 principles		Student achievement in reading
Classroom Organization Study (COS) 1977–1978		Observer ratings of lesson presentation, pupil behavior, teacher reaction to misbehavior, class climate, etc.	Counts of student levels of task engagement (e.g. on-task, academic; on-task, procedural; off-task, sanctioned or unsanctioned; off-task)	Detailed narratives of events related to managing and organizing classrooms from start of school	Teacher interviews about management practices, beliefs about student control, etc.		Student achievement in reading and math
Junior High Classroom Organization Study (JHCOS) 1989–1979		(See above)	(See above)	(See above)	(See above)		(See TJHSS)
Elementary School Pilot Study (ESP) 1978–1979		(See above)	(See above)	(See above)	Teacher interviews about their use of the manual and opinions about utility		
Classroom Management Improvement Study (CMIS) 1980–1981		(See above)	(See above)	(See above)	(See above)		
Arkansas Classroom Management Training Study (ACMTS) 1982–1983		(See above)	(See above)	Observer notes to describe classroom context, student task engagement, and time		Audiotapes of lesson content, teacher–student talk	Student performance on SRA used as a covariate with end-of-year content referenced tests
Exploration of Management Models 1984	(uses data from ACMTS) Primarily secondary analysis						

The findings of the 1979–1980 NIE study led to a refinement and expansion of the research questions in the next set of studies. One of the major questions generated was: What was the nature of classroom context in which students' perceptions of high and low amounts of differential teacher treatment were embedded, which might then contribute to students' self-expectations? To answer this question, an observational study was designed to be conducted in a subset of 12 of the 30 classrooms (in the NIMH and NIE 1980–1984 studies). These classrooms were selected from the extremes of student-perceived high- and low-differential-treatment classrooms. A model of classroom factors influencing the development of student self-evaluations was postulated (Marshall & Weinstein, 1984). This model was developed based on the earlier work of both researchers, the NIE study (1979–1980), new research findings on public–private feedback (Bossert, 1979; Blumenfeld et al., 1979), and research on single and multiple abilities of students (Cohen, 1979; Rosenholtz, 1979, in press).

This model of classroom factors affecting students' self-evaluations and a refined student mediation model served as a framework for planning and framing the next set of studies (the NIMH and NIE 1980–1983 studies). These models influenced

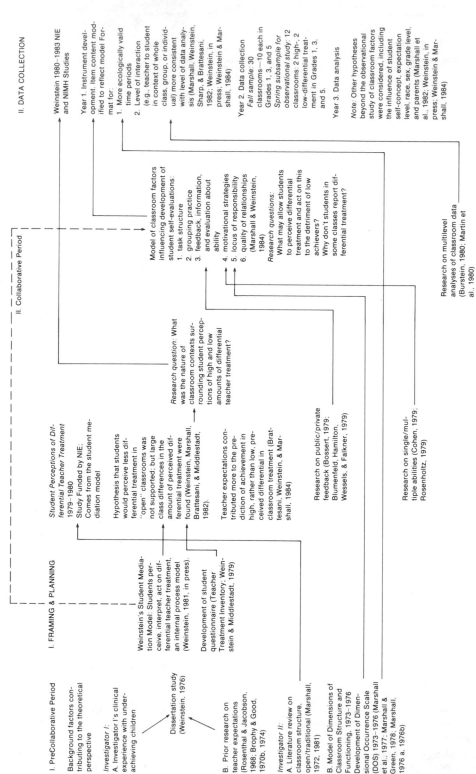

Fig. 6.7. Collaborative research cycle.

decisions about the nature of observations needed (e.g., high- and low-reading groups as well as whole-class observations). In addition three other factors contributed to the development of the observation system and to the research design: (a) the loss of information resulting from the use of categorical systems (Marshall and Green, 1978), (b) the need to use more ecologically valid observation periods (*event* rather than *time* sampling), and (c) the work by Burstein (1980) and Martin et al., (1980) on multilevel analyses of classroom data. An observation system was needed that would permit the broad-based exploration of the characteristics of classrooms where students perceived differing amounts of differential teacher treatment; therefore, given the refined questions and the new model, the Marshall instrument, the Dimension Occurrence Scale (Marshall, 1976a; Marshall et al., 1977), was modified to meet the requirements of the new studies. Both quantitative and qualitative information was collected with the modified observation system (renamed the Classroom Dimension System). Qualitative data were collected in on-line narrative records. Quantitative data were collected in three sections of the Classroom Dimension Scale (CDScale). As indicated in Figure 6.7 under "Data Collection," Part I of the CDScale was used on-line; that is, data were recorded on coding forms while the observer watched the classroom activities. This part provided an overview of the general structure of tasks, groupings, and evaluation procedures that create the context for learning during the observation period. This information provides a general picture of (a) whether students were working individually, in groups, or together, (b) where the teacher was working, (c) the subject-matter content, (d) the amount of choice that students had, and (e) the predominant types of teacher evaluation. This section consists of a nominal scale, recordings of amount of time, dichotomous variables (occurs — does not occur), counts of the exact number of cases, and a hierarchical system in which items can be coded for each level of grouping. This section, therefore, uses multiple types of data collection in order to obtain a wide view of the context on a general level.

Part II of the CDScale focuses on teachers in interaction with students or groups of students. The information obtained from this section includes: (a) types of tasks, (b) motivation strategies, (c) responsibilities, (d) evaluation and feedback, and (e) quality of the relationships. The items in this section of the CDScale are coded from narrative records, rather than live. The observer makes a narrative record (field notes) that includes the context in which the interaction occurred, the specific behaviors that occurred, and the general flow of the interaction between teacher and student. The observer records the individual student with whom the teacher interacts and whether the interaction occurs with (a) the class as a whole, (b) an individual with others around, (c) a group, (d) the individual within a group, or (e) the individual alone. The tone of the teacher's interaction is also recorded (e.g. matter-of-fact, warm). In addition, the observer also makes a second type of field note to indicate impressions and interpretations of events. Field notes are typed immediately after the observation period using a set format to permit ease of retrieval of teacher statements and interactions. After the observation period, the observer applies the Part II of the CDScale (on teachers' interactions) to the field notes. Using this combined procedure has several advantages over coding interactions on line alone or coding only after an observation period. These are: (a) an observer can count the exact number of times each behavior occurs from field records; (b) an observer can reflect on the context and consider whether the behaviors actually fit the definition as well as the nuances of behaviors not fully recorded; and (c) this approach allows accurate retrieval of instances of occurrence and discussion with other observers when checking reliability.

Part III of the CDScale is a high-inference rating scale. The observer rates the frequency and intensity of warmth and irritation conveyed to the class, the individual, and the group.

In addition to the Classroom Dimension System, student measures developed in the early Weinstein work (Teacher Treatment Inventory, Weinstein & Middlestadt, 1979), and those added in the NIE 1979 study (measures of student and teacher expectations) were modified to meet the needs and refined hypotheses of the present study. These changes included an expansion from Grade 4 to Grades 1, 3, and 5, as well as an exploration of the influence of student self-concept and level of expectation (for achievement) on (a) student perceptions of differential teacher treatment, (b) student perceptions of their teacher's expectations for them, and (c) on year-end achievement.

To ascertain a more complete picture of the classroom from other viewpoints, teachers were interviewed concerning the less observable aspects of the classroom (e.g., decisions about grouping, curriculum, evaluation) and students were interviewed concerning their perceptions of their teacher's (and mother's) attitudes and behaviors regarding the quality of their schoolwork.

The discussion above demonstrates how the work of both Weinstein and Marshall has combined to create a new approach that is an extension of the individual researcher's previous work. In addition, this work continues to develop the general framework begun by Weinstein. The question of factors that influence student learning and the effect of differential teacher treatment continue to be the thread that is consistent across studies. The process reflected in the development of the current program of research suggests that this program is interactive–reactive in the same sense as the work by Evertson and her colleagues. One study informs other studies; the ways in which observations are made are informed by previous work; and the needs of the current study (e.g., the type of setting, the age of the students, the questions under study, etc.) lead to the modification of past data collection procedures as well as the general design of the study.

The Weinstein work began with a questionnaire approach and added observation with the addition of Marshall's work. The observation system was systematically modified to include more and more contextual information. Marshall & Weinstein (1984) point out that the contextual information from the narrative records permits both exploration of variation and potential explanations for the quantitative findings. In addition, as Marshall and Weinstein (1982) suggest, the use of narratives permits retrieval of contextual information that can be used in obtaining interrater reliability and in resolving differences in perceptions of events. This type of record appears to be important when videotape records are not available, not cost effective, or not permitted by the population under study. This multiple-instrument and multiple-perspective approach permits retrieval of a wide range of information.

Example 3: A Model of Triangulation to Collect Multiple Perspectives

The third study represents a systematic effort to obtain different perspectives of the same process, discourse processes (e.g., question use in different settings: classroom, play group, home). In contrast to the presentation of the previous examples, the discussion in this section begins with the presentation of the triangulation study and then moves to a discussion of the historical roots of the various components of the study. The design of the study by Morine-Dershimer and Tenenberg (1981) is unique in that it was actually a series of preplanned contrasts and interrelated analyses of a systematically collected data set. The study involved collecting three different perspectives on each type of phenomenon: (a) teacher–student interaction in language arts lessons in which discussion was a means of instruction, (b) communication in home situations of a select set of students (families reflecting different ethnic groups), and (c) interactions in play groups outside the classroom. Figure 6.8 presents a description of this triangulation approach (Adelman & Walker, 1975). Space does not permit more than a cursory exploration of each study. Therefore, rather than focus on the studies per se, the discussion will focus on the model on a general level.

The general framework for this study was drawn from work on sociolinguistic research. The specific question focused on (a) the nature of participants' perceptions of classroom discourse; (b) the interface between and among the perceptions of different participants; (c) the relationship of students' perceptions and performance with achievement and participation in classroom events (e.g., discussion in language arts lessons); and (d) the continuity of perceptions of language functions at home, in school, and during play. One of the outcomes of this work is the identification of what is required of students in classrooms in terms of communicative participation and understandings, or, in Morine-Dershimer's words, in what it takes to be a "literate" pupil (Morine-Dershimer, 1981).

The contrasts in Triangle 1 permit exploration of the same phenomena (36 language arts lessons: 6 for each of 6 teachers in Grades 2, 3 and 4) from different sociolinguistic analytic perspectives: speech act analysis (Ramirez, 1979; cf. Smith & Coulthard, 1975), structural analysis of questions and cycle sequences (Tenenberg, 1981, in press; cf. Johnson, 1979), and analysis of language dimensions (Morine-Dershimer, Tenenberg, & Shuy, 1981; Tenenberg, Morine-Dershimer, & Shuy, 1981; Morine-Dershimer & Tenenberg, 1981). This point of triangulation is labeled "Alternative Sociolinguistic Descriptions of Classroom Discourse." The findings from this set of triangulations provided both convergent and complementary information about the nature of classroom discourse, with a special emphasis on questions (cf. Johnson, 1979; Mehan, 1979a). Taken together the information provides a more holistic picture of the nature of teacher–student interactions. This set of analyses identified teachers' use of differential questioning styles that were related to differences in student achievement.

Triangle 2, "Alternative Perceptions of Classroom Discourse," focused on perceptions of classroom discourse by teacher, student, and researcher. This triangle shares a common analysis with the previous triangle. As indicated in Figure 6.8, information was obtained using a variety of collection procedures. Videotape records were played back to teachers and pupils on the day they were taken and viewers were asked to respond to what they remembered hearing. Students and teachers were also asked to generate sentences which might be said by or to the pupil to "get someone's attention" or "get someone to do something." A sentence completion task on "rules" of discourse, constructed on the basis of pupil response to an open-ended question about "how people talk in your classroom" was also completed. Participants were asked to organize a set of three-by-five cards obtained from "what do you hear" into groups of cards that "belonged together because people were saying the same kind of thing." And finally, participants were asked to study a set of teacher questions asked in the lesson (also collected was information about teacher praise and pupil responses); they were then asked to explain who said these things, to whom, for what reason. This information was explored for convergence of perspective as well as for contrast points and relationships to achievement and participation.

Triangle 3, "Pupil Perceptions of Discourse in Alternative Settings" also explored multiple perceptions of discourse; however, in this triangle, the discourse explored was that which occurred in alternative settings (family conversations of a selected set of families, classroom discourse, and play groups discourse). Once again Triangles 2 and 3 shared a common analysis; in this instance, analysis of classroom discourse and perceptions of pupils of this discourse constituted the common analysis point.

The tasks in this triangulation were similar to those in Triangle 2. These tasks included (a) sentence completion, (b) generating sentences, (c) a "reporting-what-was-heard" task, and (d) organizing the cards on what was heard and what belonged together. This set of analyses also permitted exploration of convergence of perceptions and points of contrast in perceptions of discourse used in the three different settings (home discourse, classroom discourse, and the discourse of play).

The final triangle contrasted alternative perceptions of discourse in play settings. This triangle, "Alternative Perceptions of Discourse in Play Settings," shares a common analysis point with Triangle 3. In Triangle 3, perceptions of classmates of discourse in a play setting were contrasted with the perceptions of a group of early childhood educators (n = 10), and finally, with pupil participants' perspectives.

The decision making in this study was preplanned and the contrasts were developed on a systematic and principled basis. These contrasts guided the decision making about the data collection procedures to be used. Observations were made of three types: videotapes (a) of a set of language arts lessons in which teachers taught a series of self-selected lessons, (b) of play groups, and (c) of family interaction. The limit set by the researcher was that the language arts lessons could not contain seatwork; rather the lessons had to have some discussion so that the discourse could be explored. Stimulated recall was used in conjunction with interviews of students and teachers. These participants were shown the tapes and asked a series of questions after viewing the tapes (e.g., What do you remember hearing?). The comments were recorded by the researcher on 3 × 5 cards. The information on the cards became a source of data

Fig. 6.8. Use of triangulation to study classroom discourse: Study design and instrumentation. Adapted from Morine-Dershimer (1981).

199

(see Triangles 2 and 3). The participants were asked to organize the cards to reflect what belonged together. Finally, participants were given questions obtained from the lessons and asked to specify who said these to whom and why. This information, collected from multiple sources, provided the basis for triangulation of findings. Triangulation, therefore, is a means of exploring convergence of perception and analysis approaches. In addition, this approach permits exploration of differences in perception and/or description obtained from each perspective. This research highlights continuities and discontinuities in perceptions of various groups and various research approaches. It also identifies differential behaviors and their relationship to achievement as well as student perceptions of these differential behaviors. It is an approach that provides a broad picture of events and permits exploration of factors that can influence student performance and achievement. In this way, this study is related to the Weinstein and Marshall program in Example 2.

The discussion above focused on a single study with multiple components, but as argued previously, to fully understand a study, previous work by the researcher must be considered. Therefore, to understand why Morine-Dershimer used this particular set of collection procedures, and the specific design, the research history of this project must be considered. In the remainder of this section, an exploration of earlier work that serves as a grounding for the present study will be considered.

The Historical Grounding for the Triangulation Study. All work in classrooms undertaken by Morine-Dershimer has been designed to help teachers observe themselves and what they do

with children. The study discussed above is a logical step in a consistent program concerned with teachers' and students' thinking and the nature of instruction. Figure 6.9 provides a graphic representation of previous work.

As indicated in Figure 6.9, the studies in this past program were linked. The link was both methodological and substantive. The studies focused on building understandings of instruction and in exploring the understandings of participants in the instructional setting. What is not evident are the other aspects or premises of this body of work. The work on perception was informed and based on the work of Piaget and Taba. The procedures used considered the students' conceptions and logical ways of thinking. Piaget (Inhelder & Piaget, 1958) showed that the use of indirect procedures could lead to an understanding of children's conceptions of phenomena. Taba's (1967) work on concept formation suggested developmental issues to be considered and systematic ways to use children in instruction as well as research. This work and the resulting procedures were tied to the theory of instruction being developed by Morine-Dershimer (Morine, 1965).

The cyclic nature of the question was derived from the work of Bellack et al. (1966). This work explored question–response–reaction cycles from the perspective of the outside observer. The Bellack work suggested that a focus on question cycles would be productive.

The discussion above demonstrates how the procedures and substantive aspects of the triangulation study were related to previous work. This study, therefore, was partially theoretically driven by the theory of instruction being developed by

1965. Dissertation: A Model of Inductive Discovery for Instructional Theory (Morine, 1965) →	1969. Discovery Modes—A Criterion for Teaching Process (Morine, 1969) →	1971. Discovering New Dimensions in the Teaching Process (Morine, Spaulding, & Greenberg, 1971; Morine & Morine, 1973) →	1975. Interaction Analysis in the Classroom: Alternative Applications (Morine, 1975) →	1975. Teacher and Pupil Perceptions of Classroom Interaction (Morine & Vallance, 1975)
	Explored implications of different kinds of subject matter for instructional procedures, ways to have students try to think.	Focused on classroom observation. Development of procedures for having teachers observe their own behavior. Focused on question cycles, particularly types of teacher reactions to pupil responses.	Proposed alternative units of interactive analyses and displays of data to serve alternative purposes.	Short segments of interaction in lessons taught by different instructional methods, in unfamiliar classrooms, were shown to pupils and teachers. Asked, "What did you see happening?" Compared pupil and teacher observations.
	Premise: Process by which knowledge was developed is an important variable to consider in trying to teach the knowledge.		Raised the questions: 1. If students reported what they observed, what would the students' units be—how would they differ from those of sociolinguists?	Raised the questions: 1. What differences would pupils observe in noninstructional settings (e.g., home, play)?
			2. Would alternative approaches to description of classroom language provide complementary findings?	2. How would pupil and teacher observations compare when focused on their own classrooms?

Fig. 6.9. Historical perspective of work leading to the triangulation study.

Morine-Dershimer and partially by related work on concept development and formation. The procedures were also conceptually influenced by this theoretical frame.

One final aspect of the match between the research approach and the theory in which it is grounded should be brought out. Morine-Dershimer built this program on the notion that a particular perspective on instruction grows out of the discipline in which it is grounded. In her case, the discipline was language. Therefore, the way in which she chose to look at language had to be related to the kind of knowledge within the discipline. Since she was concerned with language in use, she grounded her work and the framework for the study in sociolinguistics. Building on the work of Stubbs (1976) she developed the planned contrasts to explore how language worked in use and what participants' perspectives were of this use. The triangulation study, therefore, was constructed within a particular theoretical framework. The framework served as a guide to all aspects of the study — the design of the study; the selection, modification, and development of instruments and procedures; and the analysis and interpretation of findings.

Example 4: An Ethnographic Program

Example 4 focuses on the ethnographic research program of Cook-Gumperz, Gumperz, and Simons (1981) and Cook-Gumperz (in press). With this example, the discussion comes full circle and returns to the interactive–reactive cycle (Hymes, 1978) described by Corsaro (1985) presented at the beginning of this section on observation as inquiry. In contrast to Examples 1 through 3 in which the interactive–reactive aspect of the research program occurred across studies, the interactive–reactive research cycle occurs within this study and is a central part of the research cycle. That is, the researcher enters with a general question that leads to the use of specific instruments, schedules of data collection, interviews, and so forth. As the researcher becomes more familiar with the setting and begins to understand the way the group under study functions, the researcher begins to focus on specific aspects of the ethnographic process. Foci are selected because they are recurrent phenomena or events or they highlight some specific area of interest (e.g., miscommunication, literacy, etc.). The cycle continues to be interactive–reactive: the questions are refined and new ones generated; new schedules are constructed; instruments are added or modified; interviews are added to obtain verification and validation, and so on. This cycle continues throughout the study (e.g., Corsaro, 1985; Heath, 1982; Pelto & Pelto, 1977; Spindler, 1982; for a synthesis of criteria and a discussion of issues related to ethnographic research in reading and other educational processes, see Green & Bloome, 1983).

The studies by Cook-Gumperz, Gumperz & Simons (1981) reflect this interactive–reactive cycle. The entire cycle is presented in Figure 6.10. While the cycle appears linear in this graphic representation, the parts interact; that is, as one moves from left to right, a history develops. Each individual part (column) has a history; that is, it is informed by what preceded it. Decisions, therefore, at any point are grounded in prior decisions and in the types of questions under study at any given point in the study. As indicated in the Corsaro (1985) quote presented earlier, the decisions are principled and part of the

demographic information about the study. The interrelationship of the parts and the decision-making process will be highlighted in the discussion that follows.

The historical context of this study is highlighted in Column 1, "Background of the Study." While this sequence of events frames this research, each of the researchers on this team had extensive experience on research in educational and other cultural settings, such as home, community (e.g., Cook-Gumperz & Corsaro, 1977; Cook-Gumperz & Gumperz, 1976; Gumperz, 1982a, 1982b; Simons & Murphy 1981). The merger of these perspectives led to the exploration of classroom processes and communicative factors that influenced assessment of student ability and student performance. The multiple perspectives are reflected in Column 2, the "Mental Frame-Grid: Assumptions guiding/driving the collection, analysis, and interpretation of data." The perspective of this research team is reflected in the following representative questions for this study, The School/Home Ethnography Project:

1. What are the continuities and discontinuities between classroom, playground, and home communication strategies?
2. How does what is said and done in the classroom influence the child's view of the learning process or goals of education?
3. How does the mismatch in discourse understanding between home experience and that in the classroom lead to miscommunication?

These questions indicate that the concern of this team was focused on the communicative environment and communicative processes of school and their relationship to home and community. The approach that this team took is generally referred to as ethnography of communication (Gumperz & Hymes, 1972). This approach to ethnography is both topic centered (Hymes, 1978) and hypothesis oriented (Sanday, 1979); that is, the project selected a focus on the classroom and used discourse theory, developmental theory, and reading theory, among other areas to guide interpretation, collection, and analysis. This study, therefore, like the studies presented earlier in this section, is part of a program of research in which prior work is used to inform the current study.

While this study has a specific conceptual and theoretical framework, this framework serves as a guide; it does not determine in advance what will be observed, collected, or counted. The determination of these factors comes from extended observation in the setting. The data collection phase took place over a 1-year period. Observation of recurrent phenomena and the expectations for participation led to the identification of a variety of loci for more specific observation. As indicated in the column entitled "Participation Observation," the observer engaged in a variety of roles: participant observer, observer participant, and aide. These roles allowed the researcher to obtain a variety of perspectives (e.g., insider and outsider) on the everyday life and events of the classroom. By observing the teacher and being a teacher's aide, the observer was able to capture different aspects of the teacher's theory of pedagogy, her rationale for organizing and managing events, and her plans and planning behavior. By focusing on the everyday events of the day from before school to after the children left, the observer

BACKGROUND OF THE STUDY 1965–1977	STAGE I FRAMING AND PLANNING THE PROJECT COMPONENTS	STAGE II DATA COLLECTION - GENERAL PARTICIPANT OBSERVATION	STAGE III TOPIC-CENTERED PARTICIPANT OBSERVATION	STAGE IV INFERENCING/ HYPOTHESIS GENERATING	STAGE V NATURAL EXPERIMENTS
1965—after the first year of Head Start, the U.S. Office of Education convened a small conference of anthropologists, linguists, psychologists, and sociologists to suggest priorities for research on children's language and its relationship to school success. Gumperz participated (Cazden et al., 1972). 1966—Follow-up conference was held. The outcome of this conference was published in *Functions of Language in the Classroom* (Cazden et al., 1972) Gumperz and Hernandez-Chavez published "Bilingualism, Bidialectalism, and Classroom Interaction" in this volume. 1974—The National Institute of Education convened a group of panels of researchers to set the research agenda for research on teaching. Gumperz participated in Panel 5, "Teaching as a Linguistic Process in a Cultural Setting" (NIE, 1974). 1977—The NIE funded a set of proposals focused on the nature of "Teaching as a Linguistic Process in a Cultural Setting" (NIE, 1977) which included a study by Cook-Gumperz, Gumperz, & Simons (1978), the one overviewed in this section.	Mental Frame Grid. Assumptions guiding/driving the collection, analysis, and interpretation of data. Assumptions are derived from theoretical and research literature, which includes work on: • discourse processes • conversational analysis • ethnography of communication • classroom organization • teaching learning processes • adult-child interactions • child language • cross-cultural communication • evaluation of performance • socialization • reading acquisition and development • metalinguistic awareness • sociolinguistics • cognitive development	**Participant Observation** Single observer assigned to each classroom. Observer assumes three roles: 1. *Participant observer:* participates in events and observes during participation—records information after event 2. *Observer participant:* primarily observes—participates only if approached by students for help 3. *Aide:* acts as aide for teacher, helps students. Each role provides a different view of events. This approach allows observers to assume an *insider's* view at times and an *outsider's* view at other times. Ongoing involvement provides time for informal interviewing, capturing developmental aspect of events, and establishing a shared perspective of events with teacher and students. **Participant Observation I:** Teacher Planning Organization — Participant Observer (PO) works with teacher before school year begins, before class at breaks, and before and after school as aide. PO is not trained teacher, is naive, and can ask questions on a "real need to know" basis; this talk is "talk for doing" job as aide. Approach is used to observe: 1. teacher plans and planning behaviors 2. teacher organizational behaviors and practices 3. teacher theory of pedagogy. **Participant Observation II:** Classroom Processes Practices — Observer participant of total day to ascertain: 1. formal segments of day 2. ways in which teacher frames activities/events 3. orchestration of events. Participant observation of events to help students and to ascertain: 1. segments of events 2. conflict/contrast points 3. expectations for behavior. Basis of segmentation: contextualization cues and participation structures, observable behaviors. — **Explicit Definition of Behaviors** Teacher definition of actions available through question and answer sequences between PO and teacher in PO's role of aide. **Implicit Definition of Behaviors** Inferred from practice and from directions given to PO as aide. Can be made explicitly during informal interviewing as part of aide's role. **Implicit Definition of Behaviors** Inferred from sequences of behavior, from actions of teacher and students working with each others behaviors and observation of contextualization cues.	*Participant Observation III:* Observe for contrastive situations/signs of discrepancy 1. Look for instances of differential learning 2. Look for events of day that reflect problem. Best site is event with high incidence of problems (e.g., miscommunication) 3. Look for atypical happenings within typical events 4. Begin to predict *type* of event that will occur, not specific event. *Participant Observation IV:* Observe and videotape select events. Observe *participation structures* and obtain rights and obligations for participation in events. Observe *verbal signals* and conventions or formulaic/ritualistic uses of language. Observe target individuals selected during earlier stages and who permit observation of contrastive behaviors.	Observe discourse strategies used within the context. Observe indications of evaluation of student performance (verbal and nonverbal). Observe students and identify differential performance and treatment within and across settings. Observe recurrent events and begin to predict occurrence of *types of* events.	Plan and execute natural experiments that permit contrast of observed phenomena with similar phenomena in controlled or contrastive settings. I. Science laboratory Lawrence Hall of Science. Explore whether the difference in participation setting and structure produce differences in performance. II. Pear stories (Chafe). Explore narrative production (oral & written) in control situation with naturally occurring narratives in classroom (e.g., sharing time). III. Storytelling task. Further explore students narrative abilities and differences in narrative style among groups of students of different language traditions. IV. Referential communication task/phonemic perception task. Explore students' ability to use decontextualized language and contrast to reading-skill performance. V. Home data collection. Collect data on narrative events in home. Work with parents to select events, have parents tape events (no PO). suggest events.

Fig. 6.10. Design of Cook-Gumperz, Gumperz, and Simon's School/Home Ethnography Project and Green's Framing and Planning Components. Part 2 of figure (Stages I–IV) from "Research on Teaching as a Linguistic Process: A State of the Art" by J. Green (1983b). Copyright 1983 by the American Educational Research Association. Reprinted by permission.

was able to obtain a picture of the segments of the day (temporal arrangement); of the ways in which the teacher framed, established, checked, maintained, suspended, and reestablished, activities, norms and so forth within and across days; and the ways in which teacher and students orchestrated and negotiated daily life. The observer had a "real need to know" in that she was a member of this social group and had roles to play in different situations.

This general observation phase led to the selection of a more focused perspective within the general perspective. That is, as the participant observer continued to collect, analyze, and interpret data, she and the other members of the research team, acting as a debriefing and analysis team, began to (a) identify recurrent patterns and phenomena; (b) generate questions for further study and hypotheses to test in later events; and (c) select new loci for observation. The latter loci would be captured on videotape as well as in field notes. Prior to this, information and descriptions were primarily obtained from field notes and observer records of various kinds. The videotape permits in-depth exploration of a preselected type of event over time. This type of record permits exploration of communicative processes involved in the event. Given the general questions listed above, the use of videotape is an important data collection procedure for it permits talk that is abstract in nature to be "frozen." That is, once talk has occurred it is not possible to remember or reconstruct how it was delivered. People frequently know what they meant, but rarely can retrieve how they said it. The frozen record, therefore, permits in-depth analysis of what talk occurred, where, when, to whom, in what ways, and for what purpose. It also permits examination of multiple perspectives (e.g., teacher, student, group, parent) and the ways in which factors such as frame of reference, linguistic abilities, expectations, and other contextualization factors (e.g., Cook-Gumperz, 1976; Corsaro, 1981) influence participation and communicative competence (Hymes, 1974).

The cycle described here begins with general participant observation (from passive to fully active). While these different types of observation continue throughout the project, a second type of data collection has been added, the collection of videotape records of selected phenomena and events. The decision about collection stems from the earlier observations and the nature of the general questions under study. As the research team gains greater and greater knowledge of the setting and social life in this setting, the questions being asked are refined and other questions are identified. Each question leads to a series of decisions about who and what to observe, how, when, where and for what purpose. One decision influences other decisions. New observation schedules within the general schedule of the school day are constructed; instruments are added; and procedures are refined, modified, and added to permit the researcher to obtain adequate information. Each decision is principled (Heath, 1982). Analysis is ongoing as is collection and interpretation. The participants' perspectives are obtained from informal interviews (e.g., as teacher aide) and from observing spontaneous comments about the events and phenomena as they occur. Specific collection periods co-occur with the more general collection procedures.

The cycle did not stop with the selection of specific events or phenomena to explore. One of the primary recurrent patterns observed had to do with the nature and function of various discourse processes (language in use). The research team decided that one process, narrative performance, would be selected as the unit of analysis. This unit was selected because it was readily identifiable and because by selecting this unit as the locus of observation the contexts in which it occurred could be allowed to vary. Therefore, the question of functional equivalence of context (Erickson & Shultz, 1981; Florio & Shultz, 1979) was not a problem for this research team. In other words, narrative was the stable unit and all other aspects were permitted to vary; the way in which factors of context influenced narrative performance could then be explored (e.g., the way in which the teacher accepted or sanctioned storytelling during group discussion or sharing time). The selection of narrative as the unit of observation also permitted exploration of differences in language use and functioning at home, in school, and on the playground.

The selection of narrative as the unit of observation also led to the inclusion of a set of natural experiments and experimental studies within the general ethnography. This set of substudies is presented in the last column of Figure 6.10. Each of these experiments was added so that different aspects of narrative performance could be explored to develop a more holistic picture of the students' narrative ability and knowledge. This information could then be contrasted with performance in everyday contexts of home and school. The ways in which teacher-student interactions supported, constrained, and/or overlooked these abilities could also be explored, as could the consequences for students of such actions. For example, findings in this project showed a difference in teacher interactions with high- and low-reading-group students (Collins, 1983), as well as differences in positive and negative sanctions of students' "sharing time" narratives (Michaels & Cook-Gumperz, 1979; Michaels, 1981). Narrative performance was shown to vary with contextual demands, with audience, and with task; narrative was also shown to be culturally patterned, and such patterns, when they did not match the expected pattern of the teacher, often led to negative assessment of ability and to sanctions of student performance (Cook-Gumperz, in press).

Conclusions and Beginnings

These representative research studies illustrate how multiple perspective approaches have evolved over the last decade. They show how decision making is both interactive and reactive. That is, changes in studies, selection of locus of observation, selection of settings, refinement of questions, and generation of new questions come from prior work, observed needs, unexplained problems or recurrent patterns within and across studies (e.g., management and organization as a locus of observation in the Evertson et al. studies; narrative as the locus of observation in the Cook-Gumperz, Gumperz, & Simons (1981) study). Each of the studies described in this section is part of a program of research. Each has a history. This history, as shown above, must be understood in order to understand the reason for the study under consideration, the procedures selected, the locus of observation, and so forth. Another way to think about the relationship of one study to previous ones within a program of research is that the individual study is part of a

CAROLYN M. EVERTSON AND JUDITH L. GREEN

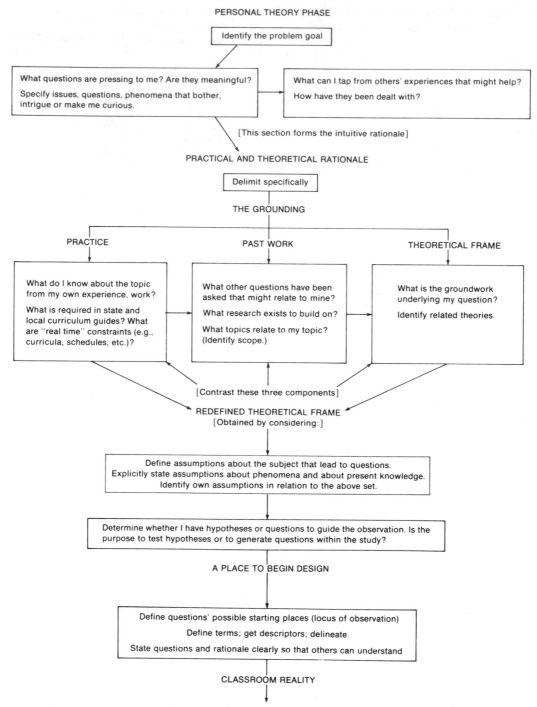

Fig. 6.11. A framework to guide decision making in observation.

larger process, even though on a general level the current study can stand alone. However, to understand what is being developed, the study must be considered in relationship to previous ones and to the related studies used to build the framework of the study and the evolving program. For example, the need to explain findings that were counter to those predicted led to the construction of projects that used a variety of qualitative and quantitative collection and analysis procedures. The reasons for the changes in methodology and questions would

not be evident without an understanding of the past history of a study.

The studies also demonstrated that qualitative and quantitative approaches are complementary. Each serves a different purpose. The use of a specific approach depends on the purpose of the study, the questions asked, and the setting in which the observations are occurring. These studies also demonstrate that any one study captures only a slice of reality. In addition, they demonstrate that different collection tools and procedures

Fig. 6.11. (*continued*)

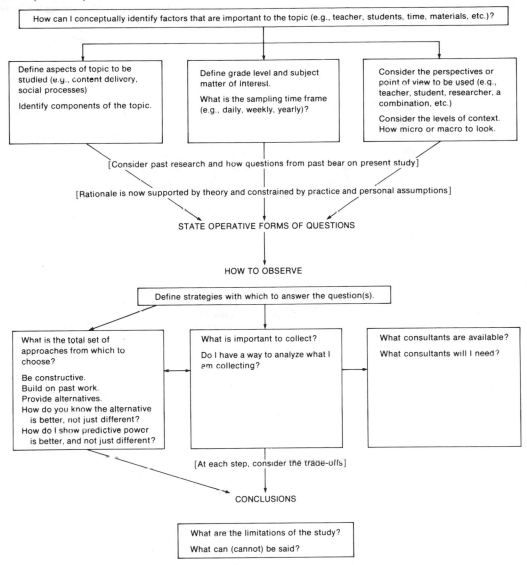

produce different and often complementary pictures of the observed phenomena.

As background for these studies, a description of the general nature of observation was presented in the first section of the chapter, which dealt with observation as method. A wide variety of factors involved in engaging in observational research were presented:

- observation as a means of representing reality
- issues of selectivity
- observation as a contextualized process
- systems for recording and storing observational data
- units of observation and aggregation of data
- issues in sampling

- representative sources of error; limits on certainty in observation
- toward criteria for adequate observation

These factors identified the issues and defined the nature of the process of observation from a generic perspective.

The two sections, when considered together, demonstrate what is involved in using observation as a systematic approach to exploring events, processes, and phenomena that occur in schools and other educational settings. In the remainder of this section, the question of how to begin will be considered. The framework that follows is meant to serve as a guide and will be presented in several formats. The formats of the framework are the product of three processes: (a) the interactions between the authors of this chapter, who represent differing research approaches suggested some of the issues to be presented; (b) the review of research involved in preparing this chapter, which also suggested some of the issues; and (c) other issues raised in research seminars on observing classroom processes at the University of Delaware and Ohio State University. The general information from Process 1 and 2 was presented in the previous section; therefore, the information and framework that define ways of considering where to begin and how to proceed, and that resulted from discussions with junior researchers, will now be considered. Once this framework has been considered, a summary framework will be presented.

The first framework was the result of a two-part process. Part 1 involved generating a list of steps to be considered when trying to design a study using observation. The participants of an observational research seminar at the University of Delaware, who had little previous experience with observation as an approach to studying teaching and learning processes (Pat Lefevre, Deborah Sardo, Deborah Smith, and Timothy Smith), generated the list presented in Table 6.10. The steps in Table 6.10 are not presented in a specific order; they are presented as they were developed over time. In Part 2, the students took these steps, ordered them, and added to them to design a framework that reflected the types of decisions involved in designing an observational study. Therefore, rather than presenting them in a fixed order, readers are invited to order these steps for themselves and to construct their own framework.

These questions demonstrate the types of decisions that need to be considered. As the seminar participants began to consider each of these statements and questions and to organize them, the relationships between and among these topics became clearer. Figure 6.11 shows how one student conceptualized the relationships between and among factors. This representation was selected because it demonstrates how a framework can be developed to approach the question of observation systematically as an inquiry process.

The junior researcher ordered the questions and topics above within six general topics. These topics move from a general identification of the question and what is in the field through a series of steps that help select the locus and make systematic decisions about what to observe, to the issue of how to observe. Observation methods are selected after decisions are made about whom to observe, what to observe, when, where, and for what purpose. Once these decisions are made on either a general or a specific level, how the observations will be made must be determined. This cycle is not rigid; rather it provides a set of steps to guide decision making. The cycle can be used both before and throughout the study. As indicated above, while the steps are viewed linearly, the components interact with each other both within and across steps.

The diagram in Figure 6.11 illustrates the variety of decisions that must be made. This framework suggests that the grounding of a study is not simple. It is mediated by personal theory and assumptions, theory and assumptions of those in the situations (practice issues), and theory and assumptions about the phenomena and process obtained from the literature on past work. In other words, the development of a framework for a particular study or the identification of the grounding of a particular study requires a form of triangulation. In addition, the

Table 6.10. Steps to be Considered in Conducting an Observational Research Study

Define question:
    What questions are pressing to me? Are they meaningful?
Define terms.
Define assumptions about the subject to be observed.
Locate past research and consider how this work bears on the question.
    Take a constructive perspective. Go beyond criticism to consider alternatives to overcome problems of past work or issues not considered. Ask: how is the present or proposed approach better? Think about how to show predictive power of the alternative approach.
Define grade level and subject matter of interest.
Define aspects of the topic (e.g., content, delivery, social aspects) that are to be studied.
What dimension of the question will be looked at in what time frame (e.g., weekly, daily, yearly)?
Define strategies with which to answer questions.
    Consider: 1. Which have been used previously?
            2. Which are available for use?
            3. What is important to collect?
            4. How is data to be analyzed?
            5. Is special training needed to use the approach or strategy?
Define next study to be done after this one. Consider the program of research.
What are the limitations of the study? What statements can or cannot be made?
Specify the issues, questions, phenomena that bother, intrigue, and/or excite curiosity.
    Identify the whole. Delimit the topic specifically.
Consider the perspectives or points of view from which to consider the question (e.g., student, teacher, observer, combination, etc.).
How can teacher, hour, materials, students, and so forth, which are important to the topic, be conceptually related?
Consider the levels of context (e.g., micro or macro).
Define terms, and get descriptors. Clearly define and delineate topic.
State questions and rationale clearly so that others can know what the question is.
Identify related theories.
What topics relate to the specific topic? Identify the scope of information needed to delimit the topic fully.
Explicitly state assumptions about the phenomena, about the knowledge we have.
    What is the groundwork underlying my question?
What other questions might relate to the question?
Determine whether hypotheses exist to be tested or the purpose of the study is to generate questions to be tested within and across studies.
What do I know about the topic? What are my own experiences? Work?
    What is required in state/local curriculum guides?
    What are "real time" constraints (e.g., curricula, schedules, access, etc.)?
What can be drawn from others' experiences that might help (e.g., other teachers, friends, etc.)?
At each step, what are the trade-offs for the decisions made?

framework suggests that as one makes different decisions the framework is modified, concepts become clarified, terms are defined, the locus of observation and focus of the study are delineated, and the limitations are identified. The selection of observation methods is made in light of the framework. These decision-making processes may be set a priori or can be used to guide actions throughout the study.

While the sample frameworks above appear linear, the process is often reflexive and recursive. Therefore, one final

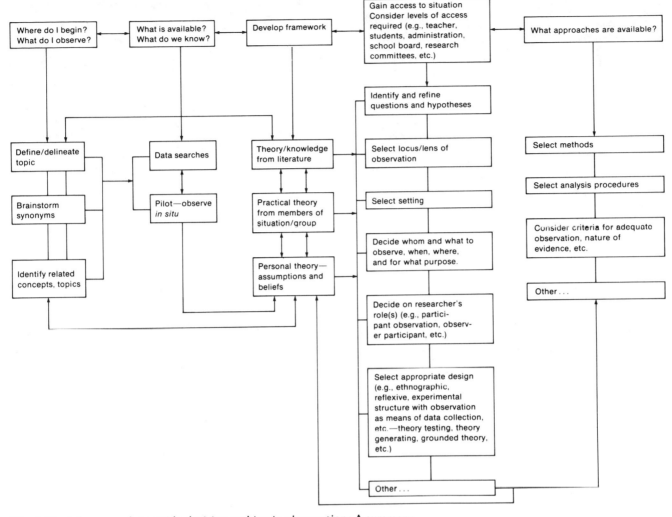

Fig. 6.12. A framework to guide decision making in observation: A summary.

framework will be presented. This framework is a synthesis of the previous work and the two main sections of this chapter and, as mentioned before, may be entered at different points. However, the different cells contained in this framework need to be considered when planning a systematic observational study and a program of research based on observation as the inquiry method.

The framework in Figure 6.12 is a general one. The authors recognize that there are different approaches to research and that each investigator will engage in observation in a different way. That is, the psychologist may observe one child in great depth or a small group of children to explore the nature of cognitive development. In contrast, the anthropologist might study a social group over time. In contrast to both of these approaches, the educational psychologist might want to observe a large number of classrooms in order to develop a normative model of how teachers manage classrooms. Each type of study may use similar observational methods; however, they will not use them in the same way for the same purpose. The framework is a place to begin; it is not a fixed guide as indicated by the

empty cells. We invite you to add to this framework, to modify it, and to restructure it. It is meant to be a heuristic device to help the person interested in using observation design a systematic study or program of research.

REFERENCES

Adelman, C. (1981). *Uttering, muttering, collecting, using, and reporting talk for social educational research.* London: Frank McIntyre.

Adelman, C., & Walker, R. (1975). Developing pictures for other frames: Action research and case study. In G. Chanan & S. Delamont (Eds.), *Frontiers of classroom research.* East Windsor, Berkshire, England: National Foundation for Educational Research.

Amidon, E., & Hough, J. (Eds.). (1967). *Interaction analysis: Theory, research, and application.* Reading, MA: Addison–Wesley.

Anderson, L. (1981). Short-term student responses to instruction. *Elementary School Journal, 82,* 97–108.

Anderson, L., Evertson, C., & Brophy, J. (1979). An experimental study of effective teaching in first grade reading groups. *Elementary School Journal, 79,* 193–223.

Au, K. (1980). Participation structures in a reading lesson with Hawaiian children. *Anthropology and Education Quarterly, 11*(2), 91–115.

Bales, R., & Strodtbeck, R. (1967). Phases in group problem-solving. In E. Amidon & J. Hough (Eds.) *Interaction analysis: Theory, research, and application.* Reading, MA: Addison–Wesley.

Barker, R. G. (1963). *The stream of behavior.* New York: Appleton-Century-Crofts.

Barker, R. G. (1968). *Ecological psychology: Concepts and methods for studying the environment of human behavior.* Stanford, CA: Stanford University Press.

Barker, R. G., & Wright, H. (1955). *Midwest and its children.* New York: Harper & Row.

Barnes, D., Britton, J., & Rosen, H. (1971). *Language, the learner, and the school* (rev. ed.). Harmondsworth, Middlesex, England: Penguin.

Barnes, D., & Todd, F. (1977). *Communication and learning in small groups.* London: Routledge & Kegan Paul.

Barr, R. (in press). Classroom interaction and curricular content. In D. Bloome (Ed.), *Literacy, language, and schooling.* Norwood, NJ: Ablex.

Barr, R., & Dreeban, R. (1983). *How schools work.* Chicago: University of Chicago Press.

Becker, H. (1970). *Sociological work.* Chicago: Aldine.

Bellack, A., Hyman, R., Smith, F., & Kliebard, H. (1966). *The language of the classroom.* New York: Columbia University Press.

Berliner, D. (1976). Impediments to the study of teacher effectiveness. *Journal of Teacher Education, 27*(1), 5–13.

Berliner, D. (1978). *Clinical studies of classroom teaching and learning.* Paper presented at the annual meeting of the American Educational Research Association, Toronto.

Berliner, D., & Koehler, V. (1983). Introduction [Special issue: Research on teaching]. *Elementary School Journal, 83*(4), 261–263.

Birdwhistell, R. (1970). *Kinesics and context: Essays on body motion communication.* Philadelphia: University of Pennsylvania Press.

Blank, M. (1973). *Teaching learning in the preschool.* Columbus, OH: Charles E. Merrill.

Bloome, D. (1981). An ethnographic approach to the study of reading activities among black junior high school students. Unpublished doctoral dissertation, Kent State University, Kent, OH.

Bloome, D. (1983). Classroom reading instruction: A socio-communicative analysis of time-on-task. *Thirty-second yearbook of the National Reading Conference.* Rochester, NY: National Reading Conference.

Bloome, D., & Green, J. (1982). The social contexts of reading: A multidisciplinary perspective. In B. Hutson (Ed.), *Advances in reading/language research* (Vol. 1). Greenwich, CT: JAI Press, Inc.

Bloome, D., & Green, J. (1984). Directions in the sociolinguistic study of reading. In D. Pearson, R. Barr, M. Kamil, & P. Mosenthal (Eds.), *Handbook of reading research.* New York: Longman.

Blumenfeld, P. C., Hamilton, V. S., Wessels, K., & Falkner, D. (1979). Teaching responsibility to first graders. *Theory into Practice, 18,* 171–180.

Blumer, H. (1969). *Symbolic interactionism: Perspective and method.* Englewood Cliffs, NJ: Prentice-Hall.

Blurton-Jones, N. (1972). In N. Blurton-Jones (Ed.), *Ethological studies of child behavior.* London: Cambridge University Press.

Borman, K. (Ed.). (1982). *The social life of children in a changing society.* Hillsdale, NJ: Lawrence Erlbaum Associates.

Bossert, S. (1979). *Tasks and social relationships in classrooms.* Cambridge: University Press.

Bracht, G., & Glass, G. (1968). The external validity of experiments. *American Educational Research Journal, 5*(4), 437–474.

Brannigan, C. R., & Humphries, D. H. (1972). Human non-verbal behavior: A means of communication. In N. Blurton-Jones (Ed.), *Ethological studies of child behavior.* Cambridge: Cambridge University Press.

Brattesani, K. A., Weinstein, R. S., & Marshall, H. H. (1984). Student perceptions of differential teacher treatment as moderators of teacher expectation effects. *Journal of Educational Psychology, 76*(2), 236–247.

Brophy, J. (1973). Stability of teacher effectiveness. *American Educational Research Journal, 10,* 245–252.

Brophy, J. (1979). Teacher praise: A functional analysis. *Review of Educational Research, 51,* 5–32.

Brophy, J. (1983). If only it were true: A response to Greer. *Educational Researcher, 12*(1), 10–13.

Brophy, J., & Evertson, C. (1974). *Process–product correlations in the Texas Teacher Effectiveness Project.* (ERIC Document Reproduction Service No. ED 091 394)

Brophy, J., & Evertson, C. (1976). *Learning from teaching: A developmental perspective.* Boston: Allyn & Bacon.

Brophy, J., & Evertson, C. (1978). Context variables in teaching. *Educational Psychologist, 12,* 310–316.

Brophy, J., & Good, T. (1970a). The Brophy—Good Dyadic Interaction System. In A. Simon & E. Boyer (Eds.), *Mirrors for behavior: An anthology of observation instruments: 1970 supplement, Vol. A.* Philadelphia: Research for Better Schools.

Brophy, J., & Good, T. (1970b). Teachers' communication of differential expectations for children's classroom performance: Some behavioral data. *Journal of Educational Psychology, 61,* 365–374.

Brophy, J., & Good, T. (1974). *Teacher–student relationships: Causes and consequences.* New York: Holt, Rinehart & Winston.

Brunswik, E. (1956). *Perception and the representative design of psychological experiments.* Berkeley: University of California Press.

Burstein, L. (1980). The analysis of multilevel data in educational research and evaluation. In D. Berliner (Ed.), *Review of research in education* (Vol. 8). Washington, DC: American Educational Research Association.

Carey, R., Harste, J., & Smith, S. (1981). Contextual constraints and discourse processes: A replication study. *Reading Research Quarterly, 16*(2), 201–212.

Cazden, C. (1976). How knowledge about language helps the classroom teacher, or does it? A personal account. *The Urban Review, 9,* 74–90.

Cazden, C. (1983). Contexts for literacy: In the mind and in the classroom. *Journal of Reading Behavior, 14*(4), 413–427.

Cazden, C., John, V., & Hymes, D. (1972). *Functions of language in the classroom.* New York: Columbia University, Teachers College Press.

Chafe, W. (1980). *The pear stories.* Norwood, NJ: Ablex.

Cochran-Smith, M. (1984). *The making of a reader.* Norwood, NJ: Ablex.

Cohen, E. (1979). *Status equalization in the desegregated school.* Paper presented at the annual meeting of the American Educational Research Assocation, San Francisco.

Cohen, J. (1960). A coefficient of agreement for nominal scales. *Educational and Psychological Measurement, 20,* 37–46.

Cole, M., Griffin, P., & Newman, D. (1979). *They're all the same in their own way* (Mid-quarter report, NIE No. G-78-0159). Washington, DC: National Institute of Education.

Coleman, J., et al. (1966). *Equality of educational opportunity.* Washington, DC: U.S. Government Printing Office.

Collins, J. (1983). *Linguistic perspectives on minority education: Discourse analysis and early literacy.* Unpublished doctoral dissertation, University of California, Berkeley.

Collins, J. (in press). Using cohesion analysis to understand access to knowledge. In D. Bloome (Ed.), *Literacy, language, and schooling.* Norwood, NJ: Ablex.

Cook-Gumperz, J. (1981). Persuasive talk: The social organization of children's talk. In J. Green & C. Wallat (Eds.), *Ethnography and language in educational settings.* Norwood, NJ: Ablex.

Cook-Gumperz, J. (Ed.). (in press). *The Social Construction of Literacy.* New York: Cambridge University Press.

Cook-Gumperz, J., & Corsaro, W. (1977). Social-ecological constraints on children's communicative competence. In J. Gumperz & J. Cook-Gumperz (Eds.), *Papers on language and context* (Working Paper No. 46). Berkeley: Language Behavior Research Laboratory. University of California.

Cook-Gumperz, J., & Gumperz, J. (1976). Context in children's speech. In J. Gumperz & J. Cook-Gumperz (Eds.), *Papers on language and context* (Working Paper No. 46). Berkeley: Language Behavior Research Laboratory. University of California.

Cook-Gumperz, J., Gumperz, J., & Simons, H. (1978). *School–home ethnography project* (Proposal). Washington, DC: National Institute of Education.

Cook-Gumperz, J., Gumperz, J., & Simons, H. (1979). *Language at school and at home: Theory, methods, and preliminary findings*

(Mid-quarter report, NIE No. G-78-0082). Washington, DC: National Institute of Education.

Cook-Gumperz, J., Gumperz, J., & Simons, H. (1981). *School–home ethnography project* (Final report, NIE No. G-78-0082). Washington, DC: National Institute of Education.

Cooper, C., Ayres-Lopez, S., & Marquis, A. (1981). *Children's discourse cooperative and didactic interaction: Developmental patterns of effective learning* (Final report, NIE No. G-78-0098). Washington, DC: National Institute of Education.

Cooper, R. (1968). How can we measure the roles which a bilingual's languages play in his everyday behavior? *Proceedings of the International Seminar on the Measurement and Description of Bilingualism.* Ottawa: Canadian Commission for UNESCO.

Corsaro, W. (1981). Entering the child's world: Research strategies for field entry and data collection. In J. Green & C. Wallat (Eds.), *Ethnography and language in educational settings.* Norwood, NJ: Ablex.

Corsaro, W. (1985). *Friendship and peer culture in the early years.* Norwood, NJ: Ablex.

Delamont, S., & Hamilton, D. (1976). Classroom research: A critique and a new approach. In M. Stubbs & S. Delamont (Eds.), *Explorations in classroom observation.* Chichester, England: John Wiley & Sons.

Denham, C., & Lieberman, A. (Eds.). (1980). *Time to learn.* Washington, DC: National Institute of Education.

Denzin, N. (1977). *The research act.* Chicago: Aldine.

DeStefano, J., & Pepinsky, H. (1981). *The learning of discourse rules of culturally different children in first grade literacy instruction* (Final report, NIE No. G-79-0032). Washington, DC: National Institute of Education.

Doyle, W. (1977). Paradigms for research on teacher effectiveness. *Review of Research in Education, 15,* 163–198.

Duncan, S., & Fiske, D. (1977). *Face-to-face interaction: Research, methods, and theory.* Hillsdale, NJ: Lawrence Erlbaum Associates.

Duncan, S., & Niederehe, G. (1974). On signalling that it's your turn to speak. *Journal of Experimental Social Psychology, 10,* 234–247.

Dunkin, M., & Biddle, B. (1974). *The study of teaching.* New York: Holt, Rinehart & Winston.

Eder, D. (1982). Differences in communicative styles across ability groups. In L. Cherry Wilkinson (Ed.), *Communicating in the classroom.* New York: Academic Press.

Edwards, A., & Furlong, V. (1978). *The language of teaching: Meaning in classroom interaction.* London: Heinemann.

Elliott, J. (1976). *Developing hypotheses about classrooms from teachers' practical constructs.* Grand Forks: North Dakota Study Group.

Emmer, E., Evertson, C., & Anderson, L. (1980). Effective classroom management at the beginning of the school year. *Elementary School Journal, 80*(5), 219–231.

Emmer, E., & Peck, R. (1973). Dimensions of classroom behavior. *Journal of Educational Psychology, 64,* 223–240.

Erickson, F. (1977). Some approaches to inquiry in school–community ethnography. *Anthropology and Education Quarterly, 8*(2), 58–69.

Erickson, F. (1979). On standards of descriptive validity in studies of classroom activity (Occasional Paper No. 16). East Lansing: Michigan State University, Institute for Research on Teaching.

Erickson, F. (1982). Classroom discourse as improvisation: Relationships between academic task structure and social participation structure in lessons. In L. Cherry Wilkinson (Ed.), *Communicating in the classroom.* New York: Academic Press.

Erickson, F., Cazden, C., Carrasco, R., & Guzman, A. (1978–1981). *Social and cultural organization of interaction in classrooms of bilingual children* (Mid-quarter report, NIE No. G-78-0099). Washington, DC: National Institute of Education.

Erickson, F., & Schultz, J. (1981). When is a context? Some issues and methods in the analysis of social competence. In J. Green & C. Wallat (Eds.), *Ethnography and language in educational settings.* Norwood, NJ: Ablex.

Erickson, F., & Wilson, J. (1982). *Sights and sounds of life in schools: A resource guide to film and videotape for research and education.* East Lansing: Michigan State University, Institute for Research on Teaching.

Evertson, C. (1984). *Taking a broad look: Quantitative analyses of classroom management training.* Paper presented to the American Educational Research Association, New Orleans.

Evertson, C., Anderson, C., Anderson, L., & Brophy, J. (1980). Relationships between classroom behaviors and student outcomes in junior high mathematics and English classes. *American Educational Research Journal, 17*(1), 43–60.

Evertson, C., Anderson, L., & Brophy, J. (1978). *The Texas Junior High School Study: Final report of process–outcome relationships.* Austin, TX: The University of Texas Research and Development Center for Teacher Education. (ERIC Document Reproduction Service No. ED 173 744)

Evertson, C., Anderson, L., & Clements, B. (1980). *Elementary school classroom organization study: Methodology and instrumentation* (Rep. No. 6002). Austin, TX: University of Texas Research and Development Center for Teacher Education. (ERIC Document Reproduction Service No. ED 205 486).

Evertson, C., & Emmer, E. (1982). Effective management at the beginning of the school year in junior high classes. *Journal of Educational Psychology, 74,* 485–498.

Evertson, C., Emmer, E., & Clements, B. (1980). *Report of methodology, rationale, and instrumentation of the Junior High School Classroom Organization Study.* (Rept. #6100) Austin, TX: The University of Texas Research and Development Center for Teacher Education (ERIC Document Reproduction Service No. ED 189 076).

Evertson, C., Emmer, E., Sanford, J., & Clements, B. (1983). Improving classroom management: An experiment in elementary school classrooms. *Elementary School Journal, 84,* 173–188.

Evertson, C., & Holley, F. (1981). Classroom observation. In J. Millman (Ed.), *Handbook of teacher evaluation.* Beverly Hills: Sage Publications.

Evertson, C., & Veldman, D. (1981). Changes over time in process measures of classroom behavior. *Journal of Educational Psychology, 73*(2), 156–163.

Fassnacht, G. (1982). *Theory and practice of observing behavior.* London: Academic Press.

Fisher, C., Berliner, D., Filby, N., Marliave, R., Cahen, L., & Dishaw, M. (1980). Teaching behaviors, academic learning time, and student achievement: An overview. In C. Denham & A. Lieberman (Eds.), *Time to learn.* Washington, DC: National Institute of Education.

Fisher, C., Berliner, D., Filby, N., Marliave, R., Cahen, L., Dishaw, M., & Moore, J. (1978). *Teaching and learning in elementary schools: A summary of the Beginning Teacher Evaluation Study.* San Francisco, CA: Far West Laboratory.

Flanders, N. (1967). Estimating reliability. In E. Amidon & J. Hough (Eds.), *Interaction analysis: Theory, research, and application.* Reading, MA: Addison–Wesley.

Flanders, N. (1970). *Analyzing teaching behavior.* Reading, MA: Addison–Wesley.

Florio, S., & Clark, C. (1982). The functions of writing in an elementary classroom. *Research in the teaching of English, 16*(2), 115–130.

Florio, S., & Schultz, J. (1979). Social competence at home and at school. *Theory into Practice, 18*(4), 234–243.

Frederiksen, C. (1975). Representing logical and semantic structure of knowledge acquired from discourse. *Cognitive Psychology, 7,* 371–458.

Frederiksen, C. (1981). Inference in pre-school children's conversations: A cognitive perspective. In J. Green & C. Wallat (Eds.), *Ethnography and language in educational settings.* Norwood, NJ: Ablex.

Frick, T., & Semmel, M. (1978). Observer agreement and reliabilities of classroom observational measures. *Review of Educational Research, 48*(1), 157–184.

Gage, N. L. (Ed.). (1963a). *Handbook of research on teaching.* Chicago: Rand McNally.

Gage, N. L. (1963b). Paradigms for research on teaching. In N. L. Gage (Ed.), *Handbook of research on teaching.* Chicago: Rand McNally.

Galloway, C. (1971). Analysis of theories and research in nonverbal communication. *Journal of the Association for the Study of Perception, 6*(2), 1–21.

Galloway, C. (1984). *Nonverbal and teacher–student relationships: An intercultural perspective.* Manuscript submitted for publication.

Garnica, O., & King, M. (Eds.). (1979). *Language, children, and society.* Elmsford, NY: Pergamon.

Genishi, C. (1983a). Observational methods for early childhood education. In B. Spodek (Ed.), *Handbook of research in early childhood education.* New York: Free Press.

Genishi, C. (1983b). *Studying classroom verbal interaction.* Paper presented to the National Conference for Research in English session at the annual meeting of the American Educational Research Association, Montreal.

Genishi, C., & Di Paolo, M. (1982). Learning through argument in a preschool. In L. Cherry Wilkinson (Ed.). *Communicating in the classroom.* New York: Academic Press.

Gilmore, P. (in press). Sulking, stepping, and tracking: The effects of attitude assessment on access to literacy. In D. Bloome (Ed.), *Literacy, language, and schooling.* Norwood, NJ: Ablex.

Gilmore, P., & Glatthorn, A. (Eds.). (1982). *Children in and out of school: Ethnography and education.* Washington, DC: Center for Applied Linguistics.

Glaser, B., & Strauss, A. (1967). *The discovery of grounded theory.* Chicago: Aldine.

Good, T. (1983). Uses and misuses of classroom observation. In W. Duckett (Ed.), *Observation and the evaluation of teaching.* Bloomington, IN: Phi Delta Kappa.

Good, T., Biddle, B., & Brophy, J. (1975). *Teachers make a difference.* New York: Holt, Rinehart & Winston.

Good, T., Cooper, H., & Blakey, S. (1980). Classroom interaction as a function of teacher expectations, student sex, and time of year. *Journal of Educational Psychology, 72,* 378–385.

Gordon, E. (Ed.). (1983). *Review of research in education* (Vol. 10). Washington, DC: American Educational Research Association.

Gordon, I., & Jester, R. (1973). Techniques of observing teaching in early childhood and outcomes of particular procedures. In R. M. W. Travers (Ed.), *Second handbook of research on teaching.* Chicago: Rand McNally.

Green, J. (1983a). Exploring classroom discourse: Linguistic perspectives on teaching-learning processes. *Educational Psychologist, 18*(3), 180–199.

Green, J. (1983b). Research on teaching as a linguistic process: A state of the art. In E. Gordon (Ed.), *Review of research in education* (Vol. 10). Washington, DC: American Educational Research Association.

Green, J., & Bloome, D. (1983). Ethnography and reading: Issues, approaches, criteria, and findings. *Thirty-second-yearbook of the National Reading Conference.* Rochester NY: National Reading Conference.

Green, J., & Harker, J. (1982). Gaining access to learning: Conversational, social, and cognitive demands of group participation. In L. Cherry Wilkinson (Ed.), *Communicating in the classrooms.* New York: Academic Press.

Green, J., Harker, J., & Wallat, C. (Eds.). (in press). *Multiple perspectives analysis in classroom discourse.* Norwood, NJ: Ablex.

Green, J., & Wallat, C. (Eds.). (1979). What is an instructional context? An exploratory analysis of conversational shifts over time. In O. Garnica & M. King (Eds.), *Language, children, and society.* New York: Pergamon.

Green, J., & Wallat, C. (Eds.). (1981a). *Ethnography and language in educational settings,* Norwood, NJ: Ablex.

Green, J., & Wallat, C. (1981b). Mapping instructional conversations. In J. Green & C. Wallat (Eds.), *Ethnography and language in educational settings.* Norwood, NJ: Ablex.

Green, J., & Weade, R. (1984). *Taking a closer look: Qualitative explorations of task management.* Paper presented at the meeting of the American Educational Research Association, New Orleans.

Griffin, P. (1977). How and when does reading occur in the classroom? *Theory into Practice, 16*(5), 376–383.

Gump, P. (1969). Intra-setting analysis: The third grade classroom as a special but instructive case. In E. Willems & H. Raush (Eds.), *Naturalistic viewpoints in psychological research.* New York: Holt, Rinehart & Winston.

Gumperz, J. (1982a). *Discourse strategies.* Cambridge: Cambridge University Press.

Gumperz, J. (1982b). *Language and social identity.* Cambridge: Cambridge University Press.

Gumperz, J., Cook-Gumperz, J., & Simons, H. (1978). *School/home eth-* *nography project. Proposal to the National Institute of Education.* Unpublished manuscript, University of California, Berkeley.

Gumperz, J., & Hernandez-Chavez, E. (1972). Bilingualism, bidialectalism, and classroom interaction. In C. Cazden, V. John, & D. Hymes (Eds.), *Functions of language in the classroom.* New York: Columbia University, Teachers College Press.

Gumperz, J., & Hymes, D. (1972). *Directions in sociolinguistics.* New York: Holt, Rinehart & Winston.

Hall, E. T. (1966). *The hidden dimension.* New York: Doubleday.

Hamilton, D. (n.d.). *Some contrasting assumptions about survey analysis and case study research.* Unpublished manuscript, University of Glasgow, Department of Education.

Hamilton, S. (1983). The social side of schooling: Ecological studies of classrooms and schools. *Elementary School Journal, 83*(4), 313–334.

Hammersley, M. (1974). The organisation of pupil participation. *Sociological Review, 22,* 355–368.

Hansen, J. F. (1979). *Sociocultural perspectives on human learning: An introduction to educational anthropology.* Englewood Cliffs, NJ: Prentice-Hall.

Harker, J. (in press). Contrasting the content of two story reading lessons: A propositional analysis. In J. Green, J. Harker, & C. Wallat (Eds.), *Multiple perspectives analysis of classroom discourse.* Norwood, NJ: Ablex.

Harper, R. G., Wiens, A. N., & Matarazzo, J. D. (1978). *Nonverbal communication: The state of the art.* New York: John Wiley.

Heap, J. (1980a). Description in ethnomethodology. *Human Studies, 3,* 87–106.

Heap, J. (1980b). What counts as reading: Limits to certainty in assessment. *Curriculum Inquiry, 10*(3), 265–292.

Heap, J. (1982). Understanding classroom events: A critique of Durkin, with an alternative. *Journal of Reading Behavior, 14*(4), 391–411.

Heap, J. (1983). *On task in discourse: Getting the right pronunciation.* Paper presented at the annual meeting of the American Educational Research Association, Montreal.

Heath, S. B. (1982). Ethnography in education: Defining the essentials. In P. Gilmore & A. Glatthorn (Eds.), *Children in and out of school.* Washington, DC: Center for Applied Linguistics.

Heath, S. B. (1983). *Ways with words: Language, life, and work in communities and classrooms.* Cambridge: Cambridge University Press.

Herbert, J., & Attridge, C. (1975). A guide for developers and users of observation systems and manuals. *American Educational Research Journal, 12*(1), 1–20.

Hough, J. B. (Ed.). (1980a). *Computer processing of data for the study of instruction.* Columbus, OH: The Ohio State University.

Hough, J. B. (Ed.). (1980b). *Concepts and categories for the study of instruction.* Columbus, OH: The Ohio State University.

Hough, J. B. (Ed.). (1980c). *Data displays and their interpretation for the study of instruction.* Columbus, OH: The Ohio State University.

Hymes, D. (1974). *Foundations in sociolinguistics: An ethnographic approach.* Philadelphia: University of Pennsylvania Press.

Hymes, D. (1977). Critique. *Anthropology and Education Quarterly. 8*(2), 91–93.

Hymes, D. (1978). *What is ethnography?* (Sociolinguistic Working Paper No. 45). Austin, TX: Southwest Educational Development Laboratory.

Hymes, D. (1981). *Ethnographic monitoring project,* (Final report, NIE No. G-78-0038). Washington, DC: National Institute of Education.

Inhelder, B., & Piaget, J. (1958). *The growth of logical thinking from childhood to adolescence,* New York: Basic Books.

Jencks, C., et al. (1972). *Inequality: A reassessment of the effect of family and schooling in America.* New York: Basic Books.

Johnson, M. C. (1979). *Discussion dynamics.* Rowley, MA: Newbury House.

Johnson, S., & Bolstad, O. (1973). Methodological issues in naturalistic observation: Some problems and solutions for field research. In L. Hammerlynk, L. Handy, & E. Mash (Eds.), *Behavior change.* Champaign, IL: Research Press.

Kimmel, A. (Ed.). (1981). *Ethics of human subject research.* San Francisco: Jossey-Bass.

Knapp, M. L. (1978). *Nonverbal communication in human interaction.* New York: Holt, Rinehart & Winston.

Koehler, V. (1978). Classroom process research: Present and future. *Journal of Classroom Interaction, 13*(2) 3–10.

Koehler, V. (in press). Issues in secondary analysis [tentative title]. In J. Green, J. Harker, & C. Wallat (Eds.), *Multiple perspectives analysis of classroom discourse.* Norwood, NJ: Ablex.

Kugle, C. (1978). *A potential source of bias in classroom observation systems: Coder drift.* Paper presented at the annual meeting of the American Educational Research Association, Toronto. (ERIC Document Reproduction Service No. ED 159 203)

Langer, I., Schultz, V., & Thun, F. (1974). *Messung komplexer Merkmale in Psychologie und Pädagogik. Ratingverfahren.* Munich: Reinhardt.

Le Compte, M., & Goetz, J. (1982). Problems of reliability and validity in ethnographic research. *Review of Educational Research, 52*(1), 31–60.

Light, R. J. (1971). Measures of response agreement for qualitative data: Some generalizations and alternatives. *Psychological Bulletin, 76*(5), 365–377.

Little, J. W. (1981). *School success and staff development: The role of staff development in urban desegregated schools* (Final report, NIE Contract No. 400-79-0049). Boulder, CO: Center for Action Research.

Little, J. W. (1982). Norms of collegiality and experimentation: Workplace conditions of school success. *American Educational Research Journal, 19*(3), 325–340.

Lorenz, K. (1981). *The foundations of ethology: The principal ideas and discoveries in animal behavior.* New York: Touchstone Books.

Lundgren, U. (1977). *Model analysis of pedagogical processes.* Stockholm: Stockholm Institute of Education, Department of Educational Research.

Marshall, H. H. (1972). Criteria for an open classroom. *Young children, 28,* 13–20

Marshall, H. H. (1976a). *Dimensional Occurrence Scale: Manual.* Berkeley: University of California, School of Education.

Marshall, H. H. (1976b). *Dimensions of classroom structure and functioning project: Final report.* Berkeley: University of California.

Marshall, H. H. (1981). Open classrooms: Has the term outlived its usefulness? *Review of Educational Research, 51,* 181–192.

Marshall, H. H., & Green, J. (1978). Context variables and purpose in the use of verbal interaction. *Journal of Classroom Interaction, 14*(2), 24–29.

Marshall, H. H., Hartsough, C., Green, J., & Lawrence, M. (1977). Stability of classroom variables as measured by a broad range observational system. *Journal of Educational Research, 70*(6), 304–311.

Marshall, H. H., & Weinstein, R. (1982). *Classroom Dimensions Observation System: Manual.* Berkeley: University of California, Psychology Department.

Marshall, H. H., & Weinstein, R. (1984). *Classrooms where students perceive high and low amounts of differential teacher treatment.* Paper presented at the annual meeting of the American Educational Research Association, New Orleans.

Marshall, H. H., & Weinstein, R. (1984). Classroom factors affecting student self evaluation: An interactional model. *Review of Educational Research, 54*(3), 301–325.

Marshall, H. H., Weinstein, R. S., Sharp, L., & Brattesani, K. A. (1982). *Students' descriptions of the ecology of the school environment for high and low achievers.* Paper presented at the meeting of the American Educational Research Association, New York.

Marston, P., & Zimmerer, L. (1979). *The effect of using more than one type of teacher observation system in the same study.* (Report No. 5070). Austin: The University of Texas Research and Development Center for Teacher Education.

Martin, J., Veldman, D., & Anderson, L. (1980). Within-class relationships between student achievement and teacher behaviors. *American Educational Research Journal, 17*(4), 479–490.

May, L. (1981). Spaulding school: Attention and styles of interaction. In D. Hymes (Ed.), *Ethnographic monitoring project* (Final report, NIE No. G-78-0038). Washington, DC: National Institute of Education.

McCall, G., & Simmons, J. (1969). *Issues in participant observation.* Reading, MA: Addison–Wesley.

McCutcheon, G. (1981). On the interpretation of classroom observations. *Educational Researcher, 10*(5), 5–10.

McDermott, R. (1976). *Kids make sense: An ethnographic account of interactional management of success and failure in one first-grade classroom.* Unpublished doctoral dissertation, Stanford University, Stanford, CA.

McDermott, R., & Hood, L. (1982). Institutionalized psychology and the ethnography of schooling. In P. Gilmore & A. Glatthorn (Eds.), *Children in and out of school.* Washington DC: Center for Applied Linguistics.

McGaw, B., Wardrop, J., & Bunda, M. (1972). Classroom observation schemes: Where are the errors? *American Educational Research Journal, 9*(1), 13–27.

Mead, M. (1975). *Blackberry winter: My early years.* New York: Pocket Books.

Medley, D., & Mitzel, H. (1963). Measuring classroom behavior by systematic observation. In N. L. Gage (Ed.), *Handbook of research on teaching.* Chicago: Rand McNally.

Medley, D., Soar, R., & Coker, H. (1984). *Measurement based evaluation of teacher performance.* New York: Longman.

Mehan, H. (1979a). *Learning lessons.* Cambridge, MA: Harvard University Press.

Mehan, H. (1979b). What time is it, Denise? Asking known information questions in classroom discourse. *Theory into Practice, 18*(4), 285–294.

Merritt, M. (1982). Distributing and directing attention in primary classrooms. In L. Cherry Wilkinson (Ed.), *Communicating in classrooms.* New York: Academic Press.

Merritt, M., & Humphrey, F. (1981). *Service-like events during the individual work time and their contribution to the nature of communication in primary classrooms* (NIE No. G-78-0159). Washington, DC: National Institute of Education.

Michaels, S. (1981). Sharing time: Children's narrative styles and differential access to literacy. *Language in Society, 10*(3), 423–442.

Michaels, S., & Cook-Gumperz, J. (1979). A study of sharing time with first grade students: Discourse narratives in the classroom. In *Proceedings of the Berkeley Linguistic Society, 5,* 87–103.

Miller, J. (1974). The nature of living systems: An overview. In *Interdisciplinary aspects of general systems theory. Proceedings of the third annual meeting of the Middle Atlantic Regional Division.* College Park, MD: Society for General Systems Research.

Mishler, E. (1984). *The discourse of medicine.* Norwood, NJ: Ablex.

Moos, R. (1976). *The human context: Environmental determinants of behavior.* New York: John Wiley.

Morine, G. (1965). *A model of inductive discovery for instructional theory.* Unpublished doctoral dissertation, Columbia University, Teachers College.

Morine, G. (1969). Discovery modes: A criterion for teaching. *Theory into Practice, 8*(1), 25–30.

Morine, G. (1975). Interaction analysis in the classroom: Alternative applications. In R. Weinberg & F. Wobds (Eds.), *Observation of pupils and teachers in mainstream and special education settings: Alternative strategies.* Minneapolis: University of Minnesota Press.

Morine, G., Spaulding, R., & Greenberg, S. (1971). *Discovering new dimensions in the teaching process.* Toronto: Intext.

Morine, G., & Vallance, E. (1975). *Teacher and pupil perceptions of classroom interaction. Beginning Teacher Evaluation Study* (Phase B). San Francisco: Far West Laboratory.

Morine, G., & Morine, G. (1973). *Discovery: A challenge to teachers.* Englewood Cliffs, NJ: Prentice-Hall.

Morine-Dershimer, G. (1981). *The literate pupil,* The J. Richard Street Lecture Series. Syracuse, NY: Syracuse University Press.

Morine-Dershimer, G. (1982). Pupil perceptions of teacher praise. *Elementary School Journal, 82*(5), 421–434.

Morine-Dershimer, G. (in press-a). Comparing systems: How do we know? In J. Green, J. Harker, & C. Wallat (Eds.), *Multiple perspective analysis of classroom discourse.* Norwood, NJ: Ablex.

Morine-Dershimer, G. (in press-b). *Talking, listening, and learning in elementary school classrooms.* New York: Longman.

Morine-Dershimer, G., & Tenenberg, M. (1981). *Participant perspectives of classroom discourse* (Executive summary, NIE No. G-78-0161). Washington, DC: National Institute of Education.

Morine-Dershimer, G., Tenenberg, M., & Shuy, R. (1981). *Why do you ask?* (Final report, Part 2, NIE No. G-78-0162). Washington, DC: National Institute of Education.

Namuddu, C. (1982). *The structure of classroom communication in some biology lessons in selected secondary schools in Kenya.* Proposal to the International Development Research Center, Ottawa.

National Institute of Education. (1974a). *Reports of panels 1–10 of the National Conference on Studies in Teaching.* Washington, DC: U.S. Office of Education.

National Institute of Education. (1974b). *Teaching as a linguistic process in a cultural context* (Panel 5 report). Washington, DC: U.S. Office of Education.

Noblit, G. W. (1982). *Not seeing the forest for the trees: The failure of synthesis for the desegregation ethnographies.* Paper presented at the meeting of the American Educational Research Association, New York.

Ober, R., Bentley, E., & Miller, E. (1971). *Systematic observation of teaching: An interaction analysis-instructional strategy approach.* Englewood Cliffs, NJ: Prentice-Hall.

Ochs, E. (1979). Transcription as theory. In E. Ochs and B. Schieffelin (Eds.), *Developmental pragmatics.* New York: Academic Press.

Ogbu, J. (1981). *Cultural ecological contexts of classroom interactions.* Paper presented at the annual meeting of the American Educational Research Association, Los Angeles.

Osgood, C. E., Suci, G. T., & Tannenbaum, P. H. (1957). *The measurement of meaning.* Urbana-Champaign: University of Illinois Press.

Pelto, P., & Pelto, G. (1977). *Anthropological research: The structure of inquiry.* New York: Harcourt Brace.

Philips, S. (1972). Participant structures and communicative competence: Warm Springs children in community and classroom. In C. Cazden, V. John, & D. Hymes (Eds.), *Functions of language in the classroom.* New York: Columbia University, Teachers College Press.

Philips, S. (1982). *The invisible culture: Communication in classroom and community on the Warm Springs Indian Reservation.* New York: Longman.

Pinnell, G. S. (1977). Language in primary classrooms. *Theory into Practice, 14*(5), 318–327.

Popkewitz, T., Tabachnick, B., & Zeichner, K. (1979). Dulling the senses: Research in teacher education. *Journal of Teacher Education, 30*(5), 52–60.

Popper, K. (1963). *Conjectures and refutations.* London: Routledge & Kegan Paul.

Power, C. (1977). A critical review of science classroom instruction studies. *Studies in Science Education, 4,* 1–30.

Ramirez, A. (1979). *Discourse patterns during composition lessons: The sequence of speech acts.* Paper presented at the annual meeting of the American Educational Research Association, San Francisco.

Ramirez, A. (in press). Analyzing speech acts. In J. Green, J. Harker, & C. Wallat (Eds.), *Multiple perspective analysis of classroom discourse.* Norwood, NJ: Ablex.

Reiss, A. (1971). Systematic observation of natural social phenomena. In H. Costner (Ed.), *Sociological methodology.* San Francisco: Jossey-Bass.

Remmers, H. H. (1963). Rating methods in research on teaching. In N. L. Gage (Ed.), *Handbook of research on teaching.* Chicago: Rand McNally.

Rentel, V. (in press). The development of cohesive harmony: A secondary analysis. In J. Green, J. Harker, & C. Wallat (Eds.), *Multiple perspectives analysis of classroom discourse.* Norwood, NJ: Ablex.

Research on teaching [Special issue]. (1983a). *Educational Psychologist, 18*(3).

Research on teaching [Special issue]. (1983b). *Elementary School Journal, 83*(4).

Richards, M., & Bernal, J. (1972). In N. Blurton-Jones (Ed.), *Ethological studies of child behavior* (pp. 175–197). London: Cambridge University Press.

Rosenholtz, S. R. (1979). *Modifying the effects of academic status: The multiple abilities classroom.* Paper presented at the meeting of the American Educational Association, San Francisco.

Rosenholtz, S. R. (in press). Treating problems of academic status. In J.

Berger & M. Zelditch. Jr. (Eds.), *Studies in expectation states theory: Pure and applied.* San Francisco: Jossey-Bass.

Rosenshine, B. (1970). The stability of teacher effects upon student achievement. *Review of Educational Research, 40,* 647–662.

Rosenshine, B., & Furst, N. (1973). The use of direct observation to study teaching. In R. M. W. Travers (Ed.), *Second handbook of research on teaching.* Chicago: Rand McNally.

Rosenthal, R., & Jacobson, L. (1968). *Pygmalion in the classroom: Teacher expectations and pupils' intellectual development.* New York: Holt, Rinehart & Winston.

Sacks, H., Schegloff, E., & Jefferson, G. (1974). A simplest systematics for the organization of turntaking for conversation. *Language, 50*(4), Part 1), 696–735.

Sanday, P. (1976). Emerging methodological developments for research design, data collection, and data analysis in anthropology and education. In C. Calhoun & F. Ianni (Eds.), *The anthropological study of education.* The Hague: Mouton.

Sanday, P. (1979). The ethnographic paradigm(s). *Administrative Science Quarterly, 24*(4), 527–538.

Sanders, D. (1981). Educational inquiry as developmental research. *Educational Researcher, 10*(3), 8–13.

Schatzman, L., & Strauss, A. (1973). *Field research: Strategies for a natural sociology.* Englewood Cliffs, NJ: Prentice-Hall.

Scheflen, A. E. (1972). *Body language and social order: Communication as behavioral control.* Englewood Cliffs, NJ: Prentice-Hall.

Scollon, R., & Scollon, S. (1984). Cooking it up and boiling it down: Abstracts of Athabaskan children's story retellings. In D. Tannen (Ed.), *Coherence in spoken and written language.* Norwood, NJ: Ablex.

Scott, W. A. (1955). Reliability of content analysis: The case of nominal scale coding. *Public Opinion Quarterly, 19,* 321–325.

Scribner, S., & Cole, M. (1981). *The psychology of literacy.* Cambridge, MA: Harvard University Press.

Sevigny, M. (1981). Triangulated inquiry—A methodology for the analysis of classroom interaction. In J. Green & C. Wallat (Eds.), *Ethnography and language in educational settings.* Norwood, NJ: Ablex.

Shavelson, R. (1983). Review of research on teachers' pedagogical judgments, plans, and decisions. *Elementary School Journal, 83*(4), 392–413.

Shavelson, R., & Dempsey-Atwood, N. (1976). Generalizability of measures of teaching behavior. *Review of Educational Research, 46*(4), 553–611.

Shaver, J. (1983). The verification of independent variables in teaching methods research. *Educational Researcher, 12*(8), 3–9.

Shulman, L. (1981). Disciplines of inquiry in education: An overview. *Educational Researcher, 10*(6), 5–12.

Shuy, R. (in press). Identifying dimensions of classroom language. In J. Green, J. Harker, & Wallat (Eds.), *Multiple perspective analysis of classroom discourse.* Norwood, NJ: Ablex.

Shuy, R., & Griffin, P. (1981). What do they do at school any day: Studying functional language. In W. P. Dickson (Ed.), *Children's oral communication skills.* New York: Academic Press.

Simon, A., & Boyer, E. G. (Eds.). (1970a). *Mirrors for behavior: An anthology of classroom observation instruments* (Vols. 7–14 and Summary). Philadelphia: Research for Better Schools. (ERIC Document Reproduction Service No. ED 031 613).

Simon, A., & Boyer, E. G. (Eds.). (1970b). *Mirrors for Behavior: An anthology of observation instruments continued, 1970 Supplement.* Vols. A & B. Philadelphia: Research for Better Schools. Inc.

Simons, H., & Murphy, S. (1981). Spoken language strategies and reading acquisition. *School–home ethnography project* (NIE No. G-78-0082). Washington, DC: National Institute of Education.

Sinclair, J. M., & Coulthard, R. M. (1975). *Toward an analysis of discourse: The English used by teachers and pupils.* London: Oxford University Press.

Smith, L., & Geoffrey, W. (1968). *Complexities of an urban classroom: An analysis toward a general theory of teaching.* New York: Holt, Rinehart & Winston.

Snow, R. (1974). Representative and quasi-representative designs for research on teaching. *Review of Educational Research, 44*(3), 265–291.

Spencer-Hall, D. (1981). Looking behind the teacher's back. *Elementary School Journal, 81*, 281–289.

Spindler, G. (1982). *Doing the ethnography of schooling: Educational anthropology in action.* New York: Holt, Rinehart & Winston.

Spradley, J. (1980). *Participant observation.* New York: Holt, Rinehart & Winston.

Stallings, J. (1977). *Learning to look: A handbook on classroom observation and teaching models.* Belmont, CA: Wadsworth.

Stallings, J. (1983). *The Stallings observation system.* Unpublished manuscript, Vanderbilt University, Peabody Center for Effective Teaching, Nashville, TN.

Stoffan-Roth, M. (1981). Conversational access strategies in instructional contexts. Unpublished doctoral dissertation, Kent State University, Kent, OH.

Stubbs, M. (1976). *Language, schools and classrooms.* London: Methuen.

Stubbs, M. (1983). *Discourse analysis; The sociolinguistic analysis of natural language.* Chicago: University of Chicago Press.

Stubbs, M., & Delamont, S. (Eds.). (1976). *Explorations in classroom observation.* Chichester, England: John Wiley.

Stubbs, M., Robinson, B., & Twite, S. (1979). *Observing classroom language* (Block 5, PE232). Stony Stratford, Milton Keynes, England: Open University Press.

Szwed, J. (1977). *The ethnography of literacy.* Paper presented to the National Institute of Education Conference on Writing, Los Angeles.

Taba, H. (1967). *Teacher's handbook for elementary social studies.* Reading, MA: Addison-Wesley.

Tannen, D. (1979). What's in a frame? Surface evidence for underlying expectations. In R. Freedle (Ed.), *Advances in discourse processing* (Vol. 2). Norwood, NJ: Ablex.

Taylor, D. (1983). *Family literacy: Young children learning to read and write.* Exeter, NH: Heinemann.

Tenenberg, M. (1981). *Cycling and recycling questions: The "when" of talking in classrooms.* Paper presented at the annual meeting of the American Educational Research Association, Los Angeles.

Tenenberg, M. (in press). Diagramming question cycle sequences. In J. Green, J. Harker, & C. Wallat (Eds.), *Multiple perspective analysis of classroom discourse.* Norwood, NJ: Ablex.

Tenenberg, M., Morine-Dershimer, G., & Shuy, R. (1981). What did anybody say? (Final report, Part I, NIE No. G-78-0162). Washington, DC: National Institute of Education.

Tikunoff, W., Ward, B., & Dasho, S. (1978). *Volume A: Three Case Studies* (Report No. 78-7). San Francisco: Far West Laboratory.

Travers, R. M. W. (Ed.). (1973). *Second handbook of research on teaching.* Chicago: Rand McNally.

Trueba, H. T., Guthrie, G. T., & Au, K. (Eds.). (1981). *Culture and the bilingual classroom: Studies in classroom ethnography.* Rowley, MA: Newbury House.

Veldman, D., & Brophy, J. (1974). Measuring teacher effects on pupil achievement. *Journal of Educational Psychology, 66*, 319–324.

Walker, D., & Shaffarzick, J. (1974). Comparing curricula. *Review of Educational Research, 44*, 83–111.

Wallat, C., & Green, J. (1979). Social rules and communicative contexts in kindergarten. *Theory into Practice, 18*(4), 275–284.

Wallat, C., & Green, J. (1982). Construction of social norms. In K. Borman (Ed.), *Social life of children in a changed society.* Hillsdale, NJ: Lawrence Erlbaum Associates.

Wallat, C., Green, J., Conlin, S., & Haramis, M. (1981). Issues related to action research in the classroom: The teacher and researcher as a team. In J. Green & C. Wallat (Eds.), *Ethnography and language in educational settings.* Norwood, NJ: Ablex.

Weinstein, R. S. (1976). Reading group membership in the first grade: Teacher behaviors and pupil experience over time. *Journal of Educational Psychology, 68*, 103–116.

Weinstein, R. S. (1981). Student perspectives on "achievement" in varied classroom environments. In P. Blumenfeld (Chair), *Student perspectives and the study of the classroom.* Symposium presented at the meeting of the American Educational Research Association, Los Angeles.

Weinstein, R. S. (1983). Student perceptions of schooling. *Elementary School Journal, 83*(4), 287–312.

Weinstein, R. S. (in press). Student mediation of classroom expectancy effects. In J. B. Dusek (Ed.), *Teacher expectancies.* Hillsdale, NJ: Lawrence Erlbaum Associates.

Weinstein, R. S., & Marshall, H. (1984). *Ecology of students' achievement expectations: Final report.* Berkeley: University of California, Psychology Department.

Weinstein, R. S., Marshall, H. H., Brattesani, K. A., & Middlestadt, S. E. (1982). Student perceptions of differential teacher treatment in open and traditional classrooms. *Journal of Educational Psychology, 74*, 678–692.

Weinstein, R. S., & Middlestadt, S. E. (1979). Student perceptions of teacher interactions with male high and low achievers. *Journal of Educational Psychology, 71*, 421–31.

Whiting, B. (1963). *Six cultures: Studies of child rearing.* New York: John Wiley.

Wilkinson, L. (Ed.). (1982). *Communicating in the classroom.* New York: Academic Press.

Wilkinson, L., & Calculator, S. (1982). Effective speakers: Student's use of language to request and obtain information and action in the classroom. In L. Cherry Wilkinson (Ed.), *Communicating in the classroom.* New York: Academic Press.

Woods, P., & Hammersley, M. (1977). *School experience: Explorations in the sociology of schooling.* London: Croom Helm.

Woolfolk, A., & Brooks, D. (1983). Nonverbal communication in teaching. In E. Gordon (Ed.), *Review of research in education,* (Vol. 10). Washington, DC: American Educational Research Association.

Wright, H. (1960). Observational child study. In P. Mussen (Ed.), *Handbook of research methods in child development.* New York: John Wiley.

Yinger, R., & Clark, C. (1981). *Reflective journal writing: Theory and practice* (Occasional Paper No. 50). East Lansing: Michigan State University, Institute for Research on Teaching.

7.

Syntheses of Research on Teaching

Herbert J. Walberg
University of Illinois at Chicago

Research synthesis makes the 1980s an extraordinary time in the history of research on teaching. The seminal contributions of Bloom (1976), Gage (1978), Glass (1977), and Light and Smith (1971) served to provide the major substantive and methodological breakthroughs in consolidating findings of educational research.

Glass, McGaw, and Smith (1981); Hedges, Giaconia, and Gage (1981); Hedges and Olkin (1981, 1983); Kulik, Kulik, and Cohen (1980), and Light and Pillemer (1982) have since provided excellent examples and insights on the synthesis of research on teaching and related educational factors (see Walberg, 1984, for a compilation and analysis). They and others are demonstrating the consistency of educational effects and are helping to put teaching on a more sound scientific basis. Before turning to an overview of this chapter that shows how this is being accomplished, several working definitions are worth considering:

Primary research, for the purpose of this chapter, reports an original analysis of raw qualitative or quantitative data. It may include a literature review, theoretical framework, and explicit hypotheses. Secondary analysis is the reanalysis of data by the original or, more often, other investigators for the same purpose for which they were collected or a different one.

Reviews are narrative commentaries about primary and secondary research. They usually summarize and evaluate studies one by one, but rarely quantitatively analyze them. Reviews often contain theoretical insights and practical recommendations, but rarely assess rival theories by their parsimonious accounting of empirical regularities.

Research synthesis explicitly applies scientific techniques and standards to the evaluation and summary of research; it not only statistically summarizes effects across studies but also provides detailed descriptions of replicable searches of literature, selection of studies, metrics of study effects, statistical procedures, and both overall and exceptional results with respect to experimental conditions, context, or subjects (Cooper & Rosenthal, 1980; Glass, 1977; Glass, McGaw, & Smith, 1981; Jackson, 1980; Light & Pillemer, 1982; and Walberg & Haertel, 1980).

Qualitative insights may be usefully combined with quantitative synthesis (Light & Pillemer, 1982); and results from multiple reviews and syntheses of the same or different topics may be compiled and compared to estimate their relative magnitudes and consistencies (Walberg, 1982b). These terms are further discussed and illustrated in subsequent sections.

The purposes of this chapter are to introduce and illustrate the methods of research synthesis, summarize recent substantive findings with respect to teaching and related factors, and to evaluate methods of reviews and synthesis. More space is devoted to substance than methods because excellent methodological sources are now widely available.

The theme of this chapter is that research synthesis and related developments have brought a new level of scientific maturity to research on teaching. The theme is illustrated in several ways by the 10 subsequent sections, which may be overviewed as follows:

1. Synthesis is the fifth of six phases of scientific research; it helps consolidate the first four phases of research before wide-scale adoption and evaluation are justified.
2. Both qualitative and quantitative methods may be used to estimate overall and categorical effects of teaching and other educational factors.
3. Reviews of research on teaching of the 1970s agree on several of the ingredients of effective teaching for measurable cognitive learning, but their procedures for arriving at conclusions are inexplicit.

The author thanks reviewers Leonard S. Cahan (Arizona State University) and Gene V Glass (University of Colorado). Thanks also to March of Dimes, the National Institute of Education, and the National Science Foundation, for supporting work on which the chapter is based.

4. Syntheses of research on educational factors completed from 1979 through early 1982 show fairly consistent and in some cases substantial effects on learning.

5. A team approach to research synthesis carried out on higher education helped settle many policy controversies on effective teaching in colleges and universities.

6. Reviews and syntheses of small-scale studies of three clusters of nine proximal factors in school learning show that its productivity may be greatly increased.

7. Syntheses of national surveys of educational effects also show consistent effects of the nine factors.

8. Four syntheses of open education research by different groups illustrate robustness of conclusions, cumulative knowledge building, and improved synthesis methods that may be expected in replicated research syntheses.

9. Syntheses of theories of instruction of the past generation also show a growing convergence on the primary factors in school learning.

10. The prospects for research synthesis to help guide educational research and practice in the next decade seem promising.

Characteristics of Applied Scientific Research

This section shows how research synthesis fits into the phases of investigation in fields with professional or practical intentions. Since research synthesis in its current form is new to educational research, it may be useful to see its place in the traditionally recognized phases of research.

Applied scientific research can be divided in a great number of ways, but the following six phases seem useful in showing the place of synthesis in the overall effort:

1. *Identification of valued outcomes.* The pure disciplines such as physics are free to seek the most fundamental phenomena; but practical fields such as medicine, agriculture, engineering, and education concern, by definition, the efficient attainment of valuable outcomes such as health, yield, and learning.

2. *Identification of plausible factors.* Substantive research seeks the causes of valued outcomes. Such causal factors and their likely bearings on effects may be sought from the following sources: common observation, practical wisdom, policy controversies, and prior research in the form of case studies, statistical correlations, and experiments. The use of parsimonious, falsifiable theory as a guide to empirical inquiry (Popper, 1959) — the modern and commonly accepted view in the natural sciences — is rare in educational and social research (Blaug, 1978; Cook & Campbell, 1979).

3. *Observation of the factors and effects.* The factors may be experimentally manipulated or only observed in their naturally occurring states. In either case, the observed covariations of factors and effects are described in case studies or numerically indexed in the form of correlations, regression weights, F-ratios, and other statistics in quantitative research.

4. *Replication of covariations.* Relationships replicated with different subjects and in a variety of circumstances can be said to be generalizable, widely confirmed, or, in Popperian spirit, unfalsified. Replication attempts by different investigators and probing theory in a program of research, however, are rare. Most research on teaching, for example, draws not on unifying theoretical paradigms and constructs but on an immense variety of somewhat incomparable constructs, empirical representations, procedures, and observation instruments (Dunkin, 1976).

5. *Research synthesis.* Comparable studies are systematically evaluated and summarized in the form of frequency distributions, means, standard deviations, and other statistics. Such analysis helps to make sense of the overall findings and classifications of them just as statistics are useful in understanding a mass of raw primary data (Glass, 1977; Glass, McGaw, & Smith, 1981).

6. *Adoption and evaluation.* Practitioners can reasonably accept the implications of research findings that syntheses prove robustly unfalsified, that are effective considering total costs, and that are without harmful side effects, although continuing local evaluation is needed. Because research syntheses published in the last several years suggest a number of consistent, worthwhile effects, educational research may be entering a new stage of scientific maturity and relevance to practice.

Methods of Research Synthesis

To indicate how synthesis may be conducted, qualitative and quantitative methods are discussed in this section. Relatively less space, however, is given to qualitative synthesis because its literature is sparse and treated elsewhere (see the chapters by Erickson and by Evertson & Green, this volume).

Qualitative Research

Aside from direct personal experience, reading anecdotes and case studies is an obvious way to learn something about little-known psychological and social phenomena. An outstanding example in educational research is Willard Waller's (1932) classic *Sociology of Teaching*. Implicitly based on case studies, it provides enduring insights on problems of teaching and becoming a teacher. A recent example of illuminating insights about teaching and learning is the issue of *Daedalus* (edited by Graubard, 1981) on America's schools, with nine replicated case studies by Robert Coles, Philip Jackson, and Sara Lightfoot of a New England preparatory school, a midwestern suburban high school, and an urban high school in Atlanta (see also the chapter by Erickson, this volume).

However valuable and vivid are such works, LeCompte and Goetz (1982) take a fairly grim view of the reliability and validity of qualitative research and find the explication of educational ethnographies "sporadic and haphazard" (p. 31). Like much quantitative research, many ethnographies have ignored theory and prior research, perhaps in an effort to have a fresh, innocent, or unbiased view of new or familiar phenomena.

There are usually questions of generalization from the sampled case to the larger universe of interest, since cases are rarely selected randomly. As long as a case study claims to be only what the term implies, that is, a study of a case, however, there is little quarrel with conventional scientific methodology. Such work continues rich humanistic traditions of inquiry in history, biography, art and literary criticism, and cultural anthropology. To this extent, case studies neither synthesize nor generalize beyond particular cases, and are beyond the scope of this chapter.

Qualitative Research Synthesis

To a larger extent, however, some qualitative researchers attempt to generalize; and they collect and analyze multiple cases or multiple studies of individual cases. The strength of their work — rich, vivid narrative — may be combined with quantitative generality and parsimony; or, case studies themselves, if sufficient in number, may be compiled and quantitatively synthesized. Light and Pillemer (1982) illustrate the combined approach and suggest quantifying qualitative information, presenting quantitative studies in narrative fashion, and tallying statistical and descriptive evidence.

Green (1982) is the only scholar known to this writer who has proposed and carried out an explicit methodology for synthesizing case studies in research on teaching. She lays out a conceptual framework for describing teaching as a linguistic process; explicates qualitative methods for its study; and tabulates the constructs and observations with respect to teaching and learning in the school, home, and community reported by 10 independent investigators in various parts of the country. Green reports many insightful and useful observations that appear generalizable across a variety of contexts and investigations. She characterizes her work as exploratory, but it seems highly promising for further development by herself and other investigators.

Quantitative Synthesis Methods

Quantitative research synthesis is not merely statistical analysis of studies. Jackson (1980) discussed six tasks comprising an integrative review or research synthesis: specifying the questions or hypotheses for investigation; selecting or sampling the studies for synthesis; coding or representing the characteristics of the primary studies; analyzing, or "meta-analyzing" (Glass, 1977; Glass, McGaw, & Smith, 1981), or statistically synthesizing the study findings; interpreting the results; and reporting them.

Although these tasks seem obviously necessary to allow replication of reviews, Jackson found that only 12 out of 87 recent reviews in prominent educational, psychological, and sociological journals provided even a cursory statement of their methods of review and synthesis. The guiding idea behind much good advice in Jackson's paper is that the methods of review and synthesis should be explicit enough to enable other investigators to attempt to replicate them.

Explicit methods of quantitative synthesis call for statistics; and two are most often employed — the vote count or box score, and the effect size (Glass, 1977). The vote count is easiest to calculate and explain to those who are unaccustomed to thinking statistically. It is simply the percentage of all studies that are positive, for example, the percentage of studies in which the experimental exceeded control groups or the independent variable correlated positively with the dependent variable.

The effect size is the difference between the means of the experimental and control groups divided by the control group standard deviation. It measures the average superiority (or inferiority, if negative) of the experimental relative to the control groups (for cases in which these statistics are unreported, Glass, McGaw, & Smith, 1981 provide a number of alternative estimation formulas).

If education had uniform or ratio variables, such as time and money, as in economics, or meters and kilograms, as in the natural sciences, effect sizes would be unnecessary. Without post hoc standardization, it could be said, for example, that the experimental groups grew .42 comprehension units in reading on average, and the control group grew .22 (see Walberg, Strykowski, Rovai, & Hung, 1984, for additional discussion and implications).

Effect sizes permit a rough calibration of comparisons across tests, contexts, subjects, and other characteristics of studies. The estimates, however, are affected by the variances in the groups, the reliabilities of the outcomes, the match of curriculum with outcome measures, and a host of other factors, whose influences, in some cases, can be estimated specifically or generally. Although effect sizes are subject to distortions, they are the only explicit means of comparing the sizes of effects in primary research that employs various outcome measures on nonuniform groups. They are likely to be necessary until an advanced theory and science of educational measurement develops ratio measures that are directly comparable across studies and populations.

Another method of estimating effects involves the calculation of overall probability of the null hypothesis from the probabilities of individual studies (Rosenthal, 1980). Perhaps because many educational studies use nonindependent units of analysis, for example, students rather than classes, and because probabilities can be calculated from vote counts and effect sizes, probability methods are less often reported.

Generalizability

The generality of the results of the synthesis can be divided into questions of extrapolation and interpolation: Do the synthesized results generalize to other populations and conditions, particularly to those that have not been studied or for whom the results are unpublished? Do the results generalize across populations and conditions for which results are available?

Extrapolation beyond published studies may be invalid because journal editors favor positive, statistically significant studies. Smith (1980) estimated from several syntheses that mean effect sizes in unpublished works, mainly doctoral dissertations, are occasionally larger but average about a third smaller than those in published studies.

Rosenthal (1980), however, showed that, given the great statistical significance of collections of published studies, the probability of null effects being established by unpublished studies is small. Furthermore, both the low reliability of educational measures and low curricular validity (correspondence between what is taught and what is tested) reduce the estimates of relations between educational means and ends. Low reliability and validity, which lead to underestimates of effects, probably more than compensate for the possible overestimation of publication bias; but more empirical and analytic work is needed on these factors to determine their general and specific distorting influences on synthesis results (see Hedges and Olkin, 1980, 1983, on these and related statistical points).

The interpolation problem can be readily solved by additional calculations of statistical tests for classified mean effects. The most obvious question in quantitative synthesis concerns the overall percentage of positive results and their average magnitude. But the next questions should concern the consistency and magnitude of results across student and teacher characteristics, educational treatments and conditions, subject matters, study outcomes, and validity factors in the studies. These questions can be answered by calculating separate results for classifications or cross-classifications of these factors.

The results may be compared by objective statistical tests such as t, F, and regression weights in general linear models. They permit conclusions on such matters as the overall effectiveness of treatments as well as their differential effectiveness on categories of students in various conditions on different outcomes. Notwithstanding the frequent claims by reviewers for differential effects on the basis of results of a few selected studies, most research syntheses yield results that are fairly robust in sign and magnitude across such categories. Such robustness is scientifically valuable because it indicates parsimonious, consistent findings. It is also educationally valuable because educators can apply robust findings more efficiently than complicated, expensive procedures, tailor made to special cases on unproven assumptions.

For further reading, a number of useful methodological writings are available. Glass (1977) provided a concise introduction to statistical methods, and Glass, McGaw, and Smith's (1981) book is a comprehensive treatment. Jackson (1980) and Cooper (1982) discussed tasks and criteria for integrative reviews and research syntheses. Light and Pillemer (1982) described methods for combining quantitative and qualitative methods. Walberg and Haertel (1980) commissioned eight methodological papers by Cahen, Cooper, Hedges, Light, Rosenthal, Smith and others, and 35 substantive papers, mostly on educational topics.

Hedges and Olkin (1980, 1983) wrote several important papers that offer new statistical footings and procedures for quantitative synthesis.

A Review of Reviews of Teaching Effects

The year 1980 marked a transition when investigators recognized the shortcomings of traditional reviews and the advantages of more objective, explicit procedures for evaluating and summarizing research. Yet traditional reviews still have a place, and this section shows that much can be learned from them (see, for example, Peterson & Walberg, 1979, and Walberg, 1982a, for recent collections of reflective reviews of various aspects of teaching and educational effects).

To investigate the methods and results of traditional reviews and how they correspond with research syntheses, Waxman and Walberg (1982) examined 19 reviews of teaching process–student outcome research that critically evaluated at least three studies and two teaching constructs. They described their methods, compared their conclusions, synthesized them, and pointed out the implications for future reviews, syntheses, and research.

The 19 reviews reflect the inexplicit and varied standards procedures in Jackson's (1980) analysis of 87 review articles in prominent educational, psychological, and sociological journals. None of the reviews, for example, described their search procedures, and only one stated explicit criteria for inclusion and exclusion of primary studies.

Comparative analysis of study selection, moreover, revealed that the reviewers failed to search diligently for primary studies or to state the reasons for excluding large parts of the research evidence. For instance, the most comprehensive of five reviews covering reinforcement (such as reward and feedback in teaching) covered only 6 studies, whereas Lysakowski and Walberg's (1981) synthesis encompassed 39 studies. Such arbitrary selection of small parts of the evidence, of course, leaves the reviews open to systematic bias. It also means that the reviews and their conclusions cannot be replicated in a strict sense because their methods are inexplicit.

Although the reviews purported to be critical, their coverage of the 33 standard threats to methodological validity (Cook & Campbell, 1979) was spotty and haphazard. In 95.4% of the

Table 7.1. Conclusions of 19 Reviews and Two Quantitative Syntheses of Research on Teaching

| Finding | Stimulation | | Engagement | Reinforcement | Management and Climate |
	Cognitive Cues	Motivational Incentives			
Number of reviews covering construct	19	5	10	13	15
Number of reviews concluding relation to learning is positive	17	5	10	9.5	13.5
Probability of an even split	.01	.10	.01	.10	.10
Mean effect sizes from quantitative synthesis	1.28		.88	.94	1.17
Probability of evidence assuming zero population effect	.01			.01	

Note. Adapted from Walberg, H. J. (1982). What makes schooling effective? *Contemporary Education Review, 1,* 1–34.

possible cases, the reviews ignored specific threats. External validity (interaction of teaching treatments with selection, setting,
and history) was relatively well covered, perhaps reflecting the
search for aptitude–treatment interactions in the 1970s; but the
serious internal validity problems such as reverse and exogenous causes in correlational studies were almost wholly ignored.
Indeed, there appeared an odd tendency to select correlational
studies and exclude experiments for review.

Despite these problems, however, a statistical tabulation of
the conclusions of the reviews (Waxman & Walberg 1982)
shows substantial and statistically significant agreement that
five broad teaching constructs—cognitive stimulation, motivational incentives, pupil engagement in learning, reinforcement,
and management and classroom climate—are positively associated with student learning outcomes (see Table 7.1). These
tabulations, moreover, are in close agreement with quantitative
syntheses of large, systematic collections of primary studies discussed in a subsequent section.

Thus, a tabulation of methods, results, and conclusions of
reviews produces reasonable statistical convergence on major
dependencies of student learning on teaching behaviors. The
results also show, however, that past narrative reviews of research on teaching often lack explicit, replicable procedures
that can be assessed by readers, and replicated by subsequent
reviewers.

Current Research Syntheses

Sixteen quantitative syntheses of educational research completed since 1979 were obtained in early 1982 by scanning publications of the American Educational Research Association
and writing to the members of "the invisible college" of about
100 scholars who meet annually to present and discuss research
on teaching. A more systematic search in late 1982 using *Dissertation Abstracts*, *Social Science Citation Index*, *Education Index*,
computer retrieval, and references in recent publications indicates that these syntheses plus those discussed in subsequent

sections of this chapter represent about half of those completed
in education at that time. (An analysis of a more complete
corpus is underway by the present author and colleagues, but
the increasing number of syntheses makes exhaustive coverage
an elusive goal.)

Table 7.2 suggests a number of instructive points for both
educational practice and research synthesis. It provides, for example, an empirical answer to the coincidence of vote counts
and effect sizes (see Hedges & Olkin, 1980, 1983, for an analytical approach). Every mean effect size that was positive also had
a vote count greater than 50%; every negative effect size had a
vote count greater than 50%. Thus, as may be expected from
normal distributions, consistently positive findings yielded
positive average results (the next section shows that much of the
variance in effects can be predicted by regression from counts).

The likely explanation for the uniform association is that
strong causes produce results in a consistent direction. Indeed,
the only cases in which the association can be reversed are
skewed distributions in which a few very large positive results
are sufficient to pull the mean above zero from a cluster of small
effects, more than half of which are negative (or vice versa).

The first two syntheses grouped under Teaching Strategies in
Table 7.2 show fairly close agreement with respect to the positive effects of cooperative learning. Johnson, Maruyama,
Johnson, Nelson, and Skon (1981) categorized their results by
comparisons of four treatment variations (cooperative, competitive, group competitive, and individualistic), whereas Slavin
(1980) categorized his results by outcomes. Cooperative learning obviously produces superior results on average; but it
would be useful if journal editors would allow research synthesists more space to report average results by greater numbers of
standard classifications of independent and dependent variables and study conditions to facilitate comparisons of replicated syntheses such as these two.

The next two syntheses raise important, unresolved methodological questions. Becker and Gersten's (1982) "synthesis"
indicated a small average effect of direct instruction in several

Table 7.2. Selected Post-1979 Quantitative Syntheses

Author	Number of Studies	Independent and Dependent Variables	Mean Correlation or Effect	Percentage Positive	Comments
Teaching Strategies					
Johnson, Maruyama, Johnson, Nelson, and Skon (1981)	122	Effects of cooperation, intergroup and interpersonal competition, and individual goal efforts on achievement and productivity	.00 .78 .37 .76 .59 .03	54 76 68 83 81 47	Cooperative vs. group competitive Cooperative vs. competitive Group competitive vs. cooperative Cooperative vs. individualistic Group competitive vs. individualistic Competitive vs. individualistic
Slavin (1980)	28	Effects of educational programs for cooperative learning		81 78 95 65	Curriculum-specific tests Standardized tests Race relations Mutual concern
Becker and Gersten (1982)	1	Effects of Direct Instruction Follow Through on later achievement (seven sites on two occasions, fifth and sixth grades)	.23	—	Effects larger for mathematics problem solving and for fifth grade

Table 7.2 *(Continued)*

Author	Number of Studies	Independent and Dependent Variables	Mean Correlation or Effect	Percentage Positive	Comments
Pflaum, Walberg, Karegianes, and Rasher (1980)	96	Effects of different methods of teaching reading on learning	.60	76	Although Hawthorne effects could be discounted, experimental groups generally did substantially better than controls; sound–symbol blending was one standard deviation higher than other treatments.
Teaching Skills					
Luiten, Ames, and Anderson (1980)	135	Effects of advance organizers on learning and retention	.23	—	Effects larger on 20+ days retention, higher achievers, college students, and when presented aurally
Redfield and Rousseau (1981)	20	Effects of higher and lower cognitive questions	.73	—	Higher questioning effects greater in training than in skills study and in more valid studies
Wilkinson (1980)	14	Effects of praise on achievement	.08	63	Praise slightly more effective for lower socioeconomic groups, primary grades, and in mathematics
Other Studies					
Butcher (1981)	47	Effects of microteaching lessons on teaching performance of secondary and elementary education students	.84 .56 .46 .35		Secondary specific skiils Secondary questioning skills Elementary specific skills Elementary questioning skills
Colosimo (1981)	24	Effects of practice and beginning teaching on self-attitudes	−.29	48	Initial experience associated with greater authoritarianism and self-doubt; inner-city experience more negative
Finley and Cooper (1981)	98	Correlations of locus of control and achievement	.18	79	Correlations higher among males; for adolescents in contrast to children and adult groups; for specific control measures; and for objective achievement
Hansford and Hattie (1982)	128	Correlation of self-concept and achievement/performance	.21	84	Correlations higher for high school students in contrast to elementary and college; higher ability students; specific rather than global self-concept; and verbal achievement measures
Carlberg and Kavale (1980)	50	Effects of special versus regular classes	−.12	—	Effects positive for learning disabled and behavior disordered and negative for slow learners and mentally retarded
Otterbacher and Cooper (1981)	43	Effects of class placement of mentally retarded students on social adjustments	.05 −.07	61 46	Special class vs. regular class Special class vs. resource class
Smith and Glass (1980)	59	Effects of class size on attitudes, climate, and instruction	.49	—	In contrast to small mean effect of .01 for achievement, moderate effects observed, which were larger on teachers than students, younger students, and for studies before 1969
Williams, Haertel, Haertel, and Walberg (1982)	23	Correlations of leisure-time television and achievement	−.05	34	Effects negative at ratio of less than 5 or greater than 15 hours per week and stronger for girls and higher ability groups
Willson and Putnam (1982)	32	Effects of pretests on outcomes	.17	57	Effects greater for cognitive and personality outcomes, for treatments lasting between 2 and 30 days, and for randomized studies

sites, but all effect sizes came from the same study. Although teachers in the various sites may have been acting independently, methodological bias can make the effects nonindependent from a statistical point of view; and independent replications by different investigators would be needed to provide a more definitive answer to the questions raised by these authors.

Pflaum, Walberg, Karegianes, and Rasher (1980) found no average superiority of different reading methods but a substantial advantage in learning outcomes of experimental over control groups no matter what the reading method employed. Although Hawthorne effects could be discounted by the synthesis, the increased energy and attention devoted to tasks by teachers in experimental groups rather than the nominal treatments themselves may partly account for superior results of treatment over control groups in teaching-methods and other educational studies.

Table 7.2 includes two replications of syntheses that indicate substantial agreement in results despite large variations in study search, selection, and numbers. Hansford and Hattie's (1982) Australian and Finley and Cooper's (1981) American syntheses of correlations of self-concept and locus of control with achievement and performance differ only slightly in the second decimal place in both the vote counts and average correlations. Carlberg and Kavale's (1980) and Otterbacher and Cooper's (1981) syntheses agree that the effects of mainstreaming (mixing regular and cognitively, emotionally, and physically handicapped children in the same classes) are inconsistent and probably near zero.

Two syntheses show curvilinear effects of independent variables on educational outcomes. Smith and Glass (1980) found that the benefits of reduced class size are larger in the range from 1 to 15 members than they are at higher ranges; for example, the measurable cognitive and affective outcome differences between classes of 20 and 60 appear trivial.

Similarly, Williams, Haertel, Haertel, and Walberg (1982) found decreasing achievement with departures in either direction from about 10 weekly hours of leisure-time television viewing such that estimated differences in achievement among children who watched 0, 10, and 20 were moderate but differences between those that watched 30 hours—an average number—and 60 hours—a large amount—are miniscule. The important substantive point, however, is that the average number of hours watched is far beyond the optimum associated with the highest grades and the highest performance on ability and achievement tests.

To cite another example of interesting and educationally important results in Table 7.2, Butcher (1981), in an excellent Australian Ph.D. thesis, showed that microteaching, now largely but unjustifiably abandoned in teacher education programs, has substantial effects on teaching skills of undergraduates in teacher training. Many fads have come and gone in education during the past few decades; but some of them, like microteaching, probably had large constructive effects. Educational research will accumulate more knowledge and help improve education more than it has if the results of old and new programs such as microteaching are synthesized.

Not all effects are consistent and positive. For example, the synthesis of pretest effects on outcomes shown last in Table 7.2 indicates that they have inconsistent effects; only 57% of the results were positive, which is near a 50–50 split. Moreover, the effects are somewhat contingent on outcomes measured, length of time between pretest and outcome, and treatment randomization.

Other effects are summarized in Table 7.2, and the reader is referred to the original syntheses for details that are not discussed here. Overall, the results indicate a large range of effects, which, if replicated in further primary research and syntheses, would have important implications for educational policies and practices.

A subsequent section provides a case study of a series of replicated and extended syntheses of open education research. Although other topics in Table 7.2 might have been chosen for illustration, the case study shows how quantitative syntheses can lead not only to a more comprehensive assessment of educational effects but also how an initial synthesis—by being explicit enough in its methods for other investigators to criticize, replicate, and extend—can lead to better subsequent syntheses, more comprehensive assessments of studies, more pointed indications for additional empirical research, and more confident conclusions and implications for the practice of education. Many of the syntheses in Table 7.2 (and additional ones that will no doubt be available soon) deserve careful study of these features, although space does not allow more extended discussion of them in this chapter.

A Team Approach to Synthesis

Chen-Lin and James Kulik lead a vigorous group of research synthesists at the University of Michigan. The group has been unusually productive of high-quality syntheses of higher education and of secondary school research. Personal communications with the group reveal that their team approach, much like that described by Shulman and Tamir (1973) in the *Second Handbook of Research on Teaching*, accounts in part for the quantity and quality of work. Researchers are likely to find their first synthesis formidable and time consuming because computer search and selection procedures, effect-size calculations, weighing techniques, and many other choices must be made and carried out for the first time. Later syntheses, however, can proceed much more efficiently because procedures can be routinized, assistants can specialize in various aspects of the work, and substantive or methodological experts can be recruited as advisors or participants in an ongoing collegial program such as that of the Kuliks.

Table 7.3 shows the results of 11 syntheses completed by the University of Michigan group by the end of 1981. Like the syntheses by other investigators discussed in the last section, those in Table 7.3 show a number of consistent moderate to large effects that can help to put high school and college teaching on a firmer scientific basis.

The Kuliks' results also permit an estimate of the mean size of effects from vote counts. The regression equation, $ES' = -.403 + .008$ (% positive), accounts for 76% of the variance in the effect sizes. The corresponding equation for the syntheses in Table 7.2 for which both indexes are available, $ES' = -.761 + .015$ (%), accounts for 59% of the effect-size variance.

Table 7.3. Major Results from Quantitative Syntheses Conducted at the University of Michigan's Center for Research on Learning and Teaching

Report	Independent Variable	Dependent Variable	Studies Number	Studies % Positive	Effect Size Mean	Effect Size SD	Comments
Bangert, Kulik, and Kulik (1981)	Individualized vs. conventional secondary teaching	Achievement on final examination	49	65	0.10	0.38	
		Attitude toward subject matter	14	64	0.14	0.27	
Cohen (1980)	Midsemester rating feedback to teacher vs. no feedback	Change on final ratings	22	91	0.38	0.41	Effects were greater when teachers received consulting help along with rating feedback.
Cohen (1981)	Class rating of instructor quality	Class achievement on final examination	67	88	0.43	0.13	Correlations were higher when teachers were faculty (not teaching assistants), when all tests were graded by a common grader, and when students rated teachers after receiving grades.
Cohen, Ebeling, and Kulik (1981)	Visual-based vs. conventional college teaching	Achievement on final examination	65	57	0.15	0.41	Achievement effects were stronger in more recent studies, in studies from universities, and when different teachers taught visual-based and control classes.
		Student rating of course quality	16	38	−0.06	0.68	
		Course completion	10	30	−0.05	0.23	
Cohen, Kulik, and Kulik (in press).	Tutorial program vs. conventional teaching	Tutee achievement on final exam	52	87	0.40	0.49	Effects on tutee achievement were stronger in studies found in journals and in studies reporting on short, structured programs, especially those emphasizing lower-level skills, in mathematics, and using local tests. Effects on tutor achievement were also clearer in studies in mathematics.
		Tutee attitude toward subject	8	100	0.29	0.21	
		Tutee self-concept	9	78	0.09	0.12	
		Tutor achievement on final exam	38	87	0.33	0.55	
		Tutor attitude toward subject	5	80	0.42	0.92	
		Tutor self-concept	16	75	0.18	0.46	
Kulik and Kulik (1981)	Ability-grouped vs. ungrouped secondary school classes	Achievement on final examination	51	71	0.10	0.32	Achievement effects were larger in studies found in journals and in studies reporting on programs for gifted and talented students.
		Self-concept	15	47	0.01	0.40	
		Attitude toward subject matter	8	88	0.37	0.32	
		Attitude toward school	11	73	0.09	0.23	
Kulik, Shwalb, and Kulik (in press)	Programed vs. conventional instruction in secondary schools	Achievement on final examination	47	49	0.08	0.47	Achievement effects were stronger in studies from the social sciences and in more recent studies.
		Attitude toward subject matter	9	44	−0.14	0.34	
Kulik, Cohen, and Ebeling (1980)	Programed vs. conventional college teaching	Achievement on final examination	56	71	0.24	0.52	Achievement effects were stronger in more recent studies.
		Course completion	9	61	−0.06	0.27	
Kulik, Kulik, and Cohen (1979a)	Personalized system of instruction vs. conventional college teaching	Achievement on final examination	61	94	0.49	0.33	Achievement effects differed by subject and were stronger when different teachers taught PSI and control classes, and when control classes contained PSI features.
		Course completion	27	37	−0.10	0.30	
		Rating of course quality	11	91	0.46	0.65	
Kulik, Kulik, and Cohen (1979b)	Audio-tutorial vs. conventional college teaching	Achievement on final examination	42	69	0.20	0.43	Achievement effects were stronger in studies found in journals.
		Course completion	22	52	−0.10	0.37	
		Rating of course quality	6	50	0.12	0.52	
Kulik, Kulik, and Cohen (1980)	Computer-based vs. conventional college teaching	Achievement on final examination	54	69	0.25	0.61	Achievement effects were stronger when different teachers taught computer-based and control classes.
		Course completion	13	46	0.01	0.30	
		Rating of course quality	11	73	0.24	0.52	

Both equations forecast near zero effect sizes for vote counts of 50%; but the higher slope for the results in Table 7.2 forecasts larger effects at the higher levels of vote counts than do the University of Michigan data; at counts of 75%, for example, the respective forecasts are about .36 and .20. Thus the regression slopes are somewhat unstable across samples, and analyses of the complete corpus of syntheses would be useful. The principle holds, however, that strong results are generally consistent.

The two data sets also permit separate empirical estimates of the distributions of vote counts and effects. The mean (and standard deviations) of the University of Michigan and other estimates of the vote counts are respectively 67 and 64 (and 19 and 16); the mean effects are respectively .17 and .22 (and .19 and .31). Assuming normal distributions of effects, empirical norms for vote counts and effect sizes can be set forth on the basis of the averages of these statistics; for example, the middle two-thirds of the effects in the recent educational research sampled range from about − .05 to .45. It could be said that effect sizes of .20 are average, and those above .45 are large and ex-

ceed about 84% of those typically found in educational research.

These norms are, of course, very rough and preliminary, but they are based on empirical results rather than opinion and may be useful in assessing present and future results until larger normative samples are analyzed. Hedges and Olkin's (1980, 1983) statistical theories are likely to put such efforts on more solid and comprehensive mathematical footings. Also, from the beginning, Glass (1977) has stressed the use of robust statistical methods to detect and remedy distributional abnormalities such as skewness and outliers.

Synthesis of Bivariate Productivity Studies

A group at the University of Illinois at Chicago has concentrated on synthesizing research on nine theoretical constructs that appear to have consistent causal influences on academic

Table 7.4. A Selective Summary of a Decade of Educational Research

Research Topics	No. of Results	Percent Positive	Research Topics	No. of Results	Percent Positive
Time on learning	25	95.4	Adjunct questions on learning:		
Innovative curricula on:			After text on recall	38	97.4
Innovative learning	45	97.8	After text on transfer	35	74.3
Traditional learning	14	35.7	Before text on recall	13	76.9
Smaller classes on learning:			Before text on transfer	17	23.5
Pre-1954 studies	53	66.0	Advance organizers on learning	32	37.5
Pre-1954 better studies	19	84.2	Analytic revision of instruction on achievement	4	100.0
Post-1954 studies	11	72.7	Direct instruction on achievement	4	100.0
All comparisons	691	60.0	Lecture vs. discussion on:		
Behavioral instruction on learning	52	98.1	Achievement	16	68.8
Personal systems of instruction on learning	103	93.2	Retention	7	100.0
Mastery learning	30	96.7	Attitudes	8	86.0
Student vs. instructor-led discussion on:			Student vs. instructor-centered discussion on:		
Achievement	10	100.0	Achievement	7	57.1
Attitude	11	100.0	Understanding	6	83.3
Factual vs. conceptual questions on achievement	4	100.0	Attitude	22	100.0
Specific teaching traits on achievement:			Factual vs. conceptual questions on achievement	4	100.0
Clarity	7	100.0	Social–psychological climate and learning:		
Flexibility	4	100.0	Cohesiveness	17	85.7
Enthusiasm	5	100.0	Satisfaction	17	100.0
Task orientation	7	85.7	Difficulty	16	86.7
Use of student ideas	8	87.5	Formality	17	64.7
Indirectness	6	83.3	Goal direction	15	73.3
Structuring	3	100.0	Democracy	14	84.6
Sparing criticism	17	70.6	Environment	15	85.7
Psychological incentives and engagement			Speed	14	53.8
Teacher cues to student	10	100.0	Diversity	14	30.8
Teacher reinforcement of student	16	87.5	Competition	9	66.7
Teacher engagement of class in lesson	6	100.0	Friction	17	0.0
Individual student engagement in lesson	15	100.0	Cliqueness	13	8.3
Open vs. traditional education on:			Apathy	15	14.3
Achievement	26	54.8	Disorganization	17	6.3
Creativity	12	100.0	Favoritism	13	10.0
Self-concept	17	88.2	Motivation and learning	232	97.8
Attitude toward school	25	92.0	Social class and learning	620	97.6
Curiosity	6	100.0	Home environment on:		
Self-determination	7	85.7	Verbal achievement	30	100.0
Independence	19	94.7	Math achievement	22	100.0
Freedom from anxiety	8	37.5	Intelligence	20	100.0
Cooperation	6	100.0	Reading gains	6	100.0
Programed instruction on learning	57	80.7	Ability	8	100.0

Note: From "What makes schooling effective?" by H. J. Walberg, 1982, *Contemporary Education Review, 1,* 1–34.

learning: student age or developmental level, ability (including prior achievement), and motivation; amount and quality of instruction; the psychological environments of the class, home, and peer group outside school; and exposure to the mass media (Walberg, 1984). The group first collected available vote counts and effect sizes in the review literature of the 1970s and then conducted more systematic syntheses directly on the nine factors. This section summarizes both efforts.

Synthesis of Reviews of the 1970s

Walberg, Schiller, and Haertel (1979) collected reviews published from 1969 to 1979 on the effects of instruction and related factors on cognitive, affective, and behavioral learning in research conducted in elementary, secondary, and college classes. The vote counts (or percent positive of all results in each review), shown in Table 7.4, should be cautiously interpreted be-

Table 7.5. Correlations and Effect Sizes for Nine Factors in Relation to School Learning

Factor	Number of Studies	Results and Comment
Instruction		
Amount	31	Correlations range from .13 to .71 with a median of .40; partial correlations controlling for ability, socioeconomic status, and other variables range from .09 to .60 with a median of .35.
Quality	95	The mean of effect sizes for reinforcement in 39 studies is 1.17, suggesting a 38-point percentile advantage over control groups, although girls and students in special schools might be somewhat more benefited; the mean effect sizes for cues, participation, and corrective feedback in 54 studies is .97, suggesting a 33-point advantage. The mean effect size of similar variables in 18 science studies is .81.
Social–Psychological environment		
Educational	12	On 19 outcomes, social–psychological climate variables added from 1 to 54 (median = 20%) to accountable variance in learning beyond ability and pretests: The signs and magnitudes of the correlations depend on specific scales, level of aggregation (classes and schools higher), nation, and grade level (later grades higher); but not on sample size, subject matter, domain of learning (cognitive, affective, or behavioral), or statistical adjustments for ability and pretests.
Home	18	Correlations of achievement, ability, and motivation with home support and stimulation range from .02 to .82 with a median of .37, multiple correlations range from .23 to .81 with a median of .44; studies of boys and girls and middle-class children in contrast to mixed groups show higher correlations (social classes correlations in 100 studies, by contrast, have a median of .25). The median correlation for three studies of home environment and learning in science is .32.
Media–TV	23	274 correlations of leisure-time television viewing and learning ranged from −.56 to .35 with a median of −.06, although effects appear increasingly deleterious from 10 to 40 hours a week and appear stronger for girls and high-IQ children.
Peer group	10	The median correlation of peer group or friend characteristics such as socioeconomic status and educational aspirations with achievement-test scores, course grades, and educational and occupational aspirations is .24; correlations are higher in urban settings and in studies of students who reported aspirations and achievements of friends. The median of two sciences studies is .24.
Aptitude		
Age–development	9	Correlations between Piaget developmental level and school achievement range from .02 to .71 with a median of .35. The mean correlation in sciences is .40.
Ability	10	From 396 correlations with learning, mean verbal intelligence measures are highest (mean = .72) followed by total ability (.71), nonverbal (.64), and quantitative (.60); correlations with achievement test scores (.70) are higher than those with grades (.57). The mean ability–learning correlation in science is .48.
Motivation	40	Mean correlation with learning is .34; correlations were higher for older samples and for combinations of subjects (mathematics) and measures, but did not depend on type of motivation nor the sex of the samples. The mean of three studies in science is .33.

Note: From "What makes schooling effective?" by H. J. Walberg, 1982, *Contemporary Education Review*, *1*, 1–34.

cause not only may journal editors more often select studies with positive results but also reviewers may select positive published studies to summarize. Neither editors nor reviewers ordinarily state their explicit policies on these important points. Subsequent, more systematic syntheses, nonetheless, have generally supported traditional reviews; and it would be wasteful to ignore the labors of the last decade of effort.

Notwithstanding the possible double bias in the vote counts (see earlier sections on counterbiases such as curriculum–test mismatch and invalidity of treatment and outcome measures), the results in Table 7.4 are impressive. A majority of the variables in the table were positively associated with learning; in 48 or 68% of the 71 tabulations, 80% or more of the comparisons or correlations are positive. Although all of the variables are candidates for synthesis using systematic search, selection, evaluation, and summary procedures, it appears that the 1970s produced reasonably consistent findings that are likely to be confirmed by more comprehensive and explicit syntheses of the present decade.

Syntheses of Productivity Factors

The group at the University of Illinois at Chicago also carried out syntheses of the nine factors using methods discussed in previous sections of this chapter. Shown in Table 7.5 are estimates made from studies of Grades Kindergarten through 12 in all curriculum areas. Also shown are separate estimates for science learning, Grades 6 through 12 from more intensive searches for unpublished work based on advice of science educators and research methodologists, which provide a semi-independent replication of the results for several of the factors.

All of the effect sizes (including mean contrasts and correlations) are in the expected direction. The mean effects for the two samples of studies are similar in magnitude, which suggests generality or robustness of effects across more and less intensive methods of synthesis. In particular, the effects of quality of instruction including cues, participation, and reinforcement of about 1.0 in general Grades K–12 and .8 in science Grades 6–12 support the conclusions of the 19 reviews discussed in a previous section (see also Table 7.1).

The syntheses in Table 7.5 provide systematic evidence that the nine factors within the three clusters — instruction, psychological environments, and student aptitude — have consistent correlations with learning. Moreover, because many of the instructional studies employed random assignment to alternative methods, and because many studies of aptitude and motivation employed longitudinal or controlled predictions, it might be said that some factors have known causal or influential directions. Despite these corroborated findings, of course, independent replications of the syntheses as well as new and probing experimental and longitudinal studies are needed.

Collections of syntheses, such as those in Tables 7.1 through 7.5, can be more useful to policymakers than traditional reviews. They show a reasonable consistency of findings in many studies and, equally important, give indications of the relative magnitudes of probable influences or effects. Because the general definitions of the factors can be made clear, and because the specific operational definitions can be traced to all original

studies, the more powerful and readily alterable factors can be selected to improve the productivity of educational practice.

Since quantitative synthesis in education is relatively new, perhaps dating from the early works of Bloom (1976) and Light and Smith (1971), the benefits for educational practice beyond those thus far discussed are difficult to document thoroughly in published literature. It can be noted, however, that the number of reviews and primary studies citing research syntheses and papers on the topic presented at the American Educational Research Association and the American Psychological Association are increasing. Moreover, in my experience, invitations to give testimony in federal courts and U.S. Congressional committees; to advise research workers outside of education as well as international, state, and local educational agencies; and to write for policy and practitioner journals such as *Daedalus*, *Educational Leadership*, and *Phi Delta Kappan* indicate growing interest in the topic beyond educational and psychological research circles.

Synthesis of Multivariate Studies

The University of Illinois at Chicago group also conducted multivariate analyses of the productivity factors in samples of from two to three thousand 13- and 17-year-old students who participated in the mathematics, social studies, and science parts of the National Assessment of Educational Progress (see, for example, Walberg, Pascarella, Haertel, Junker, and Boulanger, 1982). These survey analyses, which are summarized in Table 7.6, complement small-scale correlational and experimental studies because they provide national data on fairly comprehensive sets of the productivity factors, each of which may be statistically controlled for the others in multiple regressions of achievement and subject matter interest as dependent variables.

Such analyses allow a simultaneous assessment of qualities and amounts of instruction and the other factors in the production of learning. Since the factor levels are reported as experienced by individual students, the analyses are sensitive to microvariations in the multiple environments of the school, peer group, home, and mass media to which each student is exposed.

Although the data from the National Assessment can be used to test possible exogenous causes because they are measured and can be statistically controlled in regression equations, the measures are cross sectional for individuals. Therefore, they cannot effectively rule out reverse causation such as learning as a cause of motivation and more stimulating teaching. Another shortcoming of the data is that parental socioeconomic status serves as a proxy for ability and prior achievement.

As pointed out above, nonetheless, the strengths of the National Assessment data complement those of small-scale studies that typically control for only one or two of the factors. If syntheses of data from both sources point in the same direction, then more confidence can be placed in the conclusions.

Table 7.6 shows that the factors, when controlled for one another, are consistent in sign across subject matters, ages, operational measures of the factors, and independent national samples. For example, 95% of the weights are in the expected

Table 7.6. Standardized Regression Weights of Achievement/Attitude on Productive Factors

Subject	Age	Achievement	Attitude	Socioeconomic Status	Quality of Instruction	Quantity of Instruction	Education (Class)	Home	Peer	Homework	Media–Television	Extra-Curricular	Stimulation	Female
Science achievement	13		.0857*	.0922*	.0698		.2498**	.2268**	.0540*					
Science attitude	13	.0909*		.0300	−.2661**		.2732**	.0262	−.0980*					
Science achievement	17		.0881*	.1366**	.0746*		.2692**	.1842**	.1016**	.0921**				
Math achievement	17		.0380**	.0536**	.1696**	.1443**		.1443**			−.0546**			−.0848
Math attitude	17	.0490			.1320**			−.0940**		.1280**			.1720**	
Social studies achievement	13	.5089**	.4629**	.1488**		.0721**		.1649**						
Social studies attitude	13				.1170**	.0559*		.0590*						.0900
Social studies achievement	17	.3391**	.3238**	.1851**	.1212**	.1201**		.1360**			−.0551**			−.1502
Social studies attitude	17				.0850**	.0879**	.0902**	.0670**		.0741**		.2128**	.0551**	.1369
Reading achievement	17		.0630**	.1370**		.0527**		.1251**						
Reading attitude	17	.0522**				.2494**				.0503**				.1231
Medians		.0909	.0869	.1366	.1010	.0879	.2595	.1306	.0540	.0831	−.0548	.2128	.1136	.0900

* $p \le .05$
** $p \le .01$

225

direction. The regressions, moreover, reveal the small to moderate effects of the factors when controlled for one another (even though they are poorly measured by self-report rather than systematically observed). The squared multiple correlations also show sizeable amounts of variance accounted for even without ability and prior achievement measures in the regression equations.

In contrast to past reviews of correlational-survey research (see Walberg, 1982b, 1984 for a critical assessment), explicit tabulations of the results across studies such as those in Table 7.6 yield evidence of replicability of findings in national educational surveys. Verbal summaries of such results are difficult to assimilate and assess; but tabulations and statistical summaries help make the overall results plain to see. Although this is a step forward, it should also be acknowledged that the synthesized findings in Table 7.6 and in many other surveys are based on cross-sectional correlations and are merely a probe rather than proof of causality.

Syntheses of Open-Education Research

This section illustrates how successive syntheses can raise confidence in research conclusions and how they may improve upon one another by replication and extension just as primary studies may. The approach chosen for illustration, open education, is elusive and now dismissed by many educators, but research synthesis now illuminates it even though it may be forgotten. If education proceeds by fads rather than cumulative research, it will fail to make the great advances in productivity that have characterized agriculture and industry in this century.

Efforts to synthesize the effects of open education illustrate the dangers of basing conclusions, policies, and practices on fads and single studies no matter how large or widely publicized. It also illustrates the strengths of replication and improved methods of synthesis, and a shortcoming of much of the research discussed above that employs grades and standardized achievement as the only outcomes of teaching.

From the start, open educators tried to encourage educational outcomes that reflect school board goals such as co-operation, critical thinking, self-reliance, constructive attitudes, lifelong learning, and other objectives that evaluators seldom measure. Raven's (1981) summary of surveys in Western countries including England and the United States shows that educators, parents, and students rank these goals far above standardized test achievement and grades.

A synthesis of the relation of conventionally measured educational outcomes and adult success, moreover, shows their slight association (Samson and others, 1982). Thirty-three post-1949 studies of physicians, engineers, civil servants, teachers, adults in general, and other groups show a mean correlation of .155 of these educational outcomes with success indicators such as income; self-rated happiness; work performance and output indexes; and self-, peer, and supervisor ratings of occupational effectiveness. These results should challenge educators and researchers to seek a balance between continuing autonomy, motivation, and skills to learn new tasks as an individual or group member on one hand and mastery of teacher-chosen, textbook knowledge that may soon be obsolete or forgotten on the other.

Perhaps since Socrates, however, these have remained so polarized that educators find it difficult to stand firmly on the high middle ground of balanced or cooperative determination of the goals, means, and evaluation of learning. Progressive education, the Dalton and Winnetka plans, team teaching, the ungraded school, and other innovations in the 20th century — all of these held forth this ideal but drifted into authoritarianism, permissiveness, or confusion. They could not be sustained as idealized. Although open education, like its precursors, faded from view, it was more carefully researched. Perhaps the syntheses of this research may help educators, who want to base practice on synthesized knowledge rather than fads or to evaluate future descendants of open education.

Three Syntheses of Open Education

Horwitz (1979) first summarized about 200 abstracts of comparative studies of open and traditional education by tabulating vote counts by outcome category. Although many studies yielded nonsignificant or mixed results especially with respect to academic achievement, self-concept, anxiety, adjustment, and locus of control, more positive results were found in open education on attitudes toward school, creativity, independence, curiosity, and cooperation.

Peterson (1979) calculated effect sizes for the 45 published studies. She found about a −.1 or slightly inferior effects of open education on reading and mathematics achievement; .1 to .2 effects on creativity, attitudes toward school, and curiosity; and large .3 to .5 effects on independence and attitudes toward the teacher.

Hedges, Giaconia, and Gage (1981) synthesized 153 studies including 90 dissertations using an adjustment of Glass's effect-size estimator which is biased especially in small samples. The average effect was near zero for achievement, locus of control, self-concept, and anxiety; about .2 for adjustment, attitude towards school and teacher, curiosity, and general mental ability; and about a moderate .3 for cooperativeness, creativity, and independence.

Despite the differences in study selection and methods, the three syntheses, which cover more or less substantial parts of the corpus of research, converge roughly on the same plausible conclusion: Students in open classes do slightly or no worse in standardized achievement and slightly to substantially better on several outcomes that educators, parents, and students hold to be of great value. Unfortunately, the negative conclusion of Bennett's (1976) single study — introduced by a prominent psychologist, published by Harvard University Press, publicized by the *New York Times* and by experts that take that newspaper as their source — probably sounded the death knell of open education, even though the conclusion of the study was later retracted (Aitkin, Bennett, & Hesketh, 1981) because of obvious statistical flaws in the original analysis (Aitken, Anderson, & Hinde, 1981).

Components of Open Education

Giaconia and Hedges (1982) took another recent and constructive step in the synthesis of open education research. From their prior effect-size synthesis, they identified the studies with the largest positive and negative effects on several outcomes to differentiate more and less effective program features. They found that programs that are more effective in producing the non-achievement outcomes—attitude, creativity, and self-concept—sacrificed academic achievement on standardized measures.

These programs were characterized by emphasis on the role of the child in learning, use of diagnostic rather than norm-referenced evaluation, individualized instruction, and manipulative materials, but not three other components sometimes thought essential to open programs—multiage grouping, open space, and team teaching. Giaconia and Hedges speculate that children in the most extreme open programs may do somewhat less well on conventional achievement tests because they have little experience with them. At any rate, it appears from the two most comprehensive syntheses of effects that open classes on average enhance several nonstandard outcomes without detracting from academic achievement unless they are radically extreme.

Syntheses of Instructional Theories

As mentioned at the outset, theoretical is as important as empirical synthesis. This section illustrates the convergences of instructional models during the past 2 decades.

To specify the productivity factors in further theoretical and operational detail and to provide a more explicit framework for future primary research and synthesis, Haertel, Walberg, and Weinstein (1983) compared eight contemporary psychological models of educational performance. Each of the first four factors in Table 7.7—student ability and motivation, and quality

Table 7.7. Classification of Constructs According to the Model of Educational Productivity

Theorist	Ability	Motivation	Quality of Instruction	Quality of Instruction	Social Environment of Classroom	Home Environment	Peer Influence	Mass Media
Carroll (1963)	Aptitude Ability to comprehend instructions	Perseverance	Clarity of instruction Matching task to student characteristics	Opportunity to learn (time)				
Cooley and Leinhart (1975)	General ability Prior achievement	Motivators (internal)	Motivators (external) Structure Instructional events Attitude toward teachers	Opportunity to learn (time)	Attitudes toward school		Attitudes toward peer	
Bloom (1976)	Prior achievement Reading comprehension Verbal IQ	Attitude toward subject matter Self-concept as learner	Use of cues Reinforcement Feedback and correctives	Participation in learning task (time)	Attitudes toward school			
Harnischfeger and Wiley (1976)	Pupil background	Intrinsic motivation	Teacher activities	Pupil pursuits (seven time categories)				
Bennett (1978)	Aptitude Prior achievement	Implicit	Clarity of instruction Task difficulty and pacing	Total active learning time Quantity of schooling Time allocated to curriculum activity				
Gagné (1977)	Internal conditions of learning	Implicit	Activating motivation Informing learner of objective Directing attention Stimulating recall Providing learning guidance Enhancing retention Promoting transfer of learning Eliciting performance and providing feedback					
Glaser (1976)	Task learnings already acquired Prerequisite learnings Cognitive style Task-specific aptitudes General mediating ability	Implicit	Materials, procedures, and techniques that foster competence (e.g., knowledge structures; Learning-to-learn; Contingencies of reinforcement) Assessment of effects of instruction					
Bruner (1966)	Task-relevent skills	Predispositions	Implanting a predisposition toward learning Structuring knowledge Sequence of materials Specifying rewards and punishments					

Note. From Psychological models of educational performance by G. D. Haertel, H. W. Walberg, and T. Weinstein, 1983, *Review of Educational Research, 53,* 75–92.

and quantity of instruction — may be essential or necessary but insufficient by itself for classroom learning (age and developmental level are omitted because they are unspecified in the models).

The other four factors in Table 7.7 are less clear: Although they consistently predict outcomes, they may support or substitute for classroom learning. At any rate, it would seem useful to include all factors in future primary research to rule out exogenous causes and increase statistical precision of estimates of the effects of the essential and the other factors.

Table 7.7 shows that, among the constructs, ability and quantity of instruction are widely and relatively richly specified among the psychological models of educational performance. Explicit theoretical treatments of motivation and quantity of instruction, however, are largely confined to the Carroll tradition represented in the first four models; and the remaining factors are largely neglected even though they account for substantial blocks of children's time and variance in learning.

Table 7.7 poses theoretical questions that would be useful to answer empirically. The tension between theoretical parsimony and operational detail, for example, suggests several: Can the first four productivity constructs mediate the causal influences of the last four? Would assessments of Glaser's five student-entry behaviors allow more efficient instructional prescriptions than would, say, Carroll's, Bloom's, or Bennett's more general and more parsimonious ability subconstructs? Would less numerous subconstructs than Gagné's eight instructional qualities and Harnischfeger and Wiley's seven time categories suffice?

The theoretical formulation of educational performance models of the past two decades since the Carroll and Bruner papers has rapidly advanced. The models are explicit enough to be tested in ordinary classroom settings by experimental methods and production functions. Future empirical research and syntheses that are more comprehensive and better connected operationally to these theoretical formulations should help reach a greater degree of theoretical and empirical consensus as well as more effective educational practice.

Prospects

Research workers and educators must retain both open-mindedness and skepticism about research synthesis. Yet the 1980s do seem to be a period of quiet accomplishment. In a short time, research synthesis helped sort what is known from what needs to be known about the means and ends of education.

Agriculture, engineering, and medicine made great strides in improving human welfare as doubts arose about traditional, natural, and mystical practices, as the measurement of results intensified, as experimental findings were synthesized, and as their theoretical and practical implications were coordinated and vigorously implemented and evaluated. Education is no less open to humanistic and scientific inquiry and no lower in priority since half the workers in modern nations are in knowledge industries, and the value of investments in people is now more apparent than ever (Walberg, 1983). Although more and better research is required, synthesis points the way toward improvements that seem likely to increase teaching effectiveness and educational productivity.

REFERENCES

Aitken, M., Anderson, D., & Hinde, J. (1981). Modeling of data on teaching styles [With discussion]. *Journal of the Royal Statistical Society* (series A), *144*, 419–461.

Aitken, M., Bennett, S. N., & Hesketh, J. (1981). Teaching styles and pupil progress: A re-analysis. *British Journal of Educational Psychology, 51*.

Bangert, R. L., Kulik, J. A., & Kulik, C.-L. C. (1981). *Individualized systems of instruction in secondary schools.* Unpublished manuscript, University of Michigan, Ann Arbor.

Becker, W. C., & Gersten, R. (1982). A follow-up of Follow Through. *American Educational Research Journal, 19,* 75–92.

Bennett, S. N. (1976). *Teaching styles and pupil progress.* Shepton Mallet, Somerset, England: Open Books.

Bennett, S. N. (1978). Recent research on teaching: A dream, a belief, and a model. *British Journal of Educational Psychology, 48,* 127–147.

Blaug, M. (1978). *Economic theory in retrospect.* New York: Cambridge University Press.

Bloom, B. S. (1976). *Human characteristics and school learning.* New York: McGraw-Hill.

Bruner, J. S. (1966). *Toward a theory of instruction.* New York: W. W. Norton.

Butcher, P. M. (1981). *An experimental investigation of the effectiveness of a value claim strategy unit for use in teacher education.* Unpublished doctoral dissertation, Macquarie University, Sydney, Australia.

Cahen, L. S. (1980). Meta-analysis: A technique with promise and problems. *Evaluation in Education, 4,* 37–42.

Carlberg, C., & Kavale, K. (1980). The efficacy of special versus regular class placement for exceptional children: A meta-analysis. *Journal of Special Education, 14,* 295–309.

Carroll, J. B. (1963). A model of school learning. *Teachers College Record, 64,* 723–733.

Cohen, P. A. (1980). Effectiveness of student-rating feedback for improving college instruction. *Research in Higher Education, 13,* 321–341.

Cohen, P. A. (1981). Student ratings of instruction and student achievement. *Review of Educational Research, 51,* 281–309.

Cohen, P. A., Ebeling, B. J., & Kulik, J. A. (1981). A meta-analysis of outcome studies of visual-based instruction. *Education Communication and Technology Journal, 29,* 26–36.

Cohen, P. A., Kulik, J. A., & Kulik, C.-L. C. (1983). Educational outcomes of tutoring. *American Educational Research Journal,* in press.

Colosimo, M. L. (1981). *The effect of practice or beginning teaching on the self concepts and attitudes of teachers: A quantitative synthesis.* Unpublished doctoral dissertation, University of Chicago.

Cook, T. D., & Campbell, D. T. (1979). *Quasi-experimentation.* Chicago: Rand McNally.

Cooley, W. W., & Leinhardt, G. (1975). *The application of a model for investigating classroom processes.* Pittsburgh: University of Pittsburgh, Learning Research and Development Center.

Cooper, H. M. (1982). Scientific guidelines for conducting integrative research reviews. *Review of Educational Research, 52,* 291–302.

Cooper, H. M., & Rosenthal, R. (1980). A comparison of statistical and traditional procedures for summarizing research. *Evaluation in Education, 4,* 33–36.

Dunkin, M. J. (1976). Problems in the accumulation of process–product evidence in classroom research. *British Journal of Teacher Education, 2,* 175–187.

Finley, M. J., & Cooper, H. M. (1981). *The relation between locus of control and academic achievement.* Columbia: University of Missouri, Center for Research in Social Behavior.

Gage, N. L. (1978). *The scientific basis of the art of teaching.* New York: Columbia University, Teachers College Press.

Gagné, R. M. (1977). *The conditions of learning.* Chicago: Holt, Rinehart & Winston.

Giaconia, R. M., & Hedges, L. V. (1982). *Identifying features of open education.* Stanford, CA: Stanford University.

Glaser, R. (1976). Components of a psychological theory of instruction: Toward a science of design. *Review of Educational Research, 46,* 1–24.

Glass, G. V. (1977). Integrating findings: The meta-analysis of research. *Review of Research in Education, 5*, 351–379.

Glass, G. V., Cahen, L. S., Smith, M. L., & Filby, N. N. (1982). *School class size: Research on policy*. Beverley Hills, CA: Sage Publications.

Glass, G. V., McGaw, B., & Smith, M. L. (1981). *Meta-analysis in social research*. Beverley Hills, Sage Publications.

Graubard, S. R. (Ed.). (1981). America's schools: Portraits and perspectives. *Daedalus, 110*, 1–175.

Green, J.L. (1983). Research on teaching as a linguistic process: The state of the art. In E. Gordon (Ed.), *Review of Research in Education, 10.*

Haertel, G. D., Walberg, H. J., & Weinstein, T. (1983). Psychological models of educational performance: A theoretical synthesis of constructs. *Review of Educational Research, 53*, 75–92.

Hansford, B. C., & Hattie, J. A. (1982). The relationship between self and achievement/performance measures. *Review of Educational Research, 52*, 123–142.

Harnischfeger, A., & Wiley, D. E. (1976). The teaching–learning process in elementary schools: A synoptic view. *Curriculum Inquiry, 6*, 5–43.

Hedges, L. V., Giaconia, R. M., & Gage, N. L. (1981). *Meta-analysis of the effects of open and traditional instruction*. Stanford, CA: Stanford University, Program on Teaching Effectiveness.

Hedges, L. V., & Olkin, I. (1981). Vote counting methods in research synthesis. *Psychological Bulletin, 88*, 359–369.

Hedges, L. V., & Olkin, I. (1983). Regression models in research synthesis. *American Statistician, 37.*

Horwitz, R. A. (1979) Psychological effects of the open classroom. *Review of Educational Research, 49*, 71–86.

Jackson, G. B. (1980). Methods of integrative reviews. *Review of Educational Research, 50*, 438–460.

Johnson, D. W., Maruyama, G., Johnson, R., Nelson, D., & Skon, L. (1981). Effects of cooperative, competitive, and individualistic goal structures on achievement: A meta-analysis. *Psychological Bulletin, 89*, 47–62.

Kulik, C.-L. C., & Kulik, J. A. (1981). *Effects of ability grouping on secondary school students*. Unpublished manuscript, University of Michigan, Ann Arbor.

Kulik, C.-L. C., Shwalb, B. J., & Kulik, J. A. (   ). Programmed instruction in secondary education. *Journal of Educational Research.*

Kulik, J. A., Cohen, P. A., & Ebeling, B. J. (1980). Effectiveness of programmed instruction in higher education. *Educational Evaluation and Policy Analysis, 2*, 51–64.

Kulik, J. A., Kulik, C.-L. C., & Cohen, P. A. (1979a). A meta-analysis of outcome studies of Keller's Personalized System of Instruction. *American Psychologist, 34*, 307–318.

Kulik, J. A., Kulik, C.-L. C., & Cohen, P. A. (1979b). Research on audio-tutorial instruction. *Research in Higher Education, 11*, 321–341.

Kulik, J. A., Kulik, C.-L. C., & Cohen, P. A. (1980). Effectiveness of computer-based college teaching. *Review of Educational Research, 50*, 525–544.

LeCompte, M. D., & Goetz, J. P. (1982). Problems of reliability and validity in ethnographic research. *Review of Educational Research, 52*, 31–60.

Light, R. J., & Pillemer, D. B. (1982). Numbers and narrative: Combining their strengths in research reviews. *Harvard Educational Review, 52*, 1–26.

Light, R. J., & Smith, P. V. (1971). Accumulating evidence: Procedures for resolving contradictions among different studies. *Harvard Educational Review, 41*, 429–471.

Luiten, J., Ames, W., & Aerson, G. (1980). A meta-analysis of advance organizers on learning and retention. *American Educational Research Journal, 17*, 211–218.

Lysakowski, R. S., & Walberg, H. J. (1981). Classroom reinforcement and learning: A quantitative synthesis. *Journal of Educational Research, 75*, 69–77.

Lysakowski, R. S., & Walberg, H. J. (1983). Cues, participation, and feedback in instruction: A quantitative synthesis. *American Educational Research Journal.*

Otterbacher, K., & Cooper, H. (1981). *The effect of class placement on the social adjustment of mentally retarded children*. Columbia: University of Missouri, Center for Research in Social Behavior.

Peterson, P. L. (1979). Direct instruction reconsidered. In P. L. Peterson & H. J. Walberg (Eds.), *Research on teaching*. Berkeley, CA: McCutchan.

Peterson, P. L., & Walberg, H. J. (1979). *Research on teaching: Concepts, findings, and implications*. Berkeley, CA: McCutchan.

Pflaum, S. W., Walberg, H. J., Karegianes, M. L., & Rasher, S. (1980). Reading instruction: A quantitative synthesis. *Educational Researcher, 9*, 12–18.

Popper, K. R. (1959). *The logic of scientific discovery*. New York: Basic Books.

Raven, J. (1981). The most important problem in education is to come to terms with values. *Oxford Review of Education, 7*, 253–272.

Redfield, D. L., & Rousseau, E. W. (1981). A meta-analysis of experimental research on teacher questioning behavior. *Review of Educational Research, 51*, 237–245.

Rosenthal, R. (1980). Combining probabilities and the file drawer problem. *Evaluation in Education, 4*, 18–21.

Samson, G., Graue, M. E., Weinstein, T., & Walberg, H. J. (1982). *Academic and occupational performance: A quantitative synthesis*. Chicago: University of Illinois, Office of Evaluation Research.

Shulman, L. S., & Tamir, P. (1973). Research on teaching in the natural sciences. In R. M. W. Travers (Ed.), *Second handbook of research on teaching*. Chicago: Rand McNally.

Slavin, R. E. (1980). Cooperative learning. *Review of Educational Research, 50*, 315–342.

Smith, M. L. (1980). Publication bias and meta-analysis. *Evaluation in Education, 4*, 22–24.

Smith, M. L., & Glass, G. V. (1980). Meta-analysis of research on class size and its relationship to attitudes. *American Educational Research Journal, 17*, 419–433.

Walberg, H. J. (1980). A psychological theory of educational productivity. In F. H. Farley & N. Gordon (Eds.), *Psychology and education*. Berkeley, CA: McCutchan.

Walberg, H. J. (Ed.)(1982a). *Improving educational performance and standards: The research and evaluation basis for policy*. Berkeley, CA: McCutchan.

Walberg, H. J. (1982b). What makes schooling effective? *Contemporary Education Review, 1*, 1–34.

Walberg, H. J. (1983). Education, scientific literacy, and economic productivity. *Daedalus, 112*, 1–28.

Walberg, H. J. (1984). Improving the productivity of America's schools. *Educational Leadership, 41*, (8). 19–30.

Walberg, H. J., & Haertel, E. H. (Eds.). (1980). *Research synthesis: The state of the art, evaluation in education, 4*, 1–142.

Walberg, H. J., Pascarella, E., Haertel, G. D., Junker, L. K., & Boulanger, F. D. (1982). Probing a model of educational productivity with National Assessment samples of older adolescents. *Journal of Educational Psychology, 74*, 295–307.

Walberg, H. J., Schiller, D., & Haertel, G. D. (1979). The quiet revolution in educational research. *Phi Delta Kappan, 61*(3), 179–182.

Walberg, H. J., Strykowski, B. F., Rovai, E., & Hung, S. (1984). Exceptional performance. *Review of Educational Research, 54*, 87–112.

Waller, W. (1932). *The sociology of teaching*. New York: Longman.

Waxman, H. C., & Walberg, H. J. (1982). The relation of teaching and learning. *Contemporary Education Review, 2*, 103–120.

Wilkinson, S. S. (1980). *The relationship of teacher praise and student achievement: A meta-analysis*. Unpublished doctoral dissertation, University of Florida, Gainsville.

Williams, P. A., Haertel, E. H., Haertel, G. D., & Walberg, H. J. (1982). The impact of leisure-time television on school learning. *American Educational Research Journal, 19*, 19–50.

Willson, V. L., & Putnam, R. R. (1982). A meta-analysis of pretest sensitization effects in experimental design. *American Educational Research Journal, 19*, 249–258.

8.
Theory, Methods, Knowledge, and Research on Teaching

Bruce J. Biddle
University of Missouri

Donald S. Anderson
Australian National University

Ours is an era of great enthusiasm for research. Without the benefit of research, we are taught, our lives would be short, brutal, and mean. Research seeks to advance understanding by the application of rational thought; it enables us to substitute facts for conjecture and superstition. With research we have destroyed infectious diseases, built skyscrapers, plumbed the depths of the oceans, and landed human beings on the moon. Most of these advances have taken place in the physical and biological sciences it is true, but our enthusiasm for research extends to the social sciences as well. The enlightened policymaker seeks "facts" when planning or evaluating social programs, and to establish those "facts" we need social research. Thus, social research is seen as a practical and necessary tool for solving social problems. According to Prewitt (1981), social research has already solved innumerable problems in Western society and will continue to enrich our lives through generations of new concepts, evidence, techniques for measuring social processes, and ideas for social innovation.

Enthusiasms are often expressed for research in education, too. Green (1982, p. 5) asserts that quality education in America "cannot be achieved without relevant and responsible research," whereas a recent director of the National Institute of Education has claimed that through research "we will find ways to eliminate the effect of a student's race, sex, culture, or income on the quality of education received and on the achievement level attained" (American Sociological Association, 1978). Nor has research on teaching been exempt from such praise. Despite the fact that observational research on teaching is barely 20 years old, Dunkin and Biddle (1974) claim that it "has already developed both concepts and findings ... [that] provide useful information for educators" (p. 12), whereas Gage (1978) opines

that "in the long run, the improvement of teaching ... will come in large part from [research on teaching]" (p. 41). Moreover, accepting the broad thrust of these claims, the National Institute of Education now devotes substantial resources to research on teaching and literally hundreds of investigators are now committed to careers that involve this research field.

To say the least, belief in the social usefulness of social research is not universal. Criticisms of social research have been voiced not only by politicians and policy analysts, but by social scientists themselves, a recent example being the analysis by Scott and Shore (1979) of why sociology does not apply to public policy. Huge cuts in social research budgets have recently been mandated by reactionary governments in the United States, Australia, and other Western countries assuming that social research is either dangerous or ineffective (or perhaps both). Policy analysts such as Aaron (1978) suggest that those "not familiar with the government decision-making process are surprised and often shocked by how small a direct contribution [social] research makes." According to Berns (1981), social research simply "cannot provide the kind of hard information about human behavior that physics provides about the behavior of atoms," whereas Kristol (1981) asserts that "the methodology of the social sciences has turned out to be woefully inadequate for anything like comprehensive analysis and understanding of human affairs." Nor has research on teaching been immune to criticisms of its presumptive usefulness. According to Kerlinger (1977): "Many people think that the purpose of [social] research should be to improve the lot of mankind. Not so. Either men improve man's lot or it doesn't get improved.... There is no such thing as a science of teaching or a science of education" (pp. 5–6).

The authors thank reviewers Ernest Hilgard (Stanford University) and Kenneth Strike (Cornell University), and are indebted to Jere Brophy, Thomas Good, and Peter Hall for manuscript suggestions.

The purpose of this chapter is to address the issues raised by these contrasting reviews of the utility of social research and research on teaching. It is our contention that both the enthusiasts and detractors have adopted overly simple views of social research. Social research does not, indeed cannot, establish "facts" in any simple sense, nor do "facts" lead directly to policies or practices that improve the lot of human beings. On the other hand, social research is neither inherently "dangerous," "ineffective," or "woefully inadequate," and social scientists have a substantial role to play within the collective processes of planning, executing, and evaluating human affairs. As it turns out, that role is directly related to the assumptions and methods with which we conduct our research, so we shall have to examine the latter in some detail.

We begin our analysis by contrasting three different views of the social science enterprise. The first of these views, the *confirmatory perspective* (reviewed immediately below), represents the majority of current effort in the social sciences, presumably derives from the physical sciences in their classical stage, and assumes that social research establishes objective information that is useful for social planning. The second, a *discovery perspective* (reviewed next), assumes that the social sciences are radically different from their hard-science cousins and urges that we pay greater attention to the limitations and subjectivity of social research. The third, an *integrative perspective* (reviewed last), represents an expanded view of the research process, be it in the physical or social sciences, and stresses the key role of theory in bridging the gulfs among research activities, knowledge claims, and policy setting. Later sections of the chapter provide examples of the types of knowledge that research on teaching can generate, and focus on the appropriate use of this information in forming policy.

The Confirmatory Perspective

Much of contemporary social research presumes to establish objective information about social behavior that can be generalized. Studies conducted within this perspective give stress to careful research design, to reliable measurement of variables, to statistical manipulation of data, and to the detailed examination of evidence. Hypotheses are stated to indicate knowledge claims, and these are judged to be confirmed if they are supported by inferential statistics that reach arbitrary levels of significance. Confirmed hypotheses ("findings") are presumed to generalize to populations or contexts similar to the one studied. Simple relationships are assumed among the technical terms and concepts of the investigator, research operations, findings, and conclusions from the research. Above all, social research is regarded as offering the means for generating objective evidence and avoiding subjectivity and value judgments. Results are assumed to be independent of the investigator so that similar conclusions should be reached each time the same hypothesis is studied. The starting point for much research reflecting this perspective is a problem in the real world and is designed to provide information needed by social planners. (Such studies are termed *applied research*.) Other studies (*basic research*) are used to test theories about social behavior, but whether or not we have explained our findings with theory, social research is pre-

sumed able to generate objective information that is useful for planning policy.

Some confusion has arisen concerning the appropriate label for this dominant perspective in contemporary social research. American critics are likely to term it the "quantitative" approach and to view alternative perspectives as "qualitative" (see Filstead, 1970; or Schwartz & Jacobs, 1979), but this seems unfortunate since more issues are involved than simply dependence on precise measurement and inferential statistics. European critics seem to have settled on the "positivism" label (see Benton, 1977; Fletcher, 1974; Hughes, 1980; or Lessnoff, 1974), but those familiar with the history of philosophy may object to this use and point out that the assumptions characterizing the approach reflect classical, 19th-century physical science rather than those advanced by 20th-century logical positivists such as Mach, Schlick, Carnap, Nagel, or Bridgman (see Phillips, 1983). Our own preference is to call it the *confirmatory perspective*.

By far the bulk of current social research is confirmatory in orientation. Standards for conducting studies in this tradition are well established, and many journals now prescribe a standard format for confirmatory articles that stresses rules for presenting methods and findings but provides little guidance for stating theory or making generalizations. In the eyes of many, confirmatory research provides irreplaceable information needed for planning policy, and funding agencies usually have the confirmatory vision in mind when they award grants for research. Applied research, in particular, is funded because of its presumed relevance for policy decisions, and large portions of agency budgets are now being committed to applied studies. To illustrate, federal laws that established social programs under the Carter administration were likely to mandate evaluation of those programs by social research. Not to be outdone, the Reagan administration at one time proposed to abolish basic research centers that had been funded by the National Institute of Education in order to increase support for applied research on presumably "useful" topics (NIE Research, 1982). Plans such as these are focused on specific questions to be answered, call for unimpeachable research designs and evidence, presume simple relationships among terms, concepts, and methods, are largely atheoretical in focus, and presume direct application of research findings to policy planning. In fairness, many researchers who were trained in the confirmatory tradition would reject one or more of these emphases, and yet such emphases appear to characterize most activities of social research or those who support it.

Cross-Sectional Surveys

Two methods have dominated the confirmatory perspective in social research. The first is the *cross-sectional survey* in which data are gathered, on one occasion, often from a sample of persons taken to represent some universe of human beings in whom we are interested. How do we establish the opinions of teachers concerning a proposed curriculum change? We ask a representative sample of teachers to report their opinions to us. Information of this sort is regularly collected in Western democracies and is used as a base for planning and interpreting the effects of public policy. Cross-sectional surveys are thought to be "practical," then, and much of what we think we know about social problems is based on their evidence. Surveys enable us to answer the questions "How many?" and "How much"? Such answers are important for many reasons, but they do not tell us all that we want to know. Because surveys are limited to natural variations, they provide only weak evidence concerning causation.

There are several forms of cross-sectional surveys, of which two are intended to assess the thoughts of respondents. *Structured interviews* are surveys in which the researcher makes personal contact with respondents and asks a series of preplanned questions. Interviewing has a number of advantages: response rates tend to be high, respondent confusion can be detected and questions can be reworded so as to elicit meaningful answers, the interview can take on issues that would normally cause embarrassment or evasion among respondents, and respondents can be induced to answer large numbers of questions. Interviewing is expensive, however, and interviews are only rarely conducted with large or random samples of respondents. Many studies use interviews with small samples of respondents, and often with samples that are constructed to quota designs so as to provide specific information. Interviews have been conducted for years with teachers and others who are involved with education, and a lot of early information about teaching was generated through their use. A good recent example of the use of interviews with teachers may be found in Lortie (1975).

Given the expensiveness of interviewing, most cross-sectional surveys for assessing thought make use of *questionnaires* which are instruments for respondents to fill out themselves. Some questionnaires are administered to groups of respondents in a convenient setting. Others are mailed to potential respondents, although the latter method characteristically results in a loss of respondents from the sample. Questionnaires present a predetermined set of stimuli to the respondent which, unlike interview questions, cannot be varied in the light of responses. Psychological tests are a refined form of questionnaire in which the possible dimensions of response are even more rigidly predetermined. Questionnaires demand literacy on the part of respondents, which means that they cannot be used with very young children or respondents who are not fluent in the language in which the questionnaire is written. Their use is widespread in Western nations, however, and questionnaires are probably the cheapest way of acquiring data concerning the beliefs, attitudes, or concerns of a sample of persons — provided the issue is restricted to topics those persons have thought over and are willing to respond about. Questionnaires have also been used to collect information about teaching for years, and examples of their use for this purpose may be found in Adams et al. (1970) or Anderson, Saltet, and Vervoorn (1980).

A third form of cross-sectional survey makes use of *existing data sources*. Such sources range from newspaper accounts to governmental statistics, corporate records, archives of polling organizations, and even private documents such as diaries and files of correspondence. A good deal of social research is based on such sources, particularly in history, economics, and macrosociology. In most cases the use of existing data is justified because of their uniqueness or the fact that they are inexpensive. The social researcher who uses existing data is like the geologist or astronomer in having no control over the conditions under which those data were collected, and this provides problems of interpretation. To illustrate, more than three decades of scores are now available from the Scholastic Aptitude Test, which is administered annually to high school seniors in the United States. These scores have fallen markedly during the past decade, and this fact is sometimes interpreted as indicating a "decline in teaching standards" (Munday, 1978). Of course, many other events were also taking place in the United States during the years covered by these data, and some of the latter may also have had an effect on the achievement of high school students, so any simple interpretation of the results is suspect.

Interviews, questionnaires, and existing data sources all have substantial disadvantages when used for studying teaching. The basic reason for this is that teaching involves activities for which these three techniques provide but indirect — and often distorted — measures. Consequently, most research on teaching now makes use of a fourth method for conducting surveys, the *structured observation* of classroom processes. This last method involves collection of records from observable events that are gathered by the researcher in person or through the use of mechanical or electronic recordings. These records are then subjected to formal analysis in which types of activity are conceptualized and patterns of their appearance are counted and studied for covariance.

Sometimes researchers who have observed teaching are content to report findings generated by observational data alone. More often these data are compared with other information that is collected by use of interviews, questionnaires, or existing data sources, so that the conditions that presumably give rise to, or flow from, classroom activities are studied. Mitzel (1960) and Dunkin and Biddle (1974) note that studies of teaching normally seek to establish covariation between observed classroom processes and variables from one of three event classes: *presage variables* (which concern preexisting teacher characteristics), *context variables* (preexisting characteristics of pupils, schools, or the community), and *product variables* (evidence of pupil learning and growth). The fact that research on teaching has sought relationships between classroom process information and these three event classes tells us a good deal about the practical interests of those who conduct and finance this research. In particular, it is often assumed that significant correlations between classroom processes and pupil products suggest strategies that the teacher might use to "improve" pupil learning or attitudes. And for this reason, so-called *process–product* designs for research on teaching have been popular in the last decade.

Several examples of cross-sectional research on teaching are in order. An early and popular technique for studying teaching was pioneered by Flanders (1960, 1970). This technique made use of a single, 10-category scale for judging classroom events. Seven categories of this scale were set aside for teacher behavior, whereas three categories were used for coding pupil conduct. The investigators assumed that these categories were mutually exclusive, and data were collected by seating an observer in the back of the classroom who was to record into which category classroom events fell every three seconds. The data thus generated provided a "profile" of the lesson observed, and researchers were interested in studying covariation between these profiles and presage, context, or product information. In particular, many researchers sought to confirm the hypothesis that teachers who exhibited more "indirect" behavior (i.e., behavior that was more accepting, praising, encouraging, and questioning) would produce more pupil achievement and better pupil attitudes than teachers who were more "directive."

The Flanders technique had several advantages, and more than 100 studies were eventually published that made use of it. The technique was simple to master, and data generated with it were inexpensive, so studies within the Flanders tradition could be replicated easily and did not require grant funding. The technique was also advocated (and used) for teacher training and sensitizing. Above all, the concept of "indirect" teaching seemed a reasonable way to measure the degree to which teachers followed the tenets of progressive education, which many educators were convinced was A Better Way to Teach.

Unfortunately, the Flanders technique also suffered from several difficulties. For one, it was hard to understand why the categories of the observational instrument were mutually exclusive, and observers had difficulty making reliable observations with it. For another, observers were called upon to make judgments every three seconds rather than to respond to naturally occurring classroom events or to code leisurely from classroom recordings. In addition, the categories used for observing did not provide the information one needs to understand the import of classroom events. (To illustrate, the category system provided a code for "teacher praise," but no information was given concerning the correctness of pupil responses, so the researcher could not learn whether teachers gave praise appropriately or inappropriately.) Much of the research involved small, nonrandom samples of teachers, and it was difficult to understand why results from any given study would be expected to generalize. Finally, some researchers were so committed to confirming hypotheses about the advantages of "indirect" teaching that they failed to examine other effects generated in their study. (Indeed, according to Brophy, 1979, p. 737, "recent research from the primary grades seems to flatly contradict" the supposed advantages of "indirect teaching".) These difficulties are now widely understood, and the use of the Flanders technique has declined during the past decade.

If "indirect" teaching does not lead to hoped-for effects, then what styles of teaching are effective? Our second example illustrates a sizeable group of process–product surveys that have addressed this question. As part of Project Follow Through, Soar and Soar (1972) investigated the effectiveness of classrooms that were believed to provide a "Head Start" for minority pupils in kindergarten and first-grade classrooms. Seventy classrooms were evaluated in all, and two types of information were gathered for each classroom: observational data and pupil-achievement records. The former were generated by in-class observers who recorded a wide range of classroom activities. These data were sorted into numerous factors concerned with teacher behavior, classroom climate, and curricular emphases. Records of pupil achievement were obtained at both the beginning and ending of the year during which classrooms were observed, and the investigator used "gain scores" to indicate how much pupils had learned during the year. Two factors emerged from the gain-score data: one concerned with simple-concrete

subject matter growth, the other representing complex-abstract growth. Statistics were then calculated to see how the various factors representing classroom activities covaried with the two measures of pupil growth, and various findings appeared. Among them, simple-concrete pupil growth was found linked to "directive" teaching in a straightforward manner—the more of the latter, the more of the former. In contrast, complex-abstract pupil growth reached its maximum with a moderate amount of "directiveness" but fell off dramatically when "directiveness" was further increased.

The Soars' study illustrates several features that strong process–product surveys have in common. For one, the study involved a large sample of teachers and pupils (although the sample was not drawn from a population by random means). For another, a complex coding system was used for recording classroom activities. This generated a good deal of information so that researchers were able to examine the details of teacher-pupil interaction and to distinguish weak effects from those that were stronger. (Taken together, these features also mean that studies of this scope cannot be undertaken without substantial funding. Such funding usually comes from governmental grants to which strings are attached—a topic to which we return subsequently.) For a third, as tends to be true for most studies in the confirmatory mold, the research and its write-up were largely focused on findings; exhibited concern for research design and the strength of evidence; made extensive use of inferential statistics; presumed simple relationships among terms, concepts, and methods of measurement; offered few explanatory theories; and assumed or implied direct relationships between findings and policy impact. Finally, the major findings cited were simple relationships between classroom events and pupil achievement that applied to the sample as a whole and might, presumably, provide a basis for improving instruction in other classrooms.

Our third example represents a research tradition that began with publication of *Pygmalion in the Classroom* by Rosenthal and Jacobson (1968). Evidence offered in this seminal study suggested that when some teachers expect high levels of achievement from individual pupils, those pupils will achieve at higher levels. If this be so, then it should also be true that those teachers will treat pupils somewhat differently depending on the expectations they hold for those pupils. How, then, are teacher expectations related to teacher treatment of pupils?

A number of studies have now addressed this question, of which a good example is provided by Brophy and Evertson (1981). The latter researchers studied 27 teachers in several primary schools as they interacted with pupils. Teachers were asked to rank pupils on 13 different attributes including "calmness," "probable achievement," "maturity," "creativity," and the like. Teacher interactions with specific pupils were then observed for 10 half days for each teacher. The coding system used called for various kinds of judgment to be made for several types of interactive episodes. In all, data for 73 dimensions of teacher behavior were reported by the authors, and literally hundreds of findings were generated when these were compared with information provided by the teachers' ratings of pupils. To illustrate, the authors report that teachers tended to respond to pupils whom they "rejected" by keeping them under close surveillance, frequently reminding them of responsibilities, refusing their personal requests, treating them with impatience, and holding them up as bad examples to other pupils.

Unlike the Soars' research, the Brophy-Evertson survey was not concerned with process-product questions. It also raised explicit questions about relationships among its terms, concepts, and methods of measurement and suggested theoretical explanations for some of its findings. Apart from these differences, however, it exhibited many of the same features we have noted in the Soars' research: a large sample of teachers and pupils, a complex coding system for observing classroom activities, a focus on findings, concern for research design and strength of evidence, and the use of inferential statistics. Finally, the major findings cited were, again, relationships that might, presumably, be found in other educational contexts.

Strong cross-sectional surveys, such as those of the Soars and Brophy and Evertson, have the obvious advantage of allowing us to explore the distributions and covariations among events that occur within the samples and contexts studied. However, cross-sectional data are sometimes interpreted as if they also provided evidence for causal relationships; thus, the fact that a given pattern of teacher behavior is found associated with pupil conduct or achievements may be interpreted as if the former "caused" the latter. Such interpretations extend beyond the evidence. Cross-sectional surveys provide evidence for covariation but little information about causation, and it is quite possible that pupil characteristics will have "caused" teacher behavior, that teacher behavior and pupil characteristics interact, or that their apparent covariation is "caused" by some third factor, which was not observed in the survey.

Manipulative Experiments

A second research model favored by confirmationists is designed to provide stronger evidence for causation. *Manipulative experiments* are studies in which the investigator controls irrelevant sources of variation, manipulates an independent variable, and then observes effects in a dependent variable. In the classic, four-celled, experimental design, two groups of subjects are used. One, the *experimental group*, is manipulated, whereas the other, the *control group*, is left alone. Subjects are assigned randomly to the two groups. The dependent variable is measured twice for both groups: once at the beginning of the study, and again after the independent variable has been manipulated for the experimental group. If carefully structured, the classic experiment provides strong evidence for the causal impact of the independent variable for the subjects and context studied. Classic experiments are hard to conduct, however, and many experimental studies use weaker designs which provide less adequate evidence for judging causation (see Cook & Campbell, 1979). Manipulative experiments have greater face validity when they are performed in field conditions and use subjects that are drawn from the population of persons for whom the investigator wants to draw conclusions. Field experiments are expensive and may be impossible to conduct, however, and many experiments are presently conducted in the laboratory with university undergraduates as subjects. Needless to say, the generalizability of conclusions from such studies is often questioned. Nevertheless, laboratory experiments are convenient and are popular among social psychologists, although some widely quoted findings from that field seem never to have been confirmed outside of the laboratory context.

Manipulative experiments may be used to test hypotheses drawn from theory, and later on we discuss their use for this purpose. However, this is not their usual employment within research on teaching. Instead, investigators concerned with teaching often express dissatisfaction with the findings of surveys and use manipulative experiments to "validate" those findings. To illustrate, let us examine a study concerned with process-product relationships that was reported by Gall et al. (1978). Two experiments were conducted by the investigators, both designed to assess the impact of teaching strategies that had been found associated with pupil achievements in prior survey research. The first experiment compared the presence or absence of three teaching strategies: recitation by pupils, probing by the teacher, and redirection of teacher questions to additional pupils. The second examined the presence or absence of pupil recitation with three levels of cognitive complexity of teacher questions asked. Special, scripted lessons were prepared for sixth-grade pupils on the topic of ecology, and 12 substitute teachers were recruited who learned the scripts for each of the treatment conditions. Several hundred pupils were recruited for the study in California schools, and pupils were assigned to treatment conditions randomly. Detailed observations were conducted in the experimental classrooms to make certain that teachers made use of the teaching strategies called for in their scripts. Various types of pupil achievement were assessed, including information recall, ability to respond to higher cognitive questions, and attitudes towards the curriculum topic. Both experiments found that recitation improved pupil learning, especially information recall and higher cognitive responding. The first experiment found no effects for probing or redirection of teacher questions. The second found that low and high levels of cognitive complexity were more effective than moderate levels.

Manipulative experiments such as those of Gall et al. (1978) have a strong factorial design that separates two or more aspects of teacher behavior to examine the effects of each. They have two obvious disadvantages. For one, the methods used are somewhat artificial, and it is not clear that the recommended strategies for teaching could be implemented in actual classrooms. For the other, the effects generated are often quite weak. These disadvantages may be overcome if another experimental strategy is adopted. We illustrate the latter with an experiment reported by Good, Grouws, and Ebmeier (1983) which built on an earlier process-product survey that the authors had conducted with primary-level mathematics classes. The design of their earlier survey had enabled the researchers to isolate a set of teacher behaviors that were consistently associated with higher levels of mathematics achievement by pupils. These behaviors included daily review, proactive structuring of the lesson, the use of strategies encouraging pacing and accountability in seatwork, regular use of homework that included some review problems, and the use of special review sessions in class. Evidence favoring these and related teaching strategies was strong from the survey, but did this mean that pupil achievement would improve if a random sample of teachers was encouraged to use more of these strategies in conducting lessons?

To answer this latter question, Good et al. (1983) conducted experimental research in a major school district. Early in the academic year a large random sample of teachers was selected and each member given a package of instructional materials that described and encouraged the desired teaching strategies. A second, control group of teachers did not receive the instructional package until after the middle of the academic year. Teachers in both groups were observed to see whether the instructional program was adopted. Results showed that pupils in experimental classrooms were 5 months ahead of pupils in control classrooms by midyear, on average. Control pupils tended to "catch up" once their teachers were also exposed to the instructional package, but pupils from experimental classrooms were still significantly ahead at the end of the year. In short, the experiment had face validity and produced substantial effects. Those effects were produced by an instructional "package," however, and it is not clear from the design how each aspect of the package contributed to pupil gain.

As is true for strong surveys concerned with teaching, the manipulative experiments reported by Gall et al. (1978) and Good et al. (1983) are expensive and almost always require funding from external sources. Since they are conducted in field settings they appear to have implications for policy and practice, unless one believes that classrooms in one city are substantially different from classrooms in other cities, should not one by now be convinced that adoption of the Good et al. instructional package will also improve junior high mathematics elsewhere? (We consider this question further on.) Apart from these features, the experiments also exhibited most of the other characteristics we associate with confirmatory research: a focus on findings; concern for research design and evidence; the use of inferential statistics to validate knowledge claims; and assumptions of simple relationships among terms, concepts, and methods. (In fairness, the authors also gave stress to possible theories that might explain their results, and although the major findings cited were relationships that applied to the samples as a whole, they also discussed variations in the impact of the program on different teachers and pupils.)

In one respect, however, process–product surveys are strikingly unlike the manipulative experiments that are assumed to validate their findings. Whereas the former presume that classroom events (particularly teacher conduct) are the independent variables of teaching, the latter do not manipulate classroom events directly. Instead, experimental classrooms are exposed to various curricula or programs of teacher training, which means that presage variables are manipulated. Innumerable experimental studies appeared in earlier decades in which presage variables were manipulated and pupil learning was assessed without bothering to check whether those variables had the desired effects on classroom conduct. Recent experiments, such as those of Gall et al. (1978) and Good et al. (1983), have made this check, which increases their validity. But it is by no means certain that the effects observed in experimental classrooms are the only ones that resulted from presage manipulations. In a real sense, it is quite impossible to conduct a true, manipulative, process–product experiment. We suspect that "presage-process–product" experiments will continue to be popular, however, since they suggest things that might be done by educators to improve their products.

Reviews and Meta-Analysis

Such is the extent of social science research in the confirmatory tradition that it is difficult for consumers to keep up with the pace of publication even for a specified topic. To illustrate, Dunkin and Biddle (1974) reported reviewing approximately 500 studies concerned with research on teaching when they prepared their text. Studies that have been published since may amount to 10 times that number. How does the interested reader keep up with such voluminous research efforts?

The traditional way of solving this problem is to read reviews of the field that are published by interested scholars. Examples of such reviews for research on teaching are provided by Brophy (1979) and Good (1979). Reviews such as these provide many advantages for the reader: a convenient source of references, a conceptual orientation to the field, a discussion of methodological strengths and weaknesses found in published studies, a summary of major findings and conundrums in the data, suggestions for building explanatory theory, and an invitation to explore primary sources for additional information. Such reviews do not replace the need to read primary materials, of course. They may, however, help the neophyte to orient himor herself to the field and warn readers of weaknesses in the research conducted to date.

Recently a second technique for reviewing research has appeared called *meta-analysis* (see H. Walberg, this volume, for further discussion). This technique uses inductive statistics to assess the collective import of findings from "all" studies that have apparently investigated the same question, and a good exposition of it may be found in Glass, McGaw, and Smith (1981). Although meta-analyses can be conducted for more sophisticated reasons (such as to search for contextual effects), the primary motivation for most such studies seems to be to review evidence for making simple knowledge claims. To illustrate, Glass, Cahen, Smith, and Filby (1982) examined literally hundreds of studies concerned with the relationship of school class size and pupil achievement to see how these two variables covaried "on average." (They conclude that pupil achievement declines as class size increases.)

Meta-analysis suffers from many difficulties, of which the following are a sample. For one, most such analyses presume the confirmatory assumption of simple relationships among terms, concepts, and methods used in research. This assumption may be reasonable when one is dealing with concrete variables such as "class size." It is certainly questionable when one is dealing with an abstract variable—such as "progressive education," "teacher warmth," or "pupil self-concept"—that is called several different things by various researchers and is measured by differing techniques, conditions that are endemic in social science today. Meta-analyses generate different results depending on which studies go into the mix, and samples for such analyses will differ depending on whether they constitute studies that share the same concept and the same operation, or just happen to use a common vocabulary. Many meta-analyses take no stance on this issue and end up reviewing an ad hoc collection of studies.

Second, meta-analyses use inductive statistics for assessing knowledge claims. Such statistics assume that one is dealing with a sample from a known universe; but studies that happen

to have been published so far on a given subject do not constitute a representative sample of a common population. In fact,
any collective implication of their findings is bound to reflect
the methods, subjects, and contexts chosen for those studies,
and these are usually ignored in the meta-analytic search for
simple, universal results. To illustrate, most early research on
teaching was conducted within self-contained, white, middle-
class, American classrooms where teaching and curriculum reflected the culture of the times. Meta-analyses from such a limited universe have questionable validity if we are interested in
open classrooms, minority pupils, a working-class environment, or classrooms in France or Australia.

Third, meta-analyses normally assess "all" studies that have
appeared for a given topic, regardless of features that might
have made the evidence from those studies stronger or weaker.
Some studies involve design flaws that make their supposed
findings questionable. Others report simple correlations as a
measure of covariation between variables whereas comparable
studies report partial correlations for the same relationship in
which confounding variables have been controlled. Results
from the latter provide stronger evidence than the former, but
the two kinds of results may be blurred in meta-analysis. If
"weak" studies are numerous or involve larger samples, their
questionable results may overwhelm the more valid findings of
"strong" studies.

Fourth, most meta-analyses are conducted with collections
of published studies, but studies that are accepted for publication represent only a portion of reasearch that is conducted on
a given topic. Among other things, studies are generally easier
to publish when they use familiar methods, report findings that
achieve statistical significance, and confirm prevailing ideologies (see Glass et al., 1981, pp. 226ff.). This means that meta-
analytic conclusions are likely to reflect bias that is generated
by editorial decisions (and decisions by authors to avoid submitting certain types of results for publication).

Fifth, where meta-analyses amalgamate the data from
hundreds if not thousands of subjects, it is nearly impossible to
avoid "statistically significant" effects. Since the probability of
attaining statistical significance increases with the size of samples (until, in the limit of the universe, everything is associated
with everything else) truly small effects may attain "statistical
significance" in meta-analyses. And since the motivation for
most meta-analyses seems to be to find simple, universal effects,
the analyst is tempted to claim such effects even when they are
weak. Such claims are questionable even for isolated studies. As
Popper (1959, 1972) reminds us repeatedly, research evidence
can overturn a hypothesis unambiguously, but it can never confirm that hypothesis for all occasions in the hereafter. The
thoughtful reviewer examines previous research for clues as to
why findings might differ among studies. Only rarely would we
expect to find an effect for teaching that was both strong and
widely applicable.

Finally, meta-analyses often fail to provide those additional
features that make traditional reviews valuable: conceptual analyses, discussions of methodological strengths and weaknesses
in published studies, theoretical insights, and speculations
about deviant cases and their possible meaning. Instead, the
reader's attention is focused on one or more simple knowledge
claims and the "evidence" that apparently supports them.

These difficulties mean that many meta-analytic studies are
questionable, and the supposed findings of some have already
been contradicted by well-constructed subsequent research.
Given these difficulties, why do meta-analysis? One cannot
avoid expressing sympathy for the intentions and admiration
for the statistical competencies of those who practice this art,
but enthusiasm for meta-analysis appears to reflect many of the
questionable assumptions of confirmatory research generally.
Meta-analysis appears attractive if one is focused narrowly on
findings and strength of evidence, if one is used to working with
inferential statistics and not concerned with whether samples
are representative, if one assumes simple relationships among
terms, concepts, and methods, if one is uninterested in deviant
cases, if one is not particularly worried about theory, and—
above all—if one wants to make simple knowledge claims from
research. Once one begins to question these assumptions,
meta-analysis becomes less appealing.

Commentary

How reasonable *are* the assumptions of confirmatory research?
The basic methods of the approach—cross-sectional surveys
and manipulative experiments—have strengths that tend to
supplement one another. The former generate evidence concerning the distribution of events in a population, the latter
provide information about causation. Each suffers from weaknesses, however. It is difficult to conduct questionnaire- or in-
terview-based studies on topics that respondents do not think
about or are unwilling to discuss, and collection of some forms
of observational data is illegal, immoral, or simply too expensive. Many experiments are also impossible for similar reasons,
and manipulative experiments always run the risk of generating
conditions that are not represented in the real world.

In addition, some of the basic assumptions of confirmationism have been questioned openly. Among others, some critics
have objected to the fact that confirmatory research requires
the investigator to reduce his or her concerns to precategorized
scales. To do this, such critics say, means that we may never
discover the real concerns of those whom we are studying.
Other critics are bothered by sloppy relationships among terms,
concepts, and methods in much of confirmatory research and
claims that one can literally generate "any" finding by wording
one's question appropriately or manipulating the coding system. Thus, the findings of social research are viewed as subjective, and independent investigators studying the same
phenomena may not reach the same conclusion. Still others object to the fact that hypotheses are normally only "tested" in
confirmatory research and wonder how those hypotheses were
generated. (Indeed, if we take confirmationism seriously, how is
it possible to discover a new concept or unanticipated relationship?) And still others are concerned with the assumption implicit in confirmatory research that one can generalize from the
evidence of a single study to other, admittedly dissimilar occasions. These latter critics suggest that generalization is more
valid in the physical and biological sciences than in the social
sciences, where we rarely have enough information to know
whether a result from a given survey or experiment will or will
not generalize to another age, social class, racial group, or nationality of subjects, or to another context for behavior.

The Discovery Perspective

The latter concerns have surfaced in a series of theoretical positions that have arisen more or less independently but which share antipathy to the dominant, confirmatory position in social science. This antipathy appears in the work of symbolic interactionists, ethnomethodologists, humanistic psychologists, those advocating hermeneutics and Marxist or dialectical criticism, ethogenics, and (interestingly) a host of critical authors who have written from within the mainstream of confirmationism. For convenience, we group these rather diverse viewpoints under a single heading, the *discovery perspective*, and note that they have in common the belief that social concepts and explanations are socially constructed by both citizens and social scientists. Social knowledge and its use are both assumed to be based on values (thus, relationships between social research and policy are complex and mixed inextricably with political commitment), and "social facts" are uninterpretable outside of a theoretical, hence historical, context. Taken to its extreme, such a critical stance decries the usefulness of all social research and claims that each event in the human world is unique and unlikely to be replicated by any other event, ever. Another variant of the position views social research as the handmaiden of established privilege, and researchers as the dupes of those who pay for their efforts. (To illustrate, federal funds are more often available for studying ways to improve traditional classroom education than for exploring radical alternatives to the classroom.)

Implicit in these last arguments is the idea that at least some social science findings are illusory, and conclusions based on them are merely a restatement of the ideological commitments of researchers or their employers. Moreover, evidence can be found to support the thrust of these claims. Anyone familiar with the history of evaluation research knows of incidents in which the "findings" of research have been suppressed or "reinterpreted" to provide political support for the program evaluated. In her review of research on reading, Jeanne Chall (1967) noted that both researchers and reviewers were willing to distort their conclusions so that they matched the prevailing wisdom of the decade. Dunkin and Biddle (1974) issued a similar complaint for research on teaching, observing that some investigators held "commitments" to curricula, tests or ideologies that colored their conclusions. These distortions were not undetectable, of course. Indeed, the fact that complaints are made suggest that it is possible to detect (some kinds) of fraud or distortion within the normal procedures of confirmatory research. But it is clear that drawing conclusions from evidence is a lot more complex than the apparently simple faith of some confirmationists would have us believe. Moreover, social researchers have values, as do their employers and the human subjects they study, and these values color the topics chosen for research, the phrasing of questions, the choice of concepts and language, the ways in which research instruments are constructed, and the interpretations of results.

Ethnographic Methods

Some critics of confirmatory social research have also urged alternative research methods as means for discovering social theory that is grounded in observations of the lives of real human subjects (see Glaser & Strauss, 1967). These methods presumably enable the investigator to ask questions and discover answers that are based on the events studied rather than on the investigator's preconceptions. One model for discovery research makes use of *ethnographic methods* that were originally pioneered by anthropologists in their field studies of preliterate societies, particularly participant observation and exploratory interviewing. Participant observation is a technique in which the investigator enters the social world of those studied, observes, and tries to find out what it is like to be a member of that world. Detailed notes are taken concerning the events witnessed, and eventually these are organized and codified so that the investigator discovers the patterns of events that have appeared in that world. Exploratory interviewing involves the use of informants who can be questioned in detail concerning events and their interpretation. Characteristically, such interviews begin in an unstructured fashion, although later the investigator may also ask structured questions based on his or her growing understanding of events and the informants' construction of reality.

Three advantages are frequently cited for ethnographic methods. They do not require prior conceptualization but instead allow the discovery of truly applicable theory; they enable the investigator to understand events as they are conceived by participants; and they offer opportunity for investigations of controversial topics, in depth, or over a longer period of time than is generally possible with confirmatory methods. All three of these advantages are illustrated in the classic ethnographic study of classroom teaching that was conducted by Smith and Geoffrey (1968). In this research the primary investigator (Louis M. Smith) sat as a participant observer in the back of a junior high classroom in a working-class school in St Louis during an entire semester. During the evening he also held extensive conversations with his coinvestigator, the classroom teacher ("William Geoffrey"—actually a pseudonym), while the two researchers attempted to develop insights concerning classroom events and their meanings. Among other topics, concepts and propositions were suggested concerning the roles performed by teacher and pupils, the establishment and maintenance of classroom control, the formation of cliques, the structuring of classroom activities, decision making by the teacher, classroom pacing and skirmishing, the ebb and flow of the semester, "contracts" in teacher–pupil relationships, strategies for opening and closing lessons, and the disastrous effects of poverty and inadequate support in the school upon classroom functioning and pupil growth. Many of these insights were strikingly original—the investigators drew from their analysis of Geoffrey's thoughts about his classroom when proposing them—and some insights reflected the fact that the investigators were able to study classroom events over the course of some months.

Smith and Geoffrey's research also exemplifies the concept of *case study*, which may be defined as the intensive investigation of a single object of social inquiry such as a classroom (see Stake, 1978). Much of ethnographic research involves case studies, although a few investigations involve the comparison of two or more cases (for an example, see Carew & Lightfoot, 1979). The major advantage of the case study is that by immersing oneself in the dynamics of a single social entity one is able to uncover events or processes that one might miss with more superficial methods. For example, the researcher who uses standardized techniques for surveying classroom interaction may miss the effect of a couple of troublemakers on morale in a given classroom, but this type of effect may, indeed, be noticed by the ethnographer who spends some days in that environment. This does not mean that formal measurement must always be excluded from case studies. Test results may sometimes be used to gain understanding of pupils, or frequencies of teacher or pupil behaviors may be counted to nail down interpretations. But the case study strategy enables the investigator to adopt methods to the task of discovery rather than to impose methods that may prevent the latter.

Two problems are frequently cited for case studies. For one, the case study represents but an *N* of one, and we rarely know whether or not its findings will generalize. Limited generalizability is the price paid for the intensity of the case study method. In theory it would be possible to make case studies of representative samples, but the cost of doing so would be prohibitive. The well-written case study report rarely claims that what has been found applies to other objectives of investigation; nevertheless case studies provide an open invitation to generalize. If generalization takes the form of hypotheses to be tested by further inquiry then no damage is done. If, however, the findings from the case study are claimed to represent the state of affairs in other places or times then indeed much mischief can be created. (To illustrate, in a case study, Rist, 1973 described a teacher who was racially prejudiced in her treatment of pupils in one urban classroom. Some reviewers have assumed that this finding confirmed the existence of a general tendency for racial prejudice among primary teachers!)

For another, case studies are not objective in the sense that two investigators would necessarily generate the same insights if they studied the same case. The reason for this is that investigators inevitably come to the case study with a unique background that includes related experiences, ideological commitments, and interests in certain issues and concepts. This means that it is impossible to begin a case study without making assumptions (assertions by Glaser & Strauss, 1967, to the contrary notwithstanding). To illustrate, in planning his case studies Fensham (in press) decided to examine school characteristics, alienation, and unemployment among youth and not other phenomena. Such decisions focus attention on certain questions and lead one to ignore others. Furthermore, as the study proceeds the researcher is faced with additional choices —whether to spend more time on this topic or that, whether to talk to parents when it becomes apparent that the home is influencing what pupils do in school, whether to persist in the face of an antagonistic response, how to evaluate the effect of the researcher's presence on the phenomena being observed, how to decide when the study should end. The sensitive case researcher meets this problem by being aware of the assumptions that govern his or her decisions and by making these explicit in the report written about the study.

In the hands of competent investigators, ethnographic methods offer means for *generating theory*. By the same token, these techniques are poor ones for *testing theory*, since the data obtained by the researcher were not gathered systematically and do not represent any population of events to which the researcher may wish to generalize. Reports of ethnographic studies are normally judged to make a contribution when they generate new insights—that is, propose new concepts or suggest innovative explanations for events—and marshal evidence for those insights in the form of supportive narrative. But it is difficult to judge whether or not an ethnographic study has generated new insights, since this requires the reviewer or editor to be familiar with the bulk of related research. Consequently, published ethnographies vary greatly in quality, some people are confused between the concepts of ethnographic study and personal anecdote, and it is actually harder to detect fraud or exaggeration in ethnographic reports than in reports of confirmatory research.

To illustrate, let us distinguish between the *case study* and the *case story*. The former is an inquiry conducted according to rules of evidence. It is rigorous in its observations. Its objective is not to confirm the investigator's commitments but to investigate a problem. The latter is designed to illustrate conclusions to which the author is already committed. For example, an author might believe that teachers influence pupils through inadvertent labeling. Believing in this proposition, the author then sets out to illustrate this theme—to make a study of a classroom in order to support the labeling thesis. Instances that strengthen the conclusion are reported, and contrary instances are ignored. A skillful case story is like a good novel and provides the reader with new insights and understandings. It does not provide conclusions, however, that reflect evidence. Unfortunately, the distinction between case studies and case stories is not understood by all, and readers may have difficulty distinguishing between these two forms of endeavor in current publications. These problems are not unknown, or course, and recent authors have begun to propose formal procedures for conducting and reporting ethnographic research (see Filstead, 1970; LeCompte & Goetz, 1982; Schwartz & Jacobs, 1979; Spradley, 1979, 1980; Wilson, 1977).

Ethnographic research can be a powerful tool in the hands of a skilled investigator such as Erving Goffman, Anselm Strauss, or Louis Smith. On the other hand, it is truly difficult to do well. Many young social scientists are attracted to ethnographic methods, because they like the idea of discovering "grounded theory," because they dislike the assumptions of confirmationism, or because they despair of learning the statistical skills that confirmatory research requires. But few have the combination of theoretical sophistication, insightfulness, and writing skill necessary to complete an insightful ethnographic study. Confirmatory research is easier to conduct if one is a journeyman.

Semantic Analysis

Another method advocated by those critical of confirmationism is the semantic analysis of discourse records. Ethnomethodologists, in particular, have been active in urging the careful study of speech records as a means for uncovering the norms and customs that govern interaction and the processes through which participants evolve a shared definition of the situation. Given that classroom teaching normally takes place in a confined room, it is possible to make audio- or videotape recordings of classroom events, and these may be transcribed for formal, semantic analysis (see Cazden, John, & Hymes, 1972; or Cicourel et al., 1974).

A recent example of this method appears in the work of Hugh Mehan (1979). Mehan's study involved observation of a multigrade classroom that was part of an inner-city primary school in San Diego. In collecting data, the investigators videotaped the first hour of school activities every day for the first week of school and 1 hour per day every third week thereafter through most of the school year. Primary attention was given to teacher–pupil interaction. Building on the work of Bellack et al. (1966), Mehan views the fundamental unit of classroom discourse between teachers and pupils as a tripartite event that begins with an "initiation," continues with a "reply," and is often terminated with an "evaluation." A number of differing forms of such events were identified by Mehan, and the author used these to discuss such issues as the structuring of lessons, turn allocation, sanctioning procedures, and the ways in which linguistic and substantive competence are signaled by classroom speakers.

Well-conducted semantic studies are similar to ethnographies in their concentration on but one or a few examples of the social form of interest—in Mehan's case a single classroom. They differ in that detailed recordings are made of discourse events, and these are subjected to intensive analysis. Sometimes, as in Mehan's work, the analysis is reported informally, and extensive quotes are reported from discourse records to illustrate the insights being discussed. In other cases, such as in Bellack et al. (1966), statistical analyses of discourse-unit frequencies and sequences may be reported. In either case, semantic analysis differs from standard, ethnographic procedure in being more anchored in quantifiable data. It is more limited in scope, however, since ethnographic methods may focus on both linguistic and nonlinguistic events. Semantic analysis is a relatively new method that is as yet practiced by only a handful of researchers, and standards for publishing its work are even less fixed than for ethnographies.

Other Discovery Methods

Several other research methods are also advocated by those critical of confirmationism. One such method is *action research*, a concept that was originally proposed by Kurt Lewin as a method for harnessing the expert knowledge and desires of social scientists to contribute to social betterment. As it has evolved, action research features participation by social scientists in the processes of planning, evaluating, and adjusting social policy. Such participation is frequently found in countries whose institutions are controlled by the state, such as the Soviet Union. It occurs also in Scandinavia where social scientists are employed through semi-permanent institutions to conduct research and develop recommendations for social policy. It appears less often in countries where social policy is allowed to drift or is planned largely through political means, as in the United States, although examples of it may be found in industrial contexts, social work, and community development. Action research can also be viewed as a logical extension of the Marxist concept of "praxis" as interpreted by Habermas and the Frankfurt School (see Kemis, 1983). It is often advocated by educational theorists, and talented teachers sometimes claim to

have adopted such an orientation in their classroom practices. Moreover, formal observation of classroom events has sometimes been urged as an adjunct to in-service teacher education and action research (see Flanders, 1970). However, few systematic insights and findings seem to have been generated as yet for our understanding of teaching by means of action research.

Another method, *stimulated recall*, is sometimes used to establish the details of thoughts that persons (presumably) have entertained in interactive sequences. In its typical application to research on teaching, videotape recordings are made of a classroom lesson, and teachers are then led to view these and to recall the covert mental activity that accompanied his of her classroom participation. Such "introspective" methods have generated controversy in psychology, and it is by no means clear that teachers' reports will always match the thoughts they actually had in the classroom (see Ericsson & Simon, 1980). Nevertheless, this method has become popular among researchers concerned with studying the ways in which teachers process information and make decisions (see Shavelson & Stern, 1981).

Commentary

Research methods advocated by discovery theorists are assumed to eschew the traps of confirmatory methods. It is by no means clear, however, that they avoid all traps discussed. They share a number of common features, among them interest in the discovery of theoretical insights, the desire to learn the details of human subjects' thoughts and actions, avoidance of quantitative methods and inferential statistics, an interest in deviant cases. They tend, also, to focus on behavior over time. Discovery researchers tend to reject the assumption of unalterable social patterns, and for this reason they are wary of predicting. Social events are always changing, interacting, developing, growing. Even the publication of a finding from social research becomes the agent of its own falsification.

Those who advocate discovery research are often highly critical of confirmationism, but such criticisms may be taken with more than a grain of salt. In fact, it is inappropriate to compare the relative efficacy of these two traditions since each has different purposes; broadly these are the generation of insights on the one hand and the testing of hypotheses on the other. Although advocates for discovery decry the arid tautologies of confirmationists, and the latter express disdain for the sloppy subjectivism of discovery research, the two perspectives have complementary goals. We need them both.

An Integrative Perspective

It is possible to assemble the visions of both confirmationism and the discovery perspective into a single, expanded view of the social sciences, and several methods for social research may be said to reflect this *integrative perspective*. From this viewpoint, the activities of a science are assumed to be an extension and formalization of the ways in which we think and act in everyday life. How do we solve problems in our homes or at work? First, we look at what is going on around us and develop ideas to represent the events we observe. Next, we ponder those

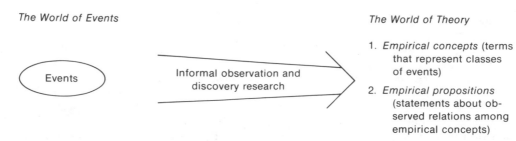

Fig. 8.1. An early stage in the development of a science.

ideas, spin out notions about why events occur, and decide what we will do about them. Finally, we take action and observe to see its effects.

So it is with science. Any form of science is based on a *theory* that is presumed to represent aspects of empirical events that we and others may observe. The theory is initially developed when an investigator looks at examples of events and tries to conceive what he or she has observed to happen—hence the need for discovery research. In its early form the theory consists only of *empirical concepts* and *propositions* that state observed relationships among those concepts. Let us represent this early, though necessary, stage in the development of a science as Figure 8.1.

Time passes, and the science with which we are concerned begins to mature by taking on two questions. First, investigators ask, how broadly applicable are its propositions? To answer this question, observations are made in a number of differing contexts. Moreover, to answer it effectively, investigators find it necessary to *agree on the methods* (or operations) they will use for making judgments about the propositions they are interested in. (In short, they must conduct cross-sectional surveys.)

Second, investigators wonder, why do the empirical propositions hold? To answer this latter question, an explanatory theo-

ry is proposed that accounts for relationships observed. That theory separates phenomena that are presumably observable (*conceptual definitions* for event classes and *empirical findings*) from phenomena that presumably explain them but are not now observed (*elements* and *postulates*). The theory is tied together by the process of *deduction* for which *axioms* (rules of logic) are also stated.

The resulting picture of our science is now more complex, and might well represent the structure of any field of inquiry up until the time of Galileo (see Figure 8.2).

Although complex, the pre-Galilean model for science suffers from defects. For one thing, as Berkeley and others have pointed out, a given set of observables may be explained by more than one set of assumptions, and the pre-Galilean model does not tell us how to sort out which is a better theory. For another, the investigator is confined to the passive task of explaining events that have already been observed. These defects may be resolved through *experimentation*, the invention of which is usually assigned to Galileo and his students. In the Galilean experiment we state an *empirical hypothesis* that is implied by theory but has not yet been tested, and then subject this hypothesis to test by examining new data to which it presumably applies. When the hypothesis is confirmed by our test, we conclude that the theory is still acceptable. When our hypothesis is

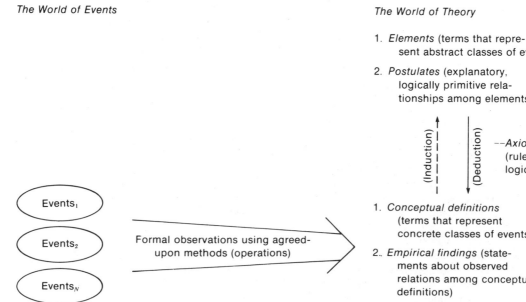

Fig. 8.2. A mature pre-Galilean science.

The World of Events

The World of Theory

1. *Elements*
2. *Postulates*

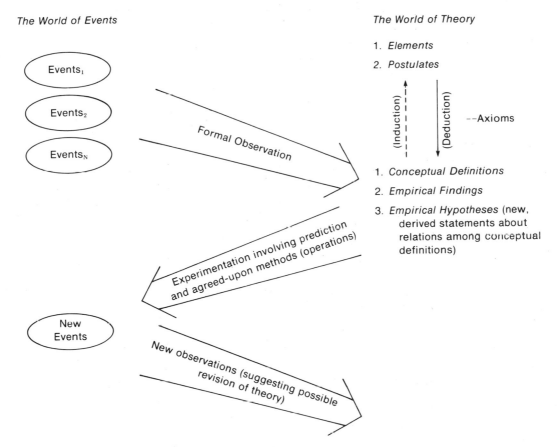

--Axioms

1. *Conceptual Definitions*
2. *Empirical Findings*
3. *Empirical Hypotheses* (new, derived statements about relations among conceptual definitions)

Fig. 8.3. A mature post-Galilean science.

not confirmed, it is time that we rethink the matter and propose a new theory (see Figure 8.3).

(Note that the concepts of manipulative experiment, discussed earlier, and Galilean experiment are not exactly the same. The former involves manipulation of independent variables by the investigator and is designed to assess causation. The latter refers to any form of investigation where the hypothesis is stated before the evidence is examined and is designed to assess theory. Some experiments are both manipulative and Galilean, but manipulative experiments are rare in certain sciences such as astronomy, geology, or economics.)

The picture we have painted gives prominence to the role of theory in scientific endeavor. By *scientific theory* we mean the system of concepts and propositions that is used to represent, think about, and predict observable events. Within a mature science that theory is also explanatory and formalized. It does not represent ultimate "truth," however; indeed, it will be superseded by other theories presently. Instead, it represents the best explanation we have, at present, for those events we have so far observed, and it is tied to those events by means of agreed-upon methods through which its concepts are measured and its propositions confirmed.

Apart from the fact that scientific activities are formalized, perhaps the most important difference between them and everyday decision making appears in the goals that they pursue. The goal of decision making is to solve problems, and when those problems are alleviated, the person turns to other tasks. The

goal of science is to satisfy curiosity, and scientific research is carried on in the hope that it will contribute to our understanding of events. To use that understanding for the solution of problems is a separate act, one of engineering, not science. Engineering is, of course, an utter necessity in our complex, technological society, and good engineering often involves research that is focused on the solving of specific problems. As we shall see below, it also involves political judgement.

Within this general view, the social sciences are presumed to differ from the physical and biological sciences in significant ways. For one thing, evidence is harder to come by in the social sciences, for many of the manipulations available to physical scientists would not be tolerated if applied to people. For another, the social world is far more complex, so much so that few formalized theories have yet emerged, and social scientists still disagree radically over the basic concepts, operations for measuring concepts, and methods appropriate for their fields. Third, much of our concern within the social sciences is with human thought, for which we have only indirect evidence at best. (Although we have direct experience of our own thinking, the thoughts of others can only be estimated by observing stimuli, behaviors, or the introspective reports of those others.)

Fourth, social scientists are part of the human condition, whether or not they are concerned with bettering it, and this affects their activities as scientists in various ways. (It influences their choice of topics for research, the ways in which they conceptualize those topics, their framing of research questions, their choice of operations, the persons whom they choose to study, and the ways in which they interpret their results.) And fifth, social behavior is meaningless out of context and therefore not amenable to study in isolation in the manner of physical or biological events. Traditional methods in the physical sciences assume that an effect obtained in a laboratory in Melbourne should also be obtainable in a laboratory in Tashkent or a production plant in Philadelphia. In contrast, a social effect observed among middle-class, native-born, American pupils in 1970 may or may not be observed among working-class, immigrant, Australian pupils in 1980, and until we know a lot more about the ways in which contexts affect human behavior, generalizations of the sort made in the physical sciences are questionable in the social realm.

These differences imply that the evidential base for the social sciences is weak. This does not mean that social research is "useless." On the contrary, any evidence is better than no evidence, some social research has direct implications for policy without concern for generalization, and social science evidence is just as useful as physical science evidence for challenging hypotheses. But it does mean that social scientists are often tempted to make generalizations that go beyond the scope of their evidence. At their best, such generalizations reflect insight and explicit (though untested) theory. At their worst, they reveal insensitivity to the limitations of context and the specific operations and research methods used to generate findings. As yet the social sciences have not developed adequate standards for monitoring the generalizations of social researchers — witness the noisy debates that have attended recent pronouncements of Arthur Jensen, James Coleman, and Daniel Moynihan. And unfortunately, many readers look only at the generalizations and are unwilling (or unable) to examine the evidence from which they were drawn.

The integrative perspective we outline has implications that are at odds with common practices in both confirmationism and the discovery perspective. When compared with confirmationism, the integrative perspective is less likely to assume that data establish "facts." Instead, data are presumed to suggest theory, and it is the purpose of social research to generate and test the latter. Integrative theorists are also less likely than confirmationists to believe that simple relationships exist among terms, operations, and concepts. Instead, relationships among these realms are accepted as problematic, and the reader must be willing to examine these relationships in order to understand the validity of findings claimed. Theory is also taken as the key to any policy implications of social research; whereas the confirmationist assumes that a finding is likely to generalize, the integrative theorist recognizes that findings are bound by context and methods, and that we must have theoretical understanding to make an effective recommendation for action. And for this reason also, integrative research is more often focused on the search for contextual variation in effects whereas confirmatory research tends to ignore issues of contextualization.

When compared with discovery research, the integrative perspective is more likely to accept the value of quantitative methods and the validity of challenging hypotheses with data. Although selection of topics for research and methods for investigation are certainly subjective decisions, hence likely to reflect the values of sponsors and researchers, the integrative theorist

holds that data generated by research tools "speak for themselves" and are quite capable of generating unexpected results. The integrative research study is also more likely to use complex designs and larger samples, and to test effects with inferential statistics. Moreover, the integrative theorist is likely to seek nomothetic generalizations about human conduct, although he or she will often agree with discovery theorists that the specifics of findings are contextually bound.

Comparative Research

Certain research methods reflect the integrative perspective. One such method is *comparative research* in which studies are designed so that they are conducted with two or more contrasting samples that represent subject variation in age, sex, race, nationality, or other context features that are presumed to matter. Several forms of comparative study can be recognized (Biddle, 1981). Some are largely descriptive and are concerned with displaying rates of occurrence for a given type of social phenomenon across contexts. Some concern the assessment of social relationships against known contextual features. Others test hypotheses that are drawn from explicit theory in two or more contexts with which the investigator is familiar. This last form of comparative research seems particularly valuable for generating insights, because the failure of simple theories to generate universal findings almost "demands" that we rewrite them so as to accommodate contextual variation. Interest in comparative research on teaching has accelerated during the past decade, and (much to the surprise of some investigators) teaching has been found to exhibit quite different forms and effects depending on grade level, subject matter, or such contextual features as the average ability or social class of classroom pupils. Indeed, one reviewer of comparative research findings (Brophy, 1979) suggests that, as of today, "there do not appear to be any universal teaching competencies...that are appropriate to all teaching circumstances" (p. 735).

To see what Brophy is referring to, we review a recent comparative study conducted by Evertson, Anderson, Anderson, and Brophy (1980). In this research the investigators observed teacher behaviors in numerous junior high classrooms. In all, 39 English instructors and 29 teachers of mathematics were observed, and data were also gathered concerning the subject matter learning of pupils as well as pupil attitudes towards their teachers. The authors report substantial differences between the behaviors of "good" teachers (i.e., those who generated both high achievement and positive attitudes among their pupils) depending on subject matter. Good mathematics teachers were active, well organized, and academically oriented. They emphasized a combination of whole-class instruction and seatwork. They were also proactive managers and were rated as more enthusiastic, nurturant, and affectionate than their less successful colleagues. The results for English teachers were more problematic and differed depending on the ability level of pupils in the classroom. Successful teachers of low-ability pupils tended to encourage self-expression, to be tolerant, to be friendly, but also to be strict disciplinarians. Teachers of high-ability pupils were often liked when they were warm, nurturant, enthusiastic, and oriented to pupils' needs, but these behaviors did not seem to be associated with greater pupil learning. (Indeed, the investigators had difficulty predicting the latter.) In short, although a few behaviors were effective in both types of lessons, the primary finding was that a "good" teacher differed sharply depending on the subject matter of the classroom.

Some comparative studies, such as that of Evertson et al. (1980), seem to have one foot in the integrative camp and one foot in confirmationism. On the one hand, their concern is clearly to expose the inpact of context on the effects of teaching. (The authors make clear that their major findings were of differences in what made a "good" teacher in the two contexts studied.) On the other, no hypotheses were stated for the study, and no theoretical interpretations were tendered for findings. As in much of confirmatory research, the focus of the report was on methods used in the study, techniques of data analysis, and on the presentation of findings. Such a study offers obvious advantages over noncomparative process–product surveys in that it suggests the need for caution when generalizing findings that are based on classrooms with but a single subject matter. But the authors appear to have missed an opportunity to suggest theoretical reasons for their findings.

It is too early yet to judge which effects of teaching are likely to apply to a broad range of classrooms and which are likely to vary sharply depending on context. Only a handful of comparative studies have yet appeared for research on teaching, despite repeated claims by educators that teaching skills are very different at the primary and secondary levels and among various subject matter fields. Teaching probably differs also depending on the grading system used in the school, physical equipment in the classroom, and the social class and ethnic background of the community in which the classroom is located, but these latter variables are only now beginning to be investigated (see Brophy & Evertson, 1976; or Good, Ebmeier, & Beckerman, 1978). Moreover, the most exciting contextual variable for comparative research — nationality — seems largely to have been ignored in teaching research to date. (As Bronfenbrenner, 1970, suggests, to study teaching cross-nationally stimulates insights about the assumptions underlying education in the various countries studied, and one of the best sources of insight for improving one's own culture is to view it through the mirror of foreign practices.) Clearly, we need a lot more comparative research in this field.

Aptitude–Treatment Interaction Research

A second method capable of contribution to the integrative perspective is *aptitude-treatment interaction* (ATI) research. This phrase seems to have been coined by Cronbach (1967; also see Cronbach & Snow, 1977) and refers to studies of the ways in which different pupils in the classroom react differentially to the common stimulus of teacher behavior. Comparative research and ATI studies are similar in their shared rejection of the proposition that the effects of teaching styles are likely to be simple and universal. They differ in that the former focus on differences among classrooms while the latter take up pupil differences within the common classroom.

ATI studies have appeared as both surveys and field experiments. To illustrate the former, we turn to the massive survey conducted in British schools by Bennett (1976). As in other Western countries, primary education in Britain has been affected by the ideology of progressive education, and Bennett set out to discover whether teachers could be identified for their adherence to "progressive" or "traditional" tenets and practices, and if so whether these made any difference to the achievements of pupils. The study began with development of a questionnaire that was administered to a large percentage of primary teachers in Northwest England. Responses to these questionnaires were cluster-analyzed, and a total of 37 teachers were chosen to represent three teaching styles: informal, mixed, and formal (the first presumably corresponding to the ideal of progressive education). Although the initial classification of teachers was made from questionnaire responses, assignment of teachers to teaching style categories was later confirmed by observation in those teachers' classrooms. Pupils in those classroom were also asked to fill out several instruments including before-and-after achievement tests in reading, mathematics, and English and a series of personality inventories. The latter were also cluster-analyzed so as to generate a set of personality types for pupils, and this information was then used to see whether differing types of pupils responded differentially to the three teaching styles studied. Bennett reported both universal and ATI effects. Among the former, gains in mathematics and English were greatest in formal classrooms, but gains in reading were (slightly) better in mixed classrooms. Informal classrooms generally did poorly when judged against subject matter gains. Among the latter, achievement differences were greater for pupils judged to be "extroverts," although ATI findings were not as impressive as those for simple effects and were not theorized about by Bennett.

Illustrations of ATI effects in experimental research are reported in a pair of studies by Peterson (1977, 1979). The first of these two studies was conducted with ninth-grade pupils who were taught a 2-week unit of social studies, the second with university undergraduates taught a 5-week educational psychology course. Four treatment conditions appeared in each experiment that varied in amount of structuring by the teacher and participation allowed for pupils or students. Lessons were observed and classroom events analyzed to establish the validity of treatment implementation. Pupils and students completed aptitude measures at the beginning of the studies and achievement and attitude instruments at their end. Three personality characteristics of pupils and students were studied for ATI effects: ability, anxiety, and independence. Substantial ATI effects appeared in both studies, and these revealed both similarities and differences in the ways in which the four treatment conditions affected achievement in the two contexts. To illustrate the former, students in both studies who were high on independence did their best in the treatment condition that combined low structuring with high participation, whereas those low on independence did best in the condition that combined high structuring with low participation. On the other hand, the best treatment condition for college students who were high on anxiety and ability was the condition low on both structuring and participation, whereas this condition was actually worst for ninth-grade pupils who were similarly high on anxiety and ability. Peterson spent some effort discussing the potential theoretical implications of these effects but shied away from propositions that would explain the contextual differences found.

Once again, it is too early to judge which effects of teaching are likely to be universal and which are likely to vary depending on pupil characteristics. Only a handful of ATI studies have yet appeared, and these have provided a mixed bag of results. Indeed, some ATI research is apparently conducted within limiting, confirmatory assumptions, and if Peterson's findings are to be taken seriously, ATI effects are also likely to vary depending on the social contexts of teaching (also see Snow, 1977). Like comparative studies, however, research on ATI has considerable ability to generate insights for theories of teaching. Interestingly, it has somewhat different practical implications. Contextualized differences in the effects of teaching may cause us to prepare somewhat different curricula of teacher training programs for pupils who come from different backgrounds or live in different communities, but ATI effects have few practical implications as long as we continue to teach in heterogeneous classrooms. Indeed, the ultimate practical implication of ATI effects is that we should abandon whole-class teaching in favor of grouped or individualized instruction (Kallós, 1975). (Somehow, this millenial state seems both questionable and unlikely.) Nevertheless, ATI research should be expanded for its theoretical potential.

Longitudinal Research

Although it is quite feasible to conduct experiments within a comparative or ATI design, the fact remains that many context presage variables that affect teaching cannot be manipulated. This does not mean that we are uninterested in the effects of such variables. On the contrary, great interest is expressed in the impact of such factors as parental expectations, community support for schools, and cultural norms on the conduct and effects of teaching. How is it possible to study these latter in a valid manner?

Perhaps the best way to study the effects of nonmanipulable variables is to conduct *longitudinal research* in which persons who are and are not exposed to a given environmental condition are examined for the subsequent effects of that exposure. To illustrate, one may observe teaching in schools that are "affluent" and "impoverished" and follow the impact of observed differences in teaching in these environments on the subsequent careers and lives of pupils. One problem with longitudinal research is, of course, that the treatment condition in which we are interested normally covaries with other environmental conditions that may also affect dependent variables. (The affluence of schools is normally tied to community affluence, and the latter may also affect subsequent pupil conduct.) Several strategies for controlling the effects of unwanted variables in longitudinal studies have now appeared, and these enable one to make a stronger case for the independent impact of environmental conditions in which we are interested (Biddle, Slavings, & Anderson, in press). A second problem concerns the practical difficulties of maintaining interest and support for the research over time and of retaining respondents in the sample for repeated collections of data. Despite these problems, longitudinal research offers an attractive alternative to experimental research for exploring causal relationships associated with teaching.

Longitudinal research that involves observation of teaching is rare to date. In contrast, longitudinal studies of the presumptive effects of teaching are published frequently. To illustrate, Crano and Mellon (1978) examined the impact of teachers' expectations on pupil achievements in a longitudinal design, and Entwisle and Hayduk (1981) studied the effects of parental and pupil expectations on achievements in a panel study. The processes of teaching were not observed in either of these investigations, however, nor were they examined in either of the extensive longitudinal studies conducted by Coleman and his colleagues (Coleman et al., 1966; Coleman, Hoffer, and Kilgore, 1982). The absence of data on teaching in these studies seems tragic. Pupils spend most of their time in school in classrooms, and evidence is now overwhelming that teaching makes a difference (Brophy, 1979; Good, 1979; Good, Biddle, & Brophy, 1975; Rosenshine, 1976, 1979). Longitudinal research that involves the observation of teaching and the comparison of its effects with those of other potent variables in the environments of pupils is clearly needed if we are to understand how teaching works and the prospects and limits of innovation through education. In addition, longitudinal designs enable us to consider research topics that cannot be investigated in cross-sectional research — such as the careers of teachers, the cumulative effects of exposure to several different teaching styles on pupils, or the impact of curricular innovations on teaching in field settings (see Popkewitz, Tabachnick, & Wehlage, 1982).

The dearth of longitudinal research on teaching probably reflects both the backgrounds and usual employments of researchers. Most investigators in the field were trained as educational psychologists and feel more comfortable with experimental design and the analysis of variance than with longitudinal design and regression techniques. In addition, most are also employed in colleges of education and share responsibility with others for the training of teachers. Within such milieus it is easy to believe that problems associated with teaching can be relieved through curricular reform or the revision of teacher training practices. Longitudinal research directs our attention to those less manipulable, less tractable variables that occur in natural settings. Although these latter enter into the lives of students and teachers, and affect the practices and effects of teaching, doing something about them in the real world may involve political reform or a reconstruction of the ways we think about and operate our educational systems. Sociologists feel more comfortable worrying about such possibilities, and longitudinal research on teaching should become more popular as more of the latter appear in the field.

Commentary

Comparative studies, ATI research, and longitudinal designs are alike in that they turn our attention away from simple assumptions concerning teaching and its effects towards an understanding of how complex these phenomena really are. This does not mean that teaching is unresearchable, of course. Teaching consists of a set of observable practices that have causes and effects that can be measured. Complexity is generated because these practices, causes, and effects are multifaceted, contextually bound, and difficult to conceptualize and study effectively. To gain understanding of these phenomena is the central purpose of research on teaching, but it is unreasonable to believe that our understanding will often be expressed as simple, universally applicable propositions. Instead, if teaching is complex, then our theories concerning it must be complex also. Moreover, any attempt to apply the results of research on teaching must surely take into consideration the contingencies those theories suggest.

Given the central role of theory in integrative research on teaching, some changes appear necessary concerning our standards for conducting and publishing research for this field. As we noted earlier, studies published in the confirmationist tradition are likely to give stress to methods and findings of research, but attempts to state theory are rare, and little control is exerted over statements of "policy implications" for results. In addition, many authors seem confused about relationships among their terms, concepts, and operations, and considerable variation in these relationships appears among articles—even those that are published in the same journal! Once it is understood that generation of theory is a major task of research, some of these practices are likely to change. One can envision a time when reviewers and editors will encourage theoretical interpretations for findings, will counsel against irresponsible statements of "policy implication," and will insist on clarification of terms, and the ways in which they are measured. But these changes will also necessitate adjustment of the grounds for supporting research and for evaluating the contributions of researchers. Fund-granting agencies will recognize that significant "improvements" which research may suggest for teaching are likely to reflect theoretical insights, and that funding dollars are better spent when they are used to support research that generates and tests such theory. University faculties will turn their attention away from counting publications towards the evaluation of contributions for their theoretical import.

Nor should we exempt the discovery tradition from criticisms. As noted, standards for publication within this tradition are vague, and serious attempts to state theory are often confused with anecdotes and personal reminiscences. Nor should it be forgotten that discovery research is useful for suggesting theory but provides only weak tests for the theory suggested. Discovery research on teaching should be published to the extent that it generates theoretical insights, and standards should be enforced that make clear the evidential base for the research and restrain authors' attempts to spin grandiose "policy implications" on minimal evidence.

Knowledge from Research on Teaching

Several years ago Graham Nuthall asked: "Is classroom interaction research worth the effort involved?" (Nuthall, 1974). We should not answer this question glibly. Good research on teaching is expensive and politically controversial, and the world might well be better off if those funds were spent composing music, eliminating cancer, or promoting nuclear disarmament. Moreover, the faith of earlier investigators that research on teaching would lead to simple and sovereign ways to improve

education has proven false. On the other hand, who will save our threatened civilization if not its educated citizens? We all have a stake in education, then, and if teaching makes a difference in the lives of pupils, we clearly must learn more about teaching. The task may be a lot more complex than we thought it was, but we do not have viable alternatives to acquisition of the knowledge that research on teaching can provide.

Granted the need, what sorts of knowledge can we expect from this research field? The integrative perspective suggests four rough categories of knowledge. Let us examine each briefly together with examples of knowledge that have already been generated through research.

Insight Generation

One type of knowledge we should expect from research is the generation of insights concerning teaching. Some research on teaching leads to new *concepts*, new ways of thinking about teaching or classifications for the events of instruction we had not thought about before. Striking examples of this type of contribution may be found in the work of Jacob Kounin (1970). In a series of studies concerned with discipline and classroom management, Kounin developed an original and fruitful vocabulary for describing strategies the teacher can pursue in gaining control over the primary classroom. Kounin's vocabulary ("momentum," "withitness," "smoothness," "group altering," "accountability," "overlappingness," "valence," and the like) is only now beginning to enter the lexicon of teachers and teacher educators, but Kounin's research has inspired a decade of investigations, and most of his concepts for classroom management have proven durable.

Other insightful studies suggest *propositions* about teaching that we have not previously thought about. Good examples of such propositions appear in Smith and Geoffrey (1968). Among other topics, these authors discuss the ways a teacher sets and enforces norms for classroom conduct. Propositions are advanced concerning the setting of limits, the use of classroom humor, the conversion of beliefs into norms for classroom conduct, and the "bargains" that are struck between the teacher and individual pupils, which evolve into differentiated classroom roles for the latter.

Conceptual and propositional insights need not have broad applicability, of course. Many of them are generated through discovery research, and their applicability may be limited. But they make us rethink our experiences with teaching and cause us to view the teaching of others with fresh perspectives. Indeed, the most significant of insights may cause us to rethink our basic ideology for teaching and to set agenda for research and teacher education for a generation or more.

Findings and Their Implications

A second type of knowledge concerns the traditional contributions of confirmatory research. Once a research topic has been set and methods have been chosen, surveys and experiments are capable of generating knowledge in the form of findings about teaching. Once again, several types of findings may be recognized. Some findings concern *existential information*—evidence about the frequencies of various forms of teaching or phenomena associated with teaching. To illustrate, a number of surveys have now examined the frequency with which teachers "praise" pupils in the classroom, and these have generally found that praise is used infrequently (Brophy, 1981). Another set of existential findings appears in the final chapter of Bellack, Kliebard, Hyman, and Smith (1966), wherein the authors discuss the "rules for playing the classroom game." The "rules" cited consist of a set of descriptive statements about the typical roles of teacher and pupils as they play out cycles of interaction in classroom exchange. (To illustrate, Bellack et al. report that teachers often "react" to pupil contributions whereas pupils rarely "react" to the teacher.)

Other findings concern *propositional relationships*, and these come in several forms. Probably the most striking of propositional findings appear when the evidence does not support a stated hypothesis. A noteworthy example of this form was also reported by Kounin (1970). Kounin began his research convinced that the key to good classroom management was to be found in the ways teachers handled pupil deviancy. The evidence did not support this proposition, however, and Kounin reported that finding and searched for other keys to unlock the management riddle. As we noted earlier, the reason why negative findings are so striking is that a hypothesis can be overturned unambiguously whereas confirmation of a hypothesis is always tentative and subject to later revision. Propositions that survive attempts at disconfirmation attract attention and status. We have already mentioned several robust propositions coming from recent research, for example that "direct" teaching (or "formal" teaching, to use Bennett's terminology) is more effective than "indirect" teaching for producing low-level subject matter learning, particularly at the primary level (Brophy, 1979; Good, 1979; Rosenshine, 1979). This particular proposition has been stated as a simple, universal effect (although further research will certainly unearth contextual limitations for it).

Knowledge in the form of findings is remarkably seductive to anyone trained in the confirmationist tradition. When looking at a graph, data table, or "statistically significant" effect it is difficult to remember that the findings reported were shaped by the questions, methods, and samples chosen for research. It is also tempting for the confirmationist to assert that findings are immediately applicable to policy decisions; however, such assertions assume that the researcher's questions are the same as the policymaker's and that the research context equates with the sociopolitical context of practice. Such is rarely the case. We return to this issue shortly.

Theory Generation

Isolated insights and findings do not a theory make. Instead, theories for teaching (or other phenomena) involve a logical structure in which abstract ideas are used to explain the specific effects that we observe in examples of teaching. If a central purpose of scientific research is to generate and test theory, then we should also expect that research on teaching will also produce knowledge in the form of theories, and so it does.

Some theories appear as common-language explanations for events. An example of this form is provided by Thomas Good.

In attempting to explain why the treatment program that he and Douglas Grouws developed for improving mathematics teaching was effective, Good (1982) suggests:

> The program had an impact because many elementary school teachers simply do not emphasize the meaning of the mathematical concepts they present to students, and they do not actively teach these concepts. Too much mathematics work in elementary schools involves some brief teacher presentation and a long period of seatwork. Such brief explanations for seatwork do not allow for meaningful and successful practice of concepts that have been taught, and the conditions necessary for students to discover or use principles on their own are also lacking. (p. 45)

Buried in such common-language explanations are assumptions about the existential characteristics of teaching and the ways in which pupils learn from classroom instruction. As Good also points out, additional research is needed to establish the validity of these assumptions. Nevertheless, theory at this level provides us with a tentative "understanding" for why things work the way they do and implies actions that we might take if we are to achieve specific effects.

Other theories are stated formally, and a few of the latter have also begun to appear for research on teaching. An early example of the latter is provided in another paper by Nuthall (n.d., p. 13). In this work, the author attempts to explain why pupils should learn during the processes of questioning and answering that characterize so many classrooms. One reason, suggested by Nuthall, is that pupils in the classroom maintain a covert responding process for which the author suggests the following propositions:

1. All pupils in a class respond covertly to each question which a teacher asks during class discussion, unless the question fails to motivate the covert response process.
2. The overt responses made by pupils during class discussion are a direct function of the covert responding processes which are activated by the teacher questions.
3. For any one pupil the covert response *condition* induced by a teacher question is a function of an interaction between the nature of the question (address, form, content) and the motivational state, memory, and response construction capabilities of that pupil.

Needless to say, many of the terms involved in these propositions (e.g., "motivation," "memory," "response construction," and the like) are given formal definitions by Nuthall, and the three propositions we have listed are but a sample of those suggested by the author.

Theories such as those advanced by Good and Nuthall serve many purposes: They provide a synthesis and explanation for findings to date, they suggest predictions that we might make for teaching contexts we have not yet examined, they make explicit the assumptions with which we think about events, and they provide tools we can use to think about and comprehend the confusing phenomena of teaching. They are invaluable; indeed it can be claimed that we cannot comprehend the meaning of an operation or finding without an implicit theory that makes those techniques and data meaningful. If this be so, better we should make that implicit theory explicit. It is certainly true that theory is necessary if we are to venture policy recommendations on the basis of research. Theoretical contributions will become more frequent as research on teaching matures.

Practical Innovations

In addition to the three types of knowledge already reviewed, research has the capacity for generating practical innovations, and two forms of the latter have already appeared from research on teaching. The first consists of devices or procedures that were originally developed for research but turn out to have applications in teacher training or classroom education. One example of this has already been cited in the use of the Flanders technique for in-service training of teachers. Another appears when instruction in the use of coding systems for studying classrooms is made part of the teacher-education curriculum. The second practical innovation form appears when curricula for classrooms or programs for teacher training are developed as an outgrowth of research. We have already described one such program developed by Good, Grouws, and Ebmeier (1983). Others that have recently evolved from research on teaching include programs by Anderson, Evertson, and Brophy (1979), Emmer, Sanford, Evertson, Clements, and Martin (1981), and Stallings, Cory, Fairweather, and Needels (1978). Practical innovations such as these have the capacity for generating change in our educational procedures that is independent of the findings and theories of research. (Indeed, programmatic innovations are sometimes adopted in contexts where they are actually counterproductive!) Nevertheless, they represent a practical and visible means by which research on teaching may make contributions to education in the here and now.

Research, Policy, and Practice

But are these or other contributions likely? At several points we have had occasion to criticize the assumption of a simple relationship between the findings of research on teaching and policy impact. To spell out the features of this assumption, many researchers (and their supporters) seem to feel that research on teaching stands apart from the society in which it is embedded but is capable of contributing to the latter. Out of affluence and enlightened but unfocused interest, the society supports research. In return, research has the capacity for generating knowledge that is then adopted by educators and policymakers who profit from that largess. To say the least, this assumption paints a questionable picture. For simplicity, we shall take up only two of its many issues here: the impact of research on policy, and the support of research on teaching.

Research and Policy in Teaching

To return to the question that prompted this chapter: What are the potential relationships between research on teaching and policy impact, and how likely are those relationships to appear? One way to answer this question is to ask where the research comes from and for whom the answers are intended. Broadly, research questions come from theoretical puzzles in the researcher's discipline or from the world of practice, and the answers may be intended for theoreticians or for practitioners. Thus, four types of research may be recognized.

First, some research on teaching is stimulated by questions from policymakers and is carried out for its explicit application to policy issues. Cross-sectional surveys may be conducted before a new curriculum is initiated to ascertain which persons feel the need for change or to establish base rates of conduct under the old curriculum. Researchers may also be asked to conduct field experiments in which a proposed innovation for teaching is pilot-tested. Evaluation research may also be undertaken to establish the impact of a program on pupils or teachers who participate in it. *Applied* studies of these types are more akin to engineering research than to research that reflects scientific questions. As such, the researcher who conducts them may make no assumptions about the generalizability of his or her results, nor will those results necessarily be published in scientific journals. In short, this type of research has only limited potential for adding to our general store of knowledge, although it is quite popular today.

Second, when research is stimulated by policy questions but is carried out, in part, for its scientific interest, useful contributions to theory can result. An example of this form appeared in the work of Soar and Soar (1972), who were asked to evaluate the effectiveness of an innovation in teaching but managed to build questions of theoretical interest into their research design. Studies of this type, which we call *grounded* (or *earthed*) research, were popular in granting agencies in the United States until quite recently. In effect, these agencies sold their budget to the Congress on the thesis that they were "solving" social problems but then encouraged researchers to be curious about results and to design studies so that they addressed both theoretical and practical questions. Interest in this form of research seems to be waning now. Researchers and their supporters seem less convinced that research ever "solves" a social problem, and reactionary politicians tend to view all social research as politically motivated. (We return to this topic below.)

Third, some research is stimulated by theoretical questions, but the answers generated are presumed to apply to policy or practice. Examples of this form may be found for such issues as the measurement of intelligence, the use of operant conditioning in the classroom, and the effects of school busing. Results from theoretically generated research have been used to argue policy recommendations for each of these issues, but such recommendations always reflect ideology. Logically, in this case it is not possible to make policy recommendations from findings alone. The questions generating the research derive from theory, and the assumptions of that theory shape the findings obtained. In addition, recommendations always presuppose cause-and-effect relationships and contextual conditions that may not apply in the community where the decision maker works. (To illustrate, findings concerning measured intelligence have one implication if we assume intelligence to be genetically determined and quite another if we assume it to be the outcome of environment.) Nevertheless, we are all familiar with researchers who conduct theoretically generated research and then make strong recommendations for policy on the basis of their findings. Such activities may be called *ideological research*.

Fourth, some studies are stimulated by theoretical questions and are conducted to answer them with no immediate policy implications in mind. Such studies, *basic research*, have been rare in research on teaching and to date have had little impact on teaching policy (although cases may be made for the work of Jacob Kounin and Louis Smith, and for Ulf Lundgren, 1972, and B. O. Smith, 1963). Studies of this form can have profound implications for policy. The impact of educational theory on teaching practices has been substantial in the past — witness the influence of Dewey, Kilpatrick, or Bruner. Research on teaching is capable of generating innovative theories, and as more of these are developed, the research effort will have more of an impact. Indeed, it can be argued that basic research has more potential for influence than any other research form (see Comroe & Dripps, 1976). However, that potential will only be realized as more basic research is conducted and as the theories developed are found to be attractive by policymakers.

It is also important to understand that conducting research and making social policy are two different forms of activity and are rarely done by the same person. Indeed, the language, traditions, reference groups, methods, and work styles of researchers and decision makers are so different that it makes sense to refer to them as two different cultures. The culture of the researcher stresses a knowledge of theory and methods, a willingness to let the data speak with honesty, and a reward system based on peer recognition. That of the policymaker is political; the person who makes policy in a democracy will have to answer to an electorate (or to someone who faces an electorate) for the outcomes of policy decisions. If the policymaker is wise, those decisions will reflect the most insightful theories and best evidence available, but the researcher does not bear the responsibility for decisions and may be resented if he or she urges policy strongly. The two cultures interface somewhat differently, depending on the form of research conducted. Applied research requires the researcher to subordinate his or her interests to those of the policymaker, and results from such studies rarely challenge the assumptions of policy. In grounded research the policymaker "tolerates" the theoretical activities of the researcher. In ideological research the investigator abandons his or her field of expertise and attempts to encourage policy. Basic research has little impact on policy until its theoretical insights are understood and integrated by the policymaker, but when the latter happens the impact of research may be profound.

Given separation between the activities of research and policymaking, it should not surprise us to discover that the former have relatively little impact on the latter. No study of the effects of research on teaching policy has yet been published, to our knowledge, but many educational innovations are adopted without benefit of research (Bennett, 1976). In one of the few surveys of the extent to which social research enters into the policy process, Caplan, Morrison, and Stambaugh (1975) interviewed 204 public servants in the executive branch of the U.S. government. They did not find much evidence of the actual use of research by policymakers; they did however uncover widely held and positive attitudes towards the social sciences in general and, in particular, to the idea that social science knowledge should be used in forming public policy. A similar combination of positive attitudes and little application has also been reported for Australia (McKinnon, 1982). (One wonders whether these findings are not partly a reflection of the limited vision of confirmationism. If we ask merely whether policymakers have been influenced by the findings of social research we may get a negative answer. If we ask, instead, to establish the degree to which they have been influenced through research-generated theories, the answer may be more positive. Be that as it may, the fact is that both researchers and policymakers believe research "ought" to have more of an impact.) Small wonder that the National Institute of Education continues to target funds for studying research impact and disseminating the findings of research.

Support of Research on Teaching

To insist that research on teaching become policy relevant is not without costs, of course. As long as researchers conduct basic research that has no immediate relevance for policy, they can make a dubious claim to immunity from the perils of political commitment. But as soon as that research is deemed relevant — once its agenda and methods are generated by social concerns as well as by theory, and once researchers or their supporters insist on output from research that can affect policy — the research process becomes politicized. Social researchers have recently been shocked in English-speaking countries when their budgets were slashed by conservative governments. (Unlike most public servants, some politicians view social research with suspicion if not hostility.) But, in fairness, researchers were willing enough to accept funds from earlier governments that espoused liberal or egalitarian goals that are clearly not shared by conservative governments. One cannot have it both ways; either research is nonrelevant and free from political constraints, or it is relevant and researchers should be prepared to stand and proclaim their values.

Given what has been said, how might we best support and encourage research on teaching? It is clearly in the public interest to support this form of endeavor. We need research on teaching, and good research in this field requires patronage. Support for some forms of social research has already been institutionalized in Western countries. It would be difficult to imagine how we would operate our economies without regular economic surveys, and our political systems are now dependent on the information provided by public opinion polls. Nevertheless, systematic research on teaching has appeared only in the last two decades, its activities are fragmented, and support for those efforts is insecure and tends to depend on unrealistic expectations for quick payoff. What is the best way of supporting research on teaching?

Several patterns of support for social research have appeared in the West. For convenience, we group these into four types that differ in their characteristic goals and the time spans for their support. One pattern is represented by the *private research corporation* that survives by selling services to clients or to governmental agencies. Such corporations range from polling agencies to profit-making research institutes that are spawned by major universities and satellite research businesses that cluster in and around national capitals. Most of the research conducted by such organizations is of an applied nature, most of it is financed through contracts, most of it is reported to clients by means of technical reports, and a little of it enters the professional domain through scientific publication. In short, this type of support is used to generate data that are presumed useful by decision makers. Such a support pattern is not very useful for generating or testing theory, however, nor does it add much to the integrated knowledge we will need to make policy decisions in the future. With increasing politicization of social research, this type of support has become popular in America during the past decade, and an example of its application to research on teaching appears in Stallings et al. (1978). It seems to be less popular in other Western countries, which may indicate the smaller scope of social research elsewhere or less enthusiasm for private enterprise.

A second support pattern appears in the *subordinate research groups* that operate as components of larger agencies that are responsible for social policy. Many such groups appear within governmental agencies in the United States, and others are operated by our larger school districts. Similarly, corporate research groups appear within major industries, particularly those with a tradition of industrial psychology or human relations interests. Subordinate research groups are often asked to generate social records. They may also assess specific problems, make recommendations for policy, conduct pilot research, or pursue evaluation studies. Given long-term support, such research groups can manage quite sophisticated research designs. Their work is also likely to be focused on "practical" problems, however, and little of it is conceived as contributions to larger issues in science. In addition, such groups normally operate within existing structural assumptions. This means that they are likely to reflect (rather than to challenge) institutional policies in the research they undertake. In addition, some social problems are unlikely to be addressed by subordinate groups because they are not clearly the responsibility of any single agency of government. An example of research on teaching from a subordinate research group appears in Solomon and Kendall (1976). This pattern is the major way in which social research is supported in the Soviet Union. It also appears in Western countries where social policies are planned by public agencies.

Within the United States, in contrast, much social research is conducted by university faculty and is supported by *grants* — a third support pattern — that are awarded by governmental agencies. Such a pattern of support has both advantages and disadvantages. University faculty are largely freed from the political constraints that apply to other civil servants, hence university-based researchers may conduct studies that challenge existing social policy. Faculty are also encouraged to be scholarly, to review related research carefully, to publish contributions in professional journals — thus, their research is usually planned for its scientific contribution. On the other hand, research that is planned for its scientific contribution alone may have little usefulness for our immediate social problems, and most grant agencies have sold themselves for presumptive ability to contribute to the solution of problems. Grant support is also usually provided on a competitive basis and for only short terms of support. This means that few faculty are able to plan longitudinal studies, and programmatic research is hard to organize and fund. In addition, the efforts of researchers are debilitated by the constant need to write grant proposals that will compete with those of other investigators for scarce resources. Faculty research efforts may also be weakened by the needs of teaching, administration, and community service that are normally expected of those who hold academic appointments. Finally, one cannot avoid the lingering suspicion that the interests of the granting agency are the tail that wags the research dog.

Moreover, if these problems were not sufficient, recent decisions by conservative governments have made it clear that this form of support is politically controversial. The former Fraser government in Australia abolished the Education Research Development Committee and curtailed information-gathering activities by the Schools Commission. Within the United States, the Reagan administration cut social science funding in the National Science Foundation and the research agencies of the Alcohol, Drug Abuse, and Mental Health Administration; and planning and funding in the National Institute of Education have become a shambles. In Britain the Thatcher government disbanded the Schools Council and curtailed social science research. One cannot avoid speculating that these actions were stimulated, in part, by persistent claims from researchers that support for research would "solve" social problems. By accepting support in response to such claims, social researchers have played a dangerous, no-win game. Either their research failed to "solve" the problem — in which case it was ineffective; or the research generated clear imperatives for social policy — in which case it became politically vulnerable. Fewer claims for immediate, practical results have generally been made for grant support in the physical and biological sciences, and funds for the latter have been less subject to political harassment. Nevertheless, and despite these many difficulties, the bulk of research on teaching to date has been conducted by isolated faculty and has been supported by grants. One wonders where support for this research effort will come from in the near future. (Empirical research on teaching seems already to be disappearing in favor of review-oriented, reflective, and hortative publication.)

The problems inherent in short-term grant support have prompted a fourth pattern of support that appears in *sponsored research centers*. Various forms of such centers have appeared, ranging from small units whose mission is to review and disseminate research for a given field, to large, multipurpose institutions that are funded with many millions of dollars. This form of support is common in Scandinavia where "permanent" research centers have been set up to conduct long-term research on social problems for which national legislation is anticipated. The Australian Council for Educational Research, a government-supported though independent organization, has provided research studies for 50 years that have influenced educational practice and contributed to knowledge in that country (Connell, 1980). Other examples appear in the Ontario Institute for Studies in Education, the many agencies that collect and analyze economic data, the Research and Development Centers that have been set up in the United States by the National Institute of Education, the occasional center for long-term social research that is funded by philanthropic foundations, and the units of the Research School of Social Science in the Australian National University, which are budget funded for full-time research.

In theory, such centers represent an ideal environment in which to conduct social research. Since their funding is long range, they are able to carry out programmatic research and complex studies. Most such centers are affiliated with universities, and their professional staffs are usually thought to be "faculty" and are encouraged to plan their research as contributions to scientific fields. Moreover, striking contributions have come from some such centers. Unfortunately, other units have failed to produce the innovative knowledge for which they were conceived. In some cases, centers have been sabotaged by political pressures; in others, resources have been siphoned away by parental institutions; again in others, the staff has been unable to find an appropriate blend of basic and applied contributions; whereas in yet others, effort has been vitiated through lack of leadership or excessive "administrivia." In short, to set up a sponsored research center does not guarantee that useful research will occur, although such centers probably represent the strongest pattern of support for social research today. Excellent research on teaching is presently being conducted within a handful of sponsored research centers in the United States and elsewhere, although support for their efforts is also threatened.

Our observations concerning support may be summarized with three recommendations. First, support through grants awarded to individual faculty and through sponsored research centers have real advantages for research on teaching and should be encouraged. Second, increased support for research on teaching is badly needed, and those who understand this need must be prepared to express it — particularly during the present crisis of disbelief in the usefulness of social research. Third, support for research on teaching has been hurt by attempts to sell it as a means for "solving" the problems of education. Within the physical and biological sciences we have developed traditions of supporting basic research. Unfortunately, such traditions are less securely established in the social sciences and almost nonexistent in educational research where nearly all effort is conceived (by both researchers and their supporters) to be useful for solving problems. With Kerlinger, we insist that educational problems will only be solved when appropriate decisions are taken by informed policymakers. Researchers can contribute knowledge to those decisions but cannot make them. Research on teaching is best sold for what it can accomplish, namely, the generation of knowledge.

In stating the latter, we stress again the many types of knowledge that social science research — including research of teaching — can contribute. Efforts from this active field have already developed insights in the forms of new concepts and propositions about teaching, findings concerning teaching and its consequences, and practical innovations in the forms of useful research tools and curricula that work. However, research on teaching is still in its infancy. It deals with a complex form of social interaction that varies depending on context, and we are only now beginning to understand those contextual effects. It has long-term, sequential characteristics and effects that we have only begun to investigate. Above all, it is only now beginning to generate its most important knowledge products — empirically based theories of teaching. Researchers trained in the confirmationist or discovery traditions of social research sometimes have but limited visions concerning the potential contributions of research on teaching, whereas philistines may expect this field to solve all of education's problems overnight or to be an utter waste of time and money. We assert that research on teaching has already developed a wide range of useful knowledge and is likely to continue doing so ... if it is supported.

Indeed, it would be difficult to find a field in social science research that is more likely to be relevant to policy than research on teaching, or one that has already produced more useful information. But this research field, like others throughout the history of science, will make its greatest contributions through development of theory.

REFERENCES

Aaron, H. J. (1978). *Politics and the Professors: The great society in perspective.* Washington, DC: The Brookings Institution.

Adams, R. S., et al. (1970). Symposium on teacher role in four English speaking countries. *Comparative Education Review, 14,* 5–64.

American Sociological Association. (1978). NIE plans new programs; plus expansion of others. *Footnotes, 6*(3), 1–3.

Anderson, D. S., Saltet, M., & Vervoorn, A. (1980). *Schools to grow in: An evaluating of secondary colleges.* Canberra: Australian National University Press.

Anderson, L. M., Evertson, C. M., & Brophy, J. E. (1979). An experimental study of effective teaching in first-grade reading groups. *Elementary School Journal, 79,* 193–223.

Bellack, A. A., Kliebard, H. M., Hyman, R. T., & Smith, F. L. (1966). *The language of the classroom.* New York: Teachers College Press, Columbia University.

Bennett, N. (1976). *Teaching styles and pupil progress.* Cambridge, MA: Harvard University Press.

Benton, T. (1977). *Philosophical foundations of the three sociologies.* London: Routledge and Kegan Paul.

Berns, W. (1981, November).Untitled. *Public Opinion,* p. 11.

Biddle, B. J. (1981). Comparative research on adolescents. *Australian Educational Researcher, 8,* 36–57.

Biddle, B. J., Slavings, R. L., & Anderson, D. S. (in press). Panel studies and causal inference. *Journal of Applied Behavioral Science.*

Bronfenbrenner, U. (1970). *Two worlds of childhood: U.S. and U.S.S.R.* New York: Russell Sage Foundation.

Brophy, J. E. (1979). Teacher behavior and its effects. *Journal of Educational Psychology, 71,* 733–750.

Brophy, J. E. (1981). Teacher praise: A functional analysis. *Review of Educational Research, 51,* 5–32.

Brophy, J. E., & Evertson, C. M. (1976). *Learning from teaching: A developmental perspective.* Boston: Allyn & Bacon.

Brophy, J. E., & Evertson, C. M. (1981). *Student characteristics and teaching.* New York: Longman.

Caplan, N., Morrison, A., & Stambaugh, R. J. (1975). *The use of social science knowledge in policy decisions at the national level.* Ann Arbor: University of Michigan, Institute for Social Research.

Carew, J. V., & Lightfoot, S. L. (1979). *Beyond bias: Perspectives on classrooms.* Cambridge, MA: Harvard University Press.

Cazden, C., John, V. P., & Hymes, D. (Eds.). (1972). *Functions of language in the classroom.* New York: Teachers College Press, Columbia University.

Chall, J. (1967). *Learning to read: The great debate.* New York: McGraw-Hill.

Cicourel, A. V., et al. (1974). *Language use and school performance.* New York: Academic Press.

Coleman, J. S., Campbell, E., Hobson, C., McPartland, J., Mood, A., Weinfield, F., & York, R. (1966). *Equality of educational opportunity.* Washington, DC: U.S. Department of Health, Education, and Welfare.

Coleman, J. S., Hoffer, T., and Kilgore, S. (1982). *High school achievement.* New York: Basic Books.

Comroe, J. H., & Dripps, R. D. (1976). Scientific basis for the support of bio-medical science. *Science, 192,* 105–111.

Connell, W. F. (1980). *The Australian Council for Educational Research: 1930–80.* Melbourne: A.C.E.R.

Cook, T. D., & Campbell, D. T. (1979). *Quasi-experimentation: Design and analysis issues for field settings.* Chicago: Rand McNally.

Crano, W. D., & Mellon, P. M. (1978). Causal influence of teachers' expectations on children's academic performance: A cross-lagged panel analysis. *Journal of Educational Psychology, 70,* 39–49.

Cronbach, L. J. (1967). How can instruction be adapted to individual differences? In R. M. Gagné (Ed.), *Learning and individual differences.* Columbus, OH: Charles E. Merrill.

Cronbach, L. J., & Snow, R. E. (1977). *Aptitudes and instructional methods.* New York: Irvington.

Dunkin, M. J., & Biddle, B. J. (1974). *The study of teaching.* New York: Holt, Rinehart & Winston.

Emmer, E. T., Sanford, J. P., Evertson, C. M., Clements, B. S., & Martin, J. (1981). *The classroom management improvement study: An experiment in elementary school classrooms.* Austin: University of Texas, R & D Center for Teacher Education.

Entwisle, D. R., & Hayduk, L. A. (1981). Academic expectations and the school attainment of young children. *Sociology of Education, 54,* 34–50.

Ericsson, K. A., & Simon, H. A. (1980). Verbal reports as data. *Psychological Review, 87,* 215–251.

Evertson, C. M., Anderson, C. W., Anderson, L. M., & Brophy, J. E. (1980). Relationships between classroom behavior and student outcomes in junior high mathematics and English classes. *American Educational Research Journal, 17,* 43–60.

Fensham, P. J. (in press). *School, alienation, and employment.* London: Routledge & Kegan Paul.

Filstead, W. J. (1970). *Qualitative methodology: Firsthand involvement with the social world.* Chicago: Markham.

Flanders, N. A. (1960). *Interaction analysis in the classroom: A manual for observers.* Ann Arbor: University of Michigan Press.

Flanders, N. A. (1970). *Analyzing teacher behavior.* Reading, MS: Addison-Wesley.

Fletcher, C. (1974). *Beneath the surface: An account of three styles of sociological research.* London: Routledge and Kegan Paul.

Gage, N. L. (1978). *The scientist basis of the art of teaching.* New York: Teachers College Press, Columbia University.

Gall, M. D., Ward, B. A., Berliner, D. C., Cahen, L. S., Winne, P. H., Elashoff, J. D., & Stanton, G. C. (1978). Effects of questioning techniques and recitation on student learning. *American Educational Research Journal, 15,* 175–199.

Glaser, B. G., & Strauss, A. L. (1967). *The discovery of grounded theory: Strategies for qualitative research.* Chicago: Aldine.

Glass, G. V., Cahen, L. S., Smith, M. L., & Filby, N. N. (1982). *School class size: Research and policy.* Beverly Hills: Sage Publications.

Glass, G. V., McGaw, B., & Smith, M. L. (1981). *Meta-analysis in social research.* Beverly Hills: Sage Publications.

Good, T. L. (1979). Teacher effectiveness in the elementary school: What we know about it now. *Journal of Teacher Education, 30,* 52–64.

Good, T. L. (1982). Classroom research. In M. Sykes and L. Shulman (Eds.), *Research and policy implications in education.* New York: Longman.

Good, T. L., Biddle, B. J., & Brophy, J. E. (1975). *Teachers make a difference.* New York: Holt, Rinehart & Winston.

Good, T. L., Ebmeier, H., & Beckerman, T. (1978). Teaching mathematics in high and low SES classrooms: An empirical comparison. *Journal of Teacher Education, 29,* 85–90.

Good, T. L., Grouws, D. A., & Ebmeier, H. (1983). *Active mathematics teaching.* New York: Longman.

Green, M. (1982). Choosing our future. *Educational Researcher, 11*(2), 4–6.

Hughes, J. (1980). *The philosophy of social research.* London: Longman.

Kallós, D. (1975). Comments on the importance of aptitude-treatment interaction research for pedagogies and for the theory and practice of teaching. In R. Schwarzer and K. Steinhagen (Eds.), *Adaptiver Unterricht: Interaktionen zwischen Hehrmethoden und Hernermerkmalen.* Munich: Kosel Verlag.

Kemis, S. (1983). Research approaches and methods: Action research. In D. S. Anderson and C. Blakers (Eds.), *Youth, transition, and social research.* Canberra: Australian National University Press.

Kerlinger, F. N. (1977). The influence of research on education practice. *Educational Researcher, 6*(8), 5–12.

Kounin, J. S. (1970). *Discipline and group management in classrooms.* New York: Holt, Rinehart & Winston.

Kristol, I. (1981, November). Untitled. *Public Opinion,* p. 12.

LeCompte, M. D., & Goetz, J. P. (1982). Problems of reliability and validity in ethnographic research. *Review of Educational Research, 52,* 31–60.

Lessnoff, M. (1974). *The structure of social science: A philosophical introduction.* London: Allen and Unwin.

Lortie, D. C. (1975). *Schoolteachers: A sociological study.* Chicago: University of Chicago Press.

Lundgren, U. (1972). *Frame factors and the teaching process: A contribution to curriculum theory and theory on teaching.* Stockholm: Almquist and Wiksell.

McKinnon, K. (1982). Policy and research: An educational policymaker's perspective. In D. S. Anderson and C. Blakers (Eds.), *Youth, transition, and social research.* Canberra: Australian National University Press.

Mehan, H. (1979). *Learning lessons: Social organization in the classroom.* Cambridge, MA: Harvard University Press.

Mitzel, H. E. (1960). Teacher effectiveness. In C. W. Harris (Ed.), *Encyclopedia of educational research* (3rd ed.). New York: Macmillan.

Munday, L. A. (1978). National decline in test scores of the college bound. *Intellect, 105,* 130.

NIE research. (1982). *Education Times, 3*(12), 6.

Nuthall, G. (1974). Is classroom interaction research worth the effort involved? *New Zealand Journal of Educational Studies, 9,* 1–17.

Nuthall, G. (n.d.). Learning in classroom discussion: A theoretical interpretation.

Peterson, P. L. (1977). Interactive effects of student anxiety, achievement orientation, and teacher behavior on student achievement and attitude. *Journal of Educational Psychology, 69,* 779–792.

Peterson, P. L. (1979). Aptitude × treatment interaction effects of teacher structuring and student participation in college instruction. *Journal of Educational Psychology, 71,* 521–533.

Phillips, D. C. (1983). After the wake: Postpositivistic educational thought. *Educational Researcher, 12*(5), 4–12.

Popkewitz, T. S., Tabachnick, B. R., & Wehlage, G. (1982). *The myth of educational reform: A study of school responses to a program of change.* Madison: University of Wisconsin Press.

Popper, K. (1959). *The logic of scientific discovery.* London: Hutchinson.

Popper, K. (1972). *Objective knowledge.* Oxford: Clarendon Press.

Prewitt, K. (1981, September/October). Early warning systems. *Society,* 3–6.

Rist, R. (1973). *The urban school: A factory for failure.* Cambridge, MA: MIT Press.

Rosenshine, B. (1976). Classroom instruction. In N. L. Gage (Ed.), *The psychology of teaching methods.* Chicago: University of Chicago Press.

Rosenshine, B. (1979). Content, time, and direct instruction. In P. L. Peterson and H. J. Walberg (Eds.), *Research on teaching: Concepts, findings, and implications.* Berkeley, CA: McCutchan.

Rosenthal, R., & Jacobson, L. (1968). *Pygmalion in the classroom: Teacher expectation and pupils' intellectual development.* New York: Holt, Rinehart & Winston.

Schwartz, H., & Jacobs, J. (1979). *Qualitative sociology: A method to the madness.* New York: Free Press.

Scott, R. A., & Shore, A. R. (1979). *Why sociology does not apply: A study of the use of sociology in public policy.* New York: Elsevier.

Shavelson, R. J., & Stern, P. (1981). Research on teachers' pedagogical thoughts, judgments, decisions, and behavior. *Review of Educational Research, 51,* 455–498.

Smith, B. O. (1963). Toward a theory of teaching. In A. A. Bellack (Ed.), *Theory and research in teaching.* Champaign: University of Illinois Press.

Smith, L. M., & Geoffrey, W. (1968). *The complexities of an urban classroom: An analysis toward a general theory of teaching.* New York: Holt, Rinehart & Winston.

Snow, R. E. (1977). Individual differences and instructional theory. *Educational Researcher, 6*(10), 11–15.

Soar, R. S., & Soar, R. M. (1972). An empirical analysis of selected Follow Through programs: An example of a process approach to evaluation. In I. Gordon (Ed.), *Early childhood education.* Chicago: National Society for the Study of Education.

Solomon, D., & Kendall, A. J. (1976). Individual characteristics and children's performance in "open" and "traditional" classroom settings. *Journal of Educational Psychology, 68,* 613–625.

Spradley, J. P. (1979). *The ethnographic interview.* New York: Holt, Rinehart & Winston.

Spradley, J. P. (1980). *Participant observation.* New York: Holt.

Stake, R. E. (1978). The case study method in social inquiry. *Educational Researcher, 7*(2), 5–8.

Stallings, J., Cory, R., Fairweather, J., & Needels, M. (1978). *A study of basic reading skills taught in secondary schools.* Palo Alto, CA: SRI International.

Wilson, S. (1977). The use of ethnographic techniques in educational research. *Review of Educational Research, 47,* 245–265.

Part 2
Research on Teaching and Teachers

9.
Teachers' Thought Processes

Christopher M. Clark
Michigan State University

Penelope L. Peterson
University of Wisconsin—Madison

The thinking, planning, and decision making of teachers constitute a large part of the psychological context of teaching. It is within this context that curriculum is interpreted and acted upon; where teachers teach and students learn. Teacher behavior is substantially influenced and even determined by teachers' thought processes. These are the fundamental assumptions behind the literature that has come to be called research on teacher thinking. Practitioners of this branch of educational research seek first to describe fully the mental lives of teachers. Second, they hope to understand and explain how and why the observable activities of teachers' professional lives take on the forms and functions that they do. They ask when and why teaching is difficult, and how human beings manage the complexity of classroom teaching. The ultimate goal of research on teachers' thought processes is to construct a portrayal of the cognitive psychology of teaching for use by educational theorists, researchers, policymakers, curriculum designers, teacher educators, school administrators, and by teachers themselves.

Our aims in this chapter are to offer a framework for organizing research on teachers' thought processes, to summarize and comment upon this diverse body of work, and to make recommendations concerning the future of research on teacher thinking. Earlier reviews of this literature (Clark & Yinger, 1979a; Posner, 1981; Shavelson & Stern, 1981) have been helpful to us in conceptualizing the organization of the field and in identifying the relevant studies. In compiling research reports for this review our main criterion was topical. That is, we searched the educational research literature for reports of research on teaching whose titles and abstracts suggested that a primary focus of the research was some aspect of teacher thinking (e.g., planning, decision making, judgment, implicit theories, expectations, attributions). The reports of research included in this review constitute a mixture of published journal articles and less widely available conference papers, technical reports, and doctoral dissertations. It is an indication of the newness of this field that the vast majority of the work has been done since 1976.

Beginnings of Research on Teachers' Thought Processes

In his book *Life in Classrooms* (1968), Philip Jackson reported the results of one of the first studies that attempted to describe and understand the mental constructs and processes that underlie teacher behavior. The descriptive character of his study was a striking departure from contemporary research on teaching and did not fit easily with the then-dominant correlational and experimental research paradigms. In 1968 it was difficult to see how description of life in a few classrooms could contribute much to the quest for teaching effectiveness. But the real power of Jackson's research was not to be found in prescriptions for teaching that might be derived from the work. Rather, Jackson's contribution to research on teaching was conceptual. He portrayed the full complexity of the teacher's task, made conceptual distinctions that fit the teacher's frame of reference (such as that between the preactive and interactive phases of teaching), and called the attention of the educational research

The authors thank reviewers Susan Florio-Ruane (Michigan State University), Gaea Leinhardt (University of Pittsburgh), and Robert Yinger (University of Cincinnati).

The two authors contributed equally to the writing of this chapter. The first author was responsible primarily for the sections on teacher planning and teachers' implicit theories. The second author was responsible primarily for the sections on teachers' interactive thoughts and decisions and teachers' attributions. The work of the first author was supported by the Institute for Research on Teaching, Michigan State University, which is funded in part by the National Institute of Education (Contract No. 400-81-0014). The work of the second author was supported by the Wisconsin Center for Education Research, which is funded in part by a grant from the National Institute of Education (Grant No. NIE-G-81-0009). The opinions expressed here are those of the authors.

community to the importance of describing the thinking and planning of teachers as a means to fuller understanding of classroom processes. In sum, Jackson's (1966) argument was the following:

> A glimpse at this "hidden" side of teaching may increase our understanding of some of the more visible and well-known features of the process.

In Sweden, Dahllof and Lundgren (1970) conducted a series of studies of the structure of the teaching process as an expression of organizational constraints. While this work was primarily concerned with the effects of contextual factors on teaching, it revealed some of the mental categories that teachers use to organize and make sense of their professional experiences. As with Jackson, the Dahllof and Lundgren contribution was primarily conceptual. Of particular significance in the Dahllof and Lundgren research was the phenomenon of the "steering group," a small subset of a class (ranging in achievement level from the 10th to 25th percentiles) that their teachers used as an informal reference group for decisions about pacing a lesson or unit. During whole-class instruction, when the students in the steering group seemed to understand what was being presented, the teacher would move the class on to a new topic. But when the teachers believed that the steering group students were not understanding or performing up to standards, the teachers slowed the pace of instruction for all. The steering group is important as a concept both because of its empirical verifiability and because it shows clearly how teachers' mental constructs can have significant pedagogical consequences.

In June 1974 the National Institute of Education convened a week-long National Conference on Studies in Teaching to create an agenda for future research on teaching. The participants in this planning conference were organized into 10 panels and each panel produced a plan for research in their area of expertise. The deliberations of Panel 6 on "Teaching as Clinical Information Processing" were of importance to the development of research on teacher thinking. Panel 6 was chaired by Lee S. Shulman and included a diverse group of experts on the psychology of human information processing, the anthropology of education, classroom interaction research, and on the practical realities of teaching. Panel 6 produced a report (National Institute of Education, 1975a) that enunciated a rationale for and defined the assumptions and the domain of a proposed program of research on teachers' thought processes. In this report the panelists argued that research on teacher thinking is necessary if we are to understand that which is uniquely human in the process of teaching:

> It is obvious that what teachers do is directed in no small measure by what they think. Moreover, it will be necessary for any innovations in the context, practices, and technology of teaching to be mediated through the minds and motives of teachers. To the extent that observed or intended teacher behavior is "thoughtless," it makes no use of the human teacher's most unique attributes. In so doing, it becomes mechanical and might well be done by a machine. If, however, teaching is done and, in all likelihood, will continue to be done by human teachers, the question of the relationships between thought and action becomes crucial. (p.1)

Beyond this logical argument for attending to teacher thinking, the Panel 6 report went on to cite research on human infor-

mation processing, which indicates that a person, when faced with a complex situation, creates a simplified model of that situation and then behaves rationally in relation to that simplified model. Simon claims that "such behavior is not even approximately optimal with respect to the real world. To predict . . . behavior we must understand the way in which this simplified model is constructed, and its construction will certainly be related to (one's) psychological properties as a perceiving, thinking, and learning animal" (Simon, 1957; cited in National Institute of Education, 1975a, p. 2). To understand, predict, and influence what teachers do, the panelists argued, researchers must study the psychological processes by which teachers perceive and define their professional responsibilities and situations.

The Panel 6 report (National Institute of Education, 1975a) is explicit about the view of the teacher that guided the panelists in their deliberations and recommendations for research:

> The Panel was oriented toward the teacher as clinician, not only in the sense of someone diagnosing specific forms of learning dysfunction or pathology and prescribing particular remedies, but more broadly as an individual responsible for (a) aggregating and making sense out of an incredible diversity of information sources about individual students and the class collectively; (b) bringing to bear a growing body of empirical and theoretical work constituting the research literature of education; somehow (c) combining all that information with the teacher's own expectations, attitudes, beliefs, purposes . . . and (d) having to respond, make judgments, render decisions, reflect, and regroup to begin again.

In short, the Panel 6 report presented an image of the teacher as a professional who has more in common with physicians, lawyers, and architects than with technicians who execute skilled performances according to prescriptions or algorithms defined by others. This view of the teacher as professional has had a profound effect on the questions asked, methods of inquiry employed, and the form of the results reported in research on teacher thinking. Moreover, the Panel 6 report influenced new initiatives in research on teaching in a more instrumental way—in 1975 the National Institute of Education issued a request for proposals for an Institute for Research on Teaching that would focus on research on teaching as clinical information processing. An Institute for Research on Teaching was established at Michigan State University in 1976, and this organization initiated the first large program of research on the thought processes of teachers.

A Model of Teacher Thought and Action

A major goal of research on teacher thought processes is to increase our understanding of how and why the process of teaching looks and works as it does. To assist the reader in visualizing how the several parts of the research literature on teacher thought processes relate to one another and how research on teacher thought processes complements the larger body of research on teaching effectiveness, we have developed the model of teacher thought and action presented in Figure 9.1. We make no claims for the empirical validity of this model, but rather offer it as a heuristic device that may be useful in making sense of the literature and as an "advance organizer"

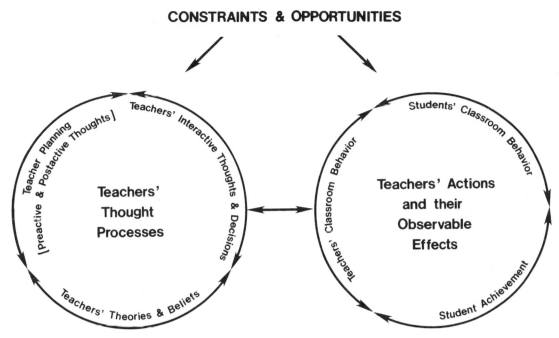

Fig. 9.1. A model of teacher thought and action.

for the topics and information that we will present in this chapter.

The model depicts two domains that are importantly involved in the process of teaching. Each domain is represented by a circle. These domains are (a) teachers' thought processes, and (b) teachers' actions and their observable effects. These two domains differ in at least two important ways. First, the domains differ in the extent to which the processes involved are observable. Teachers' thought processes occur "inside teachers' heads" and thus are unobservable. In contrast, teacher behavior, student behavior, and student achievement scores constitute observable phenomena. Thus, the phenomena involved in the teacher action domain are more easily measured and more easily subjected to empirical research methods than are the phenomena involved in the teacher thought domain. As we shall see in the next section on methods of inquiry, the domain of teachers' thought processes presents challenging methodological problems for the empirical researcher. Second, the two domains represent two paradigmatic approaches to research on teaching. Prior to 1975, the dominant research paradigm was the process–product approach to the study of teaching effectiveness. Process–product researchers have been concerned primarily with the relationship between teachers' classroom behavior, students' classroom behavior, and student achievement. In contrast, the domain of research on teachers' thought processes constitutes a paradigmatic approach to research on teaching which has only recently emerged. We will now briefly describe each domain.

Teachers' Actions and Their Observable Effects

The action domain is where classroom teaching actually takes place. Teachers behave in certain ways in the classroom and their behavior has observable effects on students. Process-pro-

duct researchers have typically assumed that causality is unidirectional, with teachers' classroom behavior affecting students' classroom behavior, which ultimately affects students' achievement (see, for example, Doyle, 1977b; Dunkin & Biddle, 1974). In the model shown in Figure 9.1, we assume that the relationships between teacher behavior, student behavior, and student achievement are reciprocal. Moreover, rather than representing the direction of causation as linear, we think that it is more accurate to represent the direction of causation as cyclical or circular. Our circular model of teachers' actions and their observable effects thus allows for the possibility that teacher behavior affects student behavior, which in turn affects teacher behavior and ultimately student achievement. Alternatively, students' achievement may cause teachers to behave differently toward the student, which then affects student behavior and subsequent student achievement.

The relationships between the three variables in the domain of teacher actions have been investigated systematically by researchers on teaching effectiveness. This research is summarized and described by Brophy and Good (this volume). Unfortunately, however, most of this research has assumed that the relationship between teachers' actions and their observable affects is a linear one and is unidirectional, and most research has not explored the possibility of reciprocal effects as we suggest in our model.

Teachers' Thought Processes

Three major categories of teachers' thought processes are encompassed within this domain: (a) teacher planning (preactive and postactive thoughts); (b) teachers' interactive thoughts and decisions; and (c) teachers' theories and beliefs. These categories reflect the researchers' conceptualization of the domain of teachers' thought processes more than an empirically derived categorization of the domain. The first two categories represent a temporal distinction between whether the thought processes occur during classroom interaction (i.e., teachers' interactive thoughts and decisions) or before or after classroom interaction (i.e., preactive and postactive thoughts). These categories follow from Jackson's (1968) distinction between the preactive, interactive, and postactive phases of teaching. These distinctions were first used by Crist, Marx, and Peterson (1974) as a way of categorizing teachers' thought processes because these researchers hypothesized that the kind of thinking that teachers do during classroom interaction would be qualitatively different from the kinds of thinking that teachers do before and after classroom interaction.

As we will see in our review of research on teachers' thought processes, the distinction between teachers' interactive thoughts and decisions and their preactive thoughts and decisions has been retained by researchers and appears to be an important one. The kind of thinking that teachers do during interactive teaching does appear to be qualitatively different from the kind of thinking they do when they are not interacting with students. In contrast, the distinction between teachers' preactive and postactive thoughts does not seem to have been retained by researchers. These two categories have been subsumed under the category of "teacher planning." Teacher planning includes the thought processes that teachers engage in prior to classroom interaction but also includes the thought processes or reflections that they engage in after classroom interaction that then guide their thinking and projections for future classroom interaction. For example, teacher planning includes the reflections that the teacher has at 3:30 p.m. at the end of a given day that then cause the teacher to plan a certain activity for the class for 8:30 a.m. the next morning. Thus, because the teaching process is a cyclical one the distinction between preactive and postactive thoughts has become blurred.

The third category, teachers' theories and beliefs, represents the rich store of knowledge that teachers have that affects their planning and their interactive thoughts and decisions. The arrows in the model indicate these effects. Of course, teachers may also develop theories and beliefs as a result of their thinking during classroom interaction and of their planning prior to and following classroom interaction. Thus, as the arrows in the model indicate, teachers' interactive thoughts and decisions and teacher planning, respectively, may also affect teachers' thoughts and beliefs.

We have included these three categories of teachers' thought processes—teacher planning, teachers' interactive thoughts and decisions, and teachers' theories and beliefs—because to date the research on teachers' thought processes has been directed toward these three major topics. In our model and in our subsequent review of the research on teachers' thought processes, we have chosen not to separate out a fourth category, teacher judgment, which has been treated as a distinct category by earlier reviewers of this research. (See, for example, Clark & Yinger, 1979a; Shavelson & Stern, 1981). We decided not to discuss research on teacher judgment as a separate category because teacher judgment is but one cognitive process that teachers use in their planning and interactive decision making. Thus, we have subsumed the research on teacher judgment under the appropriate category of teacher planning, teachers'

interactive thoughts and decisions, or teachers' theories and beliefs.

In sum, the three categories in the domain of teachers' thought processes reflect the state of the field in research on teachers' thought processes and thus reflect the researchers' conceptualizations of the field. For this reason, we have chosen to use these three categories as the organizing topics for our review of the research literature.

Constraints and Opportunities

A complete understanding of the process of teaching is not possible without an understanding of the constraints and opportunities that impinge upon the teaching process. Teachers' actions are often constrained by the physical setting or by external influences such as the school, the principal, the community, or the curriculum. Conversely, teachers may be able to behave in a certain way simply because they are given a rare opportunity to do so. Teacher's thought processes may be similarly constrained. For example, teachers may have less flexibility in their planning or perceive that they have less flexibility in their planning because certain curriculum decisions have been made already by the school district or by the principal. Alternatively, other principals may give teachers more flexibility and opportunity to engage in planning and decision making. Indeed, the extent to which responsibility and participation in the decision-making process are given to teachers (here defined as constraints and opportunities) has been shown to be an important variable that defines effective schools. (See, for example, Good and Brophy, this volume). Therefore, we deem this variable an important one that needs to be included in any model of the process of teaching. Moreover, as we shall see in our review of the research on teachers' thought processes, research findings suggest that teachers' thought processes are affected profoundly by the task demands and by the teachers' perceptions of the task. We view task demands as encompassed within constraints and opportunities.

The Relationship Between the Domains of Teacher Thought and Action

As the double-headed arrow between the domains of teacher thought and action in our model indicates, there is a reciprocal relationship between these two domains. Teachers' actions are in a large part caused by teachers' thought processes, which then in turn affect teachers' actions. However, we contend that the process of teaching will be fully understood only when these two domains are brought together and examined in relation to one another. We hope that the model presented in Figure 9.1 will serve as a useful step toward achieving such a synoptic view of the process of teaching and will also aid the reader in understanding the topics and issues that we address in the remainder of this chapter.

In the remainder of this chapter, we will review and discuss the research that has been done on teacher planning, teachers' interactive thoughts and decisions, and teachers' theories and beliefs. Before beginning our review, however, we provide a brief overview of the several methods of inquiry that have been used in research on teachers' thought processes.

Methods of Inquiry

The systematic study of the thought processes of teachers demands that researchers deal with serious technical, methodological, and epistemological challenges. This research depends heavily on various forms of self-report by teachers, and the central methodological problem deals with how to elicit and interpret valid and reliable self-reports about cognitive processes. The use of verbal reports as data has been criticized by Nisbett and Wilson (1977), and their arguments have been challenged by Ericcson and Simon (1980). Ericcson and Simon indicated that verbal reports will be most reliable and valid as data when a person is reporting on the contents of short-term memory, that is, that which he or she is currently attending to. Less reliable and valid data will result from probes that are vague and general or that require respondents to use inferential processes to complete or elaborate partially remembered information.

In the studies reviewed in this chapter, the researchers usually employed various combinations of five methods of inquiry: thinking aloud, stimulated recall, policy capturing, journal keeping and the repertory grid technique. Often these methods were supplemented by interviews, field observations, and narrative descriptions of the task, the context, and the visible behavior of the participants in a study. We will briefly describe each of these methods. (Shavelson, Webb & Burstein, this volume, discuss these methods further.)

Thinking Aloud

The thinking aloud method consists of having a teacher verbalize all of his or her thoughts while engaged in a task such as planning a lesson (e g , Peterson, Marx, & Clark, 1978) or making judgments about curriculum materials (e.g., Yinger & Clark, 1982). The teacher's verbalizations are recorded, usually on audiotape but occasionally on videotape (e.g., Smith & Sendelbach, 1979), and later transcribed to create typewritten protocols. The protocols are then subjected to various kinds of coding systems (almost always created by the investigator) to produce descriptions of the content of teacher thinking and of the sequences of cognitive processes that teachers follow while planning, making decisions, and teaching.

Stimulated Recall

The stimulated recall method was used originally by Bloom (1954) and consists of replaying a videotape or audiotape of a teaching episode to enable the viewer (usually the teacher of the episode) to recollect and report on his or her thoughts and decisions during the teaching episode. Variations in the use of stimulated recall include replaying only researcher-selected portions of the recording versus replaying the complete tape; researchers asking prespecified questions each time the tape is stopped versus soliciting open-ended commentary from the teacher; and researcher control of when to stop the tape versus teacher control or shared control. The teacher's reports and comments about thoughts and decisions while teaching are audiotaped, transcribed, and subjected to content analysis. Conners (1978a) and Tuckwell (1980a, 1980b) provide a summary, analysis, and recommendations regarding techniques

for conducting stimulated recall sessions and analyses of the resulting protocols. Calderhead (1981) offers a more theoretical and philosophical analysis of the limits and possibilities of stimulated recall in the study of teaching.

Policy Capturing

Policy capturing is a method borrowed from laboratory psychology (e.g., Hammond, 1971; Rappoport & Summers, 1973) for use in studying teacher judgment processes. In a typical policy capturing study, a teacher is presented with a series of printed descriptions of students or of hypothetical teaching situations or of curricular materials. These descriptions have been edited by the researchers so that all possible combinations of as many as five features or "cues" appear in the full set of objects to be judged. The teacher is asked to make one or more judgements or decisions about each printed description, usually recorded on a Likert scale. The goal of this approach is to produce mathematical models (usually linear regression equations) that describe the relative weightings that teachers attach to the features of the objects being judged as they make judgments about them. The resulting equations represent the "policy" of the teacher in relation to the domain in which the judgments were made (e.g., assignment of students to reading groups, selection of curricular materials). Of the several methods used to study teacher thinking, policy capturing depends least on teacher self-reports. However, the method is limited to relatively simple judgment situations that involve a small number of cues or features (typically five or fewer) that can be identified a priori by the researchers. (See Yinger and Clark, 1982 for a comparison of the strengths and limitations of policy capturing and think aloud methods in research on teaching.)

Journal Keeping

The primary application of journal keeping in research on teacher thinking has been in the study of planning. Teachers are typically asked to keep a written record of their plans for instruction as they develop, and to comment in writing on (a) the context in which their plans are made, (b) their reasons for selecting one course of action over another, and (c) their reflections on and evaluation of their plans after they are brought into action in the classroom. Journal keeping is usually supplemented by frequent interviews, both to encourage and support the teacher in the often demanding and unfamiliar process of journal keeping and to clarify and elaborate unclear or incomplete journal entries. In some cases, the researcher enters into a written dialogue with the teacher in the pages of the journal. Journal entries are subjected to content analyses and the data are used to generate descriptions and models of the planning process and the factors that influence it. (For a discussion of the use of dialogue journals see Staton, 1982.) Yinger and Clark (1981, 1985) discuss theoretical and practical issues in the use of journal writing in research on teaching.

The Repertory Grid Technique

The repertory grid technique has been used in the study of teachers' implicit theories. This technique was developed by

Kelly (1955) as a method for discovering the personal constructs that influence individual behavior. An individual is presented with a series of cards on which are written single words or statements about the domain of interest to the investigator. The subject is asked to indicate which cards are alike or different and to explain why. The resulting groupings and their associated rationales are labeled as "constructs" by the investigator. The constructs and their component elements are then arrayed in a grid format to show (either by inspection or through factor analysis) the relationships among constructs. Variations in the repertory grid technique include having the respondent generate the elements to be sorted (e.g., Munby, 1983) and involving the respondent in analysis of the relationships among components through clinical interviews (e.g., Olson, 1981).

Teacher Planning

Researchers have conceptualized teacher planning in two ways. First, they have thought of planning as a set of basic psychological processes in which a person visualizes the future, inventories means and ends, and constructs a framework to guide his or her future action. This conception of planning draws heavily on the theories and methods of cognitive psychology. Second, researchers have defined planning as "the things that teachers do when they say that they are planning." This definition suggests a phenomonological or descriptive approach to research on teacher planning, in which the teacher takes on an important role as informant or even as research collaborator.

Both of these views of teacher planning are represented in the research literature either explicitly or implicitly. These two different starting points for the study of teacher planning probably account for the variety of methods of inquiry in use and for the challenge that reviewers of this literature face in pulling together a coherent summary of what has been learned. Planning is challenging to study because it is both a psychological process and a practical activity.

We have organized our review of the research on teacher planning to address three major questions: (a) What are the types and functions of teacher planning? (b) What models have been used to describe the process of planning? and (c) What is the relationship between teacher planning and the teacher's subsequent actions in the classroom?

Types and Functions of Teacher Planning

What are the different kinds of planning that teachers do, and what purposes do they serve? The answer to both parts of this question seems to be "many." That is, many different kinds of planning are in use, and they serve many functions.

TYPES OF PLANNING

Table 9.1 summarizes the findings of eight studies in which researchers investigated the types and functions of teacher planning. Yinger (1977) and Clark and Yinger (1979b) determined that during the course of a school year, experienced teachers engaged in as many as eight different types of planning. The names of six of these eight types designate a span of time for which the planning took place: weekly, daily, long range, short range, yearly, and term planning. The remaining two types (unit and lesson planning) describe a unit of content for which the teachers planned. Judging from these empirically derived typologies of teacher planning, we would conclude that substantial teacher energy is devoted to structuring, organizing for, and managing limited classroom instructional time.

Yinger's (1977) finding that routines are a principal product of teacher planning (also supported by the work of Bromme, 1982 and Creemers & Westerhof, 1982) suggests that teachers respond to the press for simplification and efficient time management by planning. Yinger defined routines as sets of established procedures for both teacher and students that function to control and coordinate specific sequences of behavior. He identified four types of routines as products of teacher planning: (a) activity routines, (b) instructional routines, (c) management routines, and (d) executive planning routines. Routines "played such a major role in the teacher's planning behavior that [such] planning could be characterized as decision making about the selection, organization, and sequencing of routines" (1979, p. 165).

The relative importance of different types of planning was also explored by Clark and Yinger (1979b). Unit planning was cited most often by the teachers as most important, followed by weekly and daily planning. Only 7% of the teachers in this study listed lesson planning among the three most important types.

Researchers have also investigated the dynamic relationships among different types of planning. Morine-Dershimer (1977, 1979) found that teachers' written plans seldom reflect the teachers' entire plan. Rather, the few details recorded on a written plan were nested within more comprehensive planning structures, called "lesson images" by Morine-Dershimer. These lesson images, in turn, were nested within a still larger construct called the "activity flow" by Joyce (1978–1979). For elementary teachers, the activity flow encompasses the yearlong progress of a class through each particular subject matter and also is concerned with the balance of activities across subject matters in a school day or week.

Further support for the idea that teacher planning is a nested process comes from a study by Clark and Elmore (1979). Clark and Elmore interviewed and observed five elementary teachers during the first five weeks of the school year and found that teachers' planning was concerned primarily with setting up the physical environment of the classroom, assessing student abilities, and establishing the social system of the classroom. By the end of the fourth week of school, teachers had established a system of schedules, routines, and groupings for instruction. These structural and social features of the classroom then persisted throughout the school year and served as the framework within which teachers planned particular activities and units. Other studies of the first weeks of school also support the conclusion that, to a significant degree, the "problem space" (Newell & Simon, 1972) within which teacher and students operate is defined early, changes little during the course of the school year, and exerts a powerful, if subtle, influence on thought and behavior (e.g., Anderson & Evertson, 1978; Buckley & Cooper, 1978; Shultz & Florio, 1979; Tikunoff & Ward, 1978).

Table 9.1. Summary of Findings of Eight Studies of the Types and Functions of Teacher Planning

Study	Method of Inquiry	Teachers	Subject Matter	Principal Findings
Clark & Elmore (1979)	Observation, interview, and journal keeping	5 teachers of grades K–5	All	Planning early in school year focuses on establishing the physical environment and social system of the classroom.
Clark & Elmore (1981)	Think aloud during yearly planning	1 teacher of grade 2	Mathematics, science, writing	Functions of yearly planning: (a) to adapt curriculum to fit teacher's knowledge and priorities, and unique classroom situation; (b) for teacher to learn the structure and content of new curricula; (c) to develop a practical schedule for instruction.
Clark & Yinger (1979b)	Written description of plans by teachers	78 elementary teachers	All	1. Eight types of planning: weekly, daily, unit, long range, lesson, short range, yearly, term. 2. Three most important types: unit, weekly, daily. 3. Planning functions to (a) meet immediate psychological needs of the planner, (b) prepare the teacher cognitively and instrumentally for instruction, and (c) guide the interactive processes of instruction.
McCutcheon (1980)	Ethnography	12 teachers of Grades 1–6	All	1. Much teacher planning is never put on paper. 2. Functions of written lesson plans: (a) to meet administrators' demands, and (b) to be used by substitute teachers. 3. Long-range planning viewed as counterproductive because of unpredictable changes in schedule and interruptions.
Morine-Dershimer (1977)	Observation, analysis of written plans and interview	20 teachers of Grade 2; 20 teachers of Grade 5	Reading, mathematics	1. Most lesson planning done mentally rather than on paper. 2. Outline or list of topics most typical form of plan.
Morine-Dershimer (1979)	Interview, observation, and stimulated recall	10 elementary teachers		1. Mental "image" of a lesson plan used to guide teacher behavior during routine instruction. 2. Lesson plan largely abandoned when activity flow is threatened with disruption.
Smith & Sendelbach (1979)	Observation, think aloud, and stimulated recall	4 teachers of Grade 6	Science	1. Teachers depend heavily on published teacher's guides. 2. Planning produces a mental image of the unit to be taught. 3. While teaching, the teacher tries to recall and enact this mental image of the plan (with very little of the plan on paper).
Yinger (1977)	Ethnography, observation, and interview	1 teacher of combined Grades 1 & 2	All	1. Five types of planning: yearly, term, unit, weekly, and daily. 2. The "activity" was the basic unit and starting point for planning. 3. Routines are used to simplify complexity for both teacher and students.

FUNCTIONS OF PLANNING

Findings from research on teacher planning suggest that teachers have as many reasons to plan as they have types of planning. Clark and Yinger (1979b) found that teachers' written responses to a question about why they plan fell into three clus-

ters: (a) planning to meet immediate personal needs (e.g., to reduce uncertainty and anxiety, to find a sense of direction, confidence, and security); (b) planning as a means to the end of instruction (e.g., to learn the material, to collect and organize materials, to organize time and activity flow); and (c) planning to serve a direct function during instruction (e.g., to organize students, to get an activity started, to aid memory, to provide a framework for instruction and evaluation).

In an ethnographic study of the planning of 12 elementary teachers, McCutcheon (1980) confirmed that some teachers plan to meet the administrative requirement that they turn in their plans to the school principal on a regular basis. These teachers also indicated that special plans were necessary for use by substitute teachers in the event of absence of the regular teacher. These plans for substitute teachers were special both because they included a great deal of background information about how "the system" in a particular classroom and school operated and because the regular teachers tended to reserve the teaching of what they judged to be important material for themselves, and they planned filler or drill and practice activities for the substitute teachers.

PLANNING AND THE CONTENT
OF INSTRUCTION

The most obvious function of teacher planning in American schools is to transform and modify curriculum to fit the unique circumstances of each teaching situation. In one of the only studies of yearly planning, Clark and Elmore (1981) asked a second grade teacher to think aloud while doing her yearly planning for mathematics, science, and writing. The teacher reported that the primary resources that she used in her yearly planning were curriculum materials (especially the teacher's guides), memory of classroom interaction during the previous year, and the calendar for the coming school year. Her process of yearly planning, typically done during the summer months, consisted of reviewing the curriculum materials that she would be using during the coming year, rearranging the sequence of topics within curricula, and adding and deleting content to be taught. A broad outline of the content to be taught and, to a lesser extent, of how it would be taught, emerged from a process of mental review of the events of the past year, combined with adjustment of the planned sequence and pace of teaching to accommodate new curriculum materials and new ideas consistent with her implicit theory of instruction. Through her review of the past year, reflection on her satisfaction with how things went, and modifications of the content, sequence, and planned pace of instruction, the teacher's yearly planning process served to integrate her own experiences with the published materials, establishing a sense of ownership and control of content to be taught (Ben-Peretz, 1975). Yearly planning sessions satisfied this teacher that she had available the resources to provide conditions for learning that would be at least equal to those that she had provided during the previous year. For this teacher, yearly planning decreased the unpredictability and uncertainty that attend every teaching situation.

The Clark and Elmore (1981) study of yearly planning supports the idea that published curriculum materials have a powerful influence on the content and process of teaching. In a study of teacher planning for sixth grade science instruction, Smith and Sendelbach (1979) pursued this idea at the level of unit planning. Working with the Science Curriculum Improvement Study (SCIS) science curriculum, Smith and Sendelbach compared explicit directions for a unit of instruction provided in the teacher's manual with four teachers' transformations of

those directions into plans, and finally with the actual classroom behavior of one of the four teachers while teaching the unit. Observation of the four teachers during planning sessions combined with analysis of think aloud and stimulated recall interview data revealed that the principal product of a unit-planning session was a mental picture of the unit to be taught, the sequence of activities within it, and the students' probable responses. These mental plans were supplemented and cued by sketchy notes and lists of important points that the teachers wanted to be sure to remember. Smith and Sendelbach characterized the process of activating a unit plan as one of reconstructing the plan from memory, rather than of carefully following the directions provided in the teacher's guide.

Smith and Sendelbach argued that the lack of a strong connection between the published curriculum and instruction created the potential for distortions or significant omissions in the content of science instruction. From their classroom observations of one experienced teacher implementing her unit plan, they concluded that the quality of instruction was degraded somewhat by both planned and unintended deviations from the SCIS curriculum. They attributed these deviations to the teacher's limited subject matter knowledge, difficulty in finding information in the teacher's guide, and to the presence of inherently complex and confusing concepts.

SUMMARY

Three points are of special interest concerning the types and functions of teacher planning. First, researchers on teacher planning have tended to focus on a single type of planning and to study teachers at only the elementary level. To fully understand the task demands of teaching and the ways in which teachers respond to these demands, researchers need to describe the full range of kinds of planning that teachers do during the school year and the interrelationships between these kinds of planning. Second, the modest-to-insignificant role of lesson planning reported by experienced teachers is interesting. Lesson planning is the one type of planning that is addressed directly in all teacher preparation programs. Yet lesson planning is rarely claimed as an important part of the repertoire of experienced teachers. Perhaps differences between expert and novice teachers dictate that teacher education focus heavily on lesson planning. But this anomaly may also indicate that some of our teacher preparation practices bow more to the task demands of the university calendar, methods courses, and supervision models than to those of the public school environment. Finally, the functions of teacher planning that are not directly and exclusively concerned with a particular instructional episode seem to have been slighted in the research literature. Researchers and teacher educators should think more broadly about what teachers are accomplishing in their planning time, and avoid narrow comparisons of what was planned with what was taught as the major criterion for evaluation of planning quality.

Models that Describe Teacher Planning

The second major goal of researchers on teacher planning is to create models that describe the planning process. The logic of an industrial production system underlies the most widely pre-scribed model for teacher planning, first proposed by Ralph Tyler (1950). This linear model consists of a sequence of four steps: (a) specify objectives; (b) select learning activities; (c) organize learning activities; and (d) specify evaluation procedures. This linear model has been recommended for use at all levels of educational planning, and thousands of educators have been trained in its use. It was not until 1970 that researchers began to examine directly the planning processes in use by teachers and to compare what was being practiced with what was prescribed. Table 9.2 summarizes the studies conducted by these researchers.

Taylor's (1970) study of teacher planning in British secondary schools was directed toward examining how teachers planned syllabi for courses. Using group discussions with teachers, analyses of course syllabi, and a questionnaire administered to 261 teachers of English, science, and geography, Taylor came to the following general conclusions: The most common theme in the teachers' course planning was the prominence of the pupil, especially pupil needs, abilities, and interests. Following the pupil as a focus of planning, in order, of importance, were the subject matter, goals, and teaching methods. In planning for courses of study, teachers attributed little importance to evaluation and to the relationship between their own courses and the curriculum as a whole.

Taylor described the course-planning process as one in which the teacher begins with the context of teaching; next considers learning situations likely to interest and involve pupils; and only after this, considers the purposes that teaching would serve. Taylor indicated that teachers gave minor importance to the criteria and procedures for evaluating the effectiveness of their course of teaching. Taylor concluded that in curriculum planning teachers should begin with the content to be taught and accompanying important contextual considerations (e.g., time, sequencing, resources). Teachers should then consider pupil interests and attitudes, aims and purposes of the course, learning situations to be created, the philosophy of the course, the criteria for judging the course, the degree of pupil interest fostered by the course, and finally, evaluation of the course.

Zahorik (1975) continued this line of inquiry in a study in which he asked 194 teachers to list in writing the decisions that they made prior to teaching, and to indicate the order in which they made them. He classified these decisions into the following categories: objectives, content, pupil activities, materials, diagnosis, evaluation, instruction, and organization. He found that the kind of decision mentioned by the greatest number of teachers concerned pupil activities (81%). The decision most frequently made first was content (51%), followed by learning objectives (28%). Zahorik concluded that teachers' planning decisions do not always follow linearly from a specification of objectives and that, in fact, objectives are not a particularly important planning decision in terms of quantity of use.

More recently, researchers have turned their attention to describing teacher planning by observing and audiotaping teachers' thinking aloud during planning sessions. Peterson, Marx, and Clark (1978) examined planning in a laboratory situation as 12 teachers prepared to teach a new instructional unit to small groups of junior high school students with whom they had had no previous contact. During their planning periods,

teachers were instructed to think aloud, and their verbal statements were later coded into planning categories including objectives, materials, subject matter, and instructional process. The primary findings of this study were: (a) Teachers spent the largest proportion of their planning time dealing with the content to be taught; (b) after subject matter, teachers concentrated their planning efforts on instructional processes (strategies and activities); and (c) teachers spent the smallest proportion of their planning time on objectives. All three of these findings were consistent with those by Zahorik (1975) and Goodlad and Klein (1970). The third finding was also similar to results reported by Joyce and Harootunian (1964) and by Popham and Baker (1970).

In interpreting the Peterson, Marx, and Clark (1978) study, we need to consider the task demands on the teachers. The researchers provided the teachers with unfamiliar materials from which to teach, and they limited preparation time to 90 minutes immediately preceding teaching on each day of the study. Because the teachers did not know their students in advance, the teachers may have placed more emphasis on content and instructional processes in their planning than would normally be the case. Finally, the researchers provided the teachers with a list of six general teaching goals, expressed in terms of content coverage, process goals, and cognitive and attitudinal outcomes for students. Under these circumstances, it is not surprising that the teachers devoted little planning time to composing more specific objectives and used the largest part of their planning time to study the content and decide how to teach it.

Morine-Dershimer and Vallance (1976) found results consistent with those of Peterson, Marx, and Clark. Morine-Dershimer and Vallance collected written plans for two experimenter-prescribed lessons (one in mathematics and one in reading) taught by 20 teachers of second and fifth grades in their own classrooms to a small group of their students. The researchers described teachers' plans in terms of (a) specificity of written plans, (b) general format of plans, (c) statement of goals, (d) source of goal statements, (e) attention to pupil background and preparation, (f) identification of evaluation procedures, and (g) indication of possible alternative procedures. Teachers tended to be fairly specific and use an outline form in their plans. Their written plans reflected little attention to behavioral goals, diagnosis of student needs, evaluation procedures, and alternative courses of action. However, the teachers reported that writing plans for researcher-prescribed lessons was not typical of their planning, and observations of their classroom teaching behavior revealed that much of what the teachers had planned was not reflected in their written outlines (Morine-Dershimer, 1979).

In his five-month field study of one teacher, Yinger (1977) drew on his observations, interview data, and think aloud protocols to create a theoretical model of the process of teacher planning. He viewed teacher planning as taking place in three stages. The first stage is a discovery cycle in which the teacher's goal conceptions, knowledge and experience, notion of the planning dilemma, and the materials available for planning interact to produce an initial problem conception worthy of further exploration. The second stage is problem formulation and solution. Yinger proposed that the mechanism for carrying out this process is the "design cycle." He characterized problem

Table 9.2. Ten Studies of the Planning Process: Summary of Findings

Study	Method of Inquiry	Teachers	Subject Matter	Principal Findings
Clark & Yinger (1979b)	Journal keeping, interviews, and observations	5 elementary teachers	Writing	Two styles of planning consistent with the general features of Yinger's model: 1. Comprehensive planning 2. Incremental planning
Favor-Lydecker (1981)	Think aloud	7 upper elementary teachers and four undergraduates	Social studies	Five different styles of planning
McLeod (1981)	Stimulated recall	17 kindergarten teachers	Various	1. Intended learning outcomes considered during planning, while teaching, and after teaching 2. Types of intended learning outcomes: Cognitive—57.7% Social/affective—35% Psychomotor/perceptual—7.2%
Morine-Dershimer & Vallance (1976)	Analysis of written plans for an experimenter-prescribed lesson	20 teachers of second and fifth grades	Reading and mathematics	1. Outline form for most plans; fairly specific 2. Little attention to behavioral goals, diagnosis of student needs, evaluation, or alternative courses of action
Neale, Pace & Case (1983)	Questionnaire and interview	19 elementary teachers and 9 student teachers	Elementary planning	1. Attitudes toward systematic planning model favorable by teachers and student teachers 2. Belief of experienced teachers that the systematic model is useful primarily for novices and, occasionally, when planning a new unit 3. Use by student teachers of systematic planning model only when required to
Peterson, Marx, & Clark (1978)	Think aloud; teaching in laboratory setting	12 junior high school teachers	Social studies	1. Largest proportion of planning time on *content* 2. Smaller proportion on instructional strategies and activities 3. Smallest on objectives
Sardo (1982)	Observation and interview	4 junior high school teachers	English, mathematics, social studies, Spanish/French	1. Least experienced teacher planned according to Tyler linear model 2. "Content" decisions most frequently made first in planning (51%), followed by learning objectives (28%)
Taylor (1970)	Group discussions, analysis of course syllabi, and exam questions	261 British secondary teachers	English, science, geography	1. Major focus of planning, in order of importance: (a) pupil needs, abilities, and interests; (b) subject matter; (c) goals; (d) teaching methods 2. Evaluation of little importance in course planning 3. Little concern for relationship of planned course to the curriculum as a whole
Yinger (1977)	Ethnography, observation, and interview	1 teacher of combined Grades 1 & 2	All	Three-stage cyclical planning model: 1. Problem finding 2. Problem formulation and solution 3. Implementation, evaluation, and routinization
Zahorik (1975)	Questionnaire	194 elementary teachers	Elementary planning	1. "Pupil activities" the most frequently reported focus of planning (81%) 2. "Content" decisions most frequently made first in planning (51%), followed by learning objectives (28%)

solving as a design process involving progressive elaboration of plans over time. Moreover, he proposed that elaboration, investigation, and adaptation are the phases through which teachers formulate their plans. The third stage of the planning model involves implementation, evaluation, and eventual routinization of the plan. Yinger emphasized that evaluation and routinization contribute to the teacher's repertoire of knowledge and experience which in turn play a major role in the teacher's future planning deliberations.

A significant contribution of Yinger's way of conceptualizing the planning process is that he proposes a cyclical rather than a linear model. He postulates a recursive design cycle similar to the processes hypothesized to go on in the work of architects, physicians, artists, designers, and other professionals. In addition, he acknowledges that schooling is not a series of unrelated planning-teaching episodes, but that each planning event can be influenced by prior planning and teaching experiences and that, potentially, each teaching event feeds into future planning and teaching processes. He represents the cycle as a continuous, yearlong process, in which the boundaries between planning, teaching, and reflection are not sharp and distinct.

In a further investigation of the Yinger model, Clark and Yinger (1979b) asked five elementary teachers to design and plan a 2-week unit on writing that the teachers had never taught before. The teachers kept journals documenting their plans and their thinking about planning during a 3-week period, and they were interviewed twice each week. The journal keeping and interviews continued and were supplemented by observations during the 2-week period when the teachers were implementing their plans.

Clark and Yinger described the teachers' unit planning as a cyclical process, typically beginning with a general idea and moving through phases of successive elaboration. This tendency of teachers to mentally visualize, elaborate, and modify their plans was further supported by data from a later study of teacher judgment while planning (Yinger & Clark, 1982, 1983). In that study, six teachers who thought aloud while making judgments about published language arts activity descriptions were seen to change and adapt the activity descriptions to fit their own teaching situations and experiences before passing judgment about the quality and usefulness of the activities.

Visualization of the teaching activity being enacted in the specific context of their own classrooms seemed to be an essential feature of the planning process for these experienced elementary school teachers. One could hypothesize that the availability of detailed knowledge structures about a particular teaching setting provides the experienced teacher with the tools for mentally trying out learning activities and distinguishes the expert planner from the novice.

In the Clark and Yinger (1979b) study of unit planning two of the teachers' unit plans consisted of a short problem finding stage, brief unit planning, and considerable reliance on trying out activities in the classroom. Clark and Yinger referred to this approach as "incremental planning" and described teachers who employed a series of short planning steps, relying heavily on day-to-day information from the classroom. They characterized the remaining three unit plans as products of "comprehensive planning," in which the teachers developed a thoroughly specified framework for future action. When compared with in-

cremental planning, comprehensive planning involved more attention to the unit as a whole, and more time and energy invested in specifying plans as completely as possible before beginning to teach. Both approaches to unit planning seemed to work well for the teachers who used them. Incremental planning saved time and energy while staying in touch with changing student states. Comprehensive planning providing a complete and dependable guide for teacher–student interaction for the whole course of a unit, reducing uncertainty and increasing the probability of achieving prespecified learning objectives.

This notion of "planning styles" of teachers was examined further by Sardo (1982). She found a relationship between individual differences in planning style and amount of teaching experience. Sardo studied the planning of four junior high school teachers who varied in teaching experience from 2 years to 30 years. The planning of the least experienced teacher consisted primarily of daily and lesson planning and followed the Tyler linear model most closely, while the more experienced teachers tended to be less systematic planners, to spend less time planning, and to concern themselves with planning the flow of activities for an entire week rather than with the fine details of each lesson.

Similarly, Favor-Lydecker (1981) studied the social studies unit planning styles of 17 teachers of upper elementary grades (4–6) and of four advanced undergraduate elementary education majors. Each of the 21 teachers thought aloud during a 2-hour planning session for a unit on ethnic heritage. Favor-Lydecker described five different planning styles that characterized the 21 unit plans: (a) teacher–student cooperative planning, (b) brainstorming, (c) list and sequence planning, (d) culminating event in sequence planning, and (e) culminating event as goal statement planning.

One recent study tested the possibility that the reported rarity of use of the Tyler model of planning might be due to inadequate training of teachers in its use or to unsupportive contextual factors. In an interview study, Neale, Pace, and Case (1983) contrasted student teachers ($n = 9$) and experienced elementary and special education teachers ($n = 19$) in their attitudes toward and use of the Tyler systematic planning model. They found that both undergraduates and experienced teachers expressed moderately favorable attitudes toward the systematic planning model, but that experienced teachers believed that it was useful mainly for student teachers and not for themselves. Five of the 19 experienced teachers reported using the systematic planning model only when developing a new unit, and the remaining 14 teachers reported that they did not use the model at all because they believed that it took too much time, was unnecessary, or was implicitly rather than explicitly included in their informal planning. The student teachers reported that they followed the systematic planning model closely when they were required to do so in planning two sample lessons, but, when not specifically required to, most reported not using this model in planning practice teaching lessons. The results of this study contradict the hypothesis that teachers do not use the systematic planning model because they are not well trained in its use or because the organizational environment is not supportive. Novice and experienced teachers alike demonstrated knowledge of the model, and the teaching environment (a mastery learning system) was organizationally supportive of it. Yet the systematic planning model was not the approach of choice for either beginning or experienced teachers.

McLeod (1981) provided a new perspective on the role of learning objectives in planning by asking not *whether* objectives are the starting point for planning but rather *when* teachers think about objectives. Working with 17 kindergarten teachers, McLeod conducted a stimulated recall interview with each teacher, using a videotape of a 20-to 30-minute classroom activity taught by the teacher earlier that same day. The purpose of the interviews was to determine (following Pylypiw, 1974) when teachers formulated intended learning outcomes in terms of four stages:

Preactive Stage 1:   Before planning activities or selecting materials

Preactive Stage 2:   After planning but before teaching

Interactive Stage 3:   During the act of teaching

Postactive Stage 4:   During reflection after a teaching episode

The interviews were also used to determine what types of intended learning outcomes (cognitive, social, and psychomotor) teachers formulated at each stage.

Averaging the responses across the 17 teachers, McLeod found that the largest percentage of intended learning outcomes was identified during Interactive Stage 3 (45.8%). This was followed by Preactive Stage 1 (26.5%), Preactive Stage 2 (19.5%), and Postactive Stage 4 (8.2%). The data also indicated that 57.7% of the intended learning outcomes were cognitive, 35% were social or affective, and 7.2% were psychomotor or perceptual. Interestingly, teachers reported identifying social–affective intended learning outcomes primarily during the interactive stage, and cognitive outcomes predominantly during the preactive and postactive stages.

Unfortunately, in her investigation, McLeod relied primarily on stimulated recall interviews. She could have supplemented the stimulated recall data to good effect with classroom observations and with thinking aloud techniques to describe the use of learning outcomes as it was happening. However, this research does much to broaden the concept of goals, objectives, or intended learning outcomes and their roles in planning and teaching. In earlier studies researchers tended to dismiss learning objectives as a rare and, therefore, unimportant element in teacher planning, even characterizing teachers as interested only in activities rather than in outcomes. McLeod's study suggests that teachers can and do think about and act to support both specific and general learning outcomes for their students and that it is hazardous to study the process of teacher planning in isolation from interactive teaching and postactive reflection.

The role of student learning outcomes in planning and teaching has been examined by several other researchers as well (e.g., Connelly, 1972; Eisner, 1967; Eisner & Vallance, 1974; Raths, 1971; Toomey, 1977; and Wise, 1976). The concensus seems to be that planning for teaching necessarily involves the teacher's intentions for learning, but that the degree of specificity and explicitness of these intentions varies with the teacher's conception of the teaching–learning process. Toomey (1977) found, for example, that compared with more process-oriented and student-centered teachers, teachers characterized as content and teacher control oriented tended to be very specific in their articulation of and use of student learning objectives.

Teacher Planning and Teachers' Classroom Behavior

The third and final question concerns the link between teacher planning and action in the classroom. Research has demonstrated that teachers' plans influence the content of instruction and the sequence of topics (e.g., Clark & Elmore, 1981; Smith & Sendelbach, 1979), as well as the time allocations to elementary school subject matter areas (Smith, 1977). Now we turn to the few studies that have examined how teachers' plans influence what happens in the classroom. Table 9.3 presents the principal findings of these studies.

Zahorik (1970) compared the effects of structured planning with the absence of structured planning on teachers' classroom behavior. He provided 6 of 12 teachers with a partial lesson plan containing behavioral objectives and a detailed outline of content to be covered 2 weeks hence. He requested that the remaining 6 teachers reserve an hour of instructional time to carry out a task for the researchers, not telling them that they were going to be asked to teach a lesson on credit cards until

Table 9.3. Four Studies of Links Between Planning and Action: Summary of Findings

Study	Method of Inquiry	Teachers	Subject Matter	Principal Findings
Carnahan (1980)	Analysis of written plans and classroom observations	9 teachers of fifth grade	Mathematics	Positive correlation between planning statements about small-group instruction and observed use of small-group instruction
Hill, Yinger, & Robbins (1981)	Observation, interview, and analysis of written plans	6 teachers of preschool		Planning concerned with selection of materials and arrangement of physical environment of classroom
Peterson, Marx, & Clark (1978)	Think aloud, observation	12 junior high school teachers	Social studies	Positive correlations between focus of planning behavior and focus of interactive teaching behavior
Zahorik (1970)	Classroom observation	12 elementary teachers	Lesson on credit cards	Teachers given plans 2 weeks in advance noted as behaving "less sensitively toward students" than teachers not given plans

just before the appointed time. Zahorik analyzed recorded protocols of the 12 lessons focusing on "teacher behavior that is sensitive to students" (p. 144). He defined this behavior as "verbal acts of the teacher that permit, encourage, and develop pupils' ideas, thoughts, and actions" (p. 144). In comparing the protocols of the planners and nonplanners, Zahorik judged that teachers who had been given plans in advance exhibited less honest or authentic use of the pupils' ideas during the lesson. He concluded from this that the linear planning model — goals, activities and their organization, and evaluation — resulted in insensitivity to pupils on the part of the teacher.

Unfortunately, Zahorik did not determine the degree to which the teachers who received the lesson plans in advance actually planned or elaborated the lesson. A competing explanation for these findings is that the teachers who had no advance warning about what they were to teach were forced by the demands of the task to concentrate on their students' ideas and experiences, while those teachers who knew the expected topic of instruction for 2 weeks prior to teaching were influenced to focus on the content rather than on their students.

In the Peterson, Marx, and Clark (1978) laboratory study of teacher planning, teaching, and student achievement described earlier in this chapter, a number of positive relationships emerged between the focus of teachers' planning statements and their classroom behavior. For all teachers, planning on the first of three days of teaching was heavily weighted toward the content to be covered. However, the focus of their planning shifted on Days 2 and 3, with planning for instructional processes becoming more prominent. The proportion of planning statements dealing with the learner was positively related to teacher behaviors classified as "group focused." The proportion of planning statements dealing with the content was positively and significantly correlated with teacher behavior coded as "subject matter focused." These findings suggest that teacher planning was related to the general focus or tone of interactive teaching, rather than to the specific details of verbal behavior. They also suggest that the nature of the work done during the preactive planning period changes with situation-specific teaching experience. As the task demands on the teacher change, so does the nature of appropriate preparation.

Carnahan (1980) studied the planning and subsequent behavior of nine fifth grade teachers while teaching the same 2-week mathematics unit. The quality of the teachers' written plans was determined by rating plans that focused on large groups as low in quality and plans that focused on individuals or small groups as high in quality. (This criterion was chosen because the curriculum materials that the teachers were using incorporated a similar bias.) Classroom observers rated instruction for teacher clarity, use of motivation strategies, and student engagement. The main result of interest here is that Carnahan found no statistically significant relationship between his ratings of plan quality and the ratings of teaching quality. However, he did find a significant positive correlation between the total percentage of written planning statements about small groups or individuals and the observed use of small groups in the classroom. This and other findings in Carnahan's report indicate that the main relationship between written plans and subsequent classroom interaction was in the domain of organization and structuring of teaching rather than in the domain of specific verbal behavior. During interactive teaching, the responses of students are unpredictable and therefore verbal dialogue may not be a profitable focus for teacher planning.

The influence of teacher planning on classroom behavior in the teaching of preschool children seems to be somewhat different from that observed in higher grades. Hill, Yinger, and Robbins (1981) studied the planning of six teachers who constituted the staff of a university developmental preschool. During a 10-week period, the researchers observed the teachers' Friday afternoon group planning sessions, staff meetings, conferences with student teachers, materials selection from the storeroom, and their arranging of their classroom environments. They also interviewed the teachers about their planning processes and copied planning documents and records.

Hill, Yinger, and Robbins found that much of the teachers' planning consisted of selecting and arranging manipulable materials. The school storeroom was an important source of teachers' ideas for learning activities. Once the teachers identified the appropriate materials, they then focused on how to arrange these materials in the classroom for use by the children and on how to manage the transitions into and out of these activities. The teachers spent 3 or more hours per week arranging the physical environments of their classrooms. When an activity did not go well, the teacher's first improvement strategy was to rearrange the physical environment. Because teaching in this setting depended so much on the materials selected and arranged by teachers, teacher planning had a substantial influence on the nature of the children's learning opportunities. Also, the demands of teaching appear to have influenced the nature of the planning process in this setting.

These four studies, taken together, suggest that teacher planning does influence opportunity to learn, content coverage, grouping for instruction, and the general focus of classroom processes. They also highlight the fact that the finer details of classroom teaching (e.g., specific verbal behavior) are unpredictable and therefore not planned. Planning shapes the broad outline of what is possible or likely to occur while teaching and is used to manage transitions from one activity to another. But once interactive teaching begins, the teacher's plan moves to the background and interactive decision making becomes more important.

Summary of Research on Teacher Planning

Research on teacher planning provides a direct view of the cognitive activities of teachers as professionals. This literature is almost exclusively descriptive and deals primarily with the planning of experienced elementary teachers. The research indicates that there are as many as eight different types of planning that teachers engage in during the school year. These types of planning are not independent, but are nested and interact with one another.

The curriculum as published is transformed in the planning process by additions, deletions, changes in sequence and emphasis, teachers' interpretations, and misunderstandings. Other functions of teacher planning include instructional time allocation for subject matters and for individuals and groups of students, study and review of the content of instruction by teachers, organization of daily, weekly, and term schedules, meeting administrative accountability requirements, and communicating with substitute teachers. Teachers also report that the planning process produces immediate psychic rewards in the form of feelings of confidence and reduction of uncertainty. Taken together, these findings suggest that teacher planning has direct connections with variables studied in the general literature of research on teaching such as structuring, opportunity to learn, and time-on-task. Teacher planning also seems to be an appropriate topic of inquiry for researchers studying implementation of educational innovations.

The task of modeling the planning processes of teachers is far from complete. The literature is in reasonable agreement that a narrowly construed version of the linear "rational planning model" does not describe the planning behavior of experienced teachers. But it is not clear whether the several styles and models of planning described by Favor-Lydecker, Toomey, Yinger, and others are functionally superior to the rational model. Furthermore, it may be that training novice teachers in use of a version of the rational model provides them with an appropriate foundation for developing a planning style compatible with their own personal characteristics and with the task environments in which they must teach. Continued study of the planning behavior of teachers might be more profitable if researchers shift to longitudinal designs and a cognitive-developmental framework instead of continuing to accumulate descriptions of the planning of experienced teachers.

Teacher planning reduces but does not eliminate uncertainty about teacher–student interaction. Classroom teaching is a complex social process that regularly includes interruptions, surprises, and digressions. To understand fully the operation of teacher planning, researchers must look beyond the empty classroom and study the ways in which plans shape teacher and student behavior and are communicated, changed, reconstructed, or abandoned in the interactive teaching environment. It is to teachers' thinking during the process of teaching that we now turn.

Teachers' Interactive Thoughts and Decisions

Researchers on teachers' thinking have attempted to describe the thinking that teachers do while interacting with students in the classroom. More specifically, researchers have been concerned with the extent to which teachers make interactive "decisions" that lead them to change their plans or their behavior in the classroom. For example, while teaching a lesson, a teacher may make a decision to continue with the teaching strategy that he or she had planned to use, or not to continue with the strategy as a result of a decision. Researchers have attempted to "map" the interactive decisions of teachers and describe the influences on teachers' interactive decisions as well as to ascertain the influence on and the cues that the teachers use to make interactive decisions. Finally, researchers have investigated the relationship between teachers' interactive thoughts and decisions, teachers' behavior, and student outcomes. An important question here is whether teachers who are "effective" in producing positive gains in student achievement

differ in their patterns of interactive decision making from teachers who are "less effective" in promoting student achievement.

In the following sections, we will review the research on teachers' interactive thoughts and decisions that has addressed each of the above topics. We will discuss findings on the broader topic of the content of teachers' interactive thoughts and then move to a more narrow focus on findings related to teachers' interactive decision making. First, we will provide an overview of the methodology used in these studies.

Overview of Studies Using Stimulated Recall Techniques to Study Teachers' Interactive Thoughts and Decisions

Table 9.4 presents a summary of the method and procedures of 12 research studies that used stimulated recall interviews to elicit self-reports of teachers' interactive thoughts and decisions. As can be seen from Table 9.4, the 12 studies varied considerably in the grade level and experience of the participants; the number and subject matter of the lessons that were videotaped and used in the stimulated recall interview; and the actual format of the stimulated recall interview. Eleven of the 12 studies were done with elementary teachers and students from Grades 1 through 6 while 1 study was done with seventh and eighth grade students. Although most studies included several teachers, each teaching more than one lesson, Wodlinger (1980) focused on only one teacher, and several investigators taped only one lesson for each teacher (Fogarty, Wang, & Creek, 1982; Morine & Vallance, 1975; Semmel, 1977). The subject matter of the lessons that were videotaped varied considerably across the 12 studies and included reading, language arts, spelling, mathematics, social studies, and physical education. To illustrate how the format of the stimulated recall interview differed across the 12 studies, we will describe 1 study and then use it as a basis for comparison.

In a laboratory study of teachers' interactive thoughts and decisions, Peterson, Clark, and Marx (Clark & Peterson, 1981; Marx & Peterson, 1981; Peterson & Clark, 1978) had 12 experienced teachers each teach a $2\frac{1}{2}$-hour social studies lesson to three groups of seventh and eight grade students. Teachers were videotaped while they were teaching. At the end of each lesson, each teacher viewed the videotape of the first 5 minutes of the first hour of teaching and three 1–3 minute segments of each hour of instruction to "stimulate recall" of their interactive thoughts during instruction. After viewing each of these four segments, the teacher responded to the following questions:

1. What were you doing in the segment and why?
2. Were you thinking of any alternative actions or strategies at that time?
3. What were you noticing about the students?
4. How are the students responding?
5. Did any student reactions cause you to act differently than you had planned?
6. Did you have any particular objectives in mind in this segment? If so, what were they?
7. Do you remember any aspects of the situation that might have affected what you did in this segment?

In contrast to the previous study and the study by Housner and Griffey (1983), where teachers viewed only selected segments of the videotape of their lessons, teachers viewed the entire videotape in eight studies (Conners, 1978b; Fogarty, Wang, & Creek; 1982; Lowyck, 1980; Marland, 1977; McNair, 1978-1979; Morine & Vallance, 1975; Shroyer, 1981; and Wodlinger, 1980), listened to the entire audiotape of their lesson in one study (Semmel, 1977), and viewed the entire videotaped lesson twice in one study (Colker, 1982). However, even in these studies where the interviewer played the entire tape to the teacher, the procedure differed according to whether the teacher selected the videotaped segments that were the focus of the interview (as in the Lowyck, Wodlinger, & Shroyer studies), whether the teacher and interviewer were both allowed to select segments that were the focus of the interview (as in the Conners, Fogarty et al., Marland, McNair, and Morine & Vallance, studies) or whether the interviewer selected the segments that were the focus of the interview (as in the Semmel & Conners studies). Moreover, in the Peterson, Marx, and Clark study and in the studies by Colker, Housner and Griffey; McNair, Morine and Vallance; and Semmel, teachers responded to a structured interview with a prespecified set of questions. In contrast, in the studies by Conners, Lowyck, Marland, Shroyer, and Wodlinger, the format of the stimulated recall interview was a clinical one in which a few general and specific questions were predetermined by the researchers, but the actual questions varied from interview to interview as determined by the interviewer.

Although the format of the stimulated recall interviews differed considerably across the 12 studies, the coding and analysis of the stimulated recall interviews were similar in all the studies. The teachers' responses to the interview were audiotaped and coded by categorizing each of the teacher's statements or "thoughts" into one of several categories. The number of complete thoughts in each category was then tallied and compared across content categories. We turn now to the findings from these studies.

The Content of Teachers' Interactive Thoughts

Six studies have described the content of teachers' interactive thoughts. These are: Marx and Peterson (1981), McNair (1978-1979), Colker (1982), Marland (1977); Conners (1978b), and Semmel (1977). Despite the variability in the methodology used in these six studies, the findings from the studies are remarkably similar. Table 9.5 presents the percentage of teachers' interactive thoughts by content category across the six research studies. In this table, we placed similar categories side by side so as to permit comparison of the percentage of teachers' interactive thoughts in similar categories across studies.

Several findings emerge from an examination of Table 9.5. First, a relatively small portion of teachers' reports of their interactive thoughts deal with instructional objectives. Teachers mentioned objectives only 14% or less of the time across the four studies that used objectives as a category. Examples of teachers' reports of interactive thoughts about objectives include:

"I wanted them to see the connection between the 'Sh' sound and the S-H, that they all had S-H's on them."
"I wanted them to identify the senses that they were using."

Second, a relatively small percentage of teachers' statements about their interactive thoughts deal with the content or the subject matter (5% to 14% across three studies). An example of such a statement is, "At this point here I wanted to focus in on the idea of Japan being today an industrial nation, rather than an agricultural nation."

Third, a relatively larger percentage of teachers' reports of their interactive thoughts deal with the instructional process including instructional procedures and instructional strategies. The percentage was amazingly similar —20% to 30%— across the five studies that used a category like "instructional process" in their content analysis. Some examples are:

"I thought after I explained it to her, 'I didn't make that very clear.'"
"I was also thinking that I couldn't ask them to come down to the carpet one group at a time."
"I was thinking that they needed some sort of positive reinforcement."
"At this point in the lesson I felt I had reviewed what we had already talked about yesterday."
"I was trying to guide her into the sounding without actually having to do it."

Fourth, all of the six studies found that the largest percentage of teachers' reports of their interactive thoughts were concerned with the learner. Examples included the following:

"I was thinking that they don't understand what they're doing."
"I was also thinking, 'Tricia's kind of silly right now. If I ask her, I probably won't get a straight answer.'"
"I expected him to get that."
"You can't always tell with kids you know, whether they're truly inattentive or whether they're just mulling over what has been going on."
"… So they were concentrating on that."
"… and nobody was listening at all."

In the studies by Marx and Peterson, McNair, and Colker, the percentage concerned with the learner was approximately 40%. In the study by Semmel (1977), the percentage was higher (60%), perhaps because this was the only study in which teachers were dealing with exceptional children (i.e., children with a severe reading difficulty) or perhaps because in this study each teacher was teaching only one child. In contrast, Colker (1982) found no significant differences between teachers' reports of interactive thoughts about learners in a tutoring situation compared to a small-group situation or a large-group situation. Thus, the greater focus on the learner in the Semmel study is probably due to the fact that the students were exceptional children or possibly to the fact that the teachers were preservice rather than in-service teachers.

In the studies by Marland and Conners, a small percentage of teachers' reports of their interactive thoughts were categorized as "Information: pupil." However, a further analysis of their data shows that a large proportion of teachers' statements about the learner were included in their four categories entitled

Table 9.4. Twelve Studies of Teachers' Interactive Thoughts and Decisions Using Stimulated Recall Interviews

Study	Participants		Setting	Number and Type of Lesson Videotaped	Format of Stimulated Recall Interview		
	Teachers	Students			Type of Videotaped Segments Used as Stimuli	Type of Interview	Coding and Analysis of Stimulated Recall Interview
Colker (1982)	Six experienced first and second grade teachers	Intact classes of the six teachers	Classroom	Three mathematics lessons: one to a single student; one to a small group; and one to a large group	Entire tape viewed twice: teacher stopped tape during first viewing; E stopped tape during second viewing	No questions (only teacher comments) during first viewing; structured questions during second viewing	"Thought units" tallied and categorized
Conners (1978b)	Nine teachers, 1 each from Grades 1, 3, and 6 in three schools in Canada; each with 2 or more years' experience	Intact classes of the nine teachers	Classroom	One 30–60-minute language arts lesson; one 30–60-minute social studies lesson	Same as Marland, except E "played a more active role" in selecting segments	Clinical interview with some specified open-ended questions	"Thought units" tallied and categorized; ecological factors and teachers' principles, beliefs, and rules identified and tallied
Fogarty, Wang, & Creek (1982)	Eight teachers from lab school, one preschool, and two experienced first and second grade teachers; four preservice elementary and one experienced third/fourth/fifth grade teachers	Small group of 5–8 students selected from each teacher's intact class	Classroom	One 15-minute lesson (six teachers taught a reading or language arts lesson; one taught mathematics; one taught social studies)	Teacher viewed entire videotape and stopped it when recalling any thoughts or decisions; E could also stop tape	Clinical interview with some specified "probe" questions	"Decisions" identified; aspects of decisions tallied and categorized
Housner & Griffey (1983)	Eight experienced elementary physical education teachers and eight preservice elementary physical education teachers	Four children, ages 7 to 9 years, not previously acquainted with the teachers	Laboratory	Two 24-minute lessons, one on soccer and one on basketball dribbling	Six 4-minute segments of each lesson selected by experimenter	Structured interview (same questions as Peterson & Clark)	"Decisions" categorized; aspects of decisions tallied and categorized
Lowyck (1980) (Also De Corte & Lowyck, 1980)	16 fifth grade teachers in Belgium	Intact classes of the 16 teachers	Classroom	One mathematics lesson and one geography lesson; topics provided by E. (Same for all teachers)	Teacher viewed entire videotape. (Interview lasted 3–5 hours and did not occur on same day as videotaping)	Clinical interview	Content analysis (specific procedures not specified)

Study	Subjects	Students	Setting	Task	Procedure	Interview	Analysis
Marland (1977) (Also Mackay & Marland, 1978)	Six teachers, 1 each from Grades 1, 3, and 6 in two schools in canada	Intact classes of the six teachers	Classroom	One 1-hour language arts lesson and one 1-hour math lesson	Teacher viewed entire videotape and decided when to stop the videotape and reflect on thought processes; E could also stop tape	Clinical interview	"Thought units" tallied and categorized; type and aspects of decisions tallied and categorized; "principles of teaching" identified
McNair (1978–1979)	10 teachers from one school in grades 1–5 with 3 years or more experience	Two intact reading groups (1 more able; 1 less able) in each teacher's class	Classroom	One reading lesson with each of the two groups three times during the year	Teacher viewed entire videotape and stopped it when he or she "made a decision," experimenter also stopped tape, both systematically and at random	Structured interview	"Thought units" tallied and categorized
Morine & Vallance (1975)	10 "more effective" and 10 "less effective" second grade teachers; 10 "more effective" and 10 "less effective" fifth grade teachers	12 students randomly selected from within each teacher's intact class	Classroom	One 20-minute reading lesson; topic and curriculum materials provided by E	Same as McNair (1978)	Structured interview (same questions as McNair)	"Decisions" identified and categorized; aspects of decisions tallied and categorized
Peterson & Clark (1978) (Also Marx & Peterson, 1981; Clark & Peterson, 1981)	12 experienced teachers	Three groups of eight randomly assigned seventh and eighth grade students not previously acquainted with the teachers	Laboratory	One 2½-hour social studies lesson taught to each of the three groups of students; curriculum materials provided by E	First 5 minutes of the lesson and three short segments randomly selected by E	Structured interview	"Thought units" tallied and categorized; "Decision paths" identified and categorized
Semmel (1977) (Also, Semmel, Brady & Semmel, 1976)	20 preservice special education teachers	One student tutee with a severe reading deficit assigned to each teacher	Classroom	One oral reading lesson was audiotaped	Entire tape played back; E stopped tape after each pupil "miscue"	Structured interview	"Statements" tallied and categorized
Shroyer (1981)	One female fourth/ fifth grade teacher; one male and one female fifth/sixth grade teacher; each with at least four years' experience	The three teachers' intact classes	Classroom	A 1–2-week mathematics unit on rational numbers	Teacher viewed entire tape and stopped tape to reflect on thoughts, feelings, and decisions	Clinical interview (similar to Conners)	"Critical moments" identified, tallied, and categorized
Wodlinger (1980)	One female sixth grade teacher in Canada with four years of teaching experience	The teacher's intact class of 26 students	Classroom	10 30–45-minute lessons (1 language arts, 3 mathematics, 3 reading, 2 spelling lessons; 1 group discussion)	Teacher viewed entire videotape and provided running account of interactive decisions	Clinical interview with "general" and "focused" questions	Decision-related data categorized into "thought units," "decisions," and aspects of decisions tallied and categorized

Table 9.5. Percentage of Teachers' Interactive Thoughts by Content Category Across Six Research Studies

Marx & Peterson Category	%	McNair Category	%	Colker Category	%	Marland Category	%	Conners Category	%	Semmel Category	%
Objectives	13.9	Objectives	2.9			Goal statements	2.7	Objectives	5.4		
		Content: facts and ideas	13.6					Content	5.5		
Content	6.5										
Instructional procedures	30.9	Procedures and task	28.8			Tactical deliberations	23.5	Instructional moves	21.7	Instruction and/or text	19.2
Materials	6.1	Materials	8.8								
Learner	42.2	Learner	39.1	Learner	41.4	[Total learner Information:	50.0]	[Total learner Information:	44.1]	Learner	59.6
						pupil	6.8	pupil	9.7		
								Mediation: pupil	1.3		
						Perceptions	15.6	Perceptions	15.8	Reiteration of behavior	21.1
						[about learner	14.4]	[about learner	12.6]		
						Interpretations	11.9	Interpretations	16.8		
						[about learner	11.6]	[about learner	15.2]		
						Anticipations	8.6	Expectations	4.3		
						[about learner	5.6]	[about learner	4.3]		
						Reflections	18.8	Self-awareness	7.7		
						[about learner	11.6]	[about learner	1.0]		
						Information: other	6.1	Information: other	1.0		
								Beliefs	4.4		
						Feelings	5.6	Feelings	6.5		
						Fantasy	0.1				
		Other than learner	58.6								
		Time	6.6								

"perceptions," "interpretations," "anticipations" ("expectations") and "reflections" ("self-awareness"). The percentage dealing with the learner in each of these four categories is indicated in brackets in Table 9.5. If one adds together the percentages about the learner in each of these four categories with the category of pupil information, then the total percentage of teachers' reports of interactive thoughts dealing with the learner in the Marland study is 50% — a percentage that comes close to the percentages reported in the other four studies. If one conducts the same analysis on the categories in the Conners study, one finds that the total percentage of teachers' statements about the learner including perceptions about the learner, interpretations about the learner, expectations about the learner, self-awareness about the learner, information and mediation about the learner, is 44.1%.

In sum, then, *in all of the six studies, the greatest percentage of teachers' reports of interactive thoughts were concerned with the learner.* If one looks only at the studies in which normal learners were taught, the percentage of interactive thoughts reported about the learner was between 39% and 50%.

While the results in Table 9.5 present a consistent picture of the percentage of teachers' reports of interactive thoughts that fall into each of several broad categories (i.e., objectives, content, instructional process, and learner), they also suggest that it may be useful to subdivide these categories into more specific categories. In contrast to the categories used by Marx and Peterson (1981) and McNair (1978-1979), Marland's (1977)

categories reflect more of a "cognitive processes" description of teachers' interactive thoughts:

Perceptions: Units in which the teacher reported a sensory experience (e.g., one that was seen or heard).

Interpretations: Units in which the teacher attached subjective meaning to this perception.

Anticipations: Speculative thoughts or predictions made interactively about what could, or was likely to, occur in future phases of the lesson.

Reflections: Units in which the teacher was thinking about past aspects of, or events in, the lesson other than what had been done.

Conners (1978b) and Lowyck (1980) used similar categories to describe teachers' interactive thoughts. These categories come closer to describing the *processes* that teachers engage in during teaching, and, as such, move us closer to a cognitive processing analysis of teaching similar to the analyses of human problem solving and decision making that have been conducted by cognitive psychologists (see, for example, Shulman & Elstein, 1975). Moreover, these results suggest that, in the future, researchers might construct a content by processes matrix of teachers' interactive thoughts. The content would reflect *what* the teacher is thinking about during interactive teaching (e.g., objectives, subject matter, instructional process, the learner, materials, or time) and the processes would reflect *how* the teacher is thinking about it (i.e., perceiving, interpreting, anticipating, or reflecting).

All the categories in Table 9.5 reflect interactive thoughts that are directly related to the teacher's task of teaching. With the possible exception of the category "fantasy," none of the categories suggests that teachers' thoughts ever include "off-task" thoughts such as thoughts about what they are going to do after school, or thoughts about their personal problems or personal life.[1] This is in distinct contrast to the content of students' reports of interactive thoughts during a stimulated recall interview. When students are shown videotaped segments of themselves in a teaching–learning situation, they freely admit to and describe off-task interactive thoughts (see, for example, Peterson, Swing, Braverman, & Buss, 1982; Peterson, Swing, Stark, & Waas, 1983).

Because it seems unlikely that teachers' interactive thoughts are always task relevant, and it seems likely that off-task thoughts would sometimes intrude, then the high frequency of task-relevant thoughts shown in Table 9.5 may be an artifact of the stimulated recall procedures that were used in these studies. If teachers have control over stopping the videotape and talking about their interactive thoughts, then they are likely to pick only those places where they are having task-relevant interactive thoughts. Moreover, because the interviewers did not convey to the teachers that it was acceptable to have "off-task" thoughts, the demand characteristics of the situation may have been such that the teachers felt obliged to report only interactive thoughts that were "on-task." Thus, teachers may have selectively recalled or reconstructed their reports of their interactive thoughts to reflect only task-relevant thinking.

Teachers' Interactive Decisions: Definition and Frequency

While some researchers have attempted to describe the content of teachers' interactive thoughts, other researchers have attempted to identify teachers' interactive "decisions." The rationale for such a focus on teachers' interactive decision making is best summarized in the following statement by Shavelson (1973):

> Any teaching act is the result of a decision, whether conscious or unconscious, that the teacher makes after the complex cognitive processing of available information. This reasoning leads to the hypothesis that the basic teaching skill is decision making. (p. 18)

The above quote by Shavelson suggests that each action of the teacher is based on an interactive decision by the teacher. However, because of the obvious methodological problems involved in any attempt to "probe the unconscious," most researchers have restricted their definitions and defined teachers' interactive decisions as a "conscious choice" by the teacher during classroom instruction. For example, Sutcliffe and Whitfield (1979) defined a decision as a conscious act that occurs when at least two alternatives are available—the choice to change behavior and the choice not to change behavior.

Similarly, Marland (1977) defined a decision as a conscious choice. However, Marland then used a more restrictive operational definition of an interactive decision. Marland coded a teacher's report of interactive thinking as an "interactive decision" only if it included all of the following: (a) explicit reference to consideration of alternatives, (b) evidence that the teacher made a selection and became committed to one of the alternatives, and (c) evidence that the teacher followed through in the lesson with that choice of alternatives. Marland's category of a "deliberate act" appears to reflect more closely a broader conception of an interactive decision as a conscious choice. Marland categorized a teacher's interactive thoughts as a "deliberate act" whenever a teacher saw the need for some action or response but considered only one course of action or whenever a teacher reported taking a certain course of action and then stated the reason for doing so. Thus, by combining "deliberate acts" with Marland's category of "interactive decisions," we would argue that Marland (1977) and Sutcliffe and Whitfield (1979) appear to be in agreement on what constitutes an interactive decision: a teacher's conscious choice between continuing to behave as before or behaving in a different way.

Moreover, Morine and Vallance (1975), Fogarty, Wang, and Creek (1982), Wodlinger (1980), and Shroyer (1981) also agree with this definition. Morine & Vallance (1975) directed the teachers in their study to identify points on the videotape during the stimulated recall interview where the teacher remembered consciously saying to himself or herself, "Let's see, I think I'd better do *this* now," or "I guess I'll try doing this" (Morine & Vallance, 1975, p. 49). Fogarty et al. (1982) asked the teacher to stop the tape at any point where he or she recalled any thoughts or decisions.

Similarly, Wodlinger (1980) defined an interactive decision as consisting of statements or units in which the teacher's thoughts were focused upon the delivery of instructional material or student learning and in which the teacher mentioned the consideration of choice behavior as in the following:

> They weren't too sure yesterday, and they had problems with this stuff, so (I thought I would go back and ask those particular people, that were having problems yesterday.) So with Laura and Steve, you know, (I specifically asked them a question just to see if they were able to understand them from yesterday.) (p. 282)

To be coded as an interactive decision, Wodlinger indicated that the teacher must have reported a deliberate choice to implement a specific new action.

Shroyer's (1981) category of "elective action" also fits into the above definition of teachers' interactive decisions. Shroyer first identified what she called "student occlusions." She defined a student occlusion as a student difficulty or unexpected student performance in the classroom. She then argued that when confronted with a student occlusion, a teacher elects to respond with some action. She further indicated that her term "elective action" was what she meant by a decision, but that she chose this term as an alternative to "decision" because "decision has traditionally implied the consideration of alternatives, a process

---

[1] Thanks to Gregory Waas for this observation.

Table 9.6. An Analysis Across Five Studies of the Frequency of Teachers' Reported Interactive Decisions

Study	Category Name	Mean Frequency Per Lesson	Average Length of Lesson in Minutes	Estimated Number of Decisions (Acts) Per Minute	Range Across Teachers of Mean Decisions (Acts) Per Lesson	Range of Mean Decisions (Acts) Across Lessons and Teachers
Fogarty, Wang, & Creek (1982)	Interactive decisions	8.4	15	0.56	4 to 11	———[a]
Morine & Vallance (1975)	Interactive decisions	11.9	20	0.59	———[a]	———[a]
Marland (1977)	Total of interactive decisions and deliberate acts	28.3	60	0.47	10 to 36	6 to 43
Wodlinger (1980)	Interactive decisions	24.1	35	0.69	———[b]	15 to 33
Shroyer (1981)	Elective actions	22.2	45	0.49	8 to 36	———[a]

[a] Information not provided in written report.
[b] $N = 1$; no range can be computed.

for which research on interactive teacher thoughts has found little support" (Shroyer, 1981, p. 10).

These investigators have converged on a definition of an interactive decision as a deliberate choice to implement a specific action. Given this definition then, we can ask the question, "What is the frequency of teachers' reported interactive decisions?" Table 9.6 presents five studies that report results that address this question. In spite of the variations in methodology employed in these five studies (see Table 9.4), the findings reported in Table 9.6 are remarkably consistent. Across the studies, the estimated number of interactive decisions made by teachers ranged from .5 to .7 per minute. The results of these studies are consistent in suggesting that, on the average, *teachers make one interactive decision every 2 minutes.* Thus, these data suggest that the decision-making demands of classroom teaching are relatively intense.

Teachers' Consideration of Alternative Courses of Action

The above results on the prevalence of teachers' interactive decisions are in sharp contrast to statements by others, such as MacKay and Marland (1978) and Lowyck (1980), who have indicated that teachers' interactive decision making during instruction does not occur as frequently as was expected. This discrepancy may be due to the fact that, originally, some researchers such as Peterson and Clark (1978) suggested that teachers' decision making during interactive teaching involved teachers' considering two or more alternative courses of action when they observed that the lesson was not going well. This conceptualization followed from Snow's (1972) description of teacher thinking during classroom instruction as a cyclical process of observation of student behavior, followed by a judgement of whether student behavior is within desirable limits, followed, in turn, by a decision to continue the teaching process unchanged or to search memory for alternative teaching behavior that might bring student behavior back within the limits of tolerance. If no alternatives are available in memory, the teacher would continue the classroom behavior as previously; if the search yielded a plausible alternative, the teacher might decide to act on that alternative by changing the course of instruction, or might ignore the alternative and continue as before.

THE PETERSON AND CLARK MODEL

Peterson and Clark (1978) presented a model of this sequence of events. This model of a teacher's decision processes during teaching is presented in Figure 9.2. In addition, Peterson and Clark (1978) identified four alternative paths through the model. These paths are summarized in Table 9.7. In Path 1, the teacher judges students' classroom behavior to be within tolerance. In other words, the teacher judges that the students are understanding the lesson and are participating appropriately. In Path 2, the teacher judges that students' classroom behavior

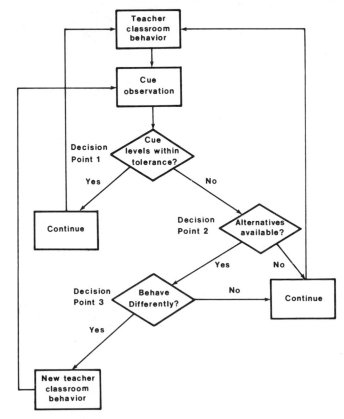

Fig. 9.2. Peterson and Clark's (1978) model of teacher interactive decision making.

Table 9.7 Four Alternative Paths for Teacher Information Processing During Instruction

Decision points	Path 1	Path 2	Path 3	Path 4
Student behavior within tolerance	Yes	No	No	No
Alternatives available?	—	No	Yes	Yes
Behave differently?	—	—	No	Yes

Note. From Peterson & Clark (1978), p.556.

is not within tolerance. For example, the teacher may judge that the students are either not understanding the lesson or perhaps are being inappropriately disruptive or withdrawn. However, there are no alternative strategies or behaviors in the teacher's behavioral repertoire. In Path 3, the teacher again judges that students' behavior is not within tolerance, and the teacher has alternative strategies or behaviors available in the teaching repertoire, but decides not to change teaching behavior to attempt to bring student behavior back within tolerance. Finally, in Path 4, the teacher judges that students' behavior is not within tolerance, but alternative teaching strategies are available, and the teacher decides to behave differently to bring student behavior back within the limits of tolerance.

Peterson and Clark (1978) categorized the reports of the cognitive processes of 12 teachers and found that the greatest majority of teachers' reports of their cognitive processes could be categorized as Path 1. The average proportion of Path 1 ranged from 71% to 61% across the 3 days of teaching. Peterson and Clark argued that because the cyclical repetition of Path 1 represented a teacher's report of conducting "business as usual," it was not surprising that teachers' reports most frequently followed this path. As one teacher put it when he was asked if he was thinking of any alternative actions or strategies, "At this point? No. None at all. It was going along. The only time I think of alternative strategies is when something startling happens" (Peterson & Clark, 1978, p. 561).

Teachers reported considering alternative strategies in only 20% to 30% of the cases across the 3 days of instruction. This latter result is consistent with the findings of other investigators. For example, of the average of 28.3 interactive decisions and deliberate acts reported by the teachers in Marland's (1977) study, only 24% (6.8) of them involved the teacher's explicit reference to considering one or more alternatives and evidence that the teacher followed through with his choice of alternatives.

Some discrepancy exists between the findings of investigators who have attempted to determine *how many* alternative courses of action teachers tend to consider when they consider changing their behavior during interactive teaching. In their study of 18 second grade teachers and 20 fifth grade teachers, Morine and Vallance (1975) found that teachers considered an average of three alternative courses of action. Marland (1977) found that in the vast majority of interactive decisions, teachers reported considering only two alternatives. In his study of one teacher, Wodlinger (1980) found that the teacher considered only one course of action for the majority of her interactive decisions.

These data on the relative infrequency with which teachers consider alternative courses of action during interactive teaching as well as the results which suggest that when teachers do consider alternative courses of action, they do not consider many alternatives, suggest that the model proposed by Peterson and Clark (1978) may not be an accurate reflection of the decision-making processes that teachers engage in during interactive teaching. Shavelson and Stern (1981) proposed an alternative model that was based on the work of Joyce (1978–1979), Peterson and Clark (1978), Shavelson (1976), and Snow (1972). This model is shown in Figure 9.3.

THE SHAVELSON AND STERN MODEL

Shavelson and Stern based their model on the assumption that teachers' interactive teaching may be characterized as carrying out well-established routines. Research on teacher planning suggests that teachers form a mental image that is activated from memory as a plan for carrying out interactive teaching. (See the section on teacher planning earlier in this chapter for a further discussion of this research.) Shavelson and Stern (1981) argue:

> These images or plans are routinized so that once begun, they typically are played out, much as a computer subroutine is. Routines minimize conscious decision making during interactive teaching and so "activity flow" is maintained. Moreover, from an information-processing perspective, the routinization of behavior makes sense. Routines reduce the information-processing load on the teacher by making the timing and sequencing of activities and students' behavior predictable within an activity flow. (p. 482)

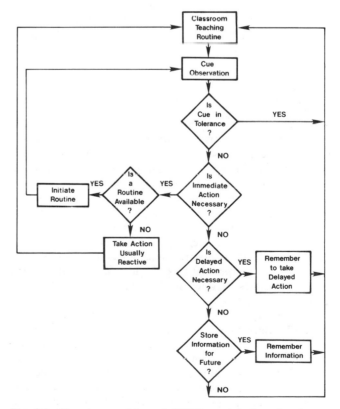

Fig. 9.3. Shavelson and Stern's (1981) model of teacher interactive decision making.

Indeed, the idea that during interactive teaching, teachers follow "routines" did not originate with Shavelson and Stern, but has been suggested by several researchers including Yinger (1977), Morine-Dershimer, (1978–1979), and Joyce (1978–1979). Shavelson and Stern's (1981) unique contribution is in presenting a model in which decision making during interactive teaching is portrayed as occurring when the teaching routine is interrupted (see Figure 9.3). As in the Peterson and Clark (1978) model, the teacher's decision-making process involves the observation of cues and the determination of whether the cues (student behaviors) are within tolerance. However, Shavelson and Stern propose that if student behavior is not within tolerance, the teacher then decides whether immediate action is necessary. If immediate action is necessary, the teacher then decides whether an alternative routine is available and if so to initiate that routine; whether delayed action may be used rather than immediate action; or whether to continue the classroom teaching routine as before.

An advantage of the Shavelson and Stern model is that it incorporates the idea of "routine" as an important concept to explain teachers' interactive teaching behavior and decision making, and it also incorporates the finding that teachers, for the most part, do not consider a large number of alternative courses of action but may consider only one alternative teaching routine as an alternative course of action. But the Shavelson and Stern model, like the Peterson and Clark (1978) model, still assumes that the only antecedent for the teacher's interactive decision is observation of student "cues" and the judgment that students' behavior is not within tolerance. We turn now to research that has investigated the antecedents of teachers' interactive decision making and examined the extent to which observation of student cues serves as the antecedent of teachers' interactive decision making.

Antecedents of Teachers' Interactive Decisions

Marland (1977) investigated the antecedents of teachers' reported interactive decisions. He found that 44% of teachers' reported interactive decisions and deliberate acts occurred in response to a judgment by the teacher that students' behavior was not within tolerance. These indications were (a) student deviance, noise, restlessness, inattentiveness, or disruption (antecedents of 20% of teachers' reported interactive decisions and deliberate acts); (b) incorrect, unsatisfactory, delayed, or incomplete student response or work (antecedents of 19.5% of teachers' reported interactive decisions and deliberate acts); and (c) students' apparent lack of understanding (antecedents of 3% of teachers' reported interactive decisions and deliberate acts).

For the purposes of this discussion, the most important point is that Marland found that the majority of teachers' reported interactive decisions occurred not in response to an observation by the teacher that student behavior was not within tolerance but rather occurred in response to other factors. Teachers reported making interactive decisions in response to a student question or a student-created contact with the teacher (19% of the reported interactive decisions); when a choice of respondent, participant, or student to be helped was needed (10%

of the decisions); when a choice of appropriate techniques was needed (6% of the decisions); when there was a transition point in the lesson from one activity to another (8% of the decisions); when the teacher anticipated a problem or a difficulty (2% of the decisions); and other miscellaneous factors including insufficient time left in the lesson (5% of the decisions), shortage of materials (4% of the decisions) and late arrival of aides (1% of the decisions). In addition, Marland found that the majority of teachers' reported deliberate acts did not occur in response to student behavior but rather in response to other factors. A large percentage of teachers' reported deliberate acts (29%) involved the teacher's selection of a student respondent or participant, selection of a specific teaching technique, or selection of appropriate examples in content. Also, a number of deliberate acts occurred in response to a student initiated comment, question, or contact (11%).

In his study of a single teacher, Wodlinger (1980) also found that 51% of the teacher's reported interactive decisions had antecedents that originated with the teacher or the environment rather than with the student. Wodlinger reported that 16% of the teacher's reported interactive decisions originated with the teacher's cognitive state or affective state. This occurred when the teacher's thoughts or feelings were the stimuli for the formulation of an interactive decision. The following excerpt from a stimulated recall protocol illustrates this category of interactive decisions: "*I was mad. I was very cross*, because, um, Michael had lost his math book and … and I was trying to decide what I was going to do about it, ah, at that point. I thought of some alternatives and thought 'Well, this isn't the time to deal with it,' so I sort of left it" (Wodlinger, 1980, p. 116).

In addition, the environment, including time constraints, interruption by another adult, and instructional material and equipment, served as antecedents for 35% of the teacher's reported interactive decisions. The antecedents for the remaining reported interactive decisions (49%) did involve observation of student cues including the teacher's assessments and estimates of student behavior, student cognition, student affect, and other student characteristics, as well as the teacher's judgment of the progress of the lesson and the lesson strategies that she was employing.

Similarly, Fogarty et al. (1982) found that, although cues from students served as antecedents for the majority of teachers' reported interactive decisions (64%), "non-student" cues served as antecedents for a large part of teachers' reported interactive decisions. Finally, although Housner and Griffey (1983) found that teachers' observations of student behavior served as antecedents of 85% of teachers' reported interactive decisions, this uncharacteristically high percentage probably reflects the fact that the stimulated recall interview included a specific question on whether teachers' observations of student behavior caused the teacher to behave differently than planned.

The results of a policy capturing study by Shavelson, Atwood, and Borko (1977) also support the conclusion that factors other than teachers' judgments about students may serve as antecedents for teachers' interactive decisions. Shavelson et al. presented 164 graduate students in education (about two-thirds of them teachers) with a description of a fictitious student named Michael. Sixteen different stories were constructed about Michael and presented to the subjects. These stories contained initial and additional information about Michael which varied in valence (Michael was portrayed as high or low in ability and effort) and in terms of reliability (the information was presented so that one could infer it was either reliable or unreliable). Each subject read only one description of Michael. After reading the description, the subject was asked to make one simulated preinstructional decision and two simulated interactive decisions. The results indicated that when subjects were asked to make an interactive decision that consisted of deciding what they would do if the student failed to answer a question during a mathematics lesson, the subjects considered the information about the student and the ability estimate irrelevant to their interactive decision. A similar picture emerged when the subject was asked to make an interactive decision about reinforcement strategies for Michael. Again, the information about the student presented in the scenario had little effect on the subjects' reported interactive decision. The authors concluded that subjects' interactive decisions depended on information that was not measured in this experiment.

Although the findings from the Shavelson et al. study support the conclusion that factors other than teachers' judgments about students may contribute to teachers' interactive decisions, these results should be interpreted with caution. Subjects' responses to a questionnaire may not bear any resemblence to teachers' interactive decision making during an actual classroom situation. In addition, in simulations of this type, subjects are limited to the information provided (in this case information on the ability and effort of Michael). By limiting the available student "cues" the researchers may have artificially restricted the natural variance in subjects' decisions. (See, e.g., Clark, Yinger, & Wildfong, 1978; Yinger & Clark, 1983.) In addition, the antecedent of a teacher's interactive decision as postulated in the Peterson and Clark model is the teacher's observation of the student's behavior rather than the teacher's judgments of the student's "states of mind" (characteristics such as ability and effort) which were the antecedents that were varied in the Shavelson et al. study. Thus, perhaps if student *behavior* had been varied, then subjects' judgments of student behavior may have affected subjects' reported interactive decisions. This hypothesis is supported by the results of a study by Cone (1978).

In a policy capturing study in which 50 teachers were presented with a description of a fictitious student, Cone (1978) found that the type of deviant student behavior had a significant effect on the teachers' reported managerial decisions. Teachers selected more severe managerial strategies for student behavior that was more severe than for student behavior that was less severe (in order from most severe to less severe: physical aggression, speaking out, out of seat, and noise). However, the way the student was characterized—as having a history of deviancy or as having no history of deviancy—also affected the teachers' reported managerial decisions. Teachers selected more severe managerial strategies for deviant students with a history of deviancy than for students with no history of deviancy. These results confirm that teachers' judgments of student behavior may be an important antecedent of teacher' interactive decisions. However, the question still remains as to why student characteristics were not importantly related to teachers' reported interactive decisions in the Shavelson et al. study, but

they were importantly related to teachers' interactive decisions in the Cone study.

A possible explanation is that students' behavior and characteristics are more importantly related to teachers' interactive decisions that are concerned with classroom management than teachers' interactive decisions that are concerned with instruction. In his study of one teacher, Wodlinger (1980) found that students were the antecedents for more of teachers' reported interactive decisions that dealt with classroom management (54%) than teachers' interactive decisions that dealt with instruction (46%). When Wodlinger examined the type of information that the teacher used in making interactive decisions, he found that observed student behavior more frequently served as information used by the teacher in making managerial decisions (34% of the time) than in making instructional decisions (17% of the time).

Toward a New Model of Teacher Interactive Decision Making

Considering the above research findings, we would suggest that neither Peterson and Clark's (1978) nor Shavelson and Stern's (1981) models of interactive decision making are sufficient. Both models need to be revised to reflect two important points. First, a model of teacher interactive decision making should reflect the definition of interactive decision making as a deliberate choice to implement a specific action rather than a choice of actions from several possible alternatives. Second, a model of teacher interactive decision making should reflect the finding that the majority of teachers' reported interactive decisions are preceded by factors other than judgments made about the student. These factors might include judgments about the environment, the teacher's state of mind, or the appropriateness of a particular teaching strategy. Thus, while a large proportion of a teacher's interactive decisions do seem to occur as a result of a teacher's judgment about student behavior, a model that focuses only on student behavior as the antecedent of teacher interactive decisions (as in the Peterson & Clark, and Shavelson & Stern models) does not accurately portray the processes involved in teacher interactive decision making.

Further specification of a model of teachers' interactive decision making requires research on the process whereby a given antecedent condition influences a teacher's interactive decisions. For example, in their models, Peterson and Clark (1978) and Shavelson and Stern (1981) assumed not only that student behavior was the sole antecedent of teachers' interactive decisions, but they also assumed a "threshold" mechanism whereby student behavior affected teachers' interactive decisions. In other words, a teacher was assumed to make an interactive decision only when student behavior was judged by the teacher to be beyond a given "threshold" at which point the teacher judged that student behavior was not within tolerance. Although in proposing their models, these researchers assumed a threshold mechanism whereby student behavior affected teacher interactive decision making, no research has been done to determine whether this is really the case. Research is needed to describe the process whereby a given antecedent condition results in an interactive decision by the teacher. Such studies might employ a process-tracing approach similar to the one used by Yinger (1977) in his study of a teacher's planning throughout a school year. Future models of teachers' interactive decision making also need to take into account the finding by Wodlinger (1980) that more than one antecedent often serves to stimulate the teacher's formulation of an interactive decision.

Specification of models of teacher interactive decision making by Peterson and Clark (1978) and Shavelson and Stern (1981) may have been premature. Calderhead (1981) suggested that such models may be overly constraining. Indeed, we now argue that these models may have led research on interactive decision making in the wrong direction because they assumed that student behavior was the only antecedent condition for teachers' interactive decisions and that teachers consider several possible alternatives, strategies, or courses of action when making an interactive decision. We would suggest, therefore, that before specifying a new model or revising the existing models of teacher interactive decision making, researchers should first do more descriptive research on how teachers make interactive decisions. Specification of a new model of teacher interactive decision making should await the findings from this research. Obviously, such an approach assumes a *descriptive* focus on teacher interactive decision making. At some point, we may want to be *prescriptive*. In other words, researchers may determine that more "effective teachers" are those who focus on student behavior as the primary antecedent condition for making an interactive decision. We turn now to this issue of teacher effectiveness and teacher interactive decision making.

Teacher Effectiveness and Teachers' Interactive Decision Making

Much research on teaching has been devoted to identifying the behaviors of effective teachers with the intent of using the findings to increase teachers' effectiveness. (See, for example, Brophy & Good, this volume; Dunkin & Biddle, 1974; Peterson & Walberg, 1979). Thus, one might ask the question, "What kinds of interactive decision making do effective teachers engage in?" or, "What constitutes effective interactive decision making by a teacher?" Although, as we shall see, little empirical research has been directed toward answering these questions, several researchers have attempted to conceptualize the interactive decision making of an effective teacher.

Doyle (1979) described an "idealized strategy" for a teacher's information processing. He suggested that at the beginning of the school year, the effective teacher consciously directs attention toward gathering information about a particular classroom group (e.g., the steering group). To gather this information, the teacher implements a limited number of activities that have become "automatized" or routinized for the teacher. Given the routinized nature of these activities, the teacher can then direct "conscious processing" of classroom events toward observing and monitoring "behavior task initiations by students" (e.g., off-task or misbehavior by students). As the students learn the classroom routines, the teacher can introduce more activities that then, in turn, become routinized. Concurrently, the teacher's conscious processing becomes fine tuned and efficient. Eventually all regular activities will be routinized, including administrative operations, recurring lessons,

and even instructional moves. The teacher's conscious processing will then be available for specialized purposes such as scanning the room periodically, monitoring particular students or groups of students in the classroom, and solving problems in areas that cannot be routinized. As Doyle (1979) put it,

> In view of the frequency and the cost — in terms of reaction time and consequences — of unexpected events, it would seem adaptive and efficient for a teacher to direct conscious processing primarily to discrepancies or anomalies. By specializing in discrepancies, a teacher can anticipate disruptions and reduce the effects of immediacy and unpredictability on task accomplishment. (pp. 62–63)

A similar picture of effective information processing during interactive teaching has been presented by Joyce (1978–1979) and Corno (1981). Corno, for example, argued that effective classroom teachers ought to be consciously engaged in information processing. Teachers should be attending to and observing students' faces, actions, behavior, and voices. They should "see, hear, and then organize and check their perceptions to pace and maintain the flow of instruction and help accomplish instructional objectives" (Corno, 1981, p. 369).

Empirical Research on the Relationship of Teachers' Interactive Decision Making to Student On-Task Behavior and Achievement. Only three empirical studies, Peterson and Clark (1978), Doyle (1977a), and Morine and Vallance (1975), have attempted to describe the thought processes and decisions of effective teachers during interactive teaching. Peterson and Clark (1978) and Morine and Vallance (1975) used the criterion that has been used typically to define effective teachers, namely, students' scores on an achievement test. In contrast, Doyle (1977a) used student classroom behavior as the criterion. He defined successful teachers as those who maintained high levels of student work involvement and low levels of disruptions in their classrooms.

The first study is the one by Peterson and Clark (1978) described previously. Peterson and Clark categorized teachers' reports of their cognitive processes during interactive teaching into one of four paths and then related teachers' scores on the paths to students' achievement scores. (See Figure 9.2 and Table 9.7.) One might argue that a more "effective" path for teacher information processing during instruction would be Path 4, while a less "effective" path for teacher information processing would be Path 3. In other words, one might hypothesize that when effective teachers observe that student behavior during classroom interaction is not within tolerance, they first consider whether alternative teaching strategies or behaviors are available in their repertoire. If so, they then decide to behave differently and to engage in new classroom behavior to bring student behavior back within the level of tolerance. This information-processing path (Path 4) appears to reflect the kind of processing that a successful classroom manager would engage in as indicated by Doyle (1979). Doyle (1979) suggested that the teacher who is a successful classroom manager recognizes "behavior task initiations" (e.g., classroom misbehavior) immediately and intervenes early. This early intervention has the advantage of neutralizing misbehavior before the student's peers in the classroom "reward" the behavior or before public consequences occur. In contrast, failure by the teacher to initiate action that would bring student behavior back within tolerance (Path 3) would define an ineffective classroom manager as described by Doyle and might be considered to constitute ineffective teaching.

In support of the latter conclusion, Peterson and Clark (1978) found that teachers' scores on Path 3 were significantly negatively related to students' achievement scores. Teachers whose reports of information processing during interactive teaching were most often categorized as Path 3 had students who achieved lower scores on a multiple choice achievement test ($r = -.50$, $p < .05$, one-tailed test) as well as on the factual content of an essay test ($r = -.64$, $p < .05$, one-tailed test). On the other hand, teachers' scores on the other paths (Path 1, Path 2, or Path 4) were not significantly related to students' achievement scores.

Interestingly, Peterson and Clark (1978) also reported information about the planning of these same teachers. They found a significant positive correlation ($r = .51$, $p < .05$), one-tailed test) between teachers' planning statements about objectives and scores on Path 3. If a teacher reported having alternative teaching strategies in mind but did not report behaving differently, it may have been because the teacher saw him or herself as pursuing an instructional objective borne in mind as the result of planning. Thus, a teacher's reported decision not to behave differently may have been a logical one based on instructional objectives that the teacher had established during planning. This interpretation is consistent with the findings of a study by Zahorik (1970) in which teachers who had 2 weeks to prepare a lesson were rated as less flexible and more rigid than teachers who had had no opportunity to plan. However, even though the teachers' information processing may have had a logical basis, the present data still indicate that teachers who reported that student behavior was outside tolerance, but who reported that they did not change their behavior, tended to be less effective teachers — to have students who achieved less.

In the second study, Doyle (1977a) observed 58 student teachers for the full duration of their student teaching assignments, which ranged from 8 to 16 weeks. He observed each student teacher for one class period each week. He used an ecological approach in taking field notes and in writing classroom descriptions. The findings showed that, compared to unsuccessful teachers, successful teachers had the following cognitive skills: (a) rapid judgement, (b) chunking, and (c) differentiation. Successful teachers learned to make rapid judgments during interactive teaching. To simplify and deal with the demands created by the complex classroom environment, successful teachers used chunking, or the ability to group discrete events into larger units, and to differentiate or discriminate among units in terms of their immediate and long-term significance.

This definition of "differentiation" is what Corno (1981) referred to as "selectivity." Corno argued that effective teachers engage in the cognitive process of selectivity — separating out important from salient incidental information — during interactive teaching. Similarly, Doyle's categories of chunking and rapid judgment are included in Corno's category of "transformation." Transformation of information involves the processes of comparison, integration, rehearsal, and elaboration. In sum,

then, the research findings from the study by Doyle (1977a) confirm the portrayal of the effective teacher as one who engages actively in cognitive processing of information during teaching but who engages in specific kinds of processes, such as chunking and differentiation, which enable the teacher to simplify and make sense of the complex classroom environment.

In support of this latter statement, Morine and Vallance (1975) found that less effective teachers mentioned specific aspects of their decisions more frequently and referred to more items of information that they used in making their decisions than did more effective teachers. In other words, less effective teachers reported having more things in mind as they discussed their interactive decisions during a stimulated recall interview. (See Table 9.4 for a description of the study and the method.) In this study, more effective teachers were defined as those whose students had higher gain scores on an achievement test, and less effective teachers were defined as those whose students had lower gain scores on an achievement test. Thus, the definition of teacher effectiveness was the one that has been used typically in process–product studies of teaching effectiveness.

Morine and Vallance reported that, compared to teachers with high student achievement gains, teachers with low student achievement gain scores tended to mention a larger number of items that they were taking into account on almost all aspects of interactive decisions that they discussed. This finding might be interpreted to mean that less effective teachers were not engaging as frequently in the cognitive processes mentioned by Corno and Doyle, such as chunking, differentiation, and selectivity, which would enable them to simplify the amount and kind of information that they were taking in during interactive teaching. Perhaps more effective teachers mentioned a smaller number of items because they had successfully "transformed the complexity of the environment into a conceptual system that enabled them to interpret discrete events and to anticipate the direction and flow of classroom activity" (Doyle, 1977a, p. 54). This conclusion is further substantiated by research comparing the interactive decision making of beginning and experienced teachers.

Studies of the Interactive Decision-Making Processes of Beginning versus Experienced Teachers. Calderhead (1981) compared the comments of beginning and experienced teachers in response to descriptions of common classroom critical incidents. Calderhead presented the critical incident orally to the teacher (e.g., "The class is working quietly when a group of children start talking amongst themselves"). He then asked the teacher: "What more do you need to know to make up your mind what to do, and what would you do?" In analyzing experienced and beginning teachers' responses to this task, Calderhead found a marked difference in the nature and sophistication of their interpretations and understanding of classroom events. He found that beginning teachers seemed to either lack the conceptual structures to make sense of classroom events or to have simple undifferentiated structures. Moreover, beginning teachers did not seem to extract the same kind or level of meaning from the description of the critical incident as did experienced teachers.

In recent years, cognitive psychologists have used the word "schema" to describe the way knowledge is stored in memory.

(See, for example, Anderson, 1977, 1984; Nisbett & Ross, 1980; Rumelhart, 1980). As Nisbett and Ross (1980) put it:

> People's generic knowledge also seems to be organized by a variety of ... *schematic*, cognitive structures (for example, the knowledge underlying one's awareness of what happens in a restaurant, one's understanding of the Good Samaritan parable, or one's conception of what an introvert is like). To describe such knowledge structures, psychologists refer to a growing list of items, including "frames," ... "scripts" ... "nuclear scenes" ... and "prototypes" ... in addition to the earlier and more generic term "schemas." (p. 28)

Although Calderhead (1981) did not discuss his findings in terms of experienced teachers having different schemata than beginning teachers, we interpret his results to suggest that experienced teachers may have better developed knowledge structures or "schemata" for phenomena related to classroom learning and teaching than do novice teachers. Similarly, we infer from the findings of Doyle (1977a) and Morine and Vallance (1975) that effective teachers may also have better developed schemata for classroom events than do ineffective teachers. Some relevant schemata for teachers might include (a) knowledge underlying their conception of what schoolchildren are like; and (b) knowledge underlying their awareness of what happens in classrooms.

Interestingly, the findings from a study by Calderhead (1983) indicate that the schemata that experienced teachers have for "schoolchildren" or "students" may differ significantly from the schemata that beginning teachers have for school children or students. Calderhead (1983) used interviews, the repertory grid technique, and stimulated recall to study the perceptions of six experienced teachers, six student teachers, and six teachers who were in their first year of teaching. He found that experienced teachers appeared to have amassed a large quantity of knowledge about children in general. As Calderhead put it, "experienced teachers in a sense 'know' their new class even before they meet them" (Calderhead, 1983, p. 5). Calderhead reported that experienced teachers knew the kinds of home backgrounds of students. They had an idea of the range of knowledge and skills to expect in their class and of the likely number of children who would need special help. They knew the types of misbehaviors and discipline problems that would occur. They knew the kinds of experiences that students tended to have had prior to school and the kinds of activities that the children engaged in outside of school.

Differences between experienced and novice teachers in another kind of schema — knowledge underlying their awareness of what happens in classrooms — may lead experienced and novice teachers to focus on different types of student cues in their interactive decision making. For example, Housner and Griffey (1983) found that while negative cues from students frequently resulted in both experienced and novice teachers' reported decisions to change their behavior (about 45% of the time), positive student cues resulted more often in experienced teachers' decisions to change their behavior than in novice teachers' decisions to change their behavior (30% and 6% of the time for experienced and novice teachers, respectively). With remarkable similarity, Fogarty et al. (1982) found that, of all the cues that led to their interactive decisions, novice teachers reported focusing on students' disruptive behavior most frequently (27% of the cues reported). In contrast, experienced teachers reported disruptive behavior infrequently in their reports of cues that led them to make interactive decisions (6% of the cues reported). These results suggest that experienced and novice teachers may differ considerably in their perceptions of classroom events as well as in their underlying schema for what constitutes an "appropriate" flow of classroom events.

Cognitive psychologists have argued that schemata affect perception, understanding, remembering, learning, and problem solving. One can well imagine that the experienced teacher would have better developed schemata as well as schemata more relevant to the teaching situation than would beginning teachers. Similarly, the schemata of "effective teachers" might differ significantly from the schemata of "ineffective" teachers. Presumably, having an appropriate schema for the conception of what a fourth grade child is like as well as an appropriate schema for events and life in a fourth grade classroom would be particularly important and useful if one were a fourth grade teacher. Such schemata would obviously affect the teacher's perception of events during interactive teaching, affect the teacher's perception of the students, enhance the teacher's understanding of events that may occur during interactive teaching, and aid the teacher in problem solving and decision making during interactive teaching.

Training Teachers in Effective Interactive Decision Making

Peterson and Clark (1978), Doyle (1977a), and Morine and Vallance (1975) investigated the relationship between variables related to teachers' interactive decision making and a criterion variable of effective teaching, such as student achievement or students' on-task behavior in class. Similarly, Calderhead's (1981, 1983) studies were descriptive studies. Thus, these studies fall within the correlational part of the correlational-experimental loop that has served as the basis for classroom research following the process–product paradigm (Rosenshine & Furst, 1973). The purpose of correlational research is to identify teaching behaviors that can then be manipulated or trained in experimental studies to determine if training teachers to engage in these "effective" behaviors leads to an increase in student achievement.

Unfortunately, no experimental studies have been undertaken in which researchers have attempted to train teachers in interactive decision-making skills and then to evaluate systematically the effects of training on students' achievement. Although some researchers have attempted to train teachers in effective decision-making skills, these researchers have not systematically evaluated the effects of training on students' achievement. For example, Bishop and Whitfield (1972) created "critical incidents" that could serve as simulation exercises for preservice teachers to practice interactive decision making. They proposed that preservice teachers should read the critical incident and then should be encouraged to develop decision-making skills by asking themselves the following questions: (a) What is the cause of the critical incident? (b) What decision areas are involved in the critical incident (e.g., cognitive learning, affective learning, pupil-teacher relationships, teacher-adult relationships, apparatus and aides, organization and administration)? (c) What criteria should be applied in making the decision? (d) What options are available? (e) Do I have enough information? (f) What is my decision? and (g) How would I evaluate my decision? Although the above model for training teachers in interactive decision making was proposed by Bishop and Whitfield in 1972, Sutcliffe and Whitfield (1979) noted that the technique had yet to be applied widely and evaluated systematically in teacher training. However, Sutcliffe and Whitfield argued that educators should train teachers in interactive decision making and, concurrently, they should evaluate the effects of training on teacher effectiveness, including the effects of training on student achievement gains.

Although we would agree that, eventually, researchers should conduct such experimental studies, we would argue that training teachers in a particular model of interactive decision making is premature. From the correlational research, we have gleaned the notion that *ineffective* teachers' interactive decision making *may* involve (a) the teacher's cognitively processing too great a variety and a quantity of information during the ongoing classroom interaction, without simplifying the information through processes such as chunking and differentiation so that the information can be used effectively in interactive decision making; and (b) a teacher's decision not to change behavior when student behavior is judged to be unacceptable, even though the teacher believes that alternative behavior or strategies are available that could change the student's behavior.

We do not have a clear idea, however, of what constitutes *effective* interactive decision making by a teacher. The teachers who in the Peterson and Clark (1978) study reported following the path that, on the face of it, would appear to be the most appropriate and effective path for a teacher's interactive decision making were not significantly more or less effective teachers than teachers who did not report following this path. On the other hand, if we can believe the findings regarding effective teachers as being better at simplifying, differentiating, and transforming the information perceived during classroom interaction, then perhaps we should focus our experimental research not on training teachers in interactive decision making but rather on training teachers to perceive, analyze, and transform their perceptions of the classroom in ways similar to those used by effective teachers.

Teachers' Theories and Beliefs

Nisbett and Ross (1980) have suggested "that people's understanding of the rapid flow of continuing social events" often depends on their "rich store of general knowledge of objects, people, events, and their characteristic relationships" (p. 28). Nisbett and Ross indicated further that some of this knowledge is organized in schematic, cognitive structures while other knowledge is represented as *beliefs* or *theories*, "that is, reasonably explicit 'propositions' about the characteristics of objects or object classes" (p. 28).

As a person whose daily task is to understand and interpret the rapid flow of social events in a classroom, the teacher obviously relies on these same kinds of knowledge structures that have been described by Nisbett and Ross (1980). We have already described how the first kind of knowledge structures or

schemata may affect teachers' information processing and behavior during planning and during classroom interaction. In this section we will discuss the second kind of knowledge, propositional knowledge, that is represented as teachers' theories or beliefs.

Teachers' Theories and Beliefs About Students: Teachers' Attributions for the Causes of a Student's Performance

Psychologists have argued that the types of theories that have the most significant and far-reaching consequences are those theories of a person that focus on the general causes of human behavior (see for example, Heider, 1958; Nisbett & Ross, 1980; and Weiner, 1974). Similarly, in considering teachers' theories and beliefs about students, some researchers have suggested that the most important beliefs that teachers have about students are those that deal with teachers' perceptions of the causes of students' behavior or, in other words, teachers' attributions for the causes of students' performance. (See, for example, Darley & Fazio, 1980; Peterson and Barger, 1984). Indeed, Darley and Fazio (1980) and Peterson and Barger (1984) have suggested that teachers' attributions for the causes of students' performance may be important in attempting to understand how teacher expectancies effect student achievement in the classroom. For these reasons, in our discussion of teachers' theories and beliefs about the student, we will focus on teachers' attributions.

Although the research literature on teachers' attributions is large, we will confine our review to research that addresses four major questions: (a) How have researchers conceptualized teachers' attributions for the causes of students' successes and failures? (b) What factors affect teachers' attributions for the causes of students' performance? (c) What is the relationship between teachers' attributions for the causes of students' performance and teachers' behavior toward these students in the classroom? and (d) What is the relationship between teachers' attributions for the causes of students' performance, teachers' planning and interactive decision making, and students' achievement? (See Peterson and Barger, 1984 for a more complete discussion of the research on teachers' attributions.)

RESEARCHERS' CONCEPTUALIZATIONS
OF ATTRIBUTIONS FOR THE
CAUSES OF STUDENTS' PERFORMANCE

Researchers have differed significantly in the category systems that they have used to describe teachers' attributions for the causes of students' performance. Table 9.8 presents four alternative category systems that have been used to describe and categorize attributions. Weiner et al. (1971), Frieze (1976), and Bar-Tal and Darom (1979) developed their categories originally to describe students' attributions for the causes of their performance. However, these categories have been used subsequently by other researchers to describe teachers' attributions. In contrast, Cooper and Burger (1980) developed their categories using teachers rather than students as respondents,

Table 9.8. A Summary of Categories Used by Researchers to Describe Students' and Teachers' Attributions for the Causes of Students' Successes and Failures

Weiner et al.'s (1971) Categories	Frieze's (1976) Categories	Bar-Tal & Darom's (1979) Categories	Cooper & Burger's (1980) Categories
Ability	Ability	Ability	Ability (academic, physical, or emotional)
Effort	Stable effort	Effort during test	Previous experience
Task difficulty	Immediate effort	Preparation at home	Acquired characteristics (habits, attitudes, self-perceptions)
Luck	Task	Interest in the subject matter	Typical effort
	Other person	Difficulty of test	Interest in the subject matter
	Mood	Difficulty of material	Immediate effort
	Luck	Conditions in the home	Attention
	Other	Teacher	Teacher (quality and kind of instruction, directions)
			Task
			Other students
			Family
			Physiological processes (mood, maturity, health)

Note. Adapted from Cooper & Burger (1980).

and they developed the categories explicitly to describe teachers' attributions for the causes of students' performance.

The four category systems in Table 9.8 also differ to the extent that they were generated a priori by the investigator or generated by the investigator in an attempt to categorize attributions that were provided by subjects in a free-response situation. Weiner et al. (1971) suggested that their experimenter-generated categories were the most common and general of the perceived causes for successes and failures. Frieze (1976) asked 51 college students to explain their own and others' successes and failures on academic and nonacademic tasks. She derived her coding scheme from the college students' open-ended responses. Bar-Tal and Darom (1979) asked 63 fifth grade students to provide explanations for their own grade that they had just received on a test. They then categorized the students' attributions for the causes of their performance into the eight categories shown in Table 9.8. Cooper and Burger (1980) asked 39 elementary and secondary teachers to list three students in their class that they expected to do well academically and three that they expected to do poorly. They then asked the teachers to list why the outcome was predicted for each student. Cooper and Burger derived their categories from the teachers' free responses.

Most researchers on teachers' attributions have tended to use some subset of the categories presented in Table 9.8 or some paraphrasing or adaptation of these categories. In addition, researchers have been concerned with some larger, more encompassing dimensions of attributions, such as whether the attribution is to a cause internal to the student (e.g., effort or ability) or external to the student (e.g., luck, task difficulty, or the teacher); whether the attribution is to a stable cause (e.g., ability, task difficulty, or typical effort) or to an unstable cause (e.g., luck or immediate effort). Furthermore, as we shall see, researchers have been concerned with whether teachers tend to attribute students' successes and failures to themselves (i.e., the teacher) and thereby take responsibility for students' performance, or whether they tend to attribute students' performance to factors other than the teacher (e.g., students' effort, ability), thereby eschewing responsibility for the students' performance.

An implicit assumption of researchers has been that if teachers fail to accept responsibility for students' successes or failures, and thus fail to see a relationship between their behavior and students' performance, they would be less likely to work to improve these students' performance in the classroom. Thus, researchers have been concerned with factors that affect teachers' attributions and, in particular, the extent to which teachers accept responsibility for students' successes or failures.

FACTORS THAT AFFECT TEACHERS' ATTRIBUTIONS: THE SELF-SERVING BIAS

Attribution theorists have hypothesized that a person's causal attributions will be affected by whether the person is an actor in the situation (i.e., one of the participants in the social interaction) or an observer (i.e., an onlooker who is uninvolved in the social interaction). (See, for example Jones & Nisbett, 1971.) Because teachers are active participants in the classroom interaction process that leads to students' successes and failures, teachers' attributions for the performance of students might be affected by or biased systematically by their role as an actor rather than as an observer. The teacher's role as an actor may lead to two different patterns of teachers' attributions: (a) ego-enhancing attributions, or (b) counter-defensive attributions. Ego-enhancing or self-serving attributions occur when, as a result of being a participant in the social interaction, teachers attribute a student's successful performance to themselves as teachers and a student's failure to factors other than the teacher. Teachers thereby enhance their egos by accepting responsibility for students' successes while blaming the students for their failures. In contrast, counter-defensive attributions occur when the teacher accepts responsibility for students' failures and gives credit to the students themselves for successes.

Research findings have been inconsistent in indicating the extent to which being an actor in the situation leads the teacher to form ego-enhancing attributions for the student's performance. Table 9.9 presents the findings from this research. Four studies have found that being an actor in the situation leads the teacher to form ego-enhancing attributions (Beckman, 1970; Brandt,

Table 9.9. Studies Investigating the "Self-Serving" Bias in Teachers' Attributions (Ego-Enhancing Attributions)

Study	Subjects	Task	Results
Ames (1975)	Undergraduate students in educational psychology	Teaching a concept classification task to a 10-year-old male confederate in one 15-minute session	"Teachers" attributed students' failure significantly more often to themselves than to the student or the situation; they attributed students' successes significantly more often to the students themselves. (nondefensive attribution.)
Beckman (1970)	Preservice teachers were the "teachers"; undergraduate psychology students were the "observers"	Teaching mathematics to two fictitious elementary schoolchildren	"Teachers" attributed a student's successful performance to themselves as teachers and a student's failure to factors other than the teacher (i.e., characteristics of student or situation). (Ego-enhancing attributions.) "Observers" attributions were not affected by student performance.
Beckman (1973)	Preservice and in-service teachers assigned randomly to be either "teacher" or "observer"	Teaching mathematics to a fictitious fifth grade student	"Teachers" attributed any change in student's performance to themselves (i.e., counterdefensive attributions) more often than did "observers."
Beckman (1976)	49 parents and 9 teachers of fourth, fifth, and sixth grade students (40% were from minority groups)	Attributions given by teachers for high-, medium-, low-performing students in their classes; parents rated their children on attributions for performance	On open-ended questions, parents of successful students were more likely to mention teaching than teachers. (Teachers never mentioned teaching as a factor on open-ended questions.) On structured questions, parents attributed performance at all levels to teacher factors as often as to child factors (ability and effort), while teachers attributed performance more often to child factors than to their own teaching.
Brandt, Hayden, & Brophy (1975)	Undergraduate students in introductory psychology	Teaching government to a fictitious fourth grade student in 4-minute lectures	"Teachers" who taught successful students assigned more responsibility to themselves (rather than to the student) than did teachers who taught unsuccessful students, (Ego-enhancing or self-serving attributions.)
Johnson, Feigenbaum, & Weiby (1964)	Preservice teachers enrolled in educational psychology course	Teaching mathematics to two fictitious fourth grade boys	Teachers attributed an improvement in students' performance to themselves as teachers; they attributed a lack of improvement to the students themselves. (Ego-enhancing attributions.)
Ross, Bierbrauer, & Polly (1974)	Preservice and in-service teachers were "teachers"; undergraduates were "teachers" or "observers"	Teaching spelling to a sixth grade confederate of the experimenter	"Teachers" attributed students' failure more often to themselves than to the student and attributed students' success more often to the students than to the teacher; this effect was more pronounced for actual teachers than for undergraduate "teachers." (Nondefensive attributions.) Undergraduate "observers" and "teachers" did not differ significantly in their attributions.
Tetlock (1980)	Undergraduate students in introductory psychology served as "observers"	Reading simulated materials from the Ross et al. study (including teachers' attributions which were varied systematically) and rating the teachers	Hypothesis was that teachers' counterdefensive (nondefensive) attributions are "self presentations" designed to create favorable impressions in others. Consistent with this hypothesis, observers rated moderately counterdefensive teachers (those in the Ross study) as significantly more competent than the moderately or highly defensive (ego-enhancing) teacher.
Wiley & Eskilson (1978)	126 elementary school teachers	Completing questionnaire after reviewing the file of a fictitious student who varied in sex, race, and past performance	Teachers were rated as playing a more important role in successful performance of a student than in unsuccessful performance. (ego-enhancing attributions.)

Hayden, & Brophy, 1975; Johnson, Feigenbaum, & Weiby, 1964; and Wiley & Eskilson, 1978). In contrast, three studies found support for a counterdefensive bias in teachers' attributions (Ames, 1975; Beckman, 1973; and Ross, Bierbrauer, & Polly, 1974). Peterson and Barger (1984) suggested that the results of these seven studies are not necessarily inconsistent and may be interpreted as indicating that teachers are less likely to make ego-enhancing attributions in more naturalistic situations. They argued that in contrast to the previous experimental studies by Johnson et al. (1964), Beckman (1970), and Beckman (1973), the studies by Ross et al. (1974) and Ames (1975) were more ecologically valid because the researchers employed an actual student confederate and permitted the "teacher" to interact during teaching with the "student." The findings of these latter two studies imply that in actual classroom settings, teachers would be more likely to make counterdefensive than ego-enhancing attributions for the causes of students' performance.

Why might teachers in an actual classroom setting be more likely to make counterdefensive attributions than self-serving attributions? Tetlock's (1980) results support the hypothesis that teachers' counterdefensive attributions are "self presentations" designed to create favorable impressions in others. (See Table 9.9). In an actual classroom setting, teachers would be likely to be concerned about the impressions that they are making on persons that they come into contact with on a daily and regular basis including students, parents, fellow teachers, and the principal. Thus, teachers would tend to make counterdefensive attributions to enhance their perceived competence. Thus, in the end, teachers' counterdefensive attributions may also be self-serving.

As an extension of this argument, Peterson and Barger (1984) proposed that in a naturalistic classroom setting teachers might even show a "humility bias" in their attributions. In the only study to date in which teachers' attributions for the cause of the performance of actual students in their own classroom were compared with parents' attributions for the same children, Beckman (1976) found that, on open-ended questions, teachers *never* mentioned teaching or the teacher as a factor determining a student's performance (see Table 9.9). Perhaps in a situation in which teachers know their students well and in which they are concerned about creating a favorable impression (in this case, with the experimenters who would read their responses and the parents of the students who also provided attributions for the cause of their child's performance), teachers may not take credit for their students' performance because they do not want to appear arrogant. A desire to create a favorable impression may have led to a "humility bias" in teachers' attributions.

Ames (1982) proposed an alternative explanation for the inconsistent findings regarding the self-serving bias in teachers' attributions. Ames proposed that teachers' attributions were affected by an additional factor — teachers' "value for responsibility." He hypothesized that a teacher's value for responsibility involves three key beliefs: (a) that teaching is an important activity, (b) that teachers engage in intentional acts to produce positive outcomes, and (c) that students' success is generally feasible given the situation and constraints. Ames predicted that high-value teachers (i.e., teachers who placed a high value on teaching) would take responsibility for their own actions and for the performance of their students (i.e., attribute students' performance and their own performance to the teacher). In contrast, Ames predicted that low-value teachers (i.e., teachers who placed a low value on teaching) would attribute students' performance to the students themselves or to situational factors. Ames did note one exception. He hypothesized that high-value teachers would attribute a successful student performance to the student because this attribution was logically consistent with the belief that good teachers reinforce their students for success to encourage the student to work hard.

Although Ames' (1982) hypotheses are appealing intuitively, little research has been done to test whether teachers' value for responsibility does indeed affect teachers' attributions. Ames (1982) reported the results of two studies that supported the hypothesized relationship between teachers' value for responsibility and teachers' attributions. However, in both these studies the findings were based on questionnaire responses from college instructors, and the obtained response rate was extremely low in both studies (39% in the first study and 31% in the second

study). Because of this low response rate, the results may not be representative; in particular, the results may be biased if, in fact, only those instructors who placed a high value on teaching (the topic of the questionnaire) were the ones who returned their questionnaires. Thus, although Ames' results are provocative, more research is needed that explores the relationship between the value that teachers place on teaching and their attributions for students' performance in the classroom.

OTHER FACTORS THAT AFFECT TEACHERS' ATTRIBUTIONS

In addition to the teacher's role in classroom interaction, researchers have hypothesized that other factors also affect teachers' attributions for the causes of students' performance. These factors include the teacher's perception of students' past performances as well as characteristics of the students, including race, social class, and sex.

Peterson and Barger (1984) concluded that research findings show that teachers use information about a student's past performance in making attributions about the causes of the student's present performance so as to maintain a "consistent" picture. Teachers are likely to attribute an "expected" outcome, such as success by a student perceived as high in ability, to a stable factor such as ability. On the other hand, teachers are likely to attribute an "unexpected" outcome, such as success by a student perceived as low in ability, to an unstable factor such as luck. One insidious outcome of this impression-maintenance attribution bias is that even students who work hard to dispel a teacher's misconception of their lack of ability might not receive full credit from the teacher for their actions.

The effects of race and social class on teachers' attributions are less clear. Researchers have hypothesized that teachers perceive that black students have less control over their successes and failures than white students and that black students' failures are due to bad luck rather than lack of ability. Findings by Wiley and Eskilson (1978) supported this hypothesis. Cooper, Baron, and Low (1975) showed that the effect of race on teachers' attributions was mediated by students' social class. In addition, Domingo-Llacuna (1976) and Feuquay (1979) found that the effects of race on social class were more complex when teachers' internal and external attributions for students of different races were broken down into specific attributions, such as ability, effort, and luck for the causes of students' successes and failures.

In contrast to the findings for race and social class, sex of student has not been shown to be a significant factor affecting teachers' attributions. For example, Wiley and Eskilson (1978) found that sex of the stimulus student in a description provided to teachers had no significant effect on the causal attributions that teachers made for students' performance. Similar nonsignificant effects of sex were reported by Hanes (1979). On the other hand, Dweck, Davidson, Nelson, and Enna (1978) reported significant sex differences in the attributional statements that teachers made to girls and boys in their classrooms. Teachers were more likely to make statements attributing failure to a lack of effort for boys than for girls. However, studies by Blumenfeld, Hamilton, Wessels, and Falkner (1977) and Heller and Parsons (1981) have failed to replicate the Dweck et al. (1978) findings.

THE RELATIONSHIP BETWEEN TEACHERS' ATTRIBUTIONS AND TEACHERS' BEHAVIOR

Attribution theorists have stated that a significant relationship exists between a teacher's attributions for the causes of a student's performance and the feedback that the teacher gives to the student. In an initial study, Weiner and Kukla (1970) found that the greater the student's success, the more positive the teacher's feedback. Students who were perceived by the teacher as expending effort were rewarded more and punished less than students who were perceived as not trying. Perceived effort was a far more important determinant of reward and punishment than perceived ability.

Most research on the relationship between teachers' attributions and their behavior has tended to support the conclusion that teachers' attributions to effort are highly predictive of the teachers' feedback to the student. Research in support of this conclusion includes studies by Cooper and Burger (1980), Covington, Spratt, and Omelich (1980), Medway (1979), Meyer (1979), Silverstein (1978). The only contrary evidence has been reported by Cooper and Baron (1977, 1979). Table 9.10 summarizes the results of the studies. Peterson and Barger (1984) concluded that the majority of the evidence suggests that students who are perceived by teachers as expending effort (i.e., teachers attribute their performance to effort) are rewarded more and punished less by teachers than students who are perceived as not really trying. (See Peterson and Barger, 1984, for a more complete discussion of the results.) They also suggested that teachers' affect or emotion may serve as a mediator between teachers' attributions and behavior. In support of this position, Prawat, Byers, and Anderson (1983) found that teachers were angry when they perceived that a student had failed due to lack of effort.

Although the majority of the research has examined the relationship between teachers' attributions and teacher feedback, two studies have explored the possibility that teachers' attributions may affect other kinds of teacher behavior. The results of a study by King (1980) suggest that teachers' attributions for the causes of a students' performance may affect the number and kind of interactions that the teacher has with the student. (See Table 9.10.) Brophy and Rohrkemper (1981) reported that teacher attributions for a student's performance affected the types of goals that the teacher sets for the student, the way in which the teacher controlled and managed the student's behavior, and the type of educational practices that the teacher used with the student. While these latter findings are suggestive rather than conclusive, they do indicate teacher behaviors that might be investigated in future studies of the relationship between teachers' attributions and teachers' behavior.

THE RELATIONSHIP BETWEEN TEACHER ATTRIBUTIONS, TEACHER PLANNING, INTERACTIVE DECISION MAKING, AND STUDENT ACHIEVEMENT.

For the most part, research on teachers' attributions has proceeded separately from research on teacher planning and teachers' interactive thoughts and decisions. Virtually no overlap exists between the names of researchers whose research we described above in the sections on teachers' planning and interactive decision making and the names of researchers who have conducted research on teachers' attributions. Even though teachers' attributions were mentioned early on as an important topic to be considered in research on teachers' thought processes (see, for example, National Institute of Education, 1975a), this research has not been integrated into the ongoing body of research on teachers' thought processes. It is not surprising, therefore, that we found no studies that investigated the relationship between teachers' attributions and teachers' planning or between teachers' attributions and teachers' interactive thoughts and decisions. Presumably, the effect of teachers' attribution on teachers' behavior would be mediated through teachers' thought processes either prior to instruction (e.g., teacher planning) or during instruction (e.g., teachers' interactive thoughts and decisions). Thus, the link between teachers' attributions and teachers' preactive and interactive thoughts and decisions remains an important one that needs to be examined.

A similar problem exists with regard to the relationship between teachers' attributions and student achievement. Although researchers on teachers' attributions have assumed implicitly that teachers' attributions for the causes of students' performance have subsequent effects on students' performance and achievement, they have not explicitly studied the relationship between teachers' attributions and student achievement. Similarly, researchers on teaching effectiveness, who have been concerned primarily with effects of teaching on student achievement, have tended not to focus on teachers' attributions although they have considered the potential effects of teachers' expectations on student achievement. (See, for example, Brophy, 1982.)

In sum, although teachers' attributions are obviously central to an understanding of the mental life of teachers, research is needed that explicates the relationship between teachers' attributions for the causes of students' performance and teachers' preactive and interactive thoughts and decision. In addition, research is needed that moves from laboratory settings in which researchers employ questionnaire and simulation methods to study teachers' attributions to real-world classroom settings in which researchers study teachers' attributions as part of the teachers' ongoing thoughts and actions during everyday teaching. In these settings, researchers also need to investigate the relationship between teachers' actual attributions for the causes of students' performance, teachers' thoughts and behavior, and students' classroom performance and achievement. Only then will we have a better understanding of the importance of teachers' beliefs about students, as represented by their attributions for the causes of students' performance.

Teachers' Implicit Theories of Teaching and Learning

Research on teachers' implicit theories constitutes the smallest and youngest part of the literature of research on teacher thinking. Yet, according to Munby (1982), inquiry into this topic is central to a complete and useful understanding of thought processes in teaching. While we may learn much that is interesting and useful from a technical point of view from research on teacher planning, interactive thinking, and teachers' attributions, we can make sense of these findings only in relation to the psychological context in which the teacher plans and decides.

Table 9.10. Studies on the Relationship Between Teachers' Attributions and Teacher Behavior

Study	Subjects	Task	Results
Cooper & Baron (1977)	Eight elementary teachers	Nine target students were selected for whom the teachers had high, medium, or low expectations, respectively. Teachers were asked to assign responsibility for each student's performance to (a) personal or (b) environmental factors. Target student–teacher behavior was observed.	Perceived responsibility for success did not predict teacher praise; perceived responsibility for failure did not predict teacher criticism. As perceived responsibility for success increased, number of negative behavior interactions decreased and frequency of child-created interactions decreased; as perceived responsibility for failure increased so did child-created procedural interactions. Performance expectations were more potent predicters of teachers' feedback than were teachers' attributions.
Cooper & Baron (1979)		Response to Meyer (1979).	(a) Effort and ability are not orthogonal in real life—they covary; (b) laboratory studies such as those done by Meyer and attribution theorists show different results than those using face-to-face interaction; (c) Meyer's own data show that low ability attributions resulted in *less*, not *more* reward.
Cooper & Burger (1980)	62 preservice teachers	A questionnaire was read in which a successful or unsuccessful student was described, with 12 causal attributions for student's performance. For each attribution teachers stated how strongly they would praise/criticize the student and whether they would work more/less with the student.	Teachers showed a greater intention to criticize failure when it was due to internal, unstable, nonteacher causes (i.e., attention, physiological processes, immediate effort). Failure caused by external events (task, teacher, other students, family) led to the *least* intention to criticize. Greater intention to praise success existed when caused by teacher influence (i.e., attention, immediate effort, interest, teacher) than when caused by little influence (i.e., psychological processes, family, other students, task).
Covington, Spratt, & Omelich (1980)	364 students enrolled in introductory psychology; half were randomly assigned to the "teacher" condition	A questionnaire described eight failure situations in terms of overall effort (high or low), stability of effort expenditure (stable or unstable) and direction of unstable low effort. "Teachers" dispersed feedback to each student.	Low student effort, regardless of stability, led to more negative teacher feedback than did high effort. Low-effort pupils were seen by teachers as less conscientious, less motivated, less persistent, more likely to procrastinate, and lazier. Indeed, punishment did *not* depend on teacher inferences about student ability but on motivational labeling. (Findings support Meyer, 1979.)
King (1980)	One sixth grade teacher, two "successful" students, and two "unsuccessful" students in the class (case study)	Interviews with and observations of students and the teacher were presented.	Student A (success attributed to ability by the teacher) was often called on by the teacher when she wanted to change pace or direction of lesson. Student B (success attributed to effort) was believed by teacher to "catch on" with merest clues. When student requested help, the teacher expected the problem to be minor. Student C (lack of success due to lack of ability) was provided additional academic support by teacher—helped her understand task requirements and worked through a problem with her. Teacher frequently interacted with Student C. Student D (lack of success due to lack of effort) was seldom interacted with by the teacher.
Medway (1979)	24 elementary teachers who had each referred a child for special education	Teachers were asked to rate the importance of each of the following factors in contributing to the student's major problems: ability; effort; adjustment or personality; home situation; educational preparation; teaching. Teachers were observed interacting with the target children.	Teachers' effort attributions were the only attributions that significantly predicted teacher's use of criticism (accounting for 32% of the overall 63% variability in teacher criticism predicted). Teachers gave more criticism to students whose performance was attributed to low versus high effort. Teachers' attributions were *not* related to teachers' use of praise.
Meyer (1979)		Criticism of Cooper and Baron (1977).	The personal responsibility measure used by Cooper and Baron was criticized for not looking specifically at ability versus effort. Attribution studies have shown that outcomes attributed to high effort receive more praise than low effort. Attributions to low ability receive more praise than attributions to high ability. Meyer also presented his own data which showed a significant positive relationship between effort and teacher reward while the relationship between ability and teacher reward varied according to ability–effort correlation.
Silverstein (1978)	96 teachers in Grades 1–12	Evaluation was made of 24 fictitious students who varied in situational dimensions, ability, effort, and outcome (within-SS design).	Significant main effect of effort was found with greater effort being evaluated more positively, regardless of ability or outcome.

For an individual teacher, this psychological context is thought to be composed of a mixture of only partially articulated theories, beliefs, and values about his or her role and about the dynamics of teaching and learning. The purpose of research on teachers' implicit theories is to make explicit and visible the frames of reference through which individual teachers perceive and process information.

Studies of teachers' implicit theories are difficult to summarize briefly. Reports of several of the studies have been published as books or reported in lengthy doctoral dissertations. Thus, our condensation of this research is necessarily selective and incomplete in its details, and might best be used as an annotated index and guide to this literature rather than as an exhaustive summary and review.

As is the case with much of teacher thinking literature, the studies of teachers' implicit theories are small-sample descriptive research. The nine studies summarized in Table 9.11 constitute those that focus on teachers' implicit theories directly. The methods of inquiry included ethnographic participant observation, clinical interviews, stimulated recall, and the repertory grid technique. The terms used to designate the topic of study included the teacher's personal perspective (Janesick, 1977), conceptual system (Duffy, 1977), principles of practice (Marland, 1977), construct system (Bussis, Chittenden, & Amarel, 1976), practical knowledge (Elbaz, 1981), and implicit theories (National Institute of Education, 1975b). Although each of these terms has a somewhat different meaning, they hold in common the idea that a teacher's cognitive and other behaviors are guided by and make sense in relation to a personally held system of beliefs, values, and principles. Prior to the researcher's intervention, these systems are typically not well specified, and the central task of the researcher is to assist the teacher in moving from an implicitly held and private belief system to an explicit description of his or her cognitive frame of reference. Because much of this domain is unexplored territory, a great deal of energy has gone into inventing and discovering appropriate language to describe teachers' implicit theories in ways that remain faithful to the teachers' own felt sense of what they believe.

Some researchers have focused on teachers' implicit theories about a particular part of the curriculum (e.g., Duffy's 1977 work on conceptions of reading). Other researchers have been concerned with teachers' general conceptions of their role (Janesick, 1977; Munby, 1983), with their beliefs about curriculum (Bussis et al., 1976), and with the principles that they use to explain their own interactive behavior (Conners, 1978b; Marland, 1977). Elbaz (1981) was more concerned with discovering the structure and content of teachers' practical knowledge than with describing the particulars of the knowledge held and used by one teacher. Ignatovich, Cusick, and Ray (1979) provide us with a striking picture of the conflicting belief systems about teaching held by teachers and administrators.

TEACHERS' PERSPECTIVES OF THEIR ROLES AS TEACHERS

In a 7-month-long ethnographic field study of a sixth grade teacher and his class, Janesick (1977) attempted to discover and describe the perspective held by that teacher about his role.

Taking a symbolic interactionist view, Janesick defined a perspective as a reflective, socially derived interpretation of experience that serves as a basis for subsequent action. The teacher's perspective combines beliefs, intentions, interpretations, and behavior that interact continually and are modified by social interaction. At any given time, teachers' perspective serves as the frame of reference within which they make sense of and interpret experience, and act rationally.

Janesick found that the broadest and most dominant aspect of the teacher's perspective was his commitment to creating and maintaining a stable and cohesive classroom group. The teacher made plans and interactive decisions and interpreted classroom events in terms of their impact on the group cohesiveness of the class. He defined the most important aspect of his teaching role as that of group leader. Group consensus and cooperation were his main criteria for a successful classroom activity.

TEACHERS' CONCEPTIONS OF READING

A study by Duffy (1977) of teachers' conceptions of reading differed from Janesick's work in several ways. Rather than building a picture of one teacher's conceptions inductively, as Janesick did, Duffy began with a typology consisting of five contrasting approaches to the teaching of reading, derived from literature review: basal text, linear skills, natural language, interest, and integrated whole. A sixth conceptual system labeled "confused/frustrated" was added later. The purposes of the Duffy study were to describe the distribution of these conceptions of the teaching of reading among teachers and, in a second phase of the study, to compare teachers' espoused beliefs with their actual classroom behavior.

Duffy had 350 teachers of beginning reading sort propositional statements about the reading process into five categories ranging from "most like me" to "least like me." Each of the six conceptions of reading listed above was represented by 6 propositions, giving a total of 36 propositional statements to be sorted. Only 37 of the 350 teachers were found to manifest strong "pure types" of conceptions of reading. This finding suggests that perhaps the conceptions that teachers do hold about the teaching of reading do not fit neatly into the research-based typology and that they may be more complex and eclectic than those of reading researchers.

In the second phase of the Duffy study, the 37 teachers who manifested strong unitary conceptions of reading completed a modified version of the Kelly Role Repertory Test to refine further and specify more clearly their beliefs about reading. Eight teachers from this group who continued to manifest clear and categorical conceptions of reading were each observed teaching reading in their own classrooms on 10 occasions. The extent to which these teachers' instructional behavior reflected their expressed conceptions of reading was determined by analysis of ethnographic field notes and postobservation interview data. Duffy (1977) reported:

Four teachers consistently employed practices which directly reflected their beliefs; these included two teachers who had structured beliefs (basal/linear skills), a teacher who had an eclectic view, and one of the teachers having an unstructured belief system (natural language/interest/integrated whole). Of those whose practices did

Table 9.11. Nine Studies of Teachers' Implicit Theories

Study	Method of Inquiry	Teachers	Findings
Bussis, Chittenden, & Amarel (1976)	Clinical interview	60 elementary teachers implementing open or informal teaching	Four contrasting orientations identified for each of four aspects of teachers' belief systems: (a) curriculum priorities, (b) role of children's needs and feelings, (c) children's interests and freedom of choice, and (d) importance of social interaction among children.
Conners (1978b)	Stimulated recall	Nine elementary teachers; 1 each from first, third and sixth grades in three schools	1. Three overarching principles of practice: a. Suppressing emotion b. Teacher authenticity c. Self-monitoring 2. Five general pedagogical principles: a. Cognitive linking b. Integration c. Closure d. General involvement e. Equality of treatment
Duffy (1977)	Repertory grid technique and observation	Eight teachers of beginning reading	Four of eight teachers behaved in ways consistent with their espoused belief systems about teaching reading. The teaching behavior of the remaining four teachers departed, to various degrees, from their espoused beliefs.
Elbaz (1981)	Clinical interview and observation	One teacher of high school English	1. Five content areas of teacher practical knowledge: a. Curriculum b. Subject matter c. Instruction d. Milieu e. Self 2. Five orientations of practical knowledge: a. Situational b. Social c. Personal d. Experiential e. Theoretical 3. Three structural forms of practical knowledge: a. Rules of practice b. Practical principles c. Images
Ignatovich, Cusick, & Ray (1979)	Q-sort	47 elementary teachers, 22 elementary principals, and 12 administrators	1. Teachers and principals had similar belief systems regarding effective teaching that stressed the humanistic, social, and group process aspects of the teacher's role. 2. Administrators implementing "rational management systems" defined effective teaching in terms of standardized test results, administrative evaluation, and the influence of outside forces on classrooms.
Janesick (1977)	Participant observation	One teacher of sixth grade	Teacher's perspective centrally concerned with creating and maintaining a stable and cohesive group.
Marland (1977)	Stimulated recall	Six elementary school teachers; language arts and math lessons by two first grade and two third grade teachers; language arts lessons only by two sixth grade teachers	Five principles of practice documented: 1. Compensation 2. Strategic leniency 3. Power sharing 4. Progressive checking 5. Suppressing emotions
Munby (1983)	Repertory grid technique	14 teachers of junior high school	1. Wide individual differences in teachers' role definitions linked to variations in curriculum implementation. 2. The number of constructs needed to describe a teacher's implicit theory ranged from three to six. 3. Five most common constructs in teachers' implicit theories: a. Student learning and developmental goals b. Student involvement c. Teacher control and authority d. Student needs and limitations e. Motivation
Olson (1981)	Repertory grid technique and interviews	Eight teachers of science in three British comprehensive secondary schools	1. High teacher classroom influence and control was the primary construct around which teachers' theories of good teaching were organized. 2. Teachers transformed and distorted new curriculum to fit their implicit theories of teaching.

not reflect their beliefs, two of the teachers having strong unstructured belief systems were found to be smuggling elements of unstructured practices into an administratively-imposed program reflecting a structured view. Two other teachers holding unstructured views, however, did not consistently reflect their beliefs; one of the teachers employed practices which, to a large degree, were counter to the unstructured belief system she espoused, while a second teacher operationalized unstructured beliefs only some of the time with some pupils and some activities. (pp. 7–8)

The Duffy study of conceptions of reading portrays a flexible and complex relationship between teachers' implicit theories and their classroom behavior. The results suggest that constraints on teacher behavior such as mandated curriculum materials, resources, time available, habits, and student abilities may interpose between theory and action and account for observed discrepancies. Because the study design began with researcher-selected categories of conceptions of reading that described only about 10% of the teachers surveyed, the results speak as much to what teachers' conceptions of reading are not as to what they are.

TEACHERS' IMPLICIT THEORIES AND BELIEFS IN OPEN EDUCATION SETTINGS

Bussis et al. (1976) described teachers' understandings of curriculum, learners, and their working environments through use of extensive clinical interviews of 60 elementary school teachers who were attempting to implement open or informal instruction. Transcripts of the interviews were coded using a coding system devised by the researchers. The Bussis et al. description of the teachers' "curriculum construct systems" revealed a tension between the press to emphasize grade-level facts and skills and the need to work toward broader developmental and process goals for learners. The researchers identified four orientations among these teachers ranging from heavy and exclusive emphasis on grade-level facts and skills to primary emphasis on broader developmental goals. The teachers' orientations concerning students' emotional needs and feelings ranged from the position that the needs and feelings of students were relatively unimportant or irrelevant as a teaching priority (20% of the teachers) to the belief that the expression of needs and feelings was integral to and inseparable from the learning process (33%). Similarly wide variance was found in teachers' beliefs about the importance of students' interests, freedom of choice in what and how they learn, and about the role of social interaction among children as a means to learning. (See Clark & Yinger, 1977, for a more extensive account of the results of the study.)

Bussis et al. moved beyond the a priori category system approach of Duffy to a coding approach derived from teachers' responses to clinical interviews. The results highlight the wide variations in teachers' belief systems even within a sample of teachers who shared a commitment to open education and informal learning.

PRINCIPLES OF PRACTICE

Two doctoral dissertations completed at the University of Alberta (Conners, 1978b; Marland, 1977), although primarily concerned with the thoughts of teachers during the interactive teaching process, also revealed much of interest about the principles that guide and explain teacher behavior. One of Marland's analyses of stimulated recall interview transcripts permitted him to derive five principles of practice that were mentioned independently by at least two of the six teachers studied or that played a powerful role in influencing the interactive behavior of one teacher. These principles of practice can be described as follows:

The principle of compensation represented an attempt on the part of the teacher to discriminate in favor of the shy, the introverted, the low-ability group, and the culturally impoverished. Two of the four teachers who applied this principle were Grade 1 teachers. This principle figured less prominently in the explanations of teachers of higher grades.

The principle of strategic leniency was a variation of the principle of compensation. Strategic leniency referred to a teacher's tendency to ignore infractions of classroom rules by children who the teacher regarded as needing special attention.

The principle of power sharing involved the teacher using the informal peer power structure to influence students. In this way, the teacher was seen as sharing both responsibility and authority with certain students. That is, the teacher would selectively reinforce the good behavior of students whom she perceived as class leaders to use their influence on their peers as an instrument for classroom management.

The principle of progressive checking involved periodically checking progress, identification of problems, and providing encouragement for low-ability-group students during seatwork. In addition to the direct assistance provided during this checking, the teacher who utilized this principle also reasoned that she was providing stimulus variation for students with short attention spans.

The principle of suppressing emotions was derived from teacher reports that they consciously suppressed the emotional feelings that they were experiencing while teaching. This principle was invoked because of the belief that, if they expressed their feelings and emotions, it might overly excite the students and encourage them to express their own feelings and emotions, thus creating a management problem.

The five principles of practice identified by Marland seem to deal primarily with student characteristics. Compensation, strategic leniency, and power sharing all require that the teacher know his or her students well enough to judge which children would benefit from the kinds of selective responses indicated by each principle. Suppressing emotions is a preventative strategy involving teacher self-management for the sake of orderly classroom management. By implication, teachers who use this principle believe that their students are emotionally volatile and that expression of emotions by students is inappropriate and constitutes a breakdown of class management. Progressive checking is, in part, a straightforward strategy for dealing with the task demands of seatwork. But the teachers also explained their instructional management behavior in terms of its appropriateness as a treatment for children with short attention spans. In Marland's analysis, conceptions of knowledge or conceptions of a particular subject matter are conspicuously absent among principles guiding interactive teacher behavior.

Conners (1978b) replicated and extended Marland's results with nine elementary teachers. His analysis of stimulated recall protocols revealed that all nine teachers used three overarching principles of practice to guide and explain their interactive teaching behavior: suppressing emotions, teacher authenticity, and self-monitoring.

The principle of suppressing emotions was similar to that described by Marland. But in addition to its use as a disruption-prevention strategy, Conners' teachers reported using what could be called "visible suppression of emotions" (e.g., remaining silent and stern-faced until the class quiets down), and also intentionally violating this principle by occasionally expressing anger or frustration to make a powerful impression on their students. This last example suggests that principles of practice can be used flexibly by teachers and even appropriately contravened in certain circumstances.

The principle of teacher authenticity involved teacher presentation of self in such a way that good personal relationships with students and a socially constructive classroom atmosphere would result. This principle was expressed as a desire to behave in ways that were open, sincere, honest, and fallible.

The principle of self-monitoring was defined as the need for teachers to remain aware of their behavior and the estimated effects of their behavior on their students. For the teachers interviewed by Connors, this principle seemed to be acted upon at a global and intuitive level of judgment, for example, by asking oneself "How am I doing ?" regularly during teaching.

Conners also identified five general pedagogical principles held by teachers: cognitive linking, integration, closure, general involvement, and equality of teatment. The first two of these principles dealt with how information to be learned should be organized and presented.

The principle of cognitive linking dictated that new information should be explicitly related by the teacher to past and future student learning experiences. *The principal of integration* called for opportunities for students to practice and apply skills and concepts learned in one subject area in other subjects and contexts in pursuit of transfer of training. *The principle of closure* involved teacher commitment to the importance of summarizing, reviewing, and tying together main points at the end of a lesson or unit. Taken together, these three principles imply a view of the student as an active learner who stores and retrieves information on the basis of meaningful connections among facts and concepts and for whom transfer and integration require explicit practice.

The final two principles claimed by Connors' teachers dealt with their commitments regarding the social dynamics and ideology of the classroom. *The principle of general involvement* was expressed as the desire to have all students participate fully in class activities, to minimize student isolation (self-selected or otherwise), and to help shy or withdrawn students to overcome their reluctance to participate. *The principle of equality of treatment* called for fair and consistent treatment of each student. It is possible to imagine classroom situations in which these last two principles would conflict, for example, violating the principle of equality of treatment to provide special attention, encouragement, or reward to withdrawn students for their full participation in a learning activity. This hypothetical example suggests that principles of practice, while useful as general guides for planning, organizing, and teaching in the classroom, are not sufficient by themselves and require artful interpretation, balance, compromise, and, occasionally, intentional violation to serve the experienced teacher well.

Elbaz (1981) examined the practical knowledge of one high school English teacher who was also developing a course on learning skills at the time of the study. Elbaz reports the particulars of this teacher's practical knowledge in great detail in her doctoral dissertation (Elbaz, 1980, 1983). For the purposes of this review, the most relevant findings of this study concern the nature of teacher practical knowledge, as summarized in Table 9.11. The five content areas of teacher practical knowledge (curriculum, subject matter, instruction, milieu, and self) are largely self-explanatory and not at all surprising. The five orientations of practical knowledge claimed by Elbaz (situational, social, personal, experiential, and theoretical), taken together, suggest that a teacher's practical knowledge is not acquired vicariously and abstractly (as in a teacher preparation course) but is learned, tested, and developed through field experience.

The three structural forms that Elbaz uses to describe teacher practical knowledge (rules of practice, practical principles, and images) provide a particularly useful framework for thinking about the research on teachers' implicit theories and about the dynamics of those theories in use. According to Elbaz, rules of practice are brief, clearly formulated statements prescribing how to behave in frequently encountered teaching situations. Implementation of a rule of practice is a simple matter of recognizing a situation and remembering the rule. In contrast, a principle of practice is a more general construct than a rule of practice, derived from personal experience, and embodying purpose in a deliberate and reflective way, which can be drawn upon to guide a teacher's actions and explain the reasons for those actions. The use of a principle of practice depends largely on teacher reflection. Thirdly, images are personally held mental pictures of how good teaching should look and feel, expressed by the teacher in terms of brief metaphoric statements or analogies. According to Elbaz, teachers work intuitively rather than analytically to realize their images of good teaching.

TEACHERS' IMPLICIT THEORIES VERSUS CURRICULUM DEVELOPERS' THEORIES.

Two related studies of teachers' implicit theories took as their starting point the problem of implementation of new curricula. Both studies employed a version of the repertory grid technique to elicit labels for constructs that the teachers used in thinking about, evaluating, and classifying teacher and student behavior. In both studies each teacher's own words were used, in large measure, to describe his or her implicit theory of teaching. In the first study, Olson (1980, 1981) presented a list of 20 teaching events, selected to reflect a wide range of science teaching methods, to eight science teachers who were implementing a new curriculum in British secondary schools. Each teacher was asked to sort and group the 20 statements, to discuss the basis for grouping with the investigator, and then to coin a label for each group. These labels were termed "constructs" by Olson. Finally, the teacher-generated construct labels (plus five construct labels supplied by Olson) were arrayed along the horizontal axis of a grid, with the 20 statements about teaching and learning arrayed along the vertical axis. Each teacher then noted the degree of relationship between each construct and each teaching–learning statement. The results of this rating process were used to describe relationships among constructs through correlational analysis and among statements about teaching and learning through factor analysis.

Olson determined that, for these teachers, the most important underlying construct in their implicit theories of teaching was classroom influence. The new science curriculum being implemented at the time of the study called for reduced teacher influence in the classroom "as a consequence of project features such as: free ranging discussion episodes; downplaying in the design the importance of content in science teaching and examination preparation; requiring teachers to instruct outside their discipline" (Olson, 1981, p. 265). According to Olson's (1981) analysis, the teachers dealt with the tension between their belief that teacher influence should be high and the curriculum developers' belief that teacher influence should be low by "domesticating" the curriculum project so that it became compatible with the teachers' implicit theories of good teaching:

> For example: discussions became lectures or recitations; intellectual skills development was translated as content memorization and examination rehearsal; the integrated design was translated as a patchwork of specialized content to be unravelled and resewn; criterion referenced assessment was translated as norm based. In short, after a period of experimentation during which they saw their influence declining, the teachers re-established influence through varied domestications of the project doctrine. (p. 265)

In a related study of the implicit theories of teaching of 14 teachers of junior high school, Munby (1983) used the repertory grid technique in two sessions, separated by 3 days. In the first session, the investigator asked each teacher to generate a set of brief statements describing what one might see during a visit to one of the teacher's classes. After generating about 20 descriptive statements (called "elements" by Munby), each teacher was asked to group the cards on which the statements were written into as many groups as made sense to the teacher. Next, each teacher was asked to discuss the bases for groupings and the distinction and other relationships between groups of statements. The investigator recorded the terms and phrases used by each teacher to explain and rationalize the groupings, and these became the "constructs" constituting the teacher's implicit theory. Finally, the "elements" and "constructs" were listed along the two axes of a grid, and the teacher was asked to consider each element in turn and rate the strength of its association with each construct.

Between the first and second interviews, Munby factor-analyzed the grid to produce construct groupings. The purpose of the second interview was to discover what beliefs and principles underlie the resultant factors. This interview and analysis process produced labels for each of the factors and teacher explanations of the relationships between the factors. From the transcripts of these second interviews, Munby identified a set of teacher statements that constituted the principles and beliefs that he characterizes as "phrases, statements, or terms which convey significant meaning to the teachers and to us about their professional activity" (Munby, 1983, p. 27).

Munby makes a forceful case that the most appropriate mode for reporting findings from his research is the case study. His report offers excerpts from 14 case studies that illustrate the wide individual differences in the implicit theories of teachers working at the same school and even within the same subject matter specializations. The existence of these idiosyncratic variations in beliefs and principles is used by Munby to explain how and why a nominally common curriculum is inevitably interpreted and implemented differently by each teacher teaching from it. In describing the general nature of teachers' implicit theories as derived from this study, Munby found that each teacher enunciated between three and six principles. The five most frequently mentioned construct categories were (a) student learning and developmental goals, (b) student involvement, (c) teacher control and authority, (d) student needs and limitations, and (e) motivation.

The Olson and Munby studies provide a sense of both the variability and consequentiality of teachers' implicit theories about teaching. Both researchers make a persuasive case for staying close to the language of practice in eliciting and describing teachers' belief systems, a position also supported by Elliott (1976). When implementing a significant curricular, organizational, or instructional change, these researchers argue that teachers' belief systems can be ignored only at the innovator's peril. These findings are supported by the results of a Q-sort study by Ignatovich et al. (1979), in which the belief systems of elementary teachers, elementary principals, and of those administrators attempting to influence classroom procedures by implementing rational management models were contrasted. They found that both teachers and elementary principals' belief systems emphasized positive relations between teachers and students, a constructive classroom social system, and humanistic approaches to instruction. In contrast, "rational management system" administrators defined effective instruction in terms of student achievement on standardized tests, abstract models of classroom learning, administrative evaluation, and the influence of outside forces on classrooms.

SUMMARY

It is difficult to synthesize a clear and unequivocal set of conclusions about teachers' implicit theories from this small and eclectic collection of studies. At the very least, we can say that teachers do seem to hold implicit theories about their work and that these conceptual systems can be made more explicit through a variety of direct and indirect inquiry techniques. Even within what appear to be relatively homogeneous groups of teachers (e.g., teachers implementing open education approaches) there is wide variation in the content and orientation of teachers' implicit theories. The several studies that describe teachers' principles of practice suggest that relatively few such principles (three to six) are needed to describe a teacher's implicit theory of teaching.

The principles of practice that teachers draw upon to explain their interactive teaching behavior deal (directly or indirectly) with student characteristics and states, teacher states, and, to a lesser extent, with the structure and organization of subject matter. Duffy's (1977) study of conceptions of reading suggests that the correspondence between teachers' espoused beliefs and classroom behavior is not always high and is moderated by circumstances that are beyond the teacher's control. This study also signaled a gradual move away from the language of researchers and toward the language of teachers in describing teachers' implicit theories.

The Ignatovich et al. (1979), Olson (1981), and Munby (1983) studies raise the possibility that conflict between teachers' implicit theories about good teaching with those of administrators or curriculum developers may explain historic and continuing difficulties in implementation of educational innovations. Elbaz's (1981) analysis of teachers' practical knowledge, especially concerning the three structural forms of practical knowledge, holds promise as an organizing conceptual system for future research and modeling of teachers' implicit theories and belief systems in use.

Conclusions

The *Second Handbook of Research on Teaching* (Travers, 1973) did not include a chapter or even a reference to research on teachers' thought processes. The research reviewed in this chapter and the view of teaching and inquiry that guide this research are new. Many of these studies raise as many questions as they answer, about method as well as about teachers' thought processes. These limitations notwithstanding, however, our review suggests a number of broad conclusions about research on teachers' thought processes.

First, the research shows that thinking plays an important part in teaching, and that the image of a teacher as a reflective professional, proposed originally by the NIE Panel 6 on Teaching as Clinical Information Processing (National Institute of Education, 1975a), is not far fetched. Teachers do plan in a rich variety of ways, and these plans have real consequences in the classroom. Teachers do have thoughts and make decisions frequently (one every 2 minutes) during interactive teaching. Teachers do have theories and belief systems that influence their perceptions, plans, and actions. This literature has given us an opportunity to broaden our appreciation for what teaching is by adding rich descriptions of the mental activities of teachers to the existing body of work that describes the visible behavior of teachers.

Because this research is so new, each study seems to break new ground. At this time, we have little that could be called a systematic and cumulative body of research. Most of the research on teachers' thought processes has been done with teachers of elementary school, and there is a conspicuous absence of attention to the thought processes of secondary school teachers. Researchers have also tended to focus on relatively discrete and isolated aspects of teachers' thoughts and actions, rather than on the whole process of teaching or on the relationships between, for example, teacher planning and interactive thoughts and action in the classroom. While a narrow focus may be useful early in a research enterprise, the time seems right for more comprehensive study of the full variety of teachers' thought processes in relationship to teachers' actions and their effects on students. Similarly, a vast majority of teachers participating in this research have been experienced teachers. The literature provides us with little sense of how teacher planning, interactive thinking and decision making, and implicit theories and beliefs develop over time, and, therefore, what kinds of interventions might help these processes along. Longitudinal studies of the development of teachers' thought processes would be one answer to this need.

The many different contexts in which these studies of teacher thinking have been done highlights the variety of task demands encountered in teaching. Teachers' thought processes seem to constitute a more or less adaptive array of responses to perceived task demands of the profession. This literature provides a reasonably good start at describing teachers' cognitive behavior, but has not done an adequate job of describing the tasks and teaching situations that call for thoughtful teaching. Researchers would do well to work simultaneously on descriptive models of teacher thought processes and on descriptive models of the tasks of teaching.

While research on teachers' thought processes is new, it has deep roots in early teaching effectiveness and curriculum research. Studies of teacher thinking are potential sources of hypotheses about and explanation of some of the puzzling and contradictory findings of process–product research on teaching and of curriculum change implementation research. For example, if teachers' implicit theory about learners or their mental image of effective teaching were contrary to that embodied in a new curriculum or an experimental teaching method, they would be unlikely to bring the innovation alive with great enthusiasm, thoroughness, and persistence. Alternatively, if an innovation or experimental treatment were introduced after a teacher's yearly and term planning were complete, it would be unlikely that the innovation would be integrated into the classroom activity flow as thoroughly as the researcher would hope. Teacher thinking, as represented in this literature, can be thought of as a set of moderating contextual factors that could influence substantially the outcomes of teacher effectiveness and curriculum effectiveness studies.

While no single study has documented every aspect of the thought processes of a teacher, from this literature we can elaborate on the picture of the teacher as a reflective and thoughtful professional that was sketched out by NIE Panel 6 (National Institute of Education, 1975a). The emerging picture of the teacher as a reflective professional is a developmental one that begins during undergraduate teacher education (or even earlier) and continues to grow and change with professional experience. The teacher education majors who would become professionals in this sense are firmly grounded in the disciplines and subject matters that they will teach. Their study of subject matter focuses on both content and on the cognitive organization of that content in ways useful to themselves and to their future students. They have had both supervised practice in using the behavioral skills and strategies of teaching and have also been initiated into the less visible aspects of teaching, including the full variety of types of planning and interactive decision making. The maturing professional teacher is one who has taken some steps toward making explicit his or her implicit theories and beliefs about learners, curriculum, subject matter, and the teacher's role. This teacher has developed a style of planning for instruction that includes several interrelated types of planning and that has become more streamlined and automatic with experience. Much of this teacher's interactive teaching consists of routines familiar to the students, thus decreasing the collective information-processing load. During teaching, the teacher attends to and intently processes academic and nonacademic sociocognitive events and cues. These experienced teachers have developed the confidence to depart from a planned course of action when they judge that to be appropriate. They reflect on and analyze the apparent effects of their own teaching and apply the results of these reflections to their future plans and actions. In short, they have become researchers on their own teaching effectiveness.

A decade of research on teachers' thought processes has taught us as much about how to think about teaching as it has about teachers' thinking. Most educators would probably have agreed with the authors of the NIE Panel 6 report that teaching is a complex and cognitively demanding human process (National Institute of Education, 1975a). The research reviewed here has begun to describe in detail the many ways in which teaching is complex, demanding, and uniquely human.

REFERENCES

Ames, R. Teachers' attributions of responsibility: Some unexpected nondefensive effects. *Journal of Educational Psychology, 67,* 668–676.

Ames, R (1982). Teachers' attributions for their own teaching. In J. M. Levine and M. C. Wang (Eds.), *Teacher and student perceptions: Implications for learning.* Hillsdale, NJ: Lawrence Erlbaum.

Anderson, L. M., & Evertson, C. M. (1978). *Classroom organization at the beginning of school: Two case studies.* Paper presented to the American Association of Colleges for Teacher Education, Chicago

Anderson, R. C. (1977). The notion of schemata and the educational enterprise. In R. C. Anderson, R. Spiro, & W. Montague (Eds.), *Schooling and the acquisition of knowledge.* Hillsdale, NJ: Lawrence Erlbaum.

Anderson, R. C. (1984, November). Some reflections on the acquisition of knowledge. *Educational Researcher, 13,* 5 10.

Bar-Tal, D., & Darom, E. (1979). Pupils' attributions of success and failure. *Child Development, 50,* 264–267.

Beckman, L. (1970). Effects of students' performance on teachers' and observers' attributions of causality. *Journal of Educational Psychology, 61,* 76–82.

Beckman, L. (1973). Teachers' and observers' perceptions of causality for a child's performance. *Journal of Educational Psychology, 65,* 198–204.

Beckman, L. J. (1976). Causal attributions of teachers and parents regarding children's performance. *Psychology in the Schools, 13,* 212–218.

Ben-Peretz, M. (1975). The concept of curriculum potential. *Curriculum Theory Network, 5,* 151–159.

Bishop, A. J., & Whitfield, R. C. (1972). *Situations in teaching.* London: McGraw-Hill.

Bloom, B. S. (1954). The thought processes of students in discussion. In S. J. French (Ed.), *Accent on teaching: Experiments in general education.* New York: Harper Brothers.

Blumenfeld, P. C., Hamilton, V. L., Wessels, K., & Falkner, D. (1977). *"You can," "You should," and "You'd better:" Teacher attributions regarding achievement and social behaviors.* Paper presented at the annual meeting of the American Psychological Association, San Francisco.

Brandt, L. J., Hayden, M. E., & Brophy, J. E. (1975). Teachers' attitudes and ascription of causation. *Journal of Educational Psychology, 67,* 677–682.

Bromme, R. (1982, March). *How to analyze routines in teachers' thinking processes during lesson planning.* Paper presented at the annual meeting of the American Educational Research Association, New York.

Brophy, J. E. (1982). *Research on the self-fulfilling prophecy and teacher expectations* (Research Series No. 119). East Lansing: Michigan State University, Institute for Research on Teaching.

Brophy, J. E., & Rohrkemper, M. M. (1981). The influence of problem ownership on teachers' perceptions of and strategies for coping with problem students. *Journal of Educational Psychology, 73,* 295–311.

Buckley, P. K., & Cooper, J. M. (1978, March). *An ethnographic study of an elementary school teacher's establishment and maintenance of group norms.* Paper presented at the annual meeting of the American Educational Research Association, Toronto, Canada.

Bussis, A. M., Chittenden, F., & Amarel, M. (1976). *Beyond surface curriculum.* Boulder, CO: Westview Press.

Calderhead, J. (1981). A psychological approach to research on teachers' classroom decision making. *British Educational Research Journal, 7,* 51–57.

Calderhead, J. (1983, April). *Research into teachers' and student teachers' cognitions: Exploring the nature of classroom practice.* Paper presented at the annual meeting of the American Educational Research Association, Montreal, Canada.

Carnahan, R. S. (1980). *The effects of teacher planning on classroom processes* (Tech. Rep. No. 541). Madison: Wisconsin R & D Center for Individualized Schooling.

Clark, C. M., & Elmore, J. L. (1979). *Teacher planning in the first weeks of school* (Research Series No. 56). East Lansing: Michigan State University, Institute for Research on Teaching.

Clark, C. M., & Elmore, J. L. (1981). *Transforming curriculum in mathematics, science, and writing: A case study of teacher yearly planning* (Research Series No. 99). East Lansing: Michigan State University, Institute for Research on Teaching.

Clark, C. M., & Peterson, P. L. (1981). Stimulated-recall. In B. R. Joyce, C. C. Brown, & L. Peck (Eds.), *Flexibility in teaching: An excursion into the nature of teaching and training.* New York: Longman.

Clark, C. M., & Yinger, R. J. (1977). Research on teacher thinking. *Curriculum Inquiry, 7*(4), 279–394).

Clark, C. M., & Yinger, R. J. (1979a). Teachers' thinking. In P. L. Peterson & H. J. Walberg (Eds.), *Research on teaching.* Berkeley, CA: McCutchan.

Clark, C. M., & Yinger, R. J. (1979b). *Three studies of teacher planning* (Research Series No. 55). East Lansing: Michigan State University.

Clark, C. M., Yinger, R. J., & Wildfong, S. C. (1978). *Identifying cues for use in studies of teacher judgment* (Research Series No. 23). East Lansing: Institute for Research on Teaching, Michigan State University.

Colker, L. (1982). *Teachers' interactive thoughts about pupil cognition.* Unpublished doctoral dissertation, University of Illinois at Urbana–Champaign.

Cone, R. (1978, March). *Teachers' decisions in managing student behavior: A laboratory simulation of interactive decision-making by teachers.* Paper presented at the annual meeting of the American Educational Research Association, Toronto, Canada.

Connelly, F. M. (1972). The functions of curriculum development. *Interchange, 3,* 161–177.

Conners, R. D. (1978a). *Using stimulated recall in naturalistic settings: Some technical procedures* (Tech. Paper No. 78-2-1). Edmonton, Canada: University of Alberta, Centre for Research in Teaching.

Conners, R. D. (1978b). *An analysis of teacher thought processes, beliefs, and principles during instruction.* Unpublished doctoral dissertation, University of Alberta, Edmonton, Canada.

Cooper, H. M., & Baron, R. M. (1977). Academic expectations and attributed responsibility as predictors of professional teachers' reinforcement behavior. *Journal of Educational Psychology, 69,* 409–418.

Cooper, H. M., & Baron, R. M. (1979). Academic expectations, attributed responsibility, and teachers' reinforcement behavior: A suggested integration of conflicting literatures. *Journal of Educational Psychology, 71,* 274–277.

Cooper, H. M., Baron, R. M., & Lowe, C. A. (1975). The importance of race and social class information in the formation of expectancies about academic performance *Journal of Educational Psychology, 67,* 312–319.

Cooper, H. M., & Burger, J. M. (1980). How teachers explain students' academic performance: A categorization of free response academic attributions. *American Educational Research Journal, 17,* 95–109.

Corno, L. (1981). Cognitive organizing in classrooms. *Curriculum Inquiry, 11,* 359–377.

Covington, M. V., Spratt, M. F., & Omelich, C. L. (1980). Is effort enough, or does diligence count too? Student and teacher reactions to effort stability in failure. *Journal of Educational Psychology, 72,* 717–729.

Creemers, B. P. M., & Westerhof, K. (1982). *Routinization of instructive and management behavior of teachers* (research paper). Haren, The Netherlands: Educational Research Institute in the North.

Crist, J., Marx, R. W., & Peterson, P. L. (1974). *Teacher behavior in the organizational domain* (Report submitted to the National Institute of Education). Stanford, CA: Stanford Center for R & D in Teaching.

Dahllof, U., & Lundgren, U. P. (1970). *Macro- and micro approaches combined for curriculum process analysis: A Swedish educational field project.* Göteborg, Sweden: University of Göteborg, Institute of Education. (Mimeo)

Darley, J. M., & Fazio, R. H. (1980). Expectancy confirmation processes arising in the social interaction sequence. *American Psychologist, 35,* 867–881.

De Corte, E., & Lowyck, J. (1980). *Analysis of cognitive processes in teaching behavior* (Report No. 24). Leuven, Belgium: Katholieke Universiteit te Leuven, Department Pedagogische Wetenschappen.

Domingo-Llacuna, E. A. (1976). The effect of pupil race, social class, speech and ability on teacher stereotypes and attributions (Doctoral dissertation, University of Illinois at Urbana–Champaign, 1976). *Dissertation Abstracts International, 37,* 2737–2738. (University Microfilms No. 76-24, 072)

Doyle, W. (1977a). Learning the classroom environment: An ecological analysis. *Journal of Teacher Education, 28,* 51–55.

Doyle, W. (1977b). Paradigms for research on teacher effectiveness. *Review of Research in Education, 5,* 163–198.

Doyle, W. (1979). Making managerial decisions in classrooms. In D. L. Duke (Ed.), *Classroom management* (Yearbook of the National Society for the Study of Education). Chicago: University of Chicago Press.

Duffy, G. (1977). *A study of teacher conceptions of reading.* Paper presented at the National Reading Conference, New Orleans.

Dunkin, M. J., & Biddle, B. J. (1974). *The study of teaching.* New York: Holt, Rinehart & Winston.

Dweck, C. S., Davidson, W., Nelson, S., & Enna, B. (1978). 1. Sex differences in learned helplessness: 2. The contingencies of evaluative feedback in the classroom; 3. An experimental analysis. *Developmental Psychology, 14,* 268–276.

Eisner, E. W. (1967). Educational objectives: Help or hindrance? *School Review, 75,* 250–260.

Eisner, E. W., & Vallance, E. (1974). *Conflicting conceptions of curriculum.* Berkeley, CA: McCutchan.

Elbaz, F. (1980). *The teacher's "practical knowledge": A case study.* Unpublished doctoral dissertation, University of Toronto.

Elbaz, F. (1981). The teacher's "practical knowledge": Report of a case study. *Curriculum Inquiry, 11,* 43–71.

Elbaz, F. (1983). *Teacher thinking: A study of practical knowledge.* New York: Nichols Publishing.

Elliot, J. (1976). *Developing hypotheses about classrooms from teachers' practical constructs.* Grand Forks: North Dakota Study Group.

Ericson, K. A., & Simon, H. A. (1980). Verbal reports as data. *Psychological Review, 87,* 215–251.

Favor-Lydecker, A. (1981, April). *Teacher planning of social studies instructional units.* Paper presented at the annual meeting of the American Educational Research Association, Los Angeles.

Feuquay, J. P. (1979). Teachers' self-attributions and their projections of student attributions under varying conditions (Doctoral dissertation, Oklahoma State University, 1979). *Dissertation Abstracts International, 40,* 4487 (University Microfilms No. 8003570)

Fogarty, J. L., Wang, M. C., & Creek, R. (1982, March). *A descriptive study of experienced and novice teachers' interactive instructional decision processes.* Paper presented at the annual meeting of the American Educational Research Association, New York City.

Frieze, I. H. (1976). Causal attributions and information-seeking to explain success and failure. *Journal of Research in Personality, 10,* 293–305.

Goodlad, J., & Klein, M. F. (1970). *Behind the classroom door.* Worthington, OH: Charles A. Jones.

Hammond, K. R. (1971). Computer graphics as an aid to learning. *Science, 172,* 903–908.

Hanes, B. F. (1979). Causal attributions by teacher-trainees for success and failure outcomes of elementary students labeled normal and gifted (Doctoral dissertation, Oklahoma State University, 1979). *Dissertation Abstracts International, 40,* 3198–31995S. (University Microfilms No. 7928212)

Heider, F. (1958). *The pscychology of interpersonal relations.* New York: Wiley.

Heller, K. A., & Parsons, J. E. (1981). Sex differences in teachers' evaluative feedback and students' expectancies for success in mathematics. *Child Development, 52,* 1015–1019.

Hill, J., Yinger, R. J., & Robbins, D. (1981, April). *Instructional planning in a developmental preschool.* Paper presented at the annual meeting of the American Educational Research Association, Los Angeles.

Housner, L. D., & Griffey, D. C. (1983, April). *Teacher cognition: Differences in planning and interactive decision making between experienced and inexperienced teachers.* Paper presented at the annual meeting of the American Educational Research Association, Montreal, Canada.

Ignatovich, F. R., Cusick, P. A., & Ray, J. E. (1979). *Value/belief patterns of teachers and those administrators engaged in attempts to influence teaching* (Research Series No. 43). East Lansing: Michigan State University, Institute for Research on Teaching.

Jackson, P. W. (1966). *The way teaching is.* Washington, DC: National Education Association.

Jackson, P. W. (1968). *Life in classrooms.* New York: Holt, Rinehart & Winston.

Janesick, V. (1977). *An ethnographic study of a teacher's classroom perspective.* Unpublished doctoral dissertation, Michigan State University, East Lansing.

Johnson, T. J., Feigenbaum, R., & Weiby, M. (1964). Some determinants and consequences of the teacher's perception of causation. *Journal of Educational Psychology, 55,* 237–246.

Jones, E. E., & Nisbett, R. E. (1971). *The actor and observer: Divergent perceptions of the causes of behavior.* Morristown, NJ: General Learning Press.

Joyce, B. R. (1978–1979). Toward a theory of information processing in teaching. *Educational Research Quarterly, 3*(4), 66–77.

Joyce, B. R., & Harootunian, B. (1964). Teaching as problem solving. *Journal of Teacher Education, 15,* 420–427.

Kelly, G. A. (1955). *The psychology of personal constructs* (2 vols.). New York: W. W. Norton.

King, L. H. (1980). *Student thought processes and the expectancy effect* (Research Rep. No. 80-1-8). Churchlands, Perth, Australia: Churchlands College of Advanced Education.

Lowyck, J. (1980). *A process analysis of teaching* (Report No. 21). Leuven, Belgium: Katholieke Universiteit te Leuven, Departement Pedagogische Wetenschappen.

MacKay, D. A., & Marland, P. W. (1978, March). *Thought processes of teachers.* Paper presented at the annual meeting of the American Educational Research Association, Toronto, Canada.

Marland, P. W. (1977). *A study of teachers' interactive thoughts.* Unpublished doctoral dissertation, University of Alberta, Edmonton, Canada.

Marx, R. W., & Peterson, P. L. (1981). The nature of teacher decision making. In B. R. Joyce, C. C. Brown, & L. Peck (Eds.), *Flexibility in teaching: An excursion into the nature of teaching and training.* New York: Longman.

McCutcheon, G. (1980). How do elementary school teachers plan? The nature of planning and influences on it. *Elementary School Journal, 81,* 4–23.

McLeod, M. A. (1981). *The identification of intended learning outcomes by early childhood teachers: An exploratory study.* Unpublished doctoral dissertation, University of Alberta, Edmonton, Canada.

McNair, K. (1978–1979). Capturing inflight decisions. *Educational Research Quarterly, 3*(4), 26–42.

Medway, F. J. (1979). Causal attributions for school-related problems: Teacher perceptions and teacher feedback. *Journal of Educational Psychology, 71,* 809–818.

Meyer, W. U. (1979). Academic expectations, attributed responsibility, and teacher's reinforcement behavior: A comment on Cooper and

Baron, with some additional data. *Journal of Educational Psychology, 71,* 269–273.

Morine, G., & Vallance, E. (1975). *Special study B: A study of teacher and pupil perceptions of classroom interaction* (Tech. Rep. No. 75-11-6). San Francisco: Far West Laboratory.

Morine-Dershimer, G. (1977, April). *What's in a plan? Stated and unstated plans for lessons.* Paper presented at the annual meeting of the American Educational Research Association, New York.

Morine-Dershimer, G. (1978–1979). Planning and classroom reality: An in-depth look. *Educational Research Quarterly, 3*(4), 83–99.

Morine-Dershimer, G. (1979). *Teacher plan and classroom reality: The South Bay study: Part 4* (Research Series No. 60). East Lansing: Michigan State University, Institute for Research on Teaching.

Morine-Dershimer, G., & Vallance, E. (1976). *Teacher planning* (Beginning Teacher Evaluation Study, Special Report C). San Francisco: Far West Laboratory.

Munby, H. (1982). The place of teachers' beliefs in research on teacher thinking and decision making, and an alternative methodology. *Instructional Science, 11,* 201–225.

Munby, H. (1983, April). *A qualitative study of teachers' beliefs and principles.* Paper presented at the annual meeting of the American Educational Research Association, Montreal.

National Institute of Education. (1975a). *Teaching as clinical information processing* (Report of Panel 6, National Conference on Studies in Teaching). Washington, DC: National Institute of Education.

National Institute of Education. (1975b). *Theory development.* (Report of Panel 10, National Conference on Studies in Teaching). Washington, DC: National Institute of Education.

Neale, D. C., Pace, A. J., & Case, A. B. (1983, April). *The influence of training, experience, and organizational environment on teachers' use of the systematic planning model.* Paper presented at the annual meeting of the American Educational Research Association, Montreal.

Newell, A., & Simon, H. A. (1972). *Human problem solving.* Englewood Cliffs, NJ: Prentice-Hall.

Nisbett, R. E., & Ross, L. (1980). *Human inference: Strategies and shortcomings of social judgment.* Englewood Cliffs, NJ: Prentice-Hall.

Nisbett, R. E., & Wilson, T. D. (1977). Telling more than we can know: Verbal reports on mental processes. *Psychological Review, 84,* 231–259.

Olson, J. K. (1980). *Innovative doctrines and practical dilemmas: A case study of curriculum translation.* Unpublished doctoral dissertation. University of Birmingham, England.

Olson, J. K. (1981). Teacher influence in the classroom. *Instructional Science, 10,* 259–275.

Peterson, P. L., & Barger, S. A. (1984). Attribution theory and teacher expectancy. In J. B. Dusek (Ed.), *Teacher expectancies* (pp. 159–184). Hillsdale, NJ: Lawrence Erlbaum.

Peterson, P. L., & Clark, C. M. (1978). Teachers' reports of their cognitive processes during teaching. *American Educational Research Journal, 15,* 555–565.

Peterson, P. L., Marx, R. W., & Clark, C. M. (1978). Teacher planning, teacher behavior, and student achievement. *American Educational Research Journal, 15,* 417–432.

Peterson, P. L., Swing, S. R., Braverman, M. T., & Buss, R. (1982). Students' aptitudes and their reports of cognitive processes during direct instruction. *Journal of Educational Psychology, 74,* 535–547.

Peterson, P. L., Swing, S. R., Stark, K. D., & Wass, G. A. (1983, April). *Students' reports of their cognitive processes and affective thoughts during classroom instruction.* Paper presented at the annual meeting of the American Educational Research Association, Montreal.

Peterson, P. L., & Walberg, H. J. (Eds.). (1979). *Research on teaching: Concepts, findings, and implications.* Berkeley, CA: McCutchan.

Popham, J. W., & Baker, E. L. (1970). *Systematic instruction.* Englewood Cliffs, NJ: Prentice-Hall.

Posner, G. (1981). New developments in curricular research: It's the thought that counts. *The Researcher* (Newsletter of the Northeastern Educational Research Association), *19,* 25–55.

Prawat, R. S., Byers, J. L., & Anderson, A. H. (1983). An attributional analysis of teachers' affective reactions to student success and failure. *American Educational Research Journal, 1,* 137–152.

Pylypiw, J. (1974). *A description of classroom curriculum development.* Unpublished doctoral dissertation, University of Alberta, Edmonton, Canada.

Rappoport, L., & Summers, D. A. (1973). *Human judgment and social interaction.* New York: Holt, Rinehart & Winston.

Raths, J. D. (1971). Teaching without specific objectives. *Educational Leadership, 28,* 714–720.

Rosenshine, B. V., & Furst, N. (1973). The use of direct observation to study teaching. In R. M. W. Travers (Ed.), *Second handbook of research on teaching.* Chicago: Rand McNally.

Ross, L., Bierbrauer, G., & Polly, S. (1974). Attribution of educational outcomes by professional and nonprofessional instructors. *Journal of Personality and Social Psychology, 29,* 609–618.

Rumelhart, D. E. (1980). Schemata: The building blocks of cognition. In R. J. Spiro, B. C. Bruce, & W. F. Brewer (Eds.), *Theoretical issues in reading comprehension: Perspectives from cognitive psychology, linguistics, artificial intelligence, and education.* Hillsdale, NJ: Lawrence Erlbaum.

Sardo, D. (1982, October). *Teacher planning styles in the middle school.* Paper presented to the Eastern Educational Research Association, Ellenville, NY.

Semmel, D. S. (1977, April). *The effects of training on teacher decision making.* Paper presented at the annual meeting of the American Educational Research Association, New York City. (ERIC Document Reproduction Service No. ED 138 558)

Semmel, M. I., Brady, M. E., & Semmel, D. S. (1976). *The development of oral reading prompting skills in a CATTS–CBTE program for preservice teachers of the mildly handicapped* (Final Rep. No. 53.5). Bloomington: Indiana University, Center for Innovation in Teaching the Handicapped. (ERIC Document Reproduction Service No. ED 162 468)

Shavelson, R. J. (1973). *The basic teaching skill: Decision making* (R & D Memorandum No. 104). Stanford, CA: Stanford University, School of Education, Center for R & D in Teaching.

Shavelson, R. J. (1976). Teachers' decision making. In N. L. Gage (Ed.), *The psychology of teaching methods* (Yearbook of the National Society for the Study of Education). Chicago: University of Chicago Press.

Shavelson, R. J., Atwood, N. K., & Borko, H. (1977). Experiments on some factors contributing to teachers' pedagogical decisions. *Cambridge Journal of Education, 7,* 51–70.

Shavelson, R. J., & Stern, P. (1981). Research on teachers' pedagogical thoughts, judgments, decisions, and behavior. *Review of Educational Research, 51,* 455–498.

Shroyer, J. C. (1981). *Critical moments in the teaching of mathematics: What makes teaching difficult?* Unpublished doctoral dissertation, Michigan State University, East Lansing.

Shulman, L. S., & Elstein, A. S. (1975). Studies of problem solving, judgment, and decision making: Implications for educational research. In F. N. Kerlinger (Ed.), *Review of Research in Education, 3,* 5–42.

Shultz, J., & Florio, S. (1979). Stop and freeze: The negotiation of social and physical space in a kindergarten/first grade classroom. *Anthropology and Education Quarterly, 10,* 166–181.

Silverstein, M. (1978). An attributional analysis of teachers' evaluative judgements (Doctoral dissertation, University of Rhode Island, 1978). *Dissertation Abstracts International, 39,* 1055–1056C. (University Microfilm No. 7813272)

Simon, H. A. (1957). *Models of man.* New York: Wiley.

Smith, E. L., & Sendelbach, N. B. (1979). *Teacher intentions for science instruction and their antecedents in program materials.* Paper presented at the annual meeting of the American Educational Research Association, San Francisco.

Smith, J. K. (1977, October). *Teacher planning for instruction* (Report No. 12). Chicago: CEMREL Studies of Educative Processes.

Snow, R. E. (1972). *A model teacher training system: An overview* (R & D Memorandum No. 92). Stanford University, School of Education, Center for R & D in Teaching. (ERIC Document Reproduction Service No. ED 066 437.)

Staton, J. (1982). *Dialogue journal writing as a communicative event* (Vol. 1). Washington, DC: Georgetown University Center for Applied Linguistics. (Mimeo)

Sutcliffe, J., & Whitfield, R. (1979). Classroom-based teaching decisions. In J. Eggleston (Ed.), *Teacher decision-making in the classroom: A collection of papers.* London: Routledge & Kegan Paul.

Taylor, P. H. (1970). *How teachers plan their courses.* Slough, Berkshire, England: National Foundation for Educational Research.

Tetlock, P. E. (1980). Explaining teacher explanations of pupil performance: A self-presentation interpretation. *Social Psychology Quarterly, 43,* 283–290.

Tikunoff, W. J., & Ward, B. A. (1978). *A naturalistic study of the initiation of students into three classroom social systems* (Report A-78-11). San Francisco: Far West Laboratory.

Toomey, R. (1977). Teachers' approaches to curriculum planning. *Curriculum Inquiry, 7,* 121–129.

Travers, R. M. W. (Ed.). (1973). *Second handbook of research on teaching.* Chicago: Rand McNally.

Tuckwell, N. B. (1980a). *Content analysis of stimulated recall protocols* (Tech. Paper No. 80-2-2). Edmonton, Canada: University of Alberta, Centre for Research in Teaching.

Tuckwell, N. B. (1980b). *Stimulated recall: Theoretical perspectives and practical and technical considerations* (Tech. Rep. No. 80-2-3). Edmonton, Canada: University of Alberta, Centre for Research in Teaching.

Tyler, R. W. (1950). *Basic principles of curriculum and instruction.* Chicago: University of Chicago Press.

Weiner, B. (Ed.). (1974). *Achievement motivation and attribution theory.* Morristown, NJ: General Learning Press.

Weiner, B., Frieze, I. H., Kukla, A., Reed, L., Rest, S., & Rosenbaum, R. M. (1971). *Perceiving the causes of success and failure.* Morristown, NJ: General Learning Press.

Weiner, B., & Kukla, A. (1970). An attributional analysis of achievement motivation. *Journal of Personality and Social Psychology, 15,* 1–20.

Wiley, M. G., & Eskilson, A. (1978). Why did you learn in school today? Teachers' perceptions of causality. *Sociology of Education, 51,* 261–269.

Wise, R. I. (1976). The use of objectives in curriculum planning. *Curriculum Theory Network, 5,* 280–289.

Wodlinger, M. G. (1980). *A study of teacher interactive decision making.* Unpublished doctoral dissertation, University of Alberta, Edmonton, Canada.

Yinger, R. J. (1977). *A study of teacher planning: Description and theory development using ethnographic and information processing methods.* Unpublished doctoral dissertation, Michigan State University, East Lansing.

Yinger, R. J. (1979). Routines in teacher planning. *Theory into Practice, 18,* 163–169.

Yinger, R. J., & Clark, C. M. (1981). *Reflective journal writing: Theory and practice* (Occasional Paper No. 50). East Lansing: Michigan State University, Institute for Research on Teaching.

Yinger, R. J., & Clark, C. M. (1982). *Understanding teachers' judgments about instruction: The task, the method, and the meaning* (Research Series No. 121). East Lansing: Michigan State University, Institute for Research on Teaching.

Yinger, R. J., & Clark, C. M. (1983). *Self-reports of teacher judgment.* (Research Series No. 134). East Lansing: Michigan State University, Institute for Research on Teaching.

Yinger, R. J., & Clark, C. M. (1985). *Using personal documents to study teacher thinking* (Occasional paper No. 84). East Lansing: Michigan State University, Institute for Research on Teaching.

Zahorik, J. A. (1970). The effects of planning on teaching. *Elementary School Journal, 71,* 143–151.

Zahorik, J. A. (1975). Teachers' planning models. *Educational Leadership, 33,* 134–139.

10.
Students' Thought Processes

Merlin C. Wittrock

University of California—Los Angeles

The recent research on students' thought processes studies the effects of teachers and instruction upon the student perceptions, expectations, attentional processes, motivations, attributions, memories, generations, understandings, beliefs, attitudes, learning strategies, and metacognitive processes that mediate achievement. The recent study of these student thought processes brings a distinctive perspective to the understanding of teachers' effects upon learning, the development of theories of teaching, and the design and analysis of teaching (Doyle, 1977, 1980; Winne & Marx, 1980; Wittrock, 1978). The distinctive perspective emphasizes the critical role that student background knowledge, perceptions of instruction, attention to the teacher, motivation and attribution for learning, affective processes, and ability to generate interpretations and understandings of instruction play in teaching and in influencing student achievement.

In contrast to research that studies how teachers or instructional processes directly contribute to student achievement, research on students' thought processes examines how teaching or teachers influence what students think, believe, feel, say, or do that affects their achievement. As a result the research designs of these studies include measures of at least two consecutive and reciprocally related links between teaching and student achievement. The first link is between teaching and student cognition. The second link is between student cognition and learning or achievement. There can often be additional links, and they can be related to one another in complex ways, such as the reciprocal relations that exist among student thoughts, achievement, and teaching. But the distinctive characteristic of the research on students' thought processes is the idea that teaching affects achievement through student thought processes. That is, teaching influences student thinking. Students' thinking mediates learning and achievement.

Perhaps teaching can also directly influence achievement, just as learning can sometimes occur without awareness. But research on students' cognitive processes examines and tests the utility of assuming otherwise, that teaching can better be understood, and improved, by knowing its effects upon the learners' thoughts that mediate achievement.

To give these statements more concrete meaning and to introduce the research findings that follow in the next sections, we will briefly discuss three often reported findings that relate teaching directly to student achievement. With each example we will contrast a simple input–output explanation of the findings with a model that interjects student thought processes as mediators between the teaching and the achievement.

First, the controversial self-fulfilling prophecy, that high or low teacher expectations regarding student achievement lead, respectively, to higher or lower student school achievement and to higher or lower student self-preceptions of academic ability, seems often, but not always, to be found in relevant empirical studies. To explore and to try to explain this phenomenon, research studies that examine student thought processes ask the following questions about the mediators of achievement. Did the teachers convey their expectations to the students? Did the students perceive the teachers' expectations? Did the students attempt to change their behavior or their self-concepts in response to the teachers' expectations? Were the students able to change their learning patterns, motivations, and expectations in response to the teaching? Did achievement change in response to these altered student cognitive and affective processes?

Research on students' thinking predicts that if these changes occurred in students' thinking, then the self-fulfilling prophecy would occur. The model implies that some students in a classroom might show these changes in thinking while other students might not show them, resulting in a teacher expectancy effect only for some students, a finding commonly reported in the literature. Another implication of this model is that the individual student, or the dyad, the teacher and the student, not the classroom, is the preferred unit to use to study the teacher expectancy effect. The reason is that student

The author thanks reviewers Penelope Peterson (University of Wisconsin—Madison) and Walter Doyle (University of Texas—Austin) for their excellent suggestions.

thoughts in response to the same teacher expectations differ from one learner to another.

Second is the often reported finding that teacher praise or reward increases learning. With this finding, a perspective that emphasizes students' thinking leads us to examine the interpretations and attributions that students construct from these rewards. To what extent do students perceive the rewards, and to what extent can students increase their information-processing skills to improve their achievement in response to the praise or reward? If students do not attribute the rewards to their own actions, or to activities over which they have some control, we would not expect the rewards to enhance learning. Teacher praise may also provide information about classroom performance to all the students who observe another student receive the praise. Praise of one student might mediate learning among a large number of students through its informational, as well as its motivational qualities. In brief, learning from teaching is not automatic. It occurs primarily through active and effortful information processing by students who must perceive and interpret teachers' actions for them to influence achievement.

Third, the time teachers allocate to learning has frequently been found to correlate directly with student achievement. The study of student cognitive processes, in this context, leads to the following hypotheses. The students' constructive use of the time, not the time per se, affects learning and achievement. Consequently, time actually devoted to the task by the students should correlate with learning more highly than should time allocated to the task by the teacher. In addition, attention, if accurately reported by the learners, should correlate with learning more highly than should time devoted to the task, as measured by observers in the classroom. The reason is that attention is an internal cognitive process that is not equivalent to externally observable activities, such as time spent looking at a book, or out a classroom window. Both of these findings are also supported in the literature on students' perceptions of attention, which will be discussed later in this chapter under the heading "Students' Perceptions of Cognitive Processes in the Classroom."

Those three examples introduce a perspective underlying the studies presented in the following sections. The following sections of this chapter illustrate but do not exhaust research on student thought processes that mediate achievement. These student thought processes include an awareness or perception of teaching, attention to it, motivation to learn, and ability to generate relations between knowledge and experience, on the one hand, and the materials or concepts to be learned, on the other hand.

These topics are discussed next. In addition, research on the teaching of learning strategies and metacognitive processes, which emphasizes awareness and control of student learning processes, is also briefly discussed. Again, the chapter introduces and illustrates the research but cannot in these few pages discuss all of the research studies in these extensive areas. Research in these areas is important for understanding how students learn how to learn and how students can be taught to improve their thought processes to facilitate knowledge acquisition, learning, and memory. Together these student thought processes and strategies comprise an organized and complementary set of cognitions. The discussion of these student thought processes represents an answer to the problem of how students' thoughts mediate learning from teaching.

Students' Perceptions and Expectations

Research on students' thought processes promises to enhance understanding of teaching and its outcomes by providing information about the instruction as it is experienced by the learners. The instruction experienced by the learners may be different from the intended instruction; or the instruction may not be understood or perceived by the learners. In these research studies, the learners' perception of the teaching is the functional instruction that influences student learning and achievement.

In the following paragraphs we begin to analyze the thought processes that contribute to the students' experience and understanding of teaching.

Students' Academic Self-Concepts and Expectations

From the beginning of elementary school, children uniformly and positively perceive their academic performance (Stipek, 1981). They often exaggerate their academic ability, using absolute rather than relative standards to evaluate their performances. As early as the first grade, high-achieving, compared with low-achieving, boys have higher expectations for success in school (Stipek & Hoffman, 1980). In the third or fourth grade, the children's perceived school performance begins to correlate positively with their teachers' estimates of their ability. By the sixth grade, children's perceived academic ability becomes more realistic and related to the performance of their classmates (Nicholls, 1979).

Teachers' feedback to children regarding their school performance seems to be related to the development of children's self-concept of ability. Kindergarten and first graders rated their own intelligence by their effort and ability to follow directions, while second and third graders emphasized their performance on specific subject matter tasks (Stipek, 1981).

These self-evaluations of ability seem to reflect the feedback the teachers often used at these grade levels. From these data, it seems that young children are capable of perceiving feedback from teachers regarding their academic performances and those of their peers in school. These perceptions also seem to influence their expectations about their future school performances.

It is too early to know the generality of these findings. But the findings suggest the early and definite effects teachers can have upon students' expectations and self-concepts of school ability.

Students' Perception of Schools, Teachers, and Teachers' Behaviors

Students also perceive school factors related to achievement, including differences among teachers and among teacher behaviors. Paton, Walberg, and Yeh (1973) found that many minority children in high school felt that they had the ability to learn. But these same children felt that luck determined achievement in school. The children felt that somebody blocked them from success, even though they had the ability to learn. These results agree with the data of the Coleman report (1966), where the feeling among students of lack of environmental control accounted for more variance in academic achievement than did any other variable.

Brookover, Beady, Flood, Schweitzer, and Wisenbaker (1977) report a related finding in the elementary school. They measured student perceptions of academic climates, and found that the belief that it was futile to pursue success in school contributed more than any other comparable variable to the variance in achievement.

These global affective processes merit further study to determine their causes, and to determine more precisely how these beliefs produce effects upon students' achievements in school. Again, the attributions students make about achievement and the sense of control they experience over their destiny in school seem to be powerful cognitive processes that mediate their school performances.

Students' perceptions of their teachers, teaching processes, and the differential treatments learners receive from teachers seem to mediate achievement in school. About at age 7, children often begin to develop more abstract and deeper perceptions of people that are based on consistent qualities that transcend observable behavior (Livesley & Bromley, 1973). Several studies have examined the qualities of a good teacher that are perceived by students. Although there is controversy over these findings, some studies find students choosing teachers who are warm, friendly, supportive and communicative, while, at the same time, orderly, highly motivating, and in charge of classroom discipline (e.g., Beck, 1967). See Weinstein (1983) for further discussions of these topics.

Students seem to discriminate differential treatments teachers give them in the classroom. In research on the teacher expectancy phenomenon, or so-called self-fulfilling prophecy, several studies examined whether students perceive differential treatment in the classroom between high- and low-achieving male students. Weinstein and Middlestadt (1979) asked two groups of children, Grades 1-3 and Grades 4-6, to rate 60 teacher behaviors as applicable or not applicable to fictional high and low achievers. The children perceived teachers to respond differently to the high achiever and to the low achiever on 15 of the 60 items. The students perceived the teachers as having high expectations and high academic demands for the high-achieving male students, to whom the teachers granted special privileges. The students saw the male low achievers as receiving fewer chances to perform in class, but as receiving greater teacher interest and concern. The high-achieving males were perceived to be more popular, friendly, competitive, attentive, independent, and successful than the low-achieving males.

In a later study, Weinstein, Marshall, Brattesani, and Middlestadt (1982) examined the perceptions of over 200 fourth through sixth graders regarding teacher behaviors toward fictional male and female high and low achievers in school. The elementary school students perceived the male and female low achievers as receiving more direction, rules, work, and negative feedback than did the male and female high achievers, whom they perceived as receiving higher teacher expectations for

performance and success, more freedom of choice, and greater opportunities. Cooper and Good (1982) report that students for whom teachers had high expectations described themselves as receiving less frequent criticism and more frequent praise than did students for whom teachers had low expectations.

Cooper (1979) presents a model, which is elaborated with some relevant data in another paper (Cooper, 1983), of the teacher expectancy effect, as mediated by student thought processes, and as studied by Weinstein and her colleagues in the two papers just described. Cooper's model suggests that high teacher expectation students frequently receive positive feedback contingent upon their effort, while students with low teacher expectations receive more noneffort-contingent negative feedback as a way to control their behavior, which teachers see as less likely to result in learning but more likely to result in classroom disturbances. As a result, low teacher expectation students are less likely to come to believe in the value of effort for attaining success in class, and therefore, to show less persistence and to experience less success. (See Cooper & Good, 1982 for further discussion.)

From these studies, it is clear that students perceive expectations by teachers and differentiate classroom treatment given to high and low expectation students. The differential treatments may induce different self-concepts of ability and different attributional patterns among students. The data on this latter issue are not extensive enough to warrant that generalization yet. However, it seems likely that the teacher expectancy effect will not be found by studying whole classrooms. Rather, teachers produce the effect with some students, who perceive differential treatment from teachers, as Weinstein's data show; but teachers may not produce the expectancy effect with other students, who do not perceive the teachers' differential and inappropriate treatment.

Research using the teacher and student dyad as the unit, rather than the classroom as the unit, seems more likely to find the teacher expectancy effect. Students do not all perceive the teacher's actions in the same, or a uniform, way.

For further discussion of these topics, see Amatora, 1952; Ames, 1981; Beam and Horvat, 1975; Blumenfeld, Hamilton, Bossert, Wessels, and Meece, 1983; Braun, 1976; Brophy, 1983; and Filby and Barnett, 1982.

Students' Perceptions of Teachers' Behavior and Classroom Instructional Processes

Children develop in their understanding of the purposes of instruction and of their teachers' motives behind classroom activities. One study suggests that first graders typically believe that the most important part of their classwork is to get it done, to get to the bottom of the page, or to get to the end of the book (Anderson, 1981). These perceptions by first graders raise fundamental questions about kindergarten and primary school teaching, which sometimes emphasizes the procedural and mechanical aspects of instruction, with less emphasis in understanding the learning involved in the classwork assignments. Are the kindergarten and first grade teachers appropriately teaching the children to focus on the mechanics of instruction, that they need to learn to facilitate understanding later? Or is the development of understanding, which might be of more interest to the pupils, being deferred inappropriately by teaching procedures that focus on behaving correctly but not necessarily on understanding what one is reading or writing in school?

In either case students learn to perceive the goals of instruction as a result of the directions they receive from their teachers. Blumenfeld et al. (1983), in their research on teacher talk and student thought, report a related finding among elementary school students. Teachers' comments and directions about academic performance, including attributions to effort as a way to succeed ("you can do better"), correlated more highly with students' thoughts than did teacher talk about social procedures and about the socialization of the child into the school and society. Apparently the teacher who focuses on the academic work and the students' responsibilities for accomplishing it through effort conveys a sense of the central importance of the intellectual activities. But perceptions of the importance of the social processes of working together are not so readily conveyed by teachers.

Students also perceive the feedback their teachers give them. As I mentioned earlier, students early in elementary school, about second grade, begin to learn from feedback about their own and their peers' relative performances in classrooms (Nicholls, 1978; Stipek, 1981). Consequently, these children learn quickly to rate themselves and their peers as high or low achievers, a consequence of teachers' behaviors that may have effects upon self-concepts, motivations, and attitudes toward peers. Filby and Barnett (1982) studied how elementary school children understand and evaluate one another's reading performance in class. They found about 90% agreement among children regarding which of them were the better readers. "Smooth error-free reading with expression sounds good to everyone" (Filby & Barnett, 1982, p. 444), at least when the whole class had opportunity to hear everyone read aloud.

Teacher praise is perceived by students somewhat differently from the ways it is intended by teachers. Wittrock (1978) distinguished, as have many other authors, two functions of teacher praise and reinforcement. First, there is the *motivational* or reinforcing function of increasing future behavior by appropriately praising or rewarding it. This function does not involve understanding or learning with awareness. Second, there is an *informational* function of teacher praise, which provides feedback about the correctness of a response.

In this much-researched area of teacher praise, the motivational function has long been considered important for teaching children to learn associations well enough to repeat them in future appropriate occasions. To accomplish this motivational or reinforcement function, teacher praise should be used frequently, discriminatively, and contingently.

However, recent classroom research finds that teacher praise does not usually function as a reinforcer or as a motivator. In several studies, Brophy (1981) found that teacher praise did not correlate with other outcomes of teaching, as one would expect if teacher praise functioned as a reinforcer.

In the same article, he also argues that teacher praise is not usually intended as a reinforcer. It is infrequently used by teachers. First grade teachers praised about 11% of the stu-

dents' correct answers in reading classes (Anderson, Evertson, & Brophy, 1979), and about 10% of the public responses in the junior high school (Evertson, Anderson, Anderson, & Brophy, 1980). In these same two studies teacher praise of student good conduct was much lower, and nearly nonexistent in the first grade.

In these studies, the teachers did not perceive or use praise as it often has been thought they did, that is, as a reinforcer. If praise functioned as a reinforcer, it would be ineffective in the typical classroom, because its infrequent use means that each student would be praised only about once every 2 hours (Brophy, 1981), and because praise is often used noncontingently.

Instead praise seems to function by providing information to all the students who *observe* the student receiving the praise. The information conveys knowledge about the answers, the desired behavior, and the teachers' expectations for performance. These findings also show reasons to study student thought processes rather than studying only direct effects of praise on learners.

Students perceive and respond differently from one another to praise, depending on their intellectual ability, cognitive style, attributions, age, and their desire to please the teacher. Many low-ability students, field-dependent students, external locus students, primary-school students, and students eager to please the teacher respond favorably to praise. For other types of students, praise can be counterproductive, for example, by changing intrinsic motivation to extrinsic motivation (Lepper, 1983) or by changing student attributions for success in school, or their perceptions of their own abilities.

Praise of a high-ability student for success on an easy task may lead to a lower self-concept of ability, or be seen as undeserved by the students. Morine-Dershimer (1982) observed elementary school students' perceptions of teacher praise. Fifty percent of these students perceived the praise to be deserved by themselves, and 23% of them reported that the praise served an instructional function, such as conveying information about correct answers, encouraging students, and making them feel good. The students high in reading achievement tended to view the praise as deserved by their performance. Students low in reading achievement viewed the praise as serving an instructional function, such as encouraging them or helping them to feel good about learning to read.

Student participation in the classroom discussions also depended upon the pupils' perception of the teachers' intent in using praise. Praise perceived as deserved led to greater participation in classroom discussions. Higher reading-achievement students, and students high in status with teachers and peers, tended to perceive praise as deserved, and also participated more frequently in classroom discussions than did lower reading-ability students. High classroom participation was correlated with reading achievement, after entering reading ability was controlled. Morine-Dershimer (1982) concludes that praise may be perceived by pupils not so much "to *reinforce the individual student* as to *give information to the group*" (p. 432, italics in original). She adds that direct instruction may be effective in that its high proportion of praised correct answers gives the entire class increased information from which all of them can learn.

From these data about perceptions of praise, it seems that praise used by teachers may serve an informational function primarily, rather than a reinforcing function. In addition, it is clear that students perceive this teacher behavior differently from one another and differently, sometimes, from the way teachers intend it to be understood.

These studies of students' perceptions of teachers' classroom behaviors revise our understanding of an important instructional procedure, suggest revisions in the use of praise to increase its informational value, and provide hypotheses about the roles of learners' thought processes in direct instruction.

Students' Perceptions of Cognitive Processes in the Classroom

Wittrock (1978) maintained that before reporting effects of students' thoughts on achievement, studies of students' thought processes in teaching and instruction should show that the students in the research actually performed the cognitive processes intended by the directions, questions, or tasks in the treatments. The students' perceptions of the instruction and teaching may be different from the teachers' intentions. The students may not engage in the thoughts intended by the teachers.

In an extensive series of studies on elementary school students' cognitive processes occuring while learning from teaching, Winne and Marx (1983) examined students' perceptions of classroom instruction and their relation to achievement. They also studied whether students could be trained to use cognitive strategies that would influence instruction. They studied three cognitive processes: (a) orienting, which involved directing students' attention; (b) operating, which included comparing, generating, and using metacognition; and (c) consolidating, which included storage and retrieval. They found that students' perceptions of instruction and the cognitive processes they used in response to it were related to achievement. They also found that they could train cognitive processes, for example through teaching note-taking strategies, that would enhance achievement on objective tests, but not on essay tests.

In another study by these two authors (Winne & Marx, 1980) university students were trained to recognize only, or to recognize and to respond to, the experimental organization or schema for learning from lectures. The learning and use of the experimental schema and the directions to take notes to facilitate learning during a lecture, rather than its recall later, interfered with learning and with the use of the students' customary, previously learned systems for acquiring knowledge during lectures. The students' perception of the new cognitive processes depended upon their previously learned strategies. Learning a new strategy involved modifying a previously learned strategy.

Their results indicate that the new strategy influenced cognitive processing. But the more important finding was that one must know and understand students' perceptions and previously learned strategies in order to teach a new strategy, and to understand how students will respond to it.

These points are elaborated in another paper by Winne and Marx (1982). In this paper they state that there is a lack of a one-to-one correspondence between instruction identified by the teacher and the cognitive processing it cues in the students (p. 513). Observation schedules probably cannot detect the instruction which actually functions for learners. Similar treatments may be perceived as quite different procedures by students, while quite different instructional methods may be perceived as similar by these same students. In addition, students' background knowledge and previously learned strategies influence the perception of teaching.

The direct effects of teacher behaviors, compared with the mediated effects of students' perceptions of the same teachers' behaviors, upon sixth grade students were studied by Stayrook, Corno, and Winne (1978). Student perceptions of teacher structuring and teacher reacting, but not of teacher soliciting, correlated more highly with achievement in this path-analytic study than did the direct effects of teacher structuring and teacher reacting. These path models did not show statistical significance. However, a reanalysis of the data, reducing error of measurement, improved the significance levels of the data.

These findings imply that research studies should include students' thought processes in their designs. The regularities that exist between teaching and student achievement involve the cognitive transformation performed by the students on the instruction they receive.

In a series of studies Peterson and her colleagues examined students' reports of their cognitive processes occurring during instruction. Peterson, Swing, Braverman, and Buss (1982), also reported in Peterson and Swing (1982), asked fifth and sixth graders, who were shown videotaped segments of their classroom instruction, to describe their thought processes that occurred during the mathematics instruction they viewed on the tapes.

Student-reported attention correlated with success on the mathematics problems more highly than did classroom observers' reports of time-off-task. With ability differences controlled, reports of understanding the lesson also correlated positively with achievement, as did students' reported use of learning strategies, such as relating the problems to experience. Students' ability to determine why and what they understood also correlated with achievement. Students' reports of using specific cognitive strategies, rather than global strategies such as thinking or listening, also correlated with achievement. These specific strategies included "relating information to prior knowledge" and "trying to understand the teacher on problem level 2" (Peterson et al., 1982, p. 544). Level 2 referred to one of the more difficult types of problems. Last, reported motivational self-thoughts correlated positively with attitudes toward mathematics.

In a related study, using similar procedures with a naturalistic classroom setting and an ethnically and socioeconomically more diverse population of fifth graders, Peterson, Swing, Stark, and Waas (1983) replicated these results and added findings about student affective thoughts during instruction. In this study classroom observation of student engagement in mathematics was unrelated to mathematics achievement, supporting Brophy and Evertson's claim (1976, p. 67) that apparent student attention (observed time-on-task) does not reliably measure anything. Students' negative self-thoughts seemed to lower both student achievement and attitudes. From these studies there is further evidence that student thought processes influence student achievement in the learning of mathematics in elementary schools.

These findings are of interest for several reasons. First, the finding that student reports of attention correlate more highly with mathematics achievement than do observers' reports of time-on-task indicates the importance and utility of obtaining measures of student cognitive processes, even when they involve self-report data. Attention is not the same as observed time-on-task, or time allotted to learning. Second, students are aware of and can recall their cognitive processes accurately enough to predict achievement, at least at a statistically significant level. Third, the more specific cognitive strategies, but not the general strategies. predict achievement. These findings imply that through the study of student thought processes we can discern the effective strategies students use in school learning. With this knowledge teachers can try to teach these strategies to other children.

These classroom studies of student reports of cognitive processes again indicate the utility of studying constructs, such as attention, for refining our understanding of the effects of teaching upon student learning. The latter studies we discussed showed the potential of attention for revising earlier conceptions about time-on-task. In the following section we explore additional implications for teaching that follow from related research literature on attention.

Attention

In the recent research literature, selective attention, voluntary attention, sustained attention, and distractability, among other types of attention, have frequently been studied in laboratories and in school settings (cf. Wittrock, in press). From these studies several components of attention have been identified, including a short-term or phasic, largely involuntary, component, sometimes called arousal or the orienting response, and a long-term or tonic, largely voluntary component. The tonic component, but usually not the phasic component, is involved in learning disabilities, behavior disorders, and in mental retardation (Zeaman & House, 1963).

From recent research on attention, educationally useful, remedial attentional training programs have been developed that help students, including learning-disabled and hyperkinetic learners, to control attention and to enhance learning from teaching. In addition, recent research on attention has led to new explanations of the ways that teacher questions, inserted questions in texts, and objectives given to learners influence classroom learning. In the following paragraphs we will explore these two lines of research, beginning with one study on selective attention, then discussing the recent findings about classroom instructional procedures, questions and objectives, and last discussing attentional training programs for learning disabled, hyperactive, and normal learners.

Willows (1974) gave good and poor readers in the sixth grade distracting words typed in red between the lines of the normal text they were asked to read. Compared with a control group not given the inserted, distracting words, the text in red distracted the poor readers more than it did the good readers. Further, the good readers focused on the meaning of the distracting text, when they did attend to it, while the poor readers focused on the surface structure, the red color of the inserted text. Distractability seems to be a type of attention that sometimes distinguishes good from poor learners.

Other data also implicate attentional problems in some reading disorders. Preston, Guthrie, and Childs (1974) found poor readers in the ninth grade to have a deficit in response to light flashes, but not to words, indicating an attentional deficit, but not an encoding or learning problem. Conners (1976) found similar results regarding reading and attention among third and fourth graders.

In research on adjunct or inserted questions, students are given texts to read with questions inserted either before the paragraphs, called prequestions, or after the paragraphs, called postquestions, that discuss the relevant answers. In these studies, the prequestions usually facilitate verbatim and factual learning, while the postquestions facilitate conceptual learning or learning of information not specific to the question (Boker, 1974).

Prior to the development of attentional models, these results were usually explained by practice, reinforcement, and the opportunity to review paragraphs provided by the postquestions. Wittrock and Lumsdaine (1977) explained these results with an attentional model. They maintained that the prequestions direct the learner's attention to a factual or specific answer. The postquestions, coming after the relevant paragraphs, direct attention only in future paragraphs to the general type of information likely to be asked after the next paragraph is read. Rickards and Denner (1978) and Andre (1979), after reviewing the literature on inserted questions, reached essentially the same conclusion, which is that the questions direct attention, at least among learners who are not already attentive to the text.

In research on the effects of giving students behavioral objectives, an attentional model again has provided a useful explanation of the findings. For many years behavioral objectives given to learners were thought to provide the teachers with readily identifiable behavior that they could easily recognize and immediately and frequently reinforce. However, Duell (1974) tested and found that behavioral objectives function by influencing selective attention. Duchastel (1979) reached the same conclusion in a study in which text of low structural importance was better learned when objectives focused it, directing students away from the text they would otherwise have studied. Kaplan and Simmons (1974) found that objectives given to learners after the text, rather than before, enhanced or broadened the learning to include information related to, but not identical to, the specific answers to the questions. In this study objectives given to learners seem to function somewhat like inserted questions, directing attention. Attention models seem useful for explaining these results and for understanding some of the cognitive effects of questions and objectives.

Attention is a student thought process that may help to explain some of the results found in studies of learning disorders, hyperactivity, and mental retardation. Learning-disabled children show a 2- or 3-year lag in development of selective attention. From 5 to 15 years of age, normally developing children show an increase in ability to focus on and to recall relevant information, with a large increment in ability occurring at ages 12 and 13. They also show no increase, or very little increase over the 5- to 15-year age span, in learning and recall of incidental information. Children apparently are learning to focus their energies on relevant information and to disregard irrelevant information, resulting in greater learning and retention of more important information, and less learning of and retention of the other information.

Other studies implicate attention in learning disabilities, and sometimes in mental retardation. Krupski (1980) found learning-disabled and mentally retarded children deficient on high-demand voluntary attention tasks, but not on short-term, involuntary attention tasks. Mentally retarded children were also more distracted, only when observed working in classrooms, than were normal children (Krupski, 1979). Outside the classroom the mentally retarded children sustained attention well. These findings imply that because voluntary, sustained attention, especially as it occurs in high-demand academic settings, is deficient in these learners, attention-training programs might ameliorate some of these learning difficulties.

The same hope has emerged from research on hyperkinetic behavior problems among children, which recently were classified by the American Psychiatric Association as attentional deficit disorders. The research indicates that hyperkinetic activity frequently responds well to stimulant drugs.

The apparent paradox of this finding is understandable, if hyperactivity involves a deficit in attention. Hyperkinetic children are often no more highly aroused than other children, nor does a stimulant drug usually reduce their arousal. Instead hyperkinetic children have a relatively flat gradient of attention, and are unable to inhibit responses well to task-relevant but distracting stimulation. When they function well, the stimulant drugs steepen this gradient, and improve the children's selective attention (Conners, 1976).

From the teacher's perspective, the hyperkinetic children given stimulant drugs seem to be quieter and less active. More probably, the children are more cognitively active in an organized, task-relevant way. Their former disorganized, task-irrelevant overt behavior subsides, which leads to the teacher's observation that their activity is reduced. Instead, their activity level probably remains high, and has probably been directed into more productive and coherent thought processes. However, the drugs are far from ideal ways to facilitate learning. In addition to the obvious and serious physical problems of drug use, hyperactive children given stimulants can come to feel that they are helpless to control their behavior, and that their learning is due to a drug, not to their effort or ability.

Recent research on attention offers a useful alternative treatment. If hyperactivity is a problem of voluntary attention, then it is possible that the teaching of cognitive strategies for consciously controlling attention might enable some children to increase attention and to enhance learning, without the physical and attributional complications that can occur with stimulant drugs (Meichenbaum & Goodman. 1971).

To explore these possibilities several attentional cognitive training programs have been developed and tested with hyperactive and normal children. Douglas, Parry, Martin, and Garson (1976) taught 7- and 8-year-old hyperactive children to use self-talk to control their attention. After 3 months of training,

their attention improved, as did their scores on the Matching Familiar Figures Test (a measure of ability to analyze details in pictures), tests of planning, and some tests of oral and listening comprehension, although reading was not taught in this program. Apparently the instruction generalized beyond the training tasks to influence ability to learn to read in the classroom.

Camp (1980), using techniques derived from Donald Meichenbaum's "stop, look, and listen" strategy, taught impulsive elementary school boys a four-step procedure to follow. Ask yourself (a) what problem you face, (b) how you will solve it (c) whether you are following your plan, and (d) how well you did with the problem. After 30 teaching sessions, the children showed gains in reading, IQ, and social behavior, which transferred to learning in the classroom.

These results show how the study of student thought processes can provide a new understanding of a learning disability that leads to cognitive training programs that might reduce or, in some cases, replace the use of stimulant drugs. This use of cognitive training programs has practical utility because the widespread use of stimulant drugs to facilitate learning is highly questionable and raises serious issues regarding its effects on children.

Using similar techniques, but with poor readers who were not hyperactive, Malamuth (1979) improved sustained attention. Reading scores also improved.

Other studies by other researchers have shown little or no effect due to strategy training programs, especially short-term programs. Generalization of training programs is also a problem, although the cognitive strategy programs, compared with behavioristic or drug programs, obtain the greatest transfer to classroom learning (Keogh & Glover, 1980). Even with these problems and caveats, these results suggest new procedures, directed at changing student thoughts, that promise practical ways to ameliorate some difficult and important learning problems. For further discussion of the educational applications of these types of cognitive training programs see Meichenbaum and Asarnow (1978).

In the earlier section on student perceptions we found that attention, as a cognitive process, offered a useful concept for explaining how time to learn leads to student achievement. Measures of attention, especially student reports of attention, correlated with achievement more highly than did measures of children's time-to-learn or observers' records of their time-on-task.

In this latter section on attention we again saw the promise and the complications that attentional constructs bring to the problem of relating teaching to achievement. From these complementary lines of cognitive research, attention, as a student thought process, deserves further study, and attentional training programs deserve further development and application. With the construct of attention inserted as a mediator between teaching and achievement our ability to predict learning from instruction increases, as does our ability to understand some of the effects of teaching upon classroom achievement and upon some learning disorders.

As a result of the increased understanding of these learning mechanisms in and out of the classroom, we can sometimes design teaching procedures, such as teachers' questions and learners' use of objectives, and remedial cognitive training programs, such as attentional programs for hyperkinetic learners of school tasks. These teaching procedures and cognitive training strategies are simple to use, inexpensive, usually easily understood by teachers, and are teachable in the classroom. Their successful application however, involves sustained, lengthy, and repeated practice in a variety of contexts that will facilitate transfer to the learning of reading, mathematics, and other subjects taught in school.

Motivation

One of the most frequently studied and useful thought processes involved in learning from teaching is motivation, the process of initiating, sustaining, and directing activity. In modern times research on motivation in teaching has focused on topics such as reinforcement, need for achievement, intrinsic and extrinsic motivation, locus of control, and most recently, attribution. As an example of how recent research on students' motivational thought processes can enhance understanding of learning from teaching we will discuss some of the recent findings and theories emerging from research on student attribution, which is the study of students' perception of the causes of their successes and failures as learners. From this research have come new explanations for the effectiveness of several concepts, such as reinforcement, teacher praise and blame, and new instructional programs in attributional retraining and in self-management skills.

Children's concepts of the causes of their successes and failures develop from a relatively undifferentiated state to a more analytic conception of the relations among ability, effort, and achievement. At about 6 years of age many children do not separate ability, effort, and achievement (Nicholls, 1978). They equate effort to intelligence, and success to smart people who work hard. At about 7 to 8 years of age they distinguish these three concepts form one another, and causally relate effort, but not ability, to achievement. At about ages 9 to 11 years, ability also becomes a cause of achievement, but they still believe that people who work hard are also intelligent or able individuals. Beginning about age 11, children realize that effort and ability are relatively independent of each other, and are causally related to achievement. This developmental progression implies that training programs designed to teach children to ascribe success and failure to effort rather than to ability are likely to be effective primarily with children who are old enough to differentiate these concepts from one another, and who realize that each of them can independently influence achievement.

Children also develop in their concept of locus of control, their belief that events they experience are under their own or internal control, rather than under the control of other people or forces outside themselves, that is, under external control. From Jean Piaget's research on causal reasoning (e.g., Piaget & Inhelder, 1975) young children often overestimate their ability to control events, including the weather and the movements of the sun and other stars.

On the other hand, researchers, such as Lefcourt (1976; 2nd ed.,1982), predict that internality, at least when measured as perceived competence, increases with age among children. Some measures of locus of control, such as Nowicki–Strickland

Internal-External Control Scale, assume a developmental increase in internality from elementary school-age children through senior high school.

The observed development in children's locus of control depends on the type of test items used to measure it. Weisz and Stipek (1982) found that "agree–disagree" scales generally found internality to increase with age, while "choice-of-attribution" scales usually show no developmental increment in internality. They explained these results by hypothesizing that perceived competence, the ability to perform activities effectively, increases with age, but perceived contingency, the perception of the relation between one's actions, including competently performed acts, and observed outcomes, such as changes in other people's behavior, or the movements of stars, declines. The two types of scales measuring locus of control seem to involve both of these two dimensions of locus of control.

These developmental findings have been presented here because they provide a context for understanding the research on attribution and its implications and limitations for understanding learning in schools, and for designing attribution change programs and self-management instructional programs.

From a background of research on need achievement and locus of control, studies and models of attribution have tried to explicate the perceived causes, the "why," or the explanations learners construct to explain their past behavior and to motivate their future behavior. Weiner (1979, 1983), who believes that locus of control consists of two dimensions, causality and controllability, separates them from each other and adds a third dimension, stability, to his model of attributional processes. Locus of causality can be either internal or external in Weiner's system. Controllability can be either uncontrollable or controllable; and stability can be either stable or unstable.

Within this three-dimensional system, the perceived causes most often researched in educational contexts are (a) ability, a stable, internal, and uncontrollable cause; (b) effort (actually immediate effort), an unstable, internal, and controllable cause; (c) luck, an unstable, external, and uncontrollable cause; and (d) task difficulty, a stable, external, and uncontrollable cause.

One hypothesis emerging from this and related models of attributional processes is that students will be highly motivated to continue to learn when they attribute success or failure to their effort, or lack of it, rather than to forces over which they have little or no control, such as their ability, luck, or other people. Although there are complications with this straightforward and useful idea, a large number of empirical studies support it and its underlying attributional model. We discuss these studies next, focusing on attributional processes involving control and locus of causality.

As I mentioned earlier in this chapter, Coleman, et al. (1966) found that, among many minority groups of children in schools, one of the most powerful variables for explaining differences in achievement was the students' perceived lack of control over events in school, although they felt they had the ability to succeed. In agreement with that finding, Nowicki and Strickland (1973) found that school achievement correlated more highly with measures of locus of control than it did with measures of intelligence. Reid and Croucher (1980) found the same type of result, using a different test of locus of control, the Crandall Intellectual Achievement Responsibility Questionnaire.

At the college level, measures of locus of control usually do not predict achievement well, although Nord, Connelly, and Diagnault (1974) found that Rotter's I–E scale, a measure of locus of control, did correlate with achievement in a complementary way to a measure of ability, an admissions test for entry into a business school. Ability and locus of control seemed to explain relatively separate or nonoverlapping portions of the variance in academic achievement. From these and other studies (see Bar-Tal, 1978, for further comment on relations between attributions and school achievement), it is clear that motivational thought processes can differentiate high and low achievers in schools and can predict learning from teaching.

Beyond their utility for predicting school achievement, motivational variables suggest how teaching processes influence the student thought processes that mediate achievement. These explanations represent attribution theory's major contribution, and lead to recently developed attributional retraining programs and self-management instructional materials, which we discuss next.

As an example of the type of explanation of teaching processes offered by attribution theory, consider how reinforcement might function to enhance learning. Attribution theory suggests that success is not enough to increase learning and achievement, which do not occur automatically or without mediation by students' thoughts. Reinforcement attributed by students to easy tasks, luck, ability, and even to excellent teachers, all internal or external factors over which the students have little control, will not increase persistence or motivation. The reason is that the students cannot or do not see that their effort contributed to the success. The theory also explains how contingent reinforcement, and sometimes teacher praise, functions to increase achievement by conveying to students that their effort produced the learning in school. Stated differently, success is not enough by itself. It must be perceived to be caused, at least in substantial part, by student effort, or other student processes under self-control and relevant to influencing learning outcomes. The theory further implies that effort invested in learning is not itself sufficient for enhancing motivation to learn. The students must perceive the causal relation between their effort and their success or failure in school.

These concepts have been studied in several educational contexts. Wang and Stiles (1976) found that students who believe their effort influences their achievement are more likely to learn than are students who believe that learning depends on teachers or other people (see also Andrews & Debus, 1978).

Dweck (1975) and Dweck, Davidson, Nelson, and Enna (1978) studied learned helplessness. Learned helplessness occurs when students feel that they cannot overcome failure. In the former study (Dweck, 1975), a group of children with learned helplessness were taught to take responsibility for their failures in school and to attribute them to lack of sufficient effort rather than lack of ability. Another group of children with learned helplessness were given a success-only training program. The children given the attribution retraining program improved, or at least maintained, their academic performance, while the success-only group of children continued to decline in school achievement. One implication of this finding is that behavior modification programs providing only success experi-ences may be insufficient for teaching children to attribute their successes to their own effort and to take responsibility for their learning.

In the second experiment, Dweck et al. (1978) studied differences in boys and girls in learned helplessness. Girls show learned helplessness more often than do boys. Perhaps because of the different feedback from teachers, girls attribute failure to lack of ability, while boys tend more often to attribute failure to lack of effort. Teachers frequently criticize boys in elementary school for nonintellectual acts, and for lack of effort, while girls are criticized almost exclusively for intellectual activities. Because of the differential criticism, boys may have more readily attributed failure to lack of effort and girls may have more readily attributed it to lack of ability.

In this study, Dweck et al. treated both boys and girls to either a teacher–boy or a teacher–girl work-related criticism. Both boys and girls who received the teacher–girl treatment came to believe that lack of ability was the cause of failure in class. (However, Heller and Parsons, 1981, did not replicate these findings.)

From Dweck's data it is possible that teachers influence learning and achievement by the way they communicate attributions differently to some boys and girls. Again, the effects of success, praise, and reinforcement depend upon the interpretations students place upon them, and upon the way they perceive them to reflect upon their performance, their ability, and their effort.

deCharms (1972) taught teachers and students, over a 2-year training program, to perceive themselves as "origins," that is, as people who can control the outcomes of teaching and can take responsibility for teaching and learning, rather than as "pawns," that is, as people who cannot control learning and teaching and cannot take responsibility for them. The origin training program increased teacher and student motivation, language skills, and arithmetic achievement. Reading was least enhanced. The program worked better with boys than with girls. The control group continued to decline in percentile rank, as it had prior to the beginning of the 2-year study, while the origin training students gained 1 year per year of enrollment in school.

In addition to these attributional retraining programs, attribution theory has led to the development of instructional programs in self-management skills, and tests of self-responsibility for learning (Wang & Stiles, 1976; Wang, 1983). These instructional programs teach students not only to exercise control and responsibility over their learning, but to set realistic goals, to manage time available to learn, and to organize information to be learned. Proficiency at these self-management skills builds a student's sense of control and responsibility and facilitates the percentage of tasks successfully completed.

From a somewhat different perspective, applying concepts about self-efficacy as well as attribution retraining, Barbara McCombs (1982, 1983) developed an extensive motivational skills training program designed to teach adult students in the military services to take responsibility for learning and to exert self-control over their strategies for acquiring information from teachers. In addition to the motivational training lessons, the program included training in metacognitive skills, including planning, monitoring and assessment, and cognitive skills such as attention, comprehension, and memory. The motivational training program increased knowledge acquisition in the technical training course, reduced absenteeism, and, by observer ratings, increased motivation to learn, when compared with a comparable control group of students.

From this sample of research on motivation, there are data to indicate that the study of student thought processes leads to new ways to predict and to understand achievement from teaching. The theory and the research also lead to useful training programs that change the ways students think about their role and responsibility in learning from teaching. These implications have already been discussed in this section. Instead of reviewing that discussion, a few comments will be provided to elaborate their meaning and their limitations.

First, the idea of student responsibility for learning does not imply a lessened teacher responsibility for teaching, as is often inappropriately inferred from these data. Rather, each participant, teacher and learner, has a distinct responsibility for achievement. Good teaching is not enough for high achievement. Good learning, the active mental contribution of the learner, is a necessary component in this model for achievement to occur. Teaching exerts its influence on achievement through students' motivational processes, which can be controlled directly by the student as well as by the teacher or other people and factors.

Second, attribution change programs that depend upon changing ability or luck for effort attributions seem to assume that learners are capable of distinguishing effort, ability, and achievement from one another. Young children in primary school often do not make these distinctions, and are not likely to learn well from attribution retraining programs that involve knowledge of the different meanings of these terms or of the implications of seeing relations develop beween effort and achievement.

Third, change to effort attributions through retraining programs or teachers' use of praise and feedback should be followed by success in school, if students are to learn that effort leads to success. One implication of this finding is that teachers must choose difficulty levels appropriately to allow effort to lead to success in schools.

Last of all, attributions themselves may involve other cognitive or affective thought processes that will lead to improved understanding of the mediation of student achievement. Attribution of success to effort may lead to enhanced self-efficacy or self-control which enhances learning. Weiner (1983) has begun to study these processes.

In another context, patients' perceived control over the onset and cause of the pain reduces its intensity (Thompson, 1981). The perceived control changes the experiences of pain, perhaps by changing attributions and by increasing a sense of self-control of efficacy. Although it does not involve students in classrooms, the finding again shows the utility of studying thought processes of people learning to solve problems.

The study of motivation has produced changes in the ways we think about student responsibility for learning, teachers' feedback, praise, reinforcement, and the students' interpretation of the causes of success and failure in school.

For the future, research in motivation should study how attribution to cognitive strategies, rather than ability or effort, might influence learning and achievement. Strategy attribution might be effective with unsuccessful but hardworking students for whom training in effort attributions would make little sense.

Learning and Memory

From the recent laboratory and classroom study of learning and knowledge acquisition we have developed a new understanding of the cognitive processes that mediate learning from teaching. From this recent research we have also developed a few useful and practical instructional methods and programs that facilitate factual learning, learning with understanding, and the direct teaching of learning strategies and metacognitive processes.

These teaching procedures and instructional programs derive from principles that emphasize the cognitive processes involved in learning and comprehension. People learn not only by associating their actions to consequences, by reinforced practice, but also by observing others, by imitating them, by generating images, inferences, plans, and analogies, by listening to a teacher, and by reading, often without practice, reward, or feedback from others.

Two of these newly studied cognitive principles of learning and memory are as old as ideas common in ancient Greece and Rome. The first principle is that one learns and remembers information by associating ideas to one another. Aristotle's (reprinted, 1964) model of memory was based on the principle of associating ideas in order, one to another, and in storing these ideas as images in long-term memory, which one could retrieve by recalling one of them; and that would lead successively to each subsequent idea in the sequence. In the paragraphs below, we will see that the Aristotelian model underlies some of the modern-day research on the facilitation of learning and remembering factual information in schools, such as the capitals of states.

A second principle of ancient origin is that learning and memory increase when learners relate information to their knowledge store and to their experience. In ancient Greece and Rome, when rhetoric was still the art of public speaking, teachers, students, lawyers, and statesmen were regularly taught to form relations between familiar objects in their homes or offices and the points they wished to make in their talks or presentations.

In modern times this same principle is again used to facilitate memory. In addition, a modification of it leads to a new way to enhance comprehension through teaching learners to relate new information to their organized knowledge, or to accommodate their knowledge to the new information. In either case, I maintain in my model of generative learning (Wittrock, 1974a, 1978, 1981) that comprehension involves learners in the generation of relations between or among the parts—the words, sentences, and ideas, for example, in the materials they are learning. Learning with understanding includes also the generation of relations between previously acquired knowledge and the information to be learned, and between or among the parts—the words, sentences and ideas, for example, in the material to be comprehended. Both learning with understanding and factual or other learning that need not lead to understanding involve learner generation of relations. However, the meaningful nature of the relations differs because of the way the information relates to other information, to the learner's experience, and the learner's organized knowledge.

One frequently studied ancient method of facilitating learning and memory, especially of factual rather than conceptual materials, involves students in the use of imagery, such as text with high-imagery words, pictures or teacher-given instructions for students to construct their own images. Prior to age 8 or 9 years, pictures and high-imagery words, but not student-generated images, facilitate learning and memory (Levin, 1981). Wittrock and Goldberg (1975) found that high imagery words facilitate memory among elementary school children and college students. Prior to ages 8 or 9, children seem to have a production deficiency; that is, they can use images given to them by others, but they cannot, upon request, construct them to facilitate their own learning and memory.

An extensive number of studies has shown the facilitating effect of imagery, especially pictures, on learning and memory. Levin, Shriberg, Miller, McCormick, and Levin (1980) found that fourth and fifth graders who had been taught an imagery mnemonic system for remembering the capitals of the states in the United States remembered considerably more of them than did a comparable group given an equal amount of time to learn them using whatever procedures they chose. In a follow-up study, Levin, Berry, Miller, and Bartell (1982, p. 386) found that for their imagery mnemonic to function properly the students must be familiar with the names of capitals. Their mnemonic is based on a "keyword" associated with the name of each capital, and an interactive image that relates the state and the keyword. Their model applies the ancient principle of associating something new with something known or familiar. In addition, they use interactive pictures, another technique taught by teachers of rhetoric in ancient Rome (Yates, 1966) to facilitate memory. Apparently the facilitation occurs by juxtaposing the familiar element, which becomes the retrieval cue, such as a piece of furniture in one's home, with the unfamiliar element, such as the first point to be delivered in the orator's speech.

In Levin's studies, the state is the familiar retrieval cue, which leads to the interactive picture, which leads to the keyword, which leads to the name of the capital, the unfamiliar word. Levin adds another element to the sequence, the keyword, but the process is basically the ancient technique.

Sweeny and Bellezza (1982) used the keyword imagery mnemonic to teach college students the definitions of unfamiliar and abstract words. Compared with a group of students who learned the same word definitions in sentences with the keyword imagery technique, recall was sizeably increased, from 23% to 35%.

With Spanish vocabulary words, Raugh and Atkinson (1975) increased college students' retention from 28% to 88% by use of the keyword imagery mnemonic. These same authors also increased retention of Russian vocabulary words from 46% to 72%, again using the keyword imagery mnemonic. Bull and Wittrock (1973) found that sixth graders remembered word definitions better when they drew their own pictures of them, rather than when a comparable group of students, given equal time to learn, memorized the dictionary definitions. Levin, Shriberg, and Berry (1983) compared three types of illustrations to facilitate learning and memory of fictitious towns: (a) separate illustrations; (b) thematic illustrations, which integrated the separate illustrations into one picture; and (c) thematic or organized illustrations supplemented with cues associated by keywords to the town's name. The organized picture supplemented with keywords produced the greatest facilitation of memory of the four characteristics or attributes, followed by the organized picture, both of which were considerably higher than the separate pictures and a control condition.

Although they have not often been used to facilitate comprehension, imagery techniques, which involve spatial juxtaposition of ideas and objects, have potential value for facilitating understanding. We saw one beginning of interest developing in research in this area with the study (Levin et al., 1983) on remembering the organization of a passage that described cities and their characteristics. See Levin (1981, in press) for further discussions of imagery and its educational implications. See Pressley, Levin, and Delaney (1982) for a review of research on the keyword method. Whether they function to increase comprehension, imagery techniques clearly have been shown to facilitate factual learning in classroom contexts, using procedures reminiscent of ancient methods. See Yates (1966) for a discussion of the memory principles that underlie the teaching functions of imagery in medieval religious art and architecture.

Verbal student thought processes have also been shown to facilitate memory of words, sometimes with dramatic gains. Bower and Clark (1969) increased college students' retention of a list of words from about 14% to about 94% by teaching them to construct simple stories from the words, keeping the words in the stories in the same order they appeared in the list. Wittrock and Carter (1975) asked college students to generate associations among hierarchically related words. Whether the words were conceptually related or only randomly ordered, the construction of relations among them sizeably increased their learning and retention.

Although many of these studies were conducted in classroom settings, we must still be cautious in applying their findings to classroom teaching because written materials or other instructional processes were often used instead of teachers.

The research on imagery and verbal processes indicates that instruction facilitates memory of factual material by either giving the learners, or asking them to generate, interactive associations among the new ideas, words, or other information they are to learn and to remember, and between these ideas and their familiar experience. When the order of the ideas or words is important, the generated associations, such as stories, should maintain the serial order of the information to be remembered. Images and verbal generations facilitate memory of ideas and information primarily by the representation they provide of the relations among the parts or elements of a written passage, and the relations they show between the passage and one's experience. With imagery mnemonics and verbal elaborations, the generated relation is between something new and something old, something familiar.

Comprehension and Knowledge Acquisition

With at least one important difference, the teaching of comprehension and knowledge also involves the generation of relations among the elements of the information, for example, the words, sentences, and paragraphs of a text, and between the information and the learners' knowledge bases, as well as their experience (Wittrock, 1974a,b; 1983). According to my model of generative learning (Wittrock, 1981) comprehension is, essentially, the generation of a structural or conceptually ordered representation of the relations among the parts of the information to be learned, and between this information or these ideas and one's knowledge base and experience. Stated somewhat differently, the imagery mnemonics called "artificial" memory by ancient scholars, which involved learners' forming arbitrary associations between familiar objects or locations in one's home or office and information to be remembered, were adequate for facilitating memory, but not necessarily for facilitating comprehension of the points to be remembered. The reason is that the associations did not involve generating conceptual relations between the learner's knowledge and the information, nor the individual ideas or points to be remembered. With both comprehension and memory, the previously acquired information, knowledge, and experience are critical in their influence. To facilitate comprehension and knowledge acquisition, a teacher must build, or rather lead the learner to build, the cognitive relations we have discussed.

A wide variety of procedures for teaching learners to construct relations between their knowledge and experience and the information or concepts to be learned, and among the concepts to be learned, has been developed and studied empirically. One of the procedures asks students to generate relations between the text they are reading and their experience and knowledge.

Using elementary school teachers with students individually assigned at random to their classes, Linden and Wittrock (1981) taught fourth graders to generate verbal and spatial relations between the text and their knowledge and experience, as they read stories in their customarily used reading books. With time held constant across all groups, the children in the two experimental groups, who generated the relations between the text and their knowledge, substantially and statistically increased their reading comprehension, to means of 31.2 and 28.6 from a mean of 17.7 for the control group, who read the stories without instructions to generate relations. All three groups were taught by the senior author, who is a trained and experienced elementary school reading teacher. Another control group, taught by the students' regular fourth grade reading teacher, allowed to teach in any manner she chose, produced a mean of 21.6 well below (p < .01) the mean achievement of the experimental groups.

In a study using intact groups of learners and their regular classroom teachers, Au (1977) taught Hawaiian primary school children, who usually achieved two standard deviations below the mean score in reading, to relate their experiences to the Hawaiian stories read to them by their reading teacher. The primary school children stated in their own words several events in their lives that related to the stories. After one year of instruction, which probably involved other differences in instructional procedures as well, the experimental group scored at the 69th percentile of the Gates–MacGinite Reading Test, while the three control groups of first graders scored at the 8th, 21st, and 27th percentiles. Lesser but still large gains were also shown for second and third graders. See Tharp (1982) for a description of the instructional program used by Au. Pichert and Anderson (1977) asked college students to read a story

about a house from the perspective of either a homebuyer or a burglar. The information the students learned and remembered depended upon the perspective they adopted. Dooling and Christiaansen (1977) told one group of college students that the story they were reading was about a familiar famous person, such as Helen Keller. The students' knowledge about the famous person led them to make inferences about the story that led to errors later, because the story was not actually about the famous person.

Familiar words and stories can also facilitate comprehension of new material, by enabling learners to generate relations between their knowledge base and the text they read. Wittrock, Marks, and Doctorow (1975) gave sixth graders a familiar story in which an undefined and unfamiliar vocabulary word was inserted into each sentence. The familiar context sizeably increased the understanding of the meaning of the vocabulary words, without defining them. In another experiment (Marks, Doctorow, & Wittrock, 1974) the substitution of one familiar word for an unfamiliar word in each sentence of a story enabled sixth graders to increase by 50% their comprehension of the texts they read. In each of these two studies, familiar ideas, either stories or words, enhanced the comprehension of unfamiliar material. These effects occurred across all different stories, tests, and student ability levels involved in the studies.

Mackenzie and White (1982) derived predictions from Wittrock's model of generative learning. They compared the effects upon ninth graders' learning induced by their actively relating the geography to concrete experiences provided by fieldwork, by active student generation of information, and by actively linking events with principles in geography. The generative, active learning group retained 90%, the passive learning group 58%, and a control group, 51% of the information they were taught.

Generating relations among the parts of the text—the sentences and the paragraphs, for example—by constructing summaries and headings, or by underlining main ideas, also facilitates comprehension and memory. Doctorow, Wittrock, and Marks (1978) gave 400 sixth graders a story to read from a commercially published reading series and asked them to generate a summary sentence for each paragraph they read, either with or without using the inserted paragraph headings. Compared with control groups given the same stories, and the same amount of time to learn, the generation of summaries, especially with use of the inserted headings, doubled comprehension. This result occurred across the two ability levels, stories, and tests used in the experiments.

Paris, Lindauer, and Cox (1977) taught 7- and 8-year-old children to construct stories and inferences about sentences they read. The construction of stories facilitated comprehension and memory of the sentences. Dee-Lucas and Di Vesta (1980) gave or had college students generate topic sentences, headings, related sentences, and unrelated sentences as they read a passage on minerals. The comprehension of the organization of the passage was facilitated most by the student generation of topic sentences. The constuction of sentences irrelevant to learning the organization of the passage, that is the so-called related sentences, reduced comprehension of the structure of the passage. Generation of topic sentences also reduced recall of factual information. It seems that generations that focus on comprehension of the organization of the passage facilitate its understanding, and reduce learning of its details. Generation of irrelevant or distracting materials reduces learning by the greatest amount, compared with teacher-given equivalents. Generation seems to be a powerful variable in these studies of verbal processes, provided the students have the age and the experience needed to perform it.

Rickards and August (1975) report a related finding with underlining of words in text, either by a teacher or by the learners. The highest learning occurred when learners underlined words they chose or words of high structural importance; while the lowest learning occurred when the learners were made to underline words of low structural importance, which was lower than that of a group that read the passage without instructions to underline words. Teacher-underlined words in the text produced results between the gains and decrements shown by the student-generated underlinings.

Again the results show a pattern that indicates the importance of actively involving students in the generation of relations among the parts of the text, when one wants to facilitate comprehension of it. Teacher-provided structure of the passage also facilitates comprehension, but not as much as does student-generated structure. Because of the power of this variable, it also produces the greatest reduction in comprehension when it is directed to irrelevant, and perhaps also to incorrect, generations of the structure of a passage. When it is done poorly, such as by students who have inadequate knowledge and ability, it can also be expected to reduce comprehension.

For these reasons the study of the students' knowledge base and ability to use learning strategies has received considerable attention recently. Pearson, Hansen, and Gordon (1979) found that second grade readers' inferential comprehension, but not factual information, of a passage about spiders depended upon their knowledge of spiders. Larkin (1981) found a difference in strategies of solving physics problems existing between experts and beginners. Chi, Glaser, and Rees (1981) found that these strategy differences involve the beginners' deficiencies in their knowledge about physics, rather than in their problem-solving strategies. The experts represent the problems more in terms of their principles of physics, while the beginners stress the surface or literal characteristics of the problem.

Roger Osborne studies the models children used to comprehend basic concepts in physical science (Osborne, 1981; Osborne & Wittrock, 1983). In research in New Zealand, Great Britain, and the United States he finds that elementary school children have basic models of scientific phenomena, such as of current flow between a battery and a light bulb connected in a simple direct current circuit, that often differ from the physicists' model of the same events. In these three countries, some children think that the electric current flows only in one half of the circuit, from the battery to the light bulb, for instance. They believe that the other wire, from the bulb to the battery, is for safety, for leakage of current. Another group of students thinks the current flows in two directions, one current from each side of the battery through its wire to the light bulb. They also think that the meeting of these opposing currents causes the light to glow. A third group of students perceives the current flow essentially as the physicists do, that it goes in one direction equal in amplitude throughout the circuit.

When children with the first two of these three models are shown data with ammeters that prove that their model is incorrect, they do not usually change their perception. Instead they often believe that outside the classroom, at home, for example, current flows the way they state that it does. Only in the classroom does current flow as the teacher thinks it does.

Children's reactions to teachers' attempts to change their models by showing them a dissonance between their belief and reality show the difficulty of teaching new theories and models. The students sometimes do not perceive a dissonance, as the teachers anticipated. The children finesse the problem by maintaining a sharp distinction between the perceived artificial school environment and the so-called real environment at home.

One implication of this finding is that teachers cannot plan on teaching only the difference between students' perceptions and scientists' models of scientific phenomena. The teaching problem involves relearning, or accommodating, students' theories and models. The first part of this teaching problem is learning the students' models. But changing these previously learned models involves more than knowing and recognizing them (Wittrock, 1963). This important area of research deserves further attention. For related findings in mathematics see Carpenter, Moser, and Romberg (1982).

In sum, from a variety of lines of research on comprehension, it seems that the generation of relations between knowledge and experience on the one hand, and the information to be learned, on the other hand, is an important mediator of teaching, as is the generation of relations among the elements of the materials to be learned. Both of these types of relations can be facilitated by either learner generation of them, when the student has the appropriate knowledge and ability, or by appropriate teacher-given structure and conceptual relations.

The teaching of new models or theories presents a complex problem that also involves the students' organized knowledge and experience. The research we have discussed implies that the learning of a new perspective or model involves the relearning or accommodation of a previously learned conception. Knowledge of that conception is a first step, but only that, toward designing instruction which must do more than simply teach the difference between students' beliefs and teachers' knowledge. The instruction should facilitate the construction of a new conceptual framework from an old preconception.

Learning Strategies and Metacognitive Processes

In this section we will discuss how students can be taught to be aware of and to control some of their thought processes, the topics studied in research on learning strategies and metacognitive processes.

However, learning strategies and metacognitive processes are the topics of a separate chapter by Weinstein and Mayer (this volume). For this reason they will not be discussed at length. Instead, to complete the theme of this chapter, I will briefly discuss some of the studies on the teaching of learning strategies and metacognitive processes to students. This discussion summarizes many of the findings already presented in this chapter.

For further discussion of learning strategies and metacognition, see Weinstein and Mayer (this volume), and Brown, Bransford, Ferrara, and Campione (1984). For further discussion of the development of metacognitive processes see Flavell (1979) and Mischel and Mischel (1983). For further discussion of research on cognitive strategies, see Pressley and Levin (1983a, 1983b).

Learning strategies, according to Weinstein and Mayer (this volume), are learners' actions and thoughts that occur during learning and that influence motivation and encoding, including acquisition, retention, and transfer.

Metacognition refers to the learners' knowledge about and control over their cognitive processes. Metacognition is a broad and loosely defined area that relates to many of the thought processes we have discussed in this chapter, which are being widely studied in education and in other fields. For example, Thompson (1981) reports that patients undergoing painful medical procedures reduced the intensity of pain they felt only when they were taught to use cognitive strategies, such as imaging situations incompatible with the pain, or thinking about the future benefits of surgery or childbirth. None of the other strategies, including behavioral and informational strategies, reduced the intensity of pain when it was actually occurring.

The teaching of learning strategies and metacognitive strategies has been found also to be effective in educational settings to facilitate attention, motivation, learning, memory, and comprehension, as well as to remediate some learning disabilities. Mischel and Baker (1975) used an attentional training program to increase delay of gratification among preschoolers, from 5 to 14 minutes, by teaching them to think of food as inedible objects. As previously discussed, Richard deCharms (1972) facilitated motivation in teachers and achievement in high school students by teaching them to think of themselves as origins rather than as pawns. Dweck (1975) enhanced motivation and achievement among "learned helpless" students by teaching them to attribute failure to lack of effort rather than to lack of ability. McCombs (1982) showed gains in learning among students in the military services as a result of a motivational training program that changed student attributions by emphasizing their responsibilities for learning through their own effort.

Learning and retention of subject matter taught in classrooms has been facilitated by learning strategy training using imagery (Levin et al., 1980, 1983; Levin, 1981), and verbal processes (Dansereau et al., 1979; C. Weinstein, 1982).

As mentioned earlier, the teaching of reading and reading comprehension has been frequently studied recently (Wittrock et al., 1975; Wittrock, 1974a). Some studies report sizeable gains in reaching comprehension due to the teaching of learning strategies or metacognitive processes (e.g., Brown et al., 1984; Doctorow et al., 1978; Linden & Wittrock, 1981; Wittrock, 1967, 1981).

Other school-taught subjects are also becoming involved in the identification and teaching of learning strategies and metacognitive processes. In the recent study of the cognitive processes of addition and subtraction, several authors (e.g., Carpenter & Moser, 1982) found that children usually begin to solve these problems by using their fingers and a "counting all with models" strategy. In this strategy they start counting in an addition problem, say 2 + 3, with the number 1, and continue using both hands to count both numbers, 2 and 3, until they reach the total. Later, they "count all without models," using the same counting technique, but not with their fingers as models. Later they "count on from the first or smaller number," and still later, they "count on from the larger number." From knowledge of this developmental progression of strategies, one could devise instruction to teach children more advanced strategies to use.

Brown and Vanlehn (1982) identified faulty strategies or "bugs" children use in subtraction problems. Knowledge of these strategies enables a teacher to understand the repeated errors children make and to provide instruction that goes beyond giving positive or negative feedback for each individual problem. The identification of the strategies also raises the possibility of teaching better strategies to facilitate subtraction.

As we saw earlier with Roger Osborne's research on children's models of science concepts, understanding children's thinking about science concepts is only the first part of designing instruction for the students. The teaching of new learning strategies to replace less effective ones poses unsolved problems.

In earlier sections of this chapter we also discussed the positive effects of Donald Meichenbaum's, Bonnie Camp's, and Virginia Douglas' metacognitive training programs for learning-disabled children. These programs enhanced student planning and self-control over learning. Each program showed transfer to learning in schools. In addition, we saw that similar self-management programs for children with reading disabilities (Malamuth, 1979) also facilitated achievement in school. In an issue of the *Journal of Topics in Learning and Learning Disabilities* "Metacognition and Learning Disabilities," (1982) the promise of instruction in metacognitive processes is discussed, including their utility for improving reading performance in school. See also Feuerstein's (1980) comprehensive cognitive training program for teaching children in school to change their thought processes and to increase achievement in reading and mathematics.

From this broad base of research on the teaching of metacognitive processes and learning strategies, the future for enhancing school achievement by use of "learning how to learn" techniques looks promising. Students can be taught learning strategies, in some instances at least, that sizeably enhance their learning. When students become aware of the processes they are using, and when they learn to control these cognitive processes, their transfer of them often increases (Brown et al., 1984).

For the future, we need research on the relation between the development of and the teaching of learning strategies and metacognitive processes. The development of learning strategies and metacognitive processes tends to follow the learner's development of relevant knowledge (Armbruster, Echols, & Brown, 1983). The teaching of these cognitive processes should involve a thorough knowledge of their development and an understanding of the students' knowledge base. With the understanding of these developmental processes and children's relevant knowledge base, it seems quite possible that instruction in learning strategies and metacognitive processes, including awareness and control of one's own learning, can facilitate achievement. It also seems possible that some of these learning strategies and metacognitive processes will generalize across different subject matters. Knowledge about learning how to learn may be useful in a variety of school-related areas, may apply across several subjects taught in school, and may be useful with different ability levels and with learning disorders.

Summary

We began this chapter with the distinctive perspective that underlies the recent research on students' thought processes. That perspective emphasizes how teaching influences achievement through student thought processes. Throughout the chapter, we discussed research on the student thought processes that represent a coherent set of cognitions centrally involved in mediating the effects of teaching. From the theory and research we reviewed, several implications for designing research on teaching and several findings relevant to understanding the effects of teaching upon student achievement were developed. Among these implications for the design of research was the finding that the study of student mediating processes provides a useful way to ask new questions about teaching, and to develop and to test hypotheses that explain, as well as predict, some of the effects of teaching.

Among the findings relevant to understanding the effects of teaching upon student achievement were the following results and explanations. In the area of student perceptions and expectations, the research indicates that student belief that success in school is possible is one of the most important factors related to school achievement. In addition, research on student perceptions and expectations finds that the teacher expectation effect, the self-fulfilling prophecy, often depends upon the individual student's ability to perceive the teacher's expectation and differential treatment of students in the classroom. The implication is that studying teacher behavior as it relates to student thought processes as mediators of achievement provides a productive way to understand results sometimes difficult to explain by correlating teacher behavior or teaching processes directly to student achievement. The research also indicates that even in intact classrooms, the individual student, or the teacher-student dyad, is the appropriate unit of statistical analysis. The reason is that student expectations differ among students in the same class given the same treatment by teachers. The students do not always sense the treatment, differential or similar, they are given by their teachers.

In the study of attention, related findings also occur. Self-report measures of attention correlate more highly with student achievement than do measures of time-to-learn or time-on-task, which do not necessarily measure student thought processes. Consequently, it seems plausible to hypothesize that measures of time-to-learn or of time-on-task predict achievement insofar as they correlate with attention, and other thought processes that may not accurately be equated to observable time-on-task, or to time-to-learn. The implication of this finding for understanding teaching is that the students' proper use of the time, not only the time "on-task" or the time allocated by the teacher to learning, influences achievement.

In the study of student motivation, the learners' attributions about the causes of their success and failure influence their interest and persistence in learning in schools. Success in school enhances motivation primarily when the students attribute the results to their own effort, rather than to other people or factors outside their control. Rewards do not seem to strengthen learning or motivation automatically, nor even primarily in the student receiving them. Instead, the rewards seem to convey information about correct answers and teacher goals and desires to many attentive students who observe the teacher and the rewarded student.

In the study of learning and memory, as well as in comprehension and knowledge acquisition, it is again the learners' generation of meaning from the teaching that influences achievement. Learning and memory are facilitated when the learners construct images and verbal representations that relate old memories to new information, especially in organized or sequenced ways.

Comprehension and knowledge acquisition are facilitated when learners incorporate new information into familiar frameworks, or revise conceptual frameworks to accommodate new information that is incompatible with the preconceptions. From this research, teaching to facilitate learning and comprehension should focus on engaging the learner in constructing relations among the elements of the subjects to be learned, and between knowledge and experience, on the one hand, and the information or conceptualizations to be learned, on the other hand.

In the study of learning strategies and metacognitive processes the effects of students' awareness and control over these thought processes have been examined. These newly emerging findings, still tentative, indicate that with some subjects taught in school, such as reading, and with some learning disorders and hyperactivity, the teaching of learning strategies and metacognitive processes can facilitate achievement.

In sum, research on student processes revises the design of studies on teaching by including in them models and data about cognitive and affective processes that mediate the effects of teaching upon student achievement. Provided the mediators are parsimoniously used and carefully measured and quantified, they can facilitate understanding of the effects of teaching upon students.

In the studies reviewed in this chapter, the results indicate some of the value of student mediating processes for explaining the effects of teaching upon achievement, and for revising our understanding of how fundamentally important teaching variables and learning processes, including reward, teacher expectations, time-on-task, success in school, learning, and knowledge acquisition, function in schools. In each case, it is the learners' generation of meaning from the teaching that mediates the achievement.

REFERENCES

Amatora, M. (1952). Can elementary school children discriminate certain traits in their teachers? *Child Development, 23,* 75–80.
Ames, C. (1981). Competitive versus cooperative reward structures: The influence of individual and group performance factors on achievement attributions and affect. *American Educational Research Journal, 18,* 273–287.
Anderson, L. (1981). Short-term student responses to classroom instruction. *Elementary School Journal, 82,* 97–108.
Anderson, L., Evertson, C., & Brophy, J. (1979). An experimental study of effective teaching in first-grade reading groups. *Elementary School Journal 79,* 193–223.

Andre, T, (1979). Does answering higher-level questions while reading facilitate productive learning? *Review of Educational Research, 49,* 280–318.

Andrews, G. R., & Debus, R. L. (1978). Persistence and causal perception of failure: Modifying cognitive attributions. *Journal of Educational Psychology, 70,* 154–166.

Aristotle. (1964). On memory and recollection. In W. S. Hett (Trans.), *On the soul (De anima); Parva naturalia; and On breath* (Appendix). Cambridge, MA: Harvard University Press, Loeb Classical Library.

Armbruster, B. B., Echols, C. H., & Brown, A. L. (1983, April). *The role of metacognition in reading to learn: A developmental perspective* (Reading Education Rep. No. 40). Champaign: University of Illinois, Center for the Study of Reading.

Au, K. (1977, December). *Cognitive training and reading achievement.* Paper presented at the meeting of the Association for the Advancement of Behavior Therapy, Atlanta, GA.

Bar-Tal, D. (1978). Attributional analysis of achievement-related behavior. *Review of Educational Research, 48,* 259–271.

Beam, K. J., & Horvat, R. E. (1975). Differences among teachers' and students' perceptions of science classroom behaviors and actual classroom behaviors. *Science Education, 59,* 333–334.

Beck, W. R. (1967). Pupils' perceptions of teacher merit: A factor analysis of five postulated dimensions. *Journal of Educational Research, 61,* 127–128.

Blumenfeld, P. C., Hamilton, V. L., Bossert, S. T., Wessels, K., & Meece, J. (1983). Teacher talk and student thought: Socialization into the student role. In J. Levine & M. C. Wang (Eds.), *Teacher and student perceptions: Implications for learning.* Hillsdale, NJ: Lawrence Erlbaum.

Boker, J. R. (1974). Immediate and delayed retention effects of interspersing questions in written instructional passages. *Journal of Educational Psychology, 66,* 96–98.

Bower, G. H., & Clark, M. C. (1969). Narrative stories as mediators for serial learning. *Psychonomic Science, 14,* 181–182.

Braun, C. (1976). Teacher-expectation: Sociopsychological dynamics. *Review of Educational Research, 46,* 185–213.

Brookover, W. B., Beady, C., Flood, P., Schweitzer, J., & Weisenbaker, J. (1977). *Schools can make a difference.* East Lansing: Michigan State University, Center for Urban Affairs.

Brophy, J. E. (1981). Teacher praise: A functional analysis. *Review of Educational Research, 51,* 5–32.

Brophy, J. E. (1983). Research on the self-fulfilling prophecy and teacher expectations. *Journal of Educational Psychology, 75,* 631–661.

Brophy, J. E., & Evertson, C. (1976). *Learning from teaching: A developmental perspective.* Boston: Allyn & Bacon.

Brown, A. L., Bransford, J. D., Ferrara, R. A., & Campione, J. C. (1984). Learning, remembering, and understanding. In J. H. Flavell & M. Markman (Eds.), *Carmichael's manual of child psychology* (Vol. 3). New York: John Wiley, pp. 77–166.

Brown, J. S., & Vanlehn, K. (1982). Towards a generative theory of "bugs." In T. P. Carpenter, J. Moser, & T. Romberg (Eds.), *Addition and subtraction: A developmental perspective.* Hillsdale, NJ: Lawrence Erlbaum.

Bull, B. L., & Wittrock, M. C. (1973). Imagery in the learning of verbal definitions. *British Journal of Educational Psychology, 43,* 289–293.

Camp, B. W. (1980). Two psychoeducational treatment programs for young aggressive boys. In C. K. Whalen and B. Henker (Eds.), *Hyperactive children, the social ecology of identification and treatment.* New York: Academic Press, pp. 191–219.

Carpenter, T. P., & Moser, J. M. (1982). The development of addition and subtraction problem solving skills. In T. P. Carpenter, J. Moser, & T. Romberg (Eds.), *Addition and subtraction: A developmental perspective.* Hillsdale, NJ: Lawrence Erlbaum.

Carpenter, T. P., Moser, J., & Romberg T. (Eds.). (1982). *Addition and subtraction: A developmental perspective.* Hillsdale, NJ: Lawrence Erlbaum.

Chi, M. T. H., Glaser, R., & Rees, E. (1981). Expertise in problem-solving. In R. Sternberg (Ed.), *Advances in the psychology of human intelligence.* Hillsdale, NJ: Lawrence Erlbaum.

Coleman, J. S., Campbell, E. Q., Hobson, C. J., McPartland, J., Mood, A. A., Weinfeld, F. S., & York, R. L. (1966). *Equality of educational opportunity* (Report from the Office of Education). Washington, DC: U.S. Government Printing Office.

Conners, C. K. (1976). Learning disabilities and stimulant drugs in children: Theoretical implications. In R. M. Knights & D. J. Bakker (Eds.), *The neuropsychology of learning disorders.* Baltimore, MD: University Park Press.

Cooper, H. (1979). Pygmalion grows up: A model for teacher expectation communication and performance influence. *Review of Educational Research, 49,* 389–410.

Cooper, H. (1983). Communication of teacher expectations to students. In J. Levine & M. C. Wang (Eds.), *Teacher and student perceptions: Implications for learning.* Hillsdale, NJ: Lawrence Erlbaum.

Cooper, H. M., & Good, T. L. (1982). *Pygmalion grows up: Studies in the expectation communication process.* New York: Longmans.

Dansereau, D. F., Collins, K. W., McDonald, B. A., Holley, C. D., Garland, J., Diekhoff, G., & Evans, S. H. (1979). Development and evaluation of a learning strategy training program. *Journal of Educational Psychology, 71,* 64–73.

deCharms, R. (1972). Personal causation training in the schools. *Journal of Applied Psychology, 2,* 95–113.

Dee Lucas, D., & DiVesta, F. J. (1980). Learner generated organizational aids: Effects on learning from text. *Journal of Educational Psychology, 72,* 304–311.

Doctorow, M. J., Wittrock, M. C., & Marks, C. B. (1978). Generative processes in reading comprehension. *Journal of Educational Psychology, 70,* 109–118.

Dooling, D. J., & Christiaansen, R. E. (1977). Episodic and semantic aspects of memory for prose. *Journal of Experimental Psychology: Human Learning and Memory, 3,* 428–436.

Douglas, V. I., Parry, P., Martin, P., & Garson, C. (1976). Assessment of a cognitive training program for hyperactive children. *Journal of Abnormal Child Psychology, 4,* 389–410.

Doyle, W. (1977). Paradigms for research on teacher effectiveness. *Review of Research in Education, 5,* 163–198.

Doyle, W. (1980). *Student mediation responses in teaching effectiveness* (Final Report). Denton, Texas: North Texas State University.

Duchastel, P. Learning objectives and the organization of prose. *Journal of Educational Psychology,* 1979, *71,* 100–106.

Duell, O. K. Effect of type of objective, level of test questions, and the judged importance of tested materials upon posttest performance. *Journal of Educational Psychology,* 1974, *66,* 225–232.

Dweck, C. (1975). The role of expectations and attributions in the alleviation of learned helplessness. *Journal of Personality and Social Psychology, 31,* 674–685.

Dweck, C. S., Davidson, W., Nelson, S., & Enna, B. (1978). Sex differences in learned helplessness: 2. The contingencies of evaluative feedback in the classroom; 3. An experiment analysis. *Developmental Psychology, 14,* 268–276.

Evertson, C., Anderson, C., Anderson, L., & Brophy, J. (1980). Relationships between classroom behaviors and student outcomes in junior high mathematics and English classes. *American Educational Research Journal, 17,* 43–60.

Feuerstein, R. (1980). *Instrumental enrichment: An instructional program for cognitive modifiability.* Baltimore, Md.: University Park Press.

Filby, N., & Barnett, B. (1982). Student perceptions of better readers in elementary classrooms. *Elementary School Journal, 82,* 435–449.

Flavell, J. H. (1979). Metacognition and cognitive monitoring: A new area of cognitive-developmental inquiry. *American Psychologist, 34,* 906–911.

Heller, K. A., & Parsons, J. E. (1981). Sex differences in teachers' evaluative feedback and students' expectations for success in mathematics. *Child Development, 52,* 1015–1019.

Kaplan, R., & Simmons, F. G. (1974). Effects of instructional objectives used as orienting stimuli or as summary/review upon prose learning. *Journal of Educational Psychology,* 614–622.

Keogh, B. K., & Glover, A. T. (1980). The generalizability and durability of cognitive training effects. *Exceptional Education Quarterly, 1,* 75–82.

Koopman, C., & Newston, D. (1981). Level of analysis in the perception of ongoing instruction. *Journal of Educational Psychology, 73,* 212–223.

Krupski, A. (1979). Are retarded children more distractable? Observational analysis of retarded and nonretarded children's classroom behavior. *American Journal of Mental Deficiency, 84,* 1–10.

Krupski, A. (1980). Attention processes: Research, theory, and implications for special education. In B. Keogh (Ed.) *Advances in Special Education,* Vol. 1, JAI Press, pp. 101–140.

Larkin, J. H. (1981). Enriching formal knowledge: A model for learning to solve textbook physics problems. In J. Anderson (Ed.), *Cognitive skills and their acquisition.* Hillsdale, NJ: Lawrence Erlbaum.

Lefcourt, H. M. (1982). *Locus of control: Current trends in theory and research.* Hillsdale, NJ: Lawrence Erlbaum. (1st ed. publshed 1976)

Lepper, M. R. (1983). Extrinsic reward and intrinsic motivation. In J. Levine & M. C. Wang (Eds.), *Teacher and student perceptions: Implications for learning.* Hillsdale, NJ.: Lawrence Erlbaum.

Levin, J. R. (1981). On functions of pictures in prose. In F. J. Pirozzolo & M. C. Wittrock (Eds.), *Neuropsychological and cognitive processes of reading.* New York: Academic Press.

Levin, J. R. (in press). Educational applications of mnemonic pictures: Possibilities beyond your wildest imagination. In A. A. Sheikh (Ed.), *Imagery and the educational process.* Farmingdale, NY: Baywood Publishing.

Levin, J. R., Berry, J. K., Miller, G. E., & Bartell, N. P. (1982). More on how (and how not) to remember the states and their captials. *The Elementary School Journal, 82,* 371–388.

Levin, J. R., Shriberg, L. K., & Berry, J. K. (1983). A concrete strategy for remembering abstract prose. *American Educational Research Journal, 20,* 277–290.

Levin, J. R., Shriberg, L. K., Miller, G. E., McCormick, C. G., & Levin, B. B. (1980). The keyword method in the classroom: How to remember the states and their capitals. *Elementary School Journal, 80,* 185–191.

Linden, M., & Wittrock, M. C. (1981). The teaching of reading comprehension according to the model of generative learning. *Reading Research Quarterly, 17,* 44–57.

Livesley, W. J., & Bromley, D. (1973). *Person perception in childhood and adolescence.* London: John Wiley.

Mackenzie, A. W., & White, R. T. (1982). Fieldwork in geography and long-term memory structures. *American Educational Research Journal, 19,* 623–632.

Malamuth, S. (1979). Self-management training for children with reading problems: Effects on reading performance and sustained attention. *Cognitive Therapy and Research, 4,* 279–289.

Marks, C. B., Doctorow, M. J., & Wittrock, M. C. (1974). Word frequency and reading comprehension. *Journal of Educational Research, 67,* 259–262.

McCombs, B. L. (1982). Transitioning learning strategies research into practice: Focus on the student in technical training. *Journal of Instructional Development, 5,* 10–17.

McCombs, B. L. (1983, April). *Motivational skills training: Helping students to adapt by taking personal responsibility and positive self-control.* Paper presented at the annual meeting of the American Educational Research Association, Montreal.

Meichenbaum, D., & Asarnow, J. (1978). Cognitive-behavior modification and metacognitive development: Implications for the classroom. In P. Kendall & S. Hollen (Eds.), *Cognitive-behavioral interventions: Theory, research, and procedures.* New York: Academic Press.

Meichenbaum, D., & Goodman, J. (1971). Training impulsive children to talk to themselves: A means of developing self-control. *Journal of Abnormal Psychology, 77,* 115–126.

"Metacognition and Learning Disabilities" [special issue]. (1982). *Topics in Learning and Learning Disabilities, 2*(1), 1–107.

Mischel, H. N., & Mischel, W. (1983). The development of children's knowledge of self-control strategies. *Child Development, 54,* 603–619.

Mischel, W., & Baker, N. (1975). Cognitive appraisals and transformations in delay behavior. *Journal of Personality and Social Psychology, 31,* 254–261.

Morine-Dershimer, G. (1982). Pupil perceptions of teacher praise. *Elementary School Journal, 82,* 421–434.

Nicholls, J. G. (1978). The development of the concepts of effort and ability, perception of academic attainment, and the understanding that difficult tasks require more ability. *Developmental Psychology, 49,* 800–814.

Nicholls, J. G. (1979). Quality and equality in intellectual development. *American Psychologist, 34,* 1071–1084.

Nord, W. R., Connelly, F., & Diagnault, G. (1974). Laws of control and aptitude test scores as predictors of academic achievement. *Journal of Educational Psychology, 66,* 956–961.

Nowicki, S., Jr., & Strickland, B. R. (1973). A locus of control scale for children. *Journal of Consulting and Clinical Psychology, 40,* 148–154.

Osborne, R. (1981). Children's ideas about electric current. *New Zealand Science Teacher, 29,* 12–19.

Osborne, R. J., & Wittrock, M. C. (1983). Learning science: A generative process. *Science Education, 67,* 489–508.

Paris, S. G., Lindauer, B. K., & Cox, G. L. (1977). The development of inferential comprehension. *Child Development, 48,* 1728–1733.

Paton, S. M., Walberg, H. J., & Yeh, E. G. (1973). Ethnicity, environmental control, and academic self-concept in Chicago. *American Educational Research Journal, 10,* 85–99.

Pearson, P. D., Hansen, J., & Gordon, C. (1979, March). *The effect of background knowledge on young children's comprehension of explicit and implicit information* (Tech. Rep. NO. 116). Urbana: University of Illinois, Center for the Study of Reading.

Peterson, P. L., & Swing, S. R. (1982). Beyond time on task: Students' reports of their thought processes during direct instruction. *Elementary School Journal, 82,* 481–491.

Peterson, P. L., Swing, S. R., Braverman, M. T., & Buss, R. (1982). Students' aptitudes and their reports of cognitive processing during instruction. *Journal of Educational Psychology. 74,* 535–547.

Peterson, P. L., Swing, S. R., Stark, K. D., & Waas, G. A. (1983, April). *Students' reports of their cognitive processes and affective thoughts during classroom instruction.* Paper presented at the annual meeting of the American Educational Research Association, Montreal.

Piaget, J., & Inhelder, B. (1975). *The origin of the idea of chance in children.* New York: W.W. Norton.

Pichert, J. W., & Anderson, R. C. (1977). Taking different perspectives on a story. *Journal of Educational Psychology, 69,* 309–315.

Pressley, M., & Levin, J. (Eds.). (1983a). *Cognitive strategy research: Educational applications.* New York: Springer Verlag.

Pressley, M., & Levin, J. (Eds.). (1983b). *Cognitive strategy research: Psychological foundations.* New York: Springer Verlag.

Pressley, M., Levin, J., & Delaney, H. (1982). The mnemonic keyword method. *Review of Educational Research, 52,* 61–91.

Preston, M.S., Guthrie, J. T., & Childs, B. (1974). Visual evoked responses in normal and disabled readers. *Psychophysiology, 11,* 452–457.

Raugh, M. R., & Atkinson, R. C. (1975). A mnemonic method for learning a second-language vocabulary. *Journal of Educational Psychology, 67,* 1–16.

Reid, I., & Croucher, A. (1980). The Crandall Intellectual Achievement Responsibility Questionnaire: A British validation study. *Educational and Psychological Measurement, 40,* 255–258.

Rickards, J. P., & August, G. J. (1975). Generative underlining strategies in prose recall. *Journal of Educational Psychology, 67,* 860–865.

Rickards, J. P., & Denner, P. R. (1978). Inserted questions as aids to reading text. *Instructional Science, 7,* 313–346.

Stayrook, N. G., Corno, L., & Winne, P. H. (1978). Path analyses relating student perceptions of teacher behavior to student achievement. *Journal of Teacher Education, 29,* 51–56.

Stipek, D. J. (1981). Children's perceptions of their own and their classmates' ability. *Journal of Educational Psychology, 73,* 404–410.

Stipek, D., & Hoffman, J. (1980). Children's achievement related expectancies as a function of academic performance histories and sex. *Journal of Educational Psychology, 72,* 861–865.

Sweeny, C. A., & Bellezza, F. S. (1982). Use of the keyword mnemonic in learning English vocabulary. *Human Learning, 1,* 155–163.

Thompson, S. C. (1981). Will it hurt less if I can control it? A complex answer to a simple question. *Psychological Bulletin, 90,* 89–101.

Tharp, R. (1982). The effective instruction of comprehension: Results and description of the Kamehameha Early Education Program. *Reading Research Quarterly, 17,* 503–527.

Wang, M. C. (1983). Development and consequences of students' sense of personal control. In J. Levine & M. C. Wang (Eds.), *Teacher and student perceptions: Implications for learning.* Hillsdale, NJ: Lawrence Erlbaum.

Wang, M. C., & Stiles, B. (1976). An investigation of children's concept of self-responsibility for their school learning. *American Educational Research Journal, 13,* 159–179.

Weiner, B. (1979). A theory of motivation for some classroom experiences. *Journal of Educational Psychology, 71,* 3–25.

Weiner, B. (1983). Speculations regarding the role of affect in achievement-change programs guided by attributional principles. In J. Levine & M. C. Wang (Eds.), *Teacher and student perceptions: Implications for learning.* Hillsdale, NJ: Lawrence Erlbaum.

Weinstein, C. E. (1982). Training students to use elaboration learning strategies. *Contemporary Educational Psychology, 7,* 301–311.

Weinstein, R. S. (1983). Student perceptions of schooling. *Elementary School Journal, 83,* 288–312.

Weinstein, R. S., Marshall, H. H., Brattesani, K. A., & Middlestadt, S. E. (1982). Student perceptions of differential teacher treatment in open and traditional classrooms. *Journal of Educational Psychology, 74,* 678–692.

Weinstein, R. S., & Middlestadt, S. E. (1979). Student perceptions of teacher interactions with male high and low achievers. *Journal of Educational Psychology, 71,* 421–431.

Weisz, J. R., & Stipek, D. (1982). Competence, contingency, and the development of perceived control. *Human Development, 25,* 250–281.

Willows, D. M. (1974). Reading between the lines: Selective attention in good and poor readers. *Child Development, 45,* 408–415.

Winne, P. H., & Marx, R. W. (1980). Matching students' cognitive responses to teaching skills. *Journal of Educational Psychology, 72,* 257–264.

Winne, P. H., & Marx, R. W. (1982). Students' and teachers' views of thinking processes for classroom learning. *Elementary School Journal, 82,* 493–518.

Winne, P. H., & Marx, R. W. (1983). *Students' cognitive processes while learning from teaching* (Final Report, NIE-G-0098). Burnaby, British Columbia: Simon Fraser University, Faculty of Education.

Wittrock, M. C. (1963) Response mode in the programming of kinetic molecular theory concepts. *Journal of Educational Psychology, 54,* 89–93,

Wittrock, M. C. (1967). Replacement and nonreplacement strategies in children's problem solving. *Journal of Educational Psychology, 58,* 69–74.

Wittrock, M. C. (1974a). Learning as a generative process. *Educational Psychologist, 11,* 87–95.

Wittrock, M. C. (1974b). A generative model of mathematics learning. *Journal for Research in Mathematics Education, 5,* 181–197.

Wittrock, M. C. (1978). The cognitive movement in instruction. *Educational Psychologist, 13,* 15–30.

Wittrock, M. C. (1981). Reading comprehension. In F. J. Pirozzolo & M. C. Wittrock (Eds.), *Neuropsychological and cognitive processes of reading.* New York: Academic Press.

Wittrock, M. C. (1983). Writing and the teaching of reading. *Language Arts, 60,* 600–606.

Wittrock, M. C. (in press). Education and recent research on attention and knowledge acquisition. In S. L. Friedman, K. A. Klivington, & R. W. Peterson (Eds.), *Brain, cognition, and education.* New York: Academic Press.

Wittrock, M. C., & Carter, J. (1975). Generative processing of hierarchically organized words. *American Journal of Psychology, 88,* 489–501.

Wittrock, M. C., & Goldberg, S. (1975). Imagery and meaningfulness in free recall; Word attributes and instructional sets. *Journal of General Psychology, 92,* 137–151.

Wittrock, M. C., & Lumsdaine, A. A. (1977). Instructional psychology. In M. R. Rosenzweig & L. W. Porter (Eds.), *Annual Review of Psychology. 28,* 417–459.

Wittrock, M. C., Marks, C. B., & Doctorow, M. J. (1975). Reading as a generative process. *Journal of Educational Psychology, 67,* 484–489.

Yates, F. (1966). *The art of memory.* London: Routledge & Kegan Paul, 1966.

Zeaman, D., & House, B. (1963). The role of attention in retardate discrimination learning. In N. Ellis, *Handbook of mental deficiency.* New York: McGraw-Hill Book Co., p. 159–223.

11.

The Teaching of Learning Strategies

Claire E. Weinstein
University of Texas, Austin

Richard E. Mayer
University of California, Santa Barbara

Introduction

In recent years increasing attention has been focused on the role of the learner as an active participant in the teaching–learning act. In particular, this view suggests that the effects of teaching depend partly on what the learner knows, such as the learner's prior knowledge, and what the learner thinks about during learning, such as the learner's active cognitive processing (Anderson, Spiro, & Montague, 1977; Cook & Mayer, 1983; Dansereau, 1985; Jones, Amiran, & Katims, 1985; Mayer, 1984; Ryan, 1981; Weinstein, 1978; Weinstein & Underwood, 1985; Wittrock, 1974, 1978).

The present paper investigates techniques that a learner can be taught to use during learning. These techniques, referred to as learning strategies, can be defined as behaviors and thoughts that a learner engages in during learning and that are intended to influence the learner's encoding process. Thus, the goal of any particular learning strategy may be to affect the learner's motivational or affective state, or the way in which the learner selects, acquires, organizes, or integrates new knowledge. For example, in preparing for a learning situation, a learner may use positive self-talk to reduce feelings of anxiety; in learning paired-associates, a learner may form a mental image to help associate the objects represented by the members of each pair; in learning from an expository passage a learner may generate summaries for each section; in learning about a scientific concept, a learner may take notes about the material. Each of these activities—coaching, imaging, summarizing, and note-taking—are examples of learning strategies.

Why should there be a chapter on "learning strategies" in a handbook of research on teaching? The rationale is that good

teaching includes teaching students how to learn, how to remember, how to think, and how to motivate themselves. Norman (1980) summarizes this argument as follows:

> It is strange that we expect students to learn yet seldom teach them about learning. We expect students to solve problems yet seldom teach them about problem solving. And, similarly, we sometimes require students to remember a considerable body of material yet seldom teach them the art of memory. It is time we made up for this lack, time that we developed the applied disciplines of learning and problem solving and memory. We need to develop the general principles of how to learn, how to remember, how to solve problems, and then to develop applied courses, and then to establish the place of these methods in an academic curriculum. (p. 97)

This argument becomes even more compelling as the lifelong learning concept continues to be defined and expanded in societal self-descriptions and educational forecasting. Helping students to develop effective ways to handle the barrage of information coming from the environment, as well as their own thinking processes, is a major goal of our educational system that will only increase in importance in the future.

This change in approach has important implications for teacher training and practice. Teachers enter the classroom with two distinctly different kinds of goals: (1) *Goals concerning the products of learning*, which focus on what students should know or be able to do as a result of learning, that is, on teaching *what* to learn. For example, when teaching addition, one goal of instruction may be that the learner acquire the number facts up to 100. (2) *Goals concerning the processes of learning*, which focus on techniques and strategies students can use to accomplish learning, that is, on teaching *how* to learn. For example,

The authors thank reviewers Judith Segal (National Institute of Education) and Barbara McCombs (University of Denver).

when teaching addition, one goal of instruction may be that the learner acquire techniques for relating new problems to existing knowledge, such as identifying that $7 + 5 = \underline{\quad}$ is the same as $6 + 6 = \underline{\quad}$. Successful teaching requires sensitivity to both types of instructional goals and skill in teaching both types of instructional objectives.

Conceptual Framework

An interest in learning strategies is the natural outgrowth of a change in orientation from behaviorist theories to cognitive theories of learning. The behaviorist (or S-R) approach to learning—as developed from the work of Hull and Spence and Skinner—focuses on how presentation of material influences behavior. As Farnham-Diggory (1977) points out, this S-R approach is based on the idea that "a stimulus goes in, a response comes out, and what happens in between is summarized by a hyphen" (p. 128).

In contrast, the cognitive approach to learning seeks to understand how incoming information is processed and structured in memory. Farnham-Diggory (1977) notes that "with the emergence of cognitive psychology in the 1960's ... now, instead of a hyphen, we have mental structures and processes" (p. 128).

The cognitive approach has changed our conception of the teaching-learning process in several ways. Instead of viewing learners as passively recording the stimuli that the teacher presents, learning is viewed as an active process that occurs within the learner and which can be influenced by the learner. Instead of viewing the outcome of learning as depending mainly on what the teacher presents, the outcome of learning is supposed to depend jointly on what information is presented and on how the learner processes that information. Hence, there are two different kinds of activities that influence the encoding process: (1) teaching strategies, such as the teacher presenting certain material at a certain time in a certain way; and (2) learning strategies, such as the learner actively organizing or elaborating or predicting about the presented material. While the traditional S-R approach has focused educators'

attention on the first kind of activity, the cognitive approach requires also focusing on the second kind of activity.

A framework for describing the teaching-learning process is presented in Table 11.1. The elements in this process include the following:

- Teacher characteristics—including the teacher's existing knowledge concerning the subject matter and how to teach, that may be required for the teaching strategy selected.
- Teaching strategies—including the teacher's performance during teaching such as what is presented, when it is presented, and how it is presented.
- Learner characteristics—including the learner's existing knowledge concerning facts, procedures, and strategies, that may be required for the learning strategy selected.
- Learning strategies—including behaviors that the learner engages in during learning that are intended to influence affective and cognitive processing during encoding.
- Encoding process—including internal cognitive processes during learning such as how the learner selects, organizes, and integrates new information.
- Learning outcome—including the newly acquired knowledge that depends on both teaching and learning strategies.
- Performance—including behavior on tests of retention and transfer.

As can be seen, instruction in learning strategies (i.e., training in how to learn) can affect learner characteristics by making specific strategies and methods available to the learner. The use of particular learning strategies during learning can affect the encoding process, which in turn affects the learning outcome and performance.

Table 11.2 lists some of the major categories of learning strategies. Each category includes methods designed to influence certain aspects of the encoding process to facilitate one or more types of learning outcome and performance. The categories listed in the table are:

- Rehearsal strategies for basic learning tasks—such as repeating the names of items in an ordered list. Common school tasks in this category include remembering the order of the planets from the sun and the order in which Shakespeare introduces the characters in the play *Hamlet*.
- Rehearsal strategies for complex learning tasks—such as copying, underlining or shadowing the material presented in class. Common school tasks in this category include underlining the main events in a story or copying portions of a lesson about the causes of World War I.

Table 11.1. Framework for Analyzing the Teaching–Learning Process

Teacher Characteristics	Learner Characteristics
What the teacher knows	What the learner knows
Teaching Strategy	Learning Strategy
What the teacher does during teaching	What the learner does during learning

Encoding Process
How information is processed

Learning Outcome
What is learned

Performance
How learning is evaluated

Table 11.2. Eight Categories of Learning Strategies

1. Basic Rehearsal Strategies
2. Complex Rehearsal Strategies
3. Basic Elaboration Strategies
4. Complex Elaboration Strategies
5. Basic Organizational Strategies
6. Complex Organizational Strategies
7. Comprehension Monitoring Strategies
8. Affective and Motivational Strategies

- Elaboration strategies for basic learning tasks—such as forming a mental image or sentence relating the items in each pair for a paired-associate list of words. Common school tasks in this category include forming a phrase or sentence relating the name of a state or its major agricultural product, or forming a mental image of a scene described by a poem.
- Elaboration strategies for complex tasks—such as paraphrasing, summarizing, or describing how new information relates to existing knowledge. Common school tasks in this category include creating an analogy between the operation of a post office and the operation of a computer, or relating the information presented about the structure of complex molecules to the information presented about the structure of simple molecules.
- Organizational strategies for basic learning tasks—such as grouping or ordering to-be-learned items from a list or a section of prose. Common school tasks in this category include organizing foreign vocabulary words into the categories for parts of speech, or creating a chronological listing of the events that led up to the Declaration of Independence.
- Organizational strategies for complex tasks—such as outlining a passage or creating a hierarchy. Common school tasks in this category include outlining assigned chapters in the textbook, or creating a diagram to show the relationship among the stress forces in a structural design.
- Comprehension monitoring strategies—such as checking for comprehension failures. Common school tasks in this category include using self-questioning to check understanding of the material presented in class and using the questions at the beginning of a section to guide one's reading behavior while studying a textbook.
- Affective strategies—such as being alert and relaxed, to help overcome test anxiety. Common school tasks in this category include reducing external distractions by studying in a quiet place, or using thought stopping to prevent thoughts of doing poorly from directing attention away from the test and toward fears of failure.

The encoding process, another element in the teaching-learning process, can be analyzed into four main components (Cook & Mayer, 1983):

- Selection—The learner actively pays attention to some of the information that is impinging on the sense receptors, and transfers this information into working memory (or "active consciousness").
- Acquisition—The learner actively transfers the information from working memory into long-term memory for permanent storage.
- Construction—The learner actively builds connections between ideas in the information that have reached working memory. This building of internal connections (Mayer, 1982, 1984) involves the development of a coherent outline organization or schema (Bransford, 1979) that holds the information together.
- Integration—The learner actively searches for prior knowledge in long-term memory and transfers this knowledge to working memory. The learner may then build external

connections (Mayer, 1982, 1984) between the incoming information and prior knowledge.

As you can see, selection and acquisition are cognitive processes that determine *how much* is learned whereas construction and integration are cognitive processes that determine the organizational coherence of *what* is learned and how it is organized.

Each of the eight learning strategies listed in Table 11.2 may be used to achieve certain goals for influencing the cognitive processes in encoding. For example, rehearsal behaviors seem to be aimed primarily at acquisition and selection of information whereas organizational and elaboration behaviors seem to be aimed primarily at construction and integration, respectively. The comprehension monitoring techniques seem related to all four processes, depending on the characteristics of the task, and affective strategies could also impact all four strategies, but may be most effective for selection and acquisition. The relationship between each learning strategy and the encoding process will be discussed in subsequent sections.

Rehearsal Strategies for Basic Learning Tasks

If you were asked to remember the names of the B vitamins, a common learning strategy you could use would be to rehearse the list of names. Rehearsing refers to the learner's actively reciting or naming the presented items during learning. The goal of this activity may be selection and acquisition of units to be transferred to working memory.

In a study by Flavell, Friedrichs, and Hoyt (1970), students' spontaneous use of rehearsal strategies during learning was found to increase with age. For example, in one experiment, subjects were given a row of windows with a button below each one. If the subject pressed a button, a light would come on for the picture in the window above the button. The light would stay on for as long as the subject kept the button pressed; as soon as the subject stopped pressing the button, the window would become blank again. The subject's job was to keep pressing the buttons, one at a time, for as long and as many times as needed, until the subject was able to recall the names for the whole series of pictures.

The results indicated large differences in the active, spontaneous rehearsal performance of children of different ages. Fourth graders were ten times more likely than nursery school children to engage in naming of objects from previous pictures and to practice by anticipating the name of an object before pressing the button. Fourth graders also engaged in repeating the name of a presented object more than twice as often as nursery school children. Apparently, by the time a child moves from nursery school to fourth grade, the child can make more use of rehearsal strategies and related techniques for memorizing new information.

A study by Hagen and Kail (1973) provides additional evidence that younger children are less likely to spontaneously rehearse as compared to older children. Flavell, Beach, and Chinsky (1966) have noted that in a list learning task almost all 10-year-olds moved their lips during learning—suggesting rehearsal—while almost no 5-year-olds moved their lips. In a training study, Kenney, Cannizzo, and Flavell (1967) identified a group of first graders who spontaneously moved their lips during learning and a group of first graders who did not give evidence of rehearsing. As expected, the "rehearsers" performed better on the memory test than the "nonrehearsers." Both groups were then given explicit training in how to rehearse a list of items, including how to name the pictures during the retention interval. This training boosted the memory performance of the "nonrehearsers" but did not affect the performance of the "rehearsers." However, on subsequent list learning tasks, the "nonrehearsers" did not continue to use the rehearsal strategy they had been taught, and their memory performance fell. Based on results such as these, Flavell (1970; Flavell & Wellman, 1977) argues that some young children have rehearsal strategies *available* to them but generally fail to spontaneously *apply* them in learning tasks. Flavell refers to this phenomenon as a "production deficiency" because the child fails to produce appropriate rehearsal strategies when they are called for.

In a related study, Appel, Cooper, McCarrell, Sims-Knight, Yussen, and Flavell (1972) presented two lists to 4-, 7-, and 11-year-olds. For one list, the children were told to look at each picture; for the other list, subjects were told to memorize the pictures. The 4-year-olds tended to behave the same for both lists; for example, they did not rehearse more for the "memorize" list, and they did not remember it better than the "look" list. The 11-year-olds did behave differently for the two lists; for the list they were asked to memorize they engaged in much more rehearsal, and also performed much better on a test of recall list. The 7-year-olds tried to engage in more rehearsal for the "memorize" list but were not successful in boosting recall performance. Appel et al. (1972) suggest a "differentiation hypothesis" in which older children are better able to use learning strategies that are appropriate for particular goals.

These studies suggest that rehearsal strategies are learned by children as they progress from nursery school to fifth or sixth grade. Below age 5, children tend not to spontaneously use rehearsal strategies in learning lists of pictures, are not distracted by activities that limit rehearsal, and do not seem to use different approaches for tasks with different requirements. Apparently, these children do not have effective rehearsal strategies available to them. By age 6 or 7, children are often able to use rehearsal strategies when explicitly instructed to do so, but may not be able to generate useful strategies spontaneously. These children seem to have rehearsal strategies available but do not seem to know how to use them. Finally, by age 11 or 12, children tend to spontaneously rehearse during learning, to be distracted by activities that interfere with rehearsal, and to modify their rehearsal behavior in line with goals of the task. While the rate of this progression is influenced by the difficulty of the task and the sophistication of the learner, there does appear to be a distinct progression in the way that children use rehearsing to enhance learning.

Rehearsal Strategies for Complex Learning Tasks

When the to-be-learned material is prose, such as a lesson from a science textbook, the rehearsal strategies can include repeating the material aloud (i.e., shadowing), copying the material, taking selective verbatim notes, and underlining the important parts of the material. In each case, the act of rehearsal involves the learner actively saying, writing, or pointing to parts of the presented material during learning. Two of the major cognitive goals of this strategy are: (1) selection—helping the learner to pay attention to important aspects of the passage, and (2) acquisition—making sure that the material is transferred into working memory for further study.

For example, in a research study, Mayer and Cook (1980) asked students to listen to a passage that described how radar works. After each phrase there was a pause, during which some students were instructed to repeat the words (shadowing group) while other students simply listened without repeating the words during each pause (control group). On a subsequent test, the shadowing group remembered more about the details and the verbatim wording of the passage, but the control group remembered more of the conceptual information and performed better on tests of creative problem solving using the radar information. Apparently, rehearsal strategies that are effective for basic learning tasks may not be as useful in some more complex tasks. One explanation of these findings is that shadowing prevented the students from actively building internal and external connections, while the control group had time to engage in these activities.

In another study, Arkes, Schumacher, and Gardner (1976) asked students to read a passage about Presidential candidates. Among the many treatment groups, some students were asked to copy the passage into their own handwriting (copy group), whereas other students were asked to perform a nonconceptual task such as circling every letter "e" (control group). Both groups were told that they would be expected to take a recall test. Results indicated that the copy group remembered approximately 50% more than the control group, but the copy group required nearly three times more study time than the control group. In another part of the study, students were not told to expect a recall test; in this case the copy group recalled approximately three times as much as the control group and also required approximately three times as much study time. Thus, while copying seems to enhance factual recall there is some reason to question its efficiency as a widely used learning strategy.

Another form of rehearsal is to copy or underline only the important parts of a lesson. For example, Rickards and August (1975) found that students who were asked to underline sentences in a passage were able to recall substantially more information than students who simply read the passage without underlining. It should be noted, however, that Brown and Smiley (1977) found that children below the sixth grade cannot adequately identify important information in prose.

Finally, Howe (1970) has found that facts that students correctly copy into their notes are far more likely to be learned than facts that are not copied into notes. For example, students were asked to take notes on a 160-word passage, and then take a recall test one week later. If a fact was in the notes, it was recalled 34% of the time; but if a fact was not in a student's notes, it was recalled less than 5% of the time. These results are consistent with the idea that rehearsal strategies serve to help the learner select information and to acquire the information. However, there is little evidence that these techniques help learners to construct internal connections or integrate the information with prior knowledge. Several of the training programs described in subsequent sections use some rehearsal strategies, but supplement these strategies with others that are aimed at other cognitive goals.

Elaboration Strategies for Basic Learning Tasks

Basic learning tasks include paired-associate learning, such as learning foreign language vocabulary; serial list learning, such as learning to recite the alphabet; and free recall list learning, such as learning to name all of the parts of the brain. Elaboration strategies that have been used for these tasks include forming a mental image or generating a sentence that connects two or more items. One major cognitive goal of elaboration strategies is construction—building of internal associations between two items (or among several items) in the to-be-learned material.

One of the most effective elaboration strategies for paired-associate learning involves using mental images to help relate and represent items in a pair. For example, to remember a word pair such as "apple-fish," a learner could form an image of a fish taking a bite out of an apple. Levin (1976) has distinguished between induced imagery strategies (in which the learner is instructed to generate and use visual imagery to associate items) and imposed imagery strategies (in which the experimenter or teacher provides an image and asks that the learner use that image to associate items). In a recent review, Reese (1977) has noted that imposed imagery tends to improve paired-associate learning performance for kindergarteners and first graders but induced imagery is better for sixth graders and adults. Apparently, younger children are not able to effectively generate images but are able to use imagery that is provided by a teacher; in contrast, older children who are able to generate their own idiosyncratic images may be distracted by the teachers' imagery suggestions.

The keyword method for acquiring foreign language vocabulary is one of the most popular attempts to teach a type of imaging strategy that also uses verbal elaboration (Atkinson, 1975; Atkinson & Raugh, 1975, Raugh & Atkinson, 1975). For example, in memorizing Spanish vocabulary such as "trigo" means "wheat," the keyword method involves two stages: first, a verbal *acoustic link* must be established in which the foreign language word is changed into an easily pronounced English "keyword." This keyword must sound like part of the foreign word; for example, "trigo" can be converted into "tree." Second, an *imagery link* must be formed between the keyword and the corresponding English word. For example, the learner could picture a tree that grows wheat stalks instead of leaves.

In a typical experiment, Raugh and Atkinson (1975) asked college students to learn 60 Spanish-to-English vocabulary pairs in 15 minutes. The experimental group was given training in the use of the keyword method; during learning the keywords were provided but subjects had to generate their own images. The control group learned the same 60 vocabulary pairs in the same amount of time, but were not given training in how to use the keyword method. The experimental group scored 88% on a recall test compared to 28% for the control group. In another study involving Russian vocabulary, students

who used the keyboard method recalled 72% compared to 46% for the control group (Atkinson & Raugh, 1975).

Levin, McCormick, Miller, Berry, and Pressley (1982) asked fourth graders to learn definitions of 12 verbs, such as "persuade." The experimental group was given a keyword for each verb—such as "purse" for "persuade"—and were given pictures that showed the keyword interacting with a definition of the vocabulary word—such as a picture of a woman being "persuaded" to buy a "purse." Control subjects were given just as much time to learn, but were not given the keyword treatment. The experimental group recalled 83% of the definitions as compared to 55% for the control group. Levin et al. (1982) also found that pictures that do not explicitly connect the vocabulary word to the keyword do not improve memory performance. In a review of research studies involving adapting the keyword method to various school tasks, Levin (1981) points out that in addition to teaching foreign language vocabulary and English vocabulary, as described above, the keyword method has been successfully applied to memorizing unfamiliar medical terms, functions of various biochemicals, cities and their products, famous people and their accomplishments, states and capitals, and U.S. presidents by number.

Pressley and his colleagues (Pressley, 1977; Pressley & Dennis-Rounds, 1980; Pressley & Levin, 1978) have found that younger children have difficulty in spontaneously generating useful keyword images, even when they are explicitly trained to do so. Thus, Levin (1981) and Pressley (1977) suggest that when the learners are children, the keyword method should be adapted to provide both keywords and pictures (showing the images). However, Jones and Hall (1982) were able to train eighth grade students to successfully carry out both steps. Students who participated in this educational treatment (five 20–30-minute sessions spaced over a 3 month interval) learned to both generate the verbal links and create effective compound images. Even more important, students who participated in this training subsequently used this strategy under appropriate task conditions and without explicit prompting. It appears that older students can learn to use this strategy effectively and to generalize its use to everyday school tasks.

In contrast to the keyword method, Beck and her colleagues (Beck, Perfetti, & McKeown, 1982) have developed an alternative method for teaching vocabulary to students. For example, in Beck's program students were given sets of related words so that they could explore the interrelationships among them. Initial results indicate that the program is useful in helping students learn the vocabulary words, and that this technique transfers well to learning of new vocabulary words. Unlike Levin's and Pressley's programs, which focus on learning of single associations, Beck's program involves the building of several associations among ideas. Thus, Beck's approach shares some of the characteristics of the organizational strategies described in the following section, and may have the effect of allowing students to build internal connections among words.

Elaboration Strategies for Complex Learning Tasks

When elaboration strategies are applied to tasks such as prose learning, the types of activities include paraphrasing, summarizing, creating analogies, generative notetaking, and question answering. The goals of these techniques include integration of presented information with prior knowledge—i.e., transferring knowledge from long-term memory into working memory and integrating the incoming information with this knowledge.

In a model of learning as a generative process developed by Wittrock (1974, 1978, 1981), the integrative processes used by the learner to relate new information to either concepts or schemas already in semantic memory, or distinctive memories of experience, are the key determinants of new learning and subsequent performance. Creating connections, or elaborations, between to-be-learned information and already established content and procedural knowledge is a major component of most knowledge acquisition frameworks based on schema theory (Schallert, 1982). Models have also been developed which relate research about levels of processing in memory to elaborative encoding (Bradshaw & Anderson, 1982).

In a recent study examining the use of summarization (Doctorow, Wittrock, & Marks, 1978), sixth graders studied commercially available reading materials. For half of the students, these materials contained paragraph headings while for the other half the entire text was presented without any inserted headings. In addition, half of the students in each of these two groups also received instructions to generate summary sentences for each paragraph right after they finished reading it. An analysis of the scores from a post-reading comprehension test indicated that students asked to generate summary sentences outperformed the control subjects. In addition, with time to learn held constant, the students receiving the passage with the inserted headings and the instructions to generate summary sentences outperformed the students in any of the other conditions.

Researchers have also investigated complex elaboration strategies singly or in combination with one or more other types of learning strategies. Weinstein (1982) examined whether students could be taught to use a variety of elaboration strategies and whether their use of these strategies would result in improvements in understanding and school performance. She created a diversified elaboration skills training program for use with ninth grade students. Instruction centered around the following five strategies: using verbal elaborators, using imaginal elaborators, creating analogies, drawing implications, creating relationships and elaborative paraphrasing (relating the material to what is already known while also restating it in one's own words). Instruction involved teaching students how to apply these strategies to a variety of learning tasks typically encountered in school, including paired-associate learning tasks, free recall learning tasks and reading comprehension tasks. The stimulus materials used during instruction were drawn from a ninth grade curriculum in science, history, English, foreign language and vocational education.

For this study, ninth grade students were randomly assigned to one of three groups: training, control, or posttest-only. The training group participated in a series of five 1-hour elaboration skill training sessions, administered at approximately 1-week intervals. Students were exposed to a set of 19 learning tasks. They were required to create a series of elaborations for each of these tasks. Experimenter-provided directions for the early tasks emphasized the properties of an effective elaboration strategy. The later training session provided opportunities for additional practice in using these skills with little or no experimenter-provided instructions. The control group was exposed to the same stimulus materials, but their task was simply to learn the information without any type of strategy prompts or directions. A posttest-only group was not exposed to the stimulus materials but did participate in the posttesting sessions. The immediate posttest was administered 1 week after the conclusion of the training, and the delayed posttest was administered approximately 1 month later. Both immediate and delayed posttests consisted of two reading comprehension tasks, two trials of paired-associate learning and serial recall, and a one-trial free recall task.

The results of the data analyses for the immediate posttest revealed significant differences between group means on the free recall task and Trial 2 of the paired-associate learning task. In each instance, the training group's performance surpassed the performance of the control and posttest-only groups, which did not differ significantly from each other. On the delayed posttest, a significant difference was obtained for the reading comprehension tasks and Trial 1 of the serial learning task. Again, these differences favored the training group.

Probably the most common form of complex rehearsal strategy involves notetaking. In a study by Carrier and Titus (1981), which is typical of much of the research in this area, high school juniors and seniors were trained to use a notetaking system developed by the Study Skills Center at the University of Minnesota. This system is designed to teach students to (a) distinguish between superordinate and subordinate information, (b) abbreviate words, (c) paraphrase in one's own words, and (d) use an outline format. Each student participating in the training listened to an explanation of the rationale for using the system and a description of each of the four components. Next, participants observed demonstrations where each component was applied in a set of model notes. Finally, the students practiced using the entire system while listening to three minilectures; the topics of these lectures included political problems in Latin America, the structure and function of cell membranes, and the characteristics of the moon. Following each minilecture, participants compared their notes to a set of model notes distributed by the experimenter and then discussed any problems they encountered or any questions they had about the task.

Students who received the training for using the notetaking system, and a control group of students who were directed to take notes just as they normally would, both listened to a 20-minute lecture describing the evolution of the brain. Prior to hearing the lecture, one-third of the students were told they would be given a multiple choice test over the material; another third were told they would have an essay test; and the final third were told only that there would be a posttest. In actuality, all students completed a 35-item objective test immediately after the lecture and a free recall test 1-week later. A notetaking efficiency score was also calculated for each participant; this score was the ratio of the number of correct information units contained in the student's notes to the total number of words recorded. Efficient notes were defined as those containing the greatest amount of information using the fewest number of words.

An analysis of the efficiency scores revealed a performance

advantage for students anticipating a multiple choice test. In addition, trained students anticipating a multiple choice test outperformed their non-trained counterparts on both types of tests. While these results lend some support to the usefulness of teaching notetaking as a learning strategy, they also highlight some of the problems with research in this area. For example, it is difficult to separate the encoding function and the storage function of notetaking. DiVesta and Gray (1972, 1973) define the encoding function as the transformation of information into more meaningful and useable forms and the storage function as the external maintenance of the information for later review. Thus, the purposes for which notes are taken and later used can have a large impact on the underlying processes used and the learning outcomes produced (Barnett, DiVesta, & Rogozinski, 1981).

Similarly, Peper and Mayer (1978) studied notetaking as a generative activity. Mayer (1980) asked college students to read a manual on a computer programming language. After each section in the manual, some subjects were asked to explain how the material related to material in another section of the manual (or to a familiar situation). These subjects performed better on tests of creative problem solving using the new language, as compared to subjects who simply read the manual without answering elaboration questions. For a critical review of the role of elaboration in prose learning, see Reder, 1980.

Organizational Strategies for Basic Learning Tasks

One strategy for remembering a list of items is to sort them into some larger organizational framework, such as grouping items into taxonomic categories. The term *clustering*, originally used by Bousfield (1953), refers to a strategy used in free recall list learning in which the learner organizes the items from a list into groups on the basis of shared characteristics or attributes. For example, although a list might be presented in the order, "table, bus, hat, van, desk, shoes, truck, belt, sofa," a learner could organize the list by taxonomic category such as, "table, desk, sofa — bus, van, truck — hat, shoes, belt." The use of this kind of an organizing strategy requires the learner to be actively involved in the task.

In a typical research study (Moely, Olson, Hawles, & Flavell, 1969), children ranging in age from 5 to 11 years were given a set of pictures to memorize. The pictures included objects from various categories such as animals, furniture, vehicles, and apparel, but no pictures from the same category were adjacent to one another in the set. The children were allowed to move and rearrange the pictures. The results indicated that children in the 5–7-year-old range did not tend to rearrange the pictures while children in the 10–11-year-old range did make strong use of the organizing strategies by rearranging the pictures by taxonomic category.

The failure of the younger children to use organizing strategies during free recall learning may be due either to lack of availability of the strategies or what Flavell (1970) has called a production deficiency. In order to examine these explanations, Moely et al. (1969), conducted an instructional study using 9-year-olds who did not spontaneously categorize. The children were readily able to rearrange pictures into categories when instructed to do so but did not normally use this strategy in a list learning task. When they were taught how to apply the organizing strategy to list learning, the students were able to do so and their recall performance was boosted. Apparently, children at this intermediate level give evidence of a production deficiency in which they possess the appropriate skill but fail to spontaneously use it during learning.

In another study, Rossi and Wittrock (1971) examined children's free recall of twelve-word lists. They found that 2-year-olds spontaneously tend to organize words most frequently on the basis of their sound (e.g., sun-fun), while 3- and 4-year-olds tend to use taxonomic category (e.g., leg-hand), and 5-year-olds tend to use serial ordering. Furthermore, rhyming reached its peak at age 2, syntactical organization (e.g., men-work) reached its peak at age 3, organization by taxonomic category reached its peak at age 4, and serial ordering reached its peak at age 5. According to the authors, although serial ordering seems to be a more elementary type of interstimulus organization than clustering by taxonomic category, its frequency and peak level at age 5 may be due to the fact that the ability to memorize 12 words is sufficiently developed that grouping them according to their common properties or common membership in one class requires more effort than memorizing them in serial order. However, longer lists may require a superior type of organization to recall all their members.

These studies suggest that there is a developmental progression in children's bases for organizing pictures during a memorization task. In general, spontaneous use of an organizing strategy based on taxonomic category seems to emerge at about age 10 or 11. However, the availability of this strategy may emerge at an earlier age, as evidenced in the study conducted by Moely et al. (1969). The same may be true in the case of list learning tasks. Although in the study conducted by Moely et al., the 9-year-old children did not normally use this strategy in a list-learning task, it seems that its availability emerges at an earlier stage as evidenced in the study conducted by Rossi and Wittrock (1971). Moreover, this latter study showed that spontaneous use of this strategy may even occur at much younger ages when the word lists are short.

In a more recent study, Bjorklund, Ornstein, and Haig (1977) focused on the structure students impose on items to be recalled at the time of study (i.e., input organization). They also examined the effects of training students to use adult sorting patterns. Three related studies were conducted using third, fifth, and seventh grade students. An analysis of the results led to the identification of four general sorting strategies: high semantic, low semantic, orthographic, and random.

The tendency to group words on the basis of meaning increased with grade level. Furthermore, the level of sophistication of a sorting style tended to predict recall performance irrespective of grade level. Subjects who grouped words on the basis of meaning showed greater recall than subjects who sorted in a random or orthographic fashion.

It was also demonstrated that children can be trained in the use of organizational techniques to aid recall. Young children, who for the most part failed to sort words into meaning-based groups in a free-sort situation, demonstrated significant improvements in recall as a result of organizational training.

Organizational Strategies for Complex Learning Tasks

A significant amount of time is spent studying from textbooks by students in the upper elementary grades, high school, and college (Cole & Sticht, 1981). Part of a student's text reading task is to identify the main ideas and important supporting details and to relate these to one another in a way that will facilitate encoding and recall. Outlining and organizing the material are commonly used to achieve these goals. Thus, two cognitive goals served by organizational strategies are selection of information to be transferred into working memory and construction of relations among ideas in working memory.

Mayer (1982, 1984) has referred to this encoding process as "building internal connections." The building of internal connections may be enhanced by explicit training in strategies for outlining and organizing items in meaningful learning tasks, such as training in the types of structural relations among ideas in a passage. Training in organizing strategies may be most important for expository prose, since most students have had much more experience in reading narrative prose (Graesser, 1981).

Outlining is a type of organizational strategy that has traditionally received much attention. In topic outlining, major and minor points are written in an abbreviated form using key words or phrases. In symbolic outlines, such as arrays, key concepts, words, or phrases are functionally related in a two-dimensional diagram. Hansell (1978) found that seventh graders could be taught to effectively outline a text passage using either a topic outline or an array. Several more specific versions of outlining are discussed below.

Dansereau and his colleagues (Dansereau, 1978; Dansereau, Collins, McDonald, Holley, Garland, Diekhoff, & Evans, 1979; Holley, Dansereau, McDonald, Garland, & Collins, 1979) have developed a technique called *networking* which trains students to identify the main internal connections among ideas in a passage. For example, six major types of links are:

- Part link. For example, the process of wound healing has three parts, namely, lag phase, fibroplasia phase, and construction phase.
- Type link. For example, two types of wounds are open and closed.
- Leads to link. For example, the growth of a scab leads to a scar.
- Analogy link. For example, a scab is like a protective bandage.
- Characteristic link. For example, an open wound involves a break in the skin.
- Evidence link. For example, an x-ray test can reveal that a bone is broken.

As can be seen, networking involves breaking a passage down into parts and then identifying the linking relations among the parts.

Holley et al. (1979) tested the effectiveness of networking training for college students. Students learned to recognize the types of links, to apply the networking procedure to sentences, to apply the networking procedure to passages, and to apply the networking procedure to their own textbooks. The training lasted about $5\frac{1}{2}$ hours spread over four sessions. On subsequent reading comprehension tests, the trained subjects outperformed nontrained subjects on remembering the main ideas. The effects of training were particularly strong for students with low GPA's, presumably because high GPA students had already developed their own techniques for organizing prose material. These results have been replicated in a learning strategy class consisting of 24 hours of training (Dansereau, 1983; Dansereau et al., 1979).

Using a somewhat different approach, Meyer (1975, 1981; Meyer, Brandt, & Bluth, 1980) has identified five top-level structures that describe the relationship among the main ideas in expository passages. Using a passage presenting information about supertankers as an example, the five structures are:

- Covariance. For example, lack of power and steering in supertankers leads to oil spills.
- Comparison. For example, ground stations for supertankers are like control towers for aircraft.
- Collection. For example, three ways to improve supertanker safety are training of officers, building safer ships, and installing ground control systems.
- Description. For example, oil spills kill wildlife as is indicated by 200,000 seabirds being killed.
- Response. For example, a problem is that supertankers spill oil and a solution is to improve their safety.

In a recent study, Meyer et al. (1980) asked ninth graders to read and recall the supertanker passage. Good readers (as measured by a standard reading achievement test) recalled the top-level structure of the passage much better than poor readers. In other words, good readers were far more likely to organize their recall for the supertanker passage around the response format. Similarly, Taylor (1980) found developmental trends in which recall of the top-level structure increases dramatically with age.

In another training study, Bartlett (1978) gave ninth graders practice in identifying four major types of top-level structures and in using these structures as aids in recall. The trained group outperformed a control group on tests of reading comprehension. Apparently, students can be taught to be sensitive to the organizational structure of expository material, and using this organization aids comprehension.

More recently, Cook (1982) has developed a training procedure to help students identify prose structures that are found in science textbooks. The five structures are:

- Generalization — The passage explains, clarifies or extends some main idea.
- Enumeration — The passage lists facts sequentially.
- Sequence — The passage describes a connected series of events or steps in a process.
- Classification — The passage groups material into categories or classes.
- Compare/contrast — The passage examines the relationship between two or more things.

These structures differ from Meyer's and Dansereau's in that Cook focused only on chemistry, biology, and physics prose.

In a preliminary study, Cook (1982) found that college students could be taught to classify passages into the five categories listed above. The next step was to develop a 10-hour training program in which students were taught to recognize the major prose structures and to outline passages from their own chemistry textbook. Trained subjects showed substantial pretest-to-posttest gains in recall of high-level material and in problem solving as compared to a control group, even though the tests involved material from unfamiliar biology and physics textbooks.

Comprehension Monitoring Strategies

The term metacognition has been used to refer to both students' knowledge about their own cognitive processes and their ability to control these processes by organizing, monitoring, and modifying them as a function of learning outcomes (Brown, 1975, 1978; Cavanaugh & Perlmutter, 1982; Flavell, 1970, 1981; Flavell & Wellman, 1977). The use of metacognitive strategies is most often operationalized as comprehension monitoring. Comprehension monitoring requires the student to establish learning goals for an instructional unit or activity, to assess the degree to which these goals are being met, and, if necessary, to modify the strategies being used to meet the goals. Comparisons of good and poor comprehenders have consistently shown that poor comprehenders are deficient in the use of active learning strategies needed to monitor understanding (Golinkoff, 1976; Meichenbaum, 1976; Ryan, 1981).

In two recent studies by Paris and Myers (1981), comprehension and memory skills of fourth grade good and poor readers were compared. The students' ability to monitor understanding of both difficult and anomalous information was measured by three different means: by spontaneous self-corrections during oral reading, by directed underlining of incomprehensible words and phrases, and by observed study behaviors. Spontaneous monitoring was measured by the percentages of anomalous words and phrases for which students hesitated, repeated, or self-corrected. Directed underlining was measured by the percentages of anomalous words and phrases underlined. In addition to observing students' study behaviors, student ratings of effectiveness were collected on 20 reading strategies that could potentially affect memory for story content. Finally, understanding was measured by responses to oral questions and a free recall test.

Comparing the performance of the good and poor readers revealed that poor readers engaged in less comprehension monitoring on all measures; these differences were also correlated with lower scores on the oral question and free recall posttests. The student ratings of perceived reading strategy effectiveness indicated that, although poor readers gave the same ratings to positive and neutral factors as did good readers, they were less aware of the detrimental influences on comprehension of negative factors. Thus, whereas many children may gradually acquire the processing skills needed for good comprehension, poor comprehenders appear to be relatively deficient in the use of active monitoring strategies.

A number of different approaches have been used to teach comprehension monitoring strategies. For example, Meichenbaum and Asarnow (1979) reviewed the research concerning training designed to teach self-control for various academic tasks. The training programs in this area are based on the use of cognitive–functional analysis of task performance to identify the processes engaged in by successful learners. These analyses are then used to diagnose the deficiencies of problem learners and to plan a course of instruction. A typical training sequence proceeds from modeling the teacher's or experimenter's instructions, to overt rehearsal, and finally to covert rehearsal. This sequence is designed to help the learner develop self-statements to use in guiding and controlling performance on target tasks. The types of performance-relevant skills focused on by these programs include (a) problem identification and definition or self-interrogation skills ("What is it I have to do?"); (b) focusing attention and response guidance which is usually the answer to the self-inquiry ("Now, carefully stop and repeat the instructions"); (c) self-reinforcement involving standard setting and self-evaluation ("Good, I'm doing fine"); and (d) coping skills and error-correction options ("That's okay ... Even if I make an error I can go slowly"). Such cognitive training is conducted across tasks, settings, and people (trainer, teacher, parent) in order to ensure that children do not develop task-specific response sets, but instead that they develop generalized strategems (Meichenbaum & Asarnow, 1979, pp. 13–14).

Bommarito and Meichenbaum (cited by Meichenbaum & Asarnow, 1979) used this model to teach seventh and eighth graders strategies they could use to monitor their reading comprehension. Thus, teaching about learning strategies needed for comprehending written material, such as finding the main ideas and elaborating on important information, was embedded in a program of self-instructional training to teach comprehension monitoring. The major instructional device used in the teaching of both types of strategies was modeling of the cognitive strategies and self-statements. The students then practiced, at first out loud and then silently, using these methods to learn from passages appropriate to their reading levels (all participants had reading scores at least one grade level below their actual academic grade).

Students who participated in the six 45-minute sessions performed better on a test of reading comprehension than did students who did not participate in the training and students who studied the learning strategies materials but did not learn to use the self-instructional technique. This superior performance was maintained after a 1 month follow-up of all students from the study. It appears that comprehension monitoring can be taught using relatively brief educational programs. Furthermore, the results seem to be stable over time. Similar results have been found by Wong and Jones (1980) and Malamuth (1979).

Other methods have also been used to teach comprehension monitoring. Smith (1973) taught seventh grade students to generate pre-reading questions to guide their reading activities. Learning disabled children's recall was improved by teaching them a strategy for identifying certain types of information while listening (Maier, 1980). Markman (1979) taught students error detection strategies to find inconsistencies in reading passages.

Affective Strategies

Many current approaches to classroom learning emphasize the role of the learner in creating, monitoring, and controlling a suitable learning environment. Research in this area has focused on the strategies learners use to focus attention, maintain concentration, manage performance anxiety, establish and maintain motivation, and manage time effectively. Prototypical of the research in this area are the studies examining performance, or test, anxiety.

For many years high test anxiety was regarded as a behavioral reaction to stress originating in the environment. Since the forces creating anxiety were presumed to be outside of a student's control, little attention was paid to the possible mediating role of the student's own thought processes. In modern conceptions of test anxiety it is the learner's perceptions or appraisals of events that make them stressful (Wine, 1980). Many students who worry about their success in school, especially about how well they will do on tests, turn their attention inward and focus on self-criticism, feelings of incompetence, and expectations of failure. Attention is directed away from learning and studying and is focused on themselves as inadequate students. This decreased attention to study and school-related tasks often produces a spiral effect where poor performances confirm students' fears and intensify their anxiety. For a recent review of this literature see Sarason (1980).

Research about methods that can be used to help students cope with debilitating performance anxiety has resulted in a number of different types of programs and interventions (Morris, Davis, & Hutchings, 1981; Phillips, Martin, & Meyers, 1972; Ribordy & Billingham, 1980; Tryon, 1980; Wildemuth, 1977). A number of these educational interventions derive from clinical approaches to anxiety treatment such as systematic desensitization (e.g., Deffenbacher & Parks, 1979), desensitization with modeling (e.g., Richardson, O'Neil, & Grant, 1977), cognitive modification (e.g., Vagg, 1977/1978), anxiety management training (Deffenbacher, Michaels, Michaels, & Daley, 1980), and rational restructuring (Osarchuk, 1976). Other approaches derive more from the traditional areas included within study skills, such as test-taking skills training (Kirkland & Hollandsworth, 1980).

In a study typical of those done with older adolescents, Goldfried, Linehan, and Smith (1978) investigated the effects of a rational restructuring strategy on the reduction of test anxiety for college students. The students who participated in the rational restructuring started out by observing a model illustrating the use of coping self-statements. These statements were designed to reduce anxiety by focusing attention away from self-deprecating thoughts and towards a simulated test. For example, instead of saying something like, "There is no way I will pass this test ... Boy! Am I stupid!," the experimenter modeled more appropriate thought such as, "O.K. It's more likely I will not fail since I did study, but even if I did fail, it does *not* mean that I am stupid." After observing the model create a number of these thinking-aloud protocols, the students were then asked to imagine a scene from a test anxiety hierarchy, to identify any negative self-statements or evaluations that came into their mind during this time, and to reduce their anxiety by substituting more rational and positive self-talk. The students were asked to visualize a total of 15 scenes.

The results of the study indicated that participants in the rational restructuring strategy training reported greater reductions on several different measures of test anxiety than did participants in either of two control groups. Thus, it appears that training designed to enhance a student's repertoire of the strategies needed to cope effectively with stress can help to reduce self-reported levels of anxiety.

Methods to teach students strategies they can use to cope effectively with performance anxiety are often embedded in other programs. For example, in the Bommarito and Meichenbaum study (cited by Meichenbaum & Asarnow, 1979) discussed in the last section, the teachers not only modeled the task-relevant statements about problem solving but also coping self-statements that could be used to reduce frustration and anxiety reactions. Anxiety reduction components can also be found in a number of the programs that will be discussed in the next section.

Implementing Learning Strategies Instructional Programs

For purposes of the present discussion we have created a taxonomy of learning strategies and have discussed prototypical research studies within each of the eight areas. It is important, however, to note that many research studies, particularly those investigating classroom applications or adjunct interventions with students, investigate study systems, alternative curriculum supplements, or experimental courses that combine one or more strategies from both within and across the different categories. The purpose of many of these research studies is to either develop specific school applications or courses, or to investigate the effectiveness of already existing methods. For example, Jones and her colleagues (Jones et al., 1983), and Sticht (1979) have focused on embedding diversified learning strategies instruction into regular reading curriculum materials. Jones' work is part of the Chicago Mastery Learning Reading Program. Strategies from each of the eight categories are taught, reinforced, and cued within the curriculum materials.

Dansereau (1985), McCombs (1981), and Weinstein (Weinstein & Underwood, 1985) have all focused on creating adjunct programs for post-secondary students in job or college settings. These experimental, integrated learning strategies instructional programs have been used to investigate strategy component interactions, instructional procedures, and generalization of teaching effects. For example, Weinstein (1982) reports substantial gains in reading comprehension, academic performance and stress reduction for college students participating in an experimental undergraduate learning strategies course.

This work has also led to the creation of experimental courses at the elementary and high school levels. For example, the Cypress-Fairbanks Independent School District in Texas is implementing a study skills curriculum for all ninth graders. The Prince George's County Public Schools in Maryland has adapted a kindergarten through grade twelve learning strategies program to be incorporated into the regular instructional programs in other content areas. The Rhode Island Department of Education has developed guidelines for implementing study skills instruction into the state's reading programs.

McCombs (1981, 1982a, 1982b) has developed self-instructional instructor-augmented learning strategies materials in the areas of time management, study skills, and self-motivation. Implementation of these materials with military technical training students led to improved test scores and lower test failure rates as well as student-reported increases in motivation and ability to take increased responsibility for learning.

It appears that learning strategies research is creating a useful data base from which applications can and will be derived. As this literature continues to mature and develop, the implications for classroom teaching, educational practice, and educational research will continue to expand.

Conclusion

In conclusion, this chapter has explored techniques for enhancing learning in basic school tasks (such as list and paired-associate learning) as well as complex school tasks (such as meaningful prose learning). The learning strategies of rehearsing, elaborating, and organizing represent three kinds of resources that may be available for an active learner. Management strategies (such as comprehension monitoring) and affective strategies (such as anxiety reduction techniques) involve the effective use of available resources. This chapter has provided evidence for the hypothesis that learning strategies can be described and taught to learners who are at appropriate levels of maturity.

Some warnings are in order, however. This chapter is concerned with explicit teaching of learning strategies, that is, general techniques for more effective learning. It should be pointed out that general techniques are just part of the arsenal of knowledge that a learner needs for effective learning. Learning is also enhanced when the learner possesses a great deal of domain-specific knowledge. Simon (1980) summarizes this point as follows: "The scissors does indeed have two blades and ... effective ... education calls for attention to both subject-matter knowledge and general skills" (p. 86). Thus, while teaching of learning skills represents an important part of an educational program, it cannot substitute for teaching of domain-specific content.

A related issue concerns the distinction between non-directed training and more directed or guided training for learning strategies. Several researchers argue for the need to make instruction more explicit and directed (see Segal, Chipman, & Glaser, 1985). In addition, these authors argue that explicit training is most useful for less skilled learners.

Another warning concerns the time costs of learning strategies. The use of any technique must take into account its time costs as well as its benefits (Anderson & Armbruster, 1982).

REFERENCES

Anderson, R. C., Spiro, R. J., & Montague, W. E. (Eds.). (1977). *Schooling and the acquisition of knowledge.* Hillsdale, N.J.: Erlbaum.

Anderson, T. H., & Armbruster, B. B. (1982). Reader and text-studying strategies. In W. Otto & S. White (Eds.), *Reading expository material.* New York: Academic Press.

Appel, L. F., Cooper, R. G., McCarrell, N., Sims-Knight, J., Yussen, S. R., & Flavell, J. H. (1972). The development of the distinction between perceiving and memorizing. *Child Development, 43,* 1365-1381.

Arkes, H., Schumacher, G., & Gardner, E. (1976). Effects of orienting tasks on the retention of prose material. *Journal of Educational Psychology, 68,* 536-545.

Atkinson, R. C. (1975). Mnemotechnics in second-language learning. *American Psychologist, 30,* 828-921.

Atkinson, R. C., & Raugh, M. R. (1975). An application of the mnemonic keyword method to the acquisition of a Russian vocabulary. *Journal of Experimental Psychology: Human Learning and Memory, 104,* 126-133.

Barnett, J. E., DiVesta, F. J., & Rogozinski, J. T. (1981). What is learned in note taking? *Journal of Educational Psychology, 73(2),* 181-192.

Bartlett, B. J. (1978). *Top-level structure as an organizational strategy for recall of classroom text.* Unpublished doctoral dissertation, Arizona State University.

Beck, I., Perfetti, C., & McKeown, J. (1982). The effects of long-term vocabulary instruction on lexical access in reading comprehension. *Journal of Educational Psychology, 75,* 506-521.

Bjorklund, D. F., Ornstein, P. A., & Haig, J. R. (1977). Developmental differences in organization and recall: Training in the use of organizational techniques. *Developmental Psychology, 13,* 175-183.

Bommarito, J., & Meichenbaum, D. (1979). Enhancing reading comprehension by means of self-instructional training. Unpublished manuscript, University of Waterloo, 1978. Cited in Meichenbaum, D., & Asarnow, J. Cognitive behavior modification and metacognitive development: Implications for the classroom. In P. Kendall & S. Hollon (Eds.), *Cognitive-behavioral interventions: Theory, research and procedures.* New York: Academic Press.

Bousfield, W. A. (1953). The occurrence of clustering in the recall of randomly arranged associates. *Journal of General Psychology, 49,* 229-240.

Bradshaw, G. L., & Anderson, J. R. (1982). Elaborative encoding as an explanation of levels of processing. *Journal of Verbal Learning and Verbal Behavior, 21,* 165-174.

Bransford, J. D. (1979). *Human cognition.* Belmont, CA: Wadsworth.

Brown, A. L. (1975). The development of memory: Knowing, knowing about knowing, and knowing how to know. In H. W. Reese (Ed.), *Advances in child development and behavior.* New York: Academic Press.

Brown, A. L. (1978). Metacognitive development and reading. In R. J. Spiro, B. C. Bruce, & G. W. F. Brewer (Eds.), *Theoretical issues in reading comprehension.* Hillsdale, N. J.: Erlbaum.

Brown, A. L., & Smiley, S. S. (1977). Rating the importance of structural units of prose passages: A problem of metacognitive development. *Child Development, 48,* 1-8.

Carrier, C. A., & Titus, A. (1981). Effects of note-taking pretraining and test mode expectations on learning from lectures. *American Educational Research Journal, 18(4),* 385-397.

Cavanaugh, J. C., & Perlmutter, M. (1982). Metamemory: A critical examination. *Child Development, 53(1),* 11-28.

Cole, J. Y., & Sticht, T. G. (1981). *The textbook in American society.* Washington: Library of Congress.

Cook, L. K. (1982). *The effects of text structure on the comprehension of scientific prose.* Unpublished doctoral dissertation, University of California, Santa Barbara.

Cook, L. K., & Mayer, R. E. (1983). Reading strategy training for meaningful learning from prose. In M. Pressley & J. Levin (Eds.), *Cognitive strategy training.* New York: Springer-Verlag.

Dansereau, D. F. (1978). The development of a learning strategies curriculum. In H. F. O'Neil, Jr. (Ed.), *Learning strategies.* New York: Academic Press.

Dansereau, D. F. (1985). Learning strategy research. In J. Segal, S. Chipman, & R. Glaser (Eds.), *Thinking and learning skills, Vol. 1. Relating instruction to research.* Hillsdale, N. J.: Erlbaum.

Dansereau, D. F., Collins, K. W., McDonald, B. A., Holley, C. C. D., Garland, J. Diekhoff, G., & Evans, S. H. (1979). Development and evaluation of a learning strategy training program. *Journal of Educational Psychology, 71,* 64-73.

Deffenbacher, J. L., Michaels, T., & Daley, P. C. (1980). Comparison of anxiety management training and self-control desensitizaton. *Journal of Counseling Psychology 27*, 232–239.

Deffenbacher, J. L., & Parks, D. H. (1979). A comparison of traditional and self-control desensitization. *Journal of Counseling Psychology, 26*, 93–97.

DiVesta, F. J., & Gray, S. G. (1972). Listening and note taking. *Journal of Educational Psychology 63*, 8–14.

DiVesta, F. J., & Gray, S. G. (1973). Listening and note taking: II. Intermediate and delayed recall as function of variations in thematic continuity, note taking, and length of listening-review intervals. *Journal of Educational Psychology, 64*, 278–287.

Doctorow, M., Wittrock, M. C., & Marks, C. (1978). Generative processes in reading comprehension. *Journal of Educational Psychology, 70*, 109–118.

Farnham-Diggory, S. (1977). The cognitive point of view. In D. J. Treffinger, J. K. Davis, & R. E. Ripple (Eds.), *Handbook of teaching educational psychology*. New York: Academic Press.

Flavell, J. H. (1970). Developmental studies of mediated memory. In H. W. Reese & L. P. Lipsitt (Eds.), *Advances in child development and behavior* (Vol. 5). New York: Academic Press.

Flavell, J. H. (1981). Cognitive monitoring. In P. Dickson (Ed.), *Children's oral communication skills*. New York: Academic Press.

Flavell, J. H., Beach, D. R., & Chinsky, J. M. (1966). Spontaneous verbal rehearsal in a memory task as a function of age. *Child Development, 37*, 283–299.

Flavell, J. H., Friedrichs, A. H., & Hoyt, J. D. (1970). Developmental changes in memorization processes. *Cognitive Psychology, 1*, 324–340.

Flavell, J. H., & Wellman, H. M. (1977). Metamemory. In R. V. Hail, Jr. & J. W. Hagen (Eds.), *Perspectives on the development of memory and cognition*. Hillsdale, N. J.: Erlbaum.

Goldfried, M. R., Linehan, M. M., & Smith, J. L. (1978). Reduction of test anxiety through cognitive restructuring. *Journal of Consulting and Clinical Psychology, 46*, 32–39.

Golinkoff, R. A. (1976). A comparison of reading comprehension processes in good and poor comprehenders. *Reading Research Quarterly, 11*, 623–659.

Graesser, A. (1981). *Prose comprehension beyond the word*. New York: Springer-Verlag.

Hagen, J. W., & Kail, R. V. 1973. Facilitation and distraction in short-term memory. *Child Development, 44*, 831–836.

Hansell, T. S. (1978). Stepping up to outlining. *Journal of Reading, 22*, 248–252.

Holley, C. D., Dansereau, D. F., McDonald, B. A., Garland, J. C., & Collins, K. W. (1979). Evaluation of a hierarchical mapping technique as an aid to prose processing. *Contemporary Educational Psychology, 4*, 227–237.

Howe, M. J. A. (1970). Using students' notes to examine the role of the individual learner in acquiring meaningful subject matter. *Journal of Educational Research, 64*, 61–63.

Jones, B. F., Amiran, M. R., & Katims, M. (1985). Embedding structural information and strategy instructions in reading and writing instructional texts: Two models of development. In J. Segal, S. Chipman, & R. Glaser (Eds.), *Thinking and learning skills, Vol. 1: Relating instruction to research*. Hillsdale, N. J.: Erlbaum.

Jones, B. F., & Hall, J. W. (1982). School applications of the mnemonic keyword method as a study strategy by eighth graders. *Journal of Educational Psychology, 74*(2), 230–237.

Kenney, T. J., Cannizzo, S. R., & Flavell, J. H. (1967). Spontaneous and induced verbal rehearsal in a recall task. *Child Development, 38*, 953–966.

Kirkland, K., & Hollandsworth, J. G. (1980). Effective test taking: Skills-acquisition versus anxiety-reduction techniques. *Journal of Consulting and Clinical Psychology, 48*, 431–439.

Klatzky, R. (1980). *Human memory*. San Francisco: Freeman.

Levin, J. R. (1976). What have we learned about maximizing what children learn? In J. R. Levin & J. L. Allen (Eds.), *Cognitive learning in children: Theories and strategies*. New York: Academic Press.

Levin, J. R. (1981). The mnemonic '80s: Keywords in the classroom. *Educational Psychologist, 16*(2), 65–82.

Levin, J. R., McCormick, C. B., Miller, G. E., Berry, J. K., & Pressley, M. (1982). Mnemonic versus nonmnemonic vocabulary-learning strategies for children. *American Educational Research Journal, 19*(1), 121–136.

Maier, A. S. (1980). The effect of focusing on the cognitive processes of learning disabled children. *Journal of Learning Disabilities, 13*, 34–38.

Malamuth, Z. (1979). Self-management training for children with reading problems: Effects on reading performance and sustained attention. *Cognitive Therapy and Research, 3*, 279–289.

Markman, E. M. (1979). Realizing that you don't understand: Elementary school children's awareness of inconsistencies. *Child Development, 50*, 643–655.

Mayer, R. E. (1980). Elaboration techniques that increase the meaningfulness of technical prose: An experimental test of the learning strategy hypothesis. *Journal of Educational Psychology, 72*, 770–784.

Mayer, R. E. (1982). Instructional variables in text processing. In A. Flammer & W. Kintsch (Eds.), *Discourse processing*. Amsterdam: North-Holland.

Mayer, R. E. (1984). Aids to prose comprehension. *Educational Psychologist, 19*, 30–42.

Mayer, R. E., & Cook, L. K. (1980). Effects of shadowing on prose comprehension and problem solving. *Memory & Cognition, 8*, 101–109.

McCombs, B. L. (1981). *Transitioning learning strategies research into practice: Focus on the student in technical training*. Paper presented at the annual meeting of the American Educational Research Association, Los Angeles.

McCombs, B. L. (1982a). Transitioning learning strategies research into practice; Focus on the student in technical training. *Journal of Instructional Development, 5*(2), 10–17.

McCombs, B. L. (1982b). Learner satisfaction and motivation: Capitalizing on strategies for positive self control. *Performance and Instruction, 21*(4), 3–6.

Meichenbaum, D. (1976). Cognitive factors as determinants of learning disabilities; A cognitive function approach. In R. Knights & D. Bakker (Eds.), *The neuropsychology of learning disorders: Theoretical approaches*. Baltimore: University Park Press.

Meichenbaum, D., & Asarnow, J. (1979). Cognitive-behavior modification and metacognitive development: Implications for the classroom. In P. C. Kendall & S. D. Hollon (Eds.), *Cognitive-behavioral interventions: Theory research and procedures*. New York: Academic Press.

Meyer, B. J. F. (1975). *The organization of prose and its effect on memory*. Amsterdam: North-Holland.

Meyer, B. J. F. (1981). Basic research on prose comprehension: A critical review. In D. F. Fisher & C. W. Peters (Eds.), *Comprehension and the competent reader*. New York: Praeger.

Meyer, B. J. F., Brandt, D. M., & Bluth, G. J. (1980). Use of top-level structure in text: Key for reading comprehension of ninth-graders. *Reading Research Quarterly, 72*, 103.

Moely, B., Olsen, F., Hawles, T., & Flavell, J. H. (1969). Production deficiency in young children's clustered recall. *Developmental Psychology, 1*, 26–34.

Morris, L. W., Davis, M. A., & Hutchings, C. H. (1981). Cognitive and emotional components of anxiety: Literature review and a revised worry-emotionality scale. *Journal of Educational Psychology, 73*(4), 541–555.

Norman, D. A. (1980). Cognitive engineering and education. In D. T. Tuma & F. Reif (Eds.), *Problem solving and education*. Hillsdale, N. J.: Erlbaum.

Osarchuk, M. M. (1976). A comparison of a cognitive, a behavior therapy, and a cognitive-and-behavior therapy treatment of test anxious college students. Doctoral dissertation, Adelphi University, New York, 1974). *Dissertation Abstracts International, 36*, 3619B. (University Microfilms No. 76-14, 25)

Paris, S. B., & Myers, M. (1981). Comprehension monitoring, memory, and study strategies of good and poor readers. *Journal of Reading Behavior, 13*(1), 5–22.

Peper, R. J., & Mayer, R. E. (1978). Note-taking as a generative activity. *Journal of Educational Psychology, 70*, 514–522.

Phillips, B. N., Martin, R. P., & Meyers, J. (1972). Interventions in relation to anxiety in school. In C. D. Spielberger (Ed.), *Anxiety: Current trends in theory and research* (Vol. 2). New York: Academic Press.

Pressley, M. (1977). Imagery and children's learning: Putting the picture in development perspective. *Review of Educational Research, 47*, 585–582.

Pressley, M., & Dennis-Rounds, J. (1980). Transfer of a mnemonic keyword strategy at two age levels. *Journal of Educational Psychology, 72*, 575–582

Pressley, M., & Levin, J. R. (1978). Development constraints associated with children's use of the keyword method of foreign language vocabulary learning. *Journal of Experimental Child Psychology, 26*, 359–373.

Raugh, M. R., & Atkinson, R. C. (1975) A mnemonic method for learning a foreign language vocabulary. *Journal of Educational Psychology 67*, 1–16.

Reder, L. M. (1980). The role of elaboration in the comprehension and retention of prose: A critical review. *Review of Educational Research, 50*, 5–53.

Reese, H. W. (1977). Imagery and associative memory. In R. V. Kail & J. W. Hagen (Eds.), *Perspectives on the development of memory and cognition*. Hillsdale, N. J.: Erlbaum.

Ribordy, S. C., & Billingham, K. A. (1980). *Test anxiety: An annotated bibliography*, Rush-Presbyterian-St. Luke's Medical Center.

Richardson, F. C., O'Neil, H. F., & Grant, R. D. (1977). Development and evaluation of an automated test anxiety reduction program for a computer-based learning environment. In J. E. Sieber, H. F. O'Neil, Jr., & S. Tobias (Eds.), *Anxiety, learning and instruction*. Hillsdale, N. J.: Erlbaum.

Rickards, J., & August, G. J. (1975). Generative underlining strategies in prose recall. *Journal of Educational Psychology, 67*, 860–865.

Rossi, S., & Wittrock, M. C. (1971). Developmental shifts in verbal recall between mental ages two and five. *Child Development. 42* 333–338.

Ryan, E. B. (1981). Identifying and remediating failures in reading comprehension: Toward an instructional approach for poor comprehension In T. G. Waller & G. E. MacKinnon (Eds.), *Advances in reading research*. New York: Academic Press.

Sarason, I. G. (1980). *Test anxiety: Theory, research, and applications*. Hillsdale, N. J.: Erlbaum.

Schallert, D. (1982). The significance of knowledge: A synthesis of research related to schema theory. In W. Otto & S. White (Eds.), *Reading expository material*. New York: Academic Press.

Segal, J. W., Chipman, S., & Glaser, R. (1985). *Thinking and learning skills, Vol. 1, Relating instruction to basic research*, Hillsdale, N. J.: Erlbaum.

Simon, H. A. (1980). Problem solving and education. In D. T. Tuma, F. Reif (Eds.), *Problem solving and education*. Hillsdale, N. J.: Erlbaum.

Smith, A. E. (1973). The effectiveness of training students to generate their own questions prior to reading. *Twenty-second Yearbook of the National Reading Conference, 1*, 71–77.

Sticht, T. G. (1979). Developing literacy and learning strategies in organizational settings. In H. F. O'Neil, Jr. & C. D. Spielberger (Eds.), *Cognitive and affective learning strategies*. New York: Academic Press.

Taylor, B. (1980). Children's memory for expository text after reading. *Reading Research Quarterly, 15*, 399–411.

Tryon, G. W. (1980) The measurement and treatment of text anxiety. *Review of Educational Research, 50*, 343–372.

Vagg, P. R. (1978). The treatment of text anxiety: A comparison of biofeedback and cognitive coping strategies (Doctoral dissertation University of Michigan, Ann Arbor, 1977). *Dissertation Abstracts International, 38*, 5599B. (University Microfilms No. 78-04, 828)

Weinstein, C. E. (1978). Teaching cognitive elaboration learning strategies. In H. F. O'Neil, Jr. (Ed.), *Learning strategies*. New York: Academic Press.

Weinstein, C. E. (1982). Training students to use elaboration learning strategies. *Contemporary Educational Psychology, 7*, 301–311.

Weinstein, C. E., & Underwood, V. L. (1985). Learning strategies: The *how* of learning. In J. Segal, S. Chipman, & R. Glaser (Eds.), *Thinking and learning skills, Vol. 1*. Hillsdale, N. J.: Erlbaum.

Wildemuth, B. (1977). *Test anxiety, an extensive bibliography*. Princeton, N.J.: Eric Clearinghouse on Tests, Measurement, and Evaluation, Educational Testing Service.

Wine, J. (1980). Cognitive-attentional theory of test anxiety. In I. G. Sarason (Ed.), *Test anxiety: Theory, research, and applications*. Hillsdale, N. J.: Erlbaum.

Wittrock, M. C. (1974). Learning as a generative process. *Educational Psychologist, 11*, 87–95.

Wittrock, M. C. (1978). The cognitive movement in instruction. *Educational Psychologist, 13*, 15–29.

Wittrock, M. C. (1981). Reading comprehension. In F. J. Pirozzolo & M. C. Wittrock (Eds.), *Neuropsychological and cognitive processes in reading*. New York: Academic Press.

Wong, B. Y. L., & Jones, W. (1982). Increasing metacomprehension in learning disabled and normally achieving students through self-questioning training. *Learning Disability Quarterly, 5*, 228–240.

12.

Teacher Behavior and Student Achievement

Jere Brophy
Michigan State University

Thomas L. Good
University of Missouri—Columbia

Introduction

This chapter reviews process–product (also called process-outcome) research linking teacher behavior to student achievement. Within this topic it stresses teacher behavior over other classroom process variables (students' interactions with peers, curriculum materials, computers, etc.) and stresses student achievement gain over other product variables (e.g., personal, social, or moral development).

The research to be discussed is concerned with teachers' effects on students, but it is a misnomer to refer to it as "teacher effectiveness" research, because this equates "effectiveness" with success in producing achievement gain. What constitutes "teacher effectiveness" is a matter of definition, and most definitions include success in socializing students and promoting their affective and personal development in addition to success in fostering their mastery of formal curricula. Consequently, we have avoided the term "teacher effectiveness" in titling the chapter and describing the research, although we use the more neutral term "teacher effects."

Developments in this field have been well documented in previous handbook chapters (Medley & Metzel, 1963; Rosenshine & Furst, 1973), and in volumes by Rosenshine (1971) and by Dunkin and Biddle (1974). This chapter, therefore, builds on these earlier reviews without overlapping them unnecessarily. It attempts to be comprehensive in covering 1973–1983 research that meets the inclusion criteria described below, emphasizing findings that conflict or seem counterintuitive over findings that seem obvious and clear-cut. Where findings conflict, we seek to identify methodological or context (subject matter, grade level, etc.) factors that may explain apparent contradictions. In this regard, the chapter has been informed by reviews and methodological commentaries published by Berliner (1976), Borich and Fenton (1977), Brophy (1979), Centra and Potter (1980), Cruickshank (1976), Denham and Lieberman (1980), Doyle (1977), Flanders and Simon (1969), Gage (1978), Good (1979), Good, Biddle, and Brophy (1975), Heath and Neilson (1974), Kyriacou and Newson (1982), Medley (1979), Peterson and Walberg (1979), Rosenshine (1976, 1979, 1983), Rosenshine and Berliner (1978), and Rosenshine and Stevens (1984).

Following this introduction, the chapter briefly reviews progress prior to 1970, describes zeitgeist trends and methodological improvements that led to the large field studies of the 1970s, details these studies and their findings, integrates these data with other data linking teacher behavior to student achievement, assesses the power and limits of the data, and discusses current trends and probable future directions.

Inclusion criteria. We have chosen to focus on research likely to generalize to typical elementary and secondary school settings, using the following criteria.

1. Focus on normal school settings with normal populations. Exclude studies conducted in laboratories, industry, the armed forces, or special facilities for special populations.

The authors thank reviewers David Berliner (University of Arizona) and Virginia Koehler (National Institute of Education).

Preparation of this chapter was supported in part through the Institute for Research on Teaching, College of Education, Michigan State University. The Institute for Research on Teaching is funded primarily by the Program for Teaching and Instruction of the National Institute of Education, United States Department of Education. The opinions expressed in this publication do not neccessarily reflect the position, policy, or endorsement of the National Institute of Education (Contract No. 400–81–0014).

2. Focus on the teacher as the vehicle of instruction. Exclude studies of programed instruction, media, text construction, and so on.

3. Focus on process-product relationships between teacher behavior and student achievement. Discuss presage and context variables that qualify or interact with process-product linkages, but exclude extended discussion of presage-process or context-process research.

4. Focus on measured achievement gain, controlled for entry level. Discuss affective or other outcomes measured in addition to achievement gain, but exclude studies that did not measure achievement gain or that failed to control or adjust for students' entering ability or achievement levels.

5. Focus on measurement of teacher behavior by trained observers, preferably using low-inference coding systems. Exclude studies restricted to teacher self-report or global ratings by students, principals, and so forth, and experiments that did not monitor treatment implementation.

6. Focus on studies that sampled from well-described, reasonably coherent populations. Exclude case studies of single classrooms and studies with little control over or description of grade level, subject matter, student populations, and so on.

7. Focus on results reported (separately) for specific teacher behaviors or clearly interpretable factor scores. Exclude data reported only in terms of typologies or unwieldy factors or clusters that combine disparate elements to mask specific process-outcome relationships, or only in terms of general systems of teacher behavior (open vs. traditional education, mastery learning, IPI, IGE, etc.).

Overlap with other chapters. Some studies that meet the above criteria nevertheless are treated briefly or excluded because they are covered elsewhere in this volume. The following criteria were adopted to avoid unnecessary overlap with other chapters.

1. Focus on elementary and secondary classrooms. Exclude research in preprimary and postsecondary classrooms.

2. Focus on the teacher or class as the unit of analysis (teacher effects). Exclude studies in which the principal, school, or curriculum is the unit of analysis, or in which individual students or subgroups within classes are being compared (ATI studies).

3. Focus on classroom management correlates of achievement outcomes, but minimize discussion of the details of effective classroom management (see Doyle, this volume).

4. Focus on teacher behaviors that appear to apply to several subject matter areas. Exclude research on teacher behavior so subject specific as to be more appropriate for the chapters on instruction within specific subject areas.

5. Focus on teachers working in naturalistic settings under ordinary conditions. Exclude studies of teachers trained to implement elaborately developed instructional systems (see Rosenshine, this volume).

6. Focus on substantive findings. Discuss observational methods and statistical analyses to the extent necessary to clarify the data, but minimize general discussion of the relative merits of different observation approaches, raw versus standardized scores, regression versus correlation, and so on.

Although exclusive in many respects, these criteria still define a broad range of research as relevant to this chapter—most studies in which objectively measured teacher behavior was linked to adjusted achievement by elementary or secondary students. Few such studies have been done, however. Using similar but looser criteria, Rosenshine (1971) located only about 50 studies linking teacher behavior to student achievement (of these, fewer than 30 meet our criteria). More recently, Medley (1977, 1979), using similar but more stringent criteria, excluded all but 14 studies (he discussed only correlations of .39 or higher). Thus, despite the importance of the topic, there has been remarkably little systematic research linking teacher behavior to student achievement.

A major reason for this lack is cost. Classroom observation is expensive. Except for a brief period in the 1970s when the National Institute of Education was able to fund several large field studies, investigators have not had the resources needed to do process-product studies that involve both large enough samples to allow the use of inferential statistics in analyzing the data and extensive enough observation in each classroom to allow comprehensive and reliable sampling of teacher behavior.

Historical Overview of the Field

In addition to the cost factor, the field was slow to develop because of historical influences on the conceptualization and measurement of teacher effectiveness which guided research on teaching. Medley (1979) has identified five successive conceptions of the effective teacher: (a) possessor of desirable personal traits; (b) user of effective methods; (c) creator of a good classroom atmosphere; (d) master of a repertoire of competencies; and (e) professional decision maker who has not only mastered needed competencies but learned when to apply them and how to orchestrate them.

Early concern with teachers' personal traits led to presage-product rather than process-product studies. Presage variables included such teacher traits as appearance, intelligence, leadership, and enthusiasm. "Product" variables were usually global ratings by supervisors or principals. This approach produced some consensus on virtues considered desirable in teachers, but no information on linkages between specific teacher behaviors and measured student achievement.

The subsequent methods focus produced experiments comparing the measured achievement of classes taught by one method with that of classes taught by another. Unfortunately, however, the majority of these studies produced inconclusive results because the differences between methods were not significant enough to produce meaningful differences in student achievement (Medley, 1979). Furthermore, the significant differences that did appear tended to contradict one another. Finally, almost all of these studies included only a few classes and inappropriately used the student rather than the class as the unit of analysis, so that effects due to methods were confounded with whatever other differences existed between the teachers (for treatments administered to intact classes, data should be aggregated and analyzed at the level of class means, and degrees of freedom should be calculated on the basis of the number of classes—not the total number of students—observed). Because of these and other difficulties, reviewers such as Morsh and Wilder (1954) and Medley and Mitzel (1963) concluded that efforts to identify effective teaching had not paid off, and that no specific teacher behavior had been linked unequivocally to student achievement.

The 1950s and 1960s brought concern about creating a good classroom climate and about the teaching competencies involved in producing student achievement. This led to an emphasis on measurement of teacher behavior through systematic observation, and to a proliferation of classroom observation systems. Some reviewers were encouraged by this progress, noting that improved process–product results could be expected if these advances in objective measurement of teacher behavior could be linked with objective measurement of student achievement. In fact, Gage (1965) and Flanders and Simon (1969) were able to report modest progress.

Other reviewers, however, were prepared to give up on this line of research, and many salient events of the 1960s and early 1970s appeared to support their point of view. One important trend was an emphasis on the curriculum over the teacher. In contrast to the research on teacher effects, studies of curriculum effects usually produced clear results indicating that students learned the content to which they were exposed (Walker & Schaffarzick, 1974). Although such curriculum effects research is silent on the question of teacher effects, it was sometimes taken to imply that teacher effects are unimportant. Furthermore, most of the highly publicized post-Sputnik federal initiatives in education concerned curriculum reform rather than teacher training. To the extent that developers considered how (not just what) to teach, they made prescriptions based on intuition or ideology rather than objective data. They seldom felt the need to experiment with ways of teaching the content, and either trained teachers to perform according to prescribed patterns or tried to develop "teacher-proof curricula" which would deliver the content to the students directly rather than depend on teachers to do so.

Early school effects research also minimized the apparent contributions of teachers. In particular, interpretations of the Coleman report (Coleman et al., 1966) and its reanalyses by Jencks et al. (1972) and by Mosteller and Moynihan (1972) seemed to indicate that teachers did not have important differential effects on student achievement. This conclusion received much more publicity than did criticisms indicating, among other things, that the study did not include systematic observation of teacher behavior and that it precluded the possibility of assessing individual teacher effects because it used the school rather than the teacher as the unit of analysis (Good et al., 1975).

Rosenshine (1970a) questioned the stability of teacher behaviors observed in process–product studies, noting that the few stability coefficients that had been reported were rather low. This called into question the meaningfulness of even low-inference measures of teacher behavior. (What is the value of improving measurement if the teacher behavior being measured is not stable?) Finally, Popham (1971) failed to find systematic differences in teacher behavior between trained instructors and comparison instructors who lacked special training, leading him to question whether teachers have any special expertise at all.

Yet, despite all this, significant progress occurred in the 1960s. Convinced of the validity of the process–product approach, Biddle, Gage, Medley, Soar, and others made important conceptual and methodological advances. Meanwhile, Bellack, Flanders, Hughes, Taba, and others contributed new observation systems and created interest in new process variables. By 1970, there were more than 100 classroom observation systems (Simon & Boyer, 1967, 1970a, 1970b). Many had been developed originally for teacher training rather than research purposes. In fact, most of the guidelines for using these systems to observe and give feedback to teachers were based on ideological commitments, and some even were contradicted by existing data (Rosenshine, 1971; Dunkin & Biddle, 1974). However, once in existence, these measurement devices and related concepts provided new tools for new process–product research.

Observation systems gradually became more sophisticated and comprehensive, especially in measuring teacher behavior related to the cognitive objectives of instruction (earlier emphasis had been mostly on affective aspects). Problems connected with reliabilities of the behaviors being measured proved solvable, at least to a degree, through increasing the amounts of observation time allocated per classroom and instituting better controls over the contexts within which observations were scheduled. Studies using the class as the unit of analysis began to show significant and sometimes stable teacher effects and process–product linkages.

Rosenshine (1971) reported that data from different investigators using different methods indicated that certain teacher behaviors were consistently correlated with student achievement gain. These correlations were not always significant, and typically were only marginal to moderate in strength even when they did reach significance. Nevertheless, the consistency in findings for certain variables was encouraging. Strong criticism of students was correlated negatively with achievement gain (mere negation of incorrect responses was unrelated or correlated positively). Positive correlates included warmth, businesslike orientation, enthusiasm, organization, variety in materials and academic activities, and high frequencies of clarity, structuring comments, probing questions asked as follow-up to initial questions, and focus on academic activities. No significant correlations were found for nonverbal expression of approval, use of student ideas, or amount of teacher talk. Mixed results were reported for verbal praise, difficulty level of instruction or of teacher questions, and amount of student talk. Rosenshine suggested that the latter variables might show inverted-U curvilinear relationships to student learning, or might interact with student individual differences.

Rosenshine's review helped pull together and define the field, and it drew attention to some important methodological and interpretive issues. Besides noting that teacher variables might have nonlinear relationships to student achievement or might interact with student individual differences, Rosenshine stressed the need to consider context or sequence factors that might affect the meanings of teacher behavior. He noted, for example, that frequency counts of teacher approval or criticism are not very useful without information about the contexts within which these teacher evaluations were delivered. Similarly, the usefulness of high- versus low-level teacher questions might be expected to vary with subject matter and grade level, so that box scores summarizing results across all studies might yield puzzling contradictions, but analyses of findings within comparable contexts might yield regularities. Finally, Rosenshine noted that qualitative distinctions in coding related but different teacher behaviors (mere feedback vs. praise or blame, brief vs. extended use of student ideas) produced more coherent results than coding with less finely differentiated categories.

Besides documenting progress, the Rosenshine (1971) review illustrated the interpretive dilemmas involved in trying to integrate and explain process–product findings. Sometimes investigators use different terminology but measure similar teacher behaviors and produce comparable findings, and sometimes they use similar terminology but measure quite different teacher behaviors and produce findings that are unrelated. If data are reported only for combination scores composed of disparate elements, it is not possible to determine whether a correlation involving the combination score holds for any particular element individually. In fact, as Rosenshine (1971) noted, different items grouped in combination scores for theoretical reasons may have contrasting patterns of correlation with achievement.

Even where clear data link reasonably specific teacher behaviors to student achievement, the causal linkages underlying the correlation remain unknown pending follow-up experimentation. For example, what are we to make of the negative relationship between frequency of severe criticism and student achievement gain? Strong teacher criticism of students rarely occurs (the correlations obtained for this variable represent the difference between teachers who seldom criticize and those who rarely or never criticize). It seems likely, then, that the correlation is due not so much to a direct negative effect of teacher criticism on student learning as to a tendency for teacher criticism to be associated with other teacher characteristics that affect student learning more directly. Perhaps criticism is more frequent among poor classroom managers who are often frustrated by student disruptions, for example, or among poor instructors who are often frustrated by student failure.

Various attempts at solving these interpretive dilemmas have been made, with varying success. Logical clustering, factor analysis, and related methods are often used for reducing the data, but these procedures will mask rather than illuminate process–product relationships if the resulting scores combine teacher behaviors that should be kept separate. We believe that analyses of process–product data should focus on identifying and coming to understand the reasons for reliable relationships. Data reduction techniques can help accomplish this when the measures being combined are aspects of the same basic teacher behavior, but otherwise, correlational patterns should be examined separately for each measure.

Coming to understand process–product data requires attention not only to correlation coefficients, but also to the means and patterns of variation in the teacher behaviors involved (as in the above example involving teacher criticism) and to context factors (grade level, subject matter, etc.) that may qualify generalization of findings. Most reviewers have tried to deal with these complexities by identifying variables studied similarly in different studies and describing general trends in the findings, perhaps adding qualifications based on context variables as well. Dunkin and Biddle (1974) formalized this approach by constructing boxes that concisely summarized the

existing research on various teacher behaviors. More recently, this general approach has been formalized still further in meta-analysis procedures developed by Glass and Smith (1978).

We have taken a different approach in this chapter. Rather than organize according to teacher behavior variables and compute box scores or meta-analyses that would largely repeat ground covered earlier by Dunkin and Biddle, Medley, Rosenshine, and others, we have decided to organize the review around what appear to be the major programmatic studies in the field, and use their common findings to induce and integrate generalities. In contrast to the box score and meta-analysis approaches, this approach focuses on the studies that seem most likely to produce valid and generalizable findings, and takes into consideration grade level, subject matter, type of teacher and classroom, amount and type of measurement of teacher behavior, and other factors unique to specific studies that may be useful in interpreting their findings. It involves more judgment and less mathematical precision than the other approaches, but we believe that it is better suited to the task of coming to understand the reasons for observed process–product relationships (and especially for resolving apparent discrepancies and explaining real discrepancies in the findings).

Progress in the 1970s

Several events occurring in the early 1970s helped to consolidate the progress of the 1960s and prepare the way for subsequent developments. One was the chapter by Rosenshine and Furst (1973) in the second edition of this handbook on the use of direct observation to study teaching. These authors noted that consistent findings had begun to accumulate and they discussed the relative merits and potential research uses of the classroom observation instruments that had accumulated and been catalogued in *Mirrors for Behavior* (Simon & Boyer, 1967, 1970a, 1970b). They also called for programmatic work on the "descriptive–correlational–experimental loop," in which classroom observation would lead to the development of instruments to measure (describe) teaching in a quantitative manner, followed by correlational studies to relate the descriptive variables to achievement, and experimental studies to test promising correlational relationships for causal effects.

Rosenshine and Furst also made methodological suggestions that foreshadowed later developments: (a) Attend to the cognitive (rather than affective) aspects of teaching, since these are the ones most likely to determine learning; (b) insure that tests reflect the content taught; (c) use more complex and varied coding systems; (d) attend to sequences of events; (e) tailor the observation system to the subject matter and context; (f) sample behavior that is representative of the teachers' typical patterns; and (g) develop a rich bank of process–process and process–product data in each study, to facilitate interpretation of the findings.

In *The Study of Teaching*, Dunkin and Biddle (1974) reviewed and critiqued all extant research that included low-inference measurement of teacher behavior. This book helped define the field of research on teaching and differentiate it from other forms of educational research. Following Mitzel (1960), Dunkin and Biddle organized the research into a model featuring presage, process, product, and context variables, and constructed boxes summarizing what was known about the frequencies of various teacher behaviors and about their relationships to context, presage, product, and other process variables. They complained of the widespread tendency to make educational prescriptions based on untested theoretical commitments rather than convincing empirical data, stating that, before attempting to implement a research finding in the schools, one would want to know:

- that the concepts used in the finding are meaningful, and that they had been measured with instruments that were valid and reliable;
- that the studies reporting the finding had used valid, uncontaminated designs;
- that the effect claimed was strong, that it was independent of other effects, and that the independent variable claimed for it was truly independent;
- that the effect applied over a wide range of teaching contexts, or if not, to what range it was limited;
- and finally that we understood why the effect took place. (p. 358)

At the time, most extant progress had taken place with regard to the first two of these concerns. This is still true, although progress in the latter three areas has also occurred in recent years, and we intend to give particular emphasis to these concerns in the present chapter (especially the last two; in regard to the third, we are not so much concerned about the strength or independence of process–product relationships as we are about describing and explaining them — whether they are weak or strong, linear or nonlinear, independent or nested within larger patterns).

Dunkin and Biddle also emphasized the need to attend to context variables — both to "build them into the design" or at least control them in selecting the teacher sample and the activities to be observed, and to suggest limits on the generalization of results. They also chided researchers for fundamental yet common mistakes (failure to sample adequately, inappropriate use of inferential statistics, failure to report basic descriptive data), and called for more comprehensive investigations designed to develop theory and explain findings rather than merely to garner support for some pet idea.

Another major factor influencing progress in the 1970s was the involvement of federal agencies, particularly the Office of Education (OE) and the National Institute of Education (NIE). In particular, OE's funding of evaluation studies of Project Follow Through and NIE's funding of several large-scale field studies and (later) experiments allowed investigators to conduct process–product research on a scale never approached previously. Furthermore, NIE convened a national conference on studies in teaching in 1974, bringing together leaders in the field to assess progress, identify needed methodological improvements, and suggest research priorities. Later, the NIE followed up by establishing the Invisible College for Research on Teaching, an informal organization of classroom researchers who gather prior to the annual AREA meetings to share state-of-the-art information. Both the agenda setting at the 1974 conference and the subsequent Invisible College activities helped pull together and unify process–product research specifically,

and research on teaching generally, as viable fields of scientific inquiry. More recently, NIE sponsored a conference to review research on teaching and summarize its implications for practitioners. The papers were later published in the March, 1983 issue of the *Elementary School Journal*.

The report of Panel 2 of the 1974 conference (National Institute of Education, 1974) produced a list of key methodological considerations for process–product researchers, identifying the following as desirable: programmatic, cumulative research designs; letting the goals of the project, and not habit or convenience, determine what and how to measure; multiple measurement of a variety of outcomes (product variables); considering nonlinear process–product relationships; considering complex interactions among variables (suppressor effects, moderator effects, etc.); eliminating or controlling entry-level differences in student ability or achievement; including both high- and low-inference measures of a variety of process behaviors; selecting samples of teachers and classrooms to insure comparability and representativeness; collecting enough data in each classroom to insure reliability and validity (or alternatively, controlling classroom events by standardizing lessons and materials); controlling for Hawthorne effects and monitoring implementation in experimental studies; insuring adequate variance and stability in relevant teacher behaviors in naturalistic studies; taking into account patterns of initiation and sequence in teacher–student interaction; and devising scoring systems that allow for more direct comparison of teachers or students than mere frequency counts provide (for example, teachers can be compared more validly using the percentages of their students' correct answers that are praised than using the rates of such praise, because percentage scores take into account differences in frequency of correct student answers).

Major Programs of Process–Product Research

No study has yet been done that includes all of these desirable characteristics, but the process-product research of the 1970s came much closer to approaching these ideals than earlier research had done, and yielded correspondingly more satisfactory results. We now turn to these findings, starting with the work of research teams who studied process-product questions programmatically in series of related studies.

Canterbury Studies

A series of studies done at the University of Canterbury in New Zealand began with a correlational study by Wright and Nuthall (1970), in which teachers taught science lessons to groups of 20 randomly selected third graders. There were no significant correlations (with achievement adjusted for IQ and general science knowledge) for total teacher or pupil talk, total teacher structuring comments, percentage of structuring that occurred immediately following questions, or starting lessons with reviews of the previous lesson; positive relationships for percentage of structuring that occurred at the ends of episodes initiated by questions, percentage of closed (rather than open) questions, praising or thanking students for their responses, asking single questions rather than two or more questions in series, and concluding lessons with reviews; and a negative relationship for student failure to respond to questions.

Redirection of the same question to another pupil following the response of the first pupil was correlated positively with achievement, but there were no significant relationships for elaborating or trying to elicit improvement on the original response. These measures were not coded separately for whether or not the original question was answered correctly, however, so their meanings are not clear.

Follow-up studies by Hughes (1973) involved experimental manipulation of pupil participation and teacher reactions to pupil response during lessons on animals taught to seventh graders. The first study involved three pupil participation treatments: random response (questions addressed to students at random), systematic response (questions addressed according to pupils' seating positions), and self-selected response (questions directed only to volunteers). The results showed no differences between treatment groups, and also no relationship between student rate of response (whether voluntary or involuntary) and adjusted achievement.

A second study involved a more extreme manipulation, in which a randomly selected half of the students in each class were asked all of the questions, while the other half were given no chances to respond at all. Once again, however, overt participation was unrelated to achievement.

A third study dealt with teacher reactions to student response. Pupils in the "reacting" group were given frequent praise for correct answers and support, along with occasional urging or mild reproach when they failed to respond correctly. Pupils in the "no reacting" group generally received little more than a statement of the correct answer. The "reacting" group outgained the "no reacting" group, both on items related to questions asked during the lesson and on other items. Taken together, Hughes's data suggest that, by seventh grade, pupils can learn effectively without overt participation in lessons, but that their learning can be affected by teachers' reactions to the responses of the students who do participate. These teacher reaction effects appear to have been motivational (mediated by the enthusiasm and demandingness communicated in the "reacting" treatment) rather than instructional (the "reacting" treatment did not involve greater opportunity to participate or get information).

Nuthall and Church (1973) describe other work done at Canterbury. In one study, teachers were asked to concentrate either on teaching conceptual knowledge or on maximizing achievement test scores. The teachers intending to teach conceptual knowledge used more open-ended questions and included more logical connectives, but did less lecturing. However, these differences were unrelated to pupil test scores, either for factual knowledge or for higher-level conceptual knowledge.

Another study (of the teaching of science concepts to 10-year-olds) involved manipulating both content coverage (how much content was introduced, to what degree of redundancy, and with how much time spent teaching it) and teacher behavior (questioning vs. lecturing). Content coverage was more closely related to achievement. With coverage held constant, there was no difference in effects on achievement between the questioning

method and the lecture method. Within the questioning method, however, contrary to Hughes's findings for seventh graders, Nuthall and Church found that students who were called on to respond learned more than those who were not called upon.

Taken together, the Canterbury studies suggest that (a) content coverage determines achievement more directly than the particular teacher behaviors used to teach the content; (b) younger students need to participate overtly in recitations and discussions, but older ones may not require such active participation; (c) questions should be asked one at a time, be clear, and be appropriate in level of difficulty so that students can understand them (most of these will be lower order); (d) teacher reactions to student response that communicate enthusiasm for the content and support (or if necessary, occasional demandingness) to the students are more motivating than matter-of-fact reactions; and (e) teacher structuring of the content, particularly in the form of reviews summarizing lesson segments, is helpful.

Flanders

Perhaps the most useful programmatic process–product research conducted prior to the 1970s was the work of Ned Flanders and his associates (Flanders, 1970), using the Flanders Interaction Analysis Categories (FIAC). Flanders believed that there was too much teacher talk and not enough student talk in most classrooms, so that teachers should be more "indirect" —should do more questioning and less lecturing, and in particular, should more often accept, praise, and make instructional use of the ideas and feelings expressed by their students. Flanders was interested primarily in the effects of teacher "indirectness" on student attitudes (liking for the teacher and the class), but he also included measures of adjusted student achievement in five studies conducted between 1959 and 1967.

The basic procedures were as follows: First, pupil attitude inventories were administered and classes located at the extremes of the distribution of pupil attitudes were selected for further study (sometimes other classes were also included). Then, entering achievement level was assessed, and the classes were observed with FIAC. The teachers worked in their regular classrooms with their regular students during these observations, but were observed teaching specially prepared experimental teaching units (similar to regular units but on different topics). This minimized the degree to which mastery of the content taught would be affected by previous school learning. Coders would observe classroom interaction for 3 seconds, then code the interaction into one of the 10 FIAC categories (shown in Table 12.1), then observe for another 3 seconds. The raw data were summed to produce frequency scores, which in turn were added to produce combination scores or divided to produce ratio scores (see Table 12.2). Flanders was most interested in the ratio of "indirect" to "direct" teaching. In his earlier work, he classified lecturing, giving directions, criticizing, and justifying authority as direct influence techniques, and asking questions, accepting and clarifying ideas or feelings, and praising or encouraging as indirect techniques. Later he eliminated lecturing and questioning from his scoring of direct and indirect teaching.

Table 12.1. Representative Data for Various Types of Junior High Classrooms Described in Terms of the Flanders Interaction Analysis Categories (FIAC)

Types of Teacher Behavior		Types of Classrooms (in percentages of total interactions observed)				
		Math (indirect)	Math (direct)	Social Studies (indirect)	Social Studies (direct)	Total
Indirect	1. Accepts feeling	.23	.11	.11	.03	.12
	2. Praises, encourages	1.69	1.06	1.25	1.14	1.28
	3. Uses pupil ideas	8.11	2.63	8.28	3.03	5.51
	Indirect subtotal	10.03	3.80	9.64	4.20	6.91
	4. Asks questions	12.52	9.53	10.75	10.80	10.90
	5. Lectures	46.72	40.83	37.45	25.67	37.67
Direct	6. Gives directions	3.38	8.64	4.29	9.86	6.54
	7. Criticizes, justifies authority	.94	4.66	1.69	5.32	3.15
	Direct subtotal	4.32	13.30	5.98	15.18	9.69
	8. Pupil talk, response	10.73	13.02	17.54	21.49	15.70
	9. Pupil talk, initiate	6.12	6.74	9.48	8.70	7.76
	10. Silence, confusion	9.56	12.79	9.16	13.94	11.36
No. of classrooms		7	9	7	8	31
No. of interactions observed		26,083	32,726	28,194	23,641	110,644

Note. From *Teacher Influence, Pupil Attitudes, and Achievement* (pp. 75-76) by N. Flanders, 1965, Washington, DC: U.S. Office of Education. Reprinted by permission.

In *Analyzing Teacher Behavior*, Flanders (1970) reviewed his own work and that of others who had used FIAC to link teacher–student interaction to student attitudes or achievement. Representative data from five of his own studies are shown in Table 12.2. Several facts about these data are noteworthy. First, they do not support the notion that teachers talk too much. In all five studies, teacher talk correlated *positively* with both achievement and attitude. Thus although about two-thirds of the talk in classrooms is teacher talk, there is no reason to believe that such talk is inappropriate or that it indicates that teachers are "oppressive," unduly "dominant," and so forth.

Second, the data generally support Flanders' hypotheses (more for attitude than for achievement), although the second grade data are systematically less supportive than the data from the other four studies. Correlations with indirectness, praise, and acceptance of student ideas tend to be positive, and correlations with restrictiveness and negative authority tend to be negative.

Third, the negative correlations for restrictiveness and criticism tend to be stronger and more consistent than the positive correlations for praise and acceptance of student ideas (especially in the data for student achievement). Furthermore, although praise and sustained acceptance are lumped together in computing indirectness scores, these teacher behaviors often correlate in opposite directions with student achievement.

Finally, the flexibility score generally correlated positively with student attitude and achievement, indicating the need to tailor techniques to the situation rather than trying to maximize indirectness at all times. Following Soar (1968), Flanders (1970) noted that teacher behavior variables may have "inverted U" curvilinear relationships or other nonlinear relationships with student achievement, so what is optimal teacher behavior may vary with the situation. He suggested that lower levels of indirectness might be appropriate for factual or skill-learning tasks, and higher levels for tasks involving abstract reasoning or creativity. We agree with these observations, and believe that they help explain the discrepant second grade data. Because most school activities in the primary grades involve low-level factual and skill learning, there is less reason to expect indirectness variables to relate to achievement in these grades in the same ways that they relate to it at higher grades.

In summary, except for the second grade data, the data shown in Table 12.2 suggest positive relationships between indirect teaching and achievement (although we have direct data only for sustained acceptance and praise; separate correlations are not given for accepting feeling, using student ideas, giving directions, or criticizing or justifying authority). Should we conclude, then, that students beyond the primary grades will achieve more if their teachers become more indirect? We think not, for several reasons.

The first, of course, is that the data are correlational. We could just as well conclude that student achievement causes teacher indirectness, or that both variables covary with some more fundamental but unmeasured third factor, Furthermore, several experimental studies comparing indirect to direct teaching failed to produce significant group differences in achievement (Rosenshine, 1970b). Thus, even when correlated with achievement, teacher indirectness variables do not necessarily cause it.

Second, as noted by Flanders (1970) himself and elaborated by Barr and Dreeben (1977), the teacher behaviors included in indirectness ratios only apply during recitations and other activities in which the teacher is instructing the whole class or a significant subgroup, and furthermore apply to only a small

Table 12.2. Correlations Between Flanders' Teacher Behavior Variables and Student Adjusted Achievement and Attitudes in Five Studies

Variable	Computation Rule	Correlations with Adjusted Achievement Study/Grade Level					Correlations with Class Attitude Study/Grade Level				
		2nd	4th	6th	7th	8th	2nd	4th	6th	7th	8th
1. Indirectness proportion ($i/i + d$)	Sum of *Accepts feeling* (1) + *Praise* (2) + *Uses pupil ideas* (3) codes divided by sum of *accepts feeling* (1) + *Praise* (2) + *Uses pupil ideas* (3) + *Gives directions* (6) + *Criticizes or justifies authority* (7) codes	−.07	.31	.22	.48*	.43*	.13	.64*	.49*	.34	.58*
2. Sustained acceptance sum	Sum of *Uses pupil ideas* (3) codes which were followed by another *Uses pupil ideas* (3) code	−.45	.19	.30	.40	.19	.13	.52*	.40*	.33	.31
3. Indirectness sum	Sum of *Accepts feeling* (1) + *Praise* (2) + *Uses pupil ideas* (3) + *Asks questions* (4) codes	.05	−.08	.26	.25	.45*	.45*	.34	.40*	.16	.51*
4. Questions sum	Sum of *Asks questions* (4) codes	.07	−.19	.11	−.06	.44*	.49*	−.06	.27	.00	.47*
5. Teacher talk sum	Sum of codes in Categories 1–7	.30	.08	.11	.02	.45*	.38	.10	.24	.15	.61*
6. Restrictiveness sum	Sum of *Gives directions* (6) + *Criticizes or justifies authority* (7) codes	−.10	−.24	−.04	−.61*	−.34	−.09	−.17	−.37*	−.43	−.66*
7. Restrictive feedback sum	Sum of *Pupil response* (8) + *Pupil initiation* (9) codes which were followed by *Gives directions* (6) or *Criticizes or justifies authority* (7) codes	.18	−.34	−.32*	−.50*	−.43*	.02	−.32	−.29	−.47*	−.62*
8. Negative authority sum	Sum of (6) codes followed by (7) codes + sum of (7) codes followed by (6) codes	.05	−.23	−.15	−.62*	−.25	−.22	−.22	−.32*	−.43	−.59*
9. Praise sum	Sum of *Praise* (2) codes	.25	−.13	.36*	−.23	.30	.08	.40	.35*	−.34	.38
10. Flexibility	The i/d ratio is computed separately for each classroom observation (sum of 1 + 2 + 3 divided by sum of 1 + 2 + 3 + 6 + 7). Then the lowest of these ratios is subtracted from the highest to obtain the range	−.07	.40*	.19	.37	.43*	.12	.08	.41*	.13	.43*
	Number of classes	15	16	30	15	16	15	16	30	15	16

* $p < .05$.

Note. Constructed from data in *Analyzing Teacher Behavior* (pp. 394–395) by Ned A. Flanders, 1970, Reading, MA: Addison-Wesley.

proportion of the interaction that occurs in these settings. The data in Table 12.1, from mathematics and social studies classes, are typical. Note that only about 7% of the codes are classified as indirect, and only about 10% as direct. Compare this with about 11% for teacher questions, 38% for lecturing, and 23% for pupil talk. Teacher indirectness behaviors subsume only a minority of classroom events, and have nothing directly to do with the quantity or quality of instruction in subject matter content. Futhermore, indirect classrooms provide only 5–6% more indirect teaching than direct classrooms, but yet provide about 9% more lecturing. It is possible that this, rather than indirectness, explains the differences in achievement (Flanders did not provide correlations specific to teacher lecturing; the teacher talk variable includes all seven of the teacher categories).

Third, note that indirectness behaviors occur in public settings in which the teacher is presenting information, conducting a recitation or drill, or leading a discussion. It may be that the "indirect" teachers elicit more achievement not so much because they are more likely to use "indirect" methods during group instruction, but because they do more group instruction in the first place (group instruction maximizes opportunities to accept feeling, praise, or use pupil ideas, and minimizes the need to give directions or criticize). "Indirect" teachers may actively instruct their students more often than "direct" teachers.

A related point is that the FIAC system requires that every 3-second observation be coded, so that procedural and conduct interactions get mixed in with academic interactions instead of being coded separately or ignored. As a result, several FIAC categories, especially 6 and 7, include significant proportions of codes based on nonacademic interaction (many of teachers' directions are procedural, and most of their criticism is for misconduct rather than incorrect answers). Teachers who frequently give procedural directions or behavioral criticism usually do so because their students are often confused, off-task, or disruptive. Thus, the FIAC system has a built-in tendency to classify as "direct" those teachers whose students spend less classroom time engaged in academic tasks.

Finally, the FIAC system did not distinguish between simple affirmative feedback and praise, nor between simple negation and criticism. Consequently, to the extent that statements coded as praise or criticism did refer to academic responses, the majority merely affirmed or negated the correctness of the student's statement. Also, the measures used were simply the summed frequencies of "praise" and "criticism" (rather than the percentages of correct answers praised and wrong answers criticized) — measures that depended in large part on how frequently the students in a class gave correct answers. In turn, this depended on pupil ability and comprehension of the material, as well as on the teachers' skill in presenting the material and posing questions that were clear and appropriate. Thus, teachers' content presentation and questioning skills may affect their "indirectness" scores.

These methodological and interpretive comments are included here not so much to criticize Flanders' work (he advanced the field and was ahead of his time in many ways), as to clarify its interpretation and its relationships to subsequent work by others. At first, Flanders' data seem to contradict some of the most common findings (reviewed further on) of the 1970s. However, Flanders' data are seen to be compatible with these later findings when it is recognized that teacher lecturing is not included in those measures of "direct" teaching that correlate negatively with achievement; relationships are curvilinear, revealing a lower optimum amount of indirectness in basic skills lessons; levels of student ability and motivation will affect the indirectness scores attributed to teachers, and teachers who spend more time actively instructing their students, and less time dealing with procedural or conduct concerns, are likely to get higher indirectness scores.

Soar and Soar

As noted above, the theorizing of Robert Soar (1968) concerning inverted-U curvilinear process-outcome relationships is useful in interpreting the Flanders (1970) data. Soar also conducted five process-outcome studies in the 1960s and 1970s, several in collaboration with Ruth Soar. These studies typically involved multiple measurement of student entry characteristics in the fall, of classroom processes in the middle of the school year (typically based on four to eight half-hour visits per class), and of student outcomes in the spring. The sample descriptions and references for these five studies are (a) 55 urban classrooms, Grades 3–6, all white and predominantly middle and upper SES (Soar, 1966); (b) 20 first grade classrooms in Project Follow Through, mixed racially but with predominantly low-SES pupils (Soar & Soar, 1972); (c) 59 fifth grade classrooms, mixed racially but with predominantly low-SES pupils (Soar & Soar, 1973, 1978); (d) 22 urban first grade classrooms, mixed racially and heterogeneous in SES (Soar & Soar, 1973, 1978); (e) 289 Follow Through and comparison classrooms in the primary grades, predominantly low in SES (Soar, 1973).

Two observation systems were used in the first study, one an elaboration of FIAC, and one concerned with nonverbal behavior and expression of affect. The other studies used four systems, two coded on the spot and two coded later from audiotapes. The first looked at classroom management, pupil response to it, and the teacher's and pupils' expression of affect. The second categorized the teacher's development of subject matter, using concepts from Dewey's experimentalism. The third characterized the cognitive level of discourse, using Bloom's taxonomy of cognitive objectives. Finally, the fourth system was the elaboration of FIAC.

Although combinations of factor analysis and rational cluster analysis were used to reduce the process data, the resultant factors usually possessed conceptual clarity and face validity as measures of specific teacher behavior. Factor scores were then entered into analyses designed to reveal both linear and nonlinear relationships with achievement, which was adjusted not only for entry level but frequently for personal characteristics such as dependency, anxiety, or cognitive style as well. The Soars (Soar, 1977; Soar & Soar, 1979) have integrated findings from the first four of the studies listed above, using some key conceptual distinctions.

CONCEPTUAL DISTINCTIONS

The first distinction is between *emotional climate* factors (positive or negative affect exhibited by teachers and students) and *teacher management* (or control) factors. These factors are independent: Highly controlling teachers are not necessarily rejecting or otherwise negative, and teachers who exert minimal control over pupil behavior are not necessarily student oriented or otherwise positive in their affect.

Within the sphere of emotional climate, the teacher's affect must be distinguished from the pupils' affect. Positive affect in the teacher does not necessarily imply positive affect in the students, or vice versa. Within the teacher management sphere, it is important to distinguish between *control of pupil behavior* (physical movement, opportunity to socialize), *control of learning tasks* (what learning tasks are selected and how they are carried out), and *control of thinking processes* (degree to which pupils are allowed or encouraged to confront the subject matter at a variety of cognitive levels or to pursue divergent ideas). Here too, there are no necessary relationships. A teacher who is highly controlling of physical movement and nonacademic behavior might or might not allow considerable pupil choice of learning activities or opportunity to engage in a variety of thinking processes.

Finally, the Soars also note that teacher control can be exercised either by establishing rules and routines (*established structure*), or by issuing directives, asking questions, or otherwise structuring pupil response through immediate face-to-face interaction (*current interaction*). Once again, these elements are independent: Teachers who control through established structure may or may not be highly controlling in their daily interactions with the students.

Emotional Climate. The Soars draw several conclusions that not only make good sense and fit the data from their own four studies, but also fit data from other investigators. First, there is a disordinal relationship between emotional climate and achievement gain. Negative emotional climate indicators (teacher criticism, teacher or pupil negative affect, pupil resistance) usually show significant negative correlations with achievement, but positive emotional climate indicators (teacher praise, positive teacher or pupil affect) usually do not show significant positive correlations. Most relationships are insignificant, and some are negative (especially in Soar's first study, where the students were from predominantly high SES backgrounds). Thus, these data do not support the notion that efficient learning requires a warm emotional climate. It is true that negative climates appear dysfunctional, but neutral climates are at least as supportive of achievement as more clearly warm climates.

Teacher Management. Measures of teacher control typically relate either positively or curvilinearly to achievement. Indicators of teacher control over student behavior (physical movement, socializing) show positive relationships. Students learn more in classrooms where teachers establish structures that limit pupil freedom of choice, physical movement, and disruption, and where there is relatively more teacher talk and teacher control of pupils' task behavior.

Indicators of high teacher control of learning tasks also correlate positively with achievement. This was seen regularly for measures of teacher-focused academic instruction (whole class or small group). In addition, the fifth grade study showed positive correlations for indicators of good management of independent seatwork time (pupils were usually engaged in their work, and alternative activities were available when they finished).

This general pattern of positive linear relationships was qualified by several curvilinear relationships, however. Inverted-U relationships were seen in one study for recitation activity, and in another for drill and for teacher-directed (vs. pupil-selected) activity. Thus, within the range of teacher control of learning tasks observed, the teachers who exerted greater control generally elicited higher achievement, but the relationship was ultimately curvilinear. Beyond an optimal level, additional teacher direction, drill, or recitation became dysfunctional (not because the extra instruction undermined existing learning, but because it was unnecessary and used up time that could have been spent moving on to new objectives).

The results for indicators of teacher control over pupil thinking varied with SES and grade level. In the study involving high SES students in Grades 3-6, achievement related positively to high-cognitive-level activities, and either positively or curvilinearly to indirect instruction. Codes for high cognitive level and indirectness are associated with discussion (rather than recitation or drill) activities. In contrast, achievement in the first grade and low-SES fifth grade classes was associated with recitation or drill, and with activities characterized by giving and receiving information and by narrow rather than broad teacher questions. Taken together, the data suggest that "... greater amounts of high cognitive-level interaction are dysfunctional for young pupils, especially those of lower ability, but may become functional for older elementary pupils, especially those of higher ability" (Soar & Soar, 1979, p. 114).

There were also indications that the optimal level of teacher control (vs. student freedom) varied with learning objectives. Within any particular study, gains on lower-level objectives were associated primarily with recitation, drill, and other low-cognitive-level, high teacher-focus activities, and gains on tests of higher-level skills were associated more with discussion and other activities offering more pupil freedom. Thus, according to Soar and Soar (1979):

> some degree of pupil freedom, within a context of teacher involvement that maintains focus, was related to gain.... For lower grade pupils, greater amounts of high cognitive-level interaction are not functional.... The amount of pupil freedom that is most functional for both learning tasks and thinking depends on the complexity of the learning task — for more complex tasks, a somewhat greater degree of freedom is functional, but even then it may be too great. (pp. 117-118)

Finally, these studies indicate that student SES interacts with the findings for emotional climate and teacher control. Positive affect appears to be more functional, and negative affect more dysfunctional, for low-SES pupils than for high-SES pupils. Also, a greater degree of teacher control and structuring appears to be functional for low-SES pupils than for high-SES pupils. The work of Brophy and Evertson and of Good and Grouws (to be described) supports similar conclusions.

The fifth study listed above (Soar, 1973), dealing with 289 Follow Through and comparison classrooms, was not included in the syntheses by Soar (1977) and by Soar and Soar (1979), but yielded generally compatible findings. That is, in these primary grade classrooms with low-SES students, achievement gain was associated with teacher structured time spent in reading and other academic activities involving drill or convergent questions. These findings are also compatible with the results of Stallings' research on Follow Through classrooms (described below).

Stallings

Research by Jane Stallings and her colleagues has included evaluation of Project Follow Through, correlational work at the third grade level, and correlational and experimental work in secondary reading instruction.

Follow Through Evaluation Study. This study (Stallings & Kaskowitz, 1974) involved 108 first grade and 58 third grade classes taught by experienced teachers who were implementing one of seven Follow Through models. Each class was observed for three consecutive days, focusing on the teacher for two days and on selected students for one day. Data collection focused on events important to the program sponsors, and included details about the physical environment, data on the time spent in various activities, and frequency counts of adult–child interaction. Program models ranged from heavy emphasis on structured teaching of basic skills to open classroom approaches stressing affective objectives and self-directed learning.

The two programs with the clearest academic focus produced the strongest gains in reading and math, although their students were below average in attendance (considered a measure of student attitude toward school) and in scores on the Raven's Coloured Progressive Matrices (a test of perceptual problem solving ability, administered only at the third grade level). This was one of several indications from 1970s work that the factors that maximize gain on standardized achievement tests are not necessarily the same factors that maximize progress toward other outcomes.

Implementation data indicated that most teachers followed the guidelines of their program sponsors. Consequently, as a sample, those classes contained much more variation in types of activities than would be observed in more traditional classes, as well as unusual combinations of program elements. For example, the Kansas program for the first grade level (Ramp & Rhine, 1981) called for frequent small-group instruction in basic skills by a teacher, an aide, and two parent volunteers; use of programed individualized learning materials at other times; and praise and tokens (backed by reinforcement menus) for good behavior and academic progress. This was the only program to use token reinforcement, and its combination of high rates of small-group instruction with high rates of individualized independent learning is unusual.

In many respects, then, the program rather than the class is the real unit for interpreting the Follow Through findings. Still, the data suggest the same general conclusions as other studies of primary grade instruction for low-SES students, and in most respects, the Follow Through data are typical of data from large field studies that employ multiple measures of teacher behavior. There are a great many findings, involving more variables than classes. For example, for the 108 first grade classes, 108 of 340 correlations were significant at the .05 level for mathematics, and 118 of 340 were significant for total reading. This clearly suggests significant process–product relationships, but the probability coefficients cannot be taken literally because the 340 process variables are neither conceptually nor statistically independent. Thus, the .05 level of statistical significance is used merely as an informal guideline for interpreting the data.

The clearest and most widespread pattern involved positive correlations with achievement for process variables related to student opportunity to learn academic content (time spent in academic activities, frequencies of small or large group lessons in basic skills, and frequencies of supervised seatwork activities), and negative correlations for time spent in nonacademic activities (story, music, dance, arts and crafts) or in teacher-student interaction patterns that were not stressed in the two academic programs (particularly, open or informal patterns in which teachers mostly worked with one or two individuals rather than teaching formal lessons to groups). Almost anything connected with the classical recitation pattern of teacher questioning (particularly direct, factual questions rather than more open questions) followed by student response followed by teacher feedback correlated positively with achievement. Instruction in small groups (up to eight students) correlated positively in first grade, and instruction in large groups (nine or more students) in third grade.

In general, the major finding was that students who spent most of their time being instructed by their teachers or working independently under teacher supervision made greater gains than students who spent a lot of time in nonacademic activities or who were expected to learn largely on their own. Furthermore, although the sample was composed mostly of low-SES (and thus relatively low-ability) students, these main effects were elaborated by interactions with student ability: Frequent instruction by the teacher was especially important for the lowest ability students.

Compared to the findings for opportunity to learn and for active instruction by the teacher, the findings for praise, criticism, and reinforcement were weaker and more mixed. Token reinforcement correlated positively with achievement in first grade, where it was used in the Kansas program, but by third grade it had been phased out. Praise for correct responses or good academic work also tended to correlate positively, but more notably in first grade than in third, more for math than for reading, and more for low-ability students than for high-ability students. Other forms of praise had mixed and mostly nonsignificant relationships. Neutral corrective feedback (involving neither praise nor criticism) usually correlated positively. Surprisingly, measures of negative corrective feedback (academic criticism) tended to correlate positively with learning gain when they did reach statistical significance (usually they did not).

Taken together, these data on academic feedback suggest several general conclusions:

1. When teacher feedback measures are expressed as raw frequencies (i.e., number of academic praise statements observed) rather than being adjusted for frequencies and types of student academic responses (i.e., proportion of correct answers observed that were praised by the teacher), their interpretation is ambiguous. All types of academic feedback occur more often during activities in which academic responses are elicited more often in the first place (i.e., drill or recitation lessons). Therefore, a positive correlation for frequency of academic praise may occur because of a linkage between achievement and the frequency of active instruction by the teacher, and not because of a more specific linkage between student achievement and teachers' tendencies to praise good academic responses when they are elicited.
2. Partly as a result, frequency measures of types of academic feedback show weaker relationships to achievement than measures of time spent in academic activities.
3. Academic praise and especially academic criticism are infrequent, and their base rates must be taken into account in interpreting their correlations with achievement.
4. Occasional praise (of perhaps 5–10% of good academic responses) tends to show weak but positive correlations with achievement, at least for younger and lower-ability students.
5. Criticism for poor academic responses sometimes also shows weak positive correlations, at least by third grade, but such criticism is rare, and the operative difference is between never criticizing and criticizing only rarely. Most such criticism is for repeated inattentiveness or carelessness, and thus represents an appropriate academic demandingness rather than an inappropriate hypercritical stance on the part of the teachers who employ it (in response to only about 1% of students' failures to respond correctly, about 0.05% of students' total academic responses).
6. These conclusions apply to academic criticism, not criticism for misconduct. The latter almost invariably correlates negatively with achievement, and indicates classroom organization and management difficulties.

California ECE Study. Stallings, Cory, Fairweather, and Needels (1977) evaluated reading instruction in the California Early

Childhood Education (ECE) program, which was intended to improve elementary education, particularly for low achievers. Observations were conducted in 45 third grade classes using methods similar to those used in the Follow Through study. The ECE program provided for extra aides and greater parent participation in school activities, and the target classes were selected from schools that fell below the 20th percentile in entry-level test scores. Thus, the students were similar to those in the Follow Through sample, although the ECE classes were taught according to local preference rather than the guidelines of program sponsors.

This study involved both school- (not considered here) and class-level analyses. The latter were not done on all available variables, but only on a subset of 49 variables selected on the basis of prior research. Of these, 33 showed significant relationships to reading achievement. A few were student–teacher ratio variables indicating that smaller classes generally made greater gains. The rest dealt with classroom activities and teacher–student interaction. Classes that made greater gains spent more time in reading and other academic activities, and less in games, group sharing, or socializing. Their teachers spent more time actively instructing in small groups, and less time uninvolved with students or involved with individuals rather than groups. They gave more instruction, asked more academic questions, and provided more feedback. Their students asked more questions of their own and initiated more verbal interactions with the teachers.

Clearly, these correlations replicate the Follow Through findings involving student opportunity to learn and active instruction by the teacher. The findings on small class size were not noted in the Follow Through study. Class size has revealed a great range of relationships with achievement in various studies, although meta-analysis suggests that achievement increases slightly as class size decreases (Smith & Glass 1980). The positive findings for small-group instruction support the first grade but contradict the third grade Follow Through data, although the contradiction disappears when the data are interpeted as reflecting the effects of active instruction rather than group size. That is, although instruction can be conducted effectively in either the small-group or the large-group setting, reading achievement gain is linked to frequent active instruction in reading by the teacher.

Another contrast with the Follow Through findings was the absence of significant correlations for level of question (factual vs. open ended), praise, or criticism. This happened in part because most measures of these variables were not included among the 49 selected for analysis. Also, as noted above, the frequency of academic questions seems to be a more important correlate than either the level of such questions or the nature of the teacher's feedback (praise, acknowledgement, criticism) to the responses that they elicit. In general, then, the Follow Through and ECE studies agree in identifying quantity of academic instruction by the teacher as the key correlate of achievement gain.

Teaching basic skills in secondary schools. Stallings, Cory, Fairweather, and Needels (1978) studied reading instruction at the secondary level in 27 junior high and 16 senior high reading classes (for low achievers and others who had not yet learned to read efficiently). Instruments were adapted to the activities occurring in these secondary classes, but the same general approach to observation and the same method of observing on 3 consecutive days were repeated.

Once again, quantity of instruction was the key correlate of achievement. Positive correlates included instructing small or large groups, reviewing or discussing assignments, having the students read aloud, praising their successes, and providing support and corrective feedback when they did not respond correctly. Negative correlates included teacher not interacting with the students; teacher getting organized rather than instructing; teacher offering students choices of activities; students working independently on silent reading or written assignments; time lost to outside intrusions or spent in social interaction; and frequency of negative interactions. In short, gains were minimal where teachers did not concentrate on reading achievement objectives, expected the students to learn mostly on their own, or lost significant instructional time due to disorganization or inability to obtain student cooperation.

Within these general trends, there were differential patterns related to the students' entry-level reading achievement. With students whose functional reading was at a primary level, the most successful teachers tended to use methods traditionally employed in the primary grades, although with more emphasis on comprehension than word-attack skills. They would work with one small group while the other students did written work or silent reading. Lessons began with development of vocabulary and concepts, followed by oral reading interspersed with questions to develop and check comprehension. Praise, support, and corrective feedback were frequent. In contrast, teachers working successfully with students who were behind only a grade level or two used methods traditionally employed in the upper grades: less oral reading, and more silent reading and written assignments. These teachers still instructed their students actively, however, and structured and monitored their seatwork rather than leaving them mostly on their own.

In summary, across three studies, Stallings and her colleagues found that gains in basic skills achievement were associated positively with active group instruction in the subject matter and negatively with emphasis on nonacademic activities, poor organization or classroom management, or approaches in which students are expected to manage their learning primarily on their own.

Training experiment (Secondary Reading Teachers). Based on the study just described, Stallings developed guidelines for secondary reading instruction (differentiated according to students' entry achievement levels). These guidelines, expressed in terms of percentage of time or frequency per class period, were developed for variables such as instructing individuals, groups, or the total class, asking questions, and reacting to students' academic responses and classroom behavior. They provided the basis for an experiment in which the achievement of students of teachers trained to follow the guidelines was compared with that of students in control classes.

Analyses indicated that although there was variation in degree of implementation (most of these secondary teachers were not accustomed to having students read aloud, for example, so that this technique was not used as much as it could have been), the treatment teachers eventually approximated the idealized guidelines much more closely than the control teachers did.

Furthermore, their students gained an average of 6 months more in reading achievement (Stallings, 1980). Although not quite statistically significant, this is a sizeable difference and provides some support for the causal efficacy of the behaviors prescribed in the guidelines.

Brophy and Evertson

Brophy, Evertson, and their colleagues completed a series of studies in the 1970s, starting with an assessment of the stability of individual teachers' differential effects on achievement.

Stability study. Brophy (1973) obtained achievement data from students taught during 3 consecutive years by 88 second grade and 77 third grade experienced teachers. Using data from the annually administered Metropolitan Achievement Test (MAT), the students in these 165 teachers' classes were assigned adjusted gain scores on the subtests of word knowledge, word discrimination, reading, arithmetic computation, and arithmetic reasoning (adjustments were based on data for all of the students tested in each year). These adjusted gain scores for individuals then were averaged by class to produce class mean adjusted gain scores for each teacher for each of 3 consecutive years.

Correlations of these mean adjusted scores from one year to the next (stability coefficients) were low to moderate, but positive and usually significant (most were in the .30s). Acland (1976) later reported slightly higher stability coefficients for fifth grade teachers (averaging .40), and Good and Grouws (1975, 1977) reported lower but still statistically significant coefficients (averaging .20) for third and fourth grade teachers. Thus, investigations of year-to-year stability in teacher effects on student achievement agree in showing that some teachers are consistently better than others at producing student learning gain.

Correlations across the five subsets within each year were considerably higher than the year-to-year stability coefficients for the same subtest. Thus, correlations of word knowledge scores from one year with word knowledge scores from the next tended to be in the .30s but correlations of word knowledge scores with scores from the other four subtests in the same year were usually much higher, typically in the .70s. Thus, factors unique to a given school year (the teacher's health and welfare, the specific composition and group dynamics of the class, testing conditions, etc.) created cohort effects observable in the achievement data.

Finally, within each class, gains usually were comparable across the two sexes and the five MAT subtests. Few teachers consistently got better results from boys than from girls (or vice versa), or consistently got better results in language arts or reading than in mathematics (or vice versa). These analyses revealed a strong tendency for teachers' effects on achievement to be generalized across the two sexes and the five MAT subtests in any given year, and a weaker but still significant tendency for these general effects to be stable from one year to the next (Brophy, 1973; Veldman & Brophy, 1974). This stability was high enough to allow the next step: process–product research on a subsample of teachers who were unusually consistent in their effects on student achievement.

The Texas Teacher Effectiveness Study. By the time this study was getting organized, achievement data were available for each of the 165 teachers for 4 consecutive years. Analyses of trends over time indicated that about half of the teachers were stable in their effects on achievement (typically this stability took the form of relative constancy in rank order among the 165 teachers studied, although for a few teachers it took the form of a linear trend indicating steady improvement or deterioration over time). Thirty-one of these consistent teachers were each observed for 10 hours in the first year of this research, and 28 (including 19 holdovers from the first year) were each observed for 30 hours in the second year.

These teachers were selected for *stability* rather than *level* of effectiveness in producing achievement; in fact, as a group they were distributed roughly normally across the range of adjusted MAT means observed in the larger sample of 165. Unfortunately, the district discontinued administration of the MAT prior to the beginning of classroom observation, so that end-of-year achievement data were not available. As a substitute, mean adjusted gain scores from the 4 preceding years (for each of the five MAT subtests) were averaged to compute achievement outcome estimates for each teacher. Thus, in this study, process measures were correlated with scores representing predicted effectiveness based on stable prior track records rather than with scores from tests administered subsequent to classroom observations.

Brophy and Evertson relied on an event sampling, in which events relevant to the coding categories are coded when they occur, but nothing is coded when no system-relevant events are occurring. Process data were expressed not only as frequency scores comparable to those used by Flanders and by Stallings, but also as proportion scores (examples: proportion of correct answers followed by praise; proportion of private contacts that dealt with academic work; proportion of these private work contacts that were initiated by the teacher).

Compared to frequency scores, these proportion scores reduce the degree to which measures intended to represent teacher behavior are affected by student behavior. For example, simple frequency scores for teacher praise of good responses are affected by the number of such responses produced. A fast-paced class of high achievers might produce 100 correct responses in an hour's lesson; a slower-paced group might produce only 40. Frequency scores might reveal that each teacher praises an average of (say) 10 times per hour. These scores will seem to equate the teachers. Proportion scores, however, will reveal that the first praises only about 10% of the students' correct responses, whereas the second praises about 25% (although the frequency data will also be needed to integrate these data fully). Thus, frequency and proportion scores provide different but complementary information.

The presage and process measures generated in this study were analyzed — separately for the two grade levels (second and third) and two levels of SES — for relationships to each of the five MAT subtests. The analyses for the two grade levels showed similar patterns of findings, and except for a few measures that were subject-specific in the first place, so did those for the five MAT subtests. However, there were distinctly contrasting patterns of correlates of learning gain for teachers working in low-SES versus high-SES classrooms. The findings are reported in the form of thousands of correlations (Brophy & Evertson, 1974a; Evertson & Brophy, 1973, 1974) and graphs of nonlinear relationships (Brophy & Evertson, 1974b), separately for the low and high-SES subsamples. Brophy and Evertson used the .10 level of significance because of the low sample sizes (18 high-SES and 13 low-SES classes in the first year; 15 and 13 in the second). However, in interpreting the findings they stressed general patterns of relationship that held up across both years of the study. Findings that met these criteria are summarized in a book (Brophy & Evertson, 1976).

Presage-outcome data revealed that the teachers who produced the most achievement were businesslike and task oriented. They enjoyed working with students but interacted with them primarily within a teacher–student relationship. They operated their classrooms as learning environments, spending most time on academic activities. Teachers who produced the least achievement usually showed either of two contrasting orientations. One was a heavily affective approach in which the teachers were more concerned with personal relationships and affective objectives than with cognitive objectives. The other (fortunately, least common) pattern was seen in disillusioned or bitter teachers who disliked their students and concentrated on authority and discipline in their interviews.

The teachers who produced the most achievement also assumed personal responsibility for doing so. Their interviews revealed feelings of efficacy and internal locus of control; a tendency to organize their classrooms and to plan activities proactively on a daily basis; and a "can do" attitude about overcoming problems. Rather than give up and make excuses for failure, these teachers would redouble their efforts, providing slower students with extra attention and more individualized instruction. Such persistence was particularly noticeable among teachers who were successful with low-SES students. Here, where there was a poor fit between students' needs and the curriculum's instructional materials and tests, the teachers would often substitute for the materials or develop their own methods of evaluation.

The process variables correlating most strongly and consistently with achievement were those suggesting maximal student engagement in academic activities and minimal time spent in transitions or dealing with procedures or conduct. In general, the successful classroom managers used the techniques described by Kounin (1970) and elaborated by Evertson, Emmer, Anderson, and their colleagues (see Doyle this volume). They demonstrated "withitness" by monitoring the entire class when they were instructing, and by moving around during seatwork time. They rarely made target errors (blaming the wrong student for a disruption) or timing errors (waiting too long to intervene), although they were more likely than other teachers to be coded as overreacting to minor incidents. Even so, they were more likely than other teachers to merely warn rather than threaten their students, and less likely to use personal criticism or punishment. They were proactive in articulating conduct expectations, vigilant in monitoring compliance, and consistent in following through with reminders or demands when necessary.

What these teachers demanded, however, was not so much compliance with authority as productive engagement in academic activities. Such activities were well prepared, and thus

run smoothly with few interruptions and only brief transitions in between. Seatwork assignments were well matched to students' abilities (this typically meant some degree of individualization). Students who needed help could get it from the teacher or some designated person (according to established expectations concerning when and how to seek help). Students were accountable for careful, complete work, because they knew that the work would be checked and followed up with additional instruction or assignments if necessary. Those who completed their assignments knew what other activity options were available.

There was a difference in emphasis between high-SES and low-SES classes. The high-SES students tended to be eager, compliant, and successful, whereas the low-SES students more often were struggling, anxious, or alienated. Consequently, in the high-SES classes it was especially important for the teachers to be intellectually stimulating and to provide interesting things for students to do when they finished their assignments, whereas in low-SES classrooms it was especially important for the teachers to give students assignments that they could handle and to see that those assignments were done.

Curvilinear relationships were observed between achievement and the percentages of teacher questions that were answered correctly. High-SES students progressed optimally when they answered about 70% of these questions correctly, and low-SES students when they answered about 80% correctly. These data suggest that learning proceeds most smoothly when material is somewhat new or challenging, yet relatively easy for the students to assimilate to their existing knowledge (even during lessons, when the teacher is present to explain the material and to correct misunderstandings and errors).

Success rates on independent seatwork were not measured, but it was noted that achievement gains were maximized when students consistently completed their work with few interruptions due to confusion or the need for help. This suggested that success rates on these seatwork assignments were high, perhaps approaching 100% (achieved by selecting appropriate tasks in the first place and explaining them thoroughly before releasing the students to work independently). This led the authors to speculate that optimal learning occurs when students move at a brisk pace but in small steps, so that they experience continuous progress and high success rates (averaging perhaps 75% during lessons when the teacher is present, and 90–100% when the students must work independently).

Again, there was a relative difference between high- and low-SES classes: In high-SES classes, where most students succeeded with relative ease, the pace could be brisker and the steps slightly larger. In low-SES classes, teachers had to move in smaller steps, with more explanation of new material, more practice with feedback, and, in general, more redundancy.

Small-group (mostly reading) and whole-class lessons and recitations were common in high-gain classes at both SES levels. These lessons often began with presentation of new material or review of old material, and these teacher presentations tended to be rated high in clarity. Then came a practice and feedback phase featuring questions, responses, and feedback. Most questions here were academic, usually low-level or fact questions rather than more open-ended process questions.

In high-SES classes, it was important to see that lessons did not become dominated by the most assertive students, by involving everyone, waiting for hesitant students to respond, and insisting that other students refrain from calling out the answers. However, it usually was not helpful to question these students repeatedly when they could not answer the original question. Given that most questions were factual and that most of these students were happy to respond if they could, probing in these situations would have amounted to pointless pumping of the students.

Such probing for improved response was effective in low-SES classes, however, where many students were anxious or lacking in confidence even when they knew the answers. Here, it was important for teachers to work for any kind of response at all from incommunicative students, and to try to improve the responses of students who spoke up but gave incorrect or incomplete answers. In these situations, giving clues (particularly phonics cues in reading) or rephrasing the question to make it easier were more successful strategies than waiting silently or merely repeating the original question. In contrast to high-SES classes where it was important to suppress unauthorized calling out, called out answers (relevant to the questions asked) correlated positively with achievement in low-SES classes.

Surprisingly, the use of patterned turns in small groups (mostly reading groups) correlated positively with achievement. That is, teachers who went around the small group in order, giving each successive student a turn, got greater gains than teachers who called on students "randomly" or called primarily on volunteers. One probable reason for this is that the patterned turns mechanism insured that all students participated regularly and roughly equally. Furthermore, in high-SES classes, it helped focus students' attention on the content of the lesson rather than on attempts to get the teacher to call on them, and in low-SES classes, it provided structure and predictability to lessons that may have been helpful to anxious students.

The correlations involving motivation variables were generally much weaker than those involving classroom management and academic instruction variables. Positive correlations were obtained in both SES levels for use of symbolic rewards, especially stars or smiling faces on papers that could be taken home to show parents. Concrete rewards or tokens were not used in any systematic way by the teachers under study. The findings for academic praise and criticism varied by SES and by teacher versus student initiation of interaction. Praise given in teacher-initiated interactions was distributed widely and correlated positively with achievement. However, praise given during student-initiated interactions went mostly to those students who frequently approached the teacher to show their work, and such praise correlated negatively with achievement. In general, measures of academic praise correlated positively but weakly in low-SES classes, but were unrelated to or negatively (and again, weakly) correlated with achievement in high-SES classes.

Criticism for poor academic responses or poor work correlated positively with such gain (in high-SES classes only). As in the Stallings work described above, such academic criticism was rare, so that the correlation is based on the difference between rarely criticizing students for working below their abilities and never doing so.

Academic praise was much more frequent than academic criticism, but this was not true for teachers' responses to student conduct. In fact, praise of good conduct was very rare and never correlated significantly with achievement. Criticism and punishment for misconduct were more frequent, however, and tended to correlate negatively with achievement. The teachers who elicited greater achievement tended to respond to misconduct with simple directives or warnings rather than with criticism or punishment. When something more was required, they tended to arrange an individual conference to discuss the problem and come to some agreement with the student about what was to be done. They were unlikely to lash out at students, to punish them impulsively, or to send them to the principal for discipline.

In general, the teachers who got the most gain in high-SES classes motivated by challenging and communicating high expectations to their students, occasionally delivering symbolic rewards when the students succeeded, and on rare occasions, criticizing them when they failed due to inattentiveness or poor effort. In contrast, the teachers who got the most gains in low-SES classes motivated primarily through gentle and positive encouragement rather than challenge or demandingness. They not only used symbolic rewards, but often praised their students within the contexts of personalized interactions with them.

The following variables failed to correlate significantly with achievement: teachers' warmth and enthusiasm; components of Flanders' indirectness (use of student ideas, frequent student-student interaction); advance organizers; ratio of divergent to convergent questions; democratic leadership style; confidence; and politeness to students. Brophy and Evertson (1976) argued that variables such as warmth and politeness should be expected to relate more to attitudes than achievement. For other variables (enthusiasm, advance organizers, indirectness), they argued that significant correlations did not appear because the data had been collected in the primary grades, where the following conditions exist: Students tend to be positively oriented toward and accepting of teachers and the curriculum (so that enthusiasm is not of great importance); presentations tend to be short and concentrated on isolated facts (so that advance organizers are less important); and instruction focuses on basic skills rather than use of these skills to deal with more abstract and intellectual content (so that instruction and supervision of practice are more important than teacher use of student ideas or stimulation of student–student discussion). In short, they argued, some of the classroom processes that are frequent and important for learning in the primary grades are infrequent and unimportant in other grades, and vice versa.

Junior High Study. These speculations about grade-level differences were tested in a follow-up study at the junior high level (seventh and eighth grade), using methods similar to those used in the second and third grade study but adapted to include measures of time spent in various activities (Evertson, Anderson, Anderson, & Brophy, 1980; Evertson, Anderson, & Brophy, 1978; Evertson, Emmer, & Brophy, 1980). Thirty-nine English and 29 mathematics teachers were observed an average of 20 times in each of two class sections (total $N = 136$ classes). These included most of the English and mathematics teachers working in 9 of the city's 11 junior high schools (the other two, which happened to be the lowest in average SES level, were excluded because they used individualized mathematics programs that could not be studied with the same methods).

Entry-level achievement was measured by the English and mathematics subtests of the California Achievement Test (CAT), given the previous spring. Achievement during the observation year was measured with specially prepared tests based on the content actually taught in these classes. The CAT scores accounted for 71% of the variance in end-of-year achievement in mathematics, and 85% in English. Students were also asked to rate how likeable and accessible the teachers were, how much they profited from the class, how likely they were to choose this teacher again, and so forth. Factor analysis of these nine ratings produced a strong first factor, which was used as a measure of student attitude. These attitude scores correlated positively (.32) with adjusted achievement in mathematics, but negatively (−.24) in English.

Because data were available on two class sections for each teacher, it was possible to compute correlations reflecting stability of teacher effects across classes within the same year. In mathematics, these correlations were .37 for adjusted achievement and .44 for attitude. When the data for five teachers whose two mathematics sections differed by more than 40 points on the CAT (approximately two grade equivalents) were removed, these correlations rose to .57 for achievement and .57 for attitudes. Thus, the stability of teacher effects on junior high mathematics achievement across class sections within the same year was higher than the stability across successive years observed earlier in the second and third grade study, and stability of effects on attitude was even higher. Also, attitude was correlated positively with achievement.

The data for the English classes were more complex. Here, stability correlations were only .05 for achievement but .82 for attitude. These rose to .29 and .83, respectively, when data from the 13 English teachers with highly contrasting class sections were removed (Emmer, Evertson, & Brophy, 1979). Thus, effects on achievement were not stable, and were correlated negatively with effects on attitudes (attitude effects were highly stable, however). Given that 85% of the variance in adjusted achievement in English was accounted for by CAT scores, there was little reliable variance left to be explained by classroom process measures. The root problem here was that a great range of academic content and activities appeared in these classes, despite their ostensible comparability. Some teachers concentrated on grammar and basic skills, others on reading comprehension or composition, and still others on poetry or drama. This range of activities minimized the degree to which the end-of-year tests could sample from a rich pool of common learning objectives. Thus, despite efforts to avoid this problem by monitoring the content taught, it was not possible to devise a test that would be both valid and discriminating for evaluating achievement in these English classes.

Only two general process–product patterns emerged in English classes: Achievement was greater where serious misbehaviors were uncommon and where teacher praise during class discussions was relatively frequent. There also were some findings that applied only to the classes that were below average in CAT scores. Greater gains were made in these lower-ability classes when the teachers (a) were friendlier and more accepting of students' social initiations and personal requests; and (b) encouraged students to express themselves, even to the extent of tolerating relatively high rates of calling out; but nevertheless (c) were relatively strict disciplinarians. As far as they go, these data from low-ability junior high English classes are similar to the data from low-SES second and third grade classes.

Students in English classes expressed positive attitudes toward teachers rated (by observers) as warm, nurturant, enthusiastic, and oriented to students' personal needs, and who provided more choice and variety in assignments. The students had less positive attitudes toward teachers who were academically demanding, used extensive discussion, asked difficult questions, or criticized or tried to improve unsatisfactory responses. In general, English classes in which the teacher was perceived as "nice" and the class as enjoyable but undemanding produced the most positive attitudes.

In mathematics, there was much more overlap between the processes associated with achievement and those associated with positive attitudes. Classroom organization and instruction variables correlated more strongly with achievement, and measures of teachers' personal qualities correlated higher with student attitudes, but in general, the correlations were in the same direction. The more popular mathematics teachers not only had good relationships with their students but were academically stimulating and demanding.

The more successful mathematics teachers were rated highly as classroom managers, even though behavior problems were observed just as often in their classes as in others. Perhaps they were better at "nipping problems in the bud" by stopping them quickly before they got out of hand. In any case, variables such as monitoring (withitness) and avoidance of target and timing errors were important, especially in the low-ability classes.

Measures of the amount and quality of instruction were even more directly related to achievement in these classes than they were in the second and third grade classes studied earlier. The more successful teachers taught more actively, spending more time lecturing, demonstrating, or leading recitation or discussion lessons. They devoted less time to seatwork, but were more instructionally active during the seatwork time they did have, being more likely to monitor and assist the students rather than leave them to work without supervision.

Concerning teacher questioning, the major difference was quantitative: The more successful teachers asked many more questions. Most of these were product rather than process questions, although in contrast to the findings from the early grades, the percentage of total questions asked that were process questions correlated positively with achievement in these junior high mathematics classes. About 24 questions were asked per 50-minute period in the high-gain classes, and 25% of these were process questions. In contrast, only about 8.5 questions were asked per period in the low-gain classes, and only about 15% of these were process questions.

There were no clear findings for difficulty level of question (as represented by the percentage of questions answered correctly rather than by the distribution of types of questions; process questions are not necessarily harder than product questions). However, student failure to make any response at all (in contrast to responding substantively but incorrectly) correlated negatively with achievement, again indicating the importance of teachers' getting some kind of response to each question asked.

Small-group instruction was virtually absent from these classes, so that the "patterned turns" variable was irrelevant. Most lessons were with the whole class, and response opportunities were usually created by calling on nonvolunteers (45%), calling on volunteers (25%), or accepting call-outs (25%). Of these, calling on volunteers correlated positively with achievement. Calling on nonvolunteers was not particularly harmful, at least when they were following the lesson and likely to know the answer. However, high rates of calling on nonvolunteers who then answered incorrectly were associated negatively with achievement. Similarly, call-outs were not particularly harmful so long as the teacher retained control over participation in the lesson. High call-out rates suggested absence of such control, but many teachers with intermediate rates used call-outs effectively to keep the class moving or to encourage student participation (especially in low-ability classes). Accepting relevant questions or comments called out by the students was associated positively with achievement in the low-ability classes.

Public praise of good answers was low-key and infrequent, but it correlated positively (although weakly) with achievement. Praise during private interactions, criticism of poor answers or poor work, and attempts to improve unsatisfactory responses were all unrelated to achievement. In general, unlike the primary grades where it is essential to take the time to work with individuals during (small group) lessons, in the upper grades it is more important to keep (whole class) lessons moving at a brisk pace.

Use of students' ideas (redirection of their questions to the class and integration of their comments into the discussion) related positively. Thus, except for student–student interaction, key elements of Flanders' concept of indirectness (teacher questions, praise, and use of student ideas) were associated positively with both achievement and attitude in this study. Note, however, that these events occurred within the context of teacher-directed, whole-class instruction on academic content. Furthermore, other positive relationships were observed for emphasis on active instruction (lecture–demonstrations, time spent in the developmental portion of the mathematics lesson). Thus, aspects of what Flanders called "indirect" instruction complement and co-occur with aspects of what others have called "direct" instruction. Both are aspects of what Good (1979) has called "active" instruction, and they contrast not so much with each other as with patterns in which the teacher does not instruct at all or expects the students to learn primarily on their own.

The more successful teachers had more frequent but shorter individualized contacts with students during seatwork times. This probably was because they did not release their students to begin the work until it had been explained thoroughly, so the students needed less reteaching later. Also, these teachers were generally "withit," and one aspect of this is keeping track of the whole class rather than becoming too involved for too long with individuals.

Correlations involving high-inference ratings indicated that the observers saw these successful mathematics classes as follows: Teacher maintains order and commands respect; teacher monitors class and enforces rules consistently; transitions are efficient and disruptions infrequent; teacher appears competent, confident, credible, enthusiastic, receptive to student input, and clear in presentations. Successful teachers were also rated higher on the following items dealing with expectations and academic orientation: academic encouragement, concern for achievement and grades, preparedness, use of available time for academic activities.

Taken together, the data from this study suggest resolutions to certain apparent discrepancies in previous findings. Along with Stallings' data on secondary remedial reading classes, these data from junior high mathematics classes show that linkages between achievement and measures of opportunity to learn, efficient classroom management, and active instruction by the teacher apply to the late elementary and secondary grades as well as to the primary grades, and to classes in all kinds of schools, not just those serving low-SES populations. On the other hand, the limited findings for the English classes remind us that these linkages do not appear for certain learning objectives or when there is poor overlap between what is taught and what is tested. They appear most clearly in studies where the objectives involve knowledge and skills that can be taught specifically and tested by requiring students to reproduce them.

The junior high mathematics data also show how classroom processes and process–product relationships vary with grade level. The primary grades stress instruction in basic skills, and it is important to see that each student participates actively in lessons and gets opportunities to practice and receive feedback. In the higher grades, more time is spent learning subject matter content, and students are more able to learn efficiently from listening to the teachers' presentations or to exchanges between the teacher and other students. There is less need for small-group instruction and for overt involvement of each student. However, it is important that teachers maintain attention to well-prepared and well-paced presentations, and that these presentations be clear and complete enough to enable the students to master key concepts and apply them in follow-up assignments. These grade level differences account for most of the apparent discrepancies in process–product findings. Few such findings are contradictory, but most need qualification by grade level and other context factors.

First Grade Reading Group Study. Brophy and Evertson and their colleagues also completed an experimental study of first grade reading instruction (Anderson, Evertson, & Brophy, 1979), using a small-group instruction model based on their own process–product work and on early childhood education programs developed by Marion Blank (1973) and by the Southwest Educational Development Laboratory (1973). The model was not specific to reading instruction; instead, it was intended for any small-group instruction that called for frequent recitation or performance by students. It consisted of 22 principles for organizing, managing, and instructing the group as a whole, and for providing feedback to individual students' answers to questions. These principles, along with brief explanations, were organized into a manual that provided the basis for the treatment. Early in the school year, each treatment group teacher met with a researcher who described the study and presented the manual. The researcher returned a week later to administer a test of the teacher's mastery of the principles, and to discuss any questions or concerns.

Classes from nine schools serving predominantly middle-class Anglo populations were assigned randomly (by school) to one of three groups (all classes in any given school were in the same group). Treatment-observed ($N = 10$) classes received the treatment and were observed periodically throughout the year. Treatment-unobserved classes ($N = 7$) received the treatment but were not observed. Control classes ($N = 10$) did not receive the treatment but were observed. Inclusion of the treatment-unobserved group allowed for assessment of the possible effects of observer presence on treatment effects, and inclusion of classroom observation in both treatment and control classes allowed for assessment of treatment implementation and process–product relationships in addition to effects on achievement (adjusted for entry-level reading readiness).

From November through April, the 10 treatment-observed classes and 10 control classes were observed about once a week, with emphasis on behaviors relevant to the principles in the model. These principles concerned managing the group efficiently, maintaining everyone's involvement, and providing for sufficient instruction, practice, and feedback for each individual within the group context. The teachers were advised to sit so that they could monitor the rest of the class while teaching the reading group; to begin transitions with a standard signal and lessons with an overview of objectives and a presentation of new words; to prepare the students for new lesson segments and for seatwork assignments; to call on each individual student for overt practice of any concept or skill considered crucial; to avoid choral responses; to apportion reading turns and response opportunities by the patterned turns method rather than by calling on volunteers; to discourage call-outs; to wait for answers; and to try to improve unsatisfactory answers when questions lent themselves to rephrasing or giving of clues.

Praise of good performance was to be used only in moderation, and was to be as specific and individualized as possible. Academic criticism (not mere negative feedback) was to be minimized, but if given, was to include specification of desirable or correct alternatives. If the students were progressing nicely through the lesson as a group, they were to be kept together. If not, the teacher was to dismiss those who had mastered the material and work more intensively with those who needed extra help.

Achievement data indicated that both treatment groups outperformed the control group, and that these treatment effects did not interact with entering readiness levels (class averages). There was no difference between the two treatment groups, indicating that the presence of classroom observers did not affect the results and was not necessary for treatment effectiveness.

The treatment was implemented unevenly. The best-implemented principles were those calling for frequent individualized opportunities for practice, minimal choral responses, use of ordered turns, frequent sustaining feedback, and moderate use of praise. In general, these well-implemented principles also correlated as expected with achievement. Not well implemented were the suggestions about beginning with an overview, repeating new words, giving clear explanations, or breaking up the group. With hindsight, some of these guidelines seem unnecessary or irrelevant to first grade reading group instruction, and others seem unlikely to be implemented without a more powerful treatment.

Process–product data revealed greater achievement gains under the following conditions: More time was spent in reading groups and in active instruction, and less time was spent dealing with misbehavior; transitions were shorter; the teacher sat so as to be able to monitor the class while teaching the small group; lessons were introduced with overviews; new words were presented with attention to relevant phonics cues; lessons included frequent opportunities for individuals to read and to answer questions about the reading; most questions called for response by an individual rather than the group; most responses resulted from ordered turns rather than volunteering or calling out; most incorrect answers were followed by attempts to improve the response through rephrasing the question or giving clues; occasional incorrect answers were followed by detailed process explanations (in effect, reteaching the point at issue); correct answers were followed by new questions about 20% of the time rather than less frequently; and praise of correct responses was infrequent but relatively more specific (although the absolute levels of specificity of praise were remarkably low, even for the treatment teachers). Group call-outs were associated positively with achievement for the lower-ability groups, and negatively for the higher-ability groups. Anderson, Evertson, and Brophy (1982) have revised and reorganized their guidelines for first grade reading-group instruction based on these findings from this study (see Table 12.3). These guidelines summarize the apparent implications of the findings for practice (see Anderson et al., 1979, for detailed presentation of the findings themselves).

Good and Grouws

Good and Grouws and their colleagues also conducted process-outcome research in different settings and then developed and tested a teaching model (in this case, for whole-class instruction in mathematics).

Stability Analyses. The work began with the collection of attitude and achievement data for two consecutive years (1972–3 and 1973–4) for most of the third and fourth grade teachers ($N = 103$) in a predominantly white, suburban school district. Year-to-year stability coefficients for adjusted achievement gain on subtests of the Iowa Tests of Basic Skills administered each fall were statistically significant but low, averaging only about .20 (Good and Grouws, 1975). These teachers did a great deal of formal and informal sharing of students, which may explain why the stability coefficients were lower than those typically obtained from classrooms in which the teachers work with the same students all day in all subjects. Stability coefficients for classroom climate (attitudes toward the teacher and the class) measured each spring were also low (averaging .22), perhaps because attitudes were generally quite positive (so the variance was restricted).

Achievement and attitude measures were uncorrelated. Consequently, the original plan to select teachers who were stable in their effects both on attitudes and on achievement in various subject matter areas had to be abandoned in favor of concentration on a single subject. Good and Grouws selected mathematics, partly because stability coefficients were somewhat higher in this subject. They identified 9 fourth grade teachers who taught mathematics to the same students throughout the year and whose classes were in the top third in adjusted

Table 12.3. Anderson, Evertson, and Brophy's (1982) Revised Principles for Small-Group Instruction in Beginning Reading

General Principles

1. Reading groups should be organized for efficient, sustained focus on the content.
2. All students should be not merely attentive but actively involved in the lesson.
3. The difficulty level of questions and tasks should be easy enough to allow the lesson to move along at a brisk pace and the students to experience consistent success.
4. Students should receive frequent opportunities to read and respond to questions, and should get clear feedback about the correctness of their performance.
5. Skills should be mastered to overlearning, with new ones gradually phased in while old ones are being mastered.
6. Although instruction takes place in the group setting, each individual should be monitored and provided with whatever instruction, feedback, or opportunities to practice that he or she requires.

Specific Principles

Programing for Continuous Progress

1. *Time.* Across the year, reading groups should average 25–30 minutes each. The length will depend on student attention level, which varies with time of year, student ability level, and the skills being taught.
2. *Academic focus.* Successful reading instruction includes not only organization and management of the reading group itself (discussed below), but effective management of the students who are working independently. Provide these students with appropriate assignments; rules and routines to follow when they need help or information (to minimize their needs to interrupt you as you work with your reading group); and activity options available when they finish their work (so they have something else to do).
3. *Pace.* Both progress through the curriculum and pacing within specific activities should be brisk, producing continuous progress achieved with relative ease (small steps, high success rate).
4. *Error rate.* Expect to get correct answers to about 80% of your questions in reading groups. More errors can be expected when students are working on new skills (perhaps 20–30%). Continue with practice and review until smooth, rapid, correct performance is achieved. Review responses should be almost completely (perhaps 95%) correct.

Organizing the Group

5. *Seating.* Arrange seating so that you can both work with the reading group and monitor the rest of the class at the same time.
6. *Transitions.* Teach the students to respond immediately to a signal to move into the reading group (bringing their books or other materials), and to make quick, orderly transitions between activities.
7. *Getting started.* Start lessons quickly once the students are in the group (have your materials prepared beforehand).

Introducing Lessons and Activities

8. *Overviews.* Begin with an overview to provide students with a mental set and help them anticipate what they will be learning.
9. *New words.* When presenting new words, do not merely say the word and move on. Usually, you should show the word and offer phonetic clues to help students learn to decode.
10. *Work assignments.* Be sure that students know what to do and how to do it. Before releasing them to work on activities independently, have them demonstrate how they will accomplish these activities.

Insuring Everyone's Participation

11. *Ask questions.* In addition to having the students read, ask them questions about the words and materials. This helps keep students attentive during classmates' reading turns, and allows you to call their attention to key concepts or meanings.
12. *Order turns.* Use a system, such as going in order around the group, to select students for reading or answering questions. This insures that all students have opportunities to participate, and it simplifies group management by eliminating handwaving and other student attempts to get you to call on them.
13. *Minimize call-outs.* In general, minimize student call-outs and emphasize that students must wait their turns and respect the turns of others. Occasionally, you may want to allow call-outs to pick up the pace or encourage interest, especially with low achievers or students who do not normally volunteer. If so, give clear instructions or devise a signal to indicate that you intend to allow call-outs at these times.
14. *Monitor individuals.* Be sure that everyone, but especially slow students, is checked, receives feedback, and achieves mastery. Ordinarily this will require questioning each individual student, and not relying on choral responses.

Teacher Questions and Student Answers

15. *Focus on academic content.* Concentrate your questions on the academic content; do not overdo questions about personal experiences. Most questions should be about word recognition or sentence or story comprehension.
16. *Use word-attack questions.* Include word-attack questions that require students to decode words or identify sounds within words.
17. *Wait for answers.* In general, wait for an answer if the student is still thinking about the question and may be able to respond. However, do not continue waiting if the student seems lost or is becoming embarrassed, or if you are losing the other students' attention.
18. *Give needed help.* If you think the student cannot respond without help but may be able to reason out the correct answer if you do help, provide help by simplifying the question, rephrasing the question, or giving clues.
19. *Give the answer when necessary.* When the student is unable to respond, give the answer or call on someone else. In general, focus the attention of the group on the answer, and not on the failure to respond.
20. *Explain the answer when necessary.* If the question requires one to develop a response by applying a chain of reasoning or step-by-step problem solving, explain the steps one goes through to arrive at the answer in addition to giving the answer itself.

When the Student Responds Correctly

21. *Acknowledge correctness (unless it is obvious).* Briefly acknowledge the correctness of responses (nod positively, repeat the answer, say "right," etc.), unless it is obvious to the students that their answers are correct (such as during fast-paced drills reviewing old material).
22. *Explain the answer when necessary.* Even after correct answers, feedback that emphasizes the method used to get answers will often be appropriate. Onlookers may need this information to understand why the answer is correct.
23. *Use follow-up questions.* Occasionally, you may want to address one or more follow-up questions to the same student. Such series of related questions can help the student to integrate relevant information. Or you may want to extend a line of questioning to its logical conclusion.

Praise and Criticism

24. *Praise in moderation.* Praise only occasionally (no more than perhaps 10% of correct responses). Frequent praise, especially if nonspecific, is probably less useful than more informative feedback.
25. *Specify what is praised.* When you do praise, specify what is being praised, if this is not obvious to the student and the onlookers.
26. *Use correction, not criticism.* Routinely inform students whenever they respond incorrectly, but in ways that focus on the academic content and include corrective feedback. When it is necessary to criticize (typically only about 1% of the time when students fail to respond correctly), be specific about what is being criticized and about desired alternative behaviors.

achievement in both years, and 9 parallel teachers whose classes were in the lower third in both years. These 18 teachers (and in fact, all fourth grade teachers in the district) used the same textbook.

Fourth Grade Naturalistic Study. The following fall (1974) these 18 teachers were each observed seven times. Mathematics achievement on the Iowa Tests of Basic Skills was measured in the fall and again in the spring. In addition, to protect the anonymity of the 18 "target" teachers, the same process and product data were collected in an additional 23 fourth grade classes. Thus, the data include correlations for the total sample of 41 classes, as well as comparisons of the nine high-scoring teachers' classes with the nine low-scoring teachers' classes. The correlational data will be discussed in a later section in conjunction with data from subsequent research in low-SES classes. For now, let us consider the data from the 18 target teachers. These teachers maintained their relative positions in the third year: Once again, the nine "highs" elicited considerably greater achievement gain than the nine "lows."

All 18 teachers used whole-class instruction followed by seatwork and homework assignments (the teachers who subdivided their classes into groups for differentiated instruction and assignments tended to elicit medium levels of achievement gain, as did some teachers who used the whole-class method). Thus, neither the whole class nor the small groups method was clearly superior. Teachers who got the best results used the whole-class method, but so did teachers who got the worst results. Good and Grouws (1975, 1977) argue that the whole-class method is more efficient for fourth grade mathematics instruction when used effectively, but note that it requires classroom management and instruction skills that many teachers do not possess.

The higher-achieving teachers had better-managed classes even though they had more students. They spent less time in transitions and disciplinary activity, and their students called out more answers, asked more questions, and initiated more private academic contacts with the teachers. Classroom climate ratings and student attitudes were more positive in these classes, even though their emphasis was clearly on academics.

The higher-achieving teachers moved through the curriculum at a brisker pace. They covered an average of 1.13 pages per day, compared to only 0.71 for the low-achieving teachers (Good, Grouws, & Beckerman, 1978). Page coverage correlated .49 with achievement.

Higher-achieving teachers instructed more clearly and introduced more new concepts in the development portions of lessons. The pace was quicker, and less time was spent going over previous assignments. In contrast, the lower-achieving teachers provided less clear instruction, so that by inference, more of their instructional attempts came in the form of corrections of unsatisfactory responses to questions or assignments.

The high-achieving teachers asked fewer questions (probably because they spent less time going over mistakes made on previous assignments). In particular, they asked fewer questions that yielded incorrect answers or failures to respond. When errors or response failures did occur, however, these teachers were twice as likely to give process feedback (explain the steps involved in developing the answer) as they were merely to supply the correct answer. Their lessons moved at a brisker pace,

then, for several reasons. First, they made clearer presentations at the beginning. Second, they "kept the ball moving" by interweaving explanations with questions, rather than relying more heavily on recitation. Third, more of their questions were direct, factual questions likely to produce immediate correct answers. Fourth, when students were confused, these teachers would revert to explanation rather than merely provide correct answers or attempt to elicit them through continued questioning.

During seatwork times, the high-achieving teachers circulated to monitor progress. Yet, they averaged only 3 teacher-initiated work contacts but 23 student-initiated work contacts per hour, compared to averages of 6 and 12, respectively, for the low-achieving teachers. Thus, they concentrated on giving help where it was most needed. Furthermore, their feedback during these private contacts was more likely to involve explanation (not just giving the answer or brief directives).

Good and Grouws (1977) describe the feedback of the high-achieving teachers as immediate, nonevaluative, and task-relevant. These teachers both praised and criticized less than the low-achieving teachers, and their evaluative responses were more contingent on quality of performance (the low-achieving teachers frequently praised students for something other than correct performance).

Summarizing their findings, Good and Grouws (1977) state that the higher-achieving classes showed the following clusters: frequent student initiation of academic interaction; whole-class instruction; clarity of instruction, with availability of information as needed (process feedback in particular); nonevaluative and relaxed, yet task-focused learning environments; higher achievement expectations (faster pace, more homework); and relative freedom from disruption. Even so, the effectiveness of these teachers was not always immediately obvious. Naive observers regularly rated the low-achieving teachers as low, but rated many of the high-achieving teachers as average rather than high. Thus, although low effectiveness is easy to spot because of poor management or lack of much instruction at all, observers may need training in what to look for in order to identify teachers who maximize achievement gain.

Fourth Grade Experimental Study. Good and Grouws (1979b) next conducted a treatment study, still in fourth grade mathematics but this time in urban schools serving primarily low-SES families. The treatment involved a set of instructional principles organized into a model (shown in summary form in Table 12.4) calling for briskly paced whole-class instruction supplemented by homework assignments.

The model prescribes more active whole-class instruction than most teachers deliver (particularly in development portions of lessons), and more frequent reviewing. Less time is allocated for going over homework and less time is spent on seatwork. The emphasis on development and review, and the inclusion of mental computation exercises, were based on previous mathematics education research suggesting that many teachers rely too much on independent seatwork (often without sufficient monitoring, accountability, or follow-up), and that students need more extensive development of concepts, better advance structuring and subsequent follow-up of assignments, and more opportunities to think about and integrate mathematical concepts. Consequently, these elements were added to

Table 12.4 Good and Grouws' (1979) Guidelines for Fourth Grade Mathematics Instruction

Summary of Key Instructional Behaviors

Daily Review (first 8 minutes except Mondays)
a) Review the concepts and skills associated with the homework
b) Collect and deal with homework assignments
c) Ask several mental computation exercises

Development (about 20 minutes)
a) Briefly focus on prerequisite skills and concepts
b) Focus on meaning and promoting student understanding by using lively explanations, demonstrations, process explanations, illustrations, and so forth
c) Assess student comprehension
   1) using process–product questions (active interaction)
   2) using controlled practice
d) Repeat and elaborate on the meaning portion as necessary

Seatwork (about 15 minutes)
a) Provide uninterrupted successful practice
b) Maintain momentum—keep the ball rolling—get everyone involved, then sustain involvement
c) Alert students to the fact that their work will be checked at the end of the period
d) Promote accountability—check the students' work

Homework Assignment
a) Should be assigned on a regular basis at the end of each math class except Fridays
b) Should involve about 15 minutes of work to be done at home
c) Should include one or two review problems

Special Reviews
a) Weekly review (maintenance)
   1) Conduct during the first 20 minutes each Monday
   2) Focus on skills and concepts covered during the previous week
b) Monthly review (maintenance)
   1) Conduct every fourth Monday
   2) Focus on skills and concepts covered since last monthly review

Note. From The Missouri Mathematics Effectiveness Project: An experimental study in fourth-grade classrooms by Thomas L. Good and Douglas A. Grouws, June, 1979, *Journal of Educational Psychology*, pp. 355–362. Copyright 1979, American Psychological Association. Reprinted by permission of the authors.

the model and integrated with elements drawn from the previous process–product study (whole-class approach, brisk pacing, programing for high success rates, active instruction, homework assignments).

Manuals explaining the model were given to the 21 treatment teachers, and were discussed in two 90-minute meetings. The investigators also met with the 19 control teachers, not to give specific guidelines about instruction, but to explain the importance of the study and to heighten their attention to and enthusiasm about their mathematics instruction. This was intended to minimize the degree to which outcomes favoring the treatment group could be attributed to Hawthorne effects associated with participating in an experiment.

From October, 1977, through late January, 1978, each treatment and control teacher was observed six times. Most (19 of 21) treatment teachers implemented most program elements.

The major exception was development, which usually was no more extensive in the treatment than in the control classes. The treatment classes outperformed the control classes both on a standardized mathematics test (SRA, Short-Form E, Blue Level) and on a criterion-referenced test of the content actually taught during the observation period. Student attitude data also favored the treatment classes.

Achievement gains were substantial. In a few months, the treatment group increased from the 27th to the 58th percentile on national norms, and the teachers who had the highest implementation scores produced the best results. The control group's performance did not match that of the treatment group, but it exceeded expectations based on previous years. This improvement may have been due to Hawthorne effects associated with the authors' attempt to develop heightened enthusiasm about mathematics instruction. Interviews revealed that the control teachers had not been exposed to the treatment nor changed their previous teaching behavior in major ways, but that they had thought more about their mathematics instruction. Of these 19 control teachers 12 used the whole-class approach and seven used small groups.

Subsequent analyses (Ebmeier & Good, 1979) indicated that main effects on achievement were elaborated by interactions with teacher (four types) and student (four types) characteristics. For example, the performance of low-achieving and dependent students (especially when taught by certain types of teachers) was particularly enhanced by the treatment, relative to that of higher-achieving and independent students. Also, teachers classified as "unsure" benefited more than those classified as "secure." Thus, the treatment was especially effective with both teachers and students who needed more structure.

Other Treatment Studies. Good and Grouws completed two more treatment studies at Grade 6 (Good & Grouws, 1979a), and at Grades 8 and 9 (Good & Grouws, 1981). In these studies, the treatment included not only the model shown in Table 12.4, but also a supplementary model for teaching verbal problem solving. These studies are not described in detail here because they are highly specific to mathematics instruction (see Romberg & Carpenter, this volume). In general, their effects were positive but weaker than those seen in the Grade 4 treatment study, mostly because treatment implementation was less consistent. This work, on what has been called the "Missouri Math Program," is summarized in *Active Mathematics Teaching* (Good, Grouws, & Ebmeier, 1983).

High-SES Versus Low-SES Comparisons. Good, Ebmeier, and Beckerman (1978) presented data from the fourth grade naturalistic study (Good & Grouws, 1977) and treatment study (Good & Grouws, 1979b) that allow comparisons with the SES difference findings reported by Brophy and Evertson (1974b, 1976), although each data set has unique aspects. The teachers in Good and Grouws's naturalistic study include the 9 consistently high-achieving and 9 consistently low-achieving teachers who used the whole-class approach, plus other teachers who were less consistent and extreme in their effects on achievement (many of whom used the small-group approach). They all taught in suburban schools. The 40 teachers in the experimental study included the 21 who were implementing the treatment model and thus behaving differently than they would have otherwise. They taught in an urban district. The Brophy and Evertson data, in contrast, included teaching in all subject areas (not just mathematics), in second and third grade, in an urban district. The teachers were stable in their effects on achievement, but distributed normally in degree of effectiveness.

Good, Ebmeier, and Beckerman (1978) note that the process–outcome correlations in their studies are generally lower than those involving similar variables from the Brophy and Evertson study. One possible reason is lower reliability of the process measures. The teachers in the two studies described by Good, Ebmeier, and Beckerman were observed for less time, and only during mathematics, so that some behaviors may not have occurred often enough to allow reliable measurement. Also, all of the teachers in the Brophy and Evertson study had demonstrated stability in effects on achievement, and may also have been unusually stable in their classroom behavior. This was true for only 18 of the teachers studied by Good and Grouws. Also, both fourth grade mathematics samples contained a majority of teachers who taught the whole class and a minority who used small groups. It is likely that ostensibly identical classroom process measures actually had different meanings and patterns of correlation with outcomes in these two types of classes.

As an example, consider the data on development portions of lessons. In the naturalistic study, the 9 high-achieving teachers spent somewhat more time in development than the 9 low-achieving teachers did, yet the correlation between development time and achievement for the sample as a whole was −.13. Similarly, although the guidelines for development time were poorly implemented in the treatment study, the correlation between development time and achievement gain here was −.14. Two factors contributed to these anomalous findings. First, the measure of development was quantitative (time). There is no necessary relationship between time spent in development and the quality of that development (clarity, completeness, focus on the right concepts at the right level of detail). Second, the teachers who used small groups were among the highest in development time, because they taught several small-group lessons that each included some introductory lecture-presentation. Much of this was redundant with what was said in their other small-group lessons, but it nevertheless counted as development time. Problems of this sort may have existed with other process measures as well.

Besides showing fewer significant relationships, these fourth grade mathematics data differed from Brophy and Evertson's data in that most relationships held up across the two SES settings. The SES differences that did appear, however, were generally similar to those reported by Brophy and Evertson. Both sets of data indicate that it was especially essential for teachers in low-SES classes to regularly monitor activity, supervise seatwork, and initiate interactions with students who needed help or supervision. Teachers in high-SES classes did not have to be quite so vigilant or initiatory, and could mostly confine themselves to responding to students who indicated a need for help. Positive affect, a relaxed learning climate, and praise of student responses were also more related to achievement in low-SES settings. An academic focus that included frequent lessons involving questioning the students was associated with achievement in both settings, although in low-SES settings it was important that most questions be factual "product" questions rather than more open-ended "process" questions. Similar findings were reported by Soar and Soar (1979).

The only clear contradiction noted by Good, Ebmeier, and Beckerman (1978) involved a set of (mostly nonsignificant) trends indicating that it was more often advisable to try to improve unsatisfactory responses to questions in the high-SES than in the low-SES classes. Brophy and Evertson found the opposite, and suggested that, given the factual nature of most questions in the early grades and the eagerness of most high-SES students to respond, most attempts to improve their response failures would amount to "pointless pumping." It is possible that by fourth grade, and especially in mathematics (a subject that is difficult for many students and lends itself well to rephrasing of questions or provision of clues), it is the bright and eager students who profit most from attempts to improve responses, and the slowest and most anxious students for whom such attempts would be "pointless pumping." In any case, issues concerning when and how teachers should try to improve responses seem unlikely to be resolved until they are attacked with qualitative rather than just quantitative measures.

Beginning Teacher Evaluation Study (BTES)

In 1970, the state of California established a commission to oversee teacher education and certification programs in the state. In 1972, the commission began planning a study to identify teaching competencies that could be used as the basis for evaluating beginning teachers. As planning progressed, however, discussion began to focus more on the need for research linking teacher behavior to student achievement. Eventually, with funding from the National Institute of Education and participation by researchers from the Educational Testing Service and the Far West Regional Laboratory for Educational Research and Development, a series of studies was conducted (Powell, 1980). Although the BTES name was applied to this series collectively, the studies involved experienced rather than beginning teachers, and concentrated on research rather than evaluation.

BTES Phase II: First Field Study. During the period 1973-1974, data were collected in 41 second grade and 54 fifth grade classes. The teachers had at least 3 years of experience, and worked in a variety of school districts. Data were collected on teachers' aptitudes, diagnostic skills, knowledge about subject matter, expectations and preparation for instruction, and teaching behavior, and on students' aptitudes, cognitive styles, expectations, and achievement. Classes were observed using two low-inference systems, one (the "RAMOS" system) focused on the teacher and the nature of the instruction occurring at the time, and the other (the "APPLE" system) focused on the activity of eight target students stratified by sex and achievement level. The RAMOS system was used during reading and mathematics instruction, and the APPLE system throughout the school day. Most teachers were observed four times, two with each system. The data are presented in a five-volume final report (McDonald & Elias, 1976a), in a summary report

(McDonald & Elias, 1976b), and in briefer publications (McDonald, 1976, 1977).

The findings are difficult to summarize and compare with data from related studies for several reasons. First, although sophisticated statistical methods (including multiple regression and path analysis) were used, the reports do not include correlations or other statistics linking each separate process variable to achievement. Instead, each analysis gives information about only a few process variables — those that added significantly to the variance in achievement accounted for by multiple correlations (i.e., those whose partial correlations with adjusted achievement remained significant when the effects of all other predictors were controlled). Second, although it picked up dyadic teacher–student interaction data comparable in some ways to the data developed in the Brophy and Evertson and the Good and Grouws studies, the APPLE system placed the student in the foreground. Detailed information about the teacher's behavior appeared only when the teacher happened to be interacting with a target student when that student was being observed. Third, most of the process variables used in the analyses were combination scores that lumped together different teacher behaviors (for example, time spent disciplining or preparing to instruct was aggregated with time spent actually instructing in a measure of "direct teaching time"). Consequently, the data from Phase II of BTES cannot be compared directly with the work reviewed so far.

Still, certain general trends are familiar. The largest adjusted achievement gains occurred in classes of teachers who were well organized, who maximized the time devoted to instruction and minimized time devoted to preparation, procedure, or discipline, and who spent most of their time actively instructing the students and monitoring their seatwork. Their students were mostly attentive to lessons and engaged in their assignments when working alone. Time spent overtly practicing specific skills (such as word attack in reading or computation in mathematics) was positively correlated with achievement in second grade. By fifth grade, time spent in these basic skills was negatively associated with achievement, but time spent in lessons on applications of these skills (reading comprehension, mathematics problem solving) was positively associated. Positive feedback and praise were positive correlates in second grade reading and fifth grade math. Variety of materials was a positive correlate in second grade reading but a negative correlate in the other three data sets.

Even though general trends could be identified, none of the teacher behavior measures was a significant predictor of achievement for both subject matters (reading, mathematics) at both grade levels (second, fifth). Thus, the data did not support a basic assumption that had led to the BTES in the first place: The notion that there are "generic" teaching skills that are appropriate and desirable in any teaching situation. Most other data also support this conclusion. Although certain abstract principles appear to be universal (e.g., match difficulty level of content to students' present achievement levels), few if any specific, concrete teacher behaviors are "generic" correlates of achievement (see Gage, 1979, on this point).

BTES Phase III-A: Ethnographic Study. During the period 1974–1975, Phase III-A of BTES included ethnographic study of the classes of 20 second grade and 20 fifth grade teachers in the BTES "known sample." This sample had been culled from larger samples of 100 teachers at each grade level, based on data from special 2-week units in reading and mathematics. The 40 teachers in the "known sample" consisted of 10 at each grade level considered to be "more effective" and 10 considered "less effective" on the basis of teacher behavior and student achievement in these special units.

Unlike most research reviewed in this chapter, in which data gathering was focused on previously specified events (usually, ongoing events were coded into categories in low-inference coding systems), this study used the thick-description "ethnographic" method in which observers record free-form, running descriptions of events as they occur (see Erickson, this volume). Heretofore, ethnographic methods have been used mostly in case studies of just one or a small number of classes. In Phase III-A of BTES, however, these methods were used in large enough samples of comparable classrooms to allow the use of inferential statistics.

This process was as follows. First, ethnographers (mostly graduate students in sociology and anthropology) were recruited, familiarized with second and fifth grade classrooms, and trained to write protocols describing reading and mathematics instruction. Then the ethnographers visited the classes for a week at a time, typically observing two more effective and two less effective teachers at the same grade level (the ethnographers were not told how the teachers had been classified). Notes from these observations were then tape-recorded and transcribed, and raters representing different types of expertise studied pairs of protocols (one from a more effective teacher and one from a less effective teacher) and generated dimensions on which the larger set of protocols might be compared. Eventually, 61 such dimensions were identifed and rated in each protocol.

The final data were generated by training new raters to consider pairs of protocols (again, one of each pair was from a more effective teacher and one from a less effective teacher, but raters did not know which was which) and determine which protocol gave more evidence of the behavior described by each of the 61 variables. There were 100 pairings possible at each grade level (each of 10 more effective teachers could be paired with each of 10 less effective teachers). Of these, randomly selected samples of 36 pairings were rated for each subject matter at each grade level. The data are presented in a technical report (Tikunoff, Berliner, & Rist, 1975) and in subsequent publications (Berliner & Tikunoff, 1976, 1977).

In contrast to the BTES Phase II data (on teachers who were not selected on the basis of previously demonstrated effectiveness), these data on the BTES "known sample" yielded many findings that held up across both grade level and subject matter. Twenty-one of the 61 variables yielded significant differences in all four data subsets (second grade reading, fifth grade reading, etc.). All 61 variables showed a significant relationship in at least one subset, and none yielded conflicting relationships (e.g., a significant positive relationship in one subset and a significant negative relationship in another).

Variables showing positive relationships with effectiveness in all four subsets indicated that the more effective teachers enjoyed teaching and were generally polite and pleasant in their daily interactions. They were more likely to call their students by name, attend carefully to what they said, accept their statements of feeling, praise their successes, and involve them in decision making. This pattern of positive teacher behavior was matched by high ratings of cooperation and work engagement on the part of the students, and high ratings of the conviviality of the classroom considered as a whole.

The more effective teachers also were less likely to ignore, belittle, harass, shame, put down, or exclude their students. Their students were less likely to defy or manipulate the teachers. Thus, the more effective classes were characterized by mutual respect, whereas the less effective classes sometimes showed evidence of conflict.

The more effective teachers also made demands on students, however. They encouraged them to work hard and take personal responsibility for academic progress, and they monitored that progress carefully and were consistent in following through on directions and demands. Thus, these teachers were pleasant but also businesslike in their interactions with students.

They were also more knowledgeable about their subject matter and effective in structuring it for the students, pacing movement through the curriculum, individualizing instruction, and adjusting to unexpected events or emergent instructional opportunities. They involved all of their students rather than concentrating on a subgroup, and they were more likely to ask open-ended questions and to wait for them to be answered. If aides or other adults were available, these teachers supplemented their own instruction by involving these extra adults in instructional roles.

The more effective teachers were less likely to make management errors such as switching abruptly back and forth between instruction and behavior management, making illogical statements, treating the whole group as one in order to maintain control, and calling attention to themselves for no apparent reason. Finally, they were less likely to kill time with busywork instead of initiating more profitable activities. Taken together, these data indicate that the more effective teachers were more committed to instructing their students in the subject matter, and more knowledgeable, active, and demanding in doing so. They were also better able to match the pace of instruction to the group's needs, and to respond to unforeseen events and to the needs of individuals. These academic skills were supported by classroom management skills and positive personal characteristics that engendered student attention, task engagement, and general cooperation, resulting in a generally convivial classroom atmosphere.

Several relationships appeared for one grade only (in both subject areas). Teacher and student mobility was greater in the more effective second grade classrooms. Most likely, this is related to findings reported by others that achievement is lower in classes where students spend a great deal of time working without teacher supervision. The variance in mobility is reduced by fifth grade, when most small-group instruction has been phased out. Several variables were negatively associated with effectiveness only at second grade: expressing distrust of students, publicly verbalizing performance expectations, moralizing, policing, rushing students to answer or finish their work, and overconcern about doing things by the clock. Most of these variables would be expected to correlate negatively with effectiveness measures whenever they did correlate significantly. Use of nonverbal signals to establish control was negatively related to effectiveness in fifth grade. This relationship was not expected, because Kounin (1970) and others have established that nonintrusive control techniques such as nonverbal signaling are usually preferable to more salient techniques that interrupt the flow of instruction. However, the measure recorded the frequency rather than the effectiveness with which such techniques were used, and high frequencies of control attempts suggest deficiencies in more fundamental management skills such as "withitness" or maintaining signal continuity.

There were two subject matter differences. Teacher concern about being liked (carried to the extent of trying to ingratiate oneself with students at the expense of instruction) was negatively associated with effectiveness only in mathematics. The reading data were in the same direction, however, and approached significance. Teacher attempts to dispense information and develop positive attitudes about different cultures were positively associated with effectiveness in reading but uncorrelated in mathematics, where there are fewer opportunities to relate the content to cultural differences.

The remaining variables had weaker relationships with effectiveness. Positive relationships were seen for exercising control by praising desirable behavior, defending students from assault, acting as a model, openly admitting mistakes or negative emotions, allowing students to teach one another, and using teacher-made materials. Negative relationships were seen for emphasizing competition, using drill activities, differentiating students on the basis of sex, and stereotyping according to SES, race, or ethnicity. None of these findings is surprising except the negative relationship for drill activities, which other investigators sometimes find positively associated with achievement.

The BTES ethnographic data both replicate the major findings from studies using low-inference coding and extend those findings in important ways. One major extension is into the affective area. Perhaps better than any others, these data show that academically effective teachers can also be warm, student oriented individuals who develop a generally positive classroom atmosphere and not merely an efficient learning environment. Concerning instruction, the data indicate the importance of pacing at a rate appropriate to the group, and within this, of responding to the needs of individuals. The following study addressed these instructional issues more specifically.

BTES Phase III-B: Second Field Study. During the period 1976–1977, another field study was done in 25 second grade and 21 fifth grade classes selected because they contained at least six "target students" (usually three boys and three girls) whose entry-level mathematics and reading scores fell between the 30th and 60th percentiles of the distributions of scores from larger samples of 50 classrooms at each grade level. The result was a racially and ethnically mixed sample weighted toward the lower half of the SES distribution. Except for their willingness to volunteer, the teachers in this study were not preselected, and nothing was known about their relative effectiveness.

Student achievement and attitudes were measured in October, December, and May. The teachers were interviewed at length in the fall and spring, and briefly each week in between. They also kept daily logs. These data were used to assess the teachers' "planning functions" of diagnosis (ability to predict the degree of difficulty that students would experience with particular content) and prescription (allocations of time to various content categories).

Classes were observed for one entire day each week for 20 weeks. Each of the six target students was coded every 4 minutes for the content being taught, level of attention or task engagement, and apparent level of success (high, moderate, or low). If the teacher happened to be interacting with the student, the teacher's behavior was coded for three "instructional interaction functions" divided into seven categories: presentation (planned explanation of content, unplanned explanation of content, or provision of structuring or directions for tasks), monitoring (observing or questioning the students), and feedback (feedback about academic responses or feedback designed to control attention or task engagement). The data are discussed in technical reports (Berliner, Fisher, Filby, & Marliave, 1978; Fisher et al., 1978), as well as in a chapter (Fisher et al., 1980) included in a larger volume (Denham & Lieberman, 1980) on the BTES Phase III-B findings and their potential policy implications.

Across all classes, only about 58% of the school day was allocated to academics (reading, mathematics, science, social studies), with 24% allocated to nonacademic activities (music, art, story time, sharing), and 18% to noninstructional activities (transitions, waiting, class business). Of the time allocated to academics, students averaged 70–75% actually engaged in academic tasks. They were directly supervised by the teacher only about 30% of the time, spending the other 70% in independent seatwork.

Achievement was associated with the amount of time that students were exposed to academic content (allocated time), the percentage of this time that they actually spent engaged in academic activities (engaged time), and the degree to which they were able to respond to these activities successfully (success rate). Thus, not just the quantity but the quality of student engaged time on task was associated with achievement.

As with the Brophy and Evertson (1974b) data, the findings on success rate varied with context and suggested that different success rates are optimal for different activities and types of student. For the sample as a whole, success rates for individual students averaged almost 50% high success (completely correct work except for occasional, chance-level errors due to carelessness), almost 50% medium success (student has general understanding of the task but makes errors at above a chance rate), and only 0–5% low success (student does not understand the task and is able to make correct responses at only a chance rate). Fifth grade math classes were somewhat more difficult, averaging only about 35% high success rates. Analyses at the individual student level regularly showed negative relationships with achievement for low success rates, and usually showed negative relationships for medium success rates and positive relationships for high success rates. Given the frequencies with which the three success rates were observed, these data imply that high achievement was associated, on the average, with a success rate mixture that approximated 65–75% high success, 25–35% medium success and 0% low success. Either or both of the following causes could explain this association between achievement and a primarily high success rate: High achievers

simply make fewer errors than low achievers (student ability effect), or some teachers are better than others at matching instruction and academic tasks to their students' current needs (teacher diagnosis/prescription effect).

Later analyses of these success rate data aggregated to the level of class means (i.e., using the teacher rather than the student as the unit of analysis) suggested that high achievement was associated more with moderate than with high success rates (Burstein, 1980). Here again, however, patterns of relationship varied by context (grade level, subject matter), and interpretation is complicated by the likelihood that teachers whose classes had the highest averages of "high success" time were those who relied most heavily on seatwork and provided less active group instruction to their students.

Taken together, the data suggest that a mixture of high and moderate success rates, with little or no time spent in low-success activities, was optimal. High success rates appeared to be important for younger students (second grade) and for students who had difficulty handling the work. Somewhat more challenge (i.e., moderate success rates) was appropriate for older students (fifth grade).

The BTES authors combined allocated time, engaged time, and success rate into the concept of academic learning time (ALT), which they defined as the time students spent engaged in academic tasks that they could perform with high success. ALT consistently showed significant positive correlations with achievement, and positive but not significant correlations with attitude. Thus, these data fit well with other data indicating that high achievement is associated with an instructional pace that is brisk but characterized by gradual movement through small steps with consistent (although not necessarily easy) success, and that a strong academic focus can be achieved without negative effects on student attitudes.

Other positive correlates of achievement included accuracy of diagnosis (ability to predict the difficulty that students would have with particular items), appropriate prescription of tasks (success rates were usually high or moderate, seldom low), frequent provision of academic feedback, emphasis on academic (rather than affective) goals, and student responsibility for academic work and cooperation with academic tasks. Reprimands for misbehavior correlated negatively. Thus, classroom organization and management skills and the teaching functions of diagnosis, prescription, and feedback were linked to achievement gain.

Variables connected with the teaching functions of presentation and monitoring did not correlate significantly with achievement, but did correlate with aspects of ALT. In particular, high success rates were associated positively with frequent teacher structuring of lessons and giving of directions for task procedures, and negatively with explanations given specifically in response to expressed need. Thus, success rates were higher when teachers gave more instruction "up front," before releasing students to work on assignments, and less in the form of help for students who had begun assignments but become confused.

Student engagement rates were associated positively with time spent in "substantive" interaction—when the teacher was giving information about academic content, monitoring work, or giving feedback. Engagement rates were especially low when students spent two-thirds or more of their time working alone. Teachers who stressed academics produced the most achievement, and teachers who stressed affective objectives produced the least. The latter teachers not only allocated less time to academics, but showed signs of poor diagnosis and prescription skills. Their classes were more likely to be given tasks that produced low success rates and (therefore?) to show lower task engagement rates. Teachers committed to both academic and affective objectives produced intermediate levels of achievement. Here again we see that although a strong academic focus can be compatible with positive student attitudes, different objectives ultimately begin to conflict when time allocated in the service of one comes at the expense of time that could be allocated in the service of another.

The BTES Phase III-B data also point up the tension that exists between attempts to maximize student engagement and attempts to maximize success rate. Engagement is generally higher during activities conducted by the teacher than during independent seatwork time. However, group activities expose everyone to the same content, and eventually result in moving too slowly for the brightest students but too quickly for the slowest. Differentiated seatwork assignments respond to this problem by making it possible for all students to achieve at high success rates, but require more teacher preparation and more complex classroom management, result in lower engagement rates despite the increased success rates, and tend to increase the differences between the highest and the lowest achievers in the class. These and other dilemmas raised by BTES Phase III-B data are discussed in the Denham and Lieberman (1980) volume.

Major contributions of this study are the ALT concept and the demonstration of great variance in allocated time, engaged time, and success rates. Across a school year, some second grade classes receive an average of 15 minutes of mathematics instruction per day, while others average 50 minutes. Whatever the allocated time, some classes are attentive to lessons or engaged in tasks only about 50% of the time, but others average 90%. Finally, some classes frequently are left to struggle with tasks that are beyond their present abilities, while others rarely are required to endure low success rates, frequently enjoy high success rates, and typically receive sufficient teacher structuring, monitoring, and feedback to enable them to cope effectively with challenging tasks that produce moderate success rates.

Stanford Studies

Throughout the past two decades, N. L. Gage and his students and colleagues at Stanford University have been conducting process-product research, especially experimental studies. In the mid 1960s, a series of dissertations (reviewed by Rosenshine, 1968) was designed to study the clarity and effectiveness of teachers' presentations. In each study, teachers were given identical material to teach (suited in difficulty level to their students, but not taught as part of the regular curriculum), and asked to present the material during brief (typically 10 minute) time periods. Lessons were videotaped for later analysis, and achievement was assessed with criterion-referenced test scores adjusted for ability.

Fortune (1967) studied student teachers working in Grades 4, 5 or 6 in English, mathematics, or social studies. High-inference ratings of teachers' skill in presenting the lesson significantly discriminated between higher- and lower-achieving teachers in all three subject areas. In addition, five low-inference measures of specific teacher behaviors discriminated in two areas, indicating that the higher-achieving teachers more frequently (a) introduced the material using an overview or analogy; (b) used review and repetition; (c) praised or repeated pupil answers; (d) were patient in waiting for responses to questions; and (e) integrated such responses into the lesson.

Two other studies used videotapes of experienced 12th grade social studies teachers' lectures on Thailand and Yugoslavia. One of these, by Rosenshine (described in Gage et al., 1968) involved counting the frequencies of various syntactic, linguistic, and gestural events in the teachers' behavior. Analyses of these codes revealed that the higher-achieving teachers used more gestures and movements, more rule–example–rule patterns of discourse, and more explaining links. In the rule–example–rule pattern, the teacher first presents a general rule, then a series of examples, and finally a restatement of the general rule. This contrasts with patterns in which teachers either never state the rule or state it only once rather than giving it both before and after the examples. Explaining links are words that denote cause, means, or purpose: because, in order to, if-then, therefore, consequently, and so forth. By making explicit the relationship between two ideas or events, teachers help insure that students remember the relationship and not merely the ideas or events themselves.

Hiller, Fisher, and Kaess (1969), using transcripts from these same twelfth grade social studies lectures, found that achievement was associated positively with verbal fluency and negatively with vagueness. Vagueness indicators included ambiguous designation (all of this, somewhere), negated intensifiers (not many, not very), approximation (almost, pretty much), "bluffing" and recovery (anyway, of course), error admission (excuse me, not sure), indeterminate qualification (some, a few), multiplicity (sorts, factors), possibility (may, could be), and probability (sometimes, often).

Structuring, Soliciting, and Reacting. Clark et al. (1979) conducted an experiment in which each of four teachers was trained to teach a nine-lesson ecology unit in eight different ways to eight different randomly assigned groups of sixth graders. The eight different lessons were developed by factorially varying two levels of structuring, two levels of soliciting, and two levels of reacting. High structuring involved reviewing the main ideas and facts covered in the lesson; stating objectives at the beginning; outlining lesson content; signaling transitions between lesson parts; indicating important points; and summarizing parts of lessons as the lessons proceeded. Low structuring involved the absence of these teaching behaviors.

High soliciting was defined as asking approximately 60% higher-order questions and 40% lower-order questions, and waiting at least 3 seconds for a response after asking a question. Low soliciting involved asking about 15% higher-order questions and 85% lower-order questions, and calling on a second student to respond if the first did not do so within 3 seconds. Higher-order questions were defined as those requiring mental processes beyond the knowledge level as defined in the *Taxonomy of Educational Objectives* (Bloom, Engelhart, Furst, Hill, & Krathwohl, 1956).

High reacting involved praising correct responses; negating incorrect responses and giving the reason for the incorrectness; prompting by providing hints when responses were incorrect or incomplete; and writing correct responses on the board. Low reacting consisted of giving neutral feedback following correct responses; negating incorrect responses but not giving the reason for the incorrectness; and probing or repeating questions following incomplete or incorrect responses, but without giving hints or clues. In all cases, questions were redirected to a second student if probing failed to elicit the correct response from the first, and the correct answer was given if neither probing nor redirecting succeeded in eliciting it.

Teachers were provided with lesson scripts exemplifying each mixture of instructional components (such as high structuring, low soliciting, and high reacting). Observation indicated that the teachers taught each series of lessons as prescribed, and that the lessons did not appear notably different from typical lessons in these classes.

Students were pretested for general abilities and for specific knowledge of the content taught in the unit, and were posttested both immediately after the unit and again three weeks later. Testing included attitude measures, an essay test, and a multiple choice test which yielded subscores for higher- versus lower-order knowledge items and for items that the students could have learned only from the teacher, versus from either the teacher or the text. As expected, the treatments showed greater effects on items that had to be learned from the teacher and on lower-level knowledge items.

The immediate posttest data showed no effects on the student attitude measure or the essay test. Low soliciting was associated with high scores on both low-level and high-level items learnable from the teacher only, and low-level items learnable from either the teacher or the text. In addition to these main effects for low soliciting, there were significant interactions indicating that the combination of low structuring with low reacting yielded low achievement on higher-order items learnable only from the teacher and on lower-order items learnable from either the text or the teacher. Finally, a nonsignificant trend suggested that high structuring was associated with high achievement on the lower-order items learnable only from the teacher.

Data from the retention tests three weeks later were similar. Once again there was no effect on attitude. There was one significant effect for the essay test, however, indicating that high scores were associated with high reacting. In addition, scores for lower-order multiple choice items learnable only from the teacher were associated with high structuring, low soliciting, and high reacting. Also, interaction effects again indicated that the combination of low structuring with low reacting was particularly dysfunctional.

In general, these data support other findings indicating the importance of teachers' structuring the content through clear presentations, providing feedback to student responses, and attempting to improve responses that are incomplete or incorrect, and indicating that a predominance of lower-order questions is associated with high achievement gain, even on items dealing with higher-order content.

Program on Teaching Effectiveness. More recently, Gage and his colleagues in the "Program on Teaching Effectiveness" at Stanford have conducted two additional studies involving training teachers to implement 22 principles suggested by 81 findings reported by others. Approximately 50% of these findings were drawn from Brophy and Evertson (1974a, 1974b), 31% from Stallings and Kaskowitz (1974), 15% from McDonald and Elias (1976a), and 4% from Soar (1973). Some were intended for use with all students, but others were targeted for students described as either "more academically oriented" (high achieving, well motivated) or "less academically oriented" (low achieving, possibly anxious or uncooperative).

Third grade teachers working in middle-SES schools were first stratified according to mean academic achievement of their students, and then randomly assigned to three groups: observation only ($N = 10$), minimal training plus observation ($N = 11$), or maximal training plus observation ($N = 12$). Minimally trained teachers were merely mailed packets discussing the principles (one packet per week for 5 weeks). Maximally trained teachers received the packets at the same rate, but also participated in a 2-hour meeting each week to discuss the recommendations. Classes in all three groups were observed for 4 full days prior to the treatment, another 4 or 5 days during November and December after the teachers received the packets, and another 7 days between January and May. Analyses indicated that about half of the training components were implemented successfully and that the means for the experimental groups typically were nearer to the prescribed guidelines than the means for the control group. Unexpectedly, the minimal-training group implemented the guidelines somewhat better than the maximal-training group.

Adjusted achievement in vocabulary for the combined treatment groups exceeded that of the control group by .69 standard deviation units, which approached but did not reach statistical significance ($p < .15$). There was no comparable effect on reading comprehension. Process–product correlations based on the total sample of 33 teachers supported the findings reported in earlier studies only about half of the time. Much of this agreement was with Brophy and Evertson's findings for high-SES students comparable to those included in the present study (Crawford et al., 1978). Thus, once again we see the need to consider student SES in interpreting process–product data from the early grades, particularly data on reading instruction.

A variation of this experiment was repeated in a subsequent study of 28 classes in Grades 4–6 in a school serving a low-SES, predominantly black population (Gage & Coladarci, 1980). All teachers experienced "minimal" training (receiving one packet per week for 5 weeks, by mail) but without any personal contact with the experimenters. Classrooms were also observed, but only for two 2-hour observations before and again after the treatment. This time, implementation was poor: The training-related behaviors of the 15 experimental teachers were not altered appreciably by the treatment, and did not differ significantly from those of the 13 control teachers. Nor did the achievement of treatment classes exceed that of control classes.

Despite this lack of treatment effect, process–product data based on the total sample of 28 classes indicated that the teacher behaviors (particularly those related to classroom management and time spent in academic activities) called for in the guidelines were correlated with achievement, as expected. These relationships were strongest in the fourth grade and weakest in the sixth grade, which was to be expected because the guidelines were based on data from the primary grades. Phonics instruction, which typically correlates positively with reading achievement in the early grades, correlated negatively in these middle grades.

Clarity Studies

The work of Rosenshine (1968) and of Hiller et al. (1969) on clarity of teacher presentations has been elaborated in recent years. Issues of definition and measurement have been discussed by McCaleb and White (1980), Cruickshank, Kennedy, Bush, and Myers (1979) and Kennedy, Cruickshank, Bush, and Myers (1978). In addition, M. L. Land and L. R. Smith and their colleagues have contributed a dozen individual studies and reviews (summarized in Smith & Land, 1981) concerning relationships between low-inference measures of teacher clarity and achievement. Most of these have been conducted with college students as subjects, although junior high and high school studies have been included. Typically, groups of students are randomly assigned to listen to and then take a test on an audio-taped lesson. Different versions of the lesson are prepared by varying the presence of elements that detract from clarity. The most commonly studied of these are the "vagueness terms" described by Hiller et al. (1969). Smith and Land (1981) report that adding vagueness terms to otherwise identical presentations reduced student achievement in all 10 of the studies in which vagueness was manipulated. Vagueness terms are italicized in the following excerpt:

> This mathematics lesson *might* enable you to understand a *little more* about *some things* we *usually* call number patterns. *Maybe* before we get to *probably* the main idea of the lesson, you should review *a few* prerequisite concepts. *Actually*, the first concept you need to review is positive integers. *As you know*, a positive integer is any whole number greater than zero.

Clarity can also be reduced by "mazes," which are false starts or halts in speech, redundantly spoken words, or tangles of words. Inclusion of mazes in presentations reduced achievement in three of four studies. Mazes are italicized in the following excerpt, as reported by Smith & Land (1981):

> This mathematics lesson *will enab…*will get you to understand *number, uh,* number patterns. Before we get to the *main idea of the,* main idea of the lesson, you need to review *four conc…* four prerequisite concepts. The first *idea, I mean, uh,* concept you need to review is positive integers. A positive *number…* integer is any whole *integer, uh,* number greater than zero. (p. 38)

A third element that can detract from clarity is discontinuity, in which the teacher interrupts the flow of the lesson by interjecting irrelevant content or by mentioning relevant content at inappropriate times. Kounin (1970) included such discontinuities among reasons for loss of lesson momentum. More recently, Land and Smith (1979) found that extra content interjected into presentations did not affect achievement, but Smith and Cotten (1980) found that interjected discontinuities signifi-

cantly reduced achievement. The latter study involved more drastic changes from the original clear presentation, which probably accounts for the difference in results.

A fourth detractor from clarity is saying "uh." This had a negative but nonsignificant relationship with achievement in the one study in which it was investigated in its own right (Smith, 1977). It also has been included along with the other three detractors (vagueness terms, mazes, and extra content) in studies that used a cluster of six variables to create high- and low-clarity treatments. Two positive elements in these clusters were emphasis on key aspects of the content to be learned and clear signaling of transitions between parts of lessons. Lessons constructed to maximize clarity by including these positive elements and avoiding the detractors discussed above typically produce greater achievement than less clear lessons (Land, 1979).

Other aspects of clarity, such as structuring and sequencing the content and explaining it understandably (see McCaleb & White, 1980) have been addressed by other researchers (even though not all of them use the term "clarity" in describing their data). In general, clarity of presentation is one of the more consistent correlates of achievement, at least in studies where exposure to the content to be tested is controlled.

Additional Studies

We have reviewed the programmatic work of several teams of investigators. Before initiating integrative discussion, we conclude the review with brief summaries of additional studies that meet the inclusion criteria stated at the beginning of the chapter.

Correlational Studies

Several correlational studies linked achievement to opportunity to learn the content included on tests. Content coverage was measured directly by asking teachers to state whether or not (or how much) they covered specified content (Borg, 1979; Chang & Raths, 1971; Comber & Keeves, 1973; Harris & Serwer, 1966; Husen, 1967), by coding the content relevance of classroom activities and questions (Smith, 1979), or by doing both (Cooley & Leinhardt, 1980). Other studies documented the same relationship indirectly by relating achievement to the percentages of time spent in academic activities rather than procedural or disciplinary interactions (Dalton & Willcocks, 1983; Emmer, Evertson, & Anderson, 1980; Evertson & Emmer, 1982; Fitz-Gibbon & Clark, 1982; Galton & Simon, 1980; Rose & Medway, 1981).

These "opportunity to learn" findings are sometimes also described as "time allocation" or "time-on-task" findings. The latter terms are less desirable because they are less accurate and specific (Borg, 1980). Furthermore, they require at least three qualifications. First, the data indicate the need to consider the quality of academic activities, and not just the time spent on them. Fisher et al. (1980) elaborate this point in discussing the BTES Phase III-B data. Second, the time-on-task that is linked most closely to achievement is time spent in teacher-directed lessons or in seatwork actively supervised by the teacher. Large amounts of time spent working without supervision are associated with low achievement gain. Finally, although measures of time allocation to academic activities (and especially, measures of time spent actually engaged in those activities) typically correlate positively with achievement (Borg, 1980), these relationships are typically only weak to moderate (Fitz-Gibbon & Clark, 1982; Karweit, 1983), and they vary according to the definition and measurement of time on task (Karweit & Slavin, 1982). Thus, efforts to determine the implications of research on teacher effects should concentrate on issues of opportunity to learn and quality of instruction. Time-on-task does not translate into achievement in any simple or direct way (Brophy, 1979; Karweit, 1983; Wyne & Stuck, 1982).

Arehart. Arehart (1979) studied 23 teachers who taught a 3-period probability unit to 26 classes in grades 8–11. All teachers taught to the same objectives using the same content outline and problem exercises, but were free to teach in their own way. Achievement correlates included content coverage by the teacher, percentage of assigned problems that were attempted by the students, and percentages of total interaction that were classified as "substantive," as teacher informing, and as teacher questioning. There was no significant relationship for pupil initiations. In general, percentage measures correlated more strongly than frequency measures, and teacher-informing measures more strongly than teacher-questioning measures. Teacher informing did not necessarily mean extended lecturing, however. More typically, it involved giving information for a minute or less and then asking a question.

Armento. Armento (1977) studied 20 preservice and 2 in-service teachers who delivered social studies lessons to students in Grades 3–5. High-inference correlates of achievement included ratings of accuracy of examples, relevance of teacher behavior to learning objectives, balance between concrete and abstract terminology, and expression of interest and enthusiasm. Low-inference correlates included giving definitions, examples, and labels for concepts, summarizing or reviewing main ideas, and general adequacy of content coverage. No significant relationships appeared for signaling changes in topic, asking questions (either lower order or higher order), repeating or rephrasing questions, asking questions in pairs, or telling students to stop irrelevant behavior.

Boak and Conklin. Boak and Conklin (1975) studied 10 mathematics teachers in Grades 7–9 and 20 language arts teachers in Grades 7 and 8. The teachers were classified as either high or low in interpersonal skills based on ratings of empathy, respect, and genuineness developed from audiotaped lesson segments, and on ratings of empathy based on their written responses to vignettes depicting student concerns. These classifications were then related to achievement gain. There was no relationship in the Grade 7 language arts classes, but the students of the higher-rated teachers made greater gains in reading comprehension in the eighth grade language arts classes, and in mathematics in the mathematics classes. Although the teacher classifications in this study were not based solely on observation of classroom behavior, the data suggest that the interpersonal skills stressed by Aspy (1969, 1972), Carkhuff (1969,

1971), and others may correlate with achievement in addition to affective outcomes.

Coker, Medley, and Soar. Coker, Medley, and Soar (1980) reported process–product data from 100 classes in Grades 1–12, 59 studied the first year and 41 the second year. The findings are difficult to evaluate because they are reported only for the sample as a whole rather than separately by grade levels, and because the process measures are combination scores that include data from both academic and nonacademic activities. Still, a few general trends are discernible in the correlations that were significant in both years. Positive correlates of achievement included selecting appropriate goals and objectives for students, involving the students in organizing and planning, giving clear, explicit directions, and listening to students and respecting their rights to speak during recitations and discussions. Negative correlates included poor classroom management, over-emphasis on praise and rewards (probably also related to poor classroom management), overemphasis on eliciting and responding to student questions (perhaps reflecting insufficient or ineffective presentation of information by the teacher), and overemphasis on student input into decision making. The latter findings seem reminiscent of the BTES Phase III findings suggesting that teachers who concentrated either on affective objectives or on ingratiating themselves with their students produced less achievement than teachers who concentrated on cognitive objectives.

Crawford. Crawford (1983) studied instruction in 79 Grade 1–8 special compensatory education classes for Title I students. These classes were small (5–10 students), intended to remediate weaknesses in basic reading and mathematics skills, and taught by specially trained teachers assisted by paraprofessional aides. Across grade level and subject matter, achievement gain was associated with allocation of high percentages of available time to academic activities, good monitoring and other classroom management techniques that maximized task engagement and minimized interruptions and transition time, and active instruction of the students. Much of this instruction was accomplished through interactions with individuals in teaching reading in the early grades, but instruction usually occurred with groups in upper grade reading classes and in mathematics classes at all grade levels. Success in the early grades (in both subject areas) was also associated with academic demandingness in the form of challenging assignments and frequent attempts to improve initially unsatisfactory answers to questions. The findings that primary grade reading achievement was associated with challenging assignments and with individualized instruction rather than group lessons contrast with most other findings for low-SES or low-ability students in these grades. They indicate that methods that are impractical in ordinary classes can be used effectively in special classes with small student–teacher ratios. In particular, teachers can move students through curricula at a faster pace, can provide more tutorial and individualized instruction, and can assign more difficult seatwork when the number of students in the class is small enough to allow them to monitor everyone's progress consistently and provide help when needed.

Dunkin. Dunkin (1978) studied 29 sixth grade teachers asked to teach 30-minute discussion lessons in social studies. Achievement correlates included content coverage; structuring (number of teacher structuring moves as defined by Bellack, Hyman, Smith, & Kliebard, 1966); percentage of total academic questions that were higher order (the average was only 25%); number of relevant pupil responses to teacher questions; and percentage of teacher reactions to student responses that were positive (praise) reactions (these averaged 16%). In addition, there was a nonsignificant negative trend for frequency of teacher vagueness terms.

Dunkin and Doenau. Dunkin and Doenau (1980) studied most of the same teachers studied earlier by Dunkin (1978), this time teaching two additional social studies lessons ($N = 28$ for Lesson 1, 26 for Lesson 2). Achievement correlates in both lessons included the following: content coverage through teacher informing statements; content coverage through teacher–student interaction; and total content coverage. Several variables correlated significantly in one lesson but not the other. Of these, positive correlates included total content repetition, percentage of total student words that were classified as vague, asking multiple secondary questions, student initiations that were not questions, student responses that were rejected, and long student utterances. Negative correlates for one lesson only were these: percentage of informing elements that were terminal rather than initial or intervening; percentage of total questions that were higher order (in this case, the average was 36%); frequency of student-initiated questions; frequency of positive reactions to student responses; and total teacher reactions to student responses. There was a nonsignificant negative trend for teacher vagueness in each lesson. Of the variables considered by Dunkin (1978) and by Dunkin and Doenau (1980), consistent relationships with achievement were found only for content covered and (less strongly) for teacher vagueness. Variables connected with teacher structuring, soliciting, and reacting or with types of pupil participation did not yield consistent patterns.

Larrivee and Algina. Larrivee and Algina (1983) observed in 118 elementary grade (K–6) classes that each contained a special education student who was being mainstreamed and would be present during reading and language arts instruction (most of these mainstreamed students were classified as learning disabled). Classrooms were observed four times with each of four instruments, concentrating on the mainstreamed student and certain other target students. The mainstreamed students' reading achievement was associated positively with higher ratings of teachers for efficient use of time, good relationships with students, supportive response to low-ability students, and high frequency of positive feedback to student performance. Negative correlates included the frequency of interventions concerning misconduct, time spent off-task, and time spent in transitions. Variables that correlated with academic learning time, although not significantly with reading achievement, included the frequency of easy questions, correct student responses, and attempts to improve incorrect responses. In general, these data on achievement correlates for mainstreamed special students parallel the findings for low-SES and low-achieving students in other elementary grade studies.

McConnell. McConnell (1977) related high-inference measures of teacher behavior to student attitude and achievement in 43 ninth grade algebra classes. Positive attitudes were associated with teacher clarity, enthusiasm, and task orientation. Low attitudes were most likely in classes that emphasized analysis (such classes were seen as harder and duller; perhaps the teachers were generally low on clarity and enthusiasm). Achievement in both computation and comprehension was correlated with teacher task orientation. Achievement in comprehension was also correlated with clarity, and achievement in analysis (the most abstract measure) was correlated with probing, enthusiasm, and teacher talk.

Solomon and Kendall. Solomon and Kendall (1979) studied 50 fourth grade classes in relatively affluent schools. They focused on interactions between teacher types and student types, and reported most data in terms of combination scores. However, they noted a main effect indicating that classes rated as controlled and orderly showed greater achievement than less controlled or disorganized classes. Interaction effects indicated that low-SES students did best in warm, encouraging classrooms, but high-SES students did best in more impersonal and academically demanding classrooms. Also, students who preferred autonomy generally did better in the more controlled classes, whereas those who preferred structure generally did better in the more permissive classes (differences between what is preferred and what maximizes achievement have also been reported by others; see Clark, 1982). Other data revealed additional interaction effects and contrasts between what correlated with achievement and what correlated with other outcomes (attitudes, motivation, creativity).

Experimental Studies

Alexander, Frankiewicz, and Williams. Alexander, Frankiewicz, and Williams (1979) studied five variations of social studies lessons taught to Grade 5–7 students. Control students were taught for 50 minutes without the use of organizers as described by Ausubel (1968). In the four experimental treatments, 10 of the 50 minutes were allocated to presentation of superordinate concepts under which the more specific material could be subsumed. In various treatments, the organizers were either visual (photographic slides) or oral–interactive (presentation followed by structured discussion), and were placed either before or after the rest of the lesson. All four organizer groups retained more content than the control group, but no organizer group differed significantly from any of the others. Most tests of Ausubel's ideas about organizers have involved advance organizers included in written materials prepared for independent study by high school or college students. The present study has shown that organizers designed to help students structure their learning can facilitate achievement even at the elementary level; take visual or oral–interactive form in addition to written form; and be effective when placed after the body of the lesson as postorganizers (not just prior to it as advance organizers).

Bettencourt et al. Bettencourt, Gillett, Gall, and Hull (1983) studied the effects of enthusiasm training in two studies involving beginning teachers in the elementary grades. The training was effective in each study in that the trained teachers were rated as more enthusiastic than control teachers in their instruction during a special experimental unit on probability and graphing. Effects on outcomes, however, were mixed. Student on-task behavior was the outcome measured in one study, and the treatment produced higher on-task percentages, not only in teacher-directed activities but also during seatwork times. However, achievement was the outcome measure in the second study, and this time the data revealed no significant differences. Thus, the enthusiasm training produced some desirable effects, but these were not strong enough to increase achievement significantly.

Blaney. Blaney (1983) essentially replicated the aspects of the Clark et al. (1979) study that dealt with teacher structuring and reacting. A single trained teacher taught four versions (high structuring/high reacting, high structuring/low reacting, low structuring/high reacting, low structuring/low reacting) of the same 4-day sequence of science lessons to groups of second graders, using semiscripted lessons to control content coverage. Lessons involving high structuring were longer than those involving low structuring, but level of structuring nevertheless was unrelated to achievement. Reacting was related, however: High reacting produced higher achievement.

Clasen. Clasen (1983) studied the effect of four different presentations (independent study, 75% low-level questions, 75% high-level questions, or 75% divergent production questions) of identical content on the achievement of gifted seventh graders in week-long science units. These contrasting treatments did not make much difference, possibly because all of the students were gifted and thus likely to learn the material if given the opportunity to do so. The lower-order question group outperformed both the independent study group and the higher-order question group on the-lower order items included in an immediate posttest. These group differences disappeared, however, on a delayed retention test. There were no group differences on either test for higher-order content items or divergent production items. The student attitude inventory revealed that students in the divergent production group had more positive attitudes toward their experiences during the unit than did students in the independent study group. There were no other group differences.

Gall et al. Gall, Ward, Berliner, Cahen, Winne, Elashoff, and Stanton (1978) studied the effects of varying recitation and questioning techniques on sixth grade students' achievement following specially prepared 2-week ecology units. In the first study, three groups were taught using 15 minutes of content presentation followed by 25 minutes of recitation. A fourth group (no recitation) engaged in ecology-related art activities following the content presentation. Within the three recitation groups, there was variation in probing (asking follow-up questions to try to improve an initial answer) and redirection (calling on another student to respond to a question answered by the first student). The three recitation groups learned more than the art activity group, but there was no evidence that recitations involving probing and redirection were superior to recitations that did not include these elements.

In the second study, the recitation treatments differed in cognitive level of questions asked. One group received 25% higher-level questions, the second group 50%, and the third group 75%. Once again, the three recitation groups outperformed the art activity group. The results for level of question were puzzling because the treatment using 50% higher-cognitive-level questions was less effective than the other two for promoting acquisition and retention of facts, but slightly more effective for promoting performance on higher-cognitive-level tasks. The scores for the 75% group were similar to, but lower than, those for the 25% group, even on higher-cognitive-level measures. Taken together, these two studies suggest that students benefit from recitations allowing them to answer questions about content previously presented by teachers, but do not support the hypothesized benefits of probing, redirection, or higher-level questions.

MacKay. MacKay (1979) conducted an experiment in third and sixth grade classes in Edmonton, Canada. Teachers were trained on 28 strategies drawn mostly from previous process-product research (a few strategies were included because they had been recommended by curriculum specialists). All teachers were observed prior to the treatments, then exposed to the treatments (either 2 or 4 half days of in-service activities) and then observed again. The treatments produced significant increases for 24 of the 28 strategies, suggesting generally good implementation. Process-product data showed no significant relationships in third grade reading, where there was very low variance in adjusted achievement scores. However, 16 of the 28 strategies showed significant process-product relationships in the third grade mathematics classes, nine in the sixth grade reading classes, and two in the sixth grade mathematics classes. This pattern of significant relationships was spotty, but all significant relationships were in the expected direction. Most of these involved classroom organization, group management, and responsiveness to students' answers to questions. (The correlates unique to second grade math included teacher acceptance and caring, academic learning time, interest value of assignments, and checking of seatwork performance.)

McKenzie and Henry. McKenzie and Henry (1979) developed experimental support for an innovation designed to make teachers' yes-no questions function as "test-like events" rather than mere "nominal stimuli" to each student in the class (not just to the student called on to respond). Third graders were randomly assigned to lessons with standardized content presentation and follow-up questions. In the control classes, individual students were called on (randomly) to answer questions while their classmates looked on (this is most teachers' typical recitation procedure). In the experimental class, however, all students were required to respond to every question (using nonverbal gestures). This approach reduced off-task behavior and increased achievement.

Madike. Madike (1980) assigned student teachers to teach 5-week mathematics units to comparable ninth grade classes. One group of student teachers had experienced a microteaching program for training them in teaching skills. A second group had been observed and given feedback by supervising teachers, but not necessarily on the skills stressed in the microteaching program. A third group was given no specific preparation for the teaching experience. Each student teacher was videotaped during a 35-minute lesson, and a 10-minute segment was rated for frequency of use of nine skills taught in the microteaching program. The microteaching group had higher frequencies of behaviors related to these nine skills, and the skills correlated positively (as expected) with achievement. Correlations were significant for questioning, closure (structuring at the ends of episodes initiated by questions), and cueing (verbally calling attention to important content), but not for stimulation, variation, reinforcement, planned repetition, recognizing student attention, using examples, or nonverbal cueing. Even though these data are frequency scores for Nigerian student teachers, developed from a very limited observation base, they correspond well with other data reviewed in this chapter.

Martin. Martin (1979) used an intensive reversal design and time series analyses to assess the impact of increases in higher-order questions during an experimental biology unit taught in a sixth grade class. A baseline period in which the teacher taught normally was followed by an initial experimental phase in which the teacher increased the frequency of higher-order questions, then by a return to baseline, and then by another increase in higher-order questions. During each phase, teacher questioning and student responding were monitored, and student achievement and attitudes were measured. Results indicated that increases in higher-order questions led to increases in higher-order responses. However, there was no effect on achievement or attitudes toward lessons, and a negative effect on attitudes toward the teacher. Thus, the treatment produced the intended changes in processes, but not in outcomes.

Ryan. Ryan (1973, 1974) conducted two studies of the effects of level of question in lessons taught to fifth and sixth graders during inquiry-oriented social science lessons. Each study involved two recitation–discussion groups and a control group that received lectures and completed assignments but were not involved in recitation–discussion activities or in the special activities included in the inquiry program. One discussion–recitation group received about 75% high-level questions, and the second received only about 5% high-level questions. The inquiry–recitation–discussion groups usually outperformed the control groups on both low-level and high-level objectives, but they never differed significantly from each other. Thus, both high-level and low-level questions were effective in promoting achievement of both high-level and low-level objectives.

Schuck. Schuck (1981) studied the effects of set induction on learning in ninth grade biology lessons. All teachers used the same materials to teach to the same objectives, but the experimental teachers began by inducing a learning set by drawing analogies between the new material and events that were already familiar to the students. Students exposed to the set induction treatment learned and retained more content than control students.

Smith and Sanders. Smith and Sanders (1981) studied the effect of high versus low structuring of fifth grade social studies content. Following Anderson (1969), they defined structure in terms of linear redundancy in the appearance of key concepts. In high-structure presentations, key concepts tend to be repeated from one sentence to the next, although new ones are gradually phased in and old ones phased out. This structure is typical of prose that moves systematically through a series of related statements. In low-structure presentations, the content was more jumbled. Key concepts were repeated just as often, but not in contiguous sentences. As a result, even though the same sentences were included in each version, the high-structure presentations were clearly recognizable as organized sequences of related facts, but the low-structure presentations sounded more like lists of unrelated facts. As expected, the high-structure presentations produced higher student achievement and ratings of effectiveness.

Tobin. Tobin (1980) studied the effect of increasing "wait-time" on learning in science classes for Australian students aged 10–13. Tobin's definition of wait-time was considerably broader than the definition used by Rowe (1974) in her investigations of the effects of pausing for several seconds after asking a question (in order to give the students time to think about the question before calling on one of them to try to answer it). Tobin's definition of wait-time included not only these pauses, but also teacher pauses following student responses or previous statements by the teacher. Thus, wait-time was defined by Tobin as the length of the pause preceding any teacher utterance.

Prior to treatment, the mean wait-time for all teachers was .5 seconds. Following treatment, these averages were 3.1 for the experimental teachers and .7 for the control teachers. There was no significant correlation between wait-time and achievement before the treatment (probably because there was no meaningful variation in wait-time), but a positive correlation afterwards. This was true even though only 8 of the 13 experimental teachers succeeded in meeting the criterion of an average wait-time of 3 seconds, and some of them did not view such long wait-time as appropriate. It should be noted that these lessons involved scientific concepts such as density and displacement. Such extended wait-time might be less appropriate in lessons involving simpler content or younger students.

Tobin and Capie. Tobin and Capie (1982) manipulated both teacher wait-time and quality of questioning (cognitive level, clarity, relevance) in middle school science lessons. There were four groups: (a) extended teacher wait-time plus high question quality; (b) extended teacher wait-time plus normal question quality; (c) normal teacher wait-time plus high question quality; (d) normal teacher wait-time plus normal question quality. Teachers in the extended wait-time groups were asked to average between 3 and 5 seconds of wait-time (again, wait-time was defined as the length of time preceding a teacher utterance). Teachers in the high question quality groups were asked to plan their questioning to be high in cognitive level, clarity, and relevance (which included both relevance to the objectives of the lesson and appropriateness of timing given the flow of the lesson). The teachers were observed and given feedback to help them maintain the specified wait-time and question quality levels.

Wait-time showed a significant positive correlation with achievement, and there were positive but nonsignificant relationships for cognitive level, clarity, and relevance of questioning (variance in question quality was low, because all teachers tended to ask questions that were high in cognitive level, clarity, and relevance, because they all were given detailed lesson plans).

Although wait-time correlated positively with achievement, it also interacted with question quality and showed a curvilinear relationship to student engagement. The interactions suggest that longer wait-times are especially important when instruction deals with higher-cognitive-level objectives, and that a mix of questions at varying cognitive levels produces the highest achievement (a ratio of approximately two higher-level questions to one lower-level question was optimal in these data). The highest rates of attending were associated with wait-times of approximately 3 seconds (as opposed to shorter or longer wait-times) combined with intermediate cognitive levels of question (as opposed to lower or higher levels).

Summary and Integration of the Findings

Earlier handbook chapters on teacher effects concentrated on issues of definition and methodology, because there were few replicated findings to discuss. However, research of the 1960s and 1970s yielded numerous replicated linkages between teacher behavior and achievement. Many of these linkages have even been validated experimentally, although it remains true that experimental findings are weaker and less consistent than correlational findings.

The emphasis here is on consistency and replication of findings, not size of correlation. Even the most generally replicated findings tend to be based on low-to-moderate correlations, and are not always strong enough to reach statistical significance (although significant findings in the opposite direction are rare or absent for the relationships summarized below). Also, many findings must be qualified by reference to grade level, student characteristics, or teaching objectives. This reflects the fact that effective instruction involves selecting (from a larger repertoire) and orchestrating those teaching behaviors that are appropriate to the context and to the teacher's goals, rather than mastering and consistently applying a few "generic" teaching skills.

Research-based conclusions about teacher behaviors that maximize student achievement are summarized below, first for general aspects of instruction and then for the handling of specific lesson components. The evidence supporting these conclusions is strongest for basic skills instruction in the primary grades, but extant data suggest that they also apply to instruction in certain subjects at all grade levels (limits and qualifications on the data are discussed in the next major section). For economy of presentation, the findings will sometimes be phrased as "teachers should" statements. Readers should bear in mind that such statements are made with reference to maximizing student achievement and not with reference to maximizing "teacher effectiveness" defined more broadly.

Quantity and Pacing of Instruction

The most consistently replicated findings link achievement to the quantity and pacing of instruction.

Opportunity to Learn/Content Covered. Amount learned is related to opportunity to learn, whether measured in terms of pages of curriculum covered or percentage of test items taught through lecture or recitation. Opportunity to learn is determined in part by length of school day and school year (assuming appropriate instruction, of course), and in part by the variables discussed below.

Role Definition/Expectations/Time Allocation. Achievement is maximized when teachers emphasize academic instruction as a major part of their own role, expect their students to master the curriculum, and allocate most of the available time to curriculum-related activities. This is seen in relationships involving presage measures of teachers' role definitions and expectations, high-inference ratings of the degree to which teachers are businesslike or task oriented, and low-inference measures of time allocated to academic activities rather than to activities with other objectives (personal adjustment, group dynamics) or with no clear objectives at all ("free time," student choice of games or pastimes).

Classroom Management/Student Engaged Time. Not all time allocated to academic activities is actually spent engaged in these activities. Engagement rates depend on the teacher's ability to organize and manage the classroom as an efficient learning environment where academic activities run smoothly, transitions are brief and orderly, and little time is spent getting organized or dealing with inattention or resistance. Key indicators of effective management include: good preparation of the classroom and installation of rules and procedures at the beginning of the year, "withitness" and overlapping in general interaction with students, smoothness and momentum in lesson pacing, variety and appropriate level of challenge in assignments, consistent accountability procedures and follow-up concerning seatwork, and clarity about when and how students can get help and about what options are available when they finish (see Doyle, this volume).

Consistent Success/Academic Learning Time. To learn efficiently, students must be engaged in activities that are appropriate in difficulty level and otherwise suited to their current achievement levels and needs. It is important not only to maximize content coverage by pacing the students briskly through the curriculum, but also to see that they make continuous progress all along the way, moving through small steps with high (or at least moderate) rates of success and minimal confusion or frustration. If lessons are to run smoothly without loss of momentum and students are to work on assignments with high levels of success, teachers must be effective in diagnosing learning needs and prescribing appropriate activities. Their questions must usually (about 75%) of the time) yield correct answers and seldom yield no response at all, and their seatwork activities must be completed with 90–100% success by most students. (Such high success rates should not be taken as suggestive of instructional overkill or assignment of pointless busywork. Appropriate seatwork will extend knowledge and provide needed practice. It will also be do-able, however, because it is pitched at the right level and because the students have been prepared for it. Thus, the high success rates result from effort and thought, not mere automatic application of already overlearned algorithms). Continuous progress at high rates of success, carried to the point that performance objectives can be met smoothly and rapidly, is especially important in the early grades and whenever students are learning basic knowledge or skills that will be applied later in higher-level activities.

In summary, then, there is a tension between the goal of maximizing content coverage by pacing the students through the curriculum as rapidly as possible and the needs to (a) move in small steps so that each new objective can be learned readily and without frustration; (b) see that the students practice the new learning until they achieve consolidated mastery marked by consistently smooth and correct responses; and (c) where necessary, see that the students learn to integrate the new learning with other concepts and skills and to apply it efficiently in problem-solving situations. The pace at which the class can move will depend on the students' abilities and developmental levels, the nature of the subject matter, the student–teacher ratio, and the teacher's managerial and instructional skills. In general, teachers should hold errors to a minimum by choosing tasks that their students can handle and explaining those tasks clearly before releasing the students to work on them. The more challenging the task, the more the teacher must be prepared to monitor performance as the students work on the task (not just to correct answers later) and to provide immediate help to those who need it.

Bennett, Desforges, Cockburn, and Wilkenson (1981) point out that not only the frequency of errors is important, but their timing and quality. Early in a unit, where new learning is occurring, relatively frequent errors may be expected. Later, however, when mastery levels are supposed to have been achieved, errors should be minimal. Also, some errors occur because students have the right general idea but make a minor miscalculation, or because they involve sound logic that is based on assumptions that are plausible but happen to be faulty. Such "high quality" errors are understandable and may even provide helpful guidance to the teacher. However, errors that suggest inattention, hopeless confusion, or alienation from the material are undesirable.

Active Teaching. Students achieve more in classes where they spend most of their time being taught or supervised by their teachers rather than working on their own (or not working at all). These classes include frequent lessons (whole class or small group, depending on grade level and subject matter) in which the teacher presents information and develops concepts through lecture and demonstration, elaborates this information in the feedback given following responses to recitation or discussion questions, prepares the students for follow-up seatwork activities by giving instructions and going through practice examples, monitors progress on assignments after releasing the students to work independently, and follows up with appropriate feedback and reteaching when necessary. The teacher carries the content to the students personally rather than depending on the curriculum materials to do so, but conveys information mostly in brief presentations followed by recitation or application opportunities. There is a great deal of teacher talk, but most of it is academic rather than procedural or managerial, and much of it involves asking questions and giving feedback rather than extended lecturing.

The findings summarized above all deal with quantity of academic activity, particularly the time spent in organized lessons and supervised seatwork. The following variables concern the form and quality of teachers' organized lessons.

Whole-Class Versus Small-Group Versus Individualized Instruction

The data do not say much about teaching the whole class versus small groups. No experimental studies compared these two lesson formats directly, and the issue was not addressed correlationally except in the Follow Through studies where it was confounded with other systematic differences. Even in the absence of definitive data, certain trade-offs are obvious. Whole-class instruction is simpler in that the teacher needs to plan only one set of lessons and is free to circulate during seatwork times (although teaching the whole class is more demanding than teaching any particular small group). The small-group approach involves preparing differentiated lessons and assignments and keeps the teacher busy instructing small groups most of the time (and thus unavailable to monitor and assist the majority of students who are working on assignments). Thus, the small-group approach requires well-chosen assignments that the students are willing to engage in and able to complete successfully, as well as rules and procedures that enable students to get help (if confused) or direction (about what to do when finished) without disrupting the momentum of the teacher's small-group lessons. Unless they have an aide, even teachers who are able to make the small-group approach work may find that it takes too much effort to be worth the trouble.

However, small-group instruction may be necessary in at least two situations. The first is beginning reading instruction, where it is essential that each individual read aloud so that the teacher can monitor progress and diagnose and correct consistent error patterns. The slow pace, repetition, and sustained attention to individuals that such instruction requires are incompatible with the brisk pacing that makes for successful whole-class lessons. Thus, grouping (although not necessarily ability grouping) is a way for teachers to accommodate the slow-paced "reading turns" that characterize beginning reading instruction. It can be phased out as reading lessons evolve from decoding to comprehension objectives.

Grouping may also be necessary in highly heterogeneous classes. Here, grouping may be based on differences in ability, achievement, or language dominance, and different groups may receive both different instruction and different assignments. This requires more complex planning and group management than whole-class instruction, and introduces the potential for undesirable expectation or labeling effects, but there may be no alternative in many classes.

In discussing grouping, a distinction must be made between grouping students for differentiated instruction and grouping students for cooperative work on assignments following (common) instruction. The preceding remarks about grouping refer to the trade-offs involved in differentiating the class to allow for separate instruction or assignments. They do not apply to the use of student teams, tournaments, and other approaches that Slavin (1980, 1983) and others have recommended for boosting motivation and increasing prosocial peer contact during work on assignments. These approaches involve introducing cooperative or competitive (not merely individualistic) reward structures to the management of seatwork, and can be used with whole-class, small-group, or individualized instruction.

The studies reviewed here do not have much to say about individualized instruction, because process-outcome researchers have concentrated on teacher-led instruction (other reviews suggest mixed findings; see Good & Brophy, 1984). In particular, these data are silent on the relative merits of specific programs of individualized instruction (IGE, IPI, etc.). However, they do show consistent positive correlations with achievement for active (whole class or small group) instruction by the teacher, and negative correlations for time spent in independent seatwork without continuing teacher supervision. Thus, although these data do not contradict the notion of individualizing instruction as a general principle, they do raise doubts about the probable effectiveness of particular programs of individualized instruction in which students are expected to learn mostly on their own, from reading curriculum materials, working on assignments, and taking tests. This approach to individualizing instruction does not appear feasible in ordinary classes, although it can work in special classes with low student-teacher ratios (cf. Crawford, 1983).

In summary, small-group instruction is more complex to implement than whole-class instruction, but it may sometimes be necessary. Available data are not very informative about when small-group instruction should be considered the method of choice, nor about how it should be designed and managed. "Individualized instruction" which relies heavily on unsupervised independent seatwork is not as effective as teacher-led instruction.

Giving Information

Variables of lesson form and quality can be divided into those that involve giving information (structuring), asking questions (soliciting), and providing feedback (reacting). The following variables apply to the function of giving information.

Structuring. Achievement is maximized when teachers not only actively present material, but structure it by beginning with overviews, advance organizers, or review of objectives; outlining the content and signaling transitions between lesson parts; calling attention to main ideas; summarizing subparts of the lesson as it proceeds; and reviewing main ideas at the end. Organizing concepts and analogies helps learners link the new to the already familiar. Overviews and outlines help them to develop learning sets to use in assimilating the content as it unfolds. Rule-example-rule patterns and internal summaries tie specific information items to integrative concepts. Summary reviews integrate and reinforce the learning of major points. Taken together, these structuring elements not only facilitate memory for the information but allow for its apprehension as an integrated whole with recognition of the relationships between parts.

Redundancy/Sequencing. Achievement is higher when information is presented with a degree of redundancy, particularly in the form of repeating and reviewing general rules and key concepts. The kind of redundancy that is involved in the sequential structuring built into the study by Smith and Sanders (1981) also appears important. In general, structuring, redundancy, and sequencing affect what is learned from listening to verbal presentations, even though they are not powerful determinants of learning from reading text.

Clarity. Clarity of presentation is a consistent correlate of achievement, whether measured by high-inference ratings or low-inference indicators such as absence of "vagueness terms" or "mazes." Knowledge about factors that detract from clarity needs to be supplemented with knowledge about positive factors that enhance clarity (for example, what kinds of analogies and examples facilitate learning, and why?) but in any case, students learn more from clear presentations than from unclear ones.

Enthusiasm. Enthusiasm, usually measured by high-inference ratings, appears to be more related to affective than to cognitive outcomes. Nevertheless, it often correlates with achievement, especially for older students.

Pacing/Wait-Time. "Pacing" usually refers to the solicitation aspects of lessons, but it can also refer to the rate of presentation of information during initial structuring. Although few studies have addressed the matter directly, data from the early grades seem to favor rapid pacing, both because this helps maintain lesson momentum (and thus minimizes inattention) and because such pacing seems to suit the basic skills learning that occurs at these grade levels. Typically, teacher presentations are short and interspersed with recitation or practice opportunities. At higher grade levels, however, where teachers make longer presentations on more abstract or complex content, it may be necessary to move at a slower pace, allowing time for each new concept to "sink in." At least, this seems to be the implication of wait-time data reported by Tobin (1980) and by Tobin and Capie (1982). Issues of pacing and wait-time during information presentation clearly need more research.

Questioning the Students

The variables in this section concern the teacher's management of public response opportunities during recitations and discussions.

Difficulty Level of Questions. Data on difficulty level of questions continue to yield mixed results. It seems clear that most (perhaps three-fourths) of teachers' questions should elicit correct answers, and that most of the rest should elicit overt, substantive reponses (incorrect or incomplete answers) rather than failures to respond at all. Beyond these generalities, optimal question difficulty probably varies with context. Basic skills instruction requires a great deal of drill and practice, and thus frequent fast-paced drill–review lessons during which most questions are answered rapidly and correctly. However, when teaching complex cognitive content, or when trying to stimulate students to generalize from, evaluate, or apply their learning, teachers will need to raise questions that few students can answer correctly (as well as questions that have no single correct answers at all).

Cognitive Level of Questions. The cognitive level of a question is conceptually separate from its difficulty level. The data reviewed here on cognitive level of question, and even meta-analyses of these and other relevant data (Winne, 1979; Redfield & Rousseau, 1981) yield inconsistent results. The data do refute the simplistic (but frequently assumed) notion that higher-level questions are categorically better than lower-level questions. Several studies indicate that lower-level questions facilitate learning, even learning of higher-level objectives. Furthermore, even when the frequency of higher-level questions correlates positively with achievement, the absolute numbers on which these correlations are based typically show that only about 25% of the questions asked were classified as higher level. Thus, in general, we should expect teachers to ask more lower-level than higher-level questions, even when dealing with higher-level content and seeking to promote higher-level objectives.

These are just frequency norms, however. To develop more useful information about cognitive level of question, researchers will have to develop more complex methods of coding that take into account the teacher's goals (it seems obvious that different kinds of questions are appropriate for different goals), the quality of the questions (clarity, relevance, etc.), and their timing and appropriateness given the flow of the activity. Research on the latter issues will require shifting from the individual question to the question sequence as the unit of analysis. For example, sequences beginning with a higher-level question and then proceeding through several lower-level follow-up questions would be appropriate for some purposes (such as asking students to suggest a possible application of an idea, and then probing for details about how the suggested application could work). A different purpose (such as trying to call students' attention to relevant facts and then stimulate them to integrate the facts and draw an important conclusion) might require a series of lower-level questions followed by a higher-level question.

Clarity of Question. Each teacher question should yield a (not necessarily correct) student answer. Teachers can train students to answer by showing a willingness to wait for the answer (instead of calling on someone else or giving the answer themselves). Clarity of question is also a factor: Students sometimes cannot respond because questions are vague or ambiguous, or because the teacher asks two or more questions without stopping to get an answer to the first one.

Postquestion Wait-Time. Studies of science instruction have shown higher achievement when teachers pause for about 3 seconds (rather than 1 second or less) after a question, to give the students time to think before calling on one of them. This variable has not been addressed in other contexts. It seems likely, however, that length of pause following questions should vary directly with their difficulty level and especially their complexity or cognitive level. A question calling for application of abstract principles should require a longer pause than a factual question.

Selecting the Respondent. Findings on this issue vary according to grade level, SES, and whole-class versus small-group setting. In the early grades, and especially during small-group lessons, it is important that all students participate overtly (and roughly equally). In small-group reading lessons, this can be accomplished by using the "patterned turns" method, training the students not to call out answers or reading words, and calling on nonvolunteers as well as volunteers. In these grades, it is important to prevent assertive students from coopting other students' response opportunities, and to insure that reticent students participate regularly even though they seldom volunteer.

Student call-outs usually correlate positively with achievement in low-SES classes but negatively in high-SES classes. This suggests the following principle: When most students are eager to respond, teachers will have to suppress their call-outs and train them to respect one another's response opportunities; however, when most students are reticent, teachers will have to encourage them to participate (which may include accepting relevant call-outs).

It is seldom feasible to have all students participate overtly in whole-class lessons, let alone to insure that all participate equally. This need not present a problem even in the lower grades in subjects such as spelling or arithmetic computation, where practice and assessment can be accomplished through written exercises. It may present a dilemma, however, for primary grade teachers working on objectives that call for overt verbal practice, and for teachers at any level who want to make assignments that call for students to make verbal presentations to the group (speeches, research reports). Here, it may be necessary to divide the class into groups or to schedule only a few presentations per day and use the rest of the period for faster-paced activities.

Except as noted in the previous paragraph, overt verbal participation in lessons does not seem to be an important achievement correlate in the upper grades. Still, rather than interact with the same few students most of the time, teachers in these grades probably should encourage volunteering (pausing after asking questions, to give students time to think and raise their hands, will help here) and call on nonvolunteers frequently (especially when they are likely to be able to respond correctly).

Waiting for the Student to Respond. Once teachers do call on students (especially nonvolunteers), they usually should wait until the students offer a substantive response, ask for help or clarification, or overtly say "I don't know." Sometimes, however, especially in whole-class lessons where lengthy pauses threaten continuity or momentum, it will be necessary for the teacher to curtail the pause by making one of the reacting moves discussed in the following section.

Reacting to Student Responses

Once the teacher has asked a question and called on a student to answer, the teacher then must monitor the student's response (or lack of it) and react to it.

Reactions to Correct Responses. Correct responses should be acknowledged as such, because even if the respondent knows that the answer is correct, some of the onlookers may not. Ordinarily (perhaps 90%) of the time) this acknowledgement should take the form of overt feedback, which may range from brief head nods through short affirmation statements ("right," "yes") or repetition of the answer, to more extensive praise or elaboration of the answer. Such overt affirmation can be omitted on occasion, such as during fast-paced drills in which the students understand that the teacher will simply move on to the next question if the previous question is answered correctly.

Although it is important for teachers to give feedback so that everyone knows that an answer was correct, it usually is not important to praise the student who supplied the answer. Such praise is often intrusive and distracting, and it may even embarrass the recipient, especially if the accomplishment was not especially praiseworthy in the first place. In any case, teachers who maximize achievement are sparing rather than effusive in praising correct answers. To the extent that such praise is effective, it is more likely to be effective when specific rather than global, and when used with low-SES or dependent/anxious students rather than with high-SES or assertive/confident students.

Reacting to Partly Correct Responses. Following responses that are incomplete or only partly correct, teachers ordinarily should affirm the correct part and then follow up by giving clues or rephrasing the question. If this does not succeed, the teacher can give the answer or call on another student.

Reacting to Incorrect Responses. Following incorrect answers, teachers should begin by indicating that the response is not correct. Almost all (99%) of the time, this negative feedback should be simple negation rather than personal criticism, although criticism may be appropriate for students who have been persistently inattentive or unprepared.

After indicating that the answer was incorrect, teachers usually should try to elicit an improved response by rephrasing the question or giving clues. Such response improvement attempts are likely to be facilitative when they are generally successful, but teachers should avoid "pointless pumping" in situations where questions cannot be broken down or the student is too confused or anxious to profit from further questioning.

Sometimes the feedback following an incorrect answer should include not only the correct answer but a more extended explanation of why the answer is correct or how it can be determined from the information given. Such extended explanation should be included in the feedback whenever the respondent (or others in the class) might not "get the point" from hearing the answer alone, as well as at times when a review or summary of part of the lesson is needed.

Reacting to "No Response." Teachers should train their students to respond overtly to questions, even if only to say "I don't know." Thus, if waiting has not produced an overt response, they should probe ("Do you know?"), elicit an overt response, and then follow up by giving feedback, supplying the answer, or calling on someone else (depending on the student's response to the probe).

Reacting to Student Questions and Comments. Teachers should answer relevant student questions or redirect them to the class, and incorporate relevant student comments into the lesson. Such use of student ideas appears to become more important with each succeeding grade level, as students become both more able to contribute useful ideas and more sensitive to whether teachers treat their ideas with interest and respect.

Handling Seatwork and Homework Assignments

Although independent seatwork is probably overused and is not a substitute for active teacher instruction or for drill–recitation–discussion opportunities, seatwork (and homework) assignments provide needed practice and application opportunities. Ideally, such assignments will be varied and interesting enough to motivate student engagement, new or challenging enough to constitute meaningful learning experiences rather than pointless busywork, and yet easy enough to allow success with reasonable effort. For assignments on which students are expected to work on their own, success rates will have to be very high–near 100%. Lower (although still generally high) success rates can be tolerated when students who need help can get it quickly.

Student success rates, and the effectiveness of seatwork assignments generally, are enhanced when teachers explain the work and go over practice examples with the students before releasing them to work independently. Furthermore, once the students are released to work independently, the work goes more smoothly if the teacher (or an aide) circulates to monitor progress and provide help when needed. If the work has been well chosen and well explained, most of these "helping" interactions will be brief, and at any given time, most students will be progressing smoothly through the assignment rather than waiting for help.

Students should know what work they are accountable for, how to get help when they need it, and what to do when they finish. Performance should be monitored for completion and accuracy, and students should receive timely and specific feedback. Where the whole class or group had the same assignment, review of the assignment can be part of the next day's lesson. Other assignments will require more individualized feedback. Where performance is poor, teachers should provide not only feedback but reteaching and follow-up assignments designed to insure that the material is mastered.

Among responses to seatwork and homework performance, feedback and follow-up are more closely related to achievement than praise or reward. Even so, positive relationships have been reported for praise, symbolic rewards, and token reinforcement (at least in the early grades). Such rewards may facilitate learning if tied to complete and correct performance on assignments.

Context-Specific Findings

Even the most widely replicated process–product relationships usually must be qualified by references to the context of instruction. Usually, these interactions with context involve minor elaborations of main trends, but occasionally, as in the Brophy and Evertson (1976) or the Solomon and Kendall (1979) studies, interactions are more powerful than main effects and suggest qualitatively different treatment for different groups of students. Certain interaction effects appear repeatedly and constitute well-established findings.

Grade Level. In the early grades, classroom management involves a great deal of instruction in desired routines and procedures. Less of this instruction is necessary in the later grades, but it becomes especially important to be clear about expectations and to follow up on accountability demands. Lessons in the early grades involve basic skills instruction, often in small groups, and it is important that each student participate overtly and often. In later grades, lessons typically are with the whole class and involve applications of basic skills or consideration of more abstract content. Overt participation is less important than factors such as teachers' structuring of the content, clarity of statements and questions, and enthusiasm. The praise and symbolic rewards that are common in the early grades give way to the more impersonal and academically centered instruction common in the later grades, although it is important for teachers in the later grades to treat students' contributions with interest and respect.

Student SES/Ability/Affect. SES is a "proxy" for a complex of correlated cognitive and affective differences between subgroups of students. The cognitive differences involve IQ, ability, or achievement levels. Interactions between process–product findings and student SES or achievement level indicate that low-SES/low-achieving students need more control and structuring from their teachers: more active instruction and feedback, more redundancy, and smaller steps with higher success rates. This will mean more review, drill, and practice, and thus more lower-level questions. Across the school year, it will mean exposure to less material, but with emphasis on mastery of the material that is taught and on moving students through the curriculum as briskly as they are able to progress.

Affective correlates of SES include the degree to which students feel secure and confident versus anxious or alienated in the classroom. High-SES students are more likely to be confident, eager to participate, and responsive to challenge. They want respect and require feedback, but usually do not require a great deal of encouragement or praise. They thrive in an atmosphere that is academically stimulating and somewhat demanding. Low-SES students are more likely to require warmth and support in addition to good instruction, and to need more encouragement for their efforts and praise for their successes. It is especially important to teach them to respond overtly rather than remain passive when asked a question, and to be accepting

of their (relevant) call-outs and other academic initiations when they do occur.

Teacher's Intentions/Objectives. What constitutes appropriate instructional behavior will vary with the teacher's objectives. This factor has rarely been studied directly, but relevant principles can be inferred easily from the data reviewed. First, as an extension of the principle of student opportunity to learn, it seems obvious that instruction designed to achieve particular objectives should include teacher presentation of, and student opportunity to practice or apply, content relevant to those objectives. This, in turn, has implications about what methods are appropriate. To the extent that the students need new information, they are likely to need group lessons featuring teacher information presentation followed by recitation or discussion opportunities. The appropriateness of follow-up practice or application opportunities would depend on the objectives. When it is sufficient that the students be able to reproduce knowledge on cue, routine seatwork assignments and tests might suffice. However, if students are expected to integrate broad patterns of learning or apply them to their everyday lives, it will be necessary to schedule activities that involve problem solving, decision making, essay composition, preparation of research reports, or construction of some product. In general, the nature and cognitive level of the information given and the questions asked during an activity should depend on the objectives being pursued and the place of the activity within the anticipated progression through the curriculum.

Other. Some findings are specific to particular contexts. For example, the principles put forth by Anderson et al. (1982) are specific to small-group instruction in the primary grades, and several studies included variables that are specific to subject matter (such as concentration on word attack versus comprehension in reading instruction). These and other context factors must be considered in attempting to generalize from any study.

Power and Limits of the Data

The last 15 years have produced an orderly knowledge base linking teacher behavior to achievement. Although just a beginning, this is a major advance over what was available previously. If applied with proper attention to its limits, this knowledge base should help improve teacher education and teaching practice. Several important limits and qualifications need to be kept in mind, however.

One is that the causal relationships that explain linkages between teacher behavior and student achievement are not always clear, and even when they are, process–product relationships do not translate directly into prescriptions for teaching practice. In the case of correlations between teacher behaviors and achievement, positive correlations do not necessarily indicate that the teacher behavior should be maximized (even within the observed range, let alone the theoretical range). Thus, it would be inappropriate to conclude that teachers should always wait at least 3 seconds for a response to a question, should never criticize students, or should never schedule independent seatwork.

To develop sensible recommendations about teacher behaviors, one must consider their means and ranges of variation. A positive correlation for a behavior that happens regularly must be interpreted differently from a positive correlation for a behavior that occurs only rarely. In addition, one must consider the contexts within which the behavior occurs, and its patterns of relationship with other teacher behaviors and with student behaviors. In what contexts is this teacher behavior an option? What other options are available in the same contexts? When is this behavior the option of choice, and why? Answering such questions requires knowledge about process–process as well as process–product relationships (and more generally, a familiarity with classrooms and how they work).

In effect, then, although it is necessary to study teacher behaviors individually in order to establish their specific relationships to achievement, and although it is necessary to strip away much of the context in which these behaviors are embedded in order to accumulate a large enough sample of comparable behaviors to allow the use of inferential statistics, interpretation of the relationships thus identified requires reconsideration of the teacher behaviors as parts of larger patterns occurring in particular contexts. Thus, in trying to develop guidelines about when and for how long teachers should wait for students to answer a question, one must consider such factors as the nature of the question, whether the student seems to be thinking about the question or is likely to profit from additional time, and whether further waiting might endanger the lesson's continuity or momentum.

Different patterns might be functionally equivalent. For example, it may make no important difference whether the three main points of a presentation are summarized at the beginning or the end of the presentation (so long as they are summarized), or whether a mathematics computation review is done with flash cards during a lesson or through a seatwork assignment afterwards. Functionally equivalent patterns such as this have rarely been considered, let alone investigated systematically (see Good & Power, 1976, for discussion of functionally equivalent classroom learning experiences).

The fact that there may be different but functionally equivalent paths to the same outcome is but one reason why data linking teacher behavior to achievement should not be used for teacher evaluation or accountability purposes. If teachers are to be evaluated according to the achievement they produce, then this achievement should be measured directly. Information on short-term outcomes such as academic learning time or performance on assignments might be of some use, but it would be inappropriate to penalize teachers for failing to follow overly rigid behavioral prescriptions if they produced as much achievement as the teachers who did follow the prescriptions.

Another reason why the data presented here cannot be used in any simple fashion for evaluating teachers is that achievement gain was the only outcome considered in detail. Teachers vary not only in their success in producing achievement, but in their success in fostering positive attitudes, personal development, and good group relations. Unfortunately, success on one of these dimensions does not necessarily imply success on the others. It is possible to optimize progress along several dimensions simultaneously to some degree, but beyond some point, further progress toward one objective will come at the expense of progress toward others. Even ideal teaching will involve trade-offs rather than optimizing in an absolute sense (Clark, 1982; Evertson, 1979; Peterson, 1979; Schofield, 1981).

Another limit to these data is that the correlational findings were based on natural variation in existing classroom practices, and even most of the experiments involved practices previously observed occurring spontaneously. Several implications follow. One is that generalization of these data is probably limited to traditionally taught classrooms (they would not apply to totally individualized approaches, for example). Another is that prescriptions for application probably should remain within the ranges of teacher behavior observed in these studies. Simple-minded extrapolations beyond those ranges (such as, if 15 minutes of homework per night are good, 2 hours per night would be eight times better) are not supported by the data and probably are counterproductive. A third point to consider is that naturalistic data reflect the practices prevalent in the time and place in which they were collected (primarily the United States in the 1970s, in this case). Compared to schools in Europe and Japan, American schools in the 1970s probably featured less active (whole class or small group) instruction by teachers, less content coverage per unit of time, and less time on task (cf. Dalton & Willcocks, 1983). Consequently, quantity of instruction and opportunity-to-learn factors were among the strongest correlates of achievement. In other countries, however, or wherever content coverage is uniformly high (and variance is low), qualitative measures of teaching might correlate more strongly with achievement than quantitative measures.

Finally, most findings must be qualified by grade level, type of objective, type of student, and other context factors. This creates dilemmas for teachers working with heterogeneous classes. Furthermore, even within context, it seems likely that all relationships are ultimately curvilinear. Too much of even a generally good thing is still too much.

At least two common themes cut across the findings, despite the need for limitations and qualifications. One is that academic learning is influenced by amount of the time that students spend engaged in appropriate academic tasks. The second is that students learn more efficiently when their teachers first structure new information for them and help them relate it to what they already know, and then monitor their performance and provide corrective feedback during recitation, drill, practice, or application activities. For a time, these generalizations seemed confined to the early grades or to basic rather than more advanced skills. However, it now appears that they apply to any body of knowledge or set of skills that has been sufficiently well organized and analyzed so that it can be presented (explained, modeled) systematically and then practiced or applied during activities that call for student performance that can be evaluated for quality and (where incorrect or imperfect) given corrective feedback.

This certainly includes aspects of reading comprehension and mathematics problem solving in addition to word attack and mathematics computation, and it probably includes aspects of complex learning that are not usually thought of as attainable through systematic teaching (developing learning-to-learn skills, creative writing, artistic expression). Even for higher-level, complex learning objectives, guidance through planned sequences of experience is likely to be more effective than unsystematic trial and error.

It should be noted that the instruction involved in such higher-level activities is often highly complex and demanding. Instead of supplying simple algorithms to be imitated or giving correct answers to factual questions, effective instructors working at higher levels must be able to do the following: develop apt analogies or examples that will enable students to relate the new to the familiar or the abstract to the concrete; identify key concepts that help to organize complex bodies of information; model problem-solving processes that involve judgment and decision making under conditions of uncertainty; and diagnose and correct subtle misconceptions in students' thinking. These are complex, demanding, and yet essential activities, and should neither be demeaned as intrusive "teacher talk" nor confused with the relatively simple "telling" or giving of "right answers" that occur in basic skills lessons in the early grades.

Finally, it should be stressed that there are no shortcuts to successful attainment of higher-level learning objectives. Such success will not be achieved with relative ease through discovery learning by the student. Instead, it will require considerable instruction from the teacher, as well as thorough mastery of basic knowledge and skills which must be integrated and applied in the process of "higher level" performance. Development of basic knowledge and skills to the necessary levels of automatic and errorless performance will require a great deal of drill and practice. Thus, drill and practice activities should not be slighted as "low level." They appear to be just as essential to complex and creative intellectual performance as they are to the performance of a virtuoso violinist.

Methodological Notes

Methodological issues were discussed in detail in an earlier section, and pertinent aspects of methodology were mentioned in discussing individual studies. Rather than repeat all of that here, we will merely call attention to a few salient points. Most of these concern the need for more targeted and refined measurement. Data compiled by forcing unselected interaction into a few general categories and then computing frequencies are not very useful. Better data will result from thought and planning devoted to issues such as the following.

What are the teacher and student behaviors of interest, and in what contexts do they occur? If they occur only in certain contexts, data collection must be planned for these contexts, and other contexts can be ignored. However, within the range of relevant contexts, behavior may vary in meaning or in patterns of correlation with other variables. Thus, the behavior may have to be measured somewhat differently in different contexts. In any case, it will be important to record the data so that tallies can be analyzed separately for each context in addition to being combined across contexts.

Within context, when is the behavior possible or likely to occur? If this question can be answered clearly, it will be possible to supplement frequency scores indicating the rate of occurrence of the behavior with percentage scores (for example, percentage of lessons begun with an overview) reflecting the relative frequency of the behavior in situations in which it could be expected. These two types of scores carry different information.

Does the behavior usually occur as part of a predictable sequence? If so, the coding should be planned to allow examination of entire sequences in addition to separate examination of the component behaviors. Patterns of initiation and reaction should be retained in the coding system, so that proactive teacher behaviors can be separated from reactive teacher behaviors that occur in response to student initiations.

Are there important distinctions concerning the quality, timing, or appropriateness of the behavior that can be built into the coding system? Even the most sophisticated contemporary coding systems use relatively crude, global category definitions that could be improved considerably through differentiation of qualitatively different subtypes or coding of the appropriateness of behaviors in addition to merely noting their occurrences. For example, Brophy (1981) reviewed a wide range of literature on teacher praise, noting that such praise has different purposes and meanings in different contexts. He concluded that the quality of teacher praise is more important than its frequency, and offered the guidelines shown in Table 12.5. Research that built some of these qualitative distinctions into the measurement of teacher praise would probably produce more orderly and meaningful results than the research done to date using cruder measures. Note that praise is just an example: Conceptualization and measurement of most of the other teacher behavior variables discussed in this chapter are equally crude and in need of elaboration.

Existing findings on quantity of instruction are stronger and more consistent than the findings on quality, because so many findings were derived from naturalistic situations where teachers varied drastically in their allocation of time to academic activities and in their classroom organization and management skills. The differences in student opportunity to learn created by these differences in time allocation and classroom management probably overwhelmed, and thus masked, the effects of whatever differences occurred in quality of instruction. To study quality differences, it will be necessary to control quantity differences, at minimum by restricting samples to teachers who are skilled in classroom management and similar in their goals and time allocations, and sometimes even by scripting or otherwise controlling the amount and nature of instruction.

How can the teacher behavior be sampled and measured reliably? If the study will rely on naturalistic observation, it will be important to observe in contexts in which the behavior appears frequently, and to observe often and long enough to build up a reliable sample of the behavior.

Is there congruence between the content taught, the categories in the observation system, and the content tested? The content taught in the different classes to be observed should be identical (otherwise, differences in curricula will be confounded with differences in methods), and the test should be a valid and reliable sampling of that content. Where relevant, the test data should allow for separate analysis of different types or levels of learning, as well as distinctions such as whether the material was specifically taught by the teacher or merely included in the text, or whether the items tapped intentional or incidental learning. In addition, the coding categories should reflect the content taught—the categories used for coding small-group reading instruction in first grade should be very different from those used for coding whole-class science instruction in twelfth grade.

How should the data be reported? At minimum, both descriptive information (means, variance) and process–product information (correlation or regression coefficients) should be provided for each separate classroom process variable. Results

Table 12.5. Guidelines for Effective Praise

Effective Praise	Ineffective Praise
1. is delivered contingently	1. is delivered randomly or unsystematically
2. specifies the particulars of the accomplishment	2. is restricted to global positive reactions
3. shows spontaneity, variety, and other signs of credibility; suggests clear attention to the student's accomplishment	3. shows a bland uniformity that suggests a conditioned response made with minimal attention
4. rewards attainment of specified performance criteria (which can include effort criteria, however)	4. rewards mere participation, without consideration of performance processes or outcomes
5. provides information to students about their competence or the value of their accomplishments	5. provides no information at all or gives students information about their status
6. orients students toward better appreciation of their own task-related behavior and thinking about problem solving	6. orients students toward comparing themselves with others and thinking about competing
7. uses students' own prior accomplishments as the context for describing present accomplishments	7. uses the accomplishments of peers as the context for describing students' present accomplishments
8. is given in recognition of noteworthy effort or success at difficult (for *this* student) tasks	8. is given without regard to the effort expended or the meaning of the accomplishment
9. attributes success to effort and ability, implying that similar successes can be expected in the future	9. attributes success to ability alone or to external factors such as luck or low task difficulty
10. fosters endogenous attributions (students believe that they expend effort on the task because they enjoy the task and/or want to develop task-relevant skills)	10. fosters exogenous attributions (students believe that they expend effort on the task for external reasons—to please the teacher, win a competition or reward, etc.)
11. focuses students' attention on their own task-relevant behavior	11. focuses students' attention on the teacher as an external authority figure who is manipulating them
12. fosters appreciation of, and desirable attributions about, task-relevant behavior after the process is completed	12. intrudes into the ongoing process, distracting attention from task-relevant behavior

Note. From Teacher praise: A functional analysis by Jere Brophy, spring 1981, *Review of Educational Research*, pp. 5–32. Copyright 1981 by the American Educational Research Association.

of multiple regression analyses and data for combination scores can be given as well, but in addition to rather than instead of basic descriptive and correlational data for each variable. Relevant context information should be supplied and mentioned as qualifiers on potential generalization of the findings, and any suggested prescriptions for teacher practice should place the teaching behaviors back into context and take into account the naturally occurring limits and variance within which the obtained correlational relationships occurred.

Next Steps in Research on Teacher Effects

To enhance its value for both theory and practice, research on teacher effects needs not only methodological improvements but expansion into new areas. For example, most existing research yields conclusions about lessons or lesson components, but little information is available on more molar structures. What are the characteristics of an effective week or unit? How are concepts learned in one unit used effectively in the next? How can units be designed to allow for distributed practice, meaningful integration of learning, and transfer or application?

A related point is that more attention is needed to consecutive sequences of instruction. How does information gathered in the process of interacting with students today affect the teacher's instructional behavior or assignments tomorrow? What changes should occur in the nature and length of lesson components (presentation of new information, recitation, drill, etc.) as teachers initiate and move through a unit? To study these issues of instructional redundancy, integration of concepts, and teachers' processing and use of information gathered during teaching, researchers will have to focus on the instructional unit rather than the lesson as their unit of analysis, and to

observe over several consecutive days rather than spread observations across the term.

More thick description and microanalysis of how lessons and lesson components are accomplished by teachers are also needed. For example, Good and Grouws (1979a, 1979b) urged teachers to include in their lessons a development phase in which they would present concepts, give examples, demonstrate through modeling, and so forth. They gave guidelines about how much time to spend in developmental phases of lessons, but not much qualitative advice, let alone step-by-step instructions, about how to accomplish development segments. One logical next step for their research would be to concentrate attention on development portions of lessons in order to become more prescriptive about the nature and sequencing of steps to include, about the effectiveness of different kinds of examples, and so on (see Good et al., 1983 for related discussion).

Attention is needed to teachers' goals and intentions. We need to know what teachers are trying to accomplish in order to interpret their behaviors, and also to make useful contextual and qualitative distinctions for coding those behaviors. Depending on the teacher's intention at the time, behavior such as asking a particular question or praising a particular student's response may or may not be appropriate.

More attention is needed to higher-level instruction (higher in terms of both grade level and cognitive level). It will be especially important to control the objectives that teachers are working toward in this context. Presently, debates on "cognitive level of instruction" seem to resolve to conflicts about curriculum (what should be taught) rather than method (how it should be taught). Progress toward resolution is unlikely until this confusion is eliminated and appropriate research is conducted. Curriculum issues should be addressed by minimizing the variation in teaching methods or at least the variance in outcomes that can be attributed to differences in teaching methods (ideally, by insuring that each curriculum is taught as well as it can be taught). Method issues must be addressed by holding curriculum constant. Productive research on teaching to higher-level objectives may require not only controlling the content taught in a general sense, but scripting teachers' behavior during lessons and controlling the curriculum materials and assignments to which the students are exposed.

Many questions about effective instruction have not been studied at all yet, or not studied appropriately: the selection and sequencing of questions to include in recitations or discussions designed to achieve particular goals; the nature of the diagnosis and feedback that should occur when teachers monitor progress while students work on assignments; the relative advantages of various accountability procedures, scoring and grading practices, and review and reteaching practices that are applied to completed seatwork assignments; qualitative aspects of teacher presentations other than clarity (usefulness of examples and analogies, density and sequencing of information, length of information-presentation segments and placement with respect to questioning or practice segments); the relative advantages of various questions, tasks, and assignments that students are to work on independently; and questions about how effective instruction might evolve during the course of a unit or a school year.

Integrating Teacher Effects Research with Other Research

Instruction and its relationships to achievement can be isolated for purposes of analysis, but in reality instruction always occurs within particular contexts. Consequently, in designing and speculating about the implications of research on teacher effects, it is useful to consider such research in conjunction with research on factors other than teacher behavior and student achievement. The following three types of research seem especially apropos.

Subject Matter Instruction. Research on instruction in topics within specific subject areas supplements the process–outcome findings reported in this chapter. Research in reading instruction, for example, has shown that concepts can be taught more effectively using certain types and sequences of examples rather than other types or sequences (Engelmann & Carnine, 1982), and that students can be taught not only factual knowledge and word-attack skills, but also the higher-level concepts and learning-to-learn skills needed for effective reading comprehension (Adams, Carnine, & Gersten, 1982; Brown, Campione, & Day, 1981).

Research in mathematics and science instruction has shown that many concepts are counterintuitive or otherwise difficult to grasp and retain, not only for students but also for teachers and other adults. Consequently, teachers with limited backgrounds in certain subject matter areas may teach incorrect content or fail to recognize and correct their students' distorted understandings (cf. Eaton, Anderson, & Smith, 1984). Clearly, the effectiveness of lessons will vary with teachers' interest in and knowledge about the content being taught.

More generally, in delineating the contexts within which instruction occurs, researchers need to pay more specific attention not only to types of lessons and lesson components (Berliner, 1983; Brophy, 1979), but also to the scope and sequence of the curriculum and to the specific subject matter goals and content taught in particular lessons (see Romberg, 1983, for examples in the area of mathematics instruction).

Student Mediation of Instruction. Teachers' instructional objectives are mediated not only by teacher behavior but by academic tasks that teachers present to students (Doyle, 1983) and by students' individualized responses to instruction and academic activities. Students will carry different meanings away from the same lecture or demonstration (Winne & Marx, 1982), respond differentially to teacher behaviors such as praise (Brophy, 1981; Morine-Dershimer, 1982; Weinstein, 1983), and demonstrate diverse needs for structure or autonomy (Ebmeier & Good, 1979; Janicki & Peterson, 1981). Students can profitably teach one another or work together under certain conditions (Slavin, 1980), although some grouping arrangements work better than others (Webb, 1980).

The effects of many teacher behaviors that appear to facilitate achievement (clear presentations, appropriate difficulty level of questions, structuring of the content, specificity of feedback and praise) are mediated via students' immediate information processing. These teacher behaviors provide students with information or engage them with content so that the new information is assimilable; short-term memory is not overloaded (which helps make assimilation possible); connections are made between existing knowledge and the new information; and "chunking" and other efficient mechanisms for processing and retaining information are developed through engagement in appropriate practice and application activities. Discussion of these short-term cognitive outcomes of instruction (changes in students' concepts or content-related information-processing abilities) may be more useful to teachers or teacher educators than discussion of scores on norm-referenced achievement tests. More generally, better articulation of research on teaching with research on students' mediation of classroom events should help us to understand the causal linkages underlying process–outcome relationships, and also to discover unintended side effects of teacher behaviors. The eventual result should be a grounded theory of teaching and its effects. See Wittrock's chapter (this volume) for further discussion of student mediation.

Other Outcome Variables. Research on producing achievement needs to be articulated with research on producing other student outcomes. Effects on student attitudes toward the teacher, the subject matter, or the class were reported in some of the studies reviewed in this chapter. Student attitudes were linked most closely to measures of teacher warmth and student orientation: praise, use of student ideas, willingness to listen to students and respect their contributions, and socializing with students in addition to instructing them. These teacher behaviors are mostly just different from rather than either similar or contradictory to the teacher behaviors associated with achievement, and the two sets of behaviors are compatible to some extent. However, students are likely to have more positive attitudes toward moderately demanding teachers than toward highly demanding teachers.

Few studies of teacher effects on achievement also gathered information on outcomes such as the development of independence, good work habits, social skills, or personal adjustment and mental health. Nor have studies concerned with these outcomes typically measured achievement. Clearly, more research that addresses these multiple outcomes simultaneously within the same study is needed to develop information about what trade-offs must be faced and about what can realistically be accomplished in typical classrooms.

Certain instructional methods have predictable effects on outcomes other than achievement. For example, achievement differences among students are more salient in classes that are subdivided into ability groups or taught routinely as whole classes involving public performance and evaluation than they are in classes that feature individualized instruction or flexible small-group assignments based on factors other than achievement (Bossert, 1979; Rosenholtz & Wilson, 1980; Weinstein, 1983). Social relationships are likely to focus on peers of similar ability level in the former classes, but to involve a broader range of peers in the latter classes. It is also true that the social aspects of education may have important effects on what is learned or how well (Florio, 1978; Eder, 1981; Rosenholtz & Cohen, 1983). Eventually, it will be necessary to integrate research on teacher effects with research on classroom composition (e.g., Bossert, 1979), classroom ecology (Doyle, 1979; Hamilton, 1983), and student perceptions (Weinstein, 1983) to develop a more complete picture of how schooling influences student outcomes.

Conclusion

Comparison of this chapter with related chapters in the first and second editions of this handbook make it clear that we now know much more about teacher effects on achievement than we did in 1963 or even 1973. The myth that teachers do not make a difference in student learning has been refuted, and programmatic research reflecting the description–correlation–experimentation loop called for by Rosenshine and Furst (1973) has begun to appear. As a result, the fund of available information on producing student achievement (especially the literature relating to the general area of classroom management and to the subject areas of elementary reading and mathematics instruction) has progressed from a collection of disappointing and inconsistent findings to a small but well-established knowledge base that includes several successful field experiments.

Although illustrating that instructional processes make a difference, this research also shows that complex instructional problems cannot be solved with simple prescriptions. In the past, when detailed information describing classroom processes and linking them to outcomes did not exist, educational change efforts were typically based on simple theoretical models and associated rhetoric calling for "solutions" that were both oversimplified and overly rigid. The data reviewed here should make it clear that no such "solution" can be effective because what constitutes effective instruction (even if attention is restricted to achievement as the sole outcome of interest) varies with context. What appears to be just the right amount of demandingness (or structuring of content, or praise, etc.) for one class might be too much for a second class but not enough for a third class. Even within the same class, what constitutes effective instruction will vary according to subject matter, group size, and the specific instructional objectives being pursued.

Elitist critics often undervalue teaching or even suggest that anyone can teach ("Those who can, do; those who can't, teach"). The data reviewed here refute this myth as well. Although it may be true that most adults could survive in the classroom, it is not true that most could teach effectively. Even trained and experienced teachers vary widely in how they organize the classroom and present instruction. Specifically, they differ in several respects: the expectations and achievement objectives they hold for themselves, their classes, and individual students; how they select and design academic tasks; and how actively they instruct and communicate with students about academic tasks. Those who do these things successfully produce significantly more achievement than those who do not, but doing them successfully demands a blend of knowledge, energy, motivation, and communication and decision-making skills that many teachers, let alone ordinary adults, do not possess.

Improvement of education must begin with recruitment of capable teachers, followed by retention of those teachers in the teacher role. Preservice and in-service teacher education in both subject matter and pedagogy are also essential, however. This includes familiarizing teachers with the findings reviewed in this chapter. This may sound gratuitous, but many teachers, even recently trained ones, are not aware of important concepts and findings from research on teaching.

It is important that this information be presented in ways that respect the uniqueness of each classroom and recognize that classrooms are complex social settings in which teachers must process a great deal of information rapidly, deal with several agendas simultaneously, and make quick decisions throughout the day. Thus, rather than trying to translate it into overly rigid or generalized prescriptions, teacher educators should present this information to teachers within a decision-making format that enables them to examine concepts critically and adapt them to the particular contexts within which they teach (for an illustration of this, see Amarel, 1981). Research on how teacher education programs can accomplish this effectively is badly needed.

Also needed, of course, is more research on teaching in general and on teacher effects in particular. Despite the successes of the 1960s and 1970s, progress has slowed noticeably of late. In part, this is because we are in a natural period of consolidation following a period of rapid development of new findings using newly developed techniques. However, reduction in support for research on teaching has been another factor. Just as a knowledge base about teaching and teacher education was finally becoming established, the budget for the National Institute of Education was being decimated repeatedly. Adjusted for inflation, federal support of educational research is now below one-third of what it was even a few years ago. We hope that this trend will be reversed, so that authors writing about teacher effects research in the next handbook will also be able to report the kind of progress that we have been able to report in this one.

REFERENCES

Acland, H. (1976). Stability of teacher effectiveness: A replication. *Journal of Educational Research, 69,* 289–292.

Adams, A., Carnine, D., & Gersten, R. (1982). Instructional strategies for studying content area texts in the intermediate grades. *Reading Research Quarterly, 18,* 27–55.

Alexander, L., Frankiewicz, R., & Williams, R. (1979). Facilitation of learning and retention of oral instruction using advance and post organizers. *Journal of Educational Psychology, 71,* 701–707.

Amarel, M. (1981, April). *Literacy: The personal dimension.* Paper presented at the annual meeting of the American Educational Research Association, Los Angeles.

Anderson, L., Evertson, C., & Brophy, J. (1979). An experimental study of effective teaching in first-grade reading groups. *Elementary School Journal, 79,* 193–223.

Anderson, L., Evertson, C., & Brophy, J. (1982). *Principles of small-group instruction in elementary reading* (Occasional Paper No. 58). East Lansing: Michigan State University, Institute for Research on Teaching.

Anderson, O. (1969). *Structure in teaching: Theory and analysis.* New York: Teachers College Press, Columbia University.

Arehart, J. (1979). Student opportunity to learn related to student achievement of objectives in a probability unit. *Journal of Educational Research, 72,* 253–269.

Armento, B. (1977). Teacher behaviors related to student achievement on a social science concept test. *Journal of Teacher Education, 28,* 46–52.

Aspy, D. (1969). The effect of teacher-offered conditions of empathy, positive regard, and congruence upon student achievement. *Florida Journal of Educational Research, 11,* 39–48.

Aspy, D. (1972). *Toward a technology for humanizing education.* Champaign, IL: Research Press.

Ausubel, D. (1968). *Educational psychology: A cognitive view.* New York: Holt, Rinehart & Winston.

Barr, R., & Dreeben, R. (1977). Instruction in classrooms. *Review of Research in Education, 5,* 89–162.

Bellack, A., Hyman, R., Smith, F., & Kliebard, H. (1966). *The language of the classroom.* New York: Columbia University Press.

Bennett, N. (1976). *Teaching styles and pupil progress.* London: Open Books.

Bennett, N., Desforges, C., Cockburn, A., & Wilkinson, B. (1981). *The quality of pupil learning experiences: Interim report.* Lancaster, England: University of Lancaster, Centre for Educational Research and Development.

Berliner, D. (1976). Impediments to the study of teacher effectiveness. *Journal of Teacher Education, 27,* 5–13.

Berliner, D. (1977). Impediments to measuring teacher effectiveness. In G. Borich and K. Fenton (Eds.), *The appraisal of teaching: Concepts and process.* Reading, Ma: Addison–Wesley.

Berliner, D. (1979). Tempus educare. In P Peterson and H. Walberg (Eds.), *Research on teaching: Concepts, findings, and implications.* Berkeley, CA: McCutchan.

Berliner, D. (1983). Developing conceptions of classroom environments: Some light on the T in classroom studies of ATI. *Educational Psychologist, 18,* 1–13.

Berliner, D., Fisher, C., Filby, N., & Marliave, R. (1978). *Executive summary of Beginning Teacher Evaluation Study.* San Francisco: Far West Laboratory.

Berliner, D., & Tikunoff, W. (1976). The California Beginning Teacher Evaluation Study: Overview of the ethnographic study. *Journal of Teacher Education, 27*(1), 24–30.

Berliner, D., & Tikunoff, W. (1977). Ethnography in the classroom. In G. Borich and K. Fenton (Eds.), *The appraisal of teaching: Concepts and process.* Reading, MA: Addison–Wesley.

Bettencourt, E., Gillett, M., Gall, M., & Hull, R. (1983). Effects of teacher enthusiasm training on student on-task behavior and achievement. *American Educational Research Journal, 20,* 435–450.

Blaney, R. (1983). Effects of teacher structuring and reacting on student achievement. *Elementary School Journal, 83,* 569–577.

Blank, M. (1973). *Teaching learning in the preschool: A dialogue approach.* Columbus, OH: Charles E. Merrill.

Bloom, B., Engelhart, M., Furst, E., Hill, W., & Krathwohl, D. (Eds.). (1956). *Taxonomy of educational objectives: Handbook 1. Cognitive domain.* New York: David McKay.

Boak, R., & Conklin, R. (1975). The effect of teachers' levels of interpersonal skills on junior high school students' achievement and anxiety. *American Educational Research Journal, 12,* 537–549.

Borg, W. (1979). Teacher coverage of academic content and pupil achievement. *Journal of Educational Psychology, 71,* 635–645.

Borg, W. (1980). Time and school learning. In C. Denham and A. Lieberman (Eds.), *Time to learn.* Washington, DC: National Institute of Education.

Borich, G., & Fenton, K. (Eds.). (1977). *The appraisal of teaching: Concepts and process.* Reading, MA: Addison–Wesley.

Bossert, S. (1979). *Task and social relationships in classrooms: A study of classroom organization and its consequences* (American Sociological Association, Arnold and Caroline Rose Monograph Series). New York: Cambridge University Press.

Brophy, J. (1973). Stability of teacher effectiveness. *American Educational Research Journal, 10,* 245–252.

Brophy, J. (1979). Teacher behavior and its effects. *Journal of Educational Psychology, 71,* 733–750.

Brophy, J. (1981). Teacher praise: A functional analysis. *Review of Educational Research, 51,* 5–32.

Brophy, J., & Evertson, C. (1974a). *Process–product correlations in the Texas Teacher Effectiveness Study: Final Report* (Research Report 74-4). Austin: University of Texas, R & D Center for Teacher Education. (ERIC Document Reproduction Service No. ED 091 094)

Brophy, J., & Evertson, C. (1974b). *The Texas Teacher Effectiveness Project: Presentation of non-linear relationships and summary discussion* (Research Report No. 74-6). Austin: University of Texas, R & D Center for Teacher Education, (ERIC Document Reproduction Service No. ED 099 345).

Brophy, J., & Evertson, C. (1976). *Learning from teaching: A Developmental perspective.* Boston: Allyn and Bacon.

Brophy, J., & Evertson, C. (1978). Context variables in teaching. *Educational Psychologist, 12,* 310–316.

Brown, A., Campione, J., & Day, J. (1981). Learning to learn: On training students to learn from texts. *Educational Researcher, 2,* 14–21.

Burstein, L. (1980). Issues in the aggregation of data. *Review of Research in Education, 8,* 158–233.

Bush, A., Kennedy, J., & Cruickshank, D. (1977). An empirical investigation of teacher clarity. *Journal of Teacher Education, 28,* 53–58.

Carkhuff, R. (1969). *Helping and human relations: A primer for lay and professional helpers: Vol. 2. Practice and research.* New York: Holt, Rinehart & Winston.

Carkhuff, R. (1971). *The development of human resources.* New York: Holt, Rinehart & Winston.

Centra, J., & Potter, D. (1980). School and teacher effects: An interrelational model. *Review of Educational Research, 50,* 273–291.

Chang, S., & Raths, J. (1971). The schools' contribution to the cumulating deficit *Journal of Educational Research, 64,* 272–276.

Clark, C., Gage, N., Marx, R., Peterson, P., Stayrook, N., & Winne, P. (1979). A factorial experiment on teacher structuring, soliciting, and reacting. *Journal of Educational Psychology, 71,* 534–552.

Clark, R. (1982). Antagonism between achievement and enjoyment in ATI studies. *Educational Psychologist, 17,* 92–101.

Clasen, D. (1983, April). *The effect of four different instructional strategies on the achievement of gifted seventh grade students.* Paper presented at the annual meeting of the American Educational Research Association, Montreal.

Coker, H., Medley, D., & Soar, R. (1980). How valid are expert opinions about effective teaching? *Phi Delta Kappan, 62,* 131–134, 149.

Coleman, J., Campbell, E., Hobson, C., McPartland, J., Mood, A., Weinfield, F., & York, R. (1966). *Equality of educational opportunity.* Washington, DC: U.S. Office of Health, Education, and Welfare.

Comber, L., & Keeves, J. (1973). *Science education in nineteen countries.* New York: Halsted Press.

Cooley, W., & Leinhardt, G. (1980). The Instructional Dimensions Study. *Educational Evaluation and Policy Analysis, 2,* 7–25.

Crawford, J. (1983). A study of instructional processes in Title I classes: 1981–82. *Journal of Research and Evaluation of the Oklahoma City Public Schools, 13* (1).

Crawford, J., Gage, N., Corno, L., Stayrook, N., Mitman, A., Schunk, D., Stallings, J., Baskin, E., Harvey, P., Austin, D., Cronin, D., & Newman, R. (1978). *An experiment on teacher effectiveness and parent-assisted instruction in the third grade* (3 vols.). Stanford, CA: Stanford University, Center for Educational Research at Stanford.

Cruickshank, D. (1976). Synthesis of selected recent research on teacher effects. *Journal of Teacher Education. 27*(1), 57–60.

Cruickshank, D., Kennedy, J., Bush, A., & Myers, B. (1979). Clear teaching: What is it? *British Journal of Teacher Education, 5*, 27–33.

Dalton, M., & Willcocks, J. (Eds.). (1983). *Moving from the primary classroom.* London: Routledge & Kegan Paul.

Denham, C., & Lieberman, A. (Eds.). (1980). *Time to learn.* Washington, DC: National Institute of Education.

Doyle, W. (1977). Paradigms for research on teacher effectiveness. *Review of Research in Education, 5*, 163–198.

Doyle, W. (1979). Classroom task and students' abilities. In P. Peterson and H. Walberg (Eds.), *Research on teaching: Concepts, findings, and implications.* Berkeley, CA: McCutchan.

Doyle, W. (1983). Academic work. *Review of Educational Research, 53*, 159–199.

Dunkin, M. (1978). Student characteristics, classroom processes, and student achievement. *Journal of Educational Psychology, 70*, 998–1009.

Dunkin, M., & Biddle, B. (1974). *The study of teaching.* New York: Holt, Rinehart & Winston.

Dunkin, M., & Doenau, S. (1980). A replication study of unique and joint contributions to variance in student achievement. *Journal of Educational Psychology, 72*, 394–403.

Eaton, J., Anderson, C., & Smith, E. (1984). Students' misconceptions interfere with science learning: Case studies of fifth-grade students. *Elementary School Journal, 84*, 365–379.

Ebmeier, H., & Good, T. (1979). The effects of instructing teachers about good teaching on the mathematics achievement of fourth grade students. *American Educational Research Journal, 16*, 1–16.

Eder, D. (1981). Ability grouping as a self-fulfilling prophecy: A micro-analysis of teacher–student interaction. *Sociology of Education, 54*, 151–173.

Emmer, E., Evertson, C., & Anderson, L. (1980). Effective classroom management at the beginning of the school year. *Elementary School Journal, 80*, 219–231.

Emmer, E., Evertson, C., & Brophy, J. (1979). Stability of teacher effects in junior high classrooms. *American Educational Research Journal, 16*, 71–75.

Engelmann, S., & Carnine, D. (1982). *Theory of instruction: Principles and applications.* New York: Irvington.

Evertson, C. (1979). *Teacher behavior, student achievement, and student attitudes: Descriptions of selected classrooms* (Report No. 4063). Austin: University of Texas, R & D Center for Teacher Education.

Evertson, C., Anderson, C., Anderson, L., & Brophy, J. (1980). Relationships between classroom behaviors and student outcomes in junior high mathematics and English classes. *American Educational Research Journal, 17*, 43–60.

Evertson, C., Anderson, L., & Brophy, J. (1978). *Texas Junior High School Study: Final report of process–outcome relationships* (Report No. 4061). Austin: University of Texas, R & D Center for Teacher Education.

Evertson, C., & Brophy, J. (1973). High-inference behavioral ratings as correlates of teaching effectiveness. *JSAS Catalog of Selected Documents in Psychology, 3*, 97. (ERIC Document Reproduction Service No. ED 095 174)

Evertson, C., & Brophy, J. (1974). *Texas Teacher Effectiveness Project: Questionnaire and interview data* (Research Report No. 74–5). Austin: University of Texas, R & D Center for Teacher Education. (ERIC Document Reproduction Service No. ED 099 346)

Evertson, C., & Emmer, E. (1982). Effective management at the beginning of the school year in junior high classes. *Journal of Educational Psychology, 74*, 485–498.

Evertson, C., Emmer, E., & Brophy, J. (1980). Predictors of effective teaching in junior high mathematics classrooms. *Journal for Research in Mathematics Education, 11*, 167–178.

Fisher, C., Berliner, D., Filby, N., Marliave, R., Cahen, L., & Dishaw, M. (1980). Teaching behaviors, academic learning time, and student achievement: An overview. In C. Denham and A. Lieberman (Eds.), *Time to learn.* Washington, DC: National Institute of Education.

Fisher, C., Filby, N., Marliave, R., Cahen L., Dishaw, M., Moore, J., & Berliner, D. (1978). *Teaching behaviors, academic learning time and student achievement: Final report of Phase III-B, Beginning Teacher Evaluation Study.* San Francisco: Far West Laboratory.

Fitz-Gibbon, C., & Clark, K. (1982). Time variables in classroom research: A study of eight urban secondary school mathematics classes. *British Journal of Educational Psychology, 52*, 301–316.

Flanders, N. (1965). *Teacher influence, pupil attitudes, and achievement* (Cooperative Research Monograph No. 12). Washington DC: U.S. Office of Education.

Flanders, N. (1970). *Analyzing teacher behavior.* Reading, MA: Addison–Wesley.

Flanders, N., & Simon, A. (1969). Teacher effectiveness. In R. Ebel (Ed.), *Encyclopedia of Educational Research* (4th ed.). New York: Macmillan.

Florio, S. (1978). *Learning how to go to school: An ethnography of interaction in a kindergarten–first-grade classroom.* Unpublished Ph.D. dissertation, Harvard University, Cambridge, MA.

Fortune, J. (1967). *A study of the generality of presenting behaviors in teaching preschool children* (Final Report for U.S. Office of Education Project No. 6-8468). Memphis, TN: Memphis State University. (ERIC Document Reproduction Service No. ED 016 285)

Gage, N. (1965). Desirable behaviors of teachers. *Urban Education, 1*, 85–95.

Gage, N. (1978). *The scientific basis of the art of teaching.* New York: Teachers College Press, Columbia University.

Gage, N. (1979). The generality of dimensions of teaching. In P. Peterson and H. Walberg (Eds.), *Research on teaching: Concepts, findings, and implications.* Berkeley, CA: McCutchan.

Gage, N. (1983). When does research on teaching yield implications for practice? *Elementary School Journal, 83*, 492–496.

Gage, N., Belgard, M., Dell, D., Hiller, J., Rosenshine, B., & Unruh, W. (1968). *Explorations of the teacher's effectiveness in explaining* (Tech. Rep. No. 4). Stanford, CA: Stanford University, Center for Research and Development in Teaching.

Gage, N., & Coladarci, T. (1980). *Replication of an experiment with a research-based inservice teacher education program.* Stanford, CA: Stanford University, Center for Educational Research at Stanford, Program on Teaching Effectiveness.

Gall, M., Ward, B., Berliner, D., Cahen, L., Winne, P., Elashoff, J., & Stanton, G. (1978). Effects of questioning techniques and recitation on student learning. *American Educational Research Journal, 15*, 175–199.

Galton, M., & Simon, B. (1980). *Progress and performance in the primary classroom.* Boston: Routledge & Kegan Paul.

Glass, G., & Smith, M. (1978). *Meta-analysis of research on the relationship of class size and achievement.* Boulder: University of Colorado, Laboratory of Educational Research.

Good, T. (1979). Teacher effectiveness in the elementary school: What we know about it now. *Journal of Teacher Education, 30*, 52–64.

Good, T., Biddle, B., & Brophy, J. (1975). *Teachers make a difference.* New York: Holt, Rinehart & Winston.

Good, T., & Brophy, J. (1984). *Looking in Classrooms* (3rd ed.). New York: Harper & Row.

Good, T., Ebmeier, H., & Beckerman, T. (1978). Teaching mathematics in high and low SES classrooms: An empirical comparison. *Journal of Teacher Education, 29*, 85–90.

Good, T., & Grouws, D. (1975). *Process–product relationship in fourth-grade mathematics classrooms* (Final Report: National Institute of Education Grant NIE-G-00-3-0123). Columbia: University of Missouri, College of Education.

Good, T., & Grouws, D. (1977). Teaching effects: A process–product study in fourth grade mathematics classrooms. *Journal of Teacher Education, 28*, 49–54.

Good, T., & Grouws, D. (1979a). *Experimental study of mathematics instruction in elementary schools* (Final Report, National Institute of Education Grant No. NIE-G-79-0103). Columbia: University of Missouri, Center for the Study of Social Behavior.

Good, T., & Grouws, D. (1979b). The Missouri Mathematics Effectiveness Project: An experimental study in fourth grade classrooms. *Journal of Educational Psychology, 71,* 355–362.

Good, T., & Grouws, D. (1981). *Experimental research in secondary mathematics* (Final Report, National Institute of Education Grant No. NIE-G-79-0103). Columbia: University of Missouri, Center for the Study of Social Behavior.

Good, T., Grouws, D., & Beckerman, T. (1978). Curriculum pacing: Some empirical data in mathematics. *Journal of Curriculum Studies, 10,* 75–81.

Good, T., Grouws, D., & Ebmeier, M. (1983). *Active mathematics teaching.* New York: Longman.

Good, T., & Power, C. (1976). Designing successful classroom environments for different types of students. *Journal of Curriculum Studies, 8,* 1–16.

Hamilton, S. (1983). The social side of schooling: Ecological studies of classrooms and schools. *Elementary School Journal, 83,* 313–334.

Harris, A., & Serwer, B. (1966). The CRAFT Project: Instructional time in reading research. *Reading Research Quarterly, 2,* 27–57.

Heath, R., & Nielson, M.(1974). The research basis for performance-based teacher education. *Review of Educational Research, 44,* 463–484.

Hiller, J., Fisher, G., & Kaess, W. (1969). A computer investigation of verbal characteristics of effective classroom lecturing. *American Educational Research Journal, 6,* 661–675.

Hughes, D. (1973). An experimental investigation of the effects of pupil responding and teacher reacting on pupil achievement. *American Educational Research Journal, 10,* 21–37.

Husen, T. (Ed.). (1967). *International study of achievement in mathematics* (Vols. 1). New York: John Wiley.

Janicki, T., & Peterson, P. (1981). Aptitude–treatment interaction effects of variations in direct instruction. *American Educational Research Journal, 18,* 63–82.

Jencks, C., Smith, M., Acland, H., Bane, M., Cohen, D., Gintis, H., Heyns, B., & Michelson, S. (1972). *Inequality: A reassessment of the effect of family and schooling in America.* New York: Basic Books.

Karweit, N. (1983). *Time on task: A research review* (Report No. 332). Baltimore, MD: Johns Hopkins University, Center for Social Organization for Schools.

Karweit, N., & Slavin, R. (1982). Time-on-task: Issues of timing, sampling, and definition. *Journal of Educational Psychology, 74,* 844–851.

Kennedy, J., Cruickshank, D., Bush, A., & Myers, B. (1978). Additional investigations into the nature of teacher clarity. *Journal of Educational Research, 72,* 3–10.

Kounin, J. (1970). *Discipline and group management in classrooms.* New York: Holt, Rinehart & Winston.

Kyriacou, C., & Newson, G. (1982). Teacher effectiveness: A consideration of research problems. *Educational Review, 34,* 3–12.

Land, M. (1979). Low-inference variables and teacher clarity: Effects on student concept learning. *Journal of Educational Psychology, 71,* 795–799.

Land, M., & Smith, L. (1979). The effect of low inference teacher clarity inhibitors on student achievement. *Journal of Teacher Education, 31,* 55–57.

Larrivee, B., & Algina, J. (1983, April). *Identification of teaching behaviors which predict success for mainstreamed students.* Paper presented at the annual meeting of the American Educational Research Association.

MacKay, A. (1979). *Project Quest: Teaching strategies and pupil achievement* (Research Report No. 79-1-3). Edmonton, Canada: University of Alberta, Centre for Research in Teaching, Faculty of Education.

Madike, F. (1980). Teacher classroom behaviors involved in microteaching and student achievement: A regression study. *Journal of Educational Psychology, 72,* 265–274.

Martin, J. (1979). Effects of teacher higher-order questions on student process and product variables in a single-classroom study. *Journal of Educational Research, 72,* 183–187.

McCaleb, J., & White, J. (1980). Critical dimensions in evaluating teacher clarity. *Journal of Classroom Interaction, 15,* 27–30.

McConnell, J. (1977). *Relationships between selected teacher behaviors and attitudes/achievements of algebra classes.* Paper presented at the Annual Meeting of the American Educational Research Association.

McDonald, F. (1976). Report on Phase II of the Beginning Teacher Evaluation Study. *Journal of Teacher Education, 27(1),* 39–42.

McDonald, F. (1977). Research on teaching: Report on Phase II of the Beginning Teacher Evaluation Study. In G. Borich and K. Fenton (Eds.), *The appraisal of teaching: Concepts and process.* Reading, MA: Addison–Wesley.

McDonald, F., & Elias, P. (1976a). *The effects of teaching performance on pupil learning. Beginning Teacher Evaluation Study, Phase II, 1974–1976* (Final report, 5 vols.). Princeton, NJ: Educational Testing Service.

McDonald, F., & Elias, P. (1976b). *Executive summary report: Beginning Teacher Evaluation Study, Phase II.* Princeton, NJ: Educational Testing Service.

McKenzie, G., & Henry, M. (1979). Effects of testlike events on on-task behavior, test anxiety, and achievement in a classroom rule-learning task. *Journal of Educational Psychology, 71,* 370–374.

Medley, D. (1977). *Teacher competency and teacher effectiveness: A review of process–product research.* Washington DC: American Association of Colleges for Teacher Education.

Medley, D. (1979). The effectiveness of teachers. In P. Peterson and H. Walberg (Eds.), *Research on teaching: Concepts, findings, and implications.* Berkeley, CA: McCutchan.

Medley, D., & Mitzel, H. (1963). Measuring classroom behavior by systematic observation. In N. L. Gage (Ed.), *Handbook of research on teaching.* Chicago: Rand McNally.

Mitzel, H. (1960). Teacher effectiveness. In C. Harris (Ed.), *Encyclopedia of educational research* (3rd ed.). New York: Macmillan.

Morine-Dershimer, G. (1982). Pupil perceptions of teacher praise. *Elementary School Journal, 82,* 421–434.

Morsh, J., & Wilder, E. (1954). *Identifying the effective instructor: A review of the quantitative studies, 1900–1952* (Research Bulletin No. AFPTRC-TR-54-44). San Antonio, TX: USAF Personnel Training Research Center, Lackland Air Force Base.

Mosteller, F., & Moynihan, D. (1972). *On equality of educational opportunity.* New York: Random House.

National Institute of Education. (1974). *Report of Panel 2 of the National Conference on Studies in Teaching: Teaching as human interaction.* Washington DC: National Institute of Education.

Nuthall, G., & Church, J. (1973). Experimental studies of teaching behaviour. In G. Chanan (Ed.), *Towards a science of teaching.* London: National Foundation for Educational Research.

Peterson, P. (1979). Direct instruction reconsidered. In P. Peterson and H. Walberg (Eds.), *Research on teaching. Concepts, findings, and implications.* Berkeley, CA: McCutchan.

Peterson, P., & Walberg, H. (Eds.). (1979). *Research on teaching: Concepts, findings, and implications.* Berkeley, CA: McCutchan.

Popham, W. (1971). Performance tests of teaching proficiency: Rationale, development, and validation. *American Educational Research Journal, 8,* 105–117.

Powell, M. (1980). The Beginning Teacher Evaluation Study: A brief history of a major research project. In C. Denham and A. Lieberman (Eds.), *Time to learn.* Washington DC: National Institute of Education.

Ramp, E., & Rhine, W. (1981). Behavior analysis model. In W. Rhine (Ed.), *Making schools more effective: New directions from Follow Through.* New York: Academic Press.

Redfield, D., & Rousseau E. (1981). A meta-analysis of experimental research on teacher questioning behavior. *Review of Educational Research, 51,* 237–245.

Romberg, T. (1983). A common curriculum for mathematics. In G. Fenstermacher and J. Goodlad (Eds.), *Individual differences and the common curriculum* (Eighty-second yearbook of the National

Society for the Study of Education, Part 1). Chicago: University of Chicago Press.

Rose, J., & Medway, F. (1981). Teacher locus of control, teacher behavior, and student behavior as determinants of student achievement. *Journal of Educational Research, 74*, 375–381.

Rosenholtz, S., & Cohen, E. (1983). Back to basics and the desegregated school. *Elementary School Journal, 83*, 515–527.

Rosenholtz, S., & Wilson, B. (1980). The effect of classroom structure on shared perceptions of ability. *American Educational Research Journal, 17*, 75–82.

Rosenshine, B. (1968). To explain: A review of research. *Educational Leadership, 26*, 275–280.

Rosenshine, B. (1970a). Evaluation of instruction. *Review of Educational Research, 40*, 279–301.

Rosenshine, B. (1970b). Experimental classroom studies of indirect teaching. *Classroom Interaction Newsletter, 5*(2), 7–11.

Rosenshine, B. (1971). *Teaching behaviours and student achievement.* London: National Foundation for Educational Research.

Rosenshine, B. (1976). Classroom instruction. In N. L. Gage (Eds.), *The psychology of teaching methods* (Seventy-seventh yearbook of the National Society for the Study of Education). Chicago: University of Chicago Press.

Rosenshine, B. (1979). Content, time, and direct instruction. In P. Peterson and H. Walberg (Eds.), *Research on teaching: Concepts, findings, and implications.* Berkeley, CA: McCutchan.

Rosenshine, B. (1983). Teaching functions in instructional programs. *Elementary School Journal, 83*, 335–351.

Rosenshine, B., & Berliner, D. (1978). Academic engaged time. *British Journal of Teacher Education, 4*, 3–16.

Rosenshine, B., & Furst, N. (1973). The use of direct observation to study teaching. In R. M. W. Travers (Ed.), *Second Handbook of Research on Teaching.* Chicago: Rand McNally.

Rosenshine, B., & Stevens, R. (1984). Classroom instruction in reading. In D. Pearson (Ed.), *Handbook of research on reading.* New York: Longman.

Rowe, M. (1974). Wait-time and rewards as instructional variables, their influence on language, logic and fate control: Part 1. Wait-time. *Journal of Research in Science Teaching. 11*, 81–94.

Ryan, F. (1973). Differentiated effects of levels of questioning on student achievement. *Elementary School Journal, 41*, 63–67.

Ryan, F. (1974). The effects on social studies achievement of multiple student responding to different levels of questioning. *Journal of Experimental Education, 42*, 71–75.

Schofield, H. (1978). Teacher effects on cognitive and affective pupil outcomes in elementary school mathematics. *Journal of Educational Psychology, 73*, 462–471.

Schuck, R. (1981). The impact of set induction on student achievement and retention. *Journal of Educational Research, 74*, 227–232.

Simon, A., & Boyer, E. (Eds.). (1967). *Mirrors for behavior: An anthology of observation instruments.* Philadelphia: Research for Better Schools.

Simon, A., & Boyer, E. (Eds.). (1970a). *Mirrors for behavior: An anthology of observation instruments continued, 1970 supplement,* Volume A. Philadelphia: Research for Better Schools.

Simon, A., & Boyer, E. (Eds.). (1970b). *Mirrors for behavior: An anthology of observation instruments continued, 1970 supplement,* Volume B. Philadelphia: Research for Better Schools.

Slavin, R. (1980). Cooperative learning. *Review of Educational Research, 50*, 315–342.

Slavin, R. (1983). *Team-assisted individualization: A cooperative learning solution for adaptive instruction in mathematics* (Report No. 340). Baltimore: Johns Hopkins University, Center for the Social Organization of Schools.

Smith, L. (1977). Aspects of teacher discourse and student achievement in mathematics. *Journal for Research in Mathematics Education, 8*, 195–204.

Smith, L. (1979). Task-oriented lessons and student achievement. *Journal of Educational Research, 73*, 16–19.

Smith, L., & Cotten, M. (1980). Effect of lesson vagueness and discontinuity on student achievement and attitudes. *Journal of Educational Psychology, 72*, 670–675.

Smith, L., & Land, M. (1981). Low-inference verbal behaviors related to teacher clarity. *Journal of Classroom Interaction, 17*, 37–42.

Smith, L., & Sanders, K. (1981). The effects on student achievement and student perception of varying structure in social studies content. *Journal of Educational Research, 74*, 333–336.

Smith, M., & Glass, G. (1980). Meta-analysis of research on class size and its relationship to attitudes and instruction. *American Educational Research Journal, 17*, 419–433.

Soar, R. S. (1966). *An integrative approach to classroom learning* (Report for NIMH Projects No. 5-R11 MH 01096 and 7-R11 MH 02045. Philadelphia: Temple University. (ERIC Document Reproduction Service No. ED 033 749).

Soar, R. S. (1968). Optimum teacher–pupil interaction for pupil growth. *Educational Leadership, 26*, 275–280.

Soar, R. S. (1973). *Follow Through classroom process measurement and pupil growth* (1970–1971, final report). Gainesville: University of Florida, Institute for Development of Human Resources. (ERIC Document Reproduction Service No. ED 106 297).

Soar, R. S. (1977). An integration of findings from four studies of teacher effectiveness. In G. Borich and K. Fenton (Eds.), *The appraisal of teaching: Concepts and process.* Reading, MA: Addison-Wesley.

Soar, R. S., & Soar, R. M. (1972). An empirical analysis of selected Follow Through programs: An example of a process approach to evaluation. In I. Gordon (Ed.), *Early Childhood Education.* Chicago: National Society for the Study of Education.

Soar, R. S., & Soar, R. M. (1973). Classroom behavior, pupil characteristics and pupil growth for the school year and the summer. Gainesville: University of Florida, Institute for Development of Human Resources.

Soar, R. S., & Soar, R. M. (1978). *Setting variables, classroom interaction, and multiple pupil outcomes* (Final report, Project No. 6-0432, Grant No. NIE-G-76-0100). Washington, DC: National Institute of Education.

Soar, R. S., & Soar, R.M. (1979). Emotional climate and management. In P. Peterson and H. Walberg (Eds.), *Research on teaching: Concepts, findings, and implications.* Berkeley, CA: McCutchan.

Solomon, D., & Kendell, A. (1979). *Children in classrooms: An investigation of person–environment interaction.* New York: Praeger.

Southwest Educational Development Laboratory. (1973). *Bilingual kindergarten program inservice manual* (Vol. 1). Austin, TX: National Educational Laboratory Publishers.

Stallings, J. (1975). Implementation and child effects of teaching practices in Follow Through classrooms. *Monographs of the Society for Research in Child Development, 40*, (7–8, Serial No. 163).

Stallings, J. (1980). Allocated academic learning time revisited, or beyond time on task. *Educational Researcher, 8*(11), 11–16.

Stallings, J., Cory, R., Fairweather, J., & Needels, M. (1977). *Early Childhood Education classroom evaluation.* Menlo Park, CA: SRI International.

Stallings, J., Cory, R., Fairweather, J., & Needels, M. (1978). *A study of basic reading skills taught in secondary schools.* Menlo Park, CA: SRI International.

Stallings, J., & Kaskowitz, D. (1974). *Follow Through classroom observation evaluation 1972–1973* (SRI Project URU-7370). Stanford, CA: Stanford Research Institute.

Stallings, J., Needels, M., & Stayrook, N. (1979). *The teaching of basic reading skills in secondary schools, Phase II and Phase III.* Menlo Park, CA: SRI International.

Tikunoff, W., Berliner, D., & Rist, R. (1975). An ethnographic study of the forty classrooms of the Beginning Teacher Evaluation Study known sample (Tech. Rep. No. 75-10-5). San Francisco: Far West Laboratory.

Tobin, K. (1980). The effect of an extended teacher wait-time on science achievement. *Journal of Research in Science Teaching, 17*, 469–475.

Tobin, K., & Capie, W. (1982). Relationships between classroom process variables and middle-school science achievement. *Journal of Educational Psychology, 74*, 441–454.

Veldman, D., & Brophy, J. (1974). Measuring teacher effects on pupil achievement. *Journal of Educational Psychology, 66*, 319–324.

Walker, D., & Schaffarzick, J. (1974). Comparing curricula. *Review of Educational Research, 44*, 83–111.

Webb, N. (1980). A process–outcome analysis of learning in group and individual settings. *Educational Psychologist, 15*, 69–83.

Weinstein, R. (1983). Student perceptions of schooling. *Elementary School Journal, 83*, 287–312.

Winne, P. (1979). Experiments relating teachers' use of higher cognitive questions to student achievement. *Review of Educational Research, 49*, 13–50.

Winne, P., & Marx, R. (1982). Students' and teachers' views of thinking processes involved in classroom learning. *Elementary School Journal, 82*, 493–518.

Wright, C., & Nuthall, G. (1970). Relationships between teacher behaviors and pupil achievement in three experimental elementary science lessons. *American Educational Research Journal, 7*, 477–491.

Wyne, M., & Stuck, G. (1982). Time and learning: Implications for the classroom teacher. *Elementary School Journal, 83*, 67–75.

13.

Teaching Functions

Barak Rosenshine and Robert Stevens
University of Illinois

Recent Experimental Studies

In recent years our understanding of successful teaching has increased considerably. There have been numerous successful experimental studies in which teachers have been trained to increase the academic achievement of their students. In these studies, which have taken place in regular classrooms, one group of teachers received training in specific instructional procedures and one group continued their regular teaching. In the successful studies, the teachers implemented the training and their students had higher achievement and/or higher academic engaged time than did students in the classrooms of the untrained teachers. Particularly noteworthy studies include:

- Texas First Grade Reading Group Study (Anderson, Evertson, & Brophy, 1979, 1982)
- Missouri Mathematics Effectiveness Study (Good & Grouws, 1979) (for math in intermediate grades)
- The Texas Elementary School Study (Evertson, Emmer, Clements, Sanford, Worsham, & Williams, 1981; Emmer, Evertson, Sanford, & Clements, 1982);
- The Texas Junior High School Study (Emmer, Evertson, Sanford, Clements, & Worsham, 1982; Emmer, Evertson, Sanford, & Clements, 1982);
- Organizing and Instructing High School Classes (Fitzpatrick, 1981, 1982)
- Exemplary Centers for Reading Instruction (ECRI) (Reid, 1978, 1979, 1980, 1981) (for reading in grades 1–5)
- Direct Instruction Follow Through Program (Becker, 1977).

The results of these studies are consistently positive and indicate that there are specific instructional procedures which teachers can be trained to follow and which can lead to increased achievement and student engagement in their classrooms.

Examples of Experimental Studies

An example of these experimental studies is the one conducted by Good and Grouws in 1979. In their study, 40 fourth grade teachers were divided into two groups. One group, of 21 teachers, received a 5-page manual which contained a system of sequential, instructional steps for teaching mathematics. The teachers read the manual, received two 90 minute training sessions, and proceeded to implement the key instructional behaviors in their teaching of mathematics. The control teachers did not receive the manual and were told to continue to instruct in their own style. During the 4 months of the program all teachers were observed six times.

The results showed that the teachers in the treatment group implemented many of the key instructional behaviors and, in many areas, behaved significantly differently from those in the control group. For example, the treatment teachers conducted review, checked homework, actively engaged students in seatwork, and made homework assignments significantly more often than control teachers. The results also showed that the test scores in mathematics for students of the treatment teachers increased significantly more than did the scores for students of the control teachers.

Fitzpatrick (1982) conducted a similar study involving ninth grade algebra and foreign language classes. Twenty teachers were divided into two groups, and the treatment group received a manual explaining and giving teaching suggestions on 13 instructional principles. The treatment group met twice to discuss the manual. The control teachers were told to continue their regular teaching. All teachers were observed five times in one of their classrooms.

The results showed that the treatment teachers implemented many of the principles more frequently than did the control teachers. For instance, the treatment teachers were rated higher in attending to inappropriate student behavior, maintaining the attention of all students, providing immediate feedback and

The authors thank reviewers David Berliner (University of Arizona), Jere Brophy (IRT, Michigan State University), and Richard Shavelson (UCLA).

evaluation, having fewer interruptions, setting clear expectations, and having a warm and supportive environment. In addition, overall student engagement was higher in the classrooms of the treatment teachers.

The other studies cited above were similar to these two: they all provided in-service teachers with manuals and training to implement the recommended instructional procedures. The manuals and training materials for these programs could be used effectively in both preservice and in-service teacher training. Four of the manuals are useful for general instruction (Emmer et al., 1982; Evertson et al., 1982; Fitzpatrick, 1982; Good & Grouws, 1979). The manual by Anderson, Evertson, and Brophy (1982) is oriented primarily toward instruction in elementary reading groups, whereas the program developed by Reid (1978–1981) and by Englemann (Becker, 1977) included both general instructional methods and highly specific procedures for the teaching of reading.

The purpose of this paper is to study those successful teacher training and student achievement programs and identify the common teaching functions which they emphasize. This information will be supplemented by correlational research whenever relevant.

In general, researchers have found that when effective teachers teach well structured subjects, they:

- Begin a lesson with a short review of previous, prerequisite learning.
- Begin a lesson with a short statement of goals.
- Present new material in small steps, with student practice after each step.
- Give clear and detailed instructions and explanations.
- Provide a high level of active practice for all students.
- Ask a large number of questions, check for student understanding, and obtain responses from all students.
- Guide students during initial practice.
- Provide systematic feedback and corrections.
- Provide explicit instruction and practice for seatwork exercises and, where necessary, monitor students during seatwork.

The major components in systematic teaching include teaching in small steps with student practice after each step, guiding students during initial practice, and providing all students with a high level of successful practice. Of course, all teachers use some of these behaviors some of the time, but the most effective teachers use most of them almost all the time.

Use and Limits of Research

It would be a mistake to claim that the teaching procedures which have emerged from this research apply to all subjects, and all learners, all the time. Rather, these procedures are most applicable for the "well-structured" (Simon, 1973) parts of any content area, and are least applicable to the "ill-structured" parts of any content area.

Most Applicable Procedures

These explicit teaching procedures are most applicable in those areas where the objective is to master a body of knowledge or learn a skill which can be taught in a step-by-step manner. Thus, these procedures apply to the teaching of facts that students are expected to master so that they can be used with new information in the future. Examples include arithmetic facts, decoding procedures, vocabulary, musical notation, English grammar, the factual parts of science and history, the vocabulary and grammar of foreign languages, and the factual and explicit parts of electronics, cooking, and accounting.

Similarly, these procedures apply to the teaching of processes or skills that students are expected to apply to new problems or situations. This includes mathematical computation, blending sounds in decoding, map reading, the mechanics of writing personal and business letters, English grammar, applying scientific laws, solving algebraic equations, or tuning an automobile engine. In these cases, the student is taught a general rule which is then applied to new situations.

Least Applicable

These findings are least applicable for teaching in areas which are "ill-structured," that is, where the skills to be taught do not follow explicit steps, or areas which lack a general skill which is applied repeatedly. Thus, the results of this research are less relevant for teaching composition and writing of term papers, analysis of literature, problem solving in specific content areas, discussion of social issues, or the development of unique or creative responses.

Almost all content areas are composed of well-structured and ill-structured parts, and explicit teaching can be used for teaching the well-structured parts. For example, when teaching a foreign language, explicit teaching can be used to teach vocabulary and grammar, but these procedures are less relevant for teaching fluency in conversation or reading comprehension. In teaching literature, there is a place for explicit teaching in teaching about the characters, setting, plot, and theme identification. But these procedures are less relevant for teaching students to appreciate the story, evaluate the ideas, or critique the style of writing.

New Developments in Explicit Instruction

As noted, explicit procedures are less applicable for those skills or processes where there is no clearly defined procedure that is learned and applied in new situations. Until the 1980s, this was the case in teaching reading comprehension. Durkin (1978–1979) noted that there is little explicit instruction when teaching reading comprehension. Rather, she noted that teachers spend most of their time asking questions, and spend very little time giving explicit or direct instructions in helping students understand the meaning of a paragraph or story. Indeed, she observed 24 fourth grade reading teachers for 5,000 minutes, and found that explicit comprehension instruction occurred less than 1% of the time. Durkin (1981) also inspected elementary reading textbooks and found a similar lack of explicit instruction.

Since 1975, investigators have developed explicit, direct procedures which have been shown to aid students in reading comprehension and study skills. In reading comprehension, these studies have involved training students in generative activities during reading (Carnine, Kuder, Salvino, & Moore, 1983; Linden & Wittrock, 1981) and teaching students strategies for comprehension skills (Carnine et al., 1983; Day, 1980; Patchings, Kameenui, Colvin, & Carnine, 1979; Raphael, 1980; Singer & Donlon, 1982). Each of these studies yielded significant effects in improved reading comprehension. Similarly, studies which train students in skills for studying texts (Dansereau, 1979; Larkin & Reif, 1976) have yielded significant results.

For Whom is This Approach Most Relevant?

The small-step approach which emerges from the research is particularly useful when teaching younger students, slower students, and students of all ages and abilities during the first stages of instruction with unfamiliar material (Berliner, 1982). Similarly, these ideas best apply when learning hierarchical material because subsequent learning builds upon well-formed prior learning. These ideas would also apply when the material is difficult, no matter how talented the learners.

In general, the amount of time spent in presentation, guided practice, and independent practice varies with the age and maturity of the students and the difficulty of the material. With younger students and/or difficult material, the presentation is fairly short and more time is spent in guided practice and supervised independent practice. With older, more mature, and faster students, and as the material becomes more familiar, more time is spent in presenting new material and less time is spent in guided practice.

No single, common term to describe this teaching has emerged as yet. Rather, a variety of terms are being used including direct instruction, systematic teaching, explicit instruction, active teaching, and effective teaching. All of these terms are useful for describing the systematic, explicit, direct procedures which will be discussed in this chapter.

Information Processing and Instruction

Another approach to understanding classroom teaching is to look at the recent research on human information processing. There is good correspondence between the results of this research and the research on effective teaching. The information processing results apply in three areas: the limits of our working memory, the importance of elaboration and practice, and the importance of continuing practice until the students are fluent.

When teachers present new information, they should be concerned with not presenting too much information at one time. Current information-processing theories suggest that we are "limited-capacity processors." That is, there are limits to the amount of information learners can attend to and process effectively (Beck, 1978; Miller, 1956). When too much information is presented at once, our working memory becomes swamped (James, 1890; Norman & Brobow, 1975). When this happens, we become confused, omit or skim material, and are unable to complete the processing correctly (Tobias, 1982).

This suggests that when teaching new or difficult material, a teacher should proceed in small steps and provide practice on one step before adding another. In this way, the learner does not have to process too much at one time and can concentrate his/her somewhat limited attention to processing manageable size pieces of information or skills.

In addition, a teacher can help students by reviewing relevant prior knowledge. Such review may provide the student with a cognitive structure for encoding the new material and thus require less processing resources than if the information were totally new (Spiro, 1981). Teachers provide this support by previewing lessons, telling students what they are going to learn; by relating the new information to what students have previously learned; and by providing organizers and outlines for the lesson.

A second finding is that we have to process new material in order to transfer it from our working memory to our long-term memory. That is, we have to elaborate, review, rehearse, summarize, or enhance the material (see Gagne, 1985). This suggests that a teacher should provide active practice for all students. This practice is facilitated if the teacher guides the necessary processing by asking questions, requiring students to summarize ideas in their own words, helping students make connections between old and new knowledge, having students tutor each other, supervising students as they practice new steps in a skill, and providing feedback on their efforts.

A third point is that new learning is easier when prior learning is readily accessible or automatic. In a large number of academic situations the student needs to apply and use the knowledge or skills that have been previously learned. Retention and application of previously learned knowledge and skills comes through overlearning, that is, practice beyond the point where the student has to work to give the correct response. This results in automatic processes which are rapidly executed and require little or no conscious attention. When prior learning is automatic, space is freed in our working memory, which can then be used for comprehension, application, and problem solving (LaBerge & Samuels, 1974; Spiro, 1981; Wagner & Sternberg, 1984).

Reading is a good example of the importance of automatic recall. Readers who do not decode automatically need to allocate much of their limited capacity to decoding and word identification, and as a result, they have little capacity left for comprehending what is read (LaBerge & Samuels, 1974; Perfetti & Lesgold, 1979). However, when learners are fluent in word recognition, they can then devote more processing capacity to comprehending the passage. Similarly, Greeno (1978) noted that mathematical problem solving is improved when the basic skills (addition, multiplication, etc.) are overlearned and become automatic, thus freeing processing capacity.

The benefits of overlearning suggest that there is value in repeating and rehearsing basic material that will be used in subsequent learning. In most fields, such basic material can include facts, concepts, skills and procedures, and specialized vocabulary.

We might summarize the above by saying that when learning new material it is important for the teacher to provide "instructional support" for the learner (Tobias, 1982). When providing such support, a teacher would (a) break the material into small steps in order to reduce confusion, (b) give the learner practice in each step before increasing complexity by adding another step, (c) provide for elaboration and enhancement in order to help the learner move the material from working memory into long term memory, and (d) provide for additional practice and overlearning of basic material and skills so that the learners are fluent and automatic in using them.

The research on information processing helps explain why students taught with structured curricula generally do better than those taught with either more individualized or discovery learning approaches. It also explains why young students who receive their instruction from a teacher usually achieve more than those who are expected to learn new material and skills on their own or from each other. When young students are expected to learn on their own, particularly in the early stages, the students run the danger of not attending to the right cues, or not processing important points, and of proceeding on to later points before they have done sufficient elaboration and practice.

A General Model of Effective Instruction

Putting together ideas from a number of sources (including those mentioned on page 1), we have developed a list of six fundamental instructional "functions" which appear below and, in more detail, in Table 13.1.

1. Review, check previous day's work (and reteach, if necessary)
2. Present new content/skills
3. Guided student practice (and check for understanding)
4. Feedback and correctives (and reteach, if necessary)
5. Independent student practice
6. Weekly and monthly reviews.

Table 13.1. Instructional Functions

1. Daily Review and Checking Homework
   Checking homework (routines for students to check each other's papers)
   Reteaching when necessary
   Reviewing relevant past learning (may include questioning)
   Review prerequisite skills (if applicable)

2. Presentation
   Provide short statement of objectives
   Provide overview and structuring
   Proceed in small steps but at a rapid pace
   Intersperse questions within the demonstration to check for understanding
   Highlight main points
   Provide sufficient illustrations and concrete examples
   Provide demonstrations and models
   When necessary, give detailed and redundant instructions and examples

3. Guided Practice
   Initial student practice takes place with teacher guidance
   High frequency of questions and overt student practice (from teacher and/or materials)
   Questions are directly relevant to the new content or skill
   Teacher checks for understanding (CFU) by evaluating student responses
   During CFU teacher gives additional explanation, process feedback, or repeats explanation—where necessary
   All students have a chance to respond and receive feedback; teacher insures that all students participate
   Prompts are provided during guided practice (where appropriate)
   Initial student practice is *sufficient* so that students can work independently
   Guided practice continues until students are firm
   Guided practice is continued (usually) until a success rate of 80% is achieved

4. Correctives and Feedback
   Quick, firm, and correct responses can be followed by another question or a short acknowledgment of correctness (i.e., "That's right").
   Hesitant correct answers might be followed by process feedback (i.e., "Yes, Linda, that's right because...").
   Student errors indicate a need for more practice.
   Monitor students for systematic errors.
   Try to obtain a substantive response to each question.
   Corrections can include sustaining feedback (i.e., simplifying the question, giving clues), explaining or reviewing steps, giving process feedback, or reteaching the last steps.
   Try to elicit an improved response when the first one is incorrect.
   Guided practice and corrections continue until the teacher feels that the group can meet the objectives of the lesson.
   Praise should be used in moderation, and specific praise is more effective than general praise.

5. Independent Practice (Seatwork)
   Sufficient practice
   Practice is directly relevant to skills/content taught
   Practice to overlearning
   Practice until responses are firm, quick, and automatic
   Ninety-five percent correct rate during independent practice
   Students alerted that seatwork will be checked
   Student held accountable for seatwork
   Actively supervise students, when possible

6. Weekly and Monthly Reviews
   Systematic review of previously learned material
   Include review in homework
   Frequent tests
   Reteaching of material missed in tests

Note: With older, more mature learners, or learners with more knowledge of the subject, the following adjustments can be made: (1) the size of the step in presentation can be larger (more material is presented at one time), (2) there is less time spent on teacher-guided practice and (3) the amount of overt practice can be decreased, replacing it with covert rehearsal, restating and reviewing.

A primary source for this list was the "key instructional behaviors" developed by Good and Grouws (1979) as part of their experimental study in fourth grade mathematics. Many of these functions appeared earlier as the elements of the "Lesson Design" developed by Hunter (Hunter & Russell, 1981), and Hunter derived her list from the "components of instruction" developed by Gagné (1970, p. 304). Interestingly, a series of steps titled "How to Instruct" developed during World War II (War Manpower Commission, 1945) is very similar to the work of Gagné, Hunter, and Good and Grouws.

This is not a hard and fast list. Rather, it is possible to enlarge, contract, and revise it; but it is intended to serve as a model, and as a basis of discussion about the nature of effective teaching.

There is some difference in the amount of time teachers spend on these functions in the upper and lower grades. In the lower grades the amount of material presented at any one time is smaller, more time is spent in guided student practice (through teacher questions and student answers), and more of the practice is overt. In the higher grades, the time spent in presentation becomes longer, and more material is presented at one time. In the higher grades the amount of overt practice is decreased and replaced with covert rehearsal, restating, and reviewing.

Although all classrooms have these components, they are not always carried out effectively. All classrooms have demonstrations, but frequently they are too short, there are too few examples, and the examples are imprecise or unclear. All classrooms have guided practice, but often it is infrequent or too brief, there are too few questions and examples, and too little checking for student understanding. All teachers also correct student errors, but frequently the corrections are uninformative, consisting of only a single word or sentence; reteaching in small steps occurs seldom; and there is insufficient systematic guided practice to ensure error-free performance. All classrooms have independent practice, too, but frequently too great a proportion of classroom time is allocated to independent practice, especially without immediate feedback, and students are expected to learn too much from worksheets. Frequently the teacher does not circulate to help students during independent practice and does not reteach when necessary. All classrooms have review, but frequently there is insufficient reteaching of material missed during review, and the review and practice does not continue until student responses are rapid and firm.

Many of these specific teaching skills can be taught fairly easily to experienced teachers. In numerous experimental studies (Anderson et al., 1979; Becker, 1977; Emmer et al., 1982; Evertson et al., 1981; Good & Grouws, 1979) where one group of teachers received training in these techniques and another group did not, investigators found that (a) the trained teachers used more of these skills in their classrooms and (b) the students of the trained teachers had higher achievement scores and/or engagement rates. For example, Good and Grouws (1979) found that the trained teachers reviewed and assigned homework more frequently than did the untrained teachers: Emmer et al. (1981) found that the trained teachers were rated higher in describing objectives clearly, giving clear directions, and giving clear explanations.

Demonstration, Guided Practice, and Independent Practice

Three of these functions form the instructional core: demonstration, guided practice, and independent practice. The first step is the *demonstration* of what is to be learned. This is followed by *guided student practice* in which the teacher leads the students in practice, provides prompts, checks for understanding, and provides corrections and repetition. When students are firm in their initial learning, the teacher moves them to *independent practice* where the students work with less guidance. The objective of the independent practice is to provide sufficient practice so that students achieve overlearning (Brophy, 1982) and demonstrate quickness and competence. A simple version

of this core is used frequently in the elementary grades when a teacher says: "I'll say it first, then you'll say it with me, and then you'll say it by yourself."

How would one teach two-digit multiplication (54 × 7) using these steps? The first step would be teacher demonstration of the steps followed in solving these types of problems. As part of the demonstration the teacher would *model* the use of the steps by doing problems on a chalkboard (or an overhead). This is followed by guided practice in which the students work two, three or more problems and the students are guided through the rules with teacher prompts. The teacher circulates and checks for student understanding as they do the problems. As the students become more proficient, the prompts are diminished. The frequency of student errors during guided practice gives the teacher an indication of whether any students need reteaching on the material. When a student or subset of students make frequent errors, the teacher would review or reteach the skill or process for those students or the entire class. When the students are firm in the guided practice, and are making few errors, they are moved to independent practice where they practice learning how to do the skill *accurately* and *rapidly*.

Sometimes the teacher may alternate quickly from brief demonstrations to guided practice, and back, making the two steps seem as one. For example, when teaching a word list a teacher could demonstrate how to pronounce the first word, then conduct guided practice, and continue this mixture of demonstration and practice. An integration of demonstration and guided practice allows one to present information in small steps, particularly when the information involves discrete pieces or steps. This would be followed either by guided practice on all of the new skills (e.g., class reads all the words on the word list) or independent practice on the new skills (e.g., students read the word list to the person next to them).

The Excitement of Effective Instruction

When this type of instruction is done well, it is an exciting thing to watch. It is exciting to watch the class or group move at a rapid pace and to watch *all* the students giving the correct response rapidly and confidently. When this instruction is done well, the demonstration part moves in small steps accompanied by checking for understanding. The guided practice continues until all the students are responding firmly. (There is a great difference between this firmness and the usual situation in which only half or three-fourths of the students are responding confidently.) Watching *all* the students learning new material and responding confidently can be quite exciting.

Across a number of studies and personal reports (Rosenshine & Stevens, 1984) there is no evidence, at this time, that systematic instruction is taught in an overbearing manner or that student attitudes toward school or self are affected adversely. Rather, such classrooms have reasonable teacher warmth and lead to reasonably positive student attitudes. These studies indicate that decent, humane, genuine interactions occur in many classrooms which are highly structured and teacher-directed. The image of the formal classroom as humorless, cold, and regimented was not found to be true. Today, teachers in formal classrooms are warm, concerned, flexible, and allow freedom of movement. But they are also task oriented and determined that children shall learn.

Let us turn, now, to a review of research in each of the six functions.

Daily Reviews and Checking Previous Work

There are two purposes for beginning a lesson with a short review: it provides additional practice and overlearning for previously learned material, and it allows the teacher to provide corrections and reteaching in areas where students are having difficulty. Checking of homework is one form of review.

There are a number of ways in which this function—reviewing and reteaching when necessary—can be carried out. Some suggestions include:

- Ask questions about concepts or skills taught in the previous lesson.
- Give a short quiz at the beginning of class on material from previous lessons or homework assignment.
- Have students correct each other's homework papers or quizzes.
- Have students meet in small groups (2 to 4 students per group) to review homework.
- Have students prepare questions about previous lessons or homework and ask them to each other or have the teacher ask them to the class.
- Have students prepare a written summary of the previous lesson.
- Have students ask the teacher about problems on homework and the teacher reviews, reteaches or provides additional practice.

The idea of beginning a lesson by checking the previous day's assignment appears in the experimental study of Good and Grouws (1979) and is found again in the work of Emmer et al. (1982). Each of these programs was designed for grades four to eight. In the primary grades, such explicit checking and reteaching is part of the Distar program (Becker, 1977) and the ECRI program (Reid, 1978). In the Distar reading program, there is daily review of new sounds and new words. In the ECRI program the teacher-led lesson always contains choral reviews of the vocabulary words from previous and future stories.

One would have thought that daily reviews and checking of homework were common practice. Yet, in the Missouri Math program (Good & Grouws, 1979), where daily review was included in the training manual given to the treatment teachers, they conducted review and checked homework 80 percent of the time, but the control teachers did so only 50 percent of the time. Thus, a daily review is a teaching function that could be done more frequently in most classrooms.

Presentation of Material to be Learned

All teachers, of course, demonstrate new skills and materials. But recent research in grades four to eight has shown that effective teachers of mathematics spend more time in demonstration than do less effective teachers (Evertson et al., 1980b;

Good & Grouws, 1979; Stallings, Needles, & Stayrook, 1979). The most effective mathematics teachers spent about 23 minutes per day in lecture, demonstration and discussion, whereas the least effective teachers spent only 11 minutes (Evertson et al., 1980b).

Good, Grouws, and Ebmeier (1983) reviewed four classroom-based experimental studies in mathematics which varied the amount of time spent on teacher-led development (development includes both presentation and teacher-guided practice) and the amount of time devoted to independent student practice. Although the results were not significant in all cases, there were a number of significant results and a consistent trend favoring spending at least 50 percent of the time on demonstration and guided practice.

When additional time is spent on demonstration and guided practice the teachers provide redundant explanations, give many examples and provide sufficient instruction so that the students can do the seatwork with minimal difficulty. These teachers also check the students' understanding of the presentation by asking questions (guided practice). When students make frequent errors, it is a sign of an inadequate presentation and reteaching is necessary.

What does one do in an effective demonstration? Summarizing ideas from the research review of Brophy (1980), the experimental study by Emmer et al., (1982) and the studies on teacher clarity by Kennedy, Bush, Cruickshank and Haefele, (1978), and Land and Smith (1979), we developed the suggestions listed in Table 13.2. These are grouped under four headings: clarity of goals and main points; step-by-step presentations; specific and concrete procedures; and checking for understanding.

Table 13.2. Aspects of Clear Presentations

1. Clarity of goals and main points
   a. State the goals or objectives of the presentation.
   b. Focus on one thought (point, direction) at a time.
   c. Avoid digressions.
   d. Avoid ambiguous phrases and pronouns.

2. Step-by-step presentations
   a. Present the material in small steps.
   b. Organize and present the material so that one point is mastered before the next point is given.
   c. Give explicit, step-by-step directions (when possible).
   d. Present an outline when the material is complex.

3. Specific and concrete procedures
   a. Model the skill or process (when appropriate).
   b. Give detailed and redundant explanations for difficult points.
   c. Provide students with concrete and varied examples.

4. Checking for students' understanding
   a. Be sure that students understand one point before proceeding to the next point.
   b. Ask the students questions to monitor their comprehension of what has been presented.
   c. Have students summarize the main points in their own words.
   d. Reteach the parts of the presentation that the students have difficulty comprehending, either by further teacher explanation or by students tutoring other students.

Beyond these general suggestions for improving teachers' techniques during the presentation of new material a number of questions remain. For example: How does one organize new material so that it can be learned most effectively? What are the characteristics of an effective demonstration? How many examples, and what kind, should teachers use? Is there a most effective way for sequencing examples? How much information should be presented at one time (i.e., how small or large should the instructional steps be)? At present there is little conclusive research on these questions, and determining the answers to them represents the next step in research on the function of presenting new material.

The quality and design of the instructional materials used can have an impact on the effectiveness of the presentation phase of teaching. Research on instructional materials is currently proceeding in two general areas, task analysis and instructional design (Resnick, 1976). Perhaps some of the questions presented above will be answered by this research (e.g., how many; what kind; and what sequence of examples). However, while there are presently many models for instructional design, these models vary, and a general model of effective instructional design has not yet been developed.

Although demonstration is a major part of instruction in areas such as mathematics, English grammar, science, and foreign language, there are some areas where, unfortunately, demonstration is used infrequently. As noted earlier, it is seldom used when teaching reading comprehension or higher-level cognitive thinking. Durkin (1978–1979) noted that there is seldom a demonstration phase in reading comprehension. As discussed previously, recent research has begun to define and explicate specific comprehension skills. Thus, current research is attempting to provide teachers with demonstration procedures in comprehension skills.

Similarly, although teachers are exhorted to ask higher-level cognitive questions (i.e., questions which require application, analysis, and synthesis), they seldom demonstrate how to answer such questions (nor are they taught how to provide this demonstration). Again, this may be due, at least in part, to the fact that we are only beginning to understand the cognitive processes that underlie these skills (particularly in the area of reading comprehension). Until recently, then, teachers have been limited to teaching these complicated skills without knowing how to provide explicit demonstrations.

In summary, it is important for teachers to state the goals of the lesson, provide students with explicit, step-by-step demonstrations of the new material, use many examples, and check to see that all the students understand the material before proceeding to the next point.

Guided Student Practice

In the successful experimental studies, demonstration is followed by guided student practice. In all of the studies, to date, this guided practice is conducted by the teacher. The purpose of guided practice is to:

- Guide initial practice
- Correct errors
- Reteach, if necessary
- Provide sufficient practice so that students can work independently

In one form of guided practice, the teacher asks questions and initially provides prompts or guides the students in responding, and gives them feedback and corrective help when they make errors. The questions provide the students an opportunity to practice the new skills in a controlled environment where mistakes can be corrected. In guided practice it seems preferable that students work no more than one question or problem at a time before getting feedback. This assures that students' errors will not go uncorrected. The guided practice continues until the students are confident and firm in their responses, at which time they are ready to begin independent practice.

Throughout the guided practice—from the initial, hesitant responses to the confident and firm responses—the teacher questions allow the teacher to *check for understanding*, that is, the student answers tell the teacher whether the students are ready to proceed to the next step, or whether additional practice and/or reteaching is necessary.

Of course, all teachers spend time in guided practice. However, the more effective teachers devote more time to it. That is, they spend more time asking questions, correcting errors, repeating the new material, and working problems with teacher guidance than do the less effective teachers.

The form of guided practice is modified to fit the material being taught. When a process is being taught, as in long division or multiplication with carrying, the guided practice frequently consists of problems worked under the teacher's supervision, and the teacher restating the steps as the students proceed (i.e., providing what Good & Grouws [1979] called process feedback). Teachers frequently have some students doing the math problems at the board, thus providing models for the entire class.

When facts are being taught—as in historical facts, scientific facts, and number facts—then there is less process feedback and more questions and answers during guided practice.

In summary, the guided practice function is usually led by the teacher who:

- Asks a large number of questions
- Guides students in practicing the new material, initially using prompts to lead students to the correct response and later reducing them when students are responding correctly
- Checks for student understanding
- Provides feedback
- Corrects errors
- Reteaches when necessary
- Provides for a large number of successful repetitions

Four topics in guided practice are considered below: frequent practice, high percentage of correct answers, checking for understanding, and organizing and conducting practice.

The Importance of Frequent Practice

Both correlational and experimental studies have shown that a high frequency of teacher-directed questions and student answers are important for instruction in basic arithmetic and reading skills in the primary grades. Stallings and Kaskowitz (1974) identified a pattern of "factual question-student response-teacher feedback" as the most functional for student achievement. Similar results favoring guided practice through teacher questions were obtained by Stallings, Cory, Fairweather and Needles (1977), Stallings, Needles and Stayrook (1979), Soar (1973) and Coker, Lorentz and Coker (1980). The significant correlational results in these studies means that although all teachers asked some questions, the effective teachers asked many while the less effective teachers asked few questions.

Similar results on the importance of a high frequency of questions have been obtained in mathematics in grades six to eight. In a correlational study of junior high school mathematics instruction (Evertson, Anderson, Anderson & Brophy, 1980a) the most effective teachers asked an average of 24 questions during the 50-minute mathematics period, whereas the least effective teachers asked an average of only 8.6 questions. For each group the majority of questions were factual, but the most effective teachers asked more process questions (i.e., "Explain how you got that answer"). The most effective teachers averaged six process questions per math period, whereas least effective teachers averaged only one or two.

Two experimental studies (Anderson et al., 1979; Good & Grouws, 1979) used guided practice as part of the experimental treatment. In each study the teachers who received the additional training were taught to follow the presentation of new material with guided practice. It consisted of questions asked by the teacher and supervised exercises. In both studies, teachers in the trained group asked more questions and had more guided practice than did the control teachers who continued their normal teaching. Also, in both studies, students in the experimental groups had higher achievement than the students of teachers in the control groups.

The critical variable appears to be a high percentage of student responses. Beck (1978) found a positive correlation between the number of times a word appeared in a reading program for the first grade students and the speed with which the students recognized the word, indicating that the more the students practiced the word the better it was learned. Elementary students need a good deal of practice and the frequency of teacher questions is one indicator that such practice is taking place. This is also important for adults. Kulik and Kulik (1979) found that students in college classes which gave weekly quizzes had final examination scores that were higher than the scores of students in classes that had only one or two quizzes during the term. Presumably, the added gain came from the additional practice associated with the weekly quizzes. This suggests that additional practice is also helpful for college students.

High Percentage of Correct Answers

The frequency of teacher questions is not the only important factor, because the percentage of correct student responses also plays a role in successful learning. The importance of a high percentage of rapid ("automatic"), correct responses is a relatively new idea resulting from recent research (Samuels, 1981). Although there are no scientific guidelines as to exactly what the percentage of correct answers should be, a reasonable recommendation at the present time (suggested by Brophy, 1980) is an 80% success rate when practicing new material. When reviewing, the success rate should be very high, perhaps 95% and student responses should be rapid, smooth and confident.

How can a teacher reduce the student error rate during practice exercises? The following suggestions derive from the research presented above.

1. Break down the instruction into smaller steps. Give the students instruction and practice to mastery on each step before proceeding to the next step.
2. Provide the students with very explicit demonstrations of the skills, whenever possible.
3. Intersperse the demonstration with questions in order to maintain students' attention and to check for student understanding.
4. Provide the students with teacher-monitored practice prior to seatwork activity so that the teacher can correct errors before they become part of the students' repertoire.
5. With especially confusing material, provide precorrections by advising the students about particularly confusing areas.
6. Provide sufficient independent practice, both in length and in number of exercises, to enable students to master skills to the point of overlearning (with additional exercises for the slower students).
7. Reteach material when necessary.

The research results support the value of frequent correct responses given rapidly and automatically. One of the major findings of the BTES study (Fisher et al., 1978) was that high percentage of correct answers (both during guided practice and independent practice) was positively correlated with achievement gain. Similarly, Anderson et al., (1979) found that the percent of academic interactions where the student gave the correct answer was positively related ($r = .49$) to achievement gain.

More specific information can be obtained from studies which compared the most effective and least effective classrooms. For example, in the study by Anderson et al., 1979, the mean percentage of correct answers during reading groups was 73% in the treatment teachers' classrooms but only 66% in the control classrooms. Gerstein, Carnine, and Williams (1981) found that teachers using the Distar program who obtained high reading achievement from their students had student accuracy rates near 90% whereas those with lower class achievement had accuracy rates of less than 75%. In a correlational study in fourth grade the more effective math teachers had a success rate of 82% whereas the least effective had a success rate of 76% (Good & Grouws, 1977). However, this result was not replicated in a study of junior high school math (Evertson et al., 1980a). Therefore, a high frequency of correct responses for all students appears to be very important in the elementary grades.

Of the variables mentioned above, there are two which seem most important. The effective programs and the effective teachers (a) teach new material in small steps so that the possibility for errors is lessened, and (b) practice until overlearning occurs (that is, they continue practice beyond the point where the children are accurate). For example, in the ECRI programs (Reid, 1980), there is daily review of new words in the stories that have been or will be read. Students repeat these words until they can say them at the rate of one per second. In the Distar program (Becker, 1977), the new words in every story are repeated by the reading group until all students are accurate *and* quick. In the instructions to teachers in their experimental study on primary reading groups, Anderson et al., (1979) stressed the importance of overlearning and of making sure that each student "is checked, receives feedback, and achieves mastery." All of the above procedures, which facilitate obtaining a high success rate, can be used with any reading series.

Checking for Understanding

Guided student practice also includes teacher "checking for understanding." This refers to frequent assessments of whether all the students understand either the content or skill being taught, or the steps in a process (such as two-digit multiplication). This instructional function appears in the teacher training materials developed for the Missouri Mathematics Effectiveness Project (Good & Grouws, 1979) and in the manual "Organizing and Managing the Junior High Classroom" (Emmer et al., 1981).

It is best that checking for understanding take place frequently so that teachers can provide corrections and reteach when necessary. Some methods for conducting checking for understanding include:

- Prepare a large number of oral questions beforehand
- Ask many brief questions on main points, supplementary points, and on the process being taught
- Call on students whose hands aren't raised in addition to those who volunteer
- Ask students to summarize the rule or process in their own words
- Have all students write the answers (on paper or chalkboard) while the teacher circulates
- Have all students write the answers and check them with a neighbor (frequently used with older students)
- At the end of a lecture/discussion (especially with older students) write the main points on the board and have the class meet in groups and summarize the main points to each other

The wrong way to check for understanding is to ask only a few questions, call on volunteers to hear their (usually correct) answers, and then assume that all of the class either understands or has now learned from hearing the volunteers' responses. Another error is to ask "are there any questions?" and, if there aren't any, assume that everybody understands. Another error (particularly with older children) is to assume that it is not necessary to check for understanding, and that simply repeating the points will be sufficient.

Organizing and Conducting Practice

A number of studies have provided some information on the issues of organizing and conducting practice. Topics include: random vs. ordered turns, accepting call-outs, and choral versus individual responding.

First in a correlational study (Brophy & Evertson, 1976) and then in an experimental study (Anderson et al., 1979) it was found that in primary grade reading groups it was better for student achievement if the teacher called on students in ordered turns. Such ordered turns were used when reading new words and when reading a story out loud. The authors say that ordered turns insure that all students have opportunities to practice and participate, and that they simplify group management by eliminating handwaving and other student attempts to be called on by the teacher.

Anderson et al. (1982) note that although the principle of ordered turns works well in small groups, it would be inappropriate to use this principle with whole class instruction in most situations. They suggest that when a teacher is working with a whole class it is usually more efficient to select certain students to respond to questions or to call on volunteers than to attempt systematic turns.

In both studies, student call-outs were usually negatively related to achievement gain among higher achieving students. However, for the lower achieving students in these studies, call-outs were positively related to achievement. This supports Brophy and Evertson's (1976) conclusion that call-outs may be desirable with students that may be alienated or fearful of responding. However, due to the lack of other studies in this area, these results are tentative.

One technique for obtaining a high frequency of responses in a minimum amount of time is through group choral response (see Becker, 1977). This technique is particularly useful when students are learning materials which need to be overlearned, such as decoding, word lists, and number facts.

A research study by McKenzie (1979) provides some evidence of the usefulness of group response. His study showed that students in teacher-led practice had significantly higher engagement rates when there was group response than they did during individual response. McKenzie reasoned that group responding gives each student more response opportunities than are possible with individual responses. Thus group or choral responding provides a way for teachers to achieve greater student attention during guided practice, as well as more practice on the new skills for each student.

Two successful programs, Distar (Becker, 1977) and ECRI (Reid, 1978–1982), make extensive use of choral responding in primary grade reading groups. In these programs, choral responses are initiated by a specific signal from the teacher so that the entire group will respond at the same time (much like a conductor and an orchestra). There is a danger that the slower students may delay their responses a fraction of a second and thus echo the faster students or not respond at all if the teacher does not instruct the class in how to respond in unison. Thus, choral responses without a signal and without a unified response have been associated with lower student achievement gain (Brophy & Evertson, 1976).

Becker (1977) argued that choral responding to a signal (a) allows the teacher to monitor the learning of all students effectively and quickly; (b) allows the teacher to correct the entire group when an error is made, thereby diminishing the potential embarrassment of the individual students who make them; and (c) makes the drill more like a game because of the whole group participation. The Oregon Direct Instruction Model suggests that teachers use a mixture of both choral responses and individual turns during the guided practice phase, with choral responding occurring about 70% of the time. The individual turns allow for testing of specific children. If the slower children in the group are "firm" (i.e., respond quickly and confidently) when questioned individually, the teacher moves the lesson forward; however, if they remain slow and hesitant during individual turns, this is a signal that the children need more practice. In this case it would also be argued that because the hesitant children are in a small group with others of the same ability, it is likely that the other children in the group could also benefit from the additional practice.

Group responding, in unison and to a signal, is also used successfully in the ECRI program. In ECRI it is used for learning new words and for reviewing lists of up to 100 old words. With this training, students learn to read the list of new words at a speed of one word per second.

Choral responding works best in small groups—where the teacher can monitor the responses of individual students. Monitoring is also facilitated by seating slower students close to the teacher. In primary grade mathematics, for example, choral responses can also be used with the whole class to review number facts such as multiplication tables. In short, choral responses can be an effective way to conduct guided practice.

Feedback and Correctives

Another major teaching function involves responding to student answers and correcting student errors. During guided practice, checking for understanding, and review, how should a teacher respond to student answers?

Simplifying a bit, four types of student responses can be identified:

- Correct, quick and firm
- Correct, but hesitant
- Incorrect, but a "careless" error
- Incorrect, suggesting lack of knowledge of facts or a process

Correct, Quick, and Firm

When a student response is correct, quick, and firm (usually occurring in the later stages of initial learning or in a review), then the research suggests that the teacher should simply ask a new question, thereby maintaining the momentum of the practice. There is also value in short statements of acknowledgement (e.g., "right") which do not disturb the momentum of the lesson.

Correct, but Hesitant

This often occurs during the initial stages of learning, that is, during guided practice, checking for understanding, or during a review of relatively new material. If students are correct but unsure of themselves, it is suggested that teachers provide short statements of feedback such as "correct" or "very good." It is also suggested that the teacher provide moderate amounts of process feedback, that is, re-explain the steps used to arrive at the correct answer (Anderson et al., 1979; Good & Grouws, 1979). Such feedback may not only help the student who is still learning the steps in the process, but may also help others who need this information to understand why the answer was correct.

Incorrect but Careless

When a student makes a careless error during review, drill, or reading, teachers should simply correct the student and move on.

Incorrect, Due to Lack of Knowledge of the Facts or the Process

Student errors made during the early stages of learning new material often indicate that the student is not firm in the facts or process being taught. The teacher has two options for remedying this problem:

1. Provide the students with prompts or hints to lead them to the correct answer
2. Reteach the material to the students who do not understand

Generally, the most effective approach during teacher-led practice is to try to guide the student to the correct answer by using hints, prompts or simpler questions. However, this is useful only when these individual contacts remain brief (e.g., 30 seconds or less). Contacts of longer duration are detrimental because the teacher loses the attention of the rest of the students. If a student cannot be guided to the correct answer through a brief contact, it is necessary to reteach the material to that student. Usually this reteaching occurs while the rest of the class is doing independent seatwork, or at some other time of the day (e.g., during recess, art, group activities or before or after school).

Both of these approaches to error correction—that is, prompting and reteaching—have been used successfully in experimental research and in effective instructional programs. Asking simpler questions or giving hints or prompts were successful when the contacts were brief in duration (Anderson et al., 1979; Stallings & Kaskowitz, 1974). Reteaching the material to the students who made errors is recommended by a number of programs (Becker, 1977; Good & Grouws, 1979; Reid, 1980). Good and Grouws (1979) instruct teachers to reteach when the error rate is high during a lesson. Reteaching, particularly during the initial stages of learning new material, is recommended by Becker (1977) and by Reid (1980). Each of these programs provide specific correction procedures for the student to use. The Distar program specifies not only correction procedures but also additional teaching to strengthen the student in any area of weakness.

When students are being instructed in ability groups (such as small groups in reading) and one or more students are making errors, it is usually beneficial to reteach the entire group (Becker, 1977; Reid, 1980). Since the students in the group are of similar ability, it is very likely that many of them are having similar difficulties. Thus a re-explanation of the material to the entire ability group will be useful to all of the students in the group.

When the initial presentation is given to the whole class, correcting errors by reteaching is more problematic. In most cases only a small portion of the students need reteaching, but finding the time for it and managing the other students during this remedial instruction is a problem. One method used by teachers is to reteach the entire lesson to students needing it during independent seatwork (Arlin & Webster, 1983). However, these students still need to engage in independent practice because it supplies the necessary repetitions to enable them to master the material. Another alternative is to provide remedial instruction to slower students (or students who have been absent) during recess, lunch, art, music, physical education, or before or after school. While these options may be useful on a short-term basis, they may not be satisfactory on a daily basis.

Another option for correcting errors that occur during whole class instruction is through peer tutoring (or reteaching within teams, Slavin, 1981). In this case faster students are selected as tutors and re-explain the material to students who have been making errors. Observations in Mastery Learning classrooms have recorded evidence of the usefulness of this technique (Arlin & Webster, 1983). Not only do the slower students get the reteaching they need, but the tutors also get useful practice explaining the process or skills in their own words (Webb, 1980). However, these peer tutoring techniques are probably most effective with older students, and primary grade teachers usually are faced with the problem of finding time to reteach the material to the slower students themselves.

In summary, whether one uses hints, prompts, or reteaching the material, the important point is that errors should not go uncorrected. In most cases, if a student makes an error, it is inappropriate to simply give the student the answer and then move on. It is also important that errors be detected and corrected early in a teaching sequence. If early errors are uncorrected they can become extremely difficult to correct later and systematic errors (or misrules) can interfere with subsequent learning.

In their review on effective college teaching, Kulik and Kulik (1979) found that instruction was more effective when (a) students received immediate feedback on their examinations, and (b) students had to do further study and take another test when their quiz scores did not reach a set criterion. Both points seem relevant to this discussion: students learn better with feedback given as immediately as possible; and errors should be corrected before they become systematic.

Independent Practice

Once students are exhibiting some proficiency on the new concepts or skills (as observed in correct responses at least 80% of the time in guided practice), they are ready to begin practicing on their own. Independent practice gives the students the repetitions they need to (a) integrate the new information or skills with previous knowledge or skills, and (b) become automatic in their use of the skills. What is merely demonstrated is likely to be forgotten if the student doesn't have the opportunity to practice overlearning. This independent activity should give the students enough practice that they become firm in their understanding and use of the new concepts or skills.

During independent practice the students usually go through two stages: unitization and automaticity (Samuels, 1981). During unitization the students are putting the skills together. They make few errors, but they are also slow and require a lot of energy to complete the task. After a good deal of practice, students reach the "automatic" stage where they are successful and rapid, and no longer have to "think through" each step. For example, when students are learning two-digit multiplication, they are in the unitization phase when they are hesitantly working the first few problems. When they have worked a sufficient number of problems correctly, and are confident, firm, and automatic in the skill, they are in the automaticity phase. The students' responses become more automatic because they have practiced the skills to the point of overlearning.

The important part of independent practice is that the students get enough successful practice to ensure overlearning which can be observed when their responses are automatic (i.e., quick and firm). Overlearning is particularly important for hierarchical materials such as mathematics and elementary reading. Unless there is overlearning to the point of automaticity, it is unlikely that the material will be retained (Brophy, 1980). Furthermore, hierarchical material requires the application of previously learned skills to subsequent new skills. The advantage of automaticity is that students who master the material can then concentrate their attention on learning new skills or applying the skills to new situations. For example, automaticity of decoding skills frees the students' attention for comprehension, just as automaticity of computation frees the students' attention for mathematical problem solving.

Managing Students During Seatwork

The most common context in which independent practice takes place is in individual seatwork. Students in grades one through seven spend more time working alone on seatwork than on any other activity (approximately 50 to 75% of their time) (Evertson et al., 1980a; Fisher et al., 1978; Stallings et al., 1977; Stallings & Kaskowitz, 1974). However, students are less engaged during seatwork than when they are in groups receiving instruction from the teacher. Therefore, it is important for teachers to learn how to maintain student engagement during seatwork.

Students' engagement during seatwork is affected by (a) the degree to which they are adequately prepared to do the seatwork exercises, and (b) the management of seatwork activity (keeping the students on task during seatwork). Fortunately, there are instructional procedures which can help increase student engagement during seatwork, including:

- The teacher spends more time in demonstration (explanation, discussion) and guided practice
- The teacher makes sure students are ready to work alone, by achieving a correct response rate of 80% or higher during guided practice
- The seatwork activity follows directly after guided practice
- The seatwork exercises are directly relevant to the demonstration and guided practice activities
- The teacher guides the students through the first few seatwork problems

There is ample support for these instructional procedures, both in research and in successful programs. Evertson et al. (1980b) found that teachers in junior high mathematics whose classes were more engaged during the seatwork prepared students for it during demonstration and guided practice. The most effective teachers spent 24 minutes (in a 50-minute period) in demonstration and guided practice, whereas the least effective teachers spent only 10 minutes on these same activities. Similarly, Fisher et al. (1978) found that teachers who had more questions and answers during group work had more engagement during seatwork. That is, another way to increase engagement during seatwork is to have more teacher-led practice during group work so that the students can be more successful during seatwork. Successful teachers also had the students work as a group on the first few seatwork problems before releasing them for individual seatwork (Anderson et al., 1979). The guided practice of Hunter and Russell (1981) and of Good and Grouws (1979) are additional examples of the importance of teacher-led guided practice before seatwork.

Another finding by Fisher et al. (1978) was that when teachers had to give a good deal of explanation during seatwork, student error rates were higher. Having to re-explain to many students during seatwork suggests that the initial explanation was not sufficient or that there was not sufficient practice and corrections *before* seatwork began. The students were not adequately prepared to work on their own. Evertson et al.'s (1980b) finding that long contacts during seatwork were negatively related to achievement suggests a replication of this negative correlation.

Another effective procedure for better preparing students for seatwork activity, and hence for improving their engagement during seatwork, is to break the instruction into smaller segments and have two or three segments of instruction and seatwork during a single period. In this way, the teacher provides an explanation (as in two-digit multiplication), then supervises and helps the students as they work a problem, then provides an explanation of the next step, and then supervises the students as they work the next problem. This procedure seems particularly effective for difficult material and/or slower students. This practice was advocated in the manual for teachers in the successful Junior High School Management Study (Emmer et al., 1982) and characterized successful teachers of lower achieving students in junior high math classes (Evertson, 1982).

In summary, although seatwork activities take place in all classrooms, the successful teachers spend a good deal more time than do average teachers in demonstrating what is being taught and in leading the students in guided practice. Students who are adequately prepared during the teacher-led activities are then more able to succeed during the seatwork. In contrast, the less successful teachers spent less time in demonstration and guided practice and relied more on self-paced, "individualized" materials, where students spent more time working alone.

A second way of improving student engagement during seatwork is to effectively manage the activity. Some useful management procedures are listed below:

- The teacher circulates among the students during seatwork, providing feedback, asking questions, and giving short explanations.
- When the teacher is instructing a small group and the rest of the class is working on seatwork, the teacher arranges the seats so s/he can face both the small group and the students working independently.

- The teacher establishes a set routine to be used during all seatwork activities which prescribes what students will do during seatwork, how they will get extra help when needed, and what they will do upon completion of the seatwork activity.

Fisher et al. (1978) found that when students have contacts with the teacher (or another adult) during seatwork their engagement rate increases by about 10%. Teachers moving around and interacting with students during seatwork is also an illustration of the "active teaching" which was successful in the experimental study of Good and Grouws (1979). The advantage of a teacher circulating and monitoring during seatwork led Good and Grouws (1979) to advocate teaching the class as a whole for fourth to eighth grade math. Such whole class teaching permits the teacher to actively circulate and interact with all students during seatwork.

How long should these contacts be? The research suggests that they should be relatively short, averaging 30 seconds or less (Evertson et al., 1980b; Scott & Bushell, 1974). Longer contacts appear to pose two difficulties: (a) the need for a long contact suggests that the initial explanation was not clearly understood, and (b) the more time a teacher spends with one student, the less time there is to monitor and help other students.

In elementary grades the teacher frequently instructs students in an ability group (e.g., reading groups) while the rest of the students are doing independent seatwork. The most effective way for teachers to monitor the seatwork activity during small group instruction is to arrange the seats so they can monitor both groups at the same time (Brophy & Evertson, 1976). In this way the students in the small group have their backs to the other students, and thus are not distracted. The teacher can also monitor the independently working students with periodic glances, thus improving students' engagement during seatwork.

Because teachers are frequently engaged in other activities while students are doing their seatwork (e.g., reteaching or small-group instruction), it is beneficial for the teacher to have a previously established routine for the students to follow during seatwork activity (Brophy, 1983). This routine should prescribe how the students are to conduct themselves during seatwork, including what activities they are to do during this time, what they are to do after they complete their exercises, and how they are to get extra help if necessary. For example, the routine might specify that:

- Students who have completed the exercises are to turn them in and work on other assignments or do free reading or enrichment exercises.
- Students are to check their exercises with prearranged "buddies."
- Students who need help are to approach the teacher between, not during, small-group activities.
- Students who need help may quietly ask preassigned peer tutors.

Teachers should instruct students in the various aspects of these seatwork routines at the beginning of the year, and see that they are followed throughout the year. The advantage of such routines is that they can minimize the need for teacher monitoring of the seatwork activity while they are engaged in small group instruction.

In summary, successful independent practice requires both adequate preparation of the students, and effective teacher management of the activity. Neither preparation nor management alone is sufficient.

Other Ways of Accomplishing the Independent Practice Function

As explained previously, the goal of independent practice is to provide practice to the point of overlearning and automaticity. Seatwork is the usual setting in which this function occurs, but there are three other ways in which independent practice can take place: teacher-led practice, independent practice with a routine of specific procedures, and student cooperative practice in groups.

TEACHER-LED PRACTICE

In the elementary grades, independent practice is often teacher-led. For example, if a teacher is leading a review of word lists, letter sounds, or number facts this activity can be called independent practice if the children are at a high success level and do not require prompts from the teacher.

In her study of successful teachers of lower achieving, junior high English classes, Evertson (1982) found that the teacher who had the highest engagement rate did not have long seatwork activities. Instead, the teacher used short presentations followed by long periods of repeated questions where the participation of all students was expected, the questions were narrow and direct, and there was a high degree of student success. This teacher led practice provided the practice to mastery that the students needed.

INDEPENDENT PRACTICE WITH ROUTINES

The ECRI program (Reid, 1978–1982), on the other hand, obtains high engagement by organizing routines to be followed when practicing each story. During independent practice all students work independently on a story for which they are trying to achieve "mastery." To achieve mastery a student has to:

- Read all new words in the story at a rate of one per second or faster;
- Spell all new words without error;
- Read any selection in the story at a predetermined rate; and
- Answer comprehension questions on the story.

During independent study students proceed through a checklist of tasks relevant to these skills. They use a stop watch or the clock to time themselves. When they are ready, students give a spelling test to each other, check each other for accuracy and speed of the word list, and/or check each other for accuracy and speed on the reading selection.

There are noteworthy advantages to these ECRI procedures. First, this series of tasks can be readily followed by the students,

because they are repeated with each story. Therefore, the teacher is not faced with the typical problem of having to prepare students for a different kind of worksheet each day. Second, the tasks are designed to insure that all students receive sufficient practice and obtain automaticity. Third, the student interaction provides a social dimension to this task, for it allows a student to get help from another student, and yet, keeps them focused on the academic task. Many of these ECRI procedures could be incorporated into existing programs. In particular, teachers might consider using the repeated reading until the students are reading rapidly and the student cooperative work.

STUDENT COOPERATIVE PRACTICE

Researchers have also developed procedures for students to help each other during seatwork (Johnson & Johnson, 1975; Sharan, 1980; Slavin, 1980a, 1980b, 1981). In some cases the students in the groups prepare a common product, such as the answer to a drill sheet (Johnson & Johnson, 1975), and in other situations the students study cooperatively in order to prepare for competition which takes place after the seatwork (Slavin, 1980a). Research using these procedures usually shows that students who do seatwork under these conditions achieve more than students who are in regular settings. Observational data indicates that students are also more engaged in these settings than are similar students in conventional settings (Johnson & Johnson, in press; Slavin, 1978, 1980b; Zeigler, 1981). Presumably, the advantages of these cooperative settings come from the social value of working in groups, and the cognitive value gained from explaining the material to someone and/or having the material explained to you. Another advantage of the common worksheet and the competition is that they keep the group focused on the academic task and diminish the possibility that there will be social conversation.

Summary

The purpose of independent practice is to provide the students with sufficient practice so that they can do the work automatically. This is usually done by having students work individually at seatwork. Suggestions from the research for improving student engagement during seatwork are:

1. Give clear instruction—explanations, questions, and feedback—and sufficient practice before the students begin their seatwork. Having to provide lengthy explanations during seatwork is troublesome for the teacher and for the student.
2. Circulate during seatwork, actively explaining, observing, asking questions, and giving feedback.
3. Have short contacts with individual students (i.e., 30 seconds or less).
4. For difficult material in whole class instruction, have a number of segments of instruction and seatwork during a single period.
5. Arrange seats to facilitate monitoring the students (e.g., face both small group and independently working students).
6. Establish a routine to use during seatwork activity which prescribes what students will do, how they will get help and what they will do when they have completed the exercises.

Although the most common organization of independent practice is seatwork with each child working alone, three other forms of organization have been successful:

1. Teacher-led student practice, as in repetition drills and question and answer sessions,
2. A routine of student activities to be followed during seatwork where the student works both alone and with another student, and
3. Procedures for cooperation within groups and competition between groups during seatwork.

Weekly and Monthly Reviews

The learning of new material is also enhanced by weekly and monthly reviews. Many of the recent instructional programs include periodic reviews and also provide for reteaching in areas in which the students are weak. In the Missouri Math Study (Good & Grouws, 1979) teachers were asked to review the previous week's work every Monday, and to conduct a monthly review every fourth Monday. The review provides additional teacher checking for student understanding, insures that the necessary prior skills are adequately learned, and is also a check on the teacher's pace. Good and Grouws recommend that the teacher proceed at a fairly rapid pace (to increase student interest). They also suggest that if a teacher is going too fast, it will be apparent in the weekly review, because students will make many errors.

Periodic reviews and recycling of instruction when there are student errors have been part of the Distar program since 1968. Extensive review is also built into the ECRI program in that slower students are reviewing new words for three weeks before they encounter the words in a story in their reader. This kind of massed learning followed by spaced reviews is also part of Hunter's program on increasing teaching effectiveness (Hunter & Russell, 1981).

Management Functions

Many of the programs cited on the first page also contain suggestions for managing transitions between activities, setting rules and consequences, alerting students during independent work and holding them accountable, giving students routines to follow when they need help but the teacher is busy, and other management functions.

The developers of these programs understand that instruction cannot be effective if the students are not well managed. However, that topic is beyond the scope of this paper. For a more detailed discussion see Brophy (1983).

Discussion

This chapter has discussed a number of teaching functions: review of previous learning; demonstration of new materials; guided practice and checking for understanding; feedback and corrections; independent practice; and periodic review. While writing this chapter, we were impressed with the fact that many different people, working independently, came up with fairly similar solutions to the problems involved in effective classroom instruction. The fact that independent researchers have reached similar conclusions and have collected student achievement data which supports their positions serves to validate each individual research study.

One advantage of this chapter is that it provides a general overview of the major functions of systematic teaching. What is missing, however, is the specific detail which is contained in the training manuals and materials developed by each of the investigators. We would hope that all teachers and teachers' trainers have a chance to study and discuss those training manuals.

The functions identified and explained in this paper are quite similar to those used by the most effective teachers. Most teachers already perform some of them, but the specific programs elaborate on how to perform all of these functions and provide more routines, procedures, and modifications than an individual teacher working alone could have developed. These programs make teachers aware of the six instructional functions, bring the set of skills to a conscious level, and enable teachers to develop strategies for consistent, systematic implementation (Bennett, 1982).

Now that we can describe the major teaching functions, we can ask whether there are a variety of ways in which they can be fulfilled. We have already seen that the independent practice function can be met in three ways; students working alone, teacher leading the practice, and students helping each other. (There are even a variety of ways for students to help each other.)

We have just begun to explore this issue of the variety of ways of meeting each function, and at present no conclusions can be drawn regarding their relative merit. It may be that each function can be met three ways: by the teacher, by a student working with other students, and by a student working alone — using written materials or a computer. Right now, however, not all functions can be met in all three ways — and we are limited in our choices by the constraints of working with 25 students in a classroom, the age and maturity of the students, the lack of efficient "courseware" for the student to use when working alone, and the lack of imaginative routines which will keep students on task and diminish the time lost when they move from activity to activity. For example, although the idea of students working together during independent practice always existed "in theory," such working together was also associated with off task behavior and socializing. We needed the routines developed by Slavin (1981), Johnson and Johnson (1975) and Reid (1981) before we could be confident that students would work together during independent practice and still be on task. Similarly, although "checking for understanding" could "theoretically" be handled by students working with materials or by students working with other students, at present we do not have effective routines for enabling this to happen in the elementary grades.

In conclusion, now that we can list the major functions or components which are necessary for systematic instruction, we can turn to exploring different ways in which these functions can be effectively fulfilled.

REFERENCES

Anderson, L. M., Evertson, C. M., & Brophy, J. E. (1979). An experimental study of effective teaching in first-grade reading groups. *The Elementary School Journal, 79*, 193–222.

Anderson, L. M., Evertson, C. M., & Brophy, J. E. (1982). *Principles of small group instruction in elementary reading.* East Lansing, Mich.: Institute for Research on Teaching, Michigan State University.

Arlin, M., & Webster, J. (1983). Time costs of mastery learning. *Journal of Educational Psychology, 75,* 187–195.

Beck, I. L. (1978). *Instructional ingredients for the development of beginning reading competence.* Pittsburgh, PA: Learning Research and Development Center, University of Pittsburgh.

Becker, W. C. (1977). Teaching reading and language to the disadvantaged—What we have learned from field research. *Harvard Educational Review, 47,* 518–543.

Berliner, D. (1982). '82 Issue: Should teachers be expected to learn and use direct instruction? *A.S.C.D. Update, 24,* 5.

Brophy, J. (1983). Classroom organization and management. *Elementary School Journal, 83,* 265–286.

Brophy, J. (1981). Teacher praise: A functional analysis. *Review of Educational Research, 51,* 5–32.

Brophy, J. (1980). *Recent research on teaching.* East Lansing, Mich.: Institute for Research on Teaching, Michigan State University.

Brophy, J. (1982). Successful teaching strategies for the inner-city child. *Phi Delta Kappa, 63,* 527–530.

Brophy, J., & Evertson, C. (1976). *Learning from teaching: A developmental perspective.* Boston: Allyn & Bacon.

Carnine, D., Kuder, J., Salvino, M., & Moore, J. (1983). The use of generative and question asking strategies for the improvement of reading comprehension. Paper presented at American Educational Research Association annual meeting, Montreal.

Coker, H., Lorentz, C. W., & Coker, J. (1980). Teacher behavior and student outcomes in the Georgia study. Paper presented to the American Educational Research Association Annual Meeting, Boston, MA.

Dansereau, D., Collins, K., McDonald, B., Holley, C., Garland, J., Dickhoff, G., & Evans, S. (1979). Development and evaluation of a learning strategy training program. *Journal of Educational Psychology, 71,* 64–73.

Day, J. D. (1980). Teaching summarization skills. Unpublished doctoral dissertation, Urbana, IL.: University of Illinois.

Durkin, D. (1978-79). What classroom observation reveals about reading comprehension instruction. *Reading Research Quarterly, 14,* 481–533.

Durkin, D. (1981). Reading comprehension instruction in five basal reading series. *Reading Research Quarterly, 4,* 515–544.

Emmer, E., Evertson, C., Sanford, J., Clements, B., & Worsham, M. (1982). *Organizing and managing the junior high classroom.* Austin, TX: Research and Development Center for Teacher Education, University of Texas.

Emmer, E. T., Evertson, C., Sanford, J. & Clements, B. S. (1982). *Improving classroom management: An experimental study in junior high classrooms.* Austin, TX: Research and Development Center for Teacher Education, University of Texas.

Evertson, C. (1982). Differences in instructional activities in higher and lower achieving junior high English and mathematics classrooms. *Elementary School Journal, 82,* 329–351.

Evertson, C., Anderson, C., Anderson, L., & Brophy, J. (1980a). Relationship between classroom behavior and student outcomes in junior high math and English classes. *American Elementary Research Journal, 17,* 43–60.

Evertson, C., Emmer, E. T., & Brophy, J. E. (1980b). Predictors of effective teaching in junior high mathematics classrooms. *Journal of Research in Mathematics Education, 11,* 167–178.

Evertson, C., Emmer, E., Clements, B., Sanford, J., Worsham, M., & Williams, E. (1981). *Organizing and managing the elementary school classroom.* Austin, TX: Research and Development Center for Teacher Education, University of Texas.

Fielding, G., Kameenui, E., & Gersten, R. (1983). A comparison of an inquiry and a direct instruction approach to teach legal concepts and applications to secondary school students. *Journal of Educational Research, 76,* 243–250.

Fisher, C. W., Berliner, D. C., Filby, N. N., Marliave, R., Cahen, L. S., & Dishaw, M. M. (1980). Teaching behaviors, academic learning time, and student achievement: An overview. In C. Denham & A. Liebersman (Eds.), *Time to learn.* Washington, D.C.: U. S. Government Printing Office.

Fisher, C. W., Filby, N. N., Marliave, R., Cahon, L. S., Dishaw, M. M., Moore, J. E., & Berliner, D. C. (1978). *Teaching behaviors, academic learning time, and student achievement: Final report of Phase III-B, Beginning Teacher Evaluation Study.* San Francisco, Far West Educational Laboratory for Educational Research and Development.

Fitzpatrick, K. A. (1981). *In investigation of secondary classroom material strategies for increasing student academic engaged time.* Doctoral dissertation, University of Illinois at Urbana-Champaign.

Fitzpatrick, K. A. (1982). The effect of a secondary classroom management training program on teacher and student behavior. Paper presented to the annual meeting of the American Educational Research Association, New York, NY.

Gagné, E. D. (1985). *The Cognitive Psychology of School Learning.* Boston: Little Brown and Co.

Gagné, R. (1970). *The conditions of learning.* New York: Holt, Rinehart and Winston.

Gersten, R. M., Carnine, D. W., & Williams, P. B. (1981). Measuring implementation of a structured educational model in an urban school district. *Educational Evaluation and Policy Analysis, 4,* 56–63.

Good, T. L., & Grouws, D. A. (1977). Teaching effects: Process-product study in fourth-grade mathematics classrooms. *Journal of Teacher Education, 28,* 49–54.

Good, T. L., & Grouws, D. A. (1979). The Missouri mathematics effectiveness project. *Journal of Educational Psychology, 71,* 355–362.

Good, T. L., Grouws, D. A., & Ebmeier, H. (1983). *Active mathematics teaching,* New York: Longman.

Greeno, J. (1978). Understanding and procedural knowledge in mathematics instruction. *Educational Psychologist, 12,* 262–283.

Hunter, M., & Russell, D. (1981). Planning for effective instruction: Lesson Design. In *Increasing your teaching effectivenesss.* Palo Alto, CA: The Learning Institute.

James, W. J. (1890). *The Principles of Psychology.* New York: Holt.

Johnson, D., & Johnson R. (1975). *Learning together and alone.* Englewood Cliffs, N.J.: Prentice Hall.

Johnson, D., & Johnson R. (in press). The integration of handicapped students into regular classrooms: Effects on cooperation and instruction. *Contemporary Educational Psychology.*

Kennedy, J. J., Bush, A. J., Cruickshank, D. R. & Haefele, D. (1978). Additional investigations into the nature of teacher clarity. Paper presented to the annual meeting of the American Educational Research Association, Toronto, Canada, March, 1978. (College of Education, The Ohio State University, Columbus, Ohio).

Kulik, J. A., & Kulik, C. C. (1979). College teaching. In P. L. Peterson & H. J. Walberg (Eds.), *Research on teaching: Concepts, findings, and implications.* Berkeley, Ca.: McCutchan.

LaBerge, D., & Samuels, S. J. (1974). Toward a theory of automatic information processing in reading. *Cognitive Psychology, 6,* 293–323.

Land, M., & Smith, L. (1979). Low inference teacher clarity variables: Effects on student achievement. Paper presented at annual meeting of American Educational Research Association, San Francisco.

Larkin, J. H., & Reif, F. (1976). Analysis and teaching of a general skill for studying scientific text. *Journal of Educational Psychology, 68,* 431–440.

Linden, M., & Wittrock, M. (1981). The teaching of reading comprehension according to the model of generative learning. *Reading Research Quarterly, 17,* 44–57.

McKenzie, G. (1979). Effects of questions and testlike events on achievement and on-task behavior in a classroom concept learning presentation. *Journal of Educational Research, 72,* 348–350.

Miller, G. A. (1956). The magic number seven, plus or minus two: Some limits on our capacity for processing information. *Psychological Review, 63,* 81–97.

Norman, D. A., & Brobow, D. G. (1975). On data-limited and resources-limited processes. *Cognitive Psychology, 7,* 44–64.

Patchings, W., Kameenui, E., Colvin, G., & Carnine, D. (1979). An investigation of the effects of using direct instruction procedures to teach three critical reading skills to skill deficient grade 5 children. Unpublished manuscript, Eugene, Oregon: University of Oregon.

Perfetti, C., & Lesgold, A. (1977). Discourse comprehension and sources of individual differences. In M. Just & P. Carpenter (Eds.) *Cognitive Processes in Comprehension*. Hillsdale, N.J.: Erlbaum and Associates.

Raphael, T. E. (1980). The effects of metacognitive strategy awareness training on students' question answering behavior. Unpublished doctoral dissertation, University of Illinois, Urbana, IL.

Reid, E. R. (1978–1982). *The Reader Newsletter*. Salt Lake City, Utah: Exemplary Center for Reading Instruction.

Resnick, L. B. (1976). Task analysis in instructional design. In D. Klahr (Ed.), *Cognition and instruction*. New Jersey: Erlbaum and Assoc.

Rosenshine, B., & Stevens, R. (1984). Classroom instruction in reading. In P. D. Pearson (Ed.), *Recent research on reading*. New York: Longman.

Samuels, S. J. (1981). Some essentials of decoding. *Exceptional Education Quarterly, 2*, 11–25.

Scott, J., & Bushell, D. Jr. (1974). The length of teacher contacts and students' off task behavior. *Journal of Applied Behavior Analysis, 7*, 39–44.

Sharan, S. (1980). Cooperative learning in small groups. *Review of Educational Research, 50*, 241–271.

Singer, H., & Donlon, D. (1982). Active comprehension: Problem-solving schema with question generation for comprehension of complex short stories. *Reading Research Quarterly, 17*, 116–186.

Slavin, R. E. (1978). Student teams and comparisons among equals: Effects on academic performance. *Journal of Educational Psychology, 70*, 532–538.

Slavin, R. E. (1980a). Cooperative learning. *Review of Educational Research, 50*, 317–343.

Slavin, R. E. (1980b) Effects on student teams and peer tutoring on academic achievement and time on task. *Journal of Experimental Education, 48*, 252–257.

Slavin, R. E. (1981). Student team learning. *Elementary School Journal, 82*, 5–17.

Slavin, R., Leavey, M., & Madden, N. (1982). *Combining cooperative learning and individualized instruction: Effects on student mathematics ach., att. and behaviors*. Baltimore, Md: Center for Social Organization of Schools, Johns Hopkins University.

Soar, R. S. (1973). *Follow-through classroom process measurement and pupil growth (1970–71): Final report*. Gainesville: College of Education, University of Florida.

Spiro, R. J. (1981). Cognitive processes in prose comprehension and recall. In R. Spiro, B. Bruce, and W. Brewer (eds.) *Theoretical issues in reading comprehension*. Hillsdale, N.J.: Lawrence Erlbaum and Associates.

Stallings, J. A., & Kaskowitz, D. (1974). *Follow through classroom observation evaluation, 1972–73*. Menlo Park, CA: Stanford Research Institute.

Stallings, J., Cory, R., Fairweather, J., & Needles, M. (1977). *Early childhood education classroom evaluation*. Menlo Park, CA: SRI International.

Stallings, J., Needles, M., & Stayrook, N. (1979). *How to change the process of teaching basic reading skills in secondary schools*. Menlo Park, CA: SRI International.

Tobias, S. (1982). When do instructional methods make a difference? *Educational Researcher, 11*, 4–10.

War Manpower Commission. (1945). *The training within industry report*. Washington, D.C.: Bureau of Training.

Webb, N. (1980). A process-outcome analysis of learning in group and individual settings. *Educational Psychologist, 15*, 69–83.

Zeigler, S. (1981). The effectiveness of classroom learning teams for increasing cross ethnic friendship: Additional evidence. *Human Organization, 40*, 264–268.

14.
Classroom Organization and Management

Walter Doyle
University of Texas—Austin

Introduction

Research on classroom management is directed to questions of how order is established and maintained in classroom environments. This relatively straightforward statement belies, however, the complexity of management processes. Conceptions of what constitutes orderliness vary across situations (e.g., snack time versus silent reading) as well as individuals (e.g., "traditionalists" versus "progressives"). The settings in which order is achieved, for example, whole-class lessons versus multiple-group arrangements, differ in their structure and complexity. The actions teachers can take to create and sustain order range from planning and organizing lessons to distributing resources, explaining rules, and reacting to individual and group behavior. Finally, the appropriateness of a particular action depends on circumstances, such as the purposes being sought, the work being done, the participants involved, and the time of the day. Understandably, then, the study of classroom management is a complicated enterprise.

Classroom Management in Research on Teaching

The topic of classroom management has always lurked in the shadows of research on teaching, despite a widespread concern for management among teachers and the public (see Alling, 1882; Coates & Thoresen, 1976; Fuller, 1969; Gallup, 1983) and a large body of practical literature in this area. Only scant attention, for example, was given to classroom organization and management in the first *Handbook of Research on Teaching* and the *Second Handbook of Research on Teaching*, a practice that was consistent with a long-standing tradition in the research-based literature on teaching (see, for example, Hyman, 1974; Joyce & Weil, 1972).

The neglect of classroom management in the study of teaching reflects in part the intellectual frameworks that have guided inquiry in this field (see Doyle, 1978). Most teaching researchers, whether experimental psychologists interested in instructional design (see Anderson & Faust, 1975; Thorndike, 1913) or effectiveness researchers (see Flanders, 1970; Gage, 1978), have tended to view classroom processes in a restricted sense as actions (explaining, prompting, reinforcing) that directly foster learning rather than as the sum total of what teachers do in classroom settings. In addition, much of this work has focused on individuals rather than on the social dimensions of classrooms. As a result, the management function has been given secondary consideration. The topic of discipline was taken up by clinical psychologists interested in counseling, mental health, and behavior modification (e.g., Dreikurs, 1957; Glasser, 1969; O'Leary & O'Leary, 1977; Symonds, 1934), but the focus here has traditionally been on ways to help individual students with behavior problems rather than how to manage classroom groups. Questions of organization and management in classrooms have been addressed by social psychologists and sociologists interested in classrooms as workplaces (e.g., Dreeben, 1973; Lortie, 1973; Sheviakov & Redl, 1944) or by specialists in educational administration (see Johnson & Brooks, 1979), literatures that have traditionally played a minor role in research on teaching. In this intellectual climate, the study of classroom management has had a difficult time finding a niche.

Since the publication of the *Second Handbook of Research on Teaching*, the study of classroom organization and management has moved from relative obscurity to a prominent place in research on teaching. During the 1970s major research programs devoted to organization and management were established, the topic appeared frequently at the annual meeting of the American Educational Research Association, and an AERA

The author thanks reviewers Paul Gump (University of Kansas) and Daniel L. Duke (Lewis and Clark College). Kathy Carter, Ian Westbury, James Hoffman, Douglas Brooks, Sherry Pittman, Paula Willis, and Randall Hickman were generous with their help, comments, and suggestions. The writing of this chapter was supported in part by the National Institute of Education, Contract OB-NIE-G-80-0116, P2, Research on Classroom Learning and Teaching Program. The opinions expressed herein are those of the author.

Special Interest Group on classroom management was organized. In addition, important collections of articles on this topic were published by the National Society for the Study of Education (Duke, 1979a) and the Association for Supervision and Curriculum Development (Duke, 1982), and major reviews of work in this area appeared (see Brophy, 1983a; Emmer & Evertson, 1981; Goss & Ingersoll, 1981).

At least three factors would seem to account for this recent surge of interest in classroom organization and management as a focus for research. First, school discipline and racial desegregation became important public issues that warranted attention from researchers, especially those working in federally sponsored programs. These themes were especially evident in the development of cooperative learning programs in which emphasis was placed on group cohesiveness and peer interactions across racial and ability categories (see Slavin, 1980). Second, specialists in teaching effectiveness research (e.g., Anderson, Evertson, & Brophy, 1979; Brophy & Evertson, 1976; Good & Grouws, 1975) began to include classroom management categories, many of which were derived from Kounin's studies, in their coding systems, and these categories tended to be related consistently to student achievement. As a result, interest developed in finding out more about effective management practices (see Emmer, Evertson, & Anderson, 1980). Finally, there was a sharp increase in the number of qualitative studies of classroom life following the pioneering work of Jackson (1968) and of Smith and Geoffrey (1968). The rich descriptions of classroom contexts and processes emerging from these reports revealed the complexity of social arrangements in classrooms and stimulated interest in knowing more about how classroom events were enacted by teachers and students (see Courtney Cazden, this volume).

Scope of the Review

This chapter, the first of its kind in this series of handbooks, is intended to serve as (a) a summary of the major lines of research on classroom organization and management, with special emphasis on studies that appeared in the 1970s and 1980s; and (b) a tool for organizing and integrating what is known about classrooms and their management. The coverage is by no means exhaustive. The emphasis, rather, has been on identifying significant themes in the research and assessing their contributions to understanding how classroom order is established and maintained.

The chapter is divided into six major units. The first section contains an analysis of the problem of order in classroom teaching. The purpose of this analysis is to provide a conceptual framework for understanding the nature of the management function in teaching. This framework is then used to organize and interpret the empirical data that have a bearing on classroom management. The second section is directed to the issue of how life in classrooms is organized. Special attention in this section is given to the types of contexts that occur in classrooms and to research on the behavior of participants within these contexts. The third section examines the programs of action that are embedded in classroom contexts, including both social participation structures and academic work struc-

tures. The fourth section is focused on the question of how order is accomplished in classrooms with particular emphasis on how activities are established at the beginning of the year, how lessons are accomplished, and how classroom management affects and is affected by academic work. The fifth section concentrates on the nature of misbehavior in classrooms and the function of teachers' interventions to stop misbehavior. The paper concludes with a summary of the major themes emerging from the review and a general assessment of the status and future directions of research on classroom organization and management.

The chapter has a clear classroom orientation. As a result, issues of school management and discipline are excluded. Without question school-level policies, practices, and beliefs affect classrooms in a variety of ways (see Bossert, Dwyer, Rowan, & Lee, 1982; Cohen, 1979; Duke & Meckel, 1980a, 1980b; Metz, 1978; PDK Commission, 1982). Nevertheless, problems of classroom order are solved within the classroom environment itself, and the boundary separating a classroom from the school blunts the effects of this context on classroom processes (see Warren, 1973). Moreover, teacher-student relationships in classrooms have a distinct flavor. Classroom contacts between teachers and students differ on such dimensions as duration, familiarity, substance, and purpose from those that occur in other school contexts. As a result, basic strategies for achieving classroom order differ in important ways from those appropriate to school management and discipline. Finally, because school effectiveness researchers seldom examine classrooms closely and classroom researchers seldom study school-level processes, little systematic research is available concerning the precise ways in which school policies and practices influence classroom events.

The study of classroom management is closely affiliated with research on effective teaching, teacher thinking, and classroom discourse. It is often difficult, for instance, to separate managerial and instructional processes, and researchers in these two domains often use similar research designs and classroom variables. Likewise, because classroom management studies tend to focus on the texture of the environment in which teachers work, they provide a rich source of knowledge about the substance of teachers' thinking and decision making. Moreover, it is difficult to talk about management processes, for example, teacher monitoring, without reference to the substance of teacher thinking and the underlying cognitive process involved in using this knowledge. Finally, sociolinguistic and microethnographic studies have generated insights into the ways concerted action is organized in classrooms and into the often subtle and complex processes through which information is communicated in social situations. These insights obviously have important implications for understanding how order is established and maintained in classrooms.

The scope of this review has been defined broadly enough to incorporate perspectives and findings from these related domains in building a broad understanding of classroom management processes. However, because the topics of effective teaching, teacher thinking, and classroom discourse are treated extensively in other chapters in this volume, an effort has been made to avoid excessive overlap and to direct readers to related chapters at appropriate points.

The Management Function in Teaching

Broadly speaking, classroom management refers to "the provisions and procedures necessary to establish and maintain an environment in which instruction and learning can occur" (Duke, 1979b, p. xii, italics removed). At this level of generality, however, the label is often ambiguous. The term is readily equated with "discipline," that is, the treatment of misbehavior in classrooms or schools. It also covers a wide range of teacher duties from distributing resources to students, accounting for student attendance and school property, enforcing compliance with rules and procedures, to grouping students for instruction, for example, individual progress plans or cooperative team arrangements (see Cohen, Intili, & Robbins, 1979). In addition, the term evokes a large array of competing ideologies that range from an emphasis on authority and conformity to a concern for individual self-expression (see Johnson & Brooks, 1979). Finally, the topic of classroom management has always had an uneasy association with instruction. Management is commonly viewed as a prerequisite to instruction, something to get out of the way so that teaching can occur. Recently, some investigators (e.g., Berliner, 1983b; Doyle, 1979b) have placed management at the center of the task of teaching. At the same time, others (e.g., Allington, 1983; Brophy, 1982; Buike, 1981; Duffy & McIntyre, 1982) have cautioned that teachers often appear to subordinate instruction to management concerns.

Given the amount of surplus meaning associated with classroom management, it has been necessary to dwell on the problem of definition. This problem is approached by first examining conceptions of the teacher's task and then specifying the management function within that task.

The Task of Teaching

The past decade has been marked by a growing interest in the distinctive properties of the classroom as a context and in the problems this context poses for teachers and students (see Abrahamson, 1974; Doyle, 1978, 1981; Erickson & Shultz, 1981; Gump, 1969; Hamilton, 1981; Jackson, 1968; Lancy, 1978; Mehan, 1979; Smith & Geoffrey, 1968; Westbury, 1973; Woods, 1979). Much of this work has focused on the demand structure of the classroom environment and the consequences of this structure for understanding the nature of the teaching task. The concept of "task" has two components: (a) a goal state or end product to be achieved; and (b) a problem space, that is, a set of instructions, conditions, and resources available to reach the goal state. From this perspective, the thoughts and actions of teachers are understood as attempts to assemble and use resources to accomplish the task of achieving educational ends in a complex social setting.

This emphasis on context is important for management research because, in a fundamental sense, classroom management is about classrooms (see Johnson & Brooks, 1979). If teachers met students individually, privately, and voluntarily, there would be little need to talk about classroom management. But teachers meet students in groups on a daily basis for extended periods of time to achieve purposes that do not necessarily coincide with the immediate interests of participants. In a general normative sense, attendance is mandatory,

and, for all practical purposes, groups are arbitrarily formed. In addition to creating various administrative duties and responsibilities for teachers (e.g., accounting for pupil attendance and school property), these social conditions in the workplace shape the daily tasks of teachers and define the skills required to accomplish these tasks (see Dreeben, 1973; LeCompte, 1978a; Lortie, 1973).

The Nature of the Classroom Environment

Doyle (1977, 1980) has argued that classroom settings have distinctive properties affecting participants regardless of how students are organized for learning or what educational philosophy the teacher espouses. There are, in other words, important elements already in place when teachers and students arrive at the classroom door. These elements include:

1. *Multidimensionality*, which refers to the large quantity of events and tasks in classrooms. A classroom is a crowded place in which many people with different preferences and abilities must use a restricted supply of resources to accomplish a broad range of social and personal objectives. Many events must be planned and orchestrated to meet special interests of members and changing circumstances throughout the year. Records must be kept, schedules met, supplies organized and stored, and student work collected and evaluated. In addition, a single event can have multiple consequences: Waiting a few extra moments for a student to answer a question can affect that student's motivation to learn as well as the pace of the lesson and the attention of other students in the class. Choices, therefore, are never simple.

2. *Simultaneity*, which refers to the fact that many things happen at once in classrooms. While helping an individual student during seatwork, a teacher must monitor the rest of the class, acknowledge other requests for assistance, handle interruptions, and keep track of time. During a discussion, a teacher must listen to student answers, watch other students for signs of comprehension or confusion, formulate the next question, and scan the class for possible misbehavior. At the same time, the teacher must attend to the pace of the discussion, the sequence of selecting students to answer, the relevance and quality of answers, and the logical development of content. When the class is divided into small groups, the number of simultaneous events increases, and the teacher must monitor and regulate several different activities at once.

3. *Immediacy*, which refers to the rapid pace of classroom events. Gump (1967) and Jackson (1968) have estimated that an elementary teacher has over 500 exchanges with individual students in a single day, and, in a study of first and fifth grade classes, Sieber (1979a) found that teachers publicly evaluated pupil conduct with either praise or reprimands on the average of 15.89 times per hour, or 87 times a day, or an estimated 16,000 times a year. In addition, Kounin (1970) found that order in classrooms depends in part upon maintaining momentum and a flow of classroom events. In most instances, therefore, teachers have little leisure time to reflect before acting.

4. *Unpredictability*, which refers to the fact that classroom events often take unexpected turns. Distractions and interruptions are frequent. In addition, events are jointly produced and thus it is often difficult to anticipate how an activity will go on a particular day with a particular group of students.

5. *Publicness*, which refers to the fact that classrooms are public places and that events, especially those involving the teacher, are often witnessed by a large portion of the students. "Teachers act in fishbowls; each child normally can see how the others are treated" (Lortie, 1975, p. 70). If a teacher either fails to notice that a student is violating a rule or actually reprimands an innocent bystander, the entire class learns important information about the management skills of the teacher. In addition, the audience for a disruption may actively encourage participants to continue or may join in once a disruption starts and thus magnify the effect of misbehavior.

6. *History*, which refers to the fact that classes meet for 5 days a week for several months and thus accumulate a common set of experiences, routines, and norms which provide a foundation for conducting activities. Early meetings often shape events for the rest of the term or year (Emmer et al., 1980), and routines and norms are established for behavior. A class is also affected by seasonal variations, periodic absences, the addition of new members, and the broad cycle of the year. Thus planning for a single event must take into account the broader context of the class's history (see Yinger, 1980).

Doyle (1980) contends that these intrinsic features of the classroom environment create constant pressures that shape the task of teaching. Although their intensity varies with particular conditions, these pressures operate in all classrooms regardless of how events are organized.

The Problem of Order in Classrooms

Broadly speaking, classroom teaching has two major task structures organized around the problems of (a) learning and (b) order. Learning is served by the instructional function, that is, by covering a specified block of the curriculum, promoting mastery of elements of that block, and instilling favorable attitudes toward content so that students will persist in their efforts to learn (see Abrahamson, 1974; Westbury, 1973). Order is served by the managerial function, that is, by organizing classroom groups, establishing rules and procedures, reacting to misbehavior, monitoring and pacing classroom events, and the like (Doyle, 1980).

Obviously the tasks of promoting learning and order are closely intertwined: Some minimal level of orderliness is necessary for instruction to occur and lessons must be sufficiently well constructed to capture and sustain student attention. Indeed, the tasks exist simultaneously so that a teacher often faces competing pressures to maximize learning and sustain order. In many instances, actions toward these ends are complementary. For example, monitoring individual progress on seatwork can afford opportunities for corrective feedback, and the proximity of the teacher can prevent inappropriate and disruptive behavior from starting. At other times, tensions can exist when, for example, attending to an individual student's questions slows down the pace of classroom events or the problems of controlling a particular group of students prevent a teacher from covering parts of the curriculum.

Before examining these interconnections between instruction and management, it is important to note that the task of learning and the task of order represent quite distinct levels of analysis. Because individuals rather than groups learn, an analysis of learning directs attention to individual processes. But order is a property of a social system and thus needs to be framed in a language of group processes.

This point was clearly demonstrated in the important program of management research conducted by Kounin and Gump (see Kounin, 1970; Kounin & Gump, 1958). These investigators began with a series of studies focused on "desists," or how teachers in a variety of settings (including elementary and secondary classrooms) handled misbehavior. Although they discovered a "ripple effect," that is, that ways of reacting to the misbehavior of one pupil can affect other members of the group, they concluded that creating and sustaining work involvement for a class was not closely tied to the quality of the teachers' desists. They then revised their question to focus more on what teachers did across time to achieve work involvement, and they were eventually able to demonstrate that involvement was a function of how teachers managed group dimensions and structures in classrooms rather than how they dealt with individual behavior.

Given the intellectual traditions of research on teaching mentioned earlier in this chapter, a considerable amount is known about the instruction function in classrooms (see Rosenshine, 1983; Brophy & Good, this volume). The development of a language of group processes appropriate to the classroom has progressed more slowly. Even within the field of classroom management, traditional conceptions of the management function have focused, in large measure, on individual student behavior. It is common, for instance, to associate classroom management with discipline (see Duke & Meckel, 1984; Jones & Jones, 1981; Tanner, 1978; Wolfgang & Glickman, 1980) and, thus, to focus on the inappropriate or disruptive behavior of individual students. Recently, studies of teaching have emphasized student engagement or time on task as a predictor of achievement (Berliner, 1979; Denham & Lieberman, 1980; Fisher et al., 1978), and engagement has been commonly used as a criterion variable in classroom management studies (see Emmer, Sanford, Clements, & Martin, 1982). This focus on engagement, although problematic (see Good, 1983; Peterson & Swing, 1982), has directed attention to work-related behavior rather than misbehavior and encouraged thinking about ways to increase and sustain involvement in classroom events.

Misbehavior and engagement are clearly germane to the task of achieving order in a classroom. Nevertheless, defining the management function in terms of handling misbehavior or eliciting and sustaining engagement tends to emphasize individual students as the target of the teacher's thinking and action and does not always capture the group dimensions of classroom management. Indeed, studies by Kounin (1970) and by Gump (1967) suggest that involvement is essentially a *by-product* of well-conceived and -orchestrated group activities. In other words, the *substance* of the management function, in contrast to instruction, is the classroom group, and the primary focus of the teacher in the pursuit of order is setting creation and maintenance (Gump, 1982) rather than individual behavior.

Toward a Language of Classroom Order

Some attempts have been made recently to develop a language to describe the group dimensions of classroom order. An explication of this language will allow for a more precise understanding of the management function in teaching.

Order does not necessarily mean passivity, absolute silence, or rigid conformity to rules, although these conditions are sometimes considered necessary for specific purposes (e.g., a major test). Order in a classroom simply means that within acceptable limits the students are *following the program of action necessary for a particular classroom event to be realized in the situation.* Programs of action differ across types of classroom *activities,* that is, a bounded segment of classroom time characterized by an identifiable arrangement of participants and materials and a specified pattern of communication (see Au, 1980; Doyle, 1979b, 1984; Gump, 1967, 1969; Philips, 1972; Ross, 1984; Stodolsky, Ferguson, & Wimpelberg, 1981; Yinger, 1980). For lectures or seatwork, for example, students are expected to work independently at their desks and attend to a single information source (see Kounin & Gump, 1974). Whole-class discussions, on the other hand, require that at least some students agree to answer the teacher's questions and students are expected to attend to multiple information sources.

According to this model, classroom order is defined and achieved within contexts and "each context makes different interactional demands on the members of the class" (Shultz & Florio, 1979, p. 169). To understand classroom order, then, it is necessary to examine the contexts of the classroom and how they are enacted by teachers and students. This point was well illustrated in the study by Hargreaves, Hestor, and Mellor (1975) of classroom rules in two British secondary schools. These investigators found that not all rules were in play all of the time. Rather, rules were tied to contexts or phases of a class session or lesson (see also Bremme & Erickson, 1977; Erickson & Shultz, 1981; Wallat & Green, 1979). The five common phases they found were entry, settling down or preparation, lesson proper, clearing up, and exit. Teachers had special rules and routines for each of these phases, and differences were noted across phases. During entry and preparation, students were to enter the room in an orderly fashion, go to their seats, and begin to get materials ready for class. Students were typically allowed to talk quietly among themselves during this phase. At a "switch-signal" from the teachers, the lesson phase began. Students were now expected to pay attention and not talk to each other. The lesson typically consisted of several subphases including teacher explanation, during which students were not to interrupt the teacher; question–answer time and/or discussion, during which students were expected to raise their hands and answer seriously and truthfully; and seatwork, during which quiet talk was often permitted (see deVoss, 1979,

for information about phases of seatwork segments in elementary classes). Finally, during the clearing up and exit phases, work ceased and students prepared to leave.

Order and Cooperation

From the perspective of order, "*cooperation*" rather than "engagement" (in the sense of involvement with content) is the minimum requirement for student behavior (see Doyle, 1979b). The term "cooperation," derived from Grice's (1975) analysis of the "Cooperation Principle" in conversations, is useful for at least two reasons. First, it is a social construct which emphasizes the fact that classroom activities are "jointly constituted" by the participants (Erickson & Shultz, 1981). That is, order, in classrooms as in conversations, is achieved *with* students and depends upon their willingness to follow along with the unfolding of the event. Second, the term acknowledges the fact that order can, and often does, rest on passive noninvolvement by at least some students. In seatwork, for instance, order exists as long as students are not interacting or distracting one another even though they may not be engaged in working with the content. A whole-class discussion can, and often does (see Adams, 1969), operate with only a few students actually interacting with the teacher and the others playing the roles of audience members or passive bystanders, that is, "sitting nicely" and listening (Sieber, 1981). Cooperation, in other words, includes both involvement in the program of action for the activity *and* passive noninvolvement. Misbehavior, on the other hand, is any action by one or more students that threatens to disrupt the activity flow or pull the class toward a program of action that threatens the safety of the group or violates norms of appropriate classroom behavior held by the teacher, the students, or the school staff (see Denscombe, 1980a; Gannaway, 1976; Hargreaves et al., 1975; Nash, 1976; Pollard, 1980). For an activity to succeed as a social event in a classroom, in other words, sufficient numbers of students must be willing to enact the participant role while the rest at least allow the activity to continue.

It is important to emphasize that the focus here is on the problem of order and not the problem of learning. For the purpose of learning, all students ideally should engage in working with content. But in the daily world of a classroom, order can, and often does, exist without full and continuous engagement by all students in learning tasks. Moreover, passive nonengagement is not necessarily problematic in establishing and sustaining order even though it may be unsatisfactory for learning.

The Concern for Order

Several investigators have noted that order and control are pervasive concerns for teachers in their planning and interactive decision making (see Pollard, 1980; West, 1975; Woods, 1976; Yinger, 1980; Clark & Peterson, this volume), and the concern for pupil control appears to increase during early experiences in the teaching role (see Willower, 1975; Willower, Eidell, & Hoy, 1973). Moreover, teachers spend a good deal of time teaching students to be responsible and to behave appropriately in classrooms (see Blumenfeld, Hamilton, Wessels, & Falkner, 1979; Cornbleth & Korth, 1983; Sieber, 1981).

The concern for control seems to be based on two major factors. First, as indicated earlier, classroom activities are enacted in extraordinarily complex settings. Second, activities are joint productions and thus subject to the vicissitudes of students' interests, abilities, and motivations (see Metz, 1978) as well as the problems of interpretation stemming from inherent complexity and ambiguity of social cues (see Cazden, this volume). Recent studies of students' perspectives in classrooms (e.g., Allen, 1983; deVoss, 1979; Lancy, 1976) suggest that many students are inclined to socialize, "fool around," and attempt other mild forms of misbehavior. Many of these actions are done surreptitiously and do not typically have major consequences for classroom order (see Sieber, 1979a). Yet they establish a prevailing pressure on the system so that the potential for disorder is always present in a classroom. It is understandable, then, that teachers' actions are directed to insuring order in these settings.

Summary

Classroom management refers to the actions and strategies teachers use to solve the problem of order in classrooms. Because order is a property of a social system, the language of management must be addressed to group dimensions of the classroom environment and to the contexts within which order is defined and achieved. Management is a complex enterprise because order is jointly accomplished by teachers and students and because a large number of immediate circumstances affect the nature of orderliness, the need for intervention, and the consequences of particular teacher and student actions.

How Life in Classrooms Is Organized

In recent years there has been considerable interest, especially among ecological psychologists (e.g., Gump, 1967, 1975, 1982; Ross, 1984) in describing the structures or behavior settings that organize classroom events and processes. In addition, microethnographers (e.g., Cazden, 1981; Erickson & Mohatt, 1982; Erickson & Shultz, 1981; Mehan, 1979) have examined closely the interactional processes involved in the enactment of events in classrooms. Finally, classroom researchers (e.g. Blumenfeld, Hamilton, Bossert, Wessels, & Meece, 1983; Doyle, 1979a, 1983; Doyle & Carter, 1984; Korth & Cornbleth, 1982) have begun to analyze the task systems that organize and direct classroom experiences.

These domains of theory and research are surveyed in this section because they provide important information about the factors teachers must take into account in achieving classroom order. Later in the chapter, attention turns more specifically to the management strategies teachers use for creating and maintaining settings. At the level of data analysis, a division between structure and strategy is difficult to make. The events described in classroom observations are a product of an interaction between the demands of an environment and the skills of a teacher in meeting these demands. Thus, the effects of structure are intertwined with the effects of strategies. Nevertheless, a distinction between structure and strategy is useful for identifying separate lines of inquiry in management research and for underscoring the central importance of the decisions teachers make in selecting activities for organizing work in classrooms.

Classroom Contexts

A clear sense of the classroom as a tangible context that people inhabit is found in ecological psychology. According to this tradition (see Gump, 1967, 1969), a classroom is a behavior setting, that is, an ecobehavioral unit composed of segments that *surround* and *regulate* behavior. A segment such as a spelling test, writing lesson, or study period, can be described in terms of several elements or what Burnett (1973, p. 293) has called "scene coordinates," including:

1. Its temporal boundaries or duration.
2. The physical milieu, that is, the shape of the site in which it occurs, the number and types of participants, the arrangement of participants in the available space, and the props or objects available to participants.
3. The behavior format or program of action for participants.
4. The focal content or concern of the segment.

IDENTIFYING SEGMENTS

Perhaps the easiest way to clarify the concept of segments is to describe how they are identified in studies (e.g., Doyle, 1984; Gump, 1967; Silverstein, 1979; Stodolsky, 1981) and to examine some of the types of segments that are studied in classroom research.

The database for ecological studies is typically a set of "chronicles" (Gump, 1967; Ross, 1984) or narrative records of classroom meetings. (Videotape [e.g., Kounin, 1970] and time-lapse photography [e.g., Gump, 1967] are sometimes used when the focus is primarily on fine gradients of behavior within settings.) A classroom chronicle is a reasonably complete description of the behavior stream (Barker, 1968; Gump, 1967) that contains information about scene coordinates (i.e., the participants, physical arrangements, props, and time) and a running account of action sequences within scenes.

The first stage of analysis involves dividing a chronicle into segments that represent natural units of organized action. Segmenting rules (see Doyle, 1984; Gump, 1967; Silverstein, 1979) typically calls attention to changes in (a) patterns for arranging participants (e.g., small-group versus whole-class presentation); (b) props and resources used or the sources of information (e.g., books versus films), what Silverstein (1979) called the perceptual task demands of an activity; (c) roles and responsibilities for carrying out immediate actions and events (e.g., oral answering versus writing workbook entries); and (d) "rules of appropriateness" (Erickson & Shultz, 1981, p. 156), that is, the kinds of behaviors that are allowed and disapproved (e.g., talking during snack time versus silence during seatwork). A change in one or more of these dimensions represents a potential change in the nature of the situation in which students and the teacher work.

Once segments have been identified, they are commonly labeled and various dimensions, such as time, focal concern, type of pacing, number of participants, involvement, and so forth, are coded for further analysis (see Grannis, 1978; Gump, 1967; Silverstein, 1979; Stodolsky et al., 1981). A review of research on segment dimensions will be taken up later. For now, the discussion turns to activities, one of the most widely studied classroom segments.

TYPES OF CLASSROOM ACTIVITIES

The basic unit of classroom organization is the activity (see Berliner, 1983a; Doyle, 1984; Gump, 1967; Kounin, 1970; Silverstein, 1979). Activities are relatively short blocks of classroom time — typically 10 to 20 minutes — during which students are arranged in a particular way. Common labels for activities reflect this organizational focus: seatwork, recitation, presentations, small groups. Sometimes activities are designated by their focal content, for example, morning song, spelling test, art, but an organizational pattern is strongly implied by these titles. Some evidence suggests that more than 30 separate activities occur each day in the average elementary school class (see Ross, 1984). In addition, overlapping or simultaneous segments occur during approximately one third of the elementary school day, although it is rare to find more than two segments occurring at the same time (see Gump, 1967). In a fifth grade study, Stodolsky (1981) found, for example, that the average number of simultaneous segments in math was 1.31 and in social studies was 2.49.

Berliner (1983a) has described 11 different types of activities found in 75 classrooms from kindergarten to sixth grade in three schools. Types were distinguished by duration, the number of students, the public or private nature of students' responses, the roles of participants, locus of control of content and processes, stability, attending, and features related to evaluation and feedback. The 11 types were: reading circle, seatwork, one-way presentation, two-way presentation, mediated presentation (involving films or tapes), silent reading, construction, games, play, transitions, and housekeeping. Most lists are quite similar to Berliner's. For instance, in a study of 58 elementary classes in 22 school districts over 2 years, Stodolsky et al. (1981) identified 17 activities: seatwork, diverse seatwork, individualized seatwork, recitation, discussion, lecture, demonstration, checking work, tests, group work, film audiovisual, contest, student reports, giving instructions, preparation, tutorial, and other. Yinger (1977), on the other hand, reported that the primary grade teacher he studied used 53 activities over a 12-week period. These activities included book reports, library, reading groups, reading labs, silent reading, math games, math units, creative writing, newspaper, spelling bees, weekly readers, science units, art in room, assembly, cooking, field trips, gym, music with music teacher, movies, treats, and some exotic ones such as mindbenders, orange suitcase (grammar), Snoopy Snews, and bucket check (desk cleanup).

The diversity implied by these data is subject to two restrictions. First, activities with different labels often have quite similar formats. Thus the structures for lectures, demonstrations, and audiovisual presentations are congruent on several dimensions. Similarly, seatwork often has a uniform shape regardless of the focal content. It is important to emphasize, however, that differences in focal content — that is, social stu-

dies versus science — are likely to be quite important for students and teachers. Second, in terms of actual use in classrooms or what Gump (1967) called student "occupancy time," a few activity types account for the bulk of classroom time. Although there are variations associated with content and student characteristics, approximately 65% of classroom time is spent in seatwork, 35% in whole-class presentation or recitation, and 15% in transitions and other housekeeping events (see Adams & Biddle, 1970; Borg, 1980; Burns, 1984; Edenhart-Pepe, Hudgins, & Miller, 1981; Gump, 1967, 1982; Rosenshine, 1980; Sanford & Evertson, 1983; Stodolsky et al., 1981). In elementary reading, teacher-led small groups are commonly used. Peer work groups, on the other hand, are rare in both American and British schools (see Stodolsky, 1984). Students generally spend their time in schools working alone or in whole-class presentations. Reports also indicate that secondary classes are characterized by less variety in format than elementary classes (see Rounds, Ward, Mergendoller, & Tikunoff, 1982).

SUBJECT MATTER DIFFERENCES

Some attempts have been made to explore differences in activities across subject matter areas. Stodolsky and her colleagues (Stodolsky, 1981; Stodolsky et al., 1981) examined such differences across fifth grade social studies and math lessons. In comparison to social studies, math sessions were characterized by recitation and long seatwork segments with an emphasis on practicing concepts and skills. Social studies lessons had fewer recitation segments than math, although the duration of recitations tended to be longer in social studies so that total amount of time spent in recitation was almost equal across subjects. Seatwork segments in social studies were shorter and occurred less often. In their place, social studies sessions contained more simultaneous small-group segments during which students worked together on assignments while the teacher served as a roving assistant. Stodolsky noted that there was more diversity in curriculum and in cognitive objectives across social studies classes than across math classes. Along similar lines, Kowatrakul (1959) found a greater task focus in math: Students in fifth and sixth grade classes were less likely to be involved in another academic area or in a nonacademic area during arithmetic than during science, social studies, or language. Finally, in a study of middle school science, English, and social studies classes, Korth and Cornbleth (1982) found more listening–viewing activities in science than in social studies and more seatwork in social studies than in English. They also found that social studies at this level was characterized by a greater amount of information-only tasks in contrast to the more diverse curriculum in English.

SEGMENT LEVELS

Although a great deal of attention has been given to the study of activities, it is important to acknowledge that other types of segments operate in classrooms. In a study of junior high school English classes, Doyle (1984) found that the 55-minute period which organizes the school day at this grade level created a *class session* effect that constrained the duration of activities within a session. For each class period, teachers were faced with the need to "come out even," to match the total length of activities to the length of the class session. The class session effect is probably less immediate in elementary grades because students remain in the same place for longer periods of time.

Doyle also found that separate activities were often bound together by a common focal content. A typical sequence was an introduction to a topic followed by seatwork and by time devoted to checking the work and calling out grades. Despite organizational differences, these separate activities seemed to constitute a single *lesson* segment. Along similar lines, Bloome (1981) described a 38-minute junior high social studies lesson that contained several activities: prelesson, getting attention, motivation, instruction, review, test, and feedback (see also Evertson, 1982; Hargreaves et al., 1975; Stebbins, 1974).

Classrooms also contain structures or programs of action to handle extralesson events such as transitions from one activity to another and routines for various housekeeping matters such as sharpening pencils, handing in papers, seeking help from the teacher, disposing of trash, leaving the room to get a drink of water or go to the restroom, and so on.

In summary, there would appear to be at least four structural levels in classrooms:

1. The class session, or the unit of time defined by the signal for students to assemble into the room and the signal for them to leave for recess, lunch, or home.
2. The lesson, or the set of activities bounded together by a common focal content.
3. The activity, or the distinctive pattern for organizing students for working for a unit of time within a lesson.
4. The routine, or the supplementary program of action for handling housekeeping matters in a classroom.

On some occasions, the first three levels or levels two and three may blend together: A lesson in a junior high school class may consist of only one activity and may take a full class session to accomplish. In addition, these levels are embedded in content and event structures for the week, the semester, and the year (see Yinger, 1980).

CONCLUSION

A central premise of ecological psychology is that the meaning, function, and effect of discrete behaviors (e.g., a process question by a teacher) are shaped by the larger contexts of activities, lessons, and class sessions. In other words, discrete behaviors contribute to processes of "creating, maintaining, and dissolving patterns of activity" (Gump, 1967, p. 56). From this perspective, aggregating frequencies of discrete behaviors across contexts is of limited utility.

Contexts and the Behavior of Participants

Over the past several years a body of research has accumulated concerning the relationships between classroom structures and the behavior of participants. Much of this work has grown out of attempts by ecologically oriented researchers to document ways in which environments regulate behavior. Particular attention in this research has been given to the regulatory behaviors of teachers and the work involvement levels of students.

ACTIVITY TYPES AND TEACHER BEHAVIOR

At a general level, teachers are very active participants in classroom events. In a study of six third grade classes, each of which was observed on two Wednesdays using classroom chronicles and time-lapse photographs, Gump (1967, 1969) calculated the total number of teacher acts, defined as the shortest meaningful unit of behavior directed toward students (e.g., "Open your books to page 147"). He found as follows (Gump, 1967):

> No teacher employed less than 1,000 acts [for the two days]; Mrs. Apple engaged in over 1,600. Over all, teachers responded at a rate of *four acts per minute.* It should be emphasized that these figures surely understate the amount of teacher activity invested in creating and managing a classroom day. Observers undoubtedly missed some acts; furthermore, activities not directed to students, such as preparing or putting away materials or bookkeeping or grading, were not included in the count. For the six teachers observed, behavioral output was high indeed. (pp. 49-53)

Gump found that approximately one half of the teachers' acts involved instruction (questions, feedback, imparting knowledge, etc.). The rest of the time the teachers were involved in organizing and arranging students for instruction and orienting them to tasks (23% average), dealing with deviant behavior (14%), and handling individual problems and social amenities (12%).

Gump also examined relationships between activity types and teacher behavior. In some instances, the relationship was obvious, if not mandatory: for example, the greatest number of recitation questions occur in recitations. There were, however, nonmandatory relationships that revealed some of the structural demands of classroom contexts. For example, Gump (1967) found that the teachers emitted substantially more acts during whole-class lessons than they did during reading groups (see also Edenhart-Pepe et al., 1981). This effect may occur because of differences in group size, as well as differences in task involvement rates and responsibilities. Moreover, when classes are grouped for reading, teachers are required to divide their attention between the reading group and the rest of the students who are typically assigned seatwork. It is difficult to supervise seatwork and be an active participant in a reading group at the same time. As a result, teachers may turn some of the work of running the reading group over to the students to be free to monitor the rest of the class.

Of particular interest for classroom management are variations across activities in the frequency with which teachers deal with deviant behavior. Gump (1967) found that acts labeled "dealing with deviant behavior" were typically more frequent in a recitation than in a reading group. In addition, the number of such acts was nearly the same in recitation and supervised study. Finally, during reading groups, the teachers seldom interacted with students in seatwork, but when they did, they were likely to be either dealing with deviant behavior or helping with an individual problem. In a study of two third grade and two fourth grade classrooms, Bossert (1979) also found that classroom structure had a powerful influence on the types of control exercised by teachers. Two of the teachers in Bossert's sample demanded strict adherence to rules and regulations, tended to dominate their classes, and used the recitation format more than the other two. Nevertheless, during recitation all four teachers tended to use dominant control strategies. In particular, desist or reprimand rates were higher during recitation than during seatwork and small groups for all of the teachers. Bossert argued that the large-group structure of recitations requires teachers to be more active in eliciting students' attention to a common target and more concerned about stopping misbehavior before it spreads.

One other general pattern of teacher behavior appears to be associated with activity type. Gump's (1967) data suggest that teachers provide individual student help most frequently during supervised seatwork. Recitations or reading groups are used primarily for group instruction, and few attempts are made to work with individual problems during these activities. This pattern may well be related to the public character of teacher and student performance during group-oriented activities. In such settings, the press is to maintain a group pace and to involve as many students as possible in each episode (see Gump, 1967, on external pacing, and Kounin, 1970, on group focus and momentum). During supervised seatwork when students are engaged in independent tasks, teacher–student interaction is less visible, and localized contacts with students do not slow down the momentum of the other students or appear to exclude them from the work at hand. On these grounds, one would expect more individualized teacher–student contacts in classes organized around supervised seatwork (see Bossert, 1979). At the same time, student engagement rates are often low and the frequency of reprimands high during seatwork (Gump, 1967), which suggests that these activities present their own problems for order and instruction (see Rosenshine, 1979, 1983).

Some attempts have been made to describe teacher behaviors in settings characterized by overlapping or simultaneous activities. Such class structures are complex because the alternative program of action can distract students, and the teacher is often unavailable to monitor behavior or provide assistance when needed (see Silverstein, 1979). In a study of two third grade and two fourth grade classes, Bossert (1979) reported that the frequency of reprimands was lower in multitask classes (i.e., classes in which students worked independently or in small groups on different tasks) than in whole-class recitations. In a study of five first grade and five fifth grade classes, Blumenfeld et al. (1983) found that teacher talk in "open activity structures" (i.e., when students were working on different tasks at the same time) was less negative, more likely to be about academic performance, less likely to be about social procedure, and likely to contain fewer informatives than teacher talk in single-task arrangements. Wilson, Rosenholtz, and Rosenholtz (1983) examined teacher behavior in nine third and fourth grade classrooms under different levels of what they called "task complexity," that is, the number of simultaneous groups operating in the class. They reported that teachers did not differ in the amount of task directions they gave to the class in low- and high-complexity situations. As complexity increased, however,

teachers gave more task directions to individual students as problems arose, although the frequency of this type of behavior was quite low under all conditions. In addition, there was more peer task talk and students worked together more often in high-complexity situations. The researchers interpreted this finding to mean that teachers delegate more authority to students when task complexity is high. It is difficult to ascertain from their data, however, whether increased peer interaction was a function of teacher delegation or activity structure.

In general, these results suggest that the teacher is less likely to be a central regulatory and instructional figure when simultaneous activities are being used. As will be seen, however, student involvement is lower when a teacher is not a member of the segment than when he or she is (Gump, 1967). Moreover, Soar and Soar (1983) have argued that multitask structures which give students options and choices are beneficial for learning, especially for middle- to high-ability students and for higher cognitive-level objectives, but only if teachers are able to maintain order.

Finally, recent studies by Arlin (Arlin, 1982; Arlin & Webster, 1983) have pointed to *time flow* as a dimension of activity systems that constrains teachers. In a series of naturalistic and experimental studies, Arlin found that mastery learning designs, in which achievement is set at mastery and the time students need in order to learn is allowed to vary, magnified the effect of learning rate differences among students in a class and created delays as teachers worked with a small portion of the class who did not achieve mastery. This disruption of activity momentum (see Kounin, 1970) generated serious problems of management and order for teachers. Arlin's findings suggested that highly differentiated instructional systems are inherently difficult to manage in classrooms.

The results surveyed here suggest that there are differences in the regulatory behavior of teachers associated in part with activity features rather than individual teacher preferences and styles. Further evidence for this association has been provided by Scott (1977). In a study of three effective and two ineffective head teachers in preschool programs for disadvantaged 5-year-olds, Scott reported that there were greater differences in the behavior of an individual teacher across settings (Morning Greeting versus Large Group Activity) than among teachers within a setting. Similarities among teachers were greater for the more structured and formal Large Group Activity than for the more informal Morning Greeting. In selecting an activity, therefore, a teacher defines in large measure a context that shapes his or her own options and actions. As will be seen in the next section, the selection of an activity also has consequences for student behavior.

ACTIVITY TYPES AND STUDENT BEHAVIOR

Work involvement or engagement is, by far, the most widely used student behavior variable in studies of classroom management. This emphasis seems reasonable since it reflects both common understandings of what classrooms are for and the general picture of what students typically do in these settings. As indicated earlier, involvement is used to label student behavior that reflects active engagement in working. Noninvolvement or off-task behavior often includes passive withdrawal, mild forms of inappropriate behavior, and more serious forms of misbehavior. From the perspective of management and order, these differences in the quality of off-task behavior can be significant (see Silverstein, 1979).

Engagement at a class level is usually measured in one of two ways: (a) by averaging engagement rates for individual students over a period of time, or (b) by averaging the number of students involved at several intervals during an activity. In general, the first measure is of more interest to investigators studying instruction and learning, and the latter to those studying classroom management and order. There are, of course, serious validity problems associated with measuring engagement by direct observation since it is not always possible to tell whether a student who appears engaged is actually engaged (see Peterson & Swing, 1982).

Gump's (1967) third grade study, using time-lapse photographs, remains one of the most thorough investigations of relationships between activity types and student involvement. In general, he found that involvement was highest for students in teacher-led small groups (around 92%) and lowest for pupil presentations (72%). Between these extremes, engagement was higher in whole-class recitations, tests, and teacher presentations (around 80%) than in supervised study and independent seatwork that was not supervised by the teacher (around 75%). Parallel figures have been reported by other investigators. Kounin (1970) found that student involvement in recitations was approximately 85% and involvement in seatwork segments averaged 65%. In a study of four classes at fourth, fifth, and sixth grade, Atwood (1983) found that student involvement was higher in recitation and mixed (recitation followed by class task) segments than in class task and multitask segments. Indeed, involvement was lowest when students worked on different assignments during seatwork. Rosenshine (1980) analyzed data from the Beginning Teacher Evaluation Study and reported that engagement in recitations averaged 84% in contrast to 68% in seatwork. Other studies reviewed by Rosenshine (1979, 1983), Ross (1984), and Burns (1984) have shown similar contrasts between recitations and seatwork and have indicated that when seatwork is used frequently, engagement is even lower. Finally, Edenhart-Pepe et al. (1981) reported that levels of student engagement were more consistent across teachers in recitations in contrast to seatwork and multitask structures in which there were larger differences among teachers.

Taking a slightly different focus, Silverstein (1979) examined relationships between environmental characteristics and levels of students' "problematic behavior," defined as behavior which a teacher perceives as inappropriate for a given activity. In a study of two fourth grade classes, Silverstein found that problematic behaviors from daydreaming and mild distractions to disruption, unnecessary movement, shouting, and fighting occurred most often during seatwork and silent pleasure reading and that nearly all students were involved in some type of problematic behavior during these segments. During small-group and whole-class formats, however, only a few instances of noninvolvement and mildly distracting behaviors occurred. Similar contrasts between settings were reported by Kounin (1970): Deviance in seatwork was four times that in recitations.

Gump (1967, 1969) analyzed variations in student involve-

ment between opening and remaining phases of activities. For seatwork and recitation he found that involvement during the beginning phase (the first 4 minutes of a segment) was significantly lower than involvement during the remainder of an activity. In addition, lowest involvement scores were recorded for the beginning phase of seatwork, and highest involvement scores occurred during the remaining phase of recitations. Variations in involvement by phases were also reported by deVoss (1979) in his study of collective student activity during major lesson segments in elementary classes. During what he called "comfortable work," students' attention to the work waned periodically and noise levels increased as students engaged in various "passing time" behaviors such as socializing, walking around the room, daydreaming, and so forth. If "passing time" became sufficiently visible, teachers would intervene to reestablish involvement, students would begin working again, and the cycle would be repeated. DeVoss also reported that if a product was required at the end of seatwork, students would "spurt" (i.e., work rapidly to finish) when there was an indication that the activity was about to conclude. The implication of this observation is that students do most of their work at the end of seatwork activities. Finally, Stebbins (1974) described variations in engagement across lesson segments — presentation, seatwork, and recapitulation — in elementary and secondary classes in Canada and Jamaica. He found that, across settings, seatwork commonly began quietly but soon moved toward a "crescendo of student conversation" (p. 49) that was then halted by an admonition from the teacher. He also noted that the endings of seatwork activities were often problematic because students finished at different times. Finally, he called attention to the special problems of disorder associated with vacations, holidays, and special events.

A contrast between teacher and student input was also clear in Gump's (1967) data. Involvement was highest in teacher-led small groups and lowest when there were prolonged student presentations (sharing, reporting, discussions). Low involvement for discussions (around 55%) was also reported by Kowatrakul (1959) in a study of fifth and sixth grade classes. Gump (1982) attributes this effect to the loss of momentum in the flow of an activity. Student contributions, especially in the elementary grades, are likely to be hesitant and redundant and, thus, to slow down classroom events. Some support for this view was found in a high school study by Mayers, Csikszentmihalyi, and Larson (1978): Students reported that they concentrated more and found it easier to concentrate when listening to the teacher rather than to a student. These findings suggest that there is a certain degree of ecological efficiency in teaching reading in small groups. Reading instruction often consists of episodes during which an individual student reads aloud for a relatively long period of time. The low involvement associated with such episodes can perhaps be offset by conducting them in teacher-led small groups in which involvement is typically high.

It is interesting to note that Gump (1967) did not find differences in involvement between supervised study and seatwork in which the teacher was occupied with a small group (e.g., during reading instruction). In other words, involvement during seatwork did not increase when the teacher was available to monitor. This result probably reflects the fact that

Gump's teachers spent considerable time during supervised study periods providing help to individual students. As a result, they were occupied in dyadic contacts. Doyle (1984) found in junior high classes that teachers who actively monitored and paced seatwork and kept individual contacts brief were more successful in maintaining engagement and minimizing inappropriate and disruptive behavior.

Finally, little research is available concerning the relationship between the sequence of activities and student involvement (see Ross, 1984). Some studies have focused on problems associated with starting academic work after students have been engaged in physical exercise. Gump (1967) found that involvement in the beginning phase of seatwork was especially low after recess. Similarly, Krantz and Risley (1977) found that off-task behavior was high (37%) when storytime occurred immediately after recess. Inserting a rest period between recess and storytime reduced off-task behavior to 14%. Taking a more general perspective, Brooks (1985) examined videotapes of first-day sessions in four seventh grade math classes and found that the sequence of activities in effective managers' classes was more systematic and logical than the sequence in classes of inexperienced and ineffective teachers. Brooks argued that sequence was a critical factor in communicating teaching competence on the first day of school. These few studies suggest that more research on sequences of activities would assist teachers in arranging activities during the school day.

THE PHYSICAL DESIGN OF SETTINGS

Ecological psychologists (e.g., Barker, 1968; Gump, 1974, 1982; Ross, 1984) have used the term "synomorphy" to refer to the compatibility between the program of action in an activity and the physical aspects of the setting. From the perspective of order, one can easily imagine how furniture arrangements (e.g., circles, U-shapes, straight rows), types of desks and chairs (e.g., tables or booths in art and laboratory rooms vs. conventional desks), and room dividers (e.g., bookcases, file cabinets) could affect the density of students, opportunities for interaction, and the visibility of behavior. Similarly, glare from overhead projectors or light through a window could well create blind spots for a teacher and thus interfere with monitoring classroom behavior. Unfortunately, only a limited amount of systematic inquiry has been done in this area of classroom management.

Weinstein (1979) has recently reviewed research on the effects of physical features of the classroom environment. The data on classroom design and furniture arrangements indicate that different patterns of spatial organization have little effect on achievement or verbal interaction but some effect on attitudes and conduct. In particular, it seems to be important to separate clearly areas serving different purposes and design traffic avenues in the room carefully. Density, which has been studied primarily at nursery school and college levels, appears to increase dissatisfaction and aggression and decrease attentiveness. In a study of fourth grade classes, Silverstein (1979) reported that density increased the likelihood that students would be distracted by the actions of other students and that students often wanted to be seated away from students who talked or interrupted them.

Perhaps the most widely known work on the effects of physical features of classrooms is that conducted by Adams (1969) and Adams and Biddle (1970) on the relationship between students' location and participation. These investigators found that students who sat in the "action zone" in the front and center of the room (seats were arranged in traditional rows) interacted most frequently with the teacher. Potter (1974) reported that this effect was especially strong for low-ability elementary students. Brooks, Silvern, and Wooten (1978) reported that secondary students in the social-consultive zone (front and center) received a more permissive and interactive style of communication from the teacher, while students in the public zone (middle and back of the room) received more lecturing and one-way communication. Sommer (1969) also reported an association between location and participation and argued that degree of visual contact with the instructor was positively related to amount of participation. Studies with high school and college students (e.g., Totusek & Staton-Spicer, 1982) indicate that there may be special characteristics of students who prefer to sit in the action zone, but Schwebel and Cherlin (1972) found that elementary students assigned to seats in the front row were more attentive than students assigned to other seats. The evidence seems to suggest that location does influence access to classroom events and, when a choice is given, some students seek locations that enable them to be active participants in these events.

Bennett and Blundell (1983) reported a field experiment in which 10- and 11-year-old students in two classes first spent 2 weeks in their normal classroom groups and were then assigned to work independently in rows before being reassigned to groups. The results indicated that the quantity of work completed increased and the quality of products remained the same when students sat in rows. The teachers also reported that there was a noticeable improvement in classroom behavior when the students were in rows. Some of the students seemed to prefer the work atmosphere of rows but complained of a loss in available work space.

A considerable amount of the research on physical dimensions of schooling has concentrated on differences between traditional enclosed classrooms and open-spaced buildings (see Weinstein, 1979). Stebbins (1974) observed 36 elementary and secondary classrooms in St. John's, Newfoundland, and 35 classrooms at the same levels in Kingston, Jamaica. In contrast to the traditional school buildings and enclosed classrooms in Canada, the Jamaican schools were constructed as clusters of small buildings, and the classrooms were often without doors or walls. Stebbins argued that the open structures of Jamaican classrooms contributed to the disorderly behavior because of the large number of distracting stimuli, direct access to disruptions and interruptions from other teachers and students who were not members of the class, and the ease with which students could slip out of the room when the teacher's back was turned to write on the chalkboard. Stebbins argued that these findings have implications for implementing open-plan schools. In particular, he emphasized the need for "enlightened teaching" to make academic work attractive to students. Solomon and Kendall (1976) reported that fourth grade students in open classrooms spent more time working together, initiating their own tasks, and working without teacher attention than students in traditional rooms. Students in traditional rooms spent more time in whole-class activities which were structured and closely monitored. In addition, there was more informality and spontaneity and more simultaneous activities in open than in traditional rooms. Finally, teachers in traditional rooms spent more time lecturing and disciplining students, whereas open-classroom teachers spent more time interacting with individuals and small groups.

Gump (1975) reviewed data concerning noise in open-space schools and concluded that noise bothered teachers more than it did students (see also Denscombe, 1980b) and that the effects of noise on attention depended upon the nature of the activity, the content of the message, and the density of the setting. Sommer (1969) has suggested that high spatial freedom creates a need for teachers to spend more time on discipline than in more restricted traditional settings. In a study of sixth grade classes, Short (1975) compared two teachers in self-contained classrooms with a teacher in an open-space classroom, and found that significantly more group-focused behaviors, especially group directions and reprimands, occurred in the self-contained rooms. Nevertheless, there were no significant differences across settings in the amounts of off-task and deviant behavior and in the number of reprimands directed to individuals.

Gump (1974) studied primary (first and second) and intermediate (fifth and sixth) grades in two open-space and two traditional school buildings. Differences between buildings were more consistent at the primary than at the intermediate levels, and the differences suggested that open-school students at the primary level occupied a greater variety of sites than primary students in the traditional schools (2.75 and 3.00 vs. 1.00 and 1.75). In addition, primary students in open schools worked with more adults than traditional school students did (2.67 vs. 1.37). At the intermediate level, one traditional school provided less variety in sites and number of adults than the other traditional school and the open schools. The data also indicated that open school students, especially at the primary level, spent more time than traditional school students in settings in which they worked together and in settings with external rather than self-pacing. The latter result may have occurred because there were more adults present in open classes. In addition, more time in open schools than in traditional schools was spent in transitions, waiting, and organizing (31% and 25% vs. 19% at the primary level). Gump reported that most delays in open schools occurred after transitions because teachers were busy closing out the previous activity or dealing with a problem from that activity. Finally, student on-task percentages were lower in one of the open schools at the primary level (73% vs. 80% for the other schools) and in both open schools at the intermediate level (76% and 78% vs. 82% and 86%). Referring to the frequent similarities in results, especially at the intermediate level, Gump concluded that construction alone did not necessarily affect the educational program in these schools.

SUMMARY

Teacher behavior is systematically related to the types of activities used in the classroom. The amount of time teachers spend organizing and directing students, interacting with individual students, and dealing with inappropriate and disruptive behavior is related to type of activity and the physical arrangements of the setting. Studies suggest that the greater the amount of student choice and mobility and the greater the complexity of the social scene, the greater the need for overt managing and controlling actions by teachers. In addition, student work involvement or engagement is higher in teacher-led, externally paced activities than in self-paced activities, a factor that may account for the frequent use of recitations in classrooms. In addition, student involvement is lower during the beginning phase than during the remaining phase of activities. Involvement is also especially low during activities in which there are prolonged student presentations.

Contexts as Programs of Action

The next stage in understanding classroom order involves seeing contexts as programs of action. According to Gump (1982), "The action structure is the heart of classroom segments" (p. 99). This statement is especially true for understanding classroom management because order is defined by the programs of action embedded in classroom activities. In addition to providing slots and sequences for participants' behavior, these programs of action have direction, momentum, and energy (see Arlin, 1979, 1982; Erickson, 1982a; Kounin, 1970). Time does not simply pass in classrooms. Rather, there is rhythmic movement toward the accomplishment of academic and social-interactional ends. In Merritt's (1982) term, classroom activities contain "vectors" that, once entered into, pull events and participants along their course.

Participation Structures

In this section, the common classroom activities of recitation, seatwork, multiple-group arrangements, and transitions are described in terms of their programs or vectors of action. Particular attention is given to recent microethnographic studies that have explicated the fine-grained details of setting enactment in classrooms. In shifting from structure to processes, attention turns from how common forms guide behavior to how activities are jointly constructed by teachers and students in time and space through processes of action, negotiation, and interpretation (see Bloome, 1983; Erickson & Shultz, 1981; Griffin & Mehan, 1979; Heap, 1980). The emphasis changes, in other words, from recitation as a common form recognizable in many classrooms to how a recitation is achieved in a particular class on a particular day through the joint actions of the teacher and students.

RECITATION

The classroom activity known as recitation has had an interesting history. In the 19th century, the term referred to an event in which a single student was required to "toe the line" and recite a lesson privately to the teacher. With the rise of class teaching and simultaneous instruction (see Hamilton, 1980, 1981), recitation came to mean a whole-class format characterized by question–answer drills over content. Although recitation still

WALTER DOYLE

involves calling on individual students, answers are given publicly before the rest of the class, and each teacher–student contact is often brief.

Despite a steady barrage of criticism, this form appears to have been quite durable during this century (see Cuban, 1982; Hoetker & Ahlbrand, 1969). At the same time, there would appear to be considerable variation in the uses of recitation and in how the general recitation structure is enacted in classrooms. In a recent study of elementary math and social studies, Stodolsky and her colleagues (Stodolsky et al., 1981) reported that approximately 35% of classroom time was spent in recitations and that this activity was used for several purposes, including review, introducing new material, checking answers to work, practice, and checking understanding. As purposes varied so did types of questions and opportunities for student participation. In a study of six third grade classes, Gump (1967) found that the general recitation format could be configured in different ways depending on grouping and task patterns. In a junior high school English study, Doyle (1984) reported a similar variety within formats: Presentations of content typically involved brief question–answer exchanges, and segments in which work was checked often contained explanations. In science, English, and social studies classes in a middle school, Korth and Cornbleth (1982) found that whole-class considerations of content occurred most frequently in an activity they called "QATE," that is, question and answer with teacher elaboration. These studies suggest that the stereotype of the "recitation" does not necessarily represent what happens during group lessons in classrooms.

Microethnographic analyses of classroom discourse (see Cazden's chapter on classroom discourse, this volume) have directed attention to a level of classroom functioning called participation structure, that is, the system of rules governing speaking, listening, and turn taking. This unit is often used to examine differences between the discourse rules of the home culture of ethnic minorities and the participation demands of classrooms (see Au, 1980; Erickson & Mohatt, 1982; Philips, 1972; Shultz & Florio, 1979). Sinclair and Coulthard (1975) and Mehan (1979) have described the participation structure of conventional classrooms in terms of a transaction or interactional sequence consisting of initiation, reply, and evaluation or follow-up. These episodes consist of the interconnected moves (see Bellack, Kliebard, Hyman, & Smith, 1966) teachers and students use in classrooms to accomplish interactional goals. Episodes are subunits of activities that describe how teacher–student contacts typically occur. The amount of such interpersonal contact obviously varies across different types of classroom activities. Classroom studies suggest, however, that the overall rate of teacher–pupil interactions is moderate for the individual student. In a study of third and fourth grade classes, Potter (1977) found that in discussions the average child raised his or her hand every 6 minutes and gave an answer once every 15 minutes. During seatwork, which is treated shortly, the average child had contact with the teacher once every 11 minutes. For the teacher, however, these rates are multiplied by a factor of more than 20 (see Gump, 1967).

Using transcripts of lessons from secondary classes in England and Australia and a general framework from the ethnography of conversations, McHoul (1978) proposed a set of rules governing turn taking in whole-class lessons. These rules represent what is essentially a grammar of group lessons rather than a description of an individual teacher's skill or even an effective pattern of interaction. As a grammar, the rules purport to summarize the interaction structures teachers in general try to hold in place in conversational lessons. Naturally there is considerable variation in the actual enactment of these rules on particular occasions. However, to the extent that these rules describe the essential features of group lessons, they depict a familiar program of action for students and teachers. Departures from this familiar pattern are likely to increase the need for interactional work to achieve order.

McHoul argued that, in contrast to natural conversations, the teacher is the only participant in a classroom lesson who can select a topic and elect to take the first turn. In addition, the variety of options for turn taking in classrooms is limited because the teacher controls the initial selection of a speaker, the duration of a turn (including his or her own turns), and the selection of the next speaker. The student speaking must either continue until the teacher has terminated the turn with a comment that the answer is sufficient, or select the teacher as the next speaker. The student speaking is not allowed, however, to select another student to speak, and other students cannot self-select a turn. Such a rule obviously accounts for the initiation–response–evaluation sequence of conversational episodes in classroom lessons (see Bellack et al., 1966; Mehan, 1979; Sinclair & Coulthard, 1975). This rule serves to minimize the possibility of overlap, that is, a situation in which a student self-selects to interrupt another student's turn before the teacher has signaled that the answer is adequate or sufficient, even when there are long pauses at the beginning of or during a turn. In natural coversations, such pauses signal possible junctures between turns. In classrooms, an individual student's turn, once it is started, is protected from intrusions by other students. The teacher may, of course, insert prompts to the selected speaker during a turn if the pause is long or the student makes a mistake that affects the meaning of the lesson (see Allington, 1980; Hoffman & Clements, 1984), and such prompts may be solicited from other students. Nevertheless, the teacher controls the scheduling of insertions, and such insertions do not terminate a turn. It is important to note that, in contrast to natural conversations, pauses between student and teacher turns are typically quite short (Rowe, 1974), perhaps because there is virtually no focal activity during these gaps.

McHoul's rules also dealt with the function of hand raising in classrooms. In addition to enabling a teacher to schedule one-at-a-time turns, this device helps with the problem of selecting a "knowing-and-willing answerer" (p. 201), that is, a student who is likely to stay on topic and have an answer. Thus, the teacher can avoid diversions away from the lesson or unnecessarily long delays in moving through the activity. Occasionally teachers open up turns (i.e., fail to designate a specific answerer) in order to solicit comments, suggestions, or guesses from several students. In addition, a teacher may open up turns when the answer requires esoteric knowledge that only a few students are likely to know. When such events lead to a jumble of answers, teachers quickly return to protected, one-at-a-time turns. Consistent with Kounin (1970), McHoul also noted that students are usually selected after questions are asked rather than before.

The latter practice starts the turn before the question is posed and thus excludes other students from the episode.

Finally, McHoul noted that in natural conversations turn taking is handled locally at each juncture. Because it is not always necessary for the next speaker to remain strictly on topic or for the conversers to remain organized as a unit, the course of a conversation is often unpredictable and schisms develop in which subgroups follow their own conversational paths. Such permutations would seem to be inconsistent with the task-orientation and content focus of classroom lessons. It is reasonable, therefore, that they are prevented in classrooms by rules that assign control of turns to the teacher.

Green and her associates (see Green & Harker, 1982; Wallat & Green, 1979) have examined ways in which kindergarten students bid for turns in classrooms and teachers accept or reject these bids. In contrast to McHoul's study, Green's kindergarten groups were typically smaller, topics were less academic, and there was more spontaneous vocal bidding for turns. The investigators found that the teacher selected speakers and protected an individual student's turn under the "one-speaker-at-a-time" rule. Bids for a turn were likely to be accepted, however, when they were thematically tied to the topic at hand *and* when they occurred at junctures between turns. Bids that did not meet these specifications were rejected overtly or covertly. As time progressed, there were fewer unsuccessful bids, indicating that students had learned the rules for gaining access to turns. Along similar lines, Mehan (1979) found that successful bids for turns in an elementary classroom had to be topically relevant and occur during junctures between initiation–response–evaluation episodes. And Eder (1982a) reported that successful bidding for turns increased as first grade students in one class became more experienced as participants in reading groups and classroom meetings.

SEATWORK

The term "seatwork" refers to two distinct types of classroom events. The first type is what Gump (1967) called "supervised study" during which all students are assigned to work independently at their desks with their own materials, although not necessarily the same material, and the teacher is free to monitor the total class. This type of seatwork is often quite interactive (Doyle, 1984). The second type consists of independent work while the teacher is involved in directing an activity at another part of the room and is therefore not available to monitor the total classroom continuously. Seatwork of this second type occurs often when elementary teachers are working with reading groups. Clearly the tasks of managing these two types of seatwork are substantially different because of the different demands on teacher attention and involvement.

Merritt (1982) has examined the processes of multiple attending and scheduling that occurred during "servicelike events," that is, student-initiated contacts with the teacher, in 10 classes from nursery school through third grade. In a language compatible with Kounin's (1970), Merritt noted that teachers and students were faced with the demand to monitor more than one vector of activity even when they were primarily involved in only one. Moreover, teachers stayed with a vector of activity until they located a point at which it was terminated or would

apparently continue without their immediate involvement (see also Scott, 1977). Thus, in a manner similar to turn taking in group lessons, student requests for teacher attention were ignored unless they occurred when the teacher was free to "slot out" for the request. Contacts, in other words, had to be appropriately timed. Students, in turn, were expected to wait until the teacher was free and to do something to fill the waiting time. Service-like events involved, therefore, a complex judgment concerning the nature and duration of the interruption and the stability at a particular moment of the vector of activity the teacher was primarily directing. Merritt also noted that teachers often used contextualization cues during service-like events to separate primary and secondary vectors and maintain the dual streams.

The demands of service-like events obviously vary with the nature of the teacher's involvement in a primary vector. During supervised seatwork, a teacher can more easily schedule requests from other students, whereas during reading groups slotting out is more narrowly constrained.

SMALL GROUPS AND COOPERATIVE LEARNING TEAMS

Small groups in which students work together on assignments are used infrequently in most classrooms (Clements, 1983; Emmer, 1983; Stodolsky, 1984), with a possible exception of social studies (Stodolsky, 1981). Recently several investigators have designed procedures to increase dramatically the amount of cooperative group work in classrooms and tested the effects of these procedures on academic achievement, social status, group cohesion, friendship patterns, race relations, and shared perceptions of ability (see Aronson, 1978; Cohen, 1979, 1980; Johnson, Maruyama, Johnson, Nelson, & Skon, 1981; Sharan, 1980; Slavin, 1980, 1982). Slavin (1980) has been especially active in developing and evaluating classroom systems for student team learning. For example, one system called Teams-Games-Tournament (TGT) is built around four- to five-member heterogeneous teams that cooperatively prepare to participate in academic games with members of other teams. For tournaments, competition is between students of equivalent ability and each student has a chance to contribute to the team's score. More recently Slavin and his colleagues (Slavin, Leavey, & Madden, 1984) have devised a system called Team Assisted Individualization in which students work together on individualized materials, and their performance contributes to team scores. In addition, students correct each other's work so that the teacher is given more time to instruct small groups and help individual students.

Studies in several subject fields and grade levels generally indicate that cooperative teams have positive effects on achievement, especially when instruction is carefully structured, individuals are accountable for performance, and a well-defined group reward system is used (see Slavin, 1980, for a review). In addition, such methods have positive effects on race relations and mutual concern among students. Unfortunately, there is little information available concerning the problems classroom teachers have in managing cooperative team learning procedures. Most reports describe experiments designed to test the effects of the systems. In these circumstances, the research team was actively involved in implementing the procedures and this involvement probably affected order in the classes. Clearly these systems require considerable time to prepare instructional materials and test items keyed to different ability levels. In addition, they represent very complex classroom arrangements that would, because of the multiple demands on attention and involvement, require well-developed classroom management skills. At the same time, developers have created carefully articulated systems for conducting cooperative learning teams in classroom settings. Given the apparent effectiveness of these techniques, more attention to management processes is certainly warranted.

TRANSITIONS AND INTERRUPTIONS

Transitions are points in social interaction when contexts change and, thus, they have been a favorite topic of researchers interested in activity structures and classroom discourse (see Erickson & Shultz, 1981; Gump, 1967). Minor transitions occur between speaking turns, and major transitions occur between activities or phases of a lesson, between lessons, and between class meetings. At each of these levels, large amounts of cueing and interactional negotiation occur to signal the onset of a change, the reorientation of focus, and the beginning of a new segment (see Bremme & Erickson, 1977; Cahir, 1978; Green & Harker, 1982; McDermott, 1976; Shultz & Florio, 1979). This cueing often creates "boundary indeterminacy" which makes it difficult to locate precise beginning and ending points for transitions between activities (see Arlin, 1979).

In general, the duration of major transitions depends upon the magnitude of the changes that must be made. A change in topic without an accompanying change in group structure, for example, is typically handled briefly by what Hargreaves and his colleagues (1975) called "switch-signals." A reconfiguration of the classroom, for example, from seatwork to small groups, takes more time, and teachers use a large number of regulatory acts to hold order in place until the next program of action is operating.

Approximately 31 major transitions occur per day in elementary classrooms, and they account for approximately 15% of classroom time (see Burns, 1984; Gump, 1967, 1982; Rosenshine, 1980). Because room arrangements in secondary classes typically remain the same across activities, major transitions take less time at this level (see Doyle, 1984; Evertson, 1982).

Interruptions, like transitions, are common extralesson events in classrooms, and they have clear consequences for order. Behnke (1979) examined "classroom distractions" (i.e., interruptions in the flow of instruction) that resulted from either internal sources such as student misbehavior or external sources such as visitors or announcements. Internal distractions were by far the most frequent type, accounting for nearly 90% of the interruption in the flow of instruction, but their effect usually lasted for only about 10 seconds. External interruptions, on the other hand, were infrequent but disrupted instruction for several minutes.

Academic Work as a Program of Action

It is becoming increasingly clear that subject matter is a significant component of the programs of action in classrooms.

Hoffman and Clements (1984) and Englert and Semmel (1983) have reported, for example, that teachers are likely to interrupt reading turns when a student's errors change the meaning of the text and ignore substitutions which are semantically equivalent to words in the text. These data suggest that teachers track the development of content as well as the flow of social interaction. Furthermore, students appear to focus a significant part of their attention in class on information about how to do the work they are assigned as well as what behavior they are to display (King, 1980, 1983). It would seem, therefore, that subject matter needs to be included more explicitly in research on classroom management. To that end, this section contains a review of some of the emerging theories and research on subject matter processes in classrooms.

STUDENTS' TASKS IN CLASSROOMS

Erickson (1982a, 1982b) has developed a compelling case for examining students' learning tasks in classrooms as a composite of a subject matter task structure and a social task structure, both of which contain action slots and sequences. He argues (1982b):

> At the level of enactment in real time as an environment, both task dimensions have a sequential organization that must be integrated across dimensions if hitches in the process of accomplishing the task are not to occur. If the subject matter task environment at hand (e.g., an addition problem being done in a classroom) requires carrying from the "ones" column across to the "tens" column, and the student is confused when at the point of carrying, if the social task environment prohibits asking another child for help (because that is defined as inappropriate in the social participation structure), the overall learning task at that point has become more complex. How is the child to get the needed information about an arithmetical operation in a socially appropriate way? This is an example of a sequentially arrived at point at which a learner gets "stuck" because of contradictory demands across the social and academic task dimensions. These sequential points of "stuckness" can become more salient for the learner than the overall task itself. (p.172)

Doyle (1979a, 1983) has utilized the notion of "academic tasks" to account for curriculum as a process variable or program of action in classrooms. According to this model, subject matter appears in classroom settings as work, that is, as products to be generated using available instructions and resources (see also Blumenfeld et al., 1983; deVoss, 1979; Korth & Cornbleth, 1982; LeCompte, 1978b). Accountability plays a key role in determining the value or significance of work in a classroom: Products that are evaluated strictly by the teacher are more likely to be seen as serious work, that is, work that "counts" (see Doyle & Carter, 1984; Florio et al., 1982; King, 1980; Morrison, 1982; Smith, 1978). At the same time, accountability affects the risk associated with various types of academic tasks. Tasks involving higher cognitive processes of understanding, reasoning, and problem formulation are high in inherent ambiguity and risk for students, that is, because the precise nature of correct answers cannot be predicted and rehearsed in advance, the possibility of failure is high. Ambiguity and risk, in turn, shape students' attitudes toward the work they do in classrooms. Mayers et al. (1978), for example, found that high school students had more positive attitudes and higher motivation in "boredom" classes in which the challenges were perceived as less than their skills, than in "worry" classes in which the challenges were perceived as greater than their skills.

Morine-Dershimer (1983) has described an interesting case of how students responded to different task demands during recitations in second, third, and fourth grade classes. When teachers asked convergent questions, frequency of student participation was correlated with academic ability. When teachers asked divergent questions that emphasized ideas and opinions, nearly all answers were accepted, and the task often became one of simply participating. In these instances, high-ability students were often reluctant to respond, and lower ability students participated more often than usual. In addition, students' attention to the comments of other students was low.

TEACHERS AND ACADEMIC WORK

For a teacher, the work students do is central to the instruction function but only one aspect of the creation and management of classroom activities. From the perspective of order, the nature of academic work influences the probability of student cooperation and involvement in a lesson and thus the complexity of the teacher's management task. If, for example, most students find the work too difficult, then few will be able to participate in carrying out the activity. In a study of three junior high school English classes taught by the same teacher, Doyle and Carter (1984) found that academic tasks involving descriptive or expository writing were difficult for the teacher to orchestrate in the classroom. Such tasks, which often extended over several class sessions, were characterized by long introductions, delays between introductions and seatwork segments as the students asked for clarification and assistance in getting started, and frequent student-initiated questions during work periods. In contrast, tasks involving recall or predictable algorithms, such as those found in vocabulary or grammar assignments, proceeded smoothly and efficiently.

Similar effects have been reported by other investigators. Atwood (1983), in a study of fourth through sixth grade students, found that work involvement in the mixed activities structure (recitation followed by seatwork) was low with procedurally complex tasks such as reports. In contrast, involvement was high with procedurally simple tasks. In a study of the difficulty level of materials used in reading instruction in 71 second through sixth grade classes, Jorgenson (1977) found that students' classroom behavior improved when the reading level of the materials assigned fell below measured ability. Finally, dramatic results were reported by Davis and McKnight (1976) in a study of high-ability secondary students who actively resisted an attempt to increase the intellectual demands of tasks in mathematics.

SUMMARY

Academic work carries the substance of classroom events for students and provides a context that guides their attention and information processing as well as their attitudes toward participation and cooperation. Academic work is, therefore, an important dimension of the program or vector of action in classrooms and a significant factor in accounting for how classroom life is organized and how order is achieved.

Pacing, Signal Systems, and Involvement

Some attempts have been made, especially by Gump and Kounin, to account for differences in student involvement among activity structures. This effort has provided useful insights into how programs of action operate in classrooms.

In generalizing across types of activities, Gump (1967, 1969) initially placed emphasis on what he called "pacing" and concluded that involvement was higher when the students' work was externally paced (recitations, tests) than when it was self-paced (supervised study and seatwork). In later work, Gump (1982) expanded the notion of pacing to include a difference between an active input of stimuli and a passive availability of materials. In the active structure, students are "pulled" along through the work; in the passive structure, pacing depends upon students' understanding of the action sequence and their own motivation. An emphasis on activity flow and pace is also reflected in Kounin's (1970) findings concerning the importance of momentum in managing classroom groups. This concept is also similar to Merritt's (1982) notion of "vector of activity."

Recently Kounin and Gump (1974) introduced the concept of *signal systems* to explain how different activity structures and tasks influence student involvement. A lesson's signal systems are defined as the provisions external to an individual student that signal action within the setting:

> These provisions include the communications of the teacher ("Let's see what sticks and what doesn't stick to a magnet.") and the props that go with the lesson (magnet, paper clips, pieces of paper and cloth, nails). A lesson also includes the standing behavior pattern that goes with the lesson (making piles of objects that stick or don't stick to the magnet, listening to a story being read). (p.556)

Signal systems are, in other words, the situational instructions for lesson behavior.

Kounin and Gump (1974) derived propositions about signal systems from a study of 596 videotaped lessons taught over a 2-year period by 36 student teachers to groups of four to eight preschool students. The lessons, which ran for less than 20 minutes, were a regular part of the daily schedule of the preschool, but there was no unifying theme or continuity in content across the separate lessons.

In defining features of signal systems, Kounin and Gump emphasized *continuity*, *insulation*, and *intrusiveness*. Continuity refers to the regularity of the flow of information or signals to the individual participant. Lessons high in continuity are those involving teacher presentations (reading books to the class, demonstrations) or phonograph records in which there is a single, continuous source of signal emission. Such lessons are predicted to have low deviance rates. Individual construction lessons contain tasks that are high in signal continuity "as one action and its immediate result provide impetus and guidance for the next" (Kounin & Gump, 1974, p. 557). In this case, involvement is high if the materials are appropriate and the student is capable of understanding the task and carrying out the steps to completion. Lessons that are low in continuity are group discussions, group projects, and role play in which there are multiple, shifting signal sources as well as inadequate signals and lags in the flow of information resulting from the faltering performances by students. Such lessons are expected to have low involvement and high off-task behavior.

Insulation refers to the degree that the individual student is isolated from signals for inappropriate behavior. In individual construction lessons, for example, the signal source, "resting as it does on the results of each child's own actions on his own materials, produces a tight, closed behavior–environment circuit. This closed circuit … shields each child from foreign inputs (distractions, other children's deviances) which may serve as stimuli to inappropriate behavior" (Kounin & Gump, 1974, p. 557). In contrast, group construction lessons during which students share materials are low in insulation. Lessons high in insulation are expected to have low off-task rates. In a related study of interpersonal conflicts in the same preschool, Houseman (1972) found the degree of workspace boundary (e.g., art has more boundaries surrounding individual work than blocks) was inversely related to the frequency of conflict.

Finally, some lessons (e.g., music or movement lessons) have continuous signals from a single source but are high in intrusiveness, that is, the stimuli used (e.g., bells, dance movements) are sufficiently intense to intrude into the student's attention and thus compete with the appropriate lesson signals. Such lessons are expected to be high in off-task behaviors.

Kounin and Gump (1974) found that individual construction had the lowest rate of off-task behavior of all of the lesson types. In such lessons students were sufficiently insulated to maintain task involvement even when the teacher conducted a recitation or discussion with another student or a small group of students (Kounin & Doyle, 1975). Moderate rates of off-task behavior were found for lessons in which students listened to the teacher or to records, or lessons involving teacher-led demonstrations. Involvement during these lessons could be maintained even when they included student participation if the duration of such public teacher–student interactions was short (Kounin & Doyle, 1975). Highest off-task levels were found for recitations, open discussions, group construction, and music and movement lessons. Indeed, music and movement lessons were high in contagious "group glee" in which students jumped, screamed joyfully, and laughed (see Sherman, 1975). Unfortunately, seatwork was not included in the lesson formats, so comparisons with this common activity are not possible.

The work on signal systems suggests that organizing work to maintain activity flow or momentum and guard against competing programs or vectors of action will promote order in classrooms. Despite the compelling logic of this model, it rests primarily on preschool data for lessons that were not part of a regular academic program and were taught on an ad hoc basis. Further research is needed to understand how the propositions of this model apply to other contexts and levels of schooling.

The Effect of Participants

Cooperation is, in part, a characteristic of students: Some students spend more time than others engaged in learning tasks. In a study of first, second, and third grade students in individualized learning programs in Israel, it was found by Levin, Libman, and Amiad (1980) that high-achieving students were actively engaged in working with learning materials almost twice as much as low achievers. In addition, low achievers were idle or engaged in a nonapproved activity almost three times as much as high achievers. Similar results were reported by Shimron (1976) in a study of individualized primary grade classrooms. He found that high achievers spent twice as much time on-task and completed three times more learning units than low achievers. Finally, Silverstein (1979) reported that lower ability students in the fourth grade classes she studied were more likely than other students to be engaged in problematic behavior during seatwork.

The consequences of students' academic ability and inclination to do schoolwork have been demonstrated dramatically in several recent classroom studies. Metz (1978) examined, through observations and interviews, high- and low-ability junior high school classes taught by the same teachers. Students in high-ability classes expected to have an active voice in shaping class events, challenged teachers in academic and intellectual areas, and misbehaved in ways that were difficult to detect or were close to the bounds of legitimacy. Low-ability classes, in contrast, had little interest in academic matters and seldom cooperated in class events. Their misbehavior was public and disruptive, and order was difficult to restore. The rhythm of classroom events for low-ability classes was slow and frequently interrupted. Finally teachers tended to follow a fixed daily routine and give more seatwork assignments to lower ability classes than they did to high-ability classes. Comparable results have been reported by Campbell (1974), who studied a low-ability group and a high-ability group in several classes in junior high school. He found that, in comparison to the high group, teachers were more direct and talked less within the low-ability class and there was more unproductive confusion in the low classes. Finally, Evertson (1982) reported that higher ability junior high school math and English classes ran more smoothly and had higher engagement than classes with lower ability students. Moreover, transitions took longer and were more problematic in lower ability than in higher ability classes.

Stodolsky et al. (1981) examined socioeconomic differences in the occurrence of recitations in fifth grade social studies and math classes. They found that recitations were used more frequently in lower than higher SES schools, especially in social studies. In addition, proportionately fewer recitation segments with small groups occurred in low-SES classes in comparison to middle- and high-SES classes. In other words, teachers were more likely to conduct whole-class recitations in low-SES classes than in other classes. Finally, seatwork was more prevalent in low-SES classes, and less time was spent checking work in high-SES classes.

Carter and Doyle (1982) analyzed differences in academic tasks across one high- and two average-ability classes taught by a junior high school English teacher. In this case, few dramatic differences in overall task structures were found between average- and high-ability classes. Nevertheless, the teacher tended to give more work to high-ability students and provided more explicit instructions to the average-ability classes. In addition, high-ability students were more skilled in interpreting tasks and extracting information from the teacher about the requirements of assignments.

Several studies in elementary classes have focused on differences between high- and low-ability reading groups (see Cazden, 1981, for a review). Allington (1983) and Eder (1982a,

1982b) found that low groups were characterized by frequent interruptions and much attention to management rather than instruction. Bozsik (1982) found that low-ability groups received more text-explicit questions and less wait-time than high ability groups and that high groups were given more discussion time, more text-implicit questions, and longer wait-times than low-ability groups. In addition, high groups provided more answers that the teachers praised and supported. In several respects, these findings parallel those from studies of differential treatment of high- and low-ability students within classes (see Brophy, 1983b; Good, 1981).

McDermott (1976) closely examined two 20-minute filmed segments, one of a high-ability reading group and one of a low-ability reading group, and described the ways in which these lessons were jointly produced by participants. He found that both high- and low-ability groups do a considerable amount of interactional work to sustain lesson segments and hold each other accountable for order. Nevertheless, lessons in the low-ability group were much less successful as reading events. Turn allocation was a more complex process and reading turns took longer in the low group than in the high group. Moreover, performance during reading turns for low students was hesitant, slow, and filled with errors that often required lengthy teacher instruction. McDermott's data suggest that problems with academic tasks rather than with social tasks accounted for the difficulties in accomplishing lessons in the low-ability group.

Evertson, Sanford, and Emmer (1981) found an effect for the degree of heterogeneity in junior high school English classes. In extremely heterogeneous classes (those with grade level equivalent ranges of up to 10 grade levels), teachers had difficulty adapting to individual instructional needs and meeting affective needs of students. In addition, task engagement and student cooperation were somewhat lower in these classes than in more homogeneous classes. These effects were particularly apparent in classes of poor managers.

These findings concerning classroom patterns for high- and low-ability students no doubt reflect aspects of teachers' management and instructional skills as well as their beliefs about whether different students can succeed. Nevertheless, the consistency of the findings suggests that the willingness and ability of students to engage in the programs of action in classroom segments influence in major ways the task of creating and sustaining order. Metz's (1978) findings are especially compelling in this regard. She found that although the same teachers were observed in both high- and low-ability classes, there was more similarity among classes of different teachers within the same tract than between classes of different levels taught by the same teacher. Finally, she observed that the tone of a class, whether low or high in ability, was set by a few active students while the rest followed or were passive.

Summary

Research reviewed in this section suggests that order depends upon the strength and durability of the primary program or vector of action that defines order in a particular classroom context. This program of action includes both a social partici-

pation dimension that defines rules for interacting in a complex and crowded environment and an academic work dimension that carries the substances of lessons. In classes composed of students who lack either the skill or the inclination to participate, the primary vector of action lacks strength and durability in a context in which alternative programs of action are plentiful. In such situations, teachers are required to expend a considerable amount of energy to nurture and protect the primary vector. Research on how such energy can be fruitfully expended is reviewed in the next section.

How Order Is Achieved in Classrooms

In the previous section, little attention was given to the processes of establishing and orchestrating activities in classrooms. But there are clear differences among teachers in the ways in which classroom structures are enacted. For example, research surveyed above indicates that student involvement tends to be low during activities with prolonged student talk. Yet Silverstein (1979) found in one fourth grade class that no problematic behavior of any sort occurred during student-presented book reports. Part of this effect appears to be related to the fact that the teacher actively directed book reports and used a system of accountability in which each presenter awarded points to other students for correct answers to questions about his or her book. Teacher effects were also reported by Campbell (1974). He found marked differences in the behavior of a low-ability group in different classes and commented that, "These problem youngsters were like a pack of hungry half-starved wolves with the math and English teachers, and like docile lambs with their science teacher" (Campbell, 1974, p. 665). Finally, at a more general level, Kounin (1983) reported that task involvement of the most successful teacher in his samples was 98.7%, whereas involvement for the least successful teacher was 25%.

The purpose of this section is to integrate information about the strategies and processses that account for the differential effectiveness of teachers in managing classrooms. In shifting from descriptions of classroom organization to management strategies, the emphasis turns to the options teachers have within classroom contexts for constructing well-formed activities.

Establishing Classroom Activities

From the perspective of classroom order, the early class sessions of a school year are of critical importance (see Ball, 1980; Doyle, 1979b; Smith & Geoffrey, 1968). During this time, order is defined and the processes and procedures that sustain order are put into place. Indeed, over 75 years ago Bagley (1907, p. 22) exhorted teachers that "the only way absolutely to insure a school against waste is to make the very first day thoroughly rigorous in all its details."

The validity of this concern for the beginning of the year has been demonstrated in a series of studies conducted at the University of Texas Research and Development Center for Teacher Education. The first study in the series (Emmer et al.,

1980) was conducted in 27 third grade classes. Observations began on the morning of the first day of school in 12 of the classes, and all 27 classes were observed at least once during the first 2 days. During the next 3 weeks, classes were observed 8 to 10 times, and, beginning in November, observations were conducted every 3 weeks for the remainder of the year. Data consisted of focused narrative records (running accounts of classroom events and processes), student engagement ratings done at 15-minute intervals, observer ratings on 34 dimensions of behavioral and instructional management, and student reading scores on the California Achievement Test. In a parallel study at the junior high school level (Evertson & Emmer, 1982), observations were made in two classes each of 26 mathematics and 25 English teachers in 11 schools. Each teacher was observed in one class on the first, second, and fourth days of the year, and three or four more times during the second and third weeks. Four or five observations were made in the second class during the first 3 weeks of the year. Each class was then observed once every 3 or 4 weeks for the rest of the year. As in the elementary study, data consisted of narrative records, engagement ratings, observer ratings, and student achievement scores. These descriptive efforts were followed by elementary (Evertson, Emmer, Sanford, & Clements, 1983) and junior high school (Emmer et al., 1982) intervention studies in which management procedures derived from the earlier research were taught to teachers and effects on teacher behavior and management success were analyzed. The results of these and related studies (see Borg & Ascione, 1982) are discussed in the following sections.

RULES AND PROCEDURES

Because classrooms are made up of groups of students assembled under crowded conditions for relatively long periods of time to accomplish specified purposes, life in these settings is governed by a variety of explicit and implicit rules and procedures (see Blumenfield et al., 1979; Hargreaves et al., 1975; Jackson, 1968). In addition to official rules of conduct, class sessions and patterns of interaction often appear to be ritualized, with specific formats for openings, closings, and the conduct of lessons (see Griffin & Mehan, 1979; Yinger, 1979), and teachers tend to use similar formats with different groups of students (see Carter & Doyle, 1982; Evertson, 1982).

Classroom rules are usually intended to regulate forms of individual conduct that are likely to disrupt activities, cause injury, or damage school property. Thus, there are rules concerning tardiness, talking during lessons, gum chewing, fighting, bringing materials to class, and the like (see Hargreaves et al., 1975; Tikunoff & Ward, 1978). In addition, there are a large number of implicit rules that affect social interaction and interpersonal relationships in classrooms (see Erickson & Shultz, 1981; McHoul, 1978). Procedures consist of approved ways of taking care of various duties and privileges in classrooms, such as handing in completed work, sharpening pencils, getting a drink of water, and going to the restroom. Bagley (1907), for example, recommended that teachers establish procedures in such areas as the passing of lines, the use of signals for attention and for routine movements in the class, going to the blackboard, distributing and collecting wraps, distributing

and collecting books and materials, the orderly arranging of books and materials in desks, maintaining the tidiness of the room, and leaving the room.

Studies at the Research and Development Center for Teacher Education (see their description in the foregoing section on establishing classroom activities) indicate that effective classroom managers in elementary and junior high school classes are especially skilled in establishing rules and procedures at the beginning of the year. In the elementary study (Emmer et al., 1980), a comparison of seven more effective and seven less effective managers (selected on the basis of student achievement gain and a composite of management indicators from data gathered from November to the end of the year) indicated that all teachers introduced rules and procedures on the first day. Effective managers, however, integrated their rules and procedures into a workable system and deliberately taught this system to the students. Rules and procedures were concrete, explicit, and functional, that is they contributed to order and work accomplishment. In addition, items were clearly explained to students, signals were used to indicate when actions were to be carried out or stopped, and time was spent rehearsing procedures. Shultz and Florio (1979) have also emphasized the importance of explicit information and signals, especially in the early grades and at the beginning of the year, as ways of helping students learn the classroom environment. In addition, effective managers avoided information overload by focusing initially on immediate concerns and then introducing more procedures as they were needed. At the same time, they appear to have anticipated possible interruptions or problems and had procedures readily available to handle these situations. The more effective managers also continued to remind students of the rules and procedures for the first weeks of school. Finally, effective managers monitored classes closely and stopped inappropriate behavior promptly. In contrast, less effective managers either failed to anticipate the need for rules and procedures covering important aspects of class operation or tended to have vague and unenforceable rules (for example, "Be in the right place at the right time," or "Never chew gum"). Moreover, they neither explained their rules and procedures clearly to students nor monitored and enforced compliance. Rather, they seemed to be preoccupied with clerical tasks and disoriented by problems and interruptions. Less effective managers were also more likely than effective managers to leave the room during the first day.

In the junior high study (Evertson & Emmer, 1982), six more effective and six less effective math teachers and seven more effective and seven less effective English teachers were selected on management and achievement criteria for comparative analysis (for analyses addressed to special subsamples of this data set, see Emmer, 1981, and Sanford & Evertson, 1981). In comparison to less effective managers, more effective managers were rated higher on clarity of directions and information, stating desired behavior and attitudes more frequently, presenting clear expectations for work standards, responding consistently to appropriate and inappropriate behavior, stopping disruptive behavior sooner, and using rules and procedures more frequently to deal with disruptive behavior. More and less effective managers did not differ significantly on the amount of unsanctioned off-task behavior during the first week of school, but such behavior increased significantly in classes of less effective teachers during the second and third weeks. There was, in other words, a deterioration in student behavior in poorly managed classes, especially in the areas of call-outs, talking in class, and movement around the room (see Doyle, 1979b). Specifically on the issue of rules and procedures, the investigators noted that all teachers presented rules and procedures at the beginning of the year and there were few differences across teachers in the time spent on these matters. Differences, were found, however, in the clarity and thoroughness of presentation, the monitoring of compliance, and the enforcement of rules and procedures. Successful managers anticipated problem areas, communicated expectations clearly, watched students closely, intervened promptly, and invoked consequences for behavior. Along similar lines, Brooks (1985, in press) found that, on the first day, experienced junior high math and science teachers had better organization, sequence, smoothness, eye contact, and visual scanning than inexperienced teachers. Evertson and Emmer (1982) pointed out that these results were consistent with those in the elementary study with the difference that less time at the junior high level was spent teaching and rehearsing rules and procedures. These results are also consistent with Moskowitz and Hayman's (1976) findings from a study of management practices at the beginning of the year in junior high school classes.

ACTIVITIES AND ACADEMIC WORK

Studies of the beginning of the year (Emmer et al., 1980; Evertson & Emmer, 1982) have also indicated that effective managers planned something for students to do when they began the first day, that is, little time was lost finding seats, getting organized, or waiting to be told what to do. Early activities had a simple, whole-class instructional structure, and the work was familiar, enjoyable, and easy to accomplish. Especially at the elementary level, effective managers did not push forward through the curriculum during the first several days of the year, in part because they apparently expected to have students added or removed from class. Nevertheless, students were not idle, and even the presentation of rules and procedures took on the character of lessons in which students were expected to be attentive. Teachers also monitored activities closely and helped students complete their assigned tasks. An academic focus was more apparent in junior high classes during the first week, and rules and procedures often covered assignments, notebooks, and grading. Successful junior high teachers often gave daily assignments (which most students could accomplish), monitored work closely, and emphasized students' responsibility and accountability for work. By junior high school, in other words, teachers rehearsed academic work formats rather than rules and procedures for handling classroom groups. Finally, at both elementary and junior high levels, instructions for assignments in well-managed classes were clear and explicit. Along similar lines, Atwood (1983) found that clarity of an assignment was positively associated with task involvement, and Kaplan and White (1980) reported that compliance to directions decreased as complexity of the statements increased.

In an intensive analysis of narrative records from junior high

school English classes, Doyle (1984) found that successful managers established an activity system early in the year and hovered over the system, ushering it along and protecting it from intrusion or disruption. During seatwork for the first 3 weeks, for example, contacts with individual students were brief, and the teachers circulated around the room while they maintained a whole-group focus. In classes with a high incidence of inappropriate and disruptive student behavior, successful managers tended to push the curriculum and talk about work rather than misbehavior. Less successful managers, on the other hand, tended to focus public attention on misbehavior by their frequent reprimands so that eventually all work ceased. November observations indicated that if a work system was effectively established, a successful teacher often spent less time orchestrating the total group and more time with individual students. By this point, the work system itself seemed to be carrying the burden of order and the teacher was free to attend more to particular aspects of classroom events. Sanford and Evertson (1981) have described a case in which this shift from whole-class to a more individualized focus occurred too abruptly and order deteriorated.

AN ILLUSTRATION OF RULE SETTING

Smith and Geoffrey (1968) described rule-setting processes in a self-contained seventh grade classroom in an inner-city school in ways that parallel the patterns found in effectiveness studies. Geoffrey began the first class session by taking roll, during which time he made brief comments to familiar students. One gets the impression that Geoffrey was known to several of these students and that his reputation — a topic largely overlooked in management research — played a role in creating order in the class. He then called a student up to the board to write his (the teacher's) name, and when the student erred, Geoffrey called on others until one agreed to correct the misspelling. This lesson-like event would seem to have communicated a clear sense of accountability in the class. Geoffrey then explicated the official rules. During this activity he often singled out individual students to respond to specific questions about rules, and he emphasized the need for "permission." The remaining time before recess was used to pass out books and materials and to assign "jobs" to various students. After recess, the teacher lectured the students on sitting up straight and then had them write a paragraph about something they did that summer. Geoffrey finished the morning by covering miscellaneous activities and procedures and talking with the students. On subsequent days, Geoffrey introduced academic work gradually by having spelling and reading lessons and describing procedures and regulations for assignments such as book reports. Smith and Geoffrey described four aspects of the process of establishing the classroom system as (a) "grooving the children," that is, having them rehearse rules and procedures; (b) communicating a sense of seriousness ("I mean it"); (c) following through when incidents occurred that involved the rules and procedures; and (d) softening the tone of the management system by using humor and drama. Additional analyses of the functions of humor and friendliness in the classroom can can be found in Denscombe (1980a), Pittman (1984), Stebbins (1980), and Woods (1979).

THE FUNCTION OF ROUTINES

The rehearsing and routinizing of procedures and activities in classrooms would seem to be an important mechanism for sustaining classroom order. Yinger (1979, 1980) has argued that routinization makes classroom activities less susceptible to breakdowns during interruptions because participants know the normal sequence of events. At a more micro level, McDermott (1976) has described how the positioning and interactional cueing displayed by participants carry along the sequence of events in familiar lesson contexts (see Woolfolk & Brooks, 1985 for a review of research on nonverbal cueing). In the language of signal system theory (Kounin & Gump, 1974), routines provide a continuous signal for organizational and interpersonal behavior, an effect not present in Kounin and Gump's data because the lessons in their sample were taught on an ad hoc basis by student teachers. Sociolinguistic researchers have argued that routines for parent-child story reading (Snow, Dubber, & de Blauw, 1980) and for group reading lessons in elementary classrooms (Au & Kawakami, 1984) provide stable and predictable slots for action and that within these ritualized contexts participants are free to deal with complex intellectual structures and processes. From this perspective, establishing routines and activity systems may not simply serve order as an end in itself but also provide a context for high-level academic work.

SUMMARY

Research on effective management at the beginning of the year suggests that classroom structures are successfully established when rules and procedures are announced, demonstrated, enforced, and routinized. In addition, successful managers hover over classroom activities at the beginning of the year and usher them along until students have learned the work system.

Rule Setting and Enactment Processes

Recent qualitative studies have underscored the complexity of rule systems and their enactment in classrooms. A brief survey of this work will provide further insights into how classroom activities are established.

Two aspects of the work on rule setting and enactment are especially interesting. First, some rules, particularly those for talking in class, are quite context specific. This point was clearly made by Hargreaves et al. (1975) in their study of classes in two British secondary schools. They identified "phase" rules, that is, rules associated with distinctive phases of a class session or lesson. For example, quiet talk among peers was allowed during entry and seatwork but not during teacher presentations or question–answer or recitation time. A similar emphasis on the relation between contexts and rules in elementary classes can be found in Bremme and Erickson (1977), Edelsky, Draper, and Smith (1983), Erickson and Shultz (1981), Shultz and Florio (1979), and Wallat and Green (1979).

Second, although teachers spend a great deal of time talking about rules and procedures in classrooms, most of the socializing of students to the classroom system seems to be indirect. Hargreaves and his colleagues (Hargreaves et. al, 1975) noted that many rules in secondary classes were never explicitly articulated but were, rather, part of the commonsense knowledge teachers and students used to interpret situations. Implicit rules became visible, however, when violations occurred and teachers reacted with reprimands and criticism. A similar emphasis on reacting to behavior rather than explicit socialization was reported for elementary classes by Blumenfeld et al. (1983).

These indirect processes of rule setting were emphasized by Tikunoff and Ward (1978) in their study of how rules were formulated in three classes of third, fourth, and fifth grade students. The teachers were nominated by peers as outstanding math teachers, and data consisted of detailed narrative observations for the first 30 days of the school year, daily summary tapes from the teachers, and interviews. The analysis focused on identifying rules that were either formally stated or invoked through teacher disapproval and reprimands and then tracing the life history of these rules. In interviews before school started, all three teachers indicated that they preferred to let rules emerge as needed to cover specific problems. Nevertheless, a large majority of the rules in each class were established during the first few days. Moreover, corrections and reprimands, that is, teacher reactions to rule violations, were frequent, especially in response to talking and off-task behavior, and appeared to play a major role in the rule-setting process. Most of the rules were related to the establishment of an instructional system, and there seemed to be an association between the number of rules and the complexity of the instructional format. A relatively structured class of high-ability students had 42 rules (26 of which were introduced during the first 7 days); a more informal class of average-ability students had 52 rules (28 of which were introduced during the first 4 days); and an individualized class of low-ability students had 135 rules (66 of which were introduced on the first 3 days). Consistent with findings by Nash (1976) and Gannaway (1976), students appeared to expect teachers to make the rules, and they seemed to adjust readily to the rule systems in the classes, although a large portion of the time during the first 30 days was spent on rule setting in the individual class. Finally, the investigators commented on the large number of delays caused by intrusions into the classes during the first 4 weeks of school, a factor that complicated the processes of rule setting.

In a further analysis of one teacher from Tikunoff and Ward's sample, Buckley and Cooper (1978) noted that although students did not participate officially in creating or challenging the teacher's rules, they did affect the application of the rules to particular cases. In general, the teacher consistently enforced the rules that the students readily accepted and conformed to. In areas where the teacher met resistance from some of the students (e.g., in talking with neighbors, raising hands to ask or answer a question, and cheating on tests), the teacher was considerably less consistent in reprimanding students for noncompliance. In a study of junior high English teachers, Doyle (1984) noted a similar pattern: The teachers seemed reluctant to engage in major struggles with students over rules at the beginning of the year and preferred to concentrate on establishing work systems. Rules that are not enforced, however, do not remain in force in the class. These analyses give some insight into the way in which classroom rule systems are jointly consititued by participants (see Mehan, 1980).

In a study of elementary classes, Sieber (1979b) also noted the informal, ad hoc manner in which rules were established through teachers' disciplinary actions in response to specific violations. He argued, however, that because many rules were unwritten and communicated informally in specific contexts, they became part of the fabric of classroom life and students were thus able to learn more easily the situational appropriateness of the rules. That is, disciplinary action by the teacher demonstrated to students the application of rules to particular situations. In addition, this informality increased the teacher's power as a rule arbiter who can flexibly enforce rules in response to specific circumstances. In other words, informality appears to increase the overall effectiveness of classroom rule systems.

A considerable amount of research has been done on the interactional competence students need to participate successfully in the complex rule systems of classroom lessons (Cook-Gumperz & Gumperz, 1982; Erickson & Shultz, 1981; Green & Harker, 1982; Mehan, 1980). Although most students appear to learn classroom rules and procedures readily (see LeCompte, 1980, for a kindergarten study), low-ability students and students from minority cultures sometimes have special problems comprehending the classroom system and recognizing changes in context in order to behave appropriately (see Eder, 1982a; Florio & Shultz, 1979; Philips, 1972). In other words, if a student's preschool or extraschool experiences do not foster understandings and behavior congruent with classroom demands, it is difficult for him or her to follow rules and procedures, gain access to instruction, or display competence. Suggestions for improving this situation include more explicit teaching of classroom rules and appropriate behavior (Cartledge & Milburn, 1978; Shultz & Florio, 1979) and the design of classroom procedures that are congruent with patterns of communication in specific cultures (Cazden, 1981; Erickson & Mohatt, 1982). One of the central features of the Kamehameha Early Education Program, for example, is the design of reading lessons to match the Hawaiian talk-story format familiar to the students (Au, 1980). More information concerning this research tradition is provided in the chapter on classroom discourse in this volume.

THE HIDDEN CURRICULUM

One final note is in order concerning the character of classroom rules and procedures and their general social significance. Many classroom rules are directed to issues of authority, responsibility, and task orientation. In an analysis of teacher behavior in four fourth grade classes in the Southwest, LeCompte (1978b) found that over 50% of the teachers' statements fell into what she called the "management core," which consisted of messages related to the acceptance of authority, orderliness, task orientation, and time orientation. In an analysis of rules in one fourth and fifth grade class, Buckley and Cooper (1978) found a heavy emphasis on following directions, accepting responsibility, working quietly, and respecting authority. In addition, they noted that nearly one third of the rules were related to occasions in which students are required to wait for something to happen, for example to go to lunch or to receive help from the teacher.

Several investigators have argued that the emphasis on authority and responsibility in classroom rules and procedures constitutes a "hidden curriculum" which socializes students to the world of work, that is, to adult roles in modern bureaucratic organizations, and some contend that classroom rules contribute to the reproduction of dominant social and cultural arrangements (see Apple, 1979; Blumenfeld et al., 1979; Bowles & Gintis, 1976; Jackson, 1968; Sharp & Green, 1975).

LeCompte (1978a) has argued that the work ethic of classrooms appears to reflect institutional constraints rather than personal preferences of teachers. This view was based on the high degree of similarity she observed across the four teachers with respect to the management core despite differences in class organization and personal orientation to teaching. "Teachers employed management behavior because they had no option as to whether or not activities kept moving in an orderly fashion in the classroom" (LeCompte, 1978a, p. 31). In other words, teachers cope with immediate problems of getting work done in complex social environments rather than attempt to socialize students deliberately to a bureaucratic or capitalistic social order (see Blumenfeld et al., 1983).

THE FUNCTIONS OF RULE SETTING

Both policy-directed and descriptive studies indicate that life in classrooms begins with the creation of a work system and the setting of rules and procedures to hold the system in place, and that a considerable amount of energy is devoted to this process. It is interesting to note that this process is repeated each year, despite the fact that most children seem to learn the classroom system during their first year or so in schools (see Blumenfeld et al., 1983; Florio & Shultz, 1979; LeCompte, 1980; Wallat & Green, 1979). It is unlikely that even third grade students are learning anything new when they encounter rules on the first day of school or that junior high students are unaware of the general requirements for acceptable behavior in classrooms. Yet the quality of rule setting, even at the secondary level, determines the degree of order that prevails in a class for the duration of a school term.

The fact that knowledge of classroom rules and procedures cannot be taken for granted suggests that rule setting has important socialization functions as an acknowledgement of the importance of order and a symbol of the level of vigilance and accountability that will prevail in a particular classroom (see Ball, 1980; Doyle, 1979b). By setting rules, a teacher communicates his or her awareness of what can happen in a classroom and demonstrates a degree of commitment to work (see Brooks, in press). Students are thus able to acquire valuable information early in the year about a teacher's approach and expectations for behavior. The more explicit the rules and the more clearly they are communicated, the more likely the teacher will care about maintaining order and not tolerate inappropriate and disruptive behavior. But simply stating the rules is not enough. A teacher must also demonstrate a willingness and an ability to act when rules are broken. For this reason, reprimands and consequences play a central role in the rule-setting process.

This analysis suggests that classroom order rests on a teacher's ability to communicate to students an understanding

of classroom events and processes and a willingness to cope
with complex situations. The teacher is the rule maker in a
class, but he or she must live up to students' expectations for
competence in handling the classroom system. This perspective
on classroom order will be developed even further in the
following analysis of processes involved in accomplishing classroom activities.

Orchestrating Classroom Activities

Attention now turns to teacher actions associated with carrying
out classroom activities in space and time. Although classroom
structures guide behavior and routines stabilize programs of
actions, classroom lessons have an improvisational character
(Erickson, 1982a; Griffin & Mehan, 1979). That is, the form of a
particular lesson is jointly negotiated and constructed by
students and the teacher, and order is thus subject to the
contingencies of multiple interpretations, preferences, and errors. As a result, delicate and complex processes of sustaining
order in classrooms must be balanced.

The section begins with a survey of research on *monitoring* as
a key process in conducting all forms of classroom activity. The
focus then shifts to processes involved in maintaining various
types of classroom activities, namely, (a) lessons involving
group interaction, for example, recitations and discussion; (b)
seatwork, both supervised and unsupervised; and (c) transitions. This section concludes with a discussion of relationships
between classroom management and academic work.

MONITORING

Kounin's (1970) widely influential study of 80 first and second
grade classes (each containing at least one emotionally disturbed child) pointed to teacher attention and monitoring as
central components of classroom management skill. Specifically, teachers in Kounin's study who had high levels of work
involvement and freedom from deviancy in their classes were
high on "withitness" and "overlapping," that is, they were
aware of what was going on in the classroom, communicated
this awareness to students, and were able to attend to two or
more events at the same time. Irving and Martin (1982)
reported a failure to replicate Kounin's findings for withitness
and raised questions about the definition and measurement of
the variable. Other investigators, however, have found that
withitness is positively associated with student achievement
(Brophy & Evertson, 1976); that situational awareness and
overlap capabilities predict the acquisition of classroom
management skills (Copeland, 1983; Schumm, 1971); and that
eye contact and group scanning increase work involvement and
order, especially at the beginning of the year (Brooks, 1985;
Emmer et al., 1980; Evertson & Emmer, 1982).

The content of monitoring—what teachers watch when
scanning the room—includes at least three dimensions. First,
teachers watch *groups* (see Clark & Yinger, 1979; Kounin,
1970). Teachers attend to what is happening in the entire room
and how well the total activity system is going. A group focus
does not preclude attention to individual students, but localized
attending must be scheduled within the broader framework of
the group activity (see Merritt, 1982). Second, teachers watch

conduct or behavior, with particular attention to discrepancies
from the intended program of action for the segment. Kounin
(1970) used the timeliness and accuracy of desists as an indication of withitness. That is, "withit" teachers noticed misbehavior early before it spread across the room and reprimanded the originator of the misbehavior rather than an
innocent bystander or a student who joined the event after it
began. Studies by Emmer and his colleagues (Emmer et al.,
1980; Evertson & Emmer, 1982) also indicate that successful
managers were able to anticipate misbehavior and stop it early.
Third, teachers monitor the *pace, rhythm, and duration* of
classroom events. Arlin (1982) has described how pressures to
keep things moving and avoid delays shape classroom events;
Kounin (1970) found that smoothness and momentum were
associated with management success; and Gump (1967) found
that hesitations and lags in the flow of activities increased off-
task behavior. Erickson and Mohatt (1982), in a videotape
study of two elementary classes on an Odawa Indian Reserve in
Northern Ontario, found an informative contrast between the
smooth and steady flow maintained by the Indian teacher and
the more rapid, abrupt, and choppy rhythm of the non-Indian
teacher. The former's cadence appears to be more suitable to
the children's native culture and more successful in maintaining
order and academic involvement.

Data suggest that decisions about pace through the curriculum are determined by monitoring the completion rates of the
"steering criterion group," that is, students between the 10th
and 25th percentiles in class ability (Arlin & Westbury, 1976;
Dahllof, 1971; Lundgren, 1972). Other studies (e.g., deVoss,
1979; Doyle, 1984) indicate that the actual duration of classroom activities is determined in part by teachers' estimates of
students' attention spans and work completion rates.

In addition to staying aware of classroom events and their
momentum, teachers must also communicate this awareness to
students. Kounin (1970) emphasized that teachers demonstrated awareness through the timeliness and accuracy of
reprimands. If the real culprit is caught early, then students
presumably learn that the teacher is aware of what is going on
in the room. Moreover, Kounin's (1970) work suggests that
communicating awareness prevents the initiation and spread of
off-task and disruptive behavior and thus reduces the need for
reprimands. Emmer and his colleagues (Emmer et al., 1980;
Evertson & Emmer, 1982) found that successful managers were
concrete, explicit, and thorough in their descriptions of rules
and procedures, and they commented frequently and accurately
on the appropriateness of students' behavior. Finally, Doyle's
(1984) analysis of junior high school English classes indicated
that teachers communicated situational awareness by commenting frequently on events as they were occurring in the
class. They used, in other words, a multiplicity of "contextualization cues" (Erickson & Shultz, 1981; Green & Harker, 1982;
Shultz & Florio, 1979) to establish and maintain classroom
events.

The image here is clearly of the teacher as "ringmaster"
(Smith & Geoffrey, 1968), and a large chunk of teachers'
attention is taken up gathering information about the movement of the group through time and space in the classroom and
communicating this information to students. From this perspective, teaching in classrooms demands a high degree of

efficiency in information processing and an ability to make decisions rapidly (see Doyle, 1979b). Obviously, the more complex the arrangement of students in the class and the greater the demands on the teacher as an actor in the work system, the more difficult monitoring and cueing become and, thus, the greater the probability of a breakdown in order.

The problems associated with monitoring and cueing can be clarified through a closer look at how lessons are accomplished. Investigators have paid particular attention to turn allocation processes in group lessons, multiple attending in seatwork segments, and the management of transitions.

GROUP LESSONS

The complexity of classroom events is especially apparent in conversational lessons like recitations and discussions. As indicated earlier in the description of programs of action, group lessons require that a teacher cope with a complex social system with multiple participants of different abilities and a discontinuous signal system to guide the flow of events, monitor the development of content in an often unpredictable pattern, and provide accurate and appropriate feedback to individual students for their answers (see Morine-Dershimer, 1983, for descriptions of such lessons).

Teachers appear to use a number of strategies to increase the predictability of group lessons. As indicated in the earlier review of classroom structures, whole-class group lessons are typically short (from 10 to 12 minutes) and tend to take the form of recitations rather than free discussions. Reading group lessons are typically longer, but materials provide focal content for the activity. In such formats, teachers set the topics and constrain the range of possible answers (see Hammersley, 1974). Moreover, teachers typically use narrowly focused rather than divergent or open-ended questions (Hoetker & Ahlbrand, 1969), a practice which also limits the range of options for student answers. Indeed, it would appear in some cases that student participation is restricted to occasional inserts into the stream of a teacher's presentation (see Hammersley, 1974). In other instances, teachers have been observed to accept virtually all answers, apparently to allow discussions to continue (see Bellack et al., 1966; MacLure & French, 1980; Mehan, 1974; Morine-Dershimer, 1983). Finally, teachers occasionally call on some students primarily to "secure a right answer from a competent respondent and thus to keep a good discussion going" (Potter, 1974, p. 87).

Group lessons involve public answers and some students are reluctant to participate, in part because they fear peer criticism for wrong answers (Potter, 1974, 1977). To accomplish such lessons and maintain order, a teacher must stimulate student participation through group alerting and accountability signals. Kounin (1970) found that successful managers posed questions in ways which maintained group attention and indicated that all students were potentially accountable for answering before an individual was selected. "Patterned turns," in which students were preselected for answering, localized the teacher's attention to a single student at a time and thus students tended not to attend to immediate events and became uninvolved in work. Indeed, elementary teachers appear to pose questions before calling on students much more often than

they call on students before asking a question (Borg & Ascione, 1982). In this regard, Anderson et al. (1979) found that the use of patterned turns in first grade reading groups was associated with higher reading achievement, and Good and Grouws (1975) found that group alerting had a curvilinear relationship to achievement in fourth grade mathematics. These findings must be interpreted cautiously, however, because there is some evidence that the use of patterned turns and group alerting is related to student ability. McDermott's (1976) analysis suggests that patterned turns are easier to use in higher ability groups in which all members are equally capable of reading any page and inattention is not likely to lead to disruptive behavior. And Eder's (1982b) research indicates that more group alerting occurs in low-ability groups than in high-ability groups.

Stimulating participation can, however, lead to another set of problems. In reporting a study of British secondary classes, Hammersley (1974) pointed out that the more successful a teacher was in stimulating participation, the more difficult the turn allocation process became. This dilemma in mobilizing participation stemmed from the fact that there was only one pupil slot for answering and frequently several bidders for the right to speak in that slot. Students were observed to use various strategies to secure an opportunity to give the right answer by shouting out or verbally soliciting teacher recognition by repeating "Sir" until they were called on.

Turn allocation would seem to be an especially difficult process to manage in classrooms. Several investigators have noted that teachers are not always consistent in enforcing rules against "call-outs," especially with low-ability groups (see Buckley & Cooper, 1978; Copeland, 1978; Eder, 1982a; Evertson, 1982; Sanford & Evertson, 1981). Studies of reading groups, in particular, have indicated that orchestrating turns with low-ability students is problematic. In contrast to higher ability students, low-ability students are less likely to participate and more inclined to make topically irrelevant comments (Eder, 1982a). In addition, shifts between turns in low-ability groups are less orderly and require a greater amount of concentrated teacher direction to accomplish (McDermott, 1976). Teachers in low-ability groups are more likely to interrupt reading turns (Allington, 1980), orient to listeners during turns (Eder, 1982b), and accept student-initiated interruptions that are topically relevant (Eder, 1982a). Finally, reading turns for low-ability students are longer and more likely to contain long pauses and errors that alter the meaning of the text (Eder, 1982a; Hoffman & Clements, 1984), qualities of performance that can lead to inattention (Gump, 1967) and confusion about content. These patterns suggest that teachers are attempting to maintain content flow, activity flow, and student attention by prompting correct responses and by group alerting. That is, they are trying to maintain the integrity of the activity against fairly strong countervailing pressures.

SEATWORK

In comparison to group lessons, considerably less is known about orchestrating seatwork, primarily because of a dominant interest among researchers in classroom interaction. Nevertheless, data reviewed earlier in this chapter indicated that seatwork occurs frequently in classes and presents special problems of management and cooperation. Although the demands of being the central actor and turn allocator are not present in seatwork as they are in group lessons, managing seatwork cannot be left to chance. A brief review of available data is therefore useful.

Although results were not completely consistent across studies, Kounin's (1970) research indicated that variety and challenge, that is, frequent shifts in focal content and high-level academic work, were associated with work involvement and freedom from deviancy in seatwork segments. There are, of course, limits to these dimensions. Doyle and Carter (1984) found that seatwork consisting of complex writing tasks was very difficult to manage in junior high school English classes. Similarly, Atwood (1983) found task complexity to be negatively associated with engagement.

Management studies indicate that during supervised seatwork effective teachers monitor the class thoroughly, inspect individual papers frequently, and generally hover over the work and usher it along (Doyle, 1984; Emmer et al., 1980; Evertson & Emmer, 1982). Under these conditions, seatwork is much more interactive than the label implies. Such actions would seem to approximate the conditions of external pacing that occur in group lessons. This degree of supervision is not possible, however, when the teacher is teaching a small group while the rest of the students are working independently at their desks. In this latter situation, a teacher can seldom leave the reading group to help seatwork students without disrupting the small-group lesson. Moreover, a teacher is likely to limit whole-class comments to reprimanding disruptive behavior and maintaining boundaries between the small group and the rest of the class (see McDermott, 1976).

TRANSITIONS

As indicated earlier in this chapter, transitions are important events in achieving order. Studies indicate that the quality of a transition sets the pace and tone of the subsequent segment (see Arlin, 1979; Cahir, 1978; Gump, 1967). Transitions are also affected by the ability level of a class. Evertson (1982) reported that there were more transitions in higher ability junior high classes, but the average length of a transition and the total time in transition were greater for low-ability classes.

Arlin (1979) and Doyle (1984) found that skilled managers marked the onset of transitions clearly, orchestrated transitions actively, and minimized the loss of momentum during these changes in activities. Less effective managers, on the other hand, tended to blend activities together, failed to monitor events during transitions, and took excessively long to complete the movement between segments (see also Kounin, 1970). Transitions appear to require considerable vigilance and teacher direction to accomplish successfully.

CLASS SESSIONS

Recently some attempts have been made to examine how teachers orchestrate class sessions, especially at the junior high school level in which class groups change every 55 minutes or so. Doyle (1984) noted that successful junior high school English teachers were able to "come out even," that is, to schedule and pace segments to fit the available time. In addi-

tion, they often used standard opening routines (such as copying down the day's assignments or writing in journals) to engage students in work almost immediately after the bell rang to begin class. If a class was split by a lunch period, successful managers often assigned work that carried over the break so that a program of action was available when students returned to class. Finally, effective managers often had official closing routines or let the ending bell interrupt the last segment rather than running out of work before the end of the period. Evertson (1982) reported that in low-ability junior high classes, teachers often ended academic work before the period was over. Similar results were reported by Emmer et al. (1980) for elementary teachers, and by Evertson and Emmer (1982) for junior high math and English teachers.

CUEING AND IMPROVISING CONTEXTS

This survey of research suggests that orchestrating classroom lessons involves a delicate balancing of a large number of forces and a selective and efficient processing of information about certain key dimensions that affect classroom structures and rhythms. A large chunk of a teacher's attention is taken up monitoring the flow of content and activity and watching for potential breakdowns in the system. In addition, a teacher must play an active role in carrying out the programs of action in classroom activities.

Erickson (1982a) has called attention to the improvisational character of classroom lessons. As students and a teacher go about the processes of achieving a context, they frequently adjust to the demands of immediately unfolding events and the multiple vectors of classroom settings. Order is held in place, however, by the redundancy of contextualization cues that participants use to tell each other what is happening (see Erickson & Mohatt, 1982; Erickson & Shultz, 1981; McDermott, 1976; Griffin & Mehan, 1979). These cues, which include verbal and nonverbal messages as well as the rhythm or cadence of actions and the direction or momentum of events, are often quite subtle and delicate. Shultz and Florio (1979), for example, reported an incident in which the teacher assumed the position for announcing a transition but was distracted from giving the verbal signal. The students, responding to the positional cue, started to move before the teacher was ready to begin the transition. This perspective on the achievement of order suggests that management functions can be easily disrupted by factors interfering with communication systems in classrooms.

Classroom Management and Academic Work: A Delicate Balance

Earlier it was established that academic work is implicated in classroom management as a significant part of the primary vector of action in classroom activities. In other words, the nature of the work students do plays a central role in getting lessons accomplished in real time. One important consequence of this connection is that academic work can be used to achieve order. Indeed, evidence reviewed previously (e.g., Doyle, 1984) suggests that effective teachers in difficult management situations push students through the curriculum as a way of achieving and sustaining order. Recently, however, increasing attention is being given to the possibility that subject matter is shaped in fundamental ways by management considerations, that the decisions teachers make to enhance order affect the quality of academic work and thus the quality of what students learn (see Buike, 1981; Doyle, Sanford, Clements, French, & Emmer, 1983; Duffy & McIntyre, 1982). Of particular concern is the possibility that teachers use academic work to achieve order in ways that defeat the purposes and the effects of the curriculum. In this section an attempt is made to review some of the research that has a bearing on tensions between management and the instructional program of a class. Special attention is given to how management processes affect the demands of academic work, the form that work takes in classrooms, and the quality of instruction students receive.

NEGOTIATING THE DEMANDS OF ACADEMIC WORK

Classroom studies indicate that the demands of academic work are shaped by a complex negotiation process between teachers and students (see Woods, 1978). This line of inquiry points to the possibility that teachers sometimes seek to achieve order by selecting only tasks that are familiar and easy for students.

In developing this line of reasoning, Doyle (1983) has argued that academic work involving higher level cognitive processes (understanding, reasoning, and problem formulation) is high in ambiguity and risk for students. Students respond to these factors by attempting to increase the explicitness of product specifications and reduce the stringency of accountability requirements (see especially Davis & McKnight, 1976). Such actions tend to slow down the flow of classroom events, reduce work involvement, and increase the frequency of misbehavior and disruption. That is, students' reactions to work create pressures on the management system. In response to these threats to order, teachers often simplify task demands and/or lower the risk for mistakes (see especially Doyle & Carter, 1984). In contrast, relatively simple and routine tasks involving memory or algorithms tend to proceed quite smoothly in class with little hesitation or resistance.

The tensions created by challenging academic work may lead experienced teachers to exclude such tasks in the first place. Jorgenson (1977) found, for example, that elementary students tended to be assigned materials that fell below their abilities and that conduct was better when assigned work was easier for students. In a preliminary analysis of academic tasks in junior high science, English, and mathematics classes, Doyle et al. (1983) found that teachers often used efficient production systems in which tasks were presented in small and heavily prompted increments. Such work systems were smooth running and high in output but low in ambiguity and in executive-level decision making by students. Finally, studies by Stodolsky and her colleagues (Stodolsky, 1981; Stodolsky et al., 1981) in fifth grade math and social studies and by Korth and Cornbleth (1982) in middle school science, English, and social studies found that tasks involving higher cognitive processes seldom occurred. Moreover, when such tasks did occur, they were scheduled during peer group projects or seatwork rather than recitations. In other words, higher level cognitive tasks were

sheltered from the public arena of classrooms and assigned to formats in which student performance was private and accountability diffuse. Such a strategy reduces the possibility that tensions will occur in the activity system because students cannot do the work. Research is needed on whether this strategy of sheltering higher level academic tasks also affects students' perceptions of the importance or seriousness of the work.

SUBJECT MATTER AS PROCEDURE

Some investigators have also suggested that subject matter is proceduralized in order to satisfy management demands, that is, academic work is reduced by teachers and students to a set of procedures to be followed in completing assignments. In such classes, the emphasis is on practice and completion, and instruction consists primarily of directions for completing worksheets. In addition, neither teachers nor students talk much about the meaning, purposes, or underlying operations of the content, and students seldom receive corrective feedback when they make errors (see Anderson, 1983; Bloome, 1981, 1983; Blumenfeld et al., 1983; Cornbleth & Korth, 1983; Duffy & McIntyre, 1982; Durkin, 1979; Leinhardt, Zigmond, & Cooley, 1981; Stake & Easley, 1978; Whitmer, 1982). Although there is often an appearance of engagement, the working is often counterfeit, that is, faked or done without understanding (Tousignant & Siedentop, 1982; Woods, 1978). In addition, lessons can move along quite smoothly without high-quality cognitive engagement with the content (see Eaton, Anderson, & Smith, 1984; Green, 1983; Harker, 1983).

In some ways, this emphasis on procedure is understandable because students spend a great deal of time in school completing products that are evaluated. In addition, lengthy and complex explanations of content which are not related to an immediate assignment are not likely to elicit student involvement. Finally, formulating process explanations for errors after a student completes an answer must be done at the end of a turn when the natural rhythm is to move to another participant. Nevertheless, excessive proceduralizing would appear to circumvent the purposes of the curriculum.

INTERFERENCE WITH INSTRUCTION AND LEARNING

Finally, investigators have documented that management processes can interfere with the quality of instruction students receive, especially in low-ability classes in which management is a prevailing theme. For example, practices of prompting student performance and alerting group attention in reading groups would appear to reduce the opportunities low-ability students have for learning to read (Allington, 1980; McDermott, 1976). Indeed, Eder (1982a) noted that the first grade teacher in her study often accepted student-initiated interruptions during reading turns for the low-ability group but reprimanded such attempts in the higher ability groups. As a result, attempts to interrupt decreased between fall and spring observations in the high groups and increased in the low group. Eder argues that because of the teacher's practice of allowing group members to participate in reading turns, the low-ability students were not learning appropriate rules for turn taking in other classroom groups.

Research on teacher expectations and differential teacher treatment of students in classes indicates that low-ability students are often not called on or are given limited opportunities to respond in whole-class settings (see Brophy, 1983b; Good, 1981). In other words, some teachers appear to solve the problem of order in large-group lessons by excluding lower ability students from participation in classroom activities. From a management perspective, such action is reasonable in the sense that it avoids conditions which threaten the activity system by slowing down activity and content flow and generating noninvolvement. At the same time, such actions can restrict the opportunities some students have to learn.

RESOLVING THE TENSIONS

Clearly academic work can be swamped by the management function in teaching, and teachers can become preoccupied with getting work accomplished rather than promoting student achievement (Allington, 1983; Anderson, 1983; Brophy, 1982; Duffy & McIntyre, 1982; Eder, 1982b). When this happens, management limits the opportunities students have for learning, even though engagement may be high. In such circumstances, a well-managed class would not necessarily be a high-achieving class. At the same time, some challenging academic tasks are difficult to manage in classrooms. When such tasks are being used, the class may not score high on such management indicators as attention and engagement. Issues such as these suggest that management studies that ignore content can be misleading, and instructional design studies that ignore management can miss an essential dimension related to the practical use of findings.

The data reviewed in this chapter suggest, however, that the solution to the tension between management and instruction may require a greater emphasis on management. For example, including low-ability students into the center of the activity and task systems of a class requires well-developed management skills that enable a teacher to compensate for the pressures such students place on the activity system (see Sanford & Evertson, 1981). In other words, solving the instructional problems of low-ability students cannot be done by deemphasizing management or by designing more complex instructional arrangements for the classroom. Indeed, such "solutions" are likely to increase the problems they are designed to rectify. A more appropriate answer to the problem would seem to involve improved knowledge and training in management so that teachers can be free to concentrate on instructional solutions to learning problems (see Good, 1983).

Evidence is also emerging that a well-ordered social system is a basic condition for instruction at higher cognitive levels. Soar and Soar (1983), for example, distinguished between teachers' control of behavior in classrooms and their control of learning tasks. The data they reviewed from elementary studies suggested that these two types of control are usually highly correlated but that they are differentially related to learning. The relationship between behavior control and achievement appears to be linear, whereas that between control of learning tasks and achievement takes the form of an inverted U,

suggesting that intermediate amounts of teacher control over academic work are the most beneficial, especially for higher ability students on demanding cognitive tasks. More direct evidence of this connection between order and the achievement of higher cognitive objectives was provided by Au and Kawakami (1984). Their description of the successful Kamehameha Early Education Program suggests that the carefully designed and rehearsed routines for reading comprehension lessons in this program provided a familiar and predictable context in which students were able to make mistakes and engage in complex interchanges that developed comprehension skills.

Misbehavior and Interventions

To this point in the review, questions of misbehavior and teacher interventions to stop misbehavior have been conveniently sidestepped. This diversionary tactic was intentional in part because of a need to separate issues of classroom management from issues of discipline and in part because misbehavior and teacher interventions can be understood only in terms of their relation to processes of orchestrating order in classrooms. In other words, misbehavior and what teachers do to stop it are not an isolated entity in a classroom. Rather they are part of the fabric of the ecological system that defines and sustains order.

It is now time to attack the issues of misbehavior and interventions directly. The first task consists of constructing a definition of misbehavior that is ecologically based, that is, tied to the components of the activity system in classrooms. The second task consists of explaining teacher interventions as attempts to repair breakdowns in classroom order.

Misbehavior

Interventions into the flow of an activity to stop misbehavior are based on complex judgments about the act, the actor, and the circumstances at a particular moment in classroom time. To understand interventions, then, it is necessary to understand the contours of misbehavior.

DEFINING MISBEHAVIOR

Popular attention is often drawn to incidents of severely disruptive behavior and crime in schools, such as violence, robbery, theft, vandalism, and drug traffic. Although traumatic when they occur, such acts are generally rare in most schools and most often occur in corridors, lunch rooms, and outside the buildings rather than in classrooms (see National Institute of Education, 1977; National Opinion Research Center, 1981). More common are tardiness, cutting classes, failure to bring supplies and books, inattentiveness, talking, call-outs, and mild forms of verbal and physical aggression (see Doyle, 1978; Silverstein, 1979). In some situations, students play complex verbal insult games and use threats of physical violence, and these events can have major consequences for order (see Foster, 1974), but these forms of misbehavior are not widespread.

Most misbehavior is related to attention, crowd control, and getting work accomplished in classrooms. Pullis and Cadwell (1982) found that primary grade teachers used information about students' task orientation to make classroom management decisions. Trenholm and Rose (1981) identified six broad categories of appropriate student behavior among interview responses of elementary teachers: (a) responding in the appropriate form to academic requests or tasks, (b) controlling impulsiveness, (c) dealing with problems and negative feedback in mature ways, (d) interacting courteously and cooperatively with peers, (e) attending to and becoming involved in classroom activities and procedures, and (f) recognizing appropriate contexts for different types of behaviors. Sieber (1981) examined the linguistic, kinesic, proxemic, and social components of "listening" in four first grade classrooms. The essential ingredient of listening was silence, but students also had to "sit nicely," keep their hands to themselves, and not be playing with pencils and other objects. Violations of any of these proper ways to display listening were usually reprimanded by the teachers.

Some student actions, for example, tardiness or wearing hats to class, fall fairly clearly into the category of misbehavior and require teacher intervention. Such actions are often governed explicitly by school-wide rules. Similarly, noise that is audible beyond the classroom is usually stopped by teachers (see Denscombe, 1980a). But in many cases, the situation is not quite so simple. That is, actions that appear to be quite similar are reacted to quite differently by teachers when performed by different students at different times or in different contexts (see Anderson-Levitt, 1984; Mehan, 1974; Mehan, Hertweck, Combs, & Flynn, 1982; Metz, 1978; Pittman, 1985; Solomon & Kendall, 1976). This differential treatment does not usually occur because of teacher incompetence or even inconsistency but rather because of the contextual specificity of rules and the differential consequences of actions in the behavior stream of classrooms (see Hargreaves et al., 1975). In other words, the discrete actions of the same form are not the same if they have (or are perceived to have) very different consequences under different circumstances.

The key to understanding misbehavior is to view what students do in the context of classroom structures. From this perspective, misbehavior is any behavior by one or more students that is perceived by the teacher to initiate a vector of action that competes with or threatens the primary vector of action at a particular moment in a classroom activity. Vectors perceived as misbehavior are likely to be (or likely to become) *public*, that is, visible to a significant portion of the class, and *contagious*, that is, capable of spreading rapidly or pulling other members of the class into them. Misbehavior, in other words, creates fractures or fissures in the program of action in a classroom. For classes or groups in which the primary vector is weak (i.e., students are easily distracted or not inclined to engage in academic work) and actions outside the primary vector are frequent, misbehavior is likely to be common (see Felmlee & Eder, 1983; Metz, 1978).

By this definition, not every infraction of a rule is necessarily misbehavior. Talking out of turn is not misbehavior if it advances the lesson at a time when moving forward is essential. Similarly, inattention during the last few minutes of a class session will often be tolerated because the vector of action is coming to a stop. On the other hand, consistent delays in reacting to directives can slow down the activity flow in a class and irritate a teacher (Brooks & Wagenhauser, 1980).

Misbehavior, then, is not a property of an action but of an "action in context" (Mehan et al., 1982, p. 313) and a considerable amount of interpretation based on what a teacher knows about the likely configuration of events in a classroom is involved in applying the label (cf. Hargreaves et al., 1975). In this light, the common suggestion that teachers should be "consistent" means not that they should always behave in the same way but that they should be able to make reliable judgments about the probable consequences of students' actions in different situations. The analysis here suggests that this type of consistency is not easy to achieve.

MISBEHAVIOR AS A STUDENT SKILL

It is important not to leave students out of the analysis of the interpretive work that goes into recognizing, producing, and controlling misbehavior in classrooms. In most instances, misbehavior is caused by only a few unruly students (see Metz, 1978; Sanford & Evertson, 1981; Sieber, 1979a; Tikunoff & Ward, 1978), while the rest of the class serves as members of an audience and as potential participants in the incident if it spreads. McDermott (1976) has documented how first grade students in both high- and low-ability reading groups work interactively to produce and sustain order and to hold each other accountable for appropriate behavior. Part of this interactive work consists of signals to the teacher when order is threatened, perhaps because the teacher is viewed as a protector against aggression and injury (see also Sieber, 1979b).

At the same time, there would seem to be a certain skillfulness associated with behavior outside the primary vector of action in classrooms. Even in the early elementary grades, some students are able to mask nonproductive time by faking involvement (see Buckley & Cooper, 1978) and concealing actions that teachers are likely to reprimand (see Hargreaves et al., 1975). Sieber (1979a) has vividly described how students in his study of first and fifth grade classes concealed play:

> Even if conversations stop at the lesson's beginning, for example, they are often resumed where they left off upon the first opportunity, as when the teacher turns her back to write on the blackboard. Pupils also attempt to conceal conversations by other means, such as speaking across aisles while holding an open book in front of their faces, or by "throwing their voices," i.e., speaking to others without turning their heads or moving mouths. Whispering, of course, is also employed in an attempt to render conversation inaudible to the teacher. Because whispering is limited, however, in the distance it allows communication to travel, passing of written "notes" is often resorted to. Children cooperate in passing these written messages back and forth across the room, each pass ideally being made while the teacher's glance is directed elsewhere. If the pause in the teacher's glance is of long enough duration, the folded message may even be more expediently thrown across the room to its intended recipient. An unnecessary trip to the pencil sharpener can also be taken, which allows a pupil to walk across the room and quietly drop the message into another's lap while passing by. (p. 228)

Along these same lines, Mehan (1980) described a case in which an elementary student was able to volunteer to check on playground equipment for the teacher and also use the trip to get food to share with her classmates. Other incidents in

Mehan's study involved collaboration among students to get preferred jobs in the class or block the teacher's ability to see actions that were against the rules. Tousignant and Siedentop (1982) found that during gym classes secondary students were often skilled in modifying tasks to fit their skills or in acting as "competent bystanders," that is, they would position themselves in games so as to avoid major player roles or they would fall back in line to avoid turns in individual performance situations.

In addition, the timing of misbehavior seems to be important. Rusnock and Brandler (1979) found differences across students in the timing of off-task behavior: High-ability students were likely to engage in off-task behavior at the end of segments or during transitions whereas low-ability students engaged in off-task behavior during the middle of segments. In the latter case, off-task behavior was more likely to be visible and to disrupt the activity. Spencer-Hall (1981) described a case of a fifth grade student (reportedly a typical case) who engaged in several types of "disruptive" behaviors but who actually won the "good citizenship" award for the school. The key to his success was that his actions outside the primary vector were done behind the teacher's back so that he was seldom caught.

One way to interpret these findings is to suggest that "misbehavior" by highly skilled students is not, strictly speaking, misbehavior at all. Although these actions are outside the primary vector and are visible to other students, they are inserted into small gaps in the behavior stream, gaps that are so small that less skilled students do not have time to join in and cannot react without appearing to misbehave. As a result, there is little spread of effect, and these actions have little consequence for classroom order. They do not, in other words, disrupt the primary vector of an activity.

This perspective on student skill in behaving outside the primary vector of action in a classroom would seem to be important in understanding teachers' efforts to communicate competence at the beginning of the year. If a teacher recognizes such behavior early when performed by a student known by the class to be skilled, then the teacher's competence is established instantly. If, however, a teacher fails to recognize such behavior in students known to be unskilled, then he or she is likely to have difficulty creating and sustaining order.

ORIGINS AND FUNCTIONS OF MISBEHAVIOR

The discussion to this point implies that misbehavior is a continuing pressure on teachers in classrooms. Why this is so is not altogether clear. Four of the most popular explanations for the origins of misbehavior have an ideological flavor: (a) school tasks are trivial and boring, so students are not motivated to engage in academic work; (b) schools are governed by the authoritarian imposition of ideas and rules, so students naturally rebel against these restrictions; (c) school staffs are weak or muddleheaded and thus unwilling or unable to assert their rightful authority to police student conduct; and (d) students act out to satisfy their need for adult and peer attention. At a more analytical level, some investigators have argued that deviance is the result of discrepancies between the middle-class expectations of the school and the cultural norms of subgroups of students. In other words, acceptable behavior

for turn taking or verbal games in homes and neighborhoods is not acceptable in classrooms (see Borman, 1978; Florio & Shultz, 1979; Henry, 1971; Moore, 1976). Other studies of elementary and secondary students' views of schooling have pointed to a clash between school and student cultures. These studies have fairly consistently found that students are interested primarily in socializing with their friends and in getting classroom work done with a minimum of energy and effort (see Allen, 1983; Cusick, Martin, & Palonsky, 1976; deVoss, 1979; Everhart, 1979; Lancy, 1976; Sieber, 1979a). As a result, they often look for or attempt to create opportunities for "goofing off." Goofing off, in turn, often initiates vectors of action that compete with or disrupt the primary vectors of lesson segments, an effect that appears to be especially strong when classroom structures allow for or encourage social interaction and free choice among students (see Cusick, 1973).

Some preliminary efforts have been made to assign various functions to misbehavior. Doyle (1979b) argued that students' attempts, especially at the beginning of the year, to initiate secondary vectors serve to test the boundaries of the teacher's management system and reveal possible openings for personal agendas. In addition to defining the stability and predictability of the social system of the class, this information can be used to estimate the stringency of academic accountability in a class. McDermott (1976) has constructed a compelling argument that students in a low-ability reading group used misbehavior to draw the teacher back to their group so that reading instruction could continue. In this instance, misbehavior functioned to prevent the teacher from ignoring the group during reading time. Finally, Doyle and Carter (1984) have presented evidence that frequent student questions and delays in getting work started functioned as means of controlling the demands of difficult academic work. It is not clear that these uses of misbehavior are conscious and deliberate. Nevertheless, there is reason to believe that "misbehavior" does contribute to the concentration of social structures and interaction in classroom groups, that is, that the periodic eruption of secondary vectors serves to define the boundaries and the strength of the primary vector and shape its direction.

Interventions

The research reviewed in this chapter indicates that students and teachers do a considerable amount of interactional work together to define and sustain order in classrooms. McDermott (1976), for example, reported that students in both high- and low-ability classes responded almost immediately to departures from the primary program of action and began to signal through positionings and glances their awareness of this "disorder." The ripple effect (Kounin, 1970), in other words, occurs early and students hold each other accountable for being orderly. Nevertheless, the teacher is the primary custodian of order in a classroom (see Gannaway, 1976; Nash, 1976) and, therefore, must decide when and how to intervene into the flow of activity to repair order, that is, to stop a competing or disruptive vector and return to the primary program of action for a segment. Research related to the intervention process itself, the form of interventions, and the decision to intervene is reviewed here. The final section consists of a brief survey of discipline strategies, that is, intervention programs designed to correct reasonably serious and persistent behavior problems.

THE INTERVENTION PROCESS

Interventions can repair temporary disturbances in classroom order, but they cannot establish order when no primary vector is operating. As a result, the frequency or even the quality of desists does not predict the degree of order in a classroom (Kounin, 1970). Indeed, Kounin (1983) recently reported that the least successful teacher in his samples achieved task involvement only 25% of the time and yet attempted to desist behavior 986 times in one day. The degree of order depends, rather, upon the strength of the primary vector and the timing of the intervention to occur before the secondary vector has gained strength (Kounin, 1970). Successful managers, in other words, create order by establishing activities, anticipating potential misbehavior, and catching misbehavior early when it occurs (see Emmer et al., 1980; Evertson & Emmer, 1982).

Interventions occur at a rate of about 16 per hour (see Sieber, 1976; White, 1975). Nevertheless, they are inherently risky because they call attention to potentially disruptive behavior and they initiate a program of action that, ironically, can pull the class further away from the primary vector and weaken its function in holding order in place. There is, in other words, a "ripple effect" of interventions (Kounin & Gump, 1958), that is, desist episodes influence witnesses and disrupt their involvement, although this effect appears to occur primarily during early class sessions and to depend upon a student's commitment to the work and liking for the teacher (see Kounin, 1970). In addition, inserting a desist into an action chain can disrupt the rhythm of interaction and slow down the flow of a classroom event (Brooks, 1985).

Because of these risk factors, successful interventions tend to have a private and fleeting quality that does not interrupt the flow of events (see Erickson & Mohatt, 1982). In addition to occurring early, they are often quite brief and do not invite further comment from the target student or students. Sieber (1976, 1979a, 1981), for instance, identified over 30 types of interventions in a study of first and fifth grade classes. Simple verbal reprimands accounted for 58% of the total intervention episodes observed. The other types included praise, prizes and surprises, manipulation of privileges, physical coercion/affection, generalized threats, isolation, seat changes, repetition of routines, "writing names," and detention. Of these, no single type accounted for more than 3% of the total observed episodes. Borman, Lippincott, Matey, and Obermiller (1978) noted that elementary teachers tend to use "soft imperatives," that is, suggestions or questions ("Why don't you put the pencil down?") to control behavior. Such indirect statements leave room for negotiation and avoid confrontations. Indeed, teachers use a variety of unobtrusive nonverbal signals, including gestures, direct eye contact, and proximity, to regulate misbehavior (see Woolfolk & Brooks, 1985).

Humphrey (1979) examined desists or "sanctions" during turn taking in 15 lessons from two kindergarten and two third grade classes. Of the 263 sanction incidents studied, 124 or 47% consisted of the "squelch" form only (e.g., "Shh," "Wait,"

"Stop," or "No") and 74 or 28% consisted of the squelch plus a brief explication (e.g., "Shh. Put your hand up if you want to say something"). Humphrey argued that the squelch form is uniquely suited to interrupting and terminating a student's utterance. In other words, the intervention is abrupt, short, and does not invite further comment or discussion from the student. As a result, the primary vector of the lesson is only minimally disturbed.

In classes in which the primary vector is weak, desists are likely to be frequent (Evertson, 1982; Metz, 1978; Sanford & Evertson, 1981). At the same time there would appear to be a delicate balance between attending to the primary vector and attending to inappropriate behavior. Doyle (1984) reported that successful junior high managers tended to push on through the curriculum and did not let misbehavior become the central topic of conversation. This practice often meant that some rules were not enforced and the level of inappropriate behavior remained high (see also Metz, 1978). Nevertheless, the primary vector was sustained. Along similar lines, Eder (1982a) reported that the teacher in her study consistently reprimanded attempts by high-ability students to interrupt during reading turns but accepted such bids during turns in the low-ability group. This policy would seem to reflect the strength of the primary vector in these settings. In the high-ability group, the lesson vector is likely to be strong and less susceptible to disruption by reprimands. In the low group, the lesson vector is protected and advanced by accepting topically related bids and avoiding reprimands.

Finally, studies of teacher decision making have indicated that teachers are reluctant to change activities when things are not going well (see Clark & Yinger, 1979), and McHoul (1978) reported that teachers returned to the standard format and procedures for turn taking when open bidding became chaotic. This policy again seems reasonable. When order becomes unstable, repairing a primary vector would seem to be more sensible than initiating a transition to a new vector because transitions, even in the best of circumstances, are difficult to manage. The one exception to this general rule would seem to be the switch to structured seatwork when order is threatened in a whole-class presentation or recitation (see Metz, 1978). Such a transition is frequently made in classrooms and involves a minimum of group reorganization. Moreover, inappropriate behavior is less public when students are directed to attend to work at their own desks.

THE DECISION TO INTERVENE

Interventions are, by their very nature, reactive. That is, they are occasioned by behaviors that signal the beginnings of a disruption. As a result, they cannot be planned in advance, that is, their timing is difficult to control and their form must be decided on the spot. Given the risks involved, the decision to intervene is quite problematic.

Several attempts have been made recently to study the intervention decisions of teachers. The results indicate that decisions concerning when and how to intervene are based on teachers' knowledge of who is misbehaving, what the misbehavior is, and when it occurs. In an experiment using written descriptions, Cone (1978) found, for instance, that elementary teachers' estimates of disruptiveness and selections of management strategies were based on information about the student's history of deviancy, the nature of the act, and the setting in which it occurred (i.e., large vs. small group). In postexperiment interviews, Cone also found that teachers were able to give a large number of additional cues concerning student characteristics and situational factors such as task at hand and the time of the day or year that they would consider in making intervention decisions. On the basis of extensive classroom observations and interviews of three first grade teachers, Pittman (1984) concluded that decisions to intervene were based on information about whether the behavior was serious and distracting, and decisions about the intensity of the intervention depended upon the student's history of inappropriate behavior. Using written descriptions, Natriello and Dornbusch (1980) found that teachers responded to academic problems with warmth and concern and to behavior problems with presentations of standards. In a survey of 16 classroom studies, White (1975) found consistent differences in teachers' rates of approval and disapproval across instructional and managerial behaviors of students. Finally, Humphrey (1979) found that third grade teachers were harsher in desisting turn-taking violations than kindergarten teachers, reflecting perhaps a difference in the teachers' expectations about the students' knowledge of appropriate classroom behavior.

The work of Hargreaves et al. (1975) suggests that actual decisions to intervene are made under conditions of considerable uncertainty. Early cues of possible misbehavior, for example, concealment, are ambiguous and yet the teacher has only a limited amount of time to form a judgment and act. To reduce uncertainty, teachers typify or categorize students in terms of such factors as their persistence and their visibility in the social structure of the group. Teachers, in other words, learn the likely configuration of events associated with actions by different students and use this information to decide whether an intervention is necessary.

In summary, the need to restore order in a classroom is a sign that the mechanisms that establish and sustain order are not working. The repair process itself is complex and risky as are the decisions concerning when and how to intervene. Successful managers appear to be able to decide early whether an act will disrupt order and to intervene in an inconspicuous way to cut off the path toward disorder. In attending to misbehavior and interventions, however, the emphasis remains on the primary vector of action as the fundamental means of holding order in place in classrooms.

DISCIPLINE AND REMEDIATION

A large body of literature has grown up around the treatment of chronic and serious behavior problems of elementary and secondary students, and several comprehensive discipline models, such as Teacher Effectiveness Training, Transactional Analysis, Assertive Discipline, Reality Therapy, Social Discipline, and Behavior Modification, have been proposed (see descriptions in Charles, 1981; Duke & Meckel, 1984; Wolfgang & Glickman, 1980). Although commonly associated with the topic of classroom management, much of this work is beyond the scope of this chapter because it deals primarily with large-

scale intervention programs rather than with classroom structures and the processes of accomplishing lessons. Moreover, with the exception of behavior modification, there is little research available concerning the implementation or the effectiveness of most discipline models. This section is limited, therefore, to a brief survey of research on teachers' orientations to discipline and on procedures for modifying students' classroom behavior.

Goldstein and Weber (1981) conducted three studies in a total of 69 elementary classes to examine the relationship between approaches to discipline and students' on-task behavior. Originally seven classroom management approaches were constructed by grouping the various discipline models and systems in the literature. The seven management approaches were: authoritarian, behavior modification, commonsense or cookbook, group process, instructional, permissive, and socioemotional climate. An eighth approach called intimidation was identified as a result of observations made in the first study of a series. Classroom observations were conducted for two full mornings in the first study and one full morning in the second and third studies. Data consisted of descriptions of "managerial episodes" (i.e., desist incidents) and samples of students' on-task behavior. Teacher behavior during episodes was subsequently coded and categorized into one of the eight management approaches, and profiles for each teacher were constructed. Across the three studies, the investigators reported that behaviors characteristic of two approaches, group process and socioemotional climate, were positively related to on-task behavior, and behaviors associated with the authoritarian approach were negatively related to on-task behavior. Results for the other approaches did not reach statistical significance. These results lend some support for models of discipline based on the works of Dreikurs and Cassel (1972), Glasser (1969), Kounin (1970), and Schmuck and Schmuck (1979).

Brophy and Rohrkemper (1981) examined how 98 elementary (K–6) teachers interpreted and stated they would cope with 12 chronic student problem types or syndromes as depicted in written vignettes. The problem types included failure syndrome, perfectionist, underachiever, low achiever, hostile aggressive, passive aggressive, defiant, hyperactive, distractible, immature, rejected by peers, and shy/withdrawn. The teachers were nominated by their principals as either outstanding or average in coping with problem students. Teachers were first observed for two half days to gain general impressions of their coping style and success, and then interviewed at length (from 2 to 10 hours) concerning their responses to the vignettes. Following Gordon (1974), problems were classified as (a) teacher owned, in which the student's behavior interferes with the teacher's needs or agenda, (b) student owned, in which the student's agenda or needs are frustrated by people or events other than the teacher, and (c) shared problems, in which the student's behavior does not directly challenge the teacher but has consequences for classroom management and control. Responses to the vignettes were coded for attributions about the students and about the teacher's own role in causing and remediating the problems.

Results of this study indicated that the teachers generally tended to see internal student factors rather than themselves as causes of the problems. The teachers saw students with teacher-owned problems as responsible for their own behavior, acting intentionally, and blameworthy for their acts. Those with student-owned problems were seen as not responsible for their problems. Results for students with shared problems were mixed with a tendency to see acts by these students as unintentional but perhaps controllable. The teachers saw themselves as capable of effecting changes with the help of others (parents, counselors, etc.). Teachers were pessimistic about changing students with teacher-owned problems and focused on immediate control strategies rather than basic personal changes. They saw students with student-owned problems as difficult to change but they were motivated to try through long-term remediation programs of support, encouragement, and extended talk. Finally, they proposed behavior modification, modeling, and close supervision for students with shared problems and were optimistic about being helpful, at least with specific problems for limited periods of time. In closing, Brophy and Rohrkemper noted that the teachers in their sample appeared to have limited knowledge and skill in the various treatment models available for these problem types and did not always see the solving of these problems as part of their duties as classroom teachers.

Several useful studies, reviews, and collections on behavior modification techniques have recently appeared (see Brophy, 1981, 1983b; Elardo, 1978; Emmer, 1984; Lahey & Rubinoff, 1981; McLaughlin, 1976; O'Leary & O'Leary, 1977; Thompson, Brassell, Persons, Tucker, & Rollins, 1974; Workman & Hector, 1978), and no attempt will be made to duplicate this work here. The weight of the evidence suggests that most of the early recommendations for elaborate and complex systems of token economies, systematic contingency management, and ignoring undesirable behavior while praising desired behavior were impractical for individual classroom teachers. Moreover, using rewards for desired behavior or academic performance can have deleterious effects on intrinsic motivation (see Leeper & Greene, 1978). Attention has recently turned to systems for teaching students social skills (Cartledge & Milburn, 1978), coping strategies (Spaulding, 1983), participation skills (Cohen, 1979), and self-monitoring and self-control strategies (Anderson & Prawat, 1983; Brophy, 1983a; McLaughlin, 1976). The emphasis, in other words, is moving toward helping students learn to cope with classroom processes rather than having teachers implement behavior modification programs in the classroom.

This brief survey of recent work on discipline suggests that there is a growing interest in understanding how teachers perceive and cope with chronic student behavior problems and in the development of behavior modification strategies that focus on working individually with students outside of the classroom setting itself. Less emphasis, in turn, is being placed on converting teachers into therapists or classrooms into treatment centers. In view of the specialized focus of classrooms and the complex processes that operate in these environments, such a shift in attention would seem to be quite appropriate.

Conclusion

The need for management is most apparent when order is threatened. As a result, interventions to stop misbehavior are often the primary focus of theory and research in classroom management. The evidence suggests, however, that such episodes are most appropriately viewed as occasions in which order is repaired rather than created. Thus, the quantity or quality of interventions will not predict the degree of order in a classroom unless a program of action has already been established. The evidence also suggests that intervention episodes involve complex decisions about the probable consequences of particular actions by particular students at specific moments in the activity flow of a class session. Finally, because misbehavior and a teacher's reaction to misbehavior represent a vector of action, attempts to stop misbehavior can themselves disrupt order. As a result, successful desists are often inserted skillfully into the activity flow, and in many cases teachers seem to prefer to intervene in the private rather than in the public sphere of classrooms. Teachers are intent, in other words, on staying with the primary vector that sustains order in classrooms.

Themes and Directions in Classroom Management Research

The sheer quantity of studies having a bearing on classroom organization and management is encouraging. Researchers from a variety of conceptual and methodological persuasions have been drawn to the complex issues of organizing and directing purposeful action in classroom environments. Moreover, progress has clearly been made in recent years in understanding how classroom events are structured and how management processes work in these settings. This body of research is beginning to provide a rich knowledge base for effective practice in this important aspect of teaching.

To provide a useful summary of the state of this knowledge base, attention turns in this final section to the common themes that appear across the various studies of classroom organization and management and to promising directions for research in this area.

Common Themes

If one stands back from the array of studies reviewed in this chapter, several themes surface which, taken together, represent a reasonably comprehensive framework for integrating knowledge about processes of classroom organization and management. These themes include the following:

1. Classroom management is fundamentally a process of solving the problem of *order* in classrooms rather than the problems of misbehavior or student engagement. These latter issues are not insignificant, but they are not primary targets of a teacher's management energies. Indeed, high engagement and low levels of inappropriate and disruptive behavior are by-products of an effective program of classroom organization and management. At its foundation, then, the teacher's management task is primarily one of establishing and maintaining work systems for classroom groups rather than spotting and punishing misbehavior, remediating behavioral disorders, or maximizing the engagement of individual students.

2. Order in classrooms is defined by the strength and durability of the program of action embedded in the activities teachers and students enact together as they accomplish work. This emphasis on programs of action underscores the dynamic quality of management processes. Since classrooms are moving systems, order is not a static condition or an absence of action. Rather, order is a harmony of action with structure and purpose. Since programs of action have direction and energy, they pull events toward their completion. Rules, procedures, routines, and reprimands all have a role to play in sustaining classroom order, but they can only supplement what teachers do to specify and orchestrate programs of action. The more complex the program of action for an activity, the more difficult the management task a teacher faces.

3. A program of action, and thus classroom order, is jointly enacted by teachers and students in settings of enormous complexity. Teachers obviously play a key role in initiating and sustaining classroom activities. Nevertheless, students contribute in substantial ways to the quality of order that prevails in any classroom. In classes in which students are inclined to cooperate and are capable of doing the work and in which the teacher is skillful in establishing and protecting the primary vector of action, order is readily achieved. In situations in which students lack either the inclination or the ability to follow the primary vector or the teacher lacks skill in steering the program of action, order is often a protracted struggle.

4. Programs of action in classroom activities are defined by both the rules for social participation and the demands of academic work. For this reason academic work is directly involved in the process of achieving classroom order and can be shaped in basic ways by a teacher's management decisions. Moreover, it is difficult and potentially misleading to study management processes without attention to curriculum or curriculum designs without attention to classroom processes.

5. Order in classrooms is context specific and held in place by balancing a large array of forces and processes. As a result, order is often fragile, a condition that can be easily disrupted by mistakes, intrusions, and unpredictable events. Order is not something teachers achieve once and for all so they can get on with the business of instruction. Rather, it is a permanent pressure on classroom life, and a teacher continuously faces the need to monitor and protect the programs of action in a class. Indeed, the use of familiar activities such as recitations and seatwork and the standard practice of routinizing most classroom procedures and activities appear to be reasonable strategies for offsetting the inherent delicacy of classroom order.

6. The key to a teacher's success in management appears to be his or her (a) understanding of the likely configuration of events in a classroom, and (b) skill in monitoring and guiding activities in light of this information. From this perspective, management effectiveness cannot be defined solely in terms of rules for behavior. Effectiveness must also include such cognitive dimensions as comprehension and interpretation, skills which are necessary for recognizing when to act and how to improvise classroom events to meet immediate circumstances.

Directions for Research

Although a considerable amount has been learned about classroom organization and management in the past several years, the present review has underscored some important areas for further attention. These strategic research areas include the following:

1. There is a need for a much closer look at the processes — monitoring, pacing, directing, routinizing, intervening — involved in creating and sustaining order in classrooms. Much has been learned about types of classroom structures and behaviors that effective managers use, but more attention needs to be given to the functions of these structures and behaviors and how they are enacted over time in classroom settings. It is one thing to identify the conditions associated with management effectiveness and another to understand how these conditions are established and maintained. Such a close look at management processes would provide a rich picture of how classroom order is achieved and would enlarge the knowledge base for interpreting classroom events and improving strategies for sustaining order in these complex environments. At present many of the best studies of classroom processes have been conducted in the microethnographic and sociolinguistic traditions which tend to focus on issues of culture or language acquisition and use. Within these frameworks, management per se is often a secondary consideration. This same level of descriptive and analytical detail needs to be incorporated in studies of management processes. Because detailed process studies tend to have small samples, generalizability from a single study or even a few studies is not possible. More studies need to be conducted, and considerable effort must be given to the careful integration of these studies to build valid conceptual frameworks.

2. Effort needs to be devoted to the development of cognitive models in classroom management, that is, frameworks for representing the understanding teachers have of management processes and classroom order. The research reviewed here strongly indicates that such understandings have a substantial impact on how management occurs in a classroom. At the present time, our capacity to represent this understanding is quite primitive (see Doyle, 1979b; Joyce, 1980). Improved cognitive models would make two important contributions. First, they would ease the formidable problems of integrating research findings across the separate disciplines and traditions that generate information about classroom structures and processes. Second, they would supply a better foundation for designing teacher education programs to enhance the management skills of beginning and experienced teachers.

3. The examination of management processes needs to be context sensitive. For example, several studies reviewed in this chapter (e.g., Kounin, 1970; McDermott, 1976) were based on data gathered in the last month or two of the school year. Investigators seldom acknowledged, however, the possibility that this time of year might have special characteristics (e.g., procedures and activities are very familiar to participants and most of the major curriculum tasks have already been introduced and accomplished) and that these characteristics might have affected their results.

4. The range of contexts studied in classroom management research needs to be expanded. The largest amounts of data have been gathered in kindergarten classrooms, reading groups in the primary school, and math, English, and social studies classes in fifth grade and junior high school classes. Only a limited amount of data are available for high school classrooms, especially in the United States. It may well be that substantial differences exist across contexts because of differences in subject matter focus, students' level of maturity, peer influences, teacher preparation, and the like. The data available at present are not sufficient for making such judgments.

5. Studies of management processes must incorporate information about the academic work that students and teachers are trying to accomplish. Isolating social interaction or organizational features from the substance and purposes of classroom events can easily distort the picture one gets of how classrooms work. Moreover, the evidence suggests that fundamental tension exists between management and instructional processes in classrooms. Because of the significance of this tension for both order and achievement, the topic warrants a position of high priority in research on classroom organization and management.

6. Research across the boundary separating classrooms and schools is needed. This topic is especially relevant to classroom management since order and student conduct are issues at both classroom and school levels. Classrooms are certainly influenced by the larger context within which they are situated, but few investigators have documented when and how these influences occur. Better information in this area would be useful in formulating school policies that support teacher effectiveness in classroom management.

7. Finally, teacher preparation and staff development in classroom management is a promising area for research. Some successful efforts to communicate research-derived principles of management to beginning and experienced teachers have been reported (see Borg & Ascione, 1982; Emmer et al., 1982; Emmer, Sanford, Evertson, Clements, & Martin, 1981; Griffin et al., 1983). At a more detailed process level, Copeland (1983) developed a computer system in which the operator is required to conduct a question–answer session in arithmetic with a small group of students while monitoring the order of turn taking, the accuracy of answers, and another student who is supposed to be engaged in a seatwork task. This system simulates the withitness and overlap demands of classroom settings, and scores on this test correlate strongly with success in learning to manage real classrooms. It is, in other words, a valid simulation of at least a part of the complexity of management processes. The device would seem to have important uses as a diagnostic tool as well as a training environment. In addition, it provides a model of how to design training systems that are keyed to the cognitive processes that are required to achieve order in classrooms. More work in this direction is likely to bring teacher education programs in line with the richness of the growing knowledge base in classroom management.

Systematic research on classroom organization and management has achieved considerable maturity in a relatively short time. As the dominant emphasis shifted from misbehavior and discipline to the classroom structures and processes that create and sustain purposeful order, studies of management became more central to the field of research on teaching. If the scope of management studies continues to broaden and the movement toward conceptual models continues, prospects for research in this area are very promising.

REFERENCES

Abrahamson, J. H. (1974). *Classroom constraints and teacher coping strategies: A way to conceptualize the teaching task.* Unpublished doctoral dissertation, University of Chicago.

Adams, R. S. (1969). Location as a feature of instructional interaction. *Merrill Parker Quarterly, 15*(4), 309–321.

Adams, R. S., & Biddle, B. J. (1970). *Realities of teaching: Exploration with videotape.* New York: Holt, Rinehart & Winston.

Allen, J. D. (1983, April). *Classroom management: Students' perspectives, goals, strategies.* Paper presented at the annual meeting of the American Educational Research Association, Montreal.

Alling, M. R. (1882). Some causes of failure among teachers. *Education, 3*, 82–93.

Allington, R. L. (1980). Teacher interruption behaviors during primary grade oral reading. *Journal of Educational Psychology, 72*, 371–377.

Allington, R. L. (1983). The reading instruction provided readers of differing reading abilities. *Elementary School Journal, 83*(5), 548–559.

Anderson, L. (1983, April). *Achievement-related differences in students' responses to seatwork.* Paper presented at the annual meeting of the American Educational Research Association, Montreal.

Anderson, L., Evertson, C., & Brophy, J. (1979). An experimental study of effective teaching in first-grade reading groups. *Elementary School Journal, 79*, 193–223.

Anderson, L., & Prawat, R. (1983). A synthesis of research on teaching self-control. *Educational Leadership, 40*, 62–66.

Anderson, R. C., & Faust, G. W. (1975). *Educational psychology: The science of instruction and learning.* New York: Dodd, Mead.

Anderson-Levitt, K. M. (1984). Teacher interpretation of student behavior: Cognitive and social processes. *Elementary School Journal, 84*(3), 315–337.

Apple, M. W. (1979). *Ideology and curriculum.* Boston: Routledge & Kegan Paul.

Arlin, M. (1979). Teacher transitions can disrupt time flow in classrooms. *American Educational Research Journal, 16*, 42–56.

Arlin, M. (1982). Teacher responses to student time differences in mastery learning. *American Journal of Education, 90*, 334–352.

Arlin, M., & Webster, J. (1983). Time costs of mastery learning. *Journal of Educational Psychology, 75*, 187–196.

Arlin, M. N., & Westbury, I. (1976). The leveling effect of teacher pacing on science content mastery. *Journal of Research in Science Teaching, 13*, 213–219.

Aronson, E. (1978). *The jigsaw classroom.* Beverly Hills: Sage Publications.

Atwood, R. (1983, April). *The interacting effects of task form and activity structure on students' task involvement and teacher evaluations.* Paper presented at the annual meeting of the American Educational Research Association, Montreal.

Au, K. H. (1980). Participation structures in a reading lesson with Hawaiian children: Analysis of a culturally appropriate instructional event. *Anthropology and Education Quarterly, 11*, 91–115.

Au, K. H., & Kawakami, A. J. (1984). Vygotskian perspectives on discussion processes in small group reading lessons. In L. C. Wilkinson, P. L. Peterson, & M. Hallinan (Eds.), *The social context of instruction.* New York: Academic Press.

Bagley, W. C. (1907). *Classroom management: Its principles and technique.* New York: Macmillan.

Ball, S. J. (1980). Initial encounters in the classroom and the process of establishment. In P. Woods (Ed.), *Pupil strategies: Explorations in the sociology of the school* (pp. 143–161). London: Croom Helm.

Barker, R. G. (1968). *Ecological psychology.* Stanford, CA: Stanford University Press.

Behnke, G. J. (1979). *Coping with classroom distractions: The formal research study* (Rep. IR & DT 79-2). San Francisco: Far West Laboratory.

Bellack, A. A., Kliebard, H. M., Hyman, R. T., & Smith, F. L. (1966). *The language of the classroom.* New York: Teachers College Press.

Bennett, N., & Blundell, D. (1983). Quantity and quality of work in rows and classroom groups. *Educational Psychology, 3,* 93–105.

Berliner, D. C. (1979). Tempus educare. In P. Peterson & H. Walberg (Eds.), *Research on Teaching.* Berkeley, CA: McCutchan.

Berliner, D. C. (1983a). Developing conceptions of classroom environments: Some light on the T in classroom studies of ATI. *Educational Psychologist, 18,* 1–13.

Berliner, D. C. (1983b). The executive who manages classrooms. In B. J. Fraser (Ed.), *Classroom management.* South Bentley: Western Australian Institute of Technology.

Bloome, D. (1981, April). *Reading and writing in a classroom: A sociolinguistic ethnography.* Paper presented at the annual meeting of the American Educational Research Association, Los Angeles.

Bloome, D. (1983, April). *Definitions and functions of reading in two middle school classrooms: A sociolinguistic ethnographic study.* Paper presented at the annual meeting of the American Educational Research Association, Montreal.

Blumenfeld, P. C., Hamilton, V. L., Bossert, S. T., Wessels, K., & Meece, J. (1983). Teacher talk and student thought: Socialization into the student role. In J. Levine & M. Wang (Eds.), *Teacher and student perceptions: Implications for learning.* Hillsdale, NJ: Erlbaum.

Blumenfeld, P. C., Hamilton, V. L., Wessels, K., & Falkner, D. (1979). Teaching responsibility to first graders. *Theory Into Practice, 18*(3), 174–180.

Borg, W. R. (1980). Time and school learning. In C. Denham & A. Lieberman (Eds.), *Time to learn.* Washington, DC: National Institute of Education.

Borg, W. R., & Ascione, F. R. (1982). Classroom management in elementary mainstreaming classrooms. *Journal of Educational Psychology, 74*(1), 85–95.

Borman, K. M. (1978). Social control and schooling: Power and process in two kindergarten settings. *Anthropology and Education Quarterly, 9,* 38–53.

Borman, K. M., Lippincott, N. S., Matey, C. M., & Obermiller, P. (1978, March). *Characteristics of family and classroom control in an urban Appalachian neighborhood.* Paper presented at the annual meeting of the American Educational Research Association, Toronto.

Bossert, S. (1979). *Tasks and social relationships in classrooms.* New York: Cambridge University Press.

Bossert, S. T., Dwyer, D. C., Rowan, B., & Lee, G. L. (1982, March). *Toward a school-level conceptualization of instructional management: The principal's role.* Paper presented at the annual meeting of the American Educational Research Association, New York.

Bowles, S., & Gintis, H. (1976). *Schooling in capitalist America.* London: Routledge & Kegan Paul.

Bozsik, B. E. (1982, March). *A study of teacher questioning and student response interaction during pre-story and post-story portions of reading comprehension lessons.* Paper presented at the annual meeting of the American Educational Research Association, New York.

Bremme, D., & Erickson, F. (1977). Relationships among verbal and non-verbal classroom behaviors. *Theory Into Practice, 5,* 153–161.

Brooks, D. M. (1985). Beginning the year in junior high: The first day of school. *Educational Leadership, 42*(8), 76–78.

Brooks, D. M. (in press). The teacher's communicative competence: The first day of school. *Theory into Practice.*

Brooks, D. M., Silvern, S. B., & Wooten, M. (1978). The ecology of teacher–pupil verbal interaction. *Journal of Classroom Interaction, 14,* 39–45.

Brooks, D. M., & Wagenhauser, B. (1980). Completion time as a nonverbal component of teacher attitude. *Elementary School Journal, 81*(1), 24–27.

Brophy, J. E. (1981). A functional analysis of praise. *Review of Educational Research, 51,* 5–32.

Brophy, J. E. (1982). How teachers influence what is taught and learned in classrooms. *Elementary School Journal, 83,* 1–13.

Brophy, J. E. (1983a). Classroom organization and management. *The Elementary School Journal, 83*(4), 265–286.

Brophy, J. E. (1983b). Research on the self-fulfilling prophecy and teacher expectations. *Journal of Educational Psychology, 75*(5), 631–661,

Brophy, J. E., & Evertson, C. (1976). *Learning from teaching: A developmental perspective.* Boston: Allyn & Bacon.

Brophy, J. E., & Rohrkemper, M. M. (1981). The influence of problem ownership on teachers' perceptions of and strategies for coping with student problems. *Journal of Educational Psychology, 73*(3), 295–311.

Buckley, P. K., & Cooper, J. M. (1978, March). *An ethnographic study of an elementary school teacher's establishment and maintenance of group norms.* Paper presented at the annual meeting of the American Educational Research Association, Toronto.

Buike, S. (1981). *The shaping of classroom practices: Teacher decisions* (Research Series No. 97). East Lansing: Michigan State University, Institute for Research on Teaching.

Burnett, J. H. (1973). Event description and analysis in the microethnography of urban classrooms. In F. A. J. Ianni & E. Storey (Eds.), *Cultural relevance and educational issues: Readings in anthropology and education.* Boston: Little, Brown.

Burns, R. B. (1984). How time is used in elementary schools: The activity structure of classrooms. In L. W. Anderson (Ed.), *Time and school learning: Theory, research and practice.* London: Croom Helm.

Cahir, S. R. (1978). *Activity between and within activity: Transition.* Unpublished doctoral dissertation, Georgetown University, Washington, DC.

Campbell, J. R. (1974). Can a teacher really make the difference? *School Science and Mathematics, 74,* 657–666.

Carter, K., & Doyle, W. (1982, March). *Variations in academic tasks in high- and average-ability classes.* Paper presented at the annual meeting of the American Educational Research Association, New York.

Cartledge, G., & Milburn, J. (1978). The case for teaching social skills in the classroom: A review. *Review of Educational Research, 48,* 133–156.

Cazden, C. B. (1981). Social contexts of learning to read. In J. T. Guthrie (Ed.), *Comprehension and teaching: Research reviews.* Newark, DE: International Reading Association.

Charles, C. M. (1981). *Building classroom discipline: From models to practice.* New York: Longman.

Clark, C., & Yinger, R. (1979). Teachers' thinking. In P. Peterson & H. Walberg (Eds.), *Research on teaching.* Berkeley, CA: McCutchan.

Clements, B. S. (1983). *Helping experienced teachers with classroom management: An experimental study* (R & D Rep. No. 6155). Austin: University of Texas, R & D Center for Teacher Education.

Coates, T. J., & Thoresen, C. E. (1976). Teacher anxiety: A review with recommendations. *Review of Educational Research, 46,* 159–184.

Cohen, E. G. (1979, April). *Status equalization in the desegregated school.* Paper presented at the annual meeting of the American Educational Research Association, San Francisco.

Cohen, E. G. (1980, September). *A multi-ability approach to the integrated classroom.* Paper presented at the annual meeting of the American Psychological Association, Montreal.

Cohen, E. G., Intili, J. K., & Robbins, S. H. (1979). Task and authority: A sociological view of classroom management. In D. L. Duke (Ed.), *Classroom management* (78th yearbook of the National Society for the Study of Education, Part 2). Chicago: University of Chicago Press.

Cone, R. (1978, March). *Teachers' decisions in managing student behavior.* Paper presented at the annual meeting of the American Educational Research Association, Toronto.

Cook-Gumperz, J., & Gumperz, J. J. (1982). Communicative competence in educational perspective. In L. C. Wilkinson (Ed.), *Communicating in classrooms* (pp. 13–24). New York: Academic Press.

Copeland, W. D. (1978). Processes mediating the relationship between cooperating-teacher and student-teacher classroom performance. *Journal of Educational Psychology, 70,* 95–100.

Copeland, W. D. (1983, April). *Classroom management and student teachers' cognitive abilities: A relationship.* Paper presented at the annual meeting of the American Educational Research Association, Montreal.

Cornbleth, C., & Korth, W. (April, 1983). *Doing the work: Teacher perspectives and meanings of responsibility.* Paper presented at the annual meeting of the American Educational Research Association, Montreal.

Cuban, L. (1982). Persistent instruction: The high school classroom, 1900–1980. *Phi Delta Kappan, 64,* 113–118.

Cusick, P. A. (1973). *Inside high school: The students' world.* New York: Holt, Rinehart & Winston.

Cusick, P. A., Martin, W., & Palonsky, S. (1976). Organizational structure and student behaviour in secondary school. *Journal of Curriculum Studies, 8*(1), 3–14.

Dahllof, U. S. (1971). *Ability grouping, content validity, and curriculum process analysis.* New York: Teachers College Press, Columbia University.

Davis, R. B., & McKnight, C. (1976). Conceptual, heuristic, and S-algorithmic approaches in mathematics teaching. *Journal of Children's Mathematical Behavior, 1*(Suppl. 1), 271–286.

Denham, C., & Lieberman, A. (Eds.). (1980). *Time to learn.* Washington, DC: National Institute of Education.

Denscombe, M. (1980a). "Keeping 'em quiet": The significance of noise for the practical activity of teaching. In P. Woods (Ed.), *Teacher strategies: Explorations in the sociology of the school* (pp. 61–83). London: Croom Helm.

Denscombe, M. (1980b). Pupil strategies and the open classroom. In P. Woods (Ed.), *Pupil strategies: Explorations in the sociology of the school* (pp. 50–73). London: Croom Helm.

deVoss, G. G. (1979). The structure of major lessons and collective student activity. *Elementary School Journal, 80,* 8–18.

Doyle, W. (1977). Paradigms for research on teacher effectiveness. In L. S. Shulman (Ed.), *Review of Research in Education, 5,* 163–199.

Doyle, W. (1978). Are students behaving worse than they used to behave? *Journal of Research and Development in Education, 2*(4), 3–16.

Doyle, W. (1979a). Classroom tasks and students' abilities. In P. L. Peterson & H. J. Walberg (Eds.), *Research on teaching: Concepts, findings and implications.* Berkeley, CA: McCutchan.

Doyle, W. (1979b). Making managerial decisions in classrooms. In D. L. Duke (Ed.), *Classroom management* (78th yearbook of the National Society for the Study of Education, Part 2). Chicago: University of Chicago Press.

Doyle, W. (1980). *Classroom management.* West Lafayette, IN: Kappa Delta Pi.

Doyle, W. (1981). Research on classroom contexts. *Journal of Teacher Education, 32*(6), 3–6.

Doyle, W. (1983). Academic work. *Review of Educational Research, 53*(2), 159–199.

Doyle, W. (1984). How order is achieved in classrooms: An interim report. *Journal of Curriculum Studies, 16*(3), 259–277.

Doyle, W., & Carter, K. (1984). Academic tasks in classrooms. *Curriculum Inquiry, 14*(2), 129–149.

Doyle, W., Sanford, J. P., Clements, B. S., French, B. S., & Emmer, E. T. (1983). *Managing academic tasks: Interim report of the junior high school study* (R & D Rep. 6186). Austin: University of Texas, R & D Center for Teacher Education, Austin.

Dreeben, R. (1973). The school as a workplace. In R. M. W. Travers (Ed.), *Second handbook of research on teaching* (pp. 450–473). Chicago: Rand McNally.

Dreikurs, R. (1957). *Psychology in the classroom: A manual for teachers.* New York: Harper & Row.

Dreikurs, R., & Cassel, P. (1972). *Discipline without tears.* New York: Hawthorn Books.

Duffy, G. G., & McIntyre, L. D. (1982). A naturalistic study of instructional assistance in primary-grade reading. *Elementary School Journal, 83*(1), 15–23.

Duke, D. L. (Ed.). (1979a). *Classroom management* (78th yearbook of the National Society for the Study of Education, Part 2). Chicago: University of Chicago Press.

Duke, D. L. (Ed.). (1979b). Editor's preface. In D. L. Duke (Ed.), *Classroom management* (78th yearbook of the National Society for the Study of Education, Part 2). Chicago: University of Chicago Press.

Duke, D. L. (Ed.). (1982). *Helping teachers manage classrooms.* Alexandria, VA: Association for Supervision and Curriculum Development.

Duke, D. L., & Meckel, A. M. (1980a). *Managing student behavior problems.* New York: Teachers College Press, Columbia University.

Duke, D. L., & Meckel, A. M. (1980b). The slow death of a public high school. *Phi Delta Kappan, 61*(10), 674–677.

Duke, D. L., & Meckel, A. M. (1984). *Teacher's guide to classroom management.* New York: Random House.

Durkin, D. (1979). What classroom observations reveal about reading comprehension instruction. *Reading Research Quarterly, 14,* 481–533.

Eaton, J. F., Anderson, C. W., & Smith, E. L. (1984). Students' misconceptions interfere with science learning: Case studies of fifth-grade students. *Elementary School Journal, 84,* 365–379.

Edelsky, C., Draper, K., & Smith, K. (1983). Hookin' 'em in at the start of school in a "whole language" classroom. *Anthropology and Education Quarterly, 14,* 257–281.

Edenhart-Pepe, M., Hudgins, B. B., & Miller, D. M. (1981, April). *Who is engaged more—teacher or students? An analysis of how activity structures affect student learning engagement.* Paper presented at the annual meeting of the American Educational Research Association, Los Angeles.

Eder, D. (1982a). Differences in communicative styles across ability groups. In L. C. Wilkinson (Ed.), *Communicating in classrooms* (pp. 245–264). New York: Academic Press.

Eder, D. (1982b). The impact of management and turn-allocation activities on student performance. *Discourse Processes, 5,* 147–159.

Elardo, R. (1978). Behavior modification in an elementary school: Problems and issues. *Phi Delta Kappan, 59,* 334–338.

Emmer, E. T. (1981). *Effective classroom management in junior high school mathematics classrooms* (R & D Rep. No. 6111). Austin: University of Texas, R & D Center for Teacher Education.

Emmer, E. T. (1983, April). *An investigation of heterogeneous elementary school classrooms.* Paper presented at the annual meeting of the American Educational Research Association, Montreal.

Emmer, E. T. (1984). *Classroom management: Research and implications* (R & D Rep. No. 6178). Austin: University of Texas, R & D Center for Teacher Education.

Emmer, E. T., & Evertson, C. M. (1981). Synthesis of research on classroom management. *Educational Leadership, 38*(4), 342–347.

Emmer, E., Evertson, C., & Anderson, L. (1980). Effective classroom management at the beginning of the school year. *Elementary School Journal, 80*(5), 219–231.

Emmer, E. T., Sanford, J. P., Clements, B. S., & Martin, J. (1982). *Improving classroom management and organization in junior high schools: An experimental investigation* (R & D Rep. No. 6153). Austin: University of Texas, R & D Center for Teacher Education.

Emmer, E. T., Sanford, J. P., Evertson, C. M., Clements, B. S., & Martin, J. (1981). *The Classroom Management Improvement Study: An experiment in elementary school classrooms* (R & D Rep. No. 6050). Austin: University of Texas, R & D Center for Teacher Education.

Englert, C. S., & Semmel, M. I. (1983). Spontaneous teacher decision making in interactive instructional contexts. *Journal of Educational Research, 77*(2), 112–121.

Erickson, F. (1982a). Classroom discourse as improvisation: Relationships between academic task structure and social participation structure in lessons. In L. C. Wilkinson (Ed.), *Communicating in classrooms* (pp. 153–181). New York: Academic Press.

Erickson, F. (1982b). Taught cognitive learning in its immediate environment: A neglected topic in the anthropology of education. *Anthropology and Education Quarterly, 13,* 149–180.

Erickson, F., & Mohatt, G. (1982). Cultural organization of participation structures in two classrooms of Indian students. In G. Spindler (Ed.), *Doing the ethnography of schooling.* New York: Holt, Rinehart & Winston.

Erickson, F., & Shultz, J. (1981). When is a context? Some issues and methods in the analysis of social competence. In J. L. Green & C. Wallat (Eds.), *Ethnography and language in educational settings.* Norwood, NJ: Ablex.

Everhart, R. B. (1979). The fabric of meaning in a junior high school. *Theory Into Practice, 18*(3), 152–157.

Evertson, C. M. (1982). Differences in instructional activities in higher- and lower-achieving junior high English and math classes. *Elementary School Journal, 82,* 329–350.

Evertson, C. M., & Emmer, E. T. (1982). Effective management at the beginning of the year in junior high classes. *Journal of Educational Psychology, 74*(4), 485–498.

Evertson, C. M., Emmer, E. T., Sanford, J. P., & Clements, B. S. (1983). Improving classroom management: An experiment in elementary classrooms. *Elementary School Journal, 84*(2), 173–188.

Evertson, C. M., Sanford, J. P., & Emmer, E. T. (1981). Effects of class heterogeneity in junior high school. *American Educational Research Journal, 18,* 219–232.

Felmlee, D., & Eder, D. (1983). Contextual effects in the classroom: The impact of ability groups on group attention. *Sociology of Education, 56,* 77–87.

Fisher, C., Berliner, D., Filby, N., Marliave, R., Cahen, L., Dishaw, M., & Moore, J. (1978). *Teaching behaviors, academic learning time and student achievement: Final report of Phase III-B, Beginning Teacher Evaluation Study* (Tech. Rep. No. V-1). San Francisco: Far West Laboratory.

Flanders, N. A. (1970). *Analyzing teacher behavior.* Reading, MA: Addison-Wesley.

Florio, S., Clark, C. M., Elmore, J. L., Martin, S. J., Maxwell, R. J., & Metheny, W. (1982, March). *What can you learn about writing in school? A case study in an elementary classroom.* Paper presented at the annual meeting of the American Educational Research Association, New York.

Florio, S., & Shultz, J. (1979). Social competence at home and at school. *Theory Into Practice, 18,* 234–243.

Foster, H. L. (1974). *Ribbin', jivin', and playin' the dozens: The unrecognized dilemma of inner-city schools.* Cambridge, MA: Ballinger.

Fuller, F. F. (1969). Concerns for teachers: A developmental conceptualization. *American Educational Research Journal, 6,* 207–226.

Gage, N. L. (1978). *The scientific basis of the art of teaching.* New York: Teachers College Press, Columbia University.

Gallup, G. H. (1983). The 15th annual Gallup poll of the public's attitudes toward the public schools. *Phi Delta Kappan, 65,* 33–47.

Gannaway, H. (1976). Making sense of school. In M. Stubbs & S. Delamont (Eds.), *Explorations in classroom observation.* London: John Wiley.

Glasser, W. (1969). *Schools without failure.* New York: Harper & Row.

Goldstein, J. M., & Weber, W. A. (1981, April). *Teacher managerial behaviors and on-task behavior: Three studies.* Paper presented at the annual meeting of the American Educational Research Association, Los Angeles.

Good, T. L. (1981). Teacher expectation and student perceptions: A decade of research. *Educational Leadership, 38,* 415–422.

Good, T. L. (1983). Classroom research: A decade of progress. *Educational Psychologist, 18*(3), 127–144.

Good, T. L., & Grouws, D. A. (1975). *Process–product relationships in fourth-grade mathematics classrooms* (Grant No. NEG-00-3-0123). Columbia: University of Missouri, College of Education.

Gordon, T. (1974). *Teacher effectiveness training.* New York: Peter H. Wyden.

Goss, S. S., & Ingersoll, G. M. (1981). *Management of disruptive and off-task behaviors: Selected resources.* Washington, DC: ERIC Clearinghouse on Teacher Education.

Grannis, J. C. (1978). Task engagement and the consistency of pedagogical controls: An ecological study of differently structured classroom settings. *Curriculum Inquiry, 8*(1), 3–36.

Green, J. L. (1983, April). *Lesson construction and student participation.* Paper presented at the annual meeting of the American Educational Research Association, Montreal.

Green, J. L., & Harker, J. O. (1982). Gaining access to learning: Conversational, social, and cognitive demands of group participation. In L. C. Wilkinson (Ed.), *Communicating in classrooms* (pp. 183–221). New York: Academic Press.

Grice, H. P. (1975). Logic and conversation. In P. Cole & J. L. Morgan (Eds.), *Syntax and semantics: Vol. 3. Speech acts.* New York: Academic Press.

Griffin, G. A., Barnes, S., O'Neal, S., Edwards, S., Defino, M. E., & Hukill, H. (1983). *Changing teacher practice: Final report of an experimental study* (R & D Rep. No. 9052). Austin: University of Texas, R & D Center for Teacher Education.

Griffin, P., & Mehan, H. (1979). Sense and ritual in classroom discourse. In F. Coulman (Ed.), *Conversational routine: Explorations in standardized communication situations and prepatterned speech.* The Hague: Mouton.

Gump, P. V. (1967). *The classroom behavior setting: Its nature and relation to student behavior* (*Final report*). Washington, DC: U.S. Office of Education, Bureau of Research. (ERIC Document Reproduction Service No. ED 015 515)

Gump, P. V. (1969). Intra-setting analysis: The third grade classroom as a special but instructive case. In E. Williams & H. Rausch (Eds.), *Naturalistic viewpoints in psychological research.* New York: Holt, Rinehart & Winston.

Gump, P. V. (1974). Operating environments in schools of open and traditional design. *School Review, 82*(4), 575–593.

Gump, P. V. (1975). *Ecological psychology and children.* Chicago: University of Chicago Press.

Gump, P. V. (1982). School settings and their keeping. In D. L. Duke (Ed.), *Helping teachers manage classrooms* (pp. 98–114). Alexandria, VA: Association for Supervision and Curriculum Development.

Hamilton, D. (1980). Adam Smith and the moral economy of the classroom system. *Journal of Curriculum Studies, 12,* 281–298.

Hamilton, D. (1981, January). *On simultaneous instruction and the early evolution of class teaching.* Unpublished manuscript, University of Glasgow.

Hammersley, M. (1974). The organization of pupil participation. *The Sociological Review, 22*(3), 355–368.

Hargreaves, D. H., Hester, S. K., & Mellor, F. J. (1975). *Deviance in classrooms.* Boston: Routledge & Kegan Paul.

Harker, J. O. (1983, April). *Contrasting the content of two story-reading lessons: A propositional analysis.* Paper presented at the annual meeting of the American Educational Research Association, Montreal.

Heap, J. L. (1980). What counts as reading: Limits to certainty in assessment. *Curriculum Inquiry, 10,* 265–292.

Henry, J. (1971). *On education.* New York: Random House.

Hoetker, J., & Ahlbrand, W. P. (1969). The persistence of the recitation. *American Educational Research Journal, 6,* 145–167.

Hoffman, J. V., & Clements, R. O. (1984). Reading miscues and teacher verbal feedback. *Elementary School Journal, 84,* 481–491.

Houseman, J. (1972). *An ecological study of interpersonal conflicts among preschool children.* Unpublished doctoral dissertation, Wayne State University, Detroit.

Humphrey, F. M. (1979). *"Shh!": A sociolinguistic study of teachers' turn-taking sanctions in primary school lessons.* Unpublished doctoral dissertation, Georgetown University, Washington, DC.

Hyman, R. T. (1974). *Teaching: Vantage points for study.* Englewood Cliffs, NJ: Prentice-Hall.

Irving, O., & Martin, J. (1982). Withitness: The confusing variable. *American Educational Research Journal, 19*(2), 313–319.

Jackson, P. (1968). *Life in classrooms.* New York: Holt, Rinehart & Winston.

Johnson, D. W., Maruyama, G., Johnson, R., Nelson, D., & Skon, L. (1981). Effects of cooperative, competitive, and individualistic goal structures on achievement: A meta-analysis. *Psychological Bulletin, 89,* 47–62.

Johnson, M., & Brooks, H. (1979). Conceptualizing classroom management. In D. L. Duke (Ed.), *Classroom management* (78th yearbook of the National Society for the Study of Education, Part 2). Chicago: University of Chicago Press.

Jones, V. F., & Jones, L. S. (1981). *Responsible classroom discipline.* Boston: Allyn & Bacon.

Jorgenson, G. W. (1977). Relationship of classroom behavior to the accuracy of the match between material difficulty and student ability. *Journal of Educational Psychology, 69*(1), 24–32.

Joyce, B. (1980). *Toward a theory of information processing in teaching* (Research Series No. 76). East Lansing: Michigan State University, Institute for Research on Teaching. (ERIC Document Reproduction Service No. ED 194 525)

Joyce, B., & Weil, M. (1972). *Models of teaching*. Englewood Cliffs, NJ: Prentice-Hall.

Kaplan, C. H., & White, M. A. (1980). Children's direction-following behavior in grades K-5. *Journal of Educational Research, 74*(1), 43–48.

King, L. H. (1980). *Student thought processes and the expectancy effect* (Research Rep. No. 80-1-8). Edmonton, Canada: University of Alberta, Centre for Research in Teaching.

King, L. H. (1983). Pupil classroom perceptions and the expectancy effect. *South Pacific Journal of Teacher Education, 11*(1), 54–70.

Korth, W., & Cornbleth, C. (1982, March). *Classroom activities as settings for cognitive learning opportunity and instruction*. Paper presented at the annual meeting of the American Educational Research Association, New York.

Kounin, J. S. (1970). *Discipline and group management in classrooms*. New York: Holt, Rinehart & Winston.

Kounin, J. S. (1983). *Classrooms: Individuals or behavior settings?* (Monographs in Teaching and Learning, No. 1) Bloomington: Indiana University, School of Education.

Kounin, J. S., & Doyle, P. H. (1975). Degree of continuity of a lesson's signal system and the task involvement of children. *Journal of Educational Psychology, 67*(2), 159–164.

Kounin, J., & Gump, P. (1958). The ripple effect in discipline. *Elementary School Journal, 59*, 158–162.

Kounin, J., & Gump, P. (1974). Signal systems of lesson settings and the task related behavior of preschool children. *Journal of Educational Psychology, 66*, 554–562.

Kowatrakul, S. (1959). Some behaviors of elementary school children related to classroom activities and subject areas. *Journal of Educational Psychology, 50*(3), 121–128.

Krantz, P. J., & Risley, T. R. (1977). Behavior ecology in the classroom. In K. D. O'Leary & S. G. O'Leary (Eds.), *Classroom management: The successful use of behavior modification* (2nd ed.). New York: Pergamon Press.

Lahey, B. B., & Rubinoff, A. (1981). Behavior therapy in education. In L. Michelson, M. Hersen, & S. M. Turner (Eds.), *Future perspectives in behavior therapy* (pp. 27–43). New York: Plenum Press.

Lancy, D. F. (1976). *The beliefs and behaviors of pupils in an experimental school: School settings*. Pittsburgh, PA: University of Pittsburgh, Learning R & D Center.

Lancy, D. F. (1978). The classroom as phenomenon. In D. Bar-Tal & L. Saxe (Eds.), *Social psychology of education* (pp. 111–132). Washington, DC: Hemisphere Publishing Corp.

LeCompte, M. D. (1978a). Establishing a workplace: Teacher control in the classroom. *Education and Urban Society, 11*, 87–106.

LeCompte, M. D. (1978b). Learning to work: The hidden curriculum of the classroom. *Anthropology and Education Quarterly, 9*(1), 22–37.

LeCompte, M. D. (1980). The civilizing of children: How young children learn to become students. In A. A. Van Fleet (Ed.), *Anthropology of education: Methods and applications* (pp. 105–127). Norman: University of Oklahoma.

Leeper, M., & Green, D. (1978). *The hidden costs of rewards: New perspective on the psychology of human motivation*. Hillsdale, NJ: Lawrence Erlbaum.

Leinhardt, G., Zigmond, N., & Cooley, W. W. (1981). Instruction in schools. *American Educational Research Journal, 18*, 343–361.

Levin, T., Libman, Z., & Amiad, R. (1980). Behavioral patterns of students under an individualized learning strategy. *Instructional Science, 9*, 85–100.

Lortie, D. C. (1973). Observations on teaching as work. In R. M. W. Travers (Ed.), *Second handbook of research on teaching*. Chicago: Rand McNally.

Lortie, D. C. (1975). *Schoolteacher*. Chicago: University of Chicago Press.

Lundgren, U. P. (1972). *Frame factors and the teaching process*. Stockholm: Elmquist and Wiksell.

MacLure, M., & French, P. (1980). Routes to right answers: On pupils' strategies for answering. In P. Woods (Ed.), *Pupil strategies: Explorations in the sociology of the school* (pp. 74–98). London: Croom Helm.

Mayers, P., Csikszentmihalyi, M., & Larson, R. (1978, March). *The daily experience of high school students*. Paper presented at the annual meeting of the American Educational Research Association, Toronto.

McDermott, R. P. (1976). *Kids make sense: An ethnographic account of the interactional management of success and failure in one first-grade classroom*. Unpublished doctoral dissertation, Stanford University, Stanford, CA.

McHoul, A. (1978). The organization of turns at formal talk in the classroom. *Language in Society, 7*(2), 183–213.

McLaughlin, T. F. (1976). Self-control in the classroom. *Review of Educational Research, 46*, 631–663.

Mehan, H. (1974). Accomplishing classroom lessons. In A. V. Cicourel, K. H. Jennings, S. H. M. Jennings, K. C. W. Leiter, R. MacKay, J. Mehan, & D. Roth (Eds.), *Language use and school performance*. New York: Academic Press.

Mehan, H. (1979). *Learning lessons: Social organization in a classroom*. Cambridge, MA: Harvard University Press.

Mehan, H. (1980). The competent student. *Anthropology and Education Quarterly, 11*(3), 131–152.

Mehan, H., Hertweck, A., Combs, S. E., & Flynn, P. J. (1982). Teachers' interpretations of students' behavior. In L. C. Wilkinson (Ed.), *Communicating in the classroom* (pp. 297–321). New York: Academic Press.

Merritt, M. (1982). Distributing and directing attention in primary classrooms. In L. C. Wilkinson (Ed.), *Communicating in the classroom* (pp. 223–244). New York: Academic Press.

Metz, M. (1978). *Classrooms and corridors*. Berkeley: University of California Press.

Moore, G. A. (1976). An anthropological view of urban education. In J. I. Roberts & K. Akinsanya (Eds.), *Educational patterns and cultural configurations*. New York: David McKay.

Morine-Dershimer, G. (1983). Instructional strategy and the "creation" of classroom status. *American Educational Research Journal, 20*, 645–661.

Morrison, B. S. (1982). *An investigation of reading as a learning activity in grade 9 social studies, science, and English classes*. Unpublished doctoral dissertation, University of Wisconsin, Madison.

Moskowitz, G., & Hayman, J. (1976). Success strategies of inner-city teachers: A year-long study. *Journal of Educational Research, 69*, 283–289.

Nash, R. (1976). Pupils' expectations of their teachers. In M. Stubbs & S. Delamont (Eds.), *Explorations in classroom observations*. London: John Wiley.

National Institute of Education. (1977). *Violent schools—safe schools: The safe school study report to the Congress*. Washington, DC: National Institute of Education.

National Opinion Research Center. (1981). *Discipline, order and student behavior in American high schools*. Washington, DC: National Center for Educational Statistics.

Natriello, G., & Dornbusch, S. M. (1980). Bringing behavior back in: The effects of student characteristics and behavior on the classroom behavior of teachers. *American Educational Research Journal, 20*(1), 29–43.

O'Leary, K. D., & O'Leary, S. G. (1977). *Classroom management: The successful use of behavior modification* (2nd ed.). New York: Pergamon.

PDK Commission on Discipline. (1982). *Handbook for developing schools with good discipline*. Bloomington, IN: Phi Delta Kappa.

Peterson, P., & Swing, S. (1982). Beyond time on task: Students' reports of their thought processes during direct instruction. *Elementary School Journal, 82*, 481–491.

Philips, S. U. (1972). Participant structures and communicative competence: Warm Springs children in community and classrooms. In C. B. Cazden, V. P. Johns, & D. Hymes (Eds.), *Functions of language in the classroom*. New York: Teachers College Press, Columbia University.

Pittman, S. I. (1984, April). *A cognitive ethnography and quantification of teachers' plans for managing students*. Paper presented at the annual meeting of the American Educational Research Association, New Orleans, LA.

Pittman, S. I. (1985). A cognitive ethnography and quantification of a first-grade teacher's selection routines for classroom management. *Elementary School Journal, 85*, 541–557.

Pollard, A. (1980). Teacher interests and changing situations of survival threat in primary school classrooms. In P. Woods (Ed.), *Teacher strategies: Explorations in the sociology of the school* (pp. 34–60). London: Croom Helm.

Potter, E. F. (1974). *Correlates of oral participation in classrooms.* Unpublished doctoral dissertation, University of Chicago.

Potter, E. F. (1977, April). *Children's expectancy of criticism for classroom achievement efforts.* Paper presented at the annual meeting of the American Educational Research Association, New York.

Pullis, M., & Cadwell, J. (1982). The influence of children's temperament characteristics on teachers' decision strategies. *American Educational Research Journal, 19*(2), 165–181.

Rosenshine, B. V. (1979). Content, time, and direct instruction. In P. L. Peterson & H. J. Walberg (Eds.), *Research on teaching.* Berkeley, CA: McCutchan.

Rosenshine, B. V. (1980). How time is spent in elementary classrooms. In C. Denham & A. Lieberman (Eds.), *Time to learn.* Washington, DC: National Institute of Education.

Rosenshine, B. V. (1983). Teaching functions in instructional programs. *Elementary School Journal, 83,* 335–351.

Ross, R. P. (1984). Classroom segments: The structuring of school time. In L. W. Anderson (Ed.), *Time and school learning: Theory, research and practice.* London: Croom Helm.

Rounds, T. S., Ward, B. A., Mergendoller, J. R., & Tikunoff, W. J. (1982). *Junior high school transition study: Vol. 2. Organization of instruction* (Rep. No. EPSSP-82-3). San Francisco: Far West Laboratory.

Rowe, M. B. (1974). Wait-time and rewards as instructional variables, their influence on language, logic, and fate control: 1. Wait-time. *Journal of Research in Science Teaching, 11,* 81–94.

Rusnock, M., & Brandler, N. (April, 1979). *Time off-task: Implications for learning.* Paper presented at the annual meeting of the American Educational Research Association, San Francisco.

Sanford, J. P., & Evertson, C. M. (1981). Classroom management in a low SES junior high: Three case studies. *Journal of Teacher Education, 32*(1), 34–38.

Sanford, J. P., & Evertson, C. M. (1983). Time use and activities in junior high classrooms. *Journal of Educational Research, 76,* 140–147.

Schmuck, R. A., & Schmuck, P. A. (1979). *Group processes in the classroom.* Dubuque, IA: William C. Brown.

Schumm, R. W. (1971). *Performances on multiple-attention measures as a predictor of the classroom management proficiency displayed by student teachers.* Unpublished doctoral dissertation, Indiana University Bloomington.

Schwebel, A. I., & Cherlin, D. L. (1972). Physical and social distancing in teacher–pupil relationships. *Journal of Educational Psychology, 63,* 543–550.

Scott, M. (1977). Some parameters of teacher effectiveness as assessed by an ecological approach. *Journal of Educational Psychology, 69*(3), 217–226.

Sharan, S. (1980). Cooperative learning in small groups: Recent methods and effects on achievement, attitudes, and ethnic relations. *Review of Educational Research, 50*(2), 241–272.

Sharp, R., & Green, A. (1975). *Education and social control: A study in progressive primary education.* London: Routledge & Kegan Paul.

Sherman, L. (1975). An ecological study of glee in a nursery school. *Child Development, 46,* 53–61.

Sheviakov, G. V., & Redl, F. (1944). *Discipline for today's children and youth.* Washington, DC: National Education Association, Department of Supervision and Curriculum Development.

Shimron, J. (1976). Learning activities in individually prescribed instruction. *Instructional Science, 5,* 391–401.

Short, B. L. (1975). *Investigation of the effects of the ecological setting of the public school classroom on student behavior.* Unpublished doctoral dissertation, University of California, San Francisco.

Shultz, J., & Florio, S. (1979). Stop and freeze: The negotiation of social and physical space in a kindergarten/first grade classroom. *Anthropology and Education Quarterly, 10*(3), 166–181.

Sieber, R. T. (1976). *Schooling in the bureaucratic classroom: Socialization and social reproduction in Chestnut Heights.* Unpublished doctoral dissertation, New York University.

Sieber, R. T. (1979a). Classmates as workmates: Informal peer activity in the elementary school. *Anthropology and Educational Quarterly, 10,* 207–235.

Sieber, R. T. (1979b). Schoolrooms, pupils, and rules: The role of informality in bureaucratic socialization. *Human Organization, 38*(3), 273–282.

Sieber, R. T. (1981). Socialization implications of school discipline, or how first-graders are taught to "listen". In R. T. Sieber & A. J. Gordon (Eds.), *Children and their organizations: Investigations in American culture* (pp. 18–43). Boston, MA: G. K. Hall.

Silverstein, J. M. (1979). *Individual and environmental correlates of pupil problematic and nonproblematic classroom behavior.* Unpublished doctoral dissertation, New York University.

Sinclair, J. M., & Coulthard, R. M. (1975). *Towards an analysis of discourse: The English used by teachers and pupils.* Oxford: Oxford University Press.

Slavin, R. E. (1980). Cooperative learning. *Review of Educational Research, 50*(2), 315–342.

Slavin, R. E. (1982, June). *When does cooperative learning increase student achievement?* (Contract No. NIE-G-80-0113). Washington, DC: National Institute of Education.

Slavin, R. E., Leavey, M., & Madden, N. A. (1984). Combining cooperative learning and individualized instruction: Effects on student mathematics achievement, attitudes, and behaviors. *Elementary School Journal, 84,* 409–422.

Smith, D. K. (1978, March). *A study of contrasting styles of teacher behavior.* Paper presented at the annual meeting of the Southwest Psychological Association, Atlanta, GA.

Smith, L. M., & Geoffrey, W. (1968). *The complexities of an urban classroom.* New York: Holt, Rinehart & Winston.

Snow, C. E., Dubber, C., & de Blauw, A. (1980). *Routines in mother–child interaction: Slots and fillers.* Unpublished manuscript, Harvard University, Graduate School of Education, Cambridge, MA.

Soar, R. S., & Soar, R. M. (1983, February). Context effects in the teaching–learning process. In D. C. Smith (Ed.), *Essential knowledge for beginning educators.* Washington, DC: American Association of Colleges for Teacher Education.

Solomon, D., & Kendall, A. J. (1976). Individual characteristics and children's performance in "open" and "traditional" classroom settings. *Journal of Educational Psychology, 68*(5), 613–625.

Sommer, R. (1969). *Personal space: The behavioral basis of design.* Englewood Cliffs, NJ: Prentice–Hall.

Spaulding, R. L. (1983, December). Applications of low-inference observation in teacher education. In D. C. Smith (Ed.), *Essential knowledge for beginning educators* (pp. 80–100). Washington, DC: American Association of Colleges for Teacher Education.

Spencer-Hall, D. A. (1981). Behind the teacher's back. *Elementary School Journal, 81,* 280–289.

Stake, R. E., & Easley J. A. (1978). *Case studies in science education* (Vols. 1 and 2). Urbana: University of Illinois, Center for Instructional Research and Curriculum Evaluation, Committee on Culture and Cognition.

Stebbins, R. A. (1974). *The disorderly classroom: Its physical and temporal conditions* (Monographs in Education No. 12). St. Johns, Canada: Memorial University of Newfoundland, Faculty of Education, Committee on Publications.

Stebbins, R. A. (1980). The role of humour in teaching: Strategy and self-expression. In P. Woods (Ed.), *Teacher strategies: Explorations in the sociology of the school* (pp. 84–97). London: Croom Helm.

Stodolsky, S. S. (1981, April). *Subject matter constraints on the ecology of classroom instruction.* Paper presented at the annual meeting of the American Educational Research Association, Los Angeles.

Stodolsky, S. S. (1984). Frameworks for studying instructional processes in peer work-groups. In P. L. Peterson, L. C. Wilkinson, & M. Hallinan (Eds.), *The social context of instruction.* New York: Academic Press.

Stodolsky, S. S., Ferguson, T. L., & Wimpelberg, K. (1981). The recitation persists, but what does it look like? *Journal of Curriculum Studies, 13,* 121–130.

Symonds, P. M. (1934). *Mental hygiene of the school child.* New York: Macmillan.

Tanner, L. N. (1978). *Classroom discipline for effective teaching and learning.* New York: Holt, Rinehart & Winston.

Thompson, M., Brassell, W., Persons, S., Tucker, R., & Rollins, H. (1974). Contingency management in the schools: How often and how well does it work? *American Educational Research Journal, 11,* 19–28.

Thorndike, E. L. (1913). *Educational psychology: The orginal nature of man* (Vol. 1). New York: Teachers College Press, Columbia University.

Tikunoff, W. J., & Ward, B. A. (1978). *A naturalistic study of the initiation of students into three classroom social systems* (Rep. No. A-78-11). San Francisco: Far West Laboratory.

Totusek, P. F., & Staton-Spicer, A. Q. (1982). Classroom seating preference as a function of student personality. *The Journal of Experimental Education, 50*(3), 159–163.

Tousignant, M., & Siedentop, D. (1982, November). *A qualitative analysis of task structures in required secondary physical education classes.* Unpublished manuscript, Université Laval, Département d'education physique, Ste-foy, Quebec.

Trenholm, S., & Rose, T. (1981). The compliant communicator: Teacher perceptions of appropriate classroom behavior. *The Western Journal of Speech Communication, 45,* 13–26.

Wallat, C., & Green, J. L. (1979). Social rules and communicative contexts in kindergarten. *Theory Into Practice, 18*(4), 275–284.

Warren, R. L. (1973). The classroom as a sanctuary for teachers: Discontinuities in social control. *American Anthropologist, 75,* 280–291.

Weinstein, C. S. (1979). The physical environment of the school: A review of the research. *Review of Educational Research, 49*(4), 557–610.

West, W. G. (1975). Participant observation research on the social construction of everyday classroom order. *Interchange, 6*(4), 35–43.

Westbury, I. (1973). Conventional classrooms, "open" classrooms and the technology of teaching. *Journal of Curriculum Studies, 5,* 99–121.

White, M. A. (1975). Natural rates of teacher approval and disapproval in the classroom. *Journal of Applied Behavior Analysis, 8,* 367–372.

Whitmer, S. P. (1982, March). *A descriptive multimethod study of teacher judgment during the marking process.* Paper presented at the annual meeting of the American Educational Research Association, New York.

Willower, D. J. (1975). Some comments on inquiries on schools and pupil control. *Teachers College Record, 77,* 219–230.

Willower, D. J., Eidell, T. L., & Hoy, W. K. (1973). *The school and pupil control ideology* (Penn State Studies No. 24). University Park: Pennsylvania State University.

Wilson, B. L., Rosenholtz, S. J., & Rosenholtz, S. H. (April, 1983). *Effect of task and authority structures on student task engagement.* Paper presented at the annual meeting of the American Educational Research Association, Montreal.

Wolfgang, C. H., & Glickman, C. D. (1980). *Solving discipline problems: Strategies for classroom teachers.* Boston: Allyn & Bacon.

Woods, P. (1976). Having a laugh: An antidote to schooling. In M. Hammersley & P. Woods (Eds.), *The process of schooling: A sociological reader* (pp. 178–187). London: Routledge & Kegan Paul.

Woods, P. (1978). Negotiating the demands of school work. *Journal of Curriculum Studies, 10,* 309–327.

Woods, P. (1979). *The divided school.* London: Routledge & Kegan Paul.

Woolfolk, A. E., & Brooks, D. M. (1985). Beyond words: The influence of teachers' nonverbal behaviors on students' perceptions and performances. *Elementary School Journal, 85,* 513–528.

Workman, E., & Hector, M. (1978). Behavioral self-control in classroom settings: A review of the literature. *Journal of School Psychology, 16,* 227–236.

Wright, H. F. (1967). *Recording and analyzing child behavior.* New York: Harper & Row.

Yinger, R. J. (1977). *A study of teacher planning: Description and theory development using ethnographic and information processing methods.* Unpublished doctoral dissertation, Michigan State University, East Lansing.

Yinger, R. J. (1979). Routines in teacher planning. *Theory Into Practice, 18* (3), 163–169.

Yinger, R. J. (1980). A study of teacher planning. *Elementary School Journal, 80,* 107–127.

15.
Classroom Discourse

Courtney B. Cazden
Harvard University

The study of linguistic phenomena in school settings should seek to answer educational questions. We are interested in linguistic forms only insofar as through them we can gain insight into the social events of the classroom and thereby into the understandings which students achieve. Our interest is in the social contexts of cognition: speech unites the cognitive and the social. The actual (as opposed to the intended) curriculum consists in the meanings enacted or realized by a particular teacher and class. In order to learn, students must use what they already know so as to give meaning to what the teacher presents to them. Speech makes available to reflection the processes by which they relate new knowledge to old. But this possibility depends on the social relationships, the communication system, which the teacher sets up.
(*National Institute of Education, 1974, p. 1*)

Introduction

The study of classroom discourse is the study of that communication system. Spoken language is the medium by which much teaching takes place and in which students demonstrate to teachers much of what they have learned. Spoken language is also an important part of the identities of all the participants.

Variation in ways of speaking is a universal fact of social life. Schools are the first larger institution to which children come from their families and home neighborhoods and are expected not only to attend (as in church) but to participate. Especially in this period of school consolidation and desegregation, and continuing migration across state and national borders, classrooms usually include people — adults and children — from different linguistic backgrounds. Differences in how something is said, and even when, can be matters of only temporary adjustment, or they can seriously impair effective teaching and accurate evaluation. It is essential, therefore, to consider the classroom communication system as a problematic medium that cannot be ignored as transparent by anyone interested in teaching or learning.

While there would be general agreement among educational researchers on the importance of spoken language in the process of education, there is not agreement on how it can best be studied and understood. Two research traditions have developed. Koehler describes both from her perspective as Director of the Division of Teaching and Learning of the National Institute of Education (NIE) (1978):

> Two types of teaching process studies have evolved: those which attempt to describe or define the process and those which attempt to determine which teaching processes are effective in relation to desired outcomes, such as student achievement. The latter type, called process–product research by Dunkin and Biddle (1974) has dominated research on teaching for the last 10 years. For example, eight chapters of Dunkin and Biddle's work (1974) were devoted to process–product studies while only one was descriptive (Chapter 7). However, interest in descriptive classroom research is increasing and has attracted to the study of classrooms researchers from a number of different disciplines: linguists, ecological psychologists, cognitive psychologists, [anthropologists,] and sociologists. (p. 3)

The author thanks reviewers Dell Hymes (Graduate School of Education, University of Pennsylvania) and Michael Stubbs (Department of Linguistics, University of Nottingham) for their critical comments, and Stubbs for his help with British references as well.

In the process-product tradition, the independent variables to which measurements of learning outcomes are related include frequencies of categories of classroom talk, for example, higher-order questions or teacher praise. Numerous category systems have been developed for such observations, of which Flanders's (1970) is the best known. In the descriptive traditions, coding systems are eschewed until it becomes clear in the course of the research which categories of behavior are meaningful to the participants themselves. As a label contrasting with process-product (P-P), I will use "sociolinguistic" (Sc), although methodologies to be discussed are more varied than that term implies.

A fundamental difference between P-P and Sc research is evident just from a glance at their research reports. Because P-P researchers code classroom talk on the spot into pre-established categories, their reports contain tables of frequencies, but include samples of classroom language only as examples of code categories, and even then not necessarily from the classroom under study. Sc researchers, by contrast, work from transcriptions of audio or video recordings of classroom life or, less often, from detailed observational notes. Their reports may also include frequency counts, but important place is given to qualitative analyses of excerpts of actual classroom talk.

The two traditions have developed in separation. When Flanders reviewed *Functions of Language in the Classroom* (Cazden, John, & Hymes, 1972), one of the first publications of Sc work, he noted that, "Having been interested in classroom communication for 25 years, my own interest in the book began with the excitement of discovering that reference was made to work which I recognized on only one page.... What we seem to be witnessing, if this book is taken as an example, is the development of quite separate disciplines concerned with language and its usage" (1974, p. 47). That separation continued, as can be seen from the publishing history of the *Journal of Classroom Interaction*, first started as the *Classroom Observation Newsletter* by Flanders and Anita Simon, one of the editors of the Mirrors for Behavior anthologies of classroom observation instruments. In all the issues from 1976, when the newsletter became a journal, through 1982, only two articles include utterances of the teacher and students being studied.

Philosophical and methodological differences between P-P and Sc research are part of a larger controversy in educational and social science research. The two perspectives are often called positivistic and "interpretive," respectively. Bellack (1978), Mishler (1979) and Geertz (1980) give clear discussions on a continuum from focus on research on teaching (Bellack) to focus on social science in general (Geertz). Bredo and Feinberg's reader (1983) adds a third tradition of "critical theory."

Because P-P research is included in other chapters, this chapter will focus on Sc research that has developed in the last 20 years in both the United States (US) and the United Kingdom (UK). As Stubbs accurately asserts with respect to my categorization of studies, many included in this chapter "are very much at the positivistic end of the spectrum" (personal communication 11/83). My primary criterion has been not philosophical perspective but the presence of qualitative analyses of actual classroom talk.

History

The history of one core strand of the US work can be chronicled from Cazden (1972), Koehler (1978) and Green (1983). It developed within a larger but only slightly older field, the ethnography of communication. (See Bauman & Sherzer, 1975, for a history and overview.)

Hymes's programmatic call for an ethnography of communication appeared in 1962. Three years later, just after the beginning of HeadStart and the rest of President Johnson's "war on poverty," the US Office of Education initiated a small interdisciplinary conference of anthropologists, linguists, psychologists and sociologists to suggest priorities for research on children's language and its relation to school success. Participants at the conference were concerned about the deficit models of minority children's language then gaining prominence, and about the undue emphasis on dialect differences in intervention programs. One theme of the conference discussion was the need for "contrastive sociolinguistic" research on differences in language use, not dialects, between home and school.

The following year, at a larger follow-up conference, Hymes gave the first presentation of his paper "On communicative competence" (1971), which has influenced much subsequent work. In 1972, *Functions of Language in the Classroom* (Cazden et al., 1972) appeared, with contributions from many of the participants at those two conferences. It was intended to report substantive knowledge, interest other researchers, and—as Hymes (1972) argued in his Introduction—encourage teachers to become their own ethnographers. As Bauman and Sherzer (1975) point out, 1972 was an important year in the larger field, bringing a still classic reader in the ethnography of communication (Gumperz & Hymes, 1972) and the beginning of the most important journal in the field, *Language in Society*.

Related to the ethnography of communication within anthropology is a subfield of sociology, ethnomethodology. Cicourel and his colleagues (1974) presented the first classroom studies from this perspective, and much subsequent research on classroom discourse has adapted methodology from the "conversational analysts," especially Sacks, Schegloff, and Jefferson (1974).

In 1974, the National Institute of Education assembled a set of panels to suggest an agenda for research on teaching. One panel was on "Teaching as a linguistic process in a cultural setting." The quote at the beginning of this chapter is the first paragraph of that panel's report. (It was actually written by UK researcher Douglas Barnes, who was prevented from attending by visa problems at the last minute.) And in 1977, NIE included in its Basic Skills Grants Announcement a request for proposals on "Teaching as a Linguistic Process." Green (1983) gives an integrated summary of the research funded at that time.

Viewing research in the UK from across the Atlantic, it is easier to see categories of people and their research interests than to understand their historical development. Four strands can be distinguished. First in time seems to be the work of teachers of English: *Language, the Learner and the School* by Barnes, Britton, and Rosen on behalf of the London Association for the Teaching of English (1969, revised edition 1971, and second revised edition in press). Chapter headings indicate the authors' concerns: "Language in secondary classrooms,"

"Talking to learn," and "Towards a language policy across the curriculum." Looking back on his own first research conducted in 1966 with a group of secondary teachers, Barnes (1971) writes:

> I saw it as a preliminary investigation of the interaction between the linguistic expectations (drawn from home and primary school experience) brought by pupils to their secondary schools, and the linguistic demands set up (implicitly or explicitly) by teachers in the classrooms. It seemed likely that extraneous barriers were introduced into children's learning (a) by linguistic forms whose function was social rather than intrinsic to the material and processes being learnt, and (b) by unfamiliar socio-linguistic demands and constraints arising in the control system of the secondary school. (p. 14)

A second strand is the "new sociology of education" represented first by Young (1971), and discussed historically in Karabel and Halsey (1976) and the Introduction to Woods and Hammersley (1977). Theory and methodology is taken from the same ethnomethodological sources as the work of Cicourel in the US. But in the UK, more than in the US, research is focused on how—within the school—social inequalities are (re)produced.

Third is the work of linguists, notably Sinclair and Coulthard (1975), who hoped to develop a comprehensive scheme for the analysis of discourse and started in the classroom:

> with a more simple type of spoken discourse [than normal conversation], one which has much more overt structure, where one participant has acknowledged responsibility for the direction of the discourse, for deciding who shall speak when, and for introducing and ending topics. We also wanted a situation where all participants were genuinely trying to communicate, and where potentially ambiguous utterances were likely to have one accepted meaning. We found the kind of situation we wanted in the classroom.

Fourth and last is the work of educational researchers who were critical of American P-P research and believed that ethnography and linguistics could contribute to the study of classroom talk. Chanan and Delamont (1975) and Stubbs and Delamont (1976) include early examples of this work; Stubbs (1983) and Delamont (1983) are revisions of work first published in 1976; and a reader by Stubbs and Hillier (1983) presents a diverse group of UK studies.

The predominance of anthropological perspectives in the US and sociological perspectives in the UK brings a difference in research focus "between a preoccupation with race and culture on the one hand, and with social class on the other" (Delamont & Atkinson, 1980, p. 148). And that in turn helps to explain the difference in grade level where most research has been done: in primary grades in the US because that is where cultural differences are expected to have their greatest impact as children first confront the culture of the school; in secondary schools in the UK where social class inequalities are most marked. (A UK study by Willes [1983] of the first few weeks of school for 5-year olds, including Asian immigrant children, is an exception to this pattern but was not available in time to be included in this chapter.)

Fortunately, awareness of research across the Atlantic is increasing on both sides. In this chapter, research will be categorized and discussed without regard for country of origin.

Assumptions and Constructs

As part of her summary of the studies funded by NIE in 1978, Green (1983) presents a set of assumptions and constructs derived from published and unpublished papers and interviews. Following is a shortened list from her discussion:

- Face-to-face interaction, between teacher and students and among students, is governed by context-specific rules.
- Activities have participation structures, with rights and obligations for participation. Contextualization cues are the verbal and nonverbal cues (pitch, stress, and intonation; gesture, facial expression and physical distance) that signal how utterances are to be understood, and inferencing is required for conversational comprehension. Rules for participation are implicit, conveyed and learned through interaction itself.
- Meaning is context specific. All instances of a behavior are not functionally equivalent, and messages can serve multiple functions.
- Frames of reference are developed over time and guide individual participation. Frame clashes result from differences in perception developed in past interactional experiences. Overt clashes are observable to participants and researchers, but covert clashes requiring a finer level of analysis can also contribute to negative evaluations of student ability.
- Complex communicative demands are placed on both teachers and students by the diversity of classroom communicative structures, and teachers evaluate student ability from observing communicative performance. (1983, Table II and pp. 174–186)

Green (1983) writes that these constructs:

> serve multiple purposes. They are the underpinnings of the emerging field in that they form a framework that guides observation, collection, and analysis; they are also the products of the analysis. That is, the findings from these studies further refine our knowledge of each construct, how it functions as a guide in observing behavior in natural situations, and how it functions within and across various classrooms and other educational settings. (p. 171)

These ideas will appear often in this chapter, but one construct—context—deserves more preliminary discussion. Historically, as Hymes (1982) points out, context has been ignored in linguistics:

> "Context" has had a constant meaning, yet a changing content. It has always been a word for what lay beyond the object of attention.... something to which to appeal, not something to analyze. Finally to incorporate the analysis of context into linguistics would transform linguistics, making it a realization of the program of the "ethnography of speaking," or other sociolinguistic perspectives. (pp. 13–14)

Research on classroom discourse, influenced as it has been by the program of the ethnography of speaking, does not ignore context. As Green's list makes clear, it is central to all this work. But when we look more closely at how context enters into analyses of classroom discourse, we find two relationships.

One relationship is more obvious. Context is the situation as the speaker finds it, antecedent to the moment of speaking; and it is the rules for speaking in such a context to which the speaker's utterances must be appropriate. If, for example the teacher asks a child, "What did we put in the soup?", referring to yesterday's cooking experience, and the child answers, "Dunno, what?" that would be an inappropriate response in the classroom context. It is not appropriate at school, as it might be at home, for the child to ask the adult to provide the answer. Much research on classroom discourse attempts to explicate the rules governing appropriate language use that children must learn.

But speakers do not only conform to rules and fit their speech appropriately to a pre-existing context. They actively speak to create and change the context. As Erickson (1975) says:

> We could see the situation as a system of rules for interaction that mediates between the person and the sociocultural system—a context for interaction to which persons adapt themselves, ... and in spite of which persons occasionally transcend the societal and the situational rules, redefining the situation itself in the process of performing it. (p. 484)

Teachers create and change contexts by means of language innumerable times each day. Within the same seating arrangement of a single group of children, for example, they change the context from sharing time (with one set of rules for participation) to planning for worktime (with another set of rules) (Dorr-Bremme, 1982). The successes and failures of classroom management can be construed as largely a matter of successes and failures in subtle aspects of this kind of creative language use.

It is easier to think of teachers as enacting this context-creating and context-changing role, and they may do so more often. But research shows students playing this role as well. In descriptions of peer teaching episodes in a primary classroom, Cazden et al. (1979) show how child tutors were more or less effective in this aspect of language use. Tutor Greg spoke appropriately (in the first meaning) to the teacher when, in setting the stage for his forthcoming tutoring, he said in a polite, indirect way, "Why don't you let 'em get a desk?" Then, as his tutees arrived, he shifted to unmitigated direct imperatives: "Come here. Get up and get on this side." To his tutees there was no context for him to speak appropriately in as there had been with the teacher. He appropriately created the context (second meaning) in which he was "in command" by how, as well as what, he said.

How any one researcher weights these two relationships between utterance and context can seem to depend on that researcher's point of view; like the reversible figures of the psychology of perception, what one sees depends on how one looks. But Bateson (1972) argues that conceiving the relationship in the first way is a heuristic error copied from the natural sciences, and that only the second is an accurate description:

> I speak of an action or utterance as occurring "in a context," and this conventional way of talking suggests that the particular action is a "dependent" variable, while the context is the "independent" or determining variable. But this view...is likely to distract the reader —as it has distracted me—from perceiving the ecology of the ideas which together constitute the small subsystem which I call "context." This heuristic error—copied like so many others from the ways of thought of the physicist and chemist—requires correction. It is important to see the particular utterance or action as part of the ecological subsystem called context and not as the product or effect of what remains of the context after the piece which we want to explain has been cut away from it. (p. 338).

Bateson's statement can encompass both relationships if we realize that speaking appropriately in the first meaning is not just passive conformity to a context that has an independent existence, but actively reaffirms, and thereby strengthens, the prevailing shared interpretation of the context all the participants are in; and conversely that action effective in changing the situation in the second meaning may be considered just as appropriate as action that serves to maintain it. See Wooton (1975, Ch. 3) for further general discussion; Lemke (1982, P–18 and passim) and Streeck (1980) for discussion with classroom examples.

Chapter Overview

The rest of this chapter is divided into the following sections:

- Events and their participation structures
- Features of the teacher-talk register
- Cultural differences and differential treatment
- Interactions among peers
- Classroom discourse and student learning
- Some decisions about methods

This list of headings is far from an elegant set. Two are defined by the unit that is the focus of attention: event or register feature; another two are defined by participants: students who are, or are treated as, different, and peers; still another considers relationships between language and learning or cognition. All the studies could be categorized in more than one way, and cross references are frequent.

Kinds of classroom discourse not discussed include: pre-school programs, second language and bilingual education, classrooms for the deaf using some combination of verbal and sign language, and tertiary classrooms where learning to talk in particular ways is an important part of vocational training. (Consider, for example, the heated controversy at Harvard Law School in 1982–3 when the faculty proposed to grade class participation, and students feared both increased competitiveness and opportunities for subtle discrimination, since speaking, unlike writing, cannot be evaluated anonomously.)

Also not discussed are powerful influences on classroom discourse—some obvious, others subtle—that come from outside the classroom walls. Speech is inherently sensitive to context, and the classroom context is not wholly of the participants' making. Examples that come quickly to mind are the effect on the cognitive level of teachers' questions of how children, and thereby teachers themselves, are evaluated; and the influence of living in a society stratified by class, race, and sex on how teachers hear children's talk and infer their abilities. Bracketing out such influences and considering classroom discourse as if it were the autonomous construction of its participants is a justifiable research strategy. But there is the attendant danger that we will continue to ignore those extra-classroom influences when we try to stimulate change.

In the areas of research that are included, giving more than usual space to the methods and findings of specific studies seemed advisable for two reasons. First, since this is the first Handbook review, reference to as many good studies as possible should make it easier for future researchers. Second, there is no single method for discourse analysis. Two new texts in the field with the same title, *Discourse Analysis* (Brown & Yule, 1983 and Stubbs, 1983), have little content in common. And many of the studies included in this chapter would probably fall outside all three authors' definition of the field and into what Stubbs calls "related studies ... from other disciplines" (1983, p. 13). Therefore, I will point to productive methods and cite their sources as we go along, and then return to more general comments on method at the end.

Throughout the chapter, the central question of understanding how "speech unites the cognitive and the social" will be kept in view.

Events and Their Participation Structures

A classroom day divides easily into events with labels familiar to participants: math lesson, reading group, etc. (though observers may deliberately and productively make "the familiar strange"—for example, by asking "when is reading" [Griffin, 1977]). Berliner (1983) calls for more precise description of the structure of these "subenvironments": the rules and norms that guide behavior in them and "the place holders in the scripts or schemas for behavior that are formed in each" (p. 12). Sc research includes analyses of talk in some of the common events: lessons (or recitations), worktime, sharing time ("show and tell" or "news"), and reading groups. Research on lessons and worktime is discussed here; research on sharing time and reading groups is included in the section on cultural differences and differential treatment.

This research can also be categorized by methodology rather than event. Some researchers develop a comprehensive system that can encompass all the talk. Other researchers focus on one aspect of events—the participation structure—without attempting to categorize each utterance. Still other researchers focus on particular slots in an event structure, such as teacher questions and responses to student answers, and student requests to an otherwise engaged teacher.

Comprehensive Analyses of Lesson Structure

Lessons are not only a common classroom speech event, they are also the best documented. Hoetker and Ahlbrand (1969) give a 50-year history, and many of the P-P coding schemes were designed for their analysis. In Sc research, five comprehensive analyses have been made: Bellack, Kliebard, Hyman, and Smith (1966) discussed in Dunkin and Biddle (1974); Sinclair and Coulthard (1975) and Mehan (1979) discussed here; Malcolm (1979, 1982) discussed in the section on cultural

differences; and Lemke (1982) discussed both here and in the section on discourse and learning.

All analyses of lessons identify as the criterial or "unmarked" discourse structure a three-part sequence of teacher initiation, student response and teacher evaluation (IRE). But they differ in analysis of the units that fit into each of these three structural slots, and in the larger units of which such sequences are a part. Mehan's work was done in one primary classroom, while Sinclair and Coulthard's was done in a larger set of older elementary grades.

MEHAN

Four aspects of Mehan's analysis are noteworthy. First, he presents a formal statement of lesson structure (Figure 15.1). Hymes (1972b) suggests two purposes of such formal statements: with respect to the event itself, "a considerable clarification of what one understood to be the structure has been demanded. The form of the events is disengaged ... from the verbal foliage obligatory in prose sentences, and can be more readily seen" and compared (p. 66). From Mehan's analysis, for example, it is easier to see similarities with homework collection in another classroom (Cazden et al, 1980) and even book reading sessions between parents and younger children (Cazden, 1983a). With respect to the communicative competence of individuals, "it is through some form of formal statement that one can commit oneself to a precise claim as to what it is a member of society knows in knowing how to participate in a speech act" (Hymes, 1972b, p. 66). In the case of classroom lessons, it is reasonable to consider the lesson structure as part of the communicative competence of the teacher, but children may be responding to more fragmentary and local cues.

Second, Mehan reports the frequency with which the discourse in his corpus of nine lessons fits his model, and discusses all the talk that doesn't fit. To a teacher, his analyses of various tactics for "getting through" may seem more true to life than the formal model. (Cf. McHoul's turn-taking model (1978) with observations from secondary classrooms in England and Australia but with no evidence about how much of the recorded talk fits the model.)

Third, because he works from videotapes, Mehan has additional nonverbal evidence for the psychological reality (at least to the teacher) of the larger unit—topically related set (TRS)—into which the IRE sequences are organized. The beginning and end of each TRS is signaled by a combination of kinesic, verbal and paralinguistic behavior.

Fourth, Mehan tracks changes over time in the children's participation. While one can say that the structure is a psychological reality to the teacher from the beginning, not so to the children. Mehan tracks their progress as they respond more appropriately (in timing and form) as well as correctly (in

Lesson ——————▶ Opening Phase + Instructional Phase + Closing Phase
Opening, Closing Phase ——————▶ Directive + Informative
Instructional Phase ——————▶ TRS + TRS
TRS ——————▶ Basic + Conditional Sequence (or Interactional Sequence)
Instructional Sequence ——————▶ Initiation + Reply + Evaluation

Fig. 15.1. Lesson components displayed as rewrite rules. From *Learning Lessons* (p. 75) by H. Mehan, 1979. Cambridge: Harvard University Press. Reprinted by permission.

content) to the teacher's questions, and as they become more effective in getting the floor with student initiations. In short, they learn to speak within the structure he describes. It is important to say "speak within the structure" rather than "learn the structure", because the children may be learning the meaning of local cues, such as the teacher's posture and intonation, rather than the structure of the speech event as a whole. (See Willes, 1983, for a study of young children's socialization into classroom discourse.)

SINCLAIR AND COULTHARD

Because Sinclair and Coulthard are linguists interested in speech act theory, an important contribution of their (1975) analysis is the discussion of form-function relationships: how particular words or utterances have particular interpretations in the classroom: for example, how the syntactic question, "Can you play the piano, John?" can be understood immediately and unequivocally as a command. Their answer is given in three rules diagrammed in Figure 15.2. In the piano playing example, the subject is the addressee, the action is not proscribed, there is a modal *can*, and the question refers to an action feasible at the moment; thus the meaning of a command. As Sinclair and Coulthard point out, preconditions for the interpretation of such indirect directives stipulated in abstract speech act theory — "B has the ability to do X" and "A has the right to tell B to do X" — are derived from the general rights and obligations of classroom participants and do not need to be invoked separately for the interpretation of a particular utterance. (See Burton, 1981, and Stubbs, 1981a, for critical comment on studies using the Sinclair and Coulthard scheme; and Sinclair and Brazil [1982, Part 1] for revisions in the 1975 model).

OTHER STUDIES OF LESSON STRUCTURE

A large study by Shuy and Griffin included analyses of lesson structure, but the only published excerpts are in pamphlets for teachers with accompanying videotapes. *Teacher Talk Works*

(Cahir & Kovac, 1981b) generally corroborates Mehan but has more on the nature of sanctions when children "speak out of turn". *It's Your Turn* (Cahir & Kovac, 1981a) also corroborates Mehan but finds additional turn-taking devices. *What's What with Questions* (Kovac & Cahir, 1981) includes clear diagrams on the relation of question intonation to meaning. Lemke (1982) describes alternatives to the IRE sequence he found in high school science lessons, such as duologs, debates, and true discussion.

Participation Structures

The construct of participation structure — the rights and obligations of participants with respect to who can say what, when, and to whom — is a necessary part of any analysis of classroom discourse. In the work of Erickson and his colleagues, it is the main focus. The construct was first introduced as "participant structure" by Philips (1972). Erickson changed the name to "participation structure" to connote a more dynamic process.

The title of Erickson and Schultz's methodological paper (1977) captions the analytical problem: "When is a context?" That is, what are the contextualization cues (Gumperz, 1977) by which we (researchers or participants) determine the implicit rules for appropriate talk operative at any moment. Contexts in the sense of these rules vary in discernible ways within, as well as between, situations. Philips contrasted patterns between situations at home and at school. Erickson et al. have also analysed within-situation changes from one phase of an event to another. The result is an even more complex picture of this aspect of discourse structure and, therefore, of the demands made on participants' communicative competence.

The analytic task is to determine, starting from the activity as a whole, the junctures between phases of the activity, the cues that mark the junctures, and the participation structure in each phase. This is done by repeated viewings of the videotape record, often supplemented by viewing sessions with the teacher. (See also Au & Mason, 1982).

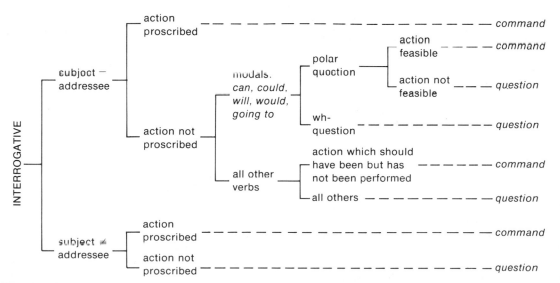

Fig. 15.2. The classification of an interrogative by situation. From *Towards an Analysis of Discourse: The English Used by Teachers and Pupils* (p. 31) by J. Sinclair and M. Coulthard, 1975. Copyright 1975 by Oxford University Press. Reprinted by permission.

This analytic method can be applied to single focus activities such as whole group meetings and to multifocus activities such as worktime, as well as to smaller units such as a tic-tac-toe game. It thus can tell us something about the structure of communication in activities that are not amenable to the kind of discourse analysis that Mehan and Sinclair and Coulthard have developed for single focus lessons.

Patterns of language use studied include the importance of nonverbal as well as verbal cues, demands on children's interactional competence, a relationship between participation structure and academic content, and evidence for the "joint construction" of discourse.

THE IMPORTANCE OF NONVERBAL CUES

In their analysis of worktime, it became clear to Shultz and Florio (1979) that the teacher enacted certain cues whenever she wanted to get all the children's attention and make an announcement. She always moved to a particular empty place in the room, a space empty of furniture where the whole group assembled for whole group meetings ("circles") and which may therefore have had a symbolic meaning as the place of teacher control; and she bent forward from the waist as she spoke. As evidence for the importance of her posture, Shultz and Florio (1979) report what happened in a negative instance in which she failed to be consistent:

> The teacher walked into the circle area, stopped, and bent forward from the waist while she was making the announcement. In the middle of the announcement, she turned out of the circle area to give directions to two students standing behind her. As she turned out of the circle area, the rest of the students began to move around, apparently thinking the announcement was over. The teacher turned back into the circle area, bent forward from the waist even more than she had done previously, and said, "Who told you to move!" The truth of the matter is that the teacher herself, by turning out of the circle area, had "told" the students to move. The students had been attending to what the teacher was doing, as much as to what she was saying. (pp. 173–174)

A similar instance occurred during one of the circles. Bremme and Erickson (1977) found that these whole group meetings were divided into what they call "teacher time" and "student time" with topics and verbal and nonverbal patterns distinct to each. Occasionally, a negative instance occurred when the teacher talked about academic content or organizational procedures as she did during teacher's time, but oriented her posture and gaze to an individual student for a relatively long time as she did during student time.

> During every instance in which the teacher performs this mixed combination of verbal and nonverbal behaviors, students begin to gaze around the room, make small shifts in their body positions and increase the amount of body movement they engage in; some may strike up brief, whispered conversations with those around them.... We infer that they read this "mixed" combination as an entirely distinct pattern. (p. 157)

These analyses carry two pieces of methodological advice. First, negative instances, when a pattern is broken, provide a natural experiment for testing hypotheses about participation structure. Second, if nonverbal cues are so important to participants (and there is no reason to think them important only to young children), they should also be important to researchers.

The latter point is forcefully made in Dore and McDermott's (1982) comparison of two analyses of a sequence of talk in a first grade reading group They present first a speech act account, using a taxonomy revised from Dore, Gearhardt, & Newman (1978), and then add an "interactional" account (derived from Scheflen, 1973, with no relationship to any coding scheme). Figure 15.3 presents both analyses for an 8-second sequence when the next turn to read is being decided.

The interactional account comes from a detailed analysis of the nonverbal "positionings" of the group of six participants "which are accomplished in concert" (p. 387). The sequence in Figure 15.3 is during a Position II — Getting a Turn to Read — when the children "are sitting up from the table, looking at the teacher or one another for cues as to who will get the next reading turn" (p. 387). From an analysis of body orientations, gaze and gaze aversion, as well as talk, Dore and McDermott argue that Rosa's remark, "I could read it" is to be interpreted — and is so interpreted by the other children and the teacher at the moment — as the opposite of its literal meaning.

More generally, Dore and McDermott argue that "the interpretation of actual utterances is a situated accomplishment" (p. 374), depending on more than knowledge of multiple levels of language structure; without reference to context in the sense shown in their interactional analysis, talk alone is "fundamentally indeterminate" (p. 375).

McDermott, Gospodinoff and Aron (1978) present an interactional account, without the speech act analysis, of another sequence from the same corpus with more extended discussion of the criteria for descriptive adequacy. McDermott and Gospodinoff (1979) present a third sequence centering on a Puerto Rican boy in the same class.

As Dore and McDermott admit, analysis at this level of detail (visible only through innumerable turns back and forth of a hand-cranked 16mm projector) is slow. Other researchers will have to decide when an educationally important question merits such labor. But even if the answer is "rarely," or even "never," the presence of this work, with its meticulously demonstrated grounds for interpretation, should make all discourse analysts pause on two questions. In general, how adequate are the grounds for our interpretations? More specifically, have we adequately considered the multiple meanings that any surface language form can have?

DEMANDS ON CHILDREN'S INTERACTIONAL COMPETENCE

Shultz (1979) describes a tic-tac-toe game embedded in the larger activity of worktime. Speech is structured around the game, here played by the teacher and three children, one of whom (C2) is a kindergartner who is being taught how to play. Shultz discovered that the three phases of the game situation — set-up, serious play, and wind-up — are organized in ways that have consequences for the talk that does and does not occur. These phases are marked by changes in the teacher's posture, by the frequency and success of attempted interruptions of the game by children who are not players, and by what

Onset Time	Speaker	Turn	Utterance	Conversational Act	Interactional Consequence
1.0	Teacher	1	All right.	Boundary Marker	Shift group focus
			Perry's ready.	Description	Nominate reader?
			Who else is ready?	Product Question	Solicit participation
				Propositionally	
				Ambiguous:	
				to read next	
				to call for a turn	
				to read along	
				to read in chorus	
3.8	Anna	2	Me.	Product Answer	Commitment to read
4.2	Jimmy	3	Not me.	Product Answer	Refusal to read
4.4	Perry	4	CA–	Compliance	Reading
4.5	Maria	5	Can I go?	Permission Request	Solicit turn
4.6	Rosa	6	YOU . . .	Compliance?	Mock-reading
6.0	Perry	7	CAN–	Compliance	Reading
6.8	Rosa	8	I could read it.		Pragmatic Counterfactual
				Illocutionarily Equivocal:	
				Answer	
				Internal Report	
				Explanation	
				Indirect Permission	
				Request	
				Claim	

Fig. 15.3. An eight-second transcript of an extended conversational sequence during a "getting-a-turn-to-read" positioning. From "Linguistic Indeterminacy and Social Context in Utterance Interpretation" by J. Dore and R. P. McDermott, 1982, *Language; 58,* 374-397. Reprinted by permission.

topics can get the floor. The teacher's posture, always leaning in during serious play, seems to be a significant contextualization cue, telling the children nonverbally "that she was very deeply engrossed in what she was doing and was therefore not available to be interrupted" (p. 282). A child's comment about a non-game topic is responded to by the teacher during the set-up phase, but a similar comment in the serious play phase is ignored. The fact that C2 attempted such a conversation at that time is seen by observers and the teacher as evidence that she is not yet a fully competent member of this classroom community.

PARTICIPATION STRUCTURE AND
ACADEMIC CONTENT

Shultz, Erickson, and Florio (1982) compare the participant structures in a math lesson with a dinner table conversation in a first grader's home. Figures 15.4 and 15.5 show the types and distribution of participation structures in both. Note that participation structures IIIA and IIIB, in which chiming in is acceptable, occur in all phases of dinner time at home but only during the instructional climax of the lesson at school.

Briefly, during the early part of a math lesson with attribute blocks, the teacher enforces a Type 1 or Type 2 structure, stopping all overlapping talk. But then, in the 20 turns leading up to the conceptual punchline of the lesson—introduction of the notion of intersecting sets—the turn allocation rules are relaxed and teacher and children overlap each other in a Type 3 structure. After the punchline, the teacher works to regain a Type 1 structure and keeps it until the end. Erickson suggests that the shift to a Type 3 structure was done by the teacher out

of awareness, a part of her implicit "pedagogical competence," and that "it simplified the task environment...allowing the children to focus mainly on the academic task structure" (Erickson, unpublished version of Shultz et al, 1982).

Demonstrations of a relationship between event structure and academic content are still rare. Lemke's study of science lessons and a deliberately designed shift in reading group structures in the Kamehameha Early Education Program are both discussed in later sections. Erickson and Catherine Pelissier are currently analyzing brief segments of discussion in a second grade that are a "fine-line between order and chaos" and that are—to both teacher and observers—the intellectual high point of the lesson (personal communication 11/83).

JOINT CONSTRUCTION OF DISCOURSE

As part of his analysis of worktime, Dorr-Bremme (1982) compared participation structures during two years with the same teacher, same overall organization of the classroom day, and even some of the same students as kindergarten children from Year 1 became first graders in Year 2. But the group as a whole was different, and this had consequences for the talk.

For example, during Year 2 student time (which is similar in function to Sharing Time), talkativeness was less evenly distributed, more children had little or nothing to say, and the most talkative children were more apt than in Year 1 to talk about topics that the teacher didn't value (like TV skits). The teacher herself was aware of these differences and considered her Year 2 group more immature, But she was not aware of the adaptive changes in her own behavior that Dorr-Bremme found on his videotapes. During Year 2, but not in Year 1, she introduced

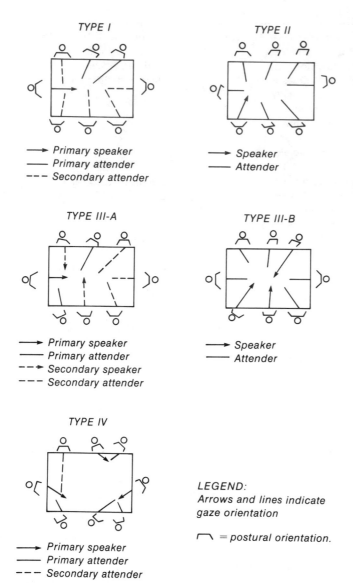

LEGEND:
Arrows and lines indicate gaze orientation

⌐ = *postural orientation.*

Fig. 15.4. Schematic representation of participation structures. From "'Where's the Floor?' Aspects of Social Relationships in Communication at Home and at School" by J. J. Shultz, F. Erickson, and S. Florio, 1982. In P. Gilmore and A. Glatthorn (Eds.), *Children in and out of School: Ethnography and Education* (p. 105). Washington: Center for Applied Linguistics. Reprinted by permission.

topics, held students to them, and herself interpolated more comments and questions. In Dorr-Bremme's (1982) words:

> It appears, in other words, that how students act can constrain the range of action choices that make sense for teachers to consider and choose. And as teachers teach (or "manage") the class in different ways, they constrain the range of actions that are appropriate and reasonable for students. But if students have a role in determining teachers' ways of doing teaching and/or "classroom management," then students play a collaborative part in structuring the classroom environment in which they are expected to learn and display what they have learned. (p. 433)

EVENT	CONSTITUENT PHASE		
	PREPARATION	FOCUS	WRAP-UP
Dinner	I, II, III-B	I, II, III-B	III-A, III-B, IV, I
Math Lesson	IV, I	I, II	I, III-A (during instructional climax) and II, IV (during clean-up)

Fig. 15.5. Distribution of participation structures across primary participant phases of the two events. For each constituent phase, participation structures are listed according to frequency of occurrence. Those participation structures that occur most often are listed first, while those that occur least often are listed last (from Shultz, Erickson, & Florio, 1982, p. 107).

Assertions about the joint construction of classroom discourse are frequent in Sc research, but the evidence is rarely as strong.

Lesson Components

All three components of the basic IRE sequence have been the focus of separate research. Most attention has been given to teacher questions because of their frequency, the pedagogical work they are intended to do, and the obvious control they exert over the talk and thereby over the enacted curriculum.

With one exception, all research on classroom discourse describes communication in the medium of face-to-face interaction. The one exception is Black, Levin, Mehan, and Quinn's comparative study (1983) of a college class (appropriately, on "classroom interaction"!) taught by Mehan to one group in a regular class and to another group who participated only via an electronic message system. Black et al. found that, in contrast to the regular classroom, discussions via computers pursued "multiple threads of discourse" rather than one at a time; had a two-part, Initiation–Reply structure without any third part for Evaluation; had a lag time of hours or days, rather than seconds, between initiations and replies; and contained minimal "back-channeling" responses. This comparison is interesting not only because it offers a glimpse of what may become a more common medium of instruction, but also because it highlights particular features of the familiar classroom, especially the effects of the necessity for immediate response. (See Rowe, 1974, for an experimental attempt to lengthen the "wait time" after teacher questions.)

TEACHER QUESTIONS

One paradox of the question/answer sequence is that pupil answers are essential for the progress of the lesson, and yet the answer expected by the teacher is rarely obvious. As French and MacLure (1981) remind us, any question—even one so seemingly simple as "Who is that?"—has many potential answers, and providing the right one requires not only knowledge but "contextualized, interpretive work" (p. 39). In videotapes of infant school classrooms collected as part of a longitudinal study of children's language development (Wells, 1981), French and MacLure find "two interactive strategies used by many teachers, which operate to give guidelines to the pupils in their attempt to get the answers teachers want" (p. 34).

One strategy is called preformulating: "teachers preface the question they want the children to answer with one or more utterances which serve to orient the children to the relevant area of experience...[and] establish as shared knowledge between herself and the child materials essential to answer her question" (p. 35):

| Preformulator | T. | Can you see what the elephant's got at the end of his trunk? |
| Nuclear utterance | | What is it? |

The second strategy is reformulating, when the initial answer is wrong. French and MacLure identify five types of reformulations, according to the degree to which they make the original question more specific (pp. 38–43):

Original Question	Reformulation
What are those people doing?	1. What are they planting?
What kind of an elephant?	2. Was he a very SAD elephant? (Here the reformulator is a wrong answer but a member of the same semantic set.)
What else did you see?	3. Did you see a chest of drawers? (Here reformulator is a right answer.)
How did they go, Gary?	4. Did they go by bus or car?
What colour have you used?	5. It's brown, isn't it?

Because these reformulators progressively decrease the cognitive task faced by the child, French and MacLure predict that teachers will prefer to use the less specific versions first, and that the above order will also be an order of sequence of use. In a footnote, they note similarities between their analysis of what teachers do, and the "simplification techniques" advocated by Blank (1973, pp. 90–97). (MacLure & French, 1980, analyse pupil strategies for answering these same questions.)

How one judges the pedagogical value of such cue-giving sequences depends on the educational philosophy of the researcher and the excerpts picked for analysis. So, McNamee (1979) construes the sequence of questions by which a kindergarten teacher talks a child through a story-retelling as a positive example of teaching in Vygotsky's zone of proximal development. But Hammersley (1977) and Edwards (1980) are critical of the concept of knowledge—something known and transmitted by an authority—that is assumed in such a discourse structure.

STUDENT RESPONSES

Asking questions that help students provide the expected answers can have three functions: enabling the lesson to proceed as planned, helping children learn how to accomplish an academic task, and helping the teacher assess their learning. Researchers often focus on one or another of these not easily separable goals.

Lundgren (1977) analyses the first function—enabling the lesson to proceed—with examples from mathematics, and shows how students can derive answers from learning the patterns of classroom discourse rather than the content of the curriculum. Here is an example (adapted from Lundgren, 1977, pp. 200–201):

T. What's four times three?
G. Eig-
T. What is two times four?
G. Eight.
T. Mm, three times four?
G. Nine, ten, eleven, twelve.
T. So, what's three times four?
G. Twelve.

While the teacher may hope that the student learns something about the relationship of addition to multiplication, the student can have learned only that the form of the teacher's final question indicates that the answer is the one immediately preceding. "The language used establishes a pattern of communication which gives the illusion that learning is actually occurring" (p. 202).

The second and third functions—learning and being assessed—are at issue in a recent controversy over literacy instruction. From an observational study in 36 intermediate grade classrooms, Durkin (1979) concluded that comprehension assessment was 25 times more frequent than comprehension instruction. She acknowledges that these conclusions depend on how teacher questions are categorized, and that "the distinction being made between interrogation that is instruction and interrogation that is assessment is not what everyone would call 'clearly apparent'". As her coding categories are defined, "if a teacher asked questions and did nothing with children's answers except, perhaps, to say they were right or wrong, that questioning would be comprehension: assessment" (1977, p. 490).

Heap (1982) argues against the unifunctionality of utterances assumed in Durkin's coding:

There is no incompatibility in claiming that a half-minute of interaction could achieve both comprehension: assessment and comprehension: instruction....The daily, routine co-participation of students in the production of lesson corpuses of knowledge has an importance which extends beyond the particular context of any one corpus. The engagement in initiation-response-feedback sequences, where teachers prod students to produce responses which they then certify, instruct students as to the type of things they should take to be relevant, relative to the texts they encounter in classroom settings (1982, p. 407).

(See Green & Bloome, in press, for a methodological discussion of ethnographic research on reading, and Cochran-Smith, in press, for an analysis of comprehension instruction/assessment in book reading sessions in a nursery school.)

TEACHER EVALUATIONS

The third part of the IRE sequence frequently does more than simply indicate whether the preceding answer was right or wrong. By commenting on a selected aspect of that answer, the teacher response can be considered not just evaluation, but "formulation." This is a category of utterance identified by ethnomethodologists Garfinkle and Sacks (see also Heritage & Watson, 1979):

> A member may treat some part of the conversation as an occasion to describe that conversation, to explain it, or characterize it, or explicate, or translate, or summarize, or furnish the gist of it, or take note of its accordance with rules, or remark on its departure from rules. That is to say, a member may use some part of a conversation to formulate the conversation. (1970, p. 350)

Griffin and Mehan give a simple example from a reading lesson:

> T. (Writes "tree" on paper attached to board) If you know what the word says, put your hand. . . .
> A. Tab.
> T. It does start with "t". Mathew?
>
> . . . [the teacher's response, "it does start with a 't'"] exemplifies a way of teaching called phonics; . . . By specifying, in fact by reifying, one of the possible interpretations of an utterance by a pupil, a teacher cooperates in the construction of that utterance as a learning of (or partial learning of, or steps toward learning) what is supposed to be learned. (1979, pp. 196, 208)

Lemke (1982) finds similar phenomena in high school science lessons. Referring to these third part utterances as "retroactively contextualizing" or "retro" for short, he finds that teacher retros can recontextualize the previous response either structurally or thematically. Structurally, for example, the teacher can reconstrue a student answer as only a bid to answer. Thematically,

> a teacher can alter or enrich the content of a student answer by retroactively placing it in a wider thematic context relevant to the thematic aims of the lesson. This seems to occur regularly, and the brevity and lack of predication in student answers may reflect their implicit collaboration in this process. (p. 21)

French and Woll (1981) follow Dore (1979) in categorizing as formulations in the same sense the "expansions" that caregivers often provide for very young children's telegraphic speech. As Brown and Bellugi (1964) said many years ago about such expansions, "It seems to us that a mother in expanding speech may be teaching more than grammar; she may be teaching something like a world-view" (p. 143).

Considering the IRE sequence as a whole, Lemke (1982) suggests that, "As a mode of thematic development the triad structure can be understood as a teacher-monolog in which some key TInform has been transformed into a TQ/SA pair, with TEval required to confirm their equivalence to the 'underlying' TInform" (p. 46).

In the end, differences of interpretation of such teacher control of classroom discourse reflect only in part unresolved empirical issues of teaching effectiveness; they also reflect philosophical and value differences about what the lesson content is worth.

Student Initiatives: Asking for Help

Many times in a school day students need to ask the teacher for help. But whereas the teacher has the right to speak to any student at any time, students have much more limited conversational access to the teacher, especially when she is already otherwise engaged.

Merritt (1982a, 1982b; Merritt & Humphrey, 1979) calls the moments when students try to get the teacher's attention "service-like events" to suggest similarities with customers getting a clerk's attention in a store or bank. Using ideas from Goffman (especially 1971), she analysed successful and unsuccesful requests for help in 10 nursery and primary classrooms, and the skills of dual processing required of both teacher and students. Here Merritt and Humphrey (1979) give one rule for success:

> The initiating child is most likely to be positively attended to if s/he makes a "nonverbal only" approach to where the teacher is "posted". . . . [perhaps because] a nonverbal initiation by the child allows the teacher to "start the talk." This prerogative means that the teacher can be "more in control" of the service-like event talk. It also means that the teacher can wait to start the service-like event talk until there is a spot in the teacher activity that can "most easily" be slotted out of. (p. 299)

Merritt's study is unusual in two respects. First, it is an analysis of educationally significant talk usually overlooked as just a side sequence, or hidden from consideration outside recording range. Second, Merritt worked from videotapes previously made as part of a different project and never herself entered the classrooms she was viewing, a rare example of such re-use. It probably worked well in this case because she came to the study with well-formed questions from an earlier study of service encounters in stores, and because her collaborator, Humphrey, had participated in making the tapes in the original research.

Where Merritt focuses on the participation structure of one event in which help is requested, Schwarz (1979) analyzes individual differences in soliciting style, using a taxonomy adapted from Bellack et al. (1966), Sinclair and Coulthard (1975), and Labov and Fanshel (1977). Her subjects are three southern-born black students in an alternative public secondary school held in a northern urban hospital. She focused on soliciting in the belief that it "is not only valuable speech behavior for all students, but particularly crucial for bicultural students with poor literacy skills" (p. 261).

The result is a set of three case studies and important advice for research. First is the importance of considering linguistic variables in combination: "The extreme distinctiveness of each student's soliciting was found in the ways in which students combined the elements of the taxonomy and not in the frequency with which they used isolated elements. . . .That variables of function, form, and topic provide significant differentiation information only when they are combined should serve as a caution to research methods that examine linguistic variables in isolation" (p. 265).

A clear example is Mary and Lottie's use of the revision solicit by which speakers ask an addressee to change a previously taken position. These acts "represent dangerous interactional ground" (p. 96), "the extreme end of the impositional scale" (p. 155). Mary and Lottie asked the same number, and both addressed 2/3 to adults. But Mary's were on factual, curricular topics and often presented evidence — for example, "They said on the news it was 3 o'clock" to the teacher who had just asserted a different time. Lottie, by contrast, used her revision solicits for procedural matters, and frequently with a paraverbal overlay of anger — for example, "I been sitting here underlining, so give me credit" to the teacher who had just given credit to a peer.

Second is the consideration of alternative explanations for solicits that failed to get compliance: "Adults tended not to comply with solicits on off-task topics, solicits in the less traditional functions, or solicits with angry paraverbal overlays. Noncompliance seemed to stem more from resisting challenging interactive meanings than not comprehending the students' resource or discourse grammar. . . . [This] emphasizes the need for observational schemes that can represent motives such as resistance" (p. 270).

Features of the Teacher-Talk Register

A "register" is a conventionalized way of speaking in a particular role, and is identified as a marker of that role. One familiar and well-studied register is the "baby-talk" (BT) that middle-class caregivers typically speak to toddlers (Snow & Ferguson, 1977). Its features include high pitch and exaggerated intonation contours, short simple sentences, and some unique lexical items (such as *pee-pee* for *urinate*). As this list makes clear, a register is not a separate level of linguistic structure, but a configuration of features at many levels.

Some shared ways of talking as a teacher are obvious — asking known answer questions and evaluating the addressee's answer, for example. But what else? There has been little research on features of the teacher-talk register, but there are some indications of what it includes and, just as importantly, what it doesn't.

Control Talk

Perhaps the most obvious feature of teacher talk is its preoccupation with matters of control — control of behavior and of talk itself. Stubbs (1976) lists eight kinds of metacommunicative talk that he found in secondary English lessons. As he says, what is special about the classroom is not that somebody talks to get others' attention, or check for understanding, but that talking in these ways is so "radically asymmetrical. . .almost never used by pupils and, when it is, it is a sign that an atypical teaching situation has arisen" (p. 162).

In secondary science lessons Lemke (1982) found examples of more complex forms of control. "I can't hear you, Ian", spoken after the nominated student Ian's turn is overlapped by another student Rosie calling out, "functions both as a request for repeat and as an admonition to Rosie" (p. 96). And "C'mon, I mean I was looking at you when you did it. Be a little subtle." said to a student who had just thrown a paper wad, invokes not only the norm against throwing things but also the "deeply implicit convention that violations done 'while teacher is looking' may be presumed deliberate challenges to teacher's authority, acts of defiance, and not just lapses from rules" (p. 91).

Other researchers have looked at stylistic variations in how control functions are enacted, especially the difference between more and less direct directives. As Sinclair and Coulthard (1975) point out, indirect forms of directive intent — such as "I can't hear you, Ian" — are conventional ways of speaking in many classrooms. Such indirection may pose interpretive problems for young children (Willes, 1983) or those of any age who are used to more direct expressions of authority (Heath, 1978, 1983).

Special Lexicon

The early work of Barnes et al. (1969) focused on "the language of secondary school teaching." Barnes categorizes the vocabulary of this language of instruction in several ways: subject-specific or more general; explicitly explained or not; and whether it has a conceptual function in making important referential distinctions or simply a sociocultural function in identifying the speaker in a certain role.

As Barnes points out, it is difficult to distinguish between the conceptual and socio-cultural functions, because the distinction may not be made in the same way by speaker (teacher) and hearers (students):

> From the point of view of the teacher, everything he says has for him a more or less important socio-cultural function in supporting his roles as teacher and as teacher-of-mathematics; yet everything he says could also (in theory) be placed on a scale for its conceptual function, according to how far it is also being used to organize the subject matter of the lesson. But this is only for the teacher; for the pupil it must be different. Each new item must first appear to have a socio-cultural function — that is, to be "the sort of thing my physics teacher says" — and then, in so far as the pupil is able to use the item in talking, thinking or writing, it will take upon itself a conceptual function. (p. 58)

Labov (1972) makes a related distinction between pretension and precision. Neither Labov nor Barnes claims there is no intellectual value to specialized ways of speaking. They ask only that we distinguish between forms that have such value and forms that don't. Barnes goes further to urge teaching strategies that can enhance student learning of the intellectually valuable forms.

Prosodic Features

Observers of teachers of young children report frequent use of high pitch and exaggerated intonation contours similar to the BT register and sometimes interpret such talk as condescending. But there is no evidence that it is so perceived by students.

Barnes (in Barnes et al., 1969) mentions in passing the intonation of markers of authority and transition such as Right and Now. But, as he says, documenting intonation requires technical transcribing skill that few educational researchers have learned. Sinclair and Brazil (1982) include a chapter on intonation, but Stubbs (in press) questions both its applicability to varied dialects and its relevance to educational questions.

Tentativeness Indicators

Feldman and Wertsch (1976) studied the frequency of stance-indicating devices: words that express a speaker's attitude toward the propositional content of an utterance—for example, "I believe" or "I know". They found that elementary teachers used fewer such devices in the classroom than in conversations with an adult interviewer. Unfortunately, they give no examples of actual classroom talk, though it was recorded on wireless microphones worn by the teacher. Instead, they quote from Mishler's (1972) study of a single teacher who responded to a student's question to which she in fact did not know the answer with a flat assertion inplying real knowledge. Mishler infers that "A qualification would put her in the same situation as the children, but the unqualified statement reinforces the knowledge and status differential between her and the children" (p. 273).

Humor

From the paucity of references to humor in research on classroom talk, one could conclude either that classes are deadpan places and absence of humor one mark of the teaching register, or that researchers consider humor irrelevant. It is more often mentioned by UK researchers, perhaps because they are more influenced by sociological perspectives, including "what most sociologists would look on as out-dated functionalism" (Walker & Goodson, 1977, p. 226).

Laughter can make institutions more human. From interviews with students, Woods (1976) notes "the importance pupils of all abilities attached to teachers being able to share a joke and have a laugh with them" (p. 178). And the folk advice to beginning teachers, "Never smile before Christmas," "clearly implies that jokes are part of the process of letting yourself become a person in the eyes of the pupils" (Walker & Goodson, 1977, p. 206).

In their study of innovative secondary school teaching, Walker and Goodson (1977) developed a set of hypotheses about humor in the classroom. For example, "Jokes between teachers and pupils mark points at which the boundaries between school-knowledge and action-knowledge are potentially negotiable" (p. 223). Not included in their list is the possible differential importance of humor in some classrooms. For example, Geoffrey (a teacher in an urban elementary school) says, "One of the most discouraging aspects of teaching in a slum school is the lack of response from pupils. . . . To have them respond in humor, within bounds, is a most acceptable way. At least they are alive" (Smith & Geoffrey, 1968, p. 58; see index for "humor" and "banter"). And a British secondary teacher says, "[There are] far more jokes among working-class kids than there are among others, so jokes are really important to them (Walker & Goodson, 1977, p. 208).

Laughter can even be informative in research on other topics, as Lemke (1982) points out:

It is a commonplace of our culture that humor is a principal "lubricant" of social interactions. Participants in these [science] lessons laugh, as we all do, at incongruities, whether seemingly "intended" or not, and thus mark for our analysis both what seems incongruous to them and those events of classroom discourse where potential friction seems to require some lubrication to smooth them over. (p. 128)

Expressions of Affect

Like humor, expressions of affect are basic to social life. Yet they are mentioned even less frequently. Goodlad's (1983) observational study of more than 1,000 classrooms found that "affect—either positive or negative—was virtually absent. What we observed could only be described as neutral, or perhaps 'flat'" (p. 467).

Absence of affect on this scale should be a "notable" absence to researchers. Goodlad's finding, coming as it does from the application of an on-the-spot coding scheme (essential for a study of this magnitude) now begs for more intense Sc research into the same phenomenon. Like humor, expressions of affect may assume special significance in some cultural settings (Kochman, 1981, Ch. 2)

Underlying Components of the Teacher-Talk Register

Both register and style are configurations of features at multiple levels of the language system, and both depend on different frequencies of such features, not their presence or absence (Hymes, 1977). But there is an important difference between the two constructs: We are apt to speak of a register, in the singular, but of styles, in the plural. It is useful to understand commonalities in the ways teachers talk, but it is also useful to understand variability; among more or less formal situations (Irvine, 1979) within a single classroom; across teachers from different cultural groups, male or female, etc. See Ferguson, 1977 for a comparable plea for research on variability in the BT register.

Research on variability can also help to validate hypotheses about underlying components of the register itself. Consider Brown's (1977) discussion of underlying components of BT. If he is right that BT is created by the conjunction of two principal components, communication-clarification (COMM) and expressive-affective (AFF), then situational variations in the importance of COMM and AFF should influence BT forms. And there is some indication that this is so. For example, Snow (1977) reports that book reading elicited more complex speech from mothers than free play, and suggests that "the extra situational support of pictures [decreasing the pressure for COMM] in the book-reading situation limits the possible topics sufficiently that the comments can be more elaborated than in the less well-defined situations" (p. 37).

Two candidates for underlying components of teacher talk are control and distance. If, for example, teacher talk is at least partly created by teachers' status as caregivers who are relative strangers (Heath, 1978), then variability in teacher talk should co-occur with differences in perceived social distance. Cazden (1979) uses Brown and Levison's (1978) comprehensive model of politeness phenomena to interpret teacher talk in one bilingual classroom.

Individual differences can be interesting too. Delamont (1976) analyses individual differences among teaching styles in a private girls' secondary school. She did a Flanders interaction analysis of 18 teachers and then a qualitative comparison, from observations and interviews, of a subset of 4. The qualitative analysis helps to explain the quantitative patterns, a demonstration of the benefit of combined modes of research.

Cultural Differences and Differential Treatment

> Without some considerable capacity of the teacher and learner to take adaptive action together in the mutual construction of learning environments, the species would not have survived and developed.... In institutions of schooling ... [that adaptive action] seem[s] to occur only between some pupils and the teacher ... [This is] the major policy issue for schooling in modern societies. (Erickson 1982a, p. 173)

Studies of cultural differences and differential treatment reflect complementary hypotheses about this issue: Because of prior experiences in their home community, students would be better served if teachers took differences into account more than they now do; and teachers now differentiate among their students in ways that may continue, even increase, inequalities of information and skills present when students start school. The two perspectives are related, as will be exemplified in the research on Sharing Time, and information on cultural differences can even contribute unwittingly to stereotypes and thereby to differential treatment (Kleinfeld, 1975, in press).

Cultural Differences

Research on cultural differences can be categorized by topic or methodology. Table 15.1 charts research studies by topic:

aspect of discourse in the rows, and group studied in the columns. The discussion that follows is organized by aspects of method: comparative research designs, problems in interpreting differences, and issues in intervention. Because of limitations of space, it does not include reference to all the studies listed in Table 15.1.

COMPARATIVE RESEARCH DESIGNS

The studies in Table 15.1 include three kinds of comparisons. The first includes observations both at home and at school. Philips's work (1972, 1983) was the pioneer. Because such research makes special demands of time and access, it is not surprising that most subsequent examples are multiyear projects.

For nine years, Heath (1983) was an ethnographer in rural black and white communities, working at the request of parents who wanted to understand why their children were having problems in school, and simultaneously a professor giving inservice courses for teachers; and she was able to integrate the two roles. For example, following her own ethnographic research on the forms and functions of questions in the children's home settings, she encouraged teachers to observe the questions they asked in their own homes and at school; and then worked with the teachers designing and trying out new patterns of classroom discourse (1982b, in press).

The Kamehameha Early Education Program (KEEP) for Polynesian children in Hawaii also evolved over about 10 years. But in contrast to solo Heath, it was the work of a large interdisciplinary team. See Calfee et al. (1981) and Tharp et al. (in press) for overviews; and Au (1979, 1980), Au and Jordan (1981), and Au and Mason (1981) on the successful reading program that can be described as a hybrid of home and school

Table 15.1. Research Studies on Cultural Differences

Aspects of Discourse Analyzed	Cultural Groups Observed						
	Black (US)	Native-American (US)	Hispanic (US)	Hawaiian (US)	Other (or several) US Groups	Non-US Cultural Groups	(White) Social-class Comparisons (US and UK)
Participant structures	Gilmore (1981) Heath (1981, 1982, 1983, in press) May (1981)	Erickson & Mohatt (1982) Lein (1975) Philips (1972, 1983) Wild et al. (1983)	McDermott & Gospodinoff (1979)	Au (1979, 1980) Au & Jordan (1981) Au & Mason (1981) Boggs (1972)	Florio & Shultz (1979) Shultz, Florio, & Erickson (1982)	McKessar & Thomas, (1978) Malcolm, (1979, 1980, 1982) Levin (1977)	Heath (1981, 1982, 1983, in press) MacLure & French (1981)
Nonverbal Synchronization	Byers & Byers (1972)	Barnhardt (1982) Collier (1979) Erickson & Mohatt (1982)			Erickson (1975) Erickson & Shultz (1982)		
Teacher register	Hollins (1982) Piestrup (1973)		Cazden (1979)			Duranti & Ochs (in press)	Walker (1978)
Content of teacher or student talk	Erickson (in press) Heath (1981, 1982, 1983, in press) Michaels (1981, 1983) Michaels & Cazden (in press)				Cazden & Hymes (1980)		Heath (1981, 1982, 1983, in press) Wells & Montgomery (1981)

participation structures, and is also an example of the principle of simplifying the participation structure in order to enhance children's attention to the academic task.

Wells's research team (1981) conducted a longitudinal study of more than 100 children in Bristol, England, equally divided into four social classes. Their comparisons of home/school conversation find few differences — primarily greater symmetry of participation rights at home (MacLure & French, 1981) and more abstract frames of reference at school (Wells & Montgomery, 1981).

A second category of studies is done only at school, and compares teachers and/or students from different cultural groups. Piestrup (1973) compared the ways black and white teachers responded to both dialect features (structural interference) and off-task behavior (functional interference) during reading instruction, and identified a group of "Black Artful" teachers who had the most successful reading lessons.

Erickson and Shultz (1982; also Erickson, 1975) relate indices of behavioral smoothness in junior college counseling interviews to the amount of helpful information received. Student/counselor pairs were categorized as same or different in ethnicity (black, Polish, etc.) or in pan-ethnicity (white ethnic or third-world). Cultural differences in interactional style affected the amount of help given, but Erickson and Shultz (1982) found that these differences could be overridden by situationally defined "comembership":

> For each counselor studied, there were encounters in which a student who differed from the counselor in ethnicity and cultural communication style received as much friendliness and special help as did a student who was similar to the counselor. But these were exceptions, and in almost every one of them, situationally relevant, particularistic comembership was established between student and counselor.... For example, if a student is Polish-American and the counselor is Italian-American, it helps if they both happen to be wrestlers and reveal themselves as such. (p. 176)

As part of the KEEP research, Au and Mason (1981) compare the reading lesson of two teachers, one who had had little experience with Polynesian children and the other who was an experienced teacher in the experimental KEEP program. On several proximal indices — amount of academically engaged time, number of reading-related and correct responses, and number of idea units and logical inferences — the same group of children performed better with the experienced teacher who held the children to academic topics but "allowed the children to speak in participation structures comfortable to them" (p. 149) in which children were freer to choose when to speak, even if it meant overlapping another child's talk.

In a third category are studies which only analyze the culturally different case and take existing literature as the standard of comparison. Malcolm, like Sinclair and Coulthard (1975) and Mehan (1979), developed a comprehensive category scheme, and then studied classrooms of Aboriginal students in Western Australia. He found speech acts "which essentially characterize Aboriginal children" (pp. 311,313):

- proxy eliciting — of the teacher by means of another child
- empty bidding — followed by silence
- deferred replying — after a longer than normal pause

- declined replying — after a direct elicitation
- shadowed replying — in the shadow of the next speaker
- unsolicited replying — without having been nominated

Malcolm (1982) analyzed the effect of these Aboriginal speech acts on the course of the lessons as distortions of idealized sequences that he calls "routines":

> The routine is a "canonical" form (cf. Wells, Montgomery, & MacLure, 1979 [and Erickson, 1982b]) for a stretch of interaction to which the participants approximate. It is like a plan for the interaction, which serves each participant as a basis for his own participation and for his expectations with regard to the participation of others.... The canonical form may not be evidenced in any single cycle, but may be inferred [cf. "prototype"] from the combined data provided by them all.... Finally, and this is of fundamental importance in this study, routines are distorted by incompletely shared acceptance or awareness of the norms of interaction by the participants. (pp. 118–119)

INTERPRETATION OF DIFFERENCES

Finding differences in patterns of interaction is not the end of the problem of interpretation but the beginning, and it is important to consider alternatives. For example, one explanation of the Aboriginal speech acts would be cultural discontinuity between home and school, and support for that interpretation comes from ethnographic descriptions of speech events in Aboriginal communities (Harris, 1980, abridged from Harris, 1977). But Malcolm (1982) offers "an additional perspective which does more justice to the active monitoring of the situation by Aboriginal pupils:"

> Aboriginal pupils are not simply incompetents in a white man's classroom; they are exercising their right as participants in a speech situation to help to "constitute" that situation (cf. Mehan, 1978, 1979).... The basics of communication to the Aboriginal pupil may well be summed up as 1. Who is this person who wants me to talk to him? 2. Who is listening in? 3. Do I want to say anything? Are my rights to noninvolvement being recognized? Have I the right to say something when I want to? If the teacher, and the school system, have treated these questions as of no account, then the Aboriginal child, by the management of his discourse role, will urge them toward acknowledging their significance. (p. 131)

While Malcolm's second interpretation may at first glance seem simply a rephrasing in other words of the construct of interference, an inference of more active response offers a resolution of one puzzling aspect of cultural discontinuity theory. We know that children can learn situationally appropriate ways of speaking and shift effectively among them at an early age. Why does that learning often fail to happen in the classroom? Or, in other words, what makes ethnic differences become ethnic borders? (McDermott & Gospodinoff, 1979, p. 192).

See Gilmore (1981) and May (1981) for other interpretations of resistance. And see Ogbu's distinction (1982) between primary cultural patterns of non-Western peoples that pre-exist entrance to Western schooling, and secondary cultural patterns of caste-like minorities in Western societies that "develop as a response to a contact situation ... and suggest not only distinctiveness from but opposition to the dominant white culture" (pp. 298, 303).

It is important to recognize that almost all analyses of classroom discourse explicitly or implicitly assume the perspective of the teacher, a perspective that Hammersley (1981) terms a kind of "normative functionalism...concerned with the norms and values that must be internalized by members of a society if that society is to function" (p. 49), and a perspective that ignores different patterns of interest among the participants. A few studies of "talk in the unofficial peer culture" that are closer to the students' perspective are discussed below.

ISSUES IN INTERVENTION

Research could continue to fill in the cells in Table 15.1 and even add columns and rows. But it will be more helpful to children and to our theories to participate with teachers in designs for change. (cf. Discussions of changes in 'setting events' in behavioral analysis: Krantz & Risely, 1977; McNaughton & Glynn, 1980).

Heath and KEEP provide positive examples. A negative contrast case is research on Black English. Labov (1982b) details the history of that research in the past twenty years and the presentation of expert testimony in a recent court case in Ann Arbor, Michigan. But there is no evidence that the plaintiff Black children have been aided by the inservice courses mandated by the judge. We have explained educational failure without being able to show how to reverse it. The losers are not only the children but our social science (Cazden, 1983b).

As a postscript, a case study in science teaching reminds us that interventions can disrupt home/school continuity as well as create it. Walker (1978) describes a charismatic black teacher in a small town in southern US—the Bible Belt:

> Perhaps most striking is the way she stresses the students' oral expression. When they read, she listens, not just for the correct answer, but for the fluency and facility with which students use scientific terminology. This combination of teaching from the text and stressing oral expression...[is] particularly developed in religious communities.... The curriculum analyst may seek the replacement of existing styles of science teaching by a "discovery" approach...[but] The effect of success in this enterprise may be to cause a disjunction between school and community. (p. 6)

It is, of course, an important value question where a goal of the school should be to maintain such continuity, and where to break it in the service of preparing students for participation in a wider world.

Differential Treatment

Like research on cultural differences, research on differential treatment can be categorized by topic and method. Table 15.2 is comparable to Table 15.1 with two differences. Because of the smaller number of studies, aspects of discourse are not separated into rows. And, unlike the columns in Table 15.1, the columns in Table 15.2 are not independent. Ability groups are not evenly or randomly constituted from different ethnic or social class groups, and reading groups in the primary grades are often not evenly constituted by sex either.

Discussion is organized under the same three headings: comparative research designs, problems in interpreting differences, and issues in intervention.

Table 15.2. Research Studies on Differential Treatment

	Groups Compared	
Ability Groups	Cultural or Social-class Groups	Boys vs. Girls
Allington (1980)	Carew & Lightfoot (1979)	See annotated bibliography in Thorne, Kramarae, & Henley (1983, pp. 287–293)
Alpert (1975)	Cazden & Hymes (1980)	
Collins (1982, 1983)	Michaels (1981, 1983)	
Eder (1981, 1982a, 1982b)	Michaels & Cazden (in press)	
Keddie (1971)	Cazden, Michaels, & Tabors, (in press)	
McDermott (1976)		

COMPARATIVE RESEARCH DESIGNS

In order to control for teacher effect, the most common design compares interactions within, rather than across, classrooms. Where the research question is a sensitive one, problems of access arise. Carew and Lightfoot (1979, Ch. 3) detail "the long search for a research sample". And problems in access in turn affect the generalizability of the results. As Carew and Lightfoot say about their own finding of no consistent evidence of differential treatment by race or sex in four first grades: "These results were not unexpected in view of the fact that the teachers had agreed to have their classrooms scrutinized by minority researchers" (1979, p. 102).

Because of both the importance of literacy instruction in the primary grades for future school success and the prevalence of homogeneous groups for reading instruction, considerable attention has been focused on differences in how high vs. low reading groups are taught. Cazden (in press-a) reviews these studies.

In secondary school, where tracking is common, within-class variation in achievement levels (and thereby often in ethnicity and social class) is reduced, and cross-classroom designs are more common. Keddie (1971), for example, compares interactional indications of what counts as "knowledge" in A vs. C stream classes that are all taught the same new humanities course. (This and Lemke, 1982, are rare studies in acknowledging the influence of Bernstein's theory [1971, 1981] of "the classification and framing of educational knowledge.") On a larger scale, Stodolsky, Ferguson, and Wimpelberg (1981) use a cross-school design to study social class differences in the distribution of elementary school recitations and discussions.

In any research on differential treatment, bias can intrude into the analysis from researchers' hypotheses (and often deep concerns). Videotapes retain information on ethnicity; and even transcripts retain information on sex unless special attention is given to their preparation (as in Cherry, 1975).

PROBLEMS IN INTERPRETATION

The most important question is whether differential treatment is helpful individualization, or detrimental bias. In Carew and

Lightfoot's words, is it "positive discrimination (discerning and responding to the individual needs of children) or negative discrimination (reacting prejudicially to children as members of low-status categories)?" (1979, p. 2).

In the case of high vs. low reading groups, Alpert (1975) argues that differential treatment is pedagogically appropriate, and that low group children will receive the high group kind of help at some later time. To test this hypothesis, we would need longitudinal studies following both the instruction and the progress of low group children. An unpublished study by Collins (reported in Cazden, in press-a) comes closest to this: a comparison of a low group lesson with a high group lesson about the same story earlier in the year.

Our interpretation of the impact of differential treatment would be enhanced by interviews with the students, especially older ones. Unfortunately, the studies included in Table 15.2 report either interviews or observations but not both. For example, Cazden and Hymes (1980) mention student reports about displays of knowledge that "get the floor" in graduate school and professors' differential response to student questions based on social science literature vs. personal experience. But whether these student reports are descriptions of actual interaction, as well as of their perceptions of it, is not known.

ISSUES IN INTERVENTION

Successful intervention depends not only on evidence that differential treatment is harmful rather than helpful, but also on understanding what produces it in the first place. Cazden (in press-a) divides contributing factors into preactive and interactive influences (after Jackson, 1968), depending on their temporal relationship to the teaching act.

In the case of differential treatment of high vs. low reading groups, preactive influences that teachers bring to their interactions with students could include preservice and inservice courses, messages about what different children need implicit in the design of curriculum materials, and the prevailing wisdom in "teachers' culture." See Hargreaves (1980) on the occupational culture of teachers as "a significant but inadequately formulated 'intervening variable' between the macro and micro levels of sociological analysis" (p. 126).

Whatever teachers' conscious pedagogical plans, differential treatment can also be maintained, even generated, in moment-to-moment "in-flight" interactions. The best laid plans may go awry because no lesson is under the teacher's unilateral control, and teacher behavior and student behavior reciprocally influence each other in complex ways. In the case of reading groups, interactive influences can include coping with children who can not keep up with the group or who have problems in attention, and teachers' need for reinforcement by hearing children read the right word (discussed in more detail in Cazden, in press-a). To the extent that the differential treatment is in some way functional in the present teaching context, it may be more productive to change that context — the "setting events" that affect the probability of teacher behavior — than to try to change teacher behavior directly.

The Case of Sharing Time

Sharing Time (ST) is a speech event in primary classrooms that is notable for the opportunity it gives children to speak at length on a topic of their choice from their out-of-school life. Research on ST focuses both on cultural differences and differential treatment. Michaels (1981) compared both the structure of narratives told by black and white children (a matter of cultural differences) and the content and timing of the questions and comments interpolated into the narratives by a white teacher (a matter of differential treatment). This research was replicated in another city (Michaels, 1983; Michaels & Cazden, in press). Michaels and Foster (in press) describe a child-run ST where attention to audience is enhanced.

Ethnic differences in children's narrative style — more "topic-centered" by white children and more "topic associating" by black students — match other descriptions of black oral style (Smitherman, 1977 and references in Erickson, in press). But relationships between these cultural differences and the teachers' differential collaboration with the children is less clear. From natural observations, it is impossible to observe a black and a white teacher responding to the same narrative.

Michaels and Cazden (in press) therefore supplemented the naturalistic observations by an experiment in which mimicked versions of both kinds of stories were played to other black and white teachers. These mimicked versions retained the child's rhythm and intonation contours (described in Michaels, 1983), but changed black dialect features to standard English and neutralized a few obvious markers of social class. The adults were asked to comment on the well-formedness of each story, and guess the probable academic success of the narrator. White adults invariably found the topic-associating stories hard to follow and were more likely to infer that the narrator was a low-achieving student; black adults were more likely to evaluate positively both kinds of stories and their narrators, noticing differences but appreciating both. In an attempt to understand why white teachers have a hard time following the topic-associating narratives, Cazden, Michaels, and Tabors (in press) analyze self-repairs in examples of both narrative styles.

Interactions Among Peers

Most research on classroom discourse has focused on interactions between students and their teacher, either because these are considered the only sites of important action or because they are easy to overhear and record. But classrooms are also contexts for interactions among peers. Potentially, children are much more available to each other than the teacher is to any of them. As a physically crowded human environment, classrooms share features with restaurants and buses, where many simultaneous conversations are the norm. But conversation among children is usually considered a nuisance, literal noise in the instructional system. And even if tolerated, the social organization of classroom life makes it a rare event (US: Goodlad, 1983; UK: Galton, Simon, & Croll, 1980).

Whatever its frequency, there are good reasons for studying peer talk, both as a potentially useful medium for official academic tasks, and as an inevitable unofficial component of classroom life. Officially, peer talk may have both cognitive and motivational benefits. To Piaget (1950, Ch.6), social interaction is an essential antidote to egocentrism; in the confrontation with alternative points of view one realizes the limitations of one's own. To Vygotsky, "The higher functions of child thought at first appear in the collective life of children in the form of argumentation and only then develop into reflection for the individual child" (1981, p. 157). Moreover, if we believe Vygotsky's theory of internalization from inter- to intrapsychological processes, then peer interactions assume special importance in school because of the asymmetry of teacher-pupil relationships. Children never give directions to teachers, and rarely ask questions except for procedures and permissions. The only context in which children can reverse interactional roles with the same intellectual content, giving directions as well as following them, and asking questions as well as answering them, is with their peers.

In addition to possible cognitive benefits, there may be motivational benefits as well, especially for students from some cultural groups. For example, see Labov (1982a) on black students, and Jordan and Tharp (1979) on Polynesian students in Hawaii. And see Charconnet (1975) for an historical account of peer tutoring around the world. After discussing peer talk around academic tasks, we turn to talk in the unofficial peer culture.

Peer Talk Around Academic Tasks

Research on peer talk has repeated the history of research on teacher–student interactions: P–P studies first, and only more recently Sc work. See Webb (1982) for a review of P–P studies, and Stodolsky (in press) for methodological comments and suggestions. We review Sc studies under three headings: spontaneous help on individual activities, collaboration on group projects, and peer tutoring where one child is asked to teach one or more peers.

Unfortunately, no descriptions could be found of a traditional Jewish practise of studying religious tests in pairs, chevrutah. Copeland's dissertation (1978) on "reading aloud in traditional Jewish text learning" mentions "groups of two simultaneously giving [the text] a sensitive oral reading and then coming together for a single reading and discussion (p. 33), and refers to chavrutot, the "study teams of two" (p. 50). But his focus is on the phenomonology of reading aloud as an important contribution to "the coincidence of intellectual, emotional, and religious experience" (p. 133) and not on the ensuing (and presumably more intellectual) discussion.

SPONTANEOUS HELP

Cooper and her colleagues have conducted a set of studies of spontaneous peer helping. As they note, the first task for interested researchers is to find a classroom where it's not considered cheating. From their first study in two classrooms, Cooper, Marquis, and Ayers-Lopez (1982) present more analysis, while Cooper, Ayers-Lopez, and Marquis (1982) give more examples. In a later study in a Montessori school, Cooper, Marquis, and Edward (in press) found both spontaneous help and group collaboration.

Episodes of spontaneous helping were identified by an opening bid for help by a "learner" or an offer of help by a "teacher." Utterances within each episode were coded for function, form, and referential specificity. Analyses include characteristics of successful episodes, developmental differences, and sociometric comparisons of the roles played by different children.

Cooper et al.'s sociometric data is particularly striking:

> In this second grade classroom, the two children who received the most unsolicited information from their peers were also the ones most frequently sought as consultants. This pattern suggests that a small number of children may be at the crossroads of learning exchanges, and are both contributing to and benefiting from these interactions, whereas others miss both the challenge of questions and the benefit of instruction from their peers (1982, p. 76).

Moreover, ability was not the only factor. Two children in the class were performing at the sixth grade level, but only one of them was sought as a consultant.

Garnica (1981) has compared the interactions of six kindergarten children who were at the bottom of the sociometric scale — called omega children — with six children picked randomly from the rest of the class. Although her focus is not just on requests for and offers of help, her findings supplement Cooper's.

Three 20-minute speech samples (collected by putting a small cassette recorder on the focal child) were analysed for each of the 12 children. Their conversational behavior was compared on seven measures:

1. Number of conversational turns in all child–child conversations;
2. Number of different child conversational partners in all child-child conversations;
3. Number of attempts to initiate a conversation to the target child;
4. Number of attempts to initiate a conversation by the target child;
5. Number of times the target child's name is used by other children;
6. Number of insults or taunts received by the target child;
7. Amount of private speech produced by the target child.

The quantitative analysis showed a significant difference between the omega children and the others on all measures except Number 6. The omega children are isolated and verbally neglected (Numbers 1–5); they talk far more to themselves (Number 7); and it appears from the qualitative analysis that the reason they do not receive more insults and taunts is that they rarely try to step out of, or challenge, their neglected status.

For her qualitative analysis, Garnica selected two episodes in which children — one omega child and one not — are coloring and need a particular magic marker. (The omega child does not get the marker; the other child does). Although the two children use different strategies in requesting markers from the other children, Garnica infers from other evidence that the difference in strategy is not the cause of the difference in results. See Rosegrant (1980) for a related study of pre-school children. She found that boys comparable in status to Garnica's omega children did in fact use higher status strategies to girls, and so their low status strategies with other boys could not be caused by an inadequate discourse repertoire.

If informal helping is important, then we need to understand not only the situations in which it works well, but how to change the status of isolated children.

COLLABORATION ON GROUP PROJECTS

Empirical support for the cognitive value of collaboration comes from a series of training studies by a group of Genevan psychologists (Perret-Clermont, 1980) in which the particular reasoning tasks, the groups assembled, and the criteria used to evaluate cognitive growth are varied. Perret-Clermont concludes from this body of work that peer interaction enhances the development of logical reasoning through a process of active cognitive reorganization induced by cognitive conflict. None of these studies analysed the interactions themselves, but such analyses have been done by Forman, and Newman, Griffin and Cole, of children working together on Piagetian-type tasks; and by Barnes and Todd in group discussions of assigned topics in a wide range of school subjects.

Forman (1981; Forman & Cazden, in press) analysed videotapes of collaborative problem-solving sessions of chemical combination tasks, and also took individual pre- and posttest measures of logical reasoning. The study provides two kinds of information about collaboration: how collaborators differ from solitary problem solvers (from a prior study), and how collaborative partnerships differ from each other in interactional patterns and cognitive growth. All procedural interactions focusing on accomplishing the assigned task were coded for type of collaboration (parallel, associative, cooperative) and type of experimentation strategy (trial-and-error, isolation of variables, combinatorial). Forman found that the collaborators solved many more problems than had the singletons in the same set of eleven sessions, and the pair who showed the most cooperative interactions and used the most combinatorial strategies also solved the most problems. But the pretest–posttest comparison did not show such clear benefits.

Qualitative analysis of the videotapes suggests that the theories of Piaget and Vygotsky apply to different aspects of the collaboration. Piaget emphasizes cognitive conflict, and that did occur later in the sessions when the experimental results were visible and the children argued about what they proved. Vygotsky emphasizes that learning consists of the internalization of social interactional processes, and that there is a period—the zone of proximal development—when children can solve problems with another that they can not yet do alone. Forman's most successful pair assumed complementary roles, giving each other support, correction, and guidance above the level that either could achieve alone.

Newman, Griffin, and Cole (in press) come to a similar conclusion in their interpretation of children's behavior on a similar task: "The intersection schema [comparable to Forman's combination strategy] is regulating the interaction among the children rather than just regulating the individual's actions."

Where both Forman's and Newman et al.'s groups collaborated on a task involving actions on objects, Barnes and Todd (1977) studied groups engaged solely in assigned talk. They also found that groups attained cognitive levels not attained by individual members. But their (1981) reflections on problems encountered in analysis stress the disappointing lack of correspondence between surface language forms and underlying social or cognitive meaning.

Barnes and Todd (1981) started out identifying three levels of analysis:

- Form—what is said, in terms of words and syntax;
- Discourse—what is done, in terms of categories such as elicitation; and
- Strategy—what is accomplished, both interactionally and cognitively.

Unlike Sinclair and Coulthard, Barnes & Todd (1981) "were not looking for those characteristics which were common to all dialogue but for those which accompanied success in carrying out cooperative learning through talk":

> We hoped to identify functional categories and then to be able to specify the forms that "realized" these functions, but we found no such simple relationship between forms and functions. For example, ... we tried to set up an "index of collaborativeness," using forms such as anaphora, subordinations, repetitions, transformations and so on. However, it turned out that enumerating these forms could not serve our purposes; ... indeed at times the distribution of the forms ... ran counter to our intuitions about the collaborativeness being shown by the children. Links between successive utterances were left implicit in our data more often than made explicit, though the nature of the link was often clear enough even to an observer as well as to participants. As Labov has shown [e.g., Labov & Fanshel, 1977], links between utterances are frequently carried out not at the Level of Form but via underlying propositions. Participants use their tacit knowledge [of both Content and Interaction] to attribute meaning to what is said. (p. 73)

Barnes and Todd here raise a critical question: can linguistic analyses illuminate the educational significance of talk? But their pessimism, while an indication of the difficulty of the work, should not be taken as the last word, and the search for more adequate linguistic models continues. Collins's analysis of collaboration in teacher-student discourse is discussed in the next section.

All three of these studies of peer collaboration worked with groups set up outside the classroom for the research. To make progress on the analytical problem of relating patterns of talk to patterns of cognitive as well as social meaning, we can benefit from such work as well as from research based more directly in the classroom.

PEER TUTORING

In the classroom analysed by Mehan (1979), videotapes were made of "instructional chains" (IC) in which the teacher taught a task—usually a reading or spelling worksheet—to one child who was then asked to instruct one or more peers. These ICs were conceived as a hybrid of informal teaching (such as Cooper analysed) and a referential communication task (Dickson, 1981). The teaching was structured by the assignment of tutor, tutee(s), task and time, but the children still had a great deal of freedom to impose on the speech event their own interactional style. Cazden et al. (1979) present case studies of four ICs taught by black students; Carrasco, Vera, and Cazden (1981) add a case study of a bilingual IC taught in English by the teacher and in Spanish by the tutor. In all cases, analysis focuses on both the interpersonal management of the role shift from peer to tutor as well as the communication of information necessary to get the task done.

Because ICs include the same task being taught first by the adult teacher and then the child tutor, a comparison of the adult and child strategies is possible. Mehan and Riel (1982) analyse a larger group of 12 ICs for this comparison. They find, for example, that both teach by example, but whereas the adult teacher elicits the examples from students by questions, the child tutors give examples to their tutees. Gumperz and Herasimchuk (1973) also compared child and adult teachers, but because the tasks were entirely different in the two situations, the result contributes more to our understanding of contextualization cues than of tutoring.

Because the differences found by Mehan and Riel are so striking, it is clear that child tutors are not simply imitating the teacher's model. It is also clear that at least these children are not enacting the kind of teaching role that appears in role-play situations. For example, Anderson (1978) found that children of the same age as the child tutors in Mehan's classroom, when asked to play a teacher puppet, exhibited behaviors clearly associated with the adult teaching register: boundary markers of authority such as "Now," "Well," "OK"; evaluative comments, even in exaggerated form: "Right, that's very right"; and first person plural pronouns: "What we're going to do is ___." These are rare in the ICs (Cazden, 1979, fn. 1). Anderson's children were middle-class and white, but beyond that cultural difference is the situational difference of role-playing someone else vs. seriously being oneself in a challenging new role.

Steinberg (1979; Steinberg & Cazden, 1979) analysed two more ICs in a school for emotionally disturbed children. Her analysis adapted methodology from Labov & Fanshel (1977) even more closely than had Cazden et al., and combined it with McDermott's analysis of nonverbal positionings. The assumption shared by both models of interaction is that coherence and sequencing in discourse depend not on the surface content of utterances but on the actions that the speech performs — actions such as making requests and putting them off, asserting some propositions and challenging others. They differ in the kind of evidence used: audio recordings by Labov and Fanshel; video tape by McDermott and Steinberg.

Talk in the Unofficial Peer Culture

Any classroom contains two interpenetrating worlds: the official world of the teacher's agenda, and the unofficial world of the peer culture. Most research is interested only in the first. Speier (1976) criticizes this bias (as Mishler, in press, criticizes a comparable bias toward the "voice of medicine" in analyses of doctor-patient interviews). To see children only in their relation to teachers and assigned tasks is to be like "colonial administrators who might be expected to write scientifically objective reports of the local populace ... by ideologically formulating only those research problems that pertain to native behaviors coming under the regulation of colonial authority" (Speier, 1976, p. 99).

One can categorize the relationship between the official and unofficial worlds in three ways: separate but equal, with children monitoring both and time-sharing between them; integrated, where for some period of time the two coincide; and in conflict. Mehan (1980) presents instances of the first two. As one example of the third, Streeck (in press) reanalyzes the IC from Cazden et al. (1979) that is least successful from the teacher's point of view to show how "The seemingly chaotic scene as a whole is a rather systematic struggle concerning the definition of the context.... The systematic production of miscommunication in this incident, then, contributes to the maintenance of a boundary between the institutional framework of the school and the more secluded social world of children." See also Willis's (1977) interview study of working-class adolescents and his (1981) response to comments on that work.

And What about Computers?

As a front page story in the Sunday New York Times says (1/2/1983), "The electronic revolution is beginning to alter social life" as well as work habits. So too in the classroom. One report on the effect of computers — in this case, LOGO — on classroom discourse found that, "Children were significantly more likely to collaborate with each other when they worked with the computers, when compared with their interaction over other classroom tasks" (Hawkins, Sheingold, Gearhart, & Berger, 1982, p. 361). In their research agenda for microcomputers, Sheingold, Kane, and Endreweit (1983) emphasize again the importance — at least during this initial phase of use — of "the social outcomes related to interaction" (p. 430), and the special role of student experts (pp. 425, 428).

Computer terminals may thus become a significant site for research on peer interaction, a new context for the exploration of how the social and the cognitive connect. But such research will pose special problems for recording technology; it will be essential to see what the children are working with on the screen as we overhear their talk.

Classroom Discourse and Student Learning

To talk about classroom discourse is to talk about interindividual communication. But education is also concerned with intraindividual change, with student learning. Research of the kind reviewed in this chapter is sometimes considered most relevant to how a class is managed and how order is maintained in the densely social nature of classroom life. But many Sc researchers share the assumption of teachers, an assumption that may itself be culture bound, as Stubbs (1976, p. 105) suggests, that discourse also affects the thought processes of each of the participants and thereby the nature of what is learned. Stubbs (1981b) presents his vision of research on the nature of that relationship:

> Much recent educational research [in the UK] has been concerned with the sociology of knowledge: with how educational knowledge is socially defined and made available to pupils. Much of this work raises "predominantly conceptual issues" (Young, 1971, p. 2) and provides no detailed specification of how knowledge is actually transmitted from teachers to pupils.... By studying discourse sequencing, one can study in empirical detail how teachers select bits of knowledge to present to pupils; how they break up topics and order their presentation; how these discrete items of knowledge are linked; how distinct topics are introduced and terminated; how pupils' responses to questions are evaluated; how pupils are made to reformulate their contributions; how bits of knowledge are paced

and allowed to emerge when the teacher considers it appropriate. I cannot see how such topics could be studied, other than in an ad hoc way, by looking at isolated utterances or features of language. But by studying the overall structure of the teacher–pupil interaction as a discourse system, these topics are inevitably studied. (pp. 127–128)

Stubbs limits his concern to how "educational knowledge is socially defined and made available to pupils," a problem for what could be called the "microsociology of knowledge." Other researchers are interested in not only the input but also the intake, not only what is made available to pupils but what they in fact learn. Among studies of the overall structure of the teacher–pupil interaction as a discourse system, only Lemke (1982) relates discourse structure to academic content (science). Mehan (1979), for example, stresses the necessary union of communicative and academic competence required for children's classroom participation, but does not discuss the implications of the particular union he found for either the social definition of knowledge or individual learning, with the exception of the infrequent category of metaprocess questions (discussed further in Fisher, 1979). Erickson (1982a) acknowledges that academic content has been ignored in most of his own research. And the studies Stubbs mentions that do address such concerns—Barnes et al. (1969) and Mishler (1972)—are less systematic and more what he sympathetically calls "insightful observation" (1981b, p. 80).

Given the general difficulty of establishing relationships between language and thought—or "speaking and thinking" as the title of Vygotsky's book (1962) should be translated—we should not be surprised that it is also difficult to verify this relationship in the classroom. Moreover, surprising as it may seem, according to Doyle (1983, p. 159), explicit attention to "how academic work is organized and accomplished in classrooms ... represents a relatively new emphasis in educational research."

In the past, the most common method for analysing classroom discourse in cognitive terms has been to categorize teacher questions on some cognitive scale. We review these attempts and then turn to more recent work.

Categorizing Teacher Questions

Bloom's *Taxonomy of educational objectives* for the cognitive domain (1956) has been the most influential scheme for categorizing questions according to their presumed cognitive level, even though it was not intended for such use. It can even be considered the prototype taxonomy, representing commonalities among the systems developed in the last 50 years (Gall, 1970). (Mehan (1979) uses a different set of categories—product, choice, process, and metaprocess—and discusses similarities between this set and Bloom and others.)

P–P research has finally validated the educational benefits of teachers asking more "higher-order" questions (Redfield & Rousseau, 1981). But the fact that it took a powerful meta-analysis to establish what teachers and researchers have believed indicates that a lot of variation in cognitive impact is not caught by frequency counts of isolated question types.

For the teacher, that variation includes the difficulties of following up more complex higher order questions with a single

student in a group lesson (Gage, 1977), and the importance of optimal placement of higher order questions in the lesson sequence (Berliner, 1976). For the researcher, there is the analytical problem of trying to decide the intent (of the teacher) and the import (to the pupil) of any question considered in isolation.

For Cole and his colleagues, categorizing the task that a particular question at a particular moment poses for a particular child is one example of the more general problem of studying "cognition in context," of "locating tasks in psychology and education" (Griffin, Cole, & Newman, 1982; Newman, Griffin, & Cole, in press). One problem is the matter of sequence: a question can be harder or easier depending on whether the answer has to be constructed or just selected, and on whether the alternatives have been used up. A second problem arises from influences on a child's response in addition to the question. How the child perceives the teacher's actions, and complex relationships with peers—"all these and more can supplement the teacher's question that is the putative locus of the task demand in such a way that the task as performed differs from what might be inferred from the question that appears to have elicited the task performance from the child" (unpublished version of Griffin et al., 1982).

Finally, there is the need for a contextual analysis of the teacher's subsequent response. Edwards and Furlong (1978) reflect on this aspect of the difficulty of making even the simple two-value distinction between open and closed questions:

Talk is not one distinct item after another. It involves what has been called "conditional relevance": the meaning of an utterance arises partly from something else which has been (or will be) said, perhaps some distance away in the interaction. ... This point, of great importance for our own analysis of classroom talk, can be illustrated by considering a problem facing many systematic researchers, that of distinguishing between closed and open questions. ... Many questions which appear to be open are closed because of the context in which they are asked (perhaps the teacher has recently provided "the" answer), or because the teacher has clear criteria of relevance or adequacy or correctness of expression to which he refers in evaluating the answers. The narrowness of the question only appears in what happens next. (p. 41)

Barnes (in Barnes et al., 1969, p. 24) calls questions that are open in form but demonstrably closed in function "pseudo-open" questions. One of his examples is:

What can you tell me about a bunsen burner, Alan?

This sounds completely open, but as the lesson ensues, it becomes clear that from all possible statements about a bunsen burner the teacher is seeking a particular statement about the conditions for luminous and non-luminous flames.

Griffin, Cole and Newman (unpublished version, 1982) point to important similarities between these difficulties in coding teacher questions and speech act analysis;

For those who have attempted to describe discourse in terms of speech acts the difficulties discussed here ought to have a familiar ring. A central difficulty in assigning utterances to a speech act category is often phrased in terms of the extremely difficult enterprise of specifying the speaker's "intent." "Intent" may be rephrased. It may be that "the function of the utterance in the stream of discourse" is what the analyst attempts to specify. How is this done? By examining the environment of the utterance in terms of preceding and following utterances, its intonation, grammatical structure and any other information the analyst can bring to bear. Despite heroic efforts, all such proposals meet with counter-interpretation and serious problems of disagreement even among those trained to do such work.

They conclude that "while we believe strongly that 'language unites the social and the cognitive' [referring to the quotation at the beginning of this chapter], we believe just as strongly that we don't have ready made procedures for specifying how this relationship works."

The conclusion seems to be that thinking about questions in terms of some scale of cognitive difficulty is probably still heuristically useful for teachers, but inherently imprecise for research.

Applying Vygotsky and Leont'ev

In Newman et al.'s continuing work (1984), there is the beginning of one alternative conception of how discourse and cognition can be related. Their work is motivated by the goal of "providing a theory of the role of culturally organized experience in the development of mind;" and they work in educational contexts in part because "education is the form of culturally organized experience that is available as a tool of government policy" (unpublished version of Newman et al., 1984).

One task selected for analysis is a problem isomorph of Piaget and Inhelder's chemical combination task: stacks of cards (at first four stacks, and then five and six), each of a different TV or movie star. In interaction with a tutor (the researcher), the child is asked to find all the ways that pairs of stars can be friends. (Presentation of the chemicals version to children in groups was mentioned above in the section on discourse among peers.) Briefly (Newman et al., in press):

> When the child had done as many pairs as possible, the researcher instituted a short tutorial before doing another trial of pair making. The child was asked to check whether all the pairs had been made. If the child did not invent a systematic procedure for checking, the tutor suggested one, asking, "Do you have all the pairs with Mork" (if Mork were the first star on the left). Then she asked about the next star to the right. These hints were designed to give the child the idea of systematically pairing each star with every other star, so as to see whether this systematic procedure [referred to by Piaget as "intersection"] carried over to the next trial at making combinations. (p. 177)

Newman et al.'s analysis of the tutor-child interaction, and especially their construal of the adult "hints" is informed by the work of Soviet psychologists Vygotsky and Leont'ev. I assume Vygotsky's theories (1962, 1978) are more familiar to readers of this chapter than Leont'ev's. Briefly, according to Leont'ev (1981) the structure of every human activity (which is energized by a motive) is composed of actions (which are directed by goals) and these actions in turn are composed of operations,

selected and carried out automatically, depending on particular conditions. Any behavior can change in status from action to operation or v.v. So, for example, shifting gears starts as a goal-directed action for a beginner; later it recedes in status to an operation, activated automatically in certain situations.

As Newman et al. say, "Implicit in [Leont'ev's] theory is the claim that instances of behavior have a property which makes them available for social negotiation and transformation. . . . We call this property of the units "non-unique analyzability" (unpublished ms.). So, for example, making pairs of cards (or chemicals) can have the status of actions in different activities to tutor and child at the same moment (synchronically), and to the same participant (diachronically) as the child's understanding develops:

> The tutor's question "How do you know you have all the pairs" presupposed that the child was trying to get all the pairs. This may have been a false presupposition but it was strategically useful (Gearhart & Newman, 1980). The question treated the child's column of pairs as if it had been produced in an attempt to get all the pairs. The teacher then invoked the intersection procedure as a means to fix up the child's "failed attempt to produce all the pairs." In other words, she appropriated the child's pair-making, turning it into an example of how to achieve the stated goal. When their own "empirical" production of pairs is retrospectively interpreted in terms of the intersection schema, children probably begin to learn the researcher's meaning of "all the pairs." (p. 190)

Newman et al. go on to suggest that, just as with the categorization of questions, there is an important difference between what's heuristic for teachers and researchers:

> In education such assumptions [by the teacher about the child's actions] may be a useful way of importing the goal into the teacher-child interaction and, from there, into the child's independent activity. The original coding scheme also treated many of the children's productions as poor strategies for getting all the pairs. In psychology, such overinterpretation may be dangerously misleading. Children are scored as doing poorly when they are not doing the task in the first place. (p. 190)

As Newman et al. apply Vygotsky and Leont'ev's theories, the process of "appropriation" (Leont'ev's term) is reciprocal and sequential. Appropriation by the teacher (as described above) is followed—at least in some tutor-child dyads—by evidence in later tasks that the action of making pairs has been appropriated by the child and transformed into an action in a new activity—namely, the systematic procedure we call "intersection."

Relatives of this way of conceiving the cognitive value of adult questions and interpretive responses appear in the discussion of formulations and expansions above; and in Cazden's discussion (1983a) of "performance before competence," Ryan's discussion (1974) of the benefits of mothers' rich interpretation of children's ambiguous one word utterances, and Vygotsky's assertion that child and adult share reference before they share meaning (1962, p. 73). Newman et al.'s contribution is in making central the "non-unique analyzability" of units of behavior. Note that this is another argument against the one-to-one correspondence between form and meaning that coding schemes assume.

Contrasting Exploratory Talk
and Final Drafts

Whereas in *Language, the Learner and the School* (1969), Barnes focused on teachers' language that may limit student learning, in *From Communication to Curriculum* (Barnes, 1976), the focus is on the positive contribution of a kind of classroom discussion in which students engage in "exploratory talk" as opposed to "final drafts."

Barnes's use of these contrasting terms is interesting for their similarity to more recent discussions of writing in which a final draft is also the end of a process that begins with more exploratory attempts. In the light of that more recent work, Barnes (1976) can be read as arguing for "classroom discourse as process." At one point he explicitly relates oral language and writing:

> The distinction between exploratory and final draft is essentially a distinction between different ways in which speech can function in the rehearsing of knowledge. In exploratory talk and writing, the learner himself takes responsibility for the adequacy of his thinking; final-draft talk and writing looks towards external criteria and distant, unknown audiences. Both uses of language have their place in education. (pp. 113–114).

Barnes recommends a teaching sequence that promotes the benefits of both kinds of talk and the relations between them, and describes an admittedly idealized example in an Environmental Studies unit that begins with an introductory presentation by the teacher, then shifts to small group discussions, and only later to a "report back" discussion with the whole class. Critical to Barnes's argument is the hypothesis that the exploratory small group talk "both strengthens class discussion and (at best) supports forms of learning which take place less readily in full class" (p. 200), but this relationship remains to be demonstrated.

More conclusive research will depend on valid indicators of exploratory talk on the one hand and final drafts on the other. Because Barnes is interested in redressing the balance in favor of more exploratory talk, he describes it in more detail. Sprinkled through the book are various possible indicators:

- hesitations, rephrasings, and false starts
- expressions of tentativeness such as "she could have gone" and "she probably felt"
- peers addressing one another directly, often by name; asking questions of each other and extending or modifying another's contributions;
- expressions of a two-way relationship between school knowledge and everyday knowledge that both helps make sense of the new and reinterprets the familiar;
- a fairly low level of explicitness.

By contrast, final draft talk should be more confident and less hesitant, and contain more explicit formulations of meanings. (cf. Och's discussion [1979a] of planned and unplanned discourse).

Relating Discourse Features
to Student Engagement

Lemke's (1982) study of high school science lessons includes an analysis of the degree of student communicative engagement (G) as indicated primarily by gaze direction and postural orientation, and the relationship of significant changes in the number of engaged students to features of the discourse. Lemke's design is "to take +G as defining interactively the perceived importance of discourse events and then to look for the local discourse features, structural and/or thematic, that are associated with such +G in more than a few isolated cases" (p. 295).

Structurally, for example, in the common three-part sequences, G rises at each new teacher question and drops with the nomination of a particular student responder. It rises at the beginning of teacher monologs but then drops monotonically during them, rises at a response to a student initiative, and stays high during a demonstration or a debate (pp 291–292).

Even more interesting is the relationship between a rise in G and violations of the norms of scientific discourse (a subject-specific register). G increased with personal reference and daily life reference, fantasy and mystery, colloquial or emotive language — at the same time as students indicated by humor and/or norm-enforcing comments that such talk was heard as violations. Lemke (1982) concludes:

> If we take +G to be a necessary condition of mastering "science" thematic systems, then the processes of science classroom discourse reflect the functional priority of the maintenance of the underlying ideology of the "science" register norms over the development of students' mastery of "science" thematic systems. (p. 297)

Analysing Collaborative Interaction

Like Barnes and Todd, Collins (1983) wanted to analyze discourse for its collaborative quality. He compared teacher–student interaction during the comprehension segments of high and low reading group lessons in a second and third grade with working and lower-middle class black children.

One measure was of "uptake": the incorporation of a student's answer into a subsequent teacher question. (This measure is similar to the "semantic contingency" of caregivers' speech to young children that has been found to be the best predictor of children's subsequent language development [Cazden, in press-b].) Here are two examples with the teacher's utterance marked + for uptake and − for its absence (Collins, 1982, pp. 151, 154):

Uptake	No Uptake
T. All right, what are they looking for?	T. Okay, when we think of a village, what do we think of? . . .
C. Signals	C. A little town.
T. What signals? (+)	T. A small town, yes. And, uh, the son's name is what? (−)

The second measure is of referential coherence: the way in which topics are introduced by a noun phrase or name and then referred to subsequently by an anaphoric pronoun. Where this is not done, and topic shifts are made with potentially ambiguous pronouns, miscommunication can occur.

Collins found that the lower reading groups in both classrooms had fewer teacher uptakes and more sequences (one or two per lesson) where referential cohesion broke down and attention was diverted from discussion of the text to communication repair. After a subsequent out-of-classroom experiment in which he elicited narratives from both high and low group children and found no group differences in the way characters were introduced and referential clarity maintained, Collins argues that the classroom differences must be produced locally, in the reading groups themselves. Possible causes are less complete text knowledge on the part of the children, and more disrupted turns.

Because Collins found linguistic indicators of collaboration does not imply that Barnes and Todd would have been more successful with Collins' measures. There is an important distinction in discourse analysis between coherence and cohesion (Brown & Yule, 1983, pp. 195-199; Stubbs, 1983, p. 9). Coherence refers to underlying semantic relations, whereas cohesion refers to the explicit realizations of these relations in such devices as repeated words (e.g., *signals* in the uptake example) and anaphoric pronouns. It is possible that interaction among peers, in contrast to that led by the teacher, is more apt to achieve its coherence from covert semantic relationships than from overt cohesive devices, and thus may be inherently harder to study.

Tracking Individual Children's Learning

Nuthall and his colleages in New Zealand are developing a methodology for studying in close detail relationships between what children say and do in classrooms and what they give later evidence of having learned. Alton-Lee and Haberfield (1982) present three such case studies of children's learning in a conservation unit in a standard two-three class (upper elementary school in the US).

Records of the focal children's involvement in the curriculum include:

- tape recordings of all class discussions;
- close monitoring of pupil activities (teacher directed, independent, and with peers), including verbatim records of talk, even to self whenever possible; and
- all written and art work.

Measurements of the concepts learned come from a 90-item test designed on the basis of a teacher planning meeting, and interviews before and after the unit and again one year later. The behavioral records were divided into files, one for the content of each of the test items, and each analysed with respect to time, activity and degree of understanding shown. Alton-Lee and Haberfield (1982) report:

> For example, an analysis of Item File 9 concerning the term "slip" (the path where stones and earth have tumbled down a mountainside) reveals the following information with respect to Diane who did not already know the term as measured by the pretest. ... During Episode 1 on Day 2 another pupil erroneously supplies the term "avalanche" and Diane fails to join a class response. She does not appear to give her full attention to the teacher until Episode 4 where he is describing a local example of a slip. The term is clearly defined by the teacher during a demonstration using sand and water in Episode 7. During Episode 8 Diane calls out "slip" in a chorus class response. By episode 16 (she misses out 5 of the teaching

episodes that occur while she is absent or in a different reading group) Diane has clearly understood the term in context as evidenced by her written response, "Rain and Wind" to an activity chart question: "What do you think was the cause of the hillside slipping down? (p. 5)

Before the immediate and delayed tests were analysed, both teacher and researcher predicted each child's learning from the file contents.

From such data, Alton-Lee and Haberfield conclude that both teacher and researcher predicted learning that did not occur, failed to predict forgetting, and failed to predict learning that occurred in the absence of any episodes in a particular file. On the last point, Diane (an average ability working class student) learned no items not in her files, while average and high ability middle class students learned two or three such items—an important insight into "how home background continues to discriminate against pupil success in school" (p. 7).

Not surprisingly, they found a positive relationship between time spent and items learned. But more important than another validation of "academic learning time" are the qualitative indications of particularly valuable ways of spending time, including verbalizations to self, and peer-interactions even during teacher-directed lessons and writing (behaviors that the researchers would have coded "off-task" on a conventional schedule). Items that were initially learned and then forgotten were associated with lack of prior experience and/or failure to clarify later misconceptions, or with lack of "any independent or group activity providing an opportunity to anchor the learning" (p. 13).

Some years ago, during discussions of appropriate evaluation for different early childhood education models (Bank Street, Bereiter-Engelman, etc.), Stodolsky (1972) hypothesized the uniqueness of each child's curriculum, especially in the more "open" models, and the consequent importance of relating any measures of learning to the actual experiences of each child. Stodolsky and Karlson (1972) showed how this could be done in a Montessori preschool. The work of Nuthall and his colleagues can be seen as a further development of this idea, here applied to older children and their interactions with teacher and peers. In a simpler but related way, Mayher and Brause (in press) describe how one teacher (influenced by Barnes's colleague, James Britton) tracked her students' appropriate or confused use of new science vocabulary during various instructional contexts. Even their conclusion about the importance of concrete experience with the concepts the words represent replicates the New Zealand work.

Some Decisions About Methods

Much has been said implicitly in all sections of this chapter about methods. Here I will not repeat or summarize, but merely highlight a few decisions, addressing them in chronological order starting with the selection of classrooms in which to work.

Selection of Classrooms

Access as well as research question will influence the selection of classrooms. And that selection can, in turn, affect what is discovered. Carew and Lightfoot (1979) commented on the effect of access on their results. Chall and Snow (1982) happened fortuitously to study some differences between volunteer and non-volunteer teachers. In a study of the development of literacy in working-class families, teachers were solicited who agreed to be interviewed and to permit observations of focal children in reading groups and other literacy instruction. Since it was a two-year study, the children moved on to other teachers who were then approached with the same research requests. Although comparison of school experiences in the two years was not a part of the original design, comments about the focal children in teacher interviews were sufficiently striking to appear in the final report. For example:

> In the first year of the study, teachers considered about one-third of both Black and white children as "better than average" in reading. In contrast, in the second year, teachers named none of the Black children and 24% of the white children as better than average (in spite of equal proportions of Black and white focal children scoring above average on standardized tests (Ch. 5, p. 56).

In this particular school system, interpretation of differences between year 1 and year 2 teachers was complicated by co-occuring influences: the passage of severe tax-cutting legislation in the state, and the beginning of a pupil-assignment integration plan in the city. But some of the difference may be due to the contrast between volunteer vs. non-volunteer teachers.

How serious this difference is depends on the researcher's views on generalizability. If one is hoping to find out something true in general, then the representativeness of classrooms studied matters very much. But if one is interested, for example, in relationships between teacher expectations as expressed in interviews and patterns of classroom discourse, then the close study of any classroom or small set of classrooms can contribute. Hymes (1982) writes at length "of a major change in the value placed on the individual instance" in the history of linguistic research (pp. 88 ff).

How to Record

Both reviewers of this chapter (Hymes and Stubbs, personal communications, 1983) point out that some Sc researchers work from observational field notes rather than tapes and transcriptions, and that all researchers may be interested in some situations where taping is impossible. A combination of methods may be the best strategy, but, given the increasingly wide availability of recording equipment and familiarity with it, reliance on field notes alone seems hard to justify. If one is to get down actual speech, not just the gist of content, then demands on the observer for transcribing speech in real time are extreme, simultaneous attention to any aspect of context is impossible, and there is no way to retrieve information (for example, about intonation) that was not noted in the first place.

A more difficult decision is what kind of recording equipment to use. The first decision is between video and audio recording. The importance of nonverbal information is asserted not only by Erickson and Shultz (1982, p. 215) who work from videotapes, but also acknowledged by Coulthard (1977, p. 106) who

does not. But serious disadvantages to videotape have to be considered as well: the greater obtrusiveness of the equipment, the more time required for analysis, and the ethical problems of privacy in any public display of the original protocols, because there is no visual analogue of a pseudonym. See Erickson and Wilson's handbook (1982) on videotaping as a research tool for extensive discussion. In the end, choice of equipment should depend on the questions one hopes to answer.

To be avoided is the determination, by the equipment being used, of the situations one can study and the questions one can ask. Erickson and Shultz (1982) point out the limitations of "focusing research attention on social situations in which talk is the central, foregrounded aspect of the activity, and consequently diverting empirical research and theory development away from considering interactional occasions in which talk is a secondary, backgrounded accompaniment to other action" (p. 215). The prevalence of lessons/recitations as research sites is as much due to the foregrounded, easily captured, talk in such settings as to their educational importance. See also Walker and Adelman (1975).

One specific decision is the kind of microphone to use. Overhead or table microphones limit recordings to events in which stationary speakers talk one at a time and background noise is minimized, situations which are usually under teacher control. To record talk in other classroom settings, some kind of wireless equipment that can be worn by focal participants is necessary. Erickson and Wilson mention only the expensive kind that broadcasts a signal to a recording deck. A cheaper alternative used by Cherry (1975) and Garnica (1981) is to attach an entire small cassette recorder on the teacher or focal child.

How to Transcribe

At some point in the analysis, transcriptions will be needed of part or all of the recordings, and decisions will have to be made about what information from the speech to retain in written form. There is no one best kind of transcription. The fact that the conventions of the conversational analysts (Sacks, Schegloff, & Jefferson, 1974) are becoming widely followed is not necessarily progress. They can be used as unthinkingly as any simpler system.

What is essential is not any specific convention, but to consider "transcription as theory" (Ochs, 1979b). The best discussions of the general problem and ways of thinking about alternative solutions are by Ochs, and Mishler (in press). The fact that Ochs is concerned with language development and Mishler with medical interviews makes their work no less relevant for analysts of classroom discourse. Both succeed "to make the task of transcription problematic, that is, to make explicit the gap between speech and text and thereby to uncover the issues involved in constructing transcripts . . . that are used as the basis for analyses and interpretations" (Mishler, in press, Ch. 2).

Related to decisions about what information to represent in the transcript are decisions about how to lay out that information on a page. Transcripts do not have to look like play scripts, and imaginative variations can serve to foreground features of the discourse focal in a particular analysis. For examples, see Mishler's use (in press) of different typefaces to foreground the voice of the patient's life world and the conflict between it and the voice of medicine; Merritt's analogous alternation (1982b) of left margins to indicate different "vectors of activity" when a teacher momentarily leaves one activity to attend to a child engaged in another; and Edelsky's experimentation (1981) with layouts in order to capture sex differences in multi-party interactions.

Whether to Interview as Well as Observe

Interviewing teachers, or holding collaborative listening or viewing sessions with them, is becoming more common. (See Florio & Walsh, 1981, jointly authored by researcher and teacher respectively, and Florio, 1981.) Helpful as such discussions can be for the teacher-researcher relationship, and possibly for the teacher's reflection on practice, the value to the discourse analysis of what teachers perceive and report is problematic.

Consider Mehan's (1974) analysis of a lesson on the comprehension and production of spatial prepositions. Although the teacher had said before the lesson that she wanted the children to produce answers that were both factually correct and grammatically complete, the actual answers varied widely. "The desired answer form [such as "The flower is under the tree."] was neither uniformly demanded nor obtained, and tokens of the same type are treated differently" (p. 106). Mehan believes that the teacher's differential treatment of children's answers, coupled with her simultaneous perceptions of uniform treatment, is a natural result of the changing moment-to-moment demands on her attention, and of her inevitably idealized memory of those moments at the time of a later account. Edwards and Furlong (1978, p. 77) refer to Mehan's work in explaining why they decided not to ask teachers and students for their interpretations.

In Mehan's later work, he deliberately eschewed interviews or viewing sessions in favor of discovering the meaning of actions to the participants through analyses of their talk and action only. McDermott, Gospodinoff, and Aron (1978) worked in the same way. In both cases, patterns were discovered in the talk that were out of awareness for the participants. The explanation lies in what Silverstein (1981) calls "the limits of awareness": the difficulty of monitoring and remembering features of speech. Most accessible to awareness and most easily remembered is the referential dimension (and not surprisingly, linguistic theories started here too); less accessible and harder to remember are details not of what was said, but how. The value of interviewing, therefore, is relative to the questions being asked and the aspects of discourse being examined.

Interviewing students is less common than interviewing teachers. Elliott (1976–77) and Adelman (1981) describe their "triangulation" among accounts of a teaching situation from three points of view—teacher, students, and observer—in an action research project whose main objective was to stimulate teachers' self-monitoring. After the teachers had been interviewed once, they were presented with the students' interpretations of the same event as a further stimulus to their reflections.

The most extensive interviewing of pupils is by Morine-Dershimer and Tenenberg (1981). In one procedure, children were individually shown videotapes of lessons they had been in earlier the same day and then asked, after the viewing, to report "what you heard anybody saying." One striking finding by Morine-Dershimer and Tenenberg (1981) was the saliency to the child viewers of the comments of their peers:

> Speech acts occurring in the answering move were reported significantly more often (proportionate to their occurrence) than acts in the opening or follow-up move ($p = .0001$). Thus pupil attention was strongly focused on the comments of other pupils. (p. 41)

Of course, the caution about not assuming identity between perceptions at the moment of acting and in a later account applies to children as well as to teachers. The pressure on children to attend to the teacher in actual lessons is totally absent in a viewing session with an outside researcher. But the greater attention to peers than to teacher could be reduced in real life and still significant. See Lemke's related finding from his *in situ* measure of engagement discussed earlier in this chapter, and see Forbes and Lubin's description (in press) of their extensive experience in interviewing children about videotapes in social cognition research.

The Role of Formal Models in Analysis

The value of formal models was discussed earlier in this chapter, but more needs to be said. Descriptions of human behavior involve both searching for repeated patterns—often called "rules"—and acknowledging, even with admiration, the inevitable improvisation. The rules can be given formal expression—of which Figures 15.1, 15.2 15.4, and 15.5 are examples; but that is only part of the story. If we were trying to describe the competence of jazz musicians, for example, we would have to attend both to their knowledge of a musical system, and to their ability to use that knowledge in creative ways at particular moments. The same is true of speakers; they know more than the general rules. (cf. Hammersley's discussion, 1981, of the need for "putting competence into action.")

So Mehan complements his rules with analyses of the teacher's ways of "getting through." And Erickson (1982b) makes improvisation more than a metaphor in his rhythmic analysis in musical notation of variations on a theme (rule) in a math lesson. Erickson's (1982b) final comment explains the methodological alternatives (of which he chose the second):

> From examination of a number of instances of the performance of a small lesson sequence, an underlying ideal model was inferred. The model outlines some salient aspects of the social participation structure and the academic task structure. . . . Looking closely at the performance of an instance of the lesson sequence, however, one sees that it is usually discrepant in some features of specific organization from the general, inferred model. If one is not simply to regard these discrepancies as random error (free variation), one has at least two options: to elaborate the formalization of the model by stating an embedded system of optional rules; or to assume that what is happening is adaptive variation, specific to the immediate circumstances of practical action in the moment of enactment. (p. 178)

The Value of Counting

At several points in this chapter (e.g., Delamont, 1976; Garnica, 1981; Mehan, 1979) the value of combining quantitative and qualitative forms of analysis has been pointed out. This distinction between P-P and Sc research is not between those who count and who don't. As Hymes says appreciatively in introducing a book of Sc research (Sankoff, 1980) that includes many statistical analyses, it is a book about "counting in context." In the same spirit, Erickson's (1977) contribution to a conference on "qualitative/quantitative research methodologies in education" applies to research on classroom discourse:

> Differences among approaches lie not in the presence or absence of quantification per se (if one thinks of quantification simply as a means of summarizing information) but in the underlying assumptions of method and proof. ... What is essential to qualitative or naturalistic research is not that it avoids the use of frequency data, but that its primary concern is with deciding what makes sense to count — with definitions of the quality of things of social life. The reluctance of many qualitatively oriented researchers to count things may be related to a theoretically based reluctance to follow Durkheim's injunction to consider social facts as things. ... The trick lies in defining carefully what the facts are in ways that are precise, reliable, and capable of quantitative summary, yet articulate with the meanings the facts have to the people engaged in everyday life. (pp. 58–59).

Finally, What do We Report Back to the Participants?

In addition to the publication of research findings as a contribution to public knowledge, researchers have an ethical responsibility to the teacher(s) observed. There seems to be a prevailing belief that the more self-knowledge the better, and that a major function of research is providing food for self-reflection. Cazden (1982) expresses one teacher's doubts on this point, doubts that apply only to information about the teacher's own behavior, not to insights about the students. Steinberg and Cazden (1979) suggest that whereas "much teacher training, preservice and inservice, focuses directly on teaching behaviors, ... perhaps a direct comparison could be made of the change value of focusing on the teacher herself vs. focusing with her on her children" (p. 265).

Concluding Remarks

In conclusion, I want to return to two phrases in the quote that opens this chapter, and then end with an issue beyond its scope.

In considering how talk unites the cognitive and the social, we have seen that "social" has two interrelated meanings: the microsociological meaning of the situation of which talk is a part, and the macrosociological meaning of stratifications within society — by class, ethnicity, sex, etc. Research on classroom discourses that can contribute to increased equity as well as increased quality needs to consider both sets of variables.

Not all the research mentioned in this chapter was designed to contribute to the improvement of practise. Some has been done by linguists, anthropologists or sociologists as a contribution to the work of their disciplines. In this first review, I have deliberately been eclectic, believing that we have much to learn about modes of analysis. But in the end, as educational researchers and not just scholars working in a classroom field site, "we are interested in linguistic forms only insofar as through them we can gain insight into the social events of the classroom and thereby into the understandings which students achieve."

But to say that does not answer difficult questions about how the understandings of researchers help the practice of teachers, about how social science knowledge gets appropriated into practitioners' knowing, about deciding who should select the research questions and who can make the best use of the answers. These questions apply not just to this chapter alone.

REFERENCES

Adelman, C. (1981). On first hearing. In C. Adelman (Ed.), *Uttering, muttering: Collecting, using and reporting talk for social and educational research.* London: Grant McIntyre.

Allington, R. L. (1980). Teacher interruption behaviors during primary grade oral reading. *Journal of Educational Psychology, 72,* 371–377.

Alpert, J. L. (1975). Do teachers adapt methods and materials to ability groups in reading? *California Journal of Educational Research, 26,* 120–123.

Alton-Lee, A., & Haberfield, R. (1982). *Understanding teaching and learning in classrooms: A predictive case study approach.* Christchurch, New Zealand: Canterbury University.

Anderson, E. S. (1978). Learning to speak with style: a study of the sociolinguistic skills of children. Unpub. doctoral dissertation, Stanford University. (University Microfilms No. 78-8755).

Au, K. H. (1979). Using the experience–text–relationship method with minority children. *The Reading Teacher, 32,* 677–679.

Au, K. H. (1980). Participation structures in a reading lesson with Hawaiian children: Analysis of a culturally appropriate instructional event. *Anthropology & Education Quarterly, 11,* 91–115.

Au, K. H-P., & Jordan, C. (1981). Teaching reading to Hawaiian children: Finding a culturally appropriate solution. In H. T. Treuba, G. P. Guthrie, & K. H-P. Au (Eds.), *Culture and the bilingual classroom: Studies in classroom ethnography.* Rowley, Mass.: Newbury House.

Au, K. H., & Mason, J. M. (1981). Social organizational factors in learning to read: The balance of rights hypothesis. *Reading Research Quarterly, 17,* 115–152.

Au, K. H-P., & Mason, J. M. (1982). *A microethnographic approach to the study of classroom reading instruction: Rationale and procedures.* Technical Report No. 237. Urbana-Champaign: Univ. of Illinois, Center for the Study of Reading.

Barnes, D. (1976). *From communication to curriculum.* London: Penguin. (Now available from Boynton/Cook, Montclair, N. J.).

Barnes, D., Britton, J., & Rosen, H. (1969). *Language, the learner and the school.* Baltimore, Md.: Penguin Books. (Revised ed., 1971; 3rd ed. in press.)

Barnes, D., & Todd, F. (1977). *Communication and learning in small groups.* London & Boston: Routledge & Kegan Paul.

Barnes, D., & Todd, F. (1981). Talk in small learning groups: Analysis of strategies. In C. Adelman (Ed.), *Uttering, muttering: Collecting, using and reporting talk for social and educational research.* London: Grant McIntyre.

Barnhardt, C. (1982). Tuning-in: Athabaskan teachers and Athabaskan students. In R. Barnhardt (Ed.), *Cross-cultural issues in Alaskan education.* Fairbanks, Alaska: Univ. of Alaska, Center for Cross-cultural Studies.

Bateson, G. (1972). *Steps to an ecology of mind.* New York: Ballantine Books.

Bauman, R., & Sherzer, J. (1975). The ethnography of speaking. *Annual Review of Anthropology, 4,* 95–119.

Bellack, A. A. (1978). *Competing ideologies in research on teaching.* Uppsala (Sweden): Uppsala Univ., Dept. of Education, Uppsala Reports on Education 1, Sept.

Bellack, A. A., Kliebard, H., Hyman, R., & Smith, F. (1966). *The language of the classroom.* New York: Teachers College Press.

Berliner, D. (1976). Impediments to the study of teacher effectiveness. *Journal of Teacher Education, 27*(1), 5–13.

Berliner, D. C. (1983). Developing conceptions of classroom environments: Some light on the T in classroom studies of ATI. *Educational Psychologist, 18,* 1–13.

Bernstein, B. (1971). On the classification and framing of educational knowledge. In *Class, Codes and Control* (Vol. 1). Beverly Hills, CA: Sage Publications.

Bernstein, B. (1981). Codes, modalities, and the process of cultural reproduction: A model. *Language in Society, 10,* 327–363.

Black, S. D., Levin, J. A., Mehan, H., & Quinn (1983). Real and non-real time interaction: Unraveling multiple threads of discourse. *Discourse Processes, 6,* 59–75.

Blank, M. (1973). *Teaching learning in the preschool: a dialogue approach.* Columbus, Ohio: Charles E. Merrill.

Bloom, B. S. (Ed.). (1956). *Taxonomy of educational objectives: Handbook I: Cognitive domain.* New York: Longmans, Green.

Boggs, S. T. (1972). The meaning of questions and narratives to Hawaiian children. In C. B. Cazden, V. P. John, & D. Hymes (Eds.), *Functions of Language in the classroom.* New York: Teachers College Press. (p. 299–327.)

Bredo, E., & Feinberg, W. (Eds.). (1983). *Knowledge and values in social and educational research.* Philadelphia: Temple University Press.

Bremme, D. W., & Erickson, F. (1977). Relationships among verbal and nonverbal classroom behaviors. *Theory into Practice, 16,* 153–161.

Brown, G. and Yule, G. (1983). *Discourse Analysis.* Cambridge (England) and New York: Cambridge University Press.

Brown, P., & Levison, S. (1978). Universals in language usage: Politeness phenomena. In E. N. Goody (Ed.), *Questions and politeness: strategies in social interaction.* Cambridge: Cambridge University Press.

Brown, R. (1977). Introduction. In C. E. Snow & C. A. Ferguson (Eds.), *Talking to children: Language input and acquisition.* New York: Cambridge University Press.

Brown, R., & Bellugi, U. (1964). Three processes in the child's acquisition of syntax. *Harvard Educ. Rev., 34,* 133–151.

Burton, D. (1981). The sociolinguistic analysis of spoken discourse. In P. French & M. MacLure (Eds.), *Adult-child conversation.* New York: St. Martins Press. (p. 21–46.)

Byers, P., & Byers, H. (1972). Nonverbal communication and the education of children. In C. B. Cazden, V. P. John, & D. Hymes (Eds.), *Functions of language in the classroom.* New York: Teachers College Press.

Cahir, S. R., & Kovac, C. (1981a). *It's your turn.* Washington, D. C.: Center for Applied Linguistics.

Cahir, S. R., & Kovac, C. (1981b). *Teacher talk works.* Washington, D. C.: Center for Applied Linguistics.

Calfee, R. C., Cazden, C. B., Duran, R. P., Griffin, M. P., Martus, M., & Willis, H. D. (1981). *Designing reading instruction for cultural minorities: The case of the Kamehameha Early Education Program.* Report to the Ford Foundation, December. (ED 215 039)

Carew, J. V., & Lightfoot, S. L. (1979). *Beyond bias: Perspectives on classrooms.* Cambridge and London: Harvard University Press.

Carrasco, R. L., Vera, A., & Cazden, C. B. (1981). Aspects of bilingual students' communicative competence in the classroom: A case study. In R. Duran (Ed.), *Latino language and communicative behavior.* Advances in discourse processes, Vol. 6. Norwood, N.J.: Ablex Pub.

Cazden, C. B. (1979). Language in education: Variation in the teacher-talk register. In J. Alatis & R. Rucker (Eds.), *Language in public life.* Washington, D.C.: Georgetown University Round Table on Languages and Linguistics.

Cazden, C. B. (1982). Four comments. In P. Gilmore & A. Glatthorn, (Eds.), *Ethnography and education: Children in and out of school.* Washington, D.C.: Center for Applied Linguistics.

Cazden, C. B. (1983a). Peekaboo as an instructional model: Discourse development at school and at home. In B. Bain (Ed.), *The sociogenesis of language and human conduct: A multi-disciplinary book of readings.* N.Y.: Plenum.

Cazden, C. B. (1983b). Can ethnographic research go beyond the status quo? *Anthropology and Education Quarterly, 14,* 33–41.

Cazden, C. B. (in press-a). Ability grouping and differential reading instruction: What happens and some possible whys. In J. Osborn & P. Wilson (Eds.), *Research foundations for a literate America.* Lexington, Mass.: Lexington Books.

Cazden, C. B. (in press-b). Environmental assistance revisited: variation and functional equivalence. In F. Kessell (Ed.), *The Development of Language and Language Researchers.* Hillsdale, N.J.: Erlbaum.

Cazden, C. B., Carrasco, R., Maldonado-Guzman, A. A., and Erickson, F. (1980). The contribution of ethnographic research to bicultural bilingual education. In J. Alatis (Ed.), *Current Issues in Bilingual Education.* Georgetown University Round Table on Language and Linguistics, Washington, D.C.: Georgetown University Press, 64–80.

Cazden, C. B., et al. (1979). "You all gonna hafta listen": Peer teaching in a primary classroom. In W. A. Collins (Ed.), *Children's language and communication.* Twelfth Annual Minnesota Symposium on Child Development. Hillsdale, N.J.: Lawrence Erlbaum.

Cazden, C., & Hymes, D. (1980). Narrative thinking and story-telling rights: A folklorist's clue to a critique of education. In D. Hymes, *Language in education: Ethnolinguistic essays.* Washington, D.C.: Center for Applied Linguistics.

Cazden, C. B., John, V. P., & Hymes, D. (Eds.). (1972). *Functions of language in the classroom.* New York: Teachers College Press.

Cazden, C. B., Michaels, S., & Tabors, P. (in press). Self-repair in Sharing Time narratives: The intersection of metalinguistic awareness, speech event and narrative style. In S. W. Freedman (Ed.), *The acquisition of writing: Revision and response.* Norwood, N.J.: Ablex.

Chall, J. & Snow, C. (Eds.). (1982). *Families and literacy: The contribution of out-of-school experiences to children's acquisition of literacy.* Final report to the National Institute of Education.

Chanan, G., & Delamont, S. (Eds.). (1975). *Frontiers of classroom research.* Slough (England): National Foundation for Educational Research.

Charconnet, M. G. (1975). Development of educational methods and techniques adapted to the specific conditions of the developing countries: Peer tutoring: Operational description of various systems and their applications. Paris: UNESCO, Div. of Methods, Materials and Techniques. (ED 136 776).

Cherry, L. J. (1975). The preschool teacher-child dyad: Sex differences in verbal interaction. *Child Development, 46,* 532–536.

Cicourel, A. V., Jennings, K. H., Jennings, S. H. H., Leiter, K. C. W., Mackay, R., Mehan, H., & Roth, D. R. (1974). *Language use and school performance.* New York: Academic Press.

Cochran-Smith, M. (in press). *The making of a reader.* Norwood, N.J.: Ablex.

Collier, M. (1979). A film study of classrooms in Western Alaska. Fairbanks, Alaska: University of Alaska at Fairbanks, Center for Cross-Cultural Studies. (ED 180 704).

Collins, J. (1982). Discourse style, classroom interaction and differential treatment. *Journal of Reading Behavior, 14,* 429–437.

Collins, J. P. (1983). A linguistic perspective on minority education: Discourse analysis and early literacy. Unpub. doctoral dissertation, Univ. of California-Berkeley.

Cooper, C. R., Ayers-Lopez, S., & Marquis, A. (1982). A children's discourse during peer learning in experimental and naturalistic situations. *Discourse Processes, 5,* 177–191.

Cooper, C. R., Marquis, A., & Ayers-Lopez, S. (1982). Peer learning in the classroom: Tracing developmental patterns and consequences of children's spontaneous interactions. In L. C. Wilkinson (Ed.), *Communicating in the classroom.* New York: Academic.

Cooper, C. R., Marquis, A., & Edward, D. (in press). Four perspectives and peer learning among elementary school children. In E. C. Mueller & C. R. Cooper (Eds.), *Process and outcome in peer relations.* New York: Academic.

Copeland, S. (1978). The effects, values and experiences of reading aloud in traditional Jewish text: A study in the coordination of form and content. Unpub. doctoral dissertation, Harvard Graduate School of Education.

Coulthard, M. (1977). *An Introduction to discourse analysis.* London: Longman.

Delamont, S. (1976). Beyond Flanders fields: The relationship of subject-matter and individuality to classroom style. In M. Stubbs & S. Delamont (Eds.), *Explorations in classroom observation.* London: John Wiley.

Delamont, S. (1983). *Interaction in the classroom.* London: Methuen.

Delamont, S., & Atkinson, P. (1980). The two traditions in educational ethnography: Sociology and anthropology compared. *British Journal of Sociology of Education. 1,* 139–152.

Dickson, W. P. (1981). Referential communication activities in research and in the curriculum: A meta-analysis. In W. P. Dickson (Ed.), *Children's oral communication skills.* New York: Academic Press.

Dore, J. (1979). Conversation and preschool language development. In P. Fletcher & M. Garman (Eds.), *Language acquisition: Studies in first language development.* New York: Cambridge University Press.

Dore, J., Gearhardt, M., & Newman, D. (1978). The structure of nursery school conversation. In K. Nelson (Ed.), *Children's language,* Vol. 1. New York: Gardner.

Dore, J., & McDermott, R. P. (1982). Linguistic indeterminacy and social context in utterance interpretation. *Language, 58,* 374–397.

Dorr-Bremme, D. W. (1982). Behaving and making sense: Creating social organization in the classroom. Unpub. doctoral dissertation, Harvard University. (UMI # 82-23, 203).

Doyle, W. (1983). Academic work. *Review of Educational Research, 53,* 159-199.

Dunkin, M. J., & Biddle, B. J. (1974). *The study of teaching.* New York: Holt, Rinehart & Winston.

Duranti, A., & Ochs, E. (in press). Literacy instruction in a Samoan village. In B. B. Schieffelin (Ed.), *Acquisition of literacy: Ethnographic perspectives.* Norwood, N.J.: Ablex.

Durkin, D. (1979). What classroom observations reveal about reading comprehension instruction. *Reading Research Quarterly, 14,* 481–533.

Edelsky, C. (1981). Who's got the floor? *Language in Society, 10,* 383–421.

Eder, D. (1981). Ability grouping as a self-fulfilling prophecy: A microanalysis of teacher-student interaction. *Sociology of Education, 54,* 151–162.

Eder, D. (1982a). The impact of management and turn-allocation activities on student performance. *Discourse Processes, 5,* 147–159.

Eder, D. (1982b). Differences in communicative styles across ability groups. In L. C. Wilkinson (Ed.), *Communicating in the classroom.* New York: Academic.

Edwards, A. D. (1980). Patterns of power and authority in classroom talk. In P. Woods (Ed.), *Teacher strategies: Explorations in the sociology of the school.* London: Croom Helm.

Edwards, A. D., & Furlong, J. J. (1978). *The language of teaching: Meaning in classroom interaction.* London: Heinemann.

Elliott, J. (1976). Developing hypotheses about classrooms from teachers' practical constructs: An account of the work of the Ford Teaching Project. *Interchange, 7*(2), 2–22.

Erickson, F. (1975). Gate-keeping and the melting pot: Interaction in counseling interviews. *Harvard Educational Review, 45,* 44–70.

Erickson, F. (1977). Some approaches to inquiry in school/community ethnography. *Anthropology and Education Quarterly, 8,* 58–69.

Erickson, F. (1982a). Taught cognitive learning in its immediate environment: A neglected topic in the anthropology of education. *Anthropology and Education Quarterly, 13,* 149–180.

Erickson, F. (1982b). Classroom discourse as improvisation: Relationships between academic task structure and social participation structures in lessons. In L. C. Wilkinson (Ed.), *Communicating in the classroom.* New York: Academic Press.

Erickson, F. (in press). Anecdote, rhapsody, and rhetoric: Devices and strategies for coherence in a discussion among Black American adolescents. In D. Tannen (Ed.), *Coherence in spoken and written discourse.* Norwood, N.J.: Ablex.

Erickson, F., & Mohatt, G. (1982). Cultural organization of participant structures in two classrooms of Indian students. In G. D. Spindler (Ed.), *Doing the ethnography of schooling: Educational anthropology in action.* New York: Holt, Rinehart & Winston.

Erickson, F., & Shultz, J. (1977). When is a context? Some issues and

methods in the analysis of social competence. *Quarterly Newsletter of the Institute for Comparative Human Development, 1*(2), 5–10. Also in J. Green & C. Wallat (Eds.), *Ethnography and language in educational settings.* Norwood, N.J.: Ablex, 1981.

Erickson, F., & Shultz, J. (1982). *The counselor as gatekeeper: Social interaction in interviews.* New York: Academic Press.

Erickson, F., & Wilson, J. (1982). *Sights and sounds of life in schools: A resource guide to film and videotape for research and education.* East Lansing: Michigan State Univer., College of Education.

Feldman, C. F., & Wertsch, J. V. (1976). Context dependent properties of teacher's speech. *Youth and Society, 7,* 227–258.

Ferguson, C. A. (1977). Baby talk as a simplified register. In C. E. Snow & C. A. Ferguson (Eds.), *Talking to children: language input and acquisition.* New York: Cambridge Univer. Press.

Fisher, S. (1979). Revealing students' reasoning practices. *Journal of Classroom Interaction, 15,* 16–24.

Flanders, N. (1970). *Analysing teacher behavior.* Reading, Mass.: Addison-Wesley.

Flanders, N. A. (1974). Review of *Functions of language in the classroom. Research in the Teaching of English, 8,* 46–48.

Florio, S. (1981). Very special natives: The evolving role of teachers as informants in educational ethnography. Occasional Paper No. 42. East Lansing: Michigan State University, The Institute for Research on Teaching. (ED 204 342).

Florio, S., & Shultz, J. (1979). Social competence at home and at school. *Theory into Practice, 18,* 234–243.

Florio, S., & Walsh, M. (1981). The teacher as colleague in classroom research. In H. T. Treuba, G. P. Guthrie, & K. H. P. Au (Ed.), *Culture and the bilingual classroom: Studies in classroom ethnography.* Rowley, Mass.: Newbury.

Forbes, D. L., & Lubin, D. A. (in press). Verbal social reasoning and observed persuasion strategies in children's social behavior. In H. Sypher & L. Applegate (Eds.), *Social cognition and social behavior.* Beverly Hills: Sage.

Forman, E. A. (1981). The role of collaboration in problem solving in children. Unpub. doctoral dissertation, Harvard University.

Forman, E. A., & Cazden, C. B. (in press). Exploring Vygotskian perspectives in education: The cognitive value of peer interaction. In J. V. Wertsch (Ed.), *Culture, communication and cognition: Vygotskian perspectives.* New York: Cambridge University Press.

French, P., & MacLure, M. (1981). Teachers' questions, pupils' answers: An investigation of questions and answers in the infant classroom. *First Language, 2,* 31–45.

French, P., & Woll, B. (1981). Context, meaning and strategy in parent-child conversation. In G. Wells (Ed.), *Learning through interaction: The study of language development.* Cambridge: Cambridge University Press.

Gage, N. L. (1977). *The scientific basis of the art of teaching.* New York: Teachers College Press.

Gall, M. D. (1970). The use of questioning in teaching. *Review of Educational Research, 40,* 707–720.

Galton, M., Simon, B., & Croll, P. (1980). *Inside the primary classroom.* Boston: Routledge & Kegan Paul.

Garfinkel, H., & Sacks, H. (1970). On formal structures of practical actions. In J. C. McKinney & E. A. Tiryakian (Eds.), *Theoretical sociology.* New York: Appleton-Century-Crofts.

Garnica, O. K. (1981). Social dominance and classroom interaction — The omega child in the classroom. In J. Green & C. Wallat (Eds.), *Ethnography and language in educational settings.* Norwood, N.J.: Ablex.

Gearhart, M., & Newman, D. (1980). Learning to draw a picture: The social context of an individual activity. *Discourse Processes, 3,* 169–184.

Geertz, C. (1980). Blurred genres: The refiguration of social thought. *American Scholar, 49,* 165–179.

Gilmore, P. (1981). Shortridge school and community: Attitudes and admission to literacy. In D. Hymes, *Ethnographic monitoring of children's acquisition of reading/language arts skills in and out of the classroom.* Final report to the National Institute of Education. (ED 208 096).

Goffman, E. (1971). *Relations in public: Microstudies of the public order.* New York: Basic Books.

Goodlad, J. I. (1983). A study of schooling: Some findings and hypotheses. *Phi Delta Kappan, 64,* 465–470.

Green, J. L. (1983). Research on teaching as a linguistic process: A state of the art. In E. W. Gordon (Ed.), *Review of research in education, Vol. 10.* Washington: American Educational Research Association.

Green, J., & Bloome, D. (in press). Ethnography and reading: Issues, approaches, criteria, and findings. *The 1983 Yearbook of the National Reading Conference.*

Griffin, P. (1977). How and when does reading occur in the classroom? *Theory Into Practice, 16,* 376–383.

Griffin, P., Cole, M., & Newman, D. (1982). Locating tasks in psychology and education. *Discourse Processes, 5,* 111–125.

Griffin, P., & Mehan, H. (1979). Sense and ritual in classroom discourse. In F. Coulmas (Ed.), *Conversational routine: Explorations in standardized communication situations and prepatterned speech.* Janua Linguarum. The Hague: Moulton.

Gumperz, J. (1977). Sociocultural knowledge in conversational inference. In M. Saville-Troike (Ed.), *Linguistics and anthropology.* Washington, D.C.: Georgetown University Press.

Gumperz, J. J., & Herasimchuk, (1973). The conversational analysis of social meaning: a study of classroom interaction. In R. W. Shuy (Ed.), *Sociolinguistics: Current trends and prospects.* 23rd Annual Round Table. Washington, D.C.: Georgetown University Press.

Gumperz, J. J., & Hymes, D. (1972). *Directions in sociolinguistics: The ethnography of communication.* New York: Holt, Rinehart & Winston.

Hall, E. T. (1961). *The silent language.* Greenwich, Conn.: Premier Books. (original, 1959).

Hammersley, M. (1977). School learning: The cultural resources required by pupils to answer a teacher's question. In P. Woods & M. Hammersley (Eds.), *School experience: Explorations in the sociology of education.* London: Croom Helm.

Hammersley, M. (1981). Putting competence into action: Some sociological notes on a model of classroom interaction. In P. French & M. MacLure (Eds.), *Adult-child conversation.* New York: St. Martins Press.

Hargreaves, D. H. (1980). The occupational culture of teachers. In P. Woods (Ed.), *Teacher strategies: Explorations in the sociology of the school.* London: Croom Helm.

Harris, S (1977) Milimgimbi Aboriginal learning contexts Unpublished doctoral dissertation, University of New Mexico.

Harris, S. (1980). Culture and learning: Tradition and education in Northeast Arnheim Land. Darwin (Australia): Northern Territory Department of Education, Professional Services Branch.

Hawkins, J., Sheingold, K., Gearhart, M., & Berger, C. (1982). Microcomputers in schools: Impact on the social life of elementary classrooms. *Journal of Applied Developmental Psychology, 3,* 361–373.

Heap, J. L. (1980). What counts as reading: Limits to certainty in assessment. *Curriculum Inquiry, 10,* 265–292.

Heap, J. L. (1982). Understanding classroom events: A critique of Durkin, with an alternative. *Journal of Reading Behavior, 14,* 391–411.

Heath, S. B. (1978). *Teacher talk: Language in the classroom.* Washington: Center for Applied Linguistics.

Heath, S. B. (1982a). What no bedtime story means: Narrative skills at home and school. *Language in Society, 11,* 49–76.

Heath, S. B. (1982b). Questioning at home and at school: A comparative study. In G. Spindler (Ed.), *Doing the ethnography of schooling: Educational anthropology in action.* New York: Holt, Rinehart & Winston.

Heath, S. B. (1983). *Ways with words: Language, life, and work in communities and classrooms.* Cambridge (England): Cambridge University Press.

Heath, S. B. (in press). A lot of talk about nothing: Preparation for academic success? *Language Arts.*

Heritage, J. C., & Watson, D. R. (1979). Formulations as conversational objects. In G. Psathas (Ed.), *Everyday language: Studies in ethnomethodology.* New York: Irvington.

Hoetker, J., & Ahlbrand, W. P. Jr. (1969). The persistence of the recitation. *American Educational Research Journal, 6,* 145–167.

Hollins, E. R. (1982). The Marva Collins story revisited: Implications for regular classroom instruction. *Journal of Teacher Education, 33,* 37–40.

Hymes, D. (1962). The ethnography of speaking. In T. Gladwin & W. C. Sturtevant (Eds.), *Anthropology and human behavior.* Washington: Anthropological Society of Washington.

Hymes, D. (1971). Competence and performance in linguistic theory. In R. Huxley & E. Ingram (Eds.), *Language acquisition: models and methods.* New York: Academic Press.

Hymes, D. (1972a). Introduction. In C. B. Cazden, V. P. John, & D. Hymes (Eds.), *Functions of language in the classroom.* New York: Teachers College Press.

Hymes, D. (1972b). Models of the interaction of language and social life. In J. J. Gumperz & D. Hymes (Eds.), *Directions in sociolinguistics: the ethnography of communication.* New York: Holt, Rinehart & Winston.

Hymes, D. H. (1977). Qualitative/quantitative research methodologies in education: a linguistic perspective. *Anthropology and education quarterly, 8,* 165–176.

Hymes, D. (1980). *Language in education: Ethnolinguistic essays.* Washington, D.C.: Center for Applied Linguistics. (ED 198 745).

Hymes, D. H. (1981). Ethnographic monitoring of children's acquisition of reading/language arts skills in and out of the classroom. Final report to the National Institute of Education. (ED 208 096).

Hymes, D. H. (1982). Ethnolinguistic study of classroom discourse. Final report to the National Institute of Education, April. (ED 217 710).

Irvine, J. T. (1979). Formality and informality in communicative events. *American Anthropologist, 81,* 773–790.

Jackson, P. W. (1968). *Life in classrooms.* New York: Holt, Rinehart & Winston.

Jordan, C., & Tharp, R. G. (1979). Culture and education. In A. J. Marsella, R. G. Tharp, & T. J. Ciborowski (Eds.), *Perspectives on cross-cultural psychology.* New York: Academic Press.

Karabel, J., & Halsey, A. H. (1976). The new sociology of education. *Theory and Society, 3,* 529–552.

Keddie, N. (1971). Classroom knowledge. In M. F. D. Young (Ed.), *Knowledge and control: New directions in the sociology of education.* London: Collier Macmillan.

Kleinfeld, J. (1975). Positive stereotyping: The cultural relativist in the classroom *Human Organization, 34,* 269–274.

Kleinfeld, J. (in press). First do no harm: A reply to Courtney Cazden. *Anthropology and Education Quarterly.*

Kochman, T. (1981). *Black and white styles in conflict.* Chicago: University of Chicago Press.

Koehler, V. (1978). Classroom process research: Present and future. *Journal of Classroom Interaction, 13*(2), 3–11.

Kovac, C., & Cahir, S. R. (1981). *What's what with questions.* Washington, D.C.: Center for Applied Linguistics.

Krantz, P. J., & Risley, T. R. (1977). Behavioral ecology in the classroom. In K. D. O'Leary (Eds.), *Classroom management. The successful use of behavior modification,* 2nd ed. New York: Pergamon

Labov, W. (1972). The logic of nonstandard English. In W. Labov, *Language in the inner city: Studies in the Black English vernacular.* Philadelphia: University of Pennsylvania Press.

Labov, W. (1982a). Competing value systems in the inner-city schools. In P. Gilmore & A. Glatthorn (Eds.), *Children in and out of school: Ethnography and education.* Washington: Center for Applied Linguistics.

Labov, W. (1982b). Objectivity and commitment in linguistic science: The case of the Black English trial in Ann Arbor. *Language in Society, 11,* 165–201.

Labov, W., & Fanshel, D. (1977). *Therapeutic discourse: Psychotherapy as conversation.* New York: Academic Press.

Lein, L. (1975). "You were talkin' though, oh yes, you was": Black American migrant children: Their speech at home and school. *Council on Anthropology and Education Quarterly, 6*(4), 6–11.

Lemke, J. L. (1982). Classroom communication of science. Final report to NSF/RISE, April. (ED 222 346).

Leont'ev, A. N. (1981). The problem of activity in psychology. In J. V. Wertsch (Ed.), *The concept of activity in Soviet psychology.* Armonk, N.Y.: M. E. Sharpe.

Levin, P. (1977). Students and teachers: A cultural analysis of Polynesian classroom interaction. Unpub. doctoral dissertation, Univ. of California–San Diego.

Lundgren, U. P. (1977). *Model analysis of pedagogical processes.* Sweden: Stockholm Institute of Education, Department of Educational Research.

McDermott, R. P. (1976). Kids make sense: an ethnographic account of the interactional management of success and failure in one first-grade classroom. Unpubl. doctoral dissert., Stanford University.

McDermott, R. P., & Gospodinoff, K. (1979). Social contexts for ethnic borders and school failure. In A. Wolfgang (Ed.), *Nonverbal behavior: Application and cultural implications.* New York: Academic Press. Also in H. T. Treuba, G. P. Guthrie, K. H-P Au (Eds.), *Culture and the bilingual classroom: Studies in classroom ethnography.* Rowley, Mass.: Newbury House, 1981.

McDermott, R. P., Gospodinoff, K., & Aron, J. (1978). Criteria for an ethnographically adequate description of concerted activities and their contexts. *Semiotica, 24,* 245–275.

McHoul, A. (1978). The organization of turns at formal talk in the classroom. *Language in Society, 7,* 183–213.

McKessar, C. J. & Thomas, D. R. (1978). Verbal and nonverbal help-seeking among urban Maori and Pakeha children. *New Zealand Journal of Educational Studies, 13,* 29–39.

MacLure, M., & French, P. (1980). Routes to right answers: On pupils' strategies for answering teachers' questions. In P. Woods (Ed.), *Pupil strategies: Explorations in the sociology of the school.* London: Croom Helm.

MacLure, M., & French, P. (1981). A comparison of talk at home and at school. In G. Wells (Ed.), *Learning through interaction: The study of language development.* Cambridge: Cambridge University Press.

McNamee, G. D. (1979). The social interactive origins of narrative skills. *Quarterly Newsletter of the Laboratory of Comparative Human Cognition, 1*(4), 63–68. (San Diego: University of California, Center for Human Information Processing).

McNaughton, S., & Glynn, T. (1980). Behavior analysis of educational settings: Current research trends in New Zealand. New Zealand Association for Research in Education, Delta Research Monographs No. 3.

Malcolm, I. (1979). The West Australian Aboriginal child and classroom interaction; A sociolinguistic approach. *Journal of Pragmatics, 3,* 305–320.

Malcolm, I. G. (1980). The discourse of the reading lesson: Sociolinguistic observations in Aboriginal classrooms. In T. Bessell-Browne et al. (Eds.), *Reading into the Eighties.* Adelaide: Australian Reading Association.

Malcolm I. (1982). Speech events of the Aboriginal classroom. *International Journal of Sociology of Language, 36,* 115–134.

May, L. (1981). Spaulding School: Attention and styles of interaction. In D. Hymes, *Ethnographic monitoring of children's acquisition of reading/language arts skills in and out of the classroom.* Final report to the National Institute of Education. (ED 208 096).

Mayher, J. S., & Brause, R. S. (in press). Teaching and learning vocabulary related to concept development. *Language Arts.*

Mehan, H. (1974). Accomplishing classroom lessons. In A. V. Cicourel et al., *Language use and school performance.* New York: Academic Press.

Mehan, H. (1978). Structuring school structure. *Harvard Educational Review, 48,* 32–64.

Mehan, H. (1979). *Learning lessons.* Cambridge: Harvard University Press.

Mehan, H. (1980). The competent student. *Anthropology and Education Quarterly, 11,* 131–152.

Mehan, H., & Riel, M. M. (1982). Teachers' and students' instructional strategies. In L. Adler (Ed.), *Cross-cultural research at issue.* New York: Academic Press.

Merritt, M. (1982a). Distributing and directing attention in primary classrooms. In L. C. Wilkinson (Ed.), *Communicating in the classroom.* New York: Academic Press.

Merritt, M. (1982b). Repeats and reformulations in primary classrooms as windows of the nature of talk engagement. *Discourse Processes, 5,* 127–145.

Merritt, M., & Humphrey, F. (1979). Teacher, talk and task: Communicative demands during individualized instruction time. *Theory into Practice, 18,* 298–303.

Michaels, S. (1981). "Sharing time": Children's narrative styles and differential access to literacy. *Language in Society, 10,* 423–442.

Michaels, S. (1983). Influences on children's narratives. *Quarterly Newsletter of the Laboratory of Comparative Human Cognition, 5,* 30–34. (San Diego: Univer. of California, Center for Human Information Processing.)

Michaels, S., & Cazden, C. B. (in press). Teacher/child collaboration as oral preparation for literacy. In B. B. Schieffelin (Ed.), *Acquisition of literacy: Ethnographic perspectives.* Norwood, N.J.: Ablex.

Michaels, S., & Foster, M. (in press). Peer-peer learning: Evidence from a kid-run sharing time. In A: Jagger & M. Smith-Burke (Eds.), *Kid watching: Observing the language learner.* Urbana, Ill.: National Council of Teachers of English.

Mishler, E. G. (1972). Implications of teacher strategies for language and cognition: Observations in first-grade classrooms. In C. B. Cazden, V. P. John, & D. Hymes (Eds.), *Functions of language in the classroom.* New York: Teachers College Press.

Mishler, E. G. (1979). Meaning in context: Is there any other kind? *Harvard Educational Review, 49,* 1–19.

Mishler, E. G. (in press). *The discourse of medicine: The dialectics of medical interviews.* Norwood, N.J.: Ablex.

Morine-Dershimer, G., & Tenenberg, M. (1981). Participant perspectives on classroom discourse. Final report to National Institute of Education, Executive summary, April. (ED 210 107).

National Institute of Education. (1974). Conference on studies in teaching. Report of Panel 5: Teaching as a linguistic process in a cultural setting. (ED 111 806).

Newman, D., Griffin, P., & Cole, M. (in press). Laboratory and classroom tasks: Social constraints and the evaluation of children's performance. In B. Rogoff & J. Lave (Eds.), *Everyday cognition: Its development in social contexts.* Cambridge: Harvard University Press.

Ochs, E. (1979a). Planned and unplanned discourse. In T. Givon (Ed.), *Syntax and Semantics: Vol. 12, Discourse and Syntax.* New York: Academic Press, 51–80.

Ochs, E. (1979b). Transcription as theory. In E. Ochs & B. B. Schieffelin (Eds.), *Developmental Pragmatics.* New York: Academic Press.

Ogbu, J. U. (1982). Cultural discontinuities and schooling. *Anthropology and Education Quarterly, 13,* 290–307.

Perret-Clermont, A. N. (1980). *Social interaction and cognitive development in children.* New York: Academic Press.

Philips, S. U. (1972). Participant structures and communicative competence: Warm Springs children in community and classroom. In C. B. Cazden, V. P. John, & D. Hymes (Eds.), *Functions of language in the classroom.* New York: Teachers College Press.

Philips, S. (1983). *The invisible culture: Communication in the classroom and community on the Warm Springs Indian Reservation.* New York & London: Longman.

Piaget, J. (1950). *The psychology of intelligence.* London: Routledge & Kegan Paul.

Piestrup, A. M. (1973). *Black Dialect Interference and Accommodation of Reading Instruction in First Grade.* California: Univ. of Calif., Berkeley. Monographs of the Language-Behavior Research Laboratory, No. 4.

Redfield, D. L., & Rousseau, E. W. (1981). A meta-analysis of experimental research on teacher questioning behavior. *Review of Educational Research, 51,* 237–245.

Rosegrant, T. J. (1980). The relationship of young children's peer group status to their use of communicative strategies. Unpublished doctoral dissertation, Univ. of Illinois at Urbana-Champaign.

Rowe, M. B. (1974, 1974) Wait time—is anybody listening? *Journal of Psycholinguistic Research, 3,* 203–224; and *Journal of Research in Science Teaching, 11,* 81–94.

Ryan, J. (1974). Early language development: Towards a communicational analysis. In M. P. M. Richards, *The integration of a child into a social world.* London: Cambridge Univ. Press.

Sacks, H., Schegloff, E. A., & Jefferson, G. (1974). A simplest systematics for the organization of turn-taking in conversation. *Language, 50,* 696–735.

Sankoff, G. (1980). *The social life of language*. Philadelphia: Univer. of Pennsylvania Press.

Scheflen, A. (1973). *Communicational structure*. Bloomington: Univ. of Indiana Press.

Schwarz, M. L. (1979). The language of access and control: Masking and mitigating by inner-city high school students. Unpublished doctoral dissertation, Columbia Univ.

Sheingold, K., Kane, J. H., & Endreweit, M. E. (1983). Microcomputer use in schools: Developing a research agenda. *Harvard Educational Review, 53*, 412–432.

Shultz, J. (1979). It's not whether you win or lose, it's how you play the game: A microethnographic analysis of game-playing in a kindergarten/first grade classroom. In O. K. Garnica & M. L. King (Eds.), *Language, children and society*. New York: Pergamon.

Shultz, J. J., Erickson, F., & Florio, S. (1982). "Where's the floor?": Aspects of social relationships in communication at home and at school. In P. Gilmore & A. Glatthorn (Eds.), *Children in and out of school: Ethnography and education*. Washington: Center for Applied Linguistics.

Shultz, J., & Florio, S. (1979). Stop and freeze: the negotiation of social and physical space in a kindergarten/first grade classroom. *Anthropology and Education Quarterly, 10*, 166–181. (ED 181 008).

Silverstein, M. (1981). The limits of awareness. Sociolinguistic Working Paper No. 84. Austin, Texas: Southwest Educational Development Laboratory.

Sinclair, J. McH., & Brazil, D. (1982). *Teacher talk*. London: Oxford Univ. Press.

Sinclair, J. McH., & Coulthard, R. M. (1975). *Towards an analysis of discourse: The English used by teachers and pupils*. London: Oxford Univ. Press.

Smith, L. M., & Geoffrey, W. (1968). *The complexities of an urban classroom: An analysis toward a general theory of teaching*. New York: Holt, Rinehart & Winston.

Smitherman, G. (1977). *Talkin' and Testifying': The language of Black America*. Boston: Houghton Mifflin.

Snow, C. E. (1977). Mothers' speech research: from input to interaction. In C. E. Snow and C. A. Ferguson (Eds.), *Talking to Children: Language Input and Acquisition*. New York: Cambridge University Press, 31–49.

Snow, C. E., & Ferguson, C. A. (Eds.), (1977). *Talking to children: Language input and acquisition*. Cambridge, England: Camb. Univ. Press.

Speier, M. (1976). The child as conversationalist: Some culture contact features of conversational interactions between adults and children. In M. Hammersley & P. Woods (Eds.), *The process of schooling: A sociological reader*. London: Routledge & Kegan Paul in association with The Open Univ.

Steinberg, Z. D. (1979). Peer teaching discourse: One peer group's negotiation of status and role in a school for the emotionally disturbed. Unpublished doctoral dissertation, Harvard Univ.

Steinberg, Z., & Cazden, C. B. (1979). Children as teachers Of peers and ourselves. *Theory Into Practice, 18*, 258–266.

Stodolsky, S. (1972). Defining treatment and outcome in early childhood education. In H. J. Wahlberg & A. T. Kopan (Eds.), *Rethinking urban education*. San Francisco: Jossey-Bass.

Stodolsky, S. (in press). Frameworks for studying instructional processes in peer work groups. In P. L. Peterson, L. C. Wilkinson, & M. T. Hallinan (Eds.), *Instructional groups in the classroom: Organization and processes*. New York: Academic.

Stodolsky, S. S., Ferguson, T. L., & Wimpelberg, K. (1981). The recitation persists, but what does it look like? *Journal of Curriculum Studies, 13*, 121–130.

Stodolsky, S. S., & Karlson, A. L. (1972). Differential outcomes of a Montessori curriculum. *Elementary School Journal, 72*, 419–433.

Streeck, J. (1980). Speech acts in interaction: A critique of Searle. *Discourse Processes, 3*, 133–154.

Streeck, J. (in press). Embodied contexts, transcontextuals, and the timing of speech acts. *Journal of Pragmatics*.

Stubbs, M. (1976). Keeping in touch: Some functions of teacher-talk. In M. Stubbs & S. Delamont (Eds.), *Explorations in classroom observation*. London: JohnWilcy. (Revised version Ch. 3 in Stubbs, 1983).

Stubbs, M. (1981a). Theory and practise: A response to Willes. In P.

French & M. MacLure (Eds.), *Adult-child conversation*. New York: St. Martins Press. (p. 81–95.)

Stubbs, M. (1981b). Scratching the surface: Linguistic data in educational research. In C. Adelman (Ed.), *Uttering, muttering: Collecting, using and reporting talk for social and educational research*. London: Grant McIntyre. (Revised version as Ch. 11 in Stubbs, 1983).

Stubbs, M. (1983a). *Discourse analysis: The sociolinguistic analysis of natural language*. Chicago: Univ. of Chicago Press.

Stubbs, M. (1983b). *Language, schools and classrooms*. London: Methuen.

Stubbs, M. (in press). Review of J. McH. Sinclair & D. Brazil (Eds.), *Teacher talk*. Applied Linguistics.

Stubbs, M., & Delamont, S. (Eds.). (1976). *Explorations in classroom observation*. London & New York: John Wiley.

Stubbs, M., & Hillier, H. (Eds.). (1983). *Language, schools and classrooms: A reader*. London: Methuen.

Tharp, R. G., Jordan, C., Speidel, G. E., Au, K. H-P., Klein, T. W., Calkins, R. P., Sloat, K. C. M., & Gallimore, R. (in press). Product and process in applied developmental research: Education and the children of a minority. *Advances in Developmental Psychology*.

Thorne, B., Kramarae, C., & Henly, N. (1983). *Language, gender and society*. Rowley, Mass.: Newbury House.

Vygotsky, L. S. (1962). *Thought and language*. Cambridge: MIT Press.

Vygotsky, L. S. (1978). *Mind in society: the development of higher psychological processes*. Cambridge: Harvard Univ. Press.

Vygotsky, L. S. (1981). The genesis of higher mental functions. In J. V. Wertsch (Ed.), *The concept of activity in Soviet psychology*. Armonk, N.Y.: M. E. Sharpe.

Walker, R. (1978). Pine City. In R. E. Stake & J. A. Easley (Eds.), *Case studies in science education, Vol 1. The case reports*. Urbana-Champaign: Univ. of Illinois, Center for Instructional Research and Curriculum Evaluation. (ED 166 058).

Walker, R., & Adelman, C. (1975). *A guide to classroom observation*. London: Methuen.

Walker, R., & Adelman, C. (1976). Strawberries. In M. Stubbs & S. Delamont (Eds.), *Eplorations in classroom observation*. London: John Wiley.

Walker, R., & Goodson, I. (1977). Humour in the classroom. In P. Woods & M. Hammersley (Eds.), *School experience: Explorations in the sociology of education*. London: Croom Helm.

Webb, N. M. (1982). Student interaction and learning in small groups. *Review of Educational Research, 52*, 421–445.

Wells, G. (Ed.). (1981). Learning through interaction: *The study of language development*. Cambridge, England and New York: Cambridge Univ. Press.

Wells, G., & Montgomery, M. (1981). Adult-child interaction at home and at school. In P. French & M. MacLure (Eds.), *Adult-child conversation*. New York: St. Martins Press.

Wells, G., Montgomery, M., & MacLure, M. (1979). Adult-child discourse: outline of a model of analysis: *Journal of Pragmatics, 3*, 337–380.

Wild, J., Nakonechny, C., & Saint-Jacques, B. (1983). Sociolinguistic aspects of Native Indian speech. *Sociolinguistics, 14*, (1), 6–8.

Willes, M. J. (1983). *Children into Pupils: A Study of Language in Early Schooling*. Boston: Routledge & Kegan Paul.

Willis, P. (1977). *Learning to labour: How working class kids get working class jobs*. Westmead, England: Saxon House. (Also Lexington, Mass.: Lexington Books, 1981.)

Willis, P. (1981). Cultural production is different from cultural reproduction is different from social reproduction is different from reproduction. *Interchange, 12*(1), 48–67.

Woods, P. (1976). Having a laugh: An antidote to schooling. In M. Hammersley & P. Woods (Eds.), *The process of schooling: A sociological reader*. London: Routledge & Kegan Paul in association with The Open University.

Woods, P., & Hammersley, M. (Eds.). (1977). *School experience: Explorations in the sociology of education*. London: Croom Helm.

Wooton, A. (1975). *Dilemmas of Discourse*. London: George Allen & Unwin.

Young. M. F. D. (Ed.). (1971). *Knowledge and control: New directions in the sociology of education*. London: Collier Macmillan.

16.
Media in Teaching

Richard E. Clark
University of Southern California

Gavriel Salomon
Tel Aviv University, Israel

Research on media in teaching has become conceptually distinguished from "instructional technology" in the past 15 years. The Commission on Instructional Technology (Tickton, 1970) defined instructional technology as "a systematic way of designing, carrying out and evaluating the total process of learning and teaching in terms of specific objectives, based on research in human learning and communication and employing a combination of human and nonhuman resources to bring about more effective instruction" (p. 12). Thus, instructional technology has been separated from the more traditional research on media in teaching.

All technologies are applications of research and experience to solve some practical problem. "Instructional technology" encompasses *all* instructional problems and thus is the technology *of* instruction. It should not be confused with the focus of this chapter which is the study of media *in* teaching. Media are part of instructional technology. They are the replicable "means," forms or vehicles by which instruction is formatted, stored, and delivered to the learner (Schwen, 1977). Thus, this chapter is concerned with the study of media when it serves instructional functions.

The need for a chapter on media in teaching springs partly from our own curiosity about its effects on children. Statistics concerning the use of various electronic media for entertainment purposes by children have alarmed many parents and educators. The basis of their concerns becomes apparent considering that the average 9-month-old child is watching an hour-and-a-half of TV a day (Holenbeck & Slaby, 1979). Children 3–4-years-old average 4 hours a day (Singer, 1983), and by the end of high school, the total amount of television-viewing time exceeds the time spent being taught in school (Morrisett, 1984). These statistics are coupled with an increased concern with the effects of the new computerized video games and the rapid addition of microcomputers to school curricula and home use (Sheingold, Kane, & Enderweit, 1983). This concern with the effects of media on young learners is not a recent phenomenon. Plato apparently expressed concern about the influence of the written delivery of instruction and recommended oral teaching instead (Saettler, 1968).

Another reason to study media in teaching is that there is a historically recurring expectation that student motivation and performance may be enhanced by them. At least since Thorndike suggested the use of pictures as labor-saving devices at the turn of the century, each new medium has created a wave of interest and positive enthusiasm on the part of educators. More recent media are widely used in classroom teaching. More than half of the school teachers in the United States use television material in class, particularly for teaching science and social sciences; 75% report using audiotapes and radio; and 62% use computers (Riccobono, 1984).

In this light, it becomes important to examine the research in the field for at least two reasons. First, we must discover what we know about the utility and effectiveness of media for instructional purposes. What in the media exerts what kinds of influence on whom and in what situational and instructional contexts? Second, the recent explosion of interest in the computer as an instructional tool requires that we examine the lessons learned from more veteran media and apply them to the study of new ones (Clark, in press; Salomon & Gardner, 1984).

The reader is cautioned that space prevents a comprehensive review of the great quantity of published material in this area. Excellent reviews and position papers are easily available. A number of articles and books exist that offer a more thorough treatment of problems than will be given here (Clark, 1983; Clark & Snow, 1975; Fleming & Levie, 1978; Heidt, 1978; Jamison, Suppes, & Welles, 1974; Kearsley, Hunter, & Seidel,

---

The authors thank reviewers George Comstock (Syracuse University) and Howard Levie (Indiana University). Thanks also to James Kulik, Robert Reiser, and William Winn for advice on earlier drafts.

1983; Leifer, 1976; Lesgold & Reif, 1983; Salomon & Clark, 1977; Salomon & Gardner, 1984; Schramm, 1977a; Sheingold, et al., 1983; Suppes, 1979; Wilkinson, 1980).

Our goal is to acknowledge and examine some of the difficulties that the field of research on media in instruction faces. We will analyze the results of past research and describe current significant changes in those questions. We will then discuss the way lessons of past media research impinge on future directions.

Review: Who Is the Fairest of Them All?

Any profession concerned with the improvement of human life, as Glaser (1982, p. 292) points out, bases its activities on beliefs about human nature. The field of media in instruction is no exception. Media research began during the behaviorist era in education, so early researchers assumed learners to be reactive, responding to external stimuli which were designed to control their behavior. Many early researchers operated on the belief that media in instruction offered great advantages in increased control of learning behaviors. Skinner's teaching machines fit this model very well, as did the early hopes voiced by audio-visual advocates (Saettler, 1968). Divergent views urging cognitive interactive questions by early researchers such as Freeman (1924, quoted by Saettler, 1968) were largely ignored.

The perceptions of learners as reactive and under stimulus control led to an intensive search for the "one best medium," a search stimulated by the great excitement that each new medium aroused and the many hopes this excitement cultivated (Clark, 1975). This early research was long on the enthusiastic advocacy of media comparison questions and short on the development of theories concerning the way media might be made to influence learning (Wartella & Reeves, 1983).

Media Comparison Studies

In the 1960s, Lumsdaine (1963) and others (e.g., Mielke, 1968) argued that gross comparisons of the influence of different media on learning might not be useful. They implied that media, when viewed as no more than collections of electromechanical devices such as television and movies, were simple delivery instruments and that when *everything else* was held constant, they would not be found to influence learning directly in and of themselves. And while it has been the case that subsequent research has borne out their suspicion, many researchers continued to search for overall learning benefits from media. But, as has become evident, learning from instruction is a much more complicated process that often involves interactions between specific tasks, particular learner traits, and various components of medium and method. In this mix, the effects of gross, undifferentiated "medium" variables could not be productive. Part of the reason for the continued reliance on media comparisons was that earlier reviewers held the door open to media influences on learning by blaming much of the lack of systematic findings in prior research on poor research design and on a lack of adequate theory.

As a result, Lumsdaine (1963), writing in the first *Handbook of Research on Teaching*, dealt primarily with adequate studies which had utilized defensible methodology, and in which significant differences were found between media treatments. With the benefit of hindsight, it is not surprising that in most of the studies he reviewed media were employed as simple vehicles for the delivery of instructional materials, and researchers manipulated such variables as text organization, size of step in programed instruction, cueing, or repeated exposures and prompting. None of these variables was generic to the media that the researchers purported to study. This is an example of what Salomon and Clark (1977) have called research *with* media, which they distinguished from research *on* media. Only in research *on* media are generic media variables examined. In the former type, media are used as mere conveyances for the treatments being examined. Although media often were not the focus of study, the results were erroneously interpreted as suggesting that learning benefits had been derived from various media.

An example of instructional research *with* media would be a study that contrasts a logically versus a randomly organized slide–tape presentation on photosynthesis (cf. Kulik, Kulik, & Cohen, 1979 for a review of a number of similar studies). Such a comparison could be carried out by any medium, thus failing to single out for study any distinguishable or unique attribute of a medium that could be expected to contribute to achievement gains.

A decade later, chapters in the *Second Handbook of Research on Teaching* by Glaser and Cooley (1973) and Levie and Dickie (1973) were cautious about the media comparison studies that were still being conducted in apparently large numbers. Levie and Dickie (1973) noted that most overall media comparison studies to that date had been fruitless and suggested that most learning objectives could be attained through "instruction presented by any of a variety of different media" (p. 859). This observation was echoed by Schramm (1977), according to whom "learning seems to be affected more by what is delivered than by the delivery system" (p. 273). At that time, televised education was still a lively topic and studies of computerized instruction were just beginning to appear. In the intervening decade, more effort has been made to analyze and refocus the results of existing comparison studies.

REVIEWS AND META-ANALYSIS OF MEDIA STUDIES

A comprehensive and often cited review by Jamison et al. (1974) surveyed comparisons of traditional instruction with instruction via computers, television, and radio. Their survey utilized a "box score" tally of existing studies, evaluations, and reviews of research. They concluded that a small number of studies reported advantages for media and others indicated more achievement with traditional instruction, but the most typical outcome was "no significant difference" between the two. As they explained, "when highly stringent controls are imposed on a study, the nature of the controls tends to force the methods of presentation into such similar formats that one can only expect the 'no significant differences' which are found" (p. 38). However, there have been criticisms of the box score method of summarizing past media research (e.g., Clark & Snow, 1975). Many of these criticisms have been accommodated by newer "meta-analytic" methods of teasing generalizations from past research (Glass, 1976). A recent series of meta-analyses of media research was conducted by James Kulik and his colleagues at the University of Michigan (Cohen, Ebling, & Kulik, 1981; Kulik, Bangert, & Williams, 1983; Kulik et al., 1979; Kulik, Kulik, & Cohen, 1980). Such meta-analyses allow for a more precise estimate of treatment effect sizes than was possible a few years ago. Meta-analytic procedures yield effect size estimates which are converted to percentage of standard deviation gains on final examination scores due to the more powerful treatment, if any. Most of the meta-analytic surveys of media research demonstrate a typical learning advantage for "newer" media of about .5 standard deviations on final examination performance, compared with "conventional" treatments. In the case of computer-based instruction studies in college environments, for example, this advantage translated to an increase from the 50th to the 66th percentile in final examinations in a variety of courses (Kulik et al. 1980). This is an impressive accomplishment if one accepts it at face value.

Confounding in Media Comparison Studies. Clark (1983) has reviewed existing meta-analysis of media research. His conclusion was that while most analyses showed positive learning effects for newer media over more conventional treatments, there was compelling evidence for confounding in the reviewed research. Two illustrations from Clark's (1983) discussion will provide an example of these two types of confounding. The sizeable effect of .5 standard deviations on final exams that has been attributed to computers in the college setting has been used to justify computer-based instruction (CBI) for teaching. However, this effect reduced to .13 standard deviations in those studies wherein one teacher planned and presented both the computer and the conventional courses. Clark (1983) claimed that this was compelling evidence that the larger effects were due to systematic but uncontrolled differences in content, novelty, and/or teaching method between conventional and media treatments but not to CBI per se. Even when the same teacher designs both treatments it is possible that slightly different and more productive presentations of content or method could be included in the computer condition which accounted for the .13 advantage. But this slight learning advantage could have been produced by any of a variety of media.

Another source of confounding, novelty, was evidenced by a decrease in the differences between media and conventional treatments over time. Clark and Snow (1975) reported that most media treatments in published studies at that time averaged about 20 minutes with a very small standard deviation. Kulik et al. (1983) reported that when computer treatments lasted less than 4 weeks, average effects were .56 standard deviations over conventional treatments. This diminished to .3 standard deviations after 5 to 8 weeks and further to .2 standard deviations after 8 weeks of student work with CBI. It is plausible to hypothesize a novelty effect in these studies and to suggest that students are becoming more familiar with the medium and expend less effort in learning from it over time. Clark (1983) has also argued that similar confoundings could

account for reports of reductions in study time for computers or other media.

A Conclusion About Media Comparisons. General media comparisons and studies pertaining to their overall instructional impact have yielded little that warrants optimism. Even in the few cases where dramatic changes in achievement or ability were found to result from the introduction of a medium such as television, as was the case in El Salvador (Schramm, 1977), it was not the medium per se that caused the change but rather the curricular reform that its introduction enabled. This in itself is an important observation, for the introduction of a new medium often allows the production of high-quality materials and novel experiences, or leads to organizational and practice changes not otherwise afforded.

One would need to distinguish here between the potential effects of a medium's generic *attributes* (e.g., ways to shape information that cultivate cognitive skills), and the effects of the medium's *introduction*. Gross media comparisons were often intended as studies of media attributes, but failing to identify and carefully manipulate specific attributes, they fell short of their goal (Clark, 1978, 1983; Clark & Snow, 1975; Levie & Dickie, 1973; Salomon, 1979; Salomon & Clark, 1977). Nor did they illuminate the process and effects of media introduction, for they focused on direct learning outcomes, not on the consequences of curricular or organizational changes in the schools.

The study of media's effects on learning precludes their treatment as unitary tools such as "television," "radio," or "computer." The common denominator of all television instances, transcending differences of content, task, method of presentation, instructional context, symbolic and formal features used, and the like, is much too narrow. It does not warrant comparisons of "televised instruction" (or, for that matter, "computer-based instruction") with an equally undifferentiated alternative. This is certainly the case with computers — whose variety of forms, usages, contents, and the activities they allow, exceeds anything known before.

The shortcomings of overall media comparisons do not render such studies useless for all purposes. The evaluation of particular products, the weighting of a medium's overall cost effectiveness, and the close monitoring of a medium's employment in practice can all benefit from one or another kind of media comparison. However, such gross comparisons have little utility for the study of those specific media attributes that may make a difference in learning for some learners on specific tasks. This lesson appears to be of special importance when applied to research on computers for, unlike TV, their instructional potential is still largely unexplored.

Cognizant of these and similar considerations, researchers shifted their attention to other types of questions. These newer approaches were based more on cognitive than behavioral approaches to learning. They were addressed at specific media attributes, assumed to be inherent to the medium under study and of potential relevance to learning-related cognitions. Hypotheses typically dealt with the interactions of particular media attributes, teaching methods, tasks, and learner traits, and focused on the cognitive consequences of different combinations for different students. While the historical vestiges of this type of question date back at least to the 1920s (e.g., Freeman, 1924, quoted by Saettler, 1968), most of the research activity has taken place in the last decade. However, as we will see, the shift to a cognitive approach has led the field away from practical research on media as it was formerly conceptualized.

The Shift of Focus: Cognitive Aspects of Media Attributes

The media comparison questions were discarded at the same time that instructional psychology was replacing behaviorist with more cognitively oriented views. In the cognitive approach, more attention is devoted to the way various media attributes, such as the visualization and imagery-evoking properties of stimuli (see review by Winn, 1981, 1982), interact with cognitive processes to influence learning. Thus, it became necessary to examine how specific elements of an instructional message might effect or activate particular cognitions for certain learners under specific task conditions. No wonder, therefore, that aptitude-treatment interaction (ATI) research has been welcomed by media researchers who expected it not only to suggest which specific media attributes were most effective for whom (e.g., Clark, 1975; Clark & Snow, 1975; Schramm, 1977), but also to indicate the kinds of cognitions that are or may become involved in the processing of differently packaged and coded materials (Salomon, 1971; 1979).

Related Questions Concerning Information Processing

There is also a growing body of research on developmental cognitive processes which are relevant to the understanding of media attributes. That research ranges from the study of reading acquisition (e.g., Resnick & Weaver, 1979) to the comprehension of stories (e.g., Stein & Glen, 1979); and from the study of how children learn to process artistic depictions (Gardner, 1980), to the study of how one learns to process narration (e.g., Collins, 1981; Jaglom & Gardner, 1981) and handle computers (e.g., Turkle, 1984).

Other literature of increasing volume is concerned with neuropsychology and the psychobiology of processing symbolic information. Unfortunately, although this research opens up a new area of interest, it still yields many contradicting interpretations, particularly in the area of hemispheric dominance or brain lateralization (Gardner, 1982). As it turns out, popular claims about an instructionally important division of labor between the two brain hemispheres are not clearly supported by research (Hellige, 1980). It is apparently the case that the left hemisphere has momentary advantage in dealing with the basic building blocks of simple, familiar, digital elements and in such logical processes as classification. The right hemisphere is the initial processor of unfamiliar, pictorial, and spatial material. Yet the right hemisphere turns out to play a role in the comprehension of stories, metaphors, puns, jokes, and other linguistic material that requires paralinguistic "scaffolding" for comprehension (Gardner, 1982). So prevailing speculations that there may be a clear hemispheric specialization for different media attributes appear to be premature.

Unlike previous research concerned with the instructional utility of media, the more current research into the way different modes of information presentation are processed and how these processing capabilities develop appear to yield important implications for instruction. Thus, for example, Anderson and Lorch (1983) have found that children attend to televised material that is comprehensible to them, implying that comprehensibility determines attention rather than the other way around. This finding suggests that instructional production techniques should be oriented to conveying comprehensible information rather than attracting attention. Newer media literacy programs are attempting to draw on this research and apply it to instructing children on how to get more selective knowledge out of mediated instruction (e.g., Dorr, Graves, & Phelps, 1980; Singer, Zuckerman, & Singer, 1980).

By and large, there were at least two results of the shift in focus in media research. First, there was the need to identify critical attributes of media which not only distinguish between media in meaningful ways but which also affect learning-relevant cognitions. This then was expected to lead to clearer distinctions between the *means* of information delivery and manipulation (e.g., radio, computers, television, books) and other components of media, notably their intrinsic modes of information presentation and the kinds of mental operations they afford. The second result was the long-overdue development of theories. The chapter turns next to a brief description of three of these theories which have evolved in the last decade and to the disputes they have generated.

GOODMANS' SYMBOL SYSTEM THEORY

The idea that media attributes or the modes of information presentation in instruction are crucial to learning has been around for some time. However, it was not until Gardner, Howard, and Perkins (1974) introduced Goodman's (1968) theory of symbol systems that the constructs of "modes of presentation" could be systematically examined.

Following Goodman (1968), Gardner et al. (1974) explained that a *symbol is anything that can be used in a referential way*, and that can be organized into systems. They offered a number of semantic and syntactic conditions to distinguish among symbol systems—including the way they are structured and the way they map upon their respective fields of reference. They offered specific dimensions of symbol systems to illustrate the way they differ.

One of the structural characteristics of symbol systems is notationality. This is the extent to which a symbol system can be unambiguously mapped onto a frame of reference. Here, for each of the system's characters there must be one, and only one, equally differentiated element in the field of reference. The system of musical notations is a prime example of notationality. Symbol systems differ in notationality. For example, verbal systems are more notational than pictorial ones, a distinction that leads to specific psychological and educational implications. Less notational symbol systems (e.g., pictures) are neither easier nor more difficult to comprehend or learn, as there is nothing inherent in these systems that makes them "easy." Nor does any system necessarily "resemble" its referents more than another. Rather, symbol systems, and hence the media of communication and tools of information manipulation that carry them, exhibit differential information biases (e.g., Meringoff, 1980) and activity biases (Salomon and Gardner, 1984). Thus, TV tends to highlight action properties of a narrative while print versions of the same material highlight figurative language. Each such presentation bias is correlated with an information pickup bias — televiewers place the narrative in a spatial imagery framework and storybook listeners place it in a temporal–descriptive one.

The introduction of a formal theory of symbol systems could potentially offer a bridge between research on media and research on cognition and symbolic behavior. Indeed, this development led to the creation of new theories and research questions by media researchers. Those theories are briefly described next. However, these new theories led away from the study of media as complex communication systems characterized by television, books, and other means of delivering messages. Current research based on symbol system theories is no longer focused on media in instruction, for as Gardner (1982) pointed out, there is no necessary one-to-one correspondence between media and symbol systems. We will return to this issue later on.

OLSON'S THEORY OF INSTRUCTIONAL MEANS

Olson bases his theory on Bruner's contention (1964) that the introduction of technologies and techniques is accompanied by the development of relevant cognitive skills, and on McLuhan's interest in the forms and structures of information media. Olson (1976; Olson & Bruner, 1974) argued that any account of human activity must begin with an understanding of the activities whereby information is picked up from the environment, mentally transformed, and stored. Different kinds of activities yield not only different aspects of the world but also engage and develop different mental skills. Olson thus distinguished between the knowledge one acquires and the skills that are involved in and are developed during the process. From observing a picture, argued Olson, one acquires knowledge about the depicted object as well as develops cognitive skills related to observation.

Olson (1976) offered a theory of instructional means. The theory attempts to show "how in . . . instruction, the content of the medium [is] related to the knowledge acquired, while the means employed (the code in which the message is represented) is related to the skills, strategies and heuristics that are called upon and developed" (1976, p. 26). Each of these elements may result in a different kind of transfer of learning: The content component results in transfer of rules and principles (a set of features that is invariant across different activities), whereas the codes or the means off instruction may result in the transfer of skills "assumed or developed in the course of relying upon that means" (1976, p. 23). These skills are the mental operations that are invariant across different contents. Each system of codes, symbols, or methods requires a different set of activities. While all such instructional means may ultimately map upon the same knowledge structure, they differ with respect to the cognitive processes they activate and cultivate (Olson & Bruner, 1974). Thus, Olson suggested (1974) that perhaps the function of

media that present new symbol systems is not so much to convey old knowledge in new forms but rather to cultivate new skills for exploration and internal representation.

One important extension of Olson's theory is his distinction between "utterance" and "text" (Olson, 1977). According to Olson (1977), oral language "is a flexible, unspecialized, all purpose instrument with a low degree of conventionalization" in which the meanings of sentences must be "negotiated in terms of the social relations, the context and the prior world knowledge of the participants" (p. 10). On the other hand, written language, "by virtue of its demands for explicitness of meaning, its permanence . . . and its realignment of social and logical function, serves the intellect in several ways" (Olson, 1977, p. 11). It serves the cultivation and maintenance of analytic, scientific, and philosophical knowledge (as contrasted with commonplace knowledge). In school, "intelligence" is skill in the medium of text. This Olson (1977) calls the "literacy bias."

Olson's distinction between cultures of utterance and text, and between similar developmental phases in a child's schooling, is of particular relevance to hypotheses concerning the cognitive effects of computer programing. Programing is a highly structured and analytic activity in a rigidly constrained symbol system (Pea & Kurland, 1985). It may — if sufficiently intense and continuous — lead to new "literacy biases" exceeding the ones attributed by Olson to texts.

SALOMON'S MEDIA ATTRIBUTES THEORY

Extending the work of Olson and Gardner, Salomon offered a theory (1979) based on the assumptions that (a) both the media and the human mind employ symbols to represent, store, and manipulate information; and (b) that some of the symbol systems employed in cognition are acquired from the symbol systems employed by media. Salomon conceptualized technologies that allow the development of unique symbol systems and combinations thereof, just as the development of the technologies of maps, films, or computers led to the development of cartography, cinematics, and programing languages. The more distinctive or contrived the symbol system used to represent information, the more distinctive the mental skills that are required and called upon. Hence, Salomon (1974a) distinguished, for example, between televised instruction that only employs the technology of television without much emphasis on the medium's unique symbolic potentialities, and televised instruction that does utilize these features fully. Only the latter might make a difference in the kind of knowledge acquired and the meanings derived from instruction as it calls upon different sets of mental skills (Salomon & Cohen, 1977).

There are a number of instructionally relevant features to the Salomon theory. He hypothesized (1979) that an instructional presentation can be "closer to" or "more distant from" the way a learner tends mentally to represent the information presented under given task requirements. The closer the match between the communicational symbol system and the content and task-specific mental representations, the easier the instructional message is to recode and comprehend. Certain symbolic modes of representation can thus "save" the learner taxing mental transformations from communicational to mental symbolic forms depending on their aptitudes, the task, and the subject matter to be learned.

A second feature of the Salomon theory is his contention that some of the symbolic features of instruction, under some conditions, can be internalized by learners and henceforth serve as "tools of mental representation." He presented evidence (Salomon, 1974a) that students deficient in cue attending are able to internalize the "zooming" of a camera lens into a stimulus field and thus increase their cue-attending skill. Another possibility here is that these same features may merely activate and strengthen partly mastered cognitive skills for other students, and in some instances such features may actually inhibit learning by preventing the use of previously acquired but more efficient skills that serve the same ends. Research following the theory has provided evidence that skill cultivation and inhibition, though limited in scope, take place under natural conditions such as exposure to a new medium like television. Salomon (1979) reported such effects on Israeli children exposed to "Sesame Street" and Schramm (1977) found similar effects on the nonverbal skills of El Salvadorean children exposed to instructional television for the first time. However, it should be remembered that Salomon's research demonstrates that symbolic features of media *can be made* to cultivate cognitive effects, not that those effects necessarily occur naturally as a result of uninvolved exposure to a medium. The occurrence of cognitive effects depends on a number of factors including the effort invested, depth of processing, and special aptitudes of individual learners (Salomon, 1983a).

OTHER SYMBOL SYSTEM THEORIES

The development of the three related theories briefly described above was paralleled by other, more symbol-system- or domain-specific theories: theories pertaining to the processing of words and pictures (e.g., Fleming, 1979; Pressley, 1977), tele-viewing and listening (Meringoff, 1980), artistic depiction (Gardner, 1980), diagrams (Winn, 1982), and more. Common to these undertakings was a growing concern with the cognitive processing of differently coded materials. Questions of instructional effectiveness were generally abandoned.

Issues Related to Symbol System Theories

Most of these newer theories have at least one important assumption in common: that cognitive representations and processing are carried out in *various* symbolic modes that are *influenced* by the symbol systems employed by media, that some of these cognitions are *unique* counterparts of communicational symbol systems, and thus can be cultivated by symbol systems. This general assumption has been challenged by critics who suggested that the type of symbolic mode employed in instructional representations may not serve any unique function in cognition and learning. Clark (1983, in press), for example, has argued that many of the different symbolic representational modes used in instruction may serve the *same basic function* in cognitive processing. If this turns out to be the case, the choice of symbol system may be less important for instruction and learning than the symbol system theories imply. Instructional

designers and curriculum planners could then choose the less expensive or more convenient medium for instruction, provided that its symbolic modes were *sufficient* to yield the necessary cognitive transformations required by the learning task and learner. This issue is similar to one currently being discussed in the larger arena of cognitive science, that is, the concern about whether images or propositions are the more "basic" representational modes for information in cognition.

Imagery and Propositions in Thought

A particularly important topic and ongoing theoretical debate in cognition was, and continues to be, concerned with the nature and foundations of images or "analogous" mental representations as contrasted with "propositions" (e.g., Anderson, 1983; Olson & Bialystock, 1983). An example of the difference between the two would be a trace image of an object in memory (an analogous representation) versus a description of the criterial attributes of the object (a proposition).

The image-versus-proposition argument to some extent replaces earlier dual trace arguments concerning whether information is stored in memory as words, pictures, or both (e.g., Paivio, 1977). It is part of the general search for a deeper understanding of information processing, a topic of special relevance to research on media in teaching since different theory and practice implications appear to follow from the two approaches. Space limitations allow only a brief description of the two approaches and their related implications.

THE DUAL-MODALITY APPROACH

Kosslyn (1981), Kosslyn and Pomerantz (1977), Paivio (1977), and Shepard (1978) have claimed that images constitute a distinct class of cognitive representations, parallel and equal in importance to semantic propositions. Shepard (1978) argued that the perception of a mental image is a process that is analogous to the perception of actual objects. Kosslyn (1981), basing his approach on computer simulation models, argued that images have both "surface representation" and "deep representation" components. Surface representations occur in a spatial mode and are a visual depiction of objects. This underlies the experience of mental imagery. The deep structure component entails a literal representation (some encoding of appearance) and a propositional element (a description of the object). The deep representation is a long-term memory trace. The trace is used spontaneously when people retrieve information about incidentally learned objects, when required to allude to physical properties of objects and when subtle comparisons are to be made. Less subtle comparisons are likely to be handled "propositionally" (Kosslyn, 1981).

The dual-modality side of this argument bears a general resemblance to media attribute theories. If images bear a direct resemblance to externally depicted objects, the acquisition of communicationally provided images of events and processes should enrich a learner's store of cognitive images and operations. Salomon's (1979) theory of the internalization of symbolic forms and Olson and Bruner's (1974) claim that intelligence is skill in a medium appear to be related to the dual-modality argument.

THE PROPOSITIONAL APPROACH

Pylyshyn (1973) denied a central role for imagery components in cognition by describing them as "epiphenomena." He relegated their alleged role in cognitive representation and processing to "abstract descriptions accessed by computationally primitive semantic interpretation functions" (Hampson & Morris, 1978). More recently, however, Pylyshyn (1981) has narrowed the debate to the question of whether images are or are not similar to what goes on when people observe corresponding events actually happening. "Similarity," he argued, is an illusory and unclear construct that is based on our commonsense knowledge. More specifically, the argument was that images are not *intrinsic* properties of the mind which are "wired in," such that they cause it to behave as it does. Rather, images are "cognitively penetrable." They are governed by conceptual, rational knowledge — by propositions — rather than exclusively by the actual features of the objects perceived. Therefore, the images we form of external reality are not determined by our direct perceptions of the features of the objects (or their pictorial representation) but by "a tacit physical theory which is good enough to predict most ordinary natural events correctly most of the time" (Pylyshyn, 1981, p. 41).

Research evidence for the propositional argument includes the finding that children who are blind from birth perform as well as sighted children on tasks that seem to require imagery (e.g., Zimler & Keenan, 1983). These findings and others challenge the dual-modality/imagery theories and suggest that the mental representations used by both the blind and the sighted take a semantic, propositional form. Additionally, one should take into account recent evidence provided by Kyllonen, Lohman, and Snow (1984), who imply that spatial thought and strategies are most useful for solving only simple problems. As problem solving (including spatial problems) becomes more difficult, learners tend to switch to the more semantic–analytical strategies.

IMPLICATIONS OF THESE APPROACHES

The dual- (or multiple-) modality approaches lead to implications similar to the ones developed earlier by Olson, Bruner, and Salomon. The propositional approach leads to different hypotheses, implying that the particular surface-symbolic appearance of a message may be relatively less consequential in learning, as it is going to be handled propositionally anyway during deeper processing. Thus, all images used in cognition may be "constructed" following propositional "rules." Imagery knowledge, and thus the symbol-system-specific cognitive skills cultivated from symbolic attributes, may only serve in the *decoding* of instruction delivered via different media.

Salomon (1983b) has recently proposed that the symbolic carriers of information mainly affect the early phases of decoding but not subsequent phases of mental elaboration of the already recoded and mentally represented material. The latter phases, he argued, include such operations as inference generation and are symbol system independent. Indeed, Salomon and Ben-Moshe have recently found that when sixth graders are taught to view television more mindfully and invest more effort in processing televised instruction, their reading comprehension scores increase significantly. This suggests that the operations involved in the deeper processing of television and print material may share a number of important procedural or strategic components.

More generally, it follows that if most basic cognitive operations rest in propositional structures, then the issue of symbol system and medium diversity in instruction may not be as important in learning as was initially assumed by the symbol system theories. We should entertain the possibility that symbol systems affect differently only initial decoding. For it is quite possible that information presented in some symbolic form is more easily recoded into (internal) propositions than when presented in another form. It is also possible that as each symbolic form offers a different information bias (highlighting selected aspects of the information), each such form may lead to different kinds of internal propositions. Thus, according to this view, media's symbolic forms may not call upon and cultivate different skills; still, they may result in easier or more difficult learning. They may also result in more or less stereotypic or varied sets of internal propositions that complement each other (Olson & Bialystock, 1983).

Another issue concerns the conditions that surround the cultivation and transfer of cognitive skills. We turn next to a brief discussion of these issues and how they might influence our understanding of media symbol system theories.

Skill Cultivation: Questions of Uniqueness and of Transfer

Salomon (1979), and more recently Greenfield (1984), have reviewed research where symbolic features of mediated experiences and instruction were shown to affect differentially the skills activated in the service of knowledge acquisition and on the mastery of these skills. Such research was inspired by Bruner's (1964) argument that internal representations and operations partly depend on learning "precisely the techniques that serve to amplify our acts, perceptions and our ratiocinative activities" (p. 2).

Such a Vygotskian view implies that unique coding or structural elements of the media (e.g., filmic causal sequences) or uniquely afforded activities (e.g., programing) may have unique effects on related mental skills. Thus, the employment of a coding element such as a close-up, or the allowance for students' manipulation of input data (e.g., Lesgold & Reif, 1983), may activate specific mental operations that facilitate the acquisition of knowledge as well as their improved mastery.

But the possibility of skill activation and cultivation from specific media attributes also raises new conceptual and empirical questions. If media's symbolic modes of information presentation can activate, even cultivate mental operations and skills, are these skills *unique*? What is their utility? *How far do they transfer, if at all*? These questions are of particular interest with respect to the use of computers in instruction (Papert, 1980; Pea & Kurland, 1985; Tikomirov, 1974), for many computer-afforded activities are rationalized in terms of their unique effects on transferable skills. Writes Papert (1980, p. 27): "By providing [a] very concrete, down-to-earth model of a particular style of thinking, work with the computer can [foster] . . . a 'style of thinking' . . . that is to say learning to think articulately about thinking."

It is very difficult to provide evidence to support the uniqueness argument since it might always be claimed that substitutions are or could be made available. More importantly, one could question the assumption implied in this approach that there is a one-to-one correspondence between coding elements and afforded activities, on the one hand, and specific modes of mental representation and operation, on the other. Wittrock's (1978) generative model of instruction suggests that when, for example, learners fail to generate relevant relationships, they should be made explicit for the learners in any means or medium available. This assumes functional equivalence between various devices for delivering instruction and various symbolic modes for representing information.

Indeed, it is possible that nominally different modes of instructional presentation (including symbolic attributes) accomplish the same function in learning, and thus activate the same operations and therefore serve instruction equally well. Blake (1977) taught chess moves to high- and low-visual-ability undergraduates using still pictures, animated arrows within pictures, or a motion film plus a narration. While all three conditions worked equally well for the higher ability learners, low visualizers learned the chess moves equally well from the arrow and motion which were significantly more effective than the static pictures. Blake's poor visualizers profited from two different operational definitions of the necessary model, animated arrows and moving chess pieces. It seems that the necessary process for learning chess moves was the visualization of the entire move allowed each piece. It could be operationalized in any of a variety of equally sufficient conditions for successful performance.

The possibility that alternative coding and structural elements, within and across symbol systems, may be functionally equivalent suggests two things. First, it suggests that research ought not to seek the unique cognitive *effects* of one or another discrete media element but rather focus on the cognitive *functions* accomplished. Filmic zooms can visually supplant part–whole relations, but so can other elements as well. And the acquisition of some sequential logic, although facilitated by computer programing, may be similarly facilitated by direct tutoring. Second, it may well be that media selection decisions (e.g., Reiser & Gagné, 1982) ought not be based on their different surface capacities to influence achievement, for a focus on surface appearance differences overlooks the possibility that whatever we think goes on is not necessarily what goes on, cognitively.

The other important issue concerns the transferability of the skills wrested from a medium's symbol system or exercised during a computer-afforded activity. One would need to distinguish between, say, the acquisition of a particular image or operation, on the one hand, and the cultivation of imagery *ability* or generalized *skill*, on the other. It is one thing if children learn from televiewing only how to become better televiewers or from programing Logo how to be better Logo programers; it is another if they show skill cultivation that transfers beyond the boundaries of that medium or activity. Work by Scribner and Cole (1981) concerning the effects of acquiring basic literacy skills in nonschool settings serves as a warning against unwarranted optimism here. Contrary to earlier claims they found no evidence to show that literacy affected

abstract thinking or, for that matter, any other generalizable ability. The Vai may have been denied what Olson (1977) has called a "culture of literacy" that may amplify the effects of basic literacy into transferable skills. For such participation would enable the literate individuals to apply the initially specific operations in a variety of complex tasks and situations, thus to allow the generalizability of these into skills.

Salomon and Perkins (1984) have recently suggested that the acquisition of knowledge and skill can potentially lead to their transfer if either one of two roads are taken: (a) The acquired skill or knowledge is mindfully and deliberately decontextualized, that is, recoded in a representational code that affords abstraction; or (b) it is practiced to the point of automaticity in a large variety of instances demanding good performance. Exposure to, say, television's codes, or extensive exploratory activity with Logo geometry could, according to this view, lead to the cultivation of transferable skills provided either one of the roads is taken. But this is not easily achieved because the first (mindful) road demands the motivated expenditure of effort, and the second (automatic) demands more and more varied practice than usually afforded in schools. Neither road was taken by the Vai tribesman studied by Scribner and Cole, hence yielding no transfer effects from their new "literacy" to other cognitive tasks. The poor transfer effects of children's (usually limited) experience with Logo (Pea & Kurland, 1984) may be explained in the same way (Clark & Voogel, in press).

The road from possible to actual transfer is fraught with difficulties. It is certainly not a matter of one-shot, brief experiences and encounters, except in the unlikely event that such mental effort is expended in reaching transferable conclusions, formulating rules, or generating guiding metacognitions. Transfer is somewhat more likely as a consequence of prolonged, continuous, and intensive application of newly developed skill and knowledge, as may be the case after years of televiewing or prolonged focused computer activity.

In all, it appears that media's symbolic forms and computers' afforded activities may have skill-cultivating effects, but that these are not necessarily unique nor easily transferable. Future research, particularly that concerned with computer-afforded learning activities will do well to ask not just whether particular skills are acquired but also how else they could be developed, and under what instructional, contextual, and psychological conditions they can be made to transfer.

A Paradigm for Future Developments

Thus far, research on media in instruction, much like all research on teaching, has centered on the *means* of instruction as independent variables and on learning outcomes in the form of knowledge or skill acquisition as dependent variables. In this respect, the basic paradigm which originates from the behavioristic assumptions about human learning has not changed even though cognitive processes have been introduced as mediators between stimuli and responses. Yet, once cognitions are seriously considered one can not escape examining them, not only as mediators but also as partial determiners of the way learners experience the stimulus.

The basic assumption here is that learners often affect the way they experience the so-called stimulus through their previously acquired attributions, personal and socially shared expectations and beliefs, personal interests, and the like. As Shulman (1980) pointed out, "The teacher's pedagogical actions merely set the task environment for pupil learning, which task environment predictably is transformed by the pupil into his or her own problem space" (p. 7).

Acknowledgement of these phenomenological inputs as factors that affect the way stimuli are experienced, thus handled, reflects the current shift of paradigms for it ascribes the learner a far more active and less externally controlled role. It examines the process of learning as an ongoing transaction or reciprocal interaction between learners and their phenomenologically perceived environment (e.g., Bandura, 1978; Olweus, 1977; Salomon, 1981; Shulman, 1980; Wittrock, 1978).

Media are thus perceived as external devices which, along with other factors, set the stage for some cognitive activities precisely because they are part of a learner's a priori anticipations. What the student thinks or believes to be the case about a particular mediated presentation or class of media can come therefore to exert at least as much influence over learning as the medium itself. This may include beliefs about the medium's difficulty level, its entertainment potential, the type of information usually presented, and typical instructional demands. Some of these anticipations are socially generated and shared. Shulman (1981), while reviewing the literature on how students invent incorrect problem-solving procedures, pointed out the role of perceived social context in influencing the way problems are treated by students: "The social context of the classroom changes the meaning of instructional tasks in significant ways. Thus, a problem-to-be-solved and an assignment-to-be-completed are psychologically quite distinct, even if the specific exercise and its attendant solutions are identical in both instances" (p. 19).

Research that uses the reciprocal paradigm is relatively new, but it carries with it a good measure of theoretical and application potential. Only a brief review, suggestive of the types of questions asked, will be attempted here because of space limitations.

Attitudes Toward Media

Hess and Tenezakis (1972) explored the affective responses of predominantly Mexican-American, low-SES seventh, eight, and ninth graders to remedial mathematics presented either by computer or teacher. Among a number of interesting findings was an unanticipated attribution of more fairness to the computer than to the teachers. The students reported that the computer treated them more equitably (kept promises, did not make decisions based on stereotypes) than some of the teachers. Students consistently trusted the computer more but found it to be less "flexible," as well as unresponsive to student desires to change the course of content of the instruction. Similarly, Stimmel, Common, McCaskill, and Durrett (1981) found a strong negative affect toward computers and computerized instruction among a large group of preservice teachers. These same teacher trainees had similar reactions to mathematics and science teaching and may have associated computers with these disciplines. It would be interesting to study how the perceptions and attitudes of computer users guide their strategies for learning from computers, how these different strategies influence learning, and how work with computers changes or maintains these perceptions reciprocally.

Perceived Learning Demands from Different Media

Presumably, differences in the qualities attributed to different media may influence learning-related behaviors of students. Ksobiech (1976) and Salomon (1981) have reported studies wherein student beliefs about the different demands placed on them by different media influenced their approach to learning tasks. Ksobiech (1976) told 60 undergraduates variously that televised and book lessons were to be evaluated by them, were to be entertaining, or were to be the subject of a test. The test group performed best on a subsequent examination with the evaluation group next best, and the students who expected to be entertained showing the poorest exam performance. Some subjects were allowed to push a button and receive more video or more narrative content from the televised treatment. The test group consistently chose more narrative (verbal) information, presumably because they believed that it was a surer route to the factual information they needed to succeed at the test. Also, the subjects who believed that a test awaited them persisted longer than the other groups.

Salomon (1981) has recently suggested a model for conceptualizing these differences in mental effort expenditure that result from different attributions to the media.

According to Salomon's model, the amount of mental effort invested in nonautomatic elaboration of material (i.e., the extent of mindful processing) depends primarily on two factors: the learners' perception of the learning-relevant characteristics of the medium and task, and their own perceived self-efficacy in elaborating the information they will receive. In a series of studies (see Salomon, 1983a for summary) he found that television is perceived to be mentally less demanding than print material of comparable content and that learners report investing less mental effort in television. This, in turn, led the more able students to generate fewer inferences from such material. Manipulating the learners' perceived task demands positively affected the amount of effort they invested and the amount of inferential learning they achieved from television. Students also came to mobilize their abilities more readily, thus moving the more able students ahead of their less able peers.

Merrill (1984) tried to affect learners' control over content, pace, display, and other input variables through the careful design of TICCIT computer-assisted instruction. None of the manipulated control variables accounted for learning differences. The only variable that did account for learning differences was an estimate of the amount of effort invested provided by the learners themselves on a posttreatment questionnaire. These findings can be taken to support the claim that learners' choices of effort investment strategies affect learning quite independently of the manipulation of instructional program features. The Merrill data suggest that effort investment, an important facilitator of nonautomatic processing of material, is very much "cognitive penetrable" and *not* totally subject to the "objective" attributes of media.

Student Choice of Media and Method

Another area that provides consistent evidence for the perceived learning demands of media is the recent literature on student choice of instructional conditions. Saracho (1982), Machula (1978–1979), and Clark (1982) reported studies wherein student enjoyment of instructional media and their subsequent achievement were negatively correlated. The results of these studies suggest that allowing students to choose the medium or method they prefer may not always result in maximum learning outcomes.

In a yearlong study involving over 250 third to sixth grade students, Saracho (1982) found that those assigned to computer-assisted instruction in basic skills liked the computer less but learned more than from other media. Similarly, Machula (1978–1979) gave instruction to over 100 undergraduates via television, voice recording, and printed text. Students liked the television less but learned more from it than from the voice recording, which they liked more.

Clark (1982) has reviewed similar studies and has suggested that students use erroneous a priori rules to choose media or methods which often result in less learning than when their aptitudes are used to assign them to instructional conditions. Students incorrectly assess the extent to which the instructional methods associated with the medium will allow them the most efficient use of their effort. Strong interactions with general ability are often found in this research. Higher ability students seem to like methods and media that they perceive as better structured and more directive because they think these demand less effort to achieve success. However, more structured methods prevent these higher ability students from employing their own considerable skills and therefore yield poorer achievements than methods that require them to structure their own learning activities. Lower ability students, on the other hand, seem to like the less structured and more discovery-oriented methods and media. They seem to want to avoid investing the effort required by the more structured approaches, which they may expect to result in failure. Since investing more effort to achieve the same disappointing results is less attractive, they prefer the unstructured approaches whereby they can control the effort they invest and remain relatively anonymous in the process. These lower ability students, however, need more structure and so they tend to achieve less with the instructional methods they prefer more.

The change we anticipate in the basic paradigm on media and technology is not from an instructionally centered ("situational") approach to a learner-centered ("personological") one. Rather, it is a shift from a unidirectional view to a reciprocal view. The instructional powers do not reside solely in the media, for the way one perceives media influences the way one treats them. Nor, however, are learners the sole power brokers, for their perceptions are founded on the kinds of media they actually encounter and the activities they are actually afforded. Research in this domain, if it is to follow a reciprocal paradigm, may benefit from the recent advances made in other fields —such as personality research (e.g., Mischel, 1984), spatial cognition (e.g., Olson & Bialystock, 1983), aptitude processes (Kyllonen et al., 1984), and person-environment interaction (Magnusson, 1981)—where such a paradigm is used.

Summary and Conclusion

The history of our experience with media in teaching has been characterized by ambivalent expectations. On the one hand, each new medium has raised our hopes for benefits to instruction and learning similar to those achieved in the entertainment, communication, and information-handling arenas. These hopes are encouraged by large industries who hope to sell newer electronic media to schools. The extraordinary development of the computer and video disc technologies in the past decade has been the most recent source of this expectation.

On the other hand, there has been a historical concern on the part of parents and educators over the impact of increased exposure to newer media. This concern carries with it a fear that children might be somehow harmed or misdirected if they spend too much time with newer mediums such as video games or television.

These expectations and fears have stimulated a great deal of research interest in the past decade and a number of attempts to build models and theories. Perhaps the most positive outcome of this effort has been a shift in the focus of research questions about media. Earlier studies, initially generated during the behavioral emphasis on external events in instruction, emphasized gross, undifferentiated comparisons of the learning impact of newer media such as television with more "traditional" media such as classroom instruction. Recent studies have exchanged the behaviorally based comparison between media with more cognitively oriented questions. We moved from asking which medium was a better teacher to a concern with which "attributes" of media might combine with learner traits under different task conditions and performance demands to produce different kinds of learning. So, for example, these newer questions ask about the possible cognitive effects of explicit filmic supplantation of cognitive operations on students' mastery of related skills; or about the relative effectiveness of animating actual object movement in teaching allowable moves in chess.

Most important during the past decade was the development of long-overdue theories and models. The theories that have attracted the most attention are those concerned with the cognitive processes activated and cultivated as a result of instruction based in media attributes. These "symbol system" theories have led to a number of engaging hypotheses such as Olson's (1977) claim that "intelligence is skill in a medium," and Salomon's (1979) expectation that student comprehension will be aided when symbolic modes of instruction more closely match student cognitive representations.

The symbol system theories have generated controversy as might be expected when the focus of a field shifts. It is interesting to note that the disputes surrounding the symbol system theories have close parallels with questions that are currently being debated in the general cognitive sciences. For example, one implicit claim of early symbol system theory inspired by Bruner (1964) was that different symbolic modes might result in the cultivation of *unique* cognitive skills. This expectation provided impetus for a now-considerable body of research. To date, the results of that research have suggested that different symbolic attributes of media can, under special conditions, cultivate cognitive skills. However, the issue of whether these skills are the unique products of media attributes or symbolic modes and whether the attributes serve *functionally* different cognitive operations is still being discussed.

The research evidence seems very similar to what has been found in the dispute between dual encoding and proposition proponents in the general cognitive literature (e.g., Kosslyn, 1981; Pylyshyn, 1981). Dual encoding research provides evidence that different types of images can have unique influences on learning and memory. Other data are offered to support an alternative view that images are coded into abstract, semantic propositions for storage and later recalled to "construct" or "reconstruct" specific images. Here a logical extension of existing arguments would suggest that many different images could be coded in the same proposition and that the form of an instructional representation has less of an effect than initially assumed.

Generally, it appears that media do not affect learning in and of themselves. Rather, some particular qualities of media may affect particular cognitions that are relevant for the learning of the knowledge or skill required by students with specific aptitude levels when learning some tasks. These cognitive effects are not necessarily unique to one or another medium or attribute of a medium. The same cognitive effect may often be obtained by other means, which suggests a measure of "functional equivalence." This implies that there may be "families" of functionally equivalent but nominally different instructional presentation forms.

It is also important to note that uniqueness is not an all-or-nothing concept. Some "families" may be relatively small and many of these functionally equivalent groups will contain forms that are more difficult or expensive to duplicate than others. For example, the kind of cognitive effects that Papert expects the programing activities "logo" to produce could, in principle, be replicated by direct teaching of logic. However, in actuality, this functional equivalence would be extremely difficult to obtain in most classrooms given current curricular realities. Moreover, direct instruction may be functionally equivalent to programing in one respect (e.g., facilitation of procedural logic) but not in others (e.g., addressing some learners' need for control).

Lessons for Future Research

As we suggested in the beginning of this chapter, there are lessons to be discerned from past research that may inform future research questions addressed at new media. It is to these lessons that we turn at last.

There is an already rapidly growing body of studies comparing computer-based instruction with more conventional means (e.g., Kulik et al., 1980 have identified over 500 such studies reminiscent of the old TV-versus-traditional-instruction question). There is also a growing interest in the cognitive effects of media-related activities such as inductive thinking skills affected by computer games (e.g., Greenfield, 1984), which is a renewal of similar questions asked in reference to television. It seems that as each new medium comes along, researchers select questions previously addressed to older media (Clark, in press; Gardner, 1982; Wartella & Reeves, 1983). Some of these questions seem, on the basis of past experience, to be more

useful than others. Our summary of some of the most important lessons and questions follows:

1. *Past research on media has shown quite clearly that no medium enhances learning more than any other medium regardless of learning task, learner traits, symbolic elements, curriculum content, or setting.*

Gross comparisons of computers or video disc technologies versus more conventional media for instruction are not likely to prove to be more useful in the future than they have been in the past. All such research to date is subject to compelling rival hypotheses concerning uncontrolled effects of instructional content, method, and novelty. We do not expect that any known or to-be-developed media will alter this expectation. However, *evaluations* of developed and developing media-based programs might usefully compare alternative forms of delivering and shaping instruction on the basis of cost efficiency, and appeal to students without making inferences about "learning" or "performance" advantages due to the medium selected. This would also suggest that future media selection schemes (e.g., Reiser & Gagné, 1982) should be based on appeal and efficiency *rather* than presumed learning benefits.

2. *Any new technology is likely to teach better than its predecessors because it generally provides better prepared instructional materials and its novelty engages learners.*

While media are not causal factors in learning, they often provide the focus for curricular reform. As each new medium is developed and gradually introduced to educational settings, it provides the opportunity for trying out novel and often engaging instructional design strategies. This is particularly true if the new medium is held in as much awe as computers.

So, as each new medium is put into educational use, researchers might consider a number of different questions. For example, we might ask about the impact of a medium's introduction on the setting (e.g., organizational climate, interactions between provider and user groups, allocation of resources), and the changes the setting undergoes (e.g., Sheingold et al., 1983). It would be useful to have more investigation of two aspects of the problem: first, the way that such innovations *naturally* influence educational settings and resources, and ways that such introductions might be *made to influence* desirable outcomes. This latter type of question is particularly important in the case of computers since their available modes of use and their actual influence on education are still far from their potential.

Aside from organizational and resource changes, newer media also *afford* convenient and often novel ways to shape instructional presentations. Of course, there is evidence from past symbol system and general cognitive science research that many different symbolic representations, such as those resulting from exposure to different media attributes, sometimes serve the same or similar functions in cognitive processing. Yet, we should notice that newer media such as computers *allow* for flexible and local construction of the conditions that facilitate skill cultivation, even though these materials might also be constructed in other ways. In this fashion, newer media serve as a *proxy* for the causal variables that influence learning and performance. Here the researcher is relatively unconcerned with the way that media attributes *naturally* influence learning. As in the case of organizational change, the concern is with the way that media attributes and the instructional presentations they afford *can be directed* in the most efficient and effective way to achieve learning goals.

Finally, researchers might wish to follow up on the issue of the "functional equivalence" between nominally different media attributes. It appears that there are "families" of attributes that may have similar cognitive consequences when they are used in instruction. It would be interesting to learn whether there are ways to predict such family "memberships" and whether these families vary in uniqueness, size, and impact. For example, does functional equivalence follow from structural similarity? Or, is structural similarity irrelevant?

Researchers should also note that few, if any, profound cognitive effects of the kind often expected from computer-afforded learning activities can be expected from *brief* exposures and occasional engagements. If, for example, essay writing on word processors is to effect essay-writing *ability* (e.g., Kane, 1983), then no short-term, out-of-context experience with the tool is likely to show much of an effect. The activity must be central, continuous, consequential, and mindfully carried out in order to render observable effects.

3. Future research on media should be conducted in the context of and with reference to similar questions in the general cognitive sciences.

One of the truly important changes to take place in media research in the past decade is the change from an externally oriented, behavioral approach to a more cognitive, interactive, reciprocal focus. Current views suggest that instructional efficacy does not reside in either external or internal events alone, but that complex interactions between events in each domain will characterize the most productive hypotheses. These newer questions, particularly those associated with the symbol system theories, bear a strong resemblance to those in various domains of cognitive sciences such as artificial intelligence, information processing, attribution theory, dual coding, and imagery, and studies of the antecedents of various kinds of transfer of learning and training. While different perspectives on the same problems have a strong and productive history in most sciences, George Mandler's recent caution (1984) is that we might find it "useful to learn more about the achievements and disasters of other scientific enterprises, lest the blinding insights that you discover at regular intervals turn out to be somebody else's old saws" (p. 314).

4. In the future, researchers might ask not only how and why a medium operates in instruction and learning, but also why it should be used at all.

The final ethical question raised by the history of media use in teaching is the pattern of its use by educators. In the past there has been a pattern of adoption by schools in response to external pressures from commercial and community special interests rather than as a result of an identified and expressed need. Most new media are not developed with educational applications as their foremost goal. Consequently, decisions to adopt them occur before there is clear evidence about their efficacy or the availability of superior materials. This was certainly the case with television and is as clearly the case with microcomputers. While the enthusiasms that surround the introduction of a new medium lend a certain currency and legitimacy to schools, they also take scarce resources away from already identified priorities. Not everything that is available for empirical study is, when seen in perspective, also desirable to study.

This is not to imply, however, that the very availability of TV or computers is in itself a poor justification for their demands on the educational system. The conscientious researcher may, on occasion, recommend that schools postpone their entry into a "higher tech" era before a number of basic questions have been addressed. For example, we need to know how media might be made to support instructional objectives and other roles it takes on, what the teachers' role will be when children receive most of their instruction from computers, and how already overburdened schools will accommodate the special demands of newer media. The study and development of media in education are aimed at the improvement of the education, not the glorification of the media. This, then, suggests a new class of questions to be asked: not only what technology, for whom, and so forth, but *why this technology now?* The lesson was best expressed by Seymour Sarason (1984), who pointed out that "Because something can be studied or developed is, in itself, an insufficient base for doing it however wondrous it appears to be in regard to understanding and controlling our world" (p. 480).

REFERENCES

Allen, W. H. (1971). Instructional media research: Past, present and future. *AV Communication Review, 19,* 5–18.

Anderson, D. R., & Lorch, E. P. (1983). Looking at television: Action or reaction. In J. Bryant and D. R. Anderson (Eds.), *Watching TV, Understanding TV.* New York: Academic Press.

Anderson, J. R. (1983). *Architecture of cognition.* Cambridge, MA: Harvard University Press.

Association for Educational Communication and Technology. (1977). *Educational technology: A glossary of terms* (Vol. 1). Washington, DC: AECT.

Bandura, A. (1978). The self system in reciprocal determinism. *American Psychologist, 33,* 344–358.

Blake, T. (1977). Motion in instructional media: Some subject–display mode interactions. *Perceptual and Motor Skills, 44,* 975–985.

Bolter, J. D. (1983). Computers for composing. In R. Case (Ed.), *Chameleon in the classroom: Developing roles for computers* (Tech. Rep. No. 22). New York: Bankstreet College.

Bransford, J. D. (1979). *Human cognition.* Belmont, CA: Wadsworth.

Brown, J. W., & Van Lehn, K. (1981). Toward a generative theory of bugs in procedural skills. In T. Romberg, T. Carpenter, & J. Moses (Eds.), *Addition and subtraction: Developmental perspectives.* Hillsdale, NJ: Lawrence Erlbaum.

Bruner, J. S. (1964). The course of cognitive growth. *American Psychologist, 19,* 1–15.

Card, S. K., Moran, T. P., & Newell, A. (1980). Computer text-editing: An information processing analysis of a routine cognitive skill. *Cognitive Psychology, 12,* 32–34.

Clark, R. E. (1975). Constructing a taxonomy of media attributes for research purposes. *AV Communication Review, 23*(2), 197–215.

Clark, R. E. (1978). Doctoral research training in educational technology. *Educational Communication and Technology Journal, 26*(2), 165–173.

Clark, R. E. (1982). Antagonism between achievement and enjoyment in ATI studies. *Educational Psychologists, 17*(2), 92–101.

Clark, R. E. (1983). Reconsidering research on learning from media. *Review of Educational Research, 53*(4), 445–460.

Clark, R. E. (in press). Confounding in educational computing research. *Journal of Educational Computing Research.*

Clark, R. E. & Snow, R. E. (1975). Alternative designs for instructional technology research. *AV Communication Review, 23*(4), 373–394.

Clark, R. E. & Voogel, A. (in press). Transfer of training principles for instructional design, *Educational Communication and Technology Journal, 33*(2).

Cohen, P., Ebling, B., and Kulik, J. (1981). A meta-analysis of outcome studies of visual based instruction. *Educational Communication and Technology Journal, 29*(1), 26–36.

Collins, A. (1981). Schemata for understanding television. In H. Kelly & H. Gardner (Eds.), *Viewing children through television.* San Francisco: Jossey-Bass.

Dixon, P., & Judd, W. (1977). A comparison of computer managed instruction and lecture modes for teaching basic statistics. *Journal of Computer Based Instruction, 4*(1), 22–25.

Dorr, A., Graves, S. B., and Phelps, E. (1980). Television literacy for young children. *Journal of Communication, 30*, 71–83.

Dweck, C. S., & Bemechat, J. (1983). Children's theories of intelligence: Consequences for learning. In S. G. Paris, G. M. Olson, & H. W. Stevenson (Eds.), *Learning and motivation in the classroom.* Hillsdale, NJ: Lawrence Erlbaum.

Fleming, M. L. (1979). On pictures in educational research. *Instructional Science, 8*, 235–251.

Fleming, M. L., & Levie, H. (1978). *Instructional message design.* Englewood Cliffs, NJ: Educational Technology Publications.

Foreman, G. E., & Edwards, C. P. (1982). *The use of stopped-action video replay to heighten theory testing in young children solving balancing tasks* (Final report). Amherst: University of Massachusetts.

Gardner, H. (1977). Senses, symbols, operations: An organization of artistry. In D. Perkins & B. Leondar (Eds.), *The arts and cognition.* Baltimore, MD: Johns Hopkins University Press.

Gardner, H. (1980). *Artful scribbles.* New York: Basic Books.

Gardner, H. (1982). *Art, mind and brain: A cognitive approach to creativity.* New York: Basic Books.

Gardner, H., Howard, V. A., and Perkins, D. (1974). Symbol systems: A philosophical, psychological and educational investigation. In D. Olson (Ed.), *Media and symbols: The forms of expression, communication and education* (73rd annual yearbook of the National Society for the Study of Education). Chicago: University of Chicago Press.

Glaser, R. (1976). Components of a psychology of instruction: Towards a science of design. *Review of Educational Research, 46*(1) 1–24.

Glaser, R. (1982). Instructional psychology: Past, present and future. *American Psychologist, 37*, 292–305.

Glaser, R., & Cooley, W. W. (1973). Instrumentation for teaching and instructional management. In R. M. W. Travers (Ed.), *Second handbook of research on teaching*, 832–857.

Glass, G. V. (1976). Primary, secondary and meta-analysis of research. *Review of Educational Research, 5*, 3–8.

Goodman, N. (1968). *Languages of art.* Indianapolis, IN: Hackett.

Greenfield, P. (1984). *Mind and media: The effects of television, video games, and computers.* Cambridge, MA: Harvard University Press.

Hampson, P. J., & Morris, P. E. (1978). Unfulfilled expectations: A criticism of Neisser's theory of imagery. *Cognition, 6*, 79–85.

Heidt, E. U. (1977). *Instructional media and the individual learner.* Hingam, MA: Kluwer Nijhoff.

Heidt, E. U. (1978). *Instructional media and the individual learner.* New York: Nichols Publishing.

Hellige, J. E. (1980). Cerebral hemisphere asymmetry: Methods, issues and impressions. *Educational Communication and Technology Journal, 28*(2), 83–98.

Herminghouse, E. (1957). Large group instruction by television. *School Review, 65*, 119–133.

Hess, R., & Tenezakis, M. (1972). The computer as a socializing agent: Some socioaffective outcomes of CAI. *AV Communication Review, 21*(3), 311–325.

Hollenbeck, A. R., & Slaby, R. G. (1979). Infant visual and vocal responses to television. *Child Development, 50*, 41–45.

Jaglom, L. M., & Gardner, H. (1981). The preschool television viewer as anthropologist. In H. Kelly & H. Gardner (Eds.), *Viewing children through television.* San Francisco: Jossey-Bass.

Jamison, D., Suppes, P., & Wells, S. (1974). The effectiveness of alternative instructional media: A survey. *Review of Educational Research, 44*, 1–68.

Kane, J. H. (1983). Computers for composing. In R. Case (Ed.), *Chameleon in the classroom: Developing roles for computers* (Tech. Rep. No. 22). New York: Bankstreet College.

Kearsley, G., Hunter, B., and Seidel, R. J. (1983). Two decades of computer based instruction: What have we learned? *T.H.E. Journal, 10*, 88–96.

Kolers, P. A. (1977). Reading pictures and reading text. In D. Perkins & B. Leondar (Eds.), *The arts and cognition.* Baltimore, MD: Johns Hopkins University Press.

Kosslyn, S. M. (1981). The medium and the message in mental imagery: A theory. *Psychological Review, 88*, 46–66.

Kosslyn, S. M., & Pomerantz, J. R. (1977). Imagery, propositions and the form of internal representations. *Cognitive Psychology, 9*, 52–76.

Ksobiech, K. (1976). The importance of perceived task and type of presentation in student response to instructional television. *AV Communication Review, 24*(4), 401–411.

Kulik, C., Kulik, J., & Cohen, P. (1980). Instructional technology and college teaching. *Teaching of Psychology, 7*(4), 199–205.

Kulik, J., Bangert, R., & Williams, G. (1983). Effects of computer-based teaching on secondary school students. *Journal of Educational Psychology, 75*(1), 19–26.

Kulik, J., Kulik, C., & Cohen, P. (1979). Research on audio-tutorial instruction: A meta-analysis of comparative studies. *Research in Higher Education, 11*(4), 321–341.

Kyllonen, P. C., Lohman, D. F., & Snow, R. E. (1984). Effects of aptitudes, strategy training, and task facets on spatial task performance. *Journal of Educational Psychology, 76*(1), 130–145.

Leifer, A. D. (1976). Teaching with television and film. In N. L. Gage (Ed.), *The psychology of teaching methods.* Chicago: University of Chicago Press.

Lesgold, A. M., & Reif, F. (1983). *Computers in education: Realizing the potential* (Report of a research conference). Philadelphia, PA: American Society of Educators.

Levie, W. H., & Dickie, K. (1973). The analysis and application of media. In R. M. W. Travers (Ed.), *Second handbook of research on teaching.* Chicago: Rand McNally.

Lumsdaine, A. (1963). Instruments and media of instruction. In N. L. Gage (Ed.), *Handbook of research on teaching.* Chicago: Rand McNally.

Machula, R. (1978–1979). Media and affect: A comparison of videotape, audiotape and print. *Journal of Educational Technology Systems, 7*(2), 167–185.

Magnusson, D. (Ed.). (1981). *Toward a psychology of situations: An interactional perspective.* Hillsdale, NJ: Lawrence Erlbaum.

Mandler, G. (1984). Cohabitation in the cognitive sciences. In W. Kintsch, J. Miller, and P. Polson (Eds.), *Methods and tactics in cognitive science.* Hillsdale, NJ: Lawrence Erlbaum.

Meringoff, L. K. (1980). Influence of the medium of children's story apprehension. *Journal of Educational Psychology, 72*, 240–249.

Merrill, M. D. (1984). Learner control and computer based learning. In B. K. Bass & C. R. Dills (Eds.), *Instructional development: The state of the art II.* Dubuque, IA: Kendall/Hunt.

Mielke, K. (1968). Questioning the questions of ETV research. *Educational Broadcasting Review, 2*, 6–15.

Mischel, W. (1984). Convergences and challenges in the search for consistency. *American Psychologist, 39*, 351–364.

Morrisett, L. (1984). Forward. In J. Murray & G. Salomon (Eds.), *The Future of Children's Television.* Boys Town, NE: Boys Town Center.

Olson, D. (1972). On a theory of instruction: Why different forms of instruction result in similar knowledge. *Interchange, 3*(1), 9–24.

Olson, D. (1974). Introduction. In D. Olson (Ed.), *Media and symbols: The forms of expression, communication, and education* (73rd yearbook of the National Society for the Study of Education). Chicago: University of Chicago Press.

Olson, D. (1976). Towards a theory of instructional means. *Educational Psychologist, 12*, 14–35.

Olson, D. (1977). Oral and written communication and the cognitive processing of children. *Journal of Communication, 27*, 10–26.

Olson, D., & Bialystock, E. (1983). *Spatial cognition.* Hillsdale, NJ: Lawrence Erlbaum.

Olson, D., & Bruner, J. (1974). Learning through experience and learning through media. In D. Olson (Ed.), *Media and symbols: The forms of expression, communication, and education* (73rd yearbook of the National Society for the Study of Education). Chicago: University of Chicago Press.

Olweus, D. (1977). A critical analysis of the "modern" interactionist position. In D. Magnusson & N. S. Endler (Eds.), *Personality at the crossroads.* Hillsdale, NJ: Lawrence Erlbaum.

Paivio, A. U. (1971). *Imagery and verbal process.* New York: Holt, Rinehart & Winston.

Paivio, A. U. (1977). Images, propositions and knowledge. In J. M. Nicholas (Ed.), *Images, perceptions and knowledge.* Dordrecht, The Netherlands: Reidel.

Papert, S. (1980). *Mindstorms: Children, computers and powerful ideas.* New York: Basic Books.

Pea, R., & Kurland, M. (1985). On the cognitive effects of learning computer programming. *New Ideas in Psychology.*

Pressley, M. (1977). Imagery and children's learning: Putting the picture in developmental perspective. *Review of Educational Research, 47*, 585–622.

Pylyshyn, Z. W. (1973). What the mind's eye tells the mind's brain: A critique of mental imagery. *Psychological Bulletin, 80*, 1024.

Pylyshyn, Z. W. (1981). The imagery debate: Analogue media versus tacit knowledge. *Psychological Review, 88*, 16–45.

Rcigcluth, C. (1983). *Instructional-design theories and models.* Hillsdale, NJ: Lawrence Erlbaum.

Reiser, R., & Gagne, R. (1982). Characteristics of media selection models. *Review of Educational Research, 52*(4), 499–512.

Resnick, L. B., & Weaver, P. A. (Eds.). (1979). *Theory and practice of early reading.* Hillsdale, NJ: Lawrence Erlbaum.

Riccobono, J. A. (1984). *Availability, use and support of instructional media, 1982–83: Corporation for Public Broadcasting.* Washington, DC: National Center for Educational Statistics.

Rice, T., Huston, A. G., & Wright, J. C. (1982). *The forms and codes of television: Effects on childrens' attention, comprehension and social behavior* (National Institute of Mental Health Update of the 1972 Report of the Surgeon General's Scientific Advisory Committee on Television and Social Behavior). Washington, DC: Surgeon General's Office.

Rumelhart, D. E., & Norman, D. A. (1981). Analogical processes in learning. In J. R. Anderson (Ed.), *Cognitive skills and their acquisition.* Hillsdale, NJ: Lawrence Erlbaum.

Saettler, P. A. (1968). *A history of instructional technology.* New York: McGraw-Hill.

Salomon, G. (1971). Heuristic models for the generation of aptitude-treatment interaction hypotheses. *Review of Educational Research, 42*, 327–343.

Salomon, G. (1974a). Internalization of filmic schematic operations in interaction with learners' aptitudes. *Journal of Educational Psychology, 66*, 499–511.

Salomon, G. (1974b). What is learned and how it is taught: The interaction between media, message, task and learner. In D. Olson (Ed.), *Media and symbols: The forms of expression, communication and education* (73rd yearbook of the National Society for the Study of Education). Chicago: University of Chicago Press.

Salomon, G. (1979). *Interaction of media, cognition and learning.* San Francisco: Jossey-Bass.

Salomon, G. (1981). *Communication and education: Social and psychological interactions.* Beverly Hills: Sage Publications.

Salomon, G. (1983a). The differential investment of mental effort in learning from different sources. *Educational Psychologist, 18*, 42–50.

Salomon, G. (1983b). Television literacy and television vs. literacy. In B.

W. Bailey & R. M. Fosheim (Eds.), *Literacy for life: The demand for reading and writing.* New York: Modern Language Association of America.

Salomon, G., & Clark, R. E. (1977). Reexamining the methodology of research on media and technology in education. *Review of Educational Research, 47*(1), 99–120.

Salomon, G., & Cohen, A. A. (1977). Television formats, mastery of mental skills, and the acquisition of knowledge. *Journal of Educational Psychology, 69*(5), 612–619.

Salomon, G., & Gardner, H. (1984). *The computer as educator: Lessons from television research.* Cambridge, MA: Harvard University, Graduate School of Education.

Salomon, G., & Perkins, D. (1984, August). *The rocky road to transfer: Rethinking mechanisms of a neglected phenomenon.* Paper presented at the Harvard Conference on Thinking, Cambridge, MA.

Saracho, O. N. (1982). The effect of a computer-assisted instruction program on basic skills achievement and attitude toward instruction of Spanish speaking migrant children. *American Educational Research Journal, 19*(2), 201–219.

Sarason, S. B. (1984). If it can be studied or developed, should it be? *American Psychologist, 39*, 477–485.

Schramm, W. (1977). *Big Media: Little Media.* Beverly Hills, CA.: Sage.

Schwarts, J. (1983). Tyranny, discipline, freedom and license: Some thoughts on educational ideology and computers. In *Education in the electronic age.* New York: WNET Media.

Schwen, T. (1977). Professional scholarship in educational technology: Criteria for inquiry. *AV Communication Review, 25*, 35–79.

Scribner, S. & Cole, M., (1981). *The psychology of literacy.* Cambridge, MA: Harvard University Press.

Sheingold, K., Kane, J. H., & Enderweit, M. E. (1983). Microcomputer use in schools: Developing a research agenda. *Harvard Education Review, 53*, 412–432.

Shepard, R. N. (1978). The mental image. *American Psychologist, 33*, 125–137.

Shulman, L. S. (1980). *Reflections on individual differences and the study of teaching.* Paper presented to the American Educational Research Association, Boston.

Shulman, L. S. (1981). Educational psychology returns to school (G. Stanley Hall Series). Paper presented at the annual meeting of the American Psychological Association, Los Angeles.

Singer, D. G. (1983). A time to reexamine the role of television in our lives. *American Psychologist, 38*, 815–816.

Singer, D. G., Zuckerman, D. M., & Singer, J. L. (1980). Helping elementary school children learn about T.V. *Journal of Communication, 30*, 84–93.

Snow, R. E., Tiffen, J., & Siebert, W. F. (1965). Individual differences and instructional film effects. *Journal of Educational Psychology, 56*(6), 315–326.

Stein, N. L., & Glen, C. G. (1979). An analysis of story comprehension in elementary school children. In R. Freedle (Ed.), *New directions in discourse comprehension.* Norwood, NJ: Ablex.

Stimmel, T., Common, J., McCaskill, B., & Durrett, H. J. (1981). Teacher resistance to computer assisted instruction. *Behavior Research Methods and Instrumentation, 13*(2), 128–130.

Suppes, P. (1979). Current trends in computer-assisted instruction. *Advances in Computers, 18*, 173–229.

Tickton, S. G. (Ed.). (1970). *To improve learning: An evaluation of instructional technology.* New York: Bowker.

Tikomirov, O. K. (1974). Man and computer: The impact of computer technology on the development of psychological processes. In D. Olson (Ed.), *Media and symbols: The forms of expression, communication, and education* (73rd yearbook of the National Society for the Study of Education). Chicago: University of Chicago Press.

Tobias, S. (1982). When do instructional methods make a difference? *Educational Researcher, 11*(4), 4–9.

Turkle, S. (1984). *The second self: Computers and the human spirit.* New York: Simon and Schuster.

Wartella, A., & Reeves, B. (1983). Recurring issues in research on children and media. *Educational Technology, 23*, 5–9.

Weizenbaum, J. (1976). *Computer power and human reason.* New York: Freeman.

Wilkinson, G. (1980). *Media in instruction: Sixty years of research.* Washington, DC: Association for Educational Communications & Technology.

Winn, W. (1981). Effect of attribute highlighting and diagrammatic organization on identification and classification. *Journal of Research in Science Teaching, 18*(1), 23–32.

Winn, W. (1982). Visualization in learning and instruction. *Educational Communication and Technology Journal, 30*(1), 3–25.

Wittrock, M. C. (1978). The cognitive movement in instruction. *Educational Psychologist, 13*, 15–31.

Wolf, T. (1977). Reading reconsidered. *Harvard Educational Review, 47*, 411–429.

Zillman, D., Williams, B. R., Bryant, J., Boyton, K. R., & Wolf, M. A. (1980). Acquisition of information from educational television programs as a function of differently paced humourous inserts. *Journal of Educational Psychology, 72*, 170–180.

Zimler, J., & Keenan, J. M. (1983). Imagery in the congenitally blind: How visual are visual images? *Journal of Experimental Psychology: Learning, Memory and Cognition, 9*, 269–282.

17.
Philosophy and Teaching

Maxine Greene
Teachers College, Columbia University

To "do" philosophy with respect to teaching is not to engage in empirical inquiry with regard to the activities involved. Rather, it is to focus upon the ideas or concepts used in studies of teaching, on the assumptions underlying research, on the "models" (Scheffler, 1967, pp. 120–134) orienting various inquiries. It is, as well, to stimulate reflectiveness about the intentions in which teaching begins, the values that are espoused, the ends that are pursued. It may take "as its point of departure concepts which are of central concern to one or the other branches of philosophy—concepts like observation, experience, understanding, imagination, appreciation, capacities, criticism, rules, habits" (Passmore, 1980, p. 16). It may originate in critical consideration of what it means to provide "the conditions which stimulate thinking" (Dewey, 1916, p. 188), to enter into a pedagogic encounter with other human beings, or to "let learn" (Heidegger, 1972), p. 15). Whether the philosopher's primary interest is in analytic or linguistic philosophy, process philosophy, experimentalism, or existential phenomenology, however, the main concern is to clarify the language used in describing or explaining the practice of teaching, to penetrate the arguments used in justifying what is done, to make visible what is presumed in the formulation of purposes and aims.

The undertaking is not to be considered an alternative to either quantitative or qualitative research. To do philosophy means to pose the kinds of questions that empower us "to think what we are doing" (Arendt, 1958, p. 5) and to locate our investigations in their historical and ideational contexts. There will, therefore, be excursions into the past throughout this chapter for the sake of finding precursors of what is being said today and of enlarging the landscapes of our own thinking. We will treat contemporary philosophical thinkers such as Hannah Arendt, Harry S. Broudy, Thomas F. Green, Jurgen Habermas, Martin Heidegger, Paul H. Hirst, Donna Kerr, James E. McClellan, Maurice Merleau-Ponty, John Passmore, Richard S. Peters, Gilbert Ryle, Jean-Paul Sartre, Israel Scheffler, Jonas F. Soltis, Alfred North Whitehead, and Ludwig Wittgenstein. Extending our perspective, we will bring to bear the ideas of philosophers such as John Dewey, William James, Immanuel Kant, John Locke, and Jean-Jacques Rousseau, as well as Aristotle, Plato, and St. Augustine. There will be more, on both sides of the time boundary and from a variety of orientations; but the point, in every case, will be to stimulate reflectiveness on inquiry into teaching and to make things somewhat more transparent, to some degree more clear.

Certain agreements mark philosophical discourse with respect to teaching today. Distinctions are made between teaching and training, teaching and conditioning, teaching and indoctrination. There is a widespread acknowledgment that teaching cannot, as B. O. Smith pointed out (1961) be assimilated to learning. In other words, there is a general recognition that "teaching is one thing and learning is quite another," even though it is agreed that teaching is an intentional act aimed at the achievement of learning, and that learning signifies a conscious coming to know (McClellan, 1976) or being able to think (Heidegger, 1972). In most instances, there is an assumption that teaching may be described as a "covert triadic relation" (Passmore, 1980, p. 22). This means that "if anyone teaches, there *must be* something he teaches and someone he teaches it to, even when these are not mentioned." Passmore calls the triadic nature of the activity "covert" because it is often overlooked and because it is not always apparent in the "grammar of our language." Nevertheless, there are few philosophers who do not pay heed to the fact that good teachers must know something about what they are teaching (or trying to let others learn), must care about it (in Peters' sense of caring about what is worthwhile [Peters, 1978]) and must be concerned about their students' learning what they are trying to teach.

Contemporary philosphers, then, tend to view most instances of teaching as intentional activities or complexes of activities aimed at moving others to take cognitive (and, perhaps, imaginative or creative) action on their own initiatives. For most, such cognitive action is norm governed or, as Thomas Green (1967) expressed it, "norm-regarding." Teaching people how to think and to inquire, how to make sense of their lived

The author thanks reviewer Gary Fenstermacher (Virginia Polytechnic Institute).

situations, is not simply a matter of creating the kinds of conditions that will arouse them to questioning. Yes, it is important that they be stimulated to pose their own questions, test out certain of their conclusions, try to validate some of their beliefs in their social and experiential milieus. But a certain "oughtness" ought to permeate the teaching–learning process, it is believed, even when it is experientially based. Donna Kerr (1981) speaks of the need to pay heed to "the structure of quality" in teaching. Most philosophers agree that teachers ought to demonstrate and to communicate a sense of how thinking *should* take place with respect to experiential issues as well as in relation to the particular disciplines. Hirst, for example, writes about the "logic" of what are often called the "forms of knowledge" (Hirst, 1965). He means the formal principles to which the terms used must conform. Principles of this sort create a "publicly accepted framework of knowledge"; and coming to understand *any* form of knowledge, he suggests, involves thinking in relations that satisfy the public criteria. Others lay their stress primarily on what is reasonable to believe or on giving "good reasons" for knowledge claims. They, too, are presuming the existence of a framework of norms or agreed-upon standards that impart relevance to the reasons given. For Scheffler, for instance, the very notion of teaching has "distinctive connotations of rational explanation and critical dialogue"; its point is "to develop a sort of learning in which the student will be capable of backing his beliefs by appropriate and sufficient means" (Scheffler, 1965, p. 10).

If it is the case that learning involves mastery of a range of "languages" or "symbol systems" for the sake of ordering experience (Goodman, 1976), or an increasingly elaborate symbolic structuring of the lived world, critical standards must be taken into account. For Hirst (1965) each set of symbolic expressions (or each "form of knowledge") is distinctive in the way it is to be tested against experience. Moreover, there is an apposite "modus operandi" associated with each way of knowing, what Gilbert Ryle called "a way of doing something," connoting more than rote or routine (Ryle, 1967), p. 114). This may be understood as something learnable; and Ryle wrote that "to have learned a method is to have learned to take care against certain specified kinds of risks, muddle, blind alley, waste, etc." (p. 115). Individual students are expected to make their own applications, to take their own risks; but each person's freedom and range of initiatives are said to be increased by learning *how* to do things, how to practice (and reflect upon practice) according to dependable norms.

John Dewey was not prone to emphasize preexisting norms or prescriptions; but he was equally concerned about taking care. Conceiving the human mind as "all the ways in which we deal consciously and expressly with the situations in which we find ourselves," he said that "mind is care in the sense of solicitude, anxiety, as well as of active looking after things that need to be tended" (Dewey, 1934, p. 263). The "mental" ought not to be thought of as a separate realm; nor ought school knowledge be segregated from the realities of everyday life. All students, he said, ought to be provided opportunities for "acquiring and testing ideas and information in active pursuits typifying important social situations," for seeing the "cross connections between the subject matter of the lesson and the wider and more direct experience of everyday life" (Dewey, 1916, p. 191). It has

been pointed out that this approach did not properly consider the criteria of evaluation for different sorts of knowledge claims; nor did Dewey place much emphasis upon the "logic" of particular subject matters. Using the scientific method as the paradigm for intelligence at its most efficient, Dewey continued to remind his readers that thoughts or ideas were always tentative. They had to be tested through application; and students always had to discover their validity for themselves. Standards, he said, were formed in any subject to the degree there was a realization of the contribution they made to the significance of an actual experience. Warning against standards taught in such a fashion that they struck students as "merely symbolic," he said that students confronted with a difficult intellectual problem that they finally managed to resolve could not but appreciate the value of clarity and definition. In such a case, the students have a standard that can be depended upon. When they simply acquire information about the processes of analyzing a subject as "standard logical functions," these are likely to mean nothing to the individual "unless it somehow comes home to him at some point as an appreciation of his own" (Dewey, 1916, p. 276). The "oughtness" that permeated teaching had to do, for Dewey, with interconnection and with experienced relevance.

In relation to this, of course, is what Dewey called the "principle of continuity of experience" (Dewey, 1963, p. 35), meaning the ways in which each experience takes up something from prior experience and alters the quality of experiences that follow. "A primary responsibility of educators," he wrote,

> is that they not only be aware of the general principle of the shaping of actual experience by environing conditions, but that they also recognize in the concrete what surroundings are conducive to having experiences that lead to growth. Above all, they should know how to utilize the surroundings, physical and social, that exist so as to extract from them all that they have to contribute to building up experiences that are worthwhile. (p. 45)

Worthwhileness, quality, even the straightforwardness and open-mindedness characteristic of a good method, were contingent upon the contributions various modes of teaching and inquiry made to a sense of increasing meaningfulness, or what Dewey often called "growth."

Peters, taking issue with this conception, recalls Plato's emphasis on "the necessity for objective standards being written into the content of education" (1965, p. 97). He writes, in fact, that "Plato's image of education as turning the eye of the soul outwards towards the light" is more convincing for him than either the authoritarian view or the "growth-theorists'" view that children ought to be allowed to learn from experience and choose for themselves. As he sees it, teachers primarily concerned about growth and self-determination pay too little heed to the transmission of worthwhile content. For him, the teacher ought deliberately to try to bring students to care about the worthwhile even as their understanding and voluntariness are assumed. This implies a certain given-ness with regard to the worthwhile: It is either resident in certain "public traditions" that are to be preserved or in the "publicly accepted framework of knowledge." It may be a function of what a particular rational community regards as valuable; it may be fundamental to the idea of justification itself.

McClellan finds a contradiction in the argument that those

who become committed to the teacher's conception of the worthwhile are free to reject it (if that is what "voluntariness" means). "To speak vulgarly," he writes, "if you start out committed to transmitting what is worthwhile to kids in such a way that the *kids* will become committed to it, you're inevitably going to violate their 'wittingness and voluntariness.' And you'll not succeed in concealing that conflict by any interspersed twaddle about 'knowledge and understanding and cognitive perspective'" (McClellan, 1976, pp. 21–22). Saying that, he raises one of the crucial issues with which philosophers have to be concerned. Most do indeed recognize that moral and political values are inescapable in the teaching enterprise. McClellan himself believes that, through education, the sense of a world-wide human community ("a rational and loving world community") should be built inside of every person. Donna Kerr writes that there can be no excellence in teaching if teachers do not bring to bear what they know and cherish (Kerr, 1981). Like others before her, she draws attention to the moral and political contexts that must be taken into account when decisions regarding subject matter and curriculum are made. It is clear enough that different social and economic systems make different demands of their schools; and, for a long time, it was sufficient in this country to justify what was taught and what methods were considered appropriate by referring to the values of liberal democracy. Dewey, for instance, continually referred to democratic values when he argued for the "ever greater utilization of scientific method in the development of the possibilities of growing, expanding experience" (Dewey, 1963, p. 89). It is obvious that he was not neutral when it came to a conceptualization of teaching; nor did he expect teachers to be neutral. He did, however, presume the existence of a moral consensus that would sustain those attempting to break with the "intellectual and moral standards of a pre-scientific age" (1963, p. 89).

Such a consensus can no longer be taken for granted in an increasingly pluralist society; nor can the association of "scientific method" with democratic values. The rise of technology, the stress on "value-free" inquiries, the spread of quantification: All have made it difficult to validate the selection of particular modes of teaching by consulting what is described as "scientific." The recognition of signal inequities in society, the acknowledgment of diverse languages and cultures, the continuing erosion of what Dewey (1954) himself had called an "articulate public" make it nearly impossible for a teacher to posit a unified public opinion that might support any specific approach to teaching. Moreover, as most philosophers would agree, teachers cannot simply draw inferences from any set of research conclusions for what they ought to do in the classroom. Indeed, it is generally considered logically impossible to infer answers to practical questions from answers to theoretical questions about what is actually the case in any given situation. As William James said with regard to psychology and the teacher, "An intermediary inventive mind must make the application, by using its originality" (James, 1906, p. 8). And it is in the course of such mediation that a teacher (or an educational researcher) may be called upon to do philosophy.

Today, the problem is complicated by prescriptions and demands that focus upon "knowing that" far more than "knowing how" (Ryle, 1949, pp. 25–32). Teachers aware of the context

in which they are working are all too frequently constrained from doing what they might call "teaching" by parental insistence that students concentrate on mastery of basic technical skills or on the accumulation of "facts" without thinking too much about what they are doing. Educators are asked to be more responsive to market demand than to accepted frameworks of knowledge or to rational norms. Those who are thoughtful, who want to be intelligent about what they are doing in the classroom, sometimes find simple pragmatic tests to validate what they are doing. Others, more philosophically inclined, recognize that practical judgments may best be made when, indeed, what they "know and cherish" is brought to bear. This means engagement in a deliberate effort to relate what research has enabled them to understand about (say) learning behaviors at different stages, the interpretations and analyses they have been able to make with regard to the meanings of disparate terms, the diagnoses they have been able to make of the social realities in which they are enmeshed, the theories of education they have learned or devised, and the values and commitments that permeate their lives. All of this can provide only a partial, perspectival view; but to "stop and think" may be all anyone can do.

There are those who believe they can take a more "objectivist" and detached approach to practical questions, who are convinced about what is "measurably" right and wrong. There are others, closer to the existential phenomenological pole, whose choice of themselves and their identities is integrally involved with the pedagogical choices they make in school. Donald Vandenberg (1971), for instance, makes focal the teacher's "way of existing." Martin Buber wrote about the teacher gathering in "the constructive forces of the world ... which the child needs for the building up of his substance." These forces, he said, must be chosen by the teacher from the world and "drawn into himself" (Buber, 1957, p. 101). For all the differences in stress, most theorists do see teaching to be an intentional undertaking and find it difficult to exclude the teacher's own believing and cherishing, the teacher's notions of what is most worthwhile. This does not signify a full agreement with Peters' idea that students must become (voluntarily) committed to the teacher's conception of the worthwhile. Of course there are those who exclude all voluntariness and attempt to impose an "official" or "normal" view of what is valuable. There are those who, laying stress upon cognitive development, discover an acknowledgment of the inherently worthwhile associated with the attainment of a high level of rationality. Still others, following Dewey, believe that students will find that certain worthwhile beliefs and commitments "work" for them and, in consequence, make them their own. Still others (mainly existential thinkers) consciously address themselves to their students' freedom and urge them (in almost total voluntariness) to "choose."

Today, what with the prevalent unease about eroding "discipline" and low achievement scores, there is a resurgent preoccupation with "excellence." Its meanings are various and vague; but educational discourse is now marked by reiterative discussion of the importance of common norms and higher standards. It is as if there were a hunger for an ideal in which diverse and confusing ideas of the worthwhile can converge. Whenever this occurs, traces of Platonic thinking seem to reappear, for all the fundamental differences with Plato on such matters as form, representation, perfection, and the "eye of the soul." Ideas having to do with certainty and permanence take on an appeal at moments of unease and sensed deficiency; and, not surprisingly, thinkers once almost forgotten are reincarnated as precursors by those in search of standards and reliable support from the past.

Plato's dialogue, the *Symposium*, is an account of friendship and human association, so convincing and eloquent as to make clear what the idea of a precursor can mean. It has to do with a gathering of Athenians, come together to celebrate *arête* or excellence in the person of Agathon who has won a prize for a tragedy. The topic of discussion is the meaning of *eros* or love; the meanings identified are multiple; and the more drinking there is, the more dissension, as the guests engage in rhetorical exercises and oratorical improvisations. At length, Socrates —who is the exemplary teacher—transforms the symposium into what it originally signified: a meeting place for a teacher and his pupils. He does so by reinterpreting the debate and by recapitulating, through the use of myth and metaphor, the phases of his own initiation into wisdom. He speaks of the questions posed to him by a wise woman named Diotima, who has drawn him to the summit of understanding. "But what," she asks, "if man had eyes to see the true beauty—the divine beauty, I mean, pure and clear and unalloyed, not clogged with the pollutions of mortality and all the colors and vanities of human life—thither looking, and holding converse with the true beauty simple and divine? Remember how in that communion only, beholding beauty with the eye of the mind, he will be enabled to bring forth, not images of beauty, but realities (for he has hold not of an image but of a reality); and bringing forth and nourishing true virtue to become the friend of God and be immortal, if mortal man may. Would that be an ignoble life?" (Plato, 1928, p. 379). Socrates is describing for those he takes to be his students the relationship between his attainment of knowledge and the emergence of his own true nature. He is trying to make them see for themselves the power of the principles of good and beauty, and the importance of making them significant in their own lives.

Philosophers today rarely think in terms of a metaphor of ascent; nor do they think of knowledge as a representation of nature or of ideal abstractions or "forms." But there remains the image of the teacher struggling to move others to become norm governed, to choose to aspire and live according to principles, to create orders in experience by means of concepts and forms. Moreover, at least for some, there remains the society, with its cacophonous voices and points of view; and there seems to be a desperate need to provoke individuals somehow to overcome self-interest, to achieve some ultimate agreement, to transcend towards the "real." The *Symposium* offers a metaphorical paradigm—perhaps of what education should be.

There are more particular notions of how teaching and knowledge are to be understood in Plato's dialogue entitled the *Meno*, and in the *Republic*; and both have affected later attempts to make ideas about teaching clear. In the *Meno*, a young man named Meno, educated by the Sophists, comes to Socrates with the question, "Can virtue be taught?" (Plato, n.d.-a, p. 11). Socrates, who believes there are no teachers who can do more than instruct in rhetoric or offer information, cannot respond directly, even though he sees virtue as a type of

knowledge. Instead, he recounts an old myth that knowledge must be viewed as a process of recollection, stimulated by a desire to recover some hidden insight and requiring an active effort on the part of the student to remember. He then performs an experiment with Meno's slave boy, who is said to know no geometry. Through the asking of leading questions, he is able to get the boy to "remember" that a square on a diagonal is twice the size of an original square. The boy does indeed admit that the square will be twice the size of the original, and Socrates admits that he did not teach him that fact. He means, of course, that knowledge cannot be imparted mechanically from without, that the student's active participation is required. Also, he wants to suggest an analogy between a person's capacity to remember and the ability to grasp the abstract concepts identified with preexisting forms. As for virtue: It cannot be taught by precept or example. Anyone who embodies it is able to teach it (as the Sophists could not), but certainly not by imposing facts about it from outside, or persuading, or using clever rhetorical devices. In the case of the slave boy, since Socrates focuses mainly on the answers to the questions, he does not enable the boy to engage in coming to know or to reason from a set of premises. He actually does not teach him to solve the problem, for all his diagrams. By demonstrating what he calls "recollection," he is acting as teacher to Meno, who had asked whether virtue could be taught.

Scheffler has suggested, however, that a model of teaching can still be found in Socrates' approach to the slave boy (Scheffler, 1967, p. 124). He calls it the "insight model," and it remains influential in our time. It is a view of knowledge as a mode of vision or insight, which must be stimulated by a teacher and what a teacher does in encounters with a student. If vision is properly stimulated, students will be likely to go off on their own initiative to think for themselves. Scheffler emphasizes the significance of language in all this and of students' efforts to grasp the meanings of the propositions presented to them through their own activity. It is up to the students, finally, to test whatever theory they can develop in real circumstances (pp. 106–107). Simply to inform someone that something is the case (as Socrates knew) is not to teach; and we are reminded again of both Dewey and Ryle. The teacher's words and sentences are intended to move students into their own conceptualizing activity. The teacher's interest ought to be in activating insight, empowering the student to find out how to interpret events and phenomena in the world.

In the *Republic*, the metaphor for this kind of self-initiated activity (in the section dealing with the myth of the cave) is an emergence out of darkness into the light. The allegory here concludes with an account of those prisoners (originally chained, inactive, mute) who have been freed to master the dialectic movement of reasoning. They have been awakened to the relization that they were living in a world of mere appearances, of illusions. Only when they become capable of understanding first principles and of grasping—through the use of intellect and the "eyes of the soul"—the unchanging forms that define reality (Plato, n.d.-b, p. 293), can they be viewed as moving beyond mere opinion, of actually coming to know.

Socrates points out to Glaucon that "certain professors of education must be wrong when they say that they can put knowledge into the soul which was not there before. . . . Whereas our argument shows that the power and capacity of learning exist in the soul already" (p. 272). This is true of all in addition to the "self-taught" philosopher-kings who have the capacity to release others to find their way. It is understandable why Werner Jaeger (along with other scholars) writes that Socrates "is the greatest teacher in European history" (Jaeger, 1943, p. 27). Setting aside Plato's dualism, we can see the significance still in those leading questions that were the heart of the "Socratic method." Jaeger adds that Socrates' idea of the aim of life is what shed a new light on the purpose of education, wherever it occurs: "Education is not the cultivation of certain abilities; it is not the communication of certain branches of knowledge.... The real essence of education is that it enables men to reach the true aim of their lives. It is thus identical with the Socratic effort to attain *phronesis*, knowledge of the good" (Jaeger, 1943, p. 69). How is the teacher to comprehend the "true aim" of students' lives? How is he or she to define the "good"?

Aristotle, in his turn, spoke of self-realization, conceived as the attainment of happiness or *eudaimonia*. Happiness is associated with the achievement of virtue for Aristotle; and he believed that education (through instruction and the cultivation of habit) is essential for the attainment of virtue and all the varieties of human excellence. "There are three things," he wrote in *Politics* (Aristotle, 1957), "which make men good and virtuous: these are nature, habit, and rational principle." Legislators are reponsible for the welfare of the polity. "All else is the work of education; we learn some things by habit and some by instruction" (p. 196). The teacher's task is to cultivate the proper dispositions and to habituate the young in moral action. Only as they act justly and temperately, only as they reflect upon those acts, will they develop moral character. Instruction is concerned, not with the shaping of dispositions, but with the development of intellect. Since the achievement of rationality is conceived to be each man's true desire and proper end, self-realization is linked to the perfecting of "intellectual intuition" and theoretical reason. There is an assumption that the living human being takes pleasure in learning, and that happiness has much to do with the actualization of potentiality, especially the potentiality of rationality or the capacity to grasp fundamental forms and principles. For Aristotle, those forms did not inhabit a separate realm, as they did for Plato. They represent the structures, as it were, of all material things; they signify the actualizations of the possibilities within all things. Actualizations or fulfillments, however, differ throughout the hierarchies of the natural world; human capacities differ, as do human potentialities. Women, children, and slaves, for instance, share in moral excellence only to the extent demanded by their functions in society. (Slaves, Aristotle believed, were "entirely without the faculty of deliberation; the woman does possess it, but in an unauthoritative way" [p. 21].)

The dominant metaphor in Aristotle's thinking was a hierarchy, a kind of pyramid arising out of inchoateness, culminating in the abstraction of pure form. We might think of Dante's later representation of it in the *Inferno*, describing the continual climbing in order "to glimpse those things whose beauty nothing mars,/Through a round opening, in the heavens enthroned,/Thence issuing, we beheld again the stars" (Dante, 1947, p. 187). All humankind "naturally" struggle upward, according to this view, strive towards their own excellence; but what that excellence is (according to Aristotle) depends upon inborn ability or *potentia* as well as upon station and function in society. Only those who attain the highest levels of rationality have any hope of reaching the pinnacle. There is, in consequence, a guiding principle of aristocracy. The culminating concern is for the kind of excellence that signifies a fully developed intellectual intuition, a capacity for contemplation and leisure, a gift for leadership in an enduring polity. The context of this kind of thinking must be an ordered cosmos, a teleological or purposeful cosmos governed by a *logos*, a principle of rational order, of unmarred form.

We can see why those who attempt to give the Aristotelian view contemporary relevance emphasize the need to identify fixed and unchanging aims for education. Students are to be enabled to will themselves to leave excessiveness, sensuality, and impulse behind and orient themselves to the absoluteness and timelessness of the true, the beautiful, and the good. Teaching may be conceived as an adaptation of Socratic questioning; it may be thought of as "instruction" in the Aristotelian sense. There may be an articulation of the meaning of a universal *paideia* (Hutchins, 1962; Adler, 1982) as alternative to relativism and fragmentation and disorder. The watchword becomes excellence when this is put forward, primarily cognitive excellence; and education is to be general education, the same for all.

But this is not the only inheritance of Aristotelianism. The emphasis upon dispositions and habits has been maintained in quite other contexts, for all the disagreements with formalism and essentialism. Dewey, for instance, wrote about the connection between the development of a reflective disposition (or the "habit" of intelligence) and the growth of character. The formation of good habits, for him, was linked to action, as it was for Aristotle. Knowledge of the good properly connected with a system of impulses and habits could not, Dewey believed, but express itself in conduct. Unlike Aristotle, he did not think that children somehow know in advance what it is to act justly. Impulse, for Dewey, had always to be linked with reflection; "the original body of impulsive tendencies" must be formed into "a voluntary self in which desires and affections center in the values which are common" (Dewey, 1960, p. 168). The view of reflectiveness differed from Aristotle's, as did the conception of knowing; but the concern for disposition, for right action, and for character remained.

The other aspect of the Aristotelian view, that associated with intellectual excellence, shows itself when R. S. Peters discusses writers in the developmental tradition who seem to presuppose normative standards of human development. "But must this be so?" Peters (1972) asks.
What he would have teachers do is intentionally to cultivate these excellences, now viewed as "general qualities of mind," (p. 122) as teachers concern themselves with the development of persons. Peters grants that these qualities of mind must show

Could not something be made of an alternative, more Greek type of approach, which singled out certain human excellences that evoke admiration in us rather than approval? These might be held up as examples of levels of development which human beings can attain by striving and by the exercise of abilities which are distinctively human—mainly connected with the use of reason. (p. 121) themselves in specific activities with their own particular standards; but he nevertheless believes that there is something common to such excellences as "being critical, creative, autonomous and the like" (p. 123). This, along with his linking of cognitive excellence to the development of a person, holds traces of the Aristotelian ideal. In seeking a way of thinking about teaching (and investigating the traces of traditional points of view in our own thinking today), we find it difficult to set all this aside.

It must be said, of course, that Dewey, Peters, and their 20th-century contemporaries do not inhabit a world dominated by classical rationalism. Plato's and Aristotle's educational ideas were much affected by the primary place of mathematics in the sphere of knowledge; indeed, mathematics, in what was conceived to be its certainty and pure abstraction, was the paradigm. Moreover, it is necessary to hold in mind that classical societies were slave-holding societies. The vivid actualities of the world of work and ordinary lived experience were relegated to those who had no place in the *polis* as citizens. Education was conceived apart from the domains of labor and work, in a sphere separated off from ordinary experience. During the medieval period, following after, theology took the place of mathematics as paradigm; feudal hierarchies overwhelmed slave-owning systems as the Christian faith (and its "City of God") eroded classical culture and the notion of citizenship in a secular public sphere.

Saint Augustine (1950), in *Concerning the Teacher*, actually said that nothing could be taught by means of signs or language. True knowledge of reality could only be gained, he thought, through direct experience with the world God had created. In addition to such "sensible" knowledge, however, there was what Augustine called "intelligible" (mathematical, logical) knowledge. This type of knowledge could be gained through the exercise of reason and intellect as illumined by the divine with an "interior light" of truth or inner vision. Scheffler (1967) uses this notion of inner vision as the source of his "insight" model of teaching, but now it has been divorced from its origin in the divine. In many respects, Augustine's view resembled the traditional classical view, especially with its emphasis on happiness as the *summum bonum* (now defined as union with God). But Augustine broke with the tradition in affirming the roles of will, desire, and love in human life. Hannah Arendt called him "the first philosopher of the Will" (Arendt, 1978, p. 84ff.) and drew attention to the connection between the will and temporality, to futuring, to the idea of what is not yet. "The freedom of spontaneity is part and parcel of the human condition," Arendt wrote. "Its mental organ is the Will" (p. 110). Not only did this signify a rejection of cyclical views of time and history; it opened the way to new ways of conceiving growth and development. It opened the possibility of imagining what it might mean to move persons voluntarily to choose to learn.

The secular city began encroaching on the "City of God" even before the medieval period ended; and, in the 16th and 17th centuries, economic, social, and political transformations gave rise to new ideas of human progress, new conceptions of science and control. René Descartes had, at least, to confront the actuality of the human being's sensory involvement with the material world, even though he could never resolve what he saw as a separation between the material and the spiritual, body and mind. Causation and other physical phenomena were only to be understood if they were translated into mathematical terms; and this led to an exclusive emphasis on training the mind and a theory of "manifest" (or revealed) truth embodied in "clear and distinct ideas" (Desartes, 1968). There was Blaise Pascal as well, another great mathematician, but one who was fundamentally ill at ease, beginning to ask what would become the existential questions about the human condition and the limits of reason (Pascal, 1958). There was Giambattista Vico, writing about a "new science" having to do with the "common sense" of humanity and the part played by cognition and language in bringing order into the world (Vico, 1948).

The Renaissance was marked by discord, diversity, and a growing sense of human dignity and power. The human being was the "paragon of animals"; and yet, asked Shakespeare's Hamlet, "What is he to me, this quintessence of dust?" Self-consciousness, doubt, an awareness of silences: These were the groundbases of the new expansiveness, as world views began changing on every side. Empirical science began gradually supplanting mathematics and logic as the paradigm of inquiry; religious and political authorities were challenged and replaced; calls for individual human rights began overwhelming the "Divine Right" of kings. The Reformation, the rise of capitalism, the beginnings of representative government, the extension of commerce: Such phenomena were transforming the climate in which people thought about how to teach their young.

John Locke (1947), in his *An Essay Concerning Human Understanding*, asserted that ideas derived from sensations, from actual experiences; they were not "innate," as Descartes had said. The mystery of mind/body relations was resolved by positing the mind as a *tabula rasa*, a blank tablet on which experience could write. The education of the young gentleman, with whom Locke was concerned, focused on the forming of mind, the settling of good habits, and the teaching of such principles as virtue and wisdom. He did not believe that the shapes of human minds could be totally altered, because each had a certain character stamped in by God, but they could be "a little mended" (Locke, 1964, p. 159). The good teacher was to focus on developing a sound mind in a sound body and, later, on knowledge of the world. Latin and language were to be considered as far less important than "virtue, and a well-tempered soul." With a right disposition, a child could be counted upon to master what he needed to know. But young people loved liberty, he thought, and had to be "brought to do the things that are fit for them, without feeling any restraint laid upon them" (p. 207). At once they all had certain "vicious habits," expressed in the desire to dominate others and take their property; and the teacher had to stress good manners, civility, and suitable human feeling.

This "empirical" view became the source of many later experiential and interactive approaches to teaching and learning. It presents a child who is malleable and receptive, whose mind is self-enclosed but open to outside influences. At once, even as that mind can associate and organize ideas, it remains capable of "intuiting" the good. Scheffler finds an "impression model" for teaching in Locke's description (Scheffler, 1967, pp. 100ff.). Here, after all, was an account of a mental structure that could process incoming information, that could—at least to a degree—be shaped from without. The teacher's responsibility, in such a view, was to select the impressions the mind received and to activate those mental powers required for making sense of the world. Scheffler takes issue, of course, with the myth of "simple ideas" and with Locke's lack of attention to language. Seeking a "verbal variant" of the model, he discusses the need to communicate to the young a verbal patterning of the sense data on which Locke relied, a translation of brute raw material into sentences. Only the teacher who can communicate in terms of statements or propositions is likely to move the student to conceptualize by means of concepts embodied in language. Otherwise, there is no way of going beyond mere "input" to thinking about untaught things.

To know is not simply to find out how, in standardized or routinized ways, to operate on what is sensed. If teaching does involve empowering people to take self-initiated cognitive action, intentional efforts must be made to engage them with the networks of concepts or the symbol systems that mark the cultural "conversation" (Oakeshott, 1962). Dewey emphasized the importance of "funded meanings," suggesting far more than mere collections of information (Dewey, 1934, p. 264). It is never enough merely to store or accumulate, any more than it is enough for a teacher simply "to convey an idea into the mind of another" by conveying "a sound into his ear" (Dewey, 1916, p. 17). A sound has to be used in a particular way; it must carry a concept, an idea. For Dewey, words get their meanings or come to be understood through being used in "action having a common interest and end" (p. 19) or through engagement in a shared activity of some kind. Viewed in this fashion, it is conceivable that much learning can take place without anyone's making a deliberate effort to explain or to demonstrate or to make clear. An intentional effort is required, however, if particular concepts are to be conveyed; and, according to Dewey, they have to be contextually communicated, to relate to shared experience in some way. They have to be grounded, others would point out, in the sensed or the perceived world, in what William James (1950) called the "sensible vividness or pungency" that is the "vital factor in reality" (p. 301). All this requires the creation of situations that stimulate students to wonder, to question, to inquire, and at length to make their own use of the concepts made available in response to cumulative interest, to problem posing, to concern. This is quite different from a mere reproduction of standard solutions or assertions. As in the case of the "decisions of principle" R. H. Hare has discussed in connection with moral action (Hare, 1964, pp. 61–63), the teacher has to provoke a degree of self-teaching. "The limit," writes Hare, "is set by the variety of conditions which may be met in doing whatever is taught." Learners have to be allowed, at some juncture, to make decisions by themselves where moral principles are concerned, and the same is true with respect to the models, the constructs, the symbol systems they are brought to understand in other domains. Only then are they likely to extend themselves in new directions, make exceptions, move into spaces the teacher can neither predict nor contain.

There are intimations of this regard for self-initiated learning in the work of another distinctive Enlightenment thinker, Jean-Jacques Rousseau. Granting his reliance upon "negative teaching" in the early years of life, granting the problematic paradigm found in botanical growth "according to nature," we can still acknowledge the importance of his resistance to mere "impression" or the stamping in of conventional social habits and patterns of belief. The orientation to experience and the phenomenal world is clearer and richer than in Locke's work, although the view of an orderly, predictable Nature is much the same. The seeds of developmental theories can be found in Rousseau's regard for the nature and needs of children at different ages. Dreading the impacts of convention, artifice, and bad habits in a society he believed to be corrupt, he recounted in *Émile* (Rousseau, 1962) a tale that may be read either as a novel or a report on a teaching experiment. However looked at, it has to do with rearing of a presumably authentic self in accord with Nature's (not the society's) demands.

For Rousseau, the young boy does not have the power to make his own use of concepts; therefore, his tutor should, in his wisdom, not try to reason with Émile, even in the manner Locke advised. "Childhood has ways of seeing, thinking, and feeling peculiar to itself; nothing can be more foolish than to seek to substitute our ways for theirs. I should expect a child of ten to be five feet in height as to be possessed of judgment" (Rousseau, 1962, p. 39). He thought that all verbal lessons should be avoided early in a student's life; the child should be left to involvement with things and to the governance of necessity (including the necessity inherent in the tutor's strength and authority). The tutor is advised, "Never be in a hurry to act" (p. 43); and the implication is that he should not himself intervene to shape proper dispositions or to communicate the "right" ideas.

It must be recognized that this type of permissivism is much at odds with contemporary definitions of teaching, like the one developed by Donna Kerr and Jonas Soltis. They deliberately tried to generate a set of "action categories which constitute teaching" (Kerr & Soltis, 1974, p. 6); and, as Thomas Green (1967) had done before them, to distinguish action from behavior. Their point is that behavior, per se, is not purposeful; and, when people teach, they cannot but intend a particular type of activity. It is not only that teachers want to bring about certain kinds of learning; they want to move the student into purposeful, conscious action. Rousseau, in contrast, may have been saying that the tutor should content himself with inculcating awareness of his mastery over the child, of the idea of property, of the importance of health, and of the lessons of nature. Since he did not believe that the boy could reason before reaching the age of twelve, he had to be left to what was called the "land of sensations."

This resembles William Blake's realm of "innocence," the green woods, the "Echoing Green" (Blake, 1967, p. 18), where children are seen to be vulnerable as well as impressionable, and where experience is undifferentiated and "wild." For Blake, however, the children are left unprotected against abusive and exploitative authorities when they are abandoned to "innocence"; there was no beneficent tutor to protect them with an authority tuned to the voice of nature. There are resemblances as well to romantic views of the child's condition, ranging from William Wordsworth's to Ralph Waldo Emerson's to John Holt's and Paul Goodman's; in each case, the child is endowed with a special spontaneity and wonder that could only be thwarted by adult interference. The "natural," as in Rousseau's work, is opposed to the "social." In Émile's case, the natural in the child has an ally and support in the person of the teacher. He is allowed to exist in a variegated and sensual world, to be exposed to a range of experiential possibilities. The point, from our present vantage point, has to do with how many of those possibilities could be realized under the "natural" conditions described. We cannot but think of Dewey once more, reminding his readers that guidance, rather than being "external imposition," may mean and ought to mean "freeing the life-process for its most adequate fulfillments" (Dewey, 1959, p. 101). The child must be deliberately empowered to cope with novelties, to solve problems, to make connections, to perceive consequences, to communicate with others, to apply the developing intelligence. Without such help and, yes, guidance, the child might well be left lost and helpless, whether on the city streets or on the green.

"Each age and state of life," wrote Rousseau, "has its own proper perfection, its own distinctive maturity. People sometimes speak about a complete man. Let us think rather of a complete child" (Rousseau, 1962, p. 65). At the age of 12, Émile is ready to enter a new stage, one that will take him in time towards manhood. Still lacking judgmental capacities, he can develop the ability to respect utility. The tutor, somewhat more active now, not only may introduce him to useful subjects like carpentry and astronomy and chemistry; he may begin the boy's moral education by introducing him to images of cooperation and mutuality (and their opposites) in the context of work activities. Émile is not yet asked or helped to conceptualize what he sees; he is simply asked to work with things, to model himself after Robinson Crusoe in planning a house and making practical use of available materials. "What is there to do when we have completed the study of such surroundings? We must convert them as much as we can to our own purposes" (p. 87). It is not a matter of getting Émile to ask questions about his surroundings nor of using the environment as a starting point for further inquiry. It is a matter of using whatever power or capability has been developed to satisfy desire — and of trying not to want any more than can be secured.

It is worth noting that what Rousseau called "our own purposes" were more specific and narrow than those Dewey had in mind when he discussed, as he so often did, the teacher's role in relation to "occupational activities." Because teachers, in Dewey's view, possess "the riper and fuller experience," they have the obligation to suggest new activities or new materials that might indicate the "intellectual possibilities of this or that course of activity — statements on the basis of carefully directed and observed experience of the questions that have arisen in connection with them and of where that knowledge can be had" (Dewey, 1959, p. 124). The idea has to do with continuity, with building up "a free body of related subject matter." The intent is educative; the direction is towards the future; the motivation has to do with becoming "different"; and there is a continuing effort to overcome the old separations between action and ideas, utility and thought. For Rousseau, the concern was mainly for equilibrium, for completeness at each stage, a putting off of the moment when ideas would have free play.

When Émile reaches the period of young manhood, free from the seductiveness of empty symbolisms and pretenses, acquainted with the concreteness of nature and the usefulness of certain phenomena, he is ready for experiences of friendship or social relationship, for reading, for the cultivation of taste. The

18th-century preoccupations emerge: the concern for temperateness, the limits set to "the misleading activity of imagination" (Rousseau, 1962, p. 119), the emphasis on the classics, the preparation for life with an "ideal woman." The paradigm of the *tabula rasa* has given way to a paradigm of the growing flower or plant, impelled to ripeness by its own *élan vital*.

Released to grow in this fashion and to develop "naturally," Emile is presumed to have achieved a balance between power and desire. Not only are his desires "good," in the sense of his having chosen properly to realize them; his powers are being properly exerted in such realization. He has attained happiness and a consciousness of well-being, by now linked to an awareness of others' well-being in the community he is finally able to join. No matter what the conditions of his future life, he can be expected to depend upon his own resources, to resist corruption, and to escape society's "chains."

We are reminded once more of the romantic and radical educational thinkers who have yearned towards the Rousseauan ideal. There are many who have argued against the coercion and compulsion identified with schooling, no matter what the efforts of the teacher. They have laid stress upon the "hidden curriculum," upon the "unequal distribution of knowledge," upon representative teachers' complicity in perpetuating inequalities by their treatment of "classroom knowledge," especially where underprivileged children are concerned (Keddie, 1982, p. 219). It is the oppressiveness rather than the artifices of society that concern such critics, as it is a process of "cultural reproduction" (Bourdieu and Passeron, 1977) that legitimates and perpetuates existing inequities and in which the teacher cannot but participate. There has been an assumption among certain libertarian thinkers, that, given existing structural conditions, if a child is left to himself without adult suggestion of any kind, that child will develop as far as he/she is capable of developing. More recently, there has been a growing concern for the nurturing of conscious "resistance" on the part of students experiencing manipulation or humiliation. Such resistance, certain critics are coming to see, is only likely to occur if appropriate "modes of pedagogy" are developed, the kinds of teaching that take "human agency seriously" (Giroux, 1983). Young people have to be deliberately empowered to "name" their own worlds and recognize the dissonances between their lived situations and experiences and the things they are being taught.

What "modes of pedagogy"? Every one of them, even those explicitly committed to what is variously thought of as "liberation," involves intervention by people intentionally engaged in teaching activities. Most philosophers today make the point that the methods used (of whatever sort) must be morally defensible: The student as free agent, as a center of consciousness, must be respected. Manipulation of the other, conditioning of the other, submission of the other to some rule of "necessity" (whether psychological or social or political) are not activities selected out by the concept of teaching. Or, to express it differently, the teacher concerned for moving others to learn to learn is morally proscribed from treating them as passive, as merely "objects." No one would deny the role of causal, indeed conditioning factors in the course of maturation and culturation; few would deny the influence of unconscious forces or disguised "hegemonic" forces in the sociopolitical environment. Nevertheless, if persons are actually to come to know or to share meanings or to comprehend the intentions of those offering explanations (or providing protocols, or making constructs accessible), they must be viewed as individuals with the potential for thinking for themselves. Or it must be presumed that the kinds of conditions necessary for such thinking can be created in classrooms.

Rousseau's work continues resonating, as it did through the 18th and into the 19th centuries. He was prized by the philosopher Immanuel Kant, wrote Ernst Cassirer (1963), because "he had distinguished more clearly than others between the mask that man wears and his actual visage" (p. 20); but Kant looked "for constancy not in what man *is* but in what he *should* be." It was in conceptualizing what man "should be" that Kant made it possible to see the connection between the freedom of "civilized" (rather than "natural") man and his rational nature. This is partly because one of the charges he set for himself was to find a way of reconciling a conception of freedom with the determinism and mechanism characteristic of 18th-century scientific descriptions of the natural order.

Determinism, Kant (1940) thought, was mitigated by the idea that human acts (which can, as physical events, indeed be explained deterministically) originate in motivation, something that can never be the object of that which was then thought of as scientific investigation. Moral agency cannot be objectively explained, even though acts can be observed and measured; therefore, the source of moral action must lie in rational life, which is free or self-determined (Kant, 1964). As a rational being, the human organism finds the good in a conscious realization of his nature as a rational being. Like the classical thinkers who came before, Kant believed in the importance of releasing man's true humanity, which he identified with his rational self. Like Rousseau, he recognized that, as physical beings, all children are part of the world of nature and must grow and act in the physical world. Since that world is a determined world, however, it is necessary to educate in order to empower individuals to use their rational capacities and, by so doing, to transcend merely physical stimulation and causation. Kant (1960) says:

Man can become man through education only. He is only what education makes him. It is to be noted that man is educated only by man, and by those men who are educated themselves. Defects, therefore, in the discipline and instruction of some men make them poor educators of their pupils. If a being of a superior nature were to assume the care of our education, we would then see what men could become. But, since education partly teaches man something and partly merely develops something within him, it cannot be known how far his natural qualities go. (p. 7)

In pursuing what Kant called the "art" of education, the teacher must discipline the child (or tame his "wildness"), instruct (in skillfulness), civilize (cultivate prudence and judiciousness), and moralize (or stimulate the development of a mind that freely chooses good aims).

Kant saw the human being as a being desiring pleasure in its many forms, including the pleasure of living in defiance of all laws. But he also saw him as capable of willing and responding to the "imperative" of particular kinds of rules (Kant, 1940, pp. 135–240). A good will, as he saw it, acts out of respect for duty or the "categorical imperative," regardless of consequences; and to will in this fashion is to select out those desires whose objects most deserve realization. Without the capacity for cognition, however, there would be no possibility of rules or action in accord with them; since it is understanding, working in association with imagination, that gives rise to rules. The power of reason allows for the unifying of the activities of understanding and imagination. It is by means of those capacities that human beings order, organize, and effect relations among the sensations that bombard them. It is by means of cognitive action and the orders it creates that persons derive their notions of things and of themselves. What is "real" for human beings, then, is a function of the categories of reason; they know what they can rationally schematize; all else is the *Ding an sich*, the unknowable, the "thing in itself." There is an "oughtness" associated with being rational, as there are an objectivity and a universality associated with rational knowledge. Crucial to the structure is the idea of rules: rules that legislate and regulate the knowing process; imperatives to which free will responds. Knowledge of the right and the voluntary ordering of desire are what distinguish human beings from animals and gods; and it is these that account for human freedom and the possibility of autonomy in a determined world.

Kant, identifying the different modes of education appropriate for the different stages of growth, believed that education should go on until the young person learns "to live as a free being." Scheffler (1967), finding a "rule model" for teaching in the Kantian philosophy suggests that the "knower," in this orientation, "must typically earn the right to confidence in his belief by acquiring the capacity to make a reasonable case for the belief in question." It is not a matter of making a case precisely as the teacher has made it, for all the fact that Scheffler has continually stressed the importance of the connection between teaching and "rational explanation and critical dialogue ... giving honest reasons and welcoming radical questions" (Scheffler, 1965, p. 10). A student capable of asking questions that literally go "to the root" of a matter will probably be one who will seek novel arguments and new perspectives. But the student will remain constrained (as the teacher is constrained) by the requirements of rationality itself. He or she will be responsive to certain rules and prescriptions having to do with the modes of justification, the use of evidence, the nature of good reasons, a regard for the truth. For Kant, concepts and understanding are defined in terms of universals that serve as rules; and this view continues to have an effect on many ways of doing philosophy with respect to teaching today.

It is the case, however, that increasingly sophisticated inquiries into cognition and the workings of the mind have rendered problematic Kant's belief that the self is a preexisting and necessary condition for all experience, a "noumenal" object transcending any possible experience. It is generally assumed, albeit from different philosophical points of view, that (as Dewey wrote) "the self is not something ready-made, but something in continuous formation through choice of action" (Dewey, 1916, p. 408). Kant's view of conceptual ordering of experience continues to exert the greatest influence, as more and more theorists of teaching call attention to the importance of introducing students, not simply to specific modes of inquiring, but to what Paul Hirst calls "networks of related concepts."

Nonetheless, we are now aware that the categories or the "transcendental schemata" in which Kant believed are neither necessary nor universal. Cultures differ; the processes of model making differ, for all the likelihood that there exist certain formal structures and sequences in the development of all human languages and thought. Jean Piaget's theory of cognitive structures (like his "genetic epistemology") involves a transformation of what Kant viewed as the changeless categories of knowledge (Piaget, 1977, pp. 765ff.). Like many philosophers, Piaget came to reject the idea of a child "simply receiving reason and the rules of right action ready-made." It is a matter of the "child achieving them with his own effort and personal experience; ... society expects more of its new generations than mere imitation; it expects enrichment" (pp. 695ff.). It is difficult to deny, however, that a basically Kantian notion of structures has permeated Piaget's distinctive structuralism, as it has many channels of educational thought.

We need but recall Noam Chomsky's belief that all languages are restricted by a set of rules that control the generation of meaningful sentences. For Chomsky (1975), there is a common structure, a "universal grammar" that underlies and restricts all particular grammars and which may be coded into all human brains. We need but think of Lawrence Kohlberg's (1971) view of the invariant formal sequences of cognitive development and the related view that the primary function of the teacher is to provoke "cognitive dissonance" in learners by stimulating them with questions that can only be answered if they move one stage beyond the one they are at. And there is Jerome Bruner with his view that "a principal task of intellect is the construction of explanatory models for the ordering of experience" (Bruner, 1973, p. 6). The problem for the teacher becomes one of inventing modes of access to the empowering skills or techniques existing in the culture. This view assumes, as Bruner writes, that for any knowledge in the culture there is "a corresponding form that is within the grasp of a young learner at the stage of development where one finds him—that any subject can be taught to anybody at any age in some form that is both interesting and honest" (Bruner, 1960, p. 33).

The emphasis upon form, on structure, now viewed as a construction of categories from the world of experience, is widespread and, indeed, fundamentally Kantian. The natural consequence is a cognitivist emphasis in teaching. Definiteness in cognition, it has been said, *is* structure; what is involved is an organization of materials around focal ideas and relationships. Many teachers, therefore, are asked to focus upon systems of notation and general ideas, or on the "forms of knowledge" we have already mentioned, the "symbol systems" or the languages by means of which we construct our worlds or, rather, "world versions," since (according to Nelson Goodman, 1978) there is no world underlying our versions of it. Although Goodman does not speak of teaching per se, there are implications for teaching in his view that "knowing is as much remaking as reporting." The processes of world making he discusses enter into knowing, as he understands it. "Perceiving motion ... often consists in producing it. Discovering laws involves drafting them. Recognizing patterns is very much a matter of inventing and imposing them. Comprehension and creation go on together."

It would appear that the many views with respect to struc-

tures and symbolic or notational orders, like the cognitive sciences generally, are in the Kantian tradition, for all the setting aside of such ideas as the "noumenal" and the "transcendental." Such work in the cognitive sciences as that done on the "language of thought" by Jerry Fodor (1980), with its emphasis on the language-like mental structures or internal representational systems that give coherence to experience, belongs in the same stream. David Dennett (1981) characteristically speaks of subsystems in association with mind and of "sub-assemblies of information processors" that eliminate the notion of a human agent with access to his or her own mind. The emphasis increasingly (especially with the growing use of microcomputers and the confidence in artificial intelligence) will be on context-free data and context-free thinking. Teaching, very likely, will be more and more oriented to the stimulation of rule-governed reasoning; computational analogies may be taken more and more seriously by students of thinking. The irony is that a tradition in so many ways rooted in Kantian thought should have become one that forces us to ponder anew the differences between human beings as objects of explanation and human beings as moral agents concerned with justifying what they do and what they know.

The Kantian stream has not, however, been the only one that has reached us from the 18th and 19th centuries. There has been an alternative tradition, far more focused on process than on structure, on the historical than on the transcendental. Originating in many senses with Georg W. F. Hegel (1967) and his commitment to the phenomenological self-reflection of knowledge, it carried with it (sometimes as tributary, sometimes as parallel stream) the thinking of Karl Marx, a number of existentialists and phenomenologists, William James, John Dewey, and others focally concerned with dialectics, development, self-consciousness, and growth. This is not to suggest that the great non-Kantians and anti-systematic thinkers were necessarily Hegelians. It is simply to say that an atmosphere was created in which more and more people, unlike Kant, came to believe, in the words of Taylor (1977), that

> our experience of things is bound up with out interaction with them; that moreover, this interaction is prior, and that what we think of as conscious human experience is an awareness that arises in a being who is already engaged with his world. From this point of view there is no level of experience that can be thought of, even as an abstraction, as pure receptivity. For our most original experience can only be understood by reference to a prior handling of or engagement with the world. (p. 107)

The Kantian dualism is rejected by such thinkers. So is the domination by mathematical logic, the connections established by rule. What is important is not the categorical structure, not the articulated rational system of imposing generic orders. It is the idea of organic relations within the totality that becomes important, and the movements within individual consciousness that lead in time to a grasp of the whole. The dialectic—the notion that we have the capacity to criticize our modes of conceiving things and to do "higher order" thinking (or critical thinking) about previously attained positions—cannot but hold implications for those who think about teaching. Hegel (1967) often spoke of the "self-formation of consciousness" as he explicated the movement beyond concrete and merely subjective knowledge to "pure" universal knowledge. His particular system, being a thought object, was presented as being certain and absolute, as any total understanding by means of thought seems absolute and necessary. Nonetheless, it proposed a historical, dialectical mode of addressing experience, for all its abstract and spiritual resolution. The "universal law" and "objective reason" that were at the heart of the system were rejected by, for instance, Karl Marx, who nevertheless retained the conceptions of the dialectic, consciousness, and history. With Friedrich Engels, he wrote in 1846: "We do not set out from what men say, imagine, conceive, nor from men as narrated, thought of, imagined, conceived, in order to arrive at men in the flesh. We set out from real, active men and on the basis of their real life process we demonstrate the development of the ideological reflexes and echoes of this life process" (Marx & Engels, 1959, p. 247).

Viewing the person as participant in a "social ensemble," Marx made possible a consideration of the social existence, indeed the cultural existence of living persons. Consciousness itself, no longer a simple interiority, was related to social experience. Moreover, he made visible the effects of ideology on thinking, a factor that cannot easily be set aside, even by teachers focused upon rules or the "forms of knowledge." Ideology may be understood as a complex of values, ideas, habits of life through which the consciousness of a particular group is expressed. As the Marxist views it, it is used to justify the status and power of the ruling class; and it is absorbed by the people as part of their ordinary education to the extent that they believe that existing arrangements, no matter how oppressive, are "natural." The ability to attribute even economic predicaments to some impersonal power (the laws of supply and demand, for example, or the will of God) is a sign, Marx wrote, of their alienation from their true life purposes. Like Rousseau, he believed that human beings are born free and potentially creative; the natural human condition was one in which people lived cooperatively together, gave their energies free play, and enjoyed the fruits of conjoint activities in understanding and harmony. Concentrating his attention on enabling people to understand the contradictions and the possibilities in their own lived lives, his concern was to awaken their class consciousness and awareness of historical necessities.

Presented with such a rendering of the human situation at a time of developing industrial capitalism, some teachers might well undertake to enable the young to break through the myths that bred false consciousness and the feeling of being mere "objects" or commodities. Such teachers might feel their primary obligation to make clear that the apparent givenness and solidity of the existing order of things were illusory. Their aims might be to help students take the kind of "scientific" view that would unveil the "realities" of the system. Associated with this would be the desire to prepare them for a transformation of that system. "The standpoint of the old materialism is 'civil' society," Marx (1959) wrote; "the standpoint of the new is *human* society, or socialized humanity. The philosophers have only *interpreted* the world, in various ways; the point, however, is to *change it*" (p. 245). The social revolution he had in mind was to be a revolution against "dehumanized life," a protest by the individual "against his isolation from that community which is the true community of man, i.e. human existence" (Schaff, 1970, p. 59).

What continues to be significant in this is the orientation to dialectical change, to a forward movement in history. What is important, too, is the linking of knowing to action, of critical reflection to transformations. The idea would take many forms in the years to come; and it still finds expression in theories of teaching. It may be taken to be a continuing challenge to the transcendental frameworks of Kantianism, to objectively given cognitive rules.

There were other adversary traditions appearing in the post-Hegelian moment, among them those associated with a developing existentialism. Self-consciousness, individuality, the sense of moral agency: Such themes became visible, for instance, in the work of Sören Kierkegaard. He, too, began as a Hegelian; but he came to reject the very idea of a universal system of thought (created, after all, by one man thinking), as he did the overcoming of the existential subject and the subject's standpoint or point of view. Attending to dimensions of modernity different from those Marx and Engels were selecting out, Kierkegaard concerned himself with the individual lost in the "crowd" or the "public," submerged and irresponsible in his or her anonymity (Kierkegaard, 1962, pp. 112–117). The paradoxes of life, he thought, were being subsumed under pieties and the search for material comforts. Even teaching was dominated by calculation and utility. The young were being trained to labor and to serve, not to think or to be.

Kierkegaard's refusal to disregard what Kant had called the "subjective private condition" of individual judgment and his personal dialectic open up dimensions of the encounter between teacher and pupil too frequently unnoticed even today. So do his discussions of ambiguity, freedom, choice, and the "courage to be." Choice is decisive for the content of personality, he wrote; but deliberation and endless "thought-experiments" too often put off the moment of choice. Too many people drift through their lives, caught in distraction and multiplicity, indifferent. "I should like to say that in making a choice it is not so much a question of choosing the right as of the energy, the earnestness, the pathos with which one chooses" (Kierkegaard, 1947, p. 105). He was talking about the possibility of commitment and engagement, surely matters of importance to those trying to empower others to learn how to learn. For all Kierkegaard's distancing himself from ordinary social life, he was—as "Individual"—communicating something about subjective experience that was not unlike what Marx was describing in another sphere. He was saying how it was for the existing person, so easily lost in aggregates of "class" and "people" and "mass." He was pointing to the depersonalization and abstractness that may mark reliance on logical prescriptions or formal principles —sometimes requiring a "dying away" from the self. For Kierkegaard, the logical thinker was never to forget that he or she was an existing individual. Otherwise, in the persistent effort to build systems, the person was likely to become "fantastical," a kind of charlatan. Preoccupied with the need for self-reflectiveness and the kind of "indirect communication" that might provoke it, Kierkegaard worked to awaken his readers to a sense of their own existence in a world lacking objective guidelines or guarantees. In the face of paradox and even absurdity, he wanted to goad them to "leap," to risk, to choose.

His religious concern, like the image of the "knight of faith," holds minor relevance for the teacher today; but the stress on striving (and even anxiety) may well have bearing on how teachers perceive their project in the world. Kierkegaard spent much of his life "trying to become a Christian," in the full knowledge that a completion of the effort or a righteous declaration that he was indeed a Christian would contradict what being a Christian entailed. So it may be with becoming a teacher. To teach, after all, is to engage in an ongoing effort to move others to learn to learn, to come to know, to think, to see. Most philosophies of teaching view this as a process, perhaps a self-correcting process, one that is itself educative without a predetermined stopping place. For people to announce that they *are* teachers with nothing further to discover or to attain might well contradict what being a teacher means. It is the unresolved dialectic that remains significant in the Kierkegaardian model, that and the attention to concreteness and particularity, to the "existing individual" without whom no theory of teaching would be complete.

Friedrich Nietzsche, with his evolutionary preoccupation and his idea of "eternal recurrence," differed in important ways with Kierkegaard; but there are resemblances that, for some, make Nietzsche's work a current in the existential stream. He also was opposed to systematizations, largely because they seemed to him to obscure what he called the "truth." All philosophic systems, in any case, ought to be seen as expressions of the ways in which certain individuals thought about their worlds; and Nietzsche wanted perpetually to question all perspectives and assumptions, "to look now out of this window, now out of that" (Nietzsche, 1967, p. 410). "Truth," for him, meant interpreted fact. Even rational thought, he said, is interpretation according to schemata or patterns we cannot throw off. For him, however, such schemata were developed in the course of history; they were not transcendent; they were not categories of human reason, as they were for Kant. There are respects in which he anticipated certain forms of pragmatic inquiry with his stress on experimental thinking in "problem situations," his conviction that truths are primarily ideas that help people live in the world. At once, he said that the truths of science abandoned human beings to a universe lacking meaning and purpose; they needed, therefore, illusions, fictions, and (especially) art. They ought to try to live their lives, he said, as works of art; but, in any event, the world can be justified eternally "only as an aesthetic phenomenon" (Nietsche, 1967, p. 554). The poet Rainer Maria Rilke (1965), writing in a Nietzschean vein, said that "we're not very much at home in the world we've expounded" (p. 3). Imagination is required if we are to create meanings or to reinvent our traditions.

Surely this remains of moment for those who ponder the process of teaching today. So, in certain respects, does Nietzsche's view of the type of person who "shall be bred, shall be willed, for being higher in value, worthier of life, more certain of a future" (Nietzsche, 1958, p. 57a). The only way to become such a person was to plumb the depths of one's own doubts and passions and, in time, to discipline them. It was not (for all the distorted readings of what Nietzsche meant by the "overman") to use one's power over others. It was to express one's powers, one's own energies in a disciplined freedom. When we recall the emphasis on excellence today, there is something suggestive in this concern for the release of energies in accord with self-reflecting choice. There may even be a connection between what

Nietzsche had in mind and Howard Gardner's notion of multiple intelligences, which gives rise to a critique of channeling, narrowing one-dimensionality where teaching is concerned. As suggestive is the idea that this person who is called "higher in value, worthier of life" represents a transition, what Heidegger called "a bridge" (Heidegger, 1972, pp. 51, 60). The real interest, in other words, is not in the finished example but in that example as a moment in a process, a transition to what is not yet.

Teaching, for such thinkers, can never be a mere matter of conveying propositions. Nor can it be only a process of involving students in critical dialogue governed by rational norms. All norms would be held to be in some measure problematic; all "forms of life" would be treated as provisional. Nonetheless, the teacher would provoke and admonish students consciously to order and interpret their experience by means of available languages or schemata, to do so from their own standpoints and in a disciplined fashion. When we consider this approach in relation to that of the so-called "cognitivists" (like Paul Hirst, say, or Richard Peters), it begins to appear that the searchlight of thought about teaching moves over similar landscapes and simply pauses in different places. The existential thinker is always more likely to make persons visible (and often audible) in their existentiality, anxious in what to them is a paradoxical freedom, always aware of their "starting point" (Cumming, 1979). The conceptual thinker is more likely to direct attention to the "forms of life" in their public expression, to the "conversation" into which students are to be initiated as, perhaps, "centers of consciousness" (Peters, 1978, p. 211), meaning consciousness of themselves as persons, centers of valuation and choice. For such thinkers, individuals develop such a consciousness when they can apply to themselves the concept of a person or what it means to *think* of themselves *as* persons. And this, in turn, depends upon the surrounding society and the importance it attaches to "individual points of view." For John Dewey, as we have seen, the existing society or the "social medium" was of even more significance as the very crucible of selfhood; but, for him, the self "is in continuous formation through choice of action." Despite all these differences (and they are considerable), the "triadic" process that is teaching involves the same terms and much of the same dynamic for all.

Martin Buber, working in the existential tradition, put special emphasis upon the paradoxes that arise when the teacher, living in a time of uncertainty, is no longer able to convey agreed-upon values and reliable truths to the young. "Aliveness" on the part of the teacher seemed to him of particular importance, along with a desire to participate in the lives of his pupils, if only through the exercise of imagination and faith. Never willing to impose even "oughts" upon his students, he continually acknowledged the significance of "norms" and said that no responsible person could be a stranger to them. "But the command inherent in a genuine norm never becomes a maxim and the fulfilment of it never a habit" (Buber, 1957, p. 115). Norms or commands, he said, remain latent in consciousness until particular situations arise that demand solutions of which the individual may have had, until that moment, no idea. A maxim, he believed, speaks in the third person, more or less abstractly; a command addresses people in the second person—speaks to, as it were, the "thou." The teacher must institute the kind of dialogue that enables students to break with the "collective" (or the peer group, we might say, or the mass audience) and establish some relation to their own selves. Only then are they likely to take their own initiatives and assume responsibility for their own learning and their own growth. For Buber (1957), the devotion to a collective or a "party" derives from a fear of being left to rely on oneself at a time when there is no more

> direction from eternal values; people want to have responsibility removed from them by an authority in which they can believe. They do not yet realize that this devotion was an escape.... But they are beginning to notice that he who no longer, with his whole being, decides what he does or does not, and assumes responsibility for it, becomes sterile in soul. And a sterile soul soon ceases to be a soul. This is where the educator can begin and should begin. (p. 115)

The language is poetic, but the relevance for a philosophy of teaching seems eminently clear. Teachers must have in their own minds and imaginations a view of what is desirable when it comes to human learning and human life. If they do, such teachers can present an image of responsibility in such a way that students will "recognize that discipline and order too are starting-points on the way towards self-responsibility." Moreover, recognizing that each individual somewhere nourishes a desire for personal wholeness or unity, and that out of an achievement of such unity may come a greater capacity to relate to others (in a manner neither totalitarianism nor bureaucracy allows), Buber chose finally to affirm that the kind of education he was describing might become "genuine education for community." In some sense, this brings him near to Dewey and those others who saw the teacher's end in view as participation in community.

There were resemblances between certain of Martin Heidegger's concerns and Dewey's as well, even as Heidegger elaborated on the ideas of project and choice. Calculative thinking, he knew, would become increasingly dominant; "computing" was likely to become the dominant mode of cognition. Acknowledging all this, he called for "meditative thinking," not as a substitute for the calculative, but as a way of regaining a sense of rootedness in nature and a more reflective awareness of cognitive agency. This kind of thinking, coupled with a renewed consciousness of what it meant to be alive and in the world, might prevent technology from dominating cognition. It might enable people to live freely with the new devices, properly used as tools to support their purposes. The point was to demystify, to "think what we are doing" (as Hannah Arendt was to say), to resist incipient "thoughtlessness." Later, Heidegger (1971) placed a particular emphasis on art and poetry to bring about the "disclosures" with which he was so concerned. In this aspect of his philosophy, he was stressing what would become of growing significance for educational thought: a hermeneutic, an interpretive approach to sense making. At once, he was calling attention to the *ground* of all human thinking, to the insistent actuality of the world.

Before proceeding to further connections between existential inquiry and philosophies of teaching and to the signal developments in existential phenomenology that have their own kind of meaning for education, we shall recall a few other contributors to what might be called the "process" tradition or the tradition

opened to contemporaneity and change. Many of the themes already opened can be found in the work of William James, particularly when he wrote of the "stream of consciousness" and objected to what he called the "constancy" of ideas (1906, pp. 15ff.). Because consciousness is selective and purposeful, because the fields of consciousness keep dissolving into one another, a teacher cannot justifiably put things before learners to learn. He or she has to try to offer ideas and objects attached to people's interests, with the expectation that interest or a sense of connection will arouse learners to the exertion of effort, the effort required if they are to learn. James (1906) called it "earthly action" and said, in connection with it: "I mean speech, I mean writing, I mean yeses and nows, and tendencies 'from' things and tendencies 'toward' things, and emotional determinations; and I mean them in the future as well as in the immediate present" (p. 27). Paying great heed to "voluntary attention," he acknowledged the focal role played by will or volition and, by extension, human choice.

Teachers, according to James, should make sure their students did not suffer from paralysis of will and retained their powers of vigorous action. He thought that education of the will would build character; and, for him, character consisted of "an organized set of habits of reaction" (p. 184). These habits depended in large measure on the stock of ideas possessed by the learner and on the habitual association of those ideas with modes of action. Like Nietzsche, he believed in looking through many windows in seach of any particular or "reasonable" idea that might feed into or become a forerunner to action. The moments of voluntary action, brief though they might be, were the critical ones; and he challenged teachers to work for these, in the full awareness that they could never be guaranteed. For all his radical empiricism and what he himself described as a materialistic view of mind, his "talks to teachers" culminated in a demand the teachers attend to the freedom of the will and students' capacity to choose. For James, too, the test of ideas and meanings and even forms of knowledge was to be found in freely initiated action, in lived life in the world.

As important as the links that tied him to existential ways of thinking were those that connected his work to that of thinkers such as Charles Sanders Peirce, George Herbert Mead, and John Dewey, especially where education was concerned. The orientation to what James called "pragmatism" suggests that all of them, despite the very real differences among them, would think of teaching in the light of its consequences for experience, for conduct, for actual practice in the world. Peirce (1955), resisting fixity or "tenacity" of belief (pp. 5–22) or the desire to avoid any change of belief, developed a theory of inquiry emphasizing "living doubt." The point of inquiry, for him, was to overcome doubt and settle opinion. He laid great stress on the uses of scientific method, which seemed to him to require a rational capacity to grasp external realities. Because it was a self-correcting capacity and involved the existence of a community of scientists, it was the most reliable method for achieving true beliefs. Where intellectual learning was concerned, logic was central, although not necessarily in nonintellectual pursuits. Late in his life, Peirce seemed to be saying that the most significant educational aim was the development of those rational ideas he associated with scientific investigation; but, at the same time, he called for the kind of education that moved people to reach beyond themselves and their own advantage, to seek out lives that would have significant consequences.

Dewey, while certainly influenced by Peirce's view of scientific method, was able to develop a notion of critical intelligence far less univocal than Peirce's concept of rationality. As we have seen, Dewey extended the concepts of "living doubt," empirical thinking, and operational tests to all the domains of human experience. He tended to view the scientific method as an instance of intelligence working at its most efficient level rather than an instance of intrinsic rationality. Peirce, however, in developing a theory of signs and insisting on the symbolic or linguistic nature of cognitive thinking (Peirce, 1955, 98–119), enriched the study of logic and language in ways that are becoming evident only today. Not only did he tie belief to action and create bridges between logic and common sense, but he shed new light on the communicative contexts in which teaching takes place, and on the connection between communication and participation in social reality.

From a different discipline and vantage point, George Herbert Mead also was investigating the relationships between communication and the development of the self. If it were not, Mead said, for the organism growing up in a social order and becoming able to internalize the attitude of the surrounding social group (or the "generalized other"), there would be no possibility of that organism's learning to be human; nor would there exist what is thought of as a self (Mead, 1934, pp. 154–156). For the self to come into being, in fact, the individual must experience himself or herself from the standpoints of other individuals in the group. It is communication that allows this to happen, "communication in the sense of significant symbols, communication which is directed not only to others but also the individual himself" (p. 139). Where teaching was concerned, Mead saw education as "conversation," belonging to a universe of discourse. He believed that subject matter should be made the "material of personal intercourse between pupils and instructors, and between the children themselves" (Petras, 1968, p. 38). Unlike Martin Buber and similar thinkers, Mead recommended that the personality of the teacher should disappear "behind the process of learning." But the teacher, as interpreter of the child's experience, should always be able to state the subject matter of instruction "in terms of the experience of the children."

Even as this social-psychological and social-philosophical view worked its way into much 20th-century thought about the connections between the teaching act and children's experience and consciousness, Peirce's more distinctively philosophic views on reason and symbolization fed into contemporary linguistic approaches. We have already seen how many philosophers now emphasize the symbol systems or the conceptual frameworks that bring intelligibility to human experience. Paul Hirst is representative when he writes that ostensibly private experiences, like emotional experiences and mental attitudes, can be made explicable only by means of conceptual frameworks that are publicly shared. Such frameworks, Hirst (1965) wrote, "can be understood only by means of the objective features with which they are associated, round which they come to be organized and built. The forms of knowledge are thus the basic articulations whereby the whole of experience has become intelligible. . . . They are the fundamental achievement of mind"

(p. 11). The fundamental achievement, then, might be said to be semiotic: the capacity to symbolize, to transmute what would otherwise be inchoate and silent into one of the many languages now available to human beings. According to this view, teaching initiates the young into what Mead called universes of discourse. It empowers them to achieve meanings by entering into conceptual frameworks that find expression through symbolic notations, each one of which is governed, as we have seen, by "accepted criteria."

We are back, it would appear, to a neo-Kantian world; but language is now thought of as a mode of cognitive action, even by those who, like R. M. Hare, concentrate on the logical or the formal properties of words. Hare (1964), discussing moral education, said that it was, at least in part, "education in the use of a language." And then:

> Thinking morally — which is one of the things that a morally educated man has to do — is only the mental correlate of speaking morally. Indeed, for obvious reasons, the speaking has to come first. We are taught to speak morally by hearing other people do it. . . . When we have learnt to use the moral words out loud, we must have learnt also to use these concepts in our thought. If we had not, we should not be using the words in our speech to others with an understanding of their meaning. (p. 173)

He was suggesting, of course, that learning to use a word in spoken communication is integrally related to using the concept in thinking.

As with Hirst, Peters, and others in the analytic school, the clarification and the understanding of meaning are of the first importance; and, if there are practical implications, they are to be found in critical, clarifying activity. Jane Roland Martin (1981), in a challenge to Hirst's views on liberal education, introduces a Deweyan reminder of the dangers of separating "reason from emotion, thought from action, education from life" (p.51). She calls for a view of liberal education that focuses on the development of a person, not simply of a mind; and she argues that "the acquisition of conceptual schemes" must play an important, but not an all-important part in planning for authentic "social and natural education." Her challenge dramatizes a growing tension in approaches to education and to teaching in contemporary philosophical thought. In one sense, it might be viewed as a tension between the pure cognitivists or the analysts and those with a more experiential or action-oriented view. It might be regarded as a resurgent struggle between those oriented to rules and norms in the Kantian tradition and those concerned with history, consciousness, and change. The tension is exacerbated by the belief on the part of some that no philosophy of teaching can be developed that does not take institutional and social contexts into account. Not only is there the problematic situation of schools existing in a nation still ridden by inequities and deprivation; there are the problems resulting from the erosion of the public, the growth of privatism, the felt lack of community. For those who take this position, it is simply not sufficient to concentrate on formal considerations, on the linguistic, on a version of what Roland Barthes (1970) called (in another connection) an "Empire of Signs." On the other hand, there is the view that the primary function of philosophy is to clarify concepts and language. Linked with this, as we have seen, is a concern for what R. S.

Peters (1975) calls "human excellences" and the unquestionable need to develop the "rational capacities to the full" (p. 125). For philosophers of this sort, the only way in which philosophy can shed light on the practice of teaching is by the elucidation of concepts and terminology.

Much elucidation of this sort originated in the work of Ludwig Wittgenstein, particularly in the later work where he concerned himself with the multiple uses of "ordinary language" and with the significance of "language games" (Wittgenstein, 1968, p. 5). It is true that he made central the elucidation of the logical syntax of language and placed great emphasis on the dangers of misusing language. Nothing, he believed, accounted for the "bewitchment of intelligence" so much as the confusion of words with things or abstract entities or forces in the universe. Once having given up the quest for a pure language that pictured atomic facts, he devoted himself to the social functions of language in the multiple situations of human life. The "forms of words," as he saw them, did not reflect the structures of an objectively existing world; they reflected, rather, certain "forms of life" which they guided and controlled. Nor, as he came to realize, did words report only on matters of fact. There were many forms of words tied to activities like morals or art, for all the dimensions of the inexpressible associated with both. He knew that feelings, too, find expression in speech and conduct. Like John Dewey, he became interested in the ways in which language served the range of human purposes in a public domain.

There are examples in his *Philosophical Investigations* that have specific reference to teaching, especially in the areas of mathematics and reading. At one point, he described the kind of "game" that required someone to write down a series of signs (natural numbers, say, in decimal notation) according to a specific rule. The teacher might originally ask a student to copy a series of numbers; but the teacher would have to realize that that student could only come to understand by going on to write the series independently. Then Wittgenstein asked his reader to imagine the student writing the numbers on his or her own initiative but randomly, or not in the right order. Or the student might make systematic mistakes. Wittgenstein then presented alternative possibilities: The teacher might try to wean the student from that systematic mistake or accept the student's way of copying and try to teach the correct method as a variant of the student's. But this, he said, would result in "our pupil's capacity to learn" coming to an end (Wittgenstein, 1968, p. 57). The reason, he wrote, that he described the phenomenon in such a fashion was that he wanted his reader to realize the possibility of imagining such a thing. "I wanted to put that picture before him, and his acceptance of the picture consists in his now being inclined to regard a given case differently; that is, to compare it with *this* rather than *that* set of pictures. I have changed his *way of looking at things.*" The point, in any case, was that the student's response, verbal or otherwise, would not provide clear evidence of understanding. Did understanding mean grasping of the system? Applying a rule? Wittgenstein warned against positing some private mental process going on in the student. And then:

What I wanted to say was: when he suddenly knew how to go on, when he understood the principle, then possibly he had a special experience—and if he is asked, "What is it? What took place when you suddenly grasped the principle?" perhaps he will describe it much as we described it above—but for us it is the circumstances under which he had such an experience that justify him in saying in such a case that he understands, that he knows how to go on. (p. 61)

Talking about reading, too, Wittgenstein stressed the experience and, at once, continually referred to his own experience, his own self-knowledge, his own awareness of the endlessly alternative possibilities. Stanley Cavell has compared Wittgenstein with Sigmund Freud and said that, like Freud's therapy, Wittgenstein's writing "wishes to prevent understanding which is unaccompanied by inner change. Both of them are intent upon unmasking the defeat of our real need in the face of self-impositions which we have not assessed or fantasies ('pictures') which we cannot escape" (Cavell, 1976, p. 72.) Perhaps more than some of his followers, Wittgenstein was concerned with discrepancies between what is said and what is actually meant; and this held signal relevance for the teacher as well. To conceive individuals as speaking subjects in this fashion, to understand the importance of engaging them in the "conversation" or the dialogue of the culture in the light of their special experiences: All this requires far more than an elucidation of syntax or meanings. Wittgenstein may not have gone on to explore what was entailed; but, throughout his later work, there is the recognition that language is the leading part of forms of activity that go beyond the linguistic. For all his rejection of private languages and hidden mental processes, his work became a kind of bridge between analysis and contemporary phenomenology.

Edmund Husserl, objecting also to psychologism (or the old tendency to reduce philosophical questions to psychological ones) and equally concerned about the unassessed and the taken for granted, began his phenomenological career with an interest in the foundations of mathematics, logic, and theory of knowledge. The initial question he confronted had to do with the ways in which persons can experience or become conscious of actual objects as opposed to the contents of their own consciousness (Husserl, 1965). As time went on, this and related issues were linked to explorations of such concepts as intentionality and the nature of consciousness itself. The idea of intentionality (Farber, 1966) has to do with the claim that consciousness is always *of* something, is always directed *to* something. "Conscious processes are also called intentional," Husserl (1960) said, "to be conscious of something; as a *cogito* to bear within itself its *cogitatum*" (p. 33). The objects of which we are conscious may be imaginary; they may be beliefs or assertions. In effect, the matter of the independent existence of objects became unimportant; what came to be of the first importance for the phenomenologist was consciousness itself. Consciousness was not, however, considered to be an inner space or pure subjectivity. Since it was viewed in terms of what Husserl called "potentialities" and "anticipations" (Husserl, 1960, section 19), meaning that what was actualized and what was perceived depended upon the standpoint of the individual perceiver, it could only be regarded as a turning *towards* phenomena or the appearances of things. Consciousness was thought to grasp what lay around through such acts as perceiving, judging, reasoning, believing, calculating. The object of each of these acts (each of these distinctive "intentions") was considered to be the meaning of that act; and the object could be an idea as well as a concrete thing (a tree, a face, a table). Associated with all this was the notion of reduction, which had to do with the presumed need to "bracket out" or put into parentheses all conventional presuppositions and ordinary ways of sense making, to "return to things themselves" (Husserl, 1962, pp. 258–260).

For our purposes, what is most relevant here is the emphasis on the need to break with what Husserl called the "natural attitude" (1965, p. 72) or the attitude that takes the outside world to be nothing more than a mass of sense data or a phenomenon conclusively defined by natural science in its most unreflective mode. He did not deny the existence of the spatiotemporal world; what he was concerned with was an understanding of the ways in which human beings related to that world, with the ways in which the faces of the world presented themselves to consciousness. In the tradition of William James and John Dewey, Husserl was rejecting dualisms, rejecting the assumption of the "givenness" of the world, existing meaningfully without reference to perspective and interpretation. The significance for the teacher lies in the stress on standpoint and interpretation, on the importance of refusing the taken-for-granted, on the recognition that reality is constituted rather than simply given. It lies as well in the recognition of the importance of the "life world" or concretely lived experience and what that signifies for the young, or *how* the world presents itself to them. Martinus Langeveld (1983) has written:

> From a phenomenological point of view, we seek the essential meanings in the human encounter, rather than in pure reflection or in speculative theories, which only pretend to have a practical import.... The realization that we will never be able to construct a form of knowledge which could tell definitively what we are to do in every conceivable circumstance has emerged only as late as the defeat of an epistemological illusion in Western consciousness. (p. 6)

The illusion he talks of has to do with the subject–object separation, or the separation between mind and the world. It is the illusion that made it impossible to conceive of the world as a lived world, a life world; and Langeveld is saying that in that life world teachers must discover and give form to their task.

Many of the Husserlian (and Langeveldian) themes are present in the work of Jean-Paul Sartre and Maurice Merleau-Ponty, who are often thought of as existential phenomenologists, and of Alfred Schutz, best identified as a social phenomenologist. Husserl, however, showed little interest in the problem of freedom or other questions raised by existentialists. Still, these concerns merged with some of his in the work of Sartre and Merleau-Ponty (and to an extent in the writings of Heidegger). Different though these thinkers were, they shared an impassioned interest in individual existence, in human freedom, and in intersubjectivity. To a greater or lesser degree as well, they were preoccupied with the problem of being (or what it actually signifies for anyone to exist). Also, in their distinctive ways, they were all committed to a view of consciousness in its intentionality and to the multiple ways in which consciousness takes hold of things. It is here and in their investigations of being-in-the-world that they have something to contribute to a philosophy of teaching, if only to pose new questions with regard to what teaching is.

Somewhat in the manner of Heidegger, Sartre turned his attention to the world and rejected the idea of dividing appearances from things or presuming that there was some reality lurking behind phenomena or, in some mysterious fashion, within the mind. Consciousness, for him too, thrusts intentionally into the world. What he called "reflective consciousness" presupposed a prereflective consciousness, an awareness of being-in-the-world that underlies the various modes of knowing (Sartre, 1956, pp. 74–79). And, indeed, his focus was on action within lived situations, the kind of action that creates projects, the kind of reflective action that creates indentity or a self by means of choice in the actual conditions of life, as those conditions are seen or undergone or interpreted by the person in the world.

A Sartrean teacher might connect the notion of "being-for-itself" or the being of possibilities (Sartre, 1956, pp. 84–89) with the challenge to learn to learn. "Being-for-itself," or the human reality in all its dynamic incompleteness, takes on much of its meaning from the idea of "being-in-itself," or the object world as it is predefined, fixed, incapable of becoming. To act on one's freedom is, in many senses, to act in a resistant world, a world threatening to label or to fix or to transmute the existing being into a thing. Sartre introduced the concept of nothingness, a concept produced by consciousness and having to do with gaps, lacks, or absences. To expect, to hope, to desire, to want to know presumes what is not yet, a deficiency to be "surpassed." Sartre (1963) wrote of human beings as going beyond situations, of a "project" (pp. 91–92) as that which is still to become, something one tries to bring into being. The "praxis" required involves "a flight and a leap ahead, at once a refusal and a realization.... Thus knowing is a moment of *praxis*, even its most fundamental one; but this knowing does not partake of an absolute Knowledge" (p. 92).

Freedom itself involves a vision of one's possibilities — or of one's "possibles" (those realizations that are reasonably attainable). More accurately, it involves a taking responsibility for and a choosing to act on what might be considered possible. (A tone-deaf child, fascinated with rock music, can hardly be encouraged to become a performer. A young person who has never seriously studied mathematics cannot be encouraged, in the senior year of high school, to become a theoretical physicist.) There is always what Sartre called "facticity": limiting conditions in one's situation or in one's capacities. One's "facticity," however, or those factors that are given, ought not to be considered as totally determinate. Nor should facticity define the emerging self. The effort ought to be to goad persons somehow to transcend, to take initiatives, to become (through learning and other modes of action) what they are not yet and might reasonably be.

Among the ways of rousing the self to wrench free of determinates is to maintain a posture of interrogation, to continue posing questions with respect to being and its limitations, since "the questioner, by the very fact that he is questioning, posits himself as in a state of indetermination; he does not know whether the reply will be affirmative or negative" (Sartre 1956, p. 6). Another way is to try to move persons to imagine a better state of things. Sartre thought freedom to be an "open project," anticipating a degree of unpredictability; but it is always possible, he said, to imagine situations being otherwise. It takes "education and reflection" (p. 435) to conceive a more satisfying, life-sustaining condition. But it is only when one can think in that way and form a project of changing the situation that one recognizes the insufficiencies in what exists and tries to repair them. If, say, a teacher can release students to imagine what might be in their lives (satisfying work; more stimulating leisure time; diverse relationships, for example), they may be enabled to see, not only what is intolerable in their present situations, but their own lack of preparation and discipline for achieving what they desire. To learn may come to mean undertaking a project of changing things or creating values by repairing such lacks. Clearly, there is another argument here for making experiences in the arts central in education; since encounters with art forms often do release imaginative powers and allow learners to envisage alternative realities. Whether it is a matter of gaining an additional perspective through looking through the lens of *Moby Dick* or Rembrandt's self-portraits, or a matter of learning another language (painting, music, dance) by means of which the learner might structure and articulate experience more variously, the realm of potential meanings cannot but expand. It is, Sartre might say, through leaning towards what is not yet, through struggling to attain new possibles, that persons discover what is lacking in their lives.

Maurice Merleau-Ponty added another dimension with his emphasis on embeddedness in the world. Unlike his contemporaries, he drew attention to the body and described consciousness as "embodied consciousness" (Merleau-Ponty, 1962, pp. 130 147). He wrote (Merleau-Ponty, 1964):

The world is not what I think but what I live through.... Unlike what classical thought told us, the relationship of subject and object is no longer that cognitive relationship in which the object always appears as constructed by the subject, but is a relationship of being, through which, to use a paradox, the subject is his body, his situation, and, in a certain sense, enters into interaction with it. (p. 52)

The ground (or what Merleau-Ponty called the primordial landscape) of all experiencing is the world as structured by perception. Rationality, as he saw it, develops on the foundation of a perceptually configured environment, whose aspects are always viewed from a particular location or perspective and are, therefore, always provisional, to some degree incomplete. It is the realization that there is something always hidden or "in reserve" or not yet known that moves people to break through the horizons of what they can grasp — to thematize, to articulate, to learn in an intersubjective world. Obviously, it requires reflection to recover contact with one's own original landscape; but Merleau-Ponty believed that, even as abstract and scientific thinking ought to be done with a clear consciousness of the experience to which it refers, so it ought to be conducted on the ground of the lived world. "Scientific thinking," he wrote (Merleau-Ponty, 1964),

a thinking which looks on from above, and thinks of the object-in-general, must return to the "there is" which underlies it, to the site, the soil of the sensible and opened world such as it is in our life and for our body — not that possible body which we may legitimately think of as an information machine but that actual body which I call mine, this sentinel standing quietly at the command of my words and my acts. Further, *associated bodies* must be brought forward along with my body ... the others who haunt me and whom I haunt, a single, present, and actual Being as habitat. (p. 160)

That "sentinel," that embodied consciousness could only emerge from the dialectical tension between itself and the determining forces of the world which made possible the achievement of freedom. Unlike Sartre, Merleau-Ponty did not believe freedom arose along with consciousness; like Dewey, he believed it had to be achieved in the course of thought and action. Also, like Dewey, he thought that the field in which freedom might be achieved was always an intersubjective one; since, for him, consciousness, or even what might be termed "subjectivity," opened out to the common. This orientation to the concrete, intersubjective world, along with his preoccupation with perspectival knowing, brings Merleau-Ponty into relation with the social phenomenologist Alfred Schutz. Schutz's work provided a seedbed for the investigation into "social reality" initiated by Peter Berger and Thomas Luckmann (1966). Also, it is in large measure the source of what Jonas Soltis calls the "sociocentric perspective" on knowledge or the view that takes into account "the cultural nature of knowledge as a communal human construction that is both formed by and forms human beings" (Soltis, 1981, p. 97).

Drawing from the work of William James, Schutz wrote of the multiplicity of what he called "provinces of meaning" (Schutz, 1967, pp. 230ff.). These include the provinces of play and dreams as well as the natural and social sciences, the humanities, the arts. Schutz saw individuals, each with his or her own biography and location in the community, sharing a commonsense reality mediated by a common vernacular. This vernacular, along with shared conventions when it came to using devices and doing things (filling fuel pumps, waiting for red lights, listening to television, taking tests in school), allowed persons (in what Husserl had called the "natural attitude") to assume that the world they inhabited was the "real" world, the normal world for everyone. It took on a givenness for them, an objective existence confirmed by the very languages they shared. Teachers, concerned as they are to induct the young into existing practices and behaviors, are usually prone to allow just such givenness to be part of the taken-for-grantedness they convey. They are likely to do little to make it in any sense "thought provoking." Seldom do they communicate the idea that what is taken for granted as normal and unchangeable is a reality humanly constructed over time. That is why so little attention is paid to the interpretive mode of knowing. It is probably why there is so little questioning of the inequities in our society, the structures and organization of schools, testing practices, regulations, and controls.

Schutz would say, however, that everyday, commonsense reality, coupled with what he called "the world of work," is crucial in everyone's experience. By the "world of work" he meant the projects, the actual activities by which people gear into their realities. Like other phenomenologists, he oriented himself to action, to involvements, to the ways in which human beings relate to others ("make music with others") and to things. The alternative to such a concern, clearly, is an acceptance of passivity, irresponsibility, "drifting" without desire to move beyond where one is. From the perspective this creates, the teacher may be viewed as one with an obligation to provoke people to "wide-awakeness" (Schutz, 1967, p. 213) with respect to the situations in which they live their lives. On one level, the teacher can call attention to the jolts experienced when, for example, students move from the world of the playground to the organized world of schoolwork, when they move from the movie theatre to the commonsense world of the street, when they awaken from dreams to the light of day. Each of these realities entails a different mode of cognition, a distinctive way of directing attention to the world; and it is in the transition from one to the other that people may become aware that there are a number of finite provinces of meaning, that the one that seems so "natural" is not all there is.

Another way of disclosing this phenomenon of what Schutz called "multiple realities" is through reminding students of what it signifies to take the perspective of the "stranger" in comparison with the perspective of the "in-group," before that stranger becomes a member. The stranger has one unquestioned scheme of reference, the in-group quite another. Both take for granted what Schutz called their "thinking as usual." When the stranger begins to participate in the in-group's activity and to enter into dialogue with other participants, both original schemes of interpretation are opened for questioning—*if* both the stranger and the in-group understand the interpretive function of each cultural pattern or scheme of reference (Schutz, 1964, pp. 97–100).

Something similar may happen when a novel is read with a degree of informed awareness. The individual student may come to see that his or her ordinary scheme of reference or "thinking as usual" does not properly apply to the situation imaginatively created by the story and has (at least for the sake of "understanding" the story) to be revised. This is partially what is implied in Joseph Conrad's *Heart of Darkness* (Conrad, 1982) when Marlow, telling about his journey into the African wilderness to a "Lawyer, an Accountant, and a Director of Companies" comfortably moored on a yawl on the Thames, burst out: "This is the worst of trying to tell. . . . Here you all are, each moored with two good addresses, like a hulk with two anchors, a butcher round one corner, a policeman round another, excellent appetites and temperature normal—you hear—normal from year's end to year's end. And you say, Absurd! Absurd be—exploded!" (p. 68). The men he is addressing have every reason to refuse his scheme of interpretation because his emphasis on wilderness and mystery and exploitation threatens a taken-for-granted grounded in a conviction of entitlement. Teachers, confronting students they intend to move to cognitive action, ought to be able to make them question their own "thinking as usual," to extend it, to go beyond.

Alternatively, a recognition of the importance of interpretation and of the many ways there are of constituting reality may lead individuals to recognize that their ordinary, conventional ways of seeing their own lived worlds may exclude or obscure important dimensions of what is there to be known. This is what is suggested in Nathaniel Hawthorne's *The Scarlet Letter* (Hawthorne, 1969) when Hester Prynne, ostracized by the Puritan community and living at the edge of the wilderness, assumes a "freedom of speculation" forbidden in the theocratic state. "For years past she had looked from this estranged point of view at human institutions, and whatever priests and legislators had established; criticizing all with hardly more reverence

than the Indian would feel for the clerical band, the judicial robe, the pillory, the gallows, the fireside, or the church" (p. 217). This does not result in inaction on her part or a cynical refusal to play a role in the community's life. Indeed, more conscious than before, more thoughtful, more wide-awake to her lived situation, she becomes a kind of paradigm of the one struggling to come to know.

There is another dimension of *The Scarlet Letter* that opens up a problem (or a "lack") unacknowledged in most of the course we have traveled in this chapter. Hawthorne wrote that "a tendency to speculation" makes a woman sad. "She discerns, it may be, such a hopeless task before her. As a first step, the whole system of society is to be torn down, and then built up anew. Then, the very nature of the opposite sex, or its long hereditary habit, which has become like nature, is to be essentially modified before woman can be allowed to assume what seems a fair and suitable position" (p. 184). It must be acknowledged that all but a few of the philosophers referred to in these pages have been males who by "long hereditary habit" have not only taken on the full responsibility for "doing" philosophy, but have apparently done so with male persons primarily in mind. The reasons for the exclusion of women from the spheres in which philosophies found public expression and publication are by now fairly clear. We can never ascertain how a female contemporary of Aristotle, Locke, Kant, or Hegel might have dealt with epistemological and ethical issues if she had been granted self-determination and regard. We can, however, affirm that, given the confinement of most women to the "private sphere," given the channels through which their energies found expression, their outlooks on the processes of coming to know and of being in the world have differed in significant respects. Not only were they limited in expectations and options, they were members of particular epistemic communities. Their lived situations differed from those of most males; their typically inferior positions could not but affect the ways in which they constituted their social realities.

As women have begun to articulate their points of view, they have mustered a fresh critical challenge to "the solipsistic bias of traditional epistemology" (Code, 1983, p. 541). Whether the vantage point is that of the psychologist Carol Gilligan emphasizing the sense in which a "morality of rights" rather than a "morality of responsibility" strikes women as dissonant with their life experiences (Gilligan, 1982) or of the philosopher Nel Noddings making "caring" more significant than rational justifications (Noddings, 1984), the importance of human connectedness and cognitive interdependence has been highlighted. Not only has this drawn attention to the impacts of historical and cultural experience on the capacities and expectations of female persons. It suggests a need to expand perspectives on human reality itself, to define new alternatives where teaching and learning are concerned, and to reflect anew on the taken-for-granted even where philosophies of teaching are concerned.

Jane Roland Martin (1982), for instance, has drawn attention to the ignoring or distorting of the accounts of women's education that have appeared in the literature of educational thought (pp. 133–148). Plato's proposal that women be given the same education as men if they were qualified for rule in the just society suggests that women seemed to Plato as capable as men when it came to high position; yet this kind of insight has been suppressed. Moreover, writes Martin, such work as Pestalozzi's, showing forth women's educative role as mothers, has been ignored. Reproductive and rearing processes, generally, have been excluded from what has been treated as the educational realm; so has the obviously educative role of the family in the transmission of cultural values. The dominant preoccupation with rationality and abstract norms has made it almost impossible to pay heed to diversely lived situations.

As has been seen, the philosophical tradition that has dealt with process, life worlds, and the overcoming of subject–object separations has often opened critical perspectives continuous with those being developed by feminist scholars. Nevertheless, with few exceptions, the image of the educated person has remained a male image; the distortions inherent in most Western languages have been ignored, as has the need to overcome the separation between private and public. More will have to be done to clarify the importance of everyday realities where persons actually live and have their being, where they act and work and struggle to understand. If it is indeed the case that, as Merleau-Ponty (1967) has said, all human beings are "condemned to meaning" (p. xix), it follows that educators must concern themselves with empowering students to made sense of, to conceptualize, to develop perspectives upon, and perhaps to transform their actually lived worlds.

In most philosophies as they bear on teaching, the empowering of persons for sense making has involved initiating them into a common vernacular or a shared universe of discourse. It is presumed that what Arendt (1958) called the "common world" (p. 57) will be sustained and enriched to the degree individuals learn to engage with one another in norm-regarding ways or by means of a reflected-upon "geography" (or the conceptual networks, the organized knowledge made accessible in schools) referring to their original "landscapes" (Vandenberg, 1971, pp. 104–107). No teacher can be oblivious to the importance of symbol systems, languages, "realms of meaning" (Phenix, 1964) or "provinces of meaning" (Schutz, 1967) when it comes to initiating the young into shared cultural life. Without some acquaintance with the schemata that have allowed members of the culture to interpret their existence and infuse their experience with meanings, individuals remain outsiders to the cultural conversation. It becomes extremely difficult even to posit a domain of intersubjectivity in which something common can be constituted. At once, if teachers are unable to communicate the notion that what is being presented as reality is to be understood as interpreted experience, if they are unable to suggest the provisional and perspectival nature of available interpretations, they are likely to become mere spokespersons for and defenders of an official view of the "way the world is." How then stimulate critical judgment or conduct critical dialogue?

Peters (1967), when he writes about the development of the educated person, reminds his readers that that person cannot be one whose "knowledge and understanding is confined to one form of thought or awareness" (p. 21). The individual with an integrated outlook is someone who has gained enough knowledge, understanding, objectivity, and sensitivity to others to participate in conversation, really to "listen to what people say

irrespective of the use he can make of it or them." Again, there is the presumption of a civilized and rational community composed of those whose experience exemplifies the processes by means of which a requisite "mastery, knowledge, and understanding has been acquired." The worthwhile things that must be taught, according to Peters, are best acquired by contact with people who have already acquired them and are patient and competent enough to initiate others into them. He makes a distinction between the formal or institutionalized authority of teachers, say, and the authority they earn by being trained in the procedures of a particular discipline necessary for its appreciation and exploration (Peters, 1978, pp. 194–198). Like Paul Hirst, he presumes the logical structure of each form of knowledge to be what defines it; and the teaching of such structures, like the emphasis on rationality, is self-justifying. The idea is that, after an individual masters the rules that govern any particular field of subject matter, then he or she may move on to "utilize" knowledge in Alfred North Whitehead's sense and to go on to relate it to life. For Whitehead (1949),

> Wisdom is the way in which knowledge is held. It concerns the handling of knowledge, its selection for the determination of relevant issues, its employment to add value to our immediate experience.... The only avenue towards wisdom is by freedom in the presence of knowledge. But the only avenue towards knowledge is by discipline in the acquirement of ordered fact. Freedom and discipline are the two essentials of education. (p. 41)

But the questions remain and will remain. Some have to do with the relation between the so-called "forms of knowledge" (or the modes of discourse through which they are conveyed) and commonsense knowledge, or what is ordinarily taken for granted by both teachers and students with respect to everyday life. It is not unusual for both teachers and students to master the terminology in a given field, while retaining a "naive" view of the experience or phenomena to which knowledge in that field refers. It is not unusual for teachers to proceed on the basis of a different set of taken-for-granted assumptions—about learning, schools, the future, the likelihood of war—than those held by their students; and dissonances in understanding (often unnoticed) are bound to occur. Just as seriously, there is likely to be an inattentiveness to the culturally different, to members of unfamiliar epistemic communities, to young persons with lived lives at variance with any their teachers know. Their perspectives and interpretations of things may be ascribed no validity; and this may be experienced as an assault on dignity or a denial of worth. All this may argue for enhanced attention to the ways in which young persons tell their own stories or articulate their own lived worlds. It may argue for a taking into account of the standpoints from which the young pose their questions, explain their expectations, identify their hopes. It may argue for more deliberate efforts to release individuals to speak in their own voices about how they actually view their own worlds.

Dewey (1916) wrote that social life is identical with communication and that to receive communication is always "to have an enlarged and changed experience" (p. 7). Moreover, if it is to be communicated, an experience has to be formulated; the speaker must move outside it, see it from others' points of view, find out the points of contact it may have with others' experiences. Experiences become meaningful to the degree they hold implications that go beyond what is consciously recognized; and communication with others, by linking the experiences of the individual with the group and allowing them to be grasped from a number of perspectives, cannot but make them more significant.

Merleau-Ponty also recognized the significance of what happens when experiences blend in this manner. Speech, he believed, is what realizes the intersubjectivity inherent in such experiences; and he spoke of the creation of speech situations in which persons could not only find out what they thought by speaking to one another, but achieve a reciprocity attainable in no other way. There is relevance in the distinction he made between linguistic meanings and those arising through speech. Speech originates in sedimented (or what Dewey called funded) meanings; it involves making explicit what is implicit in perceived reality; and it can always go beyond what might be predicted, since many people do not know what they think until they can express it in spoken words (Merleau-Ponty, 1962. pp. 174 ff.). Rules govern linguistic meanings; language "represents," it is said. The teacher may find important, not only the continuing study of language and a broadening acquaintance with the "language games" at hand, but the role of the spoken word in making visible and understandable everyday reality.

In a time of increasingly technical language, bureaucratic formulations, simulation games, and a lingua franca deriving from the media, it may become more and more necessary for teachers to create the kinds of speech situations in which and through which learners can open themselves to their lived worlds, to one another, and to themselves. Jurgen Habermas has written often about "distorted communication" and the need for "communicative competence," the kind of contextual communicative action that is based in mutual understanding and may establish a relationship of at least approximate reciprocity (Habermas, 1979, pp. 50–58, 88–90). Reciprocity, he says, "is fixed in the general structures of possible interaction. Thus the point of view of reciprocity belongs *eo ipso* to the interactive knowledge of speaking and acting subjects (p. 90). He has compared this with the rule-governed, context-free language of a rationalized social world committed to "purposive-rational action" rather than to interaction (Habermas, 1970, pp. 91–92). Even assuming that learners are to be inducted into such a world, the teacher can still encourage interactions and the reflective striving for agreements among those who can be made aware that the so-called "technicized" reality is itself a constructed one.

The problem is not to let things officially defined as objectively real overwhelm or hide the lived reality of those learning to learn. The teacher, confronting this, has also to recognize the importance of criticism and a certain degree of conflict as discussions take place in the classroom. Passmore's notion of "critico-creative thinking" entails the capacity to criticize not only cherished social values but governing rules and principles themselves. The teacher, for him, cannot suggest that rules are inherent in the nature of things without becoming an indoctrinator; nothing ought to be beyond the reach of rational criticism. This, in itself, suggests the likelihood of conflict; and Passmore realizes how unsettling this can be for a teacher "who may himself

not be convinced that a rule is a reasonable one or who may never have asked himself how it can be justified." And then he writes (Passmore, 1975):

> Anybody who sets out to teach his pupils to be critical must expect constantly to be embarrassed. He can also expect to be harrassed by his class, by his headmaster, by parents. If he gives up the idea of teaching his pupils to be critical and salves his conscience by training them in skills, this is not at all surprising. But he should at least be clear about what he is doing. (pp. 40–41)

This not only evokes Sartre's notion of interrogation; it recalls the many reminders of the importance of breaking with the natural attitude and penetrating the artificial pictures that cover over what is experienced, what is lived. For all the embarrassment of the teachers, for all the fear of failure, they cannot call themselves teachers if they are not willing to risk having students embark on new beginnings and start teaching themselves.

But the questions keep multiplying. Harry Broudy speaks of the "obstacles to rational action" in the limitations of human beings. "To serve action," he writes, "knowledge has to be organized differently than for inquiry. It has to become part of the texture of practical reasoning with its chain of purposes and consequences. It has to meet the test of credibility as well as truth" (Broudy, 1981, p. 43). The credibility of teaching, he maintains, may be regained if stress is laid, not only on the layering of meanings, but on the enabling of persons to develop interpretive perspectives by means of encounters with the disciplines. Broudy also believes that the point of developing such perspectives is to make increasing sense of lived, existential life. There remains, however, the matter of "citizenship education," what we would prefer to call the bringing into being of an "articulate public" (Dewey, 1954, p. 184).

This depends, to a large degree, on what Hirst (1965) calls a "public sharing in the symbolic systems that have been evolved" (p. 137); but it requires, at the same time, that the interpretive lenses provided by such systems be reflected upon in the light of their origin and geneses, and in terms of their relation to existing "cognitive interests" (Habermas, 1971, pp. 301–317). Moreover, they ought to be used, not merely for describing and explaining, but in the identification of insufficiencies and the development of insight into how to remedy them, to repair. The lenses, in other words, should be turned to the concrete world of actual undergoings and undertakings, where speech situations enable persons to reach out for reciprocity and the extension of such reciprocity to what James McClellan calls "a rational and loving world community."

For all their diverse stresses and preoccupations, philosophers today might achieve agreement in challenging teachers to empower young people to "come together in speech and action," as Arendt (1958, p. 25) put it and, through coming together in their plurality, create a space where freedom could be achieved and something in common brought into being. This public realm or this "common world" (p. 52) could only be constituted by people with distinctive perspectives, each granted equal regard. There is no question but that there are rules that must govern such a coming together; there are norms that must be satisfied. They have to do with fairness, mutual respect, concern, consideration for others' freedom, forgiveness, friendship, authentic expression, even love. And, yes, they have to do with clarity of language; since, without all these, there would be no space, no possibility of articulation, no possibility of a common world.

We think of Albert Camus's *The Plague* in saying that and about the evening when Tarrou and Dr. Rieux take an hour off "for friendship" from their labors in fighting the plague. Tarrou has explained to the doctor that each person on earth has the plague within him—meaning indifference, calculative attitudes, lack of care. And he tells him that it takes vigilance to maintain any sort of decency. Then he says he has concluded that "on this earth there are pestilences and there are victims, and it's up to us, as far as possible, not to join forces with the pestilences." Finally, he tells Dr. Rieux that he realizes that "all our troubles spring from our failure to use plain, clear-cut language. So I resolved to speak—and to act—quite clearly, as this was the only way of setting myself on the right track" (Camus, 1948, p. 230).

The association of friendship, sympathy, commitment, and clarity suggests what may happen when teaching is carried on for the sake of empowering persons (each a beginner, each acting on his or her own initiative) to make sense of the lived world. Questions as to what this might mean for research into the quality of teaching and the contexts of teaching, the nature of subject matter, the matter of human reality—all remain open. So do the multiple questions having to do with values and the possibility of transforming what exists. They have, clearly, to be reformulated by the empirical researcher who cares to attend to them; they have even to be recontextualized.

Meanwhile, with the unexplored confronting us, we can only continue to try to constitute something worthy of our regard in classrooms, worthy of defending in a threatening world. There are always newcomers; and that is the significant thing, whether or not the research and development are complete. There are always persons coming into the world who have to be initiated and freed to learn. Arendt (1961) wrote:

> Education is the point at which we decide whether we love the world enough to assume responsibility for it and by the same token to save it from that ruin which, except for renewal, except for the coming of the new and young, would be inevitable. And education, too, is where we decide whether we love our children enough not to expel them from our world and leave them to their own devices, nor to strike from their hands their choice of undertaking something new, something unforeseen by us, but to prepare them in advance for the task of renewing a common world. (p. 196)

Logical inferences cannot be drawn from such a statement; nor can specific implications for research plans or methodologies. The philosophic perspectives examined here do not provide guidelines for what happens in laboratories or in the situation-specific practice of teaching in the schools. They ought, however, to provoke more and more far-reaching questions, more and more examination of preconceptions and assumptions. They ought to open possibilities for further inquiry, further clarification of concepts and terms. If the "doing" of philosophy moves researchers and teachers to do more thinking about their own thinking, it is justified. If it intensifies the wonder with regard to teaching, enhances awareness of what remains unsolved, philosophers may have accomplished what they have set out to do.

REFERENCES

Adler, M. (1982). *The Paideia proposal*. New York: Macmillan.
Arendt, H. (1958). *The human condition*. Chicago: University of Chicago Press.
Arendt, H. (1961). *Between past and future*. New York: Viking Press.
Arendt, H. (1978). *Thinking*: Vol. 1. *The life of the mind*. New York: Harcourt Brace.
Aristotle. (1920). *The Nichomachean ethics* (D. P. Chase, Trans.). New York: E. P. Dutton.
Aristotle. (1957). *Aristotle's politics and poetics* (B. Jowett & T. Twining, Trans.). New York: Viking Press.
Augustine, Saint. (1950). *Concerning the teacher* (J. M. Colleran, Trans.). Westminster, MD: Newman Press.
Barthes, R. (1970). *L'empire des signes*. Geneva: University of Geneva.
Berger, P. L. & Luckmann. (1967). *The social construction of reality*. Garden City, NY: Anchor Books.
Blake, W. (1967). The echoing green. In R. F. Gleckner (ed.), *William Blake: Selected writings*. New York: Meredith.
Bourdieu J. & Passeron, J-P. (1977). *Reproduction in education, society, and culture*. London: Sage.
Broudy, H. S. (1981). *Truth and credibility: The citizen's dilemma*. New York: Longman.
Bruner, J. S. (1960). *The process of education*. Cambridge, MA: Harvard University Press.
Bruner, J. S. (1973). The perfectibility of the intellect. In J. S. Bruner, *The relevance of education*. New York: Norton Library.
Buber, M. (1957). *Between man and man*. Boston: Beacon Press.
Camus, A. (1948). *The plague* (S. Gilbert, Trans.), New York: Alfred A. Knopf.
Cassirer, E. (1963). *Rousseau, Kant, and Goethe* (J. Guttmann, P. O. Kristeller, & J. H. Randall, Jr., Trans.). New York: Harper Torchbooks.
Cavell, S. (1976). *Must we mean what we say?* Cambridge: Cambridge University Press.
Chomsky, N. (1975). *Reflections on language*. New York: Pantheon.
Code, L. B. (1983). Responsibility and the epistemic community; woman's place. *Social research, 50*(3), 536–555.
Conrad, J. (1982). *Heart of darkness*. New York: Penguin.
Cumming, R. D. (1979). *Starting point: An introduction to the dialectic of existence*. Chicago: University of Chicago Press.
Dante. (1955). Inferno. In P. Milano (Ed.), *The portable Dante*. New York: Viking Press.
Dennett, D. C. (1981). *Brainstorms: Philosophical essays on mind and psychology*. Cambridge, MA: MIT Press.
Descartes, R. (1968). *Discourse on method and other writings* (F. E. Sutcliffe, Trans.). Baltimore: Penguin.
Dewey, J. (1916). *Democracy and education*. New York: Macmillan.
Dewey, J. (1934). *Art as experience*. New York: Minton, Balch & Company.
Dewey, J. (1954). *The public and its problems*. Athens, OH: Swallow Press.
Dewey, J. (1959). The child and the curriculum. In M. S. Dworkin (Ed.), *Dewey on education*. New York: Teachers College Press, Columbia University.
Dewey, J. (1963). *Experience and education*. New York: Collier Books.
Dewey, J. (1960). Philosophies of freedom. In R. J. Bernstein (Ed.), *John Dewey on experience, nature, and freedom*. New York: Liberal Arts Press.
Farber, M. (1967). *Phenomenology and existence: Towards a philosophy within nature*. New York: Harper Torchbooks.
Freire, P. (1970). *Pedagogy of the oppressed* (M. B. Ramos, Trans.). New York: Herder and Herder.
Gilligan, C. (1982). *In a different voice*. Cambridge, MA: Harvard University Press.
Giroux, H. A. (1983). *Theory and resistance in education*. South Hadley, MA: Bergin & Garvey.
Goodman, N. (1976). *Languages of art*. Indianapolis, IN: Hackett.
Goodman, N. (1978). *Ways of worldmaking*. Indianapolis, IN: Hackett.
Green, T. F. (1967). Teaching, acting, and behaving. In I. Scheffler (Ed.) *Philosophy and education*. Boston: Allyn and Bacon.

Habermas, J. (1970). *Towards a rational society* (J. Shapiro, Trans.). Boston: Beacon Press.

Habermas, J. (1971). *Knowledge and human interests* (J. Shapiro, Trans.). Boston: Beacon Press.

Habermas, J. (1979). *Communication and the evolution of society* (T. McCarthy, Trans.). Boston: Beacon Press.

Hare, R. M. (1964). *The language of morals.* New York: Galaxy Books.

Hawthorne, N. (1969). *The scarlet letter and selected tales.* New York: Penguin.

Hegel, G. W. F. (1967). *The phenomenology of mind* (J. B. Baille, Trans.). New York: Harper Torchbooks.

Heidegger, M. (1966). *Discourse on thinking* (J. M. Anderson & E. H. Freund, Trans.). New York: Harper & Row.

Heidegger, M. (1971). *Poetry, language, thought* (A. Hofstadter, Trans.). New York: Harper and Row.

Heidegger, M. (1972). *What is called thinking?* (Gray, Trans.). New York: Harper Torchbooks.

Hirst, P. H. (1965). Liberal education and the nature of knowledge. In R. D. Archambault (Ed.), *Philosophical analysis and education.* New York: Humanities Press

Husserl, E. (1960). *Cartesian meditations* (D. Cairns, Trans.). The Hague: Martinus Nijhoff.

Husserl, E. (1962). *Ideas*: General introduction to pure phenomenology. (W. R. B. Gibson, Trans.). New York: Collier Books.

Husserl, E. (1965). *Phenomenology and the crisis of philosophy* (Q. Lauer, Trans.). New York: Harper Torchbooks.

Hutchins, R. M. (1962). *The higher learning in America.* New Haven, CT: Yale University Press.

Jaeger, W. (1943). *Paideia: The ideals of Greek culture* (G. Highet, Trans.) (Vol. II). New York: Oxford University Press.

James, W. (1906). *Talks to teachers on psychology; and to students on some of life's ideals.* New York: Henry Holt.

James, W. (1950). *The principles of psychology* (Vol. 2). New York: Dover Publications.

Kant, I. (1940). Selections from Critique of pure reason. In J. Benda (Ed.), *Kant.* Philadelphia: David McKay.

Kant, I. (1960). *Education.* Ann Arbor: University of Michigan Press.

Kant, I. (1964). *The doctrine of virtue*: Part II of the metaphysic of morals (M. J. Gregor, Trans.). New York: Harper Torchbooks.

Keddie, N. (1982). Classroom knowledge. In E. Bredo & W. Feinberg (Eds.), *Knowledge and values in social and educational research.* Philadelphia: Temple University Press.

Kerr, D. H. (1981). The structure of quality in teaching. In J. F. Soltis (Ed.), *Philosophy and education.* Chicago: University of Chicago Press.

Kerr, D. H., & Soltis, J. F. (1974). Locating teacher competency: An action description of teaching. *Educational Theory, 24,* 3–16.

Kierkegaard, S. (1947). *Either/or.* In R. Bretall (Ed.), *A Kierkegaard anthology.* Princeton, NJ: Princeton University Press.

Kierkegaard, S. (1962). *The point of view for my work as an author.* New York: Harper Torchbooks.

Kohlberg, L. (1971). States of moral development as a basis for moral education. In C. M. Beck, B. S. Crittenden, & E. V. Sullivan (Eds.), *Moral education: Interdisciplinary approaches.* New York: Newman Press.

Langeveld, M. J. (1983). Reflections on phenomenology and pedagogy. *Phenomenology and pedagogy, 1*(1), 5–7.

Locke, J. (1947). *An essay concerning human understanding.* New York: E. P. Dutton.

Locke, J. (1964). Some thoughts concerning education. In P. Gay (Ed.), *John Locke on education.* New York: Teachers College Press, Columbia University.

Martin, J. R. (1981). A new paradigm for liberal education. In J. F. Soltis (Ed.), *Philosophy and education.* Chicago: University of Chicago Press.

Martin, J. R. (1982). Excluding women from the educational realm. *Harvard Educational Review, 52*(2), 133–148.

Marx, K. (1959). *Theses on Feuerbach.* In L. S. Feuer (Ed.), *Marx and Engels: Basic writings on politics and philosophy.* Garden City, NY: Anchor Books.

Marx K., & Engels, F. (1959). Excerpts from *The German Ideology.* In L. S. Feuer (Ed.), *Basic writings on politics and philosophy.* Garden City, NY: Anchor Books.

McClellan, J. R. (1976) *Philosophy of education.* Englewood Cliffs. NJ: Prentice-Hall.

Mead, G. H. (1934). *Mind, self, and society.* Chicago: University of Chicago Press.

Merleau-Ponty, M. (1964). *The primacy of perception* (C. Dallery, Trans.). Evanston, IL: Northwestern University Press.

Merleau-Ponty, M. (1967). *Phenomenology of perception* (C. Smith, Trans.). New York: Humanities Press.

Nietzsche, F. (1958). The Antichrist. In W. Kaufmann (Ed.), *The portable Nietzsche.* New York: Viking Press.

Nietzsche, F. (1967). *The will to power* (W. Kaufmann, Trans.). New York: Random House.

Noddings, N. (1984). *Caring: A feminine approach to ethics and moral education.* Berkeley, CA: University of California Press.

Oakeshott, M. (1962). *Rationalism and politics.* London: Methuen.

Pascal, B. (1958). *Pascal's Pensées* (W. F. Trotter, Trans.). New York: E. P. Dutton.

Passmore, J. (1975). On teaching to be critical. In R. F. Dearden, P. H. Hirst, & R. S. Peters (Ed.), *Education and reason.* London: Routledge & Kegan Paul.

Passmore, J. (1980). *The philosophy of teaching.* Cambridge, MA: Harvard University Press.

Peirce, C. S. (1955). The fixation of belief. In J. Butler (Ed.), *Philosophical writings of Peirce.* New York: Dover Publications.

Peters, R. S. (1965). Education as initiation. In R. D. Archambault (Ed.), *Philosophical analysis and education.* London: Routledge & Kegan Paul.

Peters, R. S. (1967). What is an educational process? In R. S. Peters (Ed.), *The concept of education.* New York: Humanities Press.

Peters, R. S. (1975). Education and human development. In R. F. Dearden, P. H. Hirst, & R. S. Peters (Eds.), *Education and the development of reason.* Boston, MA: Routledge & Kegan Paul.

Peters, R. S. (1978). *Ethics and education.* London: George Allen and Unwin.

Petras, J. W. (1968). *George Herbert Mead: Essays on his social philosophy.* New York: Teachers College Press, Columbia University.

Phenix, P. (1964). *Realms of meaning.* New York: McGraw Hill.

Piaget, J. (1977). The multiplicity of forms of psychological explanation. In H. E. Gruber & J. J. Voneche (Eds.), *The essential Piaget.* New York: Basic Books.

Plato (n.d.-a). Meno. In B. Jowett (Trans.), *The works of Plato* (Vol. 3). New York: Tudor Publishing Co.

Plato (n.d.-b) *The republic.* In B. Jowett (Trans.), *The works of Plato* (Vol. 2). New York: Tudor Publishing Co.

Plato (1928). The symposium. In I. Edman (Ed.), *The works of Plato.* New York: Modern Library.

Rilke, R. M. (1965). *Duino Elegies* (C. F. MacIntyre, Trans.). Berkeley, CA: University of California Press.

Rousseau, J. J. (1962). *Émile.* In W. Boyd (Ed.), *The Émile of Jean Jacques Rousseau.* New York: Teachers College Press, Columbia University.

Ryle, G. (1949). *The concept of mind.* New York: Barnes & Noble.

Ryle, G. (1967). Teaching and training. In R. S. Peters (Ed.), *The concept of education.* New York: Humanities Press.

Sartre, J. P. (1956). *Being and nothingness* (H. Barnes, Trans.). New York: Philosophical Library.

Sartre, J. P. (1963). *Search for a method* (H. Barnes, Trans.). New York: Alfred A. Knopf.

Schaff, A. (1970). *Marxism and the human individual.* New York: McGraw-Hill.

Scheffler, I. (1960). *The language of education.* Springfield, IL: Charles C. Thomas.

Scheffler, I. (1965). *Conditions of knowledge.* Chicago: Scott, Foresman.

Scheffler, I. (1967). Philosophical models of teaching. In R. S. Peters (Ed.), *The concept of education.* New York: Humanities Press.

Schutz, A. (1964). *Collected papers: Vol. 2. Studies in social theory.* The Hague: Martinus Nijhoff.

Schutz, A. (1967). *Collected papers*: Vol. 1. The problem of social reality. The Hague: Martinus Nijhoff.

Smith, B. O. (1961). A concept of teaching. In B. O. Smith & R. H. Ennis (Eds.), *Language and concepts in education.* Chicago: Rand McNally.

Soltis, J. F. (1981). Education and the concept of knowledge. In J. F.

Soltis (Ed.), *Philosophy and education.* Chicago: University of Chicago Press.

Taylor, C. (1977). Interpretation and the sciences of man. In F. R. Dallmayr and T. A. McCarthy (Ed.), *Understanding and social inquiry.* Notre Dame, IN: University of Notre Dame Press.

Vandenberg, D. (1971). *Being and education.* Englewood Cliffs, NJ: Prentice-Hall.

Vico, G. (1948). *The new science* (T. G. Bergin & M. H. Fisch, Trans.). Ithaca, NY: Cornell University Press.

Whitehead, A. N. (1949). *The aims of education.* New York: Mentor Press.

Wittgenstein, L. (1968). *Philosophical investigations* (G. E. M. Anscombe, Trans.). New York: Macmillan.

Part 3
The Social and Institutional Context of Teaching

18.
The Cultures of Teaching

Sharon Feiman-Nemser and Robert E. Floden

Michigan State University

In the *Second Handbook of Research on Teaching* (Travers, 1973), Lortie (1973) calls attention to an "odd gap" in our knowledge about teachers: "We have too few studies which explore the subjective world of teachers in terms of *their* conceptions of what is salient" (p. 490). Lortie speculates that familiarity may have dulled our curiosity about the way teachers perceive themselves and their occupational lives. A decade later, this chapter considers how well that gap has been closed by drawing together research about the meaning of teaching to teachers and the origins of those meanings

The presence of a chapter on the "cultures of teaching" suggests that some new ways of looking at teaching as work have emerged over the past two decades. If we compare the focus here with related chapters in previous *Handbooks* (Charters, 1963; Lortie, 1973), we not only find new areas of inquiry (e.g., teachers' practical knowledge), but also new perspectives on familiar topics (e.g., what *women* teachers find rewarding in teaching). Most striking is a shift from trying to study the world of teaching as a public, social phenomenon to trying to understand how teachers define their own work situations. The "cultures of teaching" is a convenient label for the research we discuss even though neither our approach nor the research itself is predominantly anthropological.

In the past, many social scientists were content to study teaching from a distance, borrowing concepts mainly from psychology and sociology to explain what teaching was like. For example, in the preface to *The Nature of Teaching*, Dreeben (1970) acknowledges that he has adopted "the perspective of a somewhat cold-eyed sociological observer looking in from the outside" (p. 5). Increasingly, however, students of teaching have come to value the insider's viewpoint and to rely on teachers as informants.

The importance of asking teachers to speak for themselves about the meaning of their work is demonstrated in Nelson's (1983) research on retired Vermont schoolteachers. While these teachers worked long hours for little pay, they saw themselves as missionaries, involved in an important educational and social undertaking. An outsider might have viewed their work as exploitation. Many of the studies reviewed in this chapter seek to understand how teachers make sense of their work.

Public concern over the quality of teaching and the strong press to improve education through policy make research on the cultures of teaching particularly timely. For one thing, teachers often play the role of street-level bureaucrats (cf. Lipsky, 1980), influencing the actual implementation of policies. Knowledge about the cultures of teaching can inform predictions about how teachers are likely to respond to policy initiatives and guide efforts to shape those responses. Policies that enhance the conditions of teaching are also needed to attract and hold talented individuals and to support their best efforts. Knowledge about the cultures of teaching can help in the formulation of such policies. Finally, the practical wisdom of competent teachers remains a largely untapped source of insights for the improvement of teaching. Uncovering that knowledge is a major task in research on the cultures of teaching and can lead to policies that build on what teachers know.

In drawing policy implications from this research, however, we must not confuse cultural description with prescription. It is one thing to maintain that certain norms and sentiments exist among teachers and seem adaptive to current realities. It is quite another to assume that these norms and sentiments are worthwhile and ought to be upheld and transmitted. For example, many teachers are reluctant to request help or to offer

The authors thank reviewers Arthur Wise (Rand Corporation), Kenneth Zeichner (University of Wisconsin — Madison), and Lilian Katz (University of Illinois). Preparation of this chapter was supported by the Institute for Research on Teaching, College of Education, Michigan State University, funded primarily by the Program for Teaching and Instruction of the National Institute of Education, United States Department of Education.

guidance without being asked. The norm of noninterference may be understandable in a system where shared problem solving rarely occurs and teachers are expected to work things out on their own. Still, this cultural standard limits the possibilities for stimulation, growth, and collegial control.

Nor do we have sufficient evidence to conclude that such a standard obtains among all teachers. In fact, the question of whether even a majority of teachers shares a common culture has not been answered. It is far more likely that many cultures exist in this occupation whose members work in small towns and big cities, rich schools and poor schools, and include novices and veterans at different levels of schooling. Researchers have only begun to explore the diversity of the cultures of teaching.

We have organized this chapter around three questions that reflect the state of research on the cultures of teaching: (a) What do we know about the cultures of teaching? (b) What do we know about the origins of these cultural patterns? (c) What do we know about how teachers acquire a cultural repertoire in teaching? In so doing, we bring together bodies of work that are rarely related. We begin by discussing several methodological problems that arise in studying the cultures of teaching.

Obstacles to Studying the Cultures of Teaching

While all educational research is difficult, research on the cultures of teaching has special difficulties because of its elusive subject matter and the diversity of the teaching population. Since these conditions cannot be eliminated, researchers must consider their consequences in designing, conducting, and interpreting studies, and consumers of these studies must decide how much these problems cast doubt on the findings.

Three methodological problems have special significance for research on the cultures of teaching. First, the focus on *culture* implies inferences about knowledge, values, and norms for action, none of which can be directly observed. Second, the existence of *many* teaching cultures raises difficult questions: Which culture or cultures does a study address? How can differences among cultures and similarities within cultures be documented? Third, researchers must neither evaluate a culture by inappropriate external standards, nor fall into the relativistic trap of asserting that every aspect of that culture is good. Judgment is unavoidable in research on the cultures of teaching, where pragmatic questions about directions for change are always in the minds of researchers and policymakers.

We illustrate each of these problems with studies discussed in subsequent sections. The illustrations show not how the problems can be eliminated, but how researchers have dealt with them and with the consequences.

Describing the Unseen

A central problem in research on the cultures of teaching is how to get "inside teachers' heads" to describe their knowledge, attitudes, beliefs, and values. The difficulties of basing these descriptions on observational data are obvious — the data do not provide any direct statement of what teachers think or feel.

Merely asking teachers to tell what they know or find rewarding, however, cannot guarantee that self-reports will capture the insider's perspective. Discounting the possibility of intentional deception, it is difficult to judge how accurately people report on their own perspectives (Nisbett & Wilson, 1977). Even if people have access to accurate information about their mental lives, they may not be able to express that information clearly. We show how these difficulties affect research on the cultures of teaching by considering two of the three areas of cultural content to be discussed in this chapter: practical knowledge and occupational rewards.

Practical knowledge is difficult to describe. People often know how to do things without being able to state what they know. Furthermore, neither teachers nor researchers have an adequate vocabulary for describing practical knowledge, much of which is tacit. Philosophical and psychological talk of theories, propositions, and concepts fits codified knowledge, not tacit knowledge. To date, researchers have not gone much beyond suggesting concepts to guide the study of practical knowledge.

If teachers are pressed to give general descriptions of themselves and their work, they often use the same language that social and behavioral scientists do. These abstract descriptions may be remembered from college courses or picked up as part of the vocabulary of educated people, but they do not express teachers' own perspectives (Lampert, 1981).

Choosing guiding concepts is particularly problematic in research on the cultures of teaching. Conclusions about the rewards in teaching linked to career advancement, for example, depend on how reward and career are conceptualized. Early research on careers built on assumptions developed in research on businessmen (e.g., the assumption that a model career is an uninterrupted sequence of positions with ever-increasing responsibility). Biklen (1983) argues that these imported concepts do not accurately represent the way female teachers think about their careers. Lortie also attempts to uncover what teachers find rewarding by asking indirect questions (e.g., about occasions that make teachers feel especially proud). His inferences about occupational rewards are dependent on his assumptions about the relationship between rewards and pride.

There is no easy solution to the problem of selecting guiding concepts; concepts from academic disciplines may not capture the way teachers themselves think about their work, but teachers are seldom able to provide a set of concepts that covers a variety of situations. As Schwab (1959) has argued, the practical knowledge most appropiate for dealing with a specific teaching context will not be abstract or flexible enough to fit the variety of contexts experienced by other teachers.

Lampert (1981) directly addresses these difficulties of inference in her study of how teachers manage to teach despite the seeming contradictions that characterize their work. She met regularly with seven teachers involved as colleagues in a project designed to consider the usefulness of cognitive theory for their classroom work. Lampert was designated as a teacher advocate, responsible for seeing that the other researchers did not impose their psychological concepts on the group discussions. Forty-five meetings over the course of 2 school years, plus interviews, informal visits to classrooms, and small group meetings, gave Lampert many glimpses of teachers' "sedimented theories." Recognizing that the imposition of concepts from sociology or psychology could prevent her from describing teachers' dilemmas, she took steps to increase the chance that her formulations would be faithful to the teachers' own perceptions.

First, she used transcripts and tapes of the teachers' conversations in the research meetings as her primary source of data. By checking her interpretations against what the teachers actually said, she hoped to capture the teachers' own perspectives. Second, she restricted her attention to themes that teachers repeatedly returned to over the years of the study. Because a theme emerged in a number of different contexts, Lampert could test her understanding in a broad range of situations. Third, Lampert drew on what she had learned about the teachers through interviews and classroom visits. She attempted to make her interpretations fit everything she knew about these individuals. Because teachers returned to their work after describing their thoughts, they had a chance to check what they said against their continuing classroom practice. Finally, Lampert consciously tried to identify with the teachers, rather than with an academic discipline.

These multiple checks do not ensure the accuracy of an interpretation. As Lampert acknowledges, interpretation is based on uncertain inferences beyond the data. Checking interpretations for internal consistency may distort perspectives that are actually inconsistent or even incoherent. Ultimately, the researcher forms the concepts that guide analysis.

Finding Common Threads in a Complex Carpet

It is tempting to assume that teachers share a uniform teaching culture. Given that assumption, any sample of teachers can be chosen for intensive investigation, with the comforting belief that the culture those teachers share is *the* culture of teaching. The assumption of cultural uniformity is, however, untenable. Teachers differ in age, experience, social and cultural background, gender, marital status, subject matter, wisdom, and ability. The schools in which they work also differ in many ways, as do the groups of students they teach. All these differences may lead to differences in teaching culture. The problem facing the researcher is how to design studies and draw inferences in the light of this diversity.

Lortie (1975) bases his analysis of teaching on data from three separate studies: the Five Towns interview study, questions on the Dade County survey, and national surveys conducted by the National Education Association (NEA). The 94 teachers interviewed in the 1963 Five Towns study represent a range of socioeconomic settings and school grade levels in districts around the Boston area. The Dade County, Florida survey collected data as part of a larger 1964 survey of the professional staff in Dade County, which Lortie claims is more representative of the national teaching population than most single districts. Lortie drew on NEA surveys from the period 1960 to 1971.

Lortie's primary analysis is based on themes derived from his interview data, which are checked against the survey studies. He generally avoids conclusions about their generalizability to the teaching population as a whole. He portrays his book, *Schoolteacher*, as an attempt to propose themes for further exploration, not as an effort to describe the relative frequency with which, for example, teachers get their primary rewards from the gratitude of returning students.

Thus Lortie addresses the problem of diversity in the teaching population through a combination of careful sample selection, cross-checking against other samples, caution in claiming generality of results, and description and possible explanation of differences among different groups of teachers. For example, in discussing the rewards of teaching, he gives careful attention to differences between men and women, older and younger teachers, and married and single teachers.

While Lortie acknowledges diversity, he talks about teachers in general. Metz (1978), however, finds that diversity of teaching cultures is a central factor in the explanation of authority and control in schools. She characterizes teachers in two junior high schools as either "incorporative" or "developmental," roughly corresponding to the familiar distinction between those who emphasize teaching *subjects* and those who emphasize teaching *children*. In one school, with substantially greater student discipline problems, the teachers were sharply divided. The incorporative-developmental distinction coincided with other differences (e.g., age, style of dress, political beliefs). Metz explains the discipline problems in terms of the lack of a uniform teaching culture.

No studies of the culture of teaching can afford the large, nationally representative samples required for accurate description of every subculture. Researchers and their audiences are inevitably torn between the desire to draw general conclusions and the fear of moving beyond a relatively small sample.

That's How It Is, but Is that How It Should Be?

Early anthropological studies judged primative cultures against the template of advanced societies. One reaction to this ethnocentrism was to deny the possibility of judging any culture by external standards. In its shorter history, research on the cultures of teaching has run a similar course. Early work criticized teaching for not measuring up to the medical standard (e.g., Lortie, 1975). Recent work runs the risk of glorifying teachers' beliefs simply because they are what teachers believe. Both extremes must be avoided if research on the cultures of teaching is to guide the improvement of teaching and learning.

Maintaining the middle ground, however, is difficult. It is hard to acknowledge the special features of the teaching occupation without assuming that standing patterns of practice are desirable.

Consider Biklen's (1983) analysis of careers. Women teachers often quit their formal teaching jobs for a period of time so that they can raise a family. Biklen challenges Lortie's (1975) interpretation that teaching is "careerless," because the interpretation rests on a "corporate career model" that does not fit women teachers. How then should female careers be evaluated?

Biklen describes two women teachers who followed the standard pattern of entry and exit from formal teaching positions. Both women believe they have been continuously engaged in a career that combines family responsibilities with public school teaching. Moreover, they claim that, even when they were not teaching, they still wanted to get back to the classroom.

Biklen accepts this positive assessment without argument, concluding that the two women "are highly committed to their occupations" and "display ... consistent commitment to education" (pp. 26–27). Such a positive assessment requires justification; there may be good reasons to prefer teachers who consistently devote themselves to teaching.

In another example, Biklen provides the necessary justification. Some teachers in her study rejected promotions to administrative positions because they thought the quality of their work would suffer. These teachers placed their decision not to "advance" in their careers in a positive light; they did not view moving to an administrative position as a step up the career ladder. Biklen does not merely accept the teachers' positive assessment of their own actions. She gives reasons for calling these teachers idealistic; for example, they decided on the basis of "how they served the occupation rather than how the occupation could serve them" (p. 40).

Meeting the Methodological Challenge

The cultures of teaching are elusive. Because they vary across individuals, across schools, and over time, verbal descriptions often seem inadequate to capture them.

Still, we feel cautious optimism about the prospects for understanding the cultures of teaching. Researchers have come to terms with the inevitability of uncertain inference, and realized that such judgments are more illuminating than professions of ignorance. Acceptance of diversity has replaced the mistaken hope for universal generalizations with the more modest but attainable plan to sketch the range of diversity and suggest tentative explanations (Sarason, 1982). Recognizing the difficulty in judging aspects of the cultures of teaching is the first step towards drawing implications that respect teachers as persons without automatically endorsing their perceptions as the basis for recommended change.

Cultural Description

Teaching cultures are embodied in the work-related beliefs and knowledge teachers share — beliefs about appropriate ways of acting on the job and rewarding aspects of teaching, and knowledge that enables teachers to do their work. In describing beliefs about appropriate ways of acting, we draw on studies of the norms that govern social interactions between teachers and other role groups (e.g., principals, parents). Literature on occupational rewards in teaching forms the basis for our discussion of teachers' beliefs in that area.

Many people, including some leading educational researchers, have questioned whether teachers possess special knowledge. Does every reasonably intelligent adult know as much about teaching as most teachers? Although the question of what is needed to function effectively as a member of a teaching culture seems central to descriptive research on the

cultures of teaching, the groundwork is still being laid for research in this area.

In this section we discuss research that describes teachers' beliefs about norms for social interaction, teachers' views of the rewards in teaching, and teachers' personal, practical knowledge. Later sections on the genesis and acquisition of teaching cultures consider why it is that teachers share beliefs and knowledge.

Norms for Interaction

Norms for interaction shape the way teachers perceive their work, and especially the way they see their relationships with students, other teachers, school administrators (primarily the principal), and parents. Norms vary among different groups of teachers, and teachers within any group probably vary in how strictly they comply with a given norm. There is little research that describes or explains such variation. Below we discuss the norms that researchers most often discuss.

INTERACTIONS WITH STUDENTS

Waller's (1932) classic study of the sociology of teaching emphasizes the teacher–student relationship. Waller sees the teacher as the authority figure in the classroom and argues that teachers who do not maintain their authority run into trouble quickly. At all times, the teacher must keep a distance from the students and maintain discipline. Teachers must demonstrate to those outside the classroom that students respect them.

More recent studies of teacher socialization return to these themes of authority and discipline as guiding principles in teachers' comportment toward students. Hoy and Rees (1977) found that student teachers come to see student control as a primary goal in teaching, a goal that different teachers achieve in different ways. Ryan's (1970) accounts of beginning teachers reflect the salience of student control as a teaching concern. (See also McPherson, 1972, chapter 4.)

A second norm that governs teacher–student relationships contradicts this picture of the distant teacher because it requires teachers to form personal bonds with their students in order to motivate them to learn (Burden, 1979; Jackson, 1968; Lampert, 1984; Lortie, 1975; Sarason, 1982). The tension between these expectations for distance and closeness creates a fundamental ambiguity in the teacher's role. The problem seems most poignant for beginning teachers, but it remains a central issue for experienced teachers as well (Fountain, 1975).

Most research on the norms teachers follow in relating to students has focused on issues of authority and friendship. Increasingly, researchers are trying to find out how teachers interpret this dilemma (Lampert, 1981). Comparatively little attention has been given to the significance teachers attribute to other norms, such as treating students fairly or promoting the learning of all.

INTERACTIONS WITH OTHER TEACHERS

Silver (1973) says that teachers have peers but no colleagues. Her turn of phrase captures the norm of interaction described by many researchers (e.g., Lortie, 1975; McPherson, 1972;

Sarason, 1982). Typically teachers work in isolation, although open-space settings do make their work visible. While they see one another in the lunchroom, in staff meetings, and throughout the building, teachers seldom employ these interactions as opportunities to discuss their work or to collaborate on shared problems.

Teachers interviewed by Lortie describe the ideal colleague as someone willing to help, but never pushy. A norm against asking for help in any area of serious difficulty prevails because such a request would suggest a failing on the part of the teacher requesting assistance. A complementary norm discourages teachers from telling a peer to do something different. The only permissible exchange of information on teaching techniques is the announcement that an alternative method exists (Newberry, 1977).

While these "hands-off" norms may be prevalent, they appear to vary from one school building to the next. Little (1982), for example, describes schools where a norm of collegiality prevails. The cultures of these schools support such practices as teachers observing each other's teaching, providing suggestions for improvement, and discussing professional problems.

The "hands-off" norms need not imply that teachers within a building are not on friendly terms. In many buildings, teachers expect support from their coworkers and may socialize with them out of school (e.g., Biklen, 1983; Silver, 1973). Even so, they avoid talking about instructional practices. Commonly, lunchroom talk deals with politics, gripes, home life, and the personalities and family background of individual students, rather than curriculum, instructional content, or teaching methods (McPherson, 1972).

The teacher center movement (Devaney, 1977; Nemser & Applegate, 1983) is evidence that some teachers think they would benefit from more collegial interaction than is currently available in most schools. Perhaps working in a center with teachers from different buildings reduces the fear of revealing areas of weakness. Yet even some teachers who voluntarily attend teacher centers might use them as places to assemble teaching materials instead of as places to discuss instructional issues or seek advice on teaching difficulties (Feiman, 1975).

INTERACTIONS WITH ADMINISTRATORS

The role of the school principal has received increasing attention in the last decade (e.g., Blumberg & Greenfield, 1980; Wolcott, 1973). Studies of the principal have vacillated between raising the principal to the position of central importance in school operations (e.g., Edmonds, 1982) and declaring that the principal has little effect on school practice (e.g., Ross, 1980). How do teachers think they should treat (and be treated by) the principal?

Many teachers see themselves in an ambiguous position vis-à-vis the principal (Jackson, 1968; Lortie, 1975; McPherson, 1972; Sarason, 1982). On the one hand, they want little interference in their daily classroom routine, particularly for decisions about curriculum and instruction. On the other hand, they wish the principal would act as a buffer between themselves and outside pressures from district administrators, parents, and other community members (e.g., Biklen, 1983). In addition, they want the principal to be a strong force in maintaining student discipline—backing the teachers in their classroom discipline policies and maintaining consistent school-wide policies. In return for these services, the teachers are willing to cooperate with the principal's initiatives.

This informal system of exchange of favors was described before the increase in collective bargaining agreements, which specified teachers' (and principals') rights and responsibilities. Recent studies suggest that, while teachers' contracts have produced some change in interactions with administrators (particularly in districts just beginning collective bargaining), the change has had less effect on the daily work life of teachers than predicted. Mitchell and his colleagues (Mitchell & Kerchner, 1983; Mitchell, Kerchner, Erck, & Pryor, 1981) found a general trend toward reduction of the principal's power in the school and toward an insistence on conformity with written policies (i.e., those specified in the contract). The emphasis on explicit public policies tends to make teachers feel less dependent on the good graces of the principal and concomitantly less inclined to go along with the principal's ideas for change. Mitchell emphasizes variation among school districts.

While Johnson (1982) also notes substantial variation among districts, she found a general trend toward continuing the informal exchanges between principals and teachers, even when this departed from contract specifications. Despite explicit policies on rights and duties, teachers continued to depend on the good will of the principal for many services (e.g., equitable assignment of students to classes, buffering of parent requests and complaints). The principal relied on the good will of the teachers to maintain high educational standards. As a result, the teachers abided by the norms that preceded the contract, sometimes asking the union representatives to ignore contract violations.

INTERACTIONS WITH PARENTS

Although parents may seem to be centrally involved in and concerned with schooling, teachers typically have few interactions with parents. When students make reasonable progress, contact may not go beyond the twice yearly conference, which disappears in the upper grades.

Yet teachers and parents are continually reminded of each others' presence. Parents can see effects of school in their children; teachers can tell when parents support classroom work. Such indirect interaction produces tension, as teacher and parent (particularly female teachers and mothers, see Biklen, 1983; Lightfoot, 1978) compete for the child's attention and loyalty.

Teachers see the ideal relationship with parents as one in which the parents support teacher practices, carry out teacher requests, and do not attempt to interfere with teacher plans (Lightfoot, 1978; Lortie, 1975; McPherson, 1972). This exclusion of parents may be explained partly by teachers' desire to keep family affairs from interfering with students' performance in school. Some teachers do not want their expectations for children to be based on family background. Other teachers see some groups of parents (though perhaps not all parents) as threatening, either because their higher social status calls the

510   SHARON FEIMAN-NEMSER AND ROBERT E. FLODEN

teacher's authority into question or because the teachers see parent demands as unreasonable. Lightfoot (1978) states the matter quite strongly: Teachers, she says,

> wish to form coalitions only with parents who are obsequious, appreciative, and uncritical, or accepting of their needs for autonomy. Most parents are viewed as a critical force that, if permitted to interfere, would threaten the teachers' already insecure professional status and self-image. (p. 37)

Teachers enforce their decisions about a child's educational program by drawing on professional status and knowledge. Even though legislation requires that parents approve the programs of special education students, teachers are often able to keep parents from directing the decisions (Weatherly & Lipsky, 1977).

Concepts About the Rewards of a Career in Teaching

What rewards do teachers get from teaching? How do they envision their career prospects? Answers to these questions would increase out understanding of the satisfaction teachers derive from their work and provide direction for making that work more rewarding.

Occupational rewards are often classified as extrinsic or intrinsic rewards. Extrinsic rewards are the public benefits of high salary, short working hours, elevated status, and significant power. Intrinsic rewards, sometimes called psychic rewards or subjective rewards, are aspects of work that are valued by and visible to insiders only. To determine whether working with young people is an occupational *reward*, one must explore the perspectives of the teachers in question. Researchers have studied such intrinsic rewards as knowing that students are learning, emotional attachment to students, interaction with colleagues, satisfaction in performing a valuable service, enjoyment of teaching activities themselves, and enjoyment of learning from teaching.

Teachers vary in the importance they attach to both extrinsic and intrinsic rewards. Even the supposedly objective benefits of money and status are not valued equally by all teachers.

EXTRINSIC REWARDS

Teaching is typically portrayed as an occupation largely devoid of extrinsic rewards. While teachers aspire to professional status, they have yet to attain the associated pay, power, and prestige. Indeed, teaching may have lost ground in the past decade. How do teachers reconcile themselves to the apparent absence of extrinsic rewards?

Salary. Teachers have never been well paid; moreover, whatever salary gains were made in an era of teacher shortages and collective bargaining have been eroded. Annual teaching salaries are not competitive with salaries in fields with similar educational requirements. Futhermore, teachers' salaries rise only modestly over the course of their careers.

The psychological importance of teachers' salaries is, however, not well understood, and probably differs greatly from teacher to teacher. Hall (1982) describes two teaching couples with similar backgrounds and educational preparation where the total income of one couple is almost double that of the other couple. The high-salaried couple (from an area with a long history of support for public education) seem content with their life-style, while the low-salaried couple feel financially pressed. The psychological significance of a teaching salary may be affected by whether the teacher's spouse is in a high-paying job or the teaching salary represents half or all of the family's income. The increase in the number of single-parent families (Sweet & Jacobsen, 1983) may also bear on how different teachers perceive their earnings.

Status. The status of teaching has declined in the past decade, and teachers are sensitive to their tarnished image. Heath (cited in Fiske, 1983) has found that "teachers feel a declining sense of social status" (p. 18), and the Carnegie commission report on high schools describes secondary school teachers as "deeply troubled ... about loss of status, the bureaucratic pressures, a negative public image" (cited in Fiske, 1983, p. 18). The percentage of parents who would like their children to enter teaching continues to decline (Gallup, 1983, p. 44). From many teachers' perspectives, the low status of teaching is a significant occupational hazard.

Work Schedule. The number of hours teachers are required to be in school is small compared to the time other workers must spend at their job sites. The typical mandatory work day is less than 8 hours, and schools are not in session during the summer and other holidays. Though many teachers spend time at home preparing for work, they retain considerable flexibility in their work schedule.

This flexibility can be seen as an occupational reward. Teachers can use it to devote themselves to outside interests (other jobs, raising a family, volunteer work) without the feeling of shirking work responsibilities. Many studies report that teachers find the flexible schedule attractive (Biklen, 1983; Hall, 1982; Lortie, 1975; Nelson, 1983).

Power. While power may be a significant extrinsic reward in many occupations, it is seldom mentioned as a teaching reward. As Lortie (1975) comments, "teachers are not supposed to *enjoy* exercising power per se" (p. 102).

INTRINSIC REWARDS

Given the relative absence of extrinsic rewards, intrinsic rewards gain importance. As Lipsky (1980) points out, in a job (like teaching) where outcomes are relatively difficult to measure, the individual's own definition of what makes work worthwhile is crucially important because it influences what is actually done more than the formal goals and organizational policies. Some recent studies (e.g., Hall. 1982) suggest that the intrinsic rewards of teaching are on the wane.

Students. Most teachers find student learning and student attachment rewarding. While teachers feel pressure to increase the achievement of their entire class, they find greater rewards in the success of individual students (Jackson, 1968; Lortie,

1975; Wise, 1979). This represents a disjuncture between institutional goals and teachers' goals. Many elementary school teachers also enjoy the affection of their students. For secondary school teachers, open displays of affection are less acceptable, especially from students of the opposite sex (Hall, 1982).

Teachers in several studies have reported that rewards from students have declined (Leonard, 1983; Newman, 1978: Silver, 1973). Hall (1982), for example, found secondary school teachers frustrated by the increasing difficulty in getting students to learn and worried about the increasing danger of physical abuse by students.

Collegial Stimulation and Support. The isolation of most teachers has been frequently noted (e.g., Cohen, 1973; Lortie, 1975; McPherson, 1972; Silver, 1973; Waller, 1932). Such isolation prevents teachers from enjoying the rewards of collegial interaction—support and praise for work well done, stimulation of new ideas.

While it appears that psychic rewards in teaching come from children, not adults, some research (e.g., Cohen, 1973; Sieber, 1981) suggests that this is not universally true. There are schools with substantial collegial interaction where teachers enjoy talking shop, observing and critiquing each other's teaching, and working together to improve instruction (Little, 1982). Similarly, Cohen (1973) found that many teachers in open-space schools, where the classroom door could never be closed, were more satisfied with their jobs than teachers in schools with traditional architecture.

The emphasis on intrinsic rewards from students, rather than adults, may also be less applicable at the secondary-school level (Mann, 1976) or in schools where student achievement is low (Silver, 1973). When rewarding interactions with students are scarce, interactions with other teachers can become a primary source of intrinsic rewards.

The Glow of Service. The belief that they are providing a public service may be rewarding for many teachers. Like other government service employees, teachers tend to see themselves as performing an essential service that no one else is willing to perform (Lipsky, 1980). The service image is, however, more difficult to maintain since collective bargaining has made the public more aware of teachers' interest in their own well-being. Those entering the job market have not abandoned the ideal of public service, but teaching is less clearly an attractive service occupation (see Sykes, 1983, pp. 111-112).

Enjoyment of Teaching Activities. Teaching activities themselves can also be a source of instrinsic rewards. Mitchell and his colleagues (Mitchell, Ortiz, & Mitchell, 1982) found that teachers do not select learning activities because they lead to valued outcomes, but because they value such activities in and of themselves. Teachers vary in the kinds of classroom activities they value. Some teachers prefer activities designed to foster achievement; others, activities designed to be nurturant. Some teachers get rewards from conducting carefully planned lessons; others get satisfaction from creating a classroom environment where students have many opportunities to follow their own interests.

Plihal (1982) found that teachers who get substantial rewards from seeing the effects of their instruction get relatively little reward from the mere process of interaction, and vice versa. These preferences were related to the organization of instruction. Teachers found student learning most rewarding in math lessons, where learning goals were well defined and students worked alone at their seats. In social studies lessons, where learning goals are broad and group activities dominate, teachers found the process, rather than the outcome, most rewarding.

CONCEPTS OF CAREER

Continuity. As indicated in the preceding section, recent studies of teachers' perceptions of their careers reveal that many female teachers do not view career continuity as an important characteristic of their work. Though interruptions in employment call for explanation in a business or law career, some teachers see an in-and-out employment pattern as acceptable or even as evidence of a praiseworthy commitment to child rearing. The pattern is becoming less common, however, as women are more likely to take only a short pregnancy leave (Sweet & Jacobsen, 1983).

Vertical Advancement. With few exceptions, teachers cannot be promoted and still remain teachers. Teachers may change to other school positions (e.g., principal), but even that "promotion" is open to very few. In this respect teaching seems to be a job with little to offer the ambitious careerist. What the teacher may envision as a long-term career is a few years establishing competence and securing tenure followed by 40-odd years of performing the same job with new sets of students. In the past, teachers may have looked forward to a move from an inner-city, low-SES school to a higher SES school, either in a different part of the city, or in an affluent suburb (Becker, 1952). The shortage of teaching jobs has reduced such horizontal mobility. Cohen (1973) reports that the lack of vertical mobility is frustrating for some ambitious female elementary school teachers; other ambitious teachers wish to avoid leaving the classroom, so their desire for recognition and reward is not blocked by absence of a career ladder (though it may be blocked by absence of opportunities for public reward and recognition).

The Specialization of Teaching. Two decades ago, few distinctions could be made among teaching positions. Teachers were certified either as multisubject elementary school teachers, or as single-subject secondary school teachers. The lack of differentiation among teaching roles has frequently been cited as limiting teachers' opportunities to take on different school responsibilities.

The rise in employment of teachers' aides and specialist teachers has broken that pattern of homogeneity. Partially as a result of the availability of federal compensatory education programs, many schools hired aides to assist the regular classroom teachers. The altered staffing patterns have tended to persist even when federal funds are removed (Kirst, 1983). Though still in a minority, specialist teachers make up an increasingly larger fraction of American teachers (Kerr, 1983).

Many teachers begin their careers as specialists, but the existence of such specialist positions gives experienced classroom teachers a visible example of other possibilities for teaching employment.

The effect of this increase in the variety of teaching roles on teachers' views of their careers is largely unexplored. Kerr (1983) suggests that teachers see specialization as a way to gain autonomy, pay, and status; Milofsky (1976) describes a case wherein a specialist felt ostracized by the regular teachers in her building. The effects of specialization on the cultures of teaching deserve study.

Commitment. Commitment is one indication of the importance teachers attach to their work. Although sociological studies of work have typically concluded that teachers lack career commitment, recent research on what teaching means to teachers sheds new light on this issue. The difference in conclusions stems from the use of different definitions of "commitment" and "career." Because the search for more appropriate definitions is motivated largely by a desire to correct the male bias in previous analyses, we discuss this issue in terms of the feminization of teaching in the section on the genesis of teaching cultures.

TEACHING: WHAT'S IN IT FOR THE TEACHER?

Teaching, like other occupations, tends to attract and hold people who are initially disposed to value what the work has to offer and to be able to cope with difficulties the work presents. Thus it comes as no surprise that teaching, with a reputation as low-paid service work with children, is viewed by many teachers as rewarding in terms of interactions with students and the pleasure of serving, and not because of the pay or opportunities for advancement.

This "functional" match between job characteristics and expectations about work is likely to continue as long as the nature of the work matches what people expected when they began and as long as those outside the occupation are satisfied with those within.

Because both of these situations have recently changed, questions are being raised about the desirability of restructuring the occupation. Discussions about reforms should attend to the features of teaching that teachers have found rewarding and to how these have changed in the past decade (e.g., reductions in rewards from interacting with students). Advocates of change should, however, take care to note that if they succeed in attracting a new group of entrants into the occupation, those newcomers may expect a different mix of occupational rewards from that expected by teachers on whom most research has been conducted. If similar individuals are to continue to enter teaching, changes in teaching must attend to their expectations.

The status and attractiveness of teaching might be enhanced if teachers were seen to possess a special body of knowledge. The belief that anyone can teach makes it harder to take pride in the expertise gained through professional education and teaching experience, and may be a source of tensions between teachers, principals, and parents. As Lightfoot (1978) points out, teachers' own uncertainty about their judgment and status makes them vulnerable to parent complaints or demands for change. Uncertainty about whether they have special knowledge lowers teachers' status and makes them question their occupational choice.

Teachers' Knowledge

Teachers have not been seen as possessing a unique body of professional knowledge and expertise. The prevailing view among most researchers is that teachers have experience while academics have knowledge. Concerned about this portrait, some researchers have sought other ways to describe and analyze what teachers know. Instead of searching for professional knowledge or technical knowledge, they have looked more broadly at teachers' practical knowledge — that is, those beliefs, insights, and habits that enable teachers to do their work in schools. In so doing, they show that teachers' knowledge has the characteristics that philosophers have always attributed to practical knowledge — that it is time bound and situation specific, personally compelling and oriented toward action. They have not yet dealt with the question of why and on what grounds these beliefs, insights, and habits should be considered knowledge.

In this section, we analyze a few empirical studies of teachers' practical knowledge. The basic research strategy for gathering data on what teachers know is to get them to talk about their work in interviews (e.g., Elbaz, 1983), teacher seminars (e.g., Lampert, 1981; Lampert, 1984) or discussions of observations and classroom videotapes (e.g., Erickson, this volume). On the basis of these verbal data, researchers make inferences and claims about the content, uses, and organization of teachers' knowledge. Before illustrating this research, we consider some of the less flattering views of teachers' knowledge.

A DIM VIEW OF TEACHERS' KNOWLEDGE

Researchers have portrayed teachers' knowledge as a mixture of idiosyncratic experience and personal synthesis. For example, Lortie (1975) argues that teachers lack a technical culture, a set of commonly held, empirically derived practices and principles of pedagogy. As a result, teachers must individually develop practices consistent with their personality and experience. Jackson (1968) also implies that teachers lack professional knowledge. Teachers, he argues, are content with simple explanations. They justify their teaching on the basis of feelings and impulse rather than reflection and thought. They take strong stands against practices different from their own and rely on personal experience to defend what they do. The meanings they give to abstract terms are limited to the boundaries of their own experience.

Two explanations have been offered to account for this picture of knowledge generation and use in teaching. Lortie (1975) links the inadequacies of teacher education to the absence of a technical culture in teaching. If there is no knowledge base, then teacher education cannot transmit relevant professional knowledge. Sarason (1982) ties the fact that teachers lack a shared body of practical knowledge to teacher isolation. Because most teachers work apart from their colleagues, they have little opportunity to articulate and compare what they know. Furthermore, the need to respond continually to classroom demands is thought to foster a reliance on intuition and inpulse rather than reason (Huberman, 1983).

These explanations stem from a restricted view of knowledge in teaching. Lortie reduces problems of practice to technical choices. By limiting his notion of useful knowledge to tested relationships between ends and means, he implies that goals in teaching are givens, not things to be chosen or justified. In trying to explain teachers' reliance on intuition and impulse, Jackson implies that teaching cannot be reasonable. This claim seems untenable. On-the-spot decisions cannot be considered capricious just because they require instantaneous response in a complex and fluid environment.

The tendency to question teachers' knowledge also stems from placing a higher value on scientific knowledge than on practical and personal knowledge. Presumably scientific knowledge offers a more objective and reliable picture of classroom life because it transcends the details of specific classrooms, the biases of individual teachers, and the necessary limits of their experience. Caught up in the demands of their own work, teachers cannot solve problems in general; they must deal with specific situations. Thus their descriptions of teaching sound more like stories than theories because they are full of the particulars of their own experience. General solutions are considered better because they are not tied to a specific time and place (Schwab, 1959; Lampert, 1981).

Because practical problems are defined by these ties, this argument criticizes practical knowledge on inappropriate grounds. The close connection to practical situations where teachers' knowledge is shaped and used does not necessarily make it less valuable, just different from scientific knowledge. As Buchmann (1983a) argues, the purpose of practical knowledge is to inform wise action—not to advance general understanding. The goal of wise action and the practical contexts of teaching provide the appropriate terms for describing what teachers know, how they acquire this knowledge, and how they put it to use.

Below we discuss some empirical research on teachers' knowledge under the headings of content, uses, and organization. Looking at content implies that teachers have a substantive body of knowledge; it is, however, only by considering how this knowledge is used that we understand the sense in which it is practical. Understanding the organization of teachers' knowledge refines our appreciation of uses by showing how different forms of knowledge permit different kinds of performances.

WHAT TEACHERS KNOW

Teachers draw on diverse kinds of knowledge in carrying out their work. Still, few researchers have studied the content of teachers' knowledge. This may reflect a narrow view of teachers' knowledge or uncertainty about what kinds of knowledge to look for. By suggesting five categories of practical knowledge in teaching—knowledge of self, of the milieu of teaching, of subject matter, of curriculum development, and of instruction—Elbaz (1983) offers one way of organizing the content of teachers' knowledge. These categories, drawn from a case study of practical knowledge based on interviews with one high school English teacher named Sarah, point to areas of content

knowledge that seem relevant to teaching and may provide a useful guide for research on what teachers know.

Wheras Elbaz describes the scope of one teacher's practical knowledge, Lampert (1981; Lampert, 1984) focuses on a single category, personal knowledge, which combines Elbaz' "knowledge of self" with knowledge of students. According to Lampert, personal knowledge includes knowledge of "who the teacher is and what she cares about" (p. 204) as well as knowledge of students beyond that provided by pencil-and-paper tests. If they work together over time in a common endeavor, teachers come to know their students as people and to hold out some expectations for their "human development." The teacher's vision of what a child should become is based in what that individual teacher cares about as well as what she knows about the child. This personal knowledge is essential in accomplishing what teachers care about, what students want, and what the curriculum requires.

HOW TEACHERS USE PRACTICAL KNOWLEDGE

A unifying theme in this small body of work on teachers' knowledge is the recognition that teachers' knowledge is "actively related to the world of practice" (Elbaz, 1983). Researchers have described and conceptualized how practical knowledge is used to manage dilemmas in teaching (Lampert, 1981) or to observe and make sense of what goes on in classrooms (Erickson, in press).

Elbaz explores different ways that teachers use their practical knowledge which is formulated in response to the situations they encounter. Teachers use practical knowledge to express purposes, give shape and meaning to their experiences, and structure social realities. All these uses are conditioned by the way teachers conceive of theory, practice, and their relationship.

Separating the different uses of practical knowledge is helpful for purposes of analysis, but in practice, teachers' knowledge functions as an organized whole, orienting the teacher to her situation and allowing her to act. Elbaz illustrates this in her discussion of Sarah's decision to stop teaching English and to work in the Reading Center. As Sarah became more uncomfortable with the "back to basics" stance of the English department and with the "phony power structure" of the classroom, she found the Reading Center to be a more congenial social framework. Here she could function as a person with skills to share rather than as an authority figure. Sarah used her practical knowledge to structure a new social reality which would express her goals as a teacher and help resolve the tensions she felt from the demands of the department, her own views of literature, and the students' indifference to English.

Lampert (1981; 1984) also shows how teachers use their knowledge to resolve tensions, in this case tensions between the interpersonal and institutional aspects of teaching. Although Lampert's findings about the personal nature of teachers' knowledge accord with Lortie's and Jackson's claims, her interpretation moves in a different direction. Rather than inferring some deficiency in teachers, she argues that teachers use their personal knowledge to manage practical dilemmas. Over and over again, the teachers in her study illustrate how they managed to teach without having to make the dichotomous choices social scientists associate with the teachers's role (e.g., to satisfy either personal goals or institutional requirements; to foster either human development or academic excellence).

According to Lampert, teachers use their personal knowledge of children, what they know about a particular child, and what seems like the appropriate teacher role, to accommodate to the classroom requirements of time and curriculum as well as to a child's own knowledge, interests, and feelings. Through specific examples of encounters between teachers and students, Lampert illustrates "a complicated personal and practical process of accommodation" (p. 149) in which teachers express their responsibilites to both students and society.

Like Elbaz, Erickson (in press) shows how early elementary teachers use practical knowledge to make sense out of what happens in their classroom. Through observations, informal interviewing, and discussion of classroom videotapes, Erickson found that teachers use their knowledge of students and the yearlong curriculum to simplify their view of the classroom and to interpret specific things children do. The two teachers that Erickson studied looked at their students as multidimensional, viewing their academic work in the context of an annual curriculum cycle and attending to different aspects of an activity at different points in the year. This attention to different features of a situation over time resembles the strategy of dilemma management that Lampert describes.

By showing how teachers use their personal and practical knowledge to resolve tensions, manage dilemmas, and simplify the complexities of their work, researchers underscore the critical role of teachers' knowledge in teaching.

HOW TEACHERS' KNOWLEDGE IS ORGANIZED

Different forms of practical knowledge enable people to engage in different kinds of performances. For example, mastery of specific ways of acting in particular situations makes one less capable of responding to variable situations. Knowing the connections between different actions and their consequences provides tested ways of meeting similar situations in the future but will not help in anticipating a changing future (Schwab, 1959). In describing the structure of teachers' practical knowledge, researchers have begun to explore how practical knowledge is ordered and what uses its different structuring elements make possible.

To describe the organization of Sarah's knowledge, Elbaz distinguishes three levels that reflect varying degrees of generality: rules of practice, practical principles, and images. A rule of practice is a brief, clearly formulated statement of what to do in a particular situation. In using a rule of practice, the ends or purposes of action are taken for granted. For example, Sarah has a rule for dealing with a learning-disabled student: "he has my full attention *after* I finish all the instructions" (p. 133).

A practical principle is a broader, more inclusive statement that enbodies a rationale. The use of practical principles involves reflection. When Sarah talks of trying to make the kids happy to walk into her classroom, she states a principle regarding remedial work with students. This principle governs a variety of practices ranging from unstructured talk to coaching a student for an upcoming exam. It reflects her beliefs about the relationship between students' emotional state and their subsequent learning.

Images capture the teacher's knowledge and purposes at the most general level, orienting her overall conduct rather than directing specific actions. "The teacher's feelings, values, needs and beliefs combine as she forms images of how teaching should be, and marshals experience, theoretical knowledge, school folklore to give substance to these images" (p. 134). The image of a "window" captures the orienting purposes of Sarah's work: She wanted "to have a window onto the kids and what they are thinking" and she wanted her own window, in turn, to be more open.

The concept of images could be useful in studying teachers' practical knowledge. Images mediate between thought and action at a more general level than rules and principles and show how different kinds of knowledge and values come together in teaching. Images express the teachers' purposes. Because they are open, taking on different senses in different situations, images guide teachers intuitively, inspiring rather than determining their actions. Rules and principles embody instructional knowledge but images order all aspects of practical knowledge. Images also extend knowledge by generating new rules and principles and by helping to choose among them when they conflict.

Another structuring of teachers' knowledge that mediates between thought and action comes from Bussis, Chittenden, and Amarel's (1976) interview study of 60 teachers trying to implement more open and informal approaches in the classroom. While the researchers acknowledge that commitment to an open education philosophy is critical in implementing such an approach, they do not describe how such a commitment and the requisite knowledge, which is the focus of their study, interact. This was not their intent. Still we can imagine how the concept of image might serve to capture the way different kinds of knowledge combine with experience, values, and beliefs in creating and running an open classroom. Differences in the imagery that open-classroom teachers hold may explain some of the variation the researchers found in teachers' beliefs about children and curriculum.

The researchers conceptualized teachers' beliefs about curriculum and students in terms of classroom activities (surface content), the teacher's learning priorities for children (organizing content), and the connections between the two. A picture of the surface curriculum was reconstructed from teachers' responses to questions about a typical day, the kind of planning they did outside of school, the physical setup of the classroom, and the materials and equipment in the room. Recurring themes suggested organizing priorities. Connections were inferred when teachers' talk moved back and forth between classroom activities and organizing priorities, with specific encounters illustrating broader concerns and broader priorities related to specific instances.

The researchers found that teachers differed in the number and strength of the connections they saw between their priorities and what was going on in their classroom. For example, teachers with more and clearer priorities tended to value materials that could serve a variety of learning purposes. The researchers relate this to the knowledge a teacher uses to recognize and realize a learning priority (knowledge of materials, subject matter, children, and the learning process).

JUDGING THE WORTH OF TEACHERS' KNOWLEDGE

These studies of teachers' knowledge project an image of the teacher as someone who holds and uses knowledge to shape the work situation and guide practice. By opening up teachers' knowledge to inquiry, researchers are making a statement that the content of teachers' minds is worth investigating on its own terms. Studies of teachers' practical knowledge can greatly advance our understanding of teaching as long as researchers are sensitive to underlying epistemological issues as well as to questions about the sociology of teachers' knowledge.

Because of teachers' position in the school hierarchy, their personal knowledge often carries less authority than more objective data. The teachers in Lampert's study, for example, felt that the school's preoccupation with standardized, impersonal measures made their deepest concerns seem solipsistic and their personal knowledge unreal (p. 213).

Different forms of knowledge may be more helpful at different levels in the school system. What administrators want to know about student achievement is different from what teachers want to know (Amarel & Chittenden, 1982). Still, norms and practices that devalue teachers' knowledge contribute to their deskilling and undermine the quality of their work (Apple, 1982; see also the subsequent discussion, in this chapter, of the feminization of teaching).

Such norms and practices also ignore the critical role that personal knowledge plays in teaching. As Lampert (1981) puts it, the answer to why Johnny can't read will not be found in a book. Johnny's teacher must pull together her knowledge of learning to read with what she knows about Johnny from her personal relationship with him and decide what she wants to have happen, monitoring his progress and changing her goals and practice adaptively.

It does not follow, however, that everything a teacher believes or is willing to act on merits the label "knowledge," although that view has some support. Such a position makes the concept of knowledge as justified belief meaningless. How then can we evaluate teachers' knowledge? Buchmann (1983b, 1984) addresses this question in her analytic work on knowledge use and justification in teaching. Teachers must inevitably act on incomplete and uncertain evidence while maintaining their faith in the appropriateness of what they do. Precisely because of these conditions, it is critical that teachers' beliefs be justified on the basis of public criteria (e.g., colleagues, the curriculum, equity) rather than private ones (e.g., personal preferences) and held open to new evidence and subsequent revision.

Buchmann's arguments are well taken. Applied to research on teachers' knowledge, they raise important questions about how such knowledge develops and on what grounds it changes. Still, her analysis might be more appropriate for knowledge that comes in the form of propositions, leaving researchers with the challenge of formulating criteria that can be used to evaluate teachers' images.

Despite the diversity of teaching cultures, research on norms for interaction, occupational rewards, and teachers' knowledge has found shared ways of thinking that set groups of teachers apart from the general population. While Waller's (1932) claim that one could easily pick out the teachers in a crowd is an overstatement, experienced teachers do see their world differently. We address the questions of why teaching cultures have taken their current forms and how individuals acquire a teaching culture in the remainder of this chapter.

The Genesis of Teaching Cultures

Part of understanding the cultures of teaching involves understanding their genesis. How does it happen that teachers share certain sentiments or views of their work? What accounts for prevailing patterns of knowledge use in teaching? How do the norms that govern teachers' interactions with parents, students, and administrators evolve? How did teaching come to have low status? Why is it that common instructional practices prevail? These are questions about the origins of teaching cultures. In the previous section we were concerned with research that paints a picture of the cultures of teaching by describing shared sentiments, habits of mind, and patterns of interaction. In this section we focus on research that seeks to account for the genesis of these aspects of teaching cultures.

Some researchers have tried to explain all or part of the cultures of teaching in terms of individual characteristics. From this perspective, the fact that teachers share common outlooks simply shows that people with similar backgrounds and personalities go into teaching. While this kind of explanation may account for some of the shared meanings teachers attach to their work, it ignores the influences that stem from the contexts of teaching itself.

The most immediate context of teaching is the classroom. Since Jackson's (1968) classic study of life in classrooms, researchers have focused on how common features of the classroom environment shape common patterns of belief and behavior in teachers. Teachers not only work in classrooms, they also work in institutions which surround them with constraints and opportunities. These organizational properties represent a second source of influence on the cultures of teaching. Finally, schools function in a larger social context that shapes and is, in turn, shaped by what goes on there. Thus the cultures of teaching also reflect the influence of economic, social, and political factors.

In this section, we draw on studies that account for aspects of teaching cultures in terms of classroom, organizational, and societal influences. For example, aspects of practical knowledge and teacher–student relations have been related to the properties of classrooms; norms of interaction and rewards in teaching have been connected to school structure; and teacher status and self-image have been linked with the role of women in our society. While these examples do not cover all the external influences that researchers have studied, they do illustrate a common thesis — that the cultures of teaching are shaped by the contexts of teaching.

The Classroom Context

From an ecological perspective, classrooms have distinctive environmental properties that shape teachers' responses. Researchers have called attention to the complexity and immediacy of classroom events, and to the fact that they occur in groups, linking these features to teachers' sentiments, habits of mind, and patterns of behavior.

CLASSROOM PRESS

Classrooms are complicated and busy settings serving a variety of purposes and containing a variety of processes and events. Teachers must manage groups, deal with individual needs and responses, maintain records, evaluate student abilities, promote learning, establish routines. Jackson (1968) found that elementary teachers engage in 200–300 exchanges every hour of their working day. Not only do teachers have a variety of things to do, they must often attend to more than one thing at a time. As they help individual students, teachers must monitor the rest of the class. As they conduct lessons, they must anticipate interruptions, distribute opportunities to speak, and keep an eye on the time. Smith and Geoffrey's (1968) characterization of the teacher as a "ringmaster" seems apt.

The immediacy and complexity of classroom life have been linked with the preference of many teachers for simple explanations and practical solutions and with their resistance to proposals for change. The sheer number and pace of events call for quick and decisive actions. The workday offers little time to unravel the complex causes of the reality teachers face. Some researchers have questioned whether a deeper level of understanding would help teachers cope with the here and now (Jackson, 1968). Others have sought to uncover the tacit knowledge gained through on-the-job experience, knowledge that enables teachers to accommodate the demands of classroom life. For example, Erickson is studying how teachers' "practical ways of seeing" help reduce the complexity of classroom life and allow for selective attention to salient features of student performance. (See the foregoing discussion of teachers' practical knowledge).

Teachers' alleged conservatism has also been linked to the pressing demands of the present. Doyle and Ponder (1977) found that teachers were most receptive to proposals for change that fit with current classroom procedures and did not cause major disruptions. Those who criticize teachers for maintaining this "practicality ethic" may underestimate the added complications that flow from attempts to alter established practice and the degree to which current practices are highly adaptive to classroom realities. For example, most teachers probably find it easier to instruct the whole class than to set up and monitor multiple and simultaneous learning centers. As historians of instructional practices argue, certain formats like the recitation persist because they fit the environmental demands of classrooms (Cuban, 1984; Hoekter & Ahlbrand, 1969).

TEACHING IN A GROUP

The group-based nature of classrooms accounts for some of the fundamental ambiguities in the student–teacher relationship. (See the foregoing discussion of norms of interaction.) Unlike tutors who work with one student, teachers work with groups of 25 to 30 students. The number and diversity of students create a host of individual and group needs. Since many students do not come to school voluntarily, teachers cannot count on their willingness to do assigned tasks. Thus the teacher has the dual responsibility of maintaining attention and control over the group, while generating an openness to learning. These two tasks often seem incompatible. The former requires a certain distance, while the latter often depends on personal interest and involvement. The group context also means that actions directed toward one student are visible to others and may set a precedent. Thus in dealing with individuals, teachers must always be conscious of the message to the rest of the class (Dreeben, 1973; Waller, 1932).

The ecological argument links aspects of teaching cultures with certain properties of classroom environments. For example, the fact that classrooms contain groups of students means that teachers have both managerial and instructional responsibilities. The range of options for carrying out these responsibilities is also limited by these same classroom properties. From this perspective, parts of the cultures of teaching can be seen as the outcome of a process of adaptation to the environmental demands of classrooms. As we shall see in our discussion of how teaching cultures are acquired, this process of adaptation is particularly noticeable in the novice who must "learn the ecology of the classroom" in order to succeed as a teacher (Doyle, 1977a, 1977b; Zeichner, 1983).

Organizational Determinants of the Cultures of Teaching

While the "facts" of classroom life probably impinge most directly on teachers, the structure of schools also shape what they do and how they think about their work. Researchers have accounted for aspects of the cultures of teaching by analyzing the influence of schools as institutions. For example, the cellular structure of schools has been linked with a norm of noninterference among teachers. The authority structure has been associated with teachers' sentiments about what constitutes outside help and what feels like interference. Moreover, in discussing the sources of frustration in their work, teachers point to tensions between the job and the work of teaching. One manifestation of this tension is the incompatibility between institutional goals and teachers' goals, a common theme in teacher writing and in research on what teaching does to teachers.

CELLULAR STRUCTURE

Although teachers may work in isolation in open-space schools or work together despite physical barriers, the egg-crate architecture of many schools and the school schedule encourage teacher isolation. Teachers are cut off from their colleagues because they spend most of the day in their own classrooms. Typically teachers have (or make) few opportunities to observe each other or to talk with one another about their work. (See Little, 1982 for exceptions.) While external conditions alone do not account for teacher isolation and uncertainty, they make it harder for teachers to know how well they are doing or to see what others are doing. Sarason (1982) captures the psychological effects of the geographical properties of most schools: "The teacher is alone with problems and dilemmas, constantly thrown back on personal resources, having little or no interpersonal vehicles available for purposes of stimulation, change or control" (p. 162).

Some researchers link the cellular organization of schools with the norms of individualism and noninterference among teachers. The modal spatial arrangement encourages privacy, hence a prevailing norm of noninterference. In most schools, the classroom is considered inviolate. Teachers are not supposed to invade one another's classrooms or advise on methods or content unless directly asked. The physical isolation conveys the message that teachers ought to cope with their problems on their own, reinforcing the norm of individualism. Working it out alone comes to be accepted as the way it should be in teaching.

These effects of the cellular structure may be seen either as an unfortunate lack of mutual support or as a welcome guarantee of professional autonomy. The uncertainties of teaching are exacerbated by the fact that teachers cannot easily turn to one another for help and support. This reality is especially salient for the novice who must "sink or swim" alone (Lortie, 1975; Zeichner & Grant, 1981). The flip side of teacher isolation, however, is a certain amount of freedom. Teachers value the opportunity to run their classrooms as they see fit. A fifth grade teacher interviewed by Jackson (1968) put it bluntly: "If they made teaching too rigid or started telling me that I must use this book or that book and could not bring in supplementary materials of my own, then I'd quit" (p. 129). Still, without clear criteria for evaluating teaching and consensus about the goals of instruction, this freedom carries a heavy responsibility. While it may evoke great effort in some teachers, others can get by doing very little (Cusick, 1983).

THE PRINCIPAL'S AUTHORITY

The issue of teacher autonomy is often linked with the structure of authority relations in schools. The school assigns formal authority to the principal. Through the allocation of prized resources—materials, time, space—as well as through sanctions, the principal can exert considerable influence over teachers' working environment. As the chief administrative officer, the principal is expected to provide leadership, advice, supervision, and evaluation. The principal, however, is seldom seen as a respected expert on classroom practice (Biklen, 1983; Blumberg & Greenfield, 1980). Some teachers resent the fact that the person responsible for judging their competence observes them infrequently and knows less than they do about what is going on in their room. The fact that principals have more status and authority while teachers know more about teaching leads to feelings of ambivalence on the part of teachers toward their principal. (See the foregoing discussion of norms of interaction). When the principal places higher value on the impersonal, bureaucratic, and standardized aspects of schooling, teachers feel a conflict between the job and the work of teaching.

CONFLICTS BETWEEN THE JOB AND WORK OF TEACHING

The work of teaching includes all those aspects directly related to the realization of educational goals: motivating students,

getting to know them as individuals, assessing their understanding. The job of teaching is concerned with the realization of organizational or bureaucratic goals: maintaining order in classrooms and corridors, keeping students busy, categorizing students so that they can be processed by the administrative machinery. The tension between the organizational and personal aspects of teaching is a pervasive theme in the analytic and empirical literature on teaching (e.g., Berlak & Berlak, 1981; Dreeben, 1973; Jackson, 1968; Lortie, 1975). It also comes through when researchers describe teachers' views of their work (e.g., Biklen, 1983; Hall, 1982; Lampert, 1981; McPherson, 1972), and when teachers speak for themselves (Freedman, Jackson, & Boles, 1983).

The accumulation of administrative activities makes teaching difficult. The teacher must hold students' attention to get subject matter across, but the child coming for the attendance records, the intercom announcement of a football pep rally, and the surprise visit from a parent all break the spell (Lortie, 1975). For some teachers, these bothersome administrative tasks and interruptions reflect the low esteem that others have for them (Biklen, 1983). Wise (1979) documents the tremendous increase in administrative directives related to legal, judicial, and administrative policies that constrain teachers and take time away from teaching.

Often the tension between the job and the work of teaching is cast in terms of conflicting goals and standards. Many teachers want student learning to be based on individual needs, yet their schools expect them to improve standardized test scores, cover prescribed curricula at a set pace, and maintain an orderly classroom. Administrators and parents pay more attention to report cards and test scores than to whether students understand what they are being taught. In most schools, teachers are judged by how well their students do on standardized tests and how quietly they move through the halls, not by how well teachers know them. Teachers are supposed to provide equal educational opportunities, but school structures emphasize comparative worth and increase competition among students, teachers, and parents.

The literature on teacher socialization and teacher burnout describes the effects of this underlying tension on the cultures of teaching. (See the subsequent section on the acquisition of teaching cultures). As the job of teaching intrudes on the work of teachers, many redefine their goals in managerial terms (Lipsky, 1980). The difficulties of defining and measuring teaching success combine with institutional requirements to encourage the substitution of such goals as covering material and keeping students busy and quiet. While the phrase "teacher burnout" connotes the depletion of the individual's inner resources, Freedman et al. (1983) argue that "burnout" more accurately refers to the anger and frustration teachers feel at having to cope with conflicting institutional demands and societal expectations.

Lampert (1981) found that teachers use their personal knowledge to manage the dilemmas in their work environments. (See the foregoing discussion of teachers' knowledge). On the other hand, Gitlin (1983) shows how the use of individualized curricula with predetermined, sequential objectives keeps teachers from using their personal knowledge to influence the direction of student learning. In an ethnographic study of two teams of teachers working with such a curriculum, Gitlin found that objectives, set problems, and posttests shaped teachers' relations with students.

Teachers' integrity is threatened when school organizations ignore what they think is essential to their teaching—their personal caring and knowledge of students. As one teacher put it, teaching and learning seem incongruent in an organization that lets people who "have never met the children" make "big decisions about how they will be educated" (Lampert, 1981, p. 221).

Some teachers in Lampert's study saw the tensions between the personal standards internal to the classroom and the external measures of students' and teachers' accomplishments as a distinction between feminine and masculine perspectives on work. These teachers struggled "to bring together the individualistic and wholistic [sic] caring for human persons, which is usually associated with women's roles in the family, with their feelings about, and responsibilities for, accomplishments in their jobs, which are measured by the impersonal, task-specific, generalized standards of the workplace" (p. 240).

This struggle is part of a larger struggle that women face in a society that devalues their work. As school priorities reflect the values of the dominant society, so the cultures of teaching are shaped by the social forces that surround them. Because the quality of teaching is intimately related to a view of teaching as "women's work," and directly affected by recent changes in opportunities for women, we chose this focus to illustrate how social forces influence the cultures of teaching, and the ways social scientists have studied teachers.

Teaching as Women's Work

Most teachers are women. They represent 83% of the elementary teachers, 49% of the secondary teachers and 68% of all teachers (Feistritzer, 1983). Beyond this numerical domination is the prevailing view of teaching as women's work. This association has affected the status of teaching and the self-image of teachers. It also may explain why few scholars, until recently, have shown much interest in studying the perspectives of women who teach.

Some historians and sociologists have begun to rectify the situation by putting women teachers at the center of their inquiries. Two related lines of work can be discerned. First, historical and contemporary portraits of teaching from the inside have been gathered in order to show how gender affects the social construction of work experience (Biklen, 1983; Hall, 1982; Lightfoot, 1983; Nelson, 1983). For example, the recognition that most teachers are women leads to studies about the intersection of work and career, home and school, since it is women who carry the "double burden" in our society. This research challenges traditional social science views of teachers and offers new insights about the cultures of teaching.

A second line of work traces the origins of teacher stereotypes, linking the social devaluation of teaching to its feminization in the nineteenth century (Hoffman, 1981; Lightfoot, 1983; Richardson & Hatcher, 1983; Sugg, 1978). Beyond the social and economic factors, the low status of teaching reflects the cultural perception of teacher as woman. Given the influence of the women's movement, this imagery makes it harder for those

who teach to identify proudly with their occupation and discourages the more talented from considering it.

Under this topic, we summarize the arguments that link cultural images of teaching to the economic conditions and social roles of women in the 19th century. We show how research on elementary school teaching reflects normative expectations and cultural stereotypes of women. Finally we illustrate how new perspectives on the lives of women teachers point to new conceptualizations of the cultures of teaching.

THE "SPECIAL BUT SHADOWED" STATUS OF TEACHERS

The transformation of teaching from a temporary job for men to a "profession for women" was accompanied by a transformation in popular thinking. With the help of leaders of the common school movement, the image of the teacher shifted from "a second rate man to an exemplary women" (Hoffman, 1981). From the 1840s through the Civil War, annual reports of school superintendents extolled the special qualifications of women for teaching. Horace Mann, in his *Fourth Annual Report*, argued that "females were infinitely more fit than males to be guides and exemplars of young children" because of their "gentle manner and superior nature," their indifference to honors and future status, their desire to remain close to home rather than move out into the world (pp. 45-48, passim). Among the early image makers was Catharine Beecher, an advocate of teaching as "women's true profession," who saw the school as an extension of the domestic sphere.

These arguments were constructed in response to major social changes. Rapid urbanization and industrialization were creating new economic opportunities for men, and immigration was increasing the number of school-age children in cities. As women were needed to care for children in schools, their presumed frailties were converted into strengths (Lightfoot, 1983). Still the economic argument was probably the most compelling one to taxpayers and male school boards (Elsbree, 1939; Tyack, 1974). Women could be employed for one-half to one-third the cost of men.

Kaestle (1983) also links the feminization of teaching with the reorganization of schools. Hiring women allowed reformers to press for school innovations such as supervision and grading since gender differences fit with their view that female assistants should serve under male principal teachers, thus forming "an enduring gender-oriented hierarchy in elementary schooling" (p. 220).

The feminization of teaching had important effects on the lives of the women who taught. By the turn of the century, teaching had changed the opportunities of many young women from different social classes whose only other options included domestic service, marriage, or factory work. Still, teaching did not (and does not) have the status and respect of men's work.

THE INFLUENCE OF FEMALE STEREOTYPES

The feminization of teaching in the 19th century was accompanied by cultural stereotypes that continue to influence what others expect of teachers and how teachers view themselves. According to feminist researchers, these cultural stereotypes are perpetuated by social scientists whose perspectives on teachers reflect views of women in general.

For example, some sociologists (Geer, 1968; Dreeben, 1970; Lortie, 1975) have argued that women teachers lack a strong commitment to their work. They cite women's movement in and out of teaching to bear and raise children as evidence of low career commitment. They also assume that women have less stake than men in the economic rewards of teaching.

Teaching is considered an ideal job for women not only because it is compatible with family life, but because it draws on qualities thought to be associated with women—"the traditional womanly dimensions of nurturance, receptivity, passivity" (Lightfoot, 1978, p. 64). The historic emphasis in elementary teaching on character building rather than intellectual development is perpetuated in this idealized image.

Much research on schoolteachers takes these traditional images for granted and assumes that teaching, like other female occupations, appeals more to the emotions than the intellect (Simpson & Simpson, 1969). Jackson (1968) argues that elementary teachers exercise their feminine birthright when they base their actions on intuition and feeling rather than reason.

Teachers are not bound by this cultural imagery and the political behavior of many teachers today defies the traditional stereotype. Still, there is evidence that these expectations do affect the perspectives and behavior of many teachers. Hall (1982) found that, unlike men teachers, women teachers often played passive, submissive roles in contact with principals. "Even where principals built colleagial relations with women teachers, ... they referred to faculty as 'the girls' or expected them to cook things for school gatherings" (p. 56). (See also the discussion of the relationship between mothers and teachers in Bilken, 1983 and Lightfoot, 1978).

NEW UNDERSTANDINGS OF WOMEN TEACHERS

New scholarship on women who teach is challenging old stereotypes by raising new questions and offering new frameworks for analyzing the lives of women teachers. In their focus on the meaning of work in women's lives, researchers seek to clarify why women teach and to examine the consistency and strength of their commitment to home and school.

The traditional concept of a career as a succession of related jobs arranged in a hierarchy of prestige does not fit the realities of teaching or the way teachers view their work. Generally women do not have the luxury of concentrating on their careers in a single-minded way. The fact that women teachers have multiple commitments, however, does not necessarily mean that their work comes second (Hall, 1982). Some women integrate domestic and professional roles by choosing work that draws on characteristics and qualities traditionally associated with women (Bernard, 1974). Within a context of traditional assumptions about women and their roles, teachers could more easily integrate their commitments to home and work. For example, in country schools, teachers were allowed to bring small children with them, a flexibility that was lost in the move to consolidated and graded schools where such a practice was unthinkable (Nelson, 1983).

Biklen (1983) provides evidence of teachers' strong and consistent commitment to their work in her yearlong study of women faculty in a respected New England school serving students from a variety of social classes. The teachers she interviewed did not follow the well-integrated, planned career path associated with professionals. Still they often displayed a consistent commitment to teaching in their daily work, in their intense desire to return to teaching after periods at home with children, and in their disinterest in becoming principals. "These teachers focused their energy on the context of the work, not on its use to them for upward mobility. Hence their major frustrations came, not when their hopes for advancement were crushed, but rather when they were forced to make compromises which they felt endangered their educational vision" (p. 44). These findings underscore the need for a model that more accurately describes career commitment in a setting dominated by women.

The fact that many teachers feel a strong commitment to teaching does not mean that they identify proudly with their occupation. The social devaluation of teaching affects all teachers, even those who do not identify with the women's movement. The teachers in Biklen's study, for example, did not want teachers to be undervalued (or underpaid). They wanted the recognition that they worked hard at a challenging job and the status that such a reevaluation would bring. Many did not see that the status of elementary school teaching was related to its association with young children.

Feminism has contributed to rising expectations for women, but the social image of teachers has remained the same or perhaps has even diminished. Once the job for ordinary men, teaching is now seen as ordinary work for ordinary women. With more women in the workplace, proportionally fewer are going into teaching. Those who do have a harder time feeling good about their occupational choice. If younger teachers had to do it over again, they say they would pick a job with higher status and more pay (Biklen, 1983; Feistritzer, 1983; Lampert, 1981). This is not because young teachers dislike their job. On the contrary, many love their work, but say it does not compensate for the costs in income and self-esteem.

This review of the overlapping and often conflicting influences that shape the cultures of teaching underscores the difficulties of the job and the need to attract and retain capable individuals. A full appreciation of the impact of ecological demands, institutional expectations, and social forces should engender respect for teachers who do an excellent job and help explain why such people might want to leave teaching.

In this discussion we did not try to be exhaustive; much more could be said about the influence of other factors (economic, political, historical, and curricular) in shaping the cultures of teaching. For example, proponents of social reproduction theories view prevailing school norms and practices as mirrors of dominant social realities and as mechanisms for preserving them. From this perspective, social forces create teaching cultures in which teachers unwittingly perpetuate social inequities.

Taken together, these accounts leave little room for teachers to question the givens, make independent choices, negotiate demands. While the literature on teachers' socialization reviewed in the next section suffers from the same bias, research on teacher development assumes considerable teacher autonomy. Perhaps there is a middle ground where teachers function as policy brokers (Schwille et al., 1983), playing a role in determining how outside influences will shape what they do.

Acquiring the Cultures of Teaching

"People in a similar line of work are likely to share at least some common thoughts and feelings about that work. Such convergence can arise from the diffusion of a subculture. On the other hand, it may derive from common responses to common contingencies" (Lortie, 1975, p. 162). Although few thoughts and feelings are likely to be shared by all teachers, the existence of common perspectives, even within subgroups of teachers, calls for explanation. In the previous section we considered accounts of how the contexts of teaching influence the cultures of teaching. In this section we consider how individual teachers acquire a teaching culture.

One can ask whether individual teachers learn these views (intentionally or unintentionally) from other educators, or whether they come up with such views on their own. These alternatives suggest that some explanations will be based on the effects of socialization while others will be based on a process of development in individual teachers.

Teacher Socialization

Research on teacher socialization investigates the transmission of teacher beliefs, knowledge, attitudes, and values. Various definitions of socialization have been used, ranging from Merton's (Merton, Reader, & Kendall, 1957) inclusive definition which encompasses virtually all changes in teachers through any means (e.g., Zeichner, 1983), to narrower definitions that focus on how novice teachers, through interaction with experienced colleagues, come to hold the set of values or practices shared by that group.

Most studies of teacher socialization focus on student teaching and the first year of teaching, periods that are probably central to any process for passing on a teaching culture. During these periods, the novice imitates other teachers and learns from them about the acceptability of different ways of acting. Acquiring appropriate attitudes toward student discipline (e.g., Hoy, 1967, 1968, 1969; Hoy & Rees, 1977; Willower, 1968) is a widely described example. While experienced teachers seem overly strict with their students, new teachers may begin to imitate this model because they associate it with teaching success. At the same time, they may also experience disapproval by veteran teachers of their own more lenient approaches. Waller (1932) has written eloquently on this process, using the term "dignity" to refer to the authority role that teachers learn to maintain through interaction with their colleagues:

> Most of all is dignity enforced by one's fellow teachers. The significant people for a school teacher are other teachers, and by comparison with good standing in the fraternity the good opinion of students is a small thing and of little price. ... According to the teacher code there is no worse offense than failure to deport one's self with dignity, and the penalties exacted for the infraction of the code are severe. (p. 389)

Other groups have the potential to influence the novice, but none has been shown to play as large a role as experienced teachers. Although the formal power available to school administrators suggests their potential as powerful socializing agents (Edgar & Warren, 1969), the limited contact between teachers and principals usually limits their actual contribution (Burden, 1979; Grant & Zeichner, 1981; Isaacson, 1981). Typically the socializing power of the university is described as weak compared with the competing norms of schools; the argument that the effects of university socialization are "washed out" by school experience is described (but not endorsed) by Zeichner and Tabachnick (1981). Fellow novices play a significant role in medical socialization (e.g., Becker, Geer, Hughes, & Strauss, 1961) but they have received little attention in teacher education. Research on how student thought and action affect teaching and learning (e.g., Anderson, 1981; Doyle, 1977b; Weinstein, 1982) highlights the important role of pupils in determining teacher behaviors (Applegate, et al., 1977; Doyle, 1979; Haller, 1967; Zeichner, 1983). This research tends to focus on teachers' adaptation to classroom press rather than on how teachers acquire the expectations pupils hold for them.

While the metaphors of molding and shaping provide vivid images of the process of teacher socialization, research in the past decade raises questions about whether experienced teachers abide by a single set of norms, whether new teachers change significantly, and whether they are merely passive recipients of a teaching culture. Since different groups of teachers share different norms, beginning teachers may not encounter a unified effort to socialize them. Other factors further limit the strength of socialization forces. Lortie (1975, chapter 3) emphasizes the brevity of student teaching and the isolation of beginning teachers from their colleagues. He also argues that the absence of a technical subculture reduces the impact of socialization even if there were more interaction among teachers.

There are also problems with the common assumption that the attitudes and values teachers acquire at the university conflict with those they encounter at schools. First, the belief that university programs endorse liberal values has not been tested (Zeichner & Tabachnick, 1981). Moreover, there is some evidence that university values are congruent with those encountered in schools (e.g., Bartholomew, 1976). Tabachnick, Popkewitz, and Zeichner (1979–1980) found discrepancies between program rhetoric and the messages university faculty give students in courses and in the field.

Not only are socialization pressures weak, but beginners are not easily changed (Lacey, 1977; Power, 1981; Zeichner & Tabachnick, 1983). Following Lacey (1977), a number of researchers have focused on different ways students and beginning teachers may respond to school and university norms. Teachers may conform to expectations, believing that those expectations are appropriate. Lacey calls this internalized adjustment. They may adjust their behavior in line with expectations, but inwardly maintain reservations. He calls this strategic compliance. Finally, teachers may work to modify the expectations, strategically redefining the situation. Zeichner and Tabachnick (1983) found examples of all three strategies among the student teachers and beginning teachers they studied.

Emphasis on the resistance of beginners to the effects of the workplace may underestimate the extent to which teaching culture is transmitted from one generation of teachers to the next. Those entering teacher preparation have already had more interactions with experienced teachers than they may ever have again. Twelve or so years of elementary and secondary school provide opportunities to receive messages about what teachers do. Moreover, as pupils, teacher education students were motivated to imagine what their teachers were thinking as a way of anticipating their actions and reactions. This "apprenticeship of observation" (Lortie, 1975) may have a potent albeit undesirable effect on teacher beliefs and values. There has been some research on the effect of this apprenticeship (Tabachnick, Zeichner, Densmore, Adler, & Egan, 1982) but little attention to the process itself. Wright and Tuska (1968) are an exception, but they focus on the psychodynamic effects of family experiences rather than on the unconscious modeling effects in the classroom.

Reconsideration of the power of teacher socialization is important in placing this approach to acquiring a teaching culture in perspective. The term "socialization" itself is neutral. While researchers sometimes describe the socialization goals of schooling positively (e.g., Prawat & Anderson, 1983), *teacher* socialization often has negative connotations. Those who study the process are seen as investigating the undesirable effects of the workplace (e.g., Hoy & Rees, 1977; Lacey, 1977; Popkewitz, 1979; Waller, 1932).

There are at least two explanations for these negative overtones. First, the value of socialization depends on the value attached to the norms of the group to which the individual is being socialized. Child socialization is viewed positively because of the value placed on the learned patterns of behavior. Those who study teacher socialization often find existing practices far from ideal (e.g., Popkewitz, 1979). They believe that existing practices emphasize management and order or support current social class structures, rather than their ideals of creativity, learning, and equity. The educational ideals of the researchers shape the way they interpret teacher change, just as the researchers' views of the ideal career shape the way they describe teachers' occupational commitment. Not surprisingly, these investigators see socialization as an undesirable process because it leads to the continuation of school practices they deplore.

The early literature on medical socialization provides an interesting contrast (e.g., Becker et al., 1961; Merton et al., 1957). Here the general value Americans place on the outcome of becoming a doctor gives the process of medical socialization a positive connotation, despite some lamentable features (e.g., that students decide what they need to learn to get by, rather than respecting their professors' views of what they need to know). As problems with current medical practices gain more attention, medical socialization is viewed more critically (e.g., Freidson, 1970, 1975).

Teacher socialization might be viewed more favorably if it were looked at in the context of an exemplary group of teachers. For example, researchers might endorse the socialization that occurs in one of the "successful" schools described by Little (1982) where the norms of collegiality and experimentation prevail.

A second explanation for the undesirable connotations of socialization is that the process tends to portray the novice as a passive agent molded by outside influences. This image makes the teacher powerless, buffeted by forces beyond conscious control. Many educational researchers would prefer a more flattering image of the novice teacher as an active agent in the change process.

Models of Teacher Development

Like research on teacher socialization, research on teacher development seeks to describe and explain patterns of change in at least some sections of the teaching population. The term "development" connotes internally guided rather than externally imposed changes. The image of teachers actively directing their professional growth is an added attraction for some investigators. Under this topic, we discuss the study of teacher development in general, briefly describe three approaches to this study, then focus on the tradition that seems most capable of explaining changes related to the cultures of teaching.

In considering how studies of teacher development contribute to understanding the acquisition of teaching cultures, it is important to separate claims about existing patterns of teacher change from statements advocating particular teacher education goals or techniques. Despite statements to the contrary (e.g., Sprinthall & Thies-Sprinthall, 1983, p. 31), implications for the proper aims of teacher education do not directly flow from descriptions of development. The final stage of development is not necessarily the desired outcome of teacher education. Conversely, disagreement with the espoused development goals is not sufficient reason for rejecting the associated descriptions of patterns of change. Furthermore, because the links between developmental theories and recommended teacher education practices are often tenuous, theoretical claims and practical suggestions must be evaluated independently. One can learn about teacher change from a description of the stages many teachers pass through, without accepting the associated recommendations.

Descriptions of teacher development make it tempting to stress instruction "matched" to teachers' current stage. It is dangerous to assume, however, that observed patterns of change are the only ones possible, and even more dangerous to assume that instruction should be restricted to features central to a given stage. Just as theories of child development may serve to justify teaching practices that maintain children at their current levels of performance (e.g., Sharp & Green, 1975), theories of teacher development may lead to unwarranted acceptance of teachers' current performance.

At present no full-blown theory of teacher development exists. The developmental approaches to the study of teacher change either stop short of linking developmental theory to teacher change, or describe teacher change without offering an encompassing theory. These approaches do provide a useful contrast to socialization theories and to many conventional practices in teacher education.

At least three distinct approaches to the study of teacher development appear in the literature (Feiman & Floden, 1980): a model of changes in teacher concerns, a model based on cognitive-developmental theories, and a style of inservice education emphasizing teachers' own definitions of their needs. The first approach grows out of Fuller's (e.g., Fuller, 1969) formulation of stages teachers pass through as they gain professional experience: a survival stage when teachers are preoccupied with their own adequacy, a mastery stage when teachers concentrate on performance and concerns focus on the teaching task, and an impact stage when teachers become concerned about their effects on pupils.

A second approach, advocated by Sprinthall and his associates (e.g., Sprinthall, 1980; Sprinthall & Thies-Sprinthall, 1983) rests on theories of cognitive development. Teacher development is considered a form of adult development and effective teaching a function of higher stages. The changes considered important in this theory are described in terms of a progression through levels of ego, moral, and conceptual development as defined by Hunt (1974), Kohlberg (1969), and Loevinger (1976). In this progression, higher stages are characterized by "increased flexibility, differentiation of feelings, respect for individuality, tolerance for conflict and ambiguity, the cherishing of interpersonal ties and a broader social perspective" (Witherell & Erickson, 1978).

A third approach to teacher development, elaborated primarily by practitioners, is a style of inservice work informed by a view of professional learning as "mental growth spurred from within" (Devaney, 1978). Teachers' centers and advisory services offer a contemporary expression of this way of working (for historic parallels, see Richey, 1957), which emphasizes responding to teachers' own definitions of their learning needs, supporting teachers in their own directions of growth, and building on teachers' motivation to take curricular responsibility. In this context, teacher development is also often described in terms of stages, culminating in a teacher who takes responsibility for curricular decision making. There is a strong implication that teachers who reach the final stage will have responsive and diversified classrooms where students have many opportunities to make choices about their learning.

Of these three, the changes described in the first approach most closely match the emphasis of this chapter on how teachers view their work. The second approach considers general changes in cognitive processes, rather than changes specific to teaching. While the third approach honors teachers' views, it is more an educational intervention than a description of teacher change.

Fuller's theory was motivated by her observation that many teachers go through the same pattern of change, acquiring a common perspective. In their first experiences leading classes, many teachers worry about whether they will survive. They try to discover the parameters of the school situation and to figure out where they stand. They wonder about their "abilities to understand subject matter, to know the answers, to say 'I don't know,' to have the freedom to fail on occasion, to anticipate problems, to mobilize resources and to make changes when failures reoccur" (Fuller, 1969. pp. 220–221). They are most concerned with discovering and meeting the expectations of others. With experience, teaching concerns take over. Teachers worry whether they are presenting content appropriately, whether they are displaying the right skills. and whether they are maintaining good control over their class. In the final stage,

teachers are typically concerned about pupil progress and about their own contribution to student learning. Rather than trying to please others or to fit an externally prescribed model, they trust their own evaluation of their work. "Mature" teacher concerns include the ability to understand pupils' capacities, to specify objectives for them, to assess their gain, to recognize one's own contribution to pupils' difficulties and gains, and to evaluate oneself in terms of pupil learning (Fuller, 1969, p. 221).

Fuller explains the common developmental pattern of teacher concerns in terms of a general human tendency to be preoccupied with basic needs until they are satisfied. For beginning teachers, the most basic need is to survive. Until this need has been satisfied, concerns about student learning cannot emerge.

One problem with Fuller's description of teacher development is its generality. Presumably a teacher concerned about having students master grade-level facts and skills would be just as mature as a teacher concerned about having students become self-motivated learners. Fuller also has little to say about the factors that hinder or speed the disappearance of survival concerns or about why mastery concerns are followed by impact concerns (as opposed to concerns about salary or working conditions).

Efforts to relate research on teacher development, research on teacher socialization, and accounts of the genesis of teaching cultures could deepen our understanding of how and why teachers change in particular ways. What, for example, is the relationship between overcoming survival and mastery concerns, and learning the ecology of the classroom? Do new teachers exhibit Fuller's progression of concerns in schools where the norms of collegiality and experimentation prevail? How does the tension between the job and the work of teaching affect teacher development?

Conclusion

We conclude with a summary and analysis of what has been learned about the cultures of teaching, a discussion of implications for teacher education and educational policy, and suggestions for future research in this area.

What Has Been Learned

In many respects, descriptions of the cultures of teaching in Lortie (1975), Jackson (1968), and even Waller (1932) are still valid: teachers use little research-based technical knowledge, their rewards come from students rather than from the institution, and interactions with administrators, parents, and other teachers tend to express teachers' desire to be left to themselves. Still, research in the last decade has challenged previous claims and assumptions.

Three changes are particularly salient. First, the assumption that a uniform culture of teaching exists is now untenable. Even Lortie, who questions the existence of a shared teaching culture, tends to write as though all teachers follow certain norms (e.g., the prohibition against asking another teacher for advice). The recent work of Little (1982), Metz (1978), and Zeichner and Tabachnik (1983) repeatedly documents differences among cultures in different schools, and even differences among subgroups of teachers within a school (Metz, 1978; Parelius, 1980).

Second, the study of teaching careers using male professionals and businessmen as templates has not done justice to teaching, an occupation dominated by women. The primary importance of career ambition and single-minded devotion may be appropriate for some occupations, but these characteristics need not be desirable in all teachers. For example, it could be advantageous for successful teachers to continue working in the classroom rather than aspiring to administrative work.

Third, following the lead of several social science disciplines, research on the cultures of teaching has begun to replace the image of a passive teacher molded by bureaucracy and buffeted by external forces with an image of the teacher as an active agent, constructing perspectives and choosing actions.

While it is encouraging that a decade's research has altered some research conclusions, one must ask whether the changes add to our knowledge about the cultures of teaching or merely reflect changes in the cultures themselves. If, as Cronbach (1975) puts it, "generalizations decay," what was true in 1950 may be invalidated by social changes. How much of what has been learned in the last decade will itself be invalidated in another decade? Historical perspective can place conclusions about the cultures of teaching in a proper light. Though educational research generally focuses on change and its antecedents, recent historical studies show that some characteristics of classrooms have been remarkably stable (e.g., Cuban, 1984). The recent shifts in career opportunities for women will almost certainly affect the cultures of teaching as will schemes for merit pay if they are widely adopted.

Implications for Teacher Education and Educational Policy

What has been learned about the cultures of teaching suggests that policies and practices related to induction programs, reward structures, and teacher preparation should be reexamined.

The heterogeneity of teaching cultures makes the prospects for school change more hopeful. While academics tend to bemoan the powerful school culture which reduces the aspirations and energies of all teachers to mediocrity, school cultures are not uniform. The fact that some are inspiring, not demoralizing, shows what is possible even without major structural changes. Acknowledging differences among schools also underscores the importance of placement in the induction of prospective and beginning teachers.

Feminist perspectives on the cultures of teaching require rethinking how school districts treat teachers. For example, recent policy initiatives to address the absence of rewards in teaching may be misguided in their exclusive focus on increases in merit pay and opportunities for career advancement. These solutions assume that teachers place most value on the extrinsic rewards of money and power. In fact, many teachers may value increased opportunities for collegial interaction or job sharing. The point is to offer an array of rewards that will meet teachers' needs.

Seeing teachers as active agents rather than passive workers suggests a different role for teachers in school and district

policy. Consistent with some of the literature that indicates a loose link between formal school policies and their effects (e.g., Elmore, 1983), this view suggests that policy should seek to build and strengthen teachers' abilities to make good educational decisions, rather than seeking to control every detail of their lives. This change in mode of working with teachers would elevate their status within the educational system and perhaps increase a district's ability to attract and hold capable teachers.

Consideration of teachers' tacit knowledge suggests a shift in the balance between teacher *education* and teacher *training*. The success of behaviorally oriented research on teaching encourages a technical skills approach in teacher preparation and renewal. Though technical skills are valuable, research on the cultures of teaching suggests that much of what teachers know does not fit the means–ends statements that summarize process–product research on teaching. Teacher education must build on or rebuild what teachers and teachers-to-be already believe about their work.

The Future of Research on the Cultures of Teaching

Two striking things about research on the cultures of teaching is how little there is and how hard it is to do. The dominance of behaviorist psychology in American educational research in this century may partly explain the fact that meanings, perspectives, and beliefs have only recently become respectable objects of study. The problem of making inferences about beliefs and knowledge was one factor that led to the flight to behaviorism. While the benefits of behaviorism proved too costly, the complexities of cognitive research have not vanished. Research on the cultures of teaching is labor intensive—observations and interviews take considerable time to conduct and analyze. Even well-supported studies can seldom go beyond a small sample of teachers. The variation in teaching cultures limits the generality of conclusions from any one study. Finally, the relationship of teaching cultures to the social systems of school, community, and society makes a multidisciplinary approach particularly fruitful. Unfortunately, multidisciplinary research cuts across the grain of academic disciplines.

A wide range of topics still need attention. The existence of hetereogeneity in teaching cultures has been documented, but researchers have barely begun to describe this variation systematically. Important cultural differences may be associated with age, experience, teaching philosophy, gender, social class, school norms, location, subject matter, and grade level.

There is much speculation but little evidence on the role that teachers' organizations play in shaping the cultures of teaching. Teachers' perceptions of the proper role of such organizations would be important information for school boards, the general public, and the organizations themselves. The work of Mitchell and his associates (Mitchell & Kerchner, 1983; Mitchell et al., 1981) suggests that teachers' organizations have produced basic changes in teachers' view of their job; this deserves further investigation.

Research on teachers' knowledge has just begun. Increased understanding of what this knowledge is like, how it develops, and how it is used should clarify the place of specialized and ordinary knowledge in teaching.

Finally, the recently publicized change in the characteristics of those entering teaching deserves special attention. Many have speculated that new career opportunities for women have robbed teaching of some of its best members. Research is needed to investigate the degree to which this change in entering members has affected the cultures of teaching.

Whatever topics are investigated in the next decades, the opportunity now exists to bring a variety of research methods to bear on questions about the cultures of teaching. Recent work provides models for the use of case studies, observation, videotapes, and interviews. The educational research community currently supports multidisciplinary inquiry. That support is particularly appropriate for enlarging the scope and relevance of research on the cultures of teaching.

REFERENCES

Amarel, M., & Chittenden, E. (1982, June). *A Conceptual study of knowledge use in schools.* Princeton, NJ: Educational Testing Service.

Anderson, L. M. (1981). *Student responses to classroom instruction* (Research Series No. 109). East Lansing: Michigan State University, College of Education. Institute for Research on Teaching. (ERIC Document Reproduction Service No. ED 212 626).

Apple, M. (1982). *Education and power.* Boston: Routledge & Kegan Paul.

Applegate, J., et al. (1977). *The first-year teacher study.* Columbus: Ohio State University. (ERIC Document Reproduction Service No. ED 135 766)

Bartholomew, J. (1976). Schooling teachers: The myth of the liberal college. In G. Whitty & M. Young (Eds.), *Explorations in the politics of school knowledge.* Driffield, North Humberside, England: Nafferton.

Becker, H. (1952). The career of the Chicago public school teacher. *American Journal of Sociology, 57,* 470–477.

Becker, H., Geer, B., Hughes, E., & Strauss, A. (1961). *Boys in white.* Chicago: University of Chicago Press.

Berlak, A., & Berlak, H. (1981). *Dilemmas of schooling: Teaching and social change.* New York: Methuen.

Bernard, J. (1974). *The future of motherhood.* New York: Penguin.

Biklen, S. K. (1983). *Teaching as an occupation for women: A case study of an elementary school.* Syracuse, NY: Education Designs Group.

Blumberg, A., & Greenfield, W. (1980). *The effective principal: Perspectives on school leadership.* Boston: Allyn & Bacon.

Buchmann, M. (1983a). *Argument and conversation as discourse models of knowledge use* (Occasional Paper No. 68). East Lansing: Michigan State University, Institute for Research on Teaching.

Buchmann, M. (1983b). *Role over person: Justifying teacher action and decision* (Research Series No. 135). East Lansing: Michigan State University, Institute for Research on Teaching.

Buchmann, M. (1984). The use of research knowledge in teacher education and teaching. *American Journal of Education, 92*(4), 421–439.

Burden, P. R. (1979). Teachers' perceptions of the characteristics and influences on their personal and professional development. *Dissertation Abstracts International, 40,* 5404A. (University Microfilms No. 80-08,776)

Bussis, A., Chittenden, E., & Amarel, M. (1976). *Beyond surface curriculum: An interview study of teachers' understandings.* Boulder, CO: Westview Press.

Charters, W. W., Jr. (1963). The social background of teaching. In N. L. Gage (Ed.), *Handbook of research on teaching.* Chicago: Rand McNally.

Cohen, E. G. (1973). Open-space schools: The opportunity to become ambitious. *Sociology of Education, 46,* 143–161.

Cronbach, L. J. (1975). Beyond the two disciplines of scientific psychology. *American Psychologist, 30,* 116–127.

Cuban, L. (1984). *How teachers taught: Constancy and change in American classrooms: 1890–1980.* New York: Longman.

Cusick, P. A. (1983). *The egalitarian ideal and the American high school.* New York: Longman.

Devaney, K. (1977). *Essays on teachers' centers.* San Francisco: Far West Laboratory.

Devaney, K. (1978). On delivering staff development. *Staff Development Newsletter.* Austin, TX: Professional Development Association.

Doyle, W. (1977a). Learning the classroom environment: An ecological analysis. *Journal of Teacher Education, 28,* 51–55.

Doyle, W. (1977b). Paradigms for research on teacher effectiveness. *Review of Research in Education, 5,* 163–198.

Doyle, W. (1977c). The uses of non-verbal behaviors: Toward an ecological model of classrooms. *Merrill–Palmer Quarterly, 23,* 179–192.

Doyle, W. (1979). Classroom effects. *Theory Into Practice, 18,* 138–144.

Doyle, W., & Ponder, G. (1977). The practicality ethic in teacher decision making. *Interchange, 8*(3), 1–12.

Dreeben, R. (1970). *The nature of teaching.* Glenview, IL: Scott, Foresman.

Dreeben, R. (1973). The school as a workplace. In R. M. W. Travers (Ed.), *Second handbook of research on teaching.* Chicago: Rand McNally.

Edgar, D. E., & Warren, R. L. (1969). Power and autonomy in teacher socialization. *Sociology of Education, 42,* 386–399.

Edmonds, R. R. (1982). Programs of school improvement: An overview. *Educational Leadership, 40*(3), 4–11.

Elbaz, F. (1983). *Teacher thinking: A study of practical knowledge.* New York: Nichols.

Elmore, R. F. (1983). Complexity and control: What legislators and administrators can do about implementing public policy. In L. S. Shulman & G. Sykes (Eds.), *Handbook of teaching and policy* (pp. 342–369). New York: Longman.

Elsbree, W. S. (1939). *The American teacher.* New York: American Book Company.

Erickson, F. (in press). Tasks in Times: Objects of Study in a Natural History of Teaching. Karen Zumwalt, Ed. *ASCD Yearbook,* 1986, Association for Supervision and Curriculum Development.

Feiman, S. (1975). Patterns of teacher behavior in a teacher center. *Interchange, 6,* 56–62.

Feiman, S., & Floden, R. E. (1980). A consumer's guide to teacher development. *Journal of Staff Development, 1*(2), 126–147.

Feistritzer, C. E.. (1983). *The American teacher.* Washington, DC: Feistritzer Publications.

Fiske, E. B. (1983, October 4). Teacher fulfillment put above pay. *New York Times,* pp. 17–18.

Fountain, P. A. J. (1975). What teaching does to teachers: The teacher as worker. *Dissertation Abstracts International, 36,* 2446B. (University Microfilms No. 75-24,529)

Freedman, S., Jackson, J., & Boles, K. (1983). Teaching: An imperilled "profession." In L. S. Shulman & G. Sykes (Eds.), *Handbook of teaching and policy* (pp. 261–299). New York: Longman.

Freidson, E. (1970). *Profession of medicine.* New York: Dodd, Mead.

Freidson, E. (1975). *Doctoring together: A study of professional social control.* Chicago: University of Chicago Press.

Fuller, F. F. (1969). Concerns of teachers: A developmental characterization. *American Educational Research Journal, 6,* 207–226.

Gallup, G. H. (1983). The 15th annual Gallup poll of the public's attitudes toward the public schools. *Phi Delta Kappan, 65,* 33–47.

Geer, B. (1968). Occupational commitment and the teaching profession. In H. S. Becker, B. Geer, D. Riesman, & R. S. Weiss (Eds.), *Institutions and the person.* Chicago: Aldine.

Gitlin, A. (1983). School structure and teachers' work. In M. W. Apple & L. Weis (Eds.), *Ideology and practice in schooling.* Philadelphia: Temple University Press.

Grant, C., & Zeichner, K. (1981). Inservice support for first-year teachers: The state of the scene. *Journal of Research and Development in Education, 14,* 99–111.

Hall, D. A. S. (1982). *Teachers as persons: Case studies of the lives of women teachers.* Warrensburg: Central Missouri State University, Department of Sociology.

Haller, E. J. (1967). Pupil influence in teacher socialization: A socio-linguistic study. *Sociology of Education, 40,* 316–333.

Hoekter, J., & Ahlbrand, W. P. (1969). The persistence of the recitation. *American Educational Research Journal, 6,* 145–167.

Hoffman, N. (1981). *Women's "true" profession: Voices from the history of teaching.* New York: McGraw-Hill.

Hoy, W. (1967). Organizational socialization: The student teacher and pupil control ideology. *Journal of Educational Research, 61,* 153–155.

Hoy, W. (1968). The influence of experience on the beginning teacher. *School Review, 76,* 312–323.

Hoy, W. (1969). Pupil control ideology and organizational socialization: A further examination of the influence of experience on the beginning teacher. *School Review, 77,* 257–265.

Hoy, W., & Rees, R. (1977). The bureaucratic socialization of student teachers. *Journal of Teacher Education, 28*(1), 23–26.

Huberman, M. (1983). Recipes for busy kitchens: A situational analysis of routine knowledge use in schools. *Knowledge: Creation, Diffusion, Utilization, 4,* 478–510.

Hunt, D. (1974). *Matching models in education.* Toronto: Ontario Institute for Studies in Education.

Isaacson, N. (1981). Secondary teachers' perceptions of personal and organizational support during induction to teaching. *Dissertation Abstracts International, 42,* 35566A. (University Microfilms No. 8201839).

Jackson, P. W. (1968). *Life in classrooms.* New York: Holt, Rinehart & Winston.

Johnson, S. M. (1982). *Teacher unions and the schools.* Cambridge, MA: Harvard University, Graduate School of Education, Institute for Educational Policy Studies.

Kaestle, C. F. (1983). *Pillars of the republic: Common schools and American society: 1780–1860.* New York: Farrar, Straus.

Kerr, S. T. (1983). Teacher specialization and the growth of a bureaucratic profession. *Teachers College Record, 84,* 629–651.

Kirst, M. (1983). Teaching policy and federal categorical programs. In L. S. Shulman & G. Sykes (Eds.), *Handbook of teaching and policy* (pp. 426–448). New York: Longman.

Kohlberg, L. (1968). Stage and sequence: The cognitive-developmental approach to socialization. In D. A. Goslin (Ed.), *Handbook of socialization theory and research.* Chicago: Rand McNally.

Lacey, C. (1977). *The socialization of teachers.* London: Methuen.

Lampert, M. (1981). How teachers manage to teach: Perspectives on the unsolvable dilemmas in teaching practice. *Dissertation Abstracts International, 42,* 3122A. (University Microfilms No. 81-26,203).

Lampert, M. (1984). Teaching about thinking and thinking about teaching. *Journal of Curriculum Studies, 16,* 1–18.

Leonard, G. (1983, May). Car pool. *Esquire,* pp. 58–64, 66, 70–73.

Lightfoot, S. L. (1978). *Worlds apart: Relationships between families and schools.* New York: Basic Books.

Lightfoot, S. L. (1983). *The lives of teachers.* In L. S. Shulman & G. Sykes (Eds.), *Handbook of teaching and policy* (pp. 241–260). New York: Longman.

Lipsky, M. (1980). *Street-level bureaucracy: Dilemmas of the individual in public services.* New York: Russell Sage Foundation.

Little, J. W. (1982). Norms of collegiality and experimentation: Workplace conditions of school success. *American Educational Research Journal, 19,* 325–340.

Loevinger, J. (1976). *Ego development.* San Francisco: Jossey-Bass.

Lortie, D. (1973). Observations on teaching as work. In R. M. W. Travers (Ed.), *Second handbook of research on teaching.* Chicago: Rand McNally.

Lortie, D. (1975). *Schoolteacher.* Chicago: University of Chicago Press.

Mann, D. (1976). The politics of training teachers in schools. *Teachers College Record, 77,* 323–338.

McPherson, G. (1972). *Small town teacher.* Cambridge, MA: Harvard University Press.

Merton, R. K., Reader, G. G., & Kendall, P. L. (1957). *The student physician.* Cambridge, MA: Harvard University Press.

Metz, M. H. (1978). *Classrooms and corridors: The crisis of authority in desegregated secondary schools.* Berkeley: University of California Press.

Milofsky, C. (1976). *Special education: A sociological study of California programs.* New York: Praeger.

Mitchell, D. E., & Kerchner, C. T. (1983). Labor relations and teacher policy. In L. S. Shulman & G. Sykes (Eds.), *Handbook of teaching and policy* (pp. 214–238). New York: Longman.

Mitchell, D., Kerchner, C., Erck, W., & Pryor, G. (1981). The impact of collective bargaining on school management and policy. *American Journal of Education, 89,* 147–188.

Mitchell, D., Ortiz, F., & Mitchell, T. (1982). *Final report on controlling the impact of rewards and incentives on teacher task performance.* Riverside: University of California.

Nelson, M. K. (1983). From the one-room schoolhouse to the graded school: Teaching in Vermont, 1910–1950. *Frontiers: A Journal of Women's Studies, 7*(1), 14–20.

Nemser, S. F., & Applegate, J. H. (1983). Teacher centers. In H. E. Mitzel (Ed.), *Encyclopedia of educational research* (5th ed.). New York: Free Press.

Newberry, J. (1977, April). *The first year of experience: Influences on beginning teachers.* Paper presented at the meeting of the American Educational Research Association, New York. (ERIC Document Reproduction Service No. ED 137 299)

Newman, K. K. (1978). Middle-aged experienced teachers' perceptions of their career development. *Dissertation Abstracts International, 39,* 4885A. (University Microfilms No. 79-02, 196)

Nisbett, R. E., & Wilson, T. D. (1977). Telling more than we can know: Verbal reports on mental processes. *Psychological Review, 84,* 231–259.

Parelius, R. J. (1980, September). *Faculty cultures and instructional practices.* Unpublished manuscript, Rutgers University, Department of Sociology, New Brunswick, NJ.

Plihal, J. (1982, March). *Types of intrinsic rewards of teaching and their relationship to teacher characteristics and variables in the work setting.* Paper presented at the meeting of the American Educational Research Association, New York.

Popkewitz, T. S. (1979, April). *Teacher education as socialization: Ideology or social mission.* Paper presented at the meeting of the American Educational Research Association, San Francisco.

Power, P. G. (1981). Aspects of the transition from education student to beginning teacher. *Australian Journal of Education, 25,* 288–296.

Prawat, R. S., & Anderson, L. M. (1983). Responsibility in the classroom: A synthesis of research on teaching self-control. *Educational Leadership, 40,* 62–66.

Richardson, J. G., & Hatcher, B. W. (1983). The feminization of public school teaching. *Work and Occupations, 10,* 81–99.

Richey, H. (1957). Growth of the modern concept of inservice education. In *Inservice education for teachers, supervisors and administrators* (56th yearbook of the National Society for the Study of Education, Part 1). Chicago: University of Chicago Press.

Ross, J. A. (1980). The influence of the principal on the curriculum decisions of teachers. *Journal of Curriculum Studies, 12,* 219–230.

Ryan, K. (1970). *Don't smile until Christmas: Accounts of the first year of teaching.* Chicago: University of Chicago Press.

Sarason, S. B. (1982). *The culture of the school and the problem of change* (2nd ed.). Boston: Allyn & Bacon.

Schwab, J. J. (1959). The "impossible" role of the teacher in progressive education. *School Review, 62,* 139–159.

Schwille, J., Porter, A., Belli, G., Floden, R., Freeman, D., Knappen, L., Kuhs, T., & Schmidt, W. (1983). Teachers as policy brokers in the content of elementary school mathematics. In L. S. Shulman & G. Sykes (Eds.), *Handbook of teaching and policy* (pp. 370–391). New York: Longman.

Sharp, R., & Green, A. (1975). *Education and social control: A study in progressive primary education.* Boston: Routledge & Kegan Paul.

Sieber, S. D. (1981). Knowledge utilization in public education: Incentives and disincentives. In R. Lehming & M. Kane (Eds.), *Improving schools: Using what we know.* Beverly Hills: Sage Publications.

Silver, C. B. (1973). *Black teachers in urban schools.* New York: Praeger.

Simpson, I., & Simpson, R. (1969). Women and bureaucracy in the semi-professions. In A. Etzioni (Ed.), *The semi-professions and their organization: Teachers, nurses, and social workers.* New York: Free Press.

Smith, L. M., & Geoffrey, W. (1968). *The complexities of an urban classroom: An analysis toward a general theory of teaching.* New York: Holt, Rinehart & Winston.

Sprinthall, N. (1980). Adults as learners. In G. Hall, S. Hord, & G. Brown (Eds.), *Exploring issues in teacher education: Questions for future research.* Austin: University of Texas, R & D Center for Teacher Education.

Sprinthall, N. A., & Thies-Sprinthall, L. (1983). The teacher as an adult learner: A cognitive-developmental view. In G. A. Griffin (Ed.), *Staff development (82nd yearbook of the National Society for the Study of Education).* Chicago: University of Chicago Press.

Sugg, R. S., Jr. (1978). *Motherteacher: The feminization of American education.* Charlottesville: University Press of Virginia.

Sweet, J. A., & Jacobson, L. A. (1983). Demographic aspects of the supply and demand for teachers. In L. S. Shulman & G. Sykes (Eds.), *Handbook of teaching and policy* (pp. 192–213). New York: Longman.

Sykes, G. (1983). Public policy and the problem of teacher quality: The need for screens and magnets. In L. S. Shulman & G. Sykes (Eds.), *Handbook of teaching and policy* (pp. 97–125). New York: Longman.

Tabachnick, B., Popkewitz, T., & Zeichner, K. Teacher education and the professional perspectives of student teachers. *Interchange, 10*(4), 1979/1980, 12–29.

Tabachnick, B. R., Zeichner, K. M., Densmore, K., Adler, S., & Egan, K. (1982, March). *The impact of the student teaching experience on the development of teacher perspectives.* Paper presented at the meeting of the American Educational Research Association, New York.

Tom, A. (1984). *Teaching as a moral craft.* New York: Longman.

Travers, R. M. W. (Ed.). (1973). *Second handbook of research on teaching.* Chicago: Rand McNally.

Tyack, D. B. (1974). *The one best system: A history of American urban education.* Cambridge, MA: Harvard University Press.

Waller, W. (1932). *The sociology of teaching.* New York: Russell & Russell.

Weatherly, R., & Lipsky, M. (1977). Street-level bureaucrats and institutional innovation: Implementing special-education reform. *Harvard Educational Review, 47,* 171–197.

Weinstein, R. S. (Ed.). (1982). Students in classrooms [Special issue]. *Elementary School Journal, 82*(5).

Willower, D. J. (1968). The teacher subculture. *Samplings, 1,* 45–59.

Wise, A. (1979). *Legislated learning: The bureaucratization of the American classroom.* Berkeley: University of California Press.

Witherell, C. S., & Erickson, V. L. (1978). Teacher education as adult development. *Theory Into Practice, 17,* 229–238.

Wolcott, H. F. (1973). *The man in the principal's office: An ethnography.* New York: Holt, Rinehart & Winston.

Wright, B. D., & Tuska, S. A. (1968). From dream to life in the psychology of becoming a teacher. *School Review, 76,* 253–293.

Zeichner, K. M. (1983, March). *Individual and institutional factors related to the socialization of beginning teachers.* Paper presented at the conference "First years of teaching: What are the pertinent issues?" University of Texas, R & D Center for Teacher Education, Austin.

Zeichner, K. M., & Grant, C. A. (1981). Biography and social structure in the socialization of student teachers: A re-examination of the pupil control ideologies of student teachers. *Journal of Education for Teaching, 7,* 298–314.

Zeichner, K. M., & Tabachnick, B. R. (1981). Are the effects of university teacher education washed out by school experience? *Journal of Teacher Education, 32*(3), 7–11.

Zeichner, K. M., & Tabachnick, B. R. (1983, April). *Teacher perspectives in the face of institutional press.* Paper presented at the meeting of the American Educational Research Association, Montreal.

19.
Research on Teacher Education

Judith E. Lanier
Michigan State University

with the assistance of
Judith W. Little
Far West Laboratory

The first *Handbook of Research on Teaching* (Gage, 1963) does not devote a chapter to research on teacher education. Inquiries pertinent to the formal education of teachers are scattered throughout the volume, with part 3 giving more attention than others to teacher education issues and questions. The *Second Handbook of Research on Teaching* (Travers, 1973) does contain a chapter on teacher education, although the authors limit their review to experimental research on the process of teacher education (Peck & Tucker, p. 942). Decisions about which research receives differential attention in chapters such as these are naturally influenced by the authors' overall perspectives on the field. For purposes of this chapter, a more comprehensive view of research on teacher education has been taken than heretofore.

Chapter Content

The view expressed here assumes that the disciplinary basis of research on teacher education is broad and diverse. It assumes that teacher education is a field of multidisciplinary inquiry, if not in general conception, certainly in execution. It is no longer, and probably never was, the preserve of any one group of professional educators or social scientists. While much of the contribution still comes from psychology, more and more research on teacher education reflects disciplined inquiry that emanates from sociology, anthropology, history, philosophy, and political science. Still another part of the comprehensive

view comes from a broad definition of teacher education itself. Concerned with research on teaching prospective as well as practicing teachers, both initial and continuing teacher education is addressed. The staff development and inservice nomenclature are not prominent here, because these concepts are synonymous with continuing teacher education. Similarly, what is often referred to as preservice, precertification, or beginning teacher preparation is here referred to as initial teacher education.

The field of teacher education is recognized here as one whose problems have been generally well known since the turn of the century. Substantial improvement-oriented inquiry and developmental activity have been undertaken since then, although the troublesome circumstances remain basically unchanged. In addition, few people concerned with such matters seem to recognize the enduring nature of the problems. Those who do often become discouraged that "things never change in this field" and abandon their research and improvement efforts. After $3\frac{1}{2}$ years of research and writing, the director of the Carnegie Study of Education of Educators (Silberman, 1970) made the following observation:

Teacher education ... has been the object of recurrent investigation since the end of World War I; indeed, the preparation of teachers has been studied as frequently as the plight of the black man in America, and with as little effect. Since 1920, in fact, ten major studies of teacher education have been published, one of them running to six, another to eight, volumes. In addition, the National

The author thanks reviewers Gary Griffin (University of Illinois) and Kenneth Zeichner (University of Wisconsin).

This work was supported by the College of Education, Michigan State University, and by the Institute for Research on Teaching, College of Education, Michigan State University, funded primarily by the Program for Teaching and Instruction of the National Institute of Education, United States Department of Education (Contract No. 400-81-0014).

Society for the Study of Education, the American Association of Colleges for Teacher Education, the John Dewey Society, and the Association for Student Teaching have each devoted one or more of their annual yearbooks to the question. (p. 414)

The persistent nature of the problems of the field and the investment that has gone into their study are difficult to overlook. For purposes of this chapter, therefore, an effort is made to focus on research that not only chronicles the problems of the field once again, but highlights their enduring nature and furthers understanding of possible reasons why the troubled field is apparently so difficult to change.

This general view interacts with our observation and belief that the study of social entities such as teacher education is apt to be advanced least by adherence to the classic natural science modes of inquiry. Meaningful isolation and control of variables in complex social affairs is rarely, if ever, possible and is not recognized, therefore, as a particularly fruitful line of contemporary inquiry in teacher education.

Given these orientations, we have overlooked or given only passing attention to certain lines of research. There are, for example, a plethora of studies demonstrating that teachers can learn all sorts of things when formally taught. Emanating from an apparently defensive posture, numerous studies show that teacher education can make a significant short-term difference. Many researchers have administered pre- and postinstructional measures of knowledge and attitude in search of some selected change, following one or another instructional treatment. They find, predictably, that prospective and practicing teachers can indeed "learn new tricks," and master all sorts of subject matter knowledge and skills of the trade. They can learn to be more open-minded about particular subjects and more accepting of certain youngsters. They can come to ask all kinds of questions and to wait more or less time for student responses. They can learn "set induction," "stimulus variation," "transition signals," and all manner of task analysis and objectives preparation—and they can learn such things in more or less efficient ways through a variety of instructional formats.

Few studies of this nature are referred to or included in this chapter because we already know that teachers, like other normal human beings, are capable of learning new thoughts and behaviors in ways that conform to a set of generally accepted principles of human learning. It is hardly informative to learn that models and modeling (even if called supervising teachers or demonstration teaching) make a difference and that corrective feedback (even if referred to as coaching) enhances learning. Similarly, it is not surprising that positive and negative exemplars (even if named protocol materials) improve concept acquisition, and practice of newly acquired skills in various contexts (even if called peer or microteaching) facilitates transfer. Studies emphasizing these general themes have been systematically excluded. Rather, the emphasis is on better understanding of the chronic problems associated with teacher education, with special attention to potential reasons why they endure.

Organization of the Chapter

A major difficulty encountered in a broad review such as this one is finding a suitable conceptual framework for describing many important studies. The problem was compounded by the diversity of completed work and our desire to go beyond mere summary. It was further complicated by our sense of obligation to address questions about what the cumulative research appears to suggest for educational practice as well as research.

Although the research and practice relationship is complex and indirect in teacher education, it does exist. Therefore, we decided to organize and summarize the research in the context of how and in what ways it might inform not only researchers, but policymakers, professors, administrators, and teachers as well. The claim that the research makes no difference is avoided, as is the claim for decisive influence.

Chapter sections are organized around the heuristic Schwab (1978) provided when he referred to the "commonplace of teaching." For teaching to occur, someone (a teacher) must be teaching someone (a student) about something (a curriculum) at some place and point in time (a milieu). In teacher education, the teachers of teachers represent a diversity of roles and backgrounds—college professors, graduate assistants, public school supervisors, and others. The students are adults who are either prospective or practicing teachers. The curriculum of teacher education includes studies in general education, subject matter specialties, and pedagogy. The milieu or context of teacher education includes the general society, the university, the school district, the school, and various other contextual settings that affect teacher education in America. These four commonplaces provide the structure for the remainder of the chapter.

Studying Those Who Teach Teachers

Research on teaching teachers stands in stark contrast to research on teaching youngsters. When teaching is studied in elementary and secondary schools, teachers are considered too important to overlook. But teachers of teachers—what they are like, what they do, what they think—are typically overlooked in studies of teacher education. Even researchers are not exactly sure of who they are. While it is known that a teacher educator is one who teaches teachers, the composite of those who teach teachers is loosely defined and constantly changing. The literature suggests that finding and keeping academically strong and committed teachers of teaching is possibly even more problematic than finding and keeping qualified students of teaching. Why this problem endures and yet receives such little research attention deserves consideration.

Problems in Defining the Population: Who Are the Teacher Educators?

Teacher educators cannot be concretely identified as a group for either initial or continuing teacher education. To review the research on this commonplace meaningfully, however, the population that would reasonably be the focus of such study must be defined, at least conceptually.

One can assume that teachers of prospective teachers are those persons officially responsible for the design and delivery of the formal instructional program required of those seeking certification for elementary or secondary school teaching. Virtually all such programs contain three major components of academic work: formal course work in general–liberal studies, formal course work in each student's major and minor fields of study, and formal course work in pedagogical study. While the scope and sequence of these studies varies, depending upon whether the initial preparation occurs in a 4- or 5-year program, the three-pronged content configuration and general set of training requirements remain similar. The oversight and governance responsibility for teacher education programs is shared broadly across the institution of higher education, emanating from faculty in the various departments that make teaching contributions to these three areas. Thus most university faculty who teach undergraduate students can be considered teachers of teachers—not just those who teach specific education courses.

In this sense, the chapters in this and former handbooks discussing research on teaching in higher education (McKeachie, 1963; Trent & Cohen, 1973) should be referred to for discussion about those who teach undergraduate college students, for they are the primary teachers of teachers. But it would be misleading to leave a consideration of the research on teacher educators to these general references alone, because some of the more interesting aspects of the faculty population concern its specific relationship with the field of teacher education per se.

QUESTIONS OF PROFESSORIAL IDENTITY AND COMMITMENT

The denotative meaning of the term "teacher educator" refers to those who provide required college and university course work for prospective teachers. But most professors in the arts and sciences are perceived neither by others nor themselves as teacher educators. The connotative meaning of "teacher educator" would refer to professors of pedagogy, but the course work in pedagogical studies generally represents only about one-fifth of a secondary teacher's required program and about one-third of an elementary teacher's program. Thus the majority of faculty responsible for designing and teaching in programs for prospective teachers would be excluded if the relevant population for study were limited to those teaching pedagogy.

Another connotative meaning for "teacher educator" refers to faculty affiliated with academic units or subunits that have the word "education" in their title; yet many faculty in such units do not teach teachers. Many of them teach only students pursuing alternative school-related careers such as administration, counseling, and school psychology. Still others teach only those pursuing nonschool, though education-related, work in business, industry, government, or higher education. Thus the term "teacher educator" is not synonymous with those appointed to education units; neither is it necessarily synonymous with professors who teach an occasional course in pedagogy.

Identifying primarily with their discipline, the professors teaching foundations courses to prospective teachers (e.g., the psychology, sociology, history, or philosophy of education) tend to deny their teacher education role and identify those who teach methods courses and supervise practice teaching as the real teacher educators. But most professors teaching methods courses would disagree. Identifying with the school subjects of their expertise, they tend to consider themselves science

educators or mathematics educators or reading educators, and point to those who coordinate or supervise student teachers as the real teacher educators. Those who supervise fieldwork in the schools are probably the only faculty, as a group, who publicly identify themselves as teacher educators.

The diversity of professional associations that these respective faculty groups join and serve, as well as the professional journals to which they subscribe and contribute, give evidence of the lack of cohesion and identity among the "real" teacher educator population. While the faculty associated with programs that prepare school administrators, counselors, psychologists, and other education specialists are relatively easy to identify, such is not the case for faculty preparing teachers. Borrowman (1965a) summarized accurately the situation for faculty in institutions preparing 90% of the teachers in America: "In these institutions, the majority of faculty members have an interest in teacher education that is, at best, tangential to their most active concerns" (p. 39).

QUESTIONS OF IDENTITY AND RESPONSIBILITY BEYOND INITIAL PREPARATION

In terms of the continuing education of teachers, things are even more chaotic. Teachers teach teachers, as do principals, consultants from all kinds of state agencies and private firms, curriculum consultants, faculty from institutions of higher education, and, more recently, administrative staff referred to as staff developers. No particular or general forms of training, bodies of knowledge, or understanding of the occupation is currently required for teaching teachers. The definitional problem for researchers who seek to learn more about those who teach teachers is formidable, since teacher education is practically everyone's, and yet no one's, obvious responsibility or priority.

Skirmishes and Squabbles Among University Teacher Educators

Professors are noted for carving out and protecting their areas of academic specialization. Elaborate governance procedures guide the discourse and decision-making process in regard to academic program offerings and requirements. Although curriculum and instruction matters rest with the faculty at large, the many specialities and complexities force a division of labor, as scholars defer to one another's expertise. Single academic departments or schools are generally given primary responsibility for their own majors, and faculty in these units usually initiate and determine required and recommended program elements. They also provide guidance and oversight for students' matriculation through their programs. But this more or less standard procedure is not generally followed in teacher education. Since coming to institutions of higher education, teacher education has operated on the assumption that it should remain an all-university responsibility.

Thus a unique configuration of shared responsibility across departments or schools is generally required, and faculty concerned with teacher education are forced into constant negotiation whenever action is considered. Such negotiations are typically marked by continuing tension among professorial groups, as each seeks to retain control over one or more pieces of the program required of prospective teachers.

Although Conant's (1963) major study of teacher certification and teacher training programs is now 2 decades old, it continues to capture some of the most enduring qualities of undergraduate teacher education. After 2 years of studying the broad programs of teacher education in 77 institutions across the United States, Conant entitled the first chapter of his report "A Quarrel Among Educators." By doing so he acknowledged the broadly shared responsibility and continuing tension among teacher education faculty in institutions of higher education. Admitting that he began his study knowing from prior experience the hostility felt towards professors of education by the majority of the arts and sciences faculty, Conant completed his work with only modest explanation for the intensity of negative feeling he encountered. Hoping that the tensions were diminishing, he recognized that the quarrel among educators was not over and reported that even when interactions were not outright hostile, the gap between the two groups continued to be wide "in spite of fine words spoken by administrators about an 'all-university approach' to the education of teachers, and the existence of a committee that symbolized the approach" (p. 4).

Conant (1963) believed that much of the conflict was associated with the classic tension between schools and universities:

> Just as the professors of the academic subjects had not, in general, been willing to assume active responsibility toward the public elementary and secondary schools, they did not welcome the responsibility for the professional preparation of teachers. (p. 11)

But he interpreted the conflict primarily in terms of political power. Observing that certification regulations were imposed on the universities and colleges as the result of pressure from a coalition of State Department officials and public school people, he attributed most of the conflict to the academic faculties' resentment of any and all such external coercion. The academic faculties in turn resented the professors of education, whom they associated with the public school and State Department officials.

Yet Conant worried that he had "perhaps stated the issue too simply." He indicated that in some instances, "quarrels ostensibly about teacher education serve to mask more fundamental conflicts over economic, political, racial, or ideological issues" (p. 12), but he did not pursue these possibilities further. Sensitive, however, to the complications that surrounded the ongoing controversies, Conant (1963) was harshly critical of condemning slogans such as "those terrible teachers' colleges" or "those reactionary liberal arts professors."

> These slogans invariably represent a point of view so oversimplified as to be fundamentally invalid. This is not to say that either academic or education professors cannot be criticized. It *is* to say that neither side can be criticized to the exclusion of the other. *In the course of my investigations, I have found much to criticize strongly on both sides of the fence that separates faculties of education from those of arts and sciences.* (p. 13; emphasis in original)

Conant was probably correct in suspecting that he had "perhaps stated the issue too simply" when attributing the bulk of the problem to issues of coercive certification, although such issues do play a part. More recent evidence suggests that he may have thought too narrowly about these quarrels in at least two ways. First, the conflicts are not limited to skirmishes between education professors and liberal arts professors; similar battles go on regularly among education professors as well. Second, the fundamental conflicts likely involve a set of more basic ideological issues.

Although the population of teacher educators is difficult to identify and little research on the full population exists to guide generalization, one commonly recognized principle can be used to focus analysis of related research. There is an inverse relationship between professorial prestige and the intensity of involvement with the formal education of teachers. University faculty and their administrators remain just close enough to teacher education to avoid entrusting it to the "teacher educators," yet they remain sufficiently distant to avoid being identified with the enterprise.

It is common knowledge that professors in the arts and sciences risk a loss of academic respect, including promotion and tenure, if they assume clear interest in or responsibility for teacher education. Professors holding academic rank in education units are in even greater jeopardy of losing the respect of their academic counterparts in the university, because their close proximity makes association with teacher education more possible. And, finally, those education professors who actually supervise prospective or practicing teachers in elementary and secondary schools are indeed at the bottom of the stratification ladder.

Judge (1982) documented the low regard afforded education professors in general and those who work most closely with prospective and practicing teachers in particular. Describing how faculty in the leading American graduate schools of education sought to "distance themselves from the confused and unattractive world of teacher education" (p. 9), Judge joined a number of researchers who share this observation and have based their research on alternative explanations for the attitude.

Problems of Academic Stratification:
Why Disparage Teacher Educators?

While the most salient characteristic of teacher educators is their constant struggle with academic colleagues, their quarrels do not appear grounded in mere disputes over concrete jurisdictional boundaries as Conant suggested. Rather, their differences appear grounded in abstract views of social status, and their antagonism appears embedded in the traditions and habits of thought associated with being lower class or female. Borrowman (1965) observed, "because of their different experiences, faculty members in teacher education institutions have developed strong biases at such variance with those of their colleagues that compromise provides the only means of achieving cooperation" (p. 41). Research suggests that the "different experiences" and "strong biases" that Borrowman noted several decades ago may well be related to social class distinctions in the larger society that are simply paralleled in the university.

DIFFERENCES IN ACADEMIC LIVES AND VALUES

Recognizing that "probably no other faculty is quite so publicly criticized as that of education," and noting how they "stand out as a very different breed of the faculty on most college and university campuses," Prichard, Fen, and Buxton (1971) explored the social class origins of education faculty for possible explanatory clues. Defining social class origin in terms of father's occupational level, they found evidence "that a much larger number of incumbents enter the field of college teaching of education from homes of skilled or unskilled laborers than has been found for incumbents in other areas of academic work."

Drawing their sample from faculty in four institutions of higher learning in the Big Eight Conferences and four correspondingly smaller public institutions of higher learning in the same states, they also found that college teachers of education were underrepresented by those coming from the homes of professionals, executives, and persons in business for themselves. Examining the age of reporting faculty, they observed that the number and proportion of persons whose parents were unskilled or skilled laborers increased in representation among college teachers of education across time; they concluded that "the education faculty is increasingly being filled by incumbents from this background" (p. 225). Examination of their data on the basis of sex composition showed female professors much less represented than male professors in colleges and departments of education, with females disproportionately representing higher social class origins. Overall, their findings showed that most college teachers of education were men from lower social class backgrounds.

In discussing their work, Prichard et al. noted that the program leading to the career of college teacher of education "seems to have been designed for individuals from the lower classes who aspire to upward mobility but lack sufficient family resources" (p. 220). The doctorate in education can often be completed more quickly than the doctorate in other fields, and such programs are often set up to provide students an opportunity to pursue a livelihood by teaching or administering in elementary or secondary schools while completing much of the required graduate work. Fuller and Bown (1975, p. 29) reported similar observations and, more recently, Ducharme and Agne (1982, p. 32) validated these earlier findings.

Ducharme and Agne also found that most college of education faculty enter institutions of higher learning later than other faculty members in academia, with over 70% of them having held full-time teaching positions in elementary and secondary schools prior to their professorial duties. Other researchers have found that the persons most dissatisfied with teaching and most apt to seek alternative, upwardly mobile work in education have been men, regardless of class, and single women from middle- and upper-class backgrounds (Zeigler, 1967, Lortie, 1975). But because the majority of men teachers come from lower class backgrounds to begin with, those who get "up and out" while remaining in education are most apt to be men from the lower social classes who are studying school administration or college teaching in schools of education.

In addition to the differences between professors of education and other university professors in training and career patterns, there are differences in work responsibilities (Fuller & Bown, 1975, p. 29). A large number of faculty in institutions that prepare teachers work with elementary and secondary school personnel in a programmatic framework that requires getting the job done more than it does the pursuit of theory. Such is not the case in the arts and sciences, where faculty work in relative isolation on intellectual pursuits clearly more distant from external constraint and pressures. It is also not the case in other professional schools where fieldwork components are either absent, as in many schools of business, or given primarily to clinical faculty in nonacademic departments, as in many medical schools.

Morris' (1983) study of the characteristics and responsibilities of college of education faculty who direct student teaching experiences highlights the practical and nonacademic nature of the job requirements for these professors:

> The five most common responsibilities were establishing and maintaining public relations with off-campus personnel, placing student teachers, arriving at final decisions about problems involving student teachers, maintaining permanent records of student teachers and supervising teachers, and conferring with student teacher applicants. (p. 16)

Ducharme and Agne's findings (1982) indicate that faculty in education "have difficulty in adjusting to and accepting the norms and expectations of academe" (p. 33). Using survey and interview techniques, they sampled the views of education professors from a range of institutional types. In response to the question, "What led you to seek a position in higher education?" they found that education professors had light research and scholarship commitments and interests. Their subjects did not respond "in terms of wanting to do research, wanting to be part of the frontiers of knowledge, or wanting to lead and assist doctoral students in their research" (p. 34). Rather, the reported motivation for entering higher education was "to have an indirect impact on the place from which, in general, they have come—the lower schools" (p. 34).

Although Ducharme and Agne (1982) found a reportedly growing interest in writing and publication, Guba and Clark's research (1978) on the levels of research and development productivity of faculty in schools, departments, and colleges of education shows an extremely low record of scholarly accomplishment. Less than 20% of the 1,367 education units in higher education had faculty involved in education research and development. They found, in fact, that on a per-faculty-member basis, even in the doctoral-level schools, colleges, and departments of education, the productivity norm was basically "nonproductivity" (p. 8).

While research suggests, in general, that education professors differ from their academic counterparts in that they have less scholarly productivity and lower social class origins, one must look further to examine the possibility that these factors are related to one another or to the quarrels education professors have with other academicians. Comparing their own findings with studies of the relationship between social class origins and academic careers, Prichard et al. (1971) cite evidence in support of an observed relationship:

> Our findings, when compared with those of other studies, appear to suggest that where the field of knowledge of the incumbent is one that is largely of application or conative skills, larger numbers of individuals from the lower social classes are to be found than when the field of knowledge is one largely involving the theoretical or cognitive skills. (p. 223)

Drawing upon related work showing a disproportionate representation of middle and upper-middle classes in particular academic fields, these researchers' theoretical basis is tied to cultural background. Supposedly, middle- and upper-class backgrounds emphasize an intellectual atmosphere, emotional control, functional organization of concepts in thinking, use of fantasy in problem solving, and a lack of indoctrination in cultural concepts. Using this theoretical perspective and their own findings, Prichard and his colleagues argue that these cultural characteristics "contribute to the making of research-oriented people," and "just as the opposite occurs for incumbents in such applied areas as college teaching of education where conative–affective modes of behavior are of value" (p. 224).

Other scholars supporting this general view suggest that the relationship between cultural background and theoretical orientation goes beyond a de-emphasis of research. Even if teaching teachers is an applied area of work that includes a valuing of affective modes of behavior, and even if research is eschewed for major attention to the practice component, this may not be sufficient reason for sustained criticism and rejection by one's academic colleagues. Harry Broudy (1980) points out the need to qualify the hypothesis that it is the applied or "practice component of teacher education as such that undercuts the scholarship requirement of university status" (p. 448). If practice alone were the culprit, then other professional educators would share the image of teacher educators, and it is clear that not all of them do. Broudy (1980) suggests an alternative that indirectly lays the blame on the intellectual propensities and mental processing of teacher educators. He implies that they are excessive in their devaluing of abstract thought and decision making:

> It is only when the practice is highly routinized and demands a very low order of cognitive strain that the academic noses go up. And it is only when the practice seems divorced from a coherent body of theory on which there is considerable guild consensus that the noses stay up. (p. 448)

TEACHER EDUCATORS AND THE
INTELLECTUAL NORMS OF THE UNIVERSITY

Several historical studies suggest support for Broudy's hypothesis. Powell (1980) describes the attitude of critics across the generations as professors of education came to focus on job-oriented curricula that were seen as overly practical. Flexner, for example, apparently turned his intellectual and financial

influence to the support of teacher education after his successful upgrading of medical education. But he shifted his attitude from one of respect to one of disdain within a decade, when "atomistic training ... hostile to the development of intellectual grasp" became the norm recommended and studied by professors of education (p. 174).

Historical research also supports the idea that low status, humble social origins, and low-level knowledge and skills are related, and it emphasizes the longevity and tenacity of the problem for teacher education. Mattingly (1975) presents substantial evidence that persons concerned with the education of teachers in this country struggled to uncouple these factors when schools were first created to prepare professional teachers approximately 150 years ago. Mattingly's study describes the early struggles of education faculty in the independent normal schools who sought to construct and maintain academically respected programs of teacher education. He suggests that their battle was a losing one because the attitudes and habits of thought associated with sex and social class had an excessively strong influence.

Mattingly describes how early attempts to have professional schools for teachers reflect specific attitudes of intellectual discipline and self-possession were displaced as women and members of the lower social classes came to compose a majority of the teaching force. Even the most academic normal schools, such as the 4-year program at Bridgewater, Massachusetts, became consistently less attractive over the years as young men from the upper social strata gravitated to liberal arts colleges. The small minority of males and the 4-year course of professional study was basically eliminated by 1900. Left for women who would teach in elementary schools, the 2-year normal schools became both the norm and the bottom rung of the academic ladder. Mattingly (1975) describes the poignant curriculum shifts that accompanied this change in student body:

> At the turn of the century normal schools had been overtaken by women and by vocational training for specific skills. The curriculum had quickly lost its pretense of academic training and had gained methods which collegiate minds deemed unprofessionally mechanical. (p. 166)

Powell's historical analysis (1976), "University Schools of Education in the Twentieth Century," supports Mattingly's observations. Describing the movement toward the university and the creation of schools of education in these settings, he noted their class and sex bias as it related to substantive complexity:

> High school men wished to avoid the normals' low admissions standards and growing accessibility to persons of low social status, their emphasis on practical technique, and their rapid feminization. (p. 5)

Leading educators in 1890 believed that the establishment of teacher training opportunities in higher education, and especially in the best universities, "would raise it at once to the ranks of a learned profession, worthy to command the best talents and the loftiest intelligence, and to be entered only, like law or medicine or theology, after the amplest professional training" (Powell, 1976, p. 5). But those who avoided the normal schools and came to the university to find greater dignity and respect for themselves, teaching, and teacher education were disappointed. Expanding enrollments in the nation's schools prevented the recruitment and selection of the most elite and intellectually able into teaching, and necessitated the continued employment of women and lower-class males. Recognizing that respect would remain elusive for academically talented, upwardly mobile men so long as they continued as members of groups dominated by others of low status, education professors in the nation's leading universities sought and found an alternative means of resolving the problem of finding "positions of honor, responsibility, and authority in teaching" (Powell, 1976, p. 4). They changed the priority mission of schools of education from that of improving teacher education to that of preparing an elite minority who would become the managers of the lower status majority. Women and less able men, who would necessarily comprise the massive teaching force, could continue to receive a meager and technical preparation; the career educators, with responsibility for management and important decision making, would receive the more thorough and substantive professional education (Powell, 1976, 1980).

Powell (1976) describes how courses and programs evolved as graduate study was developed for the more "successful and ambitious teachers who look forward to promotions as principals and superintendents" (p. 7). Typically, only experienced male teachers were able to acquire the "training they needed to compete successfully for all the higher positions in the profession." He captured numerous arguments and events that led academic leaders and ambitious education faculty to shift their primary commitment from teacher education to nonteaching careers—careers that focused on specializations and management roles rather than teaching itself.

Apparently, education faculty at the university segregated themselves very early into training programs that reinforced the emerging hierarchical structure of the teaching profession. Powell uncovered, for example, a 1905 issue of the *New England Journal of Education* that spoke of growing uneasiness with the "class-conscious" character of the emerging divisions, but reported "no solution to this apparent inevitability." Such historical evidence supports the growing awareness of stratification and the expectation that serious thinking and decision making in education was to be carried out by male members of the middle and upper classes.

Mattingly's evidence (1975) also makes a persuasive case that even before the turn of the century, critical thinking and conceptual analysis and argument were selectively excluded from deliberations and constructions of the education curriculum for professional teachers. Such changes accompanied the sex and class shift in the majority membership of the teaching population. Illustrating the subtle but important changes that occurred in the norms for intellectual exchange and cognitive processing at the time of these shifts, Mattingly contrasted how differently the first and second generations of leading teacher educators thought about their work. An exemplary case in point relates to both generations' strong and shared view that social conflict and political partisanship were detrimental to professional character:

The first generation, however, differed on the point in that they *knew* the apolitical meaning originated from a political *choice*. The second generation and its successors *made a habit of their apolitical thinking* and treated the habit as a *moral principle*. (p. xiii; Italics added)

COGNITIVE COMPLEXITY, SELF-DIRECTION, AND TEACHER EDUCATION

The accumulated research suggests an interesting possibility. The reciprocal effects of personality and job conditions for those most closely associated with teacher education may have affected selective recruitment, selective retention, and, subsequently, formation of intellectual propensities and working norms that conflict with the traditional values of higher education. Such a possibility would help to explain the observed tension, as well as the disdain for and avoidance of teacher education by serious scholars both internal and external to schools of education.

Faculty in institutions of higher education are expected to value intellectual challenge, questioning, criticism, and conceptual analysis. Advancing higher learning requires that scholars enter uncharted intellectual territory, and, as they explore the not-yet-known, they must maintain a cognitive flexibility and commitment to examine alternative, sometimes competing, beliefs and assumptions. Diverse views and openness to new evidence, novel ideas, and controversial opinions are long-accepted values of the academy. Conversely, the tendency to ignore or reject competing ideas and evidence, to accept old or new ideas uncritically, or to proselytize unexamined truths are signs of academic weakness. Evidence suggests that the typical lineage of teacher educators has not prepared them to appreciate the traditional values of higher education. As Mattingly (1975) observed, "For very particular reasons the institutes of Barnard's generation attracted young men whose prominent virtues were neither intellectual self-possession nor professional daring" (p. 70). These "very particular reasons" include personality factors and job conditions that influence cognitive values and flexibility.

Personality factors associated with cognitive propensities rewarded in higher education also correlate with social stratification. Apparently, social class has a powerful influence because it represents the combined effects of child rearing, formal education, and occupation (Kohn, 1969). Kohn and Schooler's recent findings (1982) require serious attention, as they "highlight the centrality for job and personality of a mutually reinforcing triumvirate—ideational flexibility, a self-directed orientation to self and society, and occupational self-direction" (p. 1282).

Studying class-associated conditions that affect psychological functioning, Kohn found conformist values in child rearing stressed in the lower segments of the class hierarchy and more so for females than males (1969). These conformist values include a predisposition for authoritarian conservatism and other-directedness. Because most teacher educators, like teachers, are either women from middle-class or men from lower middle-class backgrounds (Fuller & Bown, 1975, p. 29), it is likely they learned conformist values as children.

The formal educational component is similarly important, insofar as it provides, or fails to provide, the intellectual flexibility and breadth of perspective so crucial to self-directed values and orientation (Kohn & Schooler 1982). The school experiences of those gravitating towards teacher education also tend to reinforce conformist values, however. Elementary and secondary schools have encouraged girls, some of whom eventually become teachers and teacher educators, to be passive, primarily followers (Pyke, 1975). Formal education has emphasized domestic roles for women in America since the 19th century; and while the traditions of female education are now changing, they have long de-emphasized intellectual prowess (Kaestle, 1983).

Studies by education sociologists also highlight the ways in which schools inadvertently contribute to the limited cognitive flexibility that children from economically disadvantaged homes bring to school. Murphy (1979) summarizes the research of a number of these scholars, whose studies suggest that teacher educators, as children of the working classes, were discouraged from developing substantive, ideational flexibility during their elementary and secondary school years.

Bordieu, for example, demonstrated an association between inequalities in the culture capital of parents from different economic backgrounds and inequalities in the school success of their children. Lower class students have less of what Bordieu calls culture capital, the ethos of the upper classes. Lacking the verbal facility, general culture, and information about the school system that brings the greatest school returns, these students simply end up with a lower quality education than their more privileged counterparts.

Perrenaud also examined sociocultural stratification and inequalities in the school success of children. Taking institutions and structural arrangements into account, he demonstrated how course, school, and program placement decisions aggravate these inequalities. Investigating these mediating variables further, Baudelot and Establet found curriculum and instruction differences also contributing to class distinctions. Moralistic and utilitarian views of knowledge encouraging conformist values and cognitive passivity were emphasized for working-class children. Children of the upper classes, on the other hand, were encouraged to value and develop more abstract thinking through music, art, pure science, mathematics, philosophy, and other studies that reinforce cognitive flexibility. Studies affirming (Anyon, 1981; McNeil, 1982) and questioning (Rehberg & Rosenthal, 1978) these generalizations continue to emerge, but a body of literature exists to suggest that schools reinforce the cognitive flexibility of those from upper class families but fail to change the conformist, other-directed thinking of those from lower class origins.

The evidence is not as convincing at the college level, but there is reason to believe that the higher education obtained by teacher educators has not been highly liberating, at least not in a way that would counter family-nurtured and school-reinforced tendencies to value cognitive conformity. Coming from modest social backgrounds, many prospective teacher educators complete their baccalaureate studies at the college nearest their homes. With monetary constraints imposing their inevitable restrictions, opportunities for rich experiential learning are, again, frequently limited.

In addition, the nonliberating nature of most undergraduate education has been criticized by scholars who have written about liberal education in the modern American university (Bestor, 1955; Borrowman, 1965a; Conant, 1963; Schwab, 1969; Silberman, 1970; Trow, 1968; Wegner, 1978). Most teacher educators did not obtain a liberating education in their own homes or schools and it is unlikely that they found it in their baccalaureate program. In addition, because most teacher educators who work closely with prospective and practicing teachers went through teacher preparation programs themselves, they likely encountered conservatively conceived studies in pedagogy. Writing in his documentary history of *Teacher Education in America*, Borrowman (1965a) speaks of the relationship between liberal education and the preparation of teachers. He describes the dominant normal school emphasis on excessive technicalism, noting that although it runs contrary to the ideals of a liberal education, it has been carried over in the minds of many who still teach teachers:

> Important leaders in American teacher education have their roots planted firmly in the normal-school tradition, large numbers of elementary- and secondary-school teachers retain the values inculcated by the normal schools, and a number of ideas central to the normal-school traditions have been institutionalized in university programs of teacher education. (p. 20)

Teacher educators might yet encounter opportunities to develop breadth of perspective, tolerance of nonconformity, and intellectual flexibility in their occupation and graduate studies. But here again, teacher educators generally acquire conservative, conformist orientations. Ducharme and Agne (1982) found that the majority of education faculty have worked 3 or more years in the lower schools, findings that are consistent with those of other studies (Joyce, Yarger & Howey, 1977; Prichard et al., 1971). The conservative nature of school settings has been well documented (Cusick, 1973; Everhart, 1984; Willis, 1980), and studies of the professionals who gather there show a conservative bias (Lortie, 1975; Zeigler, 1967). These institutional traditions, collegial relations, and the structural requirements of teaching combine to create a pervasive atmosphere of conservatism.

Studies confirm the strong impact of job conditions on psychological functioning. According to Kohn and Schooler (1982), "jobs that limit occupational self-direction decrease ideational flexibility and promote a conformist orientation to self and to society" (p. 1281). Job conditions that lead to self-directedness, on the other hand, are substantively complex; they include opportunities for reflective thinking, independent judgment, and initiative, and they are recognized for their nonroutinized activity and freedom from close supervision.

It is unlikely that the traditional structures of elementary and secondary teaching provide school teachers aspiring to careers in teacher education with sufficient opportunities to overcome existing tendencies toward other-directedness. Consequently, these prospective teacher educators have little opportunity to develop a self-directed orientation to self and society. If elementary and secondary school teaching provided more occupational self-direction than it traditionally has, prospective teacher educators would move closer to orientations that are "consistently more likely to become nonauthoritarian, to develop personally more responsible standards of morality, to become self-confident, ... less fatalistic, less anxious, and less conformist in their ideas" (Kohn & Schooler, 1982, p. 1272). But classroom teaching in the United States is not known for furthering complex intellectual development in the adults who work there (Lortie, 1975).

Similarly, the chances of encountering significant changes in cognitive habits during graduate school are little better. The financial constraints associated with humble family origins and low teacher salaries provide few opportunities for taking time off work in the pursuit of full-time graduate study. Full-time study would provide teachers with increased opportunity to become immersed in academic work, with its greater potential for intensive and deep exposure to new and stimulating ideas. In addition, possibilities of acquiring substantial external support from other sources, such as federal grants, university stipends, national fellowships, and business awards, are low. The field of education receives far less money by a wide margin than other academic and professional fields for graduate student support (Pelikan, 1983, Table 4). Most aspiring teacher educators are forced to maintain their normal, other-directed school routines, therefore, while pursuing graduate studies part-time at a nearby state university. The pattern of contextual reinforcement for conformist values and narrowness of perspective is repeated once again.

Thus the research on experiential factors associated with cognitive complexity and self-direction, combined with what is known about the lives of teacher educators who work closely with prospective and practicing teachers, suggests that their intellectual propensities may be less analytical than those traditionally held in high esteem at the university. Recently, more direct study of university supervisors has confirmed the frequent presence of this more narrow, unquestioning perspective. Reviewing the work of Stones and Morris (1972) and MacAleese (1976), Stones (1984) found supervisors to be "extremely unlikely to have given thought to the theory and practice of supervision"; he summarized findings on the methods of contemporary supervision as "atheoretical, idiosyncratic, poorly conceptualized, of doubtful efficacy, and in some cases probably 'harmful'" (p. 1). Other researchers pursuing similar questions on the thinking of those who teach methods classes and practice teaching have observed similar results. A lack of probing thought and analysis, the trademark of cognitive conservatism, seems to characterize the intellectual performance (Hogan, 1983; Katz & Raths, 1982; Zeichner & Tabachnick, 1982). The social backgrounds and occupational experiences encountered by many teacher educators are likely contributors to this nonacademic orientation. Significantly enriched intellectual opportunities for prospective and practicing teacher educators, in contrast to more condemnation and harsh criticism, can lead to constructive remedy of the problems here observed.

Summary

The body of research leading to better understanding of those who teach teachers is modest at this time. A broad search of the literature and a weaving together of circumstantial evidence was required as part of the sense-making task called for in a review of this nature. The difficult-to-locate, easy-to-overlook, and much-maligned nature of the teacher educator population lies behind the questioning perspective brought to the research studies considered in this section.

Of those responsible for teaching teachers in higher education, the most prestigious are those most removed from dealing with teacher education's problems. The thesis emerging from the research is that variables associated with social class distinctions in the larger society are simply mirrored in universities and again in colleges and departments of education. Those variables are potentially of major importance in understanding the intellectual character and social position of those most closely associated with teaching and teacher education.

A disproportionately large number of faculty teaching teachers most directly have come from lower middle-class backgrounds. It is very likely that they obtain conformist orientations and utilitarian views of knowledge from their childhood experiences at home, educational opportunities in school, and restrictive conditions of work as teachers before coming to higher education. Thus the teacher educators closest to schools and prospective and practicing teachers often assume professional work assignments and routines that demand minimal intellectual flexibility and breadth and require, instead, conformity and limited analysis. Such possibilities may partially explain why teacher educators, as some researchers have observed, "have difficulty in adjusting to and accepting the norms and expectations of academe" (Ducharme & Agne, 1982, p. 33).

The students of teacher education also have difficulty adjusting to and accepting these academic norms for many similar and some additional reasons. The school as workplace, because it is their only workplace, has an even greater impact on them than on their teachers.

Studying the Students of Teaching

Of the four commonplaces in teacher education, the students receive most attention. The student group comprises adult learners who seek formal preparation for teaching as well as those who enter teaching and become participants in various forms of continuing teacher education. More tangible than the curriculum and milieu of teacher education and certainly less threatening to study than their teachers, learners remain the primary subjects of inquiry. Lacking in power, the adult students are more readily available for study and less able to express resistance when studies of them are poorly conceptualized or interpreted.

The research on students of teaching over the past decade tends to be desultory in nature, poorly synthesized, and weakly criticized. Although there has been a good deal of data gathering and thought, there seems to be an excess of the former and a dearth of the latter. As a consequence, misrepresentation and overgeneralization of research findings has occurred in response to growing public interest. A serious need remains for improved study and scholarship.

Appropriately, however, research on prospective and practicing teachers is increasingly concerned with the teachers' intellectual competence, factors that influence their thinking abilities, and the substance and processing of their thoughts and judgments. This evolving paradigmatic shift is illustrated by the earlier handbooks' focus on research on personality and other personal qualities (Getzels & Jackson, 1963) and on behavioral performance (Peck & Tucker, 1973).

Growing researcher interest in the cognitive functioning of prospective and practicing teachers has also been accompanied by public concern (Gallup, 1983). Contemporary dissatisfaction with the intellectual performance of America's students and teachers has filled the popular press as studies reporting low test scores and other school problems have renewed interest in the qualification, competencies, expectations, and attitudes of those who teach. But contemporary interest by no means accounts for the increased research along these lines. As in all teaching situations, the composition and nature of the student group influences the nature of the teaching that occurs and accounts for a major part of the variance in learning outcomes. The cognitive processes of those choosing to become and remain teachers is and will continue to be an important area in teacher education research, therefore, even when contemporary concerns about quality subside.

Problems in Thinking About the Population: Simple Demography

The students of teaching are generally studied as members of two large groups: adult learners enrolled in higher education programs leading to recommended teaching credentials and practicing teachers receiving formal instruction meant to improve elementary and secondary education. The statistical reports of the National Education Association (1982) and the National Center for Education Statistics (Frankel & Gerald, 1982; Plisko, 1983) provide informative descriptive data, as do the synthesizing reports of Feistritzer (1983a, 1983b) and the demographic studies of Sweet and Jacobsen (1983).

But few studies place their findings in juxtaposition to comparable findings emerging from studies of meaningfully related populations. Such comparisons and contrasts are needed if misleading interpretations are to be avoided and more trustworthy perspectives created. Studies are cited, for example, showing a steady decrease in teachers' reported certainty in willingness to choose teaching if they could remake their career choice and a steady increase in teachers saying they probably or certainly would not choose teaching again (National Education Association, 1982, p. 74). Such data would be interpreted differently if the 2-decade change described for teachers was isomorphic with comparable response distributions for dentists, accountants, and business managers over the same period.

Another example of insufficient analysis is found in recent studies showing fewer women with high test scores entering teaching. Although the women's movement is often cited as the major contributor to the problem (Kerr, 1983: Schlechty & Vance, 1981), it may have had only modest effects until recently. To be sure, the women's movement provides alternatives to teaching, but it is also responsible for encouraging and enabling twice as many women to pursue careers requiring a college education as did so just 14 years ago (Astin, 1981). The more likely culprits are actual and rumored market demand, whose powerful influence would cause greater talent shifts than at present if it were not for the alleviating, as opposed to exacerbating, effects of the women's movement (Weaver, 1983, p. 46).

With some notable exceptions, the demographic studies and descriptions of the student groups do not include contrasting alternative portraits and interpretations of the population's unique characteristics important to improved understandings and expectations for America's teachers, *qua* learners. While some aspects of unique student qualities can now be considered, future research is seriously needed if teacher education policies and practices are to be significantly better informed.

TAKING SIZE FOR GRANTED

Although a number of researchers have counted prospective and practicing teachers and others have cited their numbers, few bring informed perspective to the figures. Sweet and Jacobsen (1983) at least consider the teacher work force as part of the college-educated work force, noting that, "in fact, a surprisingly large share of all college-educated workers are school teachers" (p. 192). But they do not report that even with rapid growth in the college-educated work force, teachers still accounted for more than 7.5% of this total group as recently as 1982 (Feistritzer 1983b, Table 12). With over 10% of the college-educated working women and over 4% of the college-educated working men, the occupation represents the largest single white-collar group in need of regular continuing education. As Lortie observes: Teaching is unique. No other occupation can claim a membership of over 2 million college graduates and tens of thousands with advanced degrees (p. 244).

The prospective teacher group, though reduced from earlier years, also remains formidable in size. Across the 1970s, between one-fifth and one-quarter of all college graduates in the country pursued teaching certificates (Frankel & Gerald, 1982). While bachelor's degree recipients in education declined to 12.7% in 1980 (Frankel & Gerald, 1982), education continued to rank second, behind only business and management, in total degrees conferred (Feistritzer, 1983a, p. 48). Over 265,000 bachelor's and master's degrees were granted to education majors in 1970, and approximately 222,000 in 1980.

The number of practicing elementary and secondary school teachers went well over 2 million in 1980, increasing by 1.4% across the 1970s, even while the number of pupils was dropping (Feistritzer, 1983a, p. 1). Though the number of teachers is predicted to increase by several hundred thousand by 1990 (Frankel & Gerald, 1982), projections indicate an annual need of almost 200,000 new teachers each year. The anticipated supply and demand situation is now comparable to that of the 1965–1969 period (Plisko, 1983, p. 76), when a serious teacher shortage existed. But these now-familiar numbers need more thought and consideration if the interpretations and generalizations flowing from related research on the learners are to be understood.

Consider, for example, reports that the students of teaching do not come from among the best and the brightest of the college population. Such reports are clearly misleading because many academically talented students continue to pursue careers in teaching. Whether enough of them do is a matter for analysis and judgment; but reasonable and realistic recruitment goals cannot be established until the total available talent pool is first compared with the size of the needed population and the observed proportion taken into account.

As Lortie (1975) notes, "Occupations compete for members, consciously or not, and there is a largely silent struggle between occupations as individuals choose among alternative lines of work" (p. 25). Further, the occupational struggle is not influenced by job attractions alone, because the distance down the normal curve of academic ability that must be traveled to meet the overall demand is a function of size. If a small population is needed, aspirations to obtain recruits from the very top can be realistic. As an occupation grows from 200, to 2,000, to 20,000, or to 200,000, the goal of getting recruits from the upper quartile of the college population becomes increasingly difficult.

The extent of the difficulty can be observed by looking at the year 1980 alone, when 186,000 of the 930,000 bachelor's degree graduates were in the upper quintile (Plisko, 1983, Table 4.3). If the entire talented cohort pursued teacher education, and if the usual 80% (Golladay & Noell, 1978, Table 4.6) sought jobs, there would still be a shortage of more than 30,000 teachers in light of the estimated demand for 152,000 (Plisko,1983, Table 4.2).

The size of the student group also influences the qualitative nature of instructional programs provided for learners. Effective small-group work and personalized tutorials and clerkships necessarily become costly with greater numbers. Sizeable populations provide an understandable press for less effective instructional formats that can accommodate large groups.

Group size also affects general awareness and public visibility. When even a small percentage of a large population suffers a problem like unemployment or an indignity like low test scores, it represents a relatively large absolute number. Thus even if the situation does not characterize the population as a whole, or even a significant majority, it will accurately portray reality for a substantial number. While descriptions of important characteristics of large population subsets are needed, the failure to emphasize an actual minority status when it fits many people is a common oversight, particularly when the oversight has functional value. Proportionally small, disaffected subsets of large populations can thus obtain disproportionate amounts of attention, which in turn leads people to think inappropriately that these subsets characterize the whole. An example of this phenomenon for the large teacher population over the past decade appears related to supply and demand.

Except for several unique time periods, such as the Great Depression, and particular subject fields, such as secondary social studies, jobs for teachers in the United States have been plentiful, and teachers could usually find work wherever they wanted to live. This circumstance changed across the past decade as large numbers of certified teachers, though not necessarily a large proportion, found employment less readily accessible. The illusion was created that there were few available jobs for teachers, and teacher education was naturally affected. Weaver (1983) provides some perspective:

The effect on schools of education was dramatic. The percentage of college-bound students selecting teacher education fell from its 1969 peak of 24 percent to less than 5 percent in 1982. These kinds of responses, however, are not uncommon. Engineering enrollments declined by almost one-third in the aftermath of the engineering glut of the 1969–71 market. (p. 82)

Weaver (1983) has discussed ways in which "these adjustments in opportunity and career choices also affect talent flows and institutional responses" (p. 82), helping to explain why another period of high demand now appears on the horizon. But there is reason to believe that the nation's teacher surplus of the past decade was not as severe as the public thought. The strong sense that a teacher glut existed may have been a reaction to a modest proportion, though large number, of teachers facing new occupational norms for position identification, job competition, and relocation. College graduates from most fields of study anticipate the need to compete, search widely, and possibly relocate in a less-than-preferred geographic location. Further study is needed to explore the possibility that disruptions in traditional market expectations for a segment of the teacher group overinfluenced supply and demand perceptions of the past decade.

There is no question, however, that teacher surpluses in particular subject fields and locations caused tight job markets in certain areas, just as declining public school enrollments forced layoffs. But data suggest that the popular view that teachers were not needed was exaggerated. Shortages in particular subject fields, such as science and mathematics, never ceased and were well documented and discussed (Williams, 1981, 1983). Shortages in all age and subject fields existed in various geographic locations, and although some demographers described the market shifts of the sixties and seventies in "boom to bust" terms (Sweet & Jacobsen, 1983, p. 206), such a view was generally misleading. The actual data suggest that it would be more accurate to characterize the changing national market for teachers as moving from uniformly excessive demand in the sixties to one of irregular and modest demand in the seventies.

Consider the fact that since 1970 the national demand for teachers dropped below 100,000 for 1 year only. Ranging from 99,000 to 189,000, the median number of open positions available for teachers was over 150,000 annually (Plisko, 1983, p. 182), hardly a "bust" situation. But state and regional differences in demand were large, and the social trends affecting them were studied and reported (Sweet & Jacobsen, 1983). Interest in changing market conditions actually grew across the decade, particularly when they combined with liberal certification requirements and collective bargaining pressures and contributed to an increased incidence of out-of-field teaching (Masland & Williams, July/August 1983). A North Carolina study, for example, found over 7,000 teachers teaching out of field, with over 1,100 persons not certified in science teaching science and almost 450 social studies teachers teaching math (Woolford, Presti, Gray, & Coble, 1982). The number of such studies and findings has increased, as have projections that such matters will worsen in the coming decade (Frankel & Gerald, 1982; Grant & Eiden, 1982). The public can be adequately forewarned by data collected in this demographic work, which suggests that the initial and continuing education of teachers will be increasingly needed in the years to come, particularly when the middle-age majority draws closer to retirement.

But the point of recounting the statistics gathered in these studies is not to suggest need. It is to emphasize the most salient characteristic of the student group itself: its massive size. The potential such magnitude has for both the commonness and costs of teacher education must be noted. Preparing and offering sound programs of initial and continuing teacher education in a populated country committed to equal educational opportunities for all citizens is a vast undertaking. The U.S. commitment to mass schooling makes the teaching force so large and so common, in fact, that the U.S. must look to more or less average students, as well as to the highly talented, if it is to acquire enough teachers for its classrooms. Such awareness should help people, as Broudy (1980) suggests in another context, "understand why the goal of putting an inspirational teacher in every classroom is one of the great mischievous illusions of our time" (p. 448).

SALIENT MEASURES OF CENTRAL TENDENCY

The tremendous size and diversity of the prospective and practicing teacher group suggests that its measures of central tendency must be interpreted with caution. Nonetheless, Feistritzer (1983a) uses measures reported in recent demographic studies to characterize many of today's teachers:

> A profile of the "typical" American teacher suggests a woman approaching her 40th birthday. She has taught for 12 years, mostly in her present district. Over those dozen years, she returned to her local college or university often enough to acquire enough credits for a master's degree. She is married and the mother of two children. She is white and not politically active. Her formal political affiliation, if she has one, is with the Democratic Party. She teaches in a suburban elementary school staffed largely by women. In all likelihood the school principal is male. She has about 23 pupils in her class. When counting her after-hours responsibilities, she puts in a work week slightly longer than the typical laborer, and brings home a pay check that is slightly lower. (p. 1)

A number of these general qualities have some particular meanings for teacher education. The students of teaching, that is, those entering as well as those already engaged in professional practice, remain predominantly female. Women make up over two thirds of the present teaching force and over three quarters of the prospective teacher population (Grant & Eiden, 1982). The sexes are balanced in the secondary school, but women outnumber men five to one in the elementary school. While the distribution of men and women in teaching has tended to remain constant in recent decades, the student pool now seeking initial certification has a growing proportion of women (National Education Association, 1982, p. 94). Thus to the extent that talented women acquire access to traditionally male occupations at the same time that occupations predominantly comprising women continue to be afforded less power, prestige, and pay than traditionally male occupations, the attraction and retention of highly talented persons into teacher education will grow more difficult.

Minority teachers are even more underrepresented than male teachers, as over 90% of the present teaching population is white. Recent studies show a steady decline in minority representation among prospective and practicing teachers at the very time that a rapid and significant increase in minority pupils in the nation's schools is under way (National Education Association, 1982, p. 91). It is increasingly clear that the enriching perspectives brought to teacher education by minority students from various ethnic subcultures will be lost unless more successful recruitment programs are supported.

Reductions have also occurred in both the proportion and number of younger and older teachers, suggesting that the middle-age measure of central tendency is appropriately descriptive. Parenthetically, one wonders about the extent to which this factor might relate to the apparent midlife crisis state of the occupational group itself. It suggests more straightforwardly, however, that most of today's inservice learners obtained preparation for teaching when teacher education programs were excessively large and impersonal. Further, most of them have experienced a significant amount of postbaccalaureate education, as over half already have acquired master's degrees.

Related to teachers' formal education is the nonformal education they likely received in the home. The data suggest that the educational and occupational attainments of the parents of today's teachers is still modest, though gradually increasing. As recently as 1981, almost 20% of all teachers' mothers had completed only elementary school or less, and over 70% had never attended college. While 40% of all teachers' fathers were employed in occupations that likely required higher education (professional, semiprofessional, managerial, and self-employed workers), the majority were from the ranks of skilled and unskilled laborers and clerical, sales, and farm workers (National Education Association, 1982). The lower middle-class background of persons entering and staying in teaching that became increasingly prominent in the 1950s (Zeigler, 1967) continues to characterize a significant portion of the contemporary population. Such data provide some clues to the kinds of learnings and intellectual norms that were likely emphasized in the teachers' formative years (Kohn, 1969).

Finally, there are two other statistics that should not be overlooked for their potential effect on teachers as learners. These include (a) the number and proportion of teachers reporting school year employment beyond their regular, full-time teaching responsibilities and (b) the marriage and child-rearing rates, which also suggest added work responsibility (National Education Association, 1982). Excluding summer employment, over a third of all teachers report additional work for pay either within the school system (almost 25%) or outside the school system (over 11%). Whether such work involves bus driving, coaching, bartending, child rearing, or housecleaning, it obviously reduces the time and energy available for teachers' continuing education.

The Students of Teaching: Academic Qualifications

The general impression that many persons pursuing careers in teaching are academically weak continues to be supported by research. Unfortunately, many studies using population test scores give excessive attention to measures of central tendency and insufficient attention to the range. As an unintended consequence, the illusion is created that most persons preparing for teaching are average or below average in academic ability. Attention to the distribution of talent and important differences within the population of persons seeking careers in teaching is critical if misunderstandings are to be avoided.

Serious overgeneralizations already exist in the research literature, however, and require attention if the erroneous stereotype that smart people no longer enter teaching is to be clarified. Employing more journalistic style than scholarly constraint in reporting, a number of researchers have overlooked the potentially detrimental self-fulfilling prophecy effects of exaggerated claims. In "Teaching Competence and Teacher Education," for example, Kerr (1983) concludes the following:

> As far as test scores count as proxy measures for competence, it must be said that those who are entering teaching are *relatively incompetent*. That is, *this society's brightest and best are not entering teaching.* ... In short, *the smart go elsewhere.* (pp. 127–128; italics added)

A journal article highlighting a summary statement of the Vance and Schlechty (1982) research provides another case in point; while data support the first half of their observation, they do not support the latter.

> Teaching appears to attract and retain a disproportionately high percentage of those with low measured academic ability, and *fails to attract and retain those with high ability.* (p. 22; emphasis added)

After gathering and interpreting an otherwise well-considered number of data sets, Feistritzer (1983a) also fosters the erroneous impression:

> *New opportunities for women in a wide range of professions within the United States are denying education the choice of the brightest and most creative women within the society.* (p. 60; emphasis in original)

The research in this regard is unquestionably clear. Teacher education does not fail to attract and retain persons with high ability. If there is a failure, it is that teaching does not get as many as might be hoped from the highest scoring test takers, but it does attract and retain many very bright people. Actually, the failure that is supported by data for both prospective and practicing teachers is that too many persons with excessively low scores on academic measures are allowed into teaching, but this claim needs further examination.

In order to reconcile the discrepancies encountered in various reports, two potentially confusing approaches to conceptualizing the teacher education talent pool must be distinguished. One approach first isolates the full teacher education population, counts the number from this group scoring in the upper quintile of all college graduates, and then reports the proportion that this number represents for the teacher education group as a whole. Since the overall teacher education population is very large and all fields compete for students in the upper quintile, a clear result of this approach is to come up with a relatively small proportion. Those painting a bleak picture of teacher education (e.g., Joyce & Clift, 1984) generally limit themselves to reporting data obtained from this approach.

An alternative approach used by those concerned with the talent flow in teaching starts with the academically talented population itself. Instead of beginning with all teacher education students and asking about the proportion of high scorers, they begin with all college students scoring in the upper quintile and ask about the proportion in teacher education. Like the questions that are raised, the characterizations that emerge from these two approaches differ.

When asking about the proportion of upper quintile talent going into teaching, Vance & Schlechty (1982) found that over 11% of the highest scoring college graduates on the SAT verbal and math measures went into teacher education in 1976–1979. In addition, approximately 7% of these highest scoring graduates assumed teaching positions. It would be important to know how this record of recruitment compares with those of other occupations requiring a college education, because most jobs draw from the full distribution of talent in higher education. Nevertheless, all occupations recruit from the top, and getting over one-tenth of all talented persons to enter teacher education during low demand years does not seem unreasonable; nor does getting 7% to enter teaching at this same time appear unduly low. The relevant question in need of further thought concerns what would constitute a reasonable percentage of the top quintile of college-educated persons that should pursue a career in teaching, assuming that society also wants bright and talented doctors, scientists, lawyers, and other professionals. Judgments about reasonable proportions should be made explicit before researchers and policymakers comment on the apparent shortage of academically talented persons in teacher education.

While questions remain about research findings on the top academic talent in teacher education, the case is different for the other end of the distribution. The lowest scoring subset of the college population seems to contain excessive numbers of prospective teachers; 38% of the college graduates scoring lowest on the SAT verbal and math measures were recruited to education during the 1976–1979 period, and approximately 28% of this lowest scoring subset obtained teaching positions (Vance & Schlechty, 1982). The fact that such a large number and excessive proportion of the lowest scoring college students are accepted into teacher education and subsequently recommended for certification explains the genesis of the stereotype that those in teacher education are the least academically able.

Weaver (1981) examined test data from the Educational Testing Service, the College Board, the American College Testing Program, and the National Longitudinal Study. Interested in potential changes in the mean scores of college-bound high school seniors showing a preference for teaching, he found an overall pattern of mean test-score decline in verbal and qualitative skills. The relative rank of college-bound seniors interested in teaching compared to those interested in other occupations showed little change across the decade.

Although a shifting and sorting-out process occurs after the high school preference for teaching is indicated, Weaver (1979) found the mean test scores for college seniors majoring in all education fields combined to be at roughly the 40th percentile. His data permitted the conclusion that the majority of new teacher graduates fell into the lower half of their college class on skills measured by the SAT, ACT, and NLS test battery.

Although such results hardly suggest an overwhelming below-average majority, it is a majority nevertheless, and the number and proportion at the bottom appear excessive for persons pursuing a career that is basically academic in nature. With little attention to the distribution of test scores, Weaver did note that his data showed "no larger proportion of non-white students in education than in other career fields, and the presence of minorities among graduating education seniors had virtually no effect on SAT scores" (p. 11).

Schlechty and Vance's longitudinal study (1981) of North Carolina teachers supported Weaver's conclusions. They found that as a group those entering teaching scored less well on the National Teacher Exam (NTE) than prospective teachers had in the recent past. They also found those most likely to leave teaching early and in the greatest numbers were among those obtaining the highest scores on the NTE, while those most likely to stay in teaching the longest were from the ranks of those obtaining the lowest scores on the NTE. Although one could question the use of the NTE alone, Pratt, DeLucia, and Uhl's (1979) research indicates that scores on the SAT verbal and math subtests are acceptable predictors of the NTE common examination scores.

Further work by Vance and Schlechty (1982) supported the external validity of Weaver's study as well as their own early findings. They used the National Longitudinal Study of 1972 High School Seniors to obtain their population. Drawing from those reporting an earned baccalaureate degree by 1979, they compared the SAT scores of those who majored in education, held teaching positions, or obtained teaching certificates with those who had not pursued teaching at all. Having ranked the total population into five quintiles on the basis of SAT scores, their data showed that those attracted to teaching had a proportionately larger share of the lower ranks and an appreciably smaller share of the upper ranks. In other words, the patterns from the national sample closely paralleled the patterns found among North Carolina teachers. These patterns are so regular that they ought not to be ignored.

Almost one quarter of the college graduates were recruited to education in 1979, and Vance and Schlechty's (1982) data show that the lowest ranking set of the total graduate pool contributed the greatest proportion of its members to teaching (approximately 38%). The second lowest rank contributed approximately 26% of its members to teaching, the middle rank approximately 23%, the second highest rank approximately 17%, and the highest rank about 11%.

Looking beyond high school graduates interested in teaching and college graduates recruited into education, Vance and Schlechty examined the population of college graduates who became teachers. Although 25% of all college graduates went into teacher education, only about 18% actually assumed teaching positions. But here again, the pattern of many lows and progressively fewer highs was consistent. Of the total college graduate population, the lowest ranking set had approximately 28% of its members assume teaching positions, the second-lowest rank had approximately 21%, the middle rank had approximately 18%, the second-highest rank had approximately 13%, and the highest rank had approximately 7%. Even among those who had actually taught but thought that they would subsequently leave teaching, Vance and Schlechty found

the highest percentage of potential loss among the highest ranking set (approximately 85%) and the lowest percentage of potential loss among the lowest ranking set (approximately 62%).

The research of the past decade shows that many students from the ranks of the least academically inclined, at least as judged by standardized test performance, were allowed to enter and successfully exit from professional training programs for teachers. An important perspective that must be emphasized, however, is that the phenomenon is not new or even recent in origin. The problem of too many lows in teaching, although often cast as a problem of not enough highs, has been known and a topic of expressed frustration and discussion at major educational meetings since the 1800s (Mattingly, 1975; Powell, 1980). In the mid-1900s the Carnegie Foundation for the Advancement of Teaching published a study entitled *The Student and His Knowledge* which reported the 1928–1932 high school test results for those going on to college (Learned & Wood, 1938). Their interesting introduction and conclusions highlight the enduring quality and, incidentally, the consistently sex-related nature of the research.

> The last feature of the test results that has been chosen for inclusion in this summary has to do with a group of college students who from time immemorial have been the beneficiaries of special care and attention on the part of colleges and universities. These are the students who are being prepared to teach. The results concern ... students tested in 1928 and in 1932. In both tests the teacher's average was below the average total score for the entire group and was below all other group averages except those of business, art, agriculture, and secretarial candidates. In the second test, the artists scored above the teachers.
>
> The only consolation to be drawn from these findings appears in the fact that among the prospective teachers graduating from arts colleges and technical schools the male contingent taken ranks high. In both examinations, the men scored higher than any other large occupational group except in the second test, the engineers. Unfortunately, this group of male teachers is the group with which the pupil himself comes least in contact. Their work in connection with a school is likely to assume an administrative character. The group also includes those who will teach in college and there engage partly or wholly in research. (pp. 38–39)

TOO MANY LOWS

Here the research seems unequivocal. Those who teach teachers encounter a substantial number of learners with average and high scores on standardized measures of academic ability. But the overall group norm for teacher education students falls below the average for all college students due to the larger numbers of learners scoring in the lowest ranks on such measures. The overabundance of teacher education students drawn from among the least academically inclined certainly contributes to the characterization that all prospective and practicing teachers have low intellectual ability. But the unfortunate stereotypes are not the only potentially negative consequences. An additional possibility is the discouraging effect that sustained interaction and association with large numbers of relatively slow concrete learners can have for more intellectually facile abstract learners and their teachers.

The curriculum and instruction for courses and workshops necessarily revolve around the intellectual norms of the student group. Conant (1963) argued for selection of above-average students on the grounds that "general education must not be pitched at too low a level or too slow a pace" (p. 81). Further study is needed in teacher education, assuming the student group is dominated by persons from the lowest quintiles of academic talent, on the extent to which course objectives and instructional discourse revolve around the majority's desire, if not demand, to be told rather precisely and concretely what to do and how to do it. Such concrete direction reduces cognitive strain and allows the student majority to escape from that which they are less able to enjoy or do well—think, reason, question, and analyze. It is possible that some of the long-criticized mindlessness of teacher education begins here.

In addition, a majority of adult learners tend to have a more powerful influence on their teachers and student colleagues than a majority of child learners. Not only can adult learners express dissatisfaction more directly with less fear of reprisal, they can more readily cause problems for the professor/teacher or staff developer/teacher by complaining to authorities (e.g., department chairs, school administrators, or union officials) or handing in devastating course evaluations when content seems inappropriate (e.g., too theoretical or too abstract). Negative consequences for the teachers of adults are even more apt to follow when the unhappy majority expresses their dissatisfaction as a group.

Such power and influence on the part of adult student groups is constructive when the group's academic norm is not controlled by a majority of the least able. But when that norm is dominated by lower ability students over sustained periods of time, the highly motivated and intellectually quick adult learners and teachers may well seek alternative student groups for teaching and learning. Just as adult learners have more power and influence over teachers than children do, they also have more freedom. Not captured by parental or legal authority, they can leave the classroom with relative ease when the teaching-learning situation becomes excessively uncomfortable. In addition, it is likely that talented students will help small numbers of fellow students struggle intellectually with complex knowledge and skills, but they are less likely to tolerate prolonged discussion of simplistic and surface knowledge and skill. Neither are talented adult learners apt to attempt serious conversion of the less able majority of their preservice classmates or inservice counterparts. The task is too difficult, and talented adult learners, as well as talented adult teachers, have alternatives. Opportunities for avoiding the discomfort of academic boredom and partaking of the enjoyments of intellectual challenge can be found elsewhere.

Thus if there is evidence for the hypothesis that academically talented teachers of teachers and academically talented students of teaching will tend to avoid student groups that are dominated by the least scholarly and academic, it is important that initial teacher preparation reduce the dominant proportion of lows that research shows are clustered in the student population of particular institutions (Schlechty & Vance, 1983b). Similarly, especially challenging academic opportunities in continuing education must be provided for the minority group of average and above average practicing teachers, lest they too continue the exodus from the low basic-skill levels of inservice training that now endure because of their apparent appropriateness for a less academically inclined majority.

It is also possible, given the tyranny of needs assessment approaches, that many average and above-average teachers get overlooked in continuing education decision making, since the nature of today's inservice is often determined by these majority-driven instruments. Describing the characteristics of the elementary school teacher as learner, Bierly and Berliner (1982) also seem to join the trend of generalizing needs from the apparent preferences of the below-average majority. Basing their observations on staff development evaluation reports and experience, they identify priorities that include "the need for practicality and concreteness in instruction" (p. 37), the "need for individualization and adaptation of instruction to teachers' own classroom situations" (p. 38), the "need for coaching in the classroom by observers who provide feedback," and the "need for having instructors who were or are teachers themselves" (p. 39). The press for having external experts tell or show "the concrete right way to teach" prevails. In a similar vein, but drawing from NEA surveys, McCune (1977) reports that

> the major priorities that teachers pose for the education R and D community revolve around questions such as: What are the best methods of instruction? How can I best individualize the instruction within the classroom? How can I improve my teaching effectiveness? (p. 9)

The excessively concrete and tell-me/show-me nature of such classroom-bounded concerns is made salient by the general absence of requests for more profound and thoughtful interactions and issues. Doyle and Ponder (1977–1978) also identify and discuss what they identify as the practicality ethic in teacher decision making.

While the full explanation for intellectual preferences and the press toward low-level knowledge in teacher education cannot and should not be attributed to the prospective and practicing student majority that falls significantly below the measured average of academic talent for all college-educated persons, the influence of this large below-average group must not be overlooked. These influences include the group's tendency to depress the levels of content knowledge assumed appropriate for the teacher education curriculum and to discourage talented teachers and students from being seriously committed to the improvement of teaching and teacher education.

While the need for teachers and the competition for the most talented students will continue to be strong, teacher education must look to the full distribution of college talent for its large learner population. But research and policy can shape recruitment, retention, and certification decisions so that the overall norm for the teaching force comes from the average and above, rather than from the average and below, as has historically been the case. Demographic study suggests that recent supply and demand trends would make policies to this effect possible. After the excessive demand years of the sixties, the surplus of qualified teachers available in the seventies would have permitted the screening out of the least academically inclined of the college student population. An adequate supply of qualified teacher candidates would have been available each year across the past decade, even if *all* of those in the lowest quintile had been

542

JUDITH E. LANIER AND JUDITH W. LITTLE

denied access to teacher education. It also appears that a screening policy of this or a comparable nature would be possible between now and 1990. During this time period, college graduates entering the labor force are expected to exceed jobs traditionally filled by such graduates by over 3 million (Bureau of Labor Statistics, 1980).

But students' academic ability is not everything, however, and the equally important factors of study motivation, aspiration, and expectation must also be considered. As Katherine Evans, a wise teacher education researcher from England, observed, "the ability to teach is not the same as actually bothering to do so" (cited in Crocker, 1974); to enrich this admonition still further, the realization that "the ability to teach is not the same as having the opportunity to do so" must also be added.

The Students of Teaching: Expectations and Motivations

Teacher educators encounter many learners that are not easily engaged in serious intellectual growth with the aim of improving schools and professional practice. Not only are the academic interests and abilities of the student majority low when compared with the college-educated population as a whole, but the learners' affective propensities are equally problematic. The research evidence suggests that both prospective and practicing teachers maintain low expectations for the professional knowledge aspects of their education. The desire for serious and continued learning for improvement purposes is also understandably low in light of growing declines in extrinsic and intrinsic rewards for the occupation of teaching itself. Further, aspirations to employ new understandings and intellectual insights while remaining in teaching are often perceived as dysfunctional, because opportunities to exercise informed judgment, engage in thoughtful discourse, and participate in reflective decision making are practically nonexistent as teaching is presently defined. A skeptical student attitude often prevails, therefore, in response to the very logical question, "Why bother to be a serious student of teaching if the learnings will probably not be worthwhile?"

STUDENTS' EXPECTATIONS FOR TEACHER EDUCATION

Prospective teachers' expectations for professional training are acquired indirectly from early encounters with their own elementary and secondary teachers, social norms communicated by the general public, and the existing ethos on the higher education campus. The expectations formed from these sources typically carry a negative valence and reflect an awareness that teacher education is easy to enter, intellectually weak, and possibly unnecessary.

Prospective teachers enter preservice coursework having already spent much of their lives in classrooms (Lanier & Henderson, 1973), serving what is considered an "apprenticeship of observation" (Lortie, 1975). In addition, experiences such as camp counseling, teaching Sunday school, and serving as teacher aides contribute to a conception of teaching that seems to emphasize nurturant instincts over intellectual capacity.

Book, Byers, and Freeman (1983) found that many candidates come to formal teacher preparation believing that they have little to learn. Over 40% expect to leave in less than 10 years, with almost half of this set expecting to raise a family; the others intend to change careers entirely or advance in education. In the eyes of most of the 400 students they studied, the major obligation of teacher educators was to create classroom teaching opportunities for candidates prior to their accepting paid teaching assignments. Adding to this apprentice view of teacher education was a conception on the part of many that teaching is largely "an extended form of parenting, about which there is little to learn other than through instincts and one's own experiences" (Book et al., 1983, p. 10). The summary data showed almost one-quarter of the students entering teacher education with high or complete confidence in their ability to teach prior to specialized course work. Another two-thirds were at least moderately sure of their ability at the outset, leaving almost 90% of the student group believing that professional studies had little new to offer them. Book et al. (1983) suggest that such entering views reflect the strength of the lore that there is little "need to obtain a knowledge base in pedagogy in order to become effective teachers" (p. 11).

The views that prospective and practicing teachers hold about learning to teach affect their involvement in formal programs of teacher education and their work with one another. Asked about preparation for teaching, experienced teachers insist upon the primacy of the classroom environment, arguing that teaching is inevitably learned through experience (Lortie, 1975). The expressed views of teachers that teaching is mastered on the job are more consistent and less diverse than the interpretations offered by researchers. In the research literature, one encounters a considerable degree of uncertainty about the various sources of such attitudes. The influences of prior socialization (Lortie, 1975), general university experience (Zeichner & Tabachnick, 1981), initial pedagogical preparation (Cruickshank & Broadbent, 1968; Lacey, 1977), bureaucratic and professional norms of individual schools (Hoy & Rees, 1977; Zeichner & Tabachnick, 1981, 1984), the power of significant other persons or groups (Edgar & Brod, 1970), and the peculiar ecology of the classroom (Doyle, 1977; Fuller & Bown, 1975) have all come under scrutiny.

What practicing teachers expect from teacher education is connected, understandably, to the value they assign to their own formal preparation. Unfortunately, the research on the perceived value of teacher education concentrates more on portraying teachers' general satisfaction or dissatisfaction than on probing for the sources of either. Nevertheless, the record of disappointment predominates; one recent review of the literature on teacher education and induction summarizes the descriptive literature as a "litany of woe" (Bureau of Educational Research, 1983). But while the record of teachers' disappointments is clear, insightful interpretations of the disjuncture between expectations and work and between training and on-the-job demands are less available.

One problem is that most conclusions are based on teachers' global assessments of their initial preparation and its general capacity to support them in the full range of their current responsibilities. Thus, the available literature offers little basis on which to sort out the contributions that teachers' formal preparation has made to their distinct professional capabilities.

Unique areas of preparation remain undistinguished, such as depth, rigor, and currency in subject area knowledge; sophistication in curricular and instructional judgments; broad intellectual preparation as a well-educated person; and high-quality solutions to recurring problems of student learning or classroom organization. On the whole, efforts to acknowledge the achievements of beginning teacher education or to uncover its failings have been uninformed by any clear understanding of its aspirations for teachers and teaching (Katz, 1980).

A second difficulty in judging teachers' views of their formal preparation is that the research has been largely retrospective, eliciting teachers' judgments at a time when the press of day-to-day responsibilities may submerge the intellectual dimension of their work and set a premium on technical details. A longitudinal and biographical examination of the evolving views of prospective and practicing teachers of the sort begun by Zeichner (1983) in following student teachers into their first year of teaching may help to place such judgments in context and to determine which of several competing estimates and interpretations of program effect provides greatest explanatory power (Nemser, 1983; Veenman, 1984).

Plagued by these difficulties, the available survey and case study research produces a predictably contradictory picture. In such studies, teachers give mixed reviews to the programs of beginning and continuing education in which they have participated. They are ambivalent about the capacity of such programs to build substantive competence or to serve as a route to personal self-confidence, professional prestige, and other rewards. But in the main, teachers make critical judgments. Although isolated programs receive acclaim from their graduates, the prevailing view is that the ideas and methods emphasized in beginning teacher preparation do not accord well with the challenges subsequently met in the classroom (Eddy, 1969; Fuchs, 1969; Griffin & Hukill, 1983; Little, 1981; Lortie, 1975; Ryan, 1970). In an essay probing the personal reality of learning to teach, Greene (1979) argues that such criticisms are both inevitable and, in some respects, unwarranted:

No matter how practical, how grounded our educational courses were, they suddenly appear to be totally irrelevant in the concrete situation where we find ourselves. This is because general principles never fully apply to new and special situations, especially if those principles are thought of as prescriptions or rules. Dewey spoke of principles as modes or methods of analyzing situations, tools to be used in "judging suggested courses of action." . . . We forget that, for a rule to be universally applicable, all situations must be fundamentally alike; and, as most of us know, classroom situations are always new and never twice alike. Even so, we yearn oftentimes for what might be called a "technology of teaching," for standard operating procedures that can be relied upon to "work." Devoid of these, we project our frustration back upon whatever teacher education we experienced. (pp 27–28)

Programs of continuing education come under similar attack. In a study of 50 elementary and secondary school teachers, Spencer-Hall (1982) received negative critiques on formal programs of inservice from fully half the teachers and mixed responses from almost another third. Among teachers' complaints were that programs were poorly planned, irrelevant to the demands of their work, unconnected to each other or to teachers' work over time, badly aligned with other scheduled

commitments, and implicitly or explicitly oriented toward correcting individual deficiencies. Programs were typically designed by administrators with little meaningful influence by teachers. Spencer-Hall's findings are consistent with those of other researchers (Little, 1981; Moore & Hyde, 1981). But like many of the accounts of beginning teacher preparation, the primarily disparaging views of professional development reveal only prevailing patterns, while masking the features that relate to teacher expectations and distinctions between effective and ineffective components or designs (see Vacca, Barnett, & Vacca, 1982).

Just as much of the research on elementary and secondary teaching has moved away from an emphasis on the negative toward studies of exemplary models, so is there a shift away from documenting and belaboring views of the legendary bad models that characterize the dominant modes of teacher education. A more productive approach is the study of meanings and views prospective and practicing teachers bring to and take from the most exemplary and effective teacher education practices, even if such settings represent a minority at this time. Nonetheless, present studies show that the experience of and the expectations held by contemporary participants in teacher education are, in general, predominantly negative. The ethos of low esteem for university-based and school-based teacher education is bound to influence teacher–student interactions in preservice and inservice settings.

It should also be noted that prospective and practicing teacher expectations for their professional education stand in contrast to those of persons in other professions who anticipate difficult access, hard work, a sense of academic value, and occupational continuation. Instead, prospective and practicing teachers expect simple access, easy work, minimal academic value, and occupational discontinuation. Students in other professions enter with the belief that they have much to learn. Such acknowledged unknowns become motivations to learn, and the inevitable endemic uncertainties of practice rest side by side with a respected body of collectively accepted views and practices (Fox, 1957).

Early research on the social and psychological environments of medical schools as they shape "the professional self of the student, so that he comes to think, feel, and act like a doctor" were reported by Merton, Reader, & Kendall (1957) in *The Student-Physician*. At the outset of that work, they assumed the obvious importance of the studies because "it is plainly in the professional school that the outlook and values, as well as the skills and knowledge, of practitioners are first shaped by the profession" (p. vii). No such entering assumption is possible for those studying the professional self of students coming to think, feel, and act like teachers. Learning to teach is complicated in many deceptively obvious ways (Feiman-Nemser & Buchmann, 1983), not the least of which are the students' expectations that they already have sufficient understanding and there is little more of value to be learned.

STUDENTS' MOTIVATION FOR SERIOUS STUDY OF TEACHER EDUCATION

In addition to the occasional pleasures of professional study itself, the primary rewards of initial or continuing professional education are found either in the occupation for which the study provides access or in the improved work performance that accrues as a consequence of the study. The case is no different for teacher education. Many valuable insights obtained in this regard are found in Lortie's (1975) survey work and sociological analyses reported in *Schoolteacher*. Although his specific findings are now somewhat dated, and many of his interpretations are tarnished with traditional views of women in society, the classic nature of his contributions must be taken seriously.

Lortie's data and thoughtful analyses portray a number of attractions in the work of teachers: enjoyment in working with young people; pride in performing important public service; ease of entry, exit, and re-entry; time compatibility; some modest material benefits; and psychic rewards emanating from student achievement. Importantly, Sykes (1983a, 1983b, 1984) has since updated this work by drawing on changes occurring over the past decade that appear to "undercut the classic attractions of teaching" (p. 108). He thoughtfully and often poignantly characterizes the diminishing returns: decreased enjoyment from work with less responsive and appreciative young people, a deteriorating public image of teaching as important service, a major reduction in lateral school mobility for women and upward school mobility for men, the erosion of material benefits, reduced psychic rewards from less regular student achievement, and teaching environments that all too often are disruptive, dangerous, and bureaucratic to the point of frustration.

Prospective teachers can hardly maintain the naive optimism they once held, especially in light of well-publicized declines in the job market and a spate of reports on the problems of contemporary teaching. Instead of admiration for those going into such an important field, today's citizenry wonders why those with good sense pursue it. Boyer (1983) describes the reported difficulties of students planning to enter teaching. "We are under tremendous pressure all around to constantly justify our choice of a career. Professors want to know why we are taking this course, and most of the other students think we are crazy" (p. 173).

Practicing teachers already know that rewards are few and on the decline, as are opportunities for advancement into educational administration or colleges of education. The flat career structure of teaching, combined with a great many teachers at the top of their salary schedule and in possession of a master's degree, leaves incentives for continuing education lacking in students' minds. But factors to be considered for contemporary students of continuing teacher education go beyond research on what they find missing in their work. What prolonged teaching does to their frame of mind must not be overlooked.

The Effects of Prolonged Service in Teaching

The present generation of America's teaching force, for the first time, has come to be composed of a majority of career teachers; and the research suggests that career teachers have historically been dissatisfied with and alienated from their work. Lortie (1975) described male teachers as "transient members of the

occupation, literally and psychologically" (p. 54). Yet, Zeigler (1967) found that "in actual practice, more males than females remain career teachers" (p. 16), and disgruntled ones at that; his research "produced clear and unequivocal evidence indicating there is substantial job dissatisfaction among male teachers" (p. 19). But most of the one third of the teaching force composed of men historically sought upwardly mobile work in education or alternative employment and, until recently, were generally able to be successful in this regard. But now they remain unhappily confined to what many of them perceive as a dead-end occupation.

The situation is little different for career women teachers, except that this group now includes both married and single women. Historically, the single women remaining in teaching and dedicating themselves to their work in the public's most idealized sense also became dissatisfied with the occupation (Lortie, 1975; Zeigler, 1967). Positive attitudes for both men and women deteriorate with longevity in classroom teaching and become, as Zeigler (1967) observed, "in flux if they are not firmly hostile and negative" (p. 50); Lortie (1975) agrees, noting that "persisters are relatively disadvantaged" (p. 99). Reduced up-and-out opportunities for men's traditional escape and less in-and-out job flexibility for married women seem to have provoked growing resentment.

As a group, the students of continuing teacher education are weary from the excessive demands of the occupation, dulled from their routinized work with children, and frustrated by the lack of opportunity for intellectual, purposeful exchange with adults. In response, a great many of them simply disengage from the business of teaching. Much of their teaching becomes routinized, habitual, and unenthusiastic (Sykes, 1983a). They go through the motions and they acquire second jobs or other side interests that give them something other than kids and school to think about (Cusick, 1981). While they cannot escape teaching in body, they can in mind and spirit, and these career teachers are today's majority: They are the students that teacher educators must motivate to learn to teach more effectively. The task represents an obviously formidable challenge, particularly when it must be accomplished on top of the average teacher's 46-hour work week (Sykes, 1983a).

A point of emphasis that must not be slighted, however, concerns the enduring nature of the problem here discussed. The cognitive and affective costs associated with prolonged work in teaching are not new, and two recent historical studies illustrate this reality. Dyer (Lines, 1982) was able to rescue from obscurity materials that portray the struggles of an aspiring middle-class woman teacher of the mid-19th century. In *To Raise Myself a Little: The Diaries and Letters of Jennie, a Georgia Teacher 1851–1886*, Dyer chronicles the odyssey of Amelia "Jennie" Akehurst, who moved from New York to Georgia in search of better opportunities for herself through teaching. Unsuccessful in her efforts to raise herself, she never found work that offered sufficient remuneration along with satisfactory living and working conditions. The diaries and letters that chronicle her moves portray a teacher's life in a variety of settings and point out that teaching has long held many disadvantages that even committed women found hard to endure. The dissatisfactions Jennie encountered in her career included low pay, inattentive and undisciplined students, outside interference in her classroom, and numerous other ills; like today's contemporary teachers, when her daughter followed in her footsteps, Jennie complained about the difficulties she knew awaited her.

Powell (1976), in his historical study, cites the articulate analysis of a high school teacher wrestling with the problem of attracting and keeping talented persons in teaching. As early as 1890, H. M. Willard, a Massachusetts teacher, noted that "the difficulty of recruiting the ablest and most ambitious college graduates to teaching — graduates with career options in law, medicine, business, or science — lay with the current nature of the career itself" (cited in Powell, 1976, p. 4). In striking terms, Powell draws from Willard's argument.

> In contrast with other professions in which successful individuals occupied "positions of honor, responsibility, and authority," teachers lived lives of "mechanical routine" and were subjected to a "machine of supervision, organization, classification, grading, percentages, uniformity, promotion, tests, examinations, and record-keeping." Nowhere in the school culture was there room for "individuality, ideas, independence, originality, study, investigation." Working alone and limited to their classrooms and studies, they tended to become recluses rather than "en rapport with the live issues of the day."
>
> Confined to the company of the young and powerless, teachers easily became autocratic, opinionated, and dogmatic. Their isolation extended to relationships with other teachers as well. Instead of colleagueship and cooperation, he found a "critical or jealous spirit." (p. 4)

Powell's and Dyer's work indicates that the "teaching is not what it used to be" perception on the part of many is only partially correct. In many important ways, career teaching is much as it has always been in this country. The historical and sociological research suggests that career teachers have long been rewarded inadequately and have consistently "burned out." Perhaps the major changes in the problem are ones of greater degree, increased magnitude, and general awareness of the phenomena. Continuing teacher education can help to alleviate, but will not solve, the oppressive problems of career which must be addressed, through changes in teachers' workplace, workload, and initial preparation.

Summary: Research and Better Understanding of the Learners

Those who study, set policy for, or are themselves engaged in teacher education can be increasingly informed by the growing body of research on the students of teaching. The expectations, aspirations, academic abilities, and motivation for learning that prospective and practicing teachers bring to teacher education are as influential and important as these same learner qualities in all teaching situations.

The two learner groups, preservice and inservice teachers, have both changed in important ways over the past decade. The overall size of the preservice teacher group became substantially smaller and composed of fewer academically talented and more academically weak students than heretofore. This change is of no small concern because many students of teaching, as a group, have traditionally scored in the lowest quartile of measured college student ability. Also during this past decade,

the inservice teacher group became more stable than at any time in America's past, giving this country its first generation with a majority of career teachers. The attrition that occurred at the inservice level also showed a disporportionate loss of the more academically talented teachers and a disproportionate retention of the less academically able, just as with the preservice group.

Much of the recent research documents these changes and examines the potential influences on and effects of these changes for teacher education. The other studies emanate from a variety of disciplinary perspectives and enrich the understanding of teachers as learners, although they cumulate to emphasize a clear set of challenges to teacher education.

While those who teach teachers encounter learners with a wide range of academic ability, the research cited here suggests that recruitment and retention of the more academically talented learners will become increasingly difficult. Further, although there are differences across institutions, the group norms for prospective and practicing teachers are moving toward the low-average end of the scale. Those who teach teachers also encounter learners whose motivation for learning is negatively influenced by a set of career expectations and aspirations that emanate from predominantly low professional and public regard for serious investment in teaching and teacher education. A work environment that is generally lacking in intellectual stimulation and group norms that traditionally and increasingly reflect below-average ability and interest in academic pursuits understandably influence the motivation to learn on the part of students of teaching. These problems will not only persist, but will become exacerbated if changes in the conditions of teaching are not made.

Studying the Curriculum for Teaching

Gradually acquiring more breadth and depth, the curriculum research in teacher education is more enlightening than heretofore, although many basic questions remain. In all fields the study of curriculum can be confusing because of its multiple definitions and meanings, but when several of these differences are contrasted, they illuminate the major issues and controversies surrounding curriculum research in teacher education.

One common view of curriculum study attempts to ascertain whether a selected content produces one or more effects considered desirable by academic specialists or researchers. Such studies often raise questions of input–output efficiencies and are referred to here as "expert-designed content and process studies." These studies dominate teacher education curriculum research, but their cumulated contribution to better understanding of content issues in teacher education is difficult to summarize.

An alternative to the expert-designed content and process studies is curriculum research that emanates from a broader view of curriculum itself. Curriculum studies that view curriculum as "what students have an opportunity to learn" (McCutcheon, 1982) provide more intellectual insight and challenge to the field, although less research of this order is available. Such studies raise questions about the knowledge and understandings that are either made accessible or withheld from prospective and practicing teachers. Acknowledging the moral as well as the scientific dimensions of teaching, these studies describe and analyze the problems and paradoxes of knowledge, the potentially constructive or harmful effects of learning experiences for learners (i.e., for teachers or prospective teachers in this case), and the social and cultural interests that may influence knowledge in teacher education. Because descriptive–analytic curriculum work is generally more informative for relatively young and developing fields of study like teacher education, these approaches are emphasized in this review.

What Students Have an Opportunity to Learn: Description and Analysis

Available in almost three-quarters of all 4-year colleges and universities in the nation (Plisko, 1983, Tables 4.2 and 4.9), initial teacher education conveys in its broad outlines the appearance of standardization. As an all-university responsibility, the course work for prospective teachers is organized into three familiar strands: general education, subject matter concentrations, and pedagogical study. Ordinarily, these strands include general liberal arts courses comparable to those taken by all undergraduates, courses reflecting the core knowledge in selected substantive areas, and courses meant to provide an acquaintance with the purpose and origins of schooling in America and a grasp of fundamental pedagogical principles and practices. Given such learning opportunities, initial programs are expected to prepare candidates who can assume independent classroom teaching responsibility for young students without causing undue harm. The undue harm concept implies that beginning teachers are able to do more than provide responsible oversight for the physical and emotional well-being of the children in their charge. The neophyte must also be able to provide equitable and appropriate learning opportunities for students and effectively help them acquire the content and skills common to their grade and level. But beyond these general expectations and three content categories in initial preparation, there is limited common substance to the teacher education curriculum. The course content that prospective and practicing teachers have an opportunity to learn is highly unstable and individualistic. The variation among and within courses and workshops at different institutions, as well as in the same institutions over brief periods of time, achieves almost infinite variety.

CONSISTENT CHAOS IN THE COURSE WORK

Much is said about professors of education not having agreed upon a common body of knowledge that all school teachers should possess before taking their first full-time job. But the situation is equally characteristic of other faculty groups sharing all-university responsibility for teacher education. Of the three content areas in teacher education, in fact, the two most neglected in curriculum research are the general studies and subject matter concentrations. Little is known about what prospective teachers typically encounter or learn from academic study in these areas. Conant's (1963) study of 2 decades ago stands alone as seminal work and is worthy of increased attention and follow-up.

Consider, for example, the extended-program argument that continues to rage. The only difference Conant found between 4- and 5-year programs was the number of courses available for student electives; he concluded:

To return to the California pattern, it is only fair to repeat that the issue between four-year and five-year continuous programs turns on the value one attaches to free electives. And if a parent feels that an extra year to enable the future teacher to wander about and sample academic courses is worth the cost, I should not be the person to condemn this use of money. But I would, as a taxpayer, *vigorously protest the use of tax money* for a fifth year of what I consider dubious value. (pp. 203–204; emphasis in original)

With a sample stratified for comparisons between prestige colleges and teachers' colleges, Conant found the course requirements both in subject area concentrations and in general studies in a state of disarray. After examining the depth and breadth of the subject matter concentration requirements, he reported:

Thousands of students each year wander through survey courses with only the shallowest knowledge of the subject.... It is risky to assume that a holder of a bachelor's degree from an American college has necessarily pursued a recognized subject in depth, or in a coherent pattern. (p. 106)

In his examination of the general studies, he found similar trends. A confusing disparity of offerings and requirements was present among all types of institutions in English, mathematics, social science, and the humanities. Even philosophy, which Conant considered "an essential element in any collegiate program pretending to breadth or coherence" (p. 89), was rarely a specific requirement. Conant argued for fewer electives and more requirements as a means of obtaining greater depth. Citing the practical reasons, he emphasized teachers' need for knowledge beyond their area of specialization. And Conant's arguments were not confined to classroom utility, for he strongly believed that substantive conversation with students, parents, and colleagues was also critical:

If a teacher is largely ignorant or uninformed he can do much harm. Moreover, if the teachers in a school system are to be a group of learned persons cooperating together, they should have as much intellectual experience in common as possible, and any teacher who has not studied in a variety of fields in college will always feel far out of his depth when talking with a colleague in a field other than his own.... And if teachers are to be considered learned persons in their communities, and if they are to command the respect of the professional men and women they meet, they must be prepared to discuss difficult topics. For example, to participate in any but the most superficial conversations about the impact of science on our culture, one must have at some time wrestled with the problems of the theory of knowledge. (p. 93)

Conant recommended that intensive single-subject certification as well as depth in other subjects be acquired through carefully articulated undergraduate courses. To fit this sort of depth and rigor into a 4-year teacher education program, Conant recommended the integration of professional and liberal studies and the elimination of overly simplifed, technical courses. But his logical and reasonable call for education as liberal study has been made many times before.

When higher education first assumed responsibility for teacher education, it was done in the belief that education was worthy of in-depth, scholarly study in the best university tradition. Borrowman (1965a) has documented the history of the issues and discourse that surround the general/liberal and professional studies relationship. Tracing many of America's early admonitions and recurring disappointments with education's failure to sustain the traditional values of liberal education for teachers, Borrowman emphasized the inquiring mind and spirit: A "commitment to the pursuit of knowledge for its own sake and not an undue concern for immediate results" was necessary, in addition to "problem-raising as well as problem-solving activity" (p. 11).

Bestor (cited in Borrowman, 1965a) observed that the study of education started out right, but deteriorated when the curriculum "did not offer to deepen a student's understanding of the great areas of human knowledge, nor start him off on a disciplined quest for new solutions to fundamental intellectual problems" (p. 15). Bestor, like many scholarly critics before and since, objected to preparation that offered specific practical solutions to specific practical problems instead of the knowledge teachers could use to solve problems on their own. The incessant tension and disagreement over content in teacher education continues to revolve around this basic curricular issue. Borrowman emphasized this point and urged that the crux of the argument not become confused; it is not professional education versus liberal education, but liberal–professional education versus technical–professional education.

While the research of the past decade brings perspective to this ongoing controversy, Borrowman's historical analysis continues to inform the contemporary debate over extended programs and should be reconsidered. He reported three sets of prevailing attitudes regarding the relationship between liberal and professional studies.

The first set, "that of the purists, who favor a four-year liberal education followed by a fifth year of highly professional training, has been idealized by some for a hundred years" (Borrowman, 1965a, p. 45). This purist attitude requires singleness of purpose within an institutional unit. It encourages the liberal arts faculty to ignore professional concerns, and on the professional school side it implies "that all instruction should be vigorously tested for its contribution to competence in classroom teaching" (p. 26). The professional studies, in the purist sense, are to be separated in time; that is, they are to be acquired after the general-liberal studies.

The second set of attitudes Borrowman describes is the integrated set, so called because it assumes "the distinction between liberal and professional studies to be a false one" (p. 26). Given this view, studies are selected for their concomitantly liberal and professional ends and are organized around a set of professional functions of teaching or a general social problems core.

The third set of attitudes, described as "the eclectic or ad hoc approach" (p. 39), grants a distinction between liberal and professional education but assumes that both should occur early in the student's collegiate career and continue to run parallel throughout undergraduate and graduate programs.

Borrowman's analysis refers to various initiatives and experimental programs undertaken to examine these separate and integrating positions, although little has been learned from them for some of the following reasons:

> One is that no institution has been able to attempt either plan under conditions that its advocates would consider sufficiently ideal for the experiment to be accepted as a definitive test of their basic assumptions. A second reason is that educational process is simply too involved, too little susceptible to the kind of control that scientific experimentation demands, and aimed at too many different outcomes to permit its being evaluated in terms of any single theoretical principle. (p. 40)

Consensus in favor of either extreme position has not emerged, therefore, and Borrowman notes a "widespread tendency to avoid pressing for agreement on an overarching principle" (p. 41). The purist and the ad hoc approaches prevail, in Borrowman's view, because they keep the professional and liberal studies separated. The integrated approach requires more cooperation among potentially hostile faculty and involves the risk of significant compromise. But separated approaches also tend to keep the professional education component more clearly technical and less defined as an area of liberal study. In his "Overview of Research in Teacher Education," for example, Turner (1975) builds from the prevailing common view:

> In teacher education, "training" refers to that component of preparation for which departments and schools of education are specifically responsible. Such training is thus professionally or technically oriented in the sense that the skills and knowledge taught are supposed to have a direct bearing on professional practice. (p. 97)

The professionally or technically oriented training Turner describes, when shaped by large numbers of students and faculty favoring prescriptive knowledge and skill performance, tends to slant the curriculum for teachers away from intellectually deep and rigorous study. Though this tendency has been slowed by reduced emphasis on the competency-based movement, the contemporary curriculum in teacher education continues to distance itself from a strong conceptual and intellectual orientation. The research does not suggest major curricular changes since the Conant and Borrowman studies of two decades ago, but there is growing evidence that teacher education is becoming more vocational and technical in orientation (Beyer & Zeichner, 1982).

Educational foundations, methods, and practice teaching requirements remain common to the pedagogical studies component, although great diversity remains in the amount of time given to each of these areas. In practice teaching alone, for example, Conant found a range of 90 to 300 required clock hours, and overall semester hours in elementary education ranged from 26 to 59. "With such variation," Conant noted, "the value of the median, of course, has no significance, though one often finds it quoted in surveys of teacher education" (1963, p. 129). Conant also found the translation of teaching experience into academic bookkeeping most confusing, as did Lortie (1975): "It is difficult to get precise, reliable information on what proportion of the average teacher's undergraduate study is centered on pedagogy and related courses" (p. 58).

The problems of insufficient information and ineffectual reports of central tendency continue, making it difficult to characterize the contemporary course work required of or taken by teacher education students. While some promising new efforts are under way, such as the cross-institutional transcript analysis that Shulman and Sykes have initiated at Stanford, existing data do not allow clear portraits of the explicit teacher preparation curriculum to be drawn.

Indications of general change must be inferred, therefore. Reports that field-based experience has increased (Zeichner, 1981) are supported by observations that state departments of education have mandated more time in classrooms and schools prior to student teaching (Moore, 1979). Additional reports suggest that the social and philosophical course requirements in the educational foundations sequence have been sacrificed to make room for more technical, field-oriented study (Finkelstein, 1982; Warren, 1982). What some accrediting bodies, state legislators, and other state officials sometimes do not realize is that all curricular additions require a displacement of something else; adding a reading course, for example, may mean dropping a mathematics course. If adding more general field experience across the past decade reduced social and philosophical study, it may inadvertently have increased technical education and reduced opportunity for liberal professional study. Further research is needed to assess this possibility.

Overall general descriptive work on the initial teacher education curriculum was significantly reduced across the seventies, in comparison with the extensive work completed in the sixties. But general interest in the curriculum of continuing teacher education understandably grew in concert with growing needs in this area, although little is known about the explicit curriculum here as well.

Once teachers enter professional life, their continuing education becomes difficult to trace and, like teaching itself, professional development assumes a largely private and independent character. There are no traditional content categories or required areas of study in continuing education that parallel those of the preservice institutions, and teachers' decisions to continue their professional education emanate largely from specific personal and professional circumstances. Choices about what course of professional development to pursue, how much to pursue, or even whether to pursue much of anything at all remain a matter of individual prerogative.

One descriptive inventory of teachers' continuing education activities yields radically different profiles of professional development for teachers with comparable experience and teaching assignments (Arends, 1983). A beginning high school biology teacher, characterized as an avid participant in continuing education, logged over 1600 hours in additional course work, independent research, selected conferences and workshops, and school-based decision-making groups over a 3-year period; another beginning teacher, described as a reluctant participant, logged only 29 hours of continuing education in the same 3-year period. Arends concludes:

> We are left with the impression that the whole process is a large, uncoordinated effort. We found few learning profiles that were very similar, nor could we find many instances where teachers had had the same learning experience. (p. 37)

The relatively private, eclectic, and diffuse character of continuing education thwarts attempts to understand its contribution to teachers' knowledge, competence, and enthusiasm for teaching and makes program effects difficult to evaluate (Gall, Haisley, Baker, & Perez, 1982; Stayrook, Cooperstein & Knapp, 1981). A further complication is the several functions served by programs of professional development (Little, 1981: Moore & Hyde, 1981; Schlechty & Crowell, 1983; Schlechty & Whitford, 1983), only one of which is the accummulation of technical knowledge and skill.

One function of continuing education is to serve teachers as individual members of a profession. At their best, teachers' individual pursuits add to the range, depth, and currency of subject area knowledge, contribute to the sophistication of curricular and instructional judgments, and add intellectual vigor to professional life. Necessarily, such programs also satisfy bureaucratic and career advancement purposes; they permit teachers to accumulate the record of credits and credentials associated with salary increments. In districts with declining enrollments, participation in inservice education may help teachers to preserve a competitive edge in a tight job market. Formal programs expand the range of career options by awarding credentials in administration, guidance and counseling, or various specializations.

A second and concurrent function of continuing education is to engage teachers as responsible members of a particular institution. Here, continuing education takes the form of district-sponsored staff development efforts that are frequently targeted to external requirements, including desegregation, mainstreaming, and bilingual education; generally these staff development efforts are aligned with established organizational values, priorities, programs, and traditions. While such programs may attract teachers' participation by offering college credit or other incentives, the curriculum is selected for its relevance to organizational, rather than individual, priorities (Fullan, 1982).

But regardless of purpose or function, it appears that current practice in continuing teacher education is characterized by many of the same qualities and weaknesses known to accompany initial preparation. Gall (1984) and several colleagues surveyed current staff development practices and compared them with research-based recommendations drawn from the literature. To their reported surprise (Gall, 1983), they found that "few activities reflected the sustained multi-year effort that Fullan and Pomfret found required for school improvement" (p. 3). They also found that staff development activities were relatively frequent, but "covered many topics rather than focusing on a few preeminent goals" (p. 3). Interestingly, the teachers they sampled were satisfied with 80 to 90% of their activities. Gall (1983) reported that the high rate of satisfaction could likely

> be explained by the fact that 88 percent of the inservice activities were perceived as relevant to their work; 63 percent required little new learning; 78 percent required no out-of-pocket expense; incentives were present for 55 percent; 49 percent were voluntary; and only 6 percent were assessed afterwards. (p. 3)

At the conclusion of the study Gall (1983) summarized the findings, characterizing staff development "as frequent, but fragmented and without depth" (p. 3). This observation remains consistent with both traditional and recent criticism of initial teacher preparation. Lortie (1975) described teacher education as high on general schooling and low on specialized schooling, and, compared with other professions, the "special schooling for teachers is neither intellectually nor organizationally complex" (p. 58). Comparing the mediated entry arrangements for prospective teachers to other crafts, professions, and highly skilled trades, he described it as "primitive"; practice teaching was not only brief, but "comparatively casual" (p. 59).

The research is unequivocal about the general, overall course work provided for teachers. It remains casual at best and affords a poorly conceived collage of courses across the spectrum of initial preparation and an assembly of disparate content fragments throughout continuing education. The formal offerings lack curricular articulation within and between initial and continuing teacher education, and depth of study is noticeably and consistently absent.

CURRICULUM TRADITIONS FOR A NONCAREER IN TEACHING

Some of the most promising curriculum research of the past decade examines the various opportunities for teacher learning in more detail; appropriately, it analyzes their liberal-professional consequences for teaching in contrast to those that force a more technical perspective. The growing need for teachers' lifelong learning, or at least career-long learning, makes attention to this classic issue increasingly important.

Traditional analyses of the teacher education curriculum were often restricted to criticisms of the trivial, low-level nature of required study, although notable exceptions to this trend were observed (e.g., Borrowman, 1965a; Dewey, 1904/1965; Royce, 1891/1965; Sarason, Davidson, & Blatt, 1962; Waller, 1932/1961). The typical pattern of overall description complaint and prescription seems to have been broken, however, and a more constructive and enriching trend can be observed in the past decade. Remaining appropriately critical, the more recent work gives specific and detailed consideration to numerous sins of omission as well as sins of commission in the teacher education curriculum. It often focuses on discrete components of the learning opportunities provided and combines empirical study with probing philosophical analysis. Lortie's work (1975) makes a particularly significant contribution and must be considered.

In light of the potentially deleterious effects of classroom teaching on personality and self-understanding, such as those that Waller (1932/1961) and Lightfoot (1983) observed, Lortie (1975) was "impressed by the lack of specific attention to these matters" in the teacher education curriculum:

Social workers, clinical psychologists, and psychotherapists are routinely educated to consider their own personalities and to take them into account in their work with people. Their stance is supposed to be analytic and open; one concedes and works with one's own limitations — it is hoped — in a context of self-acceptance. The tone of teacher interviews and their rhetoric reveals no such orientation; I would characterize it as moralistic rather than analytic and self-accusing rather than self-accepting. It does not appear that their work culture has come to grips with the inevitabilities of interpersonal clash and considerations of how one copes with them. (p. 159)

Lortie (1975) also observed the absence of the "shared ordeal" in teachers' education that represents an important socializing factor for professionals: "The functions performed by shared ordeal in academia — assisting occupational identity formation, encouraging collegial patterns of behavior, fostering generational trust, and enhancing self-esteem — are slighted in classroom teaching" (p. 160).

Most prospective teachers go through formal preparation programs individually, rather than as members of cohort groups. Such independent programs of study prevent sets of students taking courses in common, except at very small institutions and in some of the more innovative programs. Although all students share, in one sense, the ordeal of student teaching and the typically frightening first year of induction, they do so independently as opposed to collectively; as a consequence, these experiences do not induce "a sense of solidarity with colleagues" or "augment the 'reassurance capital' of classroom teachers" (Lortie, 1975, p. 161).

Related to the absence of shared ordeal is the presence of "eased entry" (Lortie, 1975). The time needed to qualify, the arduousness of the preparation, and the complexity of the skill and knowledge base needed for full membership in teaching are all low. The teachers Lortie interviewed described their training as easy, and he reports the absence of a single complaint "that education courses were too difficult or demanded too much effort" (p. 160). Neither did the teachers perceive their preparation as "conveying anything special — as setting them apart from others," and further, the teachers did not "consider training a key to their legitimation as teachers. That rests in experience" (p. 160).

The lack of rigorous entrance, matriculation, and exit requirements conveys a consistent message. Few applicants getting into college are denied access to teacher education, and few who wish to persist are denied recommendations for certification. The curriculum's easy access and implicit assurances of success provide the opportunity to learn that "anybody can teach." The induction period reinforces this lesson as the beginning teacher comes to learn about the underlying paradoxes in teachers' lives. Spencer-Hall (1982) contrasts the specialized knowledge that teachers are told is required for teaching and the work environment in which untrained substitutes are permitted to teach classes and in which teachers are routinely assigned to new subject areas and grade levels for which they have not been prepared.

In addition to observing the absence of self-analysis, eased access, and the lack of shared ordeal in teacher education, Lortie (1975) also noted the curriculum's lack of power in countering the three components of the teaching ethos he saw as detrimental to continued intellectual growth for teachers: conservatism, individualism, and presentism. These mutually reinforcing factors encourage intellectual dependency and discourage professional development and adaptation to change. Lortie recommended, therefore, as many scholars have before him, a strengthening of liberal-professional studies for teachers.

The implications of his research suggest screening before admission to teaching, particularly with an eye to distinguishing "between applicants who are wedded to the past and those who can revise ideas and practice in light of new experiences" (p. 230). He also encouraged teacher preparation that "could foster orientations of selectivity and personal flexibility," qualities that would require "courses and fieldwork to expand the student's ability to cope with ambiguity and complexity" (p. 230). In addition, such preparation would require a curriculum with frontal attention to the prospective teacher's early learning about teaching:

> Education students have usually internalized ... the practices of their own teachers. If teachers are to adapt their behavior to changed circumstances, they will have to be freed of unconscious influences of this kind; what they bring from the past should be as thoroughly examined as alternatives in the present. There are perplexing psychological questions in this regard; what teaching methods will be most effective in helping students to gain cognitive control over previous unconscious learning? (p. 231)

Concerned that the preparation of teachers did not "seem to result in the analytic turn of mind one finds in other occupations whose members are trained in colleges and universities," Lortie (1975) noted, in particular, the disinclination to connect knowledge of scientific method with practical teaching decisions:

> Scientific modes of reasoning and pedagogical practice seem compartmentalized ... those in other kinds of "people work" seem more inclined to connect issues with scientific modes of thought. This separation is relevant because it militates against the development of an effective culture and because its absence means that conservative doctrines receive less factual challenge; each teacher is encouraged to have a personal version of teaching truth. (p. 231)

Like many of Lortie's observations, this too concerns the need for increased professional socialization and liberal–professional study. Although he remained perplexed ("this intellectual segregation puzzles me"), he speculated that it was likely attributable to "compartmentalized instruction" and a curriculum in which education students were not expected "to apply substantive knowledge in behavioral science to practical matters" (p. 231). Although Lortie did not focus on the curriculum fragmentation problem as intensively as others (Lanier & Henderson, 1973), he indicated the need for better integration in formal preparation programs and curriculum revision that would offer significant "opportunities for countering reflexive conservatism among teachers" (p. 232).

Emphasizing the need for more intellectual exchange and enriched experience, Lortie recommended a number of ways that liberal–professional studies could be strengthened: (a) an increase in the number and diversity of classroom mentors; (b) requirements that teachers observe, evaluate, and justify their assessments of a wide variety of teacher styles and approaches; (c) expectations that teachers explicate the reasoning underlying their choices; and (d) opportunities for systematic inquiry during apprenticeship. In addition, Lortie recommended that the curriculum for practicing as well as prospective teachers contain greater opportunities for learning analytical skills and habits of thinking about serious social and educational questions; and the important means for acquiring such abilities

should be through shared discussion and analysis. In deliberations of the sort he recommended, reasons for professional action would be emphasized and compared with expressed central values in teaching and with what is known about human behavior. Such collegial discourse was important in Lortie's view because "reflexive conservatism is less readily sustained when people confront others who do things differently but well; the 'critical mass' phenomenon applies to ideas as well as to atoms" (p. 232).

Research completed since Lortie's study clearly shows that the existing curriculum for teachers is heavy with cognitive experience that reinforces the conservative, individualistic, and present-oriented intellectual tendencies he observed and reported a decade ago. A number of scholars have continued to wrestle with and focus upon the central problem Lortie raised: "how to overcome the record of intellectual dependency" when "the ethos of the occupation is tilted against engagement in pedagogical inquiry" (p. 240).

The recurring theme of the growing body of descriptive and conceptual-analytic work is grounded in the search for better understanding of ways the curriculum can facilitate sustained and continuing intellectual growth for teachers. It seeks to uncover the content and process elements of teacher education that now inhibit liberal-professional study in teaching and foster conformist, unquestioning, other-dependent orientations. In general, the findings from these more recent studies suggest that formal learning for prospective and practicing teachers is unlikely to lead to improved cognitive orientations and habits of thought until the curriculum is thoroughly reviewed and revised in such a way that the many subtle and overt lessons that foster intelligent dependency are reduced. In particular, two lines of curriculum research of the past decade better inform our understanding in this regard; they include attention to what students have an opportunity to learn from school experience, and the growing body of studies done on teaching in elementary and secondary schools.

THE CURRICULUM OF FIELD EXPERIENCE

While the study of pedagogy at the university is often viewed as having limited importance for teachers, classroom experience has been seen, traditionally, as an essential part of initial preparation. As Lortie (1975) documented, experienced teachers also stress the importance of field experience for learning practical skills. But researchers have begun to discover some unpredictably negative learnings from this curricular emphasis on experience. It now appears possible, as well as likely, that substantial amounts of field experience foster a "group management" orientation, in contrast to an "intellectual leader" orientation in teachers' thinking about their work. But this growing set of understandings needs further elaboration.

For the prospective teacher placed in the field, feeling overwhelmed is common. The press of classroom events makes it difficult for even the experienced teacher to attend to individual children (Doyle, 1977; Jackson, 1968). It is hard to tell what each child makes of the content of the day's lesson. In such a situation, the prospective teacher is likely to concentrate on the maintenance of order and on keeping the children attentive.

This circumstance has been treated lightly, heretofore, probably because the orchestration of groups of children is so commonplace in the traditions of classroom teaching. Few other professionals conduct their practice on anything other than individuals or small groups of adults. The complexities associated with teaching, where one must deliver professional expertise in a group setting of twenty to thirty youngsters simultaneously is just coming to be understood. But the research suggests that classroom experience tends to place management at the center of teaching, possibly at the expense of student learning (Hoy, 1967; Hoy & Rees, 1977).

Beginning with these initial field experiences, teachers learn to think that the way to learn more about teaching is through trial and error, not through careful thought and scholarship. What is considered most important is whether a particular technique or approach seems to give immediate practical success (Iannaccone, 1963; Jackson, 1968; Lortie, 1975; Tabachnick, Popkewitz, & Zeichner, 1979–1980).

This position has been supported by the research of Fuller (Fuller, 1969, 1970). After observing that few preservice teachers took an interest in learning about psychological theory, she began a systematic investigation of the concerns of teachers and how those concerns change over time (see also Feiman-Nemser & Floden, this volume). She found that most teachers enter their field experience predominantly concerned with their survival as teachers, and after these survival concerns have been met, teachers become chiefly concerned with curriculum and impact on students. Fuller recommended that teacher educators not work "against the tide" (Fuller, 1969, p. 223), suggesting that theoretically oriented teacher education must wait until concerns about survival have been resolved.

Thus, Fuller's work seemed to suggest that initial preparation should focus on management and practical proficiency — to do otherwise would be a violation of some developmental "law." But in fact Fuller has not shown the sequence in which teachers *must* be taught or even the sequence in which they necessarily *ought* to be taught (Floden & Feiman, 1981). Nevertheless, her research has increased the pressure on teacher educators to maintain an emphasis on technical skills.

In spite of this pressure, the difficulties of learning from field experience have been discussed since the turn of the century by scholars from Dewey (1904/1965) to the present (e.g., Feiman-Nemser & Buchman, 1984; Zeichner, 1980). Dewey, for example, described the danger and promise of field experience as a contrast between what he called the apprenticeship and laboratory approaches to curriculum in teacher education. In the apprenticeship approach, the short time available is used to give teachers the practical skills required to conduct a smooth-running class. The laboratory approach is to use the time to give the student the theoretical principles necessary to understand social and ethical issues in teaching, how children learn, how curriculum decisions might be guided, and how students' cognitions might influence teaching. But adequate opportunities for accomplishing both the laboratory and apprenticeship aims are not available in teacher education as it is presently defined.

The tension between the practical apprenticeship and the more intellectual pedagogy has continued to be resolved in favor of the technical, management approach suited for the noncareer teacher. Emphasis on mastery of management skills may well be adaptive for a teaching population where few teachers remain long in the classroom, but it appears to have serious consequences when career teachers are the norm. What is not learned, apparently, is the set of intellectual tools that would allow teachers to evaluate the quality of the education they are provided, or to critically evaluate suggestions for improvement. A model of field experience consistent with the liberal-professional approach to teacher education would strive to produce a deeper understanding of the way theoretical concepts from psychology, curriculum, and sociology are played out in classrooms. Such understanding of children, subject matter, and schools would enable teachers to provide better instruction, make better curriculum choices, and participate on a stronger footing in policy debates. Keeping the classroom under control is important, but good management alone does not focus teaching on children's higher order learning needs.

Moreover, too much emphasis on learning from experience appears to reinforce the "reflexive conservatism" that Lortie warned of (1975, p. 232), and makes it more difficult to see the range of possible decisions and actions available in teaching (Buchmann & Schwille, 1983; Floden, Buchmann, & Schwille, 1984). For teachers this emphasis often means a continuation of the teaching practices by which they were taught as well as the tendency to see the prevalent patterns of teaching as the only ones possible. It means a restriction on their views of what they might do as teachers, making it less likely that they will escape from intellectual dependency and begin to take responsibility for decisions about curriculum and students.

The problem is not that field experience cannot be valuable, but that its value is dependent on prospective teachers' being properly prepared to learn from it. Studies at the University of Wisconsin on the supervision of student teachers (Tabachnick et al., 1979–1980; Zeichner & Tabachnick, 1982) look closely at ways in which the university staff affected what was learned in field experience. Tabachnick et al. (1979–1980) found that university seminars accompanying student teaching reinforced the tendency to concentrate on mastery of technique and management, rather than encouraging careful examination of experience.

> By focusing upon *how* things are to be done in classrooms to the exclusion of *why*, the university originated discussions which tended to accept the ongoing patterns and beliefs illustrated earlier. Instead of responsibility and reflection, the actions of university personnel encouraged acquiescence and conformity to existing school routines. The latent meanings of workshops and seminars were established in a variety of ways. For example, students were continually reminded that they needed to get along if they wanted good recommendations for their job placement folders.... The content of supervisory conferences also gave legitimacy to existing classroom priorities. ... What was to be taught and for what purpose was seldom discussed between supervisors and students. Technique was treated as an end in itself and not as a means to some specified educational purpose or goal. (p. 22)

In a survey of the student teaching programs at a number of colleges and universities, Griffin (1982) similarly found little to indicate that the curriculum surrounding student teaching was arranged to provide the knowledge and inclinations needed for an intellectual career in teaching. If anything, prospective teachers were encouraged to maintain their narrow view of teaching.

It is important to note that not all researchers are critical of the emphasis on management that accompanies stress on field experience. Berliner (1982), for example, has urged that teachers be explicitly trained as managers. He hopes that, in addition to giving teachers management skills not currently included in the teacher education curriculum, calling attention to teachers' management responsibilities will move their social status closer to that of business managers. But those who do no more than manage a business suffer in the same way as teachers who are only managers—they can keep an organization going, but cannot significantly improve or redirect it.

Additional studies on how the limitations of field experience can be overcome are called for, as researchers use their expertise in ways that are increasingly consistent with the liberal–professional approach to teacher education. The learning opportunities that will help prospective and practicing teachers acquire needed technique in ways that keep management in the background and student learning in the foreground are yet to be discovered.

THE PLACE OF RESEARCH IN THE TEACHER EDUCATION CURRICULUM

The absence of a firm knowledge base for teacher education has led to a long-standing and wide-ranging search for the sort of expertise that would be helpful to the practitioner and at the same time raise the status of teacher education in the academic community. For many years, the methods and literature of educational psychology seemed to promise the most in this respect. Widespread acceptance of the diverse orientations of research psychologists fostered an instrumental view of research on teaching, a view marked by its concern for linear causal analysis, generalization across teachers, and prescription of good practice. In the hands of advocates such as Brophy, Good, Berliner, and Gage, the approach evolved into one of identifying strategic clusters of teaching behaviors and principles, analyzing their consequences for student outcomes in clearly specified contexts, ultimately designing interventions on the basis of earlier research, and evaluating the results with appropriate quantitative or qualitative methods. Brophy (1980) articulated one of the dominant presuppositions of this approach as follows: "The key to improvement has been to concentrate on developing knowledge about effective teaching and translating it into algorithms that teachers can learn and incorporate in their planning prior to teaching" (p. 3). This approach has explicitly or implicitly encouraged the idea that the findings of research on teaching could be translated directly into content to be mastered during teacher education (Zumwalt, 1982).

Research on teacher education (as opposed to research on teaching) soon followed the same tack. Studies were designed to establish the practicality of research-based teacher education and, in particular, to show that appropriate skill training alters the knowledge, skill, and attitudes of teachers (see, e.g., Anderson, Evertson, & Brophy, 1979; Crawford et al., 1977; Emmer et al., 1982; Good and Grouws, 1981). Such projects include a staff development treatment based on earlier process–product research, the latter having shown that certain principles and practices on instruction are strongly related to student learning of basic skills. Materials to support the treatment are designed and come to serve double duty as training manuals and research interventions. Initial and follow-up meetings with teachers offer researchers a method for assuring faithful implementation, while at the same time offering the teachers the opportunity to learn more thoroughly the skills being offered.

One consequence of these field experiments, skill studies, and studies of implementation has been the emergence of an unanticipated debate over how minimal a successful intervention can be. Some researchers argue that even brief, inexpensive treatments can bring about significant results (Good & Grouws, 1979), and a number of researchers have pursued related efficiency questions. Coladarci and Gage (1984) tried an extremely minimal intervention; they mailed a series of teacher training packets to teachers and then observed to see if the teachers implemented the recommendations contained in the packets. Though they found no significant change in teaching practices or student achievement, they remain hopeful of some sort of minimal intervention, in which giving teachers additional technical skills would be enough to improve both teaching practice and student achievement. Their recent search suggested needed adjustment in their minimal interventions, however. "It appears that for an intervention to be successful, the project staff must be engaged with participating teachers in some fashion" (Coladarci & Gage, 1984).

Twenty years of experimental and quasi-experimental research have confirmed that some classroom practices lend themselves well to skills training. Teachers can learn a variety of instructional skills from such projects and can demonstrate them in simulated or actual classroom situations (Joyce & Showers, 1981; Peck & Tucker, 1973). Effective features of such skills training programs include clear statements of objectives and rationales, adequate demonstration, well-designed materials, and opportunity for practice and feedback. Hypotheses about the consequences of giving teachers assistance in the classroom have also been partially tested (McFaul & Cooper, 1983; Mohlman, 1983; Showers, 1983; Wolfe, 1984).

But while this approach has been successful in terms of the limited objectives of each study, the research as a whole has not seemed to cumulate into a more coherent understanding of teaching and teacher education. Although the studies could be criticized for their methodological orientation, it has gradually become clearer that the issues are not primarily ones of choosing the best methodology for arriving at truth about teaching or teacher education, but rather in large part an ethical and epistemological matter of defining an appropriate role for the researcher, exploring the nature of appropriate relations between researchers and practitioners, and making explicit or implicit assumptions about the knowledge that practicing teachers already possess.

Insight into the nature of these issues has come from the work of other scholars in teacher education, such as Buchmann, Feiman-Nemser, Fenstermacher, Floden, and Zumwalt. They have pointed out that recent expert-designed programs for training teachers encourage practitioners to think narrowly about their work. The prescriptive approach tends to place the researcher in the role of external expert, in contrast to that of a professional colleague. The external expert role is particularly difficult for scholars engaged in research on teaching to avoid in teacher education, since the expectation from many practicing school professionals brings a "tell us what we should do" orientation.

By focusing on classroom management and low-level intellectual skills, however, the expert-designed research implicitly endorses a view of education that is most suitable for brief, technical teacher education: a curriculum possibly suitable for noncareer teachers, who have limited subject matter knowledge and a dependence upon the curriculum materials produced by others. Buchmann (1983a, 1984), Fenstermacher (1978, 1980), Kepler (1980), and Zumwalt (1982) all found that approaches in which teachers were told what to do, although perhaps effective in changing some teacher behaviors, do "not acknowledge the rationality of teachers and place the researchers in an undeservedly superior position in which teachers were not able to assess the worth of what they were being told" (Floden, in press).

This "superior position" is implicit, not only in the fact that prescriptions are given for teachers, but also in the "scientific" style in which research reports are written. Educational research, perhaps especially research on teaching, is an uncertain science. Inferences are always tentative and often dependent on implicit assumptions about the purposes of education and the criteria for judging the worth of teaching. Yet little of this uncertainty and value dependence is communicated in the typical research report that is used as part of the initial or continuing teacher education curriculum (Buchmann, 1984).

Buchmann (1983a) points out that the very emphasis the academic community places on verbal acumen makes it difficult for teachers to see themselves as competent to think through educational issues. While there is value to clear thought and careful argument, there is no need to throw out the wisdom gained from teaching simply because teachers have not been able to cast this wisdom in compelling verbal form. "We have no reason to assume that premises that need to be guessed at, terms without clear definitions, oblique references, and beliefs that are debatable must be associated with wrongheaded ideas or indefensible lines of action" (Buchmann, 1983a, p. 12). Teachers understand that teaching is context dependent and usually does not lend itself to straightforward generalization and prescription.

The critics have no wish to abandon research on teaching. They agree that research is valuable for the improvement of teaching practice, provided that there is change in the ways research impinges on practice. Fenstermacher and Zumwalt advocate using research studies as the starting point for serious discussion of educational issues. Rather than accepting the conclusions of research as prescriptions for action, teachers can compare the results to their own prior understanding. "When seemingly definitive results are contrary to one's own beliefs, the motivation to delve further is greater" (Zumwalt, 1982, p. 230).

Deliberation regarding inconsistencies between one's own beliefs and the results of research serves several purposes. It gives guidance and practice in reasoning about educational problems. It reveals the uncertainty of research results. It gives teachers the habit of calling both their own beliefs and the "conclusive" claims of researchers into question. According to Buchmann (1983a), however, an emphasis on discussion of specific research studies can be too restrictive and too much oriented toward the ideal of research, which is truth, in contrast to the ideal of practice, which is wise action.

In further countercriticism, Floden (in press) asserts that these recommendations for change in the teacher education curriculum are valuable for their emphasis on helping teachers to think independently about education, but they tend to stress independence of thought without showing how standards for reasonableness in discussion will be learned. Career teachers need to break away from their intellectual dependency, but without adopting the position that individual opinion need have no grounding in fact or argument (Buchmann, 1983b). One role for teacher educators is to strike a proper balance between encouraging independent thought and pointing out errors in reasoning or observation.

Legitimate questions are sometimes raised about the value for career teachers of a capacity for intellectual analysis and reflection, implying, at times, that support for this stand is just an ideological plea, no more worthy of attention than competing claims. But research analysts have not shunned the issue: Is it mere prejudice? What is wrong with the teacher or teacher educator who places sole emphasis on management and technique, who is satisfied for students to master low-level cognitive skills at the expense of more complex reasoning capacities?

To be sure, educators have reached no agreement on the definition of good teaching and lack of consensus. This remains an important difficulty for research on teaching teachers (for an extended discussion of this point, see Lanier & Floden 1978).

The cynic concludes that all discussions of desirable or undesirable qualities of teacher education are mere prejudice. Perhaps they are, but they may not be prejudiced in the pejorative sense. In "The Central Place of Prejudice in the Supervision of Student Teachers," Hogan (1983) suggests that prejudgment — prejudice — is the necessary basis for interpretation of all events. Such prejudgment is not unthinking partisanship, but the necessary reliance on concepts used to make sense of the world.

In thinking about teaching or teacher education, the particular starting point is open to debate. But any starting point can be the basis for worthwhile discussion and study if it is held provisionally, open to correction. For those studying and judging the education of teachers, it is "appropriate to recognize the continual possibility of bias in all our judgments and seek actively to have even our most circumspect judgments modified and corrected in our dealings with student teachers and colleagues" (Hogan, 1983, p. 41).

Hogan (1983) argues that, ideally, scholars in teacher education should model this reflective role, inviting criticism from others and recognizing the worth of what others have to say. It is a Socratic role, worthy of intellectual respect, but few teacher educators have been traditionally viewed in this manner. The obsession with technique and management continues even though its shortcomings have long been recognized. Some of the reasons the field has been effectively sidetracked for so long should not be overlooked.

Why Might the General Curriculum for Teachers Be as It Is?

Assuming that some of the more classic criticisms of the teacher education curriculum are valid, possible explanations can also be explored through research. Why, after all, should the curriculum for those responsible for educating the youth of one of the world's most technologically advanced nations remain largely arbitrary, technical, fragmented, and without depth? If the problem were unknown, or had gone unrecognized by the general public it might be less perplexing. Again, the social and historical studies (Lerner, 1979; Lortie, 1975, Mattingly, 1975; Powell, 1976; Tyack, 1967) are informative, for they suggest several major influences on the evolving development of teacher education in America. They include:

1. the rapid expansion of schooling in the late 1800s, with its accompanying high demand for elementary and secondary school personnel;
2. a social response to this demand that accommodated domestic roles for women, upward mobility aspirations of lower class men, and the institutionalization of school teaching as employment appropriate only for temporary, secondary, or part-time workers;
3. an institutional accommodation to this transient work force, which standardized brief technical training for teachers and reliance on external expertise for occupational direction; and
4. a lengthy adherence to a single dominant research paradigm in education that brought quantitative scientific study to bear on large social issues and problems of school administrators and specialists, but neglected the problems of teachers and teaching and the codification of good classroom practice.

Many of the contemporary and past problems with the teacher education curriculum originate with the deleterious effects of prolonged classroom teaching, a difficulty long recognized by career teachers in America (Lines, 1982; Mattingly, 1975; Powell, 1976). Until the nature of the job demands in teaching change, talented persons will continue to escape after only a modest period of service. Perhaps the occupation would have already undergone this needed adaptation and revision if it had not been for the rapid expansion and massive availability of schooling in America.

The extraordinarily large increase in the need for teachers around the turn of the century, that is, from a demand for 9,000 in 1890 to a demand for 42,000 by 1910, provided a temporary solution to the already recognized career problem for teachers, at least for male teachers. The educational expansion created a dual opportunity for upwardly mobile, frequently religious schoolmen who were seeking both personal advancement and social improvement. Careers in administration, supervision, and other nonteaching specializations permitted their participation in the creation of an exciting new social mission:

Schools could now hope to manage the transition of all youth to the needed adulthood of a new civilization; and schools of education could train professionals to be the managers. (Powell, 1976, p. 6)

And train managers they did, although such training soon brought unintended negative consequences for teacher education. While the expansion of administration, supervision, and other specializations provided new career opportunities for men impatient with the conditions of teaching, it also changed the investment priorities of education faculty at the university. Powell (1976) observed, "More and more these nonteaching careers, rather than teaching itself, were considered the most important careers toward which both ambitious schoolmen and ambitious schools of education should direct their principal attention" (p. 6). The consequence for the mission and curriculum in schools of education was a significant shift away from serious concern with teaching.

Primary attention was soon given to graduate training in administration and other specializations, such as research and evaluation or counseling and guidance. Of secondary importance, the education of teachers became increasingly segregated and limited to undergraduate study. Advanced periods of academic study at the university for the transient work of teaching appeared neither practical nor needed. For most women, teaching was still viewed as secondary to their "real" occupation of housekeeping and child rearing. For most men, teaching was viewed as secondary to their aspirations for more influential positions in such areas as university teaching and school management, where important policy issues in education could be decided. The resulting teacher education programs came to be affected by and subsequently came to affect the status of teaching in America; they provided, as Powell observed, "a stable organization for the education curriculum which reinforced the emerging hierarchical career structure of the profession" (p. 9).

The early norms created for teacher education at the university thus accommodated the adult society that was apparently well served by such an arrangement. The curriculum for teachers could legitimately be brief and piecemeal; to make it otherwise would mean that great energies to assure length and coherence in the curriculum would largely be in vain, given the occupation's transient membership. Needed continuity and guidance for educational policy and practice in schools could be provided by professional managers and specialists, who could, and in fact did, acquire more and better knowledge than the transient teacher majority.

The historical evidence suggests, therefore, that a norm of intellectual dependence on external expertise was established for teaching in America in the late 19th century. The low level and haphazard nature of the teacher education curriculum was unquestionably functional for the majority of teachers at that time. Fragmented, unconnected content as well as the absence of depth and professional socialization provided needed flexibility and ease of entry, exit, and re-entry for women whose primary occupational goal was domestic work. In addition, the modest investment of one's individual resources in preparation matched the modest occupational returns reasonably well. Teaching was a respectable stopping-off place for most men and women en route to doing, or already doing, what they considered to be more important work. Under such conditions, it seemed inherently sensible for teachers to turn to persons outside of the classroom for responsible, informed decision making. Borrowman's study (1965a) supports this line of reasoning and indicates how the early teacher educators rationalized the low-level intellectual needs of the teaching majority. For the period of time that teachers remained in the classroom, it was expected that they would be prepared for

teaching a curriculum prescribed by the board of education, through texts selected by that board or provided on a chance basis by parents, and according to methods suggested by master teachers or educational theorists, most of whom had been well educated in the colleges. (p. 22)

The curriculum that emerged for teachers at the university does not appear unreasonable in this light, and one can understand why, as Powell (1976) observed, "courses were given and taken for their immediate value on the job, at best, of their mobility value on transcripts, at worst" (p. 12).

With school teaching viewed as secondary in importance and primary attention assigned to administration and other specialized training, the development of the knowledge base in education was similarly affected. Although three general strategies for developing knowledge in education were originally employed in leading schools of education, one came to dominate; it was the least appropriate for addressing the problems of teaching practice (Powell, 1976).

One approach, as represented by G. Stanley Hall's work, employed elements of natural science inquiry and focused on the collection of vast amounts of data about children in school. A second sought to capture the wisdom of teaching practice by examining written and unwritten records of educational products and events that promised to inform future generations about lessons already learned. This latter approach assumed that many ideas about good practice already existed and needed to be made available through collection, synthesis, codification, and effective presentation. As in law and theology, which do not owe their professional status and knowledge base to scientific research, major efforts to discover and describe exemplary practice were meant to reduce the need to reinvent and redefine innovations with each new generation.

Notably, both of these approaches focused on the study of classroom teaching and learning. This made them vulnerable to attack and easy to dismiss with the legitimization of the scientific movement in education. Rejecting mere observation and turning to controlled experimentation, the education faculty could obtain greater status and respect at the university and could readily support the work of their primary student clientele and leading graduates—administrators and other school specialists. Powell (1976) reports that "the adoption of the laboratory method helped to eliminate the teacher as a subject of inquiry at the same time that many training programs relegated the teacher to ancillary status" (p. 10). Concomitantly, these tools of science gave added prestige and power to the policymaking leaders in the schools who quickly gathered the data they considered most important and worthwhile to their work:

Quantitative measures could assess convincingly the performance of large groups of students and thus indicate the quality of entire schools or school systems. Intelligence and achievement tests could classify large numbers of pupils quickly and thus make more defensible the increasingly specialized nature of schooling as well as

of the profession. Educational research, in short, had been enlisted to help solve the problems faced by administrators and specialists. (p. 11)

The predominantly quantitative and experimental research approach to the development of a knowledge base in education relegated description of good teaching practice to minimal status until only the past several decades. More recently, however, alternative approaches allowing for rich description and logical deduction analyses have been resurrected and focused again on the study of classroom teaching and learning. The visible shift away from a single dominant research paradigm has enriched the study of teaching practice and has begun to afford better understanding of research issues in teacher education.

Summary: Research and the Teacher Education Curriculum

The increasing proportion of career teachers makes the often-repeated call for a liberal-professional approach to teacher education all the more persuasive. The tension between liberal and technical should not be resolved by the elimination of one or the other, but preparing career teachers for their continuing education requires greater emphasis on liberal-professional studies than is presently the norm.

Unfortunately, changes in the teacher education curriculum have tended to move it in the opposite direction, giving increased dominance to the mastery of skills with immediate practical value. What is worse, studies of the curriculum of initial and continuing teacher education show it to be fragmented and shallow.

Recent research has given a more detailed picture of these weaknesses. Lortie (1975) has shown how the ease with which teachers can enter and complete their initial preparation communicates the message that little knowledge is required to be a good teacher. The way field experiences enter the curriculum pushes teacher candidates even more in the direction of a technical orientation.

The relationships between the study of teaching and the curriculum for teachers have received major attention from scholars who have examined the various intellectual consequences that alternative approaches to gathering and sharing information with teachers are apt to have. Particular attention has been given to the intellectual dependence or independence these approaches are likely to foster in teaching (Buchmann, 1983b; Fenstermacher, 1978; Kepler, 1980; Popkewitz, Tabachnick, & Zeichner, 1979; Zumwalt, 1982). This recent work also provides important perspectives on the problems associated with the all-too-common view that research provides the only key to an authoritative knowledge base for education. But teacher education is only beginning to address these complex issues in the curriculum for teachers and ample room for progress remains, particularly as it relates to the codification, preservation, and transmission of the lore of successful practice.

Slowing the process of change and adaptation is the evolutionary nature of formal education in America. In spite of the many demands for revolution and reform in teacher education, the rate and pace of the interinstitution adaptation that is required for schools and universities is apt to be slow. The curriculum for teachers is evolving from an earlier period when it was constructed to meet the needs and life-styles of a very different generation of men and women. It is now more apt to change, however, since the teaching force of today and tomorrow will likely be educated for lifelong careers in teaching. Accompanying this new challenge is the need to provide curricula that are deep, scholarly, coherent, and related to continuing a liberal education throughout one's period of professional teaching.

Milieu

Research on the social, political, and economic factors related to teacher education confirms that which is obvious to the thoughtful observer: Power and prestige are lacking. But if "schools can rise no higher than the communities that support them," as Boyer (1983, p. 6) has suggested, then better understandings of the communities responsible for teacher education are important if constructive change is to follow. The evidence suggests, overall, that communities responsible for teacher education in the United States have been derelict in the exercise of their charge to provide quality programs and public assurance of well-prepared teachers. The higher education, public school, and professional communities of which teacher education is a part maintain loose and sometimes antagonistic relationships with one another, generally accepting teacher education as a tolerable second cousin. The reasons for these general conditions are not well studied, although there is some theory and research to guide contemporary thinking on such matters.

The Higher Education Community and Support for Teacher Education

The support given to teacher education programs at the university can be understood by examining three factors: (a) the faculty effort assigned to and evaluated for making specific contributions to the program; (b) the financial resources invested to support the program; and (c) the oversight the university provides to ensure that teacher education is responsibly administered. The evidence of low support for teacher education can be readily observed when such factors are considered.

FACULTY INVESTMENT AS AN INDICATOR OF SUPPORT

Difficulties with identifying the teacher education faculty responsible for this large, uniquely administered, all-university program are treated earlier in this chapter. All but a small portion of the program faculty are involved only tangentially in program efforts. In relation to the large proportion of students pursuing careers in teaching, few faculty have official time assigned to teacher preparation, and fewer still are identified with and evaluated for their specific contributions to teacher education.

The problem of low faculty identity and participation is especially acute in the most prestigious universities and schools

of education. Commissioned by the Ford Foundation to study America's leading schools of education, Judge (1982) reported on the faculty's consistent tendency to "distance itself from the confused and unattractive world of teacher education" (p. 9).

For secondary teachers, in fact, the most influential professionals in the candidate's program are often cooperating teachers who volunteer to supervise practice teaching in the schools. These persons spend more time with the student than any other faculty and are generally provided with a token payment (possibly $50) to serve, in effect, as adjunct faculty members of the institution of higher education (Clark & Marker, 1975).

While studies have suggested that universities are supporting more teacher education faculty today than they have heretofore, such reports are misleading. Feistritzer (1984) suggests, for example, that while "enrollments in teacher education programs are dropping precipitously, the numbers of faculty teaching in them are not" (p. 34). Unfortunately, the data presented in support of this assertion are grounded in the number of full-time faculty assigned to schools, colleges, and departments of education as a whole, in contrast to the number of full-time faculty working in the all-university teacher education programs at the institution. As indicated earlier in this chapter, many faculty in academic units with the word "education" in their title never associate with teacher education programs, or have only a very minor role to play in them. Instead, many of them prepare school administrators, counselors, psychologists, media specialists, policymakers, reading diagnosticians, educational researchers, and instructors for business and industry; in effect, most of them prepare professionals for other than schoolteaching roles.

FINANCIAL INVESTMENT AS AN INDICATOR OF SUPPORT

Research conducted in the past decade also suggests that the record of financial support for teacher education is low. The institutional analyses conducted by Clark and Marker (1975) showed that "teacher training is a low prestige, low cost venture in almost all institutions of higher education" (p. 57). Peseau and Orr (1979, 1980, 1981) initiated a longitudinal study of teacher education funding in 63 leading institutions across 37 states. Their work has revealed a consistent pattern of apparent underfunding. Discussing the adequacy and equity of the 1979–1980 resource base for teacher education, Peseau (1982) reports:

> The average direct cost of instruction per year for preparing an undergraduate teacher education student was only 65 percent as much as for a public school student, and only 50 percent as much as the average cost per undergraduate student in all university disciplines; and in only 9 of 51 university teacher education programs was the direct cost of instruction as much as for a public school student in 1979–80. (p. 14)

Analysis of data from their third annual study also suggests that teacher education students pay an undue share of their higher education costs. Assuming that tuition is generally expected to cover approximately 20% of the costs of education and about 40% of the direct costs of instruction (college budgets only),

Peseau (1982) found that in 30 of the 52 universities studied during 1979–1980, teacher education students "paid 50% or more of the direct costs of instruction; 75% or more of those costs in 17 universities; 90% or more in 12 universities; and 100% or more in 8 of those universities" (p. 14).

The reasons for what Peseau (1982) calls "the outrageous underfunding of teacher education" are grounded only partially in state funding formulas, which generally place teacher education with undergraduate programs of low complexity (Orr & Peseau, 1979). Using the state of Texas formula and complexity index as a base, Peseau and Orr (1980) compared others to this model and found that "most states follow the Texas example; that is, they view teacher education programs as less complex than other university programs for funding purposes." Aspects of the Texas complexity index thus provide a base for comparison:

> At the undergraduate level the lowest of the complexity indexes is 1.00. Teacher education is indexed at 1.04; this contrasts with 1.51 for agriculture, 2.07 for engineering, and 2.74 for nursing. Indexes at the master's level range from 1.75 for law to 5.77 for veterinary medicine. Teacher education is indexed at 2.30 and compares with 3.27 for business and 5.36 for science. Differences at the post-master's level are even more dramatic. Here teacher education is indexed at 8.79; the index for business is 13.45, agriculture 16.52, nursing and engineering 17.60, fine arts 17.71, and veterinary medicine 20.53. (p. 100)

But the relatively low assignment of complexity by the state does not explain the underfunding that typically follows. The problem comes, apparently, from one of two common situations. Each state chooses to allocate resources based on its own historical pattern, which builds on traditional assumptions unfavorable to teacher education in the distribution of funds (Temple & Riggs, 1978); or, once basic financial resources are provided, university administrators reallocate funds, giving less to teacher education and more to programs that, in their judgment, either deserve or need more support (Orr & Peseau, 1979).

Clark and Marker (1975) and Kerr (1983) tie this problem of underfunding to teacher education's place in the undergraduate curriculum and reason that it is unlikely to change until teacher education is removed from this position and made a part of graduate study only. Nevertheless, it should be noted that nothing officially prevents giving more support for teacher education at the undergraduate level, just as nothing officially prevented giving it less in the beginning. Nevertheless, Kerr (1983) suggests why change at the undergraduate level is unlikely:

> The cat is left chasing its tail. Without a substantially higher allocation index, pedagogical faculties cannot possibly develop the complex and sophisticated clinical studies that teacher education sorely lacks; without highly developed and demonstrably successful clinical programs in place, universities would most likely be unwilling to adjust the index. Most certainly the index could not be increased sufficiently if it is bound to undergraduate norms. (p. 136)

Supporting this argument, Clark and Marker (1975) suggest that "the difficulty arises in trying to fit professional preparation, especially preparation that is field- and practice-oriented, into the classic mold of undergraduate lecture courses where students end up being taught to teach by being told how to teach" (p. 57).

Peseau (1982) suggests that the poor financial conditions contribute to conservative thought and behaviors on the part of faculty most closely associated with teacher education: "Financial starvation in academic programs is analogous to nutritional starvation in biological organisms. Both result in inadequate development and extreme conservatism of behavior" (p. 15). Building on their findings and years of association with education leaders involved in such studies, Peseau and Orr (1980) express frustration with the apparent means of coping with low prestige and low funding:

> Perhaps the most distressing generalization one can make about professional educators is that they tend to accept expanded responsibilities without having the resources to meet them. ... This fact reflects the profession's unwillingness to define its goals and insist on reasonable support. (p. 100)

OVERSIGHT FOR RESPONSIBLE ADMINISTRATION AS AN INDICATOR OF SUPPORT

Scholars of the past decade have brought a new level of understanding to the complexities associated with teacher education programs in higher education. Earlier interpretations of factors inhibiting effective administration and governance of teacher education programs were typically associated with the education establishment itself. Conant (1963), Koerner (1963), and Silberman (1970), for example, seemed to envision a relatively close-knit, compatible set of protective, professional groups working in concert with one another to perpetuate the status quo.

But the metaphor of a gigantic, lethargic bureaucracy in teacher education is hardly apt, since there is almost a total absence of bureaucracy functioning in teacher education. Clark and Marker's institutional analysis vividly reveals the more accurate characterization: Rather than like-minded organizations working in concert, they observed "idiosyncratic organizations, each assigned 'a piece of the action' and functioning in a state of accommodation, not to protect mutual interests but to avoid irreconcilable conflicts" (p. 74).

Analyzing the inhibitors to improvement and reform in teacher education, Lanier (1984) reported similar observations and offered an alternative metaphor to that of a unified and oppressive educational establishment:

> The major problem that makes change and improvement exceedingly difficult in teacher education is the diffuse nature of program responsibility and accountability. Too many warring factions control various small pieces of the enterprise. Consequently, each of the participating parties is weak and no single group is powerful enough to exercise responsible leadership that might significantly change the status quo. Coalitions rarely are possible, since the various actors share little mutual interest and trust. ... The situation is analogous to the current scene in war-torn Lebanon, where numerous factions with multiple, contradictory, narrow, and self-interested concerns continue to fight and further a growing anarchy. The loser, of course, is the country as a whole. (p. 2)

A college or university can provide support for teacher education by making sure that responsibility for teacher education is clearly assigned. A task for which no one is clearly responsible is unlikely to be completed well. Unless some administrative unit is given the authority and concomitant accountability, teacher education will not be well taken care of. To support teacher education, someone in the university community must oversee governance arrangements to see that someone takes charge.

Locating the administrative units responsible for the education or miseducation of America's teachers in higher education, however, is at least as difficult as attempts to locate the teacher education faculty. In their institutional analysis, Clark and Marker (1975) found, for example, the assignment of responsibility without authority and authority without responsibility, as well as resource allocations distorting functions, form determining substance, and "political compromises, external to teacher education, controlling the quality of the education of teachers" (p. 74). Their findings led them to conclude that "few organizations could survive, to say nothing of perform, with the bizarre disjunction between assigned functions, authority, and responsibility which exists in the institution of teacher education" (p. 75).

One basis for these strong conclusions is that people mistakenly have assumed that the primary responsibility and authority for the program of teacher education rest with an academic unit entitled "education." Clark and Marker, however, observed that education units provide only 15 to 20% of the preparation of secondary teachers and half of this portion is given over to the public school; and the public schools have "no formally assigned role in teacher education and its participation is dependent on its willingness as an agency, and the classroom teacher's willingness as an individual, to assume an 'extra load'" (p. 75). They emphasize how the arts and science components within institutions of higher education are organized with little, if any, thought given to the function of teacher education, even though a significant portion of their student population is in teacher education. Their evidence showed as follows:

> The bulk of the academic training of all teachers, and 80 percent of that of secondary teachers, occurs with the faculty of arts and science, but if the function is considered to be the "business" of this unit at all, it is considered an ancillary function. (p. 75)

These findings led them to conclude that the structure provides a basic framework for "organizational irresponsibility"; it not only provides "endless opportunities to avoid accountability," but also makes available to each participant in the enterprise "a rational posture to justify the avoidance." (p. 76)

In this chaotic situation, no faculty group is seen as the final authority on questions about teacher education, a situation far different from that for other academic programs at the university. In fact, the faculty most closely associated with the program, that is, the education faculty, actually are afforded the least power to effect change or exercise responsible oversight. Studies show that all-university committees and councils that were encouraged by Conant (1963) exist in the majority of institutions of higher education that prepare teachers; and the faculty composition on these councils continues to be dominated by faculty from academic units other than education (Dearmin, 1982). In her study of these all-university councils, Dearmin (1982) reported:

> No other aspect of the survey produced wider variance than responses to the query, "To whom does the council report?" Twenty-eight different reporting patterns were described. And the variance appeared as great for the councils described as very effective, as it did for the council generally. Is it possible that the university structure does not know what to do with these strange units which are neither fish nor fowl? Or are university reporting structures inherently very different across institutions? Or do councils tend to seek the level of influence the institution desires it to have? There is some evidence in the survey responses to support the latter. (p. 4)

UNDERSTANDING THE FACTORS INHIBITING QUALITY CONTROL

The reasons higher education provides such minimal support for teacher education in the manner here described are grounded in the larger social context of the general society and in the institutional traditions that have evolved in the modern American university. Part of these problems can be explained in terms of the reasons the teacher education curriculum was constructed to accommodate a short-term, part-time, noncareer orientation in teaching. These reasons were presented in the prior section of this chapter and need not be discussed here, although the low support that is attributable to the occupation's formerly high rate of turnover must not be overlooked. Nonetheless, these reasons alone do not provide sufficient understanding.

The most common argument put forward for the low support accorded teacher education is that its knowledge base is weak and questionable. Scholars have reasoned that respected professions are so recognized because of "a validated body of knowledge and skills subscribed to by the profession, passed by means of preparation programs to the inductees, and used as the basis for determining entrance to and continuance in the profession" (Howsam, Corrigan, Denemark, & Nash, 1976, p. 3). But this argument begs the question of why, traditionally, there has been such meager investment in the development of the knowledge base for teacher education itself. Few financial and human resources are provided by higher education for studying the problems or successes of teaching and learning in the nation's schools (Guba & Clark, 1978; Powell, 1976). The social context of teacher education in higher education may be better understood when the typically underplayed issues of social status, power, and displaced class conflict are taken into account.

The institution of public schooling in America remains conservative and relatively slow to accommodate a responsible, intellectual role for professional teachers; so does higher education. The maintenance of teacher education as a nonprofession is comparable to the maintenance of teaching as a noncareer. Those in power, quite naturally, support those arrangements that best serve their interests; change to accommodate the interests of others will usually be resisted (Cusick, in press).

Change is particularly difficult in teacher education because the occupation serves two groups traditionally weak in institutional influence: women and children. While legend has it that emergency situations provoke a "save the women and children" attitude, such does not seem to be the case in the more mundane activities of life, such as those encountered in teaching children and teaching teachers. Teaching in America has been and continues to be the single largest line of professional work comprised predominantly of college-educated women; and teacher education is supposed to enhance this important female-dominated occupation. However, the actual consequences of such a concentration of women are more like that discussed by Margaret Mead in one of her anthropological studies. She observed (Porter, 1983–1984):

> There are villages in which men fish and women weave and in which women fish and men weave, but in either type of village the work done by the men is valued higher than the work done by the women. (p. 2)

Even now, as various groups work to change these traditional circumstances, there is more invested in getting women access to what has traditionally been men's work than there is in upgrading the quality of that which has traditionally been women's work. Women remain concentrated in a small number of technical-skill-dominated occupations (teachers, nurses, waitresses, household workers, retail salesclerks, and secretaries). Across the board, these occupations are characterized by lower pay and less education (Bureau of Labor Statistics, March 1980).

In addition, the low status of teaching and teacher education has to do with the fact that teachers' clients are children (Geer, 1968). Other professionals and business managers gradually build up a circle of clients whom they can select to some degree. Association with this circle can raise status if the clients have high status. Continued interactions with clients outside work can give access to information and selective institutions. But teachers' clients do not bring these advantages. Teachers not only have little choice about which children will be their clients, but development of long-term relationships is also difficult because teachers typically receive a new set of students each year. Finally, as Geer (1968) observes, teachers' clients are of even lower status than teachers themselves:

> Children and adolescents (despite many cries of alarm to the contrary) are a powerless group in society, and the fact that school teachers serve minors rather than adults means that they are deprived of opportunities available to other service occupations to establish useful and prestigious relationships during their daily work. (Geer, 1968, pp. 228–229)

Status is important since teacher education operates in a competitive marketplace. Competition affects institutions in different ways. Institutions with a tradition of strong scholarship are pushed out of the business of teacher education into fields where they get better value for their work. Other institutions feel the press to maintain enrollments and some, but by no means all, respond to this press by lowering admission standards.

While a number of the leading schools Judge (1982) studied carry responsibilities for undergraduates, he observed that they "perceive themselves, and wish to be described as *graduate schools*" (p. 5; italics in original). Judge attributed this "deliberate choice ... to distance themselves from both the task of training teachers for elementary and secondary schools and that of addressing the problems and needs of schools" (p. 6) to a "series of flexible hierarchies of function and esteem" (p. 4) in which universities and colleges have come to be arranged. Observing the market-driven nature of American higher education, Judge reasoned that "an institution can survive only by being competitive" (p. 43), but in this context teacher education lacks the power and resources for obtaining a reasonable competitive edge. He described the problem as follows:

> The rules of the competition are not set by graduate schools of education, and the rules cannot be altered by the schools. Moreover, the rules are powerful in two different fields of rivalry. Education can compete with another professional school only insofar as it is linked with a powerful, organized, prestigious profession. In that sense its capacity to represent itself is limited by society's view of the status of teachers and other members of the educational profession. Similarly, its power to attract students of quality depends upon its reputation for success in advancing the careers of these students ... and bringing assured financial and professional rewards.
>
> The second field in which the rules of competition apply ... is to national comparison and ratings, which in turn are equally dependent upon scholarly achievement. The pursuit of these achievements leads to a modeling of the school on standards of research prevalent in arts and sciences and, by implication, to neglect of the more sharply professional functions of the school. (p. 44)

In other words, Judge (1982) sees the faculty in leading schools of education in the United States caught in two relatively hopeless competitions for support and respect; one competition is with the more prestigious professional schools and the other with the basic arts and sciences. Since teacher education left the normal schools and came to higher education, faculty concerned with teacher preparation have not been able to compete on an equal footing with either.

The status and power assigned to the established professions are formidable; and the rules of the game that must be followed in competition with the arts and sciences faculty press teacher educators to abandon their obligations as faculty concerned for quality professional preparation. The reward system in the prestigious institutions of higher education thus affects the career development of faculty in ways that detract from teacher education. In most such institutions, faculty are obliged to demonstrate expertise through independent inquiry, and status is not generally attached to undergraduate teaching, especially when the undergraduates are visibly associated with a low-status, low-ability group of prospective teachers (Clark & Marker, 1975; Judge, 1982).

Faculty and administrator interviews conducted by Judge (1982) reveal that faculty in the arts and sciences "regard education courses as a distraction for their abler students and freely doubt the value of the courses offered. Yet the very size of the enterprise makes it difficult to ignore; indeed, it generates resentment" (p. 46). Nevertheless, the actual size of this faculty commitment to teacher education remains a mystery because of the dispersed, all-university nature of the program. It is everyone's and no one's responsibility, and its power thus remains diffused.

While these leading institutions respond to the competitive environment by moving from teacher education into fields where they are stronger players, that option is not open to many programs, for the colleges and universities where they reside not only expect them to stay in business, but also expect them to maintain high enrollments. In an effort to maintain enrollments with a declining student population, programs are tempted to lower standards.

Empirical evidence on the effects of this competition is provided by Schlechty and Vance (1983a), who studied the institutional origins of two groups of entrants into the teacher work force in North Carolina. They found great differences in the institutions they studied. The competitive marketplace exerted more pressure at some institutions than others. The researchers concluded that "some institutions of higher education have been much more dependent than others on teacher education as a source of enrollment" (p. 95).

The teacher education programs that maintained high standards throughout the low-demand period were housed in institutions that allow scores on standardized tests to play a significant role in admissions decisions. These teacher education programs were not encouraged to offset declining enrollments with low-scoring students. But other institutions allowed their standards to drop, allowing in some cases twice as many students from the lowest quintile to enter teaching. According to Schlechty and Vance (1983a), the set of programs permitting this to happen were housed in institutions of higher education that were lacking "rigorous overall admissions standards, and thus the teacher-training programs were able to admit more low scoring students when high scoring students chose majors other than teacher education" (p. 96). They found, in fact, between 1973–1974 and 1979–1980 over a 20% increase in the market share of employed teachers from the lowest quintile of academically inclined college graduates. Lest the invidious conclusion be drawn that this represents a major increase in minority teachers, it should be noted that of the 1,242 employed teachers scoring in this lowest quintile, 172 were black teachers and 1,070 were white. It should also be noted that these 1,242 teachers were employed at the same time the United States had an excess of available talented teacher candidates.

While Schlechty and Vance (1983a) found that the type of institution did not significantly influence the decline in talent from the top quintile of high-scoring teachers, the type of institution did significantly influence the proportional increase in graduates from the bottom quintile of low-scoring teachers. Supporting the observations of Judge (1982), Sykes (1983a), Kerr (1983), and Weaver (1983), Schlechty and Vance (1983a) concluded:

> Competition for scarce resources (i.e., students) both among departments within institutions and among institutions is having an impact on the quality and quantity of teachers being produced by various institutions. (p. 98)

The pressure to maintain enrollments can be understood in terms of the roles teachers play in university life. Drawing on the work of Judge (1982) and Kerr (1983), Sykes (1983a) suggests that "the latent functions that teacher education serves within the university thoroughly confound its manifest mission" (p. 90). As Sykes (1983a) observes,

> On campus after campus, especially in the large public universities, teacher education provides a valuable source of income for the university at large, because state funding rewards enrollment, while allocation formulas favor every professional school and department *but* teacher education. (p. 90)

Hence, enrollments must be kept up.

A second latent function that teacher education programs serve is that of a holding company for students at the low end of the ability distribution. At a time when higher education enrollments are on the decline nationwide (Dearman & Plisko, 1980) and a number of institutions are admitting more students from among the less academically inclined (Schlechty & Vance, 1983a), "it is a distinct relief to all other schools and departments on campus" (Sykes, 1983a, p. 90) to have such a resource available. This form of institutional pressure, in Sykes' view (1983), "militates against both the elimination of teacher education and the raising of entrance standards (which would decrease enrollment)" (p. 90).

This effect of teacher education's serving this second latent function at the university is possibly the most detrimental of all, for it creates what Sykes (1983a) dramatically refers to as an "intellectual ghetto" with the following predictable and ironic qualities:

> Rather than forestall further slippage in the talent pool for teaching, such programs actually become part of the problem, serving as disincentives to bright students, who shun association with a major stigmatized as anti-intellectual. (p. 90)

Against this backdrop, it is easier to understand some of the likely reasons that institutions of higher education insist on maintaining an all-university approach to teacher education. The resistance to allowing schools, departments, or colleges of education to control their own destiny is not fully imbedded in authentic concern for quality teacher education and teaching quality in the nation's elementary and secondary schools. Just as the teacher education curriculum was originally constructed to accommodate low-level, technical-skill orientations tailored for noncareer, transient members of a teaching force, so are the institutional governance arrangements now locked into keeping teacher education in a state of organizational poverty and intellectual dependence.

The School Community and Support for Teacher Education

Much of the research on teacher education suggests that the dominance of practice over scholarship is supported by the belief that teachers learn good teaching mainly from experience. Hence it is important to examine schools as places in which teachers gain on-the-job experience and to ask whether the conditions that comprise this experience are in fact conducive to becoming more knowledgeable about and better at teaching.

The professional development of practicing teachers is influenced by many factors. Certainly, the ways in which the teacher's work is defined and experienced affect teachers' motivation to continue learning to teach more effectively, and to contribute to their field. Schools also influence the quality and scale of continuing teacher education through the distribution of resources and the organization of opportunity: The allocation of time, space, materials, and staff responsibilities helps to determine whether continued learning is an integral part of the obligations, opportunities, and activities of teachers.

If there are contradictions between professional ideals and workplace realities, opportunities for long-term learning by teachers are thereby undermined. In interviews with women teachers, Spencer-Hall (1982) explored the conflict that teachers perceive between exhortations to "be professional" and the working conditions they encounter in their schools. The influence that teachers exert in their own classrooms contrasts with their relative powerlessness in the organization at large. The picture drawn is of a work environment that is isolated yet crowded, intellectually arid, short on time and space, compartmentalized and yet not autonomous, and lacking in any obligation to contribute to the solution of institutional problems. New teachers, in particular, are left to their own devices. In such schools—and some would argue, in the profession at large—there is no tradition by which the ablest members of the group are recognized for their contributions to the fund of knowledge and skill for the profession. Teachers have not been organized "to promote inquiry or to add to the intellectual capital of the profession" (Lortie, 1975, p. 56). Yet, accompanying this depressing picture of professional isolation among experienced teachers and trial-and-error learning by beginning teachers are descriptions of a few exceptional schools or districts that have organized to give high priority to continuing professional development and to offer direct assistance to those just learning to teach.

LACK OF CAREER STAGES THAT SERVE TO ADVANCE LEARNING

By contrast with certain other occupations (including teaching at the university level), in which full membership in the profession is achieved in well-marked stages, elementary and secondary school teaching has been relatively "careerless" (Dalton, Thompson, & Price, 1977; Lortie, 1975; Sykes, 1983b). Little distinction is made between newcomers and others. In the responsibilities they assume, and the opportunities and rewards available to them, novice teachers are virtually indistinguishable from their more experienced colleagues. The implicit assumption is that neither the daily work of teaching nor the structure of career opportunities requires extended training and support.

Little premium is placed on cumulative mastery or professional initiative in a career that offers few rewards and opportunities based on evolving skill, sophistication, and professional standing. Efforts to characterize teachers' career stages (Christensen, Burke, Fessler, & Hagstrom, 1983; Fuller & Bown, 1975) might be more accurately seen as work to describe teachers' intellectual and social accommodation to a noncareer. Since nothing in the traditional view of teaching has led researchers to emphasize "learning to teach" as a long-term enterprise with implications for career advancement, proposals to produce career ladders could subsequently and substantially alter the research agenda on teacher education (Schlechty, 1984).

LACK OF SUPPORT FOR ENTRY INTO TEACHING

Entry into the work of teaching has been described as "abrupt" or "unstaged" with first-year teachers assuming the full responsibilities of the classroom from their very first day. The various portraits of the first year are remarkably consistent, whether drawn from the retrospective accounts of experienced teachers (Little, 1981; Lortie, 1975), from interviews and journals of beginning teachers (Fuchs, 1969; Ryan, 1970; Zeichner, 1983), or from descriptions of teacher induction programs (McDonald, 1980; Tisher, 1980; Zeichner, 1980).

For most teachers, learning by experience has been fundamentally a matter of learning alone, an exercise in unguided and unexamined trial and error. Organized inservice assistance is "measured in days and hours instead of weeks and months" (Lortie, 1975). This abrupt entry into teaching conveys the impression that teaching can be mastered in a relatively short period by persons acting independently with good sense and sufficient stamina. Researchers looking for organized programs and support and assistance during induction have been disappointed (McDonald, 1980; Zeichner, 1980). Such programs are small in number and have been unable consistently to demonstrate their superiority to the common pattern of "sink or swim" (Tisher, 1980).

Meaningful mentoring relations between experienced and beginning teachers have been the exception, not the rule (Little, 1981). Mentoring allows for mediated career entry in which novices move gradually from simple to more demanding tasks, and from modest to substantial responsibility, all under the supervision of acknowledged masters whose skill and longevity have earned them status within the occupation. Mentors are in a position to transmit valued knowledge and skill, to socialize newcomers to the institutional culture, and to influence future career opportunities. In most schools mentoring arrangements tend to be isolated, informal agreements; there is no necessary corresponding institutional agreement to lighten the load—to make the beginner's job easier by insuring "good" classes and limited additional duties (but see Tisher, 1980, for a description of systematic induction activities in Britain and Australia).

LACK OF COLLEGIAL SUPPORT FOR CONTINUED LEARNING

Whatever the provisions for induction, some workplace conditions are more conducive to professional development than others. In one study of six elementary and secondary schools, norms of collegiality and experimentation in three schools moved teaching from a private to a public enterprise. Schools in which teachers (a) routinely talked to one another about teaching, (b) were regularly observed at their work, and (c) participated in shared planning and preparation were also schools in which teachers expected to learn from and with one another on a regular basis (Little, 1981).

In a follow-up study of five secondary schools, teachers in two "avid" schools had been accorded substantial latitude for developing and testing curriculum ideas. Interested teachers joined study groups with the sole purpose of "getting smarter," and with no immediate obligation to implement new practices in the classroom. Eventually, discussions evolved in agreements to try out selected practices in classrooms, sometimes culminating in well-designed experiments involving skills training, special curricula, and comparison groups (Bird & Little, 1983). By teachers' reports, collegial work adds to the pool of available ideas and materials, the quality of solutions to curricular problems, and teachers' own confidence in their collective and individual ability to refine their work.

Involvement in professional development with colleagues stands in marked contrast to more typical involvements that are passive, brief, fragmented, and intellectually narrow. In Lortie's five towns survey, only 25% of the teachers reported "much contact" with fellow teachers in the course of their work. Amost half reported "no contact."

Research confirms that collaboration among teachers is fragile and frequently undermined by conditions of work. In a review of team work among teachers, Cohen (1981) reported that teaming was relatively unstable and short-lived in schools and that true "instructional interdependence" was rare. In a study of the effects of in-classroom coaching of teachers learning new classroom methods, Showers (1983) found that joint planning was the most valued of the coaching agreements, but was not commonly practiced in schools. Coaching was not consistent with established workplace values, habits, and schedules. Similarly, Shultze and Yinger (1983) found that their teachers' work situations did not permit use of collaborative problem-solving approaches that teachers had come to admire during inservice course work. When examining administrators' influence on teachers' professional norms, Bird and Little (1983) discovered that collegial norms were most solidly established when a "policy" of collaborative work was given material support in the form of time, space, supplies, and assigned staff.

LACK OF EFFECTIVE FORMAL ARRANGEMENTS FOR CONTINUED LEARNING

If the conditions of work and norms of collegiality do not provide an adequate basis for teachers to continue to learn about their work and vocation, it might be thought that formal programs for staff development would have high priority. But, perhaps because teaching is not viewed as a long-term career, the opposite tends to be the case. Professional development programs have been found to be programmatically isolated and politically weak (Moore & Hyde, 1981; Schlechty & Crowell, 1983). Staff development is not tied to the central obligations, opportunities, and rewards of work in the district, school, or profession and offers few career rewards to those who emerge as its leaders. "Those who run staff development," Schlechty and Crowell (1983, p. 49) point out, "seldom run schools."

In the three districts studied by Moore and Hyde (1981), responsibility for staff development was well down in the hierarchy. Staff development directors often operated with staffs of two or three, organizationally isolated from other key curriculum and program offices. At that level it was difficult to launch initiatives (i.e., to generate ideas rather than working on the ideas imposed by others), to protect them, and to grant them adequate stability and support; the programs were therefore vulnerable to varied and rapidly changing priorities at higher organizational levels (Schlechty & Whitford, 1983). Activities often operated in separate divisions and were accountable to different assistant or associate superintendents.

Responsibility for staff development was widely scattered with little attempt at coordination. From one-third to more than one-half of the program offices in each district engaged in staff development. Staff development leaders in each of these offices tended to be unaware of the activities of their counterparts in other offices, even when those activities placed demands of time and energy on the same teachers. For most, staff development was a secondary activity, a mechanism for carrying out other primary responsibilities.

Thus, the research evidence suggests that staff development has not generally been the product of coherent policy, nor has it been systematically integrated with institutional priorities for curriculum and instructional improvement. Moore and Hyde worry aloud that "commitment to staff development that is focused on specific problems is much different from a commitment to a general scheme for the improvement of instruction" (p. 110). The findings from the Vacca et al. (1982) study of professional development in six districts are similar. Administrators in only two of the six districts described a structural connection between professional development and program or teacher evaluation; in both of these instances, the connection was narrowly oriented toward the "remediation" of individual teachers rather than toward coordination of program improvement initiatives.

In many districts, staff development has grown in importance, but not in quality. McLaughlin and Marsh (1979) argue that the increased importance of staff development in the later 1970s can be traced in part to an impressive array of attempted reforms that fell short of their intended aims due in part to lack of training and assistance and in part to declining enrollments that left many districts with a corps of tenured, experienced staff. In the absence of coordination or supervision, and pressed by multiple external demands to be almost all things to almost all people, districts assembled a patchwork collection of diverse activities, rather than an orchestrated program of professional development and program improvement (Goodlad, 1984; Little, 1981; Moore & Hyde, 1981; Weinshank, Trumball, & Daly, 1983).

Ironically, the lack of effective continuing teacher education in schools is partly attributable to the absence of teachers educated for a professional teaching career that includes committed attention to district policies. If more teachers gave serious attention to the organization of district staff development programs, those programs would have greater chance for success. But districts have typically taken a needs assessment approach to involving teachers in planning staff development, leading to a fragmented program geared to the noncareer teacher. Involvement of teachers in the planning and design of professional development programs has been largely symbolic, infrequent, and inconsequential (Moore & Hyde, 1981).

Districts' inability to balance widespread decision-making

authority for professional development with substantive program direction appears unintentionally but quite systematically to erode teachers' interest in and commitment to organized programs. Themselves teachers, Weinshank et al. (1983) combine insights drawn from their own experiences with interviews of teachers and program specialists to illustrate and analyze precisely such problems of orchestration and integration. In particular, they expose some of the dilemmas associated with insecure and fleeting federal funds and the mismatch between federal regulations and teachers' judgments. But these problems, too, are not new. Referring to the cyclical mounting of inservice programs in response to educational innovations a decade ago, Cogan (1973) observed:

> It is evident that these "boom–bust–boom–bust" sequences tend to reduce teachers to a cynicism that saps their commitment to professional improvement.... What they need is more careful long-term planning for longer phases of their school-based efforts. They need programs rather than fads and episodes. (p. 225)

For teachers, involvement in professional development must compete with a host of other interests and obligations. Cusick (1983), in a description of staff relations in secondary schools, unravels a complex web of teachers' activities and involvements in and out of school. Scheduled inservice offerings take second or third place behind sponsored student activities and clubs, second jobs, or independently owned businesses, community or church activities, and family obligations.

The teachers' center movement stands as an exception to this lack of commitment, having been organized precisely to ensure teachers' influence over the content and process of continuing education and over conditions of participation (Feiman, 1978; Leiter & Cooper, 1979). However, while some centers have engaged teachers in probing investigations of fundamental problems of teaching and learning, on the whole such centers have not exerted widespread influence over the day-to-day working environments from which their participants come and to which they return (McLaughlin & Marsh, 1979).

Another alleged constraint on teachers' commitment to the accumulation and dissemination of knowledge is the union movement. Based on their two-year study of collective bargaining in California and Illinois, Mitchell and Kerchner (1983) suggest that a move toward a "laboring" definition of teachers' work has been accompanied by an increasing rationalization of tasks and a move toward closer inspection of classroom performance. A conception of teachers' work that emphasizes "labor" places less weight on teaching as craft, profession, or art—conceptions that have traditionally called forth different views of how to get members of the occupation to learn and perform.

Other research suggests that these criticisms of union contracts have been overstated. Susan Moore Johnson's (1981) study of teacher unions and the schools revealed considerable within-district variation, particularly in arenas of professional development and school improvement. Some teacher unionists have even asserted that professional organizations are taking the lead in teachers' professional development (Leiter & Cooper, 1979). Union sponsorship of teachers' centers and a three-site research and development project to translate classroom-based research into practice through the development of new staff development roles are two examples (Feiman, 1978; Rauth, Biles, Billups, & Veitch, 1982).

The use of monetary rewards for teachers to strengthen staff development is another problematic aspect of organizing teacher commitment. Sykes (1983b) suggests that the expectation of pay for participating in continuing education activities operates to isolate professional development from what are perceived to be more central aspects of teachers' work. In addition, incentive pay has been more effective in attracting teachers to inservice sessions than it has in influencing what these teachers do after the sessions. In fact, in the Rand Corporation's four-year Change Agent study, pay for attending inservice sessions was found to be inversely related to classroom implementation of the recommended practices (Berman & McLaughlin, 1978).

In short, this examination of school conditions is consistent with the thesis that teaching has been a relatively short-term, low-commitment occupation which required little by way of long-term, intensive, and coherent educational provisions. From such a perspective neither teacher nor school district could be expected to make the investments necessary to long-term payoffs. Changing work conditions in these respects could make administration of schools more difficult and expensive. For example, assistance for induction could require teachers and administrators to give more attention to the competence and potential of entering teachers. Norms of collegiality could make compatibility an important and difficult criterion in the selection of teachers. More extensive and coherent staff development programs would require giving up the notion that experience by itself is an adequate teacher of teachers. Finally, the lack of progression in the teaching career would have to be confronted and challenged, as indeed it is being challenged in many states today.

The Professional Community and Support for Teacher Education

To some observers, the notion of a profession implies that members of the profession control and determine, at least in part, the circumstances under which novices enter the profession. Thus it is important for research to consider the extent to which and the ways in which professional organizations contribute to and influence teacher education. Unfortunately, there is relatively little research on these organizations that is tightly and insightfully tied to the central issues confronting the faculty, students, and curricula of teacher education as here defined. Work on accreditation and certification, however, does provide some evidence that is largely consistent with the arguments that have been made in earlier sections of this analysis.

PROGRAM ACCREDITATION AND APPROVAL

Public and private organizations have been given responsibility for monitoring the quality of initial teacher certification programs. Each state has an agency responsible for granting or withholding approval of college and university programs; completing an approved program is the typical way for teachers to gain entry to the profession. At the national level, the National

Council for the Accreditation of Teacher Education (NCATE) is a voluntary organization that awards or denies a stamp of approval to those programs that decide to seek NCATE accreditation.

The ability of either state governments or NCATE to support the preparation of career teachers is restricted by their focus on the lowest quality programs and by questions about their effectiveness even at that level. As indicated earlier, most initial preparation programs for teachers do not provide opportunities for the most able students to prepare for a career in teaching. Yet, both state agencies and NCATE do no more than keep out the worst programs, in contrast to supporting high quality in teacher education. Political pressures on both institutions press them to define "worst" in a way that will permit approval of most programs. According to Clark and Marker (1975):

> No matter how committed the leadership of a state education agency may be, it would be politically suicidal for the state government to allow that agency to establish and attempt to maintain accreditation standards higher than it is possible for the vast majority of institutions in the state to meet.... NCATE and the regional accrediting associations are hardly in a better position. These bodies have a voluntary membership and exist ultimately at the pleasure of their institutional members. (p. 81)

Standards that the vast majority of institutions can meet are not likely to give strong support to education for a career in teaching.

The small amount of resources available to these agencies makes it difficult for them to be successful even at keeping out the worst programs. Standards for institutions are written in terms of institutional characteristics (e.g., resources in the library, inclusion of courses in specified areas), not qualities of the students completing the program. Few states have staff to make visits to institutions, so fulfillment of requirements is often checked by examining descriptions written by the programs themselves.

Clark and Marker (1975) make NCATE's accreditation process seem a bit more rigorous, though the small paid staff and extensive use of volunteers for site visits "dictates infrequent visits and routine procedures wherever possible" (p. 69). Wheeler's detailed study of NCATE's accreditation process (Wheeler, 1980) suggests that even this assessment overestimates their ability to enforce their minimal standards.

Although Wheeler (1980) found that those involved in the NCATE accreditation process took their work seriously and that many programs benefited from going through the approval process, he also found critical weaknesses. The central difficulty was that accreditation teams, instead of following the requirement that they judge whether a particular function was being performed well, looked only for whether the function was performed at all:

> This "presence-or-absence" approach to applying the Standards is pursued for many reasons, only several of which are summarized here: (1) the Standards are vague, which discourages attempts to judge the quality of programs; (2) institutions have some influence over the information made available to team and Council members, which in turn affects their availability to judge the quality of

programs; and (3) the dynamics of team visits and Council meetings virtually prelude in-depth examination of programs. (p. 6)

For example, one standard requires explicit objectives clearly related to the curriculum. In one case a final decision on this standard was delayed until the last day of the visit so that the institution could develop such objectives. Any program submitting written objectives was judged to have met this standard, without further evidence of links to the curriculum. Programs without written objectives were failed on this standard (Wheeler, 1980, p. 28).

Although NCATE continues to try to improve its operation and many states have recently tightened their program requirements, the accreditation and program approval process continues to support programs that do no more than prepare teachers for a noncareer. So long as they aim to include virtually all programs, little more can be expected.

CERTIFICATION

The profession might use the procedures for certifying teachers to support them in acquiring the knowledge and skills appropriate for a career in teaching. But fragmentation and a minimum-standards orientation prevent certification from providing such support.

In her report entitled "The Making of a Teacher," Feistritzer summarizes the current scene: "The certification of classroom teachers in the United States is a mess" (1984, p. 36). Certification requirements vary dramatically, both within a teaching specialty across states and within a state across teaching specialties. Requirements are virtually always specified in terms of courses that must be completed, but the course specifications show little rational order.

In 48 states and the District of Columbia, teachers can be certified merely by completing an approved program. Hence, the certification of most teachers is driven by political pressure to allow the majority of institutions to grant certification to their students. When program approval is the only requirement for certification, the only way in which prospective teachers must demonstrate their preparedness is by passing the required courses. In most states it is even possible to teach without completing the "required" course work. States grant emergency or substandard certificates, in some cases even to students who have not completed 4 years of college.

TEACHER ORGANIZATIONS

The teachers' associations—the National Education Association and the American Federation of Teachers—are another important part of the milieu in which teacher education operates. Their growth and strength over the past 2 decades have raised additional questions about who speaks for teacher education in the public arena (Clark & Marker, 1975), and may have changed the ways in which teachers continue their education on the job (Mitchell & Kirschner, 1983).

But, especially compared to the size and widespread influence of these organizations, little research has been conducted on their effects as part of the milieu of teacher education. Numerous topics need research attention, including the effects of collective bargaining on the public status of the teaching profession, the role teachers' organizations play in controlling how many students enter initial teacher education, the influence of teachers' organizations over requirements for initial and continuing teacher certification, and the continuing education provided by the organizations themselves.

Summary: Research and the Teacher Education Milieu

Studies of the context of teacher education at both university and K–12 levels convey one overriding impression: Institutional policies, structures, and resources that might be expected to foster the quality of teaching and teacher education appear to do the opposite. Initial and continuing teacher education are both poorly served by an institutional apparatus that belies the rhetoric of importance that, in turn, disguises the harsh realities of teaching.

Universities have never made and do not make investments in teacher education that are commensurate with talk about the importance of teacher education. Overall responsibility and accountability for these programs is absent or nominal. Research shows that the notion of a unified teacher education establishment is a myth and that lack of knowledge about teaching is by no means the sole or perhaps even the main reason for the mediocre quality of teacher education programs. The prevalence of low quality and the absence of investments to remedy the situation are not surprising, however, when one considers the low status of the client groups—teachers and children, the prevalence of women in the profession of teaching, and the current lack of public support for measures to reduce these inequalities.

The world of elementary and secondary schools has not offered a more positive environment for learning to teach. Although many would say that teachers learn best from experience, there is a growing body of research to show that the typical experience of teachers in school is noneducative at best and miseducative at worst. Staff development programs that might overcome the limitations of on-the-job experience are neither adequately organized nor sufficiently supported to meet the needs of career teachers.

Various professional organizations have been called to fill these gaps. As yet none does, although teacher organizations show increasing commitment to playing a role in both initial and continuing teacher education.

In the meantime, a system under heavy public criticism has reduced capability to resist reform. Reform, however, can be negative or positive in its consequences. To avoid repeating the mistakes that have so often been repeated in the past, clarity about and understanding of the nature of the problem is essential. This review of research on teacher education suggests that political circumstances and scholarly considerations may be converging to provide more opportunities for improvement than heretofore has been the case.

Summary: Interrelated Obstacles to Quality Teacher Education

This chapter reviews studies that potentially inform policies and practices in initial and continuing teacher education—

studies of teacher educators, studies of prospective and experienced teachers, studies of the teacher education curriculum, and studies of the milieu in which teacher education takes place. Across these four areas, mutually reinforcing factors explain why teacher education has been kept from being as academic and intellectual as it probably deserves to be, and why change is likely to be slow.

Although a number of academically talented persons pursue careers in teaching and teacher education, they remain proportionally underrepresented. Many teachers and teacher educators come from home and family backgrounds whose academic roots are often shallow and which are therefore not likely to engender strong and ingrained intellectual propensities. Persons with low measures of academic talent are allowed to dominate the field. As a result, teacher education tends to be easy and nonintellectual.

Initial and continuing teacher education goes on in an environment that makes it difficult to be scholarly and remain in teacher education. Those with a strong academic leaning find few compatriots in colleges or schools. Prospective teachers find little intellectual challenge in their professional training, and subsequently are isolated in school classrooms where low levels of knowledge are again reinforced, the rewards of work dwindle over the years, and the motivations to learn more about teaching are few. Academically capable college faculty find greater rewards when they place increasing distance between themselves and teacher education.

The deintellectualization of teacher education feeds on itself; the capable are discouraged from entering teacher education by what they see there. But other aspects of the milieu also operate to maintain the character of teacher education. Low status keeps the power to organize change out of the hands of those closest to the field. Teachers are often used only as symbols or themselves assign teacher education low priority. Researchers set themselves up as the source of leadership. Diffusion of responsibility leaves no one in charge of programs.

The picture in each domain repeats a pattern that reinforces the maintenance of teacher education as a marginal part of the university community, criticized for its lack of rigor, but discouraged from trying to be anything else. The increasingly clear descriptions of the difficulties in teacher education are themselves evidence that respectable study can be a part of teacher education. But these descriptions also show why change in teacher education, though possible, will be slow and often discouraging.

REFERENCES

Anderson, C. W. (1982). *The use of codified knowledge in five teacher education programs: A comparative analysis* (Research Series No. 118). East Lansing: Michigan State University, Institute for Research on Teaching.

Anderson, L., Evertson, C., & Brophy, J. (1979). An experimental study of effective teaching in first grade reading groups. *Elementary School Journal, 79,* 193–223.

Anyon, J. (1981). Social class and school knowledge. *Curriculum Inquiry, 11*(1), 3–41.

Arends, R. (1983). *Teachers as learners: A descriptive study of professional development activities.* Paper presented at the annual meeting of the American Educational Research Association, Montreal.

Ashton, P., Webb, R., & Doda, N. (1982). *A study of teachers' sense of efficacy.* Unpublished paper, University of Florida, Gainesville.

Astin, A. W. (1981). *The American freshman: National norms for fall 1981.* Los Angeles: University of California.

Berliner, D. C. (1978). *Changing academic learning time: Clinical interventions in four classrooms.* Paper presented at the annual meeting of the American Educational Research Association, Toronto.

Berliner, D. C. (1982). *Executive functions of teaching.* Paper presented at the annual meeting of the American Educational Research Association, New York City.

Berman, P., & McLauglin, M. W. (1978). *Implementing and sustaining innovations: Federal programs supporting educational change* (Vol. 8. Prepared for the U.S. Office of Education, DHEW). Santa Monica, CA: Rand Corporation.

Bestor, A. (1955). *The restoration of learning.* New York: Alfred A. Knopf.

Beyer, L. E., & Zeichner, K. M. (1982). Teacher training and educational foundations: A plea for discontent. *Journal of Teacher Education, 33*(3), 18–23.

Bierly, M. B., & Berliner, D. C. (1982). The elementary school teacher as learner. *Journal of Teacher Education, 33*(6), 37–40.

Bird, T. D., & Little, J. W. (1983). *Finding and founding peer coaching.* Paper presented at the annual meeting of the American Educational Research Association, Montreal.

Book, C., Byers, J., & Freeman, D. (1983). Student expectations and teacher education traditions with which we can and cannot live. *Journal of Teacher Education, 34*(1), 9–13.

Borrowman, M. L. (1965a). Liberal education and the professional education of teachers. In M. L. Borrowman (Ed.), *Teacher education in America: A documentary history* (pp. 1–53). New York, NY: Teachers College Press, Columbia University.

Borrowman, M. L. (Ed.). (1965b). *Teacher education in America: A documentary history.* New York: Teachers College Press, Columbia University.

Boyer, E. L. (1983). *High school: A report on secondary education in America.* New York: Harper & Row.

Brophy, J. E. (1980). *Teachers' cognitive activities and overt behaviors.* East Lansing: Michigan State University, College of Education.

Broudy, H. S. (1980). What do professors of education profess? *The Educational Forum, 44*(4), 441–451.

Buchmann, M. (1983a). *Argument and conversation as discourse models of knowledge use* (Occasional Paper No. 68). East Lansing: Michigan State University, Institute for Research on Teaching.

Buchmann, M. (1983b). *Role over person: Justifying teacher action and decisions* (Research Series No. 135). East Lansing: Michigan State University, Institute for Research on Teaching.

Buchmann, M. (1984). The use of research knowledge in teacher education and teaching. *American Journal of Education, 92*(4), 421–439.

Buchmann, M. & Schwille, J. (1983). Education: The overcoming of experience. *American Journal of Education, 92*(1), 30–51.

Bureau of Educational Research. (1983). *Program Design for the Virginia Beginning Teacher Assistance Program.* Charlottesville: University of Virginia, School of Education.

Bureau of Labor Statistics. (March 1980). *Occupational outlook handbook.* Washington, DC: U.S. Department of Labor.

Bureau of Labor Statistics. (September 1980). *Occupational projections and training data.* Washington, DC: U.S. Department of Labor.

Christensen, J., Burke, P., Fessler, R., & Hagstrom, D. (1983). *Stages of teachers' careers: Implications for professional development.* Washington, DC: ERIC Clearinghouse on Teacher Education.

Clark, D. L., & Marker, G. (1975). The institutionalization of teacher education. In K. Ryan (Ed.), *Teacher education* (74th yearbook of the National Society for the Study of Education, Part 2, pp. 53–86). Chicago: University of Chicago Press.

Cogan, M. L. (1973). *Clinical supervision.* Boston: Houghton Mifflin.

Cohen, E. (1981). Sociology looks at team teaching. In R. G. Corwin (Ed.), *Research in sociology of education and socialization: Vol. 2. Research on educational organizations* (pp. 163–193). Greenwich, CT: JAI Press.

Coladarci, T., & Gage, N. L. (1984). Effects of a minimal intervention on teacher behavior and student achievement. *American Educational Research Journal, 21*(3), 539–555.

Conant, J. B. (1963). *The education of American teachers.* New York: McGraw-Hill.

Crawford, J., Gage, N. L., Corno, L., Stayrook, N., Mitman, A., Schunk, D., Stallings, J., Baskin, E., Harvey, P., Austin, D., Cronin, D., & Newman, R. (1977). *An experiment on teaching effectiveness and parent-assisted instruction in the third grade.* Stanford, CA: Center for Educational Research.

Crocker, A. C. (1974). *Predicting teaching success.* Atlantic Highlands, NJ: NFER Publishing.

Cruickshank, D. R., & Broadbent, F. W. (1968). *The simulation and analysis of problems of beginning teachers.* Brockport: New York State University College. (ERIC Document Reproduction Service No. 024–637).

Cusick, P. A. (1973). *Inside high school.* New York: Holt, Rinehart & Winston.

Cusick, P. A. (1981). A study of networks among professional staffs in secondary schools. *Educational Administration Quarterly, 17*(3), 114–138.

Cusick, P. A. (1983). *The egalitarian ideal and the American high school: Studies of three schools.* New York: Longman.

Cusick, P. A. (in press). [Review of *Managers of virtue,* by D. Tyack & E. Hansot]. National Academy of Education.

Dalton, G. W., Thompson, P. H., & Price, R. L. (1977, summer). The four stages of professional careers: A new look at performance by professionals. *Organizational Dynamics, 5*(1), 19–42.

Dearman, N. B., & Plisko, V. W. (1980–1982). *The condition of education: Statistical report.* Washington, DC: U.S. Department of Education, National Center for Education Statistics.

Dearmin, E. T. (1982). *University Teacher Education Councils: Report to executive committee and faculty.* Las Vegas: University of Nevada, College of Education.

Dewey, J. (1965). The relation of theory to practice in education. In M. L. Borrowman (Ed.), *Teacher education in America: A documentary history* (pp. 140–171). New York: Teachers College Press, Columbia University. (Original work published 1904)

Doyle, W. (1977). Learning the classroom environment: An ecological analysis. *Journal of Teacher Education, 28*(6), 51–55.

Doyle, W., & Ponder, G. A. (1977–1978). The practicality ethic in teacher decision making. *Interchange, 8*(3), 1.

Ducharme, E. R., & Agne, R. M. (1982). The educational professorate: A research-based perspective. *Journal of Teacher Education, 33*(6), 30–36.

Eddy, E. M. (1969). *Becoming a teacher: The passage to professional status.* New York: Teachers College Press, Columbia University.

Edgar, D. E., & Brod, R. L. (1970). *Professional socialization and teacher autonomy.* Stanford, CA: Stanford Center for Research and Development in Teaching. (ERIC Document Reproduction Service No. ED 046–885)

Emmer, E. T., Sanford, J. P., Clements, B. S., & Martin, J. (1982). *Improving classroom management and organization in junior high schools: An experimental investigation* (R&D Rep. 6153). Austin: Research and Development Center for Teacher Education, The University of Texas at Austin.

Everhart, R. (1984). *Reading, writing, and resistance.* London: Routledge & Kegan Paul.

Feiman, S. (Ed.). (1978). *Teacher centers: What place in education?* Chicago: University of Chicago, Center for Policy Study.

Feiman-Nemser, S., & Buchmann, M. (1983). Pitfalls of experience in teacher education. In P. Tamir, A. Hofstein, & Ben-Peretz, M. (Eds.), *Preservice and inservice education of science teachers.* Philadelphia: Balaban International Science Services.

Feistritzer, C. E. (1983a). *The American teacher.* Washington, DC: Feistritzer.

Feistritzer, C. E. (1983b). *The condition of teaching: A state-by-state analysis.* Princeton, NJ: The Carnegie Foundation for the Advancement of Teaching.

Feistritzer, C. E. (1984). *The making of a teacher: A report on teacher education and certification.* Washington, DC: National Center for Educational Information.

Fenstermacher, G. D. (1978). A philosophical consideration of recent research on teacher effectiveness. In L. S. Shulman (Ed.), *Review of research in education* (Vol. 6). Itasca, IL: F. E. Peacock.

Fenstermacher, G. D. (1980). On learning to teach effectively from research on teacher effectiveness. In C. Denham & A. Lieberman (Eds.), *Time to learn*. Washington, DC: National Institute of Education.

Finkelstein, B. (1982). Technicians, mandarins, and witnesses: Searching for professional understanding. *Journal of Teacher Education, 33*(3), 25–27.

Floden, R. E. (in press). The role of rhetoric in changing teachers' beliefs. *Teaching and Teacher Education.*

Floden, R. E., Buchmann, M., & Schwille, J. R. (1984). *The case for the separation of home and school*. Paper presented at the annual meeting of the American Educational Research Association, New Orleans.

Floden, R., & Feiman, S. (1981). *A developmental approach to the study of teacher change: What's to be gained?* (Research Series No. 93). East Lansing: Michigan State University, Institute for Research on Teaching.

Fox, R. (1957). Training for uncertainty. In R. Merton, G. G. Reader, & P. L. Kendall (Eds.), *The student physician: Introductory studies in the sociology of medical education* (pp. 207–241). Cambridge, MA: Harvard University Press.

Frankel, M. M., & Gerald, D. E. (1982). *Projections of education statistics to 1990–91* (Vol. 1). Washington, DC: U. S. Department of Education, National Center for Education Statistics.

Fuchs, E. (1969). *Teachers talk: Views from inside city schools*. Garden City, NY: Doubleday.

Fullan, M. (1982). *The meaning of educational change*. New York: Teachers College Press, Columbia University.

Fuller, F. F. (1970). *Personalized teacher education for teachers: An introduction for teacher educators*. Austin: University of Texas, R & D Center for Teacher Education. (ERIC Document Reproduction Service No. ED 048-105)

Fuller, F. F. (1969). Concerns of teachers: A developmental conceptualization. *American Educational Research Journal, 6,* 207–226.

Fuller, F. F., & Bown, O. (1975). Becoming a teacher. In K. Ryan (Ed.), *Teacher education* (74th yearbook of the National Society for the Study of Education, Part 2, pp. 25–52). Chicago: University of Chicago Press.

Gage, N. L. (Ed.). (1963). *Handbook of research on teaching*. Chicago: Rand McNally.

Gall, M. D. (1983, winter). Using staff development to improve schools. *R & D Perspectives,* pp. 1–6.

Gall, M. D., Haisley, F. B., Baker, R. G., & Perez, M. (1982). *The relationship between inservice education practices and productivity of basic skills instruction*. Eugene: University of Oregon, Center for Educational Policy and Management.

Gallup, G. H. (1983). The 15th annual Gallup poll of the public's attitudes toward the public schools. *Phi Delta Kappan, 65*(1), 33–47.

Geer, B. (1968). Occupational commitment and the teaching profession. In H. S. Becker, B. Geer, D. Riesman, & R. S. Weiss (Eds.), *Institutions and the person*. Chicago: Aldine.

Getzels, J. W., & Jackson, P. W. (1963). The teacher's personality and characteristics. In N. L. Gage (Ed.), *Handbook of research on teaching*. Chicago: Rand McNally.

Golladay, M. A. & Noell, J. (1978). *The condition of education* (NCES Statistical Report). Washington, DC: U.S. Government Printing Office.

Good, T. L. & Grouws, D. A. (1979). The Missouri Mathematics Effectiveness Project: An experimental study in fourth-grade classrooms. *Journal of Educational Psychology, 71*(3), 355–362.

Good, T. L., & Grouws, D. A. (1981). *Experimental research in secondary mathematics classrooms: Working with teachers* (Final report). Columbia: University of Missouri.

Goodlad, J. (1984). *A place called school*. New York: McGraw-Hill.

Grant, W. V., & Eiden, L. J. (1982). *Digest of education statistics 1982*. Washington, DC: U.S. Department of Education, National Center for Education Statistics.

Greene, M. (1979). Teaching: The question of personal reality. In A. Lieberman & L. Miller (Eds.), *Staff development: New demands, new*

realities, new perspectives (pp. 23–35). New York: Teachers College Press, Columbia University.

Griffin, G. (1982). *Staff development* (Paper prepared for the National Institute of Education Invitational Conference, Research on Teaching: Implications for Practice, Airlie House, Virginia). Washington, DC: National Institute of Education.

Griffin, G., & Hukill, H. (Eds.). (1983). *First years of teaching: What are the pertinent issues?* Austin: University of Texas, R & D Center for Teacher Education.

Guba, E. G., & Clark, D. L. (1978). Levels of R & D productivity in schools of education. *Educational Researcher, 7*(5), 3–9.

Hogan, P. (1983). The central place of prejudice in the supervision of student teachers. *Journal of Education for Teaching, 9*(1), 30–45.

Howsam, R. B., Corrigan, D. C., Denemark, G. W., & Nash, R. J. (1976). *Educating a profession: Report of the Bicentennial Commission on Education for the Profession of Teaching*. Washington, DC: American Association of Colleges for Teacher Education.

Hoy, W. (1967). Organizational socialization: The student teacher and pupil control ideology. *Journal of Educational Research, 61,* 153–155.

Hoy, W. K., & Rees, R. (1977). The bureaucratic socialization of student teachers. *Journal of Teacher Education, 28*(1), 23–26.

Iannaccone, L. (1963). Student teaching: A transitional stage in the making of a teacher. *Theory Into Practice, 2,* 73–80.

Jackson, P. (1968). *Life in Classrooms*. New York: Holt, Rinehart & Winston.

Johnson, S. M. (1981). *Teacher unions and the schools*. Cambridge MA: Harvard University, Institute for Educational Policy Studies.

Joyce, B., & Clift, R. (1984). The Phoenix agenda: Essential reform in teacher education. *Educational Researcher, 13*(4), 5–18.

Joyce, B., & Showers, B. (1981). *Teacher training research: Working hypotheses for program design and directions for future study*. Paper presented at the annual meeting of the American Educational Research Association, Los Angeles.

Joyce, B., Yarger, S., & Howey, K. R. (1977). *Preservice teacher education*. Palo Alto, CA: Consolidated Publications.

Judge, H. (1982). *American graduate schools of education: A view from abroad* (Report to the Ford Foundation). New York: Ford Foundation.

Kaestle, C. D. (1983). *Pillars of the republic*. New York: Hill & Wang.

Katz, L. (1980). A matrix for research on teacher education. In E. Hoyle & J. Megarry (Eds.), *The professional development of teachers* (World Yearbook of Education, pp. 283–292). London: Kogan Page.

Katz, L., & Raths, J. D. (1982). The best of intentions for the education of teachers. *Action in Teacher Education* (Special issue: The role of research in education), *4*(1), 8–16.

Kepler, K. B. (1980). BTES: Implications for preservice education of teachers. In C. Denham & A. Lieberman (Eds.), *Time to learn* (pp. 139–157). Washington, DC: National Institute of Education.

Kerr, D. H. (1983). Teaching competence and teacher education in the United States. In L. S. Shulman & G. Sykes (Eds.), *Handbook of teaching and policy* (pp. 126–149). New York: Longman.

Koerner, J. D. (1963). *The miseducation of American teachers*. Boston: Houghton Mifflin.

Kohn, M. L. (1969). *Class and conformity: A study in values*. Homewood, IL: Dorsey Press.

Kohn, M. L., & Schooler, C. (1982). Job conditions and personality: A longitudinal assessment of their reciprocal effects. *American Journal of Sociology, 87*(6), 1257–1286.

Lacey, C. (1977). *The socialization of teachers*. London: Methuen.

Lanier, J. E. (1983). Tensions in teaching teachers the skills of pedagogy. In G. Griffin (Ed.), *Staff development* (82nd yearbook of the National Society for the Study of Education, pp. 118–153). Chicago: University of Chicago Press.

Lanier, J. E. (1984). *The future of teacher education: Two papers* (Occasional Paper No. 79). East Lansing: Michigan State University, Institute for Research on Teaching.

Lanier, J. E., & Floden, R. E. (1978). *Research and development needs for the advancement of teacher education* (Research Series No. 8). East Lansing: Michigan State University, Institute for Research on Teaching.

Lanier, P. E., & Henderson, J. E. (1973). The content and process of teacher education: A critique and a challenge. *New Directions for Education* (Special issue: Preparing and qualifying for admission to teaching), *1*(2), 1–102.

Learned, W. S., & Wood, B. D. (1938). *The student and his knowledge* (Bulletin No. 29). New York: Carnegie Foundation for the Advancement of Teaching.

Leiter, M., & Cooper, M. (1979). How teacher unionists view inservice education. In A. Lieberman & L. Miller (Eds.), *Staff development: New demands, new realities, new perspectives* (pp. 107–125). New York: Columbia University, Teachers College Press.

Lerner, G. (1979). *The majority finds its past: Placing women in history.* New York: Oxford University Press.

Lightfoot, S. L. (1983). The lives of teachers. In L. S. Shulman & G. Sykes (Eds.), *Handbook of Teaching and Policy* (pp. 241–260). New York: Longman.

Lines, A. A. (1982). *To raise myself a little: The diaries and letters of Jennie, a Georgia teacher, 1851–1886* (T. Dyer, Ed.). Athens: University of Georgia Press.

Little, J. W. (1981). *School success and staff development: The role of staff development in urban desegregated schools.* Boulder, CO: Center for Action Research.

Lortie, D. (1975). *Schoolteacher.* Chicago: University of Chicago Press.

MacAleese, R. (1976). A note on the free-wheeling effect in non-supervised microteaching students. *Research Intelligence, 2*(1), 20–22.

Masland, S. W., & Williams, R. T. (1983, July/August). Teacher surplus and shortage: Getting ready to accept responsibilities. *Journal of Teacher Education, 34*(4), 6–9.

Mattingly, P. H. (1975). *The classless profession.* New York: New York University Press.

McCune, S. D. (1977). *The organized teaching profession and education R and D* (Occasional Paper No. 29). Columbus, OH: Center for Vocational Education.

McCutcheon, G. (1982). What in the world is curriculum theory? *Theory Into practice, 21*(1), 18–22.

McDonald, F. J. (1980). *Study of induction programs for beginning teachers: Vol. 1. The problems of beginning teachers: A crisis in training.* Princeton NJ: Educational Testing Service.

McFaul, S., & Cooper, J. (1983). *Selected outcomes of implementing peer clinical supervision in an elementary school.* Paper presented at the annual meeting of the American Educational Research Association, Montreal.

McKeachie, W. J. (1963). Research on teaching at the college and university level. In N. L. Gage (Ed.), *Handbook of research on teaching* (pp. 1118–1172). Chicago: Rand McNally.

McLaughlin, M. W. & Marsh, D. D. (1979). Staff development and school change. In A. Lieberman & L. Miller (Eds.), *Staff development: New demands, new realities, new perspectives* (pp. 69–94). New York: Columbia University, Teachers College Press.

McNeil, L. M. (1982). *Contradictions of control: The organizational context of school knowledge* (Final report). Madison: Wisconsin Center for Public Policy.

Merton, R. K., Reader, G. G., & Kendall, P. L. (Eds.). (1957). *The student-physician: Introductory studies in the sociology of medical education.* Cambridge, MA: Harvard University Press.

Mitchell, D. E., & Kerchner, C. T. (1983). Labor relations and teacher policy. In L. Shulman & G. Sykes (Eds.), *Handbook of teaching and policy* (pp. 214–238). New York: Longman.

Mohlman, G. G. (1983). *A study of inservice training, teacher characteristics, and teacher change.* Paper presented at the annual meeting of the American Educational Research Association, Montreal.

Moore, C. (1979, November/December). National survey queries early clinical experiences. *ATE Newsletter, 12*, 3.

Moore, D. R., & Hyde, A. A. (1981). *Making sense of staff development: An analysis of staff development programs and their costs in three urban school districts.* Chicago: Designs for Change.

Morris, J. E. (1983). The director of student teaching/field experiences: Characteristics and responsibilities. *The Teacher Educator, 18*(4), 11–18.

Murphy, R. (1979). *Sociological theories of education.* Toronto: McGraw-Hill Ryerson Ltd.

National Education Association. (1982). *Status of the American public school teacher, 1980–81.* Washington, DC: National Education Association.

Nemser, S. (1983). Learning to teach. In L. S. Shulman & G. Sykes (Eds.), *Handbook of teaching and policy.* New York: Longman.

Orr, P. G., & Peseau, B. A. (1979, October). Formula funding is not the problem in teacher education. *Peabody Journal of Education, 57*(1), 61–71.

Peck, R. F., & Tucker, J. A. (1973). Research on teacher education. In R. M. W. Travers (Ed.), *Second handbook of research on teaching* (pp. 940–978). Chicago: Rand McNally.

Pelikan, J. (1983). *Scholarship and its survival: Questions on the idea of graduate education.* Princeton, NJ: Carnegie Foundation for the Advancement of Teaching.

Peseau, B. A. (1982). Developing an adequate resource base for teacher education. *Journal of Teacher Education, 33*(4), 13–15.

Peseau, B. A., & Orr, P. G. (1979). *An academic and financial study of teacher education programs through the doctoral level in public state universities and land-grant colleges.* University: University of Alabama, College of Education.

Peseau, B. A., & Orr, P. G. (1980). The outrageous underfunding of teacher education. *Phi Delta Kappan, 62*(2), 100–102.

Peseau, B. A., & Orr, P. G. (1981). *Second annual academic and financial study of teacher education programs in senior state universities and land-grant colleges, 1978–79.* Montgomery: University of Alabama, College of Education.

Plisko, V. W. (1983). *The condition of education, 1983 edition: Statistical report.* Washington, DC: U. S. Department of Education, National Center for Education Statistics.

Popkewitz, T. S., Tabachnik, R. B., & Zeichner, K. (1979). Dulling the senses: Research in teacher education. *Journal of Teacher Education, 30*(5), 52–60.

Porter, S. (1983–1984, winter). Seeking equity in the workplace. *Wingspread Journal,* p. 2.

Powell, A. G. (1976, October). University schools of education in the twentieth century. *Peabody Journal of Education, 54*(1), 3–20.

Powell, A. G. (1980). *The uncertain profession.* Cambridge, MA: Harvard University Press.

Pratt, L. K., DeLucia, S. W., & Uhl, N. P. (1979). *A study of predictors of National Teachers Examination scores at a predominantly black institution.* Paper presented at the Annual Forum of the Association for Institutional Research, San Diego. (ERIC Document Reproduction Service No. ED 174–117)

Prichard, K. W., Fen, S. N., & Buxton, T. H. (1971). Social class origins of college teachers of education. *Journal of Teacher Education, 22*(2), 219–228.

Pyke, S. W. (1975). Children's literature: Conceptions of sex roles. In R. Pike & E. Zureik (Eds.), *Socialization and values in Canadian society* (Vol. 2, pp. 51–73). Toronto: McClelland & Stewart.

Rauth, M., Biles, B., Billups, L., & Veitch, S. (1983). *Educational research and dissemination program.* Washington, DC: American Federation of Teachers.

Rehberg, R. A., & Rosenthal, E. R. (1978). *Class and merit in the American high school: An assessment of the revisionist and meritocratic arguments.* New York: Longman.

Royce, J. (1965). Is there a science of education? Reprinted in M. L. Borrowman (Ed.), *Teacher education in America: A documentary history* (pp. 100–127). New York: Teachers College Press, Columbia University. (Original work published 1891)

Ryan, K. (1970). *Don't smile until Christmas: Accounts of the first year of teaching.* Chicago: University of Chicago Press.

Sarason, S. B., Davidson, K. R., & Blatt, B. (1962). *The preparation of teachers.* New York: John Wiley.

Schlechty, P. C. (1984). *A school district revises the functions and rewards of teaching.* Paper presented at the annual meeting of the American Educational Research Association, New Orleans.

Schlechty, P. C., & Crowell, D. (1983). *Understanding and managing staff development in an urban school system.* Chapel Hill: University of North Carolina.

Schlechty, P. C., & Vance, V. S. (1981). Do academically able teachers leave education? The North Carolina case. *Phi Delta Kappan, 63*, 106–112.

Schlechty, P. C., & Vance, V. S. (1983a, October). Institutional responses to the quality/quantity issue in teacher training. *Phi Delta Kappan, 65,* 94–101.

Schlechty, P. C., & Vance, V. S. (1983b). Recruitment, selection, and retention: The shape of the teaching force. *Elementary School Journal, 83,* 469–487.

Schlechty, P. C., & Whitford, B. L. (1983). The organizational context of school systems and the functions of staff development. In G. Griffin (Ed.), *Staff development* (82nd yearbook of the National Society for the Study of Education, pp. 62–91). Chicago: University of Chicago Press.

Schwab, J. J. (1969). *College curriculum & student protest.* Chicago: University of Chicago Press.

Schwab, J. J. (1978). *Science, curriculum, and liberal education* (I. Westbury & N. J. Wilkof, Eds.). Chicago: University of Chicago Press.

Showers, B. (1983). *The transfer of training: The contributions of coaching.* Eugene, OR: R & D Center for Educational Policy and Management.

Shultz, J., & Yinger, R. (1982). *Developing inquiry skills in teachers: Some reflections on the improvement of practice.* Paper presented at the annual meeting of the American Educational Research Association, New York.

Silberman, C. (1970). *Crisis in the classroom.* New York: Random House.

Spencer-Hall, D. A. (1982). *Teachers as persons: Case studies of the lives of women teachers: Final report.* Warrensburg: Central Missouri State University.

Stayrook, N., Cooperstein, R. A., & Knapp, M. (1981). *The characteristics of Teacher Corps staff development programs and their effectiveness.* Menlo Park, CA: SRI International.

Stones, E. (1984). *Supervision in teacher education: A counseling and pedagogical approach.* London: Methuen.

Stones, E., & Morris, S. (1972). *Teaching practice: Problems and perspectives.* London: Methuen.

Sweet, J. A., & Jacobsen, L. A. (1983). Demographic aspects of supply and demand for teachers. In L. S. Shulman & G. Sykes (Eds.), *Handbook of teaching and policy* (pp. 192–213). New York: Longman.

Sykes, G. (1983a). Contradictions, ironies, and promises unfulfilled: A contemporary account of the status of teaching. *Phi Delta Kappan, 65*(2), 87–93.

Sykes, G. (1983b). Public policy and the problem of teacher quality: The need for screens and magnets. In L. Shulman & G. Sykes (Eds.), *Handbook of teaching and policy* (pp. 97–125). New York: Longman.

Sykes, G. (1984, January). The deal. *The Wilson Quarterly 8*(1), 59–77.

Tabachnick, B. R., Popkewitz, T. S., & Zeichner, K. M. (1979–1980). Teacher education and the professional perspectives of student teachers. *Interchange, 10*(4), 12–29.

Temple, C. M., & Riggs, R. O. (1978, July). The declining suitability of the formula approach to public higher education. *Peabody Journal of Education, 55*(4), 351–357.

Tisher, R. (1980). The induction of beginning teachers. In E. Hoyle & J. Mcgarry (Eds.), *The professional development of teachers* (World Yearbook of Education, pp. 69–84). London: Kogan Page.

Travers, R. M. W. (Ed.) (1973). *Second handbook of research on teaching.* Chicago: Rand McNally.

Trent, J. W., & Cohen, A. M. (1973). Research on teaching in higher education. In R. M. W. Travers (Ed.), *Second handbook of research on teaching* (pp. 997–1071). Chicago: Rand McNally.

Trow, M. (1968, May/June). Bell, book, and Berkeley. *The American Behavioral Scientist, 11*(5), 43–48.

Turner, R. L. (1975). An overview of research in teacher education. In K. Ryan (Ed.), *Teacher education* (74th yearbook of the National Society for the Study of Education, Part 2, pp. 87–110). Chicago: University of Chicago Press.

Tyack, D. B. (1967) *Turning points in American educational history.* Waltham, MA: Blaisdell.

Vacca, J., Barnett, L. J., & Vacca, R. T. (1982). *Establishing criteria for staff development personnel: Final report.* Troy, NY: Russell Sage College.

Vance, V. S., & Schlechty, P. C. (1982, September). The distribution of academic ability in the teaching force: Policy implications. *Phi Delta Kappan, 64*(1), 2–27.

Veenman, S. (1984, summer). Perceived problems of beginning teachers. *Review of Educational Research, 54*(2), 143–178.

Waller, W. (1961). *The sociology of teaching.* New York: Russell & Russell. (Original work published 1932)

Warren, D. (1982). What went wrong with the foundations and other off-center questions. *Journal of Teacher Education, 33*(3), 28–30.

Weaver, W. T. (1979). In search of quality: The need for talent in teaching. *Phi Delta Kappan, 61*(1), 29–46.

Weaver, W. T. (1981, February). *The tragedy of the commons: The effects of supply and demand on the education talent pool.* Paper presented at the meeting of the American Association of Colleges of Teacher Education, Detroit. (ERIC Document Reproduction Service No. ED 204–261)

Weaver, W. T. (1983). *America's teacher quality problem: Alternatives for reform.* New York: Praeger.

Wegner, C. (1978). *Liberal education and the modern university.* Chicago: University of Chicago Press.

Weinshank, A. B., Trumbull, E. S., & Daly, P. L. (1983). The role of the teacher in school change. In L. Shulman & G. Sykes (Eds.), *Handbook of teaching and policy* (pp. 300–314). New York: Longman.

Wheeler, C. (1980). *NCATE: Does it matter?* (Research Series No. 92). East Lansing: Michigan State University, Institute for Research on Teaching.

Williams, R. T. (1981). Beneath the surface of the mathematics teacher shortage. *Mathematics Teacher, 74*(9), 691–694.

Williams, R. T. (1983). Teacher shortages — some proposed solutions. *American Education, 19*(3), 47–51.

Willis, P. (1980). *Learning to labour.* Aldershot, Hampshire, England: Gower.

Wolfe, P. (1984). *Implementation of the Hunter Instructional Model: A staff development study.* Paper presented at the annual meeting of the American Educational Research Association, New Orleans.

Woolford, J. F., Presti, S. M., Gray, A., & Coble, R. (1982) *Teacher certification: Out-of-field teaching in grades 7–12.* Raleigh, NC: North Carolina Center for Public Policy Research.

Zeichner, K. M. (1980). Myths and realities: Field-based experiences in pre-service teacher education. *Journal of Teacher Education, 31*(6), 45–55.

Zeichner, K. M. (1981). Reflective teaching and field-based experience in teacher education. *Interchange, 12*(4), 1–22.

Zeichner, K. M. (1983). Individual and institutional factors related to the socialization of teaching. In G. Griffin & H. Hukill (Eds.), *First years of teaching: What are the pertinent issues?* Austin: University of Texas, R & D Center for Teacher Education.

Zeichner, K. M., & Tabachnick, B. R. (1981). Are the effects of university teacher education "washed out" by school experience? *Journal of Teacher Education, 32*(3), 7–11.

Zeichner, K. M., & Tabachnick, B. R. (1982). The belief systems of university supervisors in the elementary student teaching program. *Journal of Education for Teaching, 8*(1), 34–54.

Zeichner, K. M., & Tabachnick, B. R. (1984). *The development of teacher perspectives: Social strategies and institutional control in the socialization of beginning teachers.* Madison: University of Wisconsin.

Zeigler, H. (1967). *The political life of American teachers.* Englewood Cliffs, NJ: Prentice-Hall.

Zumwalt, K. K. (1982). Research on teaching: Policy implications for teacher education. In A. Lieberman & M. W. McLaughlin (Eds.), *Policy making in education* (81st yearbook of the National Society for the Study of Education, Part 1, pp. 215–248). Chicago: University of Chicago Press.

20.
School Effects

Thomas L. Good
University of Missouri-Columbia

Jere E. Brophy
Michigan State University

Introduction

This chapter discusses a topic that scholarly journals and the popular press have afforded considerable attention during the past 5 years. Although issues related to the effects of school on student achievement are salient today, interest in effective schools is recent. In 1970, Biddle noted that little systematic study of school process had occurred, and the topic of effective schools received scant attention in the *Second Handbook of Research on Teaching*. Despite considerable interest that exists in the issue today, and numerous articles that have appeared in the literature recently, we have relatively little process data to describe what takes place in schools generally or to describe how schools that influence student progress positively differ from those that have less impact.

Following the publication of the well-known Coleman et al. report in 1966, many researchers attempted to relate school inputs to school outputs; however, this research ignored what took place in schools. Extensive reviews of the input–output literature (see, for example, Averch, Carroll, Donaldson, Kiesling, and Pincus, 1974) suggest that these studies fail to provide any *consistent* evidence for a relationship between general school resources and student outcomes (such as achievement). Consequently, this chapter focuses on recent research that examines school process and its relationship to student outcomes. Readers interested in a historical overview of earlier research can find that elsewhere (e.g., Averch et al., 1974; Miller, 1983).

Research on school effects has not examined process variables in as much detail as research on teaching. Still, the 1970s were fruitful years of progress in advancing knowledge of schools and their effects on pupils.

In this chapter we describe school effectiveness research in the 1970s and 1980s — what is known about the effectiveness of public schools in terms of their ability to promote the *average academic achievement* of students they serve. We organized the chapter in this way because most research in the last decade has examined average effects of schools on students. Because of space limitations, it is impossible to review important related topics (e.g., private schools, desegregation, effects of schooling on mainstreamed students).

Although we have organized the chapter to facilitate the task of reviewing extant literature, we do not feel that extant research has explored the effects of schools on students in any systematic fashion. Indeed, later in the chapter we will raise questions about the validity of extant research and suggest other ways in which future research might proceed. At this point, it is sufficient to say that student achievement on standardized test scores cannot be equated with effectiveness per se. Schools are asked to influence many aspects of students' behavior and attitudes. Hence, information about school effects on narrow measures of student achievement is relevant and interesting but only one of many dimensions of schooling that would have to be considered in assessing the general concept of effectiveness in any real fashion. We will use the term "effective schools" frequently in this chapter despite the qualifications we have expressed about the limitations of extant findings. We do this because the literature is replete with references to effective schools. However, when we use this term we do so in a very restricted sense — to refer to schools that have obtained relatively high amounts of average student achievement.

The authors thank reviewers Steven Bossert, (University of Utah), Michael Cohen (National Association of State Boards of Education), and Marshall Smith (University of Wisconsin — Madison).

Do Schools Make a Difference in Student Achievement?

Some argue on the basis of the Coleman et al. (1966) study and subsequent input–output research that the study of schooling is pointless because the effects of schooling on student achievement are minor at best, and debate abounds concerning this topic. For example, Jencks, et al. (1972) and Rowan, Bossert, and Dwyer (1983) agree that schooling accounts for but a small percentage of variation in student achievement, but disagree markedly on the importance of such effects. Some claim that statistical procedures seriously underestimate the effects of schooling on achievement. For example, Madaus, Kellaghan, Rakow, and King (1979) argue that school-related variance in student achievement is large when one focuses on subjects actually taught in schools. Still, most research indicates that family background variables affect student achievement more than school variables, although researchers and reviewers generally agree that (a) school effects are still important and (b) school influence on student achievement is generally underestimated.

Rutter (1983) argues that the impact of schooling on achievement is underestimated because of (a) the outcome variables measured, (b) the predictor variables measured, and (c) the extent of variation of the predictor variable(s). He notes that the teaching of verbal skills (as measured in early input–output studies) is not the main objective of schooling. Accordingly, estimates of school effects have sometimes been based on measures that bear little relationship to what most schools attempt to teach. Several recent studies show that school variables account for more variance in pupil achievement on specific curriculum-based subjects and on norm-referenced tests (as opposed to general tests of verbal facility), though school variables still constitute only a small amount of the total variance (Brimer, Madaus, Chapman, Kellaghan, and Wood, 1978; Madaus et al., 1979; Postlethwaite, 1975).

Predictor variables also affect results of research on school effects. Most surveys consider a narrow range of school variables and focus on financial or physical resources rather than the internal social life of schools. There is growing evidence, however, that social and instructional variables, rather than financial variables, account for important variation among schools.

If research utilizes some average measure of an entire school, all children at that school will necessarily receive the same (school) score. As Rutter (1983) points out, this procedure involves the misleading assumption that all students in any school receive the same school experiences. Consequently, results based on such statistical analyses in many instances will underestimate the size of school effects.

However, Rutter notes that, other things being equal, a predictor variable with a wide range will account for a higher proportion of the variance than a predictor with a narrow range. This is because schools tend to be more homogeneous (with respect to certain characteristics like use of language and techniques used to discipline children) than families, and because the difference between the "best" and "worst" schools is likely to be far less than that between the best and worst homes. Aggregating data at the level of the school as the unit of analysis means averaging across students from widely contrasting types of families and also averaging across teachers who vary in instructional effectiveness, and that variance across schools is lower than the variance across both students and teachers.

Absolute Effects of Schooling

In terms of the population variance accounted for, family variables will usually have a greater effect than school variables, but schools will not necessarily have less influence than families on achievement. Rutter offers the following hypothetical example. Assume that the outcome variable is pupils' achievement in Sanskrit, that books on Sanskrit are available only to the teachers at the school, and that all schools are equally good at teaching Sanskrit. Because Sanskrit can be learned only at school, schools are necessarily the only direct influence on Sanskrit achievement. But because of variation in pupils' ability to learn (as a result of both genetic and environmental influences), some children will achieve much higher levels in Sanskrit than other children. However, because all schools teach Sanskrit equally well, schooling would account for *none* of this individual variation. In short, in this situation schools would have no effect on Sanskrit achievement in spite of the fact that all Sanskrit was necessarily learned only as a result of schooling.

It is important to understand that existing claims about the effects of schools on achievement are drawn from countries where education is compulsory (Europe, North America, Japan); hence, all students are exposed to teachers, texts, and curriculum assignments. That all students have such advantages is a factor that leads to *underestimation* of the effects of school on achievement. Heyneman and Losley (1983) examined the effect of primary-school quality on academic achievement in 29 high- and low-income countries. These researchers found that in low-income countries (where schooling is not compulsory) the predominant influence on student learning is the quality of the schools and teachers to which children are exposed (family background characteristics are considerably less important).

Heyneman and Losley argue that the skepticism of critics of American schools about the efficacy of educational investments appears to be unwarranted or at least premature. They note that when international data are used in input–output regression models (like those used by Coleman et al., 1966 and others), *school and teacher quality* appear to be the major influences on student learning around the world.

Relative Effects of Schooling

Heyneman and Losley's data suggest that attending school per se has an absolute effect that tends to be "masked" in advanced societies because virtually all students attend school. However, even in a relative sense, some forms of schooling appear to have important effects. For example, Rutter, Maughan, Mortimore, Ouston, and Smith (1979) found that after adjusting for intake characteristics, children at the most successful secondary school got an average of four times as many exam passes as children at the least successful school. Also, children in the bottom 25% of verbal ability in the most successful school on average obtained as many exam passes as children in the top 25% of verbal ability at the least successful school.

Brookover, Beady, Flood, Schweitzer, and Wisenbaker (1979) found that children in "successful" white elementary schools obtained academic achievement scores an average of about one standard deviation above those in the "unsuccessful" white elementary schools matched for intake. The difference between the successful and unsuccessful black schools was even greater. However, as Rutter notes, these were average scores and within *all* schools there are children with both superior and inferior achievement. Also, it should be emphasized that these differences are among schools at the extremes of the achievement range. Still, these data clearly show that the effects of improving the quality of the worst schools are likely to be great enough to be of considerable practical importance.

Considering that schools can have important effects on students' achievement, we now examine research on school effects that has taken place in the 1970s and 1980s. What do we know about how schools vary in instructional, organizational, and social processes and how does such variation relate to student performance?

Studies of Unusually Effective Schools

Much research in the late 1960s and early 1970s suggests that differences in school resources and practices do not relate to variations in student achievement as measured by standardized achievement tests. Klitgaard and Hall (1974) argue, however, that one of several methodological problems in earlier research (e.g., Coleman et al., 1966) was that previous studies of school effectiveness measured only general school effects (the average effect of all schools in a sample) on measurable student outcomes. They state that even if extant data are accepted (along with questionable assumptions and procedures), there could be some unusually effective individual schools. Furthermore, some unusually *ineffective schools* can also be masked when data are reported only in *group averages*, but Klitgaard and Hall did not explore this possibility.

Student progress clearly varies from school to school, but the most important issue is whether variation in achievement among schools is affected by school process or whether this variation can be explained completely in terms of student factors (e.g., aptitude). The question posed by Klitgaard and Hall is crucial and is similar to issues examined in recent process–product studies of teacher effectiveness (see chapter by Brophy & Good, this volume). If there is some meaningful variation in performance among schools, then there is reason to believe that it is possible to improve student performance in many schools.

Do Effective Schools Exist?

KLITGAARD AND HALL

We have been discussing general issues and we now turn to an examination of some of the extant literature. The first study that will be examined, Klitgaard and Hall (1974), is important

for historical as well as substantive reasons (it was the first rigorous, large-scale attempt to find effective schools).

To determine whether unusually effective schools exist, Klitgaard and Hall operationally defined effectiveness as student performance on standardized reading and mathematics achievement tests. They analyzed three data sets: the 1969–1970 and 1970–1971 Michigan assessment of fourth and seventh grades (drawn from 90% of the state's public schools); scores from Grades 2–6 from 1967–1971 in New York City; and test scores from the Project Talent high school data of 1960.

The investigators examined histograms of the residuals from a regression of achievement scores on background factors and studied a series of distributions of residuals. The investigators calculated the cumulative total for each school across years and tested to see if some schools were one standard deviation above the mean more often than chance would predict. They report that of the 161 Michigan schools that reported scores for all eight grade-year-test combinations, 15 were one standard deviation (or more) above the mean six out of eight times (less than one school would be expected by chance). Thus, about 9% of the schools in the sample increased student achievement from the 50th to the 72nd percentile (given equal student background factors).

Klitgaard and Hall report that many of the outstanding schools were rural. Nevertheless, when rural schools were excluded from the analyses, they still found schools in which students consistently overachieved.

These investigators also examined their data for unusually effective school districts. Among 627 districts studied in New York, 30 were one standard deviation above the mean at least five out of eight times (less than four districts would be expected by chance). Finally, they found little evidence of unusually effective grade levels.

Although the data support the contention that some unusually effective schools exist, the results basically support previous research which indicates that the effects of schools are small after nonschool factors (SES, aptitude) are controlled. The high-achieving schools that were identified represented only from 2% to 9% of the sample. These schools were clearly unusual and had relatively more achievement than schools with comparable populations; however, whether they were effective depends upon one's definition of effectiveness. (What performance measure is appropriate and how high does a school have to be on that measure to be considered effective?

This is an informative study that provides plausible data that at least some schools are more effective than would be predicted. However, one issue left unexamined in this study is to what extent a high-achieving school is equally effective for *all* students enrolled. That is, it may be possible for a high-achieving school to be so classified because it is unusually effective with one group of students, even though it has no special effects on the remainder of the school population. High-achieving schools could even have detrimental effects for certain students or small groups of students. This issue illustrates how relative and elusive the concept of effectiveness is. This important definitional issue will be explored later in this chapter.

Initial school effects studies (input-output studies) thus examined the average effects of schools and more recent studies concern the effects of individual schools (or groups of schools defined as effective or ineffective) on average student performance. We will argue later that researchers should now consider the effects of schools on specific types of students.

Also, it is probably easier to identify *ineffective* schools, and data from only the top half of the distribution (of residual gain scores being examined) probably underestimate the stability of school effectiveness. To our knowledge researchers have not examined ineffective schools in this way and this seems to us an important consideration.

A Study of School Processes

WEBER

In addition to being among the first to search for effective schools, Weber (1971) also conducted one of the earliest studies designed to identify the *processes* operating in effective inner-city schools. Weber believed that some inner-city schools had more positive effects on student achievement than others. He rejected the assumption that low student intelligence and a lack of funds were sufficient explanations for low-income children's failure to learn. He tested these proposals in the third grade.

To identify potentially effective inner-city schools Weber asked reading specialists, publishers, and school officials for nominations. He kept the nomination process open for over a year. He did not intend to find all of the inner-city schools that were successful in beginning reading instruction, but rather to identify enough schools so that he could describe and analyze several representative, successful schools. A total of 95 schools were nominated. Of these, only 69 seemed to be serving nonselective public school populations. To each of these 69 schools he wrote a letter asking if the principal believed that the school met the criteria (was it an inner-city school; was it successful in teaching reading?) and if the school desired an independent evaluation of reading achievement. Some principals did not respond to the letter; others replied that they were not inner-city schools or that they were not successful in beginning reading instruction in terms of the criteria employed. A number of principals refused to participate when the nature of the independent evaluation was detailed. Weber ultimately visited 17 schools in seven large cities.

Weber conducted an independent evaluation of reading achievement to eliminate the possibility (however remote) that any student coaching and manipulation of scores might occur. Because he was interested in testing the ability of poor children to read words that they already understood, Weber devised a test made up entirely of words that he thought students would understand. The test was different from nationally standardized reading achievement tests in that it did not evaluate breadth of aural vocabulary or ability to take multiple choice tests, but rather the ability to read simple American English. The final test contained 32 items and could be administered in 15 minutes.

The 17 schools participating in the project were visited between January and June of 1971, with visits lasting 2 or 3 days. Six of the 17 schools that were observed and tested met the inner-city criteria but not the reading success criteria. Seven schools met the reading success criteria but not the inner-city criteria. Four met both criteria, and Weber argues that these nonselective public schools in the central areas of large cities were attended by very poor children. The third grade median reading achievement scores of these four schools equaled or exceeded the national norm and the percentages of nonreaders were unusually low for such schools.

What, then, were the factors that distinguished these four inner-city schools from other schools that did not teach beginning reading as well? To his credit, Weber notes that it is impossible to be certain of the answer because schools do many things differently and it is difficult to determine which practices are responsible for high pupil achievement. However, he cites eight characteristics of these schools: strong leadership, high expectations, good atmosphere, emphasis on reading, additional reading personnel, use of phonics, individualization, and careful evaluation of pupil progress. Weber does not mean individualization in the narrow sense of having each child work at a different level: rather, the term implies concern for each child's progress and a willingness to modify a child's assignments if necessary.

Some of the factors *not* associated with achievement were small class size, achievement grouping (in one school all classes were heterogeneous), and physical facilities (not one of the four schools was a modern building and two were noticeably old). Two years later Weber revisited two of the four successful schools and found that one of them continued to be effective (and had even improved somewhat); however, the other school had deteriorated notably and was no longer effective. Hence, the conditions of effective schools may be only temporary, and as principals, teachers, and student cohorts change so too may the level of school effectiveness.

It is unfortunate that Weber does not explain why this one school deteriorated. Considering that many schools are presently working to increase their effectiveness, it would be important to identify factors that were associated with the decline (e.g., change in student and/or teacher population) in student achievement in this school.

The observational data in this study provide only limited information; they yield hypotheses for future testing, not clear guidelines for effective schools. To begin with, other investigators may not have described these schools as Weber did (the same behaviors, policies, and standards may constitute various types of leadership or expectations to different people). The instrument Weber used is brief, and even though it is appropriate in other respects, a 15-minute test provides limited data for assessing student knowledge. *Since the study did not include observations of ineffective schools or average schools, it is very difficult to assess whether the factors identified by Weber have any true relationship with school achievement.* Furthermore, Weber's report does not comprehensively indicate which aspects of schooling did not differentiate effective schools. Still, considering the exploratory nature of his investigation, the lack of systematic reporting of what was observed (and the procedures for such observations) is understandable. Nevertheless, this lack places limitations on the confidence with which one can rely on the process measures used in the study. Weber was very successful, however, in stimulating others to explore the issue of how schools make a difference in student achievement.

574   THOMAS L. GOOD AND JERE E. BROPHY

Two Recent Empirical Studies of School Effects

In this section of the paper we discuss two of the most rigorous and salient process–product studies of school effectiveness. Although there have been several comprehensive studies, we limit discussion here to only two of these more important and more salient studies so that we can assess more adequately the particular research strategies utilized and see more fully the strengths and weaknesses of extant research. These studies are somewhat similar to the research paradigm utilized by Klitgaard and Hall (1974); however, after identifying outlier schools the researchers attempted to explain how more and less effective schools varied in school routines and classroom practices.

A Recent Study of Effective Schools: Brookover et al. (1979)

Brookover et al. (1979) argue that the social system of a school influences the role definitions, norms, expectations, values, and beliefs that students internalize and that such socialization affects students' achievement, academic self-concepts, and other affective responses (see Figure 20.1).

The model suggests that the behavior students learn and their achievement will vary among schools and that this variation can be explained by differences among schools in inputs (quality of teachers and students), social structure, and climate. As Figure 20.1 demonstrates, Brookover et al. believe that the initial characteristics of teachers and students affect student outcomes. However, the quality of teachers and students is modified by school structures, processes, and beliefs.

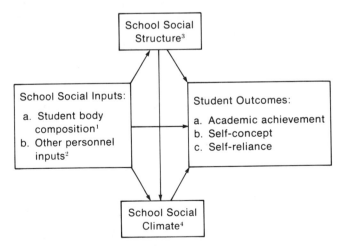

[1]measured by mean school SES and percentage white.
[2]measured by standard scores of school size, average daily attendance, professionals per 1,000 students, average years teaching experience, average tenure in school, percentage of teachers with advanced degrees, and mean teacher salary.
[3]measured by teacher satisfaction with school structure, parent involvement, differentiation in student programs, principal's report of time devoted to instruction, open-closed classroom.
[4]measured by 14 variables derived from student, teacher and principal reports of the norms, expectations, and feelings about the school.

Fig. 20.1 General model of school social system variables with hypothesized relation to student outcomes.

Brookover et al. studied 68 schools drawn from a state pool that represented a random sample of Michigan fourth and fifth grade students. Sixty-one of these schools had populations that were more than 50% white. (For some analyses the white school sample was divided at the median of the SES distribution so that high- and low-SES white schools could be compared.) The black school sample was composed of 7 schools from the state sample whose populations were more than 50% black along with 23 other majority black schools randomly selected from the population of schools with majority black populations. Data were obtained from (a) the Michigan School Assessment Reports, (b) questionnaires administered to fourth and fifth grade students, (c) questionnaires administered to teachers, and (d) school principals. Complete questionnaires can be found in Brookover et al. (1979).

INPUT VARIABLES

The major *school input* variables assessed were (a) social composition of the student body, (b) school social structure, and (c) school climate. Important *outcome* variables studied were (a) student achievement, (b) self-concept of academic ability, and (c) self-reliance. *Social composition* in this study was defined as the mean socioeconomic status of the school and the percentage of white students in the school. Other school input measures included the size of the student population, the average daily attendance of students, the number of staff per 1,000 students, and several teacher characteristics (experience, etc.).

The five factors defining the *social structure* of the school were (a) parent involvement, (b) differention of student programs (e.g., degree of ability grouping, use of students' interests in planning instruction), (c) openness of classroom organization (how often students talk and work together; how frequently seat assignments are changed), (d) time allocation (time allotted to academic, social, and administrative tasks), and (e) staff satisfaction with school structure.

In this study *school climate* was defined as the composite of norms, expectations, and beliefs about the school social system as participants perceived it.

OUTPUT VARIABLES

The measure used for *academic achievement* was the average percentage of students who mastered each of the 40 objectives in the Michigan School Assessment Test administered in the fall of 1974. Nineteen achievement objectives had been established for reading and 30 for mathematics. Brookover et al. used the mean percentage of all reading and mathematics objectives mastered to reflect achievement on a total of 245 questions.

The *self-concept of academic ability* scale focused on one aspect of self-concept — perception of self as student. The other self-concept measure was student perception of self-reliance (the extent to which students could and wanted to complete tasks or to solve problems on their own). Many of the social structure, climate, and outcome variables were assessed by questionnaires (for complete details see Brookover et al., 1979).

INTERRELATIONS AMONG INPUT VARIABLES

Three of the five variables used to define social structure were positively and significantly correlated with social composition and other input variables as well as being intercorrelated with each other (the variable "degree of differentiated programs" did not correlate in any meaningful way with other input or structural variables). Brookover et al. note that although school structure variables were related to each other and to composition measures, they were not entirely dependent on composition nor were they merely different measures of the same variable.

Some measures of school climate were highly correlated with student body composition. The authors note that such high correlations make it difficult, if not impossible, to separate the effects of climate from those of school composition on achievement. For example, students' sense of academic futility (a set of items generally identified as measuring sense of control) correlated .87 with the composition of a school's population. With the exception of differentiated programs, all input, structure, and climate variables were interrelated, at least to some degree.

INTERRELATIONS AMONG DEPENDENT VARIABLES

Perhaps most important, a negative correlation of −.55 was obtained between *mean* school achievement and *mean* self-concept of academic ability. Thus, students in lower-achieving schools actually averaged higher self-concept scores than students in higher-achieving schools. In previous research, however, Brookover et al. (1962, 1965, 1967) had found that *individual* student self-concept of ability scores correlated positively with student achievement. Here, in the 30 majority black schools there was essentially no correlation between self-concept and achievement (.004) and the same general pattern was obtained in the majority white schools (.04). There was a negative relationship between self-concept and achievement (−.23) in the white low-SES schools. In general, high achievement did not correlate with high student self-concept or self-reliance. Thus, it seems that at least in some schools different outcomes are associated with various combinations of school climate and structure variables. However, other research reviewed by Rutter (1983) suggests that effective schools can positively affect multiple criteria simultaneously.

RELATIONSHIPS BETWEEN SCHOOL SYSTEM VARIABLES AND STUDENT ACHIEVEMENT

The researchers note that except in the majority white schools (particularly the high-SES sample), less than half of the between-school variance in achievement was uniquely attributable to either input or structure variables independently. In general, more of this variance was explained by complex school social system characteristics. They suggest that their analysis does not indicate which variable or set of variables in the social system has the largest effect on achievement in all school situations, but they do argue that the small proportion of variance uniquely attributable to input variables strongly suggests that school variables are important factors affecting student achievement.

CASE STUDIES

Brookover et al. (1979) supplemented their statistical analyses with classroom observations and interviews with participants in four low-SES schools. Time spent in the schools ranged from three weeks to three months. Unfortunately, the researchers report no information about what was observed, how the data were collected, and what questions were asked of the participants. Furthermore, there is no explanation concerning the number of teachers visited in each school and no serious attention to within-school variation. Hence, it is very difficult to assess these data and their implications for practice.

The reported criteria for selecting the four schools were (a) similar racial composition, (b) similar SES levels that were significantly lower than the mean SES level for the sample, (c) achievement scores above the sample mean in one school and below the sample mean in the other within each pair, and (d) urban location. The variables used to describe differences in high- and low-achieving schools were (a) time spent in instruction, (b) write-off (percent of students not expected to master curriculum), (c) teacher expectations, (d) reinforcement practices, (e) grouping procedures, (f) teaching games, (g) principal's role, and (h) commitment of teaching and administrative staff. These variables seem to represent important aspects of schooling, but the authors do not explain why they examined these variables instead of other potential ways in which schools might differ.

Although the findings reveal some general differences that distinguished high- from low-achieving schools, there was also considerable variation in how principals and teachers in high-achieving schools obtained their effects. In brief, teachers in the higher achieving black and white schools spent more time on instruction. There were relatively few study periods, though small blocks of time were allocated for doing classroom assignments. Teachers spent as much time as was necessary to convey new concepts, problems, and so forth for each lesson. However, the teachers did not seem to spend inordinate time on lessons students had already mastered. Observations showed that academic interaction between teachers and students occurred more frequently in the white high-achieving school than in the black high-achieving school. Overall, however, academic interactions between teachers and students were more frequent in the high-achieving white and black schools than in the lower-achieving white and black schools. In most of the classes observed in the lower-achieving black and white schools, students had a great deal of time to study, read, or play while the teacher attended to administrative duties such as grading papers. In sum, more time was allocated for instruction in the high-achieving schools, although more time was spent in active teaching in the higher achieving white school than in its black counterpart. The differences in school processes across the four schools are summarized in Table 20.1.

SUMMARY

In combination, the data from this study suggest that when teachers, principals, and students believe that academic achievement is possible, school climate is conducive to learning and student achievement is higher. However, these data are

Table 20.1. Highlights of Four Case Studies: What Makes a Difference in Predominantely Black and Predominantely White High- and Low-Achieving Schools in Low-SES School Districts

	High-Achieving White School	Low-Achieving White School	High-Achieving Black School	Low-Achieving Black School
Time	Most of class time spent on instruction—except for one teacher 80–90% of time used.	Time spent on instruction varied between classrooms. In several classrooms only 10% of time spent on instruction. Several teachers had managerial problems. Many teachers who did not used low-level work to keep students involved.	Teachers did much teaching. While students were working the teachers were available for clarification and reteaching as necessary.	Most teachers attempted to keep students busy but not a lot of productive task-relevant work was achieved. Very little academic interaction with students.
Write-Offs	Few students seen as destined to fail, as hopeless cases; no remedial programs.	Usually 2–3 students per class remained outside of learning process. However, most of "slower" students less involved in work and interactions with teachers.	Teachers felt vast majority of students were capable of mastering assigned materials. Only a very few students were seen as unlikely to make it. When one strategy didn't work, teachers were willing to try other strategies.	Teachers appeared to write off large numbers of children; large numbers of students were required to attend remedial classes and such classes were seen as "dumping grounds."
Teacher Expectations	Teachers expected students to work at grade level.	Expectations for student achievement were low in general but especially for students in slow reading tracks. Grade-level achievement not seen as a realistic goal for many students.	Teachers generally reported that they expected at least 75% of their students to master assigned work and that 75% would complete high school.	Teachers generally held low performance expectations for students and teachers were unwilling to assume responsibility for student learning.
Reinforcement Practices	Appropriate reward.	Teachers varied. Some teachers used appropriate reinforcement practices but several teachers were observed to use confusing and/or totally inappropriate reinforcement practices most of the time.	Teachers tended to use reinforcement patterns that were likely to encourage higher achievement.	Many teachers in the regular classrooms used reinforcement inappropriately, often telling students they had done well when, in fact, they had not.
Grouping Procedures	No homogeneous grouping after third grade. Grouping to classrooms basically random.	Students grouped 1–6 for reading instruction. Only two groups per class—high and low. Mobility between groups very limited.	Students grouped on the basis of pretest on math and reading tests. Teachers appeared to teach with purpose of advancing students to higher groups when possible. Teachers suggested that the goal for a full year's achievement gain for all students was an academic floor and not a ceiling.	Extensive use of grouping; however, did not encourage advancing students to join higher groups and appeared to be more of a management than an instructional tool. Also, there was extensive assignment of "slow" students to remedial classes. The extensive grouping and regrouping appeared to be disruptive.

Table 20.1 (*continued*)

	High-Achieving White School	Low-Achieving White School	High-Achieving Black School	Low-Achieving Black School
Teaching Games	Reflected high expectations of teacher and appropriate reinforcement—emphasized team rather than individual learning.	No mention.	When games were used they tended to be team games. Games appeared to be used to reinforce an attitude of "try a little harder."	Teaching games seldom used in regular classes—used much in remedial classes, but tended to be individual games and not used in a way likely to stimulate achievement gain.
Principal's Role	Heavily involved in instructional issues. Provided instructional leadership. Assumed measure of responsibility for the educational functions of the school. Visited classrooms frequently.	Time shared between two buildings. Seemed to be a part-time administrator–part-time disciplinarian. Seldom visited classrooms; did not function as an educational leader. Often expressed low performance expectations for students.	Emphasized administrative duties although he did observe and critique teachers periodically. Note: the previous principal had been a more active educational leader.	Principal at this school was mainly an administrator and disciplinarian. Although the principal talked about the importance of student achievement, there was little pressure brought to bear by the principal on teachers to improve classroom performance.
Commitment	Commitment to high achievement—willing to make public announcements to one another and to parents that students could learn.	No explicit discussion.	Considerable interest in providing students with high-quality education. Much warmth directed toward individual students.	Teachers' behavior suggested that there was little they could do to increase student achievement.

Note. This table is drawn from the narrative description of Brookover et al. (1979).

interrelated and correlational; hence, it is not possible to determine whether high achievement *preceded or followed* positive expectations, or if students' high expectations for learning *preceded or followed* those of adults in the school. The data therefore do not clearly indicate how schools should initially invest limited resources available for school improvement projects. The findings do suggest, however, that improvement is possible and they indicate several variables that can be manipulated.

In summary, the Brookover et al. (1979) study is a comprehensive and successful attempt to illustrate that school inputs do not predict student outcomes (achievement, self-concept, self-reliance) independent of school process. Their case-study data suggest that schools with varying input resources will have differential effects on student achievement because of climate and structural features present in the school. Furthermore, the authors find that climate variables (although highly correlated with input variables) explain as much variation in achievement as do input variables. Although the process data collected in this study do not yield definitive statements about school process in more and less effective schools, they do suggest that schools with comparable resources can have very different climates and they provide a base on which future observational studies can build.

Another Modern Study of Effective Schools: Rutter et al. (1979)

In a 3-year study of 12 secondary schools, Rutter et al. (1979) found that some urban secondary schools were better than others in promoting students' academic and social success.

A survey of London 10-year-olds was initiated in 1970 when children were nearing the end of primary school. Assessments of intellectual level and reading attainment (as well as pupil behavior and family circumstances) were obtained for children attending primary school in one inner-London borough. All pupils were retested in 1974 at approximately age 14 during their third year of secondary school. Testing was concentrated in the 20 secondary schools that had taken the majority of the children tested in 1970 at age 10.

There were large school differences in terms of delinquency rates and achievement problems. However, the issue here was the extent to which differences were merely a reflection of input differences in the school (e.g., the proportion of difficult children admitted from primary schools). The data showed that there was not only *variation in output*, but there were also *substantial differences in input* that these 20 secondary schools had to work with (e.g., for boys, some schools admitted as few as 7% with behavior or reading problems; whereas others took as many as 48% to 50% with such problems).

Still, despite these large differences in input characteristics, after equating the pupil input of schools statistically, there were substantial and statistically significant differences between schools. Their data illustrate that schools with the most advantaged students were not necessarily those with the best outcomes and schools that had students from similar backgrounds often had vastly different outcomes. Simply put, these data illustrate that pupil behavior and delinquency rates at age 14 could not be explained by family background variables or by pupils' test or questionnaire scores at age 10. In order to study schools carefully with available resources, the investigators reduced the number of schools studied from 20 to 12.

Three main measures were collected on each student: (a) verbal reasoning scores at the age of 10, (b) parental occupation, and (c) students' scores on a behavioral questionnaire completed by their primary school teachers.

The researchers examined the extent of change in intake in student population at each of the target schools over several consecutive years. In general, they found that the population at particular schools was relatively stable, so that those schools with the most advantaged *intakes* in 1971 continued to have that advantage.

PROCESS MEASURES

The study was not designed to test a particular theory of schooling, nor was the analysis based on any preconceived ideas about which school processes are important. In general, the processes examined were derived from seven broad conceptual areas: academic emphasis, teacher actions in lessons, rewards and punishments, conditions of learning for pupils, pupils' responsibilities and participation in the school, stability of teaching, and friendship group organization. Data on processes were derived from interviews with teachers, pupils' responses to a questionnaire, and classroom observation.

OBSERVATIONAL PROCEDURES

The main series of observations consisted of one week's observation in each school, in middle-ability, third-year classes. In all, 402 lessons were tape-recorded and coded; most of these lessons (312) were in academic subjects. The investigators coded the activities of both teachers and pupils in each lesson. The observation periods were grouped into coding sections which focused first on the teacher, then on selected individual children, and finally on the whole class. Each section lasted 5 minutes and this pattern was repeated throughout the lesson. First, the coders recorded whether the teacher focused on the subject matter, pupils' behavior, or some other academic social, or administrative activity. In addition, observers noted whether the teacher interacted with children and if so, whether with the whole class or with individuals. They also coded examples of praise or punishment and any marked expressions of warmth or negative feelings toward children.

Observers noted if students appeared to be engaged in tasks set by the teacher and the frequencies of other presumably less acceptable behaviors. The coders also selected five pupils at random and recorded whether they were working appropriately. The researchers reported not only the occurrence of a behavior, but also the proportion of the class involved in it. For example, the average pupil on-task behavior was 81.5% of each lesson and about 75% of the teacher's time was spent on the subject matter of the lesson. In addition to structured, time-sampled observations, the investigators also observed playground behavior, recording pupils' activities, and noting any physical violence between children and any unofficial sanctions by staff.

OUTCOME MEASURES

The investigators used five outcome measures to assess the differential effects of individual schools: attendance, student behavior in school, examination success, employment, and delinquency. Here we will discuss only the results associated with achievement, attendance, and student behavior.

The investigators report large differences in attendance rates across schools, even after variations in school inputs were controlled. Pupil behavior (e.g., late arrival, off-task behavior, disruptive behavior) varied considerably across schools, after differences in intake were controlled. The correlation between intake and behavior was only .27, suggesting that schools with more disruptive students (as defined in terms of students' behavior in the primary school) did not necessarily have the worst classroom behavior.

Although it was difficult to compare achievement because of variation in tests and curriculum emphases across schools and the complexity of the examination system, the researchers compared academic progress across the 12 schools. Even after controlling for variations in intake it was clear that there was marked variation in achievement between schools. In general, school achievement was reasonably stable over two consecutive years (with the exception of one school). However, it was clear that marked, positive variation in achievement was a characteristic of only *two* schools in the sample (see Purkey & Smith. 1983a).

INTERRELATIONS OF OUTCOMES

Table 20.2 illustrates the schools' relative rankings in terms of attendance, academic achievement, and desirable classroom pupil behavior. It is evident that schools that tend to be high on any one of these measures tend to be high on the other two, and schools that rank low on one outcome also rank low on the other two. However, Table 20.2 shows two glaring exceptions to this pattern. In one instance, students who behaved well had poor *achievement* and attendance records. In another school students made relatively high academic progress despite relatively low attendance levels and a high amount of inappropriate classroom behavior.

As Rutter and colleagues note, variations in outcome do not necessarily prove that outcomes are influenced by what happens in schools. However, these data do strongly suggest that something more than intake measures produced the differential outcomes, and one can plausibly infer that something in the school was at work. This argument would be stronger if the researchers could demonstrate that variations in school structure, school processes, and classroom behavior were consistently associated with variations in student outcomes. We

Table 20.2. A Comparison of School Effectiveness Across Attendance, Academic Achievement, and Behavior Outcome Measures

Attendance	Academic Achievement	Behavior
1[a]	1	1
2	2	4
3	6	3
4	5	5
5	8	10
6	4	6
7	10	11
8	9	9
9	3	8
10	7	7
11	12	12
12	11	2

Note. From *Fifteen Thousand Hours: Secondary Schools and Effects on Children* by M. Rutter (p. 93). Copyright 1979 by Harvard University Press. Reprinted by permission.
[a] 1 = highest, 12 = lowest.

now discuss factors that consistently were found to be associated with more effective outcomes in the Rutter et al. study.

PROCESS FINDINGS

An academic emphasis was associated with school achievement gains. For example, schools in which teachers assigned homework frequently (and monitored the teachers to be certain that they did so) tended to have higher achievement than schools which seldom assigned homework. It is important to note, however, that the average time spent on homework (as reported by the pupils themselves) was *not* great in any of the schools and averaged only 15 to 35 minutes or so across schools. (Similar findings are also reported in classroom studies, e.g., Good, Grouws, & Ebmeier, 1983.)

These findings, of course, do not demonstrate how and why homework is associated with increased achievement. For example, it may well be that in addition to its practical value as distributed practice, homework is also of symbolic importance in emphasizing a school's concern for academic progress and its expectation that pupils have the ability to work independently.

Another aspect of academic emphasis concerns *teachers' expectations* for their pupils. Teacher expectations correlated positively and significantly with both attendance and academic outcomes. It could be argued that teachers are simply good judges of children's abilities. However, when teacher expectations were compared with student ability at intake, two of the schools in the bottom third with respect to academic expectations were in the top third with respect to initial student ability.

Furthermore, the proportion of the school week devoted to teaching was associated with more student achievement. The time actually spent teaching varied among the 12 schools from 21.9 to 24.2 hours, and was positively correlated with pupil attendance. Taken together, the findings on academic emphasis suggest that children tend to make better progress both behaviorally and academically in schools that focus on academic matters. This emphasis is reflected in a well-planned curriculum, and teachers' high academic expectations for children.

TEACHER ORIENTATION

The amount of school time spent on the lesson topic varied from 65% to over 85%; nevertheless, time spent on the lesson topic was *not* significantly associated with academic success. An attentive, well-behaved class provides the opportunity for effective teaching and productive learning. What *use* teachers make of this opportunity, however, is crucial in determining what and how much children learn.

Teachers in more successful schools spent a higher proportion of their time interacting with the *class as a whole* than with individual pupils. Lessons in the successful schools more frequently included periods of quiet work when teachers expected pupils to work by themselves.

Frequent disciplinary interventions in a school were associated with increased pupil off-task behavior. Teacher behavior that results in many interruptions of lessons and involves constant checking and reprimanding may perpetuate student behavior problems. Conversely, schools where most lessons started promptly tended to have better outcomes and better student behavior. In general, the findings on teacher management behavior in this study are remarkably similar to those reported by Kounin (1970).

REWARDS AND PUNISHMENT

Overall, the association between punishment and outcome was weak and inconsistent. The relationship between rewards (praise, appreciation) and outcome was more consistent, and all forms of reward tended to be associated with better outcomes. However, it should be noted that teachers infrequently used rewards (three or so instances of praise per lesson on average).

CONDITIONS OF LEARNING

Independent of specific rewards, schools varied in the extent to which they provided a pleasant, comfortable environment for students. One might expect good working conditions to encourage pupils to appreciate the school and perhaps to identify with its goals. To investigate this possibility, Rutter et al. developed a 14-item scale measuring general school conditions such as freedom to use the building during breaks and the lunch period, access to the telephone, and so forth. High scores on this scale were associated with higher scores on exams. As a case in point, when pupils were asked whether, if they needed to, they would talk to a member of the staff about a personal problem, a higher proportion of students in the schools with better attendance and academic achievement said that they would.

RESPONSIBILITIES AND PARTICIPATION

Pupils were asked to describe the extent to which they were encouraged to take responsibility and to help manage their school lives. The proportion of students who had some sort of school role (e.g., team captain, homework monitor, school assembly, etc.) varied greatly across schools (from 7% to 50%), and this proportion in each school correlated significantly and positively with classroom behavior and academic success.

Major Conclusions

Rutter (1983) suggests that major conclusions from his earlier work include the following:

1. Secondary schools in inner London differ markedly in the behavior and achievement shown by students.
2. Although schools varied in the proportion of behaviorally difficult or low-achieving children they admitted, these differences did not completely account for variations among schools in their pupils' subsequent behavior and attainment. This provides strong evidence that school factors affected students' behavior and achievement.
3. The variation among schools on the different pupil outcome measures was reasonably stable over periods of 4 or 5 years.
4. In general, individual schools performed fairly similarly on all outcome measures. That is, schools in which students had better-than-average behavior also had students with better achievement and less delinquency. There were some exceptions in this pattern, but the trends were substantial.
5. Differences in outcomes between schools were not due to physical factors such as size of the school or the age of the building.
6. The differences among schools in outcomes were systematically related to school characteristics (e.g., identifiable factors in academic emphasis, teacher behavior, etc.).
7. Outcomes were also influenced by factors outside teachers' immediate control. For example, examination success tended to be better in schools with a substantial nucleus of children of at least average intellectual ability, and delinquency rates were higher in schools with many of the least able pupils.
8. The effect of balance in intake was most marked with respect to delinquency and least important in the case of students' classroom behavior.
9. The association between the combined measure of overall school process and each of the outcome measures was much stronger than was the relationship between any individual process variable and outcome measure. This suggests that the cumulative effect of these various social factors may be the creation of a school ethos, or set of values, attitudes, and behaviors which characterize the school.
10. The total pattern of findings indicates a strong probability that the association between school process and outcome reflects at least a partially causal process.

This is a carefully conducted, important study. The data provided by Rutter et al. strongly suggest that school process has important effects on student outcome measures. Indeed, as noted earlier, Brookover et al. found that some white elementary schools obtained academic achievement scores an average of about one standard deviation above those in less successful white elementary schools matched for intake. The difference in achievement between the successful and unsuccessful black schools was somewhat greater.

Still, school inputs (more favorable student populations) were positively correlated with student outcomes and although strong and persuasive arguments can be made that school process affected outcomes more than did input variables (e.g., see Rutter, 1983) the data are correlational. Subsequent field experiments will help to determine if processes identified by Rutter et al. as characteristic of effective schools can be manipulated in ways that lead to improved outcomes in other schools. This study collected more process data of better quality than did other school effects studies. However, the sample of teachers observed in each school and the range of process variables studied provide only a limited view of school life. The study has nevertheless provided a solid foundation upon which subsequent experimental and observational studies can build.

Integrative Reviews of School Effects Research

Not only have there been many attempts to define and to study effective schools, there are also several literature reviews that order and integrate the studies that have been conducted. Purkey and Smith's (1983) review is one of the most comprehensive. Their review is especially instructive because it includes a wide range of research approaches representing different theoretical positions.

Purkey and Smith (1983)

These researchers argue that it is easy to conclude that the findings of recent school effects research contradict the conclusions of Colman et al., Jencks et al., and others. However, they note that new studies do *not* refute the earlier findings that easily measured structural differences among schools (library resources, etc.) are not consistently related to student achievement. Further, although recent research does not indicate that there are large differences in achievement among schools, this research has important implications for practice.

Purkey and Smith's review examines various types of school effectiveness research including outlier studies, case studies, surveys and evaluations, as well as studies of program implementation and theories of organization in schools and other institutions.

OUTLIER STUDIES

This type of school effectiveness research statistically identifies highly effective and unusually ineffective schools and then examines behavior in those schools to determine what accounts for the differences. Studies using the outlier approach included in the review were: four studies conducted by the New York State Department of Education (1974a, 1974b, 1976); a study conducted for the Maryland State Department of Education (Austin, 1978); as well as research by Lezotte, Edmonds, and Ratner (1974); Brookover and Schneider (1975); and a study of Delaware schools by Spartz, Valdes, McCormick, Myers, and Geppert (1977).

These studies generally show that the most common elements of effective schools are better control or discipline and high staff expectations for student achievement. Each of these variables was evidenced in four of the seven studies for which there are data. An emphasis on instructional leadership by the principal or another important staff member was found to be important in three studies.

Purkey and Smith note that these outlier studies are similar in some respects; however, variations in the findings from this research should serve as a caution to those who would reduce the school effects literature to five or six variables.

CASE STUDIES

Eight school case studies were reviewed: Brookover et al., 1979; Brookover and Lezotte, 1979; California State Department of Education, 1980; Glenn, 1981; Levine and Stark, 1981; Rutter et al., 1979; Venezky and Winfield, 1979; and Weber, 1971. The inherent weakness of the case study approach is the small sample size; however, the commonality of findings among these studies and the similarity of their results to findings from other kinds of studies increase their credibility.

After reviewing six of the case studies that examined a total of 43 schools (Rutter et al. and Brookover et al. were discussed separately because of their greater complexity), Purkey and Smith note that each case study focused on urban elementary schools and that the studies varied in quality of methodology and clarity of reporting.

Five factors were common to most, but not all, of the six case studies in this group: (a) strong leadership by the principal or other staff, (b) high expectations by staff for student achievement, (c) clear goals, (d) an academic emphasis for the school and an effective school-wide staff training program, and (e) a system for monitoring student progress. A focus on order and discipline was found to be important in two of the studies and a large number of factors were specific to any single study.

PROGRAM EVALUATIONS

Purkey and Smith also examined six program evaluation studies: Armor et al., 1976; Doss and Holley, 1982; Hunter, 1979; (three studies carried out by the Michigan Department of Education); and Trisman, Waller, and Wilder, 1976. They note that though these studies are methodologically stronger than the preceding two types of research, their findings are remarkably consistent with the other studies.

PORTRAIT OF AN EFFECTIVE SCHOOL

Purkey and Smith found the following variables to be important process measures of school effectiveness:

1. School-site management. A number of studies indicate that leadership and staff of the school need considerable autonomy in determining how they address problems.
2. Instructional leadership. Though the reviewers are suspicious of the "great principal" theory, it seems clear that leadership is necessary to initiate and maintain school improvement.
3. Staff stability. Once a school experiences success, retaining the staff seems to maintain effectiveness or to promote further success.
4. Curriculum articulation and organization. At the secondary level, a planned, purposeful program of courses seems to be academically more beneficial than an approach that offers many electives and few requirements.

5. School-wide staff development. Essential change involves altering people's attitudes and behavior as well as providing them with new skills and techniques.
6. Parental involvement and support. Though the evidence on this issue is mixed, it is reasonable to assume that parents need to be informed of school goals and school responsibilities.
7. School-wide recognition of academic success. The school culture is partially reflected in the ceremonies, its symbols, and the accomplishments it officially recognizes.
8. Maximized learning time. If schools emphasize academics, then a greater proportion of the school day will be devoted to academic subjects.
9. District support. Fundamental change, building level management, staff stability, and so on all depend on support from the district office.

Purkey and Smith believe that other process variables must be present as well: (a) collaborative planning and collegial relationships, (b) sense of community, (c) clear goals and high expectations, and (d) order and discipline.

Other Synthesis Reviews

COHEN

Cohen (1983) provides an overview and framework for interpreting the rapidly accumulating knowledge base concerning schooling practices that contribute to student achievement. He notes that existing summaries are fine as far as they go, but that by presenting only lists of variables, they fail to provide information on how these factors are interrelated, how they can actually be implemented, or their effects.

Cohen points out that by attempting to explain differences between schools' average level of student achievement, most previous research overlooks the important fact that most of the variance in student achievement (between 70% and 90%) actually occurs *within* schools. Also, the exclusive focus on average differences between schools assumes that all school resources are equally available to and utilized by each student in a school. Yet, within schools many students are grouped into tracks and within classes into ability groups. These groups are exposed to different teacher skills, instructional practices, curriculum materials, and social environments, all of which are believed to influence school learning.

Cohen suggests three characteristics of effective schools that can be used to organize existing research. First, school effectiveness is clearly dependent upon effective classroom teaching. Second, school effectiveness requires the careful coordination and management of the instructional program at the building level. Finally, effective schools generate a sense of shared values and culture among both students and staff.

Cohen notes that research on school practices is *not* as well developed as that on classroom practices; there are fewer studies, less frequent replication of findings across studies, and fewer concrete descriptions of specific behaviors and practices. Despite these deficiencies there are several important general research findings concerning the management and coordination of instruction. First, the curriculum and instructional programs in effective schools, especially elementary schools, are interrelated. This means that school goals, grade level and classroom instructional objectives, instructional content and activities, and measures of pupil performance are all carefully coordinated such that the instructional efforts of teachers and other instructional staff are consistent and additive.

This interconnectedness among several elements of the instructional program has several implications. First, it requires that schools have clear, public, and agreed-upon instructional goals that form the basis for selecting objectives, content, and materials. Second, the interrelationships imply that extreme differences in time allocation to the same content do not exist within a school. Cohen argues that extreme time allocation differences probably reflect the substitution of teacher preferences for the formal academic goals of the school, and result in students in various classes being exposed to functionally different curricula (see Berliner, 1979). Interrelatedness also implies that prevailing norms which grant considerable autonomy to teachers behind the closed door of the classroom carry less weight than do the shared goals of the professional staff. Furthermore, the expectations and instructional activities of nonclassroom specialists (e.g., resource teachers, reading specialists, etc.) are consistent with and supportive of the efforts of the classroom teacher. Finally, there is overlap between the content of instruction and the content included in measures of pupil performance. If textbooks and tests are not carefully coordinated (either at the school or district level), test results do not accurately reflect student learning. For an extended discussion of this problem, see Freeman et al. (1983).

According to Cohen, this argument for coordination of curriculum and instruction is *obvious*, just as a description of effective teaching practices seems *obvious*. However, coordination in schools apparently occurs infrequently. Furthermore, coordination of goals and content with performance measures suggests an image of schools that conforms closely to the classical model of bureaucracy. However, he notes that descriptions of the organization of effective schools differ notably from what is believed about schools in general. He suggests that perhaps effective schools are different from most other schools; in particular, they are better managed, their work is more frequently directed toward appropriately limited, shared goals; and instructional practices are more advanced and consistent with the most recent research.

EDMONDS

Ronald Edmonds, until his untimely death in 1983, had been one of the key figures in the school effectiveness movement. His work represented a major integrative attempt to demonstrate that schools are not interchangeable and that some schools have much more impact than others with similar resources serving similar populations. Edmonds, more than anyone, had been responsible for the communication of the belief that *schools* can and do make a difference.

In addition to the basic issue of school effectiveness (Do schools make a difference?), Edmonds spent much time dealing with (a) the investigation of pupil background characteristics that affect school effectiveness, (b) the generality of school effectiveness, (c) comparison of methods for evaluating school effectiveness, (d) the equity of proposed evaluation procedures, and (e) the comparison of effective and ineffective schools (Edmonds, 1983).

His most salient contribution was the articulation of a model for characterizing effective schools. His model underlies many of the school improvement models now being implemented in many American schools. Edmonds (1982) contended that "the correlates of effective schools are (a) the leadership of the principal characterized by substantial attention to the quality of instruction, (b) a pervasive and broadly understood instructional focus, (c) an orderly, safe climate conducive to teaching and learning, (d) teacher behaviors that convey the expectation that all students are to obtain at least minimum mastery, and (e) the use of measures of pupil achievement as the basis for program evaluation." Two of the many school improvement projects that have been stimulated in part by Edmonds' work follow.

Application of Findings from School Effects Research

At present there is clear evidence that many schools, school districts, and state departments of education are applying the results of school effectiveness research in order to improve student performance. Nevertheless, there is a paucity of data that indicate how well or in what way research findings are implemented in particular schools and how various forms and processes of implementation relate to student performance. Fortunately, however, many evaluation projects are in progress and two of these efforts will be discussed in this section.

Milwaukee's Project Rise; McCormack-Larkin and Kritek

McCormack-Larkin and Kritek (1983) note that although the quest to identify the characteristics of instructionally effective schools continues, some urban school districts are currently using available evidence to design and implement programs. One such program began in Milwaukee in March, 1979 when the school board directed the administration to develop a plan for improving achievement in 18 elementary and 2 middle schools that scored lowest on annual achievement tests. Project RISE is based upon three assumptions. First, virtually all students, regardless of their family background, race, or socioeconomic status, can acquire the basic skills. Second, inappropriate school expectations, norms, and practices account for the underachievement of many low-income and minority students. Third, the literature on effective schools and classrooms identifies expectations, norms, practices, and policies that are associated with high achievement.

In particular, the researchers believed that eight features needed to be implemented in school programs: (a) the belief among faculty and students that all students can learn and that the school is primarily responsible for their learning; (b) a strong sense of academic mission; (c) a high level of professional collegiality among staff members; (d) a strong sense of student identification and affiliation with the school; (e) grade level expectations and standards in reading, math, and language; (f) an accelerated learning program for students performing well below grade level (a component of the accelerated learning program is whole-class instruction at grade level, supplemented by small-group instruction at the student's actual skill levels); (g) increased time used for active student learning; and (h) a structured learning environment.

RISE schools abandoned the system-wide ungraded, continuous-progress school organization approach and developed grade-level objectives and standards. Grade-level standards were the prerequisites for success at the next grade level. Teachers used these standards as a guide in their planning, and students and parents were informed of them by a checklist.

Project RISE completed 3 years at the end of the 1981-1982 school year. Although the program continues, it is reasonable to ask now whether or not it has achieved its goals. Results on a standardized test administered by the school district appear in Table 20.3.

Table 20.3. Percent of Students in Milwaukee in Average or High Categories on MAT

School Year	City Avg.	RISE	Difference
Third Grade Reading			
1975–1976	73	51	22
1976–1977	68	47	21
1977–1978	70	53	17
1978–1979	74	53	21
1979–1980	76	59	17
1980–1981	77	64	13
Second Grade Reading			
1981–1982	68	64	4
Third Grade Math			
1975–1976	73	56	71
1976–1977	68	52	16
1977–1978	71	52	19
1978–1979	75	56	19
1979–1980	81	73	8
1980–1981	84	82	2
Second Grade Math			
1981–1982	80	80	0
Fifth Grade Reading			
1975–1976	65	36	29
1976–1977	64	38	26
1977–1978	65	39	26
1978–1979	66	45	21
1979–1980	68	48	20
1980–1981	72	56	16
1981–1982	71	58	13
Fifth Grade Math			
1975–1976	66	40	26
1976–1977	64	44	20
1977–1978	68	50	18
1978–1979	70	58	12
1979–1980	73	66	7
1980–1981	80	77	3
1981–1982	83	79	4

McCormack-Larkin and Kritek note that RISE schools have shown improvement in mathematics and some improvement —though not as dramatic—in reading. They note that the percentage of students in Project RISE who scored in the average or high range on the MAT has increased by about 25% in mathematics, and mathematics performance of Project RISE students is now comparable with that of other students in the district. Differences in achievement in the two subjects can possibly be attributed to the comprehensive instructional in-service programs provided by a committed group of Title I math teachers. These teachers work with classroom teachers, using the key instructional behaviors included in the eight features outlined above.

Still, the findings raise some areas of concern. Rutter et al. (1979) and Rutter (1983) argue an "ethos effect," yet when schools have uneven effects across different outcome measures and for various students, it is difficult to understand why a climate variable like ethos should have diverse outcomes in various subject areas. Clearly, presumed *general* features of effective schools cannot explain effects that are specific to subject matter.

Milwaukee school board policy has changed on two important issues, at least partly because of the influence of Project RISE. First, the schools have shifted from an ungraded primary to a graded system. As of the 1983 school year, Grades 1, 2, and 3 exist officially for the first time in approximately 40 years, and grade-level objectives have been adopted system wide. Second, schools can now retain primary students who have not mastered the skills deemed essential for the next grade level. It is possible that the retention of students in a grade may partially explain higher scores in future testing. (If a greater percentage of students repeat a grade level, part of the gain may be due to additional instruction.)

The investigators note that Project RISE has required only a small amount of money, and no new staff, new materials, and so on. Nevertheless, Project RISE appears to have achieved some success. For example, it is clear that one concrete goal of the program—that of raising district achievement—has been achieved to some extent, especially in some schools and in the area of mathematics.

New York City's School Improvement Project: Clark and McCarthy

Clark and McCarthy (1983) note that the School Improvement Project (SIP) is based on five factors derived from the school effectiveness literature, which focuses on causes of school failure (Edmonds, 1979). These five factors are administrative style, instructional emphasis on basic skills, school climate, ongoing assessment of pupil progress, and teacher expectations. SIP builds on typical school effectiveness research because it sets goals for school improvement and establishes a system for obtaining these goals. This project is a response to one criticism of the school effectiveness literature, that longitudinal studies of improvement projects in a variety of schools have not been conducted.

This school change project is also based on Edmonds' (1979) contention that schools can educate all children, regardless of family background. In June, 1979 the chancellor of the New York City public school system issued a memorandum to community school districts and all principals of elementary schools, inviting them to submit applications for participation in New York City's School Improvement Project. Of the 43 schools that applied, 10 were selected to participate in 1979–1980. Three criteria were used to select schools: voluntary participation of the principal (with the superintendent's approval), a match between school needs and SIP objectives, and a lack of other development programs in the school. An additional 9 schools from the original pool joined the project in 1980–1981. In the third year, 4 new schools entered SIP at the discretion of community superintendents.

Most students in 8 of the 10 schools in the first cohort were minority, and over half were designated as low income. From 20% to 61% of the students in a school were at or above grade level. During the first project year, SIP schools conducted a needs assessment, formed school planning committees, developed improvement plans, and reviewed and refined the plans. The plans were implemented during the second year and strengths and weaknesses were identified.

Implementation of revised plan activities in first-cohort schools was considered somewhat successful by principals and liaisons. The most successful plan activities implemented in all seven schools were reading and language arts programs and test sophistication programs in reading and mathematics. The original schools implemented an average of 14 plan components, in comparison to 21 components instituted by second-cohort schools in 1981–1982.

Preliminary student achievement data from spring 1979 to spring 1982 (see Table 20.4) indicate the percentage of students reading at and above grade level each year as measured by the California Achievement Test. For 2 of the 3 years data were analyzed, SIP schools showed greater increases than other city schools in percentage of students reading at or above grade level. For example. between spring 1980 and spring 1981, 15 SIP schools had a 6.3% increase, as compared to 3.8% for city-wide schools. Between 1981 and 1982, SIP schools continued to show increases, while city-wide schools decreased by .3%.

According to Eubanks and Levine (1983), achievement data in the New York City project are encouraging. They note that the seven schools that initiated improvement plans in 1980–1981 had an average increase of 16 points between spring 1979 and spring 1982 in the percentage of students reading at or above grade level. However, they also note that these achievement gains have stabilized and that only a few third-year schools registered noticeable gains in 1981–1982. It would be important to know more about the plans and their degree of implementation in schools where improvement continues.

The project administrators believe that vital leadership came from principals; in schools where the plan worked the principals supervised and coordinated implementation of the plan components and monitored results closely.

One implication of this project is that researchers need to obtain teachers' and principals' commitments to the SIP program. Indeed, the project now requires that principals, 60% to 70% of the staff, and the parents agree to participate through a formal vote. The program currently emphasizes that the liaison acts as a facilitator and the principal as a supervisor of the process.

Other School Improvement Efforts

The general programs discussed in the above section are but a *few* of the many school improvement projects under way. Despite many problems associated with the extant data base

Table 20.4. Student Reading Achievement in SIP Schools and City-wide: Percent At and Above Grade Level on the California Achievement Test, Grades 2 to 6, Spring 1979 to Spring 1982[a]

	Percent and Number At and Above Grade Level[b]											
	April 1979			April 1980			April 1981			April 1982	
	%	N		%	N		%	N		%	N
First-Cohort (7)	26.0	869		33.7	1,061		40.6	1,220		41.0	1,178
Gains			+7.7%			+6.9%			+0.4%		
Second-Cohort (8)[c]	—	—		33.5	1,306		39.3	1,434		44.5	1,487
Gains			—			+5.8%			+5.3%		
Combined-Cohort (15)[d]	—	—		33.6	2,367		39.9	2,654		42.8	2,665
Gains			—			+6.3%			+2.9%		
City-wide-Cohort (690)[e]	39.6	124,986		47.5	143,127		51.3	148,581		51.0	142,468
Gains			+7.9%			+3.8%			−0.3%		
Difference Between SIP and City-wide			−0.2%			+2.5%			+3.2%		

Note. From "School Improvement in New York City: The Evolution of a Project" by T. A. Clark and D. P. McCarthy, 1983, *Educational Researcher*, *12*(4), Copyright 1983 by American Educational Research Association. Reprinted by permission.

[a] Since all SIP schools are either K–5, or K–6, city-wide scores were used only through sixth grade. New York City students in Grades 2 through 9 are given the CAT annually. Many special education and certain limited-English-proficient students are excused.

[b] Because enrollments fluctuated from year to year in every school, percentages are based on actual enrollment figures for each year rather than on the same enrollment figures.

[c] The second-cohort schools started in 1980–1981, so data are not provided for 1979.

[d] Although 19 schools entered SIP (10 in 1979–1980 and 9 in 1980–1981), 4 schools dropped out during or right after the first year. Only 15 schools which completed at least 2 years are included in the combined cohort.

[e] SIP schools are not included in city-wide figures. Included are 609 elementary schools and Grades 5 and 6 in 81 intermediate schools.

available for designing school improvement plans, many projects are in progress. Unfortunately, some districts have simply taken plans developed in other districts and applied them with few, if any, modifications. However, persons who have studied the literature rightfully advocate that schools or school districts need to develop plans that are relevant to their unique needs and populations. Furthermore, districts must understand the change *process* if school effectiveness literature is to be used appropriately.

Purkey and Smith (1985) summarize the implications of recent research for schools by suggesting that it means increased involvement of teachers and other staff members in decision making, expanded opportunities for collaborative planning, and flexible change strategies that reflect the "personality" of each school.

Thus, unless districts utilize appropriate change strategies, pressure for immediate school change will lead to the attempt to improve schools through uniform policy standards (e.g., all schools will have homework, school plans, 3 years of mathematics, etc.) and may negatively affect the achievement of pupils in schools that are already most effective. Finn (1983) reasons that effective schools have become so because they have developed their own goals, norms, and expectations. He suggests that the problem is not that all schools will be required to have higher standards per se, but that the mandate to have such standards may erode the pride and the continuing commitment of good schools to seek better solutions to educational problems.

Finn (1983) argues this point:

> The schools in a given system or state are apt to be similar with respect to relatively superficial matters but dissimilar along dimensions that matter more; yet the inertial autonomy of schools *qua* schools also means that efforts to make ineffective schools more closely resemble effective schools in the ways that matter most are certain to be very difficult and quite likely to meet with little success. Moreover, policymakers seeking greater uniformity must be terribly careful lest they "level downward" through well-intentioned efforts that wind up sapping the vitality of the most effective schools rather than invigorating the others. (pp. 5–6)

Goodlad (1983) provides empirical support for Finn's contention that schools appear the same on many superficial dimensions but vary in important, subtle ways. He suggests that it is futile to attempt to improve many ineffective schools unless these schools demonstrate some basic initiative towards change. Goodlad writes:

> But the less satisfying schools described are not sufficiently in charge of their own destiny to build agenda from these data and subsequently to take action. They are not healthy organisms. They simply are not good candidates for tackling the difficult tasks of curricula and pedagogical reform. The first step is for them to become more effective in the conduct of present business and in the process to become more satisfying places for those associated with them. They need data about their present condition and considerable support and encouragement in the needed process of renewal. (pp. 269–270)

Thus, if schools do not have agreement among staff on school-wide goals, telling them to develop such goals may be irrelevant. Such schools may be able to change only after they are convinced that change is necessary, receive outside help in assessing curriculum and instruction, and in some cases, specific information on how to bring about needed change.

Many school improvement efforts begin with a needs assessment survey that solicits input from the school staff to outline school problems and general needs. However, one could argue that school staff may not be able to identify certain problems and issues, and that external review might help schools to analyze their current strengths and weaknesses. For example, the descriptions of schools provided by Jackson (1981a, 1981b) and by Lightfoot (1981a, 1981b) not only differ from each other but would likely differ from descriptions provided by the staffs of these schools. There are many views of what a school is and should be, and both internal and external assessments may be necessary in order to describe accurately a school's problems and potential.

Criteria for Evaluating School Plans

Although there has been considerable talk about the need for school plans, researchers and educators rarely describe individual school plans in journal articles or technical reports. By what criteria can we judge school plans? Implicitly, the criteria for judging plans seem to be the percentage of faculty involved in developing a plan and the number of faculty who accept the plan as valid. There can be bad plans as well as good ones, however, and some plans might constrain experimentation and growth, while others would encourage these activities. On the other hand, a school must start somewhere. Some schools will never change unless external pressure is brought on them to do so, and although staff agreement is desirable, the best that can be done in some situations is to work around those who are uncooperative but entrenched.

Data from studies of school improvement are less likely to explain *why* results are obtained or the most promising ways to develop school improvement plans. Although the plans are said to be stimulated by school effects and teacher effects research, it is often difficult to identify their research basis. In general, documentation focuses on the extent to which teachers, parents, and administrators are involved in developing the plans, and far too little attention is paid to the *validity* of the plans themselves or the extent to which they are implemented in actual practice.

Implementation of School Plans

Information is especially needed concerning the extent and quality of school plan implementation in individual classrooms. Without descriptions of *intended* and *actual* implementation of instructional, organizational, and social processes, it is difficult to assess why achievement increases in some schools and not in others. The seriousness of this question is reflected in the observation of Purkey and Smith (1983a), that only one-half of the schools participating in Milwaukee's Project RISE showed achievement increases. Were achievement increases due to motivational factors or to identifiable changes in instructional behavior?

Other school improvement projects report similar variation. For example, McCarthy, Canner, and Pershing (1983) note that 60% of the schools in the New York City project were successful. They further note that schools implemented instructional plans more successfully than plans related to improving school climate, parental participation, or school administration.

Future School Evaluation Plans

Future school evaluations must have better conceptual statements of what the school improvement program is (What is the independent variable?), improved statements of theory (Why is the program expected to work?), and more thorough observational evaluations (perferably by persons who are independent of the school district) of what takes place in schools. Too much of the current school improvement activity naively proceeds as though the existence of a school plan that is widely accepted will positively influence achievement outcomes.

The Process of Implementation

Fullan (1985) extensively examines how change processes work. He contends that an awareness of the conditions of change is critical if the effective schools literature is to be appropriately applied. His paper discusses a number of issues related to school change — Should participation be mandatory? At what level should the process be implemented (individual classroom, individual school, or district level)? How much variation should be encouraged (at classroom level, at the building level)? Should large- or small-scale approaches be used?

He contends that the process of implementation is crucial. Although it is beyond the scope of this paper to discuss the change literature, it is useful to highlight briefly the steps that Fullan recommends in helping participants to develop new skills in a manner that is satisfying and meaningful to participants:

1. Change takes place over time.
2. The initial stages of any significant change *always* involve anxiety and uncertainty.
3. Ongoing technical assistance and psychological support are crucial if the anxiety is to be coped with.
4. Change involves learning new skills through practice and feedback — it is incremental and developmental.
5. The most fundamental breakthrough occurs when people can understand the underlyilng conception and rationale with respect to "why" this new way works better.
6. Organizational conditions within the school (peer norms, administrative leadership) and in relation to the school (e.g., external administrative support and technical help) are important.
7. Successful change involves pressure, but it is pressure through *interaction* with peers and other technical and administrative leaders.

Limitations of Extant Research

Although the literature yields a number of statements concerning the characteristics of effective schools, there are several limitations that must be considered when one uses extant findings for program planning. These limitations are similar in many ways to the problems of implementing findings from teacher effects research (e.g., Berliner, 1977; Good, Biddle, & Brophy, 1983); however, the issues related to school effectiveness are more complex because there are fewer observational data that describe school processes and independent investigators have not conducted carefully controlled field experiments.

Independent Variables

To date not a single naturalistic study of effective schools provides basic data (means and standard deviations for each classroom) to demonstrate that the behavior of individual teachers in one school differs from the behavior of teachers in other schools. It will be important for future research to examine how schools vary in terms of various quantitative measures (e.g., How much homework is assigned per class?) and qualitative measures (e.g., Does homework consist largely of drill or is it designed to develop independent study skills? How do teachers use such work — do they examine it, comment on it, and use it as part of the basis for assigning a grade?).

Validity

In this chapter we have described studies that allow one to determine if and how schools influence average student performance. Although information about students' performance on criterion-referenced and norm-referenced achievement tests is valuable (if those tests are congruent with the curriculum actually used in the classroom), academic achievement is only part of what many citizens and educators mean by an effective teacher or an effective school. Most studies have examined only student achievement (studies by Brookover et al., 1979 and Rutter et al., 1979 are important and notable exceptions).

As a case in point, Miller (1983) argues and provides data to support his contention that the scientific literacy — the ability to read about, understand, and express an opinion on scientific issues — of most Americans is appallingly low. Arguments could also be made about students' performance in other areas. For example, Goodlad (1983) contends that students are very passive in their reaction to school events and that schools should help to stimulate more student thinking. Hence, there are many possible outcomes of schooling and although it is important to acknowledge and to utilize appropriately new data about effective schools, it is inadvisable to equate school effects on achievement with effectiveness per se, because many important outcomes of schooling have not been examined. (Others, too, have reached similar conclusions; see Cuban, 1983; Purkey & Smith, 1983a; Ralph & Fennessey, 1983; and Rowan et al., 1983).

Stability

It would be disturbing to go to the trouble and expense of identifying effective schools only to learn that these schools do not have stable effects on student achievement across consecutive years. This would be the equivalent of attempting to determine what makes an effective football team by identifying a football team that is outstanding during one year (e.g., the 1982 world champion San Francisco Forty Niners) and studying that team intensively the following year (e.g., policies related to scouting, drafting, training, game strategy, etc.), only to discover that the team did not even make the playoffs during the year when observational measures were collected.

Available evidence does not provide generalizable information about the stability of effective schools. It does appear that the *average* stability of school effects on student achievement is low. Rowan and Denk (1982) estimate that only about 10% of the schools drawn from a large sample were consistently effective or ineffective (i.e., in the top or bottom quartile of the residual distribution over consecutive years), and only 5% were effective or ineffective over 3 consecutive years.

Rowan and Denk (1982) used data provided by the California Assessment Program (California State Department of Education, 1977) to construct two measures of instructional effectiveness for sixth grade achievement in 810 classes from 1975–1977. The two measures they used were (a) trend analysis (Is the school improving over consecutive years?) and (b) regression-based residuals. They note that the trend analysis was biased against schools serving low-SES populations, and that decreases in scores from year to year were significantly correlated with changes in the socioeconomic composition of these schools' student bodies. Moreover, they found that this measure of effectiveness lacked stability: the correlation between gains made from 1975 to 1976 and gains from 1976 to 1977 was −.45.

These researchers also examined the bias and stability of a measure based on residuals. As expected, this measure was not correlated to measures of student background; however, the measure was relatively unstable. For example, the correlation of residuals for 1975 and 1976 was only .24; for 1976 and 1977 .19. These results are consistent with other studies of the stability of residuals (e.g., Forsythe, 1973; Jencks et al., 1972). Thus, the stability of school effectiveness measures varies according to the procedure used to estimate stability; however, all comparisons indicate that the average stability of school effects on student achievement is low.

Some data suggest that performance in "effective" schools may be more stable than in other schools. Recall that in Weber's (1971) study two of the schools (50%) maintained their effectiveness over consecutive years. Rutter et al. (1979) and Rutter (1983) report that schools that were effective (achievement, attendance, behavior) generally maintained their effectiveness over several consecutive years.

Other evidence also suggests that at least some aspects of school effects are stable over time. Reynolds, Jones, and St. Leger (1976) found a correlation of .85 for school attendance rates over 7 years and of .56 for academic attainment over the same period of time. Such stability justifies the study of effective schools and attempts to describe successful practice in these schools. However, the study of stability presents major technical and conceptual problems to those who study schools as organizational, instructional units. Why do some schools achieve highly one year but not the next? If strong principal leadership is an important variable in school achievement, how and why does achievement vary from year to year?

Multiple Criteria

In addition to questions of the stability of school effects on students' performance, there is also the issue of whether schools are generally effective or whether effectiveness is limited to a few areas of student performance. Unfortunately, this important question has received little attention; most studies of school effectiveness include only achievement measures. The data that do exist suggest that effective schools can positively influence different outcome measures simultaneously. For example, Rutter et al. (1979) found that schools that had favorable effects on student achievement also generally had positive effects on attendance and classroom behavior. (See also related evidence reviewed by Rutter, 1983.)

However, to repeat, there is little evidence directly related to the question of how general school effects are, and the outcome measures used to assess generality appear to be logically related to achievement (attendance, classroom behavior, engagement rates, etc.). Whether schools that help students to learn to express themselves well through written essays, to develop adequate computer skills, and/or to understand scientific processes well are the same schools that have high average scores on standardized achievement tests is an open question that needs to be explored.

Practical and Conceptual Issues

It seems unreasonable to include data from pupils who do not attend a school in analyses measuring school effectiveness. Despite the obvious nature of this observation, many schools with high turnover rates include in their achievement data scores of numerous students who received only limited instruction in the school. If valid and reliable measures of school effects are to be obtained, investigators must establish and report minimum instructional time periods for including students or teachers in a data set. One reason the stability of residual gain achievement scores is low in some studies may be that not enough care has been taken to determine whether a student has been "taught" in a particular school and to associate the student *with particular teachers and classes.* For example, Averch et al. (1974) note that in their extensive review of input-output studies only *one* study (Hanushek, 1970) matched student achievement with resources that teachers and students were actually exposed to.

Rowan et al. note that most studies of effective schools do not measure the instructional performance of an *entire* school. Rather, schools are labeled as effective on the basis of assessments of instructional outcomes at only one or two grade levels and in only one or two curriculum areas (for an exception, see Wellisch, MacQueen, Carriere, & Duck, 1978). Also, these authors argue that even within curriculum areas and at a single grade level, schools may not be uniformly effective for all types of students. Marco (1974) studied 70 Title I schools and found a correlation of only .32 between indexes of instructional effectiveness calculated separately for students of high and low ability (cf. Shoemaker, 1982).

Context

Only a few types of schools have been studied extensively. For example, researchers have more frequently attempted to identify effective inner-city schools and rural schools than to study effective suburban schools. Also, most attempts to improve schools have focused on elementary schools. The implications of the effective schools literature for suburban or secondary schools are therefore uncertain.

Correlational Evidence

Most of the research attempting to associate school effects with student learning is correlational. Although this information is valuable, correlational evidence only allows one to infer that two variables are associated, not that either variable directly influences the other. As Rowan et al. (1983) point out, the finding that strong principal leadership is associated with clarity of instruction and student achievement does not necessarily mean that effective principals cause teachers in their schools to be focused and systematic. It may well be that a capable teaching faculty preceded leadership and enabled the principal to assume a strong and active role.

Furthermore, correlational statements describe a relationship at one point in time. If one assumes that existing literature is valid and that certain factors are associated with effectiveness (e.g., leadership), research only indicates that principal leadership and student achievement are correlated; it does not provide evidence about how one can become a leader.

Nonlinear Relationships

Many teacher effects researchers argue that most teacher behaviors have a nonlinear relationship with student achievement (Berliner, 1977; Good, Biddle, & Brophy, 1975; and Soar & Soar, 1979). A linear relationship means that a teacher behavior and a student outcome measure are directly related—increases in the teacher behavior are accompanied by increases in student achievement. Research on teaching has often found nonlinear relationships between classroom processes and student achievement. One relatively common nonlinear pattern is an "inverted-U." In this pattern, outcome measures are associated with an optimal level of a classroom process (or teacher behavior), so that teachers who exhibit too little or too much of this process have less positive effects on students than do teachers who use the correct amount.

Many school effects variables probably have nonlinear relationships with outcomes as well, but the paucity of observational data collected in this research makes it impossible to assess the claim. Still, it seems likely that a school could have either too few or too many rules, or could assign either too much or too little homework. Even teacher expectations can be too high as well as too low (Edmonds, 1983; Good & Brophy, 1984). Unfortunately, too many advocates of change based on the school effectiveness literature assume linear relationships—if a little is good, more is certain to be better.

Averages Can Be Misleading

Studies of large samples of schools yield important profiles of more and less successful schools, but there are usually *group averages* that may or may not describe how a single effective

teacher actually behaves in a particular effective school. Persons who use research to guide practice sometimes expect all teachers' behavior to reflect the group average. Such simplistic thinking is apt to lead the literature to be too broadly and inappropriately applied.

It is also important to consider the *appropriateness* and *effects* of schooling for specific types of students. It would seem important to make mathematics (and other subjects) as interesting for girls as for boys, for example, and for minority as well as majority students (extant data on this point are not encouraging). It seems unreasonable to call a school excellent if one group of students is not making progress; however, if school effects are reported only in total averages, it will not be possible to discover whether certain groups experience poor growth in an otherwise good school.

School Plans/Teacher Autonomy

There is presently great interest in individual schools conducting needs assessments and developing their own plans. Many advocates of school improvement argue that because of unique student and teacher populations, community characteristics, histories, and resources, schools must have autonomy in developing plans. However, this same logic dictates that teachers and departments also need a degree of autonomy to chart their own directions and to record their progress. Ironically, many of those who argue most strongly for school autonomy are least interested in teacher autonomy. Although we believe that some consensus on school goals and use of resources across an entire staff is necessary, there can be too much as well as too little school-wide planning.

Whether departments in secondary schools are in agreement about curricula and instructional practices in particular subjects is also an important issue. Similarly, researchers should ask if teachers have a firm sense of improvements they are trying to effect in their classrooms. The school improvement model that many researchers and theorists advocate regards the school as an institution that establishes goals and as the mechanism that makes it likely that these goals will be realized. Another way to consider school effects, however, is as processes that encourage teachers to carefully consider what they are trying to achieve in their classrooms, to become more aware of their progress on such goals, and to make better use of other school personnel in developing their classroom strategies.

At any rate, naturalistic research does not indicate that more effective schools have more formal school plans (conduct needs assessments, etc.), but only that there is a greater informal consensus among the staff in these schools that students can learn, etc. As a strategy for building more school-wide direction and consensus, many school improvement projects emphasize the development of school-wide plans.

Lightfoot (1983) expresses a similar concern in her book, *The Good High School*. From her intensive study of six diverse but presumably good high schools, she contends:

> In all of these schools, therefore, teachers are seen as the central actors in the educational process. Their satisfaction is critical to the tone and smooth functioning of the school. Their nuturance is critical to the nurturance of students. Each school interprets teacher

rewards differently, but all of them search for a balance between the expression of teacher autonomy, initiative, and adulthood on the one hand, and the requirements of conformity, discipline, and commitments to school life on the other. (p. 341)

Sizer (1984) also addresses this point in his book, *Horace's Compromise*, which is based on his major study of American high schools. After concluding that good teachers are the critical element of successful schools, he suggests that effective schools must allow teachers autonomy but also must have standards and accountability. Hence, the issue of balance between schools' needs and teachers' needs in serving students must be addressed. Unfortunately, overapplication of the school effectiveness literature may make schools less attractive to more talented teachers.

It may be that some attention to school-wide planning and a general awareness of school goals, coupled with a focus on departmental or individual teacher plans, will be the strongest and most durable strategy for enhancing school productivity. Research and development activities need to focus on more differentiated improvement plans and plans that encourage both the coordination of school programs and initiative from individual teachers (e.g., Good & Brophy, 1984). Shulman (1983) also raises concerns about teacher autonomy in the context of applying school effectiveness research.

Who Is Responsible for Achievement?

Most persons who write about effective schools focus on teachers and principals. However, some authors suggest that the role of the student has been modified so that less is expected of students today than in the past. Further, these persons believe that too much attention is paid to the teacher, and that students need to be held accountable for learning.

Tomlinson (1981) argues that although socially imposed standards of conduct were strict and pay was meager, teachers in the 1950s were personally consoled by the public's esteem and gratitude and by their own generally unquestioned and unchallenged classroom authority. Teachers, especially as they grew older, might be viewed as a little eccentric, but seldom as ineffective. Their job was to expose students to information and to inculcate knowledge. Still, whatever they taught and however they taught it, they were rarely held responsible for how much a student learned. The responsibility for acquiring knowledge, or achievement, lay with the students themselves. It was their variable ability and motivation that determined how much they learned. Tomlinson notes that things have changed in recent times. The ability and effort of teachers have replaced the ability and labor of students as the putative determinants of achievement.

Tomlinson suggests that research generally indicates that academically effective schools are merely schools organized to pursue learning consistently. Principals, teachers, students, and parents agree upon the purpose, justification, and methods of schooling. They systematically spend their common energies on teaching and learning. They are serious about, even dedicated to, the proposition that children can and shall learn in school. No special treatment and no magic are involved, just provision of the necessary conditions for learning.

Other writers stress the importance of the home and general community in supporting learning activities (see for example, Lightfoot, 1978). Schools (and teachers) are important but not exclusive factors in facilitating students' learning. Unfortunately, many accounts of effective schools devote too little attention to the role of students, parents, and citizens in establishing and maintaining good schools.

Need for Better Measures of Student and Teacher Perceptions

We have argued that measurement of classroom processes—a careful examination of what happens in classrooms—has made the school effectiveness literature more valuable. We also believe that information about how students and teachers perceive instructional processes and opportunities in more effective schools is needed to provide clues about how to make schools more effective. Although there have been fruitful attempts to measure general reactions of teachers and students to school (e.g., Brookover et al., 1979), future research needs to focus more closely on participants' reactions to specific events, especially events believed to be central to school effectiveness.

It is also important to assess the influence of school culture and instructional processes on students' perceptions. It is one thing to say that students and teachers should hold high expectations, but another to get answers to specific questions: How do students know how hard they should work? How can students know whether they are devoting more or less effort to schoolwork than their peers? The recent work of Natriello and Dornbusch (1984) illustrates the value of measuring student perceptions, as well as the difficulty of doing this work.

Measurement of student's perceptions and observations of what they do in classes should be more central to the study of effective schools than it has been in the past. There is growing evidence that student perceptions of classroom process are valuable sources of information about schools (e.g., Cooper & Good, 1983; Peterson & Swing, 1982; Rohrkemper, 1984; Weinstein, 1983; Wittrock, this volume); however, student data are most useful when combined with process observation and contextual information. Future studies of effective schooling could make better use of student interviews in order to understand how different types of students perceive and act upon the various constraints present in more and less effective schools.

Teacher Perceptions

Similar arguments could be made about the value of measuring teacher beliefs, perceptions, and decision-making skills related to effective schooling (see Clark & Peterson, this volume). Why do some teachers believe that students can achieve curricula goals while other teachers in the same school do not? Why is it that more teachers in some schools believe that students can learn than do teachers in other schools serving similar populations? There are important data to suggest that teachers' expectations for student performance vary from school to school (see Brookover et al., 1979); however, needed now are assessments of other teacher perceptions that may help to explain why some teachers hold high expectations for student learning. Cusick (1983) provides a good description of schools from the teacher's viewpoint.

School Effects

Despite the considerable attention currently paid to school effects, few researchers have conceptualized and operationally defined school effects. As noted above, in defining an effective school researchers commonly use only a single grade level, and in studying school process they observe only a small portion of teachers in a school. Thus, observation (when it does occur) usually focuses on the classroom rather than the school. Although some studies have examined school-wide practices (e.g., school rules), many important school measures have not been examined. For example, are teachers in effective schools more aware of what other teachers do in their classrooms? Do teachers in these schools have more opportunities to learn from other teachers (e.g., to observe, to engage in formal discussion) or to receive useful feedback from them? If teachers receive more feedback, what is the nature of the feedback? Is there a shared language and emphasis among staff in how they assess the school's present strengths and weaknesses and how teachers perceive and define problems that confront the school (e.g., Spencer-Hall & Hall, 1982)?

Independence of School Effects

Researchers will have to conceptualize and isolate school effects more carefully than they have in the past. Effects on individual students are averaged to produce mean teacher effects; effects of individual teachers are averaged to produce mean school effects; and effects of individual schools are averaged to produce mean school district effects or estimates of the general effects of schooling. At each level of aggregation the variance within units probably exceeds the variance across units, so that prospects for meaningful findings at the higher levels of aggregation are limited. Attention to individual process variables makes it possible to logically separate effects on students that result from individualized (dyadic) teacher behaviors, teacher behaviors directed to the entire class, school effects representing actions of the principal or other sources of influence on the school as a whole, school district-level effects, and so forth. However, the effects of all of these on achievement are confounded in reality.

District Effects on Schools

There are a variety of ways in which school districts may encourage or restrict school effectiveness. For example, in some school districts the district office controls most money and uses it, for example, to employ curriculum coordinators throughout the district. Although individual schools may vary in the extent to which they take advantage of coordinators' skills, the variation is probably not as great as it would be if the money were available for schools to pay their own coordinators. For example, if principals were given funds to employ instructional leaders in their schools, the effects on schools of using these

leaders would probably be more apparent. Some schools would use those resources in practical ways (observing teachers and providing meaningful feedback, developing effective programs for identifying and training substitute teachers — whereas other schools might use the funds in less helpful ways (clerical tabulations).

Thus, the potential for school effects is larger in some districts than others. This observation is important, because some districts are currently decentralizing policy (e.g., individual schools set their own goals) and some school boards are redirecting control of resources from the district to the school level. As we noted above, influences at every level are confounded by resources and practices at other levels; hence, in districts in which individual schools have more power (e.g., teachers have some influence on whether principals are retained, principals can actively recruit teachers), and in which individual schools are allowed to determine how funds are spent, differential school effects are more likely to emerge.

Despite the potential impact of the district on school policy, principal leadership, and classroom processes, there has been little formal study of these effects in the past. There is now growing empirical work (see, for example, Bidwell & Kasarda, 1980; Schwille et al., 1983) and some logical argument (see Dreeban & Barr, 1983); however, more work is needed in this area. In particular, it will be important to show how decisions reached at the district level affect resources and instructional treatments that individual students or classes receive.

It is also possible to explore larger effects of the community or state on decisions and actions in particular schools. Hall and Spencer-Hall (1980) describe a case study that illustrates how an article that appeared in a newspaper was instrumental in forcing a school district to examine unanticipated issues in the area of testing policy and accountability measures. More broadly, Spencer-Hall and Hall (1982) provide a detailed analysis of two school districts they observed for about a year. They found that school problems identified in the two school districts varied in their source, duration, resolution, and negotiation. Differences between the districts in perceiving and responding to school problems could be explained in part by community context, organizational history, organizational complexity, participant efficacy, and teacher militancy. Clearly, individual schools are affected by the larger organizational and political context that surrounds them.

Parental–School Relationships

The degree of home and school cooperation is likely to be an important determinant of student achievement. However, this "obvious" possibility has received little research attention. Whether parent-school communication differs in "more" and "less" effective schools is also unclear. One might predict that home–school agreement on curriculum content and performance standards would influence student performance; however, there is also reason to suspect that parent involvement in and understanding of school programs is a complex matter.

The difficulty of understanding the potential value of parent–school relationships is due, in part, to the fact that this relationship can take many forms: understanding and supporting the school curriculum programs or discipline policies;

helping students with homework; raising money for the school; participating directly in the instructional program. As the definition changes, both the perceived (by parents and teachers) and actual benefits of parent involvement may vary considerably. Unfortunately, extant research does not provide a clear analysis of the forms nor effects of these different parent involvement activities in "more" or "less" effective schools.

Lightfoot (1978) argues persuasively that productive home–school relationships require that parents and teachers see and accept the fundamental importance of each other in the life of the child. She stresses the need for home and school to base their interaction and planning on goals of integration and cohesion rather than relationships that emphasize boundaries and individual interests. Whether the views of parents and teachers are more aligned on certain aspects of schooling in "more" than "less" effective schools is an intriguing issue that merits study.

The Role of the Principal in Program Adoption

To this point, we have reviewed research on effective schools and have made suggestions about subsequent research that needs to be conducted. We now turn to a discussion of the principal. Although the topic is logically interrelated with the issue of effective schools, we discuss the research on principals separately because research on principals has generally been conducted in a separate research tradition.

There is growing evidence that principals and other school-level factors may interact with the extent to which individual teachers adopt certain teaching practices to determine the success of program innovations. In this section of the chapter we present two examples of research that show how principal behavior can affect program adoption.

A Secondary School Example: Stallings and Mohlman (1981)

Stallings and Mohlman examined the effects of school policies on pupil outcomes in an inservice training program in eight secondary schools that included a wide variety of policies and organizational plans.

They gathered opinions about school structure from school superintendents, county coordinators of secondary schools, and Stanford University consultants who had studied a large number of Bay Area schools. School structure variables included rule clarity, rule enforcement, communication patterns, leadership style, grading systems, delinquency, and a general feeling that a school was well run or not. After potential participating schools were identified, the investigators met with principals and arranged for a meeting with teachers at the schools of eight principals who volunteered to participate early in the school year. These principals were willing to commit staff development funds for release time if their teaching staff agreed to participate.

The initial school sample was balanced in terms of ethnicity and average family income. Two of the schools had primarily white populations with students whose families had average or above-average incomes. The other six schools had large minority populations and family incomes that ranged from average to below average.

During the fall the investigators met with 10 to 12 volunteer teachers from each of the eight target schools. Three schools declined participation and three other schools replaced them. Four to seven teachers from each school ultimately participated in the training by attending seven 1–2-hour workshops.

To investigate relationships between school structure and organization, and between classroom teaching processes and school, teacher, and student outcomes, the researchers used a pretest–posttest design. Workshop training was designed to inform teachers about recent studies of effective teaching and to encourage them to use certain practices in their classrooms. Teachers were observed with a coding instrument that measured the extent to which they implemented practices believed to be correlated with student achievement. Other instruments used in the project included pupil and teacher questionnaires. The study also included interviews of principals that enabled the investigators to obtain more information about the school.

The investigators report the following major findings:

1. Schools in which policies and rules were clearer and more consistently enforced had higher teacher morale, fewer classroom intrusions, a lower absence rate, less class misbehavior, and more time-on-task.
2. Schools that had more administrative support services and fewer burdensome duties for teachers had higher teacher morale and less classroom misbehavior.
3. A more active and respected principal was associated with higher teacher morale and students who felt more friendliness.
4. In schools with more supportive principals, more teachers implemented the training program.
5. In schools where the policies and rules were clear and consistent, more teachers changed their classroom behavior as recommended.
6. Schools in which teachers implemented the effective use of time training programs had students who spent more time-on-task.
7. Findings regarding effective school policy and principal leadership style were similar for schools serving high-income and low-income students.

It is important to note that Stallings and Mohlman worked with volunteer principals and teachers and that these teachers were only a small percentage of the staff at each school. These data therefore do not yield strong statements about effective schools. The findings nevertheless provide good evidence that a principal's support is important in helping teachers to learn and use new instructional approaches, although some teachers in schools with less active principals also implemented the training information effectively.

An Elementary School Example: Hall et al. (1983)

Gene Hall and his colleagues at the Research and Development Center for Teacher Education have focused their research efforts on school organization and school change. Most recently they investigated the influence of principals as change facilitators in schools (for a review of this research see Hall, Hord, Huling, Rutherford, & Stiegelbauer, 1983). One of their studies, the Principal–Teacher Interaction Study, was an extensive examination of nine elementary school principals and their faculties who were involved in implementation and innovation at their schools.

Although the complexity and scope of Hall et al.'s (1983) work prevent us from reporting it in detail here, it is important to note that they found that the principal played a key role in successful implementation of change strategies and that successful innovation called for much time and energy from the principal. However, they also found that various principals used different leadership styles successfully. They distinguished three principal styles: *initiators* (make it happen), *managers* (help it happen), and *responders* (let it happen).

Such data suggest that there is *no* ideal style of principal leadership, even in the specific role as a change facilitator. Principals who use any one of these three general styles can be successful. Needed now are data on the quality of leadership style (How do poor initiators differ from good ones?) and the contexts in which a given style may be more or less appropriate.

An Experimental Study: Gall et al. (1984)

There is reason to believe that principals' involvement in change efforts can make a difference in program adaptation at the elementary school level. Gall et al. (1984) recently completed a field experiment to determine if the effectiveness of a staff development program for elementary teachers could be improved by training the teachers' principals in a staff development program. Although instructional leadership is considered a key skill for principals to develop, attempts to assess principals' impact on instructional programs have been rare. This project provided evidence that trained principals, on average, had a positive impact on teachers' implementation of the Missouri Mathematics Program. This study provides the first *experimental* evidence that principals' leadership behavior affects teacher behavior and student achievement. For an excellent discussion of the principal's role in staff development as well as a more general discussion of the role of staff development in the change process, see Gall et al. (1984).

The Principal as Leader

Although much school effectiveness research suggests that principals' involvement as curricula and instructional leaders is crucial, few existing data *describe* what principals do or tell how principals in more effective schools differ in their behavior from principals who head less effective schools. Fortunately, research has begun to focus on principals' behavior, and in the next decade there will likely be many observational studies of principals.

Case Studies of Five Principals: Dwyer et al. (1982)

Dwyer, Lee, Rowan, and Bossert (1982) argue that to understand leadership it is necessary to examine school processes because correlational survey studies cannot provide information about *why* some schools are more effective than others.

Dwyer et al. studied five principals for 8 weeks. These principals were selected from a larger group who had been identified as effective by superintendents and other central office administrators from Bay Area school districts. Thirty-two principals agreed to be interviewed extensively. Five of these who were most articulate in describing their jobs and seemed most interested in the study were selected for participation in the case studies. To be certain that principals of effective schools were studied, the investigators prepared 7-year school achievement score profiles. They believed that such data at least allowed them to exclude ineffective schools (in terms of achievement) from the sample.

Open-ended interviews were conducted in order to determine principals' individual philosophies of work. The five principals were observed in an unobtrusive manner, and descriptive field notes were kept of their activities. Each principal was observed during 3 full work days over an 8-week period, with these days sometimes consisting of 10 to 12 hours of observation. The day following each observation, the researchers returned and interviewed the principals about the previous day. Principals were encouraged to reflect on their decisions and activities. In addition to the interviews and observations, researchers spent 20 to 30 hours in each school observing classes, recess, lunch periods, and talking informally with teachers and students. Information such as school plans, test scores, and so forth was also obtained from each school.

Data analysis was similar to the "comparative method" framework of Glaser and Strauss (1967), with analysts generating definitions and categories from the records, searching for patterns, repetitions, and contradictions in each setting, and comparing the obtained results across settings. Narrative case studies were prepared and summarized in models that illustrated the essential qualities of a school's context, the activities that best typified the principal's management behaviors, and the expected outcome of those actions as projected by the principal. These models were then discussed with the principals in order to assess accuracy and were modified or verified on the basis of these discussions.

All the principals believed that their personal backgrounds influenced their school activities, and the observations mostly bore out these claims. For example, the democratic and egalitarian beliefs of one principal were consistent with the way in which he worked with school faculty. Dwyer et al. believe that such principal characteristics have implications for training because such knowledge could be used to match principals to schools that need specific types of leaders.

Principals' reports and the observations indicated that the community also had a significant effect on the behavior of principals. For example, one principal noted that he spent 60% of his time responding to situations that originated in the community. On the one hand, principals viewed their communities as constraining influences, or something that took time from tasks they would rather perform. However, principals also saw that the community could provide both materials and personnel, areas in which schools face serious shortages.

This study implies that institutional context both limits and provides opportunity for principals, and various administrators may react very differently to the same programs, pressures, and opportunities. In this study, principals' reactions to district-level programs varied most. Some principals were skeptical about including district goals and efforts in their school plans; other principals considered this procedure useful. Dwyer et al. found that the context of a large school (e.g., student turnover, funding cuts) often complicates the work of a school principal. However, this effect is mediated by the principal's characteristics.

In addition to principals' personality and training, situational factors also affected principals' behavior. For example, the two principals who were least obtrusive in instructional matters led faculties who had taught for 10 years or more. The more direct and intervening principals led less mature teacher faculties or ones in which more turnover occurred. Successfully leading stable, experienced teachers, then, may require different strategies than leading inexperienced teachers.

The observers reported that all five principals were active and that they were worn out after following the principals around during the day. (One wonders, however, if these principals are similar to most others.) The researchers state:

> These five principals also seemed to respond to daily cycles within their schools. First, they roam their buildings as children arrive, assessing potential problems and making sure classrooms are staffed and ready for the day. Next, they return to their offices for short-term planning, telephoning community leaders, and receiving the first round of student problems, which at this time of day are frequently related to situations in the students' homes. Then they move once again, to tour the building as recess begins, monitoring, solving problems, communicating with staff and students as they patrol. Between recesses and lunches, they commonly remain at large in the building observing classes, again talking with students and teachers as they move in and out of classrooms. Lunch periods and the hours following are frequently consumed by disciplinary problems which require interaction with students, teachers, or contacting parents with bad news. Dismissal at the end of the student day again brings these principals back to the hallways and public spaces of the building, where they admonish or praise, prompt or prohibit in rapid-fire encounters. The ensuing relative calm allows time for reflection and follow-up parent conferences, teacher conferences and staff or committee meetings of all sorts. (pp. 53–54)

These investigators suggest that daily activities enable the principal to assess how the school is functioning, to react to student misbehavior appropriately, and to suggest changes in teacher style or demonstrate new teaching styles to teachers. They speculate that the effects of these routine behaviors on the quality of instruction and on students' experiences can be substantial. In general, they found that all five principals had theories that guided their actions. All sought to understand how modifications in the structures of their schools influenced students, and all believed that their activities could and did affect how students learned.

Dwyer et al. contend that the study of these five principals produced a view of instructional leadership as accruing from routine, mundane acts related to the principals' perspectives on schooling. Furthermore, on the basis of their analyses, they argue that there are no simple ways to understand the effects of

principal behavior on schools and that more process studies are needed of principals' behavior.

This study and Wolcott's (1973) examination of one principal are the most intensive, comprehensive efforts made so far to describe in detail what principals do in their day-to-day activities. Because of their small sample sizes, however, these studies are more successful in raising issues than in resolving them. For example, the principals that Dwyer et al. studied had coherent visions of what a school should be, and they attempted to achieve these goals in their daily work. However, sampling characteristics probably made it likely that relatively more aggressive, active individuals were selected for the case studies (the five effective principals were selected largely because of their interest in the study). The energy the principals expended was impressive—they were *very active*. However, there are no data documenting that ineffective principals are less energetic and more reactive than proactive (it is too bad that average or relatively ineffective principals were not studied in this research).

Nevertheless, the Dwyer et al. study is an important initial examination of the principal's role through *observation*. At a minimum, their data suggest that there are different ways in which principals may be effective and that future research needs to examine simultaneously principals' personal beliefs, characteristics of the schools they serve (type of pupils, maturity of teaching staff), community and school district variables, and most importantly, how principals mediate conflicting sources of pressure. The work by Dwyer et al. is still in progress and as further analyses are completed and their findings are more integrated it may be possible to devise a more concrete, specific picture of the role of a relatively successful principal.

Principals in High- and Low-Achieving Schools

Brookover et al. (1979) conducted a less intensive study of four principals in two high-achieving and two low-achieving elementary schools. These researchers' major purpose was not to examine the principal's role in effective schools, but rather to determine if and how schools made a difference in student achievement (see earlier discussion of their work in this chapter).

Four case studies were completed in order to compare pairs of schools that had similar racial composition (two predominantly white; two predominantly black) and SES levels and were situated in comparable communities, but had different achievement levels (in each pair one school was comparatively high in achievement; the other school had a poor performance record). Achievement was measured by a school's mean score on the Michigan Assessment Test for 1974. Because schools within each pair were matched closely on demographic variables, it seems plausible to attribute differences in school achievement to social and process variables within schools.

Unfortunately, Brookover et al. do not describe the observational variables or procedures they used, so it is difficult to analyze their narrative reports. More information about the type of training observers received, the number and duration of observations, and so on would allow broader conclusions about the stability of the data reported. With this qualification in mind, the major findings concerning the principal's role in each school are discussed below.

The principal in the high-achieving, largely white school indicated that his primary concern was student achievement. He organized his work so that an assistant completed most of the administrative paperwork, leaving the principal time for instructional supervision. The principal's emphasis on instruction was perhaps best demonstrated by the announcement at a staff meeting that he intended to observe every teacher at least 30 times (as he had done the year before). He encouraged teachers to participate actively in inservice meetings and to discuss with him ways to improve the school. Furthermore, he wanted them to ask him for instructional advice. The researchers report that some of the teachers, especially the older ones, preferred that the principal be primarily a disciplinarian and spend less time on classroom activities. Still, all teachers seemed to respect the principal and to recognize and appreciate his interest in student achievement.

The principal in the high-achieving, largely black school was primarily an effective administrator who kept good records. He supported teachers and encouraged them to improve their instruction by attending inservice programs. Teachers in the school, however, attributed the school's effectiveness to a principal at the school 4 years earlier who had been an instructional as well as an administrative leader. For example, the former principal often led inservice training instead of merely encouraging teachers to attend. Still, the current principal periodically observed and critiqued teachers' classroom instruction; however, he believed that the primary responsibility for the quality of education in the school rested with the teachers.

The principal in the low-achieving, largely white school was the administrator of two schools and hence was only in this school on alternate mornings and afternoons. He viewed his major responsibility as dealing with problem students, and there appeared to be little interaction between the principal and the teaching staff. He spent much of his time compiling files on students with behavior problems and working with these students and their parents to solve these problems. The principal held low performance expectation for students. Furthermore, he rarely observed in classrooms, spent much time in the public areas of the school, or visited with teachers or students. In short, this administrator offered virtually no academic leadership.

The principal in the low-achieving, primarily black school served mainly as an administrator and disciplinarian. However, unlike the principal in the low-achieving, primarily white school, she was not aloof from teachers; indeed, she interacted frequently with the staff and spent much time in the teachers' lounge. At the same time, this principal had low expectations for most students. Although she expressed interest in students' achievement, she spent little time observing or critiquing teachers, and did not seem to expect a high level of teacher performance. Perhaps the most telling evidence of her lack of instructional leadership was the fact that the assistant principal was primarily responsible for observing teachers and keeping academic records, but had no power to effect change.

Results of the Dwyer et al. and Brookover et al. studies indicate that some relationship exists between the principal's role expectations and student performance. Perhaps the best way to express this relationship is that appropriate expectations on the part of a principal that students can and will learn the curriculum are necessary, but not sufficient, for effective teaching and learning to occur in a school. In addition, principals must be aware of and concerned about classroom instruction. Although it may not be necessary that principals assume direct leadership of the instructional program (e.g., Gersten, Carnine, & Green, 1982), at a minimum, they must make certain that teachers obtain information about their classroom teaching and feedback about the adequacy of their instruction.

Policy Implications of Principal Effectiveness Research

Although we have focused on two studies because of their attention to process measures, other recent studies also examine principal behavior. Indeed, Manassee (1985) reviews research on principal effectiveness and comments on the policy implications of such work. She notes that recent research (e.g., Martin & Willower, 1981; Morris & Crowson, 1981; Pitner, 1982) provides a useful description of the day-to-day behavior of principals. It is clear from her review that principals' administrative work often includes tasks that are: initiated by others, of short duration, frequently interrupted, and done in face-to-face interaction (e.g., little written communication). Considering this environment, it is little wonder that principals develop a preference for dealing with concrete, immediate, and potentially solvable problems (e.g., discussing the agenda for tonight's PTA meeting over more distant goals and more problematic activities (e.g., trying to understand the quality of teacher or student interactions). Manassee argues convincingly that the policy imperative of recent research is the need to prepare principals for their fragmented, varied, and ambiguous role and to help them develop analytical, communicative, and instructional skills in order to provide more effective leadership.

Future Research on the Principalship

Although recent studies of principals (e.g., Manassee, 1985) and their effects on teachers and students are encouraging (recent studies have started to examine what principals do), researchers have not examined many important aspects of the principal's role.

Context

It may be that a different type of principal is needed to *improve* a school's achievement than to *maintain* an already adequate school achievement record. More information is needed about the principal's role in different types of schools and about the duties of the principal in reaching goals other than those associated with basic academic achievement.

Assignment of Students and Teachers

How principals assign students to classrooms likely has a significant effect on what can be accomplished in a classroom or at a grade level within a school. Unfortunately, this variable and related student composition issues (e.g., How many honors sections will there be in a particular subject?) have been poorly defined and seldom studied systematically.

There is empirical evidence that classroom composition (the mean and range of students present in a class) affects student achievement. For example, Beckerman and Good (1981) studied the ratio of high- and low-achieving students in classrooms from a large metropolitan school district that served a middle-class population. They defined classrooms with *more favorable* teaching situations as those in which more than a third of the students were high aptitude and less than a third were low aptitude. *Less favorable* classrooms were those in which less than a third of the students were high aptitude and more than a third were low aptitude.

Beckerman and Good found that both low- and high-aptitude students in favorable classrooms had higher achievement scores than the two groups in unfavorable classrooms. Veldman and Sanford (1982) also found evidence that classroom composition is associated with student achievement. They measured classroom composition in nine junior high schools by determining the mean achievement level for each class at the beginning of the year. They found significant interaction effects, indicating that both high- and low-ability pupils do better in high-ability classes and that the effects of class ability are more pronounced with low-ability students.

Others, too, have recently explored the context effects of mean classroom ability and degree of heterogeneity on classroom outcomes. For example, Evertson, Sanford, and Emmer (1981) found that heterogeneity in students' entering achievement levels restricts classroom teachers' ability to adapt instruction to individual students' academic and affective needs. High heterogeneity was also associated with a lesser degree of student task engagement and cooperation. Leiter (1983) found, as did Beckerman and Good (1981), that students receiving instruction with high-ability classmates made substantially higher mathematics gains than did those with low-ability classmates. However, this effect did not hold in reading. Rowan and Miracle (1983) explored the effects of ability grouping on the achievement of fourth grade students in a single urban school district. They found that both within-classroom grouping for reading instruction and across-classroom ability grouping had direct effects on reading achievement, and demonstrated that ability grouping tends to reinforce initial inequalities. (However, certain aspects of within-classroom grouping had favorable effects for students in the low group.)

Dreeban and Barr (1983) demonstrated that assignment of students to classes can affect how teachers organize classes for instruction. In a study of 15 first grade classes, they found that in small classes (of about 20) with few low-aptitude students, teachers began with whole-class instruction and later reorganized classes into heterogeneous groups. Large classes (with 30 or more members) differed, both in their initial grouping arrangements and in subsequent modifications, according to the number of low-aptitude students they contained. Teachers who had fewer low-aptitude students employed a wider variety of group arrangements. Teachers with many low-aptitude students inevitably created a large low group as part of a classroom figuration consisting of three groups of equal size. The mean aptitude level of each group was the major influence on the critical instructional decision of how much material to cover over a given period of time—the pace of instruction—which in turn was a major determinant of individual learning.

It is clear that placement in a class or group with less capable students makes it more difficult for a given student to make educational progress than placement with more capable students does. Yet grouping by ability or achievement level probably is necessary under certain circumstances. The assignment of students to classes is a very important issue, though this topic has received little research attention.

Principal's Role in Assignment of Students to Classes

Although extant research has not achieved any systematic understanding of which principal beliefs lead to the assignment of students to more and less favorable classes, anecdotal evidence indicates that principals' beliefs about classroom learning are associated with their actual assignment of pupils to classes.

For example, Good and Marshall (1984) note that because of declining student enrollment in some American schools, students are grouped across grade levels in order to have sufficient numbers of students for a class. It is likely that some principals' grouping of students is influenced more by organizational or institutional needs than by concern about how best to educate students.

One of the authors observed the effects of such decision making on the school lives of some students in a small school serving a diverse population. There were enough second and third grade students to justify the formation of three classes (one mixed, one second grade, and one third grade). In this particular case, the principal decided to form the mixed class on the basis of student *maturity* (capacity to work independently) as opposed to *ability*.

The principal wanted mature third and second grade students in one classroom so that one group could work independently while the teacher worked with the other group. Had the principal formed classes according to ability, there probably would have been more pressure on the teacher to use whole-class and large-group teaching. Had the principal used more dynamic individual characteristics (sociability, works well in groups), or stressed a more social outcome (learn to work well with others who are diverse), the teacher might have made greater attempts to have second and third grade students interact.

In this case, the independent worker model and the demand characteristics communicated to the teacher by such a grouping virtually guaranteed that the teacher would instruct the second and third grade students as separate, *intact* groups (without much social or academic contact between groups), and that comparatively little social interaction would be allowed *within* groups because group work was institutionalized as individual work.

This class contained 16 second and third grade students. The four third grade girls appeared to be socially isolated, in part because of peer expectations (i.e., social interaction occurs with same-sex, same-age classmates and the teacher did little to alter this peer norm), and in part because the girls were from diverse backgrounds.

This example clearly illustrates the need to study a variety of variables if classroom life is to be understood more fully. It is likely that the principal's decision about how to assign students was influenced to some extent by his perception of the teacher's style and ability, and that the teacher's classroom strategies were influenced by her assumptions about the principal's motivation in assigning this particular composition of students. Another teacher or a different four girls might have led to different consequences.

The assignment of students to classes in secondary schools is also an important consideration. For example, in creating homerooms should a principal in a junior high or middle school with four to six feeder schools deliberately mix students from different elementary schools? What are the consequences of being an "outsider" assigned to a homeroom where most students are from the same elementary school (e.g., What are one's chances of being elected to office)? If all band members miss first-period classes, or if foreign language is taught only in the second and third periods, what consequences does this have for the composition of other classes (i.e., Does it make some easier to teach than others?). If a high school principal decides to have an honors section of mathematics, what effects does this have on instruction in other math classes? If students are assigned to sections on the basis of ability in high schools, which teachers should teach high and low sections?

Considering that well-qualified teachers in some areas (e.g., math and science) are scarce at many schools, how should these teachers be utilized? Should they teach half of the time and spend the other half working with other teachers? Should they teach beginning or advanced sections? Atkin (1983) notes that researchers have neglected the question of how truly talented and well-trained teachers should be assigned and deployed. Unfortunately, there is little information about strategies that principals use to assign teachers and students to classes or about the consequences of those strategies.

Feedback to Individual Teachers

Researchers should also examine how principals influence instructional behavior in their schools. How do they communicate expectations and establish instructional priorities? If principals encourage teachers to determine their own instructional goals, how do they become aware of each teacher's goals, and how do they monitor and provide feedback about progress? Dwyer et al. (1982) provide a helpful profile that characterizes effective principals as being *more active.* Considering that effective principals are more visible to teachers and students in their schools, it is important to know if the *quality* of their decisions and actions can be related to student progress. For example, when and how often do principals visit particular classrooms? Do successful principals spend more time with teachers they believe to be average teachers, or do they observe less capable teachers more closely? How specific is the feedback they provide to teachers? On what topics do conferences focus? Do more effective principals discuss issues of curriculum and instruction, or do they talk only about general issues of classroom management, resources, and human relations?

Because of our past interest in teacher expectation research, we have a special curiosity about principals' communication of low expectations to certain teachers. Just as some teachers expect too little from certain pupils, some principals likely expect too little from certain teachers. It would be valuable to study how principals communicate expectations to teachers (e.g., the classes or students assigned to a teacher, the committees or duties assigned, the way requests for supplies are handled, the frequency and degree of formality of observational visits, etc.) and to determine how principals vary in their ability to communicate in positive and helpful ways with teachers.

In the 1970s and early 1980s, useful literature for describing teacher planning and thinking has developed (see Clark & Peterson, this volume; Shavelson, 1983). Hopefully, the 1980s will see the development of more systematic knowledge about principals' decision making and behavior. We have discussed but two of the many areas that future research could contribute to. Needed are more detailed studies of what principals do, an understanding of why principals act as they do, and the apparent effects of their beliefs and behaviors. Research thus far indicates that effective principals are more proactive (although many aspects of proactive behavior have not been examined, e.g., Do more successful principals watch teachers teach before hiring them?) and visible, although more research is needed to validate this viewpoint.

A Synthesis of Research on Effective Schools

Nearly all studies of effective schools support the importance of principal leadership. There is far less consensus, however, on the behaviors and practices that characterize leadership on a day-to-day basis. Ironically, while principals tend to rank instructional leadership as their most important function, available evidence suggests that they have little time or opportunity to provide such leadership (Howell, 1981; McLeary & Thompson, 1979).

Rather, as Cohen (1983) notes, the work of principals is characterized by ambiguous and conflicting expectations, frequent interruptions, and crises. Principals tend to engage in short tasks or brief interactions, often as many as several hundred per day. Their interactions tend to be personal and problem centered (Morris, Crowson, Hurwitz, & Porter-Gehrie, 1981; Wolcott, 1973). Further, Salley, McPherson, and Baehr (1979) describe principals as captives of their environments, strongly influenced by the structure and organization of the school and the school district.

How, then, do principals affect school achievement? First, their goal orientation is especially important (Bossert, Dwyer, Rowan, & Lee, 1982; Greenfield, 1982). Cohen (1983) argues that effective principals emphasize achievement, set instructional goals, develop performance standards for students, and express optimism about the ability of students to meet instructional goals. He notes that, not surprisingly, in light of the inherent constraints of the role, effective principals need to be proactive, to develop and articulate a vision of the school and its future, and to project that vision in the course of numerous daily interactions with teachers (Blumberg & Greenfield, 1980; Little, 1981a, 1981b, 1982).

Compared with less effective principals, effective principals tend to take responsibility for instruction, observe teachers regularly, and discuss their work problems. It is clear that some principals have little awareness of what takes place in the classroom, so that there often are large discrepancies between recommended district policy and actual classroom practice (see, for example, Ebmeier & Ziomek, 1983). Principals can promote effective teaching by creating the conditions that enable it to occur, and by preventing or limiting intrusions once it is underway.

Cohen suggests that although it is possible to describe some of the things that principals do to contribute to instructional effectiveness, it is clear that research does *not* tell us that all effective principals engage in all of these activities, nor does it yet tell us about the conditions under which certain strategies are likely to be more or less appropriate or effective. To date, only a vague outline of a rather complex picture has emerged, and much more research needs to be done to complete the picture (see also Little, 1982). Principals must do more than provide the instructional leadership; their ability to create shared *values* and *culture* is also important. Presumably, principals in effective schools generate a strong sense of community, with commonly shared goals and high expectations for student and staff performance. Cohen notes that community in a school requires more than shared instrumental goals; it requires the creation of a moral order that entails respect for authority, genuine and pervasive caring about individuals, respect for their feelings and attitudes, mutual trust, and the consistent enforcement of norms that define and delimit acceptable behavior (see also Grant, 1982). The importance of a shared moral order should not be underestimated, because schools are fragile social institutions easily disrupted by conflict in or around them. For example, there are weak formal controls over the selection of staff, and students are involuntary clientele of the school.

Cohen argues that student and faculty norms and school "ethos" can be shaped by principals and teachers, as well as by several structural features of schools. One feature, building-level autonomy, refers to the view that circumstances among schools, even within a single district, vary considerably. Schools differ in their mix of students and staff; the characteristics of the communities they serve; the histories of their attempts at innovation and improvements; the prevailing norms, beliefs, and shared understandings; and the problems they face. From this point of view, attempts at instructional improvement will be successful only to the extent that schools are given sufficient latitude to adapt new policies or practices to their unique circumstances or to develop their own solutions to problems.

A second structural feature involves procedures for assigning students to schools. Cohen notes that the advantage some private schools appear to have in terms of creating appropriate climates may result from their procedures for recruiting new students. However, as we argued earlier in the chapter, how a principal assigns students to individual classes influences what can and does take place in the classroom.

A third structural feature of schools suggested by findings of research on school culture relates to the quantity and organization of time in schools. Simply put, shared work and collective decision making require time for teachers to talk with each other, to observe each other's classrooms, and to plan and evaluate programs. Cohen points out that policies that lengthen the school day or year could be used to free groups of teachers from classroom responsibilities during part of the school day in order to create additional time for planning and shared work.

In his conclusion, Cohen states that effective schools have become so by making headway in solving several problems that are rooted in the structure of educational organizations and the teaching profession. First, because students are involuntary clientele who bring conflicting goals to school, there needs to be a relationship of warmth and trust between teachers and students. Teachers in effective schools apparently are able to bring about the feeling in students that school achievement norms are legitimate.

Second, by their very structure, schools serve multiple social functions that compete with their instructional mission. Additionally, over the past several decades, the range of social concerns that schools have been asked to address has increased considerably. Consequently, schools are seen as having diffuse goals and little cohesion (Good et al., 1975). Effective schools, however, have been able to assert the primacy of their instructional mission around a limited set of goals, and in ways that direct and focus the allocation of resources, operating procedures and practices, and the behavior of teachers and students. The means for improving teaching effectiveness have therefore been quite limited, for without the knowledge to relate means to ends, choosing the most productive among alternative practices is difficult.

Cohen believes that the quality of research conducted over the past decade has changed this condition considerably. Practices for motivating, instructing, and controlling students in classrooms are better understood. There is now a sizeable knowledge base describing teaching practices that can be related to student learning (see Brophy & Good and Rosenshine & Stevens, this volume). Although there is still much that is not understood about teaching, the important point is that what is known is also used in effective schools, so that the technology becomes more explicit and precise, and choices about alternative practices are made more knowledgeable.

Finally, teaching is a profession in which work is typically performed in isolation from one's colleagues. Cohen suggests that this isolation has several undesirable consequences, including the limited codification of successful practices and a tendency for teachers to treat uncertainties inherent in the role as personal, rather than collective, problems. By developing collegial working relationships, effective schools tend to alleviate this problem and its consequences, and teaching becomes shared work. Teachers can thus learn from one another as well as distinguish limitations inherent in the profession itself from those related to an individual teacher's capabilities. The result is both improved teaching practices and enhanced professional self-esteem.

Summary

Prior to the mid-1960s there had been relatively little observational research that examined schooling in America. The publication of the Coleman et al. report (1966) initiated a flurry of input-output studies that attempted to examine whether school resources (e.g., the ratio of adults to children; the number of books in the library) were associated with student outcomes (typically performance on standardized achievement tests). These studies generally did not show any consistent relationship between resources and student outcomes (Averch et al., 1974).

This chapter focused on the generation of studies that followed the input-output efforts and examined studies that include measures of school process as well as school input (quality of student body or teacher staff; school resources) and school outcomes. The latter research yields findings different from those of input-output studies. First, it appears that processes associated with individual schools are related to student achievement, and suggests mechanisms through which some schools obtain more achievement than do other schools that have similar inputs. A second major finding is that some processes consistently characterize more and less successful schools. Although studies can be faulted because of methodological problems, the fact that several studies reach similar conclusions lends credibility to the claim that certain processes are associated with school effects on achievement.

Despite this consensus, however, school effects data are limited in several respects. First, most effective schools research has been conducted in urban schools, so its application to suburban schools is unknown. Second, the description of effective schools is based largely on their effectiveness in obtaining high student performance on standardized achievement tests. This is a narrow definition of school effectiveness. Although there is some evidence that schools can simultaneously achieve several goals (e.g., high attendance rates, high student engagement rates, high achievement), for the most part the question of school success on cognitive criteria other than standardized achievement (e.g., decision-making skills) has been ignored. There is no evidence that schools that teach the basic skills relatively well can also teach computer skills, science, and writing relatively well. Furthermore, process measures usually have been limited to a few global dimensions of schooling, and these examine *form* more than *quality*. Often, data are collected on only a few teachers per school, and the information about what even these teachers do is sketchy.

Future research on effective schools could better conceptualize and study school-level processes. For example, certain school practices and school-wide beliefs may make it more likely that teachers will order and use scientific equipment or take students on field trips. Rowe (1983) argues that insurance, permission, and supervision issues associated with field trips and red tape and safety considerations necessary when ordering, maintaining, and using laboratory equipment restrict teachers' use of field trips and laboratory work. It is also possible that in some schools certain administrative practices or beliefs about normative practice (the importance and necessity of lab work) may affect the frequency with which teachers take field trips and use laboratory equipment. If so, how and why are these administrative practices and beliefs created, and what maintains them?

Researchers might also ask whether in some schools it is easier for teachers to receive relevant feedback about their classroom performance from the principal or peers. Why do teachers in some schools receive more frequent and meaningful feedback about their instructional program, its consequences, and possible alternative courses of action than teachers in other schools? If in some schools teachers use other teachers more frequently as resources, what are the normative belief structures and administrative practices of those schools, how did they develop, and how are they maintained?

There is some research relevant to the issue of teachers receiving meaningful feedback about their classroom teaching (see e.g., Little, 1981b) and limited information about normative belief structures that operate in certain schools. Our point here, however, is that most effective schools research has not examined the school as a unit nor has process research been organized in order to explore issues related to the school as a unit. Research in other areas has examined the school as a unit (e.g., Metz, 1978). What we need now is an integration of such thinking and conceptualization into the effective schools research.

Another major constraint on effective schools research is that existing evidence is largely correlational. Whether active leadership precedes or follows the development of high expectations or whether student achievement precedes or follows high expectations for performance is uncertain. Still, there is growing evidence that the effective schools literature can be *translated* into practices that improve student achievement. However, as we note in this chapter, this translation often goes far beyond what the literature indicates. As a case in point, most school improvement research advocates a written and formally agreed upon (by the school staff) plan for school improvement. Correlational research provides limited evidence that teachers and administrators have more of a sense of direction and a shared consensus about what is important in high-achieving schools than in schools where achievement gains are low. It is not entirely clear whether or not a formal school plan is equivalent to the consensus and direction reached by a teaching staff through informal dialogue and day-to-day communication built up over time. A school plan is not necessarily wrong or inappropriate, but under certain conditions, a plan may force too many accommodations and achieve only superficial compliance. Here we emphasize that correlational data must be translated into practice carefully. Extant data do not indicate that one should start with a school plan (perhaps the chance to observe other science teachers or to visit other schools, for example, should precede attempts to develop a related plan). One of our qualifications for school-wide change is that school plans should be constructed so that the initiative, autonomy, and responsibility of individual teachers are preserved (the opportunity to make decisions about classroom events is one of the few things that makes teaching attractive for some teachers). Plans should also attend to the development of individual teachers (e.g., Good & Brophy, 1984; Spencer-Hall, 1984). Given extant enthusiasm in some places for master teacher plans and merit pay, and in other places for effective schools, it seems important to try to balance these two objectives.

Although it is not the focus of this chapter, there is a growing literature on organizational theory and the change process in schools, and even some useful attempts to order and apply this literature for practitioners interested in improving schools (see Fullan, in press; Purkey & Smith, 1983b). Also, the school improvement efforts currently underway will provide clues about more and less desirable ways to translate extant research, as will the emerging literature that describes the behavior of school principals (Dwyer et al., 1982).

However, we need better *process* studies of school improvement implementation if we are to understand why some school improvement plans work when apparently similar plans fail. We also need more systematic attempts to develop theoretical explanations (see Biddle & Anderson, this volume), and more basic research on other important outcomes of schooling. Although the experimentation now underway is useful, enthusiasm for application should not undermine attempts to investigate broader definitions of schooling. Research findings presently available *do not provide statements about effective schools*. The literature does yield statements about factors associated with raising students' performance on standardized achievement tests. Information about such effects is a useful step forward if educators keep in mind that extant information about effective schools cannot be equated with effective schooling.

Ironically, in the past few months a number of national commissions have examined the state of American schooling. Many of their reports recommend mechanical solutions to complex educational problems. For example, the National Commission on Excellence in Education called for longer school days. However, one wonders how more time ipso facto can improve teaching and learning in American schools. Although reports like *A Nation at Risk* have been enormously successful in generating public interest — and potentially public support — for education, they have also shifted the debate on schooling from issues of quality (what teachers and students do in classrooms to allow for understanding and application of important knowledge) to the search for standard and immediate answers (more graduation requirements). As Bossert (1983), Hall (1983), and Slavin (1983) have argued (in response to *A Nation at Risk*), issues of *quality* must be addressed if we are to improve schooling.

In this chapter we have argued that school officials need to be careful and to avoid overapplying school effects research. However, this research should not be ignored, as some policy advocates have done. It is clear that schools, even good schools, differ in subtle and important ways (Lightfoot, 1983). Calls for a longer school day in all schools because some schools need more time is a silly and costly educational prescription that will do as much harm as good.

Although certain aspects of the school effects literature may help practitioners to identify their problems and alternatives and thus allow them to think more systematically about their instructional programs, this research does not yield answers. The past decade has been an important start. The research completed to date shows that individual school variance is an important dimension that can be influenced by selected actions and resources. Despite this progress, the next step does not involve application. Rather, it requires further extending the basic knowledge in this field by completing new studies that help us to understand more the fully qualitative aspects of schooling.

REFERENCES

Armor, D., Conry-Oseguera, P., Cox, M., King, N., McDonnell, L., Pascal, A., Pauly, E., & Zellman, G. (1976). *Analysis of the school preferred reading program in selected Los Angeles minority schools.* Santa Monica, CA: Rand Corporation.

Atkin, J. M. (1983). The improvement of science teaching. *Daedalus, 112*(2), 167–187.

Austin, G. R. (1978). *Process evaluation: A comprehensive study of outliers.* Baltimore: Maryland Department of Education.

Averch, H. A., Carroll, S. J., Donaldson, T. S., Kiesling, H. J., & Pincus, J. (1974). *How effective is schooling? A critical review of research.* Santa Monica, CA: Rand Corporation.

Beckerman, T. M., & Good, T. L. (1981). The classroom ratio of high- and low-aptitude students and its effect on achievement. *American Educational Research Journal, 18*, 3, 317–327.

Berliner, D. (1977). Impediments to measuring teacher effectiveness. In G. Borich (Ed.), *The appraisal of teaching.* Reading, MA: Addision-Wesley.

Berliner, D. (1979). Tempus educare. In P. L. Peterson and H. J. Walberg (Eds.), *Research on teaching: Concepts, findings and implications.* Berkeley, CA: McCutchan.

Biddle, B. J. (1970). The institutional context. In W. Campbell (Ed.), *Scholars in context: The effects of environments on learning.* New York: John Wiley.

Bidwell, C. E., & Kasarda, J. D. (1980). Conceptualizing and measuring the effects of school and schooling. *American Journal of Education, 88*, 401–430.

Blumberg, A., & Greenfield, W. (1980). *The effective principal: Perspectives on school leadership.* Boston: Allyn & Bacon.

Bossert, S. T. (1983). New nostolgia. *Elementary School Journal, 84*(2), 138–141.

Bossert, S. T., Dwyer, D. C., Rowan, B., & Lee, G. V. (1982). The instructional management role of the principal. *Educational Administration Quarterly, 18*, 34–64.

Brimer, A., Madaus, G. F., Chapman, B., Kellaghan, T., and Wood, R. (1978). *Source of differences in school achievement.* Slough, Bucks, England: NFER.

Brookover, W. D., Beady, C., Flood, P., Schweitzer, J., & Wisenbaker, J. (1979). *School social systems and student achievement: Schools can make a difference.* New York: Praeger.

Brookover, W. B., Erickson, E., & Joiner, M. (1967). *Self-concept of ability and school achievement III* (Cooperative Research Project No. 2831). East Lansing: Michigan State University, College of Education.

Brookover, W. B., Lapere, J., Hamachek, D., Thomas, S., & Erickson, E. (1965). *Self-concept of ability and school achievement II* (Cooperative Research Project No. 1636). East Lansing: Michigan State University, College of Education.

Brookover, W. B., & Lezotte, L. W. (1979). *Changes in school characteristics coincident with changes in student achievement.* East Lansing: Michigan State University, Institute for Research on Teaching. (ERIC Document Reproduction Service No. ED 181 005).

Brookover, W. B., Paterson, A., & Thomas, S. (1962). *Self-concept of ability and school achievement* (Cooperative Research Project No. 485). East Lansing: Michigan State University, College of Education.

Brookover, W. B., & Schneider, J. M. (1975). Academic environments and elementary school achievement. *Journal of Research and Development in Education, 9*, 82–91.

California State Department of Education. (1977). *School effectiveness study: The first year.* Sacramento, CA: Office of Program Evaluation and Research.

California State Department of Education. (1980). *Report of the special studies of selected ECE schools with increasing and decreasing reading scores.* Sacramento, CA: Office of Program Evaluation and Research.

Clark, T. A., & McCarthy, D. P. (1983). School improvement in New York City: The evolution of a project. *Educational Researcher, 12*(4), 17–24.

Cohen, M. (1983). Instructional, management and social conditions in effective schools. In A. O. Webb and L. D. Webb (Eds.), *School finance and school improvement: Linkages in the 1980's.* Cambridge, MA: Ballinger.

Coleman, J., Campbell, E., Hobson, C., McPartland, J., Mood, A., Weinfield, F., & York, R. (1966). *Equality of educational opportunity.* Washington, DC: U.S. Government Printing Office.

Cooper, H. M., & Good, T. L. (1983). *Pygmalion grows up.* New York: Longman.

Cuban, L. (1983). Effective schools: A friendly but cautionary note. *Phi Delta Kappan, 64*(10), 695–696.

Cusick, P. (1983). *The egalitarian school and the American high school.* New York: Longman.

Doss, D., & Holley, F. (1982). *A cause for national pause: Title I schoolwide projects* (ORE Publication No. 81.55). Austin, TX: Austin Independent School District, Office of Research and Evaluation.

Dreeban, R., & Barr, R. (1983). Educational policy and the working of schools. In L. Shulman and G. Sykes (Eds.), *Handbook of teaching and policy.* New York: Longman.

Dwyer, D. C., Lee, G. V., Rowan, B., & Bossert, S. T. (1982). *The principal's role in instructional management: Five participant observation studies of principals in action.* San Francisco: Far West Laboratory.

Ebmeier, H. H., & Ziomek, R. L. (1983). *Student academic engagement rates* (Final report). Washington, DC: National Institute of Education.

Edmonds, R. R. (1979). Effective schools for the urban poor. *Educational Leadership, 1979, 37,* 15–27.

Edmonds, R. R. (1982). [Working paper]. East Lansing: Michigan State University, Center for School Improvement.

Edmonds, R. R. (1983). *Search for effective schools: The identification and analysis of city schools that are instructionally effective for poor children* (Unpublished final report). East Lansing: Michigan State University.

Eubanks, E. E., & Levine, D. U. (1983). A first look at effective schools projects in New York City and Milwaukee. *Phi Delta Kappan, 64*(10) 697–702.

Evertson, C. M., Sanford, J. P., & Emmer, E. T. (1981). Effects of class heterogeneity in junior high school. *American Educational Research Journal, 18*(2), 219–232.

Finn, C. (1983, June). *Toward strategic independence: Policy considerations for enhancing school effectiveness* (Final report, Grant NIE 400-79-0035). Washington, DC: National Institute of Education.

Forsythe, R. A. (1973). Some empirical results related to the stability of performance indicators in Dyer's student change model of an educational system. *Journal of Educational Measurement, 10,* 7–12.

Freeman, D. J., Kuhs, T. M., Porter, A. C., Floden, R. E., Schmidt, W. H., & Schwille, J. R. (1983). Do textbooks and tests define a national curriculum in elementary school mathematics? *Elementary School Journal, 83,* 501–513.

Fullan, M. (1985). Change processes and strategies at the local level. *Elementary School Journal, 85,* (3), 391–422.

Gall, M., Fielding, G., Schalock, D., Charters, W., & Wiczinski, J. (1984). Involving the principal in teachers' staff development: Effects on the quality of mathematics instruction in elementary schools. Eugene OR: Center for Educational Policy and Management, University of Oregon.

Gersten, R., Carnine, D., & Green, S. (1982, March). *Administrative and supervisory support functions for the implementation of effective educational programs for low income students.* Paper presented at the annual meeting of the American Educational Research Association, New York.

Glaser, B., & Strauss, A. (1967). *The discovery of grounded theory.* Chicago: Aldine.

Glenn, B. C. (1981). *What works? An examination of effective schools for poor black children.* Cambridge, MA: Harvard University, Center for Law and Education.

Good, T. L., Biddle, B. J., & Brophy, J. E. (1975). *Teachers make a difference.* New York: Holt, Rinehart & Winston.

Good, T. L., Biddle, B. J., & Brophy, J. E. (1983). *Teaching effectiveness: Research findings and policy implications* (Tech. Rep. No. 319).

Columbia: University of Missouri, Center for Research in Social Behavior.

Good, T. L., & Brophy, J. E. (1984). *Looking in classrooms* (3rd ed.). New York: Harper & Row.

Good, T. L., Grouws, D. A., & Ebmeier, H. H. (1983). *Active mathematics teaching.* New York: Longman.

Good, T. L., & Marshall, S. (1984). Do students learn more in heterogeneous or homogeneous groups? In P. Peterson & L. Cherry-Wilkinson (Eds.), *Student diversity in the organization processes.* New York: Academic Press.

Goodlad, J. (1983). *A place called school: Prospects for the future.* New York: McGraw–Hill.

Grant, G. (1982). *Education, character and American schools: Are effective schools good enough?* Syracuse, NY: Syracuse University.

Greenfield, W. D. (1982). *A synopsis of research on school principals.* Washington, DC: National Institute of Education.

Hall, G. E., Hord, S. M., Huling, L. L., Rutherford, W. L., & Stiegelbauer, S. M. (1983). *Leadership variables associated with successful school improvement.* Paper presented at the annual meeting, American Educational Research Association, Montreal.

Hall, P. M. (1983). A social construction of reality. *Elementary School Journal, 84*(2), 142–148.

Hall, P. M., & Spencer-Hall, D. A. (1980, June). *Conditions and processes of problem identification, definition, and resolution in two school systems: Toward a grounded theory* (Final report, Grant NIE-G-78-0042). Washington, DC: National Institute of Education.

Hanushek, E. (1970, December). *The value of teachers in teaching* (RM-6362-CC/RC). Santa Monica: Rand Corporation.

Heyneman, S., & Loxley, W. (1983). The effect of primary school quality on academic achievement across twenty-nine high- and low-income countries. *American Journal of Sociology, 88,* 1162–1194.

Howell, B. (1981). Profile of the principalship. *Educational Leadership, 38*(4), 333–336.

Hunter, M. G. (1979). *Final report of the Michigan cost-effectiveness study.* East Lansing: Michigan Department of Education.

Jackson, P. W. (1981a). Comprehending a well-run comprehensive school: A report on a visit to a large suburban high school. *Daedalus* (Special issue: America's Schools), *110*(4), 81–95.

Jackson, P. W. (1981b). Secondary schooling for children of the poor. *Daedalus* (Special issue: America's Schools), *110*(4), 39–57.

Jencks, C. S., Smith, M., Ackland, H., Bane, M. J., Cohen, D., Gintis, H., Heyns, B., & Michelson, S. (1972). *Inequality: A reassessment of the effect of family and schooling in America.* New York: Basic Books.

Klitgaard, R. E., & Hall, G. R. (1974). Are there unusually effective schools? *Journal of Human Resources, 74,* 90–106.

Kounin, J. S. (1970). *Discipline and group management in classrooms.* New York: Holt, Rinehart & Winston.

Leiter, J. (1983). Classroom composition and achievement gains. *Sociology of Education, 56,* 126–132.

Levine, D. U., & Stark, J. (1981, August). *Extended summary and conclusions: Institutional and organizational arrangements and processes for improving academic achievement at inner city elementary schools.* Kansas City: University of Missouri, Center for the Study of Metropolitan Problems in Education.

Lezotte, L. W., Edmonds, R., & Ratner, G. (1974). *A final report: Remedy for school failure to equitably basic school skills.* East Lansing: Michigan State University, Department of Urban and Metropolitan Studies.

Lightfoot, S. L. (1983). *The good high school: Portraits of character and culture.* New York: Basic Books.

Lightfoot, S. L. (1981a). Portraits of exemplary secondary schools: Highland Park. *Daedalus* (Special issue: America's Schools), *110*(4), 59–80.

Lightfoot, S. L. (1981b). Portraits of exemplary secondary schools: George Washington Carver comprehensive high school. *Daedalus* (Special issue: America's Schools), *110*(4), 17–37.

Lightfoot, S. L. (1978). *Worlds apart: Relationships between families and schools.* New York: Basic Books.

Little, J. W. (1981a, January). *School success and staff development: The role of staff development in urban desegregated schools* (Final report). Washington, DC: National Institute of Education.

Little, J. W. (1981b, April). *School success and staff development in urban desegregated schools: A summary of recently completed research.* Paper presented at the annual meeting of the American Educational Research Association, Los Angeles.

Little, J. W. (1982). The effective principal. *American Education, 18*(7),38–43.

Madaus, G. F., Kelleghan, T., Rakow, E. A., & King, D. J. (1979). The sensitivity of measures of school effectiveness. *Harvard Educational Review, 49,* 207–230.

Manassee, A. L. (1985). Improving conditions for principal effectiveness: Policy implications of research. *Elementary School Journal, 85,* 439–463.

Marco, G. L. (1974). A comparison of selected school effectiveness measures based on longitudinal data. *Journal of Educational Measurement, 11,* 225–234.

Martin, W., & Willower, D. (1981). The managerial behavior of high school principals. *Educational Administration Quarterly, 17,* Winter.

McCarthy, D. P., Canner, J., & Pershing, A. (1983). *Local school development project: Third annual process evaluation.* New York: Office of Educational Evaluation.

McCormack-Larkin, M., & Kritek, W. J. (1983). Milwaukee's project RISE. *Educational Leadership, 40,* 16–21.

McLeary, L. E., & Thompson, S. D. (1979). *The senior high school principalship* (Vol. 3: Summary report). Reston, VA: National Association of Secondary School Principals.

Metz, M. (1978). *Classrooms and corridors: The crisis of authority in desegregated secondary schools.* Berkeley: University of California Press.

Michigan Department of Education. (n.d.). *Questions and answers about Michigan Educational Assessment.* Lansing: Michigan Department of Education.

Miller, J. D. (1983). Scientific literacy: A conceptual and empirical review. *Daedalus, 112*(2), 29–48.

Morris, V., & Crowson, R. (1981). *The principal and instructional management.* Paper prepared for Instructional Management Program, San Francisco Far West Laboratory.

Morris, V. C., Crowson, R. L., Hurwitz, E., & Porter-Gehrie, C. (1981). *The urban principal: Discretionary decision-making in a large educational organization* (Report of an NIE-funded project). Chicago: University of Illinois.

Natriello, G., & Dornbusch, S. (1984). *Teacher evaluative standard and student effort.* New York: Longman.

New York State Department of Education. (1974a, March). *Reading achievement related to educational and environmental conditions in 12 New York City elementary schools.* Albany, NY: Division of Education and Evaluation.

New York State Department of Education. (1974b). *School factors influencing reading achievement: A case study of two inner city schools.* Albany, NY: Office of Education Performance Review. (ERIC Document Reproduction Service No. ED 089 211)

New York State Department of Education. (1976). *Three strategies for studying the effects of school process.* Albany, NY: Bureau of School Programs Evaluation.

Peterson, P., & Swing, S. (1982). Beyond time on task: Students' reports of their thought processes during classroom instruction. *Elementary School Journal, 82,* 481–491.

Pitner, N. (1982, March). *The Mintzberg method: What have we really learned.* Paper presented at the annual meeting of the American Educational Research Association, New York City.

Postlethwaite, T. H. (1975). The surveys of the International Association for the Evaluation of Educational Achievement (IEA): Implications of the IEA surveys of achievement. In A. C. Purvis and D. V. Levine (Eds.), *Educational policy and international assessment.* Berkeley, CA: McCutchan.

Purkey, S. C., & Smith, M. S. (1983a). Effective schools: A review. *Elementary School Journal, 83*(4), 427–452.

Purkey, S. C., & Smith, M. S. (1985). School reform: The district policy implications of the effective schools literature. *Elementary School Journal, 85,* 353–389.

Ralph, J. H., & Fennessey, J. (1983). Science or reform: Some questions about the effective schools model. *Phi Delta Kappan, 64*(10), 689–694.

Reynolds, D., Jones, D., and St. Leger, S. (1976). Schools do make a difference. *New Society, 37,* 223–225.

Rohrkemper, M. (1984). The influence of teacher socialization style on students' social cognition and reported interpersonal classroom behavior. *Elementary School Journal, 85,* 245–276.

Rowan, B., Bossert, S. T., & Dwyer, D. C. (1983). Research on effective schools: A cautionary note. *Educational Researcher, 12*(4), 24–31.

Rowan, B., & Denk, C. E. (1982). *Modelling the academic performance of schools using longitudinal data: An analysis of school effectiveness measures and school and principal effects on school-level achievement.* San Francisco: Far West Laboratory.

Rowan, B., & Miracle, A. W., Jr. (1983). Systems of ability grouping and the stratification of achievement in elementary schools. *Sociology of Education, 56,* 133–144.

Rowe, M. B. (1983). Scientific education: A framework for decision-makers. *Daedalus, 112*(2), 123–142.

Rutter, M. (1983). School effects on pupil progress: Research findings and policy implications. In L. S. Shulman and G. Sykes (Eds.), *Handbook of teaching and policy.* New York: Longman.

Rutter, M., Maughan, B., Mortimore, P., Ouston, J., and Smith, A. (1979). *Fifteen thousand hours: Secondary schools and their effects on children.* Cambridge, MA: Harvard University Press.

Salley, C., McPherson, R. B., & Baehr, M. E. (1979). What principals do: A preliminary occupational analysis. In D. A. Erickson and T. L. Reller (Eds.), *The principal in metropolitan schools.* Berkeley, CA: McCutchan.

Schwille, J., Porter, A., Belli, G., Floden, R., Freeman, D., Knappen, L., Kuhs, T., & Schmidt, W. (1983). Teachers as policy brokers in the content of elementary school mathematics. In L. S. Shulman and G. Sykes (Eds.), *Handbook of teaching and policy.* New York: Longman.

Shavelson, R. J. (1983). Review of research on teachers' pedagogical judgements, plans, and decisions. *Elementary School Journal, 83*(4), 392–413.

Shoemaker, J. (1982). *What are we learning? Evaluating the Connecticut school effectiveness project.* Paper presented at the annual meeting of the American Educational Research Association, New York.

Shulman, L. S. (1983). Autonomy and obligation: The remote control of teaching. In L. S. Shulman and G. Sykes (Eds.), *Handbook of teaching and policy.* New York: Longman.

Sizer, T. (1984). *Horace's compromise: The dilemma of the American high school.* Boston: Houghton Mifflin.

Slavin, R. E. (1983). Realities and remedies. *Elementary School Journal, 84*(2), 131–138.

Soar, R., & Soar, R. (1979). Emotional climate and management. In P. Peterson & H. Walberg (Eds.), *Research on teaching: Concepts, findings, and implications.* Berkeley, CA: McCutchan.

Spartz, J. L., Valdes, A. L., McCormick, W. J., Myers, J., & Geppert, W. J. (1977). *Delaware educational accountability system case studies: Elementary schools grades 1–4.* Dover: Delaware Department of Public Instruction.

Spencer D. A. (1984). The home and school lives of women teachers: Implications for staff development. *Elementary School Journal. 84* (3), 299–314.

Spencer-Hall, D. A., & Hall, P. M. (1982). Processes of problem identification and resolution in two school systems. *Studies of Symbolic Interaction, 4,* 191–216.

Stallings, J., & Mohlman, G. (1981, September). *School policy, leadership style, teacher change and student behavior in eight schools* (Final report, Grant No. NIE-G-80-0010). Washington, DC: National Institute of Education.

Tomlinson, T. (1981). The troubled years: An interpretive analysis of public schooling since 1950. *Phi Delta Kappan, 62,* 373–376.

Trisman, D. A., Waller, R. M., & Wilder, C. (1976). *A descriptive and analytic study of compensatory reading programs: Final report* (Vol. 2, PR 75-26). Princeton, NJ: Educational Testing Service.

Veldman, D., & Sanford, J. (1982). *The influence of class ability level on student achievement and classroom behavior.* Austin: University of Texas, R & D Center for Teacher Education.

Venezky, R. L., & Winfield, L. F. (1979). *Schools that succeed beyond expectations in reading* (Studies on Education Tech. Rep. No. 1). Newark: University of Delaware. (ERIC Document Reproduction Service No. ED 177 484)

Weber, G. (1971). *Inner-city children can be taught to read: Four successful schools.* Washington, DC: Council for Basic Education.

Weinstein, R. (1983). Student perceptions of schooling. *Elementary School Journal, 83,* 287–312.

Wellisch, J. B., MacQueen, A. H., Carriere, R. A., & Duck, C. A. (1978). School management and organization in successful schools. *Sociology of Education, 51,* 211–226.

Wolcott, H. (1973). *The man in the principal's office.* New York: Holt, Rinehart & Winston.

Part 4
Adapting Teaching to Differences Among Learners

21.

Adapting Teaching to Individual Differences Among Learners

Lyn Corno

Teachers College, Columbia University

Richard E. Snow

Stanford University

"The success of education depends on adapting teaching to individual differences among learners." This thought, and the admonition to teachers it carries, can be found expressed in some detail in the fourth century B.C. Chinese treatise by Yue-zheng entitled *Xue Ji*, in the ancient Hebrew Haggadah of Passover, and in the *De Institutione Oratoria* of Quintilian in first century Rome. In one form or another, it has found expression also in many of the educational theories of subsequent centuries, up to the present (see Snow, 1982a). Unfortunately, systematic procedures for accomplishing instructional adaptations of the sort envisioned through all these years have never been clearly established and validated. The theories have been vague. Professional experience has gone largely undocumented. And there have been counterproductive trends, such as the misinterpretation of Darwinian notions of adaptation, that still confuse thinking today (Cronbach & Snow, 1977).

The present chapter examines some current hypotheses about the adaptation of teaching to individual differences among learners, some of the research that supports these hypotheses, and some of the instructional programs and teaching practices that have been recommended to meet their challenge. Our review is selective, not comprehensive; its primary aim is to focus theory, research, and evaluation, and thus to aid their advance toward solid educational improvement. The history of work in this area is not reviewed, nor are the various extant programs of adaptive teaching and instruction described in detail. But the major references in this field are identified for further study by interested readers.

A Definitional Framework

At the outset we need to adopt several definitions and distinctions that will help simplify and structure discussion of alternative theories, research approaches, and practices. The individual differences among learners relevant here are called *aptitudes*. First we consider these aptitudes in relation to educational goals, and particularly to two kinds of goals — *individual* goals and *common* goals. Next we consider these aptitudes in conjunction with the structures and processes of teaching. There are two basic forms of teaching adapted to differences in student aptitude — *direct aptitude development* and *circumvention of inaptitude*. There are also two levels of adaptive teaching, called *macroadaptation* and *microadaptation*.

The Nature of Aptitude

The term *aptitude* signifies some aspect of the present state of an individual that is propaedeutic to some future achievement in some particular situation. As such, it incorporates conative and affective as well as cognitive attributes of persons that predict success in specified endeavors. It includes also prior achievement differences among persons that serve as such predictors.

Human beings differ from one another in a vast number of ways. The attributes relevant as aptitudes in a given situation are those called into play as individual differences in performance by the demands of that particular situation. The situations of primary interest in this chapter are those that are or

The authors thank reviewers Noreen Webb (UCLA Graduate School of Education), Robert Glaser (University of Pittsburg), and M. C. Wittrock (UCLA Graduate School of Education).

could be presented by *formal educational programs*. Examples of such situations are classroom learning activities at all levels of education, computer-assisted instruction in the home, technical training in the workplace, and organized educational programs in such other institutions as museums and churches. Also of interest, secondarily, are situations for which formal education endeavors to prepare persons, such as those requiring good citizenship, wise social decisions, and adaptive performance at work. *Aptitude* is thus a broad, multivariate concept and yet also a simplifying one for theory construction, under which many aspects of individual differences may be subsumed. For an elaborated justification of this view, see Cronbach and Snow (1977), Snow (1977a, 1982a), and Snow and Lohman (1984).

Educational and psychological research on aptitude has traditionally investigated three broad categories of individual difference constructs: (a) intellectual abilities, viewed as enabling cognitive skills and competencies; (b) personality characteristics, viewed as enduring affective-emotional dispositions; and (c) cognitive styles, viewed as propensities for processing information in certain ways that develop around particular ability–personality intersections. These distinctions are unfortunate. Certainly, constructs from any one of these categories are related to constructs from other categories, and individual performance in education will be a product of whatever mixture of predispositions the individual brings to that performance in interaction with the demands of the educational tasks and situations presented. It is possible that different aptitudes influence different aspects of educational performance, but it is also unlikely that there is any simple one-to-one correspondence between particular aptitudes and particular aspects of educational performance. Unfortunately, most research has studied aptitudes (or aptitude categories) taken one at a time, often using different measures to represent the same or similar constructs, and sometimes using the same measure to interpret different constructs. As a result, there has been little progress in conceptualizing or developing methods to study the complex mixtures of aptitude that educators must face and use in adapting instruction. Our discussion must retain the traditional categories of aptitude constructs, while recognizing that new combinations of constructs, and more detailed process analyses of these combinations, will eventually be needed (see also Lewis, 1976; Shuell, 1981; Snow & Farr, in press).

Aptitude and Educational Goals

Education should be seen as a long-term aptitude development effort. It seeks to foster human preparedness for later stages of life in both the individual and the collective. Especially in a rapidly changing society, the promotion of aptitudes for learning, problem solving, and future problem finding takes precedence over the teaching of today's facts and skills as a central role for education. Effective learning-to-learn and transfer, not just effective learning, is the goal. Thus, aptitude is both an important outcome of education at each step and an important preparation for the next. It is symptomatic in this regard that the ceremony usually marking completion of each major educational step, including the last, is called *commencement*.

Individual Versus Common Educational Goals

Two broad categories of educational goals must also be distinguished, following Cronbach (1967) and Glaser (1977). There are individual goals, chosen by learners (or their parents) for their own personal purposes. Schools offer a spectrum of elective courses and activities designed to provide for the selection and attainment of these individual student goals. Guidance and counseling services support this function, in part. Within a course of instruction teachers also may provide for individual student goals by allowing students choices of projects and activities that serve personal interests as well as course objectives. Individual goals are provided for by an educational program so that individuals can exercise choice in developing their own specialized aptitudes.

But there are common educational goals imposed by society to be met by each individual in the educational system. The expectation that each learner will achieve certain levels of literacy and numeracy, and certain knowledge needed for citizenship, are examples. The common goals are provided for by an educational program so that all individuals can develop the general aptitudes needed by society to preserve and advance the common good. There is a sense, too, in which individual goals feed into a common goal, because the development of a diversity of talents is a collective, common need in most modern societies.

Whereas individual goal attainment can often be served (at least at the school level) simply by diversifying programs and allowing individual choices, individual goals sometimes require and the common goals *always* require a more directive form of adaptation on the part of the educational system and also on the part of teachers. Since the passage of universal compulsory education laws, schools and teachers have been expected to teach and reach the common goals of education for all individuals, regardless of the range of human diversity that happened to present itself. Diversity among learners complicates the task of reaching common goals for all learners (Fenstermacher & Goodlad, 1983). Now, with the passage of mainstreaming laws, the range of learner diversity facing the public school teacher has been extended even further. The adaptation of teaching is primarily an attempt to meet the challenge of diversity, so this is the main focus of this chapter. Facilitating the pursuit of individual goals is an important but secondary matter.

Direct Aptitude Development Versus Circumvention of Inaptitude

Since individuals differ in aptitudes relevant to learning at the start, and since these aptitudes are multiple and imperfectly correlated, a trade-off is necessary between two basic approaches to adaptive teaching. At times, teaching can *focus directly on developing* the aptitudes needed for further instruction. Teachers can teach generalizable cognitive skills and strategies useful in later problem solving and effective decision making. At other times, teaching must find ways to *circumvent or otherwise compensate* for existing sources of inaptitude so that further instruction can proceed. Teachers can use specially trained aides as tutors, supplement regular instruction with specialized practice, and apply instructional methods that avoid demanding particular strengths that students lack. The teacher's aim will be to shift instructional demands toward areas of apparent student strength—to capitalize on some aptitudes—while avoiding other areas of apparent student weakness or inaptitude.

Which form of adaptive teaching is emphasized depends on the malleability of aptitude in a given instance and on the availability of alternative methods of teaching that differ in their reliance on particular learner aptitudes and inaptitudes. Teachers will try to develop reading comprehension and mathematical ability directly because these are common educational goals in themselves and because they are aptitudes for later instruction in fields such as social studies and science. If these aptitudes cannot be developed sufficiently for later instruction to proceed, then the later instruction must either be postponed or alternative forms of teaching science and social studies must be found that do not rely so heavily on these aptitudes. Postponement is rarely a preferable option, so the development of alternative teaching methods has become a major goal for educational research.

Macroadaptation Versus Microadaptation of Instruction

Teachers make moment-to-moment and month-to-month decisions designed to adapt instruction to the needs of different learners. Computer programs are increasingly designed to do the same. School programs can also be designed in adaptive ways, although the decisions at this level are more likely to be only of the longer term, month-to-month type. Thus, a continuum of levels of adaptation can be discerned, and the kinds of adaptation possible at each level differ from one another somewhat. It may distort this continuum to dichotomize it, but for simplicity we distinguish the month-to-month teacher and program-level decisions as macroadaptation and refer to the moment-to-moment teacher or computer adaptations as microadaptation.

The Structure and Process of Adaptive Teaching

Beyond the above distinctions, we need also to examine just what the processes of adaptation are at base, and how the adaptation of teaching can be structured to take place in schools. Extant and future research should be evaluated in this light.

The Concept of Adaptation in Teaching and Learning

Dictionary definitions of adaptation are general: "Adjustment to environmental conditions." The specific definitions become biological: "Modification of an organism or its parts that makes it more fit for existence under the conditions of its environment." Applied in human psychology, the general definitions seem to include even the momentary minutiae of sensorimotor adjustments while the biological specifications seem to apply mainly to psychophysical changes across generations in response to "natural" variations in environmental conditions. But the range of human adaptations of interest here lies between these two extremes. Also, it involves both learner adaptation *to* the environmental conditions presented and teacher adaptation *of* the environmental conditions to the learner's present state, to effect changes in that state. The teacher's goal, in other words, is to make environmental variations "nurtural" rather than merely "natural" for each learner of concern.

The basic theoretical units of this form of teacher (or computer, or educational program) adaptation can be identified and described, at either micro or macro levels, using the familiar "test-operate-test-exit" (TOTE) unit (Miller, Galanter, & Pribram, 1960) or production system (Newell & Simon, 1972) language of present-day information-processing psychology. Also of use is Glaser's (1977) language of adaptive education. There is first some assessment or test of the present state of the learner in relation to goals, including the learner's readiness to profit from each of the possible teaching operations available. Depending on the aptitudinal conditions shown to be present by this assessment, some appropriate teaching action or operation is then chosen and applied. A subsequent assessment shows whether the intended goal has been realized. If it has not, then the sequence is repeated until the goal is met. When the initial goal is met the teacher exits to the next goal. The degree to which this sequence can be considered adaptive depends on the number of alternative teaching actions available and the degree to which alternative actions are chosen to fit the assessments of learner readiness to profit from them. Indeed, when learners are simply recycled through the same teaching operations without such variations until a goal is met or not, the teaching system must be regarded as nonadaptive or only minimally adaptive, as in Glaser's Model I—learners must adapt to the given teaching system or drop out. Here, repetition is the only teaching variation that is responsive to learner differences.

When alternative teaching operations are available and applied in response to assessments of learner readiness to profit from them, however, then the teaching system can be regarded as adaptive. It may only include a single remedial loop for direct aptitude development, as in Glaser's Model II. Or, it may be made adaptive only with respect to individually chosen learner goals. Truly adaptive teaching provides alternative instructional routes to the common goals (Glaser's Model III) and includes not only a single remedial loop (Glaser's Model IV) but alternative teaching operations for the remediation of inaptitudes (see Snow, 1982a; Snow & Lohman, 1984). It also allows for individual learner goals (Glaser's Model V).

A further essential criterion for judging the adaptiveness of a teaching system concerns the degree to which the alternative teaching operations are appropriately tied to valid assessments of the states of possible learner aptitude. If differential treatment of learners is based on invalid assessments, the teaching system may become maladaptive, even discriminatory in the extreme. It is this concern that motivates most research on teacher expectancies (see Mitman & Snow, 1984).

A Formal Structure

Figure 21.1 depicts the formal structure of such an adaptive teaching system in the form of a flow chart. Although the same chart can be used to characterize both microadaptive and macroadaptive teaching, it is best initially to think only of the macro level; microadaptation involves additional complexities to be addressed separately below.

There is first an assessment of relevant aptitudes (A) with respect to the common goals (CG) of instruction and also with respect to whatever individual goals (IG) have been chosen. Thereafter, the layout of Figure 21.1 distinguishes sharply between the IG and CG branches, because the form of adaptation differs significantly between them.

In the case of IG, the system proceeds by assigning learners to individual instructional treatments (t_1, t_2, or t_3) according to the IG choices given, once there is some assurance that A is sufficient to attain the chosen goals. IG achievement is assessed periodically, as between units or beginning and more advanced courses. If success criteria are not attained, there is an option to repeat or to drop any given IG treatment. A counseling function may enter here wherein learners with aptitude patterns ill-suited to some chosen IG are aided in revising their choices. Thus, the choice to study art, music, typing, auto mechanics, or some particular history, culture, or language may be pursued, dropped, or revised as a function of aptitude or achievement in associated treatments. The typical elective courses and counseling functions in public schools today appear to work this way,

except that course trial and error more than formal assessment of aptitude seems to provide the main guide to adaptation of each student's program.

The more critical form of adaptation occurs with respect to CG, and this is our main concern in this chapter. Here there are two major sections. If A is judged sufficient to attain CG through at least one of the available alternative instructional treatments (T_1, T_2, or T_3), the learner is given whichever treatment is most likely to be effective in reaching CG. Sometimes this choice of T may be based on some combination of predicted achievement and cost for each available T. Sometimes the learner controls the choice, or aspects of it. Subsequent assessment of CG achievement determines whether or not treatment choice was successful and the learner can pass on to the next unit. If A is judged insufficient for any of the available instructional treatments, or if CG is not achieved in the treatment applied, then direct development of A is undertaken. Here, too, there will usually need to be alternative forms of direct training treatments (D_1 or D_2) tailored to the particular aptitude strengths and weaknesses of each learner (see Snow & Lohman, 1984, for examples of why this is necessary). Direct remediation of inaptitudes may or may not be successful, so the assessment needs to be diagnostic in this regard. In this direct development and assessment phase also, difficulties may be diagnosed that suggest the learner needs to be transferred to other special programs.

Although transfer to a special educational program is itself an assignment to an alternative instructional treatment T_s, the

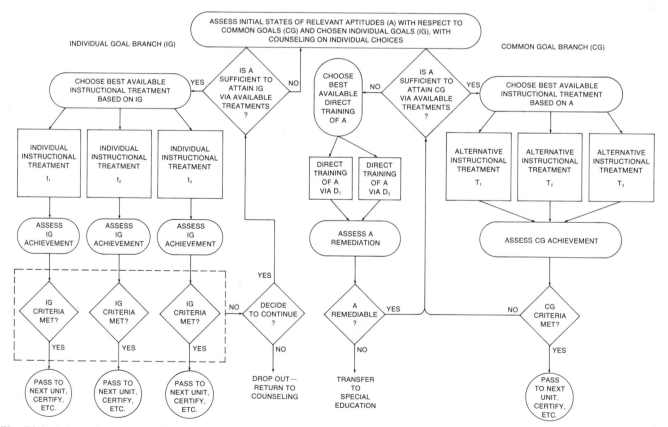

Fig. 21.1. A formal structure of adaptive teaching.

details of such programs should also be adaptive in the sense of Figure 21.1 and should be evaluated as such (Snow, 1984). Research on adaptive teaching in the context of special education, however, involves special considerations that cannot be addressed here (see MacMillan, Keogh & Jones, this volume). In some educational systems also, another kind of special decision may be taken at some aptitude assessment point to transfer "gifted" students to a special alternative treatment T_g. Such programs should also be expected to fit the pattern of Figure 21.1 (see Torrance, this volume for research in this area).

Unlike the form of adaptation used in the IG branch (which simply provides assessment, instructional electives, and counseling), adaptation in the CG branch aims at a more fundamental obligation of the teaching system — *to provide equal opportunity to reach common educational goals despite individual differences in aptitude at the start*. It seeks to accomplish this by finding or designing instructional treatments that circumvent critical learner inaptitudes, instructional treatments that remediate critical inaptitudes directly, and a set of assessments and decision rules that optimize the orchestration of these treatments. The design of such treatments — both circumvention and remediation treatments — depends on finding other learner aptitudes that can be capitalized upon. Since learner aptitudes and inaptitudes are multiple in virtually any group, adaptive teaching always requires the provision of alternative routes to common goals. And the ultimate aim in any such route is transfer — the teaching system adapts to individual differences in learners so that eventually individual learners learn to adapt themselves to new teaching situations.

A teaching system of the sort described above is of course an ideal. Perhaps no conventional school program yet resembles the pattern of Figure 21.1 in detail. While there are some approximations in existence today, and some experimental programs have been developed over the years that incorporate parts of the ideal, this type of educational reform has not yet occurred. For many years schools have expected individuals to conform to a fixed instructional treatment or drop out, and the difference between this old view and the ideal of Figure 21.1 should set the purpose of much modern research on aptitude in education. In the three remaining parts of this section we describe examples of adaptive teaching at the different levels of macro- and microadaptation, and how these approaches are used to accomplish common and individual goals.

Macroadaptation — Adaptive School Programs

At the level of *macroadaptation* is the school or training program. Here it is simplest to think of two alternative treatments, each designed to accommodate one of two particular subgroups of students. The decision rule governing the assignment of students to treatments is given by a prior analysis of aptitude-treatment interaction (ATI). Outcome is regressed on aptitude for each treatment separately in one or more valida-

tion studies. Each individual in the population thereafter receives the treatment predicted to yield the maximum outcome for that individual, among the alternative treatments available. The cost of alternative treatments can also be brought into the decision equation. Cronbach and Snow (1977) provided the procedures for ATI analyses of this sort and a review of the research literature bearing on them. Snow (1976) updated this review with respect to two principal ATI hypotheses to which we return later in this chapter.

By and large, however, schools have not attempted ATI-style macroadaptations.[1] The research evidence has shown ATI phenomena to be complex and not readily generalized (see Cronbach, 1975; Snow, 1976); it is clear that even the most studied aptitude constructs, such as intelligence or achievement motivation, are not sufficiently well understood to suggest how appropriate and practical alternative treatments should be designed in detail. And there have been many other impediments in both the research and its relation to practice (see, e.g., Good and Stipek, 1983).

Instructional designers have instead usually sought to build programs that would be adaptive mainly to the most direct manifestation of cognitive aptitude differences, namely learning rate differences; individualized pace, with repetition and special coaching for slow students has been recommended in many programs. To make instruction responsive to motivational or interest differences, programs have typically also included choice (by learner or teacher) among a variety of materials and teaching strategies to suit different students.

SOME EXISTING PROGRAMS

Variations on these themes can be seen in many of the early attempts at adaptive teaching, including especially the Dalton and Winnetka Plans of the 1920s (see Whipple, 1925). Programed instruction, developed through the 1950s, also sought to provide individualized pacing and reinforcement; its variations, such as branching, were designed especially to improve feedback and correction tailored to particular kinds of student errors. The 1960s saw the development of more comprehensive attempts with more radical redesigns of instructional formats, objectives, materials, and teacher practices. The Program for Learning in Accordance with Needs (PLAN), Individually Prescribed Instruction (IPI), Individually Guided Education (IGE), Mastery Learning (ML), and Keller's Personalized System of Instruction (PSI), are the most notable examples. The details of these programs and differences among them have been described many times so we need not use space for that here (see, e.g., Block, 1971; Block & Burns, 1976; Bloom, 1976; Henry, 1962; Keller, 1968; Klausmeier, Rossmiller, & Saily, 1977; Snow, 1982a; Wang & Lindvall, 1984; Weisgerber, 1971a, 1971b). There have also been substantial critiques and questions raised about the degree to which any of these programs fulfill all of the criteria of adaptive instruction (see, e.g., Block & Burns, 1976; Cronbach & Snow, 1977; Good & Stipek, 1983; Peterson, 1977; Wang & Lindvall, 1984).

---

[1] Two attempts to organize whole schools on an ATI pattern are known — one in elementary education in Ontario, Canada by D. E. Hunt and one in community college education at Oakland University, Detroit, Michigan, by J. Hill — but documentation of those programs and their evaluation was not available for citation at the time of this writing.

THE EVALUATION OF EXISTING PROGRAMS

The central concerns in evaluating any adaptive teaching program are threefold:

1. Are the common goals of instruction met by all students and, in particular, by those students low in initial cognitive aptitude (i.e., prior knowledge and scholastic ability) who would ordinarily be predicted not to achieve those common goals through "conventional" instruction?
2. Are there inequities preserved or produced by the program in reaching the common goals, in such areas as retention, transfer, or enrichment of learning?
3. Are there any students who are particularly ill-served by the program, relative to "conventional" instruction?

These three evaluation concerns apply in any instructional comparison, but they apply with special force in evaluating adaptive instructional programs because these programs are specifically designed to remove inequities; that is, to assure that the answers to the three above questions are "yes," "no," and "no," respectively. No evaluation of adaptive instruction can be content with average comparisons with "conventional" teaching. Whether or not an instructional program has been designed on an ATI pattern, it can be argued that its evaluation must include an ATI analysis, at least with respect to the major ATI hypotheses relevant to the instructional conditions being compared (see Snow, 1976, 1977). In brief, the argument is that whenever an instructional prescription is different for one student than for another, the implication is that both will be helped by following their own prescriptions rather than someone else's. The evaluation must verify that the prescriptions in fact result in help without any accompanying hindrances.

The optimum outcome would be the ATI regression pattern shown in Figure 21.2a. The pattern in Figure 21.2b would signify a favorable result for the first evaluation concern above if the minimally acceptable level for the common goal in this situation was clearly at point y*, rather than some higher point on the Y axis. But the positive XY slope for adaptive instruction here suggests that the second evaluation concern remains at issue — the program preserves a form of inequity and should be evaluated further, especially with respect to retention and transfer criteria. The ATI regression shown in Figure 21.2c demonstrates clear failure of the adaptive program with respect to the third concern, even given y* as the acceptable common goal level, because it appears to hold back some students relative to conventional teaching. The same conclusion would be indicated by any disordinal ATI pattern.

To be clear on these concerns, such evaluation studies will need to do more than examine ATI only with prior knowledge or scholastic ability as aptitude and common immediate achievement as outcome. Other major aptitudes to be considered in most situations include academic motivation and evaluation (test) anxiety; others may be suggested by the characteristics of the particular programs at hand. As suggested above, outcome is also multivariate; retention and transfer criteria are essential and attitude, motivation, and other aptitudes for further learning may often be appropriate additions.

Unfortunately, most evaluations of adaptive instruction have

not addressed these concerns (cf. Corno, 1980). Those that have done so sometimes find patterns like Figure 21.2c (see Snow, 1977; Snow & Lohman, 1984 give examples, including one for IPI). Some studies suggest that ML is dysfunctional for high-ability students (see Good & Stipek, 1983). But recent meta-analyses suggest that the pattern of Figure 21.2b may be most typical (see Kulik, Kulik, & Cohen, 1979, regarding PSI). Thus, achievement is improved for everyone by at least some forms of adaptive instruction but the main effects of aptitude differences are not eliminated; transfer seems not to have been studied.

Most decisions about school program adaptations are made and carried out over an extended time cycle. And such decisions are not likely to be easily reversed or altered. It is therefore important that adaptive programs at this macro level be systematically designed and evaluated. Although a school or school district might well take on this design problem itself, the

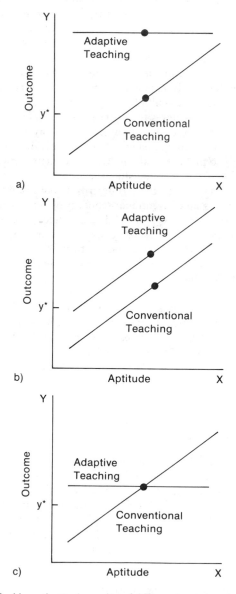

Fig. 21.2. Hypothetical results of ATI evaluations of adaptive teaching programs.

research and development, and the continuing evaluation required for such an effort, are likely to exceed the resources of all but the largest school districts. Most examples of school-level adaptation have come from research and development centers and laboratories; the schools receive the program as a package. Implementation, however, may vary significantly both within and across schools. The programs therefore must be designed with implementation in mind, and this raises a fourth concern for evaluation. It is a principal concern because even programs that show results like Figure 21.2a in tryout may end up producing the Figure 21.2c pattern in application.

TWO CURRENT SCHOOL PROGRAMS

We illustrate only two macro-level adaptive school programs in detail here. They are Individually Guided Education (IGE) and the Adaptive Learning Environments Model (ALEM).

IGE focuses on entire school environments and is seen by its designers as a comprehensive system for school reform, including school–home relations and continuing research and development. The IGE program seeks to alter not only the instructional program of a school, but also its educational assumptions and institutional traditions. At the core of the program is a model of adaptive instruction.

A school first determines instructional objectives for each student based on aptitude profiles. These profiles are derived from diagnostic assessments of achievement level in reading and mathematics, as well as stylistic motivational characteristics. Several types of instructional variations are then implemented in an effort to accommodate student individual differences. These variations include:

- Attention and guidance on the part of the teacher
- Time spent interacting with other students
- Time spent interacting with different instructional media (print, audiovisual, and direct contact materials)
- Time spent in small versus large-group activities.

Following instruction, assessment measures show how well each student attained the objectives. Depending on the outcome of this assessment, another learning cycle or a remediation cycle begins. The approach is consistent with the IG branch of our Figure 21.1.

When IGE was first developed, its technology was considered its main asset. However, it was also seen as distinct from other technology-driven instructional systems such as IPI. The name, Individually Guided Education, was chosen to reflect a belief in the importance of flexible instruction *guided* by a well-designed system but not *prescribed* by that system.

The implementation plan for IGE involves four phases: awareness of IGE, changeover to IGE, refinement of practices in IGE schools, and institutionalization (or renewal) (Klausmeier, 1977). Under the original plan, experienced teachers and principals were trained in IGE through inservice courses; now preservice teachers are trained as well. Throughout the 1970s, the program was introduced and evaluated in numerous schools nationwide. Evidence on the effects of the program continue to be disseminated by the Wisconsin Center for Individualized Schooling.

As part of the IGE evaluation studies, Popkewitz, Tabachnick, and Wehlage (1982) carried out a separate, in-depth analysis of six "exemplary" IGE schools. The intent was to follow the institutionalization process in six schools determined to be homogeneous in their self-reported implementation of the program. The schools were selected to differ in socioeconomic level and percentage of minority students, but otherwise to display similar characteristics (e.g., average standardized achievement ranges; type of school leadership).

The study used participant observation and interviews at all levels of implementation, and rotating site visitors as a constant comparative method. Analyses focused on the "meaning, use, and interpretation of IGE which characterized each of the schools" (p. 186). Results of this effort produced "portraits" of the different schools that were notable in their reflection of widely different views of IGE and, more importantly, views at variance with those intended by the IGE developers.

Although all of the schools in this sample reported full implementation of IGE, the manner and form of implementation appeared different in the different schools observed. Schools in lower socioeconomic locations were found to espouse the theory and philosophy behind IGE, and to display the IGE technologies for sociopolitical purposes, including use of the program as a means for controlling students. Schools in higher socioeconomic locations were seen to adapt IGE into a management- or efficiency-oriented program, where educational outcomes were focal, or into a more student-centered program, where the process of learning and knowledge expansion was focal. Most important was the finding that these adaptations of IGE were consistent with the observed "styles of work, conceptions of knowledge, and professional ideologies" of each school, so that implementation of this school reform program in practice actually maintained existing patterns of activity and beliefs in each school instead of reforming them (p. 4).

Popkewitz et al.'s analysis of IGE highlights the environmental constraints that operate when innovative educational programs are implemented in existing school systems, and demonstrates the manner by which practitioners may compromise developers' best-laid plans. By revising both the technology and the goals of IGE to fit their own school environments, practitioners using IGE may either fail to derive the benefits intended, or actually surpass its intended goals by creating adaptations more suited to their own unique environments. With the knowledge that such adaptations will inevitably take place, program developers can plan to assist schools in the effort and may be able to engineer more optimal adaptations. They should also build in a means of documenting these local adaptations for use in further research and development efforts and for dissemination to other similar schools.

The fourth evaluation concern noted earlier dealt with implementation. It is clear that comparative evaluations seeking answers to the first three concerns are superfluous unless the fourth concern can be satisfactorily relieved. Although IGE has benefited from much formative evaluation in its development, we do not know of a summative comparison that would provide answers to our first three questions.

A second large-scale adaptive program is the Adaptive Learning Environments Model (ALEM), developed at the Learning Research and Development Center, Pittsburgh (Wang, 1980). ALEM is a program for elementary schools explicitly designed to exemplify Glaser's (1977) model of adaptive instruction. It therefore reflects both forms of adaptation, that is, inaptitude circumvention and direct aptitude development.

The core of ALEM is a variation of IPI (Glaser, 1977). Student assignments (in reading and mathematics) are individualized based on detailed assessments of entering competencies. Each unit of instruction provides a base on which later units build. As in IGE, performance is assessed by the rate at which program objectives are mastered, and supplementary instruction is provided for faster and slower learners. ALEM updates IPI by also providing different learning activities and instruction for students with particular remedial or extension needs. That is, both pace (quantity) and type (quality) of instruction vary over students as needed. The aim is to promote basic skills development in even the least able students while also accommodating the specialized interests and needs of more able students.

ALEM also offers an organizational structure that aids school implementation of the IPI core. This structure includes (a) an instructional management system that provides guidelines on instructional time use and resource materials, (b) a home involvement effort that draws parents into the learning experiences provided at school, (c) a procedure for team teaching and work with groups of students that also maximizes time and resources, and (d) a staff development component to assist teachers in implementing and maintaining the program.

ALEM has now been evaluated in a large sample of K–3 classrooms over a full academic year (Wang & Walberg, 1983). Some 156 teachers in schools with a high percentage of economically disadvantaged students used the program as a core curriculum for reading and mathematics. The study assessed degree of implementation across classes using a specially developed assessment battery administered by trained observers three times during the year. Observation data were also obtained from a subsample of 72 first and second grade classes on the nature and sequences of teacher–student interactions, learning activities and tasks, and student time in each; individual students were the observation targets. Criterion tests accompanying the program and standardized achievement tests in reading and mathematics were administered at the end of the year. The study investigated relationships among the implementation indicators and classroom process variables, as well as implementation and student achievement.

Results showed significant differences in implementation across school sites, yet an overall degree of implementation of 92%. On individual dimensions of implementation, the sites observed rated lowest in "creating and maintaining instructional materials" and "developing student self-responsibility" (81 and 83%, respectively). These dimensions and a third, "interactive teaching," were also found to discriminate between classrooms representing high and average-low implementation levels. The three discriminating dimensions all required teachers to take responsibility for what is the heart of adaptive teaching as we have described it, and all represent deviations from mainstream classroom teaching at the elementary level.

Analyses relating implementation differences to classroom process and achievement variables showed moderate relationships in expected directions. Classroom process variables, like the implementation dimensions, showed restricted ranges that might have attenuated some relationships. The restricted ranges, however, reflect positively on ALEM, since classes were uniformly on-task, and displayed high academic teacher-student interaction. A full path analysis assessing the sequence of events from high program implementation, to consistently task-directed classroom processes, to higher student achievement, was not conducted, but could be done in reanalyses.

In general, the study demonstrated that a high average degree of implementation can be obtained for one macroadaptation program in schools with predominantly low socioeconomic status students. In turn, such an implementation can lead to favorable conditions for classroom learning in reading and mathematics on average. But again, the study did not examine relationships among student aptitudes, the ALEM program, and achievement across school sites.

So the critical questions remain: To what extent do students of different aptitude levels profit from program adaptations such as ALEM or IGE? Do these programs achieve equity in any sense, without hurting anyone? In what ways do implementation variations such as those observed in both programs affect aptitude-outcome relationships? These are ATI questions—but control sites and a radically different view of evaluation for adaptive teaching are needed to obtain the answers.

Micro- and Macroadaptation— Adaptive Teacher Variations

A wide spectrum of adaptive teaching can be observed in the behavior of many classroom teachers. The numerous classroom observation studies conducted in recent decades provide extensive evidence that teachers exhibit both *macroadaptations* and *microadaptations* (see Crawford et al., 1978 for a review; see also Brophy & Good, this volume; Gage, 1978). Some observable teacher operations seem aimed at circumventing particular inaptitudes; some seem aimed at developing particular aptitudes directly. There are distinctive teaching operations directed at particular individuals in a class, at subgroups, and at the entire class, based on teacher knowledge of each (Shavelson & Stern, 1981). There are macroadaptations often exhibited in grouping strategies within a class designed to aid the differentiation of teaching operations over units of even larger segments of instruction. An important recent advance in classroom research has been to identify empirically the different activity structures of classroom life within which different kinds of teaching adaptations may take place and different student aptitudes may be relevant (Berliner, 1983). There are then myriad teacher microadaptations observable in the minute-by-minute stream of teacher-learner interaction within each kind of classroom activity. It would appear that close observation by the teacher of the course of this continuous stream is used to modify teacher behavior as teaching proceeds.

The microadaptation of teacher classroom behavior has often been characterized as a repeated sequence of "recitation" activity (Bellack et al., 1966). The basic pattern of recitation is observable in almost all teaching; it consists of three teaching "moves" and specific acts within each. The moves are termed "structuring," "soliticing," and "reacting," referring respectively to (a) explanatory presentations of organized information, (b) monitoring and evaluating student learning, and (c) providing appropriate feedback for student responses. Teachers typically present lesson information, solicit evidence that students understand, and provide feedback on student responses. Written instruction and computerized instruction often follow this pattern as well (Gagné & Briggs, 1977).

There are many variations on this theme. Teachers may conduct classroom recitation in large or small groups, or with individual students, although most research on classroom recitation has shown it is used primarily in large-group situations (see Clark et al., 1979). Teachers may also choose from a variety of media and materials as part of the delivery. A given lesson may be preplanned in this sequence, or the sequence may occur spontaneously in response to some unexpected event, perhaps a student misunderstanding. It is instructive for our purpose to consider how the recitation might be used by a typical teacher in an imaginary circumstance that contrasts sharply with what is known about real classrooms — namely, a situation in which students are *identical in all relevant aptitudes.*

In *presenting lesson information*, there would be no need for grouping or individualization. The same instructional materials, media, and objectives could be used for all students. The manner in which material is presented (the amount of review, the number of examples, use of summaries, modeling, etc.) could be standardized. Similarly, the same amount of time could be spent with each student in interaction with the teacher and materials; all students would work at the same pace.

In *soliciting student response*, a teacher would need to be attuned to only one student — any student selected at random could provide evidence of comprehension, application, synthesis, and so forth that should hold for the entire group. There would be little response variability among students, so the questions used to solicit student response would not need to vary from one student to another. The amount of time spent in diagnostic monitoring therefore would be considerably less than is necessary with heterogeneous classes. There would be no need for attention to different skills in different students.

In *providing feedback to student responses*, the quality and quantity of feedback would not need to vary. Differential reinforcement would be unnecessary. There would be no need to distinguish "common" errors from individual errors in feedback, because all errors would be common. Here also, feedback given to one student effectively could be taken as feedback to all, saving time in the process. Learning rates in such a situation could be expected to be uniform, and the amount of instruction appropriate for a given period would be predictable. Little monitoring of progress would be required of teachers. Indeed, little understanding of students would be required of teachers; when all students are psychologically interchangeable, general principles suffice as guides to teacher behavior and individual concepts of student learning are unnecessary.

This ideal situation was thought achievable under the old theory of ability grouping. If individuals could be rank-ordered on ability to learn using some measure of intelligence or prior achievement, then simply by dividing students into three or four levels on the basis of these measures one could homogenize the teacher's task. Within groups, teaching operations could be uniform across students as above. But the research on ability grouping shows that it often results in widening gaps in academic performance between high and low achievers, stigmatization of lows, loss of self-esteem and motivation for lows, and restriction of friendship choices for cultural minorities (Calfee & Brown, 1979; Good & Stipek, 1983; Maccoby & Jacklin, 1974; Rosenholtz & Wilson, 1980). Teachers' expectations can be reflected in grouping decisions, and grouping often reinforces such expectations (Cohen, Intili, & Robbins, 1979; Weinstein, 1976). The widening gap in performance between low and high groups, moreover, may result directly from instructional differences. Some research shows that, in addition to slower pacing with lower ability groups, teachers focus more on low-level objectives and routine procedures than they do with higher ability groups (Shavelson & Stern, 1981; Weinstein, 1976). In other words, there often is a shift to different, or lower, instructional goals. Traditional ability grouping thus must be judged maladaptive, not adaptive, if the goal is to maximize each student's opportunity to reach the same common goal (cf. Slavin & Karweit, 1984). Furthermore, the teacher's task is *not* made uniform within ability groups, because students in such groups still differ in many other aptitudes for learning that are only moderately correlated, or even entirely uncorrelated with the measure used to form the groups.

Teacher adaptation is better considered at the level of individual students. Research indicates that teachers improve at their craft in part by examining whether or not they reach individual students (Good & Grouws, 1979). Other studies suggest that teachers learn to adapt across experience with successive students in tutoring situations (Clark, Snow & Shavelson, 1976). Some work further indicates that tutors develop strategies for diagnosing and operating with the multiple mental models, including incorrect models, that students generate, harbor, and use during learning (Stevens & Collins, 1980).

Our analysis thus suggests ways that teachers might successfully and spontaneously adapt both their thinking and their behavior toward differences in students, as well as develop aptitudes directly within and between individuals and also classes. Teachers can manipulate the organizational structures of the class — the groups, the learning centers, the reward structures — so long as grouping is short-term and not stigmatic. Teachers can vary the materials they choose to present information or to guide problem solving — their examples, analogies, and points of emphasis, review, and summary. They can vary the support materials they use — aides, media, and so forth, and the level and form of questions asked. They can vary reinforcement given for correct responses, the level of explanation provided for incorrect responses, the push to take a second try. They can prompt student questions in different ways to aid in diagnosis. In short, they can adjust instructional processes to individual student responses but also to their growing conception of student cognition and motivation with respect to the learning tasks at hand.

These adjustments are for the most part *qualitative* variations from one student, group, or class to another. More easily observed in classrooms are teacher's *quantitative* adjustments. They vary the amount of time spent with different students on the same problem, the amount of time students are encouraged to spend with other students or media, the number of questions asked to assess learning, the amount of feedback given for particular responses, and pacing. Unfortunately, too much research on teaching has focused only on these quantitative behavioral manifestations, without studying the qualitative cognitive and motivational content of the behavior observed. Much useful adaptive teaching may thus go undocumented. Much maladaptive teaching may also go undocumented since many teachers overdifferentiate and probably do so unsystematically.

Beyond these sorts of adaptations—adaptations that circumvent student inaptitude—teachers attempt to develop student aptitude directly. Strategies other than classroom recitation serve as examples, as well as variations on the recitation strategy. Taba's (1966) early work described an "inductive teaching" strategy that leads students through a systematic sequence of teacher questioning aimed at promoting induction of principles from facts and supporting evidence. This sequence of moves is intended to model and encourage use of an inquiry process, through which students can learn to reason through problems for themselves and then transfer these skills. A variety of other learning strategies have been identified and evaluated (see, e.g., O'Neil, 1978; O'Neil and Spielberger, 1979); these could be taught routinely by teachers to students diagnosed as needing them. Increasingly, the development of "thinking skills" has received popular (Maeroff, 1983) as well as research attention (Glaser, 1984; Lockhead & Clement, 1979). We discuss some of this work in a later section.

Teachers can similarly vary the manner in which information is presented in recitation—prompting students to organize lesson material for themselves, or to provide their own examples of principles learned. The soliciting and reacting aspects of classroom recitation can be varied by adding higher-order questions that prompt students to go beyond information given in their answers, or to use self-monitoring or self-reinforcing techniques and other aspects of self-regulation (Corno & Mandinach, 1983).

While it is clear that teachers adapt their behavior to student individual differences at virtually all levels of education, what is less clear is the underlying logic and intentionality that governs these adaptations, and whether some teachers can be characterized as "more adaptive" than others. Research on teacher decision making and planning (Clark & Peterson, this volume) initially modeled the rational decisions teachers might make. For example, considering the class average on some relevant aptitude in relation to the amount of total variability around that average, a teacher could then consider instructional objectives and the amount of available time to determine an appropriate instructional method (Snow, 1973; Shavelson, 1976). But such rationality is seldom reflected in what teachers actually do. The research shows that microadaptations in teaching tend to occur spontaneously, with little forethought. Moreover, teachers have difficulty articulating "principles" that might guide their adaptive decisions, and even identifying the variables they consider (Clark & Yinger, 1977; McNair, 1978–1979; Yinger, 1977). The studies to date do seem to indicate that only two student aptitude variables in particular are routinely identified by teachers as a basis for instructional decision making. These are generally characterized as "ability" and "motivation." But even here there is little consistency in the operational meanings individual teachers ascribe to these aptitude constructs. Until such meanings can be clarified and

teaching operations linked to them, the unsystematic kinds of teaching adaptations we have described will likely persist.

Microadaptation—Adaptive Computer Programs

Computerized instruction holds the promise to model systematic *microadaptation* more immediately than do classroom teachers. Computer programs can be made response sensitive (Atkinson, 1968), and thus adaptive, in the sense that subsequent frames are selected conditioned on the nature of a learner's response to previous frames. Depending on a student's responses to questions embedded in the instruction, supplementary instruction or remedial instruction is provided, or the student moves on to another segment of content. Since the computer is blind to differences between students apart from their responses, all students who respond similarly receive similar instruction. The computer will not tire of poor responding from students; nor will it fail to monitor each and every response a student makes. Students also develop a kind of "response sensitivity" over time when working with computerized instruction that can be seen as one component of aptitude for learning from instruction (Mandinach, 1984). Computerized instruction is thus an important vehicle for the effective application of adaptive teaching.

With the advent of intelligent computer-assisted instruction (ICAI), computers are also being programed to diagnose errors and provide correctives in ways that model effective instruction (Sleeman & Brown, 1982). By tracking error patterns across sessions of individual students as well as between students, say, in the same class, the program can determine errors most frequently made by an individual and by the entire class. Such error patterns can identify the probable sources of these "bugs," and corrective feedback can be given on a short time cycle. Given the social realities of most classrooms, this kind of systematic diagnosis and correction clearly exceeds both the cognitive and behavioral capabilities of most human teachers.

Brown and Burton (1978), for example, have developed an ICAI program to identify common errors in arithmetic. The program attempts to anticipate all possible algorithms a student could use to arrive at an answer and then classifies the students' response by matching answers to algorithms. Gradually, a model of the learner is built up as instruction proceeds that then guides the course of further instruction tailored to the individual's strengths and weaknesses (see also Jansweijer et al., 1982). Adaptive instruction thus can take the form of an "intelligent tutor," or a computer "coach"; theoretically, at least, it can perform both of the basic roles pictured in our Figure 21.1, and in addition provides a minute-to-minute feedback and correction function that serves both roles.

Goldstein (1980) has developed a computer coaching paradigm that embodies three educational roles as they interplay with the growing model of the student. These roles are labeled "expert," "psychologist," and "tutor," respectively. The expert uses a procedural representation of the skills needed to perform a particular task to specify what would be an optimal response or move in a given instance. This "move analysis" is then input to the psychologist, who judges the observed performance of the student in relation to what is known to be optimal as determined by the expert. When the student has made a move that is less than optimal, the psychologist enlists the tutor for intervention and advice. The tutor, of course, is programed with appropriate tutorial procedures and strategies. Other, quite advanced computerized instructional systems have been described by Sleeman and Brown (1982). One program, called STEAMER (Williams, Hollan, & Stevens, 1981), was developed to teach Navy personnel how to operate complicated propulsion systems and to solve problems in them when something goes wrong. The system uses detailed simulation of steam plant operations and a computer coach that "supervises." The coach questions the student, provides explanations, and enlists additional simulation tasks as needed to correct student bugs.

In theory, one can imagine both macroadaptation and microadaptation occurring within the same intelligent CAI program. Two or more macroadaptive streams might be established based on ATI evaluation. An example of this sort of CAI for the development of problem-solving skills is given by DeLeeuw (1983), who also showed how some microadaptive help-giving routines fit into the example programs. There is thus no reason, in principle, why ICAI cannot be made adaptive both with respect to aptitude information collected prior to the start of instruction and to aptitude information emerging during instruction. The latter may control choices of next frames, test items, or types of specific learning aids, but also may govern the organization or inclusion of larger chunks of instruction. The model of each learner assembled by intelligent programs is then essentially an aptitude theory of *learning in process* for each learner. The sort of intelligent coach envisioned in such work thus makes a continuum between macro and micro levels of adaptation and updates the aptitude description of each learner along the way. It remains to work out how best to evaluate the performance of such programs along this continuum. It also remains to be seen how best to use what is learned about instructional adaptation by this route in the improvement of human teacher adaptation. The early work in ICAI has benefited from the study of adaptation displayed by human tutors as teachers — we can hope that understanding gained by ICAI research also feeds back to teacher training, observation, and classroom research.

Finally, for both human teachers and computers, there is always the threat of overdifferentiation of instruction, that is, making fine distinctions among individual learners on either micro or macro levels that are unnecessary. Overdifferentiation makes adaptive instruction more costly without attendant improvements in learning outcome, and may make instruction maladaptive in some cases, particularly at the macro level.

Summary

We can summarize this section as follows:

1. At the level of macroadaptation, there is an ideal structure for the definition and organization of adaptive teaching, at least in global terms. There is a logic against which particular proposed educational programs for adapting teaching to individual differences among students can be evaluated. This is the logic of our four concerns for evaluation — (a) the extent to which common goals are met by all students,

(b) whether or not inequities are preserved or produced in reaching those goals, (c) whether or not any students are ill-served relative to other instruction, and (d) the extent to which results tried in test sites produce similar results in application. There is also a framework toward which research can aim — to provide the theory and development needed to flesh out the details of improved practical systems — the framework of ATI research.

2. At the level of microadaptation, there is a vast array of human and computer teaching behavior that reflects attempts at adaptation, or could be used to facilitate adaptation, to individual differences among students. It is not clear that teachers use a conscious logic in guiding their attempts at adaptive behavior. And it is not clear that the logic used by ICAI programs is yet the best logic. Much teaching behavior can also be maladaptive if it is not guided by sound principles, or at least evaluated by sensitive assessment *in vivo*. Research at this level, however, can apply the same framework that seems appropriate for macroadaptation, although the details of teacher (or computer) functioning that improve microadaptation may turn out to be quite different.

3. At both macro and micro levels, taxonomies of likely aptitude and instructional variables are needed to guide research. This research will need to examine carefully the possibility that practical systems can use no more than a few control variables for adaptive purposes. Overdifferentiation can be uneconomical; it can also lead to overload and hence to maladaptation, particularly at the level of minute-to-minute teacher behavior. The limit for human teacher attention may be as low as two student aptitude variables: intelligence (or general scholastic ability), and academic motivation. The limit for computerized intelligent tutors, if any, is as yet unknown.

Research Evidence and Hypotheses for Adaptive Teaching

In this section we examine some existing research evidence and hypotheses concerning adaptive teaching within the framework of a taxonomy for adaptive teaching. To focus the discussion we first discuss the main categories of aptitude constructs relevant in education.

Aptitudes

Although there are myriad aptitude constructs that might be considered in research on adaptive teaching, it has been argued that the main research effort ought to focus upon those few aptitude constructs that seem to be most centrally important in learning from instruction (Snow, 1976). It has also been argued that aptitude constructs should not be studied in isolation but rather should be juxtaposed in hopes of reaching more general conceptions of aptitude complexes (Snow, in press). In the present state of the field, however, the three categories remain distinct: academic intelligence, academic motivation, and specific prior knowledge. We attend primarily to these here, but add examples also of research dealing with various personality and cognitive style constructs to show some of the other directions in which current research is moving.

INTELLECTUAL ABILITIES

Intellectual abilities clearly hold a central position. Intelligence, defined as a complex of cognitive skills and styles of work related to effective learning and transfer, is education's most important product, as well as its most important raw material. From antiquity to modern times, educational theories have recognized intelligence as relevant to education. Indeed, most early writers in Western history *defined* differential intelligence as differential educability. Intelligence was inferred from observations about an individual's ease of learning under educational conditions (Snow, 1982a).

The fact that intercorrelations among intelligence measures and school achievement measures are significantly positive and often quite high all along the age range is a finding that influences school practices in many ways. But intelligence and learning ability are neither unitary nor identical; learning in educational settings, intellectual growth, and their correlation, represent a complex, interwoven, multivariate progression derived through experience over time and consolidated with practice. Task performance skills transfer to performances on other similar tasks and are themselves strengthened by such transfer. These cognitive skills and strategies build up and differentiate over an individual's lifetime as a function of differing experiences (especially including educational experiences; see Anastasi, 1970; Ferguson, 1954, 1956).

The correlational and factor analytic research on mental tests has provided a distinction between three major kinds of intellectual ability that is useful for continuing investigations of relations between intelligence and education. Crystallized (verbal-educational) and fluid (analytic) ability are two strongly correlated but separable general intellectual abilities (Cattell, 1963; Horn, 1978). The former seems to be developed and called upon largely under conditions of formal education. The latter seems to be developed somewhat earlier, and is associated with performance in informal learning settings as well as formal educational settings, particularly where complex reasoning and problem solving are required. A third major ability factor is visualization, specialized for processing complex figural and spatial information. Recent empirical work by Undheim (1981) and Gustafsson (in press) suggests that crystallized ability is close to what Vernon long ago called verbal-educational ability; visualization is Vernon's spatial-mechanical ability; and fluid ability is essentially the same as Spearman's *g* and Thurstone's induction factor. In other words, modern factor analytic study of intelligence seems finally to have consolidated on these distinctions.

Crystallized ability is best reflected in performance on scholastic ability and achievement tests, and seems to be relevant to learning especially where meaningful understanding of complex material is required. This kind of ability would be expected to transfer to, and be most useful for, performance in formal educational settings. Fluid ability, on the other hand, is reflected in performance on tests of analytic reasoning and problem solving that are not tied to any particular acquired learning or previously experienced tasks. While it is possible

that different environments foster these two aptitudes differentially, both kinds of intelligence are relevant to education. Crystallized ability may relate to, and benefit in interaction with, familiar and similar instructional methods and content, whereas fluid ability may relate to and benefit from learning under conditions of new or unusual methods or content —those that are different from the traditional tasks and subjects of schooling (Snow, 1982a). Spatial ability seems to be relevant to learning mainly in geometry, architecture, dentistry, mechanics, and such other subjects that depend partly, if not wholly, on specific skills in comprehending and manipulating two- and three-dimensional spatial relationships (Cronbach, 1970).

Continuing research in cognitive instructional psychology is now seeking to analyze the complex performances required in school learning and related intellectual tasks, to identify the constituent cognitive and metacognitive skills and processes involved. Developmental studies seek an understanding of the growth of these skills and processes. Both aim at promoting aptitude development through direct treatment (Snow, 1982b). The expectation is that some aspects of intellectual ability will prove relatively unalterable by direct treatment, however, at least for some individuals. Thus there will always be need for trade-off between direct development to remove inaptitudes and alternative treatments to circumvent them.

SPECIFIC PRIOR KNOWLEDGE

We consider prior knowledge an aspect of intellectual ability, particularly crystallized ability, because in most cases measures of prior knowledge will correlate highly with general scholastic aptitude and achievement measures. Also, measures of prior knowledge used as aptitudes tend to show ATI quite similar to those obtained using general or crystallized ability measures as aptitudes. The interpretations of such ATI are similar as well (Tobias, 1976, 1981).

But it is the case that knowledge about knowledge is increasing rapidly in cognitive psychology. As the cognitive theory of knowledge acquisition and organization continues to develop one can envision diagnostic measures of knowledge structure serving as guides to instruction by either teacher or computer. The models of the learner built up in intelligent CAI programs are knowledge models; they permit detailed control of instruction fit specifically to the characteristics of the present state of learner knowledge at each stage of learning. The process analyses of intellectual abilities and the structural analyses of prior knowledge should come together at some point to yield an integrated description of both the knowledge and the skill aspect of cognitive aptitude as a guide for adaptive instruction.

ACADEMIC MOTIVATION AND RELATED
PERSONALITY CHARACTERISTICS

It has long been recognized that personality factors contribute something beyond intellectual abilities to performance on academic tasks. Both the magnitude and the direction of these influences have been studied for some time (Cattell, 1965). Modern research on personality now emphasizes the importance of situational influences and the manner in which person-situation interactions might be studied (Hettema, 1979; Magnusson & Endler, 1977; Mischel, 1977, 1979; Pervin, 1980). ATI is now seen as a special case of person–situation interaction psychology.

Although there have been numerous personality factors related to academic achievement, large bodies of significant research have developed around only a few. These are personality factors that have strong conceptual links to intellectual abilities, and that lead easily to theoretical predictions concerning relationships with academic achievement. The prime example is academic motivation, although its constituents—in achievement motivation, anxiety, self-concept, and locus of control—are often the focus of separate studies. Within the research on each of these constructs, however, can be found studies that have attempted to conceptualize and integrate related factors, thus moving toward more unified theories. Research on locus of control, for example, is closely related to research on both causal attributions and learned helplessness, and has formed the basis for one integrated theory of academic motivation (see Weiner, 1980). Research on self-concept is related to research on self-esteem, self-efficacy, and competence motivation, and forms the basic for another, larger theory of motivation (see Bandura, 1982). In turn, both locus of control and self-concept are relevant to theories of achievement motivation (see Atkinson, 1981). Since studies often define constructs differently and use different measures of underlying traits, however, this literature appears more disjointed than the theories would suggest.

Among the most significant developments in modern personality theory is the conceptualization of motivational phenomena in cognitive terms. McClelland (1965) defined achievement motivation as an "affectively toned associative network," and Bandura (1982) described anxiety as "repetitive perturbing ideation." Both Weiner (1976) and Lefcourt (1976) have carried out "attributional analyses" of achievement motivation and locus of control, respectively. Bandura (1977, 1982) also has developed a cognitive theory of self-efficacy (or perceived self-competence). This shift toward the assessment of the cognitive components of motivation has led to new theoretical positions and methodologies consistent with mainstream cognitive psychology, and seems to provide a basis for merging theories of intellect and personality (see Bower, 1981; Humphreys & Revelle, 1984). While studies have related such factors to performance in education, fewer efforts have been made to consider personality and motivation in conjunction with intellectual abilities as they impact education. Nor are there many examples of theoretical integrations of these different streams of educational literature (cf. Corno & Mandinach, 1983; Thomas, 1980).

Among the most replicated results are findings concerning school-related anxiety, which show a curvilinear relationship between anxiety and performance, particularly when short-term memory demands are high (Sarason, 1980). Lens (1983) has demonstrated this same inverted U-shaped relation for both test anxiety and need for achievement. Additionally, studies by Bandura and his co-workers repeatedly (Bandura, 1980; Bandura et al., 1980) demonstrate strong positive relationships between perceived self-efficacy for different tasks and actual performance on those tasks (when self-efficacy is defined

as one's subjective estimate of probability of success). This relationship may also be curvilinear (Salomon, 1983). Finally, Weiner (1979; Weiner et al., 1983) has shown in several experiments that the manner in which academic performances are interpreted by individuals has a strong influence on subjective statements of affect, motivated behavior towards tasks, and actual task performance. Internal attributions for success (feeling like an "origin" rather than a "pawn," DeCharms, 1976) generate positive affect, increased effort towards tasks, and greater success in the future. These attributions also seem to generate higher performance expectations, which Bandura's theory moves into proximal causal position.

Much of this research has been laboratory based. More recently, hypotheses derived from attribution and self-efficacy theory have been investigated in actual classroom contexts, with teachers and students. Here, studies have shown that poor performance patterns are often the result of interactions among classroom performance demands, lowered coping capabilities (including factors like increased anxiety, lowered efficacy expectations, and attributional tendencies that reflect unfavorable self-assessments of ability), and lower levels of intellectual ability (Clifford, 1979; Covington & Beery, 1976; Nicholls, 1979; Schunk, 1981, 1982, 1983, 1984). Such hypotheses have led to development of adaptive educational programs designed to reduce performance demands for lower ability students who appear less able to cope with traditional instruction. We describe examples of such programs later on.

OTHER APTITUDES

So called "cognitive or learning styles" are also popular aptitude constructs. We associate such constructs with the overlap between individual differences in intellectual abilities and personality characteristics. This is consistent with Messick's (1982) definition of cognitive styles as "information processing regularities that develop in congenial ways around underlying personality trends" (p. 4). It also recognizes that the most studied style constructs carry ability-like definitions, are assessed using cognitive performance tests (see also Kogan, 1976), and often show correlations with ability measures high enough to raise doubts about their construct validity.

Messick (1976) has described several of the most frequently studied cognitive styles. These include field dependence–independence (a global vs analytical orientation), cognitive complexity-simplicity (the degree of "differentiation or hierarchic integration" of cognitive structures), reflectivity–impulsivity (the tendency to approach tasks with speed vs. accuracy), risk-taking (willingness to take chances in approaching goals), and convergence-divergence (the tendency to converge toward or diverge from the obvious in hypothesis generation). As with intellectual abilities, it has become increasingly important for theories and research to identify and clarify the common processes that underlie the diverse array of style constructs (Lewis, 1976). Messick's work (1976, 1984) has progressed toward this end, moving away from considering cognitive styles as solely the domain of personality theory and research (cf. Shuell, 1981).

Cognitive styles are best placed within a zone of ability–personality overlap when their definition follows Messick's emphasis on an individual's *typical propensity* for a certain manner of work in given situations. Typical propensity is hypothesized to differ from but be constrained by one's enabling competence (intellectual ability) and enduring disposition (personality). Recent empirical work supports this position. For example, Linn and Kyllonen (1981) have studied the field dependence–independence (FDI) construct, and distinguished aspects of FDI that are strongly related to measures of general fluid ability from aspects of FDI that seem to stand separately as a cognitive style. The stylistic aspects appear to represent a typical propensity to approach tasks by selecting irrelevant rather than relevant problem-solving strategies.

Also, if intellectual abilities can be viewed as largely cognitive and personality characteristics as largely affective or conative, cognitive styles might be seen as reflecting metacognitive functions for individuals—as Messick says, for organizing and controlling other information-processing and emotional responses. Studies by Sternberg (1983) have demonstrated the important role of metacognitive components in performance on verbal ability tasks. The work of Snow and Lohman (1984) has also suggested such higher-order processes in other kinds of tasks. Other research has shown metacognitive functions to be critical in a variety of learning and problem-solving situations (Brown, 1978; Flavell, 1981), including classroom learning (Corno, 1980; Corno & Mandinach, 1983; Meichenbaum & Asarnow, 1979).

As with intellectual abilities and personality characteristics, stylistic differences can be shown to relate to performance in education. For example, Lees, Kagan, and Rabson (1963) found field-independent (FI) students to have an advantage over field-dependent (FD) students in learning analytic concepts (e.g., objects with a missing leg), while FD students had an advantage in learning inferential or relational concepts (e.g., objects related to school). Witkin and Goodenough (1981) reviewed studies showing that FI students seem to perform better in certain areas of the curriculum, such as mathematics, sciences, engineering, and other analytic fields. FD students seemed to perform better in curriculum areas that have a social value focus.

Another example derives from research on cognitive complexity. One measure of cognitive complexity is a sentence-completion test in which subjects write essays on rules, criticism, parents, and other topics (Hunt & Sullivan, 1974). Other measures of cognitive complexity include variations on the Role Construct Repertory Grid (Kelly, 1955). Different measures of and names for the same construct have created conceptual confusion in this area and made integration of results difficult. However, Cronbach and Snow (1977), in reviewing several instructional studies conducted by Hunt and others, concluded that cognitive complexity (here called conceptual level) was distinguishable from general ability when both measures were obtained in research samples. And, while inconsistent across studies, some ATI with both factors appeared.

In a different vein, Snow, Wescourt, and Collins (1980) examined effects of college students' control over their own instruction when studying a programing language via computer. Results showed different performance effects, depending on "learning style profiles" derived from more discrete learning activities observed while students were on-line. Students were seen as using relatively more or less of a "rapid-fire, argumenta-

tive, quitter style," or a "slow, methodical, conscientious, checking kind of style" (Snow, 1980a; p. 156). The latter style was characteristic of better performance under learner controlled conditions.

APTITUDE–LEARNING HYPOTHESES

We consider three broad categories of aptitude variables as critical predictors of educational performance. The three categories reflect roughly the traditional distinction in psychology between cognition, conation, and affection (Snow & Farr, in press), but they do not divide aptitude cleanly into three spheres of influence on learning. The three are most certainly interrelated. And perhaps the convenient tripartite distinction even inhibits the conceptualization of new, compound aptitude constructs, called aptitude complexes, that are specially assembled for performance in particular educational situations (Snow, in press). Yet, these are the categories into which the present research literature falls. And there are strong hypotheses to the effect that variables representing these different spheres of aptitude influence different aspects of educational performance, or the same aspects in different ways.

Figure 21.3 depicts one such hypothesis within this framework. The three categories—cognition, conation, and affection—are taken to be roughly analogous to the three categories into which aptitude variables have been traditionally divided—intellectual abilities, cognitive and learning styles, and

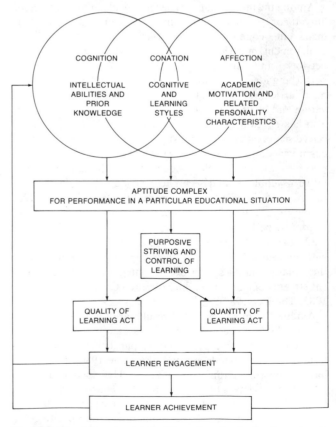

Fig 21.3 A schematic conception of aptitude for learning in relation to educational performance.

academic motivation and personality characteristics, respectively. The figure suggests that intellectual abilities as underlying cognitive processing skills have primary impact on the *quality* of educational performance — on the kinds of learning activities in which students engage as they encounter formal instruction. Personality predispositions related to academic motivation, on the other hand, may be hypothesized to exert a major impact on the *quantity* of educational performance — the persistence learners exhibit in pursuing educational goals, and their level of effort. Cognitive and learning strategies and styles, as typical propensities to process information in certain ways, derive in part from both underlying competencies and enduring dispositions, and may be hypothesized to impact that aspect of educational performance which voluntarily oversees and controls particular learning activities.

Educational aptitude complexes, that is, mixtures or compounds of these attributes for particular performance situations, will in this view also come to be associated with those several kinds of impact. The result is active learner engagement of relevant aptitudes from each category, which might be reflected in task-oriented learning behavior. "Engaged" behavior, in turn, has been shown to have consistent, positive effects on student educational achievement (see Berliner, 1979; Denham & Lieberman, 1980). This view also reflects a cycle of aptitude development wherein the continued exercise of aptitude in educational performance contributes to the continued strengthening and elaboration of aptitudes for future learning (Snow, 1982a).

A Taxonomy of Adaptive Teaching

Figure 21.4 depicts a taxonomy of adaptive teaching corresponding to the above conceptualization. To simplify the diagram we have not distinguished micro- and macroadaptation here. These would be represented as another facet in the figure. Of special interest in this taxonomy is an added dimension representing an instructional variation that can be observed across each form of adaptive teaching.

This dimension represents the extent to which the instructional environment can be said to *mediate* or act as intermediary agent in effecting student cognition and/or behavior. Much ATI research suggests that instructional treatments differ in the information-processing demands they place on learners (Cronbach & Snow, 1977). This is as true for training aimed

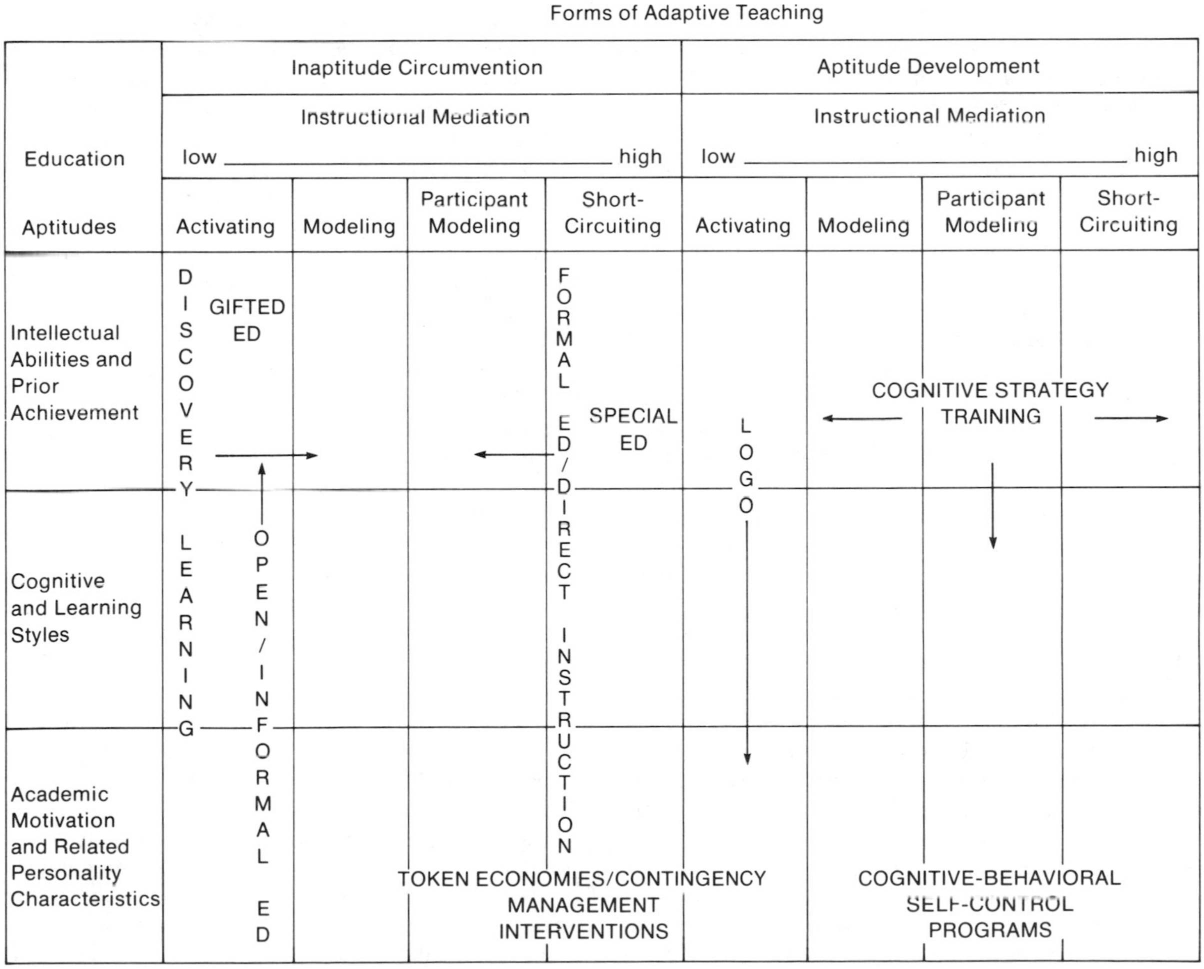

Fig. 21.4. A taxonomy of adaptive teaching.

at remediation of student inaptitudes as it is for alternative treatments adapted to student individual differences (Snow, 1982b; Snow & Lohman, 1984). Complex learning requires activity on the part of the learner. It requires at bottom appropriately invested mental effort on the part of the learner (Newell & Simon, 1972; Salomon, 1983). In different terms, it requires both metacognitive activity and cognitive processing of the information to be learned (Flavell, 1981). Teaching aids these learning activities by creating appropriate "conditions for learning" (Gagné, 1977). As instruction takes over more of the information processing burden, learning depends less on general intellectual abilities. As instruction takes over more of the burden for behavioral control, learning depends less on self-control. Thus instruction adapted to circumvent low ability will in some way reduce the processing burden, and instruction adapted to circumvent low motivation (defined here as low volition or self-control) will in some way reduce the burden of behavioral self-control. In so doing the instruction mediates (in the sense of Feuerstein, 1980) student cognition and behavior.

Little to no mediation gives learners opportunities for self-direction and discovery. More mediation demonstrates or models cognitive activity that students might imitate. Modeling plus guided practice mediates still more by its directive nature, and so may train aptitude directly. At the most intrusive end of this continuum is teaching that both directs and compensates learners in essentially a prosthetic sense — the teaching does for the students what they cannot or will not do for themselves. Salomon (1979) has described this most intrusive form of mediation as "short-circuiting" student processes and the least intrusive form as "activating" student processes. Activating mediation calls forth student capabilities and so includes the notion of capitalizing on learner aptitudes by tailoring instruction to learner capabilities or preferences. Corno and Mandinach (1983) adopted Salomon's terms in their view of classroom learning and motivation, and characterized the midrange categories of teacher mediation as "modeling" and "participant modeling" (after Bandura, 1977). We have used these terms here, although categorization distorts the implied continuum somewhat, as it does with the other dimensions.

Skilled teachers can move back and forth along a continuum of instructional mediation with the same student or different students. The range of aptitude variability in most classrooms, combined with the varied common and individual goals of education, make the need for skilled teacher judgments about appropriate mediation levels among the most problematic issues for teacher training and for research on teaching. Teaching and learning variability, in this respect, also make it difficult to locate any given educational program at some specified level of instructional mediation. We have identified in Figure 21.4 examples of teaching strategies or programs that can be seen as representing different levels, but our entries span several cells because the descriptions of the programs and our taxonomic distinctions remain crude at present.

Gifted and special education programs appear to be relatively straightforward examples of macroadaptations that function in the main to activate and short-circuit intellectual abilities, respectively. Some special education endeavors to develop aptitude directly; so-called cognitive strategy training and cognitive–behavioral self-control programs are both com-

monly used to teach the mentally retarded (Brown, 1978; Feuerstein, 1980) and the emotionally disturbed (Hewett & Blake, 1973). Such approaches seem to work for less able learners; they seem to intrude upon and interfere with the performance of more able learners. On the other hand, a common form of instruction used to teach intellectually able students is "discovery learning" (by other names, inductive teaching and inquiry teaching). Here students are led with little teacher support to discover abstract principles from concrete instances and make connections among seemingly disconnected events. In some versions of this form of instruction, the teacher even attempts to "entrap" students by intentionally leading them astray with faulty reasoning (Collins & Stevens, 1981). Such teaching places a cognitive burden on learners; students would be expected to succeed *if* their intellectual ability is up to the task. A growing body of ATI research supports this hypothesis: Discovery learning approaches tend to be effective for higher ability learners, but ineffective or even detrimental for lower ability learners (Cronbach & Snow, 1977; Snow, 1982a). Should this hypothesis continue to be substantiated, the use of discovery learning without regard to learner aptitude would be unwarranted.

As an example, consider the case argued by Seymour Papert (1980) that computer programing languages such as LOGO be taught to all students using a discovery format. In this discovery learning situation, as in others, one can expect substantial demand on the intellectual abilities of learners. Yet the subject of computer programming is different from some other subjects in the important possibility that, by learning structured programming, students will develop or improve skills in analytic and inferential reasoning. To write programs using the modern structured languages one uses both deductive and inductive reasoning (Winston & Horn, 1981). This fact has led some proponents to claim that the learning of structured programing develops general problem-solving aptitude (Papert, 1980). Preliminary research evidence, however, suggests that the realization of this aptitude development goal depends as much on how the subject is taught as it does on the nature of the subject itself. The case is similar with regard to evidence concerning the effects of learning in other subjects that manifest procedural demands — philosophy, statistics, scientific and literary inquiry, and the like. Subject matter knowledge is more or less "well-acquired" depending on teaching. For low-ability learners, discovery *de novo* can be a problematic way to learn; teacher mediation is required. Even for high-ability learners, mediation may be required to obtain the desired transfer to more general problem-solving outcomes (Sheingold, Kane, & Endreweit, 1983).

Finally, Figure 21.4 reflects an attempt to locate on the taxonomy the two popular general approaches to schooling embodied by the terms "open or informal" and "formal or direct" instruction (Bennett, 1976). Again, there is distortion because these forms of education have different features depending on the details of their application; however, open education is generally designed to encourage independent learning. It rests on an educational philosophy emphasizing the importance of discovery, experience, and free will (Neill, 1962). It also seeks to instill these qualities in the intellectual and social endeavors of students and so it spans the gamut of our aptitude dimension. In contrast, direct instruction or formal education rests on a different educational philosophy — one that emphasizes the student's need for guidance, support, and assistance in decision making. It gives teachers more control, and more justification for mediation. In formal or direct education the emphasis on the "whole person" is perhaps not as obvious as in informal education, but it seems typical for schools adopting that approach to maintain the formality outside the classroom as well (e.g., in dress codes, rules of conduct at play, etc.).

Another interpretation of our dimension of instructional mediation focuses on learner control: Low instructional mediation corresponds to high learner control. High learner control is hypothesized to serve high-ability and/or highly motivated learners best (Entwistle, 1981; Snow, 1980a). Conversely, high instructional mediation can be seen as corresponding more to "teacher direction," and thus less to learner control, at least over some aspects of the learning task. Learner control can be cognitive, behavioral, or both. As instruction can be shown to take over more of the burden for behavioral control — through, for example, behavioral monitoring and reinforcement, mediation extends beyond the cognitive domain and is more likely to interact with personality–motivation variables such as locus of control and self-efficacy (Bandura, 1982), or volitional variables such as self-regulation and purposive striving (Corno & Mandinach, 1983).

The use of this continuum of instructional mediation as a guide to adaptive teaching thus leads us to a more complete definition of adaptive teaching, which we can now state as follows:

> Adaptive teaching is teaching that arranges environmental conditions to fit learner individual differences. As learners gain in aptitude through experience with respect to the instructional goals at hand, such teaching adapts by becoming less intrusive. Less intrusion, less teacher or instructional mediation, increases the learner's information processing and/or behavioral burdens, and with this the need for more learner self-regulation. As the learner adapts, so also must the teacher.

By this definition, the instruction both adapts to the learner and allows the learner to adapt to the instruction. The teaching-learning transaction is dynamic and must be tuned to aptitude complexes in the learner that encompass intellectual abilities, personality motivation characteristics, and cognitive styles.

Selection of Example Studies

We have identified some research that seems to contribute to theory or offer hypotheses for future work on adaptive teaching as defined above. The best examples are classroom studies of carefully designed experimental treatments evaluated in an ATI framework, with measures of retention and transfer as well as of direct effects, and careful diagnosis of the teaching and learning processes that mediate between aptitude and outcome in each treatment. Such studies ask: What particular forms of instruction facilitate or interfere with learning for particular kinds of learners, and how do they do this? What aptitudes or inapti-

tudes for further learning are developed by these particular forms of instruction? Unfortunately, very little contemporary research addresses these questions directly and analytically. Most studies of adaptive teaching describe broad programs of major educational intervention, ask much simpler questions, and aim only at demonstrating average increases in educational outcomes. Since any method of teaching might serve some segment of a population more or less profitably than it serves the average, ATI hypotheses and methods are always relevant in instructional evaluations. The potential of any instructional treatment as a vehicle for adaptation cannot be determined otherwise.

The main effects of broad educational interventions are reviewed elsewhere in this volume. Also reviewed elsewhere are laboratory studies of psychological processes, and how particular psychological mechanisms are impacted by features of instruction. Such studies clearly inform research on adaptive teaching, but their implications are indirect. We limit our citations of current research to a selection of studies that exemplify more direct implications.

CURRENT RESEARCH — INAPTITUDE CIRCUMVENTION

We first examine studies representing the tradition of inaptitude circumvention. Such work suggests instructional procedures that might benefit learners with certain inaptitudes for conventional instruction. As previously stated, our hypothesis is that the degree of instructional mediation is a critical variable; inaptitudes described as low verbal ability, dysfunctional cognitive styles, and so forth may be circumvented by instruction that takes over the relevant cognitive or behavioral burdens for these learners. But there are many paths to this goal.

Earlier, Snow (1976; 1982a) reviewed research relating general intellectual abilities to teaching variations. While the review highlighted the difficulties involved in making sense of a large number of studies that differed both in characterizations of instruction and aptitude constructs, it does support the general hypothesis that instructional methods differ in information-processing burdens placed on learners and that this variation interacts with scholastic ability. The implication is that teachers can circumvent learner inability by using techniques that remove or take over some of the processing burden from less able learners. They can relieve such learners from difficult reading, analysis of complex concepts, and the necessity for substantial cognitive organizing, for example, and by so doing aid achievement and presumably also motivation, at least in the short term (see also Entwistle, 1981). In other words, the teacher specifically mediates the required cognitive processing for less able learners, while specifically not doing so for more able learners. What is not clear is how the teacher should moderate and eventually equalize this treatment difference as less able learners progress. Research has not yet followed the time course of this adaptation or examined it in systematically different classroom contexts.

But this line of research can now be merged with other significant work on school learning. First, efforts have been made by school-based researchers to work within domains of instruction over extended time periods, and to begin to develop common languages for describing that instruction. For example, from the large body of classroom research on teaching (reviewed by Brophy & Good, this volume) there has emerged a common view of the elements that constitute "direct instruction," a form of elementary school teaching that promotes on-task classroom behavior, and through it, increased academic achievement. From an adaptive teaching standpoint, direct instruction can be said to represent an effort by the teacher to monitor and control student classroom attention and persistence (to take over the process of behavioral control), rather than to permit or encourage students to control their own behavior. A second domain of effective elementary school instruction has emerged from a different theoretical and empirical base—namely "cooperative learning" (Johnson & Johnson, 1975; Slavin, 1983). While the various forms of cooperative learning have shown positive effects on academic achievement, more consistent effects have appeared on motivational outcomes, such as peer support, self-esteem, and self-attributions (Ames & Felker, 1979; Slavin, 1980). In contrast to direct instruction, which is teacher centered and large-group oriented, cooperative learning involves the use of heterogeneous student groups and more student-centered interaction.

The development of common terminology and measurement systems in each of these domains has gone a long way toward yielding consistent general conclusions. But not much of this work has asked the questions more pertinent to adaptive teaching, namely (a) To what extent does effectiveness of the method depend on the kind of student taught? (b) If effectiveness does depend on student aptitude, how might these procedures be merged, modified, or alternated to fit all the learners to be served; or (c) If effectiveness does not depend on student aptitude differences, why not?

Recent research by Peterson and her colleagues has asked these questions of direct instruction (Peterson, 1979; Peterson & Janicki, 1979). Work by Noreen Webb (1982a, 1982b, 1982c, 1983) has similarly investigated cooperative learning (see also Slavin, 1983). Results of these efforts show some ATI. For example, Janicki and Peterson (1980) found personality–instruction interactions such that students with positive attitudes and an internal locus of control performed significantly better in a small-group variation of direct instruction than in direct instruction as commonly presented to a large group.

Since cooperative learning features small-group instruction, it might not be expected to show ATI such as this. However, some studies of cooperative learning have shown mixed-ability small-group instruction to interact with student ability (prior achievement) (Lucker, Rosenfield, Sikes, & Aronson 1976; Slavin, 1980). These results favor cooperative learning as a form of instruction for circumventing student inaptitude; lower ability students performed better in the small-group approach. It is noteworthy, however, that high achievers also benefited from this form of instruction. Both Peterson, Janicki, and Swing (1981) and Webb (1982a; Webb & Kenderski, 1984) found ATI with intellectual ability to be curvilinear.

Webb's research has, in turn, helped to explain the processes by which small, mixed ability groups foster the learning of lower achievers and students low in motivation to perform. Her results show that higher ability students explain material to low-ability students, and that these explanations are generally correct. Relationships form among students as a consequence of such helping behavior, and both motivation and performance profit (Webb, 1982b, 1982c, 1983; see also Slavin, 1983).

These results serve as a different example of instructional mediation. In small, mixed-ability groups, higher ability students in effect serve as *substitute teachers* for students who have trouble learning. These higher ability peers provide the kind of instructional mediation (here by way of helping, coherent explanations) that a good teacher provides to a lower ability learner. The small-group context and group incentive structure permit more individualized attention, relationship building, and the possibility of experiencing success on a short time cycle. These aspects do not characterize the common definition of direct instruction, in which the teacher resource is not so leveraged. This current research shows also that many forms of instruction can be made to have features that aid lower achieving students. It is as possible for creative teachers to use the key features of cooperative learning in a context of direct instruction as it is for cooperative learning to manifest elements of individualization.

The hypothesis that emerges is that direct instruction facilitates learning for less able learners because it mediates and controls learning activities and processes such learners cannot control on their own, and that cooperative small groups of judiciously mixed abilities can be used to transfer some of the teacher mediation function to the more able learners in such groups. Among the many questions left for further research, however, is whether or not this adaptation promotes aptitude development in initially less able learners, so that the mediation support may eventually be withdrawn.

A provocative study by Hummel-Rossi (1981) suggests a new approach to research on adaptive teaching that brings several of these lines together. Teachers' reports of treatment directed to individual students were used to define two predominant treatment contrasts; eliciting–permissive versus directing–monitoring, and challenging versus encouraging. The first dimension in particular accounted for substantial variance in eighth grader achievement (standardized test performance and grades) along with ability tests and personality measures. ATI patterns were clearly implied:

> It appears that the teachers were highly directive and monitoring with apprehensive, insecure, and anxious students. They used more permissive techniques with self-assured, emotionally stable students. Also, they were highly directive and monitoring with the tough-minded, enthusiastic students and used eliciting–permissive methods with tender-minded, sober students. In giving feedback, teachers provided a clear intellectual challenge to emotionally stable, undemonstrative students and to bright students and gave warm encouragement to anxious, insecure students and to slow students. (p. 73)

Most importantly, the study followed the students through tenth grade achievement. The differential teacher treatments received in earlier grades were found to moderate aptitude-achievement relations observed later, suggesting important ATI relationships. The combination of teacher reports of differential treatment to students and longitudinal follow-up of students in later achievement settings demonstrates a way to use documented teacher adaptations as treatment variables in ATI research with potentially profound effects for research on teaching in general, as well as adaptive teaching.

CURRENT RESEARCH—APTITUDE DEVELOPMENT

A rather separate line of research has addressed the question of aptitude development. Snow (1982b) recently reviewed some of this literature and this section draws on that work. Since that review, however, studies in this category have burgeoned, particularly in the area of intellectual development.

Developing Intellectual Abilities and Cognitive Styles. One group of pertinent studies represents the attempt to develop general fluid ability directly, for elementary students as well as adults. Jacobs and colleagues, for example (see Jacobs, 1977; Jacobs & Vandeventer, 1968, 1972; Jacobs & White, 1971), investigated the effectiveness of training elementary students on the Raven Progressive Matrices and related reasoning tasks. Studies aimed at the Raven tasks alone showed significant but temporary improvement; however, studies aimed at training general classification skills showed increments in both performance and transfer to related tasks. These effects were also maintained for several weeks. Willis, Bliezner, and Baltes (1980) have now successfully trained and maintained training effects for fluid ability in adults. There are several other examples (Snow, 1982b).

One important outcome of these direct training efforts is the idea that training in generalizable cognitive strategies, rather than discrete cognitive skills, may have more long-lasting effects. A study by Sternberg and Weil (1980) makes this point as well. College students of different abilities were trained to use different classes of strategies for solving verbal analogy problems. In one type of training, subjects were asked to use a visualization procedure to organize statements into a spatial array. Examples were provided but subjects were able to use their own inventions as well. Another group of subjects was given an "algorithm" for solving the problems that used conditional logic to test alternatives. Each treatment group was compared to untreated controls. Results showed that the algorithm trained group solved the problems in less time. However, subjects of different abilities benefited most by using strategies consistent with their ability profiles (e.g., high spatial with visualization training, etc.). In addition, limited training such as this did little to assure that subjects would in fact do what they had been trained to do. Subjects trained to visualize, for example, were found to use that strategy and linguistic encoding as well. They did not differ from the untrained subjects in this regard. An important implication for future studies of aptitude development in this domain is that strategic differences among subjects, between verbal or spatial strategies for example, may reflect differences in relative strengths in analogous aptitudes.

Another study by Kyllonen, Lohman, and Snow (1981) trained high school students on a paper-folding spatial visualization task. Films were used to demonstrate both a folding–unfolding strategy and a verbal encoding strategy. These training conditions were compared to a practice and feedback condition

for students of different ability levels. Students high in spatial ability were found to perform best on training and transfer tasks when given the practice-feedback condition. In the terminology of adaptive teaching, this training permitted higher ability students to capitalize on (or activate) their existing aptitude for the task. Lower ability students, however, particularly those lower in both spatial and verbal ability, were helped most by the visualization training procedure (a form of modeling), at least on transfer to the related task. Again, these students seemed to derive benefit from a training approach that provided *some instructional mediation as it developed aptitude.* Thus research on direct aptitude development seems to reinforce our characterization of research within the school learning domain; direct training attempts may need to follow the same mediation principle.

Still, training in particular strategies will likely interact with aptitudes in complicated ways, just as instruction has been shown to interact with aptitudes in broader programs of education. Kyllonen, Woltz, & Lohman (1981) have shown that aptitudes and strategies not only interact, but also that students of different aptitudes may well shift strategies as tasks vary in difficulty or as experience is gained in the task. Thus, simple connections of ability and strategy, with or without training, are unlikely to reflect what learners actually do. A dynamic conception of aptitudinal adaptation is required.

The training of strategic cognitive and metacognitive activities in students has been a central focus of much additional research on the development of learning and memory skills and strategies, and strategies for learning from teaching (Brown, 1978; Corno, 1980, 1981; Meichenbaum & Asarnow, 1979; O'Neil, 1978; Pressley & Levin, 1983; Winne & Marx, 1980). Studies have also focused on special populations such as the mentally retarded (Feuerstein, 1980) and low achievers (Corno, Collins, & Capper, 1982; see also Brainin, in press). This work generally supports the position that learning and memory skills can be trained, that metacognitive awareness about learning from instruction can be developed, and that transfer to related strategic situations is possible if attention is paid in training to the generalization–transfer process (Glaser, 1984).

Developing Personality and Motivational Aptitudes. In addition to developing intellectual abilities, some research has focused on developing noncognitive aptitudes as well. Brophy (1983) has discussed teaching behavior designed to develop positive motivation for school learning in students. This is a task he argues, that must begin with counteracting the negative performance motivation that many students bring to school tasks. Low self-efficacy, high anxiety, an external locus of control, a tendency to internalize failure, and so forth all represent negative motivational patterns or lowered coping skills. Brophy writes:

> For these problems, social learning theorists would program for continuous progress and consistent success, achievement motivation theorists would train students to set challenging but achievable goals, and attribution theorists would train students to attribute poor performance to insufficient effort rather than to lack of ability. (p. 17)

As Brophy notes, while each of these recommendations has positive aspects, training in goal setting must involve appropriately realistic goals, and attribution retraining must also consider the extent to which students have been displaying errot on a task to begin with (see Clifford, 1979; Schunk, 1983; and Corno & Mandinach, 1983 for similar arguments). Each of these qualifications implies teaching adapted to different learner positions with respect to goals and task motivation.

Studies by Diener and Dweck (1978) and Schunk (1983) have shown positive effects for attribution retraining on school learning tasks. Schunk's research, in turn, has used Bandura's participant modeling instruction (Bandura, 1977) to develop self-efficacy, or positive success expectations in low-achieving students (Schunk, 1981, 1982, 1984). Other cognitive–behavioral intervention plans have been used in school settings to develop behavioral self-control (Kendall & Finch, 1979), reduce anxiety (Goldfried, 1979, and regulate anger and stress (Novaco, 1980).

Although programs of this sort have been successful in developing motivation to perform, results do not always transfer back to the classroom where conventional instruction —with its evaluative/comparative environment and large-group approach remains the norm. The student is being trained to adapt to instruction without concomitant adaptations in the instructional environment. Also, as Brophy points out, such studies do not necessarily develop motivation to *learn* — that is, to "seek to acquire the knowledge or skill that an academic activity is designed to develop" (p. 1). Development of motivation to learn is closely linked to the successful development of learning-to-learn skills, including metacognitive action control and the awareness that one *is* learning through one's own efforts and skills (Corno & Rohrkemper, in press). Put differently, it involves development of a "way" to learn in consonance with a "will" to learn, two aspects of learning that are in mutual interaction (Corno, Collins, & Capper, 1982).

One promising program for high school students with behavior problems (Sarason & Sarason, 1981) used modeling and role playing in a health course to strengthen cognitive, action control, and social skills. Control students receiving a regular health curriculum were compared with students trained in decision making in several "real world" situations: job interviewing, resisting peer pressure, asking for help in school and questions in class, cutting class, and several aspects of dealing with colleagues and authority figures. Both groups were comparable on ability measures and pretests of anxiety and problem solving. Posttests of problem solving and presentation of self in a job-interviewing situation showed trained students to outperform controls. A 1-year follow-up showed lower rates of tardiness and fewer behavior problems for the trained students as well.

From an adaptive teaching standpoint, results showed an anxiety-training interaction such that high-anxiety students benefited more from the modeling training than did low-anxiety students. The authors interpreted this result as consistent with other research showing students high in test anxiety to be particularly responsive to modeled activities in learning situations (Sarason, 1978). Snow (1977b) also discussed similar findings concerning the relationship between anxiety and school learning. Again, results support the importance of providing some environmental mediation for these students (see also Entwistle, 1981; Sieber, O'Neil, & Tobias, 1977; Solomon & Kendall, 1979). The modeling and role playing serve a participant modeling function for students who are anxious, which allows them to build coping skills as they learn (Bandura, 1982). Other school programs that fall into this category have been developed by Covington and Beery (1976) and Corno et al. (1982).

The Training and Evaluation of Adaptive Teaching

It has been said that exceptional teachers "measure students with a practiced eye" (Rubin, 1984). This simply described teacher aptitude is a complex capability; it includes such assets as alertness, "withitness," a propensity to check students' understanding continuously in a variety of ways, knowledge about how best to use what is observed, and a hesitant attitude about using any one approach with all students. These are characteristics of inquiring teachers, just as they are of inquiring individuals who seek to make sense of highly complex environments in any professional field. They are also features of intelligence broadly defined. The professional domains in which inquiry is required all have in common the need for reflection and analysis in a problem-filled environment.

As Doyle (1979) noted, classrooms have "multidimensionality, simultaneity, and unpredictability." Multidimensionality alone places great demands on teachers, and while some aspects of teaching become simpler at higher grade levels, others become more problematic. At all grade levels, the need for adaptive teaching within this complex environment persists. And the more environmental demands place information-processing and behavioral control burdens on individuals, the more effectiveness in that environment depends on general aptitudes.

What are the aptitudes for adaptive teaching, and might programs of teacher education both *develop these aptitudes* and *circumvent inaptitudes* as needed? Our view is that the training and evaluation of adaptive teaching must itself be adaptive because teachers, just as students, differ in these relevant aptitudes, however they are ultimately defined by continuing research. Unlike the learning of "basic skills" for teaching, however, the learning of adaptive teaching probably involves higher-order skills. Teachers can be readily taught to take specified actions to improve classroom management, to use both "direct" and "cooperative" kinds of instruction, or to perform in other ways that have been documented as effective. Indeed, these skills might be considered an important "common core" for teacher education. But the kind of aptitude that underlies effective adaptive teaching may require aptitude development of a rather different order.

The literature we have sampled on the training of intellectual ability again provides some implications. It is clear that attempts to develop abilities must go beyond simple practice and feedback, or coaching, or altering expectations; they must provide substantive training on the component skills involved in task performance and must also develop superordinate executive and control strategies involved in guiding performance and in generalizing and transferring skills to the classroom. Such development may be realized through long-term, regularized programs, but probably not through one-shot workshops. We also know that abilities, strategies, and methods of training interact. Attempts to develop either component skills or metacognitive strategies must fit training methods to an assessment of teachers' aptitude profiles. As before, training that is cognitively more intrusive will likely be most helpful for less able teacher trainees; such intervention could disrupt the effective strategies of those trainees initially more able. And the principle of inaptitude circumvention also includes the possibility of recognizing and capitalizing on each teacher's other strengths. By and large, research on teacher education has not yet addressed these issues.

Finally, teacher educators need to recognize that some aspects of aptitude for teaching may be developed in this manner and others not. Research on teacher education should be geared to distinguish such categories of aptitude; the results should be used to inform the selection of future teachers as well as their training. Most programs of teacher education do not approach the position of aptitude of teachers or its development in this manner, just as most educational programs for students do not approach student aptitude or its development in this manner. Yet the evaluation of adaptive teaching and the training of adaptive teachers both require an ATI perspective.

Toward a Theory of Adaptive Teaching

Students displaying aptitude for learning from conventional teaching will likely succeed in that environment. But the magnitude of aptitude variability typically confronting teachers and the evidence of strong relationship between such aptitude and achievement suggest that only some students in most classrooms will fall into this category. The majority of students will need more aptitude support than conventional teaching provides, and different kinds of specialized support will likely be needed for different kinds of students.

Available theory of aptitude for learning from teaching would hypothesize that such learning involves accessing, adapting, and applying whatever cognitive systems and structures a student already has, and inventing new systems and structures as necessary, to overcome whatever instructional impediments each student encounters. Intellectual abilities and related stylistic–personal propensities appear to represent the facilities required from both teachers and learners to accomplish this level of learning activity. The degree to which differences in these aptitudes relate to learning outcomes reflects the degree to which the teaching variations involved place demands on the learning variations involved. Analytic research toward a theory of adaptive teaching must determine how this transaction process connecting these variations takes place in a period of time, how it changes over time, and how it can be optimized to reach ultimate individual and common educational goals.

Optimization of adaptive teaching depends on transfer to the learning that occurs in other educational settings. The hypothesis is that transfer occurs by analogy among performances sharing family resemblance. What is transfered may be styles and strategies of teaching and learning, as well as acquired knowledge and skills, and research is needed to uncover the details by which this occurs.

With increasingly adaptive teaching, the cognitive, affective, and conative products of successful learning and transfer should become consolidated. Intellectual ability is reflected in consistent learning, and consistent learning is reflected in intellectual facility. Similarly, stylistic–personal aptitudes and constructive behavior and attitudes toward learning are mutually facilitating. But different forms of adaptation may breed different kinds of aptitude for further learning; they may also fail to develop certain aptitudes. One hypothesis, that fluid ability and crystallized ability, in particular, may develop from different kinds of learning and teaching experiences appears reasonable from preliminary evidence (Snow, 1982a). But longitudinal research is needed to assess this expectation — research that attends especially to transfer relations among educational experiences that may result in aptitude development and differentiation. Investigation of some of these hypotheses concerning aptitude for learning from teaching should, in turn, contribute to the theory and research on adaptive teaching we have attempted to describe and illustrate here.

Ultimately, the aim of research on teaching and on teacher training should be to show how individual teachers can best adapt to individual students. That should also be the aim of research on ICAI. Unfortunately, still today, only a small proportion of educational research addresses this issue.

REFERENCES

Ames, C., & Felker, D. (1979). An examination of children's attributions and achievement-related evaluations in competitive, cooperative, and individualistic reward structures. *Journal of Educational Psychology, 71*, 413–420.

Anastasi, A. (1970). On the formation of psychological traits. *American Psychologist, 25*, 899–910.

Atkinson, J. W. (1981). Studying personality in the content of an advanced motivational psychology. *American Psychologist, 36*, 117–129.

Atkinson, R. C. (1968). Computerized instruction and the learning process. *American Psychologist, 23*, 225–239.

Bandura, A. (1977). Self-efficacy: Toward a unifying theory of behavorial change. *Psychological Review, 84*, 191–215.

Bandura, A. (1978). The self system in reciprocal determinism. *American Psychologist, 33*, 348–358.

Bandura, A. (1980). The self and mechanisms of agency. In J. Suls (Ed.), *Psychological perspectives on the self* (Vol. 1). Hillsdale, NJ: Erlbaum.

Bandura, A. (1981). Self-referent thought: A developmental analysis of self-efficacy. In J. H. Flavell & L. D. Ross (Eds.), *Cognitive social development: Frontiers and possible futures* (pp. 200–240). NY: Cambridge University Press.

Bandura, A. (1982). Self-efficacy mechanism in human agency. *American Psychologist, 37*, 122–148.

Bandura, A., Adams, N. E., Hardy, A. B., & Howells, G. N. (1980). Tests of the generality of self-efficacy theory. *Cognitive Therapy and Research, 4*, 39–66.

Bangert, R. L., Kulik, J. A., & Kulik, C.-A. C. (1983). Individualized systems of instruction in secondary schools. *Review of Educational Research, 53*, 143–158.

Bellack, A. A., Kliebard, H. M., Hyman, R. T., & Smith, F. L. (1966). *The language of the classroom.* New York: Teachers College Press, Columbia University.

Bennett, S. N. (1976). *Teaching styles and pupil progress.* London: Open Books.

Berliner, D. C. (1979). Tempus educare. In P. L. Peterson & H. L. Walberg (Eds.), *Research on teaching* (pp. 120–136). Berkeley, CA: McCutchan.

Berliner, D. C. (1983). Developing conceptions of classroom environments: Some light on the T in classroom studies of ATI. *Educational Psychologist, 18*, 1–13.

Block, J. H. (Ed.). (1971). *Mastery learning: Theory and practice.* New York: Holt, Rinehart & Winston.

Block, J. H., and Burns, R. B. (1976). Mastery learning. *Review of Research in Education, 4*, 3–48.

Bloom, B. S. (1976). *Human characteristics and school learning.* New York: McGraw-Hill.

Bower, G. H. (1981). Mood and memory. *American Psychologist, 36*, 129–149.

Brainin, S. S. (1985, in press) Mediating learning: Pedagogic issues in the improvement of cognitive functioning. *Review of Research in Education, 12.*

Brophy, J. (1983). Conceptualizing student motivation. *Educational Psychologist, 18*, 200–215.

Brown, A. L. (1978). Knowing when, where, and how to remember: A problem of metacognition. In R. Glaser (Ed.), *Advances in instructional psychology* (Vol. 1, pp. 77–167). Hillsdale, NJ: Erlbaum.

Brown, J. S., & Burton, R. R. (1978). Diagnostic models for procedural bugs in basic mathematical skills. *Cognitive Science, 2*, 155–192.

Calfee, R., & Brown, R. (1979). Grouping students for instruction. In D. L. Duke (Ed.), *Classroom management* (78th yearbook of the National Society for the Study of Education, pp. 144–182). Chicago: University of Chicago Press.

Cattell, R. B. (1963). Theory of fluid and crystallized intelligence: A critical experiment. *Journal of Educational Psychology, 54*, 1–22.

Cattell, R. B. (1965). *The scientific analysis of personality.* Baltimore, MD: Penguin.

Clark, C. M., Gage, N. L., Marx, R. W., Peterson, P. L., Stayrock, N. G., & Winne, P. H. (1979). A factorial experiment on teacher structuring, soliciting, and reacting. *Journal of Educational Psychology, 71*, 534–553.

Clark, C. M., Snow, R. E., & Shavelson, R. J. (1976). Three experiments on learning to teach. *Journal of Teacher Education, 27*, 174–180.

Clark, C. M., & Yinger, R. J. (1977). Research on teacher thinking. *Curriculum Inquiry, 7*, 279–394.

Clifford, M. (1979). Effects of failure: Alternative explanations and possible implications. *Educational Psychologist, 14*, 44–52.

Cohen, E. G., Intili, J. K., & Robbins, S. H. (1979). Task and authority: A sociological view of classroom management. In D. L. Duke (Ed.), *Classroom management* (78th yearbook of the National Society for the Study of Education, pp. 116–144). Chicago: University of Chicago Press.

Collins, A., & Stevens, A. L. (1981). A cognitive theory of interactive teaching. In C. M. Reigeluth (Ed.), *Instructional design theories and models: An overview.* New York: Academic Press.

Corno, L. (1980). Individual and class level effects of parent-assisted instruction in classroom memory support strategies. *Journal of Educational Psychology, 74*, 278–292.

Corno, L. (1981). Cognitive organizing in classrooms. *Curriculum Inquiry, 11*, 359–377.

Corno, L., Collins, K. M., & Capper, J. (1982). *Where there's a way there's a will: Self-regulating the low achieving student.* (ERIC Document Reproduction Service No. ED 222 499 TM 820)

Corno, L., & Mandinach, E. B. (1983). The role of cognitive engagement in classroom learning and motivation. *Educational Psychologist, 18*, 88–108.

Corno, L., & Rohrkemper, M. M. (in press). The intrinsic motivation to learn in classrooms. In C. Ames & R. Ames (Eds.), *Research on motivation in education: The classroom milieu.* Orlando, FL: Academic Press.

Covington, M. W., & Beery, R. G. (1976). *Self-worth and school learning.* New York: Holt, Rinehart & Winston.

Crawford, W. J., Gage, N. L., Corno, L., Stayrook, N. G., Mitman, A. L., Schunk, D., & Stallings, J. (1978). *An experiment on teacher and parent-assisted instruction in the third grade* (Vols. 1–3). Stanford, CA: Center for Educational Research at Stanford.

Cronbach, L. J. (1967). How can instruction be adapted to individual differences? In R. M. Gagné (Ed.), *Learning and individual differences.* Columbus, OH: Charles E. Merrill.

Cronbach, L. J. (1970). *Essentials of psychological testing* (3rd ed.). New York: Harper & Row.

Cronbach, L. J. (1975). Beyond the two disciplines of scientific psychology. *American Psychologist, 30*, 116–127.

Cronbach, L. J., & Snow, R. E. (Eds.). (1977). *Aptitudes and instructional methods.* New York: Irvington/Naiburg.

DeCharms, R. (1976). *Enhancing motivation: Change in the classroom.* New York: Irvington.

DeLeeuw, L. (1983). Teaching problem solving: An ATI study of the effects of teaching algorithmic and heuristic solution methods. *Instructional Science, 12*, 1–48.

Denham, C. & Lieberman, A. (Eds.). (1980). *Time to learn.* Washington, DC: National Institute of Education.

Diener, C. I., & Dweck, C. S. (1978). An analysis of learned helplessness: Continuous changes in performance, strategy, and achievement cognitions following failures. *Journal of Personality and Social Psychology, 36*, 451–462.

Doyle, W. (1979). Learning the classroom environment: An ecological analysis. *Journal of Teacher Education, 28*, 51–55.

Entwistle, N. (1981). *Styles of learning and teaching.* New York: John Wiley.

Fenstermacher, G. D., & Goodlad, J. I. (1983). *Individual differences and the common curriculum* (82nd yearbook of the National Society for the Study of Education). Chicago: University of Chicago Press.

Ferguson, G. A. (1954). On learning and human ability. *Canadian Journal of Psychology, 8*, 95–112.

Ferguson, G. A. (1956). On transfer and the abilities of man. *Canadian Journal of Psychology, 10*, 121–131.

Feuerstein, R. (1980). *Instrumental enrichment: An intervention program for cognitive modifiability.* Baltimore, MD: University Park Press.

Flavell, J. (1981). Cognitive monitoring. In P. Dickson (Ed.), *Children's oral communication skills.* New York: Academic Press.

Gage, N. L. (1978). *The scientific basis of the art of teaching.* New York: Teachers College Press, Columbia University.

Gagné, R. M. (1977). *The conditions of learning* (3rd ed.). New York: Holt, Rinehart & Winston.

Gagné, R. M., & Briggs, L. J. (1977). *The principles of instructional design.* New York: Holt, Rinehart & Winston.

Glaser, R. (1977). *Adaptive education: Individual diversity and learning.* New York: Holt, Rinehart & Winston.

Glaser, R. (1984). Education and thinking: The role of knowledge. *American Psychologist, 39*, 93–105.

Goldfried, M. R. (1979). Anxiety reduction through cognitive-behavioral intervention. In P. C. Kendall & S. D. Hollon (Eds.). *Cognitive–behavioral interventions: Theory, research, and procedures* (pp. 177–153). New York: Academic Press.

Goldstein, I. (1980). Developing a computational representation for problem-solving skills. In D. T. Tuma & F. Reif (Eds.), *Problem solving and education: Issues in teaching and research.* Hillsdale, NJ: Erlbaum.

Good, T. L., & Grouws, D. (1979). The Missouri Mathematics Effectiveness Project: An experimental study in fourth grade classrooms. *Journal of Educational Psychology, 71*, 355–362.

Good, T. L., & Stipek, D. J. (1983). Individual differences in the classroom: A psychological perspective. In G. D. Fenstermacher & J. I. Goodlad (Eds.), *Individual differences and the common curriculum* (82nd yearbook of the National Society for the Study of Education, Part 1, pp. 9–44). Chicago: University of Chicago Press.

Gustafsson, J.-E. (in press). A unifying model for the structure of intellectual abilities. *Intelligence.*

Henry, N. B. (Ed.). (1962). *Individualizing Instruction* (61st yearbook of the National Society for the Study of Education, Part 1). Chicago: University of Chicago Press.

Hettema, P. J. (1979). *Personality and adaptation.* Amsterdam: North Holland.

Hewett, F. M., & Blake, P. R. (1973). Teaching the emotionally disturbed. In R. M. W. Travers (Ed.), *Second handbook of research on teaching.* Chicago: Rand McNally.

Horn, J. L. (1978). Human ability systems. In P. B. Baltes (Ed.), *Life-span development and behavior* (Vol. 1). New York: Academic Press.

Hummel-Rossi, B. (1981). Aptitudes as predictors of achievement moderated by teacher effect. *Measuring Human Abilities: New Directions for Testing and Measurement, 12*, 59–86.

Humphreys, M. S., & Revelle, W. (1984). Personality, motivation, and performance: A theory of the relationship between individual differences and information processing. *Psychological Review, 91*, 153–185.

Hunt, D. E., & Sullivan, E. V. (1974). *Between psychology and education.* Hinsdale, IL: Dryden.

Jacobs, P. I. (1977). *Up the IQ! How to raise your child's intelligence.* New York: Wyden Books.

Jacobs, P. I. & Vandeventer, M. (1968). Progressive matrices: An experimental developmental, non-factoral analysis. *Perceptual and Motor Skills, 27*, 759-766.

Jacobs, P. I. & Vandeventer, M. (1972). Evaluating the teaching of intelligence. *Educational and Psychological Measurement, 1972, 32*, 235–248.

Jacobs, P. I. & White, M. N. (1971). *Transfer of training in double classification skills across operations in Guilford's structure-of-intellect model* (Research Bulletin 69-20). Princeton, NJ: Educational Testing Service.

Janicki, T. C., & Peterson, P. L. (1980). *Aptitude–treatment interaction effects of variations in direct instruction* (Tech. Rep. No. 537). Madison: Wisconsin R & D Center for Individualized Schooling.

Jansweijer, W. N. H., Konst, L., Elshout, J. J., and Wieling, A. (1982). *PDP: A protocol diagnostic program for problem solving in physics.* Paper presented to the European Conference on Artificial Intelligence, Paris.

Johnson, D. W., & Johnson, R. T. (1975). *Learning together and alone.* Englewood Cliffs, NJ: Prentice–Hall.

Keller, F.S. (1968). Goodbye teacher . . . *Journal of Applied Behavior Analysis, 1*, 79–89.

Kelly, G. A. (1955). *The psychology of personal constructs.* New York: Norton.

Kendall, P. C., & Finch, A. J., Jr. (1979). Developing nonimpulsive behavior in children: Cognitive-behavioral strategies for self-control. In P. C. Kendall & S. D. Hollon (Eds.), *Cognitive–behavioral interventions: Theory, research, and procedures* (pp. 37–81). New York: Academic Press.

Klausmeier, H. J. (1977). Instructional programming for the individual student. In H. J. Klausmeier, R. A. Rossmiller, & M. Saily (Eds.). *Individually guided elementary education.* New York: Academic Press.

Klausmeier, H. J., Rossmiller, R. A., and Saily, M. (Eds.). (1977). *Individually guided elementary education: Concepts and practices.* New York: Academic Press.

Kogan, N. (1976). *Cognitive styles in infancy and early childhood.* Hillsdale, NJ: Erlbaum.

Kulik, J. A., Kulik, C.-L., & Cohen, P. A. (1979). A meta-analysis of outcome studies of Keller's Personalized System of Instruction. *American Psychologist, 34*, 307–318.

Kyllonen, P. C., Lohman, D. F., & Snow, R. E. (1981). *Effects of task facets and strategy training on spatial task performance* (Tech. Rep. No. 14). Stanford, CA: Stanford University, School of Education, Aptitude Research Project.

Kyllonen, P. C., Woltz, D. J., & Lohman, D. F. (1981). *Models of strategy and strategy–shifting in spatial visualization performance* (Tech. report 17). Stanford, CA: Stanford University, Aptitude Research Project, School of Education (NTIS No. AD-A108 003).

Lees, L. C., Kagan, J., & Rabson, A. (1963). Influence of a preference for analytic categorization upon concept acquisition. *Child Development, 34*, 433–442.

Leftcourt, H. M. (1976). *Locus of Control.* Hillsdale NJ: Erlbaum.

Lens, W. (1983). *Achievement motivation, test anxiety, and academic achievement* (Psychological Report No. 21). Leuven, Belgium: University of Leuven.

Lewis, B. M. (1976). Avoidance of aptitude–treatment trivialities. In S. Messick (Ed.), *Individuality in learning.* San Francisco: Jossey–Bass.

Linn, M. C., & Kyllonen, P. (1981). The field dependence–independence construct: Some, one, or none. *Journal of Educational Psychology, 73*, 261–273.

Lochhead, J., & Clement, J. (Eds.). (1979). *Cognitive process instruction.* Philadelphia: Franklin Institute Press.

Lucker, G. W., Rosenfield, D., Sikes, J., & Aronson, E. (1976). Performance in the interdependent classroom: A field study. *American Educational Research Journal, 13*, 115–123.

Maccoby, E. E., & Jacklin, C. N. (1974). *The psychology of sex differences.* Palo Alto, CA: Stanford University Press.

Maeroff, G. I. (1983, January 9). Teaching to think: A new emphasis. *New York Times Education Supplement*, pp. 1, 37.

Magnusson, D., & Endler, N. S. (Eds.). (1977). *Personality at the crossroads: Current issues in interactional psychology.* Hillsdale, NJ: Erlbaum.

Mandinach, E. B. (1984). *The role of strategic planning and self-regulation in learning an intellectual computer game.* Unpublished doctoral dissertation, Stanford University, School of Education.

McClelland, D. C. (1965). Toward a theory of motive acquisition. *American Psychologist, 33*, 201–211.

McNair, K. (1978-1979). Capturing inflight decisions: Thoughts while teaching. *Educational Research Quarterly, 3*, 16–25.

Meichenbaum, D., & Asarnow, J. (1979). Cognitive–behavioral modification and metacognitive development. Implications for the classroom. In P. C. Kendall & S. D. Hollon (Eds.). *Cognitive–behavioral interventions: Theory, research, and procedures* (pp. 11–37). New York: Academic Press.

Messick, S. (Ed.). (1976). *Individuality in learning: Implications of cognitive styles and creativity for human development.* San Francisco: Jossey–Bass.

Messick, S. (1984). The nature of cognitive styles: Problems and promise in educational practice. *Educational Psychologist, 19*, 59–75.

Miller, G. A., Galanter, E., & Pribram, K. (1960). *Plans and the structure of behavior.* New York: Holt, Rinehart & Winston.

Milojkovic, J. D. (1983). *Children learning computer programming: Cognitive and motivational consequences.* Unpublished doctoral dissertation, Stanford University, Stanford, CA.

Mischel, W. (1977). On the future of personality measurement. *American Psychologist, 32*, 246–254.

Mischel, W. (1979). On the interface of cognition and personality: Beyond the person–situation debate. *American Psychologist, 34*, 740–754.

Mitman, A. L., & Snow, R. E. (1984). Logical and methodological problems in teacher expectancy research. In J. B. Dusek, V. C. Hall, & W. J. Mayer (Eds.), *Teacher expectancies.* Hillsdale, NJ: Erlbaum.

Neill, A. S. (1962). *Summerhill: A radical approach to childrearing.* New York: Hart.

Newell, A., & Simon, H. A. (1972). *Human problem solving.* Englewood Cliffs, NJ: Prentice–Hall.

Nicholls, J. G. (1979). Quality and equality in intellectual development: The role of motivation in education. *American Psychologist, 34*, 1071–1085.

Novaco, R. W. (1979). The cognitive regulation of anger and stress. In P. C. Kendall & S. D. Hollon (Eds.), *Cognitive–behavioral interventions: Theory, research, and procedures.* New York: Academic Press.

O'Neil, H. F., Jr. (Ed.). (1978). *Learning strategies.* New York: Academic Press.

O'Neil, H. F., Jr., and Spielberger, C. D. (Eds.). (1979). *Cognitive and affective learning strategies.* New York: Academic Press.

Papert, S. (1980). *Mindstorms: Children, computers, and powerful ideas.* New York: Basic Books.

Pervin, L. A. (1980). *Personality: Theory, assessment, and research* (3rd ed). New York: John Wiley.

Peterson, P. L. (1977). Review of human characteristics and school learning. *American Educational Research Journal, 14*, 73–79.

Peterson, P. L. (1979). Direct instruction reconsidered. In P. L. Peterson & H. L. Walberg (Eds.) *Research on teaching: Concepts, findings, and implications* (pp. 57–70). Berkeley, CA: McCutchan.

Peterson, P. L., & Janicki, T. C. (1979). Individual characteristics and children's learning in large-group and small-group approaches. *Journal of Educational Psychology, 71*, 677–687.

Peterson, P. L., Janicki, T. C., & Swing, S. (1981). Ability × treatment interaction effects on children's learning in large group and small group approaches. *American Educational Research Journal, 18*, 453–473.

Popkewitz, T. L., Tabachick, B. R., & Wehlage, G. (1982). *The myth of educational reform.* Madison: University of Wisconsin Press.

Pressley, M., & Levin, J. R. (Eds.) (1983). *Cognitive strategy research: Educational applications.* New York: Springer-Verlag.

Rosenholtz, S. J., & Wilson, B. (1980). The effect of classroom structure on shared perceptions of ability. *American Educational Research Journal, 17,* 75–82.

Rubin, L. (1984). *Artistry in teaching.* New York: Random House.

Salomon, G. (1979). *Interaction of media, cognition and learning.* San Francisco: Jossey-Bass.

Salomon, G. (1983). The differential investment of mental effort in learning from different sources. *Educational Psychologist, 18,* 42–50.

Sarason, I. G. (1978). A cognitive social learning approach to juvenile delinquency. In R. Hare & D. Shalling (Eds.), *Psychopathic behavior: Approaches to research.* London: John Wiley.

Sarason, I. G. (Ed.). (1980). *Test anxiety: Theory, research and applications.* Hillsdale, NJ: Erlbaum.

Sarason, I. G., & Sarason, B. R. (1981). Teaching and social skills to high school students. *Journal of Consulting and Clinical Psychology, 49,* 908–918.

Schunk, D. H. (1981). Modeling and attributional effects on children's achievement. *Journal of Educational Psychology, 73,* 93–106.

Schunk, D. H. (1982). Effects of effort attributional feedback on children's perceived self-efficacy and achievement. *Journal of Educational Psychology, 74,* 548–557.

Schunk, D. H. (1983). Ability versus effort attributional feedback: Differential effects on self-efficacy and achievement. *Journal of Educational Psychology, 75,* 848–857.

Schunk, D. H. (1984). Self-efficacy perspective on achievement behavior. *Educational Psychologist, 19,* 48–58.

Shavelson, R. J. (1976). Teachers' decision making. In N. L. Gage (Ed.), *The psychology of teaching methods* (75th yearbook of the National Society for the Study of Education, pp. 372–415). Chicago: University of Chicago Press.

Shavelson, R. J., & Stern, P. (1981). Research on teachers' pedagogical thoughts, judgments, decisions, and behavior. *Review of Eductional Research, 51,* 455–498.

Sheingold, K., Kane, J. H., & Endreweit, M. E. (1983). Microcomputer use in schools: Developing a research agenda. *Harvard Educational Review, 53,* 412–433.

Shuell, T. J. (1981). Dimensions of individual differences. In F. H. Farley & N. J. Gordon (Eds.), *Psychology and education: The state of the union* (pp. 32–60). Berkeley, CA: McCutchan.

Slavin, R. E. (1980). Cooperative learning. *Review of Educational Research, 50,* 315–342.

Slavin, R. E. (1983). *Cooperative learning.* NY: Longman.

Slavin, R. E., & Karweit, N. L. (1984). *Mathematics achievement effects of three levels of individualization: Whole class, ability grouped, and individualized instruction* (Report No. 349). Baltimore, MD: Johns Hopkins University, Center for Social Organization of Schools.

Sleeman, D., & Brown, J. S. (1982). *Intelligent tutoring systems.* New York: Academic Press.

Snow, R. E. (1973). Theory construction for research on teaching. In R. M. W. Travers (Ed.), *Second handbook of research on teaching* (pp. 77–133). Chicago: Rand McNally.

Snow, R. E. (1976). Research on aptitudes: A progress report. *Review of Research in Education, 4,* 50–105.

Snow, R. E. (1977). Individual differences and instructional theory. *Educational Researcher, 6*(10), 11–15.

Snow, R. E. (1980a). Aptitude, learner control, and adaptive instruction. *Educational Psychologist, 15,* 151–158.

Snow, R. E. (1980b). Aptitude processes. In R. E. Snow, P.-A. Federico, & W. E. Montague (Eds.), *Aptitude, learning, and instruction: Vol. 2. Cognitive process analyses of learning and problem solving* (pp. 27–65). Hillsdale, NJ: Erlbaum.

Snow, R. E. [in collaboration with E. Yalow]. (1982a). Education and intelligence. In R. J. Sternberg (Ed.), *Handbook of human intelligence* (pp. 493–586). London: Cambridge University Press.

Snow, R. E. (1982b). The training of intellectual aptitude. In D. K. Detterman & R. J. Sternberg (Eds.), *How and how much can intelligence be increased?* Norwood, NJ: Ablex.

Snow, R. E. (1984). Placing children in special education: Some comments. *Educational Researcher, 13,* 12–14.

Snow, R. E. (in press). Aptitude complexes. In R. E. Snow and M. J. Farr (Eds.), *Aptitude, learning, and instruction: Vol. 3. Conative and affective process analyses.* Hillsdale, NJ: Erlbaum.

Snow, R. E., & Farr, M. J. (Eds.). (in press). *Aptitude, learning, and instruction: Vol. 3. Conative and affective process analyses.* Hillsdale, NJ: Erlbaum.

Snow, R. E., & Lohman, D. F. (1984). Toward a theory of cognitive aptitude for learning from instruction. *Journal of Educational Psychology, 76,* 347–376.

Snow, R. E., Wescourt, K., & Collins, J. (1980). *Individual differences in aptitude and learning from interactive computer-based instruction* (Tech. Rep. No. 11). Stanford, CA: Stanford University, School of Education, Aptitude Research Project.

Solomon, D., & Kendall, A. J. (1979). *Children in classrooms: An investigation of person–environment interaction.* New York: Praeger.

Sternberg, R. J. (1983). Reasoning, problem solving, and intelligence. In R. J. Sternberg (Ed.), *Handbook of human intelligence* (pp. 225–308). New York: Cambridge University Press.

Sternberg, R. J., & Weil, E. M. (1980). An aptitude-strategy interaction in linear syllogistic reasoning. *Journal of Educational Psychology, 72,* 226–234.

Stevens, A. L., & Collins, A. (1980). Multiple conceptual models of a complex system. In R. E. Snow, P.-A. Federico, & W. E. Montague (Eds.), *Aptitude, learning, and instruction: Vol. 2. Cognitive process analyses of learning and problem solving* (p. 177–199). Hillsdale, NJ: Erlbaum.

Taba, H. (1966). *Teaching strategies and cognitive functioning in elementary school children* (Cooperative Research Project 2404). San Francisco: San Francisco State College.

Thomas, J. W. (1980). Agency and achievement: Self-management and self-regard. *Review of Educational Research, 50,* 213–241.

Tobias, S. (1976). Achievement treatment interaction. *Review of Educational Research, 46,* 61–74.

Tobias, S. (1981). Adaptation to individual differences. In F. H. Farley & N. J. Gordon (Eds.), *Psychology and education: The state of the union* (pp. 60–81). Berkeley, CA: McCutchan.

Undheim, J. O. (1981). On intelligence II: A neo-Spearman model to replace Cattell's theory of fluid and crystallized intelligence. *Scandinavian Journal of Psychology, 22,* 181–187.

Wang, M. C. (1980). Adaptive instruction: Building on diversity. *Theory Into Practice, 19*(2), 122–128.

Wang, M. C., & Lindvall, C. M. (1984). Individual differences and school learning environments. *Review of Research in Education, 11,* pp. 161–225.

Wang, M. C., & Walberg, H. J. (1983). Adaptive instruction and classroom time. *American Educational Research Journal, 20,* 601–627.

Webb, N. M. (1980). A process–outcome analysis of learning in group and individual settings. *Educational Psychologist, 15,* 69–83.

Webb, N. M. (1982a). Peer interaction and learning in cooperative small groups. *Journal of Educational Psychology, 74,* 642–656.

Webb, N. M. (1982b). Student interaction and learning in small groups. *Review of Educational Research, 52,* 421–446.

Webb, N. M. (1982c). Group composition, group interaction, and achievement in cooperative small groups. *Journal of Educational Psychology, 74,* 475–485.

Webb, N. M. (1983). Predicting learning from student interaction: Defining the interaction variables. *Educational Psychologist, 18,* 33–42.

Webb, N. M., & Kenderski, C. (1984). Student interaction and learning in small group and whole class settings. In P. L. Peterson (Ed.), *Student diversity and the organization: Processes and use of instructional groups in the classrooms.* New York: Academic Press.

Weiner, B. (1976). Attribution theory, achievement motivation, and the eduational process. *Review of Educational Research, 42,* 201–215.

Weiner, B. (1979). A theory of motivation for some classroom experiences. *Journal of Educational Psychology, 71,* 3–25.

Weiner, B. (1980). *Human motivation.* New York: Holt, Rinehart & Winston.

Weiner, B., Graham, S., Taylor, S. E., & Meyer, W.-U. (1983). Social cognition in the classroom. *Educational Psychologist, 18,* 109–124.

Weinstein, R. S. (1976). Reading group membership in first grade: Teacher behaviors and pupil experience over time. *Journal of Educational Psychology, 68*, 103–116.

Weinstein, R. S. (1983). Student mediation of classroom expectancy effects. In J. B. Dusek (Ed.), *Teacher expectancies*. Hillsdale, NJ: Erlbaum.

Weisgerber, R. A. (Ed.). (1971a). *Perspectives in individualized learning*. New York: McGraw-Hill.

Weisgerber, R. A. (Ed.). (1971b). *Developmental efforts in individualized learning*. Itasca, IL: F. E. Peacock.

Whipple, G. M. (Ed.). (1925). *Adapting the schools to individual differences* (24th yearbook of the National Society for the Study of Education, Part 2). Bloomington, IL: Public School Publishing.

Williams, M. D., Hollan, J. D., & Stevens, A. (1981). An overview of STEAMER: An advanced computer-assisted instruction system for propulsion engineering. *Behavior Research Methods and Instrumentation, 13*(2), 85–90.

Willis, S. L., Blieszner, R., & Baltes, P. B. (1980). *Training research in aging: Modification of intellectual performance on a fluid ability component*. University Park: Pennsylvania State University, College of Human Development.

Winne, P. H. & Marx, R. W (1980). Matching students' cognitive responses to teaching skills. *Journal of Educational Psychology, 72*, 257–264.

Winston, P. H., & Horn, B. K. P. (1981). *LISP*. Reading, MA: Addison-Wesley.

Witkin, H. A. & Goodenough, D. R. (1981). *Cognitive styles: Essence and origins*. New York: International Universities Press.

Yinger, R. J. (1977). *A study of teacher planning: Description and theory development using ethnographic and information processing methods*. Unpublished doctoral dissertation, Michigan State University, East Lansing, MI.

22.
Teaching Creative and Gifted Learners

E. Paul Torrance
The University of Georgia

Since the publication of the *Second Handbook of Research on Teaching* (Travers, 1973), there has been an enormous increase in the literature of the teaching of creative and gifted learners. At that time, there were only two stable specialty journals in this area, the *Gifted Child Quarterly* and the *Journal of Creative Behavior*. A few articles were being published in *Exceptional Children* and *Teaching Exceptional Children* on the education of gifted and creative learners. Since then, there has emerged the *Journal for the Education of the Gifted* (an official publication of The Association for the Gifted of the Council for Exceptional Children), *Roeper Review: A Journal on Gifted Child Education*, *G/C/T* (Gifted, Creative, Talented), *Gifted Education International*, *Creative Child and Adult Quarterly*, *Gifted International*, and *Prism: A Magazine for the Gifted*. In addition, there are the popular *Gifted Children Newsletter* and the *Bulletin* of the National/State Leadership Training Institute on the Gifted and the Talented. A number of countries outside of the United States have similar newsletters, as Taiwan, Republic of South Africa, and the United Kingdom.

Several specialty publishers have emerged to develop teaching materials especially for creative and gifted learners. These include: DOK Publishers, Creative Learning Press, Trillium Press, Bearly Limited, Resources for the Gifted, Good Apple, Foxtail Press, and the National/State Leadership Training Institute on the Gifted and the Talented. The literature generated by doctoral dissertations on gifted and talented learners has reached an all-time high during the past decade, as have reports of experimental programs, demonstration or model programs, dissemination programs, and state agencies. Most of this literature is difficult to acquire and little reliance has been placed upon it in preparing this chapter.

To provide an overview of the emerging body of knowledge about teaching creative and gifted learners, an effort will be

made to summarize some of the earlier surveys. After this, the leading trends of the past decade, as revealed by the literature, will be identified and discussed.

Surveys and Compilations

In the *Second Handbook of Research on Teaching*, Getzels and Dillon (1973) identified 30 different program alternatives for teaching the gifted. These included: summer classes, nongraded primary schools, early school admission, college courses for high school students, college credit for high school courses, special classes in particular subjects, special classes in all subjects, Saturday classes, ability grouping, enrichment in regular classrooms, itinerant resource teachers, additional courses beyond a normal load, clubs and extracurricular activities, field trips, special televised courses, half-day regular and half-day enriched classrooms, acceleration, special schools, counseling, individual tutoring, independent study, student exchange, flexible progression taking advanced courses, advanced placement, honors programs, non-school programs such as libraries, museums, orchestras, etc.), new curricula, self-instructional systems (correspondence study), mentors, and parent programs.

Meanwhile, Passow (1980) in the United States and Furr (1972) in Canada have reviewed program alternatives for gifted and talented students and found diversities such as those reported by Getzels and Dillon. In 1979, one of the yearbooks of the National Society for the Study of Education was devoted to the status of knowledge about educational provisions for the gifted and talented (Passow, 1979). Among the new emphases that emerged in this review were career education; adaptations for the culturally different, disadvantaged, learning disabled, and females; Individual Education Plans (IEPs); and leader-

The author thanks reviewers Gary A. Davis (University of Wisconsin—Madison) and Donald J. Treffinger (State University College at Buffalo). Thanks also to Jack Presbury, Tammy Safter, Laura Hall, and Deborah Weiner.

ship. A compilation of 118 successful programs by the National Association for Gifted Children (Juntune, 1981) added cluster grouping, computer technology, future studies, research skills, and thinking skill development.

Although there seems to be general consensus that programs for the gifted should be an integral part of the school system (Sisk, 1980), there appears to be little agreement about how this integration should be accomplished. Surveys of what is happening in the United States in gifted education (Mitchell, 1980, 1984) indicate a strong trend away from enrichment in the regular classroom as the primary way of meeting the special needs of gifted learners. In fact, Mitchell's surveys and similar ones in specific states (Avery & Bartolini, 1979; Sloop, 1982) indicate that most programs consist of multiple alternatives instead of single ones.

In a survey of the research issues in educating the gifted, George (1983) concluded that research has continued to support the needs for: early identification of giftedness, student motivation and involvement in decisions, assistance in attaining potential, differentiated educational programs, interaction with peers of similar abilities and interests, attention to both cognitive and affective needs, homogeneous grouping by specific aptitudes, training in good study habits, long-term planning, the elimination of stereotyping, educational acceleration, and recognition of individual needs.

The most comprehensive recent survey of the status of gifted/talented education in the United States was conducted under the guidance of the Advisory Panel of the U. S. Office of Gifted and Talented by Gallagher, Weiss, Oglesby, and Thomas (1983). Although this survey was not concerned directly with matters of teaching the gifted/talented, it dealt with problems of what educational strategies are desirable to meet the special needs of this group. The parents of gifted/talented students surveyed urged that efforts be devoted to provide additional programs that would be challenging, stimulating, and individualized at both primary and secondary levels.

Examples of parental desires expressed in the Gallagher et al. survey (1983) included mentor/independent study that would be accepted by the school as valid; programs that teach such skills as communication, research, and intuitive thinking; and adequate guidance and counseling. Teachers expressed concern about making existing programs high in quality, their needs for inservice education, community support services in the form of mentors and community helpers, and specific teaching techniques for use with gifted/talented students. The administrators surveyed also expressed a recognition of the need for inservice education, community resources, and trained staff. Among administrators at the elementary school level, the most popular strategy was the resource room which combines special instruction by a specially trained teacher with experiences in the heterogeneous classroom. The second most popular preference was for the special class, with the teacher consultant strategy ranking third. At the high school level, the overwhelming preference was for the special class organized by subject matter. Independent study, the resource room, and special schools followed in that order. Enrichment was not highly favored at either the elementary or secondary level. Training in thinking skills received many favorable comments among all groups and educational levels.

Textbooks

No comprehensive review of the ways textbooks on the education of creative and gifted students deals with problems of teaching such students is possible here. However, it does seem essential to acknowledge contributions from this source. The leading textbooks, as identified by several university teachers in the field, include:

1. The third edition of Barbe and Renzulli's (1981) book of readings, *Psychology and Education of the Gifted*
2. Barbara Clark's (1979, 1983) *Growing Up Gifted*
3. James J. Gallagher's (1975) second edition of *Teaching the Gifted Child*
4. Gowan, Khatena, and Torrance's (1979) second edition of *Educating the Ablest*, a book of readings
5. Khatena's (1982) *Educational Psychology of the Gifted*
6. Maker's *Curriculum Development for the Gifted* (1982a) and *Teaching Models in Education of the Gifted* (1982b)
7. Sellin and Birch's (1980) *Educating Gifted and Talented Learners*
8. Tannenbaum's (1983) *Gifted Children: Psychological and Educational Perspective*

Trends in Program Alternatives

Radical Acceleration

Perhaps the most discussed trend in program alternatives during the past decade is Julian C. Stanley's advocacy of "radical acceleration" (Stanley, 1976, 1978a, 1978b, 1978c). Although research regarding the effects of acceleration has long been quite favorable, strong biases against it have kept it from being a popularly used option. In 1958 at the First Minnesota Conference on Gifted Children, Maynard C. Reynolds (1960) reviewed the research on acceleration and concluded that even at that time the evidence was adequate to indicate that moderately accelerated programs, applied selectively to mature and able students, are a viable alternative.

In a later survey, spanning a 50-year time period and covering 200 studies, Daurio (1979) found that not one study showed educational acceleration to be harmful or to have negative effects. Two-thirds of these studies were shown to have been beneficial. For more than a decade, Stanley and his associates (Stanley, 1976, 1978a, 1978b, 1978c; Stanley, Keating, & Fox, 1974) at Johns Hopkins University experimented with radical acceleration with mathematically precocious youths with excellent results. The program is now national in scope and has been expanded to include the verbally gifted (Fox & Durden, 1982) and other precocious groups. Many colleges and universities participated in accelerated programs by enrolling gifted, non-college youth (Solano & George, 1976; Spicker, 1982)

Mentoring

During the past decade, the use of mentors has become increasingly popular in gifted education, as reflected in an annotated bibliography (Noller & Frey, 1983) of 238 items on mentors, the popularity of the topic at professional meetings, and increased implementation of mentor programs in schools. Boston (1976); Lambert and Lambert (1982); Mattson (1983); Nash, Borman and Colson (1980); and Runions (1980) are among those who have reported successful mentor programs with gifted and creative learners.

In a 22-year longitudinal study of creative achievement, Torrance (1984a) found that having a mentor makes a statistically significant difference in creative achievement, as assessed by four criteria of success (number of publicly recognized creative achievements, number of personal or unrecognized creative achievements, judged quality of highest creative achievements, and the judged creativeness of future career images). This study questions the assumption that the mentor relationship is a brief, transitory one with a definite cutoff date; 52% of the mentor relationships reported by the study participants persisted at the time the study was conducted. The study also revealed the possible importance of helping creatively gifted young children find mentors, especially those from disadvantaged backgrounds. Torrance also found indications that a new and potentially important role may be emerging for mentors. A substantial number of the study participants attained their expertise through self-directed learning and/or a kind of apprenticeship with the assistance of a mentor. Since this expertise was not attained through a college, university, or other accrediting agency, there remained the problem of validating this expertise. In some cases, mentors were able to certify the expertise of their mentees through personal contacts or recommendations. In other cases, subjects either failed to attain this validation of their expertise or followed very circuitous paths to achieve it.

In his futuristic view of gifted child education, Plowman (1979) speculated that the changing role of the teacher will shift in the direction of mentoring. He predicted that mentors will replace certified teachers for much of education and educational planning. Mentors will determine that certain competencies have been mastered and certify that this has been done. Noller (1982) suggested that mentors use a creative problem solving process in carrying out their roles.

Self-Directed and Independent Study

A number of futurists (McHale, 1976; Rosen, 1976; Toffler, 1970) have predicted that there will be increasingly more self-directed learning at all educational levels. During the past decade, self-directed learning strategies have become rather common in teaching creative and gifted students (Torrance & Mourad, 1978). Treffinger (1975, 1980a, 1980b, 1981), Renzulli (1977), and Torrance (1979a) have been among the more outspoken advocates of this alternative. Treffinger has been especially active in developing program materials, developing guidelines for teachers and mentors or coaches, and conducting inservice workshops. Successful experiments have been reported by Bennett, Blanning, Boissere, Chang, and Collins (1971), Blanning (1978), Doherty and Evans (1981), Parke (1983), and Reiss and Cellerino (1983).

Individual Education Plans (IEPs)

For many years, arguments have been advanced in support of individual education plans for gifted students. However, it was not until IEPs were mandated for retarded, learning disabled, and other categories of handicapped learners that the practice became fairly widespread during the past decade. Among the advocates of this alternative have been Hedbring and Rubenzer (1979), Hershey (1980), Kaplan (1982), Lewis and Kanes (1979), Renzulli and Smith (1979), Stewart (1982), Treffinger (1979), and Wolf and Stephens (1979). Stewart (1982), for example, argued that both common sense and the best research available show plainly that no one type of program will meet all needs of gifted and talented learners. The very nature of programming for the gifted and talented is the art of making exceptions.

A variety of proposals have been made for implementing IEP programs and there has been considerable experimentation with IEPs in gifted education (Treffinger, 1979). Most of these plans integrate a variety of alternatives such as: regular classes with special assignments, enriched experiences, and self-directed study (Wolf & Stephens, 1979); the use of the Structure of Intellect Model (Hedbring & Rubenzer, 1979), and the Torrance Tests of Creative Thinking (Bogner, 1981) and the SOI tests (Meeker, 1979) as bases for learning activities and an accountability approach to programming for the gifted; and self-directed learning (Treffinger, 1979). Stanley (1978b) and Cox (1983a) described the use of Advanced Placement (AP) as a means of implementing individual programs and Cohn (1979) suggested a tutorial model. Cox (1983b) also described how continuous progress and nongraded systems accomplish individualization and implement IEPs.

The more inclusive instructional and program models generally emphasize the importance of individualized instruction and have built into them procedures for motivating and implementing independent study. Examples of these include: Feldhusen and Kolloff's (1978) Three-Stage Model for gifted education; Treffinger's (Treffinger & Barton, 1981) Individualized Programming Model; and Torrance's (1979c) Three Stage Incubation Model for teaching creative thinking. These models use basic principles of classroom learning and instructional design to guide development, teach subject matter knowledge, and implement individualized programming.

Renzulli's "Revolving Door" Model

A practical model that attracted widespread attention in the field of gifted education is Renzulli's "Revolving Door Model" (Renzulli, Reis, & Smith, 1981). In this plan, there are no rigid cutoff scores for admission and students may enter and leave the special program at almost any time. The upper 25% of the children in a school are designated as a talent pool. As one of the designated children generates ideas for a project and expresses strong commitment to it, he is admitted to a resource room to work on it. Prior to its widespread introduction, Renzulli and his associates conducted considerable field testing and evaluation. Research and continued evaluation of the model have been reported. For example, Delisle and Renzulli (1982) described a study of the correlates of the creative production that results from the implementation of the model. This study involved only students in the upper 25% of ability in their schools. It was found that using high rank in class as a criterion of admission would have missed a substantial percentage of students who function quite well on an independent basis. Renzulli (1982) has been concerned that real problems be used and has set forth criteria for such problems.

Counseling

During the past decade, there has been renewed and increased interest in counseling in meeting the needs of creative and gifted learners. One of the few agencies that have maintained a continuous program of service and research is located at the University of Wisconsin at Madison. For over 25 years, this agency has focused on the counseling of gifted youths. Marshall P. Sanborn (1979) of this agency, in his review concerning the counseling and guidance needs of the gifted and talented in the 1979 yearbook of the National Society for the Study of Education, emphasized the importance of recognizing the uniqueness of gifted students and the role counseling plays in dealing with the problems stemming from this uniqueness. One of the most significant books on counseling the gifted appeared in 1979 and was edited by Colangelo and Zaffran. In it, an array of distinguished authors reviewed the research evidence and advances on counseling issues such as identification, the needs of the creatively gifted, career development, the culturally diverse, black students, gifted women, families, and programming.

Van Tassell-Baska (1983) emphasized the importance of the teacher as a counselor of the gifted. Webb, Meckstroth, and Tolan (1982) dedicated themselves to the use of counseling and guidance skills with emotionally disturbed gifted students. Colangelo and Lafrenz (1981) and Frasier (1979) devoted themselves to studies of counseling the culturally diverse gifted. Brown (1978) has called attention to the dilemma of the divergent thinking gifted child and his/her need for assistance in solving adjustment problems.

Zaffran (1978) would expand the functions of counselors beyond counseling in the usual sense to include "consulting" and "research and evaluation" in work with gifted students. Kenny (1982) found that specifically designed creative writing activities can be used as a basis for guiding gifted learners to become increasingly aware of their feelings and perceptions and learn to recognize relationships between their achievements, aptitudes, interests, and goals.

Learning Styles

A considerable number of teachers of creative and gifted students saw the products resulting from research on styles of learning and thinking as a basis for adapting instruction and individual programs to the needs of the gifted. While some teachers relied upon the work of Dunn and Dunn (1975), others looked for guidance in tools growing out of the research on the specialized cerebral functions of the right and left hemispheres of the brain (McCarthy, 1980; Rubenzer, 1982). The developments associated with hemisphericity research and the differential information processing styles that flow from this

research have gripped the imaginations of teachers of the gifted and talented more than the work of Dunn and Dunn. They have also been more controversial.

At least two other learning style models have had considerable impact upon the education of gifted, creative, and talented students, both emanating from the University of Connecticut: Gregorc's (1982a, 1982b) Style Delineator and Renzulli and Smith's (1978) Learning Styles Inventory. Both of these models are instrumented by brief, easy to use, yet apparently quite powerful inventories.

Gregorc's (1982a, 1982b) Style Delineator divides thinking styles into two areas: perception and ordering. Perceptual abilities are defined as the means through which people gain information and may be abstract or concrete—through reason, emotion, and intuition or through the physical senses. Ordering abilities are the ways in which people arrange, systematize, and dispose of information. Ordering may be sequential or random—step-by step or nonlinear, simultaneous. From the concepts and measures derived, Gregorc has mapped the predictable behaviors and preferences of both teachers and students. Torrance (1982) found that Gregorc's Concrete Sequential style correlates positively and significantly (r's = .49 and .67) with the Left Hemisphere style of the Human Information Processing Survey (Torrance, Taggart, & Taggart, 1984). This scale also correlates negatively and significantly (r's = −.40 and −.35) with the Right Hemisphere scale. The Concrete Random scale correlates negatively and significantly (r's = −.41 and −.68) with the Left Hemisphere scale and positively and significantly (r's = .38 and .33) with the Right Hemisphere scale of the Human Information Processing Survey. Relationships for the Abstract Random and Abstract Sequential scales are small and less consistent than the other two scales.

Renzulli and Smith's (1978) Learning Styles Inventory is one of the instruments developed by Renzulli and his associates to guide teachers in planning learning experiences that take into account the learning style preferences of students. It yields descriptive information about student attitudes regarding the following nine general modes of instruction:

1. Projects
2. Drill and recitation
3. Peer teaching
4. Discussion
5. Teaching games
6. Independent study
7. Programmed instruction
8. Lecture
9. Simulation

This instrument seems to be easy to use and its interpretation seems to be quite straightforward and practical in its implications.

Dunn and Price (1980) reported one study involving 109 subjects identified as gifted in grades 4-8 and using the Dunn, Dunn, and Price inventory, found six variables that differentiated between gifted and nongifted students at the same educational levels. Gifted students preferred a formal design of instruction, did not need much structure, were less responsible;

preferred learning through tactile and kinesthetic senses; and had a lower preference for using auditory senses. In another study involving 170 junior high school gifted students and nongifted students, Griggs and Price (1982) found that gifted students were less teacher-motivated and more persistent and preferred quiet, learning alone, and not to use the auditory sense.

Special Schools

Just prior to the present decade, a variety of special schools for the gifted emerged as a part of the "magnet" school movement. Some of these have persisted but evaluation reports of their successes are not readily available. However, some of the older special schools have endured and have established outstanding records for serving special needs of gifted and creative learners. Cox and Daniel (1983) investigated a number of these schools as well as a variety of other kinds of programs for the gifted. They reported that there was a general disenchantment among gifted students with public schools in meeting their needs. However, the special schools seemed to be exceptions. Students in these schools stayed for hours after school and returned on weekends. They were enthusiastic, intense, and satisfied. Some of the special schools described in the literature of gifted education include: the Bronx High School of Science (Taffel, 1961; Cox & Daniel, 1983), Hunter College High School (Lawton, 1961), Yehudi Menuhin School for the Musically Gifted (Gibberd, 1966), New York City School of Music and Art (Wechsler, 1961), the Interlochen Arts Academy and National Music Camp (Cox & Daniel, 1983), and Prep-Tech (Amara & Leona, 1983), a school for academically talented students in Lexington, Massachusetts.

Saturday and Summer Programs

In many communities throughout the world, Saturday (and sometimes Sunday) and summer programs have also been popular vehicles for serving the special needs of creative and gifted students. Each year, the summer programs are listed in such media as *Gifted Children Newsletter*, *G/C/T*, and so on. The literature of gifted education is replete with descriptions of these programs. For example, Feldhusen and his associates at Purdue University have developed and described a variety of such Saturday and summer programs developed by them. Feldhusen and Wyman (1980) and Feldhusen and Sokol (1982) have reported evaluations of one of these programs and concluded that such programs do serve important needs and that the evaluations of students, teachers, and parents are quite positive. Cox (1979) investigated a number of international summer programs and consistently found positive evaluations.

Community Based Programs

The flowering of the career education movement brought renewed interest in community based educational programs and the utilization of community resources in the education of gifted students. Many of the mentor programs now in existence (Pinelli, 1977a, 1977b) were inspired by the career education

movement. Some science programs also made imaginative use of community resources and showed that such use of resources can enrich the knowledge of students, provide individualized learning in a society of specialization, and encourage the creativity of students. Colson (1980) has reported a very careful and positive evaluation of one such program. Museums appear to be a very rich resource for gifted learners (Friedman & Master, 1981). In looking to the future, Fizzell (1980) proposed that many of the special needs of gifted children might be met through community service centers. In fact similar centers are operating in Israel (Lubling & Zorman, 1982), the Republic of South Africa (Omond, 1982), and elsewhere.

Instructional Materials and Strategies

Developing Instructional Materials

During the past 10 years, an enormous amount of instructional materials has been created for use with creative and gifted students. Feldhusen and Treffinger (1980) and Karnes and Collins (1980) described and evaluated a great quantity of these materials that purport to develop creative thinking and problem-solving skills among gifted students. Feldhusen and Treffinger (1977) suggested criteria for selecting instructional materials and offered guidelines for creating teacher-planned instructional materials. Torrance and some of his associates (Black & Torrance, 1981; Torrance, 1978; Torrance & Torrance, 1978) have advocated the use of the different models of the creative problem-solving process as a basis for creating instructional materials. Torrance (1980) has also offered and implemented in a variety of settings a three-stage guide for creating lesson plans for facilitating incubation and creative problem solving. This set of guidelines has been used by at least one textbook company in preparing teacher guides, suggesting facilitative activities before, during, and after (or at the end of) a lesson.

Juntune (1979), Renzulli & Callahan (1975), and others used models of the creative problem-solving process as guides to creating curriculum materials. As evidence of the attention given to the art and science of creating instructional materials for gifted and creative learners, a 1983 issue of *Gifted Education International* contains an article from England and one from Western Australia on projects dealing with this problem. Foster (1983) described how groups of teachers in Croydon, England, collaborated to produce instructional materials for gifted primary pupils. They were evaluated following classroom testing. Print (1983) in Western Australia recommended the creation of curriculum extension packs as an effective way of coping with the needs of gifted pupils, which avoids labeling and segregation.

The section on teaching creativity will summarize data regarding curriculum packages and curriculum and administrative arrangements designed to teach creative thinking skills.

Simulations and Games

A vast literature accumulated during the past decade on simulations and games in gifted education in the form of professional articles, teacher-constructed simulation exercises and games, and commercial materials. Some leaders in gifted education have ridiculed these efforts as "fun and games" with no substantive or artistic content. While it may be true that some of the creators and/or users of these materials may have deviated from their goals at times, frequently there has been a lack of understanding of the power of simulations and games to challenge thinking, resulting in further investigation and study. Among the advocates of simulation for gifted learners has been Dorothy Sisk (1975b) who cites such advantages of simulation and games as:

1. Continuity of the natural way children gather information
2. Gives children a reason to learn
3. High level thinking is stimulated
4. Gives a valuable tool for teaching social values

To this list, Cline (1979) has added: the development of self-directed learning skills; social and affective functioning; integration of learning concepts; and risk and decision making. Kennedy and Newman (1976) studied the effects of games on the analytic and problem solving skills of young children (grades K-2) with moderately successful results. Hall (1979) studied the effects of simulation gaming on changing attitudes regarding sex roles. She found this to be a very effective means of bringing about awareness of sex-role typing, changing attitudes about sex roles, and developing open discussion. Pearson and Martfuggis (1979) found games to be an effective replacement for drills and quizzes, reviewing materials, finding out what happens in real life problems, and making these activities more exciting.

Materials in Subject Matter Fields

Although there have been no large-scale curriculum projects such as emerged in the 1960s, the past decade did see the emergence of efforts to create new instructional materials in subject matter to meet the special needs of gifted students. As in the 1960s, more effort seems to be focused on science and mathematics than any other curriculum area (Bartkovich & Mezynski, 1980; Del Giorno, 1977; Fox, 1981; George, 1976; Wheatley, 1983; Youngs, 1979). Attention has also been given to developing social studies materials (Jones, 1983; Seidman & Spain, 1983); visual arts programs (Chetelat, 1981; Szekeley, 1980); language arts (California State Department of Education, 1981; Sebesta, 1976); foreign languages (Rebbeck, 1983); human relations (Tomer, 1980); moral education (Vare, 1979); interdisciplinary materials such as language arts in science (Cravats, 1978), poetry and language arts in music (Cleveland, 1978), and even death education (Smith & Binge, 1976). The career education movement also resulted in the production and testing of materials designed for creative and gifted students (Feldhusen & Kolloff, 1979; Fox, 1976; Harding & Berger, 1979; Moore, 1979; Torrance, 1979a, 1979b).

The past decade gave considerable attention to reading as a subject matter field for the gifted. Some of the studies dealt with the extent to which provisions have been made for the gifted in the teaching of reading (McCormick & Swassing, 1982) and

whether or not junior high school gifted students need reading instruction (Dawkins, 1978). There has been continued attention to materials for developing creative reading skills (Martin & Cramond, 1983; Switzer & Nourse, 1979). Reading guides with activities to be performed before, during, and after reading have been tested with gifted students (Savage, 1983). The therapeutic and personality development aspects of reading for gifted children have also been researched (Frasier & McCannon, 1980; Korth, 1977; Pilon, 1977).

Developing Creativity and Other Tool Skills

Changing Objectives in the Education of Creative and Gifted Students

It seems obvious to the author that as civilization changes and evolves, concepts of giftedness must change. Otherwise, everyone will suffer and there will be much waste of talent, resources, and energy. Subtle changes have already taken place in the objectives of education, especially the education of the gifted and creative, in the direction of greater creativity (Torrance, 1963, 1976, 1984b). However, these changes in objectives have not been widely recognized and acknowledged. Consequently, there is considerable dissonance between what is being learned in schools and what is being evaluated. The author senses, however, that new insights are emerging among educators, the press, and the general public that may soon reduce this dissonance and move us in the direction of a new concept of giftedness in harmony with the demands of the future.

Actually, gifted students have been quite impatient with failures of educators to recognize the need for these changes. Throughout the past decade, many gifted students have said that schools as they now exist are obsolescent and are more of a tradition than a necessity (Torrance, 1976). In the 1980s, many educators in the field of gifted education have joined in this chorus and have said that schools cannot continue as centers of education unless they adapt to and plan for future developments (Weaver & Wallace, 1980) and that schools should help the gifted acquire skills of future planning, the ability to anticipate events and to respond creatively to the unexpected (Silvernail, 1980; Torrance, 1980). The future needs most frequently mentioned by scholars in the field of gifted education include: creative problem solving skills, forecasting and planning, research skills, computer skills, scientific methodology, and inventing skills.

Creativity Skills

Surveys of the status of gifted education (Mitchell, 1980, 1984) continue to show that the teaching of creativity skills is the most frequently mentioned differentiating characteristic of the teaching offered creative and gifted students. However, there have continued to be strong and vigorous opponents of these efforts (Keating, 1980; Mansfield & Busse, 1981; Stanley, 1980). There are still arguments that creative problem solving skills cannot be taught, that time devoted to the teaching of these skills is wasted and results in declines in SAT scores and failures to master the basics, and that the hundreds of experiments demonstrating the effectiveness of these efforts lack validity and have methodological flaws.

In 1972, Torrance analyzed and evaluated the results of 142 studies he was able to locate in the literature of the effects of attempts to teach creative thinking skills. When deliberate, systematic problem solving skills were taught, the percentage of successes was over 90. Using all 142 studies and all of the criteria used to assess outcomes, the overall percentage of successes was 72. There has continued to accumulate an impressive amount of evidence supporting the contention that it is possible to teach the skills of creative problem solving in such ways as to increase the chances of solving real life problems, improving performance on creativity tests, and producing products judged to be "creative."

In preparation for writing this chapter, 166 experimental studies at the elementary and secondary levels and 76 at the college and adult level conducted since the 1972 survey were located and analyzed. Table 22.1 presents a summary of successes in teaching students to think creatively according to type of training procedure for the 166 elementary and secondary studies conducted since the 1972 survey and compares these results with those revealed by the 1972 survey.

Table 22.1. Summary of Successes in Teaching Students to Think Creatively According to Type of Intervention Prior to and After 1972

Type of Intervention	Number of Studies		Number of Successes		Percentage of Successes	
	1972	1983	1972	1983	1972	1983
Osborn/Parnes CPS or modification	22	7	20.0	6.2	91	88
Other disciplined CPS procedures	5	22	4.6	16.2	92	73
Complex programs involving packages	25	31	18.0	18.7	72	60
Complex programs involving combination of strategies	—	15	—	11.5	—	77
Creative arts as vehicles	18	18	14.5	13.1	81	73
Media and reading programs	10	3	7.8	1.25	78	42
Curricular and administrative arr.	8	5	4.0	2.7	50	54
Teacher–classroom variables	26	14	14.4	8.8	55	63
Motivation, reward, competition	12	6	8.0	3.5	67	58
Facilitating testing conditions	16	20	11.0	14.1	69	70
Affective education programs	—	13	—	10.3	—	79
Altered awareness	—	6	—	4.0 d	—	67
Other conditions	—	6	—	2.8	—	47
Total (Mean)	142	166	102.3	112.6	(72)	(68)

Although there are fewer studies in the 1983 survey than in the 1972 survey using the Osborn-Parnes Creative Problem Solving procedure, the percentage of successes continues to be higher than for other categories of experimental intervention. However, this is somewhat misleading as many of the other types of training programs rely upon the Osborn-Parnes procedures as a general system and combine it with other strategies. The difficulty may be that these procedures are not taught well enough and practiced, weakening the effects. There was in 1983 a big increase in the number of studies using other disciplined approaches (from 5 to 22). However, there seems to be little or no tendency in these experimental studies to embrace such disciplined procedures as Synectics, Edward de Bono's Lateral Thinking, and the Japanese procedures such as the "KJ" and "NM" methods. Instead, the experimenters tend to devise their own disciplined procedures.

The popularity of complex programs involving packages of materials continued but the percentage of successes for these dropped somewhat (from 72 to 60%). However, a new category of complex program involving a combination of strategies emerged and the record of successes of these experiments was fairly high (77% in 15 studies). The use of the arts (drama, music, visual arts, etc.) continued to be fairly common (18 both in 1972 and 1983). The use of media and reading programs to teach creative thinking skills declined both in number and percentage of successes (from 10 to 3 studies and from 78 to 42%). The use of curricular and administrative arrangements and teacher-classroom variables remained at about the same number and level of success, as did facilitating testing conditions and the use of motivation, reward, and competition. In addition to complex programs involving a combination of strategies, two other categories emerged: affective education programs and altered awareness such as meditation, fantasy, and imagery training. The affective education programs showed a success rate of 79% and the altered awareness treatments showed one of 67%.

Table 22.2 presents a comparison of all of the elementary and secondary studies (both the 1972 and 1983 surveys) with the college and adult studies in the present survey.

There are striking differences between the elementary/secondary and college/adult studies both in type of training and in percentage of successes. As a whole, the college/adult training was somewhat more successful than the elementary/secondary training (86% compared to 70%). Especially striking is the lack of college/adult studies using complex programs involving packages of curriculum materials; media and reading; curricular and administrative arrangements; teacher/classroom variables; motivation, reward, and competition. There were also few college/adult studies involving the creative arts, and affective education programs. The most frequently used intervention at the college/adult level was the use of complex programs involving several strategies. In many courses these were courses in creative thinking or regular subject matter courses taught by creative procedures. Also, there were proportionately more studies at the college/adult level using meditation, fantasy, and other altered awareness procedures than at the elementary/secondary level. Interestingly, however, there was an absence of discussion about the appropriateness of these methods at the elementary/secondary level. However, the author is personally

Table 22.2. Comparison of Successes of Different Approaches to Teaching Creative Thinking at the Elementary/High School and College/Adult Levels

Type of Intervention	Number of Studies		Number of Successes		Percentage of Successes	
	Elem/HS	Adults	Elem/HS	Adults	Elem/HS	Adults
Osborn/Parnes CPS and modifications	29	17	26.2	15.0	90	88
Other disciplined CPS procedures	27	11	20.8	10.9	77	99
Complex programs involving packages	56	2	36.7	1.7	66	85
Complex programs combining strategies	15	26	11.5	22.7	77	87
Creative arts as vehicles	36	4	27.6	2.9	77	72
Media and reading	13	0	10.1	—	78	—
Curricular and administrative arr.	13	0	6.7	—	52	—
Teacher/classroom variables	40	0	23.2	—	58	—
Motivation, reward, competition	18	0	11.5	—	64	—
Facilitating testing conditions	36	0	25.1	—	70	—
Affective educational programs	13	2	10.3	—	79	85
Altered awareness	6	7	4.0	5.2	67	74
Other conditions	6	7	2.8	6.8	47	97
Total (Mean)	308	76	214.9	65.2	(70)	(86)

aware of studies of this nature at the elementary school level that were aborted on account of agitation by community pressure groups.

Although, there seems to be a general trend for the emergence of affective and altered state procedures, most of the training methods are highly cognitive in their approach. For example, Robert Meeker (1979) used the Structure of Intellect Model for a training program with gifted children in grades 3–6 with pre- and posttesting and experimental and control groups. The experimental groups showed statistically significant gains greater than the controls on the SOI tests of creativity. This experimental design and the results characterize a majority of the studies reported during the past decade. A new trend that seems to be emerging is the possible superiority of well-planned training programs involving music and imagery (Lowery, 1982), creative writing (Coleman, 1982), consciousness raising (Gourley, Kelly, & Zucca, 1977), practice in environmental scanning (Friedman, Raymond, & Feldhusen, 1978), and other procedures for helping students tap into their higher levels of consciousness. From the results reported in recent years, there are indications that some of these technologies for tapping into higher levels of consciousness may be at least as effective as the teaching of deliberate, systematic procedures of creative problem solving.

There has been a continuing debate as to whether creative thinking skills should be taught directly and through courses separate from the rest of the curriculum. Edward de Bono (1975, 1983) has been the leading advocate of the direct teaching of creative thinking skills (or "lateral thinking," as he calls it). His instructional materials have been rather widely adopted in England, Australia, Ireland, and Venezuela. In fact, he (de Bono, 1983) reported that 106,000 teachers in Venezuela were trained to use his program and every school child takes a course in thinking skills (2 hours of direct instruction per week). He defended the reduction in time spent in teaching information in order to focus on the direct teaching of thinking.

For some time, de Bono (1969, 1983) has attacked the fallacy that we do not need to do anything specific to help highly intelligent individuals learn how to think. He also contended that many highly intelligent people are rather ineffective thinkers. From time to time, research in gifted education has indicated that intellectually gifted students are actually poorer problem solvers than average ability students. With increased attention to the teaching of thinking skills in gifted education, it might be expected that these findings would be outdated. However, in 1982, Ludlow and Woodrum reported a study that indicates that the teaching of thinking skills in gifted education has not been very pervasive. With 20 gifted learners and 20 average learners matched for age and sex, they found that the average learners used significantly more advanced thinking strategies than the gifted learners when continued access to feedback was permitted. The gifted learners demonstrated superior performance on problems involving memory and attention but not on measures of performance efficiency and strategy selection.

Gifted education literature is replete with suggestions for teaching creative problem-solving skills to gifted children and with descriptions of program materials that have been used successfully for this purpose. Some of the more promising suggestions have been offered by Brown (1983); Callahan (1978); Davis (1971); Dirkes (1977); Firestien and Treffinger (1983); Foster (1979); Khatena (1978); Kopelman, Galasso, and Strom (1977); Shibles (1979); Torrance (1979a); Treffinger (1980b); and Wilson, Greer, and Johnson (1973). Much new material for facilitating creative thinking has emerged during the past decade (Callahan & Renzulli, 1977; de Bono, 1975, 1976; Macaranas, 1982; Manning & Brown, 1979; Myers & Torrance, 1984; Renzulli, 1973).

Two national/international curriculum and interscholastic competition projects emerged during this decade and did much to introduce and give practice in creative thinking skills in gifted education, the Future Problem Solving Program (Crabbe, 1982; Torrance, 1980) and Olympics of the Mind (Gourley, 1981). Currently, it is estimated that over 150,000 gifted students participate each year in each of these programs in the United States alone. Considerable international interest has been aroused by both of these programs.

The Future Problem Solving Program was founded in 1974 by E. Paul and Pansy Torrance (Crabbe, 1982; Torrance & Torrance, 1978) with the goals of helping gifted students to:

1. Develop richer images of the future
2. Become more creative in their thinking
3. Develop and increase their communication skills, both oral and written
4. Develop and increase their teamwork skills
5. Integrate a problem solving model into their lives
6. Develop and increase their research skills

Each year, program participants suggest topics for the next year. These suggestions are then combined into a ballot which is submitted to all participants and the five topics receiving the largest number of votes are selected for study. Three of them become topics of the practice problems for which professional feedback is given; one is used for the state bowls, and the other is used for the national/international bowl. These five problems provide the solid substantive core for the year's program and changes each year. The Osborn-Parnes Creative Problem Solving Model was chosen for use in the program. The national organization also sponsors a scenario writing program each year, an advanced program in which teams study problems submitted by cooperating government and community agencies, corporations, and the like. Some states include community involvement and visual arts programs. In the Fall of 1984, a program for primary grade students was launched. The basic program includes grades 4–12. Both objective and subjective evaluations have been quite favorable (Crabbe, 1982; Torrance, 1980).

The Olympics of the Mind program was founded by Samuel Micklus and Theodore Gourley at Glassboro State College in New Jersey and had its debut in May 1978 with 28 New Jersey schools participating. This program was designed for highly creative students capable of developing unusual ideas and insights. Identification is based on the sport's tryout method and evaluation is based on the performances of the participants. The program appeals especially to students gifted in industrial design, but also has places for students gifted in creative writing, acting, leadership, and other creative expressive and problem-solving skills. Like the Future Problem Solving Program, this program spread rapidly to include students from all 50 states of the USA, many Canadian provinces, and several countries overseas. For the World Competition, both long-term and spontaneous problems are used. Long-term problems are given to participants (who work as a team) in advance of local, district, state, or world competition. This affords teams time to prepare their own creative solutions to the problems. Spontaneous problems are given to the teams on the day of the competitions to challenge their ability to think "on their feet." The apparent success of this program demonstrated that the varsity sports model can be used to develop other types of gifted programs.

Mansfield, Busse, and Krepelka (1978) and other critics of creativity research discredited the experimental studies of the effectiveness of creativity training because of their use of divergent thinking tests to evaluate effectiveness. However, most of the studies included in their review had been published in the main journals of the American Educational Research Association and the American Psychological Association that have review procedures that would have resulted in the rejection of studies not using the objective, psychometric evidence attacked by Mansfield et al. In the wider range of studies surveyed by Torrance both in 1972 and 1984, a variety of criteria other than psychometric measures was used. Table 22.3 gives an analysis of the kinds of criteria used in the 166 elementary/secondary and 76 college/adult studies examined in preparation for writing this chapter. These data indicate that there is still a tendency to use psychometric measures such as divergent thinking or creative thinking test scores to evaluate these studies. However, there is also considerable evidence of the use of more "real life" creativity indicators, such as the

Table 22.3. Frequencies and Percentages of Each Type of Criteria Used in the Elementary/Secondary and College/Adult Studies of Effectiveness of Creativity Training

Category or Subcategory of Criteria	Elementary/ Secondary		College/Adult	
	Number	Percent	Number	Percent
Psychometric criteria:				
TTCT (Torrance tests)	126	76	29	39
SOI (Guilford tests)	9	5	11	15
Other tests, including author-develop	38	23	21	28
Non-psychometric criteria:				
Creative products	6	4	8	11
Creative behavior	14	8	28	37
Creative self-perception (self-evaluation, satisfaction, attitudes, etc.)	6	4	21	28

evaluation of creative products, creative behavior, and creative self-perceptions. This is especially true of the college/adult studies where earning money creatively, indicators of increased health and feelings of well-being, increased profits, and medical treatment techniques were among the criteria. Increased use of these more realistic criteria should help counteract common criticisms of creativity training research concerning the exclusive use of divergent thinking or creativity tests.

Forecasting and Planning Skills

Although some of the curriculum materials designed to facilitate creative problem solving have been future oriented, the importance of studying the future and cultivating forecasting and planning skills has not been widely accepted by educators. It is largely through efforts in the education of creative and gifted students that some real headway has been made in introducing the teaching of these skills. Researchers, however, recognized the needs in this area. For example, Allen and Plante described public school studies in Paterson, New Jersey, and New Haven, Connecticut, which indicate that students in school today have a greater interest in studying the future than any other academic subject. Allen and Plante pointed out that teachers are generally ill-equipped to meet this need and that few educators seem to have examined how children's images of the future affect their intellectual and emotional development. The past decade, however, has witnessed the creation of a considerable amount of materials that help teachers cope with this deficiency. For example, the Future Problem Solving Program (Crabbe, 1982) has developed handbooks and manuals for training students in the creative problem-solving process, evaluation and giving feedback on practice problems, teaching scenario writing, and getting information on the problems studied each year. Other notable efforts have been made by Bleedorn (1980, 1981), Flack and Feldhusen (1983), Kolloff (1983), Maryanopolis (1980), Stacy and Mitchell (1978), and Wooddell, Fletcher, and Dixon (1982).

Important contributions to the teaching of forecasting and planning skills have been made through the various projects generated from Calvin W. Taylor's work (1978) on multiple talent teaching. This work has been focused on teaching such abilities or talents as academic, creative, planning, communicating, forecasting, and decision-making. Among the projects that have developed and evaluated materials for teaching forecasting and planning skills have been the Talents Unlimited Project in Mobile, Alabama (Schlichter, 1979), Project REACH in Minnesota (Juntune, 1979), and Project Implode in Utah (Taylor, Lloyd, & Rollins, 1971; Taylor, 1978).

Philosophical Thinking

During the past decade, programs for teaching children philosophy seem to have made considerable impact upon the education of gifted and creative children. Perhaps the leading force in this movement has been the imaginative work of The Institute for the Advancement of Philosophy for Children, spearheaded by Matthew Lipman and his associates at Montclair State College (1974, 1979). The basic instructional material is the text for a course entitled *Harry Stottelmeier's Discovery* (Lipman et al., 1974) and an instructional manual to accompany this course material (Lipman, Sharp, & Oscanyan, 1979). The Institute also publishes a quarterly journal entitled *Thinking: A Journal of Philosophy for Children*. Each issue includes articles about new theoretical advances, classical papers of the past about philosophical thinking, new ideas for teaching philosophy to children, and evaluative studies.

The published evaluations of the use of *Harry Stottelmeier's Discovery* with the gifted/talented have been quite positive. Cinquino (1980) reported an evaluation of the program used with 53 fifth and sixth grade academically talented students. In a pre-posttest treatment study, she found that the philosophy students made statistically significant gains on the California Test of Mental Maturity's subtest on Inference, Questioning Task III (a criterion-referenced formal reasoning test), How Many Reasons? What Could You Use It For? and What Could It Be? The parents of the children participating in the program reacted quite positively to the program. An overwhelming majority of them reported that the program had provided topics for discussion at home and that their children had expressed their ideas more clearly as they used the critical and creative thinking skills taught in the program. The vast majority of the students also expressed enjoyment of the program and felt that it was worthwhile.

Burnes (1981) also reported an evaluative study of the Harry Stottelmeier program with 11 fifth and sixth grade classrooms. In a pre-posttest design, he found statistically significant gains in reading comprehension on the California Achievement Test and Questioning Task III. Yeazell (1981a) reported an evaluative study of the program involving eight fifth grade teachers and their pupils. With the comprehension subtest of the Comprehensive Test of Basic Skills, she found statistically significant gains beyond what would have been expected according to national norms. In a separate report, Yeazell (1981b) described what happened to the eight teachers who taught the philosophy program to these fifth grade pupils. Although these teachers did not improve significantly their scores on the Watson-Glaser Critical Thinking Appraisal, they showed statistically significant gains on Shostrom's Personal Orientation Inventory, affirming self-actualizing values.

Reed and Henderson (1981) reported an evaluative study involving four classes of gifted fourth graders in a pre-posttest control group design. Lipman and Shipman's Q-4 Test on reasoning skills was used to evaluate the outcomes from using the Harry Stottelmeier's Discovery materials. Statistically significant changes in thinking were found among the experimental students over their controls. The evaluation also showed that students enjoyed the program and considered it worthwhile.

Another notable curriculum for teaching philosophy to gifted students is one developed by Joe Hester and his associates at the Governor's School in Laurinburg, North Carolina, and in a local school district (Hester & Vincent, 1981; Hester, Vincent, Stahl, & Stahl, 1983). The text materials have not been available long enough to have been widely evaluated and adopted. Hester and Vincent (1981) reported exciting outcomes from using both their original materials and their adaptation of the Harry Stottelmeier Materials. The text materials developed by the Hester group make use of a variety of problems or conflicts and exercises.

Research Skills

Although there has been no burst of enthusiasm during the past decade for teaching gifted children research skills, there have been enough efforts in this area to keep alive the idea that gifted children can master many research skills, use them productively, and enjoy using them. In the late 1950s and early 1960s, Torrance became an advocate of teaching gifted children fairly sophisticated research skills as early as possible. He and his students of this period (Cunnington & Torrance, 1965; Myers, 1974; Torrance, 1972; Torrance & Myers, 1962) produced a considerable amount of teaching material and research to support this notion. Due to lack of response, most of these materials have been out of print during the past decade except for some revivals by Cunnington (1973, 1974) and Myers (1974). More recently, Kent and Esgar (1983) reported successful experiences in teaching basic research tools to gifted primary children. Riner (1983), Zuber (1980), and others described successful experiences in teaching scientific research methodology in science courses. Attention was given to teaching preschool children some of the basic skills of research by Le Rose, King, and Greenwood (1979) and Pellegrini (1982). The needs of an information society would seem to dictate renewed activity in this area. However, research methodology, statistics, and other research tools are rarely emphasized in the training of teachers of the gifted, so future developments in this area may be slow in coming.

Computer Skills

Although there is an enormous amount of activity in teaching the development and use of computer skills to gifted learners, little information about these activities has thus far appeared in the mainstream literature of gifted education. Computer courses for gifted learners offered at the University of Georgia have not been able to meet the demands in the local community. Similar reports have come to this author from many parts of the world. There are numerous reports of gifted junior high school students being employed by school boards to conduct workshops for teachers on computer utilization.

Naisbitt (1982), in his best selling *Megatrends*, maintained that success in the future will require that a person be trilingual (English, Spanish, and Computer). Thus, there seems to be a compelling need for research on the use of computers in teaching creative and gifted students.

Steele, Battista, and Krockover (1982) reported a successful experiment with gifted fifth graders, using a computer-assisted drill and practice program in mathematics. This study supplied evidence that the computer literacy of high intellectual ability students can be significantly increased by using such drill and practice with the added advantage of developing students' affective and cognitive skills. Flank (1982) pointed out that computers are tools for learning and that there are many uses for them and that not all of them are appropriate. He reported that they can be very exciting learning tools and suggested some legitimate uses of them.

William A. Beasley (1984), after an exceptionally thorough review of work concerned with microcomputer applications in the education of the gifted, found that there is very little literature specifically addressing the use of computers with the gifted, and the research is not in any way conclusive. Beasley concluded that the only area of general educational computing supported by anything approaching a conclusive body of research is the use of drill and practice and simple tutorial programs as a supplement to traditional classroom instruction. However, Beasley found ample evidence, largely from experiential data, to conclude that microcomputers are capable of playing a major role in the attainment of many of the objectives recommended by the National/State Leadership Training Institute for the Gifted and the Talented (Passow, 1982). Telecommunications, also known as networking, and computer simulations were seen as especially promising. The telecommunications would extend vastly the body of information available at the local level and the computer simulations would render the abstract as more concrete. Beasley also tried to show how computer applications might facilitate the major models in gifted education (Bloom's Taxonomy, Krathwohl's Taxonomy, Models of Creative Thinking, the Structure of Intellect Model, and Renzulli's Enrichment Triad). He pointed out ways in which computers might facilitate the learning of the gifted at all educational levels, including the preschool level.

Inventing and Other Skills

Although many creative and gifted children aspire to be inventors (about 30% of scenarios written by gifted students in the United States are an indication) and inventing by citizens of the United States has been declining since 1978 (Michaels, 1979), programs for creative and gifted children seem to have been rather unresponsive to this need. In the 1960s, the Imagi/Craft materials developed by Cunnington and Torrance (1965) stressed the development of inventing skills, encouraged children to invent, and increased motivation for careers in inventing. More recently, Hoffman (1982) described experiences with gifted students in teaching them skills of inventing.

Among the other tool skills being taught gifted children during the past decade are: debating (Lengel, 1983), creative writing (Beebe, 1979; Stoddard & Renzulli, 1983; Vida, 1979); communication skills (Sisk, 1975a); values clarification (Stahl & Stahl, 1979); media (Wedman & Jensen, 1983); and logical reasoning (Weinstein & Laughman, 1980).

Other Trends of the Decade

Several other important trends in teaching creative and gifted children worthy of inclusion have emerged during the past decade. The author had fully intended to include them. However, the volume of literature on each of them is so vast it would be impossible to do justice to them here. These include parental involvement, preschool and primary age gifted children, disadvantaged and culturally different gifted students, the learning disabled gifted, gifted girls, and the leadership gifted. The most that can be done here is to make some summary assessments and identify some of the key literature regarding each of them.

Parents as Teachers of Creative and Gifted Children

During the past 10 years, there has been greatly increased attention to the roles of parents as teachers of creative and gifted children. To satisfy this need, there has been a barrage of books, journal articles, and other materials for parents. These parents have been encouraged to organize, become informed, and to work cooperatively with school personnel to provide the best possible education for their children (Clark, 1983). *Gifted Children Newsletter* and *G/C/T* are two periodicals that attempt deliberately to supply some of the needs that have beed cited. Among the more useful books that have emerged are Ginsberg's (1976) *Is Your Child Gifted?;* Kaufmann's (1976) *Your Gifted Child and You;* Khatena's (1978) *The Creatively Gifted Child: Suggestions for Parents and Teachers;* Lewis's (1981) *How to Be a Gifted Parent;* Miller and Price's (1981) *The Gifted Child, the Family, and the Community;* Moore's (1981) *Does This Mean My Kid's a Genius?;* Tannenbaum and Newman's (1980) *Somewhere to Turn: Strategies for Parents of Gifted and Talented Children;* and Webb, Meckstroth, and Tolan's (1983) *Guiding the Gifted Child.*

Gifted Preschool and Primary Age Children

New interest has emerged in the identification and education of preschool gifted and talented children in the United States. Perhaps the three most comprehensive works in this area are Karnes' (1983) *The Underserved: Our Young Gifted Children;* Rodell, Jackson, and Robinson's (1980) *Gifted Young Children;* and the National/State Leadership Training Institute on the Gifted and the Talented's (1980) *Educating the Preschool/ Primary Gifted and Talented.*

To illustrate the nature and range of studies concerning the teaching of gifted preschool children, a few studies will be cited. Van Tassell-Baska, Schuler, and Lipschutz (1982) described an experimental program for gifted four-year-olds. This program was highly individualized and made use of small clusters, activity periods of no longer than 30 minutes, mini-assignments, and the reinforcement of strengths. The program demonstrated positive effects and developed academic skills such as mathematics and analytical skills. Harris and Bauer (1983) described a program for parents of gifted preschoolers. This program provided parents with information about giftedness and showed parents how to enrich their children's experiences at home and in the community. Reading programs for gifted children have continued to be of interest as reading at advanced levels has long created problems for many highly gifted children. Brown and Rogan (1983) believe that reading programs for gifted children should be definitely different from programs for average children. Gifted children read more widely, more creatively, and more critically.

Illustrative of the instructional models proposed for young gifted children is one described by Karnes, Shwedel, and Williams (1983). They suggested the following differentiating characteristics of such instruction:

1. Encouragement of children to pursue a chosen interest in depth

2. Learning based on needs rather than on predetermined order or sequence of instruction
3. Activities that are more complex and require more abstract and higher level thinking processes
4. Greater flexibility in the use of materials, time, and resources
5. Higher expectations for independence and persistence to tasks
6. Greater encouragement of creative and productive thinking
7. More interest in interpreting the behavior and feelings of self and others
8. More opportunities to broaden the base of knowledge and enhance language abilities

Despite evidences of increased acceptance of programs for identifying and developing gifted young children, some educators argued against identification of gifted preschoolers, contending that preschool is a better time for development than for identification. For example, Johnson (1983) advocated an enriched, child-responsive preschool environment that affords opportunities for all children to demonstrate and develop gifts specific to them. Johnson believes that doing this would meet the educational and affective needs of children who normally would have been identified as gifted, as well as the children who would have been overlooked.

Disadvantaged and Culturally Different Gifted

Throughout this decade, there has continued to be considerable ambivalence about the responsibility of education to special groups of gifted learners such as the disadvantaged and culturally different, the learning disabled, the physically handicapped, the emotionally handicapped, and girls. It is possible here to cite only a few examples of the literature concerning each of these groups.

A great deal has been said and written regarding the disadvantaged and culturally different gifted child. Perhaps the most comprehensive treatment of problems of identifying and educating this group was a book published by the Council for Exceptional Children and authored by Torrance (1977). In this book, Torrance provides a rather thorough review and analysis regarding the research and offers specific proposals for identifying and using their strengths in curriculum and career development. In 1978, the Office of Gifted and Talented of the United States Office of Education assembled a National Forum on Minority/Disadvantaged Gifted and Talented and the *Gifted Child Quarterly* devoted an entire issue to papers dealing with disadvantaged and minority gifted children (Malone, 1978). The National/State Leadership Training Institute on the Gifted and the Talented sponsored a series of national conferences on the disadvantaged gifted and the proceedings of these conferences may be obtained from LTI Publications, Ventura County Superintendent of Schools Office, Ventura, CA 93009. Despite strong arguments for developing programs to meet the needs of these groups and the imaginative proposals for accomplishing the task, very little seems to have actually been done. State department of education and other authorities have been unwilling to modify identification criteria that would make possible the inclusion of many gifted disadvantaged and cultur-ally different children who are now excluded because they do not attain specified scores in intelligence tests or similar criteria.

The Learning Disabled Gifted

It has been commonly assumed that the Learning Disabled (LD) and Gifted/Talented categories are mutually exclusive. However, as legalized criteria were applied to school popula-tions during the past decade, it was found that some children met both sets of criteria. Although this phenomenon had been observed earlier (Torrance, 1960, 1963), it had been generally ignored. Although programs for identified gifted children have generally been limited to well-adjusted, high achieving, well-rounded students, there was awareness that there were some gifted students who are also emotionally disturbed (not "well-adjusted"). For example, Rothenberg, Johnson, and Brooks (1966) described a program in which they grouped gifted children on the basis of their perceived emotional and cognitive difficulties rather than their achievement levels. They used a creative thinking approach that seemed quite open-ended and challenging. The results led the creators of the program to conclude that it helped to free the talents of the children involved. The Developmental Therapy program pioneered by Wood (1975, 1981) is a large-scale one that makes use of creative thinking and expressive, open-ended activities and attracts a number of clearly gifted youngsters.

Mary Meeker (1967) was another early advocate of attending to the needs of learning disabled gifted youngsters and referred to them as "educationally and neurologically handicapped." She stated that it would be a big step to recognize that there are children in these categories who are gifted. She suggested criteria for identifying such children and recommended that programs for them make deliberate use of more creative experiences than might be appropriate for other children. J. Elkind (1973) was among the first to maintain that educational programs for gifted children with learning disabilities should be so constructed as to capitalize on their strong learning modali-ties and at the same time strengthen those modalities that are weak. He recommended supportive reinforcement while this is being done and suggested classroom management techniques for accomplishing these goals. Eason, Smith, and Steen (1978) described techniques for teaching gifted children with what he calls the "clumsy syndrome." It involves procedures for assess-ing motor problems, activities specific to those problems, and practice strategies to promote remediation. Torrance (1982) has championed the cause of creatively gifted children with learning disabilities and, on the basis of his 22-year longitudinal study, suggested strategies for helping this special group cope with problems inherent among them.

Gifted Women and Girls

During the past decade, an enormous literature on gifted women and girls has accumulated. Blaubergs (1978) presented a comprehensive review of the literature on overcoming the sexist barriers to gifted women's achievement. In their studies of mathematically precocious youth, Stanley and his associates

(Benbow & Stanley, 1980; Fox, 1976; Fox, Benbow, & Perkins, 1983; Stanley, Keating, & Fox, 1974) have given special atten-tion to the problems of motivating and teaching mathematics to girls gifted in that discipline. On the basis of longitudinal studies conducted in 1970 and 1980 Torrance (1983a) called attention to some of the special problems in teaching creatively gifted girls.

Giftedness in Leadership

The report of the U.S. Commissioner of Education Sidney P. Marland (1972) recommended that leadership giftedness be one of the categories of gifted/talented students whose needs should be met by schools. While scattered attention had been given to this type of giftedness in the past, the profession was ill-equipped to deal with it in 1972. A few leading investigators responded to the challenge, however, and made noteworthy contributions. For example, Feldhusen (1978) developed a leadership training program for the gifted and the materials he and his associates developed have been used by numerous others. Addison (1979) also developed curriculum materials for training gifted girls in leadership. She proposed the use of simulation games as a vehicle for this purpose and suggested that simulation gaming be extended into the Renzulli Type III project. Hensel and Franklin (1983) developed leadership curri-culum materials for use with elementary and junior high school gifted students. They conducted summer training programs on leadership skills, using projects, games, and dramatics. Favor-able reactions were expressed by parents and teachers. Leader-ship curricula for the gifted were also described by Foster (1981), Kozoll and Simerly (1980), and Lindsay (1979).

Summary

The past decade has witnessed an unprecedented amount of research on teaching creative and gifted learners. There has been almost no foundation or federal government support of this type of research. Consequently there have been no large scale studies. The very existence of identified "creative" and "gifted" learners has been an invitation—a challenge—to study them. The establishment of doctoral programs with dissertation requirements to train leaders and scholars in this specialty has given impetus to research on teaching creative and gifted learners. As problems of identification and programming are solved, it may be expected that more research energy will be devoted to studying the teaching of these exceptional learners.

The large number of new publication outlets emerging dur-ing the decade may be seen as both a blessing and a curse. This wealth of publication outlets makes possible the communica-tion of new ideas, practices, and research findings. It means, however, that considerable faulty research will be disseminated. It also may mean that educators and scholars not identified professionally with gifted and creative education may remain unaware of advances in the teaching of creative and gifted learners since so little research on this topic is now being published in the more general fields of educational psychology, developmental psychology, and even in the general field of exceptional children.

There will be continuing needs for surveys of practices in teaching creative and gifted learners. As societal needs change and concepts of giftedness change in response to these changes, teaching methods, strategies, materials, goals, and the like must also change.

Many novel and exciting criteria of the effectiveness of teaching creative thinking skills have emerged. However, there seems to be a consensus that the value of special programs and teaching procedures with the creative and gifted has not been adequately demonstrated.

Radical acceleration seems to have become more generally respected but there has been no widespread rush to embrace this alternative. Mentoring as an approach to meeting some of the instructional needs of gifted and creative learners has gained momentum and so has self-directed learning, independent study, and Individual Education Plans (IEPs). Although it seems rather certain that these trends will increase and spread to other areas of education, considerable sound research support is necessary. Training in creative problem solving seems to be established rather firmly in teaching the creative and gifted learner. The continuing scarcity of teachers able to teach any systematic, disciplined method of creative problem solving has been alleviated to some extent by training programs generated by the Future Problem Solving Program and well prepared instructional materials. Less well established are increasing interests in forecasting and planning, inventing, microcomputers, philosophical thinking, research skills, and the like.

REFERENCES

Addison, L. (1979). Simulation gaming and leadership training for gifted girls. *Gifted Child Quarterly, 23,* 288–296.

Allen, D. W., & Plante, J. (1979). Looking at the future in education. *World Future Society Bulletin, 13*(2), 27–33.

Amara, J., & Leona, M. (1983). Prep-tech: A vocational school for academically talented students. *Phi Delta Kappan, 64,* 372–373.

Avery, L. D., & Bartolini, L. (1979). Survey of provisions for gifted children in Illinois: A summary paper. *Journal for the Education of the Gifted, 2,* 132–140.

Barbe, W. B., & Renzulli, J. S. (Eds.) (1981). *Psychology and education of the gifted,* (3rd. ed.) New York: Irvington Press.

Bartkovich, K. G., & Mezynski, K. (1980). Fast-paced precalculus mathematics for talented junior high students: Two recent SMPY programs. *Gifted Child Quarterly, 25* 73–80.

Beasley, W. A. (1984). Microcomputer applications in the education of the gifted. Unpublished doctoral dissertation, University of Georgia.

Beebe, R. L. (1979). Creative writing and the young gifted child. *Roeper Review, 2*(4), 27–29.

Benbow, C. P., & Stanley, J. C. (1980). Sex differences in mathematical ability: Fact or artifact. *Science, 210,* 1262–1264.

Bennett, F., Blanning, J., Boissere, M., Chang, S., & Collins, W. (1971). Potentially gifted and talented youth benefit from open study. *Gifted Child Quarterly, 15,* 96–108.

Black, R. A., & Torrance, E. P. (1981). Developing creativity instructional material according to the de Bono thinking skills model. *Creative Child and Adult Quarterly, 6,* 8–12.

Blanning, J. (1978). An independent study and seminar program for urban gifted youth. *Roeper Review, 1*(1), 15–17.

Blaubergs, M. S. (1978). Overcoming the sexist barriers to gifted women's achievement. In National/State Leadership Training Institute for the Gifted and the Talented (Ed.), *Advantage: Disadvantaged gifted.* Ventura, CA: Ventura County Superintendent of Schools Office.

Bleedorn, B. D. (1980). Future studies for the gifted. *Roeper Review, 2*(4), 25–27.

Bleedorn, B. D. (1981). *Looking ahead: Tested ideas in future studies.* Buffalo, NY: DOK publishers.

Bogner, D. (1981). Creative individual educational programs (IEPs) from creativity tests. *Creative Child and Adult Quarterly, 6,* 160–162.

Boston, B. (1976). *The sorcerer's apprentice—A case study of the role of mentoring.* Reston, VA: Council for Exceptional Children.

Brown, A. J. (1978). The dilemma of the divergent child. *Roeper Review, 1*(2), 13–16.

Brown, M. (1983). *The inventive: Innovation to ingenuity.* La Habra, CA: Foxtail Press.

Brown, W., & Rogan, J. (1983). Reading and young gifted children. *Roeper Review, 5*(3), 6–9.

Burnes, B. (1981). Harry Stottelmeier's discovery—The Minnesota experience. *Thinking, 3*(1), 8–11.

California State Department of Education. (1981). *Literature and story writing: A guide to teaching gifted and talented in the elementary and middle schools.* Sacramento, CA: California State Department of Education.

Callahan, C. M. (1978). *Developing creativity in the gifted and talented.* Reston, VA: Council for Exceptional Children.

Callahan, C. M., & Renzulli, J. S. (1977). The effectiveness of a creativity training program in the language arts. *Gifted Child Quarterly, 21,* 538–546.

Chetelat, F. J. (1981). Visual arts education for the gifted elementary level art student. *Gifted Child Quarterly, 25,* 154–158.

Cinquino, D. (1980). An evaluation of a philosophy program with 5th and 6th grade academically talented students. *Thinking, 2*(3 & 4), 79–83.

Clark, B. (1983). *Growing up gifted.* (2nd ed.) Columbus, OH: Charles E. Merrill.

Cleveland, M. E. (1978). Creative music strategies based upon poetry and the language. *Journal for the Education of the Gifted, 1,* 29–37.

Cline, S. (1979). Simulation: A teaching strategy for the gifted and talented. *Gifted Child Quarterly, 23,* 269–287.

Cohn, S. J. (1979). Individualizing science curricula for the gifted. *Gifted Child Quarterly, 23,* 317–322.

Colangelo, N., & Lafrenz, N. (1981). Counseling the culturally diverse gifted. *Gifted Child Quarterly, 25,* 27–30.

Colangelo, N., & Zaffran, R. T. (Eds.) (1979). *New voices in counseling the gifted.* Dubuque, IA: Kendall/Hunt.

Coleman, D. R. (1982). The effects of pupil use of a creative writing scale as an evaluative and instructional tool by primary gifted students. (Doctoral dissertation, Kansas State University, 1981). *Dissertation Abstracts International, 42*(8), 3409-A. (University Microfilms Order Number 8127860).

Colson, S. (1980). The evaluation of a community-based career education program for gifted and talented students. *Gifted Child Quarterly, 24,* 101–106.

Cox, J. (1979). International summer programs. *Roeper Review, 1*(4), 30–31.

Cox, J. (1983a). Advanced placement: An exemplary honors model. *G/C/T,* Issue 26, 47–51.

Cox, J. (1983b). Continuous progress and nongraded schools. *G/C/T,* Issue 25, 15–21.

Cox, J., & Daniel, N. (1983). Specialized schools for high ability students. *G/C/T,* Issue 28, 2–9.

Crabbe, A. B. (1982). Creating a brighter future: An update on the Future Problem Solving Program. *Journal for the Education of the Gifted, 5,* 2–11.

Cravats, M. (1978). Language arts in science for the gifted. *Creative Child and Adult Quarterly, 3,* 159–160.

Cunnington, B. F. (1973, 1974) *The blue crystal series.* (Two kits with cassettes, film strips, and manual) Niles, IL: United Learning.

Cunnington, B. F., & Torrance, E. P. (1965). *Imagi/craft materials.* Lexington, MA: Ginn.

Daurio, S. P. (1979). Educational enrichment versus acceleration: A review of the literature. In W. C. George, S. J. Cohn, & J. C. Stanley (Eds.), *Educating the gifted: Acceleration and enrichment.* Baltimore, MD: Johns Hopkins University Press.

Davis, G. A. (1971). Teaching for creativity: Some guiding lights. *Journal of Research and Development in Education, 4*(3), 29–34.

Davis, G. A. (1981). *Creativity is forever.* Cross Plains, WI: Badger Press.

Dawkins, B. J. (1978). Do gifted junior high school students need reading instruction? *Journal for the Education of the Gifted, 2,* 3–9.

de Bono, E. (1969). *The mechanisms of mind.* London: Jonathan Cape.

de Bono, E. (1975). *Think links.* Blandford Forum, Dorset, UK: Direct Education Services.

de Bono, E. (1976). *CoRT thinking lesson series.* Blandford Forum, Dorset, UK: Direct Education Services.

de Bono, E. (1983). The direct teaching of thinking as a skill. *Phi Delta Kappan, 64,* 703–708.

Del Giorno, B. J. (1977). RETAL as a model for developing critical and divergent thinking in gifted and talented students of science. *Gifted Child Quarterly, 21,* 58–65.

Delisle, J., & Renzulli, J. S. (1982). The revolving door identification and programming model: Correlates of creative production. *Gifted Child Quarterly, 26,* 89–95.

Dirkes, M. A. (1977). Learning through creative thinking. *Gifted Child Quarterly, 21,* 526–537.

Doherty, E., & Evans, L. (1981). Independent study process: They can think, can't they? *Journal for the Education of the Gifted, 4,* 106–110.

Dunn, H. C. (1968). Gifted children find research can be fun. *Gifted Child Quarterly, 12,* 10–13.

Dunn, R., & Dunn, K. (1975). *Educator's self teaching guide to individualizing instructional programs.* West Nyack, NY: Parker.

Dunn, R. S., & Price, G. E. (1980). The learning style characteristics of gifted students. *Gifted Child Quarterly, 24,* 33–36.

Eason, B. L., Smith, T. L., & Steen, M. F. (1978). Perceptual motor programs for the gifted-handicapped. *Journal for the Education of the Gifted, 2,* 10–21.

Elkind, J. (1973). The gifted child with learning disabilities. *Gifted Child Quarterly, 17,* 96–97.

Feldhusen, J. F. (1978). *Leadership training for the gifted.* West Lafayette, IN: Purdue University Gifted Program.

Feldhusen, J. F., & Kolloff, M. B. (1978). A three-stage model for gifted education. *G/C/T,* Issue 4, 3–5; 53–58.

Feldhusen, J. F., & Kolloff, M. B. (1979). An approach to career education for the gifted. *Roeper Review, 2*(2), 13–16.

Feldhusen, J. F., & Sokol, L. (1982). Extra-school programming to meet the needs of gifted youth: Super Saturday. *Gifted Child Quarterly, 26,* 51–56.

Feldhusen, J. F., & Treffinger, D. J. (1977). The role of instructional material in teaching creative thinking. *Gifted Child Quarterly, 21,* 450–476.

Feldhusen, J. F., & Treffinger, D. J. (1980). *Creative thinking and problem solving in gifted education.* Dubuque, IA: Kendall/Hunt.

Feldhusen, J. F., & Wyman, A. R. (1980). Super Saturday: Design and implementation of Purdue's special program for gifted children. *Gifted Child Quarterly, 24,* 15–21.

Firestien, R. L., & Treffinger, D. J. (1983). Creative problem solving: Guidelines and resources for effective facilitation. *G/C/T,* Issue 26, 2–10.

Fizzell, R. L. (1980). A schooling system for the twenty-first century. *Roeper Review, 2*(4), 22–24.

Flack, J. D., & Feldhusen, J. F. (1983). Future studies in the curricular framework of the Purdue three-stage model, *G/C/T,* Issue 27, 2–9.

Flank, S. (1982). Little hands on the computer. *G/C/T,* Issue 25, 28–29.

Foster, K. (1979). Creative problem solving. *Gifted Child Quarterly, 23,* 559–560.

Foster, L. (1983). Building materials for gifted children. *Gifted Education International, 1,* 107–113.

Foster, W. (1981). Leadership: A conceptual framework for recognizing and educating. *Gifted Child Quarterly, 25,* 17–25.

Fox, L. H. (1976). Career education for gifted preadolescents. *Gifted Child Quarterly, 20,* 262–270.

Fox, L. H. (1981). Instruction for the gifted: Some promising practices. *Journal for the Education of the Gifted, 4,* 246–254.

Fox, L. H., Benbow, C. P., & Perkins, S. (1983). In C. P. Benbow & J. C. Stanley (Eds.), *Academic precocity: Aspects of its development.* Baltimore, MD: Johns Hopkins University Press.

Fox, L. H., & Durden, W. G. (1982). *Educating verbally gifted youth.* Indianapolis, IN: Phi Delta Kappa.

Frasier, M. M. (1979). Counseling the culturally diverse gifted. In N. Colangelo & R. T. Zaffran (Eds.), *New voices in counseling the gifted.* Dubuque, IA: Kendall/Hunt.

Frasier, M. M., & McCannon, C. (1980). Using bibliotherapy with gifted children. *Gifted Child Quarterly, 25,* 81–85.

Friedman, J. M., & Master, D. (1981). School and museum: A partnership. *Gifted Child Quarterly, 25,* 43–48.

Friedman, F., Raymond, B., & Feldhusen, J. F. (1978). The effects of environmental scanning on creativity. *Gifted Child Quarterly, 22,* 248–257.

Furr, K. D. (1972). Canadian programming for the gifted. *Gifted Child Quarterly, 16,* 32–40.

Gallagher, J. J. (1975). *Teaching the gifted child.* (2nd ed.) Boston: Allyn and Bacon.

Gallagher, J. J., Weiss, P., Oglesby, K., & Thomas, T. (1983). *The status of gifted/talented education.* Ventura, CA: Ventura County Superintendent of Schools Office.

George, W. C. (1976). Accelerating mathematics instruction for the mathematically talented. *Gifted Child Quarterly, 20,* 246–261.

George, W. C. (1983). Research issues in educating America's gifted youth. *G/C/T, 27,* 20–21.

Getzels, J. W., & Dillon, J. T. (1973). The nature of giftedness and the education of the gifted. In R. M. W. Travers (Ed.), *Second handbook of research on teaching.* Chicago: Rand McNally.

Gibberd, K. (1966). A school for musically gifted children. *Gifted Child Quarterly, 10,* 194–195.

Ginsberg, G. (1976). *Is your child gifted?* New York: Simon & Schuster.

Glass, L. W. (1979). A cooperative university-high school project for talented students. *Gifted Child Quarterly, 23,* 532–537.

Gourley, T. J. (1981). Adapting the varsity sports model of nonpsycho-motor gifted students. *Gifted Child Quarterly, 25,* 164–166.

Gourley, T. J., Kelly, V., & Zucca, R. (1977). The application of a rational-psychedelic continuum concept of creativity to the classroom. *Gifted Child Quarterly, 21,* 103–108.

Gowan, J. C., Khatena, J., & Torrance, E. P. (Eds.) (1979). *Educating the ablest.* (2nd ed.) Itasca, IL: F. E. Peacock.

Gregorc, A. F. (1982a). *Gregorc Style Delineator: Development, technical and administrative manual.* Maynard, MA: Gabriel Systems.

Gregorc, A. F. (1982b). *An adult's guide to style.* Maynard, MA: Gabriel Systems.

Griggs, S. A., & Price, G. E. (1982). A comparison between the learning styles of gifted versus average suburban junior high school students. *Creative Child and Adult Quarterly, 7,* 39–42.

Hall, E. G. (1979). Simulation gaming — A device for altering attitudes about sex roles. *Gifted Child Quarterly, 23,* 356–361.

Harding, P., & Berger, P. (1979). Future images: Career images for gifted students. *Gifted and Talented Education, 1,* 134–141.

Harris, R., & Bauer, H. (1983). A program for parents of gifted preschoolers. *Roeper Review, 5*(4), 18–19.

Hedbring, C., & Rubenzer, R. (1979). Integrating the IEP and SOI with educational programming for the gifted. *Gifted Child Quarterly, 23,* 338–345.

Hensel, N., & Franklin, C. (1983). Developing emergent leadership skills in elementary and junior high students. *Roeper Review, 5*(4), 33–35.

Hershey, M. (1980). Individual educational planning for gifted students: A report from Kansas. *Journal for the Education of the Gifted, 3,* 207–213.

Hester, J., & Vincent, P. (1981). Teaching philosophy to children: A southern exposure. *Thinking, 3*(2), 39–43.

Hester, J., Vincent, P. F., Stahl, R. L., & Stahl, R. J. (1983) *Philosophy for young thinkers.* New York: Trillium Press.

Hoffman, J. G. (1982). Inventions. *G/C/T, 24,* 54–55.

Johnson, L. G. (1983). Giftedness in preschool: A better time for development than identification. *Roeper Review, 5*(4), 13–15.

Jones, H. E. (1983). Developing social studies units for the gifted: A conceptual model. *G/C/T, 28,* 32–34.

Juntune, J. (1979). Project REACH: A teacher training program for developing creative thinking skills in students. *Gifted Child Quarterly, 23,* 461–471.

Juntune, J. (Ed.) (1981). *Successful programs for the gifted and talented.* St. Paul, MN: National Association for Gifted Children.

Kaplan, S. N. (1982). Myth: There is a single curriculum for the gifted! *Gifted Child Quarterly, 26,* 32–33.

Karnes, F., & Collins, E. (1980). *Handbook of instructional resources and references for teaching the gifted.* Boston: Allyn and Bacon.

Karnes, M. B. (1983). *The underserved: Our young gifted children.* Reston, VA: Council for Exceptional Children.

Karnes, M. B., Shwedel, A. M., & Williams, M. (1983). Combining instructional models for young gifted children. *Teaching Exceptional Children, 15,* 128–135.

Kaufmann, F. (1976). *Your gifted child and you.* Reston, VA: Council for Exceptional Children.

Keating, D. P. (1980). Four faces of creativity: The continuing plight of the intellectually underserved. *Gifted Child Quarterly, 24,* 56–61.

Kennedy, B. T., & Newman, M. A. (1976). An exploratory study of the effects of games on the development of cognitive skills in young children. *Gifted Child Quarterly, 20,* 350–356.

Kenny, A. (1982). Guiding the gifted: Self awareness through creative writing. *G/C/T,* Issue 23, 9–11.

Kent, S., & Esgar, L. V. (1983). Research techniques for gifted primary students. *G/C/T,* Issue 28–29.

Khatena, J. (1978). *The creatively gifted child: Suggestions for parents and teachers.* New York: Vantage Press.

Khatena, J. (1982). *Educational psychology of the gifted.* New York: John Wiley.

Kolloff, P. B. (1983). The Center for Global Futures: Meeting the needs of gifted students in a laboratory school. *Roeper Review, 5*(3), 32–33.

Kopelman, M., Galasso, V. G., & Strom, P. (1977). A model program for the development of the creatively gifted in science. *Gifted Child Quarterly, 21,* 80–84.

Korth, V. A. (1977). The gifted in children's fiction. *Gifted Child Quarterly, 21,* 246–260.

Kozoll, C., & Simerly, R. (1980). Leadership training institute program developed by the Office of Conferences and Institutes, University of Illinois, Urbana.

Kraus, P. (1973). The accelerated. *Gifted Child Quarterly, 17,* 36–47.

Lambert, S. E., & Lambert, J. W. (1982). Mentoring — A powerful learning device. *G/C/T,* Issue 25, 12–13.

Lawton, M. T. (1961). Hunter College High School. *Gifted Child Quarterly, 5,* 65–66.

Lengel, A. L. (1983). Classroom debating in the elementary school. *G/C/T,* Issue 28, 57–60.

Le Rose, B., King, L., & Greenwood, S. (1979). The Lighthouse Project. *Gifted Child Quarterly, 23,* 472–486.

Lewis, C. L., & Kanes, L. G. (1979). Gifted IEPs: Impact of expectations and perspectives. *Journal for the Education of the Gifted, 2,* 61–69.

Lewis, D. *How to be a gifted parent.* (1981). New York: Norton.

Lindsay, B. (1979). A lamp for Diogenes: Leadership giftedness and moral education. *Roeper Review, 1*(4), 4–7.

Lipman, M. et al. (1974). *Harry Stottelmeier's discovery.* Montclair, NJ: Institute for the Advancement of Philosophy for Children, Montclair State College.

Lipman, M., Sharp, A. M., & Oscanyan, F. S. (1979). *Philosophical inquiry: An instructional manual to accompany Harry Stottelmeier's discovery.* (2nd ed.) Montclair, NJ: Institute for the Advancement of Philosophy for Children, Montclair State University.

Lowery, J. (1982). Developing creativity in gifted children. *Gifted Child Quarterly, 26,* 133–139.

Lubling, A., & Zorman, R. (1982). The educational enrichment center — A holistic community approach model. *Gifted Child Quarterly, 26,* 74–76.

Ludlow, B. L., & Woodrum, D. T. (1982). Problem solving strategies of gifted and average learners on a multiple discrimination task. *Gifted Child Quarterly, 26,* 99–104.

McCarthy, B. (1980). *The 4 MAT system: Teaching to learning style with right/left mode techniques.* Arlington Heights, IL: Excel, Inc.

McCormick, S., & Swassing, R. H. (1982). Reading instructions for the gifted: A survey of programs. *Journal for the Education of the Gifted, 5,* 34–43.

McHale, J. (1976). *The changing information environment.* Boulder, CO: Westview Press.

Macaranas, N. (1982). Fostering, experiencing, and developing creativity as a method of instruction in psychology. *Creative Child and Adult Quarterly, 7,* 15–29.

Maddy, J. E. (1963). Musically gifted children: More in less time at the Interlochen Arts Academy and National Music Camp. *Gifted Child Quarterly, 7,* 21–22.

Maker, C. J. (1982a). *Curriculum development for the gifted.* Rockville, MD: Aspen Systems.

Maker, C. J. (1982b). *Teaching models in education of the gifted.* Rockville, MD: Aspen Systems.

Malone, C. (Ed.) (1978). Disadvantaged and handicapped gifted. *Gifted Child Quarterly, 32,* 267–403.

Manning, E., & Brown, M. (1979). East Whittier city schools gifted program project: Developing divergent modes of thinking in mentally gifted minor children. *Gifted Child Quarterly, 23,* 563–578.

Mansfield, R. S., & Busse, T. V. (1981). *The psychology of creativity and discovery.* Chicago: Nelson-Hall.

Mansfield, R. S., Busse, T. V., & Krepelka, E. J. (1978). The effectiveness of creativity training. *Review of Educational Research, 48,* 517–536.

Marland, S. P., Jr. (1972). *Education of the gifted and talented: Report to the Congress of the United States.* Washington, DC: U.S. Government Printing Office.

Martin, C. E., & Cramond, B. (1983). Creative reading: Is it being taught to the gifted in elementary schools? *Journal for the Education of the Gifted, 6,* 70–79.

Maryanopolis, J. (1980). *The leading edge: A futurist workshop.* Logan, IA: Perfection Form Company.

Mattson, B. D. (1983). Mentors for the gifted and talented: Whom to seek and where to look. *G/C/T,* 27, 10–11.

Meeker, M. N. (1967). Creative experiences for the educationally and neurologically handicapped who are gifted. *Gifted Child Quarterly, 11,* 160–164.

Meeker, M. N. (1979a). *Using SOI test results: A teacher's guide.* El Segundo, CA: SOI Institute.

Meeker, R. (1979b). Can creativity be developed in gifted? *Roeper Review, 2*(1), 17–18.

Michaels, G. E. (1979). The Georgia science and engineering fair. *Georgia Journal of Science, 37*(2), 53–54.

Miller, B. S., & Price, M. (Eds.) (1981). *The gifted child, the family and the community.* New York: Walker and Company.

Mitchell, B. M. (1980). What's happening to gifted education in the U.S. today? *Roeper Review, 2*(4), 7–10.

Mitchell, B. M. (1984). An update on gifted/talented education in the U.S. *Roeper Review, 6,* 161–163.

Moore, B. A. (1979). A model career education program for gifted and disadvantaged students. *Roeper Review, 2*(2), 20–22.

Moore, L. P. (1981). *Does this mean my kid's a genius?* New York: McGraw Hill Book Company.

Myers, R. E. (1974). *Basic research skills development series.* (Two kits) Niles, IL: United Learning.

Myers, R. E., & Torrance, E. P. (1984). *Wondering: Invitations to think about the future for primary grades.* Mansfield Center, CT: Creative Learning Press.

Naisbitt, J. (1982). *Megatrends: Ten new directions transforming our lives.* New York: Warner Books.

Nash, W. R., Borman, C., Colson, S. (1980). Career education for gifted and talented students: A senior high school model. *Exceptional Children, 46,* 404–405.

National/State Leadership Training Institute on the Gifted and the Talented. (Ed.) (1979). *Developing IEPs for the gifted and talented.* Ventura, CA: Ventura County Superintendent of Schools Office.

National/State Leadership Training Institute on the Gifted and the Talented. (Ed.) (1980). *Educating the preschool/primary gifted and talented.* Ventura, CA: Ventura County Superintendent of Schools Office.

Noller, R. B. (1982). *Mentoring: A voiced scarf: An experience in creative problem solving.* Buffalo, NY: Bearly Limited.

Noller, R. B., & Frey, B. R. (1983). *Mentoring: An annotated bibliography*. Buffalo, NY: Bearly Limited.

Omond, J. (1982). Extracurricular centres for the gifted in South Africa. *Gifted Education International, 1*, 47–48.

Parke, B. N. (1983). Use of self-instructional materials with gifted primary aged students. *Gifted Child Quarterly, 27*, 29–34.

Passow, A. H. (Ed.) (1979). *The gifted and the talented*. Chicago: National Society for the Study of Education.

Passow, A. H. (1980). Secondary schools: Program alternatives for the gifted/talented. *Gifted and Talented Education, 2*, 28–40.

Passow, A. H. (1982). Curricula for the gifted. In National/State Leadership Training Institute on the Gifted and the Talented (Ed.) *Selected proceedings of the first national conference on curricula for the gifted/talented*. Ventura, CA: Ventura County Superintendent of Schools Office.

Pearson, C., & Martfuggis, J. (1979). *Creating and using learning games*. Palo Alto, CA: Learning Magazine.

Pellegrini, A. D. (1982). The effects of exploration training on young children's associative fluency. *Creative Child and Adult Quarterly, 7*, 226–233.

Pilon, B. (1977). Non-stereotyped literature for today's bright girls. *Gifted Child Quarterly, 21*, 234–238.

Pinelli, T. E. (1977a). Utilizing community resources in programming for the gifted. *Gifted Child Quarterly, 17*, 199–202.

Pinelli, T. E. (1977b). Utilizing community resources to encourage student scientific creativity in all grades. *Creative Child and Adult Quarterly, 2*, 156–163.

Plowman, P. (1979). Futuristic views of gifted child education — Images of what might be. *Gifted and Talented Education, 1*, 142–155.

Print, M. (1983). Curriculum materials for able children. *Gifted Education International, 1*, 103–106.

Rebbeck, B. J. (1983). Foreign language techniques for the gifted or watch your blooming language! *Roeper Review, 5*(4), 136–139.

Reed, R., & Henderson, A. (1981). Analytical thinking for children in Fort Worth. *Thinking, 3*(2), 27–30.

Reiss, S., & Cellerino, M. (1983). Guiding gifted students through independent study. *Teaching Exceptional Children, 15*, 136–139.

Renzulli, J. S. (1973). *New directions in creativity*. New York: Harper & Row.

Renzulli, J. S. (1976). The enrichment triad model: A guide for developing defensible programs for the gifted and the talented. *Gifted Child Quarterly, 20*, 303-326.

Renzulli, J. S. (1977). *The enrichment triad model: A guide for developing defensible programs for the gifted and talented*. Mansfield Center, CT: Creative Learning Press.

Renzulli, J. S. (1982). What makes a problem real: Stalking the illusive meaning of qualitative differences in gifted education. *Gifted Child Quarterly, 26*, 147–156.

Renzulli, J. S., & Callahan, C. (1975). Developing creativity training exercises. *Gifted Child Quarterly, 19*, 38–45.

Renzulli, J. S., Reis, S. M., & Smith, L. H. (1981). *The revolving door identification model*. Mansfield Center, CT: Creative Learning Press.

Renzulli, J. S., & Smith, L. H. (1978). *The Learning Styles Inventory: A measure of student preference for instructional techniques*. Mansfield Center, CT: Creative Learning Press.

Renzulli, J. S., & Smith, L. H. (1979). *A guidebook for developing Individual Educational Programs (IEPs) for gifted and talented students*. Mansfield Center, CT: Creative Learning Press.

Reynolds, M. C. (1960). Acceleration. In E. P. Torrance (Ed.), *Talent and education*. Minneapolis, MN: University of Minnesota Press.

Riner, P. S. (1983). Establishing scientific methodology with elementary gifted children through field biology. *G/C/T, 28*, 46–49.

Rodell, W. C., Jackson, N. E, & Robinson, H. B. (1980). *Gifted young children*. New York: Teachers College Press.

Rosen, S. (1976). *Future facts: The way things are going to work in the future*. New York: Simon & Schuster.

Rothenberg, A., Johnson, J. C., & Brooks, M. B. (1966). An approach to teaching gifted emotionally disturbed adolescents. *Gifted Child Quarterly, 10*, 90–100.

Rubenzer, R. L. (1982). *Educating the other half: Implications of left/right brain research*. Reston, VA: Council for Exceptional Children.

Runions, T. (1980). The mentor academy program: Educating the gifted/talented for the 80's. *Gifted Child Quarterly, 24*, 152–157.

Sanborn, M. P. (1979). Counseling and guidance needs of the gifted and talented. In A. H. Passow (Ed.), *The gifted and the talented: Their education and development*. Chicago: National Society for the Study of Education.

Savage, J. F. (1983). Reading guides: Effective tools for teaching the gifted. *Roeper Review, 5*(3), 9–10.

Schlichter, C. L. (1979). The multiple talent approach to the world of work. *Roeper review, 2*(2), 17–20.

Sebesta, S. L. (1976). Language arts program for the gifted. *Gifted Child Quarterly, 20*, 18–23.

Seidman, S., & Spain, M. (1983). A gifted approach to the development of a social studies unit. *Roeper Review, 5*(4), 29–30.

Sellin, D. F., & Birch, J. W. (1980). *Educating gifted and talented learners*. Rockville, MD: Aspen Systems.

Shibles, W. (1979). How to teach creativity through humor and metaphor. *Creative Child and Adult Quarterly, 4*, 243–251.

Silvernail, D. L. (1980). Gifted education for the 80's and beyond. *Roeper Review, 2*(4), 16–18.

Sisk, D. A. (1975a). Communication skills for the gifted. *Gifted Child Quarterly, 19*, 66–68.

Sisk, D. (1975b). Simulation: Learning by doing revisited. *Gifted Child Quarterly, 19*, 175–180.

Sisk, D. (1980). Issues and future directions in gifted education. *Gifted Child Quarterly, 24*, 29–32.

Sloop, E. B. (1982). A survey of selected strategies used by teachers of the gifted in Georgia. (Doctoral dissertation, University of Georgia, 1982). *Dissertation Abstracts International, 43*, 1933–A. (University Microfilms Order No. DA8225249)

Smith, D. L., & Binge, S. (1976). Death education — An urgent need for the gifted-talented-creative whose responses to life are more sensitive. *Creative Child and Adult Quarterly, 1*, 209–213.

Solano, C. H., & George, W. C. (1976). College courses and educational facilitation of the gifted. *Gifted Child Quarterly, 20*, 274–287.

Spicker, H. H. (Ed.) (1982). University-based programs for gifted children. *Journal for the Education of the Gifted, 5*, 153–224.

Stacy, M., & Mitchell, B. (1978). Preparing gifted leaders for a futuristic society. *Roeper Review, 1*(2), 19–22.

Stahl, R. L., & Stahl, R. J. (1979). Using values clarification to develop the creative potential of students: A practical approach for classroom teachers. *Roeper Review, 1*(4) 11–14.

Stanley, J. C. (1976). The case for extreme educational acceleration of intellectually brilliant youths. *Gifted Child Quarterly, 20*, 66–75.

Stanley, J. C. (1978a). Radical acceleration: Recent educational innovation at Johns Hopkins University. *Gifted Child Quarterly, 22*, 62–67.

Stanley, J. C. (1978b). Gather ye APP credits while ye may. *Gifted Child Quarterly, 22*, 129–132.

Stanley, J. C. (1980). On educating the gifted. *Educational Researcher, 9*, 8–12.

Stanley, J. C., George, W. C., & Solano, C. H. (Eds.) (1974a). *The gifted and the creative: A fifty-year perspective*. Baltimore, MD: Johns Hopkins University Press.

Stanley, J. C., Keating, D. P., & Fox, L. H. (Eds.) (1974b). *Mathematical talent: Discovery, description, and development*. Baltimore, MD: Johns Hopkins University Press.

Steele, K. J., Battista, M. T., & Krockover, G. H. (1982). The effect of microcomputer assisted instruction upon the computer literacy of high ability students. *Gifted Child Quarterly, 26*, 162–164.

Stewart, E. (1982). Myth: One program, indivisible for all. *Gifted Child Quarterly, 26*, 27–29.

Stoddard, E. P., & Renzulli, J. S. (1983). Improving the writing skills of talent pool students. *Gifted Child Quarterly, 27*, 21–27.

Switzer, C., & Nourse, M. L. (1979). Reading instruction for the gifted child in first grade. *Gifted Child Quarterly, 23*, 323–33.

Szekeley, G. (1980). The artist and the child — A model program for the artistically gifted. *Gifted Child Quarterly, 25*, 67–72.

Taffel, A. (1961). A program for the gifted at the Bronx High School of Science. *Gifted Child Quarterly, 5*, 69–70.

Tannenbaum, A. J. (1983). *Gifted Children: Psychological and educational perspectives*. New York: Macmillan.

Tannenbaum, A. J., & Newman, E. (1980). *Somewhere to turn: Strategies for parents of gifted and talented children.* New York: Teachers College Press.

Taylor, C. W. (Ed.) (1978). *Teaching for talents and gifts: 1978 status.* Washington, DC: National Institute of Education.

Taylor, C. W., Lloyd, B., & Rollins, J. (1971). Developing multiple talents in classrooms through the implementation of research. *Journal of Research and Development in Education, 4*(3), 42–50.

Toffler, A. (1970). *Future shock.* New York: Random House.

Tomer, M. (1980). Human relations in education—A rationale for a curriculum in interpersonal communication skills for gifted students—Grades K-12. *Gifted Child Quarterly, 25,* 94–97.

Torrance, E. P. (Ed.) (1960). *Talent and education.* Minneapolis, MN: University of Minnesota Press.

Torrance, E. P. (1963). *Education and the creative potential.* Minneapolis, MN: University of Minnesota Press.

Torrance, E. P. (1972). Can we teach children to think creatively? *Journal of Creative Behavior, 6,* 114–143.

Torrance, E. P. (1976). Career education and creativity—Students of the future: Their abilities, achievements, and images of the future. *Creative Child and Adult Quarterly, 1,* 76–91.

Torrance, E. P. (1977). *Discovery and nurturance of giftedness in the culturally different.* Reston, VA: Council for Exceptional Children.

Torrance, E. P. (1978). Five models for constructing creativity instructional materials. *Creative Child and Adult Quarterly, 3,* 8–14.

Torrance, E. P. (1979a). *The search for satori and creativity.* Buffalo, NY: Bearly Limited.

Torrance, E. P. (1979b). Developing creativity instructional materials according to the sociodrama model. *Creative Child and Adult Quarterly, 9,* 9–19.

Torrance, E. P. (1979c). An instructional model for enhancing incubation. *Journal of Creative Behavior, 13,* 23–35.

Torrance, E. P. (1980). More than the ten rational processes. *Creative Child and Adult Quarterly, 5,* 9–19.

Torrance, E. P. (1982a). Hemisphericity and creativity. *Journal of Research and Development in Education, 15*(3), 29–37.

Torrance, E. P. (1982b). Growing up creatively gifted with learning disabilities. In W. M. Cruickshank & J. W. Lerner (Eds.), *Coming of age.* Syracuse, NY: Syracuse University Press.

Torrance, E. P. (1983a). Status of creative women past, present, future. *Creative Child and Adult Quarterly, 8,* 135–144.

Torrance, E. P. (1984a). *Mentor relationships: How they aid creative achievement, endure, change, and die.* Buffalo, NY: Bearly Limited.

Torrance, E. P. (1984b) SAT scores go down; creativity scores go up. *Creativity Newsletter, 5*(2), 3–4.

Torrance, E. P., & Mourad, S. A. (1978). Some creativity and style of learning and thinking correlates of Guglielmino's Self Directed Learning Readiness Scale. *Psychological Reports, 43,* 1167–1171.

Torrance, E. P., & Myers, R. E. (1962). Teaching gifted elementary pupils research concepts and skills. *Gifted Child Quarterly, 6,* 1–5.

Torrance, E. P., Taggart, B., & Taggart, W. (1984). *Human Information Processing Survey.* Bensenville, IL: Scholastic Testing Service.

Torrance, E. P., & Torrance, J. P. (1978). Developing creativity instructional materials according to the Osborn-Parnes creative problem solving model. *Creative Child and Adult Quarterly, 3,* 80–90.

Travers, R. M. W. (Ed.) (1973). *Second handbook of research on teaching.* Chicago: Rand McNally.

Treffinger, D. J. (1975). Teaching for self-directed learning: A priority for the gifted and talented. *Gifted Child Quarterly, 19,* 46–59.

Treffinger, D. J. (1979). Individualized education plans for gifted and talented, and creative students. In *Developing IEPs for the gifted/talented.* Ventura, CA: Ventura County Superintendent of Schools Office.

Treffinger, D. J. (1980a). Fostering independence and creativity. *Journal for the Education of the Gifted, 3,* 214–224.

Treffinger, D. J. (1980b). *Encouraging creative learning for the gifted and talented.* Ventura, CA: Ventura County Superintendent of Schools Office.

Treffinger, D. J., & Barton, E. (1981). *Encouraging self-directed learning.* Mansfield Center, CT: Creative Learning Press.

Van Tassell-Baska, J. (1983). The teacher as counselor for the gifted. *Teaching Exceptional Children, 15,* 214–224.

Van Tassell-Baska, J., Schuler, A., & Lipschutz, J. (1982). An experimental program for gifted four-year olds. *Journal for the Education of the Gifted, 5,* 45–55.

Vare, J. W. (1979). Moral education for the gifted: A confluent model. *Gifted Child Quarterly, 23,* 487–499.

Vida, L. (1979). Children's literature for the gifted elementary school child. *Roeper Review, 1*(4), 22–24.

Weaver, R. A., & Wallace, B. (1980). Technology of the future of gifted child education. *Roeper Review, 2*(4), 19–21.

Webb, J. T., Meckstroth, E. A., & Tolan, S. S. (1982). *Guiding the gifted child: A practical source for parents and teachers.* Columbus, OH: Ohio Publishing Company.

Wechsler, L. K. (1961). The High School of Music and Art, New York city. *Gifted Child Quarterly, 5,* 67–68.

Wedman, J., & Jensen, R. A. (1983). The neglected role of media in gifted education. *G/C/T,* Issue 28, 50–53.

Weinstein, J., & Laughman, L. (1980). Teaching logical reasoning to gifted students. *Gifted Child Quarterly, 24,* 186–190.

Wheatley, G. H. (1983). A mathematics curriculum for the gifted and talented. *Gifted Child Quarterly, 27,* 77–80.

Wilson, S. H., Greer, J. F., & Johnson, R. M. (1973). Synectics, a creative problem solving technique for the gifted. *Gifted Child Quarterly, 17,* 260–267.

Wolf, J., & Stephens, T. (1979). Individualized educational planning for the gifted. *Roeper Review, 2*(2), 11–12.

Wood, M. M. (Ed.) (1975). *Developmental therapy: A textbook for teachers as therapists for emotionally disturbed young children.* Baltimore, MD: University Park Press.

Wood, M. M. (Ed.) (1981). *Developmental therapy sourcebook.* Vols. I and II. Baltimore, MD: University Park Press.

Wooddell, G. D., Fletcher, G. H., & Dixon, T. E. (1982). Future study for the adolescent gifted: A curriculum evaluation. *Journal for the Education of the Gifted, 5,* 24–33.

Yeazell, M. I. (1981a). A report of the first year of the Upshur County, West Virginia, Philosophy for Children project. *Thinking, 3*(1), 12–14.

Yeazell, M. I. (1981b). What happens to teachers who teach philosophy to children? *Thinking, 2*(3 & 4), 86–88.

Youngs, R. C. (1979). The science gifted. *Roeper Review, 2*(2), 23–24.

Zaffran, R. T. (1978). Gifted and talented students: Implications for counselors. *Roeper Review, 1*(2), 9–13.

Zuber, R. (1980). Methodology of science, artificial intelligence and the teaching of logic to gifted children. *Gifted and Talented Education, 2,* 41–59.

23.

Teaching Bilingual Learners

Lily Wong Fillmore
University of California—Berkeley

in collaboration with

Concepción Valadez
University of California—Los Angeles

Introduction

National statistics show that at present there are some 1.5 to 2.4 million American school children between the ages of 5 and 14 who are "limited in English proficiency" (LEP; O'Malley, 1982). These children present a special challenge to American educators, namely, to find more effective means of educating students who do not speak the language of school. LEP students face a high risk of not completing school in this society (National Center for Educational Statistics, 1978; Waggoner, 1981; Steinberg, Blinde, & Chan, 1982); some groups, notably those from Spanish-speaking backgrounds, are at special risk in this regard. Patterns of lower academic achievement for Mexican-American students as compared to their English speaking peers, for example, have long been apparent in lower scores in achievement tests, lower rates of promotion at school, and higher dropout rates (Manuel, 1930; Sánchez, 1932; Carter, 1970; Carter & Segura, 1979; Brown, Rosen, Hill, & Olivas, 1980). Recent figures on high school completion indicate that only 55.5% of Hispanics between ages 18 and 34 have completed high school compared to 83.9% for "white non-Hispanics" (Brown et al., 1980; Durán, 1983).

Considerable thought, effort, and funds have been devoted in the past decade and a half to seeking solutions to the many pedagogical problems presented by these students. Most of these expenditures, however, have gone into program and materials development and support, rather than into research. Until quite recently, in fact, research played a minor part in the search for solutions. There was little support for research on the kinds of problems educators face when they find themselves teaching the academic content of school to students who do not understand the language ordinarily used in school (Troike and Pérez, 1978). Not only do these students have to be taught the content of the school curriculum, they must also be taught the language of the school and the society, if they are to be prepared to participate fully in either.

In this chapter, we discuss instructional issues relating to the education of LEP students, and review the research dealing with them. Specifically, the focus of this review is bilingual education, an instructional approach in which students who do not speak the language of school are taught partly in the language of their homes, and partly in the language of the school. The issues that are discussed here are unusual in a number of ways. Unlike any other instructional approach, bilingual education has become a political matter, particularly in the United States. Discussions about it tend to be infused with political and emotional arguments that have little bearing on the complex pedagogical issues that should be of primary concern. These issues are often lost in the rhetoric that surrounds bilingual education. This review will focus on instructional issues, but because some of them are regarded as issues largely because of the social and political context in which LEP students must be educated, it is necessary to begin the review with some of the background that surrounds and often motivates the research and continuing debate on bilingual education.

Background

The problem of educating LEP students is an old one for American educators. In a society with a population composed

The author thanks reviewers Merrill Swain (The Ontario Institute for Studies in Education), Jim Cummins (The Ontario Institute for Studies in Education), Barry McLaughlin (University of California—Santa Cruz), and Charlene Rivera (Educational Testing Service).

mostly of immigrant peoples from diverse cultural and linguistic backgrounds, the school has played a special role in the naturalization process. The school has frequently been the place where these diverse groups have been exposed to the language and the common culture of the society; through this exposure, many have found the means to become assimilated into the society. In the 200 years since the U.S. became a nation, it has absorbed many millions of immigrants into its body politic through the educational process. Because of the apparent ease with which this was accomplished in the past, little notice was given to the special problems faced by immigrant students in school while they were undergoing the process. The operating assumption of the society's schools was that non-English speakers would pick up English simply by being in an all-English environment. Hence until relatively recent times, LEP students were given little in the way of instruction aimed specifically at helping them learn the school language. In fact, most of these students received no special treatment at all in the past; they were given the same instruction in school as their English-speaking classmates. The belief was that by teaching LEP students *in* English the school was providing them with the means to learn the language itself. Their exposure to English came in the form of the language used by their teachers and classmates, both in the classroom and outside of it, and by the writers of their textbooks. Many did acquire English by hearing teachers and classmates use it, by studying their textbooks, and by participating to whatever extent they could in the instructional activities conducted in the classroom and in the social life of school outside the classroom. Once these students learned English, they had the linguistic means to deal with school, and they were thereby able to take advantage of the educational opportunities available there.

But not all immigrant students were able to learn English just by being in classrooms and schools where it was spoken. Many of them had difficulty picking up the language soon enough or as well as needed to make sense of the instruction they were being given in English. Such students then had difficulty making academic progress, or in getting much out of their educational experiences at all. Cohen (1970), in a review of educational statistics from the first half of this century, found that immigrant children from non-English-speaking countries were much more likely to experience educational retardation than those from countries where English was spoken. In 1911, the retardation rates for foreign-born German children was 51%, for Russian Jews, 59.9%, and for Italians, 76.7%. For foreign-born English children, it was 29.9%, just a little higher than the 26.7% rate for native-born white children. Not coincidentally, many such LEP immigrant students left school without completing their education. Language was only one of the many complex problems facing immigrant students in American schools, and the evidence cited by Cohen indicates that other factors such as cultural background and social circumstances also influenced the ways in which different groups responded to the language differences they encountered in the classroom. Nevertheless, dropout rates among language minority students in this country have always been relatively high; until recently, however, there was virtually no way of determining the extent to which language problems were responsible. What was clear was that language minority students dropped out sooner and in greater numbers than their English monolingual classmates (Steinberg et al., 1982). This situation was not recognized as a problem in the past, perhaps because many people did not finish school. In the expanding American economy of the time there were ample job opportunities for individuals with less than a full high school education. Thus dropouts were not regarded as a problem because they never became an economic burden on the society. The situation has changed radically over the past 20 years, however. In an economy that has become increasingly technological, there are few jobs available for individuals who have less than a full education. Educational failure, whatever the cause, has become a major problem for the society; preventing it has become a major challenge for the schools. Language and related cultural differences have been identified as key factors in the educational failure of minority students, both by educators and by the courts. (For summaries and discussions of the legal decisions that have dealt with the educational problems and rights of linguistic minority students, see Leibowitz, 1982 and Teitelbaum & Hiller, 1977.)

An important ruling in this regard was made in 1974 in a legal case brought on behalf of LEP students in San Francisco's public schools in 1970. The case was based on Title VI of the Civil Rights Act of 1964, which prohibits agencies that receive federal funds from excluding anyone from participating in services provided by those funds on the basis of race, color, or national origin. Suit had been brought against the local school district on the grounds that students who did not know English were being denied access to educational services to which the law said they were entitled since those services were supported by public funds. According to the plaintiffs, these students were effectively being denied any benefit from their education since they were being instructed solely in English, a language they did not know and therefore could not understand. After a series of lower-court judgments that supported the district in its contention that LEP students were not being discriminated against since they were receiving the same education as their English-speaking classmates, the case went to the U.S. Supreme Court. There, the earlier judgments were reversed. In its ruling on the case, the court declared that the practice of instructing students in a language they did not speak or understand constituted a denial of access to the instructional services it deemed the students had a right to expect. According to the court (U.S. Supreme Court, 1974):

> There is no equality of treatment merely by providing students with the same facilities, textbooks, teachers, and curriculum; for students who do not understand English are effectively foreclosed from any meaningful education. Basic English skills are at the very core of what these public schools teach. Imposition of a requirement that, before a child can effectively participate in the educational program, he must already have acquired those basic skills is to make a mockery of public education. We know that those who do not understand English are certain to find their classroom experiences wholly incomprehensible and in no way meaningful. (U.S. Supreme Court, 414 U.S. 563).

Teitelbaum and Hiller (1977) have pointed out that the opinion in this case represents a major affirmation of the interpretation of Title VI of the Civil Rights Act that allows language discrimination to be construed as national origin discrimination when the two are associated. The court's ruling in effect says that school districts have a duty to see that students are not discriminated against because they do not speak English. Accordingly, the district was ordered to take affirmative steps in rectifying the language deficiencies that excluded LEP children from participating in its instructional programs. But while the court declared that an appropriate remedy consisted in these children being given help in overcoming their language difficulties, it did not specify by what method or in what form the help was to be given. The problem of determining the kind of instructional assistance LEP students should receive was left up to the school district and to the lower courts; HEW's Office of Civil Rights, which had the responsibility for monitoring compliance with the Lau ruling throughout the country, also played a major role in determining the precise nature of the educational remedies to be provided by the school.

Two distinctly different approaches to dealing with the special educational needs of LEP students emerged and were considered. In the first, the so-called "English as a second language" (ESL) approach, LEP students are given English instruction in special pullout classes. The objective of this approach is to make it possible for these students to cope with their regular classes, which are taught in English, by helping them learn the language in which they are being instructed. In the second, the "bilingual approach," LEP students are taught partly in English, and partly in the language spoken in their homes. Its objectives are to help students learn English by teaching them a part of the curriculum in that language, and at the same time, to make certain they get some of the subject content they should be learning in school by offering it in a language they already know.

The School District appointed a citizens' task force to consider alternative approaches and to develop a plan to address the educational needs of LEP students as required by the Court. The Office of Civil Rights appointed its own task force, this one of experts on the education of language minority students, to develop national guidelines for compliance with the ruling on the part of other school districts with significant numbers of LEP students. There was substantial agreement in the documents prepared by the two groups; both agreed in principle that the ESL approach by itself was not acceptable and that bilingual education constituted the best available solution for educational problems that stem from mismatches between home and school language use (Office of Civil Rights, 1975; San Francisco Unified School District, 1975). The OCR Guidelines which came to be known as the "Lau Remedies" are very specific in this regard: They require that bilingual instruction be provided for non-English-speaking students in which they are given subject matter instruction in their native languages until they learn enough English to get by in school without such help, and they state that ESL programs can not be offered as substitutes for bilingual instruction.

Support for this view came from proponents of bilingual education who argued that ESL deals only with the problem of teaching LEP students the language of the school, and that is just one of the many things they have to learn. They also have to acquire the basic skills and subject matter that all students should expect to learn in school. While ESL instruction might eventually give LEP students the facility in English that is needed for full participation in school, it does not offer them, during the time they are learning the language, a way to gain access to the school's curriculum (Cárdenas and Cárdenas, 1972). What such students need while they are learning English is instruction in a language they already know; they then have immediate access to the content that is being taught (Saville and Troike, 1971; TESOL, 1976; U.S. Commission on Civil Rights, 1975). Parents of LEP students have been among the most ardent supporters of bilingual education. In a study of parental opinion, Macias (1976) found that 83.9% of the Head Start parents in a predominantly Chicano neighborhood of East Los Angeles wanted bilingual education for their children. The pattern of responses provided by the 199 parents who completed questionnaires indicates that Chicano parents want their children to learn English, but not at the expense of their native language and culture. They were strongly in favor of including topics dealing with Mexican culture and history in the school's curriculum. Considerable linguistic variation exists within the Hispanic community in this country, but nevertheless this group has been unified in its support of bilingual education for its children (Macias, 1982).

Bilingual education is not a recent innovation. There have been, for example, various attempts in the past hundred or so years by German-speaking immigrant communities to establish bilingual education programs in Pennsylvania, Wisconsin, Ohio, and Nebraska (Andersson and Boyer, 1970; Leibowitz, 1970). Federal support for such programs however, is quite recent. Funds were first provided for the development and evaluation of effective models of bilingual programs in 1968 with the passage of Title VII of the Elementary and Secondary Education Act, which has come to be known as the Bilingual Education Act. This legislation made discretionary funds available to local educational agencies to start up and test out bilingual programs in their schools, but they had to compete for these funds. Such programs were entirely voluntary; there was no federal requirement that they be adopted, although it was assumed that local funding for programs that were proven effective would be forthcoming once federal support ran out. This situation changed with the Lau v. Nichols decision and the promulgation of the Lau Remedies which, in effect, required school districts to provide bilingual instruction for LEP students. Within a year, a number of states had passed legislation mandating bilingual instruction for LEP students (see Geffert, Harper, Sarmiento, & Schember, 1975, and Irizarry, n.d., for state-by-state summaries of legislative provisions). The state of Massachusetts, for example, passed a law requiring school districts with enrollments of 20 or more children of limited English-speaking ability to provide transitional bilingual programs for them. Similar legislation was soon passed in Texas, New Mexico, Illinois, New York, and California. With these legal mandates brought about through judicial rulings and legislative action, schools were required to adopt the bilingual approach to meeting the special educational needs of LEP students.

To say that these developments have been controversial is an understatement. While some educators and policymakers regard the changes bilingual education has made in our schools as improvements, other see them differently. In fact, the promulgation of bilingual education by judicial action and by changes in the law has engendered a strongly negative reaction to the use of languages other than English in our schools and in the society as a whole. Judging from the general tone of the mass media coverage of this educational development in the decade following *Lau* v. *Nichols,* there is considerable skepticism in the public mind as to whether bilingual education is an acceptable, or for that matter, a workable solution to the educational problems of LEP students in American schools. Vocal critics of bilingual education, ranging from Mexican-American writer Richard Rodríquez to Harvard sociologist Nathan Glazer, to Washington Post editor Noel Epstein, have written reviews of these programs and have concluded that (a) they prolong the "social disadvantage" of LEP students in this society by delaying their need to learn English and to assimilate into the common culture (Rodríquez, 1982); (b) they are leading to a society that is divided, not only in language and culture, but in loyalty as well (Glazer, 1980); and (c) they are not delivering the increases in academic achievement that their proponents claim for them (Epstein, 1977).

The first view reveals a largely unsupported charge that the use of their native language in school inhibits the learning of English by LEP students. Two separate misconceptions figure here: (a) that little or no English is used in these programs, and (b) that LEP students have to put aside their native languages if they are to succeed in learning English. The second view, which is related to the first, stems from a popular belief that bilingual education enables or even encourages LEP students to preserve language and cultural differences that keep them outside of the mainstream of the society; this perception has been a central theme in the continuing public debate over the wisdom of bilingual education that has been conducted in the press since *Lau* v. *Nichols.* (For an analysis of this press coverage, see Cummins, 1982.) The version of bilingual education that has engendered much of this debate is the so-called "maintenance approach," which has as a major goal the fostering and development of the native languages and cultures of minority-group children in this society. The philosophical basis for such programs is that the languages spoken by minority groups in this country constitute a national asset which should be developed rather than eradicated, a view that was endorsed by the President's Commission on Foreign Language and International Studies (1979). Maintenance bilingual programs have been controversial in two ways: Some critics object to them on the grounds that they promote linguistic and cultural pluralism which are regarded as politically and socially divisive (Glazer, 1980); others question the use of federal funds to promote the maintenance of ethnic and cultural identities of a few selected groups in this country (Epstein, 1977).

The third view arguing against the merits of bilingual education reflects a more pragmatic concern on the part of the public: Many people in the society question the pedagogical soundness of bilingual education. There is a widespread belief that the use of two languages in school leads to cognitive confusion for students, and is an inefficient way to educate students, if the goal is to teach them English. There appears to be, in fact, considerable doubt in the public mind as to whether LEP students will perform any better if they are taught in their native languages than in English. Program evaluations that have been conducted by local educational agencies in connection with Title VII funding, and those conducted by independent investigators, have done little, on the whole, to allay the public's

doubts. A well-publicized national evaluation of Spanish–English Title VII programs completed in 1977 by the American Institutes for Research (AIR) showed that participation in bilingual programs had little positive effect for the Hispanic students in the study sample (Danoff, Coles, McLaughlin, & Reynolds, 1977). They did better in mathematics than comparison students who were not in bilingual programs, but not as well in English language arts. A later analysis of a subset of the data from this study showed that the advantage in mathematics enjoyed by the bilingual students may have been illusory: Looked at more closely, the comparison students were found to outperform the bilingual students not only in English, but in mathematics as well (Danoff, 1978). The findings of this study have been challenged by bilingual education researchers largely on methodological grounds (Cárdenas, 1977; Gray, 1977; O'Malley, 1978). Gray identified several types of problems with the study: weaknesses in its pre- and posttest design with an interval of just 5 months between testing; the use of inappropriate or unreliable tests and procedures for assessing English language and reading ability; and the inappropriate aggregation of students who had received not one, but a variety of educational treatments funded by Title VII. The implementation of Title VII has been subject to local interpretation: Far from being uniform in instructional method or approach, Title VII programs are as varied as the districts that have sponsored them, the teachers whose job it has been to make them work, and the children served by them. Some of these programs are good but others are not, critics of this study have pointed out. In treating them as undifferentiated programs for evaluation, the AIR study assumed that they are more uniform than they are. As a consequence, Gray argued, any positive effects that might have been present for the exemplary bilingual programs in the sample would have been canceled out by the negative effects of programs that were bilingual in name only or were unsatisfactory in other ways. The classes that were included in the sample might have been representative of those funded by Title VII, but they were not necessarily representative of bilingual education as conceived by its supporters (Troike, 1978).

Other attempts to document the effectiveness of bilingual education programs through standard evaluation methods have had mixed results, generally. In a survey of unpublished evaluations of Title VII programs conducted by the Center for Applied Linguistics, Troike (1978) found some evidence to support the argument that properly implemented bilingual programs will show good results in academic learning and in other indicators of programmatic success. Twelve programs are cited in which participating students either outperformed comparison students, or performed at or above district and national norms. In several of the studies, students in the bilingual programs were reported to have better attendance records and to demonstrate higher self-esteem than comparison-group students. This examination of the research allowed Troike (1978) to make the following statement:

> Enough evidence has now accumulated to make it possible to say with confidence that *quality* bilingual programs *can* meet the goal of providing equal educational opportunity for students from non-English speaking backgrounds. In fact, the evidence is sufficiently strong to permit the statement that if a program is *not* producing

such results, something is wrong (though not necessarily with the program) and needs to be changed. The state of the art has progressed — at least in a few places — to the point where we should not feel it necessary to excuse bad programs just because they are bilingual: such programs are not good for students and they do the cause of bilingual education an injustice. (p. 4)

The evaluation evidence that convinced Troike that bilingual education can successfully meet the educational needs of LEP students has not convinced other reviewers of the same body of data, however. The positive evidence cited by Troike consists of a variety of success indicators; criterion-referenced tests, nationally and district-normed tests of academic achievement, reading test scores, attendance records, measures of self-concept, and the like. But as the studies that were reviewed are unpublished, the appropriateness of such measures cannot be judged, nor can the rigor of the studies be assumed. Further, since few details are provided in the discussion concerning the nature of the programs themselves, it is not easy to discover what contributed to their success.

A more recent examination of evaluations of bilingual programs conducted over the past decade led to a quite different conclusion on the part of the reviewers: That is, there is little evidence that bilingual education is effective enough to warrant its being prescribed at the federal level as the only acceptable remedy for the educational problems of LEP students (Baker and De Kanter, 1981). The aim of this study, which was carried out by staff members of the Office of Planning, Budget, and Evaluation in the U.S. Department of Education, was to assess the effectiveness of "transitional bilingual education" based on the evaluations that have been done over the years. The test of effectiveness applied in this review was whether or not the programs that had been evaluated led to better performance in English, and in "nonlanguage" subject areas. After examining several hundred studies of bilingual programs, Baker and De Kanter selected 28 for inclusion in their analysis. The others were rejected on the grounds that they did not assess performance in English or in nonlanguage subjects, or they failed the tests of methodological adequacy that were established as selection criteria for inclusion in this study. For example, studies were eliminated if they did not make use of true experimental designs with random assignment of students to treatment and control groups, or of statistical procedures to control for preexisting differences between groups when random assignment was not possible. Based on their review of the 28 studies that survived their tests (it should be noted that none of the studies reviewed by Troike appear to be among the 28 that passed inspection), Baker and De Kanter (1981) reached several conclusions that will be discussed further in the present review since they deal with instructional issues that are central concerns here. The one that is germane to the immediate discussion is this:

We conclude that TBE [transitional bilingual education] fails both tests [that is, of proven effectiveness, and of being the *only* effective approach] for justifying reliance on it as the exclusive method for instructing language minority children. There is no firm empirical evidence that TBE is uniquely effective in raising language minority students' performance in English or in non-language subject areas.

This conclusion has not gone unchallenged. Other commentators have hastened to point out that the Baker and De Kanter analysis made use of studies that were flawed in many of the same ways as those that were eliminated by application of their selectional criteria (Yates & Ortiz, 1983). The general tone of the criticisms that have been made of the Baker and De Kanter study has been that studies showing an advantage for bilingual education were generally eliminated from their analysis by unrealistic and unevenly applied selection criteria (Hernández-Chávez, Llanes, Alvarez, & Arvizu, 1981).

There has been much debate among educators and policymakers over what the federal policy should be in relation to the education of LEP students, especially since the release of the Baker and De Kanter report. Is there enough evidence to support the continued preference for bilingual education as the prescribed remedy? These debates began a year before the completion of the Baker and De Kanter study, that is, in 1980, at public hearings held throughout the country to discuss the adoption of regulations that would implement the Supreme Court's interpretation of Title VI of the Civil Rights Act of 1964 in the *Lau* v. *Nichols* case. Under the provisions of Title VI, the Department of Education had a responsibility to issue guidelines and regulations to protect "national origin minority children" from discrimination in schools that received any federal funds for support of programs.

The proposed Lau Regulations, as they came to be called, focused specifically on defining the steps that school districts should take to demonstrate compliance with Title VI; had they been adopted, they would have replaced the Lau Remedies which, technically speaking, were guidelines and not rules. As proposed originally, the Lau Regulations would have required all school districts with federally supported programs (a) to identify students whose limited proficiency in English qualified them for special help in school; (b) to provide them with instructional services that would help them learn English and would allow them to keep up in academic subjects as well; and (c) to determine through the use of assessment procedures how long these students are eligible for such services, and when they know enough English to handle instruction given exclusively in that language. The proposed rules further specified that a form of bilingual instruction be provided for students who speak English less proficiently than they do their native language. The extent to which the public disagreed on what the schools should do for these students became quite evident during the period when comments on the proposed rules could be made by interested individuals and groups at public hearings held throughout the country. Some 4,500 public comments were received (Office of Civil Rights, 1981). There was considerable disagreement over the federal government's authority to define through regulation the steps that local school districts must take to comply with Title VI. Even more controversial was the question of whether the federal government should be specifying the methods by which school districts are to educate LEP students. There were, on the one side, commentators who argued that local school districts should have options available to them, since there is little evidence that there is any one best method for educating LEP students. There is no research, it was argued, demonstrating the superiority of bilingual instruction over other methods of instruction, and none showing that it does help LEP students to perform at appropriate levels in school. According to this view, local districts are in the best position to decide what kind of services and methods are best suited to local conditions and to their students' needs. On the other side were commentators who argued that if remedies were left up to the local districts, many would elect to do nothing at all, or they were likely to concentrate their efforts on teaching LEP students English, and neglect other areas of academic development. Commentators favoring the position taken in the proposed regulations in which bilingual instruction is required for LEP students argued that it is the only approach that allows these students to participate fully in school while they are in the process of learning English, and to utilize the knowledge and experiences they already have. Responding to the issue of the apparent tenuousness of the research support for bilingual instruction, they pointed out that there is likewise little evidence that supports any of the alternatives to bilingual education. Bilingual education has not worked in many places for reasons that are unrelated to its merits. Districts that are not committed to making it work can build in many practical obstacles to the success of the program in the implementation process. These can include the placement in these programs of children whose presence greatly complicates the situation for bilingual teachers (e.g., children whose problems in school are behavioral rather than linguistic, and LEP children who speak native languages different than that spoken by the students for whom the program is intended), or the assignment of teachers to the program who do not have the necessary language skills (say, in English or in the native language of the students) that are required for teaching in the program (Office of Civil Rights, 1981).

During the period in which comments such as these were being considered, the federal administration in Washington changed hands; with it came a change in the readiness to adopt regulations concerning the federal policy on providing educational opportunities for LEP students. In February, 1981 the Department of Education announced the withdrawal of the proposed Lau Regulations. No new action has been taken subsequently to revise or resubmit the rules for reconsideration, and at present the Lau Remedies (Office of Civil Rights, 1975) continue to serve as the guide in evaluating school district compliance with Title VI.

The purpose of this background section has been to provide the reader with a perspective on the educational approach that is the focus of this chapter. In many ways, the instructional issues that are treated below tend to get lost in discussions of bilingual education, which are often emotional and philosophical rather than substantive. It is hoped that this summary of some of the events that have led to the development of bilingual education in the United States will help the reader to put into context some of the strong feelings that invariably intrude on discussions of this instructional approach.

Overview of This Chapter

The discussion that follows is organized around those issues that are, in our view, the central ones for educators to consider

in assessing the appropriateness of instructional methods to be used with LEP students. Some of these issues are general ones, and are relevant to any type of program serving LEP students; others are more specific, and are relevant particularly to programs in which LEP students receive a part of their instruction in their native language. The issues that are discussed here are directly related to two goals that the society has for LEP students, namely that of providing them with the general education that all children growing up in this society have a right to expect, and that of helping them learn English, the language of the school and society. From a strictly practical perspective, these two goals are in conflict. If the objective were solely to provide a general education for LEP students, the most practical solution would be to teach them what they have to learn in their native languages. The problem, however, is that if they were educated exclusively in their native languages these students would not learn English. The learning of English is a necessary goal if language minority students are to participate in the life of the society in which they live. On the other hand, if the school's main objective were to teach them English, the most practical solution would be to instruct LEP students solely in that language, and to concentrate on getting them to learn it as a second language. The problem then is that these students would learn little else but English in the process. Experience has shown that under this approach, many LEP students fall so far behind in school by the time they learn English that they are unable to catch up with their English-speaking classmates academically. It is possible to accomplish both goals at the same time, but to do so requires that the competition between these two sets of instructional objectives be recognized and resolved. Many of the instructional issues that are discussed in this chapter stem from the dynamic tension created by these two competing goals; thus, they provide a framework for discussing the research that is reviewed here. It should be noted that this is in no way a comprehensive review of the research in bilingual education nor of the literature related to the education of language minority students. The literature that has been examined is that which pertains to the issues at hand. The rest of this chapter is divided into three sections, each of them dealing with a major set of issues. They are issues related to language use in bilingual instruction, issues in second-language teaching and learning, and issues related to the effects of bilingualism. Within each of these sections, we will consider the nature of the instructional problem for teachers and of the learning problem for students, review representative research on aspects of the problem, and discuss directions being taken in research in that area. In the selection of studies to be reviewed, a decision was made not to include the large evaluation studies that have been concerned with assessing the *general effectiveness* of bilingual education itself. These have been discussed in the background section, and the problems with these studies are well known. Aside from that, from an instructional perspective, the question that is of interest is not whether bilingual education works as it has been implemented, but rather, how can it be implemented so it will work as it should? Thus, the evaluation research that deals with effectiveness of programs is not discussed, and only those evaluation studies that deal with instructional practices or processes are considered here.

Assumptions and Definitions

Bilingual education rests on the following assumptions:

1. Students who are less than fully proficient in the school language will have difficulty deriving academic benefit from their educational experience, since the inability to understand the language in which instruction is given precludes comprehension of the content of that instruction.

2. It takes LEP students time to acquire the level of proficiency in English that is needed to participate effectively in all-English classes. During the time it takes to learn English, they will get little out of their school experience if they are instructed exclusively in that language.

3. Instruction in the native language of LEP students allows them to participate in school, and to acquire the skills and knowledge covered in the curriculum while they are learning English. It also allows them to make use of skills, knowledge, and experiences they already have, and to build on those prior assets in school.

4. Knowledge and skills are more easily acquired by LEP students in their native language; but computational skills and many literacy skills acquired in the native language can be transferred to the new language once it is mastered. Hence time spent in learning materials in the native language is not time that is lost with respect to the coverage of subject matter in school.

5. Students need adequate exposure to the language of school in order to acquire it as a second language; this exposure to English is best when it takes place in settings in which the learners' special linguistic needs help to shape the way the language gets used. Subject matter instruction given in English can provide the exposure that LEP students need, as long as it is appropriately tailored for them. Subject matter instruction in the school language is an essential component of bilingual education.

6. Formal instruction in English as a second language (ESL) can help students get started learning the language. ESL, whether it is formal or informal, is an integral part of American bilingual education programs.

7. The academic potential of all children, including those served by bilingual programs, has the best chance of being realized when their language skills, their social and cultural experiences, and their knowledge of the world are affirmed in school; these are the foundations of academic development.

The term "bilingual education" is used in reference to a variety of instructional programs, some of which are bilingual, others of which are not. The definition of bilingual education most commonly assumed in the U.S. is the one given in the 1974 version of the Bilingual Education Act [Title VII, Elementary and Secondary Education Act]:

> The term "program of bilingual education" means a program of instruction, designed for children of limited English-speaking ability in elementary or secondary schools, in which, with respect to the years of study to which such program is applicable—"(i) there is instruction given in, and study of, English and, to the extent necessary to allow a child to progress effectively through the educational system, the native language of the children of limited

English-speaking ability, and such instruction is given with appreciation of the cultural heritage of such children, and with respect to elementary school instruction, such instruction shall, to the extent necessary, be in all courses or subjects of study which will allow a child to progress effectively through the educational system. (Sec. 703, (a) (4) (A))

Bilingual programs come in many forms, but their defining characteristics are these:

- Instruction is given in two languages; in the U.S., English is one, and the home language of the LEP students served by the program the other;
- Instruction in the language of the school is given in a way that permits students to learn it as a second language.

Programs vary considerably in the extent to which each of the two components is emphasized in their objectives, and in how they are realized. Some of this variation stems from a general confusion over the roles and functions played by language in these two aspects of bilingual programs. In particular, the distinction between *language of instruction*, that is, language used as the vehicle by which instruction and information are communicated to students in textbooks and in classrooms, and *language instruction*, that is, instruction in which language itself is the object being taught, is one that is often confused in discussions pertaining to these components.

A typology of bilingual education based in part on differing degrees of emphasis on objectives was proposed by Fishman and Lovas (1970). A similar but more complex typology was advanced by Mackey (1970), whose typology is based on the distribution of the languages with respect to the entire learning environment including home, school, area, and national goals and patterns of usage. In some cases, the primary objectives of the program are the development of English language skills, and enabling LEP students served by the program to make a shift as expeditiously as possible to an all-English program of studies. Fishman and Lovas characterize such programs as "transitional" in orientation. Transitional bilingual programs offer LEP students dual-language instruction but only until they have acquired enough English to deal with instruction given exclusively in that language. The rationale for using the students' native language in school is that it permits them to deal with school while they are learning English; the goal is reached when they can be placed in all-English classes at their appropriate grade level. Transitional programs differ from English as a second language programs in that the LEP students' native or first language (L1) is used as a language of instruction along with English, the language the students are learning as their second language (L2), whereas in ESL programs, LEP students are taught English through the exclusive use of English. The major aim of both is to help LEP students deal successfully with instruction given in English. However, transitional programs match the defining characteristics of bilingual education programs, while ESL programs do not, despite the similarity in aim. The likely outcome of transitional bilingual education is a limited bilingualism; many students shift away from the use of their L1 altogether when its use is no longer supported outside of the home.

A second major category of bilingual programs according to the Fishman and Lovas typology can be described as "maintenance" in orientation. Under the Fishman and Lovas framework, two other categories of programs can be distinguished; there are, in addition to maintenance programs, those whose aim is "monoliterate bilingualism" and those whose aim is "partial bilingualism," the differences among them having to do with the extent to which they promote literacy in the two languages of instruction. In maintenance programs, the objective is to develop full literacy skills in both languages. In monoliterate programs, the goal is to develop oral language skills in the home language, but not literacy skills, which are developed only in the societal language. In partial bilingualism programs, literacy in the home language is promoted, but not in all subject areas. In this discussion, all three are subsumed under the broadly drawn category of maintenance programs since they are not so different in their basic orientation, and the concern here is in the primary objectives and rationales that determine the nature of any given program.

Maintenance programs differ from transitional ones in that LEP students can remain in them even after they have become fully proficient in English. The students' L1 is seen as more than a temporary medium of instruction, a stopgap measure that allows them to get some benefit from school while they are learning English; it is seen as an alternative medium of instruction which serves as a legitimate means by which these students can continue to gain access to the curriculum even after they have learned English. The rationale for maintenance programs is that the continued use of both languages in school will enable the students served by these programs to develop mature skills in both languages and to achieve full bilingualism eventually. In this type of program, the emphasis is not only on the development of English language proficiency, but on maintaining and developing L1 proficiency as well. In contrast to transitional programs where bilingualism is viewed as a means by which English proficiency can be achieved, in these programs, it is seen as a worthwhile end in itself.

The differences between these two categories of programs add up to a major contrast in orientation: transitional programs are fundamentally compensatory in their orientation, while maintenance programs are augmentary in theirs. The differences between transitional and maintenance programs that have been identified here are reflected in the instructional issues that arise in each. In transitional programs, for example, questions related to establishing the levels of L2 proficiency needed to handle the exclusive use of that language in instructional materials and activities are crucial since they determine eligibility for such programs. Such questions are not as important in maintenance programs since students can remain in them even after they are proficient enough in English to handle all-English instruction. In this review, issues related to both types of programs are discussed, but the reader will find a greater emphasis on issues related to transitional programs than on those associated with maintenance programs. The reason for that is simple: Most bilingual programs are of the first type; the second is an ideal that is seldom realized. In the sections that follow, variants of these program types will be discussed in greater detail in relation to the instructional issues that figure in them.

Language Use in Bilingual Instruction

In this section we consider instructional issues that are related to the separate roles of the two languages in bilingual programs. The use of two languages in classroom instruction is a defining characteristic of bilingual programs. Questions concerning what to teach in each language and how the two languages can be used effectively are among the most complex and difficult problems associated with this instructional approach. These stem from the fact that language used in programs for LEP students must serve at least two important functions: It provides the means by which students achieve the academic and social goals of school, and it serves as the basis on which they acquire or develop skills in the language itself. It appears that how well these functions are served can depend on the form of dual language instruction that is adopted. Programs differ widely, quantitatively and qualitatively, in the separate roles and functions assigned to the two languages.

The maintenance of a balance in the use of the two languages is regarded by some to be a critical factor in achieving both objectives of bilingual programs. There must be enough L1 instruction to allow LEP students to make the progress expected of them in the school's curriculum, and enough L2 instruction to allow them to learn English. But in each case, how much is enough? Some experts believe that in order for both functions to be served, the two languages must be used in about equal parts in the teaching of subject matter. Managing this, however, is not as easy as it might appear. It is especially difficult in programs that are team taught, since the balance has to be maintained across teachers. Teachers have difficulty maintaining a balanced use of the two languages in class, since social circumstances are often more influential than pedagogical concerns in guiding language choice, even during instructional events. Teachers are inclined to switch languages whenever they sense that their LEP students are not following what is being said. Aside from that, teachers and students alike tend to use the language that seems most appropriate in any given situation, or in which it is easiest to communicate what they have to say at the time of speaking. Any rule that requires them to keep track of how much of each language they are using is unnatural and therefore, extremely difficult to follow. Programs can be designed to facilitate a balanced use of the two languages for instructional purposes, but even then there are complexities that must be considered.

Thus, the first problem to be confronted in planning a bilingual program concerns the use of the two languages of instruction. The subject matter of school is to be taught bilingually, but what does it mean in practice, to "teach bilingually"? When should teachers use Language A, and when should they use Language B? How should each be used? The question is interpreted in many different ways; it is taken as relating to the amount of time to be allocated to each language, the distribution of the two languages by subjects, the structuring of classes to facilitate bilingual instruction, or the manner in which the two languages are used in the teaching of any given subject.

The question of how the two languages are to be used instructionally figures prominently in the structuring of programs. In a survey of bilingual education projects in the United

States, Cordasco (1976) identified several organizational patterns based largely on language distribution in time. In one type, equal time is devoted to the use of the two languages, each language assigned a separate block of time. For example, classes may be conducted in Language A during morning sessions, and in Language B in the afternoon. In a second type of arrangement, the time devoted to the two languages is more or less equivalent, but there is no prearranged separation by time. Both languages are likely to be used in any given block of time. A third pattern involves the separation of the two languages over a much longer span of time. In this arrangement, instruction is initiated in the L1 of the students, and only gradually is it presented in the L2. The use of the L2 is increased as the students gain mastery over that language, and eventually the L2 replaces the L1 as the medium of instruction. A different basis for distributing the use of the two languages of instruction can be seen in Cordasco's fourth type of programs. In this type of program the L2 predominates as the medium of instruction from the beginning. The L1 is used in the teaching of some selected subjects, and as an emergency instructional aid to the students as needed. The distribution of language use is motivated in part by subject, and in part by functional necessity.

Let us examine manifestations of these organizational patterns, and of the instructional issues encountered in them.

Allocation of Language Use by Time

Practical considerations figure heavily in organizational patterns in which language use is distributed temporally. We have noted that a balanced use of the two languages is regarded as crucial to the success of bilingual programs, but keeping track of how much of each language one should be using is extremely difficult without structural support. Dividing the schedule into time blocks during which the two languages are used separately can be a simple but effective solution. In principle, it allows program planners to determine how much time is to be devoted to each language at any given point in the program, and it allows them to regulate changes in the relative usage over the course of the program.

The "alternate-days approach" whereby each of the two languages is used every other day is an example of this type of arrangement. Tucker, Sibayan, and Otanes (1970) studied the effects of this approach in an experimental bilingual education program conducted in the Philippines. The two languages in this study were Pilipino and English, both of which are official languages in the Philippines and are generally learned in school as second or third languages. Traditionally, instruction was given in Pilipino (or in the local vernacular language) during the first two years of school, and an abrupt switch was made to English at the third grade. The changeover to English was generally accompanied by transition difficulties for the students.

The purpose of the experiment described in Tucker et al. (1970) was to evaluate the relative effectiveness of plans by which students were taught monolingually in either Pilipino or English with the addition of, or switch to, the other language in Grade 3, and one in which students were taught bilingually from Grade 1. Four first grade classes were studied; two of them were taught bilingually, the other two monolingually. One of

the two monolingual classes was taught exclusively in Pilipino, while the other was conducted in English. One of the bilingual classes had had no prior school experience while the other three study classes had been in kindergarten. The two monolingual classes were taught a standard kindergarten curriculum. The bilingual classes followed the alternate days approach. Except for a language arts period, all subjects were taught in Pilipino on one day, and in English the next. Language arts was taught in the "other" language each day. The plan followed was relatively simple, and thereby workable. According to the investigators:

> The material covered on Day 2 was not simply a repetition of that covered on Day 1; but was instead a continuation of the previous day's lesson. Apparently, this switching caused no appreciable or continuing difficulty to students or teachers. A sign posted on the door of the classroom indicated *English Today*, or *Pilipino Ngayon*. (p. 284)

The investigators found the alternate-days approach to be quite effective after 1 year of treatment. Although students who had not had kindergarten did less well than those who had, the groups that were instructed bilingually generally performed as well as those who were instructed monolingually both in language and in academic content areas, thus demonstrating that they did not find the form of language alternation followed in this study confusing. Most importantly, the students in the bilingual classes appeared to be doing as well in each of the two languages as students who were being instructed monolingually in that language, suggesting that they would not find it difficult to switch to the exclusive use of either of them later on in school.

This arrangement appears to be effective because there was a clear separation between the two languages for students and for teachers. The simple rule governing language choice made it relatively easy for everyone concerned to know what language to use and to expect each day in school. However, the planning of instruction under such an arrangement can be difficult since materials are alternately taught in two languages. There must be equivalent materials in both languages in all curriculum areas, and teachers must be prepared to teach everything in both. The advantage for students under this type of plan is that they receive equivalent exposure to both languages. But there is for them the problem of acquiring reading skills in two languages at the same time, and of dealing with two sets of terms, if not ideas, for each curriculum area. These are not insurmountable problems, but they do require students to put out a greater effort than is needed when subjects are taught monolingually.

Different forms of the alternate days approach have been tried in other projects. One form that has been tried, but not studied is one in which the instructional content between the two languages is not continuous as in the Philippines project, but repeated. Hence, instruction is given in Language A on one day, and repeated in Language B the next; students receive parallel instruction in the two languages. On the face of it, this version of the alternate days approach is both cumbersome and uneconomical since twice as much time is spent on any piece of the curriculum as in the original version. A more popular and workable form of this approach involves dividing the curriculum between the two languages so that different subjects are taught on alternate days. Such programs are often team taught, with two teachers coteaching two classes of students. Typically, one teacher covers a half of the curriculum in Language A, while the other covers the rest of the curriculum in Language B. Students thus receive equivalent amounts of instruction in the two languages, but are instructed in only one language in each content area. A variant of this plan is the alternate sessions approach in which students receive instruction in a set of subjects in Language A during morning sessions, and in another set in Language B during afternoons. Both of these models have been widely used in San Francisco Unified School District, apparently with good result. Chinese-dominant LEP students in San Francisco's bilingual program in 1975–1976 were reported as performing at or above district and national norms in English and mathematics in standardized achievement tests in three out of six grades, and just 1 month below in two others (Troike, 1978).

These structural arrangements differ considerably from plans that involve the phased introduction of bilingual instruction. Mackey and Beebe (1977) discuss several such models which have been developed and tested in Dade County, Florida. Under a plan devised by Dade County school officials, LEP students at Coral Way Elementary School received instruction largely in their L1, Spanish, or in a mix of Spanish and English during the first month of school in Grade 1. They are given only 15 minutes of English instruction during this period. Gradually, over the year, the amounts of English and mixed-language instruction are increased, until the end of the year, when their combined usage exceeds the use of Spanish alone. The amount of English instruction is gradually increased until by Grade 4, the ratio of English or mixed language instruction to Spanish only is 2 to 1. By Grade 6, instructional language use is described as entirely mixed, that is, teachers and students are using both languages throughout the school day, and across the entire curriculum. Mixed instruction also referred to "combined classes of Anglos and Cubans alternating 3 weeks of each grading period working through English only, and 3 weeks working through Spanish only, in all subjects" at Grades 4 through 6, according to the time distribution plan prepared by school officials (Mackey and Beebe, 1977, p. 73). In this program, LEP students were grouped by first- and second-language ability, and were instructed accordingly. The "Anglos" were the English monolingual students in the program; they were also being instructed bilingually with a gradual increase in the amount of Spanish and bilingual instruction received over time, but under this plan, they were instructed separately. According to Mackey and Beebe, the two-way bilingual program at Coral Way School gave all of the pupils an opportunity to become "completely bilingual," with "each group learning through its own and the other's language" (p. 76).

The program was not a total success in this regard, however. Mackey and Beebe report that while the Spanish-background students eventually had equal reading proficiency and language skills at all grade levels, the English background students read significantly better in English than in Spanish. However, while the English speakers did not achieve balanced skills in their two languages, the fact that they maintained superior skills in their

native language was seen not as a failure, but as "a logical outcome of their living in an English-speaking environment" (p. 79). This point will be discussed further in the section of this chapter that is focused on language learning and teaching issues.

Bilingual programs that make use of phased introduction of the L2 vary considerably in when and how that language gets introduced. In the Coral Way program, students were given a brief ESL lesson and a short period of "mixed" instruction in art, music, and physical education at the beginning of the first grade year. Everything else during that period was presented in Spanish. The amount of English instruction was increased gradually over that year, and the amount of Spanish decreased accordingly. Another program that makes use of phased introduction of English is described by von Maltitz (1975, pp. 49–56). This program, which was conducted at a New York City school with a high concentration of Spanish speakers, differed from the Dade County program in how long it took to phase in English as a language of instruction. The decrease in the use of the L1 in the Dade County program was fairly rapid. The decrease in L1 usage in the New York program was considerably more gradual. According to von Maltitz, Puerto Rican students in the bilingual program at P.S. 25 received 85% of their instruction in Spanish, and 15% in English during the kindergarten year. The amount of instruction in English was increased slightly (by about 5 to 10%) every year or two, and the amount of Spanish decreased accordingly, until by the sixth grade, a 50–50 balance was achieved.

Evaluations indicate that this way of organizing bilingual instruction is generally effective, despite rather considerable differences in the rate by which the L2 is phased into use across instances of such programs. Students who had been in the New York City program from the first grade were reported as having performed better than students in comparison schools, particularly in the area of mathematics, whether performance was assessed in Spanish or in English. Their performance in reading as measured in the two languages was less consistent; they tended to do better in vocabulary knowledge in Spanish than in English, but they scored better in English reading comprehension than in Spanish. Their better performance in L1 reading vocabulary may be attributed to the prolonged concentration on that language in school. The fact that they did better in English reading comprehension than in Spanish would seem to indicate that they were making progress in that language nevertheless, and were, perhaps, acquiring skills that were transferable across languages.

There is research that suggests that a too-sharp shift to L2 instruction may cancel out the benefits of early native language instruction. In a study investigating the advantages of native language instruction, Baral (1979) compared the academic achievement of Mexican-American seventh and eighth grade students who had received all of their education in the United States with that of immigrant students who had received at least 2 years of schooling in Mexico before entering American schools. There have long been anecdotal reports suggesting that Mexican students who have had some educational experience in their native language before immigrating to the United States acquire English more successfully, and perform better academically than do Mexican-American students who have been educated in English from Grade 1. These reports are consistent with the findings of a study conducted in Sweden of Finnish immigrant students who entered Swedish schools after having had some of their primary instruction in Finland. Comparing the academic achievement especially in the area of Swedish language skills of these students with those of Finnish students who had received all of their education in Swedish schools, Skutnabb-Kangas and Toukomaa (1976) found this:

> Those who attended school in Finland approached the level of achievement of normal Swedish pupils ... in the written comprehension test considerably more often than those who began school in Sweden. Those who had attended school in Finland for at least three years did best. The explanation for this can perhaps be found in their better skill in their mother tongue, which laid the basis for understanding a test in Swedish. Two years in a Finnish class in Sweden did not, on the other hand, make for as good a basis for learning Swedish as the corresponding time in Finland. (pp. 65–66)

There was apparently a direct relationship between the number of years students spent in school in their native language before receiving instruction through their L2 and their eventual academic performance in the L2. According to these researchers, the findings in this study argue strongly for the proposition that the use of the L1 as the medium for early instruction can lay the foundation for later academic achievement in the L2 for linguistic minority students. It should be noted here that such findings may not generalize easily to linguistic minority students in American schools. More than L1 instruction figured in the early education of the students in these studies. Both the Finnish students studied by Skutnabb-Kangas and the Mexican students followed by Baral were educated through their L1s while living in their native countries. Thus, they were being instructed in a culturally and linguistically intact system of education, with all of the social support that comes from being in one's own native land.

Contrary to expectation, Baral found that the recent immigrants who had been placed in regular English classes from the time of arrival in American schools did not attain higher academic achievement rates as he had predicted. The native-born students consistently scored higher than the recent immigrants in reading and in mathematics. Baral's findings would appear to contradict the findings of the Skutnabb-Kangas study, but as he points out, the immigrant students in his study had attended Mexican schools for periods ranging from 2 to 4 years only. Like the Finnish students who had had less than 3 years of native language instruction, the positive effects of initial L1 instruction that might have been expected may have been canceled by a too-abrupt shift to the new language. This point appears to be well taken. Studies of immigrant students in Canada (Cummins, 1981c) have shown that it may take as many as 5 to 7 years of schooling for there to be an advantage, and for immigrant students to come up to grade norms.

The staged introduction of the L2 in programs such as the one at Coral Way School represents one type of phased bilingual instruction which is based on the premise that the transition from the language of the home to the language of the school must be made gradually to avoid educational trauma. A quite different principle is involved in a second type of program which also makes use of phased bilingual instruction. The premise on which immersion programs are based is that an immediate total immersion in the new language hastens language learning. In such programs, it is the L1 of the students that gets added to the program gradually, until a balanced use of the two languages is achieved in school. This model was developed in Quebec to introduce English-speaking students to the use of French in school. The students were not linguistic minority students, but were, instead, speakers of the primary language of the society and its schools. The ones who participated in the early experimental versions of the program were from middle-class families. They were volunteers for the program which their parents hoped would make it possible for them to acquire a second language. The development of the program was closely studied by researchers, and is perhaps one of the best-documented efforts in instructional innovation. Lambert and Tucker (1972) investigated the effects of immersion education on the academic, linguistic, social, and psychological development of the students who went through the first versions of these programs, and found that not only did they do as well in school as they would have had they been instructed exclusively in their L1, but they also achieved a level of L2 proficiency that could not be achieved under any traditional language instruction program. The positive results reported by Lambert and Tucker have been consistently supported by studies that have been done since then (e.g., Barik & Swain, 1975, 1976; Genesee, 1978; Swain, 1984). What makes these programs work?

Lambert (1984) describes the underlying rationale and the characteristics of immersion programs in the following way:

> The concept of immersion schooling was based on a very important and fundamental premise — that people learn a second (or third) language in the same way as they learn their first; that is, in contexts where they are exposed to it in its natural form and where they are motivated to communicate. From the first encounter immersion teachers use only the target language. They clearly, patiently, and repetitively focus on the development of a basic vocabulary in the new language, relying, with the youngest age groups, on plastic art materials, songs, and animated stories. But from the start, the learning of language per se is made quite incidental to learning how to make and do new and interesting things. The new language becomes a constant verbal accompaniment rather than the focus. Later, new ideas of a scientific, mathematical, or problem solving nature are given the main focus, but even then the accumulation of skill in the new language appears to be incidental, except for short daily periods of French language arts which direct students attention to the new language itself. ... The teachers' main preoccupation then is to cover fully the content subjects expected of any child in a conventional program at that grade level. Immersion programs typically consist of only anglophone pupils; thus, a whole class experiences immersion as equals, with no one having the advantage of a native speaker. (pp. 11–12)

Students are thus instructed exclusively in the L2 (French, in this case), generally through the second grade. During the second or third grade, a period of L1 (English) language arts instruction is introduced. The amount of L1 instruction, and the number of subjects taught in the L1, are gradually increased over the next several grades until a level of 60% is reached by Grades 5 or 6 (Lapkin and Cummins, 1984). Lapkin and Cummins describe several variants of immersion programs, including one described as "partial immersion" in which children begin with just half of their school day immersed in the new language. Similarly, a program variant described as "delayed immersion," which takes English monolingual students at or beyond Grade 4, has children spending only a half of their time in the L2, and the other half in their L1. The critical characteristics of these highly successful programs are the following: (a) The teachers may know both languages of instruction, but they use only the L2 in class (when the students' L1 gets added as a language of instruction, it is used by different teachers than those who use the L2); hence, (b) the two languages are kept separate, both in time and in use—teachers do not switch between the two languages in class; (c) the focus in these classes is on the teaching of subject matter rather than on language teaching; (d) the curriculum followed in these programs is the same as would be followed ordinarily; and (e) the students in these programs are mainstream children who ordinarily do well in school, and the program is voluntary for them. An important way in which Canadian immersion students differ from LEP students served by American bilingual programs is that they belong to the mainstream of that society, and are in no danger of losing either their linguistic or cultural identities by being schooled in a language they do not speak at home. For them, the learning of French represents, in Lambert's term, an "additive bilingualism": they gain a new language and add a cultural perspective without losing any ground in their first language or culture. For the LEP minority-group child, the learning of the societal language can result in what Lambert describes as "subtractive bilingualism": they gain a new language, but it is sometimes at the expense of their home language and their self-esteem, particularly when there is no support in school for either their L1 or their culture (Lambert, 1978, 1984).

The immersion approach has apparently worked as well for majority group children in the U.S. as it has in Canada. An immersion program that began as an experimental project in 1971 in Culver City, California, has been closely followed by Campbell and his UCLA colleagues over the past decade (Campbell, 1984). The students in this southern California program, like those in Canada, have been English-speaking children from mainstream families. In the Culver City project, they are immersed in Spanish, the language spoken by the large Hispanic population in the region. The program, it appears, has had good results. Campbell reports that students "have consistently performed scholastically at a level equal to or higher than their peers who have received all of their elementary school education in English" (p. 129), and like the Canadian immersion students, they have apparently maintained full proficiency in their L1, English.

By all reports, then, the immersion approach has been an effective method of educating students through a second language, judging from the academic performance of American and Canadian students who have been in these programs. It has not been an unqualified success in the area of second language education however. While the students in these programs have been able to participate in instructional activities conducted in the second language, and have made good academic progress learning, they apparently do not develop full proficiency in its use. "In spite of nearly 4,000 hours of classroom exposure, students [in the Culver City immersion program] have not acquired full command of the syntactic, morphological, lexical or phonological rules of Spanish," according to Campbell (p. 132). It is hard to say whether the Canadian children performed much better in this regard, although the test results on their language learning have generally been positive. Swain (1983) reports that after 7 years in French immersion programs, students continue to have difficulty with the grammatical, lexical, discourse, and sociolinguistic rules of the language. The reasons why students in these programs find it difficult to achieve full L2 proficiency will be discussed in the section on language learning in bilingual programs.

The findings of studies on immersion programs would suggest that it is possible to teach the entire curriculum directly in a second language, if conditions are right, and that through this experience, students can acquire both the academic content of school and the language in which it is taught simultaneously. Why should the immersion approach not work with LEP students in the United States as well? This is a question that has been raised by some of the critics of bilingual education who regard immersion education as an alternative to bilingual education. Epstein (1977), for example, concludes his examination of transitional bilingual education programs by advocating that such programs be abandoned and, in the belief that the research evidence on the Canadian immersion model demonstrates that students can be successfully taught through a second language, argues that the immersion model be adopted in this country. Baker and De Kanter (1981) came to a similar conclusion in their study of the effectiveness of bilingual education programs. They contend that the research evidence shows "structured immersion" programs to be superior to transitional bilingual education programs, and therefore argue that bilingual education should be dropped, and immersion programs or ESL programs adopted instead. It should be noted that Epstein, Baker, and De Kanter view immersion education not as a form of bilingual education, which it is, but as an alternative to it. They have in mind an educational approach in which, as Baker and De Kanter (1981) describe it,

the solution to developing English and progressing in other subjects is to teach all subjects in English at a level understood by the students. Although the curriculum assumes no prior knowledge of English, language-minority students in effect learn English as they learn math, and learn math through English instruction that is understandable at their level of English proficiency. (p. 3)

Researchers who have studied immersion education have identified some rather substantial differences between immersion programs and programs in which language minority students are taught directly through a language they do not know. Cohen and Swain (1976) note that school programs in which LEP students are schooled entirely in English contrast sharply with immersion programs in their major characteristics. In classes for LEP students, there is typically a range of L2 proficiency levels represented among them. In immersion classes, the students start out at the same level. The linguistic heterogeneity found in classes of LEP students makes the kind of teaching that immersion teachers engage in extremely difficult, if not impossible. In order to make use of the instructional practices that have worked well in immersion programs, LEP students would have to be segregated linguistically. This is likely to lead to violations of legal prohibitions against segregation by race and national origin. Furthermore, since teachers in classes for LEP students generally do not speak the L1 of the students, the students cannot make any use of their own language in school. Cohen and Swain point out that in immersion classes the teachers are bilingual. While they use only the L2 in class, they can understand the students when they use their L1. Hence it is possible in these classes for students to communicate in their L1 (although their teachers respond to them in the L2) until they are ready to use the L2. The most important difference, however, is in the role that the L1 plays in these programs. In programs for LEP students, it has at best a transitory role. The goal is to wean the students from any dependence on it as quickly as possible. In the immersion program, the goal is for the L1 to gain equal status with the L2 eventually as a medium of instruction. Given such differences, Cohen and Swain argue that L2-only instruction for language minority students is better described as "submersion" rather than immersion education. It is little different than doing nothing at all to help these students in school. The problem of low academic achievement for these students can not simply be ascribed to a mismatch between the home and school language, as Cummins (1983) has noted. There are some rather substantial social and political differences in the situations of the students in the immersion programs in Canada and in Culver City, as compared to the situations of typical LEP students in this country. Cohen and Swain and other commentators such as Hernández-Chávez (1984) have pointed out some of these differences. Some are obvious: Students in the immersion programs come from mainstream families with a tradition of educational achievement; they speak the language of the society, and are in little danger of losing their own language in the process of learning a new one. For them an immersion education results in "enrichment bilingualism," what Lambert has described as "additive bilingualism." For LEP children, who come to school with a minority status, and often from families with little education, survival rather than enrichment is the aim. The goal of the school is to move them towards English rather than towards bilingualism. The result for these students is often the loss of the home language, a kind of subtractive or "displacement bilingualism" as Hernández-Chávez describes it. A key difference, according to Hernández-Chávez, is in the social and political status of the families of the immersion students and those of LEP students. The immersion families are mostly well-educated members of the majority group who are inclined to monitor their children's educational experiences closely, and to take action when it appears that things are not going well. They can offer help with schoolwork, when help is needed. The families of LEP students are likely to be less educated, and to be unable to offer help to their children. They may also feel that they do not have any voice in how their children are to be educated at school. Such differences can add up to some rather powerful arguments against following this approach for LEP students. Cohen and Swain, however, say that the approach could work for LEP students, but only if most of the positive features of true immersion programs (for example, teachers who know the students' L1, the use of the L1 in school, clear separation of the two languages of instruction, etc.) were duplicated in programs for these students.

Allocation of Language Use by Subject

A second major way of organizing bilingual instruction is to separate the uses of the two languages by subject matter. Reading, writing, and mathematics, for example, might be taught in the students' native language, social studies, science and language arts in English. Under such a plan, the curriculum as a whole is taught bilingually, but each subject is taught monolingually. This treatment of bilingual instruction contrasts sharply with arrangements in which some or all subjects are taught in both languages, either concurrently or at different times. It should be noted, however, that while program planners may favor plans for language allocation by subject area, all too often circumstances dictate decisions concerning which language students are to be instructed in. This appears to have been the case in the bilingual program studied by Cohen (1975). The original plan in the Redwood City program was to teach all participants mathematics and science in English, and social studies, art, music, and physical education in Spanish. The goal was to enable both the Spanish- and English-speaking students in the program to become at least partially bilingual. Cohen reports that the original plan had to be altered because the LEP students were unable to follow math and science classes in English; some of them had to be taught these subjects in Spanish. Others who were reportedly just as limited in English as the ones who had to be taught in Spanish preferred continuing with English instruction because "they perceived it as more prestigious." These students were grouped with the English-speaking students in the program for instruction in these subjects.

Decisions regarding what language to teach subject matter in can reflect various concerns. The facilitation of learning is an important one. A fundamental assumption in bilingual education is that learning is easiest when it is continuous with prior linguistic, cultural, and social experience; hence, subject matter should be taught in the LEP students' L1 and in a cultural framework that is familiar to them until they have gained a familiarity with a new set of experiences at school. This premise is most clearly stated in a document prepared by the U.S. Commission on Civil Rights (1975) as a guide for school districts on developing bilingual programs:

> Without a doubt, it is easier for children to learn in a language they already understand. Native language instruction capitalizes on children's previous knowledge and maximizes the possibility that children will develop healthy self concepts and positive attitudes toward learning. Cognitive, reading and expression skills can be developed naturally, without the handicap of having to learn a new language at the same time. In addition, the second language — in this case, English — can more easily be developed if the child is also allowed to fully develop his or her native language. (p. 138)

The cognitive demands of the subject matter to be taught are another important consideration when decisions are made regarding what should be taught in each language; so is the relative ease with which the students in the program can handle the two languages. There are likely to be substantial differences in the ease with which students deal with instruction depending on the language in which it is given. Instruction given in the weaker language of the students will be harder to follow than that given in the language they know well. Macnamara (1966, 1967) found in a series of studies that students for whom the language of instruction is a second, hence weaker, language perform more poorly in subjects taught in that language than do students for whom it is a primary language. Retardation in learning was especially apparent in areas of study in which language plays a major role. In mathematics learning, Macnamara reported, bilingual students showed greater retardation in problem arithmetic, which involves verbal reasoning, than in mechanical arithmetic, which is mostly computational.

The difference, according to Macnamara, has to do with the fact that in mechanical arithmetic, instructions concerning the operations students are to use are conveyed by mathematical symbols; in problem arithmetic, they are contained in prose passages which must be read and interpreted. There has been some controversy over this point. Cummins (1977) has questioned whether the difficulty that Macnamara ascribes to the effects of instruction in a weaker language is not instead due to their having been tested in their weaker language. He contends that the immersion programs have demonstrated that students can be instructed in a weaker language without negative consequences on academic development. The question, however, is whether students who have difficulty dealing with the language they are being tested in are likely to find it easier to deal with that same language when it is used in instructional activities. Macnamara's findings suggest that curricular materials that are especially dependent on language understanding should be taught in the students' stronger language. But this raises important instructional issues. There is little in the school curriculum that is not language dependent; should everything be taught in the students' L1? To what extent are skills and content learned through the L1 transferable across languages? Can some subjects be taught in English even before students know that language? Can the two languages be used in ways that facilitate both subject matter and language learning? Let us consider these issues in relation to specific areas of the curriculum.

READING

There is no other area of the curriculum in which the arguments for beginning with native language instruction are clearer. Reading is unquestionably a language-dependent skill. It is not possible to read in a language one does not know, if reading involves the act of making intelligible to oneself written texts of any complexity beyond that of street signs. Admittedly, individuals can be taught to "decode" a printed text with a rather minimal knowledge of the language in which it is written; that is, they can be taught to reproduce the speech sounds that have been given a written representation in a language they do not know. Hence, most literate English-speaking adults could, with some training, learn to associate letters and letter combinations in written German with creditable approximations to their phonetic value, and could possibly in that way "decode" a German text. This ability is clearly distinct from knowing what the text is about. They would not find the sounds being reproduced in this way intelligible. A motivated, mature reader with good study skills presumably could go further with this type of effort and decipher the text, more or less, by looking up each word in a bilingual dictionary. This, however, is still

decoding, and not reading. Decoding is obviously an aspect of reading, but few of us would call it "reading." By reading, we refer here to the act of reconstructing the meaning of a text as intended by the writer, and through this process, gaining access to the information that is encoded in the text. What the reader must apply in this constructive process, as we have learned from studies of reading comprehension, is knowledge that is *not* encoded by the written word: knowledge of the language, of conventions of its use, of the real world, and of the topics treated in the text (e.g., Adams & Bruce, 1980; Bransford & Johnson, 1973; Fillmore, 1982; Fillmore & Kay, 1983; Tierney, Lazansky, Raphael, & Cohen, in press). A prerequisite for true reading, it would appear, is a fairly high level of knowledge of the language in which the text is written.

This was demonstrated in a study investigating differences in first and second language reading conducted on English-speaking students in Canadian schools (Cziko, 1978). The subjects in this study were four groups of seventh-graders: The first comprised beginning learners of French as a second language; the second, students who had been in a 1-year French immersion program; the third, students who had been in French immersion schools since the first grade; and the fourth, a control group of native French speakers. Students were given a cloze-type test consisting of three passages written in French, in which they were to fill in every fifth word. An analysis of the data collected on these readers showed that only the native speakers and advanced immersion students were able to make use of clues offered by the discourse constraints contained in the texts. The intermediate students were not able to make use of such contextual information. Cziko points out that the difficulties experienced by second-language readers may have been due to their inability to make use of syntactic, semantic, and discourse cues that ordinarily serve as sources of information for fluent first-language readers.

LEP students can acquire decoding skills relatively easily, even when they do not speak English. That they have considerably greater difficulty making sense of the materials they read, however, attests to the necessity of knowing the language before reading it. There have been a number of studies showing the hardly surprising result that students find it easier to learn to read in a language they already know than in one they are just learning. In a study conducted in the Chiapas highlands of Mexico, Modiano (1973) studied the effects of initial reading instruction in an L1 and in an L2. She compared a large sample of Mexican Mayan children, some of whom were being taught to read in their L1, and some in the L2, Spanish. It was found that the children who learned to read first in their L1 were more successful in becoming literate in the L2 than were those who learned to read directly in Spanish, a language they were learning at the same time. At the end of the third grade, a significant difference was found between the two groups in Spanish reading skills; the children who had learned to read initially in their L1 were apparently able to apply the skills they had acquired through their native language to the other language which they had in the meantime acquired. Modiano attributes the greater success of the L1 readers to the fact that they were able to separate the task of learning to read from that of learning a new language. The L2 readers, because they were learning the language at the same time as they were learning to read, tended to confuse the two tasks.

Rosier (1977) in a more recent study compared the effectiveness of initial reading instruction given to Navajo-speaking children in their native language with reading instruction given in English. Students who were taught reading in English were also given instruction in English as a second language. Those who were taught to read in their L1 were given help in developing oral proficiency in English, and at the second grade, were transferred to English reading. At the end of the 3-year study period which covered reading development from the first through the sixth grade, Rosier found that the group that was taught to read in their L1 scored significantly higher than the L2 reading group in the English achievement tests used in the study (the Stanford and the Metropolitan Achievement Tests). The only point at which the L1 readers did not outperform the L2 readers was at the end of the second grade. After the second grade, the L1 group either matched or outperformed the L2 group with the margin of difference between the two groups widening with each year. Rosier points out that an important conclusion to be drawn from the results of this study is that the effects of L1 instruction may not be apparent or measurable for at least 3 or 4 years. The effects of bilingual instruction appear to be cumulative, Rosier notes, with the benefits becoming more evident each year after the third grade. These studies are important in showing that initial reading instruction in the L1 has the effect of later success in L2 reading; the skill of reading, once acquired through the L1, is transferable.

Engle (1975), in an examination of the international research literature on the use of vernacular languages in early education, asked whether children who are taught subject matter in their L1 will learn to read more rapidly in an L2, and whether they will be more knowledgeable about that subject matter than children who have been taught the same materials in an L2. She considered whether under some circumstances, L2 instruction or what she refers to as the "Direct Approach" might be more advantageous than the "Native Language Approach" as advocated by UNESCO (1953). The direct approach, as Engle describes it, is instruction given in an L2, and supported by training in speaking the L2. A point-by-point comparison of the two methods, and a review of studies (including those by Modiano and by Lambert and Tucker) led Engle to conclude that neither method is clearly superior to the other, but that a number of social, cultural, and practical factors may make one preferable over the other in specific situations. The direct method gets selected at times simply because it seems to be more expeditious to teach everything in the language that the school wants the students to learn rather than wait until they have mastered the language. She notes that the research evidence shows that efforts to develop L2 literacy without oral language training are unlikely to succeed. Students taught through the native language approach may take longer to learn to read in the L2 than those in the direct method, but they may in fact make greater gains than those who have learned through the direct method over time, as Rosier later demonstrated in his study.

The question of when and how to introduce reading instruction in the L2 is an important one in bilingual education. It is, however, an instructional issue that is more often discussed than researched. Several practices are observed in programs. One is that of teaching reading in the L1 and L2 simultaneously, with students learning to read in two languages at the same time. When different writing systems or orthographies are used in the two languages, as with Chinese and English, students may be able to handle both without much interference. But where languages share the same orthography, as English and Spanish or French do, there is likely to be interference. Barik and Swain (1974) found that when English-speaking children in immersion classes who had initially been taught to read in French were given English materials to read, they did, in fact, have difficulty with interference between the two systems. Interference of this sort can be overcome in time (Barik and Swain, 1976), but it does present problems in the early stages of reading instruction. A second practice is to introduce reading instruction in the L1, but switch to L2 reading as soon as the students give evidence of being able to speak that language. This can cause difficulties for students if they have not yet learned to read in the L1 with ease, or if they have yet to reach a level of L2 proficiency that allows them to make sense of texts written in that language. A third practice is to teach L2 reading from the beginning, but use it as a kind of ESL instruction. The idea here is that the printed text can serve as the means by which students are taught the language in which the texts are written. Reading experts such as Goodman, Goodman, and Flores (1979) acknowledge that although it is usually assumed that children must have "oral proficiency" in a language before they can be taught to read in it, it is possible to introduce reading to them before they have mastered the language. Provided that students are able to deal with the new language at a receptive level, they may not need to have full productive control before they can handle reading instruction. Thus, L2 reading could expose LEP students to useful data about the new language which they would otherwise not encounter. Goodman et al. (1979) point out, however, that this works best when the learners are already literate in their L1:

> In our experience we've found that if bilingual speakers are literate in another language, their development of literacy in English will be easier than for people not literate in any language; and further, their control of English will be speeded as a result of their rapid progress in becoming literate in English. All this assumes that oral and written English are equally needed and functional and that the opportunity to use both are present. (p. 22)

Presumably, students who are not literate in their L1, or who are unable to handle the L2 at least at the receptive level, or who have no reason to learn to read in that language will not fare as well through this latter practice.

These practices, together with diverse others, are commonly referred to as "bilingual reading" in discussions of reading instruction for LEP students. That term, however, in general discussions of bilingual education, is often used equivocally. In some cases, it refers simply to reading instruction for more or less bilingual students; in others, it refers to situations in which two languages are used during reading lessons, even when the language in which students are being taught to read is English only.

The transferring of reading skills across languages has already been mentioned in connection with a number of studies of reading instruction. At issue is how easily reading skills that are initially developed in the student's L1 transfer to the L2. It is often assumed that the transfer process is fairly automatic. That seemed to be true at least for the students in the immersion programs who learned to read in the L2 initially. In this case, however, the transfer was from the L2 to the L1, the reverse of the usual situation. Thonis (1981) notes that transfer of reading skills depends on a number of factors: (a) the similarity between elements of the two systems; (b) the similarity in the ways written symbols represent linguistic forms in the two systems; and (c) the carryover of positive attitudes towards reading, and of habits of attention, concentration, and persistence that can develop through a prior successful experience with learning to read. According to Thonis, there is much that is transferable, no matter in which language reading skills are originally developed, but the greater the similarity between the writing systems of the two languages, the greater the potential for transference. She warns, however, that until an effective level of reading skills has been developed in the reader, efforts at introducing reading in another language may not necessarily result in transfer. Once readers are able to "exercise interpretative and inferential abilities of a higher order" in comprehending texts, then many of the cognitive skills learned in reading can be transferred. But if readers have achieved only that level of skill that allows them to decode and to make use of literal interpretation strategies, then the introduction of second-language reading may not tap the potential power of skill transfer. In fact, a premature switch from L1 to L2 reading is likely to interfere with the development of such higher-order reading skills.

Even when language learners are fairly good readers, an inadequate command of the L2 may cause reading problems. In a study of ESL reading, Clarke (1980) found that adult Spanish speakers who were actually competent readers in their L1 tended to revert to poor or inefficient reading strategies when they were asked to read English texts that exceeded their knowledge of the language. Clarke contends that proficient readers transfer their reading skills to the new language up to a point. A limited proficiency in the L2 can "short-circuit" the reader's system, and cause even a good reader "to revert to poor reading strategies in the new language."

MATHEMATICS

There is some difference of opinion among bilingual researchers over the question of language choice for mathematics instruction. Macnamara's research suggested that when instruction in complex subjects such as mathematics is given in the weaker language of minority students, they may have difficulty dealing with the subject matter, particularly where verbal reasoning is involved (Macnamara, 1967). Cazden (1979) appears to support that position at least in part in her discussion of criteria by which decisions on language choice should be made. Considered in terms of both the complexity of the material itself and the nature of the linguistic demands that its instruction makes on the learner, mathematics is a subject that should be taught in the students' stronger language, but science is one that can be taught in the L2, in her view. Practitioners see things differently, however.

It is often argued that subjects like mathematics are ones that can easily be taught in a weaker language since a relatively restricted set of vocabulary items is used in mathematics; because expressions such as *subtract, multiply, fraction, and exponent* have precise meanings associated with them, students can learn to use such terms even in the early stages of acquiring English. However, as Cazden points out, word problems are not presented in mathematical terms, but in ordinary language, and these have to be converted into precise mathematical expressions before they can be solved. The real difficulty for LEP students is that a rather advanced level of control of English is required for transforming word problems into mathematical terms and operations. Consider, for example, the level of linguistic knowledge called for in seeing what arithmetic operations are required to solve this problem: *A tugboat was overtaken by a speedboat that was traveling twice the speed of the tugboat. In just 2 minutes the two boats were a mile apart. How fast was the tugboat traveling?* Notice that in solving problem statements like this one, students are not told explicitly what numbers or operations to use. These facts have to be inferred from the ordinary language expressions contained in the problem; they have to be extracted from the vocabulary items used, the structural arrangements of the words, and the cohesive elements that tie the separate statements into a coherent text. Thus, to set up the problem in an arithmetic expression, they have to know the meaning of words such as *overtaken, traveling, speed* and *apart*; only then can they envision how to set up the problem. They have to recognize that terms such as *twice* which are used imprecisely in ordinary language (e.g., *I know twice as much about computers as he does*) are to be taken as precise expressions of arithmetic facts, that is, as "times two." Furthermore, word problems are typically written in a compact form with crucial information contained in relative clauses or in embedded complement structures as in our example. The extraction of meaning from sentences that are as densely packed as those used in word problems calls for a high level of language proficiency, we believe. Cazden points out that teachers can help students deal with the language used in areas of the curriculum (such as science) that lend themselves to group learning activities and discussion. She notes, however, that mathematics, unlike science, is a "solitary and silent activity" (Cazden, 1979, p. 134). It seldom involves work requiring interaction with others. Hence, students receive little external support from L2 speaking teachers and classmates in figuring out how to interpret the word problems they encounter in their workbooks. According to Cazden, "when an error is made, neither the student nor the teacher can be sure whether the problem lies in the student's inadequate comprehension of L2 or of mathematics" (p. 135). Cazden suggests that decisions concerning when to use the L2 in the teaching of mathematics to LEP students should depend at least in part on grade level. In the early years of school, much that is taught in mathematics can be communicated through nonverbal means such as through the manipulation of objects and materials. Teachers can teach in the L2 relatively early since the instructional activities allow students to figure out what is being talked about. At later stages, much of what is taught in mathematics is presented to students in the form of written materials, hence they must have adequate reading knowledge of the L2 before they can deal with mathematics instruction beyond the early years of school. In Cazden's view, LEP students should be provided with help in dealing with the "language of mathematics" in the L2 before they are required to shift to mathematics instruction which is given in that language.

Saville and Troike (1971) come to a quite different conclusion concerning the language in which students should be taught mathematics. They advise teaching mathematics to LEP students directly in English rather than in their L1 or bilingually, since individuals growing up in this society will be doing whatever advanced mathematics they have to do in English. The reason given for this advice is that learners may find it difficult to switch these skills from the L1 to the L2 later on. Saville and Troike apparently do not believe that mathematics skills are as readily transferred across languages as are reading skills, which they do advise developing initially in the L1. They do not say what evidence leads them to this conclusion, although they may be influenced by anecdotal reports that bilinguals generally find it easier to perform computations in the language through which they first learned mathematics rather than in later ones.

There are other ways to reduce potential transfer problems, however. An alternative to initiating mathematics instruction exclusively through the students' weaker language would be to teach it bilingually. LEP students could be taught to handle mathematics in the L2, using materials written in the L2, provided that they are given explanations of such materials and instructions in their use in the L1. Interference problems that might arise from students having to learn two sets of terminology for mathematics at the same time would be reduced by a functional differentiation of this type between the uses of the two languages during instruction.

There is evidence indicating that cross-language interference may not necessarily be as much of a problem in mathematics learning as Saville and Troike fear, however. Students in the Canadian immersion programs have generally not had problems transferring mathematics skills acquired in a second language to their first language. Students who were taught mathematics initially in French performed equally well, whether they were tested in English or French, according to Swain and Lapkin (1982).

The situation seems to be quite different in the case of language minority students in the U.S. Studies comparing mathematics achievement in LEP students generally indicate an advantage for those who are taught at least in part in their L1. Students who are taught mathematics exclusively in English do not do as well as those who are taught bilingually, especially in the early primary years (Elizondo de Weffer, 1972; Olesini, 1971; Treviño, 1968). Students who receive mathematics instruction in their L1 may not perform as well when tested in English, however, suggesting that skills acquired in their L1 may not transfer altogether or, perhaps, that the language used in tests may be difficult for LEP students who have not received mathematics instruction in that language. In a study evaluating the effects of bilingual instruction on the academic development of Spanish-speaking children, Skoczylas (1972) found that while a beneficial transfer across the L1 and L2 was found in academic performance generally, a positive transfer could not be found in mathematics. Students who received mathematics instruction in Spanish did not do well when measured in English. Research in Paraguay (Valadez, 1984) indicates that it

may take as many as 3 years for the effects of bilingual instruction in mathematics to be apparent. Students in experimental groups who were taught mathematics in Spanish and Guaraní did not perform better than control-group students who were taught exclusively in Spanish, their second language, until the third grade, suggesting that the benefits of bilingual instruction may be cumulative.

SCIENCE

Cazden (1979) has argued that science is a subject that can be taught to LEP students directly in the L2. It is particularly suited to serve as one of the subjects through which the L2 itself is taught to LEP students. The premise on which this is based is that students learn a language most efficiently when they are exposed to it in the context of its being used to communicate information. This works best when the situation in which the language is being used provides the learners with the means for figuring out what people are saying, and when it offers them many opportunities to practice using the language in natural communication. There are several reasons offered by Cazden for believing that science can serve this function. Science is a subject that lends itself to group activity and discussion. Much of it involves the handling of concrete objects and engagement in actions that can be understood irrespective of whether the students understand the language being spoken. It is a subject in which instructions can be demonstrated and concepts taught through activities that involve the use of objects and materials.

What little research has been done on language choice in science instruction would indicate generally that while science may be well suited as a vehicle for teaching the L2, LEP students perform better in it when it is taught at least partly in language they understand. Doebler and Mardis (1980–1981) in a study comparing the effects of English only and bilingual instruction on the academic achievement of native American children found that bilingual instruction made a significant difference in science and social science achievement. The Choctaw speakers in this study who were taught bilingually outperformed those who were taught in English in all subject areas, but it was only in these two subjects that the differences were statistically significant. There are several reasons why this should have been so. While science and social studies are subjects that lend themselves to being taught through activities and demonstration, they involve many abstract ideas and concepts that would be difficult to deal with in the weaker language of the students. The terminological precision that is required for talking about scientific concepts may be a particular problem for teachers and students alike when the subject matter is being presented in a language the students do not understand. Where they do not share the requisite language to discuss observations and experiences, teachers and students can resort to demonstration and circumlocution to some extent to talk about the subject, but such attempts at communication are often not as satisfying or as useful to the students as they would be if the discussions were conducted in language the students knew well. It would appear that even when bilingual instruction does not result in an advantage in test scores, students may nevertheless be profiting from involvement in science activities that are conducted bilingually. A study comparing bilingual and monolingual science instruction in fifth grade students found no difference between the two treatments, although the students indicated a strong preference for instruction given bilingually (Juárez, 1976). The use of their L1 apparently allowed these students to participate more freely in the discussions that were a part of the science lessons. A recent science education study conducted by Cohen, De Avila and Intili (1981) indicates that the ability to discuss one's observations and understandings has payoffs both in science and math learning, and in language development as well. Cohen et al. found that LEP students performed better in math and science when they were permitted and encouraged to talk during small-group instructional activities in the language that is the easiest for them. The freedom to talk and to write up their experiences in the language of their own choosing resulted in improved performance not only in science and math, but in language development as well for the students in this experimental study.

Concurrent Methods

In bilingual instruction, keeping the two languages separate whether by time or by subject matter makes it possible to regulate the extent to which each is used. It provides a practical way of making adjustments in usage, and ensures that enough of each is used to further the several goals of bilingual instruction. There may also be linguistic and cognitive reasons for keeping the languages separate in instruction. Bilingual educators and applied linguists have long argued against mixing languages in instructional settings on the grounds that such mixing will result in the students' inability to use either language correctly (Andersson and Boyer, 1970; Saville and Troike, 1971). Many educators believe that students who learn a second language based on mixed input will find it difficult to keep the two systems separate in their own usage. In spite of this widely held belief, the *practice* of language mixing in bilingual education occurs frequently, even in programs that have officially adopted one or another of the methods described above for keeping the languages separate. Switching momentarily to the students' L1 is an easy expedient for bilingual teachers who want to be certain that the students understand what is being said.

There are various forms of what are described here as concurrent methods. Some of these take place by design, others develop through practice. In this section, we describe the concurrent use of two languages in instruction, whether by design or by practice. At least three major types of concurrent methods can be identified. In the first, both languages are used for teaching a subject such as science or mathematics, but the two languages serve different functions and are not mixed in any way. This seems to be Saville and Troike's recommendation in their widely utilized handbook for bilingual educators (Saville and Troike, 1971) when they suggest teaching some school subjects to LEP students bilingually. They generally advocate keeping the two languages separate by subject area so that each subject is being taught exclusively in either the dominant language of the students initially or, in the case of mathematics, in English only. They suggest, however, that some areas of the curriculum such as art, music, and physical education can be taught in both languages. Even then they

advise using only one language during a given class period to reduce the interference between languages that might arise when both languages are used concurrently. The alternate days approach studied by Tucker et al. (1970) was mentioned above as a method of organizing instruction so that all subjects are taught bilingually but only one language is used during a given class period. Hence, science instruction might be given in the L1 one day, and in the L2 the next. Such a plan obviously requires equivalent sets of instructional materials in both languages, a luxury not everywhere available.

In some programs a different concurrent approach has been used, the so-called "preview/review" technique. Although details vary, in general the lesson itself is presented in the L2, but only after a preview of the new materials has been given to the students in their dominant language. This "preview" of the lesson in language they understand prepares the students to deal with the materials that are presented in the L2 during the "lesson phase." A "review" of the lesson follows the lesson itself in which a recapitulation of the materials is offered in the L1 of the students to ensure comprehension. In some versions, all three phases of the lesson occur during the same day. In others, they take place on successive days (Cohen, 1975, p. 109). An early use of this technique in a California bilingual program is described by Gonzales and Lezama (1976). They report that evaluations of the program after 2 years showed gains overall in subject matter and second-language learning for students. It is difficult to assess just how good the results were, however, since there were no control groups involved in the study. A form of the preview/review technique adopted by the Ministry of Education of Paraguay for bilingual programs in that country has been found to be highly effective (Valadez, 1984). Subject matter is taught to Guaraní speakers in the societal language, Spanish, but at the same time they are provided with a preview and review of materials in Guaraní to insure comprehension. After 3 years, students in experimental groups that have been instructed by this method outperform comparison group students in all subject areas.

A particularly fruitful use of the preview/review technique has been developed recently by Moll and Díaz (1983) who designed a series of experimental interventions using the L1, Spanish, in the case of their subjects, to help students comprehend the reading passages they were asked to read in English. The approach makes use of Vygotsky's (1978) notions of interactive learning in which children acquire problem-solving strategies in the process of being guided through complex tasks by adults. Their technique is one in which children are led through English texts, with teachers pointing out strategies for figuring out the meanings of words, and for arriving at interpretations of pieces of the text. Spanish is used selectively in this technique to ensure comprehension of the subtitles of the text. Moll and Díaz found that they were able to get their fourth grade subjects to perform at an L2 reading level equal to L1 levels by use of this technique. It should be noted that this method is one which is meant to develop reading skills in English, rather than in both languages.

The preview/review method and the alternate-days approach are concurrent methods which allow both languages of instruction to be used in the teaching of the same subject matter but which nevertheless keep them separate by time or by function.

A second type of concurrent method is far less structured, and makes no attempt at keeping the languages apart. In this type, the two languages are used alternately. Teachers switch back and forth between the two languages of instruction, either as needed or as a general practice. This approach was adopted and tested by a Texas bilingual program. Jacobson (1981) argues for language alternation as an instructional technique on the grounds that it will permit a balanced use of the two languages of instruction and help to increase the likelihood that the L1 of the students will be used enough to insure its maintenance. It will not result in interference, according to Jacobson, as long as the switches are made between sentences rather than within sentences. Presumably, language learners can separate the new language from the one they already know, provided that switches they are exposed to are made between large structures. Furthermore, since code switching is a socially accepted form of communication in the bilingual community in which the students live, the adoption of this "codeswitching strategy achieves a most desirable rapproachment between community and school" (Jacobson, 1981, pp. 148–149). On the basis of 4 years of evaluation, Jacobson claims success for the Laredo program as a "true maintenance program," although he offers no data to support that claim.

Language alternations as used in bilingual instruction take several forms. Translation is one that is particularly controversial. In this technique, information given in one language is repeated or explained in the other. Typically, the information is given first in the L2, and then given again in an L1 translation. This technique is often adopted in classes where the students are quite heterogeneous in L2 proficiency. Such appears to be the case in bilingual classrooms studied by Cohen (1975), Legarreta (1979), and Wong Fillmore (1982). In Cohen's Redwood City bilingual project, English monolinguals and Spanish speakers were grouped together for instruction generally, being segregated into linguistically homogeneous groups for language instruction only after the first year. Although the program was set up to follow an alternate days "preview/review" plan, the teachers frequently made use of translation in their teaching. According to Cohen, the teachers reported using "simultaneous translation" at such times "when they wanted to teach the same content in both languages" (p. 110). It would appear, however, that the need to do so arose because of the heterogeneous composition of the classes. No matter which language was being used on a given day, there would have been students who had difficulty understanding the content. A similar situation was observed in Wong Fillmore's (1982) study of four kindergarten classes. In classes where students were homogeneously grouped by L2 proficiency, teachers generally did not engage in translations. Where they were heterogeneously grouped, teachers tended to use translation in teaching since they were trying to make themselves understood to all of the children. The linguistic adjustments they would have had to make for the sake of the LEP students would have been inappropriate for the English monolingual students. Had they tried to teach in Spanish only the English speakers would not have been able to understand what they were saying. Hence, they adopted a translation method which guaranteed that both groups of students would understand. The problem in the translation class studied by Wong Fillmore was that the students developed a selective listening strategy, They listened only when the language they understood was being used, and tuned out otherwise. A similar strategy was adopted by the Anglo students in Cohen's (1975) study:

> When simultaneous translation was used, the Anglo children didn't have to pay close attention to the content as it was presented in Spanish, because they knew the same content would be repeated immediately in English. (p. 110)

The translation technique makes it possible for all students in a heterogeneously grouped class to have access to the materials being taught. However, as we will see later, it can negatively affect second-language learning, precisely because students tend to ignore the language they do not understand when they can count on immediate translations.

In Legarreta's (1979) investigation of language choice in bilingual classrooms, translation was used in four of the five kindergarten classes she studied. The fifth class followed an alternate-days approach. It appears that when translations are examined carefully, they are not always equivalent to the original. In fact, the two languages may come to be differentiated in use in such situations just as they are in other code-switching situations. Valdés-Fallis (1978) suggests that teachers' language attitudes are likely to be reflected in their code-switching behaviors in the classroom. Code switches in Spanish–English bilingual classes are much more frequently observed in Spanish lessons than in English. During Spanish lessons, English is frequently the language used for classroom control. The implication of the choice of English for this function, according to Valdés-Fallis, can be interpreted as a message by the students of the "power and efficiency of English as opposed to Spanish" (p. 20). In her examination of the functions of the English and Spanish used in her translation classes, Legarreta found that shifts to English tended to occur most frequently when teachers were expressing solidarity and acceptance or disciplining students. English was chosen 77% of the time on the average for expressing acceptance or solidarity, and in amplifying pupil statements. It was chosen 72% of the time when teachers were correcting students and maintaining order in the classroom. The fifth classroom which was organized as an alternate-days program was quite different. A much more balanced use of the two languages was found in this class than in the other four, but here the language chosen for acceptance and solidarity tended to be Spanish (72%) rather than English (28%). Similarly, the language used for correction and the maintenance of order was more frequently Spanish (62%) than English (38%). Legarreta argues that such choices by teachers in translation classes can be a powerful impetus for rapid change in the students. The social messages communicated to students can sometimes be even more salient than the content that is being taught.

The third major type of concurrent method used in bilingual education can be described as the functional approach. It is a technique that develops out of practice, rather than design. The chief characteristic of functional approaches is that language alternations appear to be made for communicative purposes. For example, when teachers perceive that students are having difficulty comprehending what is being said, they switch to the other language to supply a translation or clarification, or needed background information. Otherwise, the language of instruction in such classes is English. The major difference between the functional approach and the previously discussed language alternation approaches is that English is the main language of instruction in this method, whereas in language alternation classes a balanced use of the two languages is a goal if not a reality. That is, in classes that make use of functional alternations, instruction is conducted in L2, and the students' L1 is used only as needed, and generally in response to immediate feedback provided by students. This was apparently the technique used at the Miami Central Bay School in bilingual classes for English monolingual students (Mackey and Beebe, 1977):

> Spanish was to be the basic language of instruction in these bilingual classes. Whenever a student did not understand, however, the teachers repeated in English. (p. 94)

In a recently completed study of effective practices in bilingual classrooms, Tikunoff (1983) found that functional alternations between languages was a major instructional strategy. The language of instruction in the 58 classrooms that formed the study sample in the Significant Bilingual Instructional Features Study (SBIFS) was predominantly English. The sample comprised classrooms that had been identified as "successful programs" in a site selection procedure that began with nominations by parents and practitioners from around the country. Across this national sample of classrooms, Tikunoff found that the various L1s were used approximately 25% of the time and in the following manner:

> As indicated, English was used predominantly. However, when a student was not comprehending what was required or needed feedback to attain task completion, teachers frequently switched to the NES/LES student's native language in order to communicate effectively. Thus, L1 was used to seek clarification of instruction. (p. 13)

Tikunoff notes that about a half of the alternations that were observed could be categorized as "instructional development," about a third were "procedures and directions," and a fifth were "behavioral feedback to students." The chief function served by the L1 in these classrooms, apparently, was to ensure that LEP students could participate effectively in instruction given in English.

The SBIFS finding that English is used far more frequently than the L1 in bilingual education is generally supported by other studies of programs that follow concurrent methods, although the average reported (60%) is somewhat lower than those reported in other studies. Legarreta, for example, found that teachers used considerably more English in the four translation classes she studied. She found that English was used an average of 72% of the time across the four; in the alternate-days class she studied, English was used 51% of the time. In a study of language use in bilingual classrooms by Schultz (1975), English was found to be used 70% of the time. In a recent study of characteristics of bilingual education programs, Halcón (1983) found that English was the most frequently used language in 65% of the Title VII projects surveyed. Based on the data provided by project personnel, it would appear that English is used from 51% to 70% of the time in three-fifths of the classrooms studied, from 71% to 90% in another fifth, and over 90% in just 3% of the classes. It should be noted, however, that frequency of language use is difficult to assess, and can rarely be measured with precision; estimates of language use provided by participants, such as those used in the Halcón study, are even less reliable. When actual usage is measured precisely, the frequencies of L1 and L2 usage may turn out to be far different than previously reported in research. In a study of instructional practices in bilingual classes, Wong Fillmore et al. (1983) found that the L1 of the students was used no more than 10% of the time in the Chinese and Spanish bilingual classrooms they studied. In the Halcón study, percentages were based on estimates of use; in most of the other studies discussed here, the relative use of the two languages was calculated on the basis of "utterances" as the unit of measurement. In the case of the SBIF Study, the method was to measure the interval of time between language switches. Thus, timing for L1 use begins when a teacher switches from English to L1, and ends with a switch back to English. The percentage of use for each language was calculated on the basis of the amount of time spent in L1 against the total of that time plus the time spent in L2 use. In the Wong Fillmore et al. study, the method involved counting speech and silence separately. This appears to be an important distinction since teachers differ considerably in how much time they spend using any language at all during instructional activities. Nevertheless, in these classrooms as in all others where the languages of instruction are not kept separate by time blocks, English appears to be the language predominantly used for instructional purposes.

Language Learning and Teaching Through Bilingual Instruction

In this section, we discuss instructional issues and research related to second-language learning and teaching in bilingual programs. A major concern in all such programs is that of helping participation students to acquire a second language. For some, the objective is to teach English to the LEP students, and the L1 of the LEP students to the English-speaking participants. Reciprocal bilingualism was the aim of the Redwood City program studied by Cohen (1975) and the Miami programs studied by Mackey and Beebe (1977). In the Canadian and Culver City immersion programs, the main objective has been to teach a minority-group language to majority-group students. Most bilingual programs, however, focus primarily on teaching the language of the school and society to language minority students. The extent to which programs succeed in this regard depends on many factors. Students in bilingual programs, no matter what their first language, have the ability to acquire or develop second-language skills, provided they are given opportunities to hear and use the new language. How well and quickly they learn, or whether they learn at all, depends on a variety of factors. There are three major types: factors related to the social settings in which bilingual programs are conducted, those related to the instructional programs, and those related to the learners themselves. These factors affect language learning by influencing the quality and quantity of exposure to the target language that students get in the classroom, and by influencing the ways in which students deal with opportunities to use the language. It should be noted that there are many second-language issues that are not examined here. Second-language learning and teaching are separate research areas, each with an extensive literature. Hence, it is not feasible to include in this chapter a comprehensive review of the extant research literature. (See McLaughlin, 1984 and Hakuta & Cancino, 1977 for discussions of the issues and research on second-language learning in children). We deal only with those issues and studies that are relevant to language learning and teaching in bilingual education.

Social Setting Factors

Schools and classrooms vary greatly in how well they work as social settings for language learning. Language learning is, in an important sense, as much a social process as it is a cognitive one. It takes place in social settings that allow learners to come into contact with people who speak the target language well enough to help in its learning. Ideally, there are many such "speakers" available, and the setting is one that creates many occasions for the learners to interact with them. In order to learn a language, learners must be exposed to it as it is used by people who know it well. It is in the process of trying to understand what the speakers are saying and in trying to communicate with them that the learners acquire the new language. The speech samples produced by speakers contain the blueprint for the language. In their efforts to understand and to communicate with speakers, learners gradually figure out how meaning is represented through the language, and how it is used by speakers in communication. Not all instances of speech serve this function for learners, however. Researchers who have studied first- and second-language learning have observed that the speech that works as "input" for the acquisition endeavor is that which has been adjusted and modified for the sake of the learners; it is speech that has been produced with the learners' special linguistic limitations in mind (see Snow & Ferguson, 1977, for studies of "motherese," the special speech registers adults are inclined to adopt in talking to young first-language learners). Hatch (1983) analyzed samples of learner and speaker discourse reported in studies of first- and second-language learning, and found that speakers make similar adjustments for both kinds of learners; they include a slower rate of speaking, clearer enunciation, the use of concrete references, a preference for shorter and less complex structures than usual, the use of repetitions and rephrasings, and the accompaniment of speech with gestures and extralinguistic cues that aid understanding. Others have determined that this kind of speech is often produced interactively with learners influencing the level of adjustments in form and content that are chosen by speakers (Cross, 1978; Long, 1981). Through their collaborative attempts to communicate, learners and speakers "negotiate" the form of messages until they are comprehensible to the learners (Hatch, 1983). According to some researchers "comprehensibility" is a major determinant of whether or not language spoken to learners works as input (Krashen, 1981a, 1981b;

Long, 1981). Language works as input when it is serving a genuine communicative function, and when the message that is being communicated can be understood from context. Krashen (1980) has argued that linguistic development takes place when learners manage to understand input containing structures that are slightly in advance of their present level of linguistic competence. It might seem that the fine tuning this requires would be difficult to achieve, but fortunately, the inclination to modify one's speech for the sake of learners is a fairly natural process, and even children can do it if they have reason to communicate with learners (McClure, Saville-Troike, & Fritz, 1982; Wong Fillmore, 1976).

Classrooms can be ideal settings for language learning since they bring learners and speakers together for extended periods of time, and since the participants have ample reason to communicate with one another. Getting them to interact together in ways that promote language learning, however, requires that attention be given to the social climate within the setting. Learners need opportunities to hear and practice the language in order to learn it, but they have to be motivated to take advantage of those opportunities. Speakers can help in the process by talking with the learners, but they have to want to communicate with them for their speech to serve effectively as input. Hence, the structuring of the social setting in the classroom can be an important instructional issue. Enright (1982) has found in a study of interactional patterns in bilingual classrooms that the organizational structures that teachers establish for instructional events can influence the quantity and quality of the language that learners have available to them as input. Because the language used in classrooms is an important source of input for learners, there must be a careful and deliberate structuring of the instructional environment so that language serves not only the purposes of communication and instruction, but of language learning as well.

The proportion of LEP students in classrooms is one factor that requires special attention. The ideal situation is one in which there is, in addition to teachers, a balance between language learners and classmates who know the target language well enough to help in its learning, and there are many reasons for them to talk with one another. Fathman (1976) found in a study of second-language learning in 500 elementary through high school subjects that LEP students generally did not achieve well in English where they were greatly outnumbered by English speakers, or when they outnumbered English speakers. The concentration of students speaking the same L1 appeared also to affect L2 learning, with students in schools from mixed linguistic backgrounds outperforming those in schools with one language predominating. In many bilingual programs, LEP students outnumber English speakers. Some programs admit only students who speak little or no English; the LEP students in them have no English-speaking classmates to interact with, and they must base their learning of English entirely on the language used by teachers. The teacher, being the only language model available to the learners, must provide enough exposure to the target language to support the language-learning efforts of the entire class. The Canadian immersion programs have provided evidence that this can be done, but as we shall see, the L2 that is learned even in these successful programs may fall somewhat short of the target.

Students who find themselves in classrooms with high concentrations of L2 learners may have difficulty getting adequate exposure to the new language or enough practice in speaking it. They find it easier and more natural, when talking among themselves, to use their L1 rather than the language they are just learning. Hence, they tend to get little practice in the use of the L2 outside of teacher directed lessons conducted in that language. Their teachers may encourage them to use the L2 when talking to classmates, but since everyone is just learning the language, the forms they use are likely to be imperfect ones. This kind of practice may result in interim forms becoming permanent features of the L2 learners' version of the target language, a phenomenon that has been documented in the Canadian and American immersion programs. In a study of L2 learning in immersion programs, Selinker, Swain, and Dumas (1975) found that the French being learned by the immersion students was not altogether standard, but contained instead many features that could be described as interlanguage forms. Cohen (1982) reports that interlanguage forms are also present in the Spanish of the Culver City immersion students. Swain (1983) found recently that even after 7 years in immersion programs, students have not yet fully mastered the structures and usages of French. Significant differences were found between them and native speakers in their knowledge and use of spoken and written forms of French. The input on which these students have based their L2 learning has come largely from teachers. Swain argues that although they have had comprehensible input on which to base their learning of the language, it has not been sufficient to ensure their development toward a native-like version of the language. The immersion students can make themselves understood in the classroom since the same contextual information that makes the teachers' language comprehensible to them allows teachers and classmates to interpret what they are saying. They can get their message across even when they use grammatically deviant forms or sociolinguistically inappropriate forms since the situation makes clear what they are saying. As long as they are understood, they do not find it necessary to change. In order to develop towards a more native-speaker-like version of the language, learners have to have more opportunities to use the language with native speakers, since it is in the process of trying to communicate with competent speakers of the language that they discover what they need to do differently. According to Swain, advancements in language development come when learners discover that the forms they are using are not being understood. The negative feedback they are likely to get from native speakers when they have failed to communicate pushes them to be attentive to the way native speakers say things. Unless learners are motivated by a desire to communicate comprehensibly to native speakers of the target language, they may not be altogether aware of just how their version of the language differs from that spoken by others. This kind of motivation is hard to sustain, however, in social settings that do not provide frequent opportunities for learners to interact with speakers of the language.

Let us consider other ways in which aspects of the social setting can influence the extent to which classrooms work as settings for language learning. The goal of reciprocal L2 learning is one that has been highly valued by proponents of bilingual education. Programs that are set up to achieve this goal may offer English-speaking participants, for example, some subject matter instruction through the language of the LEP students along with formal language lessons. Evaluations of these programs, however, have shown that such efforts are rarely successful. In many communities with large enough numbers of LEP students to warrant bilingual programs, there exist considerable status differences between the language groups. The bilingual programs come to represent a means of fostering understanding and of reducing social differences, not just in helping the members of the language minority group learn English, but by teaching the majority-group members the language of the minority group as well. However, it is frequently the case that while the minority-group students learn English, the English speakers learn little if anything of the LEP students' language.

Such was the finding in a recent study of English-speaking children in an Arizona Spanish–English bilingual program (Edelsky and Hudelson, 1980). There were only 7 English speakers in the first grade class they studied; the rest of the 23 students in the class were Spanish dominant. Hence, there were adequate numbers of Spanish-speaking classmates available to help them learn Spanish. Spanish was used by teachers for the teaching of subjects such as social studies, music, and various other classroom activities, so the learners were hearing Spanish regularly. Edelsky and Hudelson found after a year, however, that the English speakers had learned virtually no Spanish at all. They had learned at the very most, only "one routine — rote counting, some number words, two color words, and for [one of the children], a possible understanding in [the] test setting of the word *chiquito*" (p.38). Needless to say, the Spanish speakers in the class learned considerably more English. The problem in situations like this, according to Edelsky and Hudelson, is that the members of the majority group are socially dominant even when they are outnumbered. The language of the dominant group is the norm: It is the "unmarked" code in this situation. It is regarded by all as the natural, or appropriate language for discourse in that setting while the language of the lower-status group is regarded as a "marked language," or not quite natural, by everyone concerned. The members of the lower group may find it more natural to use their own language in speaking among themselves, but they would not regard it as appropriate to use it in settings that involved speakers of the unmarked language. Hence, even when its use is encouraged in school by teachers, the learners and speakers of a marked language may find it difficult to use in talking to one another. In this study, there were no observations made in which a Spanish speaker addressed an English speaker directly in Spanish. It may have been that the English speakers did not invite the use of Spanish by indications of interest; but whatever the reason, the Spanish speakers did not in their interactions with the English speakers play their part in helping them to learn Spanish. In a case like this, it is difficult to say whether the learners did not learn because they were not motivated to do so, or because no one expected them to want to learn. Social status relationships and group attitudes, it seems, can play a major role in determining the direction language learning will take when two groups come into contact.

Researchers who have studied social factors in language learning have found that motivational differences in learners can affect the ease with which they learn second languages. Gardner and Lambert (1972) distinguish between integrative motivation and instrumental motivation. Integrative motivation is characterized as the desire to learn a language that comes from an interest in communication or association with members of the target language group; instrumental motivation represents a more practical orientation, the desire to learn a language because it would be useful or profitable for the learner to do so. What we see in cases such as that documented by Edelsky and Hudelson is evidence that motivation may be involved in negative instances of learning as well. Graham (1984) contends that in addition to the types of motivation previously identified, there is one that he describes as "assimilative," in which language learning is regarded by the learner as the equivalent of taking membership in the group that speaks the language. One learns a language if one wants to become a member of a speech community, or does not learn it if one prefers to remain outside of it. By not learning a marked language, then, the majority-group students in this case reject an association with a lower-status group. Marked languages can be learned by majority-group students, as we have seen in the Canadian and American immersion programs. In these programs, however, majority- and minority-group students are generally not brought together, so status differences are kept in the background.

Studies that have focused on patterns of language use in American classrooms have shown that when LEP students and their English-speaking classmates interact, the direction of communicative effort moves almost invariably in the direction of English. An ethnographic study of second-language learning by McClure et al. (1982) has shown that English speakers are likely to use ungrammatical "foreigner-talk" forms in trying to accommodate to the linguistic needs of their LEP interlocutors. Some of these are apparently modeled after features of utterances produced by the learners themselves in their attempts at speaking English. English speakers are unlikely to make use of any L1 forms picked up from the LEP students, however. The LEP students in the elementary school classrooms in this study generally relied on what little English they knew together with nonverbal means to communicate with their classmates. However, when they had exhausted their repertory of such tactics they sometimes did resort to their native language in trying to communicate with the English speakers. Such forms are rarely learned by the English speakers.

There is much to be learned of the social settings in which children acquire new languages, and ethnographic research methods are particularly suited for studying patterns of social and linguistic interaction between learners and teachers in bilingual classrooms (Hymes, 1979). Trueba and Wright (1980–1981), in arguing for the use of such methods, point out that only by examining the interactional patterns and structures in classrooms can educators come to see the extent to which social factors affect the academic progress of culturally different students. In fact, both their language learning and academic outcomes can be understood only when social processes are considered. This has been demonstrated in two recently completed studies of interactional patterns in bilingual classrooms. In a study investigating instructional events in third grade bilingual classrooms, Moll and Díaz (1982) found

that learner capabilities can be greatly underestimated in L2 teaching situations when teachers assume that the levels at which LEP students are able to produce English reflect their comprehension levels as well. The subjects in this study were apparently able to understand English much better than they could speak it, and their discussions of the English texts they were being asked to read indicated that they could accurately interpret what they were reading, even if they had difficulty pronouncing the words in them. Microanalyses of videotaped English reading lessons revealed that teachers may take unfamiliarity with English as indicative of decoding problems, which leads them to focus on low-level skill development, rather than on promoting the higher-order interpretive skills that students may actually be capable of handling. (For examples of ethnographic studies that document the effects of social factors on the development and organization of bilingual programs, see Peng-Guthrie, 1982 and MacDonald and Kushner, 1982.)

Another ethnographic study, this one by Erickson, Cazden, Carrasco, and Maldonado-Guzman (1983), showed that a teacher's inability to understand the L1 of LEP students can lead to interactional patterns that may negatively affect learning. Analyses of interactional patterns between an English-monolingual teacher and Spanish-speaking first grade students during instructional activities revealed that because the teacher could not understand Spanish, she sometimes failed to recognize or misinterpreted positive learning behavior on the part of the students as instances of misbehavior. The students on their side were reported to take advantage of the fact that the teacher could not understand Spanish by engaging in verbal behavior that represented serious violations of established rules of social conduct in classrooms. These same children behaved in a very different manner with a teacher who was able to understand them. Patterns of social and linguistic behavior in classrooms can influence learning profoundly, so studies of this type are invaluable for attaining a better understanding of what can happen in language learning.

Instructional Issues in Language Learning

In an earlier section of this paper, language use in bilingual programs was considered from the standpoint of efficacy in imparting subject matter. This section is concerned with the effects of language use on second-language learning. How classrooms are organized for instruction can influence the ways in which teachers and students communicate with one another; how language is used in the instructional program can have a major effect on the learning of the language skills needed for school. Let us first consider issues related to language use in bilingual instruction.

In bilingual classrooms, instructional language serves not only as the means by which students are taught the skills and information that they are supposed to learn in school; it also serves as the means by which they are to learn a second language. It is often the case that the only regular contact learners have with the language is in the classroom, so the kind of exposure they get to it there determines whether or not they learn it. Teachers in such classes have to deal with two sets of objectives which are often in conflict. There is, for each grade level and for each area of the curriculum, materials that must be covered if the students are to complete school successfully and on schedule. But if the students have difficulty understanding the language of instruction, let us say English, then the task of teaching them will not be easy. Non-English speakers can be taught directly in English, of course, and they will eventually learn some English through the experience of being instructed through it. However, they are unlikely to cover as much subject matter as they should, or to learn as well as they might if they already knew the language they were being instructed in. The solution of using the students' L1 has made the task more manageable. In a previous section, we discussed instructional approaches that have been taken in the interest of meeting the academic objectives of school. We now consider the effects of some of these practices on language learning.

Concurrent methods involving alternating use of the L1 and L2 in teaching take various forms, as noted earlier. The general approach, however, is to teach in the L2, the language the students are just learning, and to use the L1 when needed to ensure comprehension. From the standpoint of subject matter instruction, this approach appears to work well enough (see, for example, Tikunoff, 1983 and Jacobson, 1981). How well concurrent methods work for language learning may be another matter. There has been little research in which language learning has been studied in classrooms where versions of language alternation are used in teaching. At least one form of language alternation may actually work against language learning. In the translation approach, teachers switch back and forth between the L1 and the L2, usually giving L1 translations for everything that is said in the L2. What little research is available on the use of this method indicates that students may not find it easy to learn the L2 based on this kind of usage. In a study comparing methods of language use in bilingual classes, Legarreta (1975, 1979) found that the translation method was not as effective in promoting the acquisition of English as the method of teaching directly in the target language in a class organized as an alternate-days program. The young Spanish-speaking students in Legarreta's study were drawn from 17 bilingual kindergartens. Some of them received formal ESL instruction, others did not. Formal ESL instruction appeared not to make a difference in how well they learned English, but the manner in which their teachers used the two languages of instruction did. Those who were taught by the translation method did not learn as much English as did those who were taught through the alternate-sessions method in which the two languages of instruction were kept completely separate.

What is wrong with the translation method? It appears that when teachers rely on translation to make what they are presenting comprehensible to their students, the language learning process is short-circuited in at least two ways, according to a recent investigation of second-language learning in four kindergarten classrooms (Wong Fillmore, 1982). In this study, it was found that 40% of the non-English speakers in a class taught by the translation method failed to learn any English after a year of instruction. In contrast, every child in a comparison class that was taught by the direct method acquired some English. Although the children in this class varied in how much they had learned, none could be described as a non-English

speaker after a year in school. In order to learn a new language, students have to have properly adjusted input to work on, as well as samples of speech that have been carefully tailored to fit their linguistic needs, and these must be more or less comprehensible to them, as noted earlier. Learning takes place when the learners try to make sense of what is being said, when they try to relate what they think people are saying to the language they are using. As reported earlier, observations of students in translation classes reveal that they tend to pay attention when the language they already know is being used, and to tune out otherwise. It appears that when teachers give the same information in both languages, they take away the need for the learners to figure out for themselves what is being said. Hence, the learners do not carry out their part of the two-way process of learning a language. But even if the learners paid attention when the L2 is used, they might find the language they hear in such arrangements not altogether useful as input. The problem is that when teachers rely on translations, they tend not to adjust their use of the L2 as they otherwise would in talking to learners, and so the learning process is cut short at both ends.

Given the inherent difficulties involved in teaching students subject matter and a second language at the same time, should the two tasks be separated? One instructional approach that was discussed earlier involved teaching everything except ESL to LEP students in their L1 initially, and as they learn English through ESL, shift them over to English instruction. While ESL is an essential supplement to bilingual instruction, it can not by itself provide LEP students with the language skills needed for school. The kind of English-language skills that LEP students have to acquire are the ones that will allow them to deal with the language used in school. It is the set of skills that enables them to understand the instruction they receive in school, to participate orally in recitations, to ask and to answer questions, to read text materials with comprehension, and in general to formulate their ideas and thoughts in oral and written form. The only way to develop functional language skills of this or of any other kind is through use. Language instruction can help, but it can not substitute for real experiences in which language is serving genuine communicative functions for the learners. The best such experiences come in the form of instructional activities conducted in the target language in which students are encouraged to communicate with one another about interesting and involving subject matter. The language used by teachers and classmates in instructional activities plays an important part in the acquisition of such skills.

Instructional language, that is, language used as the medium of instruction, constitutes a different speech register from ordinary social language (Cazden, 1972; Edwards and Furlong, 1978). Instructional language and ordinary social language are both used in the daily life of classrooms, but the first kind, because its object is to convey information and to teach skills, tends to be more precise, more expository, and more highly propositional than the second. The second kind, whose object is to support social interaction, tends to be more informal and more formulaic than propositional, and its social meaning is as important as its ideational meaning. Language learners need to become proficient in using both kinds of language in order to function in school, but for educational purposes it is most crucial that they learn to deal with instructional language. The only way it can be mastered, however, is for the learners to be engaged in its use on a regular basis.

A distinction proposed by Cummins (1979, 1981a) is relevant to this discussion. Cummins sees language proficiency as consisting of two types of language skills. One is "cognitive" and is required for academic work; the other is "social" and figures in interpersonal communication. The two differ in important ways in how meaning is carried. In the first type, meaning is carried by linguistic forms and structures primarily, and can be understood more or less independently of the situation in which it has been produced. Cummins characterizes it as "context-reduced" language in keeping with distinctions that others such as Donaldson (1978) and Olson (1977) have made. The second type tends to be less explicit and less dependent on linguistic cues, and relatively more dependent on contextual support for interpretation since it is used in interpersonal communication where meaning is partly carried by the situation, in shared experience, and by gestures. The interpersonal type of language proficiency is acquired early in life through socializing experiences in the home, according to Cummins, and is fundamental to the development of cognitive and academic language skills. He contends that well-developed first-language skills are essential to the development of second-language skills, and in fact, students may have difficulty dealing with the academic uses of a second language if they have not yet acquired the proficiency for dealing with that level of usage in the native language (Cummins, 1979). Instructional activities conducted primarily in the L1 are essential to the development of such skills.

Let us now consider what have been found to be relatively effective ways of organizing instructional programs and of using language in teaching from the standpoint of enabling LEP students to develop the language skills they need for school. The research that has focused on this issue is not extensive, but it is consistent in showing that methods involving the teaching of subject matter directly in the target language such as that used in the Canadian immersion bilingual education programs produce the best results. While the second-language skills acquired by students have been found to be less than perfect even in the most successful of these programs (cf. Selinker, Swain, & Dumas, 1975; Swain, 1983), the methods followed in these programs have nonetheless worked exceedingly well. The immersion students have acquired L2 skills that enable them to perform as well in school as comparable students who have been taught exclusively in the L1. Studies comparing different methods of language use in bilingual instruction have found the direct method to be more effective for L2 learning than the concurrent method (Wong Fillmore, 1982; Legarreta, 1979) despite the fact that students may hear more English used in classes following the concurrent method Legarreta, 1977). The critical factor in the relatively successful programs has been that the two languages of instruction have been kept completely separate either by time or by subject matter. When the L2 is used, it is the only language used, and teachers do what they can to convey the information they are trying to impart during the lesson in whatever way they can short of resorting to the students' L1. In fact, in many ways successful bilingual classes are organized in ways that allow them to emulate immersion classes for at least a part of the day. The key characteristics of the immersion technique, as the reader will recall from previous discussions, are these: (a) The classes are linguistically homogeneous (that is, all of the students are more or less at the same L2 proficiency level); (b) although teachers are bilingual and can understand the students when they use the L1, they themselves use the L2 only when interacting with them; (c) teachers teach subject matter exclusively in the L2, making sure that students understand what is being taught by whatever means they have available to them, through games, songs, and activities that involve the student in understanding and learning by doing rather than just by listening; and (d) the new language serves a real communicative function from the very beginning, and is to be learned in the context of use. The linguistic homogeneity of these classes is critical to the success of the method. Teachers find it easiest and most natural to make the linguistic adjustments needed by learners when it is clear that everyone needs them. As we have tried to show, speech (including that used by teachers in lessons) works as input for language learning only when it has been custom-tailored to fit the linguistic needs of the learners in question. It is far more difficult to deal with the needs of heterogeneous groups because what is fitting for some students is not for others. This difficulty, it appears, accounts for why teachers sometimes resort to using translations in linguistically heterogeneous classes, as noted earlier.

The problem for bilingual teachers is that most classes are heterogeneous in L2 proficiency, even when the students are all from the same L1 background. How can instruction be organized so that language can be used in ways that promote L2 development? The solution that has been adopted in many programs has been to group the students by L2 proficiency for instruction given in that language. This allows teachers to attend to the special needs of each group of students separately, and for everyone to be on an equal linguistic footing during group instruction. In this way, teachers create periods in which immersion teaching techniques can be used effectively. This being the case, would LEP students be better served in segregated classes? We believe not. The research evidence suggests that students need the immersion type of activity that can be provided most easily in segregated groups, but they also need to have contact with classmates who are fluent speakers of the L2 in order to develop a native-like control of that language. They would profit from being in integrated classes for some part of each day. The ideal situation for language learning, according to educators who specialize in the development of language skills during the elementary school years (cf. Lindfors, 1983 and Urzua, 1981) consists of instructional activities that allow children to interact freely in the course of working on mutually involving tasks that invite discussion, questioning, responding, and so forth. A certain amount of social engineering and structuring is needed to make such activities really work for language learning, however. Left on their own, students may not be inclined to interact in ways that are helpful from the standpoint of language learning. Children may find it just as hard as teachers do to consider the linguistic needs of learners in linguistically mixed groups, or they may engage in the use of "foreigner talk," which gives the learners an erroneous idea of what the L2 is really like. It takes planning to create instructional activities that minimize such problems, and constant monitoring to make sure that such activities work as they should. Among the most promising efforts in this regard have been programs that make use of peer tutoring as a method of getting English-speaking students to interact with LEP students in bilingual programs in ways that enhance language learning (cf. Johnson and August, 1981).

Formal Language Instruction

A question that is frequently raised in bilingual education concerns the necessity of formal ESL instruction. During the early years of bilingual education, this question was a topic of much debate. The controversy, for the most part, has been political rather than pedagogical, however. ESL has been seen by those who advocate rights for language minority groups as the society's mechanism for achieving its assimilative goals. The objection to the teaching of ESL in bilingual programs stemmed from the perception that the emphasis in the early programs was on teaching LEP children English rather than on providing them with a comprehensive education in their L1s and in English. This emphasis on ESL despite the stated goals of the Title VII legislation reflected the assimilative nature of the educational model in this country which, according to some bilingual education advocates such as Kjolseth (1971), was really aimed at "the accelerated demise of the ethnic mother tongue." This perspective is reflected in the Office of Civil Rights' injunction against schools offering ESL to LEP students as a substitute for bilingual education in complying with the *Lau v. Nichols* decision (Office of Civil Rights, 1975). The arguments OCR offered against ESL as a comprehensive instructional solution focused on its ineffectiveness as a means of providing students with useful language skills, and on its lack of concern with the cultural heritage and needs of the students (U.S. Civil Rights Commission, 1975, pp. 22–28). The deeper concern that can be detected between the lines is that such an approach will ultimately deprive language minority students of their rights to have and hold onto a native language and culture. A 1968 editorial in the Hispanic publication *El Grito* is reported to have characterized ESL programs as "arrogant linguistic imperialism" (Spolsky, 1971). Although such views are less prevalent now than during the first years of the existence of bilingual programs in this country, they continue to be a source of controversy.

Educators are divided on the matter, although nearly all recognize that some form of instructional assistance must be provided to enable LEP students in bilingual programs to acquire the language skills needed for effective functioning in school (cf. TESOL, 1976; Alatis, 1979; Spolsky, 1970). The appropriate instructional choice would be ESL instruction of some sort, but some educators object to it on the grounds that it is superfluous in well-implemented bilingual programs. Functional language skills cannot be taught, we are reminded; they can only be acquired through use. Students can and will acquire them if they are being taught subject matter in the target language, hence special instruction in which the language is specifically taught is unnecessary, according to this view. The opposing view is that ESL can help to facilitate the process of learning English and ensure that the English acquired by LEP students is a grammatical and standard variety. Left on their own, students can and will manage to learn English eventually, but the task may be unnecessarily painful and frustrating, if they have to work everything out on their own. Experts on language learning and teaching believe that some formal instruction in ESL can serve as the linguistic bootstraps needed by LEP students to pull themselves beyond the difficult early stages of language learning. Christina Bratt Paulston (commentary at TESOL meeting [Summer, 1983]) argues that formal L2 instruction, particularly when it is focused on specific problems, may be just what it will take to help the students in Canadian immersion programs unlearn the ungrammatical structures they have acquired from other learners, and to move on to a more native-like command of French.

Nevertheless, while bilingual and ESL specialists alike may recognize that there is a need for language instruction, they do not generally agree as to the form it should take. As Paulston points out, in the minds of many educators, ESL has become "identified and synonymous with the audiolingual method of language teaching," in which the focus is on the learning of grammatical rules through pattern practice and drill (Paulston, 1983, p. 77). Advocates of the so-called "integrative approaches" of language instruction (e.g., Terrell, 1981) argue that "grammar-based approaches" have failed to provide students with the functional language skills needed for living in societies where the L2 is actually spoken. Methods and materials that are organized around pattern practice and language drills are nevertheless widely used in school programs, and teachers believe in them, in the absence of evidence that they do any harm. This is not to say that all ESL programs make use of such practices.

The rubric ESL covers many different approaches and methods, although they fall basically into two general categories: what might be characterized as structural, or rule-oriented approaches, and communicative or integrative approaches. In the first, the emphasis is on developing language sequentially by teaching the grammatical patterns and structural rules of the language. The syllabi for programs of this type are generally organized around matters of grammar, vocabulary, and pronunciation that build from the simple to the complex; thus students are gradually taught the forms and structural principles of the language that allow them to produce grammatically correct sentences in the language (e.g., Paulston & Bruder, 1976). In the second type of approach, the emphasis is on the development of communicative skills by teaching students conventional relationships between the forms and structures of the new language and their social and functional meanings. Syllabi of this type of language-teaching program are organized around communicative functions such as making requests and asking permission, notions of language such as expressing causal relations and making comparisons, and topics such as sports, games, and holidays (Littlewood, 1981). In the course of learning to deal with such functions and topics, students acquire a repertory of forms and structures that vary in grammatical complexity, along with strategies for using them in socially appropriate ways. Both types of programs have the same basic objective, that is, to provide learners with a working command of the language that serves at least their immediate communicative needs. What it takes to get beyond that is experience in speaking the language with native speakers, and time.

The question of what works best can be determined only by research, but to date there has been virtually nothing comparing the effectiveness of various language-teaching methods and approaches in bilingual programs. What little research has been done on ESL in relation to bilingual education has sought to determine whether ESL makes a difference. Whether or not it does would seem to depend on what is being done as ESL, on how well the program is conceived and implemented, on how well the teachers are trained in the methods used, and how committed they are to making them work. Since there is about as much variation in ESL programs as in bilingual programs, no one study can settle the question of whether ESL itself makes a difference. On a more pragmatic level, it certainly cannot hurt to provide LEP students in even the most effective bilingual programs with some ESL training. The available evidence on second-language learning in bilingual programs indicates that many LEP students get little exposure to English outside of the classroom, so they must base their learning of it on what they can get while they are in school. A part of each school day is, and should be, spent learning through the L1 to ensure subject matter mastery. Some part of it will be spent in English instruction. However, as we have seen, whether the language used in those instructional events can be used by the LEP students as input for their language learning efforts depends on a number of complex social, pedagogical, and individual factors. That being the case, ESL instruction, provided it is well designed and implemented, can reinforce the English they are getting in the course of participating in such activities, at the very least. It may even ensure that the students acquire the English skills they need to deal effectively with the subject matter instruction that they are receiving in English.

Learner Factors

Among educators, it has long been assumed that second-language learning is an easy matter for children, and the younger they are, the easier it is. In fact, language learning is taken so much for granted that it is commonly believed that as long as children are properly instructed and are given adequate exposure to English, they ought to pick up the language in a year or two at the most. Hence, the effectiveness of educational programs meant for LEP students is frequently judged on whether students can meet the schedule that others assume they should be following in mastering the new language. The assumption of rapid and easy L2 learning as a norm may be based on a model that comes from L1 learning. The home is an impressively effective language classroom since all normal children come close to mastering the intricacies of the language spoken there before they begin school. The expectation is that classrooms ought to work at least as well for ensuring L2 learning as homes do for the L1. When normal children do not learn to speak the language of the home in the expected time, it is generally assumed that parents are not providing them with an adequate home environment or with appropriate experiences. Likewise, when children do not acquire a second language in the expected time, it is assumed that there is something wrong with the educational program they are being exposed to, or with the experiences provided them in the classroom.

Evidence has been accumulating in the past several years that the process of L1 learning may be less uniform than previously thought: For those who look, variation can be found in how children make use of early opportunities to learn even their first language, and in the extent to which they have actually mastered the first language by the time they go to school. The variations found in first-language learning, however, are nothing compared to those found in second-language learning. Even the most cursory observation of the LEP students in any classroom at all will reveal startling differences across individuals in how much of a command of the L2 they have acquired in a school year. This is true no matter what kind of an educational program they are exposed to. Some programs, as we have tried to show, appear to work much better for language learning than do others. However, there is variation to be found even in the ones that can be shown to be much better than others. Obviously, in classroom programs that seem to promote successful L2 development, one finds substantially more children who make progress in learning the new language than in classrooms that are less successful in this regard. But in even the worst programs (from the standpoint of language learning), one finds in a year's time that there are some students who will have made tremendous progress in acquiring the new language. Similarly, in even the best programs one finds that some children will have made little discernible progress in the same period of time (Saville-Troike, 1983; Wong Fillmore, 1982, 1983).

There is mounting evidence that while some children can acquire a new language in, say, 2 years, the majority may take as many as 2 to 3 years longer (Cummins, 1981b, 1981c; Wong Fillmore, 1983). Indeed, there may be some who need as many as 6 to 7 years of exposure to a new language, whether they are in bilingual programs or in all-English ones. Such variation may be exacerbated by the programs learners find themselves in, or by factors related to the social setting in which the programs must operate, but they stem from differences that exist in the learners themselves. Individual characteristics of learners — their social skills and inclinations, their attitudes and motivations, and the way they handle complex cognitive tasks such as those involved in school — can greatly influence their ability to deal with the learning of a new language, whatever the circumstances. Hence, one finds in the same classrooms considerable variation in how much learners can get out of the same exposure to English. Such differences are frequently attributed to learner differences of the same sort that create variation in learning of any kind. Students who are intellectually capable and motivated to do well can be shown to perform better in school than students who are less so. Intellectual capability and motivation may contribute to successful language learning as well, but it appears not to be a major source of the differences found in children. Relationships have been established between such factors and successful language learning in adults or near adults (e.g., Carroll, 1979; Gardner & Lambert, 1972), but a relationship between these variables and language learning in children has not, to date, been convincingly established. Bright and motivated children are found among those who learn new languages most sucessfully. But it sometimes happens that students who are quite motivated to learn and use the new language, and who otherwise do well in school, experience considerable difficulty dealing with the problems of learning a new language. Other factors, it appears, can override motivation and intellectual talent in determining how capably individuals handle the business of learning a new language. Let us look at some of these.

Language learning, as we have argued, is both a social and a cognitive process. Learners cannot learn a language without the help and collaboration of those who already speak it. In order to learn the target language, there must be opportunities for learners and speakers to come into contact, and reason for them to communicate with one another in a cooperative fashion. The place where these contacts occur for LEP students is in the classrooms, a social setting that offers ample reason for children to interact with speakers of the target language. If, in addition to the teacher, there are students in the classroom who speak the target language, then the learners will find more opportunity to interact with people who can help them in learning the language, as we have already pointed out. Otherwise, the learners must rely on teachers' supplying them with all the help they need to learn the language. Whatever the social situation, however, learners play a substantial role in making sure that they get enough such help. While a certain amount of exposure to the new language is guaranteed them as long as they are actually being taught in the target language for a part of each day, it may or may not be enough to sustain the language-learning process.

Hence, to a large extent, the learners have to seek additional support for their language-learning efforts, either from teachers and L2-speaking classmates in the classroom, or from anyone they can find to help them outside of it. This means that learners must figure out ways of initiating social contacts with people with whom they do not have easy ways of interacting since they lack a common language. It takes considerable social skill and confidence to be able to manage this, and as anyone who has worked with children knows, these characteristics vary in children. Differences in social skill can stem from variation in early experience and from individual differences in personality and social style characteristics. Children who are shy or introverted will find it more difficult than those who are sociable or outgoing to participate in the interactions that provide the input and practice needed for language learning (Wong Fillmore, 1979, 1983). Learners also differ in matters of talkativeness. Those who do enjoy talking and who exercise this inclination not only get more practice using the language, they also generate much more input for themselves (Hatch, 1983; Seliger, 1977; Strong 1982). Differences in interests may incline learners to seek and engage in particular kinds of activities. Cathcart (1983) has recently shown that the language functions children use and practice depend on the type of activities they engage in.

Accumulating evidence indicates that such learner variables may indeed contribute substantially to differential results in second-language learning in children. The relationships between these learner characteristics and success in language learning are anything but simple, however. While sociability, outgoingness, and talkativeness have been found to be characteristics associated with successful language learning in some studies (e.g. Wong Fillmore, 1979), this is not always the case. For example, Swain and Burnaby (1976) found, contrary to their expectations, that the children in their Canadian immersion study who tended to be introverted and studious were better language learners than those who were outgoing and sociable. Saville-Troike (1983) likewise found that the children in her study who were the best language learners were not necessarily the most sociable and outgoing. In fact, the ones who could be described as such were among the least successful. In a study relating social style characteristics to second-language learning, Strong (1982) found that interest in interaction with native speakers of the target language did not appear to make much of a difference in how well kindergarten-age children learn a second language.

How can these contradictory findings be reconciled? In a longitudinal study of individual differences of second-language learning among young learners, Wong Fillmore (1983) found that none of these characteristics by itself can determine what happens in language learning; much depends on what kind of situation learners find themselves in, who is available for them to interact with, what kind of input they have to work with, and the like. Personal characteristics such as sociability and outgoingness which incline children to seek out and socialize with others can made a big difference in language learning in situations in which it is up to the learners to make their own contacts with speakers of the target language. However, if learners find themselves in situations where everyone is a novice in the language, then sociability does not help much. In classrooms with a high concentration of learners, as in the French immersion classes studied by Burnaby and Swain, where the teacher is the main source of input, children who are studious and introverted will do much better than those who are less so. In this kind of situation, the children who pay attention to what teachers are saying and doing are going to get much more out of the language they use than those who do not. Those who are outgoing will be inclined to socialize with classmates. Since these classmates are also speakers of the L1, they are more likely to use the L1 in their interactions than the L2, which they are all just learning. As Wong Fillmore has found, the children who, because they are gregarious, might be good learners in a different setting are as likely to be among the poorest in classrooms with high concentrations of learners. In such classes, those children who are less sociable or more adult-oriented may, in fact, be much better off since they are then open to well-formed input from the teacher, and are not spending much time practicing and acquiring imperfectly realized forms from their fellow language learners. Gregariousness and a peer orientation help only when there are speakers of the target language to interact with among one's peers, and when the members of the learner group and the target language group have an interest in interaction with one another. As pointed out earlier, language learning is a two-way process, and it can be accomplished only if both parties are willing to play their necessary roles.

Learning style differences in individuals can also be a source of variability in second-language learning. The cognitive part of the process involves learners' applying a variety of cognitive strategies to the task of discovering relationships between the things they hear speakers saying, and what they can observe of objects, events, actions, and relationships in the world within which the language is being used. They must then discover the structural principles relating linguistic forms to speaker intentions and the rules of social usage, and try out what they have learned by this process in their own speech. Once they attempt to use the language themselves they can assess whether their guesses about it have been correct. They will find that they can be understood by speakers of the language to the extent that they have been able to figure things out correctly. If they cannot be understood, their interlocutors will let them know in one way or another. Cooperative speech partners will try to guess what was meant, and in that process, they may provide the learners with additional input that helps to straighten things out. The process calls for two types of activities, then: The first is one of discerning the relationships existing between linguistic forms and their meanings and functions, and the second is one of testing and consolidating one's developing linguistic knowledge through speech. Individuals vary considerably in how they handle both types of activities. They differ, for example, in the extent to which they are inclined to look for or to see relationships that exist in the phenomena they are exposed to. Some learners are much more observant and better able to see patterns than others; they are likely to figure things out more quickly and accurately than others. Another characteristic that is likely to influence an individual's ability to figure relationships out is mental flexibility, which allows one to form hypotheses about the nature of the phenomena being observed, and to test and revise them mentally along the way. Such characteristics have been found to be important factors in adult foreign-language learning, and they appear to be major factors in child second-language learning as well (Wong Fillmore, 1983). Social characteristics of learners can interact with cognitive characteristics to produce unexpected results. It is sometimes the case that learners are fairly good at discovering patterns and rules in the language, but make slow progress in mastering the language because they lack the confidence to try out what they are learning. The fear of appearing foolish or of being wrong can slow down the language-learning process considerably, even for young children. Those who are unafraid of trying things out, and who do not mind being wrong will get considerably more practice, but whether or not they actually are good learners depends on how well they can recognize when their guesses have been on target. Much remains to be learned about the ways in which social and cognitive differences in learners influence the process of language learning.

Age is a learner variable that may also exert an influence on language learning, but not necessarily in the direction that educators believe it does. The popular view is that younger children learn second languages much more successfully than older children. The evidence ordinarily cited to support this view is the observation that many adults have considerable difficulty learning new languages and those who do rarely learn one without an "accent," whereas nearly all children who are exposed to a second language not only learn it, they generally attain a native-like level of proficiency in its use. Educators who are of this opinion object to bilingual education on the grounds that it may actually work against second-language learning by delaying the process beyond the point at which it can still be done easily and completely. Accordingly, they advise teachers in bilingual classes to use the native language as sparingly as possible, and for only as long as necessary. They also advocate

the introduction and teaching of the second language as early as possible. This notion has been challenged in Cummins' (1979, 1981b) "interdependence hypothesis," in which uninterrupted language and cognitive development are more crucial to later academic and language development than early exposure to a second language. According to Cummins, a premature switch to a second language may disrupt the development of the cognitive structures that undergird not only the first language, but any subsequent language as well. Such structures are "interdependent," and they must be stabilized in the learner's native language before they can support academic learning. Fundamental to this argument is the assumption that the development of L2 skills is contingent on well-developed L1 skills (Toukomaa and Skutnabb-Kangas, 1977). Contrary to the view that it may be too late to learn a second language if its introduction is delayed beyond the early years of school, Cummins (1979, 1980, 1981a, 1981c) argues that older learners, because they are cognitively more mature and have better developed L1 skills, are able to acquire the cognitively demanding aspects of an L2 more rapidly than younger learners. Cummins, Swain, Nakajima, Handscombe, and Green (1981) investigated the relationship between L1 and L2 proficiency in immigrant students in Canadian schools. The subjects were all upper-class Japanese students, some of whom had immigrated at a fairly young age, others at a later age. The later-immigrating students had enjoyed longer uninterrupted development in their native language, and thus had much better-developed L1 literacy and language skills than those who had immigrated at a younger age. Cummins and his colleagues found no differences between older and younger students in the acquisition of those aspects of linguistic proficiency that figure in everyday social interaction. They did find, however, that later-entering students had a distinct advantage in acquiring the more academic types of language skills: Their development of the language proficiency required for school was significantly faster than that of early-entering students.

The findings in the Canadian research appear to support ones that have come from earlier studies conducted in Sweden. A series of studies conducted over a 25-year period investigated the effect of age on second-language learning in school children. Ekstrand (1982) recently reported on a study conducted in the midsixties, with the entire population of recent immigrant students in Swedish schools participating as subjects, in which the relationship was investigated between age and length of residence (LOR) in Sweden, and the learning of Swedish as a second language. The students ranged in age from 8 to 17 years, and had been in Sweden less than 3 years. Second-language performance was measured by tests of oral and written language comprehension and production; in addition intelligence was measured by tests that had been standardized on native speakers of Swedish. Clear age effects were found with older immigrant students generally outperforming younger ones on both types of measures, leading Ekstrand to conclude that "language learning ability improves with age as does intellectual functioning." This finding appears to be consistent with that of the Cummins et al. (1981) study. Oral production was the one measure that was not significantly related to age, but was related to LOR. It appears that while older children may have a definite advantage in dealing with most aspects of language learning, it nevertheless takes them time to develop skill in expressing themselves in a new language. Length of residence, of course, was unrelated to intelligence, and was only weakly related to all measures of language proficiency except for oral production, listening comprehension, and written production, which were more clearly associated. Of the three, however, only oral production was strongly related to LOR. These three are skills that apparently take time to develop. Thus, the longer students are in school practicing and hearing the new language, the better they can understand what people are saying, and express themselves in it in both oral and written form.

These findings are consistent with research evidence from observational case studies in which young children have been compared with older ones (Ervin-Tripp, 1974), and from cross-sectional studies in which children have been compared with adults (Snow & Hoefnagel-Höhle, 1978, 1982). Altogether, the research suggests that older learners make more rapid progress in learning second languages, and appear to be more accurate in figuring out how the language works than do young learners. Ervin-Tripp ascribes the advantage enjoyed by older children to the better-developed memory heuristics and more efficient learning strategies that come with greater cognitive maturity. She points out that learners who already know how to read have developed a fairly abstract knowledge of the phonology of the language which gives them a special advantage in acquiring a new language. Snow and Hoefnagel-Höhle (1978) considered whether an advantage, if one existed, would extend across all aspects of language learning for the age group, or whether it would be divided between groups by component skills. Hence they looked for age differences by assessing language learning on a large battery of tests which separately measured production and reception of morphology, syntax, vocabulary, and phonology. The learners in this study were English speakers living in Holland, and they were learning Dutch as a second language. Snow and Hoefnagel-Höhle found that, in general, older learners had an advantage over younger ones in learning "the rule-governed aspects of a second language," that is, morphology and syntax, but little or no advantage in gaining control over the sound system of the language. Adults were better than young children in nearly all aspects of language learning, but they were not better than teenagers. Teenagers outperformed adults on morphology, vocabulary, and syntax as measured on a translation test. These findings led Snow and Hoefnagel-Höhle to conclude that although the age advantage in favor of older learners was a clear one, it was nevertheless limited.

The findings in the Dutch study may help to explain the findings in a study by Ramírez and Politzer (1978) in which Spanish-speaking elementary school-age children were compared with junior and senior high school students on their learning of English over a period of a year. The younger subjects in this study were enrolled in bilingual education programs. The older students, of whom there were two groups, were enrolled in all-English classes; one group was studied after a year of English exposure, the other after 2 years. Ramírez and Politzer found that the older students were generally better than the younger ones in learning English, although younger students did as well as the older ones in some aspects of learning

the new language. No differences, however, were found between the two groups of older students though one of them had had twice as much exposure to English as the other. This suggests that while older learners may make more rapid progress in learning a new language than younger learners, the advantage is temporary, and declines after the initial period of learning the new language. Since it takes time to learn a new language, ultimately younger learners may have an edge on older ones since they have time on their side, a point that has been demonstrated in research conducted by Krashen, Long, and Scarcella (1979). It is frequently the case that older learners (that is, those who begin learning a second language during or after adolescence) reach a point in the learning of the new language that is short of a native-like level of proficiency, and they make no further progress. As Selinker (1972) characterizes it, their language skills fossilize at an "interlanguage" state. This also happens with younger learners, but it is not nearly as common as with older ones. Thus, it is remarkable when older learners acquire a native-like control over a second language, it is remarkable when young children do not.

What instructional implications can we draw from these findings? Clearly, educators who worry about the consequences of delaying second-language instruction beyond the first years of school can be assured that their concerns are not altogether warranted. However, given the fact that age can interact with all of the other learner characteristics discussed in this section, it may be necessary to consider what sort of instructional methods might work best for helping students of different ages learn the school language. Integrative or communicative approaches might be ideal for younger students, but as McLaughlin (1982) and Paulston (1980) have argued, older learners may need and profit from instruction that focuses on the rules, patterns, and uses of the new language.

Cognitive and Social Effects of Bilingualism

The issues to be raised in this final section deal with the cognitive and social consequences of bilingual instruction. In the introductory section of this chapter, it was noted that both research and practice in bilingual instruction have been shaped to a considerable extent by the public controversy surrounding it. English has become the predominant language of instruction in bilingual classrooms, and programs everywhere are focused on the teaching of English because of the public perception that the use of the L1 in school fosters a lasting dependence on that language, and removes the need for LEP students to learn English at all. The current debate over whether the federal government ought to continue advocating bilingual education as the instructional remedy of choice in Lau-type cases puts a tremendous burden on bilingual educators to demonstrate that these programs are mainly concerned with progress in English, and the use of the L1 in school is in fact just a means to that end. Thus, the emphasis on program planning has been to design instructional services that facilitate the transition from dependence on the L1 in school to an exclusive reliance on the L2. In a sense bilingual education has had to justify its existence by denying its unique characteristic, namely that it makes it possible for children to learn through two languages, and to become truly bilingual.

Research in this area has become preoccupied with the need to prove that bilingual education does not put LEP students at an academic disadvantage, and this has been in response to charges that whatever learning is accomplished through the L1 is an academic dead end, having mainly the effect of delaying the students' proper assimilation into the school's regular program. Much of the research we have examined has focused on assessing the extent to which programs have succeeded in allowing students to learn English and to make academic progress through English. Indeed, with a few notable exceptions, the research in bilingual education has focused on academic development in the L2, with little attention paid either to the development of the L1, or to the academic progress that students are making in the L1. Even when such progress is assessed, the issue has been whether skills developed in the L1 are readily transferable to the L2; the real test of bilingual instruction has been in how well it helps students adjust to instruction in English. As we have discovered by examining the instructional research in this field, much of it has been *reactive* to criticisms rather than *active* in determining the most effective methods of educating linguistically different students in this society.

In this section, we examine research that relates to another facet of the public debate over bilingual education. While the controversy surrounding bilingual education has largely focused on the issue of English, there is perhaps an even deeper concern over the maintenance of ethnic languages by minority groups in this society. By and large, Americans take pride in being a monolingual society. Bilingualism is little valued here. This, perhaps, accounts for the general lack of interest among Americans in learning foreign languages, and the commensurate lack of understanding of the perspectives represented by groups that speak other languages. The social picture in this country might be very different if Americans were more inclined to become bilinguals themselves by adding a foreign language to their linguistic resources. Cziko, Lambert, and Gutter (1979–1980) have shown that participation in immersion programs can narrow the social gulf that has long existed between Francophones and Anglophones in Canada. It appears that as English-speaking children acquire French they generally develop more favorable attitudes towards French-speaking Canadians, and they are better able to identify with them (see also Lambert & Tucker, 1972). Other studies have shown that the best time to develop positive attitudes through bilingualism is in the early grades of school; the younger the students are when they are exposed to a foreign language, the greater the social benefits of bilingualism (e.g., Genesee, Tucker, & Lambert, 1978).

Such attitudes could well be fostered in this society as well. Too many people in the society regard those who maintain a language other than English as "outsiders." As noted in the background section, to many Americans, English represents the society itself, and the ability to speak English constitutes a symbolic attachment to the society, while minority languages represent attachments to other groups and societies. Thus, in the minds of many, bilingualism implies divided loyalty. While such perceptions are not widely discussed, they nevertheless have influenced the way bilingual education has been received in this country. The popular view seems to be that bilingualism is an abnormal state, and any program that promotes it is wrongheaded.

An even more pervasive belief has been that bilingualism may be detrimental to intellectual functioning. Such fears no doubt will seem absurd to people in societies where bilingualism and even multilingualism are commonplace, but in North America, they have engendered a substantial amount of research activity addressed at studying the cognitive consequences of knowing more than one language. Until rather recently (that is, until the sixties), much of the psychological research dealing with bilingualism was devoted to investigating the extent to which it affected normal cognitive development. Researchers and educators alike seemed to assume that the human mind could develop its potential capacity and operate under full power only if it was undivided linguistically. Bilingualism to many people meant cognitive confusion, and even worse, an incomplete knowledge or control of any language. The early research did indeed seem to confirm the most pessimistic views on this phenomenon, but as later researchers have observed, many of these studies were poorly designed and important factors such as social class and educational background were not controlled. (For reviews of the early work, see Darcy, 1953, 1963. See also Ben-Zeev, 1977a, Lambert, 1977, and Segalowitz, 1977 for discussions of this work relative to issues that have been examined in more recent research.)

These views were generally unchallenged until Peal and Lambert (1962) found through a well-designed study that French–English bilingual children in Montreal were significantly better on measures of both verbal and nonverbal intelligence than were carefully matched monolingual children. The bilingual children's patterns of performance suggested they had a more diversified structure of intelligence and greater flexibility in thought than the monolingual children. These results have been replicated, confirmed, and refined in subsequent research conducted around the world by other researchers (Lambert, 1977). Only a few of these studies will be discussed here since a through review of this research is beyond the scope of this chapter. Those discussed here are representative of studies seeking to dispel the public suspicion that tends to undermine the objectives of bilingual education, namely that learning in two languages will lead to academic confusion and language problems.

Duncan and De Avila (1979) examined the question of whether bilingualism offers a different kind of "cognitive metaset" for dealing with experience, a point they have argued elsewhere (De Avila & Duncan, 1979). They contend that in the course of dealing through two language systems, learners develop a facility for figuring out which of their available cognitive schemes are appropriate to a particular situation; this, in turn, increases their capacity for handling new problems and for integrating new intellectual strategies. In a cross-sectional study involving some 200 young Hispanic students (Grades 1–3) drawn from urban and rural communities in California, Texas, New York, and Florida, Duncan and De Avila assessed the relationship between degree of bilingualism and cognitive functioning based on measures of linguistic proficiency, intelligence, and cognitive style. Their Spanish and English language-assessment procedures subdivided their sample into 5 linguistic proficiency groupings ranging from fully proficient bilinguals to partial bilinguals and monolinguals. One group, comprising 26.5% of their total sample, were identified as being limited bilinguals, students who were proficient neither in English nor in Spanish. A small number of these (5.9% of the total sample) appeared to have serious language problems. Duncan and De Avila (1979) found across measures a positive and uniform relationship between bilingual proficiency and intellectual functioning, with the bilingual children outperforming all other groups in their tests of intellectual functioning. Limited bilingual children generally performed more poorly than monolinguals, but their patterns of performance led Duncan and De Avila to conclude that their deficiencies were linguistic rather than intellectual.

A longitudinal study investigating the relationship between bilingualism and cognitive development was completed recently by Hakuta and Díaz (in press). The authors took a quite different methodological approach in their investigation than that taken in other such studies. Instead of comparing bilinguals with monolinguals, they studied the effects of bilingualism on cognitive development by looking for evidence of change in cognitive capacity as monolingual students become bilingual. Over 120 Spanish-speaking kindergarten and first grade students enrolled in a New Haven bilingual education program were followed for the period of a school year. The subjects in this study were tested for English and Spanish proficiency at the beginning of the school year, and again at the end. They were also tested on a nonverbal cognitive ability test. Hakuta and Díaz found that as the subjects increased in degree of bilingualism, their scores on the cognitive test increased as well. The relationship between degree of bilingualism and cognitive ability over time was found to be highly significant, leading Hakuta and Díaz to argue that degree of bilingualism appears to be a causal factor in the increase in cognitive ability observed in these students.

A different approach to studying the relationship between bilingualism and intellectual functioning is exemplified by Kessler and Quinn's experimental study of the effects of bilingualism and bilingual instruction on the development of academic skills (Kessler & Quinn, 1980). In this investigation, bilingual students were compared with monolinguals on their ability to solve science problems, and to give verbal expression to their hypotheses. The subjects were students from four sixth grade classes, two of them English monolingual and two Spanish-English bilingual. There were also two control classes. The experimental groups were given 12 science lessons which were presented in English to bilingual and English monolingual groups alike. Each lesson was organized around a film session in which a science problem was depicted. Following the film presentation and lesson, students were required to write as many hypotheses as they could in a controlled period of time. Their hypotheses were rated both for scientific quality and for syntactic complexity. Kessler and Quinn found that the bilingual students consistently outperformed the monolinguals in the quality and linguistic complexity of their hypotheses. Furthermore, a positive relationship between the quality of the students' hypotheses and the complexity of the language they used was found for both groups, suggesting that the two kinds of abilities involve similar cognitive mechanisms.

A relationship between bilingualism and increased development in general verbal skills has been established in a number of studies. Ianco-Worrall (1972) has shown that young bilinguals, Afrikaans-English speakers in this study, consistently outperform monolinguals in being able to distinguish between phonetic and semantic similarities in word-analysis tasks. Cummins (1978), in studies of children in Irish-English and Ukrainian-English bilingual programs, considered whether or not bilingualism affected linguistic awareness or analytical abilites in dealing with language-related tasks. Cummins presented his subjects with a variety of tasks measuring their ability to deal with ambiguity, contradictions, arbitrariness of language, classification, and transformations. Fluent bilinguals outperformed monolingual and nonfluent subjects in tests dealing with some but not all of these aspects of linguistic awareness. The tasks in which significant main effects were found for degree of bilingualism were those involving linguistic analysis; no differences were found on tasks requiring them to make semantic discriminations or to deal with the arbitrariness of language. Overall, however, this study seems to show that bilingualism does promote higher-level verbal skill development.

Results from studies by Ben-Zeev (1972, 1977b) appear consistent with Cummins' findings in showing that while bilinguals have better-developed analytical skills in dealing with language-related tasks, they do not necessarily have a better command of the semantic aspects of language. In two separate investigations, one dealing with Hebrew and English and the other with Spanish and English, she found that bilinguals generally performed better than monolinguals on cognitive and linguistic measures calling for structural analysis and manipulation, but not on those requiring a knowledge of the semantic structure of the language. Bilinguals in both groups did not do as well as monolinguals in vocabulary tests, and produced more errors in oral language tasks than did the monolinguals. The Hebrew-English bilinguals, however, appeared to be better than their monolingual controls in more tasks than were the Spanish-English bilinguals. Ben-Zeev (1977a) suggests that the social circumstances of the community in which the Hispanic group lived may have diluted the cognitive and linguistic benefits that bilingualism offers. These children came from lower socioeconomic-level families residing in an urban neighborhood where they were exposed, as Ben-Zeev observes, to the intolerance of foreign languages that is found in many places in this country. How much this might have affected their development is not known, but these children generally reported a preference for English although they admitted that Spanish was the language they spoke better. This early shift in linguistic preference suggests that for these children, the learning of English will result eventually in what Lambert (1977) has described as "subtractive bilingualism," a condition that offers few of the benefits of knowing two languages that "additive bilingualism" offers.

This distinction is an important one to keep in mind in considering the outcome of educational programs for language minority students. Many of them continue to have problems in school even after they appear to have learned English. This can cause considerable consternation for educators who are responsible for their academic development. When these students do not speak English, it is easy enough to explain the difficulties they have in school, and it is clear what needs to be done to help them. But when their difficulties persist even after they apparently "know" English, it is not so easy to explain what the problem is, or to know what to do about it. A detailed analysis by Cummins (1981b) of over 400 teacher referral forms in which psychological assessments were requested for language minority students revealed that teachers frequently conclude that there must be something wrong with the children who continue to have difficulty in school after learning English. Cummins found that teachers often judged children to be fluent in the school language when they in fact had only a very superficial knowledge of it. Many of the children could handle English in face-to-face informal contacts but they lacked the level of skills needed to deal with the academic uses of that language in school. As Cummins has pointed out, a common response in such situations is to blame children for the school's failure to understand or to meet their educational needs.

It appears, however, that it is even more common to blame the program, but not necessarily for the right reasons. The conclusion policymakers and educators reach, on hearing that many language minority students continue to have difficulty in school despite the special programs that are provided for them, is that the programs are ineffective. Hence, they urge a change in program or argue that the programs would demonstrate a greater effectiveness by moving students through them faster. It is a common experience for LEP students to be removed from bilingual and ESL programs as soon as they have learned enough English to pass the proficiency tests that schools use for the purpose of determining eligibility for such programs. Ulibarrí, Spencer, and Rivas (1981) conducted a study to assess the effectiveness of the tests that school districts most frequently use for this purpose. They sought to establish the degree to which such tests agreed in their classification of students, and to determine how well they predicted academic achievement in school. Over a thousand Hispanic students in California schools were tested on three tests of oral proficiency. In addition, they were rated on oral language proficiency in English and Spanish, and on reading and math achievement by their teachers. Standardized achievement test data were collected on these students as well. It was found that the three tests examined in the study were not as comparable as they could be in categorizing the children by proficiency level, since they classified different proportions of the samples as fluent, limited, and non-English speaking. Further, it was found that they were much less dependable even than teacher ratings in predicting academic achievement. It appears that how long students receive the special services they require may well depend on which test is being used at their school. Given the low predictive value of most proficiency tests, it is easy to see how children can be judged to be fluent in English and still not be able to handle schoolwork that is taught entirely in that language. Not surprisingly, English for these students does not ensure educational progress in school. Access to the school's curriculum depends on the acquisition of those aspects of the language that are required for academic work, and this type of linguistic proficiency is rarely assessed in tests of proficiency.

Conclusion

In view of the controversy surrounding bilingual education, it is easy to see how its true objectives and potential benefits have become secondary to all else. It offers children a chance to survive in school without giving up their cultural identities. It allows them to become bilingual and to enjoy the social and cognitive benefits that bilingualism offers individuals. All of them will learn English eventually. However, it takes more than learning a second language to be bilingual and to get the full benefits of bilingualism. Social factors can exert a considerable influence on the outcome of the second-language learning process. In order to become true bilinguals these children must hang onto and develop their knowledge of the native language as they acquire English. In this society, however, the learning of English all too often means the loss of the L1. Countless groups have lost their languages in the process of learning English, despite their best efforts to preserve them (Fishman, 1980a, 1980b). In the research that has been discussed in this chapter, we have seen that much of the emphasis in bilingual education has been to help students learn English. However, it can be argued that with or without such help, there is little danger that LEP students who have gone through the American school system can avoid learning English. The social forces that impel them to learn English are sufficiently great that they will learn it sooner or later. English is the predominant language of the society they live in, and these students know they have to learn it. They are surrounded by it wherever they go, including the bilingual classroom, as we have seen. Any English instruction they are given there facilitates the process, but it is not, in most cases, a necessity. The real problem for these students is that they are likely to acquire English but end up nevertheless without the resources that allow them to take part in the society they are growing up in. For many of them, the price paid for learning English is the mother tongue and their cultural identity. All too often, this leads to the loss of many of the cultural resources to which that language gives them access. What is lost in surrendering the native language may be the connectedness with primary group and community that gives an individual the personal stability needed for coping with adult responsibilities and opportunities. In the long run, however, the greatest loss may be to the society. The immigrant groups whose children are the LEP students in our schools today have enormous cultural resources and talent to contribute to their adopted society. These contributions can help to invigorate and enrich the society as they have in the past. The learning of English will give LEP students access to the opportunities offered by the society, but if the unique resources that their cultures have given them are lost in the process they will have less to give back to the society as adults.

REFERENCES

Adams, M., & Bruce, B. (1980). *Background knowledge and reading comprehension* (Reading Education Report No. 13). Champaign-Urbana, IL: University of Illinois, Center for the Study of Reading.

Alatis, J. E. (1979). The role of ESL in bilingual education. *NABE Journal 3*(3), 27–37.

Andersson, T., & Bover, M. (1970). *Bilingual schooling in the United States* (2 vols.) Washington, DC: U.S. Government Printing Office. (Southwest Educational Development Laboratory, Austin, TX).

Baker, K. A., & De Kanter, A. A. (1981, September). *Effectiveness of bilingual education: A review of the literature.* Washington, DC: U.S.

Department of Education, Office of Planning, Budget, and Evaluation.

Baral, D. P. (1979). Academic achievement of recent immigrants from Mexico. *NABE Journal, 3*(3), 1–13.

Barik, H. C., & Swain, M. (1974). English–French bilingual education in the early grades: The Elguin study. *Modern Language Journal. 58,* 392–403.

Barik, H. C., & Swain, M. (1975). Three year evaluation of a large scale early grade French immersion program: The Ottawa study. *Language Learning, 25,* 1–30.

Barik, H. C., & Swain, M. (1976). English–French bilingual education in the early grades: The Elgin study through grade four. *Modern Language Journal, 60,* 3–17.

Ben-Zeev, S. (1972). *The influence of bilingualism on cognitive development and cognitive strategy.* Unpublished Ph.D. Dissertation, University of Chicago.

Ben-Zeev, S. (1977a). Mechanisms by which childhood bilingualism affects understanding of language and cognitive structures. In P. Hornby (Ed.), *Bilingualism: Psychological, social, and educational implications.* New York: Academic Press.

Ben-Zeev, S. (1977b). The effect of Spanish–English bilingualism in children from less privileged neighborhoods on cognitive development and cognitive strategy. *Working Papers on Bilingualism, 14,* 83–122.

Bilingual Education Act (Title VII, ESEA), Public Law 93-380, 20 U.S.C., 800b, (1974, August 21).

Blanco, G. (1977). The education perspective. In *Bilingual education: Current perspectives* (Vol. 4, pp. 1–63). Arlington, VA: Center for Applied Linguistics.

Bransford, J. D., & Johnson, M. K. (1973). Considerations of some problems of comprehension. In W. G. Chase (Ed.), *Visual information processing.* New York: Academic Press.

Brown, G. H., Rosen, N. L., Hill, S. T., & Olivas, M. A. (1980). *The condition of education for Hispanic Americans.* National Center for Education Statistics. Washington, DC: U. S. Printing Office.

Campbell, R. N. (1984). The immersion approach of foreign language teaching. In *Studies on immersion education: A collection for United States educators.* (pp. 114–143). Sacramento: California State Department of Education.

Cárdenas, B., and Cárdenas, J. A. (1972). *The theory of incompatibilities: A conceptual framework for responding to the educational needs of Mexican–American Children.* San Antonio, TX: Intercultural Development Research Association.

Cárdenas, J. A. (1977). *An IDRA response with summary: The AIR evaluation of the impact of ESEA Title VII Spanish/English Bilingual Education Program.* San Antonio, TX: Intercultural Development Research Associates.

Carroll, J. B. (1979). Twenty-five years of research on foreign language aptitude. In K. C. Diller (Ed.), *Individual differences and universals in language learning aptitude.* Rowley, Ma: Newbury House.

Carter, T. P. (1970). *Mexican Americans in school: A history of educational neglect.* New York: College Entrance Examination Board.

Carter, T. P., & Segura, R. D. (1979). *Mexican Americans in school: A decade of change.* New York: College Entrance Examination Board.

Cathcart, R. (1983). *Situational variability in the second language production of kindergartners.* Unpublished Ph.D. Dissertation, University of California, Berkeley.

Cazden, C. (1972). *Child language and education.* New York: Holt, Rinehart & Winston.

Cazden, C. (1979) Curriculum language contexts for bilingual education. In *Language development in a bilingual setting* (pp. 129–138). Los Angeles: National Dissemination and Assessment Center.

Clarke, M. (1980). The short circuit hypothesis of ESL reading — Or when language competence interferes with reading performance. *Modern Language Journal. 64*(2), 203–209.

Cohen, A. D. (1975). *A sociolinguistic approach to bilingual education.* Rowley, MA.: Newbury House.

Cohen, A. D. (1982). Researching the linguistic outcomes of bilingual programs. *The bilingual review, 9*(2), 97–108.

Cohen, A. D., & Swain, M. (1976). Bilingual education: The "immersion" model in the North American context. *TESOL Quarterly, 10*(1), 45–54.

Cohen, D. K. (1970). Immigrants and the schools. *Review of Educational Research, 40*(1), 13–27.

Cohen, E. S., De Avila, E. A., & Intili, J. A. (1981). *Multicultural improvement of cognitive abilities.* Report to the California State Department of Education.

Cordasco, F. (1976). *Bilingual schooling in the United States: A sourcebook for educational personnel.* New York: McGraw-Hill.

Cross, T. G. (1978). Mothers' speech and its association with rate of linguistic development in young children. In N. Waterson and C. Snow (Eds.), *The development of communication.* Chichester, England: John Wiley.

Cummins, J. (1977). Immersion education in Ireland: A Critical review of Macnamara's findings (*Working Papers in Bilingualism* No. 13). Toronto: Ontario Institute for Studies in Education.

Cummins, J. (1978). Metalinguistic development of children in bilingual education programs: Data from Irish and Canadian Ukrainian-English programs. In M. Paradis (Ed.), *The fourth LACUS forum 1977.* Columbia, SC: Hornbeam Press.

Cummins, J. (1979). Linguistic interdependence and the educational development of bilingual children. *Review of Educational Research, 49*(2), 222–251.

Cummins, J. (1980)). The cross-lingual dimensions of language proficiency: Implications for bilingual education and the optimal age issue. *TESOL Quarterly, 14*(2), 175–187.

Cummins, J. (1981a). The role of primary language development in promoting educational success for language minority students. In *Schooling and language minority students: A theoretical framework.* Los Angeles: Evaluation and Dissemination and Assessment Center.

Cummins, J. (1981b). Four misconceptions about language proficiency in bilingual education. *NABE Journal, 5*(3), 31–45.

Cummins, J. (1981c). Age on arrival and immigrant second language learning in Canada: A reassessment. *Applied Linguistics, 2*(2), 132–149.

Cummins, J. (1982). *War of words: Bilingual education and the search for American identity* (Report to the Ford Foundation). Toronto: Ontario Institute for Studies in Education.

Cummins, J. (1983). *Heritage language education: A literature review.* Toronto: Ministry of Education,

Cummins, J., Swain, S., Nakajima, K., Handscombe, J., & Green, D. (1981, March). *Linguistic interdependence among Japanese immigrant students.* Paper presented at the Language Proficiency Assessment Symposium, Airlie, VA.

Cziko, G. A. (1978). Differences in first- and second-language reading: The use of syntactic, semantic and discourse constraints. *Canadian Modern Language Review, 34,* 473–489.

Cziko, G. A., Lambert, W. E., and Gutter, R. (1979–1980). French immersion programs and students' social attitudes: A multidimensional investigation. *NABE Journal, 4*(2), 19–33.

Danoff, M. N. (1978). *Evaluation of the impact of ESEA Title VII Spanish/English Bilingual Education Program: Overview of study and findings.* Palo Alto, CA: American Institute for Research.

Danoff, M. N., Coles, G. J., McLaughlin, D. H., and Reynolds, D. J. (1977). *Evaluation of the impact of ESEA Title VII Spanish/English Bilingual Education Program: Study design and interim findings* (Vol. 1) Palo Alto, CA: American Institute for Research.

Darcy, N. T. (1953). A review of the literature on the effects of bilingualism upon the measurement of intelligence. *Journal of Genetic Psychology, 103,* 21–57.

Darcy, N. T. (1963). Bilingualism and the measurement of intelligence: Review of a decade of research. *Journal of Genetic Psychology, 103,* 259–283.

De Avila, E. A. & Duncan, S. E. (1979). Bilingualism and the metaset. *NABE Journal, 3*(2), 1–20.

Doebler, L. K., & Mardis, L. J. (1980–1981). Effects of a bilingual education program for native American children. *NABE Journal, 5*(2), 23–28.

Donaldson, M. (1978). *Children's minds.* Glasgow: Collins.

Duncan, S. E. & De Avila, E. A. (1979). Bilingualism and cognition: Some recent findings. *NABE Journal, 4*(1), 15–50.

Durán, R. P. (1983). *Hispanics' education and background: Predictors of college achievement.* New York: College Entrance Examination Board.

Edelsky, C., & Hudelson, S. (1980). Acquiring a second language when you're not the underdog. In R. Scarcella and S. Krashen (Eds.), *Research in second language acquisition,* Rowley, MA: Newbury House.

Edwards, A. D., and Furlong, V. J. (1978). *The language of teaching.* London: Heinemann.

Ekstrand, L. H. (1982). Age and length of residence as variables related to the adjustment of migrant children with special reference to second language learning. In S. D. Krashen, R. C. Scarcella, and M. H. Long (Eds.), *Child and adult differences in second language acquisition.* Rowley, MA: Newbury House.

Elizondo de Weffer, R. D. C. (1972). *Effects of first language instruction in academic and psychological development of bilingual children.* Unpublished Ph.D. Dissertation, Illinois Institute of Technology, Chicago.

Engle, P. L. (1975). *The use of vernacular languages in education* (Bilingual Education Series No. 3). Arlington, VA: Center for Applied Linguistics.

Enright, D. S. (1982). *Student language use in traditional and open bilingual classrooms.* Unpublished Ph.D. Dissertation, Stanford University, Stanford, CA.

Epstein, N. (1977). *Language, ethnicity, and the schools: Policy alternatives for bilingual–bicultural education.* Washington, DC: George Washington University, Institute for Educational Leadership.

Erickson, F., Cazden, C., Carrasco, R., & Maldonado-Guzman, A. (1983, September). *Social and cultural organization in classrooms of bilingual children* (Final report to the National Institute of Education). Unpublished manuscript.

Ervin-Tripp, S. M. (1974). Is second language learning like the first? *TESOL Quarterly, 8*(2), 111–127.

Fathman, A. K. (1976). Variables affecting the successful learning of English as a second language. *TESOL Quarterley, 10*(4), 433–441.

Fillmore, C. J. (1982). Ideal readers and real readers. In D. Tannen (Ed.), *Georgetown University Round Table on Languages and Linguistics, 1981.* Washington, DC: Georgetown University Press.

Fillmore, C. J. & Kay, P. (1983). *Text semantic analysis of reading comprehension tests* (Final report to the National Institute of Education). Berkeley: University of California. (ERIC Document Reproduction Service No. 238-908)

Fishman, J. A. (1980a). Bilingualism and biculturalism as individal and as societal phenomena. *Journal of Multilingual and Multicultural Development, 1,* 3–16.

Fishman, J. A. (1980b). Bilingual education in the United States under ethnic community auspices. In J. E. Alatis (Ed.), *Georgetown University Roundtable on Languages and Linguistics 1980.* Washington, DC: Georgetown University Press.

Fishman, J. A., & Lovas, J. (1970). Bilingual education in a sociolinguistic perspective. *TESOL Quarterly, 4*(3), 215–222.

Gardner, R. C., & Lambert, W. E. (1972). *Attitudes and motivation in second language learning.* Rowley MA: Newbury House.

Geffert, H. N., Harper, R. J. II., Sarmiento, S., & Schember, D. M. (1975). *The current status of U. S. bilingual education legislation* (Papers in Applied Linguistics: Bilingual Education Series No. 4). Arlington, VA: Center for Applied Linguistics.

Genesee, F. (1978). A longitudinal evaluation of an early immersion school program. *Canadian Journal of Education, 3*(4) 31–50.

Genesee, F., Tucker, G. R., & Lambert, W. E. (1978). The development of ethnic identity and ethnic role taking skills in children from different school settings. *International Journal of Psychology, 13,* 39–57.

Glazer, N. (1980, May). Pluralism and ethnicity. Proceedings of "The New Bilingualism," a conference sponsored by the Center for the Study of the American Experience, Annenberg School of Communications, University of Southern California, Los Angeles.

Gonzales, E., & Lezama, J. (1976). The dual language model: A practical approach to bilingual education. In J. E. Alatis and K.

Twaddell (Eds.), *English as a second language in bilingual education: Selected TESOL Papers.* Washington, DC: Teachers of English to Speakers of Other Languages.

Goodman, K., Goodman, Y., & Flores, B. (1979). *Reading in the bilingual classroom: Literacy and biliteracy.* Rosslyn, VA: National Clearinghouse for Bilingual Education.

Graham, C. R. (1984, March). *Beyond integrative motivation: The development and influence of assimilative motivation.* Paper presented at TESOL Convention, Houston, TX.

Gray, T. (1977). *Response to AIR study.* Arlington. VA: Center for Applied Linguistics.

Hakuta, K., & Cancino, H. (1977). Trends in second language acquisition research. *Harvard Educational Review, 47*(3), 294–316.

Hakuta, K., & Díaz, R. M. (in press). The relationship between degree of bilingualism and cognitive ability: Some longitudinal data. In K. E. Nelson (Ed.), *Children's language* (Vol. 6). New York: Erlbaum.

Halcón, J. J. (1983). A structural profile of basic Title VII (Spanish–English) bilingual bicultural education programs. *NABE Journal, 7*(3), 55–73.

Hatch, E. M. (1983). *Psycholinguistics: A second language perspective.* Rowley, MA: Newbury House.

Hernández-Chavez, E. (1984). The inadequacy of English immersion education as an educational approach for language minority students in the United States. In *Studies on Immersion Education: A Collection for United States Educators* (pp. 144–183). Sacramento: California State Department of Education.

Hernández-Chavez, E., Llanes, J., Alvarez, R., & Arvizu, S. (1981). *The federal policy toward language and education: Pendulum or progress?* (Monograph No. 12). Sacramento, CA: Cross Cultural Resource Center.

Hymes, D. (1979). Ethnographic monitoring. *Language development in a bilingual setting.* Los Angeles: National Dissemination and Assessment Center.

Ianco-Worrall, A. D. (1972). Bilingualism and cognitive development. *Child Development, 43,* 1390–1400.

Irizarry, R. A. (n.d.) *Bilingual education: State and federal legislative mandates.* Los Angeles: National Dissemination and Assessment Center, Center for the Study of Evaluation.

Jacobson, R. (1981). Can and should the Laredo experiment be duplicated elsewhere? The applicability of the concurrent approach in other communities. In P. C. Gonzales (Ed.), *Proceedings of the Eighth Annual International Bilingual Bicultural Education Conference.* Rosslyn, VA: National Clearinghouse for Bilingual Education.

Johnson, D. M., & August, D. (1981). Social factors in second language acquisition: Peer tutoring intervention. In P. Gonzales (Ed.), *Proceedings of the Eighth Annual International Bilingual Bicultural Education Conference.* Rosslyn, VA: National Clearinghouse for Bilingual Education.

Juárez, J. R. (1976). *Subordinate and superordinate science process skills: An experiment in science instruction using the English and Spanish language with fifth grade children in bilingual schools.* Unpublished Ph. D. Dissertation, University of Washington, Seattle.

Kessler, C., & Quinn, M. E. (1980). Positive effects of bilingualism on science problem-solving abilities. In J. E. Alatis (Ed.), *Current issues in bilingual education. Georgetown University Round Table on Languages and Linguistics 1980.* Washington, DC: Georgetown University Press.

Kjolseth, R. (1971). Bilingual education programs in the United States: For assimilation or pluralism? In B. Spolsky (Ed.), *The language education of minority children.* Rowley, MA: Newbury House.

Krashen, S. (1980). The input hypothesis. In J. E. Alatis (Ed.), *Current issues in bilingual education. Georgetown University Round Table on Languages and Linguistics 1980.* Washington, DC: Georgetown University Press.

Krashen, S. (1981a). *Second language acquisition and second language learning.* London: Pergamon.

Krashen, S. (1981b) Bilingual education and second language acquisition theory. In *Schooling and language minority students: A Theoretical framework.* Los Angeles: Evaluation and Dissemination and Assessment Center.

Krashen, S., Long, M., & Scarcella, R. (1979). Age, rate and eventual attainment in second language acquisition. *TESOL Quarterly, 13*, 573–582.

Lambert, W. E. (1977). The effects of bilingualism on the individual: Cognitive and sociocultural consequences. In P. Hornby (Ed.), *Bilingualism: Psychological, social, and educational implications.* New York: Academic Press.

Lambert, W. E. (1978). Some cognitive and sociocultural consequences of being bilingual. In J. E. Alatis (Ed.), *International dimensions of bilingual education.* Washington, DC: Georgetown University Press.

Lambert, W. E. (1984). An overview of issues in immersion education. In *Studies on immersion education: A collection for United States educators* (pp. 8–30). Sacramento: California State Department of Education.

Lambert, W. E., & Tucker, G. R. (1972). *Bilingual education of children: The St. Lambert experiment.* Rowley MA: Newbury House.

Lapkin, S., & Cummins, J. (1984). Canadian French immersion education: Current administrative and instructional practices. In *Studies on immersion education. A collection for United States educators.* Sacramento: California State Department of Education. 58–86.

Legarreta, D. (1975). *An investigation of the use or non-use of formal English as Second Language (ESL) training on the acquisition of English by Spanish-speaking kindergarten children in traditional and bilingual classrooms.* Unpublished Ph.D. Dissertation, University of California, Berkeley.

Legarreta, D. (1977). Language choice in bilingual classrooms. *TESOL Quarterly, 11*(1), 9–16.

Legarreta, D. (1979). The effects of program models on language acquisition by Spanish speaking children. *TESOL Quarterly, 13*(4), 521–534.

Leibowitz, A. H. (1970). *Educational policy and political acceptance: The imposition of English as the language of instruction in American schools.* Washington, DC: Center for Applied Linguistics.

Leibowitz, A. H. (1982). *Federal recognition of the rights of minority language groups.* Rosslyn, VA: National Clearinghouse for Bilingual Education.

Lindfors, J. (1983). Exploring in and through language. In M. A. Clarke and J. Handscombe (Eds.), *On Tesol '82: Pacific perspectives on language learning and teaching.* Washington, DC: Teachers of English to Speakers of Other Languages.

Littlewood, W. (1981). *Communicative language teaching: An introduction.* Cambridge: Cambridge University Press.

Long, M. H. (1981). Input, interaction, and second language acquisition. In H. Winitz (Ed.), Native language and foreign language acquisition [Special issue]. *Annals of the New York Academy of Sciences, 379*, 259–278.

MacDonald, B., & Kushner, S. (Eds.). (1982). *Bread and dreams: A case study of bilingual schooling in the United States* (CARE Occasional Publications No. 12). Norwich, England: Center for Applied Research in Education.

Macias, R. F. (1976). Opinions of Chicano community parents on bilingual preschool education. In A. Verdoodt and R. Kjolseth (Eds.), *Language in society.* Louvain: Institute de Linguistique de Louvain.

Macias, R. F. (1982). Language diversity among United States Hispanics: Some background considerations for schooling and for non-biased assessment. In J. Spielberg (Ed.), *Proceedings: Invitational symposium on Hispanic American diversity.* East Lansing: Michigan State Department of Education.

Mackey, W. F. (1970). A typology of bilingual education. *Foreign Language Annals, 3*, 596–608

Mackey, W. F., & Beebe, V. N. (1977). *Bilingual schools for a bilingual community: Miami's adaptation to the Cuban refugees.* Rowley MA: Newbury House.

Macnamara, J. (1966) *Bilingualism in primary education.* Edinburgh: Edinburgh University Press.

Macnamara, J. (1967). The effects of instruction in a weaker language. *Journal of Social Issues, 23*(2), 121–135.

Macnamara, J. (1970). Bilingualism and thought. In J. E. Alatis (Ed.), *Report of the twenty-first annual round table meeting on linguistics*

and language studies. Washington, DC: Georgetown University Press.

Manuel, H. T. (1930). *The education of Mexican-American and Spanish-speaking children in Texas.* Austin: University of Texas, Fund for Research in the Social Sciences.

McClure, E., Saville-Troike, M., & Fritz, M. (1982). *Children's communicative tactics across language boundaries.* Paper presented at the meeting of the Chicago Linguistic Society.

McLaughlin, B. (1984). *Second language acquisition in childhood* (Vol. 1, Preschool Children Second Edition). Hillsdale, NJ: Erlbaum Associates.

McLaughlin, B. (1982). *Language learning in bilingual education.* (Paper prepared for the National Institute of Education). Unpublished manuscript, University of California, Berkeley.

Modiano, N. (1973). *Indian education in the Chiapas highlands.* New York: Holt, Rinehart & Winston.

Moll, L., & Díaz, E. (1982). *Ethnographic pedagogy: Promoting effective bilingual instruction.* Unpublished manuscript, Laboratory of Comparative Human Cognition, University of California, San Diego.

Moll, L., & Díaz, E. (1983). *Towards an interactional pedagogical psychology: A bilingual case study.* Unpublished manuscript, Laboratory of Comparative Human Cognition, University of California, San Diego.

National Center for Educational Statistics. (1978, July). *The education of language-minority persons in the United States, Spring 1976. NCES Bulletin,* 78-B-4.

Office of Civil Rights. (1975). *Task force findings specifying remedies available for eliminating past educational practices ruled unlawful under Lau v. Nichols.* Washington, DC: Department of Health, Education, and Welfare.

Office of Civil Rights. (1981, February 27). *Analysis of public comments: August 5, 1980 civil rights language minority notice of proposed rulemaking.* Washington, DC: U.S. Department of Education.

Olesini, J. (1971). *The effect of bilingual instruction on the achievement of elementary pupils.* Unpublished Ph.D. Dissertation, East Texas State University, Commerce.

Olson, D. R. (1977). From utterance to text: The bias of language in speech and writing. *Harvard Education Review, 47*(3), 257–281.

O'Malley, J. M. (1978). Review of the evaluation of the impact of ESEA Title VII Spanish/English bilingual education programs. *Bilingual Resources, 1*(2), 6–10.

O'Malley, J. M. (1982). *Children's English and services study: Educational needs assessment for language minority children with limited English proficiency.* Rosslyn, VA: National Clearinghouse for Bilingual Education.

Paulston, C. B. (1980). *Bilingual education: Theories and issues.* Rowley, MA: Newbury House.

Paulston, C. B. (1983). Second language acquisition in school settings. In W. J. Tikunoff (Ed.), *Compatibility of the SBIF features with other research on instruction for LEP students.* San Francisco: Far West Laboratory.

Paulston, C. B., & Bruder, M. N. (1976). *Teaching English as a second language: Techniques and procedures.* Cambridge, MA: Winthrop.

Peal, E., & Lambert, W. E. (1962). The relation of bilingualism to intelligence. *Psychological Monographs, 76*, 1–23.

Peng-Guthrie, G. (1982). *An ethnography of bilingual education in a Chinese community.* Unpublished Ph.D. Dissertation. University of Illinois, Urbana–Champaign.

President's Commission on Foreign Language and International Studies. (1979). *Strength through wisdom: A critique of U.S. capability.* Washington, DC: U.S. Government Printing Office.

Ramírez, A. G., & Politzer, R. L. (1978). Comprehension and production in English as a second language by elementary school children and adolescents. In E. Hatch (Ed.), *Second language acquisition.* Rowley, MA: Newbury House.

Rodríquez, R. (1982). *Hunger of memory. The education of Richard Rodriquez.* Boston: David R. Godine.

Rosier, P. (1977). *A comparative study of two approaches of introducing initial reading to Navajo children: The direct method and the native language method.* Unpublished Ph.D. Dissertation, Northern Arizona University, Flagstaff.

San Francisco Unified School District. (1975, January 21). *Response to the mandate of Lau v. Nichols by the San Francisco unified school district: An abstract of the master plan for bilingual–bicultural education*. Unpublished Manuscript.

Sánchez, G. I. (1932). Group differences in Spanish-speaking children: A critical review. *Journal of Applied Psychology, 16*(5), 549–558.

Saville, M., & Troike, R. C. (1971). *Handbook of bilingual education*. Washington, DC: Teachers of English to Speakers of other Languages.

Saville-Troike, M. (1983, August). *What really matters in second language learning for academic achievement?* Paper presented at the TESOL Summer Institute, Toronto.

Schultz, J. (1975, March). *Language use in bilingual classrooms* (Harvard University, 1975). Paper presented at the TESOL annual convention, Los Angeles.

Segalowitz, N. (1977). Psychological perspectives on bilingual education. In B. Spolsky and R. Cooper (Eds.), *Frontiers of bilingual education*. Rowley MA: Newbury House.

Segalowitz, N., & Gatbonton, N. (1977). Studies of the nonfluent bilingual. In P. Hornby (Ed.), *Bilingualism: Psychological, social, and educational implications*. New York: Academic Press.

Seliger, H. W. (1977). Does practice make perfect? A study of interactional patterns and L2 competence. *Language Learning, 27*(2), 263–278.

Selinker, L. (1972). Interlanguage. *International Review of Applied Linguistics, 10*, 209-231.

Selinker, L., Swain, M., & Dumas, G. (1975). The interlanguage hypotheses extended to children. *Language Learning, 25*(1), 139–152.

Skoczylas, R. V. (1972). *An evaluation of some cognitive and affective aspects of a Spanish–English bilingual education program*. Unpublished Ph. D. Dissertation, University of New Mexico, Albuquerque.

Skutnabb-Kangas, T., & Toukomaa, P. (1976). *Teaching migrant children's mother tongue and learning the language of the host country in the context of the socio-cultural situation of the migrant family*. Helsinki: Finnish National Commision for UNESCO.

Snow, C. E., & Ferguson, C. A. (Eds.), (1977). *Talking to children: Language input and acquisition*. Cambridge: Cambridge University Press.

Snow, C. E., & Hoefnagel-Höhle, M. (1978). Age differences in second language acquisition. In E. Hatch (Ed.), *Second language acquisition*. Rowley, MA: Newbury House.

Snow, C. E., & Hoefnagel-Höhle, M. (1982). The critical period for language acquisition: Evidence from second language learning. In S. D. Krashen, R. C. Scarcella, & M. H. Long, *Child adult differences in second language acquisition*. Rowley, MA: Newbury House.

Spolsky, B. (1970). TESOL. In D. Lange (Ed.), *The Britannica review of foreign language education* (Vol. 2). Chicago: Encyclopaedia Brittanica.

Spolsky, B. (1971). The limits of language education. In B. Spolsky (Ed.), *The language education of minority children*. Rowley, MA: Newbury House.

Steinberg, L., Blinde, P. L., & Chan, K. S. (1982). *Dropping out among language minority youth: A review of the literature* (NCBR Working Paper No. 81-3W). Los Alamitos, CA: National Center for Bilingual Research.

Strong, M. A. (1982). *Social styles and second language acquisition among kindergartners*. Unpublished Ph.D. Dissertation, University of California, Berkeley.

Swain, M. (1983, October). *Communicative competence: Some roles of comprehensible input and comprehensible output in its development*. Paper presented at the 10th University of Michigan Conference on Applied Linguistics, Ann Arbor, MI. [To appear in S. Gass and C. Madden (Eds.), *Input in Second Language Acquisition*. Rowley, MA: Newbury House].

Swain, M. (1984). A review of immersion education in Canada: Research and evaluation studies. *Studies on Immmersion Education: A Collection for United States Educators*. Sacramento: California State Department of Education.

Swain, M., & Burnaby, B. (1976). Personality characteristics and second language learning in young children: A pilot study. *Working Papers in Bilingualism*. No. 11, 115–128.

Swain, M. & Lapkin, S. (1982). *Evaluating bilingual education: A Canadian case study*. Clevedon/Avon, England: Multilingual Matters.

Teitelbaum, H., & Hiller, R. J. (1977). The legal perspective. In *Bilingual education: Current perspectives* (Vol. 3). Arlington, VA: Center for Applied Linguistics.

Terrell, T. (1981). The natural approach in bilingual education. In California State Department of Education, *Schooling and language minority students: A theoretical framework*. Los Angeles: Evaluation and Dissemination and Assessment Center.

TESOL. (1976). *Position paper on the role of English as a second language in bilingual education*. Washington, DC: Teachers of English to Speakers of Other Languages.

Thonis, E. (1981). Reading instruction for language minority students. In *Schooling and language minority students: A theoretical framework*. Los Angeles; Evaluation and Dissemination and Assessment Center.

Tierney, R. J., Lazansky, J., Raphael, T., & Cohen, P. (in press). Author's intentions and reader's interpretation. In R. J. Tierney, P. Anders, & J. N. Mitchell (Eds.), *Understanding readers' understandings*. Hillsdale, NJ: Erlbaum.

Tikunoff, W. J. (1983). *An emerging description of successful bilingual instruction: An executive summary of Part 1 of the SBIF descriptive study*. San Francisco: Far West Laboratory.

Toukomaa, P., & Skutnabb-Kangas, T. (1977). *The intensive teaching of the mother tongue in migrant children of pre-school age and children in the lower level of comprehensive school*. Helsinki: Finnish National Commission For UNESCO.

Treviño, B. A. G. (1968). *An analysis of the effectiveness of a bilingual program in the teaching of mathematics in the primary grades*. Unpublished Ph.D. Dissertation, University of Texas, Austin.

Troike, R. C. (1978). *Research evidence for the effectiveness of bilingual education*. Rosslyn, VA: National Clearinghouse for Bilingual Education.

Troike, R. C., & Pérez, E. (1978). At the crossroads. In *Bilingual education: Current perspectives* (Vol. 5, pp. 63–81). Arlington, VA: Center for Applied Linguistics.

Trueba, H., & Wright, P. G. (1980–1981). On ethnographic studies of multicultural education. *NABE Journal, 5*(2), 29–56.

Tucker, G. R., Sibayan, B. P., & Otanes, F. T. (1970). An alternate days approach to bilingual education. In James E. Alatis (Ed.), *Report of the twenty-first annual round table meeting on linguistics and language study* (No. 23). Washington, DC: Georgetown, University Press.

Ulibarrí, D. M., Spencer, M. L., & Rivas, G. A. (1981). Language proficiency and academic achievement: A study of language proficiency tests and their relationship to school ratings as predictors of academic achievement. *NABE Journal, 5*(3), 47–80.

UNESCO. (1953). *The use of vernacular languages in education* (Monographs on Fundamental Education No. 8). Paris: UNESCO.

Urzua, C. (1981). *Talking purposefully*. Silver Springs, MD: Institute of Modern Language.

U.S. Commission on Civil Rights. (1975). *A better chance to learn: Bilingual bicultural education* (Clearinghouse Publication No. 51). Washington, DC: U.S. Government Printing Office, Number 629-984/377.

U.S. Supreme Court. (1974). Lau v. Nichols, 414 U.S. 563.

Valadez, C. M. (1984). *Informe final evaluación formativa y sumativa: Proyecto educación bilingüe, Paraguay*. Asunción: Ministry of Education and Culture (Agency for International Development).

Valdés-Fallis, G. (1978). Code switching and the classroom teacher. *Language and education: Theory and practice* (Vol. 4). Arlington, VA: Center for Applied Linguistics.

Von Maltitz, F. W. (1975). *Living and learning in two languages*. New York: McGraw-Hill.

Vygotsky, L. S. (1978). *Mind in society*. Cambridge, MA: Harvard University Press.

Waggoner, D. (1981). Educational attainment of language minorities in the United States. *NABE Journal, 6*, 41–53.

Wong Fillmore, L. (1976). *The second time around: Cognitive and social strategies in second language acquisition.* Unpublished Ph.D. Dissertation, Stanford University, Stanford, CA.

Wong Fillmore, L. (1979). Individual differences in second language acquisition. In C. J. Fillmore, W. S. Y. Wang, and D. K. Kempler (Eds.), *Individual differences in language ability and language behavior.* New York: Academic Press.

Wong Fillmore, L. (1982). Instructional language as linguistic input: Second language learning in classrooms. In L. C. Wilkinson (Ed.), *Communicating in the classroom.* New York: Academic Press.

Wong Fillmore, L. (1983). The language learner as an individual. In M. Clarke and J. Handscombe (Eds.), *On TESOL '82: Pacific perspectives on language learning and teaching.* Washington, DC: Teachers of English to Speakers of Other Languages.

Wong Fillmore, L., Ammon, P., Ammon, M. S., DeLucchi, K., Jensen, J., McLaughlin, B., & Strong, M. (1983). *Learning language through bilingual instruction: Second Year report* (Submitted to the National Institute of Education). Berkeley: University of California.

Yates, J. R., & Ortiz, A. A. (1983). Baker-deKanter Review: Inappropriate conclusions on the efficacy of bilingual education. *NABE Journal,* 7(3), 75–84.

24.

Special Educational Research on Mildly Handicapped Learners

Donald L. MacMillan
University of California—Riverside

Barbara K. Keogh
University of California—Los Angeles

Reginald L. Jones
University of California—Berkeley

Scope and Rationale

The focus of this review is on special educational research on mildly handicapped learners. By restricting coverage to this subset of children who comprise only a portion of those served in special education programs we do not mean to convey the impression that research conducted on other handicapped children (i.e., severely and/or multiply handicapped children with sensory handicaps, children with physical handicaps) is any less important or rigorous. Rather, the focus reflects both the interests of the authors and a belief that the mildly handicapped, and the research conducted on them, is of great interest and importance to the intended audience of this volume.

Our use of the term "mildly handicapped" refers to those children commonly categorized as educable mentally retarded (EMR), learning disabled (LD), behavior disordered (BD), mildly emotionally disturbed (ED), or children with minimal brain dysfunction (MBD). Whether these special educational categories constitute distinctly separate populations or are subsets of one population is a topic of concern to researchers in the field of special education (Keogh, 1982c). Even specifying population parameters for EMR or LD children has proven to

be a difficult task (MacMillan, Meyers, & Morrison, 1980). The problem is not limited to research. Service delivery programs have reflected the overlap in child characteristics. To illustrate, in California the learning handicapped (LH) category (*California Master Plan for Special Education*, 1974) combines under a single rubric children who would formerly have been differentiated as EMR, LD, or BD. Children who fit this LH category are the focus of our review—inefficient school learners whose deviations in school achievement, and possibly social adjustment, are so marked as to necessitate specialized intervention. At the same time, these are usually ablebodied, normal-appearing children whose learning problems are not compounded by physical stigmata or physical disabilities.

Our reasons for restricting this review to the children described above are, in part, due to the current emphasis on *least restriction* and *mainstreaming*. Placement of handicapped children in the least restrictive environment is a basic tenet of PL 94-142, the Education for All Handicapped Children Act of 1975, and has resulted in many handicapped children's being placed in regular grades—or in the mainstream. By far the greatest number of mainstreamed children are the mildly handicapped. For the more patently disabled, more protective

---

The reviewers for this chapter were Milton Budoff (Research Institute for Educational Problems) and Samuel Guskin (Indiana University).

placements (e.g., special classes, special schools) constitute the least restrictive placement. Hence, general educators are most likely to encounter mildly handicapped children in the name of mainstreaming.

Another reason for focusing on the mildly handicapped derives from the nature of the educational adaptations required to meet their special needs. Other chapters in this volume contain research on "traditional" content and instructional strategies encountered in general education. In mandating the education of severely handicapped individuals PL 94-142 has resulted in a revolution in the meaning of the word "education"; the term now includes the teaching of toileting, grooming, feeding, and other self-help skills. In other words, adaptations for severely handicapped children have included modifications of both *what* is taught and *how* it is taught. In contrast, the curriculum for mildly handicapped children corresponds closely to traditional general education in terms of *what* is taught; modifications occur primarily in *how* it is taught. Note that content areas such as reading, arithmetic, and social studies are included routinely as part of the curriculum for mildly handicapped children.

Zigler's position (1967, 1977) regarding a two-group approach to mental retardation is germane to the present discussion. For years Zigler has advanced the position that the mildly retarded, whom he refers to as the *familial* mentally retarded, represent the lower end of the normal distribution; as such, they are *normal* in the sense that differences between them and higher-IQ children are differences of *degree*, not *kind*. Conversely, the more severely retarded (e.g., below approximately IQ = 50) exhibit intellectual limitations that result from chromosomal anomalies or brain damage. Hence, differences in intellectual performance of this group do not reflect the effects of polygenic inheritance, but rather the effects of other influences. In this view of retardation mildly handicapped children provide a population for whom traditional "child" variables, "instructional" variables, and aptitude-treatment interactions are worthy of study in the same way that they are studied in nonhandicapped school-age subjects. A detailed exchange on the *developmental* versus *difference* or *defect* approaches to research on mentally retarded subjects may be found in Ellis (1969), Milgram (1969), Schonebaum and Zinober (1977), and Zigler (1969, 1973). More recent reviews of Piagetian research with retarded subjects provide further support for the developmental position (see Weisz & Zigler, 1979; Woodward, 1979). These authors conclude that mildly retarded children follow a "similar sequence" of Piaget's stages of cognitive development, passing through the stages in the same order, albeit at a slower pace. However, performances by subjects with brain wave abnormalities fail to support the similar-sequence hypothesis, a further argument in support of Zigler's two-group hypothesis.

Finally, mildly handicapped children, especially those categorized as EMR or LD, comprise the largest group of pupils served through special education. According to a 1980 report from the Government Accounting Office (GAO), on a national level EMRs make up 19% of pupils served in special education programs; LDs comprise 36%. Thus, because of relatively high incidence, the discontinuities in development exhibited by severely debilitated children, the greater probability of mildly handicapped children's being encountered by general educators and researchers studying nonhandicapped children, and the similarities in curricular content and instructional strategies for nonhandicapped and mildly handicapped pupils, we conclude that our focus on the mildly handicapped will be fruitful for the intended audience of this volume.

This review considers substantive research findings on mildly handicapped learners; however, we first consider several methodological issues that are important for the reader to understand in order to interpret the substantive findings appropriately. Therefore, the next few sections (i.e., recent history, issues concerning sampling, issues concerning instrumentation and documentation of program effects) provide the background for the reader concerning methodological problems in conducting research on mildly handicapped learners. After discussing these issues, the chapter contains review and discussions of substantive findings of research on learning, cognition, and noncognitive variables with mildly handicapped learners. The final two sections in the chapter contain summaries of research in two rather new directions in special education—mainstreaming and early intervention. Let us turn to consider the recent history of forces that have shaped special education, which has in turn dictated what children qualify for special education services as mildly handicapped learners.

Recent History

Within the last 10 to 15 years the complexion of special education has changed drastically. These changes have been brought about by a number of forces, including court cases, federal and state legislation, and debate within the academic and professional community. As in any enterprise such as education, one component is affected by changes in another. So it is with the general field of education, where changes in special education have exerted a definite effect on many other educational enterprises. Since publication of the *Second Handbook of Research on Teaching* (Travers, 1973), the literature on behavioral characteristics of handicapped learners has expanded rapidly and the establishment of the "rights" of handicapped persons has dramatically and rapidly changed the delivery of educational as well as other treatment services.

A major impetus for change came in the form of litigation intended to protect handicapped children from denial of constitutional rights and to promote access to educational opportunities previously denied them. Two types of lawsuits had a dramatic impact on the educational system. The first established the constitutional right to a free and appropriate public education for severely debilitated children, heretofore denied admission to public schooling because of the severity of their handicaps. The landmark case of this type was the *Pennsylvania Association for Retarded Children v. the Commonwealth of Pennsylvania* (1972) (referred to commonly as P.A.R.C.). P.A.R.C. established that every child, regardless of the severity of his or her handicap, is constitutionally guaranteed the right to a free and appropriate public education. Burt (1975, p. 294) observed that the legal theory behind the P.A.R.C. decision was that excluding retarded children from public education was "unconstitutional invidious discrimination" and that the retarded, through exclusion, were denied equal access to educational opportunity.

Important to note in P.A.R.C. is that parents acknowledged their child's handicap, but argued *for admission* to appropriate educational services — that is, special educational services. It is important to note, too, that the P.A.R.C. decision, along with subsequent legislation, dramatically changed the meaning of the word "education." Meyers, MacMillan, and Zetlin (1978) observed that the word "education" had traditionally implied an "academic" program. However, the inclusion of severely and multiply impaired children extended the definition of education to include basic self-help skills.

A second type of litigation affecting the educational system sought relief for academically low-achieving minority children often included in special education programs designed for the mildly mentally retarded. Notable cases include *Diana v. State Board of Education* (1970), *Larry P. v. Riles* (1972), and *People in Action on Special Education v. Hannon* (1980) (generally referred to as P.A.S.E.). These class action suits were brought on behalf of minority children placed in classes for the educable mentally retarded. In *Diana* the plaintiffs were Hispanic children; in *Larry P.* and *P.A.S.E.* the plaintiffs were black. Plaintiffs alleged that special education placement and programing violated the child's constitutionally guaranteed rights. The EMR programs were alleged to be inferior, and placement thereby was a denial of equal educational opportunity. It was also alleged that placement involved biased tests and a lack of parental involvement, both constituting a denial of due process. The trials revolved around the issue of bias inherent in individual tests of intelligence and their use in placement decisions for children from sociolinguistically different backgrounds. *Diana* and *Larry P.* decisions favored the plaintiffs, while the court ruled in favor of the defendants in P.A.S.E.

Plaintiffs in these cases were concerned with placement procedures and the appropriateness of the educational program provided for children identified by these means. Unlike the parents in P.A.R.C., who sought to get special education for their severely retarded children, the parents in these latter cases wanted "inappropriately identified EMR" children decertified as retarded, and sought procedural safeguards that would prevent the future inappropriate labeling of similar children as retarded. In other words, they wanted children *out* of special education. The issue of how to provide for the low achievement manifested by the children in question went unresolved except to say it should not be provided in the context of an EMR program.

Litigation such as that described above has had far-reaching effects on education. *Diana* and *P.A.R.C.* were settled by stipulation, so they do not constitute legal precedents. *Larry P.* and *P.A.S.E.*, while adjudicated, were contradictory in the findings rendered by the two judges. Nevertheless, the result, for the very publicity, has been a change in educational policy and a pronounced influence on legislators in the drafting of federal and state legislation.

Public Law 94-142 represents the culmination of the litigation, incorporating many of the rights and safeguards that emanated in a series of court cases. It is a most ambitious and in many ways a forward-looking piece of legislation. MacMillan (1982, pp. 3–4) summarized the basic rights and protections provided by PL 94-142 as follows:

1. *The right to due process.* Procedural safeguards were mandated to assure due process in classification and placement in the schools. Parents are guaranteed access to school records and the right to impartial hearings regarding their child's placement. Parents are also guaranteed the opportunity for independent evaluations of their child.
2. *Protection against discriminatory testing during assessment.* This safeguard ensures that placement will not be made on the basis of a single psychometric instrument, and requires that tests be administered in the child's native language.
3. *Placement in the least restrictive educational setting.* This provision states that handicapped children should be educated in environments resembling, as closely as possible, those in which nonhandicapped children are educated. It is intended to protect the child from the presumed detrimental effects of segregation.
4. *Individualized education programs.* Educators must prepare a written description of each child's program to ensure accountability. These programs must specify (1) the program's objectives, (2) the services to be provided, (3) the program's schedule, and (4) the criteria used to determine the program's effectiveness.

When passed, this bill was hailed by most as the "Bill of Rights for the Handicapped." However, living with it and implementing these worthwhile, if ill-defined, concepts has been difficult. Zigler and Muenchow (1979) described the IEP (individualized education program), a fundamental operational component of the law, as the "impossible education program." MacMillan and Meyers (1980) note that a test that does not discriminate (i.e., valid discrimination between those of varying ability) is a poor test, yet the law calls for "nondiscriminatory testing" without establishing criteria by which to establish its nondiscriminatory function. Nevertheless, the law as it has been implemented has resulted in marked changes in special education.

Special Education: 1965 versus 1982

When one considers the nature of special education circa 1965, several characteristics stand out. Most notable was that special education operated apart from general education. Children with handicaps were referred by teachers in general education, evaluated and placed into a special education program; general education then ceased to have any responsibility or involvement with the handicapped child. The building principal may have had "authority for" a special class located in his or her building, but in reality the special class teacher was administratively responsible to an administrator at the district level.

Handicapped children were previously categorized as belonging to one of several distinct categories, for example, educable mentally retarded (EMR), emotionally disturbed (ED), trainable mentally retarded (TMR), learning disabled (LD), behavior disordered (BD), or as blind, deaf, or physically handicapped. Programs were designed for each category, usually organized on an age/grade basis. By program we mean there were program objectives, a sequence of instructional strategies designed to promote the objectives, and instructional strategies designed to accommodate the particular handicap exhibited by children in a particular program. One underlying assumption was that handicapped children could be served best in a protective environment in which programs were modified in accordance with the handicapping conditions. Exceptions were speech-handicapped children and some of the early pull-out programs for LD children.

A second assumption had to do with the similarity of children within program categories, that is, the assumption of within-category homogeneity. Curriculum content and instructional techniques were developed on a belief that all handicapped children in a given category needed the same educational program. The assumption that children with similar handicapping conditions had similar educational needs was derived in part from the historical recognition that children with sensory handicaps (e.g., blind or deaf) required modification of instructional modes and materials in order to make information accessible. Indeed, programs for blind and deaf pupils were the first special education categories, and clearly provided needed educational services to children with specific limitations. However, the assumption of instructional homogeneity was less tenable when extended to other categories of exceptionality, especially to the mildly handicapped children classified as EMR, LD, BD, and ED, and when tested against evidence of individual differences within categories. Recognition of within-category heterogeneity, that is, of individual differences among children within similar handicapping conditions, was made explicit in PL 94–142 through the mandated individual educational program concept already described.

Attempts to comply with provisions of PL 94–142, particularly as they apply to the mildly handicapped learner, have drastically changed the ways these children are provided special educational services. Concepts like "least restriction" and "mainstreaming" have reduced the number of self-contained special classes for EMR, LD, and BD children in favor of placement in regular grades with needed services provided in the regular class or on short-term pullout to a resource room. Categorical instructional programs have been replaced by individualized education programs (IEPs), which specify objectives, services, and evaluative criteria for each child. Hence, categorical programs per se are nonexistent and no longer describe the education of a given retarded or LD child. Similarly, objectives (short- and long-term) are established individually, thus rendering criterion-referenced evaluations of "programs" difficult, if not impossible. Services needed to achieve objectives vary from child to child within category, thereby making it difficult to compare various programs for handicapped learners. There is no longer instructional homogeneity in the categorically based programs.

There has also been a drastic change in the characteristics of children labeled and served as EMR between 1965 and the present, with a corresponding change in the LD and BD population parameters. The most widely accepted definition of mental retardation is that of the American Association on Mental Deficiency (AAMD) (Grossman, 1973, 1977; Heber, 1961). Most states use a definition that corresponds to the prevalent AAMD definition, thus specifying an approximate IQ

cutoff. In the 1961 version (Heber, 1961) the upper limit of IQ for defining mental retardation was − 1 SD (or, roughly IQ 85); however, in the Grossman versions (1973, 1977) the upper limit was dropped to − 2 SDs (or, roughly IQ 70). The consequences of this change are substantial. First, compared to the later definitions EMR programs circa 1965 included far more capable children. Second, minority children constituted a disproportionately high percentage of EMR enrollments. Changes in screening, and possible trepidation in identifying minority children as retarded has reduced the disproportion somewhat, although not as dramatically as anticipated, as shown in Table 24.1. MacMillan and Borthwick (1980) concluded that changes mandated by court cases and recent legislation have resulted in an EMR population far more debilitated than that found in 1965, and one which essentially could not be integrated into regular grades. Hence, the typical EMR of 1965 was very different (i.e. more able) than the current EMR.

A corollary to change in the EMR population is change in LD, BD, and possibly ED populations. The effect is most obvious in the changes in EMR–LD ratio. The definition of LD has always included an "exclusion" provision—that is, the academic difficulties must not be due to blindness, mental retardation, and so forth. As a result, the definition of LD is automatically changed by a change in definition of mental retardation. In 1965 the lower IQ limit for LD was approximately 86, since the upper limit for mental retardation was 85. However, with the adoption of a more restrictive definition of mental retardation (Grossman, 1973) the IQ range considered "normal" expanded down to IQ 71. The extent to which children in the IQ range 70–85 have been certified as LD since 1973 is undocumented to our knowledge; however, psychometrically these children are candidates for LD certification. As discussed in a subsequent section of the review, several studies document the lowered IQ range found in programs serving LD children. Further, examination of incidence figures for EMR and LD children served suggests a decrease in number of EMR pupils accompanied by an increase in number of LD pupils (Keogh, Becker, Kukic, & Kukic, 1974).

Current sentiment clearly favors serving handicapped children in regular classes to the maximum extent possible,

Table 24.1. Proportion of Children of Relevant Ethnic Groups in EMR Classes Before and After Test Moratorium

Year	Black	Hispanic	Other White	Total % Minority
Before moratorium				
1973–1974	24.56	22.74	50.86	49.14
1974–1975	22.61	22.20	53.35	56.65
After moratorium				
1975–1976	24.75	21.93	50.89	49.09
1976–1977	25.43	22.44	49.54	50.46
1977–1978	23.22	22.64	51.66	48.34

Note: From "Psychological Evidence in *Larry P. V. Wilson Riles*: An Evaluation by a Witness for the Defense" by N. M. Lambert, 1981, *American Psychologist, 36,* p. 941. Copyright 1981 by the American Psychological Association. Reprinted by permission.

consistent with the principle of "least restriction." In some states, such as California, new categories have been forged which combine some of the more specific categories used previously, and currently used by the Office of Special Education. For example, in the 1960s, California used the category educationally handicapped (EH), which subsumed children who in other states would be classified as LD, BD, or children with minimal brain dysfunction. More recently, however, the EH category was combined with EMR to form a new, and broader, category—learning handicapped (LH) (*California Master Plan for Special Education*, 1974).

In states where these broader, more inclusive, categories have emerged, the problem for the researcher in sampling a population with known parameters is confounded. In addition, changes in definition of particular handicaps raise questions about the validity of previous research and evaluation findings when applied to the current group of children being served under each handicap rubric (MacMillan et al., 1980). The implication of these changes for research in special education deserves brief discussion.

Issues Concerning Sampling

Changes in the nature of special education from 1965 to the present have implications for both the person conducting research and evaluation and for the consumer of research and evaluation. One obvious consequence derives from the changes that have occurred in the characteristics of children served as LD, EMR, BD, and ED. Because of these definitional changes the body of research literature is of unknown validity for groups of children currently classified within these categories. Hence, consumers of previous research results—including those describing behavioral characteristics of these populations—must question the utility of such descriptions when making decisions about children presently designated as holding category membership. Furthermore, evidence suggesting that a given approach is more beneficial than some other approach requires confirmation of subject similarities. That is, does the program benefit children who are more or less able than those for whom the original benefits were demonstrated? In short, changes in population parameters of various mildly handicapped categories renders the results of research valid for only the period of time for which the definitional parameters for a category remain unchanged.

The changes in special education also have implications for efforts to compare educational programs for handicapped children by means of between-group designs. Such designs require that certain assumptions be met—namely, that there be greater homogeneity within a group or treatment than between groups or treatments being compared (see Baumeister, 1967). Current special education practices, such as the provision that an IEP be provided for each child, makes it impossible to meet this assumption. Conceivably, every EMR or LD child in a given class could have a different program, thus making it impossible to describe the "treatment" provided. Similarly, variations in the processes for identifying children make comparative studies on learning or other behaviors risky. MacMillan et al. (1980) described variations in system identification as occurring as a result of:

1. teacher referral behavior;
2. screening of referrals;
3. placement or nonplacement of eligible children;
4. ethnicity of the child being considered.

The point is that schools are in the business of supplying services—not in delineating clean research populations for behavioral scientists. As a result, researchers must be cautious in sampling from system-identified populations whose parameters are ill defined.

Subject variability is a particularly troubling issue when investigators attempt to make inferences about the nature of learning disabilities or mental retardation based on study of system-identified subjects. System identification of exceptional children may lead to overidentification of pupils with particular constellations of characteristics, while at the same time underidentifying other pupils with similar but not identical characteristics. The problem is well illustrated by consideration of referral rates for boys and girls for special education placement within school districts. For children in EMR programs sex ratios in special programs are approximately 1.2 to 1; for LD programs placement rates are often 3 or 4 to 1, sometimes higher; in both examples boys outnumber girls. The reasons for these differential rates are uncertain, but likely involve influences of professionals' perceptions as well as of actual child characteristics. In a recent study of referral patterns using simulation techniques, Reid (1982) found that when presented with identical detailed information, classroom teachers were more apt to refer boys than girls, although pupil behavior, achievement, and ability were similar for children of each sex. The research investigator who attempts to understand the nature of learning disabilities or mild retardation must consider whether the research data collected on system-identified subjects explicates something about the exceptional conditions themselves or something about the systems that identify them.

The foregoing suggests difficulty in conducting research on mildly handicapped populations using traditional research designs. Yet an examination of the research on behavioral characteristics and educational treatments reveals considerable insensitivity to such changes on the part of the research community. LD or EMR "samples" are compared to nonhandicapped samples on any number of variables, despite the fact that the two samples may overlap considerably on characteristics highly related to the characteristic serving as the dependent variable.

Sample Heterogeneity

Problems of sample heterogeneity are particularly evident in research on learning disabilities. Since its identification as a formal special education category approximately 20 years ago, the growth of intervention programs and research efforts has been dramatic. Study of learning disabilities is viewed as a legitimate research topic for investigators from a variety of professional and disciplinary backgrounds, and investigators have diverse perspectives. While diversity has added to the clinical understanding of the problems of learning disabled children, it has also added considerably to the confusion and inconsistencies about criteria for subject selection, and has limited the generalizability of results of studies and programs.

Differences in professional perspectives have been magnified by ongoing disagreements about definition. The 1967 National Advisory Committee on Handicapped Children, for example, focused on disabilities involving "understanding or in using spoken or written language" (1968). This definition, in addition to its focus on language-related problems, allowed for several etiologies but excluded problems due to mental retardation, sensory or motor handicaps, emotional disturbances, or environmental conditions. The exclusionary components have been maintained in most subsequent definitions, but the specific language disability focus has been broadened to include children with a variety of learning problems. As an example, the 1981 National Joint Committee for Learning Disabilities proposed (see Hammill, Leigh, McNutt, & Larsen, 1981) as follows:

> Learning disabilities is a generic term that refers to a heterogeneous group of disorders manifested by significant difficulties in the acquisition and use of listening, speaking, reading, writing, reasoning or mathematics abilities. These disorders are intrinsic to the individual and presumed to be due to central nervous system dysfunction. Even though a learning disability may occur concomitantly with other handicapping conditions (e.g., sensory impairment, mental retardation, social and emotional disturbance) or environmental influences (e.g., cultural differences, insufficient/inappropriate instruction, psychiatric factors), it is not the direct result of these conditions or influences. (p. 336)

This definition allows for the presence of learning disabilities along with other handicapping conditions. It may be useful as a framework for providing services to individuals with a broad band of problems. The problem, of course, is that it will probably increase, not reduce sample heterogeneity.

In this regard it may be noted that because incidence figures are in part a function of definition, the estimates of numbers of individuals with learning disabilities differ dramatically. In the original regulations for PL 94-142 the number of fundable pupils categorized as learning disabled was 1/6 of the 12% total number of handicapped children. Yet, according to the 1981 GAO report, it has been estimated that as many as 26% of school-age children are learning disabled, a figure considerably higher than the 3% used by SRI-I in its studies of PL 94-142. Both research and programs obviously have been influenced by the operational criteria used in subject selection.

As mentioned earlier, it is important to note, too, that selection criteria used for identification as learning disabled also influence identification of subjects as educable mentally retarded, behaviorally disordered, or emotionally disturbed. There is likely overlap of individuals categorized in these groupings. Given the broad array of problems or symptoms that come under the LD rubric, it is not surprising that many children identified as LD may also evidence symptoms of behavior problems or adjustment difficulties, or be of borderline intellectual ability. Describing characteristics of over 1900 children formally identified as LD and receiving educational services through the Child Service Demonstration Centers (CSDC), Norman and Zigmond (1980) found that over half of the CSDCs included children with IQs below 69. Further, only 47% of the CSDC-served pupils met the federal ability-achievement discrepancy formula. These findings were corroborated by Mann, Davis, Boyer, Metz, and Wolford (1983) in a recent review of CSDC compliance with the federal definition of learning disabilities. Clearly subject heterogeneity is a continuing and pervasive problem for LD researchers, limiting the sample population generalizations and restricting inferences about LD and other special education categories.

Addressing the sample problem directly, Keogh (1982c) has noted that two kinds of sample heterogeneity are particularly important in LD research. The first pinpoints subject differences across studies; the second relates to subject differences within a given study. As has already been noted, many disciplines claim LD as a legitimate research area, and many different operational criteria and methods are used to select subjects. Investigators with a medical perspective may diagnose as learning disabled those children who evidence particular neurological signs; investigators with an educational or psychological bent may include in study samples all children with achievement-ability discrepancies, or all children evidencing particular patterns of deficits in reading or arithmetic. Given the array of subjects included in different studies or programs, it is not surprising that particular intervention or experimental techniques often lead to different results.

The problem is compounded further when the heterogeneity of sample characteristics within studies is considered. The most usual sampling parameters in LD research, for example, IQ and achievement in selected school subjects, are loosely defined. The mean IQ for an LD sample might be "normal" but individual scores often range between 80 and 120; within the sample, level of achievement in school subjects might vary from 1–4 years behind chronological age expectancy. Thus, in any group of LD subjects we are likely to find considerable range of ability and achievement, to say nothing of variance on other child characteristics. If the program or the particular experimental manipulation being tested in a given study is influenced by ability, a possible subject-procedure confound is likely. The assumption of sample homogeneity, fundamental to most experimental paradigms, is particularly suspect in LD research.

Responses to problems of sample heterogeneity have been proposed by a number of investigators in this research area. Three different approaches are illustrative. Although the approaches differ in specific techniques, they have in common the goal of reducing subject heterogeneity by identifying reliable and conceptually reasonable subgroups within the broad LD category.

EMPIRICALLY DEFINED SUBGROUPS

As part of the UCLA Marker Variable Project, Keogh and her colleagues (Keogh, Major, Reid, Gandara, & Omori, 1978; Keogh, Major, Reid, Omori, & Gandara, 1980; Keogh, Major-Kingsley, Omori-Gordon, & Reid, 1982) developed a set of sample descriptors or "markers" useful in characterizing subjects and samples in LD research. In this project markers were defined as "descriptive 'bench marks' or common reference points" (Keogh et al., 1980) which could be used to determine sample comparability across studies or programs, and which would allow alignment of findings from different studies. In the UCLA project markers were derived after a detailed search of over 1400 data-based articles, and from conceptual and definitional perspectives on learning disabilities. Following revision and field test, four sets of markers were proposed: descriptive, substantive, topical, and background. Markers and operational techniques for assessment are included in a marker guide (Keogh et al., 1982), and provide a system for comprehensive description of subject characteristics using a common reporting format. While not all investigators of LD might have data on all markers, as in other research areas, use of a common subject description system provides the basis for determining comparability of samples across studies. Use of a marker system also allows for empirically based delineation of subgroups within samples, thus identifying and reducing the heterogeneity so characteristic of most LD research.

RATIONALLY DEFINED SUBGROUPS

A second approach to reducing sample heterogeneity is proposed by Torgesen (1982b), who calls for rationally defined subgroups in LD research. Torgesen suggests that it is necessary to develop a "systematic taxonomy of LD subtypes ... [each subgroup] ... homogeneous with regard to the major variables contributing to failure in school" (p. 114). Arguing that a common characteristic of LD children relates to problems in information processing, Torgesen has implemented a program of research focused on short-term memory. His overall research plan is to reduce sample variance by systematic selection of subjects using stringent criteria: controls on chronological age, IQ, and degree of school failure; and, importantly for the present discussion, deficiencies in short-term memory. Dual control or comparison groups include children similar to the primary sample except for intact short-term memory or adequate achievement in school.

The systematic selection of LD subgroups allows Torgesen (Torgesen & Houck, 1980) to pinpoint the effects of short-term memory on a variety of learning and memorial tasks. It also allows a clearer description of process–instruction interactions of obvious importance in school programs. Other investigators of learning disabilities might argue for study of process variables other than short-term memory. However, the goal of delineation of rationally defined subgroups as the basis for a taxonomy of learning disabilities is to be commended. Torgesen provides a theoretically based approach to dealing with the sample heterogeneity which has plagued both research and programs in this field.

CLUSTER ANALYSIS

A third promising technique for dealing with the range of subject characteristics is cluster analysis. This is a set of statistical procedures that groups or clusters individuals on the basis of their similarity on selected variables. In essence, subjects are successively matched or grouped according to their patterns of performance or profiles. The goal in the procedure is to identify homogeneous subgroups and to minimize overlap among subgroups. Cluster analysis combines statistical and clinical decisions. The clusters are usually determined statistically, but the significance or meaning of clusters requires logical decision. That is, do clusters have clinical integrity and interpretability? Two examples of cluster approaches are illustrative.

Satz and Morris (1981) described the use of cluster analysis to identify a learning-disabled group within a sample of unselected (N = 236) fifth grade pupils who had participated in the Florida Longitudinal Study. Based on a discrepancy between achievement and chronological age expectancy, these investigators identified 9 subgroups or clusters. Two subgroups (n = 89) were clinically described as learning disabled. The neuropsychological test scores of members of these groups were then subjected to further and different clustering techniques. These procedures yielded five relatively homogeneous subgroups of LD subjects who evidenced patterns of global language impairment (n = 27); specific language impairment (n = 14); global language and perceptual impairment (n = 10); visual–perceptual motor impairment (n = 23); and no neuropsychological impairment, this group called by the investigators an "unexpected learning disabled subtype" (n = 12). These statistically derived clusters were consistent with clinical subtypes identified by other investigators and, thus supported the use of this technique as a way of dealing with sample variability within the LD classification.

Further support for the use of clustering procedures comes from the work of McKinney and his colleagues (McKinney & Fisher, 1982) who used clustering techniques to identify subgroups of subjects according to diagnostic information collected when children were identified for special services. Intellectual and achievement information was combined with classroom behavior data to yield four major clusters of LD children. McKinney's clusters were not validated against other external measures, but the groupings were conceptually interpretable, and like the Satz and Morris (1981) findings, demonstrated the feasibility of the clustering approach.

While of potential use in addressing the problems of sample heterogeneity, the cluster techniques have a number of inherent limitations, not the least of which is interpretability. As noted by McKinney and Fisher (1982), statistical classification procedures may effectively group sample members into homogeneous clusters. However, the meaningfulness or the predictive value of the clusters or groups may be limited. We suggest that this is a particularly important consideration when clustering pupils for instructional or intervention purposes. There continues to be a need for clinical validation of statistically defined groups.

OTHER EXPERIMENTAL EFFORTS

Among EMR children there are at least two distinct subgroups: (a) children who are inefficient learners in all situations, and (b) children who are inefficient learners of abstract materials, but who show an ability to learn nonschool material rather efficiently. Several experimental approaches have been offered to differentiate between these presumably different subgroups of mildly retarded children; that is, the "truly retarded" and the "pseudoretarded." Jensen (1970) has used laboratory learning tasks to develop a theory of primary and secondary familial mental retardation based on two levels of learning abilities. Level I, or *associative abilities*, refers to skills tapped by tests such as digit span and serial learning; Level II, or *cognitive abilities*, refers to reasoning tasks such as the Raven's Progressive Matrices. Jensen reported that Level II abilities depend in part on Level I skills, and that Level I skills are distributed similarly for low-SES and middle-SES populations. While there is debate on the value of Level I and Level II abilities (see recent exchange, Stankov, Horn, & Roy, 1980; Jensen, 1982; Horn & Stankov, 1982), Jensen (1970) distinguished between children diagnosed as mentally retarded on the basis of being (a) low on both levels I and II, and (b) low on Level II, but not on Level I. The distinction is between

1. primary familial retardation—deficient in Levels I and II, and
2. secondary familial retardation—deficient in only Level II.

Budoff and his associates (Babad & Budoff, 1974; Budoff, 1967, 1970; Budoff, Meskin, & Harrison, 1971) also have attempted to differentiate between the *educationally* retarded but not mentally retarded and those children who are essentially unintelligent. The *learning-potential* (LP) assessment procedures consist of nonverbal reasoning problems (copying geometric designs with modified Kohs blocks), then instructing the child who scores low on principles relevant to the task, and then retesting the child. Two relevant patterns emerge for low-scoring children: (a) *Gainers* perform poorly at initial testing but improve considerably after instruction, and (b) *nongainers* do not appreciably improve after instruction. Budoff (1967) described gainers as coming from poor homes and disorganized family units, while the few middle-class subjects were nongainers. Further, LP profiles were reported to be better predictors than IQ or placement (special or regular class) of performance in a laboratory science program in electricity. The efforts of Jensen and Budoff offer experimental bases for differentiating among the mildly retarded on which subsequent research can proceed. Their initial findings confirm the clinical impressions that EMR children from poorer economic backgrounds are often more socially adept and able to learn nonacademic tasks than are the equal-IQ middle-class counterparts.

In sum, the delineation of reasonable and conceptually defensible subgroups continues to be an important goal for research investigators who study exceptional children. Sample or subject heterogeneity within any special education classification may well confound or mask real differences across categories, may dilute experimental manipulations or procedures, and may confound empirical validation of theory. Lack of comparable and replicable data across studies limits generalizations and inferences from an increasingly voluminous research literature. Whatever method used, whether a marker approach, rationally defined subgroups, statistical clustering techniques, or experimentally identified subjects, there is clear need for careful delineation of subgroups within broadly defined special education classifications.

Issues Concerning Instrumentation and Documentation of Program Effects

Appropriate instrumentation has proved a persistent problem for those concerned with assessment of mildly handicapped individuals. Questions about the appropriateness of extant instruments have been raised in regard to diagnosis and assessment for clinical purposes, as well as about research and

evaluation efforts where achievement (Jones, 1976), personality (Gardner, 1966), self-concept (MacMillan, 1982), sociometric methods (MacMillan & Morrison, 1984), and even IQ (Zigler & Trickett, 1978) serve as dependent variables or program outcomes to be tapped.

Issues surrounding the use of intelligence tests with minority children have been debated heatedly in academic and legal arenas for some time. The relative importance of genetics and environment as determinants of intelligence, and in turn EMR status, has resulted in advocates for both positions (e.g., Jensen, 1969; Mercer, 1970). Much of the exchange is pertinent only to EMR children, since a disproportionately high percentage of minority children have historically been enrolled in these programs. However, even in the LD field the commonly used criterion for defining LD children, that is, the discrepancy between aptitude and achievement, has been roundly criticized. The primary issue is the accuracy of difference scores. Salvia and Clark (1973) argue that the statistical weakness in quantifying any deficit or discrepancy (e.g., between two achievement tests, modality preferences, or aptitude-achievement) undermines the use of deficit data in educational decision making. This argument is supported by Page (1980) in a detailed review of PL 94–142 regulations having to do with LD assessment and classification. As noted by Salvia and Clark (1973), the meaning of the difference between two scores is dependent upon the reliabilities of the two tests, the size of their standard deviations, the degree of correlation between the tests, and differences between norming groups. Page suggests that the "reliability of the differences would be perfect when the test reliabilities were themselves perfect but the correlation between tests was zero" (1980, p. 447). Unfortunately, for the special educator or psychologist who must use deficit scores as the basis for classification, placement, or evaluation of program impact, the reliabilities of most commonly used tests are suspect, and the correlation between tests is often high (Ysseldyke, 1977). Further, as noted by Page (1980), because of differing reliabilities of the instruments used to measure aptitude and achievement, when corrections are made for attenuation, some currently designated LD children might be "overachievers." We will consider questions of test reliabilities in a subsequent section.

For the researcher or evaluator, however, the selection of extant instruments for measuring independent and dependent variables is fraught with another common problem—few instruments have been standardized on handicapped children. The severity of the problem is compounded for those instruments that require reading, given the common problem of language and reading across the categories of mildly handicapped children. Instrument selection is not just a problem of statistical or psychometric adequacy of tests. Efforts to document the effects of special education programs for mildly handicapped children are beset with problems of selection of outcome indices which reflect success or failure. Special education programs, early intervention programs, and mainstreaming programs have usually been evaluated in terms of cognition or achievement, occasionally according to "adjustment" (e.g., self-concept, personality, social status).

Zigler and Trickett (1978) provided an incisive analysis of the heavy reliance on intelligence (operationalized as IQ) in the evaluation of early childhood intervention programs; their observations pertain directly to other special education programs. Recognizing the concern over demonstrating the success or failure of special programs, in government circles referred to as "accountability," Zigler and Trickett noted that accountability takes two forms: (a) "process evaluation," where questions concentrate on who receives services, how many, and the nature of the services; and (b) "outcome evaluation," which attempts to document the impact of the services. In this second form of evaluation, according to Zigler and Trickett (1978),

> we encounter the government's beloved concept of "cost–benefit analysis." This elegant phrase, a creation originally of the Department of Defense, is usually translated as "how much bang do you buy per buck?" (p. 789)

Any attempt to provide cost–benefit evidence requires the selection of outcomes that will be accepted as legitimate indicators of success or failure. The most often used outcome measure for evaluating early intervention programs has been the IQ; for special classes and mainstream programs the standardized achievement test is a commonly used indicator. The reasons for the selection of these outcomes are severalfold. First, these are well-developed instruments with impressive psychometric properties which seemingly provide the user with instruments that can be defended in terms of their psychometric characteristics. Second, the instruments can be easily administered, particularly if a "short form" is selected for use. Third, the IQ and achievement scores do relate to outcomes generally accepted as important by educators and policymakers alike. The issues and limitations in the use of intelligence tests with handicapped learners have been extensively documented, and thus need no further documentation here. Zigler and Trickett (1978) suggest, however, that IQ is limited as an outcome measure of program impact. They propose instead that "social competence" is a construct of greater importance, despite the problems in defining and measuring it. We will return to consider this point later, but here will turn to the problems inherent in the use of achievement tests with mildly handicapped learners.

Achievement

Jones and MacMillan (1973) note that comparisons among and within pupils are based on expected patterns of growth and development. This requires norms for expected patterns of growth relative to age, program level, and subject matter areas. At present there are few achievement norms for mildly handicapped or other exceptional children, making it difficult to ascertain whether growth is fast, slow, or at an expected rate. Lack of a solid basis for determining expected achievement makes it difficult to demonstrate variations in program impact, the goal of outcome evaluation. It has been possible to obtain highly *reliable* achievement test data with a standardized achievement battery with mildly handicapped children through the use of out-of-level testing procedures (Yoshida, 1976). In this procedure the teacher is asked to indicate the appropriate level of the test to administer, and the children are tested in small groups. The reliability aspect does not deal with the normative issue, however.

Standardized tests of achievement have been developed on large samples of children and include items covering a range of objectives held in typical school programs. Moreover, many instruments are reported to possess adequate psychometric properties. However, mildly handicapped learners were not, in most instances, included in the standardization samples. One consequence is that phrasing of questions, vocabulary, and response formats have not received careful consideration; yet they can influence directly the performance of mildly handicapped children. Jones (1976) noted that since achievement tests are designed to provide information about the achievement of students in the middle range, the content validity for children outside this range must be questioned. This leads to problems of test reliability. Tests developed for the middle level of learners at specific age and grade levels are not reliable for subjects outside these age and grade levels, since test scores become unreliable at the extreme ends of the score distribution (Nunnaly, 1967). In an effort to deal with the effects of unreliability of test scores, Ysseldyke (1977) proposed use of regressed "true scores" rather than observed scores as the basis of decision. The use of regressed scores would be particularly effective if tests are highly unreliable, unnecessary if tests are perfectly reliable (i.e., the true and observed scores would be identical). In discussion of the use of regressed scores in decisions about LD or other handicapping classifications, Page (1980) notes that the use of regressed scores does not change the rank-ordering of subjects within the group; thus, where decisions are based on quotas (e.g., the lower 2%, the top 4%) there is no advantage to using the transformed score. However, where absolute cutoff points are used as the basis for decision (e.g., IQ below 70; achievement at 3.0 grade equivalent), the use of regressed rather than observed scores will have a direct effect on the number of selectees.

Compounding the problems, particularly with a number of EMR students, is the possible cultural bias in item content. Given the overrepresentation of ethnic minority children in EMR programs, Jones (1976) suggested that test content be scrutinized by minority scholars and test specialists and that items judged "unfair" be removed. He recommended further that differential scoring may need to be offered if items are included that reflect cultural idiosyncracies. Some efforts at different scoring procedures have been attempted in IQ testing (see Mercer & Lewis, 1977) but relatively little has been done in achievement testing.

A particular problem in the uncritical use of achievement tests to evaluate various educational treatments for mildly handicapped children is the lack of "match" between the content of the test and the curriculum in the particular special educational program. Meyers, MacMillan, and Yoshida (1980) suggest this is a major flaw in the research on the efficacy of special classes versus regular class placement. In the regular class the handicapped child is taught a traditional academic content (e.g., reading and arithmetic) by traditional instructional methods. Conversely, in the special classes greater emphasis is placed on social and prevocational skills and less emphasis is placed on academics per se. The validity of achievement test data varies dramatically between these two educational treatments; nevertheless, achievement tests are used as the common denominator in these studies.

Clearly, the uncritical use of standardized tests of achievement must be challenged and reliable alternatives sought for use with mildly handicapped children. The problems of measurement of achievement have consequences for decisions at both individual/clinical levels and at program/evaluation levels.

Adjustment

Problems are no less serious in the measurement of "adjustment" outcomes — personality, self-concept, or sociometric status of mildly handicapped pupils. Standardized measures of adjustment possess the same problems encountered in achievement tests. Gardner's (1966) comment on the use of the California Test of Personality with mildly retarded subjects is relevant today:

> It is apparent that the test items reflect a middle class set of values (e.g., Would you rather stay away from most parties? Should children be nice to people they don't like? Is it necessary to thank those who have helped you?). Should the retardate be viewed as maladjusted if he does not respond in terms of the values? In addition, other items answered realistically in terms of the typical experience of retardates, especially those who attend regular classes, would be scored as deviant responses (e.g., Do your classmates think you cannot do well in school? Is school work so hard that you are afraid you will fail? Do most of your friends and classmates think you are bright?). Again, realistic answers to these questions would lower the adjustment score of the retardate. This type of procedure would appear to be an inappropriate approach to defining and evaluating adjustment and maladjustment with the mentally retarded, especially for those who are attending regular classes. (p. 103)

These comments hold for LD children as well as mentally retarded, and they hold, in general, for other personality tests.

Research findings and methodological considerations in the study of self-concept and peer status are discussed in detail in other sections of this chapter. At issue here is the use of these adjustment indicators for program evaluation. In regard to self-concept, the fact that most scales are verbal in nature and require skills beyond many mildly handicapped persons poses a number of problems. Furthermore, Balla and Zigler (1979) observed that there are almost as many measures of self-concept as there are reported studies. This makes comparison of results difficult and questions the validity of many findings. To further complicate the situation, some scales measure a unitary self-concept, whereas others break down the construct into subscales — for example, academic and social self-concepts. Shavelson, Hubner, and Stanton (1976) have discussed potential problems in interpreting factor scores, opting for the use of total scores as reflecting stable characteristics. The stability and reliability of subscale or factor scores for interpreting self-concept of special education subjects is unknown. Further, self-concept scales seldom have norms for handicapped children, an exception being the Piers–Harris Self-Concept Scale for which norms for behaviorally disordered children are now available (Bloom, Shea, & Eun, 1979).

From a different perspective, Sternlicht and Deutsch (1972) questioned the validity of self-concept measures taken on retarded subjects, arguing that retardation is so emotionally laden that retarded individuals have difficulty in reporting and accepting their own limitations. Sternlicht and Deutsch hypothesize further that retarded people can develop needs to protect themselves from their failures and from fears of negative evaluations by others. Given this scenario, the veracity of responses given to items requiring a response that is seen as critical of one's behavior or self-esteem is questionable. One might speculate that mildly handicapped individuals overestimate their "real" self-worth because of limits of cognitive ability or because of defensive responses to feelings of inferiority.

On the basis of instrument limitations, imprecise constructs, and complex developmental interactions, interpretation of self-concept results for program evaluation purposes continues to be uncertain and to require confirmation from various sources. In evaluations of special education programs the evaluator is confronted with interpreting "high" self-concept scores for some mildly handicapped individuals — are these *unrealistic* or do they reflect program success? On the other hand, does one interpret "low" scores to indicate *realistic* scores or program failures? Self-concept continues to be an appealing but difficult topic for study, especially within the context of demonstrating program or teaching impact.

Another indicator of adjustment used frequently in evaluations of special education programs has been peer acceptance. Usually, sociometric methods are used to tap peer acceptance. Morrison (1981b) examined the information yielded by the two most common types of sociometric methods: peer nomination and roster and rating methods. She noted that variations in method and variations within a given method (e.g., format and scoring) can yield diverse findings. Peer nomination typically involves selecting three classmates on the basis of a sociometric criterion. When used in mainstreamed settings, mildly handicapped children are seldom known and therefore are not chosen often — yielding no social acceptance information on these children, yet sometimes specifying friendship patterns. The roster/rating method, conversely, does yield social acceptance information on every child in the class; it does not delineate friendships, however. Oden and Asher (1977) distinguished between the two methods and noted that peer nomination methods yield a strong friendship choice, while roster and rating methods yield a more general feeling of acceptance. At issue for the evaluator, then, is what data are more appropriate for the purposes of the evaluation.

Problems in interpreting sociometric findings are inherent when comparisons are made between classes (either special versus regular class or class A versus class B). Sociometric data are a direct function of class composition — that is, the peers who do the rating of one another; hence, a child's social status is meaningful only in the context of a given class. In studies using identical instruments it was found that the pattern of predictors of social status for mildly handicapped children differed for self-contained special classes (MacMillan & Morrison, 1980) and mainstreamed settings (Gottlieb, Semmel, & Veldman, 1978). Consider for a moment the dilemma confronting the researcher/evaluator who finds that LD children are "highly accepted" in a special class and "tolerated" in a regular class.

Still another consideration in gathering sociometric data is the response format. In roster and rating scales the raters are asked to respond on a 3- or 5-point scale (from "like" to "dislike") indicating how they feel toward each member of their class. Efforts to ensure that mildly handicapped children understand the categories available for selection have led to simplified response formats (e.g., smiling faces to indicate "like" and frowning faces to indicate "dislike"). The adequacy of these format changes and the possible influence of response mode on handicapped children's responses is essentially unknown. A related concern with the roster and rating method is the possibility that a child does not know every member in the class. A response option is usually offered for this contingency; something like "don't know." Such a response is to indicate nonacquaintance; however, we do not know how often mildly handicapped children respond with "don't know" to indicate "I do not know how I feel about them" as opposed to the intended "I do not know them."

Finally, the use of sociometrics in evaluating program adequacy requires consideration of possible reasons for selection. The interpretation problem is especially pertinent when sociometrics are used to tap peer acceptance in classes varying in socioeconomic and racial composition. When a mainstreamed EMR who is black is rejected, the reasons for rejection could be because of inappropriate behavior, social class differences from the modal level of the class, or rejection by classmates because the child is black. Efforts to elucidate the reasons for rejection in order that appropriate interventions may be implemented are necessary.

In summary, the assessment of handicapped pupils and the use of child data for purposes of documenting the impact of special education programs are plagued by continuing problems of instrumentation. There is an increasing number of tests, but many are limited by imprecise conceptualization, inadequate and/or inappropriate norms, and unacceptable psychometric properties. Measurement is a problem when applied to all educational programs; it is a particular problem when the targets of assessment are handicapped children. It is not surprising, then, that documentation of program impact is such a troublesome area for special educators.

Zigler and Trickett (1978) have argued persuasively for reconceptualizing outcome goals to include physical, social, and health domains as well as the cognitive one. They suggest that exclusive reliance on IQ as an outcome index does not allow for demonstration of the full range of program effects. This argument receives support from the work of Sheehan and Keogh (1981, 1982), who reviewed outcome information from a series of early intervention programs, concluding that where intellectual measures are used, small treatment effects are the rule rather than the exception. Sheehan and Keogh (1981) proposed several strategies to be considered when planning documentation efforts in special programs. The first relates to the substance and scope of interventions (see the section on early intervention in this chapter). The second involves the use of more powerful design and analytic techniques, including consideration of levels of program implementation. A third relates to the refinement of assessment practices, including more careful analysis of assessment information. A final point was consistent with the Zigler and Trickett argument, calling for a broader use of outcome information and methods. For many handicapped children the program effects on IQ will be

essentially negligible, yet there may be significant and powerful changes in motivation and affect, in family stability and coping, and in long-term outcomes. However, reconceptualization of appropriate and valid outcome domains carries with it new demands for the development of adequate and sound instrumentation.

Having considered some of the measurement and methodological problems inherent in research with mildly handicapped pupils, we now turn to review some of the major substantive areas of work. These include research on learning and cognition, noncognitive variables, mainstreaming, and efforts to prevent developmental problems.

Research on Learning and Cognition

Haywood, Meyers, and Switzky (1982) describe the research on learning in mental retardation prior to 1960 as being scattered theoretically and essentially atheoretical. A similar observation can be made about research in learning disabilities, as it has been only in the last 10 years that theory has systematically influenced research. The current surge of interest and activity directed at study of cognitive processes in mildly impaired individuals has its origins, in part at least, in cognitive research derived from information-processing models.

Whereas most of the theories that guided research on retardation, for example, the attention of Zeaman and House (1963, 1979) and the memory theories of Ellis (1963, 1970) and Spitz (1963, 1966, 1979), had focused on selected psychological functions, the information-processing models provided a heuristic for viewing deficits in performance within a larger cognitive system. Information-processing models proposed by Newell and Simon (1972) and Atkinson and Schiffrin (1968) and the memory model of Craik and Lockhart (1972) were developed to simulate human intelligence and to describe and explain the processing abilities of maturely functioning, unimpaired learners. The models also raised interesting and important questions for researchers who study handicapping conditions, especially mild mental retardation or learning disabilities, as the processing components could be related to characteristic patterns of deficiencies in learning and performance. Of particular importance was recognition of the need to identify functional processes that account for the transformation of information within the cognitive system, for example, control processes and strategies; and, to understand the influence of "meta" processes of metacognition and metamemory (Flavell, 1976; Flavell & Wellman, 1977).

Ann Brown's (1974, 1975, 1977, 1978) work on memory has been an important stimulus to recent research on mildly handicapped individuals, as her model combines a developmental perspective with the recognition that memory and learning must be studied within a broader view of cognition in general. In an important paper in 1975 she differentiated three knowledge dimensions: "knowing," "knowing about knowing," and "knowing how to know." The first referred to the broad memory system central to cognitive development; the second to metamemorial processes (the knowledge the individual has about his own memory skills); and the third to the kinds of strategies or skills the individual brings to bear on learning or memory tasks. In recent work Brown and Palincsar (1982) emphasized the distinction between (a) knowing about cognition, and (b) the regulation of cognition. The "twin concepts" of reflection and self-regulation may have different developmental courses (Brown & Palincsar, 1982), and it is reasonable that they may be differently affected in mildly handicapped pupils.

Brown's work was attractive to researchers in special education because in addition to identifying different dimensions of knowing, it allowed distinctions between structural and functional components of the processing system, directed study of task characteristics as well as of individual abilities, and emphasized developmental differences in performance. Brown's model thus captured information-processing and metacognitive perspectives and provided direction for research with mildly handicapped individuals. Keogh and Hall (1983) have proposed that this processing model also provides a reasonable explanation for the IQ-achievement discrepancy which is a defining characteristic of LD pupils.

The impact of the information-processing perspective is evident when the empirical work of the past 10 years is examined. Rather than a specific deficit emphasis, research has focused on the ways task variables, individual histories, cultural influences, and developmental status affect cognitive processing and performance (see Detterman, 1979; Hagen, Barclay, & Newman, 1982; Hagen, Jongward, & Kail, 1975; Hall, 1980; Torgesen & Kail, 1980, for discussion). MacMillan (1982) notes that recent memory research in mental retardation has focused on (a) the retarded child's inefficiency in organizing incoming stimuli, (b) the retarded child's inefficient use of rehearsal strategies to retain input and transfer it from short-term to long-term memory, and (c) the retarded child's inefficiency in gaining access to remembered information that bears on current situations.

These processing problems are similar to those described by investigators who study children with learning disabilities or with specific academic deficiencies such as poor reading. Based on a comprehensive review of the literature, Torgesen and Kail (1980) suggest that relative to normal readers, poor readers may be deficient in the application of strategies such as stimulus labeling and rehearsal, and may be less able to use categorization as a mnemonic tool for organizing information. Problems in strategy selection and application have also been documented in recent research carried out in several federally funded Learning Disabilities Research Institutes (see *Exceptional Education Quarterly*, 1983, for summary of Institute findings). Importantly, Institute research has not only documented LD pupils' problems in organization and strategy use, but has also demonstrated that many strategies and organizational skills are trainable.

The importance of understanding the role of process variables in learning is emphasized in the cognitive behavior modification (CBM) approach of Meichenbaum (1977) and the cognitive training programs of Douglas (1972, 1980) and Camp (1980). Drawing from her work with hyperactive children, Douglas (1980) has posited a direct link between metacognition and the mastery of knowledge requiring strategic effort. She specifically underscores the role of "executive operations," including analysis, reflection, planning, and monitoring. In a series of studies at McGill, Douglas and her colleagues (see Douglas, 1980 for review) have demonstrated the impact of

cognitive training on hyperactive children's behavior, motivation, and achievement. This work is consistent with that of Camp (1980) with behaviorally disordered boys and with that of Meichenbaum and Goodman (1969, 1971) with impulsive children.

From a number of perspectives, then, there is evidence that cognitive training approaches are useful and effective interventions for many mildly impaired learners. As noted by Keogh and Glover (1980), however, several points deserve consideration before wholesale implementation of these techniques. Age of children and specifics and intensity of procedures and program content have been found to influence results. The target of training, that is, development of skills or the selection and use of already developed skills, also may require specific training techniques. Finally, different domains of competence (personal-social, academic, or behavioral) may be differentially affected by particular procedures. Generalization across domains may occur but cannot be assumed (Keogh & Bartlett, 1980). In sum the cognitive training-information-processing approaches appear promising and useful for both research and practice with both LD and EMR pupils. A number of important research topics have been generated by the work to date.

A brief discussion of selected research on process variables may be illustrative. Let us consider first work on attention and input organization.

Attention and Input Organization

Working primarily with retarded individuals, Zeaman and House (1963) engaged in a program of research designed to uncover "process parameters" of learning which are related to differences in MA and/or IQ. To do this they used discrimination learning tasks and backward learning curves. Tasks were selected that yielded learning curves that did not differ according to level of intelligence or difficulty. In their early research Zeaman and House revealed that performance remained at chance levels for varying lengths of time, but once learning began the learning curves rose rapidly to criterion. While subjects differed in the length of time they responded at a chance level, the slopes of the learning curves were similar once learning began. Subjects with lower MAs and IQs were found to remain at a chance level of responding for a longer period of time. This was attributed to differences in attending to the relevant dimensions of the discrimination task. Hence, the retarded were viewed as being deficient in attention, rather than in learning. The distinction between problems in attention, rather than in learning, has also been a fundamental one in LD research, and has led to a large literature directed at various aspects of attentional disturbances (Hallahan & Reeve, 1980; Krupski, 1980).

In a later paper Fisher and Zeaman (1973) expanded the theoretical model to incorporate the memory theory of Atkinson and Shiffrin (1968) and thereby consider retention, or memory, as it relates to learning. Fisher and Zeaman distinguished between *structural features* and *control processes*. In their view structural features are stable and not amenable to change through training, while control processes are trainable and are optional memory strategies. In the case of retarded persons the evidence suggests that poor short-term memory is a structural feature, while rehearsal strategies are a memory process which can be trained. In the case of LD pupils, problems in short-term memory may be related more to inadequate use of strategies than to structural deficiencies, although recent work by Torgesen and Houck (1980) suggests that structural limitations, not just problems in strategy use, may contribute to the short-term memory deficiencies of some LD children. The heterogeneity of many LD research samples already noted may mask or confound possible subgroup differences in processing problems. More will be said about rehearsal strategies (mnemonic strategies) later in this section.

Also of relevance to the structural–control question is the consistent finding that there are few differences among normally developing, mentally retarded, and learning-disabled pupils in recognition memory. However, differences in speed of memory processing between mildly handicapped and normal learners have been studied. Hall and Guare (1982) and Zakreski (1982) have also documented differences in perceptual speed between LD and normal achieving children. This aspect of structural-control contributions to memory problems deserves study.

Input Organization

Closely related to the attentional question, Spitz (1963, 1966) demonstrated that retarded children are less efficient than normals at categorizing incoming data into "chunks," a finding also reported for LD pupils (Hall, 1979). By failing to categorize, mildly handicapped children rapidly overload their capacity. Spitz (1966) utilized a digit span task to test his notions regarding the possibility of improving memory of retarded children by organizing input for them. To do this, he grouped digits spatially. For example, if instead of showing the digits as 8, 3, 5, 9, the experimenter presented them as 83 59, then, instead of having to remember 4 *bits* of information (i.e., 8, 3, 5, 9), the child had to remember only 2 bits of information (ie., 83, 59). Spitz found that such spatial grouping did facilitate the recall of retarded children, but it did not appreciably benefit normals. Moreover, the spatial grouping helped 12-year-old EMRs, but not 9-year-old EMRs.

While spatial grouping improved the recall of older EMRs, other studies (MacMillan, 1972) suggested that only when retarded subjects called the grouped digits as couplets (e.g., said "eighty-four" for 84) was the grouping beneficial. Interestingly, the spatial grouping resulted in poorer performance by non-retarded subjects, suggesting that the input organization imposed by the experimenter interfered with the spontaneous strategy of these same children. Findings from studies of LD children are generally consistent with those with EMR pupils. Torgesen and Houck (1980) report that auditory recall of digits in a grouped or chunked format improved performance of both LD and normals. However, the recall of normal children and of one subset of LD children deteriorated under a forced organization condition. As with the EMR studies, an imposed organization sometimes had a negative impact on the performance of normal subjects.

The findings with digit span suggest that mildly retarded children fail to organize input in an efficient manner. When such organization is provided for them, they appear to be able to use it to improve recall, provided the strategy is one within their repertoire. Similar findings are consistently reported for investigations using associative clustering. Spitz (1966) reported that when lists of words were "presented clustered" (as opposed to random ordering of words) or when the words randomly presented were "requested clustered" (e.g., experimenter asks for "all the animals you can remember"), the performance of retarded children was enhanced. Similarly, Hall (1979) found that LD boys' performance on an associated clustering task was markedly improved when they were cued to use organizing categories. In the cued condition LDs performed as well as normal peers; however, the LDs did not use categories spontaneously. These findings are consistent with the coding studies of Bauer (1979, 1982) and Wong and Wong (1977), who found that poor readers performed adequately on simple tasks but did poorly on tasks requiring more complex organization or coding elaboration.

An aspect of input organization that has been a target of considerable research is selective attention (see Hagen, 1967; Hagen, Jongward & Kail, 1975; Pick, Frankel, & Hess, 1975). Important to the present discussion, Hallahan and Reeve (1980) suggest that there are differences between deficient learners and normal achievers in selective attention as demonstrated by performance on incidental learning tasks; that there is a developmental basis for these differences; that the problems in selective attention are linked to inability to use verbal rehearsal (control processes); and that training in verbal rehearsal improves performance on incidental learning tasks.

Taken as a whole, then, there is consistent evidence that both mildly retarded and LD children have deficient organizational skills (which may be interpreted as attention problems), but that they can be helped to use strategies to advantage. However, without external prompting they appear to employ inefficient organizational strategies, to rely on rote memory, or apparently to use no strategy at all. The growing literature on information processing and memory attests to the importance of strategy use in learning and cognition, and underscores the role of problems in strategy use by mildly handicapped learners. The "strategy or capacity deficit" controversy (Swanson, 1982) is not yet settled, however. As noted by Torgesen (1982a), the strategy research to date has been limited by subject differences, by a narrow range of tasks and settings, and by inadequate understanding of developmental antecedents. The reader is referred to Volume 2, Numbers 1 and 2, of *Topics in Learning and Learning Disabilities*; these are devoted to discussions of metacognition and the strategy–capacity questions, respectively.

Rehearsal (*Mnemonic*) Strategies

Recognition of the importance of rehearsal in memory tasks has led to extensive research on the use of rehearsal by retarded children (Glidden, 1979). Thus far the evidence suggests that while retarded children can be explicitly trained to use these strategies (Paris & Haywood, 1973), they tend to use them inefficiently when required to do so spontaneously. Even when trained to use rehearsal strategies, the effects of training appear to be limited to the specific tasks and contexts in which training occurred (Belmont & Butterfield, 1977; Borkowski &

Cavanaugh, 1979; Brown, 1974, 1978; Campione & Brown, 1977).

Retarded subjects have been shown to be able to learn rehearsal strategies and to utilize them in a number of areas successfully (Haywood et al., 1982). However, Brown (1974) concluded that retarded subjects seldom, if ever, assess the demands of a task or situation and/or efficiently select a strategy that will lead to a solution. This inability suggests a weakness in what Butterfield and Belmont (1977) called *executive control*—that is, the selection, sequence, evaluation, revision, or change of mnemonic strategies. Lack of ability to plan, to determine the need for particular strategies, and to evaluate effectiveness also characterize LD pupils. As noted by Keogh and Hall (1983), many LD pupils may have or may be trained to have an adequate repertoire of specific strategies. The problem appears to be in the strategic process "of combining or recombining particular strategies into an overall plan of organization" (p. 15). Lack of awareness of the need for planfulness and strategy application may make LD pupils appear to be "inactive learners" (Torgesen, 1982b).

Campione and Brown's (1977) distinction between *maintenance* and *generalization* may clarify wherein the greatest difficulties arise in strategy learning and use. They have proposed a detailed model for studying retarded–nonretarded differences in process variables needed to promote generalization. Retarded children have been able to use strategies when there is no change in the experimental task used (i.e., strategy maintenance); further, these strategies are maintained for considerable lengths of time. However, evidence supporting the ability of retarded children to generalize a mnemonic strategy to a novel task has not been forthcoming. In addition, while retarded children's ability to perform metamemorial tasks improves with age, it develops at a rate much slower than observed in normals (Haywood et al., 1983).

In their review of memory processes in mildly handicapped children, Torgesen and Kail (1980) specified three criteria for determining the effectiveness of training memorial strategies: durability, generalization, and minimization of normal/deficient pupil differences. The evidence to date suggests that retarded and learning-disabled persons frequently do not use mnemonic strategies spontaneously. Yet, if taught such strategies, they can use them to advantage and their performance often reaches that of normal persons; further, once learned, strategies can be maintained for considerable lengths of time. Thus far, however, the research has not demonstrated that deficient learners, specifically retarded children, generalize strategies to new tasks, although some evidence of generalization is reported with LD pupils (Brown & Palincsar, 1982; Conner, 1983; Schumaker, Deshler, Alley, & Warner, 1983). Relevant to the generalization issue, Brown and Palincsar emphasized that an "ideal training strategy" would include practice in strategy use and instruction in awareness of strategy use and control. A combination of strategy training, awareness training, and control training may enhance generalization.

For years, Herman Spitz (1963, 1966) has studied learning and memory in retarded subjects. However, recently Spitz (1979) has concluded that the distinguishing feature of mental retardation is a deficit in *reasoning*—not in learning and memory. He argues that basically, retarded children evidence problems in "thinking and reasoning." Game problems of logic and strategy were used to study these processes, and Spitz (1979) reported that retarded children perform more poorly on these tasks than do *either* CA-equal normals or MA-equal normals (who are considerably younger). On some tasks requiring stereotyped rote responses, retarded subjects outperform college students and on certain other tasks they perform at a level comparable to CA-equal normals. However, on the tasks used by Spitz (1979), calling for "logical foresight," they perform at a level below MA-equal normals. Retarded children appear to have difficulty looking ahead and considering "if--then" conditional situations.

The position taken by Spitz (1979) is consistent with those of Brown (1974) and Belmont and Butterfield (1977)—namely, that the deficit is in knowing when to utilize a strategy, and what specific strategy is efficient or inefficient. While retarded people can employ strategies efficiently, they do not appear to analyze a novel task, select an appropriate strategy, and employ it successfully. Such skills are the essence of metamemory, executive function, and reasoning as used by these theorists.

Applicability to Teaching

It is noteworthy that research on the learning and cognition of mildly handicapped learners has weighed heavily in favor of controlled, laboratory, group research designed to differentiate the handicapped from the nonhandicapped. Conversely, there is a paucity of research that derives from instructional theory. Use of the terms *molar* and *molecular* may be useful in making distinctions between two kinds of behavioral outcomes (or dependent variables) that result from empirical undertakings. MacMillan and Meyers (1984) described these terms as follows:

> Molar learning refers to those outcomes obviously related to efficient functioning in the society. Mastery of tool subjects (e.g., reading, math), vocational skills, social skills, and skills related to independent functioning are examples of molar learnings. Molecular learning refers to the fine-grained performances often thought to underlie molar learning where facilitation of this type of learning does not, in and of itself, assure greater social competence. Traditional discrimination learning, serial learning, and paired-associate learning tasks are examples of tasks that produce molecular learning. (p. 474)

In these terms, learning research with mildly handicapped learners has been mostly molecular in nature. In many instances the research has not assisted classroom teachers or pupils in special education, although one exception is the application of operant approaches.

Brooks and Baumeister (1977) suggest that there is a tendency for laboratory research to be preoccupied with internal validity with a resulting threat to external validity. For example, the tasks to be learned in laboratory research tend to be highly molecular, thus permitting the experimenter considerable control over stimuli presented. In this approach the experimenter frequently takes pains to divorce *what* is to be learned from the experiential background of the subject. In contrast, the tasks to be taught mildly handicapped children in school are molar in nature and experiential differences do, in fact, give one child an advantage over another. Further, the experimental stimuli may have little relationship to handicapped individuals' actual experiences. For example, Zeaman and House (1979) employed discrimination learning tasks requiring subjects to differentiate among physical dimensions (color, shape, size). We might ask: How do their findings apply to teachers' problems in getting retarded children to sustain attention or to discriminate between restroom signs for men and women, sidewalks and streets, and other molar adaptations required in school learning or social adaptation? The experimental findings may have implications for handicapped individuals' everyday learning, but too often the applications have not been demonstrated.

A second factor that limits the external validity of laboratory findings is the setting in which data are collected. Subjects are usually tested on a one-to-one basis in a highly structured setting in which extraneous stimuli are controlled. Generalizations to a classroom with 15 to 35 students, one teacher, and a range of extraneous stimuli must be drawn with caution. Finally, the practice of restricting variability of subject characteristics in order to isolate the effects of independent variables limits the generalizability of findings. By restricting the range of IQ, age, or SES in a sample, the investigator restricts the proportion of mildly handicapped children to whom the findings can be generalized.

Taken as a whole, the laboratory research on learning and cognition allows a number of *potential* implications. However, far too little work has been done to test the utility of these possibilities. Our point is illustrated by the Mercer and Snell (1977) text wherein the authors review extensive research under various theoretical orientations. Unfortunately the sections on "teaching implications" are restricted mostly to operant research and modeling. Some effort to move laboratory research to the classroom is evident. For example, Martin (1978) and Turnure and Thurlow (1973) have studied word recognition in EMR learners. Ross and Ross (1978) have demonstrated that EMR children could apply cognitive training to novel problem-solving situations. Some of the cognitive training approaches (Camp, 1980; Douglas, 1980) have provided evidence of "real-world" effects. Current reports from the LD Research Institutes (see *Exceptional Education Quarterly*, 1983) document the applicability and effectiveness of cognitive training techniques to LD pupils in schools. Although the various research programs focused on somewhat different age groups and/or problems, the consistency of the laboratory-developed cognitive training techniques in classrooms is encouraging.

The lack of a good *match* between laboratory research findings and instruction in special education has been recognized for some time. It is not unique to special education. The following quotation from developmental psychologist Bettye Caldwell (1974a) summarizes the state of affairs nicely:

> The schools do not need any raw theoretical solutions to their problems, only battle-tested products can hope for acceptance and adoption. Until an idea reaches that stage, the developers themselves should be working right now in the schools to learn some important facts about how their ideas will be received and what problems are likely to be encountered in the implementation. (p. 52)

MacMillan and Meyers (1984) offer the possibility that research derived from instructional theorists might prove fruitful to the field of special education—particularly research concerned with the mildly handicapped. However, we are struck by the paucity of work with handicapped learners derived from mastery teaching and learning (Block, 1974; Bloom, 1976), an approach that appears most appropriate to the mainstreaming efforts. A promising direction is found in the Kamehameha Early Education Project (KEEP; see Gallimore, Boggs, & Jordan, 1974), in which the achievement of Hawaiian children, among the lowest SES of U.S. minority children, was dramatically improved. By modifying instructional processes and materials based on naturalistic investigation of the children, their homes, and teacher–pupil interactions, Gallimore and his associates have successfully led a frontal assault on the molar learning of these formerly low-achieving children.

In summary, the research literature identifies a number of possible approaches to the learning problems of mildly handicapped learners. To date, however, the familiar gap between theory and practice has too often limited the impact of learning research in special education. As suggested in other sections of this chapter, this is unfortunate for two reasons. First, mildly handicapped learners may provide a critical test of a number of learning constructs. Second, the handicapped learner will likely benefit from the application of sound theory.

Research on Noncognitive Variables

Messick (1979) distinguished between *cognitive* and *noncognitive* measures in educational research. The former are those that predict school achievement and include qualities such as intellectual ability and information-processing skills. Noncognitive characteristics refer to many other attributes of personality that influence learning—affect, motivation, and related characteristics. These attributes may explain why persons with comparable aptitudes sometimes learn and achieve differently. Messick (1982) acknowledged that some of these noncognitive characteristics have important cognitive components as the two interact in complex ways.

Handicapped learners are thought to experience excessive failure and consequently several noncognitive characteristics (e.g., self-concept, motivation) have served frequently as outcome measures for evaluations of educational treatments. We might speculate whether low values on such measures (e.g., low self-concept) lead to academic failure or whether repeated failure results in depreciating these characteristics. Unfortunately few studies employ designs that permit causal inferences.

Self-Concept

When Heber (1964) reviewed the literature on self-concept of mentally retarded persons, he found two studies. Since that time there has been increasing activity along this line. We will consider briefly this research from three perspectives: studies on self-concept, studies on the effect of class placement on self-concept, and studies on the relationship between self-concept and achievement.

Guthrie and his associates (Guthrie, Butler, & Gorlow, 1961; Guthrie, Butler, Gorlow, & White, 1964) conducted a series of self-concept studies in which they reported that retarded persons behave in ways designed to protect themselves from painful rejection rather than to gain approval. Presumably, negative experiences prompt retarded persons to "avoid rejection" rather than "seek acceptance."

Several investigators (Fine & Caldwell, 1967; McAfee & Cleland, 1965; Ringness, 1961) reported that retarded children have unrealistically high self-concepts, or have self-concepts that do not differ from average or above-average IQ children. However, Guthrie, Butler, and Gorlow (1963) found lower self-concepts for institutionalized than noninstitutionalized retarded subjects while Piers and Harris (1964) found lower self-concepts for institutionalized retarded subjects than for public school normal children. Unfortunately, differences in age, instruments, and confounding of independent variables (e.g., retarded status plus institutionalization) preclude any definitive conclusions about the structure of self-concept in retarded subjects (Schurr, Joiner, & Towne, 1979). Although similar sampling and methodological problems also limit interpretation of self-concept research with LD pupils, there is support for the view that LD children have poor self-concept relative to their nondisabled peers (Black, 1974; Koppitz, 1971; Larsen, Parker, & Jorjorian, 1973; Yauman, 1980). Ribner (1978) found self-concept of minimally brain damaged children (often included in LD classifications) to differ from undamaged peers, a finding consistent with Rosenthal's (1973) work with dyslexic pupils.

Early research relating ability level to self-concept was influential in the debate over homogeneous and heterogeneous classes in retarded pupils. Schurr et al., (1979) reviewed these early studies which suggested that low-ability children had higher self-concepts in homogeneously grouped classes than when they were enrolled in heterogeneous classes. Such results suggested that children develop self-attitudes based on comparisons of themselves with peers in their classes. Mann (1960) reported contrary results: Children placed in low-ability groups made more negative self-evaluations than did those in regular grades. Meyerowitz (1962) reported more self-derogations by special-class EMRs compared to regular-class slow learners. These inconsistent findings suggest that self-evaluations may be related to modal level of achievement in a child's class, or that the effect may be varied, depending on the measure employed or other factors.

This interpretation receives some support from Yauman's (1980) study of LD third grade boys. Yauman compared Piers–Harris self-concept scores of three groups: LD boys in special segregated classes, LD boys in regular classes but with special tutoring, and non-LD regular-class controls. Piers–Harris self-concept scores were highest for the non-LD boys, lowest for the tutored (regular-class) LD group. When reading scores were controlled, differences in self-concept scores were not significantly different among groups. The confounding of achievement and placement status in this study makes it difficult to pull out the direct effect of placement (regular class or special class) on self-concept, but does support the poor self-concept of LD children. It is interesting to note that in Yauman's study the often reported positive correlation between self-concept and achievement was found only for the non-LD regular-class boys. This was inconsistent with a significant negative relationship between degree of reading retardation and self-concept reported by Black (1974) in his study of elementary school learning-disabled pupils. Black did not find a

significant correlation between self-concept and IQ, suggesting that for children within a normal ability range, intelligence is not a powerful contributor to self-concept. Yauman's findings are consistent with those of Ribner (1978), however, who reported higher self-concept scores for segregated rather than mainstreamed minimal-brain-damaged children.

Taken together these findings raise interesting questions about the impact of placement on self-views of problem learners. As the trend in educational planning for LD pupils has been predominantly toward mainstream placement with ancillary help, placement impact may be more easily studied with retarded pupils. However, it is clear from the few studies with EMR and LD pupils that placement in mainsteam settings does not guarantee positive self-attitudes. Possible contributors to the reported low self-concept of mainstream LD pupils, for example, peer and teacher attitudes, overly rigorous academic demands, and inadequacies in social communication skills, deserve study. A discussion of mainstream research is found in a subsequent section of this chapter.

Possibly implicated in the low self-concepts of EMR pupils in special classes is the fact that children are labeled "mentally retarded" prior to being placed, and may incorporate this negative evaluation in their self-perceptions (MacMillan, Jones, & Aloia, 1974). Towne and Joiner (1966) assessed self-concept *before* the child was labeled EMR and placed in a special class and then measured self-concept at several points in time during the first year. Children in their study showed more favorable self-concepts after being labeled and placed than they did prior to being informed that they were going into EMR classes. Self-concept scores stayed at this elevated level until the end of the first year in EMR classes, when they dropped slightly. Seven of these children were ultimately delabeled and returned to regular grades. Schurr, Towne, and Joiner (1972) tested these children prior to their return to regular classes and then one year later. Self-concept scores were significantly lower after one year in regular class than they had been just prior to removal from the special EMR class. These findings suggest that comparison to peers is a more important influence on self-evaluations than is membership in a "special class" or a "regular class," an interpretation consistent with the research on LD pupils already discussed.

A positive relationship between self-concept and achievement has been a consistent finding in the research on mildly handicapped pupils despite the restricted range in achievement scores typically found in special classes. Significant relationships between LD pupils' self-concept scores and their test-determined achievement in school subjects has been documented by Black (1974), Levitan and Kiraly (1975), and Patten (1983). Working with retarded pupils, Guthrie et al. (1963) reported positive correlations between self-concept and achievement even when the effects of intelligence were partialed out. These findings are consistent with the data reported on normals. However, the cause–effect sequence remains unclear. Purkey (1970) wrote:

> Although the data do not provide clear-cut evidence about which comes first—a positive self-concept or scholastic success, a negative self-concept or scholastic failure—it does stress a strong reciprocal relationship and gives us reason to assume that enhancing the self-concept is a vital influence in improving academic performance. (p. 27)

Peer Acceptance

The abundance of research on peer acceptance of mildly handicapped children has contrasted a mildly handicapped group (i.e., EMR or LD) to a nonhandicapped group of children in regular grades. That research will be considered later in the chapter under the discussion of mainstreaming. Here we will discuss the research concerned with possible reasons mildly handicapped children have the social status they do in certain groups.

EMR children tend to have lower social status than their nonhandicapped peers in regular grades (MacMillan & Morrison, 1984), a finding that also characterizes LD pupils (Bryan & Bryan, 1982; Garrett & Crump, 1980; Siperstein, Bopp, & Bak, 1978). While differences in peer acceptance are reliably confirmed, much of the sociometric research has been limited to comparisons of popularity within particular handicapped groups. These studies yield descriptive information regarding social status, but they do not reveal *why* a child is accepted or rejected. Moreover, comparative studies of handicapped versus nonhandicapped children have tended to be interpreted, when differences occur, in terms of the handicap. For instance, it is assumed that EMR or LD children are less popular *because* they are retarded or LD. The search for reasons handicapped children possess the social status they do has taken several directions, and a number of promising findings have emerged.

In early research Johnson (1950) found that a low-IQ group of children (mean IQ = 63.69) in regular grades were accepted less often and rejected more often on sociometric ratings than were normal-ability peers. He then asked classmates why they had rejected children, and reported that the low-IQ children were rejected for the same reasons other children were rejected, for example, swearing, teasing, and bullying. Baldwin (1958) also reported that low-IQ children (IQ range, 50–74) were rated low by classmates because of antisocial behavior. Hence, the early investigations that solicited verbal reasons from raters led to conclusions that mildly handicapped children were not rejected because of their labeled status, but rather because they exhibited behaviors judged offensive by the raters.

In a program of research directed at understanding the social problems of LD pupils (see Bryan & Bryan,1982, for review), Bryan and her colleagues documented differences in the verbal communication patterns of LD and non-LD children which appear to contribute to their low social status. In a classroom observation study Bryan, Wheeler, Felcan, and Henek (1976) reported that when compared to non-LD peers, LD children tended to make more competitive and rejecting statements and to give fewer positive/consideration comments; they were also less apt to respond to peer-initiated contact. These findings were corroborated in further classroom research by Bryan and Bryan (1978). Social communication problems of LDs are not limited to verbal skills, however. Axelrod (1982) found LD adolescents less able than non-LD peers on tests of nonverbal sensitivity and of social intelligence. J. Bryan and Sherman's (1980) work on immediate impressions has shown that naive observers are able to identify LD children on the basis of a few minutes observation of nonverbal social behavior.

For both verbal and nonverbal behaviors, then, it appears that relative to non-LD peers, LD children are socially inept, engage in more aggressive and abrasive behavior, and are likely to be rejected. Bryan and Bryan (1982) suggest that a number of child characteristics may contribute to these social difficulties: attentional problems, poor verbal communication skills, and poor ability to recognize and interpret social and emotional information conveyed by others. Their hypotheses are consistent with those of other investigators of social problems of LD children: deficits in social perception (Bruno, 1981; Wiig & Harris, 1974) and in role taking (Dickstein & Warren, 1980; Wong & Wong, 1980). The reader is referred to the comprehensive review by Bryan and Bryan (1982) and to the recent issue of *Learning Disability Quarterly* (1982) for detailed discussion of the social interaction skills of LD pupils and selected approaches to interventions. These articles reflect the range of substantive and methodological problems that characterize this research area.

Another line of research directed at specifying influences on handicapped children's social problems is exemplified by the study of Bruininks, Rynders, and Gross (1974). These investigators attempted to uncover characteristics of both the rater and the ratee that are related to sociometric choices. Sex of rater and socioeconomic status were controlled and 65 EMRs (IQ = 50–85) in elementary grades served as target subjects in two school districts — one urban and one suburban. Same-sex ratings were higher for urban EMRs than non-EMRs of both sexes, while suburban EMRs were rated lower than non-EMR children. Whether different sociometric patterns due to differing SES levels of the school districts attest to the greater tolerance of urban nonretarded children or to differences in social adeptness between the two EMR groups remains unclear. What is important is the recognition that factors independent of child characteristics influence social acceptance.

The point is well illustrated by the work of Gottlieb et al. (1978), who used a regression model to study the influence of certain variables on sociometric status. Independent variables included peer perceptions of cognitive ability and disruptive behavior, teacher perceptions of cognitive ability and disruptive behavior, and the degree of integration. These authors reported that acceptance and rejection scores (the dependent variables) were associated with different sets of independent variables. Acceptance was associated with perceptions of cognitive ability (both peer and teacher) while rejection was related to perceptions of misbehavior. MacMillan and Morrison (1980), employing the same instruments in a study of both EMR and EH children in self-contained as opposed to regular classes, found a different pattern of association between teacher and peer ratings of academic competence and misbehavior and pupils' acceptance and rejection. It seems likely that setting factors (special vs. regular, teacher–pupil ratio, modal achievement level of the class) as well as characteristics of the raters and ratees contribute to the different sets of patterns.

Given the common use of sociometric techniques in the study of social competence of mildly handicapped children, a methodological comment is in order. The analysis used by Gottlieb et al. (1978) and MacMillan and Morrison (1980) was commonality analysis, which partitions the variance of the dependent variable into shared and unique variance in an effort to identify the relative influence of the independent variables (Kerlinger &

Pedhazur, 1973). While it is tempting to draw causal inferences from these data and to base interventions on such inferences, the analysis does not permit such conclusions because of interdependency between independent variables. Moreover, the results are highly dependent on the particular type of multiple regression technique used (e.g., stepwise regression, commonality analysis). Morrison and Borthwick (1983) note that there are both methodological and substantive reasons for considering alternative approaches to describe the association between child characteristics and social status. Two approaches deserve consideration.

First, Morrison and Borthwick (1983) used a cluster analytic technique to identify groups of EMR children having similar profiles based on the following: peer and teacher perceptions of cognitive abilities and misbehavior, social acceptance, social rejection, and toleration. Ten different profiles, representing four basic types of social status profiles, were identified: (a) high acceptance — with low or average toleration and rejection scores; (b) high toleration; (c) high rejection — with low to average toleration and acceptance scores; and (d) average scores on all three social status scores. This approach provides an alternative, and more detailed, method of generating outcome measures from sociometric ratings; it provides information beyond a mere tabulation of how many acceptance or rejection nominations are received by a given child. Moreover, it recognizes that some children are either liked very much or disliked very much, a vastly different pattern than that of a child whose acceptance, tolerance, and rejection scores are distributed rectangularly. Importantly, the two profiles yield similar mean sociometric scores.

MacMillan and Morrison (1984) have challenged the significance of equal weighting to all nominations received by a child. In most sociometric schemes a nomination by the lowest-status child in the class "counts" as much as a nomination by the highest-status child. However, are these two nominations of equal significance? Another assumption underlying traditional sociometric scoring is that the more nominations a child receives, the "better" his or her acceptance. Yet, it may be that receiving 1 nomination from a child whose acceptance is highly valued is of greater consequence than receiving 10 nominations from classmates a child does not like or value. To the extent that sociometric data are used as an important evaluation outcome in evaluations of educational treatments (e.g., mainstreaming) for mildly handicapped children, we must propose that results be interpreted cautiously. What constitutes "success" for mainstreamed children in sociometric terms? Being at or above the class mean number of nominations? Receiving no rejection nominations? Being accepted by one other child whose friendship is valued by the child being rated?

A second possible approach to uncovering factors associated with social acceptance of mildly handicapped children is exemplified by a study by Morrison, Forness, and MacMillan (1983). A model of influence was hypothesized beginning with observed behavior and achievement, mediated through teacher and peer perceptions of cognitive and behavioral competence, leading to social status. This model was tested by a path analysis performed on data collected on 133 mildly retarded children enrolled in self-contained special classes. The results revealed the following causal sequence or pathway of influence: (a)

observed behavior and achievement, (b) teacher perceptions of these competencies, (c) peer perceptions of these competencies, and (d) resultant social status ratings. The teacher's influence on the peer group's perceptions of a child's achievement and behavior suggests subtle ways in which teachers in EMR classes communicate to students who thereby adopt the teacher's evaluations.

In summary, despite measurement and methodological limitations, there is a substantive literature that attests to the low social status and poor self-esteem of mildly handicapped children. Contributors to their social interactions include personal characteristics and skills of handicapped children themselves, as well as perceptions, attitudes, and attributions of nonhandicapped peers and teachers. An important line of research thus focuses on the views of those who interact with handicapped children. Attribution theory appears particularly promising in this regard, and deserves brief discussion within the context of special education.

Attribution Theory

One approach to understanding children's performance in achievement related settings is the attributional theory of achievement motivation proposed by Weiner (1974, 1976). Rooted in the naive psychology of Heider (1958), and drawing from the locus of control work of Rotter (1966), Weiner's model provides a synthesis of cognitive and motivational constructs. Said simply, attributions are viewed as efforts to "make sense of" or to interpret the causes of events; these perceived causes are presumed to determine subsequent affective responses, expectancies, and behaviors. This attributional approach is particularly useful when integrated with the decision model proposed by Shavelson (1976), as it provides a way of assessing the effects of selected child and teacher variables on teachers' educational decisions.

Weiner has focused his work on attributions within an achievement context and suggests that there are four primary perceived causes of achievement outcomes: ability, effort, task difficulty, and luck. According to this model the four perceived causes represent three dimensions: stability, locus of control, and controllability. Ability and task difficulty are considered to be stable, effort and luck unstable. The locus-of-control dimension is viewed as being either internal or external; ability and effort are internal, task difficulty and luck external. An attribution to good luck as an explanation for passing an examination would be thought of as an external, unstable attribution. An attribution to ability for the same passing grade would represent a stable, internally perceived cause for attribution. As noted by Ruble and Boggianno (1980) other attributions beyond the four proposed in Weiner's model may also be useful in explaining behavior within an achievement context. To date, however, the bulk of the research has been focused on the four attributions identified by Weiner.

Weiner's model has clear relevance to educational practice, both from the perspective of the learner and the teacher. Considering first the nature of self-attributions about success and failure in school, consistent findings confirm that mildly handicapped children tend to be self-blaming for failure (Harter

& Zigler, 1974; MacMillan & Keogh, 1971). Retarded pupils appear to interpret even neutral events (e.g., task interruption) as failure and as due to personal inadequacy, a stable and internal cause. Normally achieving children attribute task interruption to teacher interference, or to other external and unstable causes (MacMillan & Keogh, 1971). We can only speculate about the long-term consequences of stable, internal, negative attributions on perceived competence and self-concept. The point becomes especially salient given that exceptional pupils experience failure on a fairly regular basis.

By the same token, exceptional pupils' attributions about success in achievement situations need investigation, as it may well be that occasional successes have limited impact on perceived competence because the attributions are to unstable, external causes (e.g., luck or an easy task). Lahti's (1979) research provides preliminary evidence in this regard. She presented low-achieving, average-achieving, and high-achieving junior high school boys' success experiences on school-like tasks, finding differences in expectations and attributions. Specifically, low achievers made external and unstable attributions to success whereas high achievers attributed success to internal stable causes. Low achievers also reported more affective indicators of low esteem, for example, feelings of being unsure, scared, embarrassed. Lahti's work provides further support for the importance of pupils' attribution in achievement settings.

The attributions by others of importance in handicapped children's lives also deserve discussion. As has been noted already, self-perceptions of competence are, in part, a function of the attitudes and behaviors of others. Retarded children have been found to have external motivational orientations and to rely heavily on others for standards of performance and for reinforcement. It seems likely that their relative self-perceptions are built up through exposure to attitudes of parents, teachers, and peers. Parents' attributions about their children's achievement were tested directly by Lavelle (1977), who asked parents of retarded, educationally handicapped, and normally achieving children about the causes of their children's successes or failures on a series of school-like tasks. As expected, parents of normally achieving pupils attributed their children's successes to ability and effort, their failures to task difficulty and luck. Parents of educationally handicapped (LD) children attributed both successes and failures to effort. Parents of mentally retarded pupils attributed failure to ability, and success to luck. In essence the attributions about the retarded children confirmed their cognitive limitations by attributing failure to an internal and stable condition, but "wrote off" the successes through attributions to unstable and external causes. While it is true that the attributions have a reality from the view of these parents, the findings raise interesting questions about the links between attributions, expectancies, and behaviors of adults in response to handicapped children (Lavelle & Keogh, 1981).

Research in educational settings has also demonstrated clearly that there are links between expectations, attributions, and teachers' behaviors (Brophy & Evertson, 1981; Brophy & Good, 1974). Applied to LD children, Foster and Ysseldyke (1976) and Foster, Schmidt, and Sabatino (1976) found that teachers viewed "labeled" pupils more negatively and thought they would have more problems than unlabeled pupils exhibiting the same behaviors. In Jacob's (1978) study teachers made

different interpretations of a videotape of a 9-year-old boy depending on whether or not they had been told the child was LD. Palmer (1980) found that teachers made somewhat different attributions about labeled and unlabeled secondary school pupils, and importantly, that they came to different conclusions about instructional and management needs based on their attributions. This suggests that one effect of labeling may be to induce teachers to make different attributions about the causes of pupils' academic and/or social inadequacies. It seems a reasonable inference that both instructional and management decisions will vary as a function of attributions.

The point is well illustrated by the work of Weiner and Kukla (1970), who showed that teachers' attributions are linked to affective responses as well as to evaluative decisions. Using a vignette format, these investigators presented teachers with information about pupils' ability, effort, and success or failure on an examination. Teachers were asked to assign grades on the basis of this information. The most generously rewarded pupils were those with low ability who tried hard; the least positively rewarded pupils were those with high ability who did not try hard. Perceived effort was an important influence on teachers' evaluations of, and their affective responses to, pupils.

While the impact of teachers' attributions on their decisions and behaviors has been demonstrated, the constellations of pupil characteristics that form the basis of teachers' responses have not been precisely delineated. Braun's (1976) review of the teacher expectancy literature identified a number of child variables of importance, including sex, ethnicity, and attractiveness. Keogh (1982a) has discussed the impact of pupils' temperament on teachers' decisions. Based on research with over 300 primary grade pupils, Pullis and Cadwell (1982) found that pupils' temperament influenced teachers' grades, their estimates of children's ability, and their management decisions in a variety of classroom situations. Individual differences in pupils' temperament were also found to influence teachers' perceptions of teachability of LD (Keogh, 1983) and preschool children (Keogh, 1982a, 1982b).

Kornblau (1982) and Kornblau and Keogh (1980) suggest that teachers have a priori views of what characterizes "teachable" or model pupils; and that their responses to individual children vary according to how similar or dissimilar the pupil is to this model and according to the attributions about the match or mismatch. Kornblau (1982) used a pool of teacher-generated descriptions of ideal pupils as the basis for developing a Teachability Scale. Thirty-three items are included in the scale, and the items are grouped into three factors: cognitive–motivational characteristics, school-appropriate behaviors, and personal–social characteristics. Kornblau has shown that there is considerable agreement among teachers about the characteristics of teachable pupils across grade levels, preschool through junior high, although the value or weight of particular characteristics varies somewhat with grade level.

From the perspective of the special educator, attribution theory may provide a link between child characteristics and teacher behavior. As noted already, there is a large literature that describes the impact of teachers' perceptions and expectations on their instructional and personal interactions with pupils (Brophy & Evertson, 1981; Brophy & Good, 1974). Using observational techniques, Maddox-McGinty (1975) demonstrated that classroom teachers' interactions with individual children varied as a function of their perceptions of the children's teachability. One generalization emerging from these studies is that it is not just the recognition of individual differences among children, but the attributions made about the causes of these differences, that influences teachers' behavior.

Attributions of handicapped pupils about the causes of their own successes and failures also provide information of instructional importance. Dweck's (Dweck, 1975; Dweck & Goetz, 1978; Dweck & Reppucci, 1973) work on "learned helplessness," for example, suggests that poor learners often attribute achievement outcomes to influences beyond their own control; that is, they believe that outcomes are noncontingent with their own behavior. In varying degrees many mildly handicapped children evidence signs of learned helplessness; thus, for some of these students at least, attribution retraining may be an appropriate intervention.

Another motivationally based approach to achievement of relevance to special educators is the work of Susan Harter on perceived competency (Harter, 1978, 1981). This research program is of interest both substantively and methodologically, and deserves brief review within the context of mildly handicapped pupils.

Perceived Competence

Using Robert White's (1959) "concept of competence" or effectance motivation as backdrop, Harter (1978, 1981) has formulated a model of intrinsic motivation that takes into account both individual differences and developmental change, and that considers the roles of socializing agents as well as of individually focused characteristics. Harter notes that White viewed effectance motivation as a global construct, suggesting that there was an intrinsic "urge toward competence" which was reinforced and developed through successful mastery attempts (i.e., positive outcomes). While of considerable appeal, White's construct lacks precision and is difficult to test quantitatively. Harter's refinements and extensions of White's formulation consider the implications of failure for mastery motivation, document a relationship between affective response (pleasure) and task difficulty, address questions of the contributions of socializing agents and individual social histories on motivation, and lead to differentiation among domains of perceived competence. Harter's work is of interest to special educators from both conceptual and methodological perspectives.

Harter and her colleagues have identified three primary areas of competence which in their opinion are particularly relevant in understanding self-concept in elementary school children. These are cognitive competence, which emphasizes achievement or academic performance; social competence, which addresses peer relationships; and physical competence, which has to do with physical and outdoor activities. These three areas of perceived competence, along with a fourth domain, a "general sense of worth," have been operationally defined and can be measured using the Perceived Competence Scale (Harter, 1982).

Given the pervasive problems with measurement that have plagued research on self-concept, the Perceived Competence Scale deserves brief review. The Scale consists of 28 items which tap the four self-concept areas. Items are presented in a "structured alternative format," which allows a child to indicate whether a competence or a noncompetence statement is "really true for me" or "sort of true for me." In Harter's view the structured alternative format minimizes the tendency for respondents to give socially desirable responses, a serious problem in most self-report inventories.

Psychometric properties of the scale are reasonably good. The factor structure has been found to be consistent across several age groups and has been replicated with independent samples; internal consistency of scales is acceptable; and test-retest reliabilities are high. Correlations among subscales are moderate, yet there is some independence of self-perceptions of competence within the domains as defined by Harter. Children's self-reports of competence and teacher's ratings on a similar scale were significantly related, providing some evidence of convergent validity. Further, children's reports of perceived cognitive competence were found to relate to other measures including motivational orientation, preference for challenge, and curiosity (Harter, 1981). The scale has been tested in a series of studies carried out by Harter and her colleagues (see Harter, 1982 for review). Their findings support the use of the scale as a reliable and reasonable technique for assessing perceived competence of school-age children.

The factorial validity of the Harter scale deserves particular note as it relates to a problem all too common in measurement of motivational and affective variables. Harter (1981) suggests that "it is imperative that the distinctions imposed by the scale constructor correspond to distinctions perceived by the child" (p. 14). This, of course, is closely tied to issues of developmental level of respondents, as the same items or statements may be interpreted differently by children in different age groups. Further, the frame of reference used by the child respondents may be the same as that of the research investigator or scale constructor. Questions of factorial invariance thus become fundamental when drawing inference from self-report scales.

This problem is sometimes acknowledged when scales are applied across a wide age or developmental range. It is seldom considered, however, when using standard self-report measures with exceptional learners. For the most part it is assumed that exceptional learners respond within the same frame of reference as nonhandicapped learners, and that the factor structure of the scale is similar for handicapped and nonhandicapped respondents. Yet, handicapped children may interpret test items in unique and individualistic ways, and may use a frame of reference that is different from that of other nonhandicapped children as well as different from that of the scale constructor. These possible differences may limit the inferences and interpretations that can legitimately be derived from the self-report responses of handicapped children. Harter's demonstration of the consistency of the factor structure of the Perceived Competence Scale serves as reminder to those investigators whose research is focused on special education populations.

Limits of space preclude a full description of Harter's research to date. However, her work relating motivational orientations to classroom learning is particularly relevant to the present volume. In the broadest sense the goal in this line of research was to determine if components of classroom learning could be linked to intrinsic or extrinsic motivational functions. Focusing on the domain of cognitive competence, Harter (1978) found that elementary age children identified five different motivational aspects of classroom learning: preference for challenge versus preference for easy work assigned; incentive to work to satisfy one's own interest and curiosity versus working to please the teacher and obtain good grades; independent mastery attempts versus dependence on the teacher; independent judgment versus reliance on teacher's judgment; internal criteria for success/failure versus external criteria for success/failure. Following tests and revisions, the first two scales were merged into a single scale entitled Curiosity/Interest; and a separate factor, labeled Independent Judgment Versus Reliance on Teachers' Judgment, was identified.

Of particular interest were findings demonstrating changes in children's perceptions of classroom learning with age and grade. Specifically, scores on the subscales changed from third grade through junior high school. Independent Judgment Versus Reliance on Teachers' Judgment, and Internal Criteria Versus External Criteria shifted toward a more intrinsic orientation; in contrast, the other three scales (Preference for Challenge, Curiosity/Interest, and Independent Mastery) changed from an intrinsic to an extrinsic orientation. Harter has posed several interpretations of these findings, including possible developmental changes in motivation, or the possibility that schools in fact may stifle "children's intrinsic interest in school learning, particularly with regard to challenges, curiosity, and independent mastery" (1978, p. 36).

Possible effects of schooling on children's motivational characteristics may be particularly potent when we consider the educational experiences of exceptional pupils served in special education programs. Given the importance of socialization history on the development of motivational orientations and on perceived competence, it is predictable that children who are frequently failures in academic and social areas, who experience prolonged dependency on others, and who have limitations and/or distortions in interpreting the meaning or consequences of events, would have low perceived competence and would tend towards an external motivational orientation. Considerable evidence supports this interpretation. Harter and Zigler (1974) found that normally developing children were more intrinsic than were retarded children matched on mental age. Harter (1978) found differences favoring normal children in response to mastery of challenging tasks. MacMillan (1975) demonstrated that retarded and normal children were different in their response to task interruption, the retardates tending to be more self-blaming than the normals. This generalized expectancy for failure was apparent even when the meaning of interruption was defined as success or as a neutral event (MacMillan & Keogh, 1971). Testing the social history hypothesis, Keogh, Cahill, and MacMillan (1972) found that expectancy for failure and a self-blaming response to interruption were characteristic of 12-year-old but not 9-year-old educationally handicapped pupils. The older unsuccessful pupils were similar to retarded children in their interpretation of interruption, suggesting that self-blame for failure and an expectancy for failure develop, in part at least, with the experience of persistent failure on problem-solving tasks. A possible inference from these findings is that school contributes to the development of negative motivational and affective characteristics of exceptional pupils.

Implications for Research with Mildly Handicapped Children

Whether due to disenchantment with strict behavioral approaches to instruction, or because of increased sensitivity to the role of motivation in cognitive performance, the past 10 years have seen a dramatic increase in research on affective variables of importance in learning settings. The bulk of this research has been carried out outside the traditional special education arena. Yet a number of approaches have particular relevance for exceptional children who often evidence profound motivational and affective problems associated with, and likely contributing to, their primary handicapping condition. Several approaches have been reviewed as especially promising in providing a framework for analysis of affective or motivational variables that may be useful in understanding, and perhaps improving, cognitive and educational performance of exceptional children. Taken as a whole, the findings raise a number of questions that have implications for decisions about children and their instruction. What are the motivational and affective consequences of placement in mainstream or segregated programs? How can more intrinsic motivational orientations be nurtured and developed in children with cognitive or physical limitations? How pervasive and stable are the motivational consequences of limitations in a particular competence area? What is the impact of perceptions and attributions of peers and teachers on self-views of handicapped learners?

Mainstreaming

The term "mainstreaming" is an educational corollary to the Scandinavian principle of "normalization." Normalization suggests that disabled persons be exposed to, and placed in, environments that approximate normal environments to the maximum extent possible in light of their disability. One environment is the educational setting, and educators have in large numbers advocated placement of handicapped learners in the mainstream of public education (i.e., regular classes) to the maximum extent possible. Legislation (e.g., PL 94-142) incorporates the term "least restrictive" environment or alternative (LRA) instead of the term mainstreaming. LRA is a legal concept, and several authors (Semmel, Gottlieb, & Robinson, 1979) have offered a continuum of educational alternatives in an ordered manner, these including separate special schools, resource rooms, and individual tutoring. Although the concept of LRA is the foundation of integrated educational programing, such educational modifications are commonly called mainstreaming, and will be referred to as such in this chapter.

Kaufman, Gottlieb, Agard, and Kukic (1975) proposed a definition of mainstreaming that incorporated three major components: (a) integration, (b) educational planning and programing processes, and (c) clarification of responsibilities among educational personnel. It has been argued (MacMillan & Semmel, 1977) that if all three components must be present then few, if any, programs described to date meet the definition of "mainstreaming," at least for EMR pupils. The most common element used to define mainstreaming in practice is *temporal integration*, which maximizes the opportunities for handicapped children to interact with nonhandicapped children. A common figure cited for the amount of temporal integration required to constitute "mainstreaming" is 50% of the school day (Gottlieb, 1981). However, that 50% frequently includes time spent between classes in the hall, at lunch, at recess, and the like (Zigler & Muenchow, 1979).

Despite the unclear boundaries between EMR and LD classifications, it should be noted that most programs for LD pupils are regular-class based. Specialized services are provided by "pullout" programs in resource rooms for limited periods of the day and by special instruction within the regular classrooms. The mainstream issue, then, is more appropriately considered within the context of EMR rather than LD programs. Let us consider the available evidence on mainstreaming by the following topics: (a) the process, (b) academic achievement, and (c) social adjustment.

Process

A major impetus behind mainstreaming was the overrepresentation of minority children in EMR classes. This served as a basis for *Diana, Larry P.*, and *P.A.S.E.* One consideration is the impact of mainstreaming on the ethnic composition of classes. Asked directly, did mainstreaming alter the ethnic representation in EMR classes? The result of the California decertification of between 11,000 and 14,000 EMRs bears on the issue directly. Although a large percentage of decertified EMRs were ethnic minority pupils, the overall impact on the proportion of minority EMRs was not great. The percent of black EMRs in 1973–1974 was 24.56 and in 1977–1978 was 23.22. For Hispanics the percentage in 1973–1974 was 22.74 and in 1977–1978 was 22.64 (Lambert, 1981). The consistency of the percentages at the two time periods is to be noted, as decertification resulted in a 48% reduction in EMR enrollments overall (Gottlieb, 1981).

During the early 1970s the state of Texas removed mildly handicapped learners from special classes and integrated them into regular classes. Gottlieb, Agard, Kaufman, and Semmel (1976) reported on the regular classes into which the previously segregated EMR children were placed. Caucasian EMR children (n = 115) were placed in regular classes that averaged 61.1% Caucasian; black EMR children (n = 83) in classes averaging 43.8% Caucasian; and Mexican-American EMR (n = 143) children in classes that averaged 29.1% Caucasian. These figures do not suggest racial segregation in mainstream placements, since few differences were found between classroom composition and the ethnic representation of the school as a whole. Gottlieb (1981) commented regarding these figures that as long as mainstreamed EMRs attend neighborhood schools that are racially segregated, the switching of EMRs from segregated self-contained to regular classes is unlikely to alter the ethnic balance of classmates in either class setting. Data to date lead to the interpretation that mainstreaming has not had a major impact on changing the ethnic composition of classes in which these marginal students are enrolled.

A second process consideration has to do with pupil-setting match. When mainstreaming of EMR children occurs, a frequent dilemma confronting those charged with placement decisions concerns what classes in the regular program should be selected. Should EMR pupils be placed with CA peers (where they will likely be behind in achievement) or be placed with pupils of similar achievement levels (where they will be older than their classmates)? Evidence from both Project PRIME (Kaufman, Agard, & Semmel, in press) and the California decertification process (Meyers, MacMillan, & Yoshida, 1975) suggested the EMR children were placed into classes where they were about 1 year older than their classmates. PRIME data revealed further that the "normal" classmates were subaverage in both IQ and socioeconomic status (Kaufman et al., in press). Meyers et al. (1975) found that the decertified EMRs were placed into very low-achieving classes, a finding corroborated by Keogh and Levitt (1976) in their follow-up of 153 decertified junior high school students.

A third process aspect of mainstreaming has to do with instruction. Extensive observational data from Project PRIME (Kaufman et al., in press) revealed both similarities and differences in instructional characteristics between regular and special classes. In regular classes teachers spent 75.7% of the time in large-group instruction (teaching the class as a whole), while special-class teachers spent 44.8% of the time in large-group instruction. Conversely, special-class teachers engaged in individual instruction 26.7% of the time as contrasted to 12.0% of the time for regular-class teachers. Regular-class teachers reported that they spent, on average, 16% of the school day teaching reading, while special-class teachers reportedly spent 27% of the school day on reading instruction.

Similarities between regular and special classes were reported in the amount of questioning and directing, amount of time spent interacting with teachers, and the amount of time interacting with peers. With the exception of grouping arrangements for instruction and the time spent on reading instruction, the data reported by Kaufman et al. (in press) are strikingly similar for regular and special classes. In light of these similarities, Semmel et al. (1979) concluded that it is not suprising that achievement differences between children in these two settings have not been dramatic.

More will be said later about goals for mainstream education of the mildly handicapped, but in the present context it is important to note that the goals of change in racial composition of classes, reduction of the percentage of minority children in the EMR category, and the provision of different instructional climates have not been achieved (Gottlieb, 1981). Let us turn our attention now to the evidence on achievement and social adjustment differences for mildly handicapped learners in special and regular classes.

Achievement

One of the principal arguments advanced against segregated special EMR classes was their failure to promote superior academic achievement despite smaller class size and specially trained teachers (Dunn, 1968). The strong emotion attached to the issue of special classes for EMR children was not as evident for LD or ED children, largely because these two categories have not contained a disproportionate number of ethnic minority children, and because, as already noted, most LD pupils were regular-class based. An inconsistent but growing literature addresses the efficacy issue with EMR pupils.

Ten efficacy studies comparing EMR children in special classes to those in regular classes were published between 1932 and 1965. None of these studies reported significantly superior achievement by the special-class students. Five found significantly better achievement for pupils in regular-class placement (Bennett, 1932; Cassidy & Stanton, 1959; Elenbogen, 1957; Mullen & Itkin, 1961; Pertsch, 1936) and five reported no differences in achievement (Ainsworth, 1959; Blatt, 1958; Goldstein, Moss, & Jordan, 1965; Thurstone, 1959; Wrightstone, Forlano, Lepkowski, Sontag, & Edelstein, 1959). This pattern of findings led Dunn (1968) to conclude that low-IQ children were not well served by segregated special-class programs. Based on their review Semmel et al. (1979) concluded: "Not one study indicated that handicapped children achieved at higher levels in special classes than in regular grades (p. 237)." Unfortunately, the inferences to be drawn from these studies are unclear, as the studies themselves are flawed.

The efficacy studies have been roundly criticized on methodological grounds (Guskin & Spicker, 1968; Kirk, 1964). MacMillan (1971) notes the likely selective bias in sampling, that is, children who remained in regular grades were superior in achievement and thereby avoided placement in the special class; and/or the regular class sample contained unknown proportions of low-IQ children who would have avoided identification as EMR had they been in a district offering EMR programs. The possible sampling bias is also inherent in most efficacy studies of LD, ED, or BD children. That is, achievement may be confounded with social and behavioral characteristics that influence identification and placement. Thus, definitive comparisons among programs are difficult to make.

A second methodological issue concerns the appropriateness of achievement tests used as the major outcomes of importance. Special EMR classes often offer curricula that emphasize content other than reading and math per se, particularly in the early elementary years. LD or ED pupils may be in programs that target social behaviors rather than academic skills. Therefore, it should come as no surprise that one group of children taught reading and math (i.e., regular-class students) surpassed a group of children taught social skills (i.e., special-class students) on measures tapping traditional academic learnings. Finally, most studies employed children as the unit of measurement, when teacher effectiveness (not administrative arrangement) may have been the component of importance. Classes, rather than individuals, may be the appropriate unit of analysis.

A study of the efficacy of special classes for ED children was conducted by Vacc (1968); these same students were followed up some 5 years after they had entered special ED classes (Vacc, 1972). Pre- and posttest data on achievement after 1 year in special classes indicated higher achievement for the children in the special class. The follow-up data compared the performance of 11 of the original 16 special-class children who had been returned to regular classes for at least 2 years. The achievement of these 11 was not significantly different from that of ED students who had never been placed in special classes. The failure to demonstrate long-term achievement benefits for special classes may call into question the efficacy of special ED classes, but the criticisms of the EMR efficacy studies apply as well to Vacc's study.

The early efficacy studies describe how low-IQ children (usually those without concomitant serious achievement deficits) performed in regular classes without ancillary support. The more recent research that evaluates mainstreaming usually involves programs wherein some ancillary support services are provided to the child either in the form of a resource room pullout program or services delivered in the regular class. However, interpretation of results is still limited because of methodological constraints. As example, two projects (Rodee, 1971; Walker, 1974) failed to assign subjects to treatments randomly, thus leading to the suspicion that the more able children were mainstreamed while the less able remained in segregated special classes. Both of these studies reported significantly higher achievement in reading for mainstreamed children; however, no difference was found in arithmetic achievement. In one of the few studies using random assignment of EMR children to either a resource room (45 to 60 minutes each day) or a special class, Budoff and Gottlieb (1976) found no significant differences in reading or arithmetic achievement.

Bradfield, Brown, Kaplan, Rickert, and Stannard (1973) studied six EMR children — three integrated into a third grade and three into a fourth grade. Both classes were described as having low teacher–pupil ratios and as individualized; teachers of both classes were given inservice training. Although the test was not specified, the authors reported that the integrated EMRs achieved as well as control children in special classes. The achievement of the integrated EMRs' nonretarded classmates, however, was lower in certain academic subjects than was that of nonretarded children in classes with no mainstreamed EMRs. During the second year, the integrated EMRs made significantly greater gains in reading and math as compared to EMR children in special classes. Further, the nonretarded classmates in the mainstreaming class made greater gains in math than did those in classes not involved in the mainstreaming program. Other comparisons of fourth graders and all achievement comparisons of third grade nonretarded children revealed no reliable differences in reading or math. These findings provide support for mainstream placement, but are obviously limited by sample size and possible teacher–program differences.

Meyers et al. (1975) examined 12 California school districts as they integrated former EMR students back into regular grades according to the mandates in *Diana*. The study, in part, consisted of a comparison of Metropolitan Achievement Test (MAT) scores by three groups: decertified (D), EMR children remaining in special classes, and low-achieving regular-class control children (RC) matched with D subjects on the basis of class, sex, and ethnicity. An analysis of covariance (with grade level as covariate), performed on MAT reading and math scores, indicated that the three groups (decertified, EMR, regular class) differed in both subject matter areas. EMR children scored significantly lower than decertified students, who, in turn, scored significantly lower than regular-class children in both reading and math. Interestingly, decertified students' class marks from teachers in reading and math were not lower than those received by regular-class students.

Keogh and Levitt (1976) studied a sample of 267 students who had been in EMR programs as elementary school children but who had changed status in the California decertification program. When followed up in junior high school, 57% of the 267 were in regular classes; 7% had been reassigned to EMR programs; 10% were in special classes for educationally handicapped pupils; 16% had transferred, were in court placements, or suspended. It was not possible to find 56 (21%) of the original sample. Seventy percent of the decertified pupils had been placed in 6 of the 18 junior high schools in the district, mostly low-achievement schools. Each target student was matched with four classmates similar in sex and ethnicity; teachers were not told which pupils were target or comparison, yet teachers rated decertified pupils as doing less well academically and socially than their peers. Former EMR pupils also performed less well on standard achievement tests than did comparison students, although achievement in the six schools was overall below district and national norms. Despite findings that former EMR students were lower than classmates in achievement and personal social skills, teachers were unaware which pupils had previously been in special education programs, suggesting that the decertified students' overall performance in school was within the range of their classmates. The results indicate that the former EMRs had problems in academic and personal–social domains, but that they were not dramatically discrepant from peers.

Project PRIME (Kaufman et al., in press) included norm-referenced achievement measures taken on integrated and segregated EMRs as well as on regular class controls. The two EMR groups (segregated and mainstreamed) achieved at a comparable level; however, this was a lower level than that of the regular class controls. More specifically, both EMR samples achieved in the lowest one percentile on standardized achievement tests of reading and arithmetic.

In light of the research evidence on the academic achievement of mildly handicapped learners in regular and special classes, the relevant question does not appear to be whether they achieve better in one administrative arrangement or another. A major generalization is that mildly handicapped children achieve poorly in most administrative arrangements. Semmel et al. (1979), after reviewing the research on mainstreaming, wrote:

> An examination of the data from the investigations reviewed reveals one marked fact: Regardless of class placement, mentally retarded children read exceedingly poorly. When differences between class placement do occur, these differences may be statistically significant but are probably trivial insofar as they affect retarded children's overall success in school. We note that in the investigations cited, mean reading scores of EMR pupils never reached a grade level of 4.0. . . . Instructional alternatives that have been offered to date have proven relatively ineffectual regardless of the environment in which these children are taught. (p. 237)

Social Adjustment

The efficacy studies discussed previously yielded limited information about the adjustment of retarded children in school, and the criticisms leveled at the studies of achievement also pertain to those focused on adjustment. The evidence on social adjustment consists primarily of two kinds: self-concept and sociometric status. Since selected research on these topics was reviewed earlier in this chapter, only highlights of the findings will be presented here.

The widely held clinical belief that LD pupils are low in self-concept receives support from a consistent but rather limited empirical literature (see the noncognitive section of this review). Larsen et al. (1973) found LD elementary school pupils more discrepant in real–ideal perceptions than were nondisabled peers. Black (1974), working with a clinical sample of referred children, reported that LD pupils were lower in self-concept than were other subgroups. In a longitudinal study of LD adults, using an in-depth interview technique, Major-Kingsley (1982) found that the majority of her subjects reported negative self-feelings and low self-concepts as children. Interestingly, many felt these negative self-perceptions had been overcome by young adulthood. These findings as a whole are consistent with clinical observations that problem learners are likely to have low self-esteem and poor self-concepts. In Bryan and Bryan's (1982) view, poor learners feel "less worthy" in both academic and personality domains. With a few exceptions (e.g., Yauman, 1980) there has been little research that relates self-concept of LD pupils to instructional or administrative organization. The EMR literature may be more instructive in that regard.

Comparisons of self-concept scores of EMR children in regular classes with those in self-contained classes have yielded findings of no differences between groups (e.g., Budoff & Gottlieb, 1976; Walker, 1974), or differences favoring the EMRs in segregated special classes (e.g., Schurr, Towne, & Joiner, 1972). Hence, when differences are found, they suggest that EMR children profit from the protectiveness of the special class and a peer group that permits favorable self-comparisons. None of the studies reported better self-concepts in regular class EMRs.

A slightly different pattern of findings emerges from research comparing partially mainstreamed EMRs to EMRs who are totally segregated. These studies (e.g., Carroll, 1967) have yielded consistent findings that mainstreamed and partially integrated handicapped children score higher on self-concept measures than do totally segregated children. However, the designs employed in most self-concept studies do not permit ruling out a selective bias in sampling. What remains unclear is the importance of the reference group and/or the individual pupil's status in classes. That is, the reference group for handicapped segregated learners is composed of other handicapped pupils; for mainstreamed pupils the reference group includes nonhandicapped pupils. Presumably class status would be higher for a handicapped child in a self-contained special class than in a mainstreamed class. Clearly both reference group and within-class standing are influences on self-concept and must be taken into account in reviewing evidence on this topic.

Research on sociometric status of mildly handicapped learners in various classroom settings is far more extensive than that on self-concept (see MacMillan & Morrison, 1984, for an extended analysis of the EMR literature). Since Johnson's (1950) early study, the research on the social position of mildly retarded children in regular classes reveals a consistent finding of inferior social position. Gottlieb (1981) contends that one of the major factors underlying the push for mainstreaming was the hope that once nonhandicapped children had an opportunity to interact with handicapped children in the regular class, there would be a reduction in the unfamiliarity between EMR and nonretarded children. It was supposed that greater familiarity would then lead to greater acceptance. A more systematic version of the "contact hypothesis" (Christopolos & Renz, 1969) predicts that people who are initially negatively valued will become less attractive, while those initially positively valued or neutrally valued will become more highly valued. The assumption underlying mainstreaming was that EMR or LD children were neutrally valued and would be more positively valued by nonhandicapped children once they had extended contact with them in the regular classes.

Empirical support for the contact hypothesis has not been forthcoming in EMR research. When Goodman, Gottlieb, and Harrison (1972) had nonretarded children rate other nonretarded children, mainstreamed EMRs, and segregated EMRs, the nonretarded children enjoyed the highest social status. Surprisingly, nonretarded males rejected the mainstreamed EMRs significantly more often than they did the segregated EMRs. Gottlieb and Budoff (1973) studied "exposure" as a possible determinant of the social status of integrated EMRs. Nonretarded children from two schools (one traditional with enclosed rooms, the other an open school with no interior walls) rated integrated and segregated EMRs. Again, partially integrated EMRs received less favorable ratings than did segregated EMRs, regardless of the school architecture. Both EMR and nonretarded children in the open school had lower average social status ratings than did children in the traditional school. The authors attributed this to the greater visibility of the children to their peers.

Possible reasons for the lower social status of integrated EMRs include the fact that contact provides an opportunity for EMR children to exhibit inappropriate behaviors or traits associated with low ratings. Support for this position comes from attitude studies, Gottlieb, Cohen, and Goldstein (1974) reporting more favorable attitudes in schools with no retarded children, whether integrated or in special classes. A study by Gottlieb and Davis (1973) required nonretarded children to select either a nonretarded or EMR child as a partner in a ringtoss game. Three treatment conditions were employed: (a) choice between a nonretarded child and an integrated EMR, (b) choice between a nonretarded and segregated EMR child, and (c) choice between an integrated and a segregated EMR. In Conditions a and b, the nonretarded child was selected 27 of a 28 possible times. Under Condition c, where the choice was between integrated and segregated EMRs, there was no significant difference in the preferences of the nonretarded children.

A similar pattern of findings has emerged for LD children. Bryan (1974, 1976) studied the social status of LD children enrolled in regular classes, Grades 3–5. LD children were found to be accepted less often and rejected more often than were non-LD peers. Bruininks (1978a, 1978b) investigated the social status of mainstream LD children who went to a resource room for up to 45 minutes per day. She reported lower social status for LD children as compared to that of non-LD peers. Moreover, the LD children were less accurate than non-LD peers in perceptions of their own social status. Siperstein, Bopp, and

Bak (1978) studied the social status of LD children in regular fifth and sixth grades using a peer nomination technique. They found that LD children were nominated significantly less often than non-LD children. While no LD child occupied a "star" position, neither were LD children found to occupy an "isolate" position in greater proportions than did non-LD children. Overall, consistent findings of differences in sociometric status and in peer acceptance in mainstream settings (Deshler, Schumaker, Warner, Alley, & Clark, 1980; Garrett & Crump, 1980; Scranton & Ryckman, 1979) suggest that social competence of LD pupils may be an important consideration in placement decisions (Gresham, 1983).

Applied to the question of mainstreaming, the evidence on social acceptance of mildly handicapped learners, in general, fails to provide support for the hope that mainstreaming per se improves their social status. The evidence collectively portrays these children as less well known and less accepted than their nonhandicapped peers. However, according to Gottlieb (1981) undue pessimism is tempered by two considerations:

> Sociometric status scores between mainstreamed and nonretarded children indicate that about one-sixth of EMR children are as well accepted as average nonretarded children; i.e., not all retarded children are sociometrically rejected or nonaccepted. Second, there is considerable evidence that the sociometric status of mainstreamed EMR children can be improved (Ballard, Corman, Gottlieb, & Kaufman, 1978; Leyser & Gottlieb, 1980; Lilly, 1971). (p. 119)

The evidence to date does, however, testify to the fact that mere placement of mildly handicapped children into regular grades without specific treatment is likely to yield low peer acceptance for the vast majority of these children. Methodological problems with sociometric data (see earlier section of this chapter) and a lack of precise dependent measures must be addressed if the reasons for low social status are to be understood more fully. As noted recently by Bryan (1982), research on the social problems of LD pupils also requires attention to both developmental and gender influences as well. Further research providing additional documentation of the lower status of mildly handicapped children in regular grades is unnecessary. What is needed is research that unravels some of the complexities underlying the dynamics of acceptance and rejection.

Efforts to Prevent Developmental Problems Through Early Intervention

Interest in the importance of the preschool years in ultimate cognitive, emotional, and social development dates back to the early Iowa studies (e.g., Skeels & Dye, 1939; Wellman, Skeels, & Skodak, 1940). However, attempts to *prevent* mild retardation are a relatively new development. Ramey, Sparling, Bryant, and Wasik (1982) note that four trends are contributors to this prevention emphasis:

1. Hunt's (1961) book, *Intelligence and Experience*, promoted an appreciation of the potential power of early experience to modify some components of early intelligence.
2. A series of investigations (e.g., Golden, Birns, Bridger, & Moss, 1971; Ramey & Campbell, 1979) suggested that it is

during the second year that differences in cognitive abilities of children from different socioeconomic backgrounds emerge.

3. The human potential movement of the 1960s and 1970s provided a social climate that favored helping socially disadvantaged families gain access to the American educational and economic mainstream.

4. Trends toward cost–benefit analyses prompted social scientists to seek efficient ways of helping disadvantaged families and children.

Intervention programs differ in their definition of early, some beginning in infancy, others during the preschool years. Partly because of a philosophy that "earlier is better" derived from assumptions of developmental plasticity in the infancy period, and partly because preliminary evaluations of Project Headstart revealed that it did not reduce the prevalence of mild retardation (Westinghouse, 1969), there has been a shift toward infant programs. During the past 15 years early intervention has become one of the most heavily funded areas in the field of mental retardation, and it remains an area enthusiastically endorsed as a promising direction.

Robinson (1976) described two types of early intervention programs in the field of mental retardation: (a) programs for the poor, and (b) programs for the handicapped. (The reader is referred to comprehensive reviews of programs for handicapped infants and young children by Hayden & Haring, 1976, 1977; Keogh, Wilcoxen, & Bernheimer, 1983; and the volume edited by Tjossem, 1976). It is with the former type of program that we are concerned here, as these programs are directed at prevention of the mild handicapping conditions which are the focus of this chapter. Tjossem (1976) used the term "environmental risk" to describe the status of children who appear biologically sound and who have no major physical problems, but who are born into environments that are associated with a disproportionately high number of children with mild handicaps. Links between poverty environments and a host of problems in development have been clearly delineated (for reviews see Farran, Haskins, & Gallagher, 1980; Keogh et al., 1983). The impact of poverty on risk status is evidenced in a number of ways.

Compared to more advantaged groups, low-income mothers receive less prenatal care and their infants are at higher risk for pre- and postnatal complications (Kessner, Singer, Kalk, & Schlesinger, 1973; Placek, 1977). Chronic untreated health conditions, for example, vision, dental, and nutritional problems are common. According to the Select Panel Report (1981), an estimated 62% of children under age 4 living in poverty have not received full immunization for polio. Lead poisoning, a known teratogenic agent, is twice as common in poverty as in nonpoverty environments (Berwick & Komaroff, 1982). Relative to children from socioeconomically advantaged homes, poor children have substantially higher rates of school failure, and are at risk for classification as EMR.

Given the well-described relationships among SES, health, cognition, and educational status, it is ironic that prevention programs have been focused primarily in the educational arena. As discussed in subsequent sections of this review, the results of educational interventions are in general positive. This is a rather surprising finding given the complexity of risk, its many contributors, and the relatively limited scope of interventions (Keogh et al., 1983). We can speculate that the impact of intervention might have been greater had the educational programs been accompanied by comprehensive medical, social, and economic programs. What is clear is that children from poverty environments are at risk for a variety of mildly handicapping conditions, including school failure. It is likely that many of these conditions could be lessened or ameliorated given comprehensive early intervention programs. Of particular interest in the present chapter is consideration of early intervention as a step toward prevention of developmental delays, especially mild mental retardation.

Early Experience Versus Life Span Positions

At present there are two contrasting positions about the relative importance of early years on development: the *early experience position* and the *life span position*. Advocates of the early experience position argue that experiences during the early years exert a disproportionate influence on developmental outcomes. Those who advance a life span position consider early experience a necessary link in development, but do not assume that early experiences have direct, long-term effects on adult behavior. Goldhaber (1979) contrasted the two positions as follows:

> The strong early experience position views early experience as both a necessary, and in many instances, a sufficient condition for future development. The strong life span position views early experience as a necessary but not sufficient condition for future development. One should not interpret this strong life span as implying that the early years are unimportant. To say that experiences during the early years are not sufficient for future development does not make these experiences any less necessary. (p. 119)

The early experience position derives from several sources (see Bloom, 1964; Caldwell, 1974; Goldhaber, 1979; Hunt, 1969). Most of the experimental research employed infrahuman subjects exposed to extremely atypical early rearing experiences, and suggested a "critical period" during infancy where experiences, or lack thereof, exerted dramatic influences on development. These findings were interpreted to suggest that "the effects of cultural deprivation are analogous to the experimentally found effects of experiential deprivation in infancy" (Hunt, 1969, p. 47).

A second series of reports in support of the early experience position concerned children exposed to extreme environmental deprivation in early childhood (e.g., Dennis, 1960; Goldfarb, 1955). Institutional and orphanage research children were found to evidence a variety of developmental delays, often severe in nature. Reports about children coming from a "culture of poverty" (e.g., Deutsch, 1960) also seemed to suggest that the early years are a "critical period" and that irreversible harm can result from unstimulating environments. This hypothesis received support from a third line of research in which planned interventions were designed to provide experiences lacking in institutions (e.g., Skeels & Dye, 1939) and poor neighborhoods (e.g., Kirk, 1958).

The conceptual analyses of Hunt (1961, 1969) and Bloom (1964) were influential in the academic community and among politicians and policymakers. Essentially, these scholars emphasized that experience and environment are important determinants of intelligence; and that environmental intervention will have its pronounced effect before age 4. This view of the importance of early experience is challenged by others who adopt a life span perspective.

The life span position has been advanced most forcefully by the British psychologists Clarke and Clarke. They provided a review of issues such as critical periods, the durability of early experiences, the reversibility of early deprivation, and the relevance of animal research to theories of early experiences of humans. They reached the following conclusions (1976, p. 12):

1. The notion that a critical period of development exercises a powerful influence on later characteristics is not in accord with some evidence about the development of deprived children, specifically about those who later experienced significant environment change.
2. Normally, for most children, environmental changes do not occur, so the outcome of later life may be a result not merely of early experience, but of continuing experiences.
3. The results of experimental studies of extreme deprivation in animals, although important, must be extrapolated to humans cautiously.
4. Important experiments about reversing the effects of early experiences in animals have yet to be carried out.

Clearly, the life span position provides a more optimistic outlook for educators dealing with children at risk for school failure. It suggests that early intervention is insufficient, in and of itself, to assure school success. It also provides reasons for initiating interventions at a point in time after preschool years without assuming that the critical period for intellectual and achievement stimulation has passed. The life span view does not negate the importance of early experience but rather argues for the impact of experiences in all developmental periods. Let us now examine the evidence on the effectiveness of early intervention with environmentally at-risk children.

Evidence on Preventing Mild Retardation

During the Johnson administration's War on Poverty funding was provided for Head Start, a program designed to prevent developmental problems, especially school failure, in children from impoverished homes through comprehensive medical, dental, social, and educational preschool services. Because of complex economic, sociopolitical, and professional reasons, the major component of Head Start to be operationalized was the educational one. For the most part Head Start came to mean preschool education. A number of different program models were implemented, many borrowed from traditional nursery school programs and based in general developmental theory. (These models and programs are discussed in the chapter by Stallings & Stipek, this volume.)

Darlington, Royce, Snipper, Murray, and Lazar (1980) described a follow-up of 14 early intervention programs. Recently, Lazar and Darlington (1982) reported on a collaborative follow-up of 11 projects, independently conducted, whose subjects ranged from 9 to 19 years of age at the time of follow-up. The importance of these follow-up data warrants closer inspection.

CONSORTIUM FINDINGS

The Consortium for Longitudinal Studies (Darlington et al., 1980; Lazar & Darlington, 1982) pooled the data of the 11 original studies on preschool intervention for low-income families. They were able to locate 1599 children between the ages of 9 and 19 from the original total of roughly 2700 subjects. During the period 1976–1977 these children were contacted and data collected on intelligence, school records, school-administered achievement tests, attitudes and values, and the impact on the family. A description of the original programs can be found in Lazar and Darlington (1982). While all programs were concerned with promoting cognitive skills, there was considerable variability in curricula, in assignment of subjects to groups, and in the form of service delivery employed.

Lazar and Darlington (1982) concluded that the early education programs produced significant positive effects on school competence, developed abilities (including achievement), children's attitudes and values, and selected family outcomes (e.g., maternal attitudes toward school performance). Participation in the programs improved the chances of a poor child's meeting the demands of the public schools. While 29% of control-group children were assigned to special education or remediation classes, only 14% of the treatment-group children were so assigned. Whereas 31% of control-group children were retained in a grade 1 or more years, only 25% of experimental children were held back. Differences were still significant when the effects of original IQ, sex, ethnic background, and family background were controlled. Findings were even more dramatic when only experimentally designed studies were included in the analyses. For example, Darlington et al. (1980) combined special education services and grade retention into a single variable (failure to meet school requirements). The experimental groups in the four experimentally designed projects had a median failure percentage of 32% compared to the control group's 53%.

While experimental subjects maintained higher IQs for 3 to 4 years after program termination, these differences were nonsignificant by the time of follow-up. There was some evidence of improved achievement test scores for experimental subjects in elementary grades, with differences in math achievement being most pronounced. Mothers of experimental children expressed more satisfaction with their children's school performance than did mothers of control children. In addition, the mothers of experimental children had higher occupational aspirations for their children than the children had for themselves. Control mothers showed no such consistent pattern.

This ambitious effort to evaluate the long-term effects of early intervention with poverty children suggests positive effects in the molar outcomes of school success, that is, retention and special education placement. Zigler and Trickett (1978) argue for the importance of these outcomes vis-à-vis moderating variables predictive of school success (e.g., IQ). Yet, the studies pooled by Lazar and Darlington (1982) did vary widely along a number of dimensions, and other insights might be gained by examining only those projects employing greater experimental controls.

FOUR EXPERIMENTAL PROJECTS

Ramey and Bryant (1982) reviewed results from those projects meeting the following criteria: (a) began before the child was 12 months of age, (b) offered continuous services to the child and/or parents from age 1 to age 3 years, (c) reported data on the developmental status of participating children, and (d) employed a true experimental design, including random assignment of high-risk children to experimentally treated and control groups. These criteria resulted in the selection of four programs: the Milwaukee Project (Garber & Heber, 1981); the Carolina Abecedarian Project (Ramey & Haskins, 1981); the Mobile Unit for Child Health Supervision (Gutelius et al., 1977); and the Florida Parent Education Program (Gordon & Guinagh, 1978). While all four projects met the criterion for adequacy of research design, they were quite diverse in the nature and intensity of services delivered, in the specific educational treatments, and in the format for delivering educational treatments. Table 24.2 summarizes the services provided experimental and control-group families in the four projects. It is important for the reader to be sensitive to the fact that this analysis of the four projects is dependent largely on IQ data. To some, this practice is troubling and they would prefer a broader band of outcomes to be considered when evaluating early intervention programs.

Table 24.2. Services Provided to Experimental and Control Families in Four Early Intervention Programs

Project	Experimentals	Controls
Milwaukee Project (Garber & Heber, 1981)	Educational daycare Home vists Vocational training for parents Periodic assessments	Periodic assessments
Abecedarian Project (Ramey & Haskins, 1981)	Educational daycare Medical care Social work services Periodic assessments	Nutritional supplements Medical care Social work services Periodic assessments
Mobile Unit (Gutelius et al., 1977)	Home visits Medical care Iron supplements Call-in consultation Periodic assessments	Referral to public health services Periodic assessments
Florida Parent Education (Gordon & Guinagh, 1978)	Home visits Play groups Periodic assessments	Periodic assessments

Note: From "Evidence for Prevention of Developmental Retardation During Infancy" by C. T. Ramey and D. M. Bryant, 1982, *Journal of the Division for Early Childhood, 5*, p. 75. Copyright 1982 by the Council for Exceptional Children. Reprinted by permission.

Ramey and Bryant (1982) rated the projects in terms of the *intensity of treatment*, which they defined as the amount of time the project had direct contact or involvement with the children or families, plus the range and variety of services offered. According to this metric the Milwaukee Project was the most intense, followed by the Abecedarian, Gordon, and Gutelius projects in rank order. The latter two differed in that the Gordon project had more contact but the Gutelius project offered a broader range of services.

All four projects enrolled children from families with low income and limited educational levels, randomly assigned subjects to experimental and control conditions, and secured measures of mental development during the first 24 months. Finally, all projects administered the Stanford-Binet at age 36 months. Figure 24.1 depicts the Mental Development Index (MDI) or IQ results for the experimental and control groups in the four projects at various points between birth and 36 months. Evident in this figure are the following:

1. Experimental and control groups of the four projects did not differ in developmental status at the time of initial assessment, but all reported significant differences at age 36 months.
2. Among the experimental groups the mean IQs at 36 months ordered identically to the Ramey and Bryant ratings of the intensity of treatments; that is Milwaukee, Abecedarian, Gordon, and Gutelius projects.
3. At 36 months, all experimental groups surpassed all control groups on mean IQ. Moreover, the mean IQs for all experimental groups were at or above the national average, while mean IQs for all control groups were below the national average.
4. The performance of control groups can be characterized as a downward trend over time, and that of experimental groups can be described as either a less severe downward trend or, in the case of Milwaukee, a slightly rising trend.

Ramey and Bryant (1982) note that when one compares the magnitude of the discrepancy in IQ at 36 months between experimental and control groups within projects an interesting finding emerges. The magnitude of the discrepancy in IQ between experimental and control groups is related to the difference in the intensity of treatments afforded the experimental and control groups. The greatest discrepancy in IQ for groups is found in the Milwaukee Project (approximately 30 points). This project provided a very intense treatment for the experimental group and virtually no treatment for the control group. The Abecedarian Project shows a 16 IQ point discrepancy between experimental and control groups; while the treatment for experimental subjects in this project was almost as intense as that in the Milwaukee Project, the controls also received considerable services. Ramey and Bryant (1982) conclude:

Therefore, it seems parsimonious to conclude that not only is the absolute developmental level of the experimentally treated children proportional to the intensity of treatment they received, but also that the magnitude of discrepancy between treated and untreated children within each program is also proportional to the difference in intensity with which those two groups were treated. (p. 77)

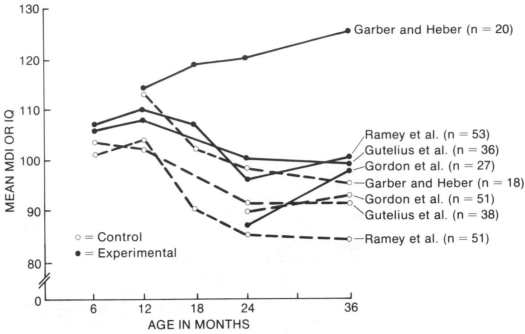

Fig. 24.1 MDI or IQ ratings of four early intervention projects.

From "Evidence for Prevention of Developmental Retardation During Infancy" by C. T. Ramey and D. M. Bryant, 1982, *Journal of the Division for Early Childhood, 5,* p. 76. Copyright 1982 by Division for Early Childhood. Reprinted by permission.

Ramey and Bryant note that the intensity of programing as an explanation awaits further verification since children were not randomly assigned to the four projects. Such a test will come in the Carolina Approach to Responsive Education (Ramey, Sparling, & Wasik, 1981) currently under way.

Of the four projects meeting the criteria of Ramey and Bryant (1982), only the Gordon subjects were included in the follow-up analysis of Lazar and Darlington (1982). The long-term effects of the various interventions provided in the other three projects must await the subjects' passage through school. Similarly, the persistence of differences between experimentals and controls will have to be studied as they relate to differences in molar outcomes such as school success.

Performance of control-group children in early intervention projects confirms the assumption that they are indeed at risk for school failure. Further, the results of well-controlled experimental projects and long-term follow-up studies suggest that intervention at an early age does prevent developmental retardation in a substantial number of cases. One question still unanswered is whether one can predict (based on either child characteristics, parent characteristics, or some combination) which cases will respond favorably to certain intervention strategies and which cases will not. Furthermore, there is need of component analysis to determine which elements of a given intervention account for the gains (or lack of deterioration) achieved by children.

To the extent that research on early intervention guides policy formulation, the interventions yielding the greatest benefits to children are those described by Ramey and Bryant (1982) as being the more *intense* and having greater *breadth of programing.* We should like to argue for an even broader

definition of intensity and breadth. That is, given the links among poverty, health, and development, it seems clear that full-scale prevention programs cannot be limited to educational interventions alone. Rather, prevention requires services directed at a number of aspects of a child's life, including medical and health-related services. It is somewhat ironic that such a program is presently mandated by federal legislation, yet is not widely implemented.

The federal program of Early and Periodic Screening, Diagnosis and Treatment (EPSDT) is a 1967 amendment to the Social Security Act which provides a mechanism for comprehensive health-related services for poverty children. The legislation contains components of outreach, screening, and treatment, and is directed at both physical and developmental problems. Although the program was to be operational in 1969, according to the Children's Defense Fund (1977), in 1974–1975 approximately 25% of Medicaid-eligible children had been screened and only about 60% of those screened had received treatment. As noted by Keogh et al. (1983) EPSDT has been plagued by administrative and implementation problems, as well as by professional controversy, so that the delivery of services is inconsistent. Reduced support for Medicaid in the last 2 years has further affected the services offered to poverty children through EPSDT; the preventive aspects of the program have been particularly curtailed.

Issues in Early Intervention

When intervention programs for lower socioeconomic children were developed nearly 2 decades ago, the interveners were rarely questioned about their motives. But in the late 1960s and thereafter minority-group social scientists as well as politicians and community leaders raised many questions about intervention philosophy, intervention methods, intended outcomes, and the possible iatrogenic effects of the intervention programs. The issues raised are part of a continuing debate and have not yet been resolved.

Gray (1971) summarized a number of ethical issues in intervention research. A first issue concerns the rights of parents. Gray notes that the parent is completely responsible for the child and has the full right to grant or withhold consent for the child's participation in any program except, possibly, in cases of extreme medical need. A more difficult issue, however, is whether parents' rights extend to decision making with respect to the intervention itself and include the right to dictate the program's goals and methods. Minority-group scholars have addressed this issue and conclude that parents and/or their representatives do indeed have the right to appraise interveners' goals and methods and to refuse to participate when the proposed procedures are judged to be not in their interests (Williams, 1980). As an example of community involvement in intervention research Williams cites the case of the Community Research Review Committee (CRRC) established by the Boston Black United Front. The purpose of CRRC was to review proposals for research in the Boston black community. Early in its existence CRRC evaluated a project that was to be conducted over a 4-year period on a group of black infants. The mothers were to be subjected to intervention over a 10-month period. Following several meetings with the principal investigators, CRRC rejected the proposals as not being in the best interests of the community and encouraged black parents to refuse to allow their babies to be used in the study. At issue in the rejection was CRRC's belief that black professionals needed to be significantly involved in the project's conceptualization and implementation. CRRC also expressed concern about the deficiency-oriented perspectives undergirding the proposed intervention.

Minority scholars have also argued that interveners are promoting a white middle-class model of what is appropriate behavior when dealing with other ethnic groups (Gray, 1971). Gray notes, for example, that developmental interveners are often accused of working with a theoretical model based on an assumption of deficiency in the subject and that while social scientists speak of cultural differences they are concerned with cultural deficiencies. In the 1970s and 1980s such perspectives have been unacceptable to minority-group scholars.

Some questions, of course, go beyond parents' and minority professionals' rights to assess proposed research and intervention programs. One criticism is that developmental interveners ignore the fact that the basic problem is the entire social system and not the young child and his family. Sroufe (1970), in commenting on a series of specific intervention projects designed for low-SES children and their parents (Bee, Nyman, Pytkowicz, Sarason, & Van Egeren, 1968; Bee et al., 1969; Streissguth, 1969), examined intervention logic, which he summarized as follows: Black people do not have equal access to the professions, general employment, or political power because they do not succeed in school, due to their inferior home environment. Sroufe (1970) observes that "at the very least,

current intervention research perpetuates the delusion that problems of black and other poor people are inherent in the ghetto, and that the solution of these problems lies in work on ghetto people" (p. 144).

Gordon (1971) similarly viewed intervention projects from a micro level. In responding to an article on parent–child centers that focused on the training of parents and services to their children (Hunt, 1971), Gordon notes that Hunt failed to consider the possibilities for improvement that might result from changes in society's maltreatment of such populations. Gordon observes, for example, that Hunt gave no attention to what changes might result from the simple introduction of more money and better life conditions. Such changes might lead to different kinds of interactions between parents and children, as well as to different courses of development. Gordon speculates that providing money or better life conditions were not considered viable interventions in that they are unlikely to be acceptable to society. Social scientists should concern themselves with proposals that society may be more willing to accept.

In a similar vein, Gray (1971) writes: "Asking a developmental intervener to work to change the whole social system is about as inappropriate as asking a thoracic surgeon why he does not give up the practice of lung surgery and instead work on outlawing cigarettes and certain pollutants in the atmosphere" (p. 83).

It is clear that there is no consensus among scholars as to what the appropriate level for developmental intervention ought to be. Most likely, intervention at both micro and macro levels will prove fruitful in the long run. The purpose of this brief section is not to provide definitive answers to this debate but rather to call the reader's attention to an often neglected literature on important ethical and philosophical issues in developmental intervention work.

Final Comments

An attempt to summarize what has been already written would be cumbersome, and so the space can be better used to consider what the research has meant to handicapped children. That is, what has been the impact of the research reviewed on the education of mildly handicapped children? To accomplish that end, we will examine the impact of research in two areas: first, changes in teaching; and second, changes in policy affecting the education of handicapped children.

A good deal of special education research dealing with mildly handicapped learners has not been concerned with "teaching." Rather, research has been influenced by cognitive and developmental psychology and the majority of variables under investigation have been within-child variables. Considerable effort has been devoted to understanding how groups of mildly handicapped children differ from groups of nonhandicapped children. Differences are defined in how they learn and how they perceive themselves, as well as in how the nonhandicapped population reacts to handicapped individuals. The research attempts designed to gain insights into these processes can be characterized as more "basic" in nature and concerned more with internal validity of the research than with the external validity of the findings. Despite the relatively limited research effort directed toward teaching, recent trends suggest more concern for instructional variables. Several examples are illustrative.

Major impetus for consideration of instructional variables came from the early work of behavioral psychologists who worked with severely impaired, often institutionalized, individuals (see MacMillan & Morrison, 1980 for review). Many of these behavioral approaches were refined and expanded to fit into special education programs in school, Hewett's (1968) "engineered classroom" being one example. The behavioral programs provided increased sensitivity to setting and motivational (i.e., reinforcement) conditions and introduced special educators to techniques and approaches that were useful across a broad range of handicapping conditions and ages. The approaches also had applicability in regular education programs, and thus drew attention from nonspecial education researchers who were interested in instructional variables.

Another major stimulant to the study of instructional variables is the information-processing–cognitive training approaches already described. Starting with more theoretical and psychologically-based questions, investigators of cognitive processing (Brown, 1977; Camp, 1980; Douglas, 1972, 1980; Meichenbaum, 1977) have become increasingly concerned with instructional components and programs. Their efforts have focused on children with somewhat different problems (e.g., impulsive, hyperactive, behaviorally disordered, or mentally retarded), yet their analyses of components of cognitive processing are useful to both regular and special education practitioners. Their contributions to theory and research have stimulated a whole series of research efforts which will likely lead to an expanded evidential base for instructional decisions.

Research that contrasts the efficacy of various administrative arrangements, including mainstreaming, has been conducted with mildly impaired learners. These studies have viewed administrative arrangements as "treatments," but have in most instances failed to consider within-program variations in curricula, materials, instructional strategies, and the like. Further, while this research permits conclusions on the consequences of *where* we deliver special education services, it fails to enlighten us much on *how* the children are taught in the various settings.

Taken as a whole we suggest that the research to date is best described as rich in *potential* implications for instructional practices. What is needed now are attempts to validate laboratory practices with learning tasks actually used in instruction under conditions encountered in school settings. The analogy of applied behavior analysis may clarify our point. Current research on learning, cognition, and noncognitive variables resembles learning developed in laboratories with infrahuman subjects. What is now needed in special education is to move the theory and principles into the applied arena as the applied behavior analysts did over a decade ago. It will then be possible to ascertain the applicability of findings of laboratory-type research for promoting more efficient learning and adjustment by mildly handicapped learners.

From another perspective, it is important to note that the historic role of special education research on instruction has been the development of materials and instructional strategies useful with both handicapped and nonhandicapped children. For example, the materials and methods of Seguin, Montessori, and Fernald have proven useful to educators in both special and general education. In short, these pioneers contributed significantly to teaching and instruction. However, the more recent line of special education research, conducted in the psychological mode and aimed at more molecular learning tasks, has moved the research to laboratory-like settings. The result is a literature that often fails to contribute directly to the teaching process. On the positive side, however, it is encouraging that investigators from a variety of disciplinary backgrounds have now begun to study special education pupils and practices.

A second approach to special education research is in terms of its impact on policy concerning the education of mildly handicapped children. Legislation funding federal agencies concerned with research in special education indicates clearly that such research is intended to be "mission oriented"—that is, designed to influence policy decisions. Yet policy in special education does not appear to follow research. Baumeister (1981) observed that current policies regarding mainstreaming, early childhood education, and deinstitutionalization cannot be defended on the basis of compelling empirical support. Rather than research directing policy, research tends to follow policy.

Baumeister (1981) argued that a policy legitimatizes research in a given area. For example, research on mainstreaming increased dramatically after passage of PL 94–142. Government agencies solicited requests for proposals (RFPs) for research on various components of PL 94–142, and mainstreaming was designated a high priority for funding. Similarly, early childhood education and education of severely handicapped children have been declared high priority areas. Research monies are allocated to investigate these areas, with the presumed intent to stimulate research that justifies the policy. This sequence of policy preceding research appears typical of the recent past of special education. We have had policy enacted through the courts and through legislation, particularly in the areas of (a) identification of mildly retarded children, (b) early intervention for at-risk children, and (c) definitions of learning disabilities. The policy decisions have stimulated research and scholarly debate on these topics. In contrast, it is difficult to identify a policy in special education precipitated by research findings.

We believe it is important to reflect on the role of research in policy formulation, or more accurately, in policy reformulation. Research findings suggest consequences that *can* result from interventions such as early intervention, mainstreaming, or early medical screening. Such programs can be shown to prevent developmental retardation, to promote higher academic achievement, or to prevent medical problems known to be associated with learning problems. However, research results do not necessarily indicate what *will* be the consequences—that is the domain of public policy. Ramey (1982) noted that Lazar and Darlington's (1982) analysis of early intervention programs demonstrated that special education placements, among other outcomes, were significantly lower for experimental than control-group children. However, whether these research-documented benefits *can* result or *will* result depends on political, economic, and social considerations. The health-related program of EPSDT is a striking case in point. Policymakers are influenced by a variety of factors. For example, economic considerations are a primary concern to policymakers and the term "cost–benefit analysis" is a key word in government circles. While it is impossible to put a dollar figure on the benefits of preventing a severe hearing loss in one child, or the raising of the average IQ of poor children by 10 points, we do know that research that demonstrates benefits to children has often failed to make its way into policy. It is time to consider when research ought to lead to policy, and to consider the implementation process a legitimate topic.

Another arena in which policy concerning special education practices has been made has been the court system. The role of research in judicial decisions and in shaping the remedy handed down by the court is perplexing. In two landmark cases (*Diana* and *Larry P.*), the Rosenthal and Jacobson (1968) study was of primary importance in convincing Judge Peckham to invoke "strict scrutiny," which required the state of California to show a "compelling state interest" for classifying children as EMR. It is interesting that a study so roundly condemned in the research community should be so influential in the court's proceedings. Further, the courts were inconsistent in the ways that considered evidence pertaining to the fairness of intelligence tests for use with black children. In *Larry P.*, Judge Peckham heard expert witnesses on both sides of the issue, and based his judgment of fairness on this testimony. Conversely, in *P.A.S.E.*, Judge Grady examined the test items himself, and based his decision on his own impressions of the items.

Finally, in prescribing the remedy in both *Diana* and *Larry P.*, Judge Peckham handed down mandates that, in some instances, were contraindicated by the extant evidence (Meyers, Sundstrom, & Yoshida, 1974). The children in question in both of these cases were marginal achievers who were not patently "mentally retarded"; yet they were clearly educationally deficient. Such children had been the target of compensatory education programs included in the budget submitted by the California legislature to both Governors Reagan and Brown. This component was "blue penciled" out of the budget by both governors. Hence, for the children in question the alternatives left for educators were: (a) do nothing and permit the academic failure to persist, and (b) label the children as EMR in order to be able to provide needed special services. Neither was an attractive option; however, the intermediate alternative represented by compensatory education (providing needed assistance without labeling) was unavailable. Judge Peckham never mentioned the possibility of mandating the state to fund compensatory education programs.

In summary, the fact that most research has not been directed specifically at the teaching process for mildly handicapped children points to an area of need for subsequent study. The evidence derived from the efficacy and mainstreaming work to date suggests that we have not been successful in teaching mildly handicapped learners, regardless of where we place them (special or regular classes), or what we call them (EMR, LD or "normal"). The challenge before us is to study the instructional process directly, rather than to continue to be preoccupied with variables such as administrative arrangements and labels, influences that account for little variance in achievement differences. The closer we get to the actual instruction, the more likely we can account for substantial proportions of variance.

The evidence concerning the apparent lack of impact of research on policy in special education suggests a need for greater sensitivity on the part of the research community. It is important that evidence be available to policymakers in a manner that is understandable and usable. Lindblom and Cohen (1979) used the term "ordinary knowledge" to describe what kind of information influences policy. They suggest that scientific knowledge can become ordinary knowledge when it filters into the public consciousness and is no longer the exclusive domain of science. If we hope that research will benefit handicapped children it is essential that our findings become ordinary knowledge and thereby be available in a manner that can influence the quality of education these children receive.

REFERENCES

Ainsworth, S. H. (1959). *An exploratory study of education, social and emotional factors in the education of educable mentally retarded children in Georgia public schools* (U. S. Office of Education Cooperative Research Program, Project No. 171). Athens: University of Georgia.

Anastasiow, N. J. (1978). Strategies and models for early childhood intervention programs in integrated settings. In M. J. Guralnick (Ed.), *Early intervention and the integration of handicapped and nonhandicapped children* (pp. 85–111). Baltimore: University Park Press.

Atkinson, R. C., & Shiffrin, R. M. (1968). Human memory: A proposed system and its control processes. In K. W. Spencer & J. T. Spence (Eds.), *The psychology of learning motivation* (Vol. 2). New York: Academic Press.

Axelrod, L. (1982). Social perception in learning disabled adolescents. *Journal of Learning Disabilities, 15*(10), 610–613.

Babad, E. Y., & Budoff, M. (1974). Sensitivity and validity of learning potential in three levels of ability. *Journal of Educational Psychology, 66*, 439–447.

Badger, E. (1976). Effects of parent education program on teenage mothers and their offspring. In K. G. Scott, T. Field, & E. Robertson (Eds.), *Teenage parents and their offspring.* New York: Grune & Stratton.

Baldwin, W. K. (1958). The educable mentally retarded child in the regular grades. *Exceptional Children, 25*, 106–108; 112.

Balla, D., & Zigler, E. (1979). Personality development in retarded persons. In N. R. Ellis (Ed.), *Handbook of mental deficiency* (2nd ed., pp. 143–168). Hillsdale, NJ: Erlbaum.

Ballard, M., Corman, L., Gottlieb, J., & Kaufman, M. J. (1978). Improving the social status of mainstreamed retarded children. *Journal of Educational Psychology, 69*, 605–611.

Bauer, R. H. (1979). Memory, acquisition, and category clustering in learning disabled children. *Journal of Experimental Child Psychology, 27*, 365–383.

Bauer, R. H. (1982). Information processing as a way of understanding and diagnosing learning disabilities. *Topics in Learning and Learning Disabilities, 2*(2), 33–45.

Baumeister, A. A. (1967). Problems in comparative studies of mental retardates and normals. *American Journal of Mental Deficiency, 71*, 869–875.

Baumeister, A. A. (1981). Mental retardation policy and research: An unfulfilled promise. *American Journal of Mental Deficiency, 85*, 449–456.

Bee, H. L., Nyman, B. A., Pytkowicz, A. R., Sarason, I. G., & Van Egeren, L. (1968). Research Report #8, Parts I & II. Seattle: University of Washington.

Bee, H. L., Streissguth, A. P., Van Egeren, L. F., Leckie, M. S., & Nyman, B. A. (1970). Deficits and value judgments: A comment on Sroufe's critique. *Developmental Psychology, 2*, 146–149.

Bee, H. L., Van Egeren, L., Pytkowicz, A. R., Nyman, B. A., & Leckie, M. S. (1969). Social class differences in maternal teaching strategies and speech patterns. *Developmental Psychology, 1*, 726–734.

Belmont, J. M., & Butterfield, E. C. (1977). The instructional approach to developmental cognitive research. In R. V. Kail & J. W. Hagen

(Eds.), *Perspectives on the development of memory and cognition* (pp. 437–481). Hillsdale, NJ: Erlbaum, 1977.

Belmont, J. M., & Butterfield, E. C. (1978). Training retarded people to generalize memorization methods across memory tasks. In P. E. Gruneberg & R. N. Sykes (Eds.), *Practical aspects of memory.* London: Academic Press.

Bennett, A. (1932). *A comparative study of subnormal children in the elementary grades.* New York: Teachers College Bureau of Publications.

Berwick, D. M., & Komaroff, A. L. (1982). Cost effectiveness of lead screening. *New England Journal of Medicine, 306*(23), 1392–1398.

Black, F. W. (1974). Self-concept as related to achievement and age in learning-disabled children. *Child Development, 45,* 1137–1140.

Blatt, B. (1958). The physical, personality, and academic status of children who are mentally retarded attending special classes as compared with children who are mentally retarded attending regular classes. *American Journal of Mental Deficiency, 62,* 810–818.

Block, J. H. (Ed.). (1974). *Schools, society, and mastery learning.* New York: Holt, Rinehart & Winston.

Bloom, B. S., (1964). *Stability and change in human characteristics.* New York: John Wiley.

Bloom, B. S. (1976). *Human characteristics and school learning.* New York: McGraw–Hill.

Bloom, R. B., Shea, R. J., & Eun, B. S. (1979). The Piers–Harris Self-Concept Scale: Norms for behaviorally disordered children. *Psychology in the Schools, 16,* 483–487.

Borkowski, J. G., & Cavanaugh, J. C. (1979). Maintenance and generalization of skills and strategies in the retarded. In N. R. Ellis (Ed.), *Handbook of mental deficiency* (2nd ed., pp. 569–612). Hillsdale, NJ: Erlbaum.

Bradfield, H. R., Brown, J., Kaplan, P., Rickert, E., & Stannard, R. (1973). The special child in the regular classroom. *Exceptional Children, 39,* 384–390.

Braun, C. (1976). Teacher expectation: Sociopsychological dynamics. *Review of Educational Research, 46*(2), 185–213.

Brooks, P. H., & Baumeister, A. A. (1977). A plea for consideration of ecological validity in the experimental psychology of mental retardation: A guest editorial. *American Journal of Mental Deficiency, 81,* 407–416.

Brophy, J., & Evertson, C. M. (1981). *Student characteristics and teaching.* New York: Longman.

Brophy, J. E., & Good, T. L. (1974). *Teacher–student relationships: Causes and consequences.* New York: Holt, Rinehart & Winston.

Brown, A. L. (1974). The role of strategic behavior in retardate memory. In N. R. Ellis (Ed.), *International review of research in mental retardation,* (Vol. 7, pp. 55–104). New York: Academic Press.

Brown, A. L. (1975). The development of memory: Knowing, knowing about knowing, and knowing how to know. In H. W. Reese (Ed.), *Advances in child development and behavior* (Vol. 10). New York: Academic Press.

Brown, A. L. (1977). Development, schooling, and the acquisition of knowledge about knowledge. In R. C. Anderson, R. J. Spiro, & W. E. Montague (Eds.), *Schooling and the acquisition of knowledge.* Hillsdale, NJ: Erlbaum.

Brown, A. L. (1978). Knowing when, where and how to remember: A problem of metacognition. In R. Glaser (Ed.), *Advances in instructional psychology.* Hillsdale, NJ: Erlbaum.

Brown, A. L. (1980). Metacognitive development and reading. In R. J. Spiro, B. Bruce, & W. F. Brewer (Eds.), *Theoretical issues in reading comprehension.* Hillsdale, NJ: Erlbaum.

Brown, A. L., & Palincsar, A. S. (1982). Inducing strategic learning from texts by means of informed, self-control training. *Topics in Learning and Learning Disabilities, 2*(1), 1–18.

Bruininks, R. H., Rynders, J. E., & Gross, J. C. (1974). Social acceptance of mildly retarded pupils in resource rooms and regular classes. *American Journal of Mental Deficiency, 78,* 377–383.

Bruininks, V. L. (1978a). Peer status and personality characteristics of learning disabled and nondisabled students. *Journal of Learning Disabilities, 11,* 29–34.

Bruininks, V. L. (1978b). Actual and perceived peer status of learning disabled students in mainstream programs. *Journal of Special Education, 12,* 51–58.

Bruno, R. M. (1981). Interpretation of pictorially presented social situations by learning disabled and normal children. *Journal of Learning Disabilities, 14,* 350–352.

Bryan, J. H., & Sherman, R. (1980). Immediate impressions of nonverbal ingratiation attempts by learning disabled. *Journal of Learning Disabilities, 3,* 19–28.

Bryan, T. H. (1974). Peer popularity of learning disabled children. *Journal of Learning Disabilities, 7,* 621–625.

Bryan, T. H. (1976). Peer popularity of learning disabled children: A replication. *Journal of Learning Disabilities, 9,* 307–311.

Bryan, T. H. (1982). Social skills of learning disabled children and youth: An overview. *Learning Disability Quarterly, 5*(4), 332–333.

Bryan, T. H., & Bryan, J. H. (1978). Social interactions of learning disabled children. *Learning Disability Quarterly, 1*(1), 33–38.

Bryan, T. H., & Bryan, J. H. (1982). Some personal and social experiences of learning disabled children. In B. K. Keogh (Ed.), *Advances in special education* (Vol. 3). Greenwich, CT: JAI Press.

Bryan, T. H., Wheeler, R., Felcan, J., & Henek, T. (1976). An observational study of children's communication. *Journal of Learning Disabilities, 9,* 661–669.

Budoff, M. (1967). Learning potential among institutionalized young adult retardates. *American Journal of Mental Deficiency, 72,* 404–411.

Budoff, M. (1970). Social and test data correlates of learning potential status in educable mental retardates. *Studies in Learning Potential, 1*(3).

Budoff, M., & Gottlieb, J. (1976). Special class EMR children mainstreamed: A study of an aptitude (learning potential) × treatment interaction. *American Journal of Mental Deficiency, 81,* 1–11.

Budoff, M., Meskin, J., & Harrison, R. H. (1971). Educational test of the learning-potential hypothesis. *American Journal of Mental Deficiency, 76,* 159–169.

Burt, R. A. (1975). Judicial action to aid the retarded. In N. Hobbs (Ed.), *Issues in the classification of children* (Vol. 2, pp. 293–318). San Francisco: Jossey–Bass.

Butterfield, E. C., & Belmont, J. M. (1977). Assessing and improving the executive functions of mentally retarded people. In I. Bialer & M. Sternlicht (Eds.), *The psychology of mental retardation: Issues and approaches.* New York: Psychological Dimensions.

Caldwell, B. M. (1974a, February). My experiences as a school principal—or two years in the salt mines. *Newsletter* (Division of Developmental Psychology, American Psychological Association), pp. 49–53.

Caldwell, B. M. (1974b). The rationale for early intervention. In R. L. Jones & D. L. MacMillan (Eds.), *Special education in transition* (pp. 195–207). Boston: Allyn & Bacon.

California master plan for special education. (1974). P. 44. Sacramento: Bureau of Publications.

Camp, B. W. (1980). Two psychoeducational programs for aggressive boys. In C. K. Whalen & B. Henker (Eds.), *Hyperactive children—The social ecology of identification and treatment.* New York: Academic Press.

Campione, J. C., & Brown, A. L. (1977). Memory and metamemory development in educable mentally retarded children. In R. V. Kail & J. W. Hagen (Eds.), *Perspectives on the development of memory and cognition.* Hillsdale, NJ: Erlbaum.

Campione, J. C., & Brown, A. L. (1978). Toward a theory of intelligence: Contributions from research with retarded children. *Intelligence, 2,* 279–304.

Carroll, A. W. (1967). The effects of segregated and partially integrated school programs on self-concepts and academic achievement of educable mental retardates. *Exceptional Children, 34,* 93–96.

Cassidy, V., & Stanton, J. (1959). *An investigation of factors involved in the educational placement of mentally retarded children.* (U. S. Office of Education Cooperative Research Program, Project Number 43). Columbus: Ohio State University.

Children's Defense Fund. (1977). *EPSDT. Does it spell health care for poor children?* Washington, DC: Washington Research Project.

Christopolos, R., & Renz, P. (1969). A critical evaluation of special education programs. *Journal of Special Education, 3,* 371–379.

Clarke, A. M., & Clarke, A. B. D. (Eds.). (1976). *Early experience: Myth and evidence.* New York: Free Press.

Comptroller General of the United States. (1981, September). Report to the Chairman, Subcommittee on Select Education, Committee on Educational Labor, House of Representatives, IEP-81-1.

Conner, F. P. (1983). Improving school instruction for learning disabled children: The Teachers College Institute. *Exceptional Education Quarterly, 4*(1), 45–74.

Controversy: Strategy or capacity deficit? [Special issue]. (1982). *Topics in Learning at Learning Disabilities, 2*(2), 1–89.

Corman, L. & Gottlieb, J. (1979). Mainstreaming mentally retarded children: A review of research. In N. R. Ellis (Ed.), *International review of research in mental retardation* (Vol. 9, pp. 251–275). New York: Academic Press.

Craik, F. I. M., & Lockhart, R. S. (1972). Levels of processing: A framework for memory research. *Journal of Verbal Learning and Verbal Behavior, 11*, 671–684.

Darlington, R. B., Royce, J. M., Snipper, A. S., Murray, H. W., & Lazar, I. (1980). Preschool programs and later school competence of children from low-income families. *Science, 208*, 202–204.

Dennis, W. (1960). Causes of retardation among institutional children. *Journal of Genetic Psychology, 96*, 47–59.

Deshler, D. D., Schumaker, J. B., Warner, M. M., Alley, G. R., & Clark, F. L. (1980). *An epidemiological study of learning disabled adolescents in secondary schools: Social status, peer relationships, activities in and out of school, and time use* (Research Report No. 18). Lawrence: University of Kansas, Institute for Research in Learning Disabilities.

Detterman, D. K. (1979). Memory in the mentally retarded. In N. R. Ellis (Ed.), *Handbook of mental deficiency* (2nd ed, pp. 737–760). Hillsdale, NJ: Erlbaum, 1979.

Deutsch, M. (1960). Minority group and class status as related to social and personality factors in scholastic achievement. *Society for Applied Anthropology*, No. 2.

Diana v. State Board of Education, C-70-37 (RFP Dist. N. Calif. 1970).

Dickstein, E.B., & Warren, D. R. (1980). Role-taking deficits in learning disabled children. *Journal of Learning Disabilities, 13*, 33–37.

Douglas, V. I. (1972). Stop, look and listen: The problem of sustained attention and impulse control in hyperactive and normal children. *Canadian Journal of Behavioral Sciences, 4*, 259–282.

Douglas, V. I. (1980). Treatment and training approaches to hyperactivity: Establishing internal and external control. In C. K. Whalen & B. Henker (Eds.), *Hyperactive children — The social ecology of identification and treatment*. New York: Academic Press.

Dunn, L. M. (1968). Special education for the mildly retarded: Is much of it justifiable? *Exceptional Children, 35*, 5–22.

Dweck, C. S. (1975). The role of expectations and attributions in the alleviation of learned helplessness. *Journal of Personality and Social Psychology, 31*, 674–685.

Dweck, C. S., & Goetz, T. E. (1978). Attribution and learned helplessness. In J. H. Harvey, W. Ickes, & R. F. Kid (Eds.), *New directions in attribution research* (Vol. 2). Hillsdale, NJ: Erlbaum.

Dweck, C. S., & Reppucci, N. D. (1973). Learned helplessness and reinforcement responsibility in children. *Journal of Personality and Social Psychology, 25*, 109–116.

Elenbogen, M. L. (1957). A comparative study of some aspects of academic and social adjustment of two groups of mentally retarded children in special classes and regular classes. *Dissertation Abstracts, 17*, 2496.

Ellis, N. R. (1963). The stimulus trace and behavioral inadequacy. In N. R. Ellis (Ed.), *Handbook of mental deficiency* (pp. 134–158). New York: McGraw-Hill.

Ellis, N. R. (1969). A behavioral research strategy in mental retardation: Defense and critique. *American Journal of Mental Deficiency, 73*, 557–566.

Ellis, N. R. (1970). Memory processes in retardates and normals. In N. R. Ellis (Ed.), *International review of research in mental retardation*, (Vol. 6, pp. 1–32). New York: Academic Press.

Exceptional Education Quarterly. (1983). "Research in Learning Disabilities" (Special Issue), *4*(1).

Farran, D., Haskins, R., & Gallagher, J. J. (1980). Poverty and mental retardation: A search for explanations. In J. J. Gallagher (Ed.), *Ecology of exceptional children*. San Francisco: Jossey-Bass.

Fine, M., & Caldwell, T. (1967). Self-evaluation of school related behavior of educable mentally retarded children — a preliminary report. *Exceptional Children, 34*, 324.

Fisher, M. A., & Zeaman, D. (1973). An attention–retention theory of retardate discrimination learning. In N. R. Ellis (Ed.), *International review of research in mental retardation* (Vol. 6, pp. 171–256). New York: Academic Press.

Flavell, J. H. (1976). Metacognitive aspects of problem solving. In L. B. Resnick (Ed.), *The nature of intelligence*. Hillsdale, NJ: Erlbaum.

Flavell, J. H., & Wellman, H. M. (1977). Metamemory. In R. V. Kail & J. W. Hagen (Eds.), *Perspectives on the development of memory and cognition*. Hillsdale, NJ: Erlbaum.

Foster, G. G., Schmidt, C. R., & Sabatino, D. (1976). Teacher expectancies and the label "learning disabilities." *Journal of Learning Disabilities, 9*, 58–66.

Foster, G. G., & Ysseldyke, J. (1976). Expectancy and halo effects as a result of artificially induced teacher bias. *Contemporary Educational Psychology, 1*, 37–45.

Fraiberg, S. (1975). Intervention in infancy: A program for blind infants. In B. Z. Friedlander, G. M. Sterritt, & G. E. Kirk, (Eds.), *Exceptional infant* (Vol. 3). New York: Brunner-Mazel.

Gallimore, R., Boggs, S., & Jordan, C. (1974). *Culture, behavior, and education: A study of Hawaiian Americans*. Beverly Hills, CA: Sage Publications.

Garber, H., & Heber, R. (1981). The efficacy of early intervention with family rehabilitation. In M. J. Begab, H. C. Haywood, & H. L. Garber (Eds.), *Psychosocial influences in retarded performance: Vol. 2. Strategies for improving competence* (pp. 71–87). Baltimore: University Park Press.

Gardner, W. I. (1966). Social and emotional adjustment of mildly retarded children and adolescents: Critical review. *Exceptional Children, 33*, 97–105.

Garrett, M. R., & Crump, W. D. (1980). Peer acceptance, teacher performances and self-appraisal of social status among learning disabled students. *Learning Disability Quarterly, 3*, 42–48.

Glidden, L. M. (1979). Training of learning and memory in retarded persons: Strategies, techniques, and teaching tools. In N. R. Ellis (Ed.), *Handbook of mental deficiency* (2nd ed., pp. 619–657). Hillsdale, NJ: Erlbaum.

Golden, M., Birns, B., Bridger, W., & Moss, A. (1971). Social-class differentiation in cognitive development among black preschool children. *Child Development, 42*, 37–45.

Goldfarb, W. (1955). Emotional and intellectual consequences of psychologic deprivation in infancy: A re-evaluation. In W. Hock & J. Zubin (Eds.), *Psychopathology of childhood* (pp. 105–119). New York: Grune & Stratton.

Goldhaber, D. (1979). Does the changing view of early experience imply a changing view of early development? In L. G. Katz (Ed.), *Current topics in early childhood education* (Vol. 2, pp. 117–140). Norwood, NJ: Ablex.

Goldstein, H., Moss, J. W., & Jordan, L. J. (1965). *The efficacy of special class training on the development of mentally retarded children* (U. S. Office of Education, Cooperative Project No. 619). Urbana: University of Illinois.

Goodman, H., Gottlieb, J., & Harrison, R. H. (1972). Social acceptance of EMRs integrated into a nongraded elementary school. *American Journal of Mental Deficiency, 76*, 412–417.

Gordon, E. W. (1971). Parent and child centers: Their basis in the behavioral and educational sciences: An invited critique. *American Journal of Orthopsychiatry, 41*, 39–42.

Gordon, I. J., & Guinagh, B. J. (1978). *A home learning center approach to early stimulation*. JSAS Catalog of Selected Documents in Psychology, 8, 6, (Ms. No. 1634). (Originally published as a final report to the National Institute of Health. Gainesville: University of Florida, Institute for Development of Human Resources) 1974.

Gottlieb, J. (1975). Public, peer, and professional attitudes toward mentally retarded persons. In M. J. Begab & S. A. Richardson (Eds.), *The mentally retarded and society: A social science perspective* (pp. 99–125). Baltimore: University Park Press.

Gottlieb, J. (1981). Mainstreaming: Fulfilling the promise? *American Journal of Mental Deficiency, 86*, 115–126.

Gottlieb, J., Agard, J. A., Kaufman, M. J., & Semmel, M. I. (1976). Retarded children mainstreamed: Practices as they affect minority group children. In R. L. Jones (Ed.), *Mainstreaming and the minority child* (pp. 195–214). Reston, VA: Council for Exceptional Children.

Gottlieb, J., & Budoff, M. (1973). Social acceptability of retarded children in nongraded schools differing in architecture. *American Journal of Mental Deficiency, 78*, 15–19.

Gottlieb, J., Cohen, L., & Goldstein, L. (1974). Social contact and personal adjustment as variables relating to attitudes towards EMR children. *Training School Bulletin, 71*, 9–16.

Gottlieb, J., & Davis, J. E. (1973). Social acceptance of EMRs during overt behavioral interaction. *American Journal of Mental Deficiency, 78*, 141–143.

Gottlieb, J., Semmel, M. I., & Veldman, D. J. (1978). Correlates of social status among mainstreamed mentally retarded children. *Journal of Educational Psychology, 70*, 396–405.

Gray, S. W. (1971, May–June). Ethical issues in research in early childhood intervention. *Children*, pp. 81–87.

Gresham, F. M. (1983). Social skills assessment as a component of mainstreaming placement decisions. *Exceptional Children, 49*(4), 331–336.

Grossman, H. J. (Ed.). (1973). *Manual on terminology and classification in mental retardation.* Washington, DC: American Association on Mental Deficiency.

Grossman, H. J. (Ed.). (1977). *Manual on terminology and classification in mental retardation.* Washington, DC: American Association on Mental Deficiency.

Guskin, S. L., & Spicker, H. H. (1968). Educational research in mental retardation. In N. R. Ellis (Ed.), *International review of research in mental retardation* (Vol. 3, pp. 217–278). New York: Academic Press.

Gutelius, M. F., Kirsch, A. D., MacDonald, S., Brooks, M. R., McErlean, T., & Newcomb, C. (1977). Controlled study of child health supervision: Behavioral results. *Pediatrics, 60*, 294–304.

Guthrie, G., Butler, A., & Gorlow, L. (1961). Patterns of self-attitudes of retardates. *American Journal of Mental Deficiency, 66*, 222–229.

Guthrie, G., Butler, A., & Gorlow, L. (1963). Personality differences between institutionalized and non-institutionalized retardates. *American Journal of Mental Deficiency, 67*, 543–548.

Guthrie, G., Butler, A., Gorlow, L., & White, G. (1964). Non-verbal expression of self-attitudes of retardates. *American Journal of Mental Deficiency, 69*, 42–49.

Hagen, J. W. (1967). The effect of distraction on selective attention. *Child Development, 38*, 685–694.

Hagen, J. W., Barclay, C. R., & Newman, R. J. (1982). Metacognition, self-knowledge, and learning disabilities: Some thoughts on knowing and doing. *Topics in Learning and Learning Disabilities, 2*(1), 19–26.

Hagen, J. W., Jongward, R. H., & Kail, R. V. Jr. (1975). Cognitive perspectives on the development of memory. In R. W. Rech (Ed.), *Advances in child development and behavior* (Vol. 10). New York: Academic Press.

Hagen, J. W., & Kail, R. V., Jr. (1975). The role of attention in perceptual and cognitive development. In W. M. Cruickshank & D. P. Hallahan (Eds.), *Perceptual and learning disabilities in children.* Syracuse, NY: Syracuse University Press.

Hall, R. J. (1979). *An information processing approach to the study of learning disabilities.* Unpublished doctoral dissertation, University of California, Los Angeles.

Hall, R. J. (1980). An information processing approach to the study of exceptional children. In B. K. Keogh (Ed.), *Advances in special education* (Vol. 2). Greenwich, CT: JAI Press.

Hall, R. J., & Guare, F. R. (1982). Decision-making speed in learning disabled and normally achieving pupils. Paper presented at the American Psychological Association Annual Convention. Washington, DC.

Hallahan, D. P., & Bryan, T. H. (1981). Learning disabilities. In J. M. Kaufman & D. P. Hallahan (Eds.), *Handbook of special education.* Englewood Cliffs, NJ: Prentice-Hall.

Hallahan, D. P., & Reeve, R. E. (1980). Selective attention and distractibility. In B. E. Keogh (Ed.), *Advances in special education* (Vol. 1). Greenwich, CT: JAI Press.

Hammill, D. D., Leigh, J. E., McNutt, G., & Larsen, S. C. (1981). A new definition of learning disabilities. *Learning Disability Quarterly, 4*(4), 336–342.

Harter, S. (1978). Effective motivation reconsidered: Toward a developmental model. *Human Development, 21*, 34–64.

Harter, S. (1981). A model of mastery motivation in children: Individual differences and developmental change. *Minnesota Symposium on Child Psychology, 14*, 215–255.

Harter, S. (1982). The perceived competence scale for children. *Child Development, 53*, 87–97.

Harter, S., & Zigler, E. (1974). The assessment of effectiveness motivation in normal and retarded children. *Developmental Psychology, 10*, 160–180.

Hayden, A., & Haring, N. (1976). Early intervention for high risk infants and young children: Programs for Down's syndrome children. In T. J. Tjossem (Ed.), *Intervention strategies for high risk infants and young children.* Baltimore: University Park Press.

Hayden, A., & Haring, N. (1977). The acceleration and maintenance of developmental gains in Down's syndrome school-age children. In P. Mittler (Ed.), *Research to practice in mental retardation* (Vol. 1). Baltimore: University Park Press.

Haywood, H. C., Meyers, C. E., & Switzky, H. N. (1982). Mental retardation. *Annual Review of Psychology, 33*, 309–342.

Heber, R. F. (1961). A manual on terminology and classification in mental retardation (Rev. ed.). *American Journal of Mental Deficiency Monograph* (Suppl. 64).

Heber, R. F. (1964). Personality. In H. A. Stevens & R. Heber (Eds.), *Mental retardation: A review of research* (pp. 143–174). Chicago: University of Chicago Press.

Heider, F. (1958). *The psychology of interpersonal relations.* New York: John Wiley.

Hewett, F. M. (1968). *The emotionally disturbed child in the classroom.* Boston: Allyn & Bacon.

Horn, J., & Stankov, L. (1982). Comments about a chameleon theory: Level I/Level II. *Journal of Educational Psychology, 74*, 874–877.

Hunt, J. McV (1961). *Intelligence and experience.* New York: Ronald Press.

Hunt, J. McV (1969). *The challenge of incompetence and poverty.* Urbana: University of Illinois.

Hunt, J. McV. (1971). Parent and child centers: Their basis in the behavioral and educational sciences. *American Journal of Orthopsychiatry, 41*, 13–38.

Jacobs, W. R. (1978). The effects of the learning disability label on classroom teachers' ability objectively to observe and interpret child behaviors. *Learning Disability Quarterly, 1*(1), 50–55.

Jensen, A. R. (1969). How much can we boost IQ and scholastic achievement? *Harvard Educational Review, 39*, 1–123.

Jensen, A. R., (1970). A theory of primary and secondary familial mental re-retardation. In N. R. Ellis (Ed.), *International review of research in mental retardation* (Vol. 4, pp. 33–105). New York: Academic Press.

Jensen, A. R. (1982). Level I/Level II: Factors or categories? *Journal of Educational Psychology, 74*, 868–873.

Johnson, G. O. (1950). A study of the social position of mentally handicapped children in the regular grades. *American Journal of Mental Deficiency, 55*, 60–89.

Jones, R. L. (1976). Evaluating mainstream programs for minority children. In R. L. Jones (Ed.), *Mainstreaming and the minority child* (pp. 235–257). Minneapolis: Leadership Training Institute/Special Education.

Jones, R. L., & Macmillan, D. L. (Eds.) (1973). *Special education in transition.* Boston: Allyn & Bacon.

Kaufman, M. J., Agard, J. A., & Semmel, M. I. (in press). *Mainstreaming: Learners and their environments.* Baltimore: University Park Press.

Kaufman, M. J., Gottlieb, J., Agard, J., & Kukic, M. (1975). Mainstreaming: Toward an explication of the construct. In E. L. Meyen, G. A. Vergason, & R. J. Whelan (Eds.), *Alternatives for teaching exceptional children.* Denver: Love Publishing.

Keogh, B. K. (1982a). Children's temperament and teachers' decisions. In R. Porter & G. M. Collins (Eds.), *Temperamental differences in infants and young children* (Ciba Foundation Symposium 89). London: Pitman.

Keogh, B. K. (1982b, June). Parent–researcher relationship: Issues and methodological concerns. Paper presented at AAMD Convention, Boston, MA.

Keogh, B. K. (1982c). Research in learning disabilities: A view of status and need. In J. P. Das, R. Mulcahey, & T. Wall (Eds.), *Learning disabilities*. New York: Plenum.

Keogh, B. K. (1983). Individual differences in temperament: A contribution to the personal–social and educational competence of learning disabled children. In J. D. McKinney & L. Feagens (Eds.), *Current topics in learning disabilities*. Norwood, NJ: Ablex.

Keogh, B. K., & Bartlett, C. J. (1980). An educational analysis of hyperactive children's achievement problems. In C. K. Whalen & B. Henker (Eds.), *Hyperactive children — the social ecology of identification and treatment*. New York: Academic Press.

Keogh, B. K., Becker, L. D., Kukic, M., & Kukic, S. (1974). Programs for EH and EMR pupils: Review and recommendations, Part I. *Academic Therapy*, *1*(3), 176–198.

Keogh, B. K., Cahill, C. W., & MacMillan, D. L. (1972). Perception of interruption by educationally handicapped children. *American Journal of Mental Deficiency*, 77, 107–108.

Keogh, B. K., & Glover, A. T. (1980). The generality and durability of cognitive training effects. *Exceptional Education*, *1*(1), 75–81.

Keogh, B. K., & Hall, R. J. (1983). Cognitive training with learning disabled pupils. In A. Meyers & W. Craighead (Eds.), *Cognitive behavior modification*. New York: Plenum.

Keogh, B. K., & Levitt, M. (1976). Special education in the mainstream: A confrontation of limitations? *Focus on Exceptional Children*, *8*(1), 2–11.

Keogh, B. K., Major, S. M., Reid, H. P., Gandara, P., & Omori, H. (1978). Marker variables: A search for comparability and generalizability in the field of learning disabilities. *Learning Disability Quarterly*, *1*(3), 5–11.

Keogh, B. K., Major, S. M., Reid, H. P., Omori, H., & Gandara, P. (1980). Proposed markers in learning disabilities research. *Journal of Abnormal Child Psychology*, *8*(1), 21–31.

Keogh, B. K., Major-Kingsley, S., Omori-Gordon, H. P., & Reid, H. (1982). *A system of marker variables for the field of learning disabilities*. New York: Syracuse University Press.

Keogh, B. K., Wilcoxen, A. G., & Bernheimer, L. (1983). Prevention services for risk children: Evidence for policy and practice. In D. C. Farran & J. D. McKinney (Eds.), *The concept of risk in intellectual and social development*. New York: Academic Press.

Kerlinger, G. N., & Pedhazur, E. J. (1973). *Multiple regression in behavioral research*. New York: Holt, Rinehart & Winston.

Kessner, D. M., Singer, J., Kalk, C. E., & Schlesinger, E. R. (1973). *Infant death: An analysis by maternal risk and health care* (Vol. 1). Washington, DC: National Academy of Sciences.

Kirk, S. A. (1958). *Early education of the mentally retarded: An experimental study*. Urbana: University of Illinois Press.

Kirk, S. A. (1964). Research in education. In H. A. Stevens & R. Heber (Eds.), *Mental retardation: A review of research* (pp. 57–99). Chicago: University of Chicago Press.

Koppitz, E. M. (1971). *Children with learning disabilities. A five year followup study*. New York: Grune & Stratton.

Kornblau, B. (1982). The teachable pupil survey: A technique for assessing teachers' perceptions of pupil attributes. *Psychology in the Schools*, *19*, 170–174.

Kornblau, B., & Keogh, B. K. (1980). Teacher perceptions and educational decisions. In J. Gallagher (Ed.), *New directions for exceptional children* (No. 1, pp. 87–102). San Francisco: Jossey-Bass.

Krupski, A. (1980). Attention processes: Research, theory, and implications for special education. In B. K. Keogh (Ed.), *Advances in special education: Vol. 1. Basic constructs and theoretical orientations*. Greenwich, CT: JAI Press.

Lahti, G. P. (1979). Causal attributions, expressions of affect, and performance change following a success experience of low achieving, average achieving, and high achieving boys. Unpublished doctoral dissertation, University of California, Los Angeles.

Lambert, N. M. (1981). Psychological evidence in *Larry P. v. Wilson Riles*: An evaluation by a witness for the defense. *American Psychologists*, *36*, 937–952.

Larry P. v. Riles. (1972). USLW 2033 (U.S. June 21).

Larsen, S. C., Parker, R., & Jorjorian, J. (1973). Differences in self-concept of normal and learning disabled children. *Perceptual and Motor Skills*, *37*, 510.

Lavelle, N. (1977). Parents' expectations and causal attributions concerning their children's performance on school-related tasks. Unpublished doctoral dissertation, University of California, Los Angeles.

Lavelle, N., & Keogh, B. K. (1981). Expectations and attributions of parents of handicapped children: A review of research. In J. J. Gallagher (Ed.), *New directions for exceptional children* (No. 4, pp. 1–27). San Francisco: Jossey-Bass.

Lazar, I., & Darlington, R. (1982). Lasting effects of early education: A report from the consortium for longitudinal studies. *Monographs of the Society for Research in Child Development 47* (Serial No. 195).

Learning Disability Quarterly. (1982, fall). "LD Students' Social Skills" (Special issue), *5*(4).

Levitan, H., & Kiraly, J. (1975). Achievement and self-concept in young LD children. *Academic Therapy*, *4*(10), 453–455.

Leyser, Y., & Gottlieb, J. (1980). Improving the social status of rejected pupils. *Exceptional Children*, *46*, 459–461.

Lilly, M. S. (1971). Improving social acceptance of low sociometric status, low achieving students. *Exceptional Children*, *37*, 341–347.

Lindblom, C. E., & Cohen, D. K. (1979). *Usable knowledge: Social science and social problem solving*. New Haven: Yale University Press.

MacMillan, D. L. (1971). Special education for the mildly retarded: Servant or savant? *Focus on Exceptional Children*, *2*, 1–11.

MacMillan, D. L. (1972). Facilitative effect on input organization as a function of verbal response to stimuli in EMR and nonretarded children. *American Journal of Mental Deficiency*, *76*, 408–411.

MacMillan, D. L. (1975). The effect of experimental success and failure on the situational expectancy of EMR and nonretarded children. *American Journal of Mental Deficiency*, *80*, 90–95.

MacMillan, D. L. (1982). *Mental retardation in school and society* (2nd ed.). Boston: Little, Brown.

MacMillan, D. L., & Borthwick, S. (1980). The new EMR population: Can they be mainstreamed? *Mental Retardation*, *18*, 155–158.

MacMillan, D. L., Jones, R. L., & Aloia, G. F. (1974). The mentally retarded label: A theoretical analysis and review of research. *American Journal of Mental Deficiency*, *79*, 241–261.

MacMillan, D. L., & Keogh, B. K. (1971). Normal and retarded children's expectancy for failure. *Developmental Psychology*, *4*, 343–348.

MacMillan, D. L., & Meyers, C. E. (1980). Larry P.: An educational interpretation. *School Psychology Review*, *9*(2), 136–148.

MacMillan, D. L., & Meyers, C. E. (1984). Molecular research and molar learning. In P. Brooks, C. McCauley, & R. Spencer (Eds.), *Learning and cognition in the mentally retarded* (pp. 473–492). Baltimore: University Park Press.

MacMillan, D. L., Meyers, C. E., & Morrison, G. M. (1980). System-identification of mildly mentally retarded children: Implications for interpreting and conducting research. *American Journal of Mental Deficiency*, *85*, 108–115.

MacMillan, D. L., & Morrison, G. M. (1979). Educational programming. In H. C. Quay & J. S. Werry (Eds.), *Psychopathological disorders of childhood* (2nd ed., pp. 411–450). New York: John Wiley.

MacMillan, D. L., & Morrison, G. M. (1980). Correlates of social status among mildly handicapped learners in self-contained special classes. *Journal of Educational Psychology*, *72*, 437–444.

MacMillan, D. L, & Morrison, G. M., (1984). Sociometric research in special education. In R. L. Jones (Ed.), *Attitude and attitude change in special education* (pp. 79–117). Reston, VA: Council for Exceptional Children.

MacMillan, D. L., & Semmel, M. I. (1977). Evaluation of mainstreaming programs. *Focus on Exceptional Children*, *9*, 1–14.

Maddox-McGinty, A. (1975). *Children's nonverbal behavior in the classroom and teachers' perceptions of teachability: An observational study*. Unpublished doctoral dissertation. University of California, Los Angeles.

Major-Kingsley, S. (1982). Learning disabled boys as young adults: Achievement, adjustment, and aspirations. Unpublished doctoral dissertation. University of California, Los Angeles.

Mann, L., Davis, C. H., Boyer, C. W., Jr., Metz, C. M., & Wolford, D. (1983). LD or not LD, that was the question: A retrospection analysis of Child Service Demonstration Centers' compliance with the federal definition of learning disabilities. *Journal of Learning Disabilities, 16*(1), 14–17.

Mann, M. (1960). What does ability grouping do to the self-concept? *Childhood Education, 36*, 357–360.

Martin, C. J. (1978). Meditational processes in the retarded: Implications for teaching reading. In N. R. Ellis (Ed.), *International review of research in mental retardation* (Vol. 9, pp. 61–84). New York: Academic Press.

McAfee, R., & Cleland, C. (1965). The discrepancy between self-concept and ideal-self as a measure of psychological adjustment in educable mentally retarded males. *American Journal of Mental Deficiency, 70*, 63–68.

McKinney, J. D. & Fisher, L. (1982, April). *The search for subtypes of specific learning disability.* Paper read at the Gatlinburg Conference on Research in Mental Retardation/Developmental Disabilities, Gatlinburg, TN.

McKinney, J. D., McClure, S., & Feagans L. (1982). Classroom behavior patterns of learning disabled and non-learning disabled children. *Learning Disability Quarterly, 5*, 45–52.

Meichenbaum, D. H. (1977). *Cognitive behavior modification.* New York: Plenum.

Meichenbaum, D. H., & Goodman, J. (1969). Reflection-impulsivity and verbal control of motor behavior. *Child Development, 40*, 785–797.

Meichenbaum, D. H, & Goodman, J. (1971). Training impulsive children to talk to themselves: A means of developing self-control. *Journal of Abnormal Psychology, 77*, 115–126.

Mercer, C. D., & Snell, M. E. (1977). *Learning theory research in mental retardation.* Columbus, OH: Charles E. Merrill.

Mercer, J. R. (1970). Sociological perspectives on mild mental retardation. In H. C. Haywood (Ed.), *Social-cultural aspects of mental retardation.* New York: Appleton-Century-Crofts.

Mercer, J. R., & Lewis, J. (1977). *System of multicultural pluralistic assessment: Parent interview manual.* New York: Psychological Corporation.

Messick, S. (1979). Potential uses of noncognitive measurement in education. *Journal of Educational Psychology, 71*, 281–292.

Messick, S. (1982). *Cognition styles in educational practice.* Paper presented at the annual meeting of the American Educational Research Association, New York.

Meta cognition and learning disabilities [Special issue]. (1982). *Topics in Learning Disabilities, 2*(1), 1–107.

Meyerowitz, J.(1962). Self-derogations in young retardates and special class placement. *Child Development, 33*, 443–451.

Meyers, C. E., MacMillan, D. L., & Yoshida, R. K. (1975). *Correlates for success in transition of MR to regular class* (Vols. 1 and 2; Appendix. Final Report). Pomona: University of California, Neuropsychiatric Institute—Pacific State Hospital. (ERIC Document Reproduction Service Nos. EC 081 038 and EC 081 039)

Meyers, C. E., MacMillan, D. L., & Yoshida, R. K. (1980). Regular class education of EMR students from efficacy to mainstreaming: A review of issues and research. In J. Gottlieb (Ed.), *Educating mentally retarded persons in the mainstream* (pp. 176–206). Baltimore: University Park Press.

Meyers, C. E., MacMillan, D. L., & Zetlin, A. (1978). Education for all handicapped children. *Pediatric Annals, 7*, 348–356.

Meyers, C. E., Sundstrom, P. E., & Yoshida, R. K. The school psychologist and assessment in special education. *School Psychology Monographs, 2*(1), 3–57.

Milgram, N. A. (1969). The rationale and irrationale of Zigler's motivational approach to mental retardation. *American Journal of Mental Deficiency, 73*, 527–532.

Morrison, G. M. (1981a). Perspectives of social status of learning-handicapped and nonhandicapped students. *American Journal of Mental Deficiency, 86*, 243–251.

Morrison, G. M. (1981b). Sociometric measurement: Methodological considerations of its use with mildly handicapped and nonhandicapped children. *Journal of Educational Psychology, 73*, 193–201.

Morrison, G. M., & Borthwick, S. (1983). Patterns of behavior, cognitive competence, and social status for educable mentally retarded children. *Journal of Special Education, 17*(4), 441–452.

Morrison, G. M., Forness, S. R., & MacMillan, D. L. (1983). Influences on sociometric ratings of mildly handicapped children: A path analysis. *Journal of Educational Psychology, 75*, 63–74.

Mullen, F., & Itkin, W. (1961). The value of special classes for the mentally handicapped. *Chicago School Journal, 42*, 353–363.

National Advisory Committee on Handicapped Children. (1968). *Special education for handicapped children: First annual report.* Washington, DC: U.S. Department of Health, Education, and Welfare.

Newell, A., & Simon, H. A. (1972). *Human problem solving.* Englewood Cliffs, NJ: Prentice-Hall.

Norman, C. A., & Zigmond, N. (1980). Characteristics of children labeled and served as learning disabled in school systems affiliated with child service demonstration centers. *Journal of Learning Disabilities, 13*(10), 542–547.

Nunnally, J. D. (1967). *Psychometric theory.* New York: McGraw-Hill.

Oden, S., & Asher, S. R. (1977). Coaching children in social skills for friendship making. *Child Development, 48*, 495–506.

Page, E. B. (1980, winter). Tests of decisions for the handicapped: A guide to evaluation under the new law. *Journal of Special Education, 14*(4), 423–483.

Palmer, D. J. (1979). Regular-classroom teachers' attributions and instructional prescription for handicapped and nonhandicapped pupils. *Journal of Special Education, 13*(3), 325–337.

Palmer, D. J. (1980). The effect of educable mental retardation descriptive information on regular classroom teachers' attribution and instructional prescriptions. *Mental Retardation, 18*, 171–175.

Paris, S. G., & Haywood, H. C. (1973). Mental retardation as a learning disorder. In H. J. Grossman (Ed.), Symposium on learning disorders [Special issue]. *The Pediatric Clinics of North America, 20*(3), 641–651.

Patten, M. D. (1983). Relationship between self-esteem, anxiety, and achievement in young learning disabled students. *Journal of Learning Disabilities, 16*(1), 43–45.

Pennsylvania Association for Retarded Children v. Commonwealth of Pennsylvania. 343 F. Supp. 279 (E.D. Pa. 1972).

People in Action on Special Education v. Hannon (E.D. Illinois 1980).

Pertsch, C. F. (1936). *A comparative study of the progress of subnormal pupils in the grades and in special classes.* New York: Teachers College, Columbia University.

Pick, A. D., Frankel, D. G., & Hess, V. L. (1975). Children's attention: The development of selectivity. In E. M. Heatherington (Ed.), *Review of child development research* (Vol. 5). Chicago: University of Chicago Press.

Piers, E., & Harris, D. (1964). Age and other correlates of self-concept in children. *Journal of Educational Psychology, 55*, 91–95.

Placek, P. J. (1977). Maternal and infant health factors associated with low birth weight: Findings from the 1972 National Natality Survey. In D. M. Reed & F. J. Stanley (Eds.), *Epidemiology of prematurity.* Baltimore, MD: Urban and Schwarnzberg.

Public Law 94-142, Education for All Handicapped Children Act (November 29, 1975).

Pullis, M. E., & Cadwell, J. (1982). The relationship between children's temperament characteristics and teachers' classroom decisions. *American Educational Research Journal, 19*, 165–181.

Purkey, W. W. (1970). *Self-concept and school achievement.* Englewood Cliffs, NJ: Prentice-Hall.

Ramey, C. T. (1982). In I. Lazar & R. Darlington. Lasting effects of early education: A report from the consortium for longitudinal studies. *Monographs of the Society for Research in Child Development, 47*(2/3), 142–151.

Ramey, C. T., & Bryant, D. M. (1982). Evidence for prevention of developmental retardation during infancy. *Journal of the Division for Early Childhood, 5*, 73–78.

Ramey, C. T., & Bryant, D. M. (in press). Preventing and treating mental retardation: Biomedical and educational interventions. In J. L. Matson & J. A. Mulick (Eds.), *Comprehensive handbook of mental retardation.* New York: Pergamon Press.

Ramey, C. T., & Campbell, F. A. (1979). Compensatory education for disadvantaged children. *School Review, 87*, 171–189.

Ramey, C. T., & Haskins, R. (1981). The causes and treatment of school failure: Insights from the Carolina Abecedarian Project. In M. J. Begab, H. C. Haywood, & H. L. Garber (Eds.), *Psychosocial influences in retarded performance: Vol. 2. Strategies for improving competence* (pp. 89–112). Baltimore: University Park Press.

Ramey, C. T., Sparling, J. J., Bryant, D. M., & Wasik, B. H. (1982). Primary prevention of developmental retardation during infancy. *Journal of Prevention and Human Services, 1,* 61-83.

Ramey, C. T., Sparling, J., & Wasik, B. H. (1981). Creating social environments to facilitate language development. In R. Schiefelbush & D. Bricker (eds.), *Early language intervention.* Baltimore: University Park Press.

Reid, H. P. (1982). Sex-related bias in teachers' decisions to refer children with potential learning disabilities. Unpublished doctoral dissertation. University of California, Los Angeles.

Ribner, S. (1978). The effects of special class placement on the self-concept of exceptional children. *Journal of Learning Disabilities, 11,* 313-323.

Ringness, T. (1961). Self-concept of children of low, average, and high intelligence. *American Journal of Mental Deficiency, 65,* 453-461.

Robinson, H., & Robinson, N. (1971). Longitudinal development of very young children in a comprehensive day-care program: The first two years. *Child Development, 42,* 1673-1683.

Robinson, N. M. (1976, June). *Prevention: The future society. The future of very early intervention and education.* Paper read at the annual convention of the American Association on Mental Deficiency, Chicago.

Rodee, M. (1971). *A study to evaluate the resource teacher concept when used with high level educable retardates at a primary level.* Unpublished doctoral dissertation, University of Iowa, Iowa City.

Rosenthal, J. H. (1973). Self-esteem in dyslexic children. *Academic Therapy, 9,* 26-32.

Rosenthal, R. & Jacobson, L. (1868). *Pygmalion in the classroom: Teacher expectation and pupil's intellectual development.* New York: Holt, Rinehart, & Winston.

Ross, D. M, & Ross, S. A. (1978). Cognitive training for EMR children: Choosing the best alternative. *American Journal of Mental Deficiency, 82,* 598-601.

Rotter, J. B. (1966). Generalized expectancies for internal vs. external control reinforcement. *Psychological Monographs, 80,* 1-28.

Ruble, D. N., & Boggianno, A. K. (1980). Optimizing motivation in an achievement context. In B. K. Keogh (Ed.), *Advances in Special Education* (Vol. 1). Greenwich, CT: JAI Press.

Salvia, J., & Clark, J. (1973). Use of deficits to identify the learning disabled. *Exceptional Children, 39*(4), 305-309.

Satz, P., & Morris, R. (1981). Learning disability subtypes: A review. In F. J. Pirozzolo & M. C. Wittrock (Eds.), *Neuropsychological and cognitive processes in reading.* New York: Academic Press.

Schonebaum, R. M., & Zinober, J. W. (1977). Learning and memory in mental retardation: The defect–developmental distinction re-evaluated. In I. Bialer & M. Sternlicht (Eds.), *The psychology of mental retardation* (pp. 243-274). New York: Psychological Dimension.

Schumaker, J. B., Deshler, D. D., Alley, Y. R., & Warner, H. M. (1983). Toward the development of an intervention model for learning disabled adolescents: The University of Kansas Institute. *Exceptional Education Quarterly, 4*(1), 45-74.

Schurr, K. T., Joiner, L. M., & Towne, R. C. (1979). Self-concept research on the mentally retarded: Review of empirical studies. *Mental Retardation, 17,* 39-43.

Schurr, K. T., Towne, R. C., & Joiner, L. M. (1972). Trends in self-concept of ability over 2 years of special class placement. *Journal of Special Education, 6,* 161-166.

Scranton, T. R., & Ryckman, D. B. (1979). Sociometric status of learning disabled children in an integrating program. *Journal of Learning Disabilities, 12,* 402-407.

Select Panel for the Promotion of Child Health. (1981). *Better health for our children: A national strategy* (4 vols., DHSS/PHS Publication No. 79 55071). Washington, DC: U. S. Government Printing Office.

Semmel, M. J., Gottlieb, J., & Robinson, N. M. (1979). Mainstreaming: Perspectives on educating handicapped children in the public schools. *Review of Research in Education, 7,* 223-279.

Shavelson, R. J. (1976). Teachers' decision making. In N. L. Gage (Ed.), *The psychology of teaching methods* (Yearbook of the NSSE, Vol. 75, Part 1). Chicago: University of Chicago Press.

Shavelson, R. J., Hubner, J. J., & Stanton, G. C. (1976). Self-concept validation of construct interpretations. *Review of Educational Research, 46,* 407-441.

Shavelson, R. J., & Stern, P. (1981). Research on teachers' pedagogical thoughts, judgments, decision, and behavior. *Review of Educational Research, 51*(4), 455-498.

Sheare, J. B. (1978). The impact of resource programs upon the self-concept and peer acceptance of learning disabled children. *Psychology in the Schools, 15,* 406-412.

Sheehan, R., & Keogh, B. K. (1981). Strategies for documenting progress of handicapped children in early education programs. *Education Evaluation and Policy Analysis, 3*(6), 59-68.

Sheehan, R., & Keogh, B. K. (1982). Design and analysis in the evaluation of early children's special education programs. *Topics in Early Childhood Special Education, 1*(4), 81-88.

Siperstein, G. N., Bopp, M. J., & Bak, J. J. (1978). Social status of learning-disabled children. *Journal of Learning Disabilities, 11*(2), 49-53.

Skeels, H. M., & Dye, H. B. (1939). A study of the effects of differential stimulation on mentally retarded children. *Proceedings of the American Association on Mental Deficiency, 44,* 114-136.

Spitz, H. H. (1963). Field theory in mental deficiency. In N. R. Ellis (Ed.), *Handbook of mental deficiency* (pp. 11-40). New York: McGraw-Hill.

Spitz, H. H. (1966). The role of input organization in the learning and memory of mental retardates. In N. R. Ellis (Ed.), *International review of research in mental retardation* (Vol. 2, pp. 29-56). New York: Academic Press.

Spitz, H. H. (1979). Beyond field theory in the study of mental deficiency. In N. R. Ellis (Ed.), *Handbook of mental deficiency* (2nd ed., pp. 121-141). Hillsdale, NJ: Erlbaum.

Sroufe, L. A. (1970). A methodological and philosophical critique of intervention-oriented research. *Developmental Psychology, 2,* 140-145.

Stankov, L., Horn, J. L., & Roy, T. (1980). On the relationship between Gf/Gc theory and Jensen's Level I/II theory. *Journal of Educational Psychology, 72,* 796-809.

Sternlicht, M., & Deutsch, M. R. (1972). *Personality development and social behavior in the mentally retarded.* Lexington, MA: Lexington Books.

Streissguth, A. P. (1969). Social class and racial differences in preschool children's cognitive functioning. Paper presented at the Biennial Meeting of the Society for Research in Child Development, Santa Monica, March.

Swanson, H. L. (1982). Forward to controversy: Strategy or capacity deficit. *Topics in Learning and Learning Disabilities, 2*(2), 10-14.

Thomas, A., & Chess, S. (1980). *The dynamics of psychological development.* New York: Brunner-Mazel.

Thurstone, T. G. (1959). *An evaluation of educating mentally handicapped children in special classes and in regular grades* (U. S. Office of Education Cooperative Research Program, Project No. OE-SAE-6452). Chapel Hill: University of North Carolina.

Tjossem, T. D. (1976). Early intervention: Issues and approaches. In T. D. Tjossem (Ed.), *Intervention strategies for high risk infants and young children* (pp. 3-33). Baltimore: University Park Press.

Torgesen, J. K. (1978). Performance of reading disabled children on serial memory tasks: A review. *Reading Research Quarterly, 19,* 57-87.

Torgesen, J. K. (1982a). The learning disabled child as an inactive learner: Educational implications. *Topics in Learning and Learning Disabilities, 2*(1), 45-52.

Torgesen, J. K. (1982b). The use of rationally defined subgroups in research on learning disabilities. In J. P. Das, R. F. Mulcahy, & A. E. Wall (Eds.), *Theory and research in learning disabilities.* New York: Plenum.

Torgesen, J. K., & Houck, G. (1980). Processing deficiencies in learning disabled children who perform poorly on the digit span test. *Journal of Educational Psychology, 72,* 141-160.

Torgesen, J., & Kail, R. V., Jr. (1980). Memory processes in exceptional children. In B. K. Keogh (Ed.), *Advances in special education* (Vol. 1). Greenwich, CT: JAI Press.

Towne, R., & Joiner, L. (1966). *The effect of special class placement on the self-concept of ability of the educable mentally retarded child* (U. S. Office of Education). East Lansing: Michigan State University.

Travers, R. M. W. (Ed.). (1973). *Second handbook of research on teaching*. Chicago: Rand McNally.

Turnbull, H. R., & Turnbull, A. (1978). *Free appropriate public education: Law and implementation*. Denver: Love Publishing Co.

Turnure, J., & Thurlow, M. (1973). Verbal elaboration and the promotion of transfer of training in educable mentally retarded children. *Journal of Experimental Child Psychology, 15*, 137–148.

Vacc, N. A. (1968). A study of emotionally disturbed children in regular and special classes. *Exceptional Children, 35*, 197–206.

Vacc, N. A. (1972). Long term effects of special class intervention for emotionally disturbed children. *Exceptional Children, 39*, 15–22.

Walker, V. (1974). The efficacy of the resource room for educating retarded children. *Exceptional Children, 40*, 288–289.

Weiner, B. (1974). *Achievement motivation and attribution theory*. Morristown, NJ: General Learning Press.

Weiner, B. (1976). An attributional approach for educational psychology. *Review of Research in Education, 4*, 179–207.

Weiner, B., & Kukla, A. (1970). An attributional analysis of achievement motivation. *Journal of Personality and Social Psychology, 5*, 1–20.

Weisz, J. R., & Zigler, E. (1979). Cognitive development in retarded and nonretarded persons: Piagetian tests of the similar sequence hypothesis. *Psychological Bulletin, 86*, 831–851.

Wellman, B. L., Skeels, H. M., & Skodak, M. (1940). Review of McNemar's critical examination of Iowa studies. *Psychological Bulletin, 38*, 93–111.

Westinghouse Learning Corporation. (1969). *The impact of Head Start: An evaluation of Head Start on children's cognitive and affective development*. Athens: OH: Ohio University.

White, R. W. (1959). Motivation reconsidered: The concept of competence. *Psychological Review, 66*, 277–333.

Wiig, E. H., & Harris, S. P. (1974). Perception and interpretation of nonverbally expressed emotions by adolescents with learning disabilities. *Perceptual and Motor Skills, 38*, 239–245.

Williams, R. L. (1980). The death of white research in the black community. In Jones, R. L. (Ed.). *Black psychology* (pp. 403–417). New York: Harper & Row.

Wong, B., & Wong, R. (1977). Recall and clustering of verbal materials among normal and poor readers. *Bulletin of the Psychonomic Society, 10*(5), 375–378.

Wong, B., & Wong, R. (1980). Role-taking skills in normal achieving and learning disabled children. *Learning Disability Quarterly, 3*, 3–11.

Woodward, W. M. (1979). Piaget's theory and the study of mental retardation. In N. R. Ellis (Ed.) *Handbook of mental deficiency* (pp. 169–195). Hillsdale, NJ: Erlbaum.

Wrightstone, J. W., Forlano, G., Lepokowski, J. R., Sontag, M., & Edelstein, J. D. (1959). *A comparison of educational outcomes under single-track and two-track plans for educable mentally retarded children* (U.S. Office of Education Cooperative Research Program, Project No. 144). New York: New York City Board of Education.

Yauman, B. E. (1980). Special education placement and the self-concept of elementary-school age children. *Learning Disability Quarterly, 3*(3), 30–35.

Yoshida, R. K. (1976). Out-of-level testing of special education students with a standardized achievement battery. *Journal of Educational Measurement, 13*, 215–221.

Ysseldyke, J. E. (1977, May). *Current issues in the assessment of learning disabled children and some proposed approaches to appropriate use of assessment information*. Paper presented at the BEH Conference on Assessment of Learning Disabilities, Atlanta, Georgia.

Zakreski, R. S. (1982). Effect of content and training on the generalization of a cognitive strategy by normally achieving and learning disabled boys. Unpublished doctoral dissertation, University of Virginia.

Zeaman, D., & House, B. J. (1979). A review of attention theory. In N. R. Ellis (Ed.), *Handbook of mental deficiency* (2nd ed. pp. 63–120). Hillsdale, NJ: Erlbaum.

Zeaman, D., & House, B. J. (1963). The role of attention in retardate discrimination learning. In N. R. Ellis (Ed.), *Handbook of mental deficiency* (pp. 159–223). New York: McGraw-Hill.

Zigler, E. (1967). Familial mental retardation: A continuing dilemma. *Science, 155*, 292–298.

Zigler, E. (1969). Developmental versus difference theories of mental retardation and the problem of motivation. *American Journal of Mental Deficiency, 73*, 536–556.

Zigler, E. (1973). The retarded child as a whole person. In D. K. Routh (Ed.), *The experimental psychology of mental retardation* (pp. 67–273). Chicago: Aldine.

Zigler, E. (1977). Dealing with retardation. *Science, 196*, 1192–1194.

Zigler, E. & Muenchow, S. (1979). Mainstreaming: The proof is in the implementation. *American Psychologist, 34*, 993–996.

Zigler, E., & Trickett, P. K. (1978). IQ, social competence, and evaluation of early childhood intervention programs. *American Psychologist, 33* 789–798.

Part 5
Research on the Teaching of Subjects and Grade Levels

25.
Research on Early Childhood and Elementary School Teaching Programs

Jane A. Stallings
Vanderbilt University

Deborah Stipek
University of California—Los Angeles

There are many points of view of what education ought to be, and what is considered the best education for children changes as the perceived needs of society change. As a result of Sputnik, mathematics and science programs were funded. The civil rights movement produced basic education programs that were funded to improve the education of low-income children. Recently, the report of the National Commission on Excellence in Education (1983) challenged educators to provide quality education for high and low achievers so that all students might reach their potential.

In the *Handbook of Research on Teaching* (Gage, 1963) the chapter on early education focused upon studies occurring during the era of Sputnik. In the *Second Handbook of Research on Teaching* (Travers, 1973) Beller described the studies originating during the civil rights era. These studies primarily examined relationships between child learning and preschool programs. Most of the programs studied were developed for use with low-income children and were federally funded in the 1960s and 1970s through Head Start as part of the War on Poverty. The hypothesis was that if intervention programs started early enough (in some cases even before birth), children from low socioeconomic groups would prosper more from the schooling they received than would children from similar circumstances who did not receive early training and opportunities to learn.

Early results indicated that children in these programs often scored higher than control children on intelligence and school readiness tests. Unfortunately these advantages diminished by the end of the first grade in school. Some Head Start graduates enrolled in National Follow Through Planned Variation programs when they entered public school. The goal of Follow Through was to provide a continuous program from kindergarten through third grade. The children in structured, academically oriented Follow Through programs continued to make academic progress and scored higher than control children on achievement tests. Children in cognitively oriented Follow Through programs scored higher on problem-solving tests than did control children (Stallings, 1975). However, the overall academic effects of Head Start and Follow Through programs were rather meager (House, Glass, McLean, & Walker, 1977) and the federal funding for these programs was drastically reduced in the late 1970s.

Refusing to believe that all of their efforts to improve the life chances of children in Head Start and Follow Through programs were in vain, several researchers launched longitudinal studies to see how graduates from their programs were prospering in the public schools. Thus, it is possible in this third *Handbook of Research on Teaching* to consider to what extent these compensatory education programs of the civil rights era have been successful in the long run.

This chapter will describe long-term studies of several preschool programs: the Consortium's longitudinal report of 12 preschool programs, a longitudinal report of 4 Head Start programs in Louisville, Kentucky, and the Perry Preschool

The authors thank reviewers Walter Doyle (University of Texas — Austin) and Evan Keislar (University of California — Los Angeles). Thanks also to Mary Wilcox, Educational Researcher, and Louise Miller (University of Louisville).

Program in Ypsilanti, Michigan. Longitudinal reports from 2 Follow Through programs are also included: the Parent Education Follow Through Program and the Direct Instruction Follow Through Model.

Since the waning of the War on Poverty, the focus of educational innovations has shifted in several noteworthy ways. Unlike the "special" programs for "special," low-income children developed in the 1960s and 1970s, more recently developed programs are usually designed to be implemented in the regular classrooms and are for the benefit of all students. Furthermore, current research no longer reflects the focus of earlier decades on preschool-age children. These shifts are consistent with recent reports on American education expressing concern about the quality of education at all levels. Thus, in the last decade we have witnessed exciting innovations designed for elementary school classrooms.

We have selected two examples of innovative programs that gained prominence in the 1970s: Mastery Learning and Cooperative Learning. We chose to review these two popular educational models because they have been implemented throughout the country and a sufficient amount of well-designed research allows us to make some conclusions regarding their effectiveness. Since Mastery Learning and Cooperative Learning are relative newcomers on the educational scene, we will not be able to assess their long-term effects. But we will be able to examine the immediate effects of these models on student achievement.

For all of the specific instructional programs included in this review, the theoretical base, the classroom implementations, and, when possible, the long-term student outcomes are described. Research studies on these instructional programs had to pass several criteria to be included in this chapter. First, the findings had to contribute to the knowledge base of research on teaching in preschool or elementary school. Second, the design and samples had to be adequate to allow confidence in the findings. Among the studies that met these criteria, the authors' priorities and knowledge base guided the final selection of research reviewed in this chapter.

Longitudinal Studies

Early Childhood Education: The Consortium's Longitudinal Study

In spite of the poor prognosis from evaluations for their programs, 12 investigators of the 1960s early education programs formed a Consortium for Longitudinal Studies. Their purpose was to study the long-term effects of the experimental Head Start programs. While the infant and preschool programs varied from teaching parents in their homes, to daycare centers, to highly structured preschools, their common purpose was to help preschool-age children develop school competence and positive attitudes toward school. Another common element of the experimental preschool programs was the belief that the parents were integral to the child's success in school. Thus, the programs' goals were to have a positive impact on the family and the child. The consortium included Kuno Beller, Cynthia Deutsch, Martin Deutsch, Ira Gordon, Susan Gray, Merle

Karnes, Phyllis Levenstein, Louise B. Miller, Francis Palmer, David Weikart, Myron Woolman, and Edward Zigler. The effects of these infant and preschool experimental programs were analyzed by Lazar, Hubbel, Murray, Rosche, and Royce (1977); Lazar, Darlington, Murray, Royce and Snipper (1982); and Meyer (1984).

By pooling their original data, these investigators hoped to locate a large enough sample of participants to estimate the long-term effects of early education upon children who had completed at least the sixth grade of school. Attrition was, of course, a great problem to the study. Another problem was the variety of tests and measurements used to assess school achievement and other student outcomes. These included: scores on intelligence tests, achievement tests, student attitudinal interviews, and parent questionnaires. In addition to these measures, ecologically valid indicators for school success were used, for example, lower retention rates, fewer assignments to special education classes, and fewer teenage pregnancies.

From this consortium of studies of the long-term effects of preschool intervention programs, Lazar et al. (1982, p. 55) reported significant effects on students' school competence, attitudes about self and school, and effects upon families. The experimental programs appeared to improve the school competence of low-income children. They were more able than control children to meet their schools' requirements for adequate performance, including reduced rates of assignment to special education and retention in grade. Only 8.6% of the experimental students required special education placement compared to 29% of the control students, and 19% of the experimental children were held back a grade compared to 24% of the control students. Meyer, in a review of these findings (1984), notes that "the one experimental group [in the study] showing the highest retention rate [almost 50%] also shows the lowest percentage of students placed into special education classes" (p. 2). This finding raises the question about the relationship between retention and placement in special education classes. Early retention in grade may increase the chances of success for the low-achieving student and thus reduce the chances that students at risk will be placed in special education classes. As Meyer (1984) points out, this positive effect of early retention raises doubt about using lower retention rates alone as a measure of a program's long-term effectiveness. While lower retention rate alone does not provide a convincing indication of effectiveness, in combination with fewer special education placements, it provides a valid long-term measure of the effectiveness of the experimental programs.

Initially, early education programs improved children's performance on achievement and intelligence tests. But 3 or 4 years after the programs, the differences between the treatment and control children often disappeared. Within most programs, children with early education had higher achievement test scores than the control children on either reading or math, but this finding did not exist for the pooled sample.

Compared with control children, there was a tendency for children with early education experience to answer questions about themselves and school in a more positive manner. However, the teenagers with preschool experience had educational and work expectations similar to those of control children.

An interesting finding regarding teenage pregnancy emerged from the Early Training Project program developed by Susan Gray. The results of Gray, Ramsey, and Klaus' 17-year follow-up report (1982) indicated that program females who became pregnant during high school were more likely than pregnant control females to continue their schooling. There was also a significant program advantage for all program females for grade retention, drop-out rate, and placement in Educable Mentally Handicapped (EMH) classrooms.

Overall, early education had a positive effect on the family. Across all projects, mothers of program graduates were more satisfied with their children's school performance and had higher occupational aspirations for their children than did control families (Lazar et al., 1982, p. 56). Another analysis of these data by Vapova and Royce (1978) indicated that programs with parent involvement, particularly those with home visit components, were more effective in improving parental attitudes toward the school, themselves, and their children than were programs without such components.

Though they are similar to one another in many ways, the programs differed in delivery mode. Lazar et al. found evidence of effectiveness for both home- and center-based programs, for programs using either professionals or paraprofessionals, and for programs for infants as well as those for older preschoolers. Further, they found no evidence that maternal education attainment, father presence, sex, or family size were crucial to the benefits of preschool (p. 65). In terms of policy, those authors conclude, "We find ourselves in the peculiar position of asserting the commonsense notion that children will benefit from good experience. The sum of our work indicates that children from low income families derive measurable educational benefits from diverse, well run, early education programs" (p. 68).

Whenever findings are summarized or averaged over several groups, the power of the statistics may be increased, but interesting and important anomalies in programs may be washed out or overlooked. Such is the case for the Lazar et al. (1982) report. Beyond the common group findings, there were some programs that distinguished themselves from others because of the types of data collected systematically over many years. Because the Perry Preschool Program stands out in having significant long-term findings beyond those collective findings reported by the Consortium for Longitudinal Studies, it merits more detailed attention. A description of this program follows.

The Perry Preschool Program

One of the 12 preschool programs included in the Consortium for Longitudinal Studies that has been particularly successful in studying its own long-term effects is David Weikart's Perry Preschool Program. It began in the mid-1960s and is still flourishing in over 1,000 preschool classrooms in the United States, South America, and Europe. The longitudinal effects of the program have been studied over the last 19 years by Schweinhart and Weikart (1980).

Weikart's cognitively oriented program began at Perry Preschool in Ypsilanti, Michigan. The longitudinal sample was drawn from children who lived in the attendance area of the Perry Elementary School on the south side of Ypsilanti. A 1952 report of the Ypsilanti Housing Commission called it one of the worst-congested slum areas in the state of Michigan. School failure and a high crime rate have been perennial problems in the area.

Fortunately for research purposes, the Ypsilanti community is quite stable. In almost 2 decades since the end of their preschool experience, subjects can still be located. Of the original 128 children, 4 moved out of the area and 1 died. Schweinhart and Weikart (1980) attributed this community stability to the automobile industry which created a contained job market. Given the early-1980s slump in auto production, it will be interesting to see whether these researchers can continue to follow the children from the Perry Preschool.

In the *Second Handbook of Research on Teaching*, Beller (1973) summarizes the initial findings of the Perry Preschool study in the following way: "It appears that Weikart found effects of preschool education on intellectual functioning to be immediate, but they lasted only a short period after preschool, that is to the end of first or second grade" (p. 560). Nevertheless, Weikart was not discouraged by the findings and continued to follow the children for the next 10 years.

The theoretical underpinnings of Weikart's Cognitive model rest firmly upon a transactional approach to the relationship between heredity and environment, between the individual and his or her field of operation (Schweinhart & Weikart, 1980, p. 5). The ongoing interaction between internal and external factors in human behavior and development is also a position taken by Dewey and Piaget (Anastasiow, 1979). The relative contributions of heredity and environment most likely shift over time as well as differ from one situation or aspect of behavior to another (Sameroff, 1979).

In explaining the transactional approach, Schweinhart and Weikart (1980) go on to say:

> For many years, it was assumed that intelligence was almost solely determined by heredity. Then early childhood intervention studies demonstrated that cognitive ability could be improved, at least temporarily. The pendulum swung back as Jensen (1969) and others interpreted the return of IQs to their pre-intervention levels as an indication that cognitive ability could not really be altered. However, a transactional interpretation of the same sequence of events is that environments did contribute to cognitive ability: a stimulating preschool environment enhanced cognitive ability; a less stimulating elementary school environment, in the midst of conditions of poverty, depressed cognitive ability. Different environments influenced cognitive ability in different ways. ... Our transactional approach seeks to balance internal, self-originated motivations, attitudes, and abilities against external indications of expectation, approval, or disapproval. (pp. 5, 7)

The transactional approach postulates a time-oriented concept of complex interactions between the child and the school environment. A rewarding environment of school achievement, commitment to schooling, and social reinforcement of the student role cybernetically controls the role performances that are conducive to success. While a change in the student role is possible, it is extremely difficult: Better to begin with a role conducive to success. Preschool represents a period of time when such a positive student role may be constructed through a high-quality educational program (Schweinhart & Weikart, p. 7).

The children in the Perry Preschool Program attended school 5 half-days every week for a full school year. Their parents were visited in their homes 1½ hours each week. Parents were encouraged to structure household activities and to include the children in accomplishing the tasks.

The curriculum at the Perry Preschool was cognitively oriented and was based upon the sequential developmental theory of Piaget. In essence, children start at the motor level of abstraction where they learn to use their own bodies to experience and learn concepts. Much of their learning at this stage occurs through touching, manipulating, tasting, and smelling. The next stage is labeling what they are exploring and experiencing. Finally, at the symbolic level, objects become very familiar and symbols can represent objects. At this stage the skills to think abstractly develop.

Thus, the materials and activities used in the classroom and homes must provide opportunities for children to experience their environment, to classify objects, to learn about the size and order of objects, and to understand temporal and spatial relationships. Weikart (Weikart, Rogers, Adcock, & McClelland, 1971) says, "Learning by the child is a product of his active involvement with the environment structured by the teacher (and the mother). Learning comes through the child's actions, not through repetition of what he has been told" (p. 5). Activities that teachers developed to promote these desired cognitive skills included sorting tasks which required discrimination in touch, smell, and taste, games that required a sequencing of items or events, and labeling games of contrasts and similarities. Sociodramatic play was used to develop concentration and to integrate scattered experiences.

To help children develop a sense of time and space and control of their impulses, a daily routine was established so that each child planned his or her activities and evaluated the product at the end of the period. The following interaction was observed at the Perry Preschool:

Teacher: "Joseph, where did you work yesterday?"
Joseph: "In the block area."
Teacher: "Where do you want to work today?"
Joseph: "In the workshop."
Teacher: "What are you going to make, Joseph?"
Joseph: "An airplane."
Teacher: "What will you do first?"
Joseph: "I'll find two pieces of wood and nail them together in the center like this." (He crosses his index fingers.) "Then I'll find another little piece of wood for the propeller."

At the end of the period the teacher will ask Joseph to evaluate his product: the good parts and those that need improvement (Stallings, 1977, p. 133).

The original sample of 128 children was homogeneous in level of mental functioning (educable mentally retarded), and socioeconomic background (black and low income). The children were randomly assigned to treatment and control groups. Children were tested before the intervention and at the end of each school year until the end of the third grade on: (a) the Stanford–Binet and the Peabody Pictorial Vocabulary Test to assess intellectual functioning, (b) the Illinois Test of Psycholinguistic Abilities to assess language development, (c) the California Achievement Test to assess academic achievement, and (d) several pupil self-reports and rating scales to assess attitudes, delinquency, work experience, and aspirations.

All together, data were collected on 48 measures. Treatment and control students were contacted almost yearly by interviewers and testers. Parents completed an initial interview and another 11 years later. From ages 3 to 10 and at age 14 the children were given IQ tests; achievement tests were given annually for children between the ages of 7 and 11 and at age 14. School records were examined from kindergarten through high school. Extensive interviews with youths in the study were conducted at ages 15 and 19.

Although the experimental and control children started with similar IQ scores in the low 80s, the Perry Preschool children exceeded the control group by 12 IQ points after 2 years of preschool, by 6 points at the end of kindergarten, and by 5 points at the end of first grade. By the end of second grade, the IQ scores of the groups were equivalent.

The Perry Preschool children were slightly superior to the controls in overall achievement. They passed between 5 and 7% more of the items on the lower primary form and the upper primary form of the California Achievement Test (CAT). At age 14 the Perry Preschool group passed 8% more of the items on the CAT (see Figure 25.1). However, this was only 36% of the items on the Level 4 form. This means both treatment and control groups were well below the National Norm. Therefore, academically the Weikart Cognitive Approach cannot be judged as effective for developing skills tested by achievement tests. Similar findings were reported for children in Weikart's Cognitively Oriented Follow Through Program (House et al., 1977). However, the goal of this model was to provide a school and home environment conducive to the development of cognitive skills, personal initiative, planning, and evaluation skills. These are attributes that are not easily measured by standardized tests of achievement or intelligence, and program effects on students are more likely to be assessed by nonobtrusive measures and seen over a period of several years.

The school records and interviews taken by the High Scope Foundation researchers over the 15 years of the study revealed some very impressive differences between the children with preschool experience and those without such experience (see Figure 25.2). Students who had been in Weikart's preschool program were 21% less likely to report that they had been arrested by age 19 than were control students. Nearly twice as many of the control students reported being involved to some extent in the court system by age 19. Fifty-five percent of the controls had dropped out of school, but only 29% were employed. The picture was a bit rosier for the Perry Preschool graduates: 65% had graduated or were still in school; 48% were currently employed (at a time when black youth unemployment had soared into the upper 60% bracket); further, 45% of those employed supported themselves (e.g., did not receive welfare). During interviews, the children with preschool education reported a greater commitment to schooling. At age 15 these children showed a greater willingness to talk to parents about school. They spent more time on homework and had a higher self-rating of school ability than the control group.

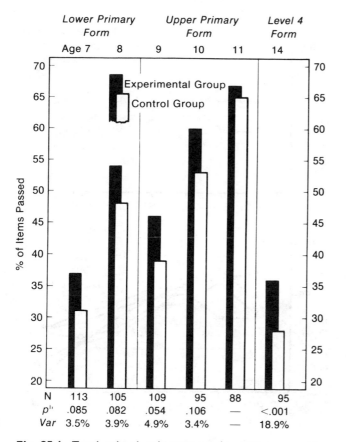

Although the students who attended the Perry Preschool functioned 12 points below the national average on the California Test of Basic Skills at age 14, there were many positive outcomes for these students. The summary of findings reported by Schweinhart and Weikart (1980) is impressive:

> Improvement in the cognitive ability at school entry of children who attended preschool is indicated by their increased IQs during kindergarten and first grade. Greater commitment to schooling is evidenced by more highly rated elementary school motivation, by a higher value placed on schooling by teenagers, and by several other aspects of school commitment. Improved school achievement for these children is shown by generally higher achievement test scores during elementary school and distinctly higher scores at eighth grade (age fourteen) than scores for control group children. Reinforcement of the student role is indicated by more highly rated social development in elementary school, fewer years spent in special education, and greater satisfaction and higher aspirations expressed by parents with respect to the schooling of their children. (p. 31)

It appears that the goals of the Cognitive Approach are met to a great extent. Given their early training in discrimination, planning, and evaluating, these students are more able to make judgments about staying in school and preparing for a productive work life than students without such early training. It is impressive that 38% are attending college or receiving job training. Further, the fact that 48% are employed at a time when poor black adolescents are primary targets for unemployment speaks positively for the program's impact on work skills.

Weikart attributes the success of the program to the improvement in cognitive ability during preschool. This had its effect upon the way the child was introduced to the school social system. The Perry Preschool children entered kindergarten with a functioning IQ of 95 compared to 84 for those children who had not attended preschool. Since IQ scores correlate highly with school success, it is not surprising that the tasks required to score higher on IQ tests are similar to those learned during preschool and relate to tasks required of kindergarten and first grade children. Then according to the transactional theory of education, the child's initial orientation

Fig. 25.1. Total school achievement by group over time. (Achievement data from California Achievement Tests. [Tiegs & Clark, 1963, 1970]. The α_t, an index of the consistency of measurement over time, was .953. The α for the age 14 test (the only one for which α was assessed) was .966. From *Young Children Grow Up: Effects of the Perry Preschool Program on Youths Through Age 15* by L. J. Schweinhart and D. P. Weikart. Copyright 1980 by High/Scope Educational Research Foundation. Reprinted by permission.

Note. ^{a}p is reported if less than .10, followed by the percent of variance accounted for by group membership.

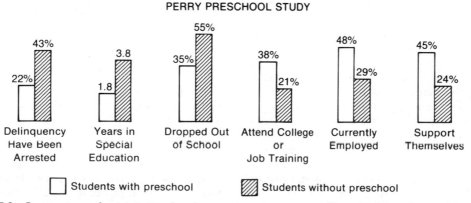

PERRY PRESCHOOL STUDY

☐ Students with preschool   ▨ Students without preschool

Fig. 25.2. Comparison of experimental and control students at age 19 in the Perry Preschool Study.

towards school tasks would be solidified by a greater commitment to schooling and by adoption of a student role consistent
to school success.

According to the findings from this study, the returns to
society for the costs of preschool education are great. The
returns include reduced costs for incarceration, reduced costs
for special education, and probably increased life earnings for
the participants.

Miller and Bizzell's Study of Four Head Start Programs

Another longitudinal study of early intervention programs was
conducted by Miller and Bizzell (1983b). They have followed
the progress of children who in 1968–1969 attended four
different Head Start Programs in Louisville, Kentucky. Ninth
and 10th grade results are reported for children who participated for 1 year in Bereiter-Engelmann's Direct Instruction
(BE), Susan Gray's DARCEE, Montessori, and traditional
prekindergarten. A control group of children not attending
Head Start was also recruited and included in the follow-up
studies.

The experimental children, predominantly low-income and
90% black, were randomly assigned to the programs. Controls
were recruited from neighborhoods in which the experimental
classes were located. Fourteen classes were developed: four each
for BE, DARCEE, and traditional; two for Montessori. At the
end of the prekindergarten year, 214 experimental children were
in the sample.

The Preschool Inventory (PSI) (Caldwell, 1968) was administered 8 weeks after the children started preschool and at the
end of the preschool year and at the end of kindergarten.
California Achievement Test scores were obtained from the
school systems at the end of 1st and 2nd grades. Stanford
Achievement Test scores were available for children in 4th
through 8th grades, and scores from the Comprehensive Test of
Basic Skills were available for children in 9th and 10th grades.
The STEP-Locator, a brief test of language and math skills, was
administered to the 9th- and 10th-graders by the research staff.
Intelligence was measured with the Stanford–Binet (Terman &
Merrill, 1960) at the beginning of the preschool experience and
at the end of preschool, 1st, 2nd, and 8th grades. Beginning
in spring, 1977, the Wechsler Intelligence Scale and the
Stanford–Binet Intelligence Test were administered in alternate
years by the research staff.

The results indicate that the academic and IQ trends established by the end of kindergarten persisted into the 9th and 10th
grade years (see Figures 25.3 and 25.4). These figures show that
only the Montessori boys were not lower in IQ at 10th grade
than at the end of prekindergarten. At the end of 10th grade, the
Montessori boys were operating above national norms academically and were within the normal range of IQ. This was
15.3 points above the 10th grade DARCEE boys who had
started at the same IQ level as Montessori boys in preschool.

IQ scores for the Montessori girls increased at the end of
preschool and then dropped off radically. The control girls and
the DARCEE girls started the study 8 to 10 points higher
academically than other girls, and for the most part maintained

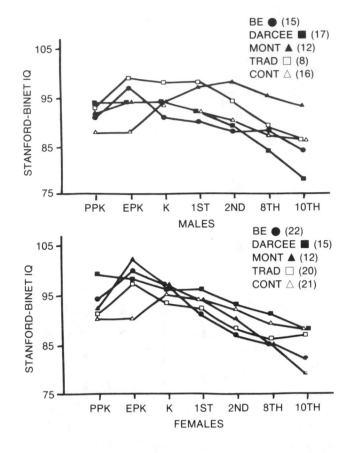

Fig. 25.3. Stanford-Binet IQ test results for students in four
Head Start programs. From "Long-Term Effects of Four
Preschool Programs: 9th and 10th Grade Results" by L. Miller
and R. Bizzell. Copyright 1983 by The Society for Research in
Child Development, Inc. Reprinted by permission.

this academic superiority throughout the study (see Figure
25.4). Only at the 6th grade did the academic scores of BE,
DARCEE, and Montessori converge.

It is possible these puzzling findings are due to chance.
However, considering the original random assignment and
considering that attrition has not been differential, the chance
factor is not a plausible explanation. In fact, Miller and Bizzell
(1983a) report that in the Montessori schools, attrition was in a
direction that lowered the probability of positive outcomes
(p. 23).

DISCUSSION OF THE MONTESSORI PROGRAM

If the Montessori preschool program had a very positive effect
upon young boys, what made the program effective for boys?
To consider this question, let us examine the Montessori
program.

Maria Montessori believed that the motivation to learn is
present at the start of life and that appropriate activities or
materials activate the motivation to learn. The fundamental
task of education is setting the child free to learn from the
environment. The educators' responsibility is to design and

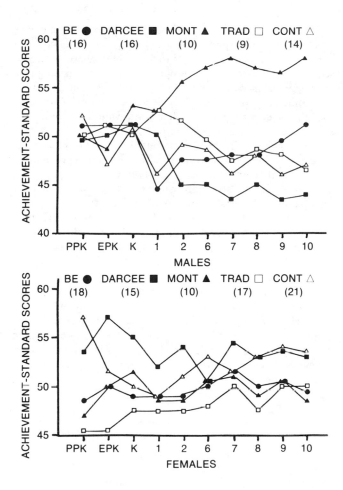

Fig. 25.4. Achievement results for students in four Head Start programs. From "Long-Term Effects of Four Preschool Programs: 9th and 10th Grade Results" by L. Miller and R. Bizzell. Copyright 1983 by The Society for Research in Child Development, Inc. Reprinted by permission.

organize the environment so that children can learn through self-correcting materials and activities. With self-correcting materials, children learn from direct experience. Teachers' judgment of success is not needed. The materials provide the feedback to the children and set them free to do their own correcting and to set their own pace.

Montessori believed that sensory experiences were directly related to the development of the child's mind. Beller (1973) summarized this theory as follows:

> Intelligence is the ability to classify. Classification consists of analyzing an object and extracting a determined attribute therefrom. If this capacity for selecting single attributes is not acquired, associations by means of similarities, synthesis and all higher work of intelligence becomes impossible. (p. 562)

The highly structured curriculum Montessori developed was based upon the assumptions about knowledge acquisition described above.

The Montessori program is dependent upon specific materials developed over the past 70 years. These same materials are

present in each Montessori classroom regardless of the geographical location or social status of the clientele. All preschools will have the same materials (e.g., the brown stairs and pink tower) which can only be assembled in one way. The child's task is to assemble the pieces in the single correct way.

During Montessori training, teacher candidates learn to organize and present these materials in a specified sequence. They also learn how to present or demonstrate the materials to individuals or small groups of children. Children are expected to attend to instruction, to finish each task and to put away their own materials.

Teachers in this model are encouraged to be supportive and facilitative: They should not develop emotional dependence in children. Their function is to be a director and monitor and to intervene as little as possible with the children. Task orientation is the focus of the relationship between children and teachers. Montessori thought that strong emotional ties were likely to interfere with task performance. Children are encouraged to control their emotionality and to become self-sufficient. With teachers modeling this behavior, mutual respect and helpfulness were expected to develop between teachers and students.

External rewards and punishments are discouraged. Montessori believed that children have an inner force that provides a stronger motivation than any extrinsic incentive. Each lesson or activity has a specific objective: The child's pleasure is derived from completing the task and meeting the objective. When children complete tasks, they inform the teacher, replace the materials, and receive a new lesson determined by the teacher. With minimal verbalization, the teacher states the objective of the new lesson. The children are not hurried through tasks or criticized for mistakes. The cornerstones of this model are to activate children's motivation to learn, and to help them develop the self-discipline to complete tasks.

Although children are at liberty to complete each activity at their own pace, the sequence of the activities is strictly controlled by the teacher. The sequencing enables the child to first discriminate between items, and to match sensory qualities such as size, color, or pitch. Next, qualities are ordered according to dimensions such as tall to short, thick or thin. Eventually the child is able to differentiate and integrate sensory dimensions. In this approach to child learning, the teacher provides minimal verbal labeling and description. The child learns through direct sensory experience.

The curriculum is meant to provide exercises for all of the senses. Thus, it includes reading, writing, numeration, weights and measures, pottery, painting, music, cooking, role playing, construction blocks, gardening, and other practical life experiences appropriate for each age group (Stodolsky, 1972).

Given these curriculum materials and experiences, and the instructional processes employed by Montessori teachers, it seems clear that this program is oriented toward the development of sorting, matching, classification skills, fine motor coordination, self-assurance, task persistence, and independence, and not so much toward verbal or social development.

It is of considerable interest that a specific program would be more beneficial to boys than to girls. Overall, the girls in the study had higher achievement levels than the boys except in the Montessori program (see Figure 25.5). The most plausible

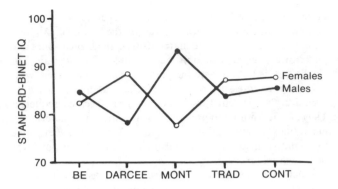

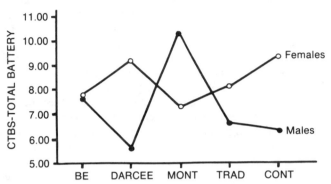

Fig. 25.5. Comparison of test results for male and female Head Start students. From "Long-Term Effects of Four Preschool Programs: 9th and 10th Grade Results" by L. Miller and R. Bizzell. Copyright 1983 by The Society for Research in Child Development, Inc. Reprinted by permission.

explanation may be found in some component of the Montessori program which is particularly beneficial for disadvantaged 4-year-old boys. Something within the structured sequencing of the self-correcting Montessori materials may have allowed the boys to develop discrimination, classification, and focusing skills. Such skills are required for taking tests and performing well in school. Perhaps the spatial qualities of the materials were more helpful to the boys than to the girls. Boys are typically less mature than girls at age 4, and it may be they were more susceptible to the effects of this individually paced, structured program than were the girls. That is, their cognitive structures were more pliable and were more influenced by their experiences than were the girls'. Perhaps there are teachable moments when children are more likely to learn through the sensory experiences that Montessori believed were so closely related to the development of the child's mind.

DISCUSSION OF THE DARCEE PROGRAM

In the DARCEE program the girls tested approximately at grade level in the 9th and 10th grades, but the boys were achieving at the 6th grade level (see Figure 25.5). Was there something in the DARCEE program that was better for girls than for boys?

The program, developed by Susan Gray at Peabody College, was based upon the premise that to succeed in school children need to develop basic concepts such as color, shape, size, and sequence. In addition, the program focused upon language development since the low-income children the program served had limited school vocabularies. School achievement was also thought to depend upon children's motivation to achieve in school.

The 31 children in the program attended a daycare center 5 days a week during the school year. The instruction provided to the 31 children in DARCEE was observed to have a greater amount of verbal instruction than other programs. Visual and manipulative materials were used, but usually in a group format. Part of the purpose of these activities was to help children learn to take turns using materials rather than learning at an individual exploratory pace. The time spent observing other children use the materials was likely to be as great as the time each child spent using the materials (Miller & Bizzell, 1983a, p. 26). This is quite a contrast from the Montessori program which provided for more individual manipulation of materials and less verbal interaction than other programs.

Since girls are known to mature faster than boys during the preschool years, Miller and Bizzell hypothesized that "between the ages of four and five when this sample entered prekindergarten the little girls were more ready to process information gained through observation and verbal instruction, particularly in the group setting, while the little boys needed more kinesthetic methods of instruction and/or more hands-on manipulation of materials in the learning of specific concepts" (p. 25).

This is a rational hypothesis, but it does not explain why the DARCEE and control girls had such similar test scores. The control girls, who did not participate in a preschool program, started with slightly higher achievement test scores, but DARCEE girls started with slightly higher IQ scores. At the 8th, 9th, and 10th grades the control and DARCEE girls were similar to each other and considerably higher than girls from the other three programs. Unless there is something special in the control children's home and grade school experiences, this finding indicates that for girls, the preschool experience had little positive academic effect in subsequent years.

DISCUSSION OF THE BEREITER—ENGELMANN (BE) PROGRAM

The BE preschool program (sometimes called Academic Preschool) provided a carefully structured, highly verbal, patterned drill and practice program. The drill occurred in small groups and focused upon learning verbal and mathematical operations. Teachers' questions and children's group responses were rhythmical and sometimes accompanied by kinesthetic activities such as counting coins into a coffee can.

The 37 children in the BE sample started preschool at approximately the same IQ level as children in the other programs, but the girls' IQ scores dropped 10 points by the end of 10th grade (see Figure 25.3). Montessori girls' IQ scores dropped a similar amount. The BE boys' scores also dropped, but not so much as the girls. The BE boys' achievement test scores hovered slightly above the 50th percentile and the BE girls' achievement test scores were slightly below that point, both at preschool and at 10th grade (see Figure 25.4). The boys' scores dropped dramatically at 1st grade but rose to slightly above the 50th percentile by 10th grade. At 10th grade, the BE boys tested higher than did DARCEE, traditional, and control boys, but the DARCEE and control girls scored higher than the BE girls.

Actually these BE children held their own in school, but progressed very little beyond their entry point. It may be that this didactic preschool program which required one teacher and at least two classroom aides constantly focusing the children's attention on fast-paced drill and practice activities was not productive in the long run. When the children entered school and did not receive this type of tightly structured program, boys in particular could not function well in the traditional classrooms.

SUMMARY AND CONCLUSIONS (CONTROL VS. PROGRAM CHILDREN)

The four Head Start programs summarized by Miller and Bizzell (1983) indicate strong and continuing program effects for Montessori boys. A possible explanation for their high scores on achievement tests may be an interaction between the individually paced, self-correcting, cognitive materials of the Montessori program and 4-year-old boys' cognitive receptivity. The Montessori program and materials require focused attention and completion of activities—skills that would serve children well in later school experiences.

Other children in the study fared less well when compared with the Montessori boys or control children who did not attend preschool. Control girls' IQ test scores dropped less than did girls' scores in the four preschool programs. Further, control girls' achievement test scores were as high as or higher than all other girls at 8th, 9th, and 10th grades (see Figures 25.3 and 25.4).

Control boys achieved at the same rate as did boys who attended traditional preschools and scored higher than the DARCEE boys from 2nd grade through 10th grade. The control boys' IQ scores were more consistent than other boys' scores throughout the study, increasing the most at the end of kindergarten. This pattern of IQ scores increasing at kindergarten was also true for control girls. Interestingly, IQ scores peaked for the children in the four preschool programs at the end of the preschool year, and tended to drop at the end of kindergarten.

This pattern suggests that experiences the children had in preschool (for program children) or in kindergarten (for control children) prepared them to score higher on the Stanford–Binet IQ test than they did prior to those experiences. This finding suggests that school experiences are closely related to the abilities examined by the Stanford–Binet. Except for the Montessori boys, the pattern for IQ scores was to drop off at the end of the children's second year in school; kindergarten for program sample and first grade for control. This finding does not suggest that students became less intelligent. They most likely scored just as well on the same IQ test items; however, their increasing age would require them to complete more items

correctly to maintain IQ scores set in the previous year, for example, a score of 90 at age 5 requires more items correct than a score of 90 at age 4. A possible explanation for the drop in IQ scores may be that school experiences and IQ test items did not continue to have the same positive relationship as they did initially. This suggests that IQ scores were a test of experience rather than intelligence. Only the Montessori boys' school experience seems to have provided them with skills or the abilities required to continue to grow cognitively, that is, complete more IQ items each year relevant to their age.

Clearly further analyses are needed to understand the interactions of sex difference, instructional programs, and test scores. Miller and Bizzell (1983) promise case studies of high- and low-ability students in each group. It would be of considerable interest to have available other outcomes of the programs such as attendance, grades, dropout rate, retentions, and placements in special education classes such as those collected in the other longitudinal studies. Standardized test scores may not be the best way to judge a program's long-term effectiveness since achievement tests and IQ scores are so much related to the curriculum and experiences children receive in the classroom.

Follow Through Longitudinal Studies

When researchers found that the gains in achievement made by Head Start children tended to drop off at the end of kindergarten or first grade, a government-funded program was initiated to allow programs to provide a continuous educational experience from kindergarten through third grade. This comprehensive program was called Follow Through. Project Follow Through was originally set up in a "planned variation" research design; that is, the goal was to examine the differential effectiveness of programs based on divergent educational and developmental theories. The program began when researchers and other educational stakeholders were invited by the government to submit plans for establishing their various programs in public schools in order to test whether their individual approaches could improve the educational achievement of economically disadvantaged children.

The overall objective of Follow Through was to improve the "life chances" of low-income children. Goodrich and St. Pierre (1980) include college attendance, future earnings, and other postschool variables as indicators of success in life. These indicators are not yet assessable for most of the Follow Through graduates. However, those authors also suggest other indicators such as attendance, special education placement, grade retention, dropout rate, grades, test scores, course selection, and discipline records as reasonable assessment variables for Follow Through classrooms (p. 2).

Twenty-two Follow Through programs were implemented in sites across the country. Of these, two Follow Through programs have been in continuous operation since 1968 and have collected excellent data subsequent to children's graduation from their programs: They are the Parent Education Follow Through Program and the Direct Instruction Follow Through Program. Other Follow Through programs are in current use but have not yet collected longitudinal data on their early participants; thus our review is limited to the two programs that follow.

PARENT EDUCATION FOLLOW THROUGH
PROGRAM (PEFTP)

Some models combined home intervention with the child's schooling. Ira Gordon's Florida Parent Program is one of these. The program was developed at the University of Florida in the 1960s. Initially it was used with infants and mothers and was subsequently developed for use in Head Start preschools and Follow Through kindergarten through third grade classrooms.

Gordon's position was that if an intervention program was to be successful, it must start early (preferably during infancy), and it must include the home environment, especially the mother, in addition to the child. The major goals of the Gordon program are to enhance the intellectual and personality development of the child, and to produce changes in the mother's self-esteem and in her conviction that she could affect what happens to her and her child (Beller, 1973). An important feature of this program has been to use women from the community as paraprofessionals trained to function as home educators. In the Head Start and Follow Through programs, these paraprofessionals assisted in the classrooms in the mornings and visited homes in the afternoons.

The theory of the Parent Education Follow Through Program developed from the belief in an ecological system of relationships between home, school, and community. This point of view is consistent with Bronfenbrenner's ecological theory of human development (1974, 1979). According to Rubin, Olmstead, and Kelly, (1981),

> A basic tenent underlying both the Gordon program and the ecological theory is that the child and his or her family do not exist in isolation, but are influenced by, and in turn influence, other systems in the environment. These reciprocal relationships among a variety of systems can be considered a transactional approach to the provision of services to children and families. (p. 176)

Although political, social, and economic systems are recognized to interact with the family and school system, the PEFTP focuses primarily upon the interaction between home and school, for example, children, parents, and school personnel. This program has been implemented in 10 communities during the past 13 years. Each of these communities works closely with the model's sponsor located now at the University of North Carolina in Chapel Hill.

The instructional practices of the PEFTP require the participation of the parents and school personnel: They are considered the key people contributing to a child's development. This program promotes a close relationship between these key people to maximize opportunities for the child to learn. Rubin et al. (1981) describe the major features as follows:

> (1) Comprehensive services (social, psychological, and medical), (2) weekly home visitations by paid paraprofessionals during which home learning activities stressing specific parental teaching behaviors are delivered, and (3) parental participation of various kinds including volunteer, employee and decision-maker. (p. 178)

In the PEFTP children learn at home and at school. A paid parent educator serves as a classroom aide in the mornings and coordinates learning activity training for mothers to use with their children in their homes in the afternoons. These visits are scheduled to occur once a week in the homes throughout the school year. A typical visit for a kindergarten parent might include presenting a set of large and small red, yellow, and green balloons and asking the child to sort out the large balloons and small balloons; to sort the red, yellow, and green balloons. A related activity might be to sort red, yellow, and green paper circles and red, yellow, and green paper squares.

A great advantage of these in-home activities is that younger children in the home also learn the concepts being taught. During a kindergarten home visit of the PEFTP, the first author observed a 3-year-old child run to a table drawer, remove some cut paper figures, and hand them to the parent educator, saying, "Red, red, red!" Indeed they were red circles left from the previous parent educator visit.

Essentially parents are guided to interact with their children in specific supportive ways that are likely to promote learning. Rubin et al. (1981, p. 179) suggest the following Desirable Teaching Behaviors for parents:

- Before starting an activity, explain what you are going to do.
- Before starting an activity, give the learner time to familiarize himself or herself with the materials.
- Ask questions which have more than one correct answer.
- Ask questions which require multiple-word answers.
- Encourage the learner to enlarge upon his or her answer.
- Get the learner to ask questions.
- Give the learner time to think about the problem: don't be too quick to help.
- Get the learner to make judgments on the basis of evidence rather than by guessing.
- Praise the learner when he or she does well or takes small steps in the right direction.
- Let the learner know when his or her answer or work is wrong, but do so in a positive or neutral manner.

Classroom teachers are also encouraged to use these procedures and techniques when interacting with children. Although the curriculum is not specified, teachers are encouraged to provide activities that are appropriate for the child's stage of development according to Piaget's definitions of stages. In this way the program is similar to that of Montessori and Weikart's Perry Preschool Program.

Gordon's infant study was carried out in small towns in rural Florida. The sample was composed of low-income mothers and their babies born between June 1966 and September 1967. There was a final sample of 193 mother and infant pairs. A large set of data was collected from the mothers and infants. This included measurements of mothers' self-esteem, attitudes, expectations, language ability; infants' Bayley Infant Scales and Griffith Mental Development Scales (GMDS). At the end of the first year of life, the experimental children were superior to the control children on scores of the GMDS. In 1972 when all of the experimental and control children had passed their fourth birthday, Gordon reported strong and consistent effects of his parent intervention program. Findings were based upon the Stanford Binet Test, the Peabody Picture Vocabulary Test, and the Leiter International Performance Scale. The highest scores were found among children who had been in the program 2 or 3 years.

The Parent Education Follow Through Program has been implemented in 10 communities around the country since 1969, serving approximately 8,000 children from kindergarten to third grade. Given that this model focuses upon the home and the parents' participation, the assessment procedures are somewhat different than those of other studies. The data reported by Rubin et al. (1981) include: (a) descriptive data which include records of quality and quantity of home visits made to participating families, parent participation, and parental classroom volunteering; (b) child achievement data from standardized achievement tests for grades kindergarten through third, data focusing on parental teaching behaviors, home environments, and child achievement, and data on vertical diffusion; and (c) case study information focusing upon the program's impact in the communities (p. 180).

Each community program required one home visit a week for each child in the program. These researchers found that 80% of the children received at least 75% of the scheduled home visits. This is impressive when we consider that 8,000 children in the program received approximately 150,000 home visits.

Involvement of these low-income parents in school activities was a goal of the program. Data presented in Tables 25.1 and 25.2 indicate that participation in Policy Advisory Committee, other school activities, and volunteering in school increased dramatically from 1974 to 1979. Another positive impact of the program was on parents' use of Desirable Teaching Behaviors (DTBs). Parents in the program were videotaped as they taught

Table 25.2. Parental Involvement Data: Percentages of Parents Who Volunteer in the Classroom (1974–1979)

Year	Lowest Community	Median Community	Highest Community
1973–1974	19	42	58
1974–1975	29	45	70
1975–1976	27	42	96
1976–1977	28	55	84
1977–1978	36	76	90
1978–1979	32	71	90

Note. The years included in this table represent all the years for which there are complete sets of data.

The lowest, median, and highest community indicate the lowest, median, and highest-achieving community during the year indicated.

From "Comprehensive Model for Child Services" by R. Rubin, P. Olmsted, and J. Kelly, 1981, *Children and Youth Services Review, 3,* p. 184. Copyright 1981 by Pergamon Press, Ltd. Reprinted by permission.

Table 25.1. Parental Involvement Data: Percentages of Parents Who Attend Policy Advisory Committee Meetings and Activities (1974–1979)

Year	Lowest Community	Median Community	Highest Community
Meetings			
1973–1974	9	27	59
1974–1975	14	28	57
1975–1976	18	34	55
1976–1977	13	33	53
1977–1978	27	41	83
1978–1979	36	50	71
Activities			
1973–1974	7	15	27
1974–1975	4	22	31
1975–1976	14	26	44
1976–1977	11	27	62
1977–1978	20	50	84
1978–1979	19	44	79

Note. The years included in this table represent all the years for which there are complete sets of data.

The lowest, median, and highest community indicate the lowest, median, and highest-achieving community during the year indicated.

From "Comprehensive Model for Child Services" by R. Rubin, P. Olmsted, and J. Kelly, 1981, *Children and Youth Services Review, 3,* p. 184. Copyright 1981 by Pergamon Press, Ltd. Reprinted by permission.

their child an activity. Control parents were also videotaped while teaching their child an activity. The results indicated that PEFTP parents had a mean of 24.0 in their use of Desirable Teaching Behaviors (DTBs) and nonprogram parents scored a mean of 14.5 DTBs. A study by Olmsted (1977) showed the number of DTBs used by a parent correlated with reading (r = .50, p < .001) and with math (r = .35, p < .05).

External evaluations of the PEFTP students' achievement by SRI International and Abt Associates (1977) and a reanalysis of these data by House et al. (1977) reported significant evidence for the effectiveness of the PEFTP. Of the 13 Follow Through programs analyzed, the PEFTP was ranked fourth in achievement effect size.

The inference made by Rubin et al. (1981) is that child achievement behavior is influenced by the involvement of parents in the roles previously mentioned and specifically by the role of parents as teachers of their own child.

To examine the longitudinal effects of the PEFTP, a study was conducted in the Richmond, Virginia, public school system. This study started in 1968 when the PEFTP was adopted. Since that time the PEFTP has been implemented in 40 classrooms in 10 elementary schools within the city of Richmond. According to researchers Halstead (1982) and Olmsted and Rubin (1982) the program in these classrooms has been consistently well implemented over the years.

The sample was drawn from children who entered the kindergarten program in 1969–1970, 1970–1971, or 1971–1972. Children were selected for study on the following basis: (a) had participated in the PEFTP for 2 or more years; (b) had a sibling between 1 and 5 years older; (c) had a complete cumulative school record as of the end of the 1980–1981 school year. The number of children in the three cohorts meeting the criteria was 122 (Rubin, Olmsted, Szegda, Wetherby, & Williams, 1983, p. 7).

Interestingly, the PEFTP researchers used older siblings of the treatment children for comparison. For each program child, the older sibling closest in age who had not participated in the program and who had a complete cumulative record was selected for the comparison sample. As stated by the researchers (Rubin et al., 1983):

> One advantage of an older-sibling comparison group design is the common backgrounds of the subjects in the two groups, including home, neighborhood or community, and school. Although evidence had been found of program effects diffusing down to younger children in the family, there has been no evidence of upward diffusion; so it is reasonably safe to conclude that there are few, if any, contaminating program effects for the comparison group. (p. 8)

Of the 122 PEFTP students in the school year 1980–1981, 61% were in Grades 7 through 12, 28% had graduated, and 10% had dropped out. By contrast, 39% of their older siblings were still in school, 28% had graduated, and 31% had dropped out. The difference in dropout rate is significant and important. In addition, PEFTP girls were retained significantly less often than other children (both PEFTP boys and older siblings) in the sample. The average number of years of placement in special education for the older sibling group was more than twice that of the PEFTP students. Achievement test data were not reported for this longitudinal study.

The early preschool studies and Follow Through studies of the PEFTP indicated that children in this parent-focused program made acceptable cognitive and achievement growth. Equally important, their school success is indicated by fewer placements in special education, fewer grade retentions, and a lower incidence of dropout from school. All of these variables affect student opportunities to become productive citizens in our society. A program of this kind benefits not only an individual child, but also the family, school system, and society by assisting its participants to become more successful members of society (Rubin et al., 1983, p. 19).

DIRECT INSTRUCTION/FOLLOW THROUGH MODEL

The Direct Instruction Follow Through model grew from the highly structured BE preschool program previously described in the Miller and Bizzell (1983b) study. This academic preschool program was an anomaly when it was created by Bereiter and Engelmann (1966). The major objectives of the BE Direct Instruction program were to help children acquire basic skills in arithmetic, to develop effective use of language, and to master visual symbols and basic color concepts. Through academic achievements, the children were expected to increase their self-esteem and develop self-confidence. The program was developed especially for children from lower-income homes who lacked language skills necessary for success in school. In Beller's (1973) words, "The academic preschool was designed as a crash program of language remediation to help four- and five-year-old lower income children catch up to middle class children" (p. 569).

Most other preschool programs of that time were developed to foster the cognitive, social, and emotional skills of children. In essence, they were responsive to the needs of the whole child. In sharp contrast, the academic preschool model specified exactly what children needed to succeed in school and dictated how teachers should modify children's behavior. This model stood out in the crowd of preschool models: It was cheered by behavioral psychologists, jeered by cognitive developmentalists. The latter group felt it unwise or even criminal to subject young children to such narrowly focused activities.

Behavior modification models grew out of the learning theories of Pavlov (1927) and Skinner (1968). These theorists submit that any healthy animal or person can be taught to perform tasks successfully if the unit of learning is small enough and if the reinforcement offered is desired by the subject. The Academic Preschool Program's curriculum and practice were based upon Skinner's operant conditioning theory. Operant conditioning is a form of learning in which a designated behavioral act is reinforced to bring about its regular occurrence. In operant conditioning, the response or behavior operates upon the environment to generate consequences. The consequences are contingent upon the emission of a response. If the response is acceptable, the consequence is pleasant and the response is reinforced. A simple example is a mother asking a child to put napkins on the table (stimulus); the child does (response); the mother says, "Thank you. You are a big girl to help mother," thus reinforcing the child's helping behavior.

In comparing the cognitive developmentalists and the behavior modifiers, Maccoby and Zellner (1970) had the following to say:

> The cognitive developmentalist, following the Piagetian theory, believes that the process of education is one of building cognitive structures in the mind of the child. The behavior modifier is wont to say that he does not know what cognitive structures are—that he believes these are fiction, myths, invented by psychologists, that serve more to hinder than to help his understanding of how the child learns. The behavior modifier conceives of education as a process of producing changes in observable behavior. Usually the changes take the form of adding new responses to the child's repertoire —like filling up an empty jar with marbles, adding one marble at a time. ... Reinforcement is the mechanism that produces this result. The behaviorist does not, of course, believe that nothing goes on inside the head—only that it is not profitable to speculate about these internal processes, since they cannot be directly observed or controlled. The only thing we can control is what we observe, and all we can observe is behavior. (p. 34)

Results over time have indicated that children who continued in this structured academic program eventually won the academic marble game.

Encouraged by their initial success with some preschool children, Bereiter and Engelmann responded to the government's request for proposals to provide educational programs for kindergarten through third grade which would aid children to maintain the gains achieved in Head Start or other preschool programs. The Academic Preschool program developed for the elementary school is now known as the Oregon Direct Instruction program. This program was awarded Follow Through Planned Variation funds and was subsequently implemented in 20 locations across the nation. In 1983 this Follow Through program could be found in 60 American cities and a number of foreign countries.

The Direct Instruction program is based upon the premise that positive reinforcement is essential to modifying student behavior and maximizing children's academic success. To implement the belief that children can be trained to succeed, a carefully sequenced curriculum and a rigidly controlled instructional process are required.

At the inception of the preschool model, Carl Bereiter and Siegfried Engelmann created sets of curriculum for reading, spelling, language arts, and mathematics. The lessons were presented in small hierarchical steps. Teachers presented a bit of information; children repeated the information; teachers asked a simple direct question about the information; children responded. If the response was correct, the children were praised. If the response was wrong, the teacher corrected the children and the process was repeated until the children repeated the right answer automatically. Then and only then did they proceed to the next sequence. The drill and practice was kept at a rapid pace with systematic and enthusiastic praise for right answers.

The Follow Through program required curricular materials for kindergarten through third grade. Thus, materials were prepared for reading, spelling, language arts, mathematics, science, and music for each of these grade levels. Since Planned Variation Follow Through was a national model, the instructional process for using the curriculum had to be made essentially teacher proof. To accomplish this, a script was prepared for each lesson to be used by teachers and classroom aides in all parts of the country.

The Follow Through approach that evolved under the direction of Siegfried Engelmann and Wesley Becker required three adults trained in Direct Instruction methods in each classroom. For reading, math, and language development, children were grouped on the basis of their ability according to criterion tests given weekly. The classroom teacher was usually responsible for the reading program; a full-time aide was responsible for the math program; and a second full-time aide was responsible for spelling and handwriting. In order for the children to receive maximum amounts of stimulation and praise during a learning session, the teachers worked with 8 to 10 children at a time and addressed most questions and praise to the group. By addressing the group, the teacher was attempting to keep all participants totally engaged all of the time. The teacher might rapidly question individuals to see if they had learned each step, but primarily the teacher addressed the entire group.

Individual learning problems were diagnosed through weekly testing and each child then received the drill and practice necessary to learn required skills. In this model, the teachers were the directors. They initiated each stimulus and quickly reinforced or modified each response. They controlled the students, keeping them on task through continuing interactions and positive reinforcement. Students and teachers shared the pleasure and the excitement of correct responses. Observations conducted by Stallings and Kaskowitz (1974) found 90% of the Direction Instruction teachers in five urban and rural locations implementing the model as specified by the developers. These findings indicated that the educational model and the teacher training program were transportable to urban and rural sites.

Early reports for the Academic Preschool program of Bereiter and Engelmann indicated that after 2 years in the academic preschool, children made greater gains on the Stanford–Binet and the Wide Range Achievement Test than children of comparison groups who had not received such intensive academic training. Upon entering the first grade, the experimental children achieved at nearly the second grade level in reading, arithmetic, and spelling. As with other preschool programs, the success of the children was short lived. At the end of the first grade year there was little academic difference between treatment and control children (Beller, 1973, p. 570).

The Academic Preschool program was then modified for use in kindergarten through third grade and was called the Oregon Direct Instruction Follow Through Program. Since its inception, the Direct Instruction Follow Through Program has been reported to have a positive effect upon children's reading and mathematics achievement test scores (Abt Associates, 1977; Stebbins, St. Pierre, Proper, Anderson, & Cerva, 1977). Of the nine major Follow Through models evaluated, Direct Instruction ranked highest in reading and mathematics. In 1977 Becker reported that the average scores for the students in the program corresponded to the 49th–50th percentile on the mathematics, language, and spelling subtests of the Metropolitan Achievement Test, and the 41st percentile in reading. Stallings (1975) also found that the first and third grade children in the Direct Instruction model scored higher in reading and mathematics than children in the six other Follow Through models in that study. On the negative side, on a test attributing responsibility for achievement success, Direct Instruction third grade children more often attributed their success to their teachers or other factors outside of themselves and attributed their failures to themselves. Another negative finding was that the Direct Instruction third grade children scored lower than children in cognitive developmental models on a test of nonverbal problem-solving abilities (Ravens Progressive Matrices). These children who spent most of their time at school in rapid-paced drill and practice activities or completing carefully sequenced worksheets had little opportunity to work with concrete materials. This lack of experience in taking things apart, putting them back together, learning relationships, and seeing how things fit together may have contributed to their low scores.

The primary question posed to all educational models is: What are the long-term effects? Will children who have learned through carefully sequenced lessons and teacher guidance during the initial stages be able to work and learn independently in classrooms that do not provide the support and consistency of the Follow Through program?

Several studies have examined the longitudinal effects of the Direct Instructional model. In these studies the researchers have tracked the original control and experimental children. Becker and Gersten (1982) found that fifth and sixth graders in five sites have scored higher than control children on the Wide Range Achievement Test in reading decoding, mathematics, and spelling. The authors noted that the magnitude of the effects was appreciably lower than it had been in third grade. A quasi-experimental follow-up study by Meyer, Gersten, and Gutkin (1984) found that New York fifth graders who had experienced 4 years of Direct Instruction scored significantly higher than did comparison children and were well above national median levels in reading on the Comprehensive Test of Basic Skills. Meyer (1984) reported that urban ninth graders, who had experienced Direct Instruction in kindergarten through third grade, scored significantly higher than comparison students, and were at ninth grade level in reading and at 8.6 grade level in mathematics. Although the findings are not consistent across sites, there is evidence to indicate that Direct Instruction ninth grade students are more likely to attend school and less likely to be retained than comparison students. It also appears that the students who experienced Direct Instruction were more likely to graduate. Of the 23 New York students who started the program in 1969, 57% graduated, compared to 35% of the 29 comparison students; 4% had been retained, compared to 7% of the controls; 39% had applied to college, compared to 10% of the controls.

In Miller and Bizzell's (1983b) comparison of the longitudinal effects of four preschool programs, 1 year of (BE) Direct Instruction was found to have little positive long-term effect upon eighth and ninth grade students. It appears that for students to benefit in the long run from this very structured program, they must be enrolled for several years during elementary school. The graduates from the (kindergarten through third grade) Direct Instruction Follow Through model now in secondary schools are achieving near to national norms and are performing better on tests of achievement than are children from Weikart's Perry Preschool, Montessori, or Parent Education Follow Through Program.

Clearly, the longitudinal findings regarding retention, attendance, and graduation have important implications for the cost effectiveness of the Direct Instruction model. While academic achievement is in itself important, it is likely that students' success in school contributes significantly to a greater commitment toward schooling. This fits with the behavioral philosophy that success reinforces success. If the goal is to have students succeed academically, then a program is needed insuring that children will succeed at a high rate and that they will eventually expect to succeed.

Summary and Implications

The longitudinal programs reviewed in this chapter indicate that the field of research on teaching and learning has made substantial progress during the last decade. Prior to this time researchers have accepted short-term effects to measure the quality of educational programs. The set of studies reviewed here provides longitudinal analyses of child learning and long-term effects of teaching strategies. This longitudinal view has allowed the researchers to go beyond the usual analyses of student gains on IQ and achievement tests.

Most of the preschool and elementary school programs that were funded and evaluated during the 1960s and 1970s aimed at improving the life chances of low-income children. These children were thought to be deprived of experiences related to success in school. Given that preschool children spend most of their time in their own homes, one goal common to the preschool programs was to have a positive impact upon the family. Most often this program component was implemented through home visits which provided parents with information, cognitive activities, and materials to use with their children. Parents were welcomed to the schools and encouraged to take part in school activities. Another common goal was to help

children develop competencies that would serve them well in school and to develop positive attitudes in children toward schooling. Such program outcomes are not very amenable to measurement by standardized tests, especially since little children are notoriously poor test takers (Stodolsky, 1972).

To examine program impact on families, the longitudinal studies compared responses of experimental and control parents to questions regarding their own lives, their child's schooling, and their expectations for their child. Indications of school competence were the rate at which these at-risk children were passed to the next grade in school, and the rate at which they remained in the mainstream of schools. Using these outcome measures, the analyses conducted by the Consortium for Longitudinal Studies generated findings that make a good case for low-income children attending preschool.

When compared with control children at sixth grade, experimental children in the twelve Consortium programs had been retained less often in grade, placed less often in special education classrooms, and had answered questions about school in a more positive manner. Across all the programs, the parents reported being more satisfied with their children's success in school and having higher aspirations for their children than control parents. These analyses and results did not identify any particular programs or teaching strategies that were most effective. Lazar et al. (1982) simply state that the sum of their work indicates that children from low-income families derive measurable educational benefits from diverse, well-run early education programs (p. 18). This statement and these findings suggest that preschool programs can follow several different formats and be effective: home based or center based, using paraprofessionals or professional staff, for infants or preschoolers. Common components should include involvement with the families and some structured, cognitive school-like activities.

Two other programs reviewed in this chapter had well-developed parent components: the Parent Education Follow Through Program (PEFTP), and the Perry Preschool Program. Researchers have followed these children into high school and report that in addition to having fewer children retained in grades and placed in special education classrooms, the program children are staying in school and are graduating at a greater rate than are control children. In the case of the Perry Preschool children, who have been tracked to age 19, more of them are employed or attending college and fewer have reported acts of delinquency that resulted in arrest compared to control children.

There were many similarities in the educational experiences of the Perry Preschool children and the PEFTP children. Both models were driven by an ecological theory, that is, that a child and his or her family influence and are influenced by the school and community. The parents in both models were visited weekly by school personnel. The visitor taught the parent how to do school-type activities with the child and encouraged the parents to participate in school programs. The parents in both experimental groups were found to have more positive attitudes toward school and higher expectations for their children than did parents who did not receive this type of attention. The instructional methods and curriculum employed by teachers in both models were responsive to the stage developmental ideas of Piaget. Teachers provided opportunities for children to gain basic cognitive concepts through materials and experience.

It is difficult to separate the effect of the intervention with the family upon the children's persistence and competence in school from the effect of the Piagetian-type educational tasks the children engaged in at school. Since neither the Perry Preschool or PEFTP researchers report consistent positive cognitive or achievement results for their students in high school, it is more likely that the family expectations explain the persistence of children to stay in school, to graduate, to get jobs, and to apply for college. Over the 15 years of the study, the home is the more constant factor. Given that the children spent only 1 year in the Perry Preschool Program, and 2 to 4 years in the PEFTP, it appears children's experiences in PEFTP and Perry Preschool did provide the basis for acceptable school performance so that they were promoted to the next grade and were not often assigned to special education classes.

The family visitation component was missing from the four Head Start programs studied by Miller and Bizzell (1983b). These researchers relied almost entirely upon change scores in IQ and achievement to assess the difference in effectiveness of the programs. An interesting pattern emerged for the IQ test scores. All of the children in the four preschool programs except Montessori boys had IQ scores that peaked at the end of the preschool year, whereas the control children, who did not attend preschool, had their scores peak at the end of kindergarten, which was their first year in school. These patterns suggest that IQ scores are quite responsive to school experiences and should not be used as a baseline to evaluate change until after children's first year in school.

The analyses of the DARCEE, Montessori, BE/Direct Instruction, traditional, and control groups were unique in separating effects for girls and boys in the programs. The control children did not attend preschool and provided interesting findings, though potentially disturbing to preschool advocates. The control girls achieved as well as or better than other girls in the study when tested in the seventh, eighth, and ninth grades. The control boys tested higher than did boys in two of the preschool programs. The researchers suggest that this higher achievement by control children was due to the fact that they were from slightly higher socioeconomic homes, since these families had not applied for entrance into the Head Start programs. However, control children's IQ scores were lower than other children's at the first testing, while their achievement test scores at the same time were higher than other children's. Unless there was something specially nurturing in the homes of these children and absent from the other homes in the study, the case for sending children to preschool in order to achieve academically in school is not strong.

Another puzzling and interesting finding from the study was that after the 1st grade, the boys who had experienced the Montessori preschool program scored significantly higher than all other children at each of the following 6-year testing points. The Montessori girls did not succeed in school in the same way. Only the girls in the traditional preschool had lower test scores than did the Montessori girls. Further, the Montessori boys' IQ scores did not drop lower by the end of the 10th grade, as did the IQ scores for children in all other groups. We can only speculate that a relationship exists between 4-year-old boys'

cognitive structure and self-paced, self-correcting materials such as those used in the Montessori preschool program. This does not suggest that only 4-year-old boys in the Montessori program will benefit from these materials. Perhaps 3-year-old girls, who mature cognitively at an earlier age, or children in their own homes, would also benefit from these materials.

The Direct Instruction Follow Through model was evaluated by a set of research studies that used longitudinal achievement data and unobtrusive measures. Apparently, children do need more than 1 year of this highly structured verbal program to succeed later in school. The children in the 1-year BE Direct Instruction group reported by Miller and Bizzell (1983a) achieved at about the same rate at the 9th and 10th grades as they did upon entering preschool. On the Comprehensive Test of Basic Skills administered at 9th grade, students scored at the 8th grade level. However, the Follow Through children who participated in the Direct Instruction program from kindergarten through 3rd grade gained academically in school so that by 9th grade they were achieving at grade level. School records revealed that these children were less likely to be retained in grades, more likely to graduate, and more likely to apply for college than were the control students. Overall, the longitudinal findings for the Direct Instruction model are very positive.

Implications from these studies for preschool and elementary educators are that family involvement activities help foster positive attitudes toward school and in turn support children to be successful in school and to be persistent enough to graduate. In 1-year preschool programs, impact on cognitive development is most likely to come from Montessori-type self-paced, self-correcting materials, especially for 4-year-old boys and perhaps for 3-year-old girls.

One implication for elementary school educators is that a structured, carefully sequenced program for low-achieving children in the lower four grades helps them to succeed academically in high school.

Elementary Educational Innovations of the 1970s

Paralleling changes in the political and social climate of the 1970s were changes in psychologists' assumptions about intellectual development. The conventional wisdom of the 1960s was that children were most responsive to educational intervention efforts before the age of 5, and if no special efforts were made to give disadvantaged children a "head start" during this critical period, they would forever be doomed to a low level of academic achievement. Educational research demonstrated that while well-organized educational intervention during the preschool years contributed toward school success and improved life chances, it was insufficient to assure disadvantaged children of academic competence for the remainder of their school years. Accordingly, recent educational innovations are less concentrated on preschool-age children or narrowly focused upon economically disadvantaged children.

Two programs characteristic of these more recently developed educational innovations are Mastery Learning and Cooperative Learning. Both of these programs gained prominence in the 1970s and can be applied to children at almost any age and at any socioeconomic level. For the most part, they are implemented in the regular classroom. Mastery Learning and Cooperative Learning were developed during the 1970s, but were not systematically funded in districts over several years through titled programs such as Head Start or Follow Through. Consequently, it is difficult to evaluate their long-term effects on learning. School districts typically grasp an innovation and try to implement it as best they can, and do not build in methods to evaluate systematically the impact of the innovation on teachers and students over time. However, these two programs have been implemented in classrooms throughout the country and considerable research by interested university-based researchers and graduate students allows us to make some conclusions about their effectiveness.

We would have liked to review a third popular educational innovation of the 1970s—the Madeline Hunter Instructional Skills program. This program is an attempt to guide teacher planning so that teachers are clear about their lessons' objectives and about their instruction. Another basic condition of the Hunter program is that lessons are appropriate for the children—not too hard and not too easy. Practice is guided with many checks for student understanding. The program has been adopted by several states as their primary instructional program, but there has been little experimental research on its implementation by teachers or on its effect upon students. There are studies under way in Pittsburgh by the Learning, Research, and Development Center, and in Napa County and Marin County in California to examine the program's effectiveness. A study by Stallings, Robbins, and Wolfe (1984) of the Napa program indicates that the prescribed instructional skills contribute significantly to students' engaged rate and achievement in mathematics. Due to the large following of this early education program, the program is merely mentioned here with the hope that it will be described in the next *Handbook for Research on Teaching*.

Mastery Learning: Theory, Practice, and Outcomes

Underlying mastery learning models is the fundamental assumption that nearly all students can learn the basic school curriculum, but that some take longer than others. Bloom popularized this notion and designed the original educational program based on it, but the theoretical basis for the strategy was developed by Carroll (1963). According to Carroll's model, amount of learning in school is a function of the amount of time spent in proportion to the amount of time needed. Thus, a child needing a considerable amount of time but given little time masters only part of the school curriculum. Bloom's (1968, 1971, 1974, 1976, 1981) solution for achieving greater equity in school learning is to vary the amount of time children spend on learning. He claimed that most students, perhaps as many as 95%, can achieve mastery if they are given the amount of instructional time they need.

While all mastery-based educational programs are designed primarily to enhance student achievement, an important assumption is that mastery-based learning enhances motivation. Because students are presumably given the time they need to achieve mastery, all students should expect success to result from their efforts, and the expectation that success can be achieved through effort has been shown by achievement motivation theorists to affect motivation positively (Dweck & Goetz, 1978; Weiner, 1979). Low-ability students (or slow learners) would be expected to benefit most from a mastery-based model because under competitive evaluative conditions, they have little hope of success, regardless of the amount of effort they expend.

Another potentially positive motivational feature of mastery-based programs is that the students have a greater role in their own evaluation. Also, errors are considered a natural part of the learning process and are consequently not a reason for embarrassment or humiliation. Theoretically, this approach should reduce the maladaptive behavior that often results from children's attempt to avoid "failure" (e.g., reluctance to ask the teacher a question for fear of revealing ignorance).

INSTRUCTIONAL PRACTICE

Introduction of the mastery learning model into a classroom does not necessarily affect the mode or the content of instruction. Varying the amount of time children spend on learning concepts or skills does not preclude, for example, whole-class instruction and lecturing, although practically it is often accompanied by more individualized instructional techniques. And it can potentially be used with almost any curriculum, although hierarchically structured programs are more easily adapted to a mastery learning approach than are others.

Clear instructional objectives are required in mastery learning programs. It is necessary to break a course or subject into small discrete units of learning to allow individualized evaluation of increments in mastery. The units are short enough to allow close monitoring of individual student's understanding, and they are organized hierarchically so that the material taught in each unit is used at increasing levels of complexity in subsequent units. Generally, each unit is introduced by the teacher in a whole-class format. The style of presentation is not prescribed in mastery learning programs, and therefore varies according to each teacher's customary style. Following the teacher's presentation, students are given instructional material to practice the application of the new concepts.

Diagnostic tests are critical to a mastery learning program. The teacher is instructed to develop brief, ungraded, student-scored, diagnostic-progress tests used for formative evaluation of students' level of understanding (Bloom, Hastings, & Madaus, 1971). These evaluations provide the teacher and child with feedback about each child's progress toward achieving the educational objectives. The child is given additional instructional material ("correctives") based on his or her specific level of mastery. The correctives are used for further instruction and should differ from the teacher's group instruction. These correctives often include cooperative small-group study sessions, peer tutoring, programed instruction, supplementary textbooks and workbooks, audiovisual materials, academic games and puzzles, and affective exercises. Children who master the unit relatively quickly are given enrichments, allowing the material covered on the formative test to be studied more intensely (vertical enrichments) or more broadly (horizontal enrichments). Students continue this diagnostic test-corrective instruction cycle until they have achieved mastery. They are supposed to do the additional studying on their own time, although practically, class time is often set aside for this purpose (Block, 1974).

A summative evaluation instrument is used to determine grades. Grading is noncompetitive in that any student who has mastered the curriculum designated for that length of instructional time is given an A. Until a child demonstrates mastery on the summative test, he or she is given an I (incomplete), indicating "mastery in the making." Ideally, all but a few students should eventually achieve the predetermined level of mastery.

Bloom's Learning for Mastery (LFM) model has been used in hundreds of classrooms throughout the United States and in as many as 20 other countries (Block, 1979). Consequently, many variations of the original model exist. Other mastery models based upon LFM are also common. Keller (1968), for example, developed an instructional model that is compatible with the basic assumptions of Bloom's model, but in practice is quite different. In Keller's Personalized System of Instruction (PSI), students proceed through a set of written curriculum materials at their own pace. The theoretical basis for this strategy lies in B. F. Skinner's operant conditioning. Students are given a stimulus via written materials; each student responds and receives reinforcement for the response. The application of the theory can be seen in the hierarchical materials and programed instruction (Block & Burns, 1976, p. 9). Thus, a visitor to a PSI classroom would see students working independently at their desks and a teacher and possibly several aides moving from student to student to offer assistance. After an initial attempt to complete the unit material, a student is given the unit mastery test by a "proctor" (who may be the teacher, a teacher's aide, or a more advanced student or classmate). If the student passes the test, he or she advances to the next unit.

Otherwise, the student uses the unit correctives to restudy the unmastered material. The cycle continues until the student demonstrates mastery on one form of the unit test.

The major difference between LFM and PSI programs is that in LFM classrooms students are expected to work on their own time to master material so that the entire class can together go on to the next unit of study. In PSI classrooms students continue to work at their own pace throughout the school year. This difference has two important implications. The LFM method theoretically should reduce the variability in achievement levels among students. Students who learn more slowly take more time to achieve mastery, but some of that additional time is their own. The LFM method has most often been used in elementary classrooms. The PSI method could actually result in increased variability in mastery because the fast learners are not at all delayed in their progress by the slower learners, as they are to some degree in traditional classrooms using whole-class instructional techniques. The PSI is more often used in secondary and college classrooms.

A second major difference in the programs concerns the role of the teacher. In LFM classrooms the teacher is more likely to use interactive verbal instruction with large or small groups as well as monitoring individuals, whereas in PSI the curriculum provides the instruction through self-paced paper-and-pencil tasks and the teacher is more a monitor of the curriculum.

OUTCOMES

The mastery-based program has been embraced by hundreds of school systems in this nation and across the world. As with many innovations, those employing the new program did not conduct research studies to measure the program effects. Block and Burns (1976) summarized six LFM studies conducted in elementary schools (see Table 25.3). Of these studies, two had nonequivalent control groups; five had posttest scores only, and one was a time series. Only the Anderson (1976a) study used

Table 25.3. LFM Cognitive Studies

Study	Grade Level	Student Type[a]	Sample Size[b]	No. of Classrooms	Subject Matter	Duration	Type of Experimental Design	Learning Measures
Anderson (1976a)	1–6	Advantaged	Exp. = 195 Con. = 195	24	Mathematics	9 months	Nonequivalent control group	Achievement, rentention (4 months)
Burrows & Okey (1975)	4–5	Advantaged & disadvantaged	Exp. = 63 Con. = 21	4	Geometry	2 weeks	Posttest only, control group	Achievement, rentention (2 weeks)
Kim et al. (1974)	2	Advantaged & disadvantaged	Exp. = 906 Con. = 576	20	Moral ed. Korean arithmetic	2–4 weeks 8 months	Posttest only, control group	Achievement
Lee et al. (1971)	5–6	Advantaged	Exp. = 7409 Con. = 5095	179	Arithmetic Science	—	Nonequivalent control group	Achievement
Okey (1974)	3–4	—	Exp. = 66 Con. = 64	5	Fractions	2 weeks	Posttest only, control group	Achievement
Okey (1975)	Primary grades	—	Exp. = 356 Con. = 356	14	Mathematics Language arts	4 weeks 1 semester	Time series	Achievement

Note. From "Mastery Learning" by J. Block and R. Burns, 1976, *Review of Research in Education, 4*, p. 15. Copyright 1976 by James Block & Robert Burns. Abbreviated version reprinted by permission.
[a] The term *advantaged* is used merely in contrast to the term *disadvantaged*; it does not imply special or superior students.
[b] Exp. = Experimental Group; Con. = Control Group.

standardized achievement tests; all of the others used criterion tests developed to assess mastery. In spite of the studies' limitations, taken as a group they represent a large sample of children and we think it appropriate to review them here.

The intervention lasted from 2 to 4 weeks for most studies. Only Anderson (1976a) and Lee et al. (1971) report the effects of the mastery program over a school year, that is, 8 or 9 months. The children in the studies were from average or above-average income homes. Only Burrows and Okey (1975) and Kim, Cho, Park & Park (1974) included disadvantaged children. The Kim et al. study was conducted in Korea and focused upon moral education. The studies in this country focused upon mathematics and science.

The goals regarding outcomes for children in mastery learning programs focus upon improved learning and retention, and reduced variability in what children learn. If mastery learning is working, then all children will master the material and the variability in what children learn will be reduced. The results of these six studies are displayed on Table 25.4. Anderson had standardized achievement test data for 18 of the 24 classrooms studied. Of these 18 classrooms, 3 performed on the achievement tests significantly better than the control classrooms (p < .05). Eight classrooms scored higher than the control group, but not statistically. On the other hand, 4 control classrooms scored significantly higher than the mastery groups and 3 control classrooms merely scored higher than the mastery classrooms. These findings indicate a positive trend for the mastery learning but not a ringing vote of confidence for mastery learning students' superiority on standardized achievement tests.

The other five studies assessed achievement by using criterion tests given at the end of the unit of study to examine students' mastery of what had been taught. Burrows and Okey (1975), Kim et al. (1974), Lee et al. (1971), and Okey (1974 and 1975) reported significant positive differences for mastery students compared to control groups.

Only Anderson (1976a) and Burrows & Okey (1975) reported retention data (see Table 25.4). Anderson's report was for five classrooms which were given criterion or unit tests. Three of these classrooms retained information significantly better than did control classrooms (p < .05) and in two mastery classrooms, retention scores were greater, but not statistically greater than nonmastery classrooms. There was less variability among students in the retention of the information in all five mastery classrooms when compared to the control group.

In Burrows and Okey's (1975) study of geometry in three mastery classrooms and one control classroom, the mastery students had significantly higher scores on the criterion test at the end of the 2-week intervention and were found to retain more information when tested at a later date. The mastery groups' achievement variance and retention variance was less than or equal to the nonmastery group. These are mild but encouraging findings.

Another of the goals of the LFM program is to reduce the variance in achievement outcomes, not by "bringing down" fast learners, but by "bringing up" slow learners. In 17 of Anderson's 18 classrooms (see Table 25.4) the mastery classrooms' achievement variance was less than or equal to the control classrooms'. However, in the studies of Kim et al. (1974) and Okey (1974 and 1975) the question of variability in students' test scores is not clearly in favor of the mastery classrooms.

To reduce variability in student test scores requires more time for some students. An important question is "How much time?" The studies reviewed by Block and Burns indicate that from 10 to 50% more study time is required for nearly all children to reach the criterion for mastery, although extra study

Table 25.4. Summary of Mastery Learning Research

| | Achievement | | | | | | Retention | | | | | |
| | Level of Learning[a] | | | | Variability of Learning | | Level of Learning | | | | Variability of Learning | |
LFM Studies	(≫)	(>)	(<)	(≪)	(≤)	(>)	(≫)	(>)	(<)	(≪)	(≤)	(>)
Anderson (1976a)	3	8	4	3	17	1	3	2	0	0	5	0
Burrows & Okey (1975)	1	0	0	0	1	0	1	0	0	0	1	0
Kim et al. (1974)	2	0	0	0	0	2						
Lee et al. (1971)	4	0	0	0	3	1						
Okey (1974)	1	4	0	0	3	2						
Okey (1975)	7	7	0	0	9	5						
LFM Total	18	19	4	3	33	11	4	2	0	0	6	0

Note. From "Mastery Learning" by J. Block and R. Burns, 1976, *Review of Research in Education, 4,* p. 20. Copyright 1976 by James Block & Robert Burns. Abbreviated version reprinted by permission.

[a] The symbols in the headings indicate the following:

Level of Learning
   (≫) Scores of mastery group statistically greater than scores of nonmastery group (p < .05).
   (>) Scores of mastery group greater, but not statistically greater, than scores of nonmastery group.
   (≪) Scores of mastery group less than, but not statistically less than, scores of nonmastery group.
   (<) Scores of mastery group statistically less than scores of nonmastery group (p < .05).

Variability of Learning
   (≤) Mastery group achievement variance less than or equal to nonmastery achievement variance.
   (>) Mastery group achievement variance greater than nonmastery achievement variance.

time seems to decrease in a program of relatively long duration. One of the main contributors to additional study time in mastery classrooms is the slower learners' tendency to procrastinate, especially when first introduced to a mastery program (Anderson, 1976b; Lloyd & Knutzen, 1969). This problem may be especially serious for young children.

The research has not directly tested the effect of the increased study time required by slow learners on the level of achievement attained by fast learners. However, if the teacher waits for all or nearly all of the students to reach mastery of a unit before going on to the next unit, and if some additional learning time comes from class time, then achievement costs to fast learners seem inevitable.

Only a few studies have explored the affective outcomes of mastery versus nonmastery programs, but their results usually favor mastery programs. Block and Burns (1976) summarize studies that have demonstrated a positive effect of mastery learning on students' interest in and attitudes toward the subject matter, self-concept (academic and more general), academic self-confidence, attitudes toward cooperative learning, and attitudes toward instruction. For example, Anderson (1976a) studied 24 first through sixth grade classrooms over a 9-month period. Children learning mathematics in mastery-based programs had a more positive attitude toward mathematics and, generally, a more positive self-concept than nonmastery-taught students.

The one negative affective outcome reported is higher test anxiety in LFM classrooms. Block and Burns attribute this outcome to the fact that a student's grade is wholly determined by performance on one summative final examination which determines whether an A or an I has been earned for the grading period.

Informal observations of mastery-based programs suggest that competitiveness is not reduced by mastery methods as much as early proponents of the model had hoped. Crockenberg and Bryant (1978) point out that booklets or units are organized hierarchically and the level is usually indicated by a salient marker, such as color. Learners can easily determine who is more or less advanced in the curriculum, and some observers claim that many children are keenly aware of where they are in comparison to their classmates. Buckholdt and Wodarski (1974) and Levine (1983) have also noted children's tendency to create a "race to the end of the curriculum." Thus, while grading is noncompetitive, children sometimes themselves create a competitive situation.

In general, the evidence available suggests that mastery learning programs have a mildly positive effect upon student achievement and attitudes. Why then are these programs controversial? Criticisms of mastery-based learning on both ideological and practical grounds are common in the educational literature. The major criticisms are discussed below.

Smith (1981) questions the fairness of mastery learning programs to brighter students. He points out that given a fixed amount of time (the school calendar), teacher time devoted to additional instruction for low-ability (or slow-learning) students is necessarily time *not* spent with high-ability students. Also, as noted above, if the teacher does not proceed to the next unit of instruction until nearly all of the students have achieved mastery of the previous unit, high-ability students will inevita-

bly experience some "waiting." Consequently, the higher level of mastery enjoyed by the slower student may require some sacrifice on the part of the high-ability students.

Note that the philosophy of individualized instruction is somewhat different from LFM in that each student is supposed to reach his or her own potential. Accordingly, PSI teachers are not instructed to spend additional instructional time with slower students, and because the program is fully individualized, fast students are not required to wait for slower students. However, teachers may themselves decide to give more attention to the slow learners.

Cohen (1981) and Spady (1981) claim that it is possible for slow learners to achieve a high level of mastery without holding back fast learners. They both suggest that this negative outcome of mastery-based learning can be avoided if the curriculum is open-ended, that is, if the fast learners are always provided new material to master. Practically, this may require a more individualized instructional method than was originally proposed by Bloom. Educators are experimenting with curricular materials that offer enrichment experiences for students who achieve mastery quickly, but the practical problems involved in assuring that nearly all children master the entire curriculum, and that high-ability students also reach their full potential, have not been resolved.

Barone (1978) expresses another ideological concern, that a too-narrow view of education is implicit in mastery learning programs. Even reading and writing, Barone argues, involve more than a set of skills that can be evaluated by a standardized test. Such aspects of education as creativity are given too little attention in a program that breaks learning down into discrete testable units.

On a more practical level, mastery-based programs have been criticized for being too structured and rigid, even mechanistic (Cox & Dunn, 1979; Groff, 1974; Horton, 1979; Jaynes, 1975). Mastery programs do require that the curriculum be dissected into small units, and teachers usually use prepackaged materials for instruction and evaluation. These self-paced materials tend to develop visual and fine motor skills but not listening or speaking skills. Block (1977) comments on another practical problem associated with the emphasis on diagnostic evaluation in mastery-based programs. He suggests that sometimes the tests orient the children "too well" to the evaluation instrument. "As the course taught for mastery unfolds, these students tend more and more to ignore any material that they perceive to be incidental to the core of their teacher's instruction" (p. 34).

The method of evaluation, according to Block (1977), poses additional problems. Some highly competitive (usually high ability) students are less motivated in a situation in which all students are able to obtain a high grade. Other students, especially those who have difficulty achieving mastery, are bothered by an evaluation system that grades only achievement outcomes and ignores their efforts. As mentioned before, many students are also anxious about having their grade depend solely on their performance on the final summative examination.

Horton (1979) criticizes mastery-based programs for the unrealistic demands made on teachers. He points out that the claim of mastery advocates that up to 95% mastery rates can be achieved with a 10 to 20% increase in time is unrealistic. In addition to this instructional demand, considerable time is required for preparing instructional materials and evaluation instruments. In such individualized materials-based programs, teachers felt they spent too much time managing the curriculum, testing, and keeping records rather than providing a variety of skill-building and thought-provoking activities (Amarel & Stallings, 1978).

SUMMARY

Although the model is not without major problems, mastery-based educational programs have been reasonably successful in achieving the goal of increasing the proportion of students who master the basic student curriculum. One of the most positive aspects of the model is the basic belief that all students can learn. A study by Good and Dembo (1973) found that more than half of the 163 inservice teachers they interviewed estimated that less than 50% of their students could "really master the material" they had to teach. The importance of teachers' expectations for student learning is well known (Good, 1981). Mastery learning advocates no doubt make an important contribution to student learning by convincing teachers that all children can master the curriculum. Indeed, the achievement gains observed for children in mastery-based programs may be explained as much by teachers' enhanced expectations, especially for the low-ability students, as by any other aspect of the program.

Cooperative Learning

Another alternative instructional format that has gained considerable prominence in recent years is cooperative learning. Like mastery learning, cooperative learning is designed to be integrated into regular elementary and secondary classrooms. Although packaged instructional programs are available, teachers can implement the principles of cooperative learning using their own instructional materials.

Cooperative learning has been implemented in various ways. This variance can be described in two dimensions. First, programs vary in terms of the *task structure*, which has implications for the amount of time children actually interact in learning tasks with each other. In some programs, children work on the task as a group. This format is presumed to encourage truly cooperative learning and peer tutoring. In other programs, the task is divided up and members of the group work independently.

Cooperative learning programs also differ in terms of the *reward contingency*. For example, the grade or reward might be contingent on a product cooperatively produced by the group, or it might be contingent upon the sum or average of the individual members' performance. In most cooperative learning models, students work in small learning groups of about four to six children and their reward or grade is based on the group's performance.

Cooperative learning models have been designed to achieve at least four purposes. First, cooperative learning is presumed to raise the perceived value of academic achievement among students and to encourage students to help and support peers in

their group rather than compete against all other classmates. The assumption is that by rewarding groups as well as individuals for their academic achievement, peer norms will favor rather than oppose high achievement. Thus, like in sports where excellence in individual performance is encouraged because it benefits the whole team, team competition in the classroom results in greater student support of each other's achievements.

A second purpose of cooperative learning rests on the belief that children can learn from each other and that cooperation can benefit both high- and low-ability children. The high-ability child achieves a higher level of understanding in the process of helping slower children, and the low-ability child benefits from the other children's assistance.

Third, from a motivational perspective, cooperative models are an alternative to the individual competitive model — characteristic of most classrooms — that can have devastating consequences for the motivation of slower learners. Individual competition can enhance the motivation of students who have some possibility of "winning," but research shows that many children, who begin the competition at a disadvantage and who expect to fare poorly no matter how hard they try, eventually cease trying (Covington & Beery, 1976; Dweck & Reppucci, 1973). A group reward structure may relieve motivation problems that many low-ability students have in individual competition situations. Evidence suggests, for example, that simply being a member of a successful group, regardless of a child's own performance, allows the child some of the advantages of success, such as high self-perceptions of ability, satisfaction, and peer esteem (Ames, 1981; Ames & Felker, 1979). Moreover, unlike the individualized competitive situation, in which some children know that they have no chance at winning regardless of their efforts, group competition presumably pits groups of equal ability against each other, and consequently maximizes motivation for *all* members of the group.

Finally, cooperative learning programs were developed in part to improve race relations in the schools. The assumption is that if children from different ethnic groups work interdependently, they will learn to appreciate each other's strengths and to develop interracial friendships.

There are many cooperative learning programs that have been studied. These include Learning Together, developed by Johnson and Johnson (1975), Group Investigation, developed by Sharan and Sharan (1976), and Team Assisted Individualization (TAI), developed by Slavin, Leavey, and Madden (1982). Research using these and other methods of cooperative learning is reviewed by Slavin (1983). We chose to review in depth three programs that stand out for the amount of systematic development and research available: Teams–Games–Tournaments (TGT), Student Teams and Achievement Divisions (STAD), and Jigsaw.

TEAMS–GAMES–TOURNAMENTS (TGT)

TGT is a supplement to the instructional approach already used by the teacher and it is often used exclusively for one or two specific subject areas. New material is initially presented by the teacher to the whole class, usually in a lecture–discussion format. Following this presentation, students are divided into four- or five-member teams. Each team is diverse in terms of the level of achievement of its members, race, or other important variables on which children in the classroom vary. Ideally, teams should be equally matched on past academic performance in the subject at hand.

Teammate practice sessions prepare students for game sessions in an ongoing tournament. After the material has been presented, teams work together on worksheets or other material. Usually, students quiz each other during these sessions, or they work problems together and correct each other's mistakes. The emphasis is on preparing the entire team for the tournament. Thus, students are encouraged to assist and support each other in their attempt to master the academic material.

DeVries and Slavin (1978) describe how the tournament functions:

> In the tournament, which takes place once or twice each week, each student is assigned to a tournament table where he or she competes individually against students from other teams. The students at each table are roughly comparable in achievement level. The tournament tables are numbered with Table "1" being the "top" table. At the end of the period, the players at each table compare their scores to determine the top, middle, and low scorers at the various game tables. The top scorer at each table receives six points, the middle scorer four points, and the low scorer two points. Team scores are then calculated by simply adding the results for teammates. These scores are added to the team's tallies from previous game sessions in the tournament, creating a cumulative score. Team standings are then formed and shared with the students. The results are publicized in a weekly classroom newsletter. ... Skill exercise sessions which focus on the current subject matter are played during the tournament. At each three-person table, students answer questions posed on card sets or game sheets to demonstrate mastery of specific skills. A basic set of rules, including a challenge rule, dictates the form of play. (p. 29)

Several features of TGT are likely to maximize motivation and learning for all students. First, teams are mixed in ability. This gives faster-learning students an opportunity to function as tutors and it provides slower learning students with additional assistance. Second, the tournament tables are composed of students performing at about the same level. This makes it possible for students of all levels of past performance to contribute maximally to their team scores. Third, after the first week, students change tables depending on their own performance in the most recent tournament. TGT therefore avoids the inflexibility that often occurs when students are grouped by ability for instruction.

TGT has been assessed in a variety of classroom situations. The research has examined its effects on academic achievement, student attitudes, and classroom social processes. At least five studies have been done at the elementary school level (see DeVries & Slavin, 1978 for a review). A study by DeVries, Mescon, and Shackman (1975) is illustrative. Fifty-three third grade students were assigned to either a TGT program or a control group for instruction in reading vocabulary and verbal analogies. The two teachers involved were rotated across treatment groups to control for teacher effects. The TGT students worked in four- or five-member teams. The tournaments were organized around 13 vocabulary games and 9 verbal analogy games. Each game consisted of between 32 and 39 items. Thus, a student at each game table read aloud the definition and three alternative answers. The student then said which alternative word correctly matched the definition and the student's opponents were told either to agree or challenge the answer. TGT tournaments were conducted twice weekly and classroom newsletters described the performance of both the student teams and the individual students. The control condition had the same curriculum objectives, but students worked by themselves and rewards (grades and student praise) were administered to individual students on a partially competitive basis. To control for a "Hawthorne effect," control students were given a variety of unusual classroom activities (e.g., games, multicolored worksheets).

Prior to implementing the program, there were no differences between the TGT and control groups on any of the dependent variables. However, TGT students scored higher than control students on a treatment-specific vocabulary test and on another vocabulary test, and a treatment-specific verbal analogies test, but not on a verbal analogies test measuring transfer effects. The TGT effect for the two vocabulary skill measures was due primarily to gains by initially low-achieving students.

In a larger study of 456 fourth and fifth grade students and their 17 teachers in five elementary schools, Slavin and Karweit (1981) assigned teachers by school to either an experimental or a control group. The experimental teachers used TGT for mathematics instruction for an entire semester. The TGT students scored higher than control students, with pretest scores controlled, on the CTBS mathematics computations subscale, but not on the mathematics concepts and applications subscale.

At least 10 other evaluations of TGT have been completed, although only 4 of them at the elementary school level. All 10 studies were done in public schools, and TGT was always administered by classroom teachers. Also, all of the studies used random assignment of classes to treatments and teachers of both experimental and control groups were given the same curriculum objectives and materials. Sample sizes have ranged from 53 to 1,742 students.

TGT was found to increase achievement significantly more than the control treatment on four of the seven standardized tests and eight of the nine treatment-specific tests used in these 10 studies (DeVries & Slavin, 1978). Positive effects for TGT on standardized achievement tests were found in 4 of the 7 studies that included them. Positive effects have also been found on measures of mutual concern, race relations (friendships between students of different races), attitudes toward school, students' perceptions of peer support for their own performance (DeVries & Slavin, 1978), and self-esteem (Slavin & Karweit, 1981).

STUDENT TEAMS AND ACHIEVEMENT DIVISIONS (STAD)

STAD programs are similar to TGT programs. Teachers present new material, usually in a lecture–discussion format, and students work together in four- or five-member heterogeneous teams. However, the function of the team in STAD programs is to prepare its members to take individual quizzes twice a week, rather than to participate in a tournament.

Students are not allowed to help each other while taking the quizzes. Nevertheless, because team scores are based on the performance of individual students, students should be just as motivated to assist and support each other in the learning process as they are in TGT programs.

In addition to teams, which are heterogeneous with regard to past performance, students are organized into "divisions" composed of students who are roughly equal in terms of past performance. The highest ranking score among that group of equals earns the maximum number of points, regardless of the relative level of achievement of the entire division. Thus, rewards are contingent upon performance within a group of children performing at about the same level, rather than upon relative performance in a classroom of students achieving at very different levels. The assumption is that such a reward structure gives every child an equal chance of attaining high rewards, and in so doing, optimizes the motivation of all children. Moreover, each child's score is based on his or her improvement since the last quiz, or relative to an individually calculated "base score." Consequently, students should be motivated to continually improve their performance so they can earn points for their team.

In the Slavin and Karweit (1981) study of 456 fourth and fifth grade students, described above, the teachers in the experimental group used STAD during an entire semester for all language arts instruction. Compared to control students, STAD students scored higher, with pretest scores controlled, on three of four CTBS language arts subscales (reading vocabulary, language mechanics, and language expression, but not on reading comprehension).

A later study (Madden & Slavin, 1983) included 183 third, fourth, and sixth graders. Forty of the students were classified as academically handicapped. Each teacher taught one control and one experimental class; the assignment to experimental or control group was made randomly for each teacher, with stratification to ensure an academic balance between both groups. The same structured mathematics curriculum was used in both the experimental and the control conditions. However, in the experimental condition, teachers used STAD, while in the control condition students worked independently on the same worksheets, and quiz scores were given individually.

One of the purposes of this study was to test the effects of cooperative groups on nonhandicapped students' acceptance of handicapped students. Nonhandicapped student responses to a questionnaire indicated that students experiencing the cooperative groups were less likely than control students to reject the academically handicapped students, but were not more likely to choose them for friends. With regard to achievement, both handicapped and nonhandicapped students in the experimental group improved their scores on a curriculum-specific test more than control students; however, the difference was significant only for the nonhandicapped students (because of the larger sample size). Positive effects of cooperative learning for the entire sample were also found on the Coopersmith Self-Esteem Inventory.

Slavin (1978a) examined the effects of STAD on academic achievement in language arts for 424 fourth grade students. The study compared four treatments: (a) team reward and peer tutoring; (b) team reward without peer tutoring; (c) individual reward with peer tutoring; and (d) individual reward without peer tutoring. In all four treatments scores were based on

ability-homogeneous achievement divisions. Control-group classes used a traditional whole-class instructional method.

After 9 weeks the four experimental groups achieved higher scores than did the control group. Team rewards produced higher achievement than individual rewards, but having peers help each other in peer tutoring sessions did not result in higher achievement than was found for students who worked individually. Thus these results are consistent with Slavin's (1984) recent summary of cooperative learning studies: "The results of the field experimental research on cooperative learning methods indicate that the positive effects of these methods on student achievement result from the use of cooperative incentives, not cooperative tasks" (p. 61).

The comparison group on which rewards are based has also been found to be an important component of STAD programs. Slavin (1978b) varied the comparison group (comparison with entire class vs. comparison with equals, i.e. the achievement division) and reward structure (team vs. individual) in a study of 205 seventh grade students in eight intact English classes. The different treatments had no effect on achievement measures. However, students whose rewards were based on comparison with equals were on-task more than students whose rewards were based on comparisons with the whole class; comparison with equals also resulted in more positive attitudes and perceptions of peer support for academic performance. Participation in teams resulted in higher scores on measures of motivation and mutual concern, and peer support for academic performance, and students working in teams spent more time on-task than students working individually.

Two additional evaluations, reported in Slavin (1978a), demonstrated that biracial teams increase the number of cross-racial friendships. Study 2 included 62 seventh grade students, 40% white and 60% black, in intact English classes. Study 4 involved 424 seventh and eighth grade students in two inner-city junior high schools. About a third of the students were black, and the remaining two-thirds were primarily white. In both of these studies, students participating in the STAD program made more cross-race selections for friends on a sociometric measure than did control students. The data on which students benefit most in terms of achievement is contradictory. In Study 2, described above, the STAD program had a highly significant and positive effect on black students' achievement, but only a marginally significant effect on white students' achievement. No academic achievement effects were found for either white or black students in Study 4.

JIGSAW

The Jigsaw method was developed to foster peer cooperation and tutoring and race relations by creating interdependence among students. In the Aronson et al. (1978) original Jigsaw method, a different portion of a learning task is assigned to each of five or six members on a team and task completion requires contingent and mutual cooperation. For example, a biography might be broken into life stages and background on the culture. Each team member would read his or her own section. Members of different teams who have studied the same section meet in "expert groups" to discuss their sections. Then students meet with their teams and take turns teaching their teammates about their section. Students are dependent on the other members of their team for those sections they did not personally cover. They are therefore motivated to listen carefully to their teammates and to support their teammates' efforts. Teachers move among the groups, offering assistance, encouragement, or direction where it is needed. Following the team reports, students may take individual quizzes covering all of the topics. All group members are therefore ultimately responsible for learning all the curriculum material.

Ziegler (1981) evaluated a variation of the Jigsaw method in a study of 146 sixth grade children representing over five different ethnic groups. She describes the program as follows:

> Children were divided into "home teams" of four to six members, depending on the number of children in the class. ... Children worked in those home teams one and one-half class periods (about eighty minutes) per week. They also worked in "expert groups" which were only somewhat heterogeneous, about forty minutes per week. ... Each child shared the research work with members of his or her expert group, with all working on the same assignment. Then, on two subsequent days that week, each child, meeting with his or her team members, taught them what he or she had learned and learned from them their assigned pieces. Weekly or biweekly quizzes were given, and an individual student's mark was a composite of the individual score, plus the average score for all members of his or her home team. (p. 265)

Compared to control children, Jigsaw children learned more and retained their knowledge to a greater degree. Observations revealed further that Jigsaw children spent more time on-task. Children in the Jigsaw program also showed evidence on a sociometric measure of greater cross-ethnic friendships than control children.

Sharan (1980) summarizes four studies assessing the effect of the Jigsaw method. In the first, Lucker, Rosenfield, Sikes, and Aronson (1976) studied the academic achievement of 493 fifth and sixth grade students of different ethnicity (Anglo, Mexican-American, and black). Children in the Jigsaw program operated daily for 45 minutes during a 2-week period. Children in the control group received traditional whole-class instruction with the same material. The Jigsaw method resulted in superior performance for minority children, but not for Anglo children. Other studies have found positive effects of Jigsaw methods on children's attitudes toward their classmates and toward school, and self-esteem (Blaney, Stephan, Rosenfield, Aronson, & Sikes, 1977; Geffner, 1978), and role-taking (Bridgeman, 1977).

CONCLUSIONS

The three cooperative learning programs reviewed here are representative of a vast number of cooperative learning experiments (see reviews by Johnson & Johnson, 1974; Sharan, 1980; Slavin, 1977, 1983, 1984). Positive effects of cooperative learning on achievement and attitudinal variables have been found in many carefully controlled studies. But the academic superiority of cooperative models is not universally found, and there are many factors that undoubtedly mediate the effectiveness of cooperative learning methods.

For example, the three studies of TGT that did not show higher achievement levels for TGT students over control students used curricular materials from social studies. Sharan (1980) questions whether social studies, or other subjects requiring a high level of cognitive functioning, may not be appropriate for study with TGT or STAD formats. Other studies have found that both the composition of the group (e.g., the ability or performance levels of its members; Laughlin, 1978; Webb, 1982) and process variables, such as the form of academic and social exchange in the group (Webb, 1980a, 1980b, 1982), mediate the effects of cooperative learning. Finally, cooperative learning may benefit some groups of children, such as low achievers (DeVries et al., 1975; Edwards, DeVries, & Snyder, 1972) or minorities (Lucker et al., 1976; Slavin, 1978a, Study 2) more than others.

A particularly noteworthy finding of research on cooperative learning is that the incentive structure is more important than opportunities for cooperation. Slavin (1983) points out that instructions to work cooperatively alone have not been found to increase student achievement more than instructions to work independently. In two studies, allowing students to work together without providing a group goal or making them dependent on one another's achievement resulted in *lower* achievement than was observed for students who worked independently (Johnson, Johnson, & Scott, 1978; Slavin, 1980a). In contrast, studies consistently show superior learning by students in cooperative groups who could earn group rewards based on group members' academic performance, over students in individualistic, competitive, or traditional control methods.

There are many possible reasons why group rewards increase achievement in cooperative learning. Students would certainly care more about the performance of their peers under this condition and would be more motivated to assist and support their teammates in the learning process. Hamblin, Hathaway, and Wodarski (1971) found that the frequency of peer tutoring and student achievement increased linearly as the proportion of students' rewards dependent on the lowest of three scores in their groups increased from 0% to 33% to 67% to 100%. These results suggest that the reward incentive has an important effect on the kind of interaction that occurs in cooperative groups. Group rewards are also likely to result in peer pressure on individual students to pay attention and maximize their own learning. Also, a group reward structure allows all students, even those who typically perform at a relatively low level, an opportunity to succeed, and this may be highly motivating for those students who, under other conditions, would most likely fail.

In conclusion, it is clear that cooperative learning can have positive effects on learning and other important attitudinal variables, but there are many factors that must be considered in a decision about whether and how to implement it. In addition to those mentioned above, the teacher's training, commitment to cooperative learning, and perception of his or her role must also be considered.

Perhaps the most important outcomes of these cooperative experiences are in the affective domain, for example, mutual concern, friendships with students of other races, liking school, and perceiving peer support. The effects of these outcomes may be found in a more productive work life and more socially responsible adults. We encourage the cooperative program researchers to plan such follow-up studies.

Summary

Many instructional innovations became prominent during the 1970s and could have been reviewed in this chapter. The two that we chose to discuss — Mastery Learning and Cooperative Learning — share several characteristics that, in our view, made them particularly deserving of special attention. First, they have been widely implemented and carefully studied. Few educational programs developed in the last decade have received so much research attention. Second, these programs are not overly prescriptive. They can be implemented in almost any classroom and teachers can preserve many aspects of their own preferred teaching style and instructional techniques. To be sure, a mastery learning curriculum has to be divided into small, hierarchically organized units; in cooperative learning programs students must be allowed to work in groups. Yet in both cases, teachers have considerable flexibility in the way they present new material, the textbooks they use, the tests they give, and in other aspects of their teaching.

Even with this considerable flexibility, neither mastery learning or cooperative learning are appropriate for all teachers, all children, and all subjects. We suggest that teachers experiment with the various programs that have been described in this chapter, try different approaches for different subject areas, and ultimately, develop their own variation of these programs — one that works for them and for their students. Researchers often lament the fact that teachers do not implement their program precisely according to the instructions. We are in sympathy with researchers who are attempting to conduct a rigorous assessment of a program's effects. But we applaud teachers who themselves assess the effectiveness of a program, and modify it to achieve the greatest amount of learning in their own classrooms.

Because mastery learning and cooperative learning are relative newcomers on the educational scene, we could not assess their long-term effects. But we can speculate on how a child might benefit, in the long run, from experience in such programs. Cooperative learning programs teach children something they rarely experience in traditional classrooms, that learning can come from shared ideas and shared work to reach a common goal. From such team efforts mutual respect for individual contributions has a chance to develop. Collegial skills are well recognized as requisites to a satisfying and successful adult work life.

Both mastery learning and cooperative learning emphasize motivation and both programs provide opportunities for all children to succeed, including those who generally fail under individual competitive and normatively evaluated conditions. Therefore, in mastery learning and cooperative learning programs children may develop greater confidence in their ability to learn and to succeed at academic tasks. By raising a child's self-image and expectations, a positive long-term impact on learning could be realized from both programs.

Admittedly, these are optimistic speculations. But we urge researchers who may study the long-term impact of these programs to include in their analysis these kinds of possible consequences.

Final Comments

The compensatory education programs developed for preschool and lower elementary in the late 1960s and 1970s were comprehensive in nature and shared the goal of improving the life chances of low-income children through an improved education. The new models specified the materials to be used, the activities to occur, and the nature of teacher–student interactions. Programs ranged in theory regarding how children learn from Skinner's stimulus–response behavior modification to Piaget's stages of development. Classroom practice attempted to make these theories concrete, for example, through hierarchically structured curricula which include ample drill, practice, and feedback, or self-correcting materials-based curricula with a problem-solving structure.

Differences in how children grew and developed were found to be related to early school experiences; for example, children in the academically oriented programs achieved higher scores on achievement tests and children in materials-oriented problem-solving programs scored higher on nonverbal problem-solving tests. Nevertheless, the results of the massive compensatory interventions were in general disappointing since most children from these programs did not continue to achieve academically in school at a better rate than did similar children who were not involved in these early childhood programs. However, there are some impressive longitudinal sets of data that suggest that children experiencing these early intervention programs demonstrated a particular brand of success in upper elementary and secondary school. Compared to control groups, they were less often retained in any grade and were less often placed in special education classes. As teenagers they were less likely to drop out of school and more likely to graduate from high school. Certainly these outcomes are indicators of school success for low-achieving children.

The University of Oregon Direct Instruction Follow Through program was the only early intervention program we examined longitudinally to have its students continue to excel over comparison groups and match national norms on achievement tests as the students continued on into high school. This continuing achievement was based upon continued contact with the program; that is, 1 year of preschool experience did not give children a lasting advantage in elementary school.

There is a similarity in theory and practice between Direct Instruction, discussed in the first section of this chapter, and the Mastery Learning, discussed in the second section. Mastery Learning evolved as a program for all children (not just low SES). Both programs are very carefully structured and require sequential curriculum materials in which students can be tested regularly and recycled through materials to gain mastery as needed. The Mastery Learning program focuses upon providing time to insure mastery by all students working either with large groups, small groups, or individuals. The Direct Instruction program also expects that all children will learn what is necessary to complete lessons correctly, and works with small groups at similar achievement levels or with individuals as needed. The Direct Instruction model, being a part of the many National Follow Through evaluations, has been systematically studied for program implementation and student effects using appropriate comparisons and pretest-posttest designs. The Mastery Learning program has a less good research base since single adopting school sites are not likely to establish control groups, nor do they systematically collect implementation data or pretest and posttest student effects data. Because there is a dearth of good information comparing mastery programs in elementary school with nonmastery programs, we encourage researchers to conduct carefully designed longitudinal studies in districts using the Mastery Learning program. The expectation that all of the children in our schools can succeed is at the heart of American educational philosophy, and we should know more about under what circumstances this outcome can occur.

The Cooperative Learning program discussed in Section 2 was intended for use in classrooms as a method or strategy to teach the curriculum. Its goal is to provide opportunities for children to work together in solving problems. So much of schooling is competitive that we applaud this attempt to develop cooperative skills. Most adult work requires a joint effort of workers to accomplish tasks, yet in schools we tend to develop only competitive attitudes and work-alone skills. The findings for increased achievement for students in Cooperative Learning programs are inconsistent, but more positive than negative. Certainly the attitudinal data regarding working with others are encouraging. It is important, we think, to conduct some longitudinal studies of children who have taken part in cooperative learning activities over several years.

Sadly lacking in early childhood education research are studies of thinking skills. The closest any of the preschool programs come to teaching these skills is the Montessori program which teaches relationship through self-corrective materials. Weikart's Perry Preschool model also teaches thinking skills through planning, evaluation, and foreseeing consequences. Some problem-solving skills are developed in cooperative learning games. However, the central problem is that adequate group tests to measure the thinking or reasoning skills of elementary and secondary students are sadly lacking. Studies by researchers in cognitive processes such as those by Bransford (1979) should be embedded in studies of classrooms where teachers attempt to teach thinking skills. We have made great strides in understanding more of the relationship between teaching young children and long-term learning effects. We hope the next decade will produce replicable studies and generalizable findings on the teaching of thinking skills in preschool and elementary school classrooms.

REFERENCES

Abt Associates. (1977). *Education as experimentation: A planned variation model.* Reports to the U.S. Office of Education, Office of Planning, Budgeting, and Evaluation (Contract No. 300-75-0134). Cambridge, MA: Abt Associates.

Amarel, M., & Stallings, J. (1978). *Perspectives on the Instructional Dimension Study* (Chapter 6: Individualized instruction). Washington, DC: National Institute of Education.

Ames, C. (1981). Competitive versus cooperative reward structure: The influence of individual and group performance factors on achievement attributions and affect. *American Educational Research Journal, 18*, 273-288.

Ames, C., & Felker, D. (1979). An examination of children's attributions and achievement-related evaluations in competitive, cooperative, and individualistic reward structures. *Journal of Educational Psychology, 71*, 413-420.

Anastasiow, N. J. (1979). John Dewey and current cognitive psychology of learning. In S. J. Meisels (Ed.), *Special education and development.* Baltimore: University Park Press.

Anderson, L. (1976a). *The effects of a mastery learning program on selected cognitive, affective and interpersonal variables in Grades 1 through 6.* Paper presented at the annual meeting of the American Educational Research Association, San Francisco.

Anderson, L. (1976b). An empirical investigation of individual differences in time to learn. *Journal of Educational Psychology, 68*, 226-233.

Arlin, M., & Webster, J. (1983). Time costs of mastery learning. *Journal of Educational Psychology, 75*, 187-195.

Aronson, E., Stephan, C., Sikes, J., Blaney, N., & Snapp, M. (1978). *The jigsaw classroom.* Beverly Hills, CA: Sage.

Barone, T. (1978). Reading, writing, and mastery learning: Are they compatible? *Educational Leadership, 36*, 187-191.

Becker, W. C., & Engelmann, S. E. (1978). *Analysis of achievement data on six cohorts of low-income children from 20 school districts in the University of Oregon Direct Instruction Follow Through model* (Tech. Rep. 78-1). Eugene, OR: University of Oregon, Follow Through Project.

Becker, W. C., & Gersten, R. (1982). A follow up of Follow Through: The later effects of the direct instruction model on children in fifth and sixth grades. *American Educational Research Journal, 19*, 75-92.

Beller, E. Kuno. (1973). "Research on organized programs of early education." In R. M. W. Travers (Ed.), *Second handbook of research on teaching.* Chicago: Rand McNally.

Bereiter, C., & Engelmann, S. (1966). *Teaching disadvantaged children in the preschool.* Englewood Cliffs, NJ: Prentice-Hall.

Blaney, J., Stephan, S., Rosenfield, D., Aronson, E., & Sikes, J. (1977). Interdependence in the classroom: A field study. *Journal of Educational Psychology, 69*, 121-128.

Block, J. (Ed.) (1974). *Schools, society, and mastery learning.* New York: Holt, Rinehart & Winston.

Block, J. (1977). Motivation, evaluation, and mastery learning. *UCLA Educator, 19*, 31-36.

Block, J. (1979). Mastery learning: The current state of the craft. *Educational Leadership, 37*, 114-117.

Block, J. & Burns, R. (1976). Mastery learning. *Review of Research in Education, 4*, 3-49.

Bloom, B. (1968). Learning for Mastery. *Evaluation Comment, 1.* UCLA Center for the Study of Evaluation, Occasional Report No. 9.

Bloom, B. (1971). Mastery learning and its implications for curriculum development. In E. W. Eisner (Ed.), *Confronting curriculum reform.* Boston: Little, Brown.

Bloom, B. (1974). An introduction to mastery learning theory. In J. H. Block (Ed.), *Schools, society, and mastery learning.* New York: Holt, Rinehart & Winston.

Bloom, B. (1976). *Human characteristics and school learning.* New York: McGraw-Hill.

Bloom, B. (1981). *All our children learning.* New York: McGraw-Hill.

Bloom, B., Hastings, J., & Madaus, G. (1971). *Handbook on formative and summative evaluation of student learning.* New York: McGraw Hill.

Bransford, J. (1979). *Human cognition: Learning, understanding and remembering.* Belmont, CA: Wadsworth.

Bridgeman, D. (1977). *The influence of cooperative, interdependent learning on role taking and moral reasoning: A theoretical and empirical field study with fifth grade students.* Unpublished doctoral dissertation, University of California, Santa Cruz.

Bronfenbrenner, J. (1974). Developmental research, public policy, and the ecology of childhood. *Child Development, 45,* 1–5.

Bronfenbrenner, J. (1979). *The ecology of human development: Experiments by nature and design.* Cambridge, MA: Harvard University Press.

Buckholdt, D. & Wodarski, J. (1974). *The effects of different reinforcement systems on cooperative behaviors exhibited by children in classroom contexts.* Paper presented at the meeting of the American Psychological Association, New Orleans, LA, 1974.

Burrows, C. K., & Okey, J. R. (1975, Mar.–Apr). *The effects of a mastery learning strategy on achievement.* Paper presented at the annual meeting of the American Educational Research Association, Washington, DC.

Caldwell, B. M. (1968). *Preschool inventory experimental edition — 1968 administration manual.* Princeton, NJ: Educational Testing Service.

Carroll, J. (1963). A model of school learning. *Teachers College Record, 64,* 723–733.

Cohen, A. (1981). *Dilemmas in the use of learner-response delivery systems.* Paper presented at the annual meeting of the American Educational Research Association, Los Angeles.

Covington, M., & Beery, R. (1976). *Self-worth and school learning.* New York: Holt, Rinehart & Winston.

Cox, W., Jr., & Dunn, T. (1979). Mastery learning: A psychological trap? *Educational Psychologist, 14,* 24–29.

Crockenberg, S., & Bryant, B. (1978). Socialization: The "implicit curriculum" of learning environments. *Journal of Research and Development in Education, 12,* 69–78.

DeVries, D., Mescon, I., & Shackman, S. (1975). *Teams-games-tournaments (TGT) effects on reading skills in the elementary grades* (Rep. No. 200). Baltimore: Johns Hopkins University, Center for Social Organization of Schools.

DeVries, D., & Slavin, R. (1978). Teams-games-tournaments (TGT): Review of ten classroom experiments. *Journal of Research and Development in Education, 12,* 28–38.

Dweck, C., & Goetz, T. (1978). Attributions and learned helplessness. In J. Harvey, W. Ickes, & R. Kidd (Eds.), *New directions in attribution research.* Hillsdale, NJ: Erlbaum.

Dweck, C., & Reppucci, N. (1973). Learned helplessness and reinforcement responsibility in children. *Journal of Personality and Social Psychology, 25,* 109–116.

Edwards, K., DeVries, D., & Snyder, J. (1972). Games and teams: A winning combination. *Simulation and Games, 3,* 247–269.

Gage, N. L. (Ed.). (1963). *Handbook of research on teaching.* Chicago: Rand McNally.

Geffner, R. (1978). *The effects of interdependent learning on self-esteem, interethnic relations, and interethnic attitudes of elementary school children: A field experiment.* Unpublished doctoral dissertation, University of California, Santa Cruz.

Gersten, R., & Carnine, D. (1983, April). *The later effects of Direct Instruction Follow Through: Preliminary findings.* Paper presented at the American Educational Research Association, Montreal.

Good, T. (1981). Teacher expectations and student perceptions: A decade of research. *Educational Leadership, 38,* 415–422.

Good, T., & Dembo, M. (1973). Teacher expectations: Self-report data. *School Review, 81,* 247–253.

Goodrich, R. L., & St. Pierre, R. G. (1980, February). *Opportunities for studying later effects of Follow Through: Executive summary* (Contract No. HEW-300-78-0443, Examination of Alternatives for Follow Through Experimentation). Cambridge, MA: Abt Associates.

Gordon, I. J. (1969). *Early childhood stimulation through parent education* (Final report to the Children's Bureau, Social and Rehabilitation Service, Dept. of Health, Education, and Welfare). Gainesville: University of Florida.

Gray, S. W., Ramsey, B. K., & Klaus, R. A. (1982). *From 3 to 20: The Early Training Project.* Baltimore: University Park Press.

Groff, P. (1974). Some criticisms of mastery learning. *Today's Education, 63,* 88–91.

Halstead, J. S. (1982). *Annual report of the Follow Through program* (Dept. of Education Grant No. G007501868). Richmond, VA: Richmond Public Schools.

Hamblin, R., Hathaway, C., & Wodarski, J. (1971). Group contingencies, peer tutoring, and accelerating academic achievement. In E.

Ramp and W. Hopkins (Eds.), *A new direction for education: Behavior analysis* (pp. 41–53). Lawrence: University of Kansas, Department of Human Development.

Horton, L. (1979). Mastery learning: Sound in theory, but … *Educational Leadership, 37,* 154–156.

House, E., Glass, G., McLean, L., & Walker, D. (1977). *No simple answer: Critique of the "Follow Through" evaluation.* Urbana: University of Illinois, Center for Instructional Research and Curriculum Evaluation.

Jaynes, J. (1975). Hello, teacher … *Contemporary Psychology, 20,* 629–631.

Johnson, D., & Johnson, R. (1974). Instructional goal structure: Cooperative, competitive, or individualistic. *Review of Educational Research, 44,* 213–240.

Johnson, D., & Johnson, R. (1975). *Learning together and alone.* Englewood Cliffs, NJ: Prentice-Hall.

Johnson, D., Johnson, R., & Scott, L. (1978). The effects of cooperative and individualized instruction on student attitudes and achievement. *Journal of Social Psychology, 104,* 207–216.

Keller, F. (1968). Goodbye, teacher … *Journal of Applied Behavior Analysis, 1,* 79–89.

Kim, Y., Cho, G., Park, J., & Park, M. (1974). *An application of a new instructional model* (Res. Rep. No. 8). Seoul: Korean Educational Development Institute.

Kulik, J., Kulik, C., & Cohen, P. (1979). A Meta-analysis of outcome studies of Keller's personalized system of instruction. *American Psychologist, 34,* 110–113.

Laughlin, P. (1978). Ability and group problem solving. *Journal of Research and Development in Education, 12,* 114–120.

Lazar, I., Darlington, R., Murray, H., Royce, J., & Snipper, A. (1982). The lasting effects of early education: A report from the Consortium for Longitudinal Studies. *Monographs of the Society for Research in Child Development, 47* (2–3, Serial No. 195).

Lazar, I., Hubell, V. R., Murray, H., Rosche, M., & Royce, J. (1977). *The persistence of preschool effects* (Publication No. [OHDS] 78-30130). Washington, DC: Department of Health, Education and Welfare.

Lee, Y., Kim, C., Kim, H., Park, B., Yoo, H., Chang S., & Kim, S. (1971). *Interaction improvement studies on the mastery learning project* (Final Report on Mastery Learning Program, April–November 1971). Seoul: Seoul National University, Educational Research Center.

Levine, J. (1983). Social comparison and education. In J. Levine & M. Wang (Eds.), *Teacher and student perceptions: Implication for learning.* Hillsdale, NJ: Erlbaum.

Lloyd, K., & Knutzen, N. (1969). A self-paced programmed undergraduate course in the experimental analysis of behavior. *Journal of Applied Behavioral Analysis, 2,* 125–133.

Lucker, G., Rosenfield, D., Sikes, J., & Aronson, E. (1976). Performance in the interdependent classroom: A field study. *American Educational Research Journal, 13,* 115–123.

Maccoby, E. E., & Zellner, M. (1970). *Experiments in primary education: Aspects of Project Follow Through.* New York: Harcourt Brace.

Madden, N., & Slavin, R. (1983). Effects of cooperative learning on the social acceptance of mainstreamed academically handicapped students. *Journal of Special Education, 17,* 171–182.

Meyer, L. (1984). Longterm academic effects of Direct Instruction Follow Through. *Elementary School Journal. 1984, 4,* 380–394.

Meyer, L., Gersten, R., & Gutkin, J. (1984). Direct Instruction: A Project Follow Through success story. *Elementary School Journal. 1984, 2,* 241–252.

Miller, L., & Bizzell, R. (1983a). Long-term effects of four preschool programs: Ninth and tenth grade results. Louisville, KY: University of Louisville.

Miller, L., & Bizzell, R. (1983b). Long-term effects of four preschool programs: Sixth, seventh, and eighth grades. *Child Development, 54,* 727–741.

National Commission on Excellence in Education. (1983). "A Nation at risk: The imperative for educational reform." Washington, DC: National Commission.

Okey, J. R. (1974). Altering teacher and pupil behavior with mastery teaching. *School Science and Mathematics, 74,* 530–535.

Okey, J. (1975, August). *Development of mastery teaching materials*

(Final Evaluation Rep., USOE G-74-2990). Bloomington: Indiana University.

Olmsted, P. P. (1977). *The relationship of program participation and parental teaching behavior with children's standardized achievement measures in two program sites.* Unpublished doctoral dissertation, University of Florida.

Olmsted, P. P., & Rubin, R. I. (1982, September). *Assistance to local Follow Through programs* (Annual Rep., Dept. of Education, Grant No. G00-770-1691). Washington, DC: U.S. Dept. of Education, Follow Through Branch.

Pavlov, I. P., (1927). *Conditioned reflexes* (G. V. Anrep, Trans.). London: Oxford University Press.

Rubin, R., Olmsted, P., & Kelly, J. (1981). Comprehensive model for child services. *Children and Youth Services Review, 3*, 175-192.

Rubin, R., Olmsted, P., Szegda, M., Wetherby, M., & Williams, D. (1983). *Long-term effects of parent education Follow Through program participation.* Paper presented at the American Educational Research Association annual meeting in Montreal, Canada, April, 1983.

Sameroff, A. J. (1979, March). *Theoretical and empirical issues in the operationalization of transactional research.* Paper presented at the biennial meeting of the Society for Research in Child Development, San Francisco.

Schweinhart, L., & Weikart, D. (1980). *Young children grow up: The effects of the Perry Preschool Program on youths through age 15* (Monograph No. 7). Ypsilanti, MI: High/Scope Educational Research Foundation.

Sharan, S., & Sharan, Y. (1976). *Small-group teaching.* Englewood Cliffs, NJ: Education Technology Publications.

Sharan, S. (1980). Cooperative learning in small groups: Recent methods and effects on achievement, attitudes, and ethnic relations. *Review of Educational Research, 50*, 241-271.

Skinner, B. F. (1968). *Technology of teaching.* New York: Appleton-Century-Crofts.

Slavin, R. (1977). Classroom reward structure: An analytical and practical review. *Review of Educational Research, 47*, 633-650.

Slavin, R. (1978a). Student teams and achievement divisions. *Journal of Research and Development in Education, 12*, 39-49.

Slavin, R. (1978b). Student teams and comparison among equals: Effects on academic performance and student attitudes. *Journal of Educational Psychology, 70*, 532-538.

Slavin, R. (1980a). Effects of student teams and peer tutoring on academic achievement and time on task. *Journal of Experimental Education, 48*, 252-257.

Slavin, R. (1980b). *Using student team learning* (rev. ed.). Baltimore: Johns Hopkins University, Center for Social Organization of Schools.

Slavin, R. (1983). *Cooperative learning.* New York: Longman.

Slavin, R. (1984). Students motivating students to excel: Cooperative incentives, cooperative tasks, and student achievement. *Elementary School Journal 1984, 85*, 53-64.

Slavin, R., & Karweit, N. (1981). Cognitive and affective outcomes of an intensive student team learning experience. *Journal of Experimental Education, 50*, 29-35.

Slavin, R., Leavey, M., & Madden, N. (1982). *Effects of student teams*

and individualized instruction on student mathematics achievement, attitudes, and behaviors. Paper presented at the annual convention of the American Educational Research Association, New York.

Smith, J. (1981). *Philosophical considerations of mastery learning theory: An empirical study.* Paper presented at the annual meeting of the American Educational Research Association, Los Angeles.

Spady, W. (1981). *Outcome-based instructional management: A sociological perspective.* Unpublished manuscript, American Association of School Administrators, Arlington, VA.

Stallings, J. (1975, December). Implementations and child effects of teaching practices in Follow Through classrooms. Monograph of the Society for Research in Child Development, *40*, 7-8.

Stallings, J. (1977). *Learning to look: A handbook on classroom observation and teaching models.* Belmont, CA: Wadsworth.

Stallings, J., & Kaskowitz, D. (1974). *Follow Through classroom observation evaluation, 1972-73.* Menlo Park, CA: SRI International.

Stallings, J., Robbins, P., & Wolfe, P. (1984). *A staff development program to increase student learning time and achievement.* Napa, CA: Unpublished student program.

Stebbins, L., St. Pierre, R. G., Proper, E. C., Anderson, R. B., & Cerva, R. R. (1977). *Education as experimentation: A planned variation model* (Vol. 4A-D). Cambridge, MA: Abt Associates.

Stodolsky, S. S. (1972). Defining treatment and outcomes in early childhood education. In H. J. Walberg & A. T. Kopan (Eds.), *Rethinking urban education.* San Francisco: Jossey-Bass.

Terman, L. W., & Merrill, M. A. (1960). *Stanford-Binet Intelligence Scale.* Cambridge, MA: Houghton Mifflin.

Tiegs, E. W., & Clark, W. W. (1963) *Manual: California Achievement Test, complete battery.* Monterey Park: California Test Bureau (McGraw-Hill).

Tiegs, E. W., & Clark, W. W. (1970) *Test coordinator's handbook: California Achievement Tests.* Monterey, California: California Test Bureau (McGraw-Hill).

Travers, R. M. W. (Ed.). (1973). *Second handbook of research on teaching.* Chicago: Rand McNally.

Vapova, J., & Royce, J. (1978, March). *Comparison of the long-term effects of infants and preschool programs on academic performance.* Paper presented at the annual meeting of the American Educational Research Association, Toronto.

Webb, N. (1980a). Group process: The key to learning in groups. *New Directions for Methodology of Social and Behavioral Science, 6*, 77-87.

Webb, N. (1980b). A process-outcome analysis of learning in groups and individual settings. *Educational Psychologist, 15*, 69-83.

Webb, N. (1982). Peer interaction and learning in cooperative small groups. *Journal of Educational Psychology, 74*, 642-655.

Weikart, D., Rogers, L., Adcock, C., McClelland, D. (1971). *The cognitively oriented curriculum: A framework for preschool teachers.* Urbana: University of Illinois—NAEYC.

Weiner, B. (1979). A theory of motivation for some classroom experiences. *Journal of Educational Psychology, 71*, 3-25.

Ziegler, S. (1981). The effectiveness of cooperative learning teams for increasing cross-ethnic friendship: Additional evidence. *Human Organization, 40*, 264-268.

26.

Research on Teaching in Higher Education

Michael J. Dunkin
The University of Sydney, Australia

with the assistance of

Jennifer Barnes
The University of Sydney, Australia

During the decade following publication of the *Second Hand-book of Research on Teaching* (Travers, 1973), several notable developments occurred in research on teaching in higher education. Innovative approaches to structuring learning experiences for students, such as computer-based teaching and the Keller Plan, generated enough research for several reviews to be written. Developments in techniques of reviewing the research and synthesizing its findings, described by Walberg (this volume), were applied to higher education. Increased interest was shown in observational research of classroom processes. Controversial issues surrounding student evaluation of instruction stimulated much research activity and research on attempts to implement knowledge about teaching in higher education in order to improve it through faculty development programs was conducted. This chapter has been designed to present and discuss the preceding developments and to suggest their implications for future research and practice in higher education.

In subsequent sections, a conceptual framework for integrating the research is suggested, and evidence pertaining to the various types of relationships involving teaching variables in higher education is summarized. The section on Research on Teaching Methods is concerned mainly with methods effectiveness experiments. The section on Research on Facets of Teaching Behavior is organized in terms of qualities of teaching behavior observed in studies of the full range of relationships involving teaching variables. Later parts of the chapter focus upon research in the evaluation and improvement of teaching in higher education. The chapter concludes with a discussion of issues arising from research reviewed in earlier sections.

A Conceptual Framework

According to Gage (1963), there are three main questions involved in research on teaching. They are: How do teachers behave? Why do they behave as they do? and What are the effects of their behavior? Information about three types of variables is required to answer those questions. First, there is teaching behavior, or the processes of teaching; the set of variables involved in all three questions and most central to research on teaching. Second, there are the causes or determinants of those processes. Finally, there are variables indicating the effects, or consequences, of teaching processes.

Teaching processes are behaviors engaged in for the purposes of promoting learning in others. They can be thought of in global terms as teaching methods, such as lecturing, leading discussions, and demonstrating. They can also be thought of as more specific teaching behaviors, such as statements of fact, particular types of questions, or categories of reactions to student behaviors. Some teaching methods involve face-to-face contact between teachers and students more than others. Lecturing, for example, is usually performed live by the teacher, but sometimes recorded lectures are presented, and some methods, for example, the Keller Plan, are designed to minimize such contact. Whether the teacher is present or absent on those occasions when learning by students is being guided, teaching processes are observable and are subject to analysis in terms of specific categories of teaching behavior. Furthermore, teaching need not always be performed by those chiefly employed for that purpose. One teaching method is peer teaching, whereby

The author thanks reviewers James Kulik (University of Michigan) and Wilbert McKeachie (University of Michigan).

students attempt to promote the learning of each other, and the Keller Plan includes senior students as proctors to assist more junior students. Again, the behavior engaged in by students in such teaching capacities is analyzable as teaching behavior. The answer to Gage's first question lies in both the teaching methods and the specific categories of teaching behavior employed by those who attempt to promote the learning of others by exerting influence upon the particular types of experiences of those others.

Determinants of teaching behavior consist of attributes of the teachers, the students, or the contexts in which they behave. Teachers perform any one set of processes in association with other sets of processes and the connection between the two sets may be causal. Teachers also behave as they do because of who they are. They possess characteristics that may predispose them to behave in some ways more than in others. Included, too, are their formal learning backgrounds, their education as teachers and researchers, and even early experiences quite remote from their positions as teachers.

Teachers behave as they do partly because of their students. Characteristics of students, some relating to formal criteria of selection into formal educational contexts, such as previous academic performance, but also other characteristics, such as student sex and ethnicity, may affect the way teachers behave. Most immediately, however, the way students present themselves, their behavior in contact with teachers, influences the latter. Student attentiveness, completion of tasks set by the teacher, and evaluations of the teaching they receive must all be assumed to be potential determinants of the teaching processes experienced.

Teachers and students come together in contexts that themselves contain the power to influence teaching and learning. Contextual factors such as the size of the institution, its resources, and whether it is public or private are relevant here. Contextual variations can range from type of teaching space and size of class to type of discipline taught, to the society and culture in which the particular institution is located. Different areas of knowledge, curricula, and programs may also be expected to have their emphases reflected in teaching processes. Inquiry-oriented learning materials should result in classroom events more consistent with inquiry than didacticism. Teaching in medical schools might be expected to differ from teaching in engineering, and teaching in advanced courses from teaching in introductory courses.

The effects of teaching in higher education, as at other levels of education, are most commonly researched in terms of academic achievements of students. Comparative studies of different teaching methods are the best examples of achievement criteria being used in research on teaching in higher education. Other criteria of effectiveness are, however, often employed. They include students' evaluations or ratings, time taken for students to complete courses, withdrawal or completion rates, and students' attitudes toward the course.

In summary, the ways in which teachers behave in higher education classrooms have been conceptualized in terms of both global teaching methods and specific categories of teaching behavior. It is these *processes* of teaching that are central to research on teaching. Sometimes research on teaching in higher education is concerned with explaining variations in the occur-

rence of these processes. Processes themselves are researched as influences upon other processes, but more often explanations of variations in them are sought in the background characteristics of teachers themselves and their students. Characteristics of teachers and students when used as possible sources of explanation of variation in process variables are referred to as *presage variables*, that is, as the bases for predictions or forecasts of classroom processes. Features of the substantive, physical, and institutional environments in which teachers and students come together are also employed as possible influences upon process variables in higher education. When used in that way, they are referred to in this chapter as *context variables*.

While teaching variables are classified as process variables and determinants of variations in teaching are called process, presage, or context variables, the effects of teaching processes when considered at a point in time are either other process variables or such outcomes as student attitudes and achievements. More commonly, however, the effects of teaching processes are sought not in subsequent processes but in the *products* taken away by the students in terms of academic or professional achievements and attitudes. Research in teaching in higher education has been more concerned with the effects of processes upon products than with any other of the possible issues involving teaching behavior.

The pursuit of Gage's three questions for research on teaching (Gage, 1963) leads in the higher education domain, as well as in others, to an elaboration of the issues and questions in terms of four classes of variables: process, presage, context, and product. These four types of variables are useful in describing research on teaching as follows:

Gage's Questions	Types of Variable and Relationships
How do teachers behave?	Process occurrence
Why do they behave as they do?	Process–Process relationships Presage–Process relationships Context–Process relationships
What are the effects of their behavior?	Process–Process relationships Process–Product relationships

It should be noted that other possible relationships such as those between presage and product variables are not included here. This is because they do not qualify as research on teaching. To do that, they must include process variables. In the rest of this chapter the preceding conceptual framework will be applied to research on teaching in higher education.

Research on Teaching Methods

This section is divided into two parts. The first part presents the conclusions of reviewers who have synthesized research on teaching methods that rely for their effectiveness mainly on interpersonal communication between teachers and students. In this part, therefore, research on lectures versus discussion, team teaching, and peer teaching is reviewed.

The second part focuses on teaching methods that rely upon highly structured learning materials, usually, but not always, involving the use of hardware, such as tape recorders, projectors, or computers, and designed to facilitate individualized learning.

One of the most rapidly expanding areas of higher education is distance education. Research on this topic is not reviewed in this chapter because it is much more than a teaching method and because most of the methods that are reviewed in the chapter are available for use in distance education. Readers interested in research in distance education will find works by Daniel, Stroud, and Thompson (1982), and Holmberg (1982) helpful.

Social Interaction Methods

There have been several reviews of research on the relative benefits of lecturing and discussion methods in higher education. McKeachie (1963) concluded his review of research comparing the two as follows: "When one is asked whether lecture is better than discussion, the appropriate counter would seem to be, For what goals?" (p. 1127). It seems that over the following 16 years, little reason for altering that conclusion emerged, for Kulik and Kulik (1979) indicated that a similar conclusion was warranted. They compared several reviews and wrote:

> These reviewers agree on some basic conclusions. First, they point out that teaching by discussion is neither more nor less effective than teaching by lecture when the criterion of effectiveness is learning of factual information. . . .
> The reviewers also agree that teaching by discussion is more effective than teaching by lecture for more ambitious cognitive objectives, such as developing problem-solving ability. . . . [Those who] reviewed research on the relative effectiveness of discussion versus lecturing in terms of changing attitudes. . . . found a third area of agreement [in favor of discussion]. . . .
> Where the reviewers disagree somewhat is in their conclusions about student satisfaction with teaching by lecture versus teaching by discussion. . . . (pp. 71–73)

Schustereit (1980) reviewed research on team teaching in higher education and accepted the definition by Johnson and Lobb (1959): "a group of two or more persons assigned to the same students at the same time for instructional purposes in a particular subject or combination of subjects" (p. 59). Schustereit divided the studies reviewed into two types, those comparing team-taught and "solitary-teacher-taught" classes, and those comparing three different teaching techniques including team-teaching. Using "box-score" methods (see Walberg, this volume) of synthesizing the research, Schustereit found inconsistent results from the 10 studies reviewed and concluded as follows: ". . . While the reviewed studies gave a plurality of support to team-teaching, a generalization that team-teaching is a superior instructional technique would not be justified based on the various studies" (p. 88).

Goldschmid and Goldschmid (1976) attempted to synthesize literature on peer teaching in higher education. After summarizing sociopsychological, pedagogical, economic, and political arguments in favor of using peer relationships to enhance learning, the authors discussed five types of peer teaching: discussion groups, seminars, or tutorial groups, as led by teaching assistants; the proctor model, as in the Keller Plan (Keller, 1968), in which senior students may assist individual students; student learning groups that are instructorless or self-directed; the learning cell, or student dyad; and "*parrainage*," or senior students counselling entering students. Clearly, the variety of procedures included in the grouping of those heterogeneous approaches made peer teaching too broad a concept for specific or confident conclusions to be reached. Moreover, only a small body of relevant research was found to exist. Goldschmid and Goldschmid (1976) concluded:

> Despite its many advantages—including its low cost—peer teaching is not a panacea for all instructional problems. In fact, it is best used together with other teaching and learning methods. It may be particularly relevant when one seeks to maximize the students' [sic] responsibility for his own learning and active participation in the learning process, and to enhance the development of skills for cooperation and social interaction. (p. 29)

Research on other teaching methods relying upon social interaction, such as clinical teaching, is reviewed in other chapters (see Dinham & Stritter, this volume), except for a few studies of special relevance to the following section on facets of teaching behavior.

The research just reviewed was predominantly process-product research. It is difficult to obtain evidence regarding the actual processes in terms of which the prescriptively defined methods were implemented. Furthermore, questions such as the extent to which presage and context variables affected those processes and, indirectly, student outcomes, were rarely addressed.

In all, it seems that university and college teachers can derive only very shaky guidance from research in choosing between lectures, discussion, team teaching, and peer teaching. At most, research might justify the choice of discussions rather than lectures where higher cognitive learnings and attitude change are the objectives. Within the samples of each of the preceding methods researched, there were instances that were highly effective and highly ineffective. Yet there has been surprisingly little research that has tried to discover the differences between those effective instances and the less effective ones. The section of this chapter on Research on Facets of Teaching Behavior discusses that approach to research.

Individualized Methods

As mentioned at the beginning of this chapter, one of the most prominent developments in research on teaching in higher education in recent years has been the application of the techniques of meta-analysis in attempts to synthesize research. This is particularly true of research on methods of instruction associated with applications of technological developments to higher education. This part is concerned with meta-analysis connected with the Center for Research on Learning and Instruction at the University of Michigan. In these studies, the Michigan team synthesized research findings concerning audio-tutorial instruction (Kulik, Kulik, & Cohen, 1979b), computer-based teaching (Kulik, Kulik, & Cohen, 1980), Keller Plan instruction (Kulik et al., 1979a; Kulik, Jaksa, & Kulik, 1978), programed instruction (Kulik, Cohen, & Ebeling, 1980), and visual-based instruction (Cohen, Ebeling, & Kulik, 1981).

The fact that a uniform set of procedures was used across the meta-analyses to identify and analyze studies makes it possible to attempt a synthesis of them here. There are also similarities among the instructional methods themselves that make treating them together reasonable. Apart from the use of technological developments, the methods generally share the attribute of being modularized in the sense that course content is divided into reasonably small, self-contained units in pursuit of well-defined learning objectives. Most of the methods are attempts to provide individualization or personalization in higher education. Third, most of the methods emphasize the provision of feedback to students on their performance on trials or tests that are taken frequently. Fourth, student activity is a common feature along with less emphasis upon the teacher in formal teaching situations, such as lectures. In these respects they form a relatively homogeneous set of teaching processes.

The Michigan meta-analyses were attempts to answer questions mainly about process–product relationships. For example, Does the innovative method prove to be more effective than conventional instruction in the typical comparative study? The influence of presage and context variables was also explored in questions such as: Do certain types of students benefit more than others from the innovative method? Under what conditions is the innovative method most effective?

PROCESS–PRODUCT RELATIONSHIPS
ACROSS METHODS

The Michigan team synthesized findings concerning the relative effectiveness of the innovative methods in relation to the following main criteria: student achievement, both shorter and longer term, where possible; student satisfaction with the instruction and the course; withdrawal rates; where sufficient data were available, time used by students in taking the course; and correlations between student aptitude and student achievement. Several types of statistics were reported, including estimated average percentage scores and percentile ranks in relation to achievement criteria, and estimated average scores on 5-point scales for satisfaction criteria. Traditional types of information regarding statistical significance were reported for most comparisons, but in all of the meta-analyses emphasis was given to effect size measures which sometimes were calculated according to procedures recommended by Glass (1976) and sometimes according to Cohen (1969). Kulik, Kulik, and Cohen (1979b) found that four different methods of calculating effect size were highly intercorrelated ($.99 \geqslant r \geqslant .83$). "Box-scores" of numbers of studies favoring innovative as against conventional methods were also reported.

Table 26.1 summarizes the results of the Michigan syntheses. It supplements Walberg's (this volume) Table 6.3. Table 26.1 indicates that for audio-tutorials, computer-based teaching, programmed instruction, and visual-based instruction, there was a small but statistically significant superiority in short-term achievement by students experiencing the innovative method over students in conventional courses. For students in Keller Plan courses, this superiority in achievement was considerably greater, as manifested in an effect of moderate size. Table 26.1 does not include information regarding longer term retention, but where such information was analyzed by the Michigan team, effect size was found to be at least as great and usually greater in the longer term in favor of the innovation. Differences in student satisfaction between innovative and conventional methods are shown in Table 26.1 to be small to negligible, with the exception, again, of the Keller Plan, in whose favor was another effect of moderate size. Differences in withdrawal rates also were shown to be negligible in all comparisons. In the few comparisons available for student time per week, statistically significant advantages were seen only for students receiving computer-based instruction.

Because mastery is a common requirement among the innovations researched, results were also reported for aptitude-achievement correlations. Bloom's model (1968) suggests that under mastery requirements, in which students of both high and low initial ability have to attain the same standard of performance to satisfy the criterion of success, the correlation between aptitude and achievement should be much smaller than in situations where mastery is not required. Table 26.1 indicates that this hypothesis was not supported in the research on innovations in higher education. Differences between the correlation coefficients in question were small in every case.

The research included in these meta-analyses was conducted in various contexts and under various design conditions, so that it was possible to investigate whether the effectiveness of a teaching method depended upon the methodological features of the research and the contexts of teaching. The Michigan team developed sets of categories for describing features of the studies. The list used in their meta-analysis of research on Keller Plan methods is presented in Table 26.2. Many of the categories were common across the several meta-analyses. One category not included for the Keller Plan meta-analysis, but included for the others, was whether or not the report was published.

The only category to make a significant difference to achievement in the audio-tutorial research was, in fact, publication status. Studies published in journals were found to report achievement results more in favor of audio-tutorials than studies reported in dissertations and unpublished papers. Year of publication had a significant effect upon results in research on both programed instruction and visual-based instruction. Whether or not the research was conducted in a doctorate-granting university made a difference in the meta-analysis of research on visual-based instruction.

In three cases, attempts to control for instructor effects appeared to be influential. In research on computer-based teaching, Keller Plan, and visual-based instruction, student achievement results more favorable to the innovation were obtained if different instructors implemented the innovative and the conventional instruction than if the same instructor implemented both.

CONTEXTUAL EFFECTS

Interestingly enough, for only two of the innovative methods were substantial effects on student achievement found to depend on variations in the instructional contexts themselves.

Table 26.1. Summary of Results of the Michigan Meta-Analyses of Research on Instructional Technology in Higher Education

	N	Student Achievement Exam Scores	Percentile Rank	N	Student Satisfaction (5-Point Scale)	N	Withdrawal Rate	N	Time Taken (Hrs/Week)	N	Aptitude Achievement Correlation
Audio-Tutorials	42	68.5%	58	6	3.56	22	19%	—	—	12	.36
Conventional instruction		66.9%	50		3.30		17%				.39
Significance level		p < .05	—		N.S.		N.S.				N.S.
Mean effect size		.20	—		.12		0.06				.02
Computer-Based teaching	54	60.6%	60	11	3.77	13	26.9%	8	2.25	7	.41
Conventional instruction		57.6%	50		3.50		27.6%		3.50		.51
Significance level		p < .01	—		—		N.S.		p < .01		N.S.
Mean effect size		.25	—		.24		−.01		—		.12
Keller Plan instruction	61	73.6%	70	11	4.19	27	13.9%	4		9	.50
Conventional instruction		65.9%	50		3.40		12.6%		Approx. equal		.50
Significance level		p < .0001	—		p < .01		N.S.		—		N.S.
Mean effect size		.49	—		.46		.10		—		0
Programmed instruction	56	67.1%	60	4	3.41	9	20.3%	9	5	19	.40
Conventional instruction		64.8%	50		3.49		19.7%		6		.48
Significance level		p < .05	—		N.S.		N.S.		N.S.		N.S.
Mean effect size		.28	—		−.10		.06		—		.09
Visual-Based instruction	65	68.4%	56	16	3.45	10	13.1%	—	—	16	.50
Conventional instruction		66.9%	50		3.48		13.2%				.45
Significance level		p < .01	—		—		N.S.				N.S.
Mean effect size		.15	—		−.06		−.05				.06

Note. A dash indicates that the information was not available. "N.S." means not statistically significant at the .05 level.

Visual-based instruction that involved using videotape to provide student teachers with feedback on their teaching performances was found to be much more effective than other uses of visual media. Keller Plan courses were more effective in mathematics, engineering, and psychology than in the physical and life sciences and other social sciences. It seemed not to matter whether audio-tutorial techniques varied somewhat from those developed by Postlethwait (Postlethwait, Novak, & Murray, 1972), or whether computer-based teaching involved using the computer to manage student learning, tutor students, conduct simulation exercises, or involve students in programing for problem solving. No advantages of linear and branching programs over each other were apparent, and the use of still-projection motion pictures, multimedia approaches, closed-circuit TV, educational TV, and film or videotape for observing classrooms in teacher education seemed to be equally effective.

PROCESS-PRODUCT RELATIONSHIPS
WITHIN KELLER PLAN

Variations within applications of the Keller Plan proved to be opportune because they provided Kulik and his colleagues with opportunities to test the contributions of the various component features of the method to its overall effectiveness (Kulik et al., 1978). The authors concluded on the basis of "box-scores" that requiring students to attain mastery on a unit before progressing leads to higher achievement without affecting withdrawal rate or student satisfaction. The mastery requirement

emerged, therefore, as an important component of the Keller Plan.

Implementations of Keller Plan principles also were found to vary in the size of the course units and in the number of quizzes students undertook. The few relevant studies on these issues contained various deficiencies in design, but were interpreted as a group to give support for smaller units and more frequent quizzing. Student retention of subject matter appeared to benefit from them, while satisfaction and study time seemed unaffected. Kulik and his colleagues also investigated various aspects of the student proctor's role in Keller Plan courses. It was pointed out that proctors performed three main functions: to score quizzes objectively, to provide immediate feedback on quiz performance to students, and to discuss course material with students. The research seemed to indicate that the amount of contact students had with proctors was unimportant, but that the timing of feedback was influential. Students' retention appeared adversely affected by delayed rather than immediate feedback. The timing of the feedback seemed to be more important than from whom it came, for students who graded their own quizzes were found to perform as well as students relying on proctors for feedback.

In relation to the student self-pacing component of the Keller Plan, Kulik et al., (1978) concluded

... self pacing in itself does not appear to make a significant difference in the level of student achievement. Self-pacing may contribute, however, to student morale and general satisfaction with

Table 26.2. Categories for Describing Study Features and Number of Studies in Each Category of Meta-Analysis of Keller Plan Research

Coding Category	Number of Studies	Coding Category	Number of Studies
Subject matter		Historical effects	
Physical and life sciences	10	Same semester	45
Mathematics and engineering	11	Different semester	3
Psychology	18	Subject assignment	
Other social sciences	6	Random	10
		Evidence of equivalence	17
Course level		No evidence of equivalence	21
Introductory	32		
Nonintroductory	15	Variations in experimental classes	
		Pure PSI	41
Type of school		Compromised PSI	7
Major research universities	9		
Other research universities	6	Authorship of examination	
Doctorate-granting universities	7	Standardized exam	9
Comprehensive colleges	17	Collaborated exam	11
Liberal arts colleges	6	Single-instructor-designed exam	17
Community colleges and special institutions	3	Scoring bias	
		Objective	26
Instructor		Blind essay	5
Same	22	Other essay	6
Different	22	Essay and objective	5
Variations in control classes		Weight toward final grade	
No PSI components	43	Same for both classes: either no weight or complete determination of grade	7
Some characteristics of PSI	5	Same for both classes: partial weight	8
		More weight for conventional exam	11

Note. PSI = personalized system of instruction.

From "A Meta-Analysis of Outcome Studies of Keller's Personalized System of Instruction" by J. A. Kulik, C-L. C. Kulik, and P. A. Cohen, 1979, *American Psychologist, 34*, p. 315. Copyright 1979 by American Psychological Association.

a course. Course policies which limit self-pacing, especially those which provide positive incentives for student progress, have successfully reduced procrastination and lowered withdrawal rates in PSI courses. (p. 10)

Regarding the remaining components of Keller Plan courses, explicit unit objectives, review units, and optional lectures for stimulation, the Michigan team found little evidence in favor of explicit objectives and none in support of the lectures. There was support for review units, but it came from only a small number of studies.

The single most significant conclusion to be reached from research on innovatory teaching methods in higher education is that the Keller Plan is clearly superior to other methods with which it has been compared. Indeed, the Keller Plan has been so consistently found superior that it must rank as the method with the greatest research support in the history of research on teaching. The other innovatory methods also receive support from research when student achievement is the criterion. However, their benefits are relatively small although statistically significant.

Another important contribution of research on the Keller Plan is that it has allowed evidence to be gathered on the relative contributions of the different components of the system. It seems that parsimony might be achieved through the use of mastery requirements, frequent quizzes, immediate feedback, and review units; but not proctor tutoring, self-pacing, explicit objectives, and occasional lecturing. Identification of the essentials and nonessentials of the innovations, as in the review by Kulik et al., (1978), might ameliorate some of the difficulties found in implementing them. For the Keller Plan, at least, it appears that one of the most troublesome components for teachers and administrators, that is, self-pacing, may not be essential for deriving the benefits of the method.

Research on Facets of Teaching Behavior

The research reviewed in this section concerns aspects, qualities, or facets of classroom behavior that might be found in any of the teaching methods described in the previous section. Rosenshine (1971), Dunkin and Biddle (1974), and Simon and Boyer (1974) delineated several facets of teaching behavior emerging from research on teaching. They included the following: a *cognitive* facet concerned with intellectual properties, such as levels of thinking required to answer different types of questions; a *socioemotional* facet associated with displays of feelings, sanctioning behaviors, such as praise and criticism, and initiation and response; a *substantive* facet to which subject-matter variations, such as the amount of content in a lecture, are relevant; and a *communication* facet involving properties of language use, such as clarity, fluency, and expressiveness. In part, these facets have been researched through the application of observational schedules to teaching as it occurs in naturalistic teaching contexts. In some cases, however, the research has been experimental in that researchers have intervened to regulate the occurrence of the behaviors concerned. Most of the facets have had long histories of research at various levels of education.

The main facets in terms of which the research reviewed in this section is organized are the cognitive and the socioemotional. The communication facet is represented by research on clarity, but research on another category of behavior within that facet, expressiveness, is postponed until a later section. Research on the substantive facet, especially that on content coverage, is also postponed until a later section. Because research on expressiveness and content coverage is better known in higher education in association with research on student evaluations of teaching, they are both discussed under that heading. The section concludes with research on combinations or syntheses of such facets as those just listed as they have been identified through the application of such statistical techniques as cluster analysis to data about specific categories of teaching behavior. Where the concerns and volume of studies and findings warrant, the discussion of research relevant to these facets is organized in terms of the frequency of occurrence of processes pertaining to the facets, and relationships involving those processes with other processes, with context variables, with characteristics of teachers and students (presage variables), and with outcomes of instruction (product variables).

Cognitive Operations in the Classroom

Research on the cognitive processes in college level classrooms was a feature of the late 1970s and early 1980s. Attempts to classify teacher behavior in the cognitive domain have relied mainly on the concepts developed by Bloom and his colleagues (Bloom, Engelhart, Furst, Hill, & Krathwohl, 1956) and by Guilford (1956). Four such studies were reviewed by Wenk and Menges (1982).

The Bloom taxonomy was developed in relation to statements of educational objectives concerning knowledge and intellectual abilities and skills. The taxonomy was arranged in a hierarchy of six major classes of cognitive objectives, defined so that the intended behaviors in one class were likely to depend upon the intended behaviors included in lower levels of the hierarchy. The six major classes were Knowledge; Comprehension (Translation, Interpretation, Extrapolation); Application; Analysis; Synthesis; and Evaluation.

Distinctions between lower- and higher-level classroom processes have been used in relation to undergraduate education courses by Baumgart (1972, 1976); to college biology by Merlino (1977); in microbiology laboratory classes by Hegarty (1978, 1979); in science laboratory classes by Shymansky and Penick (1979), and Kyle, Penick, and Shymansky (1980); in literature, history, and humanities classes by Andrews (1980); and in clinical discussions in medical education by Foster (1981). Variations in the precise definitions of higher- and lower-level processes have existed across these studies. For example, Hegarty regarded Knowledge and the Translation subcategory of Comprehension as lower level, with the Interpretation subcategory of Comprehension, together with Application, Analysis, Synthesis, and Evaluation categories being referred to as "scientific processes." By contrast, Andrews included Memorization, Comprehension, and Application in his concept of lower-level processes. Shymansky and Penick (1979) and Kyle et al. (1980) distinguished between factual recall questions and extended thought questions.

Barnes (1980) also used the Bloom taxonomy in her observations of classes across several disciplines. However, she did not dichotomize the categories into higher and lower levels. Smith (1977, 1980) used the taxonomy with classes in the humanities, social sciences, and natural sciences, but only with respect to students' reports of their out-of-class study behaviors and not in the observation of classroom processes.

Guilford's (1956) three-dimensional model of the intellect was constructed on the idea that an intellectual ability involves engaging a particular type of cognitive *operation*, upon a particular type of *content*, in order to generate a particular type of *product*. Each combination of operation, content, and product denoted a specific ability. It has been the operation facet of Guilford's model that classroom observers have found particularly useful. Guilford posited five categories of operation: Cognition, Memory, Divergent Production, Convergent Production, and Evaluation.

In classroom applications of Guilford's categories, Cognition and Memory are usually combined to form a category similar to Bloom's Knowledge category. The Cognitive–Memory category has then been rated as lower-level processing, with the remaining types constituting higher-level processing. Furthermore, the distinction between Convergent Thinking and Divergent Thinking has allowed some researchers to investigate something akin to the creativity continuum (Dunkin & Biddle, 1974).

Other systems for analyzing cognitive processes in classrooms that have been used in higher education are those devised by Bellack, Kliebard, Hyman, and Smith, (1966) and Smith (1971). The Bellack system is a complex one containing several facets, one of which was named the Substantive–Logical. Verbal behavior concerned with the substantive content of lessons was coded according to the type of logical process involved. The logical processes included were Defining, Interpreting, Fact Stating, Explaining, Opining, and Justifying. Aubrecht (1978) used these and other Bellack concepts in her study of classes in basic physics courses at a large midwestern university. The categories of Defining, Fact Stating, and Opining were regarded together as "lower" or "simpler thought processes," while Interpreting, Explaining, and Justifying were "higher" or "more complex processes" (p. 326). Powell (1974) used categories similar to the Bellack ones in his study of small group teaching methods across several disciplines. Smith's system (1971) was devised principally to observe "inquiry" as contrasted with "verification" or "investigative" behavior in science laboratory classes. Tamir (1977) used a modification of the system to compare university and high school classes.

The findings of research using the Bloom, Guilford, Bellack, and Smith categories in observing cognitive qualities of teacher and student behavior in college and university classrooms have represented the various types suggested in the "Conceptual Framework" presented here. Below they are grouped in accordance with those types as process occurrence, context-process relationships, presage-process relationships, process-process relationships, and process-product relationships.

PROCESS OCCURRENCE

In all but one (Smith, 1977; 1980) of the studies in which process occurrence data were reported, the proportion of the observational units coded as lower level was greater than the proportion coded as higher level (Baumgart, 1972; Barnes, 1980; Foster, 1981; Hegarty, 1978, 1979; Powell, 1974; Shymansky & Penick, 1979). The between-study mean for lower level was 60.63% ($N = 7$, $S.D. = 27.27$) and for higher level it was 26.88% ($N = 7$, $S.D. = 16.17$) with the rest being concerned with managerial topics. Smith's findings (1977, 1980), particularly that greater use was made of higher than lower cognitive levels by students when participating in classroom interaction, are quite different from the findings of other studies, although they did reveal an emphasis on teachers' questions at the Cognitive–Memory level. Tamir (1977) observed teacher behavior in laboratory classes in chemistry, biology, physiology, and histology at the Hebrew University in Israel. He found, with data aggregated across the four disciplines, that verification behaviors occurred twice as often as inquiry behaviors and concluded that the latter were given a low priority.

To these findings concerning the occurrence of various types of cognitive processes should be added the findings of Aubrecht (1978) to be discussed later in this chapter.

CONTEXT-PROCESS RELATIONSHIPS

Findings of this type concern differences between institutions, disciplines, and curricula within the one discipline, and types of leadership. Hegarty (1978) reported differences in cognitive levels between the two Australian universities in which she observed microbiology laboratory classes. She found quite large differences in the proportions of tutor talk to students' talk at the lower cognitive level (89% at one university and 67% at the other) and the higher cognitive level (12% and 33%) when the focus was on content. At one university there was also much more tutor-to-tutor talk at the higher cognitive level than at the other. These differences seemed to be consistent with differences between the laboratory manuals of the two institutions. When Hegarty (1978) did a detailed examination of the relationship between the cognitive emphases of the laboratory manuals and laboratory behavior in one of the universities, she found as follows:

> As the level of enquiry increased, there was a marked increase in the proportion of tutor's time spent on the development of substantive content, especially at low cognitive levels, and a concomitant marked increase in students' time spent listening to such talk. There was a slight trend towards a similar increase in the proportion of students' time spent on talk at low cognitive levels. Most importantly, there was a marked increase in time spent by students talking on scientific processes, most of which was accounted for by talk with a fellow student not a tutor, as target. (p. 50)

The results concerning tutor talk on scientific (higher-level) processes were not consistent. As the level of inquiry rose from exercises in which aims, materials, methods, and answers were all given, to those in which the aim was given but only part of the materials or part of the methods were given, with the answer left open, the percentage of time tutors talked on scientific processes increased slightly. However, when the level rose to exercises in which only the aims were given, the percentage of tutor talk on scientific processes decreased to below what it was for exercises of the lowest level of inquiry. During the more "open" exercises, there was a sharp increase in the amount of time tutors spent out of the classroom collecting and organizing materials in preparation areas and private laboratories. In her attempts to account for this finding, Hegarty considered evidence from interviews with the tutors that they sought to perform the role of resource persons rather than challengers or promoters of inquiry behavior. She also considered the possibility that tutors felt threatened by not being able to act as authorities in relation to the more open exercises, and not

having been trained in the skills required for such exercises, sought security in management activities, especially those outside the classroom.

Tamir (1977) also compared the relative occurrence of inquiry behavior in laboratory classes at the Hebrew University with their occurrence in high schools. He found that the ratio of inquiry to verification behaviors in high schools was more than twice that in the university. In the high schools inquiry behavior seemed to be elicited particularly during postlaboratory sessions, which did not occur in the university classes observed. The difference was attributed by Tamir to the university's apparent adherence to "the traditional approach in which every measure is taken to ensure smooth and safe completion of the task by providing detailed instructions, by eliminating any difficulty, and by guarding the students against any 'mistakes' that may lead them to obtain unpredicted results" (Tamir, 1977, p. 315).

Barnes (1980) found that differences across large and small, public and private colleges in the cognitive qualities of questions asked by professors were statistically significant ($\chi^2 = 27.09$, $df = 9$, $p < .01$). The two large colleges were found to have a significantly higher proportion of convergent questions than the two smaller colleges. The large private college displayed the highest incidence of divergent questions, with the small public college having the lowest percentages of both divergent and evaluative questions.

Both Barnes (1980) and Kyle et al., (1980) found question type to be independent of beginning and advanced course status, but dependent upon type of discipline. Barnes found that courses in the humanities/social science/arts disciplines had a significantly lower proportion of cognitive memory questions than courses in the mathematics/engineering/science group. Kyle et al., (1980) found differences among five science disciplines in the occurrence of both extended thought and factual recall questions. The occurrence of the former was so rare in all disciplines that the differences discovered have little meaning. Chemistry and physics tended to have higher incidences of factual recall questions than botany, geology, and zoology.

Powell (1974) found that there was more student talk in discussion groups not led by tutors than in those that were led by tutors. However, there was little or no difference in the cognitive qualities of the discussion with or without the tutor.

PRESAGE-PROCESS RELATIONSHIPS

Only two studies of those reviewed included these types of relationships. Aubrecht (1978) conducted a faculty development experiment to be described more fully later in this chapter. Foster (1981) measured students' cognitive and affective characteristics on entry to a clinical stage of a medical education program. She then explored the association between students' entry characteristics and their behavior in clinical discussion groups. Performance on the Medical College Admission Test (MCAT), the Watson–Glaser Critical Thinking Appraisal Test A (CTA-A), and the Flexibility scale of the California Psychological Inventory (CPI) accounted for significant but small proportions of the variance in students' classroom use of higher cognitive levels (4.5%, 2.9%, and 2.1%, respectively). In total, students' entry characteristics accounted for approximately

10% of the variance in student use of higher cognitive levels in classroom discussion.

PROCESS–PROCESS RELATIONSHIPS

Barnes (1980) investigated several types of process–process relationships, but either found no significant relationships or significant but very small ones between professors' questions and students' cognitive levels.

Andrews (1980) tested hypotheses involving questioning variables, drawn from both the Guilford and Bloom concepts of cognitive processes, in relation to student participation and "wait-time," the time elapsing between a teacher's question and a student response. He found that the mean number of student statements was significantly higher following divergent than following convergent questions. He also found that higher-level questions (those demanding analysis, synthesis, or evaluation) were followed by a larger mean number of student statements, but not longer wait-time, than low-level questions (those involving memorization, comprehension, and application). These findings were obtained with the individual question as the unit of statistical analysis. He also developed a concept of "teaching style" that involved using the teaching assistant as the unit of analysis. A significant positive relationship was found between teacher use of divergent questions and the mean class number of student statements (Spearman $r = .82, p < .03$). The correlation between convergent questions and student statements was sizeable, but, given a small number of teaching assistants, was not statistically significant (Spearman $r = .60, p < .15$).

With the question used as the unit of analysis, Andrews examined the combined effects of the Guilford and Bloom categorizations. He found that high-level divergent questions were followed by significantly more student statements than low-level divergent questions. However, the same difference within convergent questions was not found. Andrews suggested that the single-correct-answer nature of convergent questions might inhibit the richness of response that higher-level questions otherwise elicit.

Andrews also researched *cognitive consistency* in questions asked by teaching assistants. He noticed that sometimes, when more than one question was asked at a time, the questions varied in cognitive level, possibly creating confusion on the part of respondents. It was found that among multiple questions, those that contained logical inconsistencies were followed by significantly longer periods of wait-time, or "student thinking time," than those without inconsistencies. However, multiple consistent questions were followed by significantly more student statements. When consistency was present in both multiple and single questioning episodes, the former tended to be followed by more student statements, but shorter wait-time than the latter. Furthermore, multiple, divergent questions that were consistent were followed by significantly more student statements than multiple, inconsistent, divergent questions.

Andrews' pursuit of questioning led him, thus, to the conceptualization of four attributes: divergence/convergence; higher-level/low-level; single ("straightforward")/multiple; and consistency ("structured")/inconsistency ("vague"). Various combinations of these led further to the presentation of 11 different types of questions. Three types, which Andrews grouped together as "Structured Divergent Questions," were found to be the most productive of student statements in response, together producing nearly three times as many as the other types together.

Foster (1981) found significant positive correlations, each of about .30, between Knowledge, Comprehension, and Application types of teachers' questions and students' responses at each of those levels. At the higher levels, the coefficient for the combined Analysis, Synthesis, and Evaluation categories was .43 ($p < .01$). Significant negative correlations were found between teachers' use of Knowledge questions and students' use of Application ($r = -.36, p < .01$), and between teachers' use of Application and students' use of combined Analysis, Synthesis, and Evaluation ($r = -.28, p < .01$).

In general, therefore, it seems that the cognitive quality of teachers' questions in higher education has a marked influence on student classroom behavior. Not only does the cognitive level of students' responses tend to reflect the demands placed upon them by their teachers, so that lower-level responses tend to be elicited by lower-level questions, but also the amount of student participation seems to be affected. Andrews' elaborations in terms of the single versus multiple and the consistent versus inconsistent aspects of questioning behavior are certainly worthy of further exploration in higher education contexts.

PROCESS–PRODUCT RELATIONSHIPS

Merlino (1977) found that when teachers were grouped according to the percentage of higher level questions asked during class sessions, significant gains in the development of students' understanding of key biological concepts were found to vary positively with that percentage. In addition, the greater the proportion of higher-level questions asked, the more positive were students' evaluations of the teaching they received. Smith (1977, 1980) used canonical correlation techniques to explore relationships between several classroom behavior variables and two student product variables. The product variables consisted of class mean standardized change scores on the Watson-Glaser Test of Critical Thinking Ability and class reports of their use of various cognitive levels during out-of-class study, as measured with an instrument developed by Chickering (1972) based on the Bloom taxonomy. The set of six process variables consisted of student participation, divergent and evaluative questions, encouragement, and peer-to-peer interaction. Smith recognized disagreement among commentators on whether the unit of analysis in this type of research should be the student or the class and so decided to report results obtained when both units were used. Because Smith used the teacher as the sampling unit and did not investigate intraclass differences involving process variables, it would appear that the teacher is the more appropriate unit of analysis and so only results obtained on that basis are presented here. Unfortunately, the smallness of the sample of teachers ($N = 12$) was a severe limitation on the study.

The canonical correlation coefficient between the set of six process variables listed here and the set of seven product variables was found to be .96 ($p < .10$). When the process variables were correlated with the class mean scores on the set of six study behaviors only, a perfect coefficient of 1.00 ($p <$ .001) was obtained. These coefficients are so large as to be quite rare in research on teaching and should be accepted and interpreted with caution.

When the percentage of divergent and evaluative questions combined was studied in relation to each of the seven product variables separately, only the correlation with the use of evaluation during study was statistically significant ($r = .61$, $p < .05$). The corresponding coefficient for divergent and evaluative student responses was also statistically significant ($r = .57$, $p < .05$). Neither of these two cognitive process variables was correlated substantially or significantly with class mean change in critical thinking scores or with any of the other five types of study behaviors.

In general, and as will be seen in the section on Socioemotional Qualities later in this chapter, Smith obtained stronger results for the noncognitive classroom processes he researched. He attributed the difference mainly to the narrow range of incidence of questioning behavior observed in the 12 classes. Given Smith's results for process occurrence, the maximum encounter with teachers' questions of the combined divergent and evaluative types could only have been an average of two or three per session. It is, then, surprising that any statistically significant, let alone sizeable, results were obtained with that variable.

Foster (1981) found that presage variables represented by student medical achievement at the beginning of the year accounted for almost 57% of the variance in the product variable consisting of end-of-year scores on the NBME examination; that the presage variable, student MCAT scores, accounted for 3%; and that the process variable, student higher cognitive level talk, accounted for less than 1%. When the Watson-Glaser form B (CTA-B) scores were used as the product variable, performance on the Watson-Glaser form A test accounted for about 24% of the variance. CPI Achievement via Conformance scores and student higher cognitive level talk accounted for 5% and less than 1%, respectively. However, zero-order correlation coefficients between students' use of higher cognitive processes and the NBME and CTA-B products were .30 and .36, respectively. Apparently, the partialling out of the variance in the multiple regression analyses greatly affected the measured contributions of the student higher-level process variable.

Among her conclusions, Foster (1981) wrote that "the findings would seem to suggest ... that it is the better-prepared students who will perform better on tests and that they are incidentally the ones who talk more at the higher cognitive levels in class" (p. 839). She went on to caution against concluding that the value of clinical discussion groups is questionable, pointing out the limitations in the type of medical achievement tests used in the study and reporting that 89% of students considered the discussion groups to be valuable.

The results of the three studies of process–product relationships involving cognitive levels of classroom behavior suggest that such behaviors are positively related to achievement criteria. However, the contribution of cognitive level process variables to achievement products tended to be small in comparison with student presage variables and other process variables. Attempts to explain these small effects have suggested

that they might be due to design and measurement flaws in the research, such as insufficient variance in the process variables themselves, or inappropriate achievement tests.

In summary, observational research on cognitive operations in higher education classrooms has been based on concepts of behavior used for many years in other contexts. Acceptance of dichotomies such as higher- and lower-level questions, and convergent and divergent thought, has been accompanied by inconsistencies among the precise definitions of those terms, so that the search for an accumulation of knowledge involving them is hazardous. Except for the work of Andrews (1980), there is little evidence of concern with refining concepts relevant to the cognitive facet of classroom behavior.

As in other contexts of education, it seems that lower-level and convergent types of cognitive operations are predominant in higher education. Demands upon memorizing factual information are more apparent than demands for the complex intellectual processing of information and conventional answers seem more the norm than new and unusual ones. The balance is not, however, impervious to influence, for it seems that the cognitive quality of classrooms may be dependent upon the types of instructional materials used. For example, inquiry-oriented laboratory exercises were found to be accompanied by larger proportions of higher cognitive categories in the verbal exchanges during laboratory classes (Hegarty, 1978). Furthermore, the evidence suggests that teachers have the power to vary the intellectual climate of classrooms by asking questions that stimulate desired types of responses by students. The matter is not uncomplicated, however, and attempts to manipulate the cognitive processes of classrooms sometimes have undesirable side effects. As Hegarty implied, teachers pressed into unfamiliar roles involving higher-level processes rather than lower-level ones might respond by escaping from the presence of their students, and as Andrews (1980) found, some attempts by teachers to vary the level of thought lead to vagueness, inconsistency, and confusion. Overcoming such problems is a challenge for faculty development programs such as those discussed later in this chapter.

The findings concerning differences in cognitive processes according to type of institution and academic discipline are too few to be more than suggestive. Research that is designed to explicate the precise ways in which such variables as size or status of institution filter down to affect occurrences in classrooms is badly needed. It is to be expected that curriculum and staff development procedures and associated resources play important intermediary roles in that process. It is also an important possibility that differences in the content and structure of disciplines are manifested in the ways in which they are taught. Donald's work (1980) at McGill University in Canada is a good example of interest in this area.

It has become commonplace for researchers to report that student entry characteristics, especially prior academic ability and achievement, are more strongly associated with subsequent achievements than processes exhibited in classrooms. Gage (1978) has argued that such findings should be expected and should not be used to denigrate the value of teaching, or research on process–product relationships, for such presage variables as prior achievement are themselves likely to represent the cumulative effects of teaching over many years, especially by the time students enter higher education. The few studies that have investigated relationships between cognitive processes and student achievement in higher education have produced inconsistent results and do not permit a conclusion to be reached. Similarly, relationships between cognitive processes and other product variables, such as students' study behaviors and evaluations of teaching, have only been explored in one or two studies and so conclusions there would also be grossly premature.

Socioemotional Qualities

The most commonly used approach to the analysis of socioemotional qualities of teaching processes in higher education contexts has involved the application of the Flanders Interaction Analysis Categories (FIAC; Amidon & Flanders, 1963) or a modification of them to analyze classroom behavior by both teachers and students.

PROCESS OCCURRENCE

Smith (1977, 1980) applied a modification of FIAC to classes conducted by 12 faculty members in the humanities, social sciences, and natural sciences in a small liberal arts college in the United States. Adequate levels of intra- and interobserver agreement were attained over the four sessions observed for each teacher. Smith found that only about 4% of class time was spent on the teacher's praising, encouraging, and using students' ideas and that student talk accounted for a total of 14% of class time. By implication, the incidence of teacher criticism was less than the incidence of teacher support.

Barnes' (1980) study of teaching in four institutions found that 48% of sequences initiated by teachers' questions contained students' responses, and that 11% contained teacher acceptance or use of students' ideas. Almost two thirds of the sequences in which there were students' responses contained no reaction from the teacher other than a resumption of lecturing.

Foster (1981) found in clinical discussion groups in medicine that teacher support (encouragement and praise) occupied approximately 4% of class time, while teacher criticism occupied less than 1% of that time. Students' responses and initiations occupied about 10% and 8% of class time, respectively. Another 24% consisted of students' reports, with teachers' lecturing (46%) and teachers' questions (7%) occupying almost all of the balance.

Baumgart (1972) used a system developed by Benne and Sheats (1948) for analyzing small group discussions into *task functions* and *group building functions*. He found that group building functions including showing solidarity, encouraging, harmonizing, and compromising comprised about 16% of task and group building functions combined, while disagreeing, showing tension, and showing antagonism accounted for a total of about 5%. Baumgart also found that in these discussions 35% of the talk was from the teachers, while 65% was by the students. Teachers did about 68% of the structuring and soliciting, but 13% and 28% of the responding and reacting, respectively. Students in this context had much more active roles than the students in New York high schools observed by Bellack and his colleagues (Bellack et al., 1966), and, appar-

ently, the students in the other contexts studied in the research reviewed in this section.

Apart from Baumgart's findings, the trend from these few studies seems to be for affectivity to play a minor role in classrooms in higher education and for students to take relatively passive parts. Baumgart's data were gathered in an institution established partly on the basis of a commitment to small group teaching in which perhaps two thirds of students' class time was spent.

CONTEXT-PROCESS RELATIONSHIPS

Barnes (1980) investigated differences according to status of course (beginning versus advanced) and discipline (humanities versus math/science) in the frequency of occurrence of the five most common questioning patterns she identified. She found that advanced courses contained patterns including teacher acceptance or use of students' ideas almost twice as often as beginning courses, and that those patterns were three times as frequent in the humanities as in the math/science disciplines.

Both Barnes (1980) and Hegarty (1979) found differences in socioemotional qualities between the institutions they compared. Hegarty (1979) found in the microbiology laboratory classes she investigated that students talked 50% more at one university than at the other and that tutors at the former university talked only half as much as at the latter. At the first university tutors talked twice as much as each student, while at the second, tutors talked seven times as much as each student. At both universities, students almost never experienced or offered verbal acceptance or criticism during the laboratory classes.

Barnes found that 51% of teachers' questioning sequences contained students' responses in the two large universities, while the corresponding figure for the two small universities was 41%. In particular, a higher percentage (21%) of those sequences in larger universities contained teacher acceptance and use of students' ideas than in smaller universities (9%). Barnes found only small differences according to whether the universities were public or private.

In all, very little concern with contextual effects upon socioemotional aspects of classroom behavior is apparent in research in higher education.

PRESAGE-PROCESS RELATIONSHIPS

There appears to have been a neglect of research on relationships between college teachers' characteristics, training, and other background variables, on the one hand, and the systematically observed socioemotional qualities of their classroom behavior on the other. Indeed, the only presage-process relationship concerning socioemotional aspects of classrooms located in the present review involves students. Foster (1981) found that medical students' scores on the Flexibility scale of the California Psychological Inventory (CPI) were significantly related to individual student-initiated talk, but accounted for only about 4% of the variance in the latter.

PROCESS-PROCESS RELATIONSHIPS

In a study stimulated more by an interest in a general classroom phenomenon than in the higher education context specifically,

Klein (1971) conducted an experiment concerning student influence on teacher behavior. Her study involved as subjects 24 guest lecturers in education ranging from graduate teaching assistants to full professors in six universities in the United States. Regular undergraduate and graduate students applied the experimental treatments in the 24 classes. The students were given instructions as to when to behave normally, when to engage in positive behaviors, and when to engage in negative behaviors during predetermined periods during class times with the 24 teachers. Positive behaviors including smiling, looking at the teacher, and answering questions quickly and correctly. Negative behaviors included frowning, looking out the window, talking to other students, and disagreeing with a teacher's statement. Flanders Interaction Analysis Categories (FIAC) were applied to tape recordings of the class sessions along with live observational instruments of teacher nonverbal behavior and student behavior. Klein (1971) found that the teachers appeared to change their behavior in response to changes in student behavior. She concluded that teachers engaged more in directive and criticizing behavior during periods of negative student behavior than during periods of positive or natural student behavior, and that teachers used clarification more during positive student behavior than during negative student behavior. These findings suggested to Klein that if positive teacher behavior enhances student achievement, and if students can elicit positive teacher behavior, then "students may be encouraged to assume responsibility for their own behavior and purposely help their teachers behave more effectively" (p. 419).

As reported earlier in this chapter under *process–occurrence*, Barnes (1980) found that teachers' questions elicited students' responses only about 50% of the time and that those responses were received with acceptance and/or use by the teacher much less often. It would be interesting to know whether some qualities of students' responses were more likely than others to win such support from teachers. On the basis of Klein's evidence, that would seem likely to the extent that students might even have the potential to manipulate teachers' reactions!

PROCESS–PRODUCT RELATIONSHIPS

Smith (1977) found quite large process–product correlations involving student participation, teacher encouragement, and student-to-student interaction. However, given a sample size of only 12, many of those coefficients were not statistically significant. Both student participation and teacher encouragement correlated significantly with change in critical thinking (.63 and .62), with use of analysis (.55 and .56), and with use of synthesis (.56 and .55). Student-to-student interaction correlated .57, .52, and .53 with change in critical thinking, use of interpretation, and use of application, respectively. The three socioemotional variables together must have contributed in large proportion to the canonical correlations of .96 and 1.00 reported previously between the sets of process and product variables he researched. Again, the limitations of Smith's study suggest that caution is needed in accepting and interpreting these results.

Foster's (1981) study of clinical discussion groups in medicine found that the variables of classroom verbal behavior including student response and initiation, and teacher support

and criticism, made negligible contributions to variance in the cognitive outcome measures of medical achievement and post-test critical thinking ability, compared with the contribution of students' entry performance and pretest critical thinking ability. It would indeed have been surprising if that had not been the case, given that both outcomes were measured with alternative forms of instruments used to measure cognitive attributes on entry and the two forms of each test were probably designed to maximize the correlation between scores obtained on them.

Kounin (1970) reported a study of the phenomenon of "the ripple effect" arising from his informal observations of the effect on the audience of his reprimanding a student who was reading a newspaper during a lecture he was giving in a course in mental hygiene. As well as the target student ceasing to read the newspaper, Kounin (1970) noticed dramatic effects on the others:

> Side glances to others ceased, whispers stopped, eyes went from windows or the instructor to notebooks on the desks. The silence was heavy, as if the students were closing out the classroom and escaping to the safety of a notebook. I believe that if I had sneezed they would have written the sound in their notes.... Why were they so affected by an action of the instructor that wasn't even directed at them? (pp. 1–2)

In an experiment stimulated by the incident, two instructors, each teaching two classes in education (a total of four classes) administered a "threatening desist" in one of their classes and a "supportive desist" in the other, in each case to a "student-stooge" who came very late by arrangement with the experimenter. Checks on whether the experimental manipulation "took" confirmed that students were well aware of the two different types of reprimand ($p < .001$). With data gathered by questionnaires administered before and after each lecture, Kounin found that students' ratings of the instructors' competence, likability, nonauthoritarianism, and fairness, and their own freedom to communicate about themselves to the instructor, tended to decrease in every class where threatening desists had been applied. The same was found for supportive desists except for one of the two classes on likability and the two classes on fairness where ratings tended to increase. He also found that decreases in ratings following threatening desists were significantly greater, or nearly so, than those following supportive desists for 8 of the 10 comparisons (2 desists × 5 qualities).

However, the fact that students reported being surprised that an instructor would issue a reprimand to a latecomer, and that such behavior was not typical of either instructor, discouraged Kounin from attributing the differences in ratings to the desists themselves. Instead he recommended the "advisability of using teacher style variables that are within student expectations and that have some ecological prevalence" (Kounin, 1970, p. 7). In subsequent research on matters of discipline and group management in classrooms, Kounin sought contexts other than those in higher education and found strong support for his recommendations. It remains to be seen whether the recommended observation of natural teaching contexts, and of style variables, rather than induced incidents in experimental designs, gives greater promise of understanding such phenomena in higher education.

The study by Cranton and Hillgartner (1981) also contributed findings relevant to this section, but discussion of it is postponed until later in this chapter.

In summary, research on the socioemotional facet of classroom behavior in higher education, like that on the cognitive facet, has depended greatly upon categories of behavior developed with respect to other educational contexts much earlier. The only concepts of behavior that seem to have emerged in relation to this facet from observations commenced in higher education are "desist-techniques" and "the ripple effect" generated by Kounin and his colleagues in the 1950s. Findings regarding the incidence of such categories of teacher talk as praise, acceptance, lecturing, and questioning seem not to be generalizable across the contexts represented in the research reviewed here, where percentages of teacher talk were found to range from a low of 35% (Baumgart, 1972) to a high of 86% (Smith, 1977, 1980) and percentages of student initiation varied from a high of 32% (Baumgart, 1972) to a low of 8% (Foster, 1981). The most consistent finding was that teacher praise, encouragement, and acceptance accounted for less than 5% of total class time (Smith, 1977, 1980; Foster, 1981). Perhaps one factor that needs to be taken into account in the search for generalizable findings is that teaching in higher education occurs in formats that place limits upon the occurrence of specific categories of behavior. One of the most common of these formats is the lecture, in relation to which it would be unusual to find little more than a token amount of verbal interaction involving such processes as praise, acceptance, and questioning. On the other hand, in the format of the small group discussion, it would be surprising if student talk did not account for a sizeable proportion of the time. It would seem that Smith's (1977, 1980) research was conducted within a predominantly lecture format. Baumgart (1972) and Foster (1981), on the other hand, investigated formats that were explicitly small group discussions and in several respects obtained quite different findings from Smith's.

In addition to teaching formats, or methods, contextual factors seem to influence the occurrence of more specific classroom processes. If, as Barnes (1980) found, the incidence of teacher supportive behaviors is higher in advanced than in beginning courses, it could be because teachers and students know one another better in the former, and also because only less problematic students survive to advanced levels. These possibilities do not, however, explain why teacher supportiveness might be more frequent in the humanities than in the sciences (Barnes, 1980). Perhaps the explanation for that difference lies in the very basis for the distinction between those two, and the humanities do, after all, turn out to be more humanistic both in content and in personnel. That there are differences involving the socioemotional facet between institutions depending on size (Barnes, 1980) or laboratory manuals (Hegarty, 1978) again suggests the need for research into the processes by which institutional characteristics are mediated to students.

It comes as no surprise to learn that student behavior affects teacher behavior, but the idea that students might act in concert to manipulate teacher behavior is bound to startle even the most liberal college teachers. Yet Klein (1971) saw such potential in her findings. Barnes' less dramatic findings (1980) that teachers' questions often failed to evoke students' responses

leads to speculation about the qualities that might distinguish effective from ineffective questions. Andrews' research (1980), discussed previously, should prove valuable in that regard. Similarly, students' responses that win teacher acceptance are presumably different from those that do not. It would seem worthwhile to explore those differences together with data about teachers' criteria in distinguishing between the two in reacting positively or otherwise.

On the basis of Smith's findings (1977, 1980) that student participation, student-to-student interaction, and teacher encouragement correlated positively and quite strongly with both student growth in critical thinking ability and higher level study processes, college teachers might see value in increasing the occurrence of such processes in their classrooms. On the other hand, Foster (1981) found only trivial effects of variations in such processes. Limitations of both these studies have already been mentioned, so that a healthy skepticism is probably the most appropriate reaction to their results. Similarly, Kounin's evidence (1970) that students' ratings of the instructor were more negative after threatening desists than after supportive desists, while thoroughly plausible, was, in his view, flawed by the possibly confounding effect of students' expectations. That research, too, is in need of replication.

Again, there have been too few attempts to investigate relationships between socioemotional aspects of college and university classrooms and product variables to permit more than the listing of individual findings given here. It is interesting that while at lower levels of education, research on socioemotional qualities of classroom behavior has been voluminous, there has been only a handful of studies to review. It is as though the classrooms of higher education are not only inappropriate contexts in which to display such things as emotions, but that they are also inappropriate places in which to conduct research on emotions.

Clarity in Teaching

One of the most common aspects of teaching included in evaluation instruments is clarity. Most often the rater has been expected to supply his or her own definition of clarity and the specific behavioral components of the concept have not been explained. Rosenshine and Furst (1973) reported that in all five studies they located using the variable, significant relationships were found with student achievement. They were particularly impressed with the robustness of the variable because different rating instruments, different types of raters, and different times of rating had been used in measuring it. During the 1970s, some progress was made in identifying the low-inference correlates of clarity and in exploring their relationships with student achievement.

Land (1979) described five low-inference variables of teacher clarity which he named: vagueness terms; verbal mazes; specification and emphasis; clear transitions; and unexplained additional content. Vagueness terms were initially reported as a process variable in research on teaching by Hiller, Fisher, and Kaess (1969), who conducted analyses of transcripts of high school lessons given in a lecture format on topics in social studies. These researchers took the view that uncertainty upon the part of the teacher about the subject matter being taught manifested itself in the use of vague terms and phrases, such as "things," "about," "some," "probably," and "may be."

Hiller and his colleagues also developed a low inference measure of verbal fluency which was indicated by length of sentences, the appearance of commas in the transcript, and the use of "uhs," "ahs," and other hesitations. This last aspect of fluency was adopted by L. R. Smith (1977) and others in association with "verbal mazes," described as false starts, halts in speech, redundantly stated words, and tangles of words.

Specification and emphasis were defined by Land (1979) as "the presence of an explanation of how a concept was an example of the concept definition" (p. 796). The same author defined clear transitions as "the presence of such transitional terms as 'now' and 'the last item'" when the teacher was indicating that one part of a lecture was ending and another part beginning (pp. 796–797). Additional, unexplained content was defined as "extra terms that were related to the lesson but were not essential to the main idea of the lesson" (p. 797).

Land (1985) summarized research on these variables at the college level. He reviewed two process-product studies (Land & Smith, 1979a, 1979b) of mathematics classes at the college level which had experimentally manipulated the frequency of vagueness terms used by the teacher and had then sought effects on student achievement. In each case statistically significant ($p <$ .05) or near significant ($p <$ .07) negative effects on vagueness were found and the proportions of variance accounted for in unadjusted student achievement scores ranged from 2% to 8%.

Land (1985) also reviewed process–product studies at the college level of the effects of combinations of all the clarity variables described previously. Three such studies (Denham & Land, 1981; Land, 1979, 1980) found significant effects in favor of clear expositions with clarity accounting for 20%, 8%, and 6% of the variance in student achievement in psychology. Land and Smith (1981) found no significant effects in college level social studies for vagueness terms and verbal mazes combined, but Land (1981) found a significant effect for that combination accounting for 6% of the variance in favor of clarity in college level mathematics. In both studies, large effects of the clarity combination were found on students' perceptions of teacher clarity. The process variable, clarity, accounted for 59% of the variance in the product variable, student perceptions of clarity, in Land's 1981 study and 32% in Land and Smith's study (1981). That students were so sensitive to variations in clarity is evidence that the experimental treatment "took."

Land (1985) concluded his review of research on low-inference measures of clarity as follows:

> On the basis of natural classroom studies, low-inference variables of clarity can be broadly divided into those that inhibit learning (e.g. vagueness terms), and those that facilitate learning (e.g. signaling transitions). More is known about two of these variables—vagueness terms and verbal mazes—than is known about other low-inference clarity variables. Additional research in delineating other low-inference clarity variables and their effects (singularly and in combination) on student perception and achievement is needed. (p. 5410)

Land went on to point out the further need to apply the findings of such research in attempts to change teachers'

behavior and test the effectiveness of such change in enhancing student achievement.

In a study using a different approach to measuring clarity Hines, Cruickshank, and Kennedy (1982) obtained observer ratings on a cluster of 29 different low-inference variables thought to comprise clarity in teaching. In the college level mathematics classes studied, variations in clarity were found to account for 52% of the variance in mean class achievement ($p < .03$). That a single variable of teaching behavior should account for so much variance in mean class achievement is unusual and perhaps should be accepted with caution. Clarity as observed on the 29 variables was also found to be strongly related to students' perceptions of teacher clarity. Those perceptions, in turn, accounted for 28% of the variance in mean class achievement and related strongly to student satisfaction. It seemed as though student perceptions of clarity in teaching mediated the effects of observed clarity upon both student satisfaction and achievement.

As with research on teacher clarity in other settings, studies in the higher education context indicate that the clarity construct has both predictive and concurrent validity in terms of a variety of product criteria and when operationalized in different ways. The role of student perceptions in the research has been interesting. On the one hand, evidence that students are sensitive to variations in clarity establishes that experimental treatments, where applied, did "take." On the other hand, evidence of a similar kind has led to an elaboration of theory, such that student perceptions have been seen as mediating variables between the objectively present variations in teacher clarity and other product variables of student achievement and student evaluations of the teaching. The role thus accorded to student perceptions of variations in teaching has important implications for research on student evaluations of teaching and is discussed at greater length later in this chapter. The effects of teachers' use of vagueness terms and verbal mazes upon student achievement have been consistently negative. The implications of these findings for the improvement of teaching are, however, in need of research. It is not yet established whether vagueness terms and the elements of verbal mazes are language impediments that can be eliminated through training in verbal expression or whether the problems are rooted in teacher lack of mastery of subject matter, requiring more academic development. The study by Hiller (1971) suggested the latter, but there is a need for further study, preferably in higher education contexts. In the meantime, teachers in colleges and universities can be reasonably confident that students exposed to teaching that is high in clarity tend to achieve at a higher level and to evaluate that teaching more positively than students experiencing teaching that is low in clarity.

Syntheses of Teaching Behavior

Research on teaching in higher education contains at least three approaches to the identification and description of ways in which separate categories and facets of teaching behavior cohere or are synthesized into patterns. Such syntheses, if seen to typify the behavior of some teachers over time, would seem to underlie concepts such as teaching styles and roles. One approach is the application of system-based observational techniques to yield quantitative descriptive data about variations in the occurrence of different categories and facets of classroom behavior and then to explore the extent to which they form clusters (Baumgart, 1976). Another approach depends upon quantitative information about patterns of teaching behavior as perceived by teachers themselves and conveyed through self-reports (Brown, Bakhtar, & Youngman, 1982). A third approach is the ethnographic one (Cooper, 1981a, 1981b; Cooper, Henry, Korzenny, & Yelon, undated; Cooper, Orban, Henry, & Townsend, undated; Yelon, Cooper, Henry, Korzenny & Alexander, 1980). Only the first two approaches are represented in this subsection. The ethnographic approach as applied to higher education is still very much in its infancy and to date has yielded only a handful of case studies.

Baumgart obtained audiotapes of 50-minute meetings in 29 small groups led by 20 different tutors in nine undergraduate courses in education at a university in Sydney, Australia. After transcribing the tapes, Baumgart analyzed the transcripts using category systems devised by Bellack et al., (1966), Benne and Sheats (1948), and a system for coding cognitive level derived from the work of Bloom et al., (1956), Gallagher and Aschner (1963), and Taba and Elzey (1964). Data on a final set of 37 classroom behavior variables were obtained. Two different methods of cluster analysis were applied and both revealed similar patterns of tutor or group leader behavior. In each case six "behaviourally differentiated tutor roles" (Baumgart, 1976, p. 311) were identified as *Reflexive Judge, Data Input, Stage Setter, Elaborator, Probe,* and *Cognitive Engineer.*

Baumgart found that students tended to engage in lower proportions of utterances concerned with facts and opinions and higher proportions of utterances concerned with processes including translation, interpretation, and generalization when tutors were performing more the role of reflexive judge. When the role of probe was emphasized, students also engaged in a higher proportion of processes involving explanation, analysis, and synthesis. The two roles, reflexive judge and probe, also tended to attract higher student ratings of the worth of the small group discussions, although the result for probing might have been an artifact of its overlap with the reflexive judge role. Baumgart's report indicated that his typology was useful in teacher development activities through modeling, role playing, and videotape feedback.

Brown et al., (1982) focused their attention upon the styles of lecturing of 258 lecturers in two English universities in relation to subject areas, academic status, and years of experience. A 60-item self-report inventory was administered and the responses factor analyzed to generate six scales, labeled as follows: Information Giving; Structured Lecture; Purposive Lecture; Visualized Lecture; Self-Doubt Lecture; and Presentation. Cluster analysis was used to yield five clusters of lectures, each having a distinctive pattern of lecturing behavior. These five patterns are described as *Oral Lecturer, Exemplary Lecturer, Information Providers, Amorphous Lecturers,* and *Self-Doubters.*

Brown and his colleagues found a strong association among lecturing patterns and subject areas, with Oral Lecturers more common in the humanities and social sciences, Exemplaries more often found in biomedical sciences, and Information Providers and Amorphous Lecturers more frequent in science and engineering.

Length of experience was found to be unrelated to lecturing patterns, but a trend was noted for the Exemplary style to be more frequent among professors and for Information Providing and Amorphous styles to occur more among lecturers.

These two attempts to provide empirically based typologies of teaching style are quite different from each other in spite of the approach to statistical analysis common to both. They investigated two different teaching formats, the small group discussion and the lecture. One used system-based observational techniques to gather data about process variables, while the other used a self-report inventory yielding teachers' perceptions of themselves. Baumgart found evidence chiefly favoring the reflexive judge role, which students responded to with higher thought levels during the discussions themselves, and with more positive evaluations following them.

Brown and his associates found further evidence of differences in classroom processes among disciplines, raising again the question of the connection between structures of knowledge and ways of teaching. Their finding a relationship between academic status and lecturing pattern is unique in the research reviewed in this chapter and evokes several plausible interpretations. Are some teaching patterns more conducive to promotion than others? Does increased mastery of an academic discipline lead to the adoption of some teaching styles rather than others? Or, given the methodology of the study, do full professors merely see themselves differently from others, and if so, why?

The studies by Baumgart and by Brown and his colleagues demonstrate the potential value of research into patterns of teaching behavior in higher education. They show that such patterns can be involved importantly in several different types of relationships ranging from context-process to process-product associations. There is a need for much more research of this kind in higher education. It is especially valuable in that it provides knowledge of naturally occurring syntheses of teaching behaviors that complements knowledge about the prescriptively derived teaching methods reviewed earlier in this chapter.

Research on Evaluating and Improving Teaching

The evaluation and improvement of instruction are closely linked in research in higher education, because evaluation has been seen as an instrument for enhancing the quality of teaching. In this section, research on student evaluations of teaching is reviewed and evidence relating to their credibility and usefulness in improving teaching is emphasized. A second main concern of this section is research on other approaches to the improvement of teaching, such as small grants schemes, faculty seminars and workshops, and microteaching.

Student Evaluations of Teaching

Research in higher education in the 1970s gave particular emphasis to student evaluations of teaching. The literature on relationships between student ratings of instruction and student achievement was found to contain some hundreds of titles at the end of the decade, while comprehensive reviews of that research numbered at least a dozen (Cohen, 1981). Research concerned with other matters, including the effectiveness of feedback based on student ratings, was reviewed by Rotem and Glasman (1979), by Cohen (1980), and by Levinson-Rose and Menges (1981). Those reviews involved many additional studies.

To qualify for inclusion in this chapter, research on student evaluations of teaching should include teaching process variables in its design. However, to invoke that criterion rigorously would be to exclude most of the research conducted in this important area. Instead, some research that does not satisfy the criterion is reviewed here because it illuminates issues related to research involving teaching process variables. Research on student evaluations that includes teaching process variables is important not just because it satisfies the definition of research on teaching advanced at the beginning of this chapter. It is important mainly because it is crucial to establish just what it is specifically that students respond to when they make judgments about the worth of the teaching they experience. Presumably, student evaluations are based, at least partially, on their perceptions of the teaching they receive and, presumably, those perceptions are accurate in that they reflect the actual processes engaged in by the teachers. If these presumptions are not justified, then it is difficult to see how student evaluations can be legitimately useful except in terms of intrinsic benefits for those making them, such as in venting their spleens or expressing their pleasure.

It would be naive to expect that student evaluations would be impervious to influence also by students' characteristics and by the contexts in which they are taught. Psychological research over many decades has demonstrated clearly that personal attributes and general features of the environment do influence perceptions and judgments and there is no reason to expect that students are immune to these influences in their perceptions and evaluations of teaching. The usefulness of student evaluations does not depend on their being free of such influences, so much as in the ability to take account of them.

The several issues involved in the preceding discussion form the basis for the organization of this review of research on student evaluations of teaching in higher education. The first issues concern the relationships between teaching behaviors, on the one hand, and student perceptions and evaluations, on the other. These are process–product relationships in terms of the conceptual framework adopted in this chapter. In the course of discussing those relationships, research concerned with other types of relationships, such as between student characteristics and student evaluations (presage–product relationships) and environmental influences upon student evaluations (context–product relationships) is relevant and is summarized. The latter part of the section reviews research on the effects of feedback from student evaluations upon the improvement of teaching.

PROCESS–PRODUCT RELATIONSHIPS

Some examples of research on the sensitivity of students to variations in classroom processes was reviewed in the previous section of this chapter. Included there was the study reported by Kounin (1970) in which college students were found to be aware of experimental manipulations of threatening and non-threatening desists by teachers and to evaluate the latter accordingly. Also, there were the studies by Land (1981), Land and Smith (1981), and Hines et al. (1982) in which college students' perceptions of variations in teacher clarity were found to be positively associated with actual variations in clarity exhibited in the classroom. The study by Hines and his colleagues went one step further and demonstrated a strong relationship between student perceptions and student satisfaction. That study provided evidence along the whole chain of relationships stipulated earlier as necessary to establish the credibility of student evaluations. Variations in significant teaching processes were found related to student perceptions which were found related to student evaluations (satisfaction) and also to student achievement.

The best known investigations of student evaluations in relation to teaching processes are studies of the "Dr. Fox effect" or "educational seduction" (Abrami, Leventhal, & Perry, 1982). The first of the Dr. Fox studies was conducted by Naftulin, Ware and Donnelly (1973) who had a professional actor assume the name, Dr. Myron L. Fox, and pose as a visiting professor. The actor proceeded to lecture to three groups of experienced educators in a manner that was highly expressive but low in substantive content. The experienced educators were reported as having expressed satisfaction with the amount they had learned from the lecture, thus suggesting that expressive behavior was at least as important as content coverage in determining audience reactions, and casting doubt on the validity of audience ratings as criteria of lecture effectiveness.

Kaplan (1974) and Frey (1978) criticized the study on several grounds including lack of both internal and external validity. There followed a series of experiments in which lecturer expressiveness, content coverage, incentives to learn, and other variables were manipulated, and student ratings and learning were treated as dependent or outcome variables (Abrami, Dickens, Perry, & Leventhal, 1980; Abrami, Perry, & Leventhal, 1982; Marsh & Ware, 1982; Meier, 1977; Meier & Feldhusen, 1979; Perry, Abrami, & Leventhal, 1979; Perry, Abrami, Leventhal, & Check, 1979; Ramagli, 1979; Ramagli & Greenwood, 1980; Ware & Williams, 1975; Williams & Ware, 1976; Williams & Ware, 1977). Attempts to review and interpret such studies have been made by several authors (Frey, 1978, 1979a, 1979b; Leventhal, 1979, 1980; Leventhal, Abrami, & Perry, 1979; Marsh, 1985; McKeachie, 1979; Ware & Williams, 1979, 1980), culminating in a meta-analysis by Abrami, Leventhal, & Perry (1982). The last authors drew attention to disagreements among previous reviewers such that some concluded on the basis of the Dr. Fox studies that student ratings are invalid indicators of teacher effectiveness in enhancing student learning (e.g., Ware & Williams, 1975), while others concluded that expressiveness is an important aspect of teacher behavior which can be used to enhance student learning (e.g., Frey, 1978). Ware collaborated with Marsh (Marsh & Ware, 1982) in a reanalysis of the data from the Ware and Williams studies. A factor analysis of the original rating instrument indicated five factors or independent dimensions of the rating scores, and that instructor expressiveness seemed to affect only one factor, Instructor Enthusiasm, while content coverage seemed to affect the factor of Instructor Knowledge. Thus, it appeared that evaluations were, in fact, responsive specifically to the teaching variables manipulated, and that expressiveness was not disguising variations in content coverage, as the original results suggested.

Abrami, Leventhal, and Perry (1982) investigated main and interaction effects involving expressiveness and content coverage in relation to student ratings and achievement as criterion variables. Their results when student ratings were the criterion were as follows:

> In all [12] studies, the effect of expressiveness on summary or global ratings was significant and reasonably large (unweighted mean $\omega^2 = .285$) ...
>
> The effect of content on ratings was inconsistent and generally much smaller (unweighted mean $\omega^2 = .046$, weighted mean $\omega^2 = .038$) than the expressiveness effect, about one sixth the size or less. Smaller still was the interaction effect of expressiveness and content on ratings (unweighted mean $\omega^2 = .016$) .... (p. 452)

In a study not conducted within the Dr. Fox tradition, and not included in the Abrami, Leventhal, and Perry (1982) meta-analysis, Andersen and Withrow (1981) investigated the effects of variations in nonverbal expressiveness upon affective, behavioral, and cognitive learnings of 299 undergraduate students in a lower-division speech communication course at a large eastern U.S. university. Videotaped lectures were used to present high, medium, and low levels of nonverbal expressiveness. Significant effects were found on affective criteria with variations in nonverbal expressiveness accounting for 9%, 3%, and 6%, respectively, of the variance in students' ratings of lecturer sociability, students' attitudes toward the lecture, and students' attitudes toward the videotape. No significant or sizeable effects were found on the likelihood of students' engaging in the suggested communication strategies or of attending another lecture.

Another study of the validity of student evaluations as judged by the extent to which they relate to behavior actually engaged in by teachers in normal classroom conditions was conducted by Cranton and Hillgartner (1981), who explored this matter with 28 professors from several disciplines, using Shulman's (1975) modification of the FIAC system to observe teaching behavior. The professors were all involved in teacher improvement activities. The authors found that three general areas of teacher behavior were more closely related than others to students' ratings. They summarized their results as follows:

> (1) When instructors spent time structuring classes and explaining relationships, students gave higher ratings on logical organization items. (2) When professors praised student behavior, asked questions and clarified or elaborated on student responses, ratings on the effectiveness of discussion leading were higher. (3) When instructor time was spent in discussions, praising student behavior, and silence (waiting for answers), students tended to rate the classroom atmosphere as being one which encourages learning. (p. 73)

This type of information is not only evidence regarding an important aspect of the credibility of student ratings, but is also potentially useful to teachers wanting to know which aspects of their behavior are producing high or low student ratings.

Every one of the preceding studies found evidence that student evaluations were responsive to variations in teaching processes although the relationships were generally small to moderate in size and varied depending upon which teaching process was manipulated or observed and which attribute of the teaching was rated. Variations in the relationships give rise to the possibility that some of the teaching processes to which students are sensitive are unimportant while some to which they are insensitive are important. The Dr. Fox studies are also relevant to this issue which became one of the focal points of the meta-analysis by Abrami, Levanthal, and Perry (1982). As mentioned previously, those authors reported that student evaluations were much more responsive to variations in expressiveness than to variations in content coverage. The question then raised was: How important are expressiveness and content coverage for student achievement?

When student achievement was the criterion, Abrami, Leventhal, and Perry (1982) obtained results which they reported as follows:

> In contrast to the substantial impact of expressiveness on ratings, the effect of expressiveness on achievement was insignificant in 5 of 10 analyses, on average accounting for only 4 percent of the achievement variance. The effect of content on achievement was significant in all studies except [one].... On average, content accounted for a sizeable amount of achievement variance (unweighted mean $\omega^2 = .158$). The Expressiveness × Content interaction reached significance in only one study. ... where it accounted for less than 2 percent of the achievement variance. (p. 454)

Andersen and Withrow (1981) also investigated the effects of variations in expressiveness upon student achievement in terms of two tests of cognitive learnings and found no significant effects. In all, the results of this study were consistent with the results of the Abrami, Leventhal and Perry (1982) meta-analyses. Expressiveness was again found to be more effective in relation to students' rating of instruction than in relation to cognitive achievement.

After concluding that expressiveness had been shown to have a sizeable impact on student ratings of instruction but not on achievement, while the reverse applied for content coverage, Abrami, Leventhal, and Perry (1982) discussed limitations arising from the ways in which those two process variables had been presented in the Dr. Fox experiments. In particular, it was pointed out that the levels of expressiveness and content coverage as manipulated could not be held to be representative of the variations in expressiveness and content coverage that would be found in field studies. Therefore, it was argued, findings of the differential effects of the experimental treatments involving those variables cannot be assumed to represent the findings of effects that might be found in the field. The Dr. Fox studies were incapable, according to the authors, of telling much about the validity of student ratings as predictors of student achievement. The authors went on to advocate field research on the variations in occurrence of expressiveness, content coverage, and other characteristics.

The latter type of research would require the development of observational instruments to permit the identification and measurement of expressiveness and content coverage as they occur in the field. It would be important that such instruments be developed on the basis of the definitions and examples of such concepts of teaching behavior as have been provided in the experimental studies. Definitions of expressiveness presented in the studies mentioned in this chapter contain qualities that vary considerably in the degree of inference that would be required by an observer trying to detect their presence in a lecture. Ware's definition (1974) was the only one in the Dr. Fox experiments that included the terms *dynamism, emotional appeal, seduction,* and *stimulation.* Meier and Feldhusen (1979) alone referred to looking at notes, and smiles. Perry, Abrami, Leventhal, and Check (1979) made the only reference to eye contact. The most agreed upon ingredients of expressiveness were charisma, enthusiasm, friendliness, vocal inflection, humor, and physical movement, all of which are highly inferential concepts which probably subsume the more specific behaviors such as smiling, looking at notes, and making eye contact. Detailed analyses of the specific behaviors performed in different sets of videotapes would require the development of an observational system which could then prove useful in research on expressiveness in naturalistic field settings.

Content coverage, or "content density" as it was called by Meier and Feldhusen (1979, p. 341),was more specifically defined in the studies reviewed. In the Ware and Williams (1975) tapes, the high-content treatment contained 26 different teaching points. The medium-content and low-content treatments contained 14 and 4 points, respectively. Length of treatment was kept uniform by the insertion of unrelated examples, meaningless utterances, and circular discussion. Similar procedures were employed in the black-and-white and color videotapes prepared by Perry, Abrami, and Leventhal (1979). Variations in content, however, consist not only in the number of propositions, but also in levels of abstraction, degree of organization, and so on. It would seem important that these aspects also be investigated.

The Ware and Williams (1975) videotaped lectures were on "The Biochemistry of Learning" and were prepared for an introductory course in psychology. The black-and-white videotapes used by Perry, Abrami, and Leventhal (1979) were on impression formation and were also directed toward students in an introductory course in psychology. The color videotapes used in the second experiment by Perry, Abrami, Leventhal, and Check (1979) were on sex roles and stereotyping and they, too, were prepared for use in an introductory course in psychology. Clearly, before the relative influence of content coverage upon student outcomes is to be known, there is need for research in other disciplines than psychology.

There still remains the matter of the effects of extraneous variables upon student evaluations. Commonly expressed views are that students do not have the mastery of subject matter required to evaluate the content of instruction, that students are biased by extraneous factors such as the sex and popularity of the instructor, and that students are more negative toward more demanding courses. Marsh (1985) found weak or mixed results for claims that course level, class size, nature of discipline, instructor sex and rank, and student sex and personality influenced student ratings. He did find tendencies for classes receiving or expecting higher grades, having higher interest in the subject, and enrolled in elective rather than compulsory courses to give more positive ratings, but found ambiguities in the interpretations that might be made of those results. For example, the association between expected or actual grade and ratings might have indicated either grading leniency or superior learning. Interestingly enough, evidence did confirm an association between the workload or difficulty of a course and student ratings. However, it was a positive relationship, and so contradicted the common expectation.

Abrami, Leventhal, and Perry (1982) included in their meta-analysis tests to see whether relationships between expressiveness and/or content coverage and student evaluations and achievement were affected by extraneous factors. They found that the effects of the following were minimal: monetary or experimental credit incentives, second exposure to the lecturer, opportunity for study, stated purposes of the evaluation, instructor reputation, student personality characteristics, and instructor grading standards. Other reviewers of the literature on student evaluations include Costin, Greenough, and Menges, (1971); Kulik and McKeachie (1975); McKeachie (1979); and Menges (1979); all of whom concluded that student evaluations were not unduly affected by extraneous elements.

Finally, there is the question of the relationship between student evaluations of instruction and student achievement. Cohen's meta-analysis (1981) of research on relationships between student ratings of instruction and student achievement revealed mean correlations between student achievement and overall ratings of courses and teachers of .47 and .43, respectively. Although the correlation with student achievement tended to be higher if student ratings were obtained after students knew their grades in the course, Cohen concluded that "student ratings of instruction are a valid index of instructional effectiveness" (p. 305).

On balance, it seems from the research reviewed here that students are able to perceive variations in teaching processes, and that the latter, more than extraneous elements, affect student evaluations of teaching. There is also evidence that teaching processes vary in the size of their effects upon student evaluations. The possibility that the latter are unduly affected by unimportant teaching processes has not been adequately researched. Research on teaching in higher education provides little indication of which are important and unimportant teaching processes. Finally, student evaluations have been found generally to have moderate effects upon student achievement. It now remains to be seen whether or not student evaluations can serve as a basis for the improvement of teaching.

USEFULNESS OF STUDENT EVALUATIONS IN IMPROVING TEACHING

Student evaluations of instruction are useful to the extent that they assist in improving teaching, lead to better informed decisions about the careers of personnel, and help students to make suitable choices of courses and teachers. A fourth purpose, to serve as a variable in research on teaching, is not so often recognized and is usually neglected as a criterion for evaluating the usefulness of student ratings. The earlier sections of this chapter contain references to studies in which student ratings were found useful for this fourth purpose.

If feedback on student evaluations leads to the improvement of teaching, then presumably it does so by changing the behavior of the teachers concerned in ways that are consistent with criteria of teaching effectiveness. Thus, the question of the potential of student evaluations to improve teaching is analyzable into two separate questions: Do student evaluations bring about change in teaching processes? and Are the changes consistent with criteria of teaching effectiveness? To answer these questions, two types of studies would be required. First, there would be presage–process studies, in which feedback on student evaluations would be used as independent variables and teaching processes would be the dependent variables. Second, there would be process–product studies in which the processes shown to be changed by feedback on student evaluations would be used as independent variables and criteria of teaching effectiveness, such as subsequent student evaluations, and student achievement, would be dependent variables. Research on the usefulness of student evaluations has not been of those types, however, but has combined the two questions by omitting process variables in what are essentially presage–product studies. That is, the research has been concerned mainly with providing teachers with feedback on student evaluations at one point in time, and then exploring their relationships with second measures of students' evaluations, or student achievement measures, obtained at some later point, such as the end of the course. The reviews by Rotem and Glasman (1979); Abrami, Leventhal, and Perry (1979); Cohen (1980); and Levinson-Rose and Menges (1981) were almost exclusively conducted upon research of the presage–product type.

Rotem and Glasman (1979) concluded "that feedback from student ratings . . . does not seem to be effective for the purpose of improving the performance of university teachers" (p. 507). Nevertheless, those reviewers did not recommend dispensing with feedback from students because they thought it might be rendered more effective in the future. Abrami, Leventhal, and Perry (1979) concluded that feedback from student ratings helped some instructors to improve their subsequent student ratings, but the effect was not reliable and was of unknown size. Cohen's meta-analysis (1980) led him to conclude that feedback from student ratings had made a "modest but significant contribution to the improvement of college teaching" (p. 336). Students' end-of-course ratings of teachers' skills and of provision of feedback to students were found to increase moderately (average effect sizes .47 and .40, respectively) after teachers were informed of the results of midterm students' ratings. Students' overall ratings also increased moderately (effect size .38). All three increases were statistically significant. Students whose instructors received midterm feedback also tended to rate their own learning higher and to express more favorable attitudes toward the subject matter at the end of the course. Effects of midterm feedback were found to be much larger if it was augmented with consultation and the like.

Levinson-Rose and Menges (1981) reached similar conclusions about the importance of consultation in association with feedback on student evaluations. They also found that such feedback is likely to be more effective for teachers whose students' ratings are less favorable than their self-ratings. Such teachers were seen to be especially suitable for the investment of consultants' efforts.

None of the studies reviewed by Levinson-Rose and Menges

(1981) provided direct evidence of changes in teaching in response to feedback from students, and only five used self-reports concerning changes from teachers. Without exploration of intermediate steps in a theoretically derived process by which feedback from students might produce change that is improvement, research on the utility of student evaluations for that purpose is incomplete. Research on the processes by which feedback results in changes in teaching which in turn affect subsequent student ratings and achievement is needed to enhance understanding of teaching and learning associations in higher education.

In all, the evidence concerning the credibility of student evaluations of teaching has more often been based on associations with actual teaching processes than has the evidence of the usefulness of student evaluations in improving instruction. Indeed, there is very little research evidence on the usefulness of student evaluations in improving any of the processes thought to benefit from them. Coleman and McKeachie (1981) found some evidence that student evaluations affect students' choices of courses, but whether they improve those choices and whether they affect and improve decisions made about teaching personnel are largely unresearched issues in higher education. Much more research into the classroom processes to which students respond in forming their evaluations is needed. Until, through such research, much more is known about student evaluations, their use as bases for decisions in education needs to be cautious. Some of the issues involving student evaluations are especially complex and, it seems, cannot be resolved solely on the basis of empirical research. For example, the nonempirical issues of whether students should control the curricula of higher education or appointments of faculty are probably independent of research on the validity of student evaluations and their usefulness in improving teaching.

Other Attempts to Improve Instruction

Levinson-Rose and Menges (1981) reviewed several other approaches to the improvement of teaching in higher education. They were: grants for faculty development projects; workshops and seminars; microteaching and minicourses; and concept-based training using protocols of teaching incidents.

Grants to support development projects, commonly known as "small grants," were found in 58% of the 756 institutions surveyed by Centra (1978). These grants are usually awarded competitively, paralleling grants awarded in support of research, and are seen as incentives promoting interest in teaching. Apparently they are different from research grants at the evaluation and reporting stages because Levinson-Rose and Menges could find only one report of a study of the effectiveness of such grant schemes in improving teaching. Presumably, many reports on such projects do not include data on improving teaching. The evidence of that one study (Kozma, 1978) was that even quite small grants can encourage increase in the use of instructional innovations by university teachers.

Studies of the effectiveness of workshops and seminars in producing improvements in teaching have usually used graduate teaching assistants as subjects and have been directed toward either attitude change or skill development (Levinson-Rose & Menges, 1981). Both Goldman (1978) and Graham (1971) found evidence consistent with the hypothesis that workshops produced desired affective changes in teachers.

Where the focus of workshops and seminars was on skill development, Levinson-Rose and Menges (1981) concluded that 24 of 28 studies produced evidence supporting their effectiveness. Criteria of effectiveness employed in the studies included student ratings, ratings by trained observers, and student learning. The likelihood that evidence supported the intervention appeared unrelated to the type of criterion used. Although only one of the studies (Bray & Howard, 1980) had the design characteristics required for Levinson-Rose and Menges to have high confidence in the results, the research provides grounds for optimism that skill-oriented seminars not only influence teaching behavior in desired directions, but also through that influence, increase student learning and affect students' opinions of the teaching. The reviewers, in reaching similar conclusions, raised the issue of compulsory/voluntary participation in faculty development workshops and its implications for generalizability of research findings. Results of research conducted on interventions in which subjects are obliged to participate may not apply when participation in such activities is voluntary.

In addition to the research on workshops and seminars reviewed by Levinson-Rose and Menges (1981), there has been research on the effectiveness of whole courses or programs of learning activities, often organized in the workshop format. Among the best known of these is the research done by a team at Simon Fraser University in Vancouver (Martin, Marx, Hasell, & Ellis, 1978; Marx, Martin, Ellis, & Hasell, 1978; Marx, Ellis, & Martin, 1979). The Teaching Assistant Training Program consisted of 15 hours of instruction for 3 hours on each of 5 evenings. Its objectives were to teach participants five major areas of educational content, skills, and attitudes, as follows: (a) the incorporation of principles of learning in the design of instruction; (b) the development and use of behavioral objectives in instruction; (c) the measurement of learning; (d) effective discussion group or laboratory sessions; (e) ethical and moral dilemmas in teaching.

Four groups of teaching assistants were involved in the program, while a fifth group became the control group. Interview and questionnaire data were obtained from the participants as well as their students' perceptions, attitudes, ratings, and grades. The evaluation prompted the following conclusions among others, by the authors: (a) participants were perceived by their students to be better tutorial leaders and more willing to improve their teaching; (b) in terms of student achievement, participation for the 15 hours of the program was at least equivalent in instructional value to three semesters' teaching experience without training. Those who are responsible for organizing and conducting such training programs will find solace in the suggestion that their efforts are cost effective in comparison with the "school of hard knocks."

Levinson-Rose and Menges (1981) located only three studies of microteaching in higher education (Johnson, 1977; Perlberg, Peri, Wienreb, Nitzan & Shimron, 1972; Perry, Leventhal, & Abrami, 1979). The first two found evidence that participation in microteaching programs produced desired changes in be-havior, while the third found that instructors initially rated as highly effective had students who rated them higher and who achieved higher after the instructors participated in a modified microteaching program. No changes were observed for instructors initially rated as low-effective. More recently, Sharp (1981) reported that viewing videotaped models of lecturing skills increased short-term performance of those skills in a microteaching context, and Brown (1980) found that teachers who participated in a microteaching program on skills in explaining viewed the experience favorably and were rated favorably by trained observers on changes in the quality of their explanations.

One approach to the improvement of teaching that Levinson-Rose and Menges (1981) regarded as particularly relevant was training in the development of concepts of teaching and learning appropriate to higher education. Concept-based training is not so much concerned with enhancing repertoires of teaching behavior as is microteaching. Rather, it aims to enhance teachers' powers of thought concerning teaching, thus increasing their ability to plan, hypothesize about, make decisions about, and monitor their own teaching. The attempt by Taylor-Way (1981) at Cornell University to use the techniques of Interpersonal Process Recall (Kagan, 1973, 1975) is an example of this approach. In it teachers used microteaching contexts to study covert aspects of their teaching, with emphasis upon expression of thoughts and feelings about teaching, and the development of concepts and principles. Taylor-Way reported favorably upon the conceptual development and refinement observed in a case-study approach to the evaluation of the program.

The study by Aubrecht (1978) also involved concept development and included a case study approach, but it was based on a formal first stage in which teachers were introduced to Bellack's (Bellack et al., 1966) categories for observing classroom behavior. Aubrecht found that teachers who were provided with feedback in the form of trained observer codings of their behavior and who received unconditional support from a consultant for changes suggested by themselves subsequently behaved differently from a control group in many of the pedagogical moves and substantive–logical operations performed.

In all, those responsible for faculty development in universities and colleges might derive encouragement from the research just reviewed. So far, there is no indication of a one best way to improve teaching in higher education. On the contrary, the small amount of research that has been conducted suggests that there is a variety of effective ways and, therefore, that combined approaches have a good chance of capitalizing on the strengths of each. Research to come might explore such combinations.

In conclusion, it might be argued that research is needed that inquires into the attributes of teachers that affect their potential to benefit from teaching improvement efforts. Beliefs and attitudes toward teaching and teacher education should be profitable avenues for investigation here if research such as that by Brown and Daines (1981) and Genn (1982) is any guide. Furthermore, Menges (1980) has suggested a theoretical model, a "theory of reasoned action" (p. 5) capable of accommodating such variables along with others such as feedback and teaching behavior.

Implications for Future Research and Practice

Research on teaching in higher education as reviewed in this chapter has revealed the following strengths and weaknesses:

1. The innovatory methods of teaching discussed have in most cases been found slightly superior to conventional teaching methods, and in one case, the Keller Plan, considerably superior. Colleges and universities can be reasonably confident that careful implementation of these innovations can proceed with little risk of harm to students and with some promise of benefit. Cost-effectiveness information is however, lacking, except in the few cases where savings in student time have been found.

2. Recently applied techniques for synthesizing research findings have proved invaluable in the preparation of this chapter. Not only have they contributed greatly to knowledge about cumulative findings of research; they have also led to the identification of gaps in research and to the development of category systems that have proved useful in describing and grouping studies. Those category systems will also prove useful in designing future research. Furthermore, meta-analysis has made possible the exploration of design and contextual influences upon research findings. In doing this, meta-analyses have had to rely on fortuitously occurring variations across studies. It is hoped that in the future such variations will more often be planned.

3. There has been an increase in concern with the nature of teaching behavior as revealed through the application of observational techniques in naturalistic settings. This approach promises to enhance knowledge and understanding of teaching in higher education contexts, whether innovative or conventional. So far, concepts of behavior underlying those observations have been highly derivative of concepts used for many years at lower levels of education. Concepts that are especially applicable in higher education need to be developed and applied. There has been an almost total neglect of student academic learning behavior, both in and out of class sessions, in this research. Research at lower levels of education suggests that this is a profitable area of investigation.

4. There is now some evidence of the credibility of student evaluations of teaching in higher education in terms of their sensitivity to known variations in teaching processes. Much more research is needed to demonstrate ways in which student evaluations can be put to effective use in improving teaching. In particular, research on the effects of feedback from student ratings upon change in teaching processes is needed.

5. There is some cause for confidence that techniques for inducing desired changes in teaching behavior are effective. However, there has been little research on teaching skills in higher education, and so the efforts of faculty development agents are much in need of support from that quarter. The roles played by teachers' beliefs, values, and attitudes toward teaching and learning need to be explored in the context of teaching improvement efforts.

6. The dominant paradigm underlying research on teaching in higher education has been the process-product one. In most cases, however, the process part has been assumed on the basis of prescriptive definitions, or rated by untrained observers, rather than documented through careful observation. The process-product paradigm is limiting in the types of knowledge about teaching and learning that can be generated within it. Research on teaching in higher education might do well to explore alternative paradigms as presented in the chapter by Shulman in this volume. In particular, there would seem to be value in a paradigm of presage, context, process, and product variables elaborated so as to accommodate teacher thinking and valuing as well as student academic learning processes.

Perhaps the most surprising aspect of research on teaching in higher education is that its contribution to the improvement of teaching has not been evaluated. Studies of dissemination and diffusion of research on teaching at this level are almost nonexistent and little is known of the extent to which faculty development agencies have been able to use such research in designing and implementing their programs. It is to be expected that the next decade will see an increase in concern with the usefulness of research not only in enhancing knowledge and understanding of teaching, but also in improving it.

REFERENCES

Abrami, P. C., Dickens, W. J., Perry, R. P., & Leventhal, L. (1980). Do teacher standards for assigning grades affect student evaluations of instruction? *Journal of Educational Psychology, 72,* 107–118.

Abrami, P. C., Leventhal, L., & Perry, R. P. (1979). *Can feedback from student ratings help improve college teaching?* Paper presented at the meeting of the Fifth International Conference on Improving University Teaching, London.

Abrami, P. C., Leventhal, L., & Perry, R. P. (1982). Educational seduction. *Review of Educational Research, 52,* 446–464.

Abrami, P. C., Perry, R. P., & Leventhal, L. (1982). The relationship between student personality characteristics, teacher ratings, and student achievement. *Journal of Educational Psychology, 74,* 111–125.

Amidon, E. J., & Flanders, N. (1963). *The role of the teacher in the classroom.* Minneapolis, MN: Amidon and Associates.

Andersen, J. F., & Withrow, J. G. (1981). The impact of lecturer nonverbal expressiveness on improving mediated instruction. *Communication Education, 30,* 342–353.

Andrews, J. D. (1980). The verbal structure of teacher questions: Its impact on class discussion. *POD Quarterly, 2,* 130–163.

Aubrecht, J. D. (1978). Teacher effectiveness: Self-determined change. *American Journal of Physics, 46,* 324–328.

Barnes, C. P. (1980, April). *Questioning: The untapped resource.* Paper presented at the annual meeting of the American Educational Research Association, Boston.

Baumgart, N. L. (1972). *A study of verbal interaction in university tutorials.* Unpublished doctoral dissertation, Macquarie University, Sydney, Australia.

Baumgart, N. L. (1976). Verbal interaction in university tutorials. *Higher Education, 5,* 301–317.

Bellack, A. A., Kliebard, H. M., Hyman, R. T., & Smith, F. L. Jr. (1966). *The language of the classroom.* New York: Teachers College Press.

Benne, K. D., Sheats, P. (1948). Functional roles of group members. *Journal of Social Issues, 4,* 42–47.

Bloom, B. S. (1968). Learning for mastery. *Evaluation Comment, 1*(2).

Bloom, B. S., Engelhart, M. D., Furst, E. J., Hill, W. H., & Krathwohl, D. R. (Eds.). (1956). *Taxonomy of educational objectives: The classification of education goals, handbook I: The cognitive domain.* New York: David McKay.

Bray, J. H., & Howard, G. S. (1980). Methodological considerations in the evaluation of a teacher-training program. *Journal of Educational Psychology, 72*, 62–70.

Brown, G. A. (1980). *Explaining: Studies from the higher education context.* Final Report to the Social Science Research Council. University of Nottingham, England.

Brown, G. A., Bakhtar, M., & Youngman, M. B. (1982). *Toward a typology of lecturing styles.* University of Nottingham, England.

Brown, G. A., & Daines, J. M. (1981). Can explaining be learnt? Some lecturers' views. *Higher Education, 10*, 573–580.

Centra, J. A. (1978). Faculty development in higher education. *Teachers College Record, 80*, 188–201.

Chickering, A. (1972). Undergraduate academic experience. *Journal of Educational Psychology, 63*, 134–143.

Cohen, J. (1969). *Statistical power analysis for the behavioral sciences.* New York: Academic Press.

Cohen, P. A. (1980). Effectiveness of student-rating feedback for improving college instruction: A meta-analysis of findings. *Research in Higher Education, 13*, 321–341.

Cohen, P. A. (1981). Student ratings of instruction and student achievement: A meta-analysis of multisection validity studies. *Review of Educational Research, 51*, 281–309.

Cohen, P. A., Ebeling, B. J., & Kulik, J. A. (1981). A meta-analysis of outcome studies of visual-based instruction. *Educational Communication and Technology, 29*, 26–36.

Coleman, J., & McKeachie, W. J. (1981). Effects of instructor course evaluations on student course selections. *Journal of Educational Psychology, 73*, 224–226.

Cooper, C. R. (1981a). Different ways of being a teacher: An ethnographic study of a college instructor's academic and social roles in the classroom. *Journal of Classroom Interaction, 16*, 27–37.

Cooper, C. R. (1981b). *An ethnographic study of teaching style.* Paper presented at the Midwest-Regional Conference on Qualitative Research in Education, Kent State University, Kent, Ohio.

Cooper, C. R., Henry, R., Korzenny, S., & Yelon, S. (undated). *Procedures for studying effective college instruction.* Unpublished manuscript, Michigan State University, Learning and Evaluation Service.

Cooper, C. R., Orban, D., Henry, R., & Townsend, J. (undated). *Teaching and storytelling: An ethnographic study of the instructional process in a college classroom.* Unpublished manuscript, Michigan State University, Learning and Evaluation Service.

Costin, F., Greenough, W. T., & Menges, R. J. (1971). Student ratings of college teaching: Reliability, validity, and usefulness. *Review of Educational Research, 41*, 511–535.

Cranton, P. A., & Hillgartner, W. (1981). The relationships between student ratings and instructor behavior: Implications for improving teaching. *Canadian Journal of Higher Education, 11*, 73–81.

Daniel, J. S., Stroud, M. A., & Thompson, J. R. (Eds.). (1982). *Learning at a distance: A world perspective.* Edmonton: Athabasca University/International Council for Correspondence Education.

Denham, M. A., & Land, M. L. (1981). Research brief Effect of teacher verbal fluency and clarity on student achievement. *Technical Teachers Journal of Education, 8*, 227–229.

Donald, J. G. (1980). *Structures of knowledge and implications for teaching.* Vancouver: Centre for the Improvement of Teaching, University of British Columbia.

Dunkin, M. J., & Biddle, B. J. (1974). *The study of teaching.* New York: Holt, Rinehart & Winston.

Foster, P. J. (1981). Clinical discussion groups: Verbal participation and outcomes. *Journal of Medical Education, 56*, 831–838.

Frey, P. W. (1978). A two-dimensional analysis of student ratings of instruction. *Research in Higher Education, 9*, 60–91.

Frey, P. W. (1979a). The Dr. Fox effect and its implications. *Instructional Evaluation, 3*, 1–5.

Frey, P. W. (1979b). Dr. Fox revisited. *Instructional Evaluation, 4*, 6–12.

Gage, N. L. (Ed.). (1983). *Handbook of research on teaching.* Chicago: Rand McNally.

Gage, N. L. (1978). *The scientific "basis" of the art of teaching.* New York: Teachers College Press.

Gallagher, J. J., & Aschner, M. J. (1963). A preliminary report on analyses of classroom interaction. *Merrill-Palmer Quarterly of Behavior and Development, 9*, 183–195.

Genn, J. M. (1982, May). *The receptivity of Australian university teachers towards academic staff development programs focusing on the teaching role.* Paper presented at the annual meeting of the Higher Education Research and Development Society of Australasia, Sydney, Australia.

Glass, G. V. (1976). Primary, secondary, and meta-analysis of research. *Educational Researcher, 5*, 3–8.

Goldman, J. A. (1978). Effects of a faculty development workshop upon self-actualization. *Education, 98*, 254–258.

Goldschmid, B., & Goldschmid, M. L. (1976). Peer teaching in higher education: A review. *Higher Education, 5*, 9–33.

Graham, M. W. (1971). Development of an inservice program for geology teaching assistants to reduce role conflict and to improve skills. Unpublished doctoral dissertation, Ohio State University, Columbus, OH.

Guilford, J. P. (1956). The structure of the intellect. *Psychological Bulletin, 53*, 267–293.

Hegarty, E. H. (1978). Levels of scientific enquiry in university science laboratory classes: Implications for curriculum deliberations. *Research in Science Education, 8*, 45–57.

Hegarty, E. H. (1979). *The role of laboratory work in teaching microbiology at university level.* Unpublished doctoral dissertation, University of New South Wales, Sydney, Australia.

Hiller, J. H. (1971). Verbal response indicators of conceptual vagueness. *America Educational Research Journal, 8*, 151–161.

Hiller, J. H., Fisher, G. A., & Kaess, W. (1969). A computer investigation of verbal characteristics of effective classroom lecturing. *American Educational Research Journal, 6*, 661–675.

Hines, C. V., Cruickshank, D. R., & Kennedy, J. J. (1982, March). *Measures of teacher clarity and their relationships to student achievement and satisfaction.* Paper presented at the annual meeting of the American Educational Research Association, New York.

Holmberg, B. (1982). *Recent research into distance education.* Hagen, F. R. Germany: Fern Universitat.

Johnson, G. R. (1977). Enhancing community/junior college professors' questioning strategies and interaction with students. *Community/Junior College Research Quarterly, 2*, 47–54.

Johnson, R. H., & Lobb, M. D. (1959). completes three-year study of staffing, changing class size, programming, and scheduling. *National Association of Secondary School Principals Bulletin, 43*, 57–78.

Kagan, N. (1973). Can technology help us toward reliability in influencing human interaction? *Educational Technology, 13*, 44–51.

Kagan, N. (1975). *Interpersonal Process Recall — a method for influencing human interaction.* Michigan State University, Department of Counseling, Personal Services and Educational Psychology, East Lansing, MI.

Kaplan, R. M. (1974). Reflections on the Dr. Fox paradigm. *Journal of Medical Education, 49*, 310–312.

Keller, F. S. (1968). "Good-bye teacher . . ." *Journal of Applied Behavior Analysis, 1*, 79–89.

Klein, S. S. (1971). Student influence on teacher behavior. *American Educational Research Journal, 8*, 403–421.

Kounin, J. S. (1970). *Discipline and group management in classrooms.* New York: Holt, Rinehart & Winston.

Kozma, R. B. (1978). Faculty development and the adoption and diffusion of classroom innovations. *Journal of Higher Education, 49*, 438–449.

Kulik, J. A., Cohen, P. A., & Ebeling, B. J. (1980). Effectiveness of programmed instruction in higher education: A meta-analysis of findings. *Educational Evaluation and Policy Analysis, 2*, 51–64.

Kulik, J. A., Jaksa, P., & Kulik, C-L. C. (1978). Research on component features of Keller's Personalized System of Instruction. *Journal of Personalized Instruction, 3*, 2–14.

Kulik, J. A., & Kulik, C-L. C. (1979). College teaching. In P. L. Peterson & H. J. Walberg (Eds.), *Research on teaching: Concepts, findings, and implications.* (pp. 70–93) Berkeley, CA: McCutcheon.

Kulik, J. A., Kulik, C-L. C., & Cohen, P. A. (1979a). A meta-analysis of outcome studies of Keller's Personalized System of Instruction. *American Psychologist, 34*, 307–318.

Kulik, J. A., Kulik, C-L. C., & Cohen, P. A. (1979b). Research on audiotutorial instruction: A meta-analysis of comparative studies. *Research in Higher Education, 11*, 321–341.

Kulik, J. A., Kulik, C-L. C., & Cohen, P. A. (1980). Effectiveness of computer-based college teaching: A meta-analysis of findings. *Review of Educational Research, 50*, 525–544.

Kulik, J. A., & McKeachie, W. J. (1975). The evaluation of teachers in higher education. In F. N. Kerlinger (Ed.), *Review of Research in Education*, Vol. 3. Itasca, IL: F. E. Peacock.

Kyle, W. C., Jr., Penick, J. E., & Shymansky, J. A. (1980). Assessing and analyzing behavior strategies of instructors in college science laboratories. *Journal of Research in Science Teaching, 17*, 131–137.

Land, M. L. (1979). Low-inference variables of teacher clarity: Effects on student concept learning. *Journal of Educational Psychology, 71*, 795–799.

Land, M. L. (1980). Teacher clarity and cognitive level of questions: Effects on learning. *Journal of Experimental Education, 49*, 48–51.

Land, M. L. (1981). Combined effects of two teacher clarity variables on student achievement. *Journal of Experimental Education, 50*, 14–17.

Land, M. L. (1985). Vagueness and clarity in the classroom. In T. Husén & T. N. Postlethwaite (Eds.), *International encyclopedia of education: Research and studies*. Oxford: Pergamon Press.

Land, M. L., & Smith, L. R. (1979a). The effect of low inference teacher clarity inhibitors on student achievement. *Journal of Teacher Education, 30*, 55–57.

Land, M. L., & Smith, L. R. (1979b). Effects of a teacher clarity variable on student achievement. *Journal of Educational Research, 72*, 196–197.

Land, M. L., & Smith, L. R. (1981). College student ratings and teacher behavior: An experimental study. *Journal of Social Studies Research, 5*, 19–22.

Leventhal, L. (1979). The Doctor Fox effect: An alternative interpretation. *Instructional Evaluation, 4*, 1–6.

Leventhal, L. (1980). Alternative interpretation of the Dr. Fox effect: Reply to Frey. *Instructional Evaluation, 4*, 13–14.

Leventhal, L., Abrami, P. C., & Perry, R. P. (1979, July). *Educational seduction and the validity of student ratings — An alternative interpretation*. Paper presented at the Fifth International Conference on Improving University Teaching, London, England.

Levinson-Rose, J., & Menges, R. J. (1981). Improving college teaching: A critical review of research. *Review of Educational Research, 51*, 403–434.

McKeachie, W. J. (1963). Research on teaching at the college and university level. In N. L. Gage (Ed.), *Handbook of research on teaching*. Chicago: Rand McNally.

McKeachie, W. J. (1979). Student ratings of faculty: A reprise. *Academe, 65*, 384–397.

Marsh, H. W. (1985). Students as evaluators of teaching. In T. Husén & T. N. Postlethwaite (Eds.), *International encyclopedia of education: Research and studies*. Oxford: Pergamon Press.

Marsh, H. W., & Ware, J. E. Jr. (1982). Effects of expressiveness, content coverage, and incentive on multidimensional student rating scales: New interpretations of the Dr. Fox effect. *Journal of Educational Psychology, 74*, 126–134.

Martin, J., Marx, R. W., Hasell, J., & Ellis, J. F. (1978). Improving the instructional effectiveness of university teaching assistants: Report II. *Canadian Journal of Education, 3*, 13–26.

Marx, R. W., Ellis, J. F., & Martin, J. (1979). The training of teaching assistants in Canadian universities: A survey and case study. *The Canadian Journal of Higher Education, 9*, 56–63.

Marx, R. W., Martin, J., Ellis, J. F., & Hasell, J. (1978). Improving the instructional effectiveness of university teaching assistants: Report I. *Canadian Journal of Education, 3*, 1–12.

Meier, R. S. (1977). *Student ratings of instruction: Characteristics that influence evaluations of teachers*. Unpublished doctoral dissertation, Purdue University, West Lafayette, IN.

Meier, R. S., & Feldhusen, J. F. (1979). Another look at Dr. Fox: Effect of stated purpose for evaluation, lecturer expressiveness and density of lecture content on student ratings. *Journal of Educational Psychology, 71*, 339–345.

Menges, R. J. (1979). Evaluating teaching effectiveness: What is the proper role for students? *Liberal Education, 65*, 356–370.

Menges, R. J. (1980). *Incentives and motivation in the teaching-learning process: The role of teacher intentions*. Paper presented at the 22nd International Congress of Psychology, Leipzig, Poland.

Merlino, A. (1977). A comparison of the effectiveness of three levels of teacher questioning on the outcomes of instruction in a college biology course. (Doctoral dissertation, New York University, 1976). *Dissertation Abstracts International, 37*, 5551-A.

Naftulin, D. H., Ware, J. E. Jr., & Donnelly, F. A. (1973). The Doctor Fox lecture: A paradigm of education seduction. *Journal of Medical Education, 48*, 630–635.

Perlberg, A., Peri, J. N., Weinreb, M., Nitzan, E., & Shimron, J. (1972). Microteaching and videotape recordings: A new approach to improving teaching. *Journal of Medical Education, 47*, 43–50.

Perry, R. P., Abrami, P. C., & Leventhal, L. (1979). Educational seduction: The effect of instructor expressiveness and lecture content on student ratings and achievement. *Journal of Educational Psychology, 71*, 107–116.

Perry, R. P., Abrami, P. C., Leventhal, L., & Check, J. (1979). Instructor reputation: An expectancy relationship involving student ratings and achievement. *Journal of Educational Psychology, 71*, 776–787.

Perry, R. P., Leventhal, L., & Abrami, P. C. (1979). *An observational learning procedure for improving university instruction*. Paper presented at the meeting of the Fifth International Conference on Improving University Teaching, London, England.

Postlethwaite, S. N., Novak, J., & Murray, H. T. Jr. (1972). *The audiotutorial approach to learning*. Minneapolis: Burgess Publishing Co.

Powell, J. P. (1974). Small group teaching methods in higher education. *Educational Research, 16*, 167–171.

Ramagli, H. J. Jr. (1979). *The Doctor Fox effect: A paired lecture comparison of lecturer expressiveness and lecture content*. Unpublished doctoral dissertation, University of Florida. Gainesville, FL.

Ramagli, H. J. Jr., & Greenwood, G. E. (1980, April). *The Dr. Fox effect: A paired lecture comparison of lecturer expressiveness and lecture content*. Paper presented at the annual meeting of the American Educational Research Association, Boston.

Rosenshine, B. (1971). *Teaching behaviors and student achievement*. Slough, Bucks (U.K.): National Foundation for Educational Research.

Rosenshine, B., & Furst, N. (1973). The use of direct observation to study teaching. In R. M. W. Travers (Ed.), *Second handbook of research on teaching*. Chicago: Rand McNally.

Rotem, A., & Glasman, N. S. (1979). On the effectiveness of students' evaluative feedback to university instructors. *Review of Educational Research, 49*, 497–511.

Schustereit, R. C. (1980). Team-teaching and academic achievement. *Improving College and University Teaching, 28*, 85–89.

Sharp, G. (1981). Acquisition of lecturing skills by university teaching assistants: Some effects of interest, topic relevance, and viewing a model videotape. *American Educational Research Journal, 18*, 491–502.

Shulman, L. (1975). *Development of a category observation system for the analysis of video-taped class sessions*. Montreal, Canada: McGill University, Centre for Learning and Development.

Shymansky, J. A., & Penick, J. E. (1979). Use of systematic observations to improve college science laboratory instruction. *Science Education, 63*, 195–203.

Simon, A., & Boyer, E. G. (Eds.). (1974). *Mirrors for behavior III: An anthology of observation instruments*. Wyncote, PA: Communication Materials Center.

Smith, D. G. (1977). College classroom interactions and critical thinking. *Journal of Educational Psychology, 69*, 180–190.

Smith, D. G. (1980, April). *Instruction and outcomes in an undergraduate setting*. Paper presented at the annual meeting of the American Educational Research Association, Boston.

Smith, J. P. (1971). The development of a classroom observation instrument relevant to the earth science curriculum project. *Journal of Research in Science Teaching, 8*, 231–235.

Smith, L. R. (1977). Aspects of teacher discourse and student achievement in mathematics. *Journal of Research in Mathematics Education, 8*, 195–204.

Taba, H., & Elzey, F. F. (1964). Teaching strategies and thought processes. *Teachers College Record, 65*, 524–534.

Tamir, P. (1977). How are the laboratories used? *Journal of Research in Science Teaching, 14,* 311–316.

Taylor-Way, D. G. (1981, April). *Adaptation of Interpersonal Process Recall and a theory of educating for the improvement of college instruction.* Paper presented at the annual meeting of the American Educational Research Association, Los Angeles.

Travers, R. M. W. (Ed.). (1973). *Second handbook of research on teaching.* Chicago: Rand McNally.

Ware, J. E. (1974). *The Doctor Fox effect: A study of lecturer effectiveness and ratings of instruction.* Unpublished doctoral dissertation, Southern Illinois University, Carbondale, IL.

Ware, J. E., & Williams, R. G. (1975). The Dr. Fox effect: A study of lecture effectiveness and ratings of instruction. *Journal of Medical Education, 50,* 149–156.

Ware, J. E. Jr., & Williams, R. G. (1979). Seeing through the Doctor Fox effect: A response to Frey. *Instructional Evaluation, 3,* 6–10.

Ware, J. E. Jr., & Williams, R. G. (1980). A reanalysis of the Doctor Fox experiments. *Instructional Evaluation, 4,* 15–18.

Wenk, V. A., & Menges, R. J. (1982). *Classroom questions in postsecondary education.* Unpublished manuscript, Northwestern University, School of Education, Evanston, IL.

Williams, R. G., & Ware, J. E. (1976). Validity of student ratings of instruction under different incentive conditions: A further study of the Dr. Fox effect. *Journal of Educational Psychology, 68,* 48–56.

Williams, R. G., & Ware, J. E. (1977). An extended visit with Dr. Fox: Validity of student satisfaction with instruction ratings after repeated exposures to a lecturer. *American Educational Research Journal, 14,* 449–457.

Yelon, S., Cooper, C., Henry, R., Korzenny, S., & Alexander, G. P. (1980). *Style of teaching: An ethnographic study.* Unpublished manuscript, Michigan State University, Learning and Evaluation Service. East Lansing, MI.

27.
Research on Written Composition

Marlene Scardamalia
York University

Carl Bereiter
Ontario Institute for Studies in Education

Introduction

During the period following the publication of the *Second Handbook of Research on Teaching*, writing has risen from a relatively neglected school subject to an object of lively attention in both the popular and the academic media. Popular interest seems to have been set aflame by a *Newsweek* article (December 8, 1975) titled "Why Johnny Can't Write," a title that gives the flavor of much of the discussion that followed in the popular media. Given the short life expectancy of educational crises, it would not be appropriate in a handbook article to devote many paragraphs to analyzing the current writing crisis. There are, however, some points brought to light in the recent flurry of discussion that are important for establishing the educational significance of research to be discussed in this chapter.

Of particular interest was the extremely wide range of people thought to be in need of writing improvement. Although the most conspicuous writing difficulties were to be found among speakers of nonstandard dialects (Shaughnessy, 1977a), university students in general were found wanting (Lyons, 1976), as well as bureaucrats (Redish, in press) and business writers (Odell, 1980). It thus appears that the "writing problem" is not a matter of a minority for whom writing is especially problematic but rather a matter of the majority.

When the news media take up an instructional issue, they tend to focus on the question of whether things have gotten worse, a question that is usually unanswerable and often beside the point. Data from the National Assessment of Educational Progress (1975, 1980a, 1980b, 1980c) have, in fact, shown evidence of declines across the period 1969–1979, but not of

such magnitude as to provoke an educational crisis. Rather, it would seem that the source of the sudden dissatisfaction with writing competence is a rise in expectations. Increasing numbers of low-income and minority students have been entering higher education and seeking entry into middle-class occupations where facility with written language is expected. At the same time, with the trend in occupations toward processing information rather than material, more and more people find themselves needing to communicate through written language and depending on written communication from others (Sawyer, 1977). This situation has created a new emphasis on readability and on the informational adequacy of texts, rather than on technical correctness (Black, 1982; Hirsch, 1977; Nystrand, 1979).

Response to the "Writing Crisis"

One response to the public interest in writing was a dramatic increase in research activity. Whereas in 1974 there were no sessions at the American Educational Research Association's annual meeting presenting research on writing, by the time of the 1979 annual meeting there were 16 such sessions. There were, however, other more direct responses to the demand for writing improvement that also have relevance to research on teaching.

Evaluation. Many educational jurisdictions in the United States and Canada called for the first time for systematic evaluation of writing abilities. Writing evaluation had long been recognized as a thorny problem, characterized by uncertainties both as to

The authors thank reviewers Robert de Beaugrande (University of Florida) and Martha King (Ohio State University). The preparation of this chapter was aided by grants from the Alfred P. Sloan Foundation and by the Ontario Ministry of Education, through its block grant to the Ontario Institute for Studies in Education. Marlene Scardamalia's affiliation has changed to the Ontario Institute for Studies in Education since the publication of this volume.

the manner of obtaining data and the manner of scoring it (Diederich, 1964). The sudden need to do it anyway led to writing evaluation's becoming itself a major subject of research (Cooper & Odell, 1977).

Document Design. Not all of the concern about writing improvement was focused on instruction. In 1978 U.S. President Carter issued an executive order (E012044) calling for government regulations to be written in "plain English" that was understandable to the people who were expected to comply with the regulations. The Document Design Project, undertaken by the American Institutes for Research, provided direct guidance to public and private agencies in producing more readable documents. With the involvement of researchers from Carnegie-Mellon University, the project also carried out a substantial program of research looking into the relation between what readers do to understand and what writers do to be understood. (See, for instance, "Revising Functional Documents: The Scenario Principle" [Flower, Hayes, & Swarts, 1980].)

Instructional Improvement. The notion that something was wrong with writing instruction could hardly be said to have taken language arts educators by surprise. There was already ample evidence that most teachers from elementary school through university were ill prepared to teach writing (Morrison & Austin, 1977), that not much writing was done in schools (R. Applebee, 1966), and that much of the required writing gave little motivation or scope for the exercise of higher level composing abilities (Muller, 1967). It is probably safe to say, accordingly, that in the view of most language arts specialists the knowledge needed to improve writing instruction was presumed already to exist, so that the problems were mainly problems of implementation. The subtitle of a monograph by Donald Graves (1978), *Let Them Write,* succinctly expressed one view of how to do something straightaway about the condition of writing in the schools.

The most comprehensive effort at instructional improvement was the Bay Area Writing Project, which soon broadened into the National Writing Project (Gray & Myers, 1978). Working through the medium of teacher development seminars, this project sought to increase teachers' own interest and competence in writing and to acquaint them with the best of available teaching activities. Thus tackling the known shortcomings of writing instruction in a direct and positive manner, the Bay Area Project received widespread endorsement (see, for instance, Fadiman & Howard, 1979; Nelms, 1979).

New Focuses of Research

At least nine new educationally relevant focuses of research on writing have emerged in the past decade. At present they are largely separate, conducted by only slightly overlapping groups of researchers and with little basis for relating findings from one area to another. Possibilities for synthesis exist, however, and will be touched on in the course of this chapter.

1. *Early development of written symbolism.* At the center of this research focus is Vygotsky's contention that the child's discovery of written symbolism is a major step in the development of thinking (Vygotsky, 1978, chapter 8). The principal interest has been in how children from the very beginning construct meaning—inventing spellings and other meaningful characters to convey meanings for which they have no conventional symbols (Bissex, 1980; Clay, 1975; DeFord, 1980; Read, 1971). The practical outcome of this research has been the encouragement of writing at much earlier ages than had previously been thought feasible (Graves, 1983). This opens the possibility, currently under investigation by Graves and others, of unifying the acquisition of writing and reading skills.

2. *Discourse analysis.* Whereas earlier linguistic research on writing had focused on the sentence and its constituents (e.g., Hunt, 1965), recent research has tended to focus on principles that tie sentences to one another and to the context of action in which the language is embedded. Conceptual roots of the research are in systemic grammar, particularly the concept of cohesion (Halliday & Hasan, 1976), and in the theory of speech acts (Grice, 1975). Current research has been largely devoted to studying developmental trends in attainment of discourse competence (Bracewell, Frederiksen, & Frederiksen, 1982; Britton, Burgess, Martin, McLeod, & Rosen, 1975; King & Rentel, 1981; McCutchen & Perfetti, 1982).

3. *Story grammar.* The early age and apparent universality of children's grasp of the structure of narratives has generated widespread research interest (Mandler & Johnson, 1977; Mandler, Scribner, Cole, & DeForest, 1980; Stein & Trabasso, 1982). A thorough airing of theoretical issues is given in Beaugrande (1982b) and accompanying responses by other scholars. Most of the research has dealt with story comprehension and recall, but there have been extensions into research on children's story production (Botvin & Sutton-Smith, 1977; Bracewell et al., 1982; King & Rentel 1981) and knowledge about stories (Bereiter & Scardamalia, 1982; Stein & Policastro, 1984).

4. *Basic writers.* Whereas the preceding three focuses of research all deal with young children, another major recent focus has been on what have come to be called "basic writers," defined by Shaughnessy (1977b) as "adult beginners"—adult students displaying an extreme lack of development of writing ability. Research on basic writers has emphasized problems arising from discrepancies in uses and conventions between nonstandard spoken dialects and standard written English and other sociolinguistic factors that create barriers to college-level standards of written communication (Shaughnessy, 1977a; see also the *Journal of Basic Writing,* the first volume of which appeared in 1978).

5. *The "new" rhetoric.* One of the most interesting developments of the past decade has been the emergence of a new vein of rhetorical research oriented toward instruction (Warnock, 1976). With links to the classical idea of "invention," or the generation of novel material for compositions, this new vein of research has investigated teachable techniques for directing and elaborating thought about composition content (see Corbett, 1971; Kinneavy, 1980; Winterowd, 1975; Young, Becker, & Pike, 1970; survey by Young, 1976).

6. *Writing "apprehension."* Psychometric research on anxiety toward writing has identified a reliably measurable trait that appears to be significantly implicated in how well people write and in how they feel about writing (Daly & Miller, 1975; Faigley, Daly, & Witte, 1981).

7. *Classroom practices.* Whereas earlier research on classroom practices in the teaching of writing relied mainly on surveys (e.g., R. Applebee, 1966), a trend is now well established toward more in-depth analysis, using ethnographic and sociolinguistic methods (Florio & Clark, 1982; Pettigrew, Shaw, & Van Nostrand, 1981; Staton, Shuy, & Kreeft, 1982).

8. *"Response."* Instructional research on writing has long been concerned with the effects of different kinds of marking or correction of student writing (reviewed by Knoblauch & Brannon, 1981). A more recent research interest, however, has been in other, more highly interactive kinds of response to student writing (Freedman, 1981). Paramount among these have been "conferencing" (Graves, 1978), a procedure using brief, individual consultations at various points during composition, and interactive journal writing, in which the teacher responds individually to students' personal journal entries (Staton, 1980).

9. *The composing process.* Methods and concepts of cognitive science have been brought to bear on the question of what goes on in the mind as people compose. This active area of research has included basic theoretical studies (e.g., Hayes & Flower, 1980a; Scardamalia, Bereiter, & Goelman, 1982), developmental studies (e.g., Burtis, Bereiter, Scardamalia, & Tetroe, 1983, analysis of writing in real time (Matsuhashi, 1982), and studies comparing experts and novices (e.g., Flower & Hayes, 1980a; Perl, 1979; Sommers, 1980).

In addition to these nine new focuses of research, we should mention a potential focus — neuropsychological research related to writing (Emig, 1978). As Faigley (1982) points out, brain research currently serves primarily as a source of metaphors for people concerned with writing (see, however, Glassner, 1982).

Movements Toward Synthesis

Older reviews of research on writing customarily lamented its neglect in comparison to other major uses of language (West, 1967). Although writing still lags far behind reading as an object of research, there is now enough research relevant to the teaching of writing and composition that it cannot be adequately reviewed and synthesized in a chapter of this size. This is only partly a result of increased quantity, however. It is even more a result of the newness of the various research focuses previously described. There has not been time for the necessary cross-linkages to develop.

As an example, the work on early development of written symbolism and the work on composing processes in older children and adults should obviously tie together into a coherent picture of writing development (Gundlach, 1982). Yet the two bodies of research are at present unintegrated to the extent of being almost devoid of cross-reference. Integration will depend on evidence, currently lacking, as to what connection exists between the young child's discovery of written symboliza-

tion and the older child's development of competence in text composition.

Two general approaches seem to be currently in contention as ways to bring the many strands of writing research together. One approach might be characterized as "contextual" (Mishler, 1979), centering on the meanings that writing has for people in different contexts (Britton et al., 1975; Graves, 1981; King, 1978). The other is a cognitive science approach, drawing broadly on the contributions of various disciplines to this hybrid science (see Beaugrande, 1982a and Black, 1982 for overviews).

At present the contextual approach is clearly ascendant among language arts educators (see any issue of *Language Arts*), and possesses a marked advantage when it comes to establishing links between theory, disciplined observation, and the everyday experiences of teachers. The cognitive science approach has its main advocates among researchers, for reasons similar to those that have supported the "cognitive revolution" in many other areas dealt with in this volume. It provides pretty much the "only paradigm in town" for investigating complex mental processes, which all sides agree are of central concern in writing. Moreover, it permits writing researchers to take advantage of theoretical and methodological advances that have been made by cognitive scientists in such other areas as linguistics, psycholinguistics, developmental psychology, and cognitive anthropology, and such special research focuses as problem solving, discourse processes, social cognition, metacognition, self-regulation, emotions, dreams, and consciousness.

There is no immediate prospect of a cognitive science synthesis of the nine strands of research previously mentioned. Some cognitive research is going on in each of them, however, and Beaugrande (1984) has made a major contribution to synthesizing diverse findings within a cognitive framework. Recent indications of a drawing together of previously unconnected areas are an examination of writers' emotional blocks in terms of composing strategies (Rose, 1980) and an effort to base a major international evaluation of writing achievement on cognitive models (Purves & Takala, 1982).

Perhaps the least assimilated focus of research is the one we have labeled "response," and it has been a major focus of those taking a contextual approach. In the present chapter we will try to establish some conceptual bridges between cognitive process research and types of student–teacher interaction in writing, but it seems that a real synthesis will require research that combines cognitive and ethnomethodological perspectives (cf. Wertsch, in press).

What has been achieved so far is a fairly coherent description of mental processes that go on in writing and substantial progress toward understanding the cognitive changes involved as oral language competence gets reshaped into the ability to compose written texts. This chapter will be largely devoted to discussing progress on these fronts and its relevance to research on the teaching of writing.

Nature of the Composing Process

Research into the composing process has been greatly aided by the procedure of having subjects think aloud while composing

(Emig, 1971; Hayes & Flower, 1980a). Protocols thus obtained from skilled writers make it evident that, although there is obviously a structure to the composing process, it does not correspond to the traditional textbook picture of collecting material, organizing it, writing it out, and then revising it. Those procedures all occur, but not in such a linear manner (Hayes & Flower, 1980a; Sommers, 1980).

It should be understood that thinking aloud protocols are not presumed to give a direct record of the mental processes of composing. Many significant mental events are not available to the writer for mention (Scardamalia et al., 1982), and thinking aloud itself has been found to introduce certain distortions (Black, Galambos, & Reiser, 1984). Thinking aloud protocols are better thought of simply as data (Ericsson & Simon, 1980), to be used in conjunction with other data to make inferences about the composing process. Bereiter & Scardamalia (1983b) discuss six different levels of inquiry into the composing process that need to be coordinated in theory development. Process description, such as may be based on protocol analysis, is one such level; others include text analysis, theory-guided experimentation, and simulation (including simulation through intervention with live writers). Although in the discussion that follows it will be impossible to indicate the nature of the evidence for every conclusion cited, we try to avoid stating conclusions that are based on evidence from only one level of inquiry.

Several general models of the composing process have been put forth, each with the virtue of highlighting certain aspects of the process. Beaugrande (1984) offers a multilevel model that gives prominence to the different kinds of mental units that must be manipulated in composition, and we will appeal to that model in discussing mental representations of text. Augustine (1981) offers a model that highlights the rhetorical decisions writers must make. The model that gives the most explicit account of mental operations is that of Hayes and Flower (Flower & Hayes, 1981; Hayes & Flower, 1980a, 1980b), the gross structure of which is depicted in Figure 27.1. It is also the most widely cited model, and has tended to fix the vocabulary people use in talking about the composing process.

According to this model, the main parts of the composing process are *planning, translating, and reviewing.* The heart of planning is generating ideas, most of which are ideas for what to write. These are culled and arranged to create a plan that controls the process of actual text production, which is called translating. Some of the generated ideas, however, are ideas for goals to be pursued, and these are stored for consultation throughout the composing process. These various subprocesses sound fairly obvious, of course. The strength of the model lies in its claim to account for the amazing diversity of mental events during composition on the basis of a relatively small number of such subprocesses. This is accomplished by a control structure that permits virtually any subprocess to incorporate any other subprocess. Thus, the whole planning process may be called up in the service of editing, or the reviewing process may be called up for purposes of arriving at an organizing decision. This property of the model, sometimes called "recursion," sets it apart from the step-by-step models of composition that have commonly been explicitly or implicitly endorsed in composition textbooks (Rose, 1981).

Figure 27. 1 depicts only the general structure of a model of the composing process. One of the claims made by Hayes and Flower (1980a) is that individual differences in composing strategies may be represented by different detailed models that all fit the general structure. In a later section we will discuss a model of an immature composing process which, even though it differs markedly from the model of mature composing constructed by Hayes and Flower, nevertheless fits the general structure and may be viewed as a radically reduced version of the mature model. Caccamise (in press) obtained protocol data on students generating composition ideas that led her to propose a different detailed model of the *generating* process from that originally proposed by Hayes and Flower (1980a), but one that still fits the general structure. The general structure of the model, thus, appears to do what it is supposed to, which is to serve as a frame for working out more detailed and possibly more controversial accounts of how the mind copes with writing tasks.

The Hayes and Flower model is in the tradition of problem-solving models pioneered by Newell and Simon (1972). Recently Newell (1980) has argued that all human goal-oriented symbolic activity resembles problem solving in that it consists of a heuristic search through what Newell calls "problem spaces." A problem space contains a set of symbolic structures or knowledge states and a set of mental operations that can be applied to change one knowledge state into another. Heuristic search through the problem space consists of such mental operations being carried out under the constraints of "search control knowledge." What writing researchers typically call a "composing strategy," and the kind of thing that can be represented in the framework of the Hayes and Flower model, is what Newell calls search control knowledge. Describing a person's search control knowledge gives only a partial account of the person's writing competence. It remains to describe the symbolic structures available to the writer and to specify the operations on those structures that are within the writer's repertoire. Research on children's composing processes, to be discussed in the next section, suggests that an important key to understanding why they write the way they do is the kinds of mental representations of text that they have available to operate on.

Figure 27.2 depicts a composing process model developed by Robert de Beaugrande (1984). It is based on a synthesis of experimental findings related to the kinds of symbolic structures operated on within the course of text production. As did Figure 27.1, Figure 27.2 gives only the gross structure of the model. *Goals* comprise a variety of symbolic structures — not only representations of the intended outcome of the writing effort but also representations of the reader, of text type, and style. An *idea*, in Beaugrande's model, is "a configuration of conceptual content that acts as a *control center* for building the *text-world model* (the total configuration of knowledge activated for processing the text . . .)" (Beaugrande, 1984, P. 109). *Conceptual development* refers to the generation and integration of specific items of content that constitute the detailed representation of the ideas.

Beaugrande calls his a "parallel-stage interaction" model, indicating that the various processes of symbolic construction go on more or less simultaneously and that they are

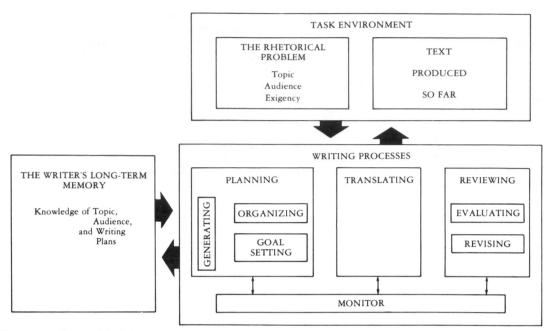

Fig. 27.1. Structure of a model of the composing process.

From "Writing as Problem Solving" by J. R. Hayes and L. S. Flower, 1980, *Visible Language, 14*(4), pp. 388–399. Copyright 1980 by Visible Language. Reprinted by permission.

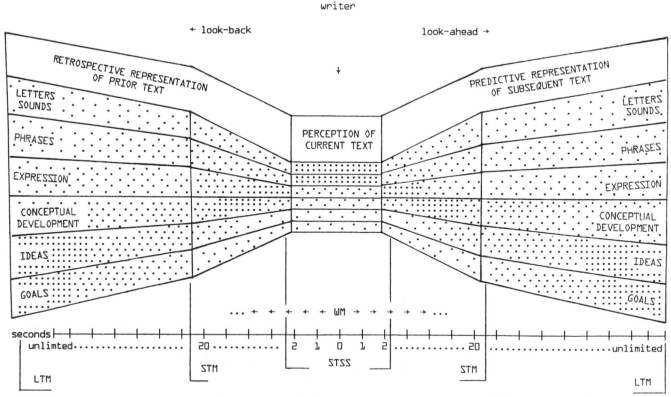

Fig. 27.2 A parallel-stage interaction model of text production. (LTM = long-term memory; STM = short-term memory; STSS = short-term sensory storage; WM = working memory.)

From *Text Production: Toward a Science of Composition* (p. 106) by R. de Beaugrande, 1984, Norwood, NJ: Ablex. Copyright 1984 by Ablex. Reprinted by permission.

interpenetrable—that is, that what happens as a result of processing at one level may alter the knowledge states current at other levels. Broadly speaking, these premises are also embodied in the Hayes and Flower model. They imply that the skilled writer must have flexible access to a wide range of mental representations of actual and intended text and of conditions bearing on plans for the text, as well as a highly sophisticated control structure for coordinating operations on these many different kinds of knowledge states.

A sense of the variety of levels at which text is mentally manipulated by mature writers may be gained from the following fairly typical excerpt from a planning protocol taken from our files. The writer was planning a short essay on the question, "Should children choose what subjects they study in school?"

> Okay, reasons why.... I'm just wondering if values [referring here to a previously generated *idea*, in Beaugrande's terms] will fit under this initial one [referring to another *idea*], which means that this initial one is really the argument [shifting now to thinking of the item in terms of *text type*], and that argument would be supported from those different subsections [a *plan*, now, for achieving the unstated *goal* of convincing the reader].

The models of the composing process developed thus far are what Kosslyn (1980) calls "protomodels." They are precursors of theory, not instantiations of theories. Theory development itself—as one might expect from the newness of the field—is embryonic. As in a number of other areas of cognitive research, however, theoretically interesting questions are starting to emerge from the analysis of differences between experts and novices or children.

What, in cognitive process terms, must be added to oral language competence in order to produce competence in written composition? Do immature writers naturally possess the basic structure of the mature composing process, needing only more sophisticated knowledge in order to write like an expert, or does the control structure itself have to be acquired? Are all of the relevant kinds of mental representations available to them, or do the very prototypes of some of them have to be constructed? Are unskilled adult writers merely lacking in some of the knowledge experts have or have they gone down a different developmental route that has led them to a different system of text production? Questions such as these, which will be taken up in the next sections, point toward matters of both theoretical and practical significance.

Problems in Learning to Write

Discussions of writing are usually organized according to outwardly visible parts of the process—gathering material, outlining, drafting text, revising, and so on. These divisions do not necessarily correspond to divisions in the underlying mental process, however. For instance, it makes little psychological sense to treat changing a sentence after it is written down as a different process from changing it before it is written. Indeed, evidence to be cited later suggests that focusing on revision as if it were a special process may lead to wasted instructional effort. In the present section, accordingly, we shall abandon the conventional categories and organize the discussion around what appear to be psychologically coherent aspects of the composing process.

There has been considerable discussion of what fundamentally distinguishes writing from oral communication (Olson, 1977; Rubin, 1980b). It is not simply the medium of expression. Many writers, past and present, have used dictation as a way of producing written text. A body of recent developmental research supports the view that competence in written composition does not consist merely of special knowledge and skills added to those of oral language ability. Rather, it involves radical conversion "from a language production system dependent at every level on inputs from a conversational partner to a system capable of functioning autonomously" (Bereiter & Scardamalia, 1982). In the following sections evidence will be examined concerning aspects of competence that appear to create special problems for the immature writer. In each case we will look first at what expert or mature writers do, then at what novices and children do, and finally at intervention studies that shed light on what is involved in moving students toward more expert-like competence.

Framing Written Discourse

Much recent research has focused on formal text structures that are believed to guide the writer in constructing a text and a reader in comprehending it (Mandler & Johnson, 1977; Stein & Glenn, 1979; Thorndyke, 1977; van Dijk, 1980). Story grammar, discourse schema, script, superstructure, and frame are terms that have been applied to such structures. We use the term framing here, to indicate the active process of creating an organizing structure for a composition (Bracewell et al., 1982). The premise shared by most investigators is that these structures are not merely characteristics that inevitably emerge in text but that they represent knowledge readers and writers possess (Mandler et al., 1980; Stein & Trabasso, 1982; but see Black & Wilensky, 1979). From this it would follow that a major requirement for competence in writing is learning the essential form of various literary types—narrative, exposition, argument, and the like.

EXPERT COMPETENCE

If one accepts the premise that discourse schemata are a significant part of writers' competence, then it follows by definition that skilled writers have a well-developed repertoire of such schemata (Bereiter, 1980). What remains an empirical question is the kind of access writers have to their discourse knowledge. Is their discourse knowledge like geographical knowledge—functioning tacitly most of the time but available for conscious inspection and application when needed? Or is it like syntactical knowledge for people unschooled in grammar—largely inaccessible, even though highly functional?

There is not much evidence on this point, but what there is suggests that skillful adults can and frequently do made conscious use of abstract knowledge of discourse forms. Olson, Mack, and Duffy (1981) had university students think aloud while reading simple narrative and expository texts. They found readers of expository texts making predictions about the kind of information forthcoming in the text—for instance, predict-ing that an example would follow, but not predicting what the content of the example would be. Examples are abstract entities, defined by their function in text; hence, predicting that an example will appear indicates explicitly thinking in terms of discourse schema knowledge.

Thinking aloud protocols we have obtained from skilled writers also show numerous examples of explicit reference to discourse schema elements. In the following example, a writer who has been periodically reformulating her approach to a composition makes a third and final recapitulation of her plan:

> I would state my opinion, my point of view, taking in the fact that some people would not agree with it; and, taking note of this position, I would go through the disadvantages, which I think obviously can be overcome, and then move on to say how. After those three major points are out of the way I would conclude by talking about the benefits.

Here we see that abstract notions such as "opinion," "position," and "major points" play an obvious function in helping the writer work out an overall structure for the text (Chafe, 1977). However, this is a rather extreme case of explicit use of discourse knowledge. In many other expert protocols discourse knowledge remains more in the background. It seems that a simple distinction between explicit and implicit or conscious and unconscious knowledge will not do. Skilled writers make all kinds of use of their discourse knowledge, with varying degrees of consciousness and explicitness.

STUDENT COMPETENCE

Most research on discourse schema knowledge in children has dealt with narrative. This research has yielded abundant evidence that implicit knowledge of narrative form guides children's comprehension of stories. After reviewing a number of such studies, Stein and Trabasso (1982) arrive at the forceful conclusion

> that the use of schematic knowledge is so powerful that listeners have little control over the types of retrieval strategies used during recall of narrative information. Even when listeners are instructed to reproduce texts in a verbatim form, they *cannot* do so when the text contains certain types of omissions or certain sequences of events. (p. 217)

Story production evidently lags behind story comprehension, but by the end of the primary grades virtually all children are producing well-formed narrative compositions (Botvin & Sut-ton-Smith, 1977; Bracewell et al., 1982; King & Rentel, 1981; Stein & Trabasso, 1982). Other standard literary genres, such as exposition and argument, have been much less extensively investigated, but in the several thousand compositions of these kinds that we have examined, we have noticed very few failures in children aged 10 years and up to conform to genre. Their discourse grammars may be simpler than those of experts, but when assigned an argument topic they produce something clearly recognizable as an argument and not a narrative or an exposition; likewise for the other genres. The deviations that do occur—usually producing narratives when some other genre

was called for—are more likely attributable to losing hold than to lack of the appropriate schema.

Nevertheless, findings from the National Assessment of Edu-cational Progress (1980a, 1980b, 1980c) indicate that students have serious weaknesses in meeting the more substantive requirements of written genres. On persuasive writing assign-ments, about 31% of 13-year-olds and 22% of 17-year-olds were rated as failing to provide even minimal support for a position. On a task calling for making up a story about a picture, about a third of 17-year-olds were rated as failing to meet the fundamental demands of fiction "either because the plot is only barely outlined, the story rambles on without structure, the story is incomplete or the story is really several unconnected stories" (National Assessment, 1980a, p. 14). Such findings raise questions about the uses to which students are able to put their implicit discourse schema knowledge.

Somewhat surprisingly, students from the age of 10 have been found to demonstrate ability to gain some conscious access to their discourse schema knowledge. Under questioning they can name discourse elements found in various genres (Bereiter & Scardamalia, 1982), and they can with some accuracy label such elements in their own and other texts (Scardamalia & Paris, 1985). Young students also appeal to schema knowledge when working on scrambled text problems, saying things like "It's about the planet...like telling the setting" (Scardamalia & Bereiter, 1984). Since it is unlikely that they were explicitly taught any of these things, it appears that they are able to draw deliberately on their implicit discourse schemata.

The fact that children can gain access to their discourse schema knowledge through special questioning or special tasks does not, however, tell us anything about the uses they are able to make of this knowledge in composition. Thinking aloud protocols by school-age writers that we have analyzed show almost no evidence of the explicit use of abstract schema knowledge found in skilled adults. The difference here, however, could be in what young writers report rather than in what they do. Discovering the actual functions of discourse knowledge in children's composing requires experimental probing, which was the purpose of the intervention studies to which we now turn.

INTERVENTIONS

In this and similar sections later, intervention studies are examined, not in terms of instructional effectiveness, but in terms of what they reveal about the nature of writing compe-tence and its development. Instructional issues per se are treated separately in other portions of the chapter.

One way to investigate children's use of discourse knowledge is to make elements of this knowledge more accessible and observe effects on composition. In one study (Paris, 1980) elementary school children were trained in recognizing ele-ments of the argument genre (statement of belief, reason, reason on other side, example, etc.). The elements were as much as possible taught out of context and no practice or suggestion was given concerning the use of them in composition. Neverthe-less the training showed some transfer to composition, resulting in increased presentation of reasons on both sides of an argument and a decline in the number of nonfunctional elements.

These results suggest that children may be able to make some decisions in writing based on abstract structural considerations rather than on concrete considerations of content. A more direct test of this possibility was made by coaching children in a composing procedure of first choosing an abstract element and then producing a sentence of the chosen kind, then choosing a next element, and so on (study by Bereiter, Scardamalia, Anderson, & Smart, reported in Bereiter & Scardamalia, 1982). The most notable result here is that 12-year-olds were able to carry out the procedure and claimed it helped them think of things to say. This testimony was supported by a test of transfer to normal writing, which showed a general increase in the number and variety of discourse elements used. Apparently, then, children can use abstract specifications of discourse elements as probes for retrieving appropriate content from memory. This is a noteworthy capability, which will figure prominently in a subsequent description of a model of immature composing processes.

In the preceding study, children made their own choices of which discourse elements to use where. A third experiment, by Bracewell and the present writers (reported in Bracewell, 1980), examined the effect of having such choices made by an expert, with the child still generating the actual content and language. Children first wrote argument essays. Then, in individual conferences, the experimenter labeled discourse elements and suggested the insertion of additional discourse elements that would make for a stronger or more sophisticated argument. Except for the increased elaboration of content, directly induced by the experimenter, the essays showed no significant change.

These studies leave much unexplained, but they do at least make it clear that there is more to competence in framing discourse than having an abstract schema in the mind that regulates what kind of element will go where. Such schemata are no doubt an important part of expert competence, clearly foreshadowed in the performance of young writers (Waters, 1980). But when a mature level of such competence is directly injected into the composing process of young writers, as in the Bracewell et al. experiment cited above, the effects are minimal. Over and above this regulative role, abstract discourse knowledge in experts appears to serve a variety of other roles in formulating goals, making strategic decisions, and constructing high-level representations of content that can be manipulated effectively during text planning (Scardamalia & Paris, 1985).

Content Generation

Thinking aloud protocols indicate that for experts and novices alike the greater part of effort in writing goes into generating content — thinking of what to say (Burtis et al., 1983; Hayes & Flower, 1980a). Mature writers, however, typically generate far more content than they will use or intend to use in their compositions, whereas for young writers finding enough content is frequently a problem and they cannot imagine discarding anything that would fit (Bereiter & Scardamalia, 1982). An obvious explanation is that young writers don't know enough

about the subjects they are asked to write on. While that is undoubtedly true (A. Applebee, 1981), young writers also have difficulty getting access to the knowledge they do have. Here the difference between composition and conversation is noteworthy. In conversation there are continual cues from other speakers that aid retrieval of relevant content. Writers, unless they are in collaboration, are left to their own resources and thus have need of strategies for self-directed memory search.

EXPERT COMPETENCE

Memory search is seldom directly revealed in protocols. Identifying memory search strategies is accordingly a highly speculative matter, resting on the general fit of hypothesis to data rather than on reconstruction of processes from individual protocols (cf. Caccamise, in press). Two processes that seem necessary to account for expert performance are metamemorial search and heuristic or goal-directed search.

Metamemorial search is search aimed at determining the availability of information in memory rather than at retrieving specific information (Bereiter & Scardamalia, 1982). In protocol data we have collected it is suggested by statements about having much or little information on a topic, as in the following:

I think I'd probably stay away from [the issue of] testing because — I'm not really sure: I think there should be something but since I don't know enough, I'd rather stay away from it so it wouldn't weaken my argument.

As the example illustrates, this kind of search can play an important part in high-level planning.

Heuristic search is a term taken from the problem-solving literature, where it stands in contrast to trial-and-error search (Hayes, 1981). It involves reducing the space of possibilities one must search through by taking advantage of partial knowledge of what it is one is looking for. Greeno (1978) observed that in composition problems generally (which include artistic creation of all sorts as well as theory construction) a large part of the problem-solving effort goes into elaborating constraints. Constraints function heuristically when they serve to direct memory search toward promising areas of content. In keeping with this analysis, Flower and Hayes (1981) found that 60% of the ideas generated by expert writers were not in response to the assigned topic or in response to preceding ideas but were in response to the writer's own elaboration of the rhetorical problem.

Caccamise (in press) presented data on content generation which she found did not fit a model of heuristic search but which rather suggested that people retrieved ideas in an associative (spreading activation) way and then edited out ones that did not fit task constraints — in other words, in a trial-and-error fashion. However, her task was one that called for exhaustive search of memory (listing all the ideas that would fit). This would tend to make heuristic search unprofitable. Indeed, the task would seem to force writers into the condition we find young writers often to be in, which is that of generating every suitable idea they can.

STUDENT COMPETENCE

Young writers show a lack of effective metamemorial search strategies for surveying the information they have available. When students in Grades 4 and 6 were asked to name topics about which they knew relatively much and relatively little, they evidenced great difficulty deciding, and few could name as many as three topics of either kind (study by Scardamalia, Bereiter, & Woodruff, summarized in Bereiter & Scardamalia, 1982).

Whereas Flower and Hayes (1981) found expert writers generating most content ideas in response to their own elaborations of the rhetorical problem, they found novice adult writers to generate 70% of their ideas in response either to the topic assignment or to the last content item considered. These results suggest that novice writers do not make the same use that experts do of search heuristics based on problem analysis, and that accordingly they must rely more on trial-and-error search, using whatever cues are available in the environment to stimulate retrieval of content from memory. Much the same conclusion was reached by Crowley (1977) from an analysis of writing diaries kept by college students.

Differences between young and old novices appear to depend on the number of constraints in the writing assignment that they employ as cues or tests. McCutchen and Perfetti (1982) have run computer simulations of memory search models differing in the number of constraints honored. Holding the knowledge base constant, they found that a one-constraint model yielded content similar to that found in second grade expository writing, a two-constraint model yielded fourth grade content, and a three-constraint model yielded content like that found in Grades 6 and 8.

INTERVENTIONS

Many of the modern educational practices used to improve student writing may be viewed as interventions that compensate for students' lacks in metamemorial and heuristic search. One of the simplest practices is permitting students to write on topics about which they already have a strong drive to express themselves. Graves (1975) found this to significantly increase the amount written by primary grade children. This practice renders metamemorial and goal-directed memory search unnecessary, by allowing the writer to make use of memory contents that have already, for one reason or other, been activated.

"Prewriting" activities (Boiarsky, 1982) — be they conferences, class discussions, films, or private exercises in reflection — have the effect of bringing a wealth of memorial content to the fore where it is available for selection and use. "Discovery" heuristics (Young et al., 1970) are prewriting procedures that typically involve nonspecific goal-directed search, as in seeking an answer to the question, "Are there different ways of interpreting X?" An interesting question, not yet systematically investigated to our knowledge, is to what extent these heuristics mirror the heuristics actually used by expert writers and to what extent they serve as substitutes, achieving somewhat the same effect but without the kind of problem analysis and goal setting carried out by experts.

In our experience with a large variety of intervention studies (Bereiter & Scardamalia, 1982), we find that no matter what the intent of the intervention, children will find a way to use the input as cues to aid memory retrieval and will enthusiastically report that the intervention helped them "think of what to say" (see also Scardamalia & Bereiter, in press-a, and Woodruff, Bereiter, & Scardamalia, 1981). Simply urging students to go on, after the point where they claimed to have written everything they could think of, was found to double their production (Scardamalia et al., 1982). If one thinks of memory as arranged in hierarchical networks, then it appears that what students normally do is recall high-level nodes and then stop (cf. McCutchen & Perfetti, 1982), as they do when recalling text (Mandler & Johnson, 1977; Meyer, 1977). Evidently urging students to go on prompts them to work further down into subordinate nodes or to move to neighboring nodes.

Another intervention that has been found to increase content generation significantly is to have children list — after they have been assigned a topic but before they begin writing — isolated words that they think they might use (Anderson, Bereiter, & Smart, summarized in Bereiter & Scardamalia, 1982). This procedure would seem even more directly to promote search through subordinate nodes. However, it is perhaps best viewed, not as a way of inducing metamemorial search but as a way of streamlining the trial-and-error procedure that young writers already use for searching through content. Content generation can also be greatly boosted by allowing young writers to dictate. It is evidently the speed of dictation rather than its freedom from mechanical demands that produces this effect, since the effect is largely lost if dictation is slowed down to the child's normal rate of writing (Scardamalia et al., 1982). This speed effect suggests that content generation by young writers is very much an associative process, depending on spreading activation (Caccamise, in press), rather than a goal-directed process of heuristic search. Although the evidence is not precisely comparable, dictation by skilled adults does not appear to have anything like the same effect on content generation (Gould, 1980).

Are there any interventions, however, that actually cast light on the ability of students to undertake metamemorial or heuristic search? Studies that we are aware of provide tenuous evidence suggesting that, when the task calls for it, young writers can undertake both kinds of search to some extent. In as-yet unreported research by the present authors, evidence of metamemorial search began to appear in the planning protocols of 12-year-old writers when they were given a general topic (such as "an interesting animal") and had to choose their own specific topic to write on. They frequently had difficulty taking inventory of the extent and appropriateness of their knowledge about various animals, and some students just plunged in and began generating content about the first animal that came to mind; but on the whole there was substantially more evidence of metamemorial search than when students were writing on an already specified topic.

The most convincing evidence of heuristic search capabilities in young writers comes from studies cited in the preceding section showing that students can generate content to fit specified genre elements — reasons, examples, arguments on the other side, and so forth. Another task that shows evidence of inducing heuristic search is the task of writing toward a prescribed ending sentence (McCutchen & Perfetti, 1982); research by Tetroe and others, reported in Bereiter & Scardamalia, 1982). There is also evidence that when children are made aware that an exhaustive presentation of content is required—as in writing instructions for playing a game (Kroll, 1978; Scardamalia, Bereiter, & McDonald, 1978)—then they search further down from memory nodes than they do in their spontaneous expository writing.

A summary position compatible with available findings would be the following: Experts and novices alike generate content partly by heuristic search, guided by knowledge of what they are looking for, and partly by associative processes that bring content spontaneously to mind. Good writing undoubtedly requires both. Novice writers, however, appear to rely more on associative processes and to lack the executive controls that would enable them to undertake heuristic searches on their own initiative. Such an analysis serves to remind us that it is the discourse production system as a whole that generates an item of text, not a particular subcomponent of it. The ability to undertake heuristic search for content depends on ability to formulate goals and plans, and those abilities in turn depend on ability to carry out purposeful searches of memory.

Written Language Production

The actual production of written text involves a host of problems that usually receive only passing attention from writing researchers. These include handwriting (or typing), spelling, punctuation, and "usage" in the various senses in which written expressions are expected to be more carefully chosen than spoken ones. In its own right, spelling has begun to receive attention both from linguists (e.g., Stubbs, 1980) and psychologists (see volume edited by Frith, 1980). At least one innovative approach to spelling instruction, based on morphemes, has appeared (Dixon, 1976) and shown evidence of effectiveness (Maggs, McMillan, Patching, & Hawke, 1981). Syntax has been a long-standing concern of writing researchers (Hunt, 1965), and the ubiquitous T-unit continues to appear as a dependent variable, even though it is frequently not relevant to the questions now being investigated.

A writing researcher who has tried to incorporate a detailed treatment of both the language-related and the content-related aspects of writing into a theoretical account is Beaugrande (1984). A key notion linking the two aspects is "linearization," which refers to a whole range of processes involved in translating ideational material that is often hierarchically or spatially organized into a linear sequence of acts that result in a text that can be read linearly. Of interest in the present discussion will be the extent to which linearization poses recognizable problems in learning to write.

Most investigators of the composing process have limited their concern with language production to two aspects: (a) its possible interference with other subprocesses or competition with them for mental resources (Perl, 1979; Scardamalia et al., 1982), and (b) the problem of establishing voluntary control over language production processes that normally run without conscious attention in conversation (Bracewell, 1980).

EXPERT COMPETENCE

With regard to the two concerns just mentioned, expert writers are assumed to enjoy the advantages of (a) having procedures such as spelling and punctuation largely automatized so that they leave mental capacity free to deal with higher level tasks; (b) having control structures that permit switching back and forth between higher and lower level demands, so that they do not have to be coped with simultaneously; and (c) possessing a repertoire of linguistic alternatives that can be put to strategic use in achieving rhetorical goals (Beaugrande, 1984). This last point is parallel to the one made about discourse schema knowledge—that experts are distinguished not so much by having the knowledge as by having it available for planning. Evidence of automaticity comes from "slips of the pen" (Hotoph, 1980), which resemble those made in speaking and suggest that writers are planning ahead at the same time that they are putting words on paper.

STUDENT COMPETENCE

The hypothesis that immature writers are handicapped by having to devote attention to writing mechanics holds, it appears, only for quite inexperienced writers. Clay (1975), studying beginning writers, observed midsentence switches in syntactic form which she attributed to difficulties in transcription. King and Rentel (1981) found the dictated stories of first and second graders to be much more fully developed than their written stories; but at this early stage in literacy, it is not clear whether one is seeing interference from writing demands or simply an inability to put all one's thoughts into writing. By Grades 4 and 6, however, Scardamalia et al. (1982) found that a small advantage in quality of dictated over written texts was reversed when children were urged to keep going. As noted previously, the slow rate of written production impeded content generation, but it was found to have offsetting advantages in coherence.

Primary grade children often subvocalize each word or letter while writing it (Simon, 1973), which suggests their attention is wholly taken up with transcription. But by Grade 4 they have begun to confine subvocalization to pauses during transcription, they begin making the same kinds of "slips of the pen" experts make, and if stopped suddenly while writing they report about five words already definitely in mind in advance of the last word written (Scardamalia et al., 1982). All of this suggests that by the end of elementary school, even though the mechanics of writing may still be quite poorly perfected, children have developed efficient executive controls for switching attention between mechanical and substantive concerns, so that interference and cognitive overload are not serious problems (Bereiter & Scardamalia, 1983b; Scardamalia et al., 1982).

What does this say about linearization as a problem? The issue is not clearly enough drawn for a definite answer, but informal observations suggest that converting nonlinear knowledge to linear text may be more a problem for mature writers than for children. One must first reckon with the astonishingly short latencies for children in starting to write once a topic has been given—ranging from an average of 3 seconds for fifth graders writing on a simple story topic (Zbrodoff, 1984) to an average of 3 minutes for high school writing assignments (A.

Applebee, 1981). Secondly, children seem to have trouble suppressing the production of linear text, as when asked to brainstorm or take notes (Bereiter & Scardamalia, 1982; Burtis et al., 1983). As we shall propose in a later section, the overall composing strategy common in young writers appears to be one that is specifically geared to linear text generation, and it is a strategy that permits them to ignore the deeper problems of linearization.

Deliberate control of language devices has mainly been investigated with respect to syntax. Kress and Bracewell (1981) found that when instructed to do so deliberately, high school students were unable to generate many of the grammatical errors that they produced spontaneously. Bracewell (1980; 1983) and Scardamalia (1981) present a variety of experimental results showing children's difficulties in exerting intentional control over syntax. In one study, children were shown different renditions of the same content, varying in amount of coordination, the extremes being the following:

A. Ernie has a dog. Grover has a cat. Grover has a canary. Grover has a dog.

B. Ernie has a dog; but Grover has three different pets, a cat, a canary, and a dog.

Children of age nine and up reliably chose Version B over Version A, and could explain why. However, when given parallel content and asked to imitate either A or B, they produced sentences with intermediate amounts of coordination instead.

It must be assumed that the children had the necessary syntactic structure for producing Version A, and so their failure to produce it implies inability to exert intentional control over their syntactic choices. Children's difficulties with intentional control of syntax fit nicely with developmental models of working memory capacity (Scardamalia, 1981).

Although syntactic alternatives are important for manipulating focus, Bock (1982) has proposed that in ordinary speech syntactic alternatives often serve the more mundane purpose of allowing the speaker to start talking before the whole sentence is planned. If this is true, then becoming able to make the strategic choices that skilled writers are assumed to make would require not only having a repertoire of alternatives but also learning to override the natural tendency to let syntax be determined by the order in which words come to mind.

A language feature that has received special attention in recent studies of student writing is cohesion, the tying together of sentences in text by means such as conjunctions, pronouns, and definite articles (Halliday & Hasan, 1976). Developmental gains in use of cohesive devices are typically found (Bracewell et al., 1982; King & Rentel, 1981; McCutchen & Perfetti, 1982). McCutchen & Perfetti (1982) show evidence, however, that the cohesive ties found in children's texts reflect developmental differences in memory search strategies giving rise to text content, and that these search strategies in turn reflect differences in children's sensitivity to coherence constraints in the writing assignment or in the existing text. Thus, in an unusually penetrating way, McCutchen and Perfetti show the interdependence of different parts of the cognitive system in text composition.

INTERVENTIONS

The dictation studies reported by Scardamalia et al. (1982) were intervention studies aimed at discovering the extent to which children's composing would become more expert-like if various low-level problems of production were eased. Although the greater speed of production made possible by dictation led to generating more text, there was nothing in the findings to suggest that quality of children's compositions was adversely affected by the mechanical difficulties of writing.

Another intervention that may free writers from demands of written language production is simply to instruct them not to pay attention to mechanics, sentence formation, and the like. Teachers often advise students to ignore such problems in first drafts, believing that it will free them to attend more to content. A formal test of this conjecture was carried out by Glynn, Britton, Muth, and Dogan (1982) with college students. Students did, in fact, generate more ideas, the more low-level requirements they were instructed to ignore. These findings are thus consistent with those from dictation studies. Rather different results were reported with 11-year-olds, however, in a 1981 master's thesis by Jeffrey Fisher (1981). When told to ignore mechanics and focus on content while revising their stories, children did produce fewer mechanical changes but not more content changes. The most content changes were produced by repeated revision with no instructions to focus on anything in particular. Although the two studies are not similar enough to draw confident conclusions, it may be that what we have in the divergence of results between adults and preadolescents is the factor of intentional control rearing its head. Fisher's results suggest that for young writers it took extra mental effort for them to ignore mechanics. With college students, on the other hand, intentional control over language processes may be sufficiently well developed that certain monitoring processes can be turned off at will, thus saving mental capacity for use on other parts of the composing task.

We are not aware of intervention studies concerned with establishing intentional control over language choices. Sentence-combining practice is evidently effective in increasing the syntactic options available to writers (O'Hare, 1973), but there is no indication that it leads to greater voluntary control of these options. Mellon's expressed intent (1969) in devising sentence combining was, in fact, that it should promote automaticity. Bracewell (1980) found that children were able to exert more intentional control over syntax when the content to be expressed was given to them in tabular form than when it was given to them in sentence form. It is interesting in this connection that many of the discovery heuristics provided for students make use of matrices or other nonlinear formats, which may have the effect of breaking up automatic processes of linearization and forcing the student to give conscious thought to the construction of sentences and sentence sequences.

Goal Formulation and Planning

Protocol analyses have served to dramatize the amount and variety of planning that goes on in composition (Flower & Hayes, 1980a). As the term is commonly used in cognitive science, "planning" refers to working through a task at an abstract level before working through it concretely (Anderson, 1980; Newell, 1980). It is thus distinguishable from rehearsal, which refers to working through a task at approximately the same level of concreteness as will eventually be used. As we shall see, composition planning in children starts out more like rehearsal and gradually comes to be carried on at levels more remote from the level of text production. A level of special importance is that of goals and subgoals. A plan for any enterprise is, in fact, likely to consist mostly of subgoals rather than actions—"get lawnmower fixed," "patch tent," and so forth. While all writers presumably have goals of some kind, not all writers are able to construct networks of subgoals leading to their main goals.

EXPERT COMPETENCE

Flower and Hayes (1981) show that expert writers very purposefully plan by translating high-level goals into subgoals —for instance, converting the goal of "Make this part interesting" into "So I'll start with a list of jobs they might consider." The result of this active construction of goals, however, is that subgoals tend to pile up, creating a potentially serious burden on working memory, which the skilled writer must accordingly have strategies for handling (Flower & Hayes, 1980b).

Skillful planning is often "opportunistic" (Hayes-Roth & Hayes-Roth, 1979). The planner recognizes when the attainment of one subgoal creates the opportunity for attaining another, and so chooses and arranges subgoals accordingly. Opportunities are often discovered in the course of writing rather than in advance, so that planning goes on throughout the composing process (Flower & Hayes, 1980a; Matsuhashi, 1982). The result is that even top-level goals may undergo change and thus have an emergent quality. Compositions often turn out in ways unanticipated by the writer (Murray, 1978), but this is not an indication of planlessness. Rather it is an indication of a very dynamic planning process that keeps adjusting decisions at every level in the light of decisions made at other levels (cf. Hayes-Roth & Hayes-Roth, 1979).

STUDENT COMPETENCE

Graves (1975) sees the beginnings of children's composition planning in their use of drawing or acting things out as a preliminary to writing. Graves aptly calls this "rehearsal," however; for although it involves working through the task in a different form, it is done at a level at least as concrete as that of the eventual writing. When fourth graders are asked to plan a composition in advance, what they do is clearly rehearsal. The material they generate either orally or in notes closely resembles the eventual product and may properly be regarded as a first draft rather than a plan (Burtis et al., 1983). Between the sixth and the eighth grade students' protocols and notes start to show evidence of working at a more abstract level than text production. Notes are more telegraphic, and sometimes refer to abstract entities like "my position" (Burtis et al., 1983). This suggests planning at the level of *conceptual development* or *ideas* in Beaugrande's model (see Figure 27.2). But there is little evidence of planning at the level of *goals*.

In 24 recently analyzed planning protocols from sixth graders we found only 1 protocol that contained as many as two references to goals; 6 contained one reference, and the remaining 17 contained no references to goals. Thus, even though these young students may have goals and occasionally allude to them, goals do not appear to enter explicitly into the planning process. Protocol data from adult novices show more references to goals, but goals still do not appear to be the highly functional symbolic entities that they are for experts, and there is an absence of formulation of subgoals (Flower & Hayes, 1981; Perl, 1979).

The problem of flexible access comes to the fore here as it does with respect to discourse schema knowledge. In order for goals to be operated on in planning it is not enough that they exist as tacit knowledge that constrains behavior; they must be mentally represented in a way that permits them to be consulted, altered, and decomposed. Evidence about goal representations is difficult to come by, but indirect evidence may be gleaned from recall protocols. Scardamalia and Paris (1985) found that when school-age writers were asked to state their main goal after writing they tended to restate the assignment or to summarize the main point they were trying to make (a representation at the level of *ideas* rather than *goals*), whereas graduate students were likely to give an elaborated goal statement much like those observed by Flower and Hayes in composing protocols. When asked to recall details of text, such as how many times they used a certain word, graduate students sometimes recalled goals as an aid to reconstructing the surface text, whereas young writers worked directly with memory of the surface text.

It is frequently pointed out as a criticism of school writing tasks that they are too meaningless to elicit much goal-directed thought on the part of students (A. Applebee, 1981; Macrorie, 1976). This might help explain why students have not developed goal-related planning processes, but it does not serve as grounds for dismissing the evidence. Skilled writers, when given a task that they consider unfitting, may complain; but once they set about composing, they start constructing goals (Bereiter & Scardamalia, 1983a). It is important, we believe, to look on goal construction as a part of writing competence and not as an externally determined precondition of good writing.

Can young writers carry out goal-related planning more successfully in narrative than in other genres? The fact that children can construct stories with plots would seem to stand as evidence that they can. Bartlett (1982) reported children by the middle school years to make use of foreshadowing statements of the "little did they know" variety, which would seem even more surely to evidence planning ahead to rhetorical targets. Not enough is known about the mental process of story construction to permit us to take these external indications as prima facie evidence, however. Children are known to have trouble with stories that occur in any but normal event order (Stein & Trabasso, 1982). The foreshadowed events in Bartlett's study were pictorially present, so that they did not have to be held in mind. Burtis (1983) compared thinking aloud protocols of young writers planning stories and arguments and found no greater evidence of high-level planning with narratives.

One story feature that would require goal-directed planning is suspense, which depends on building slowly toward a crucial

MARLENE SCARDAMALIA AND CARL BEREITER

event. Bereiter & Scardamalia (1984b) reported a study in which students in Grades 3 through 7 tried to write suspenseful stories and then rewrote them to make them more suspenseful, after having been exposed to instruction and/or a model suspense story. Only 26% of the original stories were rated as at least moderately suspenseful, and there was no increase in this percentage on revision. Although children are undoubtedly more successful in some respects with stories than with other literary forms (Hidi & Hildyard, 1983; McCutchen & Perfetti, 1982), evidence does not suggest that it is because they can carry out a higher level of planning in narrative. It is even possible that narrative, because it is so heavily constrained schematically, elicits a more concrete level of intellectual activity than other forms. Olson, Mack, and Duffy (1981) report that when reading narrative, readers tend to predict concrete content whereas with other genres they make more abstract predictions of type of content.

INTERVENTIONS

An experimental intervention that has been shown to produce increased amounts of goal-directed planning is the ending sentence task, in which students are given a sentence that their composition must lead up to (Tetroe, Bereiter, & Scardamalia, 1981). Whether this task has instructional value is a matter currently under investigation. For the present, research using ending sentence tasks has served to indicate two things: (a) students' difficulties perhaps lie more in goal construction and representation than in strategies for pursuing goals. When goals are articulated and made salient for them, problem-solving processes are brought into play; (b) there is a definite information-processing load associated with holding composition subgoals in mind. Tetroe, in thesis research summarized by Bereiter & Scardamalia (1984), varied the number of constraints imposed by ending sentences. For instance, the phrase "a crowd of angry people" was assumed to contain one more constraint than "a crowd of people." She found that the number of ending-sentence constraints children could handle was predictable from independent measures of their working memory capacity. Scardamalia (1981) presents analyses of performance on other composition tasks that also show severe limits on the number of constraints or subgoals that young writers can cope with simultaneously.

Interventions that have a significant effect on goal formulation itself remain to be demonstrated. Reports of "conferencing" indicate that teachers may often perform the function of helping children articulate goals and convert global intentions into operative subgoals (Brandt, 1982; Graves, 1978). The goal-formulating process in these cases, however, would appear to rely on executive processes in the mind of the teacher. The problem is how to induce such processes in the mind of the student. In the next section we report interventions that have been successful in increasing the amount of planning and the amount of reflective thought that goes on in planning.

Reprocessing

Reprocessing refers to the notion that whatever is produced from an episode of text processing—be it text, notes, or

thoughts—can be used as input to a further cycle of processing that does not simply add to what was produced before but transforms it. Reprocessing thus spans everything from editing for mistakes to reformulating goals. Revision is a special case of reprocessing, applied to actual text. But as Murray (1978) explains, revision itself can encompass fundamentally different kinds of reprocessing. Murray distinguishes "internal revision," in which writers try "to discover and develop what they have to say" (p. 91), from "external revision," in which text is shaped toward its intended audience.

According to Murray, revision begins with the reading of a completed first draft. Composing protocols, however, sometimes show a great deal of reprocessing of both the "internal" and the "external" type going on during the creation of a draft (see, for instance, the transcripts provided by Emig, 1971). Accordingly, the concept of reprocessing is a more suitable theoretical term than revision because it refers to what goes on mentally rather than being tied to differences in surface behavior.

Reprocessing is of interest not only because of its effect on the final composition but also because of its effect on the writer's knowledge. Discussions by writers are replete with testimonials to the effect that their understanding of what they are trying to say emerges in the course of writing rather than preceding it (Lowenthal, 1980: Murray, 1978; Odell, 1980). From an information-processing viewpoint there is nothing romantic or implausible about these claims. If knowledge consists of propositions constructed by the knower, then it stands to reason that progressive reconstruction of propositions should generate new knowledge. This "epistemic" function of writing (Bereiter, 1980) has made it seem promising to use writing as a vehicle to promote learning in subject matter courses (Lehr, 1980). However, such uses of writing presuppose that the writer is engaged in active reprocessing at the level of concepts and central ideas, something that, as we shall see, cannot be taken for granted.

EXPERT COMPETENCE

Although protocol data show instances of reconsidering, modifying, and elaborating decisions at different levels, the main evidence about the importance of reprocessing in expert competence comes from testimonials like those referred to above. Steinberg (1980) enters the cautionary note that not all expert writing is a process of discovery. On the other hand, expert writers can often turn a run-of-the-mill writing chore into one that involves discovery. We have speculated that this is done by an assimilative process of reconstructing the goal so that it incorporates both the pragmatic goal or assignment and other goals of personal importance to the writer (Scardamalia & Bereiter, 1982).

Skilled writers differ widely in overt behavior associated with reprocessing—in how many drafts they produce, in how much they fuss over the first draft, and so forth (Della-Piana, 1978; Emig, 1971; Wason, 1980). Hayes and Flower (1980a) indicate, however, that these large overt differences could be due to relatively minor "program" changes at the cognitive process level. An interesting untested hypothesis related to this is that skilled writers ought to be able to shift to a different overt behavior pattern with little difficulty and little effect on the eventual product.

STUDENT COMPETENCE

Revising by students has received a great deal of research attention, both because of its assumed importance and because students manifestly do so little of it (National Assessment of Educational Progress, 1977; Nold, 1981). Revising, even by college students, tends to be concentrated at the level of proofreading, with little revision of content (Crowley, 1977; Faigley & Witte, 1981; Sommers, 1980). However, for students at a given level of expertise, more revision is not associated with better writing (Beach, 1979; Bridwell, 1980; Faigley & Witte, 1981).

Although paucity of revision suggests paucity of reprocessing, there is evidence that certain kinds of reprocessing do go on in student writers. Momentary changes between the words students say they are about to write and the words they actually do write have been observed both at elementary (Scardamalia et al., 1982) and university levels (Beaugrande, 1984). Comparing notes taken during planning and eventual texts, Burtis et al. (1983) found that by age 14 no notes were incorporated into text without major change. Even at age 10 about half the notes eventually incorporated into text underwent some major change—elaboration, reordering, combination, or addition.

The kind of reprocessing that does not appear to go on in immature writers is that involving goals and main ideas (Perl, 1979; Sommers, 1980). This, of course, is serious, because it is reprocessing at these levels that is most likely to result in new knowledge. As we have noted previously, however, there is evidence that novices do not represent text explicitly at the level of goals and main ideas. Thus, to the extent that reprocessing consists of deliberate operation on such mental representations, novices cannot be expected to reprocess at high levels because they have not constructed the mental representations they need for reprocessing.

INTERVENTIONS

The preceding analysis would suggest that direct efforts to boost revision would not be very successful, and this has often been found to be the case (e.g., Beach, 1979; Hansen, 1978). On the other hand, with certain kinds of external support, children even in the primary grades have been reported to make substantive revisions of their compositions (Calkins, 1979; Graves, 1978). Graves is quoted (Brandt, 1982) as saying that the task of the teacher in providing this support is

> to figure out "what the kid is about, what he has in mind," and help him resee and rethink it until it's clear, not by telling him what to say but by asking questions. (p. 57)

This suggests that what the teacher is doing is providing the executive structure for reprocessing, and that accordingly what prevents students from carrying out successful revision by themselves is the lack of such an executive structure.

A series of studies by members of the Toronto Writing Research group have explored this possibility through the use of interventions that provide carefully limited forms of executive support. (See Bereiter & Scardamalia, 1983b, for a general discussion of this research strategy, under the rubric of "simulation by intervention.") The first study used a procedure in which students stopped after every sentence to execute a routine of evaluating, diagnosing, choosing a tactic, and carrying out any revision decided on (Scardamalia & Bereiter, 1983b). The second study used a procedure more oriented to the whole text, which consisted of reading the text, placing markers where problems were noted, and then diagnosing the problems and selecting remedies (Scardamalia & Bereiter, in press-a). In both cases the procedures were simplified by providing a fixed set of evaluations or diagnoses to choose from. The outstanding result in both studies was the high quality of evaluations made by the students, as judged in relation to evaluations made by professionals. The procedures also elicited higher level revisions than those normally observed, a significant majority of which were rated as positive. The second study also showed evidence of transfer. A more extended classroom trial of these kinds of "procedural facilitations" has shown significant improvements in quality of the whole text as well as in quality of individual revisions (Cohen & Scardamalia, 1983).

These results suggest that lack of an executive procedure for reprocessing is at least a contributory factor in young writers' problems with revision. Comments by the students themselves strongly supported this interpretation (Scardamalia & Bereiter, in press-b). Procedural facilitation of reprocessing has been extended to planning, through the use of cue cards that suggest reflective moves in the course of thinking aloud—"An important point I haven't considered yet is . . . ," and so forth. This intervention has been found to increase rated reflectiveness of essays and to transfer to a significant increase in the number of reflective statements in unassisted planning protocols (Scardamalia & Bereiter, in press-a; Scardamalia, Bereiter & Steinbach, 1984).

In all of these "simulation by intervention" studies the kind of reprocessing that has been observed has tended to be at what we would consider a local level—reconsidering a particular expression or point rather than one's whole approach or viewpoint. At least in the later studies, the importance of higher level reprocessing was discussed with students and they showed every indication of wanting to do it. That the majority of students had trouble doing so points again to the problem of mental representation—that without mental representations of goals and central ideas, reprocessing them is impossible. It is possible that some very general rise in the level of mental representation of problems is required, something comparable to the attainment of formal operational thought (Inhelder & Piaget, 1958). Even if this should be true, however, it would seem that written composition, carried out with as high a level of planning and reflection as children are capable of, should be an important way of fostering this overall development or representational ability.

Differences in Composing Strategies

In the preceding sections a number of seemingly major differences were noted between the composing processes of experts and immature writers. These differences were found mainly in the kinds of mental representations writers have available to work on and in their ability to exert deliberate control over subprocesses. It is not difficult, on the basis of these differences, to explain why novices do not write as well as experts. What is difficult to account for is why young people write as well as they do—why, given any reasonable writing assignment, most students can set to work immediately and produce a composition that makes sense, that is on topic, and that meets structural requirements of the appropriate genre.

The general character of expert composing strategies has already been discussed in the section on the nature of the composing process. Hayes and Flower (1980a) have aptly characterized expert composing as a form of problem solving. It is heuristic search through a space consisting of mental representations of possible text. It is, however, as Beaugrande's model (1984) emphasizes, problem solving carried on through parallel action in a number of different problem spaces, each characterized by a different kind or level of mental representation of possible text.

We have proposed that immature writers manage to cope with the difficulties of composition by using a greatly simplified version of what might be considered the *generating* component of Hayes and Flower's model. A model of this strategy, called "knowledge telling" (Bereiter & Scardamalia, in press) is presented in its crudest form in Figure 27.3. The term "knowledge telling" refers to the strategy's key simplifying feature, which consists of converting all writing tasks into tasks of telling what one knows about a topic.

This model, like all other descriptions of cognitive strategies, is a hypothetical construction, not directly observable but testable according to its ability to account for known facts. Although this model was based on studies of school-age writers, it appears to fit many college and university students as well. A description by Perl (1979) of the planning activity of novice college writers will be found to correspond closely to the first four steps in the model. And the following description by Crowley (1977) serves as a virtual exegesis of the knowledge-telling model:

> The students' model of the composing process, then, moves in a straight line from writing-as-remembering or writing-by-pattern through editing for mechanical errors. The students' writing process is strictly linear, with little or no recursive movement. Synthesis—the composing—is either automatic, a spontaneous flow of memory generated by a writing idea, or generated by the imposition of an organizational pattern—an outline of main and subordinated ideas—which dictates the flow of prose. (p. 167)

The knowledge-telling model offers a way of accounting for the ability of young people to compose even though they have access to only a limited range of mental representations. It accounts for novice writers' occasional eloquence when they strike a topic that spontaneously elicits rich material from memory. Since knowledge telling is a component of an expert composing strategy, it is understandable how, with certain kinds of guidance that provide a more sophisticated executive structure for knowledge telling to work within, young writers can exhibit expert-like planning and reprocessing. But it also explains why the typical piece of unassisted writing by students should strike evaluators as lacking plan and purpose (Larson, 1971) and showing "an innocent lack of consideration for what their readers know and do not know, and for what they are or are not interested in" (Maimon, 1979, p. 364).

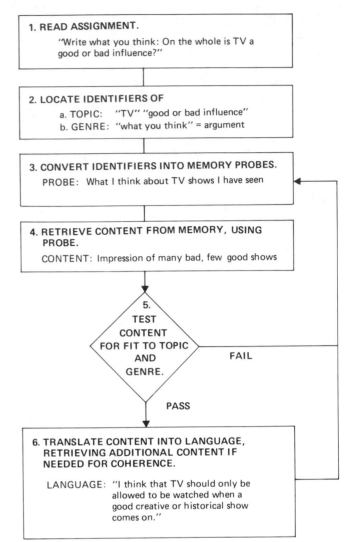

Fig. 27.3 A model of text generation according to the knowledge-telling strategy.

Knowledge telling is capable of refinement in several ways to incorporate goals and reader-related considerations. Additional test criteria may be inserted at Step 5 (Figure 27.3), so that items are rejected if they fail, for example, to meet a criterion of plausibility or interestingness. In this way young writers can achieve the kind of local-level reprocessing that was reported in the preceding section. There would seem to be a limit to the amount of refinement that can be achieved in this way, however. Caccamise's findings on idea generation (in press) indicate that as test criteria are added efficiency of memory retrieval declines and the burden on working memory increases. Thus one would expect the knowledge-telling strategy to break down when too many test criteria are added, and this could well be the cause of some student writing blocks (cf. Rose, 1980).

Another refinement of the basic strategy is to switch it from producing text as output to producing notes, which may then be subjected to further tests that do not have to be kept in mind during content generation. Protocol studies show students making this switch between Grades 4 and 10 (Burtis et al., 1983). None of these refinements, however, turn knowledge telling into a strategy that permits strategic pursuit of rhetorical goals or the reprocessing of goals and main ideas that results in growth of knowledge through writing. Thus, in some fundamental and extremely important respects, the knowledge-telling strategy appears to be a developmental dead end. In later sections we will be considering various approaches to instruction in light of their promise for inducing development beyond the knowledge-telling strategy.

Two questions need to be raised about the generalizability of the knowledge-telling model. First, although it seems to describe the performance of many students, there are documented exceptions in the form of young writers who show expert-like goal formulation and reprocessing. There does not seem to be at present any way of determining whether these cases reflect the large unexplained variations in talent found in all the arts or whether they reflect life experiences that could make most children into accomplished writers. Second, although evidence supporting the knowledge-telling model comes from many sources, the kinds of writing episodes examined are the relatively brief ones characteristic of school writing activities. Would different strategies appear in extended writing? Because extended writing by schoolchildren usually involves considerable teacher participation in the composing process (cf. Crowhurst, 1979), one cannot take performance in such situations as more than suggestive. One possibility worth investigating is that mental representations of goals and central ideas may take shape very slowly in the minds of immature writers and therefore may emerge only in extended writing.

It has frequently been suggested that the kind of strategy represented in the knowledge-telling model is an adaptive response to the peculiar social context of school writing (A. Applebee, 1981; Perl, 1979; Shaughnessy, 1977b). Bereiter and Scardamalia (in press) itemize eleven common educational practices (some of them virtually unalterable) that encourage a knowledge-telling strategy. There would seem to be fertile ground here for combined cognitive and ethnomethodological research.

Instructional Issues

Conceivably research on the composing process will lead in time to a coherent "cognitive approach" to writing instruction. Such an approach does not exist at present, however, and it is not necessarily a desirable eventuality if it means yet another approach to be put into competition with existing ones. Undoubtedly one hope motivating most people doing cognitive process research on writing is that it will lead to means of teaching expert composing processes to novices. That does not necessarily mean creating a rival method, however. Research on the composing process may also contribute to the teaching of writing by (a) improving existing approaches, (b) suggesting new or more clearly specified instructional goals, and (c) providing a generally more powerful conceptual basis for planning writing instruction. In the sections that follow, actual and potential contributions of these types will be discussed.

Contexts for School Writing

"Contexts" has become almost as much a buzz word as "process" in current talk about writing instruction. It reflects the fact that writing occurs in many different situations and under a variety of conditions, all of which contribute, for good or ill, to the child's development as a writer. Consequently, an understanding of writing development requires attending to all these contexts in which writing occurs, examining the motives for writing, the task demands, and the social supports that prevail in them (Graves, 1981; Mosenthal, 1983). The main contexts for school writing that receive attention in the educational literature may be summarized as follows:

WRITING AS A SELF-CONTAINED ACTIVITY

Here we refer to contexts in which writing is the focal activity and where it is carried out for its intrinsic satisfactions. Examples range from elaborately organized writing workshops (Crowhurst, 1979) to the perfunctory "On Friday afternoons we do creative writing." The type of writing commonly involved is "expressive" writing, which James Britton has defined as "writing that assumes an interest in the writer as well as in what he has to say about the world" (1982, p. 156). It spans the functions Florio and Clark (1982) classify as "writing to know oneself and others" and "writing to occupy free time." Among the kinds of expressive writing figuring in school activities are personal journal writing, personal experience narratives, and interpersonal exchanges, such as journal entries that form the basis for correspondence between teacher and student (Staton, 1980).

Although data collected with a view to external validity are close to nonexistent, there seems little reason to doubt the abundance of case material indicating that, given a reasonably supportive context, most children will take readily to opportunities for expressive writing (Calkins, 1983; Graves, 1983). There thus seems to be substantial merit in the current enthusiasm for expressive activity approaches to writing, especially as regards developing written language fluency and a sense of the personal satisfactions that can come from writing.

Research on composing processes raises two questions about expressive writing activities, however. The first has to do with how much expressive writing calls upon the higher processes involved in expert writing. From a processing standpoint, expressive writing would seem to have the following characteristics: (a) readily available content, so that heuristic search of memory is not required; (b) little need for intentional framing of the discourse, since content may be adequately presented in the form given to it in memory (Flower, 1979); and (c) little need for goal-related planning, since the goal of the activity is to a large extent realized through the very act of expression. All of this serves to explain why expressive writing should be easier for novices than other kinds of writing, but it also suggests that it may be limited in the kinds and levels of writing abilities it can be expected to foster. Thus there is reason, from an instructional viewpoint, to regard expressive writing as a preliminary or bridge to other kinds of writing (Britton, 1982).

The second question concerns the role of the teacher. In currently popular activity approaches to writing, the teacher serves as a collaborator rather than an instructor (Dyson & Jensen, 1981). The teacher's collaborative function is likely to include taking over certain executive functions, such as directing goal formation and memory search, and serving as the source of high-level representations of the student's text. This could be an aid or an impediment to learning, depending on what students are able to internalize from the collaborative process (see subsequent section titled "The Problem of Internalization").

WRITING AS A CONTRIBUTORY ACTIVITY

Here we refer to contexts in which writing is not the focal activity but where it is carried out as instrumental to or incidental to some other activity. In his study of writing in secondary schools, A. Applebee (1981) found that most student writing was not done as part of writing instruction but was incidental to other activities, such as taking tests or carrying out learning activities in various subjects. The "Writing Across the Curriculum" movement is dedicated to promoting and improving such contributory functions of writing (A. Applebee, 1977). Florio and Clark (1982) found that one of the main ways the elementary school teachers they studied worked writing into the curriculum was by devising ways to make it incidental to other activities — for instance, constructing posters as part of a safety campaign.

The obvious advantage of contributory contexts is realism: As in most real-life contexts, writing is directed toward some pragmatic end rather than being done for its own sake. The principal limitation is in the range of purposes that writing can serve in school. A. Applebee (1981) found that most incidental writing in high school consisted of brief written responses executed for the purpose of displaying knowledge. Thus students received little experience with the larger purposes and problems of text production (but, it would appear, received plenty of encouragement for knowledge telling).

Although occasionally more red-blooded uses of writing are possible through community action projects, consumerism, and the like, it would seem that the most realistic prospect for improving practical uses of writing in the schools lies in discovering ways that writing can contribute to the existing purposes of subject matter courses. Current instructional research that points in this direction deals with summarization as an aid to learning from texts (Brown, Campione, & Day, 1981; Christophersen, 1981; Taylor, 1982). Lehr (1980) discusses a variety of other possibilities for integrating writing with classroom instruction.

WRITING AS EXERCISE OF SKILL

In this category we place all writing activities carried out for the explicit purpose of skill development. Included is actual composition writing, when the emphasis is placed on performance rather than on inner satisfaction or practical function, and also such ancillary activities as spelling drills and sentence-combining exercises, No sharp line divides writing as an activity from writing as exercise. Clark and Florio (1981) analyze an instance of something starting out as an informal activity (diary writing) and gradually becoming formalized into an exercise, and there are no doubt also instances of an exercise capturing student interest and evolving into an intrinsically motivated activity. Nevertheless it seems important to distinguish the exercise context from other school writing contexts because of its distinctive uses and problems.

Writing exercises account for the bulk of efforts to teach writing (A. Applebee, 1981). In recent years, however, exercise has come increasingly under attack as a fundamentally unsound way to teach writing. The grounds are that it is writing carried on without the normal sense of an audience and of communicative intent, with the result that the student fails to acquire a genuine sense of what it is to be a writer (Moffett, 1968; Smith, 1982) and develops a bland, depersonalized style that Macrorie (1976) calls "Engfish." It might also be speculated that the exercise context encourages development of low processing-demand composing strategies such as knowledge telling.

Not all writing exercise consists of composition assignments, however. Sentence-combining practice, which consists of assembling simple sentences into complex ones, under the guidance of rules or cues that ensure their well-formedness (Mellon, 1969; O'Hare, 1973), has yielded a preponderance of results showing gains in "syntactic maturity," with occasional indications of benefits for other aspects of writing ability and even for reading comprehension (see Stotsky, 1975, and White & Karl, 1980, for reviews).

An exercise context that has been little used in writing is the game. Games provide a context for purposeful, rule-governed activity. Design of nontrivial games for writing depends on having a theory of the underlying processes, however, since it is these processes and not the objective conditions of writing that games have the potential to generate. It is perhaps for this reason that writing activities posing game-like challenges to rhetorical skill have only recently begun to appear (Scardamalia, Bereiter, & Fillion, 1981).

WRITING INSTRUCTION

Compared to mathematics, for instance, where there is a great deal of explaining, demonstrating, and teaching of rules, very little direct instruction goes on in the teaching of writing. What there is is largely confined to teaching conventions — punctuation rules, format conventions, and the like, and even then teachers appear to rely mainly on practice and correction (A. Applebee, 1981). Composition textbooks attempt to provide explicit principles, but the principles themselves are often of dubious validity and there are indications that students tend to take them too literally and to overextend them (Beaugrande, 1984; Harris, 1979; Rose, 1980, 1981). All of this has suggested to some that writing belongs to the category of things that can be "learned but not taught" (Elbow, 1973).

The evidence that students tend to overapply textbook principles suggests, on the contrary, that explicit instruction can have a significant effect on how students write. The trick is to make it have a positive rather than a detrimental effect. A major challenge for modern writing research is to discover teachable principles that are valid and that students can readily convert into procedural knowledge (Anderson, 1982). Progress in this direction will be discussed later under the headings of "strategy instruction" and "product-oriented instruction."

Instructional Goals Related to the Composing Process

Traditionally, the goals of writing instruction have been expressed in terms of the qualities of good writing—clarity, organization, and the like—or in terms of abilities and aptitudes. One of the prospects of research on the composing process is that it might lead to the definition of instructional goals that can more readily be evaluated as to their attainability and more readily translated into instructional subgoals. From the earlier discussion of expert and novice strategies, three different instructional goals may be identified pertaining to development of composing strategies: (a) refining the knowledge-telling strategy, (b) inducing goal-directed strategies, and (c) fostering the development of reflective planning. These goals, it will be recognized, are distinct. Attaining one goal is not necessarily a step toward attaining another.

REFINING THE KNOWLEDGE-TELLING STRATEGY

The knowledge-telling strategy, as we have noted, is capable of considerable refinement by adding test criteria that enable the writer to reject inappropriate content or language and by adopting the practice of generating and arranging notes in advance of writing. In this way knowledge tellers can produce compositions meeting ordinary standards of style and content. Most traditional writing instruction seems to be aimed at this objective. That is, it is not concerned with altering the basic way students compose but rather with bringing their performance under the control of acceptable literary standards. Two serious limitations of the knowledge-telling strategy were pointed out, however: (a) Writing carried out through this strategy is not a very powerful tool either for achieving communicative aims or for developing one's understanding. (b) Refining knowledge telling through the addition of test criteria means decreased efficiency and increased burden on working memory as the number of test criteria increases. These practical limitations might mean that most people can never become very successful writers as long as they follow a knowledge-telling strategy.

INDUCING GOAL-DIRECTED STRATEGIES

The principal weakness of a knowledge-telling strategy is that it does not contain provisions for explicit formulation and pursuit of goals, thus severely limiting the writer's ability to realize intentions through writing. A common theme in calls for improving the conditions of writing in schools is that writing should become a more purposeful activity (A. Applebee, 1981; Macrorie, 1976; Muller, 1967). A reasonable assumption supporting these views is that if students are writing in situations where they are trying to accomplish something definite through their writing and where they can find out whether they achieved it, they will naturally acquire goal-directed strategies. That, surely, is how most cognitive strategies are learned, and it serves to explain some of the highly effective writing skills that Odell and Goswami (1982) have observed in business people.

A major difficulty, as noted in previous discussion, is to find school contexts that support writing goals other than knowledge display and self-expression. In the absence of conditions that normally motivate writing to convince, to inform, and so forth, educators may need to design games or problem tasks to create the necessary goal conditions. There is also, however, the problem that an overemphasis on pragmatic goals might lead to overly pragmatic composing strategies, oriented toward fixed goals and lacking the ability to harmonize personal and externally defined objectives (Scardamalia & Bereiter, 1982).

FOSTERING REFLECTIVE PLANNING

Reflective planning refers to the reprocessing or progressive shaping of goals and ideas during composition (Scardamalia & Bereiter, in press-a). In a model proposed by Scardamalia et al. (1984), reflective processes in writing are attributed to interaction between two problem spaces—a content space, in which problems of knowledge and belief are dealt with, and a rhetorical space, in which problems of achieving goals of the composition are dealt with. An instructional experiment reported by Scardamalia et al. (1984) gave evidence that the two-way interaction between problem spaces could be fostered in elementary school children. Reflective planning is an instructional goal of such obvious importance that it warrants continued research into its teachability.

New Approaches to Writing Instruction

A search through recent journals would indicate that methods of writing instruction receiving the most attention include conferencing (Graves, 1978), freewriting (Elbow, 1973), rhetoric of invention (Young, 1976), and sentence combining (Mellon, 1969). In the present discussion, however, these will be treated as special cases of more general types of innovative approach to writing instruction. In the past, methods of writing instruction have tended to grow up piecemeal, connected to one another, if at all, only by broad philosophical premises. Research on composing processes has advanced far enough, however, that it is now possible to identify certain basic ways of trying to influence the composing process and thus to consider particular methods in terms of how they attempt to bring about such changes. The four basic approaches that will be considered here are strategy instruction (the most direct approach), procedural facilitation (a generic label for a variety of ways of helping students adopt more sophisticated composing strategies by providing external supports), product-oriented instruction (instruction that attempts to promote strategy development by providing students with clearer knowledge of goals to strive for in the written product), and inquiry learning (learning through guided experimentation and exploration).

Strategy Instruction

Textbooks have begun to appear at the college level that present writing to students as a cognitive process and provide explicit instruction in cognitive strategies (Beaugrande, 1982c; Flower, 1981). There are informal reports that college students respond well to strategy instruction but there does not yet appear to be evidence available about the effect of such instruction on students' actual composing strategies. Before-and-after protocol analyses are obviously called for.

Such studies, carried out by the Toronto Writing Research Group with younger students, suggest problems in trying to use direct teaching of composing strategies with school-age writers. In one study students were instructed briefly in what adults think about when planning a composition—audience, goals, what they know about the subject, organization, and problems. Some students were taught these as principles, some saw them demonstrated by a videotaped model thinking aloud, and some received both kinds of instruction. Ten-year-olds could not reliably identify what kind of planning the model was doing and showed no effect from any treatment; 14-year-olds could reliably identify what the model was doing and showed signs of trying to imitate the model, but only at a very superficial level (Burtis et al., 1983). In a more extended instructional study with 12-year-olds (Scardamalia et al., 1984), before-and-after protocol analyses showed a significant increase in the number of planning statements judged to indicate reflective thought, but there was no systematic change in the distribution of kinds of planning carried out. The instruction provided in this latter study, moreover, included procedural facilitation as well as direct instruction, so that the results cannot be taken as a demonstration of effects of direct strategy instruction.

The only other before-and-after research we are aware of on strategy instruction also involves procedural facilitation. This is research on teaching students heuristics of discovery (Odell, 1974; Young, 1976). Students were taught principles and procedures for developing their thoughts on subjects in advance of writing, but were also provided with formal devices for organizing the discovery process. These studies, conducted with university students, produced results similar to the study with 12-year-olds cited above, with gains being observed in the amount of reflective thought revealed in compositions.

The basic problem in strategy instruction is how to convert declarative knowledge (knowledge about the composing process) into procedural knowledge or know-how. In his theory of skill acquisition, Anderson (1982) proposes that this conversion depends on the learner's having already available a general-purpose procedure that makes it possible to convert the declarative propositions into operative subgoals. In the case of students who already have a goal-directed composing strategy, it would accordingly be expected that they could benefit from suggestions interpretable as subgoals—for instance, the suggestion in Flower (1981) to define a "projected self" to be put across in the composition. But for students whose existing procedures were limited to knowledge telling, such suggestions would be expected to be ineffective because the students would have no way to convert them to subgoals that could be operative within the structure of their composing strategies.

Procedural Facilitation

An alternative to direct teaching of composing strategies is to provide students with help in carrying out more sophisticated composing processes. In a sense, the traditional practice of teacher comments on student compositions has this aim, insofar as the teacher's comments are expected to help students take a critical view of their work, consider more sophisticated alternatives, and so forth. Such help may be called "substan-tive" facilitation (Bereiter & Scardamalia, 1982). In effect, it involves the teacher as a collaborator. In recent times this collaborative role has come to be explicitly recognized as distinct from a direct instructional role (Dyson & Jensen, 1981). Even if the collaboration is limited to subtle probes and hints (e.g., Calkins, 1979), it still constitutes substantive facilitation to the extent that it involves the teacher's responding to what the student has said or intends to say.

In contrast to substantive facilitation is "procedural" facilitation (Bereiter & Scardamalia, 1982; Scardamalia & Bereiter, in press-b). In procedural facilitation help is of a nonspecific sort, related to the student's cognitive processes, but not responsive to the actual substance of what the student is thinking or writing. Help consists of supports intended to enable students to carry out more complex composing processes by themselves.

Procedural facilitation may be quite passive, such as that provided by a word processor, which simply makes it easier to execute certain mechanical parts of the composing process, thus presumably freeing the writer to devote more mental resources to higher level parts of the process (Daiute, 1982). A more active procedural facilitation is the provision of cue cards to prompt reflection during planning (Scardamalia & Bereiter, in press-a). Researchers in the rhetoric of invention have also made use of procedural facilitations, often in the form of matrices or other standard forms to be used for aiding heuristic search of memory and information sources (Young, 1976).

Substantive and procedural facilitation are compatible and can occur in combination, but they present somewhat different instructional problems. With substantive facilitation the problem is to provide help that promotes learning rather than making learning unnecessary. In the light of modern conceptions of the composing process, which see it as going on at multiple levels and as extending from initial intentions to finished product, this problem appears as considerably more complex than it does when one views composition as restricted to what one does with pen in hand. Problems with procedural facilitation have to do with the unpredictable uses students make of extrinsic inputs. Examples have been noted in earlier sections, such as the tendency to exploit all inputs as cues to aid memory search. The problems with both kinds of facilitation may, however, be subsumed under the general problem of internalization, which will be discussed in a later section.

Procedural facilitation appears to hold promise as a way of influencing the direction of attention during composing. We have seen evidence of transfer of facilitated procedures into unassisted composition in such areas as content generation (Bereiter & Scardamalia, 1982), attention to structural elements (Paris, 1980), critical evaluation of content, and diagnosis of text difficulties (study by Cattani, Scardamalia & Bereiter, reported in Scardamalia & Bereiter, in press-a). Such use of procedural facilitation presupposes, however, that the relevant mental representations are there to be attended to. It can do little good to direct students' attention to their goals for a composition if they are not consciously able to represent such goals. There is substantial evidence that procedural facilitation can increase the level of sophistication of the composing processes students carry out within the limits imposed by the kinds of mental representations they construct. It also seems reasonable to expect that it could foster development of higher level mental representations of text; but this remains to be systematically investigated.

CONFERENCING

Conferencing, which refers to any sort of one-to-one discussion between teacher and student during the evolution of a composition, can include both substantive and procedural facilitation. The teacher who says, "What do you think your next step should be in planning this essay?" is not responding substantively to the student's work but is simply helping direct attention to a procedural decision. A combination of procedural facilitation of planning and substantive facilitation of mental representations of goals and central ideas could provide supportive conditions for students to exercise more sophisticated composing strategies.

The main drawback of conferencing currently seems to be the tendency of many teachers to take too much of the initiative, casting the student in the role of "receiver of information" (Jacob, 1982). In more expert hands, there is continual attention to the students' internalizing the planning, evaluating, and other processes that go on in the writing conference (Calkins, 1983).

COMPUTER FACILITATION OF COMPOSING

Innovative work on the application of computers to writing is at present mainly focused on the "tool" use of computers—as word processors, automated editors, dictionaries, and encyclopedias, and as components in communication networks (Anandam, Eisel, & Kotler, 1980; Bruce & Rubin, in press; Frase, Macdonald, Gingrich, Keenan, & Collymore, 1981; Levin, Boruta, & Vasconcellos, 1983. For an overview, see Daiute (1983)

Computers appear to have potential for fostering higher-order abilities in composing, but software design is currently more determined by what computers can do than by what students need. Computers make it easy to move, delete, and add to text, thereby presumably fostering revision. But executing these external parts of the revision process is orders of magnitude easier than carrying out the nonobservable goal-constructing, monitoring, and problem-solving activities that are part of the mature revising process. Although there is much talk at educational computing conferences about enhanced tools that will facilitate mental processes in writing, the prototype software that has actually appeared consists mainly of additional information-manipulating aids for the writer who already has highly sophisticated composing strategies.

Computers can, for the novice writer, take on a variety of procedural facilitative roles such as cueing, short-term memory support, and segmenting and sequencing parts of the composing task. Burns and Culp (1980) were able to computerize invention heuristics through question-asking programs. A "help" program that provided procedural prompts was enthusiastically received by junior high school students, although it had no observable short-term effect on their composing (Woodruff et al., 1981). Whereas word processors eliminate only certain mechanical burdens of writing, it is possible for instructional purposes to have the computer selectively take over other parts of the composing process, so as to direct the learner's efforts to particular problems. Story Maker, for instance, is a program that supplies sentences, leaving the user to determine events (Rubin, 1980a), and EXPLORE leaves the user to make structural and stylistic decisions, the computer doing the rest of the work of producing an essay (Woodruff, Scardamalia, & Bereiter, 1982).

To be useful as procedural facilitations, computer software must induce mental processes that are not only of a higher level than those students normally employ but that can also have an influence on students' normal composing processes. There is evidence that the Writer's Workbench (Frase et al., 1981) may meet this requirement. It contains tools for automated analysis of style in texts. Kiefer and Smith (1983) found that university students who used these tools showed transfer to stylistic revision under unassisted writing conditions,

THE PROBLEM OF INTERNALIZATION

Procedural facilitation of no matter what variety is expected to have its instructional effect by providing external support for a procedure that the student will eventually run autonomously. Vygotsky (1978) called this movement from external dependence to autonomy "internalization." The term is apt in its suggestion that the externally supported process must correspond in a fundamental way to the intended internal process.

Although it is not easily answered, the question of internalizability needs to be asked about all the kinds of facilitation we have been considering, substantive as well as procedural. Heuristic invention procedures, for instance, are often aided by matrix forms that the student fills in as a way of elaborating thoughts in an organized way. Although such devices may lead students to generate the kinds of ideas experts generate, it does not seem very plausible that what goes on in the mind of the expert bears much correspondence to the matrix format. Is the procedure, therefore, likely to be one that students will abandon as soon as external supports are removed? On first thought, conferencing would seem to be well designed for internalization; the thinking, carried out jointly at first, comes in time to be carried out in the mind of the student. But the form of the conference is dialogue, and there is no indication from research to suggest that the mature composing process has the form of an internal dialogue. A more readily internalizable form might be the "assisted monologue" (Scardamalia et al., 1984) where the talking is primarily done by the student, with the teacher inserting prompts rather than conversational turns.

Sentence combining is perhaps the most surprising instructional intervention from the standpoint of internalization. Students are provided with short sentences that often do not make sense in the order presented, but which, when combined according to rule, deliver an intelligible message (Mellon, 1969). On the face of it, such a procedure bears no relation to how people normally compose sentences, since normally we have some prior idea of what we are trying to say. Yet the empirical evidence indicates that a syntactical process of some generality is internalized from sentence-combining practice (O'Hare, 1973). One can only surmise that, in spite of the evident dissimilarities, the contrived procedures used in sentence combining correspond at some deep level to the cognitive process by which a complex sentence is synthesized (cf. Bock, 1982). At any rate, the sentence-combining story makes it clear that our current understanding of cognitive processes is not sufficient to enable us to answer questions of internalization by deductive argument. Serious research is needed to determine what students internalize from what teachers have helped or induced them to do.

Product-Oriented Instruction

Popular discourse on writing instruction has set up a somewhat artificial contrast between "product" and "process" approaches, the former concentrating on evaluating and upgrading the quality of what students write, the latter concentrating in one way or other on the composing process. As Perkins (in press) has argued, however, one of the main ways that cognitive processes develop in real life is through striving to produce an adequate product; and the more realistically learners are aware of what product characteristics they should be striving for and of how successful they are in achieving them, the more likely it is that the attendant cognitive processes will develop.

Traditionally it has been the province of rhetoric to teach, through rules and examples, the characteristics of good written products—what constitutes a tightly knit paragraph, a convincing argument, and so forth. Two kinds of current cognitive research show promise of contributing to this tradition. Both kinds, interestingly, involve connections between reading and writing. One is research on the effects of various literary devices on readers and the other is research on how students learn or fail to learn from literary models.

Included in the first category are (a) studies that show how different organizations of content in text and different signals of that organization affect ability to recall the text (e.g., Meyer, 1977), (b) studies that show how use of a narrative format improves understanding of regulations (Flower et al., 1980), and (c) studies that show how manipulations of event order and narrative viewpoint generate effects such as surprise or suspense in readers (Brewer, 1980; Brewer & Lichtenstein, 1981). Also of interest are trade-offs among effects, as when devices used to make a text more readable reduce its rememberability (Collins & Gentner, 1980).

An obvious gain from research of this kind is that it should provide students with a basis for making more goal-related choices among literary alternatives. Furthermore, in order to study empirically the effects of literary devices, researchers are forced to define these devices explicitly (so that coders can use the definitions, for instance). This should have the result of producing descriptions of literary devices and strategies that are more accessible to students than many of the descriptions derived from traditional literary scholarship. We imagine, for instance, that Brewer and Lichtenstein's account of how suspense is produced in narratives could be more readily adapted to practice by novices than more purely literary analyses.

It is widely recognized that much of what students learn about writing must come from exposure to examples (Smith, 1982). The knowledge obtained from such reading is, of course, "product" knowledge; reading typically furnishes no clue to the process by which the literary work was brought into existence. At present it is largely a matter of assumption that obtaining knowledge of writing through reading requires some special

directing of attention, distinct from that required for ordinary reading comprehension. In current doctoral research at the Ontario Institute for Studies in Education, however, Nangar Sukumar has found measures of language awareness in reading to account for an additional 10% of the variance in high school students' rated writing ability, over and above the 32% accounted for by reading comprehension and general intelligence test scores.

Research on how people extract literary knowledge from examples has only recently begun, and only the most tentative results can be suggested. Elizabeth Church (Church & Bereiter, 1983) had high school students think aloud while reading different translations of a passage from the *Divine Comedy*. When told to pay attention to the style of the translation, students were able to do so for a short time, but then tended to lose hold of the instruction and lapse into attending only to content. This suggests that attending to style was not an orientation that students could simply switch on, but that it required conscious holding in mind of a constraint, and thus a risk of cognitive overload. When students were not told what to attend to, they attended only to content on first reading, but on subsequent readings a few began to attend to literary features. Most, once they had processed the content to their satisfaction, found nothing further to attend to.

In one part of the study, students were asked to compare two translations and then to convert a passage from one translation into the style of the other. There was substantial correspondence between the kinds of features noticed in reading and the kinds captured in imitation, which suggests that the thinking aloud procedure was picking up reading events that were relevant to writing. This study, and others conducted more recently by the present authors, demonstrate that students of all levels from Grade 3 up can extract some knowledge of literary features from examining model texts. However, the knowledge they most readily pick up is knowledge that could have easily been communicated through explicit statement. It remains for more extended investigations to find out what is required for students to pick up the more elusive qualities of style and form that teachers traditionally rely on literary models to communicate.

Inquiry learning

Writing instruction has no tradition of learning through guided inquiry and experimentation the way mathematics and science instruction do. However the inquiry approach to writing described by Hillocks (1982) comes close. This approach involves students in work with a data source, such as concrete objects or texts. Problems of interpreting the data are handled concurrently with writing problems, such as how to report observations and defend conclusions about the data. Hillocks reports studies by himself and others that show strong learning effects. This inquiry approach has obvious application to the use of writing in content areas. Also, the approach may foster reflective processes by encouraging interaction between content and rhetorical problem spaces (cf. Scardamalia et al., 1984).

A quite different sort of inquiry learning is represented by children's invention of their own writing systems. Descriptive accounts indicate that, given encouragement, children who do not yet know how to read will begin producing documents containing letters or symbols that they interpret meaningfully. Through efforts to communicate with adults and peers, they gradually adopt consistent symbols, linear arrangements, ways of showing divisions between words, and eventually conventions of spelling, punctuation, and the like (Bissex, 1980; Clay, 1975).

Educational effects of encouraging invented writing are just beginning to be tested. Obviously it enables children to start writing independently at an earlier age, and this benefit could be substantial. If there is some gain from the discovery process itself, it would seem likely to be in the form of metalinguistic awareness. Children should get an idea of writing as a communicative medium, and understanding that writing conventions are conventions, and an appreciation of what such conventions are for (Graves, 1983). Interestingly, a major payoff might come in reading rather than writing. According to the case studies of Read (1971) and Bissex (1980), children trying to work out their own spelling systems eventually settle on the idea of grapheme–phoneme correspondence. Thus, by inventing spelling they also invent phonics, which provides them with a tool for independent reading.

Another possibility for learning by discovery is the composing process itself. Techniques such as thinking aloud and procedural facilitation make interpretable data on the composing process available not only to researchers but also to students. In a paper titled "Child as Coinvestigator" (Scardamalia & Bereiter, 1983a), we detail a large number of procedures that have proved workable for involving students in explorations of their cognitive processes during composition. We have favorable reports of older students' designing and conducting composing process studies of their own. Even students who dislike writing have been found to be interested in investigating their composing processes.

Prospect

We sense a great deal of optimism among language arts educators that the conditions of learning to write will soon improve dramatically. Computer euphoria is one source of this optimism, but a better grounded source is the reports of what teachers have been able to do by way of creating a social climate supportive of written expression (e.g., Calkins, 1980; Staton, 1980). One teacher we know has even managed to involve families in what she calls a "culture of writing" by keeping up interactive journals with the parents, the children serving as intermediaries and sometimes as interpreters, since many of the parents are not literate in English.

There is no doubt that if a "culture of writing" can be established, learning to write should be greatly facilitated. The same cognitive changes would have to occur as have been discussed in this chapter, but the likelihood would become greater that they could occur through informal learning. It must be recognized, however, that what has actually been observed so far has been the often heroic efforts of a relative handful of dedicated teachers, and not a massive cultural shift supportive of literacy.

Even a moderately optimistic forecast would have to allow that the teaching of writing will probably continue to take place in a relatively uncongenial cultural environment — so that there is little prospect, for instance, that children will learn to write as naturally as they learn to talk (even if there is no biological impediment to their doing so). Accordingly, there is likely to be a continuing need for instructional solutions to writing problems. The hopeful prospect offered by research on composing processes is that certain processes that are not currently teachable may become so. Thus there is ground for optimism that the job of the writing teacher may take on a more progressive character and be less tied to the endless cycle of practice and response.

REFERENCES

Anandam, K., Eisel, E., & Kotler, L. (1980). Effectiveness of a computer-based feedback system for writing. *Journal of Computer-Based Instruction, 6*(4), 125–133.

Anderson, J. R. (1980). *Cognitive psychology and its implications.* San Francisco, W. H. Freeman.

Anderson, J. R. (1982). Acquisition of cognitive skill. *Psychological Review, 89,* 369–406.

Applebee, A. N. (1977). Eric/RCS Report: Writing across the curriculum: The London projects. *English Journal, 66*(9), 81–85.

Applebee, A. N. (1981). *Writing in the secondary school: English and the content areas.* Urbana, IL: National Council of Teachers of English.

Applebee, R. K. (1966). National study of High School English programs: A record of English teaching today. *English Journal, 55,* 273–281.

Augustine, D. (1981). Geometries and words: Linguistics and philosophy: A model of the composing process. *College English, 43*(3), 221–231.

Bartlett, E. (1982). *Children's difficulties in establishing consistent voice and space/time dimensions in narrative text.* Paper presented at the meeting of the American Educational Research Association, New York.

Beach, R. (1979). The effects of between-draft teacher evaluation versus student self-evaluation on high school students' revising of rough drafts. *Research on the Teaching of English, 13,* 111–119.

Beaugrande, R. de. (1982a). Psychology and composition: Past, present, future. In M. Nystrand (Ed.), *What writers know: The language, process, and structure of written discourse* (pp. 211–267). New York: Academic Press.

Beaugrande, R. de. (1982b). The story of grammars and the grammar of stories. *Journal of Pragmatics, 6,* 383–422.

Beaugrande, R. de. (1982c). *Writing step by step.* Gainsville: University of Florida, Office of Instructional Resources.

Beaugrande, R. de. (1984). *Text production: Toward a science of composition.* Norwood, NJ: Ablex.

Bereiter, C. (1980). Development in writing. In L. W. Gregg & E. R. Steinberg (Eds.), *Cognitive processes in writing* (pp. 73–93). Hillsdale, NJ: Lawrence Erlbaum.

Bereiter, C., & Scardamalia, M. (1982). From conversation to composition: The role of instruction in a developmental process. In R. Glaser (Ed.), *Advances in instructional psychology* (Vol. 2, pp. 1–64). Hillsdale, NJ: Lawrence Erlbaum.

Bereiter, C., & Scardamalia, M. (1983a). Does learning to write have to be so difficult? In A. Freedman, I. Pringle, & J. Yalden (Eds.), *Learning to write: First language, second language* (pp. 20–33). London: Longman.

Bereiter, C., & Scardamalia, M. (1983b). Levels of inquiry in writing research. In P. Mosenthal, S. Walmsley, & L. Tamor (Eds.), *Research on writing: Principles and methods* (pp. 3–25). New York: Longman.

Bereiter, C., & Scardamalia, M. (1984a). Information processing demand of text composition. In H. Mandl, N. Stein, & T. Trabasso (Eds.), *Learning and comprehension of text* (pp. 407–428) Hillsdale, NJ: Lawrence Erlbaum.

Bereiter, C., & Scardamalia, M. (1984b). Learning about writing from reading. *Written Communication, 1*(2), 163–188.

Bereiter, C., & Scardamalia, M. (in press). Cognitive coping strategies and the problem of "inert knowledge." In S. S. Chipman, J. W. Segal, & R. Glaser (Eds.), *Thinking and learning skills: Current research and open questions* (Vol. 2). Hillsdale, NJ: Lawrence Erlbaum.

Bissex, G. L. (1980). *GYNS AT WRK: A child learns to write and read.* Cambridge, MA: Harvard University Press.

Black, J. B. (1982). Psycholinguistic processes in writing. In S. Rosenberg (Ed.), *Handbook of applied psycholinguistics: Major thrust of research and theory* (pp. 199–216). Hillsdale, NJ: Lawrence Erlbaum.

Black, J. B., Galambos, J. A., & Reiser, B. J. (1984). Coordinating discovery and verification research. In D. Kieras & M. Just (Eds.), *New methods in reading comprehension.* Hillsdale, NJ: Lawrence Erlbaum.

Black, J. B. & Wilensky, R. (1979). An evaluation of story grammars. *Cognitive Science, 3,* 213–230.

Bock, J. K. (1982). Toward a cognitive psychology of syntax: Information processing contributions to sentence formulation. *Psychological Review, 89,* 1–47.

Boiarsky, C. (1982). Prewriting is the essence of writing. *English Journal, 71*(4), 44–47.

Botvin, G. J., & Sutton-Smith, B. (1977). The development of structural complexity in children's fantasy narratives. *Developmental Psychology, 13,* 377–388.

Bracewell, R. J. (1980). Writing as a cognitive activity. *Visible Language, 14,* 400–422.

Bracewell, R. J. (1983). Investigating the control of writing skills. In P. Mosenthal, S. Walmsley, & L Tamor (Eds.), *Research on writing: Principles and methods.* (pp. 177–203). New York: Longman.

Bracewell, R. J., Frederiksen, C. H., & Frederiksen, J. F. (1982). Cognitive processes in composing and comprehending discourse. *Educational Psychologist, 17*(3), 146–164.

Brandt, A. (1982). Writing readiness. *Psychology Today, 16*(3), 55–59.

Brewer, W. F. (1980). Literary theory, rhetoric, and stylistics: Implications for psychology. In R. J. Spiro, B. C. Bruce, & W. F. Brewer (Eds.), *Theoretical issues in reading comprehension* (pp. 221–239). Hillsdale, NJ: Lawrence Erlbaum.

Brewer, W. F., & Lichtenstein, E. H. (1981). Event schemas, story schemas, and story grammars. In A. D. Baddley & J. Long (Eds.), *Attention and performance* (Vol. 9, pp. 363–379). Hillsdale, NJ: Lawrence Erlbaum.

Bridwell, L. S. (1980). Revising strategies in twelfth grade students: Transactional writing. *Research in the Teaching of English, 14,* 107–122.

Britton, J. (1982). Spectator role and the beginnings of writing. In M. Nystrand (Ed.), *What writers know: The language, process, and structure of written discourse* (pp. 149–169). New York: Academic Press, 149–169.

Britton, J., Burgess, T., Martin, N., McLeod, A., & Rosen, H. (1975). *The development of writing abilities (11–18).* London: Macmillan Education Ltd.

Brown, A. L., Campione, J. C., & Day, J. D. (1981). Learning to learn: On training students to learn from texts. *Educational Researcher, 10*(2), 14–21.

Bruce, B. C., & Rubin, A. D. (in press). What we're learning with QUILL. In M. L. Kamil & R. C. Leslie (Eds.), *Perspectives on computers and instruction for reading and writing.* Rochester, NY: National Reading Conference.

Burns, H. L., & Culp, G. H. (1980). Stimulating invention in English composition through computer-assisted instruction. *Educational Technology, 20*(8), 5–10.

Burtis, P. J. (1983). *Planning in narrative and argument writing.* Paper presented at the meeting of the American Educational Research Association, Montreal.

Burtis, P. J., Bereiter, C., Scardamalia, M., & Tetroe, J. (1983). The development of planning in writing. In G. Wells & B. M. Kroll (Eds.), *Explorations in the development of writing* (pp. 153–174). Chichester, England: John Wiley.

Caccamise, D. J. (in press). Idea generation in writing. In A. Matsuhashi (Ed.), *Writing in real time: Modelling production processes.* New York: Longman.

Calkins, L. M. (1979). Andrea learns to make writing hard. *Language Arts, 56,* 569–576.

Calkins, L. M. (1980). Research update: When children want to punctuate: Basic skills belong in context. *Language Arts, 57*(5), 567–573.

Calkins, L. M. (1983). *Lessons from a child: On the teaching and learning of writing.* Exeter, NH: Heineman Educational Books.

Chafe, W. L. (1977). Creativity in verbalization and its implications for the nature of stored knowledge. In R. O. Freedle (Ed.), *Discourse production and comprehension* (pp. 41–55). Norwood, NJ: Ablex.

Christophersen, S. L. (1981). Effects of knowledge of semantic roles on summarizing written prose. *Contemporary Educational Psychology, 6,* 59–65.

Church, E., & Bereiter, C. (1983). Reading for style. *Language Arts, 60*(4), 470–476.

Clark, C. M., & Florio, S. (1981, August). *Diary time : The life history of an occasion for writing* (Research Series No. 106). East Lansing: Michigan State University, Institute for Research on Teaching. *Resources in Education,* 1982, *17*(8), 137–138. ERIC number ED 214 648.

Clay, M. M. (1975). *What did I write: Beginning writing behaviour.* Auckland, New Zealand: Heinemann Educational Books.

Cohen, E., & Scardamalia, M. (1983). *The effects of instructional intervention in the revision of essays by grade six children.* Paper presented at the meeting of the American Educational Research Association, Montreal.

Collins, A., & Gentner, D. (1980). A framework for a cognitive theory of writing. In L. W. Gregg & E. Steinberg (Eds.), *Cognitive processes in writing: An interdisciplinary approach* (pp. 51–72). Hillsdale, NJ: Lawrence Erlbaum.

Cooper, C. R., & Odell, L. (Eds.). (1977). *Evaluating writing: Describing, measuring, judging.* Urbana, IL: National Council of Teachers of English.

Corbett, E. (1971). *Classical rhetoric for the modern student.* New York: Oxford University Press.

Crowhurst, M. (1979). The writing workshop: An experiment in peer response to writing. *Language Arts, 56*(7), 757–762.

Crowley, S. (1977). Components of the composing process. *College Composition and Communication, 28*(2), 166–169.

Daiute, C. (1982, March/April). Word processing. Can it make even good writers better? *Electronic Learning,* pp. 29–31.

Daiute, C. A. (1983). The computer as stylus and audience. *College Composition and Communication, 34,* 134–145.

Daly, J. A., & Miller, M. D. (1975). Further studies on writing apprehension: SAT scores, success expectations, willingness to take advanced courses, and sex differences. *Research in the Teaching of English, 9,* 242–249.

DeFord, D. E. (1980). Young children and their writing. *Theory Into Practice, 19*(3), 157–162.

Della-Piana, G. M. (1978). Research strategies for the study of revision processes in writing poetry. In C. R. Cooper & L. Odell (Eds.), *Research on composing: Points of departure* (pp. 105–134). Urbana, IL: National Council of Teachers of English.

Diederich, P. B. (1964). The measurement of skill in writing. *School Review, 54,* 584–592.

Dixon, R. (1976). *Morphographic spelling* (Parts 1 and 2). Chicago: Science Research Associates.

Dyson, A. H., & Jenson, J. M. (1981). "Real " writing in the elementary classroom. *Momentum, 12*(4), 11–13.

Elbow, P. (1973). *Writing without teachers.* London: Oxford University Press.

Emig, J. (1971). *The composing processes of twelfth graders* (Research Report No. 13). Champaign, IL: National Council of Teachers of English.

Emig, J. (1978). Hand, eye, brain: Some "basics" in the writing process. In C. R. Cooper & L. Odell (Eds.), *Research of composing: Points of departure* (pp. 59–71). Urbana, IL: National Council of Teachers of English.

Ericsson, K. A., & Simon, H. A. (1980). Verbal reports as data. *Psychological Review, 87,* 215–251.

Fadiman, C., & Howard, J. (1979). *Empty pages.* New York: Fearon Pitman.

Faigley, L. (1982). Review of linguistics, stylistics, and the teaching of composition. *College Composition and Communication, 33*(1), 96–98.

Faigley, L., Daly, J., & Witte, S. (1981). The role of writing apprehension in writing performance and competence. *Journal of Educational Research, 75*, 16–21.

Faigley, L., & Witte, S. (1981). Analyzing revision. *College Composition and Communication, 32*, 400–414.

Fisher, J. E. (1981). *The interference of mechanical errors in the revision of compositions by grade six children.* Unpublished master's thesis, University of Toronto, Toronto.

Florio, S., & Clark, C. M. (1982). The functions of writing in an elementary classroom. *Research in the Teaching of English, 16*, 115–130.

Flower, L. (1979, September). Writer-based prose: A cognitive basis for problems in writing. *College English, 41*(1), 19–37.

Flower, L. (1981). *Problem-solving strategies for writing.* New York: Harcourt Brace.

Flower, L., & Hayes, J. R. (1980a). The cognition of discovery: Defining a rhetorical problem. *College Composition and Communication, 31*(2), 21–32.

Flower, L., & Hayes, J. R. (1980b). The dynamics of composing: Making plans and juggling constraints. In L. W. Gregg & E. R. Steinberg (Eds.), *Cognitive processes in writing* (pp. 31–50). Hillsdale, NJ: Lawrence Erlbaum.

Flower, L., & Hayes, J. R. (1981). The pregnant pause: An inquiry into the nature of planning. *Research in the Teaching of English, 15*, 229–244.

Flower, L., Hayes, J. R., & Swarts, H. (1980). *Revising functional documents: The scenario principle* (Document Design Project Tech. Rep. No.10). Pittsburgh, PA: Carnegie–Mellon University.

Frase, L.T., Macdonald, N. H., Gingrich, P. S., Keenan, S. A., & Collymore, J. L. (1981). Computer aids for text assessment and writing instruction. *Performance and Instruction, 20*,(9), 21–24.

Freedman, S. W. (1981). Evaluation in the writing conference: An interactive process. In M. C. Hairston & C. L. Selfe (Eds.), *Selected papers from the 1981 Texas Writing Research Conference.* Austin: University of Texas.

Frith, U. (Ed.). (1980). *Cognitive processes in spelling.* London: Academic Press.

Glassner, D. (1982). *Lateral specialization of the modes of composing: An EEG study.* Unpublished doctoral dissertation, Rutgers University, New Brunswick, NJ.

Glynn, S. M., Britton, B. K., Muth, K. D., & Dogan, N. (1982). Writing and revising persuasive documents: Cognitive demands. *Journal of Educational Psychology, 74*, 557–567.

Gould, J. D. (1980). Experiments on composing letters: Some facts, some myths, and some observations. In L. W. Gregg & E. R. Steinberg (Eds.), *Cognitive processes in writing* (pp. 97–127). Hillsdale, NJ: Lawrence Erlbaum.

Graves, D. H. (1975). An examination of the writing processes of seven year old children. *Research in the Teaching of English, 9*, 227–241.

Graves, D. H. (1978). *Balance the basics: Let them write.* New York: Ford Foundation.

Graves, D. H. (1981). Research update: Writing research for the eighties: What is needed. *Language Arts, 58*,(2), 197–206.

Graves, D. H. (1983). *Writing: Teachers and children at work.* Exeter, NH: Heinemann Educational Books.

Gray, J., & Myers, M. (1978). The Bay Area Writing Project. *Phi Delta Kappan, 59*, 410–413.

Greeno, J. G. (1978). Natures of problem-solving abilities. In W. K. Estes (Ed.), *Handbook of learning and cognitive processes* (Vol. 5, pp. 239–270). Hillsdale, NJ: Lawrence Erlbaum.

Grice, H. P. (1975). Logic and conversation. In P. Cole & J. J. Morgan (Eds.), *Syntax and semantics: Vol. 3. Speech acts* (pp. 41–58). New York: Academic Press.

Gundlach, R. A. (1982). Children as writers. The beginnings of learning to write. In M. Nystrand (Ed.), *What writers know: The language, process, and structure of written discourse* (pp. 129–147). New York: Academic Press.

Halliday, M. A. K., & Hasan, R. (1976). *Cohesion in English.* London: Longman.

Hansen, B. (1978). Rewriting is a waste of time. *College English, 39*(8), 956–960.

Harris, M. (1979). Staffroom exchange: Contradictory perception of rules for writing. *College Composition and Communication, 30*, 218–220.

Hayes, J. R. (1981). *The complete problem solver.* Philadelphia: Franklin Institute Press.

Hayes, J. R., & Flower, L. S. (1980a). Identifying the organization of writing processes. In L. W. Gregg & E. R. Steinberg (Eds.), *Cognitive processes in writing* (pp. 3–30). Hillsdale, NJ: Lawrence Erlbaum.

Hayes, J. R., & Flower, L. S. (1980b). Writing as problem solving. *Visible Language, 14*(4), 388–399.

Hayes-Roth, B., & Hayes-Roth, F. (1979). A cognitive model of planning. *Cognitive Science, 3*, 275–310.

Hidi, S., & Hildyard, A. (1983). The comparison of oral and written productions of two discourse types. *Discourse Processes, 6*, 91–105.

Hillocks, G., Jr. (1982). Inquiry and the composing process. Theory and research. *College English, 44*, 659–673.

Hirsch, E. D., Jr. (1977). *The philosophy of composition.* Chicago: University of Chicago Press.

Hotopf, N. (1980). Slips of the pen. In U. Frith (Ed.), *Cognitive processes in spelling* (pp. 287–307). London: Academic Press.

Hunt, K. (1965). *Grammatical structures written at three grade levels* (Research Rep. No. 3). Champaign, IL: National Council of Teachers of English.

Inhelder, B., & Piaget, J. (1958). *The growth of logical thinking from childhood to adolescence.* New York: Basic Books.

Jacob, G. P. (1982). An ethnographic study of the writing conference: The degree of student involvement in the writing process. (Doctoral dissertation, Indiana University of Pennsylvania). *Dissertation Abstracts International., 43*, 386A. (University Microfilms No. DA 8216050).

Kiefer, K. E., & Smith, C. R. (1983). Textual analysis with computers; Tests of Bell Laboratories' computer software. *Research in the Teaching of English, 17*, 201–214.

King, M. L. (1978). Research in composition: A need for theory. *Research in the Teaching of English, 12*, 193–202.

King, M. L., & Rentel, V. M. (1981). Research update: Conveying meaning in written texts. *Language Arts, 58*(6), 721–728.

Kinneavy, J. (1980). *A theory of discourse.* New York: Norton.

Knoblauch, C. H., & Brannon, L. (1981). Teacher commentary on student writing: The state of the art. *Freshman English News, 10*(2), 1–4.

Kosslyn, S. M. (1980). *Image and mind.* Cambridge, MA: Harvard University Press.

Kress, F., & Bracewell, R. J. (1981). Taught but not learned: Reasons for grammatical errors and implications for instruction. In I. Pringle and A. Freedman (Eds.), *Teaching, writing, learning.* Ottawa: Canadian Council of Teachers of English.

Kroll, B. M. (1978). Cognitive egocentrism and the problem of audience awareness in written discourse. *Research in the Teaching of English, 12*, 269–281.

Larson, R. (1971). Toward a linear rhetoric of the essay. *College Composition and Communication, 22*, 140–145.

Lehr, F. (1980). ERIC/RCS Report: Writing as learning in the content areas. *English Journal, 69*(8), 23–25.

Levin, J. A., Boruta, M. J., & Vasconcellos, M. T. (1983). Microcomputer-based environments for writing: A writer's assistant. In A. C. Wilkinson (Ed.), *Classroom computers and cognitive science* (pp. 219–322). New York: Academic Press.

Lowenthal, D. (1980). Mixing levels of revision. *Visible Language, 14*(4), 383–387.

Lyons, G. (1976, September). The higher illiteracy. *Harper's,* pp. 33–40.

Macrorie, K. (1976). *Telling writing.* Rochelle Park, NJ: Hayden.

Maggs, A., McMillan, K., Patching, W., & Hawke, H. (1981). Accelerating spelling skills with morphographs. *Educational Psychology, 1*(1), 49–56.

Maimon, E. (1979). Talking to strangers. *College Composition and Communication, 30*, 364–369.

Mandler, J., & Johnson, N. (1977). Remembrance of things parsed: Story structure and recall. *Cognitive Psychology, 9*, 111–151.

Mandler, J. M., Scribner, S., Cole, M., & DeForest, M. (1980). Cross-cultural invariance in story recall. *Child Development, 51,* 19–26.

Matsuhashi, A. (1982). Explorations in the real-time production of written discourse. In M. Nystrand (Ed.), *What writers know: The language, process, and structure of written discourse* (pp. 269–290). New York: Academic Press.

McCutchen, D., & Perfetti, C. A. (1982). Coherence and connectedness in the development of discourse production. *Text, 2,* 113–139.

Mellon, J. C. (1969). *Transformational sentence-combining: A method for enhancing the development of syntactic fluency in English composition* (Research Rep. No. 10). Urbana, IL: National Council of Teachers of English.

Meyer, B. J. F. (1977). What is remembered from prose: A function of passage structure. In R. O. Freedle (Ed.), *Discourse production and comprehension* (Vol. 1, pp. 307–336). Norwood, NJ: Ablex.

Mishler, E. G. (1979). Meaning in context: Is there any other kind? *Harvard Educational Review, 49,* 1–19.

Moffett, J. (1968). *Teaching the universe of discourse.* Boston: Houghton Mifflin.

Morrison, C., & Austin, M. C. (1977). *The torchlighters revisited.* Newark, DE: International Reading Association.

Mosenthal, P. (1983). Defining classroom writing competence: A paradigmatic perspective. *Review of Educational Research, 53,* 217–251.

Muller, H. J. (1967). *The uses of English.* New York: Holt, Rinehart & Winston.

Murray, D. M. (1978). Internal revision: A process of discovery. In C. R. Cooper & L. Odell (Eds.), *Research on composing* (pp. 85–103). Urbana, IL: National Council of Teachers of English.

National Assessment of Educational Progress. (1975). *Writing mechanics, 1969–1974: A capsule description of changes in writing mechanics* (Report No. 05-W-01). Denver, CO: National Assessment of Educational Progress.

National Assessment of Educational Progress. (1977). *Write/rewrite: An assessment of revision skills; selected results from the second national assessment of writing.* Washington, DC: U.S. Government Printing Office. (ERIC Document Reproduction Service No. ED 141 826)

National Assessment of Educational Progress. (1980a). *Writing achievement, 1969–1979: Results from the third national writing assessment* (Vol. 1: 17-year-olds). Denver, CO: National Assessment of Educational Progress. (ERIC Document Reproduction Service No. ED 196 042)

National Assessment of Educational Progress. (1980b). *Writing achievement, 1969–1979: Results from the third national writing assessment* (Vol. 2: 13-year-olds). Denver, CO: National Assessment of Educational Progress. (ERIC Document Reproduction Service No. ED 196 043)

National Assessment of Educational Progress. (1980c). *Writing achievement, 1969–1979: Results from the third national writing assessment* (Vol. 3: 9-year-olds). Denver, CO: National Assessment of Educational Progress. (ERIC Document Reproduction Service No. ED 196 044)

Nelms, B. F. (1979). Editorial: The writing projects: Toward a new professionalism. *English Education, 10*(3), 131–133.

Newell, A. (1980). Reasoning, problem solving, and decision processes: The problem space as a fundamental category. In R. S. Nickerson (Ed.), *Attention and performance* (Vol. 8, pp. 693–718). Hillsdale, NJ: Lawrence Erlbaum.

Newell, A., & Simon, H. A. (1972). *Human problem solving.* Englewood Cliffs, NJ: Prentice-Hall.

Nold, E. W. (1981). Revising. In C. H. Frederiksen, & J. F. Dominic (Eds.), *Writing: The nature, development, and teaching of written communication* (pp. 67–79). Hillsdale, NJ: Lawrence Erlbaum.

Nystrand, M. (1979). Using readability research to investigate writing. *Research in the Teaching of English, 13*(3), 231–242.

Odell, L. (1974). Measuring the effect of instruction in prewriting. *Research in the Teaching of English, 8,* 228–240.

Odell, L. (1980). Business writing: Observations and implications for teaching composition. *Theory Into Practice, 19*(3), 225–232.

Odell, L., & Goswami, D. (1982). Writing in a non-academic setting. *Research in the Teaching of English, 16*(3), 201–223.

O'Hare, F. (1973). *Sentence combining: Improving student writing without formal grammar instruction* (Research Rep. No. 15). Urbana, IL: National Council of Teachers of English.

Olson, D. R. (1977). From utterance to text: The bias of language in speech and writing. *Harvard Educational Review, 47*(3), 257–281.

Olson, G. M., Mack, R. L., & Duffy, S. A. (1981). Cognitive aspects of genre. *Poetics, 10,* 283–315.

Paris, P. (1980). *Discourse schemata as knowledge and as regulators of text production.* Unpublished master's thesis, York University, Downsview, Canada.

Perkins, D. N. (in press). General cognitive skills: Why not? In S. S. Chipman, J. W. Segal, & R. Glaser (Eds.), *Thinking and learning skills: Current research and open issues* (Vol. 2). Hillsdale, NJ: Lawrence Erlbaum.

Perl, S. (1979). The composing process of unskilled college writers. *Research in the Teaching of English, 13,* 317–336.

Pettigrew, J., Shaw, R. A., & Van Nostrand, A. D. (1981). Collaborative analysis of writing instruction. *Research in the Teaching of English, 15,* 329–341.

Purves, A. C., & Takala, S. (Eds.), (1982). An international perspective on the evaluation of written composition. *Evaluation in Education, 5*(3), 207–390.

Read, C. (1971). Pre-school children's knowledge of English phonology. *Harvard Educational Review, 41,* 1–34.

Redish, J. C. (in press). The language of the bureaucracy. In R. Bailey (Ed.), *Literacy in the 1980's.*

Rose, M. (1980). Rigid rules, inflexible plans, and the stifling of language: A cognitivist analysis of writer's block. *College Composition and Communication, 31*(4), 389–400.

Rose, M. (1981). Sophisticated, ineffective books — The dismantling of process in composition texts. *College Composition and Communication, 32*(1), 65–74.

Rubin, A. (1980a). Making stories, making sense. *Language Arts, 57,* 285–298.

Rubin, A. (1980b). A theoretical taxonomy of the differences between oral and written language. In R. J. Spiro, B. C. Bruce, & W. F. Brewer (Eds.), *Theoretical issues in reading comprehension* (pp. 411–438). Hillsdale, NJ: Lawrence Erlbaum.

Sawyer, T. M. (1977). Why speech will not totally replace writing. *College Composition and Communication, 28*(1), 43–48.

Scardamalia, M. (1981). How children cope with the cognitive demands of writing. In C. F. Frederiksen, & J. F. Dominic (Eds.), *Writing: The nature, development and teaching of written communication* (Vol. 2, pp. 81–103). Hillsdale, NJ: Lawrence Erlbaum.

Scardamalia, M., & Bereiter, C. (1982). Assimilative processes in composition planning. *Educational Psychologist, 17*(3), 165–171.

Scardamalia, M., & Bereiter, C. (1983a). Child as co-investigator: Helping children gain insight into their own mental processes. In S. Paris, G. Olson, & H. Stevenson (Eds.), *Learning and motivation in the classroom* (pp. 61–82). Hillsdale, NJ: Lawrence Erlbaum.

Scardamalia, M., & Bereiter, C. (1983b). The development of evaluative, diagnostic and remedial capabilities in children's composing. In M. Martlew (Ed.), *The psychology of written language: Developmental and educational perspectives* (pp. 67–95). London: John Wiley.

Scardamalia, M., & Bereiter, C. (1984). Development of strategies in text processing. In H. Mandl, N. Stein, & T. Trabasso (Eds.), *Learning and comprehension of text* (pp. 379–406). Hillsdale, NJ: Lawrence Erlbaum.

Scardamalia, M., & Bereiter, C. (in press-a). The development of dialectical processes in writing. In D. Olsen, N. Torrance, & A. Hildyard (Eds.), *Literacy, language and learning: The nature and consequences of reading and writing.* Cambridge: Cambridge University Press.

Scardamalia, M., & Bereiter, C. (in press-b). Fostering the development of self-regulation in children's knowledge processing. In S. S. Chipman, J. W. Segal, & R. Glaser (Eds.), *Thinking and learning skills: Current research and open questions* (Vol. 2). Hillsdale, NJ: Lawrence Erlbaum.

Scardamalia, M., Bereiter, C., & Fillion, B. (1981). *Writing for results: A sourcebook of consequential composing activities.* Toronto: OISE Press. (Also, La Salle, IL: Open Court)

Scardamalia, M., Bereiter, C., & Goelman, H. (1982). The role of production factors in writing ability. In M. Nystrand (Ed.), *What writers know: The language, process, and structure of written discourse* (pp. 173–210). New York: Academic Press.

Scardamalia, M., Bereiter, C., & McDonald, J. D. S. (1978, August). Role-taking in written communication investigated by manipulating anticipatory knowledge. *Resources in Education.* (ERIC Document Reproduction Service No. ED 151 792)

Scardamalia, M., Bereiter, C., & Steinbach, R. (1984). Teachability of reflective processes in written composition. *Cognitive Science, 8*(2), 173–190.

Scardamalia, M., & Paris, P. (1985). The function of explicit discourse knowledge in the development of text representations and composing strategies. *Cognition and Instruction, 2*(1), 1–39.

Shaughnessy, M. P. (1977a). *Errors and expectations: A guide for the teacher of basic writing.* New York: Oxford University Press.

Shaughnessy, M. P. (1977b). Some needed research on writing. *College Composition and Communication, 28,* 317–320.

Simon, J. (1973). *La Langue écrite de l'enfant.* Paris: Presses Universitaires de France.

Smith, F. (1982). *Writing and the writer.* New York: Holt, Rinehart & Winston.

Sommers, N. (1980). Revision strategies of student writers and experienced adult writers. *College Composition and Communication, 31,* 378–388.

Staton, J. (1980). Writing and counseling: Using a dialogue journal. *Language Arts, 57*(5), 514–518.

Staton, J., Shuy, R., & Kreeft, J. (1982). *Analysis of dialogue journal writing as a communicative event* (Final report, Vols. 1 & 2). Washington, DC: Center for Applied Linguistics. (ERIC Document Reproduction Service Nos. ED 214 196, ED 214 197).

Stein, N. L., & Glenn, C. G. (1979). An analysis of story comprehension in elementary school children. In R. O. Freedle (Ed.), *New directions in discourse processing* (Vol. 2, pp. 53–120). Norwood, NJ: Ablex.

Stein, N., & Policastro, M. (1984). The concept of a story: A comparison between children's and teachers' viewpoints. In H. Mandl, N. Stein, & T. Trabasso (Eds.), *Learning and comprehension of text* (pp. 113–155). Hillsdale, NJ: Lawrence Erlbaum.

Stein, N. L., & Trabasso, T. (1982). What's in a story. An approach to comprehension and instruction. In R. Glaser (Ed.), *Advances in instructional psychology* (pp. 213–267). Hillsdale, NJ: Lawrence Erlbaum.

Steinberg, E. R. (1980). A garden of opportunities and a thicket of dangers. In L. W. Gregg & E. R. Steinberg (Eds.), *Cognitive processes in writing* (pp. 155–167). Hillsdale, NJ: Lawrence Erlbaum.

Stotsky, S. L. (1975). Sentence combining as a curriculum activity: Its effect on written language development and reading comprehension. *Research in the Teaching of English, 9*(1), 30–71.

Stubbs, M. (1980). *Language and literacy: The sociolinguistics of reading and writing.* London; Routledge and Kegan Paul.

Taylor, K. K. (1982). Can college students summarize? *Journal of Reading, 26,* 524–528.

Tetroe, J., Bereiter, C., & Scardamalia, M. (1981). *How to make a dent in the writing process.* Paper presented at the meeting of the American Educational Research Association, Los Angeles.

Thorndyke, P. W. (1977). Cognitive structures in comprehension and memory of narrative discourse. *Cognitive Psychology, 9,* 77–110.

van Dijk, T. A. (1980). *Macrostructures: An interdisciplinary study of global structures in discourse, interaction, and cognition.* Hillsdale, NJ: Lawrence Erlbaum.

Vygotsky, L. S. (1978). *Mind in society: The development of higher psychological processes.* (M. Cole, V. John-Steiner, S. Scribner, & E. Souberman, Eds. and Trans.). Cambridge, MA: Harvard University Press.

Warnock, J. (1976, fall). New rhetoric and the grammar of pedagogy. *Freshman English News, 5,* 1–4, 12–22.

Wason, P. C. (1980). Specific thoughts on the writing process. In L. W. Gregg & E. R. Steinberg (Eds.), *Cognitive processes in writing* (pp. 129–137). Hillsdale, NJ: Lawrence Erlbaum.

Waters, H. S. (1980). "Class News": A single-subject longitudinal study of prose production and schema formation during childhood. *Journal of Verbal Learning and Verbal Behaviour, 19,* 152–167.

Wertsch, J. (Ed.). (in press). *Culture, communication, and cognition: Vygotskian perspectives.* New York: Cambridge University Press.

West, W. W. (1967). Written composition. *Review of Educational Research, 37*(2), 159–167.

White, R. S., & Karl, H. (1980). Reading, writing, and sentence combining: The track record. *Reading Improvement, 17,* 226–232.

Winterowd, W. R. (Ed.). (1975). *Contemporary rhetoric.* New York: Harcourt Brace.

Woodruff, E., Bereiter, C., & Scardamalia, M. (1981). On the road to computer assisted compositions. *Journal of Educational Technology Systems, 10*(2), 133–148.

Woodruff, E., Scardamalia, M., & Bereiter, C. (1982). Computers and the composing process: An examination of computer-writer interaction. In J. Lawlor (Ed.), *Computers in composition instruction* (p. 31–45). Los Alamitos, CA. SWRL Educational Research and Development.

Young, R. E. (1976). Invention: A topographical survey. In G. Tate (Ed.), *Teaching composition: Ten bibliographical essays.* Fort Worth, TX: Christian University Press.

Young, R. W., Becker, A. L., & Pike, K. E. (1970). *Rhetoric: Discovery and change.* New York: Harcourt Brace.

Zbrodoff, N. J. (1984). *Writing stories under time and length constraints.* Unpublished doctoral dissertation, University of Toronto.

28.

Research on Teaching Reading

Robert Calfee
Stanford University

Priscilla Drum
University of California—Santa Barbara

Introduction

What should the reader expect of a chapter entitled "Research on Teaching Reading"? Because varied perspectives might be taken, we thought it advisable to attempt an explicit answer to this question. First, our readers should know what we mean by research on teaching reading, including our definitions of *reading* and *teaching*. Second, the reader should be given a framework for organizing the research literature. Third, the reader should find an account of that literature. We will not attempt a compendium, but instead will highlight samples from the past decade of research on various topics. The goal is to fashion a guide for the informed professional and for apprentices trying to comprehend a new field.

This introductory section will now continue with some contextual remarks. As experienced colleagues realize, contemporary reading research is not neutral, but reflects the social and political context in which it occurs.

The Place of Reading Instruction in American Education

Research on reading instruction needs to be viewed against the purposes for reading in a particular place and time. In the 1960s optimism prevailed, with the promises of improved schooling an important consideration underlying this spirit. A dramatic event was the 1969 announcement of the Right to Read program by Commissioner of Education James E. Allen, Jr. Proposed at the beginning of the Nixon presidency, the program might have been the primary focus of this chapter if its promise had been realized. As it turned out, Right to Read was lost in the turmoil of the 70s, and never moved beyond the initial rhetoric. The federal Right to Read office set up reading centers for adults and distributed kits of "exemplary" materials; little else was accomplished, though see Carroll and Chall (1975), quoted in the next paragraph. The program was discontinued during the early years of the Reagan administration. The National Reading Council, also established in 1970 and designed to involve the private sector in the Right to Read effort, was closed in 1973.

Before his death in 1971, Allen commissioned a report on the status of reading in the United States. The survey, prepared by John Carroll and Jeanne Chall (1975) for the National Academy of Education, gave a comprehensive and thoughtful account of the national situation at the beginning of the decade covered in this chapter. They wrote under darkening clouds of national despair and turmoil, but their mood was one of hope and urgency:

> Our national policy is that every child is expected to complete at least the twelfth grade; we ought then to expect every child to attain twelfth-grade literacy. ... The simplest and, to us, most persuasive argument for literacy is that an individual cannot participate in modern society unless he can read, and by this we mean reading at a rather high level of literacy. (pp. 9–10)

One feature of the Carroll and Chall volume deserves special notice. The report includes several case studies, brief accounts of fictional people for whom learning to read was difficult. Some individuals had to cope with difficult situations like poverty at home and in the neighborhood; some had personal problems. But the main point was that in every instance a

The authors thank reviewers Joseph R. Jenkins (University of Washington) and James R. Squire (Ginn Corporation).

teacher might have made a difference. Such was the tenor of the times.

In the late 70s and early 80s, the Right to Read was replaced by the Demand for Excellence. The mood changed dramatically: a concern for equity turned into an emphasis on standards. Minimum competency tests for high school graduation were mandated in many states and school districts. Remedial programs were provided to failing students, but the rate of high school dropouts increased for the first time in decades (U. S. Office of Education, 1984) — dropout statistics are not altogether trustworthy, to be sure, and little is known about the relation between tighter standards, remedial high school programs, and school leaving.

The shift in the societal context over the decade has been multifaceted. Emphasis on minimum standards in the basic skills (chiefly reading) shifted rapidly during the early 1980s to concern about excellence in education — increase in graduation requirements, lengthening of school days and years, and toughening of testing. Funding remained stable or actually declined (in real dollars) in some states. Research and development activities dropped to a fraction of what had been planned 2 decades before.

The institution of schooling has come under fire repeatedly in recent years. The National Commission on Excellence in Education (1983) captured the prevailing concern in its oft-quoted charge that "the educational foundations of our society are presently being eroded by a rising tide of mediocrity that threatens our very future as a Nation and a people." (p. 5). Copperman (1978) arrayed standardized test results showing that, after a brief period of hope during the post-Sputnik period (1957–1965), the quality of public education in the United States declined markedly. He pointed to the inadequacy of literacy instruction in the nation's schools as the primary cause for the declines:

> Since the mid-1960's, academic performance and standards have shown a sharp and widespread decline. ... Even in the more traditional classes, work demands and imposed standards have dropped considerably ... high-school textbooks in most subject areas have been rewritten with a sharply reduced reading level, usually one or more years lower than the grade for which they are intended. ... Federal money and intervention were supposed to solve our most pressing educational problems. Instead, they have proven to be a multi-billion dollar source of fraud and political interference. (pp. 15, 16, 21)

Other causes for the decline, in his opinion, were the loss of authority by teachers and principals, the loss of respect for "structure," the replacement of basal textbooks by "open education," and a lowering of standards to accommodate less able students. Whatever the truth of such claims, the quotation captures the prevailing spirit of polemic and concern.

As this chapter was written, a visitor to the schools would see efforts to respond to these challenges, most notably increased time in reading and mathematics. Teaching activities are defined with greater precision, since direct instruction has been associated with higher test scores in several studies. Surveys indicate that most (perhaps 95% of) elementary teachers rely on a basal series, and that they hew closely to the teacher's manual (Dixon, 1979). Student performance is monitored through standardized tests; parents, the general public, teachers and administrators, and politicians give close attention to the findings.

The results of these efforts are mixed. Reading performance in the primary grades shows improvements (NAEP, 1981), and SAT scores are steadying, but achievement in the upper grades continues to drop, especially in the more demanding literacy tasks, and in writing and the so-called content areas (chiefly social studies and science).

The preceding "snapshots" capture some aspects of reading instruction in the mid-1980s. Our goal has been to sketch the societal and historical context within which the review is framed. The field of study, the methods of research, and the expected findings all reflect this context, which has seen major fluctuations in the past two decades.

Previous Handbooks

The two previous handbooks (Gage, 1963; Travers, 1973) provide a historical perspective of a different kind. Russell and Fea (1963) wrote during a "golden era" of research on reading instruction. The nation was optimistic, support for education was increasing, and hopes were high for a bright future. Russell and Fea's announced intention was to focus on research in classroom settings, with particular emphasis on methods and materials for instruction. They expressed less interest in ancillary topics like psychology, physiology, sociology, and linguistics. In fact, however, of the three topics in their review, two were predominantly psychological — perceptual processes in word recognition and conceptual processes in comprehension. The third topic, classroom management and organization, was not unique to reading instruction. These observations are not meant to criticize — the authors dealt with the literature available at that time.

Ten years later, Della-Piana and Endo (1973) wrote at the peak of the "federal era." Research funds had increased substantially during the decade, and optimism remained high about the potential of public schooling. The stated goal of the review was to emphasize "sources that appear to be productive for methodological, theoretical or practical values in developing a body of generalizable knowledge and in improving reading instruction" (p. 883). They described the First Grade Reading Study (Bond & Dykstra, 1967) and Chall's (1967) *Learning to Read: The Great Debate*, both of which investigated variations in "the method of instruction." Should emphasis be placed on phonics or meaning? Should instruction go from part to whole or the reverse? The answer to these and other "methods" questions seemed to be "Yes" — many things help.

The review also covered the newly emerging technologies. The computer had arrived, and with it new languages and concepts; hence a section on product development. Once again, relatively little of the research examined classroom practices or the curriculum. The studies were rooted in psychological theory and relied on laboratory analogues of reading. The "methods" experiments contrasted programmatic approaches (phonics, linguistic techniques, language experience, and so on), but actual practice was seldom observed. For whatever reason, the effects of variations in methods were generally small compared with the variance between teachers and students.

An Overview of the Chapter

The substantive portion of the present chapter begins with a definition of reading that gives our perspective on the literate person. The definition provides a framework for the curricular domain by identifying four major components in skilled reading: decoding, word meaning, the comprehension of sentences and paragraphs, and the comprehension of entire texts. Next comes a section on the acquisition of literacy which contrasts stage models with learning models.

Finally come three sections on research findings: instruction in decoding, in word meaning, and in various forms of comprehension. The strategy in these sections will be to sketch each domain in broad strokes, and then select several studies to highlight methodologically and substantively.

Our selections are constrained by the available literature, of course. We will concentrate on studies that inform the dimensions of curriculum and instruction, and will emphasize examples from classroom practice where possible. Greater attention will be paid to issues and paradigms newly arrived on the scene — chief among these are advances in cognitive psychology and comprehension theory. On the other hand, as Barton (1963) noted more than 20 years ago, "It does appear ... from an analysis of manuals, texts on reading instruction, introductions to readers, and similar advice to teachers over the past 150 years [and, one might add, from reviews of the research literature], that almost all of the issues raised in the past ten years were being raised long before there was anything such as educational research" (p. 249).

The Literate Person

The aim of reading instruction is to help a person become literate. Literacy has at times meant little more than reading and writing one's name (Mathews, 1966), but modern society puts greater demands on the citizen. A literate person should be able to read almost anything in the native language, with understanding of the message or identification of the barriers to understanding. A literate person knows when a text is ambiguous, when the lexicon is unfamiliar, or when the conceptual framework for the text is unknown. How does this skill and knowledge come about, and of what does it consist? To address this question, the section will begin with a description of the curriculum domain of reading the English language. The synopsis emphasizes three facets of the curriculum — the foundation in oral language, the nature of English as a historical polyglot, and formal and informal styles of language usage.

Next comes an analysis of the psychological processes in skilled reading. Heading the list are the basic cognitive resources that underlie all thinking and behavior. Then follows a description of what goes on in the mind of a competent reader while scanning a text. These analyses provide a theoretical model of the reading process that will comprise the primary frame of reference for the remainder of the chapter.

The Curriculum of Reading

A curriculum is a course of study — the word has its roots in the notion of a racetrack or an obstacle course. Literacy is derivative of language; reading is the mastery of written language. It is therefore appropriate to say something about the foundation in spoken language for the development of literacy.

LANGUAGE

"By the age of three or four, virtually every child has learned a language." You immediately and properly understand the reference to *spoken language*. The child's linguistic performance matures through adolescence and beyond, but the essential characteristics of adult language appear in the preschooler's speech and comprehension, including a well-developed phonological system, a substantial store of morphemes and rules for adding to that store, a syntax that allows the child to parse and produce the strings of morphemes that relate ideas, and an understanding of the conventions for carrying on a conversation.

On the other hand, the preschooler's language is rooted in pragmatics, in making things happen (Halliday, 1975). The early forms of language serve the child's immediate needs in fairly economical fashion. By the fourth year, language and thought have begun to shape one another, and language has come to serve the needs of abstraction and problem solving. Children differ considerably in the extent and character of language usage, but virtually every 4-year-old has learned the most fundamental lesson about language — words stand for ideas!

Language is a complex and even mysterious phenomenon, but linguists agree on the major components. The partitioning into the categories of phonology, morphology, syntax, and some larger unit (discourse or the like) is widely accepted, and linguists are confident about examining these components independently of one another. Moreover, an individual may have problems in one element (e.g., a lisp) with no discernible influence on the other elements.

THE ENGLISH LANGUAGE

History is the key to English (Nist, 1966; Balmuth, 1982). The complexities of the language spring from our variegated heritage. Several waves of conquerors have swept across the British Isles during the past 2 millenia, each leaving an impression on the inhabitants and their speech. Some invasions were predominantly physical (the Angles, the Saxons, the Danes, and the Normans), while others were intellectual (from the 17th century on, the French and the Italians; and afterwards most of the world). There was no institution comparable to the Académie Française to protect linguistic purity; instead, the culture seemed almost to invite linguistic intrusions.

The foundation of English is Anglo-Saxon, a North German language. After their arrival during the 5 centuries after the birth of Christ until the Norman invasion, the Danes, Angles, and Saxons lived together in linguistic harmony. Over the centuries the language became simpler in its syntactic structure and more complex in its lexical system. The Battle of Hastings in 1066 marked an event that was to alter the English language greatly. The Normans, Norsemen who had lived for a time in France, spoke a variant of French, a Romance or Latinate language, which was designated after the conquest as the official language of the land. As described by Nist (1966), the Normans won the battle, but they lost the war:

> The Norman King of England and his French nobility remained utterly indifferent to the English language until about 1200. During that time the royal court patronized French literature, not English. When the court and its aristocratic supporters did finally pay attention to the native language of the land they dominated, that language was no longer the ... Teutonic and highly inflected Old English but the hybrid-becoming, Romance-importing, and inflection-dropping Middle English. (p. 107)

By the middle of the 1300s Chaucer, Duns Scotus, and Roger Bacon wrote in a form recognizable today as English. The next major event equaled the Norman conquest in linguistic impact—the Renaissance begun under Elizabeth I. It was the time of Shakespeare, Bacon, Milton, Donne, and Spenser; of Newton, Hooke, Halley; of the King James translation of the Bible; of the exploration of North America and the "rule of the waves" by the British Navy. The *word* had by then become the fundamental unit. The English language, opportunistic as ever, continued to beg, borrow, steal, and invent. Words flowed by the tens of thousands into English from the Continent and the Scholastic tradition. Thus the language acquired a word for every occasion; several, in fact, each differing subtly from the others in connotation and style (Barzun, 1977). Modern English had arrived, a polyglot of remarkable vitality, richness, and simplicity.

WRITTEN ENGLISH

The Roman alphabet used to write English traces back to Egyptian pictographs and the Phoenician syllabary, and thence to the Greek alphabet (Gelb, 1952). The Greeks invented the alphabetic principle, each letter representing a single phoneme, more or less. Spoken Greek was fairly simple and consistent, and so the alphabetic principle was a natural fit. The particular insight of the Greeks was to develop symbols for the vowels as well as for the consonants. The Romans modified the Greek alphabet to suit the relatively simple demands of Latin. The subsequent adaptation of the Roman alphabet to Anglo-Saxon speech posed a greater challenge, which will be discussed in the section on decoding.

In 1476, William Caxton introduced the printing press to England. This event, occurring just before the Elizabethan era, fixed the spelling of English during a time of turmoil in the language. As Nist (1966) put it:

> These changes in the pronunciation of English took place during the worst possible time, when the spelling of the language jelled from 1550 to 1650. Thus, for the most part, present-day English spells like a post-Chaucerian and pronounces like a post-Shakespearean.

Whatever the correspondence between spelling and pronunciation before the "changes," the match thereafter was poorer.

Reading and Formal Language

The graphic representation of speech is a remarkable invention, and analyses of literacy naturally begin with the printed aspects of reading. On the other hand, writing has influenced human thought and communication in ways other than the conversion of speech into writing. These other influences are of fundamental importance in the reading curriculum.

The contrast between spoken and written modes of expression has been emphasized by Olson (1977), who builds on previous work by Luria (1976), Vygotsky (1962), and Goody and Watt (1963), among others. The distinction has been most often expressed as the difference between *utterance* and *text*, that is, between speech and print. The characteristics of each style of expression are summarized in Table 28.1. A conversation between friends generally makes sense only in the situation in which the conversation takes place. In the language of text, little is left to chance; the writer eschews phrases like "y'know what I mean ... really." Because it is so explicit, a book's message remains fairly constant regardless of where and when the book is read. To be sure, this constancy assumes that the reader knows the conventions used in the text; the reader must conform to the writer's idea of audience. Texts are relatively unchanging over time. The reader may forget a detail or change an interpretation, but at least the words are not lost in the air.

Differences between writing and speech have been documented by both educators and behavioral scientists (Chafe & Danielwicz in press; Kroll, 1977; O'Donnell, 1974; Olson, 1977). The important contrast, however, is not between speech and print, but between *natural* and *formal* styles of thought and communication (Freedman & Calfee, 1984; Heath, 1983). Reading instruction does not simply teach the child a system for translating speech into print, but instills an understanding of the conventions for thinking and communicating in the modern world. Some scholars believe that the acquisition of the skills of literacy ensure that the individual has mastery of the formal style; for example, Goody (1977) says, "I see the acquisition of these [literate] means of communication as effectively transforming the nature of cognitive processes" (p. 18). Others question whether transfer from reading to formal style is automatic. For instance, Wells (1979) states that "literacy can be associated with important facilitating effects, ... but the [facilitation] will depend upon the uses to which literacy is habitually put, once it has been acquired" (p. 27).

The evidence supports the doubters. Scribner and Cole (1978; also see Heath, 1983, for examples closer to home), from their studies of literacy among the Vai tribespeople of West Africa, challenge the assumption that abstract thinking is an automatic consequence of literacy. Instead, they find that the conditions of acquisition determine the conditions of transfer. The Vai learn their script in situations that relate to immediate,

Table 28.1. Characteristics of Natural vs. Formal Language

Natural Language (Utterance)	Formal Language (Text)
Highly Implicit; Interactive	Highly Explicit
Context Bound	Context Free
Unique; Idiosyncratic; Personal	Repeatable; Memory-Supported
Intuitive	Logical; Rational
Sequential; Descriptive	Expository; "Context"

practical needs; they learn by doing, rather than from school-ing. They practice on commonplace tasks — writing letters, recording contributions to a funeral feast, listing donations to a religious society. The consequences, according to Scribner and Cole, seem to be that

> the effects of literacy, and perhaps schooling as well, are restricted
> ... to closely related practices. ... If the educational objective is to
> foster analytic logical reasoning, that objective should guide the
> choice of the instructional program. (pp. 457, 460)

This point is central to the goals of the reading curriculum and instruction in reading. It is not enough for the citizens of a modern country to perform at minimum levels of competence in reading and writing. The deeper learning entailed in the acquisition of a formal style of language and thought, as described by Bruner (1966), is most likely achieved when instruction fosters the acquisition of broadly generalizable analytic problem-solving skills, where the primary task for the student is to discover the principles by which spoken English is converted into written form, and how to apply those principles to novel forms of expression and communication:

> Many ... skills are taught in the subtle interaction of parent and
> child ... as in the case of language learning, where the pedagogy is
> highly unselfconscious. It is probably true that most of the primitive
> skills of manipulating and looking and attending are also taught in
> this way. It is when the society goes beyond these relatively
> primitive techniques that the less spontaneous instruction of the
> school must be relied upon. At this point the culture necessarily
> comes to rely upon its formal education as a means of providing
> skills. And insofar as there has been any innovation in tools or tool-
> using, ... the educational system is the sole means of dissemina-
> tion — the sole agent of evolution, if you will. (p. 26)

Cognitive Processes in Skilled Reading

The previous section portrayed the reading curriculum in bold strokes. This section on the cognitive structure of the skilled reader begins with a general discussion of cognitive processes, and then applies these concepts to the domain of reading. The section builds on a variety of sources, many summarized in Calfee (1981), but also see Crowder (1982) and Downing and Leong (1982) for additional background on the psychology of reading, along with Wittrock (1978) and Greeno (1980) on the cognitive movement in education.

HUMAN INFORMATION PROCESSING

What is the mind of a skilled reader like? The answer to this question can be grounded in the psychology of human informa-tion processing developed over the past quarter-century, nicely summarized by Simon (1978) as follows:

> A few basic characteristics of the human information-processing
> system shape its problem-solving efforts. Apart from its sensory
> organs, the system operates almost entirely serially, one process at a
> time, rather than in parallel fashion [many processes at a time]. This
> seriality is reflected in the narrowness of its momentary focus of
> attention. The elementary processes of the information-processing
> system are executed in tens or hundreds of milliseconds. The inputs

and outputs of these processes are held in a small short-term memory with a capacity of only a few (between, say, four and seven) familiar symbols or *chunks*. The system has access to an essentially unlimited long-term memory, but the time required to store a new chunk in that memory is on the order of seconds or tens of seconds. (p. 273)

From this perspective, the key to understanding how a person performs a skilled task like reading comes not from the mental "hardware," but from the "software," from the pack-ages of knowledge stored in long-term memory that guide the performance of routinized activities. The ability to think is shaped by the limited capacity of the attentional system. The executive homunculus that "runs the mind" can focus on only a small number of distinctive entities, and these only one at a time. How do we manage thinking that is fast and complicated, which is clearly within our capability? The answer is that the competent person has internalized a large number of highly automated routines, so that he or she can carry out complex tasks "without thinking" while simultaneously attending to a small number of matters that do require focal attention.

Automated routines, along with other knowledge, are stored in long-term memory, which is the repository of experience, facts, beliefs, skills, feelings, and so on. Human memory has a storage capacity that is, for all practical purposes, unlimited. Much of what we know requires nothing more than attending to an event. The details may be fuzzy, and we may be unable to recapture the memory unless provided a cue for recognition, but memory abides.

Long-term memory is inherently inclined to abstract and organize. Life consists of a relatively small number of recurring events, and the mind captures these patterns of recurrence. The concept of abstract mental representations has been variously labeled by cognitive psychologists, but *schema* is probably most common (Rumelhart, 1980). A schema is defined as an outline or "frame" comprising the major elements and relations, along with a set of "slots" to be filled.

The mind is not a static machine containing fixed outlines. As Estes (1980) points out it is alive:

> The human memory seems to be not at all like a storeroom, a
> library, or a computer core memory, a place where items of
> information are stored and kept until wanted, but rather presents a
> picture of a complex, dynamic system that at any given time can be
> made to deliver information concerning discrete events or items it
> has had experience with in the past. In fact, the human memory does
> not, in a literal sense, store anything; it simply changes as a function
> of experience. (p. 68)

How does the mind create a schema? Here are three answers to the question, answers that are *not* mutually exclusive. The first is a simple averaging mechanism; common features in a set of related experiences are remembered most clearly, thus form-ing a "prototype." This mechanism requires little in the way of focal attention; the individual may be quite aware of the nature of the abstraction, and the prototype may remain "nameless."

A second model links experience with a preexisting pattern; "registering for classes at the university is like going to a cafeteria," for example. While the person may be unaware of the link at times, on other occasions the analogy may depend on language and intention. Bolinger (1980) speaks elegantly of the latter possibility:

> This seeing of like and unlike, of putting together and classifying apart ... is the mechanism through which reality is organized and the whole construct of language is built. ... The world is a vast elaborated *metaphor*. ... Nature does not come to the child in ordered fashion, but the child is equipped to perceive parts of it, and is born with the intellectual capacity that surpasses all others: the ability to see resemblances. (p. 191)

The third source of mental structures is sufficiently different from the others to merit a unique label; we will designate it as a *script*. Schemata result from naturally occurring experiences and natural reactions to those experiences. No one teaches you the similarities among restaurant-like experiences; you figure them out on your own. In other instances, however, organizing structures come from rational analysis and formal instruction. The principles of Newtonian physics lead to conclusions that are counterintuitive and that seem to contradict everyday experience. Newton's derivation of the laws of physical motion was a brilliant insight, and the Three Laws of Motion stand as a prime example of a parsimonious framework for perceiving and interpreting a domain of experience—a framework of such importance that it has been placed in the curriculum, ensuring that successive generations will share this insight.

Scripts and schemata probably comprise endpoints on a continuum. The two varieties of mental structures have different characteristics, different strengths and weaknesses, and almost certainly they emerge through different sets of environmental events (see subsequent discussion of learning by doing and by knowing).

SEPARABLE PROCESSES IN READING

How should we describe the mind of a skilled reader—someone who has been taught to read English in a formal classroom setting? The student has acquired a rather complex domain of knowledge, which allows him or her to gain information from printed material.

One approach is to characterize the domain by a set of relatively independent processes (Calfee, 1976; Frederiksen, 1980; Perfetti & Lesgold, 1979; R. J. Sternberg, 1977; S. Sternberg, 1969; and Simon, 1981, who refers to "nearly decomposable" components). While each component may have a complicated internal structure, the relation between any pair of components is simple. The reading process may appear highly interactive and complicated in operation, but the underlying structure is actually quite simple—such is the gist of the separable-process assumption.

The key to understanding the reading process is the curriculum. The "ideal" reader has acquired the set of components shown in Figure 28.1. Independence of the components reflects neither physiology nor statistics, but rather the structure of knowledge used to perform the task. The components act as *stable intermediate forms* (Simon, 1981), as subparts of a larger system, with each part relatively unaffected by the other subparts. A teacher can work on vocabulary apart from decoding; the reader can analyze the grammar of a sentence without necessarily engaging the overall text structure.

The headings in Figure 28.1 resemble in some ways the top-level categories in contemporary scope-and-sequence charts and basal reading series. The components also correspond to linguistic categories for analyzing spoken languages—phonology, morphology, syntax, and various types of discourse structure. For better or worse, scope-and-sequence charts are not taken too seriously, probably just as well. In them one finds mixtures from different categories, so that word meaning objectives may be listed under vocabulary, and so on. We will take the model quite seriously in this chapter, however, and will use it to organize our presentation of the research literature.

Learning to Read

How does a child learn to speak? The answer is mysterious. Expose an infant to language, and he or she will learn to speak. No curriculum is needed; the skill is acquired without formal schooling.

How does a child learn to read? Opinions differ, but one point is clear: "Exposure" to print does not guarantee that a child will benefit from the experience. What then is the explanation?

At least four answers have been posed in response to this question: (a) Reading is acquired naturally, like learning to speak; (b) reading is acquired through a series of stages; (c) reading is learned through the mastery of a set of specific skills; and (d) reading is learned by formal instruction in a new domain of knowledge. While these answers are not mutually exclusive, they are sufficiently distinctive to warrant separate coverage.

Acquisition as a Natural Process

An extreme version of the naturalistic approach holds that exposure to reading materials is all that is required for acquisition (Goelman, Oberg, & Smith, 1984). The learning of oral language is viewed as a good model to follow. Tinkering with the natural state of affairs may lead to failure, because children will have to deal with concepts and structures that make little sense to them. Reading failure results from efforts to "teach" what children might more easily learn on their own, according to this position.

A variant of the naturalistic position stresses the importance of providing reading materials and activities with which the child is already familiar. The Language Experience method (Allen & Allen, 1966) exemplifies this position. Applebee and Langer (1983) also focus on the language task confronting the student, but propose that the instructor provide a conceptual framework or "scaffolding" to aid the student. The level of support is critical. Compare "fill in the blank" worksheets with essay questions; the first activity provides too much support and the second provides too little. Applebee and Langer recommend an intermediate level of support, giving the student only as much guidance as is needed, where the discussion of a text, the explanation of a decoding principle, the definition of a word all fit a model determined by the instructor.

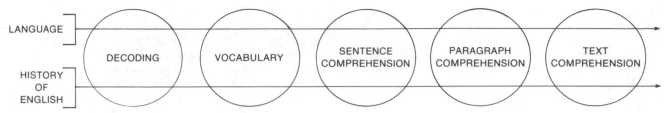

Fig. 28.1. Components of the reading process

Stage Theory

Chall (1983), a major figure in reading instruction for more than 3 decades, has proposed a six-stage model of reading acquisition that elegantly portrays this point of view. Chall likens the acquisition of reading to growth in spoken language or the development of cognition: "Like Piaget's cognitive stages, ... reading stages have a definite structure and ... generally [follow] a hierarchical progression" (p. 11). The sequential constraints are assumed to be critical; the student must move through one stage before tackling the next (pp. 55ff). Chall notes that passage from one stage to another depends on the student's interaction with the home and school environment (pp. 78ff), and she discusses in some detail the transitions from one stage to the next (pp. 40ff).

Here are the stages:

STAGE 0. PREREADING: BIRTH TO AGE 6

The numbering and the description of this stage are both unusual. It is the stage that is not a stage, yet it "covers a greater period of time and . . . a greater series of changes than any of the other stages"(p. 13). In this period fall the times of home, preschool, and kindergarten. While it is labeled the "prereading" stage, what the student is taught about reading before first grade matters greatly (see references in Chall, pp. 13–14).

STAGE 1. INITIAL READING OR DECODING: AGES 6 TO 7

For Chall, the acquisition of letter–sound correspondences is critically important for the beginning reader (e.g., Chall, 1967); unsurprisingly, the first "real" step in her reading model emphasizes this domain. Chall does not equate decoding with reading, but does emphasize that beginning readers "have to engage, at least temporarily, in what appears to be less mature reading behavior—being glued to print" (p. 18).

STAGE 2. FLUENCY: AGES 7 TO 8

With practice, the child no longer gives major attention to decoding, but begins to focus on the content. First must come the development of speed and "automatization" of decoding skills. "Stage 2 reading is not for gaining new information, but for confirming what is already known to the reader" (p. 18).

STAGE 3. READING TO LEARN: AGES ... ?

In this phase, students "start on the long course of reading to 'learn the new'" (p. 20). Reading becomes a tool for exploring subject matter areas and for handling daily affairs.

STAGE 4. MULTIPLE VIEWPOINTS: HIGH SCHOOL

Texts at this level present the youngster with more than a single point of view. Comprehension is more demanding, because the student must hold one set of ideas in mind while acquiring another comparison or expansion.

STAGE 5. RECONSTRUCTION: COLLEGE AND BEYOND

In this stage the student views from multiple perspectives—a "metareading" stage. The young adult has the knowledge and maturity to realize that text is not a God-given truth, but a collection of ideas to be examined and challenged.

As an account of current practice, Chall's stages may describe progress toward literacy for many students. But the question remains—what is being described? Is it a developmental model, in which individual students proceed through these steps because of inherent characteristics of the human mind? Is it a learning model, in which the reading curriculum requires some things to be acquired before others? Is it a curriculum model, in which experts have constructed the optimal sequence?

Chall's account does not focus on the developing child, but on the materials and the environmental conditions that surround the child. In this sense, her model is not grounded in developmental concepts. Nor does she speak to the nature of learning. There is an implicit model of "practice"; with sufficient exposure to materials, with instruction, encouragement and feedback, and with time, the child will acquire the skills and knowledge required for literacy. The psychology of learning is largely empirical.

Chall seems to be describing a curriculum model. "Many practices in the schools seem to parallel the reading stages proposed here" (p. 65). She is attentive to the organizational characteristics of the school environment through which students move, and she highlights several disjunctures—the entry to kindergarten, the jump to first grade, the changes from the early primary to the late elementary grades, and the shift to secondary school. Research and practice (for example, the fourth grade "slump," Chall, 1983, p. 67) point to the importance of these transitions.

Reading as the Mastery of Specific Skills

Dominating contemporary design of reading materials, of texts for preservice training of teachers, and of reading tests is the notion that reading is a collection of precisely defined objectives or skills (Osborn, Wilson, & Anderson, 1985). The number and character of the objectives varies with the publisher and the category. Decoding tends to be highly fractionated (e.g., /f/, as in f, ff, gh, and ph: prefixes ex-, inter-, and super-; and suffixes -ist, -ible, and -able). Vocabulary objectives are generally fewer but more diffuse (e.g., antonyms, synonyms, multiple meanings, context clues). Comprehension objectives take shape as a collection of poorly defined terms (e.g., main idea, literal and inferential comprehension, fact versus opinion).

Acquisition depends on teacher-led presentations and worksheet activities, following which students' performance is assessed by curriculum-embedded tests. A low score leads to more practice on similar activities. The learning model is implicit and empirical—practice makes perfect (or at least permanent). A typical lesson which may span two or more reading sessions, contains a variety of objectives, usually covering all of the major categories but seldom with any clear relation to one another. The lesson generally begins with a review of several words from the text, oral reading of a story, interspersed questions about details and inferences from the text, after which the student may complete worksheets on /f/, word meanings from context, and map-reading skills. The goal is to cover the skills, which may number in the thousands. The incoherence of the collection is a poor match to the known characteristics of human mental processes.

Learning as a Formal Activity

The last model to be presented combines cognitive psychology and curriculum theory. The ideas behind the proposal are more fully developed in Calfee (1981), and will be only sketched here.

The model begins with the assumption that the architecture of the mind is fundamentally simple. What makes the mind interesting and complex are its contents, the mental structures that underlie performance and knowledge. Some of those structures—for example, what we know about restaurants—occur through natural learning. Others—for example, what we know about sentence diagraming—result from formal instruction. At both ends of this continuum, the final product is a mental representation, a body of knowledge, shaped by the mind into a more or less coherent structure.

The distinction between natural and formal learning does not entail a value judgment. Both kinds of learning are important in the development of competence, and the educated person relies on both types of learning more or less consciously to support each other. John Dewey (1902) who has spoken with wisdom on virtually every educational topic, describes this interplay between learning by experience and learning by schooling:

The map is not a substitute for personal experience. The map does not take the place of the actual journey. The logically formulated material of a science or branch of learning, of a study, is no substitute for the having of individual experiences. ... But the map, a summary, an arranged and orderly view of previous experience, serves as a guide to future experience. ... Through the map every new traveler may get from his own journey the benefits of others' explorations without the waste of energy and loss of time involved in their wanderings. (pp. 20–21)

The contrast between types of learning, summarized in Table 28.2, amounts to a theory of learning. The distinctions between the two types entail significant variations both in content and conditions, both for learning and teaching. Learning-by-doing is relatively haphazard. Inefficient in the short run, it ensures practiced skills applicable to a wide range of settings. "Teaching" in this approach is incidental, little more than supervision to protect the learner from harm.

In learning-by-knowing, the content is critically important; it is the curriculum, grounded in the artifactual knowledge of the culture, in tools for thinking cherished because of their simplicity, their power, and their elegance. The criteria call to mind the separable-process model of reading presented earlier (Figure 28.1), which has coherence as the primary aim—a small number of simply related elements.

And so our foundation for reviewing the literature on instruction in reading will be the content of the reading curriculum. While instructional issues will be highlighted against this instructional backdrop, the perspective on instruction is not neutral. Just as reading is viewed as a formalism, grounded in a small number of fundamental components, so can teaching be construed. The components of teaching, as "unnatural" an act as reading (Gough & Hillinger, 1980), have been discussed elsewhere (Calfee & Shefelbine, 1981) and will only be sketched here:

- *A Conception of the Curriculum.* "What is the nature of reading?" The teacher's answer should satisfy the criteria of simplicity and coherence.
- *A Conception of the Learner.* The teacher's image of the nature of learning should transcend the subject matter, and should provide pragmatic guidance for instruction.
- *Development and Selection of Materials.* A craftsman should be master of his or her tools—instructional materials are the teacher's work kit, and so the teacher should be master of these materials.
- *Assessment Procedures.* Vital to instruction is measurement of instructional outcomes—a level of knowledge beyond the minutiae of "tests," but rooted in the basic concepts of valid evidence and interpretation.

Table 28.2. Major Distinctions Between Learning Based on Doing and Learning Based on Knowing

Doing (Schema)	Knowing (Script)
Learning comes from repeated experiences	Learning results from teaching
Acquisition takes much time and effort, with many mistakes	Acquisition may be virtually instantaneous—the "aha!" feeling
Repeated experiences eventually become organized through natural mental processes—coherence is the result of learning	Information is presented in a carefully organized manner from the beginning—coherence is the foundation for learning
Little or no awareness of the content or process of acquisition	Awareness is often an essential part of acquisition
"What is learned" can serve as basis for gaining knowledge	"What is learned" may facilitate development of skills based on practice

- *Long-Range Management.* The teacher has charge of a small business—grouping of students, allocation of resources (time, people, materials), scheduling of events, arrangement of the room—and all these matters require planning over days, weeks, months, even years.
- *Short-term Interaction.* One child strikes another; a question is asked and no one responds; a student gives an unexpected answer. In these and a thousand other moment-to-moment situations, the teacher must decide immediately on a course of action.
- *Relation to School as an Organization.* The teacher is part of a team, and the well-being of the school rests on the shoulders of the team as a whole.

To reiterate the point made earlier, our purpose in listing these teaching components is to advise the reader of the framework guiding our analysis of the "teaching" portion of "research on teaching reading." The conception of the reading curriculum, the development and selection of materials, the instruction actually presented, and the assessment procedures, all merit attention when reviewing a research paper.

Decoding

Perhaps no other topic in reading instruction provokes as much controversy as the place of phonics—should the beginning reader concentrate on spelling patterns or on the meaning of the text? After a brief review of this continuing debate, we will provide a structural description of English letter–sound correspondence. This foundation gives a perspective on the several research areas covered in the second part of the section, which examines in turn the knowledge children bring to school about words and sounds, laboratory investigations of the acquisition of spelling patterns, the roles of fluency and of context in decoding, and some classroom studies of phonics instruction.

To Decode or Not to Decode

Learning to Read: The Great Debate (Chall, 1967) argued the role and timing of decoding in reading acquisition (also see Mathews, 1966). Several issues were taken for granted in this debate, including the question: Decode or not decode? What is decoding? We will rely on a beguilingly simple definition: Decoding comprises the skills and knowledge by which a reader translates printed words into speech, that is, pronounces a written word.

TODAY'S CURRICULUM

The decoding curriculum in most contemporary basal series takes the following shape: Divide the letter–sound correspondences into specific objectives (e.g., *f*, *ff*, *gh* and *ph* make the sound /f/). Teach the child these objectives, often through seatwork. Avoid rules—they are untrustworthy (e.g., "When two vowels go walking, the first does the talking"; translated, vowel digraphs in words like *pain*, *beet*, *boat* and *fuel* take the name of the first letter—but see exceptions like *said*, *bread*, *broad*, and *language*).

The centrality of decoding in the first stages of reading acquisition is often assumed. Some scholars seem to think that to read is to decode, that the child with decoding skills will easily transfer this skill and preexisting language to printed materials.

The decoding curriculum, a skill-based, "bottom-up," drill-and-practice program, is often the first encounter with formal reading instruction. Unsurprisingly, this state of affairs has drawn fire from educators opposing what they see as inhumane and mindless. They view meaning as the goal of reading, and see decoding as secondary. The child will discover the essentials of decoding if simply given opportunities to interact freely with print. Leave the mechanics of decoding for later, if needed.

The debate has gone on for millenia, and shows no signs of slackening. Tchudi (1983) reviewed five books from the early 1980s that capture the intellectual side of the argument:

- Flesch (1981) in *Why Johnny Still Can't Read* repeats his arguments that phonics (decoding) is critical. (Copperman, 1978, also supports the Fleschian view).
- Sharp (1982) argues with equal vigor that *The "Real" Reason Why Johnny Still Can't Read* is the inconsistency of English spelling. He recommends regularizing the letter–sound system.
- Bettelheim and Zelan (1982) view mispronunciations as Freudian slips, best ignored. Expose the child to good literature (they have recommendations), help the child to find meaning, and let decoding take care of itself. Goodman (Golash, 1982) holds a similar view, though without the psychoanalytic overtones. Smith (1978), also of the Goodman persuasion, surprisingly did not have a book for review.
- Finally, Kohl (1982), in his book *Basic Skills*, stresses "using the language skillfully, ... thinking for problem solving, thinking imaginatively, understanding fellow human beings, and knowing how to learn something for oneself"—certainly not the usual back-to-basics.

On the empirical side, substantial evidence speaks to the advantages of early phonics. Chall (1967) reviewed many of these findings, to which can be added more recent findings from large-scale evaluation efforts (the First-Grade Reading Study, Bond & Dykstra, 1967; Planned Variation in Follow-Through, Stallings, 1975). Standardized tests show modest but consistent gains from direct instruction in decoding (Becker & Carnine, 1980). The student who has not acquired decoding skill by the middle of elementary school will be hindered in further academic attainments. Studies comparing good and poor readers have focused on decoding or "word identification" skills as the critical dimension (Kleiman, 1982). Doehring, Trites, Patel, and Fiedorowicz (1981) assessed a cohort of 88 students with severe reading problems and found that "the greatest reading impairment was in orally decoding nonsense words" (p. 190). In surveys, teachers emphasize the importance of decoding skill (e.g., Mason & Osborne, 1982), perhaps because they find this easier to describe than comprehension skill. Students also tend to identify decoding and oral reading fluency as the hallmark of the good reader (Johns, 1984). Small wonder that Liberman and Shankweiler (1979) state with confidence that "the child's fundamental task in learning to read is to construct a link between the arbitrary signs of print and speech" (p. 110). Glushko (1981) puts it bluntly: "Dealing with nonsense is what reading and pronunciation are fundamentally all about" (p. 61).

THE ISSUES

What is one to believe? Opinions range widely, the facts do not give any position overwhelming support, and instructional programs and practices can be found for any of the prevailing motifs and various combinations thereof. Given some truth to each point of view, but also much to argue with, it seems appropriate to present our thoughts on some issues:

- The questions are partly empirical, but not entirely. When proponents point to superior performance after phonics training, the evidence cannot be disregarded. On the other hand, empiricism has its limits. The advantage of phonics training is typically small, and many students continue to experience comprehension problems, especially in the later grades. Seldom does innovation spring from empirical studies of "what is," but rather when an innovator imagines "what might be."
- English spelling, complex on the surface, is not a simple alphabetic system, but is morphophonemic. The spelling-sound patterns track "words" from the underlying layers of of the language (Venezky, 1970; Chomsky & Halle, 1968), and become clear only when one examines the historical evolution of the spoken language and parallel developments in writing.
- Reliance on rote drill and practice as the primary vehicle for decoding instruction is probably a mistake. Rote instruction is slow in any event, but is especially problematic when "what is being learned" is complex, and when the instructional goal is transfered beyond the immediate domain of "what is taught." Kintsch (1979) remarks that "what happens in the later grades is not really a reading problem but a cognitive problem" (pp. 328–329). In fact, the intellectual demands in learning English spelling–sound relations are as significant as those in learning the structures of expository prose. The problem is aggravated by unsupervised seatwork, especially when students lack understanding of the purpose of a task (Anderson, 1982).
- "What is learned" in decoding must include fluency, but it should also encompass understanding. The competent reader can not only pronounce a world like *euchormonium* but can also explain how he or she arrived at the results.
- The acquisition of decoding skills and knowledge, while important in learning to read, need not be "the first thing taught." It is probably a mistake to design an instructional program in which one component (e.g., decoding) becomes an *unnecessary* barrier to the acquisition of other components (Resnick, 1979).

The English spelling–sound system is, in short, a domain of knowledge. While challenging in its structure, it is by no means arbitrary. Solving this problem lies within the intellectual power of virtually every youngster, given appropriate conditions. The problem does have an onionlike quality—the first

solutions provide a start in decoding, but other layers emerge along the way. It is unfortunate that decoding instruction fades at about third or fourth grade, "just when the fun starts."

The Decoding Curriculum

HISTORY AND ENGLISH SPELLING

As noted earlier, English writing reflects the history of the language (Bloomfield & Newmark, 1963; Gordon, 1972; Nist, 1966; Pei, 1968), and it is helpful to have an appreciation of how writing shaped herself to fit the history. Histories of the writing system are rare, and tend to be rather technical. Balmuth's (1982) book, designed specifically to treat the English writing system from a "phonics" perspective, provides useful information (also see Chomsky & Halle, 1968; Fries, 1962; Gelb, 1963; Venezky, 1970; Wijk, 1966). Balmuth stops short of a "nuts and bolts" of instruction, and so we will sketch the major features of the English letter–sound system below.

English spelling is fundamentally alphabetic, but this generalization becomes clearer when the language is "carved" along its historical joints (Figure 28.2). Modern English contains words from virtually every language in the world, and hence a plethora of spelling patterns. Two of the contributors are especially important in reading instruction — Anglo-Saxon and the Romance languages (primarily French and Latin); Greek is significant for scholarship as well as some other familiar aspects of daily life (*television, phonograph, microscope, dinosaur*, and so on), but will not be covered because of limitation of space.

LETTERS, SYLLABLES, AND WORDS

Decoding an unfamiliar word proceeds in three phases. Unless the word is quite short, the reader should first attempt to divide

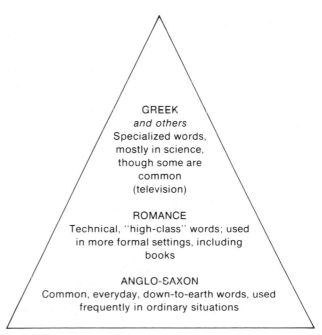

Fig. 28.2 The layers of the English language.

it into its basic *morphemes*, or meaning-bearing units. Pronunciation and meaning are both easier with parts than with wholes. Compounding, in which two or more independent units are conjoined, is common in English — *doghouse, uphold*, and so on. Another pattern is affixation, with a root word modified by prefixes or suffixes — *internationalization, thoughtfulness*, and so on. Affixes are often bound morphemes, which exist only in combinations.

The second step is to check for polysyllabic morphemes. If a morpheme has more than one vowel separated by consonants, then it is polysyllabic — *napkin, inter-, poly-*, and so on. Several strategies work about equally well for syllable division (Groff, 1971; Ruddell, 1974, p. 14).

Finally, each morpheme or syllable is divided into letters or letter combinations, to each of which a "sound" or phonetic equivalent is assigned. The importance of the previous divisions now becomes apparent. Consider how you would pronounce *nuthouse* if divided *nu-thouse* rather than *nut-house*.

Two caveats are in order: First, these stages describe the strategy of a skilled reader *who has been taught these steps* for attacking a new and difficult word. The skilled reader probably has direct access to frequently occuring words (Ehri & Roberts, 1979). Second, these steps are reversed in acquiring literacy. The young child is first taught the basic letter-sound correspondences, then techniques for handling simple polysyllabic units, and then morphographic analysis. Each new step gives the reader access to a larger set of "long words."

THE ANGLO-SAXON CORE

English is grounded in the Anglo-Saxon heritage. Commonplace words, those most frequent in speech and print, come from this base. Familiarity should not lead to contempt, however; the Anglo-Saxon base is a complex structure in its own right.

Frequently used words fall into two categories. In the first group are familiar terms comprising the stuff of everyday life, as described by Nist (1966):

No matter whether a man is American, British, Canadian, Australian, New Zealander or South African, he still *loves his mother, father, brother, sister, wife, son and daughter; lifts his hand to his head, his cup to his mouth, his eye to heaven and his heart to God; hates his foes, likes his friends, kisses his kin and buries his dead; draws his breath, eats his bread, drinks his water, stands his watch, wipes his sweat, feels his sorrow, weeps his tears and sheds his blood; and all these things he thinks about and calls both good and bad.* (p. 9)

The second category are *function words* — articles, prepositions, conjunctions, some adverbs, and certain verbs. English grammar relies on sentence frames more than word endings: word order supported by function words. These terms, which have little substantive meaning beyond their functional role, tend toward unusual spellings — *of, was, though, do, from*, and so on. The irregularities arise primarily because these oldest words in the language retained their original spellings over centuries of changing pronunciation. Frequency of use led to constancy of spelling. The meaning of these words from the Anglo-Saxon core, the most frequent words in the language, are familiar to most children on entry to school. In many programs these are

the first words taught to the beginning reader, which means that students first encounter those words with the most irregular spellings.

There is nonetheless order to Anglo-Saxon spelling patterns. Syllabic and morphographic patterns are relatively simple. Base morphemes generally contain one or two syllables — *dog, cream, often, hundred, rabbit*. Word compounds are commonplace — *doughnut, greenhouse, peanut*. Affixation also occurs. Suffixes mostly serve syntactic functions (*teacher, funny, forgivable*). Prepositions are common as prefixes (*undertake, input*) and suffixes (*blowup, knockdown*). Both prepositions and base words in these combinations are familiar as stand-alone units.

Anglo-Saxon letter-sound correspondences present some challenge. The phonology is complex, with more sounds than letters in the Roman alphabet. This mismatch was handled early in the development of English writing by (a) *digraph spellings*, with two letters representing a sound, and (b) *markers*, which cue alternate pronunciations of a spelling.

The basic pattern is laid out in Table 28.3 (Venezky, 1970). Single-letter consonant spellings are virtually invariant — each letter stands for a single sound. Consonant blends are common and regular. Consonant diagraphs, combinations with *h* in the second position, handle sounds for which no letter exists.

While consonants pose little difficulty to beginning readers, Anglo-Saxon vowels are another matter. Table 28.3 reveals that even here there is a structure. First, each single vowel spelling usually has one of two pronunciations, referred to as *long* and

Table 28.3. Basic Structure of Letter–Sound Correspondences for Anglo-Saxon Words in English

CONSONANTS

Single Letter	Blended	Digraphs
Consistent and simple correspondences, easily learned:	Combinations of single letter sounds:	Relatively few combinations, each consistent:
b a t	st a nd	ch atter
f i n	pr o ng	sh are
p i ll	spl i nt	th eir, th ing
		wh ere

VOWELS

Single Letter		Digraphs
Long vs. Short	-r and -1 Affected	
mate mat	par pare pal pall	One sound:
Pete pet	her here ___	ai/ay maid, may
pining pinning	sir ___ ___	ee meet
biter bitter	for ___ ___	oa boat
nodes nods	___ ___ ___	oi/oy foil, toy
cubed cubbed		au/aw taut, law
		eu/ew feud, few
		Two sounds:
		ea breath breathe
		oo cook food
		ou/ow {round four / cow snow}

short, or free and checked. The contrast is fundamental for decoding Anglo-Saxon vowels, and students are on their way to mastering the system when they have grasped this alternation.

The most probable pronunciation of a single vowel letter is also *marked* in Anglo-Saxon spelling, as shown in Table 28.3. The marking often designated as the "final -*e*" rule, actually operates as follows:

> If a single vowel letter is followed by a consonant-vowel combination, it takes the long pronunciation; if the single vowel spelling is followed by a terminal consonant or by two or more consonants, it takes the short pronunciation.

Thus, the -*e* in *mate, Pete, nodes* and *cubed* is a vowel marker. At one time pronounced, it is "silent," or takes a schwa pronunciation (*dozes*). The doubled consonants in *bitter, pinning* and *cubbed* mark the short pronunciation of the vowel.

Also shown under the single-letter vowel spellings are examples of a vowel plus -*r* and -*l*. These two consonants are actually semivowels, and fall between vowels and consonants in their pronunciation. Their spellings are probably best presented as combinations rather than blends.

Finally are the vowel digraphs. These spellings, complex in their origins (see Balmuth, 1982), comprise a veritable mélange, and are the most frequent source of complaints about the inconsistency of English spelling—*though, through, rough, ought, bough, bound, hour*—where is rhyme or reason? But Table 28.3 reveals order even here. One set of digraphs is consistently paired with a single sound. Digraphs in the second set take two distinctive sounds. In the latter instance, there is no pattern to the two sounds, nor are there any reliable markers for deciding between the two alternatives. Only three digraphs fall into this category, however, and the task of learning these correspondences should not be a major hurdle.

Finally a handful of idiosyncratic pronunciations fall outside this structure—*could, should, do, does, laugh, night, light, of, one, said, two, was*, along with the set of -*ough* words. Some of these "weirdos" are frequent in print. The student encounters them often and will learn them by rote. Thus, to focus on the exceptions and ignore the general consistency of the Anglo-Saxon base would seem a serious mistake.

ROMANCE WORDS

Much of what the student learns from decoding Anglo-Saxon transfers to words of Romance origins. There are a few significant modifications.

Romance words entered English in two waves. First came the Norman invasion, at a time when for 200 years French was the official language of the land. The English accepted the French vocabulary, sometimes as a commonplace, but more often as a "fancy" alternative. French spelling had been regularized by the 10th century, and so remained relatively unchanged in crossing the Channel. English usage led to significant changes in pronunciation, however, with consequences for the letter-sound correspondences.

The second wave of Romance intrusions came during the English Renaissance, when scholars and scientists "borrowed" tens of thousands of Latin (and Greek) words. These had standard spellings kept constant by the printing press. Again,

the English pronunciation varied from the original, with implications for the spelling-sound relations.

The most noticeable difference between Anglo-Saxon and Romance words is in length and apparent complexity. These are differences in morphology. Romance words tend to contain more morphemes, and include unfamiliar affixes—*a-, e-, ex-, inter-, -ion, -ual, -ity*, and so on. Transfer of word analysis strategies to Romance words is probably most likely when the student has a clearly articulated understanding of the strategy and is given some idea about the units.

Three differences between Anglo-Saxon and Romance letter-sound correspondences require note. First, long-short vowel alternations are still found, but the marking system is less consistent. Second, the stress patterns are complex. Romance words are far more likely to contain unstressed elements, in which the vowel becomes a schwa. These effects are seen in word pairs like *sane/sanity, nation/national, audit/auditory*.

The third spelling-sound difference appears in suffixes of the general form consonant-vowel-vowel-consonant, as in -*tion, -sion, -tial*, and also -*cious, -tious*. The initial consonant-consonant is pronounced /-*sh*/, the vowel digraph takes a schwa, and the final consonant is pronounced as usual. The correspondence reflects a "laziness" in English pronunciation. Aside from these suffixes, vowel digraphs are less common than in Anglo-Saxon, and tend to be quite regular.

Finally, the various languages do not operate in isolation. The declensions and conjugations of Anglo-Saxon English apply directly to words from all origins. Numerous combinations blend elements from several sources. These combinations may be viewed as poor usage, but the vitality of the language suggests that purists will lose these battles. We can expect to hear that football is *over-televised* (with or without the hyphen), and we already know that many people are *undernourished*.

Research Topics in Decoding

The preceding section attempted a broad view of two topics: (a) the current state of curriculum and instruction in decoding, and (b) a structural-historical review of English writing. The coverage was normative rather than empirical. Insofar as the generalizations have merit, a tension exists between current practice and the structural foundations of English writing. The discussion of the writing system was intended to heighten that tension, on the grounds that research and practice may rest at present on too narrow a view of the system.

The organization in the present section intentionally confounds two dimensions—(a) level of acquisition and (b) artificial versus natural settings for research. For each area, two questions merit attention: (a) Where do the studies fall on the continuum of beginning versus skilled reading? (b) Where do the studies fall on the continuum of laboratory investigation to naturalistic inquiry?

ENTRY KNOWLEDGE

What do children know when they come to school that will help them in learning to decode English writing? How does this knowledge shape the instruction offered to students, and how does it influence progress during the primary grades? A serious answer to these questions could take the entire chapter. We will hit some highlights.

A few generalizations can be attempted without data. Children come to school with a working command of a language. It may or may not match closely the language of the school. Children's capabilities include both reception and production — they can understand and they can communicate. All four linguistic functions are operative — phonology, semantics, syntax, and discourse.

Children differ in their command of the language on entry to school (Heath, 1983). Some may lisp or have other speech impediments. Vocabulary extent and precision vary widely. Familiarity with formal language also covers a broad range. The only child of educated parents is probably more skilled at "grown-up" talk than the fifth child of a single parent.

Children differ in their experience with books. Most preschoolers in modern society have seen print — if only as a signal to their favorite fast-food chain. Some children have parents reading to them in the evenings. Some are fluent readers on kindergarten entry — certain cultures view such preparation as a parental duty. Some have "picked up reading" with little or no "teaching."

Differences at school entry predict response to instruction. An early tradition in educational research was the correlational study of reading readiness (Vellutino, 1979, surveys this work, and highlights the possibilities and limitations). From one perspective, the paradigm is self-serving. Some youngsters come to school better prepared than others. Those who are "ready" are given further reading instruction; those less well prepared are assigned to readiness training (generally *not* reading instruction). The predictions are then validated at the end of the first grade — the first group does much better than the second one. To be sure, it might be advisable to allocate more effort to those youngsters who are least "ready" (Calfee & Venezky, 1969).

Intelligence is another gauge measuring differences between students. From his examination of correlational data, Jensen (1980, 1981) concluded that "the vast majority of poor readers [are poor] not because they lack decoding skills but because they are deficient in comprehension which, as measured by standard tests of reading comprehension, is largely a matter of g [generalized intelligence]" (1980, p. 325). Meta-analytic surveys suggest that the correlation may be weaker than reported by Jensen (Hammill & McNutt, 1981). Stanovich, Cunningham, and Feeman (1984) found decoding skill (including phonological awareness; subsequent discussion) more strongly correlated with reading in the primary grades than was intelligence; for older students, the pattern was more diffuse and generalized.

Then there is the "letter name" literature. The preschooler's ability to recite the letter names, in English at least, is a strong predictor of reading achievement in the primary grades (Calfee, 1977; Venezky, 1975); this correlation appears to be weakening with the advent of Head Start and "Sesame Street," and may depend on the culture (Nurses, 1979; Sulzby, 1983). Ehri (1983), in her review of this literature, highlighted instructional studies; students were taught letter names to determine any effect on reading acquisition. Little transfer was found, but flaws in the studies render any conclusion suspect.

This research is a vignette of sorts: Letter-name knowledge is correlated with success in learning to read. Why not teach letter names? Cause and effect are egregiously confused in this reasoning. Ehri (1983) concludes that "this is an empirical question to be answered with data, not logic" (p. 150). Sulzby (1983) argues that both data and logic are needed, and raises questions about the underlying causal mechanisms.

A variation on the "entry" theme is the idea that many children enter school as readers through experience with printed materials in meaningful settings, from which they have discovered for themselves how to decode. As Smith (1976) has put it, "Children learn to read by reading."

Evidence on this point is mostly anecdotal — "My child learned to read all by himself (or herself)!" The evidence varies. If a child can compose original pieces, and if the spelling contains phonetic misspellings, then the youngster has probably acquired letter–sound principles (Chomsky, 1970; Read, 1975). In contrast, the preschooler who can read a book "with closed eyes" has learned something about literacy, but not necessarily about decoding.

In a reasonably well-controlled study, Masonheimer, Drum, and Ehri (1984) showed that exposure to print did not necessarily lead to an appreciation of English writing. Preschoolers (3–5 years old) were shown 10 popular logos (e.g., McDonalds's arches); children who could identify 8 of the 10 were tested on the saliency of the printed elements in the logos. As graphic and color cues were gradually eliminated until only the stylized writing remained, the children became less able to identify the logos. Performance was bimodal; 95% of the preschoolers could read none of the isolated words, while the remaining 5% could read virtually all of them. Masonheimer et al. (1984) conclude:

> Some authorities (Goodman & Goodman, 1979; Goodman & Altwerger, 1981; Harste, Burke, & Woodward, 1982) [hold that] reading begins during the preschool years when children become able to identify print frequently seen in their environment. . . . but environmental print does not contribute to reading acquisition [when] there is no "press" on the subject to look beyond the cues which are easiest to discern and most obvious (e.g., golden arches) and begin attending to alphabetic cues. (p. 258)

Most children need some guidance in figuring out the "writing game."

THE TECHNICAL VOCABULARY OF READING

Children differ on entry to school in knowledge of technical concepts and vocabulary in decoding. The concepts of *word* and *sound* are critical. Skilled readers take for granted several conventions variously labeled "language awareness" or "metalinguistic knowledge" (Downing & Valtin, 1984). With reading, says Ehri (1984), a person gains a new perspective on language and a new technical language for discussing spoken language:

> When children learn to read printed language, they become able to visualize what they are saying and hearing. When children learn to read clocks and calendars, they acquire a visual means of representing the passage of time. [When they] learn to read music, they become able to visualize what is sung or played on an instrument. . . . Acquisition of a spatial model . . . enables the possessor to hold

onto and keep track of phenomona which themselves leave no trace or have no permanence, [and] ... imposes organization upon the phenomena by specifying units, subunits and interrelationships that might otherwise be difficult to detect or discriminate. (p. 119)

Writing and speaking differ, as noted earlier. In speech, "word" is poorly defined. Meaning-bearing elements or morphemes are not the same as words. In print, a word is a letter string bounded by blank spaces or punctuation. In speech, "sounds" or phonemes seldom come to conscious awareness; indeed, psycholinguistic analyses of the phonetic stream show that the component phonemes overlay one another, so that isolating a single phoneme is unnatural if not impossible (Liberman, Cooper, Shankweiler, & Studdert-Kennedy, 1967). In speech, phonemes and morphemes come in streams that express thoughts, overlaid by prosodic and intonational cues. In print, this stream is chopped into chunks that are only partly meaningful, and the stress patterns and pauses so vital in speech are replaced by punctuation symbols, a weak substitute at best (Bolinger, 1975).

What do children know of the technical language of writing when they come to school—sentences, words, sounds, consonants, vowels, and so on? Indeed what is their concept of *reading*? The answer seems to be that most children know little, and what they know may be wrong. Reid (1966) found from interviews that prereaders lacked "any specific expectancies of what reading was going to be like, of what the activity consisted in, of the purpose and use of it.... [Many] were not even clear whether one 'read' the pictures or other 'marks' on the page" (pp. 58, 60). Some of these concepts are relatively easy to acquire (e.g., word), but others are much more difficult to grasp.

Reviews by Downing and Valtin (1984) and Tunmer, Pratt, and Herriman (1984) provide detail on these generalizations. Valtin (1984) lists three metaconcepts in acquiring literacy: "(1) Understanding the nature of reading and writing, e.g., that written language represents ... speech; (2) grasping the alphabetic principle of our script; and (3) conscious and deliberate mastery of language" (p. 256). Tunmer et al. (1984) organize metalevel facets according to standard linguistic categories—phonological awareness, knowledge of "the word," and lexical and pragmatic awareness. They also stress the importance of general awareness of the nature of literacy. They conclude that "children who have listened to printed text read by parents or siblings are more likely to benefit from reading instruction for two reasons; they are more familiar with the use of textlike language, and they are more apt to have a clearer concept of what reading is all about" (p. 153).

Several studies show that, while prereaders know little about the "word" when they enter school, the concept is quickly acquired. Ehri (1975) studied "word consciousness" in preschoolers, kindergartners, and first-graders, using a variety of tasks and materials. The first two groups were still confused about wordness at the end of the school year, especially functional words; first-graders did much better. It appears that experience with print helps the child grasp the conventions of print. Similar findings have been reported by Downing and Oliver (1973-1974).

Bowey, Tunmer, and Pratt (1981) suggest that previous investigations may have both over- and underestimated chil-

dren's knowledge. They note (as does Henderson, 1977) that it is one thing to perform tasks requiring a tacit concept of wordness, and another matter to articulate that knowledge. In three year-end experiments with preschoolers, first-graders, and second-graders (there is apparently no kindergarten in Australia), they systematically explored children's performance on various contrasts (words versus sounds, function versus content words, and words versus phrases). After an initial assessment, students received brief training with feedback, and were then retested. With more schooling, students had less need of training even on difficult tasks. Students whose performance was initially poor improved substantially, even with short-term training. The authors conclude that "the significant training effect ... suggests that teachers may, with relatively little effort, succeed in teaching children the technical vocabulary of reading instruction" (p. 511).

Sounds were more problematic. A substantial literature now exists on tasks variously labeled as phonetic awareness or segmentation. Reviews by Downing and Valtin (1984) and Tunmer et al. (1984) cover the topic, which has also been surveyed by Lewkowicz (1980), Jorm and Share (1983), and Routh and Fox (1984). Lewkowicz' analysis is especially comprehensive.

Included under the rubric of phonetic awareness is a range of activities, from rhyming through isolation of sounds ("What is the first sound in /fish/?"), to Pig Latin. Although the tasks vary in complexity and clarity, two subsets seem particularly pertinent to decoding—segmentation and blending. Segmentation requires the student to analyze the sounds in a word; blending requires that the sounds be combined.

Several generalizations can be drawn: (a) Phonetic awareness on entry to school is correlated with later reading achievement, more strongly than virtually any other entering index except perhaps vocabulary knowledge; (b) young children have considerable difficulty in understanding what is intended on phonetic awareness tasks, unless they have already learned to read; and (c) under the right conditions training can be effective, though it is not easy to specify these conditions. Children do gain competence in segmenting and blending as they learn to read, but cause and effect are not clear—indeed, the relation may be symmetric.

Some reading series, especially those with a strong phonics component, incorporate exercises in segmentation and blending. Experimental programs (Lindamood & Lindamood, 1969; Rosner, 1972; Venezky, Green, & Leslie, 1975; Wallach & Wallach, 1976; Williams, 1980) especially emphasize these areas. Some experimental studies have been conducted (Calfee, 1977; Lewkowicz, 1980, p. 693ff), but few are definitive. Training appears more effective and efficient when articulation is invoked, when pronunciation is slowed and overemphasized, when irrelevant aspects of the problem are minimized, and when learning is supported by mnemonics.

Teachers are probably aware that children differ on this dimension; we know less about how teachers conceptualize these differences. Nor do we know about teachers' metalinguistic knowledge, their concepts of the technical aspects of the relations between sounds and print. In one survey, Pidgeon (1984) obtained data from "reception" (i.e., kindergarten and first grade) teachers in Great Britain. Among his conclusions:

Teachers mistakenly assumed that students had prior knowledge about the technical aspects of reading; they were generally more concerned with planning instructional activities than
with assessment of student learning; learning relied more on
associations than on understanding; and decoding was generally taught from sight to sound (see the printed word and
pronounce it). These generalizations are troubling if true — the
Pidgeon survey has serious limitations, but the pattern seems
consistent with other observations (Duffy & Roehler, 1982).
What is lacking in these studies is curricular specificity and a
linkage to the instructional features of the teacher's manual.

The upshot is that from the beginning of their experience in
learning to read, many students appear confused about the
fundamental nature of literacy, and especially about decoding.
They may or may not be able to distinguish the elements that
comprise words; they eventually gain some familiarity with
letters and the notion that words are letter strings; many will
never grasp what in the speech stream is to be associated with
letters. For these students, reading is the learning of words as
wholes, a strategy that eventually fails.

Some years ago Vernon (1957) expressed a concern about
reading disability that has a similar ring:

> The fundamental and basic characteristic of reading disability seems
> to be cognitive confusion [about the relations between successions
> of printed words and phonetic patterns]. The employment of
> reasoning is almost certainly involved in understanding the variable
> associations between printed and sounded letters. . . . these associa-
> tions may be acquired through rote learning. But, even if this is
> possible with very simple letter–phoneme associations, the more
> complex associations and the correct application of the rules of
> spelling necessitate intelligent comprehension. (p. 82)

The point will be reiterated at the end of this section — decoding, from the initial linkages between letters and sounds to the
articulate awareness of the underlying morphophonemic structure, is a difficult intellectual challenge. To construe this task as
the rote learning of piecemeal objectives may seriously mislead
both students and teachers.

"MINIATURE" DECODING STUDIES

Research in natural classroom settings is tough. It is understandable that investigators should turn to analogues. In miniature decoding studies, the early stages of decoding acquisition
are studied under conditions that allow careful control of
relevant factors (e.g., Jeffreys & Samuels, 1967; Silberman,
1967). These studies generally entail training of individual
students on a relatively small set of target words. The subjects
may be children, but college students have also been used.

This paradigm has its strengths and weaknesses; recent
studies show advances over earlier efforts. For instance, Dahl
(1979) factorially investigated three methods to improve the
decoding skills of below-average second-graders. The subjects'
tasks were to read passages aloud with fluency, to recognize
words presented in isolation, and to answer several sets of
comprehensive questions.

The Hypothesis/Test method required the student to combine spelling and contextual cues to generate a plausible
pronunciation for an unknown word and to test out the

hypothesis. The method resembles the approach of the skilled
reader, but slowed down. In Repeated/Readings, selections
were read and reread aloud until the student was both accurate
and fast. The Flashed/Word method amounted to rote training.
The design included eight combinations of the presence or
absence of these methods, with four students assigned to each
condition.

On most measures, the Hypothesis/Test treatment had a
large positive effect, the Flashed/Word treatment had none, and
Repeated/Reading fell in between. Analysis seemed to win out
over rote learning. The researcher had predicted matches
between treatments and measures — Hypothesis/Test should
benefit cloze and comprehension measures, Repeated/Reading
the oral reading tasks, and Flashed/Words the word identification tasks. The first two predictions held; the third did not.
Virtually no interactions were significant.

The study has promise as an experimental analogue, and the
findings provide interesting leads. To be sure, instructional time
may not have been adequately controlled, and the investigator
failed to incorporate student entry factors in the design, thus
weakening the power of the experiment and forestalling an
examination of aptitude–treatment interactions.

In a second example (Kibby, 1979), 144 first-graders were
each taught 12 words in four sessions of 3 words each. The
training factors were Method (phonics or sight-word), Practice
(recognition or production), and Instruction (no correction,
correction, and "mastery"). Materials were confounded with
method; Phonics words were *at, bat, hat, mat, rat, sat*, while the
Sight-Word list included *boy, children, farm, house, rabbit,
wagon*. A within-subject design was used; each student was
tested on all the training combinations. A variety of dependent
measures was included in the battery.

The results were somewhat complex, but several generalizations can be made. First, training performance was higher in the
Sight-Word condition, sensible given the low interitem similarity in this condition. Students learned the responses, but had
difficulty pairing them with the appropriate stimuli. (We call
this the "Pug" effect, after the difficulty experienced by a first-
grader in a phonics program; when uncertain he would regularly say "Pug," the central character of the series.)

Second, correction had only a slight positive effect on training and no transfer benefits; there were only six training trials.
The "mastery" condition entailed exposure without feedback; if
a student was already having trouble learning the list, further
training had no benefit whatsoever. Finally, student performance was lower during training under the Production condition ("say the word") than under the Recognition condition
("is it house or rabbit?"), but Production training paid off
during the transfer tests, especially when these required
production.

This study represents a significant effort to investigate the
early stages of decoding acquisition, but is also flawed in several
ways. Certain problems may be arguable; using a within-
subjects design in a learning experiment always raises the
possibility of transfer from one condition to another, though
such transfer was not evident in this study. The amount of
training was quite modest, a problem only if students fail to
master the task, as in this study. Blanchard and McNinch
(1980) note in critiquing another study that "it seems doubtful

that poor readers, as a result of a one-time, single-word decoding procedure ... can compensate for a five-year difference in reading performance." (p. 560)

More serious in both of the preceding studies is the absence of any model of the task—what was the curriculum, what pedagogy was intended, and what was the process of learning and transfer? Given the low levels of performance, one might expect the investigator to review the task for weaknesses in the instructional design. Instead, the purpose seemed limited empirical investigation of the factor set. Empiricism has its limits.

Finally, let us consider the study by Anderson, Mason, and Shirey (1984). Two observational studies are reported in the paper; we will focus on the first and more extensive of the two. The investigation is both extensive and complex, and might have been discussed elsewhere in the chapter; it is introduced here as a transition between "miniature" experimental and naturalistic studies. As the authors note, the investigation had the potential "to study the independent effects of variables that are correlated in nature, ... to get a preliminary look at the causal dynamics in reading groups, ... and to investigate the interplay of a large number of factors that converge at given moments to determine [performance]" (p. 10).

The child's task was to learn 36 rather complex sentences (Anderson et al., 1984, p. 11):

The hungry children were in the kitchen helping mother make donuts.

The old shoes were put away in the back of the closet.

Green blood ran out when the boy shot an arrow through the monster's head.

The students, more than 250 third graders, were taught in groups of 4. In the Meaning condition, the student predicted what might happen next after each sentence; oral miscues were ignored or corrected quickly and without comment. In the Accuracy condition, miscues were corrected and the student had to reread the sentence to a criterion of accuracy and fluency. Other factors in the design included the makeup of the group (homogeneous or heterogeneous), active or passive turn taking, reading ability, reading fluency, and the readability and interestingness of the sentences. The measures included sentence recall (given "old shoes" as a clue, the student recalled the rest of the sentence) and decoding performance (16 hard words from the sentences).

The data were subjected to multiple regression analyses —more than 30 main effects and interactions were assessed. Attention, consonant with the experimenters' purposes, focused on sentence recall. In general, the Meaning treatment had a positive effect on recall, especially for students at higher levels of reading achievement. Interesting sentences were better recalled than dull ones. Difficult sentences were better recalled in the Accuracy condition—students had to read these sentences several times, and so were better practiced on them. In homogeneous high-ability groups receiving the Accuracy treatment, recall was especially poor—they read each sentence quickly, and then went on to the next. Finally, fluency interacted with the treatment on the decoding measure—the Accuracy condition helped students who lacked fluency in decoding.

This investigation illustrates the costs and benefits of attempting a controlled study under conditions that approximate the regular classroom. Several of the findings are quite informative, but multicollinearity in the predictors led to some ambiguities of interpretation. In this investigation, as in Dahl's, interactions moderated certain main effects, but the structure of the findings was relatively simple.

Two limitations deserve note. First, the strong emphasis on meaning led the investigators to give less attention to the assessment of other outcomes. Students tend to learn what they are taught. If they are taught to focus on meaning, then they will typically do better on a test of meaning than if their attention is directed to the surface aspects of the material. Beginning readers need to understand what they read, but fluent and accurate decoding is also important. The task for instructional design is the creation of programs that meet both of these needs.

The second limitation is related to the adequacy of the instructional treatments. Students had opportunities for practice, but relatively little *instruction*. This limitation may explain the rather substantial aptitude–treatment interaction—the abler students gained more from the Meaning treatment. Opportunities for practice help when the student already has some understanding. As in the Kibby experiment, the present study would have been more informative if grounded in a theoretical framework of the curriculum and the pedagogy of the task.

The "miniature" studies reviewed above are clearly no longer small. In their design, in the student sample, in the tasks and measures of performance, they approach the complexity and reach of naturalistic studies, while attempting the precise control of laboratory studies. We can expect to see increasing payoff from these efforts if present trends continue.

WHAT IS LEARNED FROM DECODING INSTRUCTION?

Studies of word recognition have a long history in experimental psychology (Smith & Spoehr, 1974; Venezky, 1977). Recent years have seen a new development in efforts to relate word recognition processes to instructional experiences. The idea, often implicit, is that no single model determines word recognition, but that differences between and within subjects will reflect knowledge, skills, and strategies acquired during the elementary grades.

Two major research questions have emerged in this domain. First, when a subject "reads" a word, does the translation entail direct access to a visual pattern, or is it moderated by a phonological letter-to-sound activity, or do both processes operate? Second, in those situations in which translation is phonological, does the coding depend on spelling–sound rules or on analogies to familiar words?

The role of instruction in establishing codes should be especially marked in English writing. If students have not learned the spelling–sound patterns (perhaps because they were not taught), then one would not expect to see evidence of phonological codes. For these "Chinese" readers (Baron & Strawson, 1976; Baron, Treiman, Wilf, & Kellman, 1980), pronunciation speed should depend only on the number of times the child has previously encountered the word. The reasoning behind these hypotheses is heuristic rather than formal, but the description does fit research findings for poor readers (e.g., Carnine, Carnine, & Gersten, 1984; Lesgold & Curtis, 1981, pp. 340ff). A clearer picture awaits more precise studies of the relation between what has been taught and what appears to have been learned.

Research on visual versus phonological codes in word recognition has been reviewed by McCusker, Hillinger, and Bias (1981), and by Jorm and Share (1983). McCusker et al. (1981), from studies of skilled adult readers, conclude that "the data point to a dual access model in which high-frequency words enjoy high-speed access via a visually based representation, whereas low-frequency words are accessed using a slower, phonological recoding process" (p. 217). As a teacher might put it, some words are learned by sight (those seen often in print), while others (less frequent) are handled by word attack strategies. Students are taught both approaches, and it is reassuring to see research findings consistent with instructional practice. To be sure, these results hold for the schools' success stories (college students). This area continues to attract attention; articles by Underwood and Thwaites (1982), Taft (1984), and Rossmeisl and Theios (1982) reflect the sophistication with which researchers now determine the codes used by skilled readers in high-speed tasks.

Jorm and Share (1983), viewing the research from a developmental and instructional perspective, propose that "although phonological recoding may play a minor role in skilled adult reading, it plays a critical role in helping the child become a skilled reader" (p. 103). Their concern is primarily on the role of phonological recoding in reading acquisition, and so they give less attention to studies of visual coding in young readers. They contrast two theoretical positions: Stage theory (readers begin by using phonological recoding, and with practice resort to the faster access available through direct visual codes); and Comparator theory (a "race-horse" model in which visual and phonological codes compete with one another; the winner depends on experience and situational factors). Stage theory comes in two versions, the probabilistic version described above, and a strong version, easily rejected, in which readers move irreversibly from one stage to the next.

In presenting these models and reviewing the literature, Jorm and Share pay little attention to instructional practices. In English-speaking countries, one finds two or three dominant approaches to teaching word recognition. Present practice is typically rather eclectic; the child begins with a set of sight words learned by rote and useful in round-robin reading. Phonics instruction follows, with emphasis on word attack strategies during the midelementary grades but also stress on fluent oral reading. In the late elementary grades and onward, silent reading (fostering visual coding?) predominates. One can find variations. Some programs stress phonics from the beginning, whereas others emphasize sight recognition and "reading for meaning." The words from these latter programs typically provide the student little basis for discovering letter–sound generalizations. Finally, individual teachers may do much to reconfigure any given program.

Several studies indicate that inadequate phonological recoding may be a hallmark of the poor reader (Jorm & Share, 1983, p. 133ff). To test this skill, the subject is asked to read a synthetic or nonsense word, one that conforms to the underlying structure of English spelling but has no assigned meaning. The usual finding, mentioned later in the section, is that poor readers are at a special disadvantage with words that they have never seen before. A few studies have directly addressed the relation between how words are coded in a person's memory and the decoding instruction and other relevant experiences of the person. Each investigation has its limitations, but the overall pattern makes sense.

Nelson (1974), for instance, studied the oral reading performance of kindergartners taught by a phonics or sight-word basal series. A factor analysis of the test battery yielded two factors, one of which seemed to be a decoding index and the other a sight-word index. These factor scores were significantly different for students in the two basal programs, and in the predicted directions. (Barr, 1972, in a study to be described later, reports a similar pattern). Alegria, Pignot, and Morais (1982) assessed the phonetic segmentation skills of teachers taught in a phonics or a sight-word program. The segmentation task was quite difficult, requiring the student to reverse the sounds in a word (so that TOE became OAT). Students in the phonics program were four times more successful than those in the sight-word program. Finally, Treiman and Baron (1983), investigating the effects of phonemic awareness training on reading acquisition, also found training experiences reflected in the students' coding.

Several assessment and training studies reveal students using both visual and phonological codes, depending on their level of experience and the conditions of assessment. Waters, Seidenberg, and Bruck (1984) illustrate one approach. They note that English, like most modern written languages, relies on the alphabetic principle (hence the tendency for readers to rely on phonological coding when in need), but parallel systems exist (e.g., signs like $, %, #, and "weirdos" in English spelling), so that some words must be learned as visual codes. In their study, spellings of the test words were either regular (*best*, *dust*), exceptional (*give*, *bowl*), or "strange" (*once*, *view*); word frequency was also controlled. The subject's tasks were to pronounce each word as quickly as possible, and (in a separate block of trials) to identify each stimulus as word or nonword. Age (fourth grade, fifth grade, and adult) and reading level (high or low) were also controlled.

Our chief interest is in the pronunciation task. Familiar words, no matter how spelled, were pronounced quickly by the better readers (500 milliseconds for adults, 750 milliseconds for fourth-graders). Regularly spelled unfamiliar words were also quickly pronounced. Unfamiliar words, especially those with strange spellings, took an additional 50–100 milliseconds. Low-ability fourth-graders performed differently in several respects. First, they are much slower in general; familiar words, which they handled most quickly and without regard to spelling pattern, required 1200 milliseconds or more. Unfamiliar words took longer, even if regularly spelled (1500 milliseconds), and especially if "strange" (2500 milliseconds).

Waters et al. interpret the findings as showing "greater involvement of phonological information in the early stages of reading, ... [but] fast decoders treat a larger class of items as 'high-frequency' [i.e., familiar] items" (pp. 302ff). These conclusions are somewhat compromised by limitations in the stimulus words (all were short, Anglo-Saxon, and single syllable, and the classification of spelling patterns was rather crude), and by the presence of a floor effect for the better readers. Nonetheless, the findings do support the previous generalization about dual coding systems, depending on the reader's characteristics, the spelling patterns, and the task. The article contains a substantial number of references to earlier studies along the same lines.

Assuming that a student has been taught spelling patterns, what is acquired—rules or analogies? One might expect the answer to this question to be placed in the context of a careful analysis of what is taught. As noted earlier, patterns more than rules are emphasized in teaching. Glushko (1981) proposed that readers rely solely on analogy: "As letters in a word are identified, an entire neighborhood of words that share orthographic features is activated in memory, and the pronunciation emerges through the coordination and synthesis of many partially activated phonological representations" (p. 62). He presents findings from three "mini-experiments" to support this conclusion.

The "analogy" model has been criticized—Jorm and Share (1983) point out that the beginning reader does not have too many patterns to activate, and point to conflicting findings by Andrews (1982); Barber and Millar (1982) note flaws in Glushko's stimulus words. On the other hand, the issues raised by Glushko seem of fundamental importance—it is perhaps unfortunate that the question is posed as "What do readers do?" rather than "How can we help readers learn what they need to do?" Certainly analogy is a powerful approach for learning, and for training as well (Silberman, 1967; also see Cunningham, 1975–1976, for a demonstration of the effectiveness of the analogical approach in a "miniature" decoding study). The same can be said about rules, generalizations, and regularities. Indeed, the contrast is not either-or; analogy and rule are better construed as endpoints on a continuum. The task for assessing and training decoding would seem to be establishment of a clear and workable structure for describing the regularities, followed by empirical investigation of the conditions under which students can be taught the essentials of that structure.

FLUENCY IN DECODING

The competent reader decodes with accuracy, but with fluency as well. Perfetti and Lesgold (1979) have reviewed this area, and summarize several studies by Perfetti and his colleagues delimiting various conditions under which speed does or does not indicate competence. Rapid response is sometimes only a sign of impulsivity (Kagan, Rosman, Day, Albert, & Phillips, 1964), but it is more often a marker of competence. Curtis (1980) tested elementary students on a variety of reading skills, and found that by fifth grade any speeded task differentiated the more from the less able readers (also see Biemiller, 1977–1978.

Speed is an end in its own right, but it also is an indicator of other advantages. LaBerge and Samuels (1974) were among the first in recent times to point out the benefits of "automaticity" in decoding. Their model of the reading process incorporated several stages between the translation of letters and the final extraction of meaning; as decoding became an automatic response, intermediate stages could be bypassed, relieving demands on human attention. When decoding requires attention,

then something else (presumably comprehension) must wait. Perfetti and Lesgold (1979; also see Liberman & Shankweiler, 1979) have identified "several components in reading that, when not fully developed, could increase [sic] the working memory bottleneck...: access to long-term memory, speed and automation of decoding, and efficiency of reading strategies" (p. 59).

Reducing demands on short-term memory is certainly one advantage of fluency. Another benefit is the ease in understanding text when the rate is adequate (a related issue is the loss of prosodic and suprasegmental information when words are uttered one at a time; slow readers do not "read with meaning"). Five syllables per second is the rate of normal speech; 5 to 10 units can be retained for 10 to 15 seconds without loss. Under normal conditions the "listener" can easily organize a sentence and transfer the gist to long-term memory. When the rate is greatly reduced, problems arise: "The computation of sentence structure must take place within a certain limited period. If a sentence is uttered too slowly—say one word every 5 seconds—its structure collapses, ... [and what remains] is a string of words" (McNeill, 1968).

Poor readers are slow readers; what can be done to alleviate this problem? One answer is to "practice, practice, practice." Huey (1968) put it more elegantly: "Repetition progressively frees the mind from attention to details, makes facile the total act, shortens the time, and reduces the extent to which consciousness must concern itself with the process" (p. 104). Jenkins and Pany (1981) review several studies on this issue. The general finding seems to be that practice in pronouncing a list of words speeds performance on that list, but with little transfer to other words and few benefits for comprehension. Most of these studies used a relatively short list of words, practice did not include instruction, and training was relatively short.

Fleisher, Jenkins, and Pany (1979), for example, trained fourth- and fifth-graders on speeded pronunciation of a list of 75 words. In the first experiment, words were presented on flash cards one at a time; in the second study the words were embedded in phrases. After training, students read passages containing the words, and both reading speed and comprehension were assessed.

The training was effective. Poor readers without training read words in isolation at about half the rate of good readers; with training, this difference became negligible. The training did not totally eliminate differences; trained poor readers improved, but still performed more slowly than skilled readers when reading passages containing the words. The training had no effect on comprehension performance—none whatsoever. Students in this situation learned only what they were taught. Blanchard (1980), on the other hand, found that providing flash-card training to extremely poor readers did have a positive effects on comprehension—extent of need may also matter.

Samuels (1979; also Carver & Hoffman, 1981; C. Chomsky, 1978) proposed the method of "repeated readings" to promote fluency. The student (or perhaps another skilled reader) attempts a first reading, works on any problems, and reads it again until the result is "smooth." Dahl (1979) evaluated this method in her study, and found benefits on all measures of decoding speed and accuracy (errors were cut in half, and speed increased by 50%). Improvements in comprehension were smaller.

Finally, what happens to reading speed during silent reading? In particular, are oral and silent reading similar operations in good and poor readers? Juel and Holmes (1981) illustrate how information-processing techniques can be used to address this question (they also review the earlier literature on the topic). Second- and fifth-graders of high and low reading achievement read 64 sentences in which both word and sentence factors were systematically varied (for words, the factors included spelling–sound regularity, number of syllables, frequency, and abstractness; for sentences, the reversibility of subject and predicate nouns).

Word factors had substantial effects on oral reading, especially for the poor readers, who were much slower than the good readers (7.4 versus 3.3 seconds/sentence). The effects were less noticeable in silent reading, and the differences between poor and good readers were smaller (4.8 versus 3.2 seconds/sentence). Comprehension, as measured by a picture-recognition task, did not differ between good and poor readers, nor between oral and silent reading. The authors note that "the added attention expended on achieving oral pronunciations [does not result in] less time spent on sentence comprehension. Rather, it appears simply to increase poor readers' overall processing time" (p. 560).

The purpose of oral reading exercises is an issue worth further examination. Fluency may correlate with other performance indicators, but cause and effect are unclear. As in the case of letter names, the direct instructional approach misses the point. Training the student to "read words fast" may succeed in some purposes but fail in others. Recommendations promoting rereading and greater reliance on silent reading, however, would appear to warrant more careful investigation.

DECODING AND CONTEXT

Several studies have found that words are read aloud more quickly in the context of a sentence or passage than in isolation (e.g., Fleisher et al., 1979; Stanovich et al., 1984). Advocates of reading for meaning reinforce the point, noting that syntactic and semantic clues allow the reader to play a "psycholinguistic guessing game" (Goodman, 1970) rather than struggle with the nonsense of print.

How are decoding and comprehension related? One finds strong differences of opinion, and individual positions are not always clear. Perfetti and Lesgold (1979), for instance, state:

> Skilled reading can be partly understood as a set of interrelated component processes, ... [such that] a gain in one subskill allows gains in other subskills, that an insufficiently developed subskill may limit the apparent inadequacy of other subskills, and that the processes underlying the skills are difficult to study in isolation. (p. 57)

This statement is then qualified: "The component processes are isolable in principle although interrelated in practice, ... [and] the situation ... is one of structural independence but functional interdependence" (p. 58). Perfetti and Lesgold rely on analogy to a hi-fi music system: In operation (i.e., when a

reader is reading or a hi-fi playing) processes are likely to be complexly interrelated. Nonetheless, it is still possible to identify the distinctive functional components that underlie observable performance.

And so what does happen to decoding when words are read aloud in context? What is the character of the interaction? Perfetti and Roth (1981; Perfetti, Goldman, & Hogaboam, 1979) discuss several investigations of this question. The subjects' task was to read (or listen to or study) part of a passage, then pronounce as quickly as possible a word displayed on a visual display. The factors included context (present or not), word frequency and length, and reading achievement of the subjects (all in third to fifth grade). "A major result was that less skilled readers benefitted from story context at least to the same extent as did skilled readers. ... [In particular], less skilled readers showed very large facilitation for long low-frequency words" (pp. 273, 275). The good readers could decode all of the words very quickly (about 500 milliseconds/word), and a floor effect may exist: "Skilled readers are already so good at word identification that context is of little consequence" (Perfetti et al., 1979, p. 281).

The second experiment performed by Perfetti et al. showed that for less skilled readers the text had to be highly supportive for facilitation to occur. If the target word was not readily predictable from the context, then poor readers were not helped by context. Moreover, "subjects who were faster at word identification tended to be more accurate at predicting the next word in a story. Skilled readers thus appear to have at least two advantages. They are more efficient at context-free verbal coding and more able to use context in anticipating words" (p. 283).

The question remains—do these results indicate complex interactions between processes, or do they reflect confounded variations in students' instructional experiences? That is, if the student has difficulty in becoming a fluent decoder, then the chances may be slim that he or she will be taught comprehension strategies—thus the "double whammy."

Juel (1980; also see Juel, 1983, for a related study) also investigated the effects of context on decoding performance. She laid out the opposing theories. One position holds that skilled readers are predominantly "text-driven"; they use cues from the printed text (whether through phonological or visual cues is irrelevant). Poor readers are "concept-driven"; they rely less on print and more on their sense of contextual meaning. The contrasting position is that skilled readers make extensive use of context, turning to the printed material only when their predictions fail, whereas poor readers rely mainly on the text.

Second- and third-graders, either high or low in reading achievement, were presented words varying in spelling–sound regularity, number of syllables, and frequency, in either a strong or weak sentence context, or in isolation. The dependent measure was the percentage of correct pronunciations. When the task was to pronounce isolated words, performance was strongly influenced by all factors in the design. The differences were much smaller when supporting context was provided. This pattern was most marked for low-ability students; high ability students did not require contextual support. Moreover, low-frequency, hard-to-decode words were difficult for all groups, quite apart from context. In Stanovich et al. (1984) context was provided by coherent and random paragraphs. The subjects, first-graders, were tested in the late fall and spring. Coherent context aided both skilled and unskilled readers, but the benefits were much greater for the former and during the spring rather than fall testing. The contrast between these two sets of findings may reflect the relative skill of students and the difficulty of the words.

The preceding studies give some idea of findings from research on the effects of context on decoding. Several other investigations could be added to this list: Ehri has been active in this area, finding in one study that contextual training of function words led to a better grasp of syntactic/semantic identities (Ehri & Wilce, 1980), and in another that the same principle held for content words (Ehri & Roberts, 1979). Willows and Ryan (1981) explored the effect on oral reading of deleting words from the text or transforming text by a physical rotation (skilled readers were better at "filling the gaps"). Nemko (1984) found that training students to decode words in isolation or in context had differential transfer effects (if the goal is context-free decoding, train in isolation). Rash, Johnson, and Gleadow (1984), in a study immediately preceding Nemko's, came to the opposite conclusion (the study has serious limitations—students learned "Nicki's tooth fell out" and "Our television needs fixing" as sentences or as isolated words; not surprisingly, the two sentences were easier to learn than eight unrelated words).

This expanding body of research raises questions as well as providing some answers. The questions motivating the research are only partly illuminated by the findings. Context helps the reader in decoding under some conditions, but not others. Both good and poor readers use context; poor readers have a greater need to rely on context, but good readers seem better able to use the surrounding materials if they have a need. These conclusions guide assessment more than training—a student's decoding skills are estimated with greater validity in isolation than in context. The role of context during instruction is more problematic. Few studies address this issue, and those that do provide little guidance. There is work to be done in this area, both theoretical and pragmatic.

NATURALISTIC STUDIES OF DECODING

Perhaps because it is easier to "see" decoding instruction than other reading activities, several investigations of decoding under natural classroom conditions have been reported, some of which will be reported in this section. Several large-scale investigations are not discussed because they are covered elsewhere in the Handbook, or lack precise measures of decoding (e.g., Berliner & Rosenshine, 1977; McDonald & Elias, 1975; Stallings, 1975).

We begin with the study by Barr and Dreeben (1983), in many respects an exemplar. The data were collected by Barr in the early 1970s (Barr, 1972, 1973-1974, 1974-1975). The sample, designed to cover a range of instructional and organizational conditions, and a variety of student entry skills, included about 150 students from 15 first grade classes in six schools and three districts. Decoding was assessed in a variety of ways, the curriculum was carefully analyzed, and instruction was monitored by classroom observations.

Barr and Dreeben present a detailed secondary analysis of the data. The major focus of the report was the social organization of the classes. Students are generally not assigned at random to reading groups, and once a student is assigned to a group, several consequences ensue. One suspects that similar generalizations hold for other curriculum areas, but elementary reading may have some distinctive features in this regard. Our summary, however, will concentrate on curriculum and instructional features of the study.

The report is especially revealing about the relationship between the content covered during instruction, the nature of that content, the manner in which instruction proceeds, and student performance on decoding and comprehension tests. Also noteworthy is the nature of these relations for children of differing entry levels in different classes. The data do not provide detail on teacher-student interactions, and so less can be said about the extent to which teachers converted allocated time into productive time.

Differences in phonics coverage between classes was predictable from four factors—group phonics aptitude, difficulty of the phonics materials, time allocated to phonics instruction, and time spent in supervising learning. Teachers made significant decisions—"We observed wide differences in new word and phonics coverage among groups sharing the same relative rank among classes" (Barr & Dreeben, 1983, p. 113)—and these decisions had consequences for student learning.

The number of basal lessons covered by the teacher during the school year was a group-determined decision. Level and pace for each group of students was based primarily on the ease with which students could read aloud. Phonics coverage and pace were derivative on this decision, and were not directly related to group aptitude; "basal instruction is established, and the recommendations of the teachers' manual [and accompanying worksheets] govern phonics coverage" (p. 124).

Difficulty of the phonics materials was the strongest predictor of the amount covered, with group aptitude next in order; the two together account for almost 80% of the variability in coverage. Designers of basal series treat the textual materials independently of phonics objectives, so that knowing a student is reading materials at a given grade level tells little about phonics tasks. If the phonics worksheets happen to be especially difficult, then teachers may adjust the pace.

According to Barr and Dreeben (1983), time spent in supervision of phonics instruction by the teacher is a statistically significant predictor of coverage, and the descriptive statistics tell the tale quite dramatically:

> More phonics instruction [than basal instruction] occurs as seatwork and supervised instruction is rare. . . . Teachers allocate more time to basal reading (43 minutes) and supervise a substantial portion of that time (33 minutes). By contrast, less time is spent on phonics each day (31 minutes) and considerably less of it is supervised (8 minutes). (p. 120)

Leinhardt, Zigmond and Cooley, 1981, in a detailed study of reading in special education classrooms, report similar findings: "The teachers in this study spent only 16 minutes per day in . . . direct instructional contacts, and of that time, 14 minutes were used to give general reading instructions, 1 minute per day was spent waiting while a student completed a reading task, and only one minute per day was used to explain or model correct elements in reading" — (p. 358. These are averages; the variability was substantial.)

Barr and Dreeben found that student performances reflected coverage: "Our evidence shows that pace is a major influence on learning; the more material children cover, the more they learn" (p. 130). Moreover, achievement was fairly specific to the substance covered. Thus, the number of sight words from the basal series pronounced by the student was strongly correlated with basal coverage (r = .93), and the number of phonics objectives mastered was correlated with phonics coverage (r = .62). The off-diagonal entries of this matrix were .50 or less. Standardized achievement tests were a closer match to basal (r = .75) than to phonics coverage (r = .57), unsurprising given the omnibus content of the former measures.

Student aptitude on entry to school determined group assignment, which in turn determined coverage, which then determined standardized test performance, or so went the path analysis; "the effect of aptitude on general first grade achievement (beta = .15) is smaller than that attributable to both basal (beta = .45) and phonics (beta = .31) learning. . . . What the children have learned directly out of their basal reading materials has a greater impact on their general reading achievement than their aptitude, a finding that shows the preeminence of instructional events and their immediate outcomes over aptitude" (p. 143).

Barr and Dreeben report that children assigned to different groups, and hence with differing entry levels, benefited differently from the instructional program. In their Table 6.2, Barr and Dreeben (1983) present a careful accounting of basal and phonics coverage for each class and group. The table requires detailed study, but even a cursory glance reveals enormous disparities between classes and groups, with more than an order of magnitude separating coverage by groups that were nominally the same (i.e., low, middle, or high).

Nonetheless, and for whatever reasons, low-ability students were generally less able to transfer what they learned in one setting to other situations:

> In the low aptitude subsample [unlike the high aptitude group], phonics learning is not related to basal learning. . . . Among these children, who are the least ready to read, the acquisition of phonics skills does not occur derivatively from basal reading or in conjunction with it, but more narrowly reflects the pace of phonics instruction. In short, the low aptitude children learn the phonics they are taught and do not pick it up as a by-product of more general reading. (p. 148)

This brief account barely scratches the surface of the Barr and Dreeben presentation. The study has limits, but nonetheless provides a model of what can be attained through a carefully planned research design within the environs of the regular classroom.

A second example, the Reading Diary study, was undertaken in the mid-1970s to investigate the acquisition of decoding skills by first-graders. The first report appeared in Calfee and Piontkowski (1981; also see Piontkowski, 1981). Fifty students were selected from 10 first-grade classes in four schools, selected to represent a variety of organizational contexts and student backgrounds. None of the students could read in September, but all were judged by the teacher as likely to read by midyear. Classrooms were observed, and students were measured on prereading skills, pronunciation ability, oral reading and comprehension, and standardized test performance. Emphasis was on the development of a multifaceted test of decoding ability, designed for comprehension and efficient assessment of growth during the school year.

Calfee and Piontkowski report findings from the decoding test. The general pattern was one of rapidly expanding variability between students. In October, most students could identify rhymes, match letters to initial sounds, and name the letters. Differences in performance on these tasks were negligible. By June, some children had not advanced much beyond the skills of October, while others could decode polysyllabic words with some fluency. Nor were the variations evenly distributed over schools and classes; student scores showed some classes far more effective in promoting student growth than others.

Other analyses showed that level of decoding skill was at least partly independent of oral reading and comprehension (oral reading was assessed individually, not in the round-robin setting). Students who had mastered decoding were generally good at the reading and comprehension tasks, but other students could read a simple story even though their decoding skills were still relatively weak.

Grouping practices play an important role in reading instruction, as noted earlier. Equally important is the teacher's response to the group. Allington (1980), demonstrating another approach to naturalistic investigation, made tape recordings of round-robin sessions in 20 classrooms, a high and low group for each teacher. The purpose was to determine teacher interruptions during oral reading by high- and low-ability groups.

The results showed that "teachers are more likely to interrupt poor readers than good readers when an oral-reading error occurs, regardless of the semantic appropriateness of the error" (p. 375). Poor readers made more miscues than good readers (9.4 versus 5.8), and a larger proportion of these were semantically inappropriate (71 versus 53%). Teachers interrupted readers in good groups on only 11% of the semantically appropriate errors; readers in low groups were interrupted 55% of the time. Interruptions on semantically inappropriate miscues were 48 and 79% for good and poor readers, respectively. The overall result was that poor readers are interrupted frequently. Allington also found that when poor readers were stopped, the teacher pronounced the word for the student or made a remark about the letter–sound cues; when good readers were stopped, corrective pronunciation was also likely, but the teacher tended to emphasize semantic cues.

Direct teaching of decoding is relatively rare in basal instruction (some programs include a significant decoding component, but these are in the minority). Most children learn to "read" in the reading circle. Poor readers generally have trouble decoding, and so the teacher may be right to guide the student by interruption and correction. On the other hand, it seems equally likely that the momentary exchange serves little purpose other than to break the student's concentration on the meaning of the text, and perhaps to further convince the student that he or she lacks competence in dealing with text.

Decoding: In Summary

Whether one views decoding as the first or most essential stage of becoming literate, it clearly is a critical aspect of reading acquisition. Research on this topic is vigorous, multifaceted, and evolving. The questions raised in the past decade represent new directions from the 10 years previous, and the next decade is likely to surprise us once more.

We do find two major limitations in existing paradigms of decoding research. One is the reliance on correlational rather than experimental (i.e., interventional) approaches. Kintsch (1979) says: "If there is a moral [to the difficulty in drawing conclusions from existing research on reading], it is ... that we continually get ourselves into trouble because [or when] we do not know how to interpret correlational data" (p. 328). We need to attempt more investigations that incorporate a significant instructional component.

The second limitation is the restricted view of the decoding curriculum, or to put it another way, the piecemeal selection of stimulus words and spelling patterns. The problem exemplifies Clark's (1973) "fixed-effect" fallacy — when the materials for a study have been selected to demonstrate a particular point, then what is the extent of generalization (Cronbach, Gleser, Nanda, & Rajaratnam, 1972)?

But the question is even broader. The vision of English writing held by researchers and practitioners is remarkably unenlightened by either the history that generated the language or the linguistic principles that constrained this evolution. Future designs for selection of target words will undoubtedly include word frequency and regularity as factors. Our hope is that the accompanying prose might consider questions like "Why and how does frequency affect pronunciation skill?" and "What is meant by regularity?" (Venezky, 1976, pp. 22-23), with answers grounded in the underlying structure of the writing system.

Finally, the emphasis on instruction and structure also has implications for assessment. In a sense, instruction uses assessment as an anchor. One can teach, but in the absence of trustworthy evidence of what is being learned, the activity becomes pointless and undirected. Curtis and Glaser (1983), in their review of assessment practices in reading, note the importance of measuring fluency as well as accuracy. Implicit in this comment is the notion that actual pronunciation is probably the most trustworthy measure of decoding skills. Paper-and-pencil tasks are less direct indices.

We would also emphasize structure and understanding. The spelling patterns chosen for assessment should reflect the structural characteristics of the writing system, and should give information about the parts of the structure that have been mastered by the student. In addition, we would propose that understanding of the system should be a goal of instruction. Metacognitive research has provided insights into comprehension processes; there has been no parallel development in the area of decoding. By the end of elementary school, the student should be able to articulate a strategy for attacking novel words, a strategy that is sensitive to the morphophonemic character of English spelling, and that is grounded in the historical features of the language. Toward this end, it might be useful to determine teachers' knowledge of this domain. If researchers, curriculum designers, and teachers cannot articulate the structural features of English spelling, then we should not be surprised if students fail to acquire this competence.

Vocabulary

This section of the chapter focuses on word meaning in reading instruction. The discussion begins with an overview of the vocabulary curriculum and an account of vocabulary training as it typically occurs in the classroom. Next are segments on two topics that have been investigated rather extensively in recent years: readability, and the relation between vocabulary and comprehension. The section ends with a consideration of topics that warrant investigation in the future.

What Is the Vocabulary Curriculum?

While most reading teachers agree on the importance of vocabulary instruction, the goals are less clear. First let us attempt to simplify the question by eliminating one source of confusion — teaching vocabulary is teaching the meaning of a word, not how to pronounce it. The latter task falls under the rubric of decoding.

What does it mean to have a word in one's vocabulary, to "know" a word? This question has baffled philosophers throughout recorded history; Green (1984) has argued that "for most words, the notion 'the meaning of the word x' simply does not make sense" (p. 1). Teachers cannot afford the luxury to wait for the outcome of philosphical debate — competence in reading requires that students have an extensive vocabulary and "know" a lot of words. The teacher's job is to help students achieve that goal.

But again, what does it mean to *know a word*? Answers to the question generally include the notion of labeling a more or less well-defined concept — we use words to point to things in the world (Wittgenstein, 1958). Function words, the syntactic "mortar" that binds together ideas, serve a different role, one better discussed under the rubric of sentence comprehension. Words also serve to label abstract concepts that may transcend any effort at illustration.

Words are not neutral in this enterprise. Anyone who has played a word association game is aware that words come in structured sets. As Bransford and Nitsch (1978) point out: words are related to one another in addition to being associated with practical knowledge that gives them meaning. These relations are due in large measure, but not entirely, to the fact that practical knowledge is itself highly structured" (p. 281). Research in the last decade has converged on the nature of associative structure, and on the roles of experience and schooling on these structures (Clark & Clark, 1977; Anglin, 1977; Miller & Johnson-Laird, 1976).

What it means to know a word is determined in part by how it is related to experiences and to other words. But a word may be known in varying degrees. "Knowing a word well involves knowledge of a whole series of networks in which the word functions" (Graves, 1984). It involves depth of meaning; precise usage; facile access (think of scrabble and crossword puzzle experts); the ability to articulate one's understanding; flexibility in the application of the knowledge of a word; the appreciation of metaphor, analogy, word play; the ability to recognize a synonym, to define, to use a word expressively.

Graves (1984) has organized school learning of vocabulary under five rubrics: (a) new labels for known concepts (the injunction "Withdraw your digit from your nasal orifice!" uses novel words for a command familiar to most children); (b) new labels for new concepts, a task in the upper elementary grades and upward in virtually all subject matter areas; (c) new meanings for known labels that may or may not entail new concepts — "force" is a known label, but the meaning in physics is new to most children; (d) enriching and expanding the meanings of words already known; and (e) moving words from receptive to expressive vocabularies (we all recognize far more words than we can use expressively).

The full shape of the vocabulary curriculum remains to be determined. As the preceding comments show, one goal of vocabulary instruction may be to increase the size of the student's vocabulary, but there is also the need to ingrain a respect for words and to instill a self-awareness of the adequacy of one's capability to determine a word's meaning in a particular context.

WHAT DO PRESCHOOLERS KNOW ABOUT WORDS?

Children bring a lot of words to school with them. Estimates of "vocabulary size" vary by orders of magnitude (Anderson & Freebody, 1981; Nagy & Anderson, 1984; and references therein), with guesses ranging between 1,000 and 10,000 words, depending on the criterion for "knowing a word."

Some students know more words than others, and some know words more deeply than others. Some students know more "school" words than others (see Bruce, Rubin, Starr, & Liebling, 1983). Finally, some students are better than others at explaining what a word means.

Indicators of vocabulary knowledge are highly correlated with the construct of intelligence, which in turn is highly correlated with school success and with performance on reading tests. What do these relationships mean? The possibilities are several: (a) Some students are inherently smarter than others; (b) some students have had a richer experience than others; (c) some students have been better trained than others to handle a particular assessment; (d) some combination of the three elements listed above is operating. Anderson and Freebody (1981) point out that the first explanation, innate aptitude, implies an immutability of sorts; instruction may improve vocabulary for all students, but individual differences will remain. The other two hypotheses about individual differences are within the power of the school to change, in principle at least. "Access" or fluency of knowledge may be important (Mezynski, 1983), as may knowledge of words specific to particular text (the "instrumentalist" hypothesis).

Whatever the explanation for individual differences, prior to school entry most youngsters have acquired language naturally, through trial and error, through repeated experience, without a great deal of reflection and examination about the nature of what has been learned. Metalinguistic and metacognitive awareness is limited (Tunmer, et al., 1984, and references therein). The preschooler's vocabulary reflects the particulars of

his or her environment and the accidents of experience. It is functional and concrete — "a hole is to dig," in Ruth Krauss's words. Associations are direct and primitive. They may be based on rhyme (pig-dig), common features (cat-black) or category membership (cat-dog). Seldom are the structures highly developed, nor do systematic relations (super-, sub-, or co-ordination) appear to be part of preschool thinking. When such relations are present (some children have played "animal, vegetable, mineral"), they tend to be implicit. Many kindergartners have begun to play with words, usually in the form of outrageous puns, but they are not inclined to reflect on their knowledge of "word meaning" — indeed, the concept of "knowing a word" is poorly developed (Al Issa, 1969; Anglin, 1977; Litowitz, 1977; Nelson, 1978).

Building on What Already Exists. Preschoolers at all levels of entering ability possess language and demonstrated success at acquiring vocabulary. School is a place where students are exposed to words — to words familiar, to words unknown, in contexts that guide understanding, and in strange isolation. There has been little systematic study of "classroom" vocabulary, but our impression from observations and examination of teachers' manuals is that teacher talk tends to be "familiar," that low-frequency words are rare in both student and teacher talk.

Since preschoolers already have experience in acquiring vocabulary from context, there would seem to be value in promoting the intentionally rich use of language in the classroom. The student is continually encountering new experiences in the classroom — new concepts, if you will. The teacher, by consciously "talking about" everything that happens, can provide opportunities to learn new concepts and the labels that identify them. It is equally important that the teacher encourage "student talk"; modeling is important, but the eventual aim is for the student to gain expressive control over vocabulary.

Finally, students naturally rely on context as a substitute for precise word usage. They may have some idea of the most appropriate word to suit a given situation, but the "natural" thing when you cannot quickly find the right word is to say "You know what I mean," or "It's kinda like that," or in some other way to handle the situation by nonlinguistic means. The teacher, by example and by questioning, leads the student to more effective use of vocabulary, all of this in the course of other ongoing events and without "planning a lesson."

Acquiring New Knowledge. Systematic vocabulary instruction aims toward two goals. First is the acquisition of new concepts. As the student encounters the various disciplines and professions, new concepts abound and vocabulary becomes a critical concern. From journalism: "A story written in the *inverted pyramid* style will start with a *hook* in the *lead*, followed by details of diminishing importance so that the story can be cut from the *tail*." From biology: "The chemical process called *photosynthesis* involves the *reaction* of a plant's *chlorophyll* with *carbon dioxide* from the air and sunlight to produce *oxygen*" (examples from Konopak, 1984).

The student's task in these two passages may be generally construed as "learning vocabulary," but the demands are different in the two examples. In the journalism example, the critical words are already known to most students, but under different meanings; in the biology example, both the critical words and the concepts are likely to be unknown. In both these examples, the aim is to discern relations among ideas and activities, and within that framework to acquire the proper labels. The student who learns by rote the definitions of the key words without understanding the underlying relations may pass a vocabulary test, but to little lasting advantage. Moreover, learning in such instances is unlikely to occur through trial and error. "Discovering" biological relations is improbable for most students; for journalism, the editor may decide to wait for students to learn from experience, but the quality of the school paper and the value of the experience for the students may both suffer.

A second domain of new knowledge is the relatively small set of paradigmatic structures that account for the majority of semantic relations. The most primitive structure is the topic-centered arrangement, often referred to as a "web" by teachers (Figure 28.3). Asked for associations to a known word, students can readily respond, starting with an immediate link, pursuing a thread of thought, a break while a new connection is sought, and thence onward. The organizing principle is a central hub with radiating spokes. A more sophisticated version clusters related associations, and may even name each set, the initial steps in imposing coherence on a domain.

Matrices and hierarchies (also shown in Figure 28.3) are two other basic structures that alone or in combination undergird knowledge in the subject matters. These structures are frequent in content-area texts, but they also provide frameworks for organizing words, and familiarity with them should be an important goal of vocabulary instruction in the reading curriculum.

Acquiring New Strategies for Vocabulary. Learning from experience and analyzing semantic structures are both important goals for vocabulary instruction, but schooling can also help the student sense when to stop and examine a word, and can provide good techniques for breaking a complex word into component parts, explicit tactics for analyzing contextual clues, and knowledge of when and how to use dictionaries and other references.

These strategies represent a qualitatively different approach to the acquisition of vocabulary. They are marked by a reflectivity, by explicit analysis, and by thoughtful decisions about the techniques and resources most appropriately applied when the student is uncertain about how to interpret a word.

The first step in this process is the development of a sensitivity to such situations. Early in language acquisition parents often take time to label objects and events in their child's world. After entry to school, the youngster has fewer opportunities to pause during a discussion and ask "What does X mean?" The assumption seems to be that meaning will be made clear if necessary, and that understanding can otherwise be taken for granted.

A goal of vocabulary training is to reinstitute an inquiring and critical attitude, and a sense of how to judge whether a word needs to be examined more carefully. Studies of word deletion using the cloze procedure demonstrate that a third of the words may be deleted from some texts without significantly

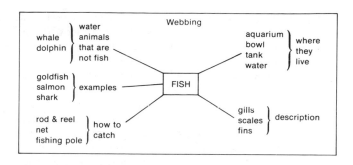

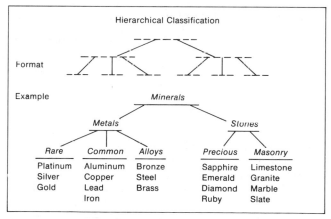

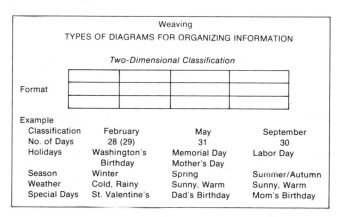

Fig. 28.3 Webbing, matrix, and hierarchical classification.

reducing understanding (Stratton & Nacke, 1974). A critical factor is the information value of a word context — under what conditions is it essential to know what a word means? This question has received relatively little attention by researchers. Even less attention has been given to students' awareness of information value, or to instruction in identifying the informativeness of a word in context. If a student has decided that a particular word contains critical information, what then? There would seem to be obvious benefit to techniques that can be applied without "leaving the text" — using context, or examining the morphological characteristics of the word. Decisions about the merits of these tactics (or perhaps more drastic steps, like consulting a dictionary) are essential elements in a strategic approach to vocabulary.

Beyond identification of word meaning sufficient for the comprehension of a passage, there is also the matter of expressive control in speaking and writing. The aim is not simply increased knowledge of "big" or unfamiliar words, but improvements in precision and richness. Slater and Graves (1984) asked Martin Mann and Teresa Redd of *Time* magazine how they would make school texts more interesting and readable. The answer was to use "action verbs, contrasts, metaphors, colloquial expressions, familiar tone, word play, alliteration, vivid adjectives, participial phrases, appositives, and a few big words." Each of these items features vocabulary as a critical element.

A REPRISE

The list of curriculum topics presented above is rather extensive, but seems reasonable given the importance of vocabulary to success in other areas of schooling. Facility in handling words is likely to become a more valuable talent in the future (Sola Pool, 1983). Molloy's (1982) advice is to learn a new word every day, and you will be perceived as better educated, more important, more powerful, taller, and morally superior (not better dressed!). Be this as it may, certainly the school should give students a good start toward an improved vocabulary, and the skills needed to sustain growth on their own. The curriculum now in place is rather more modest in its aims.

What Happens in Typical Instruction?

In this section we discuss several features in present-day instructional practice. These issues form the backdrop for research questions that have been pursued during the past decade.

BASAL INSTRUCTION

The first point about current practice in vocabulary instruction is that there is not much of it. Beck, McKeown, McCaslin, and Burke (1979) and Jenkins and Dixon (1983), after examining several basal reading series, found that direct instruction in word meaning varied from none at all to 200–500 words per year. These are small numbers to begin with, and many of the words selected for teaching were already known to most youngsters.

Vocabulary is introduced in two ways by most existing basal series. In the first, a list of words is presented for instruction at the beginning of the lesson. These may be words judged as difficult to pronounce or occurring infrequently in print at that grade level. The words are generally *not* selected on the basis of mutual semantic relations or textual importance. Instruction typically proceeds by asking students to give a meaning or make up a sentence with the word. The glossary is consulted on occasion. Most series then follow the first pass by worksheet activities—the words are matched to synonyms, placed in a sentence frame, or the like.

Beck et al. and Jenkins and Dixon also concluded that vocabulary instruction in the elementary grades lacked both "intensity and scope." The materials relied chiefly on rote practice and context as the basis for meaning. There were too few repetitions to ensure rote learning, and the context was often inadequate to clarify meaning. Other activities encountered from time to time, mainly through worksheets—dictionary practice, compound words, roots and affixes, occasionally a weblike association task—were sporadic and disconnected from the main thrust of the lesson. An exception was the program on morphographics or "word parts" in Distar (Engelmann, Haddox, Hanner, & Osborn, 1978); when these developers decide to incorporate an objective in the curriculum, training is implemented in a sustained and consistent fashion.

Teachers use the basal series, and the patterns described above are readily observed in the classroom. As Schramm (1955) noted some time ago:

> The most influential group of men in this country in the making of school texts [may be] the educational editors of our large publishing houses. Their only real competitors are the ideological leaders like Dewey and Thorndike whose concepts of what a textbook should be and how it should be made have been reflected in the efforts of hundreds of editors and authors. (p. 158)

Dewey and Thorndike have not been with us for a while, and only a few scholars have examined reading series in the past quarter-century. Some critiques have appeared recently (see Anderson, Osborn & Tierney, 1984, and references therein for work by the Center for the Study of Reading; Beck et al, 1980, for work at the Learning Research and Development Center).

ADVICE IN TEXTBOOKS

What advice is given to teachers about vocabulary instruction? One of the most popular texts is Johnson and Pearson (1984). One finds in it a large number of topics, a collage of meaning and decoding, student activities in great variety, all in all a great deal of material, a collection distinguished more by diversity than coherence. Johnson and Pearson do attempt some organization of the domain:

Classification	Multimeaning Words	Resources
Synonyms	Polysemous words	Dictionary
Antonyms	Homographs	Thesaurus
Denotation/		Etymology
Connotation		
Semantic maps		
Feature analysis		
Analogies		
Homophones		

Some structure is better than none, but these lists are not altogether satisfying as a way to "carve the turkey." This text is typical of what is found in most textbooks on reading instruction, which in turn mirror what is found in teachers' manuals.

VOCABULARY CONTROL

Students should not be expected to handle words with which they are unfamiliar; this is the principle underlying vocabulary control. Familiarity is measured by counting how often a word occurs in print. Control is imposed by limiting the words at each grade level (especially in the primary grades) to high-frequency words.

At the extreme, this reasoning leads to the advice that only a handful of commonplace words need to be taught: "Since the 300 most common words constitute 75% and the 1,000 most common constitute 90% of the words that we write, it quickly becomes clear that the population of words whose mastery teachers should seek is much smaller than formerly imagined" (Clifford, 1978, p. 140). This suggestion ignores the information value of words; it is precisely the rare words that comprise the critical core differentiating one passage from another.

The topic of readability will be examined in greater detail below. For the moment, we will simply observe that the basal materials available for reading instruction are typically constrained in vocabulary usage, especially in the primary grades. Moreover, teachers are commonly advised to determine the student's reading level (based on frequency counts), and then select textual materials matched to this level. The result is that beginning readers or those experiencing difficulty with phonics are exposed to a rather barren sample of words.

PRACTICE IN CONTEXT

The most frequent advice from researchers in recent years emphasizes that meaning is largely gained from context. School children double their vocabulary between third and seventh grade (Jenkins & Dixon, 1983), and it is assumed that this gain occurs through multiple exposures in context. Since this approach seems to work, why not simply improve on it? "Repetitions, opportunities to practice using the word, and review characterize formal vocabulary teaching" (Jenkins & Dixon, 1983, p. 5). "In general, there appear to be three important variables: (1) amount of practice given to the words, (2) breadth of training in the use of words, and (3) the degree to which active processing is encouraged" (Mezynski, 1983, p. 273).

Most accounts of "learning a word's meaning from context" have lacked exactitude. Sternberg and Powell (1983; also Sternberg, Powell, & Kay, 1983; Jenkins & Dixon, 1983) have presented the most comprehensive conception to date of the role of context in word meaning. They first distinguish context clues from the conditions that mediate their use. Consider the sentence "At dawn, *sol* arose on the horizon and shone brightly." Assume that the reader knows every word except *sol*. Clues in the surrounding text that shape the features of the unknown word include, according to Sternberg and Powell, dimensions of time, space, function description, value, cause and effect, class membership, and equivalence. These sources combine to paint a picture of the meaning of the unknown term.

Mediating conditions are dimensions such as the number of occurrences of the unknown word, the variability of the contexts in which the word is embedded, the relevance and proximity of clues, the overall difficulty of the passage, the familiarity of the topic, the number of other unknown words, and so on. Jenkins and Dixon further classify "unknownness" in the form of a matrix:

	SIMPLE SYNONYM	NO SYNONYM
CONCEPT KNOWN	*altercation* (fight)	*odometer* (the gadget that tells no. of miles)
CONCEPT NOT KNOWN	*arcane* (obscure)	*legislature* _____

These thoughts require refinement, but they appear to have value for analyzing how contexts support the growth of word meaning.

Jenkins and Dixon note that research on context and word meaning have focused on the relative importance of various types of clues on the student's success in inferring word meanings. Equally important is how these factors influence the student's use of text to infer word meaning when the primary task is to comprehend the passage: "Readers can often get by without figuring out a word's meaning, and thus may not bother to try" (Jenkins & Dixon, 1983, p. 254). Konopak (1984) notes that textual context varies greatly from the primary through the secondary grades: in the primary grades, "vocabulary development is mostly learner-based, relying on direct and indirect contextual settings to provide meaning. ... the focus [then] changes from general vocabulary to content-specific words in the higher grades" (pp. 8, 9).

WORDS

Advice in a different style comes from a small book by Lodwig and Barrett (1981) entitled *Words, Words, Words*. Designed for high schoolers and college students, the book begins, "This is a book about words and their meanings." The chapter titles differ from what one encounters in textbooks for teachers — *Words; Words and History; Word Creation; Words and Their Meanings; Changes in Word Meanings; The Development of the Dictionary*. One gets a sense of the evolution of a communications technology, of the role of words as a tool of an increasingly articulate human race. The approach to context learning differs considerably from the previous discussion: "A typical word does not have just *a* meaning; it has a cluster of meanings. ... Each of these senses of the word is appropriately used in certain contexts" (p. 76). Or as Whorf (1956) put it, "The meaning of a word is less like a dollar bill with a fixed amount than like a blank check to be filled in as required" (p. 234). Lodwig and Barrett's advice is to look for restatements of the unknown word, for contrasts, for key words, or to attempt morphological analysis — they offer six pages of specific suggestions in plain language with accompanying exercises. We mention this source because it represents an interesting contrast with the prevailing conceptions of vocabulary instruction, a contrast with implications for both research and practice.

Research Topics in Vocabulary Instruction

Not too long ago it would have been relatively difficult to identify a significant body of research on vocabulary. The past decade, however, has seen something of a renaissance in this area. We have selected two broad categories for review: readability and context effects, that is, the relation between vocabulary and comprehension. Both focus on the content of instruction more than on teaching activities, but many of the findings appear to have instructional implications. A great deal of territory in this vital domain remains unexplored.

READABILITY

The foundations of readability research were described earlier under the rubric of vocabulary control. In the first years of school the child faces many challenges. Why not reduce one of the hurdles by selecting for initial instruction only already familiar words? As skill develops, less familiar words can be gradually introduced.

How to measure word familiarity? Thorndike (1921a), in creating *The Teacher's Word Book*, relied on counts of printed words in school texts. Basal readers, when measured against these word counts, were found wanting—primers contained many words not in the 10,000 most frequent words (e.g., *baggy, Bert, bluebird,* and *crawly,* but also *baff, bannock, bight,* and *Canute;* Clifford, 1978, p. 143, after Thorndike, 1921b). Publishers began to respond to these findings, and today word counts dominate the design of basal reading systems.

Readability research (Clifford, 1978; Klare, 1963, 1974–1975) grew up around the word count paradigm. Studies showed that texts that were easier to read were more quickly read and were better comprehended if they contained a preponderance of high-frequency words. Sentence length played a secondary role in the readability equation.

Readability research is discussed here because vocabulary is the critical element in the equation. It is included in the chapter because of the importance of readability in determining the texts available for instruction, and in guiding teacher choices about the passages that are suitable for students of a given ability level. As the following selections reveal, the area remains active half a century after the appearance of the *Word Book.*

Textbook publishers frequently have to revise original passages to conform to readability requirements—how do they manage this task? Davison and Kantor (1982) examined these rewriting tactics in four texts that were lowered to fit junior high students reading 2 or 3 years below grade level. Passage length was greatly reduced (two-thirds to one-quarter of the original), sentence length dropped from 20 + to 13 words per sentence, and clauses fell from three to fewer than two per sentence. Changes in lexical usage, according to Davison and Kantor, were equally dramatic:

> In general, a lexical item may be a candidate for change under two major circumstances: if it is a proper name, technical, or specialized term with no obvious import to young readers; or if the item is vague or has fallen from current usage. [Thus] *Hippocrates recommended milk to his patients as a curative beverage* [becomes] *One of the most famous Greek doctors told his patients to drink milk to cure illness.* (p. 204)

This example and the principles espoused are not necessarily unreasonable, but the results can be unfortunate. Davison and Kantor point to a serious flaw:

> If deletion of topic sentences and splitting of longer complex sentences into shorter component sentences is done *without a view of the entire text as connected discourse,* then the adapted version may have fewer cues than the original for relating sentences and clauses. It might actually be *harder* to understand than the original. ... Readability formulas, in our opinion, fail to give any adequate characterization of readability, except in a purely statistical sense from which no particular conclusions can be drawn for *creating* readable texts. (p. 207)

The risks from formulaic application of word counts in the selection and design of reading passages were pointed out soon after the publication of the *Word Book.* Words at a common index of difficulty often present quite different conceptual demands; for instance, these pairs are at the same frequency in the original list: *inside/err, ate/elate, dirty/deem, hers/withal* (Clifford, 1978, p. 127, also reference therein). Davis (1944) found negligible correlations between word frequency and test performance, and concluded that teachers and textbook authors who employed word counts to restrict vocabulary usage "should be aware that by so doing they are probably accomplishing very little toward controlling the actual 'difficulty' of the materials" (p. 174). Good writing always takes word choice into account, but only as one of several factors. To judge the range of outcomes possible within the constraints of the readability formula and the creativity of writers, you might scan one or more basal texts for examples of Aesop's fables (they are reasonably popular), and compare basal versions with the originals.

In another example of recent developments in this area, Goodman and Bird (1984) investigated *intratext* word counts. Readability research has generally employed aggregate word counts—measures averaged over hundreds of texts. Goodman and Bird were interested in the patterns of word frequencies within a text. Their empirical findings are probably less important than the theoretical analyses.

The major point is that, even though a word is quite rare in general, it may be relatively common in a particular text. The writer does not include a word in a text because it is frequent, but because the topic calls for the word. A rare word (along with its referents) may occur several times in a passage, in which case it is not rare in the context of the passage. A word occurring only once in a text is unlikely to be significant, whether it is common or rare in the aggregate. A common word may occur frequently in a text, but still pose a challenge to understanding because it takes on a different meaning (common words tend to have more meanings than infrequent words; compare *draw* with *neurosurgeon*). "Teachers concerned about vocabulary development would do better to focus on functional use of words and terms in the context of real passages than to resort to decontextualized lists. ... A text, after all, is considerably more than the sum of its words" (Goodman & Bird, 1984, p. 144).

So what should be concluded from research on readability? On the one hand, it is probably easier for students to make their way through a text that has commonplace words and short sentences. They may not learn much from the experience, to be sure. On the other hand, a text filled with critical and unknown vocabulary can easily overwhelm the student (and even the teacher), as Thorndike (1934) points out:

> The worst, which often occurs in basic readers and supplementary reading, is to require children to read material which they cannot understand; or can understand, but do not enjoy; or cannot understand, and would not enjoy if they could understand it. ... Books do not have to be bad literature; but the vocabulary and sentence structure must not thwart comprehension of what the book tells, and that must be something that the pupil cares to be told. (p. 19)

The issues appear not to have changed greatly in 50 years.

VOCABULARY AND COMPREHENSION

Can a student understand a passage when some or many of the words are unknown? How can the student use context to gauge the meaning of unknown words? These questions have a long history. Hilliard (1926) exhorted that "training in vocabulary, with proper motivation, is a type of work well within the grasp of every teacher, and from this evidence seems to be one of the strategic points in building up comprehension" (p. 40; quoted in Clifford, 1978). Everyday experience suggests that we frequently acquire word meanings from context, not through formal instruction, but as it were "in passing."

Why discuss these topics under the rubric of vocabulary, especially given the emphasis on separability of the components of reading? In fact, most studies on this topic focus on the *words*, with less attention given to the specifics of the text, or to the relation of words to the text. Perhaps the next *Handbook of Research on Teaching* will be able to view these issues from the perspective of both word and text.

Does Studying Vocabulary Aid Comprehension? Mezynski (1983) reviews eight studies of this question. All the investigations were "instructional"—students were specially trained on words thought to be problematic, and then were tested on comprehension of a test passage. The research, spanning 2 decades, varied widely in the nature and number of the students, the amount of instruction, and the adequacy of the research design. Most students were in the upper elementary grades, however, and most of the programs lasted for several weeks; new words were introduced at the rate of about 10 per week. In "direct training" studies, the target words were from the passage, while in the "general transfer" studies training was on a large set of words, with the expectation of an overall advantage. Word knowledge and passage comprehension were measured by various combinations of recall and recognition tests.

The typical findings were that vocabulary training improved performance on vocabulary tests, but had little effect on reading comprehension. As Mezynski (1983) notes, "It is difficult to imagine how a reader could comprehend text in which most of the words are unfamiliar" (p. 253). But that is seldom the situation. Rather, readers (and listeners) may occasionally encounter words that are unknown, but only some of these are critical to understanding the text. It also matters how comprehension is measured—multiple choice tests are less sensitive indicators of instructional interventions than are free-recall measures.

The literature typifies the empirical tradition in educational research (Clifford, 1978). Lacking an overall framework, researchers work on bits and pieces of a problem. Mezynski (1983, p. 258) points out a number of serious confoundings, and notes that, given the large number of uncontrolled procedural variations, the studies are difficult to compare. She also homes in on two critical issues that may explain why effects on comprehension were negligible: (a) vocabulary knowledge may be unnecessary for comprehension of some texts (e.g., narratives), and (b) the instruction may have been inadequate to support comprehension (e.g., not enough training for automatic access, or rote training insufficient to transfer to the comprehension task).

Another perspective is gained by looking at the studies where there was an effect on comprehension. We will examine two of these, one employing "direct" training and the other "general" training.

The "direct" study is reported by Kameenui, Carnine, and Freschi (1982) as a series of two experiments asking: (a) Do difficult words make text comprehensible? (also see Marks, Doctorow, & Wittrock, 1974); (b) Does adding redundant information improve comprehension? (c) Does learning the difficult words make the text more comprehensible? and (d) Does incorporating vocabulary training in passage review lead to improved performance? These questions certainly merit attention, although the way that they are operationalized in these experiments was not entirely satisfactory.

The two experiments, both performed with upper elementary students, were virtually identical except for the passages. The texts were single paragraphs of less then 100 words. Six words were selected as targets for each passage. Training was short-term and individualized. After instruction, students were asked multiple choice questions and given a free-recall test. In one condition, familiar synonyms were substituted for the target words. In other conditions, the "hard" words were in the text and students received (a) no training, (b) no training but redundant cues in the passage, (c) rote association training, or (d) "passage-integrated" training (the student was stopped during the reading and interrogated/trained on the difficult words).

The experiment was carefully designed to yield the desired results—Kameenui et al. (1982) note that the materials were "contrived," and so they appear. Here is the text with the target words marked as Xs (unknown word meaning):

Joe and Ann went to school in Portland. They were XXXXXXXXXXs. They saw each other often. They had lots of XXXXXXXXXXs. At the end of high school, Ann XXXXXXed Joe. Then Ann moved away. Joe stayed in Portland. He got a job as a XXXXXXX. One day Joe was working, and he saw Ann. Ann did not see Joe. Ann looked XXXXXXXXXXXX. She was being XXXXXXXXXXed.

The unknown words were quite dense (10% of the total passage, and perhaps half of the substantive words). You should decide for yourself whether you "understand" the passage. Below is the version with the infrequent words in place (as in the original), and with redundant information in parentheses:

Joe and Ann went to school in Portland. They were *antogonists*. They saw each other often. They had lots of *altercations*. (They just didn't get along very well.) At the end of high school, Ann *maligned* Joe. Then Ann moved away. Joe stayed in Portland. He got a job as a *bailiff*. One day Joe was working, and he saw Ann (talking to a policeman and answering questions). Ann did not see Joe. Ann looked *apprehensive*. She was being *incarcerated*. (p. 373–374)

The second passage was similarly designed, perhaps a bit more contrived. Some questions demanded little more than syntactic knowledge; for example, in the second text, the statement "Harry said Ace was *pusillanimous*" was followed by the question "Who did Harry think was pusillanimous?"

The findings were that redundancy and vocabulary training did lead to better performance on questions where knowledge of the difficult vocabulary was critical. The effects were substantial and replicable. Viewed as a demonstration, the findings are provocative. They may be less a model for classroom practice, however, then an illustration of the persistence and ingenuity of educational researchers.

A different sort of persistence appears in a study by McKeown, Beck, Omanson, & Perfetti (1983). In a previous study (Beck, Perfetti, & McKeown, 1982), children given intensive and varied training on a list of 104 words over 5 months of schooling demonstrated their command of the words—they could define them, and were more adept in timed tasks. Performance on a story comprehension task did not distinguish trained from untrained students, however, except in one condition where students received substantial additional practice.

The replication by McKeown et al. (1983) incorporated several methodological enhancements over the original design, primarily in the methods for assessing the effects on story comprehension. Again, training focused on a target set of 104 words divided into several structured subsets (e.g., *rival*, *hermit*, *novice*, and *virtuoso* are from the "people" cluster). Training consisted of 75 half-hour lessons over 5 months. There were multiple opportunities for practice, interword relations were stressed, and students had to justify their answers about word meaning.

The training clearly affected performance on the vocabulary tests. As exposures were increased from *none* to *some* (10–18 occurrences) and then to *many* (26–40 occurrences) the percentage of correct answers grew from 34 to 71 to 80%—still not perfect. The effects on story comprehension were statistically significant—recall of central ideas increased from 16 to 33%, and multiple choice performance went from 44 to 66%. The density of target words in the test passages was quite high (about 30 per 300 running words).

The replication by McKeown et al. (1983) is good news and bad news for advocates of the "vocabulary helps comprehension" position. On the positive side, it is encouraging to see evidence of effective instruction, and transfer to a new situation. On the negative side, the cost was substantial, and the magnitude of the effect relatively slight (two-thirds of the central ideas were *not* recalled by the students). Back to the positive side, prototypical recalls (p. 14) were convincing that the trained students had undergone a significant (and not merely statistical) change in their capability to explain what they had read in a clear and articulate fashion—target words were used in recall to good effect.

It is possible, then, to find conditions in which knowledge of critical vocabulary is essential to comprehension of a passage. The training may influence basic understanding, but the student's ability to express this understanding is also important (Duin & Graves, 1984). The research thus far has been demonstrational, and lacks comprehensiveness. The character of the texts is either unknown or highly suspect. The relation of the critical vocabulary to the text is generally unspecified. While training has been quite extensive in some studies, instruction generally fell outside the regular reading activities, and so the practical applicability of the instructional techniques remains uncertain. With the exception of the Pittsburgh studies, there is little evidence of transfer. Students learn the target words, but

do not learn to learn words. All in all, this domain is best described as "promising," with much work remaining ahead.

Does Studying a Passage Improve Vocabulary? It might seem self-evident that the person who reads a great deal will thereby increase his or her vocabulary. Given the relative impoverishment of vocabulary instruction in present-day reading programs, several researchers have concluded that students' chief method for acquiring vocabulary in the elementary grades is by "default" through context.

What are the mechanisms that drive contextual learning of word meaning? What features of a text promote the acquisition of unfamiliar words? How can students be assisted in determining that they need to reflect on a particular word in a passage? What strategies are most useful in taking advantage of context? These questions have been investigated in one form or another by several researchers during the past decade. The studies have generally relied on practice rather than instruction, and the emphasis has been on variation in worksheet content and layout more than strategic training.

In one of the most frequently cited studies, Gipe (1979) varied treatment, grade, and student ability. The youngsters, third- and fifth-graders, were trained on 12 words each week for 8 weeks. Students were pretested on a list of 150 words, and the 48 least well known were selected for training. During a given week, one of four treatments was in effect: Association (rote learning—"A *barbarian* is a cruel mean person"); Category (semantic association—"Add some words to the list of bad people, starting with *mean, cruel, barbarian, robber*"); Context (target words embedded in texts, with probe questions—"Write what a *barbarian* might do at the dinner table"); and Dictionary ("Write the definition and use the word in a sentence"). Instruction consisted of worksheet exercises that lasted for 15 minutes a day; students worked on their own, with minimal teacher involvement. Assessment comprised two tests, one at the end of each week of training and a second test 1 week after the entire session.

The results supported context training as the most effective of the four treatments, with the category scheme and dictionary exercises as least effective. The differences are not great—48% correct for Context, compared with 34% for Dictionary. More notably, none of the treatments led to anything approaching mastery. At best, high-ability fifth-graders were correct on 9 out of 12 words from a list like *barbarian, colossal, graphite*, and *wretched* (the words are "eighth grade level" and hence not extraordinarily rare). The results may speak most directly to the ineffectiveness of worksheet-based methods of teaching vocabulary. The differences between the treatments are confounded in several ways, and appear differentially appropriate to the criterion tasks, both of which required analysis of meaning in context.

Jenkins, Stein, and Wysocki (1984) investigated several factors that "mediated" context effects—preexposure to a synonym prior to reading the passage, number of paragraph exposures (0 to 10), and the word sets (three different versions). The measures included "Supply Definition" (write the meaning of an underlined word in a sentence), "Select Definition" (a multiple choice test), "Sentence Completion" (multiple choice), and a comprehension test using a new passage containing six target words. The students, relatively high-ability fifth-graders, first reviewed pronunciation of the words, and then went through one of the treatment combinations using worksheet methods. The target words were rare for fifth-graders (e.g., *acquiesce, loquacious, potent, reform*(?), and *virtuoso*). Training continued for 10 days, on 0, 2, 6, or 10 of which students were asked to read paragraphs containing the target words.

The factors all had substantial main effects, ability greatest, followed by preexposure, word set (a random factor), and then the number of exposures (or paragraphs). There was a substantial jump from "0" to "2 exposures," especially for the higher-ability students, with further exposures leading to a linear increase in performance. Interactions were generally negligible.

Vocabulary learning occurred in the absence of systematic instruction, especially if preceded by a short "definition" (a synonym), and more so for higher-ability students in an above-average group. Ability level may be an important consideration in this study. These were able students, probably accustomed to learning on their own, and both the introduction of the words' pronunciation and the preexposure activities are likely to have been taken as clues about the purpose of the study. On the other hand, performance was substantially below maximum (60% correct for the "Supply Definition" task for the higher-ability students after 10 sets of paragraphs).

The significant effect of word sets raises an interesting question—it may be that the passages were not all equally facilitative of vocabulary learning. What are the critical factors? Nagy, Herman, and Anderson, (1985) carried out a study similar in several respects to Jenkins et al., in which they varied the text genre (narrative versus expository). Surprisingly, they found little difference in the contextual support provided by the two genres. Both passages were difficult, there was only a single instance of each genre, and the information value of the words to the text was not determined. More questions were raised than answered, and once again the focus is on the materials and worksheet practice.

Carnine, Kameenui, and Coyle (1984) have also investigated mediating variables in vocabulary learning. The first stage of the study was descriptive; no instructional treatments were administered. The form of context clue and the proximity were varied factorially. Three types of clues were examined: Synonym (A starfish has an *idiosyncratic* way of eating. *It certainly is strange*); Contrast (*It certainly is not normal*); and Inference (*Most animals do not eat this way*). "Close" and "distant" referred to the number of other words intervening between the target word and the contextual clues. Two words were selected for each of the six conditions for a total of 12 target words. Students were either tested on word meanings in isolation, or after reading short paragraphs in which the form and proximity factors were varied. Meaning was assessed by multiple choice tests; the item used to illustrate the test design was not especially reassuring—none of the answers to *adumbrate* was correct.

Context influenced word knowledge, almost doubling the rate of correct response. Form and proximity interacted—when the context clues were close to the target word, the form did not matter; when several words intervened, synonyms were much more usable than were the contrasts, which were in turn better than inference clues.

These findings appear quite interesting on the surface, and would seem to have implications for instructional design. But first consider the results of the second stage. An experimental paradigm was employed using the same basic materials and procedures as in the first study, but with students assigned to different instructional treatments—no training, practice on passages with a modicum of practice, or rule-plus-practice (the rule was rather spare: "When there's a hard word in the sentence, look for other words that tell you more about that word").

The results were straightforward and somewhat disturbing. The two training conditions differed from the no-training condition (75% versus 40% correct, so far so good), but not from each other (the rule was not an effective supplement to practice). However, neither the form nor proximity factors influenced performance! This failure to replicate the results of the previous descriptive study, which went unmentioned by the authors, leaves one uneasy about the trustworthiness of the findings.

Patberg, Graves, and Stibbe (in press) replicated Carnine et al. in its essentials, but with two variations. First, they employed an active teaching condition, in which the classroom teacher modeled application of various context clues, and led class discussions of the techniques. Second, they added a third test assessing transfer to a totally new set of words and passages.

When target words were tested in isolation, the two training groups (practice and active teaching) differed substantially from the no-treatment condition, but not from each other. The second test assessed target word knowledge in context—here the active teaching group showed growth, but the other two groups did not. Finally, on the transfer test, the active teaching group evidenced more change than the other two groups, but the effect was not statistically trustworthy. The researchers also varied the form and proximity factors, but did not report any of the results—a strange omission.

Once again, a review of the research domain leaves one unsatisfied—parts of the puzzle come into view, but then become fuzzy. It seems clear that, under certain circumstances, a student may learn something about the meaning of a new word from reading a passage. The nature of the passage, the relation between the words and the text, the type of assessment (and implicitly, the level of understanding of the word) are all candidates in determining the effectiveness of contextually based learning. We are still largely in the dark about the specifics of the factors. Moreover, virtually none of the research has employed robust instructional treatments. Sternberg et al. (1983) address these issues forcefully:

> The ease of use of the learning-by-context method depends upon the degree of facilitation provided by the context in which the word occurs. Some contexts (such as Gipe's) essentially define the word; others leave its meaning murky. . . . A vocabulary training program that uses learning from context is incomplete if it fails to provide instruction in how to use context. (pp. 128–129)

The problem is not a lack of concepts and practical knowledge to guide the design of research on vocabulary learning from context. Sternberg's taxonomy and variations thereon provide a starting point for the design of materials, of instructional programs, and of assessment devices. What remains is to bring the pieces together into a coherent research plan, replicated in a variety of settings and with a variety of student and teacher populations.

What does the future hold? Less than a decade ago, vocabulary was a cold topic: "Perusal of the current literature would suggest that the topic is a vanishing species," we wrote at the time (Calfee & Drum, 1978, p. 217). The situation has certainly changed. The present state of instructional practices leaves considerable room for improvement, however, and both researchers and practitioners are challenged to propose alternatives that are creative and practical. We will address some possibilities below. Assessment of vocabulary is another area where advances have been made, but work remains to be done.

Improvements in Vocabulary Instruction. One way to expand the student's vocabulary is through active study, either directly or through contextual reading. Most of the studies reviewed above show that students can learn under a variety of conditions, given enough practice. This approach, unfortunately, is quite expensive. The McKeown et al. (1983) study, probably the best example along these lines, reflects the limits of the approach. While there was a clear effect of training, mastery was not achieved on the target words and there was little evidence of transfer to words not taught.

Metalinguistic and metacognitive strategies are the "big news" of the day—put in simple language, the learner may be helped if the instructional design clearly explicates the content, the processes, and the structures of the domain. This principle is just beginning to appear in vocabulary research. Nicol, Graves, and Slater (1984) taught upper elementary students a set of eight prefixes in 3 half-hour sessions. The students remembered the prefixes and the words used to illustrate the prefixes, and were able to apply this knowledge to new words. The gains were substantial compared with a noninstructed group (80-90% correct versus 35-60%), and persisted over a 3-week delay with no sign of diminution. Jenkins, Haynes, and Stein (1983) provided explicit instruction on the use of appositive constructions in context learning ("Photosynthesis, the formation of carbohydrates in plant chlorophyll, is a vital part of the food chain"—not all students will understand that the information set off by commas defines photosynthesis). Brief instruction on the rhetorical device of apposition helped students. As another example, students taught the keyword method as an alternative to rote memorization are faster at learning a list of target words (Pressley, Levin, & Delaney, 1982).

The critical feature in these studies seems to be explicit training on strategies for handling words in general rather than training on a particular set of words. The content of training may be quite limited—eight prefixes, a set of appositives, a handful of keywords—but the student who is led to see the extensions of the methods has moved from learning words to learning to learn words.

Assessing Vocabulary Knowledge. Several of the studies reviewed above employed rather innovative approaches to vocabulary assessment, either in the design of alternatives in a multiple choice format or in the use of interview procedures to get a fuller picture of productive and explanatory competence.

Students' knowledge of a word would seem most validly determined by individual assessment of oral language skills. Printed tests require knowledge and fluency in decoding; picture vocabulary tests have other limitations (Calfee, Venezky, & Chapman, 1969). Reliance on a restricted range of tasks can easily mislead. Labov (1978), commenting on the finding that more than 35,000 Hispanic youngsters in New York City were "incompetent" in both English and Spanish, noted that one might conclude instead that "educators do not yet have the competence to determine the child's dominant language" (p. 437).

Performance can change rather dramatically when the assessment task is varied. Markman and Hutchinson (1984) showed that preschoolers gave thematic associations to target words under one set of instructions ("cow" was responded to with "milk"), whereas taxonomic responses were elicited under other instructions ("cow" was responded to with "pig"). The finding is important because it reveals that preschoolers possess the intellectual foundations for abstract categorical thought—assessment techniques have previously been uninformative on this point, and instructional programs have been founded on the assumption that children lack this capability.

The examples thus far have been from the early years of schooling, but the issues are more universal. The cloze procedure (see above) is frequently employed to assess comprehension. Several experiments have led to the conclusion that the procedure may be a poor index of comprehension when the latter is defined to be the grasp of a text structure as a coherent whole (Shanahan, Kamil, & Tobin, 1982; Kintsch & Yarborough, 1982; van Dijk & Kintsch, 1983; and references therein). The cloze test assesses students' ability to identify or select the word most appropriate to a local sentential context. If the sentences in a text are scrambled, free recall of the text is hindered, but cloze performance is relatively unchanged. Cloze performance is correlated with other measures of comprehension, but the test results are not necessarily accurate guides for instructional decisions about comprehension.

Finally, a more serious consideration of assessment procedures brings us face to face with the question that began this section: What does it mean to *know a word*? Surely more is intended than the selection of the correct alternative from a set of four choices. Yet in many respects this definition of knowledge has come to shape instructional practices and research derivative on these practices. This situation has changed somewhat in the past decade, but valid assessment remains a fundamental challenge for research on vocabulary knowledge.

Reading Comprehension

Three components are essential to any act of reading comprehension: a text, a reader of the text, and an interpretation of the text by the reader. The results for any study of reading comprehension will depend on the types of texts used, the readers' knowledge and purposes for reading, and the performance measures for evaluating the quality of the interpretation.

Psychological processes in text comprehension became a target for cognitive psychologists in the late 60s. Early work examined the effects of sentence structures as tests of generative transformation theory (Chomsky, 1957; 1965). In an advance over the paired-associate studies of previous decades, the sentence rather than the word was the object of research. Syntax was assumed to be the universal linguistic component, with the meaning conveyed by a particular syntactic structure derived from other nonlinguistic cognitive abilities. The independence of syntax and semantics was later challenged by case theory (Fillmore, 1968) and by the generative semanticists, an argument that continues to the present (Bock, 1982). In any event, basic research began to center on units larger than letters or words.

By the 1970s, reading research moved to the investigation of even larger textual units, focusing on the structure of texts more than the content. Performance, measured in early studies by multiple-choice tests, began to be assessed by free recall and protocol analysis. Interactions between reader and text were viewed as of fundamental importance. Less attention was given to educational research, following the dictum that applied research should build on basic findings (Vacca & Vacca, 1983). Durkin's (1978-1979) finding that comprehension was rarely taught in most classrooms led to increased interest in comprehension instruction, but studies are still sparse. Accordingly this section will focus on text variables rather than instructional ones.

The Text

The texts used for comprehension research covered a potpourri of types, generally dichotomized as narration or exposition. Most have been short, fewer than a thousand words. The brevity reflected the difficulty of controlling the text and analyzing the protocols. Effects for book-length materials have been confined to surveys of taste and enjoyment (Taylor, 1976; Sharon, 1973-1974). Investigations of text understanding will be reviewed first from the vantage of narrative and expository genre, and variations on these two themes. Next we look at the effects of the reader's background knowledge, and the related matter of inferential processes. Finally, a pair of contrastive studies will be examined as exemplars.

EXPOSITORY AND TECHNICAL WRITING

A text is generally defined as a coherent written message. The content, the structure or organization for presenting that content, and the situational constraints for reading are important determinants of comprehension. Examples include messages, as letters from friends requesting a favor or reporting on daily events; religious texts "read" as a devotional or cultural act; and textbooks for learning. Each genre places different requirements on the reader (Scribner & Cole, 1981; Heath, 1983). Personal letters generally take advantage of well-formed preexisting schemas: "Your first cousin (someone already known) just got married (a well-understood event)." Ritual reading may actually be antithetical to interpretation; worship is the purpose rather than evaluation. Texts for learning, in contrast, are designed to change mental structure, laying out a new script to reorganize a domain of knowledge. The content of the message

and the purpose for reading must both be considered before comprehension itself can be defined.

Situational constraints can determine the interpretation of texts, as in making a recipe, filling out a form, or assembling a machine. "Functional literacy" tasks often entail well-framed texts designed for a specific set of operations (Mikulecky, 1982). Job-training studies (Northcutt, 1975; Sticht, 1977, 1980; Murphy, 1975) rely on "how to" materials. The text is supported by graphics (charts, maps, pictures), with the text needed at a minimum to explain the procedures. Background information or elaboration of the underlying principles is omitted. The written messages are instructions to the reader to do something; subsequent actions and consequences confirm or disconfirm the reader's understanding.

MEMORY FOR SENTENCES IN BRIEF PASSAGES

Several features characterize research under this heading. The texts used to investigate comprehension have relied on brief descriptive passages. Major effort was devoted to finding a method of describing the informational base of the text in order to score recall protocols, efforts that led to increasingly complex representations of texts. After 2 decades of work dominated more or less by intrasentence analyses, the move was to intersentence connections (Crothers, 1972, 1979; Frederiksen, 1972, 1977; Grimes, 1975; Kintsch, 1974; Kintsch & Keenan, 1973; Kintsch & van Dijk, 1978; Miller & Kintsch, 1980). Comprehension was generally assessed in these investigations by word recall or responses to specific questions or cue words. One of the first signs that the research paradigm was about to shift from question answering to recall appeared in Carroll and Freedle's (1972) *Comprehension and the Acquisition of Knowledge*. The question in several papers in this volume was the psychological reality of the scheme proposed to parse sentences into information units. Did recall protocols map onto the text units?

The actual texts from this period were simple descriptions, historical and social studies materials, accounts of imaginary places (Circle Island), research reports for psychology classes, newspaper articles, and so forth. The texts were brief and had to fit normative reading patterns.

Free recall became the preferred performance measure. The goal was to predict the content and structure of recall following a single reading of the text. Texts are seldom veridically recalled under these conditions. Some information is deleted, and sentence word order is often rearranged. An occasional word is likely to be changed.

The ability to understand the contents of the texts was assumed, so comprehension of the text was not the question. Instead, the research addressed the redundancy and ordering of the information. What information was most salient for different readers given that they understood the material? What staging of that information by the writer was most facilitative for retention of the important information? Of course, what is important depends upon the author's view. In any case, more recall equaled better performance.

Text analysis schemes were text specific; for instance, Kintsch's propositional analysis laid out the units within a specific text. There was no effort to predetermine the characteristics of a well written text. The Turner and Greene (1977) algorithms for propositional analysis gave an outline of procedures. Following text analyses, one could predict the likelihood of retaining various propositions (e.g., Miller and Kintsch's "leading edge" predictions), but again these were text specific. The staging rules were used to decide what information within a particular text would be retained, not what is a good rendition of this information versus some other method of presenting the information.

The typical findings were that the most inclusive information within a passage was more likely to be remembered than the elaborative details, though often the contents of entire sentences were not retained. Better readers remembered more information, but if only one piece of information was recalled, it represented an important piece of information within all of the analytic procedures. This finding corroborated the commonality among the various text analysis procedures despite surface differences and that all of them did describe a psychologically real characteristic of information importance within these very brief, general texts, where comprehension or understanding of the information was not the question. The research paradigm was a valuable tool for handling the microstructure of a passage, but could not be readily applied to more extensive texts.

The importance of the major ideas within general-information texts may be unique to brief texts; if the subject can decode this material, then the teacher need not worry about delineating the main idea. With longer texts, chapters, or books, where the readers are expected to learn new structures of knowledge, the important informational units may not be so apparent. The Halliday and Hassan (1976) coherence definition of text as compared with a list of unrelated sentences makes the main idea (aspect of topic) so salient that retention of topic is an unavoidable consequence of exposure if one can read at all. However, this isolation of the topic appeared to be an unconscious reaction to text characteristics in younger and poorer readers, for many of them were unable to select the most important ideas, to evaluate text organization, or to rate congruence of ideas presented (Brown & Smiley, 1977; Danner, 1976; Bransford, Stein, Shelton, & Owings, 1981).

Another problem with brief texts as experimental passages is the high level of performance. What if subjects make no errors? As more time intervenes between reading the text and giving the recall, retention becomes less veridical and resembles more an outline of the major ideas. If the material is either unusual or overlearned, there will be changes from the text over time, usually reflecting prior knowledge about the topic that was not included in the original text. Error analysis or misreadings of the text information are rarely reported in recall studies. The Spilich, Vesponder, Chiesi, and Voss study (1979) is one exception, but they were examining recall for a special domain (baseball). If a reader already knows the ideas presented, then changes from the text are usually elaborations of the content. It is difficult to conceive of the limits for inference chains from these texts, or what additions should be considered misreadings.

Texts have been manipulated in a variety of ways: text scramblings (sentences, paragraphs, embedding one topic within another, and so forth), deleting information, reorganizing chunks, putting in summaries, taking out summaries, and increasing proposition density. The general results have been that text with good internal order, where the information on each topic is clustered together rather than interspersed, is more memorable.

This research has been used to speak to the readability question, to suggest that text structure should be added to the sentence length and vocabulary level variables used in readability formulas. Reading materials should be explicit and clearly organized if they are to be remembered.

NARRATIVES

Stories generally tell "what happened." Who did what to whom and why? To be sure, more complex literature can also be read to analyze and appreciate the writer's craft or vicariously to learn more about motivations, life styles, ongoing events—the stuff of human existence. Fiction can and does contain abstract ideas and technical information. When this occurs, the writing style generally changes to exposition, with an interruption in the chronology of events. For most simple stories, such as those used in the story grammar research described later, comprehension refers to accurate memory for the events of the story—digressions are seldom incorporated in the text.

MEMORY FOR SIMPLE STORIES

A substantial research literature has grown up around the individual's ability to recall the structure of simple stories. The foundation for this work was the development of story grammars by Mandler and Johnson (1977), Rumelhart (1975), and Stein and Glenn (1979), among others. These story grammarians laid out the necessary and elaborative categories of information needed to describe a story. They then used these categories and the sequencing of the information units to compare "better" and "worse" stories by their inclusion of the categorical information in "best" orders. Research has tested the validity of the categories as well as better-versus-worse story structures, with the results much as expected. Categories that were explicit were more likely to be retained, and if the essential parts of the episodic structure were not present and in the order specified by the grammar, then comprehension (recall) was impeded. Chronological sequencing was better than flashbacks or embedded structures.

The materials represented the simplest narrative styles, though the content was occasionally bizarre: a farmer trying to get his mule out of the barn, a dog dropping his bone in the water as he tries to attack his own reflection, a prince saving a fair lady from a dragon, and so forth. Many bore resemblances to the basal primers, unsurprising since the subjects sampled often included elementary students. A few stories were slightly more sophisticated: *Tales of the Decameron*, "Tar Babies" (an Apache folk tale), Aesop fables, and Japanese folk tales. Even these took the form of single-message narrations, and the sophistication came by basing the stories in a different time, place, or culture.

The range of narrative constructions is far greater than represented in the materials investigated thus far. Consider the varied devices reflected in texts like Umberto Eco's *The Name of the Rose* (1980), Desmond Bagley's *The Snow Tiger* (1975), or an Agatha Christie mystery. All are concerned with criminal acts and the discovery of the perpetrator. The settings are 14th century Italy, a town in New Zealand, and Britain, respectively. The lexicon used, the familiarity of the setting, the author's expectations for his or her readers' background knowledge and aesthetic values are some of the factors that make stories more or less difficult, but in what ways? What are the effects of differences in these few factors on the quality of interpretations by various readers? Story grammar categories may apply to these complex forms, but there is no substantiation as yet.

MEMORY FOR EXPOSITORY TEXTS

We have thus far considered comprehension of sentences, paragraphs, and simple stories. A different set of concepts are required to describe writing of informational and technical character—descriptions, sequential and process accounts, explanations, arguments, and the like. Meyer (1975, 1977, 1985) was among the first to tackle this problem. She turned to concepts from the rhetoric: (a) antecedent/consequence relations, (b) problem/solution relations, (c) compare/contrast relations (d) collection by commonality relations, and (e) description/elaboration relations. In several experiments, she altered the rhetorical structure while keeping content the same; in other studies the content was varied to determine the effects on retention of information. The findings do not show that any one type of rhetorical structure is better comprehended than any other. Instead, the findings seem often to be passage specific. Some combinations of content and structure are more difficult than others.

Various hypotheses can be entertained. One possibility is that certain content may logically fit a particular type of structure, that there is an interaction between how the information is presented (the structure) and the content of the information. The need is for studies that more systematically vary content and structure; for instance, problem/solution content presented in a number of different problem-solving structures. A further complication is the possibility that students' general ability and specific knowledge may influence the appropriateness of different "packages." Much work needs to be done in untangling this snarl.

Problems in the way of this task are numerous. First, books, chapters, and lengthy essays are poorly described at the word choice, syntactic type, or paragraph levels that are commonly employed to assess readability. The structural approaches employed presently quickly become unwieldy. A 20-page essay contains an enormous amount of language. Van Dijk and Kintsch (1983) analyzed a 2-page article from *Newsweek*; the task took the better part of their book, and even so they concluded that they had covered only a modest number of semantic and pragmatic variables. Grimes (1975) in *The Thread of Discourse* also took the better part of a book to characterize the opening paragraph of C. S. Lewis' (1943) *Out of the Silent Planet*. Counting, controlling, describing the content of extended literature would be inordinately tedious with current methods, and the findings would challenge interpretation.

The second problem with extensive texts relates to the complexity problem. What is the appropriate unit for analysis?

After reading "Verbal Comprehension in Instructional Situations" (Just & Carpenter, 1976), what should readers be able to do to show that they have understood the article? Summary measures have been suggested, with a summary defined as an outline of the major topical headings. For knowledgeable readers, such an outline would not include new learning; it is the details of the presentation that have extended their scripts for information processing concepts.

The measures used for describing comprehension must reflect the informational units contained in the text as well as the goals for learning. Novices and experts do not understand a text in the same ways nor do they glean identical information. Schooling is a means of inducing learning. Performance measures must reflect the intended goals for the particular group of learners.

A third problem in evaluating the manner of presenting information in an expository text lies in the text selection procedures. Up to the present, most researchers have relied on naturally occurring texts, and so content and structure have been joined. The organizational quality of the text has thus been confounded with the topic. Substance and form have been inextricably interwoven; the two elements have jointly determined the text quality and the character of the reader's interpretation. A quite different approach is to assume that any given topic can be presented in different structural forms (Calfee & Curley, 1984). The author, given a particular subject matter, would seem to have the option within limits of describing it as an object, explaining it in a sequence, or attempting a conceptual or argumentative essay on the matter.

The renewed interest in writing, both the processes involved and the product (what is good writing), holds promise for defining the variables for determining text quality (see Bereiter & Scardamalia, in this volume). Until there is some concerted effort on this topic, perhaps the most useful sources are books on rhetoric, such as *Prose Models* (Levin, 1978), *Modern Rhetoric* (Brooks & Warren, 1958), *Thought in English Prose* (Dent, 1930), or *A Theory of Discourse* (Kinneavy, 1971).

The Reader

The text is an important consideration in comprehension, but so is the mental apparatus brought by the reader—background knowledge, purpose in reading, and strategic approach. Some readers are relatively passive (and most of us take this stance at times—when we settle back with a "junk book" to pass some time); other readers tackle comprehension as a problem-solving task. In this section we will review the issues of background or schematic knowledge, and of active inferential processing of text.

SCHEMATA FOR COMPREHENSION

Research under the heading of schema theory focused on the organization of knowledge in the reader's head and the interplay of these representations with the text (Wittrock, Marks, & Doctorow, 1975; Wittrock, 1981). The work takes a Whorfian perspective, in which comprehension outcomes were relative to the readers' particular schemata. Texts were selected for certain audiences, such as an Indian wedding (Steffensen, Joag-dev, &

Anderson, 1979); manipulated to be deliberately ambiguous, such as "Washing Clothes," a passage from Bransford and Johnson (1972); or so general that many interpretations were possible, such as a description of a house (Pichert & Anderson, 1977). These were not the erudite, formal texts described by Olson (1977) for argument or knowledge of formal thinking. Natural events, weddings, houses, snowslides, and deaths typify the content.

The readers tested were either from the American culture in the case of the deliberately ambiguous texts, or from a select culture with a different knowledge base, such as Indian versus American college students for an Indian wedding story. The point of the research was to demonstrate that prior schematic knowledge derived from cultural experiences or from more narrow experiential bases influenced what was recalled or inferred after exposure to the text.

Not surprisingly, the results have confirmed this expectation. The experienced-based readers have less to learn. Most of the text is already known and it simply acts as a stimulus cue for recognition. Since the amount of new information is comparatively slight for those who have the appropriate background, the task is simplified. This effect is, of course, the point behind schema research. If the appropriate knowledge is known or can be learned through prior preparation, such as advance organizers, directed reading activities, or scaffolding, performance on some criterion measures will be improved.

INFERENCING ABOUT TEXTS

Readers draw inferences by bringing two given pieces of information together into a new construction. They build inference chains by extrapolating to new situations. All written messages rely on the reader's ability to supply the missing links, for no piece of writing can be sufficiently complete to negate this requirement. It is indeed difficult to think of any mental operation that does not involve inferencing. Our senses note the physical situation, the black marks on the white page, the cloud patterns in the sky, the position of the neighboring cars on the freeways, but it is within our memories of similar past situations that we find the knowledge to make sense of the present situation and to predict what is likely to happen. Yet this requisite human activity is often considered a higher-level skill.

First one learns to read a given text and then with maturation, more knowledge and experience, and greater fluency and accuracy in the reading act, the older child supposedly becomes capable of integrating the information in new ways. He or she can now add appropriate information to the text from long-term memory. The problem with this oversimplistic conception of inferencing as a higher-order ability is that it is dependent upon the specific inference expected as well as the level of text being read. The last decade of research has offered evidence that even very young children make appropriate inferences under certain conditions, conditions where they have prior schemas pertinent to the discourse information (Spiro, 1977).

Examples from the research literature include both accurate and inaccurate inferences, but age does not appear to be the distinguishing factor. Children in Grades 2 through 5 did not vary in their ability to recognize true inferences as contrasted

with false inferences for the following text (Paris & Carter, 1973):

> The bird is inside the cage,
> the cage is under the table,
> the bird is yellow.

All ages knew that *The bird is under the table* was a true inference and that *The bird is on top of the table* was false. When the content was based on children's experiential knowledge, as in *ants*, *jelly*, and *kitchens* (Moeser, 1976), or other familiar objects or events, even kindergartners were near perfect in identifying the correct choice. These inference tasks resembled those conducted with college students who were given pieces of information and who then, on forced choice or recognition tests, falsely identified as given information obvious conclusions. If you are told that there is a mountain with a village at the bottom of the mountain and that an avalanche is coming down the mountain, the inference that the town will be smothered seems reasonable — and many subjects believed that the conclusion was provided by the text (Bransford & Johnson, 1972).

The relationships between given and new information in Haviland and Clark (1974), where the authors were exploring anaphoric contingencies, also used common experience-based information, for example, *picnics*, *car trunks*, *coolers*, *beer*. This research confirmed the belief that when the subjects knew a lot about the content described within a text, they used this knowledge to fill in and elaborate the content to the point where they constructed a new representation — some portion reader based and some portion text based, a new text that was an interaction from both sources. Schemata influence inferences.

Under other conditions, this interaction, a new but logically reasonable presentation, is less likely to occur. Upper grade elementary children had difficulty in deciding whether an inference was true or indefinite after exposure to the following sentence pair:

> John has more cake than Mary.
> John ate more cake than Mary.

The acceptable answer was indefinite as John could have dropped the cake on the floor, not liked the cake, or not been hungry. However, most of the children thought this was a true inference, perhaps because if they have more of something stereotypically perceived of as good (cake), they would eat it. For the true inference, there were few errors (Hildyard & Olson, 1978):

> John has more cake than Mary.
> Mary has less cake than John.

In a second study, Hildyard and Olson examined contextual inferences for narrative passages. Fifth-graders had to decide on the appropriateness of the inferences for the particular story. Able students made more appropriate choices, a finding that is similar to that of Goetz (1979), who found that older and abler high school readers rated statements more accurately as being (a) an exact match, (b) a paraphrase, (c) implied by the story, or

(d) consistent with the story. If the prior knowledge is available, the inference will be made; thus, it is knowledge rather than inference that determines the interaction of text and reader (Omanson, Warren, & Trabasso, 1978).

Substituting the explanation of having or not having prior knowledge as the causal source for appropriate inference performance does not provide assistance in planning instruction. One vague requirement has simply replaced the preceding one. Not simply inference failures due to lack of knowledge as discussed by Anderson and Pearson (1984), but what types of inferences are difficult, for whom, and under what conditions — answers to these questions could aid in planning instruction.

For instance, children could assess the literal meaning of text when that text was in agreement with what they knew, but when the text was either indefinite or contradictory to what they knew, performance was much poorer (Hildyard & Olson, 1982). First, third, and fifth grade children were asked to decide on the appropriate relations between objects and events presented in descriptive passages. The relations were *in front-behind, before-after, on top-under, earlier-later, more-less, bigger-smaller*. First-graders could not handle neutral or counterfactual information. Third-graders did not recognize counterfactual information. Only fifth-graders performed better than chance on all three types and they were not very accurate on the latter two types. These and other listening tasks (Markham, 1979) simply confirm that children cannot assess missing links in their own knowledge structures; they do not know what they don't know (Brown, 1978).

An obvious goal of instruction is for the student to enlarge his or her personal knowledge base, to recognize the given information within a text and to integrate what is new with that which was previously known. But within a classroom there are as many different knowledge bases as there are students. The decisions concerning what preparations should be provided to help the students read with understanding and to promote the learning of new information are not easy ones. The research on advance preparation has had mixed results.

Several training studies intended to improve comprehension performance have shown that providing background knowledge (Schallert, 1976; Pearson, Hansen, & Gordon, 1979) and inference training (Hansen, 1981; Hansen & Pearson, 1983) have indeed improved the performance of the less able readers though with little effect on able readers. The reading materials are likely too simple to provide any new information for the abler students. For instance, in the Hansen and Pearson study (1983), grade-level stories (fourth grade) were used, but the average reading level for the abler students was 6.3. Rather than assuming such training was not needed by the abler readers as the authors did, one could find it enlightening to try similar training with more difficult texts.

Instructional Studies

Two instructional studies focusing on different aspects of reading comprehension are examined in some detail in this section. The studies have been selected as representative of models for studying comprehension instruction. The studies differ in several ways, and reflect quite different historical approaches to the question of how to help students understand what they read. Yet both consider characteristics of the learners, the curriculum for instruction as related to the performance measures, and the context for learning. Through the integration of subsequent studies such as these, we may find some answers to the troublesome problem of teaching students how to learn from reading texts.

STRATEGIES FOR COMPREHENDING: AN EXPERIMENTAL STUDY

Palincsar and Brown (1984) used an experimental approach to examine effects on the development of general comprehension skills in remedial seventh grade readers. The authors, noting the imprecise definitions of comprehension skills, identified from the literature six major comprehension activities:

1. understanding the purposes of reading, both explicit and implicit;
2. activating relevant background knowledge;
3. allocating attention so that concentration can be focused on the major content at the expense of trivia;
4. evaluating content critically for internal consistency, and compatibility with prior knowledge and common sense;
5. monitoring ongoing activities to see if comprehension is occurring, by engaging in such activities as periodic review and self-interrogation; and
6. drawing and testing inferences of many kinds, including interpretations, predictions, and conclusions.

For the purposes of instruction, they selected four concrete activities that could be engaged in by novice learners and that would embody the overlapping functions contained in Items 1–6 above. These were *summarizing, questioning, clarifying,* and *predicting*.

These general comprehension skills or strategies fit under the general heading of metacognitive activities, in the thinking of these researchers. The limitation of this description of the curricular foundations of the problem is that it is a general description of activities that any problem solver would go through in attacking a problem. The activities seem as pertinent to the interpretations of children acquiring their initial spoken language as to the isolation of the tectonic plate theory. In other words, these are useful problem-solving strategies for various contents. In this sense, the study follows the tradition of prior study skills work, such as the SQ3R (Survey, Question, Read, Review, Recite) approach of Robinson (1970). The central focus is on learning how to perform a mental operation prior to, while reading, or after reading any text; thus the desired goals of instruction are relatively content free. True, expository texts are the materials for instruction, the discourse units that the students are learning to manipulate; but any expository texts could serve this function.

Palincsar and Brown based their instructional model on Vygotsky's zone of proximal development (1978), that is, what a child can do with aid from a teacher, that child can be taught to do without assistance. First, the teacher models the activity, then the child and the teacher perform the activity together with the child taking on more and more of the responsibility for the activity, until finally the child becomes independent of the teacher for that activity. Basically, the children were asked to predict the passage information, to ask "teacher-type" questions about the passages, and to summarize the passage at various points.

The actual content used for the study were 13 passages of approximately 1500 words each taken from various text readers at the seventh grade readability level. Except for requirements for a range of expository topics, little attention was given to the contents or the structure of texts. These passages were used to assess performance with 45 shorter passages from the same sources used for training. Whether these subjects were being exposed to new ideas or not was not explored. Instead, the actions of summarizing, questioning, clarifying, and predicting were the goals for training.

Two sample passages used by Palincsar and Brown in the study, as well as various responses (good and bad), are presented below:

HOW CAN SNAKES BE SO FLEXIBLE

The snake's skeleton and parts of its body are very flexible—something like a rubber hose with bones. A snake's backbone can have as many as 300 vertebrae, almost ten times as many as a human's. These vertebrae are connected by loose and rubbery tissues that allow easy movement. Because of this bendable, twistable spinal construction, a snake can turn its body in almost any direction at almost any point. (p. 140)

Perhaps you are wondering where the lava and other volcanic products come from. Deep within our earth there are pockets of molten rock called *magma*. Forced upward in part by gas pressure, this molten rock continually tries to reach the surface. Eventually—by means of cracks in the crustal rocks or some similar zone of weakness—the magma may break out of the ground. It then flows from the vent as lava, or spews skyward as dense clouds of lava particles. (p. 138)

These brief excerpts from the full 1500-word essays were used to illustrate the question-asking and summarizing procedures. Each paragraph was read, then the teacher generated main idea questions and summaries by giving cues (e.g., "what happened when"), or modeling an appropriate question, and asking the student to repeat it. For instance, the following response pair is from early in the training. The student's summary was "Snakes can move forward and backward and they have a rubbery something." The ideal summary given for the same passage used the title and two details: "A snake's flexibility is due to its unusual backbone, which consists of many vertebrae connected by loose rubbery tissue" (pp. 140–142).

One essay consisted of a description of snakes: kinds, habitat, physiology, and so forth. Instead of having the pupils read the entire essay, the task was simplified into small chunks so that the students would not be intimidated. However, the authors do not indicate that eventually the pupils will learn how to evaluate an entire section. In fact, such a procedure would be another study and likely take much more time. But because of the limited text portions used for training, the task itself is quite different than learning how to study a text.

These two four-sentence paragraphs can be used only to study the structure of a paragraph. Neither selection has an explicit main idea except for the title of the "snake" paragraph.

The amount of information is naturally slight and would be difficult to retain or learn as presented because there is no larger framework in which to insert the information. One summary given at the end of training, "My summary would be that this paragraph is about magma and magma is molten rock and I wouldn't add anything else," was given a good commendation by the teacher. In truth, it is a reasonable summary for the excerpt, but it may not indicate that the student has learned how to summarize.

The information content is so slight that the student need not evaluate the information by locating major points that sum up the details presented. The student does not have to integrate several points into a macroproposition of his or her own creation. The student has simply selected the italicized word and joined it with the subject phrase of the next sentence. Both the brevity of the texts and the erratic structures limit the learning to inclusion of question words in questions and isolation of the key content words for summaries. No improvement was found in either study in evaluating the importance of information. The students were never directly taught this skill nor could they have been, for the texts used did not offer the opportunity of so doing.

Assessment was multifaceted but, except for certain transfer tests, closely related to the reciprocal teaching instruction, and certainly it reflected two of the curricular components of interest, summarizing and questioning. Both pre- and posttests consisted of reading a fifth grade expository passage and answering 10 questions on the passage. The question types, from the Pearson and Johnson (1978) classification, were: (a) text explicit (answer is in the text), (b) text implicit (answer refers to background knowledge about the topic not supplied by the text). Similar tests were used for baseline, for treatment assessment, for the transfer tests to regular science and social studies classes, and for the delayed test.

Four other transfer tests in the Palincsar and Brown (1984) reciprocal-teaching study assessed (a) summarizing, where the students received points for deleting trivia and redundancies, for writing superordinate terms for similar ideas, for identifying underlying topic sentences, and for supplying topic sentences for paragraphs that lacked them; (b) predicting questions — the students wrote 10 teacher-type questions; (c) detecting incongruities — the students had to say "yes" (this line fits the topic) or "no" (it does not) for four passages, three of which contained anomalous lines; and (d) rating of thematic importance — the students were asked to eliminate in order the least important one-fourth of the text, then the next one-fourth, and the next, leaving only the topmost information. All transfer tests with passages counterbalanced were given both prior to initiation of the study and upon "termination of the study" (p. 2). The Gates–MacGinitie standardized reading test was administered to the reciprocal-teaching students approximately 3 months after the study.

A total of 37 seventh grade students participated in the first study. The 13 average-reading-ability students served as a comparison point for any gains. The other 24 students had oral reading rates of 100 words per minute with less than two decoding errors, but with standard comprehension scores 2 years below grade and less than 40% correct on the pretest. The 21 students who participated in the regular teacher study had somewhat higher scores but were considered in need of special help in their schools particularly in reading comprehension. Their prior instruction in reading was not mentioned. Two of the teachers were resource room teachers and two were regular teachers; all received three reciprocal-teaching training sessions.

The six students in the reciprocal training groups did show marked improvement in their ability to answer comprehension questions, though no difference on type of question. Generally, these six students outperformed the locating information and the two control groups as well as raising their percentile rankings in their social studies and science classes. For the summarization transfer test, the reciprocal-teaching group were equivalent to the 13 average readers and much better than the untreated controls. Though there was no significant difference on question prediction, four of the six reciprocal students who scored poorly at the pretest did improve. They were also reliably better on detecting ambiguities than the controls. There were no differences on ratings of thematic importance, an activity which had not been taught. In the second study, there were no controls, so all comparisons are within subject comparisons. Similar results were found for the transfer tests, with no effect for teacher, indicating that all four teachers were equally able in implementing the curriculum.

The small class size, from two up to seven students, obviously limits the generalizability of the Palincsar and Brown study to normative classrooms, but the transfer to classroom work (science and social studies) is obviously impressive. However, the six students in the first study with their intensive one-on-two work with a teacher/researcher for 8 weeks did not surpass the average reading group. What prior comprehension training had both groups received? We do not know, but whatever the curriculum was, the average group had learned to summarize, to question, and to detect anomalies as well as the specially trained group. The average group had also learned how to rate passages for thematic importance, a task that the reciprocal group could not perform. Perhaps the difference is in what was taught or perhaps it was in the one-on-one attention that the small class size made possible.

This study does speak to comprehension curriculum, for these children did learn how to ask questions and to express the major idea in very brief excerpts, activities that these "poor comprehenders" could not do before the instruction. However, the intent of such instruction is to generalize reading comprehension abilities to all texts, and the ultimate test of the efficiency of this instruction will be the students' capabilities in independently handling, that is, understanding subsequent expository texts in different content domains. Thus this study raises a number of questions for instructional research. Will such training lead to better learning from extended texts, where summarizing and questioning become much more complex tasks, or will different types of instructional procedures have to be considered—procedures that consider the substance of the text and its organizational structure?

LEARNING TEXT CONCEPTS: A CASE STUDY

In the second study (Anderson & Smith, 1984; also Roth, Smith, & Anderson, 1984), the researchers have used an obser-vational, case study approach to look at learning of science concepts by fifth grade students from texts and from teacher instruction. Duffy, Roehler, and Mason (1984) refer to this as process research in contrast with the strategy research of the Palincsar and Brown (1984) study. "Process" seems here to refer to the research methods, describing the processes of teaching, rather than a learning goal for the students.

The focus in these studies is on the learning of specific scientific knowledge and on the identification of naive student beliefs that interfere with subsequent learning from either text or teacher. The information content of both the texts used and the teacher/student verbal interactions are of primary concern. From this content, student misconceptions can be identified and then mapped to the information presented by the texts and by the teacher and appropriate preparation for new learning or elaboration of current knowledge can be incorporated into the content area curriculum.

The historical tradition for this research question is that of preparation for learning, such as advance organizers (Ausubel, 1978; Mayer, 1979), adjunct questions (Anderson & Biddle, 1975; Rickards & Hatcher, 1977-1978), and development of these and other mathemagenic activities ("learning-related processes," p. 110, Rothkopf, 1982). The important measures for this type of research include the accuracy and depth of the content learned and the mental representation, the script, formed by the learner in the domain of interest.

The Anderson and Smith (1984) study consisted of observations during the first year, and both observation and intervention during the second year. The science units selected for observation included a "light" unit presented in the text, *Exploring Science*, and a unit on photosynthesis, covered in *Communities*, which requires the students to conduct investigations and record results, a form of discovery or inquiry learning that does not include an informational text. Nine teachers presenting the photosynthesis unit and five teachers presenting the light material were observed during the first year. The students were pretested and posttested on the information. Though the academic performance of these students is not as well specified in this study as in the previous one, there is precise information on what the children knew before instruction on the curricular goals. Also, detailed notes were recorded for the specific instructional episodes, and the teachers were interviewed concerning their planning for instruction and their evaluation of the outcomes. The pretests and posttests were constructed from a propositional analysis of the materials and activities used for instruction.

Here is a sample from Anderson and Smith (1984) of the "light" information from the textbook and two propositions used for testing:

> Have you ever thrown a rubber ball at something? If you have, you know that when the ball hits most things, it bounces off them. Like a rubber ball, light bounces off most things it hits. When light travels to something opaque, all the light does not stop. Some of the light bounces off. When light travels to something translucent or transparent, all the light does not pass through. Some of this light bounces. When light bounces off things and travels to your eyes, you are able to see (p. 187)

Propositions:

    (1) Light travels in a straight line.
    (2) Light bounces off most things that it hits.

Of the 200-plus children tested on this passage, fewer than one-fourth of them understood it. This result was attributed to an erroneous schema for vision rather than a confusing text. Anderson and Smith do not recommend rewriting the passage, as "the scientific schema for vision is correct" (p. 188); instead, the children should be taught the appropriate information on how vision operates so that they will "abandon (erroneous) preconceptions and replace them with more adequate scientific conceptions" (p. 189).

The requirement for conceptual change by means of instruction is, of course, a desirable goal, but we are not convinced that the text itself should not be changed. The text is poor. Nowhere is the major point made that our eyes do not see the objects but only the light waves reflected from the objects. The children are expected to derive this fact from the ball analogy, an high-level inference. The references to *opaque*, *translucent*, and *transparent* substances are trying to make a point that all kinds of objects reflect some light and that the reflected light is what we see. If the text is not going to inform the students directly of the effects of different surfaces on the quality of the light waves, then the text is unnecessarily confusing. Why bring up the different surfaces? Again the major underlying information seems to be that our eyes can only see reflected light from surfaces. Nowhere in this passage is that point made clearly and unambiguously.

This text has features of the newer, schema-based recommendations for writing "friendly" text, and, as such, shows some of the pitfalls of content-free textual recommendations. Familiar analogies are used whether they explain or not because like old shoes they are more comfortable. The recommendations of Armbruster (1984) appear more trustworthy. Text writers should (a) specify what it is they want to teach, (b) list what are the most likely erroneous preconceptions concerning this learning, and then (c) directly state their major points attacking each preconception in turn. Education has spent too many years, too much effort, and too much money in preparing materials to be easy rather than in preparing them so that the message is clearly stated. Familiarity is not a substitute for accuracy, nor is it a good way to present the appropriate scientific schema.

The results from the first year of this study are capsulized in the statement, "None of the 14 teachers we observed during the first year of the program was particularly successful in inducing conceptual change in his or her students" (p. 190). From the statement, we deduced that whatever the performance level at the pretest, there was little change at the posttest. Neither the best of the didactic teachers nor the best of those who used discovery teaching were able to bring about new mental representations for these scientific principles in the majority of their students.

For the intervention phase of this study, the second year, the program materials were modified by rewriting pertinent sections of the teacher's guide for the discovery approach (SCIS [Science Curriculum Improvement Study]) used for the photosynthesis unit, and by preparing transparencies and a teacher's guide for the *Exploring Science* textbook used for the "light"

unit. Anderson and Smith (p. 196) list three purposes guiding the preparation of the new materials:

1. We tried to describe the most common and most important student preconceptions.
2. We tried to describe conceptual goals or objectives by contrasting those common preconceptions with more acceptable scientific conceptions.
3. We tried to describe a teaching strategy which would bring about conceptual conflict and lead (hopefully) to conceptual change on the part of the students.

Ten of the original 14 teachers taught either the "light" or photosynthesis units.

The preliminary results from the teacher interviews were highly favorable. The teachers believed that they had not only learned what concepts should be taught and how to teach them but had also learned more about light and photosynthesis themselves. The percentage of children understanding the major concepts in the didactic classes also increased in Year 2 over Year 1; in one class, the percentage of children understanding that "our eyes detect reflected light (rather than detect objects directly)" changed from 35% to 81% with the new materials. From the SCIS tests the authors gained the impression that it is harder to bring about conceptual change using discovery methods, for "the results of experiments in which ten-year-old children are growing their own plants are often ambiguous, so students may never actually make observations that lead them to question their preconceptions" (p. 199).

A subsequent logical analysis of the case study research (Roth, Smith, & Anderson, 1984), pp. 286–287) resulted in a general model for content teaching based on four principles:

1. Teachers need to be sensitive to their students' misconceptions, and they need to continually consider how these misconceptions are influencing students' responses to instruction.
2. Teachers need to focus what they say and what their students are saying on the "whys" of science.
3. Teachers need to know more than just what questions to ask; they also need to know how to respond to student statements.
4. There must be a balance between open-ended verbal interactions and directed, structured discussions that lead to closure and consensus.

Basically, this study tends to confirm an old teaching adage. What the students already know about the course content (whether this knowledge be correct or erroneous) should be the basis for the instruction provided.

INSTRUCTIONAL RESEARCH

As both of these studies have shown, instructional research is a complex task. Attention has to be paid to the students, the teachers, the curriculum, and the instructional environment, but it is possible. We do have evidence that remedial readers can learn and apply strategies for comprehension, but we need to know whether these strategies can be learned in more typical classrooms and whether the strategies will transfer to independent reading in the future. An important variable for content-area teachers has been somewhat isolated; that variable is the erroneous schemata children already have for scientific concepts. We need to know the importance of this variable for older students and for other content areas. The four principles listed above seem to be valuable dicta for planning instructional programs. Instructional research for reading/discourse comprehension appears to be in a neonate phase, but at least we see a beginning.

Epilogue

In a preliminary search of the ERIC files when first beginning this chapter, we found that more than 25,000 entries were identified under the joint rubric of reading and instruction. Since that time, of course, the literature has not become any smaller.

We have not attempted to "cover" this literature in our review. In fact, many of the entries were not appropriate; they were not research based, or did not contribute to improved understanding of *reading instruction*, which we have taken as the focus of this chapter. In fact, many of the most informative reports were more or less "fugitive"; chapters in edited volumes, technical reports, and so on, and not accessible through the ERIC system.

Literacy is the foundation for lifelong learning; thus its importance in practice and in research. Our goal in this chapter has been to lay a solid foundation in the curriculum of literacy, and against this framework to examine trends in the content and methods of research on reading. In such a vigorous and vital area, it is not surprising to find variety, almost to the point of the Tower of Babel. Some of the diversity is problematic, in our opinion. There is a piecemeal character to the literature, partly because of the way that the domain has been construed, and partly because of the empirical tradition in educational research.

The new directions in this field seem to us quite promising, however. The extension of research to hard problems (comprehension) in difficult settings (the classroom) reflects a maturing of theory and method in educational research. Psychologists continue to play a major role in reading research, but the discipline is now joined by other specialists — linguists and anthropologists, to name just two categories — in genuinely collegial endeavors. In a strange way, enlarging the scope of the problem and increasing the range of actors may have led to a more coherent formulation of "reading" and "reading instruction." We have framed this review around the rhetorical foundations of the curriculum, which we see as providing a trustworthy unity. It will be interesting to read this chapter in the next edition — one thing about which we can be certain is that reading instruction will continue to be a significant field of scholarship, research, and debate.

REFERENCES

Alegria, J., Pignot, E., & Morais, J. (1982). Phonetic analysis of speech and memory codes in beginning readers. *Memory & Cognition, 10*, 451–456.

Al Issa, I. (1969). The development of word definitions in children. *Journal of Genetic Psychology, 114*, 25–28.

Allen, R. V., & Allen, C. (1966). *Language experiences in reading: Teachers' resource book.* Chicago: Encyclopedia Brittanica Press.

Allington, R. L. (1980). Teacher interruption behaviors during primary-grade oral reading. *Journal of Educational Psychology, 72*, 371–377.

Anderson, C. W., & Smith, E. L. (1984). Children's preconceptions and content-area textbooks. In G. G. Duffy, L. R. Roehler, & J. Mason (Eds.), *Comprehension instruction: Perspectives and suggestions.* New York: Longman.

Anderson, L. M. (1982). *Student responses to seatwork: Implications for the study of students' cognitive processing.* (Research Series No. 102). East Lansing: Michigan State University, Institute for Research on Teaching.

Anderson, R. C., & Biddle, W. B. (1975). On asking people questions about what they are reading. In G. Bower (Ed.), *Psychology of learning and motivation* (Vol. 9). New York: Academic Press.

Anderson, R. C., & Freebody, P. (1981). Vocabulary knowledge. In J. T. Guthrie (Ed.), *Comprehension and teaching: Research reviews.* Newark, DE: International Reading Association.

Anderson, R. C., Mason, J., & Shirey, L. (1984). The reading group: An experimental investigation of a labyrinth. *Reading Research Quarterly, 19*, 6–38.

Anderson, R. C., Osborn, J. & Tierney, R. J. (Eds.). (1984). *Learning to read in American schools: Basal readers and content texts.* Hillsdale, NJ: Erlbaum.

Anderson, R. C., & Pearson, P. D. (1984). A schema-theoretic view of basic processes in reading. In P. D. Pearson (Ed.), *Handbook of reading research.* New York: Longman.

Andrews, S. (1982). Phonological recoding: Is the regularity effect consistent? *Memory & Cognition, 10*, 565–575.

Anglin, J. M. (1977). *Word, object and conceptual development.* New York: W. W. Norton.

Applebee, A. N., & Langer, J. A. (1983). Instructional scaffolding: Reading and writing as natural language activities. *Language Arts, 60*, 168–175.

Armbruster, B. B. (1984). The problem of "inconsiderate text." In G. G. Duffy, L. R. Roehler & J. Mason (Eds.), *Comprehension instruction: Perspectives and suggestions.* New York: Longman.

Ausubel, D. P. (1978). In defense of advance organizers: A reply to the critics. *Review of Educational Research, 48*, 251–257.

Bagley, D. (1975). *The snow tiger.* New York: Harper & Row.

Balmuth, M. (1982). *The roots of phonics: A historical introduction.* New York: McGraw-Hill

Barber, P. J., & Millar, D. G. (1982). Subjective judgments of spelling-sound correspondences: Effects of word regularity and word frequency. *Memory & Cognition, 10*, 457–464.

Barr, R. C. (1972). The influence of instructional conditions on word recognition errors. *Reading Research Quarterly, 7*, 509–529.

Barr, R. C. (1973–1974). Instructional pace differences and their effect on reading acquisition. *Reading Research Quarterly, 9*, 526–554.

Barr, R. C. (1974–1975). The effect of instruction on pupil reading strategies. *Reading Research Quarterly, 10*, 555–582.

Barr, R., & Dreeben, R., with Wiratchai, N. (1983). *How schools work.* Chicago: University of Chicago Press.

Barton, A. N. (1963). Reading research and its communication: The Columbia-Carnegie project. In J. A. Figurel (Ed.), *Reading as an intellectual activity.* Newark, DE: International Reading Association.

Barzun, J. (1977). *The modern researcher* (3rd ed.). New York: Harcourt Brace Jovanovich.

Beck, I. L., McCaslin, E. S., & McKeown, M. G. (1980). *The rationale and design of a program to teach vocabulary to fourth-grade students.* Unpublished manuscript, University of Pittsburgh, Learning Research and Development Center, Pittsburgh.

Beck, I. L., McKeown, M. G., McCaslin, & Burkes, A. M. (1979). *Instructional dimensions that may affect reading comprehension: Examples from two commercial reading programs.* Unpublished manuscript, University of Pittsburgh, Learning Research and Development Center, Pittsburgh.

Beck, I. L., & Perfetti, C. A., & McKeown, M. G. (1982). Effects of long-term vocabulary instruction on lexical access and reading comprehension. *Journal of Educational Psychology, 74*, 506–521.

Becker, W. C., & Carnine, D. W. (1980). Direct instruction as an effective approach to educational intervention with disadvantaged and low performers. In B. Lahey & A. Kazdin (Eds.), *Advances in clinical child psychology* (Vol. 3). New York: Plenum Press.

Berliner, D. C., & Rosenshine, B. (1977). The acquisition of knowledge in the classroom. In R. C. Anderson, R. J. Spiro & W. E. Montague (Eds.), *Schooling and the acquisition of knowledge*. Hillsdale, NJ: Erlbaum.

Bettelheim, G., & Zelan, K. (1982). *On learning to read: The child's fascination with meaning*. New York: Alfred A. Knopf.

Biemiller, A. (1977-1978). Relationships between oral reading rates for letters, words, and simple text in the development of reading achievement. *Reading Research Quarterly, 13*, 223-253.

Blanchard, J. S. (1980). Preliminary investigation of transfer between single-word decoding ability and contextual reading comprehension by poor readers in grade six. *Perceptual and Motor Skills, 51*, 1271-1281.

Blanchard, J. S. & McNinch, G. H. (1980). Commentary: Testing the decoding sufficiency hypothesis: A response to Fleisher, Jenkins, and Pany. *Reading Research Quarterly, 15*, 559-564.

Bloomfield, M. W., & Newmark, L. (1963). *A linguistic introduction to the history of English*. New York: Alfred A. Knopf.

Bock, J. K. (1982). Toward a cognitive psychology of syntax: Information processing contributions to sentence formulation. *Psychological Review, 89*, 1-47.

Bolinger, D. L. (1975). *Aspects of language* (2nd ed.). New York: Harcourt Brace.

Bolinger, D. L. M. (1980). *Language—the loaded weapon*. New York: Longman.

Bond, G. L., & Dykstra, R. (1967). The cooperative research program in first-grade reading instruction. [Special issue]. *Reading Research Quarterly, 2*(4).

Bowey, J. A., Tunmer, W. E., & Pratt, C. (1984). The development of children's understanding of the metalinguistic term *word*. *Journal of Educational Psychology, 76*, 500-512.

Bransford, J. D., & Johnson, M. K. (1972). Contextual prerequisites for understanding: Some investigations of comprehension and recall. *Journal of Verbal Learning and Verbal Behavior, 11*, 717-726.

Bransford, J. D., & Nitsch, K. E. (1978). Coming to understand things we could not previously understand. In J. F. Kavanagh & W. Strange (Eds.), *Speech and language in the laboratory, school, and clinic*. Cambridge, MA: MIT Press.

Bransford, J. D., Stein, B. S., Shelton, T. S., & Owings, R. A. (1981). Cognition and adaptation: The importance of learning to learn. In J. Harvey (Ed.), *Cognition, social behavior, and the environment*. Hillsdale, NJ: Erlbaum.

Brooks, C., & Warren, R. P. (1958). *Modern rhetoric*. New York: Harcourt Brace.

Brown, A. L. (1978). Knowing when, where, and how to remember: A problem of metacognition. In R. Glaser, (Ed.), *Advances in instructional psychology* (Vol. 1). Hillsdale, NJ: Erlbaum.

Brown, A. L., & Smiley, S. S. (1977). Rating the importance of structural units of prose passages: A problem of metacognitive development. *Child Development, 48*, 1-8.

Bruce, B., Rubin, A., Starr, K., & Liebling, C. (1983). *Vocabulary bias in reading curricula*. (CSR Tech. Rep. No. 280). Champaign: University of Illinois.

Bruner, J. S. (1966). *Toward a theory of instruction*. Cambridge, MA: Belknap Press.

Calfee, R. C. (1976). Sources of dependency in cognitive processes. In D. Klahr (Ed.), *Cognition and instruction*. Hillsdale, NJ: Erlbaum.

Calfee, R. C. (1977). Assessment of independent reading skills: Basic research and practical applications. In A. S. Reber & D. L. Scarborough (Eds.), *Toward a psychology of reading*. Hillsdale, NJ: Erlbaum.

Calfee, R. C. (1981). Cognitive psychology and educational practice. *Review of Research in Education, 9*, 3-72.

Calfee, R. C., & Curley, R. G. (1984). Structures of prose in content areas. In J. Flood (Ed.), *Understanding reading comprehension*. Newark, DE: International Reading Association.

Calfee, R. C., & Drum, P. A. (1978). Learning to read: Theory, research, and practice. *Curriculum Inquiry, 8*, 183-249.

Calfee, R. C. & Piontkowski, D. C. (1981). The reading diary: Acquisition of decoding. *Reading Research Quarterly, 16*, 346-373.

Calfee, R. C., & Shefelbine, J. L. (1981). A structural model of teaching. In A. Lewy & D. Nevo (Eds.), *Evaluation roles in education*. New York: Gordon and Breach.

Calfee, R. C., & Venezky, R. L. (1969). Component skills in beginning reading. In K. S. Goodman & J. T. Fleming (Eds.), *Psycholinguistics and the teaching of reading*. Newark, DE: International Reading Association.

Calfee, R. C., Venezky, R. L., & Chapman, R. S. (1969). Pronunciation of synthetic words with predictable and unpredictable letter-sound correspondences (Tech. Rep. No. 71). Madison: University of Wisconsin, R&D Center for Cognitive Learning.

Carnine, L., Carnine, D., & Gersten, R. (1984). Analysis of oral reading errors made by economically disadvantaged students taught with a synthetic-phonics approach. *Reading Research Quarterly, 19*, 343-356.

Carnine, D., Kameenui, E., & Coyle, G. (1984). Utilization of contextual information in determining the meanings of unfamiliar words in context. *Reading Research Quarterly, 19*, 188-204.

Carroll, J. B., & Chall, J. S. (Eds.). (1975). *Toward a literate society*. New York: McGraw-Hill.

Carroll, J. B., & Freedle, R. O. (Eds.). (1972). *Language comprehension and the acquisition of knowledge*. Washington, DC: V. H. Winston.

Carver, R., & Hoffman, J. (1981). The effect of practice through repeated reading on gain in reading ability using a computer-based instructional system. *Reading Research Quarterly, 16*, 374-390.

Chafe, W., & Danielwicz, J. (in press). Properties of spoken and written language. In R. Horowitz & S. J. Samuels (Eds.), Comprehending oral and written language. New York: Academic Press.

Chall, J. S. (1967). *Learning to read: The great debate*. New York: McGraw-Hill.

Chall, J. S. (1983). *Stages of reading development*. NY: McGraw-Hill.

Chomsky, C. (1978). When you still can't read in third grade: After decoding, who? In S. J. Samuels (Ed.), *What research has to say about reading instruction*. Newark, DE: International Reading Association.

Chomsky, N. (1957). *Syntactic structures*. The Hague: Mouton.

Chomsky, N. (1965). *Aspects of the theory of syntax*. Cambridge, MA: MIT Press.

Chomsky, N. (1970). Phonology and reading. In H. Levin & J. P. Williams (Eds.), *Basic studies on reading*. New York: Basic Books.

Chomsky, N., & Halle, M. (1968). *Sound patterns of English*. New York: Harper & Row.

Clark, H. H. (1973). The language-as-fixed-effect fallacy: A critique of language statistics in psychological research. *Journal of Verbal Learning and Verbal Behavior, 12*, 334-359.

Clark, H. H., & Clark, E. V. (1977). *Psychology and language*. New York: Harcourt Brace Jovanovich.

Clifford, G. (1978). Words for schools: The applications in education of the vocabulary researches of Edward Thorndike. In P. Suppes (Ed.), *Impact of research on education: Some case studies*. Washington, DC: National Institute of Education.

Copperman, P. (1978). *The literacy hoax*. New York: William Morrow.

Cronbach, L. J., Gleser, G. C., Nanda, H., & Rajaratnam, J. (1972). *The dependability of behavioral measurements: Theory of generalizability for scores and profiles*. New York: John Wiley.

Crothers, E. J. (1972). Memory structure and the recall of discourse. In R. O. Freedle & J. B. Carroll (Eds.), *Language comprehension and the acquistion of knowledge*. New York: John Wiley.

Crothers, E. J., (1979). *Paragraph structures*. Norwood, NJ: Ablex.

Crowder, R. G. (1982). *The psychology of reading*. New York: Oxford University Press.

Cunningham, P. M. (1975-1976). Investigating a synthesized theory of mediated word identification. *Reading Research Quarterly, 9*, 127-143.

Curtis, M. E. (1980). Development of components of reading skill. *Journal of Educational Psychology, 72*, 656-669.

Curtis, M. E., & Glaser, R. (1983). Reading theory and the assessment of reading achievement. *Journal of Educational Measurement, 20*, 133-147.

Dahl, P. R. (1979). An experimental program for teaching high speed word recognition and comprehension skills. J. J. E. Button, T. C. Lovitt & T. D. Rowland (Eds.), *Communications research in learning disabilities and mental retardation*. Baltimore: University Park Press.

Danner, F. W. (1976). Children's understanding of intersentence organization in the recall of short descriptive passages. *Journal of Educational Psychology, 68,* 174–183.

Davis, F. B. (1944). The interpretation of frequency ratings obtained from "the teachers word book." *Journal of Educational Psychology, 36,* 169–174.

Davison, A., & Kantor, R. N. (1982). On the failure of readability formulas to define readable texts: A case study from adaptations. *Reading Research Quarterly, 18,* 187–209.

de Sola Pool, I. (1983). Tracking the flow of information. *Science, 221,* 609–613.

Della-Piana, G. M., & Endo, G. T. (1973). Reading research. In R. M. Travers (Ed.), *Second handbook of research on teaching.* Chicago: Rand McNally.

Dent, J. C. (1930). *Thought in English prose.* New York: Odyssey.

Dewey, J. (1902). *The child and the curriculum.* Chicago: University of Chicago Press.

Dixon, C. N. (1979). Selection and use of instructional materials. In R. C. Calfee & P. A. Drum (Eds.), *Teaching reading in compensatory classes.* Newark, DE: International Reading Association.

Doehring, D. G., Trites, R. L., Patel, P. G. & Fiedorowicz, C. A. M. (1981). *Reading disabilities: The interaction of reading, language, and neuropsychological deficits.* New York: Academic Press.

Downing, J., & Leong, C. K. (1982). *Psychology of reading.* New York: Macmillan.

Downing, J., & Oliver, P. (1973–1974). The child's conception of a word. *Reading Research Quarterly, 9,* 568–582.

Duffy, G. G., & Roehler, L. R. (1982). Commentary: The illusion of instruction. *Reading Research Quarterly, 17,* 438–445.

Duffy, G. G., Roehler, L. R., & Mason, J. (1984). *Comprehension instruction.* New York: Longman.

Duin, A., & Graves, M. F. (1984). *Effects of vocabulary instruction.* Unpublished manuscript, University of Minnesota, College of Education, Minneapolis.

Durkin, D. (1978–1979). What classroom observations reveal about comprehension instruction. *Reading Research Quarterly, 14,* 481–533.

Eco, U. (1980). *The name of the rose.* New York: Harcourt Brace.

Ehri, L. C. (1975). Word consciousness in readers and prereaders. *Journal of Educational Psychology, 67,* 204–212.

Ehri, L. C. (1983). A critique of five studies related to letter-name knowledge and learning to read. In L. M. Gentile, M. L. Kamil & J. S. Blanchard (Eds.), *Reading research revisited.* Columbus, OH: Merrill.

Ehri, L. C. (1984). How orthography alters spoken language competencies in children learning to read and spell. In J. Downing & R. Valtin (Eds.), *Language awareness and learning to read.* New York: Springer-Verlag.

Ehri, L. C., & Roberts, K. T. (1979). Do beginners learn printed words better in contexts or in isolation? *Child Development, 50,* 675–685.

Ehri, L. C., & Wilce, L. S. (1980). Do beginners learn to read function words better in sentences or in lists? *Reading Research Quarterly, 15,* 451–476.

Engelmann, S., Haddox, P., Hanner, S., & Osborn, J. (1978). *Thinking basics: Corrective reading program comprehension A.* Chicago: Science Research Associates.

Estes, W. K. (1980). Is human memory obsolete? *American Scientist, 68,* 62–69.

Fillmore, C. J. (1968). The case for case. In E. Bach & R. T. Harms (Eds.), *Universals in linguistic theory.* New York: Holt, Rinehart and Winston.

Fleisher, L. S., Jenkins, J. R., & Pany, D. (1979). Effects on poor readers' comprehension of training in rapid decoding. *Reading Research Quarterly, 15,* 30–48.

Flesch, R. (1981). *Why Johnny still can't read.* New York: Harper & Row.

Frederiksen, C. H. (1972). Effects of task-induced cognitive operations on comprehension and memory processes. In R. O. Freedle, & J. B. Carroll (Eds.), *Language comprehension and the acquisition of knowledge.* New York: John Wiley.

Frederiksen, C. H. (1977). Structure and process in discourse production and comprehension. In M. A. Just & P. Carpenter (Eds.), *Cognitive processes in comprehension.* Hillsdale, NJ: Erlbaum.

Frederiksen, C. H. (1980). Component skills in reading: Measurement of individual differences through chronometric analysis. In R. E. Snow, P.-A. Federico & W. E. Montague (Eds.), *Aptitude, learning, and instruction* (Vol. 1). Hillsdale, NJ: Erlbaum.

Freedman, S. W., & Calfee, R. C. (1984). Understanding and comprehending. *Written Communications, 1,* 459–490.

Fries, C. C. (1962). *Linguistics and reading.* New York: Holt, Rinehart and Winston.

Gage, N. L. (Ed.). (1963). *Handbook of research on teaching.* Chicago: Rand McNally.

Gelb, I. J. (1952). *A study of writing: The foundations of grammatology.* Chicago: University of Chicago Press.

Gelb, I. J. (1963). *A study of writing* (2nd ed.). Chicago: University of Chicago Press.

Gipe, J. (1979). Investigating techniques for teaching word meanings. *Reading Research Quarterly, 14,* 624–644.

Glushko, R. J. (1981). Principles for pronouncing print: The psychology of phonography. In A. M. Lesgold & C. A. Perfetti (Eds.), *Interactive processes in reading.* Hillsdale, NJ: Erlbaum.

Goelman, H., Oberg, A. O., & Smith, F. (Eds.). (1984). *Awakening to literacy.* London: Exeter.

Goetz, E. M. (1979). Early reading: A developmental approach. *Young Children, 34,* 4–13.

Golasch, F. V. (Ed.). (1982). *Language and literacy: The selected essays of Kenneth S. Goodman* (Vol. 1). Boston, MA: Routledge & Kegan Paul.

Goodman, K. S. (1970). Reading: A psycholinguistic guessing game. In H. Singer & R. B. Ruddell (Eds.), *Theoretical models and processes of reading.* Newark, DE: International Reading Association.

Goodman, K. S., & Goodman, Y. M. (1979). Learning to read is natural. In L. B. Resnick & P. A. Weaver (Eds.), *Theory and practice of early reading* (Vol. 1). Hillsdale, NJ: Erlbaum.

Goodman, K. S., & Bird, L. B. (1984). On the wording of texts: A study of intra-text word frequency. *Research in the Teaching of English, 18,* 119–145.

Goody, J. (1977). *The domestication of the savage mind.* London: Cambridge University Press.

Goody, J., & Watt, I. (1963). The consequences of literacy. *Comparative Studies in Society and History, 5,* 304–345.

Gordon, J. D. (1972). *The English language.* New York: Crowell.

Gough, P. B., & Hillinger, M. L. (1980). Learning to read: An unnatural act. *Bulletin of the Orton Society, 30,* 179–196.

Graves, M. F. (in press). *The roles of instruction in fostering vocabulary development.* In M. C. McKeown & M. E. Curtis (Eds.), *The nature of vocabulary acquisition.* Hillsdale, NJ: Erlbaum.

Green, G. M. (1984). *Some remarks on how words mean* (CSR Tech. Rep. No. 307) Champaign: University of Illinois.

Greeno, J. G. (1980). Psychology of learning, 1960–1980: One participant's observations. *American Psychologist, 35,* 713–728.

Grimes, J. E. (1975). *The thread of discourse.* The Hague: Mouton.

Groff, P. (1971). *The syllable: Its nature and pedagogical usefulness.* Portland, OR: Northwest Regional Educational Laboratory.

Halliday, M. A. K. (1975). *Learning how to mean: Explorations in the development of language.* London: Edward Arnold.

Halliday, M. A. K., & Hassan, R. (1976). *Cohesion in English.* London: Longman.

Hammill, D., & McNutt, G. (1981). *The correlates of reading.* Austin, TX: Pro-Ed.

Hansen, J. (1981). The effects of inference training and practice on young children's comprehension. *Reading Research Quarterly, 16,* 391–417.

Hansen, J., & Pearson, P. D. (1983). An instructional study. Improving the inferential comprehension of good and poor fourth-grade readers. *Journal of Educational Psychology, 75,* 821–829.

Haviland, S., & Clark, H. (1974). What's new? Acquiring new information as a process in comprehension. *Journal of Verbal Learning and Verbal Behavior, 13,* 512–521.

Heath, S. B. (1983). *Ways with words: Language, life, and work in communities and classrooms.* Cambridge: Cambridge University Press.

Henderson, L. (1977). Word recognition. In N. S. Sutherland (Ed.). *Tutorial essays in psychology.* Hillsdale, NJ: Erlbaum.

Hildyard, A., & Olson, D. R. (1978). Memory and inference in the comprehension of oral and written discourse. *Discourse Processes, 7,* 91–117.

Hildyard, A., & Olson, D. R. (1982). Forms of comprehension of texts. In W. Otto & S. White (Eds.), *Reading expository material.* New York: Academic Press.

Hilliard, G. H. (1926). Probable types of difficulties underlying low scores in comprehension tests. In C. L. Robbins (Ed.), *University of Iowa studies in education* (Vol. 2). Iowa City: University of Iowa Press.

Huey, E. B. (1968). *The psychology and pedagogy of reading.* Cambridge, MA: MIT Press. (Original work published 1908).

Jeffreys, W. E., Samuels, S. J. (1967). The effect of method of reading training on initial learning and transfer. *Journal of Verbal Learning and Verbal Behavior, 6,* 354–358.

Jenkins, J. R., & Dixon, R. (1983). Vocabulary learning. *Contemporary Educational Psychology, 8,* 237–260.

Jenkins, J. R., Haynes, M., & Stein, M. (1983). An evaluation of instruction on learning word meanings from context in one commercial reading program. Unpublished manuscript, University of Washington, College of Education, Seattle.

Jenkins, J. R., & Pany, D. (1981). Instructional variables in reading comprehension. In J. T. Guthrie (Ed.), *Comprehension and teaching: Research reviews.* Newark, DE: International Reading Association.

Jenkins, J. R., Stein, M. L., & Wysocki, K. (1984). Learning vocabulary through reading. *American Educational Research Journal, 21,* 767–787.

Jensen, A. (1980). *Bias in mental testing.* New York: Free Press.

Jensen, A. (1981). Raising the IQ: The Ramey and Haskins study. *Intelligence, 5,* 29–40.

Johns, J. L. (1984). Students' perceptions of reading: Insights from research and pedagogical implications. In J. Downing & R. Valtin (Eds.), *Language awareness and learning to read.* New York: Springer-Verlag.

Johnson, D. D., & Pearson, P. D. (1984). *Teaching reading vocabulary* (2nd ed.). New York: Holt, Rinehart and Winston.

Jorm, A. F., & Share, D. L. (1983). Phonological recoding and reading acquisition. *Applied Psycholinguistics, 4,* 103–147.

Juel, C. (1980). Comparison of word identification strategies with varying context, word type, and reader skill. *Reading Research Quarterly, 15,* 358–376.

Juel, C. (1983). The development and use of mediated word identification. *Reading Research Quarterly, 18,* 306–327.

Juel, C., & Holmes, B. (1981). Oral and silent reading of sentences. *Reading Research Quarterly, 16,* 545–568.

Just, M. A., & Carpenter, P. A. (1976). Verbal comprehension in instructional situations. In D. Klahr (Ed.), *Cognition and instruction.* Hillsdale, NJ: Erlbaum.

Kagan, J., Rosman, L., Day, D., Albert, J., & Phillips, W. (1964). Information processing in the child: Significance of analytic and reflective attitudes [Special issue]. *Psychological Monographs, 78.*

Kameenui, E. J., Carnine, D. W., & Freschi, R. (1982). Effects of text construction and instructional procedures for teaching word meanings on comprehension and recall. *Reading Research Quarterly, 17,* 367–388.

Kibby, M. W. (1979). The effects of certain instructional conditions and response modes on initial word learning. *Reading Research Quarterly, 15,* 147–171.

Kinneavy J. L. (1971). *A theory of discourse.* Englewood Cliffs, NJ: Prentice-Hall.

Kintsch, W. (1974). *The representation of meaning in memory.* Hillsdale, NJ: Erlbaum.

Kintsch, W. (1979). Concerning the marriage of research and practice in beginning reading instruction. In L. B. Resnick & P. A. Weaver (Eds.), *Theory and practice of early reading.* Hillsdale, NJ: Erlbaum.

Kintsch, W., & Keenan, J. M. (1973). Reading rate as a function of number of propositions in the base structure of sentences. *Cognitive Psychology, 6,* 257–274.

Kintsch, W., & van Dijk, T. A. (1978). Toward a model of text comprehension and production. *Psychological Review, 85,* 363–394.

Kintsch, W., & Yarbrough, J. C. (1982). Role of rhetorical structure in text comprehension. *Journal of Educational Psychology, 74,* 828–834.

Klare, G. R. (1963). *The measurement of readability.* Ames, IA: Iowa State University Press.

lare, G. R. (1974–1975). Assessing readability. *Reading Research Quarterly, 10,* 62–102.

Kleiman, G. M. (1982). *Comparing good and poor readers: A critique of the research* (CSR Tech. Rep. No. 246). Champaign: University of Illinois.

Kohl, H. (1982). *Basic skills: A plan for your child, a program for all children.* Boston: Little, Brown.

Konopak, B. D. (1984). *The effects of text characteristics on word meaning from high school physics texts.* Unpublished doctoral dissertation. University of California, Santa Barbara.

Kroll, B. (1977). Combining ideas in written and spoken English, In E. O. Keenan & T. L. Bennett (Eds.), *Discourse across time and space. Southern California Occasional Papers in Linguistics, 5,* 69–108.

LaBerge, D., & Samuels, S. J. (1974). Toward a theory of automatic information processing in reading. *Cognitive Psychology, 6,* 293–323.

Labov, W. (1978). Gaining acces to the dictionary (A discussion of Miller's paper). In J. F. Kavanaugh & W. Strange (Eds.), *Speech and language in the laboratory, school, and clinic.* Cambridge, MA: MIT Press.

Leinhardt, G., Zigmond, N., & Cooley, W. W. (1981). Reading instruction and its effects. *American Educational Research Journal, 18,* 343–361.

Lesgold, A. M., & Curtis, M. E. (1981). Learning to read words efficiently. In A. M. Lesgold & C. A. Perfetti (Eds.), *Interactive processes in reading.* Hillsdale, NJ: Erlbaum.

Levin, G. (1978). *Prose models* (4th ed.). New York: Harcourt Brace.

Lewis, C. S. (1943). *Out of the silent planet.* New York: Macmillan.

Lewkowicz, N. K. (1980). Phonemic awareness training: What to teach and how to teach it. *Journal of Educational Psychology, 72,* 686–700.

Liberman, A. M., Cooper, F. S., Shankweiler, D. P., & Studdert-Kennedy, M. (1967). Perception of the speech code. *Psychological Review, 74,* 431–461.

Liberman, I. Y., & Shankweiler, D. (1979). Speech, the alphabet, and teaching to read. In L. Resnick & P. Weaver (Eds.), *Theory and practice of early reading* (Vol. 3). Hillsdale, NJ: Erlbaum.

Lindamood, C. H., & Lindamood, P. C. (1969). *Auditory discrimination in depth.* Boston: Teaching Resources.

Litowitz, B. (1977). Learning to make definitions. *Journal of Child Language, 4,* 289–304.

Lodwig, R. R., & Barrett, E. F. (1981). *Words, words, words: Vocabularies and dictionaries* (rev. 2nd ed.). Montclair, NJ: Boynton/Cook.

Luria, A. R. (1976). *Cognitive development: Its cultural and social foundations.* Cambridge, MA: Harvard University Press.

Mandler, J. M., & Johnson, N. S. (1977). Remembrance of things parsed: Story structure and recall. *Cognitive Psychology, 9,* 111–191.

Markham, E. M. (1979). Realizing you don't understand: Elementary school children's awareness of inconsistencies. *Child Development, 50,* 643–655.

Markham, E. M., & Hutchinson, J. E. (1984). Children's sensitivity to constraints on word meaning: Taxonomic versus thematic relations. *Cognitive Psychology, 16,* 1–27.

Marks, C. B., Doctorow, M. J., & Wittrock, M. C. (1974). Word frequency and reading comprehension. *Journal of Educational Research, 67,* 259–262.

Mason, J., & Osborn, J. (1982). *When do children begin "reading to learn"? A survey of classroom reading instruction practices in grades two through five* (CSR Tech. Rep. No. 261). Champaign: University of Illinois.

Masonheimer, P. E., Drum, P. A., & Ehri, L. C. (1984). Does environmental print identification lead children into word reading? *Journal of Reading Behavior, 16,* 257–271.

Mathews, M. M. (1966). *Teaching to read*. Chicago: University of Chicago Press.

Mayer, R. E. (1979). Can advance organizers influence meaningful learning? *Review of Educational Research, 49*, 371–383.

McCusker, L. X., Hillinger, M. L., & Bias, R. G. (1981). Phonological recording and reading. *Psychological Bulletin, 89*, 217–245.

McDonald, F. J., & Elias, P. (1975). *Beginning teacher evaluation study: Phase II, final report* (Vol. 1, Chap. 10). Princeton, NJ: Educational Testing Service.

McKeown, M. G., Beck, I. L., Omanson, R. C., & Perfetti, C. A. (1983). The effects of long-term vocabulary instruction on reading comprehension: A replication. *Journal of Reading Behavior, 15*, 3–18.

McNeill, D. (1968). Production and perception: The view from language. *Ontario Journal of Educational Research, 10*, 181–185.

Meyer, B. J. F. (1975). *The organization of prose and its effects on memory*. Amsterdam: North Holland.

Meyer, B. J. F. (1977). The structure of prose: Effects on learning and memory and implications for educational practice. In R. C. Anderson, R. J. Spiro & W. E. Montague (Eds.), *Schooling and the acquisition of knowledge*. Hillsdale, NJ: Erlbaum.

Meyer, B. J. F. (1985). Prose analysis: Purposes, procedures, and problems. In B. K. Britton & J. B. Black (Eds.), *Understanding expository text*. Hillsdale, NJ: Erlbaum.

Mezynski, K. (1983). Issues concerning the acquisition of knowledge: Effects of vocabulary training on reading comprehension. *Review of Educational Research, 53*, 253–279.

Mikulecky, L. (1982). Job literacy: The relationship between school preparation and workplace actuality. *Reading Research Quarterly, 17*, 400–419.

Miller, G. A., & Johnson-Laird, P. N. (1976). *Language and perception*. Cambridge, MA: Belknap Press.

Miller, J. R., & Kintsch, W. (1980). Readability and recall of short prose passages: A theoretical analysis. *Journal of Experimental Psychology: Human Learning and Memory, 6*, 335–354.

Moeser, S. D. (1976). Inferential reasoning in episodic memory. *Journal of Verbal Learning and Verbal Behavior, 15*, 193–212.

Molloy, J. T. (1982). Remarks made on a talk-show in Los Angeles, CA. (Author of *Dress for success* (1975). New York: Warner Books.)

Murphy, R. T. (1975). *Adult functional reading study. Project: Targeted research and development reading program objectives* (Subparts 1, 2, 3). Princeton, NJ: Educational Testing Service.

Nagy, W. E. & Anderson, R. C. (1984). How many words are there in printed school English? *Reading Research Quarterly, 19*, 304–330.

Nagy, W. E. Herman, P. A., Anderson, R. C. (1985). Learning words from context. *Reading Research Quarterly, 20*, 233–253.

National Assessment of Educational Progress (NAEP) (1981). *Three national assessments of reading: Changes in performance 1970–80* (Rep. No. 11–R–01). Denver, CO: Education Commission of the States.

National Commission on Excellence in Education (1983). *A nation at risk: The imperative for educational reform*. Washington, DC: U.S. Government Printing Office.

Nelson, K. (1978). Semantic development and the development of semantic memory. In K. E. Nelson (Ed.), *Children's language* (Vol. 1). New York: Gardner Press.

Nemko, B. (1984). Context versus isolation: Another look at beginning readers. *Reading Research Quarterly, 19*, 461–467.

Nicol, J. E., Graves, M. F., & Slater, W. H. (1984). Building vocabulary through prefix instruction. Manuscript submitted for publication.

Nist, J. (1966). *A structural history of English*. New York: St. Martin's Press.

Northcutt, N. (1975). Functional literacy for adults. In D. Nielsen & H. Hjelm (Eds.), *Reading and career education: Perspectives on reading* No. 19). Newark, DE: International Reading Association.

Nurss, J. R. (1979). Assessment of readiness. In T. G. Waller & G. E. Mackinnon (Eds.), *Reading research, advances in theory and practice* (Vol. 1). New York: Academic Press.

O'Donnell, R. (1974). Syntactic differences between speech and writing. *American Speech, 49*, 102–110.

Olson, D. R. (1977). From utterance to text: The basis of language in speech and writing. *Harvard Educational Review, 47*, 257–281.

Omanson, R. C., Warren, W. H., & Trabasso, T. (1978). Goals, themes, inferences and memory: A developmental study. *Discourse Processes, 1*, 337–354.

Osborn, J., Wilson, P. T., & Andersen, R. C. (Eds.). (1985). *Reading education: Foundations for a literate America*. Lexington, MA: D. C. Heath.

Palincsar, A. S., & Brown, A. L. (1984). Reciprocal teaching of comprehension-fostering and monitoring activities. *Cognition and Instruction, 1*, 117–175.

Paris, S. G., & Carter, A. Y. (1973). Semantic and constructive aspects of sentence memory in children. *Developmental Psychology, 1*, 109–113.

Patberg, J. A., Graves, M. F., & Stibbe, M. A. (1984). Effects of active teaching and practice in facilitating students' use of context clues. In J. A. Niles & L. A. Harris (Eds.), *Changing perspectives in research in reading/language processing and instruction*. Rochester, NY: National Reading Conference.

Pearson, P. D., Hansen, J., & Gordon, C. (1979). The effect of background knowledge on young children's comprehension of explicit and implicit information. *Journal of Reading Behavior, 11*, 201–210.

Pearson, P. D., & Johnson, D. D. (1978). *Teaching reading comprehension*. New York: Holt, Rinehart and Winston.

Pei, M. (1968). *What's in a word? Language—yesterday, today, and tomorrow*. New York: Hawthorn.

Perfetti, C. A., Goldman, S. R., & Hogaboam, T. W. (1979). Reading skill and the identification of words in discourse context. *Memory and Cognition, 7*, 273–282.

Perfetti, C. A., & Lesgold, A. M. (1979). Coding and comprehension in skilled reading and implications for reading instruction. In L. B. Resnick & P. Weaver (Eds.), *Theory and practice in early reading* (Vol. 1). Hillsdale, NJ: Erlbaum.

Perfetti, C. A., & Roth, S. (1981). Some of the interactive processes in reading and their role in reading skill. A. M. Lesgold & C. A. Perfetti (Eds.), *Interactive processes in reading*. Hillsdale, NJ: Erlbaum.

Pichert, J., & Anderson, R. (1977). Taking different perspectives on a story. *Journal of Educational Psychology, 69*, 309–315.

Pidgeon, D. (1984). Theory and practice in learning to read. In J. Downing & R. Valtin (Eds.), *Language awareness and learning to read*. New York: Springer-Verlag

Piontkowski, D. C. (1981). A structural analysis of classroom processes in beginning reading instruction. Unpublished doctoral dissertation, Stanford University.

Pressley, M., Levin, J. R., & Delaney, H. D. (1982). The mnemonic keyword method. *Review of Educational Research, 52*, 61–91.

Rash, J., Johnson, T. D., & Gleadow, N. (1984). Acquisition and retention of written words by kindergarten children under varying learning conditions. *Reading Research Quarterly, 19*, 452–460.

Read, C. (1975). *Children's categorization of speech sounds in English*. NCTE Research Report No. 17. Urbana, IL: National Council of Teachers of English.

Reid, J. F. (1966). Learning to think about reading. *Educational Research, 9*, 56–62.

Resnick, L. B. (1979). Theories and prescription for early reading instruction. In L. B. Resnick & P. A. Weaver (Eds.), *Theory and practice of early reading* (Vol. 2). Hillsdale, NJ: Erlbaum.

Rickards, J. P., & Hatcher, C. W. (1977–1978). Interspersed meaningful learning questions as semantic cues for poor comprehenders. *Reading Research Quarterly, 13*, 538–553.

Robinson, F. P. (1970). *Effective study* (4th ed.). New York: Harper & Row.

Rosner, J. (1972). *The development and validation of an individualized perceptual skills curriculum*. (Publication 1972/7). Pittsburgh, PA: University of Pittsburgh Learning R&D Center.

Rossmeissl, P. G., & Theios, J. (1982). Identification and pronunciation effects in a verbal reaction time task for words, pseudowords, and letters. *Memory & Cognition, 10*, 443–450.

Roth, K. J., Smith, E. L., & Anderson, C. W. (1984). Verbal patterns of teachers: Comprehension instruction in the content areas. In G. G. Duffy, L. R. Roehler & J. Mason (Eds.), *Comprehension instruction: Perspectives and suggestions*. New York: Longman.

Rothkopf, E. (1982). Adjunct aids and the control of mathemagenic activities during purposeful reading. In W. Otto & S. White (Eds.), *Reading expository material*. New York: Academic Press.

Routh, D. K., & Fox, B. (1984). "M . . . is a little bit of May": Phonemes, reading, and spelling. In K. D. Gadow & I. Bialer (Eds.), *Advances in learning and behavior disabilities* (Vol. 3). Greenwich, CT: JAI.

Ruddell, R. B. (1974). *Reading-language instruction: Innovative practices*. Englewood Cliffs, NJ: Prentice-Hall.

Russell, D. H., & Fea, H. R. (1963). Research on teaching reading. In N. L. Gage (Ed.), *Handbook of research on teaching*. Chicago: Rand McNally.

Rumelhart, D. E. (1975). Notes on a schema for stories. In D. G. Bobrow & A. Collins (Eds.), *Representation and understanding*. Hillsdale, NJ: Erlbaum.

Rumelhart, D. E. (1980). Schemata: The building blocks of cognition. In R. J. Spiro, B. C. Bruce & W. F. Brewer (Eds.), *Theoretical issues in reading comprehension*. Hillsdale, NJ: Erlbaum.

Samuels, S. J. (1979). The method of repeated readings. *The Reading Teacher, 32*, 403–408.

Schallert, D. L. (1976). Improving memory for prose: The relationship between depth of processing and context. *Journal of Verbal Learning and Verbal Behavior, 15*, 621–632.

Schramm, W. (1955). The publishing process in L. J. Cronbach (Ed.), *Text materials in modern education*. Urbana, IL: University of Illinois Press.

Scribner, S., & Cole, M. (1978). Literacy without schooling: Testing for intellectual effects. *Harvard Educational Review, 48*, 448–461.

Scribner, S., & Cole, M. (1981). *The psychology of literacy*. Cambridge, MA: Harvard University Press.

Shanahan, T., Kamil, M. L., & Tobin, A. W. (1982). Cloze as a measure of intersentential comprehension. *Reading Research Quarterly, 17*, 229–255.

Sharon, A. T. (1973–1974). What do adults read? *Reading Research Quarterly, 9*, 148–169.

Sharp, S. L. (1982). *The real reason why Johnny still can't read*. New York: Exposition Press.

Silberman, H. F. (1967). Experimental analysis of a beginning reading skill. In J. P. DeCecco (Ed.), *The psychology of language, thought, and instruction*. New York: Holt, Rinehart and Winston.

Simon, H. A. (1978). Information-processing theory of human problem solving. In W. K. Estes (Ed.), *Handbook of learning and cognitive processes: Human information processing*. (Vol. 5). Hillsdale, NJ: Erlbaum.

Simon, H. A. (1981). *The sciences of the artificial*. (2nd ed.). Cambridge, MA: MIT Press.

Slater, W. H., & Graves, M. F. (1984). *In proving the comprehensibility of expository prose: A comparison and assessment of revisions made by composition instructors, text linguists, popular editors*. Symposium proposal submitted to National Reading Conference for 1984 meeting.

Smith, E. E., & Spoehr, K. T. (1974). The perception of printed English: A theoretical perception. In B. Kantowitz (Ed.), *Human information processing: Tutorials in performance and cognition*. Hillsdale, NJ: Erlbaum.

Smith, F. (1976). Learning to read by reading. *Language Arts, 53*, 297–322.

Smith, F. (1978). *Understanding reading: A psycholinguistic analysis of reading and learning to read* (2nd ed.). New York: Holt, Rinehart and Winston.

Spilich, G. J., Vesonder, G. T., Chiesi, H. L., & Voss, J. F. (1979). Text processing of domain-related information for individuals with high and low domain knowledge. *Journal of Verbal Learning and Verbal Behavior, 18*, 275–290.

Spiro, R. (1977). Remembering information from text: The "state of schema" approach. In R. C. Anderson, R. Spiro & W. Montague (Eds.), *Schooling and the acquisition of knowledge*. Hillsdale, NJ: Erlbaum.

Stallings, J. (1975). Implementation and child effects of teaching practices in Follow Through classrooms. *Monographs of the Society for Research in Child Development, 40*, (Serial No. 163).

Stanovich, K. E., Cunningham, A. E., & Feeman, D. J. (1984). Intelli-gence, cognitive skills, and early reading progress. *Reading Research Quarterly, 19*, 278–303.

Steffensen, M. S., Joag-dev, C., & Anderson, R. E. (1979). A cross-cultural perspective on reading comprehension. *Reading Research Quarterly, 15*, 10–29.

Stein, N. L., & Glenn, C. G. (1979). An analysis of story comprehension in elementary school children. In R. Freedle (Ed.), *New directions in discourse processing*. Norwood, NJ: Ablex.

Sternberg, R. J. (1977). *Intelligence, information processing, and analogical reasoning: The componential analysis of human abilities*. Hillsdale, NJ: Erlbaum.

Sternberg, R. J., & Powell, J. S. (1983). Comprehending verbal comprehensions. *American Psychologist, 8*, 878–893.

Sternberg, R. J., Powell, J. S., & Kaye, D. B. (1983). Teaching vocabulary-building skills: A contextual approach. In A. C. Wilkinson (Ed.), *Classroom computers and cognitive science*. New York: Academic Press.

Sternberg, S. (1969). The discovery of processing stages: Extensions of Donder's method. In W. G. Koster (Ed.), *Attention and performance II*. Amsterdam: North Holland.

Sticht, T. G. (1977). Comprehending reading at work. In M. A. Just & P. A. Carpenter (Eds.), *Cognitive processes in comprehension*. Hillsdale, NJ: Erlbaum.

Sticht, T. G. (1980). *Literacy and vocational competence*. (Columbus, OH, National Center for Research Rep. 2, No. 12). Washington, DC: Department of Labor.

Stratton, R. P., & Nacke, P. L. (1974). The role of vocabulary knowledge in comprehension. In P. L. Nacke (Ed.), *23rd yearbook of the National Reading Conference*. Clemson, SC: National Reading Conference.

Sulzby, E. (1983). A commentary on Ehri's critique of five studies related to letter-name knowledge and learning to read: Broadening the question. In L. M. Gentile, M. L. Kamil & J. S. Blanchard (Eds.), *Reading research revisited*. Columbus, OH: Charles E. Merrill.

Taft, M. (1984). Evidence for an abstract lexical representation of word structure. *Memory & Cognition, 12*, 264–269.

Taylor, J. (1976). The voluntary book-reading habits of secondary school pupils. *The Use of English, 25*, 5–12.

Tchudi, S. N. (1983). A range of views and some concrete proposals regarding the teaching and learning of reading. *Phi Delta Kappan*, June, 742–744 (Books section).

Thorndike, E. L. (1921a). *The teacher's word book*. New York: Teachers College Press.

Thorndike, E. L. (1921b). Word knowledge in the elementary school. *Teachers College Record, 22*, 334–370.

Thorndike, E. L. (1934). Improving the ability to read. *Teachers College Record, 36*, 1–19.

Travers, R. M. W. (1973). *Second handbook of research on teaching*. Chicago: Rand McNally.

Treiman, R., & Baron, J. (1983). Phonemic-analysis training helps children benefit from spelling-sound rules. *Memory & Cognition, 11*, 382–389.

Tunmer, W. E., Pratt, C., & Herriman, M. L. (Eds.). (1984). *Metalinguistic awareness in children: Theory, research, and implications*. New York: Springer-Verlag.

Turner, A. & Greene, E. (1977). *Construction and use of a propositional text space* (Tech. Rep. No. 63). Boulder, CO: Institute for Study of Intellectual Behavior.

Underwood, G., & Thwaites, S. (1982). Automatic phonological coding of unattended printed words. *Memory & Cognition, 10*, 434–442.

U.S. Office of Education (1984). *Digest of education statistics*. Washington, DC: National Center for Education Statistics.

Vacca, R. T., & Vacca, J. L. (1983). Two less than fortunate consequences of reading research in the 1970's. *Reading Research Quarterly, 18*, 382–383.

Valtin, R. (1984). The development of metalinguistic abilities in children learning to read and write. In J. Downing & R. Valtin (Eds.), *Language awareness and learning to read*. New York: Springer-Verlag.

van Dijk, T. A., & Kintsch, W. (1983). *Strategies of discourse comprehension*. New York: Academic Press.

Vellutino, F. R. (1979). *Dyslexia: Theory and research*. Cambridge, MA: MIT Press.

Venezky, R. L. (1970). *The structure of English orthography*. The Hague: Mouton.

Venezky, R. L. (1975). The curious role of letter names in reading instruction. *Visible Language, 9*, 7–23.

Venezky, R. L. (1976). *Theoretical and experimental base for teaching reading*. The Hague: Mouton.

Venezky, R. L. (1977). Research on reading processes: A historical perspective. *American Psychologist, 32*, 339–345.

Venezky, R. L., Green, J., & Leslie, R. (1975). *Evaluation studies of the prereading skills program* (Tech. Rep. No. 311). Madison: University of Wisconsin, R&D Center for Cognitive Learning.

Vernon, M. D. (1957). *Backwardness in reading*. London: Cambridge University Press.

Vygotsky, L. S. (1962). *Thought and language*. Cambridge, MA: MIT Press; New York: Wiley.

Vygotsky, L. S. (1978). *Mind in society: The development of higher psychological processes* (M. Cole, V. John-Steiner, S. Scribner, & E. Souberman, Eds. and Trans.). Cambridge, MA: Harvard University Press.

Wallach, M. A. & Wallach, L. (1976). *The teaching all children to read instructional kit*. Chicago: University of Chicago Press.

Waters, G. S., Seidenberg, M. S., & Bruck, M. (1984). Children's and adults' use of spelling-sound information in three reading tasks. *Memory & Cognition, 12*, 293–305.

Wells, G. (1979). Language, literacy and educational success. *New Education, 1*, 23–34.

Whorf, B. L. (1956). *Language, thought and reality*. Cambridge, MA: MIT Press.

Wijk, A. (1966). *Rules of pronunciation for the English language*. London: Oxford University Press.

Williams, J. P. (1980). Teaching decoding with an emphasis on phoneme analysis and phoneme blending. *Journal of Educational Psychology, 72*, 1-15.

Willows, D. M., & Ryan, E. B. (1981). Differential utilization of syntactic and semantic information by skilled and less skilled readers in the intermediate grades. *Journal of Educational Psychology, 73*, 607–615.

Wittgenstein, L. (1958). *Philosophical investigations* (2nd ed.). New York: Macmillan.

Wittrock, M. C. (1978). The cognitive movement in instruction. *Educational Psychologist, 13*, 25–29.

Wittrock, M. C. (1981). Reading comprehension. In F. J. Pirozzolo & M. C. Wittrock (Eds.), *Neuropsychological and cognitive processes in reading*. New York: Academic Press.

Wittrock, M. C., Marks, C. G., & Doctorow, M. J. (1975). Reading as a generative process. *Journal of Educational Psychology, 67*, 484–489.

29.

Research on Teaching and Learning Mathematics: Two Disciplines of Scientific Inquiry

Thomas A. Romberg
University of Wisconsin–Madison

Thomas P. Carpenter
University of Wisconsin–Madison

No one doubts the importance of mathematics. Of concern, however, is whether students who are currently being taught mathematics in school will have an adequate preparation for the scientific world of the twenty-first century. There is a danger that policymakers and practitioners will respond to the current crisis "without benefit of the carefully collected, sifted, analyzed, and interpreted bodies of knowledge that constitute the stuff of educational scholarship" (Shulman, 1983, p. 485). We need to rethink the content of the school mathematics program, but in doing so we need to take into account implications derived from two disciplines of scientific inquiry. The first comes from research on how students learn mathematics, and the second from research on teaching.

Since the publication of the *Second Handbook of Research on Teaching* over a decade ago, there has been a major shift in the direction of research on students' learning and thinking. A new cognitive science is emerging that is beginning to provide real insight into how students learn mathematical concepts and skills. Similarly, traditional research paradigms for the study of teaching are being challenged, and promising new directions of research on instruction are being developed. Thus, recent research both on students' learning and on teaching is begin-

ning to provide the kinds of knowledge that could significantly shape the design of instruction in mathematics. In this chapter, we attempt to synthesize the most promising directions and the potential contributions of this research. We begin by examining the current state of instruction in mathematics. We do this because, if changes are to be made, we must challenge what is now common practice (Romberg & Price, 1983). Traditional instruction is based on a metaphor of production in which students are seen as "raw material" to be transformed by "skilled technicians" (Kliebard, 1972). The views of learning and teaching upon which this metaphor is based are no longer appropriate. Next, we examine some of the directions taken by current research on children's learning and the potential contribution of that research for making decisions about mathematics instruction. Following the section on children's learning, we synthesize recent research on teaching mathematics, focusing on both conceptual issues and major findings. From the analyses of research from both disciplines, we challenge the assumptions upon which traditional schooling is based and conclude with a general discussion of the directions that we think research in mathematics education should take in the future.

The authors thank reviewers Robbie Case (Ontario Institute for Studies in Education), Douglas McLeod (San Diego State University), and Robert Seigler (Carnegie-Mellon University). Preparation of this paper was supported in part by the Wisconsin Center for Education Research which is supported in part by a grant from the National Institute of Education (Grant No. NIE-G-81-0009). The opinions expressed in this paper do not necessarily reflect the position, policy, or endorsement of the National Institute of Education. The opinions expressed are those of the authors.

The Current State of Mathematics Instruction

In 1975, the National Advisory Committee on Mathematical Education (NACOME) commissioned a study of elementary school mathematics instruction. The picture drawn from this survey is as follows (Conference Board of Mathematical Sciences, 1975):

> The "median" classroom is self-contained. The mathematics period is about 43 minutes long, and about half of this time is written work. A single text is used in whole-class instruction. The text is followed fairly closely, but students are likely to read at most one or two pages out of five pages of textual materials other than problems. It seems likely that the text, at least as far as the students are concerned, is primarily a source of problem lists. Teachers are essentially teaching the same way they were taught in school. Almost none of the concepts, methods, or big ideas of modern mathematics programs have appeared in this median classroom. (p. 77)

Additional evidence comes from three studies commissioned by the National Science Foundation. The studies included a national survey of current practices (Weiss, 1978), a review of literature (Suydam & Osborne, 1977), and a set of case studies (Stake & Easley, 1978). A synthesis of all three studies was prepared by a committee of the National Council of Teachers of Mathematics (Fey, 1979a, 1979b). While the profile and interpretation of mathematics teaching that emerges from these studies is neither simple nor consistent, the predominant pattern is "extensive teacher-directed explanation and questioning followed by student seatwork on paper-and-pencil assignments" (Fey, 1979a, p. 494).

The following remarks from one of the National Science Foundation (NSF) case studies of mathematics teaching are typical (Welch, 1978):

> In all math classes I visited, the sequence of activities was the same. First, answers were given for the previous day's assignment. The more difficult problems were worked by the teacher or a student at the chalkboard. A brief explanation, sometimes none at all, was given of the new material, and problems were assigned for the next day. The remainder of the class was devoted to working on the homework while the teacher moved about the room answering questions. The most noticeable thing about math classes was the repetition of this routine. (p. 6)

There are three serious limitations of mathematics instruction as just characterized.

First, mathematics is assumed to be a static bounded discipline. The emphasis is on teaching the concepts and skills associated with aspects of this discipline. This traditional view of mathematics perceives that there is a lot to teach. This massive "record of knowledge, independent of its place as an outcome of inquiry and a resource in further inquiry, is taken to be knowledge" (Dewey, 1916, pp. 186–187). For schools, the consequences of this traditional view of mathematics are that mathematics is divorced from science and other disciplines and then separated into subjects such as arithmetic, algebra, geometry, trigonometry, and so on. Within each subject, ideas are selected, separated, and reformulated into a rational order. This is followed by subdividing each subject into topics, each topic into studies, each study into lessons, and each lesson into specific facts and skills. This fragmentation of mathematics has divorced the subject from reality and from inquiry. Such essential characteristics of mathematics as abstracting, inventing, proving, and applying are often lost.

Second, when the record of knowledge is mistakenly taken to be knowledge, the acquisition of information becomes an end in itself, and students spend their time absorbing what other people have done, rather than in having experiences of their own. Students are treated as pieces of "registering apparatus," which store up information isolated from action and purpose (Dewey, 1916, p. 147). The daily lessons of the traditional classroom are obviously geared to absorption and not inquiry. Yet, current research indicates that acquired knowledge is not simply a collection of concepts and procedural skills filed in long-term memory. Rather, the knowledge is structured by individuals in meaningful ways, which grow and change over time.

Third, the role of teachers in the traditional classroom is managerial or procedural in that (Romberg, 1985):

> their job is to assign lessons to their classes of students, start and stop the lessons according to some schedule, explain the rules and procedures of each lesson, judge the action of the students during the lesson, and maintain order and control throughout. (p. 5)

Furthermore, the individual lessons are selected by teachers to cover an aspect of a concept or skill within a given time slot. In practice, however, teachers' decisions about what to select are often limited, in spite of apparent latitude to arrange schedules and select activities. In most schools, the mathematical concepts and skills to be taught are provided for teachers via a curriculum guide; a syllabus; or, most often, a textbook. Such materials rarely give teachers many alternatives. In this traditional classroom, the teacher's job is related neither to a conception of mathematical knowledge to be transmitted nor to an understanding of how learning occurs.

Research on Mathematics Learning

The question of how knowledge about children's learning should influence instructional practice has been a matter of debate for some time. Learning theorists like Thorndike (1922) and Skinner (1968) have argued that instruction should be based directly on theories of learning, and programs of instruction have been implemented based on their theories. On the other hand researchers on teaching like Gage (1964) have argued that learning theories have little or nothing to contribute to theories of instruction.

Although the emphasis in research on learning has changed dramatically in the last 15 years, the connection between theories of instruction and theories of learning remains an issue (Schrag, 1981). There have been attempts to draw instructional implications from recent research in cognitive science (Glaser, 1978; Klahr, 1976; Resnick, 1981a, 1983; Resnick & Ford, 1981), but most of the implications are still in the potential stage, and much of the research directly addressing questions of instruction has remained untouched by the revolution in cognitive science.

Glaser (1976a, 1976b) argued that a primary reason for the lack of success in applying theories of learning to theories of instruction is that learning theories are descriptive whereas theories of instruction are necessarily prescriptive. Learning theories describe how children learn or think; instructional theories attempt to draw conclusions about how instruction should be carried out. Glaser argued that prescriptive theories do not follow directly from descriptive theories and that research is needed to build the connection. However, although prescriptions for instruction may not follow immediately from basic research on learning or cognition, some parameters for theories of instruction are provided. Theories of instruction need to be consistent with what we know about how children learn and think.

Research on teaching is based upon a variety of assumptions, whether they are made explicit or not, about the nature of children's learning. Much of the current research on teaching makes implicit assumptions about children's learning that are not consistent with current cognitive theories of learning. We propose that a much closer integration of research on learning and research on teaching is needed. We do not suggest that such an integration is a panacea. Current learning research provides relatively little insight regarding many central problems of instruction. But research is beginning to provide a perspective on how children learn mathematics that must be reflected in research on teaching if we are going to provide an accurate picture of instruction.

In this section we examine the potential implications of current research on children's acquisition of mathematical concepts and skills for research on instruction in mathematics. We begin by characterizing recent research on children's acquisition of mathematical concepts and skills. It is not our purpose to provide a comprehensive review of this research. The research is too extensive to do justice to in the space available, and several recently published volumes provide detailed syntheses of current research in this area (Carpenter, Moser, & Romberg, 1982; Ginsburg, 1983; Lesh & Landau, 1983; Lester, 1982; Resnick & Ford, 1981; Shumway, 1980).

Cognitive Learning Theory

BACKGROUND

Some of the earliest attempts to apply learning theory have involved instruction in mathematics. In the 1920s, Thorndike's theories significantly influenced the design of the elementary arithmetic curriculum. The theories of Thorndike and more recent behaviorists generally failed, however, to account for the structure of the discipline of mathematics. Instruction based on behaviorist principles tended to fragment the curriculum into a number of isolated parts that could be learned through appropriate reinforcement. (See Cronbach & Suppes, 1969, for a discussion of the development of arithmetic programs based on the work of Thorndike; Becker & Carnine, 1980, provide an example of a more recent application of behaviorist principles.)

Initial attempts to apply behaviorism to instruction were opposed by Brownell (1935) and others, who argued that effective instruction in mathematics needed to be grounded in understanding of basic concepts of mathematics. However, although Brownell provided examples of how to teach specific skills for understanding, he did not develop a comprehensive theory that could specify criteria for developing instruction to further understanding. The principles of Gestalt psychology were also consistent with the idea that instruction should be based on understanding, but that theory also provided little direct guidance regarding the design instruction to promote understanding.

In the 1960s several theories of learning and development emerged that promised to provide a more direct link between learning theory and the teaching of mathematics. The theories of Ausubel (1968), Bruner (1960, 1966), and Gagné (1965) focused explicitly on the structure of the content to be learned. From a different perspective, Piaget (Piaget, 1952; Piaget & Inhelder, 1956; Piaget, Inhelder, & Szeminska, 1960) proposed a theory of development of the foundations of basic number, measurement, and geometry concepts. (See Shulman, 1970, for an excellent discussion of the relation between these different theories and their implications for instruction.)

Although Piaget was not explicitly concerned with problems of instruction and did not directly study the development of mathematics concepts and skills that traditionally have been in the mainstream of the mathematics curriculum, the logical operations that he described seemed on face value to underly much of the basic mathematics taught in the primary grades. Constructs such as conservation, transitivity, and class inclusion appeared to be prerequisites for understanding most basic number and measurement concepts. A number of studies attempted to empirically establish how Piagetian logical operations were related to the learning of basic mathematics concepts (Carpenter, 1980; Hiebert & Carpenter, 1982). Although performance on Piagetian tasks has consistently been found to be correlated with arithmetic achievement, Piagetian logical operations have generally not proved helpful in explaining children's ability to learn most basic mathematics concepts and skills (Hiebert & Carpenter, 1982).

The theories of Ausubel, Bruner, and Gagné could be applied more directly to the curriculum than could Piaget's theories. Although Ausubel's and Bruner's positions were probably more congruent with the current theoretical orientation than Gagné's initial neo-behaviorism, it was Gagné who provided the clearest specification of how the mathematics curriculum could be analyzed and researched (Case & Bereiter, 1982). Gagné's task analysis provided a framework for systematically organizing a content domain into a hierarchy of principles, concepts, and skills. Task analysis was used in the design of several elementary mathematics projects, including Individually Prescribed Instruction (Lindvall & Bolven, 1967) and Developing Mathematical Processes (Romberg, Harvey, Moser, & Montgomery, 1974, 1975, 1976); and the careful specification of relationships between different principles, concepts, and skills is reflected in present analyses of mathematics content. The narrow focus on observable behavioral objectives proved too limiting, however, and the emphasis has shifted so that internal cognitive processes are acknowledged. Rational task analysis, which is based on a logical analysis by experts, has evolved to empirical task analysis, which focuses on what children actually do when they solve mathematics problems.

INFORMATION PROCESSING

In the 1970s, a new approach to the study of human thinking began to gain widespread support: information processing. (See Lachman, Lachman, & Butterfield, 1979; Siegler, 1981; or Simon, 1979 for a more detailed discussion of information processing.) It is difficult to precisely define information processing, and there are significant distinctions between different information-processing approaches. What they have in common is that they describe thought processes in terms of symbol manipulation (Siegler, 1982), they focus on the processing and representation of information, and they attempt to achieve a high degree of precision in describing cognition.

Most information-processing approaches share certain assumptions about the architecture of the information-processing system. It is generally assumed that there are three structural levels of the system: a sensory or intake register, a working memory, and a long-term memory. All information enters the system through the sensory register, but it can only be held there a short period of time. To remain in the system, information must enter the working memory, where it can be combined with information from the long-term memory. All operations on information occur in the working memory. In other words, this is where conscious thinking occurs. The constraint on the working memory is that it is extremely limited in capacity and can only attend to a few chunks of information at a time. The long-term memory is potentially unlimited in capacity and contains all the information that one knows. The limitation on the long-term memory is the problem of accessing information stored there. In addition to these basic structural features of the system, most information-processing approaches assume the existence of executive or control processes that monitor the operation of the system. These include routines like rehearsal strategies for storing information in long-term memory or possibly general heuristics for problem solving.

Information-processing theories can be divided into two broad classes: those concerned explicitly with the nature of the information-processing system and those that examine how the information-processing system operates in particular situations (Siegler, 1983). The second category of research appears to have the greatest potential for understanding how mathematics is learned. Rather than build their theories on simple laboratory tasks as the behaviorists did, information-processing researchers have been concerned with more complex cognitive operations. This has made it an ideal approach for studying mathematics learning, and much of the research has focused on basic mathematics concepts and skills.

The Learning of Mathematics

The early work of Brownell (1935) and some of the problem-solving research of the Gestalt psychologists (Resnick & Ford, 1981) foreshadowed the cognitive orientation of current research on mathematics learning. But in the last 10 years, this perspective has been reinforced by the dramatic shift in basic psychological research on learning, and the focus on cognitive processes has become more prominent in mathematics education research. Wittrock (1974) was one of the first to point out

the broad implications of the developing field of cognitive science for research in mathematics education. The principles he outlined still characterize much of this research. Although not all current research on children's learning of mathematics falls directly within a broadly defined domain of information processing, much of the most promising work shares a common orientation with the information-processing approach. Two prominent features of this work are the focus on the processes that children use in doing mathematics and a careful analysis of the specific domain in which the research is conducted.

The following examples provide a perspective on different approaches to studying the learning of mathematics and some of the ways in which this research might affect instruction in mathematics. The examples are illustrative and do not constitute a comprehensive review of research in this area. The examples are selected from areas in which there exists a substantial body of supporting research, but a number of other examples could have been selected as well. Each example provides a different perspective with potentially different kinds of insight regarding instructional implications.

Invention and Stages of Development in Learning Addition and Subtraction

One of the basic assumptions underlying much current research is that children actively construct knowledge for themselves through interaction with the environment and reorganization of their own mental constructs (Steffe, vonGlasersfeld, Richards, & Cobb, 1983). Although instruction clearly affects what children learn, it does not determine it. Children are not passive recipients of knowledge; they interpret it, put structure into it, and assimilate it in light of their own mental framework (Wittrock, 1974). There is a growing body of research that suggests that children invent a great deal of their own mathematics (Resnick, 1976) and that they come to school with well developed informal systems of mathematics (Ginsburg, 1977). Some of the best examples of children's invention come from research on children's addition and subtraction strategies.

One paradigm for studying children's cognitive processes is chronometric analysis. This approach involves breaking operations down into a series of discrete steps like counting by ones. It is assumed that the time required to solve a given problem using a particular strategy is a linear function of the number of steps needed to reach the solution. By finding the best fit between response latencies for subjects solving a variety of problems and the regression equations of possible solution strategies, the most appropriate model can be inferred.

Several studies (Groen & Parkman, 1972; Suppes & Groen, 1967) have used chronometric analysis to investigate children's solutions to simple addition problems of the form $a + b = ?$, where a and b are whole numbers less than 10. The performance models used in these studies hypothesize that a mental counter is set to a particular value and incremented in units of 1. Five models hypothesized for addition problems of the form $a + b = ?$ are given in Table 29.1.

It is assumed that the time required to set the counter is independent of the value to which it is set and that each count requires the same amount of time. Thus, for each model the

Table 29.1. Hypothesized Process Models for Addition
($a + b = ?$)

Model	Strategy
ALL	The counter is set to 0, it is incremented by a units, then it is further incremented by b units.
LEFT	The counter is set to a (the left-most number) and it is incremented by b units.
RIGHT	The counter is set to b (the right-most number) and it is incremented by a units.
MAX	The counter is set to the smaller of a and b, and is incremented by the larger.
MIN	The counter is set to the larger of a and b, and is incremented by the smaller.

relative time required to solve different problems can be predicted. For the ALL addition model, the time T required to solve a given problem is represented by the equation:

$$T = k_1 + k_2 (a + b)$$

where k_1 represents the time required to initially set the counter, k_2 represents the time required to increment the counter 1 unit, and a and b are the addends of the problem. The corresponding equation for the MIN model is:

$$T = k_1 + k_2 \text{ MIN } (a, b).$$

The ALL model predicts that the same time is required to solve problems that have the same sum; the larger the sum the more time required. The MIN model predicts that the time required to solve a problem is strictly a function of the smallest addend.

To identify the best fitting model, predicted latencies are compared to the latencies observed for children solving a number of different problems. With younger children, only two models fit the data, the ALL model and MIN model. Of the two models, the MIN model provides the best fit with the data (Suppes & Groen, 1967). With the older subjects, the MIN model has consistently been found to best represent the patterns of observed latencies (Groen & Parkman, 1972).

The MIN model is more efficient than the ALL model and requires a better understanding of the addition operation (Fuson, 1982). However, the strategy is not generally taught or even encouraged in most elementary mathematics programs. This suggests that the strategy is invented by the children themselves. Further evidence that the MIN model is invented is provided by Groen and Resnick (1977), who carefully controlled the instruction of a group of kindergarten children. In spite of the fact that instruction was based exclusively on the ALL model, the responses of a number of children were best fit by the MIN model.

Similar findings have been reported for children's solutions to simple addition and subtraction word problems (Carpenter & Moser, 1983; Riley, Greeno, & Heller, 1983). The approaches that have been most commonly employed to assess the processes that children use to solve word problems are individual clinical interviews and the analysis of errors. In clinical studies of children's solutions of simple addition and subtraction problems, the interviewer can often infer the strategy a child is

using by observing the child's actions with objects or fingers and watching how the child counts. For less overt solutions, the interviewer must rely on the child's explanation of how the problem was solved or upon think-aloud protocols. The analysis of errors is based on the assumption that certain strategies will result in specific patterns of errors for different problems. By observing the pattern of errors for a particular child, the general approach that the child is using can be inferred.

This line of research is particularly concerned with distinctions between problems that result in different methods of solution. This has resulted in an analysis of addition and subtraction problems that differentiates between problem types based on semantic differences involving the action or relationships described in the problems (Carpenter & Moser, 1983; Riley et al., 1983). The four subtraction problems in Table 29.2 illustrate the kinds of distinctions drawn between problem types. Although all four problems can be represented by the mathematical sentence $13 - 5 = ?$, they present distinct interpretations of subtraction.

The first problem describes the action of removing a subset of a given set. The second, describing an additive change action, has as its unknown the size of that change. The third problem involves the comparison of two distinct sets, and the fourth is a static situation in which one of two parts of a known whole must be found. Altogether, there are six basic semantic problem types (Carpenter & Moser, 1982). For each semantic problem type, three distinct problems can be generated by varying which quantity is unknown. For example, the Separate problem in Table 29.2 could be altered as follows to produce a parallel addition problem: "Tom had some candies. He gave 5 candies to his sister Connie. If he has 8 candies left, how many candies did he have to start with?"

As with the symbolic addition problems, children initially solve word problems by counting. For subtraction problems, the strategies that children tend to use reflect the structure of the problem. The youngest children attempt to directly represent the action of relationship described in the problem using physical objects or fingers. To solve the Separate problem in Table 29.2, they make a set of 13 objects, remove 5, and count the remaining objects to find the answer. On the other hand, the Join/Missing Addend problem (Table 29.2) is solved by initially making a set of 5 objects and incrementing it until there is a total of 13 objects. The answer is found by counting the objects

Table 29.2. Classes of Subtraction Word Problems

Problem Type	Example Problem
Separate	Tom has 13 marbles. He gave 5 marbles to his sister Connie. How many marbles does Tom have left?
Join/Missing Addend	Tom had 5 marbles. His sister Connie gave him some more marbles. Now Tom has 13 marbles. How many marbles did Connie give to him?
Compare	Tom has 5 marbles. His sister Connie has 13 marbles. How many more marbles does Connie have than Tom?
Combine	There are 13 marbles in the bag. Five of them are red and the rest are blue. How many blue marbles are in the bag?

added to the initial set. The Compare problem in Table 29.2 generates a third method of solution. In this case, children tend to make two sets, put them in one-to-one correspondence, and count the unmatched objects.

The ultimate goal of the research is not just to describe different strategies that children use. The objective is to clearly describe the development of addition and subtraction concepts and skills and build models that specify the knowledge necessary for performance at each stage of development.

In the earliest stage, children can only solve problems that they can model directly with physical objects. They are unable to solve a problem like the following, in which the initial quantity is unknown, because it is impossible to represent the action in the problem except by trial and error: "John had some marbles. He lost 8 of them. Then he had 5 left. How many marbles did he have to start with?"

Children progress from this initial stage along two dimensions: They begin to adopt more abstract versions of their modeling, and they become more able to choose strategies that are not direct representations of the semantic structure of the problem. The abstract extensions of the modeling strategies are similar to the MIN strategy described for symbolic addition problems. To solve the Join/Missing Addend problem, a child at this level recognizes that it is not necessary to construct the initial set of 5 objects and simply starts counting at 5 and counts to 13, usually keeping track of the number of counts on his or her fingers. The Separate problem is represented by counting backward from 13.

The most explicit analyses of the knowledge and skills required to solve addition and subtraction word problems is provided by two computer simulation models developed by Riley et al. (1983) and Briars and Larkin (1984). The reason that computer models are generated is that human thinking is extremely complex. For even straightforward tasks like solving simple word problems, there are a number of rules that interact in a variety of ways. If a task is broken down into basic elements, it is almost impossible to chart the sequence of actions without a computer. Constructing a computer model forces one to be extremely precise, which exposes the limits of our knowledge and theories.

The two models are based on similar analyses of performance, but somewhat different characterizations of knowledge at each stage of problem solving. Riley et al., (1983) identified three basic levels of knowledge involved in problem solving: (1) problem schemata, (2) action schemata, and (3) strategic knowledge for planning solutions to problems. There are three basic problem schemata: one for Join and Separate problems, one for Combine problems, and one for Compare problems. Problems are represented as semantic networks that specify the relations between elements in the problem. Children at more advanced levels have richer problem schemata that integrate more elements of a given problem. Action schemata relate the knowledge represented in the semantic networks to the actual problem-solving procedures. These schemata essentially correspond to children's modeling and counting solution processes. Strategic knowledge is organized to permit top-down planning. When a problem is given, a goal is set. If the initial goal cannot be satisfied, subgoals are set. This process of setting goals and subgoals continues until the problem is solved.

Riley et al. (1983) identified three levels of skill for solving Change problems, and a computer simulation model was constructed for each level. Children in Level 1 are limited to external representations of problem situations using physical objects. They can solve simple addition problems and Separate subtraction problems by directly modeling the problems with counters. They cannot solve Missing Addend problems because they have no way to keep track of the double role played by some elements in the direct modeling solution.

The major advance of Level 2 over Level 1 is that it includes a schema that makes it possible to keep a mental record of the role of each piece of data in the problem. This allows children in Level 2 to solve Missing Addend problems. Level 2 children can also solve addition problems by counting on from the first number (LEFT), but they are still limited to direct representation of problem action and are unable to solve problems in which the initial quantity is unknown, because the initial set cannot be represented.

Level 3 includes a schema for representing part-whole relations that allows children to proceed in a top-down direction in order to construct a representation of the relationships among all the pieces of information in the problem before solving it. This frees children from relying on solutions that directly represent the action of the problem. Level 3 children can solve all basic addition and subtraction problems. The flexibility also allows children to count on from the larger number (MIN) to solve addition problems.

The model proposed by Briars and Larkin (1984) hypothesizes the same three levels of performance. Although the details differ, both models predict essentially the same set of cognitive mechanisms governing the first two levels. At Level 3, however, there are some fundamental differences between the models. Although both models predict the same responses for all problems, they attribute the responses to different knowledge structures. Briars and Larkin hypothesized that two schemata are required to represent problems in Level 3. There is a subset-equivalence schema, which is similar to Riley's part-whole schema, but it is more limited in its application. It allows children to interchange subsets, which provide the basis for the MIN strategy and for solving Join problems with the initial quantity unknown, but it does not provide a means for solving Separate problems with the initial quantity unknown. These solutions require a time-reversal schema, which allows joining and separating actions to be reversed in time.

IMPLICATIONS FOR INSTRUCTION

The research on addition and subtraction suggests that the current primary mathematics curriculum fails to capitalize on the rich informal mathematics that children bring to instruction. Children's invented strategies for solving addition and subtraction problems are frequently more efficient and more conceptually based than the mechanical procedures included in many mathematics programs. The research suggests that it is not necessary to defer instruction on word problems until computational skills have been mastered and that word problems can be more completely integrated into the curriculum than is currently the case. In fact, it has been proposed that word problems should be used as a basis for developing addition and subtraction concepts, rather than teaching computational skills first and then applying them to solve problems (Carpenter & Moser, 1983).

When word problems are introduced, instruction often fails to capitalize on children's natural problem-solving abilities. The semantic analysis of problems that children spontaneously use provides a much better basis to develop problem-solving skills than many of the techniques that are taught, which are based on surface characteristics of problems, such as looking for key words that are related to specific operations.

Case (1983; Case & Bereiter, 1982) argued that instruction should not only build upon the concepts and skills with which children start out; it should explicitly move children through successive stages in the development of those concepts and skills. The research on addition and subtraction has identified a progression of concepts and skills that is generally not reflected in instruction. Most instruction jumps directly from the characterization of addition and subtraction using simple physical models to the memorization of number facts, not acknowledging that there is an extended period during which children count on (MIN) and count back to solve addition and subtraction problems. Similarly, there generally is no explicit attempt to further the development of part-whole schema or other representations that are critical for analyzing more complex word problems.

There is some evidence that instruction based on these principles can be effective. Fuson (1982) has analyzed the subskills involved in counting on (MIN) and has demonstrated that direct instruction on these subskills is sufficient to teach children to count on (Secada, Fuson, & Hall, 1983), and a program that teaches children to diagram part–whole relationships has been reasonably successful in teaching children to solve word problems (Kouba & Moser, 1979).

Although there has been some success in teaching specific concepts and skills, it has not been established that instruction should necessarily reflect the natural development of concepts and skills. Exactly how instruction should be sequenced to build on children's informal mathematical knowledge is still an open question. However, the research describing children's strategies provides some insights into possible alternative instructional sequences. Furthermore, it makes available a powerful tool for evaluating children's progress at each point in the sequence.

The Analysis of Errors: Buggy Algorithms

Another approach to the analysis of errors is illustrated by the work of John Seeley Brown and associates (Brown & Burton, 1978; Brown & VanLehn, 1980, 1982; VanLehn, 1983). They argue that many errors are rule governed. They result not from failing to learn a particular algorithm, but from learning the wrong algorithm. For the subtraction algorithm, the most prevalent error of this type is subtracting the smaller digit from the larger. A number of other incorrect or "buggy" algorithms can be identified that involve the systematic misapplication of specific procedures within the subtraction algorithm (Table 29.3).

Table 29.3. Examples of Common Bugs

Computing Error	Example
Smaller-From-Larger	$\begin{array}{r} 207 \\ -169 \\ \hline 162 \end{array}$
Zero-Instead-of-Borrow	$\begin{array}{r} 207 \\ -169 \\ \hline 100 \end{array}$
Smaller-From-Larger-Instead-of-Borrow-From-Zero	$\begin{array}{r} 207 \\ -169 \\ \hline 42 \end{array}$
Zero-Instead-of-Borrow-From-Zero	$\begin{array}{r} 207 \\ -169 \\ \hline 40 \end{array}$

Note. Adopted from "On the Representation of Procedures in Repair Theory" by K. VanLehn in *The Development of Mathematical Thinking* (pp. 205, 206), edited by H. Ginsburg, 1983, New York: Academic Press. Copyright 1983 by Academic Press. Reprinted by permission.

It is not Brown and his colleagues' purpose, however, to simply identify common buggy algorithms. Their goal is to develop a generative theory of bugs that can account for how bugs are acquired. They hypothesize that bugs occur when students are confronted with problems for which the algorithms they have learned are inadequate. To resolve this impasse, they modify their existing algorithm to fit the new problem situation. If their algorithm is strictly a set of meaningless skills, their modifications or repairs often result in a buggy algorithm.

Brown and colleagues start by decomposing a skill like subtraction into its primitive elements. This may be expressed as a list or as a network of rules. By deleting one of the rules or procedures, they model the situation of a student who has forgotten or failed to learn a specific procedure. This results in an impasse that the model attempts to repair by applying one of a number of repair rules, resulting in a bug. The model also includes a set of critics that keeps it from generating bugs that never occur in practice. An example of a critic is "do not leave a blank in the middle of an answer."

Using a set of nine core procedures and four repair rules, the model generates about one-fourth of all bugs empirically identified in children's solutions to multidigit subtraction problems (Brown & VanLehn, 1980). With a somewhat less restrictive set of core procedures, almost half of the observed subtraction bugs can be generated. Although the analysis that Brown and associates have conducted focused on the subtraction algorithm, they believe that the basic theory is generalizable and applies to the acquisition of bugs in any domain. Matz (1980) has developed a similar theory to account for the acquisition of buggy procedures in algebra.

IMPLICATIONS FOR INSTRUCTION

The theory of bugs might be applied to instruction in several ways. One obvious application involves the diagnosis and remediation of students' errors. The theory provides a much clearer specification of buggy algorithms and the underlying source of bugs than is provided by other analyses of students' errors (Ashlock, 1976; Reisman, 1978). This has made it possible to construct diagnostic tests that can distinguish different bugs. In fact, Brown and colleagues have generated a minimum set of exercises that is needed to distinguish all identified bugs. Brown's analysis also makes it possible to identify the specific procedural rules that were not available and resulted in the bug. Successful remediations could focus on the acquisition of those rules. Furthermore, the theory provides a language for analyzing bugs and discussing them with the children using them. Without such a precise formulation, it is often difficult to communicate to children the reasons for their errors, even after a systematic error has been identified.

Brown and Burton (1978) have developed a computer program (BUGGY), which they have used to train teachers on the diagnostic potential of their model. The program plays the part of a student with a particular bug. The program provides one example of the bug and then asks the teacher to give it additional problems to identify the bug. When the teacher thinks the bug has been identified, the program makes up problems for the teacher to solve using the bug. Thus, the teacher is given practice both in identifying bugs and constructing appropriate problems to diagnose bugs. Brown and Burton have also used the BUGGY program with seventh- and eighth-grade students. They propose that allowing students to play diagnostician causes them to reflect upon their own procedures and enables them to analyze the underlying causes of their own errors in other areas of mathematics.

In addition to its value for diagnosis and remediation, the theory of bugs also has implications for designing instruction to keep bugs from occurring. Resnick (1982) investigated the effect of an instructional program designed for this purpose. She noted that the bugs identified by Brown and colleagues resulted from a breakdown in procedural rules. She argued that if subtraction procedures could be taught meaningfully at each step so that the students understood the basis for their procedures, then bugs would not occur. She found that students generally understood a great deal of the base 10 number system, but they were unable to correct this knowledge with the procedures they followed to subtract. She designed an instructional program using Dienes base 10 blocks that at each step in the operation produced a mapping between procedural skills and the semantics of subtraction involving the base 10 number system. In a clinical study of three children who had diagnosed buggy algorithms, the procedure was successful in eliminating existing bugs and preventing the formation of new bugs.

The Organization of Knowledge in Memory

Most recent cognitive research in mathematics has focused on the processes that children use to solve certain kinds of problems. Another important area of research deals with the organization of knowledge in long-term memory. It is generally agreed that some sort of structure is imposed on concepts stored in long-term memory (Anderson & Bower, 1973). The particular structure is important because the central problem in remembering is retrieving concepts from long-term memory. If there is a rich structure, concepts will be more accessible and can be accessed in chunks, which allows related concepts to be used more efficiently in problem solving.

The mapping of concepts in long-term memory has been used more widely to study learning in science than in mathematics (Chi, Glaser, & Rees, 1982; Stewart, 1980), but several studies have attempted to describe relationships between concepts in specified areas in mathematics (Geeslin & Shavelson, 1975; Greeno, 1976, 1978). By analyzing verbal protocols of students' problem solutions (Greeno, 1976, 1978), or using word association techniques (Geeslin & Shavelson, 1975), or teaching students to construct concept maps (Stewart, 1980), inferences can be drawn about how individual students organize and think about related concepts. From this analysis a semantic network can be constructed specifying the observed relations between concepts or propositions. These networks provide a basis for formalizing notions of understanding in an area. Greeno (1978) identified three criteria for assessing understanding, based on the structure of these semantic networks: (a) the degree of integration of related concepts, (b) the number of connections made with concepts in other areas, and (c) the correspondence of the semantic network with those proposed by experts in the field. Thus, better understanding and the ability to apply one's concepts and skills comes not from simply knowing more facts but from a better organization of the facts available.

Many studies have been concerned with differences between the ways that novices and experts organize their knowledge (Chase & Simon, 1973; Chi et al., 1982; Larkin, McDermott, Simon & Simon, 1980; Simon & Simon, 1978). Experts tend to organize their knowledge into bigger chunks than novices. Furthermore, the chunks are organized differently. Experts tend to organize knowledge based on higher-order principles, whereas novices store their knowledge in more isolated bits or sort it on the basis of surface characteristics. Chi et al. (1982) concluded that the problem-solving deficiencies of novices can be attributed primarily to limitations in their knowledge base rather than to lack of general problem-solving skills.

In general, it appears that it is important to stress relationships between concepts, especially higher-order relationships that are related to ways the concepts may be used to solve problems. The analysis of conceptual maps constructed by experts in a field provides a framework for organizing instruction to emphasize important correspondences between related concepts, and the analysis of students' conceptual maps provides a means to evaluate their level of understanding of a topic.

General Implications Based on Architectural Features

Although the most direct applications to instruction from recent research on human cognition come from research examining performance in a specific task domain, implications also follow from conclusions about the general nature of human cognition. For example, the generally accepted assumption that information is structured in long-term memory clearly argues against instruction that teaches number facts as associations between unrelated number pairs and their sums or products.

One architectural feature of the human information processor that potentially has significant implications for instruction is the limited capacity of the working memory. A theory of cognitive development was proposed by Pascual-Leone (1970) that attempted to account for observed stages of development in terms of increasing capacity of working memory.

Case (1978b, 1983) has developed a theory of intellectual development that extends Pascual-Leone's initial analysis and specifically addresses problems of instruction (Case, 1975, 1978a, 1978c; Case & Bereiter, 1982). The basic implication of this theory for instruction is that instruction should be designed to not exceed the processing capacity of the learner. This is accomplished by simplifying the structure of the strategy to be taught as much as possible without distorting it and by designing instruction so that the number of new operations introduced at each step is minimized.

Case (1983; Case & Bereiter, 1982) proposed a developmental theory of instructional design based on the following principles.

1. Identify the task to be taught and develop procedures for assessing the strategies that children at different levels of skill use on the task.
2. Use the procedures to assess the strategies used by children at a variety of ages, ranging from children who exhibit the lowest levels of performance to children who are skilled at the task.
3. Arrange the different strategies into a developmental sequence, and devise instruction that recapitulates this sequence. In other words, the instruction is designed to bring students from one level to the next. Particular attention should be given to the increase in working memory capacity at each step.
4. In order to reduce the processing demands of each new procedure, sufficient practice should be provided at each step so that the procedures already learned become automatic.

Instruction based on these principles has been effective in teaching mathematics concepts like ratio and proportion that are often difficult for young children to learn (Case, 1978c, 1983; Case & Bereiter, 1982).

Metacognition and Mathematical Problem Solving

Another line of research with implications for instruction in mathematics proposes that students' complex mathematical behavior cannot be understood strictly in terms of the processes that they use to solve problems or the knowledge they have stored in long-term memory. Schoenfeld (1980, 1983) and Silver (1982) argued that it is necessary to consider metacognitive aspects of performance as well. Metacognition refers to knowledge about one's own thought processes. This includes the monitoring and control of these processes. In almost any problem situation a large number of alternative procedures might be applied at each step of the solution. The general planning and selection of procedures is as critical as the knowledge involved in applying the procedures.

Some of the basic differences between expert and novice problem solvers can be traced to fundamental differences in how they monitor and control their own thinking. For example, experts tend to organize their knowledge based on higher-order principles, whereas novices store their knowledge in more isolated bits or sort it on the basis of surface characteristics (Chi et al., 1982). The way in which the knowledge is stored is almost certainly related to the way the knowledge was encoded when it was learned. In other words, experts try to put structure into information when they learn it; novices do not. Thus, basic differences in learning may be traced to differences in how the learning situation is perceived. There are also fundamental differences in aspects of a problem to which experts and novices attend. Krutetski (1976) and Silver (1979) have found that skilled problem solvers attend primarily to a problem's structure, whereas less-skilled problem solvers attend to surface details of the problem.

Schoenfeld (1983) has identified another basic metacognitive difference between novice and expert problem solvers. Experts have "vigilant managers" that carefully monitor problem-solving performance and strive for efficiency and accuracy. Novices, on the other hand, lack such managers and often waste the knowledge and skills that they do possess. For example, novices may spend almost all the time allocated to a given problem on a calculation that does not bring them any nearer the solution of the problem.

There is evidence that by making students conscious of their own thinking processes, learning can be enhanced. In other words, by explicitly addressing metacognitive aspects of learning and problem solving, students can be taught how to learn more effectively. For example, subjects in simple recall studies significantly increase their learning by simply being instructed to structure the information they are learning in some way (Wittrock, 1974). Schoenfeld (1980) has reported some success in explicitly teaching the managerial skills that he has found lacking in novice problem solvers, and a study by Silver, Branca, and Adams (1980) suggests that instruction that emphasizes the metacognitive aspects of problem solving can be effective in helping students to be more aware of their own thought processes.

The Application of Research on Cognition to Problems of Instruction

The specific examples just cited suggest some generalizations about the kind of instructional issues that may be productively addressed by the current approaches to research on children's learning and problem solving in mathematics. A central consideration that instructional research needs to take into account involves assumptions about the general nature of the learner. The perspective taken by current cognitive approaches assumes that children are not passive learners who simply absorb knowledge. Children come to school with rich informal systems of mathematics. They actively structure incoming information and attempt to fit it into their established cognitive framework. Furthermore, information in long-term memory possesses a definite structure.

Another important issue involves the relation between understanding and skill development. Theories of learning and teaching have often been based on assumptions about whether it is more important to develop understanding or teach skills (Resnick & Ford, 1981). Current research is beginning to provide some perspective on the intricate relationship between understanding and skill development. Research on teaching that is inconsistent with this general perspective on the nature of learning is in danger of providing a distorted perspective of the effects of instruction.

There is also a very different orientation to understanding. In the curriculum of the 1960s, the understanding issue was addressed by the use of very precise language, the clear specification of basic principles like commutativity and associativity, and the reliance on quite formal mathematical justification or proof. The research on children's learning of mathematics indicates that developing understanding needs to take into account how the learner thinks about a problem or concept. Understanding involves fitting information into the learner's existing cognitive framework. This means taking into account the knowledge of the mathematics under consideration that the learner brings to the situation, connecting semantic knowledge and procedural skills, and encouraging integration of related concepts.

In the curriculum reforms of the 1960s, the selection and sequencing of content was based almost exclusively on logical mathematical considerations. The perspective is shifting so that we now realize we must also take into account how the learner thinks about the mathematics and how the mathematics might be used to solve problems. This has lead researchers to think about the different conceptions one may have of particular content areas rather than simply attempting to construct one mathematically consistent system. The analysis of addition and subtraction word problems is one example of this level of analysis (Carpenter & Moser, 1983; Riley et al., 1983), and Kieren's (1975, 1980) analysis of fractions is another.

Most of the implications for instruction discussed in this section deal with content issues — the selection or sequencing of content or the representation of content. The reason for this emphasis is that current cognitive research most directly relates to content issues. Most cognitive research provides a perspective on what children know and how they solve problems at isolated points in time. The structure of children's knowledge and their problem-solving processes can be compared to the content of the curriculum, and inferences made and tested about how to provide the most appropriate match.

Most current theories, however, have very little to say about transitions from one stage to another. In other words, they don't directly address issues of learning. As a consequence, current theories have very little to say about classroom organization or interaction with students. In fact, even issues of how to structure practice and reinforcement, about which classical behaviorist theories had a great deal to say, are not addressed by most current cognitive research. Resnick and Ford (1981) have noted this paucity of research dealing with classical learning theory issues and have suggested that a cognitive theory of learning is needed that takes a broader perspective in addressing issues of learning than is currently the case.

Although research on children's learning of mathematics appears on the surface to have definite implications for the selection and sequencing of content, how instruction should be designed to incorporate these findings is a complex issue. There are a number of ways that instruction might be sequenced to build upon our knowledge of how concepts develop in children. Case (1983; Case & Bereiter, 1982) recommended that instruction be patterned along the lines of the observed stages of development. In other words, lead children through the stages by explicitly teaching the strategies of each succeeding stage. Case has designed successful instructions based on this principle, but other sequences are equally plausible.

An alternative would be to skip the intermediate levels and attempt to teach the most advanced procedures. If the objective is to teach the novice the strategies of the expert, it may be more efficient to directly teach the expert strategies. For example, the counting techniques of the intermediate stage in the development of addition and subtraction are not logically prerequisite for acquiring the addition and subtraction concepts and skills of a mature adult. In fact, other procedures that rely on relations between number facts may result in a better understanding and a more structured organization of number facts in long-term memory than would result from instruction emphasizing counting. Studies by Steinberg (1983) and Thornton (1978) have successfully based instruction on some of the most sophisticated strategies observed in young children's solutions to addition and subtraction problems.

Furthermore, attempting to explicitly teach invented strategies may be difficult. Groen and Resnick (1977) noted that it was difficult to give an adequate explanation of counting-on (MIN) in teaching addition. Besides, even without instruction, children appear to invent most of these strategies for themselves.

We currently know a great deal more about how children learn mathematics than we know about how to apply this knowledge to mathematics instruction. Research is clearly needed to explore how knowledge of children's learning of mathematics can be applied to the design of instruction. The learning research provides a starting point for designing instruction. It also provides extremely powerful tools for evaluating the effects of instruction. This may be the most significant implication that current cognitive research in mathematics has for research on instruction. Erlwanger (1975) has demonstrated that written tests can provide a distorted picture of children's learning and that clinical interview procedures that attempt to assess children's underlying processes and understanding provide insights that are not available using standard testing procedures. For example, the study by Resnick (1982), which bases evaluation on a substantial body of literature describing children's cognitive processes, provides much clearer insights regarding the specific effects of instruction than would otherwise be possible. In the history of science, the availability of more precise measuring instruments has often made possible significant theoretical breakthroughs. Evaluation procedures based on the growing body of research in cognitive psychology potentially provide this kind of opportunity for research on instruction.

The picture of how students learn based on recent research is quite different from that assumed in traditional classrooms. This perspective is that learners construct knowledge, they do not simply absorb what they are told. The research on teaching also provides a different perspective about classrooms.

Research on Mathematics Teaching

As with research on learning, the relationship between research on teaching mathematics and instructional practice is a matter of concern. The central question is: What information from research on teaching can guide improvement in the teaching of mathematics? Most research on teaching has not been directly related to mathematics. Furthermore, most relevant studies have focused on improving traditional mathematics teaching by making it more efficient or effective. Because such studies are based on conceptions of mathematics and learning different from those described in this chapter, even their positive findings may be irrelevant or possibly detrimental (Schrag, 1981). Nevertheless, the research, if examined with caution, does suggest some important teacher behaviors.

In addition, an examination of this past work can warn us of what not to do or emphasize and perhaps suggest methods for future inquiry. To organize this section, we have separated our summary into two sections that reflect the two ideologies or research traditions that dominate research on teaching as described by Bellack (1978). He labeled them *scientific studies* and *field-based studies*.

Scientific Studies of the Teaching of Mathematics

The logic of this line of research has been stated by Gage (1980): "Before we can know what kinds of teaching practices we ought to seek, we need to know what kinds of teaching practices are associated with the kinds of student achievement and attitudes that we want" (p. 1). Thus, the search for teaching procedures that have been demonstrated to be effective in bringing about student learning preoccupies the attention of these scholars.

Since the publication of the *Second Handbook of Research on Teaching* (Travers, 1973), literally hundreds of studies have been done following this empirical strategy. This research on teaching has been summarized by several noted scholars (e.g., Bellack, 1978; Dunkin & Biddle, 1974; Gage, 1977; Medley, 1977; Ornstein & Levine, 1981) and there is even a review of the reviews (Waxman & Walberg, 1982). These general reviews, while important because they portray the fundamental characteristics and findings of this research, do not directly address questions about the teaching of mathematics. They document that most of the research has focused only on the behaviors of teachers during instruction, not on what pupils are doing during instruction or on the content being taught. In the past decade, however, four reviews of research have focused specifically on the teaching of mathematics (Bell, Costello, & Küchemann, 1980; Cooney, 1980; Romberg, Small, & Carnahan, 1979; Suydam & Osborne, 1977). This section draws heavily on those reviews as well as a selection of studies in which mathematics was being taught. There were four conceptual aspects of these studies and seven categories of findings of particular interest.

Conceptual Issues

LACK OF THEORY

The major problem faced by the authors of the four reviews when trying to organize and synthesize past research has been

that the choice of teaching behaviors to study seems haphazard. Some researchers use different labels for the same behavior, or the same label for different behaviors, different coding procedures which yield different frequencies, and on and on. Fenstermacher (1978) argued that this is true because the paradigm "does not incorporate a conception or justification of what is ultimately worth knowing and doing" (p. 175). Also, Winne and Marx (1977) argued that this research on teaching "has been devoid of postulating a reasonable psychological foundation mapping out why certain events of teaching should influence particular learning processes in students which are manifested later in observable behavior such as test responses" (p. 670). The lack of conceptualization in this line of research occurred because the researchers have not dealt with the theoretical assumptions of why the frequency of a particular teaching behavior influences student learning. In fact, this research follows an inductive approach in order to discover relationships. The difficulty of this approach has been documented by Waxman and Walberg (1982) in their summary of reviews of teaching. They organized the findings of 19 reviews into five very general categories of behavior. Even then, they found consistent agreement in only three areas: providing cognitive cues, pupil engagement, and classroom management/climate. Each was positively related to achievement (p. 18). They considered the results "hard won knowledge" about a complex problem. It can be described as extremely disappointing given the amount of time and effort put into this kind of research.

COUNTING FREQUENCIES OF BEHAVIORS

Lacking a substantive theory of teaching, this group of researchers has focused on methodological questions. Following the notions of experimentalism, concern has been on improving research designs, providing better operational definitions of variables, or devising more adequate procedures for counting behaviors and better techniques of statistical analysis. In particular, it has been assumed that teaching practices can be described in terms of the specific observable behaviors of teachers (asking questions, giving feedback, etc.) and the variability in the frequency of such behaviors will be a good indicator of the potency of such practices. The choice and labeling of which behaviors to observe has been made by each researcher.

Initially, only teacher behaviors were coded and then related to pupil performance in studies called "process–product" studies (Dunkin & Biddle, 1974). Recognizing that teachers interact with students during instruction, dyadic interactions were then added to these studies. Finally, in addition to teacher behaviors, the actions of students were observed and coded as well for investigations called "time-on-task" or "direct instruction" studies. In all cases, the basic data-gathering procedure was to hire and train an observer who sat unobtrusively in a classroom and filled out an observational form as teaching was carried out. The data from the form were then either calibrated in terms of actual frequencies of behavior (14 neutral and 3 positive reinforcements were observed in a 30-minute time interval) or in terms of minutes in which the behavior was observed (neutral reinforcement was given in 10 out of 30 minutes). Unfortunately, this reliance on methodological procedures has limited the kinds of problems addressed and the ways they have been conceptualized (Nuthall, 1974; Romberg & Fox, 1976). Who is to say that a large number of questions posed by the teacher is more potent than a single question raised at the "right" moment in an instructional episode?

CONTENT

The ideas about the content to be taught are often ignored or assumed to be outside the scope of inquiry in most research on teaching. Romberg, Small, and Carnahan (1979) located hundreds of studies that assessed the effectiveness of almost every conceivable aspect of teaching behavior, but found few models of instruction that included a content component. Haertel, Walberg, and Weinstein (1983), in their recent review, found eight models that presented holistic conceptions of student learning in the classroom and explicitly contained a "quality of instruction" component. Such a component was usually associated with some discussion of content.

The primary model was proposed by Carroll (1963). He discussed quality of instruction as a factor in determining the amount of time pupils need to spend on a learning task. A second model, Bloom (1976), was derived from Carroll's. Bloom presented four determinants of quality: appropriate use of cues, pupil participation, effective use of reinforcement, and effective use of feedback. While both models address the concept of quality of course content, neither actually addresses the content of a lesson, let alone the mathematical content of a lesson. Only one model, by Harnischfeger and Wiley (1975), included a component called "character of instructional materials." They suggested that the structure of the material to be learned influences task organization, task complexity, pacing, and clarity of instruction. However, the structure of the content to be learned was not specified in any model. As a result Romberg, Small, and Carnahan (1979) proposed a model that considered both the structure of the content units and the way content is segmented and sequenced for instruction.

In summary, most studies of mathematics teaching are too global. As Kilpatrick (1977) argued, we must begin "with careful descriptions of a specified set of teachers teaching a specified set of topics to a specified set of pupils" (p. 98). This approach would take into account the specific content and teaching techniques unique to that content. Brophy (1977), in his reaction to Kilpatrick's position, agreed and went on to state that this strategy would

> not only specify the general kinds of teacher behavior that would be required, but in particular, should specify criteria of quality of appropriateness. This would allow observers to code not merely *what* the teacher was doing, but *how well*. (p. 49)

ASSESSMENT

To operationalize Gage's (1980) notions of achievement and attitudes, the dependent variables in this paradigm, most researchers have used standardized achievement tests. Such tests have serious problems (Berliner, 1976). They rarely reflect what was taught in any one teacher's classroom; when used with young, bilingual, or lower socioeconomic status children, they may yield biased results; and at best, they indicate only the number of correct answers produced by a student, not how a problem was worked. On the whole, off-the-shelf standardized achievement tests make poor dependent variables for studies of teaching. Their use merely compounds the problems when there is a lack of concern for the content being taught.

Tests for special curriculum units have been created by many investigators when studying mathematics teaching (for example, Berliner & Ward, 1974; Montgomery, 1973; Peterson & Janicki, 1979; Romberg & Gilbert, 1972). These are undoubtedly more valid and more reactive to classroom teaching than are standardized tests (for example, see Filby, 1976). However, studying teacher effectiveness with dependent measures tied to special teaching units may not be a fair characterization of teaching over the long haul, because different teachers may not cover the same units during a year. Also, the existing examples of such tests do not capture the learning of such mathematical processes as abstracting, inventing, proving, or applying. Nevertheless, for curriculum units, such tests are preferable to standardized tests.

Multivariate outcomes are another problem. The gain in achievement of the learner is commonly used to measure instructional outcomes. However, once concepts and skills have been achieved, considerable time is spent in most classes attempting to maintain that level of performance. A second dependent variable should be the maintenance of performance. In the same view, a third dependent variable should be "preparation for new concepts and skills" (Romberg, 1979a). This idea grows out of the notion of "savings transfer" (Cronbach, 1965). The learning of some ideas, often of limited importance in their own right, provides a basis for the acquisition of later important concepts and skills.

Finally, as noted in the previous section, recent developments in cognitive psychology are beginning to provide researchers with techniques for measuring processes used to solve problems. These techniques potentially will provide researchers with much more sensitive measures of student outcomes and hence provide a much clearer picture of the specific effects of instruction.

In summary, although student outcomes are indisputably the ultimate dependent variables in research on teaching, researchers need to question what outcomes are to be examined and how data are to be gathered and interpreted. This will be particularly important with respect to the kind of mathematics program we envision.

Major Findings

VARIABILITY

The first important but rarely discussed finding of most of the research on teaching from this perspective is that, regardless of the observational technique or scaling procedure a researcher has used, every day is different in every classroom and that every classroom is different from every other classroom, no matter what behaviors are being coded. It is also true that some behaviors in which there is both high frequency and considerable variability (e.g., percentage of time teachers talk) seem to have little effect on learning, and some happen infrequently (such as teacher structuring) but, when they occur, appear to be very powerful. This variability begins with text material. From an examination of mathematics textbooks, Schwille et al. (1983) concluded:

> Outside whole-number computation, we found substantial variation even at the marginal level of the classification (e.g., variation of emphasis on fractions, number sentences, estimation, and metric measurement). Still more variation could be seen at the specific or cell level. In the three [most widely used at fourth grade] textbooks, for example, over half of the 290 cell-level topics covered (by one or more items in one or more books) were unique to a single book. Only twenty-eight percent of these topics were covered in all three books. (p. 376)

Then, teachers choose to allocate different amounts of time to instruction. The following example is illustrative of this finding. Table 29.4 summarizes data from the Beginning Teacher Evaluation Study (Berliner, 1978) obtained from teachers' logs over an average of 90 days' instruction from October to May of the school year. The entries are number of minutes allocated to various content areas in four fifth-grade classes. The widespread variability is obvious. Classrooms 14 and 18 spent dramatically more time on division than the other two fifth-grade classes. In Classroom 18, fractions were emphasized. Word problems hardly seemed to be of interest to the teachers of Classes 3, 4, and 18 when compared with Class 14.

These differences in the content coverage in classrooms should result in differences in achievement. If these fifth-grade classes were tested on fractions, students in Classroom 18 would probably show superior performance when contrasted to similar students in the other fifth-grade classes.

Table 29.4. Beginning Teacher Evaluation Study: Pupil Time (in minutes) in Content Areas of Mathematics for Four Fifth-Grade Classes

Content Area	Classes			
	3	4	14	18
Computation				
Addition	33	234	95	26
Subtraction	77	205	248	4
Multiplication: Basic facts	40	79	89	142
Multiplication: Speed tests	34	51	8	24
Multiplication: Algorithm	341	910	720	343
Division	243	19	1548	2223
Fractions	54	370	495	2016
Other	0	82	213	0
Concepts/Application				
Computational transfer	49	24	160	147
Numerals/place value (whole number)	0	53	29	0
Word problems	58	3	322	15
Geometry: Perimeter	0	53	73	0
Geometry: Area	0	103	49	0
Geometry: Number pairs	90	40	0	0
Geometry: Lines or figures	418	126	70	280
Other	174	128	1411	68

Note. From "Allocated Time, Engaged Time and Academic Learning Time in Elementary Mathematics Instruction" by D. C. Berliner, 1978, p. 21. Reprinted by permission.

This example also illustrates the problem of using standardized achievement tests. As long as teachers choose the content they emphasize in their classroom, such tests can never be used as fair measures of teacher effectiveness because they evaluate students in areas that the teacher did not cover or emphasize. Even if teachers use the same curricular program, the number of minutes spent on a particular mathematical topic, or spent exploring, or spent with children in small groups varies considerably. For example, Romberg, Stephens, Buchanan, and Steinberg (1983) found that among eight teachers in three comparable schools, an instructional topic varied from 186 to 416 minutes, and time spent in Grade 1 for students to explore relationships varied from 91 to 258 minutes.

This picture of variability in text content, in content emphasis, and in the actions of teachers and pupils on the surface contradicts the stereotype of traditional mathematics teaching presented earlier in this chapter. Part of the reason for this is methodological, in that only constructs upon which classes vary are included in these studies, even if they have little meaning or impact on performance. A second reason is that the unit of scaling (observed behaviors in some component of time) is not totally appropriate. For example, Romberg (1983b), in a recent reanalysis of time-based observational data from 20 classrooms, found that if time spent on an aspect of instruction was adjusted in terms of overall allocated time, a consistent picture was found. The primary difference between classes at each grade level was in terms of total allocated time to mathematics and not what was emphasized. Teachers modified the program by selecting parts to be taught and how much time was then spent on each part. But, the dominant pattern was to emphasize skill development and practice via worksheets, not to select activities that encourage discussion and exploration.

Nevertheless, the existence of variability in teaching practice cannot be denied. There are some teaching behaviors that vary, and altering these behaviors potentially could improve mathematics instruction.

ALLOCATED AND ENGAGED TIME

The second important finding is about "pupil engaged time" in relation to "allocated time." The practical importance of these variables for classroom studies is well-documented (see, Borg, 1979). The wide range of allocated time to specific content areas was shown in Table 29.4. The overall allocated time and engaged time for the same fifth-grade classrooms is shown in Table 29.5. Jones and Romberg (1979) summarized three studies on the teaching of elementary school mathematics: The Beginning Teacher Education Study (BTES) (Fisher et al., 1978); Phase IV (mathematics) of the IGE Evaluation Study (Webb & Romberg, 1979); and the Coordinated Studies in Mathematics (Romberg et al., 1983). They found that "classes in which less time is allocated to mathematics instruction are likely to have relatively poorer achievement in the subject" (p. 60).

This message is clearly supported in all the studies. While there are limits on the amount of time any class teacher can allocate to mathematics instruction, the teacher who consistently devotes less time to mathematics instruction than colleagues can expect relatively poorer student achievement.

Table 29.5. Beginning Teacher Evaluation Study: Allocated and Pupil Engaged Time in Mathematics for Four Fifth-Grade Classes

Time	Classes			
	3	4	14	18
Number of days data collected	73	89	91	93
Average minutes allocated daily	23	28	61	57
Percentage of time students engaged	74	80	80	66
Engaged minutes per day	17	22	49	38

Note. From "Allocated Time, Engaged Time and Academic Learning Time in Elementary Mathematics Instruction" by D. C. Berliner, 1978, p. 21. Reprinted by permission.

Jones and Romberg (1979) also concluded that "Teachers can expect that class engagement and individual pupil engagement will be good indicators of mathematical achievement" (p. 62). Teachers have no doubt used some form of engagement as a built-in evaluation system for a long time. Nevertheless, these studies give the process legitimacy.

These implications about allocated and engaged time are well documented and directly related to elementary school classroom practices in the teaching of mathematics. However, by itself, the notion of engaged time is not meaningful because it is an indirect measure of classroom learning. Romberg (1979b) argued that three aspects of the engaged time need to be considered: content coverage, the episodic nature of instruction, and interactive engagement. Students should be engaged in activities that are reasonable and intentional. Furthermore, lessons and units have an episode structure. Like a story, a unit must have a start, a development, a climax, and a summary. The character of the pupil's engagement should be appropriate to the development of the unit. Finally, to be engaged means to be interacting with ideas. The typology of those interactions is not well-developed.

"Time-on-task" as conventionally studied fails to recognize variability in tasks. Bell et al. (1980) argued that "it is necessary first to distinguish between skills, conceptual structures and general strategies" (p. vi). These distinctions are important because different teaching methods are appropriate for each. Berliner (1983), recognizing that different teaching methods occur, has even developed a taxonomy of classroom activity structures. Unfortunately, he has yet to attempt to tie these activity structures to content or instructional intentions. Thus, the notion of "engaged time," while provocative, is vacuous in many studies.

DEVELOPMENTAL PORTION OF LESSONS

The third finding of this research comes from the Missouri Mathematics Project (Good, Grouws, & Ebmeier, 1983). We consider it to be the best example of an experimental program on mathematics teaching. Beginning with a process–product study of fourth-grade teaching, Good and Grouws (1975) found that the quality of the developmental portion of a lesson differed considerably for good and ineffective teachers. Their definition of this variable is as follows:

> The developmental portion of a mathematics period is that part of a lesson devoted to increasing comprehension of skills, concepts, and other facets of the mathematics curriculum. For example, in the area of skill development, instruction focused on why an algorithm works, how certain skills are interrelated, what properties are characteristic of a given skill, and means of estimating correct answers should be considered part of developmental work. In the area of concept development, developmental activities would include initial instruction designed to help children distinguish the given concept from other concepts. Also included would be the associating of a label with a given concept. Attempts to extend ideas and facilitate transfer of ideas are a part of developmental work. (p. 114)

Although the amount of class time teachers spent on development was very low, there were significant differences on this variable between effective and ineffective teachers. Based on this, an experiment was carried out in 1977 at the fourth-grade level (Good & Grouws, 1977). In this study, the experimental teachers were asked to spend about one half of the mathematics class time (about 20 minutes) on developmental work, and they were to increase student participation in development just prior to the practice portion of the lesson. The achievement gains for the treatment group students were quite dramatic.

Development was also a part of their experimental research in junior high mathematics classrooms. Treatment teachers were again asked to devote a large part of their instructional time to development, and there was the addition of a daily, 10-minute verbal problem-solving component. Again, they found that development was difficult to implement, just as it had been in the fourth-grade study, and treatment teachers varied considerably in amount of development time. However, their mean total development time was considerably more than the total development time for control teachers. This difference was due mainly to the extra time treatment teachers spent on verbal problem solving. The treatment student group performed significantly better than the control group on the problem-solving measure and slightly better on the general mathematics achievement measure.

The ability of a teacher to put new ideas in perspective of past and future ideas for students should help pupil engagement and achievement no matter what mathematics are being taught. Also, it is important to note that this program best illustrates the "descriptive-correlational-experimental loop" held up as the model of scientific inquiry in this line of research (Rosenshine & Furst, 1973). From the program's "atheoretical" beginnings, operational variables were derived by induction from observed data, confirmed as important by correlation, and then validated through experimentation.

INSTRUCTION IN SMALL GROUPS

The fourth important area of research on mathematics teaching from the scientific perspectives differs considerably from those previously described in that a specific aspect of instruction has been examined from a particular perspective. The set of studies is on the social interaction of students and the conditions under which they interact when learning in small groups and cooperative learning environments (Webb, 1982). This research is based on notions from social psychology, notably Deutsch's theory of cooperation and competition (1949). Many of the studies have been done using mathematical topics to be learned under collaborative or competitive situations (e.g., Davidson, 1980; Slavin, 1980; Swing & Peterson, 1982; Webb, 1982).

In general, the findings of this line of research have been that students who studied in cooperative small groups are more cooperative and less competitive than students in control groups; students in the control group seldom cooperate spontaneously; and greater group productivity is related to cooperative small groups. Furthermore, from more recent research we are beginning to understand the complex dynamics of group learning and the linkages between background characteristics, group actions, and learning (Webb, 1980).

TEACHERS' PLANNING AND DECISION MAKING

One important line of research assumes that the teacher behaviors, so carefully documented in the empirical studies, are deliberate. They are the result of purposeful, reflective plans (Yinger, 1978). Thus studies have been carried out associated with the planning process, thinking, and decision making. For example, Carnahan (1980) examined the quality of teachers' written plans with both the organizational and interactive environments in mathematics classrooms. He found that plans consistently focused on large group routines with few references to small groups or individuals (p. 105), and the quality of plans was reflected in classroom organization and clarity of presentation but not in student achievement (p. 140).

Features that influence the judgments of teachers have been examined by several researchers (e.g., Clark & Yinger, 1978). Although subject matter features have been included in such studies, teachers' reactions to mathematics have not been examined. However, in language arts only a very few instances of concern for "meaningfulness of activities" or "integration with other activities" were mentioned (p. 19). One can only guess that it would be no better for mathematics.

Shavelson (1976) and colleagues have applied statistical models of decision theory, in particular, decision making under uncertainty (Luce & Raiffa, 1967), to the actions of teachers. In this approach, it has been assumed that teachers have a number of methods available to help their students attain a goal. Teachers chose a particular strategy in an attempt to achieve a desired outcome by matching events — both within the student and within the classroom — with a particular teaching strategy. These events occur with some probability; thus, the teacher must subjectively estimate the probability of a particular event. Information about alternative teaching strategies, events and their probabilities, and outcomes resulting from pairing a single strategy with a particular event is used to make pedagogical decisions (Borko, Cone, Russo, & Shavelson, 1979).

This approach has proven useful in describing the kinds of decisions made in planning instruction, if there is sufficient time to consider alternative strategies, student characteristics, and the probable outcomes of instructional strategies (Shavelson, 1976). Unfortunately, the studies carried out using this approach have to date been simulation studies conducted in controlled laboratory conditions. The generalizability to normal classroom situations is in doubt because during interactive teaching, teachers undoubtedly are not as aware of their decisions or as deliberate about them. Nevertheless, the decision model has been shown to be important as a heuristic.

Together, these studies demonstrate that teachers' behaviors are influenced by rational and reflective actions. Their plans and what influences their thinking and decision making, however, are not based on considerations of what is to be taught.

TEACHING STRATEGIES

Another line of research holds the view that teaching behavior varies with the nature of the content as well as with the nature of the student. Thus, task variability is assumed. This premise has led to what Henderson (1976) has termed *teachable objects*, that is, those items of knowledge that teachers teach and, it is hoped, students learn. Most of the research is rooted in the notions of Smith and colleagues (Smith, Meux, Coombs, Nuthall, & Precians, 1967) who were interested in the specific teaching behaviors. Research specifically directed toward mathematics teaching following this perspective has been conducted in the Teaching Strategies Project at the University of Georgia (Cooney, 1976).

The set of teachable objects includes mathematical concepts and principles. A concept is a noun-like term whose referent is a set of objects. A principle is either a generalization or else a prescription that applies to a general mathematical procedure. Once mathematical concepts and principles have been identified, one can consider the logical ways in which such content be taught. These ways of acting are referred to as moves and have been classified in various ways (e.g., Cooney, Davis, & Henderson, 1975).

For example, there are two general categories of concept moves: characterization moves and exemplification moves. Characterization moves provide information concerning the general nature of a concept's referent set. Exemplification moves involve the identification of examples and nonexamples, perhaps with justification explaining why an object is or is not an example, and the use of counter examples when a false statement has been made about the concept's referent set (Cooney, 1976, p. 5).

It is claimed that many teachers have an impoverished, inflexible set of moves. Treatment involving extensive discussions and uses of moves and strategies suggests that teachers from such instruction "can generate more ideas on how to teach certain mathematical concepts and principles and can also generate a greater variety of questions to ascertain learning than those teachers not receiving knowledge of moves" (Cooney, 1976, p. 22).

This research program (summarized in Cooney & Bradbard, 1976) differs significantly from other experimental studies in that it begins with considerations of the content to be taught. Also, the assumption that there are different "mathematical objects" which require different teaching strategies seems plausible, no matter what conception of mathematics is held. However, the separation of mathematics into teachable objects, while perhaps more rational than behavioral objectives or rough content categories, still conceives of mathematics as bits of knowledge to be mastered.

The final topic of consideration in this section deals with the extensive research on individual differences and their lack of impact on instruction. There is no question that each individual differs in important ways from every other individual. In fact, Resnick (1981b) has argued that American psychology is based on the assumption "that differences among people are individual rather than social differences" (p. 2). Goodlad (1983) argued that three aspects of individuality should be attended to in curricular practice: developmental differences among learners of the same age; differences in modes or styles of learning; and differences in interests, goals, and life-styles (pp. 300–301). The scientific problem for educators has been to identify interactions of such individual differences with appropriate instructional treatments (Cronbach, 1957). Unfortunately, while we have been very successful in identifying, measuring, and characterizing a variety of differences among individuals, we have not been successful in adapting mathematics instruction to such differences (Cronbach & Snow, 1977; Fennema & Behr, 1980).

The later difficulty, in part, grows out of the limited knowledge of how individual differences are related to how students learn. In the past, most individual differences have been identified using psychometric procedures. For example, scores on the "hidden figures test" are used to identify "field dependence/independence." While there is ample evidence that scores on such tests vary, such variance is a very indirect indicator of how information is actually processed in instructional situations. In fact, individual differences have been identified by interest groups from differential psychology, developmental psychology, sociology, social psychology, and political science (Romberg, 1983a). Claims have been based on different information, and hence different conclusions are reached about how instruction should proceed based on that information. For example, one argument is that instruction should be adapted to "complement" differences. For example, if some students learn at a faster rate, they should be allowed (encouraged) to proceed through a program at a faster pace; or if students differ in spatial ability, activities should be adapted so that students with that ability can utilize it in learning.

A contrasting argument is that instruction on the same mathematical units should be adapted to "compensate" for differences. This is often put forward in terms of social equity. Social, cultural, and even intellectual inequities exist, but the school should not exacerbate the inequities. For example, ability grouping is seen as social class grouping. Thus, differential instruction based on "ability" would only further differentiate social classes.

The difficulty in both arguments is not that the information about differences is invalid, but that the connection between those differences and instruction and learning is unclear. Teachers can and do vary instructional practices. Some aspects of dealing with individual differences have been incorporated into the traditions of some schools. But the question still remains: How can we relate instruction to individual differ-

ences? We believe the answer lies in changing the focus of the question of differences from psychometrically or socially defined differences to differences in how information is processed.

In general, the "scientific" studies related to the teaching of mathematics have failed to provide teachers with a list of tested behaviors that will make them competent teachers and ensure that their students will learn. There are at least four problems with this line of research. First, there has been a failure to take seriously the challenge to identify "the kinds of student achievement and attitudes we want" (Gage, 1980, p. 1). "Residualized mean gain scores" have become methodological proxies for "what we want," and the standardized test has become the operational definition of what is worth knowing.

Second, even when researchers find reasonable variables such as "lesson development," which are demonstrably effective, they are only effective within the traditional conception of teaching. They can only make current teaching more efficient or effective, but they cannot make it radically different.

Third, because there is no theory underlying the causal relationships found, such claims can also only be made within that conception of teaching. Even "lesson development," unlike fertilizer in agricultural research, lacks theoretical justification for its influence on learning. The effects of fertilizer are not justified on split-plot experimental research alone, because its chemical composition actually makes for increased yields. (See Suppes, 1972 for a good discussion of this point.)

Fourth, the promise of relating instruction to individual differences is yet to be fulfilled. In general, teachers fail to consider individuals in their planning of lessons, selection of activities, judgments of responses, and so on.

In one sense, this research reflects the early stages of what Kuhn (1979) called "the route of normal science." In the absence of a paradigm or set of organizing principles, all facts that could possibly pertain to a problem area are likely to seem equally relevant. Although early fact-collecting has been essential to the origin of many significant sciences, one somehow hesitates to call the resulting literature scientific. However, some "hard-won facts" or ideas derived from this perspective are important and need to be kept in mind as new programs are developed.

Field-Based Studies

During the past decade, a number of studies about mathematics teaching have been carried out from a research approach quite different from the "scientific" orientation in the previous section. An examination of the literature of these studies, which Bellack (1978) called field-based studies, reveals two distinguishing features. First, the dominant research styles are those of the new breed of interpretive sociologists, variously calling themselves symbolic interactionists, phenomenologists, and ethnomethodologists. What is common among these studies is the concern with intentionality and the actor's subjective interpretation (or meaning) as the basis for understanding of the social world. Second, the problem of greatest concern in these studies is to gain understanding of teaching from the viewpoint of teachers and students by means of a description of the flow of classroom events as perceived and interpreted by participants (Bellack, 1978, p. 21).

To illustrate this perspective, we use seven studies on the teaching of mathematics which represent a cross section of theoretical positions that guide those who use a field-study approach to the study of schooling: first, a set of 11 case studies in science education directed by Stake and Easley (1978); second, the study of teaching and learning in English primary schools by Berlak, Berlak, Bagenstos, and Mikel (1975); third, a study by Smith and Sendelbach (1979) titled "Teacher Intentions for Science Instruction and Their Antecedents in Program Materials"; fourth, a study on the implementation of an activity based program by Stephens (1982); fifth, Brandau's (1981) paper "The Practices of an Elementary Mathematics Teacher—An Ethnographic Approach to the Study of Problem Solving"; sixth, Anyon's (1981) study "Social Class and School Knowledge"; and finally Donovan's (1983) study of an innovative mathematics program. There are two conceptual aspects of these studies and three findings of particular interest from this perspective.

Conceptual Issues

THEORETICAL ORIENTATIONS

The most significant feature distinguishing these studies from one another is their theoretical orientations. While each may be said to adopt a field-study or ethnographic approach to the study of schooling, how the particular events and actions being studied are interpreted is tied to the theoretical perspective each investigator has adopted.

In the study of classrooms, Stephens (1982) and Donovan (1983) drew upon perspectives from the sociology of knowledge and political theory. Using insights from sociologists such as Mannheim (1952) and Durkheim (1961), each explored the interplay between the institutional and cultural contexts of schooling, the influence of these factors on how the work of teachers and students is defined, and what constitutes mathematical knowledge.

The studies by Berlak et al. (1975) and Brandau (1981), by contrast, pay less attention to social, political, and cultural factors beyond the classroom and depict teachers as actively negotiating for themselves the meaning of classroom events. Both studies describe teachers' classroom behavior in terms of their beliefs and how children learn, and in terms of teachers' beliefs about their own role in children's learning. The theoretical perspective of these two studies is indebted to the theory of symbolic interactionism as articulated by Mead (1934) and Blumer (1969). This interpretative framework treats teachers' actions as components of classroom life, where the classroom itself is perceived as a miniature society in its own right, autonomous, not subject to profound change, and tending toward the harmonious resolution of conflict—as is implied by the metaphors of "dilemma," "tension," "conflict," and "resolution" which Berlak et al. (1975) employ.

The study by Smith and Sendelbach (1979) and the NSF case studies (Stake & Easley, 1978) lie between these two perspec-

tives. While many of their interpretations are in the symbolic interactionism tradition, there is a conscious effort to take us out of classroom to the school and community, but not to the extent of examining classroom actions in terms of wider social and political meanings.

To extend these differences among field studies even further, Anyon's (1981) study "Social Class and School Knowledge" is included. She employs a neo-Marxist perspective to examine the content and methodology of mathematics teaching in five elementary schools.

BEYOND RHETORIC

A common element of each study is that one is trying to penetrate the rhetoric of educational discourse in order to discern a deeper meaning of the events being studied. The term *rhetoric* is used in a nonpejorative sense, to connote commonly accepted ways of describing school events, and refers to those uses of the rhetoric of education that tend to attribute common practices and shared beliefs to schools and teachers. Sometimes, one may use the rhetoric of education to describe a group of schools as all using a specific instructional program. These uses of educational rhetoric exemplify perfectly legitimate ways of referring to certain features in common of the schools being discussed. On other occasions, the rhetoric may refer to less specific elements of school philosophy and practice, when one speaks, for example, of "open" primary schools in the context of English education. However, beneath these common labels there may exist a diversity of belief and practice and a degree of complexity in each, which tends to be obscured by the uses of educational rhetoric.

For example, the major purpose of the study by Berlak et al., (1975) was to penetrate the rhetoric of educational discourse and to ascertain how teachers actually define their own work and that of students. They examined several "informal" primary schools in England. The rhetoric of open education depicted these schools as places where children tended to make decisions about what should be learned, where children did not rely on extrinsic motivation from their teacher in carrying out their work, and where they tended also to set their own standards. They noted, however, many contradictions. Accordingly, they became increasingly certain that whatever accounted for teachers' behavior, it was not the beliefs attributed to them by the proponents of open education (Berlak et al., 1975).

Smith and Sendelbach (1979) in their study "Teacher Intentions for Science Instruction and Their Antecedents in Program Materials" focused on the extent to which the literal guidelines for the program were interpreted by teachers and incorporated into their plans for classroom instruction. Their study depicts teachers as actively engaged in giving their own meanings to a program of instruction.

Stephens (1982) studied how an activity-based mathematics program, *Developing Mathematics Processes* (DMP) (Romberg et al., 1974, 1975, 1976), was assimilated into the existing network of beliefs, purposes, and values in schools. He discovered that those elements of a given activity that were intended to provide opportunity for children to construct meaning had been abandoned or substantially modified. Often the concept or skill to be taught was presented as a task separated from the mathematical context that gave it meaning (p. 223).

In summary, one common element of such studies is that they search for the underlying meanings of educational events. They clearly demonstrate that the labels used to describe programs and procedures such as "open education" or "constructivist activities" are given different meanings by different teachers.

Major Findings

SIMILARITY AND DIVERSITY

One finding common to all the studies that gathered data in more than one classroom has been the observation that "each place was different in important ways [and] each teacher made unique contributions" (Stake & Easley, 1978, Preface). In the NSF case studies, this diversity was attributed to the selection of classrooms. The case studies were designed to provide the National Science Foundation with a portrayal of current conditions in K–12 mathematics and science classrooms to help make the foundation's programs of support for science education consistent with national needs. Eleven high schools and their feeder schools were selected to provide a diverse and balanced group of sites: rural and urban; east, west, north, and south; racially diverse; economically well-off and impoverished; constructing schools and closing schools; innovative and traditional.

Smith and Sendelbach (1979) and Berlak et al. (1975) attributed the diversity they observed to different and individual meanings given the programs by teachers. Because terms like *open education* are vague, or a program's intent is not well outlined, each teacher gives the actual program unique meanings.

Anyon (1981), however, saw the diversity in terms of "social class" differences. She depicted the teaching of mathematics in a working class school as spending a great deal of time carrying out procedures, "the purposes of which were often unexplained, and which were seemingly unconnected to thought processes or decision making" (p. 8). In a middle-class school, she discerned more flexibility in regard to the procedures that children were expected to follow. There, the teacher tended to set out several alternative methods of solving a problem and made efforts to ensure that children understood what they were doing. In a professional school, on the other hand, the teacher placed a greater emphasis on children's building up mathematical knowledge through discovery techniques or through direct experience. Finally, in an executive school, these patterns of teaching were extended even further to include explicit problem solving, testing hypotheses about mathematical variables, and encouraging pupils to justify the reasonableness of their answers.

Thus, across all these studies, classrooms differ in a variety of important ways for understandable reasons. Yet, at the same time, there were several features on which the classrooms were very similar and conformed to the stereotype of mathematics instruction discussed earlier.

CLASSROOM CONTROL

The assumption of most "scientific" research has been that teachers' acts are primarily related to getting students to learn something. For example, the notions of teacher decision making are based on making decisions related to individual learning outcomes. One outcome of several of the field-based studies is that that assumption is false. The primary concern of teachers is how to maintain order and control. Stephens (1982) gave several examples where materials were adapted not to increase the potential for learning, but so that teachers could better manage the classroom. For example, when teachers anticipated that their group would experience difficulty with a given activity, they preferred to demonstrate the uses of manipulative materials for the whole class rather than have children attempt to use manipulatives by themselves or in small groups.

Stephens (1982) concluded that:

whenever a management approach to instruction emerged in the teaching of DMP, opportunities for children to participate in the development of agreed rules for mathematical inquiry were severely curtailed; their experience of abstracting was often limited by the priorities and procedures which accompanied that perspective. (p. 231)

It was also evident that limitations were applied to the opportunities available to children for inventing, proving, and applying mathematical relationships. In fact, children's conceptions of these mathematical notions were likely to be redefined by the management approach to instruction.

Similarly, when Brandau (1981) looked at how a teacher's belief about mathematics and ideas for mathematics teaching are realized or compromised in the classroom, she found the same results. Brandau's interest was in uncovering the layers of meaning that teachers gave to their work. As well as seeing the instructional process as the medium through which teachers realized their ideals, or were led to compromise them, or experienced conflict as the process of realizing that some goals seemed to compromise others, Brandau saw the teacher, on these occasions, as engaged in problem solving by trying out new strategies and new styles of teaching. The compromises of ideals were always in the direction of maintaining control.

Both Anyon (1981) and Donovan (1983) expressed this emphasis in the broader context of social class and the control exerted over the working-class children.

OWNERSHIP OF KNOWLEDGE

Permeating all of the studies is the fact that the textbook was seen as the authority on knowledge and the guide to learning. In particular, this was observed in the NSF case studies (Stake & Easley, 1978), Stephens (1982), and Smith and Sendelbach (1979). Stake and Easley pointed out that while teachers were "relatively free to depart from district syllabus or community expectation, the teacher seldom exercised either freedom" (Preface). It might be concluded that many teachers see their job as "covering the text." Further, it was also noted that mathematics and science were seldom "taught as scientific inquiry—all subjects were presented as what experts had found to be true" (Stake & Easley, 1978, Preface). Ownership of mathematics rests with the textbook authors and not with the classroom teacher. Departures are rarely made and, if made, are done to increase classroom control, not to make the content more meaningful.

Donovan (1983) found that even when an innovative measurement program was implemented to supplement the primary syllabus, teachers relegated its exploratory activities to an aide and gave it no emphasis in assessment or grading, thus creating an illusion of expanding the children's opportunities to learn.

In summary, "field-based studies" of mathematics teaching, while considerably fewer than the "scientific" studies, are interesting in that through different conceptual lenses, different aspects of teaching are illuminated. The recitation format is reasonable, given that management is the primary concern of schools. By letting the textbook be the authority for knowledge, the teacher is able to concentrate on the group.

Finally, these studies add to our knowledge about the traditions of schooling. In particular, they illuminate aspects of the environment of classrooms overlooked in scientific studies. Some of these environmental aspects must be challenged if real change is to occur in the teaching of mathematics.

Summary

The picture of mathematics teaching drawn from both "scientific" and "field-based" studies both supports and contradicts the stereotype picture of traditional mathematics teaching. Teachers are more concerned with management and control than they are with learning; their "group" is important, not individuals within the group; mathematics is to be covered in an efficient manner; and so on.

However, it is clear there is variation in instruction. Classes differ for a variety of reasons and some of those differences —development of lessons, allocating more time, using small groups, rational planning, and ownership of knowledge—do make a difference in students' learning.

Beyond Two Disciplines

From the two disciplines examined in this chapter, cognitive science and classroom teaching, current research is beginning to establish sufficient findings so that significant changes are called for in the teaching of mathematics. The traditional classroom focuses on competition, management, and group aptitudes; the mathematics taught is assumed to be a fixed body of knowledge, and it is taught under the assumption that learners absorb what has been covered. The research shows that learning proceeds through *construction*, not *absorption*, and that good teaching involves more than management. We believe the task of this next decade will be to bring the variety of constructs from both disciplines together and relate them to an appropriate view of the mathematics to be taught. To do this, we suggest seven areas where scholars should concentrate their efforts.

1. *The scope of research on students' learning must be expanded.* In order to provide a detailed analysis of the processes that students use to solve mathematical problems, cognitive science research has generally been carried out in very structured environments, often involving the analysis of performance of a single student. This research has made a significant contribution to our understanding of how mathematical concepts and skills are acquired, and there is a continued need for research of this type. But such studies cannot provide a complete picture of how learning occurs in typical classrooms. One of the limitations of most of the research to date is that it only provides a picture of performance at isolated points in time. It does not carefully examine how or why change occurs, and it does not consider the specific effects of instruction. Furthermore, classrooms are very different environments from the laboratory settings that characterize most cognitive science research. Cognitive science research focuses on the knowledge and strategies used by individuals. But teachers are concerned with providing activities to groups of students. Furthermore, teachers are concerned with maintaining order and control, not just optimizing learning experiences.

Research is needed that blends the strengths of current cognitive science research with a concern for the realities of the classroom and focuses on students' learning from instruction over extended periods of time. The Soviet teaching experiment provides an example of this kind of research (Kieran, 1985).

2. *Teaching research should consider how learning proceeds.* Scholars doing teaching research, either from a scientific or field-based perspective, have made no assumptions about learning, or have only assumed that individuals learn by absorbing new information. In this research, learning is operationally defined in terms of "residualized mean gain scores" for the classroom group. What are needed are studies similar to those recently done by Peterson and Swing (1982) and Winne and Marx (1982). Both examined students' reports of their thought processes during classroom instruction. However, these studies did not use a cognitive science perspective of learning. The kind of teaching study that needs to be done would bring together both notions about the classroom, the teacher, and the student's role in that environment, and how individuals construct knowledge.

3. *Models bridging the learning–teaching gap need to be constructed.* In light of the preceding, we believe that it is important to develop dynamic rather than static models that are learning-based and at the same time involve components of the teaching classroom environment. What is needed for instructional research is a conceptual revolution like the constructivist revolution in the psychology of learning. We must abandon the attempts to objectively link indirectly defined "independent" variables with operationally defined "dependent" variables associated with broad samples of instruction. At present, the best learning research results from static models derived from careful descriptions of how individuals are processing information. Such models are inadequate when one is talking about change, learning, or growth. Dynamic models are needed that capture the way meaning is constructed in classroom settings on specific mathematical tasks.

4. *Mathematical content should be seriously included in such models.* A theory of learning must include a central role for what is to be learned (Resnick, 1981 b). In neither research on learning nor research on teaching has there been an adequate consideration of mathematical content. There has been little discussion

in either about what it means to know or do mathematics. The tasks in learning research and the activities in teaching research tend not to represent a complete picture of mathematics. Schoenfeld (1983) argued that their content is arithmetic, computation, or particular concept learning. This is not to deny that studies based on such tasks are important, but they are only a small part of what constitutes mathematics. In many of the learning studies, the units of mathematics used bear little resemblance to what goes on in school or what one would expect in the learning of mathematics. For example, expert versus novice problem-solving studies often use puzzle problems. To solve such tasks, little mathematical background is required.

Similarly, many of the studies of teaching select a chapter of a textbook or use a nontypical unit of mathematics. Typical text chapters simply do not provide the teacher (or the researcher) with a complete perspective for development. In addition, such research may be reinforcing a "saber-tooth curriculum" (Pediwell, 1939) rather than providing knowledge about how to teach good mathematics. Thus, whether attempting to study students' learning or instruction, research should begin with mathematically sound units of instruction.

5. *The role of computers and technology must be considered.* In the last section the issue of this "sabre-tooth curriculum" was raised. One danger of all research on the learning and teaching of mathematics is that it will continue to study current practice rather than focus on the future. The technology now available to mathematics instruction may make current texts and procedures as extinct as the saber-toothed tiger. Today it is not clear what the role of this technology will be on what constitutes mathematics, the learning of mathematics, or the teaching of mathematics. However, it is clear that this technology cannot be ignored. For example, the Conference Board of the Mathematical Sciences (1983) has recommended that calculators and computers be introduced in the mathematics classroom at the earliest grade practicable (p. 12). Because of this, they also suggest that substantially more emphasis be placed on the development of mental arithmetic, estimation, and approximation and substantially less be placed on paper and pencil execution of the arithmetic operations (p. 12). Tomorrow's mathematics class will indeed involve a different technology from the text, lecture, blackboard, worksheet procedures now in use. The potential for changing not only how instruction proceeds, but what is taught, to whom, and by whom is apparent.

6. *New assessment tools must be developed.* Given that new information about learning and teaching is now available, that mathematics as a discipline is changing, and that future instruction will take into account the new technology, new assessment techniques must be developed if research is to improve. We must give up the outdated notion that one can assess the learning of mathematics solely in terms of the ability to produce correct answers. A person's performance depends on the kind of knowledge the person has about a particular situation. What is important is that we understand how learners try to link new information to what they already know. We must understand how information is organized and connected to past experience if we are to understand how something is learned. Thus, prior knowledge and the strategies that students use as well as

production of correct answers must be assessed. This means giving up standardized tests and even objective-referenced tests for process-related tests.

Educational researchers have long assumed that comparability of measures is assured by using standardized tests. This assumption is false because the scores reflect opportunities to learn (see Table 29.4), include items on content not taught (Porter, 1978), and so on. In fact Berliner (1975) has argued that one of the major impediments to the study of teacher effectiveness was the use of standardized tests.

Objective-referenced tests are more sensitive to instruction, but are often multiple indicators of a common trait (Blaylock, 1983). Unfortunately, we rarely posit a theory that relates such reference indicators to a general variable.

Finally, both standardized and objective-referenced tests only count the number of correct responses to items. They do not assess how subjects worked the problems. Measurement procedures that identify processes used as well as correctness of answers are now needed. A process assessment methodology (e.g., Siegler, 1981) has been successfully used to classify individual children based on clinically derived information. Modifications in the procedures should be possible for the development of group-administered assessments.

7. *We need to establish research programs.* We must recognize the limits of our domain of inquiry as well as its complexity. No one study is going to answer a particular question. Chains of inquiry are built up over time by research teams collaborating on a problem area. Only if there is a group of scholars working together can we begin to find answers to important questions. In addition, our studies must be conducted over a variety of time periods. We are interested in growth and change of how students assimilate and accommodate information, acquire new concepts, include new ideas, interpret new ideas in light of prior knowledge, and so on. These concerns can only be studied by teams over time.

In conclusion, we are cautiously optimistic about the potential for meaningful change in the teaching of mathematics. The dramatic advances in technology will almost surely force change both in what mathematics is taught and in how it is taught. Research on learning and research on teaching are on the threshold of providing the kinds of knowledge that could lead to real advances in mathematics instruction. Change is inevitable. If we can build upon a solid knowledge base derived from research on teaching and learning, the change could result in real progress in the teaching and learning of mathematics.

REFERENCES

Anderson, J. R., & Bower, C. H. (1973). *Human associative memory.* Washington, DC: Winston.

Anyon, J. (1981). Social class and school knowledge. *Curriculum Inquiry, 11*(1), 3–42.

Ashlock, R. B. (1976). *Error patterns in computation* (2nd ed). Columbus, OH: Merrill.

Ausubel, D. P. (1968). *Educational psychology: A cognitive view.* New York: Holt, Rinehart, & Winston.

Becker, W. C., & Carnine, D. W. (1980). Direct instruction: An effective approach to educational intervention with the disadvantaged and performers (pp. 429–473). In B. B. Lahey & A. E. Kazdin (Eds.), *Advances in clinical psychology* (Vol. 3). New York: Plenum.

Bell, A. W., Costello, J., & Küchemann, D. E. (1980). *A review of research in mathematical education*. Nottingham, England: Shell Centre for Mathematical Education.

Bellack, A. (1978). *Competing ideologies in research on teaching* (Upsala Reports on Education No. 1). Upsala, Sweden: University of Upsala.

Berlak, A. C., Berlak, H., Bagenstos, N. T., & Mikel, E. R. (1975). A participant-observation study of teaching and learning in English primary schools. *School Review, 82*, 215–243.

Berliner, D. C. (1975, March). *Impediments to the study of teacher effectiveness*. Paper presented at the annual meeting of the National Association for Research in Science Teaching, Los Angeles, CA.

Berliner, D. C. (1976). Impediments to the study of teacher effectiveness. *Journal of Teacher Education, 27*, 5–13.

Berliner, D. C. (1978, April). *Allocated time, engaged time and academic learning time in elementary mathematics instruction*. Paper presented at the meeting of the National Council of Teachers of Mathematics, San Diego, CA.

Berliner, D. C. (1983). Developing conceptions of classroom environments: Some light on the T in classroom studies of ATI. *Educational Psychologist, 18*, 1–13.

Berliner, D. C., & Ward, B. (1974). *Proposal for phase III beginning teacher evaluation study*. San Francisco: Far West Laboratory for Educational Research and Development.

Blaylock, H. M. (1983). *Conceptualization and measurement in the social sciences*. Beverly Hills, CA: Sage.

Bloom, B. (1976). *Human characteristics and school learning*. New York: McGraw-Hill.

Blumer, H. (1969). *Social interactionism*. Englewood Cliffs, NJ: Prentice-Hall.

Borg, W. Time and school learning. (1979). In C. Denham & A. Lieberman (Eds.), *Time to learn* (pp. 33–72). Washington, DC: National Institute of Education.

Borko, H., Cone, R., Russo, N. A, & Shavelson, R. J. (1979). Teachers' decision making. In P. L. Peterson & H. J. Walberg (Eds.), *Research on teaching*. Berkeley, CA: McCutchan.

Brandau, L. (1981, April). The practices of an elementary mathematics teacher — An ethnographic approach to the study of problem solving. In *Multiple perspectives on problem solving via complementary methodologies*. Symposium conducted at the annual meeting of the American Educational Research Association, Los Angeles, CA.

Briars, D. J., & Larkin, J. H. (1984). An integrated model of skill in solving elementary word problems. *Cognition and Instruction, 1*(3), 245–296.

Brophy, J. (1977). Reaction to Kilpatrick's paper. In *Proceedings of the Research-on-teaching mathematics conference*. East Lansing, MI: Institute for Research on Teaching.

Brown, J. S., & Burton, R. R. (1978). Diagnostic models for procedural bugs in basic mathematical skills. *Cognitive Science, 2*, 153–192.

Brown, J. S., & VanLehn, K. (1980). Repair theory: A generative theory of bugs in procedural skills. *Cognitive Science, 4*, 379–426.

Brown, J. S., & VanLehn, K. (1982). Towards a generative theory of "bugs." In T. P. Carpenter, J. M. Moser, & T. A. Romberg (Eds.), *Addition and subtraction: A cognitive perspective* (pp. 117–135). Hillsdale, NJ: Erlbaum.

Brownell, W. A. (1935). Psychological considerations in the learning and the teaching of arithmetic. In W. D. Reeve (Ed.), *The teaching of arithmetic: The tenth yearbook of the National Council of Teachers of Mathematics* (pp. 1–31). New York: Teachers College Press.

Bruner, J. S. (1960). *The process of education*. Cambridge, MA: Harvard University Press.

Bruner, J. S. (1966). *Toward a theory of instruction*. Cambridge, MA: Belknap Press.

Carnahan, R. S. (1980). *The effects of teacher planning on classroom processes*. Unpublished doctoral dissertation, University of Wisconsin-Madison.

Carpenter, T. P. (1980). Cognitive development and mathematics learning. In R. Shumway (Ed.), *Research in mathematics education* (pp. 146–206). Reston, VA: National Council of Teachers of Mathematics.

Carpenter, T. P., Hiebert, J., & Moser, J. M. (1983). The effect of instruction on children's solutions of addition and subtraction word problems. *Educational Studies in Mathematics, 14*, 55–72.

Carpenter, T. P., & Moser, J. M. (1982). The development of addition and subtraction problem-solving skills. In T. P. Carpenter, J. M. Moser, & T. A. Romberg (Eds.), *Addition and subtraction: A cognitive perspective* (pp. 9–24). Hillsdale, NJ: Erlbaum.

Carpenter, T. P., & Moser, J. M. (1983). The acquisition of addition and subtraction concepts. In R. Lesh & M. Landau (Eds.), *The acquisition of mathematical concepts and processes* (pp. 7–44). New York: Academic Press.

Carpenter, T. P., Moser, J. M., & Romberg, T. A. (1982). *Addition and subtraction: A cognitive perspective*. Hillsdale, NJ: Erlbaum.

Carroll, J. (1963). A model for school learning. *Teachers College Record, 64*, 723–733.

Case, R. (1975). Gearing the demands of instruction to the developmental capacities of the learner. *Review of Educational Research, 45*, 59–87.

Case, R. (1978a). A developmentally based theory and technology of instruction. *Review of Educational Research, 48*, 339–469.

Case, R. (1978b). Intellectual development from birth to adulthood: A neo-Piagetian interpretation. In R. Siegler (Ed.), *Children's thinking: What develops?* (pp. 37–72). Hillsdale, NJ: Erlbaum.

Case, R. (1978c). Piaget and beyond: Toward a developmentally based theory and technology of instruction. In R. Glaser (Ed.), *Advances in instructional psychology* (pp. 167–228). Hillsdale, NJ: Erlbaum.

Case, R. (1983). *Intellectual development: A systematic reinterpretation*. New York: Academic Press.

Case, R., & Bereiter, C. (1982). *From behaviorism to cognitive behaviorism to cognitive development: Steps in the evolution of instructional design*. Paper presented at the Conference for Educational Technology in the 80s, Caracas, Venezuela.

Chase, W. J., & Simon, H. A. (1973). Perception in chess. *Cognitive Psychology, 4*, 55–81.

Chi, M. T. H., Glaser, R., & Rees, E. (1982). Expertise in problem solving. In R. Sternberg (Ed.), *Advances in the psychology of human intelligence* (pp. 7–75). Hillsdale, NJ: Erlbaum.

Clark, C. M., & Yinger, R. J. (1978). *Research on teaching thinking* (Research Series No. 12). East Lansing, MI: Institute for Research on Teaching.

Conference Board of Mathematical Sciences. (1975). *Overview and analysis of school mathematics, grades K–12*. Washington, DC: Author.

Conference Board of Mathematical Sciences. (1983). The mathematical sciences curriculum K–12: What is still fundamental and what is not. In National Science Board Commission on Precollege Education in Mathematics, Science, and Technology, *Interim Report to the National Science Board*. Washington, DC: National Science Board.

Cooney, T. (1976, August). *The teaching strategies project*. Paper presented at the Third International Congress on Mathematics Education, Kalsruhe, West Germany.

Cooney, T. (1980). Research on teaching and teacher education. In R. Shumway (Ed.), *Research in mathematics education* (pp. 433–474). Reston, VA: National Council of Teachers of Mathematics.

Cooney, T. J., & Bradbard, D. A. (Eds.). (1976). *Teaching strategies*. Columbus, OH: ERIC/SMEAC Center for Science, Mathematics, and Environmental Education.

Cooney, T. J., Davis, E. J., & Henderson, K. B. (1975). *Dynamics of teaching secondary school mathematics*. Boston: Houghton Mifflin.

Cronbach, L. J. (1957). The two disciplines of scientific psychology. *American Psychologist, 12*, 671–684.

Cronbach, L. J. (1965). Mathematical learning. *Monograph of Child Development, 30*, 119–124.

Cronbach, L. J., & Snow, R. E. (1977). *Aptitudes and instructional methods*. New York: Irvington.

Cronbach, L. J., & Suppes, P. (Eds.). (1969). *Research for tomorrow's schools: Disciplined inquiry for education*. New York: Macmillan.

Davidson, N. (1980). The small group discovery method: 1967–1977. In J. G. Harvey & T. A. Romberg (Eds.), *Problem solving studies in mathematics* (pp. 33–57). Madison: Wisconsin Research and Development Center for Individualized Schooling.

Deutsch, M. (1949). An experimental study of the effects of cooperation and competition upon group process. *Human Relations, 2,* 199-231.

Dewey, J. (1916). *Democracy and education.* New York: Macmillan.

Donovan, B. F. (1983). *Power and curriculum in implementation: A case study of an innovatory mathematics program.* Unpublished doctoral dissertation, Universtity of Wisconsin-Madison.

Dunkin, M. J., & Biddle, B. J. (1974). *The study of teaching.* New York: Academic Press.

Durkheim, E. (1961). *Moral education.* Glencoe, IL: The Free Press.

Erlwanger, S. H. (1975). Case studies of children's conceptions of mathematics: Part I. *Journal of Children's Mathematical Behavior, 1,* 7-26.

Fennema, E., & Behr, M. J. (1980). Individual differences and the learning of mathematics. In R. J. Shumway (Ed.), *Research in mathematics education* (pp. 324-355). Reston, VA: National Council of Teachers of Mathematics.

Fenstermacher, G. (1978). A philosophic consideration of recent research on teacher effectiveness. In L. Shulman (Ed.), *Review of research in education* (Vol.6, pp. 157-185). Itasca, IL: Peacock.

Fey, J. (1979a). Mathematics teaching today: Perspectives from three national surveys. *The Mathematics Teacher, 72,* 490-504.

Fey, J. (1979b). Mathematics teaching today: Perspectives from three national surveys (for the elementary grades). *The Arithmetic Teacher, 27,* 10-14.

Filby, N. (1976). *Progress report on reactivity analyses (October-December test data)* (Technical Note III-5). San Francisco: Beginning Teacher Evaluation Study, Far West Laboratory for Educational Research and Development.

Fisher, C., Berliner, D., Filby, N., Marliave, R., Cahen, L., Dishaw, M., & Moore, J. (1978). *Teaching and learning in elementary schools: A summary of the Beginning Teacher Evaluation Study.* San Francisco: Far West Laboratory for Educational Research and Development.

Fuson, K. (1982). An analysis of the counting-on solution procedure in addition. In T. P. Carpenter, J. M. Moser, & T. A. Romberg (Eds.), *Addition and subtraction: A cognitive perspective* (pp. 67-82). Hillsdale, NJ: Erlbaum.

Gage, N. L. (1964). Theories of teaching. In E. R. Hilgard (Ed.), *Theories of learning and instruction: Sixty third yearbook of the National Society for the Study of Education: Part 1* (pp. 268-285). Chicago: University of Chicago Press.

Gage, N. (1977). *The scientific basis of the art of teaching.* New York: Teachers College Press.

Gage, N. (1980, July). *Current research on teacher education and staff development.* Paper presented at the Teacher Education/Staff Development Research Symposium, Kent State University, Kent, OH.

Gagné, R. M. (1965). *The conditions of learning.* New York: Holt, Rinehart, & Winston.

Geeslin, W. E., & Shavelson, R. (1975). Comparison of content structure and cognitive structure in high school students' learning of probability. *Journal for Research in Mathematics Education, 6,* 109-120.

Ginsburg, H. (1977). *Children's arithmetic: The learning process.* New York: Van Nostrand.

Ginsburg, H. A. (Ed.). (1983). *The development of mathematical thinking.* New York: Academic Press.

Glaser, R. (1976a). Cognitive psychology and instructional design. In D. Klahr (Ed.), *Cognition and instruction* (pp. 303-316). Hillsdale, NJ: Erlbaum.

Glaser, R. (1976b). Components of a psychology of instruction: Toward a science of design. *Review of Educational Research, 46,* 1-24.

Glaser, R. (Ed.). (1978). *Advances in instructional psychology* (Vol. 1). Hillsdale, NJ: Erlbaum.

Good, T., & Grouws, D. (1975). *Process-product relationship in fourth grade mathematics classes.* (NIE Final Report). Columbia, MO: Center for Research in Social Behavior.

Good, T., & Grouws, D. (1977). Teaching effects: A process-product study in fourth grade mathematics classrooms. *Journal of Teacher Education, 28,* 49-54.

Good, T., Grouws, D., & Ebmeier, H. (1983). *Active mathematics teaching.* New York: Longman.

Goodlad, J. I. (1983). Individuality, commonality, and curriculum practice. In G. D. Fenstermacher & J. I. Goodlad (Eds.), *Individual differences and the common curriculum: Eighty-second yearbook of the National Society for the Study of Education* (pp. 300-318). Chicago: University of Chicago Press.

Greeno, J. G. (1976). Cognitive objectives of instruction: Theory of knowledge for solving problems and answering questions. In D. Klahr (Ed.), *Cognition and instruction* (pp. 123-160). Hillsdale, NJ: Erlbaum.

Greeno, J. G. (1978). A study of problem solving. In R. Glaser (Ed.), *Advances in instructional psychology* (Vol. 1). Hillsdale, NJ: Erlbaum.

Groen, G. J., & Parkman, J. M. (1972). A chronometric analysis of simple addition. *Psychological Review, 79,* 329-343.

Groen, G., & Resnick, L. B. (1977). Can preschool children invent addition algorithms? *Journal of Educational Psychology, 69,* 645-652.

Haertel, G. D., Walberg, H. J., & Weinstein, T. (1983). Psychological models of educational performance: A theoretical synthesis of constructs. *Review of Educational Research, 53,* 75-91.

Harnischfeger, A., & Wiley, D. (1975). *Teaching-learning processes in elementary schools: A synoptic view* (Studies of Education Processes, Report No. 9). Chicago: University of Chicago.

Henderson, K. B. (1976). Toward the development of pedagogical theory in mathematics. In T. J. Cooney & D. A. Bradbard (Eds.), *Teaching strategies: Papers from a research workshop* (pp. 35-50). Columbus, OH: ERIC/SMEAC.

Hiebert, J., & Carpenter, T. P. (1982). Piagetian tasks as readiness measures in mathematics instruction: A critical review. *Educational Studies in Mathematics, 13,* 329-345.

Jones, C. A., & Romberg, T. A. (1979). *Three "time-task" studies and their implications for teaching and teacher education* (Project Paper 79-6). Madison: Wisconsin Research and Development Center.

Kieran, C. (in press). The Soviet teaching experiment. In T. A. Romberg (Ed.), *Research methods for studies in mathematics education: Some considerations and alternatives.* Madison, WI: Wisconsin Education Research Center.

Kieren, T.E. (1975). On the mathematical, cognitive, and instructional foundations of rational numbers. In R. Lesh (Ed.), *Number and measurement* (pp. 101-144). Columbus, OH: ERIC.

Kieren, T.E. (1980). Knowing rational numbers: Ideas and symbols. In M. E. Lindquist (Ed.), *Selected issues in mathematics education* (pp. 69-81). Chicago: National Society for the Study of Education.

Kilpatrick, J. (1977). Research on teaching mathematics to the elementary pupil. In *Proceedings of the Research-on-teaching mathematics conference.* East Lansing, MI: Institute for Research on Teaching.

Klahr, D. (1976). *Cognition and instruction.* Hillsdale, NJ: Erlbaum.

Kliebard, H. M. (1972). Metaphorical roots of curriculum design. *Teachers College Record, 73,* 403-404.

Kouba, V., & Moser, J. (1979). *Development and validation of curriculum units related to initial sentence writing* (Technical Report No. 522). Madison: Wisconsin Research and Development Center for Individualized Schooling.

Krutetski, J. A. (1976). *The psychology of mathematical abilities in schoolchildren.* Chicago: University of Chicago Press.

Kuhn, T. (1979). *The structure of scientific revolutions* (2nd ed.). Chicago: The University of Chicago Press.

Lachman, R., Lachman, J., & Butterfield, E. C. (1979). *Cognitive psychology and information processing: An introduction.* Hillsdale, NJ: Erlbaum.

Larkin, J. H., McDermott, J., Simon, D. D., & Simon, H. A. (1980). Models of competence in solving physics problems. *Cognitive Science, 4,* 317-345.

Lesh, R., & Landau, M. (Eds.). (1983). *Acquisition of mathematical concepts and processes.* New York: Academic Press.

Lester, F. (Ed.). (1982). *Perspectives on research in mathematical problem solving.* Philadelphia: Franklin Institute Press.

Lindvall, C. M., & Bolvin, J. O. (1967). Programmed instruction in the schools: An application of programming principles in Individually Prescribed Instruction. In P. C. Lange (Ed.), *Programmed instruction: Sixty-sixth yearbook of the National Society for the Study of Education* (pp. 217-254). Chicago: University of Chicago Press.

Luce, R., & Raiffa, H. (1967). *Games and decisions.* New York: Wiley.

Mannheim, K. (1952). *Essays on the sociology of knowledge*. London: Routledge and Kegan Paul.

Matz, M. (1980). Towards a computational theory of algebraic competence. *The Journal of Mathematical Behavior, 3*, 93–166.

Mead, G. H. (1934). *Mind, self and society*. Chicago: University of Chicago Press.

Medley, D. (1977). *Teacher competence and teacher effectiveness*. Washington, DC: American Association of Colleges for Higher Education.

Montgomery, M. (1973). The interaction of three levels of aptitude determined by a teach-test procedure with two treatments related to area. *Journal for Research in Mathematics Education, 4*, 271–278.

Nuthall, G. (1974). Is classroom interaction worth the effort involved? *New Zealand Journal of Educational Studies, 9*, 1–17.

Ornstein, A., & Levine, D. (1981). Teacher behavior research: Overview and outlook. *Phi Delta Kappan, 62*, 592–596.

Pascual-Leone, J. (1970). A mathematical model for the transition rule in Piaget's developmental stages. *Acta Psychologica, 32*, 301–345.

Pediwell, A. (1939). *The saber-tooth curriculum*. New York: McGraw-Hill.

Peterson, P., & Janicki, T. (1979). *Individual characteristics and children's learning in large-group and small-group approaches* (Technical Report No. 496). Madison: Wisconsin Research and Development Center for Individualized Schooling.

Peterson, P. L., & Swing, S. R. (1982). Beyond time on task: Students' reports of their thought processes during classroom instruction. *Elementary School Journal, 5*, 481–491.

Piaget, J. (1952). *The child's conception of number*. New York: Humanities Press.

Piaget, J., & Inhelder, B. (1956). *The child's conception of space*. London: Routledge and Kegan Paul.

Piaget, J., Inhelder, B., & Szeminska, A. (1960). *The child's conception of geometry*. New York: Basic Books.

Porter, A. C. (1978). *Relationship between testing and the curriculum* (Occasional Paper No. 9). East Lansing, MI: Institute for Research on Teaching.

Reisman, F. K. (1978). *A guide to the diagnostic teaching of arithmetic*. Columbus, OH: Merrill.

Resnick, L. B. (1976). Task analysis in instructional design: Some cases from mathematics. In D. Klahr (Ed.), *Cognition and instruction* (pp. 51–80). Hillsdale, NJ: Erlbaum.

Resnick, L. B. (1981a). Instructional psychology. *Annual Review of Psychology 32*, 659–704.

Resnick, L. (1981b). Social assumptions as a context for science: Some reflections on psychology and education. *Educational Psychologist, 16*, 1–10.

Resnick, L. B. (1982). Syntax and semantics in learning to subtract. In T. P. Carpenter, J. M. Moser, & T. A. Romberg (Eds.), *Addition and subtraction: A cognitive perspective* (pp. 136–155). Hillsdale, NJ: Erlbaum.

Resnick, L. B. (1983). Mathematics and science learning: A new conception. *Science, 220*, 477–478.

Resnick, L. B., & Ford, W. W. (1981). *The psychology of mathematics for instruction*. Hillsdale, NJ: Erlbaum.

Riley, M. S., Greeno, J. G., & Heller, J. I. (1983). Development of children's problem-solving ability in arithmetic. In H. Ginsburg (Ed.), *The development of mathematical thinking* (pp. 153–200). New York: Academic Press.

Romberg, T. (1979a). Pupil outcomes and pupil pursuits. In T. Romberg, M. Small, & R. Cranahan, *Research on teaching from a curricular perspective* (Theoretical Paper No. 81). Madison: Wisconsin Research and Development Center for Individualized Schooling.

Romberg, T. (1979b). Salient features of the BTES framework of teacher behaviors. In C. Denham & A. Lieberman (Eds.), *Time to learn* (pp. 73–93). Washington, DC: National Institute of Education.

Romberg, T. (1983a). A common curriculum for mathematics. In J. Goodlad & G. Fenstermacher (Eds.), *Individual differences and the common curriculum: Eighty-second yearbook of the National Society for the Study of Education* (pp. 121–159). Chicago: University of Chicago Press.

Romberg, T. A. (1983b, April). *Allocated time and content covered in mathematics classrooms*. Paper presented at the annual meeting of the American Educational Research Association, Montreal.

Romberg, T. (Ed). (1985). *Toward effective schooling: The IGE experience*. Lanham, MD: University Press of America.

Romberg, T., & Fox, G. (1976). Problems in analyzing dynamic events within teacher education. In G. Fox (Ed.), *The 1975 CMTI impact study* (pp. 47–73). Madison, WI: Teacher Corps Project.

Romberg, T., & Gilbert, L. (1972). The effect of training on the performance of kindergarten children on nonstandard but related tasks. *Journal for Research in Mathematics Education, 3*(2), 69–75.

Romberg, T., Harvey, J., Moser, J., & Montgomery, M. (1974, 1975, 1976). *Developing mathematical processes*. Chicago: Rand McNally.

Romberg, T., & Price, G. (1983). Curriculum implementation and staff development as cultural change. In G. Griffin (Ed.), *Staff development: Eighty-second Yearbook of the National Society for the Study of Education* (pp. 154–184). Chicago: University of Chicago Press.

Romberg, T. A., Small, M., & Carnahan, R. (1979). *Research on teaching from a curricular perspective* (Theoretical Paper No. 81). Madison: Wisconsin Research and Development Center for Individualized Schooling.

Romberg, T. A., Stephens, W. M., Buchanan, A. E., & Steinberg, R. (1983). *Quantitative differences in content covered in mathematics classes and the relationship of those differences to pupil performance* (Project Report). Madison: Wisconsin Center for Education Research.

Rosenshine, B., & Furst, N. (1973). The use of direct observation to study teaching. In R. M. W. Travers (Ed.), *Second handbook of research on teaching*. Chicago: Rand McNally.

Schoenfeld, A. H. (1980). Teaching problem-solving skills. *American Mathematical Monthly, 87*, 794–805.

Schoenfeld, A. H. (1983). The wild, wild, wild, wild, wild world of problem solving. *For the Learning of Mathematics, 3*, 40–47.

Schrag, F. Knowing and doing. (1981). *American Journal of Education, 89*, 253–282.

Schwille, J., Porter, A., Belli, G., Floden, R., Freeman, D., Knappen, L., Kuhs, T., & Schmidt, W. (1983). Teachers as policy brokers in the content of elementary school mathematics. In L. S. Schulman & G. Sykes (Eds.), *Handbook of teaching and policy*. New York: Longman.

Secada, W. G., Fuson, K. C., & Hall, J. W. (1983). The transition from counting all to counting on in addition. *Journal for Research in Mathematics Education, 14*, 47–57.

Shavelson, R. (1976). Teachers' decision making. In N. L. Gage (Ed.), *The psychology of teaching models: Seventy-fifth yearbook of the National Society for the Study of Education*. Chicago: University of Chicago Press.

Shulman, L. S. (1970). Psychology and mathematics education. In E. G. Begle (Ed.), *Mathematics education: Sixty-ninth yearbook of the National Society for the Study of Education* (pp. 23–74). Chicago: University of Chicago Press.

Shulman, L. S. (1983). Autonomy and obligation. In S. Shulman & G. Sykes (Eds.), *Handbook of teaching and policy* (pp. 484–504). New York: Longman.

Shumway, R. (Ed.). (1980). *Research in mathematics education*. Reston, VA: National Council of Teachers of Mathematics.

Siegler, R. S. (1981). Developmental sequences within and between concepts. *Society for Research in Child Development Monographs, 46*, (Serial No. 189).

Siegler, R. S. (1983). Information processing approaches to development. In P. Mussen & W. Kassen (Eds.), *Manual of child psychology* (pp. 129–211). New York: Wiley.

Silver, E. A. (1979). Student perceptions of relatedness among mathematical verbal problems. *Journal for Research in Mathematics Education, 10*, 195–210.

Silver, E. A. (1982). *Thinking about problem solving: Toward an understanding of metacognitive aspects of mathematical problem solving*. Paper presented at the Conference on Thinking, Saba, Figi.

Silver, E. A., Branca, N. A., & Adams, V. M. (1980). Metacognition: The missing link in problem solving? In R. Karplus (Ed.), *Proceedings of* the Fourth International Conference for the Psychology of Mathematics Education (pp. 213-222). Berkeley, CA: University of California.

Simon, D. P., & Simon, H. A. (1978). Individual differences in solving physics problems. In R. S. Siegler (Ed.), Children's thinking: What develops? (325-348). Hillsdale, NJ: Erlbaum.

Simon, H. (1979). Information processing models of cognition. Annual Review of Psychology, 30, 363-396.

Skinner, B. F. (1968). The technology of teaching. New York: Appleton.

Slavin, R. (1980). Cooperative learning. Review of Educational Research, 50, 315-342.

Smith, B. O., Meux, M. O., Coombs, J., Nuthall, G., & Precians, R. (1967). A study of the strategies of teaching. Urbana: Bureau of Educational Research, College of Education, University of Illinois.

Smith, E. L., & Sendelbach, N. B. (1979, April). Teacher intentions for science instruction and their antecedents in program materials. Paper presented at the annual meeting of the American Educational Research Association, San Francisco.

Stake, R., & Easley, J. (Eds.). (1978). Case studies in science education. Urbana: University of Illinois.

Steffe, L. P., vonGlasersfeld, E., Richards, J., & Cobb, P. (1983). Children's counting types: Philosophy, theory and application. New York: Praeger.

Steinberg, R. (1983). Instruction in basic facts. Unpublished doctoral dissertation, University of Wisconsin, Madison.

Stephens, W. (1982). Mathematical knowledge and school work: A case study of the teaching of developing mathematical processes (Project Report). Madison: Wisconsin Center for Education Research.

Stewart, J. (1980). Techniques for assessing and representing information in cognitive structure. Science Education, 64, 223-235.

Suppes, P. (1972). Facts and fantasies of education (Technical Report No. 193). Stanford, CA: Institute for Mathematical Studies in the Social Sciences.

Suppes, P., & Groen, G. (1967). Some counting models for first grade performance data on simple facts. In J. M. Scandura (Ed.), Research in mathematics education (pp. 35-43). Washington, DC: National Council of Teachers of Mathematics.

Suydam, M., & Osborne, A. (1977). The status of pre-college science, mathematics, and social studies education: 1955-1975 (Vol. 2, Mathematics education). Columbus: The Ohio State University Center for Science and Mathematics Education.

Swing, S., & Peterson, P. (1982). The relationship of student ability and small group interaction to student achievement. American Educational Research Journal, 19, 259-274.

Thorndike, E. L. (1922). The psychology of arithmetic. New York: Macmillan.

Thornton, C. A. (1978). Emphasizing thinking strategies in basic fact instruction. Journal for Research in Mathematics Education, 9, 214-227.

Travers, R. (Ed.). (1973). Second handbook of research on teaching. Chicago: Rand McNally & Company.

VanLehn, K. (1983). On the representation of procedures in repair theory. In H. Ginsburg (Ed.), The development of mathematical thinking (201-253). New York: Academic Press.

Waxman, H., & Walberg, H. (1982). The relation of teaching and learning: A review of reviews of process-product research. Contemporary Education Review, 1, 103-120.

Webb, N. (1980). A process-outcome analysis of learning in group and individual settings. Educational Psychologist, 15(2), 69-83.

Webb, N. (1982). Student interaction and learning in small groups. Review of Educational Research, 52, 421-445.

Webb, N., & Romberg, T. (1979). The design of Phase IV of the IGE evaluation project (Project Paper No. 79-42). Madison: Wisconsin Research and Development Center.

Weiss, I. (1978). Report of the 1977 national survey of science, mathematics, and social studies education. Research Triangle Park, NC: Research Triangle Institute.

Welch, W. (1978). Science education in Urbanville: A case study. In R. Stake & J. Easley (Eds.), Case studies in science education (pp. 5-1-5-33). Urbana, IL: University of Illinois.

Winne, P. H., & Marx, R. (1977). Reconceptualizing research on teaching. Journal of Educational Psychology, 69, 668-678.

Winne, P. H., & Marx, R. W. (1982). Students' and teachers' views of thinking processes for classroom learning. Elementary School Journal, 5, 493-518.

Wittrock, M. C. (1974). A generative model of mathematics learning. Journal for Research in Mathematics Education, 5, 181-196.

Yinger, R. J. (1978). A study of teacher planning: Description and a model of preactive decision making (Research Series No. 19). East Lansing, MI: Institute for Research on Teaching.

30.
Research on Natural Sciences

Richard T. White
Monash University

Richard P. Tisher
Monash University

Introduction

The decade that has passed since the publication of the *Second Handbook of Research on Teaching* was one of enthusiasm and energy in research in science education. Great advances were made in sophistication of methods and depths of insight. In this introduction we outline the association these advances have with developments in the theories, concepts, and models used in research, before describing the varying extents to which they occurred in different fields.

Major themes in the sciences chapter of the *Second Handbook* (Shulman and Tamir, 1973) are the structure of knowledge and the impact of the great central curricula. We see these as the genesis of the chief themes of our chapter, namely, the learner's assimilation of knowledge and the implementation of curricula. The shift in themes marks a crucial change in style of research. The great contrast between the two periods is the emphasis that researchers in the 1970s began to place on understanding the reasons for effects. They became less content with discovering that a change in teaching procedure or in curriculum led to a change in performance without also wanting to find out how and why the effect occurred. Naturally, as can be seen in the sections of the chapter, this development went further in some fields than others.

Subtle, detailed theories are needed to explain mechanisms of effects. During the decade calls began to be made for research to be more closely associated with theory (e.g., Bowen, 1975; Lamb, 1976). Though rarely referred to earlier, in the 1970s Piaget's theory of human development became prominent, even dominant, in science education. Its appeal to science educators is that it is constructivist, dealing with the manner in which children build up their own beliefs and pictures of the world. The constructivist character is shared by information-process-

ing theories, Ausubel's cognitive psychology (Ausubel, 1968), Kelly's personal construct theory (Kelly, 1955), Wittrock's generative model of learning (Wittrock, 1974), and the conceptions of learning put forward by the University of Göteborg school (e.g., Dahlgren & Marton, 1978; Marton & Säljö, 1976). Though important, so far these theories have had a more diffuse and less substantial influence on research in science education than Piaget has had. The next decade may see a synthesis of these related but distinct theories that will have a strong effect on the course of research.

The complex forms of the detailed theories brought many new concepts, such as stages of development, levels of processing, cognitive structure, semantic and episodic memory, and cognitive style, into research. Other concepts that became prominent, such as wait-time, question types, and teaching style, may reflect a trend to take more account of teachers' experiences and their views of what is important in the classroom. A third source of new concepts was an appreciation that earlier research in curriculum had treated the practical processes of teaching and learning too simply; and so terms such as mutual adaptation and school-based curriculum development were introduced.

The increase in concepts and the new theories made research richer and more diverse. The theories and concepts people have in mind determine the model they use for the relations between the classes of variables which they see as important in the study of teaching and learning. Models in turn influence the questions researchers tackle, and the way they seek answers. Early in the last decade, most research on learning in science appeared to be based on a simple model of instruction determining performance, a model that did not encourage researchers to consider what individuals do in learning or how the instruction has its effect. The commonest form of investigation was a comparison

The authors thank reviewers Roger Osborne (University of Waikato) and Audrey Champagne (University of Pittsburgh).

of several instructional treatments with respect to their effect on groups' scores on performance measures; individuals were submerged in their groups, contributing to the mean value but having their deviations from it described, as often as not, as "error". Aptitude–treatment interaction studies did give some attention to individual characteristics, but even there the learner was seen as a member of a factorial cell and as a contributor to error variance. Although studies of that sort are still common, more have come to be based on complex models that allow attention to be given to variations between individuals and between contexts in which instruction and learning occur. The model shown in Figure 30.1, which we will use in organizing and interrelating the large body of research that we have to describe, is an example.

Inevitably, the model in Figure 30.1 represents our own notions of the relations that matter in science education. It is not put forward as the only possible, only correct, or only valuable one. We could, for instance, have followed Keeves (1975) and given more weight to the effect that social factors such as ethnicity, parental income and aspirations, and school type have on level of educational achievement. Our experiences, and our purpose of making clear the relations between many studies, are different from Keeves's, and so our model has a different form.

The model shown in Figure 30.1 has three sections. On its left are the external influences of instruction, past events, and the present context in which the learner is placed. The center contains aspects of the individual that are involved in the process of learning. The outcome of learning is the new arrangement of memory, which is determined by the external influences as well as by prior memory, abilities, and attitudes. At the right is performance, the external act which is determined by perception of context, memory, attitude state, and abilities.

Most of our discussion of the decade's research is divided into sections related to elements of the model. Studies are not easily separated into those concerned with styles of instruction, attributes of learners, or forms of performance, because any investigation may involve all three of these bases of classification. Nevertheless, the separation has been made in an attempt to illuminate important issues in science education.

Most of the elements of Figure 30.1 are covered directly by sections in the chapter, though comments on context, experiences, and types of performance are made throughout rather than in separate sections. The descriptions in the various sections attest to the complexity of research during the decade. Before we turn to them, we should comment on the other outstanding characteristic of the decade's research, namely, its quantity.

There was such a remarkable growth in amount of research that it is now far from possible for any review to be comprehensive. We have had to select topics, and unwillingly omit interesting and relevant work on the history and philosophy of science teaching, teacher education, gender differences, mastery learning and test development. Further selection was necessary within topics. Our reference to pre-1971 studies is sufficient only to indicate the course of development of research, and few conference papers and dissertations are cited. Fortunately, reviews which often included unpublished work appeared frequently throughout the decade, and the present chapter can be read as a supplement to them. Among them are bibliographies (e.g., Wilson, 1981); the annual summaries that have been published in *Science Education* since 1975; and reviews, among which meta-analyses are becoming common, on limited topics, which appear regularly in *Studies in Science Education* and occasionally in the *Journal of Research in Science Teaching* and the *Review of Educational Research*.

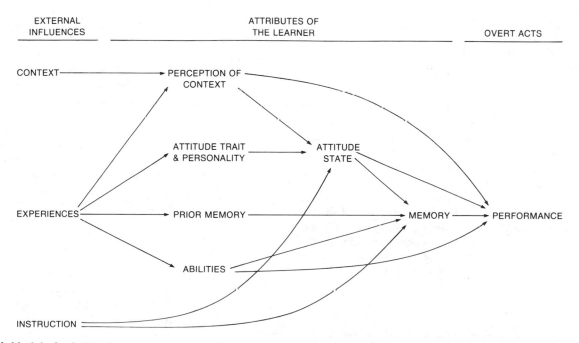

Fig. 30.1 Model of relations between external influences, characteristics of the learner, and performance.

Much of the present activity is a continuation of the growth that has long been evident in North America, where research in science education has been vigorous for many years. A more notable feature is the emergence of active groups in other countries. At the commencement of the decade nearly all science education research was concentrated in North America; no other region had a journal which was solely for reports of research on science education, and few foreign authors wrote for the American journals. The scene is different now. By the 1980s nearly a quarter of the articles in the *Journal of Research in Science Teaching* had a foreign author. The Australian Science Education Research Association held its first meeting in 1971, and the proceedings of its annual conference evolved to form the journal *Research in Science Education*. In Europe, two new journals began: *Studies in Science Education*, devoted to substantial reviews, in 1976; and the *European Journal of Science Education* in 1979; while yet another, *Research in Science and Technological Education*, is about to appear. Research centers grew in Europe, Australia, New Zealand, Israel, and Southeast Asia. These international developments are important, because as well as drawing on the American achievement they did much to foster the acceptance of theories and alternative styles of research which, as we try to show in a number of sections that follow, broadened and enriched science educators' perspectives.

Variables in Teaching

Many of the general effects of teaching are described in the sections on memory, ability, and attitude. Here we concentrate on issues of teaching that have received specialized attention in a science context, such as classroom organization, questioning, and preinstructional strategies; that we believe *should* receive attention, such as the design of texts; or that are of traditional importance in science education, such as the use of the laboratory.

The section begins with research on procedures in classrooms. Determinants of the effectiveness of teaching include the preparation of students for learning, the nature of interactions between pupils and teacher, and questioning techniques.

Preinstructional Strategies

Hartley and Davies (1976) identify four types of preinstructional technique: advance organizers, behavioral objectives, overviews, and pretests. They point out essential differences between the techniques in both form and function. They maintain that advance organizers clarify the learning task ahead by providing a conceptual framework that pupils can subsequently use; behavioral objectives inform them of what it is they are to accomplish; overviews prepare them for the learning task ahead; and pretests alert the learners to specific things they need to know. Researchers in science education have concentrated on advance organizers and behavioral objectives.

ADVANCE ORGANIZERS

Studies of advance organizers typically consist of comparing two groups, one of which receives information which it is believed will aid learners to assimilate a subsequent communication which is given to both groups.

Although most early studies showed that the advance organizer had a beneficial effect, mixed results began to appear in the past decade. A further instance of the positive effect of organizers comes from Kahle and Rastovac (1976), while no significant effect is reported by Clawson and Barnes (1973), Graber, Means, and Johnsten (1972), Kahle and Nordland (1975), and Koran and Koran (1973). After review, Hartley and Davies (1976) and Gabel, Kogan, and Sherwood (1980) concluded that advance organizers are generally advantageous, though results are not clear-cut. In contrast, Barnes and Clawson (1975), whose methods were criticized by Lawton and Wanska (1977), concluded that advance organizers generally are ineffective. Resolution of the conflict in results may lie in the suggestion by West and Fensham (1974) that advance organizers can assist learning only if they supply subsuming concepts which the students lack. West and Fensham (1976) argue that most advance organizer studies do not provide evidence about the validity of Ausubel's theory, since they do not eliminate alternative explanations for positive or negative results. West and Fensham (1976) attempted a more critical test by making two predictions: that only those learners who lack relevant prior knowledge will benefit from an advance organizer; and that the benefit can equally well be provided by remedial teaching of the relevant prior knowledge. Their results confirmed both predictions, providing strong support for at least part of Ausubel's theory.

BEHAVIORAL OBJECTIVES

The effect that behavioral objectives have on learning in science is not definitely established. Akers (1980) found that although a group that received behavioral objectives before instruction had greater achievement than a group that did not, the difference was not statistically significant. Kahle (1978) also found no significant difference in achievement, though objectives did enhance retention. In contrast, Anderson and Fowler (1978) found that behavioral objectives produced no significant improvement in retention performances, but noted an interaction between amount of prior knowledge and the cognitive level of behavioral objectives. For example, pupils high in prior knowledge who experienced a high cognitive level of behavioral objectives performed better than their lower-prior-knowledge peers on knowledge and comprehension questions in retention tests. Another example of an interaction is the observation by Hartley and Davies (1976) that pupils of middle ability appear to profit more from being given behavioral objectives than pupils of higher or lower ability.

General support for the use of objectives is available. In a meta-analysis Boulanger (1981b) clustered 11 science educational research studies dealing with several preinstructional strategies, and found that 8 of the studies on a total of 1,204 subjects yielded a statistically significant mean cognitive effect size which was favorable to the use of a preinstructional strategy. Among the strongest contributors to the large effect were the five studies on the use of behavioral objectives.

Interaction and Control in the Classroom

For convenience we have grouped the research into three conceptually interrelated categories dealing with classroom interactions, management, and structuring imposed by the teacher. All refer to aspects of the dynamics of teaching, what sorts of things teachers and students say to each other, what styles of teaching there are, what sorts of behavior students exhibit, and how the operation of the classroom is determined.

CLASSROOM INTERACTIONS

Formal instruments such as rating scales and sign and category systems are commonly used to investigate interaction patterns in science classrooms (Power, 1977), though informal procedures are sometimes employed (e.g., Hamilton, 1975). The formal instruments have been used to obtain data indirectly, from teachers' or pupils' perceptions, or directly, from live observations or recordings.

The Learning Environment Inventory (Anderson, 1971), or one of its adaptations, is often used in the indirect approach. It has been used to study general science, biology, chemistry, and physics classrooms (Walberg, 1974), self-paced science learning environments (Fraser, 1978; Power & Tisher, 1979), and kibbutzim classrooms (Sharan & Yaakobi, 1981). Walberg (1979) has compiled a comprehensive report of the findings associated with its applications around the world.

Direct observations have been conducted using a number of systems. Prior to 1973 there were about 14 schemes developed specifically to study science classrooms (Power, 1977) and others have been added since. An example is the Science Curriculum Assessment System (SCAS), which is described by Simon and Boyer (1974). It was used by Penick and Shymansky (1977) when they found that in teacher-structured classrooms the students spend more time watching teachers, following their directions, and initiating interactions with them. The Instrument for the Analysis of Science Teaching (IAST) (Hall, 1978), which focuses on processes, has been used with some success as a self-analysis tool for science teachers. Hall (1978) reports that the training module associated with IAST makes teachers more aware of their teaching behaviors, more aroused about being able to alter them, and more conscientious about planning for the kinds of teaching behaviors they wish to exhibit. The Science Teaching Observation Schedule (STOS) (Eggleston, Galton, & Jones, 1975) developed in the United Kingdom contains 23 categories which direct attention to the intellectual transactions taking place during science lessons. Although the scheme has its critics (e.g., Dunkerton & Guy, 1981), it has been used to map interactive behaviors of trainee science teachers (Dreyfus & Eggleston, 1979) and to establish typologies of science teachers that can be associated with pupil outcomes (Galton & Eggleston, 1979). The three typologies, teachers as informers, problem solvers, and enquirers, resemble those established by Tisher and Power (1978) in their studies of self-paced learning environments. Galton and Eggleston (1979) found that teachers rarely changed their style; no style was more effective with low-ability pupils; above-average pupils in physics and biology classes performed significantly better on posttests when taught by problem solvers; and the informing style was the one most often used by biology teachers. In Australia Tisher and Power (1978) used their multiple-category coding system SABIC, a Scheme for Analysing Behavior in Individualized Classrooms, to map interaction patterns and study associations between behaviors and outcomes. They found that pupil inactivity, teacher passivity, and managerial ineffectiveness were negatively related to science achievement and attitudes.

There are other schemes than those developed specifically for science lessons which have been used to study science classroom dynamics. Campbell (1977) used Flanders Interaction Categories to study verbal behavior in junior high classes, Abraham (1976) used an interaction analysis instrument based on Guilford's structure of the intellect model to study chemistry classes, and Crocker et al. (1977) and Oakley and Crocker (1980) used a modified Bellack scheme to code behaviors in elementary school classes. The rationale for the Crocker et al. (1977) project was derived from Barker's behavior setting concept (Barker, 1963) and from Bernstein's concept of strong and weak framing (Bernstein, 1971) as a way of viewing the range of options available to the pupil in the setting. This constitutes a break with much of the earlier research on classroom dynamics. Barker's ecological psychology has also provided guiding constructs for a Science Classroom Management Project in Australia where six pupil behavior codes for task involvement and deviancy and nine categories of lesson subsettings are used to describe secondary science teaching (Butler, Beasley, Buckley, & Endean, 1980). Another development is Munby's argument that novel, philosophically based conceptions are needed if classroom research is to inform practice. This leads him to the view that classroom studies should focus on the intellectual quality of teaching (Munby, 1980).

Studies of classroom dynamics provide a rich array of findings: The quality of interaction in classroom groups depends on whether the teacher elects to use homogeneous or heterogeneous groupings of pupils (Abraham, 1976); high-ability pupil groups have to wait longer than others following divergent and evaluative questions, but their contributions are used more frequently (Campbell, 1977); teacher behaviors are remarkably stable in whole-class and group settings in elementary schools (Crocker et al., 1977), but pupil behaviors differ markedly depending on the presence or absence of the teacher in the group setting (Oakley & Crocker, 1980); there is little interaction between girls and boys in science classes so the opportunity for girls to learn features of science from boys, who tend to have more knowledge, is low (Lockheed & Harris, 1982). These results highlight the complexity of science-learning environments.

So many coding schemes have been used for direct observations of classroom dynamics that there are insufficient replications of each study to allow a consolidation of knowledge about science teaching that can be generalized readily to more than one setting. It is not easy to synthesize the results from studies based on widely differing frameworks. The emergence of new frameworks derived from Barker's ecological psychology may herald a new and more cohesive approach to the study of science classrooms.

MANAGEMENT

The devotion of a N.S.S.E. (National Society for the Study of Education) yearbook (Duke, 1979) to the topic shows that there is considerable general research interest in classroom management. However, there have been few investigations of management in science education. Anderson (1980) conducted a naturalistic study of how elementary school teachers coped with the the tasks of classroom management and information structuring during science lessons. He noted that they allowed whole-class discussion to predominate. When they did allow individual work by pupils more management problems were created; for example, the amount of time spent on transitions from one activity to another increased. He also reported that there was little evidence that the teachers were truly concerned about the learning and enjoyment of pupils. If Anderson's findings are indicative of the state of science education in other elementary schools in the United States and the rest of the world, then the situation is an extremely sad one both with respect to teachers' abilities to cope and the lack of sparkle in elementary science education.

In a high school study, Nuccio (1982) looked more closely at actions of the teacher than at behavior of pupils. He defined effective teachers as those who spend more time on instruction. They devoted less time to initiating lessons or handling transitions, and more time to dealing with pupil inattention or disruption during lessons than their less effective colleagues. His findings are congruent with those in the general research literature that the more effective managers establish rules and procedures for the classroom, explain these carefully and explicitly at the beginning of the school year, use the rules and procedures consistently throughout the year, and suppress inappropriate behaviors quickly (Duke, 1979). Though further replications of management studies may be made with science classes, a more significant step educationally would be to conduct inservice and preservice programs in order to sensitize teachers to management issues and to develop their management skills. Emmer, Evertson, Clements, Sanford, and Worsham (1981) provide an example of such a program, though not in science. An evaluation of the training program could be undertaken to provide data for improvements. This type of approach involving action and evaluation departs from the traditional style of research in science education but is likely to have more effect on the practice of science teaching.

IMPOSED STRUCTURE

As well as establishing classroom rules and monitoring disruptive behavior, teachers can guide or organize what happens in the classroom by playing a dominant role in many of a lesson's activities. For example, they may curtail the proportion of time pupils talk by monopolizing the verbal discourse or they may restrict independent activities by setting pupils highly specific learning tasks. Several researchers have studied the effects that different types of teacher-imposed structure can have upon pupils' achievements, attitudes, and creativity. In Canada, Crocker, Bartlett, and Elliott (1976) compared the effect of greater teacher control within Grade 6 classes using units from a specially designed process-based elementary science curriculum with a less structured mode of using the units. In the unstructured mode pupils were provided with the necessary apparatus and the area of investigation while the structured mode was akin to a guided discovery approach. Overall the structured mode yielded better results, but it was evident that different strategies were more effective for different types of pupil.

Further studies indicate that when teacher directiveness is decreased the pupils exhibit more lesson-related behavior (Penick, Shymansky, Matthews, & Good, 1976), while in the teacher-structured environment more class time is spent listening to the teacher, following the teacher's directions, and copying peers' work (Allen, 1977). Form of structure does not greatly affect verbal creativity (Penick, 1976); and the attitude of male pupils, which is generally better than that of females, is higher with the student-structured style, whereas the attitude of females is higher with the teacher-structured (Abhyankar, 1977). It may be worth studying whether these results apply in other cultural settings since the findings from Australian research (Power & Tisher, 1976; Tisher & Power, 1975) indicate that imposed teacher structure need not lead to less desirable attitudes. However, Tisher and Power (1975) noted that under certain conditions pupils' attitude to science could be greatly depressed. This occurred where preservice teachers who did not value inquiry learning imposed additional structure in a classroom where ninth grade pupils were following a unit from the self-paced inquiry-centered Australian Science Education Project (ASEP). Their findings also indicated that moderate amounts of teacher structuring (review, overview, class discussion on salient points in each lesson) by teachers who valued the inquiry approach in ASEP led to greater gains in pupil achievement. This result complements that of Arlin and Westbury (1976), who investigated the effect of teacher pacing on high school pupils' mastery of science content. Their study indicates that teacher pacing tends to narrow the achievement variance in a class and to depress the mean class achievement by limiting the achievement of abler pupils. It is apparent that both benefits and deficits may be derived from additional levels of teacher structuring.

The Role of Questions and Skill in Questioning

Questions from the teacher are a common feature of classrooms in many parts of the world. The steady though small interest that researchers have maintained in the role of questions in science teaching may be indicative of a generally accepted belief that questioning, especially higher cognitive questioning, is an essential ingredient of inquiry and discovery and consequently should be fostered in science education. The belief persists despite general reviews of the research on questioning behaviors (Gall, 1970; Winne, 1979) which indicate that higher cognitive questions are not particularly effective in fostering pupil achievement. No doubt the recent meta-analysis by Redfield and Rousseau (1981), which concludes that higher cognitive questions have a greater effect on pupils' achievement than lower cognitive ones, will be accepted by some researchers as a vindication of their persistence.

The research on questions in science teaching is of three types. Some studies deal with the effect of questions in science texts; others with the improvement of teachers' questioning skills and the effects that new questioning skills have on pupils' achievement, critical thinking, and attitudes; and some with the effect of lengths of pauses between questions, responses, and reactions. All three types concern questions posed to the students. Brown, Campione, and Day (1981) advocate that attention should also be paid to the role of pupils' questions and to improving their skills in framing them.

QUESTIONS IN TEXT

Although early studies by Rothkopf (1970) showed that the insertion of questions in text has a positive effect on learning, recent studies in science teaching show that the result depends on attributes of the learner and may even be adverse. Holliday, Whittaker, and Loose (1978) found that the adjunct study questions made no difference to the performance of high-ability students and handicapped those of low ability. The selection of the questions is also important: Holliday (1981) found that a partial set of study questions encouraged pupils to concentrate on selected portions of critical information and resulted in inadequate processing of specialized material.

QUESTIONING SKILLS

Attempts to improve teachers' questioning skills have generally been short-term projects with preservice teachers. They indicate that training in the use of a question classification scheme can raise the cognitive level of questions that preservice teachers use (Riley, 1978), and that simple training procedures such as studying pamphlets and listening to audiotapes can improve teachers' questioning behaviors (Chewprecha, Gardner, & Sapianchai, 1980). The self-training materials produced by Chewprecha et al. (1980) and written and audiotape materials produced by Lamb (1977) were used with experienced teachers; the results support the general conclusion that—provided the teachers can be persuaded to work through them—training materials are effective in encouraging use of a wider cognitive variety of questions.

A few workers have examined the subsequent effects that new questioning strategies have in classrooms. Santiesteban (1976) noted that there were few attitudinal changes among primary pupils, although those subjected to more questions demanding classification and observation expressed more frustration with science. Ray (1979) varied the cognitive level of questions in two nondirective high school chemistry teaching strategies, and reported a higher performance on critical thinking and abstract reasoning among the pupils subjected to the higher cognitive treatment. On the other hand Tobin and Capie (1982) reported negligible effects on science achievement when they attempted to monitor and maintain high-quality questioning among teachers of Grades 6, 7, and 8. Riley (1981) found that pupils subjected to a 50–50 mix of higher cognitive and other questions did not perform as well as those who were subjected to either a low or a high proportion of higher cognitive questions. Riley (1981) compared his findings with significant studies in the general literature on questioning; this is an encouraging exception to normal practice, for few have attempted to integrate the work in science education on a research issue with that being done in other fields.

A disappointing feature of the published reports on questioning is that little detail is given about the nature and the quality of the treatments designed to improve teachers' skills. As a consequence researchers cannot replicate studies and practitioners cannot implement the training programs.

WAIT-TIME

Pauses or delays in classroom interaction patterns involving questions have received particular attention from researchers in science education. Rowe's early paper (1969) on wait-time, the length of the pauses between a teacher's question and a pupil's response or between that response and the teacher's subsequent reaction, stimulated a number of studies. Rowe summarized the first group of investigations, and discussed some of the methodological questions associated with the study of wait-time (Rowe, 1974a, 1974b). She stated that when wait-times are increased beyond a usual average of about 1 second to at least 3 to 5 seconds pupils increase the length of their responses, offer more alternative answers, ask more questions, interact more with other pupils, and appear more confident in their replies. Teachers who use longer wait-times tend to ask fewer yet more appropriate questions, demonstrate greater response flexibility, and alter their expectations of pupils (e.g., lifting those held for pupils previously rated as relatively slow).

Subsequent research dealing with the pauses between teachers' questions and pupils' responses (Wait-Time I) or with pauses between pupils' responses and teachers' reactions to these (Wait-Time II) generally supports Rowe's claims. Most wait-time studies have been conducted in elementary schools using preservice teachers and units from the Science Curriculum Improvement Study (SCIS). Usually the teachers were trained to alter the wait-times and the nature and patterning of the questions they asked. The training has involved microteaching (Anshutz, 1975; Esquivel, Lashier, & Smith, 1978), the study of instructional pamphlets (Chewprecha et al., 1980), minicourses plus analysis of written materials and classification exercises (Rice, 1977), and modeling (DeTure, 1979). It appears that the various training programs can effect the length of both wait-times, although Wait-Time II is more under the control of the teacher than Wait-Time I.

Studies of wait-time involving secondary teachers are few. In physics classes, Anderson (1978) was able to extend the wait-time between the teacher's question and pupil's response to more than 3 seconds and observed that the length of pupils' responses increased and that they perceived the lessons as being less difficult than did pupils in short wait-time classes. The pupils regarded the lessons as slow-moving and the apathy of girls increased. This research suggests that increases in wait-time interact with and affect pupils' attitudes and their perceptions of the learning environment.

Although wait-time may affect responses and attitudes, there is no compelling evidence that it is associated with pupils' science achievement. Anderson (1978) found no relation at the high school level and Anshutz (1975) reported none with third and fourth grade pupils using SCIS, though in a study of Wait-Time II in 23 Australian primary classes over a 13-week period, Tobin (1980) found that extension of pauses between pupil response and the teacher's reaction was associated with increases in achievement. He comments that the effect of wait-time on achievement is no doubt indirect. Increases in wait-times alone do not necessarily lead to increases in achievement; what counts is what the pupils are thinking during the periods of wait-time.

Tobias (1982) has discussed this point more generally. He argues that students experiencing apparently different instructional treatments may actually be employing identical cognitive processes. Altering wait-times and the nature of the associated teacher questions and reactions to pupil responses will be important only if there is heightened cognitive activity by pupils during Wait-Time I and by teachers during Wait-Time II. For example, pupil learning is more likely to be facilitated when Wait-Time I is extended if during that time they actively attempt to comprehend the teacher's question, and relate it to their prior knowledge. The research on wait-times indicates that little is known about what pupils are thinking during science instruction. Although difficult, it could be profitable to study what pupils and teachers think during pauses in order to discover how to train them to use those times more effectively.

Text Design

Texts are a common feature of schooling, but receive far less attention in science education research than many other instructional variables. Some studies of the effect of placement of questions in text were mentioned earlier, in the section on questioning. Illustrations have also been studied.

Barufaldi and Dietz (1975) showed that elementary school children perform better on observation and comparison tasks when given actual objects rather than photographs or drawings, which indicates that effort and skill are needed to process illustrations and abstract information from them. Line diagrams have been found to aid learning (Holliday, 1975; Holliday & Harvey, 1976), but when they do not (e.g., J. L. Thomas, 1978), possible interpretations are that processing did not occur because the students lacked the necessary skills or did not realize the advantage to be gained from the illustrations, or because they had such strong verbal skills that the illustration was redundant.

Dwyer (1972) presents results that are consistent with the notion of processing. Of four types of illustration, presented in black and white or color, the most effective was a simple line drawing in color, which students took most time to process. Dwyer suggested that the effect occurred because the students' experience led them to believe that line drawings are provided to teach something, while realistic drawings and photographs have the different purpose of attempting to acquaint them with reality. Requiring students to answer specific questions about an illustration should encourage processing and lead to improved learning, as Kauchak, Eggen, and Kirk (1978) found with graphs, though when Alesandrini and Rigney (1981) had undergraduates interact with illustrations on the touch-sensitive screen of a computer terminal their performance on a verbal posttest was not significantly better than that of a control group that received no pictorial assistance. Further research should follow Dwyer's practice of measuring the time learners spend on illustrations, and should attempt to discover the properties of illustrations that influence that time.

The involvement of skills is shown by a result obtained by Holliday, Brunner, and Donais (1977), when students had to learn either from colored drawings of objects, with verbal labels and arrows showing relations, or from uncolored block diagrams of printed words in rectangles and circles, with arrows. A significant difference was found only for students of low verbal aptitude, who presumably had trouble processing the greater number of words in the block diagrams. Winn (1980) provides further indication that students with higher verbal ability are better able to make use of block-word diagrams. When a diagram supplemented the text the cognitive structure, assessed by a word association method, of only the more able students was brought closer to the subject structure.

It would be useful to see whether students who appear not to benefit from illustrations can be trained in appropriate processing skills. Another line would be to see whether the layout of the text and illustrations can be arranged in ways that encourage processing. Wendt (1979) compared four arrangements of physics text and diagrams, and found that students preferred a novel double-page layout in which the first column contained basic information, the second additional explanations, the third illustrations, and the fourth peripheral information. Students who learned from that version had slightly greater achievement and took less time than the other groups. The shorter time result runs contrary to the notion of processing that was discussed in relation to Dwyer's study (1972), so investigation of the mechanism behind the various results is needed.

Although more research is needed on illustrations in text, they are relatively well studied compared with the form of the text itself. The work that Anderson (1966) originated on structure of oral communications could readily be applied to see whether variations in the structure of text affect learning. Studies of structure in oral communication appeared occasionally throughout the decade, but never became popular as a line of research. The studies may have lacked appeal because they were restricted to situations unlike those in the normal classroom, in which lectures were read from a script without the students' being able to ask questions, or because the outcome was perceived as obvious. Certainly the published studies contain few surprises. Anderson (1974) defined two indices for quantifying structure, one measuring the interlinking of terms in successive sentences and the other the rate at which important new ideas are introduced. Studies show that high values of the first index go with better acquisition of content (e.g., Lamb et al., 1979; Mathis & Schrum, 1977; Simmons, 1980). Other studies, in which fluctuations in the second index are measured throughout the communication, indicate that in effective structures main ideas are spaced through the script and each is elaborated before the next is introduced (Anderson & Lee, 1975; Lu, 1978). It should be a simple matter to check whether these results apply to large bodies of printed text.

Laboratory Work

Almost as a matter of dogma, laboratory work has long been accepted as an integral and vital part of science teaching. Nevertheless its purpose should be considered, partly so that investment in laboratories can be defended against attack from economy-seeking administrators and partly because detailed specification of aims guides both the design of laboratory exercises and the choice of dependent variables in investigations of the effectiveness of laboratory programs.

Statements about aims can be expressions of the writer's own views, or distillations from a survey. Both can be valuable. Kreitler and Kreitler (1974) provide an example of the first type. They argue from learning theory that the real value of laboratory experiments is in enabling students to check the truth of alternative notions and as a means of demonstrating concepts, and not in training students in problem solving or in evoking their curiosity. Surveys show that teachers and students do not agree with these views. Gould (1978) found that teachers now place more value on the laboratory as a means of arousing interest and in training students in problem solving, and less on it for aiding understanding, than they did 20 years ago. Students may see the use of the laboratory as different again: Osborne (1976) found that first-year undergraduates regarded laboratory studies as the most effective learning environment for creating interest in physics and for developing critical thinking, but placed it far behind tutorials, evaluation lessons, group study, self-study, and even lectures as a means of training in problem solving. Boud, Dunn, Kennedy, and Thorley (1980) support Osborne. They observed that undergraduates placed greater value than practicing scientists and recent graduates on the role of the laboratory in supporting information given in lectures and in stimulating interest, but lesser value on developing problem-solving skill. On the other hand, Ben-Zvi, Hofstein, Samuel, and Kempa (1976a) found that 10th grade students in Israel rated promotion of interest in chemistry last out of eight aims, with the provision of information and experience for the development of theory in third place; the remainder were laboratory skills.

Because opinions depend on local conditions, past experiences, reasons for being involved in the course, and so on, surveys naturally yield varying results, which must then be more useful for determining local action than as a contribution to theory. They do suggest, though, that evaluations of the laboratory should include attitudinal, cognitive, and motor outcomes.

Milson (1979) showed that giving students with reading difficulties the chance to work in the science laboratory improved their attitude to science class and to the laboratory, but not to the science teacher, the topic, or the school. It would be interesting to find whether this result holds for normal students, and, if it were replicated, why only some attitudes were affected. Johnson, Ryan, and Schroeder (1974) found laboratory work had a very positive effect on sixth grade students' attitude to science. They suggest that the determining factor may be the students' having control over their activities rather than the actual use of materials. Ben-Zvi, Hofstein, Samuel, and Kempa (1976a) make a similar comment: They found that tenth grade students preferred laboratory experiments and teacher demonstrations to film loops of experiments, which suggested to them that the factor is potential for involvement. Another possibility is that the laboratory allows greater interaction with other students and the teacher. Investigations, which might well involve interviews, are needed to test these suggestions.

Notions of control, involvement, and interaction are also involved in cognitive outcomes. Riban (1976) and Mackenzie and White (1982) applied them as principles in the design of fieldwork, though their techniques should be equally effective in the indoor laboratory. Riban developed a form of field study, applicable to all the natural sciences, in which students define their own problems for investigation, and after consulting with the teacher about their practicality, determine what data will be needed to solve them, and organize the collection by dividing responsibilities among themselves. Riban claims that the learning displayed with this method "exceeded any reasonable expectations" (p. 10). No groups of students showed poor learning, which indicates that group dynamics and the sharing of information may be responsible for the positive effect. Study of group dynamics in the laboratory and on excursions could be rewarding. Mackenzie and White (1982) found that eighth and ninth grade students retained information about the geography of coasts much better when the information was linked to episodes formed on an excursion. It was not enough merely to go on the excursion; the students had to be encouraged to process the experience through group discussions and by doing things such as observing, sketching, walking through mud, scrambling over cliff platforms, and tasting leaves.

Laboratory work that allows students the same levels of control as Riban's field study, and the same levels of involvement and interaction as it and Mackenzie and White's excursion, should be effective. That should be tested. Further, it needs to be known whether there is a lower limit to the age of children for whom the principles apply. Symington (1977) found that sixth grade students could generate their own problems for study in the laboratory, and Linn, Chen, and Thier (1977) found that fifth and sixth grade children were highly motivated and made gains (which did not quite reach conventional levels of statistical significance) in their ability to control variables when allowed to choose among a set of experiments, though few preferred to devise their own experiments. Possibly they would exercise this option if they were more accustomed to the activity.

Control and involvement may be responsible for the positive result Raghubir (1979) obtained when twelfth grade biology topics were introduced through laboratory experience, rather than the laboratory being used after lectures as a means of illustration. This method led to better cognitive performance in formulating hypotheses, making assumptions, designing investigations, understanding variables, and synthesizing new knowledge; and better attitudes in curiosity, openness, responsibility, and satisfaction. Reif and St. John (1979) used principles of interaction in an effective laboratory program. They divided the laboratory work in a college physics program into blocks, each containing five or six brief exercises done individually in which the student focused on a single topic or specific skill that would be needed in a subsequent complex experiment on which students worked in groups of four. Separating the single topics and skills allowed the students to make full and appropriate use of their interactive time on the complex experiment.

Few comparisons of the laboratory with other forms of instruction report in detail on the interactions between teacher and students (Hofstein & Lunetta, 1982), which makes it difficult to interpret results. When no difference is found between the laboratory and another method, it may be because the laboratory was so poorly organized that there was no control, involvement, or interaction, but could also occur when the compared technique encourages those processes. Cabrol and Cachet (1981) found that computer-simulated experiments, which allow control and involvement, were quite effective in training students in the principles of experimental method, though the authors warn that of course actual physical experimentation is essential for the acquisition of manipulative skills. Ben-Zvi, Hofstein, Samuel, and Kempa (1976b) showed that tenth grade students who observed experiments on film loops performed as well as students who actually did the experiments on tests of general chemistry achievement, knowledge of principles underlying chemistry experiments, and problem-solving ability in laboratory situations, and differed only on practical skills. The film loops allowed little control or interaction, but provided involvement at least as long as they were novel.

The laboratory is important for its own sake as well as for its influence on cognitive and affective outcomes. Doran (1978) provides a comprehensive review for the first part of the decade of issues and developments in the method of assessing laboratory performance. In that period techniques consisted of subjective judgments, often guided by checklists, made while observing students as they performed single operations or whole experiments. Further debate may be useful about which skills should be assessed. Eglen and Kempa (1974) specify four major skills: methodical working, experimental technique, manual dexterity, and orderliness. These may be compared with a set described by Tamir (1974), consisting of manipulation, self-reliance, observation, experimental design, communication, and reasoning. The debate about assessment would be aided by analysis of whether such sets are determined empirically, philosophically, or in response to social forces such as the demands of an examination system.

Since Doran's review there has been a new development, in accord with the criticism made by Garrett and Roberts (1982) that the classical experimental method employed in studies of the laboratory influenced researchers to ask the wrong questions. The questions were concerned solely with outcomes, not processes. By beginning with questions about what actually goes on in the laboratory and about students' perceptions of their purpose there, some researchers have been led to devise new styles of investigation. Tamir (1977a) made records of the amounts of time spent by the teacher and the students in seven types of activity such as prelab discussion and data analysis. Moreira (1980) asked Brazilian undergraduate students five questions after each of four experiments. These questions were aimed at assessing the purposefulness and degree of involvement of the students. The first question asked for the basic problem that the experiment was supposed to answer; then the key concepts in that problem were required; then a statement of the phenomena involved in the experiment, a description of the method, and finally the answer obtained to the basic problem. The results suggested that many students performed the experiments without understanding what they were doing. The same conclusion was obtained more directly by Tasker (1981) through observation of 11- to 14-year-old New Zealand children. By talking with the students during laboratory sessions, Tasker identified a number of surprising phenomena in the

conduct of the laboratory. For instance, the students perceived lessons, including laboratory sessions, as isolated events and not part of a planned sequence. They often failed to perceive the purpose of an experiment, and teachers often failed to explain it or to point out the significance of various crucial acts.

Tamir's, Moreira's, and Tasker's studies exhibit a concern for detail about students' actions and perceptions that should do much to increase understanding of the role of laboratory work in learning.

Memory Studies

This section includes studies of the effect of prior knowledge on new learning, the notion of cognitive structure, and developments in methods of probing understanding.

Prior Knowledge

First we consider prior knowledge as the repository of the general effects of language and culture, and then comment briefly on advance organizers and learning hierarchies. Other, more recent insights into the influence of prior knowledge are described under the heading of probes of understanding.

Munby (1976) describes how common language terms and forms disguise the fact that scientific statements are often intended to convey a different meaning from an everyday interpretation. What appear to be statements of fact about phenomena may be descriptions of models, which are to be discarded when further developments reduce their usefulness. Munby argues that the style of communication can determine whether students adopt realist or instrumentalist views of science, which in turn can affect attitudes to science and enrollments in science courses. Research into Munby's argument, and into the general influence of language on learning, is needed.

Some research has been done on difficulties caused by shifts in the meaning of a word between scientific and everyday contexts, and on the failure of students to comprehend the implications of logical connectives—words such as *because*, *however*, *but*, *therefore*, and *consequently*. Both types of difficulty may cause students to acquire different meanings from a communication than the teacher intended. Bell (1981) highlights problems with the word *animal*. She found that few New Zealand students between the ages of 10 and 15 accepted spiders, worms, and butterflies as animals. Many restricted *animal* to mean large four-legged mammals. Other instances of the confusion caused by everyday and specialist use of words concern force (Osborne & Gilbert, 1980b), energy (Duit, 1981), and living (Tamir, Gal-Choppin, & Nussinovitz, 1981).

Gardner (1977) reports that Grade 7 Australian students answered correctly about half the items in a test of logical connectives and Grade 10 students about three-quarters. Particular difficulty was found with connectives indicating inference, such as *therefore*, and qualified generalizations, such as *often* and *in general*. There appears to be no research into whether comprehension of connectives can be taught, and whether such teaching would improve understanding of science.

Further problems arise when the language of instruction is not an international one with well-established scientific terms. Strevens (1976) discusses the difficulties associated with absence of suitable words and concepts, unusual word orders, unfamiliarity with Latin and Greek roots, imprecise terms, and nondecimal number systems. Wilson (1981) should be consulted for a bibliography of studies on the effects of language and culture on the learning of science.

A few examples illustrate the potential that language and culture comparisons have for illuminating the processes of learning.

The same words are used in Japanese for extents of time and distance, but different words are used in Thai. Mori, Kitagawa, and Tadang (1974a) found that Thai kindergarten children, when judging the period of time a mechanical toy took to move between two points, were less affected than Japanese children by the distance between the points. Mori, Kojima, and Tadang (1976) found that Thai children's judgments of instantaneous speed were advanced beyond those of Japanese children. They relate this difference to the presence in Thai of separate words for early and fast, and for late and slow, which in Japanese have the same words.

Mori, Kitagawa, and Tadang (1974b) showed that religious beliefs affected Thai and Japanese conceptions of time. The Thais more often displayed the Buddhist notion of time as circular succession; Japanese students in Christian schools tended to see time as having a beginning and an end, and Japanese in public schools more often thought of time as linear but infinite.

At the beginning of the 1970s most work on prior knowledge was based on the theories of Ausubel and Gagné. Ausubel (1968) had written extensively on the processes of learning, describing in detail how new information is combined with old. Most research concentrated on a relatively minor part of Ausubel's theory, that is, the notion of advance organizer which was described earlier in the chapter under the heading of preinstructional strategies. Advance organizers are a simple idea, readily amenable to group experiments, while Ausubel's other ideas about assimilation of knowledge are more complex and may require detailed longitudinal studies of individuals, which so far researchers appear to have found daunting.

Ausubel's theory concerns the learning of verbal knowledge, while Gagné's is about intellectual skills. Gagné's principle of a learning hierarchy is that instruction can bring about the learning of an intellectual skill only if certain identifiable subordinate skills are present in memory. This principle was investigated from 1961 onwards, but was not finally established until the mid-1970s, following improvements in research methods by White (1974). White (1974), Linke (1974b), and Beeson (1977) confirmed that absence of a subordinate skill prevented acquisition of a higher one, and Trembath and White (1979) showed that if all the prerequisite skills were present any learner could be taught the higher skill successfully. The outcome in the Trembath and White study was limited to the students' being able to perform a skill in the form in which it was taught, which White (1979a) termed achievement and distinguished from understanding. Subsequent research on intellectual skills has been concerned with promoting their understanding, and the period of hierarchy validation appears to be over. White (1981)

provides a review of mainly Australian studies of intellectual skills which relate the hierarchy research to recent developments in cognitive structure and probes of understanding.

Cognitive Structure

In science education, cognitive structure is commonly defined as the representation of relations between elements of memory. This notion can be traced back to the work of Johnson (1964) and Deese (1962) and beyond. In the 1970s cognitive structure research was given fresh impetus by Shavelson, who used Johnson's and Deese's word association technique to compare the structure of mechanics as presented in a text with the way its constituent concepts were related in memory (Shavelson, 1972; Geeslin & Shavelson, 1975). Thro (1978) carried out a similar study.

In the word association technique, people are given the names of concepts, such as "force," and are required to respond with other names. In Shavelson's and earlier studies, the relation that the person had in mind between the stimulus name and the response was not asked for. A proximity measure, reflecting the similarity of response lists, is obtained for each pair of stimulus concepts, and these measures are used to construct a representation of the relations the people perceive among the concepts.

Shavelson (1974) discussed the use of word associations and another technique of tree construction in which a branching pattern is built up by pairing off members of a given list of concepts. Shavelson and Stanton (1975) compared word association with card-sorting and graph-building techniques, and concluded that they measure the same construct. In a further empirical study, Preece (1976b) compared two varieties of word association with tree construction and found that although they led to similar patterns of relations among concepts when responses for a whole group of people were summed, representations for an individual often differed. Preece (1976a) also compared the three alternative methods of spatial representations, nested hierarchies, and graphic networks for depicting relations between concepts. This study also produced evidence that ostensive concepts such as density and speed are integrated into cognitive structure before more abstract ones such as mass and time.

The complex methods of analysis used in Shavelson's, Preece's, and Thro's studies, which include directed graphs, proximity measures, multidimensional scaling, and cluster analysis, may have militated against wider use of the word association technique. A further negative influence is the constructive criticism by Strike and Posner (1976), Stewart (1979), and Sutton (1980), who, among other points, all comment that maps of cognitive structure tell nothing about the nature of the relation perceived between a pair of concepts. There have been two responses to this criticism: one to add nature of relations to maps of concepts; and one to represent cognitive structure by propositions, which are themselves statements of relations among concepts.

Gunstone (1980) required his respondents to a word association test to generate a sentence linking each response to its stimulus word. Gunstone showed that different forms of instruction in physics brought about different cognitive structures, even though the content was the same, and that in subsequent learning of a related topic further differences in cognitive structure appeared despite similar instruction and content. The differences in cognitive structure were reflected in differences on performance tests.

Champagne, Klopfer, DeSena, and Squires (1981) adapted the card-sorting method described by Shavelson and Stanton (1975), both to arrive at a map of cognitive structure more directly than happens with word association and to include the nature of relations between concepts. Eighth graders studying the Individualized Science unit Minerals and Rocks were given cards bearing the names of concepts such as granite, sedimentary, and magma, and were told to arrange them on a large sheet to show "how you think about the words." A researcher then asked each student why the names had been placed in that way, and as the student talked about them joined them with lines and wrote in the relation expressed by the student. The authors observed that instruction brought cognitive structures more into accord with the structure of the subject as perceived by geologists.

Pines (1977) used a very different technique to arrive at a representation of cognitive structure similar to that of Champagne et al. (1981). Through individual interviews with elementary school children, he obtained propositional statements about food chains which he converted to maps of cognitive structure. Although based on propositions, these maps consist of concepts with the propositions represented by the lines linking the concept nodes.

White (1979b) argued that concept names are not a fine enough unit to be useful, and advocated the use of propositions together with images, episodes, and intellectual skills, which he and Gagné (Gagné & White, 1978) had proposed as elements of memory, in representations of cognitive structure. White proposed that interview protocols should be scored on several dimensions to provide a vector of measures such as extent, precision, shape, and accord with authority, which would constitute a summary of an individual's cognitive structure. White and Gunstone (1980) interviewed science graduates on their knowledge of electric current and eucalypts, and found consistencies within individuals on most dimensions, implying that cognitive structure is affected by learning style as well as instruction.

Head and Sutton (1981) discuss the relation between cognitive structure and personality. They argue that individuals' affective dispositions reflect their cognitive structures, and that new insights into cognitive structure may be obtained through affect-based techniques such as sentence completion tests of ego involvement and through attending to children's spontaneous use of words when confronted with novel experiences. These interesting suggestions are too recent to have been followed up, but indicate one way in which developments in work on cognitive structure might occur.

Another possible development is foreshadowed by the observation by Sutton (1980) and White (1979b) that the language in which cognitive structure is discussed encourages the development of a static model, whereas memory may better be thought of as a dynamic property of the mind. No one has yet applied a dynamic model of cognitive structure in studies of science

learning, and it remains a distant but potentially important prospect.

Probing of Understanding

For many years now the dominant form of educational research has been the checking of a hypothesized relation between constructs. In terms of this research the measurement or description of a construct might be considered a primitive type of investigation which is long out of date. However, in recent years researchers from several countries have reported assessments of the understanding of particular scientific concepts and rules. The basic form of these studies may be primitive, but the methods that are used to probe understanding are subtle, and unexpected and challenging results have been obtained.

The studies began to appear in numbers, apparently spontaneously, in the mid-1970s, to such an extent that two conferences featuring them have been held. The proceedings are reported by Archenhold, Driver, Orton, and Wood-Robinson (1980) and Jung, Pfundt, and von Rhöneck (1982). This research may be an aspect of the general rise in interest in cognition that has been apparent since the 1960s, but there is no clear reason why the sporadic earlier appearances, for example Doran (1972), did not attract more attention or why the field began to flourish when it did. Perhaps a clue to the earlier lack of interest is provided by Coulter, Williams, and Schulz (1981), who suggest that an apparent mismatch between the capabilities of students, as assessed in terms of Piagetian stages, and the stated objectives of their science courses is tolerated because the tests their teachers use give too much weight to simple recall of facts or to well-drilled-type problems, so that the teachers are satisfied that learning is proceeding when in fact little understanding is being gained. Stewart and Dale (1981) provide further evidence that success in routine problems can mask a lack of understanding. Through interviews, they found that many students who were able to solve genetics problems by following an algorithm had incorrect or no knowledge of meiosis. Lack of understanding was not seen as a problem that existed, then, so that there was no need to probe. The Piagetian studies of level attainment that became popular in the 1970s may have suggested that there was some cause for concern, and at the same time provided, in the clinical interview, a sensitive tool for science education researchers to adapt to assessment of understanding. Debate over curricula, too, may have heightened concern for the relevance of science courses to common aspects of life, which led to studies such as Za'rour's (1976) interviews of 220 Lebanese children on their understanding of the natural phenomena of the drying of clothes, shape of the moon, rain, and falling bodies.

Whatever the reason, since the mid-1970s there have been many assessments of understanding, with students from elementary school to university, employing a variety of methods, including new techniques for group measurements as well as individual clinical interviews.

Nussbaum and Novak's (1976) study of American elementary school children's concept of the earth illustrates the sophistication of interview techniques. They arranged individual interviews with second graders, some before and some after a series of lessons on the earth, force, and gravity. The interviewer began with questions such as "What is the shape of the earth?" "Which way do we have to look in order to see the earth?" and "Why don't we see the earth as a ball?" Then the child was shown a toy figure of a girl standing on the side (equator) of a globe, and asked to draw on a diagram of the globe and girl the direction in which a rock would fall if it were dropped by the girl. Other tasks and questions followed. The sophistication of the method lies in these tasks and questions. Some children who had begun by saying that the earth is round were found to believe, for instance, that the "earth" referred to is a separate planet in the sky rather than the object on which they stood, or that it has a "bottom" somewhere past the South Pole to which things fall. In all, Nussbaum and Novak identified five notions about the earth in space, the last being the adult view. The study was replicated by Mali and Howe (1979) in Nepal, where — despite the presence of a very different cultural tradition, including the belief that the earth is flat and supported by an elephant, which may well have interfered with the instruction the children had received about the earth being round — all five notions were identified again.

One of the concerns researchers have with interviews is that they are so time consuming that only a small sample can be assessed. They need to be supplemented with a test that can be given to a group in order to check whether the conclusions obtained from the interviews hold generally. Nussbaum (1979) developed a multiple choice test, covering the five notions of the earth revealed in the Nussbaum and Novak (1976) study, and gave it to 240 students in Grades 4 to 8 in Israel. The results were consistent with the interviews, though one new notion was found.

Erickson (1979, 1980) followed the same pattern. In the first study he interviewed 10 Canadian children of ages 6 to 13 on their conceptions of heat and temperature, and then for the second study produced a Likert-scale test that incorporated the beliefs expressed in the interviews as well as the current scientific kinetic and the old caloric views, which he gave to 276 fifth-, seventh-, and ninth-graders.

By studying children of different ages, Nussbaum and Novak and Erickson were able to see gradual shifts towards scientists' conceptions. It is interesting that such a shift is necessary: Why do children develop contrary views at all, and even when they do, why do some children in a class persist in holding to a primitive view when others are prepared to accept a new one? Illumination is provided by Novick and Nussbaum (1978), who interviewed eighth-graders in Israel about their notions of the particulate nature of matter. The students displayed various conceptions of gases, including the views that they are continuous, that they are empty space, that there are particles regularly spaced, and so on. Novick and Nussbaum observed that the aspects of the scientists' model that are least assimilated are those that are hardest to reconcile with sensory perception.

Novick and Nussbaum's observation suggests that many learning difficulties arise because the student does not enter the classroom as a tabula rasa, a clean sheet on which the teacher inscribes knowledge. Nor is removal of erroneous beliefs a simple matter of cleaning mistakes from the blackboard of the mind. Instead, the students arrive with complex sets of preconceptions which, as Ausubel (1968) noted, are held strongly and are difficult to change.

Driver and Easley (1978) discussed children's formation of preconceptions, which, rather than call misconceptions, they name alternative frameworks. Driver and Easley argue that while frameworks are built up from experiences, it is important to recognize that there is a constructive element that requires creativity and imagination. The alternative frameworks are consequences of imaginative efforts to understand events. Because the frameworks are built up by the children themselves, they may be held more tenaciously than ideas their teachers give directly to them. The alternative frameworks are to be distinguished from the mistaken connections pupils make in the course of instruction.

Many investigations support the view that students construct their own frameworks. Andersson (n.d.), Fredette and Lochhead (1980), Tiberghien and Delacôte (1976) gave the same task, of arranging a battery, globe, and wire so that the globe lit up, to 7- and 12-year-olds in France, to engineering college students in the United States, and to secondary school students in Sweden. In all of these case studies, many were unable to perform the task, and a common unsuccessful effort was to place the wire between the positive terminal of the battery and the base of the globe. Andersson suggests that this may be a consequence of observing that most electrical appliances have a single lead, which people often do not realize contains more than one wire. That observation, and analogies with fuels such as gas, overrode the instruction that many of the students had had about electric circuits. Angus (1981) found that elementary school children often classified natural phenomena that involved motion, such as clouds, as living things, even though they had relatively little difficulty in classifying plants and animals. This, too, is consistent with the notion that perceptual features are used before formal instruction to develop interpretations of the world that may be difficult to alter later. Another consistent result was found by Brumby (1981) in interviews with medical students, many of whom, when asked how they would tell whether a strange-looking object they were shown was now alive or had ever been alive, suggested prodding it to see if it moved or immersing it in water to see if it gave off bubbles, while few thought of looking for cellular structure or the presence of DNA.

Investigations of understanding of mechanics, employing a range of methods, provide further instances. Helm (1980), using a multiple choice test, found that Aristotelian notions were common among South African students in 11th and 12th grades. Helm ascribed these notions to examinations, texts, and teachers, and although those may contribute, it seems that observations of the world also play a major part. Viennot (1979) discussed the formation of alternative views of mechanics, and while her results and discussion support the proposition that students develop their own scientific principles from observations of the world, she argues that the intuitive laws that she observed among French students are more like an impetus theory of motion rather than truly Aristotelian. Osborne (1980) also found alternative views, which might be called Aristotelian, to be common among New Zealand students aged from 9 to 19. Osborne probed their understanding of force in interviews centered on line drawings of situations such as a man hitting a golf ball. The technique is described by Osborne and Gilbert (1980a, 1980b), who used it in England to assess secondary school students' concepts of work and electric current. Its commonest use has been in a remarkable series of studies in the New Zealand Learning in Science Project by, for instance, K. Stead and Osborne (1981) on friction and B. Stead and Osborne (1980) on light. The LIRESPT group at the University of Paris have also used interviews extensively (e.g., Guesne, Tiberghien, & Delacôte, 1978).

Champagne, Klopfer, and Anderson (1980) developed a group technique, in which students are shown a physical situation and asked first to predict what will happen when a certain change is made, then to observe the change and its consequences, and finally to explain any discrepancy between their prediction and observation. They found that many of a large group of American undergraduate physics students had Aristotelian views about force and motion, which were relatively unaffected by instruction on Newtonian mechanics. Using the same technique, Gunstone and White (1981) obtained similar results with Australian undergraduates. In both cases the extent of the nonscientific views was surprisingly great. Gunstone and White observed that the students often made observations that accorded with their predictions, even when these were unusual. This illustrates a tendency to see the world as consistent with one's beliefs, so that once a notion of, for instance, force being necessary for motion or of the earth being flat has been formed by observation, it is difficult to change it because disconfirming instances are either not observed or are misobserved.

The next phase of research, to follow these assessments of understanding, will be to discover how alternative conceptions may be brought to conform with scientists' views. This may require careful analysis of the subject matter as well as the students' beliefs. Sexl (1981) and Duit (1981) provide an example of the sort of analysis involved. They discuss the teaching of the concept of energy. Sexl points out that energy is one physical quantity that cannot be defined operationally, and argues that its teaching should follow the same path as the historical development in which consideration of many interactions led to recognition that a quantity, later named energy, remained constant. Duit describes practical attempts to follow that path, and identifies colloquial use of the word *energy* as a factor that interferes with understanding of the conservation principle. Duit suggests that teaching build on the colloquial conception by beginning with the semantic anchor that energy is necessary when things are accelerated, lifted, illuminated, or heated, and then elaborating that anchor by discussing simple examples such as the pendulum or the flywheel.

Even with careful analysis of content and beliefs it may not be easy to change alternative conceptions. Smolicz and Nunan (1975) remind us that we should not be surprised by students' being unwilling to change beliefs in the face of evidence when scientists themselves hold to theories long after observations should have made them untenable. A preliminary attempt shows how difficult the task may be. Gunstone, Champagne, and Klopfer (1981) worked intensively for 1 day a week for 8 weeks with 12 seventh and eighth grade students who were selected for their high levels of interest and ability in science. On the first day the researchers used several methods, including the prediction–observation–explanation type described above, to establish the beliefs the students had about force and motion. In

subsequent sessions the students had experiences including weighing and dropping objects of different mass in air and water, observing them fall in vacuum, observing and measuring the motion of gliders on an air track, and operating a computer simulation of Aristotelian and Newtonian worlds. Frequent group discussions occurred. Before the final session the students showed that they had apparently acquired a satisfactory view of force and motion. However, as discussions continued it was found that most endorsed the view that velocity is proportional to force, and that they had unscientific notions of inertia. New prediction–observation–explanation tasks revealed that intuitive ideas persisted, and that most of the students retained Aristotelian notions along with their new Newtonian knowledge.

The above study shows that a major difficulty to be surmounted is the capacity humans have for storing conflicting principles. In an imaginative investigation, Dreyfus and Jungwirth (1980) showed that the context of a problem determines whether people use their scientific knowledge or their intuitive knowledge to solve it. A further instance is Brumby's (1979) study of students' choice to apply in a problem either the principles of natural selection that they had been taught or the Lamarckian views that they had developed for themselves. Unless the students are brought to acknowledge the conflict and to resolve it by reconstruction of their knowledge, this capacity to choose between conflicting views kept in separate compartments may make ineffective Driver's recommendation (1981) that teachers use laboratory activities to disprove interpretations as well as to confirm accepted ones. Stavy and Berkovitz (1980), however, were able to improve Israeli fourth-graders' conceptions of temperature by a confrontation technique. They noted that students at this level expressed the contradictory views that cold water mixed with cold water gives cold water, but that water at 10°C plus more water at 10°C gives water at 20°C. Both class teaching and individual training that made the children aware of the contradiction made them better able to solve similar problems than a control group. While this result is encouraging, it may be that further probing, with problems of a different type, would have revealed cases among the apparent successes where the contradictory views were still held, as happened with Gunstone et al. (1981).

Hewson (1982) provides one further report of success in changing deep-rooted beliefs. In order to improve the conceptions ninth grade South African students held of mass, volume, and density she combined several teaching strategies which included the use of questions and discussions to link abstract concepts with common experiences, and the provision of direct experiences that would show the learners that the new conceptions are plausible and would sharpen their definitions of terms.

Further attempts to bring about changes in learners' conceptions might well be based on the conditions that Posner, Strike, Hewson, and Gertzog (1982) have set out: The learner must be dissatisfied with his or her existing conception, and must find the new conception intelligible, plausible, and fruitful.

Ability Studies

Although many examples exist of science education studies that incorporate abilities or ability-related strategies such as serialist versus holist and deep versus surface processing, this section is restricted to those aspects of ability in which the science-oriented research is particularly prominent. Instances are attempts to identify and promote strategies used in problem solving and the study of the broad styles of processing information that are known as cognitive preferences, but by far the most popular basis for work in science education on abilities is Piaget's theory of intellectual development.

Problem-Solving Strategies

Research on problem solving is consistent with the theme pervading this chapter that mechanisms for effects should be made explicit. The strategies employed in solving problems are identified by having subjects in interviews think aloud. Thorsland and Novak (1974) used the thinking aloud technique to grade college physics students on the degrees to which they displayed analytic and intuitive strategies. The students could demonstrate both strategies, which are independent abilities and not mutually exclusive styles. Possession of the analytic strategy was found to be positively related to scholastic aptitude, but the intuitive strategy was unrelated. Through interviews, Larkin and Reif (1979) found differences in the strategies employed by novice and expert problem solvers in physics. The novice was quick to convert the problem to equations, and began manipulating them early. The expert explored the conditions of the problem more fully, making sure that the procedure was sound before putting down the equations as a group and rapidly dealing with the mathematics at the end. In a parallel observation, Wright (1979) found that people who failed at a problem said they could have been more successful if they had taken more time to sort out its crucial elements before adopting a line of solution. Wright found that training preservice teachers to attend to salient aspects of problems improved their performance at solving them.

The interview technique is practical with young students as well as adults. Mandell (1980) used it to identify strategies employed by successful problem solvers in sixth grade.

While investigations so far have attended to identifying strategies, no doubt the future will see attempts to train students in their use. An essential feature of such studies will be demonstration that the students can apply the strategies to problems quite dissimilar to those used in the training.

Cognitive Preferences

Cognitive preferences are predilections to process information in particular ways. In his seminal paper, Heath (1964) described four types, which may be summarized as preferences for principles, applications, questioning, or memorizing. Tests based on his notion consist of items requiring a choice between four correct statements, one for each of the ways of processing. The items are generally in one subject field. In one commonly used version (Atwood, 1971) the principles choice was omitted.

Brown (1975) questioned the validity of cognitive preference tests, and argued that the choice depended on the respondent's level of attainment in relation to Bloom's taxonomy (1956). Tamir (1977b) countered her arguments, though the observa-

tion that preference for memorizing is associated with poorer achievement is consistent with Brown's suggestion.

The relation between cognitive preference and learning is confused by conflicting results. Although the poorer achievers are usually those who display a preference for memorizing, there is no consistency in which of the other three preferences is found to be associated with superior performance. Sometimes it is questioning (Tamir, 1976), sometimes principles as well as questioning with applications also inferior (Kempa & Dubé, 1973; Mackay, 1972), and sometimes applications (Barnett, 1974). Further problems are caused by attempts to reduce the four preferences to two factors, when sometimes questioning and memorizing appear as opposite ends of a dimension (Kempa & Dubé, 1973) and sometimes questioning and applications (Mackay, 1972).

Some of the conflict may be due to the dimensions and relations depending on the subject matter (Mackay, 1975; Tamir, 1976). A simpler explanation is that the three preferences occasionally found to be associated with superior achievement are all reflections of a tendency to process information, in contrast to memorizing which reflects a tendency merely to accept information in the form in which it is presented. Cognitive preferences then fit well into an information-processing model.

There was a period when cognitive preferences appeared on the threshold of becoming a popular subject for research, but they now seem to be a minor though imaginative notion which might fade from view as they are overtaken by more precise formulations of the strategies used in learning. Trenchant criticism by Jungwirth (1980) of interpretations of cognitive preference scores may hasten the process.

Piagetian Studies

Piaget's work on children's development of mental strategies goes back to the 1920s. Because the strategies he studied are concerned with people's abilities to interpret the natural world and to cope with abstract representations of it, Piaget's theory is highly relevant to learning in science. However, science educators long overlooked it. In a true reflection of the state of research 10 years ago, Shulman and Tamir (1973) found it necessary to give Piaget only four passing mentions, and cited hardly any studies based on his work. That is remarkable when one contemplates the enthusiasm with which researchers in the 1970s took up Piaget's ideas to such an extent that studies based on them now dominate the science education literature.

Popularity exacts a price. Only that part of the theory which concerns stages of development has received much attention. Groen (1978) argues that Piaget's theory is too complex and interwoven for parts of it to be separated without distortion, so that when stages (which are not part of the invariant core of the theory) become the focus, new postulates have to be supplied to support them. These additions are idiosyncratic, so what is known as Piagetian theory differs from researcher to researcher. Groen's argument may explain the origin of the disagreements that occasionally occur between people who work within the Piagetian frame. Examples are the brief confrontation between Bady and Karplus (Bady, 1978), centering on whether the members of a stage are children or schemes, and the argument between Phillips and Lawson about the validity of the Karplus island puzzle and the immersed cylinders test used by Blake, Lawson, and Nordland (1976) as measures of formal operational thought (Phillips, 1977).

Another consequence of concentration on stages is lack of concern for the individual. Once people are labeled as belonging to a stage, there is a temptation to treat them as identical. Given Piaget's attention to individuals, it is ironic that, with few exceptions (e.g., Rowell & Dawson, 1977), the researchers who cite him are more concerned with treating learners as members of groups than are investigators in fields such as memory studies who have not based their work on Piagetian theory. Researchers who study the ways in which learners interact with the world and build up their own conceptions of it are more the true inheritors of the Piagetian tradition than those who concentrate on stages.

Excessive concentration on stages opens the Piagetian movement to attack from without. Novak (1977) advanced six reasons why the notion of stage should be abandoned, which consist of demonstrations that stages refer to no consistencies in behavior, that very young children are observed to think formally and the increase with age in the proportion of the population who can do this is gradual rather than stepped, that many adults do not exhibit formal thought, that throughout their period of development children demonstrate all types of thought depending on the context, and that stage is related to external factors such as socioeconomic status. Novak (1978) used those points to argue that Ausubel's theory of learning should be preferred to Piaget's developmental one. He put it as a choice: "The key issue in this paper is whether children develop general 'cognitive structures' or 'cognitive operations' to make sense out of experience, or if instead, they acquire a hierarchically organized framework of specific concepts, each of which or some combination permits them to make sense out of an experience" (pp. 3–4).

Perhaps the emphasis that many people around him were placing on stages led Novak to this position. However, it is not necessary to see Ausubel's and Piaget's theories as opposed. Indeed, Novak (1978) interprets the results of many stage studies as being consistent with Ausubel's theory, researchers within the Piagetian mould quote Ausubel with approval (e.g., Lawson, 1978), and it is not easy to devise an experiment that would provide a result supporting one of the theories and not the other. Herron (1978) discussed Novak's criticisms of stages, and suggested that both Ausubel's and Piaget's theories provide useful bases for research. The most crucial point that Herron makes is that Novak does not appear to distinguish between concepts and operations. This distinction is the key to a resolution of the Ausubelian and Piagetian positions. If it can be accepted that Ausubel is concerned with the building up of information and Piaget with the building up of generalized logical operations, both of which constructions depend on interactions of the learner with the world, then a useful synthesis is possible. This will involve more concern with specific abilities such as seriation, conservation of volume and other quantities, proportional reasoning, and control of variables, and less with stages, and consequently more attention to individuals than to groups. Our separation of abilities and memory in the model of Figure 30.1 is an attempt to speed that

acceptance and promote the synthesis.

Piaget (1964) proposed four necessary conditions for intellectual development: maturation, experience, social interaction, and equilibration. There are few studies in science education of the way these conditions operate in individuals: most involve people in groups, and shed little light on the process of development or contribute to the advance of Piagetian theory. Nearly all of the studies have one or other of four purposes: invention and validation of group tests which are to be used as alternatives to Piaget's method of clinical interview; determinations of fractions of a population in each stage, or who can perform a specific task; measurement of correlations between stage of development and other variables, particularly school achievement; and hastening the transition from one stage to the next or the acquisition of a specific ability.

PRODUCTION OF GROUP TESTS

Although the first purpose is a practical one, attempts at fulfilling it do lead to implications for theory. Interviews consume time, and require skilled, experienced people. A group test that could be administered by someone with brief training would enable larger-scale, more powerful research investigations, and would allow teachers to assess the levels of functioning of all the students in their classes. Several tests have been proposed, which diverge to varying extents from the procedure of interviews. All the tasks Piaget used in interviews involved actual objects or apparatus. In the group tests that remain closest to Piaget's procedure, such as those of Lawson (1978) and Rowell and Hoffman (1975), all subjects have their own sets of apparatus, with which they can interact as they would in an interview. The replacement of the interviewer by printed instructions and questions, and of oral responses and physical acts with written answers, inevitably causes loss of flexibility in questioning and in depth of insight. Providing individual apparatus is expensive and setting it out takes time, so in other tests the individual sets are replaced by a single demonstration, as in the tests of Robertson and Richardson (1975), Shayer and Warry (1974), and Tisher and Dale (1975) (though in practice this last test has often been used without the demonstration), or by a videotape, as in Staver and Gabel (1979). The greatest degree of divergence is in tests where no apparatus at all is used, only pencil and paper. This last group can be divided into those based on Piaget's interview tasks, such as Renner (1979), and those based on Piaget's binary operations, which his theory identifies as comprising logical thinking, such as Longeot's test (1965) and Sheehan's translated version of it (Sheehan, 1970), and Raven's (1973) test.

The group tests have to meet certain practical criteria, such as ease of administration, and must be valid. Lawson (1978) illustrates the preparation and validation of a group test. Lawson set out clear criteria for his test: It should measure concrete and formal operational reasoning, be suitable for class administration and require little time, should use physical materials and require little reading or writing, and consist of a large number of varied items to ensure reliability. The last criterion reveals one of the problems with these tests. While a greater number of items will increase reliability, greater variety generally will not. Variety supplies validity when a multidimensional construct is being measured. It seems that formal operational thinking is not a single ability, and a range of items is desirable. The problem, which is often solved arbitrarily, then is to determine what sorts of items and how many of each are to be included.

Lawson took considerable care in checking the validity of his test. He obtained face validity by having six experienced judges inspect the items, and convergent and factorial reliability by comparing the test results of 72 children with their responses in individual interviews on four Piagetian tasks. Convergent validity was indicated by a correlation of .76 between the test score and an assessment of developmental level obtained from two of the interview tasks. Factor analysis of all the data, test and interview combined, yielded three factors which Lawson interpreted as formal, concrete, and early formal reasoning. As Lawson expected that there would be only two factors, the presence of the third indicates a weakness of the stage notion. The terms "stage" and "level" inevitably imply steps, whereas the need to propose intermediate values suggests that development is better to be regarded as a ramp. This is further shown by the rather arbitrary way in which Lawson split the distribution of the test scores into three categories which were supposed to represent levels of reasoning. This is contrary to the dictum of Shayer, Adey, and Wylam (1981) that "each test should enable response to be assessed directly in terms of Piagetian level, rather than by indirect inference from total test score" (p. 158).

The awkward features of arbitrary combinations of items and arbitrary divisions and labeling of total scores are unnecessary if the notion of stage is abandoned. The individual items in Lawson's test, as in others, are sensible and provide a good assessment of a learner's possession of a specific strategy. Our argument is that there is more advantage, both in the advancement of theory and in classroom practice, in concentrating on the specific strategies rather than on the nebulous stages, though, as we discuss later, this is not to be taken as encouragement to teach directly the tested task.

Results of other investigations support the recommendation against stages. Most report moderate to low correlations between the group test scores and assessment of development based on clinical interviews. There is a tendency for the correlations to decrease as we move from a test that uses individual apparatus, Lawson's, to demonstrations and to pencil-and-paper tests. Lawson (1978) reported a correlation of .76. Shayer et al. (1981) used a demonstration and written responses to predetermined questions, but otherwise tried to preserve as many features of the clinical interview tasks as they could. For six tasks, they found correlations ranging from .55 to .85 between the test assessment of each task and the corresponding clinical interview. Staver and Gabel (1979) devised a group test with four scales, on conservation of volume by liquid displacement, separation and control of variables, combinational analysis, and proportional reasoning. The test used videotapes to present the same five cognitive tasks as were used in clinical interviews with the subjects (two tasks were used for proportional reasoning). The correlations between corresponding test and interview assessments were .07, .50, .18, and .58, comparable with the correlations of both assessments with scores on the several scales of a general ability measure, the

Cognitive Abilities Test, which had also been administered. These results led the authors to state that "little evidence for convergence between the two Piagetian methods is present" (p. 259), though surprisingly they claim the test is a valid one.

The remaining tests are pencil-and-paper types. Renner (1979) had subjects write their solutions to science problems, and estimated their intellectual development by analyzing their use of language. From an original set of 30 problems, 12 were selected as measures of intellectual development, and were given to a large number of 10th, 11th, and 12th grade students along with interviews on the four Piagetian tasks of conservation of volume, bending rods, equilibrium of the balance, and colored chemicals. The interview tasks were used to form an overall assessment of level of intellectual development. Performance on only 4 of the problems was found to be related to this assessment, and their multiple correlation with the assessment was .62.

Tschopp and Kurdek (1981) compared the performance of 27 Grade 9 and 10 Grade 11 children on an unpublished pencil-and-paper test with that on traditional Piagetian tasks administered in individual interviews. The correlations between the interview tasks and their analogous items on the group test ranged from −.20 to .35. The authors also found little consistency in performance between the parts within the test. While that may be taken as a fault of the test, the authors point out that Martorano (1977) found the same lack of consistency for clinical interview tasks that were supposed to be measuring formal operational thought. They warn "against viewing formal operations as a unitary construct. In contrast to Inhelder and Piaget (1958) we found that formal operations is not an all-or-nothing occurrence and that instruction should not be expected to generalize from one task to the next" (p. 90).

Ward, Nurrenborn, Lucas, and Herron (1981) found the correlation of Sheehan's (1970) version of the Longeot test with individual assessments of performance on Piaget's balance beam and flexible rods task to be .62 for college chemistry students. Blake (1980), however, found much lower correlations of .39 and .38 for two Australian secondary school samples between the Sheehan test and individual assessment on conservation of weight, conservation of displacement volume, separation of variables, and equilibrium in the balance. He also found moderate correlations, .55 and .48, for these samples between the Piagetian tasks and scores on the Tisher and Dale (1975) group test. Blake also measured level of reading comprehension for one sample and field dependence–independence for the other. He concluded that the Longeot test is not a good predictor of level of development for Grades 10 to 12, because reading ability affects scores below Grade 11 and field dependence–independence is generally related to performance at all grades, and that the Tisher and Dale test is not suitable below Grade 11 because reading ability then affects scores.

None of the foregoing studies reports consistently high correlations between group tests and interview assessments. Interpretation of the results is of course subjective; ours is that the group tests may be measuring some important trait, but it is not at all close to being the same thing that is assessed in individual interviews. The fault may lie in the group tests, though they appear to be carefully designed. We would also question whether the construct, level of intellectual development, as assessed by the clinical interview, is sufficiently unitary and stable to be useful as a criterion.

The second type of purpose is assessment of the proportion of a population in each developmental stage. Studies frequently combine this purpose with the third, of measuring the correlation between stage and other variables.

Most studies with the second purpose are concerned with general abilities, assessing the proportions capable of formal and concrete operational thought, though some (e.g., Carlson, 1976; Raven, 1972) deal with specific skills. Raven tested children from third to sixth grades on their achievement of the concepts of speed and acceleration. Piaget (1946/1970) had described four stages in children's development of the relations between speed, time, and distance, and Raven found that his results were very similar to Piaget's and consistent with his stages. In contrast, Carlson (1976) reported that the performance of children in Grades 1 to 6 on tasks of locating points in one, two, and three dimensions was contrary to Piaget's data and theory. Further contradictory results should promote reconsideration of the accuracy and value of Piaget's theory.

Chiappetta (1976) and Levine and Linn (1977) reviewed studies wherein the general abilities of concrete and formal operations were assessed, and as there have been few such studies since, we will not repeat their observations except to say that a common result is that far fewer people are found to demonstrate formal operational thinking than Piaget's early work indicated. In a study of thousands of 13- to 15-year-old students in the US and six European countries, Karplus, Karplus, Formisano, and Paulsen (1977) found that only about 20% used formal operations, while at college level the proportion of freshmen found to be using formal operational thinking was reported to be 25% by Killian (1979) and McKinnon and Renner (1971), 30% by Kolodiy (1975) and Griffiths (1976), and 40% by Renner and Lawson (1973). These values suggest that variations in development in an age group are so extensive that teachers and curriculum developers will encounter problems in adjusting methods or content to accommodate them.

Studies with the third purpose report relations between level of operational thought and other measures. Examples are Brown, Fournier, and Moyer (1977), Killian (1979), Kishta (1979), and Kolodiy (1977).

Kolodiy (1977) found negligible or barely significant correlations between cognitive level and "cumulative average" (presumably of school or college grade) and verbal and mathematical scholastic aptitude test scores, but most studies report significant relations between performance on Piagetian tasks and various other measures. These relations, no matter how they are calculated, are essentially correlational. They are frequently interpreted as providing support for Piaget's theory and for its application in practice. Kishta (1979) found that students who demonstrated higher cognitive levels by performance on Piagetian tasks did better than those at lower levels on the language scale of the Iowa Tests of Basic Skills, and concluded that "the

schools that encourage cognitive development of children facilitate the acquisition not only of science and math skills but also of linguistic skills. This study supports Piaget's theory that cognitive development is the bedrock upon which learning must be built" (pp. 69–70). Sayre and Ball (1975) stated that their observation that formal operational students got higher grades in school science than students at lower levels "reaffirms Jean Piaget's conceptions of the developmental growth of the intellect" (p. 171). Such strong inferences are not justified by correlational evidence, as almost any theory of learning will predict positive correlation between any pair of cognitive tests. To make a true test of Piaget's theory one needs a prediction from it that runs counter to that obtainable from other theories. These correlational studies do not provide that distinction, so have little theoretical value.

Some correlational studies have theoretical import. Lawson, Nordland, and DeVito (1975) found that the correlations between performance on Piagetian tasks and achievement in science and mathematics were similar to the correlations between the tasks and achievement in English, which they interpreted as evidence that the Piagetian tasks are substantially content-free.

On the practical side, the correlations that are observed suggest that Piagetian tests are less satisfactory for group assessment than are traditional general ability measures. Boulanger and Kremer (1981) carried out a meta-analysis of 27 studies that related age or grade and developmental level to science learning. They found that within grades the mean correlation between developmental level and science performance was .40, comparable with the value of .48 which Boulanger (1981a) had found for general ability measures and science performance. Boulanger and Kremer conclude that "Since general ability or prior achievement measures are usually available in school records, the value of administering time-consuming developmental measures for achievement prediction, in general, makes little sense unless it can be shown that developmental measures account for significant amounts of unique variance not accounted for by ability measures. However, the more common defense for the use of developmental measures is the diagnostic value of knowing student capabilities in the various kinds of theory-related logical operations. Ability measures may tap many of the same skills, but developmental measures make logical operations and student weaknesses in applying them more explicit on an individual basis" (p. 379). We take this comment as support for our view that there is no point in further measures of the correlations shown by groups between stage of development and performance on overall tests of learning in science, and that a more useful course will be to study how an individual's ability to perform specific Piagetian tasks enables him or her to acquire specific scientific knowledge or process skills.

Some correlational studies are theory based and are concerned with more specific relations. Instead of simply considering total scores on science tests, Lawson and Renner (1975) differentiated the items on physics, chemistry, and biology examinations into tests of either concrete or abstract concepts. They found that level of operational thinking was more related to performance on the abstract concepts than on the concrete ones. Lowell (1979) tested a theoretical model of abstract cognition by comparing performances on four formal operational tasks with ability to make hierarchical classifications. Preece (1978) deduced that, as much of physics involves proportionality, late development of the schema of proportionality should inhibit learning of physics. He found a weak relation between the students' performances on a pencil-and-paper test of proportional thinking and their cognitive structures in mechanics, assessed by means of word association. Nummedal and Collea (1981) found theoretical reasons to suggest that the relation between proportional reasoning and field independence would be affected by the presence of irrelevant information in the proportional reasoning task. The correlations they observed supported their hypothesis.

PROMOTION OF OPERATIONAL LEVELS

The fourth group of Piagetian studies consists of attempts to promote acquisition of strategies. Only some heeded Piaget's (1964) caution that this is a sensible pursuit only as long as the teaching is aimed at developing logical structures which transfer to many tasks and not simply at the ability to perform a single task. As Kamii and DeVries (1978) put it, "trying to teach Piagetian tasks is like trying to make the child more intelligent by teaching him to give correct answers on the Stanford–Binet Intelligence Scale" (p. 39).

The most popular teaching methods, derived from Piagetian theory, are cognitive conflict and manipulation of objects, and common outcomes are proportional reasoning and control of variables, both aspects of formal operations, and various forms of conservation. Too many studies report successful teaching for them to be cited; among the most recent are Howe and Shayer (1981) and Rowell and Dawson (1981). There are some negative reports. Nous and Raven (1973) had little success in training fifth and seventh grade students on logical operations; Blake and Nordland (1978) found that a science course had no effect on operational level; and Linn and Peterson (1973) found that the manipulative experience provided in the SCIS Material Objects unit improved the logical reasoning of culturally deprived and visually impaired children, but not that of middle class children. It is easy to interpret this last result as the filling of a deficit in the first two groups' experience.

Conflicting results have been obtained for transfer. Bredderman (1973) found that groups trained by cognitive conflict or reinforcement methods were no better than an untrained group of fifth and sixth graders at controlling variables in experimental situations that differed from those on which they had been trained. Boulanger (1976) found in one instance that instruction actually reduced children's ability at proportional reasoning on a transfer task. One of the most insightful results was obtained by Shyers and Cox (1978), who used three sets of apparatus to train college freshmen in a remedial mathematics class on proportional reasoning. The training improved the students' performance on a transfer task, but Shyers and Cox found that the effect could be ascribed to the presence of identical materials in the transfer task and one of the training tasks, rather than to development of a general proportional reasoning structure.

In sum, it appears relatively easy to train people to perform specific tasks, but that no general principles have been determined that describe how to promote the development of underlying strategies that will transfer generally. Eliciting those principles should be the aim of future studies of this type. At present there is little to build on, as there are few studies of the process of development of operational thought. Pallrand (1979) used the performance of students in three age groups on several tasks to address the questions: Is the transition from concrete to operational thought abrupt or continuous, does it occur simultaneously for different schemes, and does development of one scheme influence the development of another? In similar research, Benefield and Capie (1976), Cohen (1978), and Doyle (1980) studied the sequence of development of certain abilities by scaling them in order of difficulty. While these studies are a beginning, there is a long step between knowing that one ability is possessed by fewer people than another and understanding how they form. Other ways of investigating the developmental process are needed. One possibility is cluster analysis, which DeLuca (1981) applied to conservation, control of variables, and combinatorial reasoning tasks. Interesting gender differences appeared, which suggest that the construction of Piagetian theory relied more on male responses than female. Another possibility is closer analysis of the actions of people engaged in tasks. Smith and Padilla (1977) identified three potentially trainable basic strategies that young children use in seriating.

INTERACTION OF OPERATIONAL
LEVEL AND INSTRUCTION

In addition to studies that fit the four purposes that have now been discussed, there are a few in which operational level is regarded as a characteristic that might interact with instruction. These studies fit readily into the model of Figure 30.1, as they concern the mutual effects of instruction and ability on memory. The first two examples are about the effect of manipulation of molecular models on learning in chemistry by students exhibiting concrete, transitional, or formal levels of operational thought. Unfortunately, their results conflict. Goodstein and Howe (1978) found that concrete operational students did not profit from the use of models, though formal operational students did. Gabel and Sherwood (1980), on the other hand, found that students at all levels did better when allowed to handle the molecular models, and that there was no interaction between instructional treatment and operational level. None of the possible explanations for this difference has yet been tested.

At the other end of the school system, Smith, Trueblood, and Szabo (1981) investigated first and second grade children's skill at linear measurement. Contrary to their deduction from Piagetian theory, they found no interaction between the children's abilities to conserve length and mode of instruction that was either abstract, graphic, or manipulative.

The remaining interaction examples are complex studies. Shymansky and Yore (1980) investigated the interaction, with respect to laboratory performance and scores on quizzes of science content and processes, of treatments that differed in amount and type of guidance with three characteristics of learners, field dependence and abilities at multiple classification and control of variables. No interaction was found for the multiple classification ability, and inconsistent results across two samples were observed for the other characteristics. The pattern of results is intricate, but in general runs contrary to theory. Ward and Herron (1980) studied the three-way interaction of style of chemistry experiment, operational level of students, and type of test item. Contrary to their deduction from Piagetian theory, they observed that formal operational students did better than concrete operational students on items testing concrete thought as well as on formal items. The study was replicated over three chemical experiments, and in all cases no interaction was found between instructional treatment and operational level for concrete items, and for formal items there was a significant interaction in one experiment only. Cantu and Herron (1978) obtained similar results. No clear pattern is apparent in these examples of interaction studies, though when more are published one would hope that it should be possible to be definite about their implications. At present little can be said, except that the examples do not give much support to Piagetian theory.

Attitude Studies

In the earlier handbooks in this series, Watson (1963) and Shulman and Tamir (1973) recommended more attention to the study of attitudes to science. Research has been handicapped by absence of a mature theory encompassing the nature of attitudes and their relation to other constructs. The external boundaries of attitudes with personality attributes and with abilities are blurred, and so are the internal ones between interests, feelings, values, and appreciations. Definitions of attitude types are discussed in reviews by Aiken and Aiken (1969), Gardner (1975), and Gauld and Hukins (1980), and in the comprehensive scheme of objectives proposed by Klopfer (1971). In addition to debates about attitude types, there are unresolved issues about whether a distinction should be made between traits and states. The attitude trait is a stable characteristic of the person, and the state is a transitory consequence of the interaction of the trait and the context in which the person is placed. The distinction is incorporated in Figure 30.1 because it emphasizes the role of context, which has been neglected. Personality attributes are included with attitude traits because they, too, are stable characteristics and because they are not always easy to distinguish from attitudes.

Despite the difficulties, many researchers heeded Watson (1963) and Shulman and Tamir (1973). Some investigated and discussed how attitudes might be measured; many studied attitudes as the outcomes of instruction, context, or experience; a few looked at the influence of attitudes on achievement and performance.

Likert tests are the commonest form of attitude measure used in science teaching, but occasionally Thurstone-Chave scales, projective measures, semantic differentials, and other forms are chosen. The basis of choice is reported rarely.

Thurstone scales are less common than other types because by the nature of their construction they measure a unidimensional attribute. As attitude to science is far from unidimensional, separate Thurstone tests have to be prepared for each dimension identified. This is laborious, and difficult because theory has not advanced sufficiently for dimensions to be clear. As advance occurs, more attention could be given to Thurstone scales. The main method of progress is analysis of Likert and other potentially multidimensional tests into separate scales. Nagy (1978), for instance, used cluster analysis to divide items

on the Scientific Attitude Inventory into those which measure feelings and those which measure beliefs. Factor analysis is used more commonly. It is encouraging when the clusters or factors that emerge can be related to previously specified constructs and when the same factors appear with different populations. Skinner and Barcikowski (1973) derived similar factors from the Science Activities Checklist for the four groups of seventh and eighth grade males and females, but missed the principal factor that the authors of the test, Cooley and Reed (1961), had found. Hofstein, Ben-Zvi, Samuel, and Kempa (1977) found the same four factors in Meyer's (1969) test of interests with English students as with Israelis who did the test in translation, though the factors ran across the constructs on which the test was based. More often, as in Ormerod (1979), factors are interpreted after they emerge in the analysis and are not checked against prior constructs or factors obtained from other populations.

The format of items can affect students' assessments. Simpson, Rentz, and Shrum (1976) found that people responded differently when words in an item were replaced by others of different emotional intensity and that agreement with a positively expressed item was different in degree to disagreement with the same notion stated negatively. The implications that these effects have for the validity of attitude measures need further study.

There are many studies in which attitude to science, in one form or another, appears as an outcome. Only two determining variables appear in more than one or two studies: students' gender (Ayres & Price, 1975; Brown, Tweeton, & Pacheco, 1975; Fraser, 1980; Hofman, 1977; Novick & Duvdvani, 1976) and course of instruction (Fraser, 1980; Hasan & Billeh, 1975; Hofman, 1977; Kempa & Dubé, 1974; Krockover & Malcolm, 1978; Lazarowitz, Barufaldi, & Huntsberger, 1978; Selmes, 1973; Sherwood & Herron, 1976; Tolman & Barufaldi, 1979). Other variables are class size (Ward, 1976); grade level (Ayers & Price, 1975; Billeh & Zakhariades, 1975); teacher, intelligence, and socioeconomic status (Fraser, 1980); laboratory type (Case, 1980); grading system (Gatta, 1973); subject or topic (Hofstein et al., 1977; Sullivan, 1979); school, cultural background, achievement, and future specialization (Novick & Duvdvani, 1976); spare time activities and school location (Weltner et al., 1980); teaching method (Kauchak, 1977; Quinn, 1976); and type of student (Brown et al., 1975; Fraser & Remenyi, 1978; Willson & Horn, 1979).

Unfortunately no clear principles emerge from this mass of research. Some studies report an effect, occasionally adverse, and others none. The mechanism for attitude change remains hidden. Johnstone and Reid (1981) suggest one model of change, which should be tested. Another lead is the suggestion of Peterson and Carlson (1979) that the quest should be to identify the key elements that are present in successful influences and absent from the others. This suggestion parallels the plea made in other sections of the chapter for researchers to make explicit the detail of how an effect occurs. Case studies were advocated, and should have the same potential here.

There are few studies of the influence of attitudes on memory or performance, apart from reports of correlations in which the direction of the effect is debatable or whether both the attitude and the other variable are joint outcomes of a third, unmeasured construct.

Katz and Norris (1972) measured students' interest in a number of subjects when they were in Grade 11, and their subsequent grade achievement. They report low correlations in physical science for both males and females.

In their report on the huge study by the International Association for the Evaluation of Educational Achievement (IEA), Comber and Keeves (1973) list medians of the correlations taken over several countries for science achievement and science interests and activities. The median correlations are .04 for 10-year-olds, .27 for 14-year-olds, and .40 for students in the final year of secondary education. Comber and Keeves mention that the range of correlations across countries was wide.

In sum, the relation between attitude and achievement is low to moderate, and is affected by variables such as age, school system, and country. The details of how these variables influence the relation remain to be discovered.

There are three further examples that fit here, although the determining variables are personality aspects rather than beliefs, interests, or values.

Winsberg and Ste-Marie (1976) deduced that the need for security, one of Maslow's types of motivation (Maslow, 1968), should be negatively related to science achievement, and that both the need for esteem and the need for personal growth should be positively related. They observed correlations of the correct signs for a group of college physics students, though only the one for need for security was statistically significant.

At the beginning of a school year, Power (1973) measured the prior knowledge of science of Grade 8 Australian students, their general ability, and divergent thinking level (which would be in the abilities section of the Figure 30.1 model), and their personality and motivation (the attitude section). They were observed through the year, and at the end of the year's instruction there were tests of attitude (as an outcome) and achievement. Pupils who were initially knowledgeable, able, divergent, and who expected success received more reinforcement from their teachers and went on to greater achievement and more positive attitudes. Bright extroverts disliked the way science was taught, tended to rely on ability rather than knowledge to get by, and had only moderate achievement. Sensitive, tender-minded students often answered questions in class incorrectly, were rarely encouraged to tackle difficult questions, and attained a poor understanding of science, but maintained positive attitudes to it. The less able, individualistic students sat near the back of the class, were isolated, and neither valued nor received success.

Shymansky, Penick, Matthews, and Good (1977) investigated the effect that self-perception in relation to problem solving had on behavior in the classroom for students in Grades 1 to 5. As in Power's study (1973), the results are complex. In Grades 1 to 3 self-reliant students observed the teacher and other students less and did fewer activities than dependent students in response to directions. In Grades 4 and 5, not surprisingly, dependent students sought the teacher's attention and copied other students more than self-reliant ones did, but strangely this behavior was not present in Grades 1 to 3. The reasons behind these complex results are not obvious, which leads us again to say that an investigation of the mechanism of an effect, following its discovery, could be profitable.

Curriculum Research

The purpose of this section is to describe changes in the research associated with curriculum, rather than to provide a comprehensive listing of results. Welch (1979), who also discusses issues, gives results of much American research, and more may be found in the annual summaries published in *Science Education* (Butts, 1981; Gabel et al., 1980; Peterson & Carlson, 1979; Sipe & Farmer, 1982).

Curriculum research deals with practical situations, and is not sharply delineated from some of the naturalistic studies such as the probes of understanding of scientific concepts that were described earlier in the chapter. It could have been treated as an aspect of instruction, but we chose to separate it from that earlier section because curriculum-related research is often spoken of as if it were distinct, and because the themes we now wish to develop differ from the earlier ones.

Research on curriculum is complex. It concerns cognitive, affective, and motor outcomes of students' experiences; details of how the curriculum is produced, including how its aims, content, and basic form are determined; how it is disseminated and why it is adopted; and how it is implemented. Small parts of this complex set may be tackled usefully, though greater possibilities of understanding lie in more comprehensive studies. In practice a comprehensive study of all the aspects of a curriculum is daunting. The researchers would need to understand the nature of the curriculum, the procedures by which it was developed and implemented, and the nature of the educational system in which it is used. They should be familiar with different methods for gathering data, so that they may choose the ones most appropriate for the purpose of the evaluation and most comprehensible and useful to the audience to whom the results are to be made known. To ensure that their research has practical effect, they should possess political and interpretative skills in order to communicate their findings. Harding, Kelly, and Nicodemus (1976) argue that researchers lack experience in these matters and do not understand the complex social phenomena associated with curriculum change and evaluation. Such deficits are not surprising, since the situation is not only complex but mobile, with conditions changing sharply with time as well as place. Prescriptions of the steps researchers should follow reflect unique conditions, and are not realistic guides because they do not generalize to other situations (Lewy, 1973). Perhaps this is why, as Welch (1976) asserts, science educators have not found curriculum research an attractive activity.

Despite the difficulties, research continues, with the experiences gained in it being one factor that affects the form of later studies. Other factors are social forces and the nature of the curricula.

Research in Response to Social Forces

Research that is driven by political, economic, religious, or other social forces that are not closely related to the curriculum usually consists of a large-scale assessment of outcomes. Such assessments can be at a local level, but are more prominent when national or international. A national instance is the current Assessment of Performance in Science project in the

United Kingdom (Driver, Gott, Johnson, Worsley, & Wylie, 1982; Harlen, Black, & Johnson, 1981; Schofield, Murphy, Johnson, Worsley, &Wylie, 1982). In the United States information about the effects of science curricula is being collated in secondary analyses of data from the National Assessment of Educational Progress (e.g., Haertel, Walberg, Junker, & Pascarella, 1981). The Science Council of Canada has authorized a major study of science curricula with broader aims than assessment of outcomes; these include establishing a basis for describing the present purposes and characteristics of science teaching, conducting a historical analysis of Canadian science education, and stimulating deliberation about its future (Orpwood, 1980). Discussion papers (e.g., Aikenhead, 1980) examining science education from a variety of perspectives have been issued, and other phases will involve surveys and naturalistic case studies of teaching. The international example is the massive study by the International Association for the Evaluation of Educational Achievement (IEA), in which the science section involved over a quarter of a million students and 50,000 teachers in 19 countries (Comber & Keeves, 1973). The study represented, at the time, a substantial extension of the concept of curriculum evaluation since it included content analyses of the science courses in the participating countries as well as the employment of criterion measures.

As yet, it is not clear what effects these massive evaluations have had on the practice of science teaching.

Developments in Research Following Changes in Curricula

Other research that is more closely related to the nature of the curriculum, though still affected by social forces, is concerned not only with outcomes of student learning and the nature of the curriculum but also the procedures by which it is developed and put into practice. In this research the range and type of questions shift with changes in the nature of the curriculum, and generally increase since questions that could not have been thought of under the conditions of old curricula can, once found, be applied to old curricula as well as new. This relation between changes in curriculum and the research questions is the main theme of the curriculum section.

Changes in curricula occur in their nature and in the procedures associated with them. Nature includes characteristics such as aims, intended users, content, style, and materials; procedures are how the curricula are developed, disseminated, adopted, and implemented. Nature and procedures are interrelated; for example, a change in content often follows a change in the type of people who develop the course, and aims may determine whether teachers choose to adopt the course. Millar (1981) points out that trends in both nature and processes are shaped by social factors, among others. A specific instance is provided by Brown (1977), who identifies the outcome demands and resource constraints imposed by society among justifications that have been advanced for integrated science. More generally, Welch (1979) describes how changes in research funding policy are a consequence of larger political concerns, and shows how these affect many aspects of curriculum development and research.

CURRICULUM STEREOTYPES

In discussing how changes in the nature of courses and the associated procedures affect research, it is convenient to set out two stereotypes even though actual curricula do not fit them exactly since there are so many dimensions on which variations may occur. Dimensions include the aims of the course and its social purpose; for whom it is designed; its general philosophy, whether science is presented in an abstract, a humanistic, or a technological context, and whether science is shown as a truth to be revealed or a system to be created; the degrees of structure and flexibility in the course, whether it has a lock-step sequence or a modular format; the treatment of science as separate disciplines or an integrated whole; the extent of provision of training programs and teachers' guides; and details such as the weight given to laboratory work and the importance of textbooks.

Our stereotypes have some similarities to the stages of curricula identified by Sabar (1979). In the first stereotype, near which cluster several of the large, centrally-produced curricula of the 1950s and early 1960s such as Physical Science Study Committee (PSSC), Chemical Bond Approach (CBA), Biological Sciences Curriculum Study (BSCS), and Chem Study, the development is done by a large team in which scientists are dominant. The curriculum is to be used at the senior secondary level, and science is divided into separate disciplines, with the aim being preparation of students for tertiary study. The main emphases are on subject matter, including conceptual schemes and major principles, and on the processes of science. Consequently, both textbooks and laboratory work are important. Training programs emphasizing the structure of knowledge are run to help teachers implement the curriculum along the lines intended by its developers. The courses are designed for formal presentation and, despite rhetoric about the importance of inquiry, reception of information by students. Many ancillary teaching materials are provided. Welch (1979) describes the development and nature of curricula that approximate this stereotype.

The second stereotype is meant to reflect characteristics of courses developed later, in the 1970s. The trend towards these courses may have been spurred by the strong social forces that were evident in Western societies at the end of the 1960s, and which were manifested, among other ways, in demands and arguments about many aspects of education. Arguments for greater teacher involvement in curriculum development and for school-based curriculum development appeared in international (Organization for Economic and Cooperative Development, 1976), national (Connors, 1978; Smith, 1978; I. D. Thomas, 1978), and university (Skilbeck, 1976) publications. These arguments may have influenced as well as reflected a change in science teachers' perspectives of their role in curriculum development and implementation to something more than mere acceptors and users of someone else's package. Other instances of arguments for change are calls for the training of "curriculum proof" teachers (Zoller & Watson, 1974), for action research with science curricula (Brown & McIntyre, 1981), and for adaptations by teachers of centrally produced curricula to meet local cultural needs (Blum, 1979). Arguments for change in the nature of curricula emphasized the need for students to appreciate the relation of science to society. They include adopting an ecological approach in school biology which would involve human-centered and cybernetic structuring principles to give the curriculum greater social and interdisciplinary impact (Eulefeld, 1976; Kattman & Schaefer, 1976), while three projects in the United Kingdom are evidence of a belief that more account needs to be taken of the influence of technology in society (Dowdeswell, 1979).

The second stereotype is almost the antithesis of the first. The development team may still be large, but educational psychologists and specialists in curriculum theory and educational technology replace scientists as the dominant influence. Any elementary or secondary school level may be attended to, and science is treated as an integrated subject which has the aim of assisting students to understand themselves and their environment. Science is presented in a historical and cultural context, and its social consequences are emphasized. The course has a modular structure, without a single major textbook, so its content and sequence are flexible. It is designed for less formal presentation, with a degree of individualized learning. Teacher preparation for its use concentrates on classroom management rather than subject matter.

A real curriculum has a profile of characteristics that places it somewhere between the poles represented by the stereotypes. The PSSC course might be regarded as closer than, for instance, BSCS to the first stereotype, with Elementary School Science (ESS), Nuffield, and Australian Science Education Project (ASEP) further than both towards the second pole, near which are many of the 130 integrated science curricula located by Haggis and Adey (1979).

The large number of integrated science projects indicates a further problem confronting researchers: When the scene was dominated by a few "big" curricula it was easy to keep in touch with developments and to communicate with other researchers, but when there are many localized curricula it is difficult to find out what is happening in schools and communication is strained by the lack of common knowledge of the characteristics of the curricula. Calls have been made for a representative international network of centers to provide information about new projects (Blum, 1981).

DEVELOPMENTS IN RESEARCH ON
THE NATURE OF CURRICULA

Curricula close to the first stereotype began to be produced in the 1950s, and those close to the second considerably later. Given the emphasis in curricula that approach the first stereotype, it is consistent that early research on them dealt mainly with student outcomes, particularly tests of subject matter knowledge, process skills, attitudes to science, and laboratory techniques. Curricula were often compared to each other with respect to these outcomes. Following the appearance of second-stereotype curricula, criticisms of comparative studies became common. Walker and Schaffarzik (1974) argued that each curriculum is associated with a specific pattern of outcomes and should be judged on its own terms. Comparisons of curricula still occur, some using modern statistical techniques. An example is a meta-analysis of data from 105 studies on the effects of pre-1955 science curricula compared with post-1955 curricula

(Shymansky, Kyle, & Alport, 1983). The comparison is based on measures of achievement, attitudes, laboratory skills, critical thinking, problem solving, creativity, logical reasoning, and skills in communicating, reading, and mathematics. Shymansky, Kyle, and Alport conclude that the later curricula, which in this study include PSSC, CBA, and ESS, had a positive effect on all criteria except self-concept; that the newer chemistry curricula did less to enhance pupil performance than those in other subjects; and that the performance of mixed-sex groups was better than either predominantly male or female groups. In the view expressed here, such comparisons are a remnant of practices from the period of development of first-stereotype curricula.

As curricula closer to the second stereotype appeared, research on the nature of curricula changed. Though achievement and attitudes were still measured, new outcomes were added. Among these were pupils' perceptions of their classrooms. Fraser and Walberg (1981) review studies of the psychosocial learning environment in science classes. Other extensions of outcomes are illustrated by examinations of the effect of ESS on first grade pupils' listening skills (Barufaldi & Swift, 1980) and third and fourth grade pupils' classification skills (Vanek & Montean, 1977), of Intermediate Science Curriculum Study (ISCS) on seventh grade pupils' inquiry behaviors (Stallings & Snyder, 1977), and of ISCS (Lashier & Nieft, 1975) and an earth science syllabus (Orgren, 1977; Orgren & Doran, 1975) on teacher behavior.

Research on the nature of curricula expanded in other ways as well as in the range of outcomes. The validity of aims has been checked by seeing whether they correspond with those espoused by experts in the literature (Fraser, 1978). Investigations have been made of the ways in which curricula are individualized and the methods used in them to evaluate pupil progress (Bloch, 1977), and on the themes and content they contain. With respect to themes, science education researchers appear to favor simple procedures such as rating schemes in order to determine whether they contain, for instance, an environmental emphasis (Linke, 1974a), or the extent to which various inquiry skills are demanded in given activities and problems (Mitchell, 1978). New techniques for studying content have been advocated. Some writers (e.g., Stewart & van Kirk, 1981) argue that content analyses, especially methods that use concepts developed in the psychology of information processing and artificial intelligence, should become more common in curriculum evaluation. Carss (1975) and Clarke (1973) report on a technique wherein the distributions and co-occurrences of selected words are used to identify themes in curriculum materials. The technique was applied to a unit of the Australian Science Education Project, and fluctuations were revealed in the appearance and disappearance of themes. When the unit was rewritten so that it exhibited more structure, pupils learned more from it (Clarke, 1973). Unfortunately there has not been enough further research using thematic analysis procedures to ascertain clearly the benefits to be derived. Much remains to be learned about the structure of curricula and of their textual materials. Findings on learning from prose materials (Walker & Meyer, 1980), the notion of kinetic structure (Anderson, 1966) that was discussed in the earlier section on text design, and conceptualizations of the structure of classroom discourse

(Smith, Meux, Combs, Nuthall, & Precians, 1967) might be useful in this research.

The developments in research on the nature of curricula can be seen as consistent with the emphases in the second stereotype on the processes of learning, the role of the teacher, and the relation of science to society.

DEVELOPMENTS IN RESEARCH ON CURRICULUM PROCEDURES

The changes that appeared in research on procedures are more marked than those in research on the nature of curricula.

The purposes of evaluation broadened when curricula nearer the second stereotype began to appear in the 1970s, and the importance of the procedures of development, dissemination and adoption, and implementation was recognized. Although most evaluations continued to be designed to provide information about a finished product rather than how the curriculum might be developed and implemented, a few were used to help form the nature of the curriculum and the innovation strategies that would encourage teachers to use it. An example is the evaluation of the Individualized Science program by Klopfer and Champagne (1975). Their project involved four stages: examination of the conceptualization and planning for the Individualized Science program as well as a critical review of the curriculum materials; observations of teachers and pupils as they interacted with sets of prototype curriculum materials; a repetition of the second stage but using a larger number of teachers and pupils working with a revised set of curriculum materials and with attention being directed also to the nature of the implementation; and seeking of more comprehensive answers to questions concerning the implementation of Individualized Science and the effectiveness of the teacher preparation program. The first two stages helped form the nature of the curriculum while the other two were instrumental in shaping the nature of the innovating strategies. An important outcome of the evaluations was the development of a "Start Unit" which contained no instruction in science content but served as the pupils' introduction on how to manage the materials and assess and record their progress, which the evaluators had found could not be left to chance. Other examples are Waring's (1979) documentation of the initiation, development, and dissemination of the Nuffield Foundation Science Teaching Project and Harlen's (1975) evaluation of elementary school science in England.

There appear to be few other instances of research on development. Eventually historical analyses, including interviews with members of development teams, could lead to new insights on the positive influences and constraints that determine its course. A particular issue is the role played by the values of those who develop curricula. It is often assumed that their own educational values are congruent with those espoused by the new curriculum, but this is not always the case, as Tisher and Power (1973) found for a proportion of the developers of ASEP.

Dissemination and adoption of curricula close to the first stereotype was not studied to any extent until curricula nearer the second stereotype had appeared. When studies of these procedures did appear, they focused on the effectiveness of communication with teachers about the new curricula

(Gullickson, 1978) and on decisions to purchase new materials (Owen, 1979). The studies drew data from sample schools in local regions (Nicodemus, 1977; Willson, 1980), in several states (Gullickson (1978), or in an entire nation (Owen, 1979; Owen & Tisher, 1978). Curricula at many points between the poles of the two stereotypes were involved. In a study covering a $4\frac{1}{2}$-year period, Willson (1980) reported that when the elementary science programs AAAS (American Association for the Advancement of Science), SCIS (Science Curriculum Improvement Study), and ESS were adopted, they were used about 40% of the time, and for the secondary school programs BSCS, Earth Science Curriculum Project (ESCP), and ISCS the usage was up to 68% of the time. In a survey of 17 local education authorities in the United Kingdom, Nicodemus (1977) found that only 3 of 17 new Nuffield projects were used by three-quarters of his respondents. Tall (1981) stated that 40% to 60% of O-level biology, physics, and chemistry teachers had adopted a third or more of the Nuffield curriculum materials. In the United States, Welch (1979) found that between 30% and 39% of elementary and junior high schools used one or more of the big American curricula. In his large-scale national survey of the Australian Science Education Project, Owen (1979) documented the effectiveness of different types of communication and reported different patterns of adoption which depended on the conditions within the separate states and territories. He noted that at least some ASEP materials were used in two-thirds of Australia's secondary schools.

Independent of where the curricula are placed between the poles of the two stereotypes, questions about their adoption are essentially a second-stereotype enterprise. So are questions about implementation. In the curricula close to the first stereotype the teacher is expected to be a faithful transmitter of the curriculum that is laid down in the text and the teacher's guides, so at the time when the first stereotype curricula were disseminated the notion of studying what actually happened to the curriculum when it was placed in the teacher's hands did not arise. Conditions changed with the newer curricula near the second stereotype. Science educators who were prepared to make use of learning theories became prominent in development teams, and more attention was given to the processes of learning. These changes, and the experiences that were gained as the curricula were used, made it possible to recognize that the teacher plays a complex role in determining the form of the curriculum that is actually experienced by the students. Studies of implementation in all types of curricula could then follow.

Numerous factors affect the form of implementation of a curriculum, and each may be studied in a variety of ways. The different perspectives which teachers, pupils, curriculum developers, and outside observers may have about the implementation could be identified. The ways in which different characteristics of the curriculum such as the subject matter, classroom organization, teaching strategies, and assessment procedures influence implementation may be investigated. Different types of data might be sought, such as teachers' and pupils' opinions and frequencies and patterns of teacher and pupil behaviors. Consequently, implementation studies can vary greatly in style.

The trend towards a greater range of research styles may be a consequence of the recognition that implementation is a matter of people, rather than of materials and topics. In trying to ascertain people's views and the reasons behind their decisions, it is advantageous to have available techniques that range from the flexible and reactive to ones with greater structure. Questionnaires are an instance of a structured method. Among recent advances in their design is the Stages of Concern questionnaire which Loucks (1977) and James and Hall (1981) used to study the implementation of ISCS. Flexible and reactive procedures include interviews and case studies, of which the series edited by Stake and Easley (1978) is the most extensive example. Both the structured and flexible methods concentrate on personal perceptions of how the curriculum is being used. This is particularly clear in the case of the repertory grid technique based on Kelly's personal construct theory (Kelly, 1955), which Olson and Reid (1982) used to study the implementation of the Schools Council Integrated Science Project.

Studies of the implementation of the Australian Science Education Project provide useful illustrations of many of the developments in research on curriculum procedures. ASEP is a national project, and is one of the best-known examples of a curriculum that is near to the second stereotype. It has had a high degree of use in Australian schools, and is sharply different from the curricula it replaced. These characteristics encouraged much research on its implementation. Studies used techniques such as interviews (Owen, 1979), classroom observations (Power & Tisher, 1976), and intensive surveys of pupils, teachers, and classroom work (Northfield, 1980). They reveal that though teachers organize their classes in diverse ways, they tend to retain control over the self-paced learning environment. The pupils perceive the environment as more satisfying, less difficult, and less competitive; there is more pupil initiation of activities, more experimenting, more pupil interaction with materials, and less teacher dominance of activities than previously. However, pupils do not always perceive a self-paced learning environment as one that fosters inquiry learning (Tisher & Power, 1978) even though behavioral measures may be interpreted to indicate that the environment is an inquiry-centered one. The ASEP materials help create an environment wherein the teacher can move about the class more readily to observe, help, and counsel pupils who as a consequence perceive greater teacher surveillance.

The Australian investigations of implementation indicate that important roles can be played by the head of a science department (Owen, 1979), inservice education and collaborative decision making in a school (Northfield, 1980), and the professional and innovative climate of a school (Owen & Tisher, 1978) in the successful implementation of a new curriculum.

However, these results may not apply in another society. More needs to be learned about implementation in different cultures (Crocker, 1979; Fullan & Pomfret, 1977). Walker (1976) suggests studying the factors that account for the stability of a curriculum when it is employed in schools in communities that differ in political, cultural, and geographic characteristics.

Future Directions

Research in education is perpetually faced with two challenges. Is the form of research appropriate for the issues of moment? Do the results inform practice? We have tried to show that in the past decade researchers in science education met the first challenge well. Current research is based on the general conception that the outcomes of schooling are determined by interaction of teachers, students, and the curriculum within bounds set by a social context. The model of Figure 30.1 is a special case of the general conception, a case that reflects its period by giving particular weight to the characteristics of the learner. Although the model was used analytically in the chapter in order to aid the description of research, its real function is in synthesis, to enable researchers to make further progress in putting together complex studies that will reveal more about the processes of teaching and learning. The model also reflects the progress that has been made along the lines advocated by Hurd (1971) and Power (1976), towards recognizing that simple models and restricted methods will not provide satisfactory answers to complex problems.

Greater complexity of research has consequences that need attention. Researchers may have to heed another call by Hurd (1971) for greater risk taking, while paradoxically there should also be more routine replications in order to see how stable results are across contexts. Researchers will have to be trained to cope with a greater range of techniques, both in order to use them and to appreciate what others have done. The more complex research becomes the more difficult it is for anyone to do it adequately at the first try, so perhaps it should be made easier for graduate students and other new researchers to begin work as a member of a team that has been studying a particular issue for some time. Science education needs many more such teams.

We have less to say about the second challenge, and thereby reflect another characteristic of the decade's research. The great amount of energy that went into research did not spill over into seeing that the results affected practice. If research teams do become common, one way of coping with the challenge is for teachers to be full members of the teams. This development may lead to a different, collaborative style wherein research is done by and with, rather than on, the teacher. The research could consider how teachers' understanding about individuals, processes of learning, and curriculum affects their behavior and their role in the school. This may encourage new forms of research on pre- and inservice training and in addition could promote a wider perception of what may be achieved in teacher education.

Whether teachers are more closely involved or not, as research comes to be based on more complex models it shifts closer to the complexities of the practical school situation, and its results are more likely to be accepted as relevant. The acceptance would be hastened if more attention were given to the influence that social context has on schooling. Teachers would then see that the issues tackled in research are of real concern and do apply to their situation. Some valuable work has already been done on context, including forms as diverse as Layton's description of the historical development of science curricula in England (Layton, 1973) and the case studies edited by Stake and Easley (1978), but as in so many areas much more needs to be done.

Almost paradoxically, the observation that more needs to be done is a consequence of the progress that was made in the past decade. Understanding of science teaching advanced greatly. In order for the advance to continue, we believe that the next steps should be towards comprehensive studies that take in as many aspects as possible of the factors of context, teacher, learner, and curriculum.

REFERENCES

Abhyankar, S. B. (1977). A comparative laboratory study of the effects of two teaching strategies on sixth grade students' attitudes and self-concepts in science (Ph.D. dissertation, Florida State University, Tallahassee, 1977). *Dissertation Abstracts International, 38,* 2023A.

Abraham, M. R. (1976). The effect of grouping on verbal interaction during science inquiries. *Journal of Research in Science Teaching, 13,* 127–135.

Aiken, L. R., & Aiken, D. R. (1969). Recent research on attitudes concerning science. *Science Education, 53,* 295–305.

Aikenhead, G. S. (1980). *Science in social issues. Implications for teaching* (Discussion Paper D80/2). Ottawa: Science Council of Canada.

Akers, G. D. (1980). The effect of behavioral objectives on student achievement in Introductory Physical Science (IPS) (Doctoral dissertation, University of Maryland, College Park, 1979). *Dissertation Abstracts International, 40,* 4983A.

Alesandrini, K. L., & Rigney, J. W. (1981). Pictorial presentation and review strategies in science learning. *Journal of Research in Science Teaching, 18,* 465–474.

Allen, T. E. (1977). A study of the behaviors of two groups of disruptive children when taught with quantitatively defined strategies: Directive vs. non-directive teaching (Doctoral dissertation, Florida State University, Tallahassee, 1976). *Dissertation Abstracts International, 37,* 4252A.

Anderson, B. O. (1978). The effects of long wait-times on high school physics pupils' response length, classroom attitudes, science attitudes and achievement (Doctoral dissertation, University of Minnesota, Minneapolis, 1978). *Dissertation Abstracts International, 39,* 3493A.

Anderson, C. W. (1980). An observational study of classroom management and information structuring in elementary school science lessons (Doctoral dissertation, University of Texas, Austin, 1979). *Dissertation Abstracts International, 40,* 5810A.

Anderson, E. J., & Fowler, H. S. (1978). The effects of selected entering behaviors and different cognitive levels of behavioral objectives on learning and retention performance in a unit on population genetics. *Journal of Research in Science Teaching, 15,* 373–379.

Anderson, G. J. (1971). *The assessment of learning environments: A manual for the Learning Environment Inventory and the My Class Inventory.* Halifax: Atlantic Institute for Education.

Anderson, O. R. (1966). The strength and order of responses in a sequence as related to the degree of structure in stimuli. *Journal of Research in Science Teaching, 4,* 192–198.

Anderson, O. R. (1974). Research on structure in teaching. *Journal of Research in Science Teaching, 11,* 219–230.

Anderson, O. R., & Lee, M. T. (1975). Structure in science communications and student recall of knowledge. *Science Education, 59,* 127–138.

Andersson, B. (n.d.). *Pupils' understanding of some aspects of energy transfer.* Gothenburg, Sweden: Department of Educational Research, University of Gothenburg.

Angus, J. W. (1981). Children's conceptions of the living world. *Australian Science Teachers Journal, 27*(3), 65–68.

Anshutz, R. J. (1975). An investigation of wait time and questioning techniques as an instructional variable for science methods students microteaching elementary school children (Doctoral dissertation, University of Kansas, Lawrence, 1973). *Dissertation Abstracts International, 35,* 5978A.

Archenhold, W. F., Driver, R. H., Orton, A., & Wood-Robinson, C. (1980). *Cognitive development research in science and mathematics.* Leeds, England: University of Leeds.

Arlin, M., & Westbury, I. (1976). The leveling effect of teacher pacing on science content mastery. *Journal of Research in Science Teaching, 13,* 213–219.

Atwood, R. K. (1971). Development of a cognitive preference examination utilizing general science and social science content. *Journal of Research in Science Teaching, 8,* 273–275.

Ausubel, D. P. (1968). *Educational psychology: A cognitive view.* New York: Holt, Rinehart & Winston.

Ayers, J. B., & Price, C. O. (1975). Children's attitudes towards science. *School Science and Mathematics, 75,* 311–318.

Bady, R. J. (1978). Comments on current uses of Piaget's concept of stage. *Journal of Research in Science Teaching, 15,* 573–576.

Barker, R. G. (1963). *Ecological psychology.* Stanford: Stanford University Press.

Barnes, B. R., & Clawson, E. U. (1975). Do advance organizers facilitate learning? Recommendations for further research based on an analysis of 32 studies. *Review of Educational Research, 45,* 637–659.

Barnett, H. C. (1974). An investigation of relationships among biology achievement, perception of teacher style, and cognitive preferences. *Journal of Research in Science Teaching, 11,* 141–147.

Barufaldi, J. P., & Dietz, M. A. (1975). Effects of solid objects and two-dimensional representations of the objects on visual observation and comparison among urban children. *Journal of Research in Science Teaching, 12,* 127–132.

Barufaldi, J. P., & Swift, J. W. (1980). The influence of the BSCS-Elementary School Sciences Program instruction on first-grade students' listening skills. *Journal of Research in Science Teaching, 17,* 485–490.

Beeson, G. W. (1977). Hierarchical learning in electrical science. *Journal of Research in Science Teaching, 14,* 117–127.

Bell, B. F. (1981). When is an animal, not an animal? *Journal of Biological Education, 15,* 213–218.

Benefield, K. E., & Capie, W. (1976). An empirical derivation of hierarchies of propositions related to ten of Piaget's sixteen binary operations. *Journal of Research in Science Teaching, 13,* 193–204.

Ben-Zvi, R., Hofstein, A., Samuel, D., & Kempa, R. F. (1976b). The effectiveness of filmed experiments in high school chemical education. *Journal of Chemical Education, 53,* 518–520.

Ben-Zvi, R., Hofstein, A., Samuel, D., & Kempa, R. F. (1976a). The attitude of high school students towards the use of filmed experiments. *Journal of Chemical Education, 53,* 575–577.

Bernstein, B. (1971). *Class, codes and control.* London: Routledge & Kegan Paul.

Billeh, V. Y., & Zakhariades, G. A. (1975). The development and application of a scale for measuring scientific attitudes. *Science Education, 59,* 155–165.

Blake, A. J. D. (1980). The predictive power of two written tests of Piagetian developmental level. *Journal of Research in Science Teaching, 17,* 435–441.

Blake, A. J. D., Lawson, A. E., & Nordland, F. H. (1976). The Karplus islands puzzle: Does it measure Piagetian operations? *Journal of Research in Science Teaching, 13,* 397–404.

Blake, A. J. D., & Nordland, F. H. (1978). Science instruction and cognitive growth in college students. *Journal of Research in Science Teaching, 15,* 413–419.

Bloch, J. A. (1977). Student evaluation in "individualised" science programs. *Studies in Educational Evaluation, 3,* 95–107.

Bloom, B. S. (Ed.). (1956). *Taxonomy of educational objectives: Handbook 1. Cognitive domain.* New York: Longmans, Green.

Blum, A. (1979). Curriculum adaptation in science education: Why and how. *Science Education, 63,* 693–704.

Blum, A. (1981). The development of an integrated science curriculum information scheme. *European Journal of Science Education, 3,* 1–15.

Boud, D. J., Dunn, J., Kennedy, T., & Thorley, R. (1980). The aims of science laboratory courses: A survey of students, graduates and practicing scientists. *European Journal of Science Education, 2,* 415–428.

Boulanger, F. D. (1976). The effects of training in the proportional reasoning associated with the concept of speed. *Journal of Research in Science Teaching, 13,* 145–154.

Boulanger, F. D. (1981a). Ability and science learning: A quantitative synthesis. *Journal of Research in Science Teaching, 18,* 113–121.

Boulanger, F. D. (1981b). Instruction and science learning: A quantitative synthesis. *Journal of Research in Science Teaching, 18*, 311–327.

Boulanger, F. D., & Kremer, B. K. (1981). Age and developmental level as antecedents of science learning. *Journal of Research in Science Teaching, 18*, 371–384.

Bowen, B. L. (1975). The need for paradigms in science education research. *Science Education, 59*, 423–430.

Bredderman, T. A. (1973). The effects of training on the development of the ability to control variables. *Journal of Research in Science Teaching, 10*, 189–200.

Brown, A. L., Campione, J. C., & Day, J. D. (1981). Learning to learn: On training students to learn from texts. *Educational Researcher, 10*, (2), 14–21.

Brown, L. M., Tweeten, P. W., & Pacheco, D. (1975). Attitudinal differences among junior high school students, teachers, and parents on topics of current interest. *Science Education, 59*, 467–473.

Brown, R. L., Fournier, J. F., & Moyer, R. H. (1977). A cross-cultural study of Piagetian concrete reasoning and science concepts among rural fifth-grade Mexican- and Anglo-American students. *Journal of Research in Science Teaching, 14*, 329–334.

Brown, S. A. (1975). Cognitive preferences in science: Their nature and analysis. *Studies in Science Education, 2*, 43–65.

Brown, S. A. (1977). A review of the meanings of, and arguments for, integrated science. *Studies in Science Education, 4*, 31–62.

Brown, S. A., & McIntyre, D. (1981). An action–research approach to innovation in centralized educational systems. *European Journal of Science Education, 3*, 243–258.

Brumby, M. (1979). Problems in learning the concept of natural selection. *Journal of Biological Education, 13*, 119–122.

Brumby, M. (1981). Learning, understanding and "thinking about" the concept of life. *Australian Science Teachers Journal, 27*(3), 21–25.

Butler, J. E., Beasley, W. F., Buckley, D., & Endean, L. (1980). Pupil task involvement in secondary science classrooms. *Research in Science Education, 10*, 93–106.

Butts, D. P. (1981). A summary of research in science education — 1979. *Science Education, 65*, 337–465.

Cabrol, D., & Cachet, C. (1981). Le système ESSOR d'expérimentation scientifique simulée et ses potentialités pédagogiques. *European Journal of Science Education, 3*, 303–312.

Campbell, J. R. (1977). Science teachers' flexibility. *Journal of Research in Science Teaching, 14*, 525–532.

Cantu, L. L., & Herron, J. D. (1978). Concrete and formal Piagetian stages and science concept attainment. *Journal of Research in Science Teaching, 15*, 135–143.

Carlson, G. R. (1976). Location of a point in Euclidian space by children in grades one through six. *Journal of Research in Science Teaching, 13*, 331–336.

Carss, B. W. (1975). Thematic structural analysis applied to conceptual hierarchies. *Research in Science Education, 5*, 143–151.

Case, C. L. (1980). The influence of modified laboratory instruction on college student biology achievement. *Journal of Research in Science Teaching, 17*, 1–6.

Champagne, A. B., Klopfer, L. E., & Anderson, J. H. (1980). Factors influencing the learning of classical mechanics. *American Journal of Physics, 48*, 1074–1079.

Champagne, A. B., Klopfer, L. E., DeSena, A. T., & Squires, D. A. (1981). Structural representations of students' knowledge before and after science instruction. *Journal of Research in Science Teaching, 18*, 97–111.

Chewprecha, T., Gardner, M., & Sapianchai, N. (1980). Comparison of training methods in modifying questioning and wait time behaviors of Thai high school chemistry teachers. *Journal of Research in Science Teaching, 17*, 191–200.

Chiappetta, E. L. (1976). A review of Piagetian studies relevant to science instruction at the secondary and college level. *Science Education, 60*, 253–261.

Clarke, J. A. (1973). Ausubel and ASEP: An application of cognitive field learning theory to an ASEP unit. *Australian Science Teachers' Journal, 19*, (4), 92–97.

Clawson, E. U., & Barnes, B. R. (1973). The effects of organizers on the learning of structured anthropology materials in the elementary grades. *Journal of Experimental Education, 42*(1), 11–15.

Cohen, H. G. (1978). The scaling of six topological Piagetian groupings, as well as the effect that certain selected variables have on the attainment of these groupings and some of their homologs in the logical domain. *Journal of Research in Science Teaching, 15*, 115–125.

Comber, L. C., & Keeves, J. P. (1973). *Science education in nineteen countries.* New York: Halsted.

Connors, L. (1978). *School-based decision making* (Report on the National Conference). Canberra: Schools Commission.

Cooley, W. W., & Reed, H. B. (1961). The measurement of science interests: An operational and multidimensional approach. *Science Education, 45*, 320–326.

Coulter, D., Williams, H., & Schulz, H. (1981). Formal operational ability and the teaching of science processes. *School Science and Mathematics, 81*, 131–138.

Crocker, R. K. (1979). *From curriculum to classroom: An interview study of teacher perspectives on curriculum change in primary science.* Brisbane: Queensland State Department of Education, Curriculum Branch.

Crocker, R. K., Amaria, R. P., Banfield, H., Clark, G. W., Oakley, W. F., Rumboldt, G., & Sheppard, D. B. (1977). *Teacher control, classroom behaviors and pupil performance in elementary science classes.* St. Johns, Newfoundland: Memorial University of Newfoundland, Institute for Educational Research and Development.

Crocker, R. K., Bartlett, K. R., & Elliott, H. G. (1976). A comparison of structured and unstructured modes of teaching science process activities. *Journal of Research in Science Teaching, 13*, 267–274.

Dahlgren, L. O., & Marton, F. (1978). Students' conceptions of subject matter: An aspect of learning and teaching in higher education. *Studies in Higher Education, 3*, 25–35.

Deese, J. (1962). On the structure of associative meaning. *Psychological Review, 69*, 161–175.

DeLuca, F. P. (1981). Application of cluster analysis to the study of Piagetian stages of intellectual development. *Journal of Research in Science Teaching, 18*, 51–59.

DeTure, L. R. (1979). Relative effects of modeling on the acquisition of wait-time by preservice elementary teachers and concomitant changes in dialogue patterns. *Journal of Research in Science Teaching, 16*, 553–562.

Doran, R. L. (1972). Misconceptions of selected science concepts held by elementary school students. *Journal of Research in Science Teaching, 9*, 127–137.

Doran, R. L. (1978). Assessing the outcomes of science laboratory activities. *Science Education, 62*, 401–409.

Dowdeswell, W. H. (1979). Science and technology in the classroom. *European Journal of Science Education, 1*, 51–56.

Doyle, J. J. (1980). The order of attainment of eight projective groupings: An analysis of Piaget's spatial model. *Journal of Research in Science Teaching, 17*, 55–58.

Dreyfus, A., & Eggleston, J. F. (1979). Classroom transactions of student-teachers of science. *European Journal of Science Education, 1*, 315–325.

Dreyfus, A., & Junwirth, E. (1980). Students' perception of the logical structure of curricular as compared with everyday contexts — Study of critical thinking skills. *Science Education, 64*, 309–321.

Driver, R. (1981). Pupils' alternative frameworks in science. *European Journal of Science Education, 3*, 93–101.

Driver, R., & Easley, J. (1978). Pupils and paradigms: A review of literature related to concept development in adolescent science students. *Studies in Science Education, 5*, 61–84.

Driver, R., Gott, R., Johnson, S., Worsley, C., & Wylie, F. (1982). *Science in schools age 15: Report No. 1.* London: Her Majesty's Stationery Office.

Duit, R. (1981). Understanding energy as a conserved quantity — Remarks on the article by R. U. Sexl. *European Journal of Science Education, 3*, 291–301.

Duke, D. L. (Ed.). (1979). *Classroom management* (78th yearbook of the National Society for the Study of Education, Part 2). Chicago: University of Chicago Press.

Dunkerton, J., & Guy, J. J. (1981). The Science Teaching Observation Schedule: Is it quantitative? *European Journal of Science Education, 3*, 313–316.

Dwyer, F. M. (1972). The effect of overt responses in improving visually programed science instruction. *Journal of Research in Science Teaching, 9,* 47–55.

Eggleston, J. F., Galton, M. J., & Jones, M. (1975). *A science teaching observation schedule* (Schools Council Research Series). London: Macmillan.

Eglen, J. R., & Kempa, R. F. (1974). Assessing manipulative skills in practical chemistry. *School Science Review, 56,* 261–273.

Emmer, E. T., Evertson, C. M., Clements, B. S., Sanford, J. P., & Worsham, M. E. (1981). *Organizing and managing the junior high school classroom.* Austin: University of Texas, R & D Center for Teacher Education.

Erickson, G. L. (1979). Children's conceptions of heat and temperature. *Science Education, 63,* 221–230.

Erickson, G. L. (1980). Children's viewpoints of heat: A second look. *Science Education, 64,* 323–336.

Esquivel, J. M., Lashier, W. S., & Smith, W. S. (1978). Effect of feedback on questioning of preservice teachers in SCIS microteaching. *Science Education, 62,* 209–214.

Eulefeld, G. (1976). An ecological approach to restructuring school biology. *Journal of Biological Education, 10,* 196–202.

Fraser, B. J. (1978). Australian Science Education Project: Overview of evaluation studies. *Science Education, 62,* 417–426.

Fraser, B. J. (1980). Science teacher characteristics and student attitudinal outcomes. *School Science and Mathematics, 80,* 300–308.

Fraser, B. J., & Remenyi, A. G. (1978). Stability of the physicist's image. *American Journal of Physics, 46,* 522–524.

Fraser, B. J., & Walberg, H. J. (1981). Psychosocial learning environment in science classrooms: A review of research. *Studies in Science Education, 8,* 67–92.

Fredette, N., & Lochhead, J. (1980). Student conceptions of simple circuits. *The Physics Teacher, 18,* 194–198.

Fullan, M., & Pomfret, A. (1977). Research on curriculum and instruction implementation. *Review of Educational Research, 47,* 335–397.

Gabel, D. L., & Sherwood, R. (1980). The effect of student manipulation of molecular models on chemistry achievement according to Piagetian level. *Journal of Research in Science Teaching, 17,* 75–81.

Gabel, D. L., Kogan, M. H., & Sherwood, R. D. (1980). A summary of research in science education — 1978. *Science Education, 64,* 429–568.

Gagné, R. M., & White, R. T. (1978). Memory structures and learning outomes. *Review of Educational Research, 48,* 187–222.

Gall, M. D. (1970). The use of questions in teaching. *Review of Educational Research, 40,* 707–721.

Galton, M., & Eggleston, J. (1979). Some characteristics of effective science teaching. *European Journal of Science Education, 1,* 75–86.

Gardner, P. L. (1975). Attitudes to science: A review. *Studies in Science Education, 2,* 1–41.

Gardner, P. L. (1977). Logical connectives in science: A summary of the findings. *Research in Science Education, 7,* 9–24.

Garrett, R. M., & Roberts, I. F. (1982). Demonstration versus small group practical work in science education: A critical review of studies since 1900. *Studies in Science Education, 9,* 109–146.

Gatta, L. A. (1973). An analysis of the pass–fail grading system as compared to the conventional grading system in high school chemistry. *Journal of Research in Science Teaching, 10,* 3–12.

Gauld, C. F., & Hukins, A. A. (1980). Scientific attitudes: A review. *Studies in Science Education, 7,* 129–161.

Geeslin, W. E., & Shavelson, R. J. (1975). An exploratory analysis of the representation of a mathematical structure in students' cognitive structures. *American Educational Research Journal, 12,* 21–39.

Goodstein, M., & Howe, A. C. (1978). The use of concrete methods in secondary chemistry instruction. *Journal of Research in Science Teaching, 15,* 361–366.

Gould, C. D. (1978). Practical work in sixth-form biology. *Journal of Biological Education, 12,* 33–38.

Graber, R. A., Means, R. S., & Johnsten, T. D. (1972). The effect of subsuming concepts on student achievement on unfamiliar science learning material. *Journal of Research in Science Teaching, 9,* 277–279.

Griffiths, D. H. (1976). Physics teaching: Does it hinder intellectual development? *American Journal of Physics, 44,* 81–85.

Groen, G. J. (1978). The educational ideas of Piaget and educational practice. In P. Suppes (Ed.), *Impact of research on education: Some case studies.* Washington, DC: National Academy of Education.

Guesne, E., Tiberghien, A., & Delacôte, G. (1978). Méthodes et résultats concernant l'analyse des conceptions des élèves dans différants domaines de la physique. *Revue Francaise de Pédagogie, 45,* 25–32.

Gullickson, A. R. (1978). Elementary science curriculum dissemination in the Midwest. *Journal of Research in Science Teaching, 15,* 479–484.

Gunstone, R. F. (1980). *Structural outcomes of physics instruction.* Unpublished Ph.D. thesis, Monash University, Melbourne, Australia.

Gunstone, R. F., Champagne, A. B., & Klopfer, L. E. (1981). Instruction for understanding: A case study. *Australian Science Teachers' Journal, 27*(3), 27–32.

Gunstone, R. F., & White, R. T. (1981). Understanding of gravity. *Science Education, 65,* 291–299.

Haertel, G. D., Walberg, H. J., Junker, L., & Pascarella, E. T. (1981). Early adolescent sex differences in science learning: Evidence from the National Assessment of Educational Progress. *American Educational Research Journal, 18,* 329–341.

Haggis, S., & Adey, P. (1979). A review of integrated science education worldwide. *Studies in Science Education, 6,* 69–89.

Hall, G. E. (1978). Computer processing and feedback of interaction analysis data for teachers. *Journal of Classroom Interaction, 13,* 32–37.

Hamilton, D. (1975). *Big science, small school.* Edinburgh: Scottish Council for Research in Education.

Harding, J. M., Kelly, P. J., & Nicodemus, R. B. (1976). The study of curriculum change. *Studies in Science Education, 3,* 1–30.

Harlen, W. (1975). *Science 5–13: A formative evaluation.* London: Macmillan.

Harlen, W., Black, P., & Johnson, S. (1981). *Science in schools age 11* (Rep. No. 1). London: Her Majesty's Stationery Office.

Hartley, J., & Davies, I. K. (1976). Preinstructional strategies: The role of pretests, behavioral objectives, overviews and advance organizers. *Review of Educational Research, 46,* 239–265.

Hasan, O. E., & Billeh, V. Y. (1975). Relationship between teachers' change in attitudes toward science and some professional variables. *Journal of Research in Science Teaching, 12,* 247–253.

Head, J. O., & Sutton, C. R. (1981, April). *Structures of understanding and the ontogenesis of commitment.* Paper presented at the meeting of the American Educational Research Association, Los Angeles.

Heath, R. W. (1964). Curriculum, cognition, and educational measurement. *Educational and Psychological Measurement, 24,* 239–253.

Helm, H. (1980). Misconceptions in physics amongst South African students. *Physics Education, 15,* 92–97, 105.

Herron, J. D. (1978). Role of learning and development: Critique of Novak's comparison of Ausubel and Piaget. *Science Education, 62,* 593–605.

Hewson, M. G. A'B. (1982). *Students' existing knowledge as a factor influencing the acquisition of scientific knowledge.* Unpublished Ph.D. thesis, University of the Witwatersrand, Johannesburg, South Africa.

Hofman, H. H. (1977). An assessment of eight-year-old children's attitudes toward science. *School Science and Mathematics, 77,* 662–670.

Hofstein, A., Ben-Zvi, R., Samuel, D., & Kempa, R. F. (1977). A factoranalytic investigation of Meyer's test of interests. *Journal of Research in Science Teaching, 14,* 63–68.

Hofstein, A., Ben-Zvi, R., Samuel, D., & Tamir, P. (1977). Attitudes of Israeli high-school students toward chemistry and physics: A comparative study. *Science Education, 61,* 259–268.

Hofstein, A., & Lunetta, V. N. (1982). The role of the laboratory in science teaching: Neglected aspects of research. *Review of Educational Research, 52,* 201–217.

Holliday, W. G. (1975). The effects of verbal and adjunct pictorialverbal information in science instruction. *Journal of Research in Science Teaching, 12,* 77–83.

Holliday, W. G. (1981). Selective attentional effects of textbook study questions on student learning in science. *Journal of Research in Science Teaching, 18,* 283–289.

Holliday, W. G., Brunner, L. L., & Donais, E. L. (1977). Differential cognitive and affective responses to flow diagrams in science. *Journal of Research in Science Teaching, 14,* 129-138.

Holliday, W. G., & Harvey, D. A. (1976). Adjunct labeled drawings in teaching physics to junior high school students. *Journal of Research in Science Teaching, 13,* 37-43.

Holliday, W. G., Whittaker, H. G., & Loose, K. D. (1978, April). *Differential effects of science study questions.* Paper presented at the meeting of the National Association for Research in Science Teaching, Toronto. (ERIC Document Reproduction Service No. ED 155 058)

Howe, A. C., & Shayer, M. (1981). Sex-related differences on a task of volume and density. *Journal of Research in Science Teaching, 18,* 169-175.

Hurd, P. D. (1971). Research in science education: Planning for the future. *Journal of Research in Science Teaching, 8,* 243-249.

Inhelder, B., & Piaget, J. (1958). *The growth of logical thinking from childhood to adolescence.* New York: Basic Books.

James, R. K., & Hall, G. (1981). A study of the concerns of science teachers regarding an implementation of ISCS. *Journal of Research in Science Teaching, 18,* 479-487.

Johnson, P. E. (1964). Associative meaning of concepts in physics. *Journal of Educational Psychology, 55,* 84-88.

Johnson, R. T., Ryan, F. L., & Schroeder, H. (1974). Inquiry and the development of positive attitudes. *Science Education, 58,* 51-56.

Johnstone, A. H., & Reid, N. (1981). Towards a model for attitude change. *European Journal of Science Education, 3,* 205-212.

Jung, W., Pfundt, H., & von Rhöneck, C. (1982). *Problems concerning students' representation of physics and chemistry knowledge.* Ludwigsburg, Federal Republic of Germany: Pädagogische Hochschule Ludwigsburg.

Jungwirth, E. (1980). Alternative interpretations of findings in cognitive preference research in science education. *Science Education, 64,* 85-94.

Kahle, J. B. (1978, April). *A comparison of the effects of an advanced organizer and/or behavioral objectives on the achievement of disadvantaged biology students.* Paper presented at the meeting of the National Association for Research in Science Teaching, Toronto. (ERIC Document Reproduction Service No. ED 164 272)

Kahle, J. B., & Nordland, F. H. (1975). The effect of an advanced organizer when utilized with carefully sequenced audio-tutorial units. *Journal of Research in Science Teaching, 12,* 63-67.

Kahle, J. B., & Rastovac, J. J. (1976). The effects of a series of advanced organizers in increasing meaningful learning. *Science Education, 60,* 365-371.

Kamii, C., & DeVries, R. (1978). *Physical knowledge in preschool education: Implications of Piaget's theory.* Englewood Cliffs, NJ: Prentice-Hall.

Karplus, R., Karplus, E., Formisano, M., & Paulsen, A. C. (1977). A survey of proportional reasoning and control of variables in seven countries. *Journal of Research in Science Teaching, 14,* 411-417.

Kattmann, U., & Schaefer, G. (1976). New approaches to restructuring school biology. *Journal of Biological Education, 10,* 139-147.

Katz, M., & Norris, L. (1972). The contribution of academic interest measures to the differential prediction of marks. *Journal of Educational Measurement, 9,* 1-11.

Kauchak, D. P. (1977). The effect of essay writing on the attitudes of undergraduate science methods students. *Journal of Research in Science Teaching, 14,* 139-143.

Kauchak, D. P., Eggen, P., & Kirk, S. (1978). The effect of cue specificity on learning from graphical materials in science. *Journal of Research in Science Teaching, 15,* 499-503.

Keeves, J. P. (1975). The home, the school, and achievement in mathematics and science. *Science Education, 59,* 439-460.

Kelly, G. A. (1955). *The psychology of personal constructs.* New York: Norton.

Kempa, R. F., & Dubé, G. E. (1973). Cognitive preference orientations in students of chemistry. *British Journal of Educational Psychology, 43,* 279-288.

Kempa, R. F., & Dubé, G. E. (1974). Science interest and attitude traits in students subsequent to the study of chemistry at the ordinary level of the General Certificate of Education. *Journal of Research in Science Teaching, 11,* 361-370.

Killian, C. R. (1979). Cognitive development of college freshmen. *Journal of Research in Science Teaching, 16,* 347-350.

Kishta, M. A. (1979). Cognitive levels and linguistic abilities of elementary school children. *Journal of Research in Science Teaching, 16,* 67-71.

Klopfer, L. E. (1971). Evaluation of learning in science. In B. S. Bloom, J. T. Hastings, and G. F. Madaus (Eds.), *Handbook on formative and summative evaluation of student learning.* New York: McGraw-Hill.

Klopfer, L. E., & Champagne, A. B. (1975). Formative evaluation of the Individualized Science program. *Studies in Educational Evaluation, 1,* 109-122.

Kolodiy, G. (1975). The cognitive development of high school and college science students. *Journal of College Science Teaching, 5,* 20-22.

Kolodiy, G. O. (1977). Cognitive development and science teaching. *Journal of Research in Science Teaching, 14,* 21-26.

Koran, J. J., & Koran, M. L. (1973). Differential response to structure of advance organizers in science instruction. *Journal of Research in Science Teaching, 10,* 347-353.

Kreitler, H., & Kreitler, S. (1974). The role of the experiment in science education. *Instructional Science, 3,* 75-88.

Krockover, G. H., & Malcolm, M. D. (1978). The effects of the Science Curriculum Improvement Study upon a child's attitude toward science. *School Science and Mathematics, 78,* 575-584.

Lamb, W. G. (1976). Multiple paradigms and the infancy of science educational research. *Science Education, 60,* 413-416.

Lamb, W. G. (1977). Evaluation of a self-instructional module for training science teachers to ask a wide cognitive variety of questions. *Science Education, 61,* 29-39.

Lamb, W. G., Davis, P., Leflore, R., Hall, C., Griffin, J., & Holmes, R. (1979). The effect on student achievement of increasing kinetic structure of teachers' lectures. *Journal of Research in Science Teaching, 16,* 223-227.

Larkin, J. H., & Reif, F. (1979). Understanding and teaching problem-solving in physics. *European Journal of Science Education, 1,* 191-203.

Lashier, W. S., & Nieft, J. W. (1975). The effects of an individualized self-paced science program on selected teacher, classroom, and student variables—ISCS Level One. *Journal of Research in Science Teaching, 12,* 359-369.

Lawson, A. E. (1978). The development and validation of a classroom test of formal reasoning. *Journal of Research in Science Teaching, 15,* 11-24.

Lawson, A. E., Nordland, F. H., & DeVito, A. (1975). Relationship of formal reasoning to achievement, aptitudes, and attitudes in preservice teachers. *Journal of Research in Science Teaching, 12,* 423-431.

Lawson, A. E., & Renner, J. W. (1975). Relationships of science subject matter and developmental levels of learners. *Journal of Research in Science Teaching, 12,* 347-358.

Lawton, J. T., & Wanska, S. K. (1977). Advance organizers as a teaching strategy: A reply to Barnes and Clawson. *Review of Educational Research, 47,* 233-244.

Layton, D. (1973). *Science for the people: The origins of the school science curriculum in England.* London: Allen & Unwin.

Lazarowitz, R., Barufaldi, P. J., & Hunsberger, P. J. (1978). Student teachers' characteristics and favorable attitudes toward inquiry. *Journal of Research in Science Teaching, 15,* 559-566.

Levine, D. I., & Linn, M. C. (1977). Scientific reasoning ability in adolescence: Theoretical viewpoints and educational implications. *Journal of Research in Science Teaching, 14,* 371-384.

Lewy, A. (1973). The practice of curriculum evaluation. *Curriculum Theory Network, 11,* 6-33.

Linke, R. D. (1974a). The classification and analysis of environmental education. In P. W. Musgrave (Ed.), *Contemporary studies in the curriculum.* Sydney: Angus and Robertson.

Linke, R. D. (1974b). Influence of cultural background on hierarchical learning. *Journal of Educational Psychology, 66,* 911-918.

Linn, M. C., Chen, B., & Thier, H. D. (1977). Teaching children to control variables: Investigation of a free-choice environment. *Journal of Research in Science Teaching, 14,* 249-255.

Linn, M. C., & Peterson, R. W. (1973). The effect of direct experience with objects on middle class, culturally diverse, and visually impaired young children. *Journal of Research in Science Teaching, 10,* 83–90.

Lockheed, M., & Harris, A. (1982). *Classroom interaction and gender differences in opportunities for peer learning in science.* Paper presented at the meeting of the American Educational Research Association, New York.

Longeot, F. (1965). Analyse statistique des trois tests génétique collectifs. *Bulletin de l'Institut National D'Étude, 20,* 219–237.

Loucks, S. F. (1977). *Concerns expressed by elementary school teachers about the implementation of the SCIS curriculum.* Paper presented at the meeting of the Association for the Education of Teachers of Science, Cincinnati.

Lowell, W. E. (1979). A study of hierarchical classification in concrete and abstract thought. *Journal of Research in Science Teaching, 16,* 255–262.

Lu, P. K. (1978). Three integrative models of kinetic structure in teaching astronomy. *Journal of Research in Science Teaching, 15,* 249–255.

Mackay, L. D. (1972). Changes in cognitive preferences during two years of physics study in Victorian high schools. *Australian Science Teachers Journal, 18*(1), 63–66.

Mackay, L. D. (1975). Cognitive preferences and achievement in physics, chemistry, science and mathematics. *Research in Science Education, 5,* 49–58.

Mackenzie, A. A., & White, R. T. (1982). Fieldwork in geography and long term memory structures. *American Educational Research Journal, 19,* 623–632.

Mali, G. B., & Howe, A. (1979). Development of Earth and gravity concepts among Nepali children. *Science Education, 63,* 685–691.

Mandell, A. (1980). Problem-solving strategies of sixth-grade students who are superior problem solvers. *Science Education, 64,* 203–211.

Marton, F., & Säljö, R. (1976). On qualitative differences in learning: I. Outcome and process. *British Journal of Educational Psychology, 46,* 4–11.

Martorano, S. C. (1977). A developmental analysis of performance on Piaget's formal operations tasks. *Developmental Psychology, 13,* 666–672.

Maslow, A. H. (1968). *Toward a psychology of being.* New York: Van Nostrand Reinhold.

Mathis, P. M., & Shrum, J. W. (1977). The effect of kinetic structure on achievement and total attendance time in audio-tutorial biology. *Journal of Research in Science Teaching, 14,* 105–115.

McKinnon, J. W., & Renner, J. W. (1971). Are colleges concerned with intellectual development? *American Journal of Physics, 39,* 1047–1052.

Meyer, G. R. (1969). *A test of interests.* Milton, Queensland: Jacaranda.

Millar, R. H. (1981). Curriculum rhetoric and social control: A perspective on recent science curriculum development. *European Journal of Science Education, 3,* 271–284.

Milson, J. L. (1979). Evaluation of the effect of laboratory-oriented science curriculum materials on the attitudes of students with reading difficulties. *Science Education, 63,* 9–14.

Mitchell, D. A. (1978). The production of criteria for evaluating science curriculum materials with specific reference to criteria for inquiry and the application of these criteria to chemistry curriculum materials. *Research in Science Education, 8,* 59–69.

Moreira, M. A. (1980). A non-traditional approach to the evaluation of laboratory instruction in general physics courses. *European Journal of Science Education, 2,* 441–448.

Mori, I., Kitagawa, O., & Tadang, N. (1974a). The effect of language on a child's forming of spatio-temporal concept: On comparing Japanese and Thai children. *Science Education, 58,* 523–529.

Mori, I., Kitagawa, O., & Tadang, N. (1974b). The effect of religious ideas on a child's conception of time: A comparison of Japanese children and Thai children. *Science Education, 58,* 519–522.

Mori, I., Kojima, M., & Tadang, N. (1976). The effect of language on a child's conception of speed: A comparative study on Japanese and Thai children. *Science Education, 60,* 531–534.

Munby, A. H. (1976). Some implications of language in science education. *Science Education, 60,* 115–124.

Munby, H. (1980). Analysing teaching for intellectual independence. In H. Munby, G. Orpwood, & T. Russell (Eds.), *Seeing curriculum in a new light: Essays from science education.* Toronto: OISE Press.

Nagy, P. (1978). Subtest formation by cluster analysis of the scientific attitude inventory. *Journal of Research in Science Teaching, 15,* 355–360.

Nicodemus, R. B. (1977). Adoption and rejection of three curriculum projects. *Studies in Educational Evaluation, 3,* 67–76.

Northfield, J. R. (1980). *ASEP in Victorian secondary schools: A study of the impact and implementation of a curriculum project.* Unpublished doctoral thesis, Monash University, Melbourne, Australia.

Nous, A., & Raven, R. (1973). The effects of a structured learning sequence on children's correlative thinking about biological phenomena. *Journal of Research in Science Teaching, 10,* 251–255.

Novak, J. D. (1977). Epicycles and the homocentric Earth: Or what is wrong with *stages* of cognitive development? *Science Education, 61,* 393–395.

Novak, J. D. (1978). An alternative to Piagetian psychology for science and mathematics education. *Studies in Science Education, 5,* 1–30.

Novick, S., & Duvdvani, D. (1976). The relationship between school and student variables and the attitudes toward science of tenth-grade students in Israel. *Journal of Research in Science Teaching, 13,* 259–265.

Novick, S., & Nussbaum, J. (1978). Junior high school pupils' understanding of the particulate nature of matter: An interview study. *Science Education, 62,* 273–281.

Nuccio, E. J. (1982). *An analysis of teachers' managerial activities in secondary school science classrooms.* Paper presented at the meeting of the American Educational Research Association, New York.

Nummedal, S. G., & Collea, F. P. (1981). Field independence, task ambiguity, and performance on a proportional reasoning task. *Journal of Research in Science Teaching, 18,* 255–260.

Nussbaum, J. (1979). Children's conceptions of the Earth as a cosmic body: A cross age study. *Science Education, 63,* 83–93.

Nussbaum, J., & Novak, J. D. (1976). An assessment of children's concepts of the Earth utilizing structured interviews. *Science Education, 60,* 535–550.

Oakley, W. F., & Crocker, R. K. (1980). An exploratory study of teacher interventions in elementary science laboratory groups. *Journal of Research in Science Teaching, 17,* 407–418.

Organization for Economic and Cooperative Development (1976). *School-based curriculum development.* Paris: Centre for Educational Research and Innovation.

Olson, J. K., & Reid, W. A. (1982). Studying innovation in science teaching: The use of repertory grid techniques in developing a research strategy. *European Journal of Science Education, 4,* 193–201.

Orgren, J. (1977). The long-term effects of mandated curriculum adoption on teaching behavior. *Journal of Research in Science Teaching, 14,* 419–425.

Orgren, J., & Doran, R. L. (1975). The effects of adopting the revised New York State Regents Earth Science Syllabus on selected teacher and student variables. *Journal of Research in Science Teaching, 12,* 15–24.

Ormerod, M. B. (1979). Pupils' attitudes to the social implications of science. *European Journal of Science Education, 1,* 177–190.

Orpwood, G. W. F. (1980). Deliberative inquiry into Canadian science education. *Journal of Curriculum Studies, 12,* 363–364.

Osborne, R. J. (1976). Using student attitudes to modify instruction in physics. *Journal of Research in Science Teaching, 13,* 525–531.

Osborne, R. J. (1980). *Force* (Paper No. 16). Hamilton, New Zealand: University of Waikato, Learning in Science Project.

Osborne, R. J., & Gilbert, J. K. (1980a). A method for investigating concept understanding in science. *European Journal of Science Education, 2,* 311–321.

Osborne, R. J., & Gilbert, J. K. (1980b). A technique for exploring students' views of the world. *Physics Education, 15,* 376–379.

Owen, J. M. (1979). *The Australian Science Education Project — A study of factors affecting its adoption and implementation in schools.* Unpublished doctoral thesis, Monash University, Melbourne, Australia.

Owen, J. M., & Tisher, R. P. (1978). *Curriculum adoption: The fate of a national curriculum project in Australia*. Paper presented at the meeting of the American Educational Research Association, Toronto.

Pallrand, G. J. (1979). The transition to formal thought. *Journal of Research in Science Teaching, 16*, 445–451.

Penick, J. E. (1976). Creativity in fifth-grade science students: The effects of two patterns of instruction. *Journal of Research in Science Teaching, 13*, 307–314.

Penick, J. E., & Shymansky, J. A. (1977). The effects of teacher behavior on student behavior in fifth grade science: A replication study. *Journal of Research in Science Teaching, 14*, 427–432.

Penick, J. E., Shymansky, J. A., Matthews, C. C., & Good, R. G. (1976). Studying the effects of two quantitatively defined teaching strategies on student behavior in elementary school science using macroanalytic techniques. *Journal of Research in Science Teaching, 13*, 289–296.

Peterson, R. W., & Carlson, G. R. (1979). A summary of research in science education — 1977. *Science Education, 63*, 429–553.

Phillips, D. G. (1977). The Karplus islands puzzle, volume with metal cylinders, and other problems. *Journal of Research in Science Teaching, 14*, 361–369.

Piaget, J. (1964). Development and learning. *Journal of Research in Science Teaching, 2*, 176–186.

Piaget, J. (1970). *The child's conception of movement and speed* (G.E.T. Holloway & M. J. Mackenzie, Trans.). London: Routledge & Kegan Paul. (Original work published 1946)

Pines, A. L. (1977). *Scientific concept learning in children: The effect of prior knowledge on resulting cognitive structure subsequent to A-T instruction*. Unpublished doctoral dissertation, Cornell University.

Posner, G. J., Strike, K. A., Hewson, P. W., & Gertzog, W. A. (1982). Accommodation of a scientific conception: Toward a theory of conceptual change. *Science Education, 66*, 211–227.

Power, C. N. (1973). The unintentional consequences of science teaching. *Journal of Research in Science Teaching, 10*, 331–339.

Power, C. N. (1976). Competing paradigms in science education research. *Journal of Research in Science Teaching, 13*, 579–587.

Power, C. N. (1977). A critical review of science classroom interaction studies. *Studies in Science Education, 4*, 1–30.

Power, C. N., & Tisher, R. P. (1976). Relationships between classroom behavior and instructional outcomes in an individualized science program. *Journal of Research in Science Teaching, 13*, 489–497.

Power, C. N., & Tisher, R. P. (1979). A self-paced environment. In H. J. Walberg (Ed.), *Educational environments and effects*. Berkeley, CA: McCutchan.

Preece, P. F. W. (1976a). Associative structure of science concepts. *British Journal of Educational Psychology, 46*, 174–183.

Preece, P. F. W. (1976b). Mapping cognitive structure: A comparison of methods. *Journal of Educational Psychology, 68*, 1–8.

Preece, P. F. W. (1978). Associative structure and the schema of proportionality. *Journal of Research in Science Teaching, 15*, 395–399.

Quinn, R. E. (1976). Using value sheets to modify attitudes toward environmental problems. *Journal of Research in Science Teaching, 13*, 65–69.

Raghubir, K. P. (1979). The laboratory-investigative approach to science instruction. *Journal of Research in Science Teaching, 16*, 13–17.

Raven, R. J. (1972). The development of the concept of acceleration in elementary school children. *Journal of Research in Science Teaching, 9*, 201–206.

Raven, R. J. (1973). The development of a test of Piaget's logical operations. *Science Education, 57*, 377–385.

Ray, C. L. (1979). A comparative laboratory study of the effects of lower level and higher level questions on students' abstract reasoning and critical thinking in non-directive high school chemistry classrooms (Doctoral dissertation, Florida State University, Tallahassee, 1979). *Dissertation Abstracts International, 40*, 3220A.

Redfield, D. L., & Rousseau, E. W. (1981). A meta-analysis of experimental research on teacher questioning behavior. *Review of Educational Research, 51*, 237–245.

Reif, F., & St. John, M. (1979). Teaching physicists' thinking skills in the laboratory. *American Journal of Physics, 47*, 950–957.

Renner, J. W. (1979). The relationships between intellectual development and written responses to science questions. *Journal of Research in Science Teaching, 16*, 279–299.

Renner, J. W., & Lawson, A. E. (1973). Promoting intellectual development through science teaching. *The Physics Teacher, 11*, 273–276.

Riban, D. M. (1976). Examination of a model for field studies in science. *Science Education, 60*, 1–11.

Rice, D. R. (1977). The effect of question-asking instruction on preservice elementary science teachers. *Journal of Research in Science Teaching, 14*, 353–359.

Riley, J. P. (1978). Effects of studying a question classification system on the cognitive level of preservice teachers' questions. *Science Education, 62*, 333–338.

Riley, J. P. (1981). The effects of preservice teacher's cognitive questioning level and redirecting on student science achievement. *Journal of Research in Science Teaching, 18*, 303–309.

Robertson, W. W., & Richardson, E. (1975). The development of some physical science concepts in secondary school students. *Journal of Research in Science Teaching, 12*, 319–329.

Rothkopf, E. Z. (1970). The concept of mathemagenic activities. *Review of Educational Research, 40*, 325–336.

Rowe, M. B. (1969). Science, silence, and sanctions. *Science and Children, 6*(6), 11–13.

Rowe, M. B. (1974a). Wait-time and rewards as instructional variables, their influence on language, logic, and fate control: Part 1. Wait time. *Journal of Research in Science Teaching, 11*, 81–94.

Rowe, M. B. (1974b). Relation of wait-time and rewards to the development of language, logic, and fate control: Part 2. Rewards. *Journal of Research in Science Teaching, 11*, 291–308.

Rowell, J. A., & Dawson, C. J. (1977). Teaching about floating and sinking: Further studies toward closing the gap between cognitive psychology and classroom practice. *Science Education, 61*, 527–540.

Rowell, J. A., & Dawson, C. J. (1981). Volume, conservation and instruction: A classroom based Solomon four group study of conflict. *Journal of Research in Science Teaching, 18*, 533–546.

Rowell, J. A., & Hoffmann, P. J. (1975). Group tests for distinguishing formal from concrete thinkers. *Journal of Research in Science Teaching, 12*, 157–164.

Sabar, N. (1979). Science, curriculum, and society: Trends in science curriculum. *Science Education, 63*, 257–269.

Santiesteban, A. J. (1976). Teacher questioning performance and student affective outcomes. *Journal of Research in Science Teaching, 13*, 553–557.

Sayre, S., & Ball, D. W. (1975). Piagetian cognitive development and achievement in science. *Journal of Research in Science Teaching, 12*, 165–174.

Schofield, B., Murphy, P., Johnson, S., Worsley, C., & Wylie, F. (1982). *A.P.U. Science in schools age 13* (Rep. No. 1). London: Her Majesty's Stationery Office.

Selmes, C. (1973). Nuffield A-level biology: Attitudes to science. *Journal of Biological Education, 7*(4), 43–47.

Sexl, R. U. (1981). Some observations concerning the teaching of the energy concept. *European Journal of Science Education, 3*, 285–289.

Sharan, S., & Yaakobi, D. (1981). Classroom learning environment of city and Kibbutz biology classrooms in Israel. *European Journal of Science Education, 3*, 321–328.

Shavelson, R. J. (1972). Some aspects of the correspondence between content structure and cognitive structure in physics instruction. *Journal of Educational Psychology, 63*, 225–234.

Shavelson, R. J. (1974). Methods for examining representations of a subject-matter structure in a student's memory. *Journal of Research in Science Teaching, 11*, 231–249.

Shavelson, R. J., & Stanton, G. C. (1975). Construct validation: Methodology and application to three measures of cognitive structure. *Journal of Educational Measurement, 12*, 67–85.

Shayer, M., Adey, P., & Wylam, H. (1981). Group tests of cognitive development ideals and a realization. *Journal of Research in Science Teaching, 18*, 157–168.

Shayer, M., & Warry, D. (1974). Piaget in the classroom: Part 1. Testing a whole class at the same time. *School Science Review, 55*, 447–458.

Sheehan, D. J. (1970). The effectiveness of concrete and formal instructional procedures with concrete- and formal-operational students (Doctoral dissertation, State University of New York, Albany, 1970). *Dissertation Abstracts International, 31,* 2748A.

Sherwood, R. D., & Herron, J. D. (1976). Effect on student attitude: Individualized IAC versus conventional high school chemistry. *Science Education, 60,* 471–474.

Shulman, L. S., & Tamir, P. (1973). Research on teaching in the natural sciences. In R. M. W. Travers (Ed.), *Second handbook of research on teaching.* Chicago: Rand McNally.

Shyers, J., & Cox, D. (1978). Training for the acquisition and transfer of the concept of proportionality in remedial college students. *Journal of Research in Science Teaching, 15,* 25–36.

Shymansky, J. A., Kyle, W. C., & Alport, J. M. (1983). The effects of new science curricula on student performance. *Journal of Research in Science Teaching, 20,* 387–404.

Shymansky, J. A., Penick, J. E., Matthews, C. C., & Good, R. G. (1977). A study of student classroom behavior and self-perception as it relates to problem solving. *Journal of Research in Science Teaching, 14,* 191–198.

Shymansky, J. A., & Yore, L. D. (1980). A study of teaching strategies, student cognitive development, and cognitive style as they relate to student achievement in science. *Journal of Research in Science Teaching, 17,* 369–382.

Simmons, E. S. (1980). The influence of kinetic structure in films on biology students' achievement and attitude. *Journal of Research in Science Teaching, 17,* 67–73.

Simon, A., & Boyer, E. G. (1974). *Mirrors for behavior III: An anthology of observation instruments.* Wyncote, PA: Communication Materials Center.

Simpson, R. D., Rentz, R. R., & Shrum, J. W. (1976). Influence of instrument characteristics on student responses in attitude assessment. *Journal of Research in Science Teaching, 13,* 275–281.

Sipe, H. C., & Farmer, W. A. (1982). A summary of research in science education — 1980. *Science Education, 66,* 305–493.

Skilbeck, M. (1976). School based curriculum development. In *Supporting Curriculum Development* (Units 24–26, Open University Series on Curriculum Design and Development). Milton Keynes, England: Open University Press.

Skinner, R., & Barcikowski, R. S. (1973). Measuring specific interests in biological, physical and earth sciences in intermediate grade levels. *Journal of Research in Science Teaching, 10,* 153–158.

Smith, B. D., Meux, M., Coombs, J., Nuthall, G., & Precians, R. (1967). *A study of the strategies of teaching* (Department of Health, Education and Welfare, Office of Education, Cooperative Research Project No. 1640). Urbana: University of Illinois.

Smith, D. L. (1978). Some essentials for the effective development of school-based curriculum decision making. *Australian Science Teachers Journal, 24*(2), 55–62.

Smith, E. L., & Padilla, M. J. (1977). Strategies used by first grade children in ordering varying numbers of objects by length and weight. *Journal of Research in Science Teaching, 14,* 461–466.

Smith, S. R., Trueblood, C. R., & Szabo, M. (1981). Conservation of length and instruction in linear measurement in young children. *Journal of Research in Science Teaching, 18,* 61–68.

Smolicz, J. J., & Nunan, E. E. (1975). The philosophical and sociological foundations of science education: The demythologizing of school science. *Studies in Science Education, 2,* 101–143.

Stake, R. E., & Easley, J. A. (Eds.). (1978). *Case studies in science education.* Urbana: University of Illinois, Center for Instructional Research and Curriculum Evaluation, and Committee on Culture and Cognition.

Stallings, E. S., & Snyder, W. R. (1977). The comparison of the inquiry behavior of ISCS and non-ISCS science students as measured by the TAB science test. *Journal of Research in Science Teaching, 14,* 39–44.

Staver, J. R., & Gabel, D. L. (1979). The development and construct validation of a group-administered test of formal thought. *Journal of Research in Science Teaching, 16,* 535–544.

Stavy, R., & Berkovitz, B. (1980). Cognitive conflict as a basis for teaching quantitative aspects of the concept of temperature. *Science Education, 64,* 679–692.

Stead, B. F., & Osborne, R. J. (1980). Exploring science students'

concepts of light. *Australian Science Teachers Journal, 26*(3), 84–90.

Stead, K. E., & Osborne, R. J. (1981). What is friction? Some children's ideas. *Australian Science Teachers Journal, 27*(3), 51–57.

Stewart, J. (1979). Content and cognitive structure: Critique of assessment and representation techniques used by science education researchers. *Science Education, 63,* 395–405.

Stewart, J., & Dale, M. (1981). Solutions to genetics problems: Are they the same as correct answers? *Australian Science Teachers Journal, 27*(3), 59–64.

Stewart, J., & van Kirk, J. (1981). Content analysis in science education. *European Journal of Science Education, 3,* 171–182.

Strevens, P. (1976). Problems of learning and teaching science through a foreign language. *Studies in Science Education, 3,* 55–68.

Strike, K. A., & Posner, G. J. (1976). Epistemiological perspectives on conceptions of curriculum organization and learning. *Review of Research in Education, 4,* 106–141.

Sullivan, R. J. (1979). Students' interests in specific science topics. *Science Education, 63,* 591–598.

Sutton, C. R. (1980). The learner's prior knowledge: A critical review of techniques for probing its organization. *European Journal of Science Education, 2,* 107–120.

Symington, D. J. (1977). Class discussion as a means of generating scientific problems for primary school pupils to investigate. *Australian Science Teachers Journal, 23*(3), 63–67.

Tall, G. (1981). British science curriculum projects — How have they taken root in schools? *European Journal of Science Education, 3,* 17–38.

Tamir, P. (1974). An inquiry oriented laboratory examination. *Journal of Educational Measurement, 11,* 25–33.

Tamir, P. (1976). The relationship between achievement in biology and cognitive preference styles in high school students. *British Journal of Educational Psychology, 46,* 57–67.

Tamir, P. (1977a). How are the laboratories used? *Journal of Research in Science Teaching, 14,* 311–316.

Tamir, P. (1977b). A note on cognitive preferences in science. *Studies in Science Education, 4,* 111–121.

Tamir, P., Gal-Choppin, R., & Nussinovitz, R. (1981). How do intermediate and junior high school students conceptualize living and nonliving? *Journal of Research in Science Teaching, 18,* 241–248.

Tasker, R. (1981). Children's views and classroom experiences. *Australian Science Teachers Journal, 27*(3), 33–37.

Thomas, I. D. (1978). A decision framework for school-based decision making. *Australian Science Teachers Journal, 24*(2), 63–68.

Thomas, J. L. (1978). The influence of pictorial illustrations with written text and previous achievement on the reading comprehension of fourth grade science students. *Journal of Research in Science Teaching, 15,* 401–405.

Thorsland, M. N., & Novak, J. D. (1974). The identification and significance of intuitive and analytic problem solving approaches among college physics students. *Science Education, 58,* 245–265.

Thro, M. P. (1978). Relationships between associative and content structure of physics concepts. *Journal of Educational Psychology, 70,* 971–978.

Tiberghien, A., & Delacôte, G. (1976). Manipulation et représentations des circuits électriques simple par des enfants de 7 à 12 ans. *Revue Française de Pédagogie, 34,* 32.

Tisher, R. P., & Dale, L. G. (1975). *Understanding in Science test.* Melbourne: Australian Council for Educational Research.

Tisher, R. P., & Power, C. N. (1973). Congruency with ASEP: A study of practices and values of a group of teachers and Dip. Eds. *Australian Science Teachers Journal, 19*(3), 84–87.

Tisher, R. P., & Power, C. N. (1975). A study of the effects of teaching strategies in A.S.E.P. classrooms. *Australian Journal of Education, 19,* 127–145.

Tisher, R. P., & Power, C. N. (1978). The learning environment associated with an Australian curriculum innovation. *Journal of Curriculum Studies, 10,* 169–184.

Tobias, S. (1982). When do instructional methods make a difference? *Educational Researcher, 11*(4), 4–9.

Tobin, K. G. (1980). The effect of an extended teacher wait-time on science achievement. *Journal of Research in Science Teaching, 17,* 469–475.

Tobin, K. G., & Capie, W. (1982). Relationships between formal reasoning ability, locus of control, academic engagement and integrated process skill achievement. *Journal of Research in Science Teaching, 19*, 113 121.

Tolman, R. R., & Barufaldi, J. P. (1979). The effects of teaching the Biological Sciences Curriculum Study Elementary School Sciences Program on attitudes toward science among elementary school teachers. *Journal of Research in Science Teaching, 16*, 401–406.

Trembath, R. J., & White, R. T. (1979). Mastery achievement of intellectual skills. *Journal of Experimental Education, 47*, 247–252.

Tschopp, J. K., & Kurdeck, L. A. (1981). An assessment of the relation between traditional and paper-and-pencil formal operations tasks. *Journal of Research in Science Teaching, 18*, 87–91.

Vanek, E. P., & Montean, J. J. (1977). The effect of two science programs (ESS and Laidlaw) on student classification skills, science achievement, and attitudes. *Journal of Research in Science Teaching, 14*, 57–62.

Viennot, L. (1979). Spontaneous reasoning in elementary dynamics. *European Journal of Science Education, 1*, 205–221.

Walberg, H. J. (Ed.). (1974). *Evaluating educational performance: A sourcebook of methods, instruments, and examples.* Berkeley, CA: McCutchan.

Walberg, H. J. (Ed.). (1979). *Educational environments and effects.* Berkeley, CA: McCutchan.

Walker, C. H. & Meyer, B. J. F. (1980). Integrating information from text: An evaluation of current theories. *Review of Educational Research, 50*, 421–437.

Walker, D. F. (1976). Toward comprehension of curricular realities. *Review of Research in Education, 4*, 268–308.

Walker, D. F., & Schaffarzick, J. (1974). Comparing curricula. *Review of Educational Research, 44*, 83–111.

Ward, C. R., & Herron, J. D. (1980). Helping students understand formal chemical concepts. *Journal of Research in Science Teaching, 17*, 387–400.

Ward, C. R., Nurrenbern, S. C., Lucas, C., & Herron, J. D. (1981). Evaluation of the Longeot test of cognitive development. *Journal of Research in Science Teaching, 18*, 123–130.

Ward, W. H. (1976). A test of the association of class size to students' attitudes towards science. *Journal of Research in Science Teaching, 13*, 137–143.

Waring, M. (1979). *Social pressures and curriculum innovation: A study of the Nuffield Foundation Science Teaching Project.* London: Methuen.

Watson, F. G. (1963). Research on teaching science. In N. L. Gage (Ed.), *Handbook of research on teaching.* Chicago: Rand McNally.

Welch, W. W. (1976). Evaluating the impact of national curriculum projects. *Science Education, 60*, 475–483.

Welch, W. W. (1979). Twenty years of science curriculum development: A look back. In D. C. Berliner (Ed.) *Review of Research in Education* (Vol. 7, pp. 282–306). Washington: American Educational Research Association.

Weltner, K., Liebig, H., Halbow, D., Maichle, U., Reitz, H., & Schönfeld, G. (1980). Interest of intermediate-level secondary students in physics and technology. *European Journal of Science Education, 2*, 183–189.

Wendt, D. (1979). An experimental approach to the improvement of the typographic design of textbooks. *Visible Language, 13*, 108–133.

West, L. H. T., & Fensham, P. J. (1974). Prior knowledge and the learning of science. *Studies in Science Education, 1*, 61–81.

West, L. H. T., & Fensham, P. J. (1976). Prior knowledge or advance organizers as effective variables in chemical learning. *Journal of Research in Science Teaching, 13*, 297–306.

White, R. T. (1974). The validation of a learning hierarchy. *American Educational Research Journal, 11*, 121–136.

White, R. T. (1979a). Achievement, mastery, proficiency, competence. *Studies in Science Education, 6*, 1–22.

White, R. T. (1979b). Describing cognitive structure. In *Proceedings of the 1979 Annual Conference of the Australian Association for Research in Education*, Melbourne: AARE.

White, R. T. (1981). Achievements and directions in research on intellectual skills. *Australian Journal of Education, 25*, 224–237.

White, R. T., & Gunstone, R. F. (1980). Converting memory protocols to scores on several dimensions. In *Papers of the 1980 Annual Conference of the Australian Association for Research in Education.* Sydney: AARE.

Willson, V. L. (1980). An investigation of teachers' persistence in implementing NSF-supported science curricula. *Journal of Research in Science Teaching, 17*, 257–261.

Willson, V. L., & Horn, J. G. (1979). Differences in science teaching attitudes among secondary teachers, principals, college teacher trainers, and teacher trainees. *Journal of Research in Science Teaching, 16*, 385–389.

Wilson, B. (1981). *Cultural contexts of science and mathematics education.* Leeds, England: University of Leeds Centre for Studies in Science Education.

Winn, W. (1980). The effect of block-word diagrams on the structuring of science concepts as a function of general ability. *Journal of Research in Science Teaching, 17*, 201–211.

Winne, P. H. (1979). Experiments relating teachers' use of higher cognitive questions to student achievement. *Review of Educational Research, 49*, 13–50.

Winsberg, S., & Ste-Marie, L. (1976). The correlation of motivation and academic achievement in physics. *Journal of Research in Science Teaching, 13*, 325–329.

Wittrock, M. C. (1974). Learning as a generative process. *Educational Psychologist, 11*, 87–95.

Wright, E. L. (1979). Effect of intensive instruction in cue attendance on solving formal operational tasks. *Science Education, 63*, 381–393.

Za'rour, G. I. (1976). Interpretation of natural phenomena by Lebanese school children. *Science Education, 60*, 277–287.

Zoller, U., & Watson, F. G. (1974). Teacher training for the "second generation" of science curricula: The curriculum-proof teacher. *Science Education, 58*, 93–103.

31.

Research on Teaching Arts and Aesthetics

Beverly J. Jones
University of Oregon

June King McFee
University of Oregon

Introduction

Throughout this past decade researchers in the fields of aesthetic education, arts education, and especially visual art education and music education have engaged in explorations and dialogue regarding the content, methods, and theoretical foundations necessary to better theory and practice. Some of the important research questions which they have addressed include:

1. What are the most critical problems to be addressed?
2. What are the most appropriate methodologies with which to address the problems identified?
3. What conceptual paradigms are most useful in such research?

Important curricular questions involve the subject matter content and structure of educational programs. These questions frequently focus on the problem of integrated arts education or aesthetic education versus each of the arts taught as an independent discipline. Integral to this problem are further questions involving selection of subject matter, teaching methods, and staffing, with their concomitant theoretical, political, and economic implications.

Even a brief literature survey reveals that educational research, theory, and practice within and among the arts during the last decade were marked by divergence in philosophical and political value orientations. This divergence in value orientations has led to varying research directions both in theoretical research and in curricular questions. This may be attributed in large part to the stance taken by researchers regarding the relationship of inquiry and practice in their own particular art discipline to that of other disciplines. This includes relationships among the arts and also relationships to disciplines outside the arts such as psychology, anthropology, and sociology. The latter appears to be the result of growth of emphasis on contextual and multi- or interdisciplinary nature of research studies, particularly in visual art education and to a lesser degree in music education. Emphasis on the contextual nature of educational research is evidenced in selection of research methodologies borrowed from other disciplines and in the titles and abstracts of articles and dissertations that refer to classroom context, institutional context and — with increasing frequency — social and/or cultural context. With this proliferation of research foci among the arts and across other disciplines, there appears an increasing need for unifying theory or, at least, the use of central ideas through which to view the field of research in arts and aesthetic education. Because aesthetic theory is closely related to all of the arts, and because it is allied to general philosophy and thus can be related to the underlying philosophical base of research in other fields, it appears a useful source of central ideas to achieve interdisciplinary communication among researchers in arts and aesthetic education.

Aesthetic Education

The publication of *Guidelines: Curriculum Development in Aesthetic Education* (Barkan, Chapman, & Kern, 1970) marked the beginning of a decade of curriculum development at Central Midwestern Regional Educational Laboratory (CEMREL).

The authors thank reviewers Jessie Lovano-Kerr (Florida State University) and Ronald MacGregor (University of British Columbia).

This document represents the basis upon which much subsequent research as well as curricular development has been built. Since the publication of this document CEMREL has sponsored the publication of four yearbooks as well as other educational materials and curricular packages.

The curricular packages developed at CEMREL based upon Barkan et al. (1970) have led program reviewers to state, "CEMREL is aesthetic education in this country, it has the field to itself" (Kaelin & Ecker, 1977, p. 233). Even so, Kaelin and Ecker state:

> Without specially trained teachers to introduce the comprehensive aesthetic education program into the schools no curriculum packages, however well designed, will be an effective instrument to attain the goals now projected into the elementary and secondary schools programs. (p. 233)

Seven primary areas of research in aesthetic education are identified in the first of four yearbooks by CEMREL, *Arts and Aesthetics: An Agenda for the Future*, edited by S. Madeja (1977). The discussion of the formation of this research agenda portrays vividly the difficulties faced by researchers in this field (pp. 10–14). The items on this agenda reflect the varying academic and political views of the participants. They vary from the purely intellectual, such as "investigating the relationship of cultural values to aesthetic learning" to political policy ("preparation of an educational policy in the arts and aesthetics for the public schools"), to the politically pragmatic "establishment of a mechanism for data collection in the arts and aesthetic education that will relate to existing systems such as the National Center for Educational Statistics in the Education Division of the Department of Health, Education and Welfare" and "creation of a National Center for Research in the Arts and Aesthetics," and still further to that which may be described as wishful: "optimizing the learning experience within the schools through aesthetic education and the arts." As a national agenda for research and development in the arts this seems to illustrate confusion of directions and priorities. However, two items clearly need attention in future research: "testing and revising theories of aesthetic development in students" and "improvement of evaluation in the arts and aesthetics" (pp. 18–20). Analysis of current research suggests the former might be revised to read "formulating, testing, and revising," since with few exceptions (drawing in visual arts and some listening skills in music) there is not enough consistent research upon which to base a theory. The developmental studies conducted by researchers at Project Zero represent initial attempts to understand children's growth in aesthetic sensitivity (Gardner, 1971, 1972; Gardner, Winner, & Kirchner, 1975; Perkins & Leondar, 1977). However, these studies are not sufficiently developed to formulate theory based upon them.

Given this agenda, it might be presumed that there was some consensus within the community of art(s) educators regarding definitions, curriculum patterns, staffing, funding, and similar concerns. A brief literature survey quickly proves otherwise. Perhaps this and the resulting political and economic controversies are partially responsible for the failure of the research agenda proposed in the first yearbook to materialize substantially in an operational manner in subsequent yearbooks.

Conceptions of Aesthetic Education

In a chapter entitled "Some Reactions to a Concept of Aesthetic Education," H. S. Broudy (1977) states, "No consensus on the meaning or the usage of the term 'aesthetic education' being discernible, what follows refers pretty much to my own concept of it" (1977, p. 251). He then delineates generalizations based on his reactions toward the concept of aesthetic education by various groups. Generalizations include (a) intent to educate in more than one of the arts, hence a belief in common features among the arts which can contribute to program structure; and (b) a desire that aesthetic education be required in general education for all students. However, he states that there is disagreement on the extent to which aesthetic education should be linked with extraaesthetic values such as moral, political, economic, religious, and civic. He further states that the least agreement is found in the aesthetic and educational theories by which the objectives and approaches to aesthetic education are explicated and justified (p. 251). Broudy notes another concern present in the literature of art education and music education since the publication of the Rockefeller Report, *Coming to Our Senses* (Arts, Americans, & Education Panel, 1977), specifically,

> aesthetic education threatening the conventional performance and appreciation courses. While some proponents of aesthetic education may have such sinister intentions, most do not. On the contrary, they see aesthetic education as a form of aesthetic literacy in every art for everyone, and the work in the individual arts are elective opportunities for those who want competence in them. (p. 257)

Varying value orientations evidenced by those writing about aesthetic education lead to varying research directions and to recurring curricular questions. Among these questions are the following: Does aesthetic education involve all of the arts, and if so, are these to be taught separately, in a coordinated program, or taught together as one discipline? How is the chosen configuration to be staffed: educational specialists in each arts discipline, by a single educational specialist for all the arts, by the general classroom teacher, or by artists and performers without educational credentials? What is the subject matter focus: on aesthetic experience in all aspects including everyday life, or only on aesthetic experience in the arts? And further, if the focus is on aesthetic experience in the arts, should emphasis be placed only on exemplars, that is great works of art, or on the art forms experienced as aesthetic by students or other cultural and subcultural groups? That is, should the popular arts, folk arts, mass media, industrial design, and so forth be included as worthy of study? How should the subject matter selected be taught: in a humanities context, in a product/ performing mode, or by aiding students to emulate in turn the roles of the artist/composer/performer, historian, critic, and aesthetician? Should the program be for all students or be primarily for those self-selected or with special talents?

Even within single documents philosophical unevenness contributes to conflicting answers to these curricular questions. For example, in CEMREL's *Guidelines* (Barkan et al., 1970) the introduction is clearly slanted toward emphasis on aesthetic experience in the broadest sense following egalitarian aesthetic notions apparently derived from Dewey, whereas the later curriculum sentences in this document clearly stress exemplars of art following the mode of Hegelian idealism. While it is implied in the introduction that there should be a coordinated program consisting of all of the arts, the curricular sentences imply that specialized teachers would be needed and each art taught separately. Further, these sentences are constructed in behavioral terms, thus adding the philosophical influence of Locke for another layer of philosophical unevenness. This may be due to committee construction of the document or to lack of philosophical awareness on the part of the document's final editors. In either case, the philosophical lack of awareness apparent in this basic document sets the tone for much of the literature in the field.

Similar unevenness characterizes other major reports and projects in this area such as the Rockefeller Commission Report, *Coming to Our Senses* (Arts, Americans, & Education Panel, 1977), and the Artists in the Schools Program. A welcome exception to this may be found in the work of A. Efland (1978, 1979). He has attempted to clarify the relationship of four aesthetic theories to curricular models within and across the arts. In addition, he has critically analyzed the work of others to reveal lack of philosophical clarity (1978).

Political and Economic Implications

The implications of the various conceptions for curriculum construction, staffing, and funding are immediately apparent in the controversies generated by government funding patterns and policy statements contained in *Coming to our Senses* (Arts, Americans, & Education Panel, 1977). For example, Madeja and Smith (1982) state:

> Briefly put, the major curriculum design problem is that of maintaining the integrity of the individual arts disciplines while incorporating these disciplines into a large framework—a whole curriculum.
>
> This problem has been compounded by the position of the federal government, which in 1976 actually gave direct grants to various school systems for arts and education programs. To be eligible for this money, programs had to deal with all of the arts rather than with a single art discipline. (p. 5)

Eisner (1982) sees a direct connection between this funding policy and the move in California to replace consultants in individual art disciplines with a single arts consultant. He quotes the decline in number of visual arts consultants from 438 in 1975 to 30 in 1982 (p. 89). Concerns similar to his appeared in *Studies in Art Education*, (Chapman, 1978). This entire journal was devoted to topics and issues raised by the publication of *Coming to Our Senses*. Some art educators, agreeing with the conception of arts education contained in the report, regard it as an expression of "an idea whose time has come" (Saunders, 1978, p. 17). Others are less enthusiastic. Laura Chapman (1978) faults the panel for not consulting the professional art education association and for recommending that artists with no educational credentials be hired as teachers, and she charges that "the Panel evidently would prefer to redefine the professional field of arts education than to alter the existing federal structure for funding arts" (p. 6). V. Lanier also notes (in Lewis et al., 1978) that the "composition of the Panel includes no one—as far as one can tell from the description of the mem-

bers—who has any experience or training in the teaching of the visual arts" (p. 61). Regarding the report Efland (1978) states, "First it strongly advocates the view that the arts are basic to education then it goes on record for waiving certification for those persons teaching the arts" (p. 11). To illustrate failure to differentiate between arts educators and noncertified performing and practicing artists, June McFee (in Lewis et al., 1978) cites omissions from the report including "the well-documented efforts of music, dance, visual arts, and humanities teachers and consultants who have labored to maintain the arts in education throughout the century" (p. 57). Similar objections could be made to the Artists in the Schools Program. It represents the largest economic investment in arts education by the government, yet hires uncertified personnel. It may be viewed as a means of support for artists, but has failed to provide adequate evaluations that satisfactorily illustrate its educational value. Whether this is merely an evaluation problem, a programatic problem or a combination of both is a matter of speculation.

Shuker (1977) and Kuhn (1978) describe other programs in the nation that represent attempts to institute conceptions of aesthetic education. Perhaps future evaluations of these will provide more positive information.

Visual Arts Education

Two papers with quite different emphases stand out among the many summaries of art education research and descriptions of the field. These are K. Beittel's (1982) "Art Education," and J. McFee's (1982) paper, "Defining Art Education in the Eighties." Beittel's chapter provides a listing of the major research of recent years. McFee (1982) attempts to define the diverse field of art education identifying six facets: common operations that art educators use to reach diverse goals, current major goals, fields and disciplines drawn upon for development of goals, differing teaching methodologies or strategies, institutions in which teaching occurs, and social and political forces that affect the institutions and individuals. Both Beittel's and McFee's papers exhibit the differing theoretical orientations of their writers. In "Varieties of Art Curriculum," E. Feldman (1981) also notes the manifestation of variety in theoretical position which creates contrasting views of the correct components of an art curriculum.

The review of hundreds of articles, studies, and dissertations for this chapter with concomitant examinations of reference citations and bibliographies revealed quoting circles within the field of art education. Those quoting circles are tentatively identified as psychological, anthropological, sociocultural, political, and philosophical. The philosophical may be broken into smaller quoting circles such as phenomenology, historical philosophy, and critical theory. These seem useful distinctions because researchers in each circle quote resources outside of the field of art education as sources of information and theory. For example, Beittel (1982) emphasizes the importance of such thinkers as Habermas, Gadamer, and Dufrenne, whereas McFee (1982) incorporates terminology of cognitive and experimental psychology. The multidisciplinary character of the field emerges as additional papers are examined. One author urges attention to works in the area of sociology of knowledge, another ethnographic field studies, and yet another urges us in the direction of hermeneutic and phenomenological studies. The contrasting sources used by authors present filters through which the world of data in art education is viewed. Resulting constructs lead to contrasts of opinion in such vital questions as:

- What problems should be given priority for research?
- What are the most appropriate research methodologies for the problems identified?
- How should research be analyzed, classified, and evaluated?

Drawing Research with an Example of Contrast in Priority

The National Symposium for Research in Art was held at The University of Illinois in the fall of 1981. The title of the symposium was "Learning in Art: Representation and Metaphor." Focus of many papers was on developmental aspects of drawing. Because of this focus many of the contributors relied heavily upon quoting circles from cognitive and experimental psychology. Some of the papers from this symposium have been printed in the *Review of Research in Visual Arts Education* (Vol. 15). For example, there is an excellent paper by Lovano-Kerr and Rush (1982) reviewing the work of Gardner on Project Zero. This paper analyzes various aspects of the project that focused on "the developmental study of artistic growth" as evidenced by symbol making in drawing. A lengthy list of references to research in this area at the end of this paper indicates how important it is to researchers in the field. Golomb's paper (1981) presented at this conference, entitled "Representation and Reality: The Origin and Determinants of Young Children's Drawing," is an excellent model of research in this area. A more recent paper, "Art Ability" by McFee (1985), also focuses on the drawing of children, particularly from a cross-cultural view. She quotes not only experimental studies in the field of art education, but the papers presented at the 1978 INSEA 23rd World Congress, entitled "Arts in Cultural Diversity," and also Deregowski's (1976) book, *The Child's Representation of the World*. Another art educator whose recent work deserves mention is K. Lansing. His experimental study, "The Effect of Drawing on the Development of Mental Representation" (Lansing, 1981), leads him to question "the extent to which aesthetic education should replace laboratory work in art (drawing)" (p. 22). In direct contrast to these art educators, V. Lanier states in his article, "Conception and Priority in Art Education Research" (Lanier, 1974–1975): "Studies in artistic behavior, whether by child or adult, are by definition concerned with the wrong end of the horse" (p. 28). He further states that "the theoretical frameworks of our studies are largely either improperly conceived or inadequately ordered as to priority" (p. 30). These contrasting views may be better understood if the multidisciplinary context in which they occur is examined. Referenced quoting circles of researchers concerned with drawing include cognitive and experimental psychology with some reference to anthropology. A few studies also refer to the phenomenological aspects of drawing. Lanier's orientation may be described as primarily political. Sources of this contrasting view are apparent in his references to quotations of political scientists. His impatience with the quoting

circle of psychologists and anthropologists is evident within this article. Further, he has consistently advocated that studio-based curriculum with the artist as student model be replaced by a discussion-based curriculum with the critic as student model.

This example of contrast was selected for its glaring quality as an illustration that such disagreements are founded on sharp contrasts of value. These contrasts in value are inherent in the multidisciplinary nature of art education. It is this same characteristic that marks similar contrasts in research priority, method and evaluations, as well as contrasts of opinion regarding curricular content, construction, method, and evaluation. Some of the recommendations that end this chapter are based on the assumption that these contrasts need examination of the sort suggested by H. G. Petrie (1976, p. 42) in his plea for interdisciplinary rather than multidisciplinary efforts. This is not to suggest that the contrasts be eliminated, but rather that they should be more clearly understood as research is planned, executed, and evaluated.

Reviews and Summaries of Research: Further Contrasts in Classification and Analysis

In addition to the papers previously mentioned, several articles have been published during this decade describing, summarizing, and analyzing art education research. The *Review of Research in Visual and Environmental Education*, founded in 1973 and edited by G. Hardiman and T. Zernich, was the first journal in the field devoted exclusively to critical reviews of research. Retitled *Review of Research in Visual Arts Education*, it expanded to include original studies as well as reviews. As of fall 1982 it was further retitled *Visual Arts Research*.

In a review entitled "Research in Art Education 1970–1974," Hardiman and Zernich (1976) examined 104 doctoral dissertations for frequency of research topics. During this period the most frequent topic was aesthetic behavior, which included aesthetic preference, art attitudes, aesthetic judgments, art appreciation, and meaning in the visual arts. The second most frequent topic, instruction, included such areas as student/ teacher behaviors, teaching strategies, and motivation. They also note that during 1970–1974 over 100 psychologically oriented doctoral dissertations were reported in *Dissertation Abstracts*. Two studies mentioned in this article utilize the model of instruction based on the artist, critic, and historian. These are by Gaskin (1972) and Day (1973). They may follow the model presented in the CEMREL Guidelines (Barkan et al., 1970) in a single art discipline. Since that period Clark and Zimmerman (1974, pp. 34–49) have suggested the addition of aesthetician to this triad model of art education. Studies by Acuff (1974), Bolton (1970), Mittler (1971), Ragans (1972), and Sencer (1972) also investigate aspects of art criticism in art curriculum.

Hardiman and Zernich (1976) summarize their article with several significant statements:

A close inspection of the quantitatively oriented research done in art education reveals a body of information that is loosely structured around the theoretical controversies that proliferate the domains of anthropology, education, psychology and sociology. We draw freely from these established disciplines but offer little in return. There is little sense of progress. One finds a great deal of movement in many areas, but little development. (p. 25)

Hardiman and Zernich (1976) also note that researchers seem to have an

unreasonable amount of difficulty in separating important research questions with high transferability from trivial questions. In fact if one were to eliminate all the research in art education which has been done during the past decade, the practice of teaching art in the elementary and secondary schools would be largely unaffected. . . . Research can give us knowledge, but to be of service to the field it must be cumulative not esoteric or unique. (pp. 25–26)

Several other studies that also investigate aspects of criticism and critical theory are not included in Hardiman and Zernich's article. These are by Geahigan (1980), MacGregor (1975), Mittler (1973), and Sharer (1980).

J. C. Rush and T. R. Kratochwill (1981) analyzed and classified 529 articles published in *Studies in Art Education* from 1959 to 1979 (pp. 57–64). These articles were classified as 29% descriptive–experimental, 8% historical, 5% philosophical, 49% tests–measures, 9% issues. Of the 29% descriptive–experimental only 9% were experimental. The remainder were mostly descriptive, correlational, and causal–comparative. As stated in the article:

Only 49 studies or 9 per cent of all articles published in *Studies in Art Education* between the fall of 1959 and spring of 1979 report any kind of experimental research and most of these employ large N between-group procedures. Compared on this basis with the disciplines of psychology and education, empirical research practices in visual arts seem relatively restricted and in need of cultivation. (p. 58)

Rush and Kratochwill propose that an experimental method, time-series research, be an important component in this cultivation. It has the advantages of being suitable for school-based research designed to study behavior change resulting from teacher-student interaction on a very small scale, even that of a single subject. They state that time-series research "encourages the existence of a respectful liaison between research and teaching that is not only theoretically possible but necessary to establish credibility in the arena of educational practice" (p. 59). Research advantages of time-series designs are suggested by the authors:

Among these are studying individual variability, studying heterogeneous subject populations, evaluating change over time, the possibility of integrating research into practice and designing combined single subject and multi-subject research. (p. 59)

Beittel (1982) provides a percentage distribution of 232 articles from *Studies in Art Education*, 1969–1980, in a table similar to that of Rush and Kratochwill. He divides the articles between scientific (50%) and humanistic (50%). The scientific articles are further divided as 29.3% descriptive, 2.6% test construction, and 18.1 experimental. The humanistic are divided as 12.5% methodological, 21.1% critical-interpretive, 8.2% historical, and 8.2% philosophical (p. 59). Beittel notes

that "Rush and Kratochwill (1981) classify 77 percent of the articles as what is here called scientific." The differing categorization and counting of Beittel and Rush and Kratochwill reflect their differing theoretical orientation.

In an article entitled "Perspective and Projections: Research Synthesis and Continuity," Lovano-Kerr (1974) describes recent reviews of research. Statements in this paper include: "Kuhn (in an unpublished paper) concluded that topics of research in art education are highly ideosyncratic" (p. 59); "Most of the research in art education is of the descriptive type rather than experimental ([according to] Eisner, 1972, p. 246)" (Lovano-Kerr, p. 59); "Another limitation cited by a number of authors is that of the notable dominance of empirical studies over philosophical and historical inquiries (Davis, 1971; Eisner, 1972; Kuhn, 1974)" (Lovano-Kerr, p. 59). And later: "Eisner (1972) points to another methodological limitation in existing educational research: 'almost all research in education is statistical in nature. Although this type of information is useful, it is relevant to groups and not to individuals (p. 246).'" (Lovano-Kerr, p. 60). Also: "Notable in educational research is the problem of separation between the researcher and the classroom art teacher" (Lovano-Kerr, p. 60). As has been noted, Rush and Krotochwill's proposed experimental method could impact these problems.

Lovano-Kerr proposes a structure for research synthesis and continuity which, if implemented, would be a powerful force for correcting some of the problems of research presented in this article. The proposed structure would provide a setting in which researchers could explore their contrasting views. Possibly this would encourage interdisciplinary discussion rather than multidisciplinary presentations such as now exist.

As noted, there is little agreement about what should be studied and what methods have been used in studies. There is also little agreement about what methods are most appropriate for use. A growing emphasis on qualitative research is evident. This sometimes includes anthropological methods such as ethnographic studies; participant observer studies (Lewis, et al., 1972); phenomenological studies (Beittel, 1978; Flannery, 1980); and studies in educational criticism (Eisner, 1976; Alexander, 1980). These studies also promise to alleviate the methodological problems referred to by Eisner (1972, p. 60). The first art education dissertation relying heavily on ethnographic method was R. Degge's 1975 study. The increase in art education research using qualitative methods was documented by L. Ettinger (1983). She identified 25 studies that utilized on-site descriptive research and that were based on anthropological research techniques. Her study analyzed these studies for information regarding the sociocultural dimension. F. Anderson (1979), in an edition of *Studies in Art Education* devoted to cross-cultural research, stresses its value in understanding both variability and uniformity of cognitive (artistic) processes. Cross-cultural research is being conducted using both quantitative and qualitative methods.

Music Education

The greatest concentration of relevant studies in music education was found in the *Journal of Research in Music Education*, *The Bulletin of the Council for Research in Music Education*, and the titles and abstracts of dissertations. A summary of dissertation research in music education 1972-1977 compiled by G. Gordon (1978) appeared in the *Journal of Research in Music Education* for fall 1978. The *Journal of Music Therapy* and the *Music Educators Journal* were also examined.

Although no formal percentage count was made it seemed that the research in music education is dominated by quantitative studies based on methods derived from general education and psychology. Topics researched reveal an emphasis on skill building, particularly in performance and listening. There are, however, an increasing number of topics mentioned in formal research. There are also some studies utilizing alternative methodologies.

Recent Research

W. M. Jones (1980) analyzed trends in the function of music in music education by examining articles published in the *Music Educators Journal* between September 1968 and May 1978. In the results of this study he states:

> In the ten academic years since the Tanglewood Symposium, writers in the *Music Educators Journal* continued to advance a diversity of views regarding the functions of music in society and education. The most important of those views was that music is a means of achieving the aesthetic experience; this function was the most often stated, obtaining a mean of total yearly intensities of 22.5 and actually rose during the ten year period. The creative function of music was second in overall importance, but emphasis on creativity declined during this period. (p. 14)

He also states, "While no evidence was found that writers in music education openly disagree, it is clear that little unanimity exits regarding the relative importance of other functions." And also: "The advocacy of functions in the *Music Educators Journal* declined from 1968-69 to 1977-78. It would appear that discussion of the basic functions of music became less important to the contributors and/or editors" (p. 14).

In conclusion, Jones notes an

> advocacy of different and occasionally opposing functions. If, as it has been hypothesized, music does indeed serve all of the sixteen functions tabulated in this study, there is no evidence to demonstrate wide recognition of it among writers in the profession. (p. 19)

And finally:

> Writers in the *Music Educators Journal* continue to assert that music serves society and education in diverse ways, and they continue to develop and advocate different objectives. No evidence appeared that this diversity will not continue to operate. (p. 19)

The sixteen functions identified and tabulated by Jones are, in rank order: aesthetic experience, creativity, psychological force, cultural force, self-expression, symbolic objectification, universal language, therapy, intellectual discipline, audience development, enjoyment, leisure time, music for its own sake, historic tradition, vocational goal, and societal ritual.

The studies included in the Report on the Eighth International Seminar on Research in Music Education (1981) provide some insight into methodological directions taken in music educational research. All of these studies utilized quantitative methods derived from general education or psychology or advance theoretical positions which, it was presumed, would be experimentally tested later. Emphasized subjects of research were child development and perceptual abilities, especially in listening and performance. The title of the symposium's invited address, "For a Renewal of Scientific Agreements for Reliability and Evaluation of Experimental Musical and Psychological Research," given by D. Cristoff (1981), emphasized the experimental quantitative trend in methodology. The importance of methodology is emphasized by the prominence it is given in the overview of research in music education written by J. D. Boyle (1982). He noted that "the trend of research in the 1970s has been toward more quantification of data than in previous decades, perhaps reflecting the increased accessibility of calculators and computers that facilitate sophisticated data analysis" (p. 1287).

Musical Ability

The problem of understanding the measuring factors relating to musical ability continues to trouble music researchers. Sergeant and Roche (1973) and Funk (1976) are among those investigating developmental trends in melodic perception. Harmonic perception has been investigated by Thackray (1979), who demonstrated that it is teachable. Wassum (1980), also studying harmonic perception, relates the importance of vocal exercise, scales, and songs in the development of tonal awareness. Researchers studying rhythmic perception include Madsen (1979), Moog (1976), and Taylor (1973).

Not only are these traditionally studied aspects of musical ability of concern to contemporary music educators, but, as Boyle (1982) points out:

> Musical ability is best measured by an assessment of realistic musical skills, intellectual ability, academic achievement, environmental stimulation, and where necessary, physical attributes (Radocy & Boyle, 1979). No research-based instrument appears available at present to measure adequately that combination. Blacking's description (1973) of the Venda musical culture, in which no person is considered unmusical, is nettlesome for anyone who would use musical ability, perceptual or otherwise, as a hurdle for music education. (p. 1288)

Curricular Trends

Curriculum in music education has been heavily weighted toward the development of performance skills. The comprehensive musicianship movement, however, attempts to weight activities more evenly between analysis, creation, and performance. The aesthetic education movement also distributes activities among the role models of the composer, the performer, and the critic or historian of music. Furthermore, this movement emphasizes a multiarts or integrated arts approach to curriculum development. Although these movements form the basis for experimental programs they are not in widespread application. In assessing these programs, Lawrence (1973) compared the effects of B. Reimer's aesthetic education curriculum, G. Kyme's composition curriculum, and a traditional curriculum. His conclusions state that the aesthetic education curriculum was best for students of all ability levels.

Another trend is the focus on competency-based curriculum. In this approach a group is held to a task until mastery of the task within a set time and level of accuracy is achieved. It has primarily been used in teacher education. Stegall, Blackburn, and Coop (1978) identified 83 competencies to be used in this approach. Hofstetter (1978, 1979, 1980) has been experimenting with the use of computer-assisted instruction to aid students in achieving skills that may be measured in these terms.

Research in Music Education and Art Education Compared

Although the brief review of these two areas is not comprehensive, some areas of commonality and contrast readily emerge. A lack of agreement on goals and purposes of instruction seems evident in both art education and music education. There does, however, appear to be more agreement on appropriate methodologies to be used in research in music education than in art education. The controversy regarding separation of research from practice which is pervasive in art education is conspicuously absent in the literature of music education. Although it is only speculation, the reason for this may be that there is a better match between what is researched, that is, listening and performance skills, and what is taught. In contrast, art education research is more frequently normative, that is indicating what ought to be taught rather than analyzing the skills involved in the pervasive studio-based curriculum in public schools. A major contrast is evidenced in curricular trends toward the competency-based curriculum of music and away from strictly behavioral evaluation in art education. Use of computers is not only less in evidence in art education but also much less related to competency-based instruction and behavioral objectives. Suggested uses of computers in research also vary (Jones, 1977; Linehan, 1980).

Drama and Dance Education

There is a growing body of research in drama and dance education although it remains much smaller than that in visual arts and music education. Journals that provide resources include *Journal of Aesthetic Education; Journal of Physical Education, Recreation and Dance; American Journal of Dance Therapy; Dance Research Journal; Drama Review; Theatre Journal;* and *Theatre World.* There are also references such as *Drama in Education: The Annual Survey* (Hodson & Banham, 1972, 1973, 1975) and *Dance as Education* (Fowler, 1977). That similar controversies exist both in these disciplines and in visual art and music is evidenced in L. Carter's "A Response to Ririe: Broader Perspectives for Dance" (1981) and R. Courtney's "Microcosmos: Planning and Implementation of Drama Programs" (1981). In the latter, Courtney cites a curricular confusion deriving from disparate and frequently unexamined philosophical assumptions: "Curriculum discourse must acknowledge which frame(s) of reference is being used, yet the literature and curricular documents reveal this is rarely the case" (p. 83). Courtney indicates that unstated but differing

metaphoric and linguistic frames of reference lead to confusions of intention, goals, and assumptions, resulting in lack of clarity in curricular documents and directions.

In declaring the need to relate dance to major conceptual systems, Carter states:

> It is essential therefore that current developers of dance curriculum consider the current intellectual models of organizing knowledge, including Goodman's theory of symbols; semiotics, or the general theory of signs, as developed by Morris (1975) and others; and the expression theory of art and mind advanced by Arnheim (1974) and others (see also Sircello, 1972). Each of these theories provides a conceptual model for organizing our knowledge within a particular discipline and for comparing and contrasting modes of thought and expression in a variety of disciplines. (p. 73)

Carter contrasts this view stressing a contextualist integrative stance to that of Ririe (1981), who emphasizes dance as performance with less emphasis on context, history, criticism, or aesthetics.

Thus in all of the arts there are those stressing production/ performance and those stressing the need for history, criticism, and aesthetics. There are also in all disciplines scholars who are indicating the need for philosophical analysis of curricular decisions.

Aesthetics

A. Efland (1978), in an article entitled "Relating the Arts to Education: the History of an Idea," reviews the history of philosophy concentrating on aesthetic theory from Plato to Dewey as it relates to education in the arts. He compares philosophical positions derived from Plato, Aristotle, Kant, Schiller, and Dewey with those inherent in the Rockefeller Commission Report, *Coming to our Senses* (Arts, Americans, & Education, 1977). Efland concludes: "Though parts of the Report are compatible with this or that philosophic tradition, as a whole it reads like a 'melange' of many conflicting orientations in the arts" (p. 12). This melange of views appears characteristic of most writing in art, music, and aesthetic education. Few educators appear knowledgeable in aesthetic theory and even fewer evince an interest in applying it to their educational endeavors.

S. H. Clark (1975), in an article reviewing art education textbooks between 1960 and 1970, found that the most frequently cited philosophical aesthetic positions were those of Dewey and Langer. In the review of literature for this chapter, this was evident not only in texts, but in curricular guides, articles, and dissertations. In an indirect manner this literature frequently referred to the formalist aesthetic theories of Fry and Bell. That is, emphasis was placed on learning the formal aspects of design in art and composition in music. Infrequent references to phenomenological aesthetics appear in research articles and dissertations. This was true of art education, music education, and aesthetic education.

A glance at Margolis' review (1979b) of currents in aesthetics from the 1950s through the 1970s reveals many trends that have not made their way into education in the arts. However, Beardsley's empiricism as it is reflected in the work of Feldman seems a primary influence on the study of art criticism in art education. It has also influenced the theories of educational criticism advanced by Eisner. The *Journal of Aesthetic Education* cites the work of aestheticians and sometimes carries articles by contemporary aestheticians to a much greater extent than do the research journals of either art education or music education.

Philosophical Aesthetics

The summary article by Margolis (1979b) and its accompanying bibliography provide an excellent overview of recent currents in aesthetics. Included is a description of changes in emphasis in theory over time: the reaction in the 1950s against the idealism of Croce and Collingwood, the development in the 1960s of empiricism represented in the work of Beardsley, Sibley, and Aldrich, followed by the exploration of nonperceptual factors affecting perception itself developed by Danto, Dickie, Gombrich, Goodman, Margolis, and Wollheim in the later 1960s and 1970s. Other important contributions to aesthetic theory in recent years include phenomenology in the work of Dufrenne, Hirsch, Ingarden, and Wolff, structuralism in the work of Derrida, and Marxist aesthetics represented by Lukacs. Examination of anthologies and journals such as the *Journal of Aesthetics and Art Criticism* and the *British Journal of Aesthetics* reveals continuing interest in the theories of Wittgenstein, in formalism, and in other traditional aesthetic theories such as imitationalism and expressionism. In short, there is an abundance of variety in aesthetic theory that may be examined for philosophical matches to the theories of the various currents of thought in education in the arts. For a brief introduction to a variety of views in contemporary aesthetic theory two anthologies seem noteworthy — Dufrenne's *Main Trends in Aesthetics and the Sciences of Art* (1979) and the revised edition of Philipson and Gudel's *Aesthetics Today* (1980).

Experimental Aesthetics

Between 1960 and 1980 there was an increase in the number of studies using quantitative methodology to explore aesthetic perception in art education and music education. This was also evident in psychology. The works of D. E. Berlyne presented in *Aesthetics and Psychobiology* (1971) and in *Studies in the New Experimental Aesthetics* (1974) are excellent examples of this trend. Earlier works by Bense and Moles provide quantitative models of aesthetics, which were not as widely adopted by educators in the arts as was the type of work presented by Berlyne.

Writers in music education and art education have noted the increase in this type of study. As an example, B. Boyer's (1981) dissertation, *An Examination of Experimental Aesthetic Research from 1970 to 1980 Related to the Visual Perception of Paintings with Implications for Art Education*, identified 67 studies and 20 dissertations that utilized paintings as visual stimuli in experimental aesthetic research. The number of experimental aesthetic studies in music, art, and literature has steadily increased in the last 10 years. The founding of the *Journal of Experimental Aesthetics* is another indication of this

trend. In the preparation of this chapter over 200 studies using quantitative methods applied to aesthetic perception, motivation, preference, or judgment were examined. The majority of these studies have been done in the last decade.

The increasing availability of sophisticated statistical packages including factor analysis, multidimensional scaling, and similar techniques makes this type of experimentation much less difficult than it was previously. The development of electronic measuring devices also facilitates this research. Examples of a few biological measures used in these experiments are galvanic skin response, pupil dilation, eye movement tracking, brain wave patterns, and listening or viewing time. Also of interest to experimenters are analyses of verbal responses. Experimental aesthetic techniques seem to hold particular interest for those art(s) educators exploring perceptual and motivational aspects of the arts.

Implication of Research in Aesthetics for Art(s) Educators

Work in philosophical aesthetics and experimental aesthetics may illuminate the particular positions held by educators in the arts. For example, those interested in perceptual ability may find the work in the experimental aesthetics most helpful. Individuals interested in the nonperceptual factors influencing perceptions may find the work of philosophical aestheticians of the late 1960s and early 1970s beneficial.

Study of aesthetic theory may be seen as the unifying concern of all educators in the arts. It may be considered basic in establishing interdisciplinary dialogue within and across the arts. Efland's "Conceptions of Teaching in the Arts" (1979) analyzes four aesthetic theories for their orientation relative to psychological theories and concomitant teaching-learning orientations. He then presents examples of each in music, art, dance, and theater. His work may be viewed as an initial effort in the necessary analysis and dialogue across the arts. In drama and dance Courtney (1981) and Carter (1981) express a need for such analysis although they cite other aesthetic orientations as a basis.

Interdisciplinary Communication Recommendations

A major problem faced by educators in the arts is lack of agreement regarding functions and purposes of art(s) education. This lack of agreement leads to further conflict in research aims, curricular decisions, and so forth. This problem is manifest in communication difficulties of educators both between and within the arts. It may be profitable to examine this problem from the perspective of H. G. Petrie as expressed in "Do You See What I See? The Epistemology of Interdisciplinary Inquiry" (1976). In this article Petrie discusses the problems of interdisciplinary communication and offers analysis of both the epistemological and nonepistemological considerations necessary for successful interdisciplinary communication. For example, he sees idea dominance as a central consideration necessary for interdisciplinary success. A source of ideas considered as central concerns within and across the arts is aesthetic theory. This may provide the basis for clarifying the difference in value systems or cognitive maps of the various schools of thought on purposes and functions of the arts in education. For example, proponents of phenomenological inquiry and those with political intent will each find aesthetic theories compatible with their views. The discussion of these theories may provide a basis for clarifying differences both within and among the various theoretical orientations.

The communication thus established among proponents of various positions may permit small groups within each art discipline to agree upon identification of research topics across the arts. Examples of such topics are perceptual abilities, sociocultural components in instruction, instructional strategies for teaching historical, critical, and aesthetic aspects of the arts. This does not imply agreement regarding approach to research, merely agreement on topics to be researched. The relation of aesthetic theories adopted by various groups to their curricular decisions (reflecting what should be taught and how it should be taught) would also clarify differences in value orientation and provide a basis for discussion. Initially, this may appear to compound existing differences. However, clarification of differences, not necessarily resolution of differences, may result by placing these value orientations in the context of aesthetic theory rather than leaving them in multiple extraaesthetic contexts. These multidisciplinary contexts impede communication across quoting circles within the arts and especially across the arts. Aesthetic concerns seem the most pervasive of all values for researchers both within and across the arts. For this reason aesthetic theory seems a central topic for developing interdisciplinary dialogue and clarifying differences in research directions and developing varying but internally consistent curricula.

REFERENCES

Acuff, B. (1974). *Aesthetic inquiry and the creation of meaning: A program of instruction in the visual arts.* Unpublished doctoral dissertation, Stanford University. Stanford, CA.

Aldrich, V. (1963). *Philosophy of art.* Englewood Cliffs, NJ: Prentice-Hall.

Alexander, R. R. (1980). Mr. Jewel as a model: An educational criticism of a high school art history class. *Studies in Art Education, 21*(3), 20–30.

Anderson, F. E. (1979). Approaches to cross-cultural research in art education. *Studies in Art Education, 21*(1), 17–26.

Arnheim, R. (1974). *Art and visual perception: The new version.* Berkeley: University of California Press.

Arts, Americans, and Education Panel. (1977). *Coming to our senses: The significance of the arts for American education.* New York: McGraw-Hill.

Barkan, M., Chapman, L., & Kern, E. (1970). *Guidelines: Curriculum development in aesthetic education.* St. Louis, MO: CEMREL.

Barthes, R. (1972). *Critical essays* (R. Howard, Trans.). Evanston, IL: Northwestern University Press.

Beardsley, M. C. (1958). *Aesthetics.* New York: Harcourt Brace.

Beardsley, M. C. (1970). *The Possibility of criticism.* Detroit: Wayne State University Press.

Beittel, K. R. (1982). Art education. In H. E. Mitzel, J. H. Best & W. Rabinowitz (Eds.), *Encyclopedia of educational research* (Vol. 1, pp. 159–171). New York: Macmillan.

Beittel, K. R. (1978). Qualitative description of the qualitative. *Presentations on art education research: Phenomenological description—potential for research in art education* (No. 2, pp. 91–113). Montreal: Concordia University.

Bell, C. (1914). *Art.* London: Chatto and Windus.

Bense, M. (1954–1960). *Aesthetica* (4 vols). Stuttgart: Deutsche Verlags-Anstalt; Krefeld–Baden–Baden: Agis Verlag.

Berlyne, D. E. (1971). *Aesthetics and psychobiology.* New York: Appleton–Century–Crofts.

Berlyne, D. E. (1974). *Studies in the new experimental aesthetics.* New York: Wiley.

Blacking, J. (1973). *How musical is man?* Seattle: University of Washington Press.

Bolton, S. L. (1970). *A study of perceptual growth when using contrasting strategies in teaching art to rural deprived children.* Unpublished doctoral dissertation, University of Georgia, Athens.

Boyer, B. (1981). *An examination of experimental research from 1970 to 1980 related to the visual perception of paintings with implications for art education.* Unpublished doctoral dissertation, University of Oregon, Eugene.

Boyle, J. D. (1982). Music Education. In H. E. Mitzel, J. H. Best & W. Rabinowitz (Eds.) *Encyclopedia of educational research* (Vol. 3, pp. 1287–1299). New York: Macmillan.

Broudy, H. S. (1977). Some reactions to a concept of aesthetic education. In S. Madeja (Ed.), *Arts and aesthetics: An agenda for the future* (pp. 251–261). St. Louis MO: CEMREL.

Carter, C. L. (1981). A response to Ririe—Broader perspectives for dance. In M. Engel, J. Hausman, S. Madeja (Eds.) *Curriculum and instruction in arts and aesthetic education* (pp. 68–81). St. Louis, MO: CEMREL.

Chapman, L. (Ed.). (1978). Report of Rockefeller Panel: *Coming to Our Senses* (special issue). *Studies in Art Education. 19*(3).

Chapman, L. (1978). Coming to our senses and related matters. *Studies in Art Education, 19*(3), 3–4.

Clark, G. A., & Zimmerman, E. (1974). A walk in the right direction: A model for visual arts education. *Studies in Art Education, 19*(2), 34–49.

Clark, S. H. (1975). Modern theoretical foundations of appreciation and creation in art education textbooks, 1960–1970. *Studies in Art Education, 16*(3), 12–21.

Collingwood, R. G. (1938). *The principles of art.* London: Oxford University Press.

Conders, J., Howlett, J., & Skull, J. (Eds.). (1978). *Arts in cultural diversity: INSEA 23rd world congress.* Sydney, New York, Toronto, & London: Holt, Rinehart & Winston.

Courtney, R. (1981). Microcosmos: Planning and implementation of drama programs. In M. Engel, J. Hausman, S. Madeja (Eds.) *Curriculum and instruction in arts and aesthetic education* (pp. 82–110). St. Louis, MO: CEMREL.

Cristoff, D. (1981). For a renewal of scientific agreements for reliability and evaluation of experimental musical and psychological research. *Bulletin of the Council for Research in Music Education, 66/67,* 116–121.

Croce, B. (1922). *Aesthetics* (2nd ed. D. Ainslee, Trans.). London: Macmillan.

Danto, A. (1964). The art world. *Journal of Philosophy, 41,* 571–584.

Davis, D. J. (1971). Research in art education: An overview. *Art Education, 24*(3), 7–11.

Day, M. D. (1973). *Teaching for art appreciation: A study of effects of instruction on high school students' art preferences and art judgments.* Unpublished doctoral dissertation, Stanford University, Stanford, CA.

Degge, R. (1975). *A case study and theoretical analysis of the teaching practices in one junior high art class.* Unpublished doctoral dissertation, University of Oregon, Eugene, OR.

Deregowski, J. (1976). *The child's representation of the world.* New York: Plenum Press.

Derrida, J. (1973). *Speech and phenomena* (D. Allison, Trans.). Evanston, IL: Northwestern University Press.

Dewey, J. (1934). *Art as experience.* New York: Minton, Balch.

Dickie, G. (1974). *Art and the aesthetic.* Ithaca: Cornell University Press.

Dufrenne, M. (1973). *The phenomonology of aesthetic experience* (E. Casey et al., Trans.). Evanston, IL: Northwestern University Press.

Dufrenne, M. (Ed.). (1979). *Main trends in aesthetics and the sciences of art.* New York: Holmes & Meier.

Efland, A. (1978). Relating the arts to education: The history of an idea. *Studies in Art Education, 19*(3), 5-13.

Efland, A. (1979). Conceptions of teaching in the arts. In G. Knieter, J. Stallings, S Madeja (Eds.) *The teaching process and arts and aesthetics* (pp. 152-186). St. Louis, MO: CEMREL.

Eisner, E. W. (1972). *Educating artistic vision.* New York: Macmillan.

Eisner, E. W. (1976). Educational connoisseurship and educational criticism: Their forms and functions in educational evaluation. *Journal of Aesthetic Education, 10*, 135-150.

Eisner, E. W. (1982). Aesthetic education. In H. W. Mitzel, J. H. Best & W. Rabinowitz (Eds.), *Encyclopedia of educational research* (Vol. 1, pp. 87-94). New York, London: Macmillan.

Ettinger, L. (1983). *A comparative analysis of on-site descriptive research in art education: An initial contribution to educational ethnology.* Unpublished doctoral dissertation, University of Oregon, Eugene.

Feldman, E. (1981). Varieties of art curriculum. In M. Engel, J. Hausman, S. Madeja (Eds.) *Curriculum and instruction in arts and aesthetic education* (pp. 131-153). St. Louis, MO: CEMREL.

Flannery, M. (1980). Research methods in phenomenological aesthetics. *Review of Research in Visual Arts Education, 12*, 26-36.

Fowler, C. B. (1977). *Dance as education.* Washington, DC: National Dance Association.

Funk, J. D. (1977). *Some aspects of the development of music perception.* Unpublished doctoral dissertation, Worcester, MA: Clark University.

Gardner, H. (1971). Children's sensitivity to musical styles. *Merrill-Palmer Quarterly, 19*, 67-77.

Gardner, H. (1972). Style sensitivity in children. *Human Development, 15*, 325-338.

Gardner, H., Winner, E., & Kirchner, M. (1975). Children's conceptions of the arts. *Journal of Aesthetic Education, 9*(3), 60-77.

Gaskin, L. (1972). *Design, implementation and evaluation of an art program based upon the artist, critic, historian and teacher as exemplars of instruction.* Unpublished doctoral dissertation, Pennsylvania State University, University Park.

Geahigan, C. (1980). Metacritical inquiry in arts education. *Studies in Art Education, 21*(3), 54-67.

Golomb, C. (1981). Representations and reality: The origin and determinants of young children's drawing. *Review of Research in Visual Arts Education, 14*, 36-48.

Gombrich, E. H. (1960). *Art and illusion.* New York: Pantheon.

Goodman, N. (1969). *Languages of art.* Indianapolis: Bobbs-Merrill.

Gordon, R. D. (1978). Doctoral dissertations in music and music education, 1972-1977. *Journal of Research in Music Education, 26*, (Fall), 134-415.

Hardiman, G. W., & Zernich, T. (1976). Research in art education 1970-74: Portrayal and interpretation. *Art Education, 29*, 23-26.

Hirsch, E. D., Jr. (1967). *Validity in interpretation.* New Haven: Yale University Press.

Hodson, J., & Banham, M. (Eds.). (1972, 1973, 1975). *Drama in education: The annual survey.* London: Pilman.

Hofstetter, F. T. (1978). Computer-based recognition of perceptual patterns in harmonic dictation exercises. *Journal of Research in Music Education, 26*, 111-119.

Hofstetter, F. T. (1979). Evaluation of a competency-based approach to teaching aural interval identification. *Journal of Research in Music Education, 27*, 201-213.

Hofstetter, F. T. (1980). Computer-based recognition of perceptual patterns in chord quality dictation exercises. *Journal of Research in Music Education, 28*, 83-91.

Ingarden, R. (1973). *The literary work of art* (G. Grabowicz, Trans.). Evanston, IL: Northwestern University Press.

Jones, B. (1977). *Computer applications in art education research.* Unpublished doctoral dissertation, University of Oregon, Eugene.

Jones, W. M. (1980). Functions of music education since Tanglewood: A ten-year report. *Bulletin of the Council for Research in Music Education, 63*, 11-19.

Kaelin, E. F., & Ecker, D. W. (1977). The institutional prospects of aesthetic education. In S. Madeja (Ed.) *Arts and aesthetics: An agenda for the future* (pp. 229-241). St. Louis, MO: CEMREL.

Kuhn, M. (1974). A profile for an editor. *Studies in Art Education. 15*(3), 3.

Kuhn, M. (1978). Priorities for arts in everyday living and education. *Studies in Art Education, 19*(3), 46-49.

Langer, S. (1957). *Problems of art.* New York: Scribner's.

Lanier, V. (1974-1975). Conception and priority in art education research. *Studies in Art Education, 16*(1), 26-30.

Lansing, K. (1981). The effect of drawing on the development of mental representation. *Studies in Art Education, 22*(3),15-23.

Lawrence, V. P. (1973). *A comparison of three methods of instruction in junior high school general music.* Unpublished doctoral dissertation, Case Western Reserve University, Cleveland.

Lewis, H. P., McFee, J., Day, M., & Lanier,V. (1978). Brief commentaries on *Coming to our senses: The significance of the arts for American education. Studies in Art Education, 19*(3), 54-63.

Lewis, H. P., McFee, J. K., Stewart, W., Wilson, B., Beittel, K. R., & Pohland, P. (1972). Dialogue: Responses growing out of the paper *Participant observation as a research methodology. Studies in Art Education, 13*(3), 16-28.

Linehan, T. (1980). *A computer-mediated model for visual preference research and implications for instruction in art criticism.* Unpublished doctoral dissertation, Ohio State University, Columbus.

Lovano-Kerr, J. (1974). Research synthesis and continuity. *Studies in Art Education, 16*(1), 57-63.

Lovano-Kerr, J. & Rush, J. (1982). Project zero: The evolution of visual arts research during the seventies. *Review of Research in Visual Arts Education, 15*, 61-81.

Lukacs, G. (1962). *History and class consciousness* (R. Livingstone, Trans.). London: Merlin Press.

MacGregor, N. (1975). Concepts of criticism: implications for art education. *Studies in Art Education, 17*(1), 7-16.

Madeja, S. (Ed.). (1977). *Arts and aesthetics: An agenda for the future.* St. Louis, MO: CEMREL.

Madeja, S., & Smith, V. G. (1982, July). *Art education ASCD curriculum update.* Association for supervision and curriculum development. Alexandria, VA.

Madsen, C. K. (1979). Modulated beat discrimination among musicians and nonmusicians. *Journal of Research in Music Education, 27*, 57-67.

Margolis, J. (1979a). *Art and philosophy.* Atlantic Highlands, NJ: Humanities Press.

Margolis, J. (1979b). Recent currents in aesthetics of relevance to contemporary visual artists. *Leonardo, 12*, 111-119.

McFee, J. K. (1985). Art ability. In T. Husen & T. N. Postlethwaite (Eds.), *International encyclopedia of education.* Oxford: Pergamon Press.

McFee, J. (1982). *Defining art education in the eighties.* Reston, VA. National Art Education Association.

McFee, J. (1978). Cultural influences on aesthetic experience. In J. Conders, J. Howlett, & J. Skull (Eds.), *Arts in cultural diversity.* New York: Holt, Rinehart & Winston.

Mittler, G. A. (1971). *Utilizing counterattitudinal role playing and inconsistency as an instructional strategy in art criticism.* Unpublished doctoral dissertation, Ohio State University, Columbus.

Mittler, G. A. (1973). Experiences in critical inquiry: Approaches for use in the art methods class. *Art Education, 26*(2), 16-21.

Moles, A. (1966). *Information theory and aesthetic perception* (J. Cohen, Trans.). Urbana: University of Illinois Press.

Moog, H. (1976). The development of musical experience in children of preschool age. *Psychology of Music, 4*(2), 38-47.

Morris, C. (1975). Foundations of the theory of signs. In O. Neurath, R. Carnap, & C. Morris (Eds.), *International Encyclopedia of Unified Science* (Vol. I). Chicago: University of Chicago Press.

Perkins, D., & Leondar, B. (Eds.). (1977). *The arts and cognition.* Baltimore: Johns Hopkins University Press.

Petrie, H. G. (1976). Do you see what I see? The epistemology of interdisciplinary inquiry. *Journal of Aesthetic Education, 10*(1), 29-43.

Philipson, M., & Gudel, P. (1980). *Aesthetics today.* New York: New American Library.

Pohland, P. (1972). Participant observation as a research methodology. *Studies in Art Education, 13*(3), 4-15.

Radocy, R. E., & Boyle, J. D. (1979). *Psychological foundations of musical behavior.* Springfield, IL: Thomas.

Ragans, D. R. (1972). *The effects of instruction in a technique of art criticism upon the response of elementary students to art objects.* Unpublished doctoral dissertation, University of Georgia, Athens.

Report on the eighth international seminar on research in music education held in Dresden, Germany, Democratic Republic. (1981). *Bulletin of the Council for Research in Music Education, 66/67,* 1–121.

Ririe, S. R. (1981). Contemplating a dance program K–12. In M. Engel, J. Hausman, S. Madeja (Eds.) *Curriculum and instruction in arts and aesthetic education* (pp. 51–67). St. Louis, MO: CEMREL.

Rush, J. C., & Kratochwill, T. R. (1981). Time-series strategies for studying behavior change: Implications for research in visual arts education. *Studies in Art Education, 22*(2), 57–67.

Saunders, R. (1978). The arts — working together to make education work: An idea whose time has come. *Studies in Art Education, 19*(3), 14–19.

Sencer, Y. J. (1972). *Teaching strategies for aesthetic education based on an analysis of classroom discourse.* Unpublished doctoral dissertation, New York University.

Sergeant, D., & Roche, S. (1973). Perceptual shifts in auditory information processing of young children. *Psychology of Music, 1*(2), 39–48.

Sharer, J. W. (1980). Distinguishing justifications and explanations in judgments of art. *Studies in Art Education, 21*(2), 38–42.

Shuker, N. (Ed.). (1977). *Arts in education partners: Schools and their communities.* New York: JDR 3rd Fund.

Sibley, F. (1959). Aesthetic concepts. *Philosophical Review, 68,* 421–450.

Sircello, G. (1972). *Mind and art: An essay on the varieties of expression.* Princeton, NJ: Princeton University Press.

Stegall, J. R, Blackburn, J. E., & Coop, R. H. (1978). Administrators' ratings of competencies for an undergraduate music education curriculum. *Journal of Research in Music Education, 26,* 3–15.

Taylor, S. (1973). Musical development of children aged seven to eleven. *Psychology of Music, 1*(1), 44–49.

Thackray, R. (1979). Tests of harmonic perception. *Psychology of Music, 7,* 3–11.

Wassum, S. (1980). Elementary school children's concept of tonality. *Journal of Research in Music Education, 28,* 18–33.

Wolff, J. (1975). *Hermeneutic philosophy and the sociology of art.* London: Routledge & Kegan Paul.

Wollheim, R. (1968). *Art and its objects.* New York: Harper and Row.

32.

Moral Education and Values Education: The Discourse Perspective

Fritz K. Oser
University of Fribourg, Switzerland

Toward a Discourse Pedagogy

Introduction

Janus, the ancient Roman god, had two faces, one in front and one in back. His faces meant different things: As the god of beginnings he looked to the future and to the past; as the custodian of the gate, he noticed and controlled everyone who went in and out. There was also a Janus gate that stood open during war but closed in peacetime. In Roman times it was rarely closed. Nowadays, the Janus head symbolizes two kinds of truth and implies that there are always two sides to an issue.

The Janus head thus serves as an allegory for many twofold aspects of morality and moral education. One aspect is its subjective, the other its factual, objective part. On the one hand there are relativistic aspects to morality, on the other hand there are universal aspects. Moral education can be a positive part of teaching, but it can be an indoctrination too. The normative point of view often opposes the descriptive one. There is a rational part, but there are also emotional elements. There is a structural realm and there is the content realm of "practical" reason.[1] One can judge someone's competence or his or her performance. There is a moral point of view and value neutrality. There are technical and interactive aspects of moral education. The need for moral learning is well accepted, but many educators don't want to be concerned about it: In their view this is a subject matter too delicate to deal with. Morality

is a custodian. Wherever one goes, in or out, whatever decision is made, there is a moral dimension to it. The moral gate is almost always open.

Skeptical Attitudes Toward Morality

While theories of the acquisition of general knowledge (e.g., Aebli, 1980, 1981; Fillmore, 1971; Gage, 1981; Schank & Abelson, 1977; van Dijk, 1977), theories of structural organization of the memory (Anderson, 1976; Kintsch, 1974; Lindsay & Norman, 1972; Rumelhart, 1975; Winograd, 1972), and theories of teachers' decision making and instruction (Champagne, Klopfer, & Gunstone, 1982; Glaser, 1976; Greeno, 1976; Shavelson & Stern, 1981) are relatively well developed, there is no integrative and highly differentiated model of values and moral learning, despite a great interest in moral education. Instead there are many discrete meanings and implications of moral education, and a good many devices regarding methods and instructions for teaching morals and values.

The result often is skepticism about moral education. First, for some educators the term has a negative connotation implying churchlike and hypocritically feigned virtuous behavior. In this understanding morality means being not free, being traditional, having a puritan education, and being indoctrinated. Second, moral educational aims often seem to be in contradiction to the methods that focus on social moral values and

---

The author thanks reviewers Kevin Ryan (Ohio State University) and Richard Hersh (University of Oregon). Thanks also to J. Rest, M. Berkowitz, W. Althof, D. Garz, R. Shavelson, and M. Reich for their help and suggestions.

[1] "Practical" means here that the reason (in Kant's sense) is concerned with moral action or with the conceptualization of just action. The practical reason is the ability to choose one's actions without regard to needs of any sort. According to Kant, *Sittlichkeit* can only be a practical reason. It implies a categorical imperative and originates in the autonomy of the will (cf. Hoeffe, 1983, pp. 173ff.).

welfare. That is, many educators do believe that we should be concerned about positive social traits and values, such as cooperation, social adjustment, and democracy (Dewey, 1916/1944), or that we should promote moral development (Kohlberg, 1969, 1971, 1981b, 1984). But the actual methods of moral education of children and adolescents seem to lack coherence and power in fostering those aims. Responsible educators know that moral education often turns out as moral inculcation. (Snook, 1972). This dangerous perspective often leads educators and citizens to avoid moral education entirely in a democratic society (Attfield, 1978, p. 77) and leads therefore to a skeptical attitude towards morality. Third, even many of those educators who believe that all education must have a moral base refuse to support special moral education programs. They view philosophy and psychology, probably the two most relevant disciplines underlying moral education, as general knowledge that does not allow practical consequences in terms of aims and values promoted by teaching. Fourth, there are different concepts of moral education, such as a values clarification model, a structural development approach, and a social action model. These approaches contradict each other, criticize one another's foundations, and reproach each other for lack of empirical and theoretical accuracy. Educators fear to get lost in this variety of models, programs, and evaluative literature; they shrink from the effort of getting familiar with complex curricula and possibly apprehend wasting time and energy when using one not yet proven. Given the practical risks of each kind of program implementation, we can easily understand the temporary success of approaches which, though theoretically meager, offer recipe-like teaching strategies to be brought into action immediately (like values clarification).

We now briefly sketch the way four comprehensive overviews organize this variety of proposals for moral education. This is not to illustrate the practitioner's problems mentioned, but rather to demonstrate the "standard" way of overlooking this domain.

Our first example is the book entitled *Models of Moral Education: An Appraisal* (Hersh, Miller, & Fielding, 1980). Based on an action theory (caring, judging, acting), six models are presented, namely the *rationale-building model* developed by J. Shaver (Shaver & Strong, 1982), the *consideration model* created by P. McPhail (McPhail, Ungoed-Thomas, & Chapman, 1975), the *values clarification model* (Raths, Harmin, & Simon, 1966; Simon, Howe, & Kirschenbaum, 1972), the *value analysis model* (Coombs, 1971), the *cognitive moral development model* which is based on the theory of L. Kohlberg (1969, 1971, 1981b, 1985), and finally the *social action model* (Newmann, 1975). All these models represent differing fundamentals, differing goals, and differing educational methods.

A second example is entitled *Raising Good Children* (Lickona, 1983; see also Lickona, 1985). The author presents different educational strategies for parents, such as "foster mutual respect"; "set a good example"; "teach by telling"; "help children to think for themselves"; "help children take on real responsibilities"; "balance independence and control"; and "love children." Lickona bases his strategies on a concept of steps of naturally gradual development.

Our third example is R. T. Hall's book *Moral Education: A Handbook for Teachers* (1979). It presents five strategies for fostering moral learning: values consideration, dialogue and interaction, argumentation, concept building, and role playing. Each of these five strategies is applied to the following five topics: justice, property, truth, integrity, and personal relations.

Finally, a German-language teaching hand-book (Schneid, 1979) deals especially with values, norms, and fundamental attitudes. It presents a philosophical introduction as well as a series of methods, such as values transformation, moralization, help for personal decisions, stimulation of concrete acts, stimulation of self-education, and so forth.

These four examples share several characteristics. They present a variety of perspectives. They discuss different teaching methods and different learning materials. They criticize the models presented and they evaluate them in a practical way.

In this paper I would like to follow a somewhat different path. I want to ask: What do all these models and methods have in common? Is there any comprehensive notion of moral and values education? Is it possible to build a general framework for moral and values education? To answer these questions, four fundamental issues in moral and values education must be considered first: (a) the general desirability of moral education, (b) the notion of moral discourse, (c) the concept of moral educational situations, and (d) the distinction between moral and values education.

General Desirability of Moral Education

If we ask parents whether their children should be influenced through moral education they generally respond affirmatively, If we ask professional educators the same question there is no doubt about their agreement that everybody should be morally informed. Underlying these affirmations is the conviction that, in the professional realm, in the field of politics, in economics, in any social interaction, there is rule-guided behavior and an important part of these rules belongs to the dimensions of justice and care. Kant distinguished between perfect and imperfect duties; perfect duties are negative, for example, you must not lie, kill, nor steal, and imperfect duties are positive, for example, you should help the poor, the sick, the lonely. Both types of duties receive general acceptance from most human beings. People are aware that we can trust others only if others trust us. It is commonly accepted that our children should in general adopt rules in the sense of perfect and in many cases also of imperfect duties. Thus desirability is one important reason for the necessity of moral education.

However it is necessary to consider other and less general reasons. At the level of ordinary language, we say that children should learn to use reasons and reasoning in ambiguous decision-making situations; the philosophical grounds for morality themselves consist of this weak human competence to use rational arguments (*praktische Vernunft*) to justify norms and principles on the one hand and actions on the other. I use the word "weak" because reason is not an object, and if we rely on it we have nothing in our hands but a capacity of control which is always at stake through possible immoral contexts. The notion of personal control thus is a key characteristic of legitimacy and morality whereby control consists of the reconstruction of moral situations, of the application of rules and principles, and of the implementation of decisions. All this has to be learned in such a way that personal freedom is experienced and children attribute the origin of action to themselves. All this has to be learned by children actually doing it and having the possibility of failing and learning through failure. But perfect duties receive much more concern and imperfect duties are treated only by especially altruistic and prosocial teachers.

However, this is not all; Durkheim, for example, analyses the relationship between rationality and moral capacity of a society. He clearly states that society must protect moral and social values and not leave them to free rationalization. Values like the protection of life, the procedural forms of a democracy, and the dignity of a person cannot be reconsidered in such a way that everybody is free to choose or not to choose them. The core assumption is that nobody, as long as he is willing to be a member of a society, can reject fundamental societal and moral claims that are explicitly objects of the fundamental belief of such a society. Thus Durkheim also argues that each teacher should be able to set up a moral ideal that goes beyond a fixed system of rules and that allows the coming generation to fulfill new validity claims in the sense of more individual autonomy. This ideal has to be reconstructed by the new generation extending each moral concept to its generalizability (Durkheim, 1934, 1961, 1973). Both have to be learned; the existing morality of a society — we call it "moral consensus" (*Sittlichkeit*) — and the morality of a personal ideal which we call "moral sense" (*Moralität*). In the best cases this ideal treats imperfect duties like the perfect ones.

Finally, from a developmental perspective the reason why moral and values education should be intentionally realized lies in the assumption that a higher stage is a better stage, autonomy is better than heteronomy, and that higher moral complexity implies more role taking, a more highly developed empathy, a more deeply reflected sense of responsibility. (We return to this point more extensively in subsequent discussion.)

From this we can ask what the reasons are for the discrepancies between stated desirability and relativistic moral educational practice. A spontaneous answer could be that today morality is not limited to passivity; it seems to us that it should be possible to be professionally, politically, and socially active and effective *and* still be moral. All this carries weight with the acceptance of the fact that nowadays many belief systems, many utility concepts, many different epistemological interests coexist (Berger, 1979). However, I do not agree with A. MacIntyre's belief that all morality is relative and that reasons must be silent about ends deducible once and for all (cf. MacIntyre, 1984 especially pp. 244 ff.); rather, the term "general concept of moral and values education" alludes to a set of general moral and interactive principles that guide moral education, which initially takes an ideal form (see the following section on moral discourse).

Measured against this ideal I believe that moral education has been greatly neglected in settings such as schools, families, and workplaces. Educators fail to rely on the practical (moral) reason because practical reason, as we mentioned, is never a fixed thing, a matter guided by law, a machine of logic — it is "weak"; educators most often fail to concretize the general desirability because they lack the moral ideal in the meaning of moral sense and moral consensus. However, teachers and their students are moral philosophers, confronted every day with difficult moral problems involving honesty, truth, and the keeping of promises (Paolitto, 1977, p. 73). And reason deals with propositional truth, with validity claims, and with the integrity of each participant in a moral or value-oriented discussion. So, like Janus' head, moral education must be the beginning and the end of education because it deals with the possibility of stimulating an autonomous and self-reliant person.

Moral Discourse

I spoke about a general concept of moral education. I think that *moral discourse is the common denominator* that should encompass different elements of moral learning. Discourse is a concept first presented by Habermas (1972, 1981, 1983, 1984) in his "theory of communicative action." In a first attempt at characterization we could describe it simply as an ideal form of an open moral argumentation against which all moral argumentations should be assessed. All members participate equally, all members are assumed in advance (i.e., are presupposed) to be truthfully engaged in an attempt to construct a just solution; all members want the most justice-and-care-oriented decision. The educational theory of this moral discourse consists then in the stimulation of those elements that describe moral discourse in general. We suggest that such an educational concept has many advantages: First, moral and values education remains a cognitive, reflective enterprise, even if students have to learn certain fixed rules and norms of a specific culture. Second, moral and values education appeals to human freedom and dignity, even if its fundamental rules and principles are compulsory for the functioning of a society. Finally, indoctrination should ultimately be avoided even if we prescribe the aims and goals of moral ideals.[2]

More carefully characterized, the term moral discourse refers to an interactive ideal discussion model about problems of justice. Habermas (1982) states: "I speak of communicative actions when social interactions are co-ordinated not through the egocentric calculations of success of every individual but through co-operative achievements of understanding among participants" (p. 264). McCarthy (1978) concludes:

> What Habermas calls "communicative ethics" is grounded in the "fundamental norms of rational speech." Communication oriented

---

[2] Moral discourse is a method particularly suited to avoid indoctrination. So far it is a principle or a general guideline that guarantees and gives life to an (initially presupposed) trust in the child's social and moral capabilities. All other methods cover less ground than this fundamental principle. Kohlberg (1981), for instance, distinguishes three educational approaches. Cultural transmission has the goal of accumulating a "bag of virtues", the romantic approach aims at an uninhibited maturation of the child ("nature is good"); and the progressive approach is based on developmental stimulation which avoids indoctrination. I do not fully agree with Kohlberg's description of his own approach: Moral dilemma discussion and/or participation in a just community in itself does not guarantee interactional truthfulness and right (just) decisions, nor does it detract from strategic teaching behavior. On the other hand, even traditional methods like direct teaching must not necessarily have inculcating effects if the ensuing discourse allows for a critical stance (see also Smith, 1974).

toward reaching understanding inevitably involves the reciprocal raising and recognition of validity claims. Claims to truth and rightness, if radically challenged, can be redeemed only through argumentative discourse leading to rationally motivated consensus. (p. 325)

Applied to education this argument means that in all values and moral educational situations the claim for freedom that defines potentially autonomous self-reliant persons must be honored (Keller & Reuss 1985). More practically said: Whatever we do in moral education (transferring moral knowledge, stimulating moral action, discussing a moral problem, analyzing virtues or the moral message in a novel, etc.), the child should learn to develop his or her personal point of view and at the same time to consider the other's point of view. He or she should learn to prepare for moral decisions by capitalizing on the group discussion and making decisions, while recognizing other positions and coordinating different interpretations. Finally, the child should learn that a rational practice of communication is warranted even if disagreement persists. The educator on the other hand should learn that in every communicative moral situation he has to *presuppose* that students at each age and under every condition are reliable and truthfully looking toward a just, objective, and generalizable solution even if their logical capacity is not fully developed, even if their emotions are not fully controlled, even if their role-taking competence is still somewhat "egocentric" in a Piagetian sense, and even if they know that strategic behavior is a common fact of human life.

Through such a pedagogy based on discourse and directed to a high ethical sensibility, one proceeds from the common working out of situations, justifies possible consequences and actions, and strives toward an accepted realization of a moral decision. Keller and Reuss (1985) list the following four principles that underlie discursive ethics:

1. The principle of justification, which implies that it is necessary to justify any course of action which concerns us;
2. the principle of fairness, which guarantees a just balance in the distribution of efforts and sacrifices;
3. the principle of consequences, which implies that everybody should anticipate the consequences of actions and of omissions;
4. the principle of universalization, which implies consistency in judgment and the will to take the role of the concerned persons (Golden Rule) (cf. Keller/Reuss 1985, p. 110).

All four of these principles should be applied in moral reflections and in moral decision-making processes. Together, they lead to an autonomy which means both free expression of needs and interests and respect for other persons.

The central notion of moral discourse requires that after the presentation of moral knowledge, after the discussion of a moral or value problem, and after questioning the right way of action, the educators step back and stimulate a discussion in which the moral ideal is questioned. In this discussion "normally the orientations to truth, rightness, and truthfulness claims are combined in a syndrome that is broken up only temporarily under the pressure of problems that arise" (Habermas, 1982b, p. 235). In this sense discourses are "islands in the sea of practice, that is, improbable forms of communica-

tion; the everyday appeal to validity claims implicitly points, however, to their possibility" (p. 235). Teachers have the task of creating the conditions that give rise to the thinkability and the possibility of such islands.

The Moral Educational Situation

Let us now define what we mean by a moral educational situation. In such a situation students positively try to affect each other's moral actions, cognitive structures, values, and moral emotions through moral discourse. Further, this is a situation created for educational purposes that demand moral decisions with real consequences. But a moral decision certainly differs from other types of decision (cf. Janis & Mann, 1977; Raiffa, 1968; Shavelson, 1978; Shavelson & Stern, 1981) in which persons attempt to "optimize" the attainment of some goal given alternative courses of action, for example, in which the maximum profit or the highest efficiency is sought. Rules of altruism or rules of justice are incompatible with maximizing profit because they rely on human respect, which often sets an absolute limit for strategic or economic efficiency or even "efficiency" in terms of maximization of happiness. Imagine a politician who realizes that his political opponents are causing him troubles. This politician may have the chance to remove those adversaries. The rules of human justice and respect, however, will restrain him if he acknowledges and acts in accordance with them.

In this context moral education involves teaching the use of rules and principles, regarding justice and respect in discourse, that enable us to defer personal success in favor of another person, a community, or a society. The influence comes thus through discourse pedagogy. Competence in the use of moral discourse components enables a person to apply moral principles and rules to decision-making processes. Therefore, whatever teaching methods are intended, they have to be selected prior to the application, and with the discourse in mind, in order to be compatible. But there is a difference between the situation itself and the moral discourse. The discourse is always a step back from the reality of the situation. It is an ideal form of solving a moral problem. The moral situation is always bounded by time and other pressures; a decision must be made, an action taken. In order to act, the discourse has to be terminated and the decision has to be planned and implemented.

Moral and Values Education

Having described discourse pedagogy and our conception of a moral educational situation we should distinguish between moral education and values education in general. This distinction can be made in three ways:

First, "values education" refers to the teaching of social, political, religious, aesthetic, or other types of values. It usually points to the so-called school of values clarification (discussed subsequently), and to the Canadian research on the values curriculum (Beck, 1983). "Moral education" commonly refers to a Kantian universality-oriented conception of justice (Habermas, 1983a; Kohlberg, 1981b; Piaget, 1932/1973; Rawls, 1971, and others). According to Rest (1983) "morality" includes the following broader meanings: "(1) behavior that helps another human being, (2) behavior in conformity with social norms, (3) the internalization of social norms, (4) the arousal of empathy or guilt or both, (5) reasoning about justice, and (6) putting another's interest ahead of one's own" (p. 556). Whatever the topic of the moral discourse, the question is not whether I, as a person, am right or wrong, but rather on what kind of justification I base the claim to the rightness of my decision and what universals guide this justification.

Second, according to Habermas, one can distinguish between three classes of problems implying three types of validity claims (Furth, 1983):

> problems of facts and objective efficiency, problems of taste and subjective satisfactoriness, and problems of personal relating and social norms. . . . In Habermas's view reason is the power that allows people to make validity claims and to dispute them in a reasonable manner so as to settle the dispute. The three classes of problems engender three types of validity claims: . . . the truth of a factual statement, the truthfulness of a subjective expression, and the rightness of an interpersonal relation (pp. 182-183)

Even if the discourse principles stay the same in all three forms, the format of the content and the severity of the issues discussed change according to the importance of the value system and according to the objective, subjective, or norm-conforming cognitive orientation. Habermas' perspective illustrates the usefulness of this distinction in a sociological context.

Finally, there is another, more empirical, way to distinguish between the moral domain and social conventions. Social conventions are specific values. Turiel (1983, pp. 34 ff.) states that they are determined by the social system. Principles of justice, however, are founded intrinsically and are universally understood. Nucci and Nucci (1982a, 1982b) conducted and reviewed a number of studies showing that in a moral situation even if an authority allows "immoral" transgression, the children would say that this immoral behavior is not "just". In the case of social conventions, however, children judge transgressions differently in different social contexts. They are less severe and only functionally justified. It depends on the good taste of a person whether she or he acts in accordance with conventions.

In whatever way educational acts are analyzed, the distinction between morality and a general value system has to be made. A value can be an individual's preference for a field of human interest. Morality always relates to an a priori human point of view. It involves universal human principles which often must be reconstructed in a discourse before one can judge justly. Skinn (1980, p. 111), for example, emphasizes acculturation and exploration in values. Morality, however, must be developed through a cognitive structural transformation of a person's whole belief system. Pedagogic discourse encompasses both of them.

Elements of Moral Discourse

In this section my goal is to clarify the relationship between the discourse concept and moral situations. When the discourse concept is applied to a moral educational situation, any solution to a moral problem given by a teacher, a single student, or a group of students must be understood in terms of the four

previously mentioned principles of discursive ethics and of moral discourse pedagogy, namely (a) justification, (b) fairness, (c) consequences, and (d) universalization. The moral education situation thus is framed by an understanding of a person's circumstances, the interpretation of his or her needs, motives, and interests, and an application of contextual rules and evaluation standards. Once the situation is framed, discourse begins by first stepping back and participating in a dialogue distant from the situation. The discourse starts with the minimal morality of each situation and strives towards maximal morality, even if this maximal morality remains an ideal and a never-reached rational moral competence (see Nisan, 1985).

Now discourse pedagogy should be applied to the *different contextual elements* of educational moral situations such that for students a meaning-making process is warranted. These elements are the following:

1. The discourse should be directed to the *moral* conflict and to the stimulation of a higher level of moral judgment.
2. The discourse should be directed towards moral *role taking* and moral *empathy*.
3. The discourse should be oriented to *moral choice and action*.
4. The discourse should be directed towards *shared norms* and to a moral community (positive climate).
5. The discourse should be directed towards the *analysis* of moral situations and of value systems.
6. The discourse should be oriented towards the student's own reasoning and attitude change and psychological disposition (coping and defending).
7. The discourse should be directed towards one's theoretical moral knowledge (e.g., moral psychology, moral philosophy, etc.).

How do we know that these elements are valid and necessary? How do we justify these choices? How do we teach the seven educational moral elements to which discourse pedagogy has to be applied? Let us look at a school. We will identify the seven different elements within a concrete and complex moral educational situation. Hersh, Paolitto, and Reimer (1979) provide a useful example in the beginning of their book *Promoting Moral Growth*. They present the following moral educational situation:

> In one elementary classroom nine year old Brian, a boy with a mild case of cerebral paralysis, has become the target of abuse by others in the class. He is teased about such things as his inability to unbutton his jacket and his lack of coordination on the playground during recess. As the ridicule continues, Brian is often seen crying during class. One day, Brian is absent from school. Mrs. Warren takes this opportunity to ask her pupils to discuss what she believes is a serious problem in the class. The students seem surprised to hear that a "problem" exists, they form a discussion circle. Mrs. Warren explains, "Some people are born with a disease that prevents them from using their muscles in a normal way. It must be difficult to want to be like others and not be able to do so. I wonder what it would be like not to be able to do certain things *and* be made fun of by other children?" There is silence. The tone of Mrs. Warren's voice has not been one of anger but one of concern and sensitivity.
> One girl says, "I feel bad when Tim and Jack tease Brian." Jack answers, "I didn't mean to hurt him."

The discussion continues. Nearly every child has something to contribute. Some students see the problem from Brian's point of view. Jeff says, "I would feel angry and hurt if kids teased me like that." Janet raises the issue of fairness: "It's not fair — it's like we are cheating when we play kickball and run fast but Brian can't."

This is an emotional discussion without formal resolution. The next day, Brian returns. Several students volunteer to help him unbutton his jacket. During recess, Brian reaches base safely three times in the kickball game. As the days pass, the ridicule stops. (p. 4)

In this scene the children generated a communicative dialogue initiated by a social conflict (first element: discourse directed towards the moral conflict). In this discourse they reflected upon and judged their previous actions and asked when such a situation would be just (third element: discourse directed to the moral action). The teacher informed them about facts that give Brian's behavior a new meaning, compared to the general norms of the class (fourth element: discourse directed to shared norms). Some children developed empathy towards Brian, feeling "bad" for him. They placed themselves "in his shoes," practicing social role taking (second element: discourse directed toward empathy and role taking). Finally, the conflict was solved through a specific and real moral action which is reflected in a comparison of the students' behavior towards Brian before and after the discourse (again, third element). Let us assume that the teacher follows this conversation with related material showing the same conflict structure in literature, politics, and/or history (fifth and seventh elements: discourse oriented towards the analysis of moral material and of theoretical moral knowledge). Further, let us assume that she facilitates the students' reflections of their changes in judgment and feelings (sixth element: discourse directed towards one's own change). So in a single real life situation calling for practical justice and care we find all seven elements combined.

Thus, the analysis of the aims and means of an educational intervention, which began with a real conflict, leads to the conclusion that the discourse might very well have been directed towards the seven elements; their interrelations are produced by shared argumentation. This is an inductive way to view moral educational situations; It offers a deductive logic too if one avoids a certain fallacy. This fallacy (Kohlberg, 1978) occurs when a psychological paradigm is applied to education without considering the realities of the educational situation.

No psychological theory can be applied mechanically to an educational setting; the setting itself, its needs, and its means-end connections with the educators' general intentions must enter into the dialogue with the psychologist's theory. Hence, the seven discourse elements should be stimulated pedagogically; psychological and philosophical theories suggest how to sustain these educational acts.

By interrelating and justifying the seven elements of moral education with theory, a framework is provided for analyzing current models of moral education and the respective literature. However, rather than attempting an overview of all theories and literature on moral education, examples will be presented to demonstrate the generality of the overall frame of reference. By referring to the seven pedagogical elements, we can show how researchers have empirically evaluated similar moral education programs and indicate what kinds of theoretical and measurement problems they encountered and how research results were applied to educational practice.

Thus, these seven discourse elements also serve as a system useful for overcoming a narrow belief in one unique and exclusive theoretical position. With this conceptual system we will therefore be able to maintain an overall self-reflective perspective.

In this first section we have outlined a blueprint for moral discourse. Such discourse applies to many forms of moral education and thus frames a general program for moral and value learning, encompassing a broad variety of models and methods.

The Seven Discourse Elements of Moral Education

In the following section, the seven elements of moral discourse that have been outlined in the first section will be discussed in detail.

Discourse on Moral Conflict and the Stimulation of Moral Judgment Development

Most situations in moral education begin with a moral conflict. Two (or more) moral options (issues) compete with each other, or egoistic and altruistic values oppose one another (Oser, 1984):

> For example, the dilemma which involves the classical Salomon problem: A baby is given away for adoption because the mother is poor. The child is happy with his new parents. After some time, the mother wants her child back. She now has enough money to care for him/her. She engages the adoptive parents of her child in a court trial. This problem implies that an option for the natural rights leads to rejection of social justice and vice versa. (p. 169; also see Oser, 1981b, pp. 59 ff)

Moral conflict seems to be the paradigmatic trigger for applying contemporary moral discourse methods, as well as the basic motor for the functioning of moral systems, moral societies, and moral theories. A discourse based on these conflicts includes several important conditions:

1. presentation of the subjective truth completely and exhaustively (competence) as conceived by the participants in the conflict;
2. absence of an authority presenting an outside or observer's point of view of the "right" answer;
3. creation of a disequilibrium by presenting different arguments and different opinions to stimulate development of moral judgment on increasingly complex grounds;
4. interaction among students (discussants) coordinated in such a way that everyone reacts openly and fairly to one another's point of view (positive climate and transactional discourse);
5. linking of the principles of discourse to the principles of justice.

Kohlberg's (1958, 1969, 1976, 1980, 1981b, 1985; Kohlberg et al., 1983) cognitive developmental approach to morality and moral education is probably the best-developed available model, and so provides a good example of moral education using the discourse method. Kohlberg's work will be discussed briefly to illustrate the general pedagogy of the applied discourse method.[3]

Kohlberg's work consists of three important mutually overlapping theoretical components. The first component concerns the description and evaluation of his levels of moral judgment (see Table 32.1). The development of this theory and methodology began with the dissertation (1958) and was accomplished with the publication of the new Scoring Manual (Colby/Kohlberg, 1986). In a 20-year longitudinal study (Colby, Kohlberg, Gibbs, & Lieberman, 1983) the stage concept was tested through repeated clinical questioning (up to six times) of 58 persons in total over multiple intervals of no more than 4 years. There were but 14 regressions of the 193 transitions from one stage to another as measured on a 13-point scale. This finding strongly supports a discontinuity concept of development.

The second component of Kohlberg's work refers to the attempts to teach or to influence moral judgment. Moshe Blatt found in his dissertational work (1969) that it is possible to stimulate higher stages of moral judgment ("Blatt effect"). The first generation of this research is represented in a number of reports that appeared around 1980 (especially Cochrane & Manley-Casimir, 1980; Kuhmerker, Mentkowski, & Erickson, 1980; Mosher, 1980; also see Kohlberg, 1981b; Mosher, 1979; Munsey, 1980; and Wilson & Schochet, 1980). Kohlberg's approach is oriented neither towards teaching moral content, nor towards training virtues; rather it aims at defining development as an educational goal (cf. Kohlberg, 1981b, pp. 6 ff., pp. 49 ff.). The intention is to stimulate or to create a transformational process that will enable the subject to reach the next level through a "guided crisis."

The third part of Kohlberg's work is concerned with the just community approach, to be discussed further on.

Kohlberg's formulation led to a long series of intervention studies with the following procedures in common: In a standardized interview the starting level of moral judgment is measured. Then moral conflicts (i.e., dilemmas) are discussed. Arguments based on justification at a higher level of moral development than the subject's are presented in order to weaken the deep structure and to stimulate stage transformation (" + 1 convention"). Finally, the change in moral judgment is measured with a second standard interview.

In the first intervention study Blatt and Kohlberg (1975) demonstrated that with junior and senior high school students, 18 weekly 1-hour guided peer group discussions of moral conflicts led to significant gains in moral reasoning. Controlling for IQ they found significant effects of age and social status on moral reasoning and interactions between age and sex, but no significant effects in a follow-up interview. Unguided discussion groups did not show significant growth but did show significant follow-up gains, a fact that points to the effects of certain features of peer group interaction and discussion itself (see Berkowitz, below). This study, undertaken in the late sixties, stimulated many similar intervention studies. For example,

Sullivan (1980), in a typical evaluation study, uses different treatments such as moral discussions, counseling and empathy training, moral psychology and philosophy teaching, and educational activities, with children. The intervention resulted in a significant upward change of children's judgment on the Kohlberg scale and on the Loevinger Sentence Completion Test (1970). Colby, Kohlberg, Fenton, Speicher-Dubin, and Lieberman (1977), in a Boston and Pittsburgh comparison study, demonstrated that almost all changes in moral reasoning were toward the next stage. Interestingly no stage was skipped; the experimental classes had high levels of change, averaging a gain of 31 points on the Moral Maturity Scale (100 points = 1 full stage). Upward movements were more likely for those students who had already been at a certain stage for a while than for those who had just reached a stage (interaction between age and pretest stage). The upward movement did not appear to be due to the learning of concepts (transmitted by the teacher) but rather to the cognitive conflict and the reconstruction and the reorganization of one's moral judgments. The frequency of dilemma discussions and the way the teacher stimulated the conflict through socratic probing were significant factors for change.

Candee (1985) differentiated two types of ethical thinking: "utilitarian" and "deontologic." He shows that medical residents who demonstrated the latter type had higher moral judgments, also showed better clinical performance, and better interaction styles with patients. He used videotape feedbacks as a stimulation technique. Oser and Schlaefli (1985), working with bank apprentices in Switzerland, used a multitreatment approach to change different detailed capacities of moral judgments, for example, the sensitivity for the moral point of view, a change of value preference, the development of empathy and role-taking ability, the enhancement of moral knowledge and moral metacognition, and the use of social rules to guide interaction during moral discourse. On all measures there were significant changes. In a counseling type of study Higgins and Gordon (1985) show how the value pattern and the sociomoral development changed in two worker-owned businesses.

Finally, Boyd's (1976) dissertation warrants mention because it demonstrates how students could be led from Stage 4 to Stage 5 or 6. This is a significant achievement, since very few people develop to such high levels; Kohlberg estimated that over 80% of the adult population stay at Stages 3 or 4 on the moral judgment maturity scale.

One of the finest intervention studies was done by Berkowitz, Gibbs, and Broughton (1980), who formed same-sex undergraduate dyads based on two criteria: (a) partners had disagreed on 50% or more of the items in an opinion questionnaire; and (b) partners were at the same stage, one-third stage apart, or two-thirds to one full stage apart. The greatest development was evidenced for subjects who were only one-third stage below their partners (low disparity condition). This study is one of the few investigations directly focusing on stage transformation. Berkowitz (1985; Berkowitz & Gibbs, 1983) found that the so-called "transactive" discussion in which one's reasoning operates on the reasoning of the other is the

---

[3] The selection of studies presented in this paper is based on two criteria: (a) they are concerned with discourse, and (b) they present new aspects of a research domain.

Table 32.1. The Six Stages of Moral Judgment

Level A. Preconventional Level

Stage 1. The Stage of Punishment and Obedience

Content

Right is literal obedience to rules and authority, avoiding punishment, and not doing physical harm.

1. What is right is to avoid breaking rules, to obey for obedience' sake, and to avoid doing physical damage to people and property.
2. The reasons for doing right are avoidance of punishment and the superior power of authorities.

Social Perspective

This stage takes an egocentric point of view. A person at this stage doesn't consider the interests of others or recognize they differ from actor's, and doesn't relate two points of view. Actions are judged in terms of physical consequences rather than in terms of psychological interests of others. Authority's perspective is confused with one's own.

Stage 2. The Stage of Individual Instrumental Purpose and Exchange

Content

Right is serving one's own or other's needs and making fair deals in terms of concrete exchange.

1. What is right is following rules when it is to someone's immediate interest. Right is acting to meet one's own interests and needs and letting others do the same. Right is also what is fair, that is, what is an equal exchange, a deal, an agreement.
2. The reason for doing right is to serve one's own needs or interests in a world where one must recognize that other people have their interests, too.

Social Perspective

This stage takes a concrete individualistic perspective. A person at this stage separates own interests and points of view from those of authorities and others. He or she is aware everybody has individual interests to pursue and these conflict, so that right is relative (in the concrete individualistic sense). The person integrates or relates conflicting individual interests to one another through instrumental exchange of services, through instrumental need for the other and the other's goodwill, or through fairness giving each person the same amount.

Level B. Conventional Level

Stage 3. The Stage of Mutual Interpersonal Expectations, Relationships, and Conformity

Content

The right is playing a good (nice) role, being concerned about the other people and their feelings, keeping loyalty and trust with partners, and being motivated to follow rules and expectations.

Level C. Postconventional and Principled Level

Moral decisions are generated from rights, values, or principles that are (or could be) agreeable to all individuals composing or creating a society designed to have fair and beneficial practices.

Stage 5. The Stage of Prior Rights and Social Contract or Utility

Content

The right is upholding the basic rights, values, and legal contracts of a society, even when they conflict with the concrete rules and laws of the group.

1. What is right is being aware of the fact that people hold a variety of values and opinions, that most values and rules are relative to one's group. These "relative" rules should usually be upheld, however, in the interest of impartiality and because they are the social contract. Some nonrelative values and rights such as life and liberty, however, must be upheld in any society and regardless of majority opinion.
2. Reasons for doing right are, in general, feeling obligated to obey the law because one has made a social contract to make and abide by laws for the good of all and to protect their own rights and the rights of others. Family, friendship, trust, and work obligations are also commitments or contracts freely entered into and entail respect for the rights of others. One is concerned that laws and duties be based on rational calculation of overall utility: "the greatest good for the greatest number."

Social Perspective

This stage takes a prior-to-society perspective—that of a rational individual aware of values and rights prior to social attachments and contracts. The person integrates perspectives by formal mechanisms of agreement, contract, objective impartiality, and due process. He or she considers the moral point of view and the legal point of view, recognizes they conflict, and finds it difficult to integrate them.

Stage 6. The Stage of Universal Ethical Principles

Content

This stage assumes guidance by universal ethical principles that all humanity should follow.

1. Regarding what is right, Stage 6 is guided by universal ethical principles. Particular laws or social agreements are usually valid because they rest on such principles. When laws violate these principles, one acts in accordance with the principle. Principles are universal principles of justice: the equality of human rights and respect for the dignity of human beings as individuals. These are not merely values that are recognized, but are also principles used to generate particular decisions.
2. The reason for doing right is that, as a rational person, one has seen the validity of principles and has become committed to them.

Social Perspective

This stage takes the perspective of a moral point of view from which social arrangements derive or on which they are grounded. The perspective is that of any rational individual recognizing the nature of morality or the basic moral premise of respect for other persons as ends, not means.

---

1. What is right is living up to what is expected by people close to one or what people generally expect of people in one's role as son, sister, friend, and so on. "Being good" is important and means having good motives, showing concern about others. It also means keeping mutual relationships, maintaining trust, loyalty, respect, and gratitude.
2. Reasons for doing right are needing to be good in one's own eyes and those of others, caring for others, and because if one puts oneself in the other person's place one would want good behavior from the self (Golden Rule).

Social Perspective

This stage takes the perspective of the individual in relationship to other individuals. A person at this stage is aware of shared feelings, agreements, and expectations, which take primacy over individual interests. The person relates points of view through the "concrete Golden Rule," putting oneself in the other person's shoes. He or she does not consider generalized "system" perspective.

Stage 4. The Stage of Social System and Conscience Maintenance

Content

The right is doing one's duty in society, upholding the social order, and maintaining the welfare of society or the group.

1. What is right is fulfilling the actual duties to which one has agreed. Laws are to be upheld except in extreme cases where they conflict with other fixed social duties and rights. Right is also contributing to society, the group, or institution.
2. The reasons for doing right are to keep the institution going as a whole, self-respect or conscience as meeting one's defined obligations, or the consequences: "What if everyone did it?"

Social Perspective

This stage differentiates societal point of view from interpersonal agreement or motives. A person at this stage takes the viewpoint of the system, which defines roles and rules. He or she considers individual relations in terms of place in the system.

Level B/C Transitional Level (This level is postconventional but not yet principled.)

Content of Transition

At Stage $4\frac{1}{2}$, choice is personal and subjective. It is based on emotions, conscience is seen as arbitrary and relative, as are ideas such as "duty" and "morally right."

Transitional Social Perspective

At this stage, the perspective is that of an individual standing outside of his own society and considering himself as an individual making decisions without a generalized commitment or contract with society. One can pick and choose obligations, which are defined by particular societies, but one has no principles for such choice.

Note. From *The Philosophy of Moral Development* (pp. 409–412) by L. Kohlberg, 1981, San Francisco, Harper & Row. Copyright 1981 by Lawrence Kohlberg. Reprinted by permission.

best predictor of stage transformation. These researchers developed a system of 18 "transacts," such as integration, contradiction, refinement, and comparison, that are aspects of a communicative discourse.

Several studies of change in moral judgment have been reported in the German literature; for example, Schuhler (1980) showed that the continued development of moral judgment through moral training discussions is dependent on the nature of the group process. Groups who had undergone a Maier-type group dynamics training communicated in an easier and thematically more concentrated way, and showed greater development of moral judgment maturity.

A more complete overview on the intervention literature can be found in a number of review articles, namely, Higgins (1980), Leming (1981), Lockwood (1978), Rest (1979), Schlaefli (1984), and Schlaefli, Rest, and Thoma (1984). These reviews picture what types of interventions were conducted, which educational techniques were employed, which evaluative measures were used, and which results obtained.

The interventions designed for fostering moral development mainly use the dilemma discussion of the Blatt type (nearly all of them employ the Kohlberg Moral Judgment Interview or the Rest Defining Issues Test for assessment); other treatments include conventional social studies strategies, religious education curricula (e.g., Berkowitz & Caldwell, 1985), and so forth. There is a clear movement towards more "holistic" types of interventions, aimed not only at moral judgment development but at personal growth as a whole (cf. Rest, 1980).

Comparisons of Kohlberg-oriented and values clarification curricula reveal that the latter are far less effective, partly due to the fact that the relations between the variety of values clarification strategies and the theoretical concept are widely unclear (Leming, 1981; Lockwood, 1978). Lockwood's critical review shows that most interventions focusing on dilemma discussions were effective in advancing moral judgment approximately half a stage higher. But he also revealed that, for some subjects, the treatment could lead to a lower developmental stage, and, for others, no change. Typically most studies are concerned with treatments aimed at the transition from Stage 2 to stage 3.

Rest (1979, pp. 204-222) reviews 16 studies which were selected because they used the DIT (Defining Issue Test) for assessment. The DIT, designed by Rest (1979), measures preference for arguments pertaining to different moral stages. It offers an alternative method for assessing moral development, and it has the advantage that it can be used as a group-testing procedure. (For reviews of alternative assessment procedures, see Colby, Gibbs, Lieberman, & Kohlberg, 1983; Gibbs, Widaman, and Colby, 1982; Kuhmerker et al., 1980; Rest 1979, and (in German) Eckensberger, 1983; Lempert, 1985; Lind 1981.)

Four of these 16 studies are short-term studies without significant differences, yet only two of them utilized Kohlberg's discussion method. Another 7 studies were directed to promoting personality growth in a more complex way. Interventions of this kind implement what is often called "deliberate psychological education" (Mosher & Sprinthall, 1971). Four of these

studies showed significant effects. The last 5 studies, 3 of which had significant results, represent different programs in moral and values education.

Schlaefli, Rest and Thoma (1984) analyzed 40 more DIT studies for treatment type and duration, clearness of treatment, and effects. The authors also conducted a comprehensive quantitative meta-analysis (cf. Glass, 1981) for a systematic evaluation of the research body. They conclude that most of the studies with classical dilemma discussions are effective, while others focusing on social content (social studies curricula) are not. The "psychological education" studies, which treat moral development as one dimension among others, show good results, though it often is somewhat unclear, in multitreatment interventions, which effects are due to which particular educational strategy.

Higgins (1980), in her review on moral education, also distinguished clearly between curricula of the three mentioned types: direct moral dilemma discussion with natural groups, combined moral and "deliberate psychological" education, moral discussion programs within regular social studies curricula. Higgins finds the first group to be the most effective.

Schlaefli (1984) draws an interesting conclusion with respect to treatment duration which substantiates a suggestion of Colby et al. (1977): While short-term interventions (less than 3 weeks) definitely are not successful in changing structural features of moral cognition, there seems to be no increase of effect in programs with a duration of more than 12 weeks approximately. Schlaefli concludes that after a period of stimulation individuals' moral structures need a time of adaptation, that is, need the opportunity to validate structural steps by confrontation with manifold content elements.

The review articles we mentioned also refer partly to problems of intervention design and program evaluation. Additionally, see for this issue the contributions to Kuhmerker et al. (1980) and Oser (1981). Althof (1984) links his overview of practical approaches in moral pedagogy back to an analysis of the current status of Kohlberg-oriented moral educational theory.

Of course, the developmental approach was repeatedly criticized. One can distinguish philosophical criticisms (Aron, 1977, 1980; Habermas, 1983a; Hoeffe, 1984; Locke, 1980; Peters, 1975; Rosen, 1980), criticisms of the measurement techniques (Kurtines & Greif, 1974; Nicolayev & Phillips, 1979), conceptual criticisms (Gibbs, 1979; Kaern, 1978; Munsey, 1980). Finally you find educational criticisms (e.g., Wilson, 1979), one of the most differentiated being the one of Edelstein (1985). Edelstein discusses problems of structure and content, of judgment and action, the competence-performance hiatus, and the issue of universalism versus culturalism. There is an ongoing discussion with respect to all of these dimensions, which is very stimulating; see for instance Broughton's (1978) defense of Kohlbergian methodology against Kurtines and Greif, or Kohlberg, Levine, and Hewer's (1983) "current formulation" of the theory, which extensively responds to critics.[4]

---

[4] In recent years the body of research in progressive developmental moral education has become very impressive. For reasons of space limitation we must limit the selection of examples.

Where in the theory of stimulated moral development is discourse pedagogy located? The moral discourse method attempts precisely to stimulate higher stages of moral development. It postulates that development should be the aim of education, and that the three conditions for increasing moral judgment maturity are:

1. stimulation of a cognitive disequilibrium through presentation of real or artificial dilemmas;
2. introduction of discussion material one (respectively one-third) stage above the individual's stage of moral development (+ 1 convention) by teachers or discussion participants;
3. facilitation of the discourse by effective questioning and appropriate discussions.

However, there are many critical issues in this theoretical system. First, these conditions are necessary but not sufficient for the moral discourse pedagogy. Suppose only one of the four discourse criteria mentioned on p. 920 were fulfilled, for example, as in Kohlberg's method where only a higher stage is stimulated. In this case the discourse is strategic. For higher development is in itself not a sacred goal, and if the rationality of such a purpose is not controlled by the other three criteria we are not sure whether the "good" goal—a higher stage that is more complex, more reversible, in higher equilibrium, nearer to universal principles— has been reached through acceptable means. As a consequence a teacher has to arrange a social situation in which (a) each child has the possibility to produce his or her full subjective truth, (b) no authority can disturb the discourse by hindering it from the outside, (c) a transactive dialogue is applied to any new dilemma situation, and (d) moral principles are sought on the basis of interactional integrity. Thus the goal "stimulation to a higher stage" has to be combined with the goal "stimulation of a discourse setting." The discourse is the cognitive interactive perspective of moral growth.

Second, a major shortcoming of evaluations and measurements of educational progress within this framework is that the process of the discourse has not been sufficiently analyzed. Hence, the implementation and nature of the independent variable (that is, the moral education treatment) is uncertain. For example, most studies presented by Mosher (1980) reported increases in moral maturity from the pretest to the posttest only in one or two dimensions. Thus the dependent variable is too narrowly conceived and established. But the educational treatments are often quite different. For example, Sullivan (1980) used phasic treatments labeled as follows: "moral discussions," "counseling and empathy training," "moral psychology and philosophy," and "adolescents as moral educators". Although he measured moral development and ego development, he did not assess the nature and amount of transactional dialogue, the nature of the discourse climate, or the social involvement of a person in the discussion. There is no process–product or process–process validity in his evaluations, that is, there is no guarantee that moral discourse took place if only moral development is measured.

Nevertheless there exist a number of publications that describe techniques for introducing moral discussions and other intervention treatments into the classroom (Arbuthnot & Faust, 1981; Galbraith & Jones, 1976; Hersh et al., 1979); see also Scharf (1978) and Mosher (1980) for collections of reports on such interventions. In the German literature, Aufenanger, Garz, and Zutavern (1981) present a couple of excellent teaching strategies in the Kohlbergian sense; Pohlmann and Wolf (1982) discuss educational plans on ethics in German schools; and finally Schmidt (1983) presents a didactic of ethical instruction.

The main problem with those strategies is the complexity of the classroom or field situation. Obviously, something happens through all these forms of treatment. But what exactly is it? Two answers to this question are possible. Either research must develop a clearer model of the structural transformation process, or we accept the position that teaching implies many forms of stimulating disequilibria and the time when change occurs in one or the other pupils is unknown. The first proposition is realistic, the second pessimistic. Nevertheless the material presented by these publications is valuable.

A third problem grows out of the contradiction that education is always strategic, but moral discourse is not. If moral education must allow, or actually create, islands in the ocean of practice, achievement of the goals of moral and values education does not rely solely on the will of the teacher. It relies, in large part, on the students.

But how is it possible for students to participate in a moral discourse, that is, create islands in the ocean of practice? One possible solution to this problem is suggested by Oser's studies (1981b, 1984) of the effect of moral information about intentions and consequences, moral rules, and interaction strategies on small-group moral problem solving. Oser distinguished four hierarchical levels of small-group interaction during moral discourse: (a) action- and resolution-oriented discourse; (b) a justification discourse based on social and psychological grounds; (c) a normative and rule-oriented discourse, and (d) philosophically oriented discourse. He also distinguished three levels of "communicative compactness," which is a measure for observing how well people relate to one another. The highest level attained by 15-year-old students—level 3, normative and rule-oriented discourse—was attained with the moral rule treatment. The highest level of "communicative compactness" was reached through an interactive strategy. With both interactional strategies and moral rules provided, a statistical interaction was obtained: Both treatments yielded a tendency towards the highest possible discourse stage.

This result clearly contradicts the theory of Habermas. In his view a real discourse is possible only at the higher stages of moral development. It seems that Habermas is more concerned about an ideal form of a possible discourse. Here he neglects the cognitive-developmental aspects. According to him, on the lower stages only strategic interaction and exchange interactions are possible, but no discourse. Discourse begins only on a conventional level when persons are able to be independent from authorities and from arbitrary decisions (1983, p. 163). Yet one of Habermas's coworkers, Miller (1984a), is concerned with the ontogenesis of the discourse in children, adolescents, and young adults. For example, he tries to analyze discussions of groups of little children and to sketch the logic of their verbal interactions. This could be a way of combining educational claims with developmental realities.

The Discourse Directed Toward Moral
Role Taking and Moral Empathy

The discussion of a hypothetical moral conflict, as well as the conscious experience of actual moral situations, implies that the participant sees the issues, in part, from other persons' perspectives. But if children try to change their positions and to put themselves in the shoes of another person, they have not yet completely integrated the other's point of view. Rather they must reconstruct the other's perspective piece by piece. In this case the discourse has a different function than it has in a moral dilemma discussion. For moral utterances are based not on the logic of rational arguments but on *possibilities*, on suppositions, on alternative courses of action, and on hypotheses. The task of the group, then, is to invite the child to see the other's possibilities of thinking and of argumentation.

Assume that an individual must be punished because he has stolen money from his friend. Assume further that the adolescents involved in a discourse are at Stage 3 or 4 on Kohlberg's scale. In this case not only does the outcome of the event — right and wrong — have to be discussed, but also the intent of the act and the consequences of the act as seen by the actors. Suppose that in the case of stolen money, the thief needed the money for his sick mother, disapproved of his own act, but saw no better alternatives to pursue. Then this context has to be developed and must be related to the moral judgment about the case. The most important features of a discourse related to this role-taking process are these:

1. The validity claims of the other person should be exhaustively imagined and evaluated (subjective–subjective truth);

2. these claims must be confronted with first-hand reactions and rule-oriented decisions;

3. egoistic and altruistic claims should be brought to an equilibrium.

There is a whole range of presuppositions underlying the discourse directed towards social and moral role taking, as discussed in many studies.

The concept of "interpersonal morality" (Keller & Reuss, 1985) relates to obligations that arise from friendships, altruism, and the ability to place oneself in the other's "shoes." Selman (1980) thinks that the ego becomes merely the subject if the alter's (other's) perspective is not simply assumed. This is why varying developmental conceptions of role taking have been described as underlying this aspect of interpersonal morality. See, for example: Peters' (1982) "understanding the other" (first stage: preirrational level; second stage: egocentrism; third stage: realism; fourth stage: autonomy); Damon's (1977, 1982) distributive interactions and comprehension of social relations; Roeders' (1980) perspective taking in verbal communications; but especially Selman's (1976, 1980) social perspective stage concepts. These stages are closely related to Kohlberg's (see Table 32.2). Hoffman (1976, 1979) describes the affective dimensions of moral role taking. He argues that "empathy refers to the involuntary, at times forceful, experiencing of another person's emotional state" (1976, p. 126), that it leads to distress which stimulates the further development of empathic abilities (Stage 1: empathic distress and person permanence; Stage 2: empathic distress and role taking; Stage 3: empathic distress and identity).

Table 32.2. Issues of Interpersonal Understanding Related to Concepts of the Individual, Close Friendships, Peer Group Organizations, and Parent–Child Relations

Individual	Friendship	Peer Group	Parent–Child Relations
1. Subjectivity: covert properties of persons (thoughts, feelings, motives); conflicts between thoughts or feelings within the person	1. Formation: why (motives) and how (mechanisms) friendships are made; the ideal friend	1. Formation: why (motives) and how (mechanisms) groups are formed; the ideal member	1. Formation: motives for having children and why children need parents
2. Self-awareness: awareness of the self's ability to observe its own thoughts and actions	2. Closeness: types of friendship, ideal friendship, intimacy	2. Cohesion-loyalty: group unity	2. Love and emotional ties: between parents and children
3. Personality: stable or predictive character traits (a shy person, etc.)	3. Trust: doing things for friends; reciprocity	3. Conformity: range and rationale	3. Obedience: why children do as their parents tell them
4. Personality change: how and why people change (growing up, etc.)	4. Jealousy: feelings about intrusions into new or established friendships	4. Rules-norms: types of rules, and reasons for them	4. Punishment: the function of punishment from the parent's and the child's perspective
	5. Conflict resolution: how friends resolve problems	5. Decision-making: setting goals, resolving problems, working together	5. Conflict resolution: optimal ways for parents and children to resolve their differences
	6. Termination: how friendships break up	6. Leadership: qualities, and function to the group	
		7. Termination: why groups break up or members are excluded	

Note. From *The Growth of Interpersonal Understanding* (p. 84) by R. L. Selman, 1980, New York: Academic Press. Copyright 1980 by Academic Press. Reprinted by permission.

The measurement of empathic progress in lessons (Feschbach, 1978) and the measurement of role taking within a certain stage are still problematic. These assessments are only applicable to specific situations (e.g., film passages) and only with a limited set of standardized questions. Summaries such as Hoffman's (1977) show that not much work has been done on measurement issues. Furthermore, similarly with Kohlberg's stages, Selman's assessment of perspective-taking stages reflects a global stage score and insufficiently details the facets of children's interactional capabilities within a stage.

How do these role-taking or social perspective stages apply to the discourse? It seems that our example about the thief demands a practical discourse. In this case, too, discourse always depends on stepping back and later on including the detailed reality of the situation. Because the discourse is concerned with optimal factual truth, empathy training and role-taking training help to approach pieces of this truth. Thus the discourse must be open to the rationally conceptualized feelings for "alter" in a role-taking situation. (The role taking is the practice and the discourse the island in the ocean of that practice. For this reason in addition to the developmental dimension there also is a horizontal, goal-oriented aspect. The person becomes concerned with what I think that you think and with what you think that others feel. Oppenheimer (1980) speaks about "recursive thinking" (see also Miller, Kessel, & Flavell, 1970, "Thinking About People Thinking About People Thinking About ...: A Study of Social Cognitive Development"). The coordination of such thoughts can be done in the discourse. If the teacher uses empathy training and role playing it is important that the results of these procedures are not only discussed in developmental terms. One cannot inculcate altruistic feelings. But if they are stimulated, the children need the opportunity to step back and see themselves as the role takers—possibilities the teacher has to provide. This is the task of the discourse directed towards empathy and role taking.

In conclusion, three pedagogical aims can be derived from these perspectives:

1. enhancement of the sensitivity for the needs and feelings of others through distress experiences;
2. development of meaningful interpersonal thinking through imagining oneself in the other's "shoes" and working out similarities and differences;
3. stimulation of the discourse about the awareness of the other's perspective through role taking and through providing help and responsible care to others.

The discourse directed at role taking and empathy requires that these three aims be planned and realized, and their effects discussed. Possibly nowhere is it more apparent that it is necessary to have an open atmosphere, a feeling of sharing with other people, and a positive feeling of protection from the teacher.

Discourse Oriented to the Right Moral Act

Morality becomes effective when it generates "morally better" action. While a higher stage of moral judgment can be stimulated pedagogically, one cannot guarantee that the right moral actions will result. Rather, the higher the stage of moral development, the better the justification for actions, even if this is against conventional morality. Further, better moral knowledge about the function of the rules of justice, about the course of biographically and historically important moral situations does not necessarily lead to better moral acts. Moral action is, nevertheless, an important component of moral education. The discourse that is oriented toward moral action should educate recognition of the moral situation—its alternative courses of action and their consequences—and hence lead to a relevant decision.

Rest's procedure (1984) for analyzing actions stands out as one of the more general and comprehensive models available because he relies upon the situation as well as upon judgment, moral knowledge, moral norms, and personality variables. His four analytic steps (Rest, 1984, p. 24) are:

1. interpreting the situation and identifying a moral problem (involving empathy, role-taking, and figuring out how the participants in a situation are each affected by various actions);
2. figuring out what one ought to do, formulating a plan of action that applies the relevant moral standard or ideal (involving concepts of fairness and justice, moral judgment, application of social-moral norms);
3. evaluating the various courses of action for how they would serve moral or nonmoral values and deciding what one will actually try to do (involving decision-making processes, value integration models, defensive operations); and
4. executing and implementing the moral plan of action (involving "ego strength" and self-regulation processes).

Each of these steps can be planned and executed educationally through the discourse. The pupil learns to pass through the four steps in confronting moral situations. His analytical abilities are therefore not oriented towards the moral judgment, but rather towards the moral action and its consequences. Oser (1981b) showed empirically that in moral dilemmas (action-oriented dilemmas) the eventual action did not necessarily correspond to the conclusion drawn from the four-step analysis. This occurred because the conclusions drawn from the discussion of justice one step back from the actual situation can easily conflict with situational circumstances. This is the typical conflict between what we called moral "sense" and moral "consensus." Fifteen-year-old pupils, attempting to distribute two movie tickets among more than two people, did discuss rules of justice. But under the stress of executing the action, they abandoned their conclusion and threw away the tickets, presented them to others, or exchanged them for "cheap" concessions.

The generalization that a higher moral stage does not guarantee the realization of a "good," respectively "highly" justified act nor the suppression of morally bad acts must be understood in the context of a series of studies dealing with the relationship between moral judgment and action. From reviews by Blasi (1980), Brown & Herrnstein (1975), Kohlberg & Candee (1984), Rest (1979), the following conceptual models have emerged:

1. A model depicting the so-called "monotonic" relationship

between moral judgment and moral action: Higher stages somehow become a better guarantee, for example, for not giving electrical shocks in Milgram's classic authority study by insuring actions that are increasingly in accordance with universal principles of morality. In a typical study for this concept, Krebs and Kohlberg (1973) reported that 81% of Stage 1 people, 64% of stage 2 people, 78% of Stage 3 people, 55% of Stage 4 people, and only 20% of Stage 5 people cheated in an experimental situation. Other examples of this approach are Candee (1975), Haan, Smith, and Block (1968), Krebs and Rosenwald (1977), McNamee (1977), and Turiel and Rothman (1972).

2. A model that assumes that certain actions are influenced by different variables, such as the degree of moral justification, the orientation to moral responsibility, differences between imagined morality and described action, ego strength, situational complexity, and defense and coping mechanisms. These variables are expected to determine performance (Blasi, 1980; Brown & Herrnstein, 1975; Doebert & Nunner-Winkler, 1980, 1982; Keller, 1982; Rest, 1979).

3. A model focusing on specific situations and the degree of responsibility and obligation towards one's environment (consensual morality). Responsibility is an intervening variable between action and judgment. Higher responsibility is a guarantee for a better correspondence between judgment and action, or between moral "sense" and moral "consensus." Included in the model is the degree of ability to recognize situations as moral (Blasi, 1983; Edelstein, 1985; Gilligan, 1977, 1982; Habermas, 1983; Helkama, 1979; Keller & Reuss, 1985; Kohlberg, Levine, & Hewer, 1983; Montada, 1980; Reimer & Power, 1980; Schmitt, Dalbert, & Montada, 1980).

4. A model derived from moral action that sets performance in the context of the individual's analytic capabilities. The action itself is analyzed, and emphasis is given to mediating judgments, that is, the reflection upon the relationships between action and action possibilities, action and judgment, and action and consequences (Edelstein, 1985; Garz, 1984; Locke, 1983; Oser, 1981b; Oser & Garz, 1985; Rest, 1985). In this case persons often begin to analyze the action goals before they consider the "moral point of view." A special form of this model is so-called positive justice or prosocial behavior, which refers to the imperfect duties (Mussen & Eisenberg-Berg, 1977; Schwartz, 1973, 1977; Staub, 1979, 1984).

5. A model that entails the so-called level of "limited accepted morality" underlying each action. The model assumes that every person more or less recognizes a certain degree of socially accepted violations and consequently adjusts his or her actions (Nisan, 1985).

6. An "intervening model" for action-oriented discourse that stems from Newman's work (see Hersh et al., 1980). This model concerns environmental competence, that is, the physical ability to have impact on objects, the interpersonal ability to have an impact on persons, and the civic ability to have an impact in public affairs (Hersh et al., 1980, p. 162). This model consists of a four-step discourse method to help people engage in social action: (a) formulate common policy goals (via moral deliberation, social policy research,

etc.); (b) work for support of these goals (political-legal process knowledge, advocacy skills, group-process knowledge and skills, organization-management skills, etc.); (c) resolve philosophical concerns (commitment and openness, consideration of persons vs. causes or institutions, use of power, integrity, and personal motives vs. social justification, etc.); and (d) actual policy outcomes. The major methods to realize such a program are exploratory research of students involved in community investigation, field-related advice for information gathering, informal observation in committees, and so forth.

In conclusion, we can shed more light on these issues if we examine why certain actions are performed and why certain others are omitted. (At present the author and his associates are conducting a research study about why people evade or neglect taxes and why they have not provided financial aid in disaster situations.) In addition, we must conclude that the classic studies of Hartshorne and May (1928–1930), in which character education classes and religious instruction programs had no influence on cheating, lying, stealing, and giving, must not lead to the conclusion that traditional moral and character education is worthless. From those studies we can only say that according to traditional cheating and lying tests behavioral honesty is largely determined by immediate situational factors like good example, group approval, and the like.

Features of the discourse directed toward action are the following:

1. a decision-making process that must be open and transparent for everybody (procedural truth);
2. a comparison process between ideal and actual personally feasible action alternatives and between ideal and contextually required actions that leads to the clarification of moral acts;
3. the identification of psychological constraints (will, coping, defending, fear, responsibility) that must be related to the action chosen. For example, one must be able to explain why for one person executing an act is easy and for another person it is difficult;
4. the provision of adequate time for participants to discuss without the immediate pressure of acting in order to coordinate all points of view of possible actions.

Linking decision making in these four steps to identifying the right act — as in an artificial moral dilemma — is not sufficient to learn moral behavior. We need to provide not only a justification for the right action but also to take into consideration the means for carrying out the action, the amount of responsibility we are willing to accept, and the social consequences of the action. We must discuss the psychological and social obstacles as well as the plans for realizing our acts. This is exactly what the children in Brian's class (presented earlier) did and what the teacher was stimulating and reinforcing.

Thus the pedagogical discourse, related to moral acting, has to confront the student with a realistic moral decision-making situation in order to help him or her develop a sense of a moral action capability. Only through this enactive approach can we expect meaningful results. (See below.) Educators' task is to provide conditions in which it is possible to act responsibly.

And we accept the critical necessity to do new research in order to reach evidence that bears out this assertion.

Discourse Directed to Shared Norms and to a Moral Community Climate

In this aspect of moral education, the discourse concerns the manner or atmosphere in which morality is attained. Two trends may be distinguished. The first aims at the reduction of aggression, the maintenance of conversation rules, and the creation of a positive and warm atmosphere for all students. This is the pedagogical–psychological aspect of the discourse directed towards developing a moral climate (e.g., Anderson, 1982; Brophy & Good, 1974; Burstall, 1975; Fend, 1979; Morrison, 1979). Here the climate is a value in itself. We do not refer to these concepts because it would be a topic in itself. The second trend concerns rather the so-called "shared norms." This refers to the students' identification with the norms of the class or the school — for example, the degree to which they accept responsibility for the community in general and for finally shaping the community. This is the cognitive–psychological aspect, which was implemented in the Just Communities of the Kohlberg group in schools and jails (Colby et al., 1977; Fenton, 1978; Hickey & Scharf, 1980; Higgins & Gordon, 1985; Kohlberg, 1980, 1984; Kohlberg, Wasserman, & Richardson, 1975).

Kohlberg, Liebermann, Power, Higgins, & Codding (1981), in their curriculum evaluation of the Scarsdale Alternative School (New York), compared the effects of attending moral discussion classes in traditional high schools and in two alternative schools to control groups. The authors report that the participation in "ethical issues" courses resulted in upward stage change in each type of school, but that actually the democratic participation in the alternative schools and the experience of its moral atmosphere "appears to be a more salient source of moral stimulation than classroom moral discussion in a course" (p. 36). This means that the environmental influence of a Just Community is strong enough to promote moral development in a way that an additional increase through participation in specific ethics courses remains relatively small. We should add that moral judgment gains in alternative schools are not detrimental to regular school achievement. On standardized tests for the so-called basic skills (reading, writing, vocabulary, etc.) Just Community students perform as well as students of regular high schools (cf. Kohlberg, 1980; Strom, 1980). Four tasks emerge from these results for the initiation of intervention studies concerned with the stimulation of social-moral judgment.

1. realizing and supervising the field treatment;
2. overcoming the political and organizational conflicts of a Just Community, for example, of a school within a school, especially in Europe, where school systems are more firmly structured;
3. capturing the development from one phase to the other. It is possible to describe passages from the pre–post-design, but the process analysis approach is largely neglected;
4. individually assessing the aims mentioned above, as is the case for the aims mentioned in the other discourse domains.

It may be possible to overcome the respective problems by studying existing communities that were not experimentally created. We know very little about shared norms in good schools (Krumboltz, 1982). Nevertheless Power (1979, 1985) developed an instrument that permits identification of the "moral climate": the degree of collectiveness, the phase of the acceptance of shared norms, and the number and nature of community values in relation to certain acts like stealing, drug consumption, and so on. Power did his work at the Brookline High School (Massachusetts) in which R. Mosher created an alternative high school in 1975, but his method can also be used in other schools.

In Europe, sociological analyses relating the prerequisites for justice (or, conversely, for social inequality) to moral development and just communities primarily emphasize a model in which the social structure influences the family or school interaction, and the latter, in turn, influences individual development (Bertram, 1983).

What about the discourse related to moral climate? Having participated in a Just Community meeting with Scharf in Niantic (cf. Hickey & Scharf, 1980), in community meetings in Kohlberg's Cambridge Cluster School, and in Fenton's Pittsburgh Justice Committees, I must admit that the actual discourse tends to take sometimes an "anarchic" form. Even if there are many attempts to overcome the fact that discussions are strategic and even if many attempts are undertaken to step back and to question the ideal form of the solution to a moral or value problem there is no systematic observing and training of discourse rules.

Criteria for the discourse directed to the community would be as follows:

1. Each valid argument and any valid decision must be generalized in the sense that everybody in the community has the same claim for being treated similarly in a similar situation (truth as generalization).
2. Once a rule or a value is accepted it becomes a part of every community member's life; failure to live up to the rule and sanctions for failure must be openly regulated.
3. The whole system of moral rules and values must be analyzed and checked out from time to time. Through this discourse-based analysis the participants become aware of their own relation to the whole community system.

This community approach may further be clarified by examining the formulation of its goals and aims. The teacher should stimulate the ability to:

1. create a climate of mutual trust and remove behavior discrepancies;
2. determine behavioral rules that facilitate the moral discourse;
3. take responsibility for the class or the group;
4. initiate moral norms for the group and set sanctions;
5. enter into a contract and follow it;
6. respect moral norms in other groups, without relinquishing one's own principles.

The feasibility of a discourse aimed at shared norms depends on the realization of each of these six goals. A Just Community is not by itself a guarantee to achieve them. Teachers should consciously first introduce the discourse as a principle and then change the structure of their classroom or of their school. Mosher's Just Community is a research project; if there are constraints to such projects, educators should begin with the discourse in their own interactional field as the frame for making a community more just.

Discourse Directed to the Analysis of Moral Values and of Value-Related Texts and Curricula in Literature, Politics, and Religion

Young men and women of all ages should be given information about personal and social value systems. First, they have to analyze their own values and the value systems of peers, families, schools, and working places in their society. Second, they must examine the value systems in the literature, history, and politics of foreign cultures. This examination might involve materials that are classically collected for many moral education curricula. Some typical methods are meaning analysis of literature, direct teaching, and values clarification; intended results: imitation of and identification with ideal characters, internalization of values.

Let us begin with the second step because it is traditional in European schools. The opinion has been put forward (Habermas, 1982a) that a moral theory like Kohlberg's helps the teacher

> to structure the presentation of his subject matter more clearly, to understand students' responses, and moreover to guide classroom discussion, e.g. on dramas like Kleist's "Prinz von Homburg" or Brecht's "Kaukasischer Kreidekreis" or on Napoleon's "Code Civil", The American Civil War, Rise and Fall of the Weimar Democracy etc. The teacher would learn how to steer discussions of these topics in a way that, from a structural point of view, the moral implications of established subject-matters would come out more clearly. (p. 2)

However, these texts are not only used for stimulating moral development, but also for working out a moral point of view (cf. Baier, 1958) and the moral implications in decisive situations. To acquire moral knowledge is, in this case, an underlying goal. Among other things, the student should acquire the abilities to:

1. determine the moral standpoint in texts (moralization);
2. understand the structure of the moral action (intention, rule system, rule application, decision consequences, etc.);
3. realize that individuals apply justice norms differently;
4. know one's own moral values;
5. determine the model character of moral decision-making situations.

Working with texts from literature has two implications: First, one has to demonstrate that the writings have no status in themselves but gain significance through the particular receptions and interpretations. This is the dimension of *understanding* or hermeneutics (Kreft, 1982). Second, this approach implies a curriculum in morals that is linked to social studies, political education, history, religious education, and counseling. This is the dimension of *choosing* contents by consensus and the notion that content matter has an educational effect

(Fenton, 1975). If one looks for an effective curriculum in Europe, one realizes that there are many textbooks, teaching aids, and curricula in ethics, but hardly any empirical evaluation. Let us take as an example the volumes *Materialien zur Sozialkunde* (*Classroom material for social studies*) (Gamma et al., 1979–1980). This material was collected with great effort. A teacher's guide was prepared and proposals for didactical methods made. But the effects/results were never evaluated by research. Why is this so? One reason, but not the only one, consists in the fact that moral education in the European context is always situated in the neighborhood of philosophy and hermeneutics, or of the so-called humanistic approach to pedagogy (*Geisteswissenschaftliche Pädagogik*). Starting with Dilthey at the turn of the century, we have until today (i.e., Terhart, 1978, 1982, 1984; Oevermann, 1983; Zedler, 1983) a so-called interpretative stream in education with its background in "understanding" as philosophy. In the U.S.A. and Canada there also exist many textbooks and student materials in social studies (e.g., Fenton's collection of social studies material since 1967; Sprinthall, 1973, etc.). But there is empirical evaluation too. A good example for content-oriented work is the curriculum "Facing History and Ourselves" developed by a dedicated group of educators in the Brookline (Massachusetts) schools. One part of their work deals with the integration of a Holocaust unit into the curriculum (Stern-Strom, 1981). The project evaluation done by Lieberman (1981) focused on the assessment of interpersonal understanding and on the understanding of the content of the Holocaust curriculum, on the sense of locus of control, on the self-concept, and on other attitudes. Furthermore, changes in moral cognitions were analyzed through student journals (Bardige, 1981).

At Brookline, discourse was directed toward "objective" material and, with reference to the content of this material, correct versus incorrect actions were analyzed, presented, and discussed. The thinking and discussion elucidated the autonomy of moral acts realized by others in political, historical, literary, and other situations. (Other examples for evaluation work are Beck, Hersh, & Sullivan, 1978; Beck, Boyd, & Sullivan, 1978; Fenton, Colby, & Speicher-Dubin, 1974; Fenton, 1978.) Lieberman's evaluation of the Brookline work distinguished clearly the measurements of interpersonal understanding scores from the measurement of students correctly answering each item on the content test.

The problem with content-oriented curricula material lies in the confusing connection between (e.g., for political education) political aims, morality aims, and psychological aims (moral competence). How can moral and value education be integrated into political education if there is no understanding on an ordinary language level? Vine (1983) states:

> In the study of morality, as with other aspects of human activity, the sole task of biological and social scientists has traditionally been seen as establishing contingent and "value-free" empirical facts about how and why people come to feel, think, and behave as they do. By contrast, philosophers and moralists have assumed responsibility for elucidating the meanings of moral concepts, for specifying criteria of adequacy for alternative conceptions of morality, and for seeking to establish whether some moral ideals are objectively superior to others. But recently such comfortable doctrines and divisions of labour have increasingly come under attack. (p. 19)

With reference to political thinking, questions of ideology and morality, traditional values and morality, privacy and morality, bureaucracy and morality have to be treated under both aspects mentioned by Vine (see also Wilson & Schochet, 1980). Thus the discourse is a coordination procedure in which political life is rationally differentiated through the eyes of morality. A good European example is the moral political education concept by Hagemann, Heidbrink, and Schneider (1982), in which actual political decisions are analyzed in documents. In working with statements from newspapers and television, students learned to differentiate between consensus-oriented and success-oriented actions (see also Nipkow, 1981 and Stachel, 1982). An excellent American example for this approach is S. R. Parr's (1982) book entitled *The Moral of the Story: Literature, Values, and American Education*. Parr presents a special kind of educational device: Students are informed a priori about the value system in a given text. According to Parr:

Nathaniel Hawthorne's "The Scarlet Letter" depends upon the reader's understanding of two very different value systems: the sort of absolute moral code that New England Puritans in the seventeenth century embraced unhesitatingly and a more relativistic contemporary approach to morality in which the individual substitutes personal judgment for that of the church and community. It is in the tension between these two value systems that much of the drama of "The Scarlett Letter" lies. (p. 26)

Questions aimed at investigating the text in a shared analysis stimulate the subsequent moral discourse. The giving of information about the moral device helps to initiate and to shape the free expression of opinion.

Moral discourse, which is directed towards the analysis of actual value and moral situations through literary and historical (political) texts, depends on the following conditions:

1. There is a meaning ("objective" truth) that must be found through an interpretative analysis. No interpretation can be submitted to the class without giving the students the opportunity to participate in the truth-finding process. "Objective" means a result of an exhaustive analysis of possibilities in the texts or value systems.
2. There is a coordination concerning interpretative elements generated by other students in order to reach mutual understanding.
3. There is a content which has to be chosen, and the choice and sequence must be justified in front of the class.
4. There is an intention to present good examples in texts, but to present good examples means also to present the impact of virtues, as in the dialogue between Meno and Socrates. In this way the child sees that his or her notion of the "good" is a priori; it is in the beginning of the discussion one and the same notion of the good of others with whom he or she is bound up in the human community.
5. There must be an open understanding of texts without claiming a unilateral interpretation. Although the value systems can be criticized from a universality perspective, the person's integrity must be protected.

In this sense, dealing with examples does not mean inculcating virtues. Rather it means participating in an exhaustive analysis and pointing out the incompatibilities between the text's and one's own value system. After analyzing a given value system, a group must step back and each person must present his or her own point of view, must fully participate, and must refer to different claims and coordinate others' points of view with his or her own. This is what the word "understanding" means.

We mentioned that an important step is the educational process of analyzing the personal value system as well as that of the family, peer group, workplace and so on. For this purpose, a series of models like the values clarification concept have been developed. These models help people to become aware of their own values. The value analysis model deals with gathering and weighting the facts involved in a value judgment. The consideration model is designed to reduce suspicion, worry, defensiveness, hostility, and anxiety by instilling the values of significant people around us (cf. Hersh et al., 1980). The basic idea of the values clarification model (Harmin, 1974; Kirschenbaum, 1977; Raths et al., 1966; Simon et al., 1972), a very well known and often used model, is that people reach a conclusion about their values through an educational evaluating process. If this process does not take place, students "exhibit tendencies to be apathetic, flighty, uncertain, inconsistent, drifting, overconforming, overdissenting, and role playing" (Hersh et al., 1980, p. 76). If they learn to clarify their values they "most often exhibit the qualities of being positive, purposeful, enthusiastic, proud, and consistent" (p. 76). The authors have developed a series of written exercises (Simon et al., 1972). Their methods are moralization, modeling, laissez-faire, and teaching a how-to-live value process. The actions under investigation are thinking, feeling, deciding, communicating, and justifying. One experimental study (McKenzie, 1974, pp. 47–52) demonstrated that students who treated law cases with values clarification strategies showed "higher" justice concepts than a control group. Criticisms of this approach revolve around the relativity of claimed values, the relative lack of research, use of inculcation, and the lack of a distinction between moral and nonmoral matters and between moral and values education (see Leming, 1981; Lockwood, 1976; Stewart, 1976). In Europe only the model of McPhail deals with the analysis of value and norms underlying situations and systems that the students experience; its focus, however, is the learning of care.

The clarification of values at first sight seems an ideal form of discourse. Exercises are designed to generate consciousness about one's own value system. But to return to the description of moral discourse, values clarification does not induce a search for consensus and does not bring to bear the power of truly moral interaction. Indeed, considering the emphasis of truthfulness in values clarification, the lack of stress on truth and rightness makes morality little more than a part of the domain of aesthetic judgment. This kind of judgment is not assessed by the participants — it is only invoked; claims are made only on a private level without discussing validity claims seriously. Harrison (1976, p. 24) states: "Discussion is not recommended as a frequent activity. Raths takes the position that discussion too often leads to heated argument, partiality, overly strong influence of the group, dominance by a minority, dominance by extrinsic motives, and is to be treated warily for these reasons." Thus, there is a threefold absence of real discourse in values clarification: (a) the absence of the will to generate a common solution; (b) the absence of claims to truth and rightness; (c) the absence of a distinction between morality as a generalizable system of norms and a private aesthetic taste. The reproduction of communicative actions could be built into the values clarification model if the rationality of discourse as a means for the differentiation of the life world were considered.

Values clarification and working with texts in connection with political education, social studies, history, and so forth have the same core notion of "understanding" (hermeneutics). But both types of educational streams have to be linked to consensus-oriented action "and the implicit commitment to resolve counter claims by the power of the better argument" (Furth, 1983, p. 184).

Discourse Oriented Towards One's Own Change (Coping, Defending with Moral Values)

Little work has been done on this element of discourse which refers to a communicative "metareflection" on one's own moral reflecting and one's own moral growth (i.e., the kinds of change and trajectories of transformations that have occurred to me and the kind of psychological problems I have encountered). In the psychoanalytic tradition, researchers (Broughton, 1983; Fowler, 1980, 1981; Kegan, 1982; Noam, 1979; Noam & Kegan, 1982; Noam, Kohlberg, & Snarey, 1983) have analyzed the levels of reflection about the self and interactions, and about the quality of self-observation. Each level adds new reflection capacities, capacities that also bring about new possibilities of distortions and pathological forms of problem solving. Each level (Haan, 1977; Doobert & Nunner-Winkler, 1975, 1978) also implies new coping and defense strategies and thus new regulatory structures of the self (Edelstein & Noam, 1982). There is, however, always a relation to early childhood experiences (Doebert & Nunner-Winkler, 1983), which perturbs the judging of values and moral claims.

Three systems help to assess the self in this developmental sense: (a) the development through stages of social interaction and the making of social meaning, (b) the life phases according to Erikson (1959), and (c) the type of psychological reaction such as coping or defense. Edelstein and Noam (1982) believe that adolescents

> tend to neglect the distinction between theoretical and practical discourses. Since theoretical discourses are ... well accommodated by formal operatory structures, it is contexts of practical discourses (i.e., interpersonal conflicts involving the maintenance or disruption of communication) that lead to awareness of the insufficiency or inappropriateness of the logical formalism for maintaining the communicative system. Practical discourses thus produce the cognitive–affective dynamics required for a transition beyond the prevailing structure. (p. 412)

But Edelstein and Noam do not discuss the educational options for implementing a discourse that helps adolescents overcome the self's obligation to be caught either in rationally focused problem solving or in the pragmatics of a concrete action. The stimulation of a so-called "metalogic" of communication in which metarules help to resolve this contradiction could be a first pedagogical step. Simple discourses about disparities of view could be another one. Thus, in one of our treatment studies (Oser & Schlaefli, 1983) we worked with apprentices for one week. At the end of each day, the participants discussed their own change of values, their own transformation process, the acceptance or rejection of crises, and the quality of their own discourse. The results show that 96% of the participants thought that they were better able to discuss, 96% thought that they listened better to other people, 95% thought that they were more thoroughly reflective in their decisions, and 90% thought they were able to present their opinion with less hesitation. These data do not reflect the actual, objective mechanism that led to changes, but rather a subjective, process-oriented quantitative abstraction of the stimulating factors.

The psychoanalytic approach to reflections on personal transformation helps to use the discourse to protect the self's integrity in the face of moral reality. The defensive denial of responsibility, distortions of moral growth, and neutralizations of moral acts require a regulatory self-system which is built up by this metadiscourse. And thus, the psychoanalytic approach seems promising for further research.

With regard to metareflections, the characteristics of the discourse are:

1. The "truth" is evaluated against each person's self-regulatory system and directed to the discourse itself. We could label this "communicative truth" or "developmental truth".
2. Self-directed questions are: "What was I before?" and "How do I see the transformation of my own personality after a certain period of time or of discourse?"
3. Self-evaluative questions could be: "Can I accept my change?" "Do I refer to the change of the community?" "Does the discourse fulfill the claims made before the transformation process?"

The goals of discourse oriented toward self-change are:

1. to determine one's own moral thinking;
2. to recognize where one exhibits defense strategies in discussing matters of morality;
3. to be aware of one's style of moral argumentation;
4. to see how and why one changes one's moral arguments;
5. to analyze the moral discourse of one's group in a process-oriented way.

Such goals are not easy to reach, and evaluation of this element is extremely difficult because of the lack of appropriate data. Edelstein and Noam (1982) conclude:

> Adequacy judgments thus, in fact, entail the reconciliation of the two strands of moral reasoning, discursive idealizations and responsibility judgments. ... This reconciliation presupposes a mature self capable of interacting with other selves under the equally commanding imperatives of truth and interaction. The imperative of truth precludes the acceptance, in moral reasoning, of distortion in the service of the maintenance of interaction; the imperative of communication precludes the elimination of responsibility at the expense of truth. (p. 420)

Discourse Oriented Towards Theoretical Moral Knowledge

When information about moral philosophy or moral psychology is given in an educational situation, it can be discussed in the form of a moral discourse. This information is not given in the service of more knowledge but rather to stimulate a reconstructive thinking which enables people to deal with moral problems from a theoretical perspective. So in the philosophical domain one must study not only isolated problems (such as moral norm justifications, ethical relativism, utilitarianism, hedonism, universal principles of justice, free will and responsibility, autonomy and moral obligation, naturalistic fallacy in ethics, truth and ethics, etc.) but also schools and models of practical philosophy. In the domain of psychology and sociology of morality, the pedagogical concepts of theorists such as Durkheim, Piaget, Kohlberg, Hare, and Peters should be discussed.

Psychological and philosophical thinking have to be evaluated truthfully by students; their acceptance depends on the truth and rightness of rational arguments and on the applicability of these arguments to the person's life world. Discourse becomes the interactional instrument to develop critical competences. Thus the question is: What are students doing communicatively with the subject matter? Bok (1976) points out that instructors

> will be less concerned with presenting solutions than with carrying on an active discussion in an effort to encourage students to perceive ethical issues, wrestle with the competing arguments, discover the weaknesses in their own position, and ultimately reach thoughtful reasoned conclusions. ... With the help of carefully selected readings, students can then develop their capacity for moral reasoning by learning to sort out all of the arguments that bear upon moral problems. (p. 28)

These arguments can then be applied to the formation of certain capabilities (Bok, 1976, p. 28):

1. the capability to apply theories of moral philosophy and moral psychology to moral situations;
2. the capability to differentiate between moral and nonmoral conflict-solving theories;
3. the capability to apply moral justification procedures;
4. the capability to estimate the proper judgment within a genetically structured statement;
5. the capability to recognize the relation of moral norms, laws and principles in concrete situations;
6. the capability to develop a critical stance toward theories in general and authoritarian or unjust laws.

Such aims have been proposed for a long time, especially in the European tradition. Books such as *Principles of Ethics* by P. W. Taylor (1975) have introduced sample problems for promoting moral discussion. *Das Sokratische Gespräch* (Heckmann, 1971) intentionally stimulates the growth of the capabilities mentioned. In systematic political teaching (Hagemann 1982; Spang, 1984; Weinreich-Haste, & Locke; 1983; all in Europe) the testing of ideological positions and their moral-philosophical relevance is included as a communicative part of the instruction. A further aim is to develop a critical stance toward authoritarian or unjust moral laws. These capabilities need to be extended in the following sense: Let us say that students were informed about the developmental theory of Kohlberg. As a result, they use it as a psychological concept as well as to control and to estimate their judgment in a dilemma discourse. Evans' (1982) interesting study—one of the few direct studies in this field—found no influence of knowledge about moral psychological theory on the stages of moral development. Although this study contradicts our hypothesis, other studies—even when they did not result in increases of moral judgment stages—did report that in following such programs students felt less interactional conflict and more mutual understanding. Participants expressed the feeling that this was due to the fact that the intervention had included knowledge about the theory of moral development and meta-reflection, allowing for the measuring of one's own judgments against this theory (Oser, 1985).

In Germany, Regenbogen (1983a, 1983b) has developed a concept of "theory learning." Students learn a philosophical theory and try to apply it to different concrete situations. The author bases this learning process on each student's subjective theory, which he suggests is related to a stage of development (Stage 1: distributive justice; Stage 2: commutative justice; Stage 3: equality and equity; Stage 4: social system concept; Stage 5: norms, rights, duties in equilibration). Regenbogen demonstrates how a subject proceeds from the *justitia particularis* to the *justitia universalis*. The main problem is to explain how a preconventional or a conventional person is able to learn a postconventional theory, for instance, the Rawlsian Theory of Justice, and what happens to this theory if a person on a lower stage applies it. Regenbogen found that people on a preconventional level use theories to communicate their points of view, whereas Stage 4 persons apply philosophical theories as a means for justification, for criticism, and for reaching a consensus. Only Stage 5 persons use a philosophical theory according to its genuine criteria and for becoming clear about a moral or a value problem (cf. also Boyce and Jensen, 1978).

Oser & Schlaefli (1985), in their work with apprentices, also used information about Kohlberg's stage theory. Students were introduced inductively (with personal examples) to the dimensions of the different stages and to the stage hierarchy. Two conclusions were drawn: First, there was not much influence of theory learning on progress regarding moral sensitivity, moral stage, moral role taking, and value hierarchy. Second, as Figure 32.1 demonstrates (see also Schlaefli, 1984, p. 219), students believed they had acquired a good comprehension of the stages, but could not describe higher stages adequately, and determined their own stages (91% of the apprentices were on Stage 2, 2 1/2, or 3) less clearly than the lower or the higher stages. These results help us to understand why theory learning is a difficult matter, why in fact only the generative process of stage acquisition guarantees a reliable theoretical knowledge, and why theory learning is effective only for subjects who have already attained the higher stages.

In England, Wilson (1979, 1980) and his colleagues distinguish between (a) the rules and concepts required for a basic form of moral reasoning, and (b) getting persons to prefer to use them. Wilson believes that the "moral logic" can be learned. Knowing a rule, identifying and using the rule, and why the rule

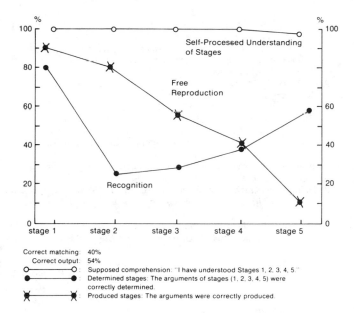

Fig. 32.1. Supposed versus "true" comprehension of the stages of argumentation. Graph shows experimental subjects' estimated percentage proportions of supposed understanding of stages, percentage proportions of correct recognition of stage items, and percentage proportions of correct free stage reproductions.

Note. From "But It Does Move: The Difficulty of Gradual Change in Moral Development" (p. 289) by F. Oser and A. Schlaefli. In M. W. Berkowitz & F. Oser (Eds.), *Moral Education: Theory and Application.* Hillsdale, NJ: Erlbaum. Copyright 1985 by Lawrence Erlbaum Associates. Reprinted by permission.

holds can be learned by philosophical teaching and are not a matter of Kohlbergian stage structure. Normative logic can be learned as a subject matter in itself. Thus "progress in moral education depends chiefly on the rejection of fantasy. The philosophical basis must be understood: It involves (a) a non-partisan approach, and (b) a grasp of moral methodology—we are to show pupils *how to get* the right answers" (1979, p. 3). So I understand Wilson's hypothesis to suggest that being able to "think" morally is a prerequisite for being able to participate in a moral discourse.

The main problem with this last type of moral educational discourse is its evaluation. In general only philosophical or psychological *knowledge* is measured, not the more important aims of this discourse element. The lack of measurement instruments relates to the fact that empirical studies are scarce and conclusions often speculative.

The form of this discourse is especially determined by these elements:

1. the objective and structured system of moral thought which should be reconstructed in a first common step (functional truth);
2. a set of theoretical assertions, applied to examples that elucidate the moral, philosophical, and psychological theories;

3. a critical attitude toward weaknesses in these systems and the development of this critical capacity;
4. an interactional discipline not based on the teacher–student relationship, but rather on the students' mutual responsibility.

Conclusions

In the first section we developed a general program of discourse pedagogy. In the second section we showed how the discourse concept could be applied to the seven elements of moral education. The seven elements served, on the one hand, to illustrate how teachers and students encounter the moral domain, and on the other hand, to present moral educational models. We have demonstrated that moral discourse enables the student to weigh against each other the many two-sided, complementary aspects of morality needed to transform the Janus situation into a balanced and mature moral identity. Because trust in the democratizing effect of school education has been weakened despite the school reforms of the last 2 decades, and because "individual impressions nourished the suspicion that the organization and 'hidden curriculum' of our schools may be inadequate for, or even adverse to, fostering democratic competence and behavior" (Lind, 1984, p. 6), there is a need to train educators in discourse pedagogy. Such discourse is the opposite of a hidden curriculum, and the opposite of an inculcation. I do not mean to imply that modeling would be impossible in moral education. The pupil has to learn to generate rational arguments, and so to practice morality. This learning is a process of progressive differentiation; students must learn to justify their actions without time pressures and without being forced to act morally under uncontrolled social pressure within a positive educational climate. Moreover, the model of moral discourse pedagogy is holistic; shared activity enables a student to develop morally. Because shared actions are consensus oriented, moral discourse forces every participant—as soon as he or she agrees to participate openly in real moral issues—to balance what we called personal morality (moral sense) with societal morality (moral consensus).

The relationship between moral discourse and elements of moral education has not been studied empirically. We need studies of the amount and quality of discourse in classrooms or families, of the relationship between discourse and other types of elements of moral education and of discourse in connection with moral educational approaches in various ages. In addition, models of social interaction like Argyris and Schoen's (1977) "theory in practice," which consists of an important distinction between ineffective and effective ideal participational systems, should be analyzed systematically in light of discourse theory.

My last thought in this paper is normative and relates to Purpel and Ryan's notion that moral education is a vast landscape of which a great part is a minefield, situated in a territory "where sages fear to tread" (Purpel & Ryan, 1975, pp. 659–662). The inescapable reality is that the school setting is always a moral enterprise; the inescapable fact is that social and political life is filled with moral content, and that history encompasses millions of moral decisions with which we as educators have to deal, not only as scientists but also as people.

This burden stands against the claim that all education should be value free (Phillips, 1979, p. 52). If we introduce moral discourse as a fundamental source of critical thinking, as a control of interactional logic, and as a motor for generating a coordination of argumentative elements, then neither inculcation nor value-free didactical teaching is acceptable. Moral discourse sets up an interaction in which teachers *and* students need to argue, and to generate by argumentation the "meta-goal" "that not all values can be reduced to preferences, that there are objective criteria on which some values really are better than others, and especially that some kinds of values are our best way of dealing with our interpersonal differences on such matters" (Boyd & Bogdan, 1984, p. 300). Such discourse implies confidence in human interactional reasoning that tends toward universal liberating morality. Thus discourse is not only related to actions, but it is an action itself.

I believe that societal morality (consensus) and personal morality (sense) *must* conflict with each other in order to make a person autonomous and, at the same time, to change society. Even if individuals promulgate a moral code of conduct and even if a society has hidden expectations for behavior that are consistent with such codes (Mehlinger, 1984, p. 189), universal theories of moral development claim a moral autonomy. The pressure towards moral conformity and the cultivation of moral autonomy contribute to the coordination and balancing of both. Science is silent on this issue. We do not know systematically under which circumstances society inhibits personal development; and we know little about the possibility of personal autonomy destroying societal moral functioning.

In conclusion, I would like to emphasize what was said in the beginning. Actually we do judge on moral issues, we do set moral rules and try to apply them; we do act morally; we do care about others and have empathetic feelings; we do defend ourselves against others' claims; educators do use examples from moral literature, film, politics, and history; and we do apply theoretical moral knowledge to concrete situations. But much work is needed to integrate these different moral discourse elements, considering differences in ages, schools, and classes. Much research has been done, but unfortunately, not enough upon which to base a comprehensive frame of moral education. To be able to teach how to solve a real moral problem, for example the integration of foreign workers in Switzerland and Germany or racial desegregation in the U.S., all seven discourse elements have to be incorporated within an educational program. With these difficult problems on our hands, we expect the Janus door to remain open.

REFERENCES

Aebli, H. (1980). *Denken, das Ordnen des Tuns: Bd. I. Kognitive Aspekte der Handlungstheorie.* Stuttgart: Klett.

Aebli, H. (1981). *Denken, das Ordnen des Tuns: Bd. II. Denkprozesse.* Stuttgart: Klett.

Althof, W. (1984). Moralerziehung in der Schule: Theorie und Praxis. Ein Literaturbericht. In A. Regenbogen, (Ed.), *Moral und Politik—Soziales Bewusstsein als Lernprozess* (pp. 148–212). Köln: Pahl-Rugenstein.

Anderson, C. S. (1982). The search for school climate: A review of the research. *Review of Educational Research 52*(3), 368–420.

Anderson, J. R. (1976). *Language, memory, and thought.* Hillsdale, NJ: Erlbaum.

Arbuthnot, J. B., & Faust, D. (1981). *Teaching moral reasoning: Theory and practice.* New York: Harper & Row.

Argyris, C., & Schoen, D. A. (1977). *Organizational learning: A theory of action and perspective.* Unpublished manuscript, Harvard University, Cambridge, MA.

Aron, I. (1977). Moral philosophy and moral education: A critique of Kohlberg's theory. *School Review, 85*(2), 197–217.

Aron, I. (1980). Moral education: The formalist tradition and the Deweyan alternative. In B. Munsey (Ed.), *Moral development, moral education, and Kohlberg: Basic issues in philosophy, religion, and education* (pp. 401–423). Birmingham, AL: Religious Education Press.

Attfield, D. G. (1978). Problems with virtues. *Journal of Moral Education, 7,* 75–80.

Aufenanger, S., Garz, D., & Zutavern, M. (Eds.). (1981). *Erziehung zur Gerechtigkeit: Unterrichtspraxis nach Lawrence Kohlberg.* München: Kösel.

Baier, K. (1958). *The moral point of view.* Ithaca, NY. [*Der Standpunkt der Moral: Eine rationale Grundlegung der Ethik.* Düsseldorf: Patmos, 1974]

Bardige, B. (1981). Facing history and ourselves: Tracing development through analysis of student journals. *Moral Education Forum, 6*(2), 42–48.

Beck, C. (1983). *Values and living: Learning materials for Grades 7 and 8.* Toronto: OISE Press.

Beck, C., Hersh, R., & Sullivan, E. (1978). *The moral education project (Year 4): 1975–76.* Toronto: The Minister of Education (Ontario) and Ontario Institute for Studies in Education.

Beck, C., Boyd, D., & Sullivan, E. (1978). *The moral education project (Year 5): Curriculum and pedagogy for reflective values education: Final report 1976–77.* Toronto: The Minister of Education (Ontario) and Ontario Institute for Studies in Education.

Berger, P. L. (1980). *The heretical imperative: Contemporary possibilities of religious affirmation.* New York: Anchor Press.

Berkowitz, M. W. (1985). The role of discussion in moral education. In M. W. Berkowitz, & F. Oser (Eds.), *Moral education: Theory and application.* (pp. 197–218). Hillsdale, NJ: Erlbaum.

Berkowitz, M. W., & Gibbs, J. C. (1983). Measuring the developmental features of moral discussion. In: *Merrill–Palmer Quarterly, 29,* 399–410.

Berkowitz, M. W., Gibbs, J. C., & Broughton, J. M. (1980). The relation of moral judgment stage disparity to developmental effects of peer dialogues. *Merrill–Palmer Quarterly, 26*(4), 341–357.

Bertram, H. (1978). *Gesellschaft, Familie und moralisches Urteil: Analysen kognitiver, familialer und sozialstruktureller Bedingungszusammenhänge moralischer Entwicklung.* Weinheim: Beltz.

Bertram, H. (1983). Ungleichheit und moralische Entwicklung. In G. Lind, H. A. Hartmann, & R. Wakenhut (Eds.), *Moralisches Urteilen und soziale Umwelt: Theoretische, methodologische und empirische Untersuchungen* (pp. 81–94). Weinheim: Beltz.

Blankertz, H. (1975). *Theorien und Modelle der Didaktik* (9th ed.). München: Juventa.

Blasi, A. (1980). Bridging moral cognition and moral action: A critical review of the literature. *Psychological Bulletin, 88,* 1–45.

Blasi, A. (1983). Moral cognition and moral action: A theoretical perspective. *Developmental Review, 3,* 178–210.

Blatt, M. (1969). *The effects of classroom discussion on the development of moral judgment.* Ph.D. dissertation, University of Chicago.

Blatt, M., & Kohlbert, L. (1975). The effects of classroom moral discussion upon children's level of moral judgment. *Journal of Moral Education, 4,* 129–161.

Bok, D. C. (1976). Can ethics be taught? *Change, 8,* 26–30.

Boyce, W. D., & Jensen, L. D. (1978). *Moral reasoning: A psychological-philosophical integration.* Lincoln, NE, and London: University of Nebraska Press.

Boyd, D. R. (1976). *Education toward principled moral judgment: An analysis of an experimental course in undergraduate moral education applying Lawrence Kohlberg's theory of moral development.* Doctoral dissertation, Harvard University, Cambridge, MA.

Boyd, D. R., & Bogdan, D. (1984). "Something" clarified, nothing of "value": A rhetorical critique of values clarification. *Educational Theory, 3*(34), 287–300.

Brophy, J. E., & Good, T. L. (1974). *Teacher-student relationships: Causes and consequences.* New York: Holt, Rinehart & Winston.

Broughton, J. M. (1978). The cognitive developmental approach to morality: A reply to Kurtines and Greif. *Journal of Moral Education, 7,* 81-96.

Broughton, J. M. (1983). The cognitive-developmental theory of adolescent self and identity. In B. Lee & G. Noam (Eds.), *Developmental approaches of the self* (pp. 215-266). New York: Plenum Press.

Brown, R., & Herrnstein, R. J. (1975). *Psychology.* Boston: Little, Brown.

Burstall, C. (1975). The Matthew effect in the classroom. *Educational Research, 21,* 19-25.

Caesar-Wolf, B. & Roethe, T. (1983). Soziologische Textinterpretation einer Interaktionssequenz zwischen Lehrer und Kind. *Bildung und Erziehung, 36,* 157-171.

Caldwell, J. A., & Berkowitz, M. W. (1985). Die Entwicklung religioesen und moralischen Denkens in einem Programm zum Religionsunterricht. In F. Oser (Ed.), *Wieviel Religion braucht der Mensch?* Zuerich: Benziger.

Candee, D. (1975). The moral psychology of Watergate. *Journal of Social Issues, 31,* 183-192.

Candee, D. (1976). Structure and choice in moral reasoning. *Journal of Personality and Social Psychology, 34,* 1293-1301.

Candee, D. (1985). Classical ethics and live patient simulations in the moral education of medical residents. In M. Berkowitz & F. Oser (Eds.), *Moral education: Theory and application.* (pp. 297-319). Hillsdale, NJ: Erlbaum.

Champagne, A. B., Klopfer, L. E., & Gunstone, R. F. (1982). Cognitive research and the design of science instruction. *Educational Psychologist, 17,* 31-53.

Cochrane, D. B., & Manley-Casimir, M. (Eds.). (1980). *Development of moral reasoning: Practical approaches.* New York: Praeger.

Colby, A., Kohlberg, L., Fenton, E., Speicher-Dubin, B., & Lieberman, M. (1977). Secondary school moral discussion programmes led by social studies teachers. *Journal of Moral Education, 6,* 90-111.

Colby, A., & Kohlberg, L. (with Gibbs, J., Candee, D., Speicher-Dubin, B., Power, C., & Lieberman, M.). (in press). *The measurement of moral judgment* (Vols. 1 & 2). New York: Cambridge University Press.

Colby, A., Kohlberg, L., Gibbs, J., & Lieberman, M. (1983). *A longitudinal study of moral judgment* (Monograph for the Society of Research in Child Development). Chicago: University of Chicago Press.

Coombs, J. (1971). Objectives of value analysis. In L. Metcalf (Ed.), *Values education: Rationale, strategies, and procedures.* Washington, DC: National Council for the Social Studies.

Damon, W. (1977). *The social world of the child.* San Francisco: Jossey-Bass.

Damon, W., & Hart, D. (1982). The development of self-understanding from infancy through adolescence. *Child Development, 53*(4), 841-864.

Dewey, J. (1944). *Democracy and education.* New York: Free Press. (Originally published 1916)

Doebert, R., & Nunner-Winkler, G. (1975). *Adoleszenzkrise und Identitätsbildung.* Frankfurt: Suhrkamp.

Doebert, R., & Nunner-Winkler, G. (1978). Performanzbestimmende Aspekte des moralischen Bewusstseins. In G. Portele (Ed.), *Sozialisation und Moral: Neuere Ansätze zur moralischen Entwicklung und Erziehung* (pp. 101-121). Weinheim: Beltz.

Doebert, R., & Nunner-Winkler, G. (1980). Jugendliche "schlagen über die Stränge": Abwehr und Bewältigungsstrategien in moralisierbaren Handlungssituationen. In L. H. Eckensberger & R. K. Silbereisen (Eds.), *Entwicklung sozialer Kognitionen: Modelle, Theorien, Methoden, Anwendung* (pp. 267-298). Stuttgart: Klett.

Doebert, R., & Nunner-Winkler, G. (1982). Formale und materiale Rollenübernahme: Das Verstehen von Selbstmordmotiven im Jugendalter. In W. Edelstein & M. Keller (Eds.), *Perspektivität und Interpretation* (pp. 320-374). Frankfurt: Suhrkamp.

Doebert, R., & Nunner-Winkler, G. (1983). Moralisches Urteilsniveau und Verlässlichkeit: Die Familie als Lernumwelt für kognitive und motivationale Aspekte des moralischen Bewusstseins in der Adoleszenz. In G. Lind, H. A. Hartmann, & R. Wakenhut (Eds.), *Moralisches Urteilen und soziale Umwelt* (pp. 95-122). Weinheim: Beltz.

Durkheim, E. (1934). *L'éducation morale.* Paris: Presse Universitaire de France.

Durkheim, E. (1961). *Moral education: A study in the theory and application of the sociology of education.* New York: Free Press.

Durkheim, E. (1973). *Erziehung, Moral und Gesellschaft.* Neuwied/Darmstadt: Luchterhand.

Eckensberger, L. H. (1983). Research on moral development in Germany. *German Journal of Psychology. 7,* 195-244.

Eckensberger, L. H., & Reinshagen, E. H. (1980) Kohlbergs Stufentheorie der Entwicklung des moralischen Urteils: Ein Versuch ihrer Reinterpretation im Bezugsrahmen handlungstheoretischer Konzepte. In L. H. Eckensberger & R. K. Silbereisen (Eds.), *Entwicklung sozialer Kognition* (pp. 65-132). Stuttgart: Klett.

Edelstein, W. (1985). Moral intervention: A skeptical note. In M. W. Berkowitz & F. Oser (Eds.), *Moral education: Theory and application.* (pp. 387-401). Hillsdale, NJ: Erlbaum.

Edelstein, W., & Noam, G. (1982). Regulatory structures of the self and 'postformal' stages in adulthood. *Human Development, 25,* 407-422.

Erikson, E. H. (1959). Identity and the life cycle. *Psychological Issues, 1*(1).

Evans, C. E. (1982). Moral stage development and knowledge of Kohlberg's theory. *Journal of Experimental Education, 51*(1), 14-17.

Fend, H. (1979). *Gesellschaftliche Bedingungen schulischer Sozialisation.* Weinheim: Beltz.

Fenton, E. (ed.). (1973-1975). *The Carnegie-Mellon social studies curriculum.* New York: Holt Rinehart & Winston.

Fenton, E. (1975). A developmental approach to civic education. In J. R. Meyer et al. (Eds.), *Values Education* (pp. 41-50). Waterloo, Ontario: Laurier.

Fenton, E. (1978). Moral education: The research findings. In P. Scharf (Ed.), *Readings in moral education* (pp. 52-59). Minneapolis: Winston Press.

Fenton, E. (1980). Moral development in the context of broad educational goals. In L. Kuhmerker, M. Mentkowski, & V. L. Erickson (Eds.), *Evaluating moral development and evaluating educational programs that have a value dimension.* New York: Character Research Press.

Fenton, E., Colby, A., & Speicher-Dubin, B. (1974). *Developing moral dilemmas for social studies classes.* Cambridge, MA: Harvard University, Moral Education and Research Foundation.

Fenton, E., & Kohlberg, L. (1976). *Moral issues in American history.* Pleasantville, NY: Guidance Associates.

Feshbach, N. D. (1978). Studies in empathic behavior in children. In B. Maher (Ed.), *Progress in Experimental Personality Research,* Vol. 8. New York: Academic Press.

Fessenden, C. L., Estrada, P., Ford, M. E., & Krumboltz, J. D. (1982). *Beyond the basics: A survey of the goals for high school students in five domains—School attitudes, interpersonal competence, moral development, health behavior, and career education.* Unpublished manuscript, Stanford University, School of Education, Project on Personal Responsibility, The Study of Stanford and the Schools. (mimeo)

Fillmore, C. J. (1971). Types of lexical information. In D. D. Sternberg & L. A. Jakobovits (Eds.), *Semantics* (pp. 370-392). Cambridge: Cambridge University Press.

Fowler, J. W. (1980). Faith and the structuring of meaning. In C. Brusselmans (Ed.), *Toward moral and religious maturity* (pp. 51-85). Morristown: Silver Burdett.

Fowler, J. W. (1981). *Stages of faith: The psychology of human development and the quest for meaning.* San Francisco: Harper & Row.

Furth, H. (1983). A developmental perspective on the societal theory of Habermas. *Human Development, 26,* 181-197.

Gage, N. L., & Giaconia, R. (1981). Teaching practices and students achievement: Causal connections. *New York University Education Quarterly 12,* 2-9.

Galbraith, R. E., & Jones, T. M. (1976). *Moral reasoning: A teaching handbook for adapting Kohlberg to the classroom.* Minneapolis, MN: Greenhaven Press.

Gamma, R., Holdener, W., Kost, F., et al. (1979–1980). *Materialien zur Sozialkunde. Bd. 1: Didaktische Grundlegung: Handlungsfeld Schule. Bd. 2: Didaktische Grundlegung: Handlungsfelder Beruf, Familie und Politik.* Basel: Beltz.

Garz, D. (1984). *Strukturgenese und Moral. Rekonstruktive Sozialisationsforschung in den Sozial- und Erziehungswissenschaften.* Opladen: Westdeutscher Verlag.

Garz, D. (1985). Urteil und Handeln — Kompetenz und Performanz — Moralität und Sittlichkeit: Ueber einige zentrale Kategorien strukturgenetischer Moralforschung. In D. Garz & F. Oser (Eds.), *Moralisches Urteil und moralisches Handeln.* Frankfurt: Suhrkamp.

Garz, D., & Kraimer, K. (Eds.). (1983). *Brauchen wir andere Forschungsmethoden?* Frankfurt: Scriptor.

Garz, D., & Oser, F. (Eds.). (1985). *Moralisches Urteil und moralisches Handeln.* Frankfurt: Suhrkamp.

Gibbs, J. C. (1979). Kohlbergs moral stage theory: A Piagetian revision. *Human Development, 22,* 89–112.

Gibbs, J. C., Widaman, K. F., & Colby, A. (1982). Construction and validation of a simplified, group-administerable equivalent to the moral judgment interview. *Child Development, 53,* 895–910.

Gilligan, C. (1977). In a different voice: Women's conceptions of self and of morality. *Harvard Educational Review, 47,* 481–517.

Gilligan, C. (1982). *In a different voice: Psychological theory and women's development.* Cambridge, MA: Harvard University Press.

Glaser, R. (1976). Components of a psychology of instruction: Toward a science of design. *Review of Educational Research, 46,* 1–24.

Glass, G. V., McGaw, B., & Smith, M. C. (1981). *Meta-analysis in social research.* Beverly Hills, CA: Sage.

Greeno, J. G. (1976). Cognitive objectives of instruction: Theory of knowledge for solving problems and answering questions. In D. Klahr (Ed.), *Cognition and instruction.* Hillsdale, NJ: Erlbaum.

Haan, N. (1977). *Coping and defending: Processes of self-environment organization.* New York: Academic Press.

Haan, N. (1978). Two moralities in action contexts. *Journal of Personality and Social Psychology, 36,* 286–305.

Haan, N., Smith, M. B., & Block, J. (1968). Moral reasoning of young adults: Political–social behavior, family background, and personality correlates. *Journal of Personality and Social Psychology, 10,* 183–201.

Habermas, J. (1972). Vorbemerkungen zu einer Theorie der kommunikativen Kompetenz. In J. Habermas & N. Luhmann. *Theorie der Gesellschaft oder Sozialtechnologie?* (pp. 101–141) Frankfurt: Suhrkamp.

Habermas, J. (1981). *Theorie des kommunikativen Handelns. Bd. 1. Handlungsrationalität und gesellschaftliche Rationalisierung. Bd. 2. Zur Kritik der funktionalistischen Vernunft.* Frankfurt: Suhrkamp.

Habermas, J. (1982a). *A communicative approach to moral theory.* Paper presented to the International Symposium on Moral Education, Fribourg.

Habermas, J. (1982b). A reply to my critics. In J. B. Thompson & D. Held (Eds.), *Habermas: Critical debates* (pp. 219–283). Cambridge: Macmillan.

Habermas, J. (1983). J. *Moralbewusstsein und kommunikatives Handeln.* Frankfurt: Suhrkamp.

Habermas, J. (1984). *Vorstudien und Ergänzungen zur Theorie des kommunikativen Handelns.* Frankfurt: Suhrkamp.

Hagemann, W., Heidbrink, H., & Schneider, M. M. (1982). *Kognition und Moralität in politischen Lernprozessen.* Opladen: Leske.

Hall, R. T. (1979). *Moral education: A handbook for teachers.* Minneapolis: Winston Press.

Harmin, M. (1974). *Making sense of our lives.* Niles, IL: Argus Communications.

Harrison, J. C. (1976). Values clarification: An appraisal. *Journal of Moral Education, 6,* 22–31.

Hartshorne, H., & May, M. A. (1928). *Studies in the nature of character. Vol. 1: Studies in deceit.* New York: Macmillan.

Hartshorne, H., May, M. A., & Maller, J. B. (1929). *Studies in the nature of character. Vol. 2: Studies in service and self-control.* New York: Macmillan.

Hartshorne, H., May, M. A., & Shuttleworth, F. K. (1930). *Studies in the nature of character. Vol. 3: Studies in the organization of character.* New York: Macmillan.

Heckmann, G. (1981). *Das sokratische Gespräch.* Hannover: Schroedel.

Helkama, K. (1979). The development of the attribution of responsibility: A critical survey of empirical research and a theoretical outline. *Research Reports* (Department of Social Psychology, University of Helsinki), *3.*

Hersh, R. H., Miller, J. P. & Fielding, G. D. (1980). *Models of moral education: An appraisal.* New York: Longman.

Hersh, R. H., Paolitto, D. P., & Reimer, J. (1979). *Promoting moral growth: From Piaget to Kohlberg.* New York: Longman.

Hickey, J. E., & Scharf, P. L. (1980). *Toward a just correctional system.* San Francisco: Jossey–Bass.

Higgins, A. (1980). Research and measurement issues in moral education interventions. In R. L. Mosher (Ed.), *Moral education: A first generation of research and development* (pp. 92–112). New York: Praeger.

Higgins, A., & Gordon, F. M. (1985). Work climate and socio-moral development in two worker-owned companies. In M. W. Berkowitz & F. Oser (Eds), *Moral education: Theory and application.* (pp. 241–268). Hillsdale, NJ: Erlbaum.

Hoeffe, O. (1974). Ethik-Unterricht in pluralistischer Gesellschaft. *Neues Hochland, 66,* 370–383.

Hoeffe, O. (1983). *Immanuel Kant.* München: Beck.

Hoeffe, O. (1985). Autonomy and generalization as moral principles. In M. W. Berkowitz & F. Oser (Eds.), *Moral education: Theory and application.* (pp. 89–107). Hillsdale, NJ: Erlbaum.

Hoffman, M. L. (1976). Empathy, role-taking, guilt, and development of altruistic motives. In T. Lickona, (Ed.), *Moral development and behavior* (pp. 124–143). New York: Holt, Rinehart & Winston.

Hoffman, M. L. (1977). Moral internalization: Current theory and research. *Advances in Experimental Psychology, 10,* 86–133.

Hoffman, M. L. (1979). Development of moral thought, feeling, and behavior. In *American Psychologist, 34,* 958–966.

Janis, I. L., & Mann, L. (1977). *Decision making: A psychological analysis of conflict, choice, and commitment.* New York: Macmillan.

Kaern, M. (1978). Vorsicht Stufe: Ein Kommentar zur Stufentheorie der moralischen Entwicklung. In G. Portele (Ed.), *Sozialisation und Moral: Neuere Ansätze zur moralischen Entwicklung und Erziehung* (pp. 81–110). Weinheim: Beltz.

Kegan, R. (1982). *The evolving self: Problem and process in human development.* Cambridge, MA: Harvard University Press.

Keller, M. (1982). Die soziale Konstitution sozialen Verstehens: Universelle und differentielle Aspekte. In W. Edelstein & M. Keller (Eds.), *Perspektivität und Interpretation: Beiträge zur Entwicklung des sozialen Verstehens* (pp. 266–285). Frankfurt: Suhrkamp.

Keller, M., & Reuss, S. (1985). The process of moral decision-making — normative and empirical conditions of participation in moral discourse. In M. Berkowitz & F. Oser (Eds.), *Moral education: Theory and application.* Hillsdale, NJ: Erlbaum, 109–123.

Kintsch, W. (1974). *The representation of meaning in memory.* Hillsdale, NJ: Erlbaum.

Kirschenbaum, H. (1977). *Advanced value clarification.* La Jolla, CA: University Associates.

Kohlberg, L. (1958). *The development of modes of moral thinking and choice in the years ten to sixteen.* Ph.D. dissertation, University of Chicago.

Kohlberg, L. (1969). Stage and sequence. The cognitive-developmental approach to socialization. In D. A. Goslin (Ed.), *Handbook of socialization theory and research* (pp. 347–480). Chicago: Rand McNally.

Kohlberg, L. (1971). Stages of moral development as a basis for moral education. In C. Beck, B. Crittenden, & E. Sullivan (Eds.), *Moral education: Interdisciplinary approaches.* Toronto: University of Toronto Press.

Kohlberg, L. (1976). Moral stages and moralization. In T. Lickona (Ed.), *Moral development and behavior: Theory, research and social issues* (pp. 2–15). New York: Holt, Rinehart & Winston.

Kohlberg, L. (1978). Foreword. In P. Scharf (Ed.), *Readings in moral education* (pp. 2–15). Oak Grove, MN: Winston Press.

Kohlberg, L. (1980). High school democracy and education for a just society. In R. L. Mosher (Ed.), *Moral education* (pp. 20–57). New York: Praeger.

Kohlberg, L. (1981a). From IS to OUGHT: How to commit the

naturalistic fallacy and get away with it in the study of moral development. In T. Mischel (Ed.), *Cognitive development and epistemology* (pp. 151–267). New York: Academic Press. [Also in: L. Kohlberg, *Essays on moral development*. (1981b). 101–189]

Kohlberg, L. (1981b). *The philosophy of moral development: Moral stages and the idea of justice* (Essays on Moral Development, Vol. 1). New York: Harper & Row.

Kohlberg, L. (1985). The just community approach to moral education in theory and practice. In M. Berkowitz & F. Oser (Eds.), *Moral education: Theory and application*. (pp. 27–87). Hillsdale, NJ: Erlbaum.

Kohlberg, L., & Candee, D. (1984). *The relationship of moral judgment to moral action*. In L. Kohlberg, *Essays on moral development. Vol. 2: The psychology of moral development* (pp. 498–581). San Francisco: Harper & Row.

Kohlberg, L., Levine, C., & Hewer, A. (1983). *Moral stages: A current formulation and a response to critics* (Contributions to Human Development 10). Basel: Karger.

Kohlberg, L., Lieberman, M., Power, C., Higgins, A., & Codding, J. (1981). Evaluating Scarsdale's "just community school" and its curriculum. Implications for the future. *Moral Education Forum* 1981, 6(4), 31–42.

Kohlberg, L., Wasserman, E., & Richardson, N. (1975). *The just community school: The theory and the Cambridge cluster school experiment*. Harvard University, Cambridge, MA: unpublished manuscript.

Krebs, D. L. (1970). Altruism — an examination of the concept and review of the literature. *Psychological Bulletin* 73(4), 258–302.

Krebs, D. L., & Rosenwald, A. (1977). Moral reasoning and moral behavior in conventional adults. *Merrill-Palmer Quarterly, 23*, 77–87.

Krebs, R., & Kohlberg, L. (1973). *Moral judgments and ego controls as determinants of resistance to cheating*. Unpublished manuscript. University of Chicago.

Kreft, J. (1982). *Moral and aesthetic development in its didactic aspect*. Paper presented to the International Symposium on Moral Education, Fribourg.

Krumboltz, I. D., Rude, S. S., Mitchell, L. K., Hamel, D. A., & Kinnier, R. (1982). Behaviors associated with "good" and "poor" outcomes in a simulated career decision. *Journal of Vocational Behavior, 2*, 349–358.

Krumboltz, J. G. (1982). Tests and guidance: What students need. In W. Schrader (Ed.), *New directions for testing and measurement: Measurement, guidance, and program improvement* (pp. 13–27). San Francisco: Jossey-Bass.

Kuhmerker, L., Mentkowski, M., & Erickson, V. L. (Eds.). (1980). *Evaluating moral development and evaluating educational programs that have a value dimension*. New York: Character Research Press.

Kurtines, W., & Greif, E. (1974). The development of moral thought: Review and evaluation of Kohlberg's approach. *Psychological Bulletin, 81*(8), 453–470.

Leming, J. S. (1981). Curricular effectiveness in moral/values education. *Journal of Moral Education, 10*(3), 147–164.

Lempert, W. (1985). Moralische Urteilsstufen und Niveaus sozialer Aggregation. Zum Verhältnis von psychischen Strukturen und sozialen Anwendungsbereichen des moralischen Bewusstseins. In F. Oser, W. Althof, D. Garz (Eds.), *Entstehung moralischer Identität*. Munich: Kindt.

Lickona, T. (1983). *Raising good children: Helping your child through the stages of moral development*. New York: Bantam.

Lickona, T. (1985). Parents as moral educators. In M. Berkowitz & F. Oser (Eds.), *Moral education: Theory and application*. (pp. 127–146). Hillsdale, NJ: Erlbaum.

Lieberman, M. (1981). Facing history and ourselves: A project evaluation. *Moral Education Forum, 6*(2), 36–41.

Lind, G. (1981). Experimental questionnaires: A new approach to personality research. In A. Kossakowski & K. Obuchowski (Eds.), *Progress in psychology of personality* (pp. 132–144). Amsterdam: North-Holland; Ost-Berlin: Deutscher Verlag der Wissenschaften.

Lind, G. (1984). *Moral competence and education in democratic society*. Final paper presented at the colloquium on conscience at Salzburg. Konstanz: Universität.

Lindsay, P. H., & Norman, D. A. (1972). *Human information processing*. New York: Academic Press.

Locke, D. (1983). Doing what comes morally. The relation between behaviour and stages of moral reasoning. *Human Development, 26*, 11–25.

Locke, D. (1980). The illusion of stage six. *Journal of Moral Education, 9*, 103–109.

Lockwood, A. L. (1976). A critical view of values clarification. In D. Purpel & K. Ryan (Eds.), *Moral education — It comes with the territory* (pp. 162–170). Berkeley, CA: McCutchan.

Lockwood, A. L. (1978). The effects of value clarification and moral development curricula on school-age subjects: A critical review of recent research. *Review of Educational Research, 48*(3), 325–364.

Loevinger, J., Wessler, R., & Redmore, C. (1970). *Measuring ego development*. San Francisco: Jossey-Bass.

MacIntyre, A. (1984). *After virtue: A study in moral theory*. Notre Dame, IN: University of Notre Dame Press.

Mauermann, L. (1978). Exemplarische Unterrichtsmodelle für die Arbeit mit Wertvorstellungen. *Pädagogische Welt, 32*, 17–23.

McCarthy, T. (1978). *The critical theory of Jürgen Habermas*. Cambridge, MIT Press.

McKenzie, G. R. (1974). A theory-based approach to inductive value clarification. *Journal of Moral Education, 1*, 47–62.

McNamee, S. (1977). Moral behaviour, moral development and motivation. *Journal of Moral Education 7*, 27–31.

McPhail, P., Ungoed-Thomas, J. R., & Chapman, H. (1975). *Learning to care*. Niles, IL: Argus Communications.

Mehlinger, H. (1984). *Place of moral values in educational programmes in depth study*. Paris: UNESCO-Papers.

Meynell, H. A. (1974). Moral education and indoctrination. *Journal of Moral Education, 4*, 17–26.

Mieth, D. (1976). Moralpädagogik zwischen Konformismus und Kreativität. Bedingungen und Ziele einer ethischen Erziehung. *Katechetische Blätter*, 34–44.

Miller, M. (1984a). *Discourse and experience*. Paper delivered at the 2nd Ringberg conference, West Germany.

Miller, M. (1984b). Zur Ontogenese des koordinierten Dissens. In W. Edelstein & J. Habermas (Eds.), *Soziale Interaktion und soziales Verstehen* (pp. 220–250). Frankfurt: Suhrkamp.

Miller, P. H., Kessel, F. S., & Flavell, J. H. (1970). Thinking about people thinking about . . .: A study of social cognitive development. *Child Development, 41*, 613–623.

Montada, L. (1980). Moralische Kompetenz: Aufbau und Aktualisierung. In L. H. Eckensberger & R. K. Silbereisen (Eds.), *Entwicklung sozialer Kognitionen* (pp. 247–266). Stuttgart: Klett.

Morrison, T. L. (1979). Classroom structure, work involvement, and social climate in elementary school classrooms. *Journal of Educational Psychology, 71*(4), 471–477.

Mosher, R. L. (Ed.), (1979). *Adolescents' development and education: A Janus knot*. Berkeley, CA: McCutchan.

Mosher, R. L. (Ed.), (1980). *Moral education. A first generation of research and development*. New York: Praeger.

Mosher, R., & Sprinthall, N. A. (1971). Psychological education: A means to promote personal development during adolescence. *The Counseling Psychologist 2*(4). 3–74.

Munsey, B. (Ed.), (1980). *Moral development, moral education and Kohlberg*. Birmingham, AL: Religious Education Press.

Mussen, P., & Eisenberg-Berg, N. (1977). *The roots of caring, sharing and helping*. San Francisco: Freeman.

Newmann, F. W. (1975). *Education for citizen action: Challenge for secondary curriculum*. Berkeley, CA: McCutchan.

Nicolayev, J., & Phillips, D. C. (1979). On assessing Kohlberg's stage theory of moral development. In D. Cochrane, C. Hamm, & A. Kazepides (Eds.), *The domain of moral education*. New York: Paulist.

Nipkow, K.-E. (1981). *Moralerziehung*. Gütersloh: Gütersloher Verlagshaus.

Nisan, M. (1985). Limited morality — A concept and its educational implications. In: M. Berkowitz & F. Oser (Eds.), *Moral education: Theory and application*. (pp. 403–420). Hillsdale, NJ: Erlbaum.

Noam, G. (1979). *Borderline psychopathology, psychoanalytic object relations theory and the structural developmental paradigm*. Unpublished manuscript, Harvard Medical School.

Noam, G. Higgins, R., & Goethals, G. (1982). Psychoanalysis as a developmental psychology. In R. Wolman (Ed.), *Handbook of developmental psychology*. Englewood Cliffs, NJ: Prentice-Hall.

Noam, G., & Kegan, R (1982). Soziale Kognition und Psychodynamik: Auf dem Wege zu einer klinischen Entwicklungspsychologie. In W. Edelstein & M. Keller (Eds.), *Perspektivität und Interpretation: Beiträge zur Entwicklung des sozialen Verstehens* (pp. 422–460). Frankfurt: Suhrkamp.

Noam, G., Kohlberg, L., & Snarey, J. (Eds.), (1983). Steps toward a model of the self. In B. Lee & G. Noam (Eds.), *Developmental approaches of the self* (pp. 59–141). New York: Plenum Press.

Nucci, L. P., & Nucci, M. S. (1982a). Children's responses to moral and social conventional transgressions in free-play settings. *Child Development, 53*, 1337–1342.

Nucci, L. P. & Nucci, M. S. (1982b). Children's social interactions in the context of moral and conventional transgressions. *Child Development, 53*, 403–412.

Oevermann, U. (1983). Hermeneutische Sinnrekonstruktion: Als Therapie und Pädagogik missverstanden, oder: Das notorische strukturtheoretische Defizit pädagogischer Wissenschaft. In D. Garz & K. Kraimer (Eds.), *Brauchen wir andere Forschungsmethoden?* (pp. 113–153). Frankfurt: Scriptor.

Oevermann, U., Allert, T., Konan, E., & Krambeck, J. (1979). Die Methodologie einer "objektiven Hermeneutik" und ihre allgemeine forschungslogische Bedeutung in den Sozialwissenschaften. In H.-G. Soeffner (Ed.), *Interpretative Verfahren in den Sozial- und Textwissenschaften* (pp. 352–434). Stuttgart: Metzler.

Oppenheimer, L. (1980). Die Beziehung zwischen rekursivem Denken und sozialer Perspektivenübernahme: Eine Entwicklungsstudie. In L. H. Eckensberger & R. K. Silbereisen (Eds.), *Entwicklung sozialer Kognitionen: Modelle, Theorien, Methoden, Anwendung* (pp. 211–228). Stuttgart: Klett.

Oser, F. (1981a). Moralische Erziehung als Intervention. *Unterrichtswissenschaft, 3*, 217–224.

Oser, F. (1981b). *Moralisches Urteil in Gruppen. Soziales Handeln—Verteilungsgerechtigkeit*. Frankfurt: Suhrkamp.

Oser, F. (1984). Cognitive stages of interaction in moral discourse. In W. M. Kurtines & J. L. Gewirtz (Eds.), *Morality, moral behavior, and moral development* (pp. 159–174). New York: Wiley.

Oser, F. (1985). Die Erziehung zu einer hoeheren Reife des religioesen Urteils. Ein Unterrichtsprojekt mit Sekundarschuelern. In F. Oser (Ed.), *Wieviel Religion braucht der Mensch?* Zuerich: Benziger.

Oser, F., & Garz, D. (1985). "Also die Annahme, dass die Welt gerecht waere, das waere sehr irrational": Eine Fallstudie. In D. Garz & F. Oser (Eds.), *Moralisches Urteil und moralisches Handeln*. Frankfurt: Suhrkamp.

Oser, F., & Schlaefli, A. (1983). *Das moralische Grenzgaengersyndrom: Eine Interventionsstudie zur Foerderung sozial-moralischer Identitaet bei Lehrlingen* (Reports on Education No. 37). Fribourg: University of Fribourg.

Oser, F., & Schlaefli, A. (1985). And it does move. In M. W. Berkowitz & F. Oser (Eds.), *Moral education: Theory and application* (pp. 269–295). Hillsdale, NJ: Erlbaum.

Paolitto, D. P. (1977). The role of the teacher in moral education. *Theory into Practice, 16*(2), 73–80.

Paolitto, D. P., & Hersch, R. H. (1976). Pedagogical implications for stimulating moral development in the classroom. In J. R. Meyer (Ed.), *Reflections on values education*. Waterloo, Ontario: Laurier.

Parr, S. R. (1982). *The moral of the story: Literature, values, and American education*. New York & London: Teachers College Press, Columbia University.

Patry, J.-L. (Ed.). (1981a). *Feldforschung: Methoden und Probleme der Sozialwissenschaften unter natürlichen Bedingungen*. Bern: Huber.

Patry, J.-L. (1981b). *Zur Validität der unabhängigen Variable in N = 1 Designs mit natürlichen Treatments*. Fribourg: Pädagogisches Institut der Universität, Arbeitsbericht.

Peters, R. S. (1975). A reply to Kohlberg. In *Phi Delta Kappan, 6*, 678.

Peters, R. S. (1982). Personales Verstehen und persönliche Beziehungen. In W. Edelstein & M. Keller (Eds.), *Subjektivität und Interpretation: Beiträge zur Entwicklung des sozialen Verstehens* (pp. 237–265). Frankfurt: Suhrkamp.

Phillips, D. Z. (1979). Is moral education really necessary? *British Journal of Educational Studies, 27*(1), 42–56.

Piaget, J. (1973). *The moral judgment of the child*. New York: Free Press. (Originally published 1932)

Pohlmann, D., & Wolf, J. (Eds.), (1982). *Moralerziehung in der Schule? Beiträge zur Entwicklung des Unterrichts: Ethik, Werte und Normen*. Göttingen: Vandenhoeck & Ruprecht.

Power, C. (1979). The moral atmosphere of the school. *Moral Education Forum, 4*(1), 9–14 (Part 1); *4*(2) 21–27 (Part 2).

Power, C. (1980). Evaluating just communities: Toward a method for assessing the moral atmosphere of the school. In L. Kuhmerker, M. Mentkowski, & V. L. Erickson (Eds.), *Evaluating moral development and evaluating educational programs that have a value dimension* (pp. 177–191). Schenectady, NY: Character Research Press.

Power, C. (1985). Democratic moral education in the large public high school. In M. W. Berkowitz & F. Oser (Eds.), *Moral education: Theory and application.* (pp. 219–238). Hillsdale, NJ: Erlbaum.

Power, C., & Reimer, J. (1978). Moral atmosphere: An educational bridge between moral judgment and action. In W. Damon (Ed.), *New directions for child development: No. 2. Moral development* (pp. 105–116). San Francisco: Jossey-Bass.

Pratt, M. W., Golding, G., & Hunter, W. J. (1983). Aging as ripening: Character and consistency of moral judgment in young, mature, and older adults. *Human Development, 26*, 277–288.

Purpel, D., & Ryan, K. (1975). Moral education: Where sages fear to tread. *Phi Delta Kappan, 56*, 659–662.

Raiffa, H. (1968). *Decision analysis*. Reading, MA: Addison-Wesley.

Raths, L. E., Harmin, M., & Simon, S. B. (1966). *Values and teaching*. Columbus, OH: Merrill.

Rawls, J. (1971). *A theory of justice*. Cambridge, MA: Belknap Press.

Regenbogen, A. (1983a). Gerechtigkeit als Lernprozess. *Osnabrücker Philosophische Schriften*, 246–322.

Regenbogen, A. (Ed.), (1983b). *Materialien: Empirische Forschungen zum Verhältnis von moralischem und politischem Bewusstsein*. Osnabrück: Universität, Fachbereich Kultur- und Geisteswissenschaften.

Regenbogen, A. (1984). Ueberlegungen zur Rationalität von moralischen Urteilen. In A. Regenbogen (Ed.), *Moral und Politik—Soziales Bewusstsein als Lernprozess* (pp. 113–122). Köln: Pahl-Rugenstein.

Reimer, J., & Power, C. (1980). Educating for a democratic community: Some unresolved dilemmas. In R. L. Mosher (Ed.), *Moral education: A first generation of research and development* (pp. 303–320). New York: Praeger.

Rest, J. R. (1979). *Development in judging moral issues*. Minneapolis, MN: University of Minnesota Press.

Rest, J. R. (1980). Basic issues in evaluating moral education programs. In L. Kuhmerker, M. Mentkowski, & V. L. Erickson (Eds.), *Evaluating moral development* (pp. 1–12). Schenectady, NY: Character Research Press.

Rest, J. R. (1983). Morality. In: J. H. Flavell & E. M. Markman (Eds.), *Handbook of child psychology. Vol. 3: Cognitive Development* (pp. 556–629). New York: Wiley.

Rest, J. R. (1984). The major components of morality. In W. M. Kurtines & J. L. Gewirtz (Eds.), *Morality, moral behavior, and moral development* (pp. 24–40). New York: Wiley.

Rest, J. R. (1985). An interdisciplinary approach to moral education. In: M. W. Berkowitz & F. Oser (Eds.), *Moral education: Theory and application* (pp. 9–25). Hillsdale, NJ: Erlbaum.

Roeders, P. (1980). Soziale Perspektivenübernahme und verbale Kommunikation. In L. H. Eckensberger & R. K. Silbereisen (Eds.), *Entwicklung sozialer Kognitionen: Modelle, Theorien, Methoden, Anwendung* (pp. 405–418). Stuttgart: Klett.

Rosen, H. (1980). *The development of sociomoral knowledge: A cognitive-structural approach*. New York: Columbia University Press.

Rosenhan, D. L. (1969). Some origins of concern for others. In P. H. Mussen et al. (Eds.), *Trends and issues in developmental psychology*. New York: Holt, Rinehart, & Winston.

Rumelhart, D. E. (1975). Notes on a schema for stories. In D. G. Bobrow & A. Collins (Eds.), *Representation and understanding* (pp. 211–236) New York: Academic Press.

Schank, R. C., & Abelson, R. P. (1977). *Scripts, plans, goals and understanding.* Hillsdale, NJ: Erlbaum.

Scharf, P. (Ed.), (1978). *Readings in moral education.* Oak Grove, MN: Winston Press.

Schlaefli, A. (1984). *Förderung der sozial-moralischen Kompetenz: Eine Interventionsstudie mit Lehrlingen.* Doctoral dissertation, University of Fribourg.

Schlaefli, A., Rest, J. R., & Thoma, S. (1984). *Does moral education improve moral judgment? A meta-analysis of intervention studies using the DIT.* (Unpublished manuscript). Minneapolis: University of Minnesota.

Schmidt, H. (1983). *Didaktik des Ethikunterrichts: Bd. 1. Grundlagen.* Stuttgart: Kohlhammer.

Schmitt, M., Dalbert, C., & Montada, L. (1983). *Interpersonale Verantwortlichkeit erwachsener Töchter ihren Müttern gegenüber: Ergebnisse der Item- und Skalenanalyse* (Bericht Nr. 23 zum Projekt "Verantwortung, Gerechtigkeit und Moral"). Universität Trier.

Schneid, K. (Ed.). (1979). *Erziehen in der Schule: Auftrag, Ziele und Methoden.* München: Oldenburg Verlag.

Schuhler, P. (1980). Effektierung von moralischen Trainingsdiskussionen. Bericht über eine empirische Untersuchung. In L. H. Eckensberger & R. K. Silbereisen (Eds.), *Entwicklung sozialer Kognitionen* (pp. 419–432). Stuttgart: Klett.

Schwartz, S. H. (1973). Normative explanations of helping behavior: A critique, proposal, and empirical test. *Journal of Experimental and Social Psychology, 9,* 349–364.

Schwartz, S. H. (1977). Normative influences on altruism. In L. Berkowitz (Ed.), *Advances in experimental social psychology* (Vol. 10). New York: Academic Press.

Selman, R. L. (1976). Social-cognitive understanding: A guide to educational and clinical practice. In T. Lickona (Ed.), *Moral development and behavior* (pp. 299–316). New York: Holt, Rinehart & Winston.

Selman, R. L. (1980). *The growth of interpersonal understanding.* New York: Academic Press.

Shavelson, R. J. (1978). *A model of teacher decision making.* Paper presented at the annual meeting of the American Educational Research Association, Toronto.

Shavelson, R. J., & Stern, P. (1981) Research on teachers' pedagogical thoughts, judgements, decisions and behavior. *Review of Educational Research, 51,* 455–498.

Shaver, J. P., & Strong, W. (1982). *Facing value decisions: Rationale-building for teachers.* New York: Teachers College Press, Columbia University.

Simon, S. B., Howe, L. W., & Kirschenbaum, H. (1972). *Values clarification: A handbook of practical strategies for teachers and students.* New York: Hart.

Simpson, E. L. (1976). A holistic approach to moral development. In T. Lickona (Ed.), *Moral development and behavior* (pp. 159–170). New York: Holt, Rinehart & Winston.

Skinn, R. L. (1980). Education in values: Acculturation and exploration. In D. Sloan (Ed.), *Education and values* (pp. 111–122). New York: Teachers College Press, Columbia University.

Smith, L. (1974). Indoctrination and intent. *Journal of Moral Education, 3,* 229–233.

Snook, I. A. (Ed.). (1972). *Concepts of indoctrination: Philosophical essays.* London: Routledge & Kegan Paul.

Spang, W. P. (1984). Moralisches und politisches Bewusstsein: Nur eine Frage des Anwendungsbereichs? In A. Regenbogen (Ed.), *Moral und Politik — Soziales Bewusstsein als Lernprozess* (pp. 51–67). Köln: Pahl-Rugenstein.

Sprinthall, N. A. (1973). A curriculum for secondary schools: Counsellors as teachers for psychological growth. *School Counsellor, 5,* 361–369.

Stachel, G. (1982). *Erfahrungen interpretieren.* Zürich: Benziger.

Stachel, G., & Mieth, D. (1978). *Ethisch handeln lernen: Zu Konzeption und Inhalt ethischer Erziehung.* Zürich: Benziger.

Staub, E. (1978). Predicting prosocial behavior: A model for specifying the nature of personality-situation and interaction. In: L. Pervin & M. Lewis (Eds.), *Internal and external determinants of behavior.* New York: Plenum.

Staub, E. (1979). *Positive social behavior and morality. Vol. 2: Socialization and development.* New York: Academic Press.

Staub, E. (1984). Steps toward a comprehensive theory of moral conduct: Goal orientation, social behavior, kindness, and cruelty. In W. M. Kurtines & J. L. Gewirtz (Eds.), *Morality, moral behavior, and moral development* (pp. 241–260). New York: Wiley.

Stewart, J. S. (1976). Problems and contradictions of values clarification. In D. Purpel & K. Ryan (Eds.), *Moral education — It comes with the territory* (pp. 136–151). Berkeley, CA: McCutchan.

Strom, M. S. (1980). Facing history and ourselves: Holocaust and human behavior. In: R. L. Mosher (Ed.), *Moral education: A first generation of research and development* (pp. 216–233). New York: Praeger.

Sullivan, P. (1980). Moral education for adolescents. In R. L. Mosher (Ed.), *Moral education: A first generation of research and development* (pp. 165–187). New York: Praeger.

Taylor, P. W. (1975). *Principles of ethics.* Encino, CA: Dickenson.

Terhart, E. (1978). *Interpretative Unterrichtsforschung.* Stuttgart: Klett.

Terhart, E. (1982). Interpretative approaches in educational research: A consideration of some theoretical issues — with particular reference to recent developments in West Germany. *Cambridge Journal of Education, 12,* 141–160.

Terhart, E. (1984). Psychologische Theorien des Lehrerhandelns. *Die Deutsche Schule, 76,* 3–18.

Thompson, J. B., & Held, D. (Eds.) (1982). *Habermas: Critical debates.* London: Macmillan.

Turiel, E. (1983). *The development of social knowledge: Morality and convention.* Cambridge: Cambridge University Press.

Turiel, E., & Rothman, G. R. (1972). The influences of reasoning on behavioral choices at different stages of moral development. *Child Development, 43,* 741–756.

Van Dijk, T. A. (1977). Semantic macro-structures and knowledge frames in discourse comprehension. In M. A. Just & P. A. Carpenter (Eds.), *Cognitive process in comprehension.* New York: Wiley.

Vine, I. (1983). The nature of moral commitments. In H. Weinreich-Haste & D. Locke (Eds.), *Morality in the making* (pp. 19–45). Chichester: John Wiley.

Weinreich-Haste, H., & Locke, D. (Eds.). (1983). *Morality in the making.* Chichester: John Wiley.

Wilson, J. (1979). Moral education: Retrospect and prospect. *Journal of Moral Education, 9,* 3–9.

Wilson, J. (1980). Understanding reasons. *Journal of Moral Education, 9,* 110–113.

Wilson, R. W., & Schochet, G. J. (Eds.). (1980). *Moral development and politics.* New York: Praeger.

Winograd, T. (1972). *Understanding natural language.* New York: Academic Press.

Zedler, P. (1983). Zur Aktualität geisteswissenschaftlicher Pädagogik. In D. Garz & K. Kraimer (Eds.), *Brauchen wir andere Forschungsmethoden?* (pp. 63–85). Frankfurt: Scriptor.

33.
Research on Teaching Social Studies

Beverly J. Armento
Georgia State University

It has been a decade since Shaver and Larkins (1973) called for a broader view of social studies research and since Van Manen (1975), going one step beyond, defined this broader view in terms of the three scholarly traditions: the empirical-analytic, interpretive, and critical sciences. Each of these three paradigms predisposes one to think about research on teaching social studies in a different way (Popkewitz & Tabachnik, 1981).

Research from an empirical-analytic perspective tends to focus on the description of correlational or causal patterns that explain social studies teaching and learning. It was this particular paradigm that dominated the social studies research referred to by Shaver and Larkins in 1973. The interpretive sciences, as well as the empirical-analytic, are concerned with description, but from this perspective the researcher focuses on gaining an understanding of how social life in classrooms is created through human action, intention, and communication. An interpretative research orientation implies examining how learners make sense of the content and experiences of instruction, or how teachers and students build meanings about themselves and social phenomena. Research from the perspective of the last of these traditions, the critical sciences, aims to make explicit the assumptions, meanings, and dynamics that underlie certain phenomena, knowledge, or ideologies. It is this orientation or goal of the critical sciences that causes them to assume a moral attitude of liberation from dominating forms of social control (Van Manen, 1975).

With the three scholarly traditions in mind, one must ask whether a broader view of social studies research indeed has been taken in the last 10 years. What appear to be the major perspectives, the problems, and the promises of research on teaching social studies? Where should efforts be directed in the future?

To answer these questions, an extensive chronological search of the professional literature data bases was conducted. This review included a computer search of ERIC resources and manual searches of *Dissertation Abstracts International* (1972–1982), *Theory and Research in Social Education* (1972–1982) and research articles in *Social Education* (1972–1982), *American Educational Research Journal, Review of Educational Research* (1972–1982), *Review of Research in Education* (1973–1983). In addition, status reports and critiques of social studies research were read (Fancett & Hawke, 1982; Fontana, 1980a, 1980b; Gross, 1972; Hertzberg, 1981; Patrick, 1982; Shaver, Davis & Helburn, 1979; Stake & Easley, 1978; Weiss, 1978; and Wiley, 1977).

Comprehensive general and topic-specific reviews of research on social studies were also surveyed (Chapin, 1974; Chapman, 1974; Ehman & Hahn, 1981; Hunkins, Ehman, Hahn, Martorella, & Tucker, 1977; Metcalf, 1963; Oswald, 1972; Shaver & Larkins, 1973; Wentworth & Lewis, 1973; and Wiley, 1977). Other citations were drawn from bibliographies or from the personal knowledge of the author.

The search for relevant theoretical and empirical work was guided by key terms commonly used in social studies education (Osborne, 1979), such as: social studies; social science; social education; citizenship education; global, economic, geographic (etc.) education; decision making; reflective inquiry; social action; and so on. Any work, theoretical or empirical in nature, that dealt with the goals of social studies or with social studies teaching–learning phenomena was read and critiqued. Omitted were content analyses of textbooks or other curricular media, curricular program evaluations, and studies on other aspects of social studies education, such as those on the adoption and diffusion of innovative programs. While valuing and moral

The author thanks reviewers Lee H. Ehman (Indiana University) and James P. Shaver (Utah State University).

development are clearly important components for most definitions of social studies, inquiries on these topics were omitted from the search and from the discussion in this chapter because another chapter in the *Handbook* is devoted to these topics.

One of the several trends that have emerged from this review of 10 years of social studies research is that an empirical-analytic orientation still seems to dominate the field; however, fundamental shifts within this type of research do appear to be occurring. These shifts follow those already made in the research on teaching mathematics and reading and have the effect of changing the psychological focus from a behavioristic to a cognitive orientation. Some interpretive work has been conducted, this mainly within the last 5 years. Research from a critical perspective has also emerged mostly within the last 5 years, with a large amount of its work being focused on theoretical issues surrounding the goals of social studies education.

This chapter is organized around these major trends. The aim of the chapter is not to review the literature in a traditional manner, but rather to examine the various ways in which issues and topics on the teaching of social studies have been studied in the last 10 years. Specific examples of research are cited for illustrative purposes; these are not intended to be exhaustive of the work in the field. The emphasis is on studies that represent emerging and promising directions.

Theoretical and Empirical Work on the Goals of Social Studies

Major philosophical and epistemological issues have marked the field of social studies education since its inception. A range of opinion exists on the basic issues of the field: the definition of the goals, the nature and role of knowledge, the scope and focus of the field, the role of the social sciences and of social issues, the appropriateness of alternative instructional methodologies, and the definition of most of the key constructs, including citizenship, decision making, reflective inquiry, and problem solving (Barr, Barth & Shermis, 1977; Hertzberg, 1981; Morrissett & Haas, 1982; Remy, 1978; Wiley, 1977).

Throughout the history of social studies reform, the central role assigned to the social studies has been that of educating citizens (Hertzberg, 1981, p. 171). Therefore, the primary concern of the social studies has tended to be defined as citizenship education and its major goals as the development of knowledge, skills, values, and social participation (Engle, 1960; Morrissett & Haas, 1982; Osborne, 1979; and Shaver, 1977). The philosophical differences existing in the field are illuminated as persons define citizenship education and the various subgoals (Foshay & Burton, 1976; Hertzberg, 1981; Shermis & Barth, 1978).

In 1977, Barr, Barth, and Shermis hypothesized that the statements people make about the purpose, methods, and content of social studies provide clues about how the field is defined. Their extensive content analysis of historical documents yielded three competing traditions: social studies taught as citizenship transmission, as social science, and as reflective inquiry. However, White's (1982) study raises questions about the validity of the three traditions. White's data indicate that a two-tradition pattern — citizenship transmission and a combination of reflective inquiry/social science — may better describe the way teachers actually view the social studies field.

Accurate descriptions of the field, however, will not substitute for what is needed: a normative conception and justification of what is important in social studies education. A normative theory of citizenship education that clarifies the conceptual components of the citizenship construct would enable hypothesis development and empirical testing of the model and would also serve as a standard for judging practical decisions.

While a comprehensive theory around which consensus could build has not been developed in the last 10 years, there have been numerous construct and model-building efforts. Stentz and Lambert (1977) refined the definition and measurement of the political efficacy construct, drawing upon related theoretical and empirical work. Guyton (1982) proposed and tested a causal model delineating the relationship of critical thinking with political participation, as mediated by self-esteem, personal control, political efficacy, and democratic attitudes. Guyton's findings suggest that critical thinking has indirect positive effects on orientations toward and on actual political participation. This linking of two major aims of social studies education has important theoretical and practical implications.

Major contributions to social studies theory building and to issue analysis have also been made through the application of the critical sciences (Cherryholmes, 1978, 1980, 1982; Giroux, 1982; Popkewitz, 1972, 1977a, 1977b; and Popkewitz, Tabachnik, & Zeichner, 1979). Here, the assumptions that underlie many current practices in social studies education are examined, normative positions are developed, and implications deriving from the alternatives are proposed.

The current practice of teaching the structures of the social science disciplines and of presenting knowledge as predetermined sets of rules, standards, and ideas, for example, is critiqued by Popkewitz (1972, 1977a, 1977b); he presents inquiry as a constructed social system in place of the view of knowledge as reproduced ideas. Cherryholmes (1980) has applied the critical theory of Habermas (1968) to the development of the definition of citizenship education as decision making. Decision making can be the "heart of the social studies" (Engle, 1960) only if ongoing, unconstrained critical discourse is at the heart of the social studies, argues Cherryholmes.

The sort of work that Popkewitz and Cherryholmes have done in the application of the critical sciences to theory building in the social studies represents a dramatic departure from prior rationale building efforts based on the ideas of such leaders as Dewey or Bruner. The various studies cited in this section represent sophisticated efforts to develop scientific knowledge about the constructs commonly used by social studies educators. The field seriously needs more work along these lines.

The Traditional Research Focus: The Teacher and Instruction

A large gap exists between the theoretical conceptualization of the goals of social studies education and the realization of those goals in day-to-day school practices. Social studies classrooms of today are little different from those of 20 years ago, despite the expenditure of millions of dollars and the involvement of many creative minds in the development of innovative curricular materials (Stake & Easley, 1978). Today, as yesterday, little attention is given to the development of systematic modes of reasoning (Fancett & Hawke, 1982). Lecture and discussion are still the most frequently used strategies in social studies classrooms, with teacher talk dominating; and the conventional textbook remains the primary instructional tool. Societal issues and controversial topics are on few classroom agendas. Not surprisingly, then, students tend to be generally apathetic toward social studies, describing their courses as boring because facts rather than ideas are emphasized (Patrick, 1982; Shaver, Davis, & Helburn, 1979; Stake & Easley, 1978; Weiss, 1978).

It is encouraging to note that Stake and Easley (1978) found teachers to be generally open to alternative teaching styles and to assistance with pedagogic problems. Would social studies teachers find pedagogic insights if they surveyed the research on the teaching of social studies? Most contemporary reviewers and critics would respond negatively and would add to this their concerns about the focus of most of the research on isolated and minor questions, the atheoretical nature of much of the current work, and the lack of accumulated knowledge after years of inquiry (Ehman & Hahn, 1981; Gross, 1972; Hunkins et al., 1977; Larkins & McKinney, 1980; Metcalf, 1963; Shaver, 1982; Shaver & Larkins, 1973; Van Manen, 1975; and Wiley, 1977). Clearly not all of the research in the field is subject to these criticisms. However, there are fundamental problems that characterize the field.

The Problems with the Traditional
Research Focus

The vast majority of the research on the teaching of social studies has examined the relationships between instructional techniques or teacher behaviors and their effects on student outcomes. These studies aim to explain stable relationships between selected educational phenomena. There is an assumption that pedagogic principles will be discovered by using an empirical-analytic orientation in the study of the social worlds of classrooms and schools.

A typical social studies investigation would examine the correlational or causal relationships existing between selected instructional techniques or particular teacher behaviors and desired student outcomes. A wide range of topics has been studied: inquiry techniques (Marsh, 1974), types of questions (McKeown, 1974; Ryan, 1973, 1974), instructional games and simulations (Van Sickle, 1977; Wentworth & Lewis, 1973), frequency of quizzes (McKenzie, 1972), teacher solicitation patterns (Smith, 1980), teacher use of concept examples and definitions (Armento, 1977), and teacher enthusiasm (Larkins & McKinney, 1982; McKinney & Larkins, 1982). Research on the instructional/teacher variables tends to reflect the general interest in the field in innovative and reflective inquiry techniques. The wide array of topics may also be reflective of the eclectic nature of the social studies as well as of the lack of consensus on a clear definition of the goals of social studies.

Student behaviors are typically viewed as outcomes of instruction; they are seldom defined as independent variables. The trend has been to measure some component of short-term cognitive gain as the product of instruction. While more attention has been given in recent years to affective outcomes, these are still studied less than the more manageable and measurable cognitive outcomes. When the affective goals are considered, they are typically conceptualized as independent of cognitive processes. A psychometric orientation dominates the current research, with outcome measures typically tapped by paper-and-pencil tests of knowledge, criterion referenced to the content of the instructional treatment.

The two most common criticisms of topics selected for social studies research are (a) that the majority of the studies focus on narrow and unimportant relationships rather than on major and fundamental issues in the field (Ehman & Hahn, 1981; Gross, 1972; Metcalf, 1963; Shaver & Larkins, 1973; and Wiley, 1977), and (b) that important omissions are made in the conceptualization of relevant factors that might influence and define learning and teaching.

There are a number of major social studies issues that could be examined. For example, given the controversy in the field over the competing approaches to social studies education (citizenship transmission, social science, and reflective inquiry), it might be informative to know if and how courses and programs operating in these alternative ways contribute to student citizenship outcomes (Shaver & Larkins, 1973; Wiley, 1977). Little work has been done on examining alternative ways of dealing with controversial issues or of dealing with the interaction of these various approaches with developmental capabilities (Gross, 1972). And little work has been done on how students derive meaning from the social world in general or from the covert aspects of the school experience.

The second major problem deals with the definitions of the variables examined in the studies. Because most of the independent variables used in instructional research are defined in terms of specific teaching techniques, little is known about how these techniques operate within comprehensive instructional approaches. Teacher questions, for example, are usually examined separately from discussion or inquiry strategies. The focus on isolated aspects of instructional approaches also ignores the range of social, cultural, economic, and psychological factors that might have relevance for learning outcomes. Dependent variables also tend to be defined as discrete elements—factual learning, concept learning, or inferential thinking, for instance. Measurement problems associated with the alternatives probably have much to do with this tendency to focus on components of learning rather than on more global outcomes. However, by concentrating on only one, usually cognitive, student outcome, researchers present an overly simplistic view of the nature of understanding. The understanding of social phenomena is better described as a network of conceptual relationships rather than as specific items of knowledge—facts, concepts, or generalizations—that are independent of one another. In addition, affective and interpersonal components of learning and intellectual development have not been adequately examined. How these elements operate together in the development of citizenship outcomes is not understood very well. To examine these relationships, a more holistic view of teaching-learning is needed.

THEORETICAL PROBLEMS

Research in the field reflects little "sustained concern with building and clarifying a theory for teaching social studies. The empirical studies have also not been the kind likely to contribute to theoretical knowledge" (Metcalf, 1963, p. 931). "The failure to apply theory is indicated by the lack of hypotheses in many research reports" (Shaver & Larkins, 1973, p. 1246). Charges of the atheoretical nature of much of the research on the teaching of social studies have formed a dominant theme in the critiques of the literature over the last 20 years. Social studies researchers, however, are not the only ones who face this problem. The field of research on teaching in general has been criticized for the lack of models or theories that might guide research. Essentially, there is a noticeable absence of any well-articulated theoretical framework for studying teaching and learning (Doyle, 1977; Forman & Chapman, 1979; Waxman & Walberg, 1982; Winne & Marx, 1977; and Woolfolk & Brooks, 1983).

Research on teaching is an applied field; by necessity researchers draw on theory and research from fields related to teaching and learning, such as social psychology, developmental psychology, cultural anthropology, cognitive psychology, and so on. Some researchers have thought that a theory of teaching would evolve from the empirical work on classrooms. However, implications for teaching derive more from the conceptualization of teaching and learning that emerges from any particular study rather than from the actual findings of that study. One of the major problems with much past social studies research is that many of those studies are not based on any explicit theoretical foundations, and fail to explain the results in the context of general theoretical principles within which the findings might make sense.

Each of the choices a researcher makes — of problem, research design, variable definition, and so on — is based on values held explicitly or implicitly. One's beliefs about the nature and aims of inquiry, the role of the investigator, the nature of learning, and the roles of teachers and students guide one's research choices (Clements, 1981; Fenstermacher, 1978; Popkewitz, 1978; Popkewitz & Tabachnik, 1982; and Popkewitz & Wehlage, 1973).

Most of the empirical work on instructional and teacher effects has been based on behavioristic assumptions about learning. According to this view, learning results as associations are formed between environmental stimuli and behavioral responses. Thus, research on teaching social studies has focused on the question of how the environment (teacher behavior, elements of instruction) directly influences student learning. Other evidence of a behavioristic orientation includes the emphasis on measurable, observable, and discrete items of behavior as learning outcomes and the emphasis on identifiable elements of instruction that direct and reinforce student behavior. For the most part, these assumptions have implicitly guided the tradition of research on teaching social studies.

METHODOLOGICAL PROBLEMS

Few reviewers of research have been willing or able to derive definitive statements of current knowledge from the literature on the teaching of social studies. Methodological flaws in several studies limit their usefulness (Shavelson & Dempsey-Atwood, 1976; Shaver & Norton, 1980). Certainly the lack of an explicit theoretical base in much of the work inhibits our ability to make sense out of some of the results. In addition, while research has been conducted on a wide range of topics, there are few "lines of inquiry" in social studies research. Where there are a number of studies on the same topic, differences in design limit applicability of the results across studies.

Heretofore, research syntheses have yielded little useful knowledge for classroom teachers of social studies. Most reviewers are pessimistic about our ability to derive principles from the studies. Recently, though, advances have been made in the methods for conducting research integrations (Cooper, 1982; Glass, 1977; Glass, McGaw, & Smith, 1981; Hedges & Olkin, 1980; Jackson, 1980; Ladas, 1980; and Waxman & Walberg, 1982). A number of the newer integrative reviewers are applying these advances and are placing their findings within theoretical frameworks. Most of these reviews draw on studies that cut across subject disciplinary lines.

An example of this new sort of integration can be seen in the synthesis of experimental research done on teacher-questioning behavior, a favorite topic for social studies investigators (see Ryan, 1973, 1974 and Kniep, 1977 for examples of studies that do build directly on one another). Two meta-analyses that included a number of social studies investigations (Andre, 1979; Redfield & Rousseau, 1981) report positive effects of higher-level questions on both reproductive and productive knowledge. The conditions under which such facilitation might occur are explained by Andre's application of an information-processing model. According to this view, questions exert only an indirect influence on learners. Thus, questions will have differential effects on learners in accordance with their prior knowledge, their ability to transform new information, and other factors. Only when the questions prompt the learner to process ideas in ways students would not have done otherwise, will the questions influence learning (Andre, 1979).

Other examples of similar integrations can be found (Martorella, 1977, on conceptual and factual learning; and Mayer, 1979, on advance organizers). Examining studies beyond those in social studies and grounding the results of the integrations in an explanatory theoretical base may increase the likelihood of developing an instructional theory, but we should proceed with caution. Generalizing research findings across subject matter studies is difficult because social studies content, processes, and outcomes are conceptually different from those in other subject areas.

A Promising Direction: Operational Research

"To achieve more productive educational research we first need better research on more important educational problems, and second, wider recognition of the special functions and limitations of research in education" (Ebel, 1982, p. 18). What we need, proposes Ebel, is not research that tries to discover how the process of education works, but rather research on creative inventions that aim to make education work better. He proposes operational research, which derives its hypotheses from experience and from previous research. These hypotheses lead to the development of procedures that have some likelihood of being effective. The outcomes of such research are the description and assessment of the developed instructional techniques.

Two examples of current social studies operational research come to mind—the work on the development of attitudes toward civil liberties by Goldenson (1978) and a study on slow learners and their study of contemporary problems by Curtis and Shaver (1980). In each case, an issue of importance to the field was selected as the research focus; creative instructional treatments were developed from syntheses of relevant areas of research. The curricular treatments represented holistic views of sound instruction, incorporating a range of teaching strategies and student activities. In each of these studies active learning was stressed, with students collecting information and analyzing community-based data. Each investigation was a rather large-scale and lengthy enterprise, with treatment and control groups in a number of schools.

A range of outcomes was also examined in each study: interest in the problem investigated, critical thinking, self-esteem, reading comprehension, and attendance in the Curtis and Shaver study; centrality and direction of attitudes toward civil liberties, and student perceptions of teacher credibility and of general classroom climate in the Goldenson study. The Goldenson and the Curtis and Shaver studies represent an important and promising departure from the typical research design that has been the trademark of research on teaching social studies.

An Emerging Research Focus: Learning and Teaching as Constructive Processes

Over 2000 years ago Greek and Roman scholars believed that instruction was effective primarily to the extent that it emphasized the internal constructive processes of the learner (Wittrock, 1977, 1978; Wittrock & Lumsdaine, 1977). Perhaps disillusioned with the failure of the traditional teacher effects paradigm to produce cumulative knowledge, some social studies researchers are now turning their attention to this ancient idea. Their movement, variously known as the intentionalist (Fenstermacher, 1978), constructivist (Magoon, 1977), or cognitive (Tobias, 1982; Wittrock, 1978) approach to the study of teaching, thus perceives the learner and the mental lives of teachers and students as being the real keys to the better understanding of classroom phenomena. The shift within the empirical-analytic research paradigm is occurring partially, perhaps, because researchers are beginning to recognize that human behavior cannot be properly studied in isolation; thoughts, intentions, and affects that prompt action must be taken into account. Underlying this movement, then, is the realization that some of the causative factors that account for one's behavior are internal.

Incoming stimuli are reorganized, these researchers believe, on the basis of the learner's prior knowledge, value orientations, and the constructive processes employed by the student in particular learning situations. It would follow from this that students and teachers are active constructors of meaning. If this is true, then studies that have "compared the external characteristics of instructional methods have obscured the most important variable accounting for learning from instruction:

macroprocesses, or the frequency and intensity with which students cognitively process instructional input" (Tobias, 1982, pp. 4–5).

It would seem, then, that any instructional method that increases students' relevant macroprocessing of the content of instruction is apt to improve achievement; any teacher behavior or any instructional variable is important to learning outcomes primarily to the extent that it stimulates students to "actively comprehend the material, to organize what is learned with what has been learned previously, and to relate it to their prior experience" (Tobias, 1982, p. 6). Thus, the same instructional technique (such as the use of games, quizzes, or higher-order questions) may be more or less successful depending on the extent to which it has stimulated student attention, motivation, image-making, and other psychological processes during instruction.

The focus for research on teaching social studies shifts from the behavioral question, "How do teachers and instruction directly influence learning?" to such questions as "How can teachers influence students to construct images and meanings of the social world? to relate prior knowledge to new data? to reorganize and elaborate upon information? to develop hierarchical systems of interrelationships? to identify and analyze social issues?" Several lines of inquiry are evolving from this constructivist perspective: the development and experimental testing of cognitive instructional theories; basic research on macroprocesses or the psychological processes employed during instruction and on students' cognitions of the social world; and interpretive work on the construction of knowledge in classrooms. This movement has only recently begun to have an effect on the research on teaching social studies. Following are several examples of social studies research that illustrate the work being conducted along the major lines of constructivist inquiry.

Theoretical and Experimental Work on a Constructivist Teaching Model

Drawing upon research conducted on the brain, on human learning, and on memory, Wittrock (1974, 1977) has developed a generative model of teaching. The generative hypothesis claims that when learners relate new information to their experiences and are required to construct images and meanings about this new information, their learning and recall will be facilitated (Wittrock, 1977).

A test of the generative hypothesis was made by MacKenzie and White (1982) as they examined the effects of three instructional methods on eighth and ninth graders' learning of geographic principles and skills. In a carefully controlled experiment, one group of students studied the social studies content in a classroom setting using a textbook–discussion format. A second group studied the same content but within the context of a natural setting, a coastal site, where the teacher could present the ideas while students could observe examples of them. The third instructional strategy was based on generative principles: while on a field trip to the coastal site, this group studied the same content as the other groups, but was given opportunities to generate data, construct records, and develop linkages between the principles learned on the field trip and other ideas already studied. Tests were given not only directly after instruction, but also 12 weeks later in order to measure retention: The classroom group demonstrated 51% retention; the traditional field trip group, 58%; and the generative field trip group, 90%. The results of this study provide evidence consistent with the generative model of teaching.

The generative model has important implications for research on teaching social studies. First of all, it provides a simple and new way of conceptualizing teaching methods. Since prior research identified instructional methods by their external discrete aspects, researchers and teachers have examined the effects of games, role plays, and discussion techniques as though they were distinctly different stimuli. But the generative mode focuses on the internal function rather than the external characteristics of a method; what is important is the way the method is used. Thus, the generative hypothesis suggests that any instructional technique has the potential to help students generate meanings, develop images of new ideas, and relate these ideas to those previously learned.

As the next logical step from its reconceptualization of methods, the generative model of teaching may provide a framework for organizing and reassessing the findings from previous research on instructional effects. The findings from these studies are important from the cognitive perspective not in and of themselves, but because from them a researcher can extrapolate the kinds of student mediating processes that do in fact make all such relationships possible (Doyle, 1977). In other words, the researcher would be interested in hypothesizing the cognitive functions served by such instructional factors as teacher enthusiasm, high-level questions, or inquiry procedures. Thus, synthesizing research within a cognitive theoretical framework can give explanatory power to past work.

Most importantly, however, this generative model serves as a viable theoretical basis for generating new, testable hypotheses for research on teaching social studies. The generative hypothesis could be examined in the context of a range of social studies outcomes, from concept learning to social inquiry. Models of teaching that have their origin in constructivist thought are compatible with the popular view within social studies education that knowledge of the social world should be generated dynamically rather than absorbed as a body of static descriptive rules. It is this compatibility that makes constructive theory a promising foundation for future social studies research.

Basic Research on Student Macroprocesses

From a constructivist perspective, social studies teaching may be viewed as a process whereby teachers facilitate the development of student psychological processes operating in social cognition and social inquiry. Little is known about these psychological processes, but a better understanding of the developmental dynamics and the psychological properties of such learning outcomes as social inquiry and social cognition should inform instructional theory-building efforts in the field.

Some research is being conducted that examines the psychological representation of knowledge structures and the critical thinking processes employed in social science problem solving. While problem solving in mathematics and physics has been rather extensively studied, little work has been conducted on social science problems or on social problems. What research has been conducted has examined the processes students employ as they solve well-defined and well-structured problems. But problems in the social sciences are not always as clearly defined as they are in mathematics or physics. Specific, agreed-upon solutions are not always readily available, if available at all. And between the time it takes to reach a solution and the time it takes to implement it, a considerable lag may occur. In addition, ethical issues, involved in problems relating to social policy, complicate the situation. For these reasons decision making in the social studies is quite different from—and, possibly, more complex than—decision making in other fields.

In order to investigate the processes used in social science problem solving, Voss, Greene, Post, and Penner (1984) and Voss, Tyler, and Yengo (1983) used protocol analysis (or a think-out-loud procedure), collecting the protocols from persons varying in training and experience. Various problems have been used. Examples include policy-making problems in which the subject might be asked to assume the role of foreign policy advisor to the president of the United States and draft a foreign policy with respect to the Soviet Union; or to play the role of the head of the USSR Ministry of Agriculture and to deal with the problem of low crop productivity.

The results of this extensive work indicate that (a) there appear to be domain-specific skills—such as declarative knowledge of the topic and particular problem-solving strategies, perhaps a historical or economic analysis—that are used within the specific problem-solving situation; (b) more sophisticated problem solvers spend a great deal of time using problem-solving strategies, such as developing a problem representation (delineating constraints and developing an orientation to the problem), identifying subproblems, and justifying and critically examining proposed solutions; and (c) more sophisticated problem solvers use a great deal of social studies-specific knowledge. Social studies-specific knowledge includes three types of structures: conceptual networks made up of facts, concepts, principles, and their interrelationships; causal relations (which aid argumentation) and hierarchical structures (which promote organization of large amounts of information). Much of the skill of social science problem solving, then, involves the learning of problem-solving strategies and also the learning and organization of a knowledge base. It is this combination of knowledge with problem-solving strategies that appears to be the key to reflective and informed problem solving.

Although the textbook is a major instructional tool, we know little about the ways in which students process written social studies material. Two sources of information interact when reading—the form and content of the material itself and the abilities and predilections the reader brings to the task (Tyler & Voss, 1982). Only a small amount of work has been done on the interaction of learner attitudinal and knowledge variables with the interpretation of written material, and there has been virtually no work done on how social studies domain-specific knowledge and attitudes influence the processing of text material.

In an experimental study, Tyler and Voss (1982) tapped subjects' knowledge of and attitude toward the Soviet Union before and after being presented with passages containing information either congruent or incongruent with expectations of USSR statements. On the basis of the results of this study and other data, Tyler and Voss proposed a model in which knowledge and attitude are viewed as integrated parts of a network-like mental structure, with "knowledge dominating text processing when passage contents are high in information value and/or disagree with the reader's expectations; [and] attitude dominat[ing] processing when passage contents are of low information value and in agreement with the reader's expectations" (Tyler & Voss, 1982, p. 524).

One major problem for research on teaching social studies conducted from a constructivist perspective is that limited information exists that can inform us of the affective and cognitive processes relevant to social studies learning. The problem-solving and text-processing studies cited here represent examples of important basic research being conducted along these lines. But much more work is needed to illuminate the unique conceptual properties of the knowledge and processes of the social studies, and to identify the psychological processes students at various developmental stages (see Farley & Gordon, 1981) employ as they construct and restructure images of the social world and deal with social issues.

Interpretive Work on the Construction of Social Knowledge

In the last several years, there has been some interpretive work conducted in social studies classrooms that aims to describe the interactive processes operating in the construction of social knowledge. White's (1981) study is an example of research conducted from an interpretive perspective. Using ethnographic data-gathering techniques (see LeCompte & Goetz, 1982) of participant observation, audiotaping of social studies lessons, interviews, and the analysis of documents and artifacts, White examined the knowledge that teachers and students constructed of different cultures while in the setting of elementary school classrooms. The view of the classroom that emerges is a minisociety where teachers and students are interrelated in an intricate maze of social transactions. Knowledge of different cultures is constructed from a framework that includes the transmission of certain values about our own society (White, 1981). Thus complete objectivity is compromised.

Further interpretive work can help us gain a better understanding of the beliefs about the social world that teachers hold, transmit, and help students to construct, and of the constructions students build from the explicit and implicit social studies curricula. The important issue of the effects of different types of studies curricula (social science, transmission, or reflective inquiry) on learner attitudes, intellectual development, and abilities might be studied using a range of qualitative and more conventional techniques. In addition to this, research conducted from an interpretive perspective can provide an understanding of the conceptions of the social world children possess at various developmental levels, and of the ways in which these mental pictures change as a function of different kinds of social studies experiences.

Focus on Ecological/Social Factors

There is an ever-growing awareness that schools, social studies classrooms, and other settings in which learners build their understandings, attitudes, and feelings about themselves and their social worlds are ecologically complex sociocultural, economic, and political systems (Doyle & Ponder, 1975; Fenstermacher, 1978; Harre & Secord, 1979; Ponder, 1981; Popkewitz, 1978; Van Sickle, 1979, 1982). The network of social and institutional phenomena within which social studies teaching and learning occur clearly influences teacher and student interactions and learning outcomes. Yet ecological factors generally have been ignored in most studies of teaching.

The major exception to this in the social studies literature has been the extensive body of work conducted on political socialization. The studies of political socialization and participation have traditionally considered such ecological factors as school and classroom climate, school political system, social status of students, and latent as well as manifest aspects of the curriculum (Ehman, 1969, 1980; Eyler, 1978; and Metzger & Barr, 1978).

Another line of inquiry that takes into account the social aspects of the classroom has been the work on goal structures or the various ways individuals relate to one another in classroom settings in the pursuit of learning outcomes. Based on social psychological theory, this body of work examines the effects of cooperative, competitive, and individualistic goal structures on a range of attitudinal and achievement outcomes. Several studies have been made using social studies content and a teams-games-tournaments instructional strategy which contains elements of cooperation, but also competition. The general results from similar studies using math, language arts, and reading content indicate that the teams-games-tournaments instructional technique promotes positive achievement outcomes. However, these results do not seem to be common across the several social studies investigations. The conflicting results from the social studies investigations may be a function of methodological problems or of differences in the social contexts of social studies classrooms (De Vries & Edwards, 1973; De Vries & Slavin, 1978; O'Neill, 1981; Sharon, 1980; Slavin, 1980). Wanted are holistic conceptualizations of social studies education that take into account both ecological factors of the school and societal factors that influence thought and action within the classroom.

Summary

Major challenges lie ahead for social studies researchers. While the theoretical and empirical work of the last 10 years illustrates a broader view in terms of the representation of the three dominant scholarly traditions, much of the work in the field remains atheoretical and therefore fragmented. To remedy this situation, a research agenda for the decade would call for (a) clarification of conceptual problems, (b) integration of theoretical principles, and (c) establishment of a broader view yet of research on teaching social studies.

A major effort must be made to clarify the conceptual problems in social studies and to advance the theoretical underpinnings of the field and of the research on teaching social studies. Methodological advances have outpaced conceptual advances in the last 10 years; sophisticated quantitative and qualitative tools cannot camouflage inadequate conceptual designs. Extension of the work begun by the critical theorists on the development of a normative theory of social studies education is needed, as well as further clarification of the field's major constructs, such as citizenship, decision making, and social inquiry. A further problem is the clarification of the conceptual properties of the knowledge and processes demanded of students by the social studies. That is, how is social studies different from other curricular areas? Theory-building efforts in social studies should particularly address the unique aspects of the field.

Also needed is the further development of theoretical models that can give power and direction to empirical-analytic research on social studies teaching while at the same time giving explanatory value to research findings. Theoretical clarity should facilitate the development of more systematic and coherent lines of inquiry in social studies; this work, in turn, should provide the basis for the continual refinement of the conceptual models.

Social studies research cannot significantly proceed if it remains isolated from the mainstream of research on teaching. Theory building and the clarifying of the unique aspects of social studies teaching and learning should aid efforts to integrate the findings of previous research across curricular areas within an explanatory framework. But to the extent that important differences exist between learning in social studies and learning in other areas, such integrations should proceed with caution. Social studies problems are not identical to the problems of mathematics and the natural sciences.

Research on teaching social studies can continue to gain intellectual power through extended use of multiple paradigms. What the field needs, as well, is broader recognition and better application of the idea that pedagogy cannot be properly studied without fully considering ecological and political institutional factors and student and teacher affective and cognitive factors. Since schools and social studies education are complex, dynamic phenomena, a multidimensional approach reflective of that reality is needed. Teams of social studies and social science researchers together with teams of researchers representing the empirical-analytic, the interpretive, and the critical sciences' perspectives might collaborate to address the most important issues in the field. By examining the quality of life in social studies classrooms from a range of perspectives and by critically proposing models congruent with a normative theory of social studies education, these researchers would advance the field theoretically and pragmatically.

REFERENCES

Andre, T. (1979). Does answering higher-level questions while reading facilitate productive learning? *Review of Educational Research, 49*(2), 280–318.

Armento, B. J. (1977). Teacher behaviors related to student achievement on a social science concept test. *Journal of Teacher Education, 28*(2), 46–52.

Barr, R. D., Barth, J. L. & Shermis, S. S. (1977). *Defining the social studies.* Arlington, VA: National Council for the Social Studies.

Chapin, J. R. (1974). *Social studies dissertations: 1969–1973.* Boulder, CO: Social Science Education Consortium. (ERIC Document Reproduction Service No. ED 098 085)

Chapman, K. (1974). *Simulation/games in the social studies: What do we know?* Boulder, CO: Social Science Education Consortium. (ERIC Document Reproduction Service No. ED 093 736)

Cherryholmes, C. H. (1978). Curriculum design as a political act: Problems and choices in teaching social justice. *Theory and Research in Social Education, 6*(4), 60–82.

Cherryholmes, C. H. (1980). Social knowledge and citizenship education: Two views of truth and criticism. *Curriculum Inquiry, 10,* 115–141.

Cherryholmes, C. H. (1982). Discourse and criticism in the social studies classroom. *Theory and Research in Social Education, 9*(4), 57–73.

Clements, M. (1981). A social paradigm: An ethical perspective. *Theory and Research in Social Education, 9*(3), 1–23.

Cooper, H. M. (1982). Scientific guidelines for conducting integrative research reviews. *Review of Educational Research, 52*(2), 291–302.

Curtis, C. K., & Shaver, J. P. (1980). Slow learners and the study of contemporary problems. *Social Education, 44*(4), 302–309.

De Vries, D. L., & Edwards, K. J. (1973). Learning games and student teams: Their effects on classroom process. *American Educational Research Journal, 10*(4), 307–318.

De Vries, D. L., & Slavin, R. (1978). Teams-games-tournaments: A research review. *Journal of Research and Development in Education, 12,* 28–38.

Doyle, W. (1977). Paradigms for research on teacher effectiveness. *Review of Research in Education, 5,* 163–198.

Doyle, W., & Ponder, G. A. (1975). Classroom ecology: Some concerns about a neglected dimension of research on teaching. *Contemporary Education, 46*(3), 183–188.

Ebel, R. (1982). The future of educational research. *Educational Researcher, 11*(8), 18–19.

Ehman, L. H. (1969). An analysis of the relationships of selected education variables with the political socialization of high school students. *American Educational Research Journal, 6,* 559–580.

Ehman, L.H. (1980). The American school in the political socialization process. *Review of Educational Research, 50*(1), 99–119.

Ehman, L. H., & Hahn, C. L. (1981). Contributions of research to social studies education. In H. D. Mehlinger & O. L. Davis (Eds.), *The social studies.* Chicago: National Society for the Study of Education.

Engle, S. H. (1960). Decision making: The heart of social studies instruction. *Social Education, 24*(7), 301–304.

Eyler, J. (1978, March). A model relating political attitudes to participation in high school activities. Paper presented at the annual meeting of the American Educational Research Association, Toronto.

Fancett, V. S., & Hawke, S. (1982). Instructional practices in social studies. In *The current state of social studies: A report of Project SPAN.* Boulder, CO: Social Science Education Consortium.

Farley, F., & Gordon, N. J. (Eds.). (1981). *Psychology and education: The state of the union.* Berkeley, CA: McCutchan.

Fenstermacher, G. D. (1978). A philosophical consideration of recent research on teacher effectiveness. *Review of Research in Education, 6,* 157–185.

Fontana, L. (1980a). *Perspectives on the social studies: Report for the Agency for Instructional Television* (Res. Rep. No. 78). Bloomington, IN: Agency for Instructional Television.

Fontana, L. (1980b). *Status of social studies teaching practices in secondary schools* (Res. Rep. No. 79). Bloomington, IN: Agency for Instructional Television.

Forman, D. C. & Chapman, D. W. (1979). Research on teaching: Why the lack of practical results? *Educational Technology, 19*(1), 37–40.

Foshay, A. W., & Burton, W. W. (1976). Citizenship as the aim of the social studies. *Theory and Research in Social Education, 4*(2), 1–22.

Giroux, H. A. (1982). Culture and rationality in Frankfurt school thought: Ideological foundations for a theory of social education. *Theory and Research in Social Education, 9*(4), 17–55.

Glass, G. V. (1977). Integrating findings: The meta-analysis of research. *Review of Research in Education, 5,* 351–379.

Glass, G. V., McGaw, B., & Smith, M. L. (1981). *Meta-analysis in social research.* Beverly Hills, CA: Sage Publications.

Goldenson, D. R. (1978). An alternative view about the role of the secondary school in political socialization: A field-experimental study of the development of civil liberties attitudes. *Theory and Research in Social Education, 6*(1), 44–72.

Gross, R. (1972). A decade of doctoral research in social science studies education. *Social Education, 36*(5), 555–560.

Guyton, E. M. (1982). *Critical thinking and political participation: The development and assessment of a causal model.* Unpublished dissertation, Georgia State University, Atlanta.

Habermas, J. (1968). *Knowledge and human interests.* Boston: Beacon Press.

Harre, R., & Secord, P. F. (1979). *The explanation of social behavior.* Totowa, NJ: Littlefield, Adams.

Hedges, L. V. & Olkin, I. (1980). Vote-counting methods in research synthesis. *Psychological Bulletin, 88*(2), 359–369.

Hertzberg, H. W. (1981). Social Studies reform — 1880–1980. *A report of Project SPAN.* Boulder, CO: Social Science Education Consortium.

Hunkins, F. P., Ehman, L. H., Hahn, C. L., Martorella, P. H., & Tucker, J. L. (1977). *Review of research in social studies education: 1970–1975.* Washington, DC: National Council for the Social Studies.

Jackson, G. B. (1980). Methods for integrative reviews. *Review of Educational Research, 50*(3), 438–460.

Kniep, W. M. (1977). Some effects of high level questions with systematic positive reinforcement on the achievement of selected social studies concepts. *Social Education, 41*(4), 340–344.

Ladas, H. (1980). Summarizing research: A case study. *Review of Educational Research, 50*(4), 597–624.

Larkins, A. G., & McKinney, C. W. (1980). Four types of theory: Implications for research in social education. *Theory and Research in Social Education, 8*(1), 9–17.

Larkins, A. G., & McKinney, C. W. (1982). Two studies of the effects of teacher enthusiasm on the social studies achievement of seventh grade students. *Theory and Research in Social Education, 10*(1), 27–41.

LeCompte, M. D., & Goetz, J. P. (1982). Problems of reliability and validity in ethnographic research. *Review of Educational Research, 52*(1), 31–60.

MacKenzie, A. A., & White, R. T. (1982). Fieldwork in geography and long-term memory structures. *American Educational Research Journal, 19*(4), 623–632.

Magoon, A. J. (1977). Constructivist approaches in educational research. *Review of Educational Research, 47,* 651–693.

Marsh, C. J. (1974). Evaluating inquiry teaching in social studies: A model of experimentation for teacher educators. *Indiana Social Studies Quarterly, 27,* 36–42.

Martorella, P. H. (1977). Research on social studies learning and instruction: Cognition. In F. P. Hunkins et al. (Eds.), *Review of research in social studies education: 1970–1975.* Washington, DC: National Council for the Social Studies.

Mayer, R. E. (1979). Can advance organizers influence meaningful learning? *Review of Educational Research, 49*(2), 371–383.

McKenzie, G. R. (1972). Some effects of frequent quizzes on inferential thinking. *American Educational Research Journal, 9*(2), 231–240.

McKeown, R. (1974). A study of the attitudinal effects of student responses to two levels of social science questions. *Theory and Research in Social Education, 2*(1), 69–77.

McKinney, C. W., & Larkins, A. G. (1982). Effects of high, normal, and low teacher enthusiasm on secondary social studies achievement. *Social Education, 46*(4), 290–292.

Metcalf, L. E. (1963). Research on teaching the social studies. In N. L. Gage (Ed.), *Handbook of research on teaching* (pp. 929–965). Chicago: Rand McNally.

Metzger, D. J., & Barr, R. D. (1978). The impact of school political systems on student political attitudes. *Theory and Research in Social Education, 6*(2), 48–79.

Morrissett, I., & Haas, J. D. (1982). Rationales, goals, and objectives in social studies. In *The current state of social studies: A report of project SPAN.* Boulder, CO: Social Science Education Consortium.

O'Neill, J. S. (1981). The effects of a teams–games–tournaments reward structure on the self-esteem and academic achievement of ninth grade social students. *Dissertation Abstracts International, 41*(12), 5053A.

Osborne, R. (1979). Revision of the NCSS Social Studies Curriculum Guidelines. *Social Education, 43*(4), 261–278.

Oswald, J. M. (1972). *Research in social studies and social science education: Introduction, analyses, and reviews of research.* Boulder, CO: Social Science Education Consortium.

Patrick, J. J. (with Hawke, S.). (1982). *Social studies curriculum materials: A report of Project SPAN.* Boulder, CO: Social Science Education Consortium.

Ponder, G. (1981). Social studies in the school: Questions of expectations and effects. In H. D. Mehlinger and O. L. Davis (Eds.), *The social studies.* Chicago: National Society for the Study of Education.

Popkewitz, T. S. (1972). The craft of study, structure, and schooling. *Teachers' College Record, 74*(2), 155–165.

Popkewitz, T. S. (1977a). Craft and community as metaphors for social inquiry curriculum. *Educational Theory, 27*(4), 310–321.

Popkewitz, T. S. (1977b). The latent values of the discipline-centered curriculum. *Theory and Research in Social Education, 5*(1), 41–60.

Popkewitz, T. S. (1978). Educational research: Values and visions of social order. *Theory and Research in Social Education, 6*(4), 20–39.

Popkewitz, T. S., & Tabachnik, B. R. (Eds.). (1981). *The study of schooling: Field based methodologies in educational research and evaluation.* New York: Praeger.

Popkewitz, T. S., & Tabachnik, B. R. (1982). Theory and social education. *Theory and Research in Social Education, 9,* iv–viii.

Popkewitz, T. S., Tabachnik, R., & Zeichner, K. M. (1979). Dulling the senses: Research in teacher education. *Journal of Teacher Education, 30*(5), 52–60.

Popkewitz, T. S., & Wehlage, G. G. (1973). Accountability: Critique and alternative perspective. *Interchange, 4*(4), 48–62.

Redfield, D. L., & Rousseau, E. W. (1981). A meta-analysis of experimental research on teacher questioning behavior. *Review of Educational Research, 51*(2), 237–245.

Remy, R. C. (1978). Social studies and citizenship education: Elements of a changing relationship. *Theory and Research in Social Education, 6*(4), 40–59.

Ryan, F. L. (1973). Differentiated effects of levels of questioning on student achievement. *Journal of Experimental Education, 41*(3), 63–67.

Ryan, F. L. (1974). The effects on social studies achievement of multiple student responding to different levels of questioning. *Journal of Experimental Education, 42*(4), 71–75.

Sharon, S. (1980). Cooperative learning in small groups: Recent methods and effects on achievement, attitudes, and ethnic relations. *Review of Educational Research, 50*(2), 241–271.

Shavelson, R. J., & Dempsey-Atwood, N. (1976). Generalizability of measures of teaching behavior. *Review of Educational Research, 46*(4), 553–611.

Shaver, J. P. (1977). A critical view of the social studies profession. *Social Education, 41*(4), 300–307.

Shaver, J. P. (1979). The usefulness of educational research in curricular/instructional decision-making in social studies. *Theory and Research in Social Education, 7*(3), 21–46.

Shaver, J. P. (1982) Reappraising the theoretical goals of research in social education. *Theory and Research in Social Education, 9*(4), 1–16.

Shaver, J. P., Davis, O. L., & Helburn, S. W. (1979). The status of social studies education: Impressions from three NSF studies. *Social Education, 43*(2), 150–153.

Shaver, J. P., & Larkins, A. G. (1973). Research on teaching social studies. In R. M. W. Travers (Ed.), *Second handbook of research on teaching.* Chicago: Rand McNally.

Shaver, J. P., & Norton, R. S. (1980). Populations, samples, randomness, and replication in two social studies journals. *Theory and Research in Social Education, 8*(2), 1–10.

Shermis, S. S., & Barth, J. (1978). Social studies and the problem of knowledge: A re-examination of Edgar Bruce Wesley's classic definition of the social studies. *Theory and Research in Social Education, 6*(1), 31–43.

Slavin, R. E. (1980). Cooperative learning. *Review of Educational Research, 50*(2), 315–342.

Smith, B. D. (1980). Influence of solicitation pattern, type of practice example, and student response on pupil behavior, commitment to discussion and concept attainment. *Theory and Research in Social Education, 7*(4), 1–17.

Stake, R. E., & Easley, J. A. (1978). *Case studies in science education.* Washington, DC: National Science Foundation.

Stentz, M., & Lambert, H. D. (1977). An empirical reformulation of political efficacy. *Theory and Research in Social Education, 5*(1), 61–85.

Tobias, S. (1982). When do instructional methods make a difference? *Educational Researcher, 11*(4), 4–9.

Tyler, S. W., & Voss, J. F. (1982). Attitude and knowledge effects in prose processing. *Journal of Verbal Learning and Verbal Behavior, 21*, 524–538.

Van Manen, M. J. M. (1975). An exploration of alternative research orientations in social education. *Theory and Research in Social Education, 3*(1), 1–28.

Van Sickle, R. L. (1977). Decision-making in simulation games. *Theory and Research in Social Education, 5*(3), 84–95.

Van Sickle, R. L. (1979). Neutralizing status constraints on student performances in small group activities. *Theory and Research in Social Education, 7*(2), 1–33.

Van Sickle, R. L. (1982). A social perspective on student learning. *Theory and Research in Social Education, 10*(2), 21–31.

Voss, J. F., Greene, T. R., Post, T. A., & Penner, B. C. (1984). Problem solving skill in the social sciences. In G. Bower (Ed.), *The psychology of learning and motivation: Advances in research theory.* New York: Academic Press.

Voss, J. F., Tyler, S. W., & Yengo, L. A. (1983). Individual differences in the solving of social science problems. In R. F. Dillon and R. R. Schnech (Eds.), *Individual differences in cognition.* New York: Academic Press.

Waxman, H., & Walberg, H. (1982). The relation of teaching learning: A review of reviews of process–product research. *Contemporary Education Review, 1*(2), 103–120.

Weiss, I. R. (1978). *Report of the 1977 National Survey of Science, Mathematics, and Social Studies Education.* Washington, DC: National Science Foundation.

Wentworth, D. R., & Lewis, D. R. (1973). A review of research on instructional games and simulations in social studies education. *Social Education, 37*(5), 432–440.

White, C. S. (1982). A validation study of the Barth-Shermis social studies preference scale. *Theory and Research in Social Education, 10*(2), 1–20.

White, J. J. (1981). An ethnographic study of the construction of knowledge about different cultures in an elementary school. *Dissertation Abstracts International, 41*(7), 3041A.

Wiley, Karen B. (1977). *The status of pre-college science, mathematics, and social science education: 1955–1975: Vol. 3. Social science education.* Washington, DC: National Science Foundation.

Winne, P. H., & Marx, R. W. (1977). Reconceptualizing research on teaching. *Journal of Educational Psychology, 69*(6), 668–678.

Wittrock, M. C. (1974). Learning as a generative process. *Educational Psychologist, 11*, 87–95.

Wittrock, M. C. (Ed.). (1977). *The human brain.* Englewood Cliffs, NJ: Prentice-Hall.

Wittrock, M. C. (1978). The cognitive movement in instruction. *Educational Psychologist, 13*, 15–29.

Wittrock, M. C. & Lumsdaine, A. A. (1977). Instructional psychology. *Annual Review of Psychology, 28*, 417–459.

Woolfolk, A. E., & Brooks, D. M. (1983). Non-verbal communication in teaching. *Review of Research in Education, 10*, 103–149.

34.

Research on Professional Education

Sarah M. Dinham
University of Arizona

Frank T. Stritter
University of North Carolina—Chapel Hill

> *The boy should ride out with his father among his tenants; should see in summer the delights of haymaking, and of harvest-home. ... The boy will see that these customs tend to ... increase the pleasure of the connexion between different classes of society, and they cement the bond of union between landlord and tenant.*
>
> (R. L. Edgeworth, 1812, on the education of a country gentleman.)

Professional Education

While it is a rare student today that pursues education like Edgeworth's for the country gentleman, professional education is nonetheless a significant component of higher education. Higher education has not, however, always been the source of professional preparation. Blauch (1962) describes three stages in the evolution of professional education: first professional training based entirely on apprenticeship—as for Edgeworth's country gentleman; second, professional training in formal settings separated from the profession's practice; and third, the current mode of theory-based programs incorporating both traditionally taught subject matter and integrated apprenticeship experiences. As Brubacker (1962) points out, although professional education may seem to have come full circle in its "return" to the apprenticeship, today's apprenticeship differs from apprenticeships of earlier eras in its reliance on theory.

Reliance on theory is among the most telling distinctions between a profession and a trade or craft. Moreover, theory development itself is one mark of a profession itself; the profession develops theories of action (Argyris & Schon, 1974) by which the profession is practiced. The profession further develops—whether by research or by custom—the theories of action by which its educational programs are practiced.

While professional education curricula vary, both among and within professions, those in higher education settings (the subject of this chapter) generally include some or all of three types (Mayhew, 1971) of educational experiences: (a) courses in the "basic arts" or "basic sciences," (b) courses addressing the profession's typical problems and activities but taught in traditional formats; and (c) the professional initiation, that is, the apprenticeship, the clinical studies, and the internship providing the link between theory and practice (Nyre & Reilly, 1979), the means by which students become practicing professionals and fill the void between professional preparation and professional practice as it is actually encountered (Thorne, 1973a).

Because these practical studies are professional education's most distinguishing feature, this chapter concentrates on the "practical," the "clinical," the "apprenticeship," the "internship" component of professional education.

After reviewing definitions of "profession" and "professional education" and describing the varied literature on professional

The authors thank reviewers Stephen Abrahamson (University of Southern California) and V. R. Neufeld (McMaster University).

education in college and university settings, this chapter concentrates on seven aspects of the professional apprenticeship, concluding with comments and recommendations on the status and future for research on professional education.

Examples of Definitions

The term "profession" may be found in most lexicons, but there the agreement ends. Thoughtful definitions of the term are offered by Becker (1962), Hughes (1973b), Mayhew (1971), and Packer and Ehrlich (1973). Cullen (1978), reviewing many writers' definitions of professionalism, analyzed selected dimensions of those definitions. In their reviews of research on professional education, Heiss, Davis and Voci (1967), Nitsch and Weller (1973), Quay (1980), and White and Burnett (1981) also suggest the broad range of definitions given to the term "profession."

Some professions distinguish between what their profession is and what it is not: "The differences between engineering and science arise from differences in purpose. An engineer is a *user* of knowledge; a scientist is a *pursuer* of knowledge" (Lancaster, 1976, p. 105). Professional education is sometimes operationally defined: In listing the essential elements in engineering education, Lancaster (1976) points out: "The engineer must have specific technical knowledge in his chosen engineering discipline. *It is this knowledge which makes him a professional*" (p. 108). The educational component known as clinical studies is occasionally defined: clinical legal studies include "law student performance on live cases or problems, or in simulation of the lawyer's role, for the mastery of basic lawyering skills and the better understanding of professional responsibility, substantive and procedural law, and the theory of legal practice" (Committee on Guidelines for Clinical Legal Education, 1980, p. 12). Other distinctions between professional and nonprofessional fields include professionals' service role requiring them to set aside their personal beliefs and preferences in favor of the client's best interests, and professionals' practice resting on their belief that by following the profession's guidelines they are acting in the best interests of their client and of society. Professional education curricula may or may not — either directly or indirectly — address these hallmarks; curricula also may vary in their relevance to the realities of clinical practice, and this correspondence between education and practice may or may not be the intent of professional education faculties.

Transmitting Professional Expertise

Professional education provides both cognitive and noncognitive indoctrination into the traditions of the field. Of the traditions in science, Jevons (1969) observes:

> Characteristics inherent in the nature of the scientific process reflect themselves quite clearly in the social organization that science has developed for itself. They form the basis and justification for the kind of apprenticeship which figures almost universally in the training of research workers. Budding scientists learn their trade by working for a time in close and active contact with an established research worker. ... Indeed ... the modern research fellow corresponds quite well to the mediaeval journeyman. (p. 35).

Kuhn (1970) describes the change of gestalt that marks the metamorphosis from novice to professional: "Looking at a bubble-chamber photograph, the student sees confused and broken lines, the physicist a record of familiar subnuclear events. Only after a number of such transformations of vision does the student become an inhabitant of the scientist's world, seeing what the scientist sees and responding as the scientist does" (p. 111).

Transforming the student's gestalt from confusion to familiarity, so the student comes to inhabit the professional world, is the business of professional education. The transformation culminates in clinical studies, the theory-based practice of an apprenticeship. Research on the educational process called the apprenticeship — principally but not exclusively clinical teaching of apprentices — is the subject of this review.

The Professional Literature on Professional Education

While in some professional fields the tradition of research on educational questions is rich, in other fields the scholarly thought about educational questions, while substantial, is not based in research. The present review of research on professional education has yielded a conjecture: A profession's educational inquiry may develop in stages. Initial attention to educational questions seems to take the forms discussed immediately below. Initial empirical research efforts then follow, and in the early stages of empiricism, certain topics tend to prevail. Later stages bring more detailed attention to educational processes themselves. The professional fields reviewed for this chapter seemed to be at various points along this continuum. Should this development conjecture be correct, for example, architectural educational inquiry will move soon from the conjectural stage to topics such as admissions prerequisites, curriculum, and post graduate assessment, with studies of teaching and learning to follow. For legal education, the coming decades will bring more detailed inquiry about both teaching and learning in law schools. And health professions educational research will continue to be refined, perhaps venturing from positivist to other paradigms and from experimental to other models. At present, however, the health professions dominate the scene and thus this chapter, not because their concerns are more profound or their educational practices more sound but because they have produced the greatest wealth of theoretically as well as generalizably useful research findings about professional education.

Concerns About Professional Education

For as long as professionals have been practicing, practitioners and teachers alike have discussed, questioned, and disagreed about educational ends and means. For many fields, however, the discussion has only recently moved into the scholarly literature. Systematic attention to teaching appears as the observations — perceptive and thoughtful but seldom empirical — of professionals deeply concerned about the direction of a profession and/or about the education of its prospective members. The young journals of education in many professions are filled with articles relating experiences and anecdotes. Such articles are often the only available reports of attempts to examine faculties' educational responsibilities and students' performance systematically and publicly.

On occasion professional conferences and scholarly works have reviewed current concerns about professional education. Turner and Rushton's 1976 volume reviews eight fields, and Northwestern University's conference (Boley, 1977) contributed the views of leaders in varied fields.

Academics as well as other onlookers have offered articulate analyses or sometimes direct criticism of educational programs. In a comprehensive overview of the then-current scene, Mayhew (1970), for example, reviewed the problems in professional education, the forces for change, the social and curricular issues, and the pressures toward more practical professional education. Mayhew elsewhere (1971) summarized the challenges in integrating clinical experience in traditional educational programs, documenting recent attempts to change curricula, and recommending measures for sound educational planning and change.

Scholarship in Professional Education

While in some professional fields empirical research on education is sparse, other serious scholarship on education often abounds. The professions differ not in their seriousness of concern about education, but in the nature of their scholarly traditions for addressing serious concerns. It is thus essential that we view serious inquiry about a profession's education in the context of that profession's scholarly traditions. Moreover, in every field the knowledge generation about educational practice mirrors the methods of thought and the rules of evidence used in each field for its own inquiry. While some fields base their knowledge generation on such strategies as controlled research studies with experimental findings aggregated into laws and ultimately theory, other fields construct knowledge otherwise, in ways that mark scholarship in those fields. Scholars whose traditions rest on empiricism often fail to realize that in these other fields the absence of traditionally defined educational research does not signify absence of careful, logical thought. Although fields such as law and architecture usually conceptualize educational problems and approach educational planning from other than empirical research premises, the traditionally trained educational researcher is wrong to criticize the methods of thought of those fields.

As an example, three recent articles offer interesting illustrations of the way some scholars in architecture have conceptualized educational problems and solutions using the paradigms of their own fields. Harris (1974) commented on educational concerns using a systems viewpoint; Jules (1973) attempted to conceptualize the student in the apprentice role, also using a systems model; and Haider (1976) offered a comprehensive architectural education model (including student expectations, teacher intentions, modifications of both, and evaluation).

In another example Cardozo (1977) offered remarks on the special nature of law schools, together with some criticisms and observations. He pointed out that while lawyers and law faculty generally feel their own training was adequate a "schizophrenia" has developed in legal education, a conflict between

those seeing needs for improvement and others finding current educational approaches perfectly satisfactory. Clinical legal education was also the subject of Thorne's (1973b) extensive overview of the exciting opportunities and myriad problems in clinical legal education, and of Swords and Walwer's (1974) analysis of clinical legal education's costs to the supervising law school and the supervising lawyer.

Is Professional Education Unresearchable?

The scholarly professional literature is laced with judgments of those who state without qualification that educational processes are incapable of systematic inquiry. For example, the anonymous scribe for an architectural education annual teachers' seminar (describing the goals of an Association of Collegiate Schools of Architecture, 1975, study funded by the Mellon Foundation) records these views:

> The ACSA study was intended to be as objective as social science knows how to make anything objective in the descriptions of the characteristics and attitudes of teachers, students, and former students, and was intended merely to provide data which is not now available because we have 30,000 students and some 3,000 teachers and God knows how many former students, some of whom are graduates and some of whom are not. There is no individual, no matter how much he moves around, who can understand the increasing diversity of this group or who can understand what the characteristic attitudes and expectations of the people who make up architectural education may be at this time. (p. 8)

Criticizing some legal scholars' firmly held conviction that teaching can neither be studied nor comprehended, Cardozo (1977) quotes an American Association of Law Schools committee exploring teaching by identified good teachers: "The 'good teacher' remains ineffable, an artist with qualities too ethereal to be susceptible to analysis or training. ... Let's complete the record; good teachers are born, not made." Cardozo goes on to observe: "Nonetheless, the AALS has three times conducted 'law teaching clinics,' aimed at helping new faculty members to become 'good teachers'" (1977, p. 47).

A different problem plagues educational research in the health professions. In a field whose clinical research rests in positivist scientific traditions, studies employing randomized clinical trials are idealized, and educational research resting on other paradigms is severely criticized or totally ignored. The observers complacently conclude that good educational research cannot be possible.

Initial Research Efforts

In early stages of research on educational questions, certain topics tend to prevail: student prerequisites and admissions, curriculum, and postgraduate education (Abrahamson, 1965).

Thoughtful attention to prerequisite coursework, academic records, and/or the student's personal experience has been given in business by the Pierson (1959) study, in law by such authors as Cardozo (1977), and in architecture by the Sanders (1963) committee. Less common, however, have been empirical studies of admissions criteria and/or personal attributes that might predict success in professional schools. Pitcher's 1962 study predicting performance in architecture was one of the first attempts by that field to assess, among other things, the field's admissions processes. In engineering, authors such as Elkins and Luetkemeyer (1974) have examined variables contributing to prediction of students' performance in university engineering programs. In medicine and other health sciences, prediction studies are more common (e.g., Carline, Cullen, Scott, Snannon, & Schaad, 1983; Meredith, Dunlap, & Baker, 1982).

In inquiry concerning educational programs themselves, the next stage usually brings such studies as surveys of curricular differences among professional schools. Mayhew (1970) studied a number of "developed" and "developing" institutions to determine their plans for expansion of graduate and professional advanced degree programs. Two historic, comprehensive surveys of business education programs are reviewed in several sources, one of the most thorough being Cheit's (1975). Over two decades ago, Muschenheim (1964) published a detailed compendium of information on foreign programs in architecture, including information on admissions procedures, curricular requirements, and degrees offered.

A third common initial research topic concerns graduates and/or postgraduate education. While in some professions the literature on postgraduate education is limited to discourses on the importance of continued lifelong learning or specifications by licensing boards for continued licensure, in a few fields research on graduates has contributed to knowledge about effects of professional educational programs (e.g., Woodward and Dinham, 1982).

The Research Literature on the Apprenticeship

Over 2 decades ago, McGlothlin (1961) observed that professions vary widely in their use of clinical experiences for teaching about professional practice. Instructors' activities and responsibilities vary significantly among professions, and characteristics learners bring to the apprenticeship vary substantially as well.

In the apprenticeship the aspiring professional learns many facets of the profession from the master, as Edgeworth's young country gentleman found. Cognitive or intellectual learning can range from the simplest levels of factual knowledge acquisition to the complexities of synthesis, evaluation, and reasoning. The learner also encounters and assimilates the rich fabric of socialization, interpersonal skills, moral reasoning, and attitudes distinguishing the profession's members. Further, a high level of technical skill must be learned for the competent professional to fulfill the profession's responsibilities. The technical skill is vital: No amount of extraordinary cognitive or psychosocial learning will substitute. The engineer, the dentist, the architect all acquire or polish skills in the apprenticeship.

Professional fields vary in their use of empirical research for assessing apprenticeship educational methods and outcomes. Further, the apprenticeship, like any complex instructional situation, includes many components and may therefore be analyzed from many perspectives. For this chapter, education through the apprenticeship includes (a) prerequisite student attributes, (b) preparatory educational experiences, (c) sites for apprenticeships, (d) characteristics and teaching behaviors of clinical instructors, (e) supplementary teaching strategies, (f) evaluation of student performance, and (g) instructional evaluation.

Prerequisite Student Attributes

Rather than addressing the attributes necessary for successful apprenticeship learning, researchers have concentrated on predicting performance in professional practice using cognitive, attitude, and skill measures. One exception has been the Council on Dental Education's requirement of manual dexterity (chalk carving and other) measures for dental school admission, a procedure with accepted validity nonetheless abandoned in 1972 for logistical reasons. A written measure used more recently to assess similar skills has questionable validity (Weinstein, 1982).

Little success has been reported for cognitive variables. Wingard and Williamson (1973) reviewed 27 articles published between 1955 and 1972 for medicine, business, education, and research professionals; none found undergraduate grades related to subsequent professional performance. Gough and Hall (1975) and Gough (1978) found that aptitude test scores (the Medical College Admission Test), premedical grades in science, and preference for science subjects were moderately related to academic performance in the first 2 years of medical school; those measures proved almost completely unrelated, however, to measures of clinical performance. A study in nursing (Kissinger & Munjas, 1982) found a relationship between three thinking process indices and students' subsequent ability to implement the nursing process (assessing, planning, intervening, and evaluating patient care). From these representative studies, it would seem that however useful they may be in the admissions process, aptitude and achievement measured with traditional psychometric techniques should not be relied upon to predict clinical performance.

In contrast, there is some evidence that attitude and value measures can predict some aspects of clinical performance. Gough and Hall (1975) reported that clinical performance was marginally predictable from medical students' personal responses to the Adjective Check List. Meredith et al., (1982) found that attitudinal characteristics of medical students as measured by comments of interviewers were correlated with clinical performance. One study showed a consistent relationship between measures of moral reasoning and performance of medical residents (Sheehan, Husted, Candee, Cooke, & Bargen, 1980), while another could not produce similar results with fourth-year dental students (Nash & Nash, 1982).

Dentistry is in the minority among professional programs in assessing technical skills prior to admission. For example, manual dexterity has been found to be at least slightly related to performance on the Perceptual Motor Ability component of the Dental Aptitude Test (Potter, McDonald, & Sagraves, 1982; Thompson, Ahlawat, & Buie, 1979).

The body of research literature on prerequisites for apprenticeship learning, while growing, is overshadowed by research linking prerequisites to earlier components—the "basic arts" and "basic sciences"—of the professional curriculum. For cognitive, affective, and skill attributes alike, the relationships with apprentice learning and clinical performance remain unclear.

Preparation for Clinical Education

Students prepare for clinical experiences by becoming knowledgeable and skillful in specific areas, the choice of areas depending on the school's curriculum. Before the apprenticeship begins, a student may learn (a) cognitive information as well as its use in situations requiring intuitive and/or analytical reasoning, (b) attitudes toward professional practice, including ethical reasoning, (c) technical skills, (d) interpersonal skills, (e) the capacity for self-initiated independent learning, and (f) characteristics of the professional role.

PROBLEM SOLVING

While factual knowledge is important in most educational programs, it is in the professional apprenticeship that knowledge must be applied in problem solving. Some assert that problem solving cannot be taught; in some fields, however, research on problem solving has suggested that the ability can be acquired. In nursing Wales and Hagerman (1979) proposed a guided design model for teaching the process, while Smeltzer (1980) has suggested a pragmatic model in which all faculty consensually agree upon application of a process model and then use it to analyze all specific nursing situations in their teaching. Elstein, Shulman, and Sprafka (1978) established that students can be helped to develop the ability, and they posed selected heuristics that can be taught; their conclusion was substantiated by Margolis, Barnoon, and Barak (1982), who used clinical algorithms to help students solve pediatric patient problems. In contrast, Neufeld, Norman, Feightner, and Barrows (1981) determined through an extensive study that the problem-solving process itself remains relatively constant through medical school and into practice; they found no process differences but substantial content differences in problem solving of student classes and practicing physicians. They recommended, therefore, that instruction be directed not at the problem-solving process itself, but at more specific behaviors that can be changed: for example, knowledge acquisition, ease with patients, and clinical data-gathering techniques.

AFFECTIVE PREREQUISITES

Personal attitudes and values that influence learning and ultimately professional behavior require attention before the apprenticeship begins. Asserting that health professionals must base decisions on consistent moral values, Davis (1981) recommended that health professions institutions must help students develop these attitudes and beliefs. The work by Sheehan et al. (1980) substantiated Davis' position by finding a correlation between moral development and medical residents' performance.

Conners (1979) demonstrated that nursing students could effectively use a modified interaction analysis to analyze videotapes of their own interactions with patients; the criteria were

sensitivity, insightfulness, and ability to work effectively with people. Fine and Therrien (1977) were similarly able to assist medical students in developing empathetic responses to patients and to attend not only to the disease but also to the patient as a unique individual with a disease symptom.

Students' attitudes toward themselves are also important. In medicine these include strategies for coping with feelings about new materials and new responsibilities, and attitudes toward such problems as illness, disease, dying, and death. Student change, whether to give up old beliefs and behaviors or to develop a new self-concept, is best facilitated by small-group discussion led by thoughtful tutors (Kahn, Lass, Hartley, and Kornreich, 1981), and/or through such programs as preclinical long-term exposure to patients in community health care services (Voorhees et al., 1977).

TECHNICAL SKILLS

Preapprenticeship courses of many types teach the technical skills—most of which are manual—required for apprentice performance. Design professions' studio courses, engineers' practical courses, and introduction to clinical medicine courses provide specific training in specific fundamental techniques of the profession.

In the health fields, some have found students inadequately prepared for patient care. Infante (1975) concluded that students are often placed in a clinical setting and given patient responsibility before they are ready, and recommended that they spend more prior time in similar settings. Elliott, Jillings, and Thorne (1982) also reported that most nursing schools have skills laboratories, but that they are not employed to the extent possible. Voight (1980) recommended that physical assessment skills of gross inspection, limited percussion, palpation, and auscultation be taught early in a nursing curriculum to build confidence, stimulate attitude, and facilitate contact with instructors. Pharmacy students learned knowledge about these skills from observing videotapes (Schwinghammer, 1981) and nursing students learned how to perform them from integrated slide–cassette programs, practice manuals, and individually evaluated performance exercises (Bauman, Cook, & Larson, 1981). Nurse practitioners have been successful in teaching medical students how to examine patients and in providing feedback on student practice (Stillman, Levinson, Ruggill, & Sabers, 1977).

In one dental school students were successfully taught motor skills in restorative dentistry in a guided systematic approach utilizing detailed checklists and extensive faculty feedback (Vann, May, & Shugars, 1981) while in another study, students learned motor skills using self-instructional materials (Dilley, Machen, Dilley, & Howden, 1978).

Self-instructional laboratories based on mechanical simulation devices have been developed to practice medical technical skills. Sajid, Lipson, and Telder (1975) described a comprehensive laboratory which included three-dimensional replicas, electronic and recorded simulations, computer-assisted encounters, self-assessment exercises, and video interactions, all accompanied by an instructional guide allowing students to practice at their own pace.

Trained patient instructors with specific physical findings

have been used very successfully; their reliability and the objective constructive feedback they provide to students are especially beneficial (Stillman, Ruggill, Rutala, & Sabers, 1980). One study has demonstrated the superiority of simulated patient training for long term (18-month) retention (Gerber, Albanese, Brown, & Mathes, 1985). The same approach has been applied to legal education in a program employing "client instructors" functioning in the multiple roles of client, teacher, and evaluator of law students' interviewing skills (Stillman, Silverman, Burpeau, & Sabers, 1982).

Development of skills for new technical procedures is less frequently discussed in the research literature. For example, preparing medical students to incorporate computer technology into patient care is only today being attempted.

INTERPERSONAL SKILLS

Communication is an essential component of any profession's functioning. Whether the nurse communicates with his patient, an engineering team with their consultants, or the architect with her client, professional success depends on communication. Even before clinical studies begin, professional communication skills can be developed.

Much of the professional communication teaching in the 1970s incorporated the use of videotape recording and playback with critique. An example is the Interpersonal Process Recall (IPR) technique, developed by Kagan and associates (1980), a method involving recall of thoughts and intentions through immediate videotape playback of a student interaction with a client or patient, integrated with open-ended questioning by a trained inquirer. IPR has been successful with both undergraduate medical students (Werner & Schneider, 1974) and medical residents (Robbins et al., 1979). Aspects of IPR have been studied for preparing students to use videotape (Finley, Kim, & Mynatt, 1979) and to demonstrate the value of objective feedback to students based on reviews of their own patient interviews (Maguire, Roe, Goldberg, Hyde, & O'Dowd, 1978).

Kahn, Cohen, and Jason (1979) reported that at least 68% of all medical schools had some type of interpersonal communications course—most taught in the preclinical years by psychiatrists and psychologists—dealing with process, information gathering, and psychological intervention skills. Carroll and Monroe (1980), in a thorough review of interviewing instruction studies, concluded: (a) Direct observation and feedback on students' interviewing behavior is a crucial instructional variable; (b) standardized presentations of illustrative patient interviews may be more effective for teaching than live spontaneous demonstrations; (c) program design should include specific statements of interviewing skills to be learned; (d) programs in communication skills should be longitudinal as opposed to being taught at one time in a curriculum; and (e) adjunct instructors can profitably be utilized as facilitators.

Sites for Apprentice Learning

While the health professions commonly base their clinical education in a hospital located on or near the university campus, other professions' apprentice education is seldom so conveniently arranged. To be sure, engineering cooperative programs offer supervised practical experience, and social work and teacher education have long incorporated practicum experiences into their curricula (Morehead, 1973), as have other professions, but the sites are typically far-flung and virtually uncontrollable. Legal clinical education has taken many forms at many sites, from campus-based legal aid clinics to practical experiences in private law offices.

As with other aspects of the apprenticeship, research examining the sites for clinical education has been conducted in health professions but not in other fields. In medicine, much of the recent literature on alternate sites has addressed the criticisms identified by Gordon, Hadac, and Smith (1977): (a) The off-campus facility has only tangential ties to the academic program; (b) multiple experiences have limited comparability; (c) there is little opportunity to monitor student experiences; and (d) adequate communication between the educational program and the off-campus site is difficult to maintain. Yet while the majority of clinical education still occurs directly under the supervision and control of the academic institution, as much as 30% of health professions education may now occur outside the institution at a site whose principal function is not education. To some extent the trend has been due to a shift toward education for primary medical care delivery, and the resulting need for sites emphasizing delivery of that care; other factors are the reduced number of hospital patients for teaching and the increase in health profession schools' enrollments.

Research on clinical sites classified as effective has resulted in a set of standards for physical therapy clinical education (Moore & Perry, 1976); the standards and methods for applying them were assessed by Barr, Gwyer, and Zippora (1982), whose work clearly established the practicality, reliability, and validity of those standards.

Criteria for nursing sites are similar (Skeath et al., 1979; Bevil & Gross, 1981). Infante (1975) focused especially on the essential elements of the clinical laboratory for nursing education, and Hawkins (1981), recognizing that well-integrated clinical experiences are essential to learning, presented a model for selecting those clinical agencies that will provide a student nurse with an optimal learning experience.

No major differences in student experiences across sites are found if the site experiences are well coordinated and communication follows the extensive suggestions offered by Ford (1978) and Pascasio (1976). Several studies using a variety of criteria have identified little difference between students who take a traditional medical clinical experience and those who take off-campus experiences (Clawson, Harris, & Garrard, 1980; Friedman, Stritter, & Talbert, 1978; Moy, Schwarz, & Zinser, 1977).

The research on characteristics of optimal clinical sites leads to several recommendations. To ensure that students have the essential exposure, experience, and instruction in a clinical setting, specific characteristics and practices are indicated. In the ideal, the instructional paradigm should stress competency so that time can be variable and achievement constant (Coble, 1981); in practice this arrangement is seldom feasible. The clinical experience should be supplemented with didactic sessions, self-teaching materials, guided readings, group sharing of student experiences, and close instructor monitoring of experiences (Philips, Rosenblatt, Gordon, & Fletcher, 1982). Interaction between student and preceptor, and between student and patient, generally facilitate learning, while problems in clinic operations can interfere (Dachelet et al., 1981).

Characteristics and Teaching Behaviors of Clinical Instructors

Research on instructor characteristics and behavior has begun to supplement the anecdotal writing of the past, although the research literature is, again, concentrated in the health professions. Even in this field, unfortunately, eagerness for research findings applicable to clinical teaching improvement has led both writers and readers to disseminate and assimilate research conclusions without sufficient critical examination of the studies' theory, methods, or criteria. The themes reviewed below are those that appear best substantiated by sound research findings.

For the health professions, Yonke (1979) and Daggett, Cassie, and Collins (1979) identified three sources of information for effective instructor characteristics and teaching behaviors: (a) Successful clinical teachers describe what has worked best, or seemed most appropriate for them; (b) students identify the teacher characteristics and behaviors that most facilitate their clinical learning; and (c) educational researchers knowledgeable about instructional psychology report their observations of clinical teaching. A fourth method, analysis of instructional outcomes, is complicated because linking cause and effect is extremely difficult when there are multiple instructors, multiple stimuli, and multiple instructional outcomes. Petzel, Harris, and Masler (1982) have, however, reported one study which does relate clinical instructors' teaching behaviors to subsequent student clinical skills performance.

Although addressing a variety of topics, the research literature on teaching behaviors concentrates on four main themes: (a) the instructor's attitudes, (b) the role model the instructor presents to students, (c) organization of the learning, and (d) practice and evaluation. The first two, attitude and role modeling, can be said to reflect the "art" of clinical teaching — talents that are difficult to teach and to learn. The review that follows can, however, sensitize clinical instructors to these dimensions' power and influence over student learning. The second two, organization and evaluation, demonstrate how the "science" of teaching can be consciously learned and modified.

The paragraphs that follow synthesize research on these four themes, drawing from a myriad of sources. Undergraduate medical education yields the greatest number of sources (e.g., Bucher & Stelling, 1977; Friberg, 1980; Gil, Rubeck, & Jones, 1982; Irby, 1978; Petzel et al., 1982; Simon, 1976; Stritter & Flair, 1980; Stritter, Hain, & Grimes, 1975) and nursing follows (e.g., Karns & Schwab, 1982; O'Shea & Parsons, 1979; Pugh, 1980; Sheahan, 1981; Wong, 1978; Weinholtz, 1983). Graduate medical education also contributes important findings (e.g., Glick & Epstein, 1977; Irby, 1979; McGlynn, Wynn & Munzenrider, 1978; Stritter & Baker, 1982), as do dentistry (e.g., Evans & Massler, 1977; MacKenzie, Heins, Holbrook, Low, & Kramer, 1979; Myers, 1977) and allied health (e.g., Scully, 1974; Steinbaugh, 1977; Westberg, Lefever, & Jason, 1980).

ATTITUDES TOWARD TEACHING AND STUDENTS

Attitudes toward teaching and interest in students are evident in an instructor's interactions. Energy, enthusiasm, and dynamism result from (a) confidence in one's teaching and professional roles, (b) excitement about the topic being taught, and (c) pure enjoyment of teaching, all of which seem to stimulate student interest and learning. The best clinical teachers have been described as supportive, humane, and encouraging rather than intimidating, insulting, and pejorative. Effective instructors show observable and personal interest in the learner's individual development and are available to students for informal contact beyond the times formally scheduled.

THE ROLE MODEL

Learners identify with clinical instructors they want to emulate; indeed, a role model's influence can extend for years. However, providing the role model as an end in itself is not sufficient. Professional competence is the first, although not the only, criterion for role models. Instructors should be able to help students observe clinical practice and to analyze it as well as to practice it themselves. They should be willing as well as able to discuss with students what they know, what they believe, and how they practice.

Beyond competence and the ability to articulate it, the instructor also models professional standards in self-confidence, leadership ability, dealing with clients or caring for patients, relationships with peers and subordinates, awareness of personal strengths and weaknesses, and ability to accept constructive criticism.

Yet clinical instructors cannot be and need not be universally expert or perfect. Rather, they are most effective if they show students their reasoning, and encourage students to question them. They should reward students for analyzing and reflecting on the model they present. They should discuss their strengths and their uncertainties, their values, and how they cope with the profession's demands. Since any one clinical instructor is unlikely to meet all a student's needs, students should be exposed to a variety of role models so they can compile a composite which expresses their sense of their own developing professional role.

ORGANIZATION

An organized clinical instructor helps the student establish a clear direction, goals, expectations, and criteria for evaluating apprenticeship learning. While the research literature on providing students with specific, organized expectations (whether established by teacher, student, or both) has not universally shown that greater learning results, clear goals seldom hinder learning. Further, instructors who ensure that expectations are articulated and activities well organized are generally positively assessed by their students. They are flexible in how they ask questions, depending upon their instructional goals and the needs of particular students.

Good clinical teachers are good question askers: they lead students through clinical problems by a nonthreatening question approach which focuses not on isolated facts but on an organized approach to the larger, more complex structure.

Because apprenticeships typically focus on practical cases immediately at hand, instructors often feel powerless in setting specific goals. They often, instead, set expectations for attendance at certain events, or state their own teaching plans rather than goals for students' learning. Students then struggle on their own to find principles explaining the very concrete, case-focused problems of their practical learning. Apprenticeship learning is likely to be more fruitful when organized expectations for student competencies—goals to be achieved—are negotiated and agreed upon in advance. As students begin practical learning the expectations can be largely instructor-determined; more mature and accomplished students can negotiate the responsbility with instructors, and acquire as well a sense of responsibility for their own learning. More intrinsic motivation for continued self-directed learning will result when, as the apprenticeship ends, students have borne a significant measure of responsibility for setting and satisfying their own expectations.

PRACTICE AND EVALUATION

Students' guided practice and careful evaluation are essential for a quality apprentice education. Evaluation in particular is essential—some would say paramount. Several principles emerge from the sources cited above.

Although clinical learning is necessarily problem, task, or issue oriented, the instructor must link students' practical work to the set of concepts or the structure defining the discipline—that is, to the theory of the profession. As students' abilities increase, their activity should move from observing the instructor/practitioner to analyzing the instructor's clinical work, to observed and supervised work, to independent unobserved clinical practice followed by instructor review. Throughout, good question-asking is essential.

To match students' clinical responsibilities with their level of achievement, instructors should assess student competence before responsibilities are assigned, negotiated, or accepted—an ideal seldom implemented. This initial assessment is but the first form of student evaluation.

Evaluation must include feedback to students, intended to help them improve their comprehension and/or performance. Whether reinforcement for correct performance or constructive criticism of errors, evaluation should be specific, it should occur frequently, it should be administered both formally and informally, and it should include explanations and remedies. Initially instructors may compare performance to some commonly accepted standard. Later, students may be asked to assess their own progress compared to that standard, in discussion with their instructor, since professional development requires self-analytical and self-critical ability.

Sadly, apprenticeship students often receive no evaluation, or they describe evaluation that was insufficient, tardy, vague, or lacked suggestions for improvement. Equally sadly, instructors also report dissatisfaction and discomfort in evaluating students.

Supplementary Teaching Strategies

Although the major apprenticeship teaching strategy is the one-on-one tutorial relationship, many other strategies are used as supplements. The supplements are necessary in part because clinical learning in apprenticeship settings is inevitably organized around the specific examples at hand, cases which taken together do not guarantee a representative spectrum by which essential knowledge, viewpoints, and skills can be taught.

Meleca, Schimpfhauser, and Witteman (1978) identified electives, conferences, demonstrations, observed student practice, programed instruction, and reading assignments as the predominant methods of supplementary health professions teaching. The research on these strategies is varied. Some authors have examined the characteristics of clinical instruction, while other studies have reported attempts to determine the effectiveness of various strategies. For example, Kissinger and Munjas (1981), studying clinical nursing teaching methods, found the combination of small-group discussion and teacher demonstration significantly *inversely* related to problem-solving test performance: Better problem solving was associated with less time in small-group discussion and observation. The authors called for increased study of simulations for teaching in clinical settings. Elements of a popular medical school clerkship were videotaped and analyzed by Foley, Smilansky, and Yonke (1979). When teaching rounds, ward rounds, lectures, patient management conferences, grand rounds, and journal club discussions were examined, medical students were found to be essentially passive, listening to instructors and residents, talking only to report facts about specific cases, while instructors and residents talked when diagnostic and management issues were addressed. The few questions to students required low-level responses: only a few asked for problem solving or reasoning.

Although these results are discouraging, Sheahan's (1980) teaching strategies model, contrasting teacher-centered activities (e.g., demonstrations, seminars, and role playing) with student-centered activities (e.g., self-study, clinical projects, and student research), could be useful for planning instruction. Several experiments support the utility of self-instructional approaches to supplement more formal instruction (Berrong, Hendricson, & Evans, 1982; Fosson, Fischer, & Patterson, 1975; Geyman & Guyton, 1974).

Small-group discussions have been successfully used to teach clinical problem solving. Among the initial efforts were focal problems (Ways, Loftus, & Jones, 1973), and small tutorial groups solving clinical problems cooperatively (Neufeld & Barrows, 1974), a strategy determined by a follow-up survey of graduates to be a major curricular strength (Woodward & Ferrier, 1982). The cognitive level of instructors' questions in small groups has been shown to be related to the level of students' critical thinking (Foster, 1981), with the higher the level of question, the higher the level of thinking and response. Weinholtz (1981) suggested a set of guidelines or "propositions" for a group leader based on ethnographic study of medical teaching rounds.

While most small-group studies are conducted within one profession, small groups have also been used for learning about working cooperatively with other health professionals (e.g., Mazur, Beeston, & Yerxa, 1979).

Simulation—closely approximating and controlling practice for accomplishing specific instructional objectives—has frequently been used in clinical settings (simulation can also be used to evaluate learner performance, as discussed below).

Simulation has four essential properties: (a) Students must respond to a stimulus, (b) aspects of the simulation should be analogous to real life, (c) the fidelity of properties and sequence of activities must transfer to real situations, and (d) students must receive feedback on the appropriateness of their actions (Hoban & Casbergue, 1978). Successful simulation approaches have included programed patients (e.g., Holzman, Singleton, Holmes, & Maatsch, 1977), mannequins (e.g., Penta & Kofman, 1973), mock clinic exercises (Sanders & Ruvolo, 1981), and the problem-based learning approach (Barrows & Tamblyn, 1977; Barrows & Tamblyn, 1980; Distlehorst & Barrows, 1982).

Evaluation of Student Performance

Clinical competence is evaluated continuously, by the student as well as by instructors. Evaluation occurs for many reasons, in differing contexts, by varying means, and on many competencies. Evaluation generally is conducted to inform a decision. Students can be evaluated diagnostically to facilitate their learning; students are evaluated summatively so instructors can move them from one educational level to another; evaluation can be formative to facilitate program development or improvement, and professional students are also evaluated terminally to provide society with a certification of competence.

Methods of systematic (versus casual) evaluation range from measures far from the actual professional role, to techniques that approximate the role, to observations of professional practice itself. Specific evaluation techniques range also from the abstract (e.g., a written multiple choice test) to the concrete (e.g., observation of practitioner interactions). A recent thorough compendium of clinical competence measures for medicine with reviews of their use and interpretation pertinent to all professions (Neufeld and Norman, 1984) would serve as a useful supplement to this chapter's brief review.

OBJECTIVE TESTS

Stiggins (1978) and other writers have defended testing with multiple choice items for clinical professional education, addressing questions of efficiency, coverage, psychometric properties, and flexibility.

The principal problem with such tests is that as they are most commonly used, they more often test recognition and lower-level cognitive abilities than the higher levels of clinical diagnosis, analysis, or problem solving. A related problem is their validity for assessing clinical performance. Written exams have, however, been integrated into well-organized and conducted educational programs (Stritter & Talbert, 1974; Levine, Daeschner, & Emery, 1977). It appears that, if every effort is made to develop tests that measure high levels of clinical ability as opposed to isolated factual recall, written objective tests — even in multiple choice format — can contribute to evaluation of clinical competence.

SIMULATIONS

The past 2 decades have brought increased interest in teaching the professional to be a problem solver. Evaluation methods simulating the clinical setting and the clinical problem to be solved have allowed examiners to infer clinical performance; Barro (1973), in her extensive review of methods for measuring physician performance, refers to simulations as indirect evidence of performance, and Vu (1979) classifies problem solving into data gathering, hypothesis development and verification, result evaluation, and final decision making. The evaluation methods reviewed below measure similar outcomes, but their approaches vary considerably.

PAPER SIMULATIONS

Rimoldi's pioneering work (1961) was successfully modified into the Patient Management Problem (PMP) by McGuire and colleagues (McGuire & Babbott, 1967; McGuire, Solomon, & Bashook, 1976). The problem cited most frequently for paper simulations is concurrent validity. For example, Norman and Feightner (1981), comparing medical student performance on a PMP with performance using a simulated patient, found a significant difference in options selected. Similarly, Page and Fielding (1980), comparing pharmacists' performance on PMPs with actual cases in the work setting, found a 66% agreement; they concluded that PMPs predict what pharmacists do, but not what they do not do. Similar findings have resulted from the work reported by Elstein et al. (1978). Despite developmental costs and validity problems, PMPs do seem to have potential for learning and evaluating some aspects of clinical performance.

COMPUTER SIMULATIONS

Simulations can successfully be presented on an interactive computer terminal. Interactive computers have largely been used for self-instructional evaluation rather than for certification. Computerized simulations are costly but flexible, and can be valid representations of the patient encounter. CASE, for example, allows the medical student to interact with a simulated patient using natural language to obtain information before proceeding with problem solving (Harless, Drennon, Marxner, Root, & Miller, 1971), while CBX, in a time-dependent simulation, evaluates students on patient risk, costs incurred, and time spent in addition to patient workup procedures (Friedman, 1973; Friedman, Korst, Schultz, Beatty, & Entine, 1978). Computer simulations have also been used successfully in dentistry to test history taking prior to conducting an actual interview with a patient (Brody, Lucacchi, Kamp, & Rozen, 1973). Computer simulation validity has been assessed in various ways. Medical residents tested by CBX indicated that it adequately approximated interaction with real patients (Friedman et al., 1978); however, Feightner and Norman (1978) determined that subjects interacting with a computer simulation elicited consistently less information on a history and physical exam than they would in actual clinical situations.

SIMULATED PATIENTS

Student interaction with a simulated patient is used widely for teaching and evaluating medical history taking and physical examination skills (Barrows, 1971; Barrows & Tamblyn, 1980; Stillman, Rutala, Stillman, & Sabers, 1982). These procedures extend the simulation process to include quality of patient interaction, a characteristic that many would argue distinguishes good from poor practice. Actors or trained patients with stable physical findings have been used successfully to evaluate medical students interviewing mothers about their children (Helfer, Black, & Helfer, 1975), medical students learning how to do a pelvic examination (Billings & Stoeckle, 1977), medical students learning how to do a complete physical examination (Stillman, Ruggill, & Sabers, 1978), medical residents performing a physical examination (Rutala, Stillman, & Sabers, 1981), and law students learning interviewing skills (Stillman et al., 1982). Samson-Fisher and Poole (1980) determined that equivalent empathy is shown to simulated patients and real patients, and students are unable to discriminate between them. Once simulated patients or clients are trained, the simulation process is replicable and can be used to provide further feedback to the student. Reliability and validity, enhanced by procedural standardization, have been satisfactorily established (Norman, Tugwell, & Feightner, 1982).

VIDEOTAPES

Videotape can present simulated interactions, present a patient problem, or record actual clinical interactions. Short presentations by actors or actual patients illustrating various clinical problems have been developed in nursing (Richards et al., 1981) and medicine (Stillman, Sabers, Redfield, & Stewart, 1977; Tardiff, 1981). Tardiff found no correlation, however, between performance on his measure and other measures of clinical competence, and concluded that something different was indeed being measured by the process. Videotapes have also been used to record and then observe a student's actual interaction with a patient. The teaching process is most successful when a resident views his own tape, when more then one session is taped, when residents receive written summaries identifying specific strengths and weaknesses, and when the program director participates in the review (Cassata, Conroe, & Clements, 1977). Another study established that videotaped patient interactions could be used reliably for assessing clinical skills if the criteria for review were developed and implemented systematically (Liu et al., 1980).

DIRECT OBSERVATION

The professional apprenticeship is unique in giving students practical experience in an environment which either simulates or is the actual working condition. Evaluation of this clinical work by direct observation is both the simplest and the most complex of clinical evaluation methods. In its simplest conceptualization, direct observation occurs continuously. But purposeful observation requires a sound theory base and sound methods.

Student professional performance has been assessed through a host of methods. Most have involved a checklist (e.g., indicating whether specific behaviors exist) and/or a rating scale (e.g., assessing performance quality). Helpful guides can be found for several health professions: medicine (Friedman, 1978; DeMers, 1978), nursing (Pearson, 1975), dentistry (MacKenzie & Harrop, 1975; Patridge & Mast, 1978), and allied health (Madigan & LaDuca, 1978). Advantages of direct observation

include ease of development and use, focus on performance, and low cost; disadvantages include difficulties with objectivity and reliability. Efforts to overcome these disadvantages have been partially successful. Crocker, Muthard, Slaymaker, and Samson (1975), for example, described a successful procedure for occupational therapy. Other writers have discussed rating scales used to certify pediatric candidates (Skakun, 1981), use of generalizability coefficients as an alternative to traditional reliability coefficients (Boodoo & O'Sullivan, 1982), training raters to increase reliability (Loustau et al., 1980), and establishing validity by analyzing student and resident performance at different educational levels (Mazucca, Cohen, & Clark, 1981). Use of direct observation rating systems for qualitative assessments can improve student performance, as long as over-quantification is avoided. Dickenson, Dimarino, and Pfitzenmair (1973) provided one response to this plea with a procedure for physical therapy clinical evaluation using narrative responses to specific relationship and treatment categories. While direct observation usually involves instructors assessing student performance, students have productively evaluated themselves (Geissler, 1973; Oratio, 1978; Cochran and Spears, 1980) and their peers (Helfer, 1972). Medical records completed by students have also been successfully assessed by instructors using specific criteria (Margolis, Sheehan, & Stickley, 1973).

MULTIPLE METHODS

Clearly no single method provides all information necessary for students to improve performance in all aspects of clinical practice. The obvious solution — combining evaluation methods for assessing various clinical abilities — has been studied in medical education settings. For example, Holmes et al. (1978) reported on a process including a written examination, tutor rating of on-the-job performance, videotaped patient interaction rated by two examiners, and a patient evaluation completed by a professional patient; the near-zero correlations among the four methods indicated that different student abilities were measured. Harden and Gleeson (1979) developed a problem-based criterion-referenced test, called the Objective Structured Clinical Examination, in which students rotate through 25-minute stations using multiple choice and free response questions to test factual information, and both static and interactive laboratory sessions to test practical skills. Newble, Elmslie, and Baxter (1978) and Petrusa, Guckian, and Perkowski (1984) have reported positive results with the procedure, which yields a profile of clinical competencies. The procedure has been demonstrated to have acceptable content and construct validity and reliability indices (Newble, Hoare, & Elmslie, 1981).

Whatever the specific format, students must develop a picture of themselves which they can compare to a standard. That picture is based on information from multiple sources: self, peers, patients and clients, and instructors. An evaluation system to establish that picture should include (a) clearly established purpose for the evaluation; (b) clear performance standards; (c) validity, reliability, and practicality of the system; (d) training for evaluators to reduce misunderstanding and increase reliability; and (e) a variety of approaches assuming that no single method will provide all information necessary.

Evaluation of Clinical Teaching

Clinical teaching, like student performance, is evaluated constantly. Judgments about clinical teaching effectiveness will always be made — often casually, sometimes meaningfully. They can be made meaningfully if the *purpose* of evaluation, the *concept* of good clinical teaching to be the standard, and the *context* in which evaluation takes place are first established. Only then will it be appropriate to determine *who* will do the evaluating of *whom,* and what *methods* will be used to collect the information on which judgments will be based.

Clinical teaching can be evaluated for formative purposes — such as providing clinical instructors with information that will help them improve what and how they teach, or for summative purposes — such as providing administrators or faculty committees with information for assignment, promotion, tenure, or salary decisions.

Teaching evaluation should be based on four premises: (a) Teaching does make a difference in what and how much students learn; (b) teaching behaviors are changeable and can, therefore, be improved; (c) evaluation of teaching is possible; and (d) one good argument is worth many individual cases (Rippey, 1981). Using these and other premises, several recent documents have reviewed the research literature on instructor evaluation, offering suggestions for developing and conducting evaluation systems. Rippey's (1981) review was most pertinent to medical education; Chambers (1977) and Mackenzie (1977) wrote about dental education; Bronstein (1979) and Serkland and Sockloff (1978) referred to allied health education; Raff, Boyle, and Stone (1977) and Norman (1978) addressed nursing education. Each of these, however, discussed teaching generally; none specifically addressed clinical teaching in the apprenticeship.

Evaluation of instruction in apprenticeships involves collection and interpretation of information from a variety of sources about teaching performance — for example, individual teachers using criteria to assess their own performance, students responding formally or informally to specific questions, faculty peers and administrators responding to similar questions, and consultants using agreed-upon criteria. As Skeff (1984) demonstrated, different data sources provide different types of information and often different interpretations of the same teaching performance.

SELF ASSESSMENT

Self-assessment is recommended when used in conjunction with another method, and when based on specific criteria agreed to by the instructor in advance. The Instrument for a Comprehensive and Relevant Education (ICARE) was developed for health educators to evaluate their own teaching. Workshops presented its use, and subsequently instructors — mostly from nursing and allied health — reported that they had used ICARE or a modification to analyze their own teaching and improved their instruction as a result (Bronstein, 1978). Schaffer's (1980) self-assessment model for allied health educators recommends that instructors evaluate themselves against consensually established standards to determine specific strengths and weaknesses, identify areas needing improvement, and develop a growth contract with their supervisors. Although it appears

to be theoretically sound, the model has not been tested empirically.

Combinations of self-assessment with other methods have been proposed for several professions. Irby (1978), suggesting that self-evaluation be coordinated with data from educational consultants and/or students, has designed the Self-Assessment Inventory for Clinical and Classroom Teaching in Medicine (Irby, 1977). Adams, Ham, Mawardi, Scali, and Weisman (1974) describe a self-assessment successfully combined with colleague group discussions. Wong and Wong (1980) suggest a useful checklist for individual use, advising nursing instructors to use it daily. An interaction analysis that objectively records interchanges between instructor and students can contribute to self-analysis based on a finite number of mutually exclusive behaviors (Drum & Cordova, 1979).

Although the empirical evidence for effectiveness of self-assessment in promoting teaching improvement is not great, it might be wise to heed Rippey's (1981) conclusion: Self-assessment is essential because one cannot improve one's teaching until personal deficiencies are recognized and the need for change internalized.

PEER EVALUATION

Whether systematic or casual, peer evaluation has always occurred in postsecondary education. Peer review underlies academic promotion and tenure processes, and some assessments of professionals' clinical competence for certification and recertification have recently employed peer reviews (Cruft, 1982). Peer review to improve teaching did not begin to appear in the research literature until the 1970s, however, and even then it was discussed principally for traditional educational programs or in preclinical topics.

Colleagues in the same specialty can provide one another with (a) insights into clinical teacher behaviors, (b) judgments on instructional materials and content appropriateness, (c) assessments of advising and evaluation procedures, and (d) appraisals of instructional development efforts (Irby, 1983). Rippey (1981) indicates that both instructor and evaluator usually benefit from the peer evaluation process.

In a comprehensive and well-researched study of peer review (Skeff, 1983), a department colleague with considerable educational expertise reviewed videotapes of clinical teaching with instructors and provided extensive feedback based on preset criteria; improvements were observed in subsequent encounters. Other studies have addressed the following: observation by a colleague and educator prior to department-meeting discussion of the conclusions (Miller, 1980); observation and discussion of medical residents' teaching by fellow residents and attending physicians (Lazerson, 1972); a one-on-one evaluation of nursing instructors by colleagues prior to a department discussion (Gorecki, 1977); and development of specific criteria embodied in an objective rating scale for use in evaluation (Sauter & Walker, 1976).

Methodological problems aside, it seems logical that peer review could be helpful in improving clinical teaching. Teachers can learn from evaluating their own teaching and that of colleagues, and both can benefit from the discussion. Peer evaluation may be optimal when (a) involved teachers participate in the system's development, (b) specific criteria are developed for the evaluation, (c) peers doing the evaluating trust one another, (d) a nonpejorative discussion is included after the evaluation, (e) a nonthreatening person facilitates the process, and (f) the effectiveness of the process is continually investigated.

STUDENT EVALUATION

Research on student ratings — the most common form of clinical teaching evaluation — shows that they can be reliable, valid, and useful, but that they have limited generalizability (Irby & Rakestraw, 1981; Rippey, 1975). Instruments used for student ratings of clinical teaching can be developed empirically based on suitable criteria and appropriate psychometric methods (Irby & Rakestraw, 1981; Kotzen and Entrekin, 1978; Purohit, Manasse, & Nelson, 1977). Such instruments are used extensively in medical schools (Lancaster, Mendelson, & Ross, 1979) and in dental schools (Chambers, 1977). Hunt (1980) found that only 75% of psychiatry residency programs used residents to evaluate faculty members' clinical teaching, that 69% relied heavily on a questionnaire, and 19% used a questionnaire in combination with an analysis of resident performance to assess the effects of teaching. Content analysis of these rating forms (Hunt, Irby, Bauer, & Loebel, 1981) revealed that categories of instructional organization and clarity appeared on 58% of the forms, instructor knowledge on 42%, group interaction skills on 41%, instructor enthusiasm on 30%, clinical supervisory skills on 25%, modeling professional characteristics on 18%, and clinical competence on 17%.

It is not clear that student feedback alone leads to improved teaching; teachers need more than student ratings. Rous, Bamford, Gromisch, Rich, Rubin, & Sall (1972) and Skeff (1983) both observed positive change in student evaluations of their medical colleagues who received only feedback from students. The Skeff study also showed greater change in attitude toward teaching when student feedback was combined with interpretation and expert consultation, while Sall, Gromisch, Rubin, and Stone (1976) found teaching improvement when the evaluations were discussed in a peer committee.

In summary, student evaluations alone cannot be expected to guarantee clinical teaching improvement. Indeed instructors often prefer to question the worth of student ratings. The criticism is unwarranted; adult students in professional fields can provide valuable information on their instruction. They can ascertain and report whether clinical instruction is helping them learn. It follows that student evaluations of clinical instruction can be useful if instructional improvement is the goal.

CONSULTATION

While clinical teaching is difficult to observe because of its fluid nature and the small numbers of students, evaluation by a consultant can be helpful in identifying problems and providing constructive feedback. The consultant generally observes instruction (either in fact or on videotape) prior to rendering suggestions; for the recommendations to be most helpful the observation should be based on preset criteria. Goin & Kline

(1974), analyzing videotaped observations by educational consultants of clinical instructors and psychiatry residents, found that the most helpful instructors focused on patient responses to residents and specific patient-care techniques rather than residents' feelings or behavior. Patridge, Harris, and Petzel (1980) reported a favorable response from clinical instructors involved in a program using consultant feedback based on observation of actual clinical teaching sessions. A program with extensive systematic observation, individualized feedback, and formal group discussion (Skeff, 1983) found observable improvements in teaching. The consultant in this study had the advantage of being both a medical colleague and an educational consultant; having both sensitivities was certainly an advantage, as Miller (1980) would agree.

SUMMARY

Because there probably is no single "best" way for clinical instructors to evaluate their teaching, multiple approaches should be used. Clinical instructors can ask students informally about their effectiveness, or they can ask more formally in writing. Students will be more apt to provide honest responses in writing, but will also do so verbally if nonthreatening rapport has been established by the instructor. Peers can help as well; most are willing to share a few minutes or even longer to observe and to provide evaluative feedback. Good educational consultants are more difficult to find, but can provide helpful feedback in short periods of time. If teaching has been guided by an instructional model (e.g., Stritter, 1982), the teaching evaluation transcends individual situations and cases. Optimally, instructors will analyze their own teaching systematically, regularly, and often. All of these suggestions require that specific questions be asked based on a consensually established definition of good clinical teaching.

Conclusions

Research on the teaching and learning processes in professional education's clinical component — the apprenticeship — is virtually nonexistent in all but the health professions. For some professional fields scholarly assessment of educational questions is not accomplished through research but instead by other approaches. For some professions where educational research is in its infancy, predictive studies, curriculum reviews, and graduate surveys predominate. Even in the health professions, attention to traditional science teaching has consumed great interest; clinical teaching investigations have gained in number and quality only in the last decade.

The preceding research review suggested the following conclusions. *First*, there is no magic formula to predict a learner's performance reliably — and much less so the complex demands of professional roles. *Second*, a learner's preparation for the practical realm must include more than merely cognitive knowledge. Not all prerequisites have received equal research attention; for example, problem solving and communication have been studied much more than have interpersonal professional attitudes or technological sophistication. *Third*, successful teaching includes both elements of the "art" of teaching (attitudes, role modeling) and the "science" of teaching (organization, practice, and evaluation). While there is some research evidence on characteristics and behaviors of successful clinical instructors, a complex environment and multiple instructors can make it difficult to isolate the impact of specific instructors and teaching behaviors. *Fourth*, because the apprenticeship depends so heavily upon the practical cases at hand, a learner's tasks can be dictated exclusively by daily work demands unless supplementary instruction, about which there is an extensive if mixed literature, is used. *Fifth*, the importance of differences among sites for clinical learning is far from known, and the research evidence about them is far from conclusive. *Sixth*, practical performance can be reliably and validly evaluated in a variety of ways, from more abstract approaches somewhat removed from the realities of professional practice to concrete approaches directly reflecting practice. *Finally*, teaching performance can — although not easily — be evaluated by self, peers, students, and consultants in an integrated approach.

Recommendations

The recommendations evolving from this discussion rest upon the special nature of research in applied disciplines, and upon the general purposes of research for theory construction.

Research in Applied Settings

While the studies reviewed above do advance our understanding of professional education, whether they can all be classified as "research" is another question. Most describe variables, or explore associations among variables; few propose causal links or offer sufficient causal evidence for prescribing action. Few are generalizable. Many studies can be classified as evaluations — of specific student groups, instructors, sites, or methods scrutinized at specific times and in specific locations. "Educational research" carried out in professional schools is usually conducted not for accumulating knowledge for theory development, but by instructors and educators whose goal is action. Its purpose is usually to improve the immediate educational process and product, not to illuminate or elucidate educational process.

Have these research and evaluation attempts employed the best strategies for answering the most pressing educational questions? Professional educational research is constrained by several forces alluded to in this chapter. First, traditions of thought and rules of evidence employed in a field's educational research generally mirror the profession's epistemology. The constraint is visible in any number of manifestations: The health professions' traditional reliance on positivist paradigms might be just as limiting, for example, as architecture's preoccupation with systems and creativity. A second force upon research is professional education's practical orientation: Because evaluation studies outnumber theory-oriented research studies, external validity and theory development have suffered.

Miller's assessment of the current research on professional education processes suggests that a hunger for new data about new efforts outweighs thoughtful study of continuing issues, and that preoccupation with small, easily isolated variables takes precedence over attention to large issues of greater meaning (1980). Indeed, professional education studies for the most part are short-term, statistically weak, and equivocally reported. Education journals in the various professional fields have often encouraged anecdotes about educational experiences and trivial studies of minute phenomena; they have not always insisted upon serious far-reaching scholarship.

Despite these problems with professional education's approach to educational research, there are promising signs. There are substantial topics to engage educators in many professions for several decades to come. Theory can be developed, and significant research questions can be addressed. Some of the more important are:

1. Are there student attributes that, in interaction with certain aspects of clinical instruction, will result in better-prepared professionals?
2. What aspects of professional education must students master prior to entering the practical environment? How can they best be taught?
3. Have the characteristics of effective practical instruction been fully identified? Can these characteristics be related to learner performance?
4. What are the optimal characteristics or logistical arrangements of sites in which practical learning takes place?
5. What are the most efficient and the most effective methods for evaluating a learner's practical performance? Which approaches can be integrated to provide a reliable, objective, and valid assessment of a learner's performance?
6. What is the best approach, or combination of approaches, for assessing clinical instruction in order to improve it?

A Research Agenda

A practical research agenda, as depicted in Figure 34.1, is suggested in this chapter's structure. The three dimensions define an array of research topics:

A. Aspects of the experience
   1. Prerequisite learner attributes
   2. Preparatory educational experiences
   3. Sites for apprenticeships
   4. Clinical instructors' characteristics and behaviors

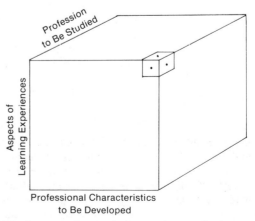

Fig. 34.1. A research agenda for professional education.

5. Supplementary teaching strategies
6. Evaluation of learner performance
7. Evaluation of teaching.
B. Professional characteristics to be developed.
1. *Cognitive* is the information base which becomes knowledge as it is transformed into a retrievable and useful form. Also included is the ability to reason with that base both intuitively and analytically.
2. *Technical* includes the physical and manipulative skills essential to the conduct of the profession.
3. *Attitudinal* are the interests, values and ethics which guide choice, argument, rationalization, action and resolution of moral problems.
4. *Psychosocial* are those aspects of interpersonal and human interaction which underly sensitivity to and communication with one's professional colleagues and/ or one's clients.
5. *Socialization* is the gradual internalization of professional values and the commitment to a professional role.
6. *Learning Skills* are important to a professional in keeping abreast of a changing field. They include the ability to decide what one needs to learn, how to learn it and when the learning has been accomplished.
C. Professions to be studied (for example)
1. Architecture
2. Business
3. Clinical psychology
4. Dentistry
5. Environmental planning
6. Forestry, etc.

Some intersects in this 3-dimensional model (e.g., A6, B1, C4) have been subjected to more scrutiny than have others. The more numerous unexplored intersects provide researchers with an almost inexhaustible supply of pressing questions.

Miller points out, however, that even questions like these, while important, are not the only questions professional educators should address (Miller, 1980). Education's relationship to society and the nature of professional practice must also be explored. For example:

1. How can the needs of practicing professionals be used to influence changes in educational programs?
2. Can the contributions of professional education be related to behavior of the professional and the effect of the service that professional provides?
3. What is the relationship between the practical component of professional education and the needs of the population to be served?
4. How can practicing professionals stay in touch with the professional educational program which gave them their beginning in the profession? How can that educational program facilitate the professional's continuing growth?
5. Can theories of professional education be developed and tested to guide not only the practice of professional education, but also research on professional education?

A research agenda for professional education must be broad both in scope and in its implications for theory. If the ultimate

purpose of research is theory construction, theory's purpose in turn is to illuminate mankind's comprehension of the world and of human action in the world. In professional education that illumination both guides practice and leads to further research, whose purpose is further theory construction.

Professional education suffers from two versions of insufficient theory. First, many professions are themselves loosely defined; their practice is based on models such as habit, the artist as hero, or craftsmanship. They suffer, in short, because there is not "theory of action" (Argyris & Schon, 1974) for the profession. And second, professional education, resting on an already tenuous theory base, suffers further because there is little educational theory of action for instruction — particularly practical instruction. In some fields apprentices are educated by methods ranging from hero worship to trial and error, while in other fields or at specific schools, students do receive planned, coordinated instruction based on educational theory.

The traditional view that research is conducted to explain, predict, and/or control natural phenomena may be insufficient for guiding research on education for professional practice. A field that is a "learned profession" an "applied science," or a "practice discipline" rests not only on the rigors of disciplined inquiry but also on a commitment to practice (Newman, 1972). Research on education for a practice discipline must reflect not only the field's disciplined inquiry but also its orientation to practice.

Dickoff, James, and Wiedenbach (1968) conceptualized theory construction for practice disciplines, proposing that research whose ultimate goal is theory for practice subsumes research at several simpler levels. They define four levels of theory: factor-isolating theory, or classification; factor-relating theory, or situation depicting; situation-relating theory, or prediction; and situation-producing theory, or prescription. Practice disciplines, they assert, should strive for prescriptive theories, which "attempt conceptualization of desired situations as well as conceptualizing the prescription under which an agent or practitioner must act in order to bring about situations of the kind conceived as desirable in the conception of the goal" (p. 420).

Yet not all research in any field, much less professional education, can be prescriptive theory-building research. Initial research on teaching in professional fields must define the essential elements or the essential factors in the young professional's education. The 3-dimensional research agenda proposed above is such a beginning. Subsequent research must draw together those factors into validated descriptions of complex learning; further research will note relationships and ultimately verify predictions — for example, predictions about aptitude-teacher interactions. Only upon this foundation can theories of practice — the ultimate goal for research on professional education — be attempted.

REFERENCES

Abrahamson, S. (1965). Professional education. *Review of Educational Research, 35*, 335–346.
Adams, W. R., Ham, T. H., Mawardi, B. H., Scali, H. A., & Weisman, R. (1974). Research on self-evaluation for clinical teachers. *Journal of Medical Education, 49*, 1166–1174.

Association of Collegiate Schools of Architecture. (1975). 1974 AIA/ACSA teachers' seminar program notes. *Journal of Architectural Education, 28,* 4–9.

Argyris, C., & Schon, D. A. (1974). *Theory in practice: Increasing professional effectiveness.* San Francisco: Jossey–Bass.

Barr, J. S., Gwyer, J., & Zippora, T. (1982). Evaluation of clinical education centers in physical therapy. *Physical Therapy, 62,* 850–861.

Barro, A. R. (1973). Survey and evaluation of approaches to physician performance measurement. *Journal of Medical Education, 48,* 1051–1093.

Barrows, H. S. (1971). *Simulated patients.* Springfield, Ill.: Thomas.

Barrows, H. S., & Tamblyn, R. M. (1977). The portable patient problem pack: A problem-based learning unit. *Journal of Medical Education, 52,* 1002–1004.

Barrows, H. S., & Tamblyn, R. M. (1980). *Problem based learning: An approach to medical education.* New York: Springer.

Bauman, K., Cook, J. & Larson, L. K. (1981). Using technology to humanize instruction: An approach to teaching nursing skills. *Journal of Nursing Education, 20*(3), 27–31.

Becker, H. S. (1962). The nature of a profession. In N. B. Henry (Ed.), *Education for the professions.* Chicago: National Society for the Study of Education.

Berrong, J. M., Hendricson, W. D., & Evans, J. J. (1982). An instructional resource center in a senior dental clinic. *Journal of Dental Education, 46,* 479–484.

Bevil, C., & Gross, L. C. (1981). Assessing the adequacy of clinical learning settings. *Nursing Outlook, 24,* 658–661.

Billings, J. A., & Stoeckle, J. D. (1977). Pelvic examination instruction and the doctor-patient relationship. *Journal of Medical Education, 52,* 834–839.

Blauch, L. E. (1962). A century of the professional school. In W. W. Brickman & S. Lehrer (Eds), *A century of higher education.* New York: Society for the Advancement of Education.

Boley, B. A. (Ed.). (1977). *Crossfire in professional education.* New York: Pergamon.

Boodoo, G. M., & O'Sullivan, P. (1982). Obtaining generalizability coefficients for clinical evaluations. *Evaluation and the Health Professions, 5,* 345–358.

Brody, H. A., Lucacchi, L. F., Kamp, M., & Rozen, R. (1973). Computer based simulated patients for teaching history-taking. *Journal of Dental Education, 37*(8), 27–31.

Bronstein, R. A. (1978). *Teacher evaluation in health professions education: A study of the impact of ICARE.* Denver: Colorado Association for Continuing Laboratory Education.

Bronstein, R. A. (1979). Teacher evaluation in the health professions. *Journal of Allied Health, 8,* 212–219.

Brubacher, J. S. (1962). The evolution of professional education. In N. B. Henry (Ed.), *Education for the professions.* Chicago: National Society for the Study of Education.

Bucher, R., & Stelling, J. G. (1977). *Becoming professional.* Beverly Hills, CA: Sage.

Cardozo, M. H. (1977). Untitled remarks. In B. A. Boley (Ed.), *Crossfire in professional education.* Elmsford, NY: Pergamon.

Carline, J. D., Cullen, T. J., Scott, C. S., Shannon, N. F., & Schaad, D. (1983). Predicting performance during clinical years from the new Medical College Admissions Test. *Journal of Medical Education, 58,* 18–25.

Carroll, J. G., & Monroe, J. (1980). Teaching clinical interviewing in the health professions. *Evaluation in the Health Professions, 3,* 21–45.

Cassata, D. M., Conroe, R. M., & Clements, P. W. (1977). A program for enhancing medical interviewing using video-tape feedback in the family practice residency. *Journal of Family Practice, 4,* 673–677.

Chambers, D. W. (1977). Faculty evaluation: Review of literature most pertinent to dental education. *Journal of Dental Education, 41,* 290–300.

Cheit, E. F. (1975). *The useful arts and the liberal tradition.* New York: McGraw-Hill.

Clawson, C. C., Harris, I. B., & Garrard, J. (1980). Effect of variations in sequencing at clinical tutorials. *Medical Education, 14,* 330–335.

Coble, D. A. (1981). The analysis of clinical instruction in a medical/ paramedical educational environment. *Dissertation Abstracts, 42,* 94A.

Cochran, S. M., & Spears, M. C. (1980). Student self assessment and instructors' ratings: A comparison. *Journal of the American Dietetic Association, 76,* 253–257.

Committee on Guidelines for Clinical Legal Education. (1980). *Clinical legal education.* Chicago: Association of American Law Schools and American Bar Association.

Conners, V. L. (1979). Teaching affective behaviors. *Journal of Nursing Education, 18*(6), 33–39.

Crocker, L.M., Muthard, J. E., Slaymaker, J. E., & Samson, L. (1975). A performance rating scale for evaluating clinical competence of occupational therapy students. *American Journal of Occupational Therapy, 29,* 81–86.

Cruft, G. E. (1982). Peer review. In J. S. Lloyd (Ed.), *Evaluation of noncognitive skills and clinical performance.* Chicago: American Board of Medical Specialties.

Cullen, J. B. (1978). *The structure of professionalism.* New York: Petrocelli.

Dachelet, C. Z., Wemett, M. F., Garling, E. J., Craig-Kuhn, K., Kent, N., & Kitzman, H. J. (1981). The critical incident technique applied to the evaluation of the clinical practicum setting. *Journal of Nursing Education, 20*(8), 15–31.

Daggett, C. J., Cassie, J. M., & Collins, G. F. (1979). Research on clinical teaching. *Review of Educational Research, 49,* 151–169.

Davis, C. M. (1981). Affective education for the health professions. *Physical Therapy, 61,* 1587–1593.

DeMers, J. L. (1978). Observational assessment of performance. In M. K. Morgan & D. M. Irby (Eds.), *Evaluating clinical competence in the health professions.* St. Louis: C. V. Mosby.

Dickinson, R., Dimarino, J., and Pfitzenmair, J. (1973). A common evaluation instrument. *Physical Therapy, 53,* 1075–1080.

Dickoff, J., James, P., and Wiedenbach, E. (1968). Theory in a practice discipline: Part I. Practice oriented theory. *Nursing Research, 17,* 415–435.

Dilley, G. J., Machen, J. B., Dilley, D. C. H., & Howden, E. F. (1978). Acquisition of psychomotor skills in tooth preparation using self-paced instruction. *Journal of Dental Education, 42,* 476–479.

Distlehorst, L., & Barrows, H. S. (1982). Problem based learning: A tool for problem based, self directed learning. *Journal of Medical Education, 57,* 486–488.

Drum, R. L., & Cordova, R. D. (1979). Analyzing and developing effective instructional behaviors for allied health educators. *Journal of Allied Health, 8,* 226–231.

Edgeworth, R. L. (1812). *Essays on professional education.* London: J. Johnson and Co.

Elkins, R. L., & Luetkemeyer, J. F. (1974). Characteristics of successful engineering students. *Engineering Education, 65,* 189–191.

Elliott, R., Jillings, C., & Thorne, S. (1982). Psychomotor skill acquisition in nursing schools in the U.S. and Canada. *The Canadian Nurse, 78,* 25–27.

Elstein, A. S., Shulman, L. S., & Sprafka, S. A. (1978). *Medical problem solving: An analysis of clinical reasoning.* Cambridge, MA: Harvard University Press.

Evans, J. R., & Massler, M. (1977). The effective clinical teacher. *Journal of Dental Education, 41,* 613–617.

Feightner, J. W., & Norman, G. R. (1978). Computer based problems as a measure of the problem solving process: Some concerns about validity. In *Proceedings, the Seventeenth Annual Conference on Research in Medical Education* (pp. 51–56). Washington, DC: Association of American Medical Colleges.

Fine, V. K., & Therrien, M. E. (1977). Empathy in the doctor-patient relationship: Skill training for medical students. *Journal of Medical Education, 52,* 752–757.

Finley, B., Kim, K. K., & Mynatt, S. (1979). Maximizing videotaped learning of IPS. *Journal of Nursing Education, 18*(1), 33–41.

Foley, R., Smilansky, J., & Yonke, A. (1979). Teacher-student interaction in a medical clerkship. *Journal of Medical Education, 54,* 622–626.

Ford, C. W. (Ed.). (1978). *Clinical education for the allied health professions.* St. Louis: C. V. Mosby.

Fosson, A., Fischer, D., & Patterson, L. (1975). Improved student learning during ambulatory pediatric clinical clerkship. *Journal of Medical Education, 50,* 398–400.

Foster, P. (1981). Clinical discussion groups: Verbal participation and outcomes. *Journal of Medical Education, 56,* 831–843.

Friberg, R. J. (1980). The role of communication and cognitive style in medical clinical education. *Dissertation Abstracts, 41,* 2462A.

Friedman, C. P., Stritter, F. T., & Talbert, L. R. (1978). A systematic comparison of teaching hospital and remote site clinical education. *Journal of Medical Education, 53,* 565–573.

Friedman, D. (1978). *The use of subjective evaluation instruments in health sciences education.* Atlanta: National Institutes of Health.

Friedman, R. B. (1973). A computer program for simulating the patient–physician encounter. *Journal of Medical Education, 48,* 92–97.

Friedman, R. B., Korst, D. R., Schultz, J. V., Beatty, E., & Entine, S. (1978). Experience with the simulated patient physician encounter. *Journal of Medical Education, 53,* 825–830.

Geissler, P. R. (1973). Student self-assessment in dental technology. *Journal of Dental Education, 37*(9), 19–21.

Gerber, W. L., Albanese, M., Brown, D., & Mathes, S. (1985). Teaching with simulated patients. *Evaluation and the Health Professions, 8,* 69–81.

Geyman, J. P., & Guyton, R. (1974). Evaluation of multimedia self-teaching programs for medical students taking community preceptorships. *Journal of Medical Education, 49,* 1062–1064.

Gil, D. H., Rubeck, R. F., & Jones, P. B. (1982). Students' perceptions of evaluative feedback. In *Proceedings, Twenty-Second Annual Conference on Research in Medical Education* (pp. 77–82). Washington, DC: Association of American Medical Colleges.

Glick, I. D., & Epstein, L. J. (1977). Increasing learning during the psychiatric residency. *Comprehensive Psychiatry, 18,* 545–549.

Goin, M. K., & Kline, F. M. (1974). Supervision observed. *Journal of Nervous and Mental Disease, 158,* 208–213.

Gordon, M. J., Hadac, R. R., & Smith, C. K. (1977). Evaluation of clinical training in the community. *Journal of Medical Education, 52,* 888–895.

Gorecki, Y. (1977). Faculty peer review. *Nursing Outlook, 25,* 439–442.

Gough, H. G. (1978). Some predictive implications of premedical scientific competence and preferences. *Journal of Medical Education, 53,* 291–300.

Gough, H. G., & Hall, W. B. (1975). The prediction of academic and clinical performance in medical school. *Research in Higher Education, 3,* 301–314.

Haider, G. (1976). An evaluative diagnostic model of education. *Journal of Architectural Education, 29,* 30–31.

Harden, R. M., & Gleeson, F. A. (1979). Assessment of clinical competence using an objective structured clinical examination. *Medical Education, 13,* 41–54.

Harless, W. G., Drennon, G. G., Marxner, J. J., Root, J. A., & Miller, G. E. (1971). CASE: A computer-aided simulation of the clinical encounter. *Journal of Medical Education, 46,* 443–448.

Harris, R. S. (1974). Into the breach. *Journal of Architectural Education, 27,* 3–4.

Hawkins, J. W. (1981). *Clinical experiences in collegiate nursing education: Selection of clinical agencies.* New York: Springer.

Heiss, A. M., Davis, A., & Voci, F. (1967). *Graduate and professional education: An annotated bibliography.* Berkeley: University of California, Center for Research and Development in Higher Education.

Helfer, R. E. (1972). Peer evaluation: Its potential usefulness in medical education. *British Journal of Medical Education, 6,* 224–231.

Helfer, R. E., Black, M. A., & Helfer, M. E. (1975). Pediatric interviewing skills taught by non physicians. *American Journal of Diseases of Children, 129,* 1053–1057.

Hoban, J. D., & Casbergue, J. P. (1978). Simulation: A technique for instruction and evaluation. In C. W. Ford (Ed.), *Clinical education for the allied health professions.* St. Louis: C. V. Mosby.

Holmes, F. F., Baker, L. H., Torian, E. C., Richardson, N. K., Glick, S., & Yarmat, A. J. (1978). Measuring clinical competence of medical students. *Medical Education, 12,* 364–368.

Holzman, G. B., Singleton, D., Holmes, T. F., & Maatsch, J. L. (1977).

Initial pelvic examination instruction: The effectiveness of three contemporary approaches. *American Journal of Obstetrics and Gynecology, 129,* 124–129.

Hughes, E. C. (Ed.). (1973a). *Education for the professions of medicine, law, theology, and social welfare.* New York: McGraw-Hill.

Hughes, E. C. (1973b). Higher education and the professions. In C. Kaysen (Ed.), *Content and context: Essays on college education.* New York: McGraw-Hill.

Hunt, D. D. (1980). Evaluation of course content and teacher effectiveness in psychiatric residencies as viewed by program chief residents. *Journal of Psychiatric Education, 4,* 124–130.

Hunt, D. D., Irby, D. M., Bauer, R., & Loebel, J. P. (1981). An appraisal of methods of evaluating training in psychiatry. *Medical Education, 15,* 332–334.

Infante, M. S. (1975). *The clinical laboratory in nursing education.* New York: John Wiley.

Irby, D. M. (1977). *Self-assessment inventory for clinical and classroom teaching in medicine.* Seattle: University of Washington School of Medicine.

Irby, D. M. (1978). Clinical faculty development. In C. W. Ford (Ed.), *Clinical education for the allied health professions.* St. Louis: C. V. Mosby.

Irby, D. M. (1978). Clinical teacher effectiveness in medicine. *Journal of Medical Education, 53,* 808–815.

Irby, D. M. (1979). Teaching and learning style preferences of family medicine preceptors and residents. *Journal of Family Practice, 8,* 1065–1087.

Irby, D. M. (1983). Peer review of teaching in medicine. *Journal of Medical Education, 58,* 457–461.

Irby, D. M., & Rakestraw, P. (1981). Evaluating clinical teaching in medicine. *Journal of Medical Education, 56,* 181–185.

Jevons, F. R. (1969). *The teaching of science.* London: Allen & Unwin.

Jules, F. A. (1973). An approach to architectural education. *Journal of Architectural Education, 26,* 114–119.

Kagan, N. (1980). Influencing human interaction: Eighteen years with IPR. In A. K. Hess (Ed.), *Psychotherapy supervision: Theory, research, and practice.* New York: John Wiley.

Kahn, E., Lass, S. L., Hartley, R., & Kornreich, H. K. (1981). Affective learning in medical education. *Journal of Medical Education, 56,* 646–652.

Kahn, G. S., Cohen, B., & Jason, H. (1979). The teaching of interpersonal skills in U.S. medical schools. *Journal of Medical Education, 54,* 29–35.

Karns, P. J., & Schwab, T. A. (1982). Therapeutic communication and clinical instruction. *Nursing Outlook, 30,* 39–43.

Kissinger, J. F., & Munjas, B. A. (1981). Nursing process, student attributes, and teaching methodologies. *Nursing Research, 4,* 242–246.

Kissinger, J. F., & Munjas, B. A. (1982). Predictors of student success. *Nursing Outlook, 30,* 53–54.

Kotzan, J. A., & Entrekin, D. N. (1978). Development and implementation of a factor analyzed faculty evaluation instrument for undergraduate pharmacy instruction. *American Journal of Pharmaceutical Education, 42,* 114–118.

Kuhn, T. S. (1970). *The structure of scientific revolutions.* Chicago: University of Chicago Press.

Lancaster, G. J., Mendelson, M. A., & Ross, G. R. (1979). The utilization of student instructional ratings in medical colleges. *Journal of Medical Education, 54,* 657–659.

Lancaster, O. E. (1976). The future of engineering education in land-grant universities. In G. L. Anderson (Ed.), *Land-grant universities and their continuing challenge.* East Lansing: Michigan State University Press.

Lazerson, A. M. (1972). Training for teaching: Psychiatry residents as teachers in an evening college. *Journal of Medical Education, 47,* 576–578.

Levine, H. G., Daeschner, C. W., & Emery, J. L. (1977). Evaluation of a modularized system of instruction in pediatrics. *Journal of Medical Education, 52,* 213–215.

Liu, P., Miller, E., Herr, G., Hardy, C., Sivarajan, M., & Willenkin, R. (1980). Videotape reliability: A method of evaluation of clinical performance examination. *Journal of Medical Education, 55,* 713–715.

Loustau, A., Lentz, M., Lee, K., McKenna, M., Hiraho, S., Walker, W. F., & Goldsmith, J. W. (1980). Using videotape to establish rater reliability. *Journal of Nursing Education, 19*(7), 10–17.

Mackenzie, R. S. (1977). Essential features of a faculty evaluation program. *Journal of Dental Education, 41,* 301–306.

Mackenzie, R. S., and Harrop, T. J. (Eds.). (1975). *An instructional information exchange of dentistry in the United States: Vol. 6. Observational measurement of clinical performance* (Publ. No. 75–70). Washington, DC: United States Department of Health, Education, and Welfare.

Mackenzie, R. S., Heins, P. J., Holbrook, W., Low, S. B., & Kramer, M. (1979). An analysis of behavioral contingencies in clinical training. *Journal of Dental Education, 43,* 578–584.

Madigan, M. J., & LaDuca, A. (1978). Higher levels of learning. In C. W. Ford (Ed.), *Clinical education in the allied health professions.* St. Louis: C. V. Mosby.

Maguire, P., Roe, P., Goldberg, D., Hyde, J. S., & O'Dowd, T. (1978). The value of feedback on teaching interviewing skills to medical students. *Psychological Medicine, 8,* 695–704.

Margolis, C. Z., Barnoon, S., & Barak, N. (1982). A required course in decision making for preclinical medical students. *Journal of Medical Education, 57,* 184–190.

Margolis, C. Z., Sheehan, T. J., & Stickley, W. T. (1973). A graded problem oriented record to evaluate clinical performance. *Pediatrics, 51,* 980–985.

Mayhew, L. B. (1970). *Graduate and professional education, 1980: A survey of institutional plans.* New York: McGraw–Hill.

Mayhew, L. B. (1971). *Changing practices in education for the professions.* Atlanta: Southern Regional Educational Board.

Mazur, H., Beeston, J. J., & Yerxa, E. J. (1979). Clinical interdisciplinary health team care: An educational experiment. *Journal of Medical Education, 54,* 703–713.

Mazzuca, S. A., Cohen, S. J., & Clark, C. M. (1981). Evaluating clinical knowledge across years of medical training. *Journal of Medical Education, 56,* 83–90.

McGlothlin, W. J. (1961). Insights from one profession which may be applied to other professions. In G. K. Smith (Ed.), *Current issues in higher education.* Washington, DC, Association for Higher Education.

McGlynn, T. J., Wynn, J. B., & Munzenrider, R. F. (1978). Resident education in primary care: How residents learn. *Journal of Medical Education, 53,* 973–981.

McGuire, C. H., & Babbott, D. (1967). Simulation technique in the measurement of problem solving skills. *Journal of Educational Measurement, 4*(1), 1–10.

McGuire, C. H., Solomon, L. M., & Bashook, P. G. (1976). *Construction and use of written simulations.* New York: Psychological Corporation.

Meleca, C. B., Schimpfauser, F. T., & Witteman, J. K. (1978). *A comprehensive and systematic assessment of clinical teaching skills and strategies in the health sciences.* Bethesda, MD: National Library of Medicine.

Meredith, K. E., Dunlap, M. R., & Baker, H. H. (1982). Subjective and objective admissions factors as predictors of clinical clerkship performance. *Journal of Medical Education, 57,* 743–751.

Miller, G. E. (1980). *Educating medical teachers.* Cambridge, MA: Harvard University Press.

Moore, M. L., & Perry, J. F. (1976). *Clinical education in physical therapy: Present status/future needs.* Washington, DC: American Physical Therapy Association.

Morehead, J. H. (1973). Professional education: The theory–practice issue reconsidered. *College Student Journal, 7*(4), 71–82.

Moy, M. L. Y., Schwartz, M. L., & Zinser, E. (1977). Evaluation of the community phase of a regionalized medical education program. In *Proceedings, the Sixteenth Annual Conference on Research in Medical Education* (pp. 42–44). Washington, DC: Association of American Medical Colleges.

Muschenheim, W. (1964). Curricula in schools of architecture: A directory. *Journal of Architectural Education, 18,* 56–62.

Myers, B. (1977). Beliefs of dental faculty and students about effective clinical teaching behaviors. *Journal of Dental Education, 41,* 68–76.

Nash, P. J., & Nash, D. A. (1982). Moral reasoning and clinical performance of student dentists. *Journal of Dental Education, 46,* 721–722.

Neufeld, V. R., & Barrows, H. S. (1974). The "McMaster philosophy": An approach to medical education. *Journal of Medical Education, 49,* 1040–1050.

Neufeld, V. R., & Norman, G. R. (Eds.). (1985). *Clinical competence: A measurement perspective.* New York: Springer.

Neufeld, V. R., Norman, G. R., Feightner, J. W., & Barrows, H. S. (1981). Clinical problem solving by medical students: A cross sectional and longitudinal analysis. *Medical Education, 15,* 315–322.

Newble, D. I., Elmslie, R. G., & Baxter, A. (1978). A problem based criterion referenced examination of clinical competence. *Journal of Medical Education, 53,* 720–726.

Newble, D. I., Hoare, J., & Elmslie, R. G. (1981). The validity and reliability of a new examination of the clinical competence of medical students. *Medical Education, 15,* 46–52.

Newman, M. A. (1972). Nursing's theoretical evolution. *Nursing Outlook, 20,* 449–453.

Nitsch, W., & Weller, W. (1973). *Social science research on higher education and universities: Part 1. Trend report.* The Hague–Paris: Mouton.

Norman, E. M. (1978). A model for judging teaching effectiveness. *Nurse Educator, 3,* 29–35.

Norman, G. R., & Feightner, J. W. (1981). A comparison of behavior on simulated patients and on PMPs. *Medical Education, 15,* 26–32.

Norman, G. R., Tugwell, P., & Feightner, J. W. (1982). A comparison of resident performance on real and simulated patients. *Journal of Medical Education, 57,* 708–715.

Nyre, G. F., & Reilly, K. C. (1979). *Professional education in the eighties: Challenges and responses* (AAHE/ERIC Higher Education Research Report #8). Washington, DC: American Association for Higher Education.

Oratio, A. R. (1978). Comparative perceptions of therapeutic effectiveness by student clinicians and clinical supervisors. *ASHA, 20,* 959–962.

O'Shea, H. J., & Parsons, M. K. (1979). Clinical Instruction: Effective and ineffective teacher behaviors. *Nursing Outlook, 27,* 411–415.

Packer, H. L., & Ehrlich, T. (1973). *New directions in legal education.* New York: McGraw–Hill.

Page, G. G., & Fielding, D. W. (1980). Performance on PMPs and performance in clinical practice: Are they related? *Journal of Medical Education, 55,* 529–537.

Pascasio, A. (1976). Clinical facilities. In C. W. Ford & M . K. Morgan (Eds.), *Teaching in the health professions.* St. Louis: C. V. Mosby Co.

Patridge, M. I., Harris, I. B., & Petzel, R. A. (1980). Implementation and evaluation of a faculty development program to improve clinical teaching. *Journal of Medical Education, 55,* 711–713.

Patridge, M. I., & Mast, T. A. (1978). Dental clinical evaluation: A review of the research. *Journal of Dental Education, 42,* 300–305.

Pearson, B. D. (1975). A model for clinical evaluation. *Nursing Outlook, 23,* 232–235.

Penta, F. B., & Kofman, S. (1973). The effectiveness of simulation devices in teaching selected skills of physical diagnosis. *Journal of Medical Education, 48,* 442–445.

Petrusa, E. R., Guckian, J. C., & Perkowski, M. S. (1984). A multiple station objective clinical evaluation. In *Proceedings, the Sixteenth Annual Conference on Research in Medical Education* (pp. 211–216). Washington, DC: Association of American Medical Colleges.

Petzel, R. A., Harris, I. B., & Masler, D. S. (1982). The empirical validation of clinical teaching strategies. *Evaluation and the Health Professions, 5,* 499–508.

Philips, W. R., Rosenblatt, R. A., Gordon, M. J., & Fletcher, R. M. (1982). Clinical content of the WAMI community clerkship in family medicine. *Journal of Medical Education, 57,* 615–620.

Pierson, F. C. (1959). *The education of American businessmen.* New York: McGraw–Hill.

Pitcher, B., Olsen, M., & Solomon, R. (1962). *A study of the prediction of academic success in architectural school.* Princeton, NJ: Educational

Testing Service.

Potter, R. H., McDonald, R. E., & Sagraves, G. D. (1982). A derived basic ability criterion for predicting dental students' performance. *Journal of Dental Education, 46,* 634–638.

Pugh, E. J. (1980). Factors influencing congruence between beliefs, intentions, and behavior in the clinical teaching of nursing. *Dissertation Abstracts, 1980, 41,* 2521A.

Purohit, A. A., Manasse, H. R., & Nelson, A. A. (1977). Critical issues in teacher and student evaluation. *American Journal of Pharmaceutical Education, 41,* 317–325.

Quay, R. H. (1980). *Index to anthologies on postsecondary education, 1960–1978.* Westport, CT: Greenwood Press.

Raff, B., Boyle, R. F., & Stone, H. L. (1977). *Evaluation of teaching effectiveness.* New York: National League for Nursing.

Richards, A., Jones, A., Nichols, K., Richardson, F., Riley, B., & Swinson, R. (1981). Videotape as an evaluation tool. *Nursing Outlook, 29,* 35–38.

Rimoldi, H. J. A. (1961). The test of diagnostic skills. *Journal of Medical Education, 36,* 73–79.

Rippey, R. M. (1975). Student evaluations of professors: Are they of value? *Journal of Medical Education, 50,* 951–958.

Rippey, R. M. (1981). *The evaluation of teaching in medical schools.* New York: Springer.

Robbins, A. S., Kauss, D. R., Heinrich, R., Abrass, I., Dreyer, J., & Clyman, B. (1979). Interpersonal skills training: Evaluation in an internal medicine residency. *Journal of Medical Education, 54,* 885–894.

Rous, S. W., Bamford, J. C., Gromisch, D., Rich, H., Rubin, S., & Sall, S. (1972). The improvement of faculty teaching through evaluation: A follow up report. *Journal of Surgical Research, 13,* 262–266.

Rutala, P. J., Stillman, P. L., & Sabers, D. L. (1981). Housestaff evaluation using patient instructors. *Evaluation and the Health Professions, 4,* 419–432.

Sajid, A., Lipson, L. F., & Telder, T. V. (1975). A simulation laboratory for medical education. *Journal of Medical Education, 50,* 970–975.

Sall, S., Gromisch, D. S., Rubin, S. H., and Stone, M. L. (1976). Improvement of faculty teaching performance in a department of obstetrics and gynecology by student evaluation. *American Journal of Obstetrics and Gynecology, 124,* 217–221.

Samson-Fisher, R. W., & Poole, A. D. (1980). Simulated patients and the assessment of medical students' interpersonal skills. *Medical Education, 14,* 249–253.

Sanders, B. R., & Ruvolo, J. F. (1981). Mock clinic: An approach to clinical education. *Physical Therapy, 61,* 1163–1167.

Sanders, W. (1963). Report of the committee on the advancement of architectural education. *Journal of Architectural Education, 18,* 19–21.

Sauter, R. C., & Walker, J. K. (1976). A theoretical model for faculty "peer" evaluation. *American Journal of Pharmaceutical Education, 40,* 165–166.

Schaffer, D. R. (1980). A faculty growth contracting model for allied health schools. *Journal of Allied Health, 9,* 233–241.

Schwinghammer, T. (1981). Videotaped introductory instruction in the physical examination for clinical clerkship students. *American Journal of Pharmaceutical Education, 45,* 33–35.

Scully, R. M. (1974). Clinical teaching of physical therapy students in clinical education. *Dissertation Abstracts, 35,* 853A.

Serkland, J. D., & Sockloff, A. L. (1976). Faculty. In C. W. Ford & M. L. Morgan, *Teaching in the Health Professions.* St. Louis: C. W. Mosby.

Sheahan, J. (1980). Some aspects of the teaching and learning of nursing. *Journal of Advanced Nursing, 5,* 491–511.

Sheahan, J. (1981). A study of the nurse tutor's role. *Journal of Advanced Nursing, 6,* 125–135.

Sheehan, T. J., Husted, S. D. R., Candee, D., Cooke, C. D., & Bargen, N. (1980). Moral judgement as a predictor of clinical performance. *Evaluation and the Health Professions, 3,* 393–404.

Simon, J. L. (1976). *A role guide and resource book for clinical preceptors* (DHEW No. HRA 77-14). Bethesda, MD: Public Health Service, Bureau of Health Manpower.

Skakun, E. N. (1981). The clinical skills assessment form. *Evaluation and the Health Professions, 4,* 330–337.

Skeath, W. A., Deadman, M. E., Gousy, S., Harvey, M., Tyrrel, S., & Yorston, S. (1979). Criteria to be used in the selection of clinical areas for basic nurse training. *Journal of Advanced Nursing, 4,* 169–180.

Skeff, K. M. (1983, September). Evaluation of a method for improving the teaching performance of the attending physician. *American Journal of Medicine, 75,* 465–470.

Skeff, K. M., Campbell, M., & Stratos, G. (1984). Evaluation of attending physicians: Three perspectives. In *Proceedings, the Sixteenth Annual Conference on Research in Medical Education* (pp. 277–282). Washington, DC: Association of American Medical Colleges.

Smeltzer, C. (1980). Teaching the nursing process—practical method. *Journal of Nursing Education, 19*(9), 31–37.

Steinbaugh, M. R. (1977). Conversational analysis: An ethnomethodological approach to the study of clinical instruction. *Dissertation Abstracts, 38,* 2126B.

Stiggins, R. J. (1978). Assessment of knowledge in the evaluation of clinical competence. In M. K. Morgan & D. M. Irby (Eds.), *Evaluating Clinical Competence in the Health Professions.* St. Louis: C. V Mosby.

Stillman, P. L., Levinson, D., Ruggill, J. S., & Sabers, D. L. (1977). The nurse practitioner as a teacher of physical examination skills. In *Proceedings, the Sixteenth Annual Conference on Research in Medical Education* (pp. 57–62). Washington, DC: Association of American Medical Colleges.

Stillman, P. L., Ruggill, J. S., Rutala, P. J., & Sabers, D. L. (1980). Patient instructors as teachers and evaluators. *Journal of Medical Education, 55,* 186–193.

Stillman, P. L., Ruggill, J. S., & Sabers, D. L. (1978). The use of practical instructors to evaluate a complete physical examination. *Evaluation and the Health Professions, 1,* 49–54.

Stillman, P. L., Rutala, P. J., Stillman, A. E., & Sabers, D. L. (1982). The use of patient instructors to evaluate the clinical competence of physicians. In J. S. Lloyd (Ed.), *Evaluation of noncognitive skills and clinical performance.* Chicago: American Board of Medical Specialties.

Stillman, P. L., Sabers, D. L., Redfield, D. L., & Stewart, D. (1977). Testing physical diagnosis skills with videotape. *Journal of Medical Education, 52,* 942–943.

Stillman, P. L., Silverman, A., Burpeau, M. Y., & Sabers, D. L. (1982). Use of client instructors to teach interviewing skills to law students. *Journal of Legal Education, 32,* 395–402.

Stritter, F. T. (1982). The learning vector—Clinical instruction and educational development of health professionals. *Nordisk Medicin, 97,* 256–257.

Stritter, F. T., & Baker, R. M. (1982). Resident preferences for the clinical teaching of ambulatory care. *Journal of Medical Education, 57,* 33–41.

Stritter, F. T., & Flair, M. D. (1980). *Effective clinical teaching.* Atlanta: National Library of Medicine.

Stritter, F. T., Hain, J. D., & Grimes, D. A. (1975). Clinical teaching reexamined. *Journal of Medical Education, 50,* 877–882.

Stritter, F. T., & Talbert, L. M. (1974). An empirical approach to instruction in obstetrics and gynecology. *Journal of Medical Education, 49,* 770–777.

Swords, P.deL., & Walwer, F. K. (1974). *The costs and resources of legal education.* New York: Columbia University Press.

Tardiff, K. (1981). A videotape technique for measuring clinical skill: Three years of experience. *Journal of Medical Education, 56,* 187–191.

Thompson, G. W., Ahlawat, K., & Buie, R. (1979). Evaluation of the dental aptitude test components as predictors of dental school performance. *Journal of the Canadian Dental Association, 45,* 407–409.

Thorne, B. (1973a). Professional education in medicine. In E. C. Hughes (Ed.), *Education for the professions of medicine, law, theology, and social welfare.* New York: McGraw-Hill.

Thorne, B. (1973b). Professional education in the law. In E. C. Hughes (Ed.), *Education for the professions of medicine, law, theology, and social welfare.* New York: McGraw-Hill.

Turner, J. D., & Rushton, J. (1976). *Education for the professions.* Manchester, England: Manchester University Press.

Vann, W. F., May, K. N., & Shugars, D. A. (1981). Acquisition of psychomotor skills in dentistry: An experimental teaching method. *Journal of Dental Education, 45,* 567–575.

Voight, J. W. (1980). Physical assessment skills in the curriculum: A pilot project and followup. *Journal of Nursing Education, 19*(2), 26–30.

Voorhees, J. D., Kaufman, A., Heffron, W., Jackson, R., DiVasto, P., Wiese, W., & Daitz, B. (1977). Teaching preclinical medical students in a clinical setting. *Journal of Family Practice, 5,* 464–465.

Vu, N. V. (1979). Medical problem solving assessment. *Evaluation and the Health Professions, 2,* 281–307.

Wales, S. K., & Hagerman, V. (1979). Guided design systems approach in nursing education. *Journal of Nursing Education, 18*(3), 38–45.

Ways, P. O., Loftus, G., & Jones, J. M. (1973). Focal problem teaching in medical education. *Journal of Medical Education, 48,* 565–571.

Weinholtz, D. A. (1983). Directing medical students' clinical care presentations. *Medical Education, 17,* 364–368.

Weinholtz, D. A. (1981). A study of instructional leadership during medical attending rounds. *Dissertation Abstracts, 42,* 3469A.

Weinstein, P. (1982). Assessing manual dexterity in dentistry. In J. S. Lloyd (Ed.), *Evaluation of noncognitive skills and clinical performance.* Chicago: American Board of Medical Specialties.

Werner, A., & Schneider, J. M. (1974). Teaching medical students interactional skills. *New England Journal of Medicine, 290,* 1232–1237.

Westberg, J., Lefever, D., & Jason, H. (1980). Clinical teaching in physician's assistant training programs. *Journal of Medical Education, 55,* 173–180.

White, J. N., & Burnett, C. W. (Eds.). (1981). *Higher education literature: An annotated bibliography.* Phoenix, AZ: Oryx.

Wingard, J. R., & Williamson, J. W. (1973). Grades as predictors of physicians' career performance: An evaluative literature review. *Journal of Medical Education, 48,* 311–322.

Wong, S. (1978). Nurse-teacher behaviors in the clinical field: Apparent effect on nursing students' learning. *Journal of Advanced Nursing, 3,* 369–372.

Wong, S., & Wong, J. (1980). The effectiveness of clinical teaching: A model for self-evaluation. *Journal of Advanced Nursing, 5,* 531–537.

Woodward, C. A., & Dinham, S. M. (1982). Methodological factors in studying medical graduates: A review of six internship performance studies. *Evaluation and the Health Professions, 5,* 95–111.

Woodward, C. A., & Ferrier, B. M. (1982). Perspectives of graduates two or five years after graduation from a three-year medical school. *Journal of Medical Education, 57,* 294–302.

Yonke, A. M. (1979). The art and science of clinical teaching. *Medical Education, 13,* 86–90.

35.

Research in Teaching in the Armed Forces

Harold F. O'Neil, Jr.
U.S. Army Research Institute

Clinton L. Anderson
Kinton Inc.

Jeanne A. Freeman
General Electric

Introduction

This chapter is the first of its topic area in this handbook. We have chosen, therefore, to provide a broad overview of our environment and attempt to show the role of teaching in a specific service, the U.S. Army. Selected research and development consistent with the demands of our environment will also be highlighted.

Military training represents a significant national investment in research, design, planning, and implementation of instruction. Although the typical academic scholar's awareness of military training increases when there is a mandatory draft or a military action that creates attention in the public media, training nevertheless goes on continuously, 24 hours a day in this country and throughout the world. The scope of the training is substantial. The three services, Army, Navy, and Air Force, together involve over 2 million people on active duty. The Reserves and the National Guard add another 1.6 million persons (Office of the Assistant Secretary of Defense, 1984). Approximately 330 thousand personnel enter military service annually and require basic training and specific job training. In addition, individuals receive refresher training, instruction to permit advancement to different or higher responsibilities, and training for coordinated unit performance rather than for only individual competencies. While the size of the training enterprise competes with some state-level educational efforts, the range of settings under which training occurs differs dramatically, from school-like classrooms, to field exercises that last weeks at a time, to sites in distant countries, sometimes under hostile or dangerous conditions. The areas of training include tasks nominally associated with the military, e.g., weapons proficiency, as well as the full range of cognitive, affective, and psychomotor abilities, including, for example, specific job training for management and leadership skills and physical fitness proficiency.

The costs of training are also enormous in scope. For example, according to the Department of Defense (DOD), the costs of running the school system alone for fiscal year 1985 (October 1,1984 to September 30, 1985) are 17.9 billion dollars (Office of the Assistant Secretary of Defense, 1984). Included in these costs are student and instructor salaries and the cost of transporting personnel to other sites for training. These costs are comparatively higher than civilian training because of the cost of paying trainees, because of the high instructor-to-student ratios, and because of the relatively high cost of specialized equipment.

Nor is training a once-and-never-again proposition. Modernization of weapon systems and technological advances require considerable updating and skills maintenance. A further requirement is that all trained personnel function in an integrated team-like way. Thus, the transfer or rotation of personnel from

The authors thank reviewers Walter Dick (Florida State University) and Frank Hart (General Electric Information Services Company). The views expressed in this chapter are solely those of the authors. Harold O'Neil's affiliation has changed to the University of Southern California as of Fall, 1985.

site to site or to new positions of authority demands constant retraining and refinement of collective performance.

It might well be asked, however, what the relevance of the military training mission is to the general topic of research on teaching. Throughout this chapter, obvious similarities to and differences from more traditional educational settings will emerge. Yet the very history of the interaction of the field of psychology of instruction with the military context makes the appropriateness of this topic for this volume clear. Consider only the well known areas and individuals connected at one time with the military training mission. Intelligence testing, achievement testing, task analysis, programed instruction, learning strategies, and computer-based instruction are but a few areas whose impetus has been in this context. A catalog of names of researchers who devoted substantial parts of their careers to work on military problems further demonstrates the interconnection among general education and military sectors. Cook, Flanagan, Glaser, Gagné, Kendall, Merrill, Norman, Popham, Resnick, Snow, Sullivan, Tyler, and Wittrock represent a few of the prominent actors in research on teaching. There is reason to suspect that current research in military training will produce a comparably impressive list of future contributors to research on teaching.

This chapter is organized along the following lines: First, a comparison between public education and military training environments is drawn. This comparison includes features such as general background, including the nature of the educational context from which the military selects its students, curriculum, staffing, and instructional approaches (including technology use). Areas receiving most attention are staffing and instructional approach, those areas most connected to teaching. The next section focuses on the types of skills toward which military training is directed. The bulk of the chapter is devoted to reporting research and development activity in three significant research domains for which military support is provided and for which military applications are extant and are of interest to the civilian sector: computer-based instruction, learning strategies, and intelligent computer-assisted instruction.

Military and Civilian Public Education: Background

Education and training in the military environment is influenced by many of the same sources as civilian society. For example, the advent of information technology and of a service-oriented society both influence subsequent job opportunities and job requirements. The Task Force on Education for Economic Growth finds that jobs which offer upward mobility will require more and more creative use of technology (Hunt, du Pont, & Cary, 1983). The Office of Technology Assessment (OTA, 1982) reports that trends in automation and the growth of the information sector of the economy will likely cause severe manpower training problems over the next 10 years. Besides a persistent demand for more highly trained scientists, engineers, and specialists, there is a strong requirement for a "more technologically literate work force." If these requirements are not met, increasingly severe economic and social penalties may be felt (OTA, 1982).

Top-level management must view its human resource development in the light of several well documented trends: growth of the total U.S. population based on longer life span and introduction of large numbers of immigrants into the United States; a 24% reduction in the 17–20-year-old group between 1980 and 1993; a possible increase in retirement age; an increased participation rate by women in the labor force; and a possible increased use of robotics to accomplish unskilled jobs (Lord & Barnes, 1983).

Many within the Armed Forces recognize the changing society and the penalties for not responding to its demands. For example, in a survey of 600 American colleges, the Task Force on Education for Economic Growth (1983) found that between 1971 and 1980 there was a 64% decline in the number of secondary school science teachers being prepared and a 78% drop in the number of mathematics teachers. Also, it was noted that the average 1982 Scholastic Aptitude Test scores for students preparing to be teachers were 80 points below the national average. Over half of the current elementary school teachers reported that they had no undergraduate training in science. This task force attributed this situation to the low levels of pay and esteem accorded to teachers. It found that the average salary of a beginning mathematics teacher with a bachelor's degree is only 60% of the beginning salary offered by private industry to bachelor's degree candidates in mathematics and statistics (Hunt et al., 1983).

The "teacher gap" in the education base reveals itself in problems with student achievement. As documented in Hunt et al. (1983), The National Assessment of Educational Progress recently reported the following findings: (a) 13% of 17-year-old students could not perform reading tasks considered to be minimal for functional literacy; (b) 28% could not answer questions testing their literal comprehension of what they read; (c) 53% could not write a letter correcting a billing error; and (d) only 21% could write a persuasive statement in 1974 (this dropped to 15% in 1979).

These findings are of concern as high school graduates are the prime recruiting market for DOD. Further insights into problems of student achievement appear when students look for employment in the military services. For example, the military services used the Armed Services Vocational Aptitude Battery (ASVAB) (McLaughlin, Rossmeissl, Wise, Brandt, & Wang, in press) to determine eligibility for enlistment and qualifications for assignment to specific military jobs. Four ASVAB subtests, i.e., word knowledge, paragraph comprehension, arithmetic reasoning, and numerical operations, are combined to form the Armed Forces Qualification Test (AFQT), a general measure of trainability and the primary criterion of enlistment eligibility. An AFQT score of 50 is considered average. In 1980, the Office of the Assistant Secretary of Defense (1982) authorized a one-time administration of the ASVAB to a nationwide sample of American youth. The 1980 youth population subgroup analysis revealed that the median AFQT score for white youth was 59, considerably higher than that of either Hispanic youth (23) or Blacks (17). These findings tend to substantiate the principal conclusion in Hunter and Harman's (1982) book that a "major shift in national education policy is needed to serve the educational needs of disadvantaged adults" (p. 104).

Although all sectors of society are affected by national shifts in demography, economic productivity, and political climate, the educational enterprise depends directly on the numbers of students anticipated for instruction and the sense of national priorities toward which such instruction is directed. The actual form of educational service varies enormously: formal or informal, voluntary or compulsory, free or fee-based, connection to economic incentives, and so on. With respect to the public schools as part of education and the military training enterprise, a contrastive analysis demonstrates that, while there are many clear distinctions, the two educational systems share features of intent and process. The nominal differences between systems remain; for instance, students in one system wear uniforms and are trained for collective goals rather then exclusively for individual achievement. Yet an explicit comparison can be useful in thinking about what research issues and initiatives might have the most power to affect both systems. In the next section, selected features of both civilian and military education and training will be reviewed briefly. These characteristics recur in discussions in subsequent sections of this chapter as they particularly constrain or are influenced by R&D options in the training area.

Characteristics of Civilian Versus Military Educational Systems

The characteristics of educational systems can be categorized into an arbitrary set of classes (e.g., organization, curriculum, staffing, and instructional approaches), each of which influences the role and utility of research on instruction and learning. Briefly, the organization of the public sector is decentralized; military education and training is centralized in schools where individual skills are taught and decentralized in units where collective skills are taught. The curriculum sources in the public sector are diffuse. They come in large measure from the available commercial material and from texts published by the private sector. Most of the curriculum, and the objectives that operationalize it, reflects the notion that education is a long-term enterprise and that its impact can be known fully only years after actual schooling. In contrast, curriculum sources in the military sector are systematic and represent specific job skills.

The major classes that distinguish military education and training are staffing and instructional approaches.

Staffing

The *staffing* of the teaching system in the public sector is based on certification with emphasis on general education (i.e., a college degree and academic major) rather than on skills pertinent to the particular teaching task itself. The movement is toward greater certification of teachers' competence, including their achievement in basic skills, their knowledge of the subject matter to be communicated, and their general understanding of and skills in education. Most certification is preservice, with some movement for recertification based on time or for additional evaluation based on merit incentives. The teachers

themselves have power to influence the system, including curriculum and instructional practice, not only by their private behavior as teachers but through their collective action as union members. In such organizations they also may directly affect policy by differential support of candidates for election.

The military services use a wide variety of teachers and teaching mechanisms. In-house formal schools and training centers employ full-time instructors, aides, and other support personnel. The U.S. Army, Navy, and Air Force have major commands dedicated to formal training functions. In addition, the military services contract out some of their education and training functions to colleges, universities, technical schools, and other teaching organizations. Much teaching is done by first-line supervisors and other lower- and middle-echelon corporate management personnel who train individual and collective skills on-the-job. In addition, there is affective learning resulting directly from peer instruction.

To provide a clear example of the role of teachers for the enlisted force in the U.S. Army, we will describe the training program of its principal teachers, the Non-Commissioned Officer (NCO) Corps. Potential NCOs begin their Army careers with initial entry training and are assigned to duty stations as lower grade enlisted personnel. After attaining the grade of E-4 (which means enlisted personnel, 2–4 years in service, the rank below sergeant), they are eligible to enter the Non-Commissioned Officer Educational System (NCOES). Army Regulation 351-1 (Department of the Army, 1981) lists the first objective of NCOES: to train NCOs to be trainers and leaders of the soldiers who will work and fight under their supervision. Another major objective is to improve unit readiness and collective mission proficiency through individual proficiency of NCOs and subordinate soldiers, clearly an additional training role.

NCOES is designed to be an integrated system of resident training, that is, service school and NCO Academy, supervised on-the-job training, self-study, and on-the-job experience, which provides job-related training for NCOs and specialists throughout their careers. The core of NCOES is a series of four courses which serve as an important element in the career ladder. The courses correspond to various grade levels which reflect seniority: (a) Primary (Grade E-4), (b) Basic (Grade E-5), (c) Advanced (Grade E-6), and (d) Senior (First Sergeant's Course Grades E-7 and E-8).

The U.S. Army Sergeants Major Academy is the capstone of enlisted training. It trains selected Master and First Sergeants for positions of highest Army NCO responsibility to provide first-line teaching throughout the Army establishment.

Although plans and programs for NCO training and education (Department of the Army, 1980) look extremely promising and thorough, their implementation, as in public education, varies. For example, even though NCOES by regulation is centrally managed, the Army has yet to establish core curriculum for its courses and to develop servicewide standards of teacher competence. Army service schools have developed and are offering courses of differing quality (U.S. General Accounting Office, 1982). Both headquarters, Department of the Army, and the U.S. Army Training and Doctrine Command (TRADOC) recognize these implementation gaps and problems and are taking steps to improve the system.

Instructional Approaches

Instructional approaches in public education are at once diverse and routinized (Goodlad, 1984; Boyer, 1983). The setting for instruction is fairly standard. Instruction takes place in a 1:25 + environment (i.e., one teacher for 25 or more students). Teaching approach is largely a matter of individual preference based upon training, resource availability, or personal exploration. Although standard texts are required, often with many options, such as workbooks, the manner of their use is not specified. The studies of teaching per se as reviewed in other chapters of this volume are the best sources for descriptions of how teaching occurs. The role of systematically developed instructional materials in public schools, using an Instructional Systems Development (ISD) approach, is now minimal.

In contrast, the instructional approach used in the Army is more prescriptive. The Armed Forces have taken giant steps to develop and implement such a systems approach to training. Instructional Systems Development (ISD) involves the systematic analysis, design, development, implementation, and evaluation of training programs and training support materials (O'Neil, 1979).

For example, evaluation in ISD is not considered simply as the process following implementation of the training program. The term "evaluate" is used in the general judgmental sense of the continuous monitoring of a program, or of the training function as a whole, and involves both verification and validation. The process, at the heart of ISD, consists of internally evaluating the training program during each phase of its preparation (at least to the degree that fiscal and manpower resources and time permit) while concurrently externally evaluating the overall training function. Thus, following implementation, feedback is used to evaluate the program, to assess the quality of job performance, and to check the organization's overall responsiveness to training needs. (See Figure 1 of "A Model for a Systems Approach to Training," U.S. Army Training and Doctrine Command, 1982).

Evaluation policy is in place, but the actual collection and availability of training evaluation data are not as common as one would expect. Because findings may be sensitive, some results are not widely disseminated in the open literature. In addition, there are few incentives to publish in most organizations, since experience on the job is generally valued above contributions to the outside professional community. Lately, there appears to be a skepticism about the utility of research and evaluation, labeled as impractical, vague, and "academic." This view results, in part, in the inability of evaluation proponents to communicate or to sell their ideas to Army management.

In the public and military sectors, the use of technology in instruction, particularly computers, is on the rise, but the systematic selection of technology for the delivery of effective instruction against given goals is still rare. Isolated uses of other technology and media (e.g., close circuit television, real-time interactive video, and videodisc/computer options) can be found. Estimates of quality of available educational programming for technology, including courseware, are low, though a thriving cottage industry may develop some special cases. The adoption of computer programs intended for other uses than teaching (e.g., VisiCalc or word processing programs) shows promise. Computer-Based Instruction (CBI) also has only moderate use in influencing instruction. An extended discussion of the R&D base for Army technology applications to training occurs later in this chapter. Other "innovations," such as the use of aides or adjunct instructional staff, peer teaching, ungraded schools, and relatively pure competency rather than time-driven programs, can be found, but no general trends. Probably the safest conclusion, in both sectors, is that teacher mediation of instruction, along with teachers lecturing, leading discussions, answering questions, and posing tasks, is the dominant form of instruction. Unfortunately, the range of teaching options does not imply that these options are used adaptively to solve some of the persistent problems of student individual and group differences in learning. In fact, recent work (Goodlad, 1984) shows a trend toward greater tracking of students, that is, the identification of sets of students with certain levels of ultimate educational achievement. This tracking is practically influenced by the increasing salience of achievement testing, particularly competency testing (now in 39 states), in highlighting student differences. These competencies are designed to help people function in "life."

Education and training in the military tends also to be "tracked" based on ASVAB aptitude scores. The difference is that military students often have immediate job goals or career advancement dependent upon their specific achievements derived from training and education. For example, in the Non-Commissioned Officer Education System (NCOES), already referenced in terms of teacher preparation, training performance is linked to promotions, reenlistments, retention, and elimination from the service. For example, poor performance results in dismissal from the Army, with little recourse. These direct incentives have a positive effect on student discipline and student work habits to meet the established standards, in some contrast to public education's future orientation. However, like the civilian sector, personal problems such as drug or alcohol abuse, financial or family difficulties, and other sources of external stress take their toll on student productivity. For the Army, these costs are particularly high since students are paid to go to school, in contrast to much of higher education where students pay to go to school.

In summary, the public education and military training systems share some features but differ in large measure. Probably the most salient distinction between military and civilian education is the focus on job proficiency rather than general educational benefits, that is, education and training are a means to an end, not an end in themselves. Training is to result in useful, demonstrable learning that is related to the accomplishment of specific jobs.

Research and Development

To continue the civilian–military comparison, let us turn to the specific topic of this volume, research in teaching (thus learning). Let us first consider how the two systems compare in research organization.

Schools in the public sector conduct relatively little activity in R&D except that which is categorized as curriculum development and mandatory evaluation. Their sights are very aptly set on the short-term improvement of the schooling enterprise rather than the long-term contribution to knowledge. At the federal level, R&D in education is conducted primarily by the National Institute of Education, created in 1972. The vast majority of its budget currently goes to supporting outside contractors and grantees, who only partly represent interests directly related to teaching and learning. In the military sector, applied R&D in training and education is conducted by service R&D laboratories such as the Air Force Human Resources Laboratory (AFHRL), the U.S. Army Research Institute (ARI), and the Navy Personnel Research and Development Center (NPRDC). DOD sponsors of basic and applied research in training also include the Defense Advance Research Projects Agency (DARPA), the Air Force Office of Scientific Research (AFOSR), the Office of Naval Research (ONR), and the Naval Training Equipment Center (NTEC). For example, the total mission of ARI is to maximize combat effectiveness through R&D on the acquisition, development, training, and utilization of soldiers in military systems. The organizational precursor to the Army Research Institute for the Behavioral and Social Sciences began in 1917 and marked the advent of military psychology. In 1972, the present organization was reconfigured and named ARI by order of the Chief of Research and Development within the Department of the Army. Since then, ARI has been responsible for the U.S. Army's human resources research program. With over 200 highly trained professionals distributed among three laboratories (Manpower and Personnel Research, Systems Research, and Training Research), ARI's major focus is to assist in manning, equipping, and training the Army. This assistance is to be accomplished through the development of a technological base program of behavioral research, much of which is conducted by ARI staff themselves. Research is funded through four major categories. (The categories of this research are defined in Army Regulation 70-1, Department of the Army, 1984.) A brief description of these categories follows: (a) Basic Research (6.1) is the scientific study and experimentation directed toward increasing fundamental knowledge and understanding for solution of military problems; (b) Exploratory Development (6.2) includes efforts directed toward solving specific military problems and toward developing and evaluating the feasibility and practicability of proposed solutions; (c) Advanced Development (6.3) includes development of nonmaterial techniques or components, subsystems, technology demonstrators, and nonmateriel technological demonstrators; and (d) Engineering Development (6.4) includes those more advanced development programs being refined for military use, but not yet approved for procurement or operation.

To what ends are these categories of research funds directed? Because the claim has been made in an earlier section that military education focuses on specific goals, what are the types of knowledge and skill that training research is used to enhance? Education and training provided by the military services can be grouped into three broad skills areas: foundation skills, individual job skills, and collective skills.

Foundation Skills

The taxonomy of "Basic Skills and Competencies for Productive Employment," contained in the Appendix of *Action for Excellence* (Hunt et al., 1983) lists essential foundation skills not only in the reading, writing, spelling, and mathematical areas, but also includes competencies needed in science, reasoning, interpersonal relations, economics, and computer literacy. Problems in public sector student accomplishment clearly show that many students leave the secondary school system without these essential foundation skills. Although new selection and assignment devices may be available for the military to identify and classify recruits better, employment standards and job classifications are, ultimately, chained to the availability of manpower. The decreasing youth manpower pool, large immigration of low-proficiency, non-English-speaking personnel, coupled with serious quality problems in the secondary school systems and high minority youth unemployment rate, weigh heavily against screening out and denying employment to all personnel with foundation skill deficiencies. The problem is further complicated by introduction of new high-technology equipment systems in the military services. Thus, training of these skills must be a priority of both the public and military sectors. One research attempt to deal with these issues is the Army's Job Skills Education Program which will be discussed later in this chapter.

Individual Job Skills

The military services have elaborate and expensive initial job training and periods of orientation, inservice training, individual skills refresher courses, and technical courses in professional development training. The military services have the most visible and well-defined individual training systems. In fiscal year 1985 (October 1, 1984–September 30, 1985), for example, the Department of Defense has a spending plan of approximately $17.9 billion on individual training. These expenditures cover:

- Recruit training (orientation and basic training) for approximately 363,356 students per year at a cost of $1.3 billion.
- Specialized skills training for approximately 1,340,352 students per year at a cost of $4.5 billion.
- One-Station Unit Training (combined recruit and specialized skills training in the Army) for approximately 92,499 students per year at a cost of $429 million.
- Flight training for approximately 15,646 students per year at a cost of approximately $2.3 billion.

Other costs included some officer acquisition costs, professional development education, medical training, and overhead (i.e., support, management, travel, and pay) (Office of the Assistant Secretary of Defense, 1984).

Much of the individual training occurs in a school-like format setting, yet some is conducted once individuals have begun their jobs at permanent duty locations. First-line supervisors and middle management personnel complain from time to time that individuals who proceed through initial job training still arrive at the job poorly prepared. This situation usually stems from problems in student accomplishment and from training compromises that have been made based on budgeting and time constraints. The Army's initial job training is an example of individual training geared to familiarization and mastery of a minimum number of the most critical tasks determined by task analysis at the entry level.

Collective Skills

However well trained individuals are to do specific jobs, it is only when workers are organized into teams, crews, or units that the mission can be accomplished. These collectives have a common mission to which each worker brings his/her own special capabilities. Those inexperienced workers who arrive in their permanent work place fresh from initial job training with a minimum level of individual proficiency must be provided the necessary on-the-job experience and seasoning in the immediate work setting in order to perform in a proficient manner. Most of this experience is gained through a molding process whereby workers become functioning teams integral to the parent unit.

Significant Training Research Domains

Because of the wide range of activity in the military, including gaming, simulation, high technology, human factors, and psychometry, it is necessary to limit the areas of training research described in this chapter.

Three areas will be described: (a) computer-based instruction (CBI), in part derived from earlier noted ISD models; (b) learning strategies, developed from cognitive and behavioral techniques for learning; and (c) intelligent computer-assisted instruction (ICAI), which represents an intersect of CBI, cognitive science, computer science, and linguistic disciplines. These fields are reported because support by military funding sources has been dominant in the development of productive research lines. They are also included because they represent areas where significant progress in both basic and applied work has resulted and for which the future is bright. Issues of learning and instruction are central to all three areas. Finally, they illustrate research venues which can be shared with and improved by coordinate R&D in the civilian sector.

Computer-Based Instruction

Computer-based instruction (CBI) is an approach to training and education that has come out of the need for people to master an increased variety of complicated subjects with an increased set of sophisticated skills and to perform these skills at higher standards. CBI's goal is to produce instructional systems that lead to more proficient performance at a reduced cost (O'Neil and Paris, 1981). With respect to reducing costs, the following advantages are noted: reduced training time; reduced reliance on trained instructors; reduced need for using expensive or possibly dangerous operational equipment; and rapid update of instructional material. With respect to increasing effectiveness, the following advantages are noted: consistent and high quality instruction on a large scale; high-quality training at remote sites; hands-on, performance-oriented instruction; individualization of instruction; rapid expansion of a high-quality training program (i.e., during mobilization); and 24-hour use capability.

The DOD has historically pursued CBI as a major R&D area. Orlansky and String (1979) document 30 evaluation studies of CBI conducted by the military services from 1968 to 1978. The studies sample a wide variety of technical training (e.g., basic electronics to recipe conversion), cognitive skills (facts and procedures), and performance-oriented skills (e.g.,

Table 35.1. CBI Student Achievement Compared to Conventional Instruction

Method of Instruction	Number of Comparisons	Student Achievement at School		
		Inferior	Same	Superior
CAI	40	1	24	15
CMI	8	0	8	0

Note. Adapted from *Cost Effectiveness of Computer-Based Instruction* by J. Orlansky and J. String. Copyright 1979 by the Institute for Defense Analysis. Reprinted by permission.

hands-on maintenance) as well as a wide range of time (e.g., a few hours to up to a year). They compared conventional instruction (group-paced, lectures, and discussions) with CAI (stores and provides instructional materials to students individually via interactive terminals, tests and guides students, and self-paced) and CMI (instructional materials and tests provided away from terminal, computer scores tests and guides students, self-paced). Their 30 studies produced 48 sets of data. About 70% of the data on CAI came from experiments with few students (up to 50) and limited course materials (1 day to 1 week). There were fewer studies of CMI but these involved more students (600 to 2,500) and longer courses (2 to 10 months). A student day would be approximately 7 hours of instruction. All of the studies report effectiveness while only 8 report some cost data. The cost data are too incomplete to generalize as to the cost-effectiveness of these systems. While effectiveness of training should be measured by how well course graduates perform specific jobs in operational units, all studies use student achievement in school as a measure of effectiveness. Data were usually provided on length of time required to complete a course as well as on student attitudes. Instructor attitudes were measured infrequently. In all cases, results were confounded due to a combination of a thorough ISD for CBI with a comparison of a conventional course with a less thorough ISD. Thus, self-pacing, computer support, amount of revision, and possibly reduced amounts of course materials are confounded.

The data from this collection of studies are consistent. As is shown in Table 35.1, student achievement is either the same or superior for CAI/CMI as compared to conventional instruction. However, in DOD training these differences in instruction do not have practical significance. The results for the amount of student training time saved by CAI/CMI are shown in Table

Table 35.2. Amounts of Student Training Time Saved by CAI and CMI, Compared to Conventional Instruction

Method of Instruction	Number of Comparisons	Student Time Savings Compared to Conventional Instruction (in percent)	
		Median	Range
CAI	40	29	−31 to 89
CMI	8	44	12 to 69
Combined	48	32	−31 to 89

Note. From *Cost Effectiveness of Computer-Based Instruction* by J. Orlansky and J. String. Copyright 1979 by the Institute for Defense Analysis. Reprinted by permission.

Table 35.3. Attitudes of Student and Instructors Comparing CAI or CMI to Conventional Instruction

Attitude to CAI/CMI	Students		Instructors	
	CAI	CMI	CAI	CMI
Favorable	29	8	1	—
No difference	1	—	—	—
Unfavorable	1	—	4	4
No report	1	—	27	4
Total	32	8	32	8

Note. Adapted from *Cost Effectiveness of Computer-Based Instruction* by J. Orlansky and J. String. Copyright 1979 by the Institute for Defense Analysis. Reprinted by permission.

35.2. The median time saved in the combined studies was 32%. These findings are important in that, unlike the civilian sector, students are paid to go to school. Also, the time savings with equivalent performance (Table 35.1) indicate the possibility of getting students to the job site faster with the equivalent level of mastery.

The attitudes of students and instructors are shown in Table 35.3. In general, student attitudes are positive while instructor attitudes are negative. The latter findings, although disturbing, are plausible in that in all cases these instructors were not provided meaningful instructor training on how to interact in this new environment.

An additional observation is that courseware for these CAI/CMI systems is expensive. As is shown in Table 35.4, the personhours to develop one hour of courseware ranged from 77 to 714 hours. Expert opinion would indicate that in today's dollars an hour of courseware costs approximately $10,000.

In summary, these data indicate that as compared to traditional instruction, CAI/CMI provides equivalent or superior achievement, with a 32% time savings. Student attitudes are positive while instructor attitudes are negative. Finally, courseware costs are high, although life cycle costs are unknown for these systems.

Similar findings are reported for CAI/CMI in the civilian sector. The seminal work in this area has been conducted by Kulik and his colleagues at the University of Michigan (Kulik, Bangert & Williams, 1983). Before their meta-analysis study, reviews of CAI/CMI were the box score review type (used by Orlanski and String, 1979). Based on Glass's meta-analysis (Glass, McGaw & Smith, 1981), Kulik et al., (1983) took a more quantitative approach to this task. For example, Kulik, Kulik, & Cohen (1980) used meta-analysis to investigate the effectiveness of computer-based college teaching. They found that computer-based instruction raised the examination scores of college students by approximately a .25 standard deviation. Computer-based teaching also had a moderate effect on attitudes of students toward instruction and toward the subject they were studying. Finally, they reported, as did Orlanksy and String (1979), that computer-based instruction reduced substantially the amount of time needed for instruction. In the 1983 article they focused on the effectiveness of computer-based teaching at the secondary level. In general, their analysis showed that computer-based teaching raised student scores on final exams by approximately a .32 standard deviation, or from the 50th to the 63rd percentile. In addition, students in CBI felt very positive toward the computer and toward the courses they were taking. They also reported that the amount of time students needed for learning was substantially less than traditional instruction. These findings are strikingly consistent with results in the military sector.

Table 35.4 Cost of Computer-Based Instruction

Method of Instruction	System	Instructional Hours Developed	Man-Hours per Instructional Hour			References
			Programming	Coding	Total	
CAI	PLATO IV	39.0	27 to 248	50 to 467	77 to 714	Hurlock & Slough (1976)
		6.0			156	Kribs (1976)
		2.0			400	Kribs (1976)
		30.0			284	U.S. Army Ordnance Center & School (1975)
		20.0			100 & 200	Dallman, DeLeo et al. (1977)
		32.0	141	81	222	Himwich (1977a)
		315.0			80	Grimes (1975)
	TICCIT	10.0			200	Kribs (1976)
		3.0			400	Kribs (1976)
		32.0	150	96	246	Himwich (1977b)
	LTS-3	30.0			175	Keesler AFB (1973)
	IBM-1500	3.5	356	119	475	Rogers & Weinstein (1974)
	Unspecified CAI	Unknown			150 & 200	Middleton, Papetti & Michell (1974)
CMI	Navy CMI	50.0	100	10	110	Carson, Graham et al. (1975)
		300.0			30 & 60	Hansen, Ross et al. (1975)
		Unknown	(293)[a]	(25)[a]	(318)[a]	Poloyn, Baudhuin et al. (1977)

[a] Requirements were given in terms of dollars per instructional hour and have been converted on the assumption of $10 per hour for military labor.

Note. Adapted from *Cost Effectiveness of Computer-Based Instruction* by J. Orlansky and J. String. Copyright 1979 by the Institute for Defense Analysis. Reprinted by permission.

In general, Kulik et al., 1983 report findings that the effects of computer-based instruction seem to be strongest at the elementary level, still strong at the secondary level, and tend to be equivalent at the college level. Finally, they reported that features of computer-based instruction tend to have little impact on student achievement. They made an interesting comment that the year of publication was related to the size of the effect, i.e., studies reported later in time (1980 vs. 1970s) indicated that CBI had a greater impact on achievement. Hartley (1977) also noticed this tendency in studies of programed instruction at the elementary and secondary level, and Kulik et al., 1983 also noticed the same effect on two separate meta-analyses of findings on programed instruction at the secondary and collegiate level. They suggest, and we believe that it seems likely, that recent improvements in instructional technology have led to more systematic and more effective instruction across time.

The general trend in the mid-seventies to early eighties for CAI/CMI research sponsored by the Department of Defense has been to either investigate the key characteristics of CAI/CMI or application of CBI to solve a pressing DOD problem. An example of the former would be Robinson, Tomblin, and Houston (1981). They provided additional information on student and instructor attitudes in a Navy CMI course. They administered attitudinal questionnaires to 100 instructors and 255 trainees in five schools taught under a Navy CMI system. In general, these questionnaires contained items exploring attitudes towards CMI, and attitudes of students and instructors. They found, as had Orlansky and String (1979), that trainee attitudes toward the CMI system in general were quite favorable, while those of instructors were generally unfavorable.

A partial solution to this negativity of military instructors in CBI environments is provided by McCombs and Dobrovolny (1980). They first provided a theoretical view of what instructor roles are appropriate for CBI classrooms. They emphasize high-level management functions such as counselor/advisor, learning strategies expert, and tutor/counselor. They kept detailed records of the activities of instructors in a CMI format, which included kind of activity observed, the factors that initiated the activity, and time devoted to each episode of the activity. In general, they found that instructors spend most of their time on relatively routine transactions. Based on their rationale, they developed an instructor training package for use of instructors in CBI environments. Subsequent research by McCombs and Dobrovolny (1982) indicated that such instructors given this training have more positive attitudes toward CBI.

Another representative approach to research in computer-based instruction during this time period was provided by Frederico (1982, 1983). In a series of studies he investigated the relationship between individual difference variables and success in Navy CMI courses. Individual difference variables were of cognitive styles (field independence vs. field dependence) and cognitive abilities and aptitudes such as general reasoning ability. In general, he found that such individual difference variables predicted positive achievement in a Navy CMI course and also varied as a function of type of instruction (fact vs. rule vs. procedure).

A complementary line of research has been conducted by Hall and Freda (1982) at the Navy's Training and Analysis Group. In their work, they were interested in how measures of student ability, a general ability measure (Armed Services Aptitude Battery), and a specific ability measure were related to the effectiveness/efficiency measures for particular CMI courses. As in the Orlansky and String (1979) study, student end-of-course grades were used as an internal criterion for training effectiveness. Hall and Freda utilized fleet supervisor ratings of adequacy of training as their external criterion of effectiveness. It should be noted, however, that specific on-the-job measures were not utilized. The training efficiency measure was the amount of student time necessary to complete training. Their study, a correlational one, looked at approximately 5,800 graduates of a CMI system utilizing five CMI courses. They found an inverse relationship between general ability and training time, that is, higher ability was associated with shorter training time, and that higher ability sailors received higher grades in CMI courses than in conventional courses. Thus, it seems from this study "the rich get richer." A general conclusion of the study was that higher aptitude personnel perform better in CMI courses, whereas there is no relationship between aptitude and achievement in conventional courses. They also found no relationship between fleet supervisor ratings of school training adequacy whether trainees were in individualized (self-paced) or conventional classes.

A rather recent interesting source for computer-based instruction in the Department of Defense is found in a special issue of the *Journal of Computer-Based Instruction*. In this issue, O'Neil and Evans (1983) provide a thumbnail sketch of CBI research being conducted in the Army, Air Force, and Navy. In general, the studies continue evolutionary development of this technology into specialized courses in specific target areas.

The Army Research Institute is currently developing a series of projects using CBI technology. For example, in a computer-based reserve maintenance training project (Goldberg, 1984), microprocessor-based courseware for reserve component tank maintenance personnel will be completed in 1986. The program will support maintenance training of reserve personnel for the latest Army tank, the MI. The intent of this program is to overcome reserve component training problems such as unavailability of new weapon systems to train on and limited training preparation time (i.e., less than 57 days of training time/year). In the Unit Management System (UMS), a microprocessor-based, networked decision support system has been designed to improve the unit commander's ability to manage all personnel, logistics, and training functions from individual through battalion level. The prototype system is operational and undergoing evaluation. This new concept is referenced through a letter of agreement between the Army Research Institute and the Army Development and Employment Agency. Table 35.5 provides a thumbnail picture of additional representative ongoing activities.

The Job Skills Education Program (JSEP), which will be completed in 1986, illustrates a variety of innovations in teaching. The intent of this effort is to provide a foundation of basic job-oriented learning skills that will permit lower aptitude soldiers to complete training successfully in both school and unit settings, thereby allowing them to perform satisfactorily on

Table 35.5. Representative ARI CBI Projects

Project/Objectives	Reference
Computerized Tutor: design develop and evaluate a low-cost hand-held computerized device to teach job-oriented vocabulary.	Bridgeman and Wisher (in press).
Data Management System for Basic Skills Education: evaluate the effectiveness of a computer-based interactive video-disc system in improving study skills, test taking strategies, anxiety management, spatial orientation and navigational skills.	Seidel and Wagner (1983).
Basic Skills Resource Center—Learning Strategies: investigate computer assisted approaches for transforming information to improve comprehension, retention, generation of imaginal and verbal elaborations, English as a second language and self-motivational skills.	Russo (in press).
Army Education Information System: develop and test a computer based educational and vocational information system.	Berkowitz and Barsom (1984).
Army Maintenance Training and Evaluation Simulation System (AMTESS): evaluate the transfer of maintenance training to operational equipment from versions of simulators incorporating various configurations of display and three dimensional hardware subsystems (e.g., passive vs. interactive video).	Unger, Swezey, Hayes, and Mirabella (1984).
Training Methods for the Combat Arms Leader: develop computer wargaming techniques allowing platoon leaders to practice tactical decision making, command, communication and control tasks and to exercise tactical doctrine against intelligent opposing force.	Zagorski and Travis (in press).
Psychological Map of Video Games: determine motivational characteristics of video games or user preferences which may affect instructional game effectiveness.	Bubko and Davis (in press).

the job and to proceed up the military career ladder.

The first phase of developing JSEP was the responsibility of the U.S. Army Training and Doctrine Command (TRADOC). It consisted of analyzing military occupational specialties and common tasks required of all soldiers to determine the prerequisite basic skills and knowledge needed for recruits to engage in initial-entry training and for enlisted soldiers to assimilate training at permanent duty stations up to the rank of Staff Sergeant, Grade E-6. Based on the results of this analysis, assessment instruments were developed and validated which accurately identified specific basic skills deficiencies in soldiers. TRADOC has completed analysis on 116 specialties and all

common tasks. These efforts cover all Army occupations that have over 200 new entrants per year. This analysis has produced a refined taxonomy containing 203 specific basic skills (Rayner, Wilson, & Farr in press). Based on the task analysis work, assessment instruments were developed and are currently undergoing validation.

The second phase, a responsibility of ARI, consists of prototype curriculum development. A 34-month contract was awarded by the Army in September 1982 to Florida State University and their subcontractor, the Hazeltine Corporation. They will, first, determine the usability of the TRADOC-developed taxonomy and tests and make modifications as necessary. Second, they will develop 420 hours of instruction designed to correct soldier deficiencies in any of the 203 basic skills. Third, they will conduct field trials at four Army sites. Revision of the prototype program will be predicated upon the formative evaluation of these field trials.

JSEP will be computer-based and run on both PLATO IV (Avner, 1979) and MicroTICCIT CBI systems (Wilson, 1984). It is anticipated that the majority of the materials developed will be modularized to facilitate open entry/open exit. A Cost Training Effectiveness Analysis (CTEA) will be conducted. In addition, learning strategies will be a key component of JSEP. Summative third-party evaluation will be performed as part of the multi-year ongoing evaluation of the Army Basic Skills Education Program being conducted by the American Institutes for Research, also under contract to ARI.

The third stage will be the Army-wide implemetation of JSEP beginning in 1987. The Adjutant General's Office, Headquarters, Department of the Army, is the program proponent and plans to operate the program through the 369 Army education centers and subcenters.

Many of the efforts presented above are in various stages of development. Therefore, it is currently difficult to refer readers to specific publications. There are, however, several ways researchers can obtain either specific publications, information about publications (e.g., bibliographies), or information about ARI's research efforts.

If one has a contract or grant with a DOD agency, publications and information about publications can be obtained, for a fee, from the Defense Technical Information Center, Cameron Station, Alexandria, VA 22314.

If one does not have a contract or grant with a DOD agency, the above service (also for a fee) can be obtained from the National Technical Information Services, 5285 Port Royal Road, Springfield, VA 22161.

For additional information about the U.S. Army Research Institute, contact the Chief, Plans, Programs and Operations, U.S. Army Research Institute, 5001 Eisenhower Avenue, Alexandria, VA 22333.

Learning Strategies

The second research field, learning strategies, has a more traditional learning and instructional research paradigm at its core. It seeks to answer a particular question: Given a relatively complex learning environment, how can an individual make the most of the available resources, both internal and external, to acquire and use information and skills in an efficient manner? This is the central question underlying learning strategies research. Unlike instructional strategies where an authority, such as the teacher or computer, manipulates the learning situation in some fashion, the learning strategist teaches skills that allow an individual to manipulate the learning situation. This focus on learning strategies, as opposed to instructional strategies, has received increased attention during the last decade. In addition to focused DOD funding, a partial explanation for this shift may be the broader integration of cognitive and educational psychology. With the emphasis in cognitive psychology on the mental processes that operate on information, it was only natural that educationally inclined researchers would become more concerned with the strategies students use to learn new material (see Dansereau, 1978; Wittrock, 1978).

As noted by Brooks, Simutis and O'Neil (in press), learning strategies can be seen as a collection of those techniques that an individual consciously controls and that typically are beneficial to the individual's acquisition, retention, and use of information. This definition could include prelearning activities such as mood modification via relaxation techniques, learning activities such as summarization, and postlearning activities such as reinforcing oneself for studying for 2 hours. Somewhat in line with this broad view of learning strategies is Dansereau's (1978) definition of an effective learning strategy as a "set of processes or steps that can be used by an individual to facilitate the acquisition, storage, and/or utilization of information" (p. 4).

An example of a coherent set of learning strategies would be Dansereau's MURDER system (Dansereau et al., 1979). Because this particular system incorporates techniques common to many learning strategy systems, it will be described in some detail. The system was developed by Dansereau and his colleagues as an omnibus studying system that could be used by college students. In many ways MURDER can be seen as an expansion of Robinson's (1946) SQ3R system. The main differences between the two systems are that (a) the MURDER system specifies exact methods for using various study strategies, and (b) the MURDER technique includes affective/conative components.

The first component of MURDER is Mood. This step consists of a number of techniques for creating a positive and relaxed internal environment for the student. It was borrowed from the work of Meichenbaum (Meichenbaum & Goodman, 1971) on positive self-talk, Ellis (1963) on rational behavior therapy, and Wolpe (1969) on systematic desensitization. The second step is Understand. In this phase the student is encouraged to identify those portions of the text that are meaningful and those portions of text that require further processing by the student to be meaningful. While this aspect of the MURDER strategy is not well defined, it appears similar to what others refer to as metacognitive strategies (Brown, Armbruster and Baker, in press). In other words, students are to identify the information they understand, as well as the information they do not understand. The next step is the Recall stage, during which the student engages in the active use of specific text-processing strategies. For example, the student is instructed to network the text to make the relationships among the various topics clearer. The final three steps in the MURDER system are Digest, Expand, and Review. In these phases the learner is asked to

further expand her or his knowledge base by finding out what information is easy to remember and what information is hard to remember. Question-asking and explicit feedback are two of the suggested techniques to use in expanding the student's understanding and memory of the text. Finally, the learner is asked to adjust his or her study techniques on the basis of test results in class (Dansereau, et al., 1983).

Dansereau (1978) has also characterized learning strategies as either primary strategies or support strategies. Examples of direct strategies are Holley, Dansereau, and Fenker's (1981) networking and Anderson's (1979) mapping strategies. Both of these techniques require the student to construct a spatial outline of text that consists of a number of idea nodes representing the major and minor concepts, facts, and so on in the passage. The idea nodes are connected by means of relational links which represent a variety of different relationships among the nodes.

Indirect strategies may deal with the learner's affective/ emotional and conative/motivational strategies for studying. Particularly popular in this area are methods for dealing with test anxiety. According to researchers such as Sarason (1960) and Spielberger (e.g., Spielberger, Gonzalez & Fletcher, 1979), test anxiety is a situation-specific trait that is characterized by feelings of tension and apprehension, self-centered worry, and activation of the autonomic nervous system. An example of one approach to dealing with test anxiety is Meichenbaum's (e.g., Meichenbaum & Butler, 1980) cognitive modification strategy system (see also O'Neil and Richardson, 1980).

Strategies that are less inclusive in scope include imagery, mnemonic, and keyword techniques. Weinstein and Mayer (this volume) have referred to these techniques as basic elaboration strategies. Mnemonics and other similar techniques are frequently used as aids in remembering lists of items (such as the familiar "every good boy does fine" to aid in remembering the names of musical notes on the treble cleff). Considerable attention has been paid to the use of mnemonics in the acquisition of a second language (e.g., Paivio & Desroches, 1981). One of the more popular techniques in this area is the keyword method developed by Atkinson (e.g., Atkinson, 1975). This method consists of associating a mediator word with the word to be learned, and then creating a mental image of the object referred to by the mediator interacting with the object referred to by the to-be-learned word.

McCombs and Dobrovolny (1980) investigated the relevance of conative affective and cognitive skill variables to a computer-managed instructional system for the Air Force. Based on analysis of a number of individual difference variables and on instructor and student interviews, they found that the following characteristics discriminated poor learners from effective learners: (a) conative variables: poor learners exhibited low motivation to learn, few professional and/or personal goals, little self discipline and responsibility, and low vocational maturity; (b) affective variables: poor learners exhibited high test anxiety and lack of skills for dealing with stress and anxiety; and (c) cognitive variables: poor learners exhibited a lack of reading comprehension and problem solving skills.

McCombs and Dobrovolny (1980) constructed a battery of individual difference measures based on these variables to discriminate between effective and noneffective learners. They constructed eight scales consisting of 140 items covering both conative and affective domains, plus reasoning. These items were administered to two groups of military trainees to predict which students would perform satisfactorily and unsatisfactorily in their military courses. It was found that approximately 80% of students could be correctly classified.

Finally, McCombs and Dobrovolny (1980) developed seven training modules covering the strategies that previous research has indicated are effective. Six of the training modules cover the following areas: (a) career development, (b) values clarification, (c) goal setting, (d) assertiveness, (e) stress, and (f) management and problem solving. An introductory module was also developed to act as an advance organizer (see Mayer, 1978). Results concerning an evaluation of these modules indicate the modules were highly effective in reducing drop-out rates from Air Force training.

Learning strategies may also vary in their modifiability, or the degree to which they can be changed to meet the needs of a particular learning situation. Dansereau (in press) referred to the extremes of this dimension as algorithmic strategies, which are relatively inflexible, and heuristic strategies, which are easily modifiable. An example of an algorithmic strategy would be Atkinson's (1975) keyword method or Brook and Dansereau's (1983) structural schema training. Both of these strategies require that the learner perform similar or identical procedures across learning situations. On the other hand, heuristic strategies, such as those outlined by Rigney, Munro, and Crook (1979), allow the learners to adapt their studying procedures to the learning environment. Rigney et al. (1979) developed a generalized learning system called Aids. This system is computer-based and offers the student guidelines to break down complex learning tasks into simpler components. One reason that this system is heuristic in nature is that the learner helps to identify what subtasks must be performed in order to complete the overall task. This characteristic allows the learner to use the system in a relatively flexible manner.

Another area of important R&D in the domain of learning strategies is research on learning strategies and motor skills (Singer, 1978; Singer & Gerson, 1979). Singer (1978) argues that similar processes are involved in the learning of verbal and motor strategies and skills. If this is the case, it may be that the strategies that are currently being developed primarily as cognitive text-processing strategies will, at least in generic form, transfer across a wide variety of motor learning situations. Finally, ongoing promising work in learning strategies consists of collaborative techniques to teach learning strategies (Dansereau, 1984), learning strategies to teach reading comprehension (Wittrock, this volume) and application of learning strategies to teach Hispanic students English as a second language (Chamot, 1984).

Learning Strategies Curriculum

As applied researchers at the Army Research Institute, the context of our own research as well as our ongoing contract program in learning strategies is the development of a research base on which to build a learning strategies curriculum for training soldiers.

Ideally, an integrated learning strategies curriculum would be comprised of several components: metacognitive, cognitive, and motivation. Table 35.6 shows the breakdown and contents of this ideal learning strategic curriculum. Within the metacognitive component, students would be taught strategies for self-assessment/evaluation, setting performance standards/criteria,

Table 35.6. Integrated Learning Strategies Curriculum

Area	Module Number	Content	Number of Hours
Introduction	1.	Establishing Rationale and Benefits of Curriculum a. Understanding the role of learning strategies in self-development and learning achievement b. Previewing curriculum and learning strategies areas and their effects/benefits/utility	2
	2.	Understanding Approach and Format of Curriculum a. Knowing expectations for students in curriculum (student's role) b. Knowing general format and approach	2
Metacognitive	3.	Self-Assessment/Evaluation a. Examining strategies and skills repertoire b. Listing perceived strengths and weaknesses	3
	4.	Setting Performance Standards/Criteria a. Gathering performance information about self, others, and task demands b. Analyzing information about above c. Picking realistic standards d. Choosing or identifying measurement criteria which reflect achievement of standards	3
	5.	Planning a. Breaking into steps b. Identifying resources and strategies for reaching goals (standards) c. Establishing timeline d. Anticipating problems e. Generating alternative strategies for handling problems	3
	6.	Self-Monitoring/Evaluation a. Deciding when and how to check b. Self-testing c. Analyzing/summarizing information about performance	3

(continued)

Table 35.6 (*continued*)

Area	Module Number	Content	Number of Hours	Area	Module Number	Content	Number of Hours
		7. Self-correction 　a. Recognizing need for change 　b. Selection of appropriate alternative strategy	3			14. Values/Knowing Yourself 　a. Knowing yourself through your values and beliefs 　b. Identifying value conflicts	3
		8. Self-Determination of Rewards 　a. Timing and scheduling of rewards 　b. Generating list of rewards 　c. Selecting appropriate reward(s)	3			15. Career Exploration 　a. Knowing career interests and skills 　b. Acquiring decision making skills 　c. Setting career goals 　d. Knowing how the Army career system works	3
Cognitive		9. Attention 　a. Managing concentration 　　1. monitoring moods 　　2. being your own coach (self-talk, images) 　　3. scheduling breaks 　b. Setting specific study goals 　　1. time management 　　2. self-contracts 　　3. self-rewards	4			16. Goal Setting 　a. Understanding the purpose of goals 　b. Learning a systematic goal setting process 　c. Setting short- and long-term goals	3
		10. Comprehension 　a. Identifying main ideas 　b. Outlining (hierarchical, networking) 　c. Summarizing main points 　d. Recognizing text structure 　e. Relating text to experience 　f. Developing self-testing questions	4			17. Stress Management 　a. Understanding stress and sources of stress 　b. Practicing general "Do, Think, Say" strategies 　c. Managing performance (test) anxiety	3
		11. Reasoning 　a. Inferencing (deduction, induction) 　b. Evaluating ideas 　c. Test-wiseness	4			18. Effective Communication 　a. Knowing your communication style 　b. Effective listening 　c. Effective talking	3
		12. Memory 　a. Building associations/using prior knowledge 　　(1) visual imagery 　　(2) elaborations 　　(3) other neumonic strategies (e.g., creating analogies, categorizing information) 　b. Recognizing memory	4			19. Problem Solving 　a. Understanding the role of problem solving skills in each learning strategy area 　b. Applying general problem solving model in realistic situations	
Motivation		13. Taking Control 　a. Understanding the concept of personal responsibility 　b. Practicing general self-control strategies (e.g., self-talk, imagery, attribution) 　c. Dealing with procrastination	3	Summary		20. Strategy Maintenance and Generalization 　a. Knowing your role in strategy maintenance and generalization (self-management) 　b. Knowing how to use other resources in strategy maintenance and generalization (e.g., instructors) 　c. Practicing maintenance and generalization strategies	2

Total Modules: 20			Total Hours: 60

Note. From "Motivational Skills Training: Helping Students Adapt by Taking Personal Responsibility And Positive Self-Control" by B. L. McCombs & K. Lockhart. *Paper presented at American Educational Research*, Association, April, 1983.

planning, self-monitoring/evaluation, self-correction, and self-determination of rewards. Within the cognitive component, students would be taught strategies for maintaining attention, reading comprehension, reasoning, and remembering. Within the motivation component, students would be taught strategies for taking control and exercising personal responsibility, for knowing themselves and their values, for exploring their career interests, for goal setting, for stress management, for effective communication, and for problem solving. The curriculum would also include an introduction to the role of learning strategies in self-development and learning achievement, to the contents of the learning strategies curriculum and its benefits, and to the approach and format of the curriculum. In addition, a summary to the curriculum would be provided and would emphasize strategy maintenance and generalization approaches.

Summary

Why is the military supporting learning strategy research when our earlier analysis contrasted the civilian and military education goals? Weren't military training goals job-specific and concrete, while civilian goals were long-term and general? The learning strategies research reported above provides a general level training, that is, to think and to organize time, rather than a specific skill related to firing a weapon or repairing a vehicle. One reason the military wishes to focus on learning strategies is to develop a system for making all training more effective and efficient. And given the reality that new jobs will be created by new technology of all types introduced into the military services, the training problem, if treated as 100 or 1,000 new task requirements, is sure to be difficult, particularly in light of fewer available personnel and generally declining academic levels of entry recruits. The learning strategies approach may be the only way to provide a common set of skills that will be useful in a variety of unexpected situations a young soldier, for instance, may be faced with, including the need to be able to use or repair equipment not even designed as of now. Learning strategies probably represent "the new basic skills." It could be the common curriculum that has eluded both military and civilian education.

Intelligent Computer-Assisted Instruction (ICAI)

The third field that illustrates the military training research enterprise is a new area, publicized but relatively arcane, that of intelligent computer-assisted instruction (ICAI). ICAI is the application of artificial intelligence to computer-assisted instruction. Artificial intelligence, a branch of computer science, is making computers smart in order to (a) make them more useful and (b) understand intelligence (Winston, 1975). Topic areas have included natural language processing (Schank, 1980), vision (Winston, 1975), knowledge representation (Woods, 1983), spoken language (Lea, 1980), planning (Hayes-Roth, 1980), and expert systems (Buchanan, 1981). The field has matured in both hardware and software. The most commonly used language in the field is LISP (List Processing). A major development in the hardware area is that personal LISP machines are now available at a relatively low cost (20–50K)

with the power of prior mainframes. In the software area two advances stand out: (a) programing support environments such as LOOPS (Bobrow, 1983) and (b) expert systems. The application of "expert systems" technology to a host of real-world problems, ranging from medical diagnosis (Clancey, 1981), to mineral prospecting (Duda & Gaschnig, 1981), have demonstrated utility of artificial intelligence techniques in a very dramatic style. Finally, the current state-of-the-art in cognitive science has advanced to the stage where it is now possible to model soldier–task–instructor characteristics with fidelity in a machine.

ICAI systems use artificial intelligence to teach a range of subject matters addressed by these systems. Representative types of subjects include: (a) collection of facts (e.g., South American geography in SCHOLAR [Carbonell & Collins, 1973]; (b) complete system models (e.g., a ship propulsion system in STEAMER [Stevens & Steinberg, 1981] and a power supply in SOPHIE [Brown & Burton, 1978]); (c) completely described procedural rules (e.g., strategy learning in WEST [Brown, Burton and de Kleer, 1982] or arithmetic in BUGGY [Brown, Burton, & Larkin, 1977]); (d) partially described procedural rules (e.g., computer programing in BIP [Barr & Atkinson, 1977] and PROUST [Johnson & Solloway, 1983] or diagnosis of infectious diseases in GUIDON [Clancey, 1979]; and (e) an imperfectly understood complex domain, causes of rainfall in WHY [Stevens, Collins, & Goldin, 1978]). An excellent review by Barr and Feigenbaum (1982) documents many of these ICAI systems.

With respect to cognitive science, progress has been made in an analysis of misconceptions or "bugs" (Clement, Lockhead, & Solloway, 1980), the use of learning strategies (O'Neil & Spielberger, 1979), and expert versus novice distinctions (Larkin, 1983). The key components of an ICAI system consist of a knowledge base: that is, (a) what the student is to learn, (b) a student model, either where the student is now with respect to subject matter or how student characteristics interact with subject matter; and (c) a tutor, that is, instructional techniques for getting the student from one point of knowledge to another. These components are described in more detail by Fletcher (1985).

Knowledge Base

This is the "expert" part of the system. Ideally, this component must represent the relevant knowledge domain. In effect, it must contain the knowledge and understanding of a subject matter expert and incorporate what McCarthy and Hayes (1969) described as the epistemological aspect of human intelligence. It must be able to generate problem solutions from situations never before encountered and not anticipated by the training system designers. It must be able to infer the true state of the system from incomplete and/or inaccurate measurements. It must be able to solve problems based on this knowledge base.

Student Model

This component must represent the learner's capabilities and needs. Just as the knowledge base must "understand" the subject matter, so the student model must understand and be able to model the learner. Some systems emphasize a student's knowledge/gaps in his knowledge base; others emphasize students' or users' misconceptions. Few do both of these very well; however, none of the current ICAI systems represent the role of traditional individual differences (i.e., smart students learn faster than not-so-smart students [Sternberg, 1982]).

Tutor

This component must be able to apply the appropriate instructional tactics at the appropriate times. This capability implies the presence of both a large repertoire of instructional tactics and a strategic understanding of how best to use them. In short, this component must represent an expert tutor (i.e., teacher). It must know what to say to the learner/user and when to say it. In addition to knowing the subject matter and the knowledge level of the user, it must know how to take the learner from one stage of skill to another and how to help the user, given his current state of knowledge. However, little of instructional research-based design considerations (e.g., Merrill & Tennyson, 1977) are reflected in ICAI tutors.

In ICAI several promising lines of attack have emerged: the GUIDON work at Stanford, ICAI R&D at Xerox Parc, and the PROUST work at Yale. At Stanford, the original project, an expert system called MYCIN, dealt with the diagnosis and treatment of organisms that infect blood or cause meningitis (Buchanan, 1981). In direct tests it has achieved performance comparable with experts in the field (Yu, 1979). Further, it has spawned a whole family of expert systems. By removing the specific medical knowledge domain, a shell of essential or empty MYCIN has been formed called EMYCIN (van Melle, 1980). Given a new problem domain, EMYCIN provides help in constructing an expert system to solve the problem. EMYCIN assumes an appropriate representation format for the new knowledge base (production systems rules) and a goal-directed, backward chaining approach as the appropriate inference mechanism. Production systems are simply collections of if--then rules. Combining EMYCIN with new knowledge domains has yielded useful expert systems for pulmonary diseases (PUFF [Kunz, 1978]) and structural analysis (SACON [Bennett and Engelmore, 1979]). Of special interest is their articulate expert for explaining its rationale. This system is called GUIDON (Clancey, 1979). In a project jointly funded by ARI and ONR, support was provided to reconfigure the production rules in MYCIN so that they became more psychologically plausible as the basis for reasoning diagnostically. This capability allows GUIDON to provide test cases to students, allows students to analyze GUIDON'S diagnosis and by interpreting the student's analysis, builds up student models of the knowledge base in diagnostic reasoning abilities. Since GUIDON2 is being designed to serve as an instructional system for any AI-based expert program using the NEOMYCIN rule-based architecture, the research will include an evaluation of GUIDON2 interacting with an expert system for diagnosing faults in electronic or mechanical systems.

Probably the most interesting work in the ICAI domain is being conducted at Xerox Parc (Sleeman & Brown, 1982).

Their fundamental thesis is that the sophisticated symbolic environments provided in personal LISP machines can expand the use and effectiveness of an instructional strategy of learning-by-doing through guided discovery learning. Learning-by-doing environments can provide a tremendous indirect opportunity for students to learn about their own thinking processes (metacognition). As an example, Brown and Burton (1979) capitalized on the current computer game mania by creating a computer coach for PLATO's "How the West Was Won" (Dugdale and Kibbey, 1977) called, simply, "West." West can watch two people playing each other and decide on its own when to interrupt politely. It can then point out to the player that if he had paid more attention to his opponent's moves he might have discovered a strategy he did not possess. The obvious strength of this coach is that it can make use of the skills of the opponents without having to create unique scenarios for tutoring. It can in fact facilitate peer tutoring.

Current work at Xerox Parc, funded by ARI, focuses on (a) designing, developing, and evaluating an ICAI system to train diagnostic maintenance skills for complex, interactive technologies such as those found in top-of-the-line Xerox machines; and (b) creating a fully developed testbed for developing knowledge that will be applicable to maintaining future high technology Army systems.

They will use Interlisp-D personal LISP machines to create causal models of selected parts of a complex reprographics machine. This smart technology training testbed will be used to train high-level diagnostic and troubleshooting skills for repair of electronic, mechanical, chemical, and electro-optic components. The electro-optical reprographic system selected for conceptual modeling and training provides a stable, fully developed high technology testbed for developing new knowledge that will be applicable to these Army systems of the 1990s. This effort will use artificial intelligence to teach semantically based procedural skills in a way that combines active, practice-based learning with instruction in appropriate mental models of equipment function. This technology-based apprenticeship approach through learning by doing, guided by expert tutorial, will accelerate the learning of the kinds of skills that expert maintenance personnel acquire slowly through years of practice, and decrease the Army's current problems with field and organizational maintenance.

PROUST (Johnson & Soloway, 1983) was founded on an empirically based psychological theory of programing knowledge that (a) identifies specific knowledge differences between programers and non-programers; (b) considers that people have natural strategies facilitated by programing language constructs; (c) considers that people confuse new knowledge with similar knowledge already learned, such as the confusion between algebra's "equals" (=) sign with the assignment operator in programing; and (d) considers that tacit knowledge plays a role in problem solving.

PROUST matches the expert program against the input novice program. PROUST constructs a program in order to analyze a student program. PROUST assumes that misconceptions are a variant of expert knowledge. It is based on a preliminary theory of high-level plan knowledge and the importance of the programer's intent and categorization of bugs. PROUST will have two components: a programing expert and a pedagogical expert. As of July 1984, the PROUST programing expert had been built and field tested with students in a Pascal introductory course. What is needed but not yet built is an intelligent tutoring system (pedagogical expert). PROUST itself was tested using only the first syntactically correct program from each of 206 students. PROUST's proven capability is to identify bugs assessed, not improve student learning. In other words, PROUST performance was measured only as a bug finder not as a meter of student performance.

However, none of these ICAI projects has been evaluated in any rigorous fashion. In a sense they have all been toy systems for research and demonstration. They have all raised a good deal of excitement and enthusiasm about their likelihood of being effective instructional environments. Ongoing applications of this ICAI research at ARI will be to move a demonstration test of such technology into a weapons system.

Summary

In this chapter, we have attempted to show the relationship between research and development in the military training environment and the teaching activities in public education. Although different in a number of ways, not the least of which is public perception, these areas share some common problems. Among these are character of student pool; training opportunities for staff, management, and students; and curriculum development. The military training environment differs from public education in its embracing long-range planning, early implementation of technology (including instructional systems development [ISD], and computer-based instruction (CBI). The most important difference, however, seems to be in the military training enterprise's emphasis on concrete, job-related skills, as opposed to the longer term, more general educational goals of the public system.

Three areas in which military training has provided the impetus for substantial research were described: (a) computer-based instruction (b) learning strategies, and (c) intelligent computer-assisted instruction (ICAI). All three of these areas depend upon research and development bases. All three are areas likely to have strong impact in the public education arena.

If this chapter is successful, it will have allowed the reader to perceive the fuzzy boundaries between military and public education research endeavors. It will have suggested that research issues and approaches are common to both enterprises, as well as demonstrate that similar "new" ideas are grown from both military and civilian education gardens. At a practical level, it should encourage regular interest and reading of military-based instructional research and development findings published in government documents, some of which are not disseminated in the standard research press. In order to find such publications, use the system that is accessible through any major university library system.

REFERENCES

Anderson, T. H. (1979). Study skills and learning strategies. In H. F. O'Neil, Jr. (Ed.), *Learning strategies.* New York: Academic Press.

Atkinson, R. C. (1975). Mnemotechniques in second-language learning. *American Psychologist, 30,* 821–828.

Avner, R. A. (1979). Production of computer-based instruction materials. In H. F. O'Neil, Jr. (Ed.), *Issues in instructional systems development* (pp. 133–180). New York: Academic Press.

Barr, A., & Atkinson, R. C. (1977). Adaptive instructional strategies. In H. Spada and W. Kempf (Eds.), *Structural models of thinking and learning.* Bern: Hans Huber.

Barr, A., & Feigenbaum, E. A. (Eds.) (1982). *The handbook of artificial intelligence* (Vol. 2). Los Altos, CA: William Kaufmann.

Bennett, J. S., & Engelmore, R. M. (1979). *SACON: A knowledge-based consultant in structural analysis.* Report number HPP–78–23, Computer Science Department, Stanford University.

Berkowitz, M. F., & Barsom, H. F. (1984, May). Computer-based career guidance system for the Army. Paper presented at the meeting for the Association for the Development of Computer-Based Instructional Systems, Columbus, OH.

Bobko, P., & Davis, Mark A. (in press). *A multidimensional scaling of video games.* An Army Research Institute Report.

Bobrow, D. G., & Stefik, M. (1983). *The LOOPS Manual.* Palo Alto: Xerox.

Boyer, E. L. (1983). *High school: A report on secondary education in America.* (The Carnegie Foundation for the Advancement of Teaching Report). New York: Harper-Row.

Bridgeman, B., & Wisher, R. A. (1985). The development of a hand-held computerized vocabulary tutor. *Journal of Machine-Mediated Learning, 1*(3).

Brooks, L. W., & Dansereau, D. F. (1983). Effects of structural schema training and text organization on expository prose processing. *Journal of Educational Psychology, 75,* 811–820.

Brooks, L. W., Simutis, Z. M., & O'Neil, H. F., Jr. (in press). Individual differences in learning strategies research. In R. Dillon (Ed.), *Individual differences in cognition,* Vol. II. New York: Academic Press.

Brown, A. L., Armbruster, B. B., & Baker, L. (in press). The role of metacognition in reading and studying. In J. Orasanu (Ed.), *Reading comprehension: From research to practice.* Hillsdale, NJ: Lawrence Erlbaum.

Brown, J. S., & Burton, R. R. (1979). An investigation of computer coaching for informal learning activities. *International Journal of Man-Machine Studies, 11,* 5–24.

Brown, J. S., Burton, R. R., & de Kleer, J. (1982). Knowledge engineering and pedagogical techniques in Sophie I, II, and III. In D. Sleeman & J. S. Brown (Eds.), *Intelligent tutoring systems.* New York: Academic Press.

Brown, J. S., Burton, R. R., & Larkin, K. M. (1977). *Representing and using procedural bugs for educational purposes.* Seattle: 1977 ACM Conference Proceedings, 247–255.

Buchanan, B. G. (1981). *Research on expert systems.* Report number CS–81–837, Computer Science Department, Stanford University.

Carbonell, J. R., & Collins, A. (1973). Natural semantics in artificial intelligence. *International Journal of Computer Aided Instruction, 3,* 344–351.

Carson, S. B., Graham, L. L., Harding, L. G., Johnson, K. A., Mayo, G. D., & Salop, P. A. (1975). *An evaluation of computer-managed instruction in Navy technical training* (Report No. TR 75–38). San Diego, CA: Navy Personnel Research and Development Center.

Chamot, A. U. (1984). *Language learning strategies for Hispanic students: Matching the strategy to the task* (Contract No. 903–82–C–0169). Alexandria, VA: Army Research Institute.

Clancey, W. J. (1979). *Transfer of rule-based expertise through tutorial dialogue.* Report number CS–769, Computer Science Department, Stanford University.

Clancey, W. J. (1981). *The epistemology of a rule-based expert system: A framework for explanation.* Report number CS–81–896, Computer Science Department, Stanford University.

Clement, J., Lockhead, J., & Soloway, E. (1980). *Positive effects of computer programming on students' understanding of variables and equations.* Proceedings of the National Association for Computing Machinery, Nashville.

Dallman, B. E., De Leo, P. J., Main, P. S., & Gillman, D. C. (1977). *Evaluation of PLATO IV in vehicle maintenance training* (Report No. AFGRL-TR77–59). Lowry Air Force Base, Colorado: Air Force Human Research Laboratory.

Dansereau, D. F. (1978). The development of a learning strategies curriculum. In H. F. O'Neil, Jr. (Ed.), *Learning Strategies.* New York: Academic Press.

Dansereau, D. F. (1984). *Computer-based learning strategy training modules: A progress report.* Alexandria, VA: Army Research Institute.

Dansereau, D. F. (in press). Learning strategy research. In J. Segal, S. Chipman and R. Glaser (Eds.), *Thinking and learning skills: Relating instruction to basic research.* Hillsdale, NJ: Lawrence Erlbaum Associates.

Dansereau, D. F., Brooks, L. W., Holley, C. D., & Collins, K. W. (1983). Learning strategies training: Effects of sequencing. *The Journal of Experimental Education, 51,* 102–108.

Dansereau, D. F., McDonald, B. A., Collins, K. W., Garland, J., Holley, C. D., Diekhoff, G. M., & Evans, S. H. (1979). Evaluation of a learning strategy system. In H. F. O'Neil, Jr. & C. D. Spielberger (Eds.), *Cognitive and affective learning strategies.* New York: Academic Press.

Department of the Army (1984). *Army Regulation No. 70–1: Systems acquisition policy and procedure* (AR 70-1). Washington, DC: Author.

Department of the Army (1980). *Army Regulation No. 350–17: Non commissioned officer development program* (*NCODP*) (AR 350-17). Washington, DC: Author.

Department of the Army (1981). *Army Regulation No. 351–1: Individual military education and training* (AR 351-1). Washington, DC: Author.

Duda, R. O., & Gaschnig, J. G. (1981). Knowledge-based expert systems come of age. *BYTE, 6,* 238–281.

Dugdale, S., & Kibbey, D. (1977). *Elementary mathematics with PLATO.* Computer-Based Education Research Laboratory, University of Illinois.

Ellis, A. (1963). *Reason and emotion in psychotherapy.* New York: Lyle Stuart.

Federico, P. A. (1982). Individual differences in cognitive characteristics and computer-managed mastery learning. *Journal of Computer-Based Instruction, 9*(1), 10–18.

Federico, P. A. (1983). Adaptive instruction. In R. E. Snow, P. A. Federico, & W. E. Montague (Eds.), *Aptitude, learning, and instruction. Vol. I Cognitive process analyses of aptitude.* Hillsdale, NJ: Lawrence Erlbaum Associates.

Fletcher, J. D. (1985). Intelligent instructional systems in training. In S. A. Andriole (Ed.), *Applications in artificial intelligence.* Princeton N.J.: Petrocelli.

Glass, G. V., McGaw, B., & Smith, M. L. (1981). *Meta-analysis in social research.* Beverly Hills, CA: Sage Publications.

Goldberg, S. (1984, May). *Model training program for reserve component units.* Paper presented at the Association for the Development of Computerized Instructional Systems, Columbus, OH.

Goodlad, J. L. (1984). *A place called school: Prospects for the future.* New York: McGraw-Hill.

Grimes, G. (1975). *Cost of initial development of PLATO instruction in veterinary medicine.* (Computer-Based Education Research Laboratory). Urbana, IL: University of Illinois.

Hall, E. & Freda, J. (1982). *A comparison of individualized and conventional instruction in Navy technical training.* Orlando, FL: Department of the Navy Training Analysis and Evaluation Group.

Hansen, D., Ross, S., Bowman, H., & Thurmond, P. (1975). *Navy computer-managed instruction: Past, present and future* (Report No. IR002671). Memphis, TN: Memphis State University, Bureau of Educational Research and Services, Foundations of Education (ERIC Documentation Reproduction Service No. ED 114 051).

Hartley S. S. (1977). *Meta-analysis of the effects of individually paced instruction in mathematics* (Doctoral dissertation, University of Colorado, 1977). Dissertation Abstracts International, 1978, *38*(7-A), 4003. (University Microfilms No. 77-29, 926.)

Hayes-Roth, B. (1980). Human planning processes. Report number R-2670, The Rand Corporation, Santa Monica, CA.

Himwich, H. A. (1977a). The Chanute Air Force Base PLATO service test: Site history and management. In H. A. Himwich (Ed.), *Critique and summary of the Chanute A.F.B. computer-based education project*

(NTC Report No. 14). Urbana, IL: Computer-Based Education Research Laboratory, University of Illinois.

Himwich, H. A. (1977b). Some aspects of project establishment and management. In H. A. Himwich (Ed.), *Summary and analysis of Aberdeen CBE project.* Urbana, IL: Computer-Based Education Research Laboratory, University of Illinois.

Holley, C. D., Dansereau, D. F., & Fenker, R. M. (1981). Some data and comments regarding educational set theory. *Journal of Educational Psychology, 73,* 494–504.

Hunt, J., du Pont., P. & Cary, F. (1983). *Action for excellence.* Summary of Transcript of Proceedings, Education Commission of the States, Task Force on Education for Economic Growth, Washington, DC.

Hurlock, R. E., & Slough, D. A. (1976). *Experimental evaluation of PLATO IV technology: Final report* (Report No. NPRDC TR76 TQ-44). San Diego, CA: Navy Personnel Research and Development Center.

Johnson, W. L., & Soloway, E. (1983). *PROUST: Knowledge-based program understanding.* Report No. 285, Computer Science Department, Yale University.

Kessler Air Force Base (1973). *Supplementary study of peer training with the Lincoln Training System* (Report No. KE PR 73–123). Kessler AFB, MS: Kessler AFB.

Kribs, H. D. (1976). *Computer-based instruction for TRIDENT FBM training* (Special Report No. 76-11). San Diego, CA: Navy Personnel Research and Development Center).

Kulik, J. A., Bangert, R. L., & Williams, G. W. (1983). Effects of computer-based teachings on secondary school students. *Journal of Educational Psychology, 75*(1), 19–26.

Kulik, J. A., Kulik, C. L., & Cohen, P. A. (1980). Effectiveness of computer-based college teaching: A meta-analysis of findings. *Review of Education Research, 50,* 525–544.

Kunz, J. (1978). *A physiological rule-based system for interpreting pulmonary function tests.* Report No. HPP–78–19, Computer Science Department, Stanford University.

Larkin, J. H. (1983). The new science education. In A. Lesgold and F. Reif (Eds.), *Computers in Education: Realizing the Potential.* Washington, DC: U.S. Government Printing Office.

Lea, W. (Ed.) (1980). *Trends in Speech Recognition.* Englewood Cliffs, NJ: Prentice-Hall.

Lord, L., & Barnes, D. (1983). *Personnel assessment 2002 (P. A. 2002)* (Personnel Plans and System Directorate Report). Washington, DC: Deputy Chief of Staff for the Department of the Army.

Mayer, R. E. (1978). Can advanced organizers influence meaningful learning? *Review of Educational Research, 49,* 371–383.

McCarthy, J., & Hayes, P. J. (1969). Some philosophical problems from the standpoint of artificial intelligence. In D. Michie and B. Meltzer (Eds.) *Machine Intelligence* 4. Edinburgh: Edinburgh University Press.

McCombs, B. L. & Lockhart, K. (1983, April). *Motivational skills training: Helping students adapt by taking personal responsibility and positive self-control.* Paper presented at the American Educational Research Association, Montreal, Canada.

McCombs, B. L., & Dobrovolny, J. L. (1980). *Rationale for the design of specific types of student skills training in the conative, affective, and cognitive skill domains.* Air Force Human Resources Laboratory, Lowry Air Force Base, CO.

McCombs, B. L., & Dobrovolny, J. L. (1982). *Student motivational skill training package: Evaluation for Air Force technical training.* Air Force Human Resources Laboratory, Lowry Air Force Base, CO.

McLaughlin, D. H., Rossmeissl, P. G., Wise, L. L., Brandt, D. A., & Wang, M. (in press). *Validation of current and alternative ASVAB area composites, based on training and SQT information on FY 1981 and FY 1982 enlisted accessions.* Alexandria, VA: Army Research Institute.

Meichenbaum, D. H., & Butler, L. (1980). Toward a conceptual model for the treatment of test anxiety: Implications for research and treatment. In I. G. Sarason (Ed.), *Test anxiety, theory, research and applications.* Hillsdale, NJ: Lawrence Erlbaum Associates.

Meichenbaum, D. H., & Goodman, J. (1971). Training impulsive children to talk to themselves: A means of self-control. *Journal of Abnormal Psychology, 77,* 115–126.

Merrill, M. D. & Tennyson, R. D. (1977). *Teaching concepts: An instructional design guide*. Englewood Cliffs, NJ: Educational Technology.

Middleton, M. G., Papetti, C. J., & Micheli, G. S. (1974). *Computer Managed Instruction in Navy Training*. (TAEG Report No. 14). Orlando, FL: Training Analysis and Evaluation Group.

Navy Personnel Research and Development Center (1984). *Annual Report FY 1984* (NPRDC Publication Annual Report FY 1984). San Diego, CA: Author.

Office of the Assistant Secretary of Defense (Manpower, Installations and Logistics) (1984). *Military manpower training report* (DOD Publication Volume IV: Force Readiness Report). Washington, DC: Department of Defense.

Office of the Secretary of Defense for Manpower, Reserve Affairs, and Logistics (1982). *Profile of American youth: 1980 nationwide administration of the Armed Services Vocational Aptitude Battery* (MRA&L Report, March 1982). Washington, DC: Department of Defense.

Office of Technology Assessment (1982). *Informational technology and its impact on American education* (OTA Report, September 1982). Washington, DC: Office of Technology Assessment.

O'Neil, H. F., Jr. (Ed.). (1979). *Issues in instructional systems development*. New York: Academic Press.

O'Neil, H. F., Jr., & Evans, R. A. (1983). Introduction to computer-based instruction in defense. *Journal of Computer-Based Instruction, 10*(3/4) 58.

O'Neil, H. F., Jr., & Paris, J. (1981). Introduction and overview of computer-based instruction. In H. F. O'Neil, Jr. (Ed.), *Computer-Based Instruction* (pp. 1–21). New York: Academic Press.

O'Neil, H. F., JR., & Richardson, F. C. (1980). Test anxiety reduction and computer-based learning environments. In I. G. Sarason (Ed.), *Test anxiety: Theory, research, and applications* (pp. 311–319). Hillsdale, NJ: Lawrence Erlbaum Associates.

O'Neil, H. F. Jr., & Spielberger, C. D. (Eds.). (1979). *Cognitive and affective learning strategies*. New York: Academic Press.

Orlansky, J., & String, J. (1979). *Cost effectiveness of computer-based instruction and military training*. (IDA Report No. P-1375). Alexandria, VA: Institute for Defense Analysis.

Paivio, A., & Desroches, A. (1981). Mnemonic techniques in second-language learning. *Journal of Educational Psychology, 73*, 780–795.

Poloyn, K.A., Baudhuin, E. S., Brekka, L., Hoyt, M., Klisen, E. E., Kennelly, D. and Rudwick, E. H. (1977). *Computer-Managed Instruction at Remote Sites: Phases II–III, A Demonstration Design* (TAEG Report No. 499. Orlando, FL: Training Analysis and Evaluation Group.

Rayner, G. T., Wilson, L. S., & Farr, B. J. (in press). *Job skills education program: Design specifications*. Alexandria VA: Army Research Institute.

Rigney, J. W., Munroe, A. & Crook, D. E. (1979). Teaching task-oriented selective reading: A learning strategy. In H. F. O'Neil, J. & C. D. Spielberger (Eds.), *Cognitive and affective learning strategies*. New York: Academic Press.

Robinson, C. A., Tomblin, E. A., & Huston, A. (1981). *Computer-managed instruction in Navy technical training: An attitudinal survey*. NPRDC technical report 82-19, San Diego, CA., NPRDC.

Robinson, F. P. (1946). *Effective study*. New York: Harper.

Russo, R. P. (in press). *Basic skills resource center: Report on the preliminary research findings*. R. P. Russo (Ed.) Alexandria, VA: Army Research Institute.

Sarason, I. G. (1960). Empirical findings and theoretical problems in the use of anxiety scales. *Psychological Bulletin, 57*, 403–415.

Schank, R. C. (1980). Language and memory. *Cognitive Science, 4*, 243–284.

Seidel, R. J., & Wagner, H. (1983). Evaluation of a spatial data management system for basic skills education. *Journal of Videodisc/Videotape, 3*(1), 69–70.

Singer, R. N. (1978). Motor skills and learning strategies. In H. F. O'Neil, Jr. (Ed.), *Learning Strategies*. New York: Academic Press.

Singer, R.N., & Gerson, R. F. (1979). Learning strategies, cognitive processes, and motor learning. In H. F. O'Neil, Jr. and C. D. Spielberger (Eds.), *Cognitive and affective learning strategies*. New York: Academic Press.

Sleeman, D., & Brown, J. S. (1982). *Intelligent tutoring systems*. New York: Academic Press.

Spielberger, C. D., Gonzalez, H. P., & Fletcher, T. (1979). Test anxiety reduction, learning strategies, and academic performance. In H. F. O'Neil, Jr. and C. D. Spielberger (Eds.), *Cognitive and affective learning strategies*. New York: Academic Press.

Sternberg, R. (Ed.). (1982). *Advances in the Psychology of Human Intelligence*. Hillsdale, NJ: Lawrence Erlbaum Associates.

Stevens, A. L., Collins, A., & Goldin, S. (1978). *Diagnosing students' misconceptions in causal models*. Report number 3786, Cambridge, Massachusetts: Bolt, Beranek, and Newman.

Stevens, A., & Steinberg, C. (1981). Project STEAMER, NPRDC Technical Note Number 81-21. San Diego: Navy Personnel Research and Development Center.

U.S. Army Ordnance Center and School (1975). *Evaluation of the PLATO IV Systems in a Military Training Environment* (Vols. 1–2). Aberdeen Proving Ground, MD: U.S. Army Ordnance Center and School.

U.S. Army Training and Doctrine Command (1982). *TRADOC regulation no. 350–7: A systems approach to training*. Ft. Monroe, VA: Author.

U.S. General Accounting Office (1982). *The Army needs to modify its system for measuring individual soldier proficiency* (GAO Publication No. FPCD-82-28). Washington, DC: Author.

Unger, K. W. Swezey, R. W., Hayes, R. T., & Mirabella, A. (1984). *Army maintenance training and evaluation simulation system (AMTESS) device evaluation: Vol 1, overview of the effort* (ARI Technical Report 642). Alexandria, VA: Army Research Institute.

van Melle, W. (1980). *A domain independent system that aids in constructing consultation programs*. Report number CS-80-820, Computer Science Department, Stanford University.

Wilson, L. S. (1984). Presenting TICCIT: State-of-the-art computer-based instruction. *Training Technology Journal, 1*(2), 26–37.

Winston, P. H. (Ed.). (1975). *The Psychology of Computer Vision*. New York: McGraw-Hill.

Wittrock, M. C. (1978). The cognitive movement in instruction. *Educational Psychologist, 13*, 15–29.

Wolpe, J. (1969). *The practice of behavioral therapy*. New York: Pergamon.

Woods, W. A. (1983). What's important about knowledge representation? *Computer, 16*, 22–29.

Yu, V. L. (1979). Antimicrobial selection by a computer: A blinded evaluation by infectious disease experts. *Journal of the American Medical Association, 242*, 1279–1282.

Zagorski, H. J., & Travis, K. M. (in press). *Tank platoon leader tactical training methods: Vol. I, concise description of findings, Vol. II, detailed description of findings* (ARI Technical Report). Alexandria, VA: Army Research Institute.

About the Contributors

Clinton L. Anderson is Educational Training Consultant for Kinton Incorporated. He formerly served as Chief of Programs and Operations, Education Directorate, Headquarters, Department of the U.S. Army.

Donald S. Anderson is Professorial Fellow in the Department of Sociology, Institute of Advanced Studies at The Australian National University. His current research projects concern professional socialization, the sociology of private schooling, and the relation of social science, theory, research, and practice. He is President of the Australian Association for Education Research and a Fellow of the Australian College of Education. He has chaired several government inquiries into education. Recent publications include *Access to Privilege* (a study of students in higher education), *Schools to Grow In*, and *Youth, Transition, and Social Research*, which he edited with Catherine Blakers.

Beverly J. Armento is Associate Professor of Social Studies Education and Director of the Center for Business and Economic Education at Georgia State University, Atlanta, Georgia. She is President of the National Association of Economic Educators, Chair of the Research in Social Studies Special Interest Group, AERA, and a former Chair of the Social Studies College and University Assembly. Her work on concept learning, teacher effectiveness, and theory-based economic education has appeared in numerous journals.

Carl Bereiter is Professor of Applied Psychology at the Ontario Institute for Studies in Education in Toronto. He is the author, with Marlen Scardamalia, of the forthcoming book *Psychology of Written Composition*. His primary areas of interest include research on cognition and instruction, text processing, and intentional learning.

Bruce J. Biddle is Professor of Psychology and of Sociology and Director of the Center for Research in Social Behavior at the University of Missouri—Columbia. A social psychologist, he has conducted research on the study of teaching, the role of the teacher, and social influence among youth. His most recent book is *Role Theory: Expectations, Identities, and Behaviors*.

Jere Brophy is Co-Director of the Institute for Research on Teaching and Professor in the Departments of Teacher Education and of Counseling, Educational Psychology, and Special Education at Michigan State University. His research interests include teacher expectations, teacher effects, classroom management, student motivation, and the dynamics of teacher-student interaction. He was the recipient of AERA's Palmer O. Johnson Award in 1983 for his article entitled "Teacher Praise: A Functional Analysis." He is author or co-author of nine books and over 100 other publications, including *Teacher-Student Relationships: Causes and Consequences*, *Looking in Classrooms* (both with Thomas L. Good), *Learning from Teaching: A Developmental Perspective*, and *Student Characteristics and Teaching* (both with Carolyn M. Evertson).

Leigh Burstein is Professor in the Research Methods and Evaluation Specialization of the Graduate School of Education and Faculty Associate in the Center for the Study of Evaluation at the University of California, Los Angeles. He is former Editor of the *Journal of Educational Measurement*. His primary research interests are in methodology for analyzing multilevel problems in educational research and program evaluation, secondary data issues, information systems in local school improvement, and educational quality indicators. He is Co-Editor of *Issues in Aggregation* and *Collecting Evaluation Data: Problems and Solutions*, and author of *Analysis of Multilevel Data in Educational Research and Evaluation*.

Robert C. Calfee is Professor of Education and Psychology at Stanford University. An experimental cognitive psychologist, he is Associate Director of the Study of Stanford and the Schools, and is currently the Editor of the *Journal of Educational Psychology*. He is the author of *Experimental Methods in Psychology*, *Human Experimental Psychology*, and *The Development of Reading*.

Thomas P. Carpenter is Professor of Curriculum and Instruction at the University of Wisconsin-Madison and Research Associate at the Wisconsin Center for Education Research. His current research deals with the development of number concepts in young children. He is Co-Editor of the book *Addition and Subtraction: A Cognitive Perspective*, and has written chapters in *The Acquisition of Mathematical Concepts and Principles*; *Problem Solving: Multiple Research Perspectives*; and *Research in Mathematics Education*.

Courtney B. Cazden Is Professor of Education at Harvard University. Her major research interests are in the development of children's verbal ability in and out of school and the functions of language in all educational settings. She is currently President of the American Association for Applied Linguistics, Past President of the Council on Anthropology and Education, a former member of the Executive Board and Council of the American Educational Research Association, and has been a Fellow at the Center for Advanced Study in the Behavioral Sciences. Recent research articles include: "Contexts for Literacy: In the Mind and in the Classroom"; "Can Ethnographic Research Go Beyond the Status Quo?"; "Effective Instructional Practices in Bilingual Education"; and "Environmental Assistance Revisited: Variation and Functional Equivalence."

Christopher M. Clark is Professor of Educational Psychology and Senior Researcher at the Institute for Research on Teaching at Michigan State University. He is a Spencer Fellow of the National Academy of Education and recipient of the 1980 Palmer O. Johnson Award of the American Educational Research Association. He chairs the special interest group on Teacher and Student Cognitions. His published work includes journal articles and book chapters on teacher thinking ("Teachers' Reports of Their Cognitive Processes During Teaching," "Teacher Planning: An Inventory of the Knowledge Base"), on the teaching of school writing ("Understanding Writing in School"), and on the relationship between research and practice ("Research in the Service of Teaching").

Richard E. Clarke is Professor of Educational Psychology and Technology and Director of the Center for Instructional Research, Development, and Training at the University of Southern California. He has served as Director of Instructional Media for the Stanford University Center for Research and Development in Teaching and was Chair of the Graduate Program in Instructional Technology at Syracuse University. He currently serves as an editorial consultant to seven journals and is Associate Editor for *Educational Communication and Technology Journal* and *Performance and Instruction Journal*. His recent publications include "Reconsidering Research on Learning from Media" and "The Transfer of Instructional Technology Between Nations."

Lyn Corno is Associate Professor of Education, specializing in educational psychology, at Columbia University's Teachers College in New York City. She is an Advisory Editor of the *Journal of Educational Psychology*, and has served on several committees of the American Educational Research Association and the American Psychological Association. Publications include articles in the *American Educational Research Journal*, the *Journal of Educational Psychology*, the *Educational Psychologist*, the *Journal of Educational Measurement*, and *Curriculum Inquiry*. Professor Corno has written a curriculum for parent-assisted instruction in memory support and chapters in several books.

Sarah M. Dinham is Associate Professor of Educational Psychology at the University of Arizona, where her areas of specialization include postsecondary academic affairs, professional education, and educational evaluation. She has been Chairman of the University of Arizona Faculty and Vice

President (for Division I, Education in the Professions) of the American Educational Research Association.

Walter Doyle is Research Scientist and Director of the Research on Classroom Learning and Teaching Program in the Research and Development Center for Teacher Education at the University of Texas at Austin. He is a specialist in classroom research with interests in classroom management, academic work, and teacher comprehension. He is Associate Editor of the *Elementary School Journal*, author of *Classroom Management*, and Co-Editor of *Focus on Teaching*. His articles have appeared in *Review of Research in Education, Review of Educational Research, Curriculum Inquiry, Journal of Curriculum Studies, Journal of Teacher Education*, and other publications.

Michael J. Dunkin is Director of the Centre for Teaching and Learning at the University of Sydney and was formerly Associate Professor in Education, Macquarie University, Sydney, Australia. He has been elected President of the Australian Association for Research on Education. His writings include the well-known book *The Study of Teaching* (with Bruce Biddle). He is the Co-Editor of the section on Teaching and Teacher Education of the *International Encyclopedia of Education: Research and Studies*. He is Associate Editor of the new international journal *Teaching and Teacher Education: An International Journal of Research and Studies*.

Priscilla A. Drum is Associate Professor in Language Development and Reading, Educational Psychology Program, Graduate School of Education, University of California, Santa Barbara. She has served as Chair of Basic Research on Reading, a special interest group of the American Educational Research Association, and as Publications Chair for the National Reading Conference. Her recent writings include "Retention of Text Information by Grade, Ability, and Study" in *Discourse Processes* and "Learning Word Meanings from Written Context" in *The Nature of Vocabulary Acquisition*.

Frederick Erickson is Professor of Teacher Education and of Pediatrics and Human Development at Michigan State University. An anthropologist of education, he is interested in relationships between the organization of diversity in society (along the lines of race, class, ethnicity, language, and culture) and the organization and conduct of schooling. His special interests lie in the sociolinguistic analyses of face-to-face interaction, and he is a pioneer in the use of cinema, film, and video tape together with participant observational fieldwork in such research. His publications include (with Jeffrey Schultz) *The Counselor as Gatekeeper: Social Interaction in Interviews*, and "Cultural Organization of Participation Structures in Two Classrooms of Indian Students." He is Past President of the Council for Anthropology in Education and is Editor of that society's journal, *Anthropology and Education Quarterly*.

Carolyn M. Evertson is Professor of Education, Peabody College, Vanderbilt University. She has conducted numerous observational studies of classroom processes, effective teaching, and teacher-student relationships. Her publications include

"Learning from Teaching: A Developmental Perspective," "Student Characteristics and Teaching" (with Jere Brophy), and two books on classroom management for teachers.

Sharon Feiman-Nemser is Senior Researcher at the Institute for Research on Teaching and Associate Professor of Teacher Education at Michigan State University's College of Education. Her publications include *Teacher Centers: What Place in Education?*; *A Consumer's Guide to Teacher Development*; and *Learning to Teach*.

Gary D Fenstermacher is Dean of the College of Education, University of Arizona, Tucson. His field of specialization is philosophy of education, with emphasis on the relation between theory and practice. He was formerly a member of the faculties at the University of California, Los Angeles, and Virginia Polytechnic Institute and State University. He has received numerous awards for teaching excellence and was recently awarded the Excellence in Professional Writing Award by the American Association of Colleges for Teacher Education. His work appears in many journals and anthologies in the field of education.

Lilly Wong Fillmore is currently an Associate Professor in the Graduate School of Education at the University of California at Berkeley. She specializes in second language learning, teaching research, and bilingual education research. Her publications in second language acquisition, which focus on learners' social and cognitive strategies and individual differences, include "Individual Differences in Second Language Learning" and "The Language Learner as an Individual." Her publications in bilingual education and in second language teaching, which are concerned with the effects of instructional practices and language use on the learning process, include "Instructional Language as Linguistic Input: Second Language Learning in Classrooms."

Robert E. Floden is Senior Researcher at the Institute for Research on Teaching and Associate Professor of Teacher Education and Educational Psychology at the College of Education, Michigan State University. His journal contributions include "Rationality to Ritual: The Multiple Roles of Evaluations in Governmental Processes" (with S. S. Weiner); "Flexner, Accreditation, and Evaluation"; "The Logic of Information-Processing Psychology in Education"; and "The Role of Rhetoric in Changing Teachers' Beliefs."

Jeanne A. Freeman is Director of Management Training for General Electric Information Services. She was formerly with Mobil Oil Corporation and the Xerox Corporation.

Thomas L. Good is Professor of Curriculum and Instruction and a Research Associate at the Center for Research in Social Behavior at the University of Missouri—Columbia. He specializes in the analysis of instructional behavior and has written many books and articles examining teacher and student behavior in classroom settings. Among his works are *Looking in Classrooms*, written with Jere E. Brophy. Professor Good is a member of the American Educational Research Association and Fellow (Division of Educational Psychology) of the American Psychological Association.

Judith L. Green is Associate Professor of Education, The Ohio State University. She has written widely on communicative competence and the ethnography of communication in classrooms. Her writings include "Research on Teaching as a Linguistic Process: A State of the Art" and "Directions in Sociolinguistics" (with David Bloome). She has also edited *Ethnography and Language in the Classroom* (with Cynthia Wallat) and *Multiple Perspectives Analysis of Classroom Discourse* (with Judith Harker and Cynthia Wallat).

Maxine Greene is Professor of Philosophy and Education and the William F. Russell Professor in the Foundations of Education at Teachers College, Columbia University. She is Past President of the American Educational Research Association, the Philosophy of Education Society, and the American Educational Studies Association. She has a D.H.L. from Lehigh University and an honorary degree from Hofstra University. Her major writings have dealt with ethics, aesthetic education, educational reform, and curriculum. Her books include *Teacher as Stranger* and *Landscapes of Learning*. Her Dewey Lecture, *The Dialectics of Freedom*, is soon to be published.

Beverly J. Jones is Associate Professor of Art Education at the University of Oregon, Eugene, Oregon. Her interests include multidisciplinary research in aesthetics and computer applications in the arts and humanities. She received the 1982 Mary J. Rouse Award for research leadership in art education.

Reginald L. Jones is Professor and Chair, Department of Afro-American Studies and Professor, School of Education, University of California, Berkeley. He specializes in the psychology and education of exceptional children and Afro-American psychology. He has held appointments as Professor and Vice Chair, Department of Philosophy, The Ohio State University; Professor and Chair, Department of Education, University of California, Riverside; and Professor and Director, University Testing Center, Haile Sellassie I University (Ethiopia). He is a Past President of the Association of Black Psychologists and is a recipient of the Council for Exceptional Children's J. Wallace Wallin Award, the Association of Black Psychologists Scholarship Award, and a Citation for Distinguished Achievement from Ohio State. His publications include *New Directions in Special Education*; *Problems and Issues in the Education of Exceptional Children*; *Special Education in Transition*; *Mainstreaming and the Minority Child*; *Black Psychology*, and *Attitudes and Attitude Change in Special Education: Theory and Practice*.

Barbara K. Keogh is Professor of Education at the University of California, Los Angeles. A licensed clinical psychologist and former member of the National Advisory Committee on the Handicapped, she is active in research on children with learning problems. She is a Fellow of the American Psychological Association and the International Academy for Research in Learning Disabilities. She is Editor of the series *Advances in Special Education* and is the senior author of *A System of Marker Variables for the Field of Learning Disabilities*.

Judith E. Lanier, Professor of Education, is Dean of the College of Education at Michigan State University. Founding Co-Director of the Institute for Research on Teaching, she continues as Associate Director concerned with the relationship between research and practice. She currently serves as the first Vice President of the recently formed Division K—Teaching and Teacher Education for the American Educational Research Association. A classroom teacher and teacher educator prior to recent administrative work, her scholarly activity focuses on the nexus between professional study in schools of education and professional practice in the elementary and secondary sector. Her chapter in the *Eighty-Second Yearbook of the National Society for the Study of Education, 1983*, entitled "Tensions in Teaching Teachers the Skills of Pedagogy," exemplifies this line of work.

Robert L. Linn is Professor of Educational Psychology and of Psychology at the University of Illinois at Urbana-Champaign. He is the Vice President for the Measurement and Research Methodology Division of the American Educational Research Association and a Past President of the National Council on Measurement in Education and of the Division on Evaluation and Measurement of the American Psychological Association. He is the Editor of *Education Measurement, Third Edition* and the author of more than 100 articles on measurement and research methodology.

Judith Warren Little is Senior Program Director at the Far West Laboratory for Educational Research and Development, San Francisco. Her research and writings have concentrated on problems of professional development, the professional environment of schools, and the structure of the teaching profession. Some publications related to these areas include "Seductive Images and Organizational Realities in Professional Development"; "Teachers as Professional Colleagues"; "Norms of Collegiality and Experimentation: Workplace Conditions of School Success"; and "Contributions of Staff Development to Principals' Instructional Leadership Practices: Gleanings from One Case Study."

Donald L. MacMillan is Professor of Education at the University of California, Riverside. He is a Fellow of the American Psychological Association and the American Association on Mental Deficiency. His research has focused on motivational characteristics and social competence in environmentally at-risk and mildly handicapped children. He has written over 70 publications, including *Mental Retardation in School and Society.*

Richard E. Mayer is Professor of Psychology at the University of California, Santa Barbara. His research areas include human learning and problem solving, with special focus on learning from science prose, mathematical problem solving, and learning computer programming. He is Editor of *Educational Psychologist* and Co-Editor of *Instructional Science*, as well as a member of the editorial board of the *Journal of Educational Psychology*. He is the author of several books, including *Thinking, Problem Solving, and Cognition* and *The Promise of Cognitive Psychology.*

June King McFee is Professor of Art Education Emeritus, The University of Oregon. She is a Distinguished Fellow of the National Art Education Association and former Editor of *Studies in Art Education*. Her areas of specialization are human behavior and cross cultural impacts in teaching art. She is the author of *Art, Culture and Environment; Art Ability;* and *Cultural Dimensions in the Teaching of Art.*

Harold F. O'Neil, Jr. is the Director of the Training Research Laboratory of the Army Research Institute. He has edited several volumes, including *Computer Based Instruction: A State of the Art Assessment.*

Fritz Oser is Professor of General Science Education, Faculty of Philosophy, at the University of Fribourg (Switzerland), and Chairman of the Swiss Educational Research Association. He has written several books and a number of articles on moral and religious development and education, mostly in his native German language. The article "Cognitive Stages of Interaction in Moral Discourse" is one of his major contributions in English. He is Co-Editor (along with M. W. Berkowitz) of *Moral Education; Theory and Applications.* He also is Editor of a series on the science of religion which reports on current research in this field. He is currently constructing and validating a theory of moral discourse pedagogy and is studying the issue of how the morality of teachers influences their general professional performance.

Penelope L. Peterson is Professor of Educational Psychology at the University of Wisconsin-Madison. She has published numerous articles and book chapters on classroom teaching and learning and edited the volume *Research on Teaching: Concepts, Findings, and Implications.* For her article on teacher decision-making during interactive classroom teaching, she received in 1980 the Palmer O. Johnson Award from the American Educational Research Association for the best research article in AERA journals. She is currently Editor of *Review of Educational Research*, a journal of the American Educational Research Association.

Thomas A. Romberg is Professor in the Department of Curriculum and Instruction at the University of Wisconsin-Madison and Faculty Associate at the Wisconsin Center for Education Research. His primary research interest is in the structure and engineering of school mathematics curricula, curriculum reform, and classroom adaptations of curricula. He was Coordinator of Research and Test Development for the School Mathematics Study Group at Stanford University. At the University of Wisconsin he has directed several major research projects including the Analysis of Mathematics Instruction Project, which produced the K-6 mathematics program *Developing Mathematical Processes*, the IGE Evaluation Project, and the Ford Foundation Urban Collaborative Network Monitoring. His major publications include *Individually Guided Mathematics; Toward Effective Schooling; The IGE Experience; Learning to Add and Subtract: The Sandy Bay Studies* (with Kevin Collins); "Curriculum Implementation and Staff Development as Cultural Change: A Common Curriculum for Mathematics."

Barak Rosenshine is Professor of Educational Psychology at the University of Illinois. He obtained his Ph.D. in Education from Stanford University. His areas of specialization are classroom instruction and instructional programs. He was the winner of the 1984 AERA Interpretive Scholarship Award and is co-author of "Classroom Instruction in Reading" (with Robert Stevens) in the *Handbook of Reading Research*.

Gavriel Salomon is Professor of Education at the University of Tel Aviv, Israel, where he heads the Center of Communication and Technology in Education. He wrote *Interaction of Media, Cognition, and Learning*, which received the first James W. Brown Publication Award in 1981. He is also the author of *Communication and Education* and many studies investigating the psychological effects of media. Dr. Salomon was Professor of Education and Chairperson of the Educational Psychology Department at the Hebrew University of Jerusalem and Howard R. Marsh Professor of Communication at the University of Michigan. He has also served as a visiting faculty member at Harvard, The Open University (England), University of Southern California, Stanford University, The Universidad Ibero Americana (Mexico), and Indiana University. He is a Fellow of the Division of Educational Psychology of the American Psychological Association, and the Editor of the educational entries in the *International Encyclopedia of Communication*.

Marlene Scardamalia is Head, Center for Applied Cognitive Science, and Professor in the Department of Measurement, Evaluation, and Computer Applications at the Ontario Institute for Studies in Education in Toronto. She is the author, with Carl Bereiter, of the forthcoming book, *Psychology of Written Composition*. Her primary areas of interest include research on text processing, intentional learning, and computer aids to higher order processing.

Richard J. Shavelson is Professor of Education at the University of California, Los Angeles and Director of the Education and Human Resources Programs at The Rand Corporation. He teaches courses in measurement, statistics and research design, and conducts methodological, psychological, and policy research. His writings include *Statistical Reasoning for the Behavioral Sciences; Generalizability Theory, Self Concept: Interplay of Theory and Methods; Review of Research on Teachers' Pedagogical Thoughts, Judgements, Decisions, and Behavior; and Teaching Mathematics and Science: Patterns of Microcomputer Use*.

Lee S. Shulman is Professor of Education and an Affiliated Professor of Psychology, Stanford University. He did undergraduate and graduate work at the University of Chicago, where he received a Ph.D. in educational psychology. From 1963 to 1982 he was a member of the faculty at Michigan State University, serving as Professor of Educational Psychology and Medical Education and as Co-Director of the Institute for Research on Teaching. His research interests are in the study of teaching, professional education in both teaching and medicine, and the psychology of instruction. He is a member of the National Academy of Education. His writings include *Medical Problem Solving* (with Elstein and Sprafka), and the *Handbook of Teaching and Policy* (edited with Sykes).

Richard E. Snow is Professor of Education and Psychology at Stanford University. His areas of research specialization include the study of individual differences in human information processing, and relationships among aptitudes, instruction, and performance outcomes. Professor Snow has served as a Divisional President for both the American Psychological Association and the American Educational Research Association, and has been a Professor in Residence at the University of Leiden, Netherlands, a Fellow at the Center for Advanced Study in the Behavioral Sciences, and, most recently, Liaison Scientist for the U.S. Office of Naval Research in London. He is a co-author of the books *Aptitudes and Instructional Methods* and *Pygmalion Reconsidered*, and Co-Editor of the series *Aptitude, Learning, and Instruction*.

Jane Stallings is Director of the Peabody Center for Effective Teaching at Vanderbilt University, Nashville, Tennessee. She has conducted seminal observation studies of teaching and learning in family day care, Head Start, Follow Through, and secondary classrooms. She is a pioneer in the translation of findings from research on teaching into effective staff development models for inservice teachers. Dr. Stallings is the author of *Learning to Look: A Handbook for Observation and Models of Teaching*, as well as numerous articles and chapters, including "An Accountability Model for Teacher Education"; "Implications from the Research on Teaching for Teacher Preparation"; "Effective Use of Classroom Time"; and "Instructional Time and Staff Development: How Useful Is the Research on Time to Teachers?"

Robert Stevens is Research Associate at the Center for Social Organization of Schools at The Johns Hopkins University. He received his Ph.D. in educational psychology from the University of Illinois. His major areas of interest are classroom instruction and cognitive task analysis. He is co-author of a chapter entitled "Classroom Instruction in Reading." He is currently helping to develop a program for elementary language arts.

Deborah Stipek is Associate Professor in the Graduate School of Education at the University of California, Los Angeles. She is head of the Developmental Studies in Education specialization.

Frank T. Stritter is Professor in the Schools of Medicine, Education and Public Health at the University of North Carolina at Chapel Hill and Director of the Office of Research and Development for Education in the Health Professions. His areas of interest are curriculum, instruction, and faculty development in higher education, with an emphasis on health professions education. He has been National Chairman of the Association of American Medical Colleges' Group on Medical Education and Program Chairman for Division I, Professional Education at the American Educational Research Association. He has written *Effective Clinical Instruction* and contributed to *The Handbook of Health Professions Education, The Handbook for the Academic Physician*, and *Teaching Quality Assurance and Cost Containment in Health Care*.

Richard P. Tisher is Professor of Education at Monash University in Australia and Head of the division dealing with research and evaluation in curriculum and teaching and with science education. His research interests include science education, effective teaching strategies, curriculum evaluation, and professional development of teachers. He has published in national and international books and journals and is especially known for his part in an Australian national study of teacher induction. He has been a Senior Australian-American Fulbright Scholar, President of the Queensland Science Teachers Association, Vice President of the Victorian Institute of Educational Research, and President of the Australian Association for Research in Education. He was the Founding Editor of *Research in Science Education*, the journal of the Australian Science Education Research Association and has resumed editorship of that publication since 1983. He is a co-author of *Fundamental Issues in Science Education*.

Ellis Paul Torrance is Alumni Foundation Distinguished Professor Emeritus of Educational Psychology at the University of Georgia at Athens. He is the author of over 30 books and 1,500 articles, as well as chapters in books and reports. He has received awards from The National Association for the Gifted, the American Personnel and Guidance Association, the Creative Education Foundation, The Future Problem Solving Program, The Olympics of the Mind, and numerous other professional organizations. The University of Georgia has established in his honor the Torrance Studies of Gifted, Creative, and Future Behaviors. Dr. Torrance is best known for *Guiding Creative Talent; The Search for Satori and Creativity; Mentor Relationships;* and *The Torrance Tests of Creative Thinking*. Now in press are *Why Fly: The Philosophy of Creativity; The Blazing Drive: Creative Persons; Learning to Fly: Creative Learning and Development; Sociodrama as a Creative Problem Solving Process; Save Tommorow for the Children;* and *Helping Students Get Beyond Aha*.

Concepción M. Valadez is Associate Professor of Education, University of California, Los Angeles. Her areas of specialization include language development, curriculum design, and teacher education. She has been Chair of the AERA special interest group Research on Bilingual Education, Associate Editor of the *CABE Journal* (California Association of Bilingual Education), and member of the Joint Committee to Develop Technical Standards in Educational and Psychological Testing. She is Associate Editor of the *NABE Journal* (National Association of Bilingual Education) and author of numerous publications on bilingual education and literacy. Her works include *Basic Skills in Urban Schools: A view from the Bilingual Classroom; The Hispanic NES/LES Children in the Los Angeles School Desegregation Plan: A Study of Five Schools; Identity, Power, and Writing Skills: The Case of the Bilingual Student*.

Herbert J. Walberg is Research Professor of Education at the University of Illinois at Chicago, one of four such professors at his institution devoted full-time to research. An educational psychologist, he is interested in the social-psychological causes and effects of learning. In the last decade, he has written on the subject of educational productivity and related topics. He was elected Fellow of the American Association for the Advancement of Science, Fellow of the Royal Statistical Society (London), Fellow of the American Psychological Association, and Visiting Fellow of the Australian Association for Research in Education. He wrote the lead article "Scientific Literacy and Economic Productivity in International Perspective" in a special issue of *Daedalus*, and edited *Evaluating Educational Performance: Educational Environments and Effects*, and *Research on Teaching* (with Penelope L. Peterson).

Noreen M. Webb is Associate Professor of Education at the University of California, Los Angeles. She teaches courses in measurement, statistics, research design, and human abilities, and conducts research on methodology and educational psychology. Her writings include "Generalizability Theory 1973-1980"; "Student Interaction and Learning in Small Groups"; and "Microcomputer Learning in Small Groups: Cognitive Requirements and Group Processes."

Claire E. Weinstein is Associate Professor and Chair in the area of learning, cognition, and instruction in the Department of Educational Psychology at the University of Texas at Austin. Her major area of specialization is human information processing and learning strategies. She is currently President of the Southwest Educational Research Association and Secretary/Treasurer of the International Association of Applied Psychology. Recent honors include a Spencer Fellowship for the National Academy of Education and the 1982 Outstanding Teacher Award from the College of Education at the University of Texas. Her publications include *Training Students to Use Elaborate Learning Strategies; Learning Strategies: The How of Learning;* and *How to Help Your Child Achieve Better in School* (with M. C. Wittrock, V. L. Underwood, & A. C. Schulte).

Richard T. White is Professor of Education at Monash University in Australia. He is Chair of Educational Psychology and specializes in the learning of science. He was President of the Australian Association for Research in Education in 1982.

Merlin C. Wittrock is Professor of Educational Psychology and Chair of the Learning and Instruction specialization in the Graduate School of Education at the University of California, Los Angeles. He is President of the Division of Education Psychology of the American Psychological Association. He is a Fellow of the American Psychological Association and the American Association for the Advancement of Science and past Fellow at the Center for Advanced Study in the Behavioral Sciences. His primary research interests are in the cognitive and affective processes involved in teaching reading, writing, science, and mathematics. He is author or editor of seven books and more than 200 articles, chapters, and papers, including *Learning and Instruction, The Human Brain,* "Reading Comprehension," "Learning as Generative Process," "The Cognitive Movement in Instruction," "The Teaching of Reading Comprehension According to the Model of Generative Learning" (with M. Linden), and "Writing and Teaching of Reading."

Indexes

Subject Index

Subject Index

Name Index

Name Index